Compact Oxford–Hachette French Dictionary

French → English
English → French

Chief Editor
Marie-Hélène Corréard

OXFORD UNIVERSITY PRESS

OXFORD
UNIVERSITY PRESS
Great Clarendon Street, Oxford, OX2 6DP,
United Kingdom

Oxford University Press is a department of the University of Oxford. It furthers the University's objective of excellence in research, scholarship, and education by publishing worldwide. Oxford is a registered trade mark of Oxford University Press in the UK and in certain other countries

First Edition published in 2013
Impression: 1

British Library Cataloguing in Publication Data
Data available

ISBN 978–0–19–966311–8

Printed in Great Britain by Clays Ltd, St Ives plc

2838136657096091

Preface

This first edition of the *Compact Oxford–Hachette French Dictionary* provides comprehensive coverage of core vocabulary across a broad spectrum of contemporary written and spoken language. It incorporates many idiomatic phrases and expressions and includes recent additions to both the French and English languages. The most appropriate new English words and senses have been selected from those sourced for recent updates to Oxford's English dictionary range, which draws on the two-billion-word Oxford English Corpus. New words and senses have been sourced by means of an exciting initiative, the Oxford Languages Tracker, which enables us to follow the latest developments in French and other modern languages. Approximately 2,000 of the commonest words in each language have been marked with a 'key' symbol.

Essential information on grammar, style, and pronunciation is provided in a convenient and accessible format, making the dictionary an ideal reference tool and study aid. The user is guided in selecting appropriate translations by clear examples of usage and construction and by information on the register of language, where required.

All grammatical terms used are explained in a glossary at the back of the dictionary, and French verbs are cross-referenced to a set of verb tables.

This new dictionary also includes an A–Z of French life and culture, providing information on contemporary French society, a calendar of traditions, festivals, and holidays in France, a practical guide to writing letters and emails in French, a guide to text messaging, and a section on navigating online services in French. A *Phrasefinder* section enables the user to communicate in commonly encountered situations such as travel, shopping, eating out, and organizing leisure activities.

Designed to meet the needs of a wide range of users, from the student at intermediate level and above to the enthusiastic traveller or business professional, the *Compact Oxford–Hachette French Dictionary* is an invaluable practical resource for learners of contemporary, idiomatic French in the 21st century.

The Editors

Préface

Cette première édition du Dictionnaire compact français Oxford–Hachette couvre l'essentiel du vocabulaire de la langue contemporaine écrite et parlée. On y trouve de nombreux idiomes et expressions ainsi que des additions récentes de l'Anglais et du Français. Ces mots et sens nouveaux ont été sélectionnés grâce à une initiative innovatrice connue sous le nom d'Oxford Language Tracker qui permet de suivre et d'enregistrer l'évolution récente non seulement de la langue française mais aussi d'autres langues vivantes. Les nouveaux mots et sens anglais les plus utiles ont été sélectionnés parmi ceux ajoutés, lors de récentes mises à jour, à la nomenclature des Dictionnaires anglais Oxford qui eux-mêmes bénéficient, pour leur élaboration, du Corpus anglais Oxford, fort de deux milliards de mots. Environ 2 000 mots, parmi les plus usités de chacune des deux langues, sont signalisés par un symbole représentant une clef.

L'information essentielle sur la grammaire, le style et la prononciation est fournie dans un format pratique et accessible, faisant du dictionnaire à la fois un ouvrage de référence et un outil indispensable à l'étude du français. L'utilisateur est guidé dans son choix des traductions les plus appropriées grâce aux exemples illustrant l'usage et la construction et à l'information sur le niveau de langue, le cas échéant.

Tous les termes grammaticaux utilisés sont définis dans le glossaire se trouvant à la fin du dictionnaire. Chaque verbe français est renvoyé à un tableau de conjugaison.

Ce nouveau dictionnaire comporte aussi un abécédaire de la culture française offrant une mine d'informations sur la société française contemporaine, un calendrier des traditions, festivals et fêtes de France, un guide pratique de correspondance pour écrire lettres et courriels en français, un guide du langage SMS, une section sur la navigation sur l'Internet de langue française, un Guide de Conversation qui permet de faciliter la communication dans les situations courantes: en voyage, dans les magasins, au restaurant et pour l'organisation des loisirs.

Conçu pour répondre aux besoins d'un grand nombre d'utilisateurs: de l'étudiant, à partir du niveau moyen, jusqu'au voyageur enthousiaste ou au professionnel, le Dictionnaire compact français Oxford–Hachette est une ressource pratique et inestimable pour tous ceux qui désirent apprendre le français idiomatique et contemporain du XXIe siècle.

Les éditeurs

Contents

The structure of French-English entries

headword

délice /delis/ *m* delight

délicieusement /delisjøzmɑ̃/ *adv*
1 deliciously

délicieux, **-ieuse** /delisjø, øz/ *adj*
1 delicious

feminine form of the headword

demandeur¹, **-euse** /dəmɑ̃dœʀ, øz/ *mf*
applicant
■ ~ **d'asile** asylum seeker; ~ **d'emploi** job-seeker

compounds in block at end of entry

words marked with this key symbol are among the most frequent 2000 words in French

⚷ **épaule** /epol/ *f* shoulder
IDIOMS **changer son fusil d'~** to change one's tactics; **avoir la tête sur les ~s** to have one's head screwed on (fam)

idioms in block at end of entry

épicier, **-ière** /episje, ɛʀ/ *mf* grocer

pronunciation in IPA

grammatical categories

francophone /fʀɑ̃kɔfɔn/ **A** *adj* French-speaking; ‹*literature*› in the French language
B *mf* French speaker

part of speech plus gender

free-lance /fʀilɑ̃s/ *mf* freelance, freelancer;

juguler /ʒygyle/ [**v1**] *vt* to stamp out

number of verb group referring to the French verb tables at the end of the dictionary

sense categories

liquider /likide/ [**v1**] *vt* **1** to settle ‹*accounts*›; to liquidate ‹*company, business*›
2 to clear ‹*goods, stock*›

lot /lo/ *m* **1** (of inheritance) share; (of land) plot
2 (in lottery) prize; **gagner le gros ~** to hit the jackpot

sense indicators

field labels for specialist terms

luth /lyt/ *m* **1** (Mus) lute
2 (Zool) leatherback

magner: **se magner** /maɲe/ [**v1**] *v refl* (+ *v être*) (pop) to get a move on (fam)

style labels

grammatical information

pomponner: **se pomponner** /pɔ̃pɔne/ [**v1**] *v refl* (+ *v être*) to get dolled up

⚷ **précédent**, **~e** /pʀesedɑ̃, ɑ̃t/ **A** *adj* previous
B *mf* **le ~, la ~e** the previous one

translations

typical collocates – words used with the headword, shown to help select the right translation

profaner /pʀɔfane/ [**v1**] *vt* to desecrate ‹*temple*›; to defile ‹*memory*›; to debase ‹*institution*›

RN /ɛʀɛn/ *f* (*abbr* = **route nationale**) ≈ A road (BrE), highway (AmE)

approximate translation

examples, with a swung dash representing the headword

⚷ **souci** /susi/ *m* **1 se faire du ~** to worry
2 problem; **j'ai d'autres ~s (en tête)** I've got other things to worry about

transfusé, **~e** /tʀɑ̃sfyze/ **A** *pp* ▶ **transfuser**

cross-reference

The structure of English-French entries

headword

battery /'bætərɪ/ *n* pile *f*; (in car) batterie *f*

battery charger *n* chargeur *m* de batteries

battery farming *n* élevage *m* en batterie

separate entries for compounds

words marked with this key symbol are among the most frequent 2000 words in English

⚷ **beat** /bi:t/ A *n* **1** (of drum, heart) battement *m*

▪ **beat back** repousser ‹*group, flames*›

▪ **beat down** ‹*rain*› tomber à verse (**on** sur); ‹*sun*› taper (**on** sur)

phrasal verbs

⚷ **cat** /kæt/ *n* (domestic) chat *m*; (female) chatte *f*; **the big ~s** les grands félins *mpl*

IDIOMS **to let the ~ out of the bag** vendre la mèche; **to rain ~s and dogs** pleuvoir des cordes

idioms in block at end of entry

grammatical categories and parts of speech

clutter /'klʌtə(r)/ **A** *n* désordre *m* **B** *vt* (*also* ~ **up**) encombrer

⚷ **edge** /edʒ/ A *n* **1** (outer limit) bord *m*; (of wood, clearing) lisière *f*; **the film had us on the ~ of our seats** le film nous a tenus en haleine **2** (of blade) tranchant *m*

sense categories

sense indicators

⚷ **especially** /ɪ'speʃəlɪ/ *adv* **1** (above all) surtout, en particulier; **him ~** lui en particulier; **~ as it's so hot** d'autant plus qu'il fait si chaud **2** (on purpose) exprès, spécialement

fishy /'fɪʃɪ/ *adj* **1** ‹*smell, taste*› de poisson **2** (fam) (suspect) louche (fam)

style labels

field labels for specialist terms

message window *n* (Comput) feuille *f* de message

mushroom /'mʌʃrʊm, -ru:m/ *n* **1** (Bot, Culin) champignon *m*

non-smoking // *adj* non fumeur *inv*

grammatical information

translations

nuisance /'nju:sns, (AmE) 'nu:-/ *n* (gen) embêtement *m*; (Law) nuisance *f*; **what a ~!** que c'est agaçant!

⚷ **official** /ə'fɪʃl/ A *n* fonctionnaire *mf*; (of party, union) officiel/-ielle *m/f*; (at town hall) employé/-e *m/f*

feminine ending in translation

typical collocates – words used with the headword, shown to help select the right translation

plump /plʌmp/ *adj* ‹*person, arm, leg*› potelé/-e; ‹*cheek, face*› rond/-e, plein/-e

plunge /plʌndʒ/ A *vt* plonger (**into** dans) B *vi* ‹*road, cliff, waterfall*› plonger; ‹*bird, plane*› piquer

secondary school *n* ≈ école *f* secondaire

approximate translation equivalent

examples, with a swung dash representing the headword

⚷ **shut** /ʃʌt/ A *adj* fermé/-e; **her eyes were ~** elle avait les yeux fermés; **to slam the door ~** claquer la porte (pour bien la fermer); **to keep one's mouth** (fam) **~** se taire

these /ði:z/ ▶ **this**

cross-reference

The pronunciation of French

Vowels

a	*as in*	*patte*	/pat/
ɑ		*pâte*	/pɑt/
ã		*clan*	/klã/
e		*dé*	/de/
ɛ		*belle*	/bɛl/
ɛ̃		*lin*	/lɛ̃/
ə		*demain*	/dəmɛ̃/
i		*gris*	/gʀi/
o		*gros*	/gʀo/
ɔ		*corps*	/kɔʀ/
ɔ̃		*long*	/lɔ̃/
œ		*leur*	/lœʀ/
œ̃		*brun*	/bʀœ̃/
ø		*deux*	/dø/
u		*fou*	/fu/
y		*pur*	/pyʀ/

Semi-vowels

j	*as in*	*fille*	/fij/
ɥ		*huit*	/ɥit/
w		*oui*	/wi/

Consonants

b	*as in*	*bal*	/bal/
d		*dent*	/dã/
f		*foire*	/fwaʀ/
g		*gomme*	/gɔm/
k		*clé*	/kle/
l		*lien*	/ljɛ̃/
m		*mer*	/mɛʀ/
n		*nage*	/naʒ/
ɲ		*gnon*	/ɲɔ̃/
ŋ		*dancing*	/dãsiŋ/
p		*porte*	/pɔʀt/
ʀ		*rire*	/ʀiʀ/
s		*sang*	/sã/
ʃ		*chien*	/ʃjɛ̃/
t		*train*	/tʀɛ̃/
v		*voile*	/vwal/
z		*zèbre*	/zɛbʀ/
ʒ		*jeune*	/ʒœn/

The symbols used in this dictionary for the pronunciation of French are those of the IPA (International Phonetic Alphabet). Certain differences in pronunciation are shown in the phonetic transcription, although many speakers do not observe them—e.g. the long 'a' /ɑ/ in *pâte* and the short 'a' /a/ in *patte*, or the difference between the nasal vowels 'un' /œ̃/ as in *brun* and 'in' /ɛ̃/ as in *brin*.

Transcription

Each entry is followed by its phonetic transcription between slashes, with a few exceptions.

Morphological variations

The phonetic transcription of the plural and feminine forms of certain nouns and adjectives does not repeat the root, but shows only the change in ending. Therefore, in certain cases, the presentation of the entry does not correspond to that of the phonetic transcripton e.g. *électricien, -ienne* /elɛktʀisjɛ̃, ɛn/.

Phrases

Full phonetic transcription is given for adverbial or prepositional phrases which are shown in alphabetical order within the main headword e.g. *emblée, d'emblée* /dɑ̃ble/, *plain-pied, de plain-pied* /d(ə)plɛ̃pje/.

Consonants

Aspiration of 'h'

Where it is impossible to make a liaison this is indicated by /ˈ/ immediately after the slash e.g. *haine* /ˈɛn/.

Assimilation

A voiced consonant can become unvoiced when it is followed by an unvoiced consonant within a word e.g. *absorber* /apsɔʀbe/.

Vowels

Open 'e' and closed 'e'

A clear distinction is made at the end of a word between a closed 'e' and an open 'e' e.g. *pré* /pʀe/ and *près* /pʀɛ/, *complet* /kɔ̃plɛ/ and *combler* /kɔ̃ble/.

Within a word the following rules apply:

- 'e' is always open in a syllable followed by a syllable containing a mute 'e' e.g. *règle* /ʀɛgl/, *réglementaire* /ʀɛgləmɑ̃tɛʀ/
- in careful speech 'e' is pronounced as a closed 'e' when it is followed by a syllable containing a closed vowel (y, i, e) e.g. *pressé* /pʀese/
- 'e' is pronounced as an open 'e' when it is followed by a syllable containing an open vowel e.g. *pressant* /pʀɛsɑ̃/.

Mute 'e'

The pronunciation of mute 'e' varies considerably depending on the level of language used and on the region from which the speaker originates. As a general rule it is only pronounced at the end of a word in the South of France or in poetry and it is, therefore, not shown. In an isolated word the mute 'e' preceded by a single consonant is dropped e.g. *parfaitement* /paʀfɛtmɑ̃/, but *probablement* /pʀɔbabləmɑ̃/. In many cases the pronunciation of the mute 'e' depends on the surrounding context. Thus one would say *une reconnaissance de dette* /ynʀəkɔnɛsɑ̃sdədɛt/, but, *ma reconnaissance est éternelle* /maʀkɔnɛsɑ̃sɛtetɛʀnɛl/. The mute 'e' is shown in brackets in order to account for this phenomenon.

Stress

There is no real stress as such in French. In normal unemphasized speech a slight stress falls on the final syllable of a word or group of words, providing that it does not contain a mute 'e'. This is not shown in the phonetic transcription of individual entries.

Abbreviations

abbr	abbreviation
adj	adjective
adv	adverb
AmE	American English
Anat	anatomy
Archit	architecture
Aut	automobile
aux	auxiliary
Bot	botany
BrE	British English
colloq	colloquial
Comput	computing
conj	conjunction
Culin	culinary
dem pron	demonstrative pronoun
det	determiner
Econ	economy
excl	exclamation
fam	familiar
f	feminine noun
Fr	French
gen	generally
Hist	history, historical
indic	indicative
inv	invariable
liter	literary
m	masculine noun
Med	medicine
mf	masculine and feminine noun
m,f	masculine and feminine noun
Mil	military
Mus	music
n	noun
Naut	nautical
phr	phrase
pl	plural
Pol	politics
pop	populaire (very informal)
pp	past participle
pp adj	past participle adjective
pr n	proper noun
pref	prefix
prep	preposition
pres p adj	present participle adjective
pron	pronoun
qch	quelque chose (something)
qn	quelqu'un (somebody)
quantif	quantifier
®	registered trademark
rel pron	relative pronoun
sb	somebody
Sch	school
sg	singular
sth	something
subj	subjunctive
Tech	technology
Univ	university
v	verb
v aux	auxiliary verb
vi	intransitive verb
v impers	impersonal verb
v inf	very informal
v refl	reflexive verb
vt	transitive verb
Zool	zoology

Note on proprietary status

This dictionary includes some words which have, or are asserted to have, proprietary status as trademarks or otherwise. Their inclusion does not imply that they have acquired for legal purposes a non-proprietary or general significance, nor any other judgement concerning their legal status. In cases where the editorial staff have some evidence that a word has proprietary status this is indicated in the entry for that word by the symbol ®, but no judgement concerning the legal status of such words is made or implied thereby.

Aa

a[1], **A** /a, ɑ/ **A** *m inv* a, A; **démontrer qch à qn par A plus B** to demonstrate sth conclusively to sb
B **A** *f* (*abbr* = **autoroute**) motorway (BrE), freeway (AmE)

a[2] /a/ ▶ **avoir**[1]

à /a/ *prep*

> You will find translations for expressions such as *machine à écrire, aller à la pêche* etc, at the entries **machine, pêche,** etc.
> For the uses of *à* with the verbs *aller, être, avoir, penser* etc, see the entries for these verbs.

1 to; **aller ~ Paris** to go to Paris; **se rendre au travail** to go to work **2** at; in; **~ la maison** at home; **être ~ Paris** to be in Paris; **au printemps** in (the) spring; **~ midi** at midday; **~ quatre kilomètres d'ici** four kilometres (BrE) from here; **~ 100 kilomètres-heure** at 100 kilometres (BrE) per *or* an hour; **un timbre ~ 0,46 euros** a 0.46 euro stamp; **(de) huit ~ dix heures par jour** between eight and ten hours a day **3** with; **le garçon aux cheveux bruns** the boy with dark hair **4 ~ qui est cette montre?** whose is this watch?; **elle est ~ elle** it's hers; **je suis ~ vous tout de suite** I'll be with you in a minute; **c'est ~ qui de jouer?** whose turn is it? **5 il est ~ plaindre** he's to be pitied **6 ~ nous tous on devrait y arriver** between all of us we should be able to manage; **~ trois on est serrés** with three people it's a squash **7 ~ ce qu'il paraît** apparently; **~ ta santé, ~ la tienne!** cheers!; **~ tes souhaits!** bless you!

abaisser /abese/ [**v1**] **A** *vt* to pull down ‹*lever*›; to lower ‹*safety curtain, window*›
B **s'abaisser** *v refl* (+ *v être*) **1** ‹*stage curtain*› to fall
2 s'~ à faire to stoop to doing

abandon /abɑ̃dɔ̃/ *m* **1 être à l'~** ‹*house*› to be abandoned; ‹*garden*› to be neglected
2 (of project, method) abandonment; (of right) relinquishment
3 (from race, competition) withdrawal

abandonné, **~e** /abɑ̃dɔne/ **A** *pp* ▶ **abandonner**
B *pp adj* **1** ‹*spouse, friend, cause*› deserted; ‹*vehicle, house, nation*› abandoned
2 ‹*path, factory*› disused

abandonner /abɑ̃dɔne/ [**v1**] *vt* **1** (gen) to give up; (in school) to drop ‹*subject*›
2 (from game, tournament) to withdraw; to retire
3 to leave ‹*person, place*›; to abandon ‹*car, object*›
4 to abandon ‹*child, animal*›; to desert ‹*home, post, cause*›
5 ‹*courage, chance*› to fail ‹*person*›

abat-jour /abaʒuʀ/ *m inv* lampshade

abats /aba/ *mpl* offal; (of poultry) giblets

abattement /abatmɑ̃/ *m* **1** despondency
2 ~ fiscal tax allowance (BrE) *or* deduction (AmE)

abattoir /abatwaʀ/ *m* abattoir, slaughterhouse

abattre /abatʀ/ [**v61**] **A** *vt* **1** to shoot [sb] down ‹*person*›; to shoot ‹*animal*›; to slaughter ‹*cattle, sheep*›
2 to pull down ‹*building*›; to knock down ‹*wall*›; ‹*person*› to fell ‹*tree*›; ‹*storm*› to bring down ‹*tree*›
3 to show ‹*card, hand*›
4 to demoralize
5 ~ de la besogne to get through a lot of work
B **s'abattre** *v refl* (+ *v être*) **s'~ sur** ‹*storm*› to break over; ‹*rain*› to beat down on; ‹*bird of prey*› to swoop down on

abbaye /abei/ *f* abbey

abbé /abe/ *m* **1** priest
2 abbot

abc /ɑbese/ *m* ABC, rudiments

abcès /apsɛ/ *m inv* abscess; **crever l'~** to resolve a crisis

abdication /abdikasjɔ̃/ *f* abdication

abdiquer /abdike/ [**v1**] *vi* ‹*sovereign*› to abdicate

abdomen /abdɔmɛn/ *m* abdomen, stomach

abdominal, **~e**, *mpl* **-aux** /abdɔminal, o/
A *adj* abdominal
B **abdominaux** *mpl* abdominal muscles

abeille /abɛj/ *f* bee

aberrant, **~e** /abɛʀɑ̃, ɑ̃t/ *adj* **1** absurd
2 aberrant

aberration /abɛʀasjɔ̃/ *f* aberration

abêtir /abetiʀ/ [**v3**], **s'abêtir** *v refl* (+ *v être*) to become stupid

abêtissant, **~e** /abetisɑ̃, ɑ̃t/ *adj* mindless

abîme /abim/ *m* **1** abyss
2 (fig) gulf

abîmer /abime/ [**v1**] **A** *vt* to damage
B **s'abîmer** *v refl* (+ *v être*) ‹*object*› to get damaged; ‹*fruit*› to spoil

abject, **~e** /abʒɛkt/ *adj* despicable, abject

ablation /ablasjɔ̃/ *f* excision, removal

abnégation /abnegasjɔ̃/ *f* self-sacrifice

aboiement /abwamɑ̃/ *m* barking

abolir /abɔliʀ/ [**v3**] *vt* to abolish

abominable /abɔminabl/ *adj* abominable

abomination /abɔminɑsjɔ̃/ *f* abomination

abondamment /abɔ̃damɑ̃/ *adv* ‹*drink*› a lot; ‹*illustrate*› amply; **rincer ~** rinse thoroughly

abondance /abɔ̃dɑ̃s/ *f* **1** (of information) wealth; (of resources) abundance
2 affluence

abondant, **~e** /abɔ̃dɑ̃, ɑ̃t/ *adj* ‹*food*› plentiful; ‹*illustrations*› numerous; ‹*vegetation*› lush

abonder /abɔ̃de/ [**v1**] *vi* to be plentiful; to abound
IDIOM **~ dans le sens de qn** to agree wholeheartedly with sb

abonné, **~e** /abɔne/ **A** *pp* ▸ **abonner**
B *mf* **1** subscriber
2 season ticket holder

abonnement /abɔnmɑ̃/ *m* **1** subscription
2 (carte d')~ season ticket

abonner /abɔne/ [**v1**] **A** *vt* **~ qn à qch** (to magazine) to take out a subscription to sth for sb; (for theatre) to buy sb a season ticket for sth
B s'abonner *v refl* (+ *v être*) to subscribe (**à** to); to buy a season ticket (**à** for)

abord /abɔʀ/ **A** *m* **1 elle est d'un ~ difficile** she is rather unapproachable
2 être d'un ~ aisé ‹*subject, book*› to be accessible
3 au premier ~ at first sight
B d'abord *phr* first; **tout d'~** first of all
C abords *mpl* surrounding area, area around

abordable /abɔʀdabl/ *adj* ‹*product, price*› affordable; ‹*text*› accessible

abordage /abɔʀdaʒ/ *m* (by pirates) boarding

aborder /abɔʀde/ [**v1**] **A** *vt* **1** to tackle ‹*problem*›
2 to approach ‹*person*›
3 to reach ‹*place, shore*›
B *vi* ‹*traveller, ship*› to land

aboutir /abutiʀ/ [**v3**] **A aboutir à** *v+prep* to lead to
B *vi* ‹*negotiations, project*› to succeed

aboutissants /abutisɑ̃/ *mpl* **les tenants et les ~ de qch** the ins and outs of sth

aboutissement /abutismɑ̃/ *m*
1 culmination
2 (successful) outcome

aboyer /abwaje/ [**v23**] *vi* ‹*dog*› to bark (**après** at)

abracadabrant, **~e** /abʀakadabʀɑ̃, ɑ̃t/ *adj* bizarre

abrasif, **-ive** /abʀazif, iv/ *adj* abrasive

abrégé /abʀeʒe/ *m* (book) concise guide

abréger /abʀeʒe/ [**v15**] *vt* **1** to shorten ‹*word, expression*›
2 to cut short ‹*visit, career*›

abreuver: **s'abreuver** /abʀøve/ [**v1**] *v refl* (+ *v être*) ‹*animal*› to drink

abreuvoir /abʀøvwaʀ/ *m* drinking trough

abréviation /abʀevjasjɔ̃/ *f* abbreviation

abri /abʀi/ *m* **1** shelter; **à l'~ de** sheltered from; (fig) safe from
2 shed

abricot /abʀiko/ *m* apricot

abricotier /abʀikɔtje/ *m* apricot tree

abriter /abʀite/ [**v1**] **A** *vt* **1** ‹*building*› to shelter ‹*people, animals*›
2 ‹*country, region*› to provide a habitat for ‹*animals, plant life*›
B s'abriter *v refl* (+ *v être*) to take shelter

abrogation /abʀɔgasjɔ̃/ *f* repeal

abroger /abʀɔʒe/ [**v13**] *vt* to repeal

abrupt, **~e** /abʀypt/ *adj* **1** ‹*hill, road*› steep; ‹*cliff*› sheer
2 ‹*person, tone*› abrupt

abruti, **~e** /abʀyti/ *mf* (offensive) moron (fam)

abrutir /abʀytiʀ/ [**v3**] **A** *vt* ‹*noise*› to deafen; ‹*alcohol, medication, fatigue*› to have a numbing effect on; ‹*blow*› to stun
B s'abrutir *v refl* (+ *v être*) **1** to become dull-witted
2 s'~ de travail to wear oneself out with work

abrutissant, **~e** /abʀytisɑ̃, ɑ̃t/ *adj* ‹*music, noise*› deafening; ‹*job*› mind-numbing

absence /apsɑ̃s/ *f* **1** absence
2 lack; **l'~ de pluie** the lack of rain

absent, **~e** /apsɑ̃, ɑ̃t/ **A** *adj* **1 être ~** to be away; (for brief spell) to be out
2 ‹*pupil, employee*› absent
3 (missing) absent (**de** from)
4 absent-minded
B *mf* absentee

absentéisme /apsɑ̃teism/ *m* absenteeism

absenter: **s'absenter** /apsɑ̃te/ [**v1**] *v refl* (+ *v être*) to go away; to go out

absolu, **~e** /apsɔly/ *adj* absolute; ‹*rule*› hard and fast

absolument /apsɔlymɑ̃/ *adv* absolutely

absolution /apsɔlysjɔ̃/ *f* absolution

absolutisme /apsɔlytism/ *m* absolutism

absorbant, **~e** /apsɔʀbɑ̃, ɑ̃t/ *adj*
1 ‹*substance*› absorbent
2 ‹*job, work*› absorbing

absorber /apsɔʀbe/ [**v1**] *vt* **1** ‹*material, plant*› to absorb
2 to take ‹*food, medicine*›
3 to occupy ‹*mind*›

absorption /apsɔʀpsjɔ̃/ *f* **1** (of liquid) absorption
2 (of food, medicine) taking

abstenir: **s'abstenir** /apstəniʀ/ [**v36**] *v refl* (+ *v être*) **1** (from voting) to abstain
2 s'~ de faire to refrain from doing

abstention /apstɑ̃sjɔ̃/ *f* abstention

abstinence /apstinɑ̃s/ *f* abstinence

---

key word

abstraction /apstʀaksjɔ̃/ *f* abstraction; **faire ~ de** to set aside

abstrait, **~e** /apstʀɛ, ɛt/ **A** *adj* abstract **B** *m* (gen) abstract; (art) abstract art

absurde /apsyʀd/ *adj*, *m* absurd

absurdité /apsyʀdite/ *f* absurdity

abus /aby/ *m inv* abuse

abuser /abyze/ [**v1**] **A** *vt* to fool **B abuser de** *v+prep* **1 ~ de l'alcool** to drink to excess
2 ~ de to exploit ‹*situation, credibility*›
3 ~ de qn to sexually abuse sb
C *vi* to go too far; **je ne voudrais pas ~** I don't want to impose
D s'abuser *v refl* (+ *v être*) **si je ne m'abuse** if I'm not mistaken

abusif, **-ive** /abyzif, iv/ *adj* **1** excessive
2 unfair
3 improper
4 over-possessive

acabit /akabi/ *m* **du même ~** of that sort

acacia /akasja/ *m* **1** (European) **(faux) ~** locust tree
2 (tropical) acacia

académicien, **-ienne** /akademisjɛ̃, ɛn/ *mf* academician

académie /akademi/ *f* (Sch) ≈ local education authority (BrE), school district (AmE)

académique /akademik/ *adj* **1** (gen) academic; of the Académie française
2 (Sch, Univ) ≈ of the local education authority (BrE) *or* school district (AmE)
3 (in art) academic

acajou /akaʒu/ *m* mahogany

acariâtre /akaʀjɑtʀ/ *adj* cantankerous

accablant, **~e** /akablɑ̃, ɑ̃t/ *adj* **1** ‹*heat, silence*› oppressive
2 ‹*evidence, testimony*› damning

accabler /akable/ [**v1**] *vt* **1** ‹*bad news*› to devastate; **être accablé par** to be overcome by ‹*heat, grief*›
2 ‹*testimony, person*› to condemn

accalmie /akalmi/ *f* **1** lull
2 slack period

accaparant, **~e** /akapaʀɑ̃, ɑ̃t/ *adj* very demanding

accaparer /akapaʀe/ [**v1**] *vt* to corner ‹*market*›; to monopolize ‹*person, power*›

accédant, **~e** /aksedɑ̃, ɑ̃t/ *mf* **~ à la propriété** home-buyer

accéder /aksede/ [**v14**] *v+prep* **1 ~ à** to reach ‹*place*›
2 ~ à to achieve ‹*fame, glory*›; to obtain ‹*job*›; to rise to ‹*high office*›

accélérateur /akseleʀatœʀ/ *m* accelerator

accélération /akseleʀasjɔ̃/ *f* acceleration

accélérer /akseleʀe/ [**v14**] **A** *vt* to speed up ‹*rhythm, process*›; **~ le pas** to quicken one's step
B *vi* ‹*driver*› to accelerate
C s'accélérer *v refl* (+ *v être*) ‹*pulse, movement*› to become faster; ‹*phenomenon*› to accelerate

accent /aksɑ̃/ *m* **1** (of person, region) accent
2 (on a letter) accent
3 (on a syllable) **~ tonique** stress; **mettre l'~ sur qch** to emphasize sth, to put the emphasis on sth
4 ~ de sincérité hint of sincerity

accentuer /aksɑ̃tɥe/ [**v1**] **A** *vt* **1** (gen) to emphasize, to accentuate
2 to heighten ‹*tension*›; to increase ‹*tendency*›
3 (in pronouncing) to stress ‹*syllable*›
B s'accentuer *v refl* (+ *v être*) to become more marked

acceptable /aksɛptabl/ *adj* **1** acceptable
2 passable; satisfactory

acceptation /aksɛptasjɔ̃/ *f* acceptance

⚷ **accepter** /aksɛpte/ [**v1**] *vt* to accept; to agree to

acception /aksɛpsjɔ̃/ *f* sense; **dans toute l'~ du terme** *or* **mot** in every sense of the word

⚷ **accès** /aksɛ/ *m inv* **1** access; **d'un ~ facile** ‹*place*› easy to get to; **'~ aux quais'** 'to the trains'; **'~ interdit'** 'no entry'; **l'~ à** access to ‹*profession, course*›; admission to ‹*club, school*›
2 ~ de colère fit of anger; **~ de fièvre** bout of fever; **par ~** by fits and starts
3 (Comput) access

accessible /aksesibl/ *adj* **1** ‹*place, book, information*› accessible
2 ~ à ‹*job*› open to
3 ‹*price, fare*› affordable

accession /aksesjɔ̃/ *f* **~ à** accession to ‹*throne, power*›; attainment of ‹*independence*›

accessoire /akseswaʀ/ **A** *adj* incidental **B** *m* **1** accessory; attachment; **~s de toilette** toilet requisites
2 (in the theatre) **~s** props

accessoirement /akseswaʀmɑ̃/ *adv* **1** incidentally, as it happens
2 if desired

accessoiriste /akseswaʀist/ *mf* props man/woman

⚷ **accident** /aksidɑ̃/ *m* **1** accident
2 hitch; mishap; **~ de parcours** (fam) hitch
■ **~ domestique** accident in the home

accidenté, **~e** /aksidɑ̃te/ **A** *adj* **1** ‹*person*› injured; ‹*car*› involved in an accident
2 ‹*road, ground*› uneven
B *mf* accident victim

accidentel, **-elle** /aksidɑ̃tɛl/ *adj* accidental

accidentellement /aksidɑ̃tɛlmɑ̃/ *adv* **1** in an accident
2 by accident, accidentally

acclamation /aklamasjɔ̃/ *f* cheering

acclamer /aklame/ [**v1**] *vt* to cheer, to acclaim

acclimater /aklimate/ [**v1**] **A** *vt* to acclimatize

a

B **s'acclimater** *v refl* (+ *v être*) to become acclimatized; to adapt

accointances /akwɛ̃tɑ̃s/ *fpl* contacts

accolade /akɔlad/ *f* embrace

accommoder /akɔmɔde/ [**v1**] **A** *vt* to prepare
B *vi* ‹*eyes*› to focus
C **s'accommoder** *v refl* (+ *v être*) **s'~ de qch** to make the best of sth; to put up with sth

accompagnateur, -trice /akɔ̃paɲatœʀ, tʀis/ *mf* **1** (Mus) accompanist
2 (with children) accompanying adult; (with tourists) courier

accompagnement /akɔ̃paɲmɑ̃/ *m* accompaniment

🗝 **accompagner** /akɔ̃paɲe/ [**v1**] *vt* **1** ‹*person*› to accompany, to go with, to come with
2 to accompany ‹*phenomenon, event*›
3 (Mus) to accompany
4 ‹*wine*› to be served with

🗝 **accomplir** /akɔ̃pliʀ/ [**v3**] **A** *vt* to accomplish ‹*task*›; to fulfil (BrE) ‹*obligation*›
B **s'accomplir** *v refl* (+ *v être*) to be fulfilled

accomplissement /akɔ̃plismɑ̃/ *m* (of mission) accomplishment, fulfilment (BrE); (of ambition, aim) realization, achievement

🗝 **accord** /akɔʀ/ *m* **1** agreement; (tacit) understanding; **d'~** all right, OK (fam); **je suis d'~** I agree (**avec** with); **se mettre** *or* **tomber d'~** to come to an agreement
2 harmony
3 (in grammar) **~ en genre/en nombre** gender/number agreement
4 (Mus) chord

accordéon /akɔʀdeɔ̃/ *m* accordion

🗝 **accorder** /akɔʀde/ [**v1**] **A** *vt* **1 ~ qch à qn** to grant sb sth ‹*favour, loan, interview, permission, right*›; to give sb sth ‹*grant, reduction, chance*›; **il n'a pas entièrement tort, je te l'accorde** he's not entirely wrong, I'll give you that
2 to attach ‹*importance, value*› (**à** to); to pay ‹*attention*›
3 (Mus) to tune ‹*instrument*›
4 to make [sth] agree ‹*word, adjective*›
B **s'accorder** *v refl* (+ *v être*) **1** to give oneself ‹*rest, time off*›
2 to agree (**sur** about, on)
3 ‹*colours, clothes*› to go (together) well
4 ‹*adjective, verb*› to agree (**avec** with)

accordeur /akɔʀdœʀ/ *m* tuner

accostage /akɔstaʒ/ *m* docking

accoster /akɔste/ [**v1**] **A** *vt* to accost ‹*person*›
B *vi* ‹*ship*› to dock

accotement /akɔtmɑ̃/ *m* verge

accouchement /akuʃmɑ̃/ *m* delivery

accoucher /akuʃe/ [**v1**] *vi* to give birth (**de** to)

accoucheur /akuʃœʀ/ *m* obstetrician

accouder: **s'accouder** /akude/ [**v1**] *v refl* (+ *v être*) to lean on one's elbows

accoudoir /akudwaʀ/ *m* arm-rest

accouplement /akupləmɑ̃/ *m* mating

accourir /akuʀiʀ/ [**v26**] *vi* to run up

accoutrement /akutʀəmɑ̃/ *m* get-up (fam)

accoutrer: **s'accoutrer** /akutʀe/ [**v1**] *v refl* (+ *v être*) to get oneself up (**de** in)

accoutumance /akutymɑ̃s/ *f* addiction

accoutumer /akutyme/ [**v1**] **A** *vt* to accustom (**à** to)
B **s'accoutumer** *v refl* (+ *v être*) to grow accustomed (**à** to)

accrédité, ~e /akʀedite/ *adj* authorized; accredited

accréditer /akʀedite/ [**v1**] *vt* **1** to give credence to ‹*rumour*›
2 to accredit ‹*ambassador*›

accro /akʀo/ *adj* (fam) hooked (fam) (**à** on)

accroc /akʀo/ *m* tear (**à** in)

accrochage /akʀɔʃaʒ/ *m* (between people) clash; (between vehicles) collision

accrocher /akʀɔʃe/ [**v1**] **A** *vt* **1** to hang (**à** from)
2 to hook [sth] on (**à** to)
3 to catch ‹*stocking, sweater*› (**à** on)
4 to catch ‹*eye, attention*›
B **s'accrocher** *v refl* (+ *v être*) **1** (to ledge) to hang on; (to post) to cling (**à** to)
2 ‹*person*› **s'~ à qn** to cling to sb
3 l'hameçon s'est accroché à ma veste the hook got caught in my jacket
4 (fam) **s'~ pour faire** to try hard to do
IDIOM **avoir le cœur** *or* **l'estomac bien accroché** to have a strong stomach

accrocheur, -euse /akʀɔʃœʀ, øz/ *adj* ‹*song, tune*› catchy; ‹*picture, title*› eye-catching

accroissement /akʀwasmɑ̃/ *m* growth

accroître /akʀwɑtʀ/ [**v72**] *vt*, **s'accroître** *v refl* (+ *v être*) to increase

accroupir: **s'accroupir** /akʀupiʀ/ [**v3**] *v refl* (+ *v être*) to squat (down); to crouch (down)

accru, ~e /akʀy/ ▸ **accroître**

🗝 **accueil** /akœj/ *m* **1** welcome
2 reception desk

accueillant, ~e /akœjɑ̃, ɑ̃t/ *adj* **1** hospitable, welcoming
2 homely (BrE), homey (AmE)

🗝 **accueillir** /akœjiʀ/ [**v27**] *vt* **1** to welcome
2 to receive, to greet
3 ‹*room, hotel*› to accommodate
4 ‹*hospital, organization*› to cater for

accumulation /akymylasjɔ̃/ *f* **1** accumulation
2 storage

accumuler /akymyle/ [**v1**] **A** *vt* **1** to store (up) ‹*things*›; to accumulate ‹*capital*›; to make a succession of ‹*mistakes*›
2 to store (up) ‹*energy*›
B **s'accumuler** *v refl* (+ *v être*) ‹*snow,*

🗝 key word

rubbish› to pile up; ‹*stocks, debts*› to accrue

accusateur, **-trice** /akyzatœʀ, tʀis/ **A** *adj* ‹*silence, finger*› accusing; ‹*presence, speech*› accusatory
B *mf* accuser; **~ public** public prosecutor

accusation /akyzasjɔ̃/ *f* **1** accusation; (Law) charge
2 l'~ the prosecution

accusé, **~e** /akyze/ **A** *pp* ▶ **accuser**
B *pp adj* ‹*wrinkles*› deep; ‹*relief*› marked
C *mf* defendant; **les ~s** the accused
■ **~ de réception** acknowledgement (of receipt)

accuser /akyze/ [**v1**] **A** *vt* **1** to accuse ‹*person*›; to blame ‹*fate*›; ‹*evidence*› to point to ‹*person*›; ‹*judge*› to charge ‹*defendant*› (**de** with)
2 to show, to register ‹*fall, deficit*›
B s'accuser *v refl* (+ *v être*) **1** ‹*person*› to take the blame
2 to become more marked
IDIOM **~ le coup** to be visibly shaken

acerbe /asɛʀb/ *adj* acerbic

acéré, **~e** /aseʀe/ *adj* sharp

acharné, **~e** /aʃaʀne/ *adj* ‹*supporter*› passionate; ‹*work*› unremitting; ‹*struggle*› fierce

acharnement /aʃaʀnəmɑ̃/ *m* furious energy

acharner: **s'acharner** /aʃaʀne/ [**v1**] *v refl* (+ *v être*) **1** to persevere; **s'~ contre** to fight against ‹*project*›
2 s'~ sur ‹*person, animal*› to keep going at ‹*victim, prey*›; (fig) to hound ‹*person*›; **la malchance s'acharne contre lui** he is dogged by bad luck

achat /aʃa/ *m* purchase

acheminement /aʃ(ə)minmɑ̃/ *m* transportation

acheminer /aʃ(ə)mine/ [**v1**] **A** *vt* to transport
B s'acheminer *v refl* (+ *v être*) **s'~ vers** to make one's way toward(s); to move toward(s)

acheter /aʃte/ [**v18**] **A** *vt* to buy; **~ qch à qn** to buy sth from sb; to buy sth for sb
B s'acheter *v refl* (+ *v être*) **1 s'~ qch** to buy oneself sth
2 cela s'achète où? where can you get it?

acheteur, **-euse** /aʃtœʀ, øz/ *mf* buyer

acheteur personnel, **-euse personnelle** *mf* personal shopper

achever /aʃve/ [**v16**] **A** *vt* **1** to finish ‹*work*›; to conclude ‹*discussions*›; to complete ‹*project, inquiry*›; to end ‹*life*›
2 to destroy ‹*animal*›; to finish off ‹*person*›
B s'achever *v refl* (+ *v être*) to end

achoppement /aʃɔpmɑ̃/ *m* **pierre d'~** stumbling block

acide /asid/ *adj*, *m* acid

acidité /asidite/ *f* acidity, tartness, sharpness

acidulé, **~e** /asidyle/ *adj* slightly acid; tangy

acier /asje/ **A** *adj inv* steel(y)
B *m* steel; **d'~** ‹*girder, column*› steel; ‹*nerves*› of steel

aciérie /asjeʀi/ *f* steelworks

acné /akne/ *f* acne; **~ juvénile** teenage acne

acolyte /akɔlit/ *mf* henchman, acolyte

acompte /akɔ̃t/ *m* **1** deposit
2 part payment

acoquiner: **s'acoquiner** /akɔkine/ [**v1**] *v refl* (+ *v être*) **s'~ avec qn** to get thick (fam) with sb

à-côté, *pl* **~s** /akote/ *m* **1** perk
2 extra expense
3 extra profit

à-coup, *pl* **~s** /aku/ *m* jolt; **par ~s** by fits and starts

acoustique /akustik/ **A** *adj* acoustic
B *f* acoustics

acquéreur /akeʀœʀ/ *m* buyer, purchaser

acquérir /akeʀiʀ/ [**v35**] *vt* **1** to acquire; (by buying) to purchase
2 to acquire ‹*reputation*›

acquiescement /akjɛsmɑ̃/ *m* **donner son ~ à** to acquiesce to

acquiescer /akjese/ [**v12**] *vi* to acquiesce

acquis, **~e** /aki, iz/ **A** *pp* ▶ **acquérir**
B *pp adj* **1** ‹*skills*› acquired
2 ‹*principle, right*› accepted, established; **les avantages ~** the gains made; **tenir qch pour ~** to take sth for granted
C *m inv* **1** acquired knowledge
2 ~ sociaux social benefits
IDIOM **bien mal ~ ne profite jamais** (Proverb) ill-gotten gains never prosper

acquisition /akizisjɔ̃/ *f* **1** purchase
2 acquisition

acquit /aki/ *m* **je le ferai par ~ de conscience** I'll do it to put my mind at rest

acquittement /akitmɑ̃/ *m* (Law) acquittal

acquitter /akite/ [**v1**] **A** *vt* (Law) to acquit
B s'acquitter *v refl* (+ *v être*) **s'~ de son devoir** to do one's duty; **s'~ d'une dette** to pay off a debt

acre /akʀ/ *f* acre

âcre /ɑkʀ/ *adj* ‹*taste*› sharp; ‹*smell*› acrid

acrobate /akʀɔbat/ *mf* acrobat

acrobatie /akʀɔbasi/ *f* acrobatics

acronyme /akʀɔnim/ *m* acronym

acrylique /akʀilik/ *adj*, *m* acrylic

acte /akt/ *m* **1** act; **~ manqué** Freudian slip; **être libre de ses ~s** to do as one wishes; **faire ~ de candidature** to put oneself forward as a candidate
2 (Law) deed; **~ de naissance** birth certificate
3 (in play) act

acteur, **-trice** /aktœʀ, tʀis/ *mf* **1** actor/actress
2 protagonist

actif, **-ive** /aktif, iv/ **A** *adj* (gen) active; ‹*market*› buoyant; **la vie active** working life
B *m* **1 l'~** the assets

2 à l'~ de qn in sb's favour (BrE)

🔑 **action** /aksjɔ̃/ *f* **1** action, act; **une bonne ~** a good deed
2 l'~ action; **moyens d'~** courses of action; **en ~** in operation
3 effect; **l'~ de qn sur** sb's influence on
4 ~ en justice legal action
5 (in finance) share

actionnaire /aksjɔnɛʀ/ *mf* shareholder

actionner /aksjɔne/ [**v1**] *vt* to activate

activement /aktivmɑ̃/ *adv* actively

activer /aktive/ [**v1**] **A** *vt* **1** to speed up ‹*work*›; to stimulate ‹*digestion*›
2 ‹*wind*› to stir up ‹*flames*›
3 to stoke ‹*fire*›
B s'activer *v refl* (+ *v être*) (fam) to hurry up

activiste /aktivist/ *adj, mf* activist

🔑 **activité** /aktivite/ *f* **1** activity; **~ professionnelle** occupation
2 être en pleine ~ ‹*street*› to be bustling with activity; ‹*person*› to be very busy; **volcan en ~** active volcano

actrice ▶ **acteur**

actualisation /aktɥalizasjɔ̃/ *f* (process) updating; (result) update

actualiser /aktɥalize/ [**v1**] *vt* to update

actualité /aktɥalite/ **A** *f* **1** current affairs; **l'~ culturelle** cultural events
2 d'~ topical; **toujours d'~** still relevant today
B actualités *fpl* **1** news
2 newsreel

🔑 **actuel, -elle** /aktɥɛl/ *adj* **1** present, current
2 ‹*film, discussion*› topical

🔑 **actuellement** /aktɥɛlmɑ̃/ *adv* **1** at the moment
2 currently

actus /akty/ *fpl* (TV, Radio), (fam) news

acuité /akɥite/ *f* **1** acuity
2 shrillness
3 (of pain) intensity

acupuncteur, -trice /akypɔ̃ktœʀ, tʀis/ *mf* acupuncturist

acupuncture /akypɔ̃ktyʀ/ *f* acupuncture

adage /adaʒ/ *m* saying, adage

adaptable /adaptabl/ *adj* **1** (flexible) adaptable (**à** to)
2 ‹*height, pressure*› adjustable; **~ à toutes les circonstances** *or* **tous les besoins** all-purpose

adaptateur, -trice /adaptatœʀ, tʀis/ **A** *mf* (for cinema, theatre) adapter
B *m* (Tech) adapter

adaptation /adaptasjɔ̃/ *f* adaptation

adapté, ~e /adapte/ *adj* **1** suitable
2 ~ à ‹*solution*› suited to
3 (for TV, stage) adapted

🔑 **adapter** /adapte/ [**v1**] **A** *vt* **1** to fit (**à** to)
2 to adapt ‹*equipment*›
3 to adapt ‹*novel*›
B s'adapter *v refl* (+ *v être*) **1** ‹*tool, part*› to fit
2 to adapt, to adjust (**à** to)

addition /adisjɔ̃/ *f* **1** addition
2 bill (BrE), check (AmE)

additionner /adisjɔne/ [**v1**] *vt* to add up

adduction /adyksjɔ̃/ *f* adduction; **~ d'eau** water conveyance

adepte /adɛpt/ *mf* **1** (of theory) supporter; (of person) disciple
2 enthusiast

adéquat, ~e /adekwa, at/ *adj* **1** appropriate, suitable
2 adequate

adéquation /adekwasjɔ̃/ *f* **1** (correspondence) appropriateness (**à, avec** to)
2 (of model) adequacy (**à** to)

adhérence /adeʀɑ̃s/ *f* (of tyre, sole) grip

adhérent, ~e /adeʀɑ̃, ɑ̃t/ *mf* member

adhérer /adeʀe/ [**v14**] *v+prep* **1 ~ à** ‹*glue*› to stick to; ‹*tyre*› to grip
2 ~ à to join

adhésif, -ive /adezif, iv/ *adj* adhesive

adhésion /adezjɔ̃/ *f* **1** membership
2 support

adieu, *pl* **~x** /adjø/ *m* goodbye, farewell

adipeux, -euse /adipø, øz/ *adj* fatty

adjectif /adʒɛktif/ *m* adjective

adjoint, ~e /adʒwɛ̃, ɛ̃t/ *mf* assistant; deputy; **~ au maire** deputy mayor

adjudant /adʒydɑ̃/ *m* ≈ warrant officer

adjudication /adʒydikasjɔ̃/ *f* auction; **~ judiciaire** sale by order of the court

adjuger /adʒyʒe/ [**v13**] *vt* to auction; **une fois, deux fois, adjugé!** going, going, gone!

adjuvant /adʒyvɑ̃/ *m* additive

ADM /adeɛm/ *fpl* (*abbr* = **armes de destruction massive**) WMD

🔑 **admettre** /admɛtʀ/ [**v60**] *vt* **1** to accept, to admit ‹*fact*›
2 to admit ‹*person, student*›; **être admis à un examen** to pass an exam
3 ~ que to suppose (that)

administrateur, -trice /administʀatœʀ, tʀis/ *mf* **1** administrator
2 director
3 trustee

administratif, -ive /administʀatif, iv/ *adj*
1 ‹*staff, building*› administrative
2 ‹*report*› official

🔑 **administration** /administʀasjɔ̃/ *f*
1 administration
2 civil service
3 être placé sous ~ judiciaire to go into receivership
4 management
5 (of drugs, sacrament) administration, giving

administrer /administʀe/ [**v1**] *vt* **1** to administer ‹*funds*›; to run ‹*company*›
2 to administer, to give ‹*drug, sacrament*›

🔑 key word

admirable /admiʀabl/ *adj* admirable

admirablement /admiʀabləmɑ̃/ *adv* ‹*do*› admirably; ‹*done*› superbly

admirateur, **-trice** /admiʀatœʀ, tʀis/ *mf* admirer

admiration /admiʀasjɔ̃/ *f* admiration

admirer /admiʀe/ [**v1**] *vt* to admire

admis, **~e** /admi, iz/ **A** *pp* ▶ **admettre**
B *pp adj* accepted; ‹*candidate*› successful

admissible /admisibl/ *adj* **1** acceptable
2 eligible

admission /admisjɔ̃/ *f* admission; **service des ~s** reception

ado /adɔ/ *mf* (fam) teenager

adolescence /adɔlesɑ̃s/ *f* adolescence

adolescent, **~e** /adɔlesɑ̃, ɑ̃t/ **A** *adj* teenage
B *mf* teenager, adolescent

adonner: **s'adonner** /adɔne/ [**v1**] *v refl* (+ *v être*) **s'~ à** to devote all one's time to; **il s'adonne à la boisson** he drinks too much

adopter /adɔpte/ [**v1**] *vt* to adopt ‹*child, method*›; to pass ‹*law*›

adoptif, **-ive** /adɔptif, iv/ *adj* **1** ‹*child, country*› adopted
2 ‹*parent*› adoptive

adoption /adɔpsjɔ̃/ *f* **1** adoption
2 passing

adorable /adɔʀabl/ *adj* adorable

adorateur, **-trice** /adɔʀatœʀ, tʀis/ *mf* worshipper (BrE)

adoration /adɔʀasjɔ̃/ *f* worship, adoration

adorer /adɔʀe/ [**v1**] *vt* to adore, to worship

adosser: **s'adosser** /adose/ [**v1**] *v refl* (+ *v être*) **s'~ à** to lean back on

adoucir /adusiʀ/ [**v3**] **A** *vt* to soften ‹*skin, water*›; to moderate ‹*tone of voice*›; to soothe ‹*throat*›; to ease ‹*suffering*›
B **s'adoucir** *v refl* (+ *v être*) ‹*temperature*› to become milder; ‹*slope*› to become more gentle

adoucissant, **~e** /adusisɑ̃, ɑ̃t/ **A** *adj* soothing
B *m* softener

adrénaline /adʀenalin/ *f* adrenalin

adresse /adʀɛs/ *f* **1** address; **se tromper d'~** to get the wrong address; (fig) to pick the wrong person; **remarque lancée à l'~ de qn** remark directed at sb
2 dexterity
3 skill
■ **~ email** email address

adresser /adʀese/ [**v1**] **A** *vt* **1** to direct ‹*criticism*› (**à** at); to make ‹*request, declaration, appeal*›; to deliver ‹*ultimatum*›; to present ‹*petition*›; to aim ‹*blow*›; **~ la parole à qn** to speak to sb
2 to send ‹*letter*›
3 to refer [sb] (**à** to)
B **s'adresser** *v refl* (+ *v être*) **1** **s'~ à qn** to speak to sb
2 **s'~ à** to contact ‹*embassy*›; **s'~ au guichet 8** to go to window 8
3 **s'~ à** ‹*measure*› to be aimed at

adroit, **~e** /adʀwa, at/ *adj* skilful (BrE)

ADSL /adeɛsɛl/ *fpl* (*abbr* = **asymmetrical digital subscriber line**) ADSL

adulte /adylt/ *adj, mf* adult

adultère /adyltɛʀ/ **A** *adj* adulterous
B *m* adultery

advenir /advəniʀ/ [**v36**] *v impers* **1** to happen; **advienne que pourra** come what may
2 **~ de** to become of

adverbe /advɛʀb/ *m* adverb

adversaire /advɛʀsɛʀ/ *mf* (gen) opponent; (Mil) adversary

adverse /advɛʀs/ *adj* **1** opposing
2 opposite

adversité /advɛʀsite/ *f* adversity

aérer /aeʀe/ [**v14**] **A** *vt* **1** to air
2 to space out
B **s'aérer** *v refl* (+ *v être*) to get some fresh air

aérien, **-ienne** /aeʀjɛ̃, ɛn/ *adj* ‹*transport*› air; ‹*photography*› aerial; **métro ~** elevated section of the underground (BrE), elevated railroad (AmE)

aéro-club, *pl* **~s** /aeʀoklœb/ *m* flying club

aérodrome /aeʀodʀom/ *m* aerodrome (BrE), (small) airfield

aérodynamique /aeʀodinamik/ *adj* aerodynamic

aérogare /aeʀogaʀ/ *f* air terminal

aéroglisseur /aeʀoglisœʀ/ *m* hovercraft

aéronautique /aeʀonotik/ *f* aeronautics

aérophagie /aeʀɔfaʒi/ *f* aerophagy

aéroport /aeʀɔpɔʀ/ *m* airport

aéroporté, **~e** /aeʀɔpɔʀte/ *adj* ‹*troops*› airborne; ‹*equipment*› transported by air

aérosol /aeʀɔsɔl/ *m* **1** aerosol
2 spray

aérospatiale /aeʀɔspasjal/ *f* aerospace industry

affabulation /afabylasjɔ̃/ *f* fabrication

affaiblir /afebliʀ/ [**v3**] **A** *vt* to weaken
B **s'affaiblir** *v refl* (+ *v être*) to get weaker

affaiblissement /afeblismɑ̃/ *m* **1** weakening
2 weakened state

affaire /afɛʀ/ **A** *f* **1** affair; (political) crisis, affair; (moral) scandal; (legal) case
2 affair, matter; **une ~ délicate** a delicate matter; **c'est l'~ de quelques jours** it'll only take a few days; **j'en fais mon ~** I'll deal with it; **c'est une autre ~** that's another matter; **c'est une ~ d'argent** there's money involved; **et voilà toute l'~** and that's that; **c'est toute une ~, ce n'est pas une petite ~** it's quite a business
3 (skill, trade) **il connaît bien son ~** he knows his job; **la mécanique, c'est leur ~** mechanics is their thing

4 deal; **faire ~ avec** to do a deal with; **avoir ~ à** to be dealing with
5 bargain; **la belle ~!** (fam) big deal (fam); **ça fera l'~** that'll do
6 business, concern
7 (difficulty) **être tiré d'~** to be out of danger
B **affaires** *fpl* **1** business
2 (personal) business affairs; **occupe-toi de tes ~s!** mind your own business!
3 things, belongings
■ **~s courantes** daily business

affairer: **s'affairer** /afeʀe/ [**v1**] *v refl* (+ *v être*) to bustle about (**à faire** doing)

affairisme /afeʀism/ *m* wheeling and dealing (fam)

affaisser: **s'affaisser** /afese/ [**v1**] *v refl* (+ *v être*) **1** to subside
2 ‹*shoulders, roof*› to sag
3 ‹*person*› to collapse

affaler: **s'affaler** /afale/ [**v1**] *v refl* (+ *v être*)
1 to collapse
2 (fam) to fall

affamé, **~e** /afame/ **A** *pp* ▶ **affamer**
B *pp adj* **1** starving
2 **~ de** hungry for

affamer /afame/ [**v1**] *vt* to starve

affectation /afɛktasjɔ̃/ *f* **1** allocation (**à** to)
2 appointment (**à** to); posting (**à** to)
3 affectation

affecter /afɛkte/ [**v1**] *vt* **1** to feign, to affect ‹*interest*›; to affect ‹*behaviour*›; **~ de faire/d'être** to pretend to do/to be
2 to allocate ‹*funds*› (**à** to)
3 to appoint (**à** to); to post (**à**, **en** to)
4 to affect ‹*market, person*›

affectif, **-ive** /afɛktif, iv/ *adj* **1** emotional
2 affective

affection /afɛksjɔ̃/ *f* **1** affection; **prendre qn en ~** to become fond of sb
2 (Med) disease

affectionner /afɛksjɔne/ [**v1**] *vt* to be fond of

affectivité /afɛktivite/ *f* feelings

affectueusement /afɛktɥøzmɑ̃/ *adv* affectionately, fondly

affectueux, **-euse** /afɛktɥø, øz/ *adj* affectionate

affermir /afɛʀmiʀ/ [**v3**] **A** *vt* to strengthen ‹*will*›; to consolidate ‹*power*›; to firm up ‹*muscles*›
B **s'affermir** *v refl* (+ *v être*) ‹*power*› to be consolidated; ‹*voice*› to become stronger; ‹*muscles*› to firm up; ‹*ground*› to become firmer

affermissement /afɛʀmismɑ̃/ *m* (of power, recovery) consolidation; (of will, muscles, voice) strengthening; (economic) improvement (**de** in)

affichage /afiʃaʒ/ *m* **1** billsticking; **campagne d'~** poster campaign
2 (Comput) display
■ **~ à cristaux liquides** liquid crystal display, LCD

affiche /afiʃ/ *f* poster; (official) notice; **à l'~** ‹*film*› now showing; ‹*play*› on; **quitter l'~** to come off
■ **~ de théâtre** playbill

affiché, **~e** /afiʃe/ **A** *pp* ▶ **afficher**
B *pp adj* **1** ‹*ad, picture*› (put) up; ‹*information*› posted (up)
2 ‹*result*› published
3 ‹*optimism, opinion*› declared
4 (Comput) ‹*data*› displayed

afficher /afiʃe/ [**v1**] **A** *vt* **1** to put up ‹*poster, notice*›
2 to display ‹*prices, result*›; **~ complet** ‹*film, play*› to be sold out; ‹*hotel*› to be fully booked
3 ‹*market*› to show ‹*rise*›
4 to declare ‹*ambitions*›; to display ‹*scorn*›; to flaunt ‹*opinions, liaison*›
B **s'afficher** *v refl* (+ *v être*) **1** to flaunt oneself
2 ‹*smile*› to appear (**sur** on)

afficheur /afiʃœʀ/ *m* **1** poster (BrE) *or* billboard (AmE) sticker
2 (Comput) visual display unit, VDU

affichiste /afiʃist/ *mf* poster artist

affilé, **~e** /afile/ *adj* ‹*blade*› sharpened

affilée: **d'affilée** /dafile/ *phr* in a row

affiler /afile/ [**v1**] *vt* to sharpen

affilier: **s'affilier** /afilje/ [**v2**] *v refl* (+ *v être*) to become affiliated

affiner /afine/ [**v1**] **A** *vt* **1** to hone ‹*style*›
2 to slim down ‹*waistline*›
B **s'affiner** *v refl* (+ *v être*) **1** ‹*style, taste*› to become (more) refined
2 ‹*waistline*› to slim down

affinité /afinite/ *f* affinity

affirmatif, **-ive** /afiʀmatif, iv/ *adj* affirmative; **faire un signe de tête ~** to nod agreement

affirmation /afiʀmasjɔ̃/ *f* assertion; **l'~ de soi** assertiveness

affirmative /afiʀmativ/ **A** *adj f* ▶ **affirmatif**
B *f* affirmative

🔑 **affirmer** /afiʀme/ [**v1**] **A** *vt* **1** to maintain; **~ faire** to claim to do
2 to assert ‹*talent, authority*›
3 to declare, to affirm ‹*will*›
B **s'affirmer** *v refl* (+ *v être*) ‹*tendency*› to become apparent; ‹*personality*› to assert itself

affleurer /aflœʀe/ [**v1**] *vi* ‹*reef*› to show on the surface; ‹*rock*› to come through the soil

affligeant, **~e** /afliʒɑ̃, ɑ̃t/ *adj* pathetic

affliger /afliʒe/ [**v13**] *vt* **1** to afflict (**de** with)
2 to distress

affluence /aflyɑ̃s/ *f* crowd(s)

affluent /aflyɑ̃/ *m* tributary

affluer /aflye/ [**v1**] *vi* ‹*people*› to flock (**à**, **vers** to); ‹*letters*› to pour in

affolant, **~e** /afɔlɑ̃, ɑ̃t/ *adj* (fam) frightening

🔑 key word

affolement /afɔlmɑ̃/ *m* panic

affoler /afɔle/ [**v1**] **A** *vt* to throw [sb] into a panic
B s'affoler *v refl* (+ *v être*) to panic

affranchi, **~e** /afʀɑ̃ʃi/ *mf* emancipated slave

affranchir /afʀɑ̃ʃiʀ/ [**v3**] **A** *vt* **1** to stamp ‹*letter*›
2 to free ‹*slave, country*›
B s'affranchir *v refl* (+ *v être*) to free oneself

affranchissement /afʀɑ̃ʃismɑ̃/ *m*
1 stamping; (cost) postage
2 liberation; freeing

affres /afʀ/ *fpl* (of pain) agony; (of hunger) pangs; (of jealousy) throes; **les ~ de la mort** death throes

affréter /afʀete/ [**v14**] *vt* to charter

affréteur /afʀetœʀ/ *m* charter company

affreusement /afʀøzmɑ̃/ *adv* (fam) terribly

affreux, **-euse** /afʀø, øz/ *adj* **1** hideous
2 awful, dreadful

affront /afʀɔ̃/ *m* affront

affrontement /afʀɔ̃tmɑ̃/ *m* confrontation

affronter /afʀɔ̃te/ [**v1**] *vt* to face ‹*situation*›; to brave ‹*weather*›

affubler /afyble/ [**v1**] *vt* **~ qn de** to deck sb out in ‹*clothes*›; to saddle sb with ‹*nickname*›

affût /afy/ *m* **se tenir** *or* **être à l'~** to lie in wait; (fig) to be on the lookout (**de** for)

affûter /afyte/ [**v1**] *vt* **1** to sharpen
2 to grind

afin /afɛ̃/ **A afin de** *phr* **~ de faire** in order to do
B afin que *phr* so that

AFP /aɛfpe/ *f* (*abbr* = **Agence France-Presse**) AFP (*French news agency*)

africain, **~e** /afʀikɛ̃, ɛn/ *adj* African

Afrique /afʀik/ *pr f* Africa

AG /aʒe/ *f*: *abbr* ▶ **assemblée**

agaçant, **~e** /agasɑ̃, ɑ̃t/ *adj* annoying

agacement /agasmɑ̃/ *m* irritation

agacer /agase/ [**v12**] *vt* to annoy, to irritate

agapes /agap/ *fpl* feast, banquet

agate /agat/ *f* **1** agate
2 marble

âge /ɑʒ/ *m* **1** age; **faire son ~** to look one's age; **un homme d'un certain ~** a middle-aged man
2 old age; **avec l'~** as one gets older; **prendre de l'~** to grow old
3 age, era
■ **l'~ bête** *or* **ingrat** the awkward *or* difficult age; **l'~ mûr** maturity

âgé, **~e** /ɑʒe/ *adj* old

agence /aʒɑ̃s/ *f* **1** agency
2 (of bank) branch
■ **~ immobilière** estate agents (BrE), real estate agency (AmE); **Agence nationale pour l'emploi, ANPE** *French national employment agency*; **~ de placement** employment agency

agencer /aʒɑ̃se/ [**v12**] *vt* to lay out ‹*room*›

agenda /aʒɛ̃da/ *m* diary

agenouiller: **s'agenouiller** /aʒnuje/ [**v1**] *v refl* (+ *v être*) to kneel (down)

agent /aʒɑ̃/ *m* **1** officer, official
2 agent
3 employee
■ **~ de change** stockbroker; **~ de la circulation** traffic policeman; **~ commercial** sales representative; **~ de police** policeman

agglomération /aglɔmeʀasjɔ̃/ *f* town; village; **l'~ lyonnaise** Lyons and its suburbs

aggloméré /aglɔmeʀe/ *m* chipboard

agglomérer /aglɔmeʀe/ [**v14**] **A** *vt* to agglomerate
B s'agglomérer *v refl* (+ *v être*) ‹*people*› to gather together; ‹*houses*› to be grouped together

agglutiner: **s'agglutiner** /aglytine/ [**v1**] *v refl* (+ *v être*) ‹*onlookers*› to crowd together (**à** at); ‹*insects*› to cluster together

aggravation /agʀavasjɔ̃/ *f* (of situation) worsening; (in debt) increase

aggraver /agʀave/ [**v1**] **A** *vt* to aggravate, to make [sth] worse
B s'aggraver *v refl* (+ *v être*) to get worse

agile /aʒil/ *adj* agile, nimble

agilité /aʒilite/ *f* agility

agios /aʒjo/ *mpl* bank charges

agir /aʒiʀ/ [**v3**] **A** *vi* **1** to act
2 to behave; **~ en lâche** to act like a coward
3 ‹*medicine*› to take effect, to work
B s'agir de *v impers* (+ *v être*) **de quoi s'agit-il?** what is it about?; **il s'agit de votre mari** it's about your husband; **mais il ne s'agit pas de ça!** but that's not the point!; **il s'agit de faire vite** we must act quickly

âgisme /ɑʒism/ *m* ageism

agissements /aʒismɑ̃/ *mpl* activities

agitateur, **-trice** /aʒitatœʀ, tʀis/ *mf* agitator

agitation /aʒitasjɔ̃/ *f* **1** restlessness
2 bustle (**de** in); activity
3 unrest

agité, **~e** /aʒite/ *adj* **1** ‹*sea*› rough, choppy; ‹*sleep*› troubled; ‹*period*› turbulent; ‹*night*› restless
2 ‹*street*› bustling; ‹*life*› hectic

agiter /aʒite/ [**v1**] **A** *vt* to wave ‹*hand*›; to shake ‹*can*›; to shake up ‹*liquid*›
B s'agiter *v refl* (+ *v être*) **1** to fidget; (in bed) to toss and turn
2 to sway (in the wind)
3 to bustle about
4 to become restless

agneau, *pl* **~x** /aɲo/ *m* **1** lamb
2 lambskin

agonie /agɔni/ *f* death throes

agonir /agɔniʀ/ [**v3**] *vt* **~ qn d'injures** to hurl insults at sb; **en rentrant, il s'est fait ~** when he got home he was told off soundly

agoniser /agɔnize/ [**v1**] *vi* to be dying

agrafe /agʀaf/ *f* **1** (for paper) staple
2 (on waistband, bra) hook
3 (Med) skin clip

agrafer /agʀafe/ [**v1**] *vt* **1** to staple [sth] (together)
2 to fasten

agrafeuse /agʀaføz/ *f* stapler

agraire /agʀɛʀ/ *adj* agrarian; **réforme ~** land reform

agrandir /agʀɑ̃diʀ/ [**v3**] **A** *vt* **1** to enlarge ‹*town, photo*›; to extend ‹*house*›
2 to expand ‹*organization*›
B **s'agrandir** *v refl* (+ *v être*) ‹*hole*› to get bigger; ‹*town, family*› to expand; ‹*eyes*› to widen

agrandissement /agʀɑ̃dismɑ̃/ *m* enlargement

agréable /agʀeabl/ *adj* nice, pleasant; **~ à vivre** ‹*person*› pleasant to be with

agréer /agʀee/ [**v11**] *vt* **1** to agree to ‹*request*›; **veuillez ~ mes salutations distinguées** yours faithfully; yours sincerely
2 to register ‹*taxi, doctor*›; **agent agréé** authorized dealer

agrégat /agʀega/ *m* aggregate; (fig) jumble

agrégation /agʀegasjɔ̃/ *f*: *high-level competitive examination for the recruitment of teachers*

agrément /agʀemɑ̃/ *m* **1** charm; **plein d'~** very pleasant; full of charm; **sans ~** dull; unattractive; cheerless; **voyage d'~** pleasure trip
2 (by official body) approval

agrémenter /agʀemɑ̃te/ [**v1**] *vt* to liven up ‹*story*›; to brighten up ‹*garden*›

agrès /agʀɛ/ *mpl* (Sport) apparatus

agresser /agʀese/ [**v1**] *vt* **1** to attack
2 to mug
3 to be aggressive with

agresseur /agʀesœʀ/ *m* **1** attacker
2 (in war) aggressor

agressif, **-ive** /agʀesif, iv/ *adj* **1** aggressive
2 violent; ear-splitting; harsh

agression /agʀesjɔ̃/ *f* **1** attack
2 mugging
3 act of aggression

agressivité /agʀesivite/ *f* aggressiveness, aggression

agricole /agʀikɔl/ *adj* **produit ~** farm produce; **coopérative ~** farming cooperative

agriculteur, **-trice** /agʀikyltœʀ, tʀis/ *mf* farmer

agriculture /agʀikyltyʀ/ *f* farming

agripper /agʀipe/ [**v1**] **A** *vt* to grab
B **s'agripper** *v refl* (+ *v être*) to cling (à to)

agro-alimentaire, *pl* **~s** /agʀoalimɑ̃tɛʀ/ *adj* food processing

agrocarburant /agʀokaʀbyʀɑ̃/ *m* biofuel

agrochimie /agʀoʃimi/ *f* agro-chemistry

agronomie /agʀɔnɔmi/ *f* agronomy

agrume /agʀym/ *m* citrus fruit

aguerrir /ageʀiʀ/ [**v3**] **A** *vt* to harden ‹*person*›
B **s'aguerrir** *v refl* (+ *v être*) to become hardened

aguets: **aux aguets** /ozagɛ/ *phr* **être aux ~** to be on one's guard

aguicher /agiʃe/ [**v1**] *vt* to lead [sb] on

aguicheur, **-euse** /agiʃœʀ, øz/ *adj* alluring

ah /ɑ/ *excl* oh!; **~ oui?**, **~ bon?** really?

ahuri, **~e** /ayʀi/ *adj* **1** dazed
2 stunned

ahurissant, **~e** /ayʀisɑ̃, ɑ̃t/ *adj* ‹*news, strength*› incredible; ‹*figure*› staggering

ai /ɛ/ ▶ **avoir**[1]

aide[1] /ɛd/ **A** *mf* assistant
B **aide-** (*combining form*) **~-soignant** nursing auxiliary (BrE), nurse's aide (AmE)
■ **~ à domicile** carer, home help; **~ familiale** mother's help

aide[2] /ɛd/ *f* **1** (from individual, group) help, assistance; (from state) assistance; **apporter son ~ à qn** to help sb
2 (financial) aid; **~ au développement** foreign aid; **~ judiciaire** legal aid
■ **~ en ligne** online help

aide-éducateur, **-trice** /ɛdedykatœʀ, tʀis/ *mf* classroom assistant

Aïd el-Fitr /aidɛlfitʀ/ *m* Eid ul-Fitr

Aïd el-Kebir /aidɛlkebiʀ/ *m* Eid al-Adha

aider /ede/ [**v1**] **A** *vt* **1** to help (**à faire** to do)
2 to aid; to give aid to
B **aider à** *v+prep* to help toward(s) ‹*understanding, funding*›
C **s'aider** *v refl* (+ *v être*) **1 s'~ de** to use ‹*dictionary, tool*›
2 to help each other

aie /ɛ/ ▶ **avoir**[1]

aïe /ɑj/ *excl* (in pain) ouch!; (in concern) **~ (~ ~), que se passe-t-il?** oh dear, what's going on?; (in anticipation) **~ ~ ~!...** oh *no*!...

aient /ɛ/ ▶ **avoir**[1]

aies /ɛ/ ▶ **avoir**[1]

aïeul, **~e** /ɑjœl/ *mf* grandfather/ grandmother

aïeux /ɑjø/ *mpl* ancestors

aigle /ɛgl/ *m, f* eagle

aiglefin /ɛgləfɛ̃/ *m* haddock

aigre /ɛgʀ/ *adj* ‹*smell, taste*› sour

aigre-doux, **-douce**, *pl* **aigres-doux**, **aigres-douces** /ɛgʀədu, dus/ *adj* (Culin) ‹*fruit, taste*› bitter-sweet; ‹*sauce*› sweet and sour

aigrette /ɛgʀɛt/ *f* (Zool) (bird) egret; (plumes) crest

aigreur /ɛgʀœʀ/ *f* **1** sourness; sharpness
2 **~s d'estomac** heartburn
3 (fig) bitterness

key word

aigrir /egRiR/ [**v3**] *vt* to embitter

aigu, **aiguë** /egy/ **A** *adj* **1** ‹*sound, voice*› high-pitched
2 ‹*pain, symptom*› acute
3 ‹*sense*› keen
B *m* (Mus) treble; high notes

aigue-marine, *pl* **aigues-marines** /ɛgmaRin/ *f* aquamarine

aiguillage /egɥijaʒ/ *m* (for trains) points (BrE), switch (AmE); **une erreur d'~** a signalling (BrE) error

aiguille /egɥij/ *f* **1** needle; **~ à coudre** sewing needle
2 (of watch, chronometer) hand; (of gauge) needle; (of weighing scales) pointer; **dans le sens des ~s d'une montre** clockwise

aiguiller /egɥije/ [**v1**] *vt* **1** to direct ‹*person*›; to send ‹*mail*›
2 (towards career) to guide ‹*person*›

aiguilleur /egɥijœR/ *m* **~ du ciel** air traffic controller

aiguillonner /egɥijɔne/ [**v1**] *vt* **1** to spur ‹*person*›; to stimulate ‹*ambition*›; **la faim m'aiguillonnant...** driven by hunger...
2 to goad ‹*ox*›

aiguiser /egize/ [**v1**] *vt* **1** to sharpen ‹*knife*›
2 to whet ‹*appetite*›; to arouse ‹*curiosity*›

aiguiseur /egizœR/ *m* knife grinder

ail, *pl* **~s** *or* **aulx** /aj, o/ *m* garlic

aile /ɛl/ *f* (gen) wing; (of windmill) sail; (of car) wing (BrE), fender (AmE); (of army) flank
IDIOMS **battre de l'~** to be in a bad way; **se sentir pousser des ~s** to feel exhilarated; **prendre un coup dans l'~** to suffer a setback; **voler de ses propres ~s** to stand on one's own two feet

aileron /ɛlRɔ̃/ *m* (of bird) wing tip; (of shark) fin; (of plane) aileron; (of ship) fin

ailier /elje/ *m* (in football) winger; (in rugby) wing three-quarter

ailleurs /ajœR/ **A** *adv* elsewhere
B **d'ailleurs** *phr* besides, moreover
C **par ailleurs** *phr* **ils se sont par ~ engagés à faire** they have also undertaken to do
IDIOM **être ~** to be miles away

aimable /ɛmabl/ *adj* **1** ‹*word*› kind
2 ‹*remark*› polite

aimablement /ɛmabləmɑ̃/ *adv* politely; kindly

aimant, **~e** /ɛmɑ̃, ɑ̃t/ **A** *pp* ▸ **aimer**
B *pp adj* affectionate
C *m* magnet

aimé, **~e** /eme/ ▸ **aimer**

aimer /eme/ [**v1**] **A** *vt* **1** to love ‹*person*›; **~ qn à la folie** to adore sb
2 to like, to be fond of ‹*person, activity, thing*›; **~ faire** to like doing; **il aime autant le vin que la bière** he likes wine as much as he likes beer; **j'aime autant te dire que** I may as well tell you that; **~ mieux** to prefer; **il n'a rien de cassé? j'aime mieux ça!** (in relief) nothing's broken? thank goodness!; **j'aime mieux ça!** (threateningly) that's more like it!
B **s'aimer** *v refl* (+ *v être*) **1** to love each other
2 to like each other

aine /ɛn/ *f* groin

aîné, **~e** /ene/ **A** *adj* elder; eldest
B *mf* **1** elder son/daughter, elder child
2 eldest son/daughter, eldest child
3 elder brother/sister
4 elder; oldest

ainsi /ɛ̃si/ **A** *adv* **1** thus; **le mélange ~ obtenu** the mixture obtained in this way; **Charlotte, c'est ~ qu'on m'appelait** Charlotte, that's what they used to call me; **s'il en est ~** if that's the way it is; **le jury se compose ~** the panel is made up as follows; **~ soit-il** amen
2 thus, so
B **ainsi que** *phr* **1** as well as
2 as; **~ que nous en avions convenu** as we had agreed

air /ɛR/ *m* **1** air; **le bon ~** clean air; **concert en plein ~** open-air concert; **activités de plein ~** outdoor activities; **aller prendre l'~** to go and get some fresh air; **on manque d'~ ici** it's stuffy in here; **être dans l'~** ‹*reform, idea*› to be in the air; **regarder en l'~** to look up; **avoir le nez en l'~** to daydream; **en l'~** ‹*threat, words*› empty; ‹*plan, idea*› vague; **tout mettre en l'~** (fam) to make a dreadful mess; **de l'~!** (fam) get lost (fam)
2 **il y a de l'~** (in room) there's a draught (BrE) *or* draft (AmE); (outside) there's a breeze; **il n'y a pas d'~** there's no wind; **un courant d'~** a draught (BrE) *or* draft (AmE)
3 manner; expression; **avoir un drôle d'~** to look odd; **d'un ~ fâché** angrily; **il y a un ~ de famille entre vous deux** you two share a family likeness; **cela m'en a tout l'~** it seems like it to me; **j'aurais l'~ de quoi?** I'd look a right idiot!; **cela a l'~ d'être une usine** it looks like a factory; **il a l'~ de vouloir faire beau** it looks as if it's going to be fine
4 tune; **un ~ d'opéra** an aria
IDIOMS **il ne manque pas d'~!** (fam) he's got a nerve!; **se donner de grands ~s** to put on airs; **j'ai besoin de changer d'~** I need a change of scene

aire /ɛR/ *f* **1** (surface) area
2 eyrie
■ **~ d'atterrissage** (for plane) landing strip; (for helicopter) landing pad; **~ de jeu** playground; **~ de services** motorway (BrE) *or* freeway (AmE) service station; **~ de stationnement** parking area

airelle /ɛRɛl/ *f* **1** bilberry
2 cranberry

aisance /ɛzɑ̃s/ *f* **1** ease
2 affluence, comfort

aise /ɛz/ **A** **aises** *fpl* **aimer ses ~s** to like one's creature comforts; **il prenait ses ~s**

a

sur le canapé he was stretched out on the sofa
B à l'aise *phr* **être à l'~** *or* **à son ~** (physically) to be comfortable; (financially) to be comfortably off; (psychologically) to be at ease; **mal à l'~** ill at ease; **à votre ~!** as you wish *or* like!

aisé, ~e /eze/ *adj* **1** easy
2 wealthy

aisément /ezemɑ̃/ *adv* easily

aisselle /ɛsɛl/ *f* armpit

ait /ɛ/ ▶ **avoir**[1]

Aix-la-Chapelle /ɛkslaʃapɛl/ *pr n* Aachen

ajonc /aʒɔ̃/ *m* gorse bush

ajouré, ~e /aʒuʀe/ *adj* ‹*tablecloth*› openwork; ‹*edge, border*› hemstitched

ajournement /aʒuʀnəmɑ̃/ *m* (of decision) postponement; (of trial) adjournment

ajourner /aʒuʀne/ [**v1**] *vt* to postpone ‹*decision, plan*›; to adjourn ‹*debate, trial*›

ajout /aʒu/ *m* addition
■ **~ de mémoire** memory upgrade

🗝 **ajouter** /aʒute/ [**v1**] **A** *vt* to add (**à** to)
B s'ajouter *v refl* (+ *v être*) **s'~ à** to be added to

ajustement /aʒystəmɑ̃/ *m* **1** (Tech) fit
2 adjustment; **~ des prix** price adjustment

ajuster /aʒyste/ [**v1**] *vt* **1** to adjust ‹*strap, price, timetable*›; to alter ‹*garment*› (**à** to); to calibrate ‹*weighing scales*›; **~ qch à** *or* **sur qch** to make sth fit sth; **corsage ajusté** close-fitting bodice
2 to arrange ‹*hair*›; to straighten ‹*hat, tie*›
3 ~ son tir to adjust one's aim

ajusteur /aʒystœʀ/ *m* fitter

alaise ▶ **alèse**

alambic /alɑ̃bik/ *m* still

alambiqué, ~e /alɑ̃bike/ *adj* ‹*expression, style*› convoluted; ‹*explanation*› tortuous

alangui, ~e /alɑ̃gi/ *adj* **1** languid
2 listless

alarmant, ~e /alaʀmɑ̃, ɑ̃t/ *adj* alarming

alarme /alaʀm/ *f* alarm

alarmer /alaʀme/ [**v1**] **A** *vt* to alarm
B s'alarmer *v refl* (+ *v être*) to become alarmed (**de qch** about sth)

albanais, ~e /albanɛ, ɛz/ **A** *adj* Albanian
B *m* (language) Albanian

Albanie /albani/ *pr f* Albania

albâtre /albɑtʀ/ *m* alabaster

albatros /albatʀos/ *m inv* albatross

albinos /albinos/ *adj inv*, *mf inv* albino

album /albɔm/ *m* **1** illustrated book; **~ de bandes dessinées** comic strip book
2 album
■ **~ à colorier** colouring (BrE) book

albumine /albymin/ *f* albumin

alchimie /alʃimi/ *f* alchemy

🗝 key word

alcool /alkɔl/ *m* **1** alcohol; **~ de poire** pear brandy; **teneur en ~** alcohol content
2 drink; **l'~ au volant** drink-driving
3 un ~ a spirit
■ **~ à brûler** methylated spirits; **~ à 90°** ≈ surgical spirit (BrE), rubbing alcohol (AmE)

alcoolémie /alkɔlemi/ *f* presence of alcohol in the blood

alcoolique /alkɔlik/ *adj*, *mf* alcoholic

alcoolisé, ~e /alkɔlize/ *adj* alcoholic

alcoolisme /alkɔlism/ *m* alcoholism

alcootest /alkɔtɛst/ *m* **1** Breathalyzer®
2 breath test

alcôve /alkov/ *f* alcove

aléas /alea/ *mpl* vagaries; (financial) hazards

aléatoire /aleatwaʀ/ *adj* **1** ‹*events*› unpredictable; ‹*profession*› insecure
2 ‹*number*› random

alentours /alɑ̃tuʀ/ *mpl* surrounding area

alerte /alɛʀt/ **A** *adj* alert; lively
B *f* alert; **donner l'~** to raise the alarm; **~ générale** full alert
■ **~ à la bombe** bomb scare

alerter /alɛʀte/ [**v1**] *vt* to alert (**sur** to)

alèse /alɛz/ *f* undersheet, mattress protector

alexandrin /alɛksɑ̃dʀɛ̃/ *adj m*, *m* alexandrine

algèbre /alʒɛbʀ/ *f* algebra

Algérie /alʒeʀi/ *pr f* Algeria

algérien, -ienne /alʒeʀjɛ̃, ɛn/ *adj* Algerian

algue /alg/ *f* **1 des ~s** algae
2 seaweed

alias **A** *m* (Comput) alias
B *adv* alias

alibi /alibi/ *m* **1** (Law) alibi
2 excuse

aliénation /aljenasjɔ̃/ *f* alienation

aliéné, ~e /aljene/ *mf* insane person

alignement /aliɲ(ə)mɑ̃/ *m* **1** row, line
2 alignment
3 ~ de qch sur qch ‹*currency, salaries*› bringing into line of sth with sth

aligner /aliɲe/ [**v1**] **A** *vt* **1** to line [sth] up
2 ~ qch sur qch to bring sth into line with sth
3 to give a list of ‹*figures*›
4 to line up ‹*players*›
B s'aligner *v refl* (+ *v être*) **1** ‹*houses, trees*› to be in a line
2 ‹*people*› to line up
3 s'~ sur to align oneself with ‹*country, party, ideas*›

aliment /alimɑ̃/ *m* (gen) food; (for farm animals) feed; (for plants) nutrient

alimentaire /alimɑ̃tɛʀ/ *adj* ‹*needs, habits*› dietary; ‹*industry, shortage*› food; **régime ~** diet

alimentation /alimɑ̃tasjɔ̃/ *f* **1** diet
2 feeding
3 food; **magasin d'~** food shop
4 food industry

5 supply, feeding; **l'~ en eau** the water supply

alimenter /alimɑ̃te/ [**v1**] **A** *vt* **1** to feed ‹*person, animal*›
2 to feed, to supply ‹*engine, boiler*›
3 to fuel ‹*conversation, hostility*›
B s'alimenter *v refl* (+ *v être*) **1** ‹*person*› to eat; ‹*animal*› to feed
2 (with water, gas) **s'~ en** to be supplied with

alinéa /alinea/ *m* **1** indentation
2 indented line
3 paragraph

alité, **~e** /alite/ *adj* **être ~** to be confined to bed

alla /ala/ ▶ **aller**[1]

allai /alɛ/ ▶ **aller**[1]

allaient /alɛ/ ▶ **aller**[1]

allais /alɛ/ ▶ **aller**[1]

allait /alɛ/ ▶ **aller**[1]

allaitement /alɛtmɑ̃/ *m* **1** breast-feeding
2 suckling

allaiter /alete/ [**v1**] *vt* **1** to breast-feed
2 to suckle

allâmes /alɑm/ ▶ **aller**[1]

allant, **~e** /alɑ̃, ɑ̃t/ **A** *pp* ▶ **aller**[1]
B *adj* active, lively
C *m* drive, bounce; **avoir de l'~, être plein d'~** to have plenty of drive, to be full of bounce; **perdre son ~** to run out of steam

allâtes /alɑt/ ▶ **aller**[1]

allé, **~e** /ale/ ▶ **aller**[1]

allécher /aleʃe/ [**v14**] *vt* to tempt (**avec** with)

allée /ale/ **A** *f* **1** (in garden, wood) path; (leading to house) drive; (in town) avenue
2 aisle
B allées *fpl* **~s et venues** comings and goings

allégé, **~e** /aleʒe/ **A** *pp* ▶ **alléger**
B *pp adj* low-fat; ‹*chocolate*› diet

allégeance /aleʒɑ̃s/ *f* allegiance

allégement /alɛʒmɑ̃/ *m* (of charges) reduction; (of restrictions, controls) relaxing; **~ fiscal** tax relief

alléger /aleʒe/ [**v15**] **A** *vt* **1** to lighten ‹*load, weight*›
2 to reduce ‹*debt*› (**de** by); to cut ‹*taxes*›; to relax ‹*control, restrictions*›
B s'alléger *v refl* (+ *v être*) **1** ‹*load*› to get lighter
2 ‹*debt, taxation*› to be reduced; ‹*embargo*› to be relaxed

allégorie /alegɔʀi/ *f* allegory

allègre /alɛgʀ/ *adj* ‹*style*› light; ‹*tone*› light-hearted; ‹*step, mood*› buoyant

allégrement /alegʀəmɑ̃/ *adv* joyfully; (ironic) blithely

allégresse /alegʀɛs/ *f* joy

allegro /alegʀo/ *adv* allegro

alléguer /alege/ [**v14**] *vt* **1** to invoke
2 to allege

Allemagne /almaɲ/ *pr f* Germany

allemand, **~e** /almɑ̃, ɑ̃d/ **A** *adj* German
B *m* (language) German

aller[1] /ale/ [**v9**] **A** *v aux* **je vais apprendre l'italien** I'm going to learn Italian; **j'allais partir quand il est arrivé** I was about to leave when he arrived; **il est allé voir l'exposition** he went to see the exhibition; **va leur parler** go and speak to them
B *vi* (+ *v être*) **1 comment vas-tu, comment ça va?** how are you?; **ça va (bien)** I'm fine; **~ beaucoup mieux** to be much better; **bois ça, ça ira mieux** drink this, you'll feel better; **les affaires vont bien** business is good; **qu'est-ce qui ne va pas?** what's the matter?; **ne pas ~ sans peine** *or* **mal** not to be easy; **ça devrait ~ de soi** it should be obvious; **ça va pas non?** (fam), **ça va pas la tête?** (fam) are you crazy? (fam)
2 to go; **où vas-tu?** where are you going?; **~ nager/au travail** to go swimming/to work; **vas-y, demande-leur!** go on, ask them!; **allons-y!** let's go!; **allons!, allez!** come on!; **~ et venir** to pace up and down; to run in and out; **les nouvelles vont vite** news travels fast; **j'y vais** (answering phone, door) I'll get it; (when leaving) (fam) I'm off (fam); **~ contre la loi** to break the law; to be against the law
3 ça va, ça ira (fam), **ça peut aller** (fam) that'll do; it'll do; **ça va comme ça** it's all right as it is; **ça ne va pas du tout** that's no good at all; **lundi ça (te) va?** would Monday suit you?
4 ~ à qn to fit sb
5 ~ à qn to suit sb; **ta cravate ne va pas avec ta chemise** your tie doesn't go with your shirt
6 ~ jusqu'à tuer to go as far as to kill; **la voiture peut ~ jusqu'à 200 km/h** the car can do up to 200 km/h; **la période qui va de 1918 à 1939** the period between 1918 and 1939; **~ sur ses 17 ans** to be going on 17
7 y ~ de sa petite larme to shed a little tear
C s'en aller *v refl* (+ *v être*) **1 s'en aller** to go, to leave, to be off; to go away
2 la tache ne s'en va pas the stain won't come out
3 (fml) to pass away, to die
D *v impers* **1 il y va de ma réputation** my reputation is at stake
2 il en va de même pour toi that goes for you too

aller[2] /ale/ *m* **1 j'ai pris le bus à l'~** I took the bus there; I took the bus here; **il n'arrête pas de faire des ~s et retours entre chez lui et son bureau** he's always going to and fro between the house and the office
2 ~ (simple) single (ticket) (BrE), one-way ticket (**pour** to); **~ retour** return ticket, round trip (AmE)
3 (Sport) **(match) ~** first leg

allèrent /alɛʀ/ ▶ **aller**[1]

allergie /alɛʀʒi/ *f* (Med) allergy

allergique /alɛʀʒik/ *adj* allergic (**à** to)

allergologue /alɛʀgɔlɔg/ *mf* allergist

aller-retour /aleʀ(ə)tuʀ/ *m* return ticket

a

allez /ale/ ▶ **aller**[1]
alliage /aljaʒ/ *m* **1** alloy
2 (fig) combination
alliance /aljɑ̃s/ *f* **1** wedding ring
2 alliance
allié, **~e** /alje/ **A** *pp* ▶ **allier**
B *pp adj* allied
C *mf* **1** ally; **les ~s** the Allies
2 relative
allier /alje/ [**v2**] **A** *vt* **1** to combine (**et, à** with)
2 (Tech) to alloy ‹*metals*› (**à, avec** with)
B s'allier *v refl* (+ *v être*) to form an alliance
alliez /alje/ ▶ **aller**[1]
alligator /aligatɔʀ/ *m* alligator
allions /aljɔ̃/ ▶ **aller**[1]
allô /alo/ *excl* hello!, hallo!
allocation /al(l)ɔkasjɔ̃/ *f* **1** allocation, granting
2 benefit (BrE), benefits (AmE)
■ **~ chômage** unemployment benefit (BrE) *or* benefits (AmE); **~s familiales** family allowance
allocution /al(l)ɔkysjɔ̃/ *f* address
allongé, **~e** /alɔ̃ʒe/ *adj* **1 être ~** ‹*person*› to be lying down; to be reclining
2 elongated
allonger /alɔ̃ʒe/ [**v13**] **A** *vt* **1** to lay [sb] down
2 to extend ‹*list, holiday*›; **cette coiffure t'allonge le visage** that hairstyle makes your face look longer
3 to water [sth] down ‹*coffee*›
B s'allonger *v refl* (+ *v être*) **1** to lie down
2 to get longer
allons /alɔ̃/ ▶ **aller**[1]
allouer /alwe/ [**v1**] *vt* to allocate ‹*sum, allowance, budget*›; to grant ‹*loan*›; to allot ‹*time*›
allumage /alymaʒ/ *m* (Aut) ignition
allumé, **~e** /alyme/ *adj* (fam) **1** mad (fam)
2 tipsy (fam)
allume-gaz /alymgaz/ *m inv* gas lighter
allumer /alyme/ [**v1**] **A** *vt* **1** to light ‹*candle, gas*›; to start ‹*fire*›
2 to switch [sth] on, to turn [sth] on; **laisser ses phares allumés** to leave one's headlights on
B s'allumer *v refl* (+ *v être*) **1** ‹*heating, radio, lighting*› to come on
2 son regard s'alluma his face lit up
allumette /alymɛt/ *f* match, matchstick
allumeur, **-euse** /alymœʀ, øz/ *mf* (fam) tease
allure /alyʀ/ *f* **1** (of walker) pace; (of vehicle) speed; **ralentir son ~** to slow down; **à toute ~** at top speed; **à cette ~** at this rate
2 (of animal) gait
3 (of person) appearance
4 style; **avoir de l'~** to have style
allusif, **-ive** /alyzif, iv/ *adj* ‹*remark*› allusive; ‹*person*› indirect
allusion /alyzjɔ̃/ *f* allusion (**à** to); **faire ~ à** to allude to
alluvial, **~e**, *mpl* **-iaux** /alyvjal, o/ *adj* alluvial
alluvion /alyvjɔ̃/ *f* alluvium; **des ~s** alluvia
almanach /almana(k)/ *m* almanac
aloi /alwɑ/ *m* **un succès de bon ~** a well-deserved success; **une plaisanterie de mauvais ~** a tasteless joke; **une gaieté de bon ~** a simple cheerfulness
⚷ **alors** /alɔʀ/ **A** *adv* **1** then; **il avait ~ 18 ans** he was 18 at the time; **la mode d'~** the fashion in those days; **jusqu'~** until then
2 then; **(mais) ~ cela change tout!** but that changes everything!; **et (puis) ~?** so what?
3 so; **il y avait une grève des trains, ~ j'ai pris l'autobus** there was a train strike, so I took the bus
4 ou ~ or else
5 (fam) so; **~ il me dit...** so he said to me...
6 non mais ~! honestly!
B alors que *phr* **1** while
2 when
C alors même que *phr* even though
alouette /alwɛt/ *f* lark
alourdir /aluʀdiʀ/ [**v3**] **A** *vt* **1** to weigh [sb] down ‹*person*›; to make [sth] tense ‹*atmosphere*›
2 to increase ‹*tax, charges*›
B s'alourdir *v refl* (+ *v être*) ‹*eyelids*› to begin to droop; ‹*air*› to grow heavy
alourdissement /aluʀdismɑ̃/ *m* (of tax, deduction) increase (**de** in)
alpestre /alpɛstʀ/ *adj* alpine
alphabet /alfabɛ/ *m* alphabet
alphabétique /alfabetik/ *adj* alphabetical
alphabétiser /alfabetize/ [**v1**] *vt* to teach [sb] to read and write
alpin, **~e** /alpɛ̃, in/ *adj* alpine
alpinisme /alpinism/ *m* mountaineering
alpiniste /alpinist/ *mf* mountaineer, climber
altération /alteʀasjɔ̃/ *f* (of faculties) impairment (**de** of); (of foodstuff) spoiling (**de** of); (in environment) deterioration (**de** in)
altérer /alteʀe/ [**v14**] *vt* **1** to affect ‹*taste, health*›
2 to spoil ‹*foodstuff*›; to fade ‹*colour*›
3 to distort ‹*text*›; to adulterate ‹*substance*›
alternance /altɛʀnɑ̃s/ *f* alternation; **en ~ avec** alternately with
alternateur /altɛʀnatœʀ/ *m* alternator
alternatif, **-ive** /altɛʀnatif, iv/ *adj* **1** (gen) alternate
2 ‹*current*› alternating
3 ‹*culture, theatre*› alternative
alternative /altɛʀnativ/ **A** *adj f* ▶ **alternatif**
B *f* alternative
alterner /altɛʀne/ [**v1**] **A** *vt* to alternate

⚷ key word

B *vi* **1** to alternate
2 ~ avec qn pour faire to take turns with sb (at) doing

altérophobie /alteʀofɔbi/ *f* alterophobia

altesse /altɛs/ *f* **1** highness
2 prince/princess

altier, **-ière** /altje, ɛʀ/ *adj* haughty

altitude /altityd/ *f* altitude; **en ~** high up (in the mountains)

alto /alto/ **A** *adj* alto
B *m* **1** (instrument) viola
2 viola player (BrE), violin (AmE)
3 (voice) alto

altruiste /altʀɥist/ *adj* altruistic

aluminium /alyminjɔm/, **alu** (fam) /aly/ *m* aluminium (BrE), aluminum (AmE)

alvéole /alveɔl/ *f* **1** (in honeycomb) cell
2 (in rock) cavity

alvéolé, **~e** /alveɔle/ *adj* honeycombed

amabilité /amabilite/ *f* **1** kindness
2 courtesy

amadouer /amadwe/ [**v1**] *vt* to coax, to cajole

amaigrir /amegʀiʀ/ [**v3**] *vt* to make [sb] thinner

amaigrissant, **~e** /amegʀisɑ̃, ɑ̃t/ *adj* slimming

amalgame /amalgam/ *m* **1** (gen) mixture
2 (in dentistry, chemistry) amalgam

amalgamer /amalgame/ [**v1**] *vt* **1** to lump together ‹*problems*›; to mix ‹*feelings, people*›
2 to blend, to amalgamate ‹*ingredients*›

amande /amɑ̃d/ *f* **1** almond
2 kernel

amanite /amanit/ *f* Amanita; **~ phalloïde** death cap

amant /amɑ̃/ *m* lover

amarre /amaʀ/ *f* rope; **les ~s** moorings

amarrer /amaʀe/ [**v1**] *vt* **1** to moor ‹*boat*›
2 to tie (**à**, **sur** to)

amas /ama/ *m inv* pile; heap

amasser /amase/ [**v1**] **A** *vt* to amass, to accumulate ‹*fortune, books*›; to collect ‹*proof*›
B s'amasser *v refl* (+ *v être*) ‹*snow, objects*› to pile up; ‹*proof, evidence*› to build up

amateur /amatœʀ/ **A** *adj inv* amateur
B *m* **1** (non-professional) amateur
2 (of sport, photography) enthusiast; (of wine) connoisseur
3 il vend sa voiture, vous êtes ~? he's selling his car, are you interested?

amazone /amazon/ *f* **en ~** sidesaddle

ambassade /ɑ̃basad/ *f* embassy

ambassadeur /ɑ̃basadœʀ/ *m* ambassador

ambassadrice /ɑ̃basadʀis/ *f* **1** ambassador
2 ambassador's wife

ambiance /ɑ̃bjɑ̃s/ *f* atmosphere

ambiant, **~e** /ɑ̃bjɑ̃, ɑ̃t/ *adj* **1** ‹*air*› surrounding; **à température ~e** at room temperature
2 prevailing

ambigu, **ambiguë** /ɑ̃bigy/ *adj* ‹*remark, situation*› ambiguous; ‹*feeling, attitude*› ambivalent

ambiguïté /ɑ̃bigɥite/ *f* ambiguity; enigmatic nature; ambivalence

ambitieux, **-ieuse** /ɑ̃bisjø, øz/ *adj* ambitious

ambition /ɑ̃bisjɔ̃/ *f* ambition

ambitionner /ɑ̃bisjɔne/ [**v1**] *vt* to aspire to

ambivalent, **~e** /ɑ̃bivalɑ̃, ɑ̃t/ *adj* ambivalent

ambre /ɑ̃bʀ/ *m* **1 ~ (jaune)** amber
2 ~ (gris) ambergris

ambulance /ɑ̃bylɑ̃s/ *f* ambulance

ambulancier, **-ière** /ɑ̃bylɑ̃sje, ɛʀ/ *mf* ambulance driver

ambulant, **~e** /ɑ̃bylɑ̃, ɑ̃t/ *adj* ‹*circus*› travelling (BrE); **vendeur ~** (in station) snack trolley man; **un cadavre ~** (fam) a walking skeleton (fam)

âme /ɑm/ *f* soul; **Dieu ait son ~** God rest his/her soul; **socialiste dans l'~** a socialist to the core; **en mon ~ et conscience** in all honesty; **pas ~ qui vive** not a (single) soul; **~ sœur** soul mate

amélioration /ameljɔʀasjɔ̃/ *f* improvement

améliorer /ameljɔʀe/ [**v1**] *vt*, **s'améliorer** *v refl* (+ *v être*) to improve

amen /amɛn/ *m inv* amen

aménagé, **~e** /amenaʒe/ **A** *pp* ▸ **aménager**
B *pp adj* **1** converted
2 equipped

aménagement /amenaʒmɑ̃/ *m* **1** (of region, town) development
2 (of roads) construction; (of parks, green spaces) creation
3 (of house, boat) fitting
4 (of timetable) adjustment; **l'~ du temps de travail** flexible working hours

aménager /amenaʒe/ [**v13**] *vt* **1** to convert; to do up ‹*house, attic*›
2 to equip ‹*kitchen*›; to develop ‹*region*›
3 to create ‹*parks, green spaces*›; to build ‹*road*›; to lay out ‹*garden*›
4 to arrange ‹*timetable*›; to adjust ‹*regulations*›

amende /amɑ̃d/ *f* fine

amendement /amɑ̃dmɑ̃/ *m* **1** (in law) amendment (**à** to, **sur** on)
2 (of soil) enrichment

amener /amne/ [**v16**] *vt* **1 ~ qn quelque part** to take sb somewhere
2 (accompany) **~ qn (quelque part)** to bring sb (somewhere)
3 (controversial) **~ qch (à qn)** to bring (sb) sth
4 to cause ‹*problems, illness*›; to bring ‹*rain, fame*›
5 to bring up ‹*issue, subject*›; **être bien**

a

amené ‹*conclusion*› to be well-presented
6 ~ qn à qch/faire to lead sb to sth/to do

amenuiser: **s'amenuiser** /amənɥize/ [**v1**] *v refl* (+ *v être*) ‹*supplies*› to dwindle; ‹*risk*› to lessen

amer, **-ère** /amɛʀ/ *adj* bitter

✓ **américain**, **~e** /ameʀikɛ̃, ɛn/ **A** *adj* American; **à l'~e** (gen) in the American style; (Culin) à l'américaine
B *m* American English

Amérindien, **-ienne** /ameʀɛ̃djɛ̃, ɛn/ *mf* Amerindian, American Indian

Amérique /ameʀik/ *pr f* America

amerrir /ameʀiʀ/ [**v3**] *vi* ‹*hydroplane*› to land (on water); ‹*spacecraft*› to splash down

amertume /amɛʀtym/ *f* bitterness

ameublement /amœbləmɑ̃/ *m* **1** furniture
2 furniture trade
3 (of room, house) furnishing

ameuter /amøte/ [**v1**] *vt* **1** ‹*person, noise*› to bring [sb] out
2 to stir [sb] up

✓ **ami**, **~e** /ami/ **A** *adj* friendly
B *mf* friend; **en ~** as a friend; **un ~ des bêtes** an animal lover; ▶ **faux**[1]
IDIOM **les bons comptes font les bons ~s** (Proverb) a debt paid is a friend kept

amiable: **à l'amiable** /alamjabl/ *phr* ‹*separate*› on friendly terms; ‹*separation*› amicable; ‹*divorce*› by mutual consent; ▶ **constat**

amiante /amjɑ̃t/ *m* asbestos

amical, **~e** *mpl* **-aux** /amikal, o/ *adj* friendly

amicale /amikal/ *f* association

amicalement /amikalmɑ̃/ *adv* **1** ‹*greet, receive*› warmly; ‹*compete*› in a friendly way
2 (at end of letter) **(bien) ~** best wishes

amidon /amidɔ̃/ *m* starch

amincir /amɛ̃siʀ/ [**v3**] *vt* to make [sb] look slimmer

amiral *mpl* **-aux** /amiʀal, o/ *m* admiral

✓ **amitié** /amitje/ **A** *f* friendship; **se lier d'~ avec qn** to strike up a friendship with sb
B **amitiés** *fpl* (at end of letter) kindest regards

ammoniac /amɔnjak/ *m* (gas) ammonia

ammoniaque /amɔnjak/ *f* ammonia

amnésie /amnezi/ *f* amnesia

amnésique /amnezik/ *adj* amnesic

amnistie /amnisti/ *f* amnesty

amocher /amɔʃe/ [**v1**] (fam) **A** *vt* to bash (fam) [sb/sth] up ‹*person, car*›
B **s'amocher** *v refl* (+ *v être*) to bash oneself up (fam); **s'~ le nez** to bash up (fam) one's nose

amoindrir /amwɛ̃dʀiʀ/ [**v3**] *vt* to reduce ‹*resistance*›; to weaken ‹*person*›

✓ key word

amonceler /amɔ̃sle/ [**v19**] **A** *vt* to pile up
B **s'amonceler** *v refl* (+ *v être*) ‹*clouds, snow*› to build up; ‹*evidence, problems*› to pile up

amoncellement /amɔ̃sɛlmɑ̃/ *m* pile; mass

amont /amɔ̃/ *m* (of river) upper reaches; **en ~** upstream (**de** from); **naviguer d'~ en aval** to sail downstream

amoral, **~e**, *mpl* **-aux** /amɔʀal, o/ *adj* amoral

amorce /amɔʀs/ *f* **1** (of discussion) initiation
2 bait
3 (of explosive) cap, primer; (of gun) cap

amorcer /amɔʀse/ [**v12**] *vt* **1** to begin
2 to prime

amorphe /amɔʀf/ *adj* apathetic

amortir /amɔʀtiʀ/ [**v3**] *vt* **1** to deaden ‹*noise*›; to absorb ‹*shock, impact*›; to break ‹*fall*›
2 to pay off ‹*debt*›
3 **j'ai amorti mon ordinateur en quelques mois** my computer paid for itself in a few months

amortissement /amɔʀtismɑ̃/ *m* **1** (of noise) deadening; (of shock) absorption; (of fall) cushioning
2 (of debt) paying off
3 (of equipment) depreciation

amortisseur /amɔʀtisœʀ/ *m* shock absorber

✓ **amour** /amuʀ/ **A** *m* love; **pour l'~ de** for the sake of; out of love for; **c'était un ~ de jeunesse** it was a youthful romance
B **amours** *m pl or f pl* **1** (Zool) mating
2 love affairs; **à tes ~s!** (to somebody sneezing) bless you!

amouracher: **s'amouracher** /amuʀaʃe/ [**v1**] *v refl* (+ *v être*) **s'~ de** to become infatuated with

amourette /amuʀɛt/ *f* passing infatuation

✓ **amoureux**, **-euse** /amuʀø, øz/ *adj* in love

amour-propre /amuʀpʀɔpʀ/ *m* self-esteem; pride

amovible /amɔvibl/ *adj* detachable; removable

ampère /ɑ̃pɛʀ/ *m* amp, ampere

amphibie /ɑ̃fibi/ *adj* (Zool, Aut) amphibious

amphithéâtre /ɑ̃fiteɑtʀ/ *m* **1** (natural, ancient) amphitheatre (BrE)
2 (at university) lecture hall

amphore /ɑ̃fɔʀ/ *f* amphora

ample /ɑ̃pl/ *adj* **1** ‹*coat, dress*› loose-fitting; ‹*skirt, sleeve*› full; ‹*gesture*› sweeping
2 ‹*quantity*› ample; ‹*harvest*› abundant; ‹*details*› full

amplement /ɑ̃pləmɑ̃/ *adv* fully; **c'est ~ suffisant** that's more than enough!

ampleur /ɑ̃plœʀ/ *f* (of problem) size; (of project, subject, survey) scope; (of event, disaster, task) scale; (of damage, reaction) extent

amplificateur /ɑ̃plifikatœʀ/ *m* amplifier

amplification /ɑ̃plifikasjɔ̃/ *f* **1** (in physics) amplification
2 (extension) (of relations) development; (of strike) escalation; (of debate) expansion

amplifier /ɑ̃plifje/ [**v2**] **A** *vt* to amplify ‹*sound, current*›; to magnify ‹*rumour*›
B s'amplifier *v refl* (+ *v être*) ‹*sound*› to grow louder; ‹*trade*› to increase; ‹*strike*› to intensify

ampoule /ɑ̃pul/ *f* **1** ~ **(électrique)** (light) bulb
2 (Med) (drinkable) phial; (injectable) ampoule
3 blister

ampoulé, **~e** /ɑ̃pule/ *adj* bombastic

amputation /ɑ̃pytasjɔ̃/ *f* amputation

amputer /ɑ̃pyte/ [**v1**] *vt* **1** (Med) to amputate ‹*limb*›; to perform an amputation on ‹*person*›
2 to cut [sth] drastically ‹*budget*›

amusant, **~e** /amyzɑ̃, ɑ̃t/ *adj* **1** entertaining
2 funny

amuse-gueule /amyzgœl/ *m inv* cocktail snack (BrE), munchies (AmE)

amusement /amyzmɑ̃/ *m* entertainment

amuser /amyze/ [**v1**] **A** *vt* **1** to entertain; to amuse
2 to distract
B s'amuser *v refl* (+ *v être*) **1** to play; **pour s'~** for fun
2 bien s'~ to have a good time

amuseur, **-euse** /amyzœʀ, øz/ *mf* entertainer

amygdale /amidal/ *f* tonsil

an /ɑ̃/ *m* year; **avoir huit ~s** to be eight (years old); **en l'~ deux mille** in the year two thousand; **l'~ 55 avant J.-C./après J.-C.** 55 BC/AD
IDIOM **bon ~, mal ~** year in, year out

anabolisant /anabolizɑ̃/ *m* anabolic steroid

anachronique /anakʀɔnik/ *adj* anachronistic

anachronisme /anakʀɔnism/ *m* anachronism

anal, **~e**, *mpl* **-aux** /anal, o/ *adj* anal

analogie /analɔʒi/ *f* analogy

analogue /analɔg/ *adj* similar (**à** to)

analphabète /analfabɛt/ *adj, mf* illiterate

analphabétisme /analfabetism/ *m* illiteracy

analyse /analiz/ *f* **1** analysis; **faire l'~ de qch** to analyse (BrE) sth
2 (Med) test
3 psychoanalysis
■ **~ coût-efficacité** cost-benefit analysis

analyser /analize/ [**v1**] *vt* **1** (gen) to analyse (BrE)
2 (Med) to test ‹*blood, urine*›

ananas /anana(s)/ *m inv* pineapple

anarchie /anaʀʃi/ *f* anarchy

anarchiste /anaʀʃist/ **A** *adj* anarchistic
B *mf* anarchist

anatomie /anatɔmi/ *f* anatomy

ancêtre /ɑ̃sɛtʀ/ *mf* ancestor

anchois /ɑ̃ʃwa/ *m inv* anchovy

ancien, **-ienne** /ɑ̃sjɛ̃, ɛn/ **A** *adj*
1 ‹*champion, president, capital*› former
2 ‹*history, language*› ancient
3 ‹*style, book, building*› old; ‹*car*› vintage; ‹*piece of furniture*› antique
4 c'est lui le plus ~ (in job) he's been here longest
B *m* **1** (in tribe, congregation) elder; (in company) senior member; **les ~s** the older people
2 old member; former student
3 l'~ older property; (furniture) antiques
■ **~ combattant** veteran

ancienne: **à l'ancienne** /alɑ̃sjɛn/ *phr* ‹*jam, piece of furniture*› traditional-style

anciennement /ɑ̃sjɛnmɑ̃/ *adv* formerly

ancienneté /ɑ̃sjɛnte/ *f* **1** (of person) seniority; **trois ans d'~** three years' service
2 (of tradition, relic) antiquity; (of building) age

ancre /ɑ̃kʀ/ *f* (Naut) anchor

ancrer /ɑ̃kʀe/ [**v1**] **A** *vt* **1** to anchor ‹*ship*›
2 to fix ‹*idea*›; to establish ‹*custom*›
B s'ancrer *v refl* (+ *v être*) **1** to anchor
2 ‹*idea*› to become fixed; ‹*custom*› to become established

Andorre /ɑ̃dɔʀ/ *pr f* Andorra

andouille /ɑ̃duj/ *f* **1** (Culin) andouille
2 (fam) fool

âne /ɑn/ *m* **1** (Zool) donkey, ass
2 (fam) dimwit (fam)
IDIOM **faire l'~ pour avoir du son** to act dumb to find out more

anéantir /aneɑ̃tiʀ/ [**v3**] *vt* **1** to ruin ‹*crops, harvest*›; to lay waste to ‹*town*›; to shatter ‹*hopes*›
2 ‹*news*› to crush; ‹*strain*› to exhaust

anéantissement /aneɑ̃tismɑ̃/ *m*
1 destruction, devastation
2 (of hope) shattering
3 (of person) total collapse

anecdote /anɛkdɔt/ *f* anecdote

anémie /anemi/ *f* **1** anaemia
2 weakness

anémier /anemje/ [**v2**] **A** *vt* **1** (Med) to make [sb] anaemic ‹*person*›
2 (fig) to weaken
B s'anémier *v refl* (+ *v être*) **1** (Med) to become anaemic
2 (fig) to grow feeble

anémique /anemik/ *adj* **1** anaemic
2 weak

anémone /anemɔn/ *f* anemone

ânerie /ɑnʀi/ *f* **1** silly remark
2 silly blunder

ânesse /anɛs/ *f* she-ass, female donkey

anesthésie /anɛstezi/ *f* anaesthesia

aneth /anɛt/ *m* dill

anfractuosité /ɑ̃fʀaktɥɔzite/ *f* crevice

ange /ɑ̃ʒ/ *m* angel
IDIOM **être aux ~s** to be in (one's) seventh heaven

a

angélique¹ /ɑ̃ʒelik/ *adj* angelic

angélique² /ɑ̃ʒelik/ *f* angelica

angelot /ɑ̃ʒlo/ *m* cherub

angine /ɑ̃ʒin/ *f* throat infection

🔑 **anglais**, **~e** /ɑ̃glɛ, ɛz/ **A** *adj* English
B *m* (language) English

Anglais, **~e** /ɑ̃glɛ, ɛz/ *mf* Englishman/ Englishwoman

anglaise /ɑ̃glɛz/ **A** *adj f* ▸ **anglais A**
B *f* ringlet

angle /ɑ̃gl/ *m* **1** angle
2 corner

Angleterre /ɑ̃glətɛʀ/ *pr f* England

anglo-américain, **~e**, *mpl* **~s** /ɑ̃gloameʀikɛ̃, ɛn/ **A** *adj* **1** Anglo-American
2 American English
B *m* (language) American English

anglo-normand, **~e**, *mpl* **~s** /ɑ̃glonɔʀmɑ̃, ɑ̃d/ *adj* Anglo-Norman

Anglo-Normande /ɑ̃glonɔʀmɑ̃d/ *adj f* **les îles ~s** the Channel Islands

anglophone /ɑ̃glɔfɔn/ **A** *adj* English-speaking
B *mf* English speaker; Anglophone

anglo-saxon, **-onne**, *mpl* **~s** /ɑ̃glosaksɔ̃, ɔn/ *adj* Anglo-Saxon

angoissant, **~e** /ɑ̃gwasɑ̃, ɑ̃t/ *adj* ‹*prospect*› alarming; ‹*film, silence*› frightening

angoisse /ɑ̃gwas/ *f* anxiety

angoissé, **~e** /ɑ̃gwase/ *adj* anxious

angoisser /ɑ̃gwase/ [**v1**] **A** *vt* to worry
B *vi* (fam) to be anxious, to be nervous

anguille /ɑ̃gij/ *f* eel

angulaire /ɑ̃gylɛʀ/ *adj* angular

anicroche /anikʀɔʃ/ *f* hitch; **sans ~(s)** without a hitch

🔑 **animal**, **~e**, *mpl* **-aux** /animal, o/ **A** *adj* animal
B *m* animal; **~ familier** pet; **~ domestique** domestic animal; **~ nuisible** pest

animalier, **-ière** /animalje, ɛʀ/ **A** *adj* wildlife
B *mf* (in a lab) animal keeper
C *m* wildlife artist

animateur, **-trice** /animatœʀ, tʀis/ *mf*
1 (of group of holidaymakers, club) coordinator; (of association) leader; (of festival) organizer
2 presenter

animation /animasjɔ̃/ *f* **1** (of group, exhibition, festival) organization; (of sales) coordination
2 life, liveliness; **ville qui manque d'~** dull town
3 (of street, market) hustle and bustle; (of people) excitement

animé, **~e** /anime/ *adj* **1** animated; lively; busy
2 **~ de mauvaises intentions** spurred on by bad intentions

🔑 **animer** /anime/ [**v1**] **A** *vt* **1** to lead ‹*discussion, group*›; to run ‹*course, show*›; to present ‹*programme*›
2 to liven up ‹*town, story, meeting*›
B **s'animer** *v refl* (+ *v être*)
1 ‹*conversation*› to become lively; ‹*meeting*› to liven up; ‹*face*› to light up
2 ‹*statue*› to come to life

animosité /animɔzite/ *f* animosity (**envers** toward(s), **entre** between)

anis /ani/ *m inv* **1** anise
2 aniseed

ankyloser: **s'ankyloser** /ɑ̃kiloze/ [**v1**] *v refl* (+ *v être*) to get stiff

annales /anal/ *fpl* **1** annals
2 (of exams) (book of) past papers

anneau, *pl* **~x** /ano/ *m* ring

🔑 **année** /ane/ *f* year; **l'~ en cours** this year, the current year; **avec les ~s** over the years; **d'~ en ~** year by year; **ces dix dernières ~s** over the last ten years; **souhaiter la bonne ~ à qn** to wish sb a happy new year; **(dans) les ~s 80** (in) the eighties; **location à l'~** annual rent
■ **~ bissextile** leap year; **~ civile** calendar year; **~ universitaire** academic year

année-lumière, *pl* **années-lumière** /anelymjɛʀ/ *f* light year

annexe¹ /anɛks/ *adj* **1** ‹*room*› adjoining
2 ‹*questions*› additional; ‹*file, document*› attached

annexe² /anɛks/ *f* **1** (building) annexe (BrE), annex (AmE)
2 (document) appendix

annexer /anɛkse/ [**v1**] *vt* to annex

annihiler /aniile/ [**v1**] *vt* to destroy ‹*efforts, hopes*›; to cancel out ‹*effect, results*›

anniversaire /anivɛʀsɛʀ/ **A** *adj* **date** *or* **jour ~ de** anniversary of
B *m* **1** birthday
2 anniversary

annonce /anɔ̃s/ *f* **1** announcement
2 advertisement, ad (fam); **petite ~** classified advertisement
3 declaration; **faire une ~** (in bridge) to bid
4 sign

🔑 **annoncer** /anɔ̃se/ [**v12**] **A** *vt* **1** to announce
2 to forecast ‹*rain, event*›
3 ‹*event, signal*› to herald
B **s'annoncer** *v refl* (+ *v être*) **1** ‹*crisis, storm*› to be brewing
2 **la récolte 92 s'annonce excellente** the '92 harvest promises to be very good

annonciateur, **-trice** /anɔ̃sjatœʀ, tʀis/ *adj* ‹*sign, signal*› warning

annoter /anɔte/ [**v1**] *vt* to annotate ‹*work*›; to write notes on ‹*worksheet, homework*›

annuaire /anɥɛʀ/ *m* **1** directory
2 yearbook

annuel, **-elle** /anɥɛl/ *adj* (gen) annual, yearly; ‹*contract*› one-year

annulaire /anylɛʀ/ *m* ring finger

🔑 key word

annulation /anylasjɔ̃/ *f* **1** (gen) cancellation; (of law) repeal
2 (Law) (of verdict) quashing; (of elections) cancellation (BrE); (of marriage) annulment

annuler /anyle/ [**v1**] **A** *vt* **1** to cancel ‹*appointment, trip*›; to write off ‹*debt*›; to discount ‹*result of match*›
2 (Law) to declare [sth] void ‹*elections*›; to quash ‹*verdict*›
B s'annuler *v refl* (+ *v être*) to cancel each other out

anodin, **~e** /anɔdɛ̃, in/ *adj* ‹*subject*› safe, neutral; ‹*question, joke*› innocent

anomalie /anɔmali/ *f* **1** anomaly
2 fault

anonymat /anɔnima/ *m* **1** anonymity
2 confidentiality

anonyme /anɔnim/ *adj* anonymous

anorexie /anɔʀɛksi/ *f* anorexia

anormal, **~e**, *mpl* **-aux** /anɔʀmal, o/ *adj* abnormal

ANPE /aɛnpeœ/ *f* (*abbr* = **Agence nationale pour l'emploi**) *French national employment agency*

anse /ɑ̃s/ *f* (of cup, basket) handle

antagoniste /ɑ̃tagɔnist/ *adj* ‹*groups*› opposing; ‹*interests*› conflicting

antan: **d'antan** /dɑ̃tɑ̃/ *phr* ‹*wars, festivals*› of old; ‹*prestige*› former; **les métiers d'~** the old trades; **le Lyon d'~** the Lyons of yesteryear

antarctique /ɑ̃taʀktik/ *adj* Antarctic

Antarctique /ɑ̃taʀktik/ *pr m* **1** Antarctic; **océan ~** Antarctic Ocean
2 Antarctica

antécédent, **~e** /ɑ̃tesedɑ̃, ɑ̃t/ **A** *adj* previous
B *m* **1** past history
2 medical history
3 (in grammar, mathematics) antecedent

antenne /ɑ̃tɛn/ *f* **1** (of radio, television) aerial; (of radar, satellite) antenna; **passer à l'~** ‹*programme, person*› to go on the air
2 (of organization, service) branch
3 (of insect, shrimp) antenna; **avoir des ~s** (fig) to have a sixth sense

antérieur, **~e** /ɑ̃teʀjœʀ/ *adj* **1** ‹*situation, work*› previous
2 ‹*limb, ligament*› anterior

anthracite /ɑ̃tʀasit/ *adj inv* charcoal grey (BrE), charcoal gray (AmE)

anthropologie /ɑ̃tʀɔpɔlɔʒi/ *f* anthropology

anthropophage /ɑ̃tʀɔpɔfaʒ/ *mf* cannibal

antiaérien, **-ienne** /ɑ̃tiaeʀjɛ̃, ɛn/ *adj* anti-aircraft

antiatomique /ɑ̃tiatɔmik/ *adj* (anti-)radiation; **abri ~** nuclear shelter

antibiotique /ɑ̃tibjɔtik/ *adj*, *m* antibiotic

antibrouillard /ɑ̃tibʀujaʀ/ *adj inv* **phare ~** fog light

antibruit /ɑ̃tibʀɥi/ *adj inv* soundproof

antichambre /ɑ̃tiʃɑ̃bʀ/ *f* anteroom

antichoc /ɑ̃tiʃɔk/ *adj inv* **1 casque ~** crash helmet
2 ‹*watch*› shockproof

anticipation /ɑ̃tisipasjɔ̃/ *f* anticipation; **roman d'~** science fiction novel

anticipé, **~e** /ɑ̃tisipe/ *adj* early

anticiper /ɑ̃tisipe/ [**v1**] **A** *vt* to anticipate ‹*reaction, change, movement*›
B *vi* **1** to get ahead of oneself
2 to think ahead

anticonformiste /ɑ̃tikɔ̃fɔʀmist/ *adj*, *mf* nonconformist

anticorps /ɑ̃tikɔʀ/ *m inv* antibody

antidater /ɑ̃tidate/ [**v1**] *vt* to backdate

antidémocratique /ɑ̃tidemɔkʀatik/ *adj* undemocratic

antidérapant, **~e** /ɑ̃tideʀapɑ̃, ɑ̃t/ *adj* ‹*tyre*› non-skid; ‹*sole*› non-slip

antidopage /ɑ̃tidɔpaʒ/ *adj* ‹*measure*› anti-doping; **contrôle ~** dope test

antidote /ɑ̃tidɔt/ *m* antidote

antigang /ɑ̃tigɑ̃g/ *adj inv* **brigade ~** crime squad

antigel /ɑ̃tiʒɛl/ *adj inv*, *m* antifreeze

anti-inflammatoire, *pl* **~s** /ɑ̃tiɛ̃flamatwaʀ/ *adj*, *m* anti-inflammatory

antillais, **~e** /ɑ̃tijɛ, ɛz/ *adj* West Indian

Antilles /ɑ̃tij/ *pr f pl* **les ~** the West Indies; **les Petites/Grandes ~** the Lesser/Greater Antilles

antilope /ɑ̃tilɔp/ *f* antelope

antimite /ɑ̃timit/ *adj*, *m* moth-repellent

antimondialisme /ɑ̃timɔ̃djalism/ *m* anti-globalization

antipathie /ɑ̃tipati/ *f* antipathy

antipathique /ɑ̃tipatik/ *adj* unpleasant

antipelliculaire /ɑ̃tipɛlikylɛʀ/ *adj* anti-dandruff

antipoison /ɑ̃tipwazɔ̃/ *adj inv* **centre ~** poisons unit

antiquaire /ɑ̃tikɛʀ/ *mf* antique dealer

antique /ɑ̃tik/ *adj* ancient

antiquité /ɑ̃tikite/ **A** *f* antique
B antiquités *fpl* antiquities

Antiquité /ɑ̃tikite/ *f* antiquity

antireflet /ɑ̃tiʀəflɛ/ *adj inv* non-reflective; (in photography) anti-glare

antirouille /ɑ̃tiʀuj/ *adj inv* **1** rust-proofing
2 rust-removing

antisèche /ɑ̃tisɛʃ/ *f* (fam) crib (fam)

antisémite /ɑ̃tisemit/ **A** *adj* anti-Semitic
B *mf* anti-Semite

antitabac /ɑ̃titaba/ *adj inv* anti-smoking

antiterrorisme /ɑ̃titɛʀɔʀism/ *m* antiterrorism

antiterroriste /ɑ̃titɛʀɔʀist/ *adj* **lutte ~** fight against terrorism

antithèse /ɑ̃titɛz/ *f* antithesis

antituberculeux, -euse /ɑ̃titybɛʀkylø, øz/ *adj* **vaccin ~** tuberculosis vaccine
antivirus /ɑ̃tiviʀys/ *m* antivirus software
antivol /ɑ̃tivɔl/ *m* (of bicycle, motorbike) lock; (of car) anti-theft device
anus /anys/ *m inv* anus
Anvers /ɑ̃vɛʀ/ *pr n* Antwerp
anxiété /ɑ̃ksjete/ *f* anxiety
anxieux, -ieuse /ɑ̃ksjø, øz/ *adj* ‹*person*› anxious; ‹*attitude*› concerned
aorte /aɔʀt/ *f* aorta
🔑 **août** /u(t)/ *m* August
apaisant, ~e /apɛzɑ̃, ɑ̃t/ *adj* **1** soothing
2 calming
apaiser /apeze/ [**v1**] **A** *vt* **1** to pacify, to appease
2 to ease ‹*conflict*›
3 to calm ‹*rage*›
B **s'apaiser** *v refl* (+ *v être*) **1** to die down
2 to calm down
apanage /apanaʒ/ *m* **être l'~ de qch/qn** to be the prerogative of sth/sb
aparté /apaʀte/ *m* **en ~** in private; (in a play) in an aside
apathie /apati/ *f* **1** apathy
2 stagnation
apatride /apatʀid/ *adj* stateless
APEC /apɛk/ *f* (*abbr* = **Agence pour l'emploi des cadres**) *executive employment agency*
🔑 **apercevoir** /apɛʀsəvwaʀ/ [**v5**] **A** *vt* **1** to make out
2 to catch sight of
B **s'apercevoir** *v refl* (+ *v être*) **1** **s'~ que** to realize that; **s'~ de** to notice ‹*mistake*›
2 to catch sight of each other
3 to meet briefly
aperçu /apɛʀsy/ **A** *pp* ▶ **apercevoir**
B *m* **1** glimpse
2 outline
3 insight
apéritif /apeʀitif/ *m* drink
apesanteur /apəzɑ̃tœʀ/ *f* weightlessness
à-peu-près /apøpʀɛ/ *m inv* vague approximation
apeuré, ~e /apœʀe/ *adj* (scared) frightened; (shy) timid
aphone /afɔn/ *adj* **être ~** to have lost one's voice
aphte /aft/ *m* mouth ulcer
apiculture /apikyltyʀ/ *f* beekeeping
apitoiement /apitwamɑ̃/ *m* pity (**sur** for)
apitoyer /apitwaje/ [**v23**] **A** *vt* to move [sb] to pity
B **s'apitoyer** *v refl* (+ *v être*) **s'~ sur (le sort de) qn** to feel sorry for sb
aplanir /aplaniʀ/ [**v3**] *vt* to level
aplati, ~e /aplati/ **A** *pp* ▶ **aplatir**
B *pp adj* **1** flattened
2 ‹*nose*› flat
aplatir /aplatiʀ/ [**v3**] *vt* **1** to flatten
2 to smooth out ‹*cushion*›; to smooth down ‹*hair*›
3 to press ‹*seams*›
aplomb /aplɔ̃/ **A** *m* **1** confidence; **vous ne manquez pas d'~!** you've got a nerve!
2 plumb, perpendicularity
B **d'aplomb** *phr* **1** **être d'~** to be straight, to be plumb vertical
2 (fam) **ça va te remettre d'~** it will put you back on your feet
apocalypse /apɔkalips/ *f* apocalypse
apogée /apɔʒe/ *m* **1** (of moon, satellite) apogee
2 (of career, empire) peak
apologie /apɔlɔʒi/ *f* panegyric; apologia; **faire l'~ de** to justify; to praise
a posteriori /apɔsteʀjɔʀi/ *phr* after the event
apostolat /apɔstɔla/ *m* **1** apostolate
2 (fig) apostolic mission
apostrophe /apɔstʀɔf/ *f* apostrophe
apostropher /apɔstʀɔfe/ [**v1**] *vt* to heckle
apothéose /apɔteoz/ *f* **1** (of show) high point
2 (of career, work) culmination
apôtre /apotʀ/ *m* apostle
🔑 **apparaître** /apaʀɛtʀ/ [**v73**] **A** *vi* (+ *v être*)
1 ‹*person, problem*› to appear; ‹*sun, moon*› to come out
2 **laisser** *or* **faire ~** to show
3 to seem
B *v impers* **il apparaît que** it appears that
apparat /apaʀa/ *m* grandeur; **d'~** ceremonial
🔑 **appareil** /apaʀɛj/ *m* **1** device
2 appliance
3 telephone; **qui est à l'~?** who's calling please?
4 aircraft
5 system; **l'~ digestif** the digestive system
6 apparatus; **l'~ du parti** the party apparatus
■ **~ auditif** hearing aid; **~ (dentaire)** brace (BrE), braces (AmE); **~ à sous** slot machine; **~ photo** camera
IDIOM **être dans son plus simple ~** to be in one's birthday suit
appareiller /apaʀeje/ [**v1**] *vi* to cast off
apparemment /apaʀamɑ̃/ *adv*
1 apparently
2 seemingly
🔑 **apparence** /apaʀɑ̃s/ *f* appearance
apparent, ~e /apaʀɑ̃, ɑ̃t/ *adj* **1** visible
2 ‹*embarrassment*› apparent
3 seeming, apparent
apparenté, ~e /apaʀɑ̃te/ *adj* **1** ‹*person*› related (**à** to)
2 ‹*company*› allied
apparenter: **s'apparenter** /apaʀɑ̃te/ [**v1**] *v refl* (+ *v être*) **s'~ à** to resemble
apparition /apaʀisjɔ̃/ *f* **1** (of product) appearance; (of problem) emergence
2 apparition

🔑 key word

⚷ **appartement** /apaʀtəmɑ̃/ *m* flat (BrE), apartment; **~ témoin** show flat (BrE), show apartment (AmE)

appartenance /apaʀtənɑ̃s/ *f* membership (à of)

⚷ **appartenir** /apaʀtəniʀ/ [**v36**] **A** **appartenir à** *v+prep* **1** **~ à** to belong to
2 **~ à** to be a member of
B *v impers* **il appartient à qn de faire** it is up to sb to do

appât /apɑ/ *m* **1** bait
2 lure

appâter /apɑte/ [**v1**] *vt* **1** to bait
2 to lure

appauvrir /apovʀiʀ/ [**v3**] **A** *vt* to impoverish
B **s'appauvrir** *v refl* (+ *v être*) to become impoverished

⚷ **appel** /apɛl/ *m* **1** call; (urgent) appeal; **~ à** call for ‹*solidarity*›; appeal for ‹*calm*›; **~ au secours** call for help; cry for help; **faire ~ à** to appeal to ‹*person*›; to call ‹*fire brigade*›; ‹*task*› to call for ‹*skills*›
2 roll call; (Sch) registration
3 (Mil) call up (BrE), draft (AmE)
4 (Law) appeal; **faire ~** to appeal
5 (Sport) take off
■ **~ d'air** draught (BrE), draft (AmE); **~ de phares** flash of headlights (BrE) *or* high beams (AmE)

appelé, **~e** /aple/ **A** *pp* ▸ **appeler**
B *pp adj* **~ à qch/à faire** destined for sth/to do
C *m* (Mil) conscript, draftee (AmE)

⚷ **appeler** /aple/ [**v19**] **A** *vt* **1** to call; **~ (qn) à l'aide** to call (to sb) for help
2 to phone (BrE), to call
3 to call ‹*doctor, taxi*›; to send for ‹*pupil*›; **~ qn sous les drapeaux** (Mil) to call sb up
4 **~ qn à faire** to call on sb to do; **~ à la grève** to call for strike action
5 **mon travail m'appelle à beaucoup voyager** my work involves a lot of travel
B **en appeler à** *v+prep* to appeal to
C **s'appeler** *v refl* (+ *v être*) to be called; **comment t'appelles-tu?** what's your name?; **je m'appelle Vladimir** my name is Vladimir; **voilà ce qui s'appelle une belle voiture!** now, that's what you call a nice car!
IDIOM **~ les choses par leur nom**, **~ un chat un chat** to call a spade a spade

appellation /apɛlɑsjɔ̃/ *f* name, appellation

appendice /apɛ̃dis/ *m* (Anat) appendix

appendicite /apɛ̃disit/ *f* appendicitis

appesantir: **s'appesantir** /apəzɑ̃tiʀ/ [**v3**] *v refl* (+ *v être*) **s'~ sur** to dwell on

appétissant, **~e** /apetisɑ̃, ɑ̃t/ *adj* appetizing

appétit /apeti/ *m* appetite

applaudir /aplodiʀ/ [**v3**] **A** *vt* to applaud
B *vi* **1** to applaud, to clap
2 (fig) to approve; **~ des deux mains** to approve heartily

applaudissement /aplodismɑ̃/ *m*
1 applause
2 acclaim

applicateur /aplikatœʀ/ *m* applicator

⚷ **application** /aplikasjɔ̃/ *f* **1** care; **il manque d'~** he doesn't apply himself
2 implementation, enforcement; **mettre en ~** to apply ‹*theory*›; to implement ‹*law*›
3 (of device, program) **~s** applications
4 (of ointment) application
5 (Comput) application program

applique /aplik/ *f* wall light

appliqué, **~e** /aplike/ *adj* **1** hardworking
2 ‹*work*› careful
3 ‹*science*› applied

⚷ **appliquer** /aplike/ [**v1**] **A** *vt* **1** to apply ‹*ointment*› (**sur** to); to put ‹*stamp*› (**sur** on)
2 to implement ‹*policy, law*›
3 to apply ‹*technique*› (**à** to)
B **s'appliquer** *v refl* (+ *v être*) **1** to take great care (**à faire** to do)
2 **s'~ à qn/qch** ‹*law, remark*› to apply to sb/sth

appoint /apwɛ̃/ *m* **1** exact change; **faire l'~** to give the exact change
2 **d'~** ‹*salary*› supplementary; ‹*heating*› additional

appointements /apwɛ̃tmɑ̃/ *mpl* salary

apport /apɔʀ/ *m* **1** provision
2 contribution

⚷ **apporter** /apɔʀte/ [**v1**] *vt* **1** to bring ‹*improvement, news*›; to bring in ‹*revenue*›; to bring about ‹*change*›; **~ qch à qn** to bring sb sth, to take sb sth
2 to give ‹*support, explanation*›

apposer /apoze/ [**v1**] *vt* to affix (**sur** on)

apposition /apozisjɔ̃/ *f* apposition

appréciable /apʀesjabl/ *adj* **1** substantial
2 **c'est ~** it's nice

appréciatif, **-ive** /apʀesjatif, iv/ *adj*
1 appreciative
2 appraising

appréciation /apʀesjasjɔ̃/ *f* **1** (of quantity) estimate
2 (financial) evaluation
3 (of quality) assessment; **être laissé à l'~ de qn** to be left to sb's discretion

⚷ **apprécier** /apʀesje/ [**v2**] *vt* **1** to appreciate ‹*art*›; to like ‹*person*›
2 (financially) to value
3 to estimate ‹*distance*›
4 to assess ‹*situation*›

appréhender /apʀeɑ̃de/ [**v1**] *vt* **1** to arrest
2 to dread
3 to comprehend, to understand

appréhension /apʀeɑ̃sjɔ̃/ *f* apprehension

⚷ **apprendre** /apʀɑ̃dʀ/ [**v52**] *vt* **1** to learn (**à faire** to do)
2 to learn ‹*truth*›; to hear (about) ‹*news*›
3 to teach
4 **~ qch à qn** to tell sb sth

apprenti, **~e** /apʀɑ̃ti/ *mf* **1** apprentice, trainee
2 novice; **~ poète** novice poet

⚷ **apprentissage** /apʀɑ̃tisaʒ/ *m* **1** training, apprenticeship
2 learning

apprêté, **~e** /apʀete/ **A** *pp* ▶ **apprêter**
B *pp adj* **1** affected
2 ‹*hairstyle*› fussy

apprêter: **s'apprêter** /apʀete/ [**v1**] *v refl* (+ *v être*) **s'~ à faire** to get ready to do

apprivoiser /apʀivwaze/ [**v1**] *vt* to tame

approbateur, **-trice** /apʀɔbatœʀ, tʀis/ *adj* **sourire ~** smile of approval

approbation /apʀɔbasjɔ̃/ *f* approval

⚷ **approche** /apʀɔʃ/ *f* approach

⚷ **approcher** /apʀɔʃe/ [**v1**] **A** *vt* **1 ~ qch de la fenêtre** to move sth near to the window
2 to go up to; to come up to
3 to come into contact with
B approcher de *v+prep* to be (getting) close to
C *vi* to approach
D s'approcher *v refl* (+ *v être*) **s'~ de** to go near; to come near

approfondi, **~e** /apʀɔfɔ̃di/ **A** *pp* ▶ **approfondir**
B *pp adj* detailed, in-depth

approfondir /apʀɔfɔ̃diʀ/ [**v3**] *vt* **1** to go into [sth] in depth
2 ~ ses connaissances en français to improve one's knowledge of French
3 to make [sth] deeper

approprié, **~e** /apʀɔpʀije/ *adj* appropriate

approprier: **s'approprier** /apʀɔpʀije/ [**v2**] *v refl* (+ *v être*) **1** to take, to appropriate ‹*object, idea*›
2 to seize ‹*power*›

approuver /apʀuve/ [**v1**] *vt* **1** to approve of; **je t'approuve d'avoir accepté** I think you were right to accept
2 to approve ‹*budget*›

approvisionnement /apʀɔvizjɔnmɑ̃/ *m* supply (**en** of)

approvisionner /apʀɔvizjɔne/ [**v1**] **A** *vt* **1** to supply (**en** with); **mal approvisionné** ‹*shop*› badly stocked
2 to pay money into ‹*account*›
B s'approvisionner *v refl* (+ *v être*) **1 s'~ en** to get one's supplies of (**auprès de** from)
2 to stock up (**en** on, with)

approximatif, **-ive** /apʀɔksimatif, iv/ *adj* ‹*estimate, translation*› rough

approximation /apʀɔksimasjɔ̃/ *f* **1** rough estimate
2 approximation

appui /apɥi/ *m* support; **à l'~ de** in support of ‹*theory*›; **prendre ~ sur** to lean on

appui-tête, *pl* **appuis-tête** /apɥitɛt/ *m* headrest

appuyé, **~e** /apɥije/ **A** *pp* ▶ **appuyer**
B *pp adj* **1** ‹*look*› intent
2 ‹*joke*› laboured (BrE)

⚷ **appuyer** /apɥije/ [**v22**] **A** *vt* **1** to rest (**sur** on); to lean (**sur** on)
2 to press (**contre** against)
3 to support, to back (up)
B *vi* **1 ~ sur** to press ‹*switch*›; to put one's foot on ‹*brake*›
2 ~ sur to stress ‹*word*›
C s'appuyer *v refl* (+ *v être*) **1** to lean (**sur** on, **contre** against)
2 s'~ sur to rely on ‹*theory*›; to draw on ‹*report*›

âpre /ɑpʀ/ *adj* **1** ‹*taste, cold*› bitter
2 ‹*voice*› harsh
3 ‹*struggle*› fierce; ‹*argument*› bitter

⚷ **après** /apʀɛ/ **A** *adv* afterward, afterwards, after; later; **peu/bien ~** shortly/long afterwards; **une heure ~** one hour later; **peu ~ il y a un lac** a bit further on there's a lake; **et ~?** and then what?; so what? (fam)
B *prep* after; **~ mon départ** after I leave; after I left; **~ coup** afterwards; **il est toujours ~ son fils** (fam) he's always on at his son (fam)
C d'après *phr* **1 d'~ moi** in my opinion; **d'~ lui/la météo** according to him/the weather forecast; **d'~ ma montre** by my watch
2 from; based on; **d'~ un dessin de Gauguin** from a drawing by Gauguin
3 l'année d'~ the year after; **la fois d'~** the next time
D après que *phr* after; **~ qu'il a parlé** after he had spoken
E après- (*combining form*) **l'~-guerre** the postwar years

après-demain /apʀɛdmɛ̃/ *adv* the day after tomorrow

après-midi /apʀɛmidi/ *m inv or f inv* afternoon

après-rasage, *pl* **~s** /apʀɛʀazaʒ/ *adj inv*, *m* after-shave

après-shampooing /apʀɛʃɑ̃pwɛ̃/ *m* conditioner

après-ski /apʀɛski/ *m inv* snow boot

après-vente /apʀɛvɑ̃t/ *adj inv* after-sales

a priori /apʀijɔʀi/ **A** *phr* a priori
B *phr* **~, ça ne devrait pas poser de problèmes** on the face of it there shouldn't be any problems

à-propos /apʀɔpo/ *m inv* **intervenir avec ~** to make an apposite remark; **agir avec ~** to do the right thing

apte /apt/ *adj* **~ à qch/à faire** capable of sth/of doing; fit for sth/to do

aptitude /aptityd/ *f* aptitude; fitness

aquarelle /akwaʀɛl/ *f* **1** watercolours (BrE)
2 watercolour (BrE)

⚷ key word

aquarium /akwaʀjɔm/ *m* aquarium, fish tank

aquatique /akwatik/ *adj* **1** aquatic
2 sport ~ water sport

aqueduc /akdyk/ *m* aqueduct

aquilin /akilɛ̃/ *adj m* aquiline

aquitain, **~e** /akitɛ̃, ɛn/ *adj* of Aquitaine; **le bassin ~** the Aquitaine Basin

arabe /aʀab/ **A** *adj* **1** Arab
2 Arabic
B *m* (language) Arabic

Arabe /aʀab/ *mf* Arab

arabesque /aʀabɛsk/ *f* arabesque

Arabie /aʀabi/ *pr f* Arabia
■ **~ Saoudite** Saudi Arabia

arabique /aʀabik/ *adj* Arabian

arachide /aʀaʃid/ *f* groundnut, peanut

araignée /aʀeɲe/ *f* spider
■ **~ de mer** spider crab
IDIOM **avoir une ~ au plafond** (fam) to have a screw loose (fam)

arbalète /aʀbalɛt/ *f* crossbow

arbitraire /aʀbitʀɛʀ/ *adj* arbitrary

arbitrairement /aʀbitʀɛʀmɑ̃/ *adv* arbitrarily

arbitre /aʀbitʀ/ *m* **1** referee, umpire
2 arbitrator

arbitrer /aʀbitʀe/ [**v1**] **A** *vt* **1** to referee, to umpire
2 to arbitrate in
B *vi* to arbitrate (**entre** between)

arborer /aʀbɔʀe/ [**v1**] *vt* **1** to wear ‹*smile*›; to sport ‹*badge*›
2 to bear ‹*banner*›; to fly ‹*flag*›

arboriculture /aʀbɔʀikyltyʀ/ *f* arboriculture

arbre /aʀbʀ/ *m* **1** tree
2 (Tech) shaft
■ **~ généalogique** family tree

arbrisseau, *pl* **~x** /aʀbʀiso/ *m* small tree

arbuste /aʀbyst/ *m* shrub

arc /aʀk/ *m* **1** (Sport) bow
2 arc
3 arch

arcade /aʀkad/ *f* arcade; **~s** archways
■ **~ sourcilière** arch of the eyebrow

arc-bouter: **s'arc-bouter** /aʀkbute/ [**v1**] *v refl* (+ *v être*) to brace oneself

arceau, *pl* **~x** /aʀso/ *m* **1** arch
2 (in croquet) hoop
3 (in car) roll bar

arc-en-ciel, *pl* **arcs-en-ciel** /aʀkɑ̃sjɛl/ *m* rainbow

archaïque /aʀkaik/ *adj* archaic

archange /aʀkɑ̃ʒ/ *m* archangel

arche /aʀʃ/ *f* arch; **~ de Noé** Noah's Ark

archéologie /aʀkeɔlɔʒi/ *f* archaeology

archéologique /aʀkeɔlɔʒik/ *adj* archaeological

archet /aʀʃɛ/ *m* (Mus) bow

archétype /aʀketip/ *m* archetype

archevêché /aʀʃəveʃe/ *m* **1** archdiocese
2 archbishop's palace

archevêque /aʀʃəvɛk/ *m* archbishop

archi /aʀʃi/ *pref* (fam) **~connu** really well-known

archipel /aʀʃipɛl/ *m* archipelago

architecte /aʀʃitɛkt/ *mf* architect

architecture /aʀʃitɛktyʀ/ *f* **1** architecture
2 structure

archives /aʀʃiv/ *fpl* archives, records

arctique /aʀktik/ *adj* arctic

Arctique /aʀktik/ *pr m* Arctic

ardemment /aʀdamɑ̃/ *adv* passionately

ardent, **~e** /aʀdɑ̃, ɑ̃t/ *adj* **1** ‹*ember*› glowing; ‹*sun*› blazing
2 ‹*faith*› burning; ‹*patriot*› fervent; ‹*speech*› impassioned; ‹*nature*› passionate

ardeur /aʀdœʀ/ *f* (of person) ardour (BrE); (of beliefs) fervour (BrE); (of beginner) enthusiasm

ardoise /aʀdwaz/ *f* **1** slate
2 (fam) account

ardu, **~e** /aʀdy/ *adj* **1** arduous
2 taxing

arène /aʀɛn/ *f* **1** arena
2 bullring
3 ~s amphitheatre (BrE)

arête /aʀɛt/ *f* **1** fish bone
2 (of roof, mountain) ridge; (of prism) edge; (of nose) bridge

argent /aʀʒɑ̃/ *m* **1** money
2 silver
■ **~ liquide** cash
IDIOM **prendre qch pour ~ comptant** to take sth at face value

argenté, **~e** /aʀʒɑ̃te/ *adj* **1** silver-plated
2 (in colour) silvery

argenterie /aʀʒɑ̃tʀi/ *f* silverware, silver

Argentine /aʀʒɑ̃tin/ *pr f* Argentina

argile /aʀʒil/ *f* clay

argot /aʀgo/ *m* slang

arguer /aʀge/ [**v1**] **A** *vt* **~ que** to claim that
B arguer de *v+prep* to give [sth] as a reason

argument /aʀgymɑ̃/ *m* argument

argumentation /aʀgymɑ̃tasjɔ̃/ *f* line of argument

argumenter /aʀgymɑ̃te/ [**v1**] *vi* to argue

argus /aʀgys/ *m inv: used car prices guide*

aride /aʀid/ *adj* arid

aridité /aʀidite/ *f* aridity

aristocratie /aʀistɔkʀasi/ *f* aristocracy

aristocratique /aʀistɔkʀatik/ *adj* aristocratic

arithmétique /aʀitmetik/ **A** *adj* arithmetical
B *f* arithmetic

arlequin /aʀləkɛ̃/ *m* harlequin

armateur /aʀmatœʀ/ *m* shipowner

armature /aʀmatyʀ/ *f* **1** (of tent) frame

2 (in construction) framework

🗝 **arme** /aʀm/ **A** *f* **1** weapon; **charger une ~** to load a gun; **rendre les ~s** to surrender; **en ~s** armed; **à ~s égales** on equal terms; **faire ses premières ~s dans l'enseignement** to start out as a teacher
2 branch of the armed services
B **armes** *fpl* coat of arms
■ **~ blanche** *weapon with a blade*; **~ de destruction massive** weapon of mass destruction; **~ à feu** firearm

armé, **~e** /aʀme/ **A** *pp* ▸ **armer**
B *pp adj* **1** armed; **vol à main ~e** armed robbery
2 equipped (**de** with, **contre** against)

🗝 **armée** /aʀme/ *f* army
■ **~ de l'air** air force; **l'~ de réserve** the reserves; **l'~ de terre** the army

armement /aʀməmɑ̃/ *m* **1** armament; arming
2 arms, weapons
3 (of rifle) cocking; (of camera) winding on
4 (of ship) fitting out

🗝 **armer** /aʀme/ [**v1**] **A** *vt* **1** to arm (**de** with, **contre** against)
2 to fit out ‹*ship*›
3 to wind on ‹*camera*›; to cock ‹*rifle*›
B **s'armer** *v refl* (+ *v être*) to arm oneself

armistice /aʀmistis/ *m* armistice

armoire /aʀmwaʀ/ *f* **1** cupboard
2 wardrobe
■ **~ à glace** wardrobe with a full length mirror; **c'est une ~ à glace** (fam) he/she is built like a tank (fam); **~ métallique** metal locker; **~ à pharmacie** medicine cabinet; **~ de toilette** bathroom cabinet

armoiries /aʀmwaʀi/ *fpl* arms

armure /aʀmyʀ/ *f* armour (BrE)

armurier /aʀmyʀje/ *m* **1** gunsmith
2 armourer (BrE)

arobas(e) /aʀɔbɑs, -bɑz/ *m* (Comput) at sign

aromates /aʀɔmat/ *mpl* herbs and spices

aromathérapeute /aʀɔmateʀapøt/ *mf* aromatherapist

aromatique /aʀɔmatik/ *adj* aromatic

aromatiser /aʀɔmatize/ [**v1**] *vt* to flavour (BrE)

arôme /aʀom/ *m* **1** aroma
2 flavouring (BrE)

arpège /aʀpɛʒ/ *m* arpeggio

arpenter /aʀpɑ̃te/ [**v1**] *vt* **1** to stride along
2 to pace up and down
3 to survey ‹*piece of land*›

arqué, **~e** /aʀke/ *adj* ‹*brows*› arched; ‹*nose*› hooked; ‹*legs*› bandy

arquer /aʀke/ [**v1**] **A** *vt* to bend ‹*bar*›
B **s'arquer** *v refl* (+ *v être*) to become bowed

arrachage /aʀaʃaʒ/ *m* (of crop) picking; (of tooth, post) pulling out; (of scrub, root) digging out; **~ des mauvaises herbes** weeding

arraché /aʀaʃe/ *m* snatch; **obtenir à l'~** to snatch ‹*victory*›; **vol à l'~** bag snatching

arrache-pied: **d'arrache-pied** /daʀaʃpje/ *phr* ‹*work*› flat out

🗝 **arracher** /aʀaʃe/ [**v1**] **A** *vt* **1** to pull up *or* dig up ‹*weeds*›; to pull out ‹*tooth*›; to tear down ‹*poster*›; to rip out ‹*page*›; to tear off ‹*mask*›; to uproot ‹*tree*›; to blow off ‹*tiles*›
2 **~ à qn** to snatch [sth] from sb ‹*bag, victory*›; to extract [sth] from sb ‹*promise*›; to get [sth] from sb ‹*smile*›
3 **~ qn à** to uproot sb from ‹*home*›; to drag sb away from ‹*work*›; to rouse sb from ‹*thoughts*›; to rescue sb from ‹*poverty*›
B **s'arracher** *v refl* (+ *v être*) **1** **~ qch** to fight over sth
2 **s'~ à** to rouse oneself from ‹*thoughts*›; to tear oneself away from ‹*work*›
IDIOMS **c'est à s'~ les cheveux!** (fam) it's enough to make you tear your hair out!; **~ les yeux à** *or* **de qn** to scratch sb's eyes out

arracheur /aʀaʃœʀ/ *m* **mentir comme un ~ de dents** to be a born liar

arraisonner /aʀɛzɔne/ [**v1**] *vt* to board and inspect

arrangeant, **~e** /aʀɑ̃ʒɑ̃, ɑ̃t/ *adj* obliging

arrangement /aʀɑ̃ʒmɑ̃/ *m* arrangement

arranger /aʀɑ̃ʒe/ [**v13**] **A** *vt* **1** to arrange, to organize
2 to sort out; **pour ne rien ~, pour tout ~** to make matters worse
3 to arrange ‹*flowers*›
4 to tidy ‹*hair*›; to straighten ‹*skirt*›
5 (Mus) to arrange
6 ‹*events*› to suit ‹*person*›
B **s'arranger** *v refl* (+ *v être*) **1** to get better, to improve
2 **s'~ avec qn** to arrange it with sb
3 to manage
4 **on s'arrangera après** we'll sort it out later
5 (fam) **elle ne sait pas s'~** she doesn't know how to make the most of herself

arrangeur, **-euse** /aʀɑ̃ʒœʀ, øz/ *mf* (Mus) arranger

arrestation /aʀɛstasjɔ̃/ *f* arrest

🗝 **arrêt** /aʀɛ/ *m* **1** (gen) stopping; (of conflict) cessation; (of delivery) cancellation; (in production) halt
2 stop; **sans ~** ‹*travel*› non-stop; ‹*interrupt*› constantly; **à l'~** ‹*vehicle*› stationary; ‹*machine*› idle; ‹*electrical appliance*› off; **marquer un temps d'~** to pause; **être aux ~s** (Mil) to be under arrest
3 stop; **un ~ de bus** a bus stop
4 (Law) ruling
■ **~ du cœur** heart failure; **~ sur image** freeze-frame, still; **~ de jeu** stoppage time; **~ de mort** death sentence; **~ de travail** stoppage of work; sick leave; sick note

arrêté, **~e** /aʀete/ **A** *pp* ▸ **arrêter**
B *pp adj* **1** ‹*matter*› settled
2 ‹*ideas*› fixed
C *m* order, decree

🗝 key word

arrêter /aʀete/ [v1] **A** *vt* **1** to stop (**de faire** doing); **être arrêté pour trois semaines** to be given a sick note for three weeks
2 to switch off ‹*machine*›; to halt ‹*process*›
3 to give up (**de faire** doing)
4 to arrest
5 to decide on ‹*plan*›
B *vi* to stop; **arrête!** stop it!
C **s'arrêter** *v refl* (+ *v être*) **1** to stop
2 to give up (**de faire** doing)
3 to end
4 **s'~ sur** to dwell on; **s'~ à** to focus on

arrhes /aʀ/ *fpl* deposit

arrière /aʀjɛʀ/ **A** *adj inv* back; rear
B *m* **1** rear; **à l'~** (in car) in the back; (on plane, train, ship) at the rear; **en ~** backward(s); (position) behind; **pencher la tête en ~** to tilt one's head back; **revenir en ~** ‹*person*› to turn back; (fig) to take a backward step; (on tape) to rewind
2 (Sport) fullback

arriéré, **~e** /aʀjeʀe/ **A** *adj* **1** outdated
2 backward
3 behind the times
B *m* arrears

arrière-cour, *pl* **~s** /aʀjɛʀkuʀ/ *f* backyard

arrière-goût, *pl* **~s** /aʀjɛʀgu/ *m* aftertaste

arrière-grand-mère, *pl* **arrière-grands-mères** /aʀjɛʀgʀɑ̃mɛʀ/ *f* great-grandmother

arrière-grand-père, *pl* **arrière-grands-pères** /aʀjɛʀgʀɑ̃pɛʀ/ *m* great-grandfather

arrière-grands-parents /aʀjɛʀgʀɑ̃paʀɑ̃/ *mpl* great-grandparents

arrière-pays /aʀjɛʀpei/ *m inv* hinterland

arrière-pensée, *pl* **~s** /aʀjɛʀpɑ̃se/ *f*
1 ulterior motive
2 **sans ~** without reservation

arrière-petits-enfants /aʀjɛʀpətizɑ̃fɑ̃/ *mpl* great-grandchildren

arrière-plan, *pl* **~s** /aʀjɛʀplɑ̃/ *m* (of picture) background

arrière-saison, *pl* **~s** /aʀjɛʀsɛzɔ̃/ *f* late autumn (BrE), late fall (AmE)

arrière-train, *pl* **~s** /aʀjɛʀtʀɛ̃/ *m* hindquarters

arrimer /aʀime/ [v1] *vt* **1** to fasten
2 (Naut) to stow

arrivage /aʀivaʒ/ *m* delivery, consignment

arrivant, **~e** /aʀivɑ̃, ɑ̃t/ *mf* **un nouvel ~** a newcomer

arrivé, **~e** /aʀive/ **A** *pp* ▶ **arriver**
B *pp adj* **1** **le premier ~** the first person to arrive
2 **être ~** to have made it (socially)

arrivée /aʀive/ *f* **1** arrival; **trains à l'~** arrivals
2 (in race) finish
3 (Tech) inlet

arriver /aʀive/ [v1] (+ *v être*) **A** *vi* **1** (gen) to arrive; (Sport) to finish; **~ à/de Paris** to arrive in/from Paris
2 to come; **~ en courant** to come running up
3 **~ à** to reach ‹*level, agreement*›; to find ‹*solution*›; **~ (jusqu')à qn** to reach sb
4 **~ à faire** to manage to do; **je n'y arrive pas** I can't do it; **~ à ses fins** to achieve one's ends
5 **en ~ à** to come to
6 to happen
B *v impers* **qu'est-il arrivé?** what happened? (à to); **il m'arrive d'y aller, il arrive que j'y aille** I sometimes go there

arrivisme /aʀivism/ *m* ruthless ambition

arrogance /aʀɔgɑ̃s/ *f* arrogance

arrogant, **~e** /aʀɔgɑ̃, ɑ̃t/ *adj* arrogant

arroger: **s'arroger** /aʀɔʒe/ [v13] *v refl* (+ *v être*) to appropriate ‹*title*›; to assume ‹*right, role*›

arrondi, **~e** /aʀɔ̃di/ **A** *adj* rounded; round
B *m* (of face) roundness; (of shoulder) curve

arrondir /aʀɔ̃diʀ/ [v3] **A** *vt* **1** to round off ‹*edge*›; **coiffure qui arrondit le visage** hairstyle that makes one's face look round
2 to open wide ‹*eyes*›
3 to round off ‹*figure*› (à to)
B **s'arrondir** *v refl* (+ *v être*) **1** ‹*object*› to become round(ed); ‹*eyes*› to widen
2 ‹*face*› to fill out
3 ‹*fortune*› to be growing
IDIOM **~ les angles** to smooth the rough edges

arrondissement /aʀɔ̃dismɑ̃/ *m* **1** (in city) arrondissement
2 (region) *administrative division in France*

arrosage /aʀozaʒ/ *m* watering

arroser /aʀoze/ [v1] **A** *vt* **1** to water, to spray; **on va se faire ~!** (fam) we're going to get soaked!
2 to baste ‹*meat*›; to sprinkle ‹*cake*›
3 to drink to
4 **repas arrosé au bourgogne** meal washed down with Burgundy
B **s'arroser** *v refl* (+ *v être*) (fam) **ça s'arrose** that calls for a drink

arroseur /aʀozœʀ/ *m* sprinkler

arrosoir /aʀozwaʀ/ *m* watering can

arsenal, *pl* **-aux** /aʀsənal, o/ *m* **1** naval shipyard
2 arsenal
3 (fam) gear

art /aʀ/ *m* **1** art
2 art, skill; **avoir l'~ de faire** to have a knack of doing
■ **~ dramatique** drama; **~ lyrique** opera; **~ de vivre** art of living; **~s ménagers** home economics; **~s plastiques** plastic arts

Artaban /aʀtabɑ̃/ *pr n* **fier comme ~** proud as a peacock

artère /aʀtɛʀ/ *f* **1** (Anat) artery
2 arterial road
3 main street

artériel, **-ielle** /aʀteʀjɛl/ *adj* arterial

arthrite /aʀtʀit/ *f* arthritis

arthrose /aʀtʀoz/ *f* osteoarthritis

a

artichaut /aʀtiʃo/ *m* (globe) artichoke
IDIOM **avoir un cœur d'~** to be fickle (*in love*)

✓ **article** /aʀtikl/ *m* **1** (in paper, law) article; (in contract) clause
2 (in grammar) article
3 item; **~s de consommation courante** basic consumer goods; **faire l'~ à qn** to give sb the sales pitch
IDIOM **être à l'~ de la mort** to be at death's door

articulaire /aʀtikylɛʀ/ *adj* articular

articulation /aʀtikylasjɔ̃/ *f* **1** (Anat) joint
2 (of lamp, sunshade) mobile joint
3 (in phonetics) articulation
4 (in sentence) link
5 (of speech, essay) structure

✓ **articuler** /aʀtikyle/ [**v1**] **A** *vt* **1** to articulate; **articule!** speak clearly!
2 to utter
3 to structure ‹*ideas*›
B **s'articuler** *v refl* (+ *v être*) **s'~ autour de** to be based on, to hinge on

artifice /aʀtifis/ *m* **1** trick
2 device; **les ~s du style** stylistic devices
3 sans ~ unpretentious

artificiel, **-ielle** /aʀtifisjɛl/ *adj* **1** artificial; man-made
2 superficial; forced

artificier /aʀtifisje/ *m* **1** bomb disposal expert
2 explosives manufacturer
3 fireworks manufacturer

artillerie /aʀtijʀi/ *f* artillery

artisan /aʀtizɑ̃/ *m* **1** artisan, craftsman
2 architect, author

artisanal, **~e**, *mpl* **-aux** /aʀtizanal, o/ *adj* ‹*method*› traditional; **de fabrication ~e** hand-crafted; home-made

artisanat /aʀtizana/ *m* **1** craft industry, cottage industry
2 artisans
■ **~ d'art** arts and crafts

✓ **artiste** /aʀtist/ **A** *adj* **1** artistic
2 il est un peu ~ he's a bit of a dreamer
B *mf* **1** artist; **~ peintre** painter
2 (on stage) performer; (in music hall) artiste; **~ lyrique** opera singer

artistique /aʀtistik/ *adj* artistic

as¹ /a/ ▶ **avoir¹**

as² /ɑs/ *m inv* ace
IDIOMS **être plein aux ~** (fam) to be loaded (fam); **passer à l'~** (fam) ‹*money*› to go down the drain; ‹*holidays*› to go by the board; **être fagoté comme l'~ de pique** (fam) to look a mess

ascendance /asɑ̃dɑ̃s/ *f* descent, ancestry

ascendant, **~e** /asɑ̃dɑ̃, ɑ̃t/ **A** *adj* ‹*curve*› rising; ‹*movement*› upward; ‹*star*› ascending
B *m* **1** influence (**sur** over)
2 (Law) ascendant

ascenseur /asɑ̃sœʀ/ *m* lift (BrE), elevator (AmE)
IDIOM **renvoyer l'~** to return the favour (BrE)

ascension /asɑ̃sjɔ̃/ *f* **1** ascent; **faire l'~ de** to climb
2 (fig) rise

ascensionnel, **-elle** /asɑ̃sjɔnɛl/ *adj* ‹*movement*› upward; **parachute ~** parascending

ascète /asɛt/ *mf* ascetic

ascétisme /asetism/ *m* asceticism

aseptique /asɛptik/ *adj* aseptic

aseptisé, **~e** /aseptize/ *adj* ‹*art*› sanitized; ‹*world*› sterile; ‹*decor*› impersonal

aseptiser /asɛptize/ [**v1**] *vt* to disinfect ‹*wound*›; to sterilize ‹*instrument*›

asexué, **~e** /asɛksɥe/ *adj* asexual

asiatique /azjatik/ *adj* Asian

Asie /azi/ *pr f* Asia; **~ Mineure** Asia Minor

asile /azil/ *m* **1** refuge; **chercher ~** to seek refuge
2 (political) asylum
3 ~ de vieillards old people's home; **~ de nuit** night shelter

asocial, **~e**, *mpl* **-iaux** /asɔsjal, o/ **A** *adj* antisocial
B *mf* social misfit

✓ **aspect** /aspɛ/ *m* **1** side; **voir qch sous son ~ positif** to see the good side of sth
2 aspect; **par bien des ~s** in many respects
3 appearance

asperge /aspɛʀʒ/ *f* **1** asparagus
2 (fam) beanpole (fam), string bean (AmE)

asperger /aspɛʀʒe/ [**v13**] *vt* to spray; to splash

aspérité /aspeʀite/ *f* (in terrain) bump

asphalte /asfalt/ *m* asphalt

asphyxiant, **~e** /asfiksjɑ̃, ɑ̃t/ *adj* asphyxiating

asphyxie /asfiksi/ *f* asphyxiation

asphyxier /asfiksje/ [**v2**] **A** *vt* **1** to asphyxiate ‹*person*›
2 to paralyse ‹*network, company*›
B **s'asphyxier** *v refl* (+ *v être*) **1** to suffocate to death
2 to gas oneself
3 ‹*network, company*› to become paralysed

aspirateur /aspiʀatœʀ/ *m* vacuum cleaner, hoover® (BrE)

aspiration /aspiʀasjɔ̃/ *f* **1** aspiration (**à** for)
2 sucking up, drawing up
3 inhalation

aspirer /aspiʀe/ [**v1**] **A** *vt* **1** to breathe in, to inhale
2 to suck [sth] up
3 consonne aspirée aspirated consonant
B **aspirer à** *v+prep* to yearn for; to aspire to

aspirine® /aspiʀin/ *f* aspirin

✓ key word

IDIOM **être blanc comme un cachet d'~** to be lily white

assagir: **s'assagir** /asaʒiʀ/ [**v3**] *v refl* (+ *v être*) to quieten down (BrE), to quiet down (AmE)

assaillant, **~e** /asajɑ̃, ɑ̃t/ *mf* **1** attacker
2 (Mil) **les ~s** the attacking forces

assaillir /asajiʀ/ [**v28**] *vt* **1** to attack
2 to plague; **~ qn de questions** to bombard sb with questions

assainir /aseniʀ/ [**v3**] *vt* **1** to clean up
2 to stabilize ‹*economy*›; to streamline ‹*company*›

assainissement /asenismɑ̃/ *m* **1** cleaning up
2 (of economy) stabilization; (of company) streamlining

assaisonnement /asɛzɔnmɑ̃/ *m* (Culin) seasoning; (on salad) dressing

assaisonner /asɛzɔne/ [**v1**] *vt* to season ‹*dish*›; to dress ‹*salad*›

assassin, **~e** /asasɛ̃, in/ **A** *adj* **1** murderous
2 ‹*campaign*› vicious
B *m* **1** murderer
2 assassin

assassinat /asasina/ *m* **1** murder
2 assassination

assassiner /asasine/ [**v1**] *vt* **1** to murder
2 to assassinate
3 (fam) to slate (fam)

assaut /aso/ *m* attack, assault; **se lancer** *or* **monter à l'~ de** to launch an attack on; **prendre d'~** to storm; **les ~s du froid** the onslaught of cold weather

assécher /aseʃe/ [**v14**] *vt* **1** to drain
2 ‹*heat*› to dry up

ASSEDIC /asedik/ *f* (*abbr* = **Association pour l'emploi dans l'industrie et le commerce**) *organization managing unemployment contributions and payments*

assemblage /asɑ̃blaʒ/ *m* **1** (of motor) assembly (**de** of)
2 (of ideas) assemblage; (of objects) collection; (of colours) combination

assemblée /asɑ̃ble/ *f* **1** gathering
2 meeting
3 assembly
■ **~ générale**, **AG** general meeting; **l'Assemblée nationale** the French National Assembly

assembler /asɑ̃ble/ [**v1**] **A** *vt* to assemble, to put together
B s'assembler *v refl* (+ *v être*) ‹*crowd*› to gather; ‹*ministers*› to assemble
IDIOM **qui se ressemble s'assemble** (Proverb) birds of a feather flock together

asséner /asene/ [**v14**] *vt* **~ un coup à qn/qch** to deal sb/sth a blow

assentiment /asɑ̃timɑ̃/ *m* assent, consent

asseoir /aswaʀ/ [**v41**] **A** *vt* **1** to sit [sb] down; (in bed) to sit [sb] up; **faire ~ qn** to make sb sit down; (politely) to offer a seat to sb
2 to establish ‹*reputation*›
3 (fam) to stagger, to astound
B s'asseoir *v refl* (+ *v être*) to sit (down); (in bed) to sit up

assermenté, **~e** /asɛʀmɑ̃te/ *adj* sworn, on oath

assertion /asɛʀsjɔ̃/ *f* assertion

asservir /asɛʀviʀ/ [**v3**] *vt* **1** to enslave ‹*person*›
2 to subjugate ‹*country*›

asservissement /asɛʀvismɑ̃/ *m* **1** (of country, people) subjugation
2 subjection
3 subservience

assesseur /asesœʀ/ *m* magistrate's assistant

assez /ase/ *adv* **1** enough; **~ fort** strong enough; **j'en ai ~** I've got enough; I'm fed up (fam)
2 quite; **je suis ~ pressé** I'm in rather a hurry; **je suis ~ d'accord** I tend to agree

assidu, **~e** /asidy/ *adj* **1** diligent
2 ‹*care*› constant
3 ‹*presence, visits*› regular
4 devoted

assiduité /asidɥite/ *f* **1** diligence; **avec ~** ‹*work*› diligently; ‹*train*› assiduously; ‹*read*› regularly
2 regular attendance
3 ~s assiduities

assiégeant, **~e** /asjeʒɑ̃, ɑ̃t/ *mf* besieger

assiéger /asjeʒe/ [**v15**] *vt* to besiege

assiette /asjɛt/ *f* **1** (for food) plate
2 ~ (fiscale) tax base
■ **~ anglaise** assorted cold meats; **~ en carton** paper plate; **~ creuse** soup plate; **~ à dessert** dessert plate
IDIOM **ne pas être dans son ~** to be out of sorts

assignation /asiɲasjɔ̃/ *f* **1** allocation
2 (Law) summons

assigner /asiɲe/ [**v1**] *vt* **1** to assign ‹*task*›
2 to set ‹*objective*›
3 to ascribe ‹*value, role*› (**à** to)
4 (Law) **~ à comparaître** to summons; **~ qn à résidence** to put sb under house arrest

assimilation /asimilasjɔ̃/ *f* **1** comparison
2 assimilation

assimilé, **~e** /asimile/ *adj* similar

assimiler /asimile/ [**v1**] **A** *vt* **1** to assimilate; **être assimilé cadre** to have executive status
2 ~ qn/qch à to liken sb/sth to
B s'assimiler *v refl* (+ *v être*) **1 s'~ à** ‹*method*› to be comparable to; ‹*person*› to compare oneself to
2 ‹*minority*› to become assimilated; ‹*substances*› to be assimilated

assis, **~e** /asi, iz/ **A** *pp* ▶ **asseoir**
B *pp adj* **1** seated; **être ~** to be sitting down; (in bed) to be sitting up; **reste ~** don't get up; (as reprimand) sit still
2 ‹*reputation*› well-established
3 (fam) staggered

assise /asiz/ *f* basis, foundation

assises /asiz/ *fpl* **1** meeting
2 (Law) assizes

assistanat /asistana/ *m* **1** (Univ) assistantship
2 (state aid) (derog) charity

assistance /asistɑ̃s/ *f* **1** assistance; aid
2 audience
3 attendance (**à** at)
■ **∼ respiratoire** artificial respiration; **l'Assistance publique** ≈ welfare services

assistant, **∼e** /asistɑ̃, ɑ̃t/ *mf* assistant
■ **∼ social** social worker

assisté, **∼e** /asiste/ **A** *pp* ▶ **assister**
B *pp adj* **1** assisted (**de** by)
2 receiving benefit (BrE), on welfare (AmE)
3 ∼ par ordinateur computer-aided
4 direction ∼e power steering
C *mf: person receiving benefit* (BrE) *or welfare* (AmE)

🔑 **assister** /asiste/ [**v1**] **A** *vt* to assist; to aid
B assister à *v+prep* **1 ∼ à** to be at, to attend
2 ∼ à to witness

associatif, **-ive** /asɔsjatif, iv/ *adj*
1 ‹*memory*› associative
2 vie associative community life

🔑 **association** /asɔsjasjɔ̃/ *f* **1** association
2 combination

associé, **∼e** /asɔsje/ **A** *adj* ‹*member*› associate; ‹*companies*› associated
B *mf* associate, partner

🔑 **associer** /asɔsje/ [**v2**] **A** *vt* **1 ∼ qn à** to include sb in ‹*success*›; to make sb a partner in ‹*business*›; to give sb a share of ‹*profits*›
2 ∼ qch à to combine sth with; to associate sth with
B s'associer *v refl* (+ *v être*) **1** to go into partnership, to link up; **s'∼ pour faire** to join forces to do
2 s'∼ à to join ‹*movement*›; to share in ‹*grief*›
3 to combine

assoiffé, **∼e** /aswafe/ *adj* **1** thirsty
2 ∼ de thirsting for

assombrir /asɔ̃bʀiʀ/ [**v3**] **A** *vt* **1** to make [sth] dark, to darken
2 to spoil; **la tristesse assombrit son visage** his/her face clouded
B s'assombrir *v refl* (+ *v être*) **1** ‹*sky*› to darken
2 ‹*face*› to become gloomy

assommant, **∼e** /asɔmɑ̃, ɑ̃t/ *adj* (fam)
1 (dull) deadly boring (fam)
2 (irritating) **tu es ∼ avec tes questions** you're a real pain (fam) with your questions

assommer /asɔme/ [**v1**] *vt* **1** to knock [sb] senseless
2 (fam) **∼ qn** to get on sb's nerves
3 (fam) ‹*news*› to stagger; ‹*heat*› to overcome

🔑 key word

assorti, **∼e** /asɔʀti/ *adj* **1** matching
2 assorted

assortiment /asɔʀtimɑ̃/ *m* **1** set
2 assortment, selection
3 (in shop) stock

assortir /asɔʀtiʀ/ [**v3**] **A** *vt* **1** to match (**à** to, **avec** with)
2 ∼ qch de qch to add sth to sth
B s'assortir *v refl* (+ *v être*) **1 s'∼ à** *or* **avec** to match
2 s'∼ de to come with

assoupir /asupiʀ/ [**v3**] **A** *vt* **1** to make [sb] drowsy
2 to dull ‹*senses, passion*›
B s'assoupir *v refl* (+ *v être*) to doze off

assoupissement /asupismɑ̃/ *m* drowsiness; (sleep) doze

assouplir /asupliʀ/ [**v3**] **A** *vt* **1** to soften ‹*washing*›
2 to make [sth] more supple ‹*body, leather*›
3 to relax ‹*rule*›
B s'assouplir *v refl* (+ *v être*) **1** to get softer
2 to become more supple
3 ‹*person, rule*› to become more flexible

assouplissant /asuplisɑ̃/ *m* fabric softener

assouplissement /asuplismɑ̃/ *m* **1** (of leather, woollens) softening; (of washing) conditioning
2 (Sport) **faire des ∼s** *or* **des exercices d'∼** to limber up
3 (of rules, policy, attitude) relaxing

assouplisseur /asuplisœʀ/ *m* fabric conditioner

assourdir /asuʀdiʀ/ [**v3**] *vt* **1** to deafen
2 to muffle

assouvir /asuviʀ/ [**v3**] *vt* to satisfy ‹*hunger*›; to assuage ‹*anger*›

assouvissement /asuvismɑ̃/ *m* **1** (of hunger) satisfying; (of anger) assuaging
2 satisfaction

assujetti, **∼e** /asyʒeti/ *adj* **∼ à** liable for ‹*tax*›; subject to ‹*rule*›

assujettir /asyʒetiʀ/ [**v3**] **A** *vt* **1** to subject (**à** to)
2 to subjugate, to subdue
3 to secure
B s'assujettir *v refl* (+ *v être*) ‹*person*› to submit (**à** to)

assumer /asyme/ [**v1**] **A** *vt* **1** to take ‹*responsibility*›; to hold ‹*post*›; to meet ‹*costs*›
2 to come to terms with ‹*conditions, identity, past*›; to accept ‹*consequences*›
B s'assumer *v refl* (+ *v être*) **1** to take responsibility for oneself
2 to come to terms with oneself

assurable /asyʀabl/ *adj* insurable

assurance /asyʀɑ̃s/ *f* **1** (self-)confidence, assurance; **avec ∼** confidently
2 assurance; **donner à qn l'∼ que** to assure sb that
3 insurance (policy)

4 insurance company
5 insurance (premium)
6 insurance (sector)
7 benefit (BrE), benefits (AmE)
■ **~ au tiers** third-party insurance; **~ maladie** health insurance; sickness benefit (BrE) *or* benefits (AmE); **~ tous risques** comprehensive insurance; **~s sociales** social insurance

assurance-crédit, *pl* **assurances-crédit** /asyʀɑ̃skʀedi/ *f* credit insurance

assurance-vie, *pl* **assurances-vie** /asyʀɑ̃svi/ *f* life insurance

assuré, **~e** /asyʀe/ **A** *pp* ▶ **assurer**
B *pp adj* **1** sure, certain (**de faire** of doing); **soyez ~ de ma reconnaissance** I am very grateful to you
2 insured
C *adj* **1** ‹*step, air*› confident; ‹*hand*› steady; **mal ~** ‹*step, voice*› faltering; ‹*gesture*› nervous
2 certain, assured
D *mf* insured party
■ **~ social** social insurance contributor

assurément /asyʀemɑ̃/ *adv* **1** definitely
2 most certainly

assurer /asyʀe/ [**v1**] **A** *vt* **1 ~ à qn que** to assure sb that; **ce n'est pas drôle, je t'assure** believe me, it's no joke
2 ~ qn de to assure sb of ‹*support*›
3 to insure ‹*property, goods*›
4 to carry out ‹*maintenance*›; to provide ‹*service*›; **~ la liaison entre** ‹*train, bus, ferry*› to operate between; **~ la gestion de** to manage
5 to ensure ‹*victory*›; to secure ‹*right, post*› (**à qn** for sb); to assure ‹*future*›; **~ un revenu à qn** to give sb an income; **~ ses vieux jours** to provide for one's old age
6 to secure ‹*rope*›; to belay ‹*climber*›
B s'assurer *v refl* (+ *v être*) **1 s'~ de qch** to make sure of sth
2 to secure ‹*advantage, help*›
3 to take out insurance
4 (fig) **s'~ contre** to insure against ‹*eventuality, risk*›

assureur /asyʀœʀ/ *m* **1** insurance agent
2 insurance company

astérisque /asteʀisk/ *m* asterisk

asthmatique /asmatik/ *adj, mf* asthmatic

asthme /asm/ *m* asthma

asticot /astiko/ *m* maggot

astigmate /astigmat/ *adj* astigmatic

astiquer /astike/ [**v1**] *vt* to polish

astral, **~e**, *mpl* **-aux** /astʀal, o/ *adj* astral

astre /astʀ/ *m* star

astreindre /astʀɛ̃dʀ/ [**v55**] **A** *vt* **~ qn à qch** ‹*person*› to force sth upon sb; ‹*rule*› to bind sb to sth; **~ qn à faire** to compel sb to do
B s'astreindre *v refl* (+ *v être*) **s'~ à qch** to subject oneself to sth

astringent, **~e** /astʀɛ̃ʒɑ̃, ɑ̃t/ *adj* astringent

astrologie /astʀɔlɔʒi/ *f* astrology

astrologique /astʀɔlɔʒik/ *adj* astrological

astrologue /astʀɔlɔg/ *mf* astrologer

astronaute /astʀɔnot/ *mf* astronaut

astronautique /astʀɔnotik/ *f* astronautics

astronomie /astʀɔnɔmi/ *f* astronomy

astronomique /astʀɔnɔmik/ *adj* astronomical

astrophysique /astʀofizik/ *f* astrophysics

astuce /astys/ *f* **1** cleverness
2 shrewdness, astuteness
3 trick
4 pun; joke

astucieux, **-ieuse** /astysjø, øz/ *adj* **1** clever
2 shrewd, sharp

asymétrique /asimetʀik/ *adj* asymmetrical

atchoum /atʃum/ *m* atishoo

atelier /atəlje/ *m* **1** (place) workshop; (artist's) studio
2 working group
3 (seminar) workshop

atermoyer /atɛʀmwaje/ [**v23**] *vi* to procrastinate

athée /ate/ **A** *adj* atheistic
B *mf* atheist

athéisme /ateism/ *m* atheism

athénien, **-ienne** /atenjɛ̃, ɛn/ *adj* Athenian

athlète /atlɛt/ *mf* athlete

athlétique /atletik/ *adj* athletic

athlétisme /atletism/ *m* athletics (BrE), track and field events

Atlantique /atlɑ̃tik/ *pr m* **l'~** the Atlantic

atlas /atlas/ *m inv* atlas

atmosphère /atmɔsfɛʀ/ *f* atmosphere

atoll /atɔl/ *m* atoll

atome /atom/ *m* atom
IDIOM **avoir des ~s crochus avec qn** (fam) to get on well with sb

atomique /atɔmik/ *adj* atomic

atomiseur /atɔmizœʀ/ *m* spray, atomizer

atone /atɔn/ *adj* **1** lifeless, apathetic
2 ‹*syllable*› unstressed

atours /atuʀ/ *mpl* finery

atout /atu/ *m* **1** trump (card); trumps
2 (fig) asset; trump card; **mettre tous les ~s dans son jeu** to leave nothing to chance

âtre /atʀ/ *m* hearth

atroce /atʀɔs/ *adj* atrocious, dreadful, terrible

atrocité /atʀɔsite/ *f* **1** atrocity
2 monstrosity

atrophie /atʀɔfi/ *f* atrophy

atrophier: **s'atrophier** /atʀɔfje/ [**v2**] *v refl* (+ *v être*) to atrophy; **bras atrophié** wasted arm

attabler: **s'attabler** /atable/ [**v1**] *v refl* (+ *v être*) to sit down at (the) table

attachant, **~e** /ataʃɑ̃, ɑ̃t/ *adj* engaging

attache /ataʃ/ *f* **1** tie; string; rope; strap; **~s familiales** family ties

a

2 avoir des ~s fines to have delicate ankles and wrists

attaché, ~e /ataʃe/ *mf* attaché
■ **~ de presse** press attaché

attachement /ataʃmɑ̃/ *m* **1** (to person) attachment
2 (to principle, cause) commitment

attacher /ataʃe/ [**v1**] **A** *vt* **1** to tie ‹*person, hands, laces*› (**à** to); to tether ‹*horse, goat*›; to chain ‹*dog*› (**à** to); to lock ‹*bicycle*› (**à** to); to tie up ‹*person, parcel*›
2 to fasten ‹*belt*›
3 to attach ‹*importance*›
4 les privilèges attachés à un poste the privileges attached to a post
B s'attacher *v refl* (+ *v être*) **1** to fasten
2 s'~ à qn/qch to become attached to sb/sth

attaquable /atakabl/ *adj* **1** ‹*place*› **facilement ~** easy to attack
2 ‹*theory, position*› shaky
3 ‹*will*› contestable

attaquant, ~e /atakɑ̃, ɑ̃t/ *mf* attacker

attaque /atak/ **A** *f* **1** attack; (on bank) raid; **passer à l'~** to move into the attack; (fig) to go on the attack; **~ à main armée** armed raid
2 (Med) stroke; **~ cardiaque** heart attack
B d'attaque *phr* (fam) on (BrE) *or* in (AmE) form; **être d'~ pour faire** to feel up to doing

attaquer /atake/ [**v1**] **A** *vt* **1** to attack; to raid ‹*bank*›
2 (Law) to contest ‹*contract, will*›; **~ qn en justice** to bring a lawsuit against sb
3 to tackle ‹*problem*›
B *vi* **1** (in tennis, golf) to drive
2 ‹*speaker*› to begin (brusquely)
C s'attaquer *v refl* (+ *v être*) **s'~ à** to attack ‹*person, policy*›; to tackle ‹*problem*›

attardé, ~e /ataʀde/ (offensive) **A** *adj* retarded (offensive)
B *mf* person with special needs

attarder: **s'attarder** /ataʀde/ [**v1**] *v refl* (+ *v être*) **1** to stay until late; to linger
2 s'~ sur to dwell on ‹*point*›

atteindre /atɛ̃dʀ/ [**v55**] **A** *vt* **1** to reach ‹*place, age, level, target*›; to achieve ‹*aim*›
2 ‹*projectile, marksman*› to hit ‹*target*›
3 ‹*illness*› to affect
B atteindre à *v+prep* to reach; to achieve

atteint, ~e /atɛ̃, ɛ̃t/ **A** *pp* ▸ **atteindre**
B *pp adj* **1** affected (**de, par** by); **être ~ de** to be suffering from ‹*illness*›
2 hit (**de, par** by)

atteinte /atɛ̃t/ **A** *f* **~ à** attack on; **porter ~ à** to undermine ‹*prestige*›; to damage ‹*reputation*›; to endanger ‹*security*›; to infringe ‹*right*›; **~ à la vie privée** breach of privacy
B hors d'atteinte *phr* **hors d'~** ‹*person*› beyond reach; ‹*target*› out of range

key word

attelage /atlaʒ/ *m* **1** (of horse) harness; (of oxen) yoke; (of wagon) coupling; (of trailer) towing attachment
2 (animals) team; (of oxen) yoke
3 horse-drawn carriage

atteler /atle/ [**v19**] **A** *vt* to harness ‹*horse*›; to yoke ‹*oxen*›; to couple ‹*wagon*›
B s'atteler *v refl* (+ *v être*) **s'~ à une tâche** to get down to a job

attelle /atɛl/ *f* (Med) splint

attenant, ~e /atnɑ̃, ɑ̃t/ *adj* adjacent

attendre /atɑ̃dʀ/ [**v6**] **A** *vt* **1** to wait for ‹*person, event*›; **j'attends de voir pour le croire** I'll believe it when I see it; **se faire ~** to keep people waiting; **la réaction ne se fit pas ~** the reaction was instantaneous; **~ son jour** *or* **heure** to bide one's time; **en attendant mieux** until something better turns up; **on ne t'attendait plus!** we'd given up on you!
2 to await, to be in store for ‹*person*›
3 to expect; **~ qch de qn/qch** to expect sth from sb/sth; **elle attend un bébé** she's expecting a baby
B *vi* to wait; (on phone) to hold; **faire ~ qn** to keep sb waiting; **en attendant** in the meantime; all the same, nonetheless; **tu ne perds rien pour ~!** (fam) I'll get you (fam), just you wait!
C s'attendre *v refl* (+ *v être*) **s'~ à qch** to expect sth; **s'~ à ce que qn fasse** to expect sb to do

attendrir /atɑ̃dʀiʀ/ [**v3**] **A** *vt* to touch, to move ‹*person*›; **se laisser ~** to soften
B s'attendrir *v refl* (+ *v être*) to feel moved

attendrissant, ~e /atɑ̃dʀisɑ̃, ɑ̃t/ *adj* touching, moving; ‹*innocence*› endearing

attendrissement /atɑ̃dʀismɑ̃/ *m* emotion

attendu[1]: **attendu que** /atɑ̃dy/ *phr*
1 given *or* considering that
2 (Law) whereas

attendu[2], ~e /atɑ̃dy/ *adj* **1** expected
2 le jour (tant) ~ the long-awaited day

attentat /atɑ̃ta/ *m* assassination attempt, attack; **~ à la bombe** bomb attack
■ **~ à la pudeur** (Law) indecent assault; **~ suicide** suicide attack

attente /atɑ̃t/ *f* **1** waiting; wait; **mon ~ a été vaine** I waited in vain; **dans l'~ de vous lire** looking forward to hearing from you; **en ~** ‹*passenger*› waiting; ‹*file*› pending; ‹*call*› on hold
2 expectation; **répondre à l'~ de qn** to come up to sb's expectations

attenter /atɑ̃te/ [**v1**] *v+prep* **~ à ses jours** to attempt suicide; **~ à la vie de qn** to make an attempt on sb's life

attentif, -ive /atɑ̃tif, iv/ *adj* attentive; **sous l'œil ~ de leur mère** under the watchful eye of their mother

attention /atɑ̃sjɔ̃/ **A** *f* **1** attention; **faire ~ à qch** to mind ‹*cars, step*›; to watch out

for ‹*black ice*›; to take care of ‹*clothes, belongings*›; to watch ‹*diet, health*›; to pay attention to ‹*fashion, details*›; **faire ~ à qn** to pay attention to sb; to keep an eye on sb; to take notice of sb
2 kind gesture; **être plein d'~s pour qn** to be very attentive to sb
B *excl* **1** (cry) look out!, watch out!; (written) attention!; (in case of danger) warning!; (on road sign) caution!
2 ~, je ne veux pas dire... don't get me wrong, I don't mean...

attentionné, **~e** /atɑ̃sjɔne/ *adj* attentive, considerate

attentisme /atɑ̃tism/ *m* wait-and-see attitude

attentivement /atɑ̃tivmɑ̃/ *adv*
1 attentively
2 carefully

atténuantes /atenɥɑ̃t/ *adj f pl* **circonstances ~** (Law) mitigating circumstances

atténuer /atenɥe/ [**v1**] **A** *vt* to ease ‹*pain, distress*›; to lessen ‹*impact*›; to smooth over ‹*differences*›; to weaken ‹*effect*›; to soften ‹*blow*›; to reduce ‹*inequalities*›; to dim ‹*light*›; to make [sth] less strong ‹*smell, taste*›
B s'atténuer *v refl* (+ *v être*) ‹*pain*› to ease; ‹*anger, grief*› to subside; ‹*corruption, pessimism*› to lessen; ‹*gaps*› to be reduced; ‹*wrinkles, colour*› to fade; ‹*storm, noise*› to die down

atterrant, **~e** /aterɑ̃, ɑ̃t/ *adj* **1** appalling
2 shattering

atterré, **~e** /atere/ *adj* **1** appalled
2 shattered

atterrir /ateriʀ/ [**v3**] *vi* to land

atterrissage /aterisaʒ/ *m* landing

attestation /atɛstasjɔ̃/ *f* **1** attestation
2 certificate

attester /atɛste/ [**v1**] *vt* **1** to vouch for; to testify to
2 to prove, to attest to

attirail /atiʀaj/ *m* gear, equipment

attirance /atiʀɑ̃s/ *f* attraction

attirant, **~e** /atiʀɑ̃, ɑ̃t/ *adj* attractive

✓ **attirer** /atiʀe/ [**v1**] **A** *vt* **1** to attract ‹*person, capital*›; to draw ‹*crowd, attention*›; **~ qn dans un coin** to take sb into a corner; **~ qn dans un piège** to lure sb into a trap
2 ‹*country, profession*› to appeal to
3 to bring ‹*shame, anger*›; **~ des ennuis à qn** to cause sb problems
B s'attirer *v refl* (+ *v être*) **s'~ le soutien de qn** to win sb's support; **s'~ des ennuis** to get into trouble

attiser /atize/ [**v1**] *vt* **1** to kindle ‹*feeling*›; to fuel ‹*discord*›; to stir up ‹*hatred*›
2 to fan ‹*fire*›

attitré, **~e** /atitʀe/ *adj* **1** ‹*chauffeur*› official
2 ‹*customer*› regular

✓ **attitude** /atityd/ *f* **1** bearing; posture
2 attitude

attouchement /atuʃmɑ̃/ *m* **1** molesting
2 fondling
3 (by healer) laying on of hands

attractif, **-ive** /atʀaktif, iv/ *adj* attractive

attraction /atʀaksjɔ̃/ *f* attraction
■ **~ terrestre** earth's gravity; **~ universelle** gravitation

attrait /atʀɛ/ *m* **1** appeal, attraction; lure
2 l'~ de qn pour qn/qch sb's liking for sb/sth

attraper /atʀape/ [**v1**] *vt* **1** to catch; **se faire ~** to get caught; **attrapez-le!** stop him!
2 to catch hold of ‹*rope, hand, leg*›
3 (fam) to catch ‹*cold, illness*›
4 (fam) to tell [sb] off

attrayant, **~e** /atʀɛjɑ̃, ɑ̃t/ *adj* **1** attractive
2 pleasant

✓ **attribuer** /atʀibɥe/ [**v1**] **A** *vt* **1** to allocate ‹*seat, task*›; to grant ‹*right*›; to award ‹*prize*›; to lend ‹*importance*›; **~ qch à la fatigue** to put sth down to tiredness
2 ~ qch à qn to credit sb with sth ‹*quality*›; to attribute sth to sb ‹*work*›
B s'attribuer *v refl* (+ *v être*) **s'~ la meilleure part** to give oneself the largest share; **s'~ tout le mérite** to take all the credit

attribut /atʀiby/ *m* **1** (quality, symbol) attribute
2 (in grammar) complement; **adjectif ~** predicative adjective; **nom ~** complement

attribution /atʀibysjɔ̃/ **A** *f* **1** allocation
2 awarding
B attributions *fpl* (of individual) remit; (of court) competence

attristant, **~e** /atʀistɑ̃, ɑ̃t/ *adj*
1 distressing, upsetting
2 depressing; **d'une bêtise ~e** depressingly stupid

attrister /atʀiste/ [**v1**] *vt* to sadden; **j'ai été attristé d'apprendre** I was sorry to hear

attroupement /atʀupmɑ̃/ *m* gathering

attrouper: **s'attrouper** /atʀupe/ [**v1**] *v refl* (+ *v être*) to gather

✓ **au** /o/ (= **à le**) ▶ **à**

aubade /obad/ *f* dawn serenade

aubaine /obɛn/ *f* **1** godsend
2 bargain

aube /ob/ *f* **1** dawn
2 alb; cassock

aubépine /obepin/ *f* hawthorn

auberge /obɛʀʒ/ *f* inn; **~ de jeunesse** youth hostel
IDIOM **tu n'es pas sorti de l'~!** (fam) you're not out of the woods yet!

aubergine /obɛʀʒin/ *f* aubergine, eggplant

aubergiste /obɛʀʒist/ *mf* innkeeper

✓ **aucun**, **~e** /okœ̃, yn/ **A** *adj* no, not any; **en ~ cas** under no circumstances
B *pron* none; **je n'ai lu ~ de vos livres**

a

I haven't read any of your books; ~ **de ses arguments n'est convaincant** none of his arguments are convincing

aucunement /okynmɑ̃/ *adv* in no way

audace /odas/ *f* **1** boldness
2 daring
3 audacity, nerve (fam); impudence

audacieux, **-ieuse** /odasjø, øz/ *adj* **1** bold
2 audacious, daring

au-delà /od(ə)la/ **A** *m* **l'~** the hereafter
B *adv* beyond; **jusqu'à 150 euros mais pas ~** up to 150 euros but no more
C **au-delà de** *phr* beyond; over

au-dessous /odəsu/ **A** *adv* **1** below
2 under; **les enfants de dix ans et ~** children of ten years and under
B **au-dessous de** *phr* below; **être ~ de tout** (fam) to be absolutely useless

au-dessus /odəsy/ **A** *adv* above; **les enfants de 10 ans et ~** children of 10 and over; **la taille ~** the next size up
B **au-dessus de** *phr* above; **~ de chez moi** in the apartment above mine; **un pont ~ de la rivière** a bridge over the river; **se pencher ~ de la table** to lean across the table

au-devant: **au-devant de** /odəvɑ̃də/ *phr* **aller ~ de qn** to go to meet sb; **aller ~ des ennuis** to let oneself in for trouble

audible /odibl/ *adj* audible

audience /odjɑ̃s/ *f* **1** (Law) hearing; **salle d'~** courtroom
2 (interview) audience
3 (public) audience

Audimat® /odimat/ *m* audience ratings

audiovisuel, **-elle** /odjɔvisɥel/ **A** *adj*
1 broadcasting
2 audiovisual
B *m* **1** broadcasting
2 audiovisual equipment
3 audiovisual methods

audit /odit/ *m* audit

auditeur, **-trice** /oditœʀ, tʀis/ *mf* listener

auditif, **-ive** /oditif, iv/ *adj* ‹*nerve*› auditory; ‹*problems*› hearing; ‹*memory*› aural

audition /odisjɔ̃/ *f* **1** (sense) hearing
2 audition
3 (Law) hearing, examination

auditionner /odisjɔne/ [**v1**] *vt*, *vi* to audition

auditoire /oditwaʀ/ *m* audience

auge /oʒ/ *f* (for animal feed) trough

augmentation /ogmɑ̃tasjɔ̃/ *f* increase; **une ~ (de salaire)** a pay rise (BrE) *or* raise (AmE)

🔑 **augmenter** /ogmɑ̃te/ [**v1**] **A** *vt* to raise, to increase; to extend; **~ le loyer de qn** to put sb's rent up
B *vi* to increase, to go up, to rise

augure /ogyʀ/ *m* **1** omen
2 augury

augurer /ogyʀe/ [**v1**] *vt* **que peut-on ~ de cette attitude?** what should we expect from this attitude?

auguste /ogyst/ *adj* august, noble

🔑 **aujourd'hui** /oʒuʀdɥi/ *adv* **1** today
2 nowadays, today; **la France d'~** present-day France

aulne /on/ *m* alder

aumône /omon/ *f* hand-out, alms; **demander l'~** to ask for charity

aumônerie /omonʀi/ *f* chaplaincy

aumônier /omonje/ *m* chaplain

aune /on/ ▶ **aulne**

🔑 **auparavant** /opaʀavɑ̃/ *adv* before; beforehand; previously; formerly

🔑 **auprès**: **auprès de** /opʀɛdə/ *phr* **1** next to, beside; **il s'est rendu ~ de sa tante** he went to see his aunt
2 compared with
3 **s'excuser ~ de qn** to apologize to sb; **renseigne-toi ~ de la mairie** ask for information at the town hall; **représentant ~ de l'ONU** representative to the UN

🔑 **auquel** ▶ **lequel**

aura /ɔʀa/ ▶ **avoir¹**

aurai /ɔʀɛ/ ▶ **avoir¹**

auras /ɔʀa/ ▶ **avoir¹**

auréole /ɔʀeɔl/ *f* **1** (stain) ring
2 halo

auréolé, **~e** /ɔʀeɔle/ *adj* **~ de** basking in the glow of

aurez /ɔʀe/ ▶ **avoir¹**

auriculaire /ɔʀikylɛʀ/ **A** *adj* auricular
B *m* little finger, pinkie

aurifère /ɔʀifɛʀ/ *adj* **1** ‹*mineral*› auriferous
2 **valeurs ~s** gold stocks

aurons /ɔʀɔ̃/ ▶ **avoir¹**

auront /ɔʀɔ̃/ ▶ **avoir¹**

aurore /ɔʀɔʀ/ *f* dawn; **~ boréale** Northern Lights, aurora borealis

auscultation /ɔskyltasjɔ̃/ *f* examination

ausculter /ɔskylte/ [**v1**] *vt* (Med) to examine

auspices /ospis/ *mpl* auspices

🔑 **aussi** /osi/ **A** *adv* **1** too, as well, also; **il sera absent et moi ~** he'll be away and so will I
2 **~ bien que** as well as; **~ âgé que** as old as
3 so; **je ne savais pas qu'il était ~ vieux** I didn't know he was so old; **dans une ~ belle maison** in such a nice house
B *conj* so, consequently

🔑 **aussitôt** /osito/ **A** *adv* **1** immediately, straight away
2 **~ arrivé** as soon as he arrived; **~ dit ~ fait** no sooner said than done
B **aussitôt que** *phr* as soon as

austère /ɔstɛʀ, ostɛʀ/ *adj* austere; severe

austérité /osteʀite/ *f* austerity; severity

austral, **~e**, *mpl* **~s** /ostʀal/ *adj* southern, south

Australie /ostʀali/ *pr f* Australia

🔑 key word

australien, **-ienne** /ostʀaljɛ̃, ɛn/ *adj* Australian

autant /otɑ̃/ **A** *adv* **il n'a jamais ~ neigé** it has never snowed so much; **je t'aime toujours ~** I still love you as much; **essaie d'en faire ~** try and do the same; **je les hais tous ~ qu'ils sont** I hate every single one of them; **j'aime ~ partir tout de suite** I'd rather leave straight away; **~ dire que la réunion est annulée** in other words the meeting is cancelled (BrE); **~ parler à un mur** you might as well be talking to the wall; **~ que je sache** as far as I know; **~ que tu peux** as much as you can
B autant de *quantif* **1 ~ de cadeaux** so many presents; **il y a ~ de femmes que d'hommes** there are as many women as (there are) men
2 ~ de gentillesse such kindness; **je n'ai pas eu ~ de chance que lui** I haven't had as much luck as he has
C d'autant *phr* **cela va permettre de réduire d'~ les coûts de production** this will allow an equivalent reduction in production costs; **d'~ plus!** all the more reason!; **d'~ moins** even less, all the less; **d'~ que** all the more so as
D pour autant *phr* for all that; **sans pour ~ tout modifier** without necessarily changing everything; **pour ~ que je sache** as far as I know

autarcie /otaʀsi/ *f* autarky; **vivre en ~** to be self-sufficient

autel /otɛl/ *m* altar

auteur /otœʀ/ *m* **1** author
2 creator; (of song) composer; (of crime) perpetrator
■ **~ dramatique** playwright

auteur-compositeur, *pl* **auteurs-compositeurs** /otœʀkɔ̃pozitœʀ/ *m* songwriter

authenticité /otɑ̃tisite/ *f* authenticity

authentifier /otɑ̃tifje/ [**v2**] *vt* to authenticate

authentique /otɑ̃tik/ *adj* ‹*story*› true; ‹*painting, document*› authentic; ‹*feeling*› genuine

autiste /otist/ *mf* autistic person

auto /oto/ *f* car, automobile (AmE)
■ **~ tamponneuse** bumper car, dodgem

autobiographie /otobjogʀafi/ *f* autobiography

autobus /otɔbys/ *m inv* bus

autocar /otɔkaʀ/ *m* coach (BrE), bus (AmE)

autochtone /otɔkton/ *adj, mf* native

autocollant, **~e** /otɔkɔlɑ̃, ɑ̃t/ **A** *adj* self-adhesive
B *m* sticker

autocuiseur /otokɥizœʀ/ *m* pressure cooker

autodéfense /otodefɑ̃s/ *f* self-defence (BrE)

autodestructeur, **-trice** /otodɛstʀyktœʀ, tʀis/ *adj* self-destructive

autodestruction /otodɛstʀyksjɔ̃/ *f* self-destruction

autodétruire: **s'autodétruire** /otodetʀɥiʀ/ [**v69**] *v refl* (+ *v être*) ‹*person*› to destroy oneself; ‹*tape*› to self-destruct; ‹*missile*› to autodestruct

autodidacte /otodidakt/ *mf* self-educated person

auto-école, *pl* **~s** /otoekɔl/ *f* driving school

autogérer: **s'autogérer** /otoʒeʀe/ [**v14**] *v refl* (+ *v être*) ‹*company*› to be run on a cooperative basis

autographe /otɔgʀaf/ *adj, m* autograph

automate /otɔmat/ *m* robot, automaton

automatique /otɔmatik/ **A** *adj*
1 automatic
2 inevitable
B *m* **1** automatic (revolver)
2 automatic camera

automatiquement /otɔmatikmɑ̃/ *adv*
1 automatically
2 (fam) inevitably

automatiser /otɔmatize/ [**v1**] *vt* to automate

automatisme /otɔmatism/ *m* automatism; automatic functioning; **acquérir des ~s** to acquire automatic reflexes

automne /otɔn/ *m* autumn (BrE), fall (AmE)

automobile /otomɔbil/ **A** *adj* **1** car
2 (Sport) ‹*racing*› motor; ‹*circuit*› motor racing
B *f* **1** (motor) car, automobile (AmE)
2 the motor (BrE) *or* automobile (AmE) industry

automobiliste /otomɔbilist/ *mf* motorist

autonome /otɔnɔm/ *adj* autonomous; independent; self-sufficient

autonomie /otɔnɔmi/ *f* **1** autonomy
2 (of car, plane) range; **~ de vol** flight range

autonomiste /otɔnɔmist/ *adj, mf* separatist

autoportrait /otopɔʀtʀɛ/ *m* self-portrait

autopsie /otɔpsi/ *f* postmortem (examination)

autoradio /otoʀadjo/ *m* car radio

autorisation /otɔʀizasjɔ̃/ *f* **1** permission; authorization
2 permit

autorisé, **~e** /otɔʀize/ *adj* authorized; legal; accredited; permitted

autoriser /otɔʀize/ [**v1**] *vt* **1** to allow, to authorize
2 ~ qn à faire to entitle sb to do
3 to make [sth] possible

autoritaire /otɔʀitɛʀ/ *adj, mf* authoritarian

autorité /otɔʀite/ *f* **1** authority; **faire qch d'~** to do sth without consultation; **il n'a aucune ~ sur ses enfants** he has no control over his children; **faire ~** ‹*person*› to be an

authority; ‹*work*› to be authoritative
2 (person) authority, expert

autoroute /otoʀut/ *f* motorway (BrE), freeway (AmE); **~ à péage** toll motorway
■ **~ de l'information** information highway

autoroutier, **-ière** /otoʀutje, ɛʀ/ *adj* motorway (BrE), freeway (AmE)

auto-stop /otostɔp/ *m* hitchhiking

auto-stoppeur, **-euse**, *mpl* **~s** /otostɔpœʀ, øz/ *mf* hitchhiker

🗝 **autour** /otuʀ/ **A** *adv* **un parterre de fleurs avec des pierres ~** a flower bed with stones around it; **tout ~** all around
B **autour de** *phr* **1** around, round (BrE); **~ de la table** around the table
2 around, about; **~ de 10 heures** around 10 o'clock
3 about, on; **un débat ~ du thème du pouvoir** a debate on the theme of power

🗝 **autre** /otʀ/ **A** *det* **1** other; **une ~ histoire** another story; **rien d'~** nothing else; **l'effet obtenu est tout ~** the effect produced is completely different
2 (fam) **nous ~s professeurs/Français** we teachers/French
B *pron* **1** **où sont les ~s?** where are the other ones?; **je t'ai pris pour un ~** I mistook you for someone else; **ils se respectent les uns les ~s** they respect each other; **chez lui c'est tout l'un ou tout l'~** with him it's all or nothing; **à d'~s!** (fam) pull the other one! (fam)
2 **prends-en un ~** have another one; **si je peux je t'en apporterai d'~s** if I can I'll bring you some more
C **autre part** *phr* somewhere else

🗝 **autrefois** /otʀəfwa/ *adv* in the past; before, formerly; in the old days; **~, quand Paris s'appelait Lutèce** long ago, when Paris was called Lutetia; **les légendes d'~** old legends

🗝 **autrement** /otʀəmɑ̃/ *adv* **1** differently, in a different way; **c'est comme ça, et pas ~** that's just the way it is; **je n'ai pas pu faire ~ que de les inviter** I had no alternative but to invite them; **on ne peut y accéder ~ que par bateau** you can only get there by boat; **je ne l'ai jamais vue ~ qu'en jean** I've never seen her in anything but jeans; **~ dit** in other words
2 otherwise
3 (fam) **~ grave** (much) more serious; **il n'était pas ~ impressionné** he wasn't particularly impressed

Autriche /otʀiʃ/ *pr f* Austria

autrichien, **-ienne** /otʀiʃjɛ̃, ɛn/ *adj* Austrian

autruche /otʀyʃ/ *f* ostrich
IDIOM **pratiquer la politique de l'~** to bury one's head in the sand

autrui /otʀɥi/ *pron* others, other people

auvent /ovɑ̃/ *m* **1** canopy
2 awning

aux /o/ (= **à les**) ▶ **à**

auxiliaire /oksiljɛʀ/ **A** *adj* **1** ‹*verb*› auxiliary
2 ‹*equipment, service*› auxiliary; ‹*motor*› back-up
3 **maître ~** assistant teacher; **infirmier ~** nursing auxiliary (BrE), nurse's aide (AmE)
B *mf* assistant, helper
C *m* auxiliary (verb)

auxquels, **auxquelles** ▶ **lequel**

avachir: **s'avachir** /avaʃiʀ/ [**v3**] *v refl* (+ *v être*) **1** ‹*chair*› to sag
2 ‹*person*› to let oneself go

avaient /avɛ/ ▶ **avoir**[1]

avais /avɛ/ ▶ **avoir**[1]

avait /avɛ/ ▶ **avoir**[1]

aval /aval/ *m* **1** (of river) lower reaches; **en ~** downstream
2 approval

avalanche /avalɑ̃ʃ/ *f* avalanche

avaler /avale/ [**v1**] *vt* **1** to swallow; **'ne pas ~'** (Med) 'not to be taken internally'
2 to inhale ‹*smoke, fumes*›

avaleur /avalœʀ/ *m* **~ de sabres** sword swallower

à-valoir /avalwaʀ/ *m inv* instalment (BrE)

🗝 **avance** /avɑ̃s/ **A** *f* **1** advance
2 lead; **avoir/prendre de l'~ sur** to be/pull ahead of
3 **une ~ (sur salaire)** an advance (on one's salary)
B **à l'avance** *phr* in advance
C **d'avance** *phr* in advance; **avoir cinq minutes d'~** to be five minutes early
D **en avance** *phr* **1** early
2 **être en ~ sur qn** to be ahead of sb
3 **il est en ~ pour son âge** he's advanced for his age
E **avances** *fpl* advances

avancé, **~e** /avɑ̃se/ **A** *pp* ▶ **avancer**
B *pp adj* ‹*ideas*› progressive; **la saison est bien ~e** it's late in the season; **te voilà bien ~!** that's done you a lot of good!

avancée /avɑ̃se/ *f* (of roof, rock) overhang

avancement /avɑ̃smɑ̃/ *m* **1** promotion
2 progress
3 **~ de l'âge de la retraite** lowering of the retirement age

🗝 **avancer** /avɑ̃se/ [**v12**] **A** *vt* **1** to move [sth] forward ‹*object*›; to push [sth] forward ‹*plate*›
2 to bring forward ‹*trip, meeting*›
3 **~ sa montre de cinq minutes** to put one's watch forward (by) five minutes
4 to get ahead with ‹*work*›; **cela ne nous avance à rien** that doesn't get us anywhere
5 **~ de l'argent à qn** ‹*bank*› to advance money to sb
6 to put forward ‹*argument, theory*›; to propose ‹*figure*›
B *vi* **1** ‹*person, vehicle*› to move (forward); ‹*army*› to advance; **elle avança vers le guichet** she went up to the ticket office

🗝 key word

2 to make progress, to progress; **faire ~ la science** to further science
3 ma montre avance de deux minutes my watch is two minutes fast
4 ‹*teeth, chin*› to stick out; ‹*peninsula*› to jut out
C s'avancer *v refl* (+ *v être*) **1 s'~ vers qch** to move toward(s) sth; **s'~ vers qn** to go toward(s) sb; to come up to sb
2 to get ahead
3 to jut out, to protrude
4 je me suis un peu avancé en lui promettant le dossier pour demain I shouldn't have committed myself by promising him/her I'd have the file ready for tomorrow

avant[1] /avɑ̃/ **A** *adv* before; first; **bien ~** long before; **il l'a mentionné ~ dans l'introduction** he mentioned it earlier in the introduction
B *prep* before; **~ mon retour** before I get back; before I got back; **~ le 1er juillet** by 1 July; **~ peu** shortly; **~ tout, ~ toute chose** above all; first and foremost
C d'avant *phr* **la séance d'~** the previous performance; **la fois d'~ nous nous étions déjà perdus** we got lost the last time as well
D avant de *phr* **~ de faire** before doing
E avant que *phr* before
F en avant *phr* forward(s); **en ~ toute!** full steam ahead!; **mettre en ~ le fait que** to point out the fact that; **se mettre en ~** to push oneself forward
G en avant de *phr* ahead of ‹*group*›

avant[2] /avɑ̃/ **A** *adj inv* ‹*wheel, seat, paw*› front
B *m* **1 l'~** the front; **aller de l'~** to forge ahead
2 (Sport) forward
C avant- (*combining form*) **l'~-Thatcher** the pre-Thatcher era

avantage /avɑ̃taʒ/ *m* **1** advantage; **tirer ~ de qch** to take advantage of sth; **paraître à son ~** to look one's best
2 benefit; **~ fiscaux** tax benefits

avantager /avɑ̃taʒe/ [**v13**] *vt* **1** ‹*person*› to favour (BrE); ‹*situation*› to be to the advantage of
2 ‹*clothes*› to show [sb/sth] off to advantage

avantageusement /avɑ̃taʒøzmɑ̃/ *adv* favourably (BrE)

avantageux, **-euse** /avɑ̃taʒø, øz/ *adj* **1** ‹*conditions, offer*› favourable (BrE), advantageous; ‹*rate, price*› attractive; **tirer un parti ~ de qch** to use sth to one's advantage
2 ‹*description, outfit*› flattering

avant-bras /avɑ̃bʀa/ *m inv* forearm

avant-centre, *pl* **avants-centres** /avɑ̃sɑ̃tʀ/ *m* centre (BrE) forward; **jouer ~** to play centre (BrE) forward

avant-coureur, *pl* **~s** /avɑ̃kuʀœʀ/ *adj* **signes ~s** early warning signs

avant-dernier, **-ière**, *pl* **~s** /avɑ̃dɛʀnje, ɛʀ/ **A** *adj* penultimate; **l'~ jour** the last day but one
B *mf* the last but one; **l'~ d'une famille de cinq** the second youngest of five children

avant-garde, *pl* **~s** /avɑ̃gaʀd/ *f* **1** avant-garde
2 vanguard; **à l'~** in the vanguard

avant-goût, *pl* **~s** /avɑ̃gu/ *m* foretaste

avant-guerre, *pl* **~s** /avɑ̃gɛʀ/ *mf* **l'~** the pre-war period; **l'Espagne d'~** pre-war Spain

avant-hier /avɑ̃tjɛʀ/ *adv* the day before yesterday

avant-poste, *pl* **~s** /avɑ̃pɔst/ *m* (Mil) outpost; **être aux ~s** to be in the vanguard

avant-première, *pl* **~s** /avɑ̃pʀəmjɛʀ/ *f* preview

avant-propos /avɑ̃pʀɔpo/ *m inv* foreword

avant-veille, *pl* **~s** /avɑ̃vɛj/ *f* two days before

avare /avaʀ/ **A** *adj* mean, miserly; **~ de** sparing with
B *mf* miser

avarice /avaʀis/ *f* meanness (BrE), miserliness

avarier: **s'avarier** /avaʀje/ [**v2**] *v refl* (+ *v être*) ‹*meat, fish*› to go rotten

avatar /avataʀ/ *m* **1** mishap
2 change

avec /avɛk/ **A** *adv* (fam) **elle est partie ~** she went off with it
B *prep* with; **~ attention** carefully; **et ~ cela, que désirez-vous?** what else would you like?; **je fais tout son travail et ~ ça il n'est pas content!** I do all his work and he's still not happy!; **sa séparation d'~ sa femme** his separation from his wife

avenant, **~e** /avnɑ̃, ɑt/ **A** *adj* pleasant
B à l'avenant *phr* in keeping

avènement /avɛnmɑ̃/ *m* **1** (of monarch) accession; (of politician, era) advent; **~ au trône** accession to the throne
2 Advent

avenir /avniʀ/ *m* future; **d'~** ‹*job*› with a future; ‹*technique, science*› of the future

aventure /avɑ̃tyʀ/ *f* **1** adventure
2 il m'est arrivé une drôle d'~ something strange happened to me
3 venture
4 (love) affair
IDIOM **dire la bonne ~ à qn** to tell sb's fortune

aventurer: **s'aventurer** /avɑ̃tyʀe/ [**v1**] *v refl* (+ *v être*) to venture

aventurier, **-ière** /avɑ̃tyʀje, ɛʀ/ *mf* adventurer/adventuress

avenue /avny/ *f* avenue

avérer: **s'avérer** /aveʀe/ [**v14**] *v refl* (+ *v être*) **s'~ utile** to prove useful; **il s'avère que** it turns out that

averse /avɛʀs/ *f* shower

aversion /avɛʀsjɔ̃/ *f* aversion; **avoir qn/qch en ~** to loathe sb/sth

averti, **~e** /avɛʀti/ **A** *pp* ▶ **avertir**
B *pp adj* **1** ‹*reader*› informed
2 experienced
avertir /avɛʀtiʀ/ [**v3**] *vt* **1** to inform
2 to warn
avertissement /avɛʀtismɑ̃/ *m* **1** warning
2 (Sport) caution
3 (in book) foreword
avertisseur /avɛʀtisœʀ/ *m* **1** alarm
2 (of car) horn
aveu, *pl* **~x** /avø/ *m* confession; admission
aveuglant, **~e** /avœglɑ̃, ɑ̃t/ *adj* blinding
aveugle /avœgl/ **A** *adj* **1** blind
2 ‹*faith, love*› blind; ‹*violence*› indiscriminate
B *mf* blind person; **les ~s** the blind
aveuglement /avœgləmɑ̃/ *m* blindness
aveuglément /avœglemɑ̃/ *adv* blindly
aveugler /avœgle/ [**v1**] *vt* to blind
aveuglette: **à l'aveuglette** /alavœglɛt/ *phr* **1** blindly
2 at random
avez /ave/ ▶ **avoir**[1]
aviateur /avjatœʀ/ *m* airman
aviation /avjasjɔ̃/ *f* **1** aviation
2 aircraft industry
3 l'~ the air force
aviatrice /avjatʀis/ *f* woman pilot
aviculteur, **-trice** /avikyltœʀ, tʀis/ *mf*
1 (of fowl) poultry farmer
2 (of birds) aviculturist
aviculture /avikyltyʀ/ *f* **1** (of fowl) poultry farming
2 (of birds) aviculture
avide /avid/ *adj* **1** greedy
2 ~ de avid for, eager for
avidement /avidmɑ̃/ *adv* ‹*eat*› greedily; ‹*read*› avidly; ‹*look, search*› eagerly
avidité /avidite/ *f* **1** greed
2 eagerness
aviez /avje/ ▶ **avoir**[1]
avilir /aviliʀ/ [**v3**] *vt* to demean
avilissant, **~e** /avilisɑ̃, ɑ̃t/ *adj* demeaning
avilissement /avilismɑ̃/ *m* degradation
aviné, **~e** /avine/ *adj* ‹*person*› inebriated; ‹*look, face*› drunken
⚷ **avion** /avjɔ̃/ *m* **1** (aero)plane (BrE), airplane (AmE), aircraft; **aller à Rome en ~** to fly to Rome; **'par ~'** 'by air mail'
2 flight
■ **~ de chasse** fighter; **~ à réaction** jet; **~ de tourisme** light passenger aircraft
avions /avjɔ̃/ ▶ **avoir**[1]
aviron /aviʀɔ̃/ *m* **1** rowing
2 oar
⚷ **avis** /avi/ *m inv* **1** opinion; **je suis de ton ~** I agree with you; **changer d'~** to change one's mind
2 advice; **sauf ~ contraire** unless otherwise informed
3 (of jury, commission) recommendation
4 notice; **lancer un ~ de recherche** to issue a description of a missing person/wanted person
■ **~ au lecteur** foreword; **~ de passage** calling card (*left by postman etc.*)
avisé, **~e** /avize/ *adj* sensible; **être bien/mal ~** to be well-/ill-advised
aviser /avize/ [**v1**] **A** *vt* to notify
B *vi* to decide
C s'aviser *v refl* (+ *v être*) **ne t'avise pas de recommencer** don't dare do that again
aviver /avive/ [**v1**] **A** *vt* **1** to intensify ‹*feeling*›; to stir up ‹*quarrel*›; to make [sth] more acute ‹*pain*›
2 to liven up ‹*colour*›
3 to kindle ‹*fire*›
B s'aviver *v refl* (+ *v être*) ‹*desire, anger*› to grow; ‹*pain, grief*› to become more acute
⚷ **avocat** /avɔka/ *m* **1** lawyer, solicitor (BrE), attorney (at law) (AmE)
2 barrister (BrE), (trial) lawyer (AmE); **~ de l'accusation** counsel for the prosecution
3 (of idea) advocate; (of cause, person) champion
4 avocado (pear)
avocate /avɔkat/ *f* woman lawyer
avoine /avwan/ *f* oats
⚷ **avoir**[1] /avwaʀ/ [**v8**]

> You will find translations for expressions such as *avoir raison, avoir beau, en avoir marre* etc, at the entries **raison, beau, marre** etc.

A *v aux* to have; **j'ai perdu mon briquet** I've lost my lighter; **il aurait aimé te parler** he would have liked to speak to you
B *vt* **1** to have (got) ‹*child, book, room, time*›; **elle avait les larmes aux yeux** there were tears in her eyes
2 to get ‹*object, job*›; to catch ‹*train, plane*›; (on the phone) **j'ai réussi à l'~** I managed to get through to him
3 to wear, to have [sth] on
4 to feel; **~ du chagrin** to feel sad; **qu'est-ce que tu as?** what's wrong with you?
5 avoir faim/froid/20 ans to be hungry/cold/20 years old
6 to beat; to have (fam), to con (fam); **j'ai été eu** I've been had
C avoir à *v+prep* to have to; **tu n'as pas à le critiquer** you shouldn't criticize him; **j'ai beaucoup à faire** I have a lot to do; **tu n'as qu'à leur écrire** all you have to do is write to them
D en avoir pour *v+prep* **1 vous en avez pour combien de temps?** how long will it take you?; how long are you going to be?
2 j'en ai eu pour 75 euros it cost me 75 euros
E il y a *v impers* **1** there is/there are; **qu'est-ce qu'il y a?** what's wrong?; **il y a qu'elle m'énerve** she's getting on my nerves, that's what's wrong; **il y a à manger pour quatre** there's enough food for four; **il y en a toujours qui se plaignent** there's

⚷ key word

always someone who complains; **il n'y en a que pour leur chien** their dog comes first
2 il y a longtemps a long time ago; **il n'y a que cinq ans que j'habite ici** I have only been living here for five years
3 combien y a-t-il jusqu'à la gare? how far is it to the station?; **il y a au moins 15 kilomètres** it's at least 15 kilometres (BrE) away

avoir² /avwaʀ/ *m* **1** credit
2 credit note
3 assets, holdings

avoisinant, **~e** /avwazinɑ̃, ɑ̃t/ *adj* neighbouring (BrE)

avoisiner /avwazine/ [**v1**] *vt* **1** ‹*costs, sum*› to be close to, to be about
2 ‹*place*› to be near

avons /avɔ̃/ ▸ **avoir¹**

avortement /avɔʀtəmɑ̃/ *m* (Med) abortion

avorter /avɔʀte/ [**v1**] *vi* **1** (Med) to have an abortion
2 ‹*cow, ewe*› to abort, to miscarry
3 ‹*plan*› to be aborted; ‹*uprising*› to fail

avorton /avɔʀtɔ̃/ *m* runt

avouable /avwabl/ *adj* worthy; respectable

avoué, **~e** /avwe/ **A** *pp* ▸ **avouer**
B *pp adj* ‹*enemy*› declared; ‹*intention*› avowed
C *m* ≈ solicitor (BrE), attorney(AmE)

✓ **avouer** /avwe/ [**v1**] **A** *vt* to confess, to admit
B *vi* to confess; to own up
C s'avouer *v refl* (+ *v être*) **s'~ rassuré** to say one feels reassured; **s'~ vaincu** to admit defeat

✓ **avril** /avʀil/ *m* April

axe /aks/ *m* **1** axis
2 (Tech) axle
3 major road
4 dans l'~ du bâtiment in a line with the building; **la cible est dans l'~ du viseur** the target is lined up in the sights

axer /akse/ [**v1**] *vt* **1** to centre (BrE) ‹*screw*›; to line up ‹*part*›
2 to base, to centre (BrE) (**sur** on)

axiome /aksjom/ *m* axiom

ayant /ɛjɑ̃/ ▸ **avoir¹**

ayant droit, *pl* **ayants droit** /ɛyɑ̃dʀwa/ *m* **1** legal claimant, beneficiary
2 assignee

ayez /aje/ ▸ **avoir¹**

ayons /ajɔ̃/ ▸ **avoir¹**

azalée /azale/ *f* azalea

Azerbaïdjan /azɛʀbajdʒɑ̃/ *pr m* Azerbaijan

azimut /azimyt/ *m* **1** (in astronomy) azimuth
2 (fig) **une offensive tous ~s** an all-out offensive; **dans tous les ~s** everywhere

azote /azɔt/ *m* nitrogen

aztèque /astɛk/ *adj* Aztec

azur /azyʀ/ *m* azure

azyme /azim/ *adj* unleavened

Bb

b, **B** /be/ *m inv* b, B; **le b a ba** the rudiments

baba /baba/ *adj inv* (fam) **en être** *or* **rester ~** to be flabbergasted (fam)

babillage /babijaʒ/ *m* babbling

babiller /babije/ [**v1**] *vi* to babble, to chatter

babines /babin/ *fpl* lips; **retrousser les ~** ‹*dog*› to bare its teeth; **se lécher les ~** to lick one's chops

babiole /babjɔl/ *f* **1** trinket
2 trifle

bâbord /babɔʀ/ *m* port (side)

babouche /babuʃ/ *f* oriental slipper

babouin /babwɛ̃/ *m* baboon

baby-foot /babifut/ *m inv* table football (BrE), table soccer

bac /bak/ *m* **1** (fam) *abbr* = **baccalauréat**
2 ferry
3 tub; **évier à deux ~s** double sink
■ **~ à sable** sandpit (BrE), sandbox (AmE)

baccalauréat /bakalɔʀea/ *m* baccalaureate (*school-leaving certificate taken at 17–18*); **~ professionnel** vocational baccalaureate (*vocationally oriented school-leaving certificate*)

bâche /bɑʃ/ *f* tarpaulin

bachelier, **-ière** /baʃəlje, ɛʀ/ *mf: holder of the baccalaureate*

bâcher /bɑʃe/ [**v1**] *vt* to cover [sth] with tarpaulin ‹*vehicle*›; **un camion bâché** a covered truck

bachotage /baʃɔtaʒ/ *m* (Sch), (fam) cramming

bâcler /bakle/ [**v1**] *vt* to dash [sth] off ‹*piece of work*›; to rush through ‹*ceremony*›

bactérie /bakteʀi/ *f* bacterium

badaud, **~e** /bado, od/ *mf* **1** passerby
2 onlooker

badigeonner /badiʒɔne/ [**v1**] *vt* **1** to paint

2 to daub (**de** with)
3 (Culin) to brush (**de** with)

b

badin, **~e** /badɛ̃, in/ *adj* ‹*tone*› bantering

baffe /baf/ *f* (fam) clout, slap

baffle /bafl/ *m* **1** speaker
2 baffle

bafouille /bafuj/ *f* (fam) letter

bafouiller /bafuje/ [**v1**] *vt*, *vi* to mumble

bagage /bagaʒ/ *m* piece of luggage; **faire ses ~s** to pack
IDIOM **plier ~** (fam) to pack up and go

bagagiste /bagaʒist/ *m* baggage handler

bagarre /bagaʀ/ *f* fight, scuffle

bagarrer: **se bagarrer** /bagaʀe/ [**v1**] *v refl* (+ *v être*) (fam) to fight

bagarreur, **-euse** /bagaʀœʀ, øz/ *adj* (fam) aggressive

bagatelle /bagatɛl/ *f* **1** trifle, triviality
2 **pour la ~ de** (ironic) for the trifling sum of

bagne /baɲ/ *m* penal colony

bagou /bagu/ *m also* **bagout** (fam) **avoir du ~** to have the gift of the gab

bague /bag/ *f* **1** ring
2 (around pipe) collar

baguette /bagɛt/ *f* **1** baguette, French stick
2 stick; **mener qn à la ~** to rule sb with a rod of iron; **~ de chef d'orchestre** conductor's baton
3 drumstick
4 chopstick
■ **~ magique** magic wand

bahut /bay/ *m* **1** sideboard
2 (sl) school
3 (fam) truck

bai, **~e** /bɛ/ *adj* bay

baie /bɛ/ *f* **1** bay
2 berry
3 **~ (vitrée)** picture window

baignade /bɛɲad/ *f* swimming

baigner /beɲe/ [**v1**] **A** *vt* **1** to give [sb] a bath
2 to bathe ‹*wound*›
B *vi* **~ dans l'huile** to be swimming in grease
C **se baigner** *v refl* (+ *v être*) to go swimming
IDIOM **ça baigne** (fam) things are going fine

baigneur, **-euse** /bɛɲœʀ, øz/ *mf* swimmer

baignoire /bɛɲwaʀ/ *f* bathtub; **~ sabot** hip bath

bail, *pl* **baux** /baj, bo/ *m* lease; **ça fait un ~** (fam) it's been ages (**que** since)

bâiller /bɑje/ [**v1**] *vi* **1** to yawn
2 to gape (open)

bailleur, **bailleresse** /bajœʀ, bajʀɛs/ *mf* lessor
■ **~ de fonds** backer, silent partner

bâillon /bɑjɔ̃/ *m* gag

🗝 **bain** /bɛ̃/ *m* **1** bath
2 swim
3 **grand/petit ~** deep/shallow pool
■ **~ de bouche** mouthwash; **~ de foule** walkabout; **prendre un ~ de soleil** to sunbathe
IDIOM **se remettre dans le ~** to get back into the swing of things

baïonnette /bajɔnɛt/ *f* bayonet

baiser /beze/ *m* kiss

baisse /bɛs/ *f* **1** (gen) fall; **en ~** falling
2 (Econ) (of power, sales) decline; (of prices) cut; **la ~ du dollar** the fall in the value of the dollar; **une ~ des loyers de 2%** a 2% drop in rents; **être en ~** ‹*rates, stocks, shares*› to be going down; ‹*results*› to be decreasing; **le marché est à la ~** (Econ) the market is bearish; **revoir des prévisions à la ~** to revise estimates downward(s); **spéculations à la ~** bear speculations
3 (of light) fading

🗝 **baisser** /bese/ [**v1**] **A** *vt* **1** to lower ‹*blind*›; to wind [sth] down ‹*window*›; to turn down ‹*collar*›; **~ les bras** (fig) to give up; **~ le nez** (fig) to hang one's head
2 to turn down ‹*volume*›; to dim ‹*light*›; to cut ‹*prices*›
B *vi* to go down, to fall, to drop (**à** to, **de** by); (drop in value) ‹*price, profit, rates, production*› to fall; ‹*wages, shares*› to go down; ‹*purchasing power, unemployment*› to decrease; ‹*productivity, market*› to decline; ‹*budget*› to be cut; ‹*currency*› to slide; ‹*water*› to subside; ‹*sight*› to fail; ‹*hearing*› to deteriorate; **~ d'un ton** (fam) ‹*person*› to calm down
C **se baisser** *v refl* (+ *v être*) **1** to bend down
2 to duck
3 to go down

baissier, **-ière** /besje, ɛʀ/ **A** *adj* bearish
B *m* (on stock exchange) bear

bajoue /baʒu/ *f* cheek

bal /bal/ *m* **1** ball, dance
2 dancehall

balade /balad/ *f* walk; ride

balader /balade/ [**v1**] (fam) **A** *vt* **1** to take [sb] for a walk/drive
2 to carry [sth] around
B **se balader** *v refl* (+ *v être*) to go for a walk/ride/drive
IDIOM **envoyer qn ~** (fam) to send sb packing (fam)

baladeur /baladœʀ/ *m* Walkman®, personal stereo
■ **~ MP3** MP3 player; **~ multimédia** portable media player

balafre /balafʀ/ *f* **1** scar
2 slash, gash

balai /balɛ/ *m* broom; **passer le ~** to sweep the floor; **du ~!** (fam) go away!

balance /balɑ̃s/ *f* **1** (weighing) scales; **faire pencher la ~** (fig) to tip the scales
2 (Econ) balance; **~ commerciale** balance of trade; **~ des comptes**, **~ des paiements**

🗝 key word

balance of payments
Balance /balɑ̃s/ *pr f* Libra
balancelle /balɑ̃sɛl/ *f* swing seat
balancement /balɑ̃smɑ̃/ *m* swaying; swinging
balancer /balɑ̃se/ [**v12**] **A** *vt* **1** to sway; to swing
2 (fam) to chuck (fam) (**sur** at); to chuck out (fam) ‹*old clothes, junk*›
3 (fam) to squeal on (fam)
B *vi* **1** to sway
2 to hesitate
C **se balancer** *v refl* (+ *v être*) **1** ‹*person*› to sway; ‹*boat*› to rock
2 (fam) **je m'en balance** I couldn't care less
balancier /balɑ̃sje/ *m* pendulum
balançoire /balɑ̃swaʀ/ *f* swing
balayer /baleje/ [**v21**] *vt* **1** to sweep (up); **~ le sol** ‹*coat*› to brush the ground
2 to brush [sth] aside ‹*objections*›
3 ‹*radar*› to scan
balayette /balɛjɛt/ *f* (short-handled) brush
balayeur, **-euse** /balɛjœʀ, øz/ *mf* road sweeper
balbutiement /balbysimɑ̃/ *m* **les ~s du cinéma** the early days of the cinema
balbutier /balbysje/ [**v2**] *vt, vi* to mumble
balcon /balkɔ̃/ *m* **1** balcony
2 (in theatre, cinema) balcony, circle
Bâle /bɑl/ *pr n* Basel
baleine /balɛn/ *f* **1** whale
2 whalebone; stay; rib
balisage /balizaʒ/ *m* (in port, channel) beaconing; (on path) marking
balise /baliz/ *f* **1** beacon
2 signpost, waymark
3 (Comput) tag
baliser /balize/ [**v1**] *vt* **1** to mark [sth] out with beacons
2 to signpost, to waymark
3 (Comput) to tag ‹*text*›
balistique /balistik/ *f* ballistics
baliverne /balivɛʀn/ *f* nonsense
ballade /balad/ *f* ballad; ballade
balle /bal/ *f* **1** ball; **renvoyer la ~ (à qn)** (fig) to retort (to sb); **se renvoyer la ~** to keep up an animated discussion; to keep passing the buck
2 (in ball games) shot; **faire des ~s** to knock the ball around; **~ de jeu** game point
3 bullet
4 (fam) franc
ballerine /balʀin/ *f* **1** ballerina
2 ballet pump
ballet /balɛ/ *m* ballet
✓ **ballon** /balɔ̃/ *m* **1** ball
2 balloon
3 wine glass
4 ~ (alcootest) Breathalyzer®
■ **~ dirigeable** airship (BrE), blimp (AmE); **~ d'eau chaude** hot water tank; **~ ovale** rugby ball; **~ rond** soccer ball
ballonnement /balɔnmɑ̃/ *m* bloating
ballot /balo/ *m* (fam) nerd (fam), fool
ballottage /balɔtaʒ/ *m: absence of an absolute majority in the first round of an election*
ballotter /balɔte/ [**v1**] *vt* **1** ‹*sea*› to toss [sb/sth] around; ‹*movement*› to jolt
2 être ballotté entre sa famille et son travail to be torn between one's family and one's job
balluchon ▶ **baluchon**
balnéaire /balneɛʀ/ *adj* ‹*resort*› seaside
balte /balt/ *adj* Baltic; **les pays ~s** the Baltic States
baluchon /balyʃɔ̃/ *m* bundle
balustrade /balystʀad/ *f* **1** parapet
2 railing
3 balustrade
bambin, **~e** /bɑ̃bɛ̃, in/ *mf* kid (fam), child
bambou /bɑ̃bu/ *m* bamboo
ban /bɑ̃/ **A** *m* round of applause
B bans *mpl* banns
IDIOM **mettre qn au ~ de la société** to ostracize sb
banal, **~e** /banal/ *adj* **1** commonplace, ordinary; **peu ~** unusual
2 trivial, trite
banalisation /banalizɑsjɔ̃/ *f* **la ~ de l'informatique** the way in which computing has become part of everyday life
banaliser /banalize/ [**v1**] *vt* **1** to make [sth] commonplace
2 voiture banalisée unmarked car
banalité /banalite/ *f* **1** ordinariness
2 triteness
3 trite remark
banane /banan/ *f* **1** banana
2 quiff
3 bumbag (BrE), fanny pack (AmE)
banc /bɑ̃/ *m* **1** bench
2 (of fish) shoal
■ **~ des accusés** dock; **~ d'essai** test bench; testing ground; **~ de sable** sandbank
bancaire /bɑ̃kɛʀ/ *adj* **1** ‹*business*› banking
2 ‹*card*› bank
bancal, **~e** /bɑ̃kal/ *adj* **1** ‹*chair*› rickety
2 ‹*solution*› unsatisfactory
bancarisation /bɑ̃kaʀizasjɔ̃/ *f percentage of the population holding a bank account*; **le taux de ~ en France est élevé** a high percentage of the French population hold a bank account
✓ **bande** /bɑ̃d/ *f* **1** gang; group; **~ de crétins!** you bunch of idiots!; **ils font ~ à part** they don't join in
2 (of animals) pack
3 (of material, paper) strip; band
4 bandage
5 broad stripe
6 (for recording) tape
■ **~ d'arrêt d'urgence, BAU** hard shoulder; **~ dessinée, BD** (fam) comic strip; comic book;

b

~ **de fréquences** waveband; ~ **originale** (of film) original soundtrack
bande-annonce, *pl* **bandes-annonces** /bɑ̃danɔ̃s/ *f* trailer
bandeau, *pl* ~**x** /bɑ̃do/ *m* **1** blindfold
2 eye patch
3 headband
bandelette /bɑ̃dlɛt/ *f* bandage
bander /bɑ̃de/ [**v1**] *vt* **1** to bandage
2 ~ **les yeux à qn** to blindfold sb
banderole /bɑ̃dʀɔl/ *f* banner
bande-son, *pl* **bandes-son** /bɑ̃dsɔ̃/ *m* soundtrack
bandit /bɑ̃di/ *m* **1** bandit; ~ **de grand chemin** highwayman
2 crook
3 rascal
banditisme /bɑ̃ditism/ *m* **le (grand)** ~ (organized) crime
bandoulière /bɑ̃duljɛʀ/ *f* shoulder strap
bang /bɑ̃g/ *m* sonic boom
banlieue /bɑ̃ljø/ *f* **1** suburbs; **de** ~ suburban
2 suburb
banlieusard, ~**e** /bɑ̃ljøzaʀ, aʀd/ *mf* suburbanite
bannière /banjɛʀ/ *f* banner; **la** ~ **étoilée** the star-spangled banner
IDIOM **c'est la croix et la** ~ it's hell (**pour faire** doing)
bannir /baniʀ/ [**v3**] *vt* **1** to banish (**de** from)
2 to ban
bannissement /banismɑ̃/ *m* banishment (**de** from)
✓ **banque** /bɑ̃k/ *f* **1** bank
2 banking
■ ~ **de données** data bank
banqueroute /bɑ̃kʀut/ *f* bankruptcy
banquet /bɑ̃kɛ/ *m* **1** banquet
2 feast
banquette /bɑ̃kɛt/ *f* (in cafe) wall seat; (in car, train) seat
banquier /bɑ̃kje/ *m* banker
banquise /bɑ̃kiz/ *f* ice floe
baptême /batɛm/ *m* **1** baptism, christening
2 (of ship) christening; (of bell) blessing
■ ~ **de l'air** first flight
baptiser /batize/ [**v1**] *vt* **1** to baptize, to christen
2 to call, to name; to nickname
3 to christen ‹*ship*›; to bless ‹*bell*›
bar /baʀ/ *m* **1** bar
2 (Zool) sea bass
baragouiner /baʀagwine/ [**v1**] *vt* (fam) to gabble ‹*sentence*›; to speak [sth] badly ‹*language*›
baraka /baʀaka/ *f* (fam) luck
baraque /baʀak/ *f* **1** shack
2 (fam) pad (fam), house

✓ key word

baraqué, ~**e** /baʀake/ *adj* (fam) hefty
baraquement /baʀakmɑ̃/ *m* **1** group of huts
2 hut
3 army camp
baratin /baʀatɛ̃/ *m* (fam) **1** sales pitch
2 sweet-talk; smooth talk (BrE) (fam)
baratiner /baʀatine/ [**v1**] *vt* (fam) **1** to give [sb] the spiel (fam)
2 to chat [sb] up (fam)
3 to try to persuade
baratineur, **-euse** /baʀatinœʀ, øz/ *mf* (fam) smooth talker (fam); (dishonest) liar
barbant, ~**e** /baʀbɑ̃, ɑ̃t/ *adj* (fam) boring
barbare /baʀbaʀ/ **A** *adj* barbaric; barbarian
B *mf* barbarian
barbarie /baʀbaʀi/ *f* barbarity, barbarism
✓ **barbe** /baʀb/ **A** *f* beard; ~ **naissante** stubble
B *excl* (fam) **la** ~**!** I've had enough!; **la** ~ **avec leurs consignes!** to hell with their orders (fam)
■ ~ **à papa** candyfloss (BrE), cotton candy (AmE)
IDIOM **à la** ~ **de qn** under sb's nose
barbelé /baʀbəle/ *m* barbed wire (BrE), barbwire (AmE)
barbiche /baʀbiʃ/ *f* **1** goatee (beard)
2 (on goat) (small) beard
barbier /baʀbje/ *m* barber
barbiturique /baʀbityʀik/ *m* barbiturate
barboteuse /baʀbɔtøz/ *f* romper suit
barbouiller /baʀbuje/ [**v1**] **A** *vt* **1** to smear (**de** with)
2 to daub (**de** with)
3 ~ **des toiles** to do daubs; ~ **du papier** to write drivel
4 être barbouillé to feel queasy
B se barbouiller *v refl* (+ *v être*) **se** ~ **le visage de qch** to get one's face all covered in sth
barbu, ~**e** /baʀby/ *adj* bearded; **il est** ~ he has a beard
barde /baʀd/ *f* thin slice of bacon, bard
bardé, ~**e** /baʀde/ *adj* covered (**de** in)
barème /baʀɛm/ *m* scale; ~ **des prix** price list; ~ **d'imposition** tax schedule *or* scale
baril /baʀil/ *m* barrel, cask; keg; drum
barillet /baʀijɛ/ *m* cylinder
bariolé, ~**e** /baʀjɔle/ *adj* multicoloured (BrE)
baromètre /baʀɔmɛtʀ/ *m* barometer
baron /baʀɔ̃/ *m* baron
baronne /baʀɔn/ *f* baroness
baroque /baʀɔk/ *adj* **1** baroque
2 bizarre
baroudeur /baʀudœʀ/ *m* **1** fighter, warrior
2 adventurer
barque /baʀk/ *f* (small) boat
barquette /baʀkɛt/ *f* punnet (BrE), basket (AmE); tub; container

barrage /baʀaʒ/ *m* **1** dam
2 roadblock; barricade; **faire ~ à** to block

barre /baʀ/ *f* **1** bar, rod
2 (of chocolate) piece
3 tiller, helm
4 band, stripe
5 stroke; **la ~ du t** the cross on the t
6 (of goal) crossbar; (in high jump) bar
7 (in ballet practice) barre
8 (Law) bar; ≈ witness box (BrE), witness stand (AmE)
9 mark; **franchir la ~ des 13%** to go over the 13% mark
■ **~ fixe** horizontal bar; **~ oblique** slash; **~ des tâches** (Comput) task bar
IDIOM **avoir un coup de ~** (fam) to feel drained all of a sudden

barreau, *pl* **~x** /baʀo/ *m* **1** (of cage) bar
2 rung
3 (Law) **le ~** the Bar

barrer /baʀe/ [**v1**] *vt* **1** to block ‹*way*›; **'route barrée'** 'road closed'
2 to cross out

barrette /baʀɛt/ *f* (hair) slide (BrE), barrette (AmE)

barreur, -euse /baʀœʀ, øz/ *mf* (gen) helmsman; (in rowing) cox; **avec ~** coxed; **sans ~** coxless

barricade /baʀikad/ *f* barricade

barrière /baʀjɛʀ/ *f* **1** fence
2 gate
3 barrier

barrique /baʀik/ *f* barrel

barrir /baʀiʀ/ [**v3**] *vi* ‹*elephant*› to trumpet

bar-tabac, *pl* **bars-tabac** /baʀtaba/ *m* cafe (*selling stamps and cigarettes*)

baryton /baʀitɔ̃/ *adj, m* baritone

bas, basse /bɑ, bɑs/ **A** *adj* low; ‹*room*› low-ceilinged; ‹*land*› low-lying; **le ciel est ~** the sky is overcast; **un enfant en ~ âge** a very young child; **être au plus ~** ‹*prices*› to have reached rock bottom; **les cours sont au plus ~** (en Bourse) prices have reached rock bottom
B *adv* **1** low; **comment peut-on tomber si ~!** how can one sink so low!
2 **voir plus ~** see below
3 quietly; **tout ~** ‹*speak*› in a whisper; ‹*sing*› softly
4 **être au plus ~** to be extremely weak; to be at one's lowest
C *m inv* **1** bottom; **le ~ du visage** the lower part of the face; **les pièces du ~** the downstairs rooms
2 stocking
D **en bas** *phr* downstairs; down below; at the bottom
■ **~ de gamme** **A** *adj* low-quality
B *m* lower end of the market; **~ morceaux** (Culin) cheap cuts; **basse saison** low season
IDIOMS **avoir des hauts et des ~** to have one's ups and downs; **à ~ les tyrans!** down with tyranny!

basané, ~e /bazane/ *adj* swarthy

bas-côté, *pl* **~s** /bɑkote/ *m* **1** verge (BrE), shoulder (AmE)
2 (side) aisle

basculant, ~e /baskylɑ̃, ɑ̃t/ *adj* **pont ~** bascule bridge; **camion à benne ~e** dump truck

bascule /baskyl/ *f* **fauteuil à ~** rocking chair

basculer /baskyle/ [**v1**] **A** *vt* to transfer ‹*call*›
B *vi* **1** to topple over; **faire ~** to tip up ‹*skip*›; to tip out ‹*load*›; to knock [sb] off balance ‹*person*›
2 (fig) to change radically

base /bɑz/ *f* **1** base; **le riz forme la ~ de leur alimentation** rice is their staple diet
2 basis; **reposer sur des ~s solides** to rest on a firm foundation; **à la ~ de qch** at the root *or* heart of sth; **salaire de ~** basic salary; **repartir sur de nouvelles ~s** to make a fresh start
3 (in politics) **la ~** the rank and file
■ **~ de données** database; **~ de lancement** launching site

baser /bɑze/ [**v1**] **A** *vt* to base (**sur** on)
B **se baser** *v refl* (+ *v être*) **se ~ sur qch** to go by sth

bas-fond, *pl* **~s** /bɑfɔ̃/ **A** *m* **1** shallows
2 dip
B **bas-fonds** *mpl* seedy areas

basilic /bazilik/ *m* basil

basilique /bazilik/ *f* basilica

basket /baskɛt/ *m* **1** basketball
2 trainer (BrE), sneaker (AmE)
IDIOM **être bien** *or* **à l'aise dans ses ~s** (fam) to be very together (fam)

basque /bask/ *adj, m* Basque

basse /bɑs/ **A** *adj* ▶ **bas A**
B *f* (Mus) bass

basse-cour, *pl* **basses-cours** /bɑskuʀ/ *f* **1** poultry yard
2 poultry

bassement /bɑsmɑ̃/ *adv* basely

bassesse /bɑsɛs/ *f* **1** baseness
2 base act

bassin /basɛ̃/ *m* **1** pond; fountain; pool
2 (in geography) basin
3 pelvis
4 bedpan
■ **~ houiller** coal field

bassine /basin/ *f* bowl; basin

bassiste /bɑsist/ *mf* bass player

bastingage /bastɛ̃gaʒ/ *m* ship's rail

bas-ventre, *pl* **~s** /bɑvɑ̃tʀ/ *m* lower abdomen

bât /bɑ/ *m* pack-saddle
IDIOM **c'est là que le ~ blesse** that's where the shoe pinches

bataille /batɑj/ **A** *f* **1** battle
2 fight
B **en bataille** *phr* ‹*hair*› dishevelled (BrE); ‹*eyebrows*› bushy

b

batailler /batɑje/ [**v1**] *vi* to fight, to battle

bataillon /batɑjɔ̃/ *m* battalion; **Dupont?, inconnu au ~** Dupont?, never heard of him

bâtard, **~e** /bɑtaʀ, aʀd/ **A** *adj* **1** ‹*dog*› mongrel
2 ‹*work, style*› hybrid
3 (offensive) ‹*child*› bastard
B *mf* **1** mongrel
2 (offensive) bastard

✓ **bateau**, *pl* **~x** /bato/ **A** *adj inv* hackneyed
B *m* **1** boat, ship; **~ à voile/moteur/vapeur** sailing/motor/steam boat; **faire du ~** to go boating; to go sailing
2 dropped kerb (BrE) *or* curb (AmE)
■ **~ amiral** flagship; **~ pneumatique** rubber dinghy; **~ de sauvetage** lifeboat

bateau-école, *pl* **bateaux-écoles** /batoekɔl/ *m* training ship

bateau-mouche, *pl* **bateaux-mouches** /batomuʃ/ *m: large river boat for sightseeing*

bateleur, **-euse** /batlœʀ, øz/ *mf* tumbler, juggler

batelier, **-ière** /batəlje, ɛʀ/ *mf* boatman/ boatwoman

bâti, **~e** /bɑti/ **A** *pp* ▶ **bâtir**
B *pp adj* **1** built; **terrain ~** developed site
2 un homme bien ~ a well-built man

batifoler /batifɔle/ [**v1**] *vi* **1** to romp about
2 to flirt

✓ **bâtiment** /bɑtimɑ̃/ *m* **1** building
2 building trade
3 ship

bâtir /bɑtiʀ/ [**v3**] *vt* **1** to build
2 to tack ‹*hem*›

bâtisse /bɑtis/ *f* (dwelling) house; (structure) building

bâtisseur, **-euse** /bɑtisœʀ, øz/ *mf* master builder; (fig) builder

bâton /bɑtɔ̃/ *m* **1** stick
2 vertical stroke
3 (Hist), (fam) ten thousand francs
■ **~ de rouge (à lèvres)** lipstick
IDIOMS **discuter à ~s rompus** to talk about this and that; **mettre des ~s dans les roues de qn** to put a spoke in sb's wheel

bâtonnet /bɑtɔnɛ/ *m* stick
■ **~ de poisson** fish finger (BrE), fish stick (AmE)

batracien /batʀasjɛ̃/ *m* batrachian

battage /bataʒ/ *m* (fam) publicity, hype (fam)

battant, **~e** /batɑ̃, ɑ̃t/ **A** *adj* **le cœur ~** with a beating heart
B *mf* fighter
C *m* **porte à deux ~s** double door

batte /bat/ *f* (Sport) bat (BrE), paddle (AmE)

battement /batmɑ̃/ *m* **1** beating; beat; fluttering; flutter
2 break, gap; wait

batterie /batʀi/ *f* **1** percussion section
2 drum kit
3 battery
■ **~ de cuisine** pots and pans

batteur /batœʀ/ *m* **1** percussionist
2 drummer
3 whisk

✓ **battre** /batʀ/ [**v61**] **A** *vt* **1** (defeat) to beat ‹*opponent*›; to break ‹*record*›
2 (hit) to beat ‹*person, animal, carpet*›; to thresh ‹*corn*›
3 ‹*rain, sea*› to beat against
4 to whisk ‹*eggs*›; to whip ‹*cream*›
5 to shuffle ‹*cards*›
6 (Mus) **~ la mesure** to beat time
7 to scour ‹*countryside*›
B battre de *v+prep* **~ des ailes** to flap its wings; **~ des cils** to flutter one's eyelashes; **~ des mains** to clap (one's hands)
C *vi* **1** ‹*heart, pulse*› to beat
2 ‹*door*› to bang
D se battre *v refl* (+ *v être*) to fight
IDIOMS **~ en retraite devant qch** to retreat before sth; **~ son plein** to be in full swing

battu, **~e** /baty/ **A** *pp* ▶ **battre**
B *pp adj* ‹*child, wife*› battered

BAU /beay/ *f*: *abbr* ▶ **bande**

baudet /bodɛ/ *m* (fam) donkey, ass

baume /bom/ *m* balm, balsam

baux /bo/ ▶ **bail**

bavard, **~e** /bavaʀ, aʀd/ **A** *adj* **1** talkative
2 indiscreet
3 long-winded
B *mf* **1** chatterbox
2 blabbermouth (fam)

bavardage /bavaʀdaʒ/ *m* **1** gossip
2 idle chatter

bavarder /bavaʀde/ [**v1**] *vi* **1** to talk, to chatter
2 to chat
3 to gossip (**sur** about)

bavarois, **~e** /bavaʀwa, az/ **A** *adj* Bavarian
B *m* (Culin) Bavarian cream, bavarois

bave /bav/ *f* dribble; spittle; slaver; slime

baver /bave/ [**v1**] *vi* **1** ‹*person*› to dribble; ‹*animal*› to slaver
2 ‹*pen*› to leak; ‹*brush*› to drip; ‹*ink, paint*› to run
IDIOM **il leur en a fait ~** (fam) he gave them a hard time

bavette /bavɛt/ *f* **1** bib
2 (Culin) flank

bavoir /bavwaʀ/ *m* bib

bavure /bavyʀ/ *f* **1** smudge
2 blunder

bazar /bazaʀ/ *m* **1** general store
2 (fam) mess
3 (fam) clutter
4 bazaar

bazarder /bazaʀde/ [**v1**] *vi* (fam) to throw out

BCBG /besebeʒe/ *adj* (fam) (*abbr* = **bon chic bon genre**) chic and conservative, Sloaney (BrE)

BCG /beseʒe/ *m* (*abbr* = **bacille bilié de Calmette et Guérin**) BCG

✓ key word

BD /bede/ (fam) *abbr* ▶ **bande**

béant, **~e** /beɑ̃, ɑ̃t/ *adj* gaping

béat, **~e** /bea, at/ *adj* ‹*person*› blissfully happy; ‹*smile*› blissful, beatific

beau (**bel** *before vowel or mute h*), **belle**, *mpl* **~x** /bo, bɛl/ **A** *adj* **1** beautiful; handsome; **se faire ~** to do oneself up; **ce n'est pas ~ à voir!** (fam) it's not a pretty sight!
2 good; fine; nice; lovely; **un ~ geste** a noble gesture; **fais de ~x rêves!** sweet dreams!; **au ~ milieu de** right in the middle of; **c'est bien ~ tout ça, mais...** (fam) that's all well and good, but...
3 ‹*sum*› tidy; ‹*salary*› very nice
B *m* **qu'est-ce que tu as fait de ~?** done anything interesting?
C avoir beau *phr* **j'ai ~ essayer, je n'y arrive pas** it's no good my trying, I can't do it
D bel et bien *phr* **1** well and truly
2 definitely
■ **~ fixe** fine weather; **~x jours** fine weather; good days
IDIOMS **faire le ~** ‹*dog*› to sit up and beg; **c'est du ~!** (fam) (ironic) lovely!

beaucoup /boku/ **A** *adv* **1** a lot; much; **c'est ~ dire** that's going a bit far; **c'est déjà ~ qu'elle soit venue** it's already quite something that she came; **~ moins de livres** far fewer books; **c'est ~ trop** it's far too much; **~ trop longtemps** far too long, much too long
2 ~ de a lot of, a great deal of; much; many; **il ne reste plus ~ de pain** there isn't much bread left; **avec ~ de soin** very carefully; **~ d'entre eux** many of them
B de beaucoup *phr* by far
C pour beaucoup *phr* **être pour ~ dans** to have a lot to do with

beauf /bof/ *m* (fam) **1** (*abbr* = **beau-frère**) brother-in-law
2 (yokel) boor (fam); boor (fam)

beau-fils, *pl* **beaux-fils** /bofis/ *m* **1** son-in-law
2 stepson

beau-frère, *pl* **beaux-frères** /bofʀɛʀ/ *m* brother-in-law

beau-parent, *pl* **beaux-parents** /bopaʀɑ̃/ *m* **1** parent-in-law
2 step-parent

beau-père, *pl* **beaux-pères** /bopɛʀ/ *m*
1 father-in-law
2 stepfather

beauté /bote/ *f* beauty; **se faire une ~** to do oneself up; **finir en ~** to end with a flourish

beaux-arts /bozaʀ/ *mpl* fine arts and architecture

bébé /bebe/ *m* baby

bec /bɛk/ *m* **1** beak; **donner des coups de ~** to peck; **il a toujours la cigarette au ~** (fam) he's always got a cigarette stuck in his mouth
2 (of jug) lip; (of teapot) spout; (of wind instrument) mouthpiece; **~ verseur** spout
IDIOMS **clouer le ~ à qn** (fam) to shut sb up (fam); **tomber sur un ~** (fam) to come across a snag

bécane /bekan/ *f* (fam) bike, bicycle

bécasse /bekas/ *f* woodcock

bec-de-lièvre, *pl* **becs-de-lièvre** /bɛkdəljɛvʀ/ *m* harelip

bêche /bɛʃ/ *f* **1** spade
2 garden fork

bêcher /beʃe/ [**v1**] *vt* to dig (with a spade)

becquée /beke/ *f* beakful; **donner la ~ à** to feed ‹*fledgling*›

bedaine /bədɛn/ *f* (fam) paunch

bédéphile /bedefil/ *mf* comic strip fan

bedonnant, **~e** /bədɔnɑ̃, ɑ̃t/ *adj* (fam) ‹*person*› paunchy

bée /be/ *adj f* **être bouche ~** to stand open-mouthed *or* gaping

beffroi /befʀwɑ/ *m* belfry

bégaiement /begɛmɑ̃/ *m* stammer, stutter

bégayer /begeje/ [**v21**] *vt*, *vi* to stammer

bègue /bɛg/ *adj* **être ~** to stammer

béguin /begɛ̃/ *m* (fam) **avoir le ~ pour qn** to have a crush on sb

beige /bɛʒ/ *adj*, *m* beige

beignet /bɛɲɛ/ *m* **1** fritter
2 doughnut, donut (AmE) (fam)

bel ▶ **beau A, D**

bêler /bɛle/ [**v1**] *vi* to bleat

belette /bəlɛt/ *f* weasel

belge /bɛlʒ/ *adj* Belgian

Belgique /bɛlʒik/ *pr f* Belgium

bélier /belje/ *m* **1** ram
2 battering ram

Bélier /belje/ *pr m* Aries

belle /bɛl/ **A** *adj f* ▶ **beau A**
B *f* decider, deciding game
C de plus belle *phr* with renewed vigour (BrE)
IDIOMS **(se) faire la ~** (fam) to do a bunk (BrE) (fam), to take a powder (AmE) (fam); **en faire voir de ~s à qn** (fam) to give sb a hard time

belle-famille, *pl* **belles-familles** /bɛlfamij/ *f* in-laws

belle-fille, *pl* **belles-filles** /bɛlfij/ *f*
1 daughter-in-law
2 stepdaughter

belle-mère, *pl* **belles-mères** /bɛlmɛʀ/ *f*
1 mother-in-law
2 stepmother

belle-sœur, *pl* **belles-sœurs** /bɛlsœʀ/ *f* sister-in-law

belligérant /bɛliʒeʀɑ̃/ *m* **1** belligerent, warring party
2 combatant

belliqueux, **-euse** /bɛlikø, øz/ *adj* aggressive

bémol /bemɔl/ *m* (Mus) flat; **mi ~** E flat

bénédiction /benediksjɔ̃/ *f* blessing

bénéfice /benefis/ *m* **1** profit
2 benefit, beneficial effect
3 advantage

bénéficiaire /benefisjɛʀ/ *mf* beneficiary

🔑 **bénéficier** /benefisje/ [**v2**] *v+prep* **~ de** to receive ‹*help*›; to enjoy ‹*immunity*›; to get ‹*special treatment*›

bénéfique /benefik/ *adj* beneficial

Bénélux /benelyks/ *pr m* Benelux

benêt /bənɛ/ *m* half-wit

bénévolat /benevɔla/ *m* voluntary work

bénévole /benevɔl/ **A** *adj* voluntary
B *mf* voluntary worker

bénévolement /benevɔlmɑ̃/ *adv* on a voluntary basis

bénin, **-igne** /benɛ̃, iɲ/ *adj* minor; benign

béni-oui-oui /beniwiwi/ *m inv* (fam) yes-man

bénir /beniʀ/ [**v3**] *vt* to bless

bénit, **~e** /beni, it/ *adj* blessed; holy

bénitier /benitje/ *m* holy water font

benjamin, **~e** /bɛ̃ʒamɛ̃, in/ *mf* youngest child

benne /bɛn/ *f* **1** skip (BrE), dumpster® (AmE)
2 (colliery) wagon
3 (cable) car

BEPC /beəpese, bɛps/ *m* (*abbr* = **Brevet d'études du premier cycle**) *former examination at the end of the first stage of secondary education*

béquille /bekij/ *f* **1** crutch
2 kickstand

bercail /bɛʀkaj/ *m* (fam) home

berceau, *pl* **~x** /bɛʀso/ *m* cradle

bercer /bɛʀse/ [**v12**] **A** *vt* to rock ‹*baby*›
B se bercer *v refl* (+ *v être*) **se ~ d'illusions** to delude oneself

berceuse /bɛʀsøz/ *f* lullaby

béret /beʀɛ/ *m* beret

bergamote /bɛʀgamɔt/ *f* bergamot

berge /bɛʀʒ/ *f* (of river, canal) bank

berger, **-ère** /bɛʀʒe, ɛʀ/ *mf* shepherd/shepherdess
■ **~ allemand** Alsatian (BrE), German shepherd

bergerie /bɛʀʒəʀi/ *f* sheepfold

berlue /bɛʀly/ *f* (fam) **avoir la ~** to be seeing things

bermuda /bɛʀmyda/ *m* Bermudas

Bermudes /bɛʀmyd/ *pr f pl* **les ~s** Bermuda

berner /bɛʀne/ [**v1**] *vt* to fool, to deceive

besace /bəzas/ *f* pouch

besogne /bəzɔɲ/ *f* job

🔑 **besoin** /bəzwɛ̃/ **A** *m* need (**de** for, **de faire** to do); **avoir ~ de** to need; **répondre à un ~** to meet a need; **au ~** if need be; **pour les ~s de la cause** for the good of the cause; **être dans le ~** to be in need
B besoins *mpl* needs; **subvenir aux ~s de qn** to provide for sb
IDIOM **faire ses ~s** (fam) ‹*person*› to relieve oneself; ‹*animal*› to do its business

bestial, **~e**, *mpl* **-iaux** /bɛstjal, o/ *adj* brutish, bestial

bestiaux /bɛstjo/ *mpl* **1** livestock
2 cattle

bestiole /bɛstjɔl/ *f* (fam) **1** creepy-crawly (fam), bug
2 animal

bétail /betaj/ *m* livestock; cattle

🔑 **bête** /bɛt/ **A** *adj* stupid, silly; **je suis restée toute ~** I was dumbfounded
B *f* creature; animal
■ **~ à bon Dieu** ladybird (BrE), ladybug (AmE); **~ noire** bête noire (BrE), pet hate
IDIOMS **il est ~ comme ses pieds** (fam) he's as dumb as can be; **chercher la petite ~** (fam) to nit-pick (fam); **reprendre du poil de la ~** (fam) to perk up; **travailler comme une ~** (fam) to work like crazy (fam)

bêtement /bɛtmɑ̃/ *adv* stupidly; **il suffit (tout) ~ de faire** you simply need to do

bêtise /betiz/ *f* **la ~** stupidity; **faire une ~** to do something stupid; **dire des ~s** to talk nonsense; **surtout pas de ~s!** be good now!

bêtisier /betizje/ *m* collection of howlers (fam)

béton /betɔ̃/ *m* concrete; (fig) watertight
■ **~ armé** reinforced concrete

bétonnière /betɔnjɛʀ/ *f* concrete mixer

betterave /bɛtʀav/ *f* beet; **~ rouge** beetroot; **~ sucrière** sugar beet

beugler /bøgle/ [**v1**] *vi* to moo; to bellow

beur /bœʀ/ *mf* (fam) second-generation North African (*living in France*)

beurette /bœʀɛt/ *f* (fam) second-generation North African (*living in France*)

🔑 **beurre** /bœʀ/ *m* butter; **~ doux** unsalted butter
■ **~ d'escargot** garlic and parsley butter; **~ noir** black butter; **œil au ~ noir** (fam) black eye
IDIOMS **faire son ~** (fam) to make a packet (fam); **compter pour du ~** (fam) to count for nothing; **vouloir le ~ et l'argent du ~** (fam) to want to have one's cake and eat it

beurré, **~e** /bœʀe/ *adj* (fam) drunk, plastered (fam)

beurrer /bœʀe/ [**v1**] *vt* to butter

beurrier /bœʀje/ *m* butter dish

beuverie /bœvʀi/ *f* drinking session

biais /bjɛ/ **A** *m inv* **1** (of material) bias
2 way; **par le ~ de qn** through sb; **par le ~ de qch** by means of sth
B de biais, **en biais** *phr* **couper une étoffe en ~** to cut material on the cross

biaiser /bjeze/ [**v1**] *vi* to hedge

bibelot /biblo/ *m* ornament

biberon /bibʀɔ̃/ *m* (baby's) bottle (BrE), (nursing) bottle (AmE)

bible /bibl/ *f* bible; **la Bible** the Bible

🔑 key word

bibliographie /biblijɔgʀafi/ *f* bibliography
bibliographique /biblijɔgʀafik/ *adj* bibliographical
bibliothécaire /biblijɔtekɛʀ/ *mf* librarian
bibliothèque /biblijɔtɛk/ *f* **1** library
2 bookcase
biblique /biblik/ *adj* biblical
bic® /bik/ *m* biro®
bicarbonate /bikaʀbɔnat/ *m* bicarbonate
bicentenaire /bisɑ̃tnɛʀ/ *m* bicentenary, bicentennial
biceps /bisɛps/ *m inv* biceps
biche /biʃ/ *f* doe
bichonner /biʃɔne/ [**v1**] *vt* (fam) to pamper
bicolore /bikɔlɔʀ/ *adj* ‹*flag*› two-coloured (BrE); ‹*fabric*› two-tone
bicoque /bikɔk/ *f* (fam) dump (fam), house
bicyclette /bisiklɛt/ *f* **1** bicycle
2 cycling
bidasse /bidas/ *m* (fam) soldier
bidet /bidɛ/ *m* bidet
bidon /bidɔ̃/ **A** *adj inv* (fam) bogus; phoney (fam)
B *m* **1** can; drum; flask
2 (fam) stomach, paunch
3 (fam) **c'est du ~** it is a load of hogwash (fam)
bidonner: **se bidonner** /bidɔne/ [**v1**] *v refl* (+ *v être*) (fam) to laugh, to fall about (fam)
bidonville /bidɔ̃vil/ *m* shanty town
bidule /bidyl/ *m* (fam) thingy (BrE) (fam), thingamajig (fam)
bielle /bjɛl/ *f* connecting rod
bien /bjɛ̃/ **A** *adj inv* **1 être ~ dans un rôle** to be good in a part; **être ~ de sa personne** to be good-looking; **ce n'est pas ~ de mentir** it's not nice to lie; **ça fait ~ d'aller à l'opéra** (fam) it's the done thing to go to the opera
2 well; **ne pas se sentir ~** not to feel well; **t'es pas ~!** (fam) you're out of your mind (fam)
3 je suis ~ dans ces bottes these boots are comfortable; **on est ~ au soleil!** isn't it nice in the sun!
4 (fam) **un quartier ~** a nice district; **des gens ~** respectable people
B *adv* **1** well; ‹*function*› properly; ‹*interpret*› correctly; **~ joué!** well done!; **aller ~** ‹*person*› to be well; ‹*business*› to go well; **ni ~ ni mal** so-so; **j'ai cru ~ faire** I thought I was doing the right thing; **c'est ~ fait pour elle!** it serves her right!; **tu ferais ~ d'y aller** it would be a good idea for you to go
2 ‹*mix*› thoroughly; ‹*fill*› completely; ‹*listen*› carefully
3 ‹*presented*› well; ‹*furnished*› tastefully; ‹*live*› comfortably; **femme ~ faite** shapely woman; **aller ~ ensemble** to go well together; **aller ~ à qn** to suit sb; **~ prendre une remarque** to take a remark in good part
4 ‹*nice, sad*› very; ‹*fear, enjoy*› very much; ‹*simple, true*› quite; **il y a ~ longtemps** a very long time ago; **merci ~** thank you very much; **~ rire** to have a good laugh; **c'est ~ compris?** is that clear?; **~ au contraire** on the contrary; **~ mieux** much *or* far better; **~ sûr** of course; **~ entendu** *or* **évidemment** naturally; **il y a ~ des années** a good many years ago; **~ des fois** often, many a time
5 je veux ~ t'aider I don't mind helping you; **j'aimerais ~ essayer** I would love to try
6 il faut ~ que ça finisse it has just got to come to an end
7 ça montre ~ que it just goes to show that; **je sais ~ que** I know that; **insiste ~** make sure you insist; **on verra ~** well, we'll see; **il le fait ~ lui, pourquoi pas moi?** if he can do it, why can't I?; **tu peux très ~ le faire toi-même** you can easily do it yourself; **que peut-il ~ faire à Paris?** what on earth can he be doing in Paris?
8 definitely; **c'est ~ ce qu'il a dit** that's exactly what he said; **tu as ~ pris les clés?** are you sure you've got the keys?; **c'est ~ de lui!** it's just like him!; **c'est ~ le moment!** (ironic) great timing!; **c'est ~ le moment de partir!** (ironic) what a time to leave!
9 at least; **elle a ~ 40 ans** she's at least 40
C *m* **1** good; **le ~ et le mal** good and evil; **ça fait du ~ aux enfants** it's good for the children; **vouloir le ~ de qn** to have sb's best interests at heart; **vouloir du ~ à qn** to wish sb well; **dire du ~/le plus grand ~ de qn** to speak well/very highly of sb
2 possession; **des ~s considérables** substantial assets
D bien que *phr* although
■ **~s de consommation** consumer goods; **~s immobiliers** real estate; **~s mobiliers** personal property; **~s personnels** private property
bien-être /bjɛ̃nɛtʀ/ *m* **1** well-being
2 welfare
3 comforts
bienfaisance /bjɛ̃fəzɑ̃s/ *f* charity
bienfaisant, **~e** /bjɛ̃fəzɑ̃, ɑ̃t/ *adj* beneficial, beneficent
bienfait /bjɛ̃fɛ/ *m* **1** kind deed; **~ du ciel** godsend
2 beneficial effect
bienfaiteur, **-trice** /bjɛ̃fɛtœʀ, tʀis/ *mf* benefactor/benefactress
bien-fondé /bjɛ̃fɔ̃de/ *m* (of idea) validity; (of claim) legitimacy
bien-pensant, **~e**, *mpl* **~s** /bjɛ̃pɑ̃sɑ̃, ɑ̃t/ *adj* **1** right-thinking
2 self-righteous
bienséance /bjɛ̃seɑ̃s/ *f* propriety; **les règles de la ~** the rules of polite society
bientôt /bjɛ̃to/ *adv* soon; **à ~** see you soon
bienveillant, **~e** /bjɛ̃vɛjɑ̃, ɑ̃t/ *adj* benevolent
bienvenu, **~e** /bjɛ̃vəny/ *adj* welcome
bienvenue /bjɛ̃vəny/ *f* welcome

b

bière /bjɛʀ/ *f* **1** beer; ~ **(à la) pression** draught (BrE) *or* draft (AmE) beer
2 coffin, casket (AmE)
■ ~ **blonde** lager; ~ **brune** ≈ stout; ~ **rousse** brown ale

bifteck /biftɛk/ *m* steak
IDIOM **gagner son** ~ (fam) to earn a living

bifurcation /bifyʀkasjɔ̃/ *f* (in road) fork

bifurquer /bifyʀke/ [**v1**] *vi* **1** ‹*road*› to fork
2 ‹*driver*› to turn off
3 (in career) to change tack

bigame /bigam/ *adj* bigamous

bigamie /bigami/ *f* bigamy

bigarré, ~**e** /bigaʀe/ *adj* **1** multicoloured (BrE)
2 ‹*crowd*› colourful (BrE)

bigleux, **-euse** /biglø, øz/ *adj* (derog, fam) poor-sighted; **complètement** ~ as blind as a bat (fam)

bigorneau, *pl* ~**x** /bigɔʀno/ *m* winkle

bigot, ~**e** /bigo, ɔt/ *mf* religious zealot

bigoudi /bigudi/ *m* roller, curler

bijou, *pl* ~**x** /biʒu/ *m* **1** piece of jewellery (BrE) *or* jewelry (AmE)
2 jewel; (fig) gem

bijouterie /biʒutʀi/ *f* (shop) jeweller's (BrE), jewelry store (AmE)

bilan /bilɑ̃/ *m* **1** balance sheet; **déposer son** ~ to file a petition in bankruptcy
2 outcome
3 (after disaster) toll
4 assessment; ~ **de santé** check-up
5 report

bilatéral, ~**e**, *mpl* **-aux** /bilateʀal, o/ *adj* bilateral

bile /bil/ *f* bile
IDIOM **se faire de la** ~ (fam) to worry

bilingue /bilɛ̃g/ *adj* bilingual

billard /bijaʀ/ *m* **1** billiards
2 billiard table
■ ~ **américain** pool; ~ **anglais** snooker
IDIOM **passer sur le** ~ (fam) to have an operation

bille /bij/ *f* **1** marble
2 (billiard) ball

✓ **billet** /bijɛ/ *m* **1** banknote, note (BrE), bill (AmE)
2 ticket
■ ~ **doux** love letter

billetterie /bijɛtʀi/ *f* cash dispenser

billion /biljɔ̃/ *m* billion (BrE), trillion (AmE)

bimensuel /bimɑ̃sɥɛl/ *m* fortnightly magazine (BrE), semi-monthly (AmE)

bimoteur /bimɔtœʀ/ *m* twin-engined plane

binaire /binɛʀ/ *adj* binary

biniou /binju/ *m* Breton bagpipes

binocles /binɔkl/ *fpl* (fam) specs (fam), glasses

bio /bjo/ **A** *adj inv* (natural) **aliments** ~ health foods; **produits** ~ organic produce; **yaourt** ~ bio yoghurt
B *f* (fam) biography

biocarburant /bjokaʀbyʀɑ̃/ *m* biofuel

biochimie /bjoʃimi/ *f* biochemistry

biodégradable /bjodegʀadabl/ *adj* biodegradable

biodiversité /bjodivɛʀsite/ *f* biodiversity

biographie /bjɔgʀafi/ *f* biography

biologie /bjɔlɔʒi/ *f* biology

biométrique /bjɔmetʀik/ *adj* biometric

biophysique /bjofizik/ *f* biophysics

biotransformation /bjotʀɑ̃sfɔʀmasjɔ̃/ *f* (Biol) biotransformation

bip /bip/ *m* beep; ~ **sonore** tone

bipède /bipɛd/ *m* biped

biplace /biplas/ *adj*, *m* two-seater

bique /bik/ *f* (fam) **une vieille** ~ an old bag (fam)

biréacteur /biʀeaktœʀ/ *m* twin-engined jet

bis[1], ~**e** /bi, biz/ *adj* greyish (BrE) *or* grayish (AmE) brown

bis[2] /bis/ *adv* **1** (in address) bis; **33** ~ **rue Juliette Lamber** 33 bis rue Juliette Lamber
2 (at show, concert) encore

bisannuel, **-elle** /bizanɥɛl/ *adj* biennial

biscornu, ~**e** /biskɔʀny/ *adj* quirky

biscotte /biskɔt/ *f* continental toast

biscuit /biskɥi/ *m* biscuit (BrE), cookie (AmE)
■ ~ **à la cuillère** sponge finger (BrE), ladyfinger (AmE); ~ **salé** cracker

bise /biz/ **A** *adj f* ▸ **bis[1]**
B *f* **1** (fam) kiss; **faire la** ~ **à qn** to kiss sb on the cheeks
2 North wind

biseau, *pl* ~**x** /bizo/ *m* **1** bevel (edge); **tailler en** ~ to bevel
2 (tool) bevel

bison /bizɔ̃/ *m* **1** bison
2 buffalo

bissextile /bisɛkstil/ *adj* **année** ~ leap year

bistouri /bistuʀi/ *m* (Med) bistoury

bistro /bistʀo/ *m also* **bistrot** (fam) bistro, cafe

bit /bit/ *m* bit

BIT /beite/ *m* (*abbr* = **Bureau international du travail**) ILO

bitume /bitym/ *m* (on road) asphalt

bivouac /bivwak/ *m* bivouac

bizarre /bizaʀ/ *adj* odd, strange

blafard, ~**e** /blafaʀ, aʀd/ *adj* pale

blague /blag/ *f* (fam) **1** joke; ~ **à part** seriously
2 fib (fam)
3 trick; **faire une** ~ **à qn** to play a trick on sb

blaguer /blage/ [**v1**] *vi* (fam) to joke

blagueur, **-euse** /blagœʀ, øz/ *mf* (fam) joker

blaireau, *pl* ~**x** /blɛʀo/ *m* **1** badger
2 shaving brush

blâmer /blɑme/ [**v1**] *vt* to criticize; to blame

blanc, **blanche** /blɑ̃, blɑ̃ʃ/ **A** *adj* (gen) white; ‹*page*› blank; ~ **cassé** off-white
B *m* **1** white; **habillé/peint en** ~ dressed in/painted white
2 household linen
3 white meat
4 (egg) white
5 blank; gap; **j'ai eu un** ~ my mind went blank
6 (fam) correction fluid
7 tirer à ~ to fire blanks
C blancs *mpl* (in chess, draughts) white

Blanc, **Blanche** /blɑ̃, blɑ̃ʃ/ *mf* white man/woman

blanc-bec, *pl* **blancs-becs** /blɑ̃bɛk/ *m* greenhorn

blanchâtre /blɑ̃ʃɑtʀ/ *adj* whitish

blanche /blɑ̃ʃ/ **A** *adj f* ▶ **blanc A**
B *f* (Mus) minim (BrE), half note (AmE)

blanchiment /blɑ̃ʃimɑ̃/ *m* **1** (of money) laundering
2 (of fabric, paper, pulp) bleaching

blanchir /blɑ̃ʃiʀ/ [**v3**] **A** *vt* **1** to whiten ‹*shoes*›
2 to clear ‹*name*›
3 to launder ‹*money*›
B *vi* **1** to turn grey (BrE) *or* gray (AmE)
2 faire ~ to blanch ‹*vegetables*›
C se blanchir *v refl* (+ *v être*) to clear oneself

blanchisserie /blɑ̃ʃisʀi/ *f* laundry

blanchisseur /blɑ̃ʃisœʀ/ *m* (shop) laundry

blanchisseuse /blɑ̃ʃisøz/ *f* laundress

blasé, ~**e** /blaze/ *adj* blasé

blason /blazɔ̃/ *m* coat of arms
IDIOM **redorer son** ~ to restore one's reputation

blasphème /blasfɛm/ *m* blasphemy

blasphémer /blasfeme/ [**v14**] *vi* to blaspheme

blatte /blat/ *f* cockroach

blé /ble/ *m* wheat; ~ **noir** buckwheat

bled /blɛd/ *m* (fam) village

blême /blɛm/ *adj* pale

blessant, ~**e** /blesɑ̃, ɑ̃t/ *adj* ‹*remark*› cutting

blessé, ~**e** /blese/ *mf* injured *or* wounded man/woman; casualty

blesser /blese/ [**v1**] **A** *vt* **1** to injure, to hurt; to wound; **il a été blessé à la tête** he sustained head injuries
2 to hurt ‹*person, feelings*›; to wound ‹*pride*›
B se blesser *v refl* (+ *v être*) to hurt oneself

blessure /blesyʀ/ *f* injury; wound

blet, **blette** /blɛ, blɛt/ *adj* overripe

bleu, ~**e** /blø/ **A** *adj* **1** blue
2 ‹*steak*› very rare
B *m* **1** blue
2 bruise
3 ~ **de travail** overalls
4 blue cheese
IDIOM **avoir une peur** ~**e de qch** to be scared stiff (fam) of sth

bleuâtre /bløɑtʀ/ *adj* bluish

bleuet /bløɛ/ *m* (Bot) cornflower

blindé, ~**e** /blɛ̃de/ *adj* armoured (BrE)

blinder /blɛ̃de/ [**v1**] *vt* to put security fittings on ‹*door*›; to armour-plate (BrE) ‹*car*›

blizzard /blizaʀ/ *m* blizzard

bloc A *m* **1** block; **faire** ~ **avec/contre qn** to side with/unite against sb
2 notepad; ~ **de papier à lettres** writing pad
3 (Comput) block
B à bloc *phr* ‹*screw*› tightly; ‹*inflate*› fully
C en bloc *phr* ‹*deny*› outright
■ ~ **opératoire** surgical unit

blocage /blɔkaʒ/ *m* blocking; ~ **des salaires** wage freeze

blockhaus /blɔkos/ *m inv* blockhouse

bloc-notes, *pl* **blocs-notes** /blɔknɔt/ *m* notepad

blocus /blɔkys/ *m inv* blockade

blog, **blogue** /blɔg/ *m* blog

blogger /blɔgœʀ/ *m* blogger

blond, ~**e** /blɔ̃, ɔ̃d/ **A** *adj* **1** blonde (BrE), blond (AmE)
2 ‹*wheat*› golden; ‹*tobacco*› light
B *mf* (female) blonde (BrE), blond (AmE); (male) blond

bloqué, ~**e** /blɔke/ **A** *pp* ▶ **bloquer**
B *pp adj* **1** blocked
2 ‹*mechanism, door*› jammed; **elle/la voiture est** ~**e** she/the car is stuck
3 être ~ ‹*activity*› to be at a standstill; ‹*situation*› to be deadlocked

bloquer /blɔke/ [**v1**] **A** *vt* **1** to block ‹*road*›
2 to lock ‹*steering wheel*›; to wedge ‹*door*›; (accidentally) to jam ‹*mechanism, door*›
3 to stop ‹*vehicle, traveller*›
4 to freeze ‹*prices*›
5 to stop ‹*project*›
6 to lump [sth] together ‹*days*›
B se bloquer *v refl* (+ *v être*) **1** ‹*brakes, door*› to jam; ‹*wheel*› to lock
2 to retreat

blottir: **se blottir** /blɔtiʀ/ [**v3**] *v refl* (+ *v être*) **se** ~ **contre** to huddle up against; to snuggle up against

blouse /bluz/ *f* **1** overall
2 coat; ~ **blanche** white coat
3 blouse

blouson /bluzɔ̃/ *m* **1** blouson; ~ **d'aviateur** bomber jacket
2 ~ **noir** ≈ rocker

blue-jean, *pl* ~**s** /bludʒin/ *m* jeans

bluffer /blœfe/ [**v1**] *vt, vi* (fam) to bluff

BN /beɛn/ *f* (*abbr* = **Bibliothèque nationale**) *national library in Paris*

boa /bɔa/ *m* boa

bobard /bɔbaʀ/ *m* (fam) fib (fam), tall story

bobine /bɔbin/ *f* (of film, cable) reel

bobo /bobo/ *m* (fam, baby talk) **1** pain
2 scratch

bocage /bɔkaʒ/ *m* hedged farmland

bocal, *pl* **-aux** /bɔkal, o/ *m* jar; bowl

bœuf /bœf/, *pl* /bø/ *m* **1** bullock (BrE), steer (AmE)
2 ox
3 beef
IDIOM **faire un effet ~** (fam) to make a fantastic (fam) impression

bof /bɔf/ *excl* (fam) **'tu préfères la mer ou la montagne?'—'~!'** 'which do you prefer, the sea or the mountains?'—'I don't mind'

bogue /bɔg/ *f or m* (Comput) bug

bohème /bɔɛm/ **A** *adj* bohemian
B *f* **la ~** bohemia

bohémien, -ienne /bɔemjɛ̃, ɛn/ *mf* Romany, gypsy

boire /bwaʀ/ [**v70**] **A** *vt* **1** to drink
2 ‹*paper*› to soak up
B se boire *v refl* (+ *v être*) **ce vin se boit frais** this wine should be drunk chilled
IDIOMS **~ comme un trou** (fam) to drink like a fish (fam); **il y a à ~ et à manger dans leur théorie** there's both good and bad in their theory

bois /bwa/ **A** *m inv* wood; **en ~** ‹*chair*› wooden; ‹*cheque*› dud (fam); **~ mort** firewood
B *mpl* **1** antlers
2 woodwind section
IDIOMS **être de ~** to be insensitive; **il va voir de quel ~ je me chauffe** (fam) I'll show him

boisé, ~e /bwaze/ *adj* wooded

boiserie /bwazʀi/ *f* **~(s)** panelling (BrE)

boisson /bwasɔ̃/ *f* drink

boîte /bwat/ *f* **1** (container) box
2 (for food) tin (BrE), can; **petits pois en ~** canned peas
3 (club) **~ (de nuit)** nightclub
4 (fam) (company) firm; office
■ **~ crânienne** cranium; **~ à gants** glove compartment; **~ à** *or* **aux lettres** post box (BrE), mailbox (AmE); **~ à** *or* **aux lettres électronique** (Comput) electronic mailbox; **~ à musique** musical box (BrE), music box (AmE); **~ noire** black box; **~ à outils** toolbox; **~ postale, BP** PO Box; **~ de vitesses** gearbox
IDIOM **mettre qn en ~** (fam) to tease sb

boiter /bwate/ [**v1**] *vi* to limp

boiteux, -euse /bwatø, øz/ **A** *adj* **1** lame
2 ‹*chair*› wobbly
3 ‹*argument, alliance*› shaky
B *mf* lame person (offensive)

boîtier /bwatje/ *m* (gen) case; (of camera) body

boitiller /bwatije/ [**v1**] *vi* to limp slightly

bol /bɔl/ *m* **1** bowl; **~ d'air** breath of fresh air
2 (fam) luck; **coup de ~** stroke of luck

bolée /bɔle/ *f* **~ de cidre** bowl of cider

key word

bolide /bɔlid/ *m* high-powered car

bombage /bɔ̃baʒ/ *m* (action) graffiti spraying; (result) (sprayed) graffiti

bombardement /bɔ̃baʀdəmɑ̃/ *m* (Mil) bombardment; bombing; shelling; **~ aérien** air raid

bombarder /bɔ̃baʀde/ [**v1**] *vt* **1** to bombard; to bomb; to shell
2 ~ qn de questions to bombard sb with questions
3 (fam) **~ qn à un poste** to catapult sb into a job

bombardier /bɔ̃baʀdje/ *m* **1** bomber
2 bombardier

bombe /bɔ̃b/ *f* **1** bomb; **faire l'effet d'une ~** to come as a bombshell
2 ~ (aérosol) spray
3 riding hat
IDIOM **partir à toute ~** (fam) to rush off

bombé, ~e /bɔ̃be/ *adj* **1** ‹*forehead*› domed; ‹*shape*› rounded
2 ‹*road*› cambered

bomber /bɔ̃be/ [**v1**] **A** *vt* **~ le torse** to thrust out one's chest; (fig) to swell with pride
B *vi* **1** ‹*plank*› to bulge out
2 (fam) to belt along (fam)

bon, bonne /bɔ̃, bɔn/ **A** *adj* **1** good; **prends un ~ pull** take a warm jumper; **elle est (bien) bonne!** (fam) that's a good one!; (indignantly) I like that!; **voilà une bonne chose de faite!** that's that out of the way!; **nous sommes ~s derniers** we're well and truly last; **il n'est pas ~ à grand-chose** he's pretty useless; **il serait ~ qu'elle le sache** she ought to know; **à quoi ~?** what's the point?
2 ‹*person, words*› kind; ‹*smile*› nice; **avoir ~ cœur** to be good-hearted
3 ‹*time, answer*› right; **c'est ~, vous pouvez y aller** it's OK, you can go
4 ‹*ticket*› valid; **tu es ~ pour la vaisselle, ce soir!** you're in line for the dishes tonight!
5 bonne nuit/chance good night/luck
B *mf* **les ~s et les méchants** good people and bad people; (in films) the good guys and the bad guys (fam)
C *m* **1** coupon; voucher
2 il y a du ~ dans cet article there are some good things in this article
D *adv* **ça sent ~!** that smells good!; **il fait ~** the weather's mild; **il fait ~ dans ta chambre** it's nice and warm in your room
E pour de bon *phr* **1** really; **tu dis ça pour de ~?** are you serious?
2 for good
■ **~ de commande** order form; **~ enfant** good-natured; **~ de garantie** guarantee slip; **~ marché** cheap; **~ mot** witticism; **~ à rien** good-for-nothing; **~ sens** common sense; **~ du Trésor** Treasury bond; **~ vivant** bon viveur; **bonne action** good deed; **bonne femme** (derog, fam) woman, dame (AmE) (fam);

wife, old lady (fam); **bonne pâte** good sort; **bonne sœur** (fam) nun

bonbon /bɔ̃bɔ̃/ *m* sweet (BrE), candy (AmE)

bonbonne /bɔ̃bɔn/ *f* **1** demijohn; (bigger) carboy
2 (for gas) cylinder

bond /bɔ̃/ *m* **1** leap; **se lever d'un ~** to leap to one's feet
2 (in time) jump
3 (in profits, exports) leap; (in prices) jump (**de** in); **la médecine a fait un ~ en avant avec cette découverte** this discovery was a medical breakthrough
(IDIOMS) **saisir la balle au ~** to seize the opportunity; **faire faux ~ à qn** to let sb down

bonde /bɔ̃d/ *f* **1** (of swimming pool) outlet; (of sink) plughole
2 (stopper) (in pool) outlet cover; (in sink) plug

bondé, **~e** /bɔ̃de/ *adj* packed (**de** with)

bondir /bɔ̃diʀ/ [**v3**] *vi* **1** to leap; **~ de joie** to jump for joy
2 ~ sur qn/qch to pounce on sb/sth
3 ‹*animal*› to leap about
4 ça m'a fait ~ I was absolutely furious (about it)

bonheur /bɔnœʀ/ *m* **1** happiness
2 pleasure; **faire le ~ de qn** ‹*present*› to make sb happy; ‹*event, exhibition*› to delight sb
3 par ~ fortunately; **au petit ~ (la chance)** at random; **tu ne connais pas ton ~!** you don't realize how lucky you are!
(IDIOM) **alors, tu as trouvé ton ~?** (fam) did you find what you wanted?

bonhomie /bɔnɔmi/ *f* good nature

bonhomme, *pl* **~s**, **bonshommes** /bɔnɔm, bɔ̃zɔm/ **A** *adj* good-natured
B *m* (fam) **1** fellow, chap (fam)
2 husband, old man (fam)
■ **~ de neige** snowman
(IDIOM) **aller** *or* **suivre son petit ~ de chemin** to go peacefully along

bonification /bɔnifikasjɔ̃/ *f* **1** (in sport) bonus points
2 (financial) bonus

boniments /bɔnimɑ̃/ *mpl* stories; **raconter des ~ à qn** to give sb some story (fam) (**à propos de** about); to smooth-talk sb

bonjour /bɔ̃ʒuʀ/ *m, excl* hello
(IDIOM) **être simple comme ~** (fam) to be very easy

bonne /bɔn/ **A** *adj f* ▶ **bon A**
B *f* **1** maid, servant
2 tu en as de ~s, toi! you must be joking!
■ **~ d'enfants** nanny

bonnement /bɔnmɑ̃/ *adv* **tout ~** (quite) simply

bonnet /bɔnɛ/ *m* **1** hat; (for baby) bonnet
2 (on bra) cup
■ **~ de nuit** nightcap; (fig) wet blanket (fam)

bonneterie /bɔnɛtʀi/ *f* hosiery

bonshommes ▶ **bonhomme**

bonsoir /bɔ̃swaʀ/ *m, excl* good evening, good night

bonté /bɔ̃te/ *f* **1** kindness
2 (of God) goodness

bonus /bɔnys/ *m inv* no-claims bonus

bookmaker /bukmɛkœʀ/ *m* bookmaker

boom /bum/ *m* boom; **en plein ~** booming

bord /bɔʀ/ *m* **1** (of plate, bed) edge; (of road) side; (of river) bank; **au ~ de** on *or* at the edge of; (fig) on the verge of; **au ~ de la mer** at the seaside; by the sea; **~ à ~** edge to edge
2 (of cup) rim; (of hat) brim
3 à ~ ‹*work*› on board; **de ~** ‹*instruments, staff*› on board; **on fera** (fam) **avec les moyens du ~** we'll make do with what we've got
4 side; **être du même ~** to be on the same side

bordeaux /bɔʀdo/ **A** *adj inv* burgundy
B *m* Bordeaux; **~ rouge** claret

border /bɔʀde/ [**v1**] *vt* **1** to line (**de** with)
2 ‹*plants*› to border ‹*lake*›
3 to tuck [sb] in
4 to edge ‹*garment*› (**de** with)

bordereau, *pl* **~x** /bɔʀdəʀo/ *m* form, slip

bordure /bɔʀdyʀ/ **A** *f* **1** (of sports ground, carpet) border
2 (of road, platform) edge
B en bordure de *phr* **1** next to ‹*park, canal, track*›
2 on the edge of ‹*park*›; on the side of ‹*road*›
3 just outside ‹*village*›

boréal, **~e**, *mpl* **-aux** /bɔʀeal, o/ *adj* boreal

borgne /bɔʀɲ/ *adj* one-eyed

borne /bɔʀn/ **A** *f* **1 ~ (kilométrique)** kilometre (BrE) marker
2 bollard (BrE), post (AmE)
3 (fam) kilometre (BrE)
4 (for electricity) terminal
B bornes *fpl* **leur ambition est sans ~s** their ambition knows no bounds
■ **~ téléphonique** emergency telephone; taxi stand telephone

borné, **~e** /bɔʀne/ *adj* narrow-minded

borner: **se borner** /bɔʀne/ [**v1**] *v refl* (+ *v être*) **1 se ~ à faire** to content oneself with doing
2 se ~ à faire to be limited to doing

bornette /bɔʀnɛt/ *f: docking station for a hired bicycle*

bosquet /bɔskɛ/ *m* grove

bosse /bɔs/ *f* **1** hump
2 bump
3 dent
(IDIOMS) **avoir la ~ de** (fam) to have a flair for; **rouler sa ~** to knock about

bosseler /bɔsle/ [**v19**] *vt* to dent; (in metalwork) to emboss

bosser /bɔse/ [**v1**] *vi* (fam) to work

bossu, **~e** /bɔsy/ *adj* hunchbacked

b

bot /bo/ *adj m* **pied ~** club foot
botanique /bɔtanik/ **A** *adj* botanical
B *f* botany
botte /bɔt/ *f* **1** boot
2 (of flowers) bunch; (of hay) bale
■ **~s de caoutchouc** wellington boots
botter /bɔte/ [**v1**] *vt* **1 ça le botte!** (fam) he loves it!
2 to kick
bottin® /bɔtɛ̃/ *m* telephone directory
bottine /bɔtin/ *f* ankle boot
bouc /buk/ *m* **1** billy goat
2 goatee
■ **~ émissaire** scapegoat
boucan /bukɑ̃/ *m* (fam) din, racket (fam)
bouche /buʃ/ *f* mouth; **faire la fine ~ devant qch** to turn one's nose up at sth
■ **~ d'aération** air vent; **~ d'égout** manhole; **~ d'incendie** fire hydrant; **~ de métro** tube (BrE) *or* subway (AmE) entrance
bouché, **~e** /buʃe/ **A** *pp* ▶ **boucher**[1]
B *pp adj* **1** blocked
2 ‹*profession*› oversubscribed
3 (fam) dim (fam)
4 cidre ~ bottled cider
bouche-à-bouche /buʃabuʃ/ *m inv* mouth-to-mouth resuscitation
bouche-à-oreille /buʃaɔʀɛj/ *m inv* **le ~** word of mouth
bouchée /buʃe/ *f* mouthful; **pour une ~ de pain** for next to nothing; **mettre les ~s doubles** to double one's efforts
boucher[1] /buʃe/ [**v1**] **A** *vt* **1** to cork
2 to block; to clog (up)
3 to fill ‹*crack*›
B se boucher *v refl* (+ *v être*) **1 se ~ le nez** to hold one's nose; **se ~ les oreilles** to put one's fingers in one's ears
2 to get blocked
IDIOM **en ~ un coin à qn** (fam) to amaze sb
boucher[2], **-ère** /buʃe, ɛʀ/ *mf* butcher
boucherie /buʃʀi/ *f* **1** butcher's shop
2 butcher's trade
3 slaughter
bouchon /buʃɔ̃/ *m* **1** cork
2 (screw)cap
3 (of wax) plug
4 traffic jam
5 (in fishing) float
boucle /bukl/ *f* **1** buckle; **~ d'oreille** earring
2 curl
3 loop
4 (Comput) loop
bouclé, **~e** /bukle/ *adj* curly
boucler /bukle/ [**v1**] *vt* **1** to fasten ‹*belt*›
2 (fam) to lock ‹*door*›
3 (fam) to cordon off ‹*district*›
4 (fam) to complete ‹*investigation*›
5 (fam) to lock [sb] up
IDIOMS **la ~** (fam) to shut up; **~ la boucle** to come full circle
bouclier /buklije/ *m* shield
bouclier humain *m* human shield
bouddhisme /budism/ *m* Buddhism
bouder /bude/ [**v1**] *vi* to sulk
bouderie /budʀi/ *f* sulking
boudin /budɛ̃/ *m* ≈ blood sausage
boudiné, **~e** /budine/ *adj* podgy
boudiner /budine/ [**v1**] *vt* **être boudiné dans qch** to be squeezed into sth
boue /bu/ *f* **1** (gen, fig) mud
2 silt
bouée /bwe/ *f* **1** rubber ring
2 buoy
■ **~ de sauvetage** *or* **de secours** lifebelt (BrE), life preserver (AmE)
boueux, **-euse** /buø, øz/ *adj* muddy
bouffant, **~e** /bufɑ̃, ɑ̃t/ *adj* **1** baggy
2 ‹*sleeves*› puffed
3 ‹*hairstyle*› bouffant
bouffe /buf/ *f* (fam) **1** eating
2 food
3 meal
bouffée /bufe/ *f* (of tobacco, steam) puff; **une ~ d'air frais** a breath of fresh air
■ **~ de chaleur** hot flush (BrE), hot flash (AmE)
bouffer /bufe/ (fam) [**v1**] **A** *vt* to eat
B *vi* to eat; (greedily) to stuff oneself (fam)
bouffi, **~e** /bufi/ *adj* puffy
bouffon /bufɔ̃/ *m* **1** clown
2 jester; buffoon
bouffonnerie /bufɔnʀi/ *f* **1** (actions) antics
2 (for comic effect) buffoonery
3 (intrinsic stupidity) ridiculousness
4 (in theatre) farce
bougeoir /buʒwaʀ/ *m* **1** candleholder
2 candlestick
bougeotte /buʒɔt/ *f* (fam) **avoir la ~** to be restless
bouger /buʒe/ [**v13**] **A** *vt* to move
B *vi* **1** to move
2 (fam) ‹*sector, company*› to be on the move
3 (fam) **ville qui bouge** lively town
C se bouger *v refl* (+ *v être*) (fam) **1** to get a move on (fam)
2 to put some effort in
bougie /buʒi/ *f* **1** candle
2 (Tech) spark plug
bougonner /bugɔne/ [**v1**] *vi* to grumble
bouillabaisse /bujabɛs/ *f* fish soup
bouillant, **~e** /bujɑ̃, ɑ̃t/ *adj* boiling (hot)
bouille /buj/ *f* (fam) face
bouilli, **~e** /buji/ ▶ **bouillir**
bouillie /buji/ *f* **1** gruel; **en ~** mushy; **mettre qn/qch en ~** to reduce sb/sth to a pulp
2 baby cereal
bouillir /bujiʀ/ [**v31**] *vi* **1** to boil
2 to be seething (**de** with)
bouilloire /bujwaʀ/ *f* kettle
bouillon /bujɔ̃/ *m* **1** broth
2 (Culin) stock

key word

3 bouillir à gros ~s to boil fiercely

bouillonnant, ~e /bujɔnɑ̃, ɑ̃t/ *adj* ‹*water*› foaming; ‹*person*› lively

bouillonner /bujɔne/ [**v1**] *vi* **1** to bubble
2 ~ d'activité to be bustling with activity

bouillotte /bujɔt/ *f* hot-water bottle

boulanger, -ère /bulɑ̃ʒe, ɛʀ/ *mf* baker

boulangerie /bulɑ̃ʒʀi/ *f* bakery

boulangerie-pâtisserie, *pl* **boulangeries-pâtisseries** /bulɑ̃ʒʀipɑtisʀi/ *f* bakery (*selling cakes and pastries*)

boule /bul/ *f* (gen) ball; (in bowling) bowl; **mettre qch en ~** to roll sth up into a ball
■ **~ de neige** snowball; **~ Quiès®** earplug
IDIOMS **il a perdu la ~** (fam) he's gone mad; **mettre qn en ~** (fam) to make sb furious

bouleau, *pl* **~x** /bulo/ *m* birch

bouledogue /buldɔg/ *m* bulldog

boulet /bulɛ/ *m* **1 ~ (de canon)** cannonball
2 ball and chain
3 (fig) millstone

boulette /bulɛt/ *f* **1** (of bread, paper) pellet
2 ~ de viande meatball
3 (fam) blunder

boulevard /bulvaʀ/ *m* boulevard
■ **~ périphérique** ring road (BrE), beltway (AmE)

bouleversant, ~e /bulvɛʀsɑ̃, ɑ̃t/ *adj* deeply moving

bouleversement /bulvɛʀsəmɑ̃/ *m* upheaval

bouleverser /bulvɛʀse/ [**v1**] *vt* **1** to move [sb] deeply
2 ‹*experience*› to shatter
3 to turn [sth] upside down ‹*house, files*›
4 to disrupt ‹*schedule*›
5 to change [sth] dramatically ‹*lifestyle*›

boulier /bulje/ *m* abacus

boulimie /bulimi/ *f* bulimia

boulon /bulɔ̃/ *m* bolt

boulot, -otte /bulo, ɔt/ **A** *adj* tubby
B *m* (fam) **1** work
2 job

boulotter /bulɔte/ [**v1**] *vt, vi* (fam) to eat

boum[1] /bum/ *m* **1** bang
2 (fam) **en plein ~** ‹*business*› booming; **faire un ~** ‹*birth rates*› to soar

boum[2] /bum/ *f* party

bouquet /bukɛ/ *m* **1 ~ (de fleurs)** bunch of flowers; bouquet
2 (of firework display) final flourish; **c'est le ~!** (fam) (fig) that's the limit! (fam)

bouquin /bukɛ̃/ *m* (fam) book

bouquiner /bukine/ [**v1**] *vt, vi* (fam) to read

bourbier /buʀbje/ *m* quagmire

bourde /buʀd/ *f* blunder

bourdon /buʀdɔ̃/ *m* bumblebee

bourdonnement /buʀdɔnmɑ̃/ *m* (of insect) buzzing; (of engine) hum; (of plane) drone

bourdonner /buʀdɔne/ [**v1**] *vi* to buzz; to hum

bourg /buʀ/ *m* market town

bourgeois, ~e /buʀʒwa, az/ **A** *adj* bourgeois
B *mf* **1** middle-class person
2 (in Ancien Regime) bourgeois
3 burgher

bourgeoisie /buʀʒwazi/ *f* **1** middle classes
2 bourgeoisie

bourgeon /buʀʒɔ̃/ *m* bud; **en ~s** in bud

bourgeonner /buʀʒɔne/ [**v1**] *vi* to bud

bourrage /buʀaʒ/ *m* **~ de crâne** brainwashing

bourrasque /buʀask/ *f* (of wind) gust

bourratif, -ive /buʀatif, iv/ *adj* very filling, stodgy

bourre /buʀ/ *f* (fam) **être à la ~** to be pushed for time

bourré, ~e /buʀe/ *adj* ‹*train, museum*› packed; ‹*case, bag*› bulging (**de** with); **~ de fric** (fam) stinking rich (fam)

bourreau, *pl* **~x** /buʀo/ *m* executioner

bourrelet /buʀlɛ/ *m* roll of fat

bourrer /buʀe/ [**v1**] *vt* **1** to cram [sth] full; to fill ‹*pipe*›
2 (fam) **~ qn de** to dose sb up with ‹*medicine*›

bourricot /buʀiko/ *m* donkey

bourrique /buʀik/ *f* **1** donkey
2 (fam) pig-headed person

bourru, ~e /buʀy/ *adj* gruff

bourse /buʀs/ *f* **1** grant (BrE), scholarship (AmE)
2 purse

Bourse /buʀs/ *f* **1** stock exchange
2 shares; **une société de ~** a broking (BrE) or brokerage (AmE) firm

boursicoter /buʀsikɔte/ [**v1**] *vi* to dabble in stocks and shares

boursier, -ière /buʀsje, ɛʀ/ **A** *adj* **le marché ~** share prices
B *mf* grant holder (BrE), scholarship student (AmE)

boursouflé, ~e /buʀsufle/ *adj* **1** blistered
2 puffy
3 ‹*body*› bloated

bousculade /buskylad/ *f* **1** jostling; (accidental) crush
2 rush

bousculer /buskyle/ [**v1**] **A** *vt* **1** to push, to jostle ‹*person*›
2 to rush
B se bousculer *v refl* (+ *v être*) to fall over each other (**pour faire** to do)

bouse /buz/ *f* **une ~ (de vache)** a cowpat

bousiller /buzije/ [**v1**] *vt* (fam) to wreck ‹*engine*›; to smash up ‹*car*›

boussole /busɔl/ *f* compass

bout /bu/ *m* **1** end; tip; (of shoe) toe; **au ~ du jardin** at the bottom of the garden; **aller jusqu'au ~** to go all the way; **aller (jusqu') au ~ de** to follow through ‹*idea, demand*›;

elle est à ~ she can't take any more; **ne me pousse pas à ~** don't push me; **être à ~ d'arguments** to have run out of arguments; **venir à ~ de** to overcome ‹*difficulty*›; to get through ‹*task, meal*›; **au ~ du compte** in the end; **à ~ portant** at point-blank range
2 (of bread, paper) piece; (of land) bit
■ **~ de chou** (fam) sweet little thing (fam); **~ d'essai** screen test
IDIOMS **tenir le bon ~** (fam) to be on the right track; **ne pas être au ~ de ses peines** not to be out of the woods yet

boutade /butad/ *f* witticism

boute-en-train /butɑ̃tʀɛ̃/ *mf inv* live wire (fig)

bouteille /butɛj/ *f* (gen) bottle; (of gas) cylinder
IDIOM **prendre de la ~** (fam) to be getting on (a bit)

boutique /butik/ *f* shop (BrE), store (AmE)

boutiquier, **-ière** /butikje, ɛʀ/ *mf* shopkeeper

bouton /butɔ̃/ *m* **1** (on clothes) button
2 knob; button
3 (Med) spot (BrE), pimple (AmE)
4 (flower) bud
■ **~ démarrer** (Comput) start button; **~ de fièvre** cold sore; **~ de manchette** cuff link; **~ d'or** buttercup; **~ de porte** doorknob; **~ retour** (Comput) back button

boutonner /butɔne/ [**v1**] *vt*, **se boutonner** *v refl* (+ *v être*) to button up

boutonneux, **-euse** /butɔnø, øz/ *adj* spotty (BrE), pimply (AmE)

boutonnière /butɔnjɛʀ/ *f* buttonhole

bouture /butyʀ/ *f* cutting

bovin, **~e** /bɔvɛ̃, in/ **A** *adj* bovine
B *m* bovine; **des ~s** cattle

box, *pl* **boxes** /bɔks/ *m* **1** lock-up garage
2 (for horse) stall
3 (in bar) alcove
■ **~ des accusés** (Law) dock

boxe /bɔks/ *f* (Sport) boxing; **~ française** savate

boxer /bɔkse/ [**v1**] *vi* (Sport) to box

boxeur /bɔksœʀ/ *m* (Sport) boxer

boyau, *pl* **~x** /bwajo/ *m* **1** gut
2 catgut
3 (for sausage) casing
4 tubeless tyre (BrE) *or* tire (AmE)

boycotter /bɔjkɔte/ [**v1**] *vt* to boycott

BP *written abbr* ▶ **boîte**

bracelet /bʀaslɛ/ *m* **1** bracelet; bangle
2 wristband; **~ de montre** watch strap

braconnier /bʀakɔnje/ *m* poacher

brader /bʀade/ [**v1**] *vt* **1** to sell cheaply
2 to sell off

braderie /bʀadʀi/ *f* **1** street market
2 discount store
3 clearance sale

braguette /bʀagɛt/ *f* flies (BrE), fly (AmE)

braille /bʀaj/ *m* Braille

brailler /bʀaje/ [**v1**] *vi* (fam) **1** to yell
2 ‹*child, singer*› to bawl

braire /bʀɛʀ/ [**v58**] *vi* to bray

braise /bʀɛz/ *f* live embers

brancard /bʀɑ̃kaʀ/ *m* stretcher

branchage /bʀɑ̃ʃaʒ/ *m* branches

⚷ **branche** /bʀɑ̃ʃ/ *f* **1** (of tree) branch
2 **céleri en ~s** sticks of celery
3 field, sector
4 (of family) branch
5 (of candelabra) branch; (of spectacles) arm; (of star) point

branché, **~e** /bʀɑ̃ʃe/ *adj* (fam) trendy (fam)

branchement /bʀɑ̃ʃmɑ̃/ *m* **1** (electrical) connection
2 (for water) branch pipe; (for electricity) lead (BrE), cable (AmE)

brancher /bʀɑ̃ʃe/ [**v1**] *vt* **1** to plug in
2 to connect (up) ‹*water, electricity*›
3 (fam) **~ qn sur** to get sb onto ‹*topic*›
4 (fam) **je vais au cinéma, ça te branche?** I'm going to the cinema, are you interested?

branchie /bʀɑ̃ʃi/ *f* (of fish) gill

brandir /bʀɑ̃diʀ/ [**v3**] *vt* to brandish

branlant, **~e** /bʀɑ̃lɑ̃, ɑ̃t/ *adj* ‹*chair*› rickety; ‹*tooth*› loose; ‹*argument*› shaky

branle /bʀɑ̃l/ *m* **mettre qch en ~** to set [sth] in motion ‹*project, convoy*›

branle-bas /bʀɑ̃lbɑ/ *m inv* commotion
■ **~ de combat** (Mil) action stations

branler /bʀɑ̃le/ [**v1**] *vi* ‹*wall*› to wobble; ‹*chair*› to be rickety; ‹*tooth*› to be loose

braquage /bʀakaʒ/ *m* (fam) robbery

braquer /bʀake/ [**v1**] **A** *vt* **1** to point ‹*gun, camera*› (**sur, vers** at); to turn *or* fix ‹*eyes*› (**sur, vers** on)
2 **~ à gauche/droite** to turn hard left/right
3 (fam) to point a gun at
4 (fam) to rob ‹*bank*›
5 (fam) **~ qn contre qn/qch** to turn sb against sb/sth
B *vi* ‹*driver*› to turn the wheel full lock (BrE) *or* all the way (AmE)
C **se braquer** *v refl* (+ *v être*) to dig one's heels in

⚷ **bras** /bʀa/ *m inv* **1** arm; **~ dessus ~ dessous** arm in arm; **porter qch à bout de ~** (fig) to keep sth afloat; **en ~ de chemise** in one's shirtsleeves
2 manpower, labour (BrE)
3 (of river) branch; **~ de mer** sound
4 (of armchair) arm
■ **~ droit** right hand man; **~ de fer** arm wrestling; (fig) trial of strength
IDIOMS **les ~ m'en tombent** I'm absolutely speechless; **avoir le ~ long** to have a lot of influence

brasier /bʀazje/ *m* inferno

bras-le-corps: **à bras-le-corps** /abʀalkɔʀ/ *phr* ‹*lift*› bodily

---
⚷ key word

brassage /bʀasaʒ/ *m* **1** (of beer) brewing
2 (mixing) (of people) intermingling; (of ideas, cultures) cross-fertilization

brassard /bʀasaʀ/ *m* armband

brasse /bʀas/ *f* (Sport) breaststroke

brasser /bʀase/ [**v1**] *vt* **1** to toss around ‹*ideas*›; to shuffle around ‹*papers*›; to intermingle ‹*population*›; **il brasse des millions** he handles big money
2 to brew ‹*beer*›

brasserie /bʀasʀi/ *f* **1** brasserie
2 brewery

brasseur, **-euse** /bʀasœʀ, øz/ *mf* brewer

brassière /bʀasjɛʀ/ *f* **1** baby's top
2 crop top

brave /bʀav/ *adj* **1** nice; **un ~ homme** a nice man
2 brave; **un homme ~** a brave man

braver /bʀave/ [**v1**] *vt* to defy ‹*person*›; to brave ‹*storm*›

bravo /bʀavo/ *excl* bravo!; well done!

bravoure /bʀavuʀ/ *f* bravery

break /bʀɛk/ *m* estate car (BrE), station wagon (AmE)

brebis /bʀəbi/ *f inv* ewe

brèche /bʀɛʃ/ *f* **1** hole, gap
2 (Mil) breach

bréchet /bʀeʃɛ/ *m* wishbone

bredouille /bʀəduj/ *adj* empty-handed

bredouiller /bʀəduje/ [**v1**] *vt*, *vi* to mumble

bref, **brève** /bʀɛf, bʀɛv/ **A** *adj* brief; short
B *adv* **(en) ~** in short

breloque /bʀəlɔk/ *f* (on bracelet) charm

Brésil /bʀezil/ *pr m* Brazil

Bretagne /bʀətaɲ/ *pr f* Brittany

bretelle /bʀətɛl/ **A** *f* **1** (gen) strap
2 slip road (BrE), ramp (AmE)
B **bretelles** *fpl* braces

breton, **-onne** /bʀətɔ̃, ɔn/ **A** *adj* Breton
B *m* (language) Breton

breuvage /bʀœvaʒ/ *m* beverage

brève /bʀɛv/ **A** *adj f* ▸ **bref A**
B *f* news flash

brevet /bʀəvɛ/ *m* **~ (d'invention)** patent
■ **~ de pilote** pilot's licence (BrE); **~ de secourisme** first aid certificate; **~ de technicien supérieur**, **BTS** *advanced vocational diploma*

breveter /bʀəvte/ [**v20**] *vt* **(faire) ~** to patent

bréviaire /bʀevjɛʀ/ *m* breviary

bribes /bʀib/ *fpl* (of conversation) snatches

bric: **de bric et de broc** /dəbʀiked(ə)bʀɔk/ *phr* ‹*furnished*› with bits and pieces

bric-à-brac /bʀikabʀak/ *m inv* bric-a-brac

bricolage /bʀikɔlaʒ/ *m* DIY (BrE), do-it-yourself

bricole /bʀikɔl/ *f* **acheter une ~** to buy a little something; **des ~s** bits and pieces

bricoler /bʀikɔle/ [**v1**] **A** *vt* (fam) **1** to tinker with
2 to throw [sth] together
B *vi* to do DIY (BrE), to fix things (AmE)

bride /bʀid/ *f* **1** bridle
2 button loop
IDIOMS **partir à ~ abattue** to dash off; **avoir la ~ sur le cou** to have free rein

bridé, **~e** /bʀide/ *adj* **yeux ~s** slanting eyes

brièvement /bʀijɛvmɑ̃/ *adv* briefly

brigade /bʀigad/ *f* **1** (Mil) brigade
2 (in police) squad

brigadier /bʀigadje/ *m* **1** ≈ corporal
2 fire chief

brigand /bʀigɑ̃/ *m* brigand, bandit

brillamment /bʀijamɑ̃/ *adv* brilliantly

brillant, **~e** /bʀijɑ̃, ɑ̃t/ **A** *adj* **1** bright; shiny; glistening
2 brilliant
B *m* (cut) diamond, brilliant

briller /bʀije/ [**v1**] *vi* **1** ‹*sun*› to shine; ‹*flame*› to burn brightly; ‹*gem*› to sparkle; ‹*nose*› to be shiny
2 ~ de ‹*eyes*› to blaze with ‹*anger*›
3 ‹*person*› to shine; **elle brille par son esprit** she's extremely witty

brimade /bʀimad/ *f* bullying

brimer /bʀime/ [**v1**] *vt* **1** to bully
2 se sentir brimé to feel picked on

brin /bʀɛ̃/ *m* **1** (of parsley) sprig; (of straw) wisp; (of grass) blade
2 un ~ de a bit of

brindille /bʀɛ̃dij/ *f* twig

bringue /bʀɛ̃g/ *f* (fam) **1** drinking party
2 rave-up (fam)
3 (girl) **(grande) ~** beanpole

brinquebaler /bʀɛ̃kbale/ [**v1**] *vi* ‹*load*› to rattle about; ‹*vehicle*› to jolt along

brio /bʀijo/ *m* brilliance; (Mus) brio

brioche /bʀijɔʃ/ *f* **1** brioche, (sweet) bun
2 (fam) paunch

brioché, **~e** /bʀijɔʃe/ *adj* (Culin) brioche

brique /bʀik/ *f* **1** brick
2 (for milk, juice) carton

briquer /bʀike/ [**v1**] *vt* to polish [sth] up

briquet /bʀikɛ/ *m* (cigarette) lighter

brise /bʀiz/ *f* breeze; **bonne ~** fresh breeze

brise-glace /bʀizglas/ *m inv* ice-breaker

briser /bʀize/ [**v1**] **A** *vt* **1** (gen) to break; to break down ‹*resistance*›
2 to shatter ‹*dream*›
3 to destroy ‹*organization*›; to break ‹*person*›; to wreck ‹*career*›
B **se briser** *v refl* (+ *v être*) **1** to break
2 ‹*dream*› to be shattered
3 ‹*voice*› to break

brise-tout /bʀiztu/ *m inv* (person) butterfingers

briseur, **-euse** /bʀizœʀ, øz/ *mf* wrecker
■ **~ de grève** strike breaker

brisure /bʀizyʀ/ *f* **1** crack
2 fragment

britannique /bʀitanik/ *adj* British

Britannique /bʀitanik/ *mf* **un/une ~** a British man/woman; **les ~s** the British (people)

broc /bʀo/ *m* ewer

brocante /bʀɔkɑ̃t/ *f* **1** bric-a-brac trade
2 flea market

broche /bʀɔʃ/ *f* **1** brooch
2 (for roasting) spit
3 (in surgery) pin

brocher /bʀɔʃe/ [**v1**] *vt* to bind [sth] (with paper) ‹*book*›; **livre broché** paperback

brochet /bʀɔʃɛ/ *m* (Zool) pike

brochette /bʀɔʃɛt/ *f* **1** skewer
2 kebab

brochure /bʀɔʃyʀ/ *f* **1** booklet
2 (travel) brochure

brocoli /bʀɔkɔli/ *m* broccoli

broder /bʀɔde/ [**v1**] *vt, vi* to embroider

broderie /bʀɔdʀi/ *f* embroidery

bromure /bʀɔmyʀ/ *m* bromide

bronche /bʀɔ̃ʃ/ *f* **les ~s** the bronchial tubes

broncher /bʀɔ̃ʃe/ [**v1**] *vi* **sans ~** without turning a hair

bronchite /bʀɔ̃ʃit/ *f* bronchitis

bronzage /bʀɔ̃zaʒ/ *m* (sun)tan

bronze /bʀɔ̃z/ *m* bronze

bronzé, **~e** /bʀɔ̃ze/ *adj* ‹*person*› suntanned

bronzer /bʀɔ̃ze/ [**v1**] *vi* to get a tan, to go brown

brossage /bʀɔsaʒ/ *m* (of hair, teeth) brushing

brosse /bʀɔs/ *f* brush; **donner un coup de ~ à qch** to give sth a brush; **avoir les cheveux (taillés) en ~** to have a crew cut

brosser /bʀɔse/ [**v1**] **A** *vt* **1** to brush; to scrub
2 to give a quick outline of
B se brosser *v refl* (+ *v être*) to brush oneself down; **se ~ les dents** to brush one's teeth

brouette /bʀuɛt/ *f* wheelbarrow

brouhaha /bʀuaa/ *m* hubbub

brouillard /bʀujaʀ/ *m* fog

brouille /bʀuj/ *f* **1** quarrel
2 rift

brouiller /bʀuje/ [**v1**] **A** *vt* **1** to make [sth] cloudy ‹*liquid*›; to blur ‹*text, vision*›; **~ les cartes** to confuse *or* cloud the issue
2 to jam ‹*signal*›; to interfere with ‹*reception*›
B se brouiller *v refl* (+ *v être*) **1** to fall out (**avec** with)
2 ‹*liquid*› to become cloudy; ‹*vision*› to become blurred; ‹*mind*› to become confused; **avoir le teint brouillé** to look ill

brouillon, **-onne** /bʀujɔ̃, ɔn/ **A** *adj*
1 untidy
2 disorganized
3 muddled
B *m* **1** rough draft
2 rough paper

broussaille /bʀusaj/ *f* **1** undergrowth
2 scrub
3 bushes

brousse /bʀus/ *f* bush; **en pleine ~** (fam) in the sticks (fam)

brouter /bʀute/ [**v1**] *vt* to nibble; to graze

brouteur, **-euse** /bʀutœʀ, øz/ *mf* browser

broyer /bʀwaje/ [**v23**] *vt* **1** to grind ‹*wheat*›
2 to crush
IDIOM **~ du noir** to brood

broyeur /bʀwajœʀ/ *m* (machine) crusher, grinder

bru /bʀy/ *f* daughter-in-law

brugnon /bʀyɲɔ̃/ *m* nectarine

bruiner /bʀɥine/ [**v1**] *v impers* to drizzle

bruissement /bʀɥismɑ̃/ *m* (of leaves) rustle; (of brook) babbling

bruit /bʀɥi/ *m* **1** noise; **~ étouffé** thud; **un ~ de ferraille** a clang
2 noise, din; **~ infernal** *or* **d'enfer** awful racket; **sans ~** silently
3 le film a fait beaucoup de ~ the film attracted a lot of attention
4 ~ (de couloir) rumour (BrE)

bruitage /bʀɥitaʒ/ *m* sound effects

bruiteur /bʀɥitœʀ/ *m* sound effects engineer

brûlant, **~e** /bʀylɑ̃, ɑ̃t/ *adj* **1** ‹*tea*› boiling hot; ‹*sand, radiator, person*› burning hot; ‹*sun*› blazing
2 ‹*issue*› burning
3 ‹*passion*› burning

brûlé, **~e** /bʀyle/ **A** *mf* **un grand ~** a third degree burns victim; **service des grands ~s** burns unit
B *m* **ça sent le ~** there's a smell of burning

brûle-parfum /bʀylpaʀfœ̃/ *m inv also* **brûle-parfums** incense burner

brûle-pourpoint: **à brûle-pourpoint** /abʀylpuʀpwɛ̃/ *phr* point-blank

brûler /bʀyle/ [**v1**] **A** *vt* **1** to burn ‹*papers*›; to set fire to ‹*house*›
2 to burn ‹*fuel*›; to use ‹*electricity*›
3 ‹*acid*› to burn; ‹*water*› to scald; **j'ai les yeux qui me brûlent** my eyes are stinging
4 (fam) **~ un feu (rouge)** to jump (fam) the lights
B *vi* **1** ‹*wood*› to burn; ‹*forest, town*› to be on fire
2 ~ (d'envie) de faire to be longing to do
C se brûler *v refl* (+ *v être*) to burn oneself

brûlure /bʀylyʀ/ *f* **1** burn; **~s d'estomac** heartburn
2 burn mark

brume /bʀym/ *f* mist; fog; haze

brumeux, **-euse** /bʀymø, øz/ *adj* **1** hazy; misty
2 ‹*idea*› hazy

brun, **~e** /bʀœ̃, bʀyn/ **A** *adj* brown, dark; dark-haired

key word

B *mf* dark-haired man/woman
C *m* brown
brunir /bʀyniʀ/ [**v3**] *vi* **1** ‹*skin*› to tan
2 (Culin) to brown
brushing /bʀœʃiŋ/ *m* blow-dry
brusque /bʀysk/ *adj* **1** ‹*tone, person*› abrupt
2 ‹*movement*› sudden; ‹*bend*› sharp
brusquement /bʀyskəmɑ̃/ *adv* **1** abruptly
2 suddenly; ‹*brake*› sharply
brusquer /bʀyske/ [**v1**] *vt* **1** to be brusque with
2 to rush
brut, **~e** /bʀyt/ *adj* **1** ‹*material*› raw; ‹*oil*› crude; ‹*stone*› rough; ‹*sugar*› unrefined
2 ‹*cider, champagne*› dry
3 ‹*salary*› gross
brutal, **~e**, *mpl* **-aux** /bʀytal, o/ *adj*
1 ‹*blow*› violent; ‹*pain, death*› sudden
2 ‹*tone*› brutal; ‹*gesture, temper*› violent
3 stark
brutalement /bʀytalmɑ̃/ *adv* **1** ‹*repress*› brutally; ‹*close*› violently
2 ‹*die, stop*› suddenly
brutaliser /bʀytalize/ [**v1**] *vt* to ill-treat
brutalité /bʀytalite/ *f* **1** brutality
2 suddenness
brute /bʀyt/ **A** *adj f* ▶ **brut**
B *f* brute; **comme une ~** ‹*hit*› savagely
Bruxelles /bʀysɛl/ *pr n* Brussels
bruyant, **~e** /bʀɥijɑ̃, ɑ̃t/ *adj* **1** noisy; loud
2 resounding
BTS /beteɛs/ *m: abbr* ▶ **brevet**
bu, **~e** /by/ ▶ **boire**
buanderie /bɥɑ̃dʀi/ *f* laundry room
buccal, **~e**, *mpl* **-aux** /bykal, o/ *adj* oral
bûche /byʃ/ *f* **1** log (of wood)
2 (fam) tumble, fall
3 (Culin) **~ de Noël** yule log
bûcher[1] /byʃe/ [**v1**] *vi* (fam) to slog away (fam)
bûcher[2] /byʃe/ *m* **1 le ~** the stake
2 (funeral) pyre
bûcheron /byʃʀɔ̃/ *m* lumberjack
bûchette /byʃɛt/ *f* (for fire) stick
bucolique /bykɔlik/ *adj* bucolic, pastoral
budget /bydʒɛ/ *m* budget
budgétaire /bydʒetɛʀ/ *adj* ‹*deficit*› budget; ‹*year*› financial (BrE), fiscal (AmE)
budgétiser /bydʒetize/ [**v1**] *vt* to include [sth] in the budget
buée /bɥe/ *f* **1** condensation
2 steam
buffet /byfɛ/ *m* **1** sideboard
2 dresser
3 (station) buffet
4 (Culin) buffet
buffle /byfl/ *m* buffalo
buis /bɥi/ *m* **1** box tree
2 boxwood
buisson /bɥisɔ̃/ *m* **1** bush
2 shrub
buissonnière /bɥisɔnjɛʀ/ *adj f* **faire l'école ~** to play truant (BrE), to play hooky (AmE) (fam)
bulbe /bylb/ *m* (Bot) bulb
bulgare /bylgaʀ/ *adj*, *m* Bulgarian
Bulgarie /bylgaʀi/ *pr f* Bulgaria
bulldozer /byldozœʀ/ *m* bulldozer
bulle /byl/ *f* **1** bubble
2 speech bubble
bulletin /byltɛ̃/ *m* **1** bulletin, report; **~ de santé** medical bulletin
2 certificate; **~ de naissance** birth certificate
3 form; **~ de salaire** payslip; **~ de participation** entry form
4 bulletin, official publication
5 ballot *or* voting paper; **~ de vote d'un (électeur) absent** absentee ballot
bulletin-réponse, *pl* **bulletins-réponse** /byltɛ̃ʀepɔ̃s/ *m* reply coupon
bulot /bylo/ *m* whelk
buraliste /byʀalist/ *mf* **1** (for smokers' supplies) tobacconist; (for cigarettes and newspapers) newsagent (BrE), news dealer (AmE)
2 (counter staff) clerk
⚷ **bureau**, *pl* **~x** /byʀo/ *m* **1** desk
2 study
3 office
4 board
5 (Comput) desktop
■ **~ d'accueil** reception; **Bureau international du travail**, **BIT** International Labour Office, ILO; **~ de poste** post office; **~ de tabac** tobacconist's; **~ de vote** polling station
bureaucratie /byʀokʀasi/ *f* bureaucracy
bureautique /byʀotik/ *f* office automation
burin /byʀɛ̃/ *m* chisel
buriné, **~e** /byʀine/ *adj* ‹*face*› craggy
burlesque /byʀlɛsk/ *adj* ludicrous; farcical
bus /bys/ *m inv* bus
buse /byz/ *f* **1** buzzard
2 (fam) clot (BrE) (fam), clod (fam)
business /biznɛs/ *m inv* (commercial) business; (private) affairs
busqué, **~e** /byske/ *adj* ‹*nose*› hooked
buste /byst/ *m* **1** (in sculpture) bust
2 (Anat) chest
3 bust, breasts
bustier /bystje/ *m* **1** long-line bra
2 bustier
⚷ **but** /by(t)/ *m* **1** goal; aim, purpose; **aller droit au ~** to go straight to the point
2 (in football) goal
3 (in archery) target
IDIOM **déclarer de ~ en blanc** to declare point-blank
buté, **~e** /byte/ *adj* stubborn, obstinate
buter /byte/ [**v1**] *vi* **~ contre qch** to trip over sth; to bump into sth; **~ sur** *or* **contre** to come up against ‹*obstacle*›
butin /bytɛ̃/ *m* (from robbery) haul

b c

butiner /bytine/ [v1] *vi* to gather pollen
butte /byt/ *f* mound
IDIOM **être en ~ à** to come up against ‹*difficulties*›; to be the butt of ‹*jokes*›
buvable /byvabl/ *adj* **1** ‹*medicine*› to be taken orally
2 drinkable
buvard /byvaʀ/ *m* **(papier) ~** blotting paper
buvette /byvɛt/ *f* refreshment area
buveur, **-euse** /byvœʀ, øz/ *mf* drinker; **c'est un gros ~** he's a heavy drinker; **un ~ de thé/bière** a tea/beer drinker

Cc

c, **C** /se/ *m inv* c, C; **c cédille** c cedilla
c' ▸ **ce B**
CA *written abbr* ▸ **chiffre**
⚷ **ça** /sa/ *pron* **1** that; this; **c'est pour ~ qu'il est parti** that's why he left; **sans ~** otherwise; **~, c'est bizarre** that's strange; **la rue a ~ de bien qu'elle est calme** one good thing about the street is that it's quiet
2 it; that; **~ fait mal** it hurts; that hurts; **~ criait de tous les côtés** there was shouting everywhere
IDIOMS **~ alors!** well I never! (fam); **~, oui!** (fam) definitely!; **elle est bête et méchante avec ~** she's stupid and what's more she's nasty; **et avec ~?** anything else?; **rien que ~!** (ironic) is that all!; **c'est ~!** that's right!; **~ y est, ~ recommence!** here we go again!; **~ y est, j'ai fini!** that's it, I've finished!
caban /kabɑ̃/ *m* sailor's jacket
cabane /kaban/ *f* **1** hut
2 shed
3 (pop) prison
cabaret /kabaʀɛ/ *m* cabaret
cabas /kaba/ *m* shopping bag
cabillaud /kabijo/ *m* cod
cabine /kabin/ *f* cabin; cab; booth; cubicle
■ **~ d'essayage** fitting room; **~ de pilotage** cockpit; **~ téléphonique** phone box (BrE), phone booth
cabinet /kabinɛ/ **A** *m* **1** (gen) office; (of doctor, dentist) surgery (BrE), office (AmE); (of judge) chambers
2 practice; **~ de médecins** medical practice; **ouvrir un ~** to set up in practice
3 agency
4 (Pol) cabinet; **~ ministériel** minister's personal staff
B **cabinets** *mpl* toilet
■ **~ de toilette** bathroom
cabinet-conseil, *pl* **cabinets-conseil** /kabinɛkɔ̃sɛj/ *m* firm of consultants
câble /kɑbl/ *m* **1** cable; rope
2 cable television
câbler /kɑble/ [v1] *vt* **1** to install cable television in ‹*house, town*›
2 to cable ‹*message*›
cabochard, **~e** /kabɔʃaʀ, aʀd/ *adj* (fam) stubborn
caboche /kabɔʃ/ *f* (fam) head
cabosser /kabɔse/ [v1] *vt* to dent
cabot /kabo/ *m* (fam) dog, mutt (fam)
cabotin, **~e** /kabɔtɛ̃, in/ *adj* **être ~** to like playing to the gallery
cabrer: **se cabrer** /kabʀe/ [v1] *v refl* (+ *v être*) **1** ‹*horse*› to rear (**devant** at)
2 ‹*person*› to jib
cabri /kabʀi/ *m* (Zool) kid
cabriole /kabʀijɔl/ *f* (of clown, child) caper
CAC® /kak/ *m* (*abbr* = **Compagnie des agents de change**) **indice ~ 40**, **~ 40** Paris Stock Exchange index
caca /kaka/ *m* (baby talk) poo (BrE) (fam), poop (AmE) (fam)
cacahuète /kakawɛt/ *f* peanut
cacao /kakao/ *m* cocoa
cacatoès /kakatɔɛs/ *m* cockatoo
cachalot /kaʃalo/ *m* sperm whale
cache¹ /kaʃ/ *m* **se servir d'un ~ pour apprendre une liste de vocabulaire** to cover up the answers while learning a list of vocabulary
cache² /kaʃ/ *f* **~ d'armes** arms cache
caché, **~e** /kaʃe/ **A** *pp* ▸ **cacher**
B *pp adj* ‹*beauty, sense*› hidden; ‹*pain, desire*› secret
cache-cache /kaʃkaʃ/ *m inv* hide and seek (BrE), hide and go seek (AmE)
cache-col /kaʃkɔl/ *m inv* scarf
cachemire /kaʃmiʀ/ *m* cashmere
cache-nez /kaʃne/ *m inv* scarf, muffler
cache-pot /kaʃpo/ *m inv* flowerpot holder
⚷ **cacher** /kaʃe/ [v1] **A** *vt* to hide; **~ son jeu** (fig) to keep one's cards close to one's chest; **~ qch à qn** to conceal sth from sb
B **se cacher** *v refl* (+ *v être*) **1** to hide;

⚷ key word

(temporarily) to go into hiding; **il ne s'en cache pas** he makes no secret of it
2 ‹*sun*› to disappear

cache-sexe /kaʃsɛks/ *m inv* G-string

cachet /kaʃɛ/ *m* **1** tablet
2 (for letter) stamp; seal; **~ de la poste** postmark
3 (of actor) fee

cacheter /kaʃte/ [**v20**] *vt* to seal

cachette /kaʃɛt/ *f* hiding place; **en ~** on the sly

cachot /kaʃo/ *m* **1** prison cell
2 dungeon

cachotterie /kaʃɔtʀi/ *f* little secret

cachottier, **-ière** /kaʃɔtje, ɛʀ/ *adj* secretive

cachou /kaʃu/ *m* cachou

cacophonie /kakɔfɔni/ *f* cacophony

cactus /kaktys/ *m inv* cactus

c-à-d (*written abbr* = **c'est-à-dire**) ie

cadastre /kadastʀ/ *m* **1** land register
2 land registry

cadavérique /kadaveʀik/ *adj* ‹*complexion*› deathly pale

cadavre /kadavʀ/ *m* corpse, body

caddie® /kadi/ *m* shopping trolley

cadeau, *pl* **~x** /kado/ **A** *m* present, gift; **faire un ~ à qn** to give sb a present; **il ne fait pas de ~x** (examiner, judge) he's very strict
B **(-)cadeau** (*combining form*) gift; **papier(-)~** wrapping paper

cadenas /kadna/ *m* padlock

cadence /kadɑ̃s/ *f* **1** rhythm
2 (of work) rate

cadet, **-ette** /kadɛ, ɛt/ **A** *adj* **1** younger
2 youngest
B *mf* **1** younger son/daughter, younger child
2 youngest child
3 younger brother/sister
4 (Sport) *athlete between the ages of 15 and 17*
IDIOM **c'est le ~ de mes soucis** it's the least of my worries

cadrage /kadʀaʒ/ *m* **1** framing
2 composition

cadran /kadʀɑ̃/ *m* (of watch) face; (of meter) dial; **~ solaire** sundial

cadre /kadʀ/ **A** *m* **1** frame
2 setting; surroundings
3 cela sort du ~ de mes fonctions that's not part of my duties
4 framework
5 executive; **~ supérieur** senior executive; **les ~s moyens** middle management
6 faire partie des ~s to be on the company's books
7 (of bicycle) frame
8 (on form) space, box
B dans le cadre de *phr* **1** on the occasion of
2 (of negotiations) within the framework of; (of campaign, plan) as part of

cadrer /kadʀe/ [**v1**] **A** *vt* to centre (BrE) ‹*picture*›
B *vi* to tally, to fit (**avec** with)

cadreur /kadʀœʀ/ *m* cameraman

caduc, **caduque** /kadyk/ *adj* **1** obsolete
2 (Law) null and void
3 ‹*leaf*› deciduous

cætera ▸ **et cætera**

cafard /kafaʀ/ *m* **1** (fam) depression; **avoir le ~** to be down in the dumps (fam)
2 cockroach

cafardeux, **-euse** /kafaʀdø, øz/ *adj* glum; gloomy

café /kafe/ *m* **1** coffee; **~ en grains** coffee beans; **~ soluble** instant coffee
2 café
■ **~ crème** espresso with milk; **~ au lait** coffee with milk; **peau ~ au lait** coffee-coloured (BrE) skin

café-concert, *pl* **cafés-concerts** /kafekɔ̃sɛʀ/ *m* cafe with live music

caféine /kafein/ *f* caffeine

cafétéria /kafeteʀja/ *f* cafeteria

cafetière /kaftjɛʀ/ *f* coffee pot; coffee maker

cafouillage /kafujaʒ/ *m* (fam) bungling (fam)

cafouiller /kafuje/ [**v1**] *vi* (fam) ‹*person*› to get flustered; ‹*machine*› to be on the blink (fam); ‹*organization*› to get in a muddle

cage /kaʒ/ *f* **1** cage
2 (Sport), (fam) goal
■ **~ d'ascenseur** lift (BrE) *or* elevator (AmE) shaft; **~ d'escalier** stairwell; **~ à lapins** rabbit hutch; **~ thoracique** rib cage

cageot /kaʒo/ *m* crate

cagette /kaʒɛt/ *f* tray

cagibi /kaʒibi/ *m* store cupboard

cagnotte /kaɲɔt/ *f* **1** kitty
2 jackpot

cagoule /kagul/ *f* balaclava; hood

cahier /kaje/ *m* **1** notebook; (Sch) exercise book
2 (in printing) section
■ **~ de brouillon** rough book; **~ de textes** homework notebook

cahin-caha /kaɛ̃kaa/ *adv* (fam) with difficulty

cahot /kao/ *m* jolt

cahoter /kaɔte/ [**v1**] *vi* ‹*vehicle*› to bounce along

cahoteux, **-euse** /kaɔtø, -øz/ *adj* ‹*road*› rough, bumpy

cahute /kayt/ *f* hut, shack

caïd /kaid/ *m* (in criminal underworld) boss; **jouer les ~s** to act tough

caillasse /kajas/ *f* stones

caille /kɑj/ *f* (Zool) quail

cailler /kɑje/ [**v1**] **A se cailler** *v refl* (+ *v être*) **1** ‹*milk*› to curdle

C

2 (fam) ‹*person*› to be freezing
B *v impers* (fam) **ça caille** it's freezing

caillot /kajo/ *m* clot

caillou, *pl* **~x** /kaju/ *m* **1** pebble; **gros ~** stone
2 (fam) nut (fam); **ne plus avoir un poil sur le ~** to be as bald as a coot (fam)

caillouteux, **-euse** /kajutø, øz/ *adj* stony

caïman /kaimɑ̃/ *m* cayman

Caire /kɛʀ/ *pr n* **le ~** Cairo

caisse /kɛs/ *f* **1** crate
2 (of car) shell, body
3 (pop) car
4 (for money) till; cash register; cash box; **les ~s de l'État** the Treasury coffers; **voler la ~** to steal the takings
5 cash desk; (in supermarket) checkout (counter); (in bank) cashier's desk
6 fund
■ **~ d'épargne** ≈ savings bank; **~ noire** slush fund; **~ à outils** toolbox

caissette /kɛsɛt/ *f* small box *or* case

caissier, **-ière** /kesje, ɛʀ/ *mf* cashier

cajoler /kaʒɔle/ [**v1**] *vt* to cuddle ‹*child*›

cajoleur, **-euse** /kaʒɔlœʀ, øz/ *adj* affectionate

cajou /kaʒu/ *m* **noix de ~** cashew nut

cake /kɛk/ *m* fruit cake

cal /kal/ *m* callus

calamar /kalamaʀ/ *m* squid

calamité /kalamite/ *f* disaster, calamity

calandre /kalɑ̃dʀ/ *f* (Aut) (radiator) grille (BrE)

calcaire /kalkɛʀ/ **A** *adj* ‹*water*› hard; ‹*soil*› chalky; ‹*rock*› limestone
B *m* **1** limestone
2 fur (BrE), sediment (AmE)

calciner /kalsine/ [**v1**] *vt* **1** to char; (in oven) to burn [sth] to a crisp
2 (in chemistry) to calcine

calcium /kalsjɔm/ *m* calcium

calcul /kalkyl/ *m* **1** calculation; **faire le ~ de qch** to calculate sth
2 arithmetic; **~ mental** mental arithmetic
3 (scheming) calculation; **agir par ~** to act out of self-interest
4 (Med) stone

calculateur, **-trice** /kalkylatœʀ, tʀis/ *adj* calculating

calculatrice /kalkylatʀis/ *f* (pocket) calculator

calculer /kalkyle/ [**v1**] **A** *vt* **1** to calculate, to work out
2 to weigh up ‹*advantages, chances*›; **tout bien calculé** all things considered
3 ~ son coup to plan one's move
B *vi* to calculate, to compute

calculette /kalkylɛt/ *f* pocket calculator

cale /kal/ *f* **1** wedge; (for wheel) chock; (for raising vehicle) block
2 (Naut) (ship's) hold

calé, **~e** /kale/ *adj* (fam) bright; **~ en qch** brilliant at sth

calebasse /kalbas/ *f* calabash, gourd

calèche /kalɛʃ/ *f* barouche, carriage

caleçon /kalsɔ̃/ *m* **1** boxer shorts; **~ long** long johns (fam)
2 (for woman) leggings

calédonien, **-ienne** /kaledɔnjɛ̃, ɛn/ *adj* **1** New Caledonian
2 Caledonian

calembour /kalɑ̃buʀ/ *m* pun, play on words

calendrier /kalɑ̃dʀije/ *m* **1** calendar
2 schedule
3 dates

cale-pied, *pl* **~s** /kalpje/ *m* toe clip

calepin /kalpɛ̃/ *m* notebook

caler /kale/ [**v1**] **A** *vt* **1** to wedge ‹*wheel*›; to steady ‹*piece of furniture*›; to support ‹*row of books*›; **bien calé dans mon fauteuil** ensconced in my armchair
2 (fam) **ça cale** it fills you up
B *vi* ‹*car*› to stall
C se caler *v refl* (+ *v être*) to settle (**dans** in)

calfeutrer /kalføtʀe/ [**v1**] **A** *vt* to stop up ‹*crack*›; to draughtproof ‹*door*›
B se calfeutrer *v refl* (+ *v être*) to shut oneself away

calibre /kalibʀ/ *m* **1** (of gun) bore, calibre (BrE); (of pipe, cable) diameter; **arme de gros ~** large-bore weapon
2 (of eggs, fruit) size, grade
3 gauge

calibrer /kalibʀe/ [**v1**] *vt* **1** (Tech) to calibrate
2 to grade, to size ‹*eggs, fruit*›

calice /kalis/ *m* chalice

calife /kalif/ *m* caliph

califourchon: **à califourchon** /akalifuʀʃɔ̃/ *phr* astride

câlin, **~e** /kɑlɛ̃, in/ **A** *adj* affectionate
B *m* cuddle

câliner /kaline/ [**v1**] *vt* to cuddle

calleux, **-euse** /kalø, øz/ *adj* calloused

calligraphie /kaligʀafi/ *f* calligraphy

calligraphier /kaligʀafje/ [**v2**] *vt* to write [sth] in a decorative hand

callosité /kalozite/ *f* callus

calmant, **~e** /kalmɑ̃, ɑ̃t/ **A** *adj* soothing
B *m* sedative

calmar /kalmaʀ/ *m* squid

⚷ **calme** /kalm/ **A** *adj* **1** ‹*sea, situation*› calm; ‹*night*› still; ‹*place, life*› quiet
2 ‹*person*› calm
B *m* **1** peace (and quiet)
2 calm; (of crowd) calmness; (of night) stillness; **dans le ~** peacefully
3 composure; **conserver son ~** to keep calm; **du ~!** calm down!; quiet!

calmement /kalməmɑ̃/ *adv* calmly

calmer /kalme/ [**v1**] **A** *vt* **1** to calm down ‹*person*›; to calm ‹*stock market*›; to defuse

⚷ key word

‹situation›; to tone down *‹discussion›*; ~ **les esprits** to calm people down
2 to ease *‹pain›*; to take the edge off *‹hunger›*; to quench *‹thirst›*
B se calmer *v refl* (+ *v être*) **1** *‹person, situation›* to calm down; *‹agitation, storm›* to die down; *‹debate›* to quieten (BrE) *or* quiet (AmE) down; *‹ardour›* to cool
2 *‹pain›* to ease

calomnie /kalɔmni/ *f* slander

calomnier /kalɔmnje/ [**v2**] *vt* to slander

calorie /kalɔʀi/ *f* calorie

calorifère /kalɔʀifɛʀ/ *adj* heat-conveying

calorique /kalɔʀik/ *adj* calorie; **ration/valeur ~** calorie intake/content

calotte /kalɔt/ *f* **1** skull cap
2 (fam) slap
3 ~ glaciaire ice cap

calque /kalk/ *m* **1** tracing
2 tracing paper
3 replica

calquer /kalke/ [**v1**] *vt* **1** to copy *‹behaviour›*
2 to trace *‹pattern, design›* (**sur** from)

calumet /kalymɛ/ *m* **~ de la paix** peace pipe

calvados /kalvados/ *m* Calvados (*apple brandy distilled in Normandy*)

calvaire /kalvɛʀ/ *m* **1** ordeal
2 (monument) wayside cross
3 Calvary

calvitie /kalvisi/ *f* baldness

camaïeu /kamajø/ *m* monochrome

camarade /kamaʀad/ *mf* **1** friend; **~ d'atelier** workmate
2 comrade

camaraderie /kamaʀadʀi/ *f* comradeship

Cambodge /kɑ̃bɔdʒ/ *pr m* Cambodia

cambouis /kɑ̃bwi/ *m* dirty grease

cambré, **~e** /kɑ̃bʀe/ *adj ‹back›* arched; *‹foot, shoe›* with a high instep

cambrer /kɑ̃bʀe/ [**v1**] **A** *vt* to curve, to arch
B se cambrer *v refl* (+ *v être*) to arch one's back

cambriolage /kɑ̃bʀijɔlaʒ/ *m* burglary

cambrioler /kɑ̃bʀijɔle/ [**v1**] *vt* to burgle (BrE), to burglarize (AmE)

cambrioleur, **-euse** /kɑ̃bʀijɔlœʀ, øz/ *mf* burglar

cambrousse /kɑ̃bʀus/ *f* (fam) **la ~** the sticks (fam), the country; **en pleine ~** in the middle of nowhere

cambrure /kɑ̃bʀyʀ/ *f* curve; (of foot) arch
■ **~ des pieds** instep; **~ des reins** small of the back

camée /kame/ *m* cameo

caméléon /kameleɔ̃/ *m* chameleon

camelote /kamlɔt/ *f* (fam) junk (fam)

camembert /kamɑ̃bɛʀ/ *m* **1** (Culin) Camembert
2 (fam) pie chart

camer: **se camer** /kame/ [**v1**] *v refl* (+ *v être*) (sl) to be on drugs

caméra /kameʀa/ *f* (cine-)camera (BrE), movie camera (AmE)

caméscope® /kameskɔp/ *m* camcorder

camion /kamjɔ̃/ *m* truck

camion-citerne, *pl* **camions-citernes** /kamjɔ̃sitɛʀn/ *m* tanker

camionnette /kamjɔnɛt/ *f* van

camionneur /kamjɔnœʀ/ *m* truck driver

camisole /kamizɔl/ *f* camisole; **~ de force** straitjacket

camomille /kamɔmij/ *f* camomile

camouflage /kamuflaʒ/ *m* **1** (Mil) camouflage
2 (fig) concealing; disguising (**en** as)

camoufler /kamufle/ [**v1**] *vt* **1** (Mil) to camouflage
2 to cover up *‹crime, mistake, truth›*; to conceal *‹intention, feelings›*
3 to hide *‹money›*

camp /kɑ̃/ *m* **1** (gen) camp
2 (Sport, Pol) side
IDIOM **ficher** (fam) **le ~** to split (fam), to leave

campagnard, **~e** /kɑ̃paɲaʀ, aʀd/ **A** *adj* country, rustic
B *mf* country person

campagne /kɑ̃paɲ/ *f* **1** country; (open) countryside
2 campaign; **faire ~** to campaign

campanule /kɑ̃panyl/ *f* bellflower

campement /kɑ̃pmɑ̃/ *m* camp, encampment

camper /kɑ̃pe/ [**v1**] **A** *vt* to portray *‹character›*; to depict *‹landscape, scene›*
B *vi* to camp
C se camper *v refl* (+ *v être*) **se ~ devant qn/qch** to stand squarely in front of sb/sth

campeur, **-euse** /kɑ̃pœʀ, øz/ *mf* camper

camphre /kɑ̃fʀ/ *m* camphor

camping /kɑ̃piŋ/ *m* **1** camping; **faire du ~ sauvage** to camp rough
2 campsite (BrE), campground (AmE)

camping-car, *pl* **~s** /kɑ̃piŋkaʀ/ *m* camper, camper van (BrE)

camping-gaz® /kɑ̃piŋgaz/ *m inv* (gas) camping stove

campus /kɑ̃pys/ *m inv* campus

Canada /kanada/ *pr m* Canada

Canadair® /kanadɛʀ/ *m* water bomber

canadien, **-ienne** /kanadjɛ̃, ɛn/ *adj* Canadian

canadienne /kanadjɛn/ *f* **1** sheepskin-lined jacket
2 ridge tent

canal, *pl* **-aux** /kanal, o/ *m* **1** canal
2 channel
3 (Anat) duct

canalisation /kanalizasjɔ̃/ *f* **1** pipe
2 mains

canaliser /kanalize/ [**v1**] *vt* **1** to canalize *‹river›*

C

2 (fig) to channel
canapé /kanape/ *m* **1** sofa; ~ **convertible** sofa bed
2 (Culin) canapé
canaque /kanak/ *adj* Kanak
canard /kanaʀ/ *m* **1** duck; ~ **laqué** Peking duck
2 (fam) rag (fam), newspaper
3 (Mus) wrong note
IDIOM **ça ne casse pas trois pattes à un** ~ (fam) it's nothing to write home about
canarder /kanaʀde/ [**v1**] *vt* (fam) to snipe at
canari /kanaʀi/ *m* canary
canasson /kanasɔ̃/ *m* (pop) nag (fam), horse
cancan /kɑ̃kɑ̃/ *m* **1** (fam) gossip
2 cancan
cancaner /kɑ̃kane/ [**v1**] *vi* (fam) to gossip
cancer /kɑ̃sɛʀ/ *m* cancer
Cancer /kɑ̃sɛʀ/ *pr m* Cancer
cancéreux, **-euse** /kɑ̃seʀø, øz/ *adj* ‹*cell*› cancerous; ‹*person*› with cancer
cancérigène /kɑ̃seʀiʒɛn/ *adj* carcinogenic
cancérologie /kɑ̃seʀɔlɔʒi/ *f* cancer research; **service de** ~ cancer ward
cancre /kɑ̃kʀ/ *m* dunce
cancrelat /kɑ̃kʀəla/ *m* cockroach
candeur /kɑ̃dœʀ/ *f* ingenuousness
candi /kɑ̃di/ *adj m* **sucre** ~ sugar candy
candidat, ~**e** /kɑ̃dida, at/ *mf* (Pol) candidate; (for job) applicant; (in competition) contestant; **être** ~ **aux élections** to stand for election (BrE), to run for office (AmE); **être** ~ **(à un poste)** to apply (for a post); **pour la vaisselle, il n'y a pas beaucoup de** ~**s!** (hum) when it comes to doing the dishes, there aren't many takers
candidature /kɑ̃didatyʀ/ *f* **1** candidature, candidacy; **retirer sa** ~ to stand down (BrE), to drop out (AmE)
2 (for a post) application; **faire acte de** ~ to apply
candide /kɑ̃did/ *adj* ingenuous
cane /kan/ *f* (female) duck
caneton /kantɔ̃/ *m* duckling
canette /kanɛt/ *f* **1** ~ **(de bière)** (small) bottle of beer
2 can; ~ **de bière** can of beer
3 (of sewing machine) spool
canevas /kanva/ *m inv* **1** canvas
2 tapestry work
3 (fig) framework
caniche /kaniʃ/ *m* poodle
canicule /kanikyl/ *f* **1** scorching heat
2 heatwave
canif /kanif/ *m* penknife
canin, ~**e** /kanɛ̃, in/ *adj* canine
canine /kanin/ *f* canine (tooth)
caniveau, *pl* ~**x** /kanivo/ *m* gutter
cannabis /kanabis/ *m* cannabis

key word

canne /kan/ *f* **1** (walking) stick
2 (Bot) cane
■ ~ **à pêche** fishing rod
canneberge /kanbɛʀʒ/ *f* cranberry
cannelle /kanɛl/ *f* cinnamon
cannette ▸ **canette**
cannibale /kanibal/ *adj*, *mf* cannibal
canoë /kanɔe/ *m* **1** canoe
2 canoeing
canoë-kayak /kanɔekajak/ *m* canoeing
canon /kanɔ̃/ **A** *adj m inv* **droit** ~ canon law
B *m* **1** (big) gun; cannon; **tirer un coup de** ~ to fire a gun; **entendre des coups de** ~ to hear cannon fire
2 (of firearm) barrel
3 (Mus) canon; **chanter en** ~ to sing in a round
4 (rule, principle) canon
5 (in religion) canon
canonique /kanɔnik/ *adj* **droit** ~ canon law; **d'âge** ~ (hum) of a venerable age
canoniser /kanɔnize/ [**v1**] *vt* to canonize
canot /kano/ *m* (small) boat, dinghy; ~ **pneumatique** rubber dinghy; ~ **de sauvetage** (on ship) lifeboat; (on plane) life raft
canotier /kanɔtje/ *m* boater
canson® /kɑ̃sɔ̃/ *m* drawing paper
cantaloup /kɑ̃talu/ *m* cantaloupe melon
cantate /kɑ̃tat/ *f* cantata
cantatrice /kɑ̃tatʀis/ *f* (opera) singer
cantine /kɑ̃tin/ *f* **1** canteen (BrE), cafeteria; **manger à la** ~ ‹*child*› to have school dinners
2 tin trunk
cantique /kɑ̃tik/ *m* hymn, canticle
canton /kɑ̃tɔ̃/ *m* canton
cantonade: **à la cantonade** /alakɑ̃tɔnad/ *phr* **parler à la** ~ to speak to no one in particular
cantonais, ~**e** /kɑ̃tɔnɛ, ɛz/ **A** *adj* Cantonese
B *m* (language) Cantonese
cantonal, ~**e**, *mpl* **-aux** /kɑ̃tɔnal, o/ *adj* cantonal
cantonner /kɑ̃tɔne/ [**v1**] *vt* ~ **qn dans un lieu** to confine sb to a place; ~ **qn dans le rôle de** to reduce sb to the role of
cantonnier /kɑ̃tɔnje/ *m* road mender
cantonnière /kɑ̃tɔnjɛʀ/ *f* pelmet
canular /kanylaʀ/ *m* hoax
canule /kanyl/ *f* cannula
canyon ▸ **cañon**
cañon /kanjɔ̃, kanjɔn/ *m* canyon
caoutchouc /kautʃu/ *m* **1** rubber
2 rubber plant
3 rubber band
caoutchouteux, **-euse** /kautʃutø, øz/ *adj* rubbery
cap /kap/ *m* **1** (in geography) cape
2 mark; **passer le** ~ **de la cinquantaine** to

pass the fifty mark
3 (direction) course; **maintenir le ~** to hold one's course; **mettre le ~ sur** to head for

Cap /kap/ *pr n* **le ~** Cape Town

CAP /seape/ *m*: *abbr* ▶ **certificat**

capable /kapabl/ *adj* capable (**de faire** of doing); **ils sont bien ~s de nous mentir** I wouldn't put it past them to lie to us

capacité /kapasite/ **A** *f* **1** ability
2 capacity
B **capacités** *fpl* (talent) abilities

cape /kap/ *f* cape; cloak
IDIOM **rire sous ~** to laugh up one's sleeve

capeline /kaplin/ *f* wide-brimmed hat

CAPES /kapɛs/ *m* (*abbr* = **certificat d'aptitude professionnelle à l'enseignement secondaire**) *secondary school teaching qualification*

capharnaüm /kafaʀnaɔm/ *m* shambles (fam)

capillaire /kapilɛʀ/ **A** *adj* **1** capillary
2 soins ~s hair care
B *m* capillary

capitaine /kapitɛn/ *m* **1** (Mil) (in army, navy) ≈ captain
2 (Sport) captain

capitainerie /kapitɛnʀi/ *f* port authority

capital, **~e**, *mpl* **-aux** /kapital, o/ **A** *adj*
1 ‹*importance*› major; ‹*role, question*› key; **il est ~ de faire** it's essential to do
2 ‹*letter*› capital
3 peine ~e capital punishment
B *m* **1** capital
2 le ~ humain/industriel human/industrial resources
C **capitaux** *mpl* capital, funds

capitale /kapital/ *f* **1** capital (city)
2 capital (letter); **en ~s d'imprimerie** in block capitals

capitalisation /kapitalizasjɔ̃/ *f* capitalization

capitaliser /kapitalize/ [**v1**] *vt* to capitalize

capitalisme /kapitalism/ *m* capitalism

capitaliste /kapitalist/ *adj*, *mf* capitalist

capitonner /kapitɔne/ [**v1**] *vt* to pad

capitulation /kapitylasjɔ̃/ *f* capitulation (**devant** to); **~ sans conditions** unconditional surrender

capituler /kapityle/ [**v1**] *vi* to capitulate

caporal, *pl* **-aux** /kapɔʀal, o/ *m* (Mil) (in army) ≈ corporal

caporalisation /kapɔʀalizasjɔ̃/ *f creating petty authoritarianism*; **la ~ du corps enseignant** the authoritarianism of the teaching profession

capot /kapo/ *m* (Aut) bonnet (BrE), hood (AmE)

capotage /kapɔtaʒ/ *m* collapse

capote /kapɔt/ *f* **1** great-coat
2 (of car, pram) hood (BrE), top
3 (fam) **~ (anglaise)** condom

capoter /kapɔte/ [**v1**] *vi* **1** to collapse
2 ‹*car*› to overturn

câpre /kɑpʀ/ *f* caper

caprice /kapʀis/ *m* **1** (of person) whim; **céder aux ~s de qn** to indulge sb's whims; **c'est un ~ de la nature** (of plant, animal) it's a freak of nature
2 faire un ~ to throw a tantrum

capricieusement /kapʀisjøzmɑ̃/ *adv* capriciously; whimsically

capricieux, **-ieuse** /kapʀisjø, øz/ *adj* ‹*person*› capricious; ‹*machine*› temperamental; ‹*weather*› changeable; ‹*destiny*› fickle

capricorne /kapʀikɔʀn/ *m* capricorn beetle

Capricorne /kapʀikɔʀn/ *pr m* Capricorn

capsule /kapsyl/ *f* **1** (of bottle) cap; top
2 (Med) capsule
3 ~ spatiale space capsule

capter /kapte/ [**v1**] *vt* **1** to get ‹*channel, programme*›; to pick up ‹*signal*›
2 to catch ‹*attention*›
3 to soak up ‹*light*›

captif, **-ive** /kaptif, iv/ *adj*, *mf* captive

captivant, **~e** /kaptivɑ̃, ɑ̃t/ *adj* enthralling; gripping; riveting; captivating

captiver /kaptive/ [**v1**] *vt* ‹*beauty*› to captivate; ‹*music*› to enthrall; ‹*story, person*› to fascinate

captivité /kaptivite/ *f* captivity

capture /kaptyʀ/ *f* capture

capturer /kaptyʀe/ [**v1**] *vt* to capture

capuche /kapyʃ/ *f* hood; **à ~** with a hood

capuchon /kapyʃɔ̃/ *m* **1** (of garment) hood
2 (of pen) cap

capucine /kapysin/ *f* nasturtium

caquet /kakɛ/ *m* prattle; **rabattre le ~ à qn** (fam) to put sb in his/her place

caqueter /kakte/ [**v20**] *vi* ‹*hen*› to cackle

car[1] /kaʀ/ *conj* because, for

car[2] /kaʀ/ *m* bus; **~ de police** police van; **~ (de ramassage) scolaire** school bus

carabine /kaʀabin/ *f* rifle

carabiné, **~e** /kaʀabine/ *adj* (fam) ‹*fever*› raging; ‹*cold*› stinking (fam)

caracoler /kaʀakɔle/ [**v1**] *vi* **1** to be well ahead
2 ‹*horse*› to prance; ‹*rider*› to parade

caractère /kaʀaktɛʀ/ *m* **1** (written) character; **~s d'imprimerie** block capitals; **en petits/gros ~s** in small/large print
2 nature, temperament; **avoir mauvais ~** to be bad-tempered
3 (personality) character; **il n'a aucun ~** he's got no backbone
4 (of house, place) character
5 characteristic
6 nature; **à ~ commercial** of a commercial nature
IDIOM **avoir un ~ de cochon** (fam), **avoir un sale ~** to have a vile temper

caractériel, **-ielle** /kaʀakteʀjɛl/ *adj* ‹*problems*› emotional; ‹*person*› disturbed
caractériser /kaʀakteʀize/ [**v1**] **A** *vt* to characterize
B **se caractériser** *v refl* (+ *v être*) to be characterized
C
caractéristique /kaʀakteʀistik/ **A** *adj* characteristic
B *f* characteristics
carafe /kaʀaf/ *f* carafe
caraïbe /kaʀaib/ *adj* Caribbean
Caraïbes /kaʀaib/ *pr f pl* Caribbean (islands)
carambolage /kaʀɑ̃bɔlaʒ/ *m* pile-up
caramboler /kaʀɑ̃bɔle/ [**v1**] *vt* to collide with
caramel /kaʀamɛl/ *m* **1** caramel
2 toffee (BrE), toffy (AmE); **~ mou** ≈ fudge
carapace /kaʀapas/ *f* shell, carapace
carat /kaʀa/ *m* carat; **or 18 ~s** 18-carat gold
caravane /kaʀavan/ *f* **1** caravan (BrE), trailer (AmE)
2 (convoy) caravan
caravelle /kaʀavɛl/ *f* (boat) caravel
carbone /kaʀbɔn/ *m* **1** carbon
2 carbon paper
3 sheet of carbon paper
carbonique /kaʀbɔnik/ *adj* carbonic; **neige ~** dry ice
carbonisé, **~e** /kaʀbɔnize/ *adj* burned-out; charred; burned to a cinder
carboniser /kaʀbɔnize/ [**v1**] *vt* **1** to carbonize
2 to reduce [sth] to ashes
carburant /kaʀbyʀɑ̃/ *m* fuel
carburateur /kaʀbyʀatœʀ/ *m* carburettor (BrE), carburetor (AmE)
carburer /kaʀbyʀe/ [**v1**] *vi* **1** **il carbure au vin rouge** he runs on red wine
2 to work flat out
carcan /kaʀkɑ̃/ *m* **1** (device) iron collar
2 **~ administratif** administrative constraints
carcasse /kaʀkas/ *f* carcass
carcéral, **~e**, *mpl* **-aux** /kaʀseʀal, o/ *adj* prison
cardan /kaʀdɑ̃/ *m* universal joint
cardiaque /kaʀdjak/ *adj* **être ~** to have a heart condition; **crise ~** heart attack
cardinal, **~e**, *mpl* **-aux** /kaʀdinal, o/ **A** *adj* cardinal
B *m* **1** cardinal
2 cardinal number
cardiologie /kaʀdjɔlɔʒi/ *f* cardiology
cardiologue /kaʀdjɔlɔg/ *mf* cardiologist
carême /kaʀɛm/ *m* **le ~** Lent
carence /kaʀɑ̃s/ *f* **1** (Med) deficiency
2 lack
3 **les ~s de la loi** the shortcomings of the law

carène /kaʀɛn/ *f* hull (*below the waterline*)
caressant, **~e** /kaʀɛsɑ̃, ɑ̃t/ *adj* affectionate; soft
caresse /kaʀɛs/ *f* caress, stroke; **faire une ~** *or* **des ~s à** to stroke
caresser /kaʀese/ [**v1**] *vt* **1** to stroke, to caress; **~ qn du regard** to look at sb lovingly
2 to entertain ‹*hope, idea*›; to cherish ‹*dream*›
IDIOM **~ qn dans le sens du poil** to stay on the right side of sb
cargaison /kaʀgɛzɔ̃/ *f* **1** cargo
2 (fam) load
cargo /kaʀgo/ *m* (Naut) freighter, cargo ship
caricatural, **~e**, *mpl* **-aux** /kaʀikatyʀal, o/ *adj* **1** grotesque
2 caricatural
caricature /kaʀikatyʀ/ *f* caricature; **c'est une ~ de procès** it's a mockery of a trial
caricaturer /kaʀikatyʀe/ [**v1**] *vt* to caricature
caricaturiste /kaʀikatyʀist/ *mf* caricaturist
carie /kaʀi/ *f* **la ~ (dentaire)** (tooth) decay; **avoir une carie** to have a hole in one's tooth
carié, **~e** /kaʀje/ *adj* decayed
carier: **se carier** /kaʀje/ [**v2**] *v refl* (+ *v être*) ‹*tooth*› to decay
carillon /kaʀijɔ̃/ *m* **1** (of church) (set of) bells; (tune) chimes
2 (chiming) clock; (sound) chimes
3 (door) chimes
carillonner /kaʀijɔne/ [**v1**] *vi* **1** ‹*bells*› to ring out, to peal out
2 (at door) to ring (loudly)
caritatif, **-ive** /kaʀitatif, iv/ *adj* charitable; **une association caritative** a charity
carlingue /kaʀlɛ̃g/ *f* (of plane) cabin
carmin /kaʀmɛ̃/ *m*, *adj inv* carmine
carnage /kaʀnaʒ/ *m* carnage, massacre
carnassier, **-ière** /kaʀnasje, ɛʀ/ *adj* carnivorous
carnaval, *pl* **~s** /kaʀnaval/ *m* carnival
carnet /kaʀnɛ/ *m* **1** notebook
2 (of tickets, vouchers, stamps) book
■ **~ de chèques** chequebook (BrE), checkbook (AmE); **~ de correspondance** (Sch) mark book; **~ de santé** health record
carnivore /kaʀnivɔʀ/ **A** *adj* carnivorous
B *m* carnivore
carotide /kaʀɔtid/ *adj*, *f* carotid
carotte /kaʀɔt/ *f* carrot
IDIOM **manier la ~ et le bâton** to use stick-and-carrot tactics
caroube /kaʀub/ *f* carob
carpe¹ /kaʀp/ *m* (Anat) carpus
carpe² /kaʀp/ *f* (fish) carp
IDIOM **il est resté muet comme une ~** he never said a word
carpette /kaʀpɛt/ *f* **1** rug
2 (fam) doormat (fam)

key word

carré, **~e** /kaʀe/ **A** *adj* **1** ‹*shape*› square; **il est ~ d'épaules** he has broad shoulders
2 ‹*metre, root*› square
B *m* **1** square
2 (of sky, ground) patch; (of chocolate) piece; **avoir une coupe au ~** to have one's hair cut in a bob; **~ blanc** 'suitable for adults only' sign on French TV
3 (in mathematics) square
4 **~ d'agneau** rack of lamb

carreau, *pl* **~x** /kaʀo/ *m* **1** (floor) tile; (wall) tile
2 window-pane; **faire les ~x** to clean the windows
3 (on paper) square; (on fabric) check
4 (in cards) diamonds
IDIOMS **rester sur le ~** (fam) to be left high and dry (fam); **se tenir à ~** (fam) to watch one's step

carrefour /kaʀfuʀ/ *m* **1** junction; crossroads
2 (fig) crossroads

carrelage /kaʀlaʒ/ *m* **1** tiled floor
2 tiles

carreler /kaʀle/ [**v19**] *vt* to tile

carrelet /kaʀlɛ/ *m* plaice

carrément /kaʀemɑ̃/ *adv* **1** **la situation devient ~ inquiétante** quite frankly the situation is becoming worrying; **il vaut ~ mieux les jeter** it would be better just to throw them out
2 completely; **dans un cas pareil, appelle ~ la police** in such a case, don't hesitate to call the police
3 ‹*ask, say*› straight out; ‹*express*› clearly
4 **allez-y ~!** go straight ahead!

carrière /kaʀjɛʀ/ *f* **1** career; **faire ~ dans** to make a career in
2 quarry; **~ de sable** sandpit

carriole /kaʀjɔl/ *f* **1** cart
2 (fam) jalopy (fam), car

carrossable /kaʀɔsabl/ *adj* suitable for motor vehicles

carrosse /kaʀɔs/ *m* (horse-drawn) coach

carrosserie /kaʀɔsʀi/ *f* **1** bodywork
2 coachbuilding
3 body repair work

carrossier /kaʀɔsje/ *m* coachbuilder

carrousel /kaʀusɛl/ *m* merry-go-round, carousel

carrure /kaʀyʀ/ *f* **1** shoulders
2 calibre (BrE)

cartable /kaʀtabl/ *m* **1** school bag, satchel
2 briefcase

carte /kaʀt/ *f* **1** card; **~ à jouer** playing card
2 pass
3 map; chart
4 **~ génétique** genetic map
5 menu; **repas à la ~** à la carte meal
■ **~ d'abonnement** season ticket; **~ d'adhérent** membership card; **~ bleue**® credit card; **~ de crédit** credit card; **~ grise** logbook; **~ d'identité** ID card; **~ orange**® season ticket (*in the Paris region*); **~ postale** postcard; **~ à puce** smart card; **~ de réduction** discount card; **~ de retrait (automatique)** cash card; **~ de séjour** resident's permit; **~ SIM** SIM card; **~ vermeil**® senior citizen's railcard; **~ des vins** wine list; **~ de visite** (social) visiting card; (professional) business card; **~ vitale** *social insurance smart card*; **~ de vœux** greetings card

cartel /kaʀtɛl/ *m* **1** cartel
2 coalition

carter /kaʀtɛʀ/ *m* (of engine) crankcase; (of gearbox) casing

cartilage /kaʀtilaʒ/ *m* **1** (Anat, Zool) cartilage
2 (Culin) gristle

cartomancie /kaʀtɔmɑ̃si/ *f* fortune-telling

cartomancien, **-ienne** /kaʀtɔmɑ̃sjɛ̃, ɛn/ *mf* fortune-teller

carton /kaʀtɔ̃/ *m* **1** cardboard; **en ~** ‹*folder*› cardboard; ‹*cups*› paper
2 (cardboard) box
3 card
■ **~ à dessin** portfolio
IDIOM **faire un ~** (fam) to do great (fam)

cartonné, **~e** /kaʀtɔne/ *adj* **couverture ~e** (of book) hard cover

cartonner /kaʀtɔne/ (fam) [**v1**] *vi* **1** (Sport) to score
2 (do well) ‹*film*› to be extremely successful

carton-pâte /kaʀtɔ̃pɑt/ *m inv* pasteboard

cartouche /kaʀtuʃ/ *f* **1** cartridge; (of gas) refill
2 **~ de cigarettes** carton of cigarettes

cas /kɑ/ **A** *m inv* case; **auquel ~** in which case; **au ~ où il viendrait** in case he comes; **prends ta voiture, au ~ où** take your car, just in case; **en ~ de besoin** if necessary; **en ~ de décès** in the event of death; **le ~ échéant** if need be; **dans le ~ contraire, vous devrez...** should the opposite occur, you will have to...; **dans le meilleur/pire des ~** at best/worst; **en aucun ~** under no circumstances; **c'est le ~ de le dire!** you can say that again!; **être dans le même ~ que qn** to be in the same position as sb; **n'aggrave pas ton ~** don't make things worse for yourself; **un ~ rare** a rare occurrence; **c'est un ~ de renvoi** it's grounds for dismissal
B **en tout cas**, **en tous les cas** *phr* **1** in any case, at any rate
2 at least
■ **~ de conscience** moral dilemma; **~ social** socially disadvantaged person
IDIOM **il a fait grand ~ de son avancement** he made a big thing of his promotion

casanier, **-ière** /kazanje, ɛʀ/ *adj* ‹*person*› stay-at-home; ‹*existence*› unadventurous

casaque /kazak/ *f* (of jockey) jersey, silk

cascade /kaskad/ *f* **1** waterfall
2 stunt

cascadeur, **-euse** /kaskadœʀ, øz/ *mf* stuntman/stuntwoman

case /kɑz/ *f* **1** hut, cabin
2 (in board games) square

3 (on form) box
■ ~ **départ** (in board game) start; **retour à la ~ départ** (fig) back to square one
IDIOM **il lui manque une ~** (fam) he's got a screw loose (fam)

caser /kɑze/ (fam) [**v1**] **A** *vt* **1** to put, to stick (fam)
2 to marry off
3 to find a place *or* job for
B **se caser** *v refl* (+ *v être*) to get married

caserne /kazɛʀn/ *f* barracks
■ ~ **de sapeurs-pompiers** fire station

casher /kaʃɛʀ/ *adj inv* kosher

casier /kɑzje/ *m* **1** (in gym) locker
2 pigeonhole
3 ~ **judiciaire** police record

casino /kazino/ *m* casino

casque /kask/ *m* **1** helmet; crash helmet; safety helmet
2 headphones
3 hairdryer

casqué, **~e** /kaske/ *adj* helmeted

casquette /kaskɛt/ *f* cap; **porter plusieurs ~s** (fig) to wear several hats

cassant, **~e** /kasɑ̃, ɑ̃t/ *adj* **1** brittle
2 curt, abrupt

casse¹ /kɑs/ *m* (pop) break-in, heist (AmE) (fam)

casse² /kɑs/ *f* **1** breakage
2 breaker's yard, scrap yard; **mettre à la ~** to scrap

cassé, **~e** /kase/ *adj* ‹*voice*› hoarse

casse-cou /kasku/ *mf inv* daredevil

casse-croûte /kaskʀut/ *m inv* snack

casse-noisettes /kasnwazɛt/, **casse-noix** /kasnwa/ *m inv* nutcrackers

🔑 **casser** /kase/ [**v1**] **A** *vt* to break ‹*object, bone*›; to crack ‹*nut*›; ~ **les prix** to slash prices; ~ **la figure** (fam) **à qn** to beat sb up (fam)
B *vi* **1** to break
2 (fam) ‹*couple*› to split up
C **se casser** *v refl* (+ *v être*) **1** to break
2 se ~ une *or* **la jambe** to break one's leg; **se ~ la figure** (fam) ‹*pedestrian*› to fall over (BrE) *or* down; ‹*venture*› to fail; ‹*people*› to have a scrap (fam); **il ne s'est pas cassé la tête** (fam) he didn't exactly strain himself
3 (fam) to go away
IDIOMS ~ **les pieds** (fam) **à qn** to annoy sb; ~ **la croûte** to eat; **ça te prendra trois heures, à tout ~** (fam) it'll take you three hours at the very most

casserole /kasʀɔl/ *f* saucepan, pan
IDIOM **chanter comme une ~** (fam) to sing atrociously

casse-tête /kastɛt/ *m inv* **1** headache, problem
2 puzzle

cassette /kasɛt/ *f* **1** tape, cassette
2 casket

casseur /kasœʀ/ *m* **1** scrap dealer
2 rioting demonstrator

cassis /kasis/ *m inv* **1** blackcurrant
2 (in road) dip

cassonade /kasɔnad/ *f* soft brown sugar

cassoulet /kasulɛ/ *m: meat and bean stew*

cassure /kasyʀ/ *f* **1** break
2 split

castagnettes /kastaɲɛt/ *fpl* castanets

caste /kast/ *f* **1** caste
2 (derog) (social) class

castor /kastɔʀ/ *m* beaver

castrer /kastʀe/ [**v1**] *vt* to castrate

cataclysme /kataklism/ *m* cataclysm

catacombes /katakɔ̃b/ *fpl* catacombs

catadioptre /katadjɔptʀ/ *m* reflector

catalepsie /katalɛpsi/ *f* catalepsy

catalogue /katalɔg/ *m* catalogue (BrE); **acheter sur ~** to buy by mail order

cataloguer /katalɔge/ [**v1**] *vt* **1** to catalogue (BrE) ‹*objects*›
2 to label ‹*people*›

catalyse /kataliz/ *f* catalysis

catalytique /katalitik/ *adj* catalytic

catamaran /katamaʀɑ̃/ *m* catamaran

cataplasme /kataplasm/ *m* poultice

catapulter /katapylte/ [**v1**] *vt* to catapult

cataracte /kataʀakt/ *f* cataract

catastrophe /katastʀɔf/ *f* disaster; **en ~** in a panic; **atterrissage en ~** crash landing

catastropher /katastʀɔfe/ [**v1**] *vt* to devastate

catastrophique /katastʀɔfik/ *adj* disastrous

catch /katʃ/ *m* wrestling

catcheur, **-euse** /katʃœʀ, øz/ *mf* wrestler

catéchisme /kateʃism/ *m* catechism

🔑 **catégorie** /kategɔʀi/ *f* **1** category; **de première/deuxième ~** top-/low-grade
2 (of staff) grade
3 (in sociology) group
4 (Sport) class

catégorique /kategɔʀik/ *adj* categorical

cathédrale /katedʀal/ *f* cathedral

cathode /katɔd/ *f* cathode

catholicisme /katɔlisism/ *m* (Roman) Catholicism

🔑 **catholique** /katɔlik/ *adj*, *mf* Catholic; **ce n'est pas très ~** (hum, fam) it's a bit unorthodox

cauchemar /koʃmaʀ/ *m* nightmare

causant, **~e** /kozɑ̃, ɑ̃t/ *adj* (fam) talkative

🔑 **cause** /koz/ *f* **1** cause; **pour la ~ de la liberté** in the cause of freedom
2 reason; **pour ~ de maladie** because of illness; **avoir pour ~ qch** to be caused by sth; **à ~ de** because of
3 case; **être en ~** ‹*system, fact*› to be at issue; ‹*person*› to be involved; **mettre hors de ~** (gen) to clear; **remettre en ~** to call

🔑 key word

[sth] into question ‹*policy, right*›; to cast doubt on ‹*project, efficiency*›; to undermine ‹*efforts*›; **remise en ~** (of system) reappraisal; **avoir gain de ~** to win one's case
IDIOM **en toute connaissance de ~** in full knowledge of the facts

causer /koze/ [**v1**] **A** *vt* **1** to cause; **~ des soucis** to give cause for concern
2 (fam) to talk about; **~ travail** to talk shop
B causer de *v+prep* to talk about
C *vi* to talk; to chat

causette /kozɛt/ *f* (fam) chat; **faire la ~** to have a little chat

caustique /kostik/ *adj* caustic

cautériser /koteʀize/ [**v1**] *vt* to cauterize

caution /kosjɔ̃/ *f* **1** (when renting) deposit; (in finance) guarantee, security; (Law) bail
2 support

cautionner /kosjɔne/ [**v1**] *vt* **1** to give one's support to
2 to stand surety for

cavalcade /kavalkad/ *f* **1** stampede, rush
2 cavalcade

cavale /kaval/ *f* (fam) escape; **en ~** on the run

cavaler /kavale/ [**v1**] *vi* (fam) to rush about

cavalerie /kavalʀi/ *f* cavalry

cavaleur, **-euse** /kavalœʀ, øz/ *adj* (fam) **être ~** to be a womanizer/man chaser

cavalier, **-ière** /kavalje, ɛʀ/ **A** *adj* cavalier
B *mf* **1** (horse) rider; **être bon ~** to be a good rider
2 (dancing) partner
C *m* **1** cavalryman
2 (in chess) knight
IDIOM **faire ~ seul** to go it alone

cave /kav/ *f* cellar; **avoir une bonne ~** to have good wines

caveau, *pl* **~x** /kavo/ *m* vault

caverne /kavɛʀn/ *f* cavern

caviar /kavjaʀ/ *m* caviar

cavité /kavite/ *f* cavity

CCP /sesepe/ *m*: *abbr* ▶ **compte**

CD /sede/ *m* (*abbr* = **compact disc**) CD

CD-I /sedei/ *m inv* (*abbr* = **compact disc interactif**) CD-I

ce /sə/ **A** (**cet** /sɛt/ *before vowel or mute h*, **cette** /sɛt/, *pl* **ces** /se/) *adj* **1** this; that; **~ crayon(-ci)** this pencil; **~ livre(-là)** that book; **cette nuit** tonight; last night; **un de ces jours** one of these days
2 (fam) **cet entretien, ça s'est bien passé?** how did the interview go?
3 et pour ces dames? what are the ladies having?
4 elle a eu cette chance que la corde a tenu she was lucky in that the rope held
5 cette arrogance! what arrogance!; **j'ai un de ces rhumes!** I've got an awful cold!
B (**c'** *before e*) *pron* **qui est-~?** who's that?; who is it?; **~ faisant** in so doing; **c'est tout dire** that says it all; **fais ~ que tu veux** do what you like; **c'est ~ à quoi il a fait allusion** that's what he was alluding to; **il a fait faillite, ~ qui n'est pas surprenant** he's gone bankrupt, which is hardly surprising; **il tient à ~ que vous veniez** he's very keen that you should come; **~ que c'est grand!** it's so big!

CE /seə/ *m*: *abbr* ▶ **cours**

CEAM *f* (*abbr* = **Carte Européenne d'Assurance Maladie**) EHIC

ceci /səsi/ *pron* this; **à ~ près que** except that; **cet hôtel a ~ de bien que...** one good thing about this hotel is that...

cécité /sesite/ *f* blindness

céder /sede/ [**v14**] **A** *vt* **1** to give up ‹*seat, share*›; to yield ‹*right*›; to make over ‹*property*›; **~ le passage** to give way; **~ la place** (fig) to give way
2 to sell
B céder à *v+prep* to give in to, to yield to
C *vi* **1** to give in
2 ‹*beam*› to give way; ‹*handle*› to break off; ‹*door*› to yield

cédille /sedij/ *f* cedilla

cèdre /sɛdʀ/ *m* cedar

CEE /seəə/ *f*: *abbr* ▶ **communauté**

CEEA /seəəa/ *f* (*abbr* = **Communauté européenne de l'énergie atomique**) EAEC

CEI /seəi/ *f*: *abbr* ▶ **communauté**

ceinture /sɛ̃tyʀ/ *f* **1** belt
2 waistband
3 girdle
4 waist; **avoir de l'eau jusqu'à la ~** to be waist-deep in water
5 (Sport) waist hold; **~ noire** black belt
6 ring
■ **~ de sauvetage** lifebelt; **~ de sécurité** safety *or* seat belt
IDIOMS **faire ~** (fam) to go without; **se serrer la ~** to tighten one's belt

ceinturer /sɛ̃tyʀe/ [**v1**] *vt* to encircle

ceinturon /sɛ̃tyʀɔ̃/ *m* belt

cela /səla/ *pron*

> *cela* and *ça* are equivalent in many cases. See the entry *ça* for more information.
> *Cela* is used in formal contexts and in the expressions shown below.

1 it; that; **quant à ~** as for that; **~ dit** having said that
2 ~ va sans dire it *or* that goes without saying; **voyez-vous ~!** did you ever hear of such a thing!

célébration /selebʀasjɔ̃/ *f* celebration

célèbre /selɛbʀ/ *adj* famous

célébrer /selebʀe/ [**v14**] *vt* **1** to celebrate ‹*event, mass*›; to perform ‹*rite*›
2 to praise ‹*person*›

célébrité /selebʀite/ *f* **1** fame
2 celebrity

céleri /sɛlʀi/ *m* **1** celery
2 celeriac

C

céleri-rave, *pl* **céleris-raves** /selʀiʀav/ *m* celeriac

céleste /selɛst/ *adj* celestial; heavenly; divine

célibat /seliba/ *m* **1** single status
2 celibacy

célibataire /selibatɛʀ/ **A** *adj* single
B *mf* bachelor/single woman

celle ▶ **celui**

celle-ci ▶ **celui-ci**

celle-là ▶ **celui-là**

celles-ci ▶ **celui-ci**

celles-là ▶ **celui-là**

cellier /selje/ *m* cellar

cellophane® /selɔfan/ *f* cellophane®

cellulaire /selylɛʀ/ *adj* cell; cellular

cellule /selyl/ *f* **1** cell
2 unit; ~ **familiale** family unit

cellulite /selylit/ *f* **1** cellulite
2 cellulitis

celte /sɛlt/ *adj*, *m* Celtic

Celte /sɛlt/ *mf* Celt

⚷ **celui** /səlɥi/, **celle** /sɛl/, *mpl* **ceux** /sø/, *fpl* **celles** /sɛl/ *pron* the one; **le train du matin ou ~ du soir?** the morning train or the evening one?; **ceux, celles** those; the ones; **ceux d'entre vous qui veulent partir** those of you who want to leave; **ceux qu'il a vendus** the ones he sold; **faire ~ qui n'entend pas** to pretend not to hear

celui-ci /səlɥisi/, **celle-ci** /sɛlsi/, *mpl* **ceux-ci** /søsi/, *fpl* **celles-ci** /sɛlsi/ *pron* **1** this one; **ceux-ci, celles-ci** these
2 je n'ai qu'une chose à dire et c'est celle-ci I have only one thing to say and it's this
3 elle essaya la fenêtre mais celle-ci était coincée she tried the window but it was jammed; **il entra, suivi de son père et de son frère; ~ portait un paquet** he came in, followed by his father and his brother; the latter was carrying a parcel

celui-là /səlɥila/, **celle-là** /sɛlla/, *mpl* **ceux-là** /søla/, *fpl* **celles-là** /sɛlla/ *pron* **1** that one; **ceux-là, celles-là** those (ones)
2 si je n'ai qu'un conseil à te donner, c'est ~ if I only have one piece of advice for you, it's this
3 the former
4 il fit une autre proposition, plus réaliste celle-là he made another proposal, a more realistic one this time
5 (fam) **il exagère, ~!** that guy's pushing it a bit! (fam)
6 (fam) **elle est bien bonne, celle-là!** that's a good one!; **je ne m'attendais pas à celle-là** I didn't expect that!; **~ même** the very one

cendre /sɑ̃dʀ/ *f* ash

cendré, **~e** /sɑ̃dʀe/ *adj* **blond ~** ash blond

cendrier /sɑ̃dʀije/ *m* ashtray

Cène /sɛn/ *f* **la ~** the Last Supper

censé, **~e** /sɑ̃se/ *adj* **être ~ faire** to be supposed to do

censeur /sɑ̃sœʀ/ *m* (Sch) *school official in charge of discipline*

censure /sɑ̃syʀ/ *f* **1** censorship
2 board of censors
3 censure

censurer /sɑ̃syʀe/ [**v1**] *vt* **1** to censor
2 to ban

⚷ **cent** /sɑ̃/ **A** *adj* a hundred, one hundred
B *m* **1** hundred
2 (division of euro) (cent)
C pour cent *phr* per cent
IDIOMS **faire les ~ pas** to pace up and down; **être aux ~ coups** (fam) to be worried sick (fam); **attendre ~ sept ans** (fam) to wait for ages

⚷ **centaine** /sɑ̃tɛn/ *f* **1** hundred
2 une ~ about a hundred

centenaire /sɑ̃tnɛʀ/ **A** *adj* hundred year-old, centenarian
B *mf* **c'est une ~** she's a hundred years old
C *m* centenary, centennial

centième /sɑ̃tjɛm/ *adj* hundredth

centilitre /sɑ̃tilitʀ/ *m* centilitre (BrE)

centime /sɑ̃tim/ *m* (Hist) centime; **~ (d'euro)** cent

centimètre /sɑ̃timɛtʀ/ *m* **1** centimetre (BrE)
2 ne pas avancer d'un ~ not to move an inch
3 tape measure

⚷ **central**, **~e** *mpl* **-aux** /sɑ̃tʀal, o/ **A** *adj* **1** central; **court ~** (in tennis) centre (BrE) court; **ordinateur ~** host computer
2 main
B *m* **~ (téléphonique)** (telephone) exchange

centrale /sɑ̃tʀal/ *f* **1** power station
2 prison

centraliser /sɑ̃tʀalize/ [**v1**] *vt* to centralize

centralisme /sɑ̃tʀalism/ *m* centralism

⚷ **centre** /sɑ̃tʀ/ *m* centre (BrE); **il se prend pour le ~ du monde** he thinks the whole world revolves around him
■ **~ aéré** children's outdoor activity centre (BrE); **~ commercial** shopping centre (BrE); **~ de documentation et d'information, CDI** learning resources centre (BrE); **~ hospitalier** hospital complex; **~ hospitalier universitaire, CHU** ≈ teaching hospital

centrer /sɑ̃tʀe/ [**v1**] *vt* to centre (BrE)

centre-ville, *pl* **centres-villes** /sɑ̃tʀəvil/ *m* town centre (BrE), city centre (BrE)

centrifuge /sɑ̃tʀifyʒ/ *adj* centrifugal

centrifugeuse /sɑ̃tʀifyʒøz/ *f* **1** juice extractor
2 centrifuge

centriste /sɑ̃tʀist/ *adj*, *mf* centrist

centuple /sɑ̃typl/ *m* **dix mille est le ~ de cent** ten thousand is a hundred times one hundred; **au ~** a hundred times over

cep /sɛp/ *m* **~ (de vigne)** vine stock

⚷ key word

cépage /sepaʒ/ *m* grape variety; **~ cabernet** Cabernet grape

cèpe /sɛp/ *m* cep

cependant /səpɑ̃dɑ̃/ **A** *conj* yet, however **B cependant que** *phr* whereas, while

céramique /seʀamik/ *f* **1** ceramic **2** ceramics

cerceau, *pl* **~x** /sɛʀso/ *m* hoop

cercle /sɛʀkl/ *m* **1** circle; **en ~** in a circle; **décrire des ~s** ‹*plane, bird*› to circle (overhead); **le ~ de famille** the family circle **2** circle, society; club **3** hoop

cercler /sɛʀkle/ [**v1**] *vt* to hoop ‹*barrel*›; **les noms cerclés en rouge** the names circled in red

cercueil /sɛʀkœj/ *m* coffin

céréale /seʀeal/ *f* cereal, grain

céréalier, **-ière** /seʀealje, ɛʀ/ *adj* ‹*production*› cereal; ‹*region*› cereal-growing

cérébral, **~e**, *mpl* **-aux** /seʀebʀal, o/ *adj* **1** cerebral **2** intellectual

cérémonial, *pl* **~s** /seʀemɔnjal/ *m* ceremonial

cérémonie /seʀemɔni/ **A** *f* ceremony; **tenue** *or* **habit de ~** ceremonial dress **B cérémonies** *fpl* ceremony; **faire des ~s** to stand on ceremony; **sans ~s** ‹*dinner, invitation*› informal; ‹*receive*› informally

cérémonieux, **-ieuse** /seʀemɔnjø, øz/ *adj* ceremonious; **d'un air ~** ceremoniously

cerf /sɛʀ/ *m* stag

cerfeuil /sɛʀfœj/ *m* chervil

cerf-volant, *pl* **cerfs-volants** /sɛʀvɔlɑ̃/ *m* **1** kite **2** stag beetle

cerise /s(ə)ʀiz/ *f* cherry

cerisier /s(ə)ʀizje/ *m* cherry (tree)

cerne /sɛʀn/ *m* ring

cerné, **~e** /sɛʀne/ *adj* **avoir les yeux ~s** to have rings under one's eyes

cerner /sɛʀne/ [**v1**] *vt* **1** to surround **2** to define ‹*problem*›; to figure out ‹*person*›; to determine ‹*personality*› **3** to outline ‹*drawing*›

certain, **~e** /sɛʀtɛ̃, ɛn/ **A** *adj* **1 être ~ de** to be certain *or* sure of **2** ‹*fact*› certain, sure; ‹*date, price, influence*› definite; ‹*rate*› fixed **B** *det* **elle restera un ~ temps** she'll stay for some time; **un ~ nombre d'erreurs** a certain number of mistakes; **d'une ~e manière** in a way; **il avait déjà un ~ âge** he was already getting on in years **C certains**, **certaines** *det pl* some; **à ~s moments** sometimes, at times **D certains**, **certaines** *pron pl* some people; **~s d'entre eux** some of them

certainement /sɛʀtɛnmɑ̃/ *adv* **1** most probably **2** certainly; **mais ~!** certainly!, of course!

certes /sɛʀt/ *adv* **ce ne sera ~ pas facile mais...** admittedly it won't be easy but...

certificat /sɛʀtifika/ *m* **1** certificate **2** testimonial
■ **~ d'aptitude professionnelle, CAP** *vocational training qualification*; **~ de décès** death certificate; **~ médical** medical certificate; **~ de résidence** proof of residence; **~ de scolarité** proof of attendance (*at school or university*); **~ de travail** *document from a previous employer giving dates and nature of employment*

certifié, **~e** /sɛʀtifje/ *adj* **professeur ~** fully qualified teacher

certifier /sɛʀtifje/ [**v2**] *vt* **1** to certify; **copie certifiée conforme** certified copy **2 elle m'a certifié que** she assured me that

certitude /sɛʀtityd/ *f* **1** certainty; **on sait avec ~ que** we know for certain that **2 avoir la ~ que** to be certain that

cérumen /seʀymɛn/ *m* earwax

cerveau, *pl* **~x** /sɛʀvo/ *m* **1** brain **2** mind **3** (person) brain (fam); **exode** *or* **fuite des ~x** brain drain; **c'est un ~** he/she has an outstanding mind **4** brains; nerve centre (BrE)
IDIOM **avoir le ~ dérangé** to be deranged

cervelas /sɛʀvəla/ *m* saveloy

cervelet /sɛʀvəlɛ/ *m* cerebellum

cervelle /sɛʀvɛl/ *f* **1** brains; **~ de veau** (Culin) calf's brains **2** (fam) **il n'a rien dans la ~** he's brainless; **~ d'oiseau** birdbrain (fam)

cervical, **~e**, *mpl* **-aux** /sɛʀvikal, o/ *adj* cervical

ces ▸ **ce A**

CES /seəɛs/ *m*: *abbr* ▸ **collège**

césar /sezaʀ/ *m* César (*film award*)

césarienne /sezaʀjɛn/ *f* Caesarian (section)

cessation /sesasjɔ̃/ *f* suspension

cesse /sɛs/ *f* **sans ~** constantly

cesser /sese/ [**v1**] **A** *vt* to stop, to cease; to end; **~ de faire** to stop doing; to give up doing **B** *vi* ‹*activity*› to cease; ‹*wind*› to drop; ‹*rain*› to stop; **faire ~** to put an end *or* a stop to, to end

cessez-le-feu /seselfø/ *m inv* ceasefire

cession /sesjɔ̃/ *f* transfer

c'est-à-dire /setadiʀ/ *phr* **1** that is (to say) **2 ~ que** which means (that); **'le travail est trop dur'—'~?'** 'the work is too hard'—'what do you mean?'

cet ▸ **ce A**

CET /seəte/ *m*: *abbr* ▸ **collège**

cette ▸ **ce A**

ceux ▸ **celui**

ceux-ci ▸ **celui-ci**

ceux-là ▶ celui-là

CFDT /seɛfdete/ *f* (*abbr* = **Confédération française démocratique du travail**) CFDT (*French trade union*)

CGC /seʒese/ *f* (*abbr* = **Confédération générale des cadres**) CGC (*French trade union*)

CGT /seʒete/ *f* (*abbr* = **Confédération générale du travail**) *French trade union*

chacal, *pl* **~s** /ʃakal/ *m* jackal

⚷ **chacun**, **~e** /ʃakœ̃, yn/ *pron* **1** each (one); **ils ont ~ sa** *or* **leur chambre** they each have their own room
2 everyone; **~ pour soi** every man for himself

chagrin, **~e** /ʃagʀɛ̃, in/ **A** *adj* despondent
B *m* grief; **faire du ~ à qn** to cause sb grief; **avoir du ~** to be sad; **avoir un gros ~** to be very upset; **~ d'amour** unhappy love affair

chagriner /ʃagʀine/ [**v1**] *vt* **1** to pain, to grieve
2 to worry

chahut /ʃay/ *m* racket (fam)

chahuter /ʃayte/ [**v1**] **A** *vt* to play up ‹*teacher*›; to heckle ‹*speaker*›
B *vi* to mess around

⚷ **chaîne** /ʃɛn/ **A** *f* **1** chain; **attacher qn avec des ~s** to chain sb up; **des catastrophes en ~** a series of disasters; **réaction en ~** chain reaction
2 assembly line; **produire (qch) à la ~** to mass-produce (sth)
3 network; **~ de solidarité** support network
4 **~ (de télévision)** (television) channel
5 **~ hi-fi/stéréo** hi-fi/stereo system
B **chaînes** *fpl* snow chains
■ **~ de fabrication** production line

chaînette /ʃɛnɛt/ *f* chain

chaînon /ʃɛnɔ̃/ *m* link; **~ manquant** missing link

⚷ **chair** /ʃɛʀ/ **A** *adj inv* flesh-coloured (BrE)
B *f* flesh; meat; **bien en ~** plump
■ **~ de poule** gooseflesh, goose pimples; **donner la ~ de poule à qn** ‹*cold*› to give sb gooseflesh; ‹*fear*› to make sb's flesh creep

chaire /ʃɛʀ/ *f* **1** pulpit
2 (at university) chair
3 rostrum

⚷ **chaise** /ʃɛz/ *f* chair
■ **~ haute** high chair; **~ longue** deckchair; **~ roulante** wheelchair
IDIOM **être assis entre deux ~s** to be in an awkward position

châle /ʃɑl/ *m* shawl

chalet /ʃalɛ/ *m* chalet

⚷ **chaleur** /ʃalœʀ/ **A** *f* **1** heat; warmth; **coup de ~** heat stroke; **~ animale** body heat
2 (of person, welcome, colour) warmth
3 (Zool) **(être) en ~** (to be) on heat
B **chaleurs** *fpl* **les grandes ~s** the hot season

chaleureusement /ʃaløʀøzmɑ̃/ *adv* warmly; wholeheartedly

chaleureux, **-euse** /ʃaløʀø, øz/ *adj* ‹*person, greeting*› warm; ‹*audience*› enthusiastic

challenge /ʃalɑ̃ʒ/ *m* **1** (Sport) tournament
2 trophy

challenger /ʃalɑ̃ʒœʀ/ *m also* **challengeur** challenger

chaloupe /ʃalup/ *f* **1** rowing boat (BrE), rowboat (AmE)
2 (motor) launch

chalumeau, *pl* **~x** /ʃalymo/ *m* blowtorch

chalut /ʃaly/ *m* trawl

chalutier /ʃalytje/ *m* **1** trawler
2 trawlerman

chamailler: se chamailler /ʃamaje/ [**v1**] *v refl* (+ *v être*) (fam) to squabble

chamarré, **~e** /ʃamaʀe/ *adj* **1** richly ornamented
2 brightly coloured (BrE)

chambard /ʃɑ̃baʀ/ *m* (fam) din, racket (fam)

chambardement /ʃɑ̃baʀdəmɑ̃/ *m* (fam) **1** shake-up (fam)
2 mess

chambouler /ʃɑ̃bule/ [**v1**] *vt* (fam) **1** to upset ‹*plans, routine*›
2 to turn [sth] upside down ‹*house*›; to mess [sth] up ‹*papers*›

chambranle /ʃɑ̃bʀɑ̃l/ *m* frame

⚷ **chambre** /ʃɑ̃bʀ/ *f* **1** bedroom; room; **~ pour une personne** single room; **~ à deux lits** twin room; **faire ~ à part** to sleep in separate rooms
2 **musique de ~** chamber music
3 (in parliament) house
4 (in administration) chamber
■ **~ à air** inner tube; **~ d'amis** guest room; **~ de commerce** chamber of commerce; **~ à coucher** bedroom; bedroom suite; **'~s d'hôte'** 'bed and breakfast'; **~ noire** camera obscura; darkroom

chambrée /ʃɑ̃bʀe/ *f* (Mil) soldiers occupying barrack room

chambrer /ʃɑ̃bʀe/ [**v1**] *vt* **1** to bring [sth] to room temperature
2 (fam) (mock) to tease

chameau, *pl* **~x** /ʃamo/ *m* (Zool) camel

chamelier /ʃaməlje/ *m* camel driver

chamelle /ʃamɛl/ *f* she-camel

chamois /ʃamwa/ *m* (Zool) chamois

⚷ **champ** /ʃɑ̃/ **A** *m* field; (fig) field, domain; **en pleins ~s** in open country; **avoir le ~ libre** to have a free hand
B **à tout bout de champ** *phr* (fam) all the time
■ **~ de courses** racetrack

champagne /ʃɑ̃paɲ/ *m* champagne

champagnisé /ʃɑ̃paɲize/ *adj* **vin ~** sparkling wine

champenois, **~e** /ʃɑ̃pənwa, az/ *adj* **1** of the Champagne region
2 **méthode ~e** champagne method

⚷ key word

champêtre /ʃɑ̃pɛtʀ/ *adj* ‹*scene*› rural; **bal ~** village dance; **déjeuner ~** country picnic

champignon /ʃɑ̃piɲɔ̃/ *m* **1** (Culin) mushroom; **~ vénéneux** toadstool
2 (Bot, Med) fungus
3 (fam) throttle, accelerator
■ **~ atomique** mushroom cloud; **~ de Paris** button mushroom (BrE), champignon (AmE)

champion, **-ionne** /ʃɑ̃pjɔ̃, ɔn/ *mf* champion; **le ~ en titre** the title-holder

championnat /ʃɑ̃pjɔna/ *m* championship

chance /ʃɑ̃s/ *f* **1** (good) luck; **coup de ~** stroke of luck; **avoir de la ~** to be lucky; **avoir la ~ de trouver une maison** to be lucky enough to find a house; **par ~** luckily, fortunately; **tenter** *or* **courir sa ~** to try one's luck
2 chance (**de** of); **il y a de fortes ~s (pour) que** there's every chance that; **il a ses ~s** he stands a good chance; **mettre toutes les ~s de son côté** to take no chances; **'il va pleuvoir?'—'il y a des ~s'** 'is it going to rain?'—'probably'
3 chance, opportunity

chancelant, **~e** /ʃɑ̃slɑ̃, ɑ̃t/ *adj* **1** ‹*gait*› unsteady; ‹*object*› rickety, shaky; ‹*person*› staggering; **d'un pas ~** unsteadily
2 ‹*courage, faith*› wavering; ‹*empire*› tottering

chanceler /ʃɑ̃sle/ [**v19**] *vi* **1** ‹*person*› to stagger; ‹*object*› to wobble
2 ‹*courage*› to waver
3 ‹*empire*› to totter; ‹*health*› to be precarious

chancelier /ʃɑ̃səlje/ *m* chancellor

chancellerie /ʃɑ̃sɛlʀi/ *f* Ministry of Justice

chanceux, **-euse** /ʃɑ̃sø, øz/ *adj* lucky

chandail /ʃɑ̃daj/ *m* sweater, jumper (BrE)

chandelier /ʃɑ̃dəlje/ *m* candelabra (BrE)

chandelle /ʃɑ̃dɛl/ *f* **1** candle; **un dîner aux ~s** a candlelit dinner
2 (Sport) shoulder stand
IDIOMS **devoir une fière ~ à** to be hugely indebted to; **faire des économies de bouts de ~s** to make cheese-paring economies

change /ʃɑ̃ʒ/ *m* **1** exchange rate
2 (foreign) exchange; **perdre au ~** (fig) to lose out

changeant, **~e** /ʃɑ̃ʒɑ̃, ɑ̃t/ *adj* changeable

changement /ʃɑ̃ʒmɑ̃/ *m* change; **~ en mieux/pire** change for the better/worse
■ **~ climatique** climate change

changer /ʃɑ̃ʒe/ [**v13**] **A** *vt* **1** to exchange ‹*object*›; to change ‹*secretary, job*›
2 to change ‹*money*›; to cash ‹*traveller's cheque*›
3 to change ‹*purchased item*›
4 ~ qch de place to move sth
5 to change ‹*situation, appearance*›; **cette coiffure te change** you look different with your hair like that; **qu'est-ce que ça change?** what difference does it make?; **cela ne change rien au fait que** that doesn't alter the fact that
6 ~ qn/qch en to turn sb/sth into
7 cela nous change de la pluie it makes a change from the rain; **pour ne pas ~** as usual
8 to change ‹*baby*›
B changer de *v+prep* to change; **~ d'avis** to change one's mind; **~ de domicile** to move house; **~ de trottoir** to cross over to the other side of the road; **nous avons changé de route au retour** we came back by a different route
C *vi* to change
D se changer *v refl* (+ *v être*) **1** to get changed
2 se ~ en to turn *or* change into

changeur, **-euse** /ʃɑ̃ʒœʀ, øz/ **A** *mf* money changer
B *m* change machine

chanoine /ʃanwan/ *m* canon

chanson /ʃɑ̃sɔ̃/ *f* **1** song; **vedette de la ~** singing star
2 c'est toujours la même ~ (fam) it's always the same old story; **je connais la ~** (fam) I've heard it all before

chansonnier, **-ière** /ʃɑ̃sɔnje, ɛʀ/ *mf* cabaret artist

chant /ʃɑ̃/ *m* **1** singing
2 (of bird, whale) song; (of cock) crow(ing); (of cricket) chirp(ing); (of cicada) shrilling
3 song
4 ode; canto
■ **~ de Noël** Christmas carol

chantage /ʃɑ̃taʒ/ *m* blackmail

chantant, **~e** /ʃɑ̃tɑ̃, ɑ̃t/ *adj* singsong

chanter /ʃɑ̃te/ [**v1**] **A** *vt* **1** to sing
2 (fam) **qu'est-ce qu'il nous chante?** what's he talking about?
B chanter à *v+prep* (fam) **ça te chante d'y aller?** do you fancy (fam) going?
C *vi* **1** to sing; **~ juste/faux** to sing in tune/ out of tune
2 ‹*bird*› to sing; ‹*cock*› to crow
3 faire ~ qn to blackmail sb

chanteur, **-euse** /ʃɑ̃tœʀ, øz/ *mf* singer

chantier /ʃɑ̃tje/ *m* **1** building site; **en ~** ‹*building*› under construction; **notre maison sera en ~ tout l'hiver** the work on our house will go on all winter; **mettre en ~** to undertake ‹*project*›
2 builder's yard
3 (fam) mess

chantonner /ʃɑ̃tɔne/ [**v1**] *vt*, *vi* to hum

chantre /ʃɑ̃tʀ/ *m* eulogist (**de** of); (poet) bard

chanvre /ʃɑ̃vʀ/ *m* hemp

chaos /kao/ *m inv* chaos

chaotique /kaɔtik/ *adj* chaotic

chaparder /ʃapaʀde/ [**v1**] *vt* (fam) to pinch (fam)

chape /ʃap/ *f* **~ de béton** concrete screed

chapeau, *pl* **~x** /ʃapo/ **A** *m* hat
B *excl* (fam) well done!

■ **~ haut de forme** top hat; **~ melon** bowler (hat) (BrE), derby (hat) (AmE); **~ de roue** (Aut) hubcap; **démarrer sur les ~x de roues** (fam) ‹*car, driver*› to shoot off at top speed

IDIOM **tirer son ~ à** to take one's hat off to

chapeauter /ʃapote/ [**v1**] *vt* (fam) to head; **le ministère chapeaute notre équipe** our team works under the ministry

chapelet /ʃaplɛ/ *m* **1** rosary
2 (of onions, insults, islands) string

chapelier, **-ière** /ʃapəlje, ɛʀ/ *mf* hatter

chapelle /ʃapɛl/ *f* **1** chapel
2 clique, coterie

chapelure /ʃaplyʀ/ *f* breadcrumbs

chaperon /ʃapʀɔ̃/ *m* chaperon(e)

chapiteau, *pl* **~x** /ʃapito/ *m* **1** marquee (BrE), tent; (of circus) big top
2 (of pillar) capital

⚷ **chapitre** /ʃapitʀ/ *m* **1** (of book) chapter
2 subject

IDIOM **avoir voix au ~** to have a say in the matter

chapka /ʃapka/ *f* fur hat

⚷ **chaque** /ʃak/ *det* each, every

char /ʃaʀ/ *m* **1** (Mil) tank
2 chariot
3 (in carnival) float
■ **~ d'assaut** (Mil) tank; **~ à bœufs** ox cart; **~ à voile** (Sport) sand yacht; ice yacht

charabia /ʃaʀabja/ *m* (fam) gobbledygook (fam)

charade /ʃaʀad/ *f* riddle

charbon /ʃaʀbɔ̃/ *m* coal; **~ de bois** charcoal

IDIOM **être sur des ~s ardents** to be like a cat on a hot tin roof

charcuter /ʃaʀkyte/ [**v1**] *vt* (fam) to hack [sb] about

charcuterie /ʃaʀkytʀi/ *f* **1** cooked pork meats
2 pork butcher's

charcutier, **-ière** /ʃaʀkytje, ɛʀ/ *mf* pork butcher

chardon /ʃaʀdɔ̃/ *m* thistle

charentais, **~e** /ʃaʀɑ̃tɛ, ɛz/ *adj* from the Charente region

charentaise /ʃaʀɑ̃tɛz/ *f* carpet slipper

⚷ **charge** /ʃaʀʒ/ **A** *f* **1** burden, load; (of vehicle) load; (of ship) cargo, freight; **prise en ~** (in taxi) minimum fare
2 avoir la ~ de qn/qch to be responsible for sb/sth; **avoir trois enfants à ~** to have three children to support; **prendre en ~** ‹*guardian*› to take charge of ‹*child*›; ‹*social security system*› to accept financial responsibility for ‹*sick person*›; to take care of ‹*fees*›
3 ~ de notaire ≈ solicitor's office
4 (legal) charge
5 (Mil) charge
B charges *fpl* **1** expenses, costs
2 (payable by tenant) **~s (locatives)** service charges
■ **~s patronales** employer's social security contributions

IDIOM **revenir à la ~** to try again

chargé, **~e** /ʃaʀʒe/ **A** *pp* ▶ **charger**
B *pp adj* **être ~ de** to be heavy *or* laden (down) with; **un regard ~ de menaces** a threatening look; **être ~ de famille** to have dependents
C *adj* ‹*person, vehicle*› loaded; ‹*day*› busy; **avoir un casier judiciaire ~** to have had several previous convictions
■ **~ d'affaires** chargé d'affaires; **~ de cours** part-time lecturer; **~ de mission** representative

chargement /ʃaʀʒəmɑ̃/ *m* **1** (goods) load; cargo
2 (action) loading

⚷ **charger** /ʃaʀʒe/ [**v13**] **A** *vt* **1** to load
2 to charge ‹*battery*›
3 ~ qn de faire to give sb the responsibility of doing; **c'est lui qui est chargé de l'enquête** he is in charge of the investigation
4 to bring evidence against ‹*accused*›
5 ‹*police*› to charge at ‹*crowd*›
B se charger *v refl* (+ *v être*) **se ~ de** to take responsibility for; **je m'en charge** I'll see to it

chargeur /ʃaʀʒœʀ/ *m* **1** (Mil) magazine
2 (of camera) cartridge
3 (Comput) loader

chariot /ʃaʀjo/ *m* **1** trolley (BrE), cart (AmE)
2 truck
3 waggon (BrE)
4 (of typewriter) carriage

charisme /kaʀism/ *m* charisma

charitable /ʃaʀitabl/ *adj* charitable

charitablement /ʃaʀitabləmɑ̃/ *adv* charitably; kindly

charité /ʃaʀite/ *f* **1** charity
2 par (pure) ~ out of the kindness of one's heart

charlatan /ʃaʀlatɑ̃/ *m* **1** quack (fam)
2 con man
3 (politician) fraud

charlot /ʃaʀlo/ *m* (fam) clown

charlotte /ʃaʀlɔt/ *f* **1** (Culin) charlotte
2 mob cap

charmant, **~e** /ʃaʀmɑ̃, ɑ̃t/ *adj* charming

charme /ʃaʀm/ **A** *m* **1** charm; **faire du ~ à qn** to make eyes at sb; **cela ne manque pas de ~** (lifestyle, novel) it's not without its charms; (proposition) it's not unattractive
2 spell
B charmes *mpl* (euph) physical attributes

IDIOM **se porter comme un ~** to be as fit as a fiddle

charmer /ʃaʀme/ [**v1**] *vt* to charm

charmeur, **-euse** /ʃaʀmœʀ, øz/ **A** *adj* winning, engaging
B *mf* charmer

charnel, **-elle** /ʃaʀnɛl/ *adj* carnal

⚷ key word

charnier /ʃaʀnje/ *m* mass grave

charnière /ʃaʀnjɛʀ/ *f* **1** hinge
2 (fig) bridge; junction; **rôle(-)~** pivotal role

charnu, **~e** /ʃaʀny/ *adj* ‹*lip*› fleshy, thick

charogne /ʃaʀɔɲ/ *f* rotting carcass

charpente /ʃaʀpɑ̃t/ *f* (of roof) roof structure; (of building) framework; (of person) build

charpentier /ʃaʀpɑ̃tje/ *m* carpenter

charpie /ʃaʀpi/ *f* **réduire** *or* **mettre qch en ~** to tear sth to shreds

charretier /ʃaʀtje/ *m* carter
IDIOM **jurer comme un ~** to swear like a trooper

charrette /ʃaʀɛt/ *f* cart; **~ à bras** handcart

charrier /ʃaʀje/ [**v2**] **A** *vt* **1** to carry, to haul
2 ‹*river*› to carry [sth] along
3 (fam) to tease [sb] unmercifully
B *vi* (fam) to go too far

charrue /ʃaʀy/ *f* plough (BrE), plow (AmE)
IDIOM **mettre la ~ avant les bœufs** to put the cart before the horse

charte /ʃaʀt/ *f* charter

charter /ʃaʀtɛʀ/ *adj inv* ‹*plane*› charter

chasse /ʃas/ *f* **1** hunting; shooting; **~ au trésor** treasure hunt; **la ~ est ouverte** it's the open season
2 ~ gardée private hunting (ground); (fig) preserve
3 donner la ~ à, prendre en ~ to chase
■ **~ à courre** hunting; **~ d'eau** (toilet) flush; **tirer la ~** to pull the chain
IDIOM **qui va à la ~ perd sa place** (Proverb) leave your place and you lose it

chassé-croisé, *pl* **chassés-croisés** /ʃasekʀwɑze/ *m* continual coming and going

chasse-neige /ʃasnɛʒ/ *m inv* snowplough (BrE), snowplow (AmE)

chasser /ʃase/ [**v1**] **A** *vt* **1** ‹*animal*› to hunt ‹*prey*›
2 ‹*hunter*› to shoot (BrE), to hunt
3 ‹*person*› to chase away ‹*animal, intruder*›; ‹*rain*› to drive away ‹*tourists*›; to fire ‹*domestic servant*›
4 to dispel ‹*smoke, doubt*›
B *vi* to go hunting

chasseur, **-euse** /ʃasœʀ, øz/ **A** *mf* hunter
B *m* **1** (Mil) fighter (aircraft); fighter pilot
2 ((in hotel)) bellboy
■ **~ alpin** *soldier trained for mountainous terrain*; **~ de têtes** head-hunter

châssis /ʃɑsi/ *m inv* **1** (of window) frame
2 (Aut) chassis

chaste /ʃast/ *adj* (gen) chaste; ‹*person*› celibate

chasteté /ʃastəte/ *f* chastity

chat¹ /ʃa/ *m* cat; tomcat
■ **~ de gouttière** ordinary cat; alley cat; **~ perché** off-ground tag
IDIOMS **donner sa langue au ~** to give in; **il n'y a pas un ~** the place is deserted; **avoir un ~ dans la gorge** to have a frog in one's throat; **il ne faut pas réveiller le ~ qui dort** (Proverb) let sleeping dogs lie; **s'entendre comme chien et ~** to fight like cat and dog

chat² /tʃat/ *m* (on mobile) chat
■ **~ video** ▶ **tchat vidéo**

châtaigne /ʃɑtɛɲ/ *f* (sweet) chestnut

châtaignier /ʃɑteɲe/ *m* (sweet) chestnut (tree); **une table de** *or* **en ~** a chestnut table

châtain /ʃɑtɛ̃/ *adj m* ‹*hair*› brown

château, *pl* **~x** /ʃato/ *m* **1** castle
2 palace
3 mansion
■ **~ de cartes** house of cards; **~ d'eau** water tower; **~ fort** fortified castle
IDIOM **mener la vie de ~** to live the life of Riley (BrE), to live like a prince

châtelain, **~e** /ʃatlɛ̃, ɛn/ *mf* **1** lord/lady of the manor
2 owner of a manor

châtier /ʃɑtje/ [**v2**] *vt* to punish

chatière /ʃatjɛʀ/ *f* cat flap

châtiment /ʃɑtimɑ̃/ *m* punishment

chatoiement /ʃatwamɑ̃/ *m* shimmering

chaton /ʃatɔ̃/ *m* **1** kitten
2 catkin

chatouille /ʃatuj/ *f* (fam) tickle

chatouiller /ʃatuje/ [**v1**] *vt* to tickle
IDIOM **~ les côtes à qn** (euph) to tan sb's hide

chatouilleux, **-euse** /ʃatujø, øz/ *adj*
1 ticklish
2 touchy (**sur** about)

chatoyant, **~e** /ʃatwajɑ̃, ɑ̃t/ *adj* shimmering; iridescent

chatoyer /ʃatwaje/ [**v23**] *vi* to shimmer

châtrer /ʃɑtʀe/ [**v1**] *vt* to castrate

chatte /ʃat/ *f* (female) cat

chaud, **~e** /ʃo, ʃod/ **A** *adj* **1** hot; warm
2 ‹*colour, voice*› warm
3 ils n'ont pas été très ~s pour faire they were not very keen on doing
4 ‹*region*› turbulent; ‹*discussion*› heated; **un des points ~s du globe** one of the flash points of the world
5 quartier ~ (fam) red light district
B *adv* **il fait ~** it's warm; it's hot; **ça ne me fait ni ~ ni froid** it doesn't matter one way or the other to me
C *m* heat; **avoir ~** to be warm; to be hot; **nous avons eu ~** (fig) we had a narrow escape; **se tenir ~** to keep warm
D à chaud *phr* **à ~** ‹*analyse*› on the spot; ‹*reaction*› immediate
■ **~ et froid** (Med) chill

chaudement /ʃodmɑ̃/ *adv* (gen) warmly; ‹*recommend*› heartily

chaudière /ʃodjɛʀ/ *f* boiler

chaudron /ʃodʀɔ̃/ *m* cauldron

chaudronnerie /ʃodʀɔnʀi/ *f* boiler-making industry; boiler works

chaudronnier, **-ière** /ʃodʀɔnje, ɛʀ/ *mf* boilermaker

chauffage /ʃofaʒ/ *m* **1** heating
2 heater

chauffagiste /ʃofaʒist/ *mf* heating engineer

chauffant, **~e** /ʃofɑ̃, ɑ̃t/ *adj* heating

chauffard /ʃofaʀ/ *m* (fam) reckless driver

chauffe /ʃof/ *f* (Tech) fire chamber

chauffe-eau /ʃofo/ *m inv* water heater

chauffe-plat /ʃofpla/ *m inv* dish warmer

chauffer /ʃofe/ [**v1**] **A** *vt* **1** to heat ‹*house*›; to heat (up) ‹*object, meal*›
2 ‹*sun*› to warm
B *vi* **1** ‹*food, oven*› to heat up; ‹*engine*› to warm up; to overheat
2 ‹*radiator*› to give out heat
3 (fam) **ça va ~!** there's going to be big trouble!
C **se chauffer** *v refl* (+ *v être*) **1 se ~ au soleil** to bask in the sun
2 se ~ au charbon to have coal-fired heating

chaufferie /ʃofʀi/ *f* **1** boiler room
2 (in boat) stokehold

chauffeur /ʃofœʀ/ *m* **1** driver
2 chauffeur

chauffeuse /ʃoføz/ *f* low armless easy chair

chaume /ʃom/ *m* **1** (in field) stubble
2 thatch

chaumière /ʃomjɛʀ/ *f* **1** thatched cottage
2 faire jaser dans les ~s to cause tongues to wag

chaussée /ʃose/ *f* **1** roadway, highway; (in town) street
2 (road) surface
3 causeway

chausse-pied, *pl* **~s** /ʃospje/ *m* shoehorn

chausser /ʃose/ [**v1**] **A** *vt* to put [sth] on ‹*shoes, spectacles*›
B *vi* **je chausse du 41** I take a (size) 41
C **se chausser** *v refl* (+ *v être*) **1** to put (one's) shoes on
2 to buy (one's) shoes

chaussette /ʃosɛt/ *f* sock
(IDIOM) **laisser tomber qn comme une vieille ~** (fam) to cast sb off like an old rag

chausseur /ʃosœʀ/ *m* shoe shop manager; shoemaker

chausson /ʃosɔ̃/ *m* **1** slipper
2 bootee
3 ballet shoe
■ **~ aux pommes** (Culin) apple turnover

🔑 **chaussure** /ʃosyʀ/ *f* shoe; **~ montante** ankle boot
(IDIOM) **trouver ~ à son pied** ‹*man, woman*› to find the right person

chauve /ʃov/ *adj* bald

chauve-souris, *pl* **chauves-souris** /ʃovsuʀi/ *f* (Zool) bat

chauvin, **~e** /ʃovɛ̃, in/ *adj* chauvinistic

chaux /ʃo/ *f* lime

chavirer /ʃaviʀe/ [**v1**] **A** *vt* to overwhelm
B *vi* **1** ‹*boat*› to capsize
2 faire ~ les cœurs to be a heartbreaker
3 ‹*objects*› to tip over

🔑 **chef** /ʃɛf/ *m* **1** leader
2 superior, boss (fam)
3 head; (of sales department) manager; **architecte en ~** chief architect
4 ~ cuisinier *or* **de cuisine** chef
5 (fam) ace; **se débrouiller comme un ~** to manage splendidly
6 de mon/leur (propre) ~ on my/their own initiative
7 au premier ~ primarily, first and foremost
■ **~ d'accusation** (Law) count of indictment; **~ d'atelier** (shop) foreman; **~ d'équipe** foreman; (Sport) team captain; (of seasonal workers) (derog) gangmaster; **~ d'État** head of state; **~ de gare** stationmaster

chef-d'œuvre, *pl* **chefs-d'œuvre** /ʃɛdœvʀ/ *m* masterpiece

chef-lieu, *pl* **chefs-lieux** /ʃɛfljø/ *m* administrative centre

🔑 **chemin** /ʃ(ə)mɛ̃/ *m* **1** country road; lane; **~ (de terre)** dirt track; path
2 way; **sur le ~ du retour** on the way back; **reprendre le ~ du bureau** to go back to work; **on a fait un bout de ~ ensemble** we walked along together for a while; **~ faisant**, **en ~** on *or* along the way; **l'idée fait son ~** the idea is gaining ground; **prendre le ~ de la faillite** to be heading for bankruptcy; **s'arrêter en ~** to stop off on the way; (fig) to stop
■ **~ de fer** railway (BrE), railroad (AmE)

cheminée /ʃ(ə)mine/ *f* **1** chimney; chimney stack
2 fireplace
3 mantelpiece
4 (of ship) funnel

cheminement /ʃ(ə)minmɑ̃/ *m* **1** slow progression
2 le ~ de sa pensée his/her train of thought

cheminer /ʃ(ə)mine/ [**v1**] *vi* **1** to walk (along)
2 ‹*idea*› to progress, to develop

cheminot /ʃ(ə)mino/ *m* railway worker (BrE), railroader (AmE)

🔑 **chemise** /ʃ(ə)miz/ *f* **1** shirt
2 folder
■ **~ de nuit** nightgown; (for man) nightshirt
(IDIOMS) **je m'en moque comme de ma première ~** (fam) I don't give two hoots (BrE) (fam) *or* a hoot (AmE); **changer d'avis comme de ~** (fam) to change one's mind at the drop of a hat

chemiserie /ʃ(ə)mizʀi/ *f* shirt-making trade; shirt factory; shirt shop

chemisier /ʃ(ə)mizje/ *m* blouse

chenal, *pl* **-aux** /ʃənal, o/ *m* channel, fairway

chenapan /ʃənapɑ̃/ *m* scallywag (fam), rascal

🔑 key word

chêne /ʃɛn/ *m* **1** oak (tree)
2 oak

chenet /ʃənɛ/ *m* firedog, andiron

chenil /ʃənil/ *m* **1** (dog) kennel
2 kennels

chenille /ʃənij/ *f* (Aut, Zool) caterpillar

cheptel /ʃɛptɛl/ *m* ~ **(vif)** livestock

chèque /ʃɛk/ *m* cheque (BrE), check (AmE)
■ ~ **en blanc** blank cheque (BrE) *or* check (AmE); ~ **en bois** (fam) rubber cheque (BrE) (fam) *or* check (AmE); ~ **sans provision** bad cheque (BrE) *or* check (AmE); ~ **de voyage** traveller's cheque (BrE), traveler's check (AmE)

chèque-cadeau, *pl* **chèques-cadeaux** /ʃɛkkado/ *m* gift token

chèque-voyage, *pl* **chèques-voyage** /ʃɛkvwajaʒ/ *m* traveller's cheque (BrE), traveler's check (AmE)

chéquier /ʃekje/ *m* chequebook (BrE), checkbook (AmE)

cher, **chère** /ʃɛʀ/ **A** *adj* **1** dear; beloved; **un être** ~ a loved one
2 (as term of address) dear
3 expensive; **pas** ~ cheap
B *mf* **mon ~/ma chère** my dear
C *adv* **1** a lot (of money); **coûter plus/moins** ~ to cost more/less; **acheter** ~ to buy at a high price
2 (fig) ‹*pay, cost*› dearly
IDIOM **ne pas donner ~ de la peau de qn** (fam) not to rate sb's chances highly

chercher /ʃɛʀʃe/ [**v1**] **A** *vt* **1** to look for ‹*person, object, trouble*›; to try to find ‹*answer, ideas*›; to try to remember ‹*name*›; ~ **fortune** to seek one's fortune; ~ **qn du regard** to look about for sb
2 ~ **à faire** to try to do
3 aller ~ qn/qch to go and get sb/sth; to pick sb/sth up
4 où est-il allé ~ cela? what made him think that?
5 une maison dans ce quartier, ça va ~ dans les 200 000 euros a house in this area must fetch (BrE) *or* get (AmE) about 200,000 euros
B se chercher *v refl* (+ *v être*) **1** to try to find oneself
2 se ~ des excuses to try to find excuses for oneself
3 (fam) to be out to get each other (fam)

chercheur, **-euse** /ʃɛʀʃœʀ, øz/ *mf* researcher
■ ~ **d'or** gold-digger

chère /ʃɛʀ/ **A** *adj f* ▶ **cher**
B *f* **faire bonne** ~ to eat well

chèrement /ʃɛʀmɑ̃/ *adv* ~ **acquise** gained at great cost

chéri, ~**e** /ʃeʀi/ **A** *pp* ▶ **chérir**
B *pp adj* beloved
C *mf* **1** darling
2 (fam) boyfriend/girlfriend

chérir /ʃeʀiʀ/ [**v3**] *vt* to cherish ‹*person*›; to hold [sth] dear ‹*idea*›

chérubin /ʃeʀybɛ̃/ *m* cherub

chétif, **-ive** /ʃetif, iv/ *adj* ‹*child*› puny

cheval, *pl* **-aux** /ʃ(ə)val, o/ **A** *m* **1** horse; **monter à** ~ to ride a horse; **remède de** ~ strong medicine; **fièvre de** ~ raging fever
2 (Sport) horse riding
3 horsemeat
B à cheval sur *phr* **1** astride
2 spanning
3 in between
4 être à ~ sur qch to be a stickler for sth
■ ~ **à bascule** rocking horse; ~ **de bataille** hobby horse; **chevaux de bois** merry-go-round horses

chevaleresque /ʃ(ə)valʀɛsk/ *adj*
1 ‹*literature*› courtly
2 ‹*person*› chivalrous

chevalerie /ʃ(ə)valʀi/ *f* chivalry

chevalet /ʃ(ə)valɛ/ *m* easel

chevalier /ʃ(ə)valje/ *m* knight

chevalière /ʃ(ə)valjɛʀ/ *f* signet ring

cheval-vapeur, *pl* **chevaux-vapeur** /ʃ(ə)valvapœʀ, ʃ(ə)vovapœʀ/ *m* horsepower

chevauchée /ʃ(ə)voʃe/ *f* ride

chevaucher /ʃ(ə)voʃe/ [**v1**] **A** *vt* **1** to sit astride ‹*animal, chair*›
2 to overlap
B se chevaucher *v refl* (+ *v être*) to overlap

chevelu, ~**e** /ʃəvly/ *adj* long-haired

chevelure /ʃəvlyʀ/ *f* hair

chevet /ʃəvɛ/ *m* bedhead; **être au ~ de qn** to be at sb's bedside

cheveu, *pl* ~**x** /ʃəvø/ **A** *m* hair; **être à un ~ de** to be within a hair's breadth of; **ne tenir qu'à un** ~ to hang by a thread
B cheveux *mpl* hair
IDIOMS **avoir un ~ sur la langue** to have a lisp; **venir comme un ~ sur la soupe** to come at an awkward moment; **se faire des ~x (blancs)** (fam) to worry oneself to death; **couper les ~x en quatre** to split hairs; **être tiré par les ~x** to be far-fetched

cheville /ʃ(ə)vij/ *f* **1** (Anat) ankle
2 Rawlplug®; peg; dowel
IDIOMS **il n'arrive pas à la ~ de Paul** he can't hold a candle to Paul; **être en ~ avec qn** (fam) to be in cahoots with sb (fam)

chèvre[1] /ʃɛvʀ/ *m* goat's cheese

chèvre[2] /ʃɛvʀ/ *f* goat; nanny goat
IDIOM **devenir** ~ (fam) to go nuts (sl)

chevreau, *pl* ~**x** /ʃəvʀo/ *m* (Zool) kid

chèvrefeuille /ʃɛvʀəfœj/ *m* honeysuckle

chevreuil /ʃəvʀœj/ *m* **1** roe (deer); roebuck
2 (Culin) venison

chevronné, ~**e** /ʃəvʀɔne/ *adj* ‹*person*› experienced

chevrotant, ~**e** /ʃəvʀɔtɑ̃, ɑ̃t/ *adj* ‹*voice*› quavering

chevroter /ʃəvʀɔte/ [**v1**] *vt, vi* to quaver

chevrotine /ʃəvʀɔtin/ *f* buckshot

chez /ʃe/ *prep* **1** ~ **qn** at sb's place; **rentre**

~ **toi** go home; **de ~ qn** ‹*telephone*› from sb's place; **fais comme ~ toi** make yourself at home
2 (referring to shop, office) **aller ~ le boucher** to go to the butcher's; **être convoqué ~ le patron** to be called in before the boss
3 (referring to a region) **~ nous** where I come from; where I live
4 among; **~ l'animal** in animals
5 **ce que j'aime ~ elle, c'est son humour** what I like about her is her sense of humour (BrE)
6 in; **~ Cocteau** in Cocteau

chic /ʃik/ **A** *adj* **1** smart (BrE), chic
2 (fam) chic, fashionable
3 (fam) ‹*person*› nice
B *m* chic; **avoir le ~ pour faire** to have a knack for doing; **avec ~** with style

chicane /ʃikan/ *f* chicane; (on road, ski slope) double bend; **en ~** on alternate sides

chicaner /ʃikane/ [**v1**] *vi* to squabble

chiche /ʃiʃ/ **A** *adj* **1** mean (BrE), stingy
2 être ~ de faire (fam) to be quite capable of doing
B *excl* **'je vais le faire'—'~!'** (fam) 'I'll do it'—'I dare you!'

chichement /ʃiʃmɑ̃/ *adv* ‹*live*› frugally; ‹*give*› stingily; ‹*pay*› poorly

chichi /ʃiʃi/ *m* fuss

chicon /ʃikɔ̃/ *m* chicory

chicorée /ʃikɔʀe/ *f* **1** (plant) chicory; (salad vegetable) endive (BrE), chicory (AmE)
2 (Culin) (powder) chicory; (drink) chicory coffee

⚷ **chien**, **chienne** /ʃjɛ̃, ʃjɛn/ **A** *adj* (fam) **ne pas être ~** not to be too hard
B *m* **1** dog
2 (of rifle) hammer
C de chien *phr* (fam) ‹*job, weather*› rotten; **ça me fait un mal de ~** it hurts like hell (fam)
■ **~ d'aveugle** guide dog; **~ de berger** sheepdog; **~ de garde** guard dog; (fig) watchdog; **~ de race** pedigree dog
IDIOMS **être couché en ~ de fusil** to be curled up; **ce n'est pas fait pour les ~s** (fam) it's there to be used

chiendent /ʃjɛ̃dɑ̃/ *m* couch grass; **brosse de ~** scrubbing brush

chienlit /ʃjɑ̃li/ *f* havoc, chaos

chien-loup, *pl* **chiens-loups** /ʃjɛ̃lu/ *m* Alsatian (BrE), German shepherd

chienne /ʃjɛn/ **A** *adj f* ▶ **chien**
B *f* (animal) bitch

chiffon /ʃifɔ̃/ *m* **1** rag, (piece of) cloth; **parler ~s** to talk (about) clothes
2 duster

chiffonné, **~e** /ʃifɔne/ *adj* **1** ‹*face*› tired looking
2 (fam) ‹*person*› troubled, ruffled

chiffonner /ʃifɔne/ [**v1**] **A** *vt* **1** to crease, to crumple
2 (fam) to bother ‹*person*›
B se chiffonner *v refl* (+ *v être*) to crease

chiffonnier /ʃifɔnje/ *m* **se battre comme des ~s** to fight like cat and dog

chiffrable /ʃifʀabl/ *adj* calculable; **les pertes ne sont pas ~s** it's impossible to put a figure on the losses

⚷ **chiffre** /ʃifʀ/ *m* **1** figure
2 monogram
■ **~ d'affaires, CA** turnover (BrE), sales (AmE); **~ arabe** Arabic numeral; **~ romain** Roman numeral; **~ de vente** sales (figures)

chiffrer /ʃifʀe/ [**v1**] **A** *vt* **1** to put a figure on ‹*cost, loss*›; to cost ‹*job*›; **~ à** to put the cost of [sth] at ‹*job*›
2 to encode ‹*message*›
B *vi* (fam) to add up; **ça chiffre vite** it soon adds up
C se chiffrer *v refl* (+ *v être*) **se ~ à** to amount to, to come to

chignole /ʃiɲɔl/ *f* hand drill

chignon /ʃiɲɔ̃/ *m* bun; chignon

chiisme /ʃiizm/ *m* Shiism

chiite /ʃiit/ *adj, mf* Shiite

Chili /ʃili/ *pr m* Chile

chimère /ʃimɛʀ/ *f* **1** pipe dream
2 (in mythology) Chimaera

chimérique /ʃimeʀik/ *adj* ‹*hope*› wild; ‹*person*› fanciful

chimie /ʃimi/ *f* chemistry

chimiothèque /ʃimjotɛk/ *f* (Chem) chemical library

chimiothérapie /ʃimjoteʀapi/ *f* chemotherapy

chimique /ʃimik/ *adj* **1** chemical; ‹*fibre*› man-made
2 ‹*food, taste*› synthetic

chimiste /ʃimist/ *mf* chemist

chimpanzé /ʃɛ̃pɑ̃ze/ *m* chimpanzee

Chine /ʃin/ *pr f* China

chiné, **~e** /ʃine/ *adj* chiné

chiner /ʃine/ [**v1**] *vi* (fam) to bargain-hunt, to antique (AmE)

⚷ **chinois**, **~e** /ʃinwa, az/ **A** *adj* Chinese
B *m* (language) Chinese
IDIOM **pour moi c'est du ~** it's double Dutch (BrE) *or* Greek to me

chiot /ʃjo/ *m* puppy, pup

chiper /ʃipe/ [**v1**] *vt* (fam) to pinch (fam)

chipie /ʃipi/ *f* (fam) little monkey (fam)

chipoter /ʃipɔte/ [**v1**] *vi* (fam) **1** to quibble (**sur** over)
2 to pick at one's food

chipoteur, **-euse** /ʃipɔtœʀ, øz/ *adj* (fam)
1 difficult
2 fussy

chips /ʃips/ *f inv* crisp (BrE), potato chip (AmE)

chique /ʃik/ *f* plug (of tobacco)

⚷ key word

(IDIOM) **couper la ~ à qn** to shut sb up (fam)

chiqué /ʃike/ *m* (fam) **1 c'est du ~** it's a put-on
2 faire du ~ to put on *or* give oneself airs

chiquenaude /ʃiknod/ *f* flick

chiquer /ʃike/ [**v1**] *vt* **tabac à ~** chewing tobacco

chiromancie /kiʀomɑ̃si/ *f* palmistry

chirurgical, **~e**, *mpl* **-aux** /ʃiʀyʀʒikal, o/ *adj* surgical

chirurgie /ʃiʀyʀʒi/ *f* surgery

chirurgien /ʃiʀyʀʒjɛ̃/ *m* surgeon

chlore /klɔʀ/ *m* chlorine

chlorer /klɔʀe/ [**v1**] *vt* to chlorinate

chlorhydrique /klɔʀidʀik/ *adj* hydrochloric

chloroforme /klɔʀɔfɔʀm/ *m* chloroform

chlorophylle /klɔʀɔfil/ *f* chlorophyll

chlorure /klɔʀyʀ/ *m* chloride

choc /ʃɔk/ **A** *adj inv* **'prix ~!'** 'huge reductions'
B *m* **1** impact, shock; collision; **sous le ~** under the impact
2 (noise) crash, smash; thud; clang; chink
3 (confrontation) (gen), (Mil) clash; (Sport) encounter; **de ~** ‹*journalist*› ace (fam)
4 (emotional, physical) shock

chocolat /ʃɔkɔla/ *m* chocolate; **~ noir** *or* **à croquer** plain (BrE) *or* dark (AmE) chocolate

chœur /kœʀ/ *m* **1** choir; (in opera, play) chorus; (fig) chorus (**de** of); **en ~** ‹*say*› in unison; ‹*laugh*› all together
2 (in church) chancel, choir

choir /ʃwaʀ/ [**v51**] *vi* to fall; **laisser ~ qn** to drop sb

choisir /ʃwaziʀ/ [**v3**] *vt* to choose

choix /ʃwa/ *m inv* **1** choice; **arrêter son ~ sur** to settle *or* decide on
2 de ~ ‹*item*› choice; ‹*candidate*› first-rate; **les places de ~** the best seats; **un morceau de ~** (of meat) a prime cut; **de second ~** of inferior quality

choléra /kɔleʀa/ *m* cholera

cholestérol /kɔlɛsteʀɔl/ *m* cholesterol

chômage /ʃomaʒ/ *m* unemployment; **mettre qn au ~** to make sb redundant (BrE), to lay sb off
■ **~ technique** layoffs

chômé, **~e** /ʃome/ *adj* **jour ~** day off; **fête ~e** national holiday

chômer /ʃome/ [**v1**] *vi* **1** to be idle
2 to be out of work

chômeur, **-euse** /ʃomœʀ, øz/ *mf* unemployed person

chope /ʃɔp/ *f* beer mug, tankard

choquant, **~e** /ʃɔkɑ̃, ɑ̃t/ *adj* shocking

choquer /ʃɔke/ [**v1**] *vt* **1** to shock ‹*person*›; to offend ‹*sight, sensibility*›
2 ‹*news*› to shake ‹*person*›; ‹*accident*› to shake [sb] (up)

chorale /kɔʀal/ *f* choir

chorégraphie /kɔʀegʀafi/ *f* choreography

choriste /kɔʀist/ *mf* chorister; member of the choir; member of the chorus

chorus /kɔʀys/ *m inv* chorus; **faire ~ avec qn** (fig) to join in with sb

chose /ʃoz/ *f* **1** (object, abstract) thing; **de deux ~s l'une** it's got to be one thing or the other; **une ~ communément admise** a widely accepted fact; **en mettant les ~s au mieux** at best; **mettre les ~s au point** to clear things up; **avant toute ~** before anything else; above all else
2 matter; **la ~ en question** the matter in hand
3 être un peu porté sur la ~ (fam) to be keen on sex

chou, *pl* **~x** /ʃu/ *m* **1** cabbage
2 choux bun (BrE), pastry shell (AmE)
3 dear, darling
■ **~ de Bruxelles** Brussels sprout; **~ à la crème** cream puff; **~ rave** kohlrabi
(IDIOMS) **bête comme ~** really easy; **faire ~ blanc** (fam) to draw a blank; **faire ses ~x gras de qch** (fam) to use sth to one's advantage; **rentrer dans le ~ de qn** (fam) to beat sb up; to give sb a piece of one's mind

choucas /ʃuka/ *m* jackdaw

chouchou /ʃuʃu/ *m* (fam) **1** (teacher's) pet; (of adoring public) darling
2 (for hair) scrunchie

chouchouter /ʃuʃute/ [**v1**] *vt* (fam) to pamper

choucroute /ʃukʀut/ *f* **1** (vegetable) sauerkraut
2 (hairstyle) beehive

chouette /ʃwɛt/ **A** *adj* (fam) great (fam), neat (AmE) (fam)
B *f* **1** owl
2 vieille ~ old harridan

chou-fleur, *pl* **choux-fleurs** /ʃuflœʀ/ *m* cauliflower

chourer /ʃuʀe/ [**v1**] *vt* (fam) to pinch (fam); **se faire ~ qch** to have sth pinched

choyer /ʃwaje/ [**v23**] *vt* to pamper

chrétien, **-ienne** /kʀetjɛ̃, ɛn/ *adj*, *mf* Christian

chrétienté /kʀetjɛ̃te/ *f* **la ~** Christendom

Christ /kʀist/ *pr n* **le ~** Christ

christianisme /kʀistjanism/ *m* Christianity

chromatique /kʀɔmatik/ *adj* chromatic

chrome /kʀom/ *m* chromium

chromosome /kʀɔmozom/ *m* chromosome

chronique /kʀɔnik/ **A** *adj* chronic
B *f* (in newspaper) column, page

chroniqueur, **-euse** /kʀɔnikœʀ, øz/ *mf* columnist, editor

chronologie /kʀɔnɔlɔʒi/ *f* chronology

chronologique /kʀɔnɔlɔʒik/ *adj* chronological

chronomètre /kʀɔnɔmɛtʀ/ *m* stopwatch

chronométrer /kʀɔnɔmetʀe/ [**v14**] *vt* to time

chrysalide /kʀizalid/ *f* chrysalis

ch'ti, *pl* **ch'tis** /ʃti/ (fam) **A** *adj* from Northern France
B *mf* person from Northern France

chu ▶ **choir**

CHU /seaʃy/ *m: abbr* ▶ **centre**

chuchotement /ʃyʃɔtmɑ̃/ *m* whisper

chuchoter /ʃyʃɔte/ [**v1**] *vt, vi* to whisper

chuchoteur, **-euse** /ʃyʃɔtœʀ, øz/ *mf* whisperer; ~ **équin** horse whisperer

chuintant, ~**e** /ʃɥɛ̃tɑ̃, ɑ̃t/ *adj* **bruit** ~ hissing sound

chuinter /ʃɥɛ̃te/ [**v1**] *vi* ‹*steam*› to hiss gently; ‹*tyre*› to swish

chum /tʃœm/ *m* (fam) friend; boyfriend

chut /ʃyt/ *excl* shh!, hush!

🔑 **chute** /ʃyt/ *f* **1** (gen) fall; (of empire) collapse; (of hair) loss; (of pressure) drop
2 (of film) ending; (of story) punch line
3 (of cloth) offcut
■ ~ **d'eau** waterfall; **la** ~ **des reins** the small of the back

Chypre /ʃipʀ/ *pr f* Cyprus

🔑 **ci** /si/ **A** *det* **cette page-**~ this page; **ces jours-**~ (past) these last few days; (future) in the next few days; (present) at the moment
B *pron* this; ~ **et ça** this and that

ci-après /siapʀɛ/ *adv* below

cible /sibl/ *f* target

cibler /sible/ [**v1**] *vt* to target

ciboulette /sibulɛt/ *f* (Bot) chive; (Culin) chives

cicatrice /sikatʀis/ *f* scar

cicatrisant, ~**e** /sikatʀizɑ̃, ɑ̃t/ *adj* healing

cicatrisation /sikatʀizasjɔ̃/ *f* healing

cicatriser /sikatʀize/ [**v1**] *vt*, **se cicatriser** *v refl* (+ *v être*) to heal

ci-contre /sikɔ̃tʀ/ *adv* opposite

ci-dessous /sidəsu/ *adv* below

ci-dessus /sidəsy/ *adv* above

cidre /sidʀ/ *m* cider

cidrerie /sidʀəʀi/ *f* cider works

🔑 **ciel** /sjɛl/, *pl* **cieux** /sjø/ *m* **1** sky; **carte du** ~ star chart; **à** ~ **ouvert** ‹*pool*› open-air; ‹*sewer*› open
2 heaven; **c'est le** ~ **qui t'envoie** you're a godsend

cierge /sjɛʀʒ/ *m* (church) candle

cieux ▶ **ciel**

cigale /sigal/ *f* cicada

cigare /sigaʀ/ *m* cigar

cigarette /sigaʀɛt/ *f* cigarette
■ ~ **électronique** electronic cigarette, e-cigarette

ci-gît /siʒi/ *phr* here lies

cigogne /sigɔɲ/ *f* stork

ci-inclus, ~**e** /siɛ̃kly, yz/ *adj, adv* enclosed

ci-joint, ~**e** /siʒwɛ̃, ɛ̃t/ *adj, adv* enclosed

cil /sil/ *m* eyelash

ciller /sije/ [**v1**] *vi* ~ **(des yeux)** to blink; **sans** ~ without batting an eyelid (BrE) *or* eyelash (AmE)

cime /sim/ *f* (tree)top

ciment /simɑ̃/ *m* cement

cimenter /simɑ̃te/ [**v1**] **A** *vt* to cement
B se cimenter (+ *v être*) *v refl* ‹*friendship*› to grow stronger

cimenterie /simɑ̃tʀi/ *f* cement works

cimetière /simtjɛʀ/ *m* cemetery, graveyard

cinéaste /sineast/ *mf* film director

ciné-club, *pl* ~**s** /sineklœb/ *m* film club

🔑 **cinéma** /sinema/ *m* **1 (salle de)** ~ cinema (BrE), movie theater (AmE)
2 cinema; film industry; **faire du** ~ to be in films
3 (fig, fam) **arrête ton** ~ cut out the play-acting; stop making such a fuss (fam)
■ ~ **d'art et d'essai** cinema showing art films (BrE), art house (AmE)

cinémathèque /sinematɛk/ *f* film archive

cinématographique /sinematɔgʀafik/ *adj* film (BrE), movie (AmE)

cinéphile /sinefil/ *mf* cinema enthusiast

cinglant, ~**e** /sɛ̃glɑ̃, ɑ̃t/ *adj* **1** ‹*wind*› biting; ‹*rain*› driving
2 ‹*remark, irony*› scathing

cinglé, ~**e** /sɛ̃gle/ *adj* (fam) mad (fam), crazy (fam)

cingler /sɛ̃gle/ [**v1**] *vt* **1** ‹*rain, wind*› to sting ‹*face*›
2 (with whip) to lash

cinoche /sinɔʃ/ *m* (fam) cinema, (BrE), movie theater (AmE)

🔑 **cinq** /sɛ̃k/ *adj inv, pron, m inv* five

cinquantaine /sɛ̃kɑ̃tɛn/ *f* **une** ~ about fifty

cinquante /sɛ̃kɑ̃t/ *adj inv, pron, m inv* fifty

cinquantenaire /sɛ̃kɑ̃tnɛʀ/ *m* fiftieth anniversary

cinquantième /sɛ̃kɑ̃tjɛm/ *adj* fiftieth

cinquième /sɛ̃kjɛm/ **A** *adj* fifth
B *f* **1** (Sch) *second year of secondary school, age 12–13*
2 (Aut) fifth (gear)

cintre /sɛ̃tʀ/ *m* **1** (clothes) hanger
2 (in architecture) curve

cintré, ~**e** /sɛ̃tʀe/ *adj* ‹*coat*› waisted; ‹*shirt*› tailored

cirage /siʀaʒ/ *m* (shoe) polish
IDIOM **être dans le** ~ (fam) to be half-conscious

circoncire /siʀkɔ̃siʀ/ [**v64**] *vt* to circumcise

circoncision /siʀkɔ̃sizjɔ̃/ *f* male circumcision

circonférence /siʀkɔ̃feʀɑ̃s/ *f* circumference

circonflexe /siʀkɔ̃flɛks/ *adj* **accent** ~ circumflex (accent)

circonscription /siʀkɔ̃skʀipsjɔ̃/ *f* district

circonscrire /siʀkɔ̃skʀiʀ/ [**v67**] *vt* **1** to contain ‹*fire, epidemic*›; to limit ‹*subject*›
2 to define

🔑 key word

circonspection /siʀkɔ̃spɛksjɔ̃/ *f* caution

circonstance /siʀkɔ̃stɑ̃s/ **A** *f*
1 circumstance
2 situation; **en toute ~** in any event; **pour la ~** for the occasion
B de circonstance *phr* ‹*poem*› for the occasion; **faire une tête de ~** to assume a suitable expression
■ **~s atténuantes** (Law) extenuating *or* mitigating circumstances

circuit /siʀkɥi/ *m* **1** (Sport, Tech) circuit
2 (in tourism) tour
3 (fig) **être mis hors ~** ‹*person*› to be put on the sidelines; **vivre en ~ fermé** to live in a closed world

circulaire /siʀkylɛʀ/ *adj, f* circular

circulation /siʀkylasjɔ̃/ *f* **1** traffic; **~ alternée** contraflow
2 circulation; **la libre ~ des personnes** the free movement of people; **disparaître de la ~** to go out of circulation

circulatoire /siʀkylatwaʀ/ *adj* circulatory

circuler /siʀkyle/ [**v1**] *vi* **1** ‹*train, bus*› to run
2 ‹*person*› to get around; to move about; (by car) to travel
3 ‹*banknotes, rumour, information*› to circulate; **faire ~** to circulate; to spread ‹*rumour*›
4 ‹*blood, air*› to circulate

cire /siʀ/ *f* wax

ciré /siʀe/ *m* oilskin

cirer /siʀe/ [**v1**] *vt* to polish ‹*shoes, floor*›

cirque /siʀk/ *m* **1** circus
2 (fig, fam) racket (fam); **arrête ton ~!** stop your nonsense!

cirrhose /siʀoz/ *f* cirrhosis

cisaille /sizɑj/ *f* pair of shears; **~s** shears

cisailler /sizɑje/ [**v1**] *vt* **1** to shear; to cut
2 to shear off

ciseau, *pl* **~x** /sizo/ **A** *m* **1** (Tech) chisel
2 (Sport) scissors jump; scissors hold
B ciseaux *mpl* scissors

ciseler /sizle/ [**v17**] *vt* to chisel

ciselure /sizlyʀ/ *f* chasing

citadelle /sitadɛl/ *f* citadel

citadin, **~e** /sitadɛ̃, in/ **A** *adj* city
B *mf* city dweller

citation /sitasjɔ̃/ *f* quotation

cité /site/ *f* **1** (gen) city; town
2 housing estate
■ **~ universitaire** student halls of residence (BrE), dormitories (AmE)

citer /site/ [**v1**] *vt* **1** to quote ‹*author, passage*›
2 to name ‹*title, book*›; to cite ‹*person, example, fact*›
3 (Law) to summon ‹*witness*›

citerne /sitɛʀn/ *f* tank

citoyen, -enne /sitwajɛ̃, ɛn/ *mf* citizen

citoyenneté /sitwajɛnte/ *f* citizenship

citrique /sitʀik/ *adj* citric

citron /sitʀɔ̃/ *m* **1** lemon
2 (fam) head, nut (fam)
■ **~ givré** lemon sorbet; **~ vert** lime

citronnade /sitʀɔnad/ *f* lemon squash (BrE), lemonade (AmE)

citronnelle /sitʀɔnɛl/ *f* (Bot) citronella

citronnier /sitʀɔnje/ *m* lemon tree

citrouille /sitʀuj/ *f* pumpkin

civet /sivɛ/ *m* ≈ stew

civière /sivjɛʀ/ *f* stretcher

civil, **~e** /sivil/ **A** *adj* (gen) civilian; ‹*marriage*› civil; ‹*funeral*› non religious
B *m* civilian; **en ~** in civilian clothes; in plain clothes; **dans le ~** in civilian life

civilisation /sivilizasjɔ̃/ *f* civilization

civiliser /sivilize/ [**v1**] *vt* to civilize

civilité /sivilite/ *f* **1** (status) title (*Mr, Mrs, Ms*)
2 (dated) (politeness) civility

civique /sivik/ *adj* civic

claie /klɛ/ *f* **1** wicker rack
2 fence, hurdle

clair, **~e** /klɛʀ/ **A** *adj* **1** ‹*colour*› light; ‹*complexion*› fair
2 ‹*room*› bright
3 ‹*weather, water*› clear
4 ‹*text*› clear; **passer le plus ~ de son temps** to spend most of one's time
B *adv* ‹*speak*› clearly; **il faisait ~** it was already light; **voir ~** to see well
C *m* **1** light; **mettre ses idées au ~** to get one's ideas straight; **tirer une affaire au ~** to get to the bottom of things
2 light colours (BrE)
■ **~ de lune** moonlight
IDIOM **c'est ~ comme de l'eau de roche** it's crystal clear

clairement /klɛʀmɑ/ *adv* clearly

clairière /klɛʀjɛʀ/ *f* clearing, glade

clairon /klɛʀɔ̃/ *m* **1** bugle
2 bugler

claironnant, **~e** /klɛʀɔnɑ̃, ɑ̃t/ *adj* strident

claironner /klɛʀɔne/ [**v1**] *vt* to shout [sth] from the rooftops

clairsemé, **~e** /klɛʀsəme/ *adj* ‹*houses*› scattered; ‹*hair*› thin; ‹*population*› sparse

clairvoyance /klɛʀvwajɑ̃s/ *f* perceptiveness

clairvoyant, **~e** /klɛʀvwajɑ̃, ɑ̃t/ *adj* perceptive

clamer /klame/ [**v1**] *vt* to proclaim

clameur /klamœʀ/ *f* roar

clan /klɑ̃/ *m* clan

clandestin, **~e** /klɑ̃dɛstɛ̃, in/ *adj* ‹*organization*› underground; ‹*immigration*› illegal; **passager ~** stowaway

clandestinement /klɑ̃dɛstinmɑ̃/ *adv* illegally

clandestinité /klɑ̃dɛstinite/ *f* secret *or* clandestine nature; **dans la ~** ‹*live*› in hiding; ‹*operate*› in secret

clap /klap/ *m* clapperboard

clapet /klapɛ/ *m* **1** valve
2 (fam) mouth, trap (fam)

c

C

clapier /klapje/ *m* rabbit hutch

clapoter /klapɔte/ [**v1**] *vi* to lap

claquage /klakaʒ/ *m* pulled *or* strained muscle

claque /klak/ *f* **1** slap
2 (fam) slap in the face
3 (in theatre) claque
IDIOM **en avoir sa ~** (fam) to be fed up

claqué, **~e** /klake/ *adj* (fam) knackered (pop), done in (fam)

claquement /klakmɑ̃/ *m* (of door) bang; (of whip) crack; (of tongue) click; (of flag) flapping

claquemurer: **se claquemurer** /klakmyʀe/ [**v1**] *v refl* (+ *v être*) to shut oneself away (**dans** in)

claquer /klake/ [**v1**] **A** *vt* **1** to slam ‹*door*›
2 (fam) to exhaust ‹*person*›
3 (fam) to blow (fam) ‹*money*›
B *vi* ‹*door*› to bang; (closing) to slam shut; ‹*flag*› to flap; **elle claque des dents** her teeth are chattering
C **se claquer** *v refl* (+ *v être*) **se ~ un muscle** to pull *or* strain a muscle

claquettes /klakɛt/ *fpl* tap dancing

clarifier /klaʀifje/ [**v2**] *vt* to clarify

clarinette /klaʀinɛt/ *f* clarinet

clarté /klaʀte/ *f* **1** light
2 (of water) clarity; (of complexion) fairness
3 (of style) clarity

⚷ **classe** /klas/ *f* **1** (Sch) (group) class, form (BrE); (level) year, form (BrE), grade (AmE); **après la ~** after school
2 (Sch) classroom
3 (in society, transport) class; **les ~s sociales** social classes
4 **avoir de la ~** to have class
5 (Mil) **faire ses ~s** to do one's basic training
■ **~ d'âge** age group; **~ verte** *educational school trip to the countryside*; **~s préparatoires (aux grandes écoles)** *preparatory classes for entrance to Grandes Écoles*

classement /klasmɑ̃/ *m* **1** classification
2 filing; **faire du ~ dans ses papiers** to sort one's papers out
3 grading; **~ trimestriel** (Sch) termly position (in class)
4 (Sport) ranking; **en tête du ~** in first place
5 (of hotel) rating

classer /klase/ [**v1**] **A** *vt* **1** to classify
2 to file (away) ‹*documents*›
3 (Law) to close ‹*case*›
4 to list ‹*old building*›
5 to class ‹*country, pupils*›; to rank ‹*song, player*›
6 (fam) to size [sb] up
B **se classer** *v refl* (+ *v être*) to rank

classeur /klasœʀ/ *m* **1** ring binder
2 file

classicisme /klasisism/ *m* **1** (in art) classicism
2 (in clothes, tastes) traditionalism

classification /klasifikasjɔ̃/ *f* classification

classifier /klasifje/ [**v2**] *vt* to classify

⚷ **classique** /klasik/ **A** *adj* **1** classical; **faire des études ~s** (Sch) to do classics
2 classic; ‹*method*› classic, standard; ‹*consequence*› usual; **de coupe ~** of classic cut; **c'est ~!** (fam) it's typical!; **c'est le coup ~!** (fam) it's the same old story!
B *m* classic

clause /kloz/ *f* clause

claustrophobie /klostʀɔfɔbi/ *f* claustrophobia

clavecin /klavsɛ̃/ *m* harpsichord

clavicule /klavikyl/ *f* collarbone

clavier /klavje/ *m* keyboard; **~ numérique** numeric keypad

claviste /klavist/ *mf* **1** typesetter
2 (Comput) keyboarder

⚷ **clé** /kle/ **A** *f* **1** (of lock, tin) key; **sous ~** under lock and key; **fermer à ~** to lock; **prix ~s en main** ‹*car*› on the road price (BrE), sticker price (AmE); **usine ~s en main** turnkey factory
2 (solution) key (**de** to)
3 spanner (BrE), wrench
4 (of flute) key; (of violin) peg; **~ de fa** bass clef
B **(-)clé** (*combining form*) **poste/mot(-)~** key post/word
C **à la clé** *phr* at stake; **avec, à la ~, une récompense** with a reward thrown in
■ **~ anglaise**, **~ à molette** adjustable spanner (BrE) *or* wrench (AmE); **~ USB** USB key

clef ▸ **clé**

clément, **~e** /klemɑ̃, ɑ̃t/ *adj* **1** ‹*judge*› lenient
2 ‹*temperature, winter*› mild

clémentine /klemɑ̃tin/ *f* clementine

cleptomanie /klɛptɔmani/ *f* kleptomania

clerc /klɛʀ/ *m* (Law) clerk

clergé /klɛʀʒe/ *m* clergy

cliché /kliʃe/ *m* **1** snapshot
2 cliché

⚷ **client**, **~e** /klijɑ̃, ɑ̃t/ *mf* (of shop) customer; (of solicitor) client; (of hotel) guest; (in taxi) fare
IDIOM **c'est à la tête du ~** it depends whether they like the look of you

clientèle /klijɑ̃tɛl/ *f* (of shop) customers; (of solicitor) clients; (of doctor) patients; **se faire une ~** to build up a clientele

cligner /kliɲe/ [**v1**] *v+prep* **~ des yeux** to blink; **~ de l'œil** to wink

clignotant /kliɲɔtɑ̃/ *m* (Aut) indicator (BrE), blinker (AmE)

clignoter /kliɲɔte/ [**v1**] *vi* ‹*light*› to flash; to flash on and off; ‹*star*› to twinkle

climat /klima/ *m* climate

climatique /klimatik/ *adj* climatic

climatisation /klimatizasjɔ̃/ *f* air conditioning

⚷ key word

climatiser /klimatize/ [**v1**] *vt* to air condition

climatiseur /klimatizœʀ/ *m* air conditioner

clin /klɛ̃/ *m* **~ d'œil** wink; (fig) allusion; **en un ~ d'œil** in a flash

clinique /klinik/ **A** *adj* clinical
B *f* private hospital; **~ vétérinaire** veterinary clinic

clinquant, **~e** /klɛ̃kɑ̃, ɑ̃t/ *adj* flashy (fam)

clip /klip/ *m* **1** pop video
2 clip-on (earring)

clique /klik/ *f* clique; **prendre ses ~s et ses claques** to pack up and go

cliquer /klike/ [**v1**] *vi* (Comput) to click (**sur** on); **~ à droite/gauche** to right-click/left-click

cliqueter /klikte/ [**v20**] *vi* ‹*keys*› to jingle; ‹*chain, machine*› to rattle

clitoris /klitɔʀis/ *m* clitoris

clivage /klivaʒ/ *m* divide; **~ d'opinion** division of opinion

clochard, **~e** /klɔʃaʀ, aʀd/ *mf* tramp

cloche /klɔʃ/ *f* **1** bell
2 (fam) clod (fam), idiot
3 ~ à fromage cover of cheese dish
IDIOMS **entendre plusieurs sons de ~** to hear several versions; **sonner les ~s à qn** to bawl sb out (fam)

cloche-pied: **à cloche-pied** /aklɔʃpje/ *phr* **sauter à ~** to hop

clocher¹ /klɔʃe/ [**v1**] *vi* (fam) **il y a quelque chose qui cloche** there's something wrong

clocher² /klɔʃe/ *m* steeple; church *or* bell tower; **querelle de ~** local quarrel

clochette /klɔʃɛt/ *f* (little) bell

cloison /klwazɔ̃/ *f* **1** partition
2 screen; **~ extensible** folding room divider

cloisonner /klwazɔne/ [**v1**] *vt* **1** to partition ‹*room*›; to divide up ‹*space*›
2 to divide up ‹*society*›; to compartmentalize ‹*administration*›

cloître /klwɑtʀ/ *m* cloister

cloîtrer /klwatʀe/ [**v1**] **A** *vt* to shut [sb] away
B se cloîtrer *v refl* (+ *v être*) to shut oneself away

clone /klon/ *m* clone

clope /klɔp/ *mf* (fam) fag (BrE) (fam), ciggy (fam), cigarette

clopin-clopant /klɔpɛ̃klɔpɑ̃/ *phr* (fam) **aller ~** to hobble along

cloporte /klɔpɔʀt/ *m* woodlouse

cloque /klɔk/ *f* blister

clore /klɔʀ/ [**v79**] **A** *vt* **1** to close ‹*debate*›
2 to end, to conclude ‹*programme*›
3 to close ‹*eyes*›
B se clore *v refl* (+ *v être*) to end (**par** with)

clos, **~e** /klo, oz/ **A** *pp* ▸ **clore**
B *pp adj* ‹*system*› closed; ‹*area*› enclosed; **monde ~** self-contained world

clôture /klotyʀ/ *f* **1** fence; wire fence; railings
2 (of debate, session) close; (of subscription) closing; **discours de ~** closing speech

clôturer /klotyʀe/ [**v1**] *vt* **1** to fence in ‹*land*›
2 to close ‹*list*›; to end ‹*debate*›

clou /klu/ **A** *m* **1** nail; stud
2 (of show) star attraction; (of evening) high point
3 (Med) boil
B clous *mpl* **1** pedestrian crossing (BrE), crosswalk (AmE)
2 (fam) **des ~s!** no way!
■ **~ de girofle** (Bot, Culin) clove
IDIOM **enfoncer le ~** to drive the point home

clouer /klue/ [**v1**] *vt* to nail down ‹*lid*›; to nail together ‹*planks*›; **~ au sol** (fig) to pin [sb] down; **être cloué au lit** to be confined to bed

clown /klun/ *m* clown

clownerie /klunʀi/ *f* clowning; **arrête tes ~s** stop clowning about

club /klœb/ *m* **1** club
2 ~ de vacances holiday camp

CM /seɛm/ *m*: *abbr* ▸ **cours**

CMU /seɛmy/ *n* (*abbr* = **Couverture Médicale Universelle**) *free health care for people on low incomes*

CNPF /seɛnpeɛf/ *m* (*abbr* = **Conseil national du patronat français**) *national council of French employers*

CNRS /seɛnɛʀɛs/ *m* (*abbr* = **Centre national de la recherche scientifique**) *national centre for scientific research*

coaguler /kɔagyle/ [**v1**] *vi*, **se coaguler** *v refl* (+ *v être*) ‹*blood*› to coagulate

coalition /kɔalisjɔ̃/ *f* coalition

coasser /kɔase/ [**v1**] *vi* to croak

cobaye /kɔbaj/ *m* guinea pig

cobra /kɔbʀa/ *m* cobra

cocaïne /kɔkain/ *f* cocaine

cocarde /kɔkaʀd/ *f* **1** rosette; (on uniform) cockade
2 (on vehicle) official badge

cocasse /kɔkas/ *adj* comical

coccinelle /kɔksinɛl/ *f* ladybird (BrE), ladybug (AmE)

coccyx /kɔksis/ *m* coccyx

coche /kɔʃ/ *m* (stage)coach
IDIOM **manquer le ~** to miss the boat

cocher¹ /kɔʃe/ [**v1**] *vt* to tick (BrE), to check (AmE)

cocher² /kɔʃe/ *m* coachman; cabman

cochère /kɔʃɛʀ/ *adj f* **porte ~** carriage entrance

cochon, **-onne** /kɔʃɔ̃, ɔn/ **A** *adj* (fam)
1 ‹*film*› dirty; ‹*person*› dirty-minded
2 ‹*person*› messy, dirty
B *mf* (fam) **1** pig (fam), slob (fam); **de ~** ‹*job*› botched; ‹*weather*› lousy (fam)
2 sex maniac
C *m* **1** (Zool) pig, hog
2 (Culin) pork

■ ~ **d'Inde** Guinea pig; ~ **de lait** sucking pig

cochonnaille /kɔʃɔnɑj/ *f* (fam) *products made from pork such as salami, bacon, pâté and ham*

cochonnerie /kɔʃɔnʀi/ *f* (fam) **1** junk (fam); **il ne mange que des ~s** he only eats junk food
2 mess; **faire des ~s** to make a mess

C

cocker /kɔkɛʀ/ *m* (cocker) spaniel

cocktail /kɔktɛl/ *m* **1** cocktail
2 (fig) mixture
3 cocktail party

coco /koko/ *m* coconut

cocon /kɔkɔ̃/ *m* cocoon

cocorico /kɔkɔʀiko/ *m* cock a doodle do

cocotier /kɔkɔtje/ *m* coconut palm

cocotte /kɔkɔt/ *f* **1** (fam, baby talk) hen
2 (fam) **ma ~** honey (fam)
3 (Culin) casserole (BrE), pot

cocotte-minute®, *pl* **cocottes-minute** /kɔkɔtminyt/ *f* pressure cooker

codage /kɔdaʒ/ *m* coding, encoding

✓ **code** /kɔd/ **A** *m* code
B codes *mpl* (of vehicle) dipped (BrE) *or* dimmed (AmE) (head)lights, low beam
■ ~ **accès** password; ~ **agence** sort code (BrE), routing number (AmE); ~ **(à) barres** bar code; ~ **confidentiel** personal identification number, PIN; ~ **guichet** ▶ **code agence**; ~ **de la nationalité** regulations as to nationality; ~ **postal** post code (BrE), zip code (AmE); ~ **de la route** (Aut) highway code (BrE), rules of the road (AmE); **passer son ~** (fam) to take the written part of a driving test

coder /kɔde/ [**v1**] *vt* to code, to encode

codétenu, **~e** /kodetny/ *mf* fellow prisoner

codifier /kɔdifje/ [**v2**] *vt* to codify ‹*laws*›; to standardize ‹*language, custom*›

codirecteur, **-trice** /kodiʀɛktœʀ, tʀis/ *mf* joint manager; joint director

coefficient /kɔefisjɑ̃/ *m* **1** ratio
2 margin
3 *weighting factor in an exam*; **la chimie est au ~ 4** chemistry results are multiplied by 4
4 (in arithmetic, physics) coefficient

coéquipier, **-ière** /koekipje, ɛʀ/ *mf* team mate

✓ **cœur** /kœʀ/ **A** *m* **1** heart; **il a le ~ malade** he has a heart condition; **serrer qn sur** *or* **contre son ~** to hold sb close; **écouter son ~** to go with one's feelings; **aller droit au ~ de qn** to touch sb deeply; **avoir un coup de ~ pour qch** to fall in love with sth; **ça me fait mal au ~ de voir** it sickens me to see; **problème de ~** emotional problem; **parler à ~ ouvert** to speak openly; **avoir bon ~** to be kind-hearted; **je n'ai plus le ~ à rien** I don't feel like doing anything any more
2 (Culin) heart
3 (fig) (of fruit, rock) core; (of problem, debate) heart; **au ~ de** (of region, town) in the middle of; (of building, problem, system) at the heart of; **au ~ de l'hiver** in the dead of winter
4 (person) **mon (petit) ~** sweetheart
5 courage; **le ~ m'a manqué** my courage failed me; **redonner du ~ à qn** to give sb new heart
6 (Games) (card) heart; (suit) hearts
B à cœur *phr* **avoir à ~ de faire** to be intent on doing; **prendre qch à ~** to take sth seriously
C de bon cœur *phr* willingly; **rire de bon ~** to laugh heartily
D par cœur *phr* by heart; **connaître qn par ~** to know sb inside out
IDIOMS **avoir mal au ~** to feel sick (BrE) *or* nauseous (AmE); **avoir du ~ au ventre** to be brave; **avoir le ~ sur la main** to be open-handed; **il ne le porte pas dans son ~** he's not his favourite (BrE) person; **j'irai mais le ~ n'y est pas** I'll go but my heart isn't in it; **si le ~ t'en dit** if you feel like it; **avoir qch sur le ~** to be resentful about sth

coexister /koegziste/ [**v1**] *vi* to coexist

coffre /kɔfʀ/ *m* **1** chest; **~ à jouets** toy box
2 (for valuables) safe; (individual) safety deposit box; **la salle des ~s** the strongroom
3 (of car) boot (BrE), trunk (AmE)
IDIOM **avoir du ~** (fam) to have a powerful voice

coffre-fort, *pl* **coffres-forts** /kɔfʀəfɔʀ/ *m* safe

coffret /kɔfʀɛ/ *m* **1** casket; **~ à bijoux** jewellery (BrE) *or* jewelry (AmE) box
2 (of records, cassettes, books) boxed set

cogérer /koʒeʀe/ [**v14**] *vt* to co-manage

cogestion /koʒɛstjɔ̃/ *f* joint management

cogiter /kɔʒite/ [**v1**] *vi* to cogitate, to think

cognac /kɔɲak/ *m* cognac (*brandy from the Cognac area*)

cogner /kɔɲe/ [**v1**] **A** *vt* to knock
B *vi* **1 ~ contre** ‹*shutter*› to bang against; ‹*branch*› to knock against; ‹*projectile*› to hit; **~ à la porte** to bang on the door
2 (fam) ‹*boxer*› to hit out
3 ‹*heart*› to pound
C se cogner *v refl* (+ *v être*) to bump into something; **se ~ le pied contre une pierre** to stub one's toe on a stone

cognitif, **-ive** /kɔgnitif, iv/ *adj* cognitive

cohabitation /koabitasjɔ̃/ *f* **1** living with somebody
2 *situation where the French President is in political opposition to the government*

cohabiter /koabite/ [**v1**] *vi* ‹*people*› to live together; ‹*things*› to coexist

cohérence /kɔeʀɑ̃s/ *f* **1** coherence; consistency
2 (in physics) cohesion

cohérent, **~e** /kɔeʀɑ̃, ɑ̃t/ *adj* coherent; consistent

cohéritier, **-ière** /koeʀitje, ɛʀ/ *mf* joint heir

✓ key word

cohésion /kɔezjɔ̃/ *f* cohesion
cohorte /koɔʀt/ *f* (fam) crowd, group
cohue /kɔy/ *f* crowd; **c'est la ~** it's a crush
coi, **coite** /kwa, kwat/ *adj* **se tenir ~** to remain quiet
coiffant, **~e** /kwafɑ̃, ɑ̃t/ *adj* **gel ~** styling gel
coiffe /kwaf/ *f* (gen) headgear; (of nun) wimple
coiffer /kwafe/ [**v1**] **A** *vt* **1 ~ qn** to do sb's hair; to comb sb's hair
2 coiffé d'une casquette wearing a cap
B se coiffer *v refl* (+ *v être*) **1** to do *or* comb one's hair
2 se ~ de qch to put sth on
IDIOM **~ qn au poteau** (fam) *or* **sur le fil** (fam) to beat sb by a whisker
coiffeur, **-euse** /kwafœʀ, øz/ *mf* hairdresser
coiffeuse /kwaføz/ *f* dressing table
coiffure /kwafyʀ/ *f* **1** hairstyle
2 hairdressing
3 headgear
coin /kwɛ̃/ **A** *m* **1** corner; **à tous les ~s de rue** everywhere; **aux quatre ~s de la ville** all over the town; **aller au ~** (as punishment) to go and stand in the corner; **j'ai dû poser mon sac dans un ~** I must have put my bag down somewhere; **au ~ du feu** by the fire
2 (of eye, mouth) corner; **un sourire en ~** a half smile; **un regard en ~** a sidelong glance
3 (of ground) plot; (of lawn) patch; **un ~ de paradis** an idyllic spot
4 (in region) **un ~ de France** a part of France; **dans le ~** around here, in these parts; around there, in those parts; **le café du ~** the local cafe; **les gens du ~** the locals; **connaître les bons ~s pour manger** to know all the good places to eat
5 (for photograph) corner; (for file) reinforcing corner
6 (Tech) wedge
B coin(-) (*combining form*) **~-repas/-salon** dining/living area
coincé, **~e** /kwɛ̃se/ **A** *pp* ▶ **coincer**
B *pp adj* **1** stuck; trapped; **~ entre** ‹*house*› wedged between
2 (fam) **j'ai le dos ~, je suis ~** my back has gone (fam)
3 (fig, fam) stuck (fam)
4 (fam) ill at ease
5 (fam) uptight (fam)
coincer /kwɛ̃se/ [**v12**] **A** *vt* **1** to wedge ‹*object*›; to wedge [sth] open/shut ‹*door*›; ‹*snow*› to trap ‹*person*›
2 to jam ‹*drawer, zip*›
3 (fam) to catch ‹*person*›; **se faire ~ par** to get caught by
4 (fam) to catch [sb] out ‹*person*›
B *vi* **1** ‹*zip, drawer*› to stick
2 (fam) **ça coince** there's a problem
C se coincer *v refl* (+ *v être*) **1** ‹*object*› to get stuck *or* jammed
2 se ~ les doigts to get one's fingers caught
coïncidence /kɔɛ̃sidɑ̃s/ *f* coincidence
coïncider /kɔɛ̃side/ [**v1**] *vi* to coincide
coing /kwɛ̃/ *m* quince
coite ▶ **coi**
col /kɔl/ *m* **1** collar
2 (in mountains) pass
3 (of bottle) neck
4 (Anat) neck
■ **~ blanc** white-collar worker
colère /kɔlɛʀ/ *f* **1** anger; **être en ~** to be angry; **passer sa ~ sur qn** to take out *or* vent one's anger on sb; **sous le coup de la ~** in a fit of anger
2 faire *or* **piquer** (fam) **une ~** to have a fit; to throw a tantrum
coléreux, **-euse** /kɔleʀø, øz/ *adj* ‹*person*› quick-tempered
colifichet /kɔlifiʃɛ/ *m* trinket; knick-knack
colimaçon /kɔlimasɔ̃/ *m* snail; **escalier en ~** spiral staircase
colin /kɔlɛ̃/ *m* (fish) hake; coley
colin-maillard /kɔlɛ̃majaʀ/ *m* **jouer à ~** to play blind man's buff
colique /kɔlik/ *f* **1** diarrhoea
2 stomach pain; (in babies) colic
colis /kɔli/ *m* parcel
■ **~ piégé** parcel bomb; **~ postal** parcel sent by mail
colite /kɔlit/ *f* colitis
collaborateur, **-trice** /kɔlabɔʀatœʀ, tʀis/ *mf* **1** colleague; assistant
2 employee
3 (journalist) contributor
4 (derog) collaborator
collaboration /kɔlabɔʀasjɔ̃/ *f* **1** (to newspaper) contribution; (work on project) collaboration
2 (in Second World War) collaboration
collaborer /kɔlabɔʀe/ [**v1**] *vi* **1 ~ à** to contribute to ‹*newspaper*›; to collaborate on ‹*project*›
2 (as working partner) to collaborate
collage /kɔlaʒ/ *m* collage; (in photography) montage
collant, **~e** /kɔlɑ̃, ɑ̃t/ **A** *adj* **1** ‹*substance, object*› sticky
2 ‹*dress*› skintight
B *m* tights (BrE), panty hose (AmE)
collation /kɔlasjɔ̃/ *f* light meal
colle /kɔl/ *f* **1** glue; (wallpaper) paste
2 (fam) (hard question) poser (fam); test
3 (fam) detention
collecte /kɔlɛkt/ *f* **1** collection; **faire une ~** to raise funds
2 (prayer) collect
collecter /kɔlɛkte/ [**v1**] *vt* to collect
collecteur, **-trice** /kɔlɛktœʀ, tʀis/ *mf* collector
■ **~ de fonds** fundraiser; **~ d'impôts** tax collector

⚷ **collectif**, **-ive** /kɔlɛktif, iv/ **A** *adj* collective; ‹*dismissals*› mass; ‹*heating*› shared; ‹*ticket*› group
B *m* **1** collective
2 action group

⚷ **collection** /kɔlɛksjɔ̃/ *f* **1** collection; **~ de timbres** stamp collection
2 (of books) series; (by same author) set

collectionner /kɔlɛksjɔne/ [**v1**] *vt* **1** to collect
2 (fig) **~ les erreurs** to make one mistake after another

collectionneur, **-euse** /kɔlɛksjɔnœʀ, øz/ *mf* collector

collectivement /kɔlɛktivmɑ̃/ *adv* (gen) collectively; ‹*resign*› en masse, as a body

collectivité /kɔlɛktivite/ *f* **1** group
2 community
■ **~ locale** local authority (BrE), local government (AmE)

⚷ **collège** /kɔlɛʒ/ *m* **1** secondary school (BrE), junior high school (AmE) (*up to age 16*)
2 college; **~ électoral** (Pol) electoral college
■ **~ d'enseignement secondaire, CES** secondary school (BrE), junior high school (AmE); **~ d'enseignement technique, CET** *technical secondary school in France*

collégial, **~e**, *mpl* **-iaux** /kɔleʒjal, o/ *adj* ‹*church*› collegial; ‹*system*› collegiate

collégien, **-ienne** /kɔleʒjɛ̃, ɛn/ *mf* schoolboy/schoolgirl

collègue /kɔlɛg/ *mf* colleague

coller /kɔle/ [**v1**] **A** *vt* **1** to stick, to glue ‹*wood, paper*›; to paste up ‹*poster*›; to hang ‹*wallpaper*›; to stick [sth] on ‹*label*›; to stick down ‹*envelope*›
2 **~ qch contre** *or* **à qch** to press sth against sth; **il la colla contre le parapet** he pushed her up against the parapet
3 (fam) to stick (fam); **je leur ai collé la facture sous le nez** I stuck the bill (right) under their noses; **~ une amende/une gifle à qn** to fine/slap sb
4 (fam) (in exam) **se faire ~** to fail
5 (fam) to give [sb] detention ‹*pupil*›
B *vi* **1** to stick
2 (fam) **~ avec** to fit *or* be consistent with
C **se coller** *v refl* (+ *v être*) **1** **se ~ à** *or* **contre qn/qch** to press oneself against sb/sth
2 (fam) **dès qu'il rentre, il se colle devant son ordinateur** as soon as he comes in he's glued (fam) to his computer

collerette /kɔlʀɛt/ *f* **1** ruff
2 ruffle

collet /kɔlɛ/ *m* **être ~ monté** to be prim

collier /kɔlje/ *m* **1** necklace; **~ de perles** string of pearls
2 (of animal) collar
3 beard
(IDIOM) **donner un coup de ~** to get one's head down; to put one's back into it

collimateur /kɔlimatœʀ/ *m* **avoir qn dans le ~** (fam) to have it in for sb (fam)

colline /kɔlin/ *f* hill

collision /kɔlizjɔ̃/ *f* collision

colloque /kɔl(l)ɔk/ *m* conference, symposium

collyre /kɔliʀ/ *m* eye drops

colmater /kɔlmate/ [**v1**] *vt* to plug, to seal off ‹*leak*›; to seal ‹*crack*›

colocation /kɔlɔkasjɔ̃/ *f* (in an apartment) flat-sharing; (in a house) house-sharing

colombe /kɔlɔ̃b/ *f* dove

colombier /kɔlɔ̃bje/ *m* dovecote

colon /kɔlɔ̃/ *m* colonist

côlon /kolɔ̃, kɔlɔ̃/ *m* colon

colonel /kɔlɔnɛl/ *m* (Mil) (in army) ≈ colonel; (in air force) ≈ group captain (BrE), ≈ colonel (AmE)

colonial, **~e**, *mpl* **-iaux** /kɔlɔnjal, o/ *adj*, *mf* colonial

colonialisme /kɔlɔnjalism/ *m* colonialism

colonie /kɔlɔni/ *f* (gen) colony; **~ (de vacances)** holiday camp (*for children*)

colonnade /kɔlɔnad/ *f* colonnade

colonne /kɔlɔn/ *f* column
■ **~ vertébrale** (Anat) spinal column

colorant, **~e** /kɔlɔʀɑ̃, ɑ̃t/ **A** *adj* colouring (BrE)
B *m* **1** colouring (BrE) agent
2 dye
3 (in chemistry) stain
4 (Culin) colouring (BrE)

coloration /kɔlɔʀasjɔ̃/ *f* **1** colouring (BrE); dyeing; staining; tinting
2 colour (BrE)

coloré, **~e** /kɔlɔʀe/ *adj* **1** (gen) coloured (BrE)
2 ‹*life, crowd*› colourful (BrE); ‹*style*› lively

colorer /kɔlɔʀe/ [**v1**] *vt* to colour (BrE); to tint; to stain; to dye

colorier /kɔlɔʀje/ [**v2**] *vt* to colour in (BrE), to color (AmE)

coloris /kɔlɔʀi/ *m inv* colour (BrE); shade

colossal, **~e**, *mpl* **-aux** /kɔlɔsal, o/ *adj* colossal, huge

colosse /kɔlɔs/ *m* giant

colporter /kɔlpɔʀte/ [**v1**] *vt* **1** to spread ‹*news*›
2 to peddle ‹*goods*›

coltiner: **se coltiner** /kɔltine/ [**v1**] *v refl* (+ *v être*) (fam) **1** to lug (fam) ‹*heavy object*›
2 to get stuck with (fam) ‹*chore, person*›

colza /kɔlza/ *m* rape

coma /kɔma/ *m* coma

comateux, **-euse** /kɔmatø, øz/ *adj* comatose

⚷ **combat** /kɔ̃ba/ *m* **1** (Mil) fighting; **~s aériens** air battles; **mettre hors de ~** to disable
2 (in politics) struggle; **livrer un ~** to campaign
3 (Sport) bout; **hors de ~** out of action
■ **~ de coqs** cock fight

⚷ key word

combatif, **-ive** /kɔ̃batif, iv/ *adj* **1** assertive
2 aggressive

combativité /kɔ̃bativite/ *f* fighting spirit

combattant, **~e** /kɔ̃batɑ̃, ɑ̃t/ *mf* combatant

combattre /kɔ̃batʀ/ [**v61**] *vt, vi* to fight

combien[1] /kɔ̃bjɛ̃/ **A** *adv* **1** **~ mesure le salon?** how big is the lounge?; **j'aimerais savoir ~ il a payé son costume** I'd like to know how much he paid for that suit; **~ êtes-vous?** how many of you are there?
2 (to what extent) **je ne saurais te dire ~ il me manque** I can't tell you how much I miss him
B **combien de** *det* **1** how many, how much
2 **~ de temps faut-il?** how long does it take?

combien[2] /kɔ̃bjɛ̃/ *mf inv* **1** **tu es le/la ~?** (in queue) how many people are before you?
2 **le ~ sommes-nous?** what's the date today?
3 (for measurements) **tu chausses du ~?** what size shoes do you take?
4 **tu le vois tous les ~?** how often do you see him?

combinaison /kɔ̃binɛzɔ̃/ *f* **1** combining; combination
2 (of safe) combination
3 (full-length) slip
4 jumpsuit
5 overalls (BrE), coveralls (AmE)
■ **~ de plongée** wetsuit

combine /kɔ̃bin/ *f* (fam) trick (fam); scheme

combiné /kɔ̃bine/ *m* handset, receiver

combiner /kɔ̃bine/ [**v1**] *vt* **1** to combine
2 to work out ‹*plan*›

comble /kɔ̃bl/ **A** *adj* ‹*room*› packed
B *m* **1** **le ~ de l'injustice/du mauvais goût** the height of injustice/of bad taste; **pour ~ de malchance j'ai...** to crown it all, I...; **c'est un** *or* **le ~!** (fam) that's the limit!
2 roof space; **de fond en ~** from top to bottom; completely
C **combles** *mpl* attic

combler /kɔ̃ble/ [**v1**] *vt* **1** to fill (in) ‹*ditch*›
2 to fill in ‹*gaps*›; to make up ‹*deficit*›
3 to fulfil (BrE) ‹*need, desire*›; **la vie m'a comblé** I've had a wonderful life; **~ qn** to fill sb with joy

combustible /kɔ̃bystibl/ **A** *adj* combustible
B *m* fuel; **~ nucléaire** nuclear fuel

combustion /kɔ̃bystjɔ̃/ *f* combustion

comédie /kɔmedi/ *f* **1** comedy
2 play-acting; **jouer la ~** to put on an act
3 (fam) scene; **faire une ~** to make a scene
■ **~ musicale** musical

comédien, **-ienne** /kɔmedjɛ̃, ɛn/ **A** *adj* **il est (un peu) ~** (fig) he puts it on
B *mf* actor/actress

comestible /kɔmɛstibl/ **A** *adj* edible
B **comestibles** *mpl* food

comète /kɔmɛt/ *f* comet

comique /kɔmik/ **A** *adj* **1** comic
2 funny
B *mf* comic actor/actress; comedian
C *m* **1** clown
2 comedy

comité /kɔmite/ *m* **1** committee
2 group

commandant /kɔmɑ̃dɑ̃/ *m* (in army) ≈ major; (in air force) ≈ squadron leader (BrE), ≈ major (AmE)
■ **~ de bord** captain

commande /kɔmɑ̃d/ *f* **1** order
2 commission; **passer ~ de qch à qn** to commission sb to do sth
3 (Tech) control; **levier de ~** control lever; **être aux** *or* **tenir les ~s** to be at the controls; (fig) to be in control
4 (Comput) command

commandement /kɔmɑ̃dmɑ̃/ *m* **1** (Mil) command
2 (in religion) commandment

commander /kɔmɑ̃de/ [**v1**] **A** *vt* **1** to order [sth] (**à qn** from sb)
2 to commission ‹*book, survey*›
3 (Mil) to command ‹*army*›; to order ‹*attack*›
4 **~ qn** to order sb about
5 **les circonstances commandent la prudence** the circumstances call for caution
6 ‹*machine*› to control ‹*mechanism*›
B **commander à** *v+prep* **1** **~ à** to be in command of
2 **~ à** to order, to command
C *vi* to give the orders, to be in charge
D **se commander** *v refl* (+ *v être*) **ça ne se commande pas** it's not something you can control

commanditer /kɔmɑ̃dite/ [**v1**] *vt* **1** to finance ‹*company*›
2 to sponsor ‹*project*›
3 to be behind ‹*crime*›

commando /kɔmɑ̃do/ *m* commando

comme /kɔm/ **A** *adv* how
B *conj* **1** as; **ici ~ en Italie** here as in Italy; **il est paresseux, ~ sa sœur d'ailleurs** he's lazy, just like his sister; **jolie ~ tout** really pretty
2 (in comparisons) **il est grand ~ sa sœur** he's as tall as his sister; **c'est tout ~** (fam) it comes to the same thing; **elle me traite ~ un enfant** she treats me like a child
3 like; **un manteau ~ le tien** a coat like yours; **~ ça** like that; **puisque c'est ~ ça** if that's the way it is
4 as if, as though; **~ pour faire** as if to do
5 (fam) **elle a eu ~ un évanouissement** she sort of fainted
6 **avare ~ il est, il ne te donnera rien** he's so mean, he won't give you anything
7 as; **travailler ~ jardinier** to work as a gardener
8 as, since; **~ elle était seule** as *or* since she was alone
9 as; **~ il traversait la rue** as he was crossing the road

c

C

(IDIOMS) **~ quoi!** which just shows!; **~ ci ~ ça** (fam) so-so (fam)

commémoration /kɔmemɔʀasjɔ̃/ *f* commemoration

commémorer /kɔmemɔʀe/ [**v1**] *vt* to commemorate

commencement /kɔmɑ̃smɑ̃/ *m* beginning

⚷ **commencer** /kɔmɑ̃se/ [**v12**] **A** *vt* **1** to start, to begin
2 ~ à *or* **de faire** to start *or* begin to do; **ça commence à bien faire!** (fam) it's getting to be a bit much!
B *vi* to start, to begin; **pour ~** for a start; **vous êtes tous coupables à ~ par toi** you're all guilty starting with you
C *v impers* **il commence à neiger** it's starting *or* beginning to snow

⚷ **comment** /kɔmɑ̃/ *adv* **1** how; **~ faire?** how can it be done?; **~ t'appelles-tu?** what's your name?; **~ ça se fait?** (fam) how come? (fam)
2 ~? qu'est-ce que tu dis? pardon? what did you say?; **Paul ~?** Paul who?
3 ~ est leur maison/fils? what's their house/son like?; **~ trouvez-vous ma robe?** what do you think of my dress?
4 ~ cela? what do you mean?; **~ donc!** but of course!; **et ~ (donc)!** (fam) and how! (fam); **'c'était bon?'—'et ~!'** (fam) 'was it nice?'—'it certainly was!'

⚷ **commentaire** /kɔmmɑ̃tɛʀ/ *m* **1** comment
2 commentary

commentateur, **-trice** /kɔmmɑ̃tatœʀ, tʀis/ *mf* commentator

commenter /kɔmmɑ̃te/ [**v1**] *vt* **1** to comment on ‹*decision, event*›
2 to give a commentary on ‹*film, visit*›
3 to commentate on ‹*match*›

commérage /kɔmeʀaʒ/ *m* gossip

commerçant, **~e** /kɔmɛʀsɑ̃, ɑ̃t/ **A** *adj* ‹*street*› shopping; ‹*nation*› trading
B *mf* shopkeeper, storekeeper (AmE); retailer

⚷ **commerce** /kɔmɛʀs/ *m* **1** shop, store (AmE); **dans le ~** in the shops *or* stores (AmE)
2 business
3 trade; **faire le ~ de** to trade in; **faire ~ de** to sell; **faire du ~** to be in business

⚷ **commercial**, **~e**, *mpl* **-iaux** /kɔmɛʀsjal, o/ **A** *adj* **1** commercial; **carrière ~e** career in sales and marketing
2 trade
B *mf* sales and marketing person

commercialisation /kɔmɛʀsjalizasjɔ̃/ *f* marketing

commercialiser /kɔmɛʀsjalize/ [**v1**] *vt* to market

commère /kɔmɛʀ/ *f* gossip

⚷ **commettre** /kɔmɛtʀ/ [**v60**] *vt* to make ‹*error*›; to commit ‹*crime*›; to carry out ‹*attack*›

commis /kɔmi/ *m* **1** (in office) clerk
2 shop assistant (BrE), sales clerk (AmE)

commissaire /kɔmisɛʀ/ *m* **1 ~ (de police)** ≈ police superintendent
2 commissioner
3 (of sports event) steward; (of exhibition) organizer

commissaire-priseur, *pl* **commissaires-priseurs** /kɔmisɛʀpʀizœʀ/ *m* auctioneer

commissariat /kɔmisaʀja/ *m* **~ (de police)** police station

⚷ **commission** /kɔmisjɔ̃/ **A** *f* **1** committee
2 commission; **payé à la ~** paid on a commission basis
3 errand
4 faire la ~ à qn to give sb the message
B commissions *fpl* (fam) shopping

commissionnaire /kɔmisjɔnɛʀ/ *m* (Econ) agent, broker

commissure /kɔmisyʀ/ *f* corner

commode /kɔmɔd/ **A** *adj* **1** (gen) convenient; ‹*tool*› handy
2 easy
3 ne pas être (très) ~ to be strict; to be difficult (to deal with)
B *f* chest of drawers

commodité /kɔmɔdite/ *f* convenience

commotion /kɔmosjɔ̃/ *f* **1 ~ (cérébrale)** concussion (*of the brain*)
2 (fig) shock

⚷ **commun**, **~e** /kɔmœ̃, yn/ **A** *adj* **1** common; ‹*policy, property*› joint; ‹*friend*› mutual; ‹*room, memories, experience*› shared; **d'un ~ accord** by mutual agreement; **après dix ans de vie ~e** after living together for ten years
2 ‹*person, tastes*› common; ‹*face*› plain
3 elle est d'une beauté peu ~e she's uncommonly beautiful
B *m* ordinary; **le ~ des mortels** ordinary mortals; **hors du ~** exceptional
C en commun *phr* ‹*work, write*› jointly, together; **avoir qch en ~** to have sth in common; **nous mettons tout en ~** we share everything

communal, **~e**, *mpl* **-aux** /kɔmynal, o/ *adj* ‹*budget, resources*› local council (BrE), local government (AmE); ‹*building*› local council (BrE), community (AmE)

communautaire /kɔmynotɛʀ/ *adj* **1** (referring to the EC) ‹*budget, law*› Community
2 la vie ~ life in a community

⚷ **communauté** /kɔmynote/ *f* **1** community
2 commune; **vivre en ~** to live in a commune

■ **Communauté économique européenne, CEE** European Economic Community, EEC; **Communauté des États indépendants, CEI** Commonwealth of Independent States, CIS

⚷ **commune** /kɔmyn/ **A** *f* village; town
B communes *fpl* **la Chambre des ~s** the (House of) Commons

⚷ key word

communément /kɔmynemɑ̃/ *adv* generally

communicatif, **-ive** /kɔmynikatif, iv/ *adj*
1 ‹*person*› talkative
2 ‹*gaiety*› infectious

communication /kɔmynikasjɔ̃/ *f* **1** **~ (téléphonique)** (telephone) call; **mettre qn en ~ avec qn** to put sb through to sb
2 report; (at conference) paper
3 demander ~ d'un dossier à qn to ask sb for a file
4 (between people) communication, contact
5 (media) communications
6 (by phone, radio) **moyens de ~** communications

communier /kɔmynje/ [**v2**] *vi* to receive Communion

communion /kɔmynjɔ̃/ *f* **1** Communion
2 (fig) communion
■ **~ (privée)** first communion

communiqué /kɔmynike/ *m*
1 communiqué, press release
2 statement

communiquer /kɔmynike/ [**v1**] **A** *vt* **1** to announce ‹*date, result*›; to give ‹*address*›
2 ‹*person*› to pass on ‹*document*›; to convey ‹*idea*›
B *vi* **1** to communicate
2 ‹*rooms*› to be adjoining
C se communiquer *v refl* (+ *v être*)
1 ‹*people*› to pass [sth] on to each other
2 ‹*fire, disease*› to spread

communisme /kɔmynism/ *m* communism

commutateur /kɔmytatœʀ/ *m* switch

commuter /kɔmyte/ [**v1**] *vt* to commute

compact, **~e** /kɔ̃pakt/ *adj* **1** ‹*fog, crowd*› dense; ‹*earth*› compact
2 ‹*car*› compact

compagne /kɔ̃paɲ/ *f* **1** (female) companion
2 (female animal) mate

compagnie /kɔ̃paɲi/ *f* **1** company; **en ~ de** together with
2 salut la ~! hello everybody!
3 (commercial) company
4 theatre company
■ **~ aérienne** airline; **~ d'assurance** insurance company; **~ pétrolière** oil company

compagnon /kɔ̃paɲɔ̃/ *m* **1** companion
2 partner
3 mate
4 journeyman
■ **~ de route** fellow traveller (BrE)

comparable /kɔ̃paʀabl/ *adj* comparable

comparaison /kɔ̃paʀɛzɔ̃/ *f* **1** comparison; **c'est sans ~ le plus confortable** it's far and away the most comfortable
2 simile
3 adjectif de ~ comparative adjective

comparaître /kɔ̃paʀɛtʀ/ [**v73**] *vi* (Law) to appear

comparatif, **-ive** /kɔ̃paʀatif, iv/ *adj* comparative

comparé, **~e** /kɔ̃paʀe/ *adj* ‹*literature, law*› comparative

comparer /kɔ̃paʀe/ [**v1**] **A** *vt* to compare
B se comparer *v refl* (+ *v être*) **1 se ~ à qn/qch** to compare oneself with sb/sth
2 to be comparable

comparse /kɔ̃paʀs/ *mf* **1** (in theatre) extra
2 sidekick (fam)

compartiment /kɔ̃paʀtimɑ̃/ *m* compartment

compartimenter /kɔ̃paʀtimɑ̃te/ [**v1**] *vt*
1 **~ un grenier** to divide up a loft with partitions
2 (fig) to compartmentalize ‹*administration*›

compas /kɔ̃pa/ *m* compass

compassion /kɔ̃pasjɔ̃/ *f* compassion

compatible /kɔ̃patibl/ *adj* compatible

compatir /kɔ̃patiʀ/ [**v3**] *vi* to sympathize

compatissant, **~e** /kɔ̃patisɑ̃, ɑ̃t/ *adj* compassionate

compatriote /kɔ̃patʀiɔt/ *mf* fellow countryman/countrywoman, compatriot

compensation /kɔ̃pɑ̃sasjɔ̃/ *f* compensation

compensation carbone *f* carbon offsetting

compensé, **~e** /kɔ̃pɑ̃se/ *adj* **1 semelle ~e** wedge heel
2 (Med) compensated

compenser /kɔ̃pɑ̃se/ [**v1**] *vt* to compensate for; to make up for; to offset

compère /kɔ̃pɛʀ/ *m* partner; accomplice

compétence /kɔ̃petɑ̃s/ *f* **1** ability; competence, skill
2 (Law) competence; **relever de la ~ de qn** to fall within the competence of sb
3 domain

compétent, **~e** /kɔ̃petɑ̃, ɑ̃t/ *adj* competent

compétitif, **-ive** /kɔ̃petitif, iv/ *adj* competitive

compétition /kɔ̃petisjɔ̃/ *f* competition; **en ~ pour** competing for; **faire de la ~** to compete; **sport de ~** competitive sport

complaire: **se complaire** /kɔ̃plɛʀ/ [**v59**] *v refl* (+ *v être*) **se ~ à faire** to take pleasure in doing

complaisance /kɔ̃plɛzɑ̃s/ *f* **1** kindness
2 (derog) soft attitude; **décrire la situation sans ~** to give an objective assessment of the situation
3 (derog) complacency

complaisant, **~e** /kɔ̃plɛzɑ̃, ɑ̃t/ *adj*
1 obliging
2 (derog) indulgent
3 (derog) complacent, self-satisfied

complément /kɔ̃plemɑ̃/ *m* **1** **~ de salaire** extra payment
2 (to funding, programme) supplement
3 **~ de nom** possessive phrase; **~ d'objet direct/indirect** direct/indirect object

complémentaire /kɔ̃plemɑ̃tɛʀ/ *adj*
1 ‹*training, information*› further; ‹*activity,*

amount› supplementary
2 complementary

🔑 **complet**, **-ète** /kɔ̃plɛ, ɛt/ **A** *adj* **1** (gen) complete; ‹*failure*› total; ‹*inquiry, range*› full; ‹*survey*› comprehensive
2 ‹*train, hotel*› full; **être (réuni) au (grand) ~** to be all present
B *m* suit; **~ veston** two-/three-piece suit

🔑 **complètement** /kɔ̃plɛtmɑ̃/ *adv* completely; ‹*read*› right through; **~ réveillé** fully awake

compléter /kɔ̃plete/ [**v14**] **A** *vt* **1** to complete ‹*collection*›; to top up ‹*sum*›
2 ‹*person*› to complement ‹*person*›
3 to complete ‹*sentence*›
B **se compléter** *v refl* (+ *v être*) ‹*elements, people*› to complement each other

🔑 **complexe** /kɔ̃plɛks/ **A** *adj* complex
B *m* **1** (psychological) complex; **il n'a pas de ~** he has no inhibitions
2 (place) complex; **un ~ sportif** a sports complex

complexer /kɔ̃plekse/ [**v1**] *vt* (fam) to give [sb] a complex

complexité /kɔ̃plɛksite/ *f* complexity

complication /kɔ̃plikasjɔ̃/ *f* complication

complice /kɔ̃plis/ **A** *adj* **1 être ~ de qch** to be a party to sth
2 ‹*air*› of complicity
B *mf* accomplice

complicité /kɔ̃plisite/ *f* **1** complicity
2 bond

compliment /kɔ̃plimɑ̃/ **A** *m* compliment
B **compliments** *mpl* (gen) compliments; **(tous) mes ~s!** congratulations!

complimenter /kɔ̃plimɑ̃te/ [**v1**] *vt* to compliment

compliqué, **~e** /kɔ̃plike/ *adj* complicated; ‹*mind*› tortuous

compliquer /kɔ̃plike/ [**v1**] **A** *vt* to complicate
B **se compliquer** *v refl* (+ *v être*) **1** to become more complicated
2 se ~ la vie *or* **l'existence** to make life difficult for oneself

complot /kɔ̃plo/ *m* plot

comploter /kɔ̃plɔte/ [**v1**] *vt, vi* to plot

🔑 **comportement** /kɔ̃pɔʀtəmɑ̃/ *m* **1** (gen) behaviour (BrE)
2 (of sportsman, car) performance

comportementaliste /kɔ̃pɔʀtəmɑ̃talist/ *mf* behaviourist

🔑 **comporter** /kɔ̃pɔʀte/ [**v1**] **A** *vt* **1** to include
2 to comprise, to consist of
3 to entail, to involve
B **se comporter** *v refl* (+ *v être*) **1** to behave, to act
2 ‹*sportsman, car*› to perform

composant /kɔ̃pozɑ̃/ *m* (Tech) component

composante /kɔ̃pozɑ̃t/ *f* element; component

composé, **~e** /kɔ̃poze/ **A** *adj* ‹*salad*› mixed
B *m* (in chemistry) compound

🔑 **composer** /kɔ̃poze/ [**v1**] **A** *vt* **1** ‹*elements, people*› to make up
2 ‹*person*› to put [sth] together ‹*programme, menu*›; to select ‹*team*›; to make up ‹*bouquet*›
3 ‹*artist*› to compose ‹*piece of music*›; to paint ‹*picture*›
4 to dial ‹*number*›
B **se composer** *v refl* (+ *v être*) **se ~ de** to be made up of

compositeur, **-trice** /kɔ̃pozitœʀ, tʀis/ *mf* **1** (Mus) composer
2 typesetter

composition /kɔ̃pozisjɔ̃/ *f* **1** (of government, delegation) make-up; (of team) line-up; (of product) ingredients; (of drug) composition
2 (of government) formation; (of team) selection; (of list, menu) drawing up; **de ma ~** of my invention
3 (of piece of music, picture) composition; (of letter) writing
4 (Sch) end-of-term test
5 typesetting
IDIOM **être de bonne ~** to be good-natured

composter /kɔ̃pɔste/ [**v1**] *vt* to (date)stamp; to punch ‹*ticket*›

compote /kɔ̃pɔt/ *f* (Culin) stewed fruit, compote

compréhensible /kɔ̃pʀeɑ̃sibl/ *adj* **1** understandable
2 comprehensible

compréhensif, **-ive** /kɔ̃pʀeɑ̃sif, iv/ *adj* understanding

compréhension /kɔ̃pʀeɑ̃sjɔ̃/ *f* understanding; comprehension

🔑 **comprendre** /kɔ̃pʀɑ̃dʀ/ [**v52**] **A** *vt* **1** to understand; **c'est à n'y rien ~** it's completely baffling; **mal ~** to misunderstand; **être compris comme une menace** to be interpreted as a threat; **se faire ~** to make oneself understood
2 to consist of, to comprise
3 to include
B **se comprendre** *v refl* (+ *v être*) **1** ‹*people*› to understand each other *or* one another
2 je me comprends I know what I'm trying to say
3 ‹*attitude*› to be understandable

compresse /kɔ̃pʀɛs/ *f* compress

compresser /kɔ̃pʀese/ [**v1**] *vt* to compress

compression /kɔ̃pʀɛsjɔ̃/ *f* **1** (Tech) compression
2 reduction
3 cut; **~s budgétaires** budget cuts

comprimé /kɔ̃pʀime/ *m* tablet

comprimer /kɔ̃pʀime/ [**v1**] *vt* **1** to constrict; to squeeze ‹*tube*›
2 (Med) to compress

3 (Tech) **air comprimé** compressed air

compris, **~e** /kɔ̃pʀi, iz/ **A** *pp* ▸ **comprendre**
B *pp adj* including; **service ~/non ~** service included/not included
C **tout compris** *phr* in total, all in (BrE) (fam)
D **y compris** *phr* including

compromettant, **~e** /kɔ̃pʀɔmetɑ̃, ɑ̃t/ *adj* compromising

compromettre /kɔ̃pʀɔmɛtʀ/ [**v60**] **A** *vt*
1 to endanger, to jeopardize
2 to compromise ‹*person*›; to damage ‹*reputation*›
B **se compromettre** *v refl* (+ *v être*) to compromise oneself

compromis /kɔ̃pʀɔmi/ *m* compromise

comptabiliser /kɔ̃tabilize/ [**v1**] *vt* to count

comptabilité /kɔ̃tabilite/ *f* **1** accountancy
2 bookkeeping; **faire sa ~** to do one's accounts
3 accounts department

comptable /kɔ̃tabl/ **A** *adj* **1** ‹*year*› accounting; ‹*department*› accounts
2 ‹*noun*› countable
B *mf* accountant; bookkeeper

comptant /kɔ̃tɑ̃/ *adv* cash

compte /kɔ̃t/ **A** *m* **1** count; **faire le ~ de qch** to work out ‹*expenditure*›; to count (up) ‹*objects*›; **comment fais-tu ton ~ pour faire...?** (fig) how do you manage to do...?; **tout ~ fait** all things considered; **en fin de ~** at the end of the day
2 (of money) amount; (of objects, people) number; **il n'y a pas le ~** that's not the right amount; that's not the right number; **il a son ~** (fam) he's done for (fam); (drunk) he's had a drop too much; **nous avons eu notre ~ d'ennuis** (fig) we've had more than our fair share of problems; **à ce ~-là** in that case
3 **prendre qch en ~**, **tenir ~ de qch** to take sth into account
4 **être** *or* **travailler à son ~** to be self-employed; **pour le ~ de qn** on behalf of sb; **y trouver son ~** to get something out of it
5 account; **~ en banque** bank account; **mettre qch sur le ~ de qn** to charge sth to sb's account; (fig) to put sth down to sb
6 **rendre ~ de qch à qn** to give an account of sth to sb; to account for sth to sb; **devoir rendre des ~s à qn** to be answerable to sb; **demander des ~s à qn** to ask for an explanation from sb
7 **se rendre ~ de** to realize; to notice
8 **dire qch sur le ~ de qn** to say sth about sb
9 (in boxing) count
B **à bon compte** *phr* **s'en tirer à bon ~** to get off lightly
■ **~ chèques** current account (BrE), checking account (AmE); **~ d'épargne** savings account; **~ épargne logement** savings account (for purchasing a property); **~ chèque postal**, **CCP** post office account; **~ joint** joint account; **~ à rebours** countdown

compte-gouttes /kɔ̃tgut/ *m inv* dropper; **au ~** (fig) sparingly

compter /kɔ̃te/ [**v1**] **A** *vt* **1** to count; **on compte deux millions de chômeurs** there is a total of two million unemployed; **il a toujours compté ses sous** he has always watched the pennies; **sans ~** ‹*give, spend*› freely; **ses jours sont comptés** his/her days are numbered
2 **~ une bouteille pour trois** to allow a bottle between three people
3 (as fee, price) **~ qch à qn** to charge sb for sth
4 to count, to include; **sans ~ les soucis** not to mention the worry
5 to have; **notre club compte des gens célèbres** our club has some well-known people among its members
6 **~ faire** to intend to do
7 **il comptait que je lui prête de l'argent** he expected me to lend him some money
B *vi* **1** to count; **~ au nombre de, ~ parmi** to be counted among
2 to matter; **c'est l'intention qui compte** it's the thought that counts; **ça compte beaucoup pour moi** it means a lot to me
3 to count; **ça ne compte pas, il a triché** it doesn't count, he cheated
4 **~ avec** to reckon with; to take [sb/sth] into account; **~ sans** not to take [sb/sth] into account
5 **~ sur** to count on ‹*person, help*›; (for support) to rely on ‹*person, resource*›; (in anticipation) to reckon on ‹*sum, income*›
C **se compter** *v refl* (+ *v être*) **leurs victoires se comptent par douzaines** they have had dozens of victories
D **à compter de** *phr* as from
E **sans compter que** *phr* and what is more; especially as

compte rendu, *pl* **comptes rendus** /kɔ̃tʀɑ̃dy/ *m* (gen) report; (of book) review

compteur /kɔ̃tœʀ/ *m* meter; clock
■ **~ kilométrique** ≈ milometer; **~ de vitesse** speedometer

comptine /kɔ̃tin/ *f* nursery rhyme

comptoir /kɔ̃twaʀ/ *m* **1** (of cafe) bar
2 (of shop) counter

comte /kɔ̃t/ *m* (title) count; earl

comté /kɔ̃te/ *m* county

comtesse /kɔ̃tɛs/ *f* countess

con, **conne** /kɔ̃, kɔn/ *mf* (vulg) bloody idiot (BrE) (sl), stupid jerk (fam); **idée à la ~** lousy idea (fam)

concasser /kɔ̃kase/ [**v1**] *vt* (Culin, Tech) to crush

concave /kɔ̃kav/ *adj* concave

concéder /kɔ̃sede/ [**v14**] *vt* to concede

concentration /kɔ̃sɑ̃tʀasjɔ̃/ *f* concentration

concentré, **~e** /kɔ̃sɑ̃tʀe/ **A** *pp* ▸ **concentrer**
B *pp adj* **1** **un air ~** a look of concentration

2 concentrated; ‹*lait*› condensed
C *m* (Culin) **~ de tomate** tomato purée (BrE) *or* paste (AmE)

concentrer /kɔ̃sɑ̃tʀe/ [**v1**] **A** *vt* to concentrate
B **se concentrer** *v refl* (+ *v être*) to concentrate; ‹*attention*› to be concentrated

🔑 **concept** /kɔ̃sɛpt/ *m* concept

🔑 **conception** /kɔ̃sɛpsjɔ̃/ *f* **1** conception
2 design
3 idea

concernant /kɔ̃sɛʀnɑ̃/ *prep* **1** concerning
2 as regards, with regard to

🔑 **concerner** /kɔ̃sɛʀne/ [**v1**] *vt* **1** to concern
2 to affect

concert /kɔ̃sɛʀ/ **A** *m* (Mus) concert
B **de concert** *phr* **ils ont agi de ~** they worked together

concertation /kɔ̃sɛʀtasjɔ̃/ *f* **1** consultation
2 cooperation

concerté, **~e** /kɔ̃sɛʀte/ *adj* concerted

concerter: **se concerter** /kɔ̃sɛʀte/ [**v1**] *v refl* (+ *v être*) to consult each other

concerto /kɔ̃sɛʀto/ *m* concerto

concession /kɔ̃sesjɔ̃/ *f* **1** (compromise) concession; **film sans ~s** uncompromising film
2 (awarding of right) concession (**de** of)
3 (right, contract) (of mine, site) concession; (Aut) dealership

concessionnaire /kɔ̃sesjɔnɛʀ/ *mf* (commercial) agent; (Aut) dealer

🔑 **concevoir** /kɔ̃s(ə)vwaʀ/ [**v5**] **A** *vt* **1** to design ‹*product, system*›
2 to conceive ‹*child*›
3 to understand ‹*attitude*›
4 to see ‹*phenomenon, activity*›
5 (fml) to conceive ‹*hatred*›
B **se concevoir** *v refl* (+ *v être*) **1** to be conceivable
2 to be understandable

concierge /kɔ̃sjɛʀʒ/ *mf* caretaker (BrE), superintendent (AmE)

concile /kɔ̃sil/ *m* council

conciliabule /kɔ̃siljabyl/ *m* consultation, confab (fam)

conciliant, **~e** /kɔ̃siljɑ̃, ɑ̃t/ *adj* conciliatory

conciliation /kɔ̃siljasjɔ̃/ *f* conciliation

concilier /kɔ̃silje/ [**v2**] *vt* to reconcile

concis, **~e** /kɔ̃si, iz/ *adj* concise

concision /kɔ̃sizjɔ̃/ *f* conciseness

concitoyen, **-enne** /kɔ̃sitwajɛ̃, ɛn/ *mf* fellow citizen

conclave /kɔ̃klav/ *m* conclave

conclu, **~e** /kɔ̃kly/ ▶ **conclure**

concluant, **~e** /kɔ̃klyɑ̃, ɑ̃t/ *adj* conclusive

🔑 **conclure** /kɔ̃klyʀ/ [**v78**] *vt* **1** to conclude (**que** that)
2 to conclude ‹*deal, agreement*›; **'marché conclu!'** 'it's a deal!'
3 ‹*person*› to conclude ‹*speech*›
4 to bring [sth] to a close ‹*festival*›

🔑 **conclusion** /kɔ̃klyzjɔ̃/ **A** *f* **1** conclusion; **tirer les ~s d'une expérience** to learn from an experience; **ne tire pas de ~s hâtives** don't jump to conclusions
2 (of deal, treaty) conclusion
3 (of speech, session) close
B **conclusions** *fpl* **1** (of analysis, autopsy) results; (of inquiry) findings
2 (Law) (of expert) opinion; (of jury) verdict; (of plaintiff) pleadings

concocter /kɔ̃kɔkte/ [**v1**] *vt* (fam) to concoct ‹*dish*›; to devise ‹*programme*›

concombre /kɔ̃kɔ̃bʀ/ *m* cucumber

concordance /kɔ̃kɔʀdɑ̃s/ *f* concordance; compatibility
■ **~ des temps** sequence of tenses

concorder /kɔ̃kɔʀde/ [**v1**] *vi* ‹*results, evidence*› to tally; ‹*estimates*› to agree

concourir /kɔ̃kuʀiʀ/ [**v26**] **A** *vi* to compete
B **concourir à** *v+prep* **~ à qch/à faire** ‹*factors*› to combine to bring about sth/to do; ‹*factor, person*› to help bring about sth/do

concours /kɔ̃kuʀ/ *m inv* **1** (gen) competition; (agricultural) show; **~ de beauté** beauty contest
2 competitive examination; **~ d'entrée** entrance examination
3 help, assistance; support; cooperation
■ **~ de circonstances** combination of circumstances

concret, **-ète** /kɔ̃kʀɛ, ɛt/ *adj* **1** ‹*result*› concrete
2 ‹*mind, person*› practical

concrètement /kɔ̃kʀɛtmɑ̃/ *adv* **1** in concrete terms
2 in practical terms

concrétisation /kɔ̃kʀetizasjɔ̃/ *f* concrete expression; fulfilment (BrE); achievement

concrétiser /kɔ̃kʀetize/ [**v1**] **A** *vt* to make [sth] a reality ‹*plan, project*›
B **se concrétiser** *v refl* (+ *v être*) ‹*dream*› to become a reality; ‹*offer*› to materialize

concubin, **~e** /kɔ̃kybɛ̃, in/ *mf* common law husband/wife

concubinage /kɔ̃kybinaʒ/ *m* cohabitation

concurrence /kɔ̃kyʀɑ̃s/ *f* competition; **prix défiant toute ~** unbeatable price; **jusqu'à ~ de** up to a limit of

concurrencer /kɔ̃kyʀɑ̃se/ [**v12**] *vt* to compete with

concurrent, **~e** /kɔ̃kyʀɑ̃, ɑ̃t/ **A** *adj* rival
B *mf* (for a job) rival; (Sport) competitor; (in competitive examination) candidate

concurrentiel, **-ielle** /kɔ̃kyʀɑ̃sjɛl/ *adj* competitive

condamnable /kɔ̃danabl/ *adj* reprehensible

condamnation /kɔ̃danasjɔ̃/ *f* **1** (Law) conviction; sentence

🔑 key word

2 condemnation

condamné, **~e** /kɔ̃dane/ **A** *adj* **1** ‹*person*› terminally ill
2 ‹*door*› sealed up
B *mf* convicted prisoner

condamner /kɔ̃dane/ [**v1**] *vt* **1** (Law) to sentence; **~ qn à une amende** to fine sb; **~ qn pour vol** to convict sb of theft
2 ‹*law*› to punish ‹*thieving, smuggling*›
3 ‹*person, country*› to condemn ‹*act, decision*›
4 ~ qn à faire to compel sb to do
5 to seal up ‹*window*›; to shut up ‹*room*›
6 (fig) to spell death for ‹*society, industry*›
7 les médecins l'ont condamné the doctors have given up hope of saving him

condensation /kɔ̃dɑ̃sasjɔ̃/ *f* condensation

condensé /kɔ̃dɑ̃se/ *m* summary; digest

condenser /kɔ̃dɑ̃se/ [**v1**] *vt*, **se condenser** *v refl* (+ *v être*) to condense

condescendance /kɔ̃desɑ̃dɑ̃s/ *f* condescension

condescendant, **~e** /kɔ̃desɑ̃dɑ̃, ɑ̃t/ *adj* condescending

condiment /kɔ̃dimɑ̃/ *m* (Culin) seasoning; condiment

condisciple /kɔ̃disipl/ *mf* fellow student

condition /kɔ̃disjɔ̃/ **A** *f* **1** condition; **à ~ d'avoir le temps** provided (that) one has the time; **sous ~** ‹*freed*› conditionally; **sans ~(s)** ‹*acceptance*› unconditional; ‹*accept*› unconditionally; **imposer ses ~s** to impose one's own terms; **~ préalable** precondition
2 (Law) (of contract, treaty) term
3 la ~ ouvrière (the conditions of) working-class life
4 ~ (sociale) social status
B conditions *fpl* **1** conditions; **dans ces ~s** in these conditions; in that case
2 terms

conditionnel, **-elle** /kɔ̃disjɔnɛl/ **A** *adj* conditional
B *m* conditional

conditionnement /kɔ̃disjɔnmɑ̃/ *m* **1** conditioning
2 packaging
■ **~ sous vide** vacuum packing

conditionner /kɔ̃disjɔne/ [**v1**] *vt* **1** to condition
2 to package

condoléances /kɔ̃dɔleɑ̃s/ *fpl* condolences

condom /kɔ̃dɔm/ *m* condom

condor /kɔ̃dɔʀ/ *m* condor

conducteur, **-trice** /kɔ̃dyktœʀ, tʀis/ **A** *adj* **1** conductive
2 ‹*principle*› guiding
B *mf* (of vehicle) driver
C *m* conductor

conduire /kɔ̃dɥiʀ/ [**v69**] **A** *vt* **1** to take ‹*person*›; (in car) to drive
2 ‹*leader, studies*› to lead; **la route qui conduit à Oxford** the road that goes to Oxford; **~ qn au désespoir** to drive sb to despair
3 to drive ‹*car, train*›; to ride ‹*motorbike*›
4 to conduct ‹*research*›; to carry out ‹*project*›; to run ‹*business*›
5 to conduct ‹*electricity, heat*›
B se conduire *v refl* (+ *v être*) to behave

conduit¹, **~e** /kɔ̃dɥi, ɥit/ ▶ **conduire**

conduit² /kɔ̃dɥi/ *m* **1** conduit
2 (Anat) canal
■ **~ de fumée** flue; **~ de ventilation** ventilation shaft

conduite /kɔ̃dɥit/ *f* **1** behaviour (BrE); (of pupil) conduct
2 (of inquiry) conducting; (of building works) supervision; (of company) management
3 (of vehicle) driving; (of motorbike) riding
4 (Aut) **voiture avec ~ à gauche** left-hand drive car
5 (exam) driving test
6 pipe

cône /kon/ *m* cone

confection /kɔ̃fɛksjɔ̃/ *f* **1** clothing industry
2 making

confectionner /kɔ̃fɛksjɔne/ [**v1**] *vt* (gen) to make; to prepare ‹*meal*›

confédération /kɔ̃fedeʀasjɔ̃/ *f* confederation
■ **la Confédération helvétique** Switzerland

confédéré, **~e** /kɔ̃fedeʀe/ *adj* confederate

conférence /kɔ̃feʀɑ̃s/ *f* **1** lecture
2 conference
3 debate
■ **~ au sommet** summit meeting

conférencier, **-ière** /kɔ̃feʀɑ̃sje, ɛʀ/ *mf* speaker; lecturer

conférer /kɔ̃feʀe/ [**v14**] *vt* to give; to confer

confesser /kɔ̃fese/ [**v1**] **A** *vt* **1** to confess ‹*sin*›
2 ~ qn to hear sb's confession
B se confesser *v refl* (+ *v être*) **1** to go to confession
2 se ~ à un ami to confide in a friend

confession /kɔ̃fesjɔ̃/ *f* **1** confession
2 faith

confessionnal, *pl* **-aux** /kɔ̃fesjɔnal, o/ *m* confessional

confetti /kɔ̃feti/ *m* confetti

confiance /kɔ̃fjɑ̃s/ *f* **1** trust; **de ~** ‹*person*› trustworthy; ‹*mission*› which requires trust; **avoir ~ en qn, faire ~ à qn** to trust sb; **mettre qn en ~** to win sb's trust
2 (in ability, self) confidence; **~ en soi** (self-)confidence

confiant, **~e** /kɔ̃fjɑ̃, ɑ̃t/ *adj* **1** confident
2 (self-)confident
3 trusting

confidence /kɔ̃fidɑ̃s/ *f* secret, confidence; **être dans la ~** to be in on the secret

confident, **~e** /kɔ̃fidɑ̃, ɑ̃t/ *mf* confidant/ confidante

confidentialité /kɔ̃fidɑ̃sjalite/ *f* confidentiality

confidentiel, **-ielle** /kɔ̃fidɑ̃sjɛl/ *adj* confidential

⚷ **confier** /kɔ̃fje/ [**v2**] **A** *vt* **1 ~ qch à qn** to entrust sb with sth ‹*mission*›; to entrust sth to sb ‹*money, letters*›
2 ~ qch à qn to confide sth to sb ‹*intentions*›
B se confier *v refl* (+ *v être*) to confide

configuration /kɔ̃figyʀasjɔ̃/ *f* **1** shape; **la ~ des lieux** the layout of the premises
2 configuration
3 set-up

configurer /kɔ̃figyʀe/ *vt* to configure

confiné, **~e** /kɔ̃fine/ *adj* **1** ‹*atmosphere*› stuffy; ‹*air*› stale
2 ‹*space*› confined, restricted

confiner /kɔ̃fine/ [**v1**] **A** *vt* to confine
B confiner à *v+prep* to border on
C se confiner *v refl* (+ *v être*) to shut oneself away *or* up

confins /kɔ̃fɛ̃/ *mpl* boundaries

confirmation /kɔ̃fiʀmasjɔ̃/ *f* confirmation

⚷ **confirmer** /kɔ̃fiʀme/ [**v1**] **A** *vt* to confirm ‹*order, fact*›; to uphold ‹*decision*›; to be evidence of ‹*attitude, quality*›; to affirm ‹*intention*›
B se confirmer *v refl* (+ *v être*) ‹*news*› to be confirmed; ‹*testimony*› to be corroborated

confiserie /kɔ̃fizʀi/ *f* **1** confectioner's (shop)
2 confectionery

confisquer /kɔ̃fiske/ [**v1**] *vt* to confiscate, to seize

confit, **~e** /kɔ̃fi, it/ **A** *adj* ‹*fruits*› crystallized
B *m* confit; **~ de canard** confit of duck

confiture /kɔ̃fityʀ/ *f* (Culin) jam, preserve; marmalade
(IDIOM) **donner de la ~ aux cochons** to cast pearls before swine

conflictuel, **-elle** /kɔ̃fliktɥɛl/ *adj* ‹*subject*› controversial; ‹*relationship*› confrontational

⚷ **conflit** /kɔ̃fli/ *m* conflict
■ **~ de générations** generation gap; **~ social** industrial strife

confluence /kɔ̃flyɑ̃s/ *f* confluence; (fig) convergence

confluent /kɔ̃flyɑ̃/ *m* confluence

⚷ **confondre** /kɔ̃fɔ̃dʀ/ [**v53**] **A** *vt* **1** to mix up, to confuse; **tous secteurs confondus** all sectors taken together
2 to merge
3 (fml) to stagger, to amaze
4 to expose ‹*traitor*›
B se confondre *v refl* (+ *v être*)
1 ‹*shapes, colours*› to merge; ‹*events, facts*› to become confused
2 ‹*interests, hopes*› to coincide
3 (fml) **se ~ en excuses** to apologize profusely

conforme /kɔ̃fɔʀm/ *adj* **1 être ~ à** to comply with ‹*regulations*›
2 être ~ à l'original to conform to the original

conformément /kɔ̃fɔʀmemɑ̃/ *adv* **~ à** in accordance with

conformer: **se conformer** /kɔ̃fɔʀme/ [**v1**] *v refl* (+ *v être*) to comply with ‹*regulations*›

conformisme /kɔ̃fɔʀmism/ *m* conformity

conformiste /kɔ̃fɔʀmist/ *adj*, *mf* conformist

conformité /kɔ̃fɔʀmite/ *f* **1 ~ à la loi** compliance with the law; **en ~ avec** ‹*act*› in accordance with
2 similarity; **vérifier la ~ de la traduction à l'original** to check that the translation is faithful to the original
3 (of tastes, points of view) correspondence

confort /kɔ̃fɔʀ/ *m* comfort; **maison tout ~** house with all mod cons (BrE) (fam) *or* modern conveniences

confortable /kɔ̃fɔʀtabl/ *adj* comfortable

confortablement /kɔ̃fɔʀtabləmɑ̃/ *adv* comfortably

conforter /kɔ̃fɔʀte/ [**v1**] *vt* to consolidate ‹*position*›; to reinforce ‹*situation*›

confrère /kɔ̃fʀɛʀ/ *m* (at work) colleague; (in association) fellow member

confrérie /kɔ̃fʀeʀi/ *f* brotherhood

confrontation /kɔ̃fʀɔ̃tasjɔ̃/ *f* **1** (of ideas, witnesses) confrontation; (of texts) comparison
2 (between people) debate; clash

confronter /kɔ̃fʀɔ̃te/ [**v1**] *vt* **1** to confront ‹*witnesses*›
2 to compare ‹*texts*›

confus, **~e** /kɔ̃fy, yz/ *adj* **1** confused
2 ‹*feeling, fear*› vague
3 sorry; embarrassed

confusément /kɔ̃fyzemɑ̃/ *adv* ‹*explain*› confusedly; ‹*feel*› vaguely

confusion /kɔ̃fyzjɔ̃/ *f* **1** confusion
2 embarrassment
3 mix-up

congé /kɔ̃ʒe/ *m* **1** leave; **prendre quatre jours de ~** to take four days off; **être en ~ de maladie** to be on sick leave
2 notice; **donner (son) ~ à qn** to give sb notice
3 prendre ~ de qn to take leave of sb

congédier /kɔ̃ʒedje/ [**v2**] *vt* to dismiss

congélateur /kɔ̃ʒelatœʀ/ *m* freezer; (in refrigerator) freezer compartment

congelé, **~e** /kɔ̃ʒle/ *adj* frozen; **produits ~s** frozen foods

congeler /kɔ̃ʒle/ [**v17**] **A** *vt* to freeze
B se congeler *v refl* (+ *v être*) to freeze

⚷ key word

congénital, **~e**, *mpl* **-aux** /kɔ̃ʒenital, o/ *adj* congenital

congère /kɔ̃ʒɛʀ/ *f* snowdrift

congestion /kɔ̃ʒɛstjɔ̃/ *f* congestion
■ **~ cérébrale** stroke

congestionner /kɔ̃ʒɛstjɔne/ [**v1**] *vt* **1 il est tout congestionné** he's all flushed
2 to congest ‹*street*›

conglomérat /kɔ̃glɔmeʀa/ *m*
1 conglomerate
2 (mixture) conglomeration

congrégation /kɔ̃gʀegasjɔ̃/ *f* congregation; (hum) assembly

congrès /kɔ̃gʀɛ/ *m* conference; **le Congrès** (AmE) Congress

congressiste /kɔ̃gʀesist/ *mf* (conference) delegate

conifère /kɔnifɛʀ/ *m* conifer

conique /kɔnik/ *adj* cone-shaped

conjecture /kɔ̃ʒɛktyʀ/ *f* conjecture; **vaines ~s** idle speculation

conjecturer /kɔ̃ʒɛktyʀe/ [**v1**] *vt* to speculate

conjoint, **~e** /kɔ̃ʒwɛ̃, ɛ̃t/ **A** *adj* ‹*action*› joint; ‹*questions*› linked
B *mf* spouse; **les ~s** the husband and wife

conjointement /kɔ̃ʒwɛ̃tmɑ̃/ *adv* **1** jointly
2 at the same time

conjonction /kɔ̃ʒɔ̃ksjɔ̃/ *f* conjunction

conjonctivite /kɔ̃ʒɔ̃ktivit/ *f* conjunctivitis

conjoncture /kɔ̃ʒɔ̃ktyʀ/ *f* situation; circumstances

conjoncturel, **-elle** /kɔ̃ʒɔ̃ktyʀɛl/ *adj* ‹*situation*› economic

conjugaison /kɔ̃ʒygɛzɔ̃/ *f* **1** (of verb) conjugation
2 (fig) combination

conjugal, **~e**, *mpl* **-aux** /kɔ̃ʒygal, o/ *adj* ‹*love*› conjugal; ‹*life*› married

conjugalement /kɔ̃ʒygalmɑ̃/ *adv* ‹*live*› as man and wife

conjuguer /kɔ̃ʒyge/ [**v1**] *vt* **1** to conjugate ‹*verb*›
2 to combine ‹*efforts*›

conjuration /kɔ̃ʒyʀasjɔ̃/ *f* **1** conspiracy
2 (of evil spirits) conjuration

conjurer /kɔ̃ʒyʀe/ [**v1**] *vt* **1** to avert ‹*crisis*›; to ward off ‹*danger*›
2 je vous en conjure I beg you

connaissance /kɔnɛsɑ̃s/ *f* **1** knowledge; **prendre ~ d'un texte** to acquaint oneself with a text; **en ~ de cause** with full knowledge of the facts
2 consciousness; **sans ~** unconscious
3 acquaintance; **faire (plus ample) ~ avec qn** to get to know sb (better); **en pays de ~** among familiar faces; on familiar ground

connaisseur, **-euse** /kɔnɛsœʀ, øz/ *mf* connoisseur, expert

connaître /kɔnɛtʀ/ [**v73**] **A** *vt* **1** to know; **faire ~ à qn** to make [sth] known to sb ‹*decision*›; to introduce sb to ‹*music*›; **je l'ai connu en Chine** I met him in China; **tu connais la nouvelle?** have you heard the news?
2 to experience ‹*hunger, failure*›; to enjoy ‹*success*›; to have ‹*difficulties*›; **~ une forte croissance** to show a rapid growth
B se connaître *v refl* (+ *v être*) **1** to know oneself
2 to know each other; **ils se sont connus à Rome** they met in Rome
3 s'y ~ en vin to know all about wine
IDIOMS **on connaît la chanson** *or* **musique!** we've heard it all before!; **~ qch comme sa poche** to know sth like the back of one's hand

conne (vulg) ▶ **con**

connecter /kɔnɛkte/ [**v1**] *vt* to connect

connexion /kɔnɛksjɔ̃/ *f* connection

connivence /kɔnivɑ̃s/ *f* connivance; **signe de ~** sign of complicity

connotation /kɔnɔtasjɔ̃/ *f* connotation

connu, **~e** /kɔny/ ▶ **connaître**

conquérant, **~e** /kɔ̃keʀɑ̃, ɑ̃t/ *mf* conqueror

conquérir /kɔ̃keʀiʀ/ [**v35**] *vt* to conquer; to capture ‹*market*›; to win over ‹*audience*›
IDIOM **se croire en pays** *or* **terrain conquis** to lord it over everyone

conquête /kɔ̃kɛt/ *f* conquest

conquis, **~e** ▶ **conquérir**

consacré, **~e** /kɔ̃sakʀe/ *adj* **formule ~e** time-honoured (BrE) expression; **artiste ~** recognized artist

consacrer /kɔ̃sakʀe/ [**v1**] **A** *vt* **1** to devote; **pouvez-vous me ~ un instant?** can you spare me a moment?
2 to sanction
3 to consecrate
B se consacrer *v refl* (+ *v être*) **se ~ à** to devote oneself to

consanguin, **~e** /kɔ̃sɑ̃gɛ̃, in/ *adj* ‹*marriage*› between blood relations

consciemment /kɔ̃sjamɑ̃/ *adv* consciously

conscience /kɔ̃sjɑ̃s/ *f* **1** conscience; **avoir bonne/mauvaise ~** to have a clear/a guilty conscience
2 awareness; **prendre ~ de** to become aware of; **prise de ~** realization; **perdre ~** to lose consciousness
■ **~ professionnelle** conscientiousness

consciencieusement /kɔ̃sjɑ̃sjøzmɑ̃/ *adv*
1 conscientiously
2 dutifully

consciencieux, **-ieuse** /kɔ̃sjɑ̃sjø, øz/ *adj* conscientious

conscient, **~e** /kɔ̃sjɑ̃, ɑ̃t/ *adj* **1** aware
2 conscious

conscrit /kɔ̃skʀi/ *m* conscript (BrE), draftee (AmE)

consécration /kɔ̃sekʀasjɔ̃/ *f* **1** (of author) recognition
2 consecration

C

consécutif, -ive /kɔ̃sekytif, iv/ *adj* consecutive; ~ à resulting from; following

consécutivement /kɔ̃sekytivmɑ̃/ *adv* consecutively

🔑 **conseil** /kɔ̃sɛj/ *m* **1** advice; **quelques ~s de prudence** a few words of warning; **il est de bon ~** he always gives good advice; **~s d'entretien** cleaning *or* care instructions
2 council
3 consultant
■ **~ d'administration** board of directors; **~ de classe** (Sch) staff meeting; **~ de discipline** disciplinary committee; **~ général** *council of a French department*

🔑 **conseiller[1], -ère** /kɔ̃seje, ɛʀ/ **A** *mf*
1 adviser (BrE)
2 counsellor (BrE)
B *m* councillor (BrE)
■ **~ commercial** commercial counsellor (BrE); **~ culturel** cultural counsellor (BrE); **~ en développement personnel** life coach; **~ d'État** member of the Council of State; **~ général** *councillor* (BrE) *for a French department*; **~ municipal** town councillor (BrE); **~ d'orientation** careers adviser

conseiller[2] /kɔ̃seje/ [**v1**] *vt* to recommend; to advise; **~ à qn de faire** to advise sb to do

consensus /kɔ̃sɛ̃sys/ *m inv* consensus

consentant, ~e /kɔ̃sɑ̃tɑ̃, ɑ̃t/ *adj* willing; (Law) consenting

consentement /kɔ̃sɑ̃tmɑ̃/ *m* consent

consentir /kɔ̃sɑ̃tiʀ/ [**v30**] **A** *vt* to grant; to allow
B consentir à *v+prep* **~ à qch/à faire** to agree to sth/to do

🔑 **conséquence** /kɔ̃sekɑ̃s/ *f* consequence; **être lourd de ~s** to have serious consequences; **sans ~(s)** of no consequence; **ne pas tirer à ~** to be of no consequence; **avoir pour ~ le chômage** to result in unemployment; **agir en ~** to act accordingly; **avoir des qualifications et un salaire en ~** to have qualifications and a corresponding salary

🔑 **conséquent, ~e** /kɔ̃sekɑ̃, ɑ̃t/ **A** *adj*
1 substantial
2 consistent
B par conséquent *phr* therefore, as a result

conservateur, -trice /kɔ̃sɛʀvatœʀ, tʀis/
A *adj* **1** conservative
2 produit ~ preservative
B *mf* **1** conservative
2 (museum) curator

conservation /kɔ̃sɛʀvasjɔ̃/ *f* conservation; preservation; **lait longue ~** long-life milk (BrE)

conservatoire /kɔ̃sɛʀvatwaʀ/ *m* academy; **~ de musique** conservatoire

conserve /kɔ̃sɛʀv/ **A** *f* **1 la ~, les ~s** canned food; **boîte de ~** can
2 preserve
B de conserve *phr* ‹*act*› in concert

🔑 **conserver** /kɔ̃sɛʀve/ [**v1**] *vt* **1** to keep; to retain; **~ l'anonymat** to remain anonymous
2 (Culin) to preserve; (in vinegar) to pickle
3 ‹*activity*› to keep [sb] young

conserverie /kɔ̃sɛʀvəʀi/ *f* **1** cannery, canning plant
2 canning industry

considérable /kɔ̃sideʀabl/ *adj* considerable, significant; **l'enjeu est ~** the stakes are high

considération /kɔ̃sideʀasjɔ̃/ *f*
1 consideration; **prendre qch en ~** to consider sth, to take sth into account; **en ~ de** in view of; **sans ~ de** irrespective of
2 consideration, factor
3 respect, esteem

🔑 **considérer** /kɔ̃sideʀe/ [**v14**] **A** *vt* **1** to consider, to take into account
2 to consider, to regard; **~ qn/qch comme (étant)** to consider sb/sth to be, to regard sb/sth (as being); **être bien considéré** to be highly regarded
B se considérer *v refl* (+ *v être*) **1 se ~ (comme)**; to consider oneself (to be)
2 se ~ (comme); to regard one another as being

consignation /kɔ̃siɲasjɔ̃/ *f* **1** deposit
2 en ~ on consignment

consigne /kɔ̃siɲ/ *f* **1** orders, instructions; **passer la ~ à qn** to pass the word on to sb; **'~s à suivre en cas d'incendie'** 'fire regulations'
2 left luggage office (BrE), baggage checkroom (AmE)
3 (on bottle) deposit
■ **~ automatique** left luggage lockers (BrE), baggage lockers (AmE)

consigné, ~e /kɔ̃siɲe/ *adj* ‹*bottle*› returnable

consigner /kɔ̃siɲe/ [**v1**] *vt* **1** to record, to write down
2 to confine ‹*soldier*›; to give [sb] detention ‹*pupil*›

consistance /kɔ̃sistɑ̃s/ *f* **1** consistency; **avoir de la/manquer de ~** to be quite thick/ to be too runny
2 substance, weight; **sans ~** ‹*person*› spineless; ‹*rumour*› groundless

consistant, ~e /kɔ̃sistɑ̃, ɑ̃t/ *adj* ‹*meal, investment*› substantial; ‹*dish*› nourishing

🔑 **consister** /kɔ̃siste/ [**v1**] *vi* **1 ~ en** *or* **dans** to consist in; **~ à faire** to consist in doing
2 ~ en to consist of, to be made up of; **en quoi consiste cette aide?** what form does this aid take?

consœur /kɔ̃sœʀ/ *f* **1** female colleague
2 counterpart

consolant, ~e /kɔ̃sɔlɑ̃, ɑ̃t/ *adj* comforting

consolation /kɔ̃sɔlasjɔ̃/ *f* consolation

console /kɔ̃sɔl/ *f* console; **~ de jeu vidéo** games console

🔑 key word

consoler /kɔ̃sɔle/ [**v1**] **A** *vt* to console; **si ça peut te ~** if it is any comfort to you
B **se consoler** *v refl* (+ *v être*) to find consolation; **se ~ de** to get over

consolidable /kɔ̃sɔlidabl/ *adj* **1** ‹*debt*› fundable
2 ‹*structure*› reinforceable

consolidation /kɔ̃sɔlidasjɔ̃/ *f* **1** (of wall) strengthening; (of position) consolidation
2 (of debt) consolidation, funding; (of turnover, balance sheet) consolidation; (of currency) strengthening

consolider /kɔ̃sɔlide/ [**v1**] **A** *vt* to consolidate, to strengthen
B **se consolider** *v refl* (+ *v être*) **1** to grow stronger, to be strengthened
2 to consolidate

consommable /kɔ̃sɔmabl/ **A** *adj* edible; drinkable
B **consommables** *mpl* (Econ, Comput) consumables

consommateur, **-trice** /kɔ̃sɔmatœʀ, tʀis/ *mf* **1** consumer
2 (in bar) customer

consommation /kɔ̃sɔmasjɔ̃/ *f*
1 consumption; **faire une grande ~ de** to use a lot of; **de ~** ‹*goods, society*› consumer
2 drink
3 consummation

consommé /kɔ̃sɔme/ *m* consommé

consommer /kɔ̃sɔme/ [**v1**] *vt* **1** to consume; to use
2 to eat ‹*food*›; to drink ‹*tea*›; to take ‹*drugs*›

consonance /kɔ̃sɔnɑ̃s/ *f* consonance; **mot aux ~s étrangères** foreign-sounding word

consonne /kɔ̃sɔn/ *f* consonant

conspirateur, **-trice** /kɔ̃spiʀatœʀ, tʀis/ *mf* conspirator

conspiration /kɔ̃spiʀasjɔ̃/ *f* conspiracy

conspirer /kɔ̃spiʀe/ [**v1**] **A** *vi* to conspire, to plot
B **conspirer à** *v+prep* to conspire to bring about; **~ à faire** to conspire to do

constamment /kɔ̃stamɑ̃/ *adv* constantly

constance /kɔ̃stɑ̃s/ *f* **1** consistency; constancy
2 steadfastness

constant, **~e** /kɔ̃stɑ̃, ɑ̃t/ *adj* **1** constant; consistent
2 continuous; continual

constante /kɔ̃stɑ̃t/ *f* constant

constat /kɔ̃sta/ *m* certified *or* official report
■ **~ (à l')amiable** *accident report drawn up by the parties involved*; **~ d'échec** admission of failure

constatation /kɔ̃statasjɔ̃/ *f* observation

constater /kɔ̃state/ [**v1**] *vt* **1** to notice, to note; **~ (par) soi-même** to see for oneself
2 to ascertain, to establish
3 to record

constellation /kɔ̃stelasjɔ̃/ *f* constellation

constellé, **~e** /kɔ̃stelle/ *adj* **~ de** spangled with; riddled with; spotted with

consternant, **~e** /kɔ̃stɛʀnɑ̃, ɑ̃t/ *adj*
1 distressing
2 appalling

consternation /kɔ̃stɛʀnasjɔ̃/ *f* consternation

consterner /kɔ̃stɛʀne/ [**v1**] *vt* to fill [sb] with consternation, to dismay

constipation /kɔ̃stipasjɔ̃/ *f* constipation

constipé, **~e** /kɔ̃stipe/ *adj* constipated

constiper /kɔ̃stipe/ [**v1**] *vt* to make [sb] constipated

constitué, **~e** /kɔ̃stitɥe/ *adj* **1 personne bien/mal ~e** person of sound/unsound constitution
2 constituted

constituer /kɔ̃stitɥe/ [**v1**] **A** *vt* **1** to be, to constitute ‹*crime, reason*›
2 to form, to set up ‹*team, commission*›
3 to make up ‹*whole*›
4 (Law) to settle; **~ qn héritier** to appoint sb as heir
B **se constituer** *v refl* (+ *v être*) **1** to build up ‹*network, reserve*›
2 se ~ en to form ‹*party*›
3 se ~ prisonnier to give oneself up

constitutif, **-ive** /kɔ̃stitytif, iv/ *adj* **1** (basic) constituent
2 (Pol) founding; constitutional

constitution /kɔ̃stitysjɔ̃/ *f* **1** (of company) setting up; (of capital) accumulation; (of application) preparing
2 constitution

constructeur, **-trice** /kɔ̃stʀyktœʀ, tʀis/ *mf*
1 (car) manufacturer
2 builder

constructif, **-ive** /kɔ̃stʀyktif, iv/ *adj* constructive

construction /kɔ̃stʀyksjɔ̃/ *f* **1** construction; building; **en ~** under construction; **de ~ japonaise** Japanese built
2 la ~ the construction industry; **~ navale** shipbuilding

construire /kɔ̃stʀɥiʀ/ [**v69**] **A** *vt* to build; to construct
B **se construire** *v refl* (+ *v être*) **1 ça s'est beaucoup construit par ici** there's been a lot of building here
2 se ~ avec le subjonctif to take the subjunctive

consul /kɔ̃syl/ *m* consul

consulat /kɔ̃syla/ *m* consulate

consultant, **~e** /kɔ̃syltɑ̃, ɑ̃t/ *mf* consultant

consultation /kɔ̃syltasjɔ̃/ *f* **1** consultation; consulting; **~ électorale** election
2 surgery hours (BrE), office hours (AmE)

consulter /kɔ̃sylte/ [**v1**] **A** *vt* to consult; **~ le peuple** to hold a general election
B *vi* ‹*doctor*› to see patients
C **se consulter** *v refl* (+ *v être*) to consult together; **se ~ du regard** to exchange glances

consumer /kɔ̃syme/ [**v1**] **A** *vt* ‹*fire*› to consume
B **se consumer** *v refl* (+ *v être*) to burn

🔑 **contact** /kɔ̃takt/ *m* **1** contact; **garder le ~** to keep in touch; **entrer en ~ avec** to get in touch with; **elle est devenue plus sociable à ton ~** she's become more sociable through spending time with you
2 mettre/couper le ~ to switch on/switch off the ignition

contacter /kɔ̃takte/ [**v1**] *vt* to contact, to get in touch with

contagieux, **-ieuse** /kɔ̃taʒjø, øz/ *adj*
1 contagious
2 ‹*laughter*› infectious

contagion /kɔ̃taʒjɔ̃/ *f* contagion

contamination /kɔ̃taminasjɔ̃/ *f* contamination

contaminer /kɔ̃tamine/ [**v1**] *vt* to contaminate; to infect

conte /kɔ̃t/ *m* tale, story

contemplatif, **-ive** /kɔ̃tɑ̃platif, iv/ *adj* contemplative

contemplation /kɔ̃tɑ̃plasjɔ̃/ *f* contemplation

contempler /kɔ̃tɑ̃ple/ [**v1**] *vt* to survey; to contemplate; to look at

🔑 **contemporain**, **~e** /kɔ̃tɑ̃pɔʀɛ̃, ɛn/ *adj*, *mf* contemporary

contenance /kɔ̃t(ə)nɑ̃s/ *f* **1** (of container) capacity
2 bearing, attitude; **perdre ~** to lose one's composure

contenant /kɔ̃t(ə)nɑ̃/ *m* packaging

conteneur /kɔ̃t(ə)nœʀ/ *m* container
■ **~ vert** (for bottles) bottle bank

🔑 **contenir** /kɔ̃t(ə)niʀ/ [**v36**] **A** *vt* **1** to contain ‹*substance, error*›
2 ‹*container*› to hold; ‹*hall*› to accommodate ‹*spectators*›
3 to contain ‹*crowd*›
B **se contenir** *v refl* (+ *v être*) to contain oneself

🔑 **content**, **~e** /kɔ̃tɑ̃, ɑ̃t/ **A** *adj* happy, pleased, glad; **~ de soi** pleased with oneself
B *m* **avoir son ~ de** to have had one's fill of

contentement /kɔ̃tɑ̃tmɑ̃/ *m* contentment

🔑 **contenter** /kɔ̃tɑ̃te/ [**v1**] **A** *vt* to satisfy ‹*customer, curiosity*›; **facile à ~** easy to please
B **se contenter** *v refl* (+ *v être*) **se ~ de qch** to content oneself with sth

contentieux /kɔ̃tɑ̃sjø/ *m* **1** bone of contention
2 legal department
3 litigation

🔑 **contenu**, **~e** /kɔ̃t(ə)ny/ **A** *pp* ▸ **contenir**
B *pp adj* restrained; suppressed
C *m* contents; content

conter /kɔ̃te/ [**v1**] *vt* to tell, to recount

contestable /kɔ̃tɛstabl/ *adj* questionable

contestataire /kɔ̃tɛstatɛʀ/ **A** *adj* anti-authority
B *mf* protester

contestation /kɔ̃tɛstasjɔ̃/ *f* **1** protest
2 challenging; **être sujet à ~**, **prêter à ~** to be questionable; **sans ~ possible** beyond dispute
3 la ~ dissent

conteste: **sans conteste** /sɑ̃kɔ̃tɛst/ *phr* unquestionably

contesté, **~e** /kɔ̃tɛste/ *adj* controversial

contester /kɔ̃tɛste/ [**v1**] **A** *vt* to question; to contest; to dispute; to challenge
B *vi* **1** to raise objections
2 to protest

🔑 **contexte** /kɔ̃tɛkst/ *m* context

contextuel, **-elle** /kɔ̃tɛkstɥɛl/ *adj* **menu ~** pop-up menu

contigu, **-uë** /kɔ̃tigy/ *adj* ‹*rooms*› adjoining

continent, **~e** /kɔ̃tinɑ̃, ɑ̃t/ **A** *adj* continent
B *m* **1** continent
2 mainland

continental, **~e**, *mpl* **-aux** /kɔ̃tinɑ̃tal, o/ *adj* **1** continental
2 mainland

contingent /kɔ̃tɛ̃ʒɑ̃/ *m* **1** contingent; (Mil) conscripts, draft (AmE)
2 quota
3 (Law), (fig) share

continu, **~e** /kɔ̃tiny/ *adj* continuous

continuation /kɔ̃tinɥasjɔ̃/ *f* continuation

continuel, **-elle** /kɔ̃tinɥɛl/ *adj* continual

🔑 **continuer** /kɔ̃tinɥe/ [**v1**] **A** *vt* to continue
B *vi* to continue, to go on

continuité /kɔ̃tinɥite/ *f* continuity

contondant, **~e** /kɔ̃tɔ̃dɑ̃, ɑ̃t/ *adj* blunt

contorsion /kɔ̃tɔʀsjɔ̃/ *f* contortion

contorsionner: **se contorsionner** /kɔ̃tɔʀsjɔne/ [**v1**] *v refl* (+ *v être*) to tie oneself in knots

contorsionniste /kɔ̃tɔʀsjɔnist/ *mf* contortionist

contour /kɔ̃tuʀ/ *m* **1** outline, contour
2 ~s (of road, river) twists and turns

contourner /kɔ̃tuʀne/ [**v1**] *vt* to go round; to by-pass ‹*town*›; to get round ‹*problem*›

contraceptif, **-ive** /kɔ̃tʀasɛptif, iv/ **A** *adj* contraceptive
B *m* contraceptive

contraception /kɔ̃tʀasɛpsjɔ̃/ *f* contraception

contractant, **~e** /kɔ̃tʀaktɑ̃, ɑ̃t/ **A** *adj* contracting
B *mf* contracting party

contracter /kɔ̃tʀakte/ [**v1**] **A** *vt* **1** to tense ‹*muscle*›
2 to incur ‹*debt*›; to take out ‹*loan*›
3 to contract ‹*disease*›
B **se contracter** *v refl* (+ *v être*) ‹*muscle, word*› to contract; ‹*face, person*› to tense up

🔑 key word

contraction /kɔ̃tʀaksjɔ̃/ *f* **1** tenseness
2 contraction

contractuel, **-elle** /kɔ̃tʀaktɥɛl/ **A** *adj* contractual; **personnel ~** contract staff
B *mf* **1** contract employee
2 traffic warden (BrE), meter reader (AmE)

contradiction /kɔ̃tʀadiksjɔ̃/ *f* contradiction

contradictoire /kɔ̃tʀadiktwaʀ/ *adj* contradictory; **~ à** in contradiction to

contraignant, **~e** /kɔ̃tʀɛɲɑ̃, ɑ̃t/ *adj* restrictive

contraindre /kɔ̃tʀɛ̃dʀ/ [**v54**] **A** *vt* **1 ~ qn à faire** to force sb to do
2 to restrain, to curb
B se contraindre *v refl* (+ *v être*) **se ~ à** to force oneself to

contraint, **~e** /kɔ̃tʀɛ̃, ɛ̃t/ *adj* **1 ~ et forcé** (Law) under duress
2 strained, forced

contrainte /kɔ̃tʀɛ̃t/ *f* **1** pressure; coercion
2 constraint
3 sans ~ without restraint, freely

contraire /kɔ̃tʀɛʀ/ **A** *adj* **1** opposite; contrary; ‹*interests*› conflicting; **être ~ aux usages** to be contrary to custom; **dans le cas ~** (should it be) otherwise
2 adverse
B *m* **le ~** the opposite, the contrary; **ne dites pas le ~** don't deny it; **au ~!** on the contrary!

contrairement /kɔ̃tʀɛʀmɑ̃/ *adv* **~ à ce qu'on pourrait penser** contrary to what one might think; **~ à qn** unlike sb

contrariant, **~e** /kɔ̃tʀaʀjɑ̃, ɑ̃t/ *adj*
1 ‹*person*› contrary
2 ‹*event*› annoying

contrarier /kɔ̃tʀaʀje/ [**v2**] *vt* **1** to upset
2 to annoy
3 to frustrate, to thwart

contrariété /kɔ̃tʀaʀjete/ *f* vexation

contraste /kɔ̃tʀast/ *m* contrast

contrasté, **~e** /kɔ̃tʀaste/ *adj* **1** contrasting
2 ‹*photo*› with good contrast
3 ‹*results*› uneven

contraster /kɔ̃tʀaste/ [**v1**] **A** *vt* to contrast ‹*colours*›; to give contrast to ‹*photo*›
B *vi* to contrast

contrat /kɔ̃tʀa/ *m* contract
■ **~ emploi solidarité, CES** part-time low-paid work for the long-term unemployed

contravention /kɔ̃tʀavɑ̃sjɔ̃/ *f* **1** parking ticket; speeding ticket; fine
2 minor offence (BrE)

contre[1] /kɔ̃tʀ/ **A** *prep* **1** against; **22% ~ 18% hier** 22% as against 18% yesterday; **allongés l'un ~ l'autre** lying side by side
2 versus
3 (in exchange) for; **échange-la ~ une bleue** exchange it for a blue one
B par contre *phr* on the other hand

contre[2] /kɔ̃tʀ/ **A** *m* **1 le pour et le ~** the pros and cons
2 (Sport) counter-attack
B *pref* counter

contre-accusation, *pl* **~s** /kɔ̃tʀakyzasjɔ̃/ *f* counter-charge

contre-allée, *pl* **~s** /kɔ̃tʀale/ *f* service road; side path

contre-attaque, *pl* **~s** /kɔ̃tʀatak/ *f* counter-attack

contrebalancer /kɔ̃tʀəbalɑ̃se/ [**v12**] *vt* **1** to counterbalance
2 to offset

contrebande /kɔ̃tʀəbɑ̃d/ *f* **1** smuggling
2 smuggled goods, contraband

contrebandier, **-ière** /kɔ̃tʀəbɑ̃dje, ɛʀ/ *mf* smuggler

contrebas: **en contrebas** /ɑ̃kɔ̃tʀəba/ *phr* (down) below; **en ~ de** below

contrebasse /kɔ̃tʀəbas/ *f* double bass

contrecarrer /kɔ̃tʀəkaʀe/ [**v1**] *vt* to thwart, to foil; to counteract

contrechamp /kɔ̃tʀəʃɑ̃/ *m* reverse shot

contrecœur: **à contrecœur** /akɔ̃tʀəkœʀ/ *phr* reluctantly

contrecoup /kɔ̃tʀəku/ *m* effects; after-effects; **par ~** as a result

contre-courant, *pl* **~s** /kɔ̃tʀəkuʀɑ̃/ *m* counter-current; **nager à ~** to swim against the current; **aller à ~ de la mode** to go against the fashion

contredire /kɔ̃tʀədiʀ/ [**v65**] **A** *vt* to contradict
B se contredire *v refl* (+ *v être*) **1** to contradict oneself
2 to contradict each other

contrée /kɔ̃tʀe/ *f* **1** land
2 region

contre-enquête, *pl* **~s** /kɔ̃tʀɑ̃kɛt/ *f* second enquiry (BrE)

contre-espionnage, *pl* **~s** /kɔ̃tʀɛspjɔnaʒ/ *m* counter-intelligence

contre-expertise, *pl* **~s** /kɔ̃tʀɛkspɛʀtiz/ *f* second opinion

contrefaçon /kɔ̃tʀəfasɔ̃/ *f* **1** forging, counterfeiting
2 forgery, counterfeit

contrefacteur /kɔ̃tʀəfaktœʀ/ *m* (of notes, credit cards, paintings) forger; (of coins) counterfeiter; (of software, invention) pirate

contrefaire /kɔ̃tʀəfɛʀ/ [**v10**] *vt* **1** to forge, to counterfeit
2 to imitate
3 to disguise

contrefort /kɔ̃tʀəfɔʀ/ *m* **1** foothills
2 buttress
3 (of shoe) back

contre-indiqué, **~e**, *mpl* **~s** /kɔ̃tʀɛ̃dike/ *adj* contraindicated; inadvisable

contre-interrogatoire, *pl* **~s** /kɔ̃tʀɛ̃teʀɔgatwaʀ/ *m* cross-examination

contre-jour, *pl* **~s** /kɔ̃tʀəʒuʀ/ *m* backlighting; **à ~** against *or* into the light

C

C

contremaître, **-esse** /kɔ̃tʀəmɛtʀ, kɔ̃tʀəmɛtʀɛs/ *mf* foreman/forewoman

contrepartie /kɔ̃tʀəpaʀti/ *f* **1** equivalent
2 compensation; **en ∼** in compensation; in return; **mais la ∼ est que le salaire est élevé** but this is offset by the high salary

contre-pied, *pl* **∼s** /kɔ̃tʀəpje/ *m* **prendre le ∼ de ce que dit qn** to say the opposite of what sb says

contreplaqué /kɔ̃tʀəplake/ *m* plywood

contrepoids /kɔ̃tʀəpwa/ *m* counterweight

contrer /kɔ̃tʀe/ [**v1**] *vt* to counter; to block

contresens /kɔ̃tʀəsɑ̃s/ *m*
1 misinterpretation
2 mistranslation
3 à ∼ in the opposite direction; the wrong way; against the grain

contretemps /kɔ̃tʀətɑ̃/ *m inv* **1** setback, contretemps
2 à ∼ (Mus) on the off-beat; out of time; (fig) at the wrong moment

contre-valeur, *pl* **∼s** /kɔ̃tʀəvalœʀ/ *f* exchange value

contrevenir /kɔ̃tʀəvəniʀ/ [**v36**] *v+prep* **∼ à** to contravene

contribuable /kɔ̃tʀibɥabl/ *mf* taxpayer

⚷ **contribuer** /kɔ̃tʀibɥe/ [**v1**] *v+prep* **∼ à** to contribute to; to pay one's share of; **cela y a beaucoup contribué** it was a major factor

contribution /kɔ̃tʀibysjɔ̃/ *f* **1** contribution; **mettre qn à ∼** to call upon sb's services
2 ∼s taxes; tax office

contrit, **∼e** /kɔ̃tʀi, it/ *adj* contrite, apologetic

⚷ **contrôle** /kɔ̃tʀol/ *m* **1** control
2 check; **∼ de police** police check; **∼ des billets** ticket inspection
3 (Sch) test; **∼ de géographie** geography test
4 check-up
5 monitoring; **sous ∼ médical** under medical supervision
■ **∼ continu (des connaissances)** continuous assessment; **∼ fiscal** tax investigation; **∼ technique (des véhicules)** MOT (test)

⚷ **contrôler** /kɔ̃tʀole/ [**v1**] **A** *vt* **1** to control
2 to monitor
3 to check; to inspect; to test
B se contrôler *v refl* (+ *v être*) to control oneself

contrôleur, **-euse** /kɔ̃tʀolœʀ, øz/ *mf* inspector; **∼ aérien** air traffic controller

contrordre /kɔ̃tʀɔʀdʀ/ *m* **1 ordres et ∼s** conflicting orders; **j'irai vendredi, sauf ∼** I'll go on Friday, unless I hear to the contrary
2 counter command

controverse /kɔ̃tʀɔvɛʀs/ *f* controversy

controversé, **∼e** /kɔ̃tʀɔvɛʀse/ *adj* controversial

contusion /kɔ̃tyzjɔ̃/ *f* bruise

convaincant, **∼e** /kɔ̃vɛ̃kɑ̃, ɑ̃t/ *adj*
1 convincing
2 persuasive

⚷ **convaincre** /kɔ̃vɛ̃kʀ/ [**v57**] **A** *vt* to convince; to persuade
B se convaincre *v refl* (+ *v être*) to convince oneself

convaincu, **∼e** /kɔ̃vɛ̃ky/ **A** *pp* ▸ **convaincre**
B *pp adj* **1** convinced; **d'un ton ∼** with conviction
2 ‹*supporter*› staunch

convalescence /kɔ̃valesɑ̃s/ *f* convalescence

convalescent, **∼e** /kɔ̃valesɑ̃, ɑ̃t/ *adj, mf* convalescent

convenable /kɔ̃vnabl/ *adj* **1** suitable
2 reasonable
3 decent; proper; respectable

convenablement /kɔ̃vnabləmɑ̃/ *adv* properly; reasonably well; decently

convenance /kɔ̃vnɑ̃s/ *f* **1 pour ∼ personnelle** for personal reasons; **à votre ∼** at your convenience
2 ∼s (social) conventions

⚷ **convenir** /kɔ̃vniʀ/ [**v36**] **A** *vt* **1** to admit
2 to agree
B convenir à *v+prep* to suit; to be suitable for
C convenir de *v+prep* **1 ∼ de** to admit, to acknowledge
2 ∼ de to agree on
D *v impers* **1 il convient de faire/que vous fassiez** one/you should do
2 ce qu'il est convenu d'appeler le réalisme what is commonly called realism; **comme convenu** as agreed

⚷ **convention** /kɔ̃vɑ̃sjɔ̃/ *f* **1** agreement
2 convention; **de ∼** conventional

conventionné, **∼e** /kɔ̃vɑ̃sjɔne/ *adj* ‹*doctor, costs*› national health service; ‹*clinic*› registered; **médecin non ∼** private doctor

conventionnel, **-elle** /kɔ̃vɑ̃sjɔnɛl/ *adj*
1 conventional
2 contractual

convenu, **∼e** /kɔ̃v(ə)ny/ **A** *pp* ▸ **convenir**
B *pp adj* **1** ‹*date, terms*› agreed
2 ‹*phrase*› conventional; ‹*smile*› polite

convergence /kɔ̃vɛʀʒɑ̃s/ *f* convergence

converger /kɔ̃vɛʀʒe/ [**v13**] *vi* to converge

⚷ **conversation** /kɔ̃vɛʀsasjɔ̃/ *f* conversation; **avoir de la ∼** to be a good conversationalist; **dans la ∼ courante** in everyday speech

converser /kɔ̃vɛʀse/ [**v1**] *vi* to converse

conversion /kɔ̃vɛʀsjɔ̃/ *f* conversion

converti, **∼e** /kɔ̃vɛʀti/ **A** *pp* ▸ **convertir**
B *mf* convert

convertible /kɔ̃vɛʀtibl/ *adj* **1** convertible
2 canapé ∼ sofa bed

convertir /kɔ̃vɛʀtiʀ/ [**v3**] **A** *vt* to convert
B se convertir *v refl* (+ *v être*) to convert; ‹*company*› to change product

convertisseur /kɔ̃vɛʀtisœʀ/ *m* converter

⚷ key word

convexe /kɔ̃vɛks/ *adj* convex
conviction /kɔ̃viksjɔ̃/ *f* conviction
convier /kɔ̃vje/ [**v2**] *vt* to invite ‹*person*›
convive /kɔ̃viv/ *mf* guest
convivial, **~e**, *mpl* **-iaux** /kɔ̃vivjal, o/ *adj* **1** convivial
2 user-friendly
convivialité /kɔ̃vivjalite/ *f* **1** friendliness; conviviality
2 user-friendliness
convocation /kɔ̃vɔkasjɔ̃/ *f* **1** (of meeting) convening; (of person) summoning; (Mil) calling up
2 notice to attend; (Law) summons; **~ aux examens** notification of examination timetables
convoi /kɔ̃vwa/ *m* **1** convoy; **'~ exceptionnel'** (Aut) 'wide *or* dangerous load'
2 train
convoiter /kɔ̃vwate/ [**v1**] *vt* to covet
convoitise /kɔ̃vwatiz/ *f* **la ~** covetousness; **~ de** lust for
convoquer /kɔ̃vɔke/ [**v1**] *vt* to call, to convene ‹*meeting*›; to send for ‹*pupil*›; to summon ‹*witness*›; to call up ‹*soldier*›; **être convoqué à un examen** to be asked to attend an exam
convoyer /kɔ̃vwaje/ [**v23**] *vt* to escort
convoyeur, **-euse** /kɔ̃vwajœʀ, øz/ *mf* **1** prison escort
2 courier; **~ de fonds** security guard
convulsif, **-ive** /kɔ̃vylsif, iv/ *adj* **1** convulsive
2 ‹*laughter*› nervous
convulsion /kɔ̃vylsjɔ̃/ *f* convulsion
convulsionner /kɔ̃vylsjɔne/ [**v1**] *vt* to convulse
coopératif, **-ive** /kɔɔpeʀatif, iv/ **A** *adj* cooperative
B **coopérative** *f* cooperative
coopération /kɔɔpeʀasjɔ̃/ *f* **1** cooperation
2 cultural/technical aid
coopérer /kɔɔpeʀe/ [**v14**] *vi* to cooperate
coordinateur, **-trice** /kɔɔʀdinatœʀ, tʀis/ **A** *adj* coordinating
B *mf* coordinator
coordination /kɔɔʀdinasjɔ̃/ *f* **1** coordination
2 joint committee
coordonné, **~e** /kɔɔʀdɔne/ **A** *pp* ▸ **coordonner**
B *pp adj* coordinated; coordinating
C **coordonnés** *mpl* (in fashion) coordinates
coordonnées /kɔɔʀdɔne/ *fpl* **1** (on graph, map) coordinates
2 information
3 address and telephone number
coordonner /kɔɔʀdɔne/ [**v1**] *vt* to coordinate
copain, **copine** /kɔpɛ̃, in/ **A** *adj* pally (BrE) (fam), chummy (fam)
B *mf* **1** friend
2 boyfriend/girlfriend
copeau, *pl* **~x** /kɔpo/ *m* shaving
Copenhague /kopɛnag/ *pr n* Copenhagen
copie /kɔpi/ *f* **1** copying; copy
2 (Sch) paper
copier /kɔpje/ [**v2**] *vt* **1** to copy
2 (Sch) **~ sur qn** to copy *or* crib from sb
copier-coller /kɔpjekɔle/ [**v1**] *vt* (Comput) to copy and paste
copieur, **-ieuse** /kɔpjœʀ, øz/ **A** *mf* (Sch) cheat
B *m* photocopier
copieusement /kɔpjøzmɑ̃/ *adv* heartily; lavishly; copiously
copieux, **-ieuse** /kɔpjø, øz/ *adj* ‹*meal*› hearty; ‹*portion*› generous; ‹*notes*› copious
copilote /kopilɔt/ *mf* co-pilot; co-driver
copine ▸ **copain**
coprésident, **~e** /kopʀezidɑ̃, ɑ̃t/ *mf* joint president; co-chair
coproduction /kopʀɔdyksjɔ̃/ *f* co-production
copropriété /kopʀɔpʀijete/ *f* joint ownership; co-ownership
coq /kɔk/ *m* cockerel, rooster; cock; **au chant du ~** at cockcrow; **le ~ du village** (fig) the local Casanova
■ **~ de bruyère** grouse
IDIOMS **être comme un ~ en pâte** to be in clover; **sauter du ~ à l'âne** to hop from one subject to another
coque /kɔk/ *f* **1** (of boat) hull; (of hydroplane) fuselage; (of car) body
2 cockle
3 (of nut) shell
coquelicot /kɔkliko/ *m* poppy
coqueluche /kɔklyʃ/ *f* **1** whooping cough
2 (fam) idol
coquet, **-ette** /kɔkɛ, ɛt/ *adj* **1** **être ~** to be particular about one's appearance
2 pretty
3 (fam) ‹*sum*› tidy (fam)
coquetier /kɔktje/ *m* egg cup
coquetterie /kɔkɛtʀi/ *f* interest in one's appearance; vanity; **par ~** out of vanity
coquillage /kɔkijaʒ/ *m* **1** shellfish
2 shell
coquille /kɔkij/ *f* **1** shell
2 scallop-shaped dish; **~ de saumon** salmon served in a shell
3 misprint
4 (Med) spinal jacket
■ **~ Saint-Jacques** scallop; scallop shell
coquillette /kɔkijɛt/ *f* small macaroni
coquin, **~e** /kɔkɛ̃, in/ **A** *adj* **1** mischievous
2 naughty, saucy
B *mf* rascal
cor /kɔʀ/ *m* **1** (Mus) horn
2 (Med) corn
IDIOM **réclamer *or* demander qch à ~ et à cri** to clamour (BrE) for sth
corail, *pl* **-aux** /kɔʀaj, o/ *adj inv*, *m* coral

C

Coran /kɔʀɑ̃/ *pr m* **le ~** the Koran
corbeau, *pl* **~x** /kɔʀbo/ *m* **1** crow; **grand ~** raven
2 (fam) writer of a poison pen letter
corbeille /kɔʀbɛj/ *f* **1** basket
2 dress circle
corbillard /kɔʀbijaʀ/ *m* hearse
⚷ **corde** /kɔʀd/ *f* **1** rope
2 ~ (à sauter) skipping rope
3 (of racket, instrument) string
■ **~ à linge** clothes line; **~ raide** tightrope; **~s vocales** vocal chords
IDIOMS **mériter la ~** to deserve to be hanged; **pleuvoir** *or* **tomber des ~s** to be raining cats and dogs (fam); **tirer sur la ~** to push one's luck; **faire jouer la ~ sensible** to tug at the heartstrings; **usé jusqu'à la ~** threadbare
cordée /kɔʀde/ *f* roped party (of climbers)
cordelière /kɔʀdəljɛʀ/ *f* cord
cordial, **~e**, *mpl* **-iaux** /kɔʀdjal, o/ *adj* cordial; warm-hearted; warm
cordialement /kɔʀdjalmɑ̃/ *adv* warmly; **~ (vôtre** *or* **à vous)** yours sincerely
cordialité /kɔʀdjalite/ *f* warmth; friendliness
cordillère /kɔʀdijɛʀ/ *f* cordillera
cordon /kɔʀdɔ̃/ *m* **1** cord; string; lace
2 flex (BrE), cord (AmE)
3 cordon
4 row
5 ribbon
■ **~ ombilical** umbilical cord
cordonnerie /kɔʀdɔnʀi/ *f* **1** shoemaking
2 shoe repairing
3 cobbler's
cordonnier /kɔʀdɔnje/ *m* cobbler
IDIOM **les ~s sont toujours les plus mal chaussés** it's always the baker's children who have no bread
Corée /kɔʀe/ *pr f* Korea
coriace /kɔʀjas/ *adj* tough
coriandre /kɔʀjɑ̃dʀ/ *f* coriander
Corinthe /kɔʀɛ̃t/ *pr n* **raisins de ~** currants
corne /kɔʀn/ *f* **1** horn; antler; **à ~s** horned; **blesser d'un coup de ~** to gore
2 (Mus) horn
3 (fam) **avoir de la ~ aux pieds** to have calluses on one's feet
■ **~ d'abondance** horn of plenty, cornucopia; **~ de brume** foghorn
cornée /kɔʀne/ *f* cornea
corneille /kɔʀnɛj/ *f* crow
cornemuse /kɔʀnəmyz/ *f* bagpipes
corner /kɔʀne/ [**v1**] *vt* to turn down the corner of ‹*page*›; **page cornée** dog-eared page
cornet /kɔʀnɛ/ *m* **1** (paper) cone
2 (ice-cream) cone, cornet (BrE)
■ **~ à dés** dice cup; **~ à pistons** cornet

⚷ key word

corniche /kɔʀniʃ/ *f* **1** cornice
2 moulding (BrE), molding (AmE)
3 ledge (of rock)
4 cliff road
cornichon /kɔʀniʃɔ̃/ *m* gherkin
Cornouailles /kɔʀnuɑj/ *pr f* Cornwall
corollaire /kɔʀɔlɛʀ/ *m* corollary
corolle /kɔʀɔl/ *f* **1** corolla
2 en ~ ‹*skirt*› flared
coron /kɔʀɔ̃/ *m* miners' terraced houses
corporatif, **-ive** /kɔʀpɔʀatif, iv/ *adj* corporate
corporation /kɔʀpɔʀasjɔ̃/ *f* corporation
corporel, **-elle** /kɔʀpɔʀɛl/ *adj* ‹*needs*› bodily; ‹*punishment*› corporal
⚷ **corps** /kɔʀ/ *m inv* body; **(combat) ~ à ~** hand-to-hand combat; **se donner ~ et âme à** to give oneself body and soul to; **faire ~ avec** ‹*person*› to stand solidly behind; ‹*building*› to be joined to; **prendre ~** to take shape
■ **~ enseignant** teaching profession; **~ et biens** (to sink) with all hands; **~ expéditionnaire** expeditionary force; **~ gras** fatty substance; **~ médical** medical profession
IDIOM **tenir au ~** to be nourishing
corpulence /kɔʀpylɑ̃s/ *f* stoutness
corpulent, **~e** /kɔʀpylɑ̃, ɑ̃t/ *adj* stout, corpulent
correct, **~e** /kɔʀɛkt/ *adj* **1** ‹*calculation*› correct; ‹*copy*› accurate
2 ‹*outfit*› proper; ‹*conduct*› correct
3 (fam) ‹*result, wine*› reasonable, decent
4 ‹*person*› polite; fair, correct
correctement /kɔʀɛktəmɑ̃/ *adv* **1** correctly
2 properly
3 decently, reasonably well
correcteur, **-trice** /kɔʀɛktœʀ, tʀis/ **A** *adj* corrective
B *mf* **1** examiner (BrE), grader (AmE)
2 proofreader
correction /kɔʀɛksjɔ̃/ *f* **1** correcting; proofreading; marking (BrE), grading (AmE)
2 correction
3 thrashing
4 correctness; good manners
correctionnel, **-elle** /kɔʀɛksjɔnɛl/ *adj* **tribunal ~** magistrate's court
correctionnelle /kɔʀɛksjɔnɛl/ *f* magistrate's court
corrélation /kɔʀelasjɔ̃/ *f* correlation; **être en ~ avec qn** to be related to sth
correspondance /kɔʀɛspɔ̃dɑ̃s/ *f* **1** letters; mail; correspondence; **faire sa ~** to write some letters; **vendu par ~** available by mail order
2 correspondence
3 connection; **trains/vols en ~** connecting trains/flights
correspondant, **~e** /kɔʀɛspɔ̃dɑ̃, ɑ̃t/ **A** *adj* corresponding
B *mf* correspondent; (Sch) pen pal

correspondre /kɔʀɛspɔ̃dʀ/ [**v6**]
A correspondre à *v+prep* to correspond to; to match; to suit ‹*tastes*›
B *vi* to correspond, to write
C se correspondre *v refl* (+ *v être*) to correspond

corrida /kɔʀida/ *f* bullfight

corridor /kɔʀidɔʀ/ *m* corridor

corrigé /kɔʀiʒe/ *m* (Sch) correct version

corriger /kɔʀiʒe/ [**v13**] **A** *vt* **1** to correct; to proofread ‹*manuscript*›; to mark (BrE), to grade (AmE) ‹*exam papers*›; to redress ‹*situation*›
2 to adjust ‹*position*›; to modify ‹*theory*›; **~ le tir** (Mil) to alter one's aim; (fig) to adjust one's tactics
3 to give [sb] a hiding (fam); to spank ‹*child*›
B se corriger *v refl* (+ *v être*) **1** to correct oneself
2 se ~ d'un défaut to cure oneself of a fault

corroborer /kɔʀɔbɔʀe/ [**v1**] *vt* to corroborate

corroder /kɔʀɔde/ [**v1**] *vt* to corrode

corrompre /kɔʀɔ̃pʀ/ [**v53**] *vt* **1** to bribe
2 to corrupt

corrompu, **~e** /kɔʀɔ̃py/ **A** *pp* ▶ **corrompre**
B *pp adj* corrupt

corrosif, **-ive** /kɔʀɔzif, iv/ *adj* **1** ‹*substance*› corrosive
2 ‹*humour*› caustic

corrosion /kɔʀɔzjɔ̃/ *f* corrosion

corruption /kɔʀypsjɔ̃/ *f* **1** corruption
2 bribery

corsage /kɔʀsaʒ/ *m* **1** blouse
2 bodice

corsaire /kɔʀsɛʀ/ *m* **1** corsair
2 pedal pushers

corse /kɔʀs/ *adj, m* Corsican

Corse /kɔʀs/ *pr f* Corsica

corsé, **~e** /kɔʀse/ *adj* ‹*coffee*› strong; ‹*sauce, story*› spicy; ‹*problem*› tough; ‹*bill*› steep

corser /kɔʀse/ [**v1**] **A** *vt* **1** to make [sth] more difficult; **pour ~ l'affaire** (just) to complicate matters
2 to make [sth] spicier ‹*sauce*›
B se corser *v refl* (+ *v être*) to get more complicated

corset /kɔʀsɛ/ *m* corset

corso /kɔʀso/ *m* **~ fleuri** procession of floral floats

cortège /kɔʀtɛʒ/ *m* procession

corvée /kɔʀve/ *f* chore; (Mil) fatigue (duty)

cosmétique /kɔsmetik/ *adj, m* cosmetic

cosmique /kɔsmik/ *adj* cosmic

cosmonaute /kɔsmɔnot/ *mf* cosmonaut

cosmopolite /kɔsmɔpɔlit/ *adj* cosmopolitan

cosse /kɔs/ *f* (of pea) pod; (of grain) husk

cossu, **~e** /kɔsy/ *adj* ‹*person*› well-to-do; ‹*interior*› plush; ‹*house*› smart

costaud /kɔsto/ *adj* (fam) strong, sturdy; hefty (fam)

costume /kɔstym/ *m* **1** suit
2 costume; **répétition en ~** dress rehearsal

costumer: **se costumer** /kɔstyme/ [**v1**] *v refl* (+ *v être*) **se ~ en** to dress up as; **soirée costumée** fancy-dress party

cotation /kɔtasjɔ̃/ *f* quotation

cote /kɔt/ *f* **1** (of stocks, commodities) quotation; (stock exchange) list
2 (of stamp) quoted value
3 (at races) odds
4 (of person, film) rating; **avoir la ~** (fam) **auprès de** to be popular with; to be well thought of by
5 (on plan) dimension
6 (on map) spot height
■ **~ d'alerte** flood level; (fig) danger level; **~ de popularité** popularity rating

côte /kot/ **A** *f* **1** coast
2 hill; **dans une ~** on a hill
3 rib
4 chop; **~ de bœuf** rib roast
B côte à côte *phr* side by side
■ **Côte d'Azur** French riviera

coté, **~e** /kɔte/ **A** *pp* ▶ **coter**
B *pp adj* **être ~** to be well thought of

côté /kote/ **A** *m* **1** side; **du ~ droit/gauche** on the right-hand/left-hand side; **chambre ~ rue** room overlooking the street; **par certains ~s** in some respects; **~ santé** health-wise; **de mon ~, je pense que...** for my part, I think that...; **d'un ~... d'un autre ~...** on the one hand... on the other hand...
2 way, direction; **de tous ~s** ‹*come*› from all directions; ‹*run*› all over the place; **du ~ de Nice** ‹*live*› near Nice; **aller du ~ de Dijon** to head for Dijon
B à côté *phr* **1** nearby; **les gens d'à ~** the people next door; **à ~ de** next to; **le ballon est passé à ~ (du but)** the ball went wide (of the goal); **répondre à ~** (by mistake) to miss the point; (on purpose) to sidestep the question
2 by comparison
3 on the side; **elle est étudiante et travaille à ~** she's a student and works on the side
C de côté *phr* **1** sideways
2 aside; **mettre qch de ~** to put sth aside ‹*money, object*›
D aux côtés de *phr* **aux ~s de qn** ‹*to be*› at sb's side; ‹*to work*› alongside sb

coteau, *pl* **~x** /kɔto/ *m* **1** hillside
2 hill
3 (sloping) vineyard

côtelette /kotlɛt/ *f* (Culin) chop

coter /kɔte/ [**v1**] *vt* **1** to quote, to list ‹*shares*›; to price ‹*car*›
2 to rate ‹*film*›

côtier, **-ière** /kotje, ɛʀ/ *adj* coastal; inshore

cotisation /kɔtizasjɔ̃/ *f* **1** contribution
2 subscription

cotiser /kɔtize/ [**v1**] **A** *vi* **1** to pay one's contributions
2 to pay one's subscription (**à** to)
B se cotiser *v refl* (+ *v être*) to club together (BrE), to go in together

C

co-titulaire /kotitylɛʀ/ *mf* joint account-holder

coton /kɔtɔ̃/ *m* **1** cotton
2 thread
3 cotton wool (BrE), cotton (AmE)
IDIOMS **filer un mauvais ~** to be in a bad way; **élever un enfant dans du ~** to give a child a very sheltered upbringing; **j'ai les jambes en ~** (after shock) my legs have turned to jelly

cotonnade /kɔtɔnad/ *f* cotton fabric

cotonneux, **-euse** /kɔtɔnø, øz/ *adj* ‹*fog*› like cotton wool; ‹*cloud*› fleecy

côtoyer /kotwaje/ [**v23**] **A** *vt* to walk alongside ‹*river*›; to move in ‹*milieu*›; to mix with ‹*people*›; to be in close contact with ‹*death*›
B se côtoyer *v refl* (+ *v être*) ‹*people*› to mix

cotte /kɔt/ *f* overalls
■ **~ de mailles** coat of mail

⚷ **cou** /ku/ *m* neck; **être endetté jusqu'au ~** to be up to one's eyes in debt

couchage /kuʃaʒ/ *m* bedding; **un studio avec ~ pour six** a studio that sleeps six

couchant /kuʃɑ̃/ **A** *adj* **au soleil ~** at sunset
B *m* **1** sunset
2 west

⚷ **couche** /kuʃ/ *f* **1** layer; (of paint) coat
2 nappy (BrE), diaper (AmE)
3 class, sector

couché, **~e** /kuʃe/ **A** *pp* ▶ **coucher**
B *pp adj* ‹*grass*› flattened; ‹*writing*› sloping

couche-culotte, *pl* **couches-culottes** /kuʃkylɔt/ *f* disposable nappy (BrE) *or* diaper (AmE)

⚷ **coucher** /kuʃe/ [**v1**] **A** *m* bedtime
B *vt* **1** to put [sb] to bed; to lay out ‹*wounded person*›
2 to lay [sth] on its side; to lay [sth] down
3 to flatten ‹*grass*›
C *vi* to sleep; **~ sous les ponts** to sleep rough (BrE) *or* outdoors
D se coucher *v refl* (+ *v être*) **1** to lie (down)
2 to go to bed
3 ‹*stem*› to bend; ‹*boat*› to list; **se ~ sur** ‹*cyclist*› to lean forward over ‹*handlebars*›
4 ‹*sun*› to set
■ **~ de soleil** sunset

couchette /kuʃɛt/ *f* couchette, berth

couci-couça /kusikusa/ *adv* (fam) so-so (fam)

coucou /kuku/ **A** *m* **1** cuckoo
2 cowslip
3 (fam) (old) crate (fam), plane
4 cuckoo clock
B *excl* (fam) **1** cooee!
2 peekaboo!

coude /kud/ *m* **1** elbow; **travailler ~ à ~** to work shoulder to shoulder
2 (in river, pipe) bend
IDIOM **se serrer les ~s** to stick together

coudé, **~e** /kude/ *adj* bent at an angle

coudée /kude/ *f* **avoir les ~s franches** to have elbow room

cou-de-pied, *pl* **cous-de-pied** /kudpje/ *m* instep

couder /kude/ [**v1**] *vt* to bend

coudre /kudʀ/ [**v76**] *vt* to sew; to sew [sth] on; to stitch [sth] on; to stitch (up)
IDIOM **leur histoire est cousue de fil blanc** you can see right through their story

couenne /kwan/ *f* (bacon) rind

couette /kwɛt/ *f* duvet

couffin /kufɛ̃/ *m* Moses basket (BrE), bassinet (AmE)

couiner /kwine/ [**v1**] *vi* to squeak, to squeal

coulant, **~e** /kulɑ̃, ɑ̃t/ *adj* ‹*Camembert*› runny; ‹*person*› easy-going

coulée /kule/ *f* (of lava) flow; (of paint) drip

⚷ **couler** /kule/ [**v1**] **A** *vt* **1** to cast ‹*metal, statue*›; to pour ‹*concrete*›
2 to sink ‹*ship*›
3 (fam) to put [sth] out of business; to bring [sb] down
B *vi* **1** ‹*blood*› to flow; ‹*paint, cheese*› to run; **faire ~ qch** to run ‹*bath*›
2 ‹*tap, pen*› to leak; ‹*nose*› to run
3 ‹*boat*› to sink; ‹*company*› to go under
C se couler *v refl* (+ *v être*) **se ~ dans/entre** to slip into/between

⚷ **couleur** /kulœʀ/ *f* **1** colour (BrE); **de ~** ‹*person*› coloured (BrE); **sans ~** colourless (BrE); **plein de ~** colourful (BrE)
2 paint
3 les ~s (washing) coloureds (BrE); (flag) the colours (BrE)
4 (in cards) suit
5 sous ~ de faire while pretending to do
IDIOMS **ne pas voir la ~ de qch** (fam) never to get a sniff of sth (fam); **il m'en a fait voir de toutes les ~s** (fam) he put me through the mill

couleuvre /kulœvʀ/ *f* grass snake
IDIOM **avaler des ~s** (fam) to believe anything one is told

coulissant, **~e** /kulisɑ̃, ɑ̃t/ *adj* sliding

coulisse /kulis/ *f* **1 les ~s, la ~** the wings; **en ~** backstage; (fig) behind the scenes
2 runner

coulisser /kulise/ [**v1**] *vi* to slide

couloir /kulwaʀ/ *m* **1** corridor (BrE), hallway; passage; **bruits de ~s** rumours (BrE)
2 lane; **~ aérien** air (traffic) lane

⚷ **coup** /ku/ *m* **1** knock; blow; **~ à la porte** knock at the door; **à ~s de bâton** with a stick; **donner un ~ de qch à qn** to hit sb with sth; **donner un ~ de poing à qn** to

---

⚷ key word

punch sb; **porter un ~ (sévère) à** (fig) to deal [sb/sth] a (severe) blow; **sa fierté en a pris un ~** it was a blow to his/her pride; **sous le ~ de la colère** in (a fit of) anger; **être sous le ~ d'une forte émotion** to be in a highly emotional state
2 (noise) knock; bang; thump, thud; **au douzième ~ de minuit** on the last stroke of midnight; **sur le ~ de dix heures** (fam) around ten; **~ de sifflet** whistle blast
3 un (petit) ~ de chiffon a (quick) wipe; **un ~ de peinture** a lick of paint
4 (in tennis, golf, cricket) stroke; shot; (in chess) move; (with dice) throw; (in boxing) punch; **tous les ~s sont permis** no holds barred
5 ~ de feu/fusil (gun)shot/(rifle) shot
6 (fam) job (fam), racket (fam); trick (fam); **monter un ~** to plan a job (fam); **il a raté son ~** (fam) he blew it (fam); **être dans le ~** to be in on it; to be up to date; **qui a fait le ~?** who did it?
7 time; **du premier ~** first time; **à tous les ~s** every time; **ce ~-ci** this time; **du ~** (fam) as a result; **après ~** afterwards; **~ sur ~** in succession; **tout d'un ~, tout à ~** suddenly, all of a sudden; **d'un ~, d'un seul ~** just like that; **en un seul ~** in one go (fam); **sur le ~** at the time; instantly, on the spot; **pleurer un bon ~** to have a good cry
8 à ~s de subventions by means of subsidies
9 (fam) drink
■ **~ bas** blow below the belt; **~s et blessures** assault and battery; **~ dur** blow; **~ franc** free kick; **~ monté** put-up job; **~ de tête** *or* **de boule** (fam) headbutt

> For translations of expressions such as *coup d'envoi*, *coup de fil* etc, look up the entries at **envoi**, **fil** etc.

IDIOMS **tenir le ~** ‹*shoes*› to last out; ‹*repair*› to hold; ‹*person*› to hold on; **être aux cent ~s** (fam) to be worried sick (fam); **faire les quatre cents ~s** (fam) to be a real tearaway; **attraper le ~ pour faire** (fam) to get the knack of doing

coupable /kupabl/ **A** *adj* guilty; ‹*negligence*› culpable; ‹*indifference*› shameful
B *mf* culprit

coupant, ~e /kupɑ̃, ɑ̃t/ *adj* sharp

coup-de-poing, *pl* **coups-de-poing** /kudpwɛ̃/ *m* **~ américain** knuckle-duster (BrE), brass knuckles (AmE)

coupe /kup/ *f* **1** cutting; cutting out; cut
2 haircut
3 (Sport) cup; **la ~ du Monde** the World Cup
4 (fruit) bowl; (champagne) glass
5 section; **~ transversale** cross section
■ **~ en brosse** crew cut
IDIOMS **la ~ est pleine** enough is enough; **être sous la ~ de qn** to be under sb's control

coupe-feu /kupfø/ *m inv* firebreak

coupe-gorge /kupgɔʀʒ/ *m inv* rough place; rough area

coupe-papier /kuppapje/ *m inv* paper knife

couper /kupe/ [v1] **A** *vt* **1** to cut; to cut down; to chop; to cut out; to cut off; **~ qch en tranches** to slice sth
2 ‹*road*› to cut across; **~ la route à qn** to cut in on sb
3 to cut off ‹*road, supplies*›; to spoil ‹*appetite*›; to take the edge off ‹*hunger*›; to turn off ‹*water*›; **~ le souffle à qn** to take sb's breath away; **~ la parole à qn** to interrupt sb
4 ~ qn de qn/qch to cut sb off from sb/sth
5 to dilute ‹*wine*›
6 (in cards) to cut ‹*pack*›; to trump ‹*card*›
B *vi* **attention ça coupe!** be careful, it's sharp; **~ à travers champs** to cut across country
C se couper *v refl* (+ *v être*) to cut oneself
IDIOM **c'est ton tour de faire à manger, tu n'y couperas pas** it's your turn to cook, you won't get out of it

couper-coller /kupekɔle/ [v1] *vt* (Comput) to cut and paste

couperet /kupʀɛ/ *m* cleaver; (of guillotine) blade; **la nouvelle est tombée comme un ~** the news came as a bolt from the blue

couperose /kupʀoz/ *f* broken veins

coupe-vent /kupvɑ̃/ *m inv* **1** windcheater (BrE), windbreaker (AmE)
2 windbreak

couple /kupl/ *m* **1** couple; pair
2 relationship

couplet /kuplɛ/ *m* **1** verse
2 couplet

coupole /kupɔl/ *f* cupola, dome

coupon /kupɔ̃/ *m* **1** remnant
2 ticket voucher
3 multi-use ticket (*in travel pass*)

coupon-réponse, *pl* **coupons-réponses** /kupɔ̃ʀepɔ̃s/ *m* reply coupon

coupure /kupyʀ/ *f* **1** cut; **~ d'électricité** *or* **de courant** power cut
2 break
3 gap
4 (bank)note (BrE), bill (AmE)
■ **~ de journal** *or* **de presse** (newspaper) cutting

cour /kuʀ/ *f* **1** courtyard; (school) playground; (farm) yard
2 (of sovereign) court; (of celebrity) entourage
3 courtship
4 (Law) court
■ **~ d'arrivée** arrivals area; **~ de départ** departures area; **~ martiale** court-martial; **~ de récréation** playground

courage /kuʀaʒ/ *m* **1** courage, bravery; **avoir du ~** to be brave
2 energy; **je n'ai même pas le ~ de me doucher** I don't even have the energy to

have a shower; **bon ~!** good luck!; **perdre ~** to lose heart; **je n'ai pas eu le ~ de dire non** I didn't have the heart to say no

courageusement /kuʀaʒøzmɑ̃/ *adv* courageously, bravely

courageux, -euse /kuʀaʒø, øz/ *adj* courageous, brave

couramment /kuʀamɑ̃/ *adv* **1** fluently
2 ‹*used*› widely; **cela se fait ~** it's very common

courant¹ /kuʀɑ̃/ *prep* **~ janvier** (some time) in January

courant², ~e /kuʀɑ̃, ɑ̃t/ **A** *adj* **1** ‹*word, practice, mistake*› common
2 ‹*language*› everyday; ‹*procedure*› usual, ordinary; ‹*size*› standard
3 ‹*month, price*› current; **le 15 du mois ~** the 15th of this month
B *m* **1** current; **il n'y a plus de ~** the power has gone off
2 trend; **un ~ politique** a political trend
3 dans le ~ de in the course of
C au courant *phr* **être au ~ de** to know about ‹*news*›; to be up to date on ‹*technique*›; **mettre qn au ~** to put sb in the picture; **tenir qn au ~** to keep sb posted
■ **~ d'air** draught (BrE), draft (AmE)

courbatu, ~e /kuʀbaty/ *adj* stiff

courbature /kuʀbatyʀ/ *f* ache; **avoir des ~s** to be stiff

courbaturé, ~e /kuʀbatyʀe/ *adj* stiff; aching

courbe /kuʀb/ **A** *adj* curved
B *f* **1** curve
2 bend
■ **~ de température** temperature chart; **~ d'apprentissage** learning curve

courber /kuʀbe/ [**v1**] *vt* to bend; **~ le dos** (fig) to bow down

courbette /kuʀbɛt/ *f* (low) bow; **faire des ~s** (fig) to bow and scrape

courbure /kuʀbyʀ/ *f* curve

coureur, -euse /kuʀœʀ, øz/ *mf* runner; **~ automobile** racing driver; **~ de jupons** philanderer

courge /kuʀʒ/ *f* (fruit) gourd; (vegetable) (vegetable) marrow

courgette /kuʀʒɛt/ *f* courgette (BrE), zucchini (AmE)

courir /kuʀiʀ/ [**v26**] **A** *vt* **1** to compete in ‹*trials*›
2 ~ le monde to roam the world
3 ~ les cocktails to do the round of the cocktail parties; **~ les boutiques** to go round the shops (BrE) *or* stores (AmE)
4 ~ un (grand) danger to be in (great) danger; **~ un (gros) risque** to run a (big) risk; **faire ~ un risque à qn** to put sb at risk
5 (fam) **~ les filles** to chase after girls
B *vi* **1** to run; to race; **~ après qn/qch** to run after sb/sth; to chase after sb/sth; **les voleurs courent toujours** the thieves are still at large; **~ à la catastrophe** to be heading for disaster
2 ‹*rumour*› to go around
IDIOMS **tu peux toujours ~!** (fam) you can go whistle for it! (fam); **laisser ~** (fam) to let things ride

couronne /kuʀɔn/ *f* **1** crown
2 ~ de fleurs garland; wreath
3 ring-shaped loaf
4 (in Paris) **la petite/grande ~** *the inner/outer suburbs*

couronnement /kuʀɔnmɑ̃/ *m* coronation

couronner /kuʀɔne/ [**v1**] *vt* to crown

courre /kuʀ/ *vt* **chasse à ~** hunting

courriel /kuʀjɛl/ *m* email

courrier /kuʀje/ *m* **1** mail, post (BrE); **faire son ~** to write letters
2 ~ du cœur problem page; **~ électronique** electronic mail; **~ des lecteurs** letters to the editor

courroie /kuʀwa/ *f* **1** strap
2 (on machine) belt

cours /kuʀ/ *m inv* **1** lesson, class; **avoir ~** to have a class; **faire ~** to teach
2 course book, textbook
3 school; **~ de théâtre** drama school
4 price; exchange rate
5 (of river) course
6 (of tale, events) course; (of ideas) flow; **la vie reprend son ~** life returns to normal; **donner libre ~ à** to give free rein to ‹*imagination*›; **au** *or* **dans le ~ de** in the course of, during; **en ~** ‹*month*› current; ‹*project*› under way; ‹*work*› in progress; **en ~ de journée** in the course of the day
■ **~ d'eau** watercourse; **~ élémentaire première année, CE1** *second year of primary school, age 7–8*; **~ moyen première année, CM1** *fourth year of primary school, age 9–10*; **~ particulier(s)** private tuition (BrE), private tutoring (AmE); **~ préparatoire, CP** *first year of primary school, age 6–7*

course /kuʀs/ *f* **1** running; run; racing; race; **faire la ~ avec qn** to race sb; **c'est la ~ tous les matins pour me préparer** I'm always in a rush in the morning to get ready
2 (in taxi) journey; **c'est 10 euros la ~** the fare is 10 euros
3 faire une ~ to run an errand; **faire les ~s** to do the shopping
4 (of star, planet) path; (of clouds) passage
■ **~ de haies** (in athletics) hurdles; (for horses) steeplechase; **~ d'obstacles** obstacle race; (fig) obstacle course; **~ de vitesse** (in athletics) sprint; (on motorbikes) speedway race
IDIOMS **ne plus être dans la ~** to be out of touch; **être à bout de ~** to be worn out

coursier, -ière /kuʀsje, ɛʀ/ *mf* messenger

court, ~e /kuʀ, kuʀt/ **A** *adj* **1** short; **de ~e durée** short-lived; short-term; **avoir le souffle ~** to get out of breath easily
2 ‹*defeat, victory, majority*› narrow
B *adv* **couper ~ à qch** to put paid to sth;

s'arrêter ~ to stop short
C *m* ~ **de tennis** tennis court
■ ~ **métrage** short (film); ~**e échelle: faire la** ~**e échelle à qn** to give sb a leg up (fam)
IDIOMS **être à** ~ **de** to be short of ‹*money*›; **prendre qn de** ~ to catch sb unprepared

court-circuit, *pl* ~**s** /kuʀsiʀkɥi/ *m* short circuit

courtier, **-ière** /kuʀtje, ɛʀ/ *mf* broker

courtiser /kuʀtize/ [**v1**] *vt* to woo

courtois, ~**e** /kuʀtwa, az/ *adj* ‹*person, tone*› courteous; ‹*genre, tradition*› courtly

courtoisie /kuʀtwazi/ *f* courtesy

couru, ~**e** /kuʀy/ **A** *pp* ▸ **courir**
B *pp adj* ‹*place*› popular
IDIOM **c'est** ~ **d'avance** (fam) it's a foregone conclusion

cousin, ~**e** /kuzɛ̃, in/ *mf* cousin

coussin /kusɛ̃/ *m* cushion

cousu, ~**e** /kuzy/ ▸ **coudre**

coût /ku/ *m* cost; ~ **de la vie** cost of living

coûtant /kutɑ̃/ *adj m* **prix** ~ cost price

couteau, *pl* ~**x** /kuto/ *m* **1** knife; **donner un coup de** ~ **à qn** to stab sb
2 razor shell (BrE) *or* clam (AmE)
3 knife edge
IDIOMS **être à** ~**x tirés avec qn** to be at daggers drawn with sb; **avoir le** ~ **sous la gorge** to have a pistol to one's head

coûter /kute/ [**v1**] **A** *vt* to cost
B *vi* to cost; ~ **cher** to be expensive; **ça m'a coûté de m'excuser** it was hard for me to apologize
C *v impers* **il t'en coûtera d'avoir fait cela** you will pay for doing this; **coûte que coûte, quoi qu'il en coûte** at all costs
IDIOM ~ **les yeux de la tête** to cost an arm and a leg (fam)

coûteux, **-euse** /kutø, øz/ *adj* costly

coutume /kutym/ *f* custom; **avoir** ~ **de faire** to be in the habit of doing
IDIOM **une fois n'est pas** ~ it does no harm just this once

coutumier, **-ière** /kutymje, ɛʀ/ *adj* customary

couture /kutyʀ/ *f* **1** sewing; dressmaking; **faire de la** ~ to sew
2 seam
IDIOMS **sous toutes les** ~**s** from every angle; **battre qn à plates** ~**s** to beat sb hollow

couturier /kutyʀje/ *m* dress designer

couturière /kutyʀjɛʀ/ *f* dressmaker

couvent /kuvɑ̃/ *m* convent

couver /kuve/ [**v1**] **A** *vt* **1** to sit on ‹*eggs*›; **la poule couve** the hen is brooding
2 to overprotect; ~ **qn/qch du regard** to look fondly at sb/sth; to gaze longingly at sb/sth
3 to be coming down with ‹*illness*›
B *vi* ‹*rebellion*› to brew; ‹*fire, anger*› to smoulder (BrE), to smolder (AmE)

couvercle /kuvɛʀkl/ *m* **1** lid
2 screw-top

couvert, ~**e** /kuvɛʀ, ɛʀt/ **A** *pp* ▸ **couvrir**
B *pp adj* **1** covered (**de** in, with); **être** ~ **de diplômes** to have a lot of qualifications
2 ‹*pool*› indoor; ‹*market*› covered
3 ‹*sky*› overcast
C *m* **1** place setting; **mettre le** ~ to lay the table; **un** ~ **en argent** a silver knife, fork and spoon
2 cover charge
D **à couvert** *phr* **se mettre à** ~ to take cover
E **sous le couvert de** *phr* under the pretence (BrE) of; **sous** ~ **de la plaisanterie** under the guise of a joke

couverture /kuvɛʀtyʀ/ *f* **1** blanket; (small) rug (BrE), lap robe (AmE)
2 (of book, magazine) cover
3 (media, mobile phone) coverage
IDIOM **tirer la** ~ **à soi** to turn a situation to one's own advantage

couveuse /kuvøz/ *f* incubator

couvre-feu, *pl* ~**x** /kuvʀəfø/ *m* curfew

couvre-lit, *pl* ~**s** /kuvʀəli/ *m* bedspread

couvreur /kuvʀœʀ/ *m* roofer

couvrir /kuvʀiʀ/ [**v32**] **A** *vt* **1** to cover ‹*furniture, wall, fire, card*›; to roof ‹*house*›; ~ **qn de qch** (with blows, jewels, compliments) to shower sb with sth
2 ‹*sound*› to drown out
3 ‹*transmitter, inspector*› to cover ‹*region*›
4 to wrap [sb] up; to cover [sb] up
5 to cover up for ‹*mistake, person*›
6 (with gun) to cover ‹*soldier*›
7 to cover ‹*distance*›
8 ‹*book, journalist*› to cover ‹*story, event*›
9 ‹*sum*› to cover ‹*expenses*›
B **se couvrir** *v refl* (+ *v être*) **1** to wrap up; to put on a hat
2 ‹*sky*› to become overcast
3 **se** ~ **de** to become covered with
4 (against accusations) to cover oneself

CP /sepe/ *m*: *abbr* ▸ **cours**

crabe /kʀab/ *m* crab

crachat /kʀaʃa/ *m* spit

crachement /kʀaʃmɑ̃/ *m* **1** spitting
2 crackling

cracher /kʀaʃe/ [**v1**] **A** *vt* **1** to spit out; **c'est le portrait de sa mère tout craché** (fam) she's the spitting image of her mother
2 to belch (out) ‹*flames, smoke*›
B *vi* to spit; **je ne cracherais pas dessus** (fam) I wouldn't turn up my nose at it

cracheur /kʀaʃœʀ/ *m* ~ **de feu** fire-eater

crachin /kʀaʃɛ̃/ *m* drizzle

crachoir /kʀaʃwaʀ/ *m* spittoon

crachoter /kʀaʃɔte/ [**v1**] *vi* **1** to cough and splutter
2 to crackle

crack /kʀak/ *m* **1** (genius) ace
2 (fam) (drug) crack (fam)

craie /kʀɛ/ *f* chalk

⚷ **craindre** /kʀɛ̃dʀ/ [**v54**] *vt* **1** to fear, to be afraid of
2 to be sensitive to ‹*cold*›; to dislike ‹*sun*›

craint, **~e** /kʀɛ̃, ɛ̃t/ ▶ **craindre**

⚷ **crainte** /kʀɛ̃t/ *f* fear; **avoir des ~s au sujet de qn** to be worried about sb; **n'ayez ~, soyez sans ~** have no fear

craintif, **-ive** /kʀɛ̃tif, iv/ *adj* timorous, timid

cramoisi, **~e** /kʀamwazi/ *adj* crimson

crampe /kʀɑ̃p/ *f* cramp

crampon /kʀɑ̃pɔ̃/ *m* crampon; **chaussures à ~s** (for football) boots with studs (BrE) *or* cleats (AmE); (for running) spiked shoes

cramponner: **se cramponner** /kʀɑ̃pɔne/ [**v1**] *v refl* (+ *v être*) to hold on tightly

cran /kʀɑ̃/ **A** *m* **1** notch; (in belt) hole; **monter d'un ~** to move up a notch
2 nick
3 (fam) **avoir du ~** to have guts (fam)
4 (in hair) wave
B **à cran** *phr* **être à ~** to be on edge
■ **~ d'arrêt** flick knife (BrE), switchblade (AmE); **~ de sûreté** safety catch

crâne /kʀɑn/ *m* **1** skull
2 (fam) head; **ne rien avoir dans le ~** to have no brains; **bourrer le ~ à qn** (fam) to brainwash sb

crânement /kʀɑnmɑ̃/ *adv* gallantly; proudly

crânien, **-ienne** /kʀɑnjɛ̃, ɛn/ *adj* cranial; **boîte crânienne** cranium

crapaud /kʀapo/ *m* toad

crapule /kʀapyl/ *f* crook

crapuleux, **-euse** /kʀapylø, øz/ *adj* villainous

craqueler: **se craqueler** /kʀakle/ [**v19**] *v refl* (+ *v être*) to crack

craquement /kʀakmɑ̃/ *m* **1** creaking sound, creak
2 cracking sound, crack

craquer /kʀake/ [**v1**] **A** *vt* **1** to split ‹*trousers*›
2 to strike ‹*match*›
B *vi* **1** ‹*seam*› to split; ‹*branch*› to crack
2 ‹*floor*› to creak
3 (fam) ‹*person*› to crack up (fam)

crasher: **se crasher** /kʀaʃe/ [**v1**] *v refl* (+ *v être*) ‹*computer*› to crash

crasse /kʀas/ *f* grime, filth

crasseux, **-euse** /kʀasø, øz/ *adj* filthy, grimy

cratère /kʀatɛʀ/ *m* crater

cravache /kʀavaʃ/ *f* whip

cravate /kʀavat/ *f* tie

crawl /kʀol/ *m* crawl

⚷ **crayon** /kʀɛjɔ̃/ *m* pencil; **~ noir** lead pencil; **~ optique** light pen

créance /kʀeɑ̃s/ *f* **1** debt (*owed by a debtor*)
2 letter of credit

créancier, **-ière** /kʀeɑ̃sje, ɛʀ/ *mf* creditor

créateur, **-trice** /kʀeatœʀ, tʀis/ *mf* creator; designer

créatif, **-ive** /kʀeatif, iv/ *adj* creative

⚷ **création** /kʀeasjɔ̃/ *f* **1** creation; **la ~ d'une entreprise** the setting up of a company; **la ~ d'un nouveau produit** the development of a new product; **tous les livres de la ~** all the books in the world
2 (work of art) creation; (play) first production; (commercial) new product

créativité /kʀeativite/ *f* creativity

⚷ **créature** /kʀeatyʀ/ *f* creature

crèche /kʀɛʃ/ *f* **1** crèche (BrE), day nursery
2 (at Christmas) crib (BrE), crèche (AmE)

crédibilité /kʀedibilite/ *f* credibility

crédible /kʀedibl/ *adj* credible

crédit /kʀedi/ *m* **1** funds; **les ~s de la recherche** research funding
2 credit; **accorder un ~** to grant credit terms; **faire ~ à qn** to give sb credit; **porter une somme au ~ d'un compte** to credit sb's account with a sum of money; **mettre** *or* **porter qch au ~ de qn** (fig) to give sb credit for sth

créditer /kʀedite/ [**v1**] *vt* to credit

créditeur, **-trice** /kʀeditœʀ, tʀis/ *adj* **être ~** to be in credit

credo /kʀedo/ *m* creed

crédule /kʀedyl/ *adj* gullible, credulous

⚷ **créer** /kʀee/ [**v11**] **A** *vt* (gen) to create; to develop ‹*new product*›; to set up ‹*company*›
B **se créer** *v refl* (+ *v être*) **se ~ des problèmes** to bring trouble on oneself

crémaillère /kʀemajɛʀ/ *f* **pendre la ~** to have a house-warming (party)

crémation /kʀemasjɔ̃/ *f* cremation

crématoire /kʀematwaʀ/ *m* crematorium

crème[1] /kʀɛm/ *adj inv* cream

crème[2] /kʀɛm/ *f* **1** cream
2 cream dessert
3 (fam) **la ~ des linguistes** the very best linguists
■ **~ Chantilly** whipped cream; **~ glacée** dairy ice cream; **~ de marrons** chestnut spread; **~ renversée** caramel custard

crémerie /kʀɛmʀi/ *f* cheese shop (BrE) *or* store (AmE)

crémeux, **-euse** /kʀemø, øz/ *adj* creamy

créneau, *pl* **~x** /kʀeno/ *m* **1** parallel parking
2 (Econ) market
3 gap, niche
4 crenel; **les ~x** crenellations
■ **~ horaire** time slot; **~ publicitaire** advertising slot

créole /kʀeɔl/ *adj*, *m* Creole

crêpe[1] /kʀɛp/ *m* **1** crepe
2 black veil

crêpe[2] /kʀɛp/ *f* pancake, crêpe

⚷ key word

crêper /kʀepe/ [**v1**] *vt* to backcomb (BrE), to tease ‹*hair*›

crépi /kʀepi/ *m* rendering

crépitement /kʀepitmɑ̃/ *m* crackling, crackle; sizzling

crépiter /kʀepite/ [**v1**] *vi* ‹*fire*› to crackle; ‹*oil*› to sizzle; ‹*rain*› to patter

crépon /kʀepɔ̃/ *m* crepe paper

crépu, **~e** /kʀepy/ *adj* frizzy

crépuscule /kʀepyskyl/ *m* twilight, dusk

crescendo /kʀeʃendo/ **A** *adv* **aller ~** ‹*noise*› to intensify
B *m* crescendo

cresson /kʀesɔ̃, kʀəsɔ̃/ *m* watercress

crête /kʀɛt/ *f* **1** (of cock) comb; (of bird) crest
2 (of mountain, wave) crest; (of roof) ridge

crétin, **~e** /kʀetɛ̃, in/ *mf* moron (fam)

creusement /kʀøzmɑ̃/ *m* **1** (de sol) digging
2 (augmentation) widening
3 (de déficit, dette, inégalités) increase

creuser /kʀøze/ [**v1**] **A** *vt* **1** to dig a hole in ‹*ground*›; to drill a hole in ‹*tooth*›; to dig into ‹*rock*›
2 to dig ‹*hole, canal, grave*›; to sink ‹*well*›
3 ‹*wrinkles*› to furrow ‹*face*›; **~ les reins** to arch one's back
4 to deepen, to increase ‹*deficit, inequalities*›
5 to go into [sth] in depth ‹*question, subject*›
B **se creuser** *v refl* (+ *v être*) **1** ‹*cheeks*› to become hollow
2 ‹*gap*› to widen
3 ‹*deficit, debt*› to increase
IDIOMS **ça creuse** (fam) it really gives you an appetite; **se ~ (la tête** *or* **la cervelle)** (fam) to rack one's brains

creux, **-euse** /kʀø, øz/ **A** *adj* **1** ‹*trunk, tooth, sound, cheeks*› hollow; ‹*stomach, speech*› empty; ‹*analysis*› shallow; **un plat ~** a shallow dish; **assiette creuse** soup dish
2 ‹*day, period*› slack, off-peak
B *adv* **sonner ~** to make a hollow sound
C *m* **1** hollow; **le ~ des reins** the small of the back; **le ~ de l'aisselle** the armpit; **le ~ de la vague** the trough of the wave; **être au ~ de la vague** (fig) to be at rock bottom
2 (fam) **avoir un petit ~** to have the munchies (fam)

crevaison /kʀəvɛzɔ̃/ *f* puncture

crevasse /kʀəvas/ *f* **1** crevasse
2 crack, fissure
3 chapped skin

crève /kʀɛv/ *f* (fam) chill; **attraper la ~** to catch a chill *or* one's death (of cold)

crever /kʀəve/ [**v16**] **A** *vt* to puncture, to burst; **~ les yeux de qn** to blind sb; to poke sb's eyes out; **ça crève les yeux** it's blindingly obvious; **ça crève le cœur** it's heartbreaking
B *vi* **1** to burst; to burst open
2 to die; **~ de faim** to be starving
3 ~ d'envie to be eaten up with envy; **~ d'orgueil** to be terribly full of oneself
C **se crever** *v refl* (+ *v être*) **il s'est crevé un œil** he put one of his eyes out
IDIOM **marche ou crève** sink or swim

crevette /kʀəvɛt/ *f* **~ grise** shrimp; **~ rose** prawn

cri /kʀi/ *m* **1** cry; shout; scream; **un ~ aigu** a shriek; **à grands ~s** loudly; **pousser les hauts ~s** to protest loudly
2 (of bird) call

criant, **~e** /kʀijɑ̃, ɑ̃t/ *adj* clear, striking

criard, **~e** /kʀiaʀ, aʀd/ *adj* ‹*voice*› shrill; ‹*colour*› garish

crible /kʀibl/ *m* (for minerals) screen; (for sand) riddle; **passer au ~** (fig) to sift through

cribler /kʀible/ [**v1**] *vt* **1 ~ qn/qch de balles** to riddle sb/sth with bullets
2 ~ qn de reproches to heap reproaches on sb

cric /kʀik/ *m* (for car) jack

criée /kʀije/ *f* **(vente à la) ~** auction

crier /kʀije/ [**v2**] **A** *vt* **1** to shout
2 to proclaim; to protest ‹*innocence*›
B **crier à** *v+prep* **on a crié au scandale quand...** there was an outcry when...
C *vi* **1** to shout; to cry; to scream
2 ‹*animal*› to give a cry; ‹*monkey*› to chatter; ‹*gull*› to cry; ‹*pig*› to squeal

crieur, **-ieuse** /kʀijœʀ, øz/ *mf* **~ de journaux** news vendor

crime /kʀim/ *m* **1** crime
2 murder; **~ crapuleux** murder for money

criminalité /kʀiminalite/ *f* crime

criminel, **-elle** /kʀiminɛl/ **A** *adj* criminal
B *mf* **1** criminal
2 murderer

crin /kʀɛ̃/ *m* horsehair; **à tout ~** (fig) dyed-in-the-wool

crinière /kʀinjɛʀ/ *f* mane

crique /kʀik/ *f* cove

criquet /kʀikɛ/ *m* locust

crise /kʀiz/ *f* **1** crisis; **~ agricole** crisis in the agricultural industry; **la ~** the economic crisis, the slump
2 shortage; **~ de l'emploi** job shortage
3 (Med) attack; **~ d'appendicite** appendicitis; **~ de toux** coughing fit
4 fit; **~ de colère** fit of rage; **faire une ~** to have a tantrum; to have a fit (fam)
■ **~ cardiaque** heart attack; **~ de foie** indigestion; **~ de nerfs** hysterics

crisper /kʀispe/ [**v1**] **A** *vt* **l'angoisse crispait son visage** his/her face was tense with worry
B **se crisper** *v refl* (+ *v être*) ‹*hands*› to clench; ‹*face, person*› to tense (up); ‹*smile*› to freeze

crisser /kʀise/ [**v1**] *vi* ‹*shoes, chalk*› to squeak; ‹*snow*› to crunch; ‹*tyres, brakes*› to screech

cristal, *pl* **-aux** /kʀistal, o/ *m* crystal

C

cristallin, **~e** /kʀistalɛ̃, in/ **A** *adj*
1 crystalline
2 crystal clear
B *m* (of eye) (crystalline) lens

cristalliser /kʀistalize/ [**v1**] *vt*, *vi*, **se cristalliser** *v refl* (+ *v être*) to crystallize

critère /kʀitɛʀ/ *m* **1** criterion; **~s de gestion/de confort** standards of management/comfort; **le ~ déterminant** the crucial factor
2 specification; **remplir les ~s d'âge et de diplôme** to meet the requirements as far as age and qualifications are concerned

critiquable /kʀitikabl/ *adj* questionable

critique[1] /kʀitik/ **A** *adj* critical
B *mf* critic

✓ **critique**[2] /kʀitik/ *f* **1** criticism; **faire une ~ à qn** to criticize sb
2 review; **faire la ~ d'un film** to review a film
3 la ~ littéraire literary criticism

critiquer /kʀitike/ [**v1**] *vt* to criticize

croasser /kʀɔase/ [**v1**] *vi* to caw

croc /kʀo/ *m* fang

croche /kʀɔʃ/ *f* quaver (BrE), eighth note (AmE); **double ~** semiquaver (BrE), sixteenth note (AmE)

croche-pied, *pl* **~s** /kʀɔʃpje/ *m* (fam) **faire un ~ à qn** to trip sb up

crochet /kʀɔʃɛ/ *m* **1** hook
2 picklock
3 crochet hook; **faire du ~** to crochet
4 square bracket
5 faire un ~ to make a detour
6 (in boxing) hook
7 fang

IDIOM **vivre aux ~s de qn** (fam) to sponge off sb (fam)

crocheter /kʀɔʃte/ [**v18**] *vt* to pick ‹*lock*›

crochu, **~e** /kʀɔʃy/ *adj* ‹*nose*› hooked; ‹*hands*› clawed

crocodile /kʀɔkɔdil/ *m* crocodile

✓ **croire** /kʀwaʀ/ [**v71**] **A** *vt* **1** to believe; **faire ~ à qn** to make sb believe
2 to think; **je crois savoir que** I happen to know that; **il est malin, faut pas ~!** (fam) he's clever, believe me!; **tu ne crois pas si bien dire** you don't know how right you are; **on croirait de la soie** it looks *or* feels like silk
3 si l'on en croit l'auteur, à en ~ l'auteur if we are to believe the author; **crois-en mon expérience** take my word for it
B croire à *v+prep* to believe ‹*story*›; to believe in ‹*ghosts*›
C croire en *v+prep* to believe in
D se croire *v refl* (+ *v être*) **il se croit beau** he thinks he's handsome

croisade /kʀwazad/ *f* crusade

croisé, **~e** /kʀwaze/ **A** *pp* ▶ **croiser**
B *pp adj* **1** ‹*legs*› crossed; ‹*arms*› folded
2 cross-bred
3 ‹*agreements*› reciprocal

croisée /kʀwaze/ *f* **1** junction; **à la ~ des chemins** at the crossroads
2 window

croisement /kʀwazmɑ̃/ *m* **1** crossroads; crossing, junction
2 (of threads, straps) crossing
3 cross-breeding; hybrid, cross(breed)

✓ **croiser** /kʀwaze/ [**v1**] **A** *vt* **1** to cross; **~ les bras** to fold one's arms
2 ~ qn/qch to pass sb/sth (coming the other way)
3 to meet; **mon regard croisa le sien** our eyes met
4 to cross(breed)
B se croiser *v refl* (+ *v être*) ‹*cars*› to pass each other; ‹*letters*› to cross in the post (BrE) *or* mail (AmE); ‹*roads*› to intersect; ‹*lines*› to cross

croisière /kʀwazjɛʀ/ *f* cruise

croissance /kʀwasɑ̃s/ *f* growth

croissant /kʀwasɑ̃/ *m* **1** croissant
2 crescent; **~ de lune** crescent moon

Croissant-Rouge /kʀwasɑ̃ʀuʒ/ *m* **le ~** Red Crescent

croître /kʀwatʀ/ [**v72**] *vi* **1** to grow; **faire ~** to grow
2 ‹*noise*› to get *or* grow louder

croix /kʀwa/ *f* cross; **bras en ~** arms out on either side of the body

IDIOMS **ton argent, tu peux faire une ~ dessus** (fam) you can kiss your money goodbye; **un jour à marquer d'une ~** a red-letter day

Croix-Rouge /kʀwaʀuʒ/ *f* **la ~** the Red Cross

croquant, **~e** /kʀɔkɑ̃, ɑ̃t/ *adj* crunchy

croque-madame /kʀɔkmadam/ *m inv*: *toasted ham and cheese sandwich topped with a fried egg*

croque-monsieur /kʀɔkməsjø/ *m inv*: *toasted ham and cheese sandwich*

croque-mort, *pl* **~s** /kʀɔkmɔʀ/ *m* (fam) undertaker

croquer /kʀɔke/ [**v1**] **A** *vt* **1** to crunch
2 to sketch; **belle à ~** as pretty as a picture
B *vi* **1** to be crunchy
2 ~ dans une pomme to bite into an apple

croquette /kʀɔkɛt/ *f* croquette

croquis /kʀɔki/ *m* sketch

crosse /kʀɔs/ *f* **1** (of rifle) butt
2 (of cane) crook
3 (Sport) stick

crotte /kʀɔt/ *f* dropping; **c'est de la ~ de chien** it's dog mess

crotter /kʀɔte/ [**v1**] *vt* to muddy; **bottes crottées** muddy boots

crottin /kʀɔtɛ̃/ *m* **1** dung
2 (small round) goat's cheese

crouler /kʀule/ [**v1**] *vi* **1** to collapse; to crumble
2 ~ sous to be weighed down by ‹*parcels,*

✓ key word

debts, work›; ~ **sous le poids de** ‹*table*› to groan under the weight of ‹*books*›

croupe /kʀup/ *f* (of horse) croup

croupi, **~e** /kʀupi/ *adj* stagnant

croupier /kʀupje/ *m* croupier

croupir /kʀupiʀ/ [**v3**] *vi* **1** ‹*water*› to stagnate
2 ~ **en prison** to rot in jail

croustillant, **~e** /kʀustijɑ̃, ɑ̃t/ *adj* **1** crispy; crunchy
2 ‹*story, details*› spicy

croustiller /kʀustije/ [**v1**] *vi* ‹*bread*› to be crusty; ‹*chocolate*› to be crunchy

croûte /kʀut/ *f* **1** (of bread) crust; (of cheese) rind; **casser la** ~ (fam) to have a bite to eat
2 (Culin) **pâté en** ~ pâté en croute *or* in pastry
3 (Med) scab
4 (fam) daub, bad painting

croûton /kʀutɔ̃/ *m* **1** crust
2 (Culin) crouton

croyance /kʀwajɑ̃s/ *f* belief

croyant, **~e** /kʀwajɑ̃, ɑ̃t/ *adj* **être** ~ to be a believer

CRS /seɛʀɛs/ *m* (*abbr* = **compagnie républicaine de sécurité**) **un** ~ *a member of the French riot police*

cru¹, **~e** /kʀy/ ▶ **croire**

cru², **~e** /kʀy/ **A** *adj* **1** raw; uncooked; ‹*milk*› unpasteurized; **se faire manger tout** ~ (fam) to be eaten alive (fam)
2 ‹*light, colour*› harsh
3 ‹*language*› crude
B *m* vineyard; vintage; vintage year; **du meilleur** ~ ‹*collection*› vintage; **du** ~ ‹*wine, author*› local

crû, **crue** /kʀy/ ▶ **croître**

cruauté /kʀyote/ *f* cruelty

cruche /kʀyʃ/ *f* jug (BrE), pitcher (AmE)

crucial, **~e**, *mpl* **-iaux** /kʀysjal, o/ *adj* crucial

crucifier /kʀysifje/ [**v2**] *vt* to crucify

crucifix /kʀysifi/ *m* crucifix

crudité /kʀydite/ *f* **~s** raw vegetables, crudités

crue /kʀy/ **A** *adj f* ▶ **cru² A**
B *f* rise in water level; flood; **en** ~ in spate

cruel, **-elle** /kʀyɛl/ *adj* cruel

cruellement /kʀyɛlmɑ̃/ *adv* **1** cruelly
2 manquer ~ **de qch** to be desperately short of sth
3 terribly; **la pénurie de carburant se fait** ~ **sentir** the fuel shortage is being sorely felt

crûment /kʀymɑ̃/ *adv* **1** bluntly
2 crudely

crustacé /kʀystase/ *m* shellfish

crypte /kʀipt(ə)/ *f* crypt

crypté, **~e** /kʀipte/ *adj* coded; encrypted

cube /kyb/ **A** *adj* cubic
B *m* **1** cube
2 building block

cubique /kybik/ *adj* **1** cubic
2 cube-shaped

cucul /kyky/ *adj* (fam) corny (fam); silly

cueillette /kœjɛt/ *f* **1** (of fruits, flowers) picking
2 crop

cueilli, **~e** /kœji/ ▶ **cueillir**

cueillir /kœjiʀ/ [**v27**] *vt* **1** to pick ‹*fruit, flowers*›
2 (fam) to arrest ‹*criminal*›

cuiller, **cuillère** /kɥijɛʀ/ *f* spoon; spoonful; ~ **à café** teaspoon; coffee spoon
IDIOMS **il n'y va pas avec le dos de la** ~ (fam) he doesn't do things by halves; **en deux coups de** ~ **à pot** in two shakes of a lamb's tail (fam)

cuillerée /kɥij(ə)ʀe/ *f* spoonful

cuir /kɥiʀ/ *m* **1** leather
2 rawhide; hide
■ ~ **chevelu** scalp

cuirassé /kɥiʀase/ *m* battleship

cuire /kɥiʀ/ [**v69**] **A** *vt* **1** to cook; to bake; to roast; ~ **à la vapeur** to steam; **à** ~ ‹*apple*› cooking
2 to fire ‹*porcelain*›
B *vi* **1** ‹*food*› to cook; to be cooking; **laissez** ~ **à petit feu** allow to simmer gently
2 (fam) **on cuit sur la plage** it's baking (hot) on the beach
3 ‹*graze*› to sting; **ça me cuit** it stings

cuisant, **~e** /kɥizɑ̃, ɑ̃t/ *adj* **1** ‹*defeat, regret*› bitter; ‹*remark*› stinging
2 ‹*pain*› burning

cuisine /kɥizin/ *f* **1** kitchen
2 galley
3 kitchen furniture
4 cooking
5 (fam) intrigues

cuisiner /kɥizine/ [**v1**] *vt, vi* to cook

cuisinier, **-ière** /kɥizinje, ɛʀ/ *mf* cook; chef

cuisinière /kɥizinjɛʀ/ *f* cooker

cuissarde /kɥisaʀd/ *f* wader; thigh boot

cuisse /kɥis/ *f* thigh; **des ~s de grenouille** frogs' legs

cuisson /kɥisɔ̃/ *f* **1** cooking; baking; roasting
2 (of pottery) firing

cuistot /kɥisto/ *m* (fam) cook

cuit, **~e** /kɥi, kɥit/ ▶ **cuire**
IDIOMS **c'est** ~ (fam) we've had it (fam); **c'est du tout** ~ (fam) it's a piece of cake (fam); it's in the bag (fam); **elle attend que ça (lui) tombe tout** ~ (fam) she expects things to fall straight into her lap

cuite /kɥit/ *f* **tenir une** ~ to be plastered (fam)

cuivre /kɥivʀ/ **A** *m* **1** ~ **(rouge)** copper
2 ~ **(jaune)** brass
B cuivres *mpl* **1** copperware
2 brass
3 (Mus) **les ~s** the brass

cul /ky/ *m* **1** (pop) bottom, arse (BrE) (vulg), ass (AmE) (sl)
2 (of bottle) bottom; ~ **sec!** (fam) bottoms up! (fam)

culasse /kylas/ *f* **1** cylinder head
2 breechblock

culbute /kylbyt/ *f* somersault

culbuter /kylbyte/ [**v1**] *vi* ‹*person*› to take a tumble; ‹*vehicle*› to overturn

cul-cul (fam) ▶ **cucul**

cul-de-jatte, *pl* **culs-de-jatte** /kydʒat/ *mf* person who has had both legs amputated

cul-de-sac, *pl* **culs-de-sac** /kydsak/ *m*
1 cul-de-sac
2 dead end

culinaire /kylinɛʀ/ *adj* culinary

culminant, **~e** /kylminɑ̃, ɑ̃t/ *adj* **point ~** (of mountain) highest point *or* peak; (of career) peak; (of crisis) height; (of holiday) high point

culminer /kylmine/ [**v1**] *vi* **1 ~ au-dessus de qch** to tower above sth
2 ‹*inflation, unemployment*› to reach its peak

culot /kylo/ *m* (fam) cheek (fam); **y aller au ~** to bluff

culotte /kylɔt/ *f* **1** pants (BrE), panties (AmE)
2 en ~(s) courte(s) in short trousers (BrE) *or* pants (AmE)

culotté, **~e** /kylɔte/ *adj* (fam) cheeky

culpabilisation /kylpabilizasjɔ̃/ *f* making guilty; feeling of guilt

culpabiliser /kylpabilize/ [**v1**] **A** *vt* to make [sb] feel guilty
B *vi* to feel guilty

culpabilité /kylpabilite/ *f* guilt

culte /kylt/ *m* **1** cult
2 religion

cultivateur, **-trice** /kyltivatœʀ, tʀis/ *mf* farmer

cultiver /kyltive/ [**v1**] **A** *vt* to grow; to cultivate
B se cultiver *v refl* (+ *v être*) to improve one's mind

✓ **culture** /kyltyʀ/ **A** *f* **1** cultivation; **la ~ du blé** wheat growing
2 crop; **~ d'hiver** winter crop
3 (in biology) culture
4 (of society) culture; **~ de masse** mass culture
5 knowledge; **~ classique** classical education
6 arts; **subventionner la ~** to subsidize the arts
B cultures *fpl* cultivated land
■ **~ physique** physical exercise

✓ **culturel**, **-elle** /kyltyʀɛl/ *adj* cultural

culturisme /kyltyʀism/ *m* body-building

cumin /kymɛ̃/ *m* cumin

cumul /kymyl/ *m* **1 ~ de fonctions** holding of several posts concurrently
2 (Law) **~ des peines** ≈ sentences to be served consecutively

cumuler /kymyle/ [**v1**] *vt* **1** to hold [sth] concurrently ‹*offices*›; to draw [sth] concurrently ‹*salaries*›
2 to accumulate ‹*handicaps, degrees*›
3 to combine ‹*results*›; to add up ‹*amounts*›

cumulus /kymylys/ *m inv* cumulus

cupide /kypid/ *adj* grasping

cupidité /kypidite/ *f* avarice, greed, cupidity

cure /kyʀ/ *f* **faire une ~** to go for a course of treatment in a spa
■ **~ d'amaigrissement** slimming course (BrE), reducing treatment (AmE); **~ de sommeil** sleep therapy

curé /kyʀe/ *m* (parish) priest

cure-dents /kyʀdɑ̃/ *m inv* toothpick

curer /kyʀe/ [**v1**] **A** *vt* to clean out ‹*pipe, pond*›
B se curer *v refl* (+ *v être*) **se ~ les ongles** to clean one's nails

curieusement /kyʀjøzmɑ̃/ *adv* **1** oddly, strangely
2 oddly enough

✓ **curieux**, **-ieuse** /kyʀjø, øz/ **A** *adj*
1 inquisitive, curious
2 strange
3 esprit ~ person with an enquiring mind; **être ~ d'apprendre** to be keen to learn
B *mf* onlooker

curiosité /kyʀjozite/ *f* curiosity

curriculum vitae /kyʀikylɔmvite/ *m inv* curriculum vitae, résumé (AmE)

curry /kyʀi/ *m* **1** curry powder
2 curry

curseur /kyʀsœʀ/ *m* cursor

cursus /kyʀsys/ *m inv* course

cutané, **~e** /kytane/ *adj* ‹*irritation*› skin

cutter /kytœʀ/ *m* Stanley knife®

cuve /kyv/ *f* vat; tank

cuvée /kyve/ *f* vatful; **la ~ 1959** the 1959 vintage; **~ du patron** house wine

cuvette /kyvɛt/ *f* **1** bowl; **~ des wc** lavatory bowl *or* pan
2 (in land) basin

CV /seve/ *m* **1** (*abbr* = **curriculum vitae**) CV (BrE), résumé (AmE)
2 (*written abbr* = **cheval-vapeur**) HP

cyberattaque /sibɛʀatak/ *f* cyberattack

cybercafé /sibɛʀkafe/ *m* cybercafe

cyberdépendance /sibɛʀdepɑ̃dɑ̃s/ *f* (Comp) addiction to the Internet

cyberdépendant, **~e** /sibɛʀdepɑ̃dɑ̃, ɑ̃t/ *adj* (Comp) addicted to the Internet

cyber-harcèlement /sibɛʀaʀsɛlmɑ̃/ *m* cyberbullying

cyberjargon /sibɛʀʒaʀgɔ̃/ *m* netspeak

cybermilitant, **~e** /sibɛʀmilitɑ̃, ɑ̃t/ *mf* (Comp) cyberactivist, hacktivist

cyberterrorisme /sibɛʀtɛʀɔʀism/ *m* (Comp) cyberterrorism

cyclable /siklabl/ *adj* **piste ~** cycle track

cycle /sikl/ *m* **1** cycle; **~ infernal** vicious cycle
2 series
3 (Sch) **premier ~** *first two years of a*

✓ key word

university degree course leading to a diploma; **deuxième ~** *final two years of a university degree course*; **troisième ~** postgraduate (BrE) *or* graduate (AmE) studies
4 (bi)cycle

cyclique /siklik/ *adj* cyclic

cyclisme /siklism/ *m* cycling; cycle racing

cycliste /siklist/ **A** *adj* ‹*club*› cycling; ‹*race*› cycle; **coureur ~** racing cyclist
B *mf* cyclist; **short de ~** cycling shorts

cyclone /siklon/ *m* **1** cyclone
2 (in weather) depression

cygne /siɲ/ *m* swan; **~ mâle** cob; **~ femelle** pen; **jeune ~** cygnet

cylindre /silɛ̃dʀ/ *m* **1** cylinder
2 roller

cylindrée /silɛ̃dʀe/ *f* capacity, size; **~ de 1200 cm^3** 1200 cc engine

cymbale /sɛ̃bal/ *m* cymbal

cynique /sinik/ *adj* cynical

cynisme /sinism/ *m* cynicism

cyprès /sipʀɛ/ *m* cypress

cystite /sistit/ *f* cystitis

Dd

d, D /de/ *m inv* d, D

d' ▸ **de**

DAB /deabe/ *m* (*abbr* = **distributeur automatique de billets**) automatic teller machine, ATM

dactylographie /daktilɔgʀafi/ *f* typing

dada /dada/ *m* (fam) **1** (baby talk) horsie (fam)
2 hobby
3 hobby horse

dadais /dadɛ/ *m inv* (fam) clumsy youth; **espèce de grand ~!** you great oaf!

daigner /deɲe/ [**v1**] *vt* to deign (**faire** to do)

daim /dɛ̃/ *m* **1** (fallow) deer
2 venison
3 buckskin
4 suede

dallage /dalaʒ/ *m* paving

dalle /dal/ *f* **1** slab
2 flagstone
3 concrete foundation slab
IDIOMS **avoir la ~** (fam) to be ravenous; **que ~** (pop) nothing at all, zilch (fam)

daller /dale/ [**v1**] *vt* to pave

daltonien, -ienne /daltɔnjɛ̃, ɛn/ *adj* colourblind (BrE), colorblind (AmE)

dam /dɑ̃, dɑm/ *m* **au grand ~ de** to the great displeasure of

dame /dam/ **A** *f* **1** lady
2 (in cards, chess) queen; (in draughts) King
B dames *fpl* draughts (BrE), checkers (AmE)

damier /damje/ *m* draughtboard (BrE), checkerboard (AmE)

damnation /danasjɔ̃/ *f* damnation

damner /dɑne/ [**v1**] **A** *vt* to damn
B se damner *v refl* (+ *v être*) to damn oneself; **se ~ pour qch** (fam) to sell one's soul for sth

dancing /dɑ̃siŋ/ *m* dance hall

dandiner: **se dandiner** /dɑ̃dine/ [**v1**] *v refl* (+ *v être*) ‹*duck*› to waddle

Danemark /danmaʀk/ *pr m* Denmark

danger /dɑ̃ʒe/ *m* danger
■ **~ public** danger to the public; (fig) menace

dangereusement /dɑ̃ʒʀøzmɑ̃/ *adv* dangerously

dangereux, -euse /dɑ̃ʒʀø, øz/ *adj* dangerous

danois, ~e /danwa, az/ **A** *adj* Danish
B *m* **1** (language) Danish
2 (dog) Great Dane

dans /dɑ̃/ *prep* **1** in; **être ~ la cuisine** to be in the kitchen; **être ~ un avion/bateau** to be on a plane/boat
2 into; **entrer ~ une pièce** to go into a room; **monter ~ un avion** to get on a plane
3 boire ~ un verre to drink out of a glass; **prendre qch ~ un placard** to take sth out of a cupboard
4 ~ deux heures in two hours; **fait ~ les deux heures** done within two hours; **je t'appellerai ~ la journée** I'll phone you during the day
5 ~ les 30 euros about 30 euros

danse /dɑ̃s/ *f* **1** dance
2 dancing; **faire de la ~** to take dancing classes
■ **~ classique** classical ballet

danser /dɑ̃se/ [**v1**] *vt, vi* to dance
IDIOM **ne pas savoir sur quel pied ~** not to know what to do

danseur, -euse /dɑ̃sœʀ, øz/ *mf* dancer; **~ étoile** principal dancer

dard /daʀ/ *m* **1** (Zool) sting
2 spear

dare-dare /daʀdaʀ/ *adv* (fam) double quick

darne /daʀn/ *f* (fish) steak
dartre /daʀtʀ/ *f* scurf patch
✓ **date** /dat/ *f* **1** date; **~ limite** deadline; **~ limite de vente** sell-by date
2 time; **depuis cette ~** from that time; **un ami de longue ~** a long-standing friend; **le dernier scandale en ~** the latest scandal
dater /date/ [**v1**] **A** *vt* to date; **à ~ du 31 juillet** as from 31 July
B *vi* **1 ~ de** to date from
2 to be dated
dation /dasjɔ̃/ *f* **~ (en paiement)** payment in kind
datte /dat/ *f* (Bot, Culin) date
dattier /datje/ *m* date palm
daube /dob/ *f* **bœuf en ~** beef casserole
dauphin /dofɛ̃/ *m* **1** dolphin
2 heir apparent
3 dauphin
daurade /dɔʀad/ *f* (sea) bream
✓ **davantage** /davɑ̃taʒ/ *adv* **1** more
2 longer; **rester ~** to stay longer
DCA /desea/ *f* (*abbr* = **défense contre les aéronefs**) anti-aircraft defence (BrE)
DDASS /das/ *f* (*abbr* = **Direction départementale de l'action sanitaire et sociale**) regional social services department
✓ **de** /də/, **d'** *before vowel or mute h* /d/

> You will find translations for expressions such as *d'abord, de travers, pomme de terre, chemin de fer* etc, at the entries **abord, travers, pomme, chemin** etc.

A *prep* **1** from; **venir ~ Paris** to come from Paris; **il est ~ père italien** his father is Italian
2 by; **un poème ~ Victor Hugo** a poem by Victor Hugo
3 of; **les chapeaux ~ Paul** Paul's hats; **le 20 du mois** the 20th of the month; **deux heures d'attente** a two hour wait; **deux heures ~ libres** two hours free
4 than; **plus/moins ~ dix** more/less than ten
5 in; **d'un ton monocorde** in a monotone
6 with; **pousser qch du pied** to push sth aside with one's foot
7 travailler ~ nuit to work at night; **ne rien faire ~ la journée** to do nothing all day
8 être content ~ faire to be happy to do
B *det* **de, de l', de la, du** some; any; **voulez-vous ~ la bière?** would you like some beer?; **je n'ai pas d'argent** I haven't got any money
dé /de/ *m* **1** dice; **les ~s sont jetés** the die is cast
2 ~ (à coudre) thimble
DEA /deəa/ *m* (*abbr* = **diplôme d'études approfondies**) postgraduate certificate (*prior to doctoral thesis*)
déambulateur /deɑ̃bylatœʀ/ *m* Zimmer® (frame)
déambuler /deɑ̃byle/ [**v1**] *vi* to wander (about)
débâcle /debɑkl/ *f* **1** (Mil) rout
2 (fig) collapse
déballage /debalaʒ/ *m* (fam) jumble; outpouring
déballer /debale/ [**v1**] *vt* **1** to unpack
2 to display
débandade /debɑ̃dad/ *f* **1** stampede
2 disarray
débarbouiller /debaʀbuje/ [**v1**] **A** *vt* to wash
B se débarbouiller *v refl* (+ *v être*) to wash one's face
débarcadère /debaʀkadɛʀ/ *m* landing stage, jetty
débardeur /debaʀdœʀ/ *m* tank top
débarquement /debaʀkəmɑ̃/ *m* **1** (of goods) unloading
2 (of passengers) disembarkation
3 (Mil) landing
débarquer /debaʀke/ [**v1**] **A** *vt* to unload ‹*goods*›
B *vi* **1** to disembark
2 (Mil) to land
3 (fam) to turn up (fam) (**chez qn** at sb's place)
débarras /debaʀa/ *m inv* **1** junk room
2 bon ~! (fam) good riddance!
débarrasser /debaʀase/ [**v1**] **A** *vt* **1** to clear (out)
2 ~ qn de to free sb from ‹*complex*›; **~ qn (de son manteau)** to take sb's coat
B se débarrasser *v refl* (+ *v être*) **se ~ de** to get rid of; to dispose of
IDIOM **~ le plancher** (fam) to clear off (fam)
✓ **débat** /deba/ *m* debate
débattre /debatʀ/ [**v61**] **A** *vt* to negotiate
B débattre de *or* **sur** *v+prep* **1 ~ de** *or* **sur** to discuss
2 ~ de *or* **sur** to debate
C se débattre *v refl* (+ *v être*) to struggle
débauche /deboʃ/ *f* **1** debauchery
2 profusion
débaucher /deboʃe/ [**v1**] *vt* **1** to corrupt
2 to lay [sb] off
3 (fam) to tempt [sb] away
débile /debil/ **A** *adj* (fam) daft (fam)
B *mf* **~ mental** (Med) person with intellectual disabilities
débilité /debilite/ *f* **1** debility
2 (fam) stupidity
débiner /debine/ (fam) [**v1**] **A** *vt* to badmouth (fam)
B se débiner *v refl* (+ *v être*) to clear off (fam); to make oneself scarce (fam)
débit /debi/ *m* **1** debit; **la somme est inscrite au ~** the sum has been debited
2 (when speaking) delivery
3 (of river) rate of flow
4 (of liquid) flow; (of gas) output
5 (Comput) **haut ~** broadband

✓ key word

■ ~ **de boissons** bar

débiter /debite/ [**v1**] *vt* **1** to debit
2 to reel [sth] off; ~ **des bêtises** to talk a lot of nonsense
3 to cut [sth] up

débiteur, **-trice** /debitœʀ, tʀis/ **A** *adj* **compte** ~ debit account; **pays** ~ debtor nation
B *mf* debtor

déblayer /debleje/ [**v21**] *vt* **1** to clear away ‹*earth, snow*›
2 to clear ‹*place*›

débloquer /deblɔke/ [**v1**] **A** *vt* **1** to unlock ‹*steering wheel*›; to unjam ‹*mechanism*›
2 to unfreeze ‹*prices*›; to end the deadlock in ‹*situation*›
3 to make [sth] available ‹*credit*›
B *vi* (fam) to be off one's rocker (fam)

déboires /debwaʀ/ *mpl* **1** disappointments
2 trials, difficulties
3 setbacks

déboiser /debwaze/ [**v1**] *vt* to deforest

déboîter /debwate/ [**v1**] **A** *vt* to disconnect ‹*tubes*›
B *vi* ‹*car*› to pull out
C se déboîter *v refl* (+ *v être*) **se** ~ **le genou** to dislocate one's knee

débonnaire /debɔnɛʀ/ *adj* good-humoured (BrE); kindly

débordant, ~**e** /debɔʀdɑ̃, ɑ̃t/ *adj*
1 ‹*imagination*› overactive
2 ~ **de** brimming with ‹*energy*›; bursting with ‹*health*›

débordé, ~**e** /debɔʀde/ **A** *pp* ▶ **déborder**
B *pp adj* **1** overwhelmed
2 overloaded

débordement /debɔʀdəmɑ̃/ *m* (of protest) flood; (of enthusiasm) excess; **parking de** ~ overflow car park

déborder /debɔʀde/ [**v1**] **A** *vt* **1** ‹*problem, feeling*› to go beyond
2 se laisser ~ to let oneself be overwhelmed
3 (Mil, Sport) to outflank
B déborder de *v+prep* to be brimming over with; to be bursting with
C *vi* **1** ‹*river*› to overflow
2 ‹*liquid*› to overflow; to boil over
3 to jut out

débouché /debuʃe/ *m* **1** market; ~**s à l'exportation** export outlets
2 job opportunity

déboucher /debuʃe/ [**v1**] **A** *vt* **1** to unblock
2 to open; to uncork
B *vi* ~ **sur** ‹*street*› to open onto; ‹*talks*› to lead to
C se déboucher *v refl* (+ *v être*) **1** to come unblocked
2 ‹*ears*› to pop
3 se ~ **les oreilles/le nez** to unblock one's ears/nose

débouler /debule/ [**v1**] **A** *vt* to charge down
B *vi* **1** to tumble down
2 (fam) to turn up

déboulonner /debulɔne/ [**v1**] *vt* to unbolt

débourser /debuʀse/ [**v1**] *vt* to pay out

déboussoler /debusɔle/ [**v1**] *vt* (fam) to confuse

✓ **debout** /dəbu/ **A** *adj inv, adv* **1** standing; ‹*object*› upright; **se mettre** ~ to stand up; **je ne tiens plus** ~ I'm falling asleep on my feet
2 ton histoire tient ~ (fam) your story seems likely
3 (out of bed) **être** ~ to be up
B *excl* get up!

déboutonner /debutɔne/ [**v1**] **A** *vt* to unbutton
B se déboutonner *v refl* (+ *v être*) to come undone

débraillé, ~**e** /debʀɑje/ *adj* ‹*person*› dishevelled (BrE); ‹*clothes, style*› sloppy

débrancher /debʀɑ̃ʃe/ [**v1**] *vt* to unplug ‹*appliance*›; to disconnect ‹*alarm system*›

débrayer /debʀeje/ [**v21**] *vi* (Aut) to declutch

débridé, ~**e** /debʀide/ *adj* unbridled

débris /debʀi/ *m inv* **1** fragment; **des** ~ **de verre** broken glass
2 piece of wreckage

débrouillard, ~**e** /debʀujaʀ, aʀd/ *adj* resourceful

débrouiller /debʀuje/ [**v1**] **A** *vt* **1** to disentangle ‹*threads*›
2 to solve ‹*riddle*›
B se débrouiller *v refl* (+ *v être*) **1** to manage
2 to get by; **il se débrouille bien en espagnol** he speaks good Spanish

débroussailler /debʀusaje/ [**v1**] *vt* to clear the undergrowth from; (fig) to do the groundwork on

débusquer /debyske/ [**v1**] *vt* to flush [sb/sth] out

✓ **début** /deby/ **A** *m* beginning; start
B débuts *mpl* **1** debut
2 early stages

débutant, ~**e** /debytɑ̃, ɑ̃t/ **A** *adj* ‹*driver, skier*› novice; ‹*engineer*› recently qualified
B *mf* beginner

débuter /debyte/ [**v1**] *vi* **1** ‹*day, novel*› to begin, to start; ‹*person*› to start off
2 to start out (**comme** as)
3 ‹*performer*› to make one's debut

deçà /dəsa/ **A** *adv* ~, **delà** here and there
B en deçà *phr* **1** on this side
2 below

décacheter /dekaʃte/ [**v20**] *vt* to unseal

décade /dekad/ *f* **1** 10-day period
2 (controversial) decade

décadence /dekadɑ̃s/ *f* decadence; decline

décadent, ~**e** /dekadɑ̃, ɑ̃t/ *adj* **1** decadent
2 in decline

décaféiné, ~**e** /dekafeine/ *adj* decaffeinated

décalage /dekalaʒ/ *m* **1** gap
2 discrepancy
3 interval, time lag
4 shift
■ **~ horaire** time difference
décalcomanie /dekalkɔmani/ *f* transfer
décaler /dekale/ [**v1**] **A** *vt* **1** to bring forward ‹*date, departure time*›
2 to put (BrE) *or* move (AmE) back
3 to move [sth] forward ‹*object*›
4 to move [sth] back ‹*object*›
B se décaler *v refl* (+ *v être*) **se ~ sur la droite** to move *or* shift to the right
décalquer /dekalke/ [**v1**] *vt* **1** to trace (**sur** from)
2 to transfer (**sur** onto)
décamper /dekɑ̃pe/ [**v1**] *vi* (fam) to run off
décanter /dekɑ̃te/ [**v1**] **A** *vt* to allow [sth] to settle ‹*liquid*›; to clarify ‹*waste water*›
B se décanter *v refl* (+ *v être*) **1** ‹*liquid*› to settle
2 ‹*situation, ideas*› to become clearer
décapant, **~e** /dekapɑ̃, ɑ̃t/ *adj* **1** scouring
2 (fam) ‹*humour*› abrasive, caustic
décaper /dekape/ [**v1**] *vt* **1** to clean
2 to strip ‹*furniture*›; **~ avec un abrasif** to scour
3 (fam) ‹*alcohol, soap*› to be harsh
décapitation /dekapitasjɔ̃/ *f* decapitation; beheading
décapiter /dekapite/ [**v1**] *vt* to behead; to decapitate
décapotable /dekapɔtabl/ *adj* **une (voiture) ~** a convertible
décapsuler /dekapsyle/ [**v1**] *vt* to take the top off
décapsuleur /dekapsylœʀ/ *m* bottle opener
décathlon /dekatlɔ̃/ *m* decathlon
décéder /desede/ [**v14**] *vi* (+ *v être*) to die
décelable /deslabl/ *adj* detectable
déceler /desle/ [**v17**] *vt* **1** to detect
2 to reveal ‹*anomaly, feeling*›
3 to indicate ‹*presence*›
⚷ **décembre** /desɑ̃bʀ/ *m* December
décemment /desamɑ̃/ *adv* decently
décence /desɑ̃s/ *f* decency
décennie /deseni/ *f* decade
décent, **~e** /desɑ̃, ɑ̃t/ *adj* **1** decent
2 proper
décentraliser /desɑ̃tʀalize/ [**v1**] *vt* to decentralize
décentrer /desɑ̃tʀe/ [**v1**] *vt* to move away from the centre (BrE)
déception /desɛpsjɔ̃/ *f* disappointment
décerner /desɛʀne/ [**v1**] *vt* to award
décès /desɛ/ *m inv* death
décevant, **~e** /desəvɑ̃, ɑ̃t/ *adj* disappointing
décevoir /desəvwaʀ/ [**v5**] *vt* **1** to disappoint
2 to fail to fulfil (BrE) ‹*hope*›

⚷ key word

déchaîné, **~e** /deʃene/ **A** *pp* ▸ **déchaîner**
B *pp adj* stirred up; **~ contre** furious with
déchaîner /deʃene/ [**v1**] **A** *vt* to rouse ‹*feelings*›; to excite ‹*people*›
B se déchaîner *v refl* (+ *v être*) **1** ‹*sea*› to rage; ‹*feelings*› to burst out
2 to go wild
déchanter /deʃɑ̃te/ [**v1**] *vi* to become disenchanted
décharge /deʃaʀʒ/ *f* **1** (of firearm) discharge
2 ~ municipale (municipal) dump
3 ~ électrique electric shock
4 (Law) acquittal
décharger /deʃaʀʒe/ [**v13**] **A** *vt* **1** to unload ‹*vessel, goods*›
2 to unload ‹*firearm*›
3 to fire ‹*gun*›
4 ~ qn de to relieve sb of ‹*task*›
5 to discharge ‹*battery*›
6 to unburden ‹*conscience*›
B se décharger *v refl* (+ *v être*) **1 se ~ de qch** to off-load sth
2 ‹*battery*› to run down
décharné, **~e** /deʃaʀne/ *adj* ‹*body*› emaciated; ‹*finger*› bony
déchausser: **se déchausser** /deʃose/ [**v1**] *v refl* (+ *v être*) **1** to take off one's shoes
2 ‹*teeth*› to work loose due to receding gums
dèche /dɛʃ/ *f* (fam) **être dans la ~** to be broke (fam)
déchéance /deʃeɑ̃s/ *f* **1** decline
2 degeneration
déchet /deʃɛ/ **A** *m* **1** scrap
2 waste
3 wreck
B déchets *mpl* waste material, waste; **~s industriels** industrial waste; **~s nucléaires** nuclear waste
déchetterie /deʃɛtʀi/ *f* waste reception centre (BrE)
déchiffrer /deʃifʀe/ [**v1**] *vt* **1** to decipher
2 (Mus) to sight-read
déchiqueté, **~e** /deʃikte/ **A** *pp* ▸ **déchiqueter**
B *pp adj* jagged, ragged
déchiqueter /deʃikte/ [**v20**] *vt* **1** to tear [sth] to shreds
2 ‹*machine, animal*› to tear to pieces
déchirant, **~e** /deʃiʀɑ̃, ɑ̃t/ *adj* **1** heart-rending
2 agonizing
déchirer /deʃiʀe/ [**v1**] **A** *vt* **1** to tear up ‹*paper, material*›
2 to tear ‹*garment*›
3 to split ‹*group*›; **déchiré entre X et Y** torn between X and Y
B se déchirer *v refl* (+ *v être*) **1** to tear
2 se ~ un muscle to tear a muscle
3 to tear each other apart
déchirure /deʃiʀyʀ/ *f* (gen), (Med) tear
déchoir /deʃwaʀ/ [**v51**] *vi* to demean oneself; **~ de son rang** to come down in the world

déchu, **∼e** /deʃy/ **A** *pp* ▶ **déchoir**
B *adj* ‹*monarch*› deposed; ‹*angel*› fallen

décibel /desibɛl/ *m* decibel

décidé, **∼e** /deside/ **A** *pp* ▶ **décider**
B *pp adj* determined; resolute

décidément /desidemɑ̃/ *adv* really

décider /deside/ [**v1**] **A** *vt* **1** to decide; **c'est décidé** it's settled
2 to persuade (**à faire** to do)
B **décider de** *v+prep* to decide on; to fix
C **se décider** *v refl* (+ *v être*) **1** to make up one's mind
2 **se ∼ pour** to decide on

décideur /desidœʀ/ *m* decision-maker

décimal, **∼e** *mpl* **-aux** /desimal, o/ *adj* decimal

décimale /desimal/ *f* decimal

décimer /desime/ [**v1**] *vt* to decimate

décisif, **-ive** /desizif, iv/ *adj* **1** decisive
2 conclusive

décision /desizjɔ̃/ *f* **1** decision
2 decisiveness

déclamer /deklame/ [**v1**] *vt* to declaim

déclaration /deklaʀasjɔ̃/ *f* **1** statement; declaration
2 notification
3 (Law) statement; **∼ de vol/perte** report of theft/loss
■ **∼ d'impôts** (income) tax return

déclaré, **∼e** /deklaʀe/ *adj* ‹*enemy*› avowed; ‹*hatred*› professed

déclarer /deklaʀe/ [**v1**] **A** *vt* **1** to declare; **il a été déclaré coupable** he was found guilty
2 to declare ‹*goods, revenue*›; to report ‹*theft*›; to register ‹*birth*›; **non déclaré** undeclared; illegal
B **se déclarer** *v refl* (+ *v être*) **1** ‹*fire, epidemic*› to break out; ‹*fever*› to start
2 **se ∼ pour/contre** to come out for/against

déclenchement /deklɑ̃ʃmɑ̃/ *m* (of mechanism) release; (of illness) onset; (of reaction) start

déclencher /deklɑ̃ʃe/ [**v1**] **A** *vt* **1** to spark (off) ‹*protest*›; to cause ‹*reaction, explosion*›; to start ‹*avalanche*›
2 to launch ‹*offensive*›; to start ‹*strike, debate*›
3 to set off ‹*mechanism*›
B **se déclencher** *v refl* (+ *v être*) **1** to go off; to be activated
2 to break out; to begin

déclic /deklik/ *m* **1** trigger
2 (of camera) click

déclin /deklɛ̃/ *m* decline

déclinaison /deklinɛzɔ̃/ *f* declension

décliner /dekline/ [**v1**] **A** *vt* **1** to decline; to turn [sth] down
2 **∼ son identité** to give one's name
3 to decline
B *vi* ‹*light, talent*› to fade; ‹*health*› to deteriorate; ‹*enthusiasm*› to wane; ‹*sun*› to go down
C **se décliner** *v refl* (+ *v être*) to decline

décocher /dekɔʃe/ [**v1**] *vt* to shoot ‹*arrow*›

décoder /dekɔde/ [**v1**] *vt* to decode

décodeur /dekɔdœʀ/ *m* decoder

décoiffer /dekwafe/ [**v1**] *vt* **∼ qn** to ruffle sb's hair

décoincer /dekwɛ̃se/ [**v12**] *vt* to unjam ‹*mechanism, door*›; to free ‹*key*›

décollage /dekɔlaʒ/ *m* take-off

décoller /dekɔle/ [**v1**] **A** *vt* to peel off ‹*sticker*›
B *vi* ‹*plane*› to take off
C **se décoller** *v refl* (+ *v être*) to come off

décolleté, **∼e** /dekɔlte/ **A** *adj* low-cut
B *m* low neckline

décolleuse /dekɔløz/ *f* steam stripper

décolonisation /dekɔlɔnizasjɔ̃/ *f* decolonization

décolorant, **∼e** /dekɔlɔʀɑ̃, ɑ̃t/ *adj* bleaching

décolorer /dekɔlɔʀe/ [**v1**] *vt* **1** to bleach
2 to cause to fade

décombres /dekɔ̃bʀ/ *mpl* rubble

décommander /dekɔmɑ̃de/ [**v1**] **A** *vt* to call [sth] off
B **se décommander** *v refl* (+ *v être*) to cry off (BrE), to beg off

décomposer /dekɔ̃poze/ [**v1**] **A** *vt* **1** to break down ‹*argument, water*›
2 to distort ‹*features*›
B **se décomposer** *v refl* (+ *v être*) **1** to decompose
2 to fall apart

décomposition /dekɔ̃pozisjɔ̃/ *f* **1** decomposition
2 disintegration

décompte /dekɔ̃t/ *m* **1** discount
2 count; **faire le ∼ de** to count [sth] up ‹*votes, points*›

décompter /dekɔ̃te/ [**v1**] *vt* **1** to deduct (**de** from)
2 to count ‹*votes, points*›

déconcentrer /dekɔ̃sɑ̃tʀe/ [**v1**] *vt* to distract

déconcertant, **∼e** /dekɔ̃sɛʀtɑ̃, ɑ̃t/ *adj* disconcerting; **d'une facilité ∼e** ridiculously easy

déconcerter /dekɔ̃sɛʀte/ [**v1**] *vt* to disconcert

déconfit, **∼e** /dekɔ̃fi, it/ *adj* crestfallen

déconfiture /dekɔ̃fityʀ/ *f* **1** (of person) failure; (of party, team) defeat
2 (of company) collapse

décongeler /dekɔ̃ʒle/ [**v17**] *vt*, *vi* to defrost

décongestionner /dekɔ̃ʒɛstjɔne/ [**v1**]
A *vt* **1** to ease the pressure on ‹*university, services*›; ‹*motorway*› to relieve congestion in ‹*street, town*›
2 to clear ‹*nose*›
B **se décongestionner** *v refl* (+ *v être*) to clear

d

déconnecter /dekɔnɛkte/ [**v1**] *vt* **1** to disconnect ‹*appliance*›
2 to dissociate

déconner /dekɔne/ [**v1**] *vi* (pop) **1** to kid around (fam); **faut pas ~!** come off it! (fam)
2 to mess around (fam); to piss around (BrE) (sl)
3 to play up (fam)

déconseiller /dekɔ̃seje/ [**v1**] *vt* to advise against

déconsidérer /dekɔ̃sideʀe/ [**v14**] **A** *vt* to discredit
B **se déconsidérer** *v refl* (+ *v être*) **tu t'es déconsidéré** it was unworthy of you

décontenancer /dekɔ̃tnɑ̃se/ [**v12**] *vt* to disconcert

décontracté, **~e** /dekɔ̃tʀakte/ **A** *pp* ▶ **décontracter**
B *pp adj* **1** relaxed
2 casual
3 laid-back (fam)

décontracter /dekɔ̃tʀakte/ [**v1**] *vt*, **se décontracter** *v refl* (+ *v être*) to relax

décontraction /dekɔ̃tʀaksjɔ̃/ *f* **1** relaxation
2 ease
3 casual attitude

déconvenue /dekɔ̃vəny/ *f* disappointment

décor /dekɔʀ/ *m* **1** decor
2 setting; **j'ai besoin de changer de ~** I need a change of scene; **partir dans le ~** (fam) to drive off the road
3 (of film) set; **tourné en ~ naturel** shot on location

décorateur, **-trice** /dekɔʀatœʀ, tʀis/ *mf*
1 interior decorator
2 set designer

décoratif, **-ive** /dekɔʀatif, iv/ *adj*
1 ornamental
2 decorative

décoration /dekɔʀasjɔ̃/ *f* **1** decorating
2 (gen), (Mil) decoration
3 interior design

décorer /dekɔʀe/ [**v1**] *vt* to decorate

décortiquer /dekɔʀtike/ [**v1**] *vt* to shell ‹*nut*›; to peel ‹*prawn*›

décote /dekɔt/ *f* (Econ) drop

découcher /dekuʃe/ [**v1**] *vi* to spend the night away from home

découdre /dekudʀ/ [**v76**] **A** *vt* to undo, to unpick (BrE) ‹*hem, seam*›
B *vi* **en ~** to have a fight (**avec** with)

découler /dekule/ [**v1**] *vi* **1** to follow (**de** from)
2 to result (**de** from)

découpage /dekupaʒ/ *m* cut-out

découper /dekupe/ [**v1**] *vt* to cut up ‹*tart*›; to carve ‹*roast*›; to divide up ‹*land*›

découragé, **~e** /dekuʀaʒe/ *adj* ‹*person*› disheartened; ‹*expression*› despondent; ‹*tone*› dejected

décourageant, **~e** /dekuʀaʒɑ̃, ɑ̃t/ *adj* disheartening

découragement /dekuʀaʒmɑ̃/ *m* discouragement, despondency

décourager /dekuʀaʒe/ [**v13**] *vt* **1** to dishearten
2 to discourage
3 to deter

décousu, **~e** /dekuzy/ **A** *pp* ▶ **découdre**
B *pp adj* ‹*hem*› which has come undone
C *adj* ‹*story*› rambling; ‹*conversation*› casual

découvert, **~e** /dekuvɛʀ, ɛʀt/ **A** *pp* ▶ **découvrir**
B *pp adj* **1** bare; **avoir la tête ~e** to be bare-headed
2 ‹*truck*› open; ‹*car*› open-topped
C *m* overdraft; **être à ~** to be overdrawn

🔑 **découverte** /dekuvɛʀt/ *f* discovery

🔑 **découvrir** /dekuvʀiʀ/ [**v32**] **A** *vt* **1** to discover; **faire ~ qch à qn** to introduce sb to sth
2 to show ‹*arm, back*›
3 to leave [sth] exposed ‹*border*›
B **se découvrir** *v refl* (+ *v être*) **1** to remove one's hat
2 **elle s'est découvert un talent** she found she had a talent

décrasser /dekʀase/ [**v1**] *vt* to get [sb/sth] clean

décrépit, **~e** /dekʀepi, it/ *adj* ‹*person*› decrepit; ‹*building*› dilapidated; ‹*wall*› crumbling

décrépitude /dekʀepityd/ *f* degeneration; decay; decrepitude

décret /dekʀɛ/ *m* decree

décréter /dekʀete/ [**v14**] *vt* **1** to order
2 to decree (**que** that)
3 to declare (**que** that)

🔑 **décrire** /dekʀiʀ/ [**v67**] *vt* **1** to describe
2 to follow

décrocher /dekʀɔʃe/ [**v1**] **A** *vt* **1** to take down ‹*picture*›
2 to uncouple ‹*wagon*›
3 **~ son téléphone** to pick up the receiver; to take the phone off the hook
4 (fam) to get ‹*contract*›
B *vi* to give up
IDIOM **~ le gros lot** to hit the jackpot

décroissant, **~e** /dekʀwasɑ̃, ɑ̃t/ *adj* fading; lessening; **par** *or* **en ordre ~** in descending order

décroître /dekʀwɑtʀ/ [**v72**] *vi* ‹*level*› to fall; ‹*moon*› to wane; ‹*day*› to get shorter; ‹*light, noise*› to fade; ‹*inflation*› to go down

décrypter /dekʀipte/ [**v1**] *vt* **1** to decipher ‹*signs*›
2 to interpret ‹*statement*›

déçu, **~e** /desy/ ▶ **décevoir**

déculpabiliser /dekylpabilize/ [**v1**] *vt* to free [sb] of guilt

🔑 key word

décupler /dekyple/ [**v1**] *vt, vi* to increase tenfold

dédaigner /dedeɲe/ [**v1**] *vt* to despise

dédaigneux, **-euse** /dedɛɲø, øz/ *adj* disdainful, scornful; **être ∼ du danger** to be unmindful of danger

dédain /dedɛ̃/ *m* contempt, disdain

dédale /dedal/ *m* **1** (of buildings) maze
2 (of laws, formalities) labyrinth

dedans /dədɑ̃/ **A** *adv* inside
B en dedans *phr* inside

dédicace /dedikas/ *f* **1** dedication (**à qn** to sb)
2 inscription

dédicacer /dedikase/ [**v12**] *vt* **1** to dedicate ‹*book*› (**à** to)
2 to sign ‹*book, photo*›

dédier /dedje/ [**v2**] *vt* **1** to dedicate ‹*novel*› (**à** to)
2 to devote ‹*life*› (**à** to)

dédire: **se dédire** /dediʀ/ [**v65**] *v refl* (+ *v être*) to back out

dédommagement /dedɔmaʒmɑ̃/ *m* compensation

dédommager /dedɔmaʒe/ [**v13**] *vt* **1** to compensate
2 ∼ qn de qch to make it up to sb for sth

dédouaner /dedwane/ [**v1**] *vt* to clear through customs

dédoubler: **se dédoubler** /deduble/ [**v1**] *v refl* (+ *v être*) ‹*nail*› to split; ‹*image*› to split in two; ‹*cable*› to come apart

dédramatiser /dedʀamatize/ [**v1**] *vi* to play things down

déductible /dedyktibl/ *adj* deductible (**de** from); **∼ des impôts** tax-deductible

déduction /dedyksjɔ̃/ *f* deduction

déduire /dedɥiʀ/ [**v69**] **A** *vt* **1** to deduce
2 to infer
3 to deduct
B se déduire *v refl* (+ *v être*) **1** to be inferred
2 to be deduced
3 to be deducted

déesse /deɛs/ *f* goddess

défaillance /defajɑ̃s/ *f* failure

défaillant, **∼e** /defajɑ̃, ɑ̃t/ *adj* **1** ‹*motor, system*› faulty
2 ‹*organization*› inefficient
3 ‹*health, memory*› failing; ‹*person*› fainting

défaillir /defajiʀ/ [**v28**] *vi* **1** to faint; **se sentir ∼** to feel faint
2 ‹*health, memory*› to fail; **soutenir qn sans ∼** to show unflinching support for sb

défaire /defɛʀ/ [**v10**] **A** *vt* to undo; to untie
B se défaire *v refl* (+ *v être*) **1** to come undone
2 se ∼ de to get rid of; to part with; to rid oneself of
3 ‹*face*› to fall; **avoir la mine défaite** to look haggard

défaite /defɛt/ *f* defeat

défaut /defo/ **A** *m* **1** fault, failing; **prendre qn en ∼** to catch sb out
2 defect; flaw; **présenter des ∼s** to be faulty; **∼ de fabrication** manufacturing fault; **∼ de prononciation** speech impediment
3 shortage; **faire ∼** ‹*money, resources*› to be lacking
B à défaut de *phr* **à ∼ de (quoi)** failing (which); **à ∼ de pouvoir acheter, elle loue** since she can't buy, she has to rent

défaveur /defavœʀ/ *f* **il s'est trompé de 5 euros en ma ∼** he overcharged me by 5 euros

défavorable /defavɔʀabl/ *adj* ‹*situation*› unfavourable (BrE) (**à** to); ‹*person*› opposed (**à** to)

défavorisé, **∼e** /defavɔʀize/ *adj*
1 underprivileged
2 disadvantaged

défavoriser /defavɔʀize/ [**v1**] *vt* **1** to discriminate against
2 to put [sb] at a disadvantage

défection /defɛksjɔ̃/ *f* **1** defection
2 non-appearance
3 (of friends) desertion

défectueux, **-euse** /defɛktɥø, øz/ *adj* ‹*material*› faulty, defective; ‹*reasoning*› flawed

défendre /defɑ̃dʀ/ [**v6**] **A** *vt* **1 ∼ à qn de faire** to forbid sb to do
2 to defend ‹*person, country, interests*›
3 to fight for ‹*right*›; to stand up for ‹*friend, principle*›; **∼ une cause** to champion a cause
4 (Law, Sport) to defend
B se défendre *v refl* (+ *v être*) **1** to defend oneself; to stand up for oneself
2 to be tenable
3 to protect oneself
4 (fam) to get by
5 on ne peut se ∼ de penser que... one can't help thinking that...

défense /defɑ̃s/ *f* **1 '∼ de fumer'** 'no smoking'; **∼ d'en parler devant lui** don't mention it in front of him
2 (Med, Mil, Sport) defence (BrE)
3 protection; **sans ∼** helpless; unprotected; **la ∼ de l'environnement** the protection of the environment; **prendre la ∼ de** to stand up for
4 (Zool) tusk

défenseur /defɑ̃sœʀ/ *m* defender

défensive /defɑ̃siv/ *f* **sur la ∼** on the defensive

déférence /defeʀɑ̃s/ *f* **marques de ∼** marks of respect

déferler /defɛʀle/ [**v1**] *vi* **1** ‹*wave*› to break (**sur** on)
2 ‹*violence*› to erupt
3 ∼ sur ‹*people*› to pour into ‹*country, town*›

d

défi /defi/ *m* **1** challenge; **mettre qn au ~ de faire** to challenge sb to do
2 air de ~ defiant look

défiance /defjɑ̃s/ *f* distrust, mistrust

défiant, **~e** /defjɑ̃, ɑ̃t/ *adj* distrustful, wary

déficience /defisjɑ̃s/ *f* deficiency

déficit /defisit/ *m* **1** deficit
2 (Med) deficiency

déficitaire /defisitɛʀ/ *adj* showing a deficit; showing a loss; showing a shortfall

défier /defje/ [**v2**] *vt* **1** to challenge ‹*rival*›
2 to defy ‹*danger, death*›; **prix défiant toute concurrence** unbeatable price

défigurer /defigyʀe/ [**v1**] *vt* to disfigure

défilé /defile/ *m* **1** parade
2 (protest) march
3 (of visitors, candidates) stream
4 gorge
■ **~ aérien** flypast (BrE), flyover (AmE); **~ militaire** march-past; **~ de mode** fashion show

défiler /defile/ [**v1**] **A** *vi* **1** to parade; ‹*protesters*› to march
2 ‹*people*› to come and go
3 ‹*images, landscape*› to unfold
4 (Comput) to scroll
B se défiler *v refl* (+ *v être*) (fam) to wriggle out of it

🔑 **définir** /definiʀ/ [**v3**] *vt* to define

définitif, **-ive** /definitif, iv/ **A** *adj* ‹*accounts, report*› final; ‹*edition*› definitive; ‹*refusal*› flat
B en définitive *phr* at the end of the day

🔑 **définition** /definisjɔ̃/ *f* definition

définitivement /definitivmɑ̃/ *adv* for good

défiscalisation /defiskalizasjɔ̃/ *m* (Fin) tax reduction, tax exemption

défiscalisé, **~e** /defiskalize/ *adj* tax-exempt

déflagration /deflagʀasjɔ̃/ *f* detonation

défoncer /defɔ̃se/ [**v12**] *vt* to break down ‹*door*›; to smash in ‹*back of a car*›

déformation /defɔʀmasjɔ̃/ *f* **1** distortion
2 deformity
3 c'est de la ~ professionnelle it's a habit that comes from the job

déformé, **~e** /defɔʀme/ *adj* ‹*face, image, truth*› distorted; ‹*object, mind*› warped; **chaussée ~e** uneven (road) surface

déformer /defɔʀme/ [**v1**] **A** *vt* **1** to bend [sth] (out of shape)
2 to distort
3 on a déformé mes propos my words have been twisted
B se déformer *v refl* (+ *v être*) to lose its shape

défoulement /defulmɑ̃/ *m* letting off steam

défouler /defule/ [**v1**] **A** *vt* **ça me défoule** it helps me (to) unwind
B se défouler *v refl* (+ *v être*) **1** to let off steam
2 se ~ sur qn to take it out on sb

défraîchi, **~e** /defʀeʃi/ *adj* ‹*garment, curtain*› worn; ‹*material, beauty*› faded

défrayer /defʀeje/ [**v21**] *vt* **1 ~ la chronique** to be the talk of the town
2 ~ qn to pay *or* meet sb's expenses

défricher /defʀiʃe/ [**v1**] *vt* to clear, to reclaim

défriser /defʀize/ [**v1**] *vt* to straighten

défroisser /defʀwase/ [**v1**] *vt* to smooth out

défunt, **~e** /defœ̃, œ̃t/ **A** *adj* **1** former
2 late
B *mf* **le ~** the deceased

dégagé, **~e** /degaʒe/ *adj* **1** ‹*road, sky*› clear; ‹*forehead*› bare
2 ‹*look*› casual

dégagement /degaʒmɑ̃/ *m* **1** clearing
2 (in football) clearance

🔑 **dégager** /degaʒe/ [**v13**] **A** *vt* **1** to free; **~ qn d'une responsabilité** to relieve sb of a responsibility; **~ des crédits** to make funds available
2 to unblock ‹*nose*›
3 to clear ‹*way*›; **'dégagez, s'il vous plaît'** 'move along please'; **dégage!** (fam) get lost! (fam)
4 to find ‹*idea, sense*›
5 to emit ‹*odour, gas*›; **~ de la chaleur** to give off heat
B se dégager *v refl* (+ *v être*) **1** to free oneself/itself
2 ‹*weather, sky*› to clear
3 se ~ de to come out of
4 to become clear

dégaine /degɛn/ *f* (fam) odd appearance

dégainer /degene/ [**v1**] *vt* to draw ‹*gun*›

dégarnir: **se dégarnir** /degaʀniʀ/ [**v3**] *v refl* (+ *v être*) to be going bald

dégât /degɑ/ *m* damage

dégel /deʒɛl/ *m* thaw

dégeler /deʒle/ [**v17**] **A** *vt* **1** to improve ‹*relations*›
2 to unfreeze ‹*credit*›
B *vi* to thaw (out)
C se dégeler *v refl* (+ *v être*) **1** ‹*relations, situation*› to thaw
2 ‹*audience*› to warm up

dégénérer /deʒeneʀe/ [**v14**] *vi* **1** ‹*incident*› to get out of hand; **~ en** to degenerate into
2 ‹*plant, species*› to degenerate

dégingandé, **~e** /deʒɛ̃gɑ̃de/ *adj* lanky

dégivrer /deʒivʀe/ [**v1**] *vt* **1** to de-ice ‹*windscreen*›
2 to defrost ‹*fridge*›

déglingué, **~e** /deglɛ̃ge/ *adj* (fam) dilapidated

déglutir /deglytiʀ/ [**v3**] *vt, vi* to swallow

dégonflé, **~e** **A** *adj* ‹*balloon*› deflated; ‹*tyre*› flat

---

🔑 key word

B *mf* (fam) chicken (fam), coward

dégonfler /degɔ̃fle/ [**v1**] **A** *vt* to deflate ‹*tyre*›
B *vi* ‹*swelling, bump*› to go down
C **se dégonfler** *v refl* (+ *v être*) **1** to deflate; to go down
2 (fam) to chicken out (fam)

dégoter /degɔte/ [**v1**] *vt also* **dégotter** (fam) to find

dégouliner /deguline/ [**v1**] *vi* **1** to trickle
2 to drip (**de** with)

dégoupiller /degupije/ [**v1**] *vt* **~ une grenade** to pull the pin out of a grenade

dégourdi, **~e** /deguʀdi/ *adj* smart

dégourdir: **se dégourdir** /deguʀdiʀ/ [**v3**] *v refl* (+ *v être*) **se ~ les jambes** to stretch one's legs

dégoût /degu/ *m* disgust

dégoûtant, **~e** /degutɑ̃, ɑ̃t/ *adj* **1** filthy
2 (fam) disgusting; revolting

dégoûté, **~e** /degute/ *adj* disgusted; **faire le ~** to turn one's nose up

dégoûter /degute/ [**v1**] *vt* **1** to disgust
2 to make [sb] feel sick
3 ~ qn de qch/de faire to put sb off sth/off doing

dégradant, **~e** /degʀadɑ̃, ɑ̃t/ *adj* degrading

dégradation /degʀadasjɔ̃/ *f* **1** damage
2 deterioration
3 decline; **la ~ des conditions de vie** the deterioration in the standard of living; **la ~ du pouvoir d'achat** the erosion in purchasing power

dégradé, **~e** /degʀade/ **A** *adj* **tons ~s** shaded tones; **coupe ~e** layered cut
B *m* (in colours) gradation

dégrader /degʀade/ [**v1**] **A** *vt* **1** to damage
2 (Mil) to cashier ‹*officer*›
3 to degrade ‹*person*›
B **se dégrader** *v refl* (+ *v être*) to deteriorate

dégrafer /degʀafe/ [**v1**] **A** *vt* to undo
B **se dégrafer** *v refl* (+ *v être*) to come undone

dégraisser /degʀese/ [**v1**] *vt* to trim the fat off

⚷ **degré** /dəgʀe/ *m* **1** degree; **par ~s** gradually; **à un moindre ~** to a lesser extent; **susceptible au plus haut ~** extremely touchy; **brûlures du premier ~** first-degree burns; **~ de parenté** degree of kinship
2 step; **enseignement du second ~** secondary education; **c'est à prendre au deuxième ~** it is not to be taken literally
3 titrer 40° d'alcool ≈ to be 70% proof
■ **~ Celsius** degree Celsius; **~ Fahrenheit** degree Fahrenheit

dégressif, **-ive** /degʀesif, iv/ *adj* ‹*tax*› graduated; **tarifs ~s** tapering charges

dégringolade /degʀɛ̃gɔlad/ *f* (fam) **1** (gen) fall
2 (Econ) collapse

dégringoler /degʀɛ̃gɔle/ (fam) [**v1**] **A** *vt* to race down ‹*stairs, hill*›
B *vi* **1** ‹*person*› to take a tumble; ‹*books*› to tumble down
2 to drop sharply

dégriser /degʀize/ [**v1**] *vt* **1** to sober [sb] up
2 to bring [sb] to his/her senses

déguerpir /degɛʀpiʀ/ [**v3**] *vi* to leave

déguisé, **~e** /degize/ *adj* **1** in fancy dress; in disguise
2 ‹*party*› fancy-dress
3 ‹*attempt*› concealed; ‹*compliment*› disguised

déguisement /degizmɑ̃/ *m* costume

déguiser /degize/ [**v1**] **A** *vt* **1** to dress [sb] up (**en** as)
2 to disguise
B **se déguiser** *v refl* (+ *v être*) **1** to dress up
2 to disguise oneself

dégustation /degystasjɔ̃/ *f* tasting

déguster /degyste/ [**v1**] *vt* to savour (BrE) ‹*drink, victory*›; to enjoy ‹*performance*›

déhanchement /deɑ̃ʃmɑ̃/ *m* **1** swaying hips
2 lopsidedness

déhancher: **se déhancher** /deɑ̃ʃe/ [**v1**] *v refl* (+ *v être*) to wiggle one's hips

⚷ **dehors** /dəɔʀ/ **A** *adv* outside; **mettre qn ~** to throw sb out; to fire sb; to expel sb
B *excl* get out!
C **en dehors de** *phr* **1** outside
2 apart from

⚷ **déjà** /deʒa/ *adv* **1** already
2 before, already; **je te l'ai ~ dit** I've told you before
3 (fam) **il s'est excusé, c'est ~ quelque chose** he apologized, that's something at least; **elle est ~ assez riche!** she's rich enough as it is; **c'est combien, ~?** how much was it again?

déjà-vu /deʒavy/ *m inv* déjà vu; **c'est du ~** (fam) we've seen it all before

déjeuner[1] /deʒœne/ [**v1**] *vi* to have lunch

⚷ **déjeuner**[2] /deʒœne/ *m* lunch

déjouer /deʒwe/ [**v1**] *vt* to frustrate ‹*precaution, manoeuvre*›; to foil ‹*plan*›; to evade ‹*inspection*›

⚷ **delà** /dəla/ *adv* **deçà** *or* **de-ci, ~** here and there

délabré, **~e** /delabʀe/ *adj* ‹*house, equipment*› dilapidated; ‹*health*› damaged

délabrement /delabʀəmɑ̃/ *m* dilapidation

délabrer /delabʀe/ [**v1**] **A** *vt* to ruin
B **se délabrer** *v refl* (+ *v être*) ‹*house*› to become run-down; ‹*business, country*› to go to rack and ruin; ‹*health*› to deteriorate

délacer /delase/ [**v12**] *vt* to undo; to unlace

délai /delɛ/ *m* **1 dans un ~ de 24 heures** within 24 hours; **respecter un ~** to meet a deadline; **dans les meilleurs ~s** as soon as possible

2 extension; **demander un ∼** to ask for extra time

■ **∼ de livraison** delivery *or* lead time

délaisser /delese/ [**v1**] *vt* **1** to abandon ‹*activity*›
2 to neglect ‹*friends*›

délassement /delɑsmɑ̃/ *m* relaxation

délasser /delɑse/ [**v1**] *vt, v refl* (+ *v être*) to relax; **ça délasse** it's relaxing

d

délateur, **-trice** /delatœʀ, tʀis/ *mf* informer

délation /delɑsjɔ̃/ *f* informing

délavé, **∼e** /delave/ *adj* **1** ‹*colour, sky*› washed-out; ‹*jeans*› faded
2 waterlogged

délayer /deleje/ [**v21**] *vt* to thin ‹*paint*›; to mix ‹*flour*›

délectation /delɛktasjɔ̃/ *f* delight

délecter: **se délecter** /delɛkte/ [**v1**] *v refl* (+ *v être*) **se ∼ à faire/en faisant** to delight in doing

délégation /delegasjɔ̃/ *f* delegation

délégué, **∼e** /delege/ *mf* delegate

■ **∼ syndical** union representative

déléguer /delege/ [**v14**] *vt* **1** to appoint [sb] as a delegate
2 to delegate ‹*responsibility, power*›

délestage /delɛstaʒ/ *m* **parking de ∼** overflow car park

délester /delɛste/ [**v1**] *vt* **1** to get rid of the ballast from
2 to divert traffic away from

délibération /delibeʀasjɔ̃/ *f* deliberation; **mettre qch en ∼** to debate sth

délibéré, **∼e** /delibeʀe/ *adj* ‹*act, violation*› deliberate; ‹*choice, policy*› conscious

délibérément /delibeʀemɑ̃/ *adv* ‹*wound, provoke*› deliberately; ‹*accept, choose*› consciously

délibérer /delibeʀe/ [**v14**] **A** **délibérer de** *or* **sur** *v+prep* to discuss
B *vi* to be in session

délicat, **∼e** /delika, at/ *adj* **1** ‹*dish*› subtle; ‹*person*› refined
2 tactful
3 thoughtful; **des procédés peu ∼s** unscrupulous means
4 ‹*balance, task*› delicate; ‹*business, moment*› sensitive; ‹*mission*› tricky
5 ‹*skin*› delicate

délicatement /delikatmɑ̃/ *adv* **1** delicately
2 tactfully

délicatesse /delikatɛs/ *f* **1** delicacy; **la ∼ de ses traits** his/her fine features
2 sensitivity
3 delicacy, trickiness

délice /delis/ *m* delight

délicieusement /delisjøzmɑ̃/ *adv*
1 deliciously
2 delightfully

délicieux, **-ieuse** /delisjø, øz/ *adj*
1 delicious
2 ‹*feeling, music*› delightful; ‹*joy*› exquisite

délié, **∼e** /delje/ *adj* **1** ‹*waist*› slender
2 ‹*movement*› loose
3 ‹*mind*› nimble

délier /delje/ [**v2**] *vt* to untie; **∼ qn de** to release sb from] ‹*promise*›

IDIOM **∼ la langue à qn** to loosen sb's tongue

délimiter /delimite/ [**v1**] *vt* **1** to mark the boundary of
2 to form the boundary of
3 to define ‹*role*›; to define the scope of ‹*subject*›

délinquance /delɛ̃kɑ̃s/ *f* crime; **la ∼ juvénile** juvenile delinquency

délinquant, **∼e** /delɛ̃kɑ̃, ɑ̃t/ **A** *adj* delinquent
B *mf* offender

déliquescence /delikesɑ̃s/ *f* decline

délirant, **∼e** /deliʀɑ̃, ɑ̃t/ *adj* **1** ‹*welcome*› ecstatic
2 (fam) ‹*scenario*› crazy (fam)

délire /deliʀ/ *m* **1** (Med) delirium
2 (fam) madness
3 frenzy; **salle en ∼** ecstatic audience

délirer /deliʀe/ [**v1**] *vi* **1** (Med) to be delirious
2 (fam) to be mad

délit /deli/ *m* offence (BrE)

■ **∼ de fuite** hit-and-run offence; **∼ d'initié** insider dealing

délivrance /delivʀɑ̃s/ *f* relief

délivrer /delivʀe/ [**v1**] *vt* **1** to free, to liberate; **∼ qn de** to relieve sb of
2 to issue ‹*passport*›

délocalisation /delɔkalizasjɔ̃/ *f* relocation; **∼ industrielle** relocation in search of cheap labour

délocaliser /delɔkalize/ *vt* to offshore

déloger /delɔʒe/ [**v13**] *vt* **1** to evict ‹*tenant*›
2 to flush out ‹*rebels, game*›
3 to remove ‹*dust*›

déloyal, **∼e**, *mpl* **-aux** /delwajal, o/ *adj* ‹*person*› disloyal; ‹*competition*› unfair

deltaplane /dɛltaplan/ *m* hang-glider

déluge /delyʒ/ *m* downpour; **∼ de** flood of ‹*tears, complaints*›; **le Déluge** the Flood

IDIOM **après moi le ∼** I don't care what happens after I'm gone

déluré, **∼e** /delyʀe/ *adj* **1** smart, resourceful
2 forward

démagogie /demagɔʒi/ *f* demagoguery, demagogy; **faire de la ∼** to try to gain popularity

démagogique /demagɔʒik/ *adj* demagogic

🗝 **demain** /dəmɛ̃/ *adv* tomorrow; **l'Europe de ∼** the Europe of the future

IDIOMS **∼ il fera jour** tomorrow is another day; **ce n'est pas ∼ la veille!** that's not going to happen in a hurry!

🗝 key word

démancher: **se démancher** /demɑ̃ʃe/ [**v1**] *v refl* (+ *v être*) ‹*tool*› to come off its handle

demande /dəmɑ̃d/ *f* **1** request, application, claim (**de** for); **~ de dommages et intérêts** claim for damages; **faire une ~ de mutation** to apply for a transfer
2 (in economics) demand
3 application form
■ **~ d'emploi** job application; **'~s d'emploi'** 'situations wanted'; **~ en mariage** marriage proposal

demandé, **~e** /dəmɑ̃de/ *adj* **très ~** ‹*destination*› very popular; ‹*product*› in great demand

demander /dəmɑ̃de/ [**v1**] **A** *vt* **1** to ask for ‹*advice, money, help*›; to apply for ‹*nationality*›; to claim ‹*damages*›; **~ le divorce** to sue for divorce; **~ en mariage** to propose to; **'on demande un plombier'** 'plumber wanted'; **fais ce qu'on te demande!** do as you're told!; **je ne demande pas mieux** there's nothing I would like better
2 ~ qch à qn to ask sb sth; **il m'a demandé de tes nouvelles** he asked after you
3 to send for ‹*priest*›; to dial ‹*number*›; **le patron vous demande** the boss wants to see you
4 to call for ‹*reforms*›; to require ‹*effort, qualification*›; to need ‹*attention*›
B se demander *v refl* (+ *v être*) to wonder

demandeur[1], **-euse** /dəmɑ̃dœʀ, øz/ *mf* applicant
■ **~ d'asile** asylum seeker; **~ d'emploi** job-seeker

demandeur[2], **-eresse** /dəmɑ̃dœʀ, d(ə)ʀɛs/ *mf* (Law) plaintiff

démangeaison /demɑ̃ʒɛzɔ̃/ *f* itch

démanger /demɑ̃ʒe/ [**v13**] *vt* **ça me démange** it itches, it's itching; **l'envie de le gifler me démangeait** I was itching to slap him

démanteler /demɑ̃tle/ [**v17**] *vt* to dismantle; to break up

démaquillage /demakijaʒ/ *m* make-up removal

démaquillant, **~e** /demakijɑ̃, ɑ̃t/ **A** *adj* ‹*milk*› cleansing
B *m* make-up remover

démaquiller: **se démaquiller** /demakije/ [**v1**] *v refl* (+ *v être*) to remove one's make-up

démarcation /demaʀkasjɔ̃/ *f* demarcation

démarchage /demaʀʃaʒ/ *m* door-to-door selling; **~ électoral** canvassing; **~ téléphonique** cold calling

démarche /demaʀʃ/ *f* **1** walk
2 step; **faire une ~ auprès de qn** to approach sb; **faire des ~s pour obtenir qch** to take steps to obtain sth
3 reasoning; **~ de la pensée** thought process

démarcher /demaʀʃe/ [**v1**] *vt* **1** to sell door-to-door
2 to canvass

démarque /demaʀk/ *f* (of goods) mark-down (**de** of)

démarquer /demaʀke/ [**v1**] **A** *vt* to mark down ‹*goods*›
B se démarquer *v refl* (+ *v être*) **1 se ~ de** to distance oneself from
2 (Sport) to get free of one's marker

démarrage /demaʀaʒ/ *m* **1** starting up
2 spurt
■ **~ en côte** hill start

démarrer /demaʀe/ [**v1**] **A** *vt* to start (up)
B *vi* **1** ‹*vehicle*› to pull away; ‹*engine*› to start; ‹*driver*› to drive off; ‹*business*› to start up; ‹*campaign*› to get under way; ‹*person*› to start off
2 (Sport) to put on a spurt

démarreur /demaʀœʀ/ *m* (in car) starter

démasquer /demaske/ [**v1**] *vt* to unmask ‹*person*›; to uncover ‹*plot*›

démazouter /demazute/ [**v1**] *vt* to clean the oil from ‹*beach*›

démêlé /demele/ *m* wrangle; **avoir des ~s avec la justice** to get into trouble with the law

démêler /demele/ [**v1**] *vt* **1** to disentangle; to untangle
2 to sort out ‹*situation*›

démembrement /demɑ̃bʀəmɑ̃/ *m* **1** break-up, dismemberment
2 (of estate) division

démembrer /demɑ̃bʀe/ [**v1**] *vt* to divide up, to dismember

déménagement /demenaʒmɑ̃/ *m* **1** moving house; move
2 removal; **entreprise de ~s** removals firm (BrE), moving company (AmE)

déménager /demenaʒe/ [**v13**] **A** *vt* **1** to move ‹*furniture*›; to relocate ‹*offices*›
2 to clear ‹*room*›
B *vi* **1** to move (house)
2 (fam) to push off (fam)
3 (fam) to be off one's rocker (fam)

déménageur /demenaʒœʀ/ *m* removal (BrE) *or* moving (AmE) man

démence /demɑ̃s/ *f* **1** insanity
2 dementia

démener: **se démener** /dem(ə)ne/ [**v16**] *v refl* (+ *v être*) **1** to thrash about
2 to put oneself out, to exert oneself

dément, **~e** /demɑ̃, ɑ̃t/ *adj* **1** insane, mad
2 (fam) terrific (fam)

démenti /demɑ̃ti/ *m* denial

démentiel, **-ielle** /demɑ̃sjɛl/ *adj* insane

démentir /demɑ̃tiʀ/ [**v30**] *vt* **1** to deny
2 ‹*person*› to refute ‹*statement*›; ‹*fact*› to give the lie to ‹*statement*›; to belie ‹*appearance*›

démesure /deməzyʀ/ *f* **1** (of ambition) excesses
2 excessive size

démesuré, **~e** /deməzyʀe/ *adj* excessive, immoderate

démettre /demɛtʀ/ [**v60**] **A** *vt* **1** to dislocate ‹*joint*›
2 to dismiss ‹*employee*›
B se démettre *v refl* (+ *v être*) **se ~ l'épaule** to dislocate one's shoulder

d

demeurant: **au demeurant** /odəmœʀɑ̃/ *phr* as it happens, for all that

demeure /dəmœʀ/ **A** *f* **1** residence
2 mettre qn en ~ de faire to require sb to do
B à demeure *phr* permanently; permanent
IDIOM **il n'y a pas péril en la ~** there's no rush

demeuré, **~e** /dəmœʀe/ *adj* retarded (offensive)

demeurer /dəmœʀe/ [**v1**] **A** *vi* **1** (+ *v avoir*) to reside, to live
2 (+ *v être*) to remain
B *v impers* **il n'en demeure pas moins que** nonetheless, the fact remains that

demi, **~e** /d(ə)mi/ **A et demi**, **et demie** *phr* and a half; **il est trois heures et ~e** it's half past three
B *mf* half
C *m* **1** glass of beer
2 (Sport) **~ de mêlée/d'ouverture** scrum/stand-off half
D à demi *phr* half; **à ~ éveillé** half awake
E demi- (*combining form*) **1** half; **une ~-pomme** half an apple
2 partial; **une ~-victoire** a partial victory

demi-cercle, *pl* **~s** /d(ə)misɛʀkl/ *m* semicircle

demie /d(ə)mi/ **A** *adj* ▶ **demi A, B**
B *f* **il est déjà la ~** it's already half past

demi-écrémé, **~e**, *mpl* **~s** /d(ə)miekʀeme/ *adj* semi-skimmed

demi-finale, *pl* **~s** /d(ə)mifinal/ *f* semi-final

demi-fond, *pl* **~s** /d(ə)mifɔ̃/ *m* middle-distance running

demi-frère, *pl* **~s** /d(ə)mifʀɛʀ/ *m* half-brother; stepbrother

demi-gros /d(ə)migʀo/ *m inv* wholesale direct to the public

demi-heure, *pl* **~s** /d(ə)mijœʀ/ *f* half an hour

demi-journée, *pl* **~s** /d(ə)miʒuʀne/ *f* half a day; **à la ~** on a half-day basis

démilitariser /demilitaʀize/ [**v1**] *vt* to demilitarize

demi-litre, *pl* **~s** /d(ə)militʀ/ *m* half a litre (BrE)

demi-mesure, *pl* **~s** /d(ə)mim(ə)zyʀ/ *f* half measure

demi-mot: **à demi-mot** /ad(ə)mimo/ *phr* **j'ai compris à ~** I didn't need to have it spelt out

✓ key word

déminer /demine/ [**v1**] *vt* to clear [sth] of mines

demi-pension /d(ə)mipɑ̃sjɔ̃/ *f* half board

demi-pensionnaire, *pl* **~s** /d(ə)mipɑ̃sjɔnɛʀ/ *mf* (Sch) pupil who has school lunches

démis, **~e** /demi, iz/ **A** *pp* ▶ **démettre**
B *pp adj* dislocated

demi-sel /d(ə)misɛl/ *adj* ‹*butter*› slightly salted

demi-sœur, *pl* **~s** /d(ə)misœʀ/ *f* half-sister; stepsister

démission /demisjɔ̃/ *f* **1** resignation (**de** from)
2 (fig) failure to take responsibility

démissionner /demisjɔne/ [**v1**] *vi* **1** to resign (**de** from)
2 to abdicate one's responsibilities

demi-tarif, *pl* **~s** /d(ə)mitaʀif/ **A** *adj* half-price
B *adv* half-price
C *m* half-price ticket

demi-tour, *pl* **~s** /d(ə)mituʀ/ *m* half turn; **faire ~** to turn back

démobiliser /demɔbilize/ [**v1**] *vt* **1** to demobilize
2 to demotivate

démocrate /demɔkʀat/ **A** *adj* democratic
B *mf* democrat

démocratie /demɔkʀasi/ *f* democracy

démocratique /demɔkʀatik/ *adj* democratic

démocratiser: **se démocratiser** /demɔkʀatize/ [**v1**] *v refl* (+ *v être*) **1** to become more democratic
2 to become more accessible

démodé, **~e** /demɔde/ *adj* old-fashioned

démoder: **se démoder** /demɔde/ [**v1**] *v refl* (+ *v être*) to go out of fashion

démographie /demɔgʀafi/ *f* demography

démographique /demɔgʀafik/ *adj* demographic

demoiselle /d(ə)mwazɛl/ *f* **1** young lady
2 single woman
■ **~ d'honneur** bridesmaid

démolir /demɔliʀ/ [**v3**] *vt* to demolish; to wreck; to destroy

démolition /demɔlisjɔ̃/ *f* demolition

démon /demɔ̃/ *m* demon, devil
■ **~ de midi** ≈ middle-age lust

démoniaque /demɔnjak/ *adj* demonic

démonstrateur, **-trice** /demɔ̃stʀatœʀ, tʀis/ *mf* (for products) demonstrator

démonstratif, **-ive** /demɔ̃stʀatif, iv/ *adj* demonstrative

démonstration /demɔ̃stʀasjɔ̃/ *f* **1** display; **~ de courage** display of courage; **~s d'amitié** a show of friendship
2 demonstration
3 (of theory) demonstration, proof

démontable /demɔ̃tabl/ *adj* ‹*furniture*› that can be taken apart

démonté, **~e** /demɔ̃te/ *adj* ‹*sea*› stormy
démonte-pneu, *pl* **~s** /demɔ̃t(ə)pnø/ *m* tyre lever (BrE), tire iron (AmE)
démonter /demɔ̃te/ [**v1**] **A** *vt* **1** to dismantle, to take [sth] to pieces ‹*machine*›; to remove ‹*wheel*›
2 (fam) to fluster; **ne pas se laisser ~** to remain unruffled
B se démonter *v refl* (+ *v être*)
1 ‹*furniture*› to come apart
2 (fam) ‹*person*› to become flustered
démontrer /demɔ̃tʀe/ [**v1**] *vt* to demonstrate, to prove
démoralisant, **~e** /demɔʀalizɑ̃, ɑ̃t/ *adj* demoralizing
démoraliser /demɔʀalize/ [**v1**] *vt* to demoralize
démordre /demɔʀdʀ/ [**v6**] *v+prep* **il n'en démord pas** he sticks by it, he's sticking to it
démotiver /demɔtive/ *vt* demotivate
démouler /demule/ [**v1**] *vt* to turn [sth] out of the tin (BrE) *or* pan (AmE) ‹*cake*›; to remove [sth] from the mould (BrE) *or* mold (AmE) ‹*statue*›
démultiplier /demyltiplije/ [**v2**] *vt* **1** to reduce ‹*speed*›
2 to increase ‹*powers, capacity*›
démuni, **~e** /demyni/ *adj* destitute; penniless; **~ de** devoid of, without ‹*talent*›
démunir /demyniʀ/ [**v3**] **A** *vt* to divest (**de** of)
B se démunir *v refl* (+ *v être*) **se ~ de qch** to leave oneself without sth
démystifier /demistifje/ [**v2**] *vt* **1 ~ qn** to dispel sb's illusions
2 to demystify
démythifier /demitifje/ [**v2**] *vt* to demythologize
dénatalité /denatalite/ *f* fall in the birth rate
dénationaliser /denasjɔnalize/ [**v1**] *vt* to denationalize
dénaturé, **~e** /denatyʀe/ *adj* **1** ‹*alcohol*› denatured
2 ‹*tastes*› warped; ‹*parents*› unnatural
dénaturer /denatyʀe/ [**v1**] *vt* **1** to denature
2 to distort ‹*facts*›
3 to spoil ‹*taste, sauce*›
dénicher /deniʃe/ [**v1**] *vt* **1** (fam) to dig out (fam) ‹*object*›; to track down ‹*person*›; to find ‹*right address*›
2 to flush out ‹*thief, animal*›
dénier /denje/ [**v2**] *vt* to deny
deniers /dənje/ *mpl* money; **~s publics** *or* **de l'État** public funds
dénigrement /denigʀəmɑ̃/ *m* denigration
dénigrer /denigʀe/ [**v1**] *vt* to denigrate
dénivellation /denivɛlasjɔ̃/ *f* **1** difference in level
2 gradient
dénombrable /denɔ̃bʀabl/ *adj* countable; **non ~** uncountable
dénombrement /denɔ̃bʀəmɑ̃/ *m* count
dénombrer /denɔ̃bʀe/ [**v1**] *vt* to count
dénomination /denɔminasjɔ̃/ *f* name, designation
dénommer /denɔme/ [**v1**] *vt* to name
dénoncer /denɔ̃se/ [**v12**] **A** *vt* to denounce
B se dénoncer *v refl* (+ *v être*) to give oneself up
dénonciation /denɔ̃sjasjɔ̃/ *f* denunciation
dénoter /denɔte/ [**v1**] *vt* denote
dénouement /denumɑ̃/ *m* **1** denouement
2 outcome
dénouer /denwe/ [**v1**] **A** *vt* **1** to undo ‹*knot*›
2 to unravel ‹*intrigue*›; to resolve ‹*crisis*›
B se dénouer *v refl* (+ *v être*) **1** ‹*laces*› to come undone
2 ‹*crisis*› to resolve itself
dénoyauter /denwajote/ [**v1**] *vt* to stone (BrE), to pit (AmE)
denrée /dɑ̃ʀe/ *f* **1** foodstuff; **~ de base** staple
2 commodity
dense /dɑ̃s/ *adj* dense; concentrated; heavy
densité /dɑ̃site/ *f* **1** density
2 denseness
dent /dɑ̃/ *f* **1** tooth; **à pleines** *or* **belles ~s** with relish; **ne rien avoir à se mettre sous la ~** to have nothing to eat
2 (of comb) tooth; (of fork) prong; **en ~s de scie** ‹*blade*› serrated; ‹*results*› which go up and down
3 crag
■ **~ de lait** milk tooth
IDIOMS **avoir une ~ contre qn** to bear sb a grudge; **avoir les ~s longues** to be ambitious
dentaire /dɑ̃tɛʀ/ *adj* dental
denté, **~e** /dɑ̃te/ *adj* **1** toothed
2 dentate
dentelé, **~e** /dɑ̃t(ə)le/ *adj* ‹*coast*› indented; ‹*crest*› jagged; ‹*stamp*› perforated; ‹*leaf*› dentate
dentelle /dɑ̃tɛl/ *f* lace
IDIOM **il ne fait pas dans la ~** he's not one to bother with niceties
dentelure /dɑ̃tlyʀ/ *f* (of stamp) perforation; (of crest) jagged outline; (of leaf) serration
dentier /dɑ̃tje/ *m* dentures
dentifrice /dɑ̃tifʀis/ *m* toothpaste
dentiste /dɑ̃tist/ *mf* dentist
dentition /dɑ̃tisjɔ̃/ *f* dentition
dénuder /denyde/ [**v1**] **A** *vt* to strip
B se dénuder *v refl* (+ *v être*) **1** to strip (off)
2 to become bare
dénué, **~e** /denɥe/ *adj* **~ de** lacking in; **~ de sens** senseless
dénuement /denymɑ̃/ *m* destitution; bareness

d

déodorant, **~e** /deɔdɔʀɑ̃, ɑ̃t/ **A** *adj* deodorant
B *m* deodorant

déontologie /deɔ̃tɔlɔʒi/ *f* (professional) ethics

dépannage /depanaʒ/ *m* repair

dépanner /depane/ [**v1**] *vt* **1** to fix ‹*car, machine*›
2 to tow away
3 (fam) to help [sb] out

dépanneur, **-euse** /depanœʀ, øz/ *mf* engineer

dépanneuse /depanøz/ *f* breakdown truck (BrE), tow truck (AmE)

dépareillé, **~e** /depaʀeje/ *adj* **1** odd; **articles ~s** oddments
2 incomplete

déparer /depaʀe/ [**v1**] *vt* to spoil, to mar

départ /depaʀ/ *m* **1** departure; **~ des grandes lignes** main line departures; **téléphone avant ton ~** phone before you leave; **être sur le ~** to be about to leave
2 resignation; **le ~ en retraite** retirement
3 (gen), (Sport) start; **donner le (signal du) ~ aux coureurs** to start the race; **prendre un nouveau ~** (fig) to make a fresh start; **au ~** at first; at the outset; **de ~** initial; ‹*language*› source; ‹*salary*› starting

départager /depaʀtaʒe/ [**v13**] *vt* to decide between ‹*competitors*›

département /depaʀtəmɑ̃/ *m* department

départemental, **~e**, *mpl* **-aux** /depaʀtəmɑ̃tal, o/ *adj* ‹*election*› local; ‹*road*› secondary

dépassé, **~e** /depɑse/ *adj* **1** outdated, outmoded
2 (fam) overwhelmed

dépassement /depɑsmɑ̃/ *m* **1** overtaking
2 overrun; **~ d'horaire** overrunning the schedule; **le ~ de la dose prescrite** exceeding the stated dose
3 ~ de soi surpassing oneself
■ **~ budgétaire** cost overrun; **~ de capacité** (Comput) overflow

dépasser /depɑse/ [**v1**] **A** *vt* **1** to overtake (BrE), to pass (AmE) ‹*car, pedestrian*›; to go past ‹*place*›
2 to exceed ‹*figure, dose, limit*›; **elle le dépasse de cinq centimètres** she's five centimetres (BrE) taller than him; **il a dépassé la cinquantaine** he's over *or* past fifty; **~ la mesure** *or* **les bornes** to go too far
3 to be ahead of, to outstrip ‹*rival*›; **ça me dépasse!** it's beyond me!
B *vi* to jut *or* stick out; ‹*underskirt*› to show

dépassionner /depasjɔne/ [**v1**] *vt* to defuse ‹*discussion*›

dépatouiller: **se dépatouiller** /depatuje/ [**v1**] *v refl* (+ *v être*) (fam) to get by

key word

dépaysé, **~e** /depeize/ *adj* **il est complètement ~** he's like a fish out of water; **il n'est pas ~ ici** he feels at home here

dépaysement /depeizmɑ̃/ *m* **1** change of scenery
2 disorientation

dépayser /depeize/ [**v1**] *vt* **1** to provide [sb] with a pleasant change of scenery
2 to disorient

dépecer /dep(ə)se/ [**v16**] *vt* to tear apart, to cut up

dépêche /depɛʃ/ *f* dispatch

dépêcher /depeʃe/ [**v16**] **A** *vt* to dispatch (à to)
B se dépêcher *v refl* (+ *v être*) to hurry up

dépeigné, **~e** /depeɲe/ *adj* dishevelled (BrE)

dépeindre /depɛ̃dʀ/ [**v55**] *vt* to depict

dépenaillé, **~e** /depənaje/ *adj* ragged

dépénaliser /depenalize/ [**v1**] *vt* to decriminalize

dépendance /depɑ̃dɑ̃s/ *f* **1** dependence, dependency
2 outbuilding
3 dependency, dependent territory

dépendant, **~e** /depɑ̃dɑ̃, ɑ̃t/ *adj* dependent (**de** on); **~s l'un de l'autre** interdependent

dépendre /depɑ̃dʀ/ [**v6**] *v+prep* **1 ~ de** to depend on
2 ~ de to be dependent on
3 ~ de ‹*organization*› to come under the control of; ‹*employee*› to be responsible to
4 ~ de ‹*environment*› to be the responsibility of
5 ~ de ‹*territory*› to be a dependency of
6 ~ de ‹*building, land*› to belong to

dépens /depɑ̃/ *mpl* **aux ~ de** at the expense of; **vivre aux ~ des autres** to live off other people

dépense /depɑ̃s/ *f* **1** spending, expenditure; **~s publiques** public expenditure
2 expense; **réduire ses ~s** to cut down on expenses
3 outlay; **une ~ de 300 euros** an outlay of 300 euros
4 consumption; **~ d'énergie physique** expenditure of physical energy

dépenser /depɑ̃se/ [**v1**] **A** *vt* to spend ‹*money, time*›; to use up ‹*energy, fuel*›
B se dépenser *v refl* (+ *v être*) to get (enough) exercise

dépensier, **-ière** /depɑ̃sje, ɛʀ/ *adj* extravagant

déperdition /depɛʀdisjɔ̃/ *f* loss

dépérir /depeʀiʀ/ [**v3**] *vi* ‹*person*› to waste away; ‹*plant*› to wilt; ‹*economy*› to be on the decline

dépêtrer: **se dépêtrer** /depɛtʀe/ [**v1**] *v refl* (+ *v être*) **se ~ de** to extricate oneself from

dépeuplement /depœpləmɑ̃/ *m* depopulation

dépeupler /depœple/ [**v1**] *vt* to depopulate ‹*region*›; to reduce the wildlife in ‹*forest*›

déphasé, **~e** /defaze/ *adj* **1** (fam) out of step **2** out of phase

dépiauter /depjote/ [**v1**] *vt* (fam) to skin ‹*animal*›

dépilation /depilasjɔ̃/ *f* hair removal

dépilatoire /depilatwaʀ/ *adj* depilatory, hair-removing

dépistable /depistabl/ *adj* detectable

dépistage /depistaʒ/ *m* screening (**de** for); **test de ~ du sida** Aids test

dépister /depiste/ [**v1**] *vt* **1** to track down ‹*criminal, game*› **2** to detect ‹*illness*›

dépit /depi/ **A** *m* pique; **par ~** out of pique **B en dépit de** *phr* in spite of; **en ~ du bon sens** in a very illogical way

dépité, **~e** /depite/ *adj* piqued (**de** at)

déplacé, **~e** /deplase/ *adj* inappropriate; **c'est ~** it's out of place; it's uncalled for

déplacement /deplasmɑ̃/ *m* **1** trip; **ça vaut le ~!** it's worth the trip!; **frais de ~** travelling (BrE) expenses **2** moving; shifting; transfer (**vers** to) **3** displacement
■ **~ de vertèbre** slipped disc

déplacer /deplase/ [**v12**] **A** *vt* to move ‹*object, person*›; to displace ‹*population*›; to shift ‹*attention*›; to change ‹*issue*› **B se déplacer** *v refl* (+ *v être*) **1** to move; **se ~ une vertèbre** to slip a disc **2** to get about; to travel **3** ‹*doctor*› to go out on call

déplaire /deplɛʀ/ [**v59**] **A** *vi* **le spectacle a déplu** the show was not well received **B déplaire à** *v+prep* **cela m'a déplu** I didn't like it; **la situation n'est pas pour me ~** the situation quite suits me **C** *v impers* **ne vous en déplaise** (ironic) whether you like it or not

déplaisant, **~e** /deplɛzɑ̃, ɑ̃t/ *adj* unpleasant

déplâtrer /deplɑtʀe/ [**v1**] *vt* to remove the cast from ‹*limb*›

dépliant /deplijɑ̃/ *m* **1** leaflet **2** fold-out page

déplier /deplije/ [**v2**] *vt* to unfold ‹*newspaper*›; to open out ‹*map*›

déploiement /deplwamɑ̃/ *m* **1** display; array **2** deployment

déplorable /deplɔʀabl/ *adj* **1** regrettable **2** appalling, deplorable

déplorer /deplɔʀe/ [**v1**] *vt* to deplore

déployer /deplwaje/ [**v23**] *vt* **1** to display ‹*talent, wealth*›; to expend ‹*energy*› **2** to deploy ‹*troops*› **3** to spread ‹*wings*›; to unfurl ‹*sail*›

déplumer: **se déplumer** /deplyme/ [**v1**] *v refl* (+ *v être*) ‹*bird*› to lose its feathers

dépoli, **~e** /depɔli/ *adj* **verre ~** frosted glass

dépolitiser /depɔlitize/ [**v1**] *vt* to depoliticize

dépolluer /depɔlɥe/ [**v1**] *vt* to rid [sth] of pollution, to clean up

dépollution /depɔlysjɔ̃/ *f* clean-up

dépopulation /depɔpylasjɔ̃/ *f* depopulation

déportation /depɔʀtasjɔ̃/ *f* **1** internment in a concentration camp **2** deportation

déporté, **~e** /depɔʀte/ *mf* **1** prisoner interned in a concentration camp **2** transported convict

déporter /depɔʀte/ [**v1**] **A** *vt* **1** to send [sb] to a concentration camp **2** to deport **B se déporter** *v refl* (+ *v être*) to swerve

déposant, **~e** /depozɑ̃, ɑ̃t/ *mf* **1** depositor **2** deponent

déposer /depoze/ [**v1**] **A** *vt* **1** to dump ‹*rubbish*›; to lay ‹*wreath*›; to drop off, to leave ‹*parcel, passenger*›; to deposit ‹*money*›; **~ les armes** to lay down one's arms **2** to register ‹*trademark*›; to submit ‹*file, offer*›; to lodge ‹*complaint*›; **~ son bilan** to file a bankruptcy petition **3** ‹*river*› to deposit ‹*alluvium*› **B** *vi* (Law) to make a statement, to testify **C se déposer** *v refl* (+ *v être*) ‹*dust*› to settle; ‹*deposit*› to collect

dépositaire /depozitɛʀ/ *mf* **1** agent; **~ agréé** authorized dealer **2** trustee

déposition /depozisjɔ̃/ *f* (Law) statement; deposition; evidence

déposséder /depɔsede/ [**v14**] *vt* to dispossess

dépôt /depo/ *m* **1** warehouse; depot **2** outlet; **l'épicerie fait ~ de pain** the grocer's sells bread **3** (of trademark) registration; (of bill) introduction **4 date limite de ~ des déclarations d'impôt** deadline for income tax returns **5** deposit **6** police cells
■ **~ de bilan** voluntary liquidation; **~ d'ordures** (rubbish) tip *or* dump (BrE); garbage dump (AmE)

dépotoir /depɔtwaʀ/ *m* **1** dump **2** (fam) shambles (fam)

dépôt-vente, *pl* **dépôts-ventes** /depovɑ̃t/ *m* second-hand shop (BrE) *or* store (*where goods are sold on commission*)

dépouille /depuj/ *f* **1** skin, hide **2** body; **~ mortelle** mortal remains **3 ~s** spoils

dépouillé, **~e** /depuje/ *adj* **1** ‹*style*› spare **2** ‹*tree*› bare

dépouillement /depujmɑ̃/ *m* **1** (of votes) counting, count; (of mail) going through **2** asceticism **3** (of style) sobriety

dépouiller /depuje/ [**v1**] *vt* **1** to skin ‹*animal*›
2 to lay [sth] bare ‹*region*›
3 to rob ‹*person*›
4 to count ‹*votes*›; to go through ‹*mail*›

dépourvu, **~e** /depuʀvy/ **A** *adj* **~ de** devoid of ‹*interest, charm*›; without ‹*heating*›
B *m* **prendre qn au ~** to take sb by surprise

dépoussiérer /depusjeʀe/ [**v14**] *vt* to dust; (fig) to revamp

dépravation /depʀavasjɔ̃/ *f* depravity

dépraver /depʀave/ [**v1**] *vt* to deprave

dépréciation /depʀesjasjɔ̃/ *f* depreciation

déprécier /depʀesje/ [**v2**] *vt* **1** to depreciate
2 to disparage, to depreciate

déprédateur, **-trice** /depʀedatœʀ, tʀis/ *mf* vandal

déprédations /depʀedasjɔ̃/ *fpl* damage

dépressif, **-ive** /depʀesif, iv/ *adj*, *mf* depressive

dépression /depʀesjɔ̃/ *f* depression; **~ nerveuse** nervous breakdown

dépressurisation /depʀesyʀizasjɔ̃/ *f*
1 depressurization
2 loss of pressure

déprimant, **~e** /depʀimɑ̃, ɑ̃t/ *adj* depressing

déprime /depʀim/ *f* (fam) depression

déprimer /depʀime/ [**v1**] **A** *vt* to depress
B *vi* (fam) to be depressed

déprogrammer /depʀɔgʀame/ [**v1**] *vt* to cancel

🔑 **depuis** /dəpɥi/ **A** *adv* since; **~ je n'ai plus de nouvelles** since then I haven't had any news
B *prep* **1** since; **~ quand vis-tu là-bas?** how long have you been living there?; **~ le début jusqu'à la fin** from start to finish
2 for; **il pleut ~ trois jours** it's been raining for three days; **~ quand?** how long?; **~ peu** recently; **~ toujours** always
3 from; **~ ma fenêtre** from my window
C **depuis que** *phr* since, ever since; **il pleut ~ que nous sommes arrivés** it's been raining ever since we arrived

député /depyte/ *m* **1** (in politics) deputy; (in GB) member of Parliament; **être ~ au Parlement européen** to be a Euro-MP *or* member of the European Parliament
2 representative

député-maire, *pl* **députés-maires** /depytemɛʀ/ *m* deputy and mayor

déqualifier /dekalifje/ [**v2**] *vt* to deskill

der /dɛʀ/ *f* (fam) last; **la ~ des ~s** the war to end all wars

déraciné, **~e** /deʀasine/ *mf* uprooted person

déracinement /deʀasinmɑ̃/ *m* **1** uprooting
2 rootlessness

🔑 key word

déraciner /deʀasine/ [**v1**] *vt* **1** to uproot
2 to eradicate ‹*prejudice*›

déraillement /deʀɑjmɑ̃/ *m* derailment

dérailler /deʀɑje/ [**v1**] *vi* **1** to be derailed; **faire ~ un train** to derail a train
2 (fam) to lose one's marbles (fam); to talk through one's hat (fam)

dérailleur /deʀɑjœʀ/ *m* derailleur

déraisonnable /deʀɛzɔnabl/ *adj* unrealistic; senseless; unreasonable

déraisonner /deʀɛzɔne/ [**v1**] *vi* to talk nonsense

dérangé, **~e** /deʀɑ̃ʒe/ *adj* **1** upset
2 (fam) deranged

dérangeant, **~e** /deʀɑ̃ʒɑ̃, ɑ̃t/ *adj* disturbing

dérangement /deʀɑ̃ʒmɑ̃/ *m* **1** trouble, inconvenience
2 **~ intestinal** stomach upset
3 **être en ~** ‹*lift, phone*› to be out of order

déranger /deʀɑ̃ʒe/ [**v13**] **A** *vt* to disturb ‹*person*›; to upset ‹*routine, plans*›; to affect ‹*mind*›; **excusez-moi de vous ~** (I'm) sorry to bother you; **est-ce que la fumée vous dérange?** do you mind if I smoke?
B **se déranger** *v refl* (+ *v être*) **1** to go out, to come out; **je me suis dérangé pour rien, c'était fermé** I wasted my time going there, it was shut
2 to get up; to move
3 to put oneself out

dérapage /deʀapaʒ/ *m* **1** skid
2 blunder
3 loss of control

déraper /deʀape/ [**v1**] *vi* **1** ‹*prices, discussion*› to get out of control
2 ‹*knife*› to slip
3 to skid
4 ‹*skier*› to side-slip

dératisation /deʀatizasjɔ̃/ *f* pest control (*for rats*)

déréglé, **~e** /deʀegle/ *adj* ‹*mind*› unbalanced; ‹*life*› irregular; ‹*mechanism*› out, disturbed

dérèglement /deʀɛgləmɑ̃/ *m* **1** (in machine) fault
2 disorder

déréglementer /deʀegləmɑ̃te/ [**v1**] *vt* to deregulate

dérégler /deʀegle/ [**v14**] *vt* to affect ‹*weather, organ*›; to upset ‹*process, mechanism*›; **~ la radio** to lose the station on the radio; **~ le réveil** to set the alarm clock wrong

dérider /deʀide/ [**v1**] **A** *vt* to cheer [sb] up
B **se dérider** *v refl* (+ *v être*) to start smiling

dérision /deʀizjɔ̃/ *f* scorn, derision; **tourner qn/qch en ~** to ridicule sb/sth

dérisoire /deʀizwaʀ/ *adj* pathetic; trivial

dérivatif, **-ive** /deʀivatif, iv/ **A** *adj* derivative

B *m* **1** diversion (à from)
2 (Med) derivative

dérivation /deʀivasjɔ̃/ *f* diversion (BrE), detour

dérive /deʀiv/ *f* drift; **à la ~** adrift

dérivé, **~e** /deʀive/ *m* by-product

dériver /deʀive/ [**v1**] **A** **dériver de** *v+prep*
1 ~ de to stem from
2 ~ de to be derived from
B *vi* to drift

dermatologie /dɛʀmatɔlɔʒi/ *f* dermatology

derme /dɛʀm/ *m* dermis

dernier, **-ière** /dɛʀnje, ɛʀ/ **A** *adj* **1** last; ‹*floor, shelf*› top; **je les veux jeudi ~ délai** I want them by Thursday at the latest
2 latest; **les dernières nouvelles** the latest news; **ces ~ temps** recently
3 du ~ ridicule utterly ridiculous; **c'était la dernière chose à faire** it was the worst possible thing to do
B *mf* last; **arriver le ~** to arrive last; **c'est bien le ~ de mes soucis** that is the least of my worries; **être le ~ de la classe** to be bottom of the class; **le petit ~** the youngest child; **ce ~** the latter; **le ~ des ~s** the lowest of the low
C **en dernier** *phr* last; **j'irai chez eux en ~** I'll go to them last
■ **~ cri** latest fashion; **dernières volontés** last requests

dernière /dɛʀnjɛʀ/ *f* **1 la ~** the latest
2 last performance

dernièrement /dɛʀnjɛʀmɑ̃/ *adv* recently

dernier-né, **dernière-née**, *mpl* **derniers-nés** /dɛʀnjene, dɛʀnjɛʀne/ *mf*
1 youngest (child)
2 latest model

dérobade /deʀɔbad/ *f* evasion

dérobé, **~e** /deʀɔbe/ **A** *adj* ‹*door, stairs*› concealed
B **à la dérobée** *phr* furtively

dérober /deʀɔbe/ [**v1**] **A** *vt* to steal
B **se dérober** *v refl* (+ *v être*) **1** to be evasive
2 to shirk responsibility
3 se ~ à to shirk ‹*duty*›
4 ‹*ground, knees*› to give way

dérogation /deʀɔgasjɔ̃/ *f* **1** (special) dispensation
2 infringement (à of)

dérogatoire /deʀɔgatwaʀ/ *adj* special; **clause ~** derogation clause

déroger /deʀɔʒe/ [**v13**] *v+prep* **~ à** to infringe ‹*law*›; to depart from ‹*principles*›; to ignore ‹*obligation*›; to break with ‹*tradition*›

dérouiller /deʀuje/ [**v1**] (fam) *vi* to get a hiding (fam) or beating; to suffer

déroulant /deʀulɑ̃/ *adj* **menu ~** pop-up menu

déroulement /deʀulmɑ̃/ *m* **1 le ~ des événements** the sequence of events; **veiller au bon ~ de** to make sure [sth] goes smoothly; **~ de carrière** career development
2 uncoiling, unwinding

dérouler /deʀule/ [**v1**] **A** *vt* to unroll ‹*carpet*›; to uncoil ‹*rope*›; to unwind ‹*wire, film*›
B **se dérouler** *v refl* (+ *v être*) **1** to take place
2 ‹*negotiations*› to proceed; ‹*story*› to unfold

déroutant, **~e** /deʀutɑ̃, ɑ̃t/ *adj* puzzling

déroute /deʀut/ *f* crushing defeat, rout; **mettre en ~** to rout; **en ~** in disarray

dérouter /deʀute/ [**v1**] *vt* **1** to puzzle
2 to divert

derrière¹ /dɛʀjɛʀ/ **A** *prep* behind; **~ les apparences** beneath the surface; **il faut toujours être ~ son dos** you have to keep after him
B *adv* behind; (of room) at the back; (in car) in the back

derrière² /dɛʀjɛʀ/ *m* **1** (of house, object) back; **de ~** ‹*bedroom*› back
2 (fam) behind (fam), backside (fam)

des /de/ **A** *det* ▶ **un A**
B *det* ▶ **de**

dès /dɛ/ **A** *prep* from; **~ (l'âge de) huit ans** from the age of eight; **~ maintenant** straight away; **je vous téléphone ~ mon arrivée** I'll phone you as soon as I arrive; **~ Versailles il y a des embouteillages** there are traffic jams from Versailles onwards
B **dès que** *phr* as soon as
C **dès lors** *phr* **1** from then on, from that time on, henceforth
2 therefore, consequently
D **dès lors que** *phr* **1** once, from the moment that
2 since

désabonner: **se désabonner** /dezabɔne/ [**v1**] *v refl* (+ *v être*) (gen) to cancel one's subscription (**à** to); (Comput) to unsubscribe

désabusé, **~e** /dezabyze/ *adj* disillusioned; cynical

désaccord /dezakɔʀ/ *m* disagreement; **être en ~** to disagree (**avec** with, **sur** over)

désaccordé, **~e** /dezakɔʀde/ *adj* out of tune

désaccoutumer: **se désaccoutumer** /dezakutyme/ [**v1**] *v refl* (+ *v être*) **se ~ de qch** to break one's dependence on sth

désactiver /dezaktive/ *vt* to deactivate

désaffecté, **~e** /dezafɛkte/ *adj* disused

désaffection /dezafɛksjɔ̃/ *f* disaffection (**pour** with)

désagréable /dezagʀeabl/ *adj* unpleasant

désagrégation /dezagʀegasjɔ̃/ *f* disintegration, break-up, collapse

désagréger: **se désagréger** /dezagʀeʒe/ [**v15**] *v refl* (+ *v être*) to disintegrate, to break up

désagrément /dezagʀemɑ̃/ *m* inconvenience

désaltérant, **~e** /dezalteʀɑ̃, ɑ̃t/ *adj* thirst-quenching

désaltérer /dezalteʀe/ [**v14**] **A** *vt* **~ qn** to quench sb's thirst
B **se désaltérer** *v refl* (+ *v être*) to quench one's thirst

désamorcer /dezamɔʀse/ [**v12**] *vt* to defuse ‹*explosive, crisis*›; to drain ‹*pump*›

désappointement /dezapwɛ̃tmɑ̃/ *m* disappointment

désappointer /dezapwɛ̃te/ [**v1**] *vt* to disappoint

désapprobateur, **-trice** /dezapʀɔbatœʀ, tʀis/ *adj* disapproving

désapprobation /dezapʀɔbasjɔ̃/ *f* disapproval

désapprouver /dezapʀuve/ [**v1**] *vt* to disapprove of

désarçonner /dezaʀsɔne/ [**v1**] *vt* **1** to throw ‹*rider*›
2 to take [sb] aback

désargenté, **~e** /dezaʀʒɑ̃te/ *adj* (fam) hard up (fam), penniless

désarmant, **~e** /dezaʀmɑ̃, ɑ̃t/ *adj* disarming

désarmé, **~e** /dezaʀme/ **A** *pp* ▸ **désarmer**
B *pp adj* **1** disarmed
2 ‹*ship*› laid up

désarmement /dezaʀməmɑ̃/ *m*
1 disarmament
2 (of ship) laying up

désarmer /dezaʀme/ [**v1**] **A** *vt* **1** to disarm
2 to lay up ‹*ship*›
B *vi* **1** to disarm
2 ‹*person*› to give up the fight; ‹*anger*› to abate

désarroi /dezaʀwa/ *m* distress; confusion

désarticulé, **~e** /dezaʀtikyle/ *adj* ‹*chair*› wrecked; ‹*puppet*› with broken joints

désastre /dezastʀ/ *m* disaster

désastreux, **-euse** /dezastʀø, øz/ *adj* disastrous

désavantage /dezavɑ̃taʒ/ *m*
1 disadvantage
2 drawback, disadvantage

désavantager /dezavɑ̃taʒe/ [**v13**] *vt* to put [sb/sth] at a disadvantage, to disadvantage

désavantageux, **-euse** /dezavɑ̃taʒø, øz/ *adj* unfavourable (BrE), disadvantageous

désaveu /dezavø/ *m* **1** denial
2 rejection

désavouer /dezavwe/ [**v1**] *vt* **1** to deny
2 to disown

désaxé, **~e** /dezakse/ **A** *pp* ▸ **désaxer**
B *pp adj* deranged
C *mf* deranged person

désaxer /dezakse/ [**v1**] *vt* **1** to put [sth] out of true ‹*wheel*›
2 to unbalance ‹*person*›

desceller /desele/ [**v1**] **A** *vt* to work [sth] free
B **se desceller** *v refl* (+ *v être*) to work loose

descendance /desɑ̃dɑ̃s/ *f* descendants

descendant, **~e** /desɑ̃dɑ̃, ɑ̃t/ *mf* descendant

🔑 **descendre** /dɛsɑ̃dʀ/ [**v6**] **A** *vt* (+ *v avoir*)
1 to take [sb/sth] down (**à** to); to bring [sb/sth] down (**de** from)
2 to lower ‹*shelf, blind*›; to wind [sth] down ‹*window*›
3 to go down, to come down ‹*road, steps, river*›; **~ la rivière à la nage** to swim down the river
4 (fam) to bump off (fam) ‹*person*›; to shoot down ‹*plane*›
5 (fam) to down ‹*bottle*›
B *vi* (+ *v être*) **1** to go down (**à** to); to come down (**de** from); ‹*night*› to fall; **tu es descendu à pied?** did you walk down?; **la route descend en pente douce** the road slopes down gently
2 **~ de** to step off ‹*step*›; to get off ‹*train, bike, horse*›; to get out of ‹*car*›
3 ‹*temperature, prices*› to drop, to go down; ‹*tide*› to go out
4 **~ dans le Midi** to go down to the South (of France)
5 **~ dans un hôtel** to stay at a hotel
6 **~ de** to be descended from

descente /desɑ̃t/ *f* **1** descent; **la ~ a pris une heure** it took an hour to come down
2 **à ma ~ du train** when I got off the train
3 **~ de police** police raid; **la police a fait une ~ dans l'immeuble** the police raided the building
4 (in skiing) downhill (event)
■ **~ de lit** (bedside) rug

descriptif, **-ive** /deskʀiptif, iv/ *adj* descriptive

🔑 **description** /deskʀipsjɔ̃/ *f* description; **faire une ~ de qch** to describe sth

désembuer /dezɑ̃bye/ [**v1**] *vt* to demist (BrE), to defog (AmE)

désemparé, **~e** /dezɑ̃paʀe/ **A** *pp* ▸ **désemparer**
B *pp adj* distraught, at a loss

désemparer /dezɑ̃paʀe/ [**v1**] *vt* to throw [sb] into confusion

désemplir /dezɑ̃pliʀ/ [**v3**] *vi* **ne pas ~** to be always full

désenchanté, **~e** /dezɑ̃ʃɑ̃te/ *adj* disillusioned, disenchanted (**de** with)

désenchantement /dezɑ̃ʃɑ̃tmɑ̃/ *m* disillusionment, disenchantment

désenclaver /dezɑ̃klave/ [**v1**] *vt* to open up ‹*region*›

désendettement /dezɑ̃dɛtmɑ̃/ *m* reduction of the debt

désenfler /dezɑ̃fle/ [**v1**] *vi* to become less swollen, to go down

🔑 key word

désengagement /dezɑ̃gaʒmɑ̃/ *m* **1** (Econ) disengagement
2 withdrawal (**de** from)

désengager: **se désengager** /dezɑ̃gaʒe/ [**v13**] *v refl* (+ *v être*) to withdraw (**de** from)

désensibiliser /desɑ̃sibilize/ [**v1**] *vt* to desensitize

désenvoûter /dezɑ̃vute/ [**v1**] *vt* to break the spell on

désépaissir /dezepɛsiʀ/ [**v3**] *vt* **1** to thin ‹*sauce*›
2 to thin [sth] out ‹*hair*›

déséquilibre /dezekilibʀ/ *m* **1** unsteadiness; **en ~** ‹*table*› unstable; ‹*person*› off balance
2 imbalance
3 derangement

déséquilibré, **~e** /dezekilibʀe/ **A** *pp* ▶ **déséquilibrer**
B *pp adj* (Med) unbalanced
C *mf* lunatic

déséquilibrer /dezekilibʀe/ [**v1**] *vt* **1** to make [sb] lose their balance; to make [sth] unstable
2 to destabilize ‹*country*›
3 (Med) to unbalance

désert, **~e** /dezɛʀ, ɛʀt/ **A** *adj* **1** uninhabited; **île ~e** desert island
2 deserted
B *m* desert

déserter /dezɛʀte/ [**v1**] *vt*, *vi* to desert

déserteur /dezɛʀtœʀ/ *m* deserter

désertion /dezɛʀsjɔ̃/ *f* **1** desertion
2 defection

désertique /dezɛʀtik/ *adj* **1** ‹*climate, region*› desert
2 barren

désespérant, **~e** /dezɛspeʀɑ̃, ɑ̃t/ *adj* ‹*person, situation*› hopeless

désespéré, **~e** /dezɛspeʀe/ **A** *pp* ▶ **désespérer**
B *pp adj* ‹*person*› in despair; ‹*situation*› hopeless; ‹*attempt*› desperate; **cri ~** cry of despair

désespérément /dezɛspeʀemɑ̃/ *adv* despairingly; desperately; hopelessly

désespérer /dezɛspeʀe/ [**v14**] **A** *vt* to drive [sb] to despair
B **désespérer de** *v+prep* **~ de qn** to despair of sb; **il ne désespère pas de le sauver** he hasn't given up hope of saving him
C *vi* to despair, to lose hope
D **se désespérer** *v refl* (+ *v être*) to despair

désespoir /dezɛspwaʀ/ *m* despair; **mettre** *or* **réduire qn au ~** to drive sb to despair

déshabillé /dezabije/ *m* negligee

déshabiller /dezabije/ [**v1**] **A** *vt* to undress
B **se déshabiller** *v refl* (+ *v être*) **1** to undress
2 to take one's coat off

déshabituer /dezabitɥe/ [**v1**] *vt* **~ qn du tabac** to get sb out of the habit of smoking

désherbant /dezɛʀbɑ̃/ *m* weedkiller

désherber /dezɛʀbe/ [**v1**] *vt* to weed

déshérité /dezeʀite/ **A** *pp* ▶ **déshériter**
B *pp adj* underprivileged; disadvantaged; deprived
C *mf* **les ~s** the underprivileged

déshériter /dezeʀite/ [**v1**] *vt* to disinherit

déshonorant, **~e** /dezɔnɔʀɑ̃, ɑ̃t/ *adj* dishonourable (BrE), degrading

déshonorer /dezɔnɔʀe/ [**v1**] **A** *vt* to bring disgrace on ‹*family*›; to bring [sth] into disrepute ‹*profession*›
B **se déshonorer** *v refl* (+ *v être*) to disgrace oneself

déshumaniser /dezymanize/ [**v1**] **A** *vt* to dehumanize
B **se déshumaniser** *v refl* (+ *v être*) to become dehumanized

déshydratation /dezidʀatasjɔ̃/ *f* **1** dehydration
2 drying

déshydrater /dezidʀate/ [**v1**] *vt* to dehydrate

desiderata /dezideʀata/ *mpl* wishes

désignation /deziɲasjɔ̃/ *f* designation

désigner /deziɲe/ [**v1**] *vt* **1** ‹*word*› to designate; ‹*triangle*› to represent
2 to point out
3 to choose; **être tout désigné pour** to be just right for

désillusion /dezil(l)yzjɔ̃/ *f* disillusion

désimlocker /desimlɔke/ [**v1**] *vt* to unblock ‹*mobile phone*›

désincarcérer /dezɛ̃kaʀseʀe/ [**v14**] *vt* to free

désincarné, **~e** /dezɛ̃kaʀne/ *adj* disembodied

désinence /dezinɑ̃s/ *f* ending

désinfectant, **~e** /dezɛ̃fɛktɑ̃, ɑ̃t/ **A** *adj* disinfecting
B *m* disinfectant

désinfecter /dezɛ̃fɛkte/ [**v1**] *vt* to disinfect

désintégrer: **se désintégrer** /dezɛ̃tegʀe/ [**v14**] *v refl* (+ *v être*) to disintegrate

désintéressé, **~e** /dezɛ̃teʀese/ **A** *pp* ▶ **désintéresser**
B *pp adj* ‹*person, act*› selfless, unselfish; ‹*advice*› disinterested

désintéressement /dezɛ̃teʀɛsmɑ̃/ *m* **1** disinterestedness; **agir avec ~** to act disinterestedly
2 (Econ) paying off

désintéresser: **se désintéresser** /dezɛ̃teʀese/ [**v1**] *v refl* (+ *v être*) **se ~ de** to lose interest in

désintérêt /dezɛ̃teʀɛ/ *m* lack of interest

désintoxiquer /dezɛ̃tɔksike/ [**v1**] *vt* to detoxify; **se faire ~** to undergo detoxification

d

désinviter /dezɛ̃vite/ *vt* disinvite

désinvolte /dezɛ̃vɔlt/ *adj* casual, offhand

désinvolture /dezɛ̃vɔltyʀ/ *f* casual manner

⚷ **désir** /deziʀ/ *m* wish, desire; **prendre ses ~s pour des réalités** to delude oneself

désirable /deziʀabl/ *adj* desirable

⚷ **désirer** /deziʀe/ [**v1**] *vt* to want; **effets non désirés** unwanted effects; **que désirez-vous?** what would you like?; **laisser à ~** to leave something to be desired

désistement /dezistəmɑ̃/ *m* withdrawal

désister: **se désister** /deziste/ [**v1**] *v refl* (+ *v être*) to stand down (BrE), to withdraw

désobéir /dezɔbeiʀ/ [**v3**] *v+prep* to disobey; **~ à qn** to disobey sb

désobéissance /dezɔbeisɑ̃s/ *f* disobedience

désobéissant, **~e** /dezɔbeisɑ̃, ɑ̃t/ *adj* disobedient

désobligeant, **~e** /dezɔbliʒɑ̃, ɑ̃t/ *adj* discourteous

désobliger /dezɔbliʒe/ [**v13**] *vt* to offend

désodorisant /dezɔdɔʀizɑ̃/ *m* deodorant

désodoriser /dezɔdɔʀize/ [**v1**] *vt* to freshen

désœuvré, **~e** /dezœvʀe/ *adj* at a loose end (BrE) (fam), at loose ends (AmE) (fam)

désœuvrement /dezœvʀəmɑ̃/ *m* **par ~** for lack of anything better to do

désolation /dezɔlasjɔ̃/ *f* **1** grief
2 desolation

désolé, **~e** /dezɔle/ **A** *pp* ▸ **désoler**
B *pp adj* **1** sorry
2 desolate

désoler /dezɔle/ [**v1**] **A** *vt* **1** to upset, to distress
2 to depress; **tu me désoles!** I despair of you!
B **se désoler** *v refl* (+ *v être*) to be upset

désopilant, **~e** /dezɔpilɑ̃, ɑ̃t/ *adj* hilarious

désordonné, **~e** /dezɔʀdɔne/ *adj* ‹*person*› untidy; ‹*meeting*› disorderly; ‹*movements*› uncoordinated; ‹*existence*› wild

désordre /dezɔʀdʀ/ **A** *adj inv* (fam) **faire ~** to look untidy *or* messy
B *m* **1** untidiness; mess; **pièce en ~** untidy room; **il a tout mis en ~** he made such a mess
2 chaos; **semer le ~** to cause chaos
3 dans le ~ in any order; **gagner dans le ~** (at races) to win with a combination forecast
4 disorder; **~s mentaux** mental disorders

désorganisation /dezɔʀganizasjɔ̃/ *f* disruption; disorganization

désorganisé, **~e** /dezɔʀganize/ *adj* disorganized

désorienter /dezɔʀjɑ̃te/ [**v1**] *vt* **1** to disorientate (BrE)
2 to confuse, to bewilder

désormais /dezɔʀmɛ/ *adv* **1** from now on
2 from then on

désosser /dezɔse/ [**v1**] *vt* (Culin) to bone

⚷ key word

despote /dɛspɔt/ *m* despot

despotique /dɛspɔtik/ *adj* despotic

desquelles ▸ **lequel**

desquels ▸ **lequel**

DESS /deəɛsɛs/ *m* (*abbr* = **diplôme d'études supérieures spécialisées**) *postgraduate degree taken after a Master's*

dessaisir /desɛziʀ/ [**v3**] **A** *vt* **1 ~ qn de** to relieve sb of ‹*responsibility*›
2 ~ qn de to divest sb of ‹*property*›
B **se dessaisir** *v refl* (+ *v être*) **se ~ de** to relinquish

dessaler /desale/ [**v1**] *vt* **1** to desalinate
2 (Culin) to desalt

dessécher /deseʃe/ [**v14**] **A** *vt* to dry [sth] out; **arbre desséché** withered tree
B **se dessécher** *v refl* (+ *v être*) ‹*hair*› to become dry; ‹*tree*› to wither; ‹*ground*› to dry out

dessein /desɛ̃/ *m* design, intention; **à ~** deliberately

desserré, **~e** /deseʀe/ *adj* loose

desserrement /desɛʀmɑ̃/ *m* **1** loosening
2 (Econ) relaxation; **~ du crédit** relaxation of credit

desserrer /deseʀe/ [**v1**] **A** *vt* **1** to loosen; to release; to undo
2 to relax ‹*grip, credit*›
B **se desserrer** *v refl* (+ *v être*) ‹*screw*› to work loose; ‹*knot*› to come undone

IDIOM **il n'a pas desserré les dents** he never once opened his mouth

dessert /desɛʀ/ *m* dessert

desserte /desɛʀt/ *f* **1** (transport) service; **la ~ d'une ville par les transports en commun** public transport services to and from a city
2 sideboard

desservir /desɛʀviʀ/ [**v30**] *vt* **1** ‹*train*› to serve ‹*town*›
2 to lead to ‹*room, floor*›
3 ‹*hospital*› to serve

⚷ **dessin** /desɛ̃/ *m* **1** drawing; **tu veux que je te fasse un ~?** (fam) do I have to spell it out for you?
2 design
3 pattern
4 outline
■ **~ animé** cartoon

dessinateur, **-trice** /desinatœʀ, tʀis/ *mf* **1** draughtsman (BrE), draftsman (AmE)
2 designer
■ **~ de bande dessinée** (strip) cartoonist

⚷ **dessiner** /desine/ [**v1**] **A** *vt* **1** to draw
2 to design ‹*material, decor*›; to draw up ‹*plans*›
B *vi* to draw
C **se dessiner** *v refl* (+ *v être*) **1** ‹*future*› to take shape
2 se ~ à l'horizon to appear on the horizon; **il se dessinait nettement dans la lumière** he was clearly outlined in the light

dessoûler /desule/ [**v1**] *vt* to sober up

dessous¹ /dəsu/ **A** *adv* underneath
B **en dessous** *phr* **1** underneath; **il habite juste en ~** he lives on the floor below
2 **la taille en ~** the next size down
C **en dessous de** *phr* below; **les enfants en ~ de 13 ans** children under 13

dessous² /dəsu/ **A** *m inv* (of plate, tongue) underside; (of arm) inside (part); **le ~ du pied** the sole of the foot; **l'étagère de** *or* **du ~** the shelf below; the bottom shelf
B *mpl* **1** underwear
2 inside story

dessous-de-plat /d(ə)sudpla/ *m inv*
1 table mat
2 plate stand
3 trivet

dessous-de-table /d(ə)sudtabl/ *m inv* backhanders (fam (BrE), bribes

dessus¹ /dəsy/ *adv* on top; **le prix est marqué ~** the price is on it; **passe ~** go over it; **compte ~** count on it; **'ton rapport est fini?'—'non, je travaille** *or* **suis ~'** 'is your report finished?'—'no, I'm working on it'

dessus² /dəsy/ *m inv* (of shoe) upper; (of table, head) top; (of hand) back; **les voisins du ~** the people who live on the floor above
IDIOM **reprendre le ~** to regain the upper hand; (after illness) to get back on one's feet

dessus-de-lit /d(ə)sydli/ *m inv* bedspread

déstabiliser /destabilize/ [**v1**] *vt* to unsettle ‹*person*›; to destabilize ‹*country*›

destin /dɛstɛ̃/ *m* **1** fate
2 destiny

destinataire /dɛstinatɛʀ/ *mf* **1** addressee
2 beneficiary
3 payee

destination /dɛstinasjɔ̃/ **A** *f* destination
B **à destination de** *phr* ‹*train*› bound for

destinée /dɛstine/ *f* destiny

destiner /dɛstine/ [**v1**] **A** *vt* **1** **~ qch à qn** to design sth for sb; **être destiné à faire** to be designed *or* intended to do; to be destined to do
2 **la lettre ne leur était pas destinée** the letter wasn't for them
B **se destiner** *v refl* (+ *v être*) **elle se destine à une carrière de juriste** she's decided on a legal career

destituer /dɛstitɥe/ [**v1**] *vt* to discharge ‹*officer*›; to depose ‹*monarch*›

destitution /dɛstitysjɔ̃/ *f* discharge; deposition

destructeur, **-trice** /dɛstʀyktœʀ, tʀis/ *adj* destructive

destruction /dɛstʀyksjɔ̃/ *f* destruction

désuet, **-ète** /dezɥɛ, ɛt/ *adj* ‹*decor*› old-world; ‹*style*› old-fashioned; ‹*word*› obsolete

désunion /dezynjɔ̃/ *f* **1** division
2 discord

désunir /dezyniʀ/ [**v3**] *vt* to divide, to break up

détachant /detaʃɑ̃/ *m* stain remover

détaché, **~e** /detaʃe/ **A** *pp* ▶ **détacher**
B *pp adj* **1** detached, unconcerned
2 ‹*teacher, diplomat*› on secondment (BrE), transferred

détachement /detaʃmɑ̃/ *m* **1** detachment (**de** from)
2 (Mil) detachment
3 secondment

détacher /detaʃe/ [**v1**] **A** *vt* **1** to untie; to unfasten; to undo
2 to take down ‹*poster*›
3 **~ les yeux** *or* **le regard de qch** to take one's eyes off sth
4 to second (BrE), to transfer
5 to remove the stain(s) from
B **se détacher** *v refl* (+ *v être*)
1 ‹*prisoner, animal*› to break loose; ‹*boat*› to come untied
2 to come undone
3 ‹*coupon*› to come out; ‹*wallpaper*› to come away
4 to grow away from ‹*person*›
5 ‹*pattern*› to stand out
6 **se ~ de** to detach oneself from; to pull away from

détail /detaj/ *m* **1** detail
2 breakdown; **analyse de ~** detailed analysis
3 retail; **acheter (qch) au ~** to buy (sth) retail

détailler /detaje/ [**v1**] *vt* **1** to detail; to itemize
2 to scrutinize

détartrer /detaʀtʀe/ [**v1**] *vt* **1** to descale ‹*kettle*›
2 to scale ‹*teeth*›

détaxe /detaks/ *f* **1** tax removal
2 tax refund
3 export rebate

détecter /detɛkte/ [**v1**] *vt* to detect

détecteur /detɛktœʀ/ *m* detector; **~ de mines** mine detector

détection /detɛksjɔ̃/ *f* detection

détective /detɛktiv/ *m* detective

déteindre /detɛ̃dʀ/ [**v55**] *vi* **1** ‹*garment*› to fade
2 ‹*colour*› to run
3 (fig) to rub off

détendre /detɑ̃dʀ/ [**v6**] **A** *vt* **1** to release ‹*spring*›
2 to slacken ‹*rope, spring*›
3 to relax ‹*muscle*›; to calm ‹*atmosphere, mind*›
B *vi* **1** to be relaxing
2 to be entertaining
C **se détendre** *v refl* (+ *v être*) **1** ‹*rope, spring*› to slacken
2 ‹*person, muscle*› to relax

détendu, **~e** /detɑ̃dy/ **A** *pp* ▶ **détendre**
B *pp adj* **1** relaxed
2 slack

détenir /det(ə)niʀ/ [**v36**] *vt* **1** to keep ‹*objects*›; to hold ‹*power, record*›; to possess ‹*arms*›; to have ‹*secret, evidence*›
2 to detain ‹*suspect*›

détente /detɑ̃t/ *f* **1** relaxation
2 détente
3 (on gun) trigger
IDIOM **être lent** *or* **dur à la ~** (fam) to be slow on the uptake

d

détention /detɑ̃sjɔ̃/ *f* **1** (of passport, drugs, record) holding; (of arms, secret) possession
2 detention; **~ préventive** custody

détenu, **~e** /detəny/ *mf* prisoner

détergent /detɛʀʒɑ̃/ *m* detergent

détériorer /deteʀjɔʀe/ [**v1**] **A** *vt* to damage
B se détériorer *v refl* (+ *v être*) ‹*situation, weather*› to deteriorate; ‹*foodstuff*› to go bad

déterminant, **~e** /detɛʀminɑ̃, ɑ̃t/ *adj* ‹*role, factor*› decisive

détermination /detɛʀminasjɔ̃/ *f* determination

déterminé, **~e** /detɛʀmine/ **A** *pp* ▸ **déterminer**
B *pp adj* **1** determined
2 given

déterminer /detɛʀmine/ [**v1**] *vt* **1** to determine ‹*reason, responsibility*›
2 to work out ‹*policy, terms*›
3 to determine ‹*attitude, decision*›
4 ~ qn à faire to make sb decide to do

déterrer /deteʀe/ [**v1**] *vt* to dig [sb/sth] up

détestable /detɛstabl/ *adj* ‹*style, weather*› appalling; ‹*habits*› revolting; ‹*person*› hateful

détester /detɛste/ [**v1**] *vt* **1** to detest, to loathe ‹*person*›
2 to hate

détonateur /detɔnatœʀ/ *m* **1** detonator
2 (fig) catalyst

détonation /detɔnasjɔ̃/ *f* detonation

détonner /detɔne/ [**v1**] *vi* to be out of place

détordre /detɔʀdʀ/ [**v6**] *vt* to straighten ‹*iron bar*›; to unwind ‹*cable*›

détour /detuʀ/ *m* **1** detour; **ça vaut le ~** it's worth the trip
2 roundabout means
3 circumlocution; **il me l'a dit sans ~s** he told me straight
4 (in road, river) bend

détourné, **~e** /detuʀne/ **A** *pp* ▸ **détourner**
B *pp adj* ‹*reference*› oblique; ‹*means*› indirect

détournement /detuʀnəmɑ̃/ *m*
1 misappropriation
2 hijacking
3 (of traffic) diversion
■ **~ de mineur** (Law) corruption of a minor

détourner /detuʀne/ [**v1**] **A** *vt* **1** to divert ‹*attention*›
2 ~ les yeux *or* **le regard** *or* **la tête** to look away
3 to divert ‹*traffic, river, flight*›; **~ la conversation** to change the subject
4 to hijack ‹*plane, ship*›; to misappropriate ‹*funds*›
B se détourner *v refl* (+ *v être*) **1 se ~ de** to turn away from ‹*friend*›
2 to look away

détracteur, **-trice** /detʀaktœʀ, tʀis/ *mf* detractor

détraqué, **~e** /detʀake/ *mf* (fam) deranged person

détraquer /detʀake/ [**v1**] **A** *vt* **1** to bust [sth] (fam); to make [sth] go wrong
2 (fam) ‹*medicine*› to upset ‹*stomach*›; to damage ‹*health*›
B se détraquer *v refl* (+ *v être*) ‹*mechanism*› to break down; ‹*weather*› to break

détremper /detʀɑ̃pe/ [**v1**] *vt* to saturate ‹*ground*›; to soak ‹*garment*›

détresse /detʀɛs/ *f* distress

détriment: **au détriment de** /odetʀimɑ̃də/ *phr* to the detriment of

détritus /detʀity(s)/ *mpl* refuse, rubbish (BrE), garbage (AmE)

détroit /detʀwɑ/ *m* straits

détromper /detʀɔ̃pe/ [**v1**] **A** *vt* to set [sb] straight
B se détromper *v refl* (+ *v être*) **détrompez-vous!** don't you believe it!

détrôner /detʀone/ [**v1**] *vt* to dethrone

détruire /detʀɥiʀ/ [**v69**] *vt* to destroy

dette /dɛt/ *f* debt; **avoir une ~ envers qn** to be indebted to sb

DEUG /dœg/ *m* (*abbr* = **diplôme d'études universitaires générales**) *university diploma taken after two years' study*

deuil /dœj/ *m* **1** bereavement
2 mourning, grief
IDIOM **faire son ~ de qch** (fam) to kiss sth goodbye (fam)

deux /dø/ **A** *adj inv* **1** two; **~ fois** twice; **des ~ côtés de la rue** on either side *or* both sides of the street; **tous les ~ jours** every other day; **à nous ~** I'm all yours; (to enemy) it's just you and me now
2 a few, a couple of
3 second; **le deux mai** the second of May (BrE), May second (AmE)
B *pron* **elles sont venues toutes les ~** they both came
C *m inv* two
IDIOMS **faire ~ poids, ~ mesures** to have double standards; **un tiens vaut mieux que ~ tu l'auras** (Proverb) a bird in the hand is worth two in the bush; **en ~ temps, trois mouvements** very quickly; **je n'ai fait ni une ni ~** I didn't have a second's hesitation

deuxième /døzjɛm/ **A** *adj* second; **dans un ~ temps nous étudierons...** secondly, we

key word

will study...
B *mf* second
■ **~ classe** second class, standard class (BrE)

deuxièmement /døzjɛmmɑ̃/ *adv* secondly

deux-points /døpwɛ̃/ *m inv* colon

deux-roues /døʀu/ *m inv* two-wheeled vehicle

dévaler /devale/ [**v1**] *vt* to hurtle down; to tear down

dévaliser /devalize/ [**v1**] *vt* **1** to rob ‹*person, bank, safe*›
2 to clean out (fam) ‹*shop, larder*›

dévaloriser /devalɔʀize/ [**v1**] **A** *vt* **1** to depreciate
2 to belittle
B se dévaloriser *v refl* (+ *v être*) **1** to lose value; to lose prestige
2 to put oneself down

dévaluation /devalɥasjɔ̃/ *f* devaluation

dévaluer /devalɥe/ [**v1**] *vt* to devalue

devancer /dəvɑ̃se/ [**v12**] *vt* **1** to be ahead of, to outstrip ‹*competitor*›
2 to anticipate ‹*demand, desire*›; to forestall ‹*attack, criticisms*›

devant¹ /dəvɑ̃/ **A** *prep* **1** in front of; **tous les hommes sont égaux ~ la loi** all men are equal in the eyes of the law; **fuir ~ le danger** to run away from danger; **le bus est passé ~ moi sans s'arrêter** the bus went straight past me without stopping
2 outside; **il attendait ~ la porte** he was waiting outside the door; he was waiting by the door
3 ahead of; **la voiture ~ nous** the car ahead *or* in front of us; **laisser passer quelqu'un ~ (soi)** to let somebody go first; **avoir toute la vie ~ soi** to have one's whole life ahead of one
B *adv* **1 'où est la poste?'—'tu es juste ~'** 'where's the post office?'—'you're right in front of it'
2 pars ~, je te rejoins go ahead, I'll catch up with you
3 (of hall, theatre) at the front; (in car) in the front

devant² /dəvɑ̃/ *m* front
IDIOM **prendre les ~s** to take the initiative

devanture /dəvɑ̃tyʀ/ *f* **1** (shop)front
2 shop *or* store (AmE) window

dévastation /devastasjɔ̃/ *f* devastation

dévaster /devaste/ [**v1**] *vt* **1** ‹*army*› to lay waste to; ‹*storm, fire*› to destroy
2 ‹*burglar*› to wreck

déveine /devɛn/ *f* (fam) rotten luck (fam), bad luck

développement /devlɔpmɑ̃/ *m*
1 development; **pays en voie de ~** developing nation *or* country
2 (in photography) developing

développer /devlɔpe/ [**v1**] **A** *vt* to develop
B se développer *v refl* (+ *v être*) ‹*body, ability*› to develop; ‹*plant, company, town*› to grow

devenir¹ /dəvniʀ/ [**v36**] *vi* (+ *v être*) to become; **et Paul, qu'est-ce qu'il devient?** and what is Paul up to these days?

devenir² /dəvniʀ/ *m* future

dévergonder: **se dévergonder** /devɛʀgɔ̃de/ [**v1**] *v refl* (+ *v être*) to be going to the bad

déverser /devɛʀse/ [**v1**] **A** *vt* to pour ‹*liquid*›; to drop ‹*bombs*›; to dump ‹*refuse, sand*›; to discharge ‹*waste*›; to disgorge ‹*crowd*›; **~ du pétrole** to dump oil; to spill oil
B se déverser *v refl* (+ *v être*) ‹*river*› to flow; ‹*sewer, crowd*› to pour

dévêtir /devɛtiʀ/ [**v33**] **A** *vt* to undress
B se dévêtir *v refl* (+ *v être*) to get undressed

déviation /devjasjɔ̃/ *f* **1** diversion (BrE), detour (AmE)
2 departure, deviation
3 (of compass) deviation
4 (of light) deflection

dévider /devide/ [**v1**] *vt* to unwind ‹*cable*›

dévier /devje/ [**v2**] **A** *vt* to deflect ‹*ball, trajectory*›; to divert ‹*traffic*›
B *vi* **1** ‹*bullet, ball*› to deflect; ‹*vehicle*› to veer off course
2 ~ de to deviate from ‹*plan*›
3 ‹*tool*› to slip
4 ‹*conversation*› to drift

devin /dəvɛ̃/ *m* soothsayer, seer

deviner /dəvine/ [**v1**] *vt* **1** to guess ‹*secret*›; to foresee, to tell ‹*future*›
2 to sense ‹*danger*›
3 to make out, to discern

devinette /dəvinɛt/ *f* riddle

devis /d(ə)vi/ *m inv* estimate, quote

dévisager /devizaʒe/ [**v13**] *vt* to stare at

devise /dəviz/ *f* **1** currency
2 (foreign) currency
3 motto

deviser /dəvize/ [**v1**] *vi* to converse

dévisser /devise/ [**v1**] *vt* to unscrew

dévoiler /devwale/ [**v1**] *vt* **1** to unveil
2 to reveal; to uncover

devoir¹ /dəvwaʀ/ [**v44**] **A** *v aux* **1** to have to; **je dois aller au travail** I've got to *or* I must go to work; **il a dû accepter** he had to accept; **il aurait dû partir** he should have left
2 il a dû accepter he must have accepted; **elle doit avoir 13 ans** she must be about 13 years old
3 cela devait arriver it was bound to happen; **un incident qui devait avoir de graves conséquences** an incident which was to have serious consequences; **ils doivent arriver vers 10 heures** they're due to arrive around 10 o'clock
B *vt* to owe; **il me doit des excuses** he owes me an apology
C se devoir *v refl* (+ *v être*) **1 je me dois de le faire** it's my duty to do it
2 les époux se doivent fidélité spouses owe

it to each other to be faithful
3 un homme de son rang se doit d'avoir un chauffeur a man of his standing has to have a chauffeur
D comme il se doit *phr* **1 agir comme il se doit** to behave in the correct way
2 comme il se doit, elle est en retard! as you might expect, she's late!

devoir² /dəvwaʀ/ *m* **1** duty; **il est de mon ~ de** it's my duty to
2 test; homework

dévolu /devɔly/ *m* **jeter son ~ sur** to set one's heart on ‹*object*›; to set one's cap at ‹*person*›

dévorant, **~e** /devɔʀɑ̃, ɑ̃t/ *adj* ‹*hunger*› voracious; ‹*flames, passion*› all-consuming

dévorer /devɔʀe/ [**v1**] *vt* **1** to devour ‹*food, book*›; **~ qn de baisers** to smother sb with kisses
2 ‹*obsession*› to consume

dévot, **~e** /devo, ɔt/ *adj* devout

dévotion /devosjɔ̃/ *f* **1** devoutness
2 (religious) devotion (**à** to)
3 passion (**pour** for)

dévoué, **~e** /devwe/ *adj* devoted (**à** to)

dévouement /devumɑ̃/ *m* devotion

dévouer: **se dévouer** /devwe/ [**v1**] *v refl* (+ *v être*) **1** to devote *or* dedicate oneself
2 to put oneself out

dévoyer /devwaje/ [**v23**] **A** *vt* to deprave [sb], to lead [sb] astray
B se dévoyer *v refl* (+ *v être*) to go astray

dextérité /dɛksteʀite/ *f* dexterity, skill

dézipper /dezipe/ [**v1**] *vt* (Comput) to unzip

diabète /djabɛt/ *m* diabetes

diabétique /djabetik/ *adj*, *mf* diabetic

diable /djɑbl/ **A** *m* **1** devil; **en ~** diabolically; fiendishly; **un (petit) ~** a little devil
2 two-wheeled trolley (BrE), hand truck (AmE)
B *excl* my God!; **pourquoi ~** why on earth
IDIOMS **habiter au ~** to live miles from anywhere; **que le ~ t'emporte!** to hell with you!; **ce n'est pas le ~!** it's not that difficult!; **avoir le ~ au corps** to be like someone possessed; **tirer le ~ par la queue** to live from hand to mouth

diablement /djɑbləmɑ̃/ *adv* terrifically

diabolique /djabɔlik/ *adj* **1** diabolic; ‹*invention*› fiendish
2 ‹*person*› demonic; ‹*scheme, smile*› devilish
3 ‹*precision*› uncanny

diabolo /djabɔlo/ *m* **~ menthe** mint cordial and lemonade (BrE) *or* soda (AmE)

diadème /djadɛm/ *m* **1** tiara
2 diadem

diagnostic /djagnɔstik/ *m* (gen), (Med) diagnosis

diagnostiquer /djagnɔstike/ [**v1**] *vt* to diagnose

diagonal, **~e** *mpl* **-aux** /djagɔnal, o/ *adj* diagonal

diagonale /djagɔnal/ *f* diagonal; **lire qch en ~** to skim through sth

diagramme /djagʀam/ *m* graph

dialecte /djalɛkt/ *m* dialect

⚷ **dialogue** /djalɔg/ *m* dialogue (BrE)

dialoguer /djalɔge/ [**v1**] *vi* to have talks

dialoguiste /djalɔgist/ *mf* screenwriter

dialyse /djaliz/ *f* dialysis

diamant /djamɑ̃/ *m* diamond

diamantaire /djamɑ̃tɛʀ/ *m* **1** diamond cutter
2 diamond merchant

diamétralement /djametʀalmɑ̃/ *adv* diametrically

diamètre /djamɛtʀ/ *m* diameter

diapason /djapazɔ̃/ *m* **1** (note) diapason
2 tuning fork
IDIOM **se mettre au ~** to fall in step

diaphragme /djafʀagm/ *m* diaphragm

diapo /djapo/ *f* (fam) slide

diaporama /djapoʀama/ *m* slide show

diapositive /djapozitiv/ *f* slide, transparency

diarrhée /djaʀe/ *f* diarrhoea

dico /diko/ *m* (fam) dictionary

dictateur /diktatœʀ/ *m* dictator

dictature /diktatyʀ/ *f* dictatorship

dictée /dikte/ *f* dictation

dicter /dikte/ [**v1**] *vt* **1** to dictate
2 to motivate

diction /diksjɔ̃/ *f* diction; elocution

dictionnaire /diksjɔnɛʀ/ *m* dictionary

dicton /diktɔ̃/ *m* saying

didacticiel /didaktisjɛl/ *m* educational software program

didactique /didaktik/ *adj* **1** ‹*work, tone*› didactic
2 ‹*term, language*› technical, specialist

dièse /djɛz/ **A** *adj* sharp
B *m* **1** (Mus) **do ~** C sharp
2 (on phone) **la touche ~** the hash key (BrE), the pound key (AmE)

diesel /djezɛl/ *m* diesel

diète /djɛt/ *f* (Med) light diet

diététicien, **-ienne** /djetetisjɛ̃, ɛn/ *mf* dietitian

diététique /djetetik/ **A** *adj* dietary; **produits ~s** health foods; **magasin ~** health food shop
B *f* dietetics

⚷ **dieu**, *pl* **~x** /djø/ *m* **1** god
2 sur le terrain c'est un ~ he's brilliant on the sports field
IDIOMS **nager comme un ~** to be a superb swimmer; **être dans le secret des ~x** to be privy to the secrets of those on high

---

⚷ key word

Dieu /djø/ *m* God
IDIOMS **se prendre pour ∼ le père** to think one is God Almighty; **chaque jour que ∼ fait** day in, day out; **il vaut mieux s'adresser à ∼ qu'à ses saints** (Proverb) always go straight to the top
diffamation /difamasjɔ̃/ *f* slander; (Law) libel
diffamatoire /difamatwaʀ/ *adj* (in writing) libellous; (verbally) slanderous; **écrit ∼** libel
diffamer /difame/ [**v1**] *vt* (gen) to slander, to defame; (Law) to libel
différé, **∼e** /difeʀe/ **A** *pp* ▸ **différer**
B *pp adj* **1** postponed
2 ‹*payment*› deferred
3 ‹*programme*› pre-recorded
C *m* (of match, event) recording
différemment /difeʀamɑ̃/ *adv* differently
différence /difeʀɑ̃s/ *f* difference; **à la ∼ de** unlike; **le droit à la ∼** the right to be different
différenciation /difeʀɑ̃sjasjɔ̃/ *f* differentiation
différencier /difeʀɑ̃sje/ [**v2**] **A** *vt* **1** to differentiate; **rien ne les différencie** there's no way of telling them apart
2 to make [sb/sth] different
B se différencier *v refl* (+ *v être*)
1 ‹*person, organization*› to differentiate oneself
2 to differ
3 to become different
différend /difeʀɑ̃/ *m* disagreement
différent, **∼e** /difeʀɑ̃, ɑ̃t/ *adj* different, various; **pour ∼es raisons** for various reasons
différentiel, **-ielle** /difeʀɑ̃sjɛl/ *adj* differential
différer /difeʀe/ [**v14**] **A** *vt* to postpone ‹*departure, meeting*›; to defer ‹*payment*›
B *vi* to differ
difficile /difisil/ *adj* **1** (gen) difficult; ‹*victory*› hard-won; **le plus ∼ reste à faire** the worst is yet to come
2 ‹*person, personality*› difficult
3 fussy (**sur** about); **tu n'es pas ∼!** you're easy to please!
difficilement /difisilmɑ̃/ *adv* with difficulty; **∼ supportable** hard to bear
difficulté /difikylte/ *f* difficulty
difforme /difɔʀm/ *adj* ‹*body, limb*› deformed; ‹*object*› strangely shaped; ‹*tree*› twisted
difformité /difɔʀmite/ *f* deformity
diffus, **∼e** /dify, yz/ *adj* ‹*light, heat*› diffuse; ‹*feeling*› vague
diffuser /difyze/ [**v1**] *vt* **1** to broadcast
2 to spread; **∼ le signalement de qn** to send out a description of sb
3 to distribute ‹*article, book*›
4 to diffuse ‹*light, heat*›
diffusion /difyzjɔ̃/ *f* **1** broadcasting; **la ∼ du film** the showing of the film
2 dissemination, diffusion
3 (commercial) distribution
4 (of newspaper) circulation
digérer /diʒeʀe/ [**v14**] *vt* **1** to digest
2 (fam) to swallow ‹*insult*›; to stomach ‹*defeat*›
digeste /diʒɛst/ *adj* easily digestible
digestif, **-ive** /diʒɛstif, iv/ **A** *adj* digestive
B *m* liqueur (*taken after dinner*); brandy
digestion /diʒɛstjɔ̃/ *f* digestion
digicode® /diʒikɔd/ *m* digital (access) lock
digital, **∼e**, *mpl* **-aux** /diʒital, o/ *adj* digital
digne /diɲ/ *adj* **1** dignified
2 worthy; **∼ de confiance** *or* **de foi** trustworthy
dignement /diɲmɑ̃/ *adv* **1** with dignity
2 fittingly
dignité /diɲite/ *f* **1** dignity; **avoir sa ∼** to have one's pride
2 (title) dignity
digression /digʀesjɔ̃/ *f* digression
digue /dig/ *f* **1** sea wall
2 dyke (BrE), dike (AmE)
3 harbour (BrE) wall
dilapider /dilapide/ [**v1**] *vt* to squander
dilatation /dilatasjɔ̃/ *f* **1** (of gas) expansion
2 (Med) dilation
dilater /dilate/ [**v1**] *vt* **1** to dilate ‹*pupil, cervix*›; to distend ‹*stomach*›
2 to expand ‹*gas*›
dilemme /dilɛm/ *m* dilemma
dilettante /dilɛtɑ̃t/ *mf* amateur
dilettantisme /dilɛtɑ̃tism/ *m* amateurism; (derog) dilettantism
diligence /diliʒɑ̃s/ *f* **1** stagecoach
2 haste
diligent, **∼e** /diliʒɑ̃, ɑ̃t/ *adj* diligent
diluant /dilɥɑ̃/ *m* thinner
diluer /dilɥe/ [**v1**] *vt* **1** to dilute
2 to thin [sth] down
diluvien, **-ienne** /dilyvjɛ̃, ɛn/ *adj* **pluies diluviennes** torrential rain
dimanche /dimɑ̃ʃ/ *m* Sunday
IDIOM **ce n'est pas tous les jours ∼** not every day is a holiday
dimension /dimɑ̃sjɔ̃/ *f* **1** dimension
2 size
3 dimension, aspect
4 (of problem) dimensions
diminué, **∼e** /diminɥe/ **A** *pp* ▸ **diminuer**
B *pp adj* ‹*person*› weak
diminuer /diminɥe/ [**v1**] **A** *vt* **1** to reduce; to lower
2 to dampen ‹*enthusiasm, courage*›
3 to belittle ‹*person, achievement*›
4 to weaken ‹*person*›; to sap ‹*strength*›
B *vi* **1** to come *or* go down; to be reduced; to fall; to decrease; **les jours diminuent** the days are getting shorter
2 ‹*activity, violence*› to fall off; ‹*tension*› to decrease; ‹*noise, flames, rumours*› to die

down; ‹*strength*› to diminish

diminutif /diminytif/ *m* **1** diminutive
2 pet name

diminution /diminysjɔ̃/ *f* decrease; reduction; (in production, trade) fall-off

dinde /dɛ̃d/ *f* turkey (hen)

dindon /dɛ̃dɔ̃/ *m* turkey (cock)
IDIOM **être le ~ de la farce** to be fooled *or* duped

d

dindonneau, *pl* **~x** /dɛ̃dɔno/ *m* turkey

dîner[1] /dine/ [**v1**] *vi* to have dinner
IDIOM **qui dort dîne** (Proverb) when you're asleep you don't feel hungry

✓ **dîner**[2] /dine/ *m* dinner

dînette /dinɛt/ *f* doll's tea set

dingo /dɛ̃go/ *adj inv* (fam) crazy (fam)

dingue **A** *adj* **1** ‹*person*› crazy (fam)
2 ‹*noise, success*› wild; ‹*price, speed*› ridiculous
B *mf* **1** nutcase (fam)
2 un ~ de musique a music freak (fam)

dinosaure /dinozɔʀ/ *m* dinosaur

diocèse /djɔsɛz/ *m* diocese

dioxyde /dijɔksid/ *m* dioxide

diphtongue /diftɔ̃g/ *f* diphthong

diplomate /diplɔmat/ **A** *adj* diplomatic
B *mf* diplomat

diplomatie /diplɔmasi/ *f* diplomacy

diplomatique /diplɔmatik/ *adj* diplomatic

diplôme /diplom/ *m* **1** certificate, diploma; **il n'a aucun ~** he hasn't got any qualifications
2 (at university) degree; diploma
3 (in army, police) staff exam

diplômé, **~e** /diplome/ **A** *adj* **une infirmière ~e** a qualified nurse
B *mf* graduate

✓ **dire**[1] /diʀ/ [**v65**] **A** *vt* **1** to say ‹*words, prayer*›; to read ‹*lesson*›; to tell ‹*story, joke*›; **~ qch entre ses dents** to mutter sth
2 to tell; **c'est ce qu'on m'a dit** so I've been told; **faire ~ à qn que** to let sb know that...; **je me suis laissé ~ que...** I heard that...; **c'est pas pour ~, mais...** (fam) I don't want to make a big deal of it, but... (fam); **à qui le dites-vous!** (fam) don't I know it!; **je ne vous le fais pas ~!** (fam) you don't need to tell me!; **dis donc, où tu te crois?** (fam) hey! where do you think you are?
3 to say (**que** that); **on dit que...** it is said that...; **si l'on peut ~** if one might say so; **autant ~ que...** you might as well say that...; **si j'ose ~** if I may say so; **c'est (tout) ~!** need I say more?; **cela dit** having said that; **tu peux le ~!** (fam) you can say that again! (fam); **à vrai ~** actually; **entre nous soit dit** between you and me; **soit dit en passant** incidentally; **c'est ~ si j'ai raison** it just goes to show I'm right; **c'est beaucoup ~** that's going a bit far; **c'est vite dit** that's easy for you to say; **ce n'est pas dit** I'm not that sure; **comment ~?** how shall I put it?; **pour ainsi ~** so to speak; **autrement dit** in other words; **comme dirait l'autre** (fam) as they say; **il n'y a pas à ~, elle est belle** (fam) you have to admit, she's beautiful
4 ‹*law*› to state; ‹*measuring device*› to show; **vouloir ~** to mean
5 ~ à qn de faire to tell sb to do
6 to think; **on dirait de l'estragon** it looks *or* tastes like tarragon; **ça ne me dit rien de faire** I don't feel like doing; **notre nouveau jardinier ne me dit rien (qui vaille)** I don't think much of our new gardener
B **se dire** *v refl* (+ *v être*) **1** to tell oneself; **il faut (bien) se ~ que...** one must realize that...
2 to exchange ‹*insults*›; **se ~ adieu** to say goodbye to each other
3 to claim to be
4 ça ne se dit pas you can't say that
C **se dire** *v impers* **il ne s'est rien dit d'intéressant à la réunion** nothing of interest was said during the meeting

dire[2] /diʀ/ *m* **au ~ de, selon les ~s de** according to

✓ **direct** /diʀɛkt/ **A** *adj* **1** ‹*contact, descendant, tax*› direct; ‹*superior*› immediate
2 ‹*route, access*› direct; **ce train est ~ pour Lille** this train is nonstop to Lille
3 direct, frank
B *m* **1** live broadcasting; **en ~ de** live from
2 (in boxing) jab; **~ du gauche** left jab
3 express (train)

✓ **directement** /diʀɛktəmɑ̃/ *adv* **1** ‹*travel, go*› straight
2 directly

✓ **directeur**, **-trice** /diʀɛktœʀ, tʀis/ **A** *adj* **principe ~** guiding principle; **idée directrice d'un ouvrage** central theme of a book
B *mf* **1** headmaster/headmistress (BrE), principal (AmE); (of private school) principal
2 (of hotel, cinema) manager/manageress
3 director; head
■ **~ de banque** bank manager; **~ général** managing director (BrE), chief executive officer (AmE); **~ de prison** prison governor (BrE), warden (AmE); **~ sportif** (team) manager

✓ **direction** /diʀɛksjɔ̃/ *f* **1** direction; **il a pris la ~ du nord** he headed north; **en ~ de** toward(s); **indiquer la ~ à qn** to tell sb the way; **prenez la ~ Nation** take the train going to 'Nation'
2 (gen) management; supervision; (of newspaper) editorship; (of movement) leadership; **orchestre sous la ~ de** orchestra conducted by
3 management; **la ~ et les ouvriers** management and workers
4 manager's office; head office
5 (Aut) steering

directive /diʀɛktiv/ *f* directive

directrice ▸ **directeur**

✓ key word

dirigeable /diʀiʒabl/ *adj, m* dirigible

dirigeant, **~e** /diʀiʒɑ̃, ɑ̃t/ **A** *adj ‹class›* ruling
B *m* leader

diriger /diʀiʒe/ [**v13**] **A** *vt* **1** to be in charge of *‹people›*; to run *‹service, party›*; to manage *‹company›*; to lead *‹investigation›*; to direct *‹operation›*
2 to steer; to pilot; **il vous dirigera dans la ville** he'll guide you around the town
3 to turn *‹light, jet›* (**sur** on); to point *‹gun, telescope›* (**sur** at)
4 to dispatch *‹goods›*; to direct *‹convoy›*
5 (Mus) to conduct
6 to direct *‹actors›*; to manage *‹theatre company›*
B se diriger *v refl* (+ *v être*) **se ~ vers** to make for; **avoir du mal à se ~ dans le noir** to have difficulty finding one's way in the dark

dirigisme /diʀiʒism/ *m* planned economy

discale /diskal/ *adj f* **hernie ~** slipped disc

discernement /disɛʀnəmɑ̃/ *m* judgement

discerner /disɛʀne/ [**v1**] *vt* **1** to detect *‹sign, smell, expression›*; to make out *‹shape, noise›*
2 to make out *‹motives›*; **~ le vrai du faux** to discriminate between truth and untruth

disciple /disipl/ *mf* **1** follower
2 disciple

disciplinaire /disiplinɛʀ/ *adj* disciplinary

discipline /disiplin/ *f* **1** discipline
2 discipline, specialism
3 (Sch) subject
4 sport

discipliner /disipline/ [**v1**] *vt* **1** to discipline
2 to control *‹troops›*; to discipline *‹thoughts, feelings›*
3 to keep [sth] under control *‹hair›*

disco /disko/ **A** *adj inv* disco
B *m* disco music

discontinu, **~e** /diskɔ̃tiny/ *adj ‹movement›* intermittent; *‹line›* broken

discordance /diskɔʀdɑ̃s/ *f* **1** (of opinions) conflict
2 (of colours) clash
3 (of sounds) dissonance

discordant, **~e** /diskɔʀdɑ̃, ɑ̃t/ *adj* **1** *‹sound, instrument›* discordant; *‹voice›* strident
2 *‹colours›* clashing
3 *‹opinions›* conflicting

discorde /diskɔʀd/ *f* discord, dissension

discothèque /diskɔtɛk/ *f* **1** music library
2 record collection
3 discotheque

discourir /diskuʀiʀ/ [**v26**] *vi* **~ de** *or* **sur qch** to hold forth on sth

discours /diskuʀ/ *m inv* **1** speech (**sur** on)
2 talk; **assez de ~, des actes!** let's have less talk and more action!
3 views; **il tient toujours le même ~** his views haven't changed
4 (in linguistics) speech; discourse

discrédit /diskʀedi/ *m* disrepute; **jeter le ~ sur** to discredit

discréditer /diskʀedite/ [**v1**] *vt* to discredit

discret, **-ète** /diskʀɛ, ɛt/ *adj* **1** *‹person›* unassuming; *‹colour›* sober; *‹charm›* subtle; *‹lighting›* subdued; *‹smile, perfume›* discreet; *‹place›* quiet
2 discreet (**sur** about)
3 not inquisitive

discrètement /diskʀɛtmɑ̃/ *adv* discreetly; soberly; quietly

discrétion /diskʀesjɔ̃/ **A** *f* discretion; **dans la plus grande ~** in the greatest secrecy
B à discrétion *phr* **il y avait à boire à ~** you could drink as much as you liked
C à la discrétion de *phr* at the discretion of

discrimination /diskʀiminasjɔ̃/ *f* discrimination

discriminatoire /diskʀiminatwaʀ/ *adj* discriminatory (**à l'encontre de** against)

discriminer /diskʀimine/ [**v1**] *vt* to discriminate between *‹things, people›*

disculper /diskylpe/ [**v1**] **A** *vt* to exculpate
B se disculper *v refl* (+ *v être*) to vindicate oneself (**auprès de qn** in the eyes of sb)

discussion /diskysjɔ̃/ *f* **1** discussion; **relancer la ~** to revive the debate
2 argument

discutable /diskytabl/ *adj* debatable; questionable

discuté, **~e** /diskyte/ **A** *pp* ▶ **discuter**
B *pp adj* controversial

discuter /diskyte/ [**v1**] **A** *vt* **1** to discuss, to debate
2 to question
B discuter de *v+prep* to discuss
C *vi* **1** to talk (**avec qn** to sb)
2 to argue
D se discuter *v refl* (+ *v être*) **ça se discute, ça peut se ~** that's debatable

diseur, **-euse** /dizœʀ, øz/ *mf* **~ de bonne aventure** fortune-teller

disgrâce /disgʀɑs/ *f* disgrace

disgracieux, **-ieuse** /disgʀasjø, øz/ *adj* ugly; unsightly

disjoindre /disʒwɛ̃dʀ/ [**v56**] **A** *vt* **1** to loosen
2 to separate
B se disjoindre *v refl* (+ *v être*) to come loose

disjoncter /disʒɔ̃kte/ [**v1**] *vi* **ça a disjoncté** the trip switch has gone

disjoncteur /disʒɔ̃ktœʀ/ *m* circuit breaker

dislocation /dislɔkasjɔ̃/ *f* **1** dismemberment
2 ~ (articulaire) dislocation (of a joint)

disloquer /dislɔke/ [**v1**] *vt* **1** to dismember *‹empire, state›*
2 to dislocate *‹shoulder, arm›*

disparaître /dispaʀɛtʀ/ [**v73**] *vi* **1** to disappear; to vanish; **disparaissez!** out

of my sight!; **des centaines de personnes disparaissent chaque année** hundreds of people go missing every year
2 ‹*pain, smell*› to go; ‹*stain*› to come out; ‹*fever*› to subside; **faire ~** to get rid of ‹*pain, dandruff*›; to remove ‹*stain*›
3 (euph) to die; to die out; to become extinct; **voir ~** to witness the end of ‹*civilization*›

d

disparate /disparat/ *adj* ill-assorted; mixed

disparition /disparisjɔ̃/ *f* **1** disappearance; (of species) extinction; **une espèce en voie de ~** an endangered species
2 (euph) death

disparu, **~e** /dispary/ **A** *pp* ▶ **disparaître**
B *pp adj* **1** missing; **porté ~** (Mil) missing in action
2 ‹*civilization, traditions*› lost; ‹*species*› extinct
3 (euph) dead
C *mf* **1** missing person
2 les ~s the dead

dispendieux, **-ieuse** /dispɑ̃djø, øz/ *adj* expensive, extravagant

dispense /dispɑ̃s/ *f* **1** exemption (**de** from)
2 certificate of exemption

dispenser /dispɑ̃se/ [**v1**] **A** *vt* **1** to give ‹*lessons, advice*›
2 ~ qn de (faire) qch to exempt sb from (doing) sth; to excuse sb from (doing) sth; **je vous dispense de commentaire** I don't need any comment from you
B se dispenser *v refl* (+ *v être*) **se ~ de (faire) qch** to spare oneself (the trouble of doing) sth

disperser /disperse/ [**v1**] **A** *vt* to scatter ‹*objects, family*›; to disperse ‹*crowd, smoke*›; to break up ‹*gathering, collection*›
B se disperser *v refl* (+ *v être*) to disperse; to scatter; to break up

disponibilité /dispɔnibilite/ **A** *f* availability
B disponibilités *fpl* available funds

🔑 **disponible** /dispɔnibl/ *adj* available

dispos, **~e** /dispo, oz/ *adj* **frais et ~** fresh as a daisy

disposé, **~e** /dispoze/ **A** *pp* ▶ **disposer**
B *pp adj* **1** arranged; laid out
2 ~ à faire willing to do
3 être bien ~ to be in a good mood; **être bien ~ à l'égard de** *or* **envers qn** to be well-disposed toward(s) sb

🔑 **disposer** /dispoze/ [**v1**] **A** *vt* **1** to arrange; to position
2 les machines dont nous disposons the machines we have at our disposal
B se disposer *v refl* (+ *v être*) **1 se ~ à faire** to be about to do
2 se ~ en cercle autour de qn to form a circle around sb

dispositif /dispozitif/ *m* **1** device; system
2 operation; **~ policier** police operation

🔑 **disposition** /dispozisjɔ̃/ **A** *f*
1 arrangement; layout; position
2 disposal; **à la ~ du public** for public use
3 measure, step
B dispositions *fpl* aptitude

disproportionné, **~e** /disprɔpɔrsjɔne/ *adj* ‹*effort, demand*› disproportionate; ‹*head*› out of proportion with one's body

dispute /dispyt/ *f* argument

disputé, **~e** /dispyte/ *adj* **1** ‹*title, match*› keenly contested
2 ‹*place, person*› sought-after (**de** by)
3 ‹*issue, plan*› controversial

disputer /dispyte/ [**v1**] **A** *vt* **1** to compete in ‹*competition*›; to compete for ‹*cup*›; to play ‹*match*›; to run ‹*race*›
2 (fam) to tell [sb] off
B se disputer *v refl* (+ *v être*) **1** to argue (**sur** about, **pour** over); **nous nous sommes disputés** we had an argument
2 to fight over ‹*inheritance, bone*›
3 ‹*tournament*› to take place

disquaire /disker/ *mf* record dealer

disqualifier /diskalifje/ [**v2**] **A** *vt* to disqualify; **se faire ~ (par)** to be disqualified (by)
B se disqualifier *v refl* (+ *v être*) to discredit oneself (**en faisant** by doing)

🔑 **disque** /disk/ *m* **1** record; **passer un ~** to play a record
2 (gen), (Tech) disc; (Comput) disk
3 (Sport) discus
■ **~ compact** compact disc; **~ dur** hard disk; **~ souple** flexi-disc; floppy disk; **~ de stationnement** parking disc

disquette /diskɛt/ *f* diskette, floppy disk

dissection /disɛksjɔ̃/ *f* dissection

dissemblable /disɑ̃blabl/ *adj* dissimilar, different

dissémination /diseminasjɔ̃/ *f* spread; dispersal; scattering; dissemination

disséminer /disemine/ [**v1**] **A** *vt* to spread ‹*germs, ideas*›; to disperse ‹*pollen*›
B se disséminer *v refl* (+ *v être*) ‹*people*› to scatter; ‹*germs, ideas*› to spread

dissension /disɑ̃sjɔ̃/ *f* disagreement (**au sein de** within)

disséquer /diseke/ [**v14**] *vt* to dissect

dissert /disɛr/ *f* essay

dissertation /disɛrtasjɔ̃/ *f* essay

disserter /disɛrte/ [**v1**] *vi* to speak (**sur** on)

dissidence /disidɑ̃s/ *f* **1** dissent; dissidence; rebellion
2 la ~ the dissidents

dissident, **~e** /disidɑ̃, ɑ̃t/ **A** *adj* dissident
B *mf* **1** dissident
2 dissenter

dissimulation /disimylasjɔ̃/ *f* concealment

dissimuler /disimyle/ [**v1**] *vt* to conceal (**qch à qn** sth from sb)

🔑 key word

dissipation /disipasjɔ̃/ *f* **1** (of misunderstanding) clearing up
2 (of fog, clouds) clearing
3 (of attention) wandering
4 restlessness

dissipé, **~e** /disipe/ *adj* ‹*pupil*› badly behaved; ‹*life*› dissipated

dissiper /disipe/ [**v1**] **A** *vt* **1** to dispel ‹*doubt*›; to clear up ‹*misunderstanding*›; to disperse ‹*smoke*›
2 to distract ‹*person*›
B se dissiper *v refl* (+ *v être*) **1** ‹*doubt*› to vanish; ‹*misunderstanding*› to be cleared up; ‹*mist*› to clear
2 to behave badly

dissocier /disɔsje/ [**v2**] *vt* to separate (**de** from)

dissolu, **~e** /disɔly/ *adj* ‹*life*› dissolute; ‹*morals*› loose

dissolution /disɔlysjɔ̃/ *f* dissolution

dissolvant, **~e** /disɔlvɑ̃, ɑ̃t/ **A** *adj* solvent
B *m* **1** nail varnish
2 solvent

dissonance /disɔnɑ̃s/ *f* dissonance

dissonant, **~e** /disɔnɑ̃, ɑ̃t/ *adj* ‹*voice*› dissonant; ‹*colours*› clashing

dissoudre /disudʀ/ [**v75**] **A** *vt* **1** to dissolve ‹*assembly*›; to disband ‹*movement*›
2 to dissolve ‹*substance*›
B se dissoudre *v refl* (+ *v être*)
1 ‹*organization*› to disband
2 ‹*substance*› to dissolve

dissous, **-oute** /disu, ut/ ▶ **dissoudre**

dissuader /disɥade/ [**v1**] *vt* to dissuade; to put [sb] off; to deter

dissuasif, **-ive** /disɥazif, iv/ *adj*
1 dissuasive; deterrent
2 prohibitive

dissuasion /disɥazjɔ̃/ *f* (Mil) deterrence

dissymétrie /disimetʀi/ *f* asymmetry

distance /distɑ̃s/ *f* **1** distance; **Paris est à quelle ~ de Londres?** how far is Paris from London?; **j'ai couru sur une ~ de deux kilomètres** I ran for two kilometres (BrE); **être à faible ~ de** not to be far (away) from; **prendre ses ~s avec** to distance oneself from; **tenir** *or* **garder ses ~s** to stand aloof; **tenir la ~** ‹*runner*› to stay the course; **à ~** from a distance; **commande à ~** remote control
2 gap; **à une semaine de ~** one week apart

distancer /distɑ̃se/ [**v12**] *vt* to outdistance; to outrun; **se laisser ~** to get left behind

distancier: **se distancier** /distɑ̃sje/ [**v2**] *v refl* (+ *v être*) to distance oneself (**de** from)

distant, **~e** /distɑ̃, ɑ̃t/ *adj* **1** ‹*place, noise*› distant; **~s de trois kilomètres** three kilometres (BrE) apart
2 ‹*person*› distant; ‹*attitude*› reserved; ‹*relations*› cool

distendre **A** *vt* **1** to distend ‹*stomach*›; to stretch ‹*skin, cable*›
2 to weaken ‹*bond, tie*›
B se distendre *v refl* (+ *v être*) **1** to slacken
2 to cool

distiller /distile/ [**v1**] *vt* to distil (BrE)

distillerie /distilʀi/ *f* **1** distillery
2 distilling

distinct, **~e** /distɛ̃, ɛ̃kt/ *adj* **1** distinct (**de** from)
2 ‹*sound*› distinct; ‹*voice*› clear
3 ‹*firm*› separate

distinctif, **-ive** /distɛ̃ktif, iv/ *adj* ‹*mark*› distinguishing; ‹*feature*› distinctive

distinction /distɛ̃ksjɔ̃/ *f* **1** distinction; **sans ~** without discrimination; indiscriminately
2 honour (BrE); **~ honorifique** award
3 refinement

distingué, **~e** /distɛ̃ge/ *adj* distinguished

distinguer /distɛ̃ge/ [**v1**] **A** *vt* **1** to distinguish between; **il est difficile de les ~** it's difficult to tell them apart
2 to distinguish, to make out
3 to discern
4 to set [sb] apart; to make [sth] different
5 to single [sb] out for an honour (BrE)
B se distinguer *v refl* (+ *v être*) **1 se ~ de** to differ from; to set oneself apart from
2 to distinguish oneself
3 to be distinguishable
4 to draw attention to oneself

distordre /distɔʀdʀ/ **A** *vt* to contort; **distordu par** contorted with
B se distordre *v refl* (+ *v être*) to become contorted

distorsion /distɔʀsjɔ̃/ *f* distortion

distraction /distʀaksjɔ̃/ *f* **1** leisure, entertainment; **les ~s sont rares ici** there's not much to do around here
2 recreation
3 absent-mindedness

distraire /distʀɛʀ/ [**v58**] **A** *vt* **1** to amuse; to entertain
2 ~ qn de qch to take sb's mind off sth
3 to distract (**de** from, **par** by)
B se distraire *v refl* (+ *v être*) **1** to amuse oneself; to enjoy oneself
2 j'ai besoin de me ~ I need to take my mind off things

distrait, **~e** /distʀɛ, ɛt/ *adj* ‹*person*› absent-minded; inattentive; ‹*air*› distracted; ‹*look*› vague

distraitement /distʀɛtmɑ̃/ *adv* absent-mindedly; **regarder ~ qch** to look vaguely at sth; **écouter ~** to listen with half an ear

distrayant, **~e** /distʀɛjɑ̃, ɑ̃t/ *adj* entertaining

distribuer /distʀibɥe/ [**v1**] *vt* **1** to distribute (**à** to); to allocate (**à** to); **~ les cartes** to deal; **~ le courrier** to deliver the mail
2 to supply ‹*water, heat*›

distributeur, **-trice** /distʀibytœʀ, tʀis/ **A** *mf* distributor

d

d

B *m* **1** dispenser; vending machine; **~ de tickets** ticket machine; **~ de billets (de banque)** cash dispenser
2 retailing group
■ **~ automatique de billets, DAB** automatic teller machine, ATM

distribution /distʀibysjɔ̃/ *f* **1** (sector) retailing
2 (in commerce) distribution
3 (of water, electricity) supply
4 (supplying) distribution, handing out; (of jobs, duties) allocation
5 (geographically) distribution, layout
6 (of actors) casting; cast
■ **~ d'actions gratuites** allocation of bonus shares; **~ automatique** automatic dispensing; **~ du courrier** postal delivery

dithyrambique /ditiʀɑ̃bik/ *adj ‹speech, comments›* ecstatic; *‹praise›* extravagant

diurétique /djyʀetik/ *adj, m* diuretic

divagation /divagasjɔ̃/ *f* ravings; rambling

divaguer /divage/ [**v1**] *vi* **1** to rave; **la fièvre le fait ~** he's delirious with fever
2 to ramble; to talk nonsense
3 to stray

divan /divɑ̃/ *m* divan; couch

divergence /divɛʀʒɑ̃s/ *f* divergence; difference

divergent, **~e** /divɛʀʒɑ̃, ɑ̃t/ *adj* divergent

diverger /divɛʀʒe/ [**v13**] *vi* to diverge (**de** from); to differ (**de** from)

divers, **~e** /divɛʀ, ɛʀs/ *adj* **1** various; **les gens les plus ~** all sorts of people
2 miscellaneous

diversement /divɛʀsəmɑ̃/ *adv* variously, in different ways

diversification /divɛʀsifikasjɔ̃/ *f* diversification; **une entreprise en voie de ~** a company in the process of diversifying; **une ~ de la clientèle** targeting a wider clientele

diversifier /divɛʀsifje/ [**v2**] *vt* to widen the range of; to diversify

diversion /divɛʀsjɔ̃/ *f* (Mil) diversion

diversité /divɛʀsite/ *f* diversity; variety

divertir /divɛʀtiʀ/ [**v3**] **A** *vt* to entertain; to amuse
B se divertir *v refl* (+ *v être*) to amuse oneself; **pour se ~** for fun

divertissant, **~e** /divɛʀtisɑ̃, ɑ̃t/ *adj* amusing; entertaining; enjoyable

divertissement /divɛʀtismɑ̃/ *m* entertainment; recreation

dividende /dividɑ̃d/ *m* dividend

divin, **~e** /divɛ̃, in/ *adj* divine

divinité /divinite/ *f* deity; divinity

diviser /divize/ [**v1**] **A** *vt* to divide
B se diviser *v refl* (+ *v être*) **1** to become divided (**sur** over)
2 to be divided
3 to be divisible
4 to divide; to fork

divisible /divizibl/ *adj* divisible

division /divizjɔ̃/ *f* division

divisionnaire /divizjɔnɛʀ/ *adj* **commissaire ~** Chief Superintendent

divorce /divɔʀs/ *m* divorce (**d'avec** from); **prononcer le ~ entre deux époux** to grant a divorce to a couple

divorcé, **~e** /divɔʀse/ *mf* divorcee

divorcer /divɔʀse/ [**v12**] *vi* to get divorced

divulgation /divylgasjɔ̃/ *f* disclosure

divulguer /divylge/ [**v1**] *vt* to disclose

dix /dis/, *but before consonant* /di/, *before vowel or mute h* /diz/ *adj inv, pron, m inv* ten
IDIOMS **ne rien savoir faire de ses ~ doigts** to be useless; **un de perdu, ~ de retrouvés** (Proverb) there's plenty more fish in the sea

dix-huit /dizɥit/ *adj inv, pron, m inv* eighteen

dix-huitième /dizɥitjɛm/ *adj* eighteenth

dixième /dizjɛm/ *adj* tenth

dix-neuf /diznœf/ *adj inv, pron, m inv* nineteen

dix-neuvième /diznœvjɛm/ *adj* nineteenth

dix-sept /dis(s)ɛt/ *adj inv, pron, m inv* seventeen

dix-septième /dis(s)ɛtjɛm/ *adj* seventeenth

dizaine /dizɛn/ *f* **1** ten
2 une ~ about ten; **des ~s de personnes** dozens of people

do /do/ *m inv* (Mus) (note) C; (in sol-fa) doh

docile /dɔsil/ *adj ‹animal, person›* docile

dock /dɔk/ *m* **1** dock
2 warehouse

docteur /dɔktœʀ/ *m* doctor; **jouer au ~** to play doctors and nurses

doctorat /dɔktɔʀa/ *m* PhD, doctorate

doctrinaire /dɔktʀinɛʀ/ *adj ‹attitude›* doctrinaire; *‹tone›* sententious

doctrine /dɔktʀin/ *f* doctrine

document /dɔkymɑ̃/ *m* **1** document; **~ sonore** audio material; **avec ~s à l'appui** with documentary evidence
2 document, paper

documentaire /dɔkymɑ̃tɛʀ/ **A** *adj* documentary; **à titre ~** for your information
B *m* documentary (**sur** on, about)

documentaliste /dɔkymɑ̃talist/ *mf* information officer; (school) librarian

documentation /dɔkymɑ̃tasjɔ̃/ *f*
1 material (**sur** on)
2 research
3 brochures
4 centre de ~ resource centre (BrE)

documenter: **se documenter** /dɔkymɑ̃te/ [**v1**] *v refl* (+ *v être*) **se ~ sur qch** to research sth

key word

dodeliner /dɔdline/ [**v1**] *vi* **il dodelinait de la tête** his head was nodding

dodo /dodo/ *m* (baby talk) **faire ~** to sleep

dodu, **-e** /dɔdy/ *adj* plump

dogmatique /dɔgmatik/ *adj* dogmatic

dogme /dɔgm/ *m* dogma

dogue /dɔg/ *m* mastiff

doigt /dwa/ *m* finger; **petit ~** little finger (BrE), pinkie; **bout des ~s** fingertips; **du bout des ~s** (fig) reluctantly; **connaître une ville sur le bout des ~s** to know a city like the back of one's hand; **montrer du ~** to point at; (fig) to point the finger at
■ **~ de pied** toe
IDIOMS **se brûler les ~s** to get one's fingers burned; **être à deux ~s de** to be a whisker away from; **filer entre les ~s de qn** ‹*money, thief*› to slip through sb's fingers; **se faire taper sur les ~s** to get one's knuckles rapped; **lever le ~** to put one's hand up

doigté /dwate/ *m* **1** tact
2 (of pianist) fingering

doléance /dɔleɑ̃s/ *f* complaint

dollar /dɔlaʀ/ *m* dollar

DOM /dɔm/ *m inv* (*abbr* = **département d'outre-mer**) *French overseas (administrative) department*

domaine /dɔmɛn/ *m* **1** estate
2 field, domain
3 territory

domanial, **~e**, *mpl* **-iaux** /dɔmanjal, o/ *adj* state-owned

dôme /dom/ *m* dome

domestique /dɔmɛstik/ **A** *adj* **1** ‹*staff, animal*› domestic
2 ‹*market*› domestic, home
B *mf* servant

domestiquer /dɔmɛstike/ [**v1**] *vt* to domesticate ‹*animal*›

domicile /dɔmisil/ **A** *m* place of residence; (of company) registered address
B à domicile *phr* **travail à ~** working at *or* from home; **'livraisons à ~'** 'home deliveries'

domicilié, **~e** /dɔmisilje/ *adj* **1 être ~ à Arras** to live in Arras
2 j'habite à Paris, mais je suis ~e à Rennes I live in Paris, but my official address is in Rennes

dominance /dɔminɑ̃s/ *f* dominance

dominant, **~e** /dɔminɑ̃, ɑ̃t/ *adj* **1** ‹*colour, gene*› dominant; ‹*wind, tendency*› prevailing; ‹*feature, idea*› main
2 ‹*class*› ruling

dominante /dɔminɑ̃t/ *f* **1** dominant feature
2 (Univ) main subject, major

dominateur, **-trice** /dɔminatœʀ, tʀis/ *adj* domineering; overbearing; imperious

domination /dɔminasjɔ̃/ *f* domination; **être sous la ~ de** to be dominated by

dominer /dɔmine/ [**v1**] **A** *vt* **1** to dominate; to tower above; **de là, on domine toute la vallée** from there you get a view of the whole valley
2 to dominate ‹*match, sector*›
3 ‹*theme*› to dominate
4 to master ‹*subject*›; to overcome ‹*fear*›; **~ la situation** to be in control of the situation
B *vi* **1** to rule, to hold sway
2 to be in the lead
3 ‹*impression*› to prevail; ‹*taste*› to stand out
C se dominer *v refl* (+ *v être*) to control oneself

dominical, **~e**, *mpl* **-aux** /dɔminikal, o/ *adj* ‹*walk, mass*› Sunday

domino /dɔmino/ *m* domino

dommage /dɔmaʒ/ *m* **1 c'est ~** it's a shame *or* pity
2 damage
3 (Law) tort
■ **~s corporels** personal injury; **~s et intérêts** damages

dommageable /dɔmaʒabl/ *adj* harmful (**pour** to)

dommages-intérêts /dɔmaʒɛ̃teʀɛ/ *mpl* damages; **5 000 euros de ~** 5,000 euros in damages

dompter /dɔ̃te/ [**v1**] *vt* to tame ‹*wild animal*›; to bring [sb] to heel ‹*unruly person*›; to subdue ‹*insurgents*›; to overcome ‹*passion*›

dompteur, **-euse** /dɔ̃tœʀ, øz/ *mf* tamer

DOM-TOM /dɔmtɔm/ *mpl* (*abbr* = **départements et territoires d'outre-mer**) *French overseas departments and territories*

don /dɔ̃/ *m* **1** donation; **faire ~ de** to give (à to); **~ de soi** self-sacrifice
2 gift; **avoir le ~ de faire** to have a talent for doing
■ **~ du sang** blood donation

donation /dɔnasjɔ̃/ *f* **1** donation
2 (Law) gift

donc /dɔ̃k/ *conj* so, therefore; **j'étais ~ en train de lire, lorsque...** so I was reading, when...; **je disais ~ que...** as I was saying...; **entrez ~!** do come in!; **mais où est-il ~ passé?** where on earth has he gone?

donjon /dɔ̃ʒɔ̃/ *m* (of castle) keep

donne /dɔn/ *f* (in cards) deal

donné, **~e** /dɔne/ **A** *pp* ▶ **donner**
B *pp adj* **1 il n'est pas ~ à tout le monde de faire** not everyone can do
2 given; **à un moment ~** at one point; all of a sudden
3 cheap
C étant donné (que) *phr* given (that)

donnée /dɔne/ *f* **1** fact, element
2 data

donner /dɔne/ [**v1**] **A** *vt* **1** to give ‹*present, headache, advice, dinner, lesson*›; **~ l'heure à qn** to tell sb the time; **je lui donne 40 ans** I'd say he/she was 40; **~ faim à qn** to make

d

d

sb feel hungry; **elle donne sa fille à garder à mes parents** she has my parents look after her daughter; **j'ai donné ma voiture à réparer** I've taken my car in to be repaired; **les sondages le donnent en tête** the polls put him in the lead
2 to show ‹*film*›; to put on ‹*play*›; to give ‹*performance*›
3 to produce, to yield ‹*fruit, juice*›; to produce ‹*results*›
4 to show ‹*signs*›
5 (fam) to inform on ‹*accomplice*›
B *vi* **1 le poirier va bien ~ cette année** the pear tree will yield a good crop this year
2 ne plus savoir où ~ de la tête (fig) not to know which way to turn
3 ~ sur ‹*room, window*› to overlook; ‹*door*› to give onto; **~ au nord** to face north; **la cuisine donne dans le salon** the kitchen leads into the living room
4 ~ dans to tend toward(s)
5 ~ de sa personne to give of oneself
C se donner *v refl* (+ *v être*) **1 se ~ à** to devote oneself to
2 se ~ le temps de faire to give oneself time to do
3 se ~ pour but de faire to make it one's aim to do
4 se ~ de grands airs to put on airs
5 se ~ des coups to exchange blows; **se ~ le mot** to pass the word on
IDIOMS **donnant donnant: je fais la cuisine, tu fais la vaisselle** fair's fair: I cook, you do the washing-up; **avec lui, c'est donnant donnant** he never does anything for nothing

donneur, **-euse** /dɔnœʀ, øz/ *mf* (Med) donor

dont /dɔ̃/ *rel pron* **1** whose, of which; **la jeune fille ~ on nous disait qu'elle avait 20 ans** the girl who they said was 20; **Sylvaine est quelqu'un ~ on se souvient** Sylvaine is somebody (that) you remember; **la maladie ~ il souffre** the illness which he's suffering from; **la façon ~ il a été traité** the way in which he has been treated
2 il y a eu plusieurs victimes ~ mon père there were several victims, one of whom was my father; **des boîtes ~ la plupart sont vides** boxes, most of which are empty

dopage /dɔpaʒ/ *m* **1** (of horses) doping
2 illegal drug-taking

doper /dɔpe/ [**v1**] *vt* to dope

dorade /dɔʀad/ *f* (sea) bream

doré, **~e** /dɔʀe/ **A** *pp* ▸ **dorer**
B *pp adj* **1** ‹*paint*› gold; ‹*frame*› gilt; ‹*dome*› gilded; ‹*hair*› golden; ‹*skin*› tanned; ‹*bread*› golden brown; **~ à l'or fin** gilded
2 ‹*exile*› luxurious; **jeunesse ~e** gilded youth
C *m* gilt

dorénavant /dɔʀenavɑ̃/ *adv* from now on

dorer /dɔʀe/ [**v1**] **A** *vt* **1** to gild
2 (Culin) to glaze
B *vi* (Culin) to brown
C se dorer *v refl* (+ *v être*) **se ~ au soleil** to sunbathe

dorloter /dɔʀlɔte/ [**v1**] *vt* to pamper

dormeur, **-euse** /dɔʀmœʀ, øz/ *mf* sleeper; **c'est un gros ~** he sleeps a lot

dormir /dɔʀmiʀ/ [**v30**] *vi* **1** to sleep; **~ debout** (fig) to be dead on one's feet; **ça m'empêche de ~** it keeps me awake; **il n'en dort plus** he's losing sleep over it
2 ‹*money*› to lie idle
IDIOMS **ne ~ que d'un œil** to sleep with one eye open; **~ sur ses deux oreilles**, **~ tranquille** to rest easy; **~ comme un loir** to sleep like a log; **~ à poings fermés** to be fast asleep

dorsal, **~e**, *mpl* **-aux** /dɔʀsal, o/ *adj* ‹*pain*› back; ‹*fin*› dorsal

dortoir /dɔʀtwaʀ/ **A** *m* dormitory
B (-)dortoir (*combining form*) **ville-~** dormitory town

dorure /dɔʀyʀ/ *f* gilt

dos /do/ *m inv* **1** back; **avoir le ~ rond** *or* **voûté** to stoop; **mal de ~** backache; **voir qn de ~** to see sb from behind; **robe décolletée dans le ~** dress with a low back; **il n'a rien sur le ~** (fam) he's wearing hardly anything; **tourner le ~ à** to have one's back to; to turn one's back to; (fig) to turn one's back on
2 (of book) spine; (of blade) blunt edge
IDIOMS **mettre qch sur le ~ de** (fam) to blame sth on; **il a bon ~ le réveil!** (fam) it's easy to blame it on the alarm clock!

dosage /dozaʒ/ *m* **1** amount; measurement
2 mix; mixing
3 proportions

dos-d'âne /dodɑn/ *m inv* hump

dose /doz/ *f* **1** dose; **forcer la ~** (fam) to go a bit far (fam)
2 measure

doser /doze/ [**v1**] *vt* **1** to measure
2 to use [sth] in a controlled way

dossard /dosaʀ/ *m* number *(worn by an athlete)*

dossier /dosje/ *m* **1** file, dossier; **~ médical** medical records; **~ d'inscription** (Sch) registration form; **sélection sur ~** selection by written application
2 (Law) file; case
3 le ~ brûlant de la pollution the controversial problem of pollution
4 file, folder
5 (of chair) back

dot /dɔt/ *f* dowry

dotation /dɔtasjɔ̃/ *f* allocation; endowment

doter /dote/ [**v1**] *vt* **1 ~ qn de qch** to allocate sth to sb
2 ~ qn/qch de to equip sb/sth with
3 ~ qn/qch de to endow sb/sth with

douane /dwan/ *f* **1** customs
2 (on goods) duty

key word

douanier, **-ière** /dwanje, ɛʀ/ **A** *adj* customs
B *m* customs officer

double /dubl/ **A** *adj* double; **l'avantage est ~** the advantage is twofold; **valise à ~ fond** suitcase with a false bottom; **~ nationalité** dual nationality; **avoir le don de ~ vue** to have second sight; **en ~ exemplaire** in duplicate
B *adv* double
C *m* **1** double; **leur piscine fait le ~ de la nôtre** their swimming pool is twice as big as ours
2 copy; **un ~ des clés** a spare set of keys
3 (in tennis) doubles

doublé, **~e** /duble/ **A** *pp* ▶ **doubler**
B *pp adj* **1** ‹*coat*› lined
2 ‹*film*› dubbed

doublement /dubləmɑ̃/ **A** *adv* in two ways; **il est ~ coupable** he's guilty on two counts
B *m* (of quantity) doubling

doubler /duble/ [**v1**] **A** *vt* **1** to double
2 to line (**de** with)
3 to dub ‹*film*›; to stand in for ‹*actor*›
4 to overtake (BrE), to pass (AmE); **'défense de ~'** 'no overtaking' (BrE), 'no passing' (AmE)
B *vi* to double
C **se doubler** *v refl* (+ *v être*) **se ~ de qch** to be coupled with sth

doublure /dublyʀ/ *f* **1** lining
2 (for actor) double

douce ▶ **doux**

douceâtre /dusɑtʀ/ *adj* sickly sweet

doucement /dusmɑ̃/ *adv* **1** gently; **~ avec le vin!** go easy on the wine!
2 quietly
3 slowly

doucereux, **-euse** /dusʀø, øz/ *adj* ‹*person*› smooth; ‹*words*› sugary; ‹*smile*› unctuous

douceur /dusœʀ/ **A** *f* **1** softness; mildness; mellowness; smoothness; gentleness; **~ de vivre** relaxed rhythm of life; **avec ~** gently
2 sweet (BrE), candy (AmE)
B **en douceur** *phr* **1** smoothly; **atterrissage en ~** smooth landing
2 **shampooing qui lave en ~** mild shampoo

douche /duʃ/ *f* shower; **~ froide** cold shower; (fig) let-down (fam)
■ **~ écossaise** alternating hot and cold shower; (fig) bucket of cold water

doucher /duʃe/ [**v1**] **A** *vt* **1** to give [sb] a shower
2 (fam) to dampen ‹*enthusiasm*›
B **se doucher** *v refl* (+ *v être*) to take a shower

doué, **~e** /dwe/ *adj* **1** gifted, talented; **être ~ pour** to have a gift for
2 **~ de** endowed with, gifted with

douille /duj/ *f* **1** cartridge (case)
2 (light) socket

douillet, **-ette** /dujɛ, ɛt/ *adj* **1** oversensitive to pain
2 cosy (BrE), cozy (AmE)

douleur /dulœʀ/ *f* **1** pain; **médicament contre la ~** painkiller
2 grief

douloureuse ▶ **douloureux**

douloureusement /duluʀøzmɑ̃/ *adv*
1 grievously; terribly
2 painfully

douloureux, **-euse** /duluʀø, øz/ *adj*
1 painful
2 ‹*event*› distressing; ‹*question*› painful

doute /dut/ **A** *m* doubt; **laisser qn dans le ~** to leave sb in a state of uncertainty; **mettre qch en ~** to call sth into question; **dans le ~, j'ai préféré ne rien dire** not being sure I didn't say anything; **il fait peu de ~ que** there's little doubt that; **nul ~ que** there's no doubt that
B **sans doute** *phr* probably; **sans aucun ~** without any doubt

douter /dute/ [**v1**] **A** *vt* **1** **~ que** to doubt that *or* whether
2 **~ de qch** to have doubts about sth; **elle l'affirme mais j'en doute** she says it's true but I have my doubts; **elle ne doute de rien!** (fam) (ironic) she's so sure of herself!
B *vi* to doubt
C **se douter** *v refl* (+ *v être*) **se ~ de** to suspect; **je m'en doutais!** I thought so!; **je me doute (bien) qu'il devait être furieux** I can (well) imagine that he was furious; **nous étions loin de nous ~ que** we didn't have the least idea that

douteux, **-euse** /dutø, øz/ *adj* **1** uncertain
2 ambiguous
3 dubious
4 ‹*deal, character*› shady

douve /duv/ *f* moat

Douvres /duvʀ/ *pr n* Dover

doux, **douce** /du, dus/ *adj* ‹*light, voice, substance*› soft; ‹*cider*› sweet; ‹*cheese, shampoo, weather*› mild; ‹*person, slope*› gentle
IDIOMS **filer ~** (fam) to keep a low profile; **se la couler douce** (fam) to take it easy; **en douce** (fam) on the sly

douzaine /duzɛn/ *f* **1** dozen; **à la ~** by the dozen
2 **une ~** about twelve, a dozen or so

douze /duz/ *adj inv, pron, m inv* twelve

douzième /duzjɛm/ *adj* twelfth

doyen, **-enne** /dwajɛ̃, ɛn/ *mf* **1** oldest person
2 the (most) senior member
3 dean

Dr (*written abbr* = **docteur**) Dr

draconien, **-ienne** /dʀakɔnjɛ̃, ɛn/ *adj* draconian; very strict

dragée /dʀaʒe/ *f* **1** sugared almond
2 sugar-coated pill

dragon /dʀagɔ̃/ *m* **1** dragon
2 (Mil) dragoon

draguer /dʀage/ [**v1**] *vt* **1** (fam) to come on to (fam)
2 to dredge, to drag ‹*river, canal*›

d

dragueur, **-euse** /dʀagœʀ, øz/ *mf* (fam) **c'est un drôle de ~** (fam) he's a terrible flirt

drain /dʀɛ̃/ *m* drain

drainage /dʀɛnaʒ/ *m* **1** drainage
2 (Med) draining (off)

drainer /dʀɛne/ [**v1**] *vt* to drain

dramatique /dʀamatik/ *adj* **1** tragic; **ce n'est pas ~** it's not the end of the world
2 dramatic; **art ~** drama; **auteur ~** playwright

dramatiquement /dʀamatikmɑ̃/ *adv* tragically

dramatiser /dʀamatize/ [**v1**] *vt* to dramatize

dramaturge /dʀamatyʀʒ/ *mf* playwright

drame /dʀam/ *m* **1** tragedy; **tourner au ~** to take a tragic turn
2 drama; play; **~ lyrique** opera

drap /dʀa/ *m* **1** sheet
2 woollen (BrE) cloth
■ **~ de plage** beach towel
IDIOM **se mettre dans de beaux ~s** to land oneself in a fine mess

drapeau, *pl* **~x** /dʀapo/ *m* flag; **être sous les ~x** to be doing military service

drap-housse, *pl* **draps-housses** /dʀaus/ *m* fitted sheet

dressage /dʀɛsaʒ/ *m* **1** training; (of horse) breaking in
2 dressage

dresser /dʀese/ [**v1**] **A** *vt* **1** to train ‹*animal*›; to break in ‹*horse*›; to teach [sb] how to behave ‹*person*›
2 to put up ‹*scaffolding*›
3 to prick up ‹*ears*›
4 to lay out ‹*buffet*›
5 to draw up ‹*list*›; **~ un procès-verbal à qn** to give sb a ticket
6 ~ qn contre to set sb against
B se dresser *v refl* (+ *v être*) **1** to stand up
2 se ~ contre to rebel against
3 ‹*statue, obstacle*› to stand; to tower up

dresseur, **-euse** /dʀɛsœʀ, øz/ *mf* trainer

dribbler /dʀible/ [**v1**] *vi* to dribble

drogue /dʀɔg/ *f* drug; **la ~** drugs; **c'est devenu une ~** it has become an addiction

drogué, **~e** /dʀɔge/ *mf* drug addict

droguer /dʀɔge/ [**v1**] **A** *vt* **1** ‹*doctor*› to dope
2 to dope ‹*animal, sportsman*›; to drug ‹*victim*›; to doctor ‹*drink*›
B se droguer *v refl* (+ *v être*) **1** to dope oneself (**à**, **de** with)
2 to take drugs

droguerie /dʀɔgʀi/ *f* hardware shop (BrE) *or* store (AmE)

droguiste /dʀɔgist/ *mf* owner of a hardware shop

droit, **~e** /dʀwa, at/ **A** *adj* **1** ‹*line, road, nose*› straight; ‹*writing*› upright; **se tenir ~** to stand up straight; to sit up straight; **s'écarter du ~ chemin** to stray from the straight and narrow
2 right; **du côté ~** on the right-hand side
3 ‹*person*› straight(forward)
4 ‹*skirt*› straight
5 ‹*angle*› right
B *adv* straight; **continuez tout ~** carry straight on; **marcher ~** to toe the line
C *m* **1** right; **être dans son (bon) ~** to be within one's rights; **cela leur revient de ~** it's theirs by right; **avoir ~ à** to be entitled to; **il a eu ~ à une amende** (ironic) he got a fine; **avoir le ~ de faire** to be allowed to do; to have the right to do; **avoir le ~ de vie ou de mort sur qn** to have power of life and death over sb; **il s'imagine qu'il a tous les ~s** he thinks he can do whatever he likes; **être en ~ de** to be entitled to
2 le ~ law; **faire son ~** to study law
3 fee
4 (in boxing) right
■ **(prisonnier de) ~ commun** non-political prisoner; **~ d'entrée** entrance fee; **~ de passage** right of way (BrE), easement (AmE); **un ~ de regard sur** a say in; **~s d'auteur** royalties; **~s de douane** customs duties; **les ~s de l'homme** human rights; **~s de succession** inheritance tax

droite /dʀwat/ *f* **1** right; **la porte de ~** the door on the right; **à ta ~** on your right; **demander à ~ et à gauche** to ask everywhere; to ask everybody
2 voter à ~ to vote for the right; **de ~** right-wing
3 straight line

droite-droite /dʀwatdʀwat/ *f* extreme right-wing

droitier, **-ière** /dʀwatje, ɛʀ/ *mf* right-hander

droitisation /dʀwatizasjɔ̃/ *f* (Pol) shift to the right; **la ~ de l'électorat** the electorate's shift to the right

droiture /dʀwatyʀ/ *f* honesty, uprightness

drôle /dʀol/ *adj* **1** funny, odd; **faire (tout) ~ à qn** to give sb a funny feeling; **faire une ~ de tête** to make a bit of a face
2 funny, amusing
3 (fam) **un ~ de courage** a lot of courage
IDIOMS **j'en ai entendu de ~s** I heard some funny things; **en faire voir de ~s à qn** to lead sb a merry dance

drôlement /dʀolmɑ̃/ *adv* **1** (fam) really
2 oddly

drôlerie /dʀolʀi/ *f* **avec ~** amusingly

dromadaire /dʀɔmadɛʀ/ *m* dromedary

dru, **~e** /dʀy/ **A** *adj* ‹*hair*› thick
B *adv* **1** ‹*grow*› thickly
2 la pluie tombait ~ it was raining heavily

druide /dʀɥid/ *m* Druid

DS /deɛs/ *f*: *Citroën car of the 1950s*

DST /deɛste/ *f* (*abbr* = **Direction de la surveillance du territoire**) *French counter-intelligence agency*

du /dy/ ▶ **de**

dû, **due**, *mpl* **dus** /dy/ **A** *pp* ▶ **devoir**[1]

key word

B *pp adj* **1** owed, owing, due (à to); **en bonne et due forme** in due form
2 ~ **à** due to
C *m* **réclamer son** ~ to claim one's due

dualité /dɥalite/ *f* duality

dubitatif, -ive /dybitatif, iv/ *adj* sceptical (BrE), skeptical (AmE)

duc /dyk/ *m* duke

duchesse /dyʃɛs/ *f* duchess

duel /dɥɛl/ *m* duel (à with); (fig) battle

dulcinée /dylsine/ *f* lady-love

dune /dyn/ *f* dune

duo /dyo, dɥo/ *m* **1** duet; **en** ~ as a duo
2 double act (BrE), duo (AmE)
3 (fam) pair

dupe /dyp/ **A** *adj* **être** ~ to be taken in *or* fooled
B *f* dupe; **un marché de** ~**s** a fool's bargain

duper /dype/ [**v1**] *vt* to fool; **facile à** ~ gullible

duperie /dypʀi/ *f* trickery

duplex /dyplɛks/ *m inv* maisonette (BrE), duplex apartment (AmE)

duplicata /dyplikata/ *m inv* duplicate

duquel ▶ **lequel**

dur, ~e /dyʀ/ **A** *adj* **1** ‹*ground, toothbrush, bread*› hard; ‹*meat*› tough; ‹*brush, cardboard*› stiff; ‹*plastic*› rigid
2 ‹*zip, handle, pedal*› stiff; ‹*steering*› heavy
3 ‹*sound, light, colour*› harsh
4 ‹*face, expression*› severe
5 ‹*parents, boss*› hard; harsh; ‹*policy*› hardline
6 ‹*living conditions*› harsh
7 ‹*job, sport*› hard; tough; ‹*climate, necessity*› harsh
8 ‹*exam*› hard, difficult
9 ‹*water*› hard
B *mf* **1** tough nut (fam); **jouer les** ~**s** to act tough
2 hardliner
C *adv* ‹*work, hit*› hard
D *m* **construction en** ~ permanent structure
E **à la dure** *phr* **élevé à la** ~**e** brought up the hard way

IDIOMS ~ **d'oreille** hard of hearing; **avoir la tête** ~**e** to be stubborn; to be dense; **avoir la vie** ~**e** ‹*habit*› to die hard; **mener la vie** ~**e à qn** to give sb a hard time

durable /dyʀabl/ *adj* ‹*impression*› lasting; ‹*interest*› enduring; ‹*material*› durable

durablement /dyʀabləmɑ̃/ *adv* on a permanent basis

durant /dyʀɑ̃/ *prep* **1** for; **des heures** ~ for hours and hours
2 during

durcir /dyʀsiʀ/ [**v3**] **A** *vt* **1** to harden ‹*ground, features, position*›
2 to step up ‹*strike action*›; ~ **sa politique en matière de** to take a harder line on
B *vi* ‹*clay, artery*› to harden; ‹*cement, glue*› to set; ‹*bread*› to go hard
C **se durcir** *v refl* (+ *v être*) **1** to harden
2 to become harsher; to intensify

durcissement /dyʀsismɑ̃/ *m* **1** hardening
2 intensification

durée /dyʀe/ *f* **1** (of reign, studies) length; (of contract) term; (of cassette) playing time; **séjour d'une** ~ **de trois mois** three-month stay; **contrat à** ~ **déterminée** fixed-term contract; **de courte** ~ ‹*peace*› short-lived; ‹*absence*› brief; ‹*loan*› short-term
2 ~ **(de vie)** life; **pile longue** ~ long-life battery

durement /dyʀmɑ̃/ *adv* **1** badly
2 harshly
3 ‹*look*› severely
4 ‹*hit*› hard

durer /dyʀe/ [**v1**] *vi* **1** to last
2 to go on; **ça ne peut plus** ~ it can't go on any longer; **faire** ~ to prolong ‹*meeting*›; **faire** ~ **le plaisir** (ironic) to prolong the agony
3 ‹*festival*› to run

dures /dyʀ/ *fpl* **en faire voir de** ~ **à ses parents** to give one's parents a hard time

dureté /dyʀte/ *f* **1** (of material, face) hardness; (of meat) toughness; (of brush) stiffness
2 (of expression, tone, climate) harshness; (of look) severity; **avec** ~ ‹*look*› severely; ‹*punish*› harshly

durillon /dyʀijɔ̃/ *m* callus

durite /dyʀit/ *f* radiator hose

DUT /deyte/ *m* (*abbr* = **diplôme universitaire de technologie**) *two-year diploma from a university institute of technology*

duvet /dyvɛ/ *m* **1** (of bird) down
2 sleeping bag

duveteux, -euse /dyvtø, øz/ *adj* downy

DVD /devede/ *m* DVD

dynamique /dinamik/ **A** *adj* dynamic, lively
B *f* **1** dynamics
2 process

dynamiser /dinamize/ [**v1**] *vt* to make [sb/sth] more dynamic; to revitalize

dynamisme /dinamism/ *m* dynamism; **être plein de** ~ to be very dynamic

dynamite /dinamit/ *f* dynamite

dynamiter /dinamite/ [**v1**] *vt* to dynamite; (fig) to destroy

dynastie /dinasti/ *f* dynasty

dysenterie /disɑ̃tʀi/ *f* dysentery

dysfonctionnement /disfɔ̃ksjɔnmɑ̃/ *m* **1** (Med) dysfunction
2 malfunctioning

dyslexie /dislɛksi/ *f* dyslexia

Ee

e, **E** /ə/ *m inv* e, E; **e dans l'o** o and e joined together

⚷ **eau**, *pl* **~x** /o/ **A** *f* **1** water; **l'~ de source** spring water; **prendre l'~** ‹*shoe*› to let in water; **être en ~** to be dripping with sweat; **mettre à l'~** to launch ‹*ship*›; **se jeter à l'~** to throw oneself into the water; (fig) to take the plunge; **tomber à l'~** (fig) to fall through; **nettoyer le sol à grande ~** to sluice the floor down
2 rain
B eaux *fpl* **1** water; waters
2 (Med) waters
■ **~ bénite** holy water; **~ de chaux** lime water; **~ douce** fresh water; **~ de Javel** ≈ (chloride) bleach; **~ de mer** seawater; **~ oxygénée** hydrogen peroxide; **~ plate** plain water; still mineral water; **~ de rose: à l'~ de rose** ‹*novel*› sentimental; **~x et forêts** forestry commission; **~x usées** waste water
IDIOMS **mettre l'~ à la bouche de qn** to make sb's mouth water; **ou dans ces ~x-là** (fam) or thereabouts; **vivre d'amour et d'~ fraîche** to live on love alone

EAU *written abbr* ▶ **Émirats**

eau-de-vie, *pl* **eaux-de-vie** /odvi/ *f* brandy, eau de vie; **à l'~** in brandy

ébahir /ebaiʀ/ [**v3**] **A** *vt* to dumbfound
B s'ébahir *v refl* (+ *v être*) to be dumbfounded

ébattre: **s'ébattre** /ebatʀ/ [**v61**] *v refl* (+ *v être*) to frolic (about); to frisk about; to splash about

ébauche /eboʃ/ *f* **1** (for sculpture) rough shape; (for picture) preliminary sketch; (of novel) preliminary draft; **être encore à l'état d'~** to be still at an early stage
2 l'~ d'un sourire a hint of a smile

ébaucher /eboʃe/ [**v1**] **A** *vt* to sketch out ‹*picture, solution*›; to draft ‹*novel, plan*›; to rough-hew ‹*statue*›; to begin ‹*conversation*›
B s'ébaucher *v refl* (+ *v être*) ‹*solution, novel*› to begin to take shape; ‹*friendship*› to begin to develop; ‹*talks*› to start

ébène /ebɛn/ *f* ebony

ébéniste /ebenist/ *mf* cabinetmaker

éberluer /ebɛʀlɥe/ [**v1**] *vt* to dumbfound

éblouir /ebluiʀ/ [**v3**] *vt* to dazzle

éblouissement /ebluismɑ̃/ *m* **1** dazzle
2 dizzy spell

éborgner /ebɔʀɲe/ [**v1**] *vt* **~ qn** to blind sb in one eye; (hum) to poke sb's eye out

éboueur /ebuœʀ/ *m* dustman (BrE), garbage man (AmE)

ébouillanter /ebujɑ̃te/ [**v1**] *vt* **1** to scald
2 to blanch ‹*vegetables*›

éboulement /ebulmɑ̃/ *m* (of wall, cliff) collapse; **~ (de rochers)** rockfall

éboulis /ebuli/ *m inv* mass of fallen rocks; heap of fallen earth

ébouriffer /ebuʀife/ [**v1**] *vt* to tousle; to ruffle

ébranler /ebʀɑ̃le/ [**v1**] *vt* **1** to rattle ‹*windowpane*›; to shake ‹*house*›; to weaken ‹*building*›
2 to shake ‹*person, confidence*›

ébrécher /ebʀeʃe/ [**v14**] *vt* to chip ‹*cup*›

ébriété /ebʀijete/ *f* intoxication

ébrouer: **s'ébrouer** /ebʀue/ [**v1**] *v refl* (+ *v être*) **1** ‹*horse*› to snort
2 ‹*person, dog*› to shake oneself/itself; ‹*bird*› to flap its wings

ébruiter /ebʀɥite/ [**v1**] **A** *vt* to divulge
B s'ébruiter *v refl* (+ *v être*) ‹*news*› to get out

ébullition /ebylisjɔ̃/ *f* (Culin) boiling
IDIOM **être en ~** ‹*crowd*› to be in a fever of excitement; ‹*country, brain*› to be in a ferment

écaille /ekaj/ *f* **1** (on fish, reptile) scale; (on oyster) shell
2 tortoiseshell; **lunettes en ~** horn-rimmed glasses
3 flake

écailler /ekaje/ [**v1**] **A** *vt* **1** (Culin) to scale ‹*fish*›; to open ‹*oyster*›
2 ~ qch to chip [sth] off
B s'écailler *v refl* (+ *v être*) to flake away

écarlate /ekaʀlat/ *adj* scarlet

écart /ekaʀ/ **A** *m* **1** (between objects) distance, gap; (between dates) interval; (between ideas) gap
2 (between versions, in prices) difference; **~ des salaires** pay differential
3 faire un ~ ‹*horse*› to shy; ‹*car*› to swerve
4 lapse; **~s de langage** bad language
B à l'écart *phr* **être à l'~** to be isolated; **se tenir à l'~** to stand apart; to keep oneself to oneself; not to join in; **mettre qn à l'~** to push sb aside; to ostracize sb; **entraîner qn à l'~** to take sb aside
C à l'écart de *phr* away from; **tenir qn à l'~ de** to keep sb away from ‹*place*›; to keep sb out of ‹*activity, talks*›

écarté, **~e** /ekaʀte/ **A** *pp* ▶ **écarter**
B *pp adj* **1** ‹*fingers*› spread; ‹*knees, legs*›

⚷ key word

apart; ‹*teeth*› widely spaced
2 ‹*place*› isolated

écarteler /ekaʀtəle/ [**v17**] *vt* (kill) to quarter [sb]

écartement /ekaʀtəmɑ̃/ *m* distance, space

écarter /ekaʀte/ [**v1**] **A** *vt* **1** to move [sth] further apart ‹*objects*›; to open ‹*curtains*›; to spread ‹*fingers, legs*›
2 to move [sth] aside ‹*chair*›; to remove ‹*obstacle*›; to push [sb] aside; to move [sb] on
3 to dispel ‹*suspicion*›; to eliminate ‹*risk, rival*›
4 to reject ‹*idea*›; to rule out ‹*possibility*›
B s'écarter *v refl* (+ *v être*) **1** ‹*crowd, clouds*› to part; ‹*shutters*› to open
2 to move away; **s'~ de** to move away from ‹*direction, standard*›; to stray from ‹*path, subject*›

ecchymose /ekimoz/ *f* bruise

ecclésiastique /eklezjastik/ *m* cleric

écervelé, **~e** /esɛʀvəle/ *mf* feather-brain

échafaud /eʃafo/ *m* **1** scaffold
2 guillotine

échafaudage /eʃafodaʒ/ *m* scaffolding

échafauder /eʃafode/ [**v1**] *vt* to put [sth] together ‹*plan*›; to develop ‹*theory*›

échalas /eʃala/ *m inv* **1** cane, stake
2 (fam) beanpole (fam)

échalote /eʃalɔt/ *f* shallot

échancré, **~e** /eʃɑ̃kʀe/ *adj* **1** ‹*dress*› low-cut; ‹*briefs*› high-cut; **trop ~** ‹*sleeve*› cut too wide
2 ‹*blouse*› open-necked
3 ‹*coast*› indented

échange /eʃɑ̃ʒ/ **A** *m* **1** exchange; **elles ont fait l'~ de leurs manteaux** they've swapped coats
2 trade; **~s commerciaux** trade
3 (cultural, linguistic) exchange
4 (Sport) rally
B en échange *phr* in exchange, in return
C en échange de *phr* in exchange for, in return for
■ **~ de bons procédés** quid pro quo

échanger /eʃɑ̃ʒe/ [**v13**] *vt* **1** to exchange; **~ des insultes** to trade insults
2 (Sport) **~ des balles** to rally

échangeur /eʃɑ̃ʒœʀ/ *m* interchange (BrE), grade separation (AmE)

échantillon /eʃɑ̃tijɔ̃/ *m* sample

échappatoire /eʃapatwaʀ/ *f* way out (**à** of)

échappement /eʃapmɑ̃/ *m* (Aut) **(tuyau d')~** exhaust (pipe)

échapper /eʃape/ [**v1**] **A échapper à** *v+prep* **1 ~ à** to get away from; (cleverly) to elude
2 ~ à to escape ‹*death, failure*›; (to manage) to avoid ‹*accident*›
3 ~ à to escape from ‹*social background*›; **je sens qu'il m'échappe** ‹*partner*› I feel he is drifting away from me; ‹*child*› I feel he's growing away from me
4 ~ à qn *or* **des mains de qn** to slip out of sb's hands
5 un soupir m'a échappé I let out a sigh
6 le titre m'échappe the title escapes me
7 ~ à to defy ‹*logic*›; **~ à la règle** to be an exception to the rule
B s'échapper *v refl* (+ *v être*) **1** to run away; to fly away; to escape; to get away
2 ‹*gas, smoke*› to escape
3 to get away; **s'~ pour quelques jours** to get away for a few days
IDIOM **l'~ belle** to have a narrow escape

écharde /eʃaʀd/ *f* splinter

écharpe /eʃaʀp/ *f* **1** scarf
2 sash

échasse /eʃɑs/ *f* stilt

échauder /eʃode/ [**v1**] *vt* to put [sb] off
IDIOM **chat échaudé craint l'eau froide** (Proverb) once bitten, twice shy

échauffement /eʃofmɑ̃/ *m* (Sport) warm-up

échauffer /eʃofe/ [**v1**] *vt* **1** (Sport) to warm up
2 to stir ‹*imagination*›; to stir up ‹*person, debate*›
3 to start [sth] fermenting
IDIOM **~ les oreilles de qn** to vex sb

échéance /eʃeɑ̃s/ *f* **1** (of debt) due date; (of share, policy) maturity date; (of loan) redemption date; **arriver à ~** ‹*payment*› to fall due; ‹*investment, policy*› to mature
2 expiry date
3 à longue/brève ~ ‹*forecast*› long-/short-term; ‹*strengthen, change*› in the long/short term
4 payment; repayment
5 date; deadline

échéancier /eʃeɑ̃sje/ *m* schedule of due dates; schedule of repayments

échéant: **le cas échéant** /ləkazeʃeɑ̃/ *phr* if need be, should the case arise

échec /eʃɛk/ **A** *m* **1** failure; setback; **faire ~ à qn** to thwart sb
2 (gen), (Mil) defeat
3 faire ~ au roi to put the king in check
B échecs *mpl* **les ~s** chess; chess set

échelle /eʃɛl/ *f* **1** ladder; **~ coulissante** extending ladder (BrE), extension ladder (AmE); **faire la courte ~ à qn** to give sb a leg up
2 (of map, model) scale; **plan à l'~** scale plan; **à l'~ mondiale** on a worldwide scale; **~ des salaires** pay scale
3 (fam) (in stocking) ladder

échelon /eʃlɔ̃/ *m* **1** (of ladder) rung
2 grade; **sauter les ~s** to get accelerated promotion
3 level

échelonner /eʃlɔne/ [**v1**] **A** *vt* **1** to space [sth] out ‹*objects*›
2 to spread ‹*payments, work*›; to stagger ‹*holidays*›
3 to grade ‹*exercises*›
B s'échelonner *v refl* (+ *v être*) **1** to be positioned at intervals

2 ‹*payments*› to be spread; ‹*departures*› to be staggered

écheveau, *pl* **~x** /eʃvo/ *m* hank, skein

échevelé, **~e** /eʃəvle/ *adj* **1** tousled
2 ‹*rhythm*› frenzied; ‹*romanticism*› unbridled

échine /eʃin/ *f* **1** (Anat) spine
2 (Culin) ≈ spare rib
IDIOM **courber l'~ devant** to submit to

échiquier /eʃikje/ *m* **1** chessboard
2 chequered (BrE) *or* checkered (AmE) pattern

Échiquier /eʃikje/ *pr m* **l'~** the Exchequer, the Treasury

écho /eko/ *m* **1** echo; **faire ~ à qch, se faire l'~ de qch** to echo sth
2 response; **nous n'avons eu aucun ~ des pourparlers** we have heard nothing about the talks

échographie /ekɔgʀafi/ *f* (Med) scan

échoir /eʃwaʀ/ [**v51**] *vi* (+ *v être*) ‹*rent*› to fall due; ‹*draft*› to be payable

échoppe /eʃɔp/ *f* stall

échouer /eʃwe/ [**v1**] **A** *vt* to beach ‹*boat*›
B **échouer à** *v+prep* to fail ‹*exam, test*›
C *vi* **1** ‹*person, attempt*› to fail
2 to end up (**dans** in)
D **s'échouer** *v refl* (+ *v être*) ‹*boat*› to run aground; ‹*whale*› to be beached

échu, **~e** /eʃy/ **A** *pp* ▶ **échoir**
B *adj* expired; **payer à terme ~** to pay in arrears

e-cigarette /isigaʀɛt/ *f* ▶ **cigarette électronique**

éclabousser /eklabuse/ [**v1**] *vt* **1** to splash
2 **il a été éclaboussé par ces rumeurs** the rumours (BrE) have damaged his reputation

éclair /eklɛʀ/ **A** *adj inv* **rencontre ~** brief meeting; **attaque ~** lightning strike; **guerre ~** blitzkrieg
B *m* **1** flash of lightning; **passer comme un ~** to flash past
2 (of explosion, diamonds) flash; (of eyes) glint
3 (of lucidity, triumph) moment; **il a eu un ~ de génie** he had a brainwave (BrE) *or* brainstorm (AmE)
4 (Culin) eclair

éclairage /eklɛʀaʒ/ *m* lighting; light; **~ au gaz** gaslight

éclairagiste /eklɛʀaʒist/ *m* (in theatre, films) electrician

éclairant, **~e** /eklɛʀɑ̃, ɑ̃t/ *adj* flare

éclaircie /eklɛʀsi/ *f* sunny spell

éclaircir /eklɛʀsiʀ/ [**v3**] **A** *vt* **1** to lighten ‹*colour*›; to lighten the colour (BrE) of ‹*paint, hair*›
2 to shed light on [sth]
B **s'éclaircir** *v refl* (+ *v être*) **1** ‹*weather*› to clear; **l'horizon s'éclaircit** (fig) the outlook is getting brighter
2 ‹*colour*› to fade; ‹*hair*› to get lighter
3 ‹*situation, mystery*› to become clearer
4 ‹*crowd, forest*› to thin out
5 **s'~ les cheveux** to lighten one's hair; **s'~ la voix** *or* **la gorge** to clear one's throat

éclaircissement /eklɛʀsismɑ̃/ *m*
1 explanation
2 clarification

éclairé, **~e** /ekleʀe/ *adj* ‹*person, advice*› enlightened; ‹*art lover*› well-informed

🔑 **éclairer** /ekleʀe/ [**v1**] **A** *vt* **1** to light ‹*street, room*›; ‹*sun*› to light up ‹*place, object*›
2 to give [sb] some light
3 ‹*remark*› to throw light on ‹*text, situation*›
4 to enlighten [sb]
B *vi* ‹*lamp, candle*› to give out light
C **s'éclairer** *v refl* (+ *v être*) **1** ‹*screen, face*› to light up
2 **s'~ à l'électricité** to have electric lighting

éclaireur /eklɛʀœʀ/ *m* **1** scout (BrE), Boy Scout (AmE)
2 (Mil) scout

éclaireuse /eklɛʀøz/ *f* guide (BrE), Girl Guide (AmE)

🔑 **éclat** /ekla/ *m* **1** splinter; **un ~ d'obus** a piece of shrapnel; **voler en ~s** to shatter
2 (of light, star) brightness; (of spotlight) glare; (of snow) sparkle
3 (of colour, material) brilliance; (of hair, plumage) shine; (of metal) lustre (BrE)
4 (of face, smile) radiance; (of eyes) sparkle; **sans ~** ‹*eyes*› dull; ‹*beauty*› lifeless
5 splendour (BrE); **manquer d'~** ‹*ceremony*› to lack sparkle
6 scene, fuss; **faire un ~** to make a scene
■ **~ de colère** fit of anger; **~ de rire** roar of laughter; **des ~s de voix** raised voices
IDIOM **rire aux ~s** to roar with laughter

éclatant, **~e** /eklatɑ̃, ɑ̃t/ *adj* **1** ‹*light*› dazzling; ‹*sun*› blazing
2 ‹*colour, plumage*› bright; **d'une blancheur ~e** sparkling white
3 ‹*beauty, smile*› radiant; ‹*victory*› brilliant
4 ‹*proof*› striking
5 ‹*laughter*› ringing

éclaté, **~e** /eklate/ *adj* (gen) fragmented; ‹*family*› divided

éclatement /eklatmɑ̃/ *m* **1** bursting
2 explosion
3 break-up (**en** into)

🔑 **éclater** /eklate/ [**v1**] *vi* **1** ‹*tyre, bubble*› to burst; ‹*shell, firework*› to explode; ‹*bottle*› to shatter; **faire ~** to burst ‹*bubble*›; to detonate ‹*bomb*›
2 ‹*pipe, boil*› to burst
3 ‹*laughter, firing*› to break out; ‹*shot*› to ring out
4 ‹*scandal, news*› to break; ‹*truth*› to come out
5 ‹*war*› to break out; ‹*storm*› to break
6 **laisser ~ sa joie** to be wild with joy
7 ‹*coalition*› to break up (**en** into); ‹*party*› to split

---

🔑 key word

8 to lose one's temper; **~ de rire** to burst out laughing

éclectique /eklɛktik/ *adj* eclectic

éclipse /eklips/ *f* eclipse

éclipser /eklipse/ [**v1**] **A** *vt* **1** to eclipse
2 to obscure
3 to outshine
B s'éclipser *v refl* (+ *v être*) (fam) to slip away

éclopé, ~e /eklɔpe/ *adj* injured, lame

éclore /eklɔʀ/ [**v79**] *vi* **1** ‹*chick, egg*› to hatch; ‹*flower*› to bloom; **faire ~ un œuf** to incubate an egg
2 ‹*idea*› to dawn; ‹*talent*› to bloom

écluse /eklyz/ *f* lock

écœurant, ~e /ekœʀɑ̃, ɑ̃t/ *adj* **1** ‹*food, smell*› sickly
2 nauseating
3 (hum) sickening

écœurement /ekœʀmɑ̃/ *m* nausea

écœurer /ekœʀe/ [**v1**] *vt* **1** to make [sb] feel sick
2 (fig) to sicken

éco-guerrier, -ière /ekogɛʀje, ɛʀ/ *mf* eco-warrior

école /ekɔl/ *f* **1** school
2 education system
3 (grande) ~ *higher education institution with competitive entrance examination*; **une ~ de commerce** a business school
4 training (**de** in); **être à bonne ~** to be in good hands
5 (of art) school; **faire ~** to gain a following
■ **~ élémentaire** primary school; **~ d'infirmières** nursing college; **~ maternelle** nursery school; **~ normale** primary teacher training college; **~ primaire** primary school; **École nationale d'administration, ENA** *Grande École for top civil servants*; **École normale supérieure, ENS** *Grande École from which the educational élite is recruited*

écolier, -ière /ekɔlje, ɛʀ/ *mf* schoolboy/schoolgirl

écologie /ekɔlɔʒi/ *f* ecology

écologique /ekɔlɔʒik/ *adj* ecological; ‹*speech*› on the environment; ‹*interest*› environmental; ‹*product*› environmentally friendly

écologiste /ekɔlɔʒist/ **A** *adj* **1** ‹*candidate*› Green
2 ‹*measure*› ecological
B *mf* **1** environmentalist
2 Green (candidate)
3 ecologist

écomusée /ekomyze/ *m* ≈ open air museum

éconduire /ekɔ̃dɥiʀ/ [**v69**] *vt* to turn [sb] away

économat /ekɔnɔma/ *m* bursar's office

économe /ekɔnɔm/ **A** *adj* thrifty
B *m* (Culin) potato peeler

économie /ekɔnɔmi/ **A** *f* **1** (of country) economy
2 (discipline) economics
3 (amount saved) saving; **faire l'~ de** to save the cost of ‹*trip*›
4 economy, thrift; **par ~** in order to save money; **s'exprimer avec une grande ~ de paroles** to express oneself succinctly
B économies *fpl* savings; **faire des ~s** to save up; to save money
■ **~ d'entreprise** managerial economics; **~ de marché** free market (economy)
IDIOM **il n'y a pas de petites ~s** every little helps

économique /ekɔnɔmik/ *adj* **1** ‹*policy, crisis*› economic
2 economical

économiser /ekɔnɔmize/ [**v1**] *vt* **1** to save (up) ‹*money*›; **~ ses forces** to pace oneself
2 to save ‹*petrol, water, energy*›
3 to economize

économiste /ekɔnɔmist/ *mf* economist

écoper /ekɔpe/ [**v1**] *vt* to bail out

écoproduit /ekopʀɔdɥi/ *m* eco-product

écorce /ekɔʀs/ *f* (of tree) bark; (of fruit) peel; (of chestnut) skin
■ **~ terrestre** earth's crust

écorché, ~e /ekɔʀʃe/ *adj* **~ (vif)** hypersensitive

écorcher /ekɔʀʃe/ [**v1**] *vt* **1** to skin ‹*animal*›; to flay ‹*person*›
2 to graze ‹*face, leg*›
3 to mispronounce ‹*word*›

écorchure /ekɔʀʃyʀ/ *f* graze

écossais, ~e /ekɔsɛ, ɛz/ **A** *adj* Scottish; ‹*whisky*› Scotch; ‹*language*› Scots; ‹*skirt*› tartan
B *m* **1** (dialect) Scots
2 (Scottish) Gaelic
3 tartan (cloth)

Écossais, ~e /ekɔsɛ, ɛz/ *mf* Scotsman/Scotswoman, Scot

Écosse /ekɔs/ *pr f* Scotland

écosser /ekɔse/ [**v1**] *vt* to shell

écot /eko/ *m* share

écotouriste /ekotuʀist/ *mf* ecotourist

écoulement /ekulmɑ̃/ *m* **1** (of water, traffic) flow; (of time) passing
2 (Med) discharge
3 (of banknotes, drugs) circulation

écouler /ekule/ [**v1**] **A** *vt* **1** to sell ‹*product*›; **les stocks sont écoulés** stocks are exhausted
2 to fence ‹*stolen goods*›; to pass ‹*banknote*›
B s'écouler *v refl* (+ *v être*) **1** ‹*time, life*› to pass
2 ‹*river*› to flow
3 ‹*oil, water*› to escape
4 ‹*water*› to drain away
5 ‹*product*› to move

écourter /ekuʀte/ [**v1**] *vt* to cut short ‹*stay*›

écoute /ekut/ *f* **1 être à l'~ de** to be listening to ‹*programme*›; to be (always) ready to listen to ‹*problems*›

2 audience; **heure de grande ~** peak listening time; peak viewing time
3 un centre d'~(s) monitoring centre (BrE); **je suis sur ~(s)** my phone is being tapped

⚷ **écouter** /ekute/ [**v1**] **A** *vt* **1** to listen to [sb/sth]; **~ qn chanter** to listen to sb singing; **~ aux portes** to eavesdrop
2 ~ son cœur to follow one's own inclination
B s'écouter *v refl* (+ *v être*) **1 s'~ parler** to like the sound of one's own voice
2 to cosset oneself
3 si je m'écoutais if it was up to me

écouteur /ekutœʀ/ *m* **1** (on phone) earpiece
2 earphones
3 headphones

écoutille /ekutij/ *f* (Naut) hatch

écrabouiller /ekʀabuje/ [**v1**] *vt* (fam) to squash

⚷ **écran** /ekʀɑ̃/ *m* **1** (gen) screen; **crever l'~** ‹*actor*› to have a great screen presence; **une vedette du petit ~** a TV star
2 cinema (BrE), movie theater (AmE)
3 (on machine) display
4 crème ~ total sun block
■ **~ antibruit** soundproofing; **~ de contrôle** monitor; **~ à cristaux de liquide** liquid crystal display, LCD; **~ solaire** sunscreen; **~ tactile** touch screen; **~ de visualisation** VDU screen

écrasant, **~e** /ekʀazɑ̃, ɑ̃t/ *adj* **1** ‹*weight*› enormous
2 ‹*heat*› sweltering; ‹*victory*› resounding; ‹*responsibility*› heavy

écraser /ekʀɑze/ [**v1**] **A** *vt* **1** to crush ‹*finger, person*›; to squash, to crush ‹*insect, hat, fruit, box*›; ‹*driver*› to run over ‹*person, animal*›; **se faire ~** to get run over
2 to flatten ‹*vegetation*›
3 (Culin) to mash ‹*fruit*›
4 ~ sa cigarette to stub out one's cigarette; **~ une larme** to wipe away a tear
5 to press ‹*nose, face*› (**contre** against)
6 to crush ‹*rebellion*›; to thrash (fam) ‹*opponent*›
7 to outshine
8 to put [sb] down
9 ‹*fatigue, heat*› to overcome
B s'écraser *v refl* (+ *v être*) **1** ‹*car, train*› to crash; ‹*driver, motorcyclist*› to have a crash; ‹*insect*› to splatter (**contre** on)
2 (fam) to shut up (fam)
3 (fam) to keep one's head down

écrémé, **~e** /ekʀeme/ *adj* skimmed

écrémer /ekʀeme/ [**v14**] *vt* **1** to skim ‹*milk*›
2 to cream off the best of ‹*candidates*›

écrevisse /ekʀəvis/ *f* crayfish (BrE), crawfish (AmE)

écrier: **s'écrier** /ekʀije/ [**v2**] *v refl* (+ *v être*) to exclaim

écrin /ekʀɛ̃/ *m* (for jewellery) case

⚷ key word

⚷ **écrire** /ekʀiʀ/ [**v67**] **A** *vt* **1** to write
2 to spell
B *vi* to write
C s'écrire *v refl* (+ *v être*) **1** to be written
2 to be spelled

écrit, **~e** /ekʀi, it/ **A** *pp* ▶ **écrire**
B *pp adj* written; **c'était ~** it was bound to happen
C *m* **1** work, piece of writing
2 document; **par ~** in writing
3 written examination
IDIOM **les paroles s'envolent, les ~s restent** never put anything in writing; (as security) get it in writing

écriteau, *pl* **~x** /ekʀito/ *m* sign

écritoire /ekʀitwaʀ/ *f* writing case

⚷ **écriture** /ekʀityʀ/ **A** *f* **1** handwriting
2 (in printing) hand
3 (text, activity) writing
4 script; **~ phonétique** phonetic script
B écritures *fpl* accounts; **tenir les ~s** to do the books

Écriture /ekʀityʀ/ *f* **les (saintes) ~s** the Scriptures; **l'~ sainte** Holy Writ

⚷ **écrivain** /ekʀivɛ̃/ *m* writer

écrou /ekʀu/ *m* (Tech) nut

écrouer /ekʀue/ [**v1**] *vt* (Law) to commit [sb] to prison

écroulé, **~e** /ekʀule/ *adj* overwhelmed; **~ de rire** (fam) doubled up with laughter

écrouler: **s'écrouler** /ekʀule/ [**v1**] *v refl* (+ *v être*) to collapse; to fade; to crumble

écru, **~e** /ekʀy/ *adj* **1** ‹*canvas*› unbleached; ‹*wool*› undyed; ‹*silk*› raw
2 (colour) ecru

écu /eky/ *m* **1** (Hist) (in EU) ecu
2 ≈ crown
3 shield

écueil /ekœj/ *m* **1** reef
2 (fig) pitfall

écuelle /ekɥɛl/ *f* **1** bowl
2 bowlful

écume /ekym/ *f* **1** (on water) foam; (on beer) froth; (on metal) dross
2 (at mouth) foam, froth

écumer /ekyme/ [**v1**] **A** *vt* **1** to skim
2 to scour, to search
B *vi* ‹*sea*› to foam; ‹*wine*› to froth

écumoire /ekymwaʀ/ *f* skimming ladle

écureuil /ekyʀœj/ *m* squirrel

écurie /ekyʀi/ *f* **1** stable
2 (Sport) stable
3 (fig) pigsty

écusson /ekysɔ̃/ *m* **1** (Mil) flash (BrE)
2 (of school) crest, badge; (of club, movement) badge; (of car) insignia
3 (in heraldry) coat of arms

écuyer, **-ère** /ekɥije, ɛʀ/ **A** *mf* **1** horseman/horsewoman
2 riding instructor
3 bareback rider

B *m* **1** squire
2 equerry
eczéma /egzema/ *m* eczema
éden /edɛn/ *m* paradise
Éden /edɛn/ *pr m* Eden
édenté, **~e** /edɑ̃te/ *adj* **1** toothless
2 gap-toothed
3 ‹*comb*› broken
EDF /œdeɛf/ *f* (*abbr* = **Électricité de France**) *French electricity board*
édicter /edikte/ [**v1**] *vt* to enact ‹*law*›
édifiant, **~e** /edifjɑ̃, ɑ̃t/ *adj* **1** edifying
2 enlightening
édifice /edifis/ *m* **1** building
2 structure
édifier /edifje/ [**v2**] *vt* **1** to build [sth]
2 to build ‹*empire*›
3 to edify
4 to enlighten
Édimbourg /edɛ̃buʀ/ *pr n* Edinburgh
édit /edi/ *m* edict
éditer /edite/ [**v1**] *vt* **1** to publish ‹*book, author*›; to release ‹*record*›
2 (Comput) to edit
éditeur, **-trice** /editœʀ, tʀis/ **A** *mf* editor
B *m* **1** publisher
2 (Comput) editor
édition /edisjɔ̃/ **A** *f* **1** (of book) publication; (of record) release
2 (book, print) edition; (record) release
3 publishing; **société d'~** publishing firm
4 editing
5 (paper) **~ du soir** evening edition
B **éditions** *fpl* **les ~s de la Roulotte** la Roulotte (Publishing Company)
éditorial, **~e**, *mpl* **-iaux** /editɔʀjal, o/ **A** *adj* ‹*policy, service*› editorial
B *m* editorial, leader
édredon /edʀədɔ̃/ *m* eiderdown
éducateur, **-trice** /edykatœʀ, tʀis/ **A** *adj* educational
B *mf* youth worker
éducatif, **-ive** /edykatif, iv/ *adj* educational
éducation /edykasjɔ̃/ *f* **1** education; **faire l'~ de qn** to educate sb
2 training
3 manners
■ **Éducation nationale, EN** Ministry of Education; (system) state education
édulcorer /edylkɔʀe/ [**v1**] *vt* **1** to sweeten
2 to tone down ‹*letter, remark*›
éduquer /edyke/ [**v1**] *vt* to educate; to train
effacé, **~e** /efase/ *adj* retiring
effacement /efasmɑ̃/ *m* **1** deletion
2 (of cassette) erasure
3 self-effacement
effacer /efase/ [**v12**] **A** *vt* **1** to rub out; to delete; to erase
2 to wipe ‹*tape*›; to clear ‹*file*›; to clean ‹*blackboard*›
3 ‹*rain*› to erase ‹*tracks*›; ‹*snow*› to cover (up) ‹*tracks*›; ‹*cream*› to remove ‹*wrinkles*›
4 to blot out ‹*memory*›; to remove ‹*differences*›
5 to write off ‹*debt*›
B **s'effacer** *v refl* (+ *v être*) **1 ça s'efface** you can rub it out
2 ‹*inscription, drawing, memory*› to fade; ‹*impression*› to wear off; ‹*fear*› to disappear
3 to step aside
4 to stay in the background
effaceur /efasœʀ/ *m* correction pen
effarant, **~e** /efaʀɑ̃, ɑ̃t/ *adj* astounding
effarer /efaʀe/ [**v1**] *vt* to alarm
effaroucher /efaʀuʃe/ [**v1**] *vt* **1** to frighten [sb/sth] away
2 to alarm
effectif, **-ive** /efɛktif, iv/ **A** *adj* real
B *m* (of school) number of pupils; (of university) number of students; (of company) workforce; (of army) strength
effectivement /efɛktivmɑ̃/ *adv* **1** indeed
2 actually, really
effectuer /efɛktɥe/ [**v1**] *vt* to do ‹*work, repairs*›; to make ‹*payment, trip*›; to carry out ‹*transaction*›; to conduct ‹*survey*›; to serve ‹*sentence*›
efféminé, **~e** /efemine/ *adj* effeminate
effervescence /efɛʀvesɑ̃s/ *f*
1 effervescence
2 turmoil
effervescent, **~e** /efɛʀvesɑ̃, ɑ̃t/ *adj*
1 effervescent
2 (fig) ‹*crowd*› seething; ‹*personality*› effervescent
effet /efɛ/ **A** *m* **1** effect; **prendre ~** ‹*measure, law*› to take effect; **sous l'~ de l'alcool** under the influence of alcohol; **couper tous ses ~s à qn** to steal sb's thunder
2 impression; **être du plus mauvais ~** to be in the worst possible taste; **faire un drôle d'~** to make one feel strange; **un ~ de surprise** an element of surprise
3 à cet ~ for that purpose
B **en effet** *phr* indeed
C **effets** *mpl* things, clothes
■ **~ de serre** greenhouse effect; **~s secondaires** (Med) side effects
efficace /efikas/ *adj* effective; efficient
efficacement /efikasmɑ̃/ *adv* efficiently; effectively
efficacité /efikasite/ *f* (of action, remedy) effectiveness; (of person, device) efficiency
effigie /efiʒi/ *f* **1** effigy; **à l'~ de** ‹*medal, stamp*› with the head of
2 logo
effilé, **~e** /efile/ *adj* ‹*almonds*› flaked
effiler /efile/ [**v1**] **A** *vt* **1** to sharpen
2 to string ‹*green beans*›
B **s'effiler** *v refl* (+ *v être*) to fray
effilocher /efilɔʃe/ [**v1**] **A** *vt* to shred
B **s'effilocher** *v refl* (+ *v être*) to fray
efflanqué, **~e** /eflɑ̃ke/ *adj* emaciated

e

effleurer /eflœʀe/ [**v1**] *vt* to touch lightly, to brush (against); **l'idée ne m'a même pas effleuré** the idea didn't even cross my mind

effluent /eflyɑ̃/ *m* effluent

effluve /eflyv/ *m* **1** unpleasant smell **2** fragrance

effondrement /efɔ̃dʀəmɑ̃/ *m* **1** collapse **2** subsidence

effondrer: **s'effondrer** /efɔ̃dʀe/ [**v1**] *v refl* (+ *v être*) **1** ‹*roof, person*› to collapse; ‹*dream*› to crumble; ‹*hopes*› to fall **2 être effondré par la nouvelle** to be distraught at the news

efforcer: **s'efforcer** /efɔʀse/ [**v12**] *v refl* (+ *v être*) to try hard (**de faire** to do)

🗝 **effort** /efɔʀ/ *m* **1** effort; **fais un petit ~ d'imagination!** use a bit of imagination!; **avec mon dos, je ne peux pas faire d'~** with this back of mine, I can't do anything strenuous **2** (in physics) stress; strain

effraction /efʀaksjɔ̃/ *f* breaking and entering
■ **~ informatique** computer hacking

effrayant, **~e** /efʀɛjɑ̃, ɑ̃t/ *adj* ‹*sight, ugliness*› frightening; ‹*thinness, paleness*› dreadful

effrayer /efʀɛje/ [**v21**] *vt* **1** to frighten; to alarm **2** ‹*difficulty, price*› to put [sb] off

effréné, **~e** /efʀene/ *adj* ‹*rhythm, competition*› frenzied; ‹*ambition*› wild

effriter /efʀite/ [**v1**] **A** *vt* to crumble; to break up
B s'effriter *v refl* (+ *v être*) to crumble (away)

effroi /efʀwɑ/ *m* dread, terror

effronté, **~e** /efʀɔ̃te/ *adj* cheeky; shameless

effroyable /efʀwɑjabl/ *adj* dreadful

effroyablement /efʀwɑjabləmɑ̃/ *adv* **1** horribly **2** (fam) terribly

effusion /efyzjɔ̃/ *f* effusion
■ **~ de sang** bloodshed

🗝 **égal**, **~e**, *mpl* **-aux** /egal, o/ **A** *adj* **1** equal (à to); **à prix ~, je préfère celui-là** if the price is the same, I'd rather have that one **2** ‹*ground*› level; ‹*light*› even; ‹*colour*› uniform; ‹*weather*› settled; ‹*pulse, breathing*› steady; **d'un pas ~** at an even pace **3 ça m'est ~** I don't mind (either way); I don't care
B *mf* equal; **traiter d'~ à ~ avec qn** to deal with sb as an equal

IDIOMS **rester ~ à soi-même** to be one's usual self; **combattre à armes ~es** to be on an equal footing

égalable /egalabl/ *adj* **difficilement ~** unparalleled; incomparably superior

🗝 **également** /egalmɑ̃/ *adv* **1** also, too **2** equally

égaler /egale/ [**v1**] *vt* **1** to equal ‹*record*›; to be as good as ‹*person*›; to be as high as ‹*price*› **2 trois plus trois égalent six** three plus three equals six *or* is six

égalisation /egalizasjɔ̃/ *f* **1** levelling (BrE) out **2** (Sport) **le penalty a permis l'~** the penalty evened (BrE) *or* tied (AmE) the score

égaliser /egalize/ [**v1**] **A** *vt* **1** to level ‹*ground*› **2** to make [sth] the same size ‹*planks*›
B *vi* (Sport) to equalize (BrE), to tie (AmE)

égalitaire /egalitɛʀ/ *adj*, *mf* egalitarian

🗝 **égalité** /egalite/ *f* **1** equality **2** (Sport) **être à ~** to be level (BrE), to be tied (AmE); **~!** deuce!

🗝 **égard** /egaʀ/ **A** *m* **1** consideration; **sans ~ pour** without regard for **2 à l'~ de qn** toward(s) sb; **à cet ~** in this respect
B égards *mpl* **avec des ~s** with respect; **être plein d'~s envers qn** to be attentive to sb's every need

égaré, **~e** /egaʀe/ *adj* **1** stray **2** ‹*look*› wild

égarement /egaʀmɑ̃/ *m* **1** distraction, madness **2** confusion **3** erratic behaviour (BrE)

égarer /egaʀe/ [**v1**] **A** *vt* **1** to lead [sb] astray **2** to mislay
B s'égarer *v refl* (+ *v être*) **1** to get lost **2** (fig) ‹*mind*› to wander; ‹*person*› to ramble

égayer /egeje/ [**v21**] *vt* to enliven; to lighten; to brighten; to cheer [sb] up

égérie /eʒeʀi/ *f* muse

égide /eʒid/ *f* aegis

églantine /eglɑ̃tin/ *f* wild rose, dog rose

églefin /egləfɛ̃/ *m* haddock

🗝 **église** /egliz/ *f* church

ego /ego/ *m inv* ego

égocentrique /egosɑ̃tʀik/ *adj*, *mf* egocentric

égoïsme /egɔism/ *m* selfishness

égoïste /egɔist/ *adj* selfish

égorger /egɔʀʒe/ [**v13**] *vt* **~ qn** to cut sb's throat

égosiller: **s'égosiller** /egozije/ [**v1**] *v refl* (+ *v être*) **1** to shout oneself hoarse **2** to sing at the top of one's voice **3** to yell

égout /egu/ *m* sewer

égoutter /egute/ [**v1**] **A** *vt* to drain
B s'égoutter *v refl* (+ *v être*) ‹*dishes, rice, vegetables*› to drain; ‹*washing*› to drip dry

égouttoir /egutwaʀ/ *m* draining rack (BrE), (dish) drainer (AmE)

égratigner /egʀatiɲe/ [**v1**] **A** *vt* to scratch, to graze

🗝 key word

B **s'égratigner** *v refl* (+ *v être*) to scratch oneself; to graze oneself

égratignure /egʀatiɲyʀ/ *f* scratch; graze

égrener /egʀəne/ [**v16**] *vt* **1** to shell ‹*peas*›; to remove the seeds from ‹*melon*›
2 to chime out ‹*notes*›; **~ son chapelet** to tell one's beads

Égypte /eʒipt/ *pr f* Egypt

égyptien, **-ienne** /eʒipsjɛ̃, ɛn/ **A** *adj* Egyptian
B *m* (language) Egyptian

éhonté, **~e** /eɔ̃te/ *adj* ‹*liar, lie*› brazen

Éire /ɛʀ/ *pr n* Éire, Republic of Ireland

éjectable /eʒɛktabl/ *adj* **siège ~** ejector seat (BrE), ejection seat (AmE)

éjecter /eʒɛkte/ [**v1**] *vt* **1** (in accident) to throw [sb/sth] out
2 (Tech) to eject

élaboration /elabɔʀasjɔ̃/ *f* development; working out; drafting; putting together

élaboré, **~e** /elabɔʀe/ *adj* sophisticated; elaborate

élaborer /elabɔʀe/ [**v1**] *vt* to work [sth] out; to draw [sth] up; to put [sth] together

élaguer /elage/ [**v1**] *vt* to prune

élan /elɑ̃/ *m* **1** (Sport) run up; **saut sans ~** standing jump
2 momentum
3 impetus
4 enthusiasm; **~ patriotique** patriotic fervour (BrE)
5 impulse; **~ de tendresse** surge of tenderness
6 (Zool) elk

élancé, **~e** /elɑ̃se/ *adj* slender

élancement /elɑ̃smɑ̃/ *m* throbbing pain

élancer: **s'élancer** /elɑ̃se/ [**v12**] *v refl* (+ *v être*) **1** to dash forward
2 s'~ vers le ciel ‹*tree, spire*› to soar up toward(s) the sky

élargi, **~e** /elaʀʒi/ *adj* enlarged; expanded

élargir /elaʀʒiʀ/ [**v3**] **A** *vt* **1** to widen ‹*road*›; to let out ‹*garment*›
2 to stretch ‹*shoes, sweater*›
3 to extend ‹*contacts, law*›; to broaden ‹*knowledge*›; to increase ‹*majority*›
B **s'élargir** *v refl* (+ *v être*) ‹*group*› to expand; ‹*gap*› to increase; ‹*road*› to widen; ‹*person*› to fill out; ‹*garment*› to stretch

élastique /elastik/ **A** *adj* **1** ‹*waistband*› elasticated (BrE), elasticized (AmE)
2 ‹*gas, fibre*› elastic
3 ‹*rule, timetable*› flexible; ‹*budget*› elastic
B *m* **1** rubber band
2 (in haberdashery) elastic
3 (Sport) bungee cord
(IDIOM) **les lâcher avec un ~** (fam) to be tight-fisted

élastomère /elastɔmɛʀ/ *m* elastomer

électeur, **-trice** /elɛktœʀ, tʀis/ *mf* voter

élection /elɛksjɔ̃/ *f* **1** election
2 choice; **mon pays d'~** my chosen country

électoral, **~e**, *mpl* **-aux** /elɛktɔʀal, o/ *adj* electoral; election

électorat /elɛktɔʀa/ *m* electorate, voters

électricien, **-ienne** /elɛktʀisjɛ̃, ɛn/ *mf* electrician

électricité /elɛktʀisite/ *f* electricity

électrifier /elɛktʀifje/ [**v2**] *vt* to electrify ‹*rail tracks*›

électrique /elɛktʀik/ *adj* **1** electrical
2 (fig) ‹*atmosphere*› electric

électriser /elɛktʀize/ [**v1**] *vt* to electrify

électro /elɛktʀo/ *pref also* **électro-** electro; **~cardiogramme** electrocardiogram

électrochoc /elɛktʀoʃɔk/ *m* **~s** electroshock therapy, EST

électrocuter: **s'électrocuter** /elɛktʀɔkyte/ [**v1**] *v refl* (+ *v être*) to be electrocuted

électrode /elɛktʀɔd/ *f* electrode

électrogène /elɛktʀɔʒɛn/ *adj* **groupe ~** (electricity) generator

électromécanicien, **-ienne** /elɛktʀomekanisjɛ̃, ɛn/ *mf* electrical engineer

électroménager /elɛktʀomenaʒe/ **A** *adj m* **appareil ~** household appliance
B *m* **1** domestic electrical appliances
2 electrical goods industry

électron /elɛktʀɔ̃/ *m* electron

électronicien, **-ienne** /elɛktʀɔnisjɛ̃, ɛn/ *mf* electronics engineer

électronique /elɛktʀɔnik/ **A** *adj* **1** ‹*circuit*› electronic
2 ‹*microscope*› electron
B *f* electronics

électrophone /elɛktʀɔfɔn/ *m* record player

élégamment /elegamɑ̃/ *adv* ‹*dress*› elegantly

élégance /elegɑ̃s/ *f* elegance; **avec ~** ‹*dress*› elegantly; ‹*lose*› gracefully; ‹*behave*› honourably (BrE); ‹*resolve problem*› neatly

élégant, **~e** /elegɑ̃, ɑ̃t/ *adj* elegant; **ce n'est pas très ~ de ta part** it's not very decent of you

élément /elemɑ̃/ **A** *m* **1** (in structure, ensemble) element; (in device) component; **~ moteur** driving force
2 factor, element; **l'~-clé de** the key element in
3 (of furniture) unit
4 fact; **disposer de tous les ~s** to have all the facts
5 (person) **bon ~** good pupil; good player
6 (chemical) element
B **éléments** *mpl* elements

élémentaire /elemɑ̃tɛʀ/ *adj* **1** ‹*principle*› basic
2 elementary

éléphant /elefɑ̃/ *m* elephant

éléphanteau, *pl* **~x** /elefɑ̃to/ *m* (elephant) calf

e

élevage /elvaʒ/ *m* **1** livestock farming; **faire de l'~ de porcs** to breed pigs; **d'~** ‹*oysters*› farmed; ‹*pheasant*› captive-bred
2 farm; **un ~ de visons** a mink farm
3 stock (**de** of)

élévateur /elevatœʀ/ *m* elevator

élévation /elevasjɔ̃/ *f* **1** rise (**de** in)
2 (to rank) elevation
3 (in architecture) elevation

⚷ **élève** /elɛv/ *mf* (gen) student; (Sch) pupil; **~ officier** trainee officer

élevé, ~e /elve/ *adj* **1** ‹*level, price, rank*› high
2 ‹*plateau*› high
3 ‹*sentiment*› fine; ‹*principles*› high; ‹*ideal*› lofty; ‹*language*› elevated

⚷ **élever** /elve/ [**v16**] **A** *vt* **1** to put up, to erect
2 to raise ‹*temperature, level*›
3 to lift, to raise ‹*load*›
4 la poésie élève l'âme poetry is elevating *or* uplifting
5 to raise ‹*objection*›
6 to bring [sb] up; **c'est mal élevé** it's bad manners (**de faire** to do)
7 to rear ‹*cattle*›; to keep ‹*bees*›
B s'élever *v refl* (+ *v être*) **1** ‹*rate*› to rise
2 s'~ à ‹*expenses*› to come to; ‹*death toll*› to stand at
3 to rise (up); **s'~ dans les airs** ‹*smoke*› to rise up into the air; ‹*bird*› to soar into the air
4 ‹*voice, protests*› to be heard
5 s'~ contre qch to protest against sth
6 ‹*statue*› to stand; **s'~ au-dessus de qch** to rise above sth

éleveur, -euse /elvœʀ, øz/ *mf* breeder

elfe /ɛlf/ *m* elf

élider /elide/ [**v1**] *vt* to elide

éligible /eliʒibl/ *adj* eligible for office

élimé, ~e /elime/ *adj* threadbare

élimer /elime/ [**v1**] **A** *vt* to wear [sth] thin
B s'élimer *v refl* (+ *v être*) to wear thin

élimination /eliminasjɔ̃/ *f* **1** (gen) elimination, defeat
2 (of stain) removal; **~ des déchets** waste disposal

éliminatoire /eliminatwaʀ/ *adj* ‹*question, match*› qualifying; ‹*mark*› eliminatory

éliminer /elimine/ [**v1**] *vt* to eliminate

élire /eliʀ/ [**v66**] *vt* to elect; **se faire ~** to be elected; **~ domicile** to take up residence

élision /elizjɔ̃/ *f* elision

élite /elit/ *f* **l'~** the elite; **d'~** ‹*troops*› elite, crack; ‹*student*› high-flying; ‹*athlete*› top

élitisme /elitism/ *m* elitism

élixir /eliksiʀ/ *m* elixir

⚷ **elle** /ɛl/ *pron f* she; it; **~s** they; **je les vois plus souvent qu'~** I see them more often than she does; I see them more often than (I see) her; **le bol bleu est à ~** the blue bowl is hers

ellébore /elebɔʀ/ *m* hellebore

elle-même, *pl* **elles-mêmes** /ɛlmɛm/ *pron* herself; itself; **elles-mêmes** themselves; **'Mme Roc?'—'~'** 'Mrs Roc?'—'speaking'

elles ▸ **elle**

ellipse /elips/ *f* ellipsis

elliptique /eliptik/ *adj* **1** elliptical
2 elliptic

élocution /elɔkysjɔ̃/ *f* diction; **défaut d'~** speech impediment

éloge /elɔʒ/ *m* **1** praise; **être tout à l'~ de qn** to do sb great credit
2 eulogy; **~ funèbre** funeral oration

élogieux, -ieuse /elɔʒjø, øz/ *adj* full of praise; laudatory

éloigné, ~e /elwaɲe/ *adj* **1** distant; **~ de tout** remote; **deux usines ~es de cinq kilomètres** two factories five kilometres (BrE) apart
2 ‹*memories*› distant; ‹*event*› remote; **~ dans le temps** distant (in time)
3 ‹*cousin*› distant

éloignement /elwaɲmɑ̃/ *m* **1** distance
2 remoteness

⚷ **éloigner** /elwaɲe/ [**v1**] **A** *vt* **1** to move [sb/sth] away
2 ils font tout pour l'~ de moi they are doing everything to drive us apart
B s'éloigner *v refl* (+ *v être*) **1** to move away; **ne t'éloigne pas trop** don't go too far away
2 s'~ de to move away from ‹*party line*›; to stray from ‹*subject*›

élongation /elɔ̃gasjɔ̃/ *f* (Med) pulled muscle

éloquence /elɔkɑ̃s/ *f* eloquence

éloquent, ~e /elɔkɑ̃, ɑ̃t/ *adj* eloquent

élu, ~e /ely/ *mf* **1** elected representative
2 beloved
3 (in religion) **les ~s** the Chosen Ones

élucider /elyside/ [**v1**] *vt* to solve ‹*crime, problem*›; to clarify ‹*circumstances*›

élucubrations /elykybʀasjɔ̃/ *fpl* rantings

éluder /elyde/ [**v1**] *vt* to evade

Élysée /elize/ *pr m* **(palais de) l'~** *the official residence of the French President*

émacier: **s'émacier** /emasje/ [**v2**] *v refl* (+ *v être*) to become emaciated

émail, *pl* **-aux** /emaj, o/ *m* enamel

e-mail /imɛ(j)l/ *m* email

émaillé, ~e /emaje/ *adj* ‹*utensil*› enamel; ‹*metal*› enamelled

émanation /emanasjɔ̃/ *f* emanation; **~s de gaz** gas fumes

émancipation /emɑ̃sipasjɔ̃/ *f* emancipation

émanciper /emɑ̃sipe/ [**v1**] **A** *vt* to emancipate ‹*people*›; to liberate ‹*country*›
B s'émanciper *v refl* (+ *v être*) to become emancipated; **femme émancipée** liberated woman

⚷ key word

émaner /emane/ [**v1**] **A** *vi* **~ de** to emanate from; to come from
B *v impers* **il émane d'elle un charme fou** she exudes charm

émaux ▸ **émail**

emballage /ɑ̃balaʒ/ *m* packaging; wrapping; packing
■ **~ sous vide** vacuum packing

emballant, **~e** /ɑ̃balɑ̃, ɑ̃t/ *adj* (fam) exciting

emballer /ɑ̃bale/ [**v1**] **A** *vt* **1** to pack, to wrap
2 (fam) **être emballé par** to be taken with
B **s'emballer** *v refl* (+ *v être*) **1** ‹*horse*› to bolt
2 (fam) to get carried away
3 to get all worked up (fam)
4 (fam) ‹*engine*› to race
5 ‹*prices, inflation*› to shoot up; ‹*currency*› to shoot up in value

embarcadère /ɑ̃barkadɛr/ *m* pier; wharf

embarcation /ɑ̃barkasjɔ̃/ *f* boat

embardée /ɑ̃barde/ *f* (of car) swerve

embargo /ɑ̃bargo/ *m* embargo

embarquement /ɑ̃barkəmɑ̃/ *m* boarding

embarquer /ɑ̃barke/ [**v1**] **A** *vt* **1** to load ‹*goods*›; to take [sb] on board
2 (fam) to take ‹*object*›; ‹*police*› to pick up ‹*criminal*›
B *vi* **1** to board
2 to sail (**pour** for)
C **s'embarquer** *v refl* (+ *v être*) **1** to board
2 (fam) **s'~ dans** to launch into ‹*explanation*›

embarras /ɑ̃bara/ *m inv* **1** embarrassment
2 awkward position; difficult situation
3 n'avoir que l'~ du choix to have too much to choose from

embarrassant, **~e** /ɑ̃barasɑ̃, ɑ̃t/ *adj* **1** awkward; embarrassing
2 cumbersome

embarrassé, **~e** /ɑ̃barase/ **A** *pp* ▸ **embarrasser**
B *pp adj* **1** embarrassed; **être bien ~ pour répondre** to be at a loss for an answer
2 ‹*room*› cluttered; **~ d'une grosse valise** weighed down with a large suitcase

embarrasser /ɑ̃barase/ [**v1**] **A** *vt* **1** to embarrass
2 to clutter [sth] (up); **cette armoire m'embarrasse plutôt qu'autre chose** this wardrobe is more of a nuisance than anything else
B **s'embarrasser** *v refl* (+ *v être*) **s'~ de** to burden oneself with ‹*baggage, person*›

embauche /ɑ̃boʃ/ *f* appointment (BrE), hiring (AmE); **salaire d'~** starting salary

embaucher /ɑ̃boʃe/ [**v1**] *vt* **1** to take on (BrE), to hire
2 (fam) to recruit

embaumer /ɑ̃bome/ [**v1**] **A** *vt* **1** ‹*smell*› to fill ‹*place*›; ‹*place*› to smell of ‹*wax*›
2 to embalm
B *vi* to be fragrant

embaumeur, **-euse** /ɑ̃bomœr, øz/ *mf* embalmer

embellir /ɑ̃belir/ [**v3**] **A** *vt* **1** to improve [sth]; to make [sb] more attractive
2 to embellish ‹*story, truth*›
B *vi* to become more attractive

embellissement /ɑ̃belismɑ̃/ *m* (of house) improving; **travaux d'~** improvements

emberlificoter /ɑ̃bɛrlifikɔte/ [**v1**] (fam)
A *vt* **1** to entangle
2 to take [sb] in (fam)
B **s'emberlificoter** *v refl* (+ *v être*) to get entangled; to get tangled up (**dans** in)

embêtant, **~e** /ɑ̃betɑ̃, ɑ̃t/ *adj* **1** annoying
2 boring

embêtement /ɑ̃betmɑ̃/ *m* problem

embêter /ɑ̃bete/ [**v1**] **A** *vt* **1** to bother
2 to pester; to annoy
3 to bore
B **s'embêter** *v refl* (+ *v être*) **1** to be bored
2 s'~ à faire to go to the bother of doing

emblée: **d'emblée** /dɑ̃ble/ *phr*
1 straightaway
2 at first sight

emblématique /ɑ̃blematik/ *adj* emblematic; symbolic

emblème /ɑ̃blɛm/ *m* emblem

embobiner /ɑ̃bɔbine/ [**v1**] *vt* (fam) to hoodwink

emboîter /ɑ̃bwate/ [**v1**] **A** *vt* to fit [sth] together; **~ qch dans** to fit sth into
B **s'emboîter** *v refl* (+ *v être*) ‹*part*› to fit (**dans** into); ‹*parts*› to fit together
IDIOM **~ le pas à qn** to fall in behind sb

embonpoint /ɑ̃bɔ̃pwɛ̃/ *m* stoutness; **avoir de l'~** to be stout

embouché, **~e** /ɑ̃buʃe/ *adj* **mal ~** coarse; in a foul mood

embouchure /ɑ̃buʃyr/ *f* (of river) mouth; (of instrument) mouthpiece; (of pipe) opening

embourber: **s'embourber** /ɑ̃burbe/ [**v1**] *v refl* (+ *v être*) **1** to get stuck in the mud
2 to get bogged down

embourgeoiser: **s'embourgeoiser** /ɑburʒwaze/ [**v1**] *v refl* (+ *v être*) ‹*person*› to become middle-class; ‹*area*› to become gentrified

embout /ɑ̃bu/ *m* (of cigar, cane) tip; (of hosepipe) nozzle; (of pipe) mouthpiece

embouteillage /ɑ̃butɛjaʒ/ *m* traffic jam

emboutir /ɑ̃butir/ [**v3**] *vt* **1** to stamp, to press ‹*part, metal*›
2 (fam) to crash into ‹*vehicle*›

embranchement /ɑ̃brɑ̃ʃmɑ̃/ *m* **1** junction
2 side road
3 (on railways) branch line

embrasé, **~e** /ɑ̃braze/ *adj* **1** burning
2 glowing

embrasement /ɑ̃brazmɑ̃/ *m* **1** blaze

2 dazzling illumination
3 unrest

embraser /ɑ̃bʀaze/ [**v1**] **A** *vt* **1** to set [sth] ablaze
2 to set [sth] alight ‹*country*›
B **s'embraser** *v refl* (+ *v être*) **1** to catch fire
2 ‹*country*› to erupt into violence
3 ‹*sky*› to be set ablaze
4 to burn with desire

⚷ **embrasser** /ɑ̃bʀase/ [**v1**] **A** *vt* **1** to kiss; **je t'embrasse** lots of love
2 to embrace; to hug
3 to take up ‹*career, cause*›
B **s'embrasser** *v refl* (+ *v être*) **1** to kiss (each other)
2 to embrace; to hug
IDIOM ~ **qn comme du bon pain** to hug sb warmly

embrasure /ɑ̃bʀazyʀ/ *f* ~ **de fenêtre** window; ~ **de porte** doorway

embrayage /ɑ̃bʀɛjaʒ/ *m* **1** clutch
2 clutch pedal

embrayer /ɑ̃bʀeje/ [**v21**] *vi* ‹*driver*› to engage the clutch; (Tech) to engage

embrigader /ɑ̃bʀigade/ [**v1**] *vt* **1** to recruit
2 (Mil) to brigade

embrouillamini /ɑ̃bʀujamini/ *m* (fam) muddle

embrouille /ɑ̃bʀuj/ *f* (fam) shady goings-on (fam)

embrouiller /ɑ̃bʀuje/ [**v1**] **A** *vt* **1** to tangle ‹*wires*›
2 to confuse ‹*matter, person*›
B **s'embrouiller** *v refl* (+ *v être*) **1** to become tangled
2 ‹*ideas, person*› to become confused

embroussaillé, **~e** /ɑ̃bʀusaje/ *adj* ‹*path*› overgrown; ‹*hair*› bushy

embrumé, **~e** /ɑ̃bʀyme/ *adj* **1** misty
2 ‹*mind*› befuddled; ‹*look*› glazed

embruns /ɑ̃bʀœ̃/ *mpl* spray

embryon /ɑ̃bʀijɔ̃/ *m* embryo

embûche /ɑ̃byʃ/ *f* **1** trap; **dresser des ~s** to set traps
2 hazard; pitfall; **semé d'~s** hazardous; (fig) fraught with pitfalls

embuer /ɑ̃bɥe/ [**v1**] **A** *vt* to mist up, to fog up
B **s'embuer** *v refl* (+ *v être*) ‹*window*› to mist up, to fog up; ‹*eyes*› to mist over

embuscade /ɑ̃byskad/ *f* ambush

embusquer: **s'embusquer** /ɑ̃byske/ [**v1**] *v refl* (+ *v être*) to lie in ambush

éméché, **~e** /emeʃe/ *adj* (fam) tipsy

émeraude /emʀod/ *f* emerald

émergence /emɛʀʒɑ̃s/ *f* emergence

émerger /emɛʀʒe/ [**v13**] *vi* to emerge

émeri /emʀi/ *m* emery

émérite /emeʀit/ *adj* **1** outstanding
2 **professeur ~** emeritus professor

émerveiller /emɛʀveje/ [**v1**] **A** *vt* **~ qn** to fill sb with wonder
B **s'émerveiller** *v refl* (+ *v être*) **s'~ de** *or* **devant qch** to marvel at sth

émetteur, **-trice** /emetœʀ, tʀis/ **A** *adj*
1 ‹*station*› broadcasting
2 ‹*bank*› issuing
B *m* **1** transmitter
2 (of loan, card) issuer

émettre /emɛtʀ/ [**v60**] *vt* **1** to express ‹*opinion, wish*›; to put forward ‹*hypothesis*›
2 to utter ‹*cry*›; to produce ‹*sound, heat*›
3 to issue ‹*document*›
4 to broadcast ‹*programme*›
5 to send out ‹*signal*›
6 to emit ‹*radiation*›

émeute /emøt/ *f* riot

émietter /emjete/ [**v1**] **A** *vt* to crumble [sth]
B **s'émietter** *v refl* (+ *v être*) to crumble

émigrant, **~e** /emigʀɑ̃, ɑ̃t/ *mf* emigrant

émigration /emigʀasjɔ̃/ *f* emigration

émigré, **~e** /emigʀe/ *mf* emigrant; émigré

émigrer /emigʀe/ [**v1**] *vi* **1** to emigrate
2 ‹*bird*› to migrate

émincer /emɛ̃se/ [**v12**] *vt* to slice [sth] thinly

éminemment /eminamɑ̃/ *adv* eminently

éminence /eminɑ̃s/ *f* **1** hillock
2 (Anat) protuberance

Éminence /eminɑ̃s/ *f* Eminence

éminent, **~e** /eminɑ̃, ɑ̃t/ *adj* distinguished, eminent

émirat /emiʀa/ *m* emirate

Émirats /emiʀa/ *pr m pl* **~ arabes unis, EAU** United Arab Emirates

émis, **~e** /emi, iz/ ▶ **émettre**

émissaire /emisɛʀ/ *m* emissary

⚷ **émission** /emisjɔ̃/ *f* **1** programme (BrE)
2 (of document) issue
3 (of waves, signals) emission

emmagasiner /ɑ̃magazine/ [**v1**] *vt* **1** to store
2 to stockpile ‹*goods*›; to store up ‹*knowledge*›

emmanchure /ɑ̃mɑ̃ʃyʀ/ *f* armhole

emmêler /ɑ̃mɛle/ [**v1**] **A** *vt* **1** to tangle
2 to confuse ‹*matter*›
B **s'emmêler** *v refl* (+ *v être*) to get tangled up; **s'~ les pieds dans** to get one's feet caught in

emménagement /ɑ̃menaʒmɑ̃/ *m* moving in

emménager /ɑ̃menaʒe/ [**v13**] *vi* to move in

emmener /ɑ̃mne/ [**v16**] *vt* **1** to take ‹*person*› (**à, jusqu'à** to); **veux-tu que je t'emmène en voiture?** do you want a lift (BrE) *or* a ride (AmE)?
2 (fam, controversial) to take [sth] with one ‹*object*›
3 to take [sb] away

emmerder /ɑ̃mɛʀde/ [**v1**] (pop) **A** *vt* to annoy, to hassle (fam); **~ le monde** to be a

⚷ key word

pain in the arse (BrE) (fam) or ass (AmE) (sl)
B **s'emmerder** *v refl* (+ *v être*) **1** to be bored stiff (fam)
2 **s'~ à faire** to go to the trouble of doing; **tu t'emmerdes pas!** you're doing all right for yourself!; you've got a nerve!

emmitoufler /ɑ̃mitufle/ [**v1**] **A** *vt* to wrap [sb/sth] up warmly
B **s'emmitoufler** *v refl* (+ *v être*) to wrap (oneself) up warmly

émoi /emwa/ *m* agitation, turmoil

émoluments /emolymɑ̃/ *mpl* remuneration

émonder /emɔ̃de/ [**v1**] *vt* to prune

émotif, **-ive** /emɔtif, iv/ *adj* emotional

émotion /emosjɔ̃/ *f* emotion

émotivité /emɔtivite/ *f* **enfant d'une grande ~** highly emotional child

émousser /emuse/ [**v1**] **A** *vt* **1** to blunt
2 to dull ‹*curiosity, sensitivity*›
B **s'émousser** *v refl* (+ *v être*) **1** to become blunt
2 ‹*curiosity*› to become dulled

émoustiller /emustije/ [**v1**] *vt* **1** to exhilarate
2 to titillate

émouvant, **~e** /emuvɑ̃, ɑ̃t/ *adj* moving

émouvoir /emuvwaʀ/ [**v43**] **A** *vt* to move, to touch; **~ l'opinion** to cause a stir
B **s'émouvoir** *v refl* (+ *v être*) **1** to be touched *or* moved
2 **s'~ de** to become concerned about; to be bothered by

empailler /ɑ̃pɑje/ [**v1**] *vt* to stuff

empailleur, **-euse** /ɑ̃pɑjœʀ, øz/ *mf* taxidermist

empaler /ɑ̃pale/ [**v1**] **A** *vt* to impale
B **s'empaler** *v refl* (+ *v être*) to become impaled

empaqueter /ɑ̃pakte/ [**v20**] *vt* to package; to wrap [sth] up

emparer: **s'emparer** /ɑ̃paʀe/ [**v1**] *v refl* (+ *v être*) **1** **s'~ de** (gen) to get hold of, to seize; to take over ‹*town*›; to seize ‹*power*›
2 **s'~ de** ‹*feeling*› to take hold of [sb]

empâter: **s'empâter** /ɑ̃pɑte/ [**v1**] *v refl* (+ *v être*) to become puffy; to put on weight

empêchement /ɑ̃pɛʃmɑ̃/ *m* unforeseen difficulty; **j'ai un ~** something's cropped up

empêcher /ɑ̃peʃe/ [**v1**] **A** *vt* to prevent, to stop; **~ qn de faire** to prevent sb (from) doing
B **s'empêcher** *v refl* (+ *v être*) **je n'ai pas pu m'~ de rire** I couldn't help laughing
C *v impers* **(il) n'empêche** all the same; **il n'empêche que** the fact remains that

empereur /ɑ̃pʀœʀ/ *m* emperor

empesé, **~e** /ɑ̃pəze/ *adj* ‹*collar*› starched; ‹*person, manner*› starchy

empester /ɑ̃pɛste/ [**v16**] **A** *vt* to stink [sth] out (BrE), to stink up (AmE)
B *vi* to stink

empêtrer: **s'empêtrer** /ɑ̃petʀe/ [**v1**] *v refl* (+ *v être*) **s'~ dans** to get entangled in ‹*briars*›; to get tangled up in ‹*lies*›

emphase /ɑ̃fɑz/ *f* **1** grandiloquence
2 emphasis

emphatique /ɑ̃fatik/ *adj* **1** grandiloquent
2 emphatic

empiècement /ɑ̃pjɛsmɑ̃/ *m* (of garment) yoke

empiéter /ɑ̃pjete/ [**v14**] *vi* to encroach

empiffrer: **s'empiffrer** /ɑ̃pifʀe/ [**v1**] *v refl* (+ *v être*) (fam) to stuff oneself

empiler /ɑ̃pile/ [**v1**] **A** *vt* to pile [sth] (up)
B **s'empiler** *v refl* (+ *v être*) to pile up

empire /ɑ̃piʀ/ *m* empire

Empire /ɑ̃piʀ/ *m* **l'~** the Empire
■ **l'~ d'Orient** the Byzantine Empire; **l'~ d'Occident** the Western Empire

empirer /ɑ̃piʀe/ [**v1**] *vi* to get worse

empirique /ɑ̃piʀik/ *adj* empirical

empirisme /ɑ̃piʀism/ *m* empiricism

emplacement /ɑ̃plasmɑ̃/ *m* **1** site
2 parking space

emplette /ɑ̃plɛt/ *f* purchase

emplir /ɑ̃pliʀ/ [**v3**] *vt*, **s'emplir** *v refl* (+ *v être*) to fill (**de** with)

emploi /ɑ̃plwɑ/ *m* **1** job
2 employment
3 use; **téléviseur couleur à vendre, cause double ~** colour (BrE) TV for sale, surplus to requirements
4 usage
■ **~ du temps** timetable
IDIOM **avoir la tête de l'~** to look the part

employé, **~e** /ɑ̃plwaje/ *mf* employee
■ **~ de banque** bank clerk; **~ municipal** local authority employee

employer /ɑ̃plwaje/ [**v23**] **A** *vt* to employ ‹*person*›; to use ‹*word, product*›
B **s'employer** *v refl* (+ *v être*) **1** to be used
2 **s'~ à faire** to apply oneself to doing

employeur, **-euse** /ɑ̃plwajœʀ, øz/ *mf* employer

empocher /ɑ̃pɔʃe/ [**v1**] *vt* to pocket

empoigner /ɑ̃pwaɲe/ [**v1**] *vt* to grab (hold of)

empoisonnant, **~e** /ɑ̃pwazɔnɑ̃, ɑ̃t/ *adj* (fam) annoying, irritating

empoisonné, **~e** /ɑ̃pwazɔne/ **A** *pp* ▶ **empoisonner**
B *pp adj* ‹*foodstuff*› poisoned; ‹*atmosphere*› sour

empoisonnement /ɑ̃pwazɔnmɑ̃/ *m* **1** poisoning
2 (fam) trouble

empoisonner /ɑ̃pwazɔne/ [**v1**] **A** *vt* to poison; **~ la vie de qn** to make sb's life a misery
B **s'empoisonner** *v refl* (+ *v être*) to poison oneself; **il s'est empoisonné avec une huître pas fraîche** he got food poisoning from eating a bad oyster

e

empoisonneur, **-euse** /ɑ̃pwazɔnœʀ, øz/ *mf* **1** poisoner
2 (fam) nuisance

emportement /ɑ̃pɔʀtəmɑ̃/ *m* fit of anger; **avec ~** angrily

🔑 **emporter** /ɑ̃pɔʀte/ [**v1**] **A** *vt* **1** to take ‹*object*›; **pizzas à ~** takeaway pizzas (BrE), pizzas to go (AmE)
2 ‹*ambulance*› to take [sb] away; ‹*plane*› to carry [sb] away
3 ‹*wind, river*› to sweep [sb/sth] away; ‹*shell, bullet*› to take ‹*ear, leg*›
4 une leucémie l'a emporté he died of leukaemia
5 to take ‹*position*›
6 l'~ to win; to prevail; **l'~ sur qch** to overcome sth
B s'emporter *v refl* (+ *v être*) to lose one's temper

empoté, **~e** /ɑ̃pɔte/ *adj* (fam) clumsy, awkward

empreindre: **s'empreindre** /ɑ̃pʀɛ̃dʀ/ [**v55**] *v refl* (+ *v être*) to become marked (**de** with), to become imbued (**de** with)

empreinte /ɑ̃pʀɛ̃t/ *f* **1** footprint; track
2 stamp, mark
■ **~ écologique** carbon footprint; **~s digitales** fingerprints

empressement /ɑ̃pʀɛsmɑ̃/ *m* **1** eagerness; **avec ~** eagerly
2 attentiveness

empresser: **s'empresser** /ɑ̃pʀese/ [**v1**] *v refl* (+ *v être*) **s'~ de faire** to hasten to do; **s'~ autour** *or* **auprès de qn** to fuss over sb

emprise /ɑ̃pʀiz/ *f* hold, influence

emprisonnement /ɑ̃pʀizɔnmɑ̃/ *m* imprisonment; **peine d'~** prison sentence

emprisonner /ɑ̃pʀizɔne/ [**v1**] *vt* **1** to imprison (**à, dans** in)
2 to keep [sb] prisoner

emprunt /ɑ̃pʀœ̃/ *m* **1** (money) loan; **faire un ~** to take out a loan
2 borrowing; **d'~** ‹*car, name*› borrowed
3 (object, book) loan; **c'est un ~ fait à un musée** it's on loan from a museum
4 (of idea, word) borrowing

emprunté, **~e** /ɑ̃pʀœ̃te/ *adj* awkward

emprunter /ɑ̃pʀœ̃te/ [**v1**] *vt* **1** to borrow
2 to take ‹*road*›

empuantir /ɑ̃pyɑ̃tiʀ/ [**v3**] *vt* to stink out (BrE), to stink up (AmE)

ému, **~e** /emy/ **A** *pp* ▶ **émouvoir**
B *pp adj* moved; touched; nervous; **trop ~ pour parler** too overcome to speak
C *adj* ‹*words*› full of emotion; ‹*memory*› fond

émulation /emylasjɔ̃/ *f* competitiveness

émule /emyl/ *mf* imitator; **être l'~ de qn** to model oneself on sb

émulsifiant /emylsifjɑ̃/ *m* emulsifier

émulsion /emylsjɔ̃/ *f* emulsion

🔑 **en** /ɑ̃/ **A** *prep* **1** in; into; to; **vivre ~ ville** to live in town; **aller ~ Allemagne** to go to Germany; **~ hiver/1991** in winter/1991; **~ semaine** during the week; **voyager ~ train** to travel by train
2 il est toujours ~ manteau he always wears a coat
3 as; **je vous parle ~ ami** I'm speaking (to you) as a friend
4 into; **traduire ~ anglais** to translate into English
5 c'est ~ or it's (made of) gold; **le même ~ bleu/plus grand** the same in blue/only bigger; **~ hauteur, le mur fait trois mètres** the wall is three metres (BrE) high
6 (*used with gerund*) **je l'ai croisé ~ sortant** I met him as I was leaving; **prends un café ~ attendant** have a cup of coffee while you're waiting; **l'enfant se réveilla ~ hurlant** the child woke up screaming; **ouvrez cette caisse ~ soulevant le couvercle** open this box by lifting the lid; **tu aurais moins chaud ~ enlevant ta veste** you'd be cooler if you took your jacket off
B *pron* **1** (indicating means) **il sortit son épée et l'~ transperça** he took out his sword and ran him/her through
2 (indicating cause) **ça l'a tellement bouleversé qu'il ~ est tombé malade** it distressed him so much that he fell ill (BrE) *or* became sick (AmE)
3 (representing person) **ils aiment leurs enfants et ils ~ sont aimés** they love their children and they are loved by them
4 (representing thing) **'veux-tu du vin?'—'oui, j'~ veux'** 'would you like some wine?'—'yes, I'd like some'; **il n'~ reste pas beaucoup** there isn't much (of it) left; there aren't many left; **j'~ suis fier** I'm proud of it
5 (fam) **tu ~ as un beau chapeau!** what a nice hat you've got!

en live /ɑ̃lajv/ *loc adv* (Radio, TV, Internet) live; **elle regarde la télévision ~ sur Internet** she watches live TV on the Internet

ENA /ena/ *f*: *abbr* ▶ **école**

énarchie /enaʀʃi/ *f network of graduates of the École nationale d'administration (ENA)*

énarque /enaʀk/ *mf* graduate of the ENA

encadré /ɑ̃kadʀe/ *m* (in newspaper) box

encadrement /ɑ̃kadʀəmɑ̃/ *m*
1 supervision
2 supervisory staff; managerial staff; (Mil) officers
3 (of picture) frame

encadrer /ɑ̃kadʀe/ [**v1**] *vt* **1** to supervise ‹*staff*›; to train ‹*soldier*›
2 to flank ‹*person*›; to frame ‹*face, window*›; **~ de rouge** to outline [sth] in red
3 to frame ‹*picture*›

encaisser /ɑ̃kese/ [**v1**] *vt* **1** to cash ‹*cheque, sum of money*›
2 (fam) to take ‹*blow, defeat*›; **je ne peux pas**

🔑 key word

~ **ton frère** I can't stand your brother
IDIOM ~ **le coup** (fam) to take it all in one's stride

encart /ɑ̃kaʀ/ *m* insert; ~ **publicitaire** promotional insert

en-cas /ɑ̃kɑ/ *m inv* snack

encastrer /ɑ̃kastʀe/ [**v1**] **A** *vt* to build in ‹*oven, refrigerator*›; to fit ‹*sink, hotplate*›; **baignoire encastrée** sunken bath
B s'encastrer *v refl* (+ *v être*) to fit (**dans** into)

encaustique /ɑ̃kɔstik/ *f* wax polish

enceinte /ɑ̃sɛ̃t/ **A** *adj f* ‹*woman*› pregnant
B *f* **1** (**mur d'**)~ surrounding wall
2 (of prison, palace) compound; (of church) interior

encens /ɑ̃sɑ̃/ *m inv* incense

encenser /ɑ̃sɑ̃se/ [**v1**] *vt* to sing the praises of ‹*person*›; to acclaim ‹*work of art*›

encercler /ɑ̃sɛʀkle/ [**v1**] *vt* **1** to surround, to encircle
2 (with pen) to circle

enchaînement /ɑ̃ʃɛnmɑ̃/ *m* **1** (of events) chain
2 sequence
3 (in music, sport) transition

enchaîner /ɑ̃ʃene/ [**v1**] **A** *vt* to chain up ‹*person, animal*›; ~ **à** to chain to
B *vi* to go on; ~ **avec une nouvelle chanson** to move on to a new song
C s'enchaîner *v refl* (+ *v être*) ‹*shots, sequences in film*› to follow on

enchantement /ɑ̃ʃɑ̃tmɑ̃/ *m* enchantment, spell; **comme par** ~ as if by magic

enchanter /ɑ̃ʃɑ̃te/ [**v1**] *vt* **1** to delight; **ça ne m'enchante guère** it doesn't exactly thrill me; **enchanté (de faire votre connaissance)!** how do you do!
2 forêt enchantée enchanted forest

enchanteur, **-eresse** /ɑ̃ʃɑ̃tœʀ, tʀɛs/ **A** *adj* enchanting
B *mf* **1** enchanter/enchantress
2 (fig) charmer

enchère /ɑ̃ʃɛʀ/ **A** *f* bid
B enchères *fpl* **vente aux** ~**s** auction

enchérir /ɑ̃ʃeʀiʀ/ [**v3**] *vi* to bid; ~ **sur qn** to bid more than sb; ~ **sur une offre** to make a higher bid

enchevêtrement /ɑ̃ʃ(ə)vɛtʀəmɑ̃/ *m* (of threads) tangle; (of corridors, streets) labyrinth

enchevêtrer /ɑ̃ʃ(ə)vetʀe/ [**v1**] **A** *vt* **1** to tangle [sth] up ‹*threads*›
2 être enchevêtré ‹*sentence, plot*› to be muddled; ‹*case*› to be complicated
B s'enchevêtrer *v refl* (+ *v être*)
1 ‹*branches, threads*› to get tangled
2 ‹*phrases, ideas*› to become muddled

enclave /ɑ̃klav/ *f* enclave

enclencher /ɑ̃klɑ̃ʃe/ [**v1**] **A** *vt* **1** to set [sth] in motion ‹*process*›
2 to engage ‹*mechanism*›
B s'enclencher *v refl* (+ *v être*)
1 ‹*process*› to get under way
2 ‹*mechanism*› to engage

enclin, ~**e** /ɑ̃klɛ̃, in/ *adj* inclined (**à** to)

enclos /ɑ̃klo/ *m inv* (gen) enclosure; (for animals) pen

enclume /ɑ̃klym/ *f* (Tech, Anat) anvil

encoche /ɑ̃kɔʃ/ *f* notch

encoder /ɑ̃kɔde/ [**v1**] *vt* to encode

encodeur /ɑ̃kɔdœʀ/ *m* (Comput) encoder

encolure /ɑ̃kɔlyʀ/ *f* **1** (of garment) neckline
2 collar size
3 (of animal) neck

encombrant, ~**e** /ɑ̃kɔ̃bʀɑ̃, ɑ̃t/ *adj* **1** bulky; cumbersome
2 ‹*person, matter*› troublesome

encombre: **sans encombre** /sɑ̃zɑ̃kɔ̃bʀ/ *phr* without a hitch

encombré, ~**e** /ɑ̃kɔ̃bʀe/ *adj* ‹*road, sky*› congested (**de** with); ‹*room*› cluttered

encombrement /ɑ̃kɔ̃bʀəmɑ̃/ *m* **1** traffic congestion
2 (of switchboard) jamming
3 (of room) cluttering
4 (of furniture) bulk

encombrer /ɑ̃kɔ̃bʀe/ [**v1**] **A** *vt* **1** ‹*object, people*› to clutter up ‹*room*›; to obstruct ‹*road, path*›
2 to jam ‹*switchboard*›; to clutter up ‹*mind*›
B s'encombrer *v refl* (+ *v être*) **s'**~ **de** to burden oneself with; **s'**~ **l'esprit** to clutter up one's mind (**de** with)

encontre: **à l'encontre de** /alɑ̃kɔ̃tʀədə/ *phr* **1** counter to
2 against
3 toward(s)

encorder: **s'encorder** /ɑ̃kɔʀde/ [**v1**] *v refl* (+ *v être*) to rope up

encore /ɑ̃kɔʀ/ **A** *adv* **1** still; **il n'est** ~ **que midi** it's only midday; **tu en es** ~ **là?** haven't you got (BrE) *or* gotten (AmE) beyond that by now?; **qu'il soit impoli passe** ~**, mais...** the fact that he's rude is one thing, but...
2 pas ~ not yet; **il n'est pas** ~ **rentré** he hasn't come home yet; he still hasn't come home; **cela ne s'est** ~ **jamais vu** it has never been seen before
3 again; ~ **toi!** you again!; ~**!** encore!, more!; ~ **une fois** once more, once again; **qu'est-ce que j'ai** ~ **fait?** what have I done now?
4 more; **mange** ~ **un peu** have some more to eat; **c'est** ~ **mieux** it's even better
5 ~ **un gâteau?** another cake?; **pendant** ~ **trois jours** for another three days; **qu'est-ce qu'il te faut** ~**?** what more do you need?
6 ~ **faut-il qu'elle accepte** but she still has to accept; **si** ~ **il était généreux!** if he were at least generous!
7 only, just; **il y a** ~ **trois mois** only three months ago
B et encore *phr* if that; **c'est tout au plus mangeable, et** ~**!** it's only just edible, if that!
C encore que *phr* even though

encourageant, **~e** /ɑ̃kuʀaʒɑ̃, ɑ̃t/ *adj* encouraging

encouragement /ɑ̃kuʀaʒmɑ̃/ *m* encouragement

✎ **encourager** /ɑ̃kuʀaʒe/ [**v13**] *vt* **1** to encourage (**à faire** to do)
2 to cheer [sb] on

encourir /ɑ̃kuʀiʀ/ [**v26**] *vt* to incur

encrasser /ɑ̃kʀase/ [**v1**] *vt* **1** to clog [sth] (up) ‹*filter, artery*›; to make [sth] sooty ‹*chimney*›
2 to dirty; (Aut) to foul up ‹*spark plugs*›

e

encre /ɑ̃kʀ/ *f* ink
■ **~ de Chine** Indian (BrE) *or* India (AmE) ink; **~ sympathique** invisible ink
IDIOMS **cela a fait couler beaucoup d'~** a lot of ink has been spilled over this; **se faire un sang d'~** to be worried sick

encrier /ɑ̃kʀije/ *m* inkwell; ink pot

encroûter: **s'encroûter** /ɑ̃kʀute/ [**v1**] *v refl* (+ *v être*) (fam) to get in a rut

encyclopédie /ɑ̃siklɔpedi/ *f* encyclopedia

endetté, **~e** /ɑ̃dete/ *adj* in debt

endettement /ɑ̃dɛtmɑ̃/ *m* debt

endetter /ɑ̃dete/ [**v1**] **A** *vt* to put [sb] into debt
B **s'endetter** *v refl* (+ *v être*) to get into debt

endiablé, **~e** /ɑ̃djable/ *adj* ‹*rhythm*› furious

endiguer /ɑ̃dige/ [**v1**] *vt* to confine ‹*river*›; to contain ‹*demonstrators*›; to curb ‹*speculation*›

endimanché, **~e** /ɑ̃dimɑ̃ʃe/ *adj* in one's Sunday best

endive /ɑ̃div/ *f* chicory (BrE), endive (AmE)

endoctriner /ɑ̃dɔktʀine/ [**v1**] *vt* to indoctrinate

endolori, **~e** /ɑ̃dɔlɔʀi/ *adj* aching

endolorir /ɑ̃dɔlɔʀiʀ/ [**v3**] *vt* to make [sb/sth] ache

endommager /ɑ̃dɔmaʒe/ [**v13**] *vt* to damage

endormi, **~e** /ɑ̃dɔʀmi/ *adj* **1** ‹*person, animal*› sleeping, asleep
2 ‹*village, mind*› sleepy

✎ **endormir** /ɑ̃dɔʀmiʀ/ [**v30**] **A** *vt* **1** to send [sb] to sleep ‹*child*›; ‹*person, substance*› to put [sb] to sleep ‹*patient*›
2 (from boredom) ‹*person, lecture*› to send [sb] to sleep ‹*person*›
3 to dupe ‹*person, opinion, enemy*›
4 to allay ‹*suspicion*›; to numb ‹*faculties*›
B **s'endormir** *v refl* (+ *v être*) **1** to fall asleep
2 to get to sleep
3 (fig) to sit back

endossable /ɑ̃dosabl/ *adj* ‹*cheque*› endorsable

endosser /ɑ̃dose/ [**v1**] *vt* **1** to take on ‹*role, responsibility*›
2 to endorse ‹*cheque*›

✎ **endroit** /ɑ̃dʀwa/ **A** *m* **1** place; **par ~s** in places; **à quel ~?** where?
2 (of fabric) right side; **à l'~** (of object) the right way up; (of garment) the right way round (BrE) *or* around (AmE)
B **à l'endroit de** *phr* toward(s)

enduire /ɑ̃dɥiʀ/ [**v69**] **A** *vt* to coat (**de** with)
B **s'enduire** *v refl* (+ *v être*) **s'~ de** to put [sth] on

enduit /ɑ̃dɥi/ *m* **1** coating
2 filler

endurance /ɑ̃dyʀɑ̃s/ *f* **1** (of person) stamina; **~ à** resistance to
2 (of engine) endurance

endurant, **~e** /ɑ̃dyʀɑ̃, ɑ̃t/ *adj* ‹*person, athlete*› tough; ‹*engine, vehicle*› hard-wearing

endurcir /ɑ̃dyʀsiʀ/ [**v3**] **A** *vt* **1** ‹*sport, hard work*› to strengthen ‹*body, character*›
2 ‹*ordeal*› to harden ‹*person*›
B **s'endurcir** *v refl* (+ *v être*) **1** to become stronger
2 to become hardened

endurer /ɑ̃dyʀe/ [**v1**] *vt* **1** to endure; **faire ~ qch à qn** to put sb through sth
2 to put up with

énergétique /enɛʀʒetik/ *adj* **1** ‹*needs, resources*› energy
2 ‹*food*› high-calorie

✎ **énergie** /enɛʀʒi/ *f* energy; **faire des économies d'~** to save energy; **trouver des ~s douces** to find safe energy sources; **avec l'~ du désespoir** driven on by despair; **avec ~** ‹*work*› energetically; ‹*protest*› strongly
■ **~ éolienne** windpower; **~ nucléaire** nuclear power *ou* energy; **~ solaire** solar power; **~ de substitution** alternative energy

énergique /enɛʀʒik/ *adj* **1** ‹*person, gesture*› energetic; ‹*handshake*› vigorous; ‹*face, expression*› resolute
2 ‹*action*› tough; ‹*protest*› strong; ‹*refusal*› firm; ‹*intervention*› forceful

énergumène /enɛʀgymɛn/ *mf* oddball

énervant, **~e** /enɛʀvɑ̃, ɑ̃t/ *adj* irritating

énervé, **~e** /enɛʀve/ *adj* **1** irritated
2 nervous; ‹*child*› overexcited

énervement /enɛʀvəmɑ̃/ *m* **1** irritation
2 agitation; **elle pleura d'~** she was so on edge that she cried

énerver /enɛʀve/ [**v1**] **A** *vt* **1** to put [sb] on edge
2 **~ qn** to get on sb's nerves, to irritate sb
B **s'énerver** *v refl* (+ *v être*) to get worked up

✎ **enfance** /ɑ̃fɑ̃s/ *f* childhood; **la petite ~** early childhood
IDIOM **c'est l'~ de l'art** it's child's play

✎ **enfant** /ɑ̃fɑ̃/ *mf* child; infant; **être ~ unique**

✎ key word

to be an only child
■ ~ **de chœur** altar boy; **ce n'est pas un ~ de chœur** (fig) he's no angel

enfanter /ɑ̃fɑ̃te/ [**v1**] *vt* to give birth to

enfantillage /ɑ̃fɑ̃tijaʒ/ *m* childishness

enfantin, **~e** /ɑ̃fɑ̃tɛ̃, in/ *adj* **1** simple, easy
2 mode ~e children's fashion
3 childish

enfer /ɑ̃fɛʀ/ *m* Hell; (fig) hell; **aller à un train d'~** (fam) to go hell for leather (fam); **soirée d'~** (fam) hell of a party (fam)

enfermer /ɑ̃fɛʀme/ [**v1**] **A** *vt* **1** to shut [sth] in ‹*animal*›; to lock [sth] up ‹*money, jewellery*›; to lock [sb] up ‹*person*›; **elle est bonne à ~** (fam) she's stark raving mad (fam)
2 ~ qn dans un rôle to confine sb to a role; **~ qn dans une situation** to trap sb in a situation
B s'enfermer *v refl* (+ *v être*) **1** (gen) to lock oneself in; (accidentally) to get locked in; (in order to be alone) to shut oneself away; **ne reste pas enfermé toute la journée!** don't stay cooped up indoors all day!
2 s'~ dans to retreat into; **s'~ dans le mutisme** to remain obstinately silent

enfiévré, **~e** /ɑ̃fjevʀe/ *adj* ‹*imagination*› fevered; ‹*atmosphere*› feverish; ‹*speech*› fiery

enfilade /ɑ̃filad/ *f* (of traps) succession; (of houses, tables) row

enfiler /ɑ̃file/ [**v1**] **A** *vt* **1** to slip on
2 to thread ‹*piece of thread, needle*›
B s'enfiler *v refl* (+ *v être*) **1** (fam) to guzzle down
2 s'~ dans to take ‹*street*›

enfin /ɑ̃fɛ̃/ *adv* finally; lastly; **~ et surtout** last but not least; **~ seuls!** alone at last!; **mais ~, cessez de vous disputer!** for heaven's sake, stop arguing!; **il pleut tous les jours, ~ presque** it rains every day, well almost

enflammé, **~e** /ɑ̃flame/ *adj* **1** burning, on fire
2 ‹*person, declaration*› passionate; ‹*speech*› impassioned
3 (Med) ‹*throat, wound*› inflamed
4 ‹*sky*› ablaze

enflammer /ɑ̃flame/ [**v1**] **A** *vt* **1** to set fire to [sth]
2 to inflame ‹*public opinion, mind*›; to fire ‹*imagination*›; to fuel ‹*anger*›
B s'enflammer *v refl* (+ *v être*) **1** ‹*house, paper*› to go up in flames; ‹*wood*› to catch fire
2 ‹*eyes*› to blaze; ‹*imagination*› to be fired (**de** with, **à la vue de** by); ‹*country*› to explode; **s'~ pour qn** to become passionate about sb; **s'~ pour qch** to get carried away by sth

enfler /ɑ̃fle/ [**v1**] **A** *vt* to exaggerate ‹*story, event*›
B *vi* **1** ‹*part of body*› to swell (up); ‹*river, sea*› to swell
2 ‹*rumour, anger*› to spread
C s'enfler *v refl* (+ *v être*) ‹*anger*› to mount; ‹*voice*› to rise; ‹*rumour*› to grow

enfoncement /ɑ̃fɔ̃smɑ̃/ *m* **1** recess; dip
2 l'~ du pays dans la récession the country's slide into recession

enfoncer /ɑ̃fɔ̃se/ [**v12**] **A** *vt* **1** to push in ‹*cork, stake*›; **~ ses mains dans ses poches** to dig one's hands into one's pockets; **~ son doigt dans** to stick one's finger into; **~ un clou dans qch** to knock a nail into sth
2 to break down ‹*door*›; to break through ‹*enemy lines*›; **~ des portes ouvertes** to state the obvious
3 ne m'enfonce pas davantage don't rub it in
B s'enfoncer *v refl* (+ *v être*) **1 s'~ dans la neige** to sink in the snow; **s'~ dans l'erreur** to make error after error; **les piquets s'enfoncent facilement** the posts go in easily; **s'~ une épine dans le doigt** to get a thorn in one's finger; **s'~ dans la forêt** to go into the forest
2 (fam) to make things worse for oneself

enfouir /ɑ̃fwiʀ/ [**v3**] **A** *vt* **1** to bury
2 ~ qch dans un sac to shove sth into a bag
B s'enfouir *v refl* (+ *v être*) **s'~ sous les couvertures** to burrow under the blankets

enfourcher /ɑ̃fuʀʃe/ [**v1**] *vt* to mount ‹*horse*›; to get on ‹*motorbike*›

enfourner /ɑ̃fuʀne/ [**v1**] *vt* **1** to put [sth] in the oven
2 (fam) to stuff down ‹*food*›

enfreindre /ɑ̃fʀɛ̃dʀ/ [**v55**] *vt* to infringe

enfuir: **s'enfuir** /ɑ̃fɥiʀ/ [**v9**] *v refl* (+ *v être*) **1** to run away; ‹*bird*› to fly away
2 to escape

enfumer /ɑ̃fyme/ [**v1**] *vt* to fill [sth] with smoke; **tu nous enfumes avec tes cigares!** you're smoking us out with your cigars!

engagé, **~e** /ɑ̃gaʒe/ *mf* enlisted man/woman

engageant, **~e** /ɑ̃gaʒɑ̃, ɑ̃t/ *adj* ‹*person, manner*› welcoming; ‹*dish, place*› inviting

engagement /ɑ̃gaʒmɑ̃/ *m* **1** commitment; **prendre l'~ de faire** to undertake to do
2 involvement
3 (Mil) enlistment

engager /ɑ̃gaʒe/ [**v13**] **A** *vt* **1** to hire ‹*staff*›; to enlist ‹*soldier*›; to engage ‹*artist*›
2 to begin ‹*process, reform policy*›; **nous avons engagé la conversation** we struck up a conversation
3 to commit, to bind ‹*person*›
4 to stake ‹*honour*›; **~ sa parole** to give one's word
5 ~ qch dans to put sth in
6 to lay out ‹*capital*›
7 ~ qn à faire to urge sb to do
8 (Sport) **~ qn dans une compétition** to enter sb for a competition
9 to pawn ‹*valuables*›

B **s'engager** *v refl* (+ *v être*) **1** to promise (**à faire** to do); **s'~ vis-à-vis de qn** to make a commitment to sb
2 **s'~ dans un projet** to embark on a project
3 to get involved
4 **s'~ sur une route** to go into a road
5 ‹*lawsuit*› to begin
6 **s'~ dans l'armée** to join the army

engelure /ɑ̃ʒlyʀ/ *f* chilblain

engendrer /ɑ̃ʒɑ̃dʀe/ [**v1**] *vt* **1** to engender
2 ‹*woman*› to give birth to; ‹*man*› to father

engin /ɑ̃ʒɛ̃/ *m* **1** device
2 vehicle
3 piece of equipment

englober /ɑ̃glɔbe/ [**v1**] *vt* to include

engloutir /ɑ̃glutiʀ/ [**v3**] *vt* **1** ‹*sea, storm, fog*› to engulf, to swallow up
2 (fam) to gulp [sth] down
3 ‹*person*› to squander ‹*money*›

engoncé, **~e** /ɑ̃gɔ̃se/ *adj* **il était ~ dans une veste trop étroite** he was squeezed into a tight jacket

engorger /ɑ̃gɔʀʒe/ [**v13**] *vt* **1** to block (up) ‹*pipes, drains*›
2 to clog up ‹*roads*›

engouement /ɑ̃gumɑ̃/ *m* (for thing, activity) passion; (for person) infatuation

engouer: **s'engouer** /ɑ̃gwe/ [**v1**] *v refl* (+ *v être*) **s'~ de** to develop a passion for

engouffrer: **s'engouffrer** /ɑ̃gufʀe/ [**v1**] *v refl* (+ *v être*) (into a room) to rush; (into a taxi) to dive

engourdi, **~e** /ɑ̃guʀdi/ *adj* ‹*limb, body*› numb (**par, de** with); ‹*person*› drowsy; ‹*town*› sleepy; ‹*mind*› dull(ed)

engourdir: **s'engourdir** /ɑ̃guʀdiʀ/ [**v3**] *v refl* (+ *v être*) ‹*limb*› to go numb; ‹*mind*› to grow dull

engourdissement /ɑ̃guʀdismɑ̃/ *m*
1 (physical) numbness; (mental) drowsiness
2 (of body) numbing; (of mind) dulling

engrais /ɑ̃gʀɛ/ *m inv* manure; fertilizer

engraisser /ɑ̃gʀese/ [**v1**] **A** *vt* **1** to fatten ‹*cattle*›
2 to fertilize ‹*soil*›
B *vi* to get fat
C **s'engraisser** *v refl* (+ *v être*) (fam) **s'~ (sur le dos de qn)** to grow fat (off sb's back) (fam)

engranger /ɑ̃gʀɑ̃ʒe/ [**v13**] *vt* to gather in ‹*harvest*›; (fig) to store; to store up

engrenage /ɑ̃gʀənaʒ/ *m* **1** gears
2 (fig) (of violence) spiral

engueuler /ɑ̃gœle/ (pop) [**v1**] **A** *vt* to tell [sb] off; to give [sb] an earful (fam)
B **s'engueuler** *v refl* (+ *v être*) to have a row

enhardir: **s'enhardir** /ɑ̃aʀdiʀ/ [**v3**] *v refl* (+ *v être*) to become bolder

énième /ɛnjɛm/ *adj* umpteenth

énigmatique /enigmatik/ *adj* enigmatic

énigme /enigm/ *f* **1** enigma, mystery
2 riddle; **parler par ~s** to speak in riddles

enivrant, **~e** /ɑ̃nivʀɑ̃, ɑ̃t/ *adj* intoxicating

enivrement /ɑ̃nivʀəmɑ̃/ *m* intoxication

enivrer /ɑ̃nivʀe/ [**v1**] **A** *vt* **1** to make [sb] drunk
2 **~ qn** ‹*success*› to go to sb's head
B **s'enivrer** *v refl* (+ *v être*) to get drunk

enjambée /ɑ̃ʒɑ̃be/ *f* stride; **avancer/s'éloigner à grandes ~s** to stride forward/off

enjamber /ɑ̃ʒɑ̃be/ [**v1**] *vt* to step over ‹*obstacle*›

enjeu, *pl* **~x** /ɑ̃ʒø/ *m* (Games) stake; **analyser l'~ des élections** to analyse (BrE) what is at stake in the elections

enjoindre /ɑ̃ʒwɛ̃dʀ/ [**v56**] *vt* **~ à qn de faire** to enjoin sb to do

enjôler /ɑ̃ʒole/ [**v1**] *vt* to beguile

enjoliver /ɑ̃ʒɔlive/ [**v1**] *vt* to embellish

enjoliveur /ɑ̃ʒɔlivœʀ/ *m* hubcap

enjoué, **~e** /ɑ̃ʒwe/ *adj* ‹*character*› cheerful; ‹*tone*› light-hearted

enlacer /ɑ̃lase/ [**v12**] **A** *vt* to embrace; ‹*snake*› to wrap itself around ‹*prey*›
B **s'enlacer** *v refl* (+ *v être*) ‹*people*› to embrace; ‹*body*› to intertwine

enlaidir /ɑ̃lediʀ/ [**v3**] *vt* to spoil ‹*landscape*›; to make [sb] look ugly ‹*person*›

enlevé, **~e** /ɑ̃lve/ *adj* lively

enlèvement /ɑ̃lɛvmɑ̃/ *m* kidnapping (BrE), abduction

⚷ **enlever** /ɑ̃lve/ [**v16**] **A** *vt* **1** to take [sth] away, to remove ‹*piece of furniture, book*›; to take [sth] down ‹*curtains, pictures*›; to take [sth] off ‹*garment*›; to move, to remove ‹*vehicle*›
2 to remove ‹*stain, paint*›
3 to take ‹*person, object*› away; **~ à qn l'envie de partir** to put sb off going
4 to kidnap; to carry [sb] off
5 to carry [sth] off ‹*trophy*›; to capture ‹*market*›
B **s'enlever** *v refl* (+ *v être*) **1** ‹*varnish*› to come off; ‹*stain*› to come out
2 ‹*part, section*› to be detachable
3 (fam) **enlève-toi de là** get off (fam)

enlisement /ɑ̃lizmɑ̃/ *m* sinking; (of negotiations) stalemate; (of movement) collapse

enliser /ɑ̃lize/ [**v1**] **A** *vt* to get [sth] stuck
B **s'enliser** *v refl* (+ *v être*) **1** ‹*boat, vehicle*› to get stuck
2 ‹*inquiry, negotiations*› to drag on

enluminure /ɑ̃lyminyʀ/ *f* illumination

enneigé, **~e** /ɑ̃neʒe/ *adj* ‹*summit*› snowy; ‹*road*› covered in snow

enneigement /ɑ̃nɛʒmɑ̃/ *m* **bulletin d'~** snow report

⚷ **ennemi**, **~e** /ɛnmi/ **A** *adj* **1** (Mil) enemy
2 (gen) hostile

⚷ key word

B *mf* enemy
C *m* (Mil) enemy; **passer à l'~** to go over to the enemy

ennui /ɑ̃nɥi/ *m* **1** boredom; **tromper l'~** to escape from boredom; **quel ~!** what a bore!
2 problem; **avoir des ~s** to have problems; **j'ai des ~s avec la police** I'm in trouble with the police; **s'attirer des ~s** to get into trouble

ennuyé, **~e** /ɑ̃nɥije/ *adj* **1** bored
2 embarrassed; **j'étais très ~ de laisser les enfants seuls** I felt awful about leaving the children on their own
3 j'aurais été très ~ si je n'avais pas eu la clé I would have been in real trouble if I hadn't had the key

ennuyer /ɑ̃nɥije/ [**v22**] **A** *vt* **1** to bore
2 to bother; **si ça ne vous ennuie pas trop** if you don't mind
3 to annoy
4 to hassle (fam)
B s'ennuyer *v refl* (+ *v être*) **1** to be bored; to get bored
2 s'~ de to miss ‹*friend*›

ennuyeux, **-euse** /ɑ̃nɥijø, øz/ *adj* **1** boring
2 tedious
3 annoying
IDIOM **être ~ comme la pluie** to be as dull as ditchwater

énoncé /enɔ̃se/ *m* **1** (of exam subject) wording (**de** of); **l'~ d'une théorie** the exposition of a theory
2 (of fact) statement (**de** of)

énoncer /enɔ̃se/ [**v12**] *vt* to pronounce ‹*verdict*›; to set out, to state ‹*facts*›; to expound ‹*theory*›

enorgueillir: **s'enorgueillir** /ɑ̃nɔʀgœjiʀ/ [**v3**] *v refl* (+ *v être*) to pride oneself (**de** on)

énorme /enɔʀm/ *adj* **1** ‹*object, person*› huge, enormous
2 ‹*success, effort*› tremendous; ‹*mistake*› terrible; ‹*lie*› outrageous

énormément /enɔʀmemɑ̃/ *adv* a tremendous amount; a great deal; **~ de temps** a tremendous amount of time; **ça m'a ~ plu** I liked it immensely

énormité /enɔʀmite/ *f* **1** (of figure, size) hugeness; (of lie) enormity
2 outrageous remark

enquérir: **s'enquérir** /ɑ̃keʀiʀ/ [**v35**] *v refl* (+ *v être*) **s'~ de** to enquire about

enquête /ɑ̃kɛt/ *f* **1** (Law) inquiry, investigation; (into a death) inquest; **~ de police** police investigation
2 (by journalist) investigation
3 (by sociologist) survey

enquêter /ɑ̃kete/ [**v1**] *vi* ‹*policeman*› to carry out an investigation; ‹*expert*› to hold an inquiry

enquêteur, **-trice** /ɑ̃ketœʀ, tʀis/ *mf*
1 investigating officer
2 pollster
3 interviewer

enquiquinant, **~e** /ɑ̃kikinɑ̃, ɑ̃t/ *adj* (fam) annoying; boring

enquiquiner /ɑ̃kikine/ [**v1**] **A** *vt* **~ qn** to get on sb's nerves; to pester sb
B s'enquiquiner *v refl* (+ *v être*) **s'~ à faire** to go to the trouble of doing

enraciner: **s'enraciner** /ɑ̃ʀasine/ [**v1**] *v refl* (+ *v être*) **1** to take root
2 (fig) ‹*person*› to put down roots; ‹*custom, idea*› to take root

enragé, **~e** /ɑ̃ʀaʒe/ *adj* **1** fanatical
2 enraged
3 (Med) rabid
IDIOM **manger de la vache ~e** (fam) to go through hard times

enrageant, **~e** /ɑ̃ʀaʒɑ̃, ɑ̃t/ *adj* infuriating

enrager /ɑ̃ʀaʒe/ [**v13**] *vi* to be furious; **faire ~ qn** to tease sb

enrayer /ɑ̃ʀeje/ [**v21**] **A** *vt* **1** to check ‹*epidemic, development*›; to curb ‹*inflation*›; to stop [sth] escalating ‹*crisis*›
2 to jam ‹*mechanism, gun*›
B s'enrayer *v refl* (+ *v être*) to get jammed

enregistrement /ɑ̃ʀəʒistʀəmɑ̃/ *m* **1** (of music) recording
2 (of data) recording; (of order) taking down
3 (of baggage) check-in

enregistrer /ɑ̃ʀəʒistʀe/ [**v1**] *vt* **1** to record ‹*cassette, album*›
2 to note ‹*progress, failure*›; to record ‹*rise, drop*›
3 to make a record of ‹*expenses*›; to take ‹*order*›; to record ‹*data*›; to set ‹*record*›
4 to register ‹*birth, claim*›
5 to check in ‹*baggage*›
6 c'est enregistré, j'enregistre (fam) I've made a mental note of it

enregistreur DVD /ɑ̃ʀəʒistʀœʀ devede/ *m* DVD writer

enrhumer: **s'enrhumer** /ɑ̃ʀyme/ [**v1**] *v refl* (+ *v être*) to catch a cold

enrichir /ɑ̃ʀiʃiʀ/ [**v3**] **A** *vt* **1** to make [sb] rich ‹*person*›; to bring wealth to ‹*country*›
2 to enrich, to enhance ‹*collection, book*›
B s'enrichir *v refl* (+ *v être*) **1** ‹*person*› to become *or* grow rich
2 to be enriched

enrichissant, **~e** /ɑ̃ʀiʃisɑ̃, ɑ̃t/ *adj* ‹*experience*› rewarding; ‹*relationship*› fulfilling

enrober /ɑ̃ʀɔbe/ [**v1**] *vt* **1** to coat
2 (fig) to wrap up ‹*news*›

enrôlement /ɑ̃ʀolmɑ̃/ *m* (in the army) enlistment; (in political party) enrolment (BrE)

enrôler /ɑ̃ʀole/ [**v1**] **A** *vt* to recruit
B s'enrôler *v refl* (+ *v être*) to enlist

enrouer: **s'enrouer** /ɑ̃ʀwe/ [**v1**] *v refl* (+ *v être*) ‹*voice*› to go hoarse; ‹*person*› to make oneself hoarse; **d'une voix enrouée** hoarsely

enrouler /ɑ̃ʀule/ [**v1**] **A** *vt* **1** to wind
2 to wrap
B s'enrouler *v refl* (+ *v être*) **1** ‹*thread,*

tape› to wind
2 ‹*person, animal*› to curl up

ENS /œnɛs/ *f*: *abbr* ▸ **école**

ensabler: **s'ensabler** /ɑ̃sɑble/ [**v1**] *v refl* (+ *v être*) ‹*vehicle*› to get stuck in the sand; ‹*boat*› to get stranded (*on a sandbank*)

ensanglanter /ɑ̃sɑ̃glɑ̃te/ [**v1**] *vt* **1** to cover [sth] with blood
2 to bring bloodshed to ‹*country*›

✎ **enseignant**, **~e** /ɑ̃sɛɲɑ̃, ɑ̃t/ **A** *adj* **corps ~** teaching profession
B *mf* (Sch) teacher; (at university) lecturer

enseigne /ɑ̃sɛɲ/ *f* **1** (shop) sign; **~ lumineuse** neon sign
2 (Mil, Naut) ensign
(IDIOM) **nous sommes logés à la même ~** we are in the same boat

✎ **enseignement** /ɑ̃sɛɲmɑ̃/ *m* **1** education; **l'~ supérieur** higher education
2 teaching; **méthodes d'~** teaching methods
3 lesson
■ **~ par correspondance** distance learning; **~ professionnel** vocational training; **~ religieux** religious instruction

✎ **enseigner** /ɑ̃seɲe/ [**v1**] *vt* to teach

✎ **ensemble** /ɑ̃sɑ̃bl/ **A** *adv* **1** together
2 at the same time
B *m* **1** group; **un ~ de personnes** a group of people; **une vue d'~** an overall view; **plan d'~ d'une ville** general plan of a town; **dans l'~** by and large; **dans l'~ de** throughout; **dans son** *or* **leur ~** as a whole
2 (of luggage, measures) set
3 unity, cohesion; **former un bel ~** to form a harmonious whole
4 (of gestures) coordination; (of sounds) unison; **un mouvement d'~** a coordinated movement
5 (in mathematics) set
6 (Mus) ensemble
7 (of offices) complex; **~ hôtelier** hotel complex; **~ industriel** industrial estate (BrE) *or* park (AmE)
8 (set of clothes) outfit; suit

ensevelir /ɑ̃səvəliʀ/ [**v3**] *vt* to bury

ensoleillé, **~e** /ɑ̃sɔleje/ *adj* sunny

ensommeillé, **~e** /ɑ̃sɔmeje/ *adj* sleepy

ensorcelé, **~e** /ɑ̃sɔʀsəle/ *adj* enchanted

ensorceler /ɑ̃sɔʀsəle/ [**v19**] *vt* **1** to cast *or* to put a spell on
2 to bewitch, to enchant

ensorceleur, **-euse** /ɑ̃sɔʀsəlœʀ, øz/ *mf* charmer

✎ **ensuite** /ɑ̃sɥit/ *adv* **1** then; after; next; **très bien, mais ~?** fine, but then what?; **il ne me l'a dit qu'~** he only told me later
2 secondly

ensuivre: **s'ensuivre** /ɑ̃sɥivʀ/ [**v19**] *v refl* (+ *v être*) to follow, to ensue

entacher /ɑ̃taʃe/ [**v1**] *vt* to mar ‹*relations*›

entaille /ɑ̃taj/ *f* **1** cut; gash
2 notch

entailler /ɑ̃taje/ [**v1**] **A** *vt* to cut into; (deeply) to make a gash in
B **s'entailler** *v refl* (+ *v être*) **s'~ le doigt** to cut one's finger, to gash one's finger

entame /ɑ̃tam/ *f* **1** (Culin) first slice
2 (in cards) lead

entamer /ɑ̃tame/ [**v1**] *vt* **1** to start ‹*day, activity*›; to initiate ‹*procedure*›; to open ‹*negotiations*›
2 to undermine ‹*credibility*›
3 to eat into ‹*savings*›
4 to cut into ‹*loaf, roast*›; to open ‹*bottle, jar*›; to start eating ‹*dessert*›
5 to cut into ‹*skin, wood*›
6 to eat into ‹*metal*›

entartrer /ɑ̃taʀtʀe/ [**v1**] **A** *vt* to fur up (BrE), to scale up
B **s'entartrer** *v refl* (+ *v être*) to scale up; ‹*teeth*› to be covered in tartar

entassement /ɑ̃tasmɑ̃/ *m* **1** piling up; cramming together
2 pile; heap

entasser /ɑ̃tase/ [**v1**] **A** *vt* **1** to pile ‹*books, clothes*›
2 to hoard ‹*money, old things*›
3 to pack, to cram ‹*people, objects*› (**dans** into)
B **s'entasser** *v refl* (+ *v être*) ‹*objects*› to pile up; ‹*people*› to squeeze (**dans** into, **sur** onto)

entendement /ɑ̃tɑ̃dmɑ̃/ *m* understanding; **cela dépasse l'~** it's beyond belief

✎ **entendre** /ɑ̃tɑ̃dʀ/ [**v6**] **A** *vt* **1** to hear ‹*noise, word*›; **faire ~ un cri** to give a cry; **je n'en ai jamais entendu parler** I've never heard of it; **on n'entend plus parler de lui** his name is not mentioned any more
2 ‹*judge*› to hear ‹*witness*›; **à t'~, tout va bien** according to you, everything is fine; **elle ne veut rien ~** she won't listen
3 to understand; **il agit comme il l'entend** he does as he likes; **elle a laissé ~ que** she intimated that; **ils ne l'entendent pas de cette oreille** they don't see it that way
4 to mean; **qu'entends-tu par là?** what do you mean by that?
5 **~ faire** to intend doing; **j'entends qu'on fasse ce que je dis** I expect people to do what I say
B **s'entendre** *v refl* (+ *v être*) **1** to get on *or* along
2 to agree (**sur** on)
3 ‹*noise*› to be heard
4 to hear oneself; ‹*two or more people*› to hear each other
5 **phrase qui peut s'~ de plusieurs façons** sentence which can be understood in several ways

entendu, **~e** /ɑ̃tɑ̃dy/ **A** *pp* ▸ **entendre**
B *pp adj* **1** **'tu viens demain?'—'~!'** 'will you come tomorrow?'—'OK!' (fam)

✎ key word

2 d'un air ~ with a knowing look
C bien entendu *phr* of course

entente /ɑ̃tɑ̃t/ *f* **1** harmony; **vivre en bonne ~ avec qn** to be on good terms with sb
2 understanding
3 arrangement

entériner /ɑ̃teʀine/ [**v1**] *vt* **1** to ratify
2 to confirm

enterré, **~e** /ɑ̃teʀe/ *adj* buried; **mort et ~** dead and buried

enterrement /ɑ̃tɛʀmɑ̃/ *m* **1** burial
2 funeral; **faire une tête d'~** (fam) to look gloomy

enterrer /ɑ̃teʀe/ [**v1**] *vt* to bury
IDIOM **~ sa vie de garçon** to have a stag party

entêtant, **~e** /ɑ̃tetɑ̃, ɑ̃t/ *adj* ‹*aroma*› heady; ‹*music*› insistent

en-tête, *pl* **~s** /ɑ̃tɛt/ *m* heading

entêtement /ɑ̃tɛtmɑ̃/ *m* stubbornness

entêter: **s'entêter** /ɑ̃tete/ [**v1**] *v refl* (+ *v être*) **1** to be stubborn
2 to persist

enthousiasme /ɑ̃tuzjasm/ *m* enthusiasm

enthousiasmer /ɑ̃tuzjasme/ [**v1**] *vt* to fill [sb] with enthusiasm

enthousiaste /ɑ̃tuzjast/ *adj* enthusiastic

enticher: **s'enticher** /ɑ̃tiʃe/ [**v1**] *v refl* (+ *v être*) **s'~ de** to become infatuated with ‹*person*›

✓ **entier**, **-ière** /ɑ̃tje, ɛʀ/ **A** *adj* **1** whole; **manger un pain ~** to eat a whole loaf; **des heures entières** for hours on end; **lait ~** full-fat milk
2 ‹*success, satisfaction*› complete; **avoir l'entière responsabilité de qch** to have full responsibility for sth
3 ‹*object, reputation*› intact; **le mystère reste ~** the mystery remains unsolved
4 avoir un caractère ~ to be thoroughgoing
B *m* (in mathematics) integer

✓ **entièrement** /ɑ̃tjɛʀmɑ̃/ *adv* entirely, completely; **~ équipé** fully equipped

entonner /ɑ̃tɔne/ [**v1**] *vt* to start singing ‹*song*›

entonnoir /ɑ̃tɔnwaʀ/ *m* **1** funnel
2 crater

entorse /ɑ̃tɔʀs/ *f* **1** (Med) sprain
2 (fig) infringement (**à** of); **faire une ~ au règlement** to bend the rules

entortiller /ɑ̃tɔʀtije/ [**v1**] **A** *vt* **1** to wind (**autour de qch** round (BrE) sth)
2 to tangle up
B s'entortiller *v refl* (+ *v être*) ‹*thread, wool*› to get entangled (**dans** in)

entourage /ɑ̃tuʀaʒ/ *m* **1** family circle
2 circle (of friends); **on dit dans son ~ que** people close to him/her say that

entouré, **~e** /ɑ̃tuʀe/ **A** *pp* ▶ **entourer**
B *adj* **1** ‹*person*› popular
2 nos patients sont très ~s our patients are well looked after

✓ **entourer** /ɑ̃tuʀe/ [**v1**] **A** *vt* **1** to surround
2 ~ qch de qch to put sth around sth; **~ qch de mystère** to shroud sth in mystery
3 to rally round (BrE) *or* around (AmE) ‹*sick person*›
B s'entourer *v refl* (+ *v être*) **s'~ d'objets** to surround oneself with things; **s'~ de précautions** to take every possible precaution

entracte /ɑ̃tʀakt/ *m* intermission

entraider: **s'entraider** /ɑ̃tʀede/ [**v1**] *v refl* (+ *v être*) to help each other *or* one another

entrailles /ɑ̃tʀɑj/ *fpl* (of animal) innards

entrain /ɑ̃tʀɛ̃/ *m* **1** (of person) spirit, go (BrE) (fam); **retrouver son ~** to cheer up
2 (of party, discussion) liveliness; **sans ~** half-hearted

entraînant, **~e** /ɑ̃tʀɛnɑ̃, ɑ̃t/ *adj* lively

entraînement /ɑ̃tʀɛnmɑ̃/ *m* **1** training, coaching
2 practice (BrE); **avoir de l'~** to be highly trained; **l'~ à la lecture** reading practice (BrE)
3 training session

✓ **entraîner** /ɑ̃tʀene/ [**v1**] **A** *vt* **1** to lead to; **une panne a entraîné l'arrêt de la production** a breakdown brought production to a standstill
2 ‹*river, current*› to carry [sb/sth] away ‹*swimmer, boat*›; **il a entraîné qn/qch dans sa chute** he dragged sb/sth down with him
3 to take, to lead ‹*person*›; **~ qn à faire** ‹*person*› to make sb do; ‹*circumstances*› to lead sb to do
4 (fig) to carry [sb] away ‹*person, group*›
5 to train, to coach ‹*athlete, team*› (**à** for); to train ‹*horse, soldier*› (**à** for)
6 ‹*engine, piston*› to drive ‹*machine, wheel, turbine*›
B s'entraîner *v refl* (+ *v être*) **1** ‹*player, soldiers*› to train
2 to prepare oneself

entraîneur /ɑ̃tʀɛnœʀ/ *m* (of athlete) coach

entrave /ɑ̃tʀav/ *f* hindrance; (on freedom) restriction

entraver /ɑ̃tʀave/ [**v1**] *vt* to hinder, to impede

✓ **entre** /ɑ̃tʀ/ *prep*

> You will find translations for expressions such as *entre parenthèses*, *entre nous* etc, at the entries **parenthèse**, **nous** etc.

1 between; **~ midi et deux** at lunchtime; **'doux ou très épicé?'—'~ les deux'** 'mild or very spicy?'—'in between'; **~ son travail et l'informatique, il n'a pas le temps de sortir** what with work and his computer he doesn't have time to go out
2 among; **organiser une soirée ~ amis** to organize a party among friends; **chacune d'~ elles** each of them; **~ hommes** as one man to another; **~ nous** between you and me; **nous sommes ~ nous** there's just the two of us; we're among friends; **les enfants**

sont souvent cruels ~ eux children are often cruel to each other

entrebâillement /ɑ̃tʀəbɑjmɑ̃/ *m* (in door, shutter, window) gap (**de** in)

entrebâiller /ɑ̃tʀəbɑje/ [**v1**] *vt* to half-open

entrechoquer /ɑ̃tʀəʃɔke/ [**v1**] **A** *vt* to clatter ‹*saucepans*›; to clink ‹*glasses*›
B s'entrechoquer *v refl* (+ *v être*)
1 ‹*glasses*› to clink
2 ‹*ideas, interests*› to clash

entrecôte /ɑ̃tʀəkot/ *f* **1** entrecôte (steak)
2 rib steak

entrecouper /ɑ̃tʀəkupe/ [**v1**] **A** *vt* to punctuate
B s'entrecouper *v refl* (+ *v être*) to intersect

entrecroiser /ɑ̃tʀəkʀwaze/ [**v1**] *vt* to intertwine

entre-deux-guerres /ɑ̃tʀədøgɛʀ/ *m or f inv* interwar period

✓ **entrée** /ɑ̃tʀe/ *f* **1** entrance (**de** to); **se retrouver à l'~ du bureau** to meet outside the office
2 (on motorway) (entry) slip road (BrE), on-ramp (AmE)
3 (in house) hall; (in hotel) lobby; (door) entry
4 l'~ dans la récession the beginning of the recession; **d'~ (de jeu)** from the very start
5 l'~ d'un pays dans une organisation the entry of a country into an organization; **'~ libre'** 'admission free'; **'~ interdite'** 'no entry'
6 ticket; **deux ~s gratuites** two free tickets
7 (of person) entrance; **réussir son ~** ‹*actor*› to enter on cue
8 (Culin) starter
9 (in bookkeeping) **~s** receipts
■ **~ des artistes** stage door; **~ en matière** introduction

entrée-sortie, *pl* **entrées-sorties** /ɑ̃tʀesɔʀti/ *f* (Comput) input-output

entrefaites: **sur ces entrefaites** /syʀsezɑ̃tʀəfɛt/ *phr* at that moment, just then

entrefilet /ɑ̃tʀəfilɛ/ *m* brief article

entrejambes /ɑ̃tʀəʒɑ̃b/ *m inv* crotch

entrelacer /ɑ̃tʀəlase/ [**v12**] *vt*, **s'entrelacer** *v refl* (+ *v être*) to intertwine, to interlace

entremêler: **s'entremêler** /ɑ̃tʀəmele/ [**v1**] *v refl* (+ *v être*) (gen) to be mixed; ‹*hair, branches*› to get tangled

entremets /ɑ̃tʀəmɛ/ *m* dessert

entremetteur, **-euse** /ɑ̃tʀəmɛtœʀ, øz/ *mf*
1 matchmaker
2 go-between

entremise /ɑ̃tʀəmiz/ *f* intervention; **il l'a su par mon ~** he heard of it through me

entreposer /ɑ̃tʀəpoze/ [**v1**] *vt* to store

entrepôt /ɑ̃tʀəpo/ *m* **1** warehouse
2 stockroom

entreprenant, **~e** /ɑ̃tʀəpʀənɑ̃, ɑ̃t/ *adj* enterprising

✓ **entreprendre** /ɑ̃tʀəpʀɑ̃dʀ/ [**v52**] *vt* **1** to start, to undertake; **~ de faire** to set about doing; to undertake to do
2 ~ qn sur un sujet to engage sb in conversation about sth

entrepreneur, **-euse** /ɑ̃tʀəpʀənœʀ, øz/ *mf*
1 builder
2 contractor
3 owner-manager (*of a small firm*)

✓ **entreprise** /ɑ̃tʀəpʀiz/ *f* **1** firm, business; **petites et moyennes ~s** small and medium-sized businesses
2 business, industry; **la libre ~** free enterprise
3 undertaking; venture
■ **~ unipersonnelle à responsabilité limitée, EURL** company owned by a sole proprietor

✓ **entrer** /ɑ̃tʀe/ [**v1**] **A** *vt* (+ *v avoir*) **1** to bring [sth] in; to take [sth] in
2 (in computing) to enter
B *vi* (+ *v être*) **1** to get in, to enter; to go in; to come in; **fais-la ~** show her in; **'défense d'~'** (on door) 'no entry'; (on gate) 'no trespassing'; **je ne fais qu'~ et sortir** I can only stay a minute
2 to fit (in); **je n'arrive pas à faire ~ la pièce dans la fente** I can't get the coin into the slot
3 ~ dans to enter ‹*period, debate*›; to join ‹*company, army, party*›; **~ à** to enter ‹*school, charts*›; to get into ‹*university*›; **~ en** to enter into ‹*negotiations*›; **~ dans la vie de qn** to come into sb's life; **~ dans la légende** ‹*person*› to become a legend; ‹*fact*› to become legendary; **cela n'entre pas dans mes attributions** it's not part of my duties; **~ dans une colère noire** to fly into a blind rage

entresol /ɑ̃tʀəsɔl/ *m* mezzanine

entre-temps /ɑ̃tʀətɑ̃/ *adv* meanwhile

✓ **entretenir** /ɑ̃tʀətniʀ/ [**v36**] **A** *vt* **1** to look after ‹*garment, house*›; to maintain ‹*road*›; **~ sa forme** to keep in shape
2 to support ‹*family*›; to keep ‹*mistress*›
3 to keep [sth] going ‹*conversation, fire*›; to keep [sth] alive ‹*friendship*›
4 ~ qn de qch to speak to sb about sth
B s'entretenir *v refl* (+ *v être*) **1 s'~ de qch** to discuss sth
2 s'~ facilement ‹*house, fabric*› to be easy to look after

✓ **entretien** /ɑ̃tʀətjɛ̃/ *m* **1** (of house) upkeep; (of car, road) maintenance; (of plant, skin) care
2 cleaning
3 (gen) discussion; (for a job) interview; (in newspaper) interview

entre-tuer: **s'entre-tuer** /ɑ̃tʀətɥe/ [**v1**] *v refl* (+ *v être*) to kill each other

entrevoir /ɑ̃tʀəvwaʀ/ [**v46**] *vt* **1** to catch a glimpse of; (indistinctly) to make out

---

✓ key word

2 to glimpse ‹*truth, solution*›
3 to foresee ‹*difficulty*›; **laisser ~ qch** ‹*result, sign*› to point to sth

entrevue /ɑ̃tʀəvy/ *f* meeting; (Pol) talks

entrouvrir /ɑ̃tʀuvʀiʀ/ [**v32**] **A** *vt* to open [sth] a little
B s'entrouvrir *v refl* (+ *v être*) (gen) ‹*door, country*› to half-open; ‹*lips*› to part

énumération /enymeʀasjɔ̃/ *f* **1** listing
2 catalogue (BrE)

énumérer /enymeʀe/ [**v14**] *vt* to enumerate

envahir /ɑ̃vaiʀ/ [**v3**] *vt* **1** ‹*troops, crowd*› to invade; ‹*animal*› to overrun
2 to flood ‹*market*›

envahissant, ~e /ɑ̃vaisɑ̃, ɑ̃t/ *adj*
1 intrusive
2 pervasive; invasive

envahisseur /ɑ̃vaisœʀ/ *m* invader

enveloppe /ɑ̃vlɔp/ *f* **1** (for letter) envelope; **sous ~** in an envelope
2 (for parcel) wrapping; (of grains) husk; (of peas, beans) pod
■ **~ budgétaire** budget

enveloppé, ~e /ɑ̃vlɔpe/ *adj* ‹*person*› plump

envelopper /ɑ̃vlɔpe/ [**v1**] **A** *vt* **1** ‹*person*› to wrap [sb/sth] (up); ‹*sheet*› to cover
2 ‹*fog, silence*› to envelop; ‹*mystery*› to surround
B s'envelopper *v refl* (+ *v être*) to wrap oneself (up)

envenimer /ɑ̃vnime/ [**v1**] **A** *vt* to inflame ‹*debate*›; to aggravate ‹*situation*›
B s'envenimer *v refl* (+ *v être*) ‹*dispute*› to worsen; ‹*situation*› to turn ugly

envergure /ɑ̃vɛʀgyʀ/ *f* **1** (of plane) wingspan
2 (fig) (of person) stature; (of project) scale; **un projet d'~** a substantial project; **sans ~** ‹*project*› limited; ‹*person*› of no account

envers¹ /ɑ̃vɛʀ/ *prep* toward(s), to
IDIOM **~ et contre tous/tout** in spite of everyone/everything

envers² /ɑ̃vɛʀ/ **A** *m inv* (of sheet of paper) back; (of piece of cloth) wrong side; (of garment) inside; (of coin) reverse
B à l'envers *phr* **1** the wrong way
2 upside down
3 inside out
4 back to front
5 the wrong way round (BrE) *or* around (AmE); **mettre ses chaussures à l'~** to put one's shoes on the wrong feet
6 passer un film à l'~ to run a film backward(s)

envie /ɑ̃vi/ *f* **1** (gen) urge (**de faire** to do); (for food) craving; **avoir ~ de qch** to feel like sth; **avoir ~ de dormir** to want to go to bed; **mourir d'~ de faire** to be dying to do (fam); **donner (l')~ à qn de faire** to make sb want to do
2 envy; **il te fait ~ ce jouet?** would you like that toy?
3 birthmark

envier /ɑ̃vje/ [**v2**] *vt* to envy

envieux, -ieuse /ɑ̃vjø, øz/ **A** *adj* envious
B *mf* **faire des ~** to make people jealous

environ /ɑ̃viʀɔ̃/ *adv* about

environnant, ~e /ɑ̃viʀɔnɑ̃, ɑ̃t/ *adj* surrounding

environnement /ɑ̃viʀɔnmɑ̃/ *m* environment

environner /ɑ̃viʀɔne/ [**v1**] *vt* to surround

environs /ɑ̃viʀɔ̃/ *mpl* **être des ~** to be from the area; **aux ~ de** (place) in the vicinity of; (time, moment) around; (amount) in the region of

envisageable /ɑ̃vizaʒabl/ *adj* possible

envisager /ɑ̃vizaʒe/ [**v13**] *vt* **1** to plan (**de faire** to do)
2 to envisage ‹*hypothesis, situation*›; to foresee ‹*problem, possibility*›; **~ le pire** to imagine the worst
3 to consider

envoi /ɑ̃vwa/ *m* **1 tous les ~s de colis sont suspendus** parcel post is suspended; **faire un ~ de** to send ‹*flowers, books*›
2 demander l'~ (immédiat) de troupes to ask for troops to be dispatched (immediately)
3 l'~ de la fusée the rocket launch; **donner le coup d'~ de** to kick off ‹*match*›; to open ‹*festival*›
■ **~ recommandé** registered post (BrE) *or* mail (AmE); **~ contre remboursement** cash on delivery

envol /ɑ̃vɔl/ *m* (of bird) flight; (of plane) takeoff

envolée /ɑ̃vɔle/ *f* **1** flight of fancy
2 (in prices) surge (**de** in); (of political party) rise

envoler: s'envoler /ɑ̃vɔle/ [**v1**] *v refl* (+ *v être*) **1** ‹*bird*› to fly off; ‹*plane, passenger*› to take off; ‹*paper, hat*› to be blown away
2 ‹*prices*› to soar
3 to vanish
4 (fam) to do a runner (fam)

envoûtement /ɑ̃vutmɑ̃/ *m* **1** bewitchment
2 spell

envoûter /ɑ̃vute/ [**v1**] *vt* to bewitch

envoyé, ~e /ɑ̃vwaje/ **A** *adj* **ça c'est (bien) ~!** (fam) well said!
B *mf* envoy; **~ spécial** special correspondent

envoyer /ɑ̃vwaje/ [**v24**] **A** *vt* **1** to send; **~ qn étudier à Genève** to send sb off to study in Geneva
2 to throw ‹*pebble*›; to fire ‹*missile*›; **~ qch dans l'œil de qn** to hit sb in the eye with sth; **~ le ballon dans les buts** to put the ball in the net
B s'envoyer *v refl* (+ *v être*) to exchange; **s'~ des baisers** to blow each other kisses
IDIOMS **~ qn promener** (fam) to send sb packing (fam); **tout ~ promener** (fam) to drop the lot (fam); **il ne me l'a pas envoyé dire** (fam) and he told me in no uncertain terms

enzyme /ɑ̃zim/ *mf* enzyme

éolien, -ienne /eɔljɛ̃, ɛn/ *adj* ‹*generator*› wind

éolienne /eɔlyɛn/ *f* **1** (aeolian) windmill
2 wind turbine

épagneul /epaɲœl/ *m* spaniel

épais, épaisse /epɛ, ɛs/ **A** *adj* **1** thick; **il n'est pas bien ∼ ce petit!** (fam) he's a skinny little fellow!
2 ‹*mind*› dull
3 ‹*night*› deep
B *adv* a lot, much

e

épaisseur /epɛsœʀ/ *f* **1** thickness; **couper qch dans (le sens de) l'∼** to cut sth sideways
2 layer

épaissir /epesiʀ/ [**v3**] **A** *vt* **1** to thicken
2 to deepen ‹*mystery*›
B *vi* **1** ‹*sauce*› to thicken; ‹*jelly*› to set
2 to put on weight
C **s'épaissir** *v refl* (+ *v être*) ‹*sauce, waist, mist*› to thicken; ‹*mystery*› to deepen

épancher: **s'épancher** /epɑ̃ʃe/ [**v1**] *v refl* (+ *v être*) to open one's heart (**auprès de** to)

épanoui, ∼e /epanwi/ *adj* ‹*flower*› in full bloom; ‹*smile*› beaming; ‹*person*› well-adjusted

épanouir /epanwiʀ/ [**v3**] **A** *vt* **1** ‹*sun*› to open (out) ‹*flower*›; ‹*joy*› to light up ‹*face*›
2 (fig) to make [sb/sth] blossom
B **s'épanouir** *v refl* (+ *v être*) ‹*flower*› to bloom; ‹*face*› to light up; ‹*person*› to blossom

épanouissant, ∼e /epanwisɑ̃, ɑ̃t/ *adj* fulfilling

épanouissement /epanwismɑ̃/ *m* **1** (of flower) blooming
2 (of person) development; (of talent) flowering

épargnant, ∼e /epaʀɲɑ̃, ɑ̃t/ *mf* saver

épargne /epaʀɲ/ *f* savings

épargner /epaʀɲe/ [**v1**] **A** *vt* **1** to save ‹*money*›
2 to spare; **∼ qch à qn** to spare sb sth
B *vi* to save
C **s'épargner** *v refl* (+ *v être*) to save oneself

éparpiller /epaʀpije/ [**v1**] *vt*, **s'éparpiller** *v refl* (+ *v être*) to scatter

épars, ∼e /epaʀ, aʀs/ *adj* scattered

épatant, ∼e /epatɑ̃, ɑ̃t/ *adj* (fam) marvellous (BrE)

épate /epat/ *f* (fam) **faire de l'∼** to show off

épaté, ∼e /epate/ *adj* **1** **nez ∼** pug nose, flat nose
2 (fam) amazed (**de** by)

épater /epate/ [**v1**] *vt* (fam) **1** to impress; **ça t'épate, hein?** surprised, aren't you?
2 to amaze

✓ **épaule** /epol/ *f* shoulder
IDIOMS **changer son fusil d'∼** to change one's tactics; **avoir la tête sur les ∼s** to have one's head screwed on (fam)

épauler /epole/ [**v1**] **A** *vt* **1** to help
2 to take aim with ‹*rifle*›
B *vi* to take aim

épaulette /epolɛt/ *f* **1** shoulder pad
2 (shoulder) strap
3 (Mil) epaulette

épave /epav/ *f* **1** wreck
2 (car) (gen) wreck; (after accident) write-off (fam); write-off (fam)
3 (person) wreck

épée /epe/ *f* sword; **c'est un coup d'∼ dans l'eau** it was a complete waste of effort

épeler /eple/ [**v19**] *vt* to spell ‹*word*›

éperdu, ∼e /epɛʀdy/ *adj* ‹*need, desire*› overwhelming; ‹*glance*› desperate; ‹*love*› boundless

éperdument /epɛʀdymɑ̃/ *adv* ‹*in love*› madly; **je me moque ∼ de ce qu'il pense** I couldn't care less what he thinks

éperon /epʀɔ̃/ *m* spur

épervier /epɛʀvje/ *m* (Zool) sparrowhawk

éphémère /efemɛʀ/ *adj* ephemeral; fleeting; short-lived

épi /epi/ *m* **1** (of corn) ear; (of flower) spike; **∼ de maïs** corn cob
2 cow's lick (BrE), cow lick (AmE)

épice /epis/ *f* spice

épicé, ∼e /epise/ *adj* spicy; hot

épicentre /episɑ̃tʀ/ *m* epicentre (BrE)

épicer /epise/ [**v12**] *vt* to spice; to add spice to

✓ **épicerie** /episʀi/ *f* **1** grocer's (shop) (BrE), grocery (store) (AmE); **∼ fine** delicatessen
2 grocery trade
3 groceries

épicier, -ière /episje, ɛʀ/ *mf* grocer

épidémie /epidemi/ *f* epidemic

épiderme /epidɛʀm/ *m* skin

épidermique /epidɛʀmik/ *adj* skin; ‹*sensitivity*› extreme; **réaction ∼** gut reaction

épier /epje/ [**v2**] *vt* **1** to spy on ‹*person, behaviour*›
2 to be on the lookout for

épilation /epilasjɔ̃/ *f* removal of unwanted hair

épilepsie /epilɛpsi/ *f* **crise d'∼** epileptic fit

épiler /epile/ [**v1**] *vt* to remove unwanted hair from; to wax ‹*leg*›; to pluck ‹*eyebrows*›

épilogue /epilɔg/ *m* epilogue (BrE)

épiloguer /epilɔge/ [**v1**] *vi* to go on and on (**sur** about)

épinard /epinaʀ/ *m* spinach
IDIOM **ça met du beurre dans les ∼s** (fam) it brings in a nice bit of extra money

épine /epin/ *f* thorn; **∼ dorsale** spine
IDIOM **ôter à qn une ∼ du pied** to take a weight off sb's shoulders

épineux, -euse /epinø, øz/ *adj* ‹*stem, character*› prickly; ‹*problem*› tricky; ‹*question*› vexed

---
✓ key word

épingle /epɛ̃gl/ *f* pin; **~ de** *or* **à nourrice, ~ de sûreté** safety pin
IDIOMS **monter qch en ~** to blow sth up out of proportion; **être tiré à quatre ~s** (fam) to be immaculately dressed; **tirer son ~ du jeu** to get out while the going is good

épinière /epinjɛʀ/ *adj f* **moelle ~** spinal cord

épique /epik/ *adj* epic; **c'était ~** (hum, fam) it was quite something (fam)

épisode /epizɔd/ *m* episode; **roman à ~s** serialized novel

épisodique /epizɔdik/ *adj* sporadic

épistolaire /epistɔlɛʀ/ *adj* epistolary; **ils ont des relations ~s** they correspond

épitaphe /epitaf/ *f* epitaph

épithète /epitɛt/ *f* attributive adjective

éploré, **~e** /eplɔʀe/ *adj* **1** grief-stricken
2 tearful

éplucher /eplyʃe/ [**v1**] *vt* to peel; (fig) to go through [sth] with a fine-tooth comb

épluchure /eplyʃyʀ/ *f* **~s** peelings

éponge /epɔ̃ʒ/ *f* **1** sponge
2 terry towelling
IDIOM **passer l'~** to forget the past

éponger /epɔ̃ʒe/ [**v13**] *vt* **1** to mop (up)
2 to absorb ‹*deficit*›; to pay off ‹*debts*›

épopée /epɔpe/ *f* **1** epic
2 saga

époque /epɔk/ *f* **1** time; **vivre avec son ~** to move with the times; **quelle ~!** what's the world coming to!; **à mon ~** in my day
2 (historical) era
3 en costume d'~ in period costume; **des meubles d'~** antique furniture

épouse /epuz/ *f* wife, spouse

épouser /epuze/ [**v1**] *vt* **1** to marry ‹*person*›
2 to adopt ‹*cause, idea*›

épousseter /epuste/ [**v20**] *vt* to dust

époustoufler /epustufle/ [**v1**] *vt* (fam) to amaze

épouvantable /epuvɑ̃tabl/ *adj* **1** (gen) dreadful
2 appalling

épouvantail /epuvɑ̃taj/ *m* **1** scarecrow
2 (fam) (ugly person) fright
3 spectre (BrE)

épouvante /epuvɑ̃t/ *f* **1** terror
2 horror

épouvanter /epuvɑ̃te/ [**v1**] *vt* **1** to terrify
2 to horrify

époux /epu/ **A** *m inv* husband
B *mpl* **les ~** the (married) couple

éprendre: **s'éprendre** /epʀɑ̃dʀ/ [**v52**] *v refl* (+ *v être*) **s'~ de qn** to become enamoured of sb

épreuve /epʀœv/ *f* **1** ordeal
2 test; **mettre à rude ~** to put [sb] to a severe test ‹*person*›; to be very hard on ‹*car, shoes*›; to tax ‹*patience, nerves*›; **à toute ~** unfailing; **l'~ du feu** ordeal by fire; **à l'~ du feu/des balles** fire-/bullet-proof
3 (part of an) examination; **~ écrite** written examination
4 (Sport) **~ d'athlétisme** athletics event
5 (photograph, print) proof

épris, **~e** /epʀi, iz/ *adj* in love (**de** with)

éprouvant, **~e** /epʀuvɑ̃, ɑ̃t/ *adj* gruelling (BrE); trying

éprouver /epʀuve/ [**v1**] *vt* **1** to feel ‹*regret, love*›; to have ‹*sensation, difficulty*›; **~ de la jalousie** to be jealous
2 to test
3 ‹*death, event*› to distress ‹*person*›; ‹*storm*› to hit ‹*region*›

éprouvette /epʀuvɛt/ *f* **1** test tube
2 sample

EPS /œpeɛs/ *f* (*abbr* = **éducation physique et sportive**) PE

épuisant, **~e** /epɥizɑ̃, ɑ̃t/ *adj* exhausting

épuisé, **~e** /epɥize/ **A** *pp* ▸ **épuiser**
B *pp adj* **1** exhausted, worn out
2 ‹*publication, book*› out of print; ‹*item*› out of stock

épuisement /epɥizmɑ̃/ *m* **1** exhaustion
2 jusqu'à ~ des stocks while stocks last

épuiser /epɥize/ [**v1**] **A** *vt* **1** to exhaust, to wear [sb] out
2 to exhaust ‹*subject, mine*›
B s'épuiser *v refl* (+ *v être*) **1** to exhaust oneself
2 ‹*stocks, provisions*› to be running out

épuisette /epɥizɛt/ *f* **1** landing net
2 shrimp net

épurateur /epyʀatœʀ/ *m* purifier

épuration /epyʀasjɔ̃/ *f* **1** (of gas, liquid) purification; (of sewage) treatment
2 purge

épurer /epyʀe/ [**v1**] *vt* **1** to purify ‹*water, gas*›
2 to purge ‹*party*›
3 to expurgate ‹*text*›

équateur /ekwatœʀ/ *m* equator

équation /ekwɑsjɔ̃/ *f* equation

équerre /ekɛʀ/ *f* **1** set square; **en** *or* **d'~** at right angles
2 flat angle bracket

équestre /ekɛstʀ/ *adj* equestrian; **centre ~** riding school

équilibre /ekilibʀ/ *m* **1** balance; **être en ~ sur** ‹*object*› to be balanced on; ‹*person*› to balance on
2 equilibrium; **manquer d'~** to be unstable; **retrouver son ~** to get back to normal

équilibrer /ekilibʀe/ [**v1**] *vt* to balance

équilibriste /ekilibʀist/ *mf* acrobat

équinoxe /ekinɔks/ *m* equinox

équipage /ekipaʒ/ *m* crew

équipe /ekip/ *f* team; crew; shift; **travailler en ~** to work as a team; **~ de tournage** film crew; **l'~ de nuit** the night shift

équipé, **~e** /ekipe/ **A** *pp* ▸ **équiper**
B *pp adj* **bien/mal ~** well-/ill-equipped; **cuisine ~e** fitted kitchen

équipée /ekipe/ *f* escapade
équipement /ekipmɑ̃/ *m* **1** equipment; kit
2 **~s** facilities
équiper /ekipe/ [**v1**] **A** *vt* to equip ‹*hospital, vehicle*›; to provide ‹*town*›; to fit out ‹*person*›
B **s'équiper** *v refl* (+ *v être*) to equip oneself
équipier, **-ière** /ekipje, ɛʀ/ *mf* **1** team member
2 crew member
équitable /ekitabl/ *adj* fair-minded; fair
équitablement /ekitabləmɑ̃/ *adv* equitably, fairly
équitation /ekitasjɔ̃/ *f* (horse) riding
équité /ekite/ *f* equity
équivalence /ekivalɑ̃s/ *f* **1** equivalence
2 **titre admis en ~** recognized qualification
équivalent, **~e** /ekivalɑ̃, ɑ̃t/ *adj*
1 equivalent
2 identical
équivaloir /ekivalwaʀ/ [**v45**] *v+prep* **~ à** to be equivalent to ‹*quantity*›; to amount to ‹*effect*›
équivoque /ekivɔk/ **A** *adj* **1** ambiguous
2 ‹*reputation*› dubious; ‹*behaviour*› questionable
B *f* ambiguity; **sans ~** ‹*reply*› unequivocal; ‹*condemn*› unequivocally
érable /eʀabl/ *m* maple (tree)
érafler /eʀafle/ [**v1**] **A** *vt* to scratch
B **s'érafler** *v refl* (+ *v être*) to scratch oneself
érailler: **s'érailler** /eʀaje/ [**v1**] *v refl* (+ *v être*) to become hoarse
ère /ɛʀ/ *f* **1** era; **en l'an 10 de notre ~** in the year 10 AD
2 age; **à l'~ atomique** in the nuclear age
érection /eʀɛksjɔ̃/ *f* erection
éreinter /eʀɛ̃te/ [**v1**] *vt* (fam) to exhaust
ergot /ɛʀgo/ *m* **1** (of cock) spur; (of dog) dewclaw
2 ergot
ergoter /ɛʀgɔte/ [**v1**] *vi* to split hairs
ériger /eʀiʒe/ [**v13**] **A** *vt* to erect ‹*statue*›
B **s'ériger** *v refl* (+ *v être*) **s'~ en** to set oneself up as
ermite /ɛʀmit/ *m* **1** hermit
2 recluse
éroder /eʀɔde/ [**v1**] *vt* to erode
érosion /eʀozjɔ̃/ *f* erosion
érotique /eʀɔtik/ *adj* erotic
érotisme /eʀɔtism/ *m* eroticism
errance /ɛʀɑ̃s/ *f* restless wandering
errant, **~e** /ɛʀɑ̃, ɑ̃t/ *adj* wandering; rootless; **chien ~** stray dog
errer /ɛʀe/ [**v1**] *vi* ‹*person, gaze*› to wander; ‹*animal*› to roam
✓ **erreur** /ɛʀœʀ/ *f* **1** mistake; **~ de judgement** error of judgment; **induire qn en ~** to mislead sb; **sauf ~ de ma part** if I'm not mistaken
2 (Law) error
erroné, **~e** /ɛʀɔne/ *adj* incorrect, erroneous
ersatz /ɛʀzats/ *m* ersatz
érudit, **~e** /eʀydi, it/ *mf* scholar
érudition /eʀydisjɔ̃/ *f* erudition, scholarship
éruption /eʀypsjɔ̃/ *f* eruption
es /ɛ/ ▸ **être**[1]
ès /ɛs/ *prep* **licence ~ lettres** ≈ arts degree, B.A. (degree)
esbroufe /ɛzbʀuf/ *f* (fam) **faire de l'~** to swank (fam), to show off
escabeau, *pl* **~x** /ɛskabo/ *m* stepladder
escadrille /ɛskadʀij/ *f* squadron
escadron /ɛskadʀɔ̃/ *m* (Mil) company; **~ de la mort** death squad
escalade /ɛskalad/ *f* **1** (Sport) climbing; ascent
2 escalation
escalader /ɛskalade/ [**v1**] *vt* to scale ‹*wall*›; to climb ‹*mountain*›
escale /ɛskal/ *f* (gen) stopover; (for ship) port of call; **~ technique** (for plane) refuelling (BrE) stop; (for ship) overhaul
✓ **escalier** /ɛskalje/ *m* **1** staircase
2 stairs
■ **~ mécanique** *or* **roulant** escalator; **~ de service** backstairs
escalope /ɛskalɔp/ *f* escalope
escamotable /ɛskamɔtabl/ *adj* ‹*landing gear*› retractable; ‹*ladder*› foldaway
escamoter /ɛskamɔte/ [**v1**] *vt* **1** ‹*magician*› to make [sth] disappear
2 to evade ‹*issue*›
escampette /ɛskɑ̃pɛt/ *f* (fam) **prendre la poudre d'~** to scarper (fam), to skedaddle (fam)
escapade /ɛskapad/ *f* escapade
escargot /ɛskaʀgo/ *m* snail
escarpé, **~e** /ɛskaʀpe/ *adj* **1** steep
2 craggy
escarpement /ɛskaʀpəmɑ̃/ *m* steep slope
escarpin /ɛskaʀpɛ̃/ *m* court shoe (BrE), pump (AmE)
escarre /ɛskaʀ/ *f* bedsore
escient /ɛsjɑ̃/ *m* **à bon ~** wittingly; **à mauvais ~** ill-advisedly
esclaffer: **s'esclaffer** /ɛsklafe/ [**v1**] *v refl* (+ *v être*) to guffaw
esclandre /ɛsklɑ̃dʀ/ *m* scene
esclavage /ɛsklavaʒ/ *m* slavery; (fig) tyranny
✓ **esclave** /ɛsklav/ *mf* slave
escompte /ɛskɔ̃t/ *m* discount
escompter /ɛskɔ̃te/ [**v1**] *vt* to anticipate; **~ faire** to count on doing, to hope to do
escorte /ɛskɔʀt/ *f* escort

✓ key word

escorter /ɛskɔʀte/ [**v1**] *vt* to escort
escrime /ɛskʀim/ *f* fencing
escrimer: **s'escrimer** /ɛskʀime/ [**v1**] *v refl* (+ *v être*) (fam) **s' ~ à faire** to knock oneself out trying to do (fam)
escroc /ɛskʀo/ *m* swindler, crook
escroquer /ɛskʀɔke/ [**v1**] *vt* to swindle
escroquerie /ɛskʀɔkʀi/ *f* **1** fraud, swindling; **tentative d'~** attempted fraud
2 swindle
ésotérique /ezɔteʀik/ *adj* esoteric
espace /ɛspas/ *m* **1** space
2 ~ de loisirs leisure complex
3 gap
4 en l'~ de in the space of; **l'~ d'un instant** for a moment
■ **~ vert** open space; **~ vital** living space
espacer /ɛspase/ [**v12**] **A** *vt* to space [sth] out
B s'espacer *v refl* (+ *v être*) to become less frequent
espadon /ɛspadɔ̃/ *m* swordfish
espadrille /ɛspadʀij/ *f* espadrille
Espagne /ɛspaɲ/ *pr f* Spain
IDIOM **bâtir des châteaux en ~** to build castles in the air
espagnol, **~e** /ɛspaɲɔl/ **A** *adj* Spanish
B *m* (language) Spanish
espalier /ɛspalje/ *m* **1** espalier
2 fruit wall
espèce /ɛspɛs/ **A** *f* **1** species; **l'~ humaine** mankind
2 kind
B espèces *fpl* **en ~s** in cash
espérance /ɛspeʀɑ̃s/ *f* hope; **~ de vie** life expectancy
espérer /ɛspeʀe/ [**v14**] **A** *vt* **1 ~ qch** to hope for sth
2 to expect; **je n'en espérais pas tant** it's more than I expected
B *vi* to hope
espiègle /ɛspjɛgl/ *adj* mischievous
espion, **-ionne** /ɛspjɔ̃, ɔn/ *mf* spy
espionnage /ɛspjɔnaʒ/ *m* espionage, spying
espionner /ɛspjɔne/ [**v1**] *vt* to spy on
esplanade /ɛsplanad/ *f* esplanade
espoir /ɛspwaʀ/ *m* hope; **reprendre ~** to feel hopeful again; **avec ~** hopefully
esprit /ɛspʀi/ *m* **1** mind; **avoir l'~ mal placé** to have a dirty mind (fam); **avoir un ~ de synthèse** to be good at synthesizing information; **avoir l'~ de contradiction** to be contrary; **dans mon ~ c'était facile** the way I saw it, it was easy; **cela ne t'est jamais venu à l'~?** didn't it ever occur to you?; **avoir l'~ ailleurs** to be miles away; **les choses de l'~** spiritual matters
2 wit; **faire de l'~** to try to be witty; **~ d'à-propos** ready wit
3 dans un ~ de vengeance in a spirit of revenge; **ils ont l'~ de famille** they're a very close family
4 l'un des plus grands ~s de son temps one of the greatest minds of his/her time; **calmer les ~s** to calm people down; **les ~s sont échauffés** feelings are running high
5 spirit; **croire aux ~s** to believe in ghosts
■ **~ de corps** solidarity; **~ d'équipe** team spirit
IDIOMS **perdre ses ~s** to faint; **les grands ~s se rencontrent** great minds think alike
esquimau, **-aude**, *mpl* **~x** /ɛskimo, od/
A *adj* Eskimo; **chien ~** husky
B *m* **1** Eskimo
2 ® chocolate-covered ice lolly (BrE), ice-cream bar (AmE)
esquinter /ɛskɛ̃te/ [**v1**] *vt* (fam) to damage
esquisse /ɛskis/ *f* **1** sketch
2 outline
esquisser /ɛskise/ [**v1**] *vt* to sketch ‹*portrait*›; to outline ‹*programme*›
esquiver /ɛskive/ [**v1**] **A** *vt* to dodge, to duck ‹*blow*›; to sidestep ‹*issue*›
B s'esquiver *v refl* (+ *v être*) to slip away
essai /esɛ/ **A** *m* **1** (Tech, Med) trial; test; **être à l'~** to undergo trials; to be tested; **~ sur route** road test
2 try, attempt; **un coup d'~** a try; **prendre qn à l'~** to give sb a try-out
3 essay
4 (in rugby) try
B essais *mpl* (Aut, Sport) qualifying round
essaim /esɛ̃/ *m* swarm
essayage /esɛjaʒ/ *m* fitting
essayer /eseje/ [**v21**] **A** *vt* **1** to try; **~ sa force** to test one's strength
2 to test ‹*weapon, product*›; to run trials on ‹*car*›
3 to try on ‹*clothes*›; to try ‹*size, colour*›; to try out ‹*car*›
B *vi* to try; **~ à la poste** to try the post office; **j'essaierai que tout se passe bien** I'll try to make sure everything goes all right
C s'essayer *v refl* (+ *v être*) **s'~ à** to have a go at, to try one's hand at
essayiste /esɛjist/ *mf* essayist
essence /esɑ̃s/ *f* **1** petrol (BrE), gasoline (AmE)
2 essential oil
3 tree species
■ **~ à briquet** lighter fuel (BrE), lighter fluid (AmE); **~ ordinaire** ≈ 2-star petrol (BrE), regular gasoline (AmE); **~ sans plomb** unleaded (petrol) (BrE), unleaded gasoline (AmE); **~ super** ≈ 4-star petrol (BrE), premium gasoline (AmE)
essentiel, **-ielle** /esɑ̃sjɛl/ **A** *adj* essential
B *m* **c'est l'~** that's the main thing; **aller à l'~** to get to the heart of the matter; **l'~ des voix** the bulk of the vote; **pour l'~** mainly; **en voyage je n'emporte que l'~** when I travel I only take the bare essentials
essentiellement /esɑ̃sjɛlmɑ̃/ *adv* **1** mainly
2 essentially
esseulé, **~e** /esœle/ *adj* forlorn

essieu, *pl* **~x** /esjø/ *m* axle

essor /esɔʀ/ *m* (of technology, area) development; **être en plein ~** to be booming

essorage /esɔʀaʒ/ *m* wringing; spin-drying

essorer /esɔʀe/ [**v1**] *vt* **1** to wring
2 to spin-dry ‹*washing*›; to spin ‹*lettuce*›

essoufflement /esufləmɑ̃/ *m* breathlessness; (fig) loss of impetus

essouffler /esufle/ [**v1**] **A** *vt* to leave [sb] breathless; **être essoufflé** to be out of breath
B **s'essouffler** *v refl* (+ *v être*) **1** to get breathless
2 to run out of steam

essuie-glace, *pl* **~s** /esɥiglas/ *m* windscreen wiper (BrE), windshield wiper (AmE)

essuie-mains /esɥimɛ̃/ *m inv* hand towel

essuie-tout /esɥitu/ *m inv* kitchen roll, kitchen paper

essuyer /esɥije/ [**v22**] **A** *vt* **1** to dry ‹*glass, hands*›; to wipe ‹*table*›; **~ la vaisselle** to dry up; **~ ses larmes** to wipe away one's tears
2 to suffer ‹*defeat, losses*›; to meet with ‹*failure*›
B **s'essuyer** *v refl* (+ *v être*) to dry oneself; **s'~ les mains** to dry one's hands

🔑 **est¹** /ɛ/ ▸ **être¹**

🔑 **est²** /ɛst/ **A** *adj inv* east; eastern
B *m* **1** east; **un vent d'~** an easterly wind
2 **l'Est** the East; **de l'Est** eastern

estafette® /ɛstafɛt/ *f* van

estampe /ɛstɑ̃p/ *f* **1** engraving
2 print

estamper /ɛstɑ̃pe/ [**v1**] *vt* (fam) to rip [sb] off (fam)

esthète /ɛstɛt/ *mf* aesthete

esthéticienne /ɛstetisjɛn/ *f* beautician

esthétique /ɛstetik/ **A** *adj* aesthetic; ‹*decor*› aesthetically pleasing; ‹*pose*› graceful
B *f* aesthetics

estimable /ɛstimabl/ *adj* **1** worthy
2 laudable
3 **difficilement ~** hard to estimate

estimation /ɛstimasjɔ̃/ *f* estimate; valuation

estime /ɛstim/ *f* respect

🔑 **estimer** /ɛstime/ [**v1**] *vt* **1** to feel; **~ nécessaire de faire** to consider it necessary to do
2 to think highly of ‹*friend, artist*›
3 to value ‹*painting*›; to assess ‹*damage*›; **une vitesse estimée à 150 km/h** an estimated speed of 150 kph
4 to reckon

estival, **~e**, *mpl* **-aux** /ɛstival, o/ *adj*
1 summer
2 summery

estivant, **~e** /ɛstivɑ̃, ɑ̃t/ *mf* summer visitor

estomac /ɛstɔma/ *m* stomach; **avoir l'~ bien accroché** to have a strong stomach
IDIOM **avoir l'~ dans les talons** (fam) to be famished

estomper /ɛstɔ̃pe/ [**v1**] **A** *vt* to blur ‹*shape*›; to gloss over ‹*details*›
B **s'estomper** *v refl* (+ *v être*) ‹*landscape*› to become blurred; ‹*hatred, memories*› to fade

estrade /ɛstʀad/ *f* platform

estragon /ɛstʀagɔ̃/ *m* tarragon

estropié, **~e** /ɛstʀɔpje/ *mf* cripple

estropier /ɛstʀɔpje/ [**v2**] **A** *vt* to maim
B **s'estropier** *v refl* (+ *v être*) to maim oneself

estuaire /ɛstɥɛʀ/ *m* estuary

esturgeon /ɛstyʀʒɔ̃/ *m* sturgeon

🔑 **et** /e/ *conj* and; **~ voilà qu'il sort un couteau de sa poche!** and next thing he whips a knife out of his pocket!; **~ alors?** so what?

étable /etabl/ *f* cowshed

établi, **~e** /etabli/ **A** *pp* ▸ **établir**
B *pp adj* **1** ‹*reputation, use*› established
2 ‹*power, regime*› ruling; ‹*order*› established
C *m* workbench

🔑 **établir** /etabliʀ/ [**v3**] **A** *vt* **1** to set up ‹*home*›
2 to establish ‹*rule, link, reputation, innocence, fact*›; to introduce ‹*tax, discipline*›; to set ‹*record, standard*›
3 to draw up ‹*list, plan, budget, file*›; to make out ‹*cheque, bill*›; to prepare ‹*quote*›; to make ‹*diagnosis*›; to draw ‹*parallel*›
B **s'établir** *v refl* (+ *v être*) **1** ‹*person*› to settle (**à, en** in); **s'~ à son compte** to set up one's own business
2 ‹*links*› to develop

🔑 **établissement** /etablismɑ̃/ *m*
1 organization; **~ bancaire** banking institution
2 (of relations, regime) establishment; (of tax, sanctions) introduction
3 premises
■ **~ commercial** commercial establishment; **~ de crédit** finance company; **~ d'enseignement supérieur** higher education institution; **~ scolaire** school

🔑 **étage** /etaʒ/ *m* **1** floor; **le premier ~** the first floor (BrE), the second floor (AmE); **à l'~** upstairs
2 (of tower) level; (of aqueduct, cake) tier

étagère /etaʒɛʀ/ *f* shelf

étaient /etɛ/ ▸ **être¹**

étain /etɛ̃/ *m* **1** tin
2 pewter

étais /etɛ/ ▸ **être¹**

était /etɛ/ ▸ **être¹**

étal /etal/ *m* **1** (market) stall
2 butcher's block

étalage /etalaʒ/ *m* **1** window display
2 display; **faire ~ de ses connaissances** to flaunt one's knowledge

🔑 key word

étalagiste /etalaʒist/ *mf* window dresser

étalement /etalmɑ̃/ *m* (of holidays) staggering; (of payments) spreading

étaler /etale/ [**v1**] **A** *vt* **1** to spread out ‹*sheet*›; to roll [sth] out ‹*pastry*›
2 to scatter
3 to spread ‹*butter, glue*›; to apply ‹*paint, ointment*›
4 to spread ‹*work, payments*›; to stagger ‹*departures*›
5 to flaunt ‹*wealth, knowledge*›; to display ‹*merchandise*›; **~ qch au grand jour** to bring sth out into the open
B s'étaler *v refl* (+ *v être*) **1** ‹*butter, paint*› to spread
2 ‹*person*› to sprawl, to spread out
3 (fam) **s'~ de tout son long** to fall flat on one's face; **s'~** *or* **se faire ~ à un examen** to fail an exam

étalon /etalɔ̃/ *m* **1** stallion
2 standard

étalon-or /etalɔ̃ɔʀ/ *m inv* gold standard

étamine /etamin/ *f* stamen

étanche /etɑ̃ʃ/ *adj* **~ (à l'eau)** waterproof; watertight; **~ (à l'air)** airtight

étanchéité /etɑ̃ʃeite/ *f* waterproofness; watertightness; airtightness

étancher /etɑ̃ʃe/ [**v1**] *vt* to quench ‹*thirst*›

étang /etɑ̃/ *m* pond

étant /etɑ̃/ ▶ **donné C, être**[1]

⚷ **étape** /etap/ *f* **1** stop
2 (in journey) stage; (in race) leg
3 (fig) stage, step; **brûler les ~s** to go too far too fast

⚷ **état** /eta/ **A** *m* **1** condition; **mettre qn hors d'~ de nuire** to put sb out of harm's way; **leur ~ de santé est excellent** they're in excellent health; **maintenir qch en ~ de marche** to keep sth in working order; **hors d'~ de marche** ‹*car*› off the road; ‹*machine*› out of order; **j'ai laissé les choses en l'~** I left everything as it was
2 state; **être dans un drôle d'~** (fam) to be in a hell of a state (fam); **être dans un ~ second** to be in a trance; **ce n'est encore qu'à l'~ de projet** it's still only at the planning stage
3 statement
B faire ~ de *phr* **1** to cite ‹*document*›
2 to mention ‹*conversation*›
3 to state ‹*preferences*›
4 to make a point of mentioning ‹*success*›
■ **~ d'âme** qualm; feeling; **~ civil** registry office (BrE); civil status; **~ d'esprit** state of mind; **~ de fait** fact; **~ des lieux** inventory and report on state of repair; **~s de service** service record
(IDIOM) **être/se mettre dans tous ses ~s** (fam) to be in/to get into a state (fam)

État /eta/ *m* **1** state, State
2 state, government

étatique /etatik/ *adj* state (BrE), public (AmE)

état-major, *pl* **états-majors** /etamaʒɔʀ/ *m* **1** (Mil) staff
2 headquarters

États-Unis /etazyni/ *pr m pl* **~ (d'Amérique)** United States (of America)

étau, *pl* **~x** /eto/ *m* vice (BrE), vise (AmE); (fig) **l'~ se resserre** the net is tightening

étayer /eteje/ [**v21**] *vt* **1** to prop up
2 (fig) to support ‹*theory*›

et cætera, et cetera, etcétera /ɛtseteʀa/ *loc adv* et cetera

⚷ **été**[1] /ete/ ▶ **être**[1]

⚷ **été**[2] /ete/ *m* summer

e

⚷ **éteindre** /etɛ̃dʀ/ [**v55**] **A** *vt* **1** to put out ‹*fire, cigarette*›; to blow out ‹*candle*›
2 to switch off ‹*light, TV, oven*›; to turn off ‹*gas*›
B s'éteindre *v refl* (+ *v être*) **1** ‹*cigarette, fire, light*› to go out; ‹*radio*› to go off
2 (euph) to pass away *or* on
3 ‹*desire, passion*› to fade

éteint, **~e** /etɛ̃, ɛ̃t/ **A** *pp* ▶ **éteindre**
B *pp adj* **1** ‹*gaze*› dull
2 ‹*volcano*› extinct; ‹*star*› extinct, dead

étendard /etɑ̃daʀ/ *m* standard, flag

⚷ **étendre** /etɑ̃dʀ/ [**v6**] **A** *vt* **1** to stretch ‹*arms, legs*›
2 to spread (out) ‹*cloth*›; **~ le linge** to hang out the washing
3 to extend ‹*embargo*›
B s'étendre *v refl* (+ *v être*) **1** ‹*land, forest*› to stretch
2 ‹*strike, epidemic*› to spread; ‹*town*› to expand, to grow
3 ‹*law, measure*› **s'~ à** to apply to
4 ‹*period, work*› to stretch, to last
5 to lie down
6 s'~ sur to dwell on

étendu, **~e** /etɑ̃dy/ **A** *pp* ▶ **étendre**
B *pp adj* ‹*city*› sprawling; ‹*region, plain*› vast; ‹*vocabulary, knowledge, damage*› extensive

étendue /etɑ̃dy/ *f* **1** expanse
2 size
3 scale, extent; range

⚷ **éternel**, **-elle** /etɛʀnɛl/ *adj* endless; eternal

éternellement /etɛʀnɛlmɑ̃/ *adv* **1** forever
2 permanently
3 perpetually
4 eternally

éterniser: **s'éterniser** /etɛʀnize/ [**v1**] *v refl* (+ *v être*) to drag on; ‹*visitor*› to stay for ages (fam)

éternité /etɛʀnite/ *f* eternity

éternuement /etɛʀnymɑ̃/ *m* sneeze

éternuer /etɛʀnɥe/ [**v1**] *vi* to sneeze

êtes /ɛt/ ▶ **être**[1]

éther /etɛʀ/ *m* ether

éthique /etik/ **A** *adj* ethical
B *f* **1** ethics
2 code of ethics

ethnie /ɛtni/ *f* ethnic group

ethnique /ɛtnik/ *adj* ethnic

ethnologie /ɛtnɔlɔʒi/ *f* ethnology

éthylique /etilik/ *adj, mf* alcoholic
éthylisme /etilism/ *m* alcoholism
éthylomètre /etilɔmɛtʀ/ *m* breathalyzer (BrE), Breathalyzer® (AmE)
éthylotest /etilɔtɛst/ *m* breath test
étiez /etje/ ▶ **être**¹
étincelant, **∼e** /etɛ̃slɑ̃, ɑ̃t/ *adj* ‹*sun*› blazing; ‹*star*› twinkling; ‹*gemstone, glass*› sparkling; ‹*feathers, colour*› brilliant
étinceler /etɛ̃sle/ [**v19**] *vi* to twinkle; to sparkle
étincelle /etɛ̃sɛl/ *f* spark; **jeter des ∼s** to glitter; **faire des ∼s** to do brilliantly
étioler: **s'étioler** /etjɔle/ [**v1**] *v refl* (+ *v être*) to wilt
étions /etjɔ̃/ ▶ **être**¹
étiquetage /etiktaʒ/ *m* labelling (BrE)
■ **∼ écologique** eco-labelling; **∼ génétique** gene tagging
étiqueter /etikte/ [**v20**] *vt* to label
étiquette /etikɛt/ *f* **1** label
2 tag; **porter une ∼** to be labelled (BrE); **candidat sans ∼** independent candidate
3 etiquette
étirer /etiʀe/ [**v1**] **A** *vt* to stretch
B **s'étirer** *v refl* (+ *v être*) **1** ‹*person*› to stretch
2 ‹*procession, road*› to stretch out
étoffe /etɔf/ *f* **1** fabric
2 (fig) substance; **avoir l'∼ d'un grand homme** to have the makings of a great man
étoffer /etɔfe/ [**v1**] **A** *vt* to expand
B **s'étoffer** *v refl* (+ *v être*) to put on weight
✓ **étoile** /etwal/ *f* star
■ **∼ filante** shooting star; **∼ de mer** starfish; **∼ polaire** Pole Star
(IDIOM) **coucher** *or* **dormir à la belle ∼** to sleep out in the open
étoilé, **∼e** /etwale/ *adj* **1** starry
2 ‹*glass, windscreen*› crazed
étole /etɔl/ *f* stole
étonnamment /etɔnamɑ̃/ *adv* surprisingly
étonnant, **∼e** /etɔnɑ̃, ɑ̃t/ *adj* **1** surprising
2 amazing
étonnement /etɔnmɑ̃/ *m* surprise
✓ **étonner** /etɔne/ [**v1**] **A** *vt* to surprise
B **s'étonner** *v refl* (+ *v être*) to be surprised
étouffant, **∼e** /etufɑ̃, ɑ̃t/ *adj* **1** stifling
2 oppressive
étouffé, **∼e** /etufe/ *adj* **1** ‹*sound, voice*› muffled
2 ‹*sob*› choked; ‹*laughter*› suppressed
étouffement /etufmɑ̃/ *m* asphyxiation
étouffer /etufe/ [**v1**] **A** *vt* **1** to suppress ‹*protest*›
2 to hush up ‹*scandal*›
3 to suffocate ‹*person*›; to choke ‹*plant*›; **la générosité ne les étouffe pas** generosity is not their middle name
4 to smother ‹*fire*›
5 to stifle ‹*yawn*›; to hold back ‹*sigh*›
6 to deaden ‹*noise*›
B *vi* to feel stifled; **on étouffe ici!** (fam) it's stifling in here!; **mourir étouffé** to die of suffocation
C **s'étouffer** *v refl* (+ *v être*) to choke
étourderie /etuʀdəʀi/ *f* absent-mindedness
étourdi, **∼e** /etuʀdi/ *adj* **1** absent-minded
2 unthinking
étourdir /etuʀdiʀ/ [**v3**] **A** *vt* **1** to stun, to daze
2 ∼ qn ‹*noise*› to make sb's head spin
B **s'étourdir** *v refl* (+ *v être*) **s'∼ de paroles** to become intoxicated with words
étourdissant, **∼e** /etuʀdisɑ̃, ɑ̃t/ *adj* ‹*noise*› deafening; ‹*speed*› dizzying
étourdissement /etuʀdismɑ̃/ *m* **avoir un ∼** to feel dizzy
✓ **étrange** /etʀɑ̃ʒ/ **A** *adj* strange; **chose ∼ elle n'a pas répondu** strangely enough she didn't answer
B *m* **1** strangeness
2 l'∼ the bizarre
étrangement /etʀɑ̃ʒmɑ̃/ *adv* **1** curiously; **vous me rappelez ∼ un ami** it's strange but you remind me of a friend
2 surprisingly
✓ **étranger**, **-ère** /etʀɑ̃ʒe, ɛʀ/ **A** *adj* **1** foreign
2 ∼ à ‹*person*› not involved in ‹*case*›; outside ‹*group*›; ‹*fact*› with no bearing on ‹*problem*›; **se sentir ∼** to feel like an outsider
3 unfamiliar
B *mf* **1** foreigner
2 outsider
3 stranger
C *m* **à l'∼** abroad
étrangeté /etʀɑ̃ʒte/ *f* strangeness
étranglé, **∼e** /etʀɑ̃gle/ *adj* **1** ‹*voice*› choked; ‹*sound*› muffled
2 ‹*street*› narrow
étranglement /etʀɑ̃gləmɑ̃/ *m*
1 strangulation
2 (of road, valley) narrow section
étrangler /etʀɑ̃gle/ [**v1**] **A** *vt* **1** to strangle
2 to choke
B **s'étrangler** *v refl* (+ *v être*) **1** to strangle oneself
2 to choke
étrangleur, **-euse** /etʀɑ̃glœʀ, øz/ *mf* strangler
✓ **être**¹ /ɛtʀ/ [**v7**] *vi* (+ *v avoir*)

> You will find translations for fixed phrases using *être* such as *être en train de*, *être sur le point de*, *quoi qu'il en soit*, *étant donné* etc, at the entries **train**, **point**, **quoi**, **donné** etc.

1 to be; **nous sommes pauvres** we are poor
2 (as auxiliary verb) **elles sont tombées** they

✓ key word

have fallen; they fell; **elle s'était vengée** she had taken her revenge
3 (to go) **je n'ai jamais été en Chine** I've never been to China
4 (with *ce*) **est-ce leur voiture?** is it their car?; **c'est grave?** is it serious?; **qui est-ce?** who is he/she?; who is that?; who is it?; **est-ce que tu parles russe?** do you speak Russian?; **qu'est-ce que c'est?** what is it?; **ce sont mes enfants** these are my children; they are my children; **c'est cela** that's right; **c'est à Pierre/lui de choisir** it's Pierre's/his turn to choose; it's up to Pierre/to him to choose; **il aurait pu s'excuser, ne serait-ce qu'en envoyant un mot** he could have apologized if only by sending a note
5 (with *il*) **il est facile de critiquer** it is easy to criticize; **il n'est pas jusqu'à l'Antarctique qui ne soit pollué** even the Antarctic is polluted; **il n'en est rien** this isn't at all the case
6 (with *en*) **où en étais-je?** where was I?; **je ne sais plus où j'en suis** I'm lost; **'où en es-tu de tes recherches?'—'j'en suis à mi-chemin'** 'how far have you got in your research?'—'I'm halfway through'; **j'en suis à me demander si...** I'm beginning to wonder whether...; **~ en uniforme** to be wearing a uniform
7 (with *y*) **j'y suis** I'm with you, I get it (fam); **je n'y suis pas** I don't get it (fam); **nous partons, vous y êtes?** we're leaving, are you ready?
8 (with *à* and *de*) **ce livre est à moi/à mon frère** this book is mine/my brother's; **à qui est ce chien?** whose dog is this?; **je suis à vous tout de suite** I'll be with you right away; **je suis à vous** I'm all yours; **~ à ce qu'on fait** to have one's mind on what one is doing; **elle est d'un ridicule!** she's so ridiculous!

être[2] /ɛtʀ/ *m* **1 ~ humain** human being; **les ~s animés et inanimés** animate and inanimate things; **un ~ sans défense** a defenceless (BrE) creature
2 person; **un ~ cher** a loved one
3 de tout son ~ with one's whole being; **blessé au plus profond de son ~** hurt to the core

étreindre /etʀɛ̃dʀ/ [**v55**] *vt* to embrace, to hug ‹*friend*›; to clasp ‹*opponent*›

étreinte /etʀɛ̃t/ *f* embrace; grip

étrenner /etʀene/ [**v1**] *vt* to use [sth] for the first time

étrennes /etʀɛn/ *fpl* **1** gift
2 money

étrier /etʀije/ *m* stirrup
IDIOM **mettre à qn le pied à l'~** (fig) to get sb started

étriper /etʀipe/ [**v1**] *vt* (fig, fam) **~ qn** to skin sb alive

étriqué, ~e /etʀike/ *adj* ‹*jacket*› skimpy; ‹*life*› restricted

étroit, ~e /etʀwa, at/ **A** *adj* **1** narrow; **avoir l'esprit ~** to be narrow-minded
2 ‹*links*› close; **en ~e collaboration** closely
B à l'étroit *phr* **nous sommes un peu à l'~** we're a bit cramped; **je me sens un peu à l'~ dans cette jupe** this skirt feels a bit too tight

étroitement /etʀwatmɑ̃/ *adv* closely

étroitesse /etʀwatɛs/ *f* narrowness

étude /etyd/ **A** *f* **1** study
2 survey
3 (mise à l')~ consideration; **à l'~** under consideration
4 (of lawyer) office
5 (Sch) study room (BrE), study hall (AmE)
6 study period
B études *fpl* studies; **faire des ~s** to be a student; **je n'ai pas fait d'~s (supérieures)** I didn't go to university *or* college
■ **~ de marché** market research

étudiant, ~e /etydjɑ̃, ɑ̃t/ *mf* student

étudié, ~e /etydje/ *adj* **1** carefully prepared
2 studied

étudier /etydje/ [**v2**] **A** *vt* to study; to examine ‹*file, situation*›; to learn ‹*lesson*›
B *vi* **1** to be a student
2 to be studying

étui /etɥi/ *m* case; **~ à revolver** holster

étuve /etyv/ *f* **1** steam room; **le grenier est une ~** (fig) the attic is like an oven
2 incubator

étymologie /etimɔlɔʒi/ *f* etymology

eu, ~e /y/ ▶ **avoir[1]**

eucalyptus /økaliptys/ *m inv* eucalyptus

eucharistie /økaʀisti/ *f* **1** Eucharist
2 Sacrament

eûmes /ym/ ▶ **avoir[1]**

eunuque /ønyk/ *m* eunuch

euphémisme /øfemism/ *m* euphemism

euphorie /øfɔʀi/ *f* euphoria

euphorique /øfɔʀik/ *adj* euphoric

euphorisant, ~e /øfɔʀizɑ̃, ɑ̃t/ **A** *adj* stimulating; uplifting; euphoriant
B *m* (Med) stimulant

eurasien, -ienne /øʀazjɛ̃, ɛn/ *adj* Eurasian

Euratom /øʀatɔm/ *f* (*abbr* = **European atomic energy commission**) Euratom

eurent /yʀ/ ▶ **avoir[1]**

EURL /œyɛʀɛl/ *f*: *abbr* ▶ **entreprise**

euro /øʀo/ *m* (currency) euro

eurochèque /øʀoʃɛk/ *m* Eurocheque

euroconnecteur /øʀokɔnɛktœʀ/ *m* Scart socket; Scart plug

eurocrate /øʀokʀat/ *mf* Eurocrat

eurodéputé, -e /øʀodepyte/ *mf* Euro MP

euromarché /øʀomaʀʃe/ *m* Euromarket

Europe /øʀɔp/ *pr f* Europe; **l'~ communautaire** the European community

européaniser /øʀɔpeanize/ [**v1**] **A** *vt* to Europeanize; **~ un débat** to broaden a debate to a European level
B s'européaniser *v refl* (+ *v être*) ‹*country*› to become Europeanized; ‹*economy*› to become adapted to a European framework

e

✐ **européen**, **-éenne** /øʀɔpeɛ̃, ɛn/ *adj* European

eurosceptique /øʀosɛptik/ *mf* Eurosceptic

Eurotunnel /øʀotynɛl/ *m* Eurotunnel

Eurozone /øʀozon/ *f* Eurozone

eus /y/ ▶ **avoir**[1]

eusse /ys/ ▶ **avoir**[1]

eussent /ys/ ▶ **avoir**[1]

eusses /ys/ ▶ **avoir**[1]

eussiez /ysje/ ▶ **avoir**[1]

eussions /ysjɔ̃/ ▶ **avoir**[1]

eut /y/ ▶ **avoir**[1]

eût /yt/ ▶ **avoir**[1]

eûtes /yt/ ▶ **avoir**[1]

euthanasie /øtanazi/ *f* euthanasia

✐ **eux** /ø/ *pron* **1** they; **je sais que ce n'est pas ∼ qui ont fait ça** I know they weren't the ones who did it
2 them; **les inviter, ∼, quelle idée!** invite *them*, what an idea!; **c'est à ∼** it's theirs

eux-mêmes /ømɛm/ *pron* themselves; **les experts ∼ reconnaissent que...** even the experts admit that...

évacuation /evakɥasjɔ̃/ *f* **1** evacuation
2 discharge; **il y a un problème d'∼ de l'eau** the water doesn't drain away

évacuer /evakɥe/ [**v1**] *vt* **1** to evacuate
2 to drain off
3 (fig) to shrug off ‹*problem*›

évader: **s'évader** /evade/ [**v1**] *v refl* (+ *v être*) **1** to escape; **faire ∼ qn** to help sb to escape
2 (fig) to get away (**de** from)

évaluable /evalɥabl/ *adj* assessable

évaluation /evalɥasjɔ̃/ *f* **1** (of collection, house) valuation; **faire l'∼ de** to value
2 (of costs, damages) assessment; estimate, appraisal (AmE)
3 (of staff) appraisal

✐ **évaluer** /evalɥe/ [**v1**] *vt* **1** to estimate ‹*size, length*›; to assess ‹*risks, costs*›
2 to value ‹*inheritance*›
3 to assess ‹*employee, student*›

Évangile /evɑ̃ʒil/ *m* Gospel

évanouir: **s'évanouir** /evanwiʀ/ [**v3**] *v refl* (+ *v être*) **1** to faint
2 ‹*feeling*› to fade

évanouissement /evanwismɑ̃/ *m*
1 blackout, fainting fit
2 fading

évaporation /evapɔʀasjɔ̃/ *f* evaporation

évaporer: **s'évaporer** /evapɔʀe/ [**v1**] *v refl* (+ *v être*) **1** to evaporate
2 (fam) to vanish

évaser /evaze/ [**v1**] **A** *vt* to flare
B **s'évaser** *v refl* (+ *v être*) ‹*duct*› to open out; ‹*skirt*› to be flared

évasif, **-ive** /evazif, iv/ *adj* evasive

évasion /evazjɔ̃/ *f* escape

✐ key word

Ève /ɛv/ *pr f* Eve; **en tenue d'∼** in her birthday suit
IDIOM **elle ne le connaît ni d'∼ ni d'Adam** she doesn't know him from Adam

évêché /eveʃe/ *m* **1** diocese
2 bishop's palace

éveil /evɛj/ *m* awakening

éveiller /eveje/ [**v1**] **A** *vt* **1** to arouse ‹*curiosity, suspicions*›; to stimulate ‹*intelligence*›; to awaken ‹*conscience*›; **un enfant éveillé** a bright child
2 to wake (up) ‹*sleeper*›; **être éveillé** to be awake
B **s'éveiller** *v refl* (+ *v être*) **1** to wake up
2 ‹*imagination*› to start to develop

✐ **événement** /evenmɑ̃/ *m* event

événementiel, **-ielle** /evenmɑ̃sjɛl/ *adj* factual

éventail /evɑ̃taj/ *m* **1** fan
2 range

éventaire /evɑ̃tɛʀ/ *m* stall

éventer: **s'éventer** /evɑ̃te/ [**v1**] *v refl* (+ *v être*) ‹*perfume, coffee*› to go off; ‹*wine*› to pass its best; ‹*beer, lemonade*› to go flat

éventrer /evɑ̃tʀe/ [**v1**] *vt* **1** ‹*person*› to disembowel; ‹*bull*› to gore
2 to rip open

éventualité /evɑ̃tɥalite/ *f* **1** eventuality
2 possibility; **dans l'∼ de** in the event of

éventuel, **-elle** /evɑ̃tɥɛl/ *adj* possible

éventuellement /evɑ̃tɥɛlmɑ̃/ *adv*
1 possibly
2 if necessary

évêque /evɛk/ *m* bishop (**de** of)

évertuer: **s'évertuer** /evɛʀtɥe/ [**v1**] *v refl* (+ *v être*) to try one's best (**à faire** to do)

éviction /eviksjɔ̃/ *f* **1** ousting (**de** from)
2 (Law) eviction

✐ **évidemment** /evidamɑ̃/ *adv* of course

✐ **évidence** /evidɑ̃s/ **A** *f* **1** obviousness
2 obvious fact; **se rendre à l'∼** to face the facts; **de toute ∼, à l'∼** obviously
B **en évidence** *phr* **laisser qch en ∼** to leave sth in an obvious place; **mettre en ∼** to highlight ‹*feature*›

✐ **évident**, **∼e** /evidɑ̃, ɑ̃t/ *adj* obvious; **ce n'est pas ∼** (fam) not necessarily; it's not so easy

évider /evide/ [**v1**] *vt* to hollow out; to scoop out

évier /evje/ *m* sink

évincer /evɛ̃se/ [**v12**] *vt* to oust ‹*rival*›

évitable /evitabl/ *adj* avoidable

✐ **éviter** /evite/ [**v1**] *vt* **1** to avoid; **∼ à qn de faire** to save sb (from) doing
2 to dodge ‹*bullet, blow*›

évocation /evɔkasjɔ̃/ *f* **1** evocation; reminiscence
2 mention (**de** of)

évolué, **∼e** /evɔlɥe/ *adj* **1** civilized
2 evolved

évoluer /evɔlɥe/ [**v1**] *vi* **1** to evolve, to change

2 to develop
3 to glide

évolutif, **-ive** /evɔlytif, iv/ *adj* progressive

évolution /evɔlysjɔ̃/ *f* **1** evolution
2 development
3 progress
4 progression
5 change; **en pleine ~** undergoing rapid change

évolutionniste /evɔlysjɔnist/ *adj* evolutionary

évoquer /evɔke/ [**v1**] *vt* **1** to recall
2 to mention, to bring up
3 to bring back ‹*memory*›; to be reminiscent of ‹*childhood*›
4 to evoke

ex /ɛks/ *m* **1** (*written abbr* = **exemple**) eg
2 (*written abbr* = **exemplaire**) copy

ex- /ɛks/ *pref* **~champion** former champion

exacerber /ɛgzasɛʀbe/ [**v1**] *vt* to exacerbate

exact, **~e** /ɛgza(kt), akt/ *adj* **1** correct
2 accurate
3 exact
4 punctual

exactement /ɛgzaktəmɑ̃/ *adv* exactly

exactitude /ɛgzaktityd/ *f* **1** correctness
2 accuracy
3 exactness
4 punctuality

ex æquo /ɛgzeko/ *adv* **ils sont premiers ~** they've tied for first place

exagération /ɛgzaʒeʀasjɔ̃/ *f* exaggeration

exagéré, **~e** /ɛgzaʒeʀe/ *adj* **1** exaggerated
2 excessive; **d'une sensibilité ~e** oversensitive

exagérément /ɛgzaʒeʀemɑ̃/ *adv* excessively

exagérer /ɛgzaʒeʀe/ [**v14**] **A** *vt* to exaggerate
B *vi* to go too far

exaltant, **~e** /ɛgzaltɑ̃, ɑ̃t/ *adj* thrilling; inspiring

exaltation /ɛgzaltasjɔ̃/ *f* **1** elation
2 stimulation
3 glorification

exalté, **~e** /ɛgzalte/ **A** *pp* ▶ **exalter**
B *pp adj* impassioned

exalter /ɛgzalte/ [**v1**] *vt* **1** to glorify
2 to heighten
3 to elate, to thrill

examen /ɛgzamɛ̃/ *m* **1** (Sch, Univ) examination, exam; **passer un ~** to take an exam; **~ de rattrapage** retake, resit (BrE)
2 (Med) examination
3 examination; consideration; review; **être en cours d'~** to be under review; to be under consideration
4 inspection
■ **~ blanc** mock (exam), practice exam; **~ de conscience** self-examination; **~ spécial d'entrée à l'université**, **ESEU** *university entrance exam for students not having the baccalaureate*

examinateur, **-trice** /ɛgzaminatœʀ, tʀis/ *mf* examiner

examiner /ɛgzamine/ [**v1**] *vt* **1** to examine; to review; **~ qch de près** to have a close look at sth
2 (Med) to examine ‹*patient, wound*›

exaspération /ɛgzaspeʀasjɔ̃/ *f*
1 exasperation
2 intensification

exaspérer /ɛgzaspeʀe/ [**v14**] *vt* **1** to exasperate, to infuriate
2 to exacerbate

exaucer /ɛgzose/ [**v12**] *vt* to grant

excavatrice /ɛkskavatʀis/ *f* excavator

excédant, **~e** /ɛksedɑ̃, ɑ̃t/ *adj* exasperating, infuriating

excédent /ɛksedɑ̃/ *m* surplus; **~ de bagages** excess baggage

excédentaire /ɛksedɑ̃tɛʀ/ *adj* surplus

excéder /ɛksede/ [**v14**] *vt* **1** to exceed
2 to infuriate

excellence /ɛksɛlɑ̃s/ *f* excellence

Excellence /ɛksɛlɑ̃s/ *f* **Son ~** His/Her Excellency

excellent, **~e** /ɛksɛlɑ̃, ɑ̃t/ *adj* excellent

exceller /ɛksele/ [**v1**] *vi* to excel

excentré, **~e** /ɛksɑ̃tʀe/ *adj* **1** ‹*area*› outlying
2 être ~ ‹*axis*› to be off-centre (BrE)

excentricité /ɛksɑ̃tʀisite/ *f* eccentricity

excentrique /ɛksɑ̃tʀik/ *adj*, *mf* eccentric

excepté, **~e** /ɛksɛpte/ **A** *pp* ▶ **excepter**
B *prep* except
C excepté que *phr* except that

excepter /ɛksɛpte/ [**v1**] *vt* **si l'on excepte** except for, apart from

exception /ɛksɛpsjɔ̃/ *f* exception; **faire ~** to be an exception; **à l'~ de**, **~ faite de** except for; **sauf ~** with the occasional exception; **d'~** ‹*person*› exceptional; ‹*law*› emergency

exceptionnel, **-elle** /ɛksɛpsjɔnɛl/ *adj* (gen) exceptional; ‹*price*› bargain; ‹*meeting*› extraordinary

exceptionnellement /ɛksɛpsjɔnɛlmɑ̃/ *adv* exceptionally

excès /ɛksɛ/ *m inv* excess; **commettre des ~** to go too far; **des ~ de langage** bad language; **tomber dans l'~ inverse** to go to the opposite extreme; **~ de confiance/zèle** overconfidence/overzealousness
■ **~ de vitesse** speeding

excessif, **-ive** /ɛksesif, iv/ *adj* **1** excessive
2 extreme; **il est ~** he is a man of extremes

excision /ɛksizjɔ̃/ *f* **1** excision
2 female circumcision

excitant, **~e** /ɛksitɑ̃, ɑ̃t/ **A** *adj*
1 ‹*substance*› stimulating
2 exciting; thrilling
B *m* stimulant

excitation /ɛksitasjɔ̃/ *f* **1** excitement

2 arousal
3 stimulation

excité, **~e** /ɛksite/ **A** *adj* **1** ‹*crowd*› in a frenzy; ‹*atmosphere*› frenzied
2 ‹*person*› thrilled, excited
3 (sexually) aroused
B *mf* **1** rowdy
2 fanatic
3 neurotic
IDIOM **être ~ comme une puce** (fam) to be like a cat on a hot tin roof

e

exciter /ɛksite/ [**v1**] **A** *vt* **1** to arouse ‹*anger*›; to kindle ‹*desire*›
2 to thrill
3 to arouse
4 to tease ‹*animal*›; to get [sb] excited ‹*child*›; ‹*coffee*› to get [sb] hyped up
5 to stimulate ‹*palate*›
B **s'exciter** *v refl* (+ *v être*) to get excited

exclamatif, **-ive** /ɛksklamatif, iv/ *adj* exclamatory

exclamation /ɛksklamasjɔ̃/ *f* exclamation

exclamer: **s'exclamer** /ɛksklame/ [**v1**] *v refl* (+ *v être*) to exclaim

exclu, **~e** /ɛkskly/ **A** *pp* ▶ **exclure**
B *pp adj* excluded; **c'est exclu!** it's out of the question!; **se sentir ~** to feel left out

exclure /ɛksklyʀ/ [**v78**] *vt* **1** to exclude ‹*person*›; to rule out ‹*possibility*›
2 to expel ‹*member*›

exclusif, **-ive** /ɛksklyzif, iv/ *adj* exclusive; **concessionnaire ~** sole agent

exclusion /ɛksklyzjɔ̃/ **A** *f* **1** exclusion; **~ sociale** social exclusion
2 expulsion
3 suspension
B **à l'exclusion de** *phr* with the exception of

exclusivité /ɛksklyzivite/ *f* exclusive rights; **en ~** ‹*publish*› exclusively; ‹*product*› exclusive

excommunier /ɛkskɔmynje/ [**v2**] *vt* to excommunicate

excrément /ɛkskʀemɑ̃/ *m* excrement

excrétion /ɛkskʀesjɔ̃/ *f* excretion

excroissance /ɛkskʀwasɑ̃s/ *f* **1** (Med) growth, excrescence
2 (in botany) outgrowth

excursion /ɛkskyʀsjɔ̃/ *f* excursion, trip

excuse /ɛkskyz/ *f* **1** excuse
2 apology

excuser /ɛkskyze/ [**v1**] **A** *vt* to forgive; to pardon; to excuse; **excusez-moi** I'm sorry; **vous êtes tout excusé** it's quite all right
B **s'excuser** *v refl* (+ *v être*) to apologize

exécrable /ɛgzekʀabl/ *adj* loathsome; dreadful; detestable

exécrer /ɛgzekʀe/ [**v14**] *vt* to loathe

exécutant, **~e** /ɛgzekytɑ̃, ɑ̃t/ *mf*
1 performer
2 **il dit n'avoir été qu'un ~** he claims he was only obeying orders

⚷ **exécuter** /ɛgzekyte/ [**v1**] **A** *vt* **1** to carry out ‹*task, mission*›; to do ‹*exercise*›
2 to carry out ‹*orders, threat*›; to fulfil (BrE) ‹*contract*›; to enforce ‹*law, ruling*›
3 to execute ‹*prisoner*›; to kill ‹*victim*›
4 (Mus) to perform
B **s'exécuter** *v refl* (+ *v être*) to comply

exécutif, **-ive** /ɛgzekytif, ive/ *adj* executive

exécution /ɛgzekysjɔ̃/ *f* **1** execution, carrying out; enforcement; fulfilment (BrE); **mettre à ~** to carry out ‹*threat*›; **travaux en cours d'~** work in progress; **veiller à la bonne ~ d'une tâche** to see that a job is done well
2 execution; **~ capitale** capital punishment

exemplaire /ɛgzɑ̃plɛʀ/ **A** *adj* **1** exemplary; **élève ~** model pupil
2 (Law) exemplary
B *m* **1** copy; print
2 specimen

exemplarité /ɛgzɑ̃plaʀite/ *f* deterrent nature (**de** of)

⚷ **exemple** /ɛgzɑ̃pl/ **A** *m* **1** example; **sans ~** unprecedented; **être l'~ de la gentillesse** to be a model of kindness; **donner qn en ~** to hold sb up as an example
2 warning (**pour** to)
B **par exemple** *phr* for example; **ça par ~!** how amazing!; well, honestly!

exemplifier /ɛgzɑ̃plifje/ [**v2**] *vt* to exemplify

exempt, **~e** /ɛgzɑ̃, ɑ̃t/ *adj* exempt; **~ d'impôt** tax-free

exempter /ɛgzɑ̃te/ [**v1**] *vt* to exempt

⚷ **exercer** /ɛgzɛʀse/ [**v12**] **A** *vt* **1** to exercise ‹*right*›; to exert ‹*authority*›
2 to exercise ‹*profession*›; to practise (BrE) ‹*art*›
3 to exercise ‹*body*›
B **s'exercer** *v refl* (+ *v être*) **1** ‹*athlete*› to train; ‹*musician*› to practise (BrE)
2 ‹*influence, force*› to be exerted

⚷ **exercice** /ɛgzɛʀsis/ *m* exercise; **faire de l'~** to get some exercise; **dans l'~ de ses fonctions** in the course of one's duty; while at work; **en ~** ‹*minister, president*› incumbent; **entrer en ~** to take up one's duties

exergue /ɛgzɛʀg/ *m* **1** epigraph
2 inscription

exhaler /ɛgzale/ [**v1**] *vt* to exhale

exhausser /ɛgzose/ [**v1**] *vt* to raise

exhaustif, **-ive** /ɛgzostif, iv/ *adj* exhaustive

exhiber /ɛgzibe/ [**v1**] **A** *vt* to flaunt ‹*wealth*›; to show ‹*animal*›; to expose ‹*body*›
B **s'exhiber** *v refl* (+ *v être*) **1** to expose oneself
2 to flaunt oneself

exhibition /ɛgzibisjɔ̃/ *f* **1** (of animals) show; exhibition

⚷ key word

2 (Sport) demonstration, display
3 (of wealth) parade; (of emotion) display
exhibitionniste /ɛgzibisjɔnist/ *adj, mf* exhibitionist
exhortation /ɛgzɔʀtasjɔ̃/ *f* exhortation; **~ au calme** call for calm
exhorter /ɛgzɔʀte/ [**v1**] *vt* to motivate; **~ qn à faire** to urge *or* exhort sb to do
exhumer /ɛgzyme/ [**v1**] *vt* **1** to exhume
2 to excavate
exigeant, **~e** /ɛgziʒɑ̃, ɑ̃t/ *adj* demanding
exigence /ɛgziʒɑ̃s/ *f* demand (**de qch** for sth)
✓ **exiger** /ɛgziʒe/ [**v13**] *vt* **1** to demand ‹*answer, reforms*›
2 to require
exigibilité /ɛgziʒibilite/ *f* (of tax, bill) payability; (of debt) repayability
exigible /ɛgziʒibl/ *adj* due
exigu, **-uë** /ɛgzigy/ *adj* ‹*room*› cramped; ‹*entrance*› narrow; ‹*space*› confined
exil /ɛgzil/ *m* exile; **en ~** in exile
exilé, **~e** /ɛgzile/ *mf* exile
exiler /ɛgzile/ [**v1**] **A** *vt* to exile
B s'exiler *v refl* (+ *v être*) to go into exile
✓ **existence** /ɛgzistɑ̃s/ *f* **1** existence
2 (fam) life
existentialisme /ɛgzistɑ̃sjalism/ *m* existentialism
✓ **exister** /ɛgziste/ [**v1**] *vi* to exist; **si le paradis existe** if there is a heaven; **la maison existe encore** the house is still standing
exode /ɛgzɔd/ *m* exodus; **~ rural** rural depopulation
exonération /ɛgzɔneʀasjɔ̃/ *f* exemption
exonérer /ɛgzɔneʀe/ [**v14**] *vt* to exempt
exorbitant, **~e** /ɛgzɔʀbitɑ̃, ɑ̃t/ *adj* ‹*price*› exorbitant; ‹*demands*› outrageous
exorbité, **~e** /ɛgzɔʀbite/ *adj* bulging
exorciser /ɛgzɔʀsize/ [**v1**] *vt* to exorcise
exotique /ɛgzɔtik/ *adj* exotic
exotisme /ɛgzɔtism/ *m* exoticism
expansif, **-ive** /ɛkspɑ̃sif, iv/ *adj* communicative, outgoing
expansion /ɛkspɑ̃sjɔ̃/ *f* **1** growth; **en (pleine) ~** (rapidly) growing
2 expansion
expansivité /ɛkspɑ̃sivite/ *f* expansiveness
expatriation /ɛkspatʀijasjɔ̃/ *f* expatriation
expatrié, **~e** /ɛkspatʀije/ *adj, mf* expatriate
expatrier /ɛkspatʀije/ [**v2**] **A** *vt* to deport
B s'expatrier *v refl* (+ *v être*) to emigrate
expectative /ɛkspɛktativ/ *f* **rester dans l'~** to wait and see
expédient /ɛkspedjɑ̃/ *m* expedient; **vivre d'~s** to live by one's wits
expédier /ɛkspedje/ [**v2**] *vt* **1** to send; to post (BrE), to mail (AmE); **~ qch à qn** to send sb sth
2 to get rid of ‹*person*›; to polish off ‹*work, meal*›; **~ un procès en une heure** to get a trial over within one hour
expéditeur, **-trice** /ɛkspeditœʀ, tʀis/ *mf* sender
expéditif, **-ive** /ɛkspeditif, iv/ *adj* ‹*person*› brisk; ‹*method*› cursory; **une justice expéditive** summary justice
expédition /ɛkspedisjɔ̃/ *f* expedition
expéditionnaire /ɛkspedisjɔnɛʀ/ **A** *adj* expeditionary
B *mf* **1** forwarding agent
2 copyist
✓ **expérience** /ɛkspeʀjɑ̃s/ *f* **1** experience; **avoir de l'~** to be experienced; **j'en ai fait l'~ à mes dépens** I learned that lesson to my cost
2 experiment
expérimental, **~e**, *mpl* **-aux** /ɛkspeʀimɑ̃tal, o/ *adj* experimental
expérimentation /ɛkspeʀimɑ̃tasjɔ̃/ *f* experimentation
■ **~ animale** experiments on animals
expérimenté, **~e** /ɛkspeʀimɑ̃te/ *adj* experienced
expérimenter /ɛkspeʀimɑ̃te/ [**v1**] *vt* to test
expert /ɛkspɛʀ/ *m* **1** expert (**en** on); **l'avis d'un ~** expert advice
2 adjuster
expert-comptable, *pl* **experts-comptables** /ɛkspɛʀkɔ̃tabl/ *m* ≈ chartered accountant (BrE), certified public accountant (AmE)
expert-conseil, *pl* **experts-conseils** /ɛkspɛʀkɔ̃sɛj/ *m* consultant
expertise /ɛkspɛʀtiz/ *f* **1** valuation (BrE), appraisal (AmE); assessment
2 expertise
expertiser /ɛkspɛʀtize/ [**v1**] *vt* to value (BrE), to appraise (AmE) ‹*jewellery*›; to assess ‹*damages*›
expier /ɛkspje/ [**v2**] *vt* to atone for, to expiate
expiration /ɛkspiʀasjɔ̃/ *f* **1** exhalation
2 expiry (BrE), expiration (AmE)
expirer /ɛkspiʀe/ [**v1**] **A** *vt* to exhale
B *vi* **1** ‹*contract*› to expire
2 to breathe out
explicatif, **-ive** /ɛksplikatif, iv/ *adj* explanatory
✓ **explication** /ɛksplikasjɔ̃/ *f* explanation; **nous avons eu une bonne ~** we've talked things through
explicite /ɛksplisit/ *adj* ‹*text, film*› explicit; ‹*answer*› definite
explicitement /ɛksplisitmɑ̃/ *adv* ‹*mention*› explicitly; ‹*condemn*› unequivocally; ‹*ask*› specifically
expliciter /ɛksplisite/ [**v1**] *vt* to clarify
✓ **expliquer** /ɛksplike/ [**v1**] **A** *vt* **1** to explain
2 (Sch) to analyse (BrE) ‹*text*›
B s'expliquer *v refl* (+ *v être*) **s'~ qch** to understand sth; **tout finira par s'~**

everything will become clear

exploit /ɛksplwɑ/ *m* exploit, feat

exploitant, **~e** /ɛksplwatɑ̃, ɑ̃t/ *mf* **~ agricole** farmer

exploitation /ɛksplwatasjɔ̃/ *f* **1** exploitation
2 ~ agricole farm; **~ commerciale** business concern
3 (of land, forest) exploitation; (of airline, shipping line) operation

exploiter /ɛksplwate/ [**v1**] *vt* **1** to exploit ‹*person*›
2 to work ‹*mine*›; to mine ‹*coal*›; to exploit ‹*forest*›; to run ‹*firm*›; to operate ‹*airline*›
3 to make the most of ‹*gift, knowledge*›

explorateur, **-trice** /ɛksplɔʀatœʀ, tʀis/ *mf* explorer

exploration /ɛksplɔʀasjɔ̃/ *f* exploration

explorer /ɛksplɔʀe/ [**v1**] *vt* to explore

exploser /ɛksploze/ [**v1**] *vi* to explode; to blow up; **faire ~** to blow up; to explode; to cause [sth] to blow up

explosif, **-ive** /ɛksplozif, iv/ **A** *adj* explosive
B *m* explosive; **attentat à l'~** bomb attack

explosion /ɛksplozjɔ̃/ *f* **1** explosion
2 outburst
3 (in market) boom

export /ɛkspɔʀ/ *m* export

exportateur, **-trice** /ɛkspɔʀtatœʀ, tʀis/ *mf* exporter

exportation /ɛkspɔʀtasjɔ̃/ *f* export

exporter /ɛkspɔʀte/ [**v1**] *vt* to export

exposé, **~e** /ɛkspoze/ **A** *pp* ▶ **exposer**
B *pp adj* **1** exposed; **maison ~e au sud** south-facing house
2 on show; on display
C *m* **1 ~ de** account of; **faire un** *or* **l'~ des faits** to give a statement of the facts
2 (Sch) talk; **faire un ~** to give a talk

🔑 **exposer** /ɛkspoze/ [**v1**] **A** *vt* **1** to exhibit ‹*art*›; to display, to put [sth] on display ‹*goods*›
2 to state ‹*facts*›; to outline ‹*idea, plan*›; to explain ‹*situation*›
3 to risk ‹*life, reputation*›
4 to expose ‹*skin, body*›; **ne reste pas exposé au soleil** stay out of the sun
B s'exposer *v refl* (+ *v être*) **1** to put oneself at risk; **s'~ à** to lay oneself open to ‹*criticism*›
2 s'~ au soleil to go out in the sun

exposition /ɛkspozisjɔ̃/ *f* **1** (of art) exhibition; (of animals, plants) show; (for trade) fair
2 (in shop) display
3 (of situation, facts) exposition
4 (of house) aspect
5 (to light, radiation) exposure

exprès¹ /ɛkspʀɛ/ *adv* **1** deliberately, on purpose; **comme par un fait ~** as bad luck would have it
2 specially

exprès², **-esse** /ɛkspʀɛs/ **A** *adj* express
B exprès *adj inv* **envoyer qch en** *or* **par ~** to send sth special delivery *or* express

express /ɛkspʀɛs/ **A** *adj inv* express
B *m inv* **1** express (train)
2 espresso

expressément /ɛkspʀesemɑ̃/ *adv* expressly

expressif, **-ive** /ɛkspʀesif, iv/ *adj* expressive

🔑 **expression** /ɛkspʀesjɔ̃/ *f* expression; **réduire qch à sa plus simple ~** (fig) to reduce sth to a minimum
■ **~ corporelle** self-expression through movement

expressivité /ɛkspʀesivite/ *f* expressiveness

exprimable /ɛkspʀimabl/ *adj* **difficilement ~** hard to express

🔑 **exprimer** /ɛkspʀime/ [**v1**] **A** *vt* to express
B s'exprimer *v refl* (+ *v être*) **1** to express oneself; **si j'ose m'~ ainsi** if I may put it that way
2 to be expressed

expropriation /ɛkspʀɔpʀijasjɔ̃/ *f* compulsory purchase; expropriation

exproprier /ɛkspʀɔpʀije/ [**v2**] *vt* **~ qn** to put a compulsory purchase order on sb's property

expulser /ɛkspylse/ [**v1**] *vt* **1** to evict
2 to deport
3 to expel
4 (Sport) to send [sb] off

expulsion /ɛkspylsjɔ̃/ *f* **1** eviction
2 deportation
3 expulsion

expurger /ɛkspyʀʒe/ [**v13**] *vt* to purge

exquis, **~e** /ɛkski, iz/ *adj* exquisite; delightful

exsangue /ɛgzɑ̃g/ *adj* bloodless

exsuder /ɛksyde/ [**v1**] **A** *vt* to exude
B *vi* to ooze (**de** from)

extase /ɛkstɑz/ *f* ecstasy

extasier: **s'extasier** /ɛkstazje/ [**v2**] *v refl* (+ *v être*) to go into ecstasy *or* raptures

extatique /ɛkstatik/ *adj* ecstatic

extensible /ɛkstɑ̃sibl/ *adj* **1** extensible
2 extendable

extensif, **-ive** /ɛkstɑ̃sif, iv/ *adj* **1** extensive
2 extended

extension /ɛkstɑ̃sjɔ̃/ *f* extension; **prendre de l'~** ‹*industry*› to expand; ‹*strike*› to spread

exténuer /ɛkstenɥe/ [**v1**] *vt* to exhaust

🔑 **extérieur**, **~e** /ɛksteʀjœʀ/ **A** *adj* **1** outside
2 outer
3 foreign
4 outward
B *m* **1** outside; **à l'~** outside, outdoors; **d'~** outdoor
2 exterior, appearance
3 en ~ ‹*filmed*› on location

extérieurement /ɛksteʀjœʀmɑ̃/ *adv* **1** on the outside
2 outwardly

🔑 key word

extérioriser /ɛksteʀjɔʀize/ [**v1**] *vt* to show
extermination /ɛkstɛʀminasjɔ̃/ *f* extermination
exterminer /ɛkstɛʀmine/ [**v1**] *vt* to exterminate; to wipe out
externalisation /ɛkstɛʀnalizasjɔ̃/ *f* outsourcing
externaliser /ɛkstɛʀnalize/ *vt* to outsource
externat /ɛkstɛʀna/ *m* **1** (Sch) day school
2 préparer l'~ to prepare for medical school entrance exams; **faire son ~** to be a non-resident student doctor (in a hospital)
externe /ɛkstɛʀn/ **A** *adj* external; outside; exterior
B *mf* **1** (Sch) day pupil
2 (Med) non-residential medical student (BrE), extern (AmE)
extincteur /ɛkstɛ̃ktœʀ/ *m* fire extinguisher
extinction /ɛkstɛ̃ksjɔ̃/ *f* **1** (Med) **avoir une ~ de voix** to have lost one's voice
2 extinction; **espèce en voie d'~** endangered species
3 après l'~ de l'incendie after the fire was put out; **après l'~ des feux** after lights out
extirper /ɛkstiʀpe/ [**v1**] *vt* **1** to eradicate
2 (fam) to drag ‹*person*› (**de** out of, from)
extorquer /ɛkstɔʀke/ [**v1**] *vt* to extort
extorsion /ɛkstɔʀsjɔ̃/ *f* extortion
extra /ɛkstʀa/ **A** *adj inv* **1** (fam) great (fam)
2 ‹*product*› of superior quality
B *m inv* **1** extra; **se payer un petit ~** to have a little treat
2 faire des ~ to do a few extra jobs
3 extra worker
extracommunautaire, *pl* **~s** /ɛkstʀakɔmynotɛʀ/ *adj* non-EEC
extraction /ɛkstʀaksjɔ̃/ *f* **1** (of oil, gas) extraction; (of coal, diamonds) mining; (of marble, slate) quarrying
2 (of bullet, tooth) extraction
extrader /ɛkstʀade/ [**v1**] *vt* to extradite
⚷ **extraire** /ɛkstʀɛʀ/ [**v58**] *vt* **1** to extract ‹*mineral*›; to mine ‹*gold, coal*›; to quarry ‹*slate, marble*›
2 to extract; to pull out; to remove
extrait /ɛkstʀɛ/ *m* **1** (from book, film) extract, excerpt; (from speech) extract
2 essence, extract; **~ de viande** meat extract
■ **~ (d'acte) de naissance** birth certificate; **~ de casier judiciaire (de qn)** copy of (sb's) criminal record; **~ de compte** abstract of accounts
extra-long, **-longue**, *mpl* **~s** /ɛkstʀalɔ̃, ɔ̃g/ *adj* ‹*cigarette*› king-size; ‹*clothing*› extra long
extralucide /ɛkstʀalysid/ *adj* clairvoyant
⚷ **extraordinaire** /ɛkstʀaɔʀdinɛʀ/ *adj*
1 extraordinary, amazing, remarkable; **c'est quand même ~!** it's incredible!
2 ‹*expenses, measures*› extraordinary
extraordinairement /ɛkstʀaɔʀdinɛʀmɑ̃/ *adv* amazingly, extraordinarily
extrapoler /ɛkstʀapɔle/ [**v1**] *vt, vi* to extrapolate
extrascolaire /ɛkstʀaskɔlɛʀ/ *adj* extracurricular
extraterrestre /ɛkstʀatɛʀɛstʀ/ *mf* extraterrestrial, alien
extra-utérin, **~e**, *mpl* **~s** /ɛkstʀayteʀɛ̃, in/ *adj* **grossesse ~e** ectopic pregnancy
extravagance /ɛkstʀavagɑ̃s/ *f*
1 eccentricity
2 extravagance
extravagant, **~e** /ɛkstʀavagɑ̃, ɑ̃t/ *adj*
1 eccentric
2 extravagant
3 exorbitant
extraverti, **~e** /ɛkstʀavɛʀti/ *adj, mf* extrovert
⚷ **extrême** /ɛkstʀɛm/ **A** *adj* **1** furthest; **dans l'~ nord/sud du pays** in the extreme North/South of the country
2 extreme
3 drastic
B *m* extreme; **c'est pousser la logique à l'~** that's taking logic to extremes; **à l'~ inverse** at the other extreme
extrêmement /ɛkstʀɛmmɑ̃/ *adv* extremely
Extrême-Orient /ɛkstʀɛmɔʀjɑ̃/ *pr m* **l'~** the Far East
extrémiste /ɛkstʀemist/ *adj, mf* extremist
extrémité /ɛkstʀemite/ *f* **1** end; (of finger) tip; (of mast) top; (of town, field) edge; **aux deux ~s** at both ends
2 extreme
exubérance /egzybeʀɑ̃s/ *f* exuberance
exubérant, **~e** /egzybeʀɑ̃, ɑ̃t/ *adj* exuberant
exultation /egzyltasjɔ̃/ *f* exultation
exulter /egzylte/ [**v1**] *vi* to be exultant, to exult (**de** with), to exult (**de faire** at doing)
exutoire /egzytwaʀ/ *m* outlet

e

Ff

f, **F** /ɛf/ *m inv* **1** (letter) f, F
2 **F3** two-bedroom flat (BrE) *or* apartment
3 (Hist) (*written abbr* = **franc**) **50 F** 50 F

fa /fa/ *m inv* (Mus) (note) F; (in sol-fa) fa

fable /fɑbl/ *f* **1** tale
2 fable
3 tall story

fabricant /fabʀikɑ̃/ *m* manufacturer

fabrication /fabʀikasjɔ̃/ *f* making; manufacture; **~ en série** mass production
■ **~ assistée par ordinateur, FAO** computer-aided manufacturing, CAM

fabrique /fabʀik/ *f* factory

⚷ **fabriquer** /fabʀike/ [**v1**] *vt* **1** to make; to manufacture
2 to invent ‹*alibi*›; **qu'est-ce que tu fabriques?** (fam) what are you up to?

fabulateur, **-trice** /fabylatœʀ, tʀis/ *mf* compulsive liar

fabuler /fabyle/ [**v1**] *vi* **1** to make things up
2 to confabulate

fabuleusement /fabyløzmɑ̃/ *adv* fabulously

fabuleux, **-euse** /fabylø, øz/ *adj* ‹*beauty*› fabulous; ‹*sum*› fantastic; ‹*creature*› mythical

fac /fak/ *f* (fam) **1** faculty
2 university

façade /fasad/ *f* **1** (of building) front; **~ nord** north side
2 facade

⚷ **face** /fas/ **A** *f* **1** face
2 side; **le côté ~ d'une pièce** the heads side of a coin
3 **faire ~** to face up to things; **se faire ~** to face each other; to be opposite one another; **faire ~ à** to face ‹*place*›; (fig) to face ‹*adversary, challenge*›; to cope with ‹*spending*›; to meet ‹*demand*›
B **de face** *phr* ‹*photo*› full-face; ‹*lighting*› frontal
C **en face** *phr* **il habite en ~** he lives opposite; **voir les choses en ~** to see things as they are; **l'équipe d'en ~** the opposing team
D **en face de** *phr* **1** **en ~ de l'église** opposite the church (BrE), across from the church
2 compared with
E **face à** *phr* **1** **mon lit est ~ à la fenêtre** my bed faces the window
2 **~ à cette situation** in view of this situation
(IDIOM) **se voiler la ~** not to face facts

face-à-face /fasafas/ *m inv* **1** one-to-one debate (BrE), one-on-one debate (AmE)
2 encounter

facétie /fasesi/ *f* facetious remark; practical joke

facétieux, **-ieuse** /fasesjø, øz/ *adj* mischievous

facette /fasɛt/ *f* facet

fâché, **~e** /fɑʃe/ **A** *pp* ▶ **fâcher**
B *pp adj* angry; **être ~ avec qn** to have fallen out with sb

fâcher: **se fâcher** /fɑʃe/ [**v1**] *v refl* (+ *v être*)
1 to get angry
2 to fall out

fâcheux, **-euse** /fɑʃø, øz/ *adj* ‹*influence*› detrimental; ‹*delay*› unfortunate; ‹*news*› distressing

facial, **~e**, *mpl* **-iaux** /fasjal, o/ *adj* facial

faciès /fasjɛs/ *m inv* **1** facies
2 face

⚷ **facile** /fasil/ **A** *adj* **1** easy; **avoir la larme ~** to be quick to cry
2 easy-going
B *adv* (fam) easily

⚷ **facilement** /fasilmɑ̃/ *adv* **1** easily
2 (fam) **j'ai mis ~ deux heures pour venir** it took me a good two hours to get here

facilité /fasilite/ **A** *f* **1** (of work) easiness; (of use, maintenance) ease
2 fluency
B **facilités** *fpl* **1** **donner toutes ~s pour faire** to afford every opportunity to do
2 **~s (de paiement)** easy terms

faciliter /fasilite/ [**v1**] *vt* to make [sth] easier

⚷ **façon** /fasɔ̃/ **A** *f* **1** way; **de toute ~, de toutes les ~s** anyway; **de ~ à faire** in order to do; in such a way as to do; **de ~ (à ce) qu'elle fasse** so (that) she does; **elle nous a joué un tour à sa ~** she played a trick of her own on us; **~ de parler** so to speak
2 **un peigne ~ ivoire** an imitation ivory comb
3 (of garment) making-up
B **façons** *fpl* **en voilà des ~s!** what a way to behave!; **sans ~s** ‹*meal*› informal; ‹*person*› unpretentious

façonner /fasɔne/ [**v1**] *vt* **1** to manufacture; to make
2 to hew ‹*wood*›; to fashion ‹*clay*›
3 to shape, to mould (BrE), to mold (AmE)

fac-similé, *pl* **~s** /faksimile/ *m* facsimile

⚷ **facteur**, **-trice** /faktœʀ, tʀis/ **A** *mf*

⚷ key word

postman/postwoman
B *m* factor
factice /faktis/ *adj* ‹*smile*› forced; ‹*jewellery*› imitation; ‹*flower, beauty*› artificial
faction /faksjɔ̃/ *f* **1** faction
2 (Mil) guard duty
factrice ▶ **facteur A**
factuel, **-elle** /faktɥɛl/ *adj* factual
facturation /faktyʀasjɔ̃/ *f* **1** invoicing
2 invoicing department
facture /faktyʀ/ *f* bill; invoice
facturer /faktyʀe/ [**v1**] *vt* to invoice ‹*goods*›
facturette /faktyʀɛt/ *f* credit card slip
facturier, **-ière** /faktyʀje, ɛʀ/ **A** *mf* invoice clerk
B *m* invoice book
facturière /faktyʀjɛʀ/ *f* invoicing machine
facultatif, **-ive** /fakyltatif, iv/ *adj* optional
faculté /fakylte/ *f* **1** (mental) faculty; ability
2 option
3 (at university) faculty
4 (Law) right
fade /fad/ *adj* ‹*person, book*› dull; ‹*food, taste*› tasteless; ‹*colour*› drab
fadette /fadɛt/ *f* (Journ) *abbr* (= **facture détaillée**) itemised bill
fadeur /fadœʀ/ *f* blandness; dreariness
fagot /fago/ *m* bundle of firewood
fagoter /fagɔte/ [**v1**] **A** *vt* to do [sb] up (fam)
B se fagoter *v refl* (+ *v être*) to do oneself up (fam); **(être) mal fagoté** (to be) badly dressed
faible /fɛbl/ **A** *adj* **1** (gen) weak; ‹*sight*› poor; ‹*constitution*› frail; **être ~ avec qn** to be too soft on sb
2 ‹*proportion, increase*› small; ‹*income, speed*› low; ‹*means, impact*› limited; ‹*chance*› slim
3 ‹*noise, glow*› faint; ‹*lighting*› dim; ‹*wind, rain*› light
4 ‹*result*› poor; ‹*argument*› feeble
5 ‹*pupil, class*› slow; **~ d'esprit** feeble-minded
6 le mot est ~! that's putting it mildly!
B *mf* weak-willed person
C *m* weakness; **avoir un ~ pour qn** to have a soft spot for sb
faiblement /fɛbləmɑ̃/ *adv* weakly; ‹*influence, increase*› slightly; ‹*lit*› dimly
faiblesse /fɛblɛs/ *f* **1** weakness; (of invalid) frailty
2 inadequacy
3 (of voice) faintness; (of lighting) dimness
faiblir /fɛbliʀ/ [**v3**] *vi* **1** ‹*person, pulse*› to get weaker; ‹*sight*› to be failing
2 ‹*person, currency*› to weaken
3 ‹*athlete*› to flag; ‹*plot*› to decline; ‹*interest*› to wane; ‹*speed*› to slacken
4 ‹*storm*› to abate; ‹*noise*› to grow faint
faïence /fajɑ̃s/ *f* earthenware
IDIOM **se regarder en chiens de ~** to look daggers at each other

faille /fɑj/ *f* **1** (in geology) fault
2 flaw; **sans ~** unfailing
3 rift
faillir /fajiʀ/ [**v28**] *vi* **1 elle a failli le gifler** she almost *or* (very) nearly slapped him
2 sans ~ unfailingly
faillite /fajit/ *f* **1** bankruptcy
2 failure
faim /fɛ̃/ *f* hunger; **avoir ~** to be hungry; **mourir de ~** to die of starvation; (fig) to be starving; **je suis resté sur ma ~** I was disappointed
fainéant, **~e** /feneɑ̃, ɑ̃t/ *adj* lazy
fainéantise /feneɑ̃tiz/ *f* laziness
faire /fɛʀ/ [**v10**]

> You will find the translations for expressions such as *faire peur*, *faire semblant* etc, at the entries **peur**, **semblant**, etc.

A *vt* **1** to make; **~ son lit/une faute** to make one's bed/a mistake; **~ des jaloux** to make people jealous; **deux et deux font quatre** two and two is four
2 to do; **~ de la recherche** to do research; **j'ai à ~** I have things to do; **que fait-il?** what does he do?; what is he doing?; **que veux-tu que j'y fasse?** what do you want me to do about it?; **~ médecine/du violon** to do *or* study medicine/to study *or* play the violin; **~ une école de commerce** to go to business school; **~ un numéro de téléphone/une lettre** to dial a number/to write a letter; **~ du tennis/de la couture** to play tennis/to sew; **~ un poulet** to do *or* cook a chicken
3 to do ‹*distance, journey*›; to go round ‹*shops*›; to do (fam) ‹*region, museums*›; **j'ai fait tous les tiroirs mais je ne l'ai pas trouvé** I went through all the drawers but I couldn't find it
4 (fam) to have ‹*diabetes, complex*›
5 ~ le malade to pretend to be ill
6 leur départ ne m'a rien fait their departure didn't affect me at all; **ça y fait** (fam) it has an effect; **pour ce que ça fait!** (fam) for all the good it does!
7 to say; **'bien sûr,' fit-elle** 'of course,' she said; **le canard fait 'coin-coin'** ducks go 'quack'
8 ça m'a fait rire it made me laugh; **~ manger un bébé** to feed a baby; **fais voir** show me; **fais-leur prendre un rendez-vous** get them to make an appointment; **~ traverser la rue à un vieillard** to help an old man across the road
9 ~ réparer sa voiture to have *or* get one's car repaired
10 je n'en ai rien à ~ (fam) I couldn't care less; **ça ne fait rien!** it doesn't matter!; **qu'est-ce que ça peut bien te ~?** (fam) what is it to you?; **il sait y ~** he's got the knack; **il ne fait que pleuvoir** it never stops raining; **je ne fais qu'obéir aux ordres** I'm only obeying orders
B *vi* **1** to do, to act; **fais comme tu veux** do as you like

2 to look; ~ **jeune** to look young
3 ça fait 15 ans que j'habite ici I've been living here for 15 years; **ça fait 2 mètres de long** it's 2 metres (BrE) long
4 to go (to the toilet); **tu as fait?** have you been?
5 (fam) ~ **avec** to make do with; to put up with
C se faire *v refl* (+ *v être*) **1 se ~ un café** to make oneself a coffee; **se ~ comprendre** to make oneself understood
2 to get, to become; **il se fait tard** it's getting late
3 s'en ~ to worry; **il ne s'en fait pas!** he's not the sort of person to worry about things!; (as criticism) he's got a nerve!
4 se ~ à to get used to
5 ça se fait encore ici it's still done here; **ça ne se fait pas** it's not the done thing
6 ‹*colour, style*› to be in (fashion)
7 c'est ce qui se fait de mieux it's the best there is
8 comment se fait-il que...? how is it that...?, how come...?

faire-part /fɛʀpaʀ/ *m inv* announcement

faire-valoir /fɛʀvalwaʀ/ *m inv* **être le ~ de** ‹*actor*› to be a foil for

fais /fɛ/ ▶ **faire**

faisaient /fəzɛ/ ▶ **faire**

faisais /fəzɛ/ ▶ **faire**

faisait /fəzɛ/ ▶ **faire**

faisan /fəzɑ̃/ *m* (cock) pheasant

faisane /fəzan/ *f* **(poule) ~** hen pheasant

faisant /fəzɑ̃/ ▶ **faire**

faisceau, *pl* **~x** /fɛso/ *m* **1** beam; **~ lumineux** beam of light
2 bundle

faisiez /fəzje/ ▶ **faire**

faisions /fəzjɔ̃/ ▶ **faire**

faisons /fəzɔ̃/ ▶ **faire**

⚷ **fait**, **~e** /fɛ, fɛt/ **A** *pp* ▶ **faire**
B *pp adj* **1** done; **c'en est ~ de** that's the end of; **c'est bien ~ (pour toi)!** (fam) it serves you right!
2 ~ de *or* **en** made (up) of; **idée toute ~e** ready-made idea; **elle est bien ~e** she's got a great figure; **la vie est mal ~e** life is unfair
3 ~ pour qch/pour faire meant for sth/to do
4 ‹*programme, device*› designed
5 (fam) done for
6 un fromage bien ~ a ripe cheese
C *m* **1** fact; **le ~ est là** *or* **les ~s sont là, il t'a trompé** the fact (of the matter) is that he cheated you; **les ~s et gestes de qn** sb's movements
2 de ce ~ because of this *or* that; **être le ~ de qn** to be due to sb
3 event
4 aller droit au ~ to go straight to the point
D au fait /ofɛt/ *phr* by the way
E de fait *phr* **1** ‹*situation*› de facto
2 ‹*exist, result in*› effectively
3 indeed
F en fait *phr* in fact, actually
G en fait de *phr* as regards
■ **~ divers** (short) news item; **~ de société** fact of life
IDIOMS **être au ~ de** to be informed about; **prendre qn sur le ~** to catch sb in the act

faîte /fɛt/ *m* (of mountain) summit; (of house) rooftop; (of tree) top

faites /fɛt/ ▶ **faire**

falaise /falɛz/ *f* cliff

fallacieux, **-ieuse** /falasjø, øz/ *adj* ‹*argument*› fallacious; ‹*pretext*› false

⚷ **falloir** /falwaʀ/ [**v50**] **A** *v impers* **1 il faut qn/qch** we need sb/sth; sb/sth is needed; **il va ~ deux jours/du courage** it will take two days/courage; **il me/te/leur faut qch** I/you/they need sth; **il me faut ce livre!** I've got to have that book!
2 il faut faire we/you etc have (got) to do; we/you etc must do; we/you etc should do; **il ne faut pas la déranger** she mustn't be disturbed; **il fallait le faire** it had to be done; **faut le faire!** (fam) (admiring) it takes a bit of doing!; (critical) would you believe it?; **comme il faut** ‹*behave*› properly
3 il faut que tu fasses you have (got) to do, you must do; you should do
B s'en falloir *v refl* (+ *v être*) **peu s'en faut** very nearly; **elle a perdu, mais il s'en est fallu de peu** she lost, but only just
IDIOMS **il faut ce qu'il faut!** there's no point in skimping!; **en moins de temps qu'il ne faut pour le dire** before you could say Jack Robinson

fallu /faly/ ▶ **falloir**

falsification /falsifikasjɔ̃/ *f* **1** falsification
2 forging

falsifier /falsifje/ [**v2**] *vt* **1** to falsify, to tamper with ‹*document*›; to distort ‹*facts*›
2 to forge

famé, **~e** /fame/ *adj* **un quartier mal ~** a disreputable *or* seedy area

famélique /famelik/ *adj* emaciated, scrawny

⚷ **fameux**, **-euse** /famø, øz/ *adj* **1** much talked about
2 famous
3 excellent

⚷ **familial**, **~e**, *mpl* **-iaux** /familjal, o/ *adj*
1 ‹*meal, life, firm*› family
2 voiture ~e estate car (BrE), station wagon (AmE)

familiariser /familjaʀize/ [**v1**] *vt* to familiarize

familiarité /familjaʀite/ *f* familiarity

familier, **-ière** /familje, ɛʀ/ *adj* **1** ‹*face, landscape*› familiar
2 ‹*word*› informal, colloquial
3 ‹*attitude*› informal; ‹*person, gesture*› familiar

⚷ key word

4 animal ~ pet

familièrement /familjɛʀmɑ̃/ *adv*
1 commonly
2 informally
3 with undue familiarity

famille /famij/ *f* family; **c'est de ~** it runs in the family

famine /famin/ *f* famine

fanatique /fanatik/ **A** *adj* ‹*believer*› fanatical; ‹*admiration, love*› ardent
B *mf* **1** fanatic
2 (fam) enthusiast, freak (fam)

fanatisme /fanatism/ *m* fanaticism

faner /fane/ [**v1**] **A** *vi* **1** to wither
2 to make hay
B se faner *v refl* (+ *v être*) **1** ‹*plant*› to wither, to wilt
2 ‹*beauty, colour*› to fade

fanfare /fɑ̃faʀ/ *f* brass band; **annoncer qch en ~** to trumpet sth

fanfaron, -onne /fɑ̃faʀɔ̃, ɔn/ *mf* boaster, swaggerer; **faire le ~** to boast

fanfaronner /fɑ̃faʀɔne/ [**v1**] *vi* to boast

fanion /fanjɔ̃/ *m* pennant

fantaisie /fɑ̃tezi/ *f* **1** imaginativeness; **manquer de ~** ‹*person*› to be staid; ‹*life*› to be dull
2 whim, fancy
3 s'offrir une petite ~ to spoil oneself; **un bijou ~** a piece of costume jewellery (BrE) *or* jewelry (AmE)

fantaisiste /fɑ̃tezist/ *adj* **1** ‹*person*› unreliable; ‹*figures*› doubtful
2 ‹*idea*› far-fetched

fantasme /fɑ̃tasm/ *m* fantasy

fantasque /fɑ̃task/ *adj* ‹*character*› unpredictable; ‹*tale*› fanciful

fantassin /fɑ̃tasɛ̃/ *m* infantryman, foot soldier

fantastique /fɑ̃tastik/ **A** *adj* fantastic
B *m* **le ~** fantasy

fantoche /fɑ̃tɔʃ/ *adj* puppet

fantôme /fɑ̃tom/ **A** *m* ghost
B (-)fantôme (*combining form*) ‹*train, city*› ghost; **image(-)~** (on screen) ghost; **société(-)~** (Law) dummy company

FAO /ɛfao/ *f* (Comput) (*abbr* = **fabrication assistée par ordinateur**) CAM

faon /fɑ̃/ *m* (Zool) fawn

faramineux, -euse /faʀaminø, øz/ *adj* (fam) colossal, staggering; incredible

farandole /faʀɑ̃dɔl/ *f* (dance) farandole; ≈ conga

farce /faʀs/ *f* **1** practical joke; **magasin de ~s et attrapes** joke shop (BrE), novelty store (AmE)
2 joke
3 (in theatre) farce
4 stuffing, forcemeat

farceur, -euse /faʀsœʀ, øz/ *mf* practical joker

farcir /faʀsiʀ/ [**v3**] *vt* (Culin) to stuff

fard /faʀ/ *m* make-up; **sans ~** ‹*beauty*› natural; ‹*truth*› simple
■ **~ à joues** blusher; **~ à paupières** eye-shadow
IDIOM **piquer un ~** (fam) to go as red as a beetroot (BrE), to turn as red as a beet (AmE)

fardeau, *pl* **~x** /faʀdo/ *m* burden

farder /faʀde/ [**v1**] **A** *vt* to disguise ‹*truth*›
B se farder *v refl* (+ *v être*) ‹*actor*› to make up; ‹*woman*› to use make-up

farfelu, ~e /faʀfəly/ *adj* (fam) ‹*idea*› hare-brained (fam); ‹*person*› scatter-brained (fam); ‹*show*› bizarre

farfouiller /faʀfuje/ [**v1**] *vi* (fam) to rummage around *or* about (**dans** in)

farine /faʀin/ *f* **1** flour
2 baby cereal
■ **~ d'avoine** oatmeal
IDIOM **se faire rouler dans la ~** (fam) to be had (fam)

farineux, -euse /faʀinø, øz/ *adj* ‹*food*› starchy; ‹*potato*› floury

farniente /faʀnjɛnte/ *m* **le ~** lazing about, lazing around

farouche /faʀuʃ/ *adj* **1** ‹*child, animal*› timid, shy; ‹*adult*› unsociable
2 ‹*look, warrior*› fierce
3 ‹*enemy, hatred*› bitter; ‹*adversary*› fierce; ‹*supporter*› staunch; ‹*will*› iron

farouchement /faʀuʃmɑ̃/ *adv* ‹*opposed, independent*› fiercely; ‹*refuse*› doggedly

fascicule /fasikyl/ *m* **1** booklet
2 fascicule

fascinant, ~e /fasinɑ̃, ɑ̃t/ *adj* ‹*person, film*› fascinating; ‹*charm, music*› spellbinding

fascination /fasinasjɔ̃/ *f* fascination

fasciner /fasine/ [**v1**] *vt* ‹*speaker, music*› to hold [sb] spellbound; ‹*sea, person*› to fascinate

fascisant, ~e /faʃizɑ̃, ɑ̃t/ *adj* fascistic

fascisme /faʃism/ *m* fascism

fasse /fas/ ▸ **faire**

fassent /fas/ ▸ **faire**

fasses /fas/ ▸ **faire**

fassiez /fasje/ ▸ **faire**

fassions /fasjɔ̃/ ▸ **faire**

faste /fast/ **A** *adj* auspicious
B *m* splendour (BrE), pomp; **avec ~** with pomp

fastidieux, -ieuse /fastidjø, øz/ *adj* tedious

fatal, ~e /fatal/ *adj* **1** inevitable
2 fatal, disastrous
3 ‹*moment, day*› fateful

fatalement /fatalmɑ̃/ *adv* inevitably

fatalisme /fatalism/ *m* fatalism

fatalité /fatalite/ *f* **1 la ~** fate
2 mischance
3 inevitability

fatidique /fatidik/ *adj* fateful

fatigant, ~e /fatigɑ̃, ɑ̃t/ *adj* **1** ‹*sport, journey*› tiring; ‹*climate*› wearing
2 ‹*work*› arduous

3 ‹*person*› tiresome; ‹*film, conversation*› tedious

fatigue /fatig/ *f* **1** tiredness; **être mort de ~, tomber de ~** to be dead tired
2 (Med) fatigue; **~ visuelle** eye strain

fatigué, ~e /fatige/ **A** *pp* ▸ **fatiguer**
B *pp adj* ‹*voice*› strained; ‹*eyes, smile*› weary

fatiguer /fatige/ [**v1**] **A** *vt* **1** to make [sb/sth] tired; to strain ‹*eyes*›
2 to tire [sb] out
3 to wear [sb] out
4 to wear out ‹*engine*›
B *vi* **1** (fam) to get tired
2 ‹*engine, car*› to be labouring (BrE)
C se fatiguer *v refl* (+ *v être*) **1** to get tired
2 to tire oneself out
3 se ~ les yeux to strain one's eyes
4 se ~ à faire to bother doing

fatras /fatʀa/ *m inv* jumble

faubourg /fobuʀ/ *m* working class area (*on the outskirts*)

fauché, ~e /foʃe/ *adj* (fam) broke (fam), penniless

faucher /foʃe/ [**v1**] *vt* **1** to mow; to scythe
2 ‹*car, bullet*› to mow [sb] down
3 (fam) to steal

faucheuse /foʃøz/ *f* mowing machine

faucille /fosij/ *f* sickle

faucon /fokɔ̃/ *m* falcon, hawk (AmE)

faudra ▸ **falloir**

faufiler /fofile/ [**v1**] **A** *vt* to baste
B se faufiler *v refl* (+ *v être*) **1 se ~ à l'extérieur** to slip out
2 se ~ dans ‹*mistakes*› to creep into ‹*text*›
3 ‹*route*› to snake in and out

faune /fon/ *f* **1** wildlife, fauna; **la ~ marine** marine life
2 (derog) set, crowd

faussaire /fosɛʀ/ *mf* forger

fausse ▸ **faux[1] A**

faussement /fosmɑ̃/ *adv* **1** falsely, wrongfully
2 deceptively

fausser /fose/ [**v1**] *vt* to distort ‹*result, mechanism*›; to damage ‹*lock*›; to buckle ‹*blade*›
IDIOM **~ compagnie à qn** to give sb the slip

faut ▸ **falloir**

faute /fot/ *f* **1** mistake, error; **il a fait un (parcours) sans ~** he's never put a foot wrong
2 (gen) misdemeanour (BrE); (Law) civil wrong; **être en ~** to be at fault; **prendre qn en ~** to catch sb out
3 fault; **c'est (de) ma ~** it's my fault; **par la ~ de qn** because of sb; **rejeter la ~ sur qn** to lay the blame on sb
4 ~ de temps through lack of time; **~ de mieux** for want of anything better; **~ de quoi** otherwise, failing which; **sans ~** without fail
5 (Sport) foul; (in tennis) fault

fauteuil /fotœj/ *m* **1** chair, armchair
2 (in theatre) seat

fauteur /fotœʀ/ *m* **~ de troubles** troublemaker; **~ de guerre** warmonger

fautif, -ive /fotif, iv/ **A** *adj* **1** at fault
2 ‹*memory*› faulty; ‹*reference*› inaccurate
B *mf* culprit

fauve /fov/ **A** *adj* tawny
B *m* **1** wild animal
2 big cat
3 (colour) fawn

fauvette /fovɛt/ *f* warbler

faux[1], fausse /fo, fos/ **A** *adj* **1** ‹*result, number, idea*› wrong; ‹*impression, promise, accusation*› false
2 ‹*beard, tooth, eyelashes*› false
3 ‹*wood, marble, diamonds*› imitation, fake; ‹*door, drawer*› false
4 ‹*passport, money*› forged
5 ‹*policeman, bishop*› bogus; ‹*candour, humility*› feigned
6 ‹*hope*› false; ‹*fear*› groundless
7 deceitful
B *adv* ‹*play, sing*› out of tune
C *m inv* **1 le ~** falsehood
2 fake; forgery
■ **fausse couche** (Med) miscarriage; **fausse facture** bogus invoice; **fausse fenêtre** blind window; **fausse joie** ill-founded joy; **faire une fausse joie à qn** to raise sb's hopes in vain; **fausse monnaie** forged *or* counterfeit currency; **fausse monnaie** forged *or* counterfeit currency; **fausse note** jarring note; **fausse piste** wrong track; **~ ami** *foreign word which looks deceptively like a word in one's own language*; **~ en écriture(s)** falsification of accounts; **~ frais** extras, incidental expenses; **~ jeton** (fam) two-faced person; **~ nom** assumed name; **~ pas** slip; mistake; faux pas; **~ pli** crease; **~ témoignage** perjury

faux[2] /fo/ *f inv* scythe

faux-filet, *pl* **~s** /fofilɛ/ *m* sirloin

faux-monnayeur, *pl* **~s** /fomɔnɛjœʀ/ *m* forger, counterfeiter

faux-semblant, *pl* **~s** /fosɑ̃blɑ̃/ *m* **les ~s** pretence (BrE)

faveur /favœʀ/ **A** *f* favour (BrE); **régime** *or* **traitement de ~** preferential treatment; **des mesures en ~ des handicapés** measures to help the disabled; **intervenir en ~ de qn** to intervene on sb's behalf
B à la faveur de *phr* thanks to; **à la ~ de la nuit** under cover of darkness

favorable /favɔʀabl/ *adj* favourable (BrE); **être ~ à qch** to be in favour (BrE) of sth

favori, -ite /favɔʀi, it/ **A** *adj, mf* favourite (BrE)
B favoris *mpl* sideburns

favoriser /favɔʀize/ [**v1**] *vt* **1** to favour (BrE); **les milieux favorisés** the privileged classes
2 to encourage, to promote

favorite ▶ **favori A**

favoritisme /favɔʀitism/ *m* favouritism (BrE)

fax /faks/ *m inv* **1** fax
2 fax machine

fayot¹ /fajo/ *m* (fam) bean

fayot², **-otte** /fajo, ɔt/ *mf* (fam) creep (fam), crawler (fam)

FB (Hist) (*written abbr* = **franc belge**) BFr

fébrile /febʀil/ *adj* **1** ‹*emotion, gesture*› feverish; ‹*person*› nervous
2 (Med) feverish

fébrilité /febʀilite/ *f* **1** agitation; **avec ~** agitatedly
2 nervousness

fécal, **~e**, *mpl* **-aux** /fekal, o/ *adj* faecal

fécond, **~e** /fekɔ̃, ɔ̃d/ *adj* **1** fertile
2 fruitful

fécondation /fekɔ̃dasjɔ̃/ *f* (of female) impregnation; (of plant) pollination; (of egg) fertilization

féconder /fekɔ̃de/ [**v1**] *vt* to impregnate ‹*female*›; to inseminate ‹*animal*›; to pollinate ‹*plant*›; to fertilize ‹*egg, ovum*›

fécondité /fekɔ̃dite/ *f* **1** fertility
2 (of author) productivity

fécule /fekyl/ *f* starch

féculent /fekylɑ̃/ *m* starch; starchy food

fédéral, **~e**, *mpl* **-aux** /fedeʀal, o/ *adj* federal

fédéralisme /fedeʀalism/ *m* federalism

fédératif, **-ive** /fedeʀatif, iv/ *adj* federal

fédération /fedeʀasjɔ̃/ *f* federation

fée /fe/ *f* fairy; **~ du logis** perfect housewife
IDIOM **avoir des doigts de ~** to have nimble fingers

féerie /fe(e)ʀi/ *f* **1 c'est une vraie ~** it's magical
2 extravaganza

féerique /fe(e)ʀik/ *adj* ‹*beauty*› enchanting; ‹*landscape, moment*› enchanted

feignant, **~e** /fɛɲɑ̃, ɑ̃t/ ▶ **fainéant**

feindre /fɛ̃dʀ/ [**v55**] *vt* to feign; **~ de faire/d'être** to pretend to do/to be

feinte /fɛ̃t/ *f* **1** feint; **faire une ~** (in football, rugby) to dummy (BrE), to fake (AmE)
2 (fam) trick, ruse

fêlé, **~e** /fɛle/ *adj* (fam) cracked (fam)

fêler /fɛle/ [**v1**] *vt*, **se fêler** *v refl* (+ *v être*) to crack

félicitations /felisitasjɔ̃/ *fpl* congratulations

féliciter /felisite/ [**v1**] **A** *vt* to congratulate
B se féliciter *v refl* (+ *v être*) **se ~ de qch** to be very pleased about sth

félin, **~e** /felɛ̃, in/ **A** *adj* **1** feline; **exposition ~e** cat show
2 ‹*grace*› feline; ‹*eyes*› catlike
B *m* feline; **les ~s** felines, the cat family

fêlure /fɛlyʀ/ *f* crack

femelle /fəmɛl/ **A** *adj* female; **éléphant ~** cow elephant; **moineau ~** hen sparrow
B *f* female; (in pair) mate

féminin, **~e** /feminɛ̃, in/ **A** *adj* ‹*sex, occupation*› female; ‹*magazine, record*› women's; ‹*team, club*› ladies'; ‹*appearance*› feminine
B *m* feminine; **au ~** in the feminine

féminiser: **se féminiser** /feminize/ [**v1**] *v refl* (+ *v être*) ‹*profession*› to become more open to women; to become predominantly female

féministe /feminist/ *adj, mf* feminist

féminité /feminite/ *f* femininity

femme /fam/ *f* **1** woman
2 wife
■ **~ d'affaires** businesswoman; **~ de chambre** chambermaid; **~ au foyer** housewife; **~ d'intérieur** homemaker; **~ de service** cleaner, cleaning lady; **~ de tête** assertive woman; ▶ **bon, jeune**
IDIOM **souvent ~ varie** woman is fickle

fémur /femyʀ/ *m* thigh bone; **se casser le col du ~** to break one's hip

FEN /fɛn/ *f* (*abbr* = **Fédération de l'éducation nationale**) FEN (*French teachers' union*)

fendiller: **se fendiller** /fɑ̃dije/ [**v1**] *v refl* (+ *v être*) ‹*lips*› to chap; ‹*earth*› to craze over; ‹*wood*› to crack

fendre /fɑ̃dʀ/ [**v6**] **A** *vt* **1** to chop ‹*wood*›; to slit ‹*material*›
2 to crack ‹*wall, stone*›; to split ‹*lip*›
3 ~ le cœur à qn to break sb's heart
4 ~ l'air to slice through the air; **~ la foule** to push one's way through the crowd
B se fendre *v refl* (+ *v être*) **1** to crack
2 (fam) to cough up (fam) ‹*money*›; **tu ne t'es pas fendu!** that didn't break the bank!
IDIOMS **se ~ la pêche** (fam) to split one's sides (fam); **avoir la bouche fendue jusqu'aux oreilles** to be grinning from ear to ear

fenêtre /fənɛtʀ/ *f* window
■ **~ à guillotine** sash window
IDIOM **jeter l'argent par les ~s** to throw money away

fenouil /fənuj/ *m* fennel

fente /fɑ̃t/ *f* **1** slit; (for coin, card) slot; (of jacket) vent
2 crack; (in wood) split; (in rock) crevice

féodal, **~e**, *mpl* **-aux** /feɔdal, o/ *adj* feudal

fer /fɛʀ/ *m* **1** iron; **de ~** ‹*discipline, fist, will*› iron
2 (on shoe) steel tip
3 branding iron
4 croiser le ~ avec to cross swords with
■ **~ à cheval** horseshoe; **~ forgé** wrought iron; **~ à repasser** iron
IDIOMS **croire dur comme ~** to believe wholeheartedly; **tomber les quatre ~s en**

l'air (fam) to fall flat on one's back

fera /fəʀa/ ▶ **faire**

ferai /fəʀɛ/ ▶ **faire**

feraient /fəʀɛ/ ▶ **faire**

ferais /fəʀɛ/ ▶ **faire**

ferait /fəʀɛ/ ▶ **faire**

feras /fəʀa/ ▶ **faire**

fer-blanc, *pl* **fers-blancs** /fɛʀblɑ̃/ *m* tinplate

ferez /fəʀe/ ▶ **faire**

férié, **~e** /feʀje/ *adj* **jour ~** public holiday (BrE), holiday (AmE)

f

feriez /fəʀje/ ▶ **faire**

ferions /fəʀjɔ̃/ ▶ **faire**

⚷ **ferme**[1] /fɛʀm/ **A** *adj* **1** firm
2 (Law) **peine de prison ~** custodial sentence
B *adv* ‹*argue, campaign*› vigorously; ‹*believe*› firmly; **tenir ~** to stand one's ground
IDIOM **attendre de pied ~** to be ready and waiting

⚷ **ferme**[2] /fɛʀm/ *f* farm, farmhouse
■ **~ éolienne** wind farm; **~ solaire** solar farm

fermement /fɛʀməmɑ̃/ *adv* firmly

ferment /fɛʀmɑ̃/ *m* ferment

fermenter /fɛʀmɑ̃te/ [**v1**] *vi* to ferment

⚷ **fermer** /fɛʀme/ [**v1**] **A** *vt* **1** to close, to shut ‹*door, book, eyes*›; to clench ‹*fist*›; to draw ‹*curtain*›; to turn off ‹*tap, gas, radio*›; to do up ‹*jacket*›; **~ à clé** to lock (up)
2 to close ‹*shop, airport, road*›; (definitively) to close [sth] down
B *vi* to close (down)
C se fermer *v refl* (+ *v être*) **1** ‹*door*› to shut; ‹*flower*› to close up; ‹*coat, bracelet*› to fasten
2 ‹*person*› to clam up; ‹*face*› to harden
IDIOM **~ les yeux sur** to turn a blind eye to

fermeté /fɛʀməte/ *f* firmness

fermette /fɛʀmɛt/ *f* farmhouse-style cottage

fermeture /fɛʀmətyʀ/ *f* **1** (of business, account) closing; (definitive) closure, closing down
2 (on handbag) clasp; (on garment) fastening
■ **~ éclair®**, **~ à glissière** zip (BrE), zipper (AmE)

fermier, **-ière** /fɛʀmje, ɛʀ/ **A** *adj* free-range
B *mf* farmer

fermoir /fɛʀmwaʀ/ *m* (on necklace, bag) clasp

féroce /feʀɔs/ *adj* **1** fierce; ferocious
2 ‹*appetite*› voracious

férocité /feʀɔsite/ *f* **1** (of animal) ferociousness
2 (of remark) savagery
3 (of person) fierceness

ferons /fəʀɔ̃/ ▶ **faire**

feront /fəʀɔ̃/ ▶ **faire**

ferraille /feʀɑj/ *f* **1** scrap metal
2 scrapheap
3 (fam) small change

ferrailleur /feʀɑjœʀ/ *m* scrap (metal) dealer

ferronnerie /feʀɔnʀi/ *f* **1** ironworks
2 wrought iron work
3 iron work

ferroviaire /feʀɔvjɛʀ/ *adj* ‹*transport, collision*› rail; ‹*station, tunnel*› railway (BrE), railroad (AmE)

fertile /fɛʀtil/ *adj* fertile; ‹*year*› productive

fertilisant /fɛʀtilizɑ̃/ *m* fertilizer

fertilité /fɛʀtilite/ *f* fertility

fervent, **~e** /fɛʀvɑ̃, ɑ̃t/ *adj* ‹*believer*› fervent; ‹*admirer*› ardent

ferveur /fɛʀvœʀ/ *f* (of prayer) fervour (BrE); (of love) ardour (BrE)

fesse /fɛs/ *f* buttock
IDIOM **coûter la peau des ~s** (fam) to cost an arm and a leg (fam)

fessée /fese/ *f* smack on the bottom, spanking

festin /fɛstɛ̃/ *m* feast

festival /fɛstival/ *m* festival

festivités /fɛstivite/ *fpl* festivities

festoyer /fɛstwaje/ [**v23**] *vi* to feast

fêtard, **~e** /fɛtaʀ, aʀd/ *mf* (fam) reveller

⚷ **fête** /fɛt/ *f* **1** public holiday (BrE), holiday (AmE)
2 (saint's) name day; **ça va être ma ~!** (fam) I'm going to cop it! (fam)
3 festival
4 (day of) celebration
5 party; **faire la ~** to live it up (fam)
6 fête, fair, celebrations
■ **~ foraine** funfair; **~ du travail** May Day, Labour Day (BrE)
IDIOM **faire sa ~ à qn** (fam) to give sb a working over (fam)

fêter /fete/ [**v1**] *vt* to celebrate ‹*event*›

fétiche /fetiʃ/ **A** *adj* lucky
B *m* **1** mascot
2 fetish

fétide /fetid/ *adj* foul; foul-smelling

feu[1], **~e** /fø/ *adj* late; **~ la reine, la ~e reine** the late queen

⚷ **feu**[2], *pl* **~x** /fø/ *m* **1** fire ▶ **huile**
2 light; **sous le ~ des projecteurs** under the glare of the spotlights; (fig) in the spotlight
3 traffic light; **j'ai le ~ vert de mon patron** my boss has given me the go-ahead
4 (on cooker) ring (BrE), burner (AmE); **faire cuire à petit ~** cook over a gentle heat
5 avez-vous du ~? have you got a light?
6 passion; **dans le ~ de la discussion** in the heat of the discussion
7 ~! (Mil) fire!; **faire ~** to fire; **coup de ~** shot
8 (Mil) action
■ **~ d'artifice** fireworks display; firework; **~ de cheminée** chimney fire; open fire; **~ follet**

will-o'-the-wisp; ~ **de joie** bonfire; ~ **roulant** (Mil) continuous fire; (fig) **le ~ roulant des questions du public** the continuous barrage of audience questions; ~ **de signalisation**, ~ **tricolore** traffic light; ~**x de croisement** dipped (BrE) *or* dimmed (AmE) headlights; ~**x de détresse** warning lights; ~**x de route** headlights

IDIOMS **il n'y a pas le ~!** (fam) there's no rush!; **ne pas faire long ~** (fam) not to last long; **il n'y a vu que du ~** (fam) he fell for it; **mourir à petit ~** to die a slow death

feuillage /fœjaʒ/ *m* foliage, leaves

feuille /fœj/ *f* **1** (Bot) leaf
2 (of paper, metal) sheet
■ ~ **de chou** (fam) rag (fam), newspaper; ~ **d'impôts** tax return; ~ **de maladie** *a form for reclaiming medical expenses from the social security office*; ~ **de paie** payslip (BrE), pay stub (AmE)

feuillet /fœjɛ/ *m* **1** (in book) leaf
2 page

feuilleté, ~**e** /fœjte/ *adj* **pâte** ~**e** puff pastry

feuilleter /fœjte/ [**v20**] *vt* to leaf through [sth]

feuilleton /fœjtɔ̃/ *m* serial; soap (opera)

feutre /føtʀ/ *m* **1** felt
2 felt-tip (pen)

feutré, ~**e** /føtʀe/ *adj* ‹*atmosphere*› hushed; ‹*sound*› muffled

fève /fɛv/ *f* **1** broad bean
2 lucky charm (*hidden in Twelfth Night cake*)

février /fevʀije/ *m* February

FF (Hist) (*written abbr* = **franc français**) FFr

fiabilité /fjabilite/ *f* reliability

fiable /fjabl/ *adj* reliable

fiançailles /fjɑ̃saj/ *fpl* engagement

fiancé, ~**e** /fjɑ̃se/ *mf* fiancé/fiancée

fiancer: **se fiancer** /fjɑ̃se/ [**v12**] *v refl* (+ *v être*) to get engaged

fibre /fibʀ/ *f* fibre (BrE)

ficeler /fisle/ [**v19**] *vt* to tie up ‹*parcel*›

ficelle /fisɛl/ *f* **1** string
2 trick; **la ~ est un peu grosse** it's a bit obvious
3 thin baguette

IDIOM **tirer sur la ~** to push one's luck

fiche /fiʃ/ *f* **1** index card; slip
2 form; ~ **d'inscription** enrolment (BrE) form
3 plug; **prise à trois** ~**s** three-pin plug
■ ~ **d'état civil** *record of personal details for administrative purposes*; ~ **de paie** payslip (BrE), pay stub (AmE)

ficher /fiʃe/ [**v1**] **A** *vt* **1** to put [sth] on a file; to open a file on [sb]; **être fiché (par la police)** to be on police files
2 to drive ‹*stake, nail*›
3 (fam) to do; **qu'est-ce que tu fiches?** what the heck are you doing? (fam); **n'en avoir rien à ~** not to give a damn (fam)
4 (fam) ~ **un coup à qn** (fig) to be a real blow to sb; ~ **la paix à qn** to leave sb alone
5 (fam) ~ **qch quelque part** to chuck sth somewhere (fam); ~ **qn dehors** to kick sb out (fam)
B se ficher *v refl* (+ *v être*) **1** ‹*arrow, knife*› to stick
2 (fam) **se ~ de qn** to make fun of sb; **se ~ du monde** to have a hell of a nerve (fam)
3 (fam) **se ~ de ce que qn fait** not to give a damn (about) what sb does (fam)

fichier /fiʃje/ *m* file; (in library) index

fichu **A** *pp* ▶ **ficher A3, A4, A5, B**
B *adj* **1** ‹*weather, job*› rotten (fam); ‹*rain*› dreadful; ‹*car, TV*› damned (fam)
2 ‹*person, car*› done for (fam); **s'il pleut c'est ~** if it rains that's the end of that
3 être bien ~ to be well designed; ‹*book*› to be well laid out; **je suis mal ~** I feel lousy (fam)
4 être ~ de faire to be quite capable of doing

fictif, **-ive** /fiktif, iv/ *adj* imaginary; false

fiction /fiksjɔ̃/ *f* **1** fiction
2 (on TV) drama

fidèle /fidɛl/ **A** *adj* **1** ‹*person, dog*› faithful; **être ~ au poste** to be always there
2 loyal
3 true (**à** to)
4 ‹*translation*› faithful
B *mf* **1** loyal supporter
2 les ~s the faithful

fidèlement /fidɛlmɑ̃/ *adv* **1** faithfully
2 loyally

fidéliser /fidelize/ [**v1**] *vt* to secure the loyalty of ‹*clients*›

fidélité /fidelite/ *f* **1** fidelity
2 loyalty
3 (of translation) accuracy

fiduciaire /fidysjɛʀ/ *adj* fiduciary; **société ~** trust company

fief /fjɛf/ *m* **1** fief
2 (fig) territory; (of party) stronghold

fieffé, ~**e** /fjefe/ *adj* ~ **menteur** incorrigible liar

fier[1], **fière** /fjɛʀ/ *adj* proud; **avoir fière allure** to cut a fine figure

fier[2]: **se fier** /fje/ [**v2**] *v refl* (+ *v être*) **1 se ~ à** to trust ‹*person, promise*›
2 se ~ à to rely on ‹*person, instrument*›; to trust to ‹*chance*›

fierté /fjɛʀte/ *f* pride

fièvre /fjɛvʀ/ *f* **1** (high) temperature; **avoir de la ~** to have a (high) temperature
2 frenzy
3 fervour (BrE); ~ **électorale** election fever
■ ~ **de cheval** (fam) raging fever

fiévreusement /fjevʀøzmɑ̃/ *adv* frantically; feverishly

fiévreux, **-euse** /fjevʀø, øz/ *adj* **1** (Med) feverish

2 (agitated) frantic
3 (passionate) feverish

figer /fiʒe/ [**v13**] **A** *vt* to congeal ‹*grease*›; to thicken ‹*sauce*›; to clot ‹*blood*›
B se figer *v refl* (+ *v être*) **1** ‹*smile, person*› to freeze
2 ‹*grease*› to congeal; ‹*blood*› to clot

fignoler /fiɲɔle/ [**v1**] **A** *vt* **1** to put the finishing touches to
2 to take great pains over
B *vi* to fiddle about

figue /fig/ *f* fig; ~ **de Barbarie** prickly pear

figuier /figje/ *m* fig tree

figurant, ~**e** /figyʀɑ̃, ɑ̃t/ *mf* (in films) extra; (in theatre) bit player

figuratif, **-ive** /figyʀatif, iv/ *adj* figurative, representational; **artiste non** ~ abstract artist

figuration /figyʀasjɔ̃/ *f* **faire de la** ~ (in films) to be an extra; (fig) to have a token role

figure /figyʀ/ *f* **1** face
2 faire ~ **d'amateur** to look like an amateur; **reprendre** ~ **humaine** to look half human again
3 (in history, politics) figure
4 (in drawing) figure
IDIOMS **prendre** ~ to take shape; **faire bonne** ~ to keep an air of composure; to make the right impression; to do well

figurer /figyʀe/ [**v1**] **A** *vt* to represent
B *vi* ‹*name, object*› to appear
C se figurer *v refl* (+ *v être*) to imagine

figurine /figyʀin/ *f* figurine

fil /fil/ **A** *m* **1** thread; ▶ **coudre**
2 yarn
3 string; ~ **de fer** wire
4 wire; (on appliance) flex (BrE), cord (AmE); (on phone) lead; **coup de** ~ (fam) (phone) call; **au bout du** ~ (fam) on the phone
5 (of conversation, text) thread; **perdre le** ~ **des événements** to lose track of events
6 (of razor) edge
B au fil de *phr* in the course of; **au** ~ **des ans** over the years; **aller au** ~ **de l'eau** to go with the flow
■ ~ **conducteur** (of heat) conductor; (of novel) thread; (of inquiry) lead; ~ **directeur** guiding principle
IDIOM **ne tenir qu'à un** ~ to hang by a thread

filament /filamɑ̃/ *m* filament

filature /filatyʀ/ *f* **1** textile mill
2 spinning
3 prendre qn en ~ to tail sb (fam)

file /fil/ *f* **1** ~ **(d'attente)** queue (BrE), line (AmE)
2 line; ~ **indienne** single file
3 lane; **se garer en double** ~ to double-park

filer /file/ [**v1**] **A** *vt* **1** to spin ‹*wool, cotton*›
2 to spin ‹*web, cocoon*›
3 to ladder (BrE), to get a run in ‹*tights*›
4 to tail [sb] (fam)
5 (fam) to give [sth] (**à qn** to sb)
B *vi* (fam) **1** to go off, to leave
2 to rush
3 ‹*time*› to fly by; ‹*prisoner*› to get away; ~ **entre les mains** to slip through one's fingers

filet /filɛ/ *m* **1** net; ~ **à provisions** string bag; **coup de** ~ (police) raid
2 fillet
3 (of water) trickle; (of smoke) wisp; ~ **de citron** dash of lemon juice

filial, ~**e** *mpl* **-iaux** /filjal, o/ *adj* filial

filiale /filjal/ *f* subsidiary

filiation /filjasjɔ̃/ *f* filiation

filière /filjɛʀ/ *f* **1** (Sch) course of study
2 (Econ) field
3 suivre la ~ **habituelle** to climb up the usual career ladder
4 official channels
5 ~ **(clandestine) de la drogue** drugs ring

filiforme /filifɔʀm/ *adj* spindly; thread-like

filigrane /filigʀan/ *m* filigree

filin /filɛ̃/ *m* rope

fille /fij/ *f* **1** daughter
2 girl; ~ **mère** unmarried mother

fillette /fijɛt/ *f* **1** little girl
2 (fam) half bottle

filleul /fijœl/ *m* godson, godchild

filleule /fijœl/ *f* goddaughter, godchild

film /film/ *m* **1** film (BrE), movie (AmE)
2 (thin) film
■ ~ **d'animation** cartoon

filmer /filme/ [**v1**] *vt* to film

filmique /filmik/ *adj* film; cinematic

filon /filɔ̃/ *m* vein, seam

filou /filu/ *m* crook; cheat; rascal

fils /fis/ *m inv* son; **Dupont** ~ Dupont Junior

filtre /filtʀ/ *m* filter

filtrer /filtʀe/ [**v1**] **A** *vt* **1** to filter
2 to screen ‹*visitors, calls*›
B *vi* ‹*information*› to leak out; ‹*idea, liquid*› to filter through

fîmes /fim/ ▶ **faire**

fin[1], **fine** /fɛ̃, fin/ **A** *adj* **1** ‹*rain, sand, brush*› fine; ‹*slice, layer*› thin
2 ‹*ankle, waist*› slender; ‹*features*› fine; ‹*dish*› delicate
3 ‹*person*› perceptive; ‹*taste, humour*› subtle; **vraiment c'est** ~**!** that's really clever!; **jouer au plus** ~ **avec qn** to try to outsmart sb; **avoir l'air** ~ (fam) to look a fool
4 avoir l'ouïe ~**e** to have a keen sense of hearing
5 au ~ **fond de** in the remotest part of ‹*country*›; **le** ~ **mot de l'histoire** the truth of the matter
B *adv* **1 être** ~ **prêt** to be all set
2 ‹*write, grind*› finely; ‹*slice*› thinly
C *m* **le** ~ **du** ~ the ultimate

key word

■ **~e mouche** sly customer (fam); **~es herbes** mixed herbs

fin² /fɛ̃/ *f* **1** end, ending; **à la ~ des années 70** in the late '70s; **tu vas te taire à la ~!** (fam) for God's sake, be quiet!; **chômeur en ~ de droits** unemployed person no longer entitled to benefit
2 end, death
3 end, aim, purpose
■ **~ de série** oddment

final, **~e** *mpl* **-aux** /final, o/ *adj* final

finale /final/ *f* (Sport) final

finalement /finalmɑ̃/ *adv* **1** in the end, finally
2 in fact, actually

finaliser /finalize/ [**v1**] *vt* to finalize; to complete

finalité /finalite/ *f* **1** purpose, aim
2 finality

finance /finɑ̃s/ **A** *f* **1 la ~** finance
2 financiers
B finances *fpl* **les ~s** finances; **moyennant ~s** for a consideration

financement /finɑ̃smɑ̃/ *m* financing

financer /finɑ̃se/ [**v12**] *vt* to finance

financier, **-ière** /finɑ̃sje, ɛʀ/ **A** *adj* financial
B *m* **1** financier
2 small cake

finaud, **-e** /fino, od/ *mf* (Comput) hacker

finesse /finɛs/ *f* **1** (of thread, writing) fineness; (of layer, paper) thinness
2 (of dish) delicacy; (of face) fineness; (of waist) slenderness
3 (of remark, person) perceptiveness; (of actor) sensitivity
4 (of senses) keenness
5 les ~s d'une langue the subtleties of a language

fini, **~e** /fini/ **A** *pp* ▶ **finir**
B *pp adj* **être ~** to be over, to be finished
C *m* finish

finir /finiʀ/ [**v3**] **A** *vt* **1** to finish (off), to complete; to end ‹*day*›
2 to use up ‹*supplies*›
B *vi* to finish, to end; ‹*contract, lease*› to run out; **le film finit bien** the film has a happy ending; **ça va mal ~!** it'll end in tears!; **~ par faire** to end up doing; **ils finiront bien par céder** they're bound to give in in the end; **en ~ avec qn/qch** to have done with sb/sth; **finissons-en!** let's get it over with!

finissant /finisɑ̃/ ▶ **finir**

finition /finisjɔ̃/ *f* **1** finishing
2 finish

finlandais, **~e** /fɛ̃lɑ̃dɛ, ɛz/ *adj* Finnish

Finlandais, **~e** /fɛ̃lɑ̃dɛ, ɛz/ *mf* Finn

Finlande /fɛ̃lɑ̃d/ *pr f* Finland

finnois, **~e** /finwa, az/ **A** *adj* Finnish
B *m* (language) Finnish

fioriture /fjɔʀityʀ/ *f* embellishment

fioul /fjul/ *m* fuel oil

firent /fiʀ/ ▶ **faire**

firme /fiʀm/ *f* firm

fis /fi/ ▶ **faire**

fisc /fisk/ *m* tax office

fiscal, **~e**, *mpl* **-aux** /fiskal, o/ *adj* fiscal, tax

fiscaliser /fiskalize/ [**v1**] *vt* **1** to tax
2 to fund [sth] by taxation

fiscalité /fiskalite/ *f* **1** taxation
2 tax system

fisse /fis/ ▶ **faire**

fissent /fis/ ▶ **faire**

fisses /fis/ ▶ **faire**

fissible /fisibl/ *adj* fissionable, fissile

fissiez /fisje/ ▶ **faire**

fission /fisjɔ̃/ *f* fission; **~ nucléaire** nuclear fission

fissionner /fisjɔne/ [**v1**] *vt*, *vi* to split

fissions /fisjɔ̃/ ▶ **faire**

fissure /fisyʀ/ *f* **1** crack
2 (Anat) fissure

fissurer /fisyʀe/ [**v1**] *vt* to crack, to fissure

fit /fi/ ▶ **faire**

fîtes /fit/ ▶ **faire**

fixation /fiksasjɔ̃/ *f* **1** fixing; fastening
2 (on ski) binding
3 fixation

fixe /fiks/ *adj* **1** fixed
2 permanent

fixé, **~e** /fikse/ **A** *pp* ▶ **fixer**
B *pp adj* **1 tu es ~ maintenant!** you've got the picture now! (fam)
2 nous ne sommes pas encore très ~s we haven't really decided yet

fixer /fikse/ [**v1**] **A** *vt* **1** to fix (**à** to)
2 to set ‹*date, price*›; to establish ‹*boundaries*›; **~ son choix sur** to decide on
3 to fix ‹*colour, emulsion*›
4 to focus ‹*attention*›; to stare at ‹*person*›
B se fixer *v refl* (+ *v être*) **1** ‹*part*› to be attached
2 to set oneself ‹*goal, limit*›

flacon /flakɔ̃/ *m* **1** (small) bottle
2 decanter
3 (in laboratory) flask

flagada /flagada/ *adj inv* (fam) weary

flageller /flaʒele/ [**v1**] *vt* to flog; (as religious punishment) to flagellate

flageoler /flaʒɔle/ [**v1**] *vi* **avoir les jambes qui flageolent** to feel wobbly

flageolet /flaʒɔlɛ/ *m* flageolet

flagrant, **~e** /flagʀɑ̃, ɑ̃t/ *adj* ‹*difference*› obvious; ‹*injustice*› flagrant; ‹*lie*› blatant; **prendre qn en ~ délit** to catch sb red-handed

flair /flɛʀ/ *m* **1** sense of smell, nose
2 intuition

flairer /fleʀe/ [**v1**] *vt* **1** to sniff ‹*object*›; **le chien a flairé une piste** the dog has picked up a scent
2 ‹*animal*› to scent; ‹*person*› to smell
3 to sense ‹*danger*›

flamand, **~e** /flamɑ̃, ɑ̃d/ **A** *adj* Flemish
B *m* (language) Flemish

flamant /flamɑ̃/ *m* flamingo

flambant /flɑ̃bɑ̃/ *adv* **~ neuf** brand new

flambeau, *pl* **~x** /flɑ̃bo/ *m* torch

flambée /flɑ̃be/ *f* **1** fire; **faire une ~** to light a fire
2 (of hatred) flare-up; (of prices) explosion

flamber /flɑ̃be/ [**v1**] **A** *vt* to flambé ‹*pancake*›
B *vi* to burn

flamboyant, **~e** /flɑ̃bwajɑ̃, ɑ̃t/ *adj* ‹*fire, light*› blazing; ‹*colour*› flaming

flamme /flɑm/ *f* **1** flame; **en ~s** on fire
2 love, passion
IDIOMS **descendre en ~s** to shoot down; **être tout feu tout ~** to be wildly enthusiastic

flan /flɑ̃/ *m* (Culin) custard tart (BrE) *or* flan (AmE)
IDIOM **en rester comme deux ronds de ~** (fam) to be dumbfounded

flanc /flɑ̃/ *m* (of person, mountain) side; (of animal) flank; **être sur le ~** (fam) to be exhausted

flancher /flɑ̃ʃe/ [**v1**] *vi* (fam) **1** to lose one's nerve
2 to crack up
3 ‹*heart, engine*› to give out

flanelle /flanɛl/ *f* flannel

flâner /flɑne/ [**v1**] *vi* to stroll; to loaf around (fam)

flâneur, **-euse** /flɑnœʀ, øz/ *mf* **1** stroller
2 loafer (fam), idler

flanquer /flɑ̃ke/ [**v1**] **A** *vt* **1** to flank; **il est toujours flanqué de son adjoint** his assistant never leaves his side
2 (fam) to give ‹*blow, fine*›; **~ qch par terre** to throw sth to the ground; to drop sth; to knock sth to the ground
B se flanquer *v refl* (+ *v être*) (fam) **se ~ dans** to run into

flapi, **~e** /flapi/ *adj* (fam) worn out

flaque /flak/ *f* **~ (d'eau)** puddle; **~ d'huile** pool of oil

flash, *pl* **~es** /flaʃ/ *m* **1** (on camera) flash
2 ~ (d'information) news headlines; **~ publicitaire** advert (BrE), commercial (AmE)

flasque[1] /flask/ *adj* ‹*skin, flesh*› flabby

flasque[2] /flask/ *f* flask

flatter /flate/ [**v1**] **A** *vt* to flatter
B se flatter *v refl* (+ *v être*) to pride oneself

flatterie /flatʀi/ *f* flattery

flatteur, **-euse** /flatœʀ, øz/ *adj* **1** ‹*portrait*› flattering
2 ‹*person, remarks*› sycophantic

flatulence /flatylɑ̃s/ *f* wind, flatulence

fléau, *pl* **~x** /fleo/ *m* **1** scourge
2 (fig) curse, plague
3 (person) pest

flèche /flɛʃ/ *f* **1** arrow; **partir en ~** to shoot off; **monter en ~** ‹*prices*› to soar
2 barbed remark
3 spire

flécher /fleʃe/ [**v14**] *vt* to signpost

fléchette /fleʃɛt/ *f* **1** dart
2 (game) darts

fléchir /fleʃiʀ/ [**v3**] **A** *vt* **1** to bend
2 to sway ‹*person, opinion*›; to weaken ‹*will*›
B *vi* **1** ‹*knees*› to bend; ‹*legs*› to give way
2 ‹*attention*› to flag; ‹*courage*› to waver; ‹*will*› to weaken; ‹*demand*› to fall off

flegmatique /flɛgmatik/ *adj* phlegmatic

flegme /flɛgm/ *m* phlegm, composure

flemmard, **~e** /flemaʀ, aʀd/ *mf* (fam) lazybones (fam), lazy devil (fam)

flemme /flɛm/ *f* (fam) laziness

flétan /fletɑ̃/ *m* halibut

flétrir /fletʀiʀ/ [**v3**] **A** *vt* to blacken ‹*reputation*›
B se flétrir *v refl* (+ *v être*) ‹*plant*› to wither; ‹*flower, beauty*› to fade; ‹*fruit*› to shrivel

fleur /flœʀ/ *f* **1** flower; **être en ~s** ‹*garden*› to be full of flowers; ‹*plant, shrub*› to be in bloom; ‹*tree, lilac*› to be in blossom; **à ~s** flowery
2 à ~ d'eau just above the water
■ **~ des champs** wild flower; **~ de lys** fleur-de-lis
IDIOMS **être ~ bleue** to be romantic; **avoir une sensibilité à ~ de peau** to be hypersensitive; **avoir les nerfs à ~ de peau** to be a bundle of nerves; **faire une ~ à qn** (fam) to do sb a favour (BrE)

fleuret /flœʀɛ/ *m* (sword) foil

fleurette /flœʀɛt/ *f* (Culin) **crème ~** whipping cream

fleuri, **~e** /flœʀi/ **A** *pp* ▶ **fleurir**
B *pp adj* **1** ‹*garden*› full of flowers; ‹*tree*› in blossom; in bloom
2 ‹*table*› decorated with flowers
3 ‹*wallpaper*› flowery

fleurir /flœʀiʀ/ [**v3**] *vi* **1** ‹*rose bush*› to flower; ‹*cherry tree*› to blossom
2 ‹*new buildings*› to spring up; ‹*posters*› to appear
3 to thrive, to flourish

fleuriste /flœʀist/ *mf* **1** florist
2 flower shop

fleuve /flœv/ **A** *m* river
B (-)fleuve (*combining form*) interminable; ▶ **roman-fleuve**

flexible /flɛksibl/ *adj* **1** ‹*blade, tube*› flexible; ‹*body*› supple
2 ‹*person, timetable*› flexible

flexion /flɛksjɔ̃/ *f* (of object) bending; (of arm, leg) flexing

flic /flik/ *m* (fam) cop (fam), policeman

flipper /flipœʀ/ *m* (Games) **1** pinball machine

key word

2 (device in machine) flipper
3 (game) pinball

flirter /flœʀte/ [**v1**] *vi* to flirt

flocon /flɔkɔ̃/ *m* (of snow) flake; (of dust) speck; (of wool) bit; **~s d'avoine** oat flakes (BrE), oatmeal (AmE)

flop /flɔp/ *m* (fam) flop

flopée /flɔpe/ *f* (fam) **(toute) une ~ de gamins** masses of kids (fam)

floraison /flɔʀɛzɔ̃/ *f* flowering

floral, **~e**, *mpl* **-aux** /flɔʀal, o/ *adj* floral

floralies /flɔʀali/ *fpl* flower show

flore /flɔʀ/ *f* flora

florilège /flɔʀilɛʒ/ *m* anthology

florin /flɔʀɛ̃/ *m* (Dutch currency) guilder

florissant, **~e** /flɔʀisɑ̃, ɑ̃t/ *adj* **1** ‹*activity*› thriving
2 ‹*complexion*› ruddy

flot /flo/ **A** *m* **1** (of letters, refugees) flood; (of visitors) stream
2 les ~s the deep, the sea
B à flot *phr* **couler à ~(s)** to flow

flottant, **~e** /flɔtɑ̃, ɑ̃t/ *adj* ‹*wood, line*› floating; ‹*clothes, hair*› flowing

flotte /flɔt/ *f* **1** fleet
2 (fam) rain
3 (fam) water

flottement /flɔtmɑ̃/ *m* **1** wavering
2 (of currency) floating

flotter /flɔte/ [**v1**] **A** *vi* **1** to float; **~ à la dérive** to drift
2 ‹*mist*› to drift; ‹*flag*› to fly; **~ au vent** to flutter in the wind; **elle flotte dans ses vêtements** her clothes are hanging off her
3 ‹*currency*› to float
B *v impers* (fam) to rain

flotteur /flɔtœʀ/ *m* float

flou, **~e** /flu/ **A** *adj* **1** ‹*outline*› blurred
2 (fig) vague, hazy
B *m* **1** fuzziness
2 (fig) vagueness
■ **~ artistique** soft focus; (fig) artistry

flouer /flue/ [**v1**] *vt* (fam) to cheat; **se faire ~** to be had (fam)

fluctuant, **~e** /flyktɥɑ̃, ɑ̃t/ *adj* ‹*prices, opinions*› fluctuating; ‹*person*› fickle

fluet, **-ette** /flyɛ, ɛt/ *adj* ‹*body, person*› slight; ‹*voice*› thin, reedy

fluide /flɥid/ **A** *adj* **1** ‹*oil, paint*› fluid
2 ‹*style*› fluent; ‹*traffic*› moving freely
B *m* **1** (in physics) fluid
2 (of clairvoyant) (psychic) powers

fluo /flyo/ *adj inv* (fam) fluorescent

fluor /flyɔʀ/ *m* fluorine

fluorescent, **~e** /flyɔʀɛsɑ̃, ɑ̃t/ *adj* fluorescent

flûte /flyt/ **A** *f* **1** (Mus) flute; **petite ~** piccolo
2 (champagne) flute
3 French stick
B *excl* (fam) damn! (fam), darn it! (fam)
■ **~ à bec** recorder; **~ de Pan** panpipes

fluvial, **~e**, *mpl* **-iaux** /flyvjal, o/ *adj* fluvial, river

flux /fly/ *m inv* **1** (gen), (Econ) flow
2 (in physics) flux
3 le ~ et le reflux flood tide and ebb tide; (fig) the ebb and flow
4 influx

FMI /ɛfɛmi/ *m*: *abbr* ▶ **fonds**

foc /fɔk/ *m* jib

focal, **~e**, *mpl* **-aux** /fɔkal, o/ *adj* focal

focaliser /fɔkalize/ [**v1**] *vt* to focus ‹*rays*›; to focalize ‹*electron beam*›

fœtus /fetys/ *m inv* foetus

f

foi /fwa/ *f* **1** faith; **avoir la ~** to be a believer
2 ma ~ oui well yes; **en toute bonne ~ je crois que** in all sincerity, I believe that; **il est de mauvaise ~** he doesn't mean a word of it
3 sur la ~ de témoins on the evidence of witnesses; **qui fait** *or* **faisant ~** ‹*text, signature*› authentic; **sous la ~ du serment** under oath
IDIOM **sans ~ ni loi** fearing neither God nor man

foie /fwa/ *m* liver; **crise de ~** indigestion

foin /fwɛ̃/ *m* hay; **tas de ~** haystack; **la saison des ~s** the haymaking season

foire /fwaʀ/ *f* **1** fair; **~ du livre** book fair
2 fun fair
3 (fam) bedlam; **faire la ~** (fam) to live it up (fam)

fois /fwa/ **A** *f inv* time; **une ~** once; **deux ~** twice; **quatre ~ trois font douze** four times three is twelve; **l'autre ~** last time; **une (bonne) ~ pour toutes** once and for all; **une ~ sur deux** half the time; **une ~ sur trois** every third time; **deux ~ sur cinq** two times out of five; **toutes les ~ que** every time (that); **deux ~ plus petit** half as big; **c'est dix ~ trop lourd!** it's far too heavy!; **régler en trois ~** to pay in three instalments (BrE); **pour la énième ~** for the hundredth time; **(à) la première ~** the first time; **la première ~ que je vous ai parlé** when I first talked to you
B à la fois *phr* **deux à la ~** two at a time; **elle est à la ~ intelligente et travailleuse** she's both clever and hardworking
C des fois *phr* (fam) sometimes; **tu n'as pas vu mon chien, des ~?** you wouldn't have seen my dog, by any chance?
D des fois que *phr* (fam) in case
IDIOM **il était une ~** once upon a time there was

foisonner /fwazɔne/ [**v1**] *vi* to abound

fol ▶ **fou A**

folâtrer /fɔlɑtʀe/ [**v1**] *vi* to romp about; to frisk

folichon, **-onne** /fɔliʃɔ̃, ɔn/ *adj* (fam) **pas ~** far from brilliant

folie /fɔli/ *f* **1** madness; **aimer qn/qch à la ~** to be mad (BrE) *or* crazy about sb/sth
2 act of folly; **elle a fait une ~ en acceptant** she was mad to accept

3 extravagance
■ **~ des grandeurs** delusions of grandeur

folk /fɔlk/ *m* folk music

folklo /fɔlklo/ *adj* (fam) eccentric, crazy (fam)

folklore /fɔlklɔʀ/ *m* **1** folklore
2 (fam) razzmatazz (fam)

folklorique /fɔlklɔʀik/ *adj* **1** ‹*music*› folk; ‹*costume*› traditional
2 (fam) eccentric

folle ▶ **fou A, B**

follement /fɔlmɑ̃/ *adv* **s'amuser ~** to have a terrific time

follet /fɔlɛ/ *adj m* **feu ~** will-o'-the-wisp

fomenter /fɔmɑ̃te/ [**v1**] *vt* to instigate

foncé, **~e** /fɔ̃se/ *adj* ‹*colour*› dark; ‹*pink*› deep

foncer /fɔ̃se/ [**v12**] **A** *vt* **1** to make [sth] darker *or* deeper ‹*colour*›
2 (Culin) to line
B *vi* **1** (fam) ‹*person, vehicle*› to tear along (fam); **fonce!** get a move on! (fam); **~ vers/dans** to rush toward(s)/into; **~ sur qch/vers la sortie** to make a dash for sth/for the exit; **~ sur qn** to charge at sb; **~ à New York** to dash over to New York
2 ‹*colour*› (gen) to darken; ‹*pink, mauve*› to deepen; ‹*fabric*› to go darker

fonceur, **-euse** /fɔ̃sœʀ, øz/ (fam) **A** *adj* dynamic
B *mf* go-getter (fam)

foncier, **-ière** /fɔ̃sje, ɛʀ/ *adj* ‹*income*› from land; **impôt ~** property tax

foncièrement /fɔ̃sjɛʀmɑ̃/ *adv* fundamentally

🔑 **fonction** /fɔ̃ksjɔ̃/ *f* **1** (in administration, company) post; duties; **dans l'exercice de leurs ~s** while carrying out their duties; **occuper la ~ de** to hold the position of; **voiture de ~** company car
2 en ~ de according to
3 function; **avoir pour ~ de faire** to be designed to do; **faire ~ de** to serve as
4 profession; **~ enseignante** teaching profession
■ **~ publique** civil service

fonctionnaire /fɔ̃ksjɔnɛʀ/ *mf* civil servant; (higher ranking) government official

fonctionnalité /fɔ̃ksjɔnalite/ *f* functionality

fonctionnel, **-elle** /fɔ̃ksjɔnɛl/ *adj* functional

🔑 **fonctionnement** /fɔ̃ksjɔnmɑ̃/ *m* **1** (of institution) functioning
2 (of machinery) working; **mauvais ~** malfunction; **en ~** in service

🔑 **fonctionner** /fɔ̃ksjɔne/ [**v1**] *vi* to work; **~ à l'essence** to run on petrol (BrE) *or* gas (AmE)

🔑 **fond** /fɔ̃/ **A** *m* **1** (of vessel, lake, valley) bottom; (of cupboard, wardrobe) back; **~ de la mer** seabed; **~ de l'océan** ocean floor; **toucher le ~** (in water) to touch the bottom; (fig) to hit rock bottom
2 (of shop, yard) back; (of corridor, room) far end; **la chambre du ~** the back bedroom; **au ~ des bois** deep in the woods; **de ~ en comble** from top to bottom
3 les problèmes de ~ the basic problems; **un débat de ~** an in-depth debate; **au ~** *or* **dans le ~, le problème est simple** basically, the problem is simple
4 (of text) content
5 regarder qn au ~ des yeux (suspiciously) to give sb a searching look; **elle a un bon ~** she's very good at heart
6 background; **~ musical** background music
7 un ~ de porto a drop of port
8 (Naut) **il y a 20 mètres de ~** the water is 20 metres (BrE) deep
9 (Sport) **épreuve de ~** long-distance event
B à fond *phr* **1 connaître qch à ~** to be an expert in sth; **être à ~ pour** (fam) to support wholeheartedly; **respirer à ~** to breathe deeply; **mettre la radio à ~** to turn the radio right up
2 (fam) **rouler à ~** to drive at top speed
■ **~ d'artichaut** artichoke bottom; **~ de teint** foundation (BrE), make-up base (AmE)

🔑 **fondamental**, **~e**, *mpl* **-aux** /fɔ̃damɑ̃tal, o/ *adj* **1** basic, fundamental
2 essential

fondamentalement /fɔ̃damɑ̃talmɑ̃/ *adv* **1** fundamentally
2 radically

fondamentaliste /fɔ̃damɑ̃talist/ *m* fundamentalist

fondant, **~e** /fɔ̃dɑ̃, ɑ̃t/ *adj* **1** ‹*ice*› melting
2 ‹*pear*› which melts in the mouth

fondateur, **-trice** /fɔ̃datœʀ, tʀis/ *mf* founder; **groupe ~** founding group

fondation /fɔ̃dasjɔ̃/ **A** *f* foundation
B fondations *fpl* foundations

fondé, **~e** /fɔ̃de/ **A** *pp* ▶ **fonder**
B *pp adj* justifiable, well-founded, legitimate; **non ~, mal ~** ‹*accusation*› groundless
■ **~ de pouvoir** (of company) authorized representative; (of bank) senior banking executive

fondement /fɔ̃dmɑ̃/ *m* foundation; **être sans** *or* **dénué de ~** to be unfounded

🔑 **fonder** /fɔ̃de/ [**v1**] **A** *vt* **1** to found
2 to base
B se fonder *v refl* (+ *v être*) **se ~ sur** ‹*theory, method*› to be based on; ‹*person*› to go on

fonderie /fɔ̃dʀi/ *f* **1** foundry
2 casting

fondre /fɔ̃dʀ/ [**v6**] **A** *vt* **1** to melt down ‹*metal*›; to smelt ‹*mineral*›
2 to cast ‹*statue*›
B *vi* **1** ‹*snow, butter*› to melt
2 ‹*sugar*› to dissolve
3 ‹*savings*› to melt away

🔑 key word

4 (emotionally) to soften; ~ **en larmes** to dissolve into tears
C **se fondre** *v refl* (+ *v être*) **se ~ dans** ‹*person, figure*› to blend in with

fonds /fɔ̃/ **A** *m inv* **1** (in gallery, museum) collection
2 fund
B *mpl* funds
■ ~ **d'amortissement** sinking fund; ~ **bloqués** frozen assets; ~ **de commerce** business; ~ **de placement** investment fund; ~ **de prévoyance** provident fund; ~ **propres** equity capital; ~ **de roulement** working capital; ~ **de solidarité** mutual aid fund; **Fonds monétaire international, FMI** International Monetary Fund, IMF

fondu, **~e** /fɔ̃dy/ **A** *pp* ▶ **fondre**
B *pp adj* ‹*butter*› melted; ‹*metal*› molten

fondue /fɔ̃dy/ *f* (Culin) fondue; ~ **savoyarde** cheese fondue; ~ **bourguignonne** fondue bourguignonne (*meat dipped in hot oil*)

font /fɔ̃/ ▶ **faire**

fontaine /fɔ̃tɛn/ *f* **1** fountain
2 spring

fonte /fɔ̃t/ *f* **1** cast iron
2 melting down, smelting
3 thawing; ~ **des neiges** thaw

fonts /fɔ̃/ *mpl* ~ **baptismaux** font

foot /fut/ (fam) ▶ **football**

football /futbol/ *m* football (BrE), soccer

footballeur, **-euse** /futbolœʀ, øz/ *mf* football *or* soccer player

footing /futiŋ/ *m* jogging

forage /fɔʀaʒ/ *m* drilling

forain, **-aine** /fɔʀɛ̃, ɛn/ **A** *adj* fairground
B *m* stallkeeper; **les ~s** fairground people

forçat /fɔʀsa/ *m* **1** convict
2 galley slave

force /fɔʀs/ **A** *f* **1** strength; **~s** strength; **avoir de la ~** to be strong; **c'est au-dessus de mes ~s** it's too much for me; **de toutes ses ~s** with all one's might; **ils sont de ~ égale aux échecs** they are evenly matched at chess
2 force; **de ~** by force; **faire manger de ~** to force [sb] to eat; **entrer de ~ dans un lieu** to force one's way into a place
3 ~ **de vente** sales force; **~s** (Mil) forces; **d'importantes ~s de police** large numbers of police
B **à force** *phr* (fam) **à ~, elle l'a cassé** she ended up breaking it
C **à force de** *phr* **réussir à ~ de travail** to succeed by dint of hard work; **il est aphone à ~ de crier** he's been shouting so much (that) he's lost his voice
■ ~ **de dissuasion** (Mil) deterrent force; ~ **de frappe** nuclear weapons; **~s de l'ordre** forces of law and order

forcé, **~e** /fɔʀse/ **A** *pp* ▶ **forcer**
B *pp adj* **1** (gen) forced
2 ‹*consequence*› inevitable; **c'est~!** (fam) there's no way around it! (fam)

forcément /fɔʀsemɑ̃/ *adv* inevitably; **pas ~** not necessarily

forcené, **~e** /fɔʀsəne/ **A** *adj* ‹*rhythm*› furious; ‹*activity*› frenzied
B *mf* **1** maniac
2 crazed gunman

forcer /fɔʀse/ [**v12**] **A** *vt* **1** to force
2 to break through ‹*fence, enclosure*›; ~ **la porte de qn** to force one's way into sb's house; ~ **le passage** to force one's way through
B **forcer sur** *v+prep* to overdo ‹*salt, colour*›
C *vi* **1** to overdo it
2 serrez sans ~ do not tighten too much; **ne force pas!** don't force it!
D **se forcer** *v refl* (+ *v être*) to force oneself
IDIOM ~ **la main à qn** to force sb's hand

forcing /fɔʀsiŋ/ *m* (fam) **faire du ~** to go all out

forer /fɔʀe/ [**v1**] *vt* to drill

forestier, **-ière** /fɔʀɛstje, ɛʀ/ *adj* ‹*area*› forested; **chemin ~** forest path; **exploitation forestière** (place) forestry plantation

foret /fɔʀɛ/ *m* drill

forêt /fɔʀɛ/ *f* forest; ~ **tropicale** rain forest
IDIOM **c'est l'arbre qui cache la ~** you can't see the wood for the trees

forfait /fɔʀfɛ/ *m* **1** fixed rate; **un ~ de 8 euros** a fixed price of 8 euros
2 package; ~ **avion-auto** fly-drive package
3 ~ **skieur** ski pass
4 (of player) withdrawal; **déclarer ~** to give up; (Sport) to withdraw

forfaitaire /fɔʀfɛtɛʀ/ *adj* **prix ~** contract *or* all-inclusive price; **indemnité ~** basic allowance

forge /fɔʀʒ/ *f* **1** forge
2 ironworks

forgé, **~e** /fɔʀʒe/ **A** *pp* ▶ **forger**
B *pp adj* ‹*object, metal*› wrought

forger /fɔʀʒe/ [**v13**] *vt* **1** to forge
2 to form ‹*character*›

forgeron /fɔʀʒəʀɔ̃/ *m* blacksmith
IDIOM **c'est en forgeant qu'on devient ~** (Proverb) practice makes perfect

formaliser: **se formaliser** /fɔʀmalize/ [**v1**] *v refl* (+ *v être*) to take offence (BrE)

formalité /fɔʀmalite/ *f* formality; **les ~s à accomplir pour obtenir un visa** the necessary procedure to obtain a visa; **par pure ~** as a matter of form

format /fɔʀma/ *m* format, size

formatage /fɔʀmataʒ/ *m* (Comput) formatting; **faire un ~** to format

formateur, **-trice** /fɔʀmatœʀ, tʀis/ *adj* formative

formation /fɔʀmasjɔ̃/ *f* **1** education; training; **avoir une ~ littéraire** to have an arts background; **en ~** undergoing training
2 training course

3 (of government, team) forming
4 group
■ **~ continue, ~ permanente** adult continuing education; **~ professionnelle** professional training

⚷ **forme** /fɔʀm/ **A** *f* **1** shape; form; **en ~ de** in the shape of; **sous ~ de** in the form of; **sans ~** shapeless; **pour la ~** as a matter of form
2 (of payment) method
3 (physical condition) form; **en pleine ~** in great shape
B formes *fpl* **1** (of person) figure
2 (of object, building) lines
3 faire qch dans les ~s to do sth in the correct manner; **y mettre les ~s** to be tactful

formé, ~e /fɔʀme/ **A** *pp* ▶ **former**
B *pp adj* **1** made up; formed
2 educated; trained
3 ‹*writing, sentence*› formed

formel, -elle /fɔʀmɛl/ *adj* **1** ‹*refusal, denial, person*› categorical; ‹*order*› strict; **être ~ sur qch** ‹*person*› to be definite about sth
2 c'est purement ~ it's just a formality

formellement /fɔʀmɛlmɑ̃/ *adv*
1 categorically; strictly
2 officially; **~ identifié** clearly identified

⚷ **former** /fɔʀme/ [**v1**] **A** *vt* **1** to form ‹*circle, rectangle*›
2 to form, to constitute
3 to train ‹*staff*›; to educate ‹*person, tastes*›; to develop ‹*intelligence*›
4 to form ‹*abscess, film*›
B se former *v refl* (+ *v être*) **1** to form
2 to be formed
3 to train, to be trained
4 ‹*character, style*› to develop

formidable /fɔʀmidabl/ *adj* **1** ‹*force*› tremendous
2 (fam) great, marvellous (BrE)
3 (fam) incredible

formol /fɔʀmɔl/ *m* formalin

formulaire /fɔʀmylɛʀ/ *m* form

formulation /fɔʀmylasjɔ̃/ *f* formulation; wording; **la ~ de cette idée est difficile** it's not easy to express that idea

⚷ **formule** /fɔʀmyl/ *f* **1** expression; **~ toute faite** set phrase
2 (in travel, tourism) option; **~ à 75€** (in restaurant) set menu at 75€
3 method
4 concept
5 (in science) formula
6 (of car) **~ un** Formula One
7 (of magazine) format
■ **~ magique** magic words

formuler /fɔʀmyle/ [**v1**] *vt* (gen) to express; to put [sth] into words ‹*idea*›

⚷ **fort, ~e** /fɔʀ, fɔʀt/ **A** *adj* **1** strong; **armée ~e de 10 000 hommes** 10,000-strong army; **~ d'un chiffre d'affaires en hausse** boasting an increased turnover
2 ‹*noise*› loud; ‹*light*› bright; ‹*heat, activity*› intense; ‹*temperature, fever, rate*› high; ‹*blow, jolt*› hard; ‹*rain*› heavy; ‹*spice*› hot; ‹*majority*› large; ‹*lack, shortage*› great; ‹*drop, increase*› sharp; **~e émigration** high level of emigration
3 (at school subject) good
4 ‹*person*› stout; ‹*hips*› broad; ‹*bust*› large; ‹*thighs*› big
5 (fam) **c'est un peu ~!** that's a bit much! (fam)
B *adv* **1** extremely, very
2 ‹*doubt*› very much; **avoir ~ à faire** (fam) to have a lot to do
3 ‹*hit*› hard; ‹*squeeze*› tight; ‹*breathe*› deeply; ‹*speak*› loudly; **y aller un peu ~** (fam) to go a bit too far
4 il ne va pas très ~ he's not very well
C *m* **1** fort
2 strong person
D au plus fort de *phr* **au plus ~ de l'été** at the height of summer
■ **~e tête** rebel
IDIOM **c'est plus ~ que moi/qu'elle** I/she just can't help it

fortement /fɔʀtəmɑ̃/ *adv* ‹*criticize*› strongly; ‹*rise*› sharply; ‹*industrialized*› highly; ‹*shaken*› deeply; ‹*damaged*› badly; ‹*displease, dislike*› greatly; ‹*armed*› heavily; **il est ~ question de...** it is highly likely that...

forteresse /fɔʀtəʀɛs/ *f* stronghold

fortiche /fɔʀtiʃ/ *adj* (fam) smart, clever (en at)

fortifiant /fɔʀtifjɑ̃/ *m* (Med) tonic

fortification /fɔʀtifikasjɔ̃/ *f* fortification

fortifier /fɔʀtifje/ [**v2**] *vt* **1** to strengthen ‹*nails, hair*›
2 ‹*meal*› to fortify; ‹*holiday, vitamins*› to do [sb] good
3 to reinforce ‹*construction*›

fortuit, ~e /fɔʀtɥi, it/ *adj* ‹*meeting*› accidental; ‹*incident, discovery*› fortuitous

⚷ **fortune** /fɔʀtyn/ *f* **1** fortune
2 de ~ makeshift
IDIOM **faire contre mauvaise ~ bon cœur** to put on a brave face

fortuné, ~e /fɔʀtyne/ *adj* wealthy

forum de discussion *m* (Comput) discussion board

fosse /fos/ *f* **1** pit
2 grave
3 sandpit
■ **~ commune** communal grave; **~ septique** septic tank

fossé /fɔse/ *m* **1** (gen) ditch; (of castle) moat
2 (fig) gap; rift

fossette /fɔsɛt/ *f* dimple

fossile /fɔsil/ *adj, m* fossil

fossiliser /fɔsilize/ [**v1**] *vt*, **se fossiliser** *v refl* (+ *v être*) to fossilize

fossoyeur /fɔswajœʀ/ *m* gravedigger

⚷ key word

fou, **fol** *before vowel or mute h*, **folle** /fu, fɔl/ **A** *adj* **1** (insane) mad; **devenir ~** to go mad; **un tueur ~** a crazed killer
2 ‹*person, idea*› mad (BrE), crazy; ‹*look*› wild; ‹*story*› crazy; **être ~ furieux** (fam) to be raving mad; **être ~ à lier** (fam) to be stark raving mad (fam); **entre eux c'est l'amour ~** they're madly in love; **~ de qn** crazy about sb
3 ‹*success*› huge; **un monde ~** a huge crowd; **avoir un mal ~ à faire** to find it incredibly difficult to do
4 ‹*vehicle, horse*› runaway; ‹*lock of hair*› stray; **avoir le ~ rire** to have a fit of the giggles
B *mf* madman/madwoman; **envoyer qn chez les ~s** (fam) to send sb to the nuthouse (fam); **courir comme un ~** to run like mad; **c'est un ~ d'art contemporain** he's mad about contemporary art
C *m* **1** fool, court jester
2 (in chess) bishop
IDIOMS **faire les ~s** (fam) to fool about; **plus on est de ~s plus on rit** (fam) the more the merrier

foudre /fudʀ/ *f* lightning; **coup de ~** love at first sight; **avoir le coup de ~ pour** to be really taken with

foudroyant, **~e** /fudʀwajɑ̃, ɑ̃t/ *adj* ‹*attack*› lightning; ‹*look*› furious; ‹*death*› sudden

foudroyer /fudʀwaje/ [**v23**] *vt* **1** to strike ‹*tree*›; **mort foudroyé** struck dead by lightning; **~ qn du regard** to look daggers at sb (fam)
2 ‹*bad news*› to devastate

fouet /fwɛ/ *m* **1** whip; **dix coups de ~** ten lashes of the whip; **le grand air m'a donné un coup de ~** the fresh air invigorated me; **se heurter de plein ~** to collide head-on
2 (Culin) whisk; **~ mécanique** hand whisk

fouetter /fwɛte/ [**v1**] *vt* **1** to whip, to flog ‹*person*›; to whip ‹*animal*›
2 la pluie leur fouettait le visage the rain lashed their faces
IDIOMS **il n'y a pas de quoi ~ un chat** (fam) it's no big deal (fam); **avoir d'autres chats à ~** (fam) to have other fish to fry

foufou, **fofolle** /fufu, fɔfɔl/ *adj* (fam) scatterbrained

fougère /fuʒɛʀ/ *f* **1** fern
2 bracken

fougue /fug/ *f* enthusiasm

fougueusement /fugøzmɑ̃/ *adv* enthusiastically

fougueux, **-euse** /fugø, øz/ *adj* spirited; enthusiastic

fouille /fuj/ *f* **1** (of place, person, baggage) search
2 excavation

fouillé, **~e** /fuje/ **A** *pp* ▶ **fouiller**
B *pp adj* ‹*study, portrait, piece of work*› detailed; ‹*style*› elaborate

fouiller /fuje/ [**v1**] **A** *vt* **1** to search; to frisk
2 to dig ‹*site*›
B *vi* **~ dans** (gen) to rummage through; to search ‹*memory*›; to delve into ‹*past*›

fouillis /fuji/ *m inv* mess; jumble

fouine /fwin/ *f* (Zool) stone marten

fouiner /fwine/ [**v1**] *vi* **1** to forage about
2 ~ dans to rummage through ‹*objects, papers*›; to poke one's nose into ‹*life, past*›

foulard /fulaʀ/ *m* scarf, headscarf

foule /ful/ *f* **1** crowd; mob; **il y avait ~ à la réunion** there were masses of people at the meeting; **venir en ~ à** to flock to
2 mass

foulée /fule/ *f* (of horse, athlete) stride; **courir dans la ~ de qn** (Sport) to tail sb; **dans la ~ il a...** while he was at it, he...

fouler /fule/ [**v1**] **A** *vt* to tread ‹*grapes*›
B se fouler *v refl* (+ *v être*) **1** (Med) **se ~ le poignet** to sprain one's wrist
2 (fam) **tu ne t'es pas foulé** you didn't kill yourself (fam)

foulure /fulyʀ/ *f* sprain

four /fuʀ/ *m* **1** oven; **cuire au ~** to roast, to bake
2 furnace; kiln
■ **~ crématoire** crematory (furnace); **~ à micro-ondes** microwave oven

fourbu, **~e** /fuʀby/ *adj* exhausted

fourche /fuʀʃ/ *f* fork; **faire une ~** to fork

fourcher /fuʀʃe/ [**v1**] *vi* **ma langue a fourché** it was a slip of the tongue

fourchette /fuʀʃɛt/ *f* **1** fork
2 (of prices, temperature) range; (of income) bracket; **~ horaire** period

fourchu, **~e** /fuʀʃy/ *adj* ‹*branch*› forked; **cheveux ~s** split ends

fourgon /fuʀgɔ̃/ *m* **1** van
2 (of train) goods wagon (BrE), freight car (AmE)
■ **~ à bestiaux** cattle truck

fourgonnette /fuʀgɔnɛt/ *f* (small) van

fourguer /fuʀge/ (pop) [**v1**] *vt* to flog (fam) (à to), to sell [sth] off (à to)

fourmi /fuʀmi/ *f* (Zool) ant; **travail de ~** laborious task
IDIOM **avoir des ~s dans les jambes** to have pins and needles in one's legs

fourmilier /fuʀmilje/ *m* anteater

fourmilière /fuʀmiljɛʀ/ *f* ant hill

fourmillement /fuʀmijmɑ̃/ *m* **1 un ~ de gens** a mass of people
2 tingling sensation

fourmiller /fuʀmije/ [**v1**] **A fourmiller de** *v+prep* to be chock-full of ‹*mistakes*›; to be swarming with ‹*visitors*›
B *vi* to abound

fournaise /fuʀnɛz/ *f* blaze; **la ville est une ~ en été** the town is baking hot in summer

fourneau, *pl* **~x** /fuʀno/ *m* **1** (Tech) furnace
2 stove

fournée /fuʀne/ *f* batch

fourni, **~e** /fuʀni/ **A** *pp* ▶ **fournir**
B *pp adj* ‹*hair*› thick; ‹*grass*› lush

f

fournir /furnir/ [**v3**] **A** *vt* to supply ‹*document, equipment*›; to provide ‹*energy*›; to contribute ‹*effort*›; to produce ‹*proof*›
B **se fournir** *v refl* (+ *v être*) **se ~ chez** *or* **auprès de** to get [sth] from

fournisseur, **-euse** /furnisœr, øz/ **A** *adj* **pays ~** exporting country
B *m* supplier; **~ de drogue** drug dealer
■ **~ d'accès** (Comput) service provider

fourniture /furnityr/ *f* **1** supply, provision
2 ~s scolaires/de bureau school/office stationery; **~s de laboratoire** laboratory equipment

fourrage /furaʒ/ *m* forage; **~ sec** fodder

fourré, **~e** /fure/ **A** *pp* ▸ **fourrer**
B *pp adj* **1** (Culin) filled
2 fur-lined; lined
3 (fam) **toujours ~ au café** always hanging about at the cafe
C *m* thicket

fourrer /fure/ [**v1**] **A** *vt* **1** (fam) to stick (fam); **~ qch dans la tête de qn** to put sth into sb's head
2 (Culin) to fill
3 to line ‹*garment*›
B **se fourrer** *v refl* (+ *v être*) (fam) **1 se ~ dans un coin** to get into a corner
2 se ~ une idée dans la tête to get an idea into one's head

fourre-tout /furtu/ *adj inv* **sac ~** holdall (BrE), carryall (AmE)

fourreur /furœr/ *m* furrier

fourrière /furjɛr/ *f* pound; **mettre une voiture à la ~** to impound a car

fourrure /furyr/ *f* fur, coat

fourvoyer: **se fourvoyer** /furvwaje/ [**v23**] *v refl* (+ *v être*) to make a mistake

foutoir /futwar/ *m* (pop) shambles (fam); complete chaos

foutre /futr/ [**v6**] (pop) **A** *vt* **1 n'en avoir rien à ~** not to give a damn (fam)
2 ~ qch quelque part to stick sth somewhere (fam)
B **se foutre** *v refl* (+ *v être*) **1 il ne s'est pas foutu de toi!** he's been very generous!; **se ~ du monde** to have a bloody (BrE) *or* hell of a (AmE) nerve (sl)
2 not to give a damn (fam)
IDIOM **~ le camp** to bugger off (BrE) (fam), to split (AmE) (fam)

foutu, **~e** /futy/ (pop) **A** *pp* ▸ **foutre**
B *pp adj* **1** (*before n*) bloody awful (BrE) (sl), damned (AmE)
2 être ~ ‹*person, garment*› to have had it (fam)
3 être mal ~ to be unattractive; to feel lousy (fam)
4 être ~ de faire to be totally capable of doing

foyer /fwaje/ *m* **1** home; **fonder un ~** to get married
2 (family) household
3 hostel
4 club
5 (for fire) hearth
6 (of resistance) pocket; **un ~ d'incendie** a fire
7 (of rebellion) seat; (of epidemic) source
8 (in optics) focus; **lunettes à double ~** bifocals
■ **~ fiscal** household for tax purposes; **~ de placement** foster home

fracas /fraka/ *m inv* (of falling object) crash; (of waves) roar; (of town, battle) din

fracassant, **~e** /frakasɑ̃, ɑ̃t/ *adj* ‹*noise*› deafening; ‹*news*› sensational; ‹*success*› stunning

fracasser /frakase/ [**v1**] **A** *vt* to smash
B **se fracasser** *v refl* (+ *v être*) to crash

fraction /fraksjɔ̃/ *f* **1** (in mathematics) fraction
2 (of sum of money) part; (of company) section; **en une ~ de seconde** in a split second

fractionnement /fraksjɔnmɑ̃/ *m* division; fragmentation

fractionner /fraksjɔne/ [**v1**] *vt* to divide up ‹*work, group*›; to split ‹*party*›

fracture /fraktyr/ *f* fracture; **~ du poignet** fractured wrist

fracturer /fraktyre/ [**v1**] **A** *vt* to break down ‹*door*›; to break ‹*window*›; to force ‹*safe*›
B **se fracturer** *v refl* (+ *v être*) **se ~ la cheville** to break one's ankle

fragile /fraʒil/ *adj* **1** fragile
2 ‹*person*› frail; ‹*eye*› sensitive; ‹*heart*› weak

fragiliser /fraʒilize/ [**v1**] *vt* to weaken

fragilité /fraʒilite/ *f* **1** fragility
2 frailty

fragment /fragmɑ̃/ *m* **1** (of cup, bone) fragment
2 (of book, novel) passage

fragmentaire /fragmɑ̃tɛr/ *adj* patchy; sketchy; sporadic

fragmentation /fragmɑ̃tasjɔ̃/ *f* **1** division; splitting up
2 fragmentation

fragmenter /fragmɑ̃te/ [**v1**] *vt* to break up ‹*substance*›; to divide up ‹*work*›

fraîche ▸ **frais E, A**

fraîchement /frɛʃmɑ̃/ *adv* **1** freshly, newly
2 coldly; **elle a été ~ accueillie** she was given a cool reception

fraîcheur /frɛʃœr/ *f* **1** coolness; coldness; **la ~ du soir** the cold evening air
2 freshness

frais, **fraîche** /frɛ, frɛʃ/ **A** *adj* **1** cool; cold; **'servir ~'** 'serve chilled'
2 ‹*news, snow*› fresh; ‹*paint*› wet
3 ‹*complexion*› fresh
4 ‹*troops*› fresh; **de l'argent ~** more money
B *adv* **il fait ~** it's cool
C *m* **prendre le ~** to get some fresh air; **mettre au ~** to put in a cool place; to put to cool

---

key word

D *mpl* **1** expenses; **aux ~ de l'entreprise** paid for by the company; **rentrer dans ses ~** to cover one's expenses; **faire les ~ de qch** to bear the brunt of sth
2 fees
3 costs
E **à la fraîche** *phr* in the cool of the morning; in the cool of the evening
■ **~ d'annulation** cancellation fees; **~ de déplacement** (of employee) travel expenses; (for repairman) call-out charge; **~ divers** miscellaneous costs; **~ d'expédition** (for parcel) postage and packing; **~ de fonctionnement** running costs; **~ de garde** childminding fees; **~ d'inscription** (gen) registration fees; (for school) school fees (BrE), tuition fees (AmE); (at university) tuition fees; **~ de port** postage; **~ professionnels** professional expenses; **~ de scolarité** tuition fees, school fees (BrE)

fraise /fʀɛz/ *f* **1** strawberry; **~ des bois** wild strawberry
2 (tool, instrument) reamer; milling cutter; (of dentist) drill
IDIOM **ramener sa ~** (fam) to stick one's nose in (fam)

fraiseur, -euse /fʀɛzœʀ, øz/ *mf* cutter

fraiseuse /fʀɛzøz/ *f* milling machine

fraisier /fʀɛzje/ *m* **1** strawberry plant
2 strawberry gateau

framboise /fʀɑ̃bwaz/ *f* **1** raspberry
2 raspberry liqueur

framboisier /fʀɑ̃bwazje/ *m* raspberry cane; raspberry bush

franc, franche /fʀɑ̃, fʀɑ̃ʃ/ **A** *adj* **1** ‹*person*› frank, straight; ‹*reply*› straight; ‹*laughter, expression*› open, honest; **jouer ~ jeu** to play fair
2 duty-free; **~ de port** postage paid
B *m* (currency) franc; **~ lourd** (Hist) new franc

français, ~e /fʀɑ̃sɛ, ɛz/ **A** *adj* French
B *m* (language) French

Français, ~e /fʀɑ̃sɛ, ɛz/ *mf* Frenchman/ Frenchwoman

France /fʀɑ̃s/ *pr f* France

franche ▸ **franc A**

franchement /fʀɑ̃ʃmɑ̃/ *adv* **1** frankly, candidly; **je lui ai demandé ~** I asked him straight out
2 ‹*lean*› firmly; ‹*enter*› boldly
3 really; **il m'a franchement agacé** he really annoyed me; **~!** (well) really!

franchir /fʀɑ̃ʃiʀ/ [**v3**] *vt* to cross ‹*line*›; to get over ‹*fence*›; to cover ‹*distance*›

franchise /fʀɑ̃ʃiz/ *f* **1** frankness, sincerity
2 exemption
3 (in insurance) excess (BrE), deductible (AmE)
4 (to sell goods) franchise
■ **~ de bagages** baggage allowance; **~ fiscale** tax exemption; **~ postale** 'postage paid'; **en ~ postale** post free

franchiser /fʀɑ̃ʃize/ [**v1**] *vt* to franchise

franchissement /fʀɑ̃ʃismɑ̃/ *m* crossing; clearing; **~ de la ligne continue** crossing the white line

franciser /fʀɑ̃size/ [**v1**] *vt* to Gallicize

franc-jeu /fʀɑ̃ʒø/ *m* fair play

franc-maçon, -onne, *pl* **francs-maçons, franc-maçonnes** /fʀɑ̃masɔ̃, ɔn/ *mf* Freemason

franc-maçonnerie, *pl* **~s** /fʀɑ̃masɔnʀi/ *f* **la ~** Freemasonry

franco /fʀɑ̃ko/ *adv* **1 ~ de port** postage paid, carriage paid
2 (fam) **y aller ~** to go right ahead

francophone /fʀɑ̃kɔfɔn/ **A** *adj* French-speaking; ‹*literature*› in the French language
B *mf* French speaker

francophonie /fʀɑ̃kɔfɔni/ *f* French-speaking world

franc-parler /fʀɑ̃paʀle/ *m* **avoir son ~** to speak one's mind

frange /fʀɑ̃ʒ/ *f* **1** (on rug, curtain, garment) fringe
2 (hair) fringe (BrE), bangs (AmE)

frangin /fʀɑ̃ʒɛ̃/ *m* (fam) brother

frangine /fʀɑ̃ʒin/ *f* (fam) sister

franglais /fʀɑ̃glɛ/ *m* Franglais

franquette: **à la bonne franquette** /alabɔnfʀɑ̃kɛt/ *phr* (fam) **recevoir qn à la bonne ~** to have sb over for an informal meal

frappé, ~e /fʀape/ **A** *pp* ▸ **frapper**
B *pp adj* ‹*cocktail*› frappé; ‹*coffee*› iced

frapper /fʀape/ [**v1**] **A** *vt* **1** (gen) to hit, to strike; **~ à coups de pied** to kick; **~ à coups de poing** to punch; **~ un grand coup** (gen) to hit hard; (on door) to knock
2 to strike ‹*coin*›
3 ‹*unemployment, epidemic*› to hit ‹*region*›; **les taxes qui frappent les produits français** duties imposed on French goods
4 ce qui m'a frappé c'est... what struck me was...; **j'ai été frappé de voir que...** I was amazed to see that...
B *vi* **1** to hit, to strike; **~ dans ses mains** to clap one's hands
2 to knock; **on a frappé** there was a knock at the door
3 ‹*criminals*› to strike

frasque /fʀask/ *f* escapade

fraternel, -elle /fʀatɛʀnɛl/ *adj* fraternal, brotherly

fraternellement /fʀatɛʀnɛlmɑ̃/ *adv* in a brotherly fashion

fraternisation /fʀatɛʀnizasjɔ̃/ *f* fraternizing

fraterniser /fʀatɛʀnize/ [**v1**] *vi* to fraternize

fraternité /fʀatɛʀnite/ *f* fraternity

fraude /fʀod/ *f* (Law) fraud; **~ fiscale** tax fraud; **~ électorale** vote *or* election rigging; **en ~** ‹*enter*› illegally

f

frauder /fʀode/ [**v1**] *vi* (on public transport) to travel without a ticket; (in cinema) to slip in without paying

fraudeur, -euse /fʀodœʀ, øz/ *mf* swindler; tax evader; cheat

frauduleux, -euse /fʀodylø, øz/ *adj* fraudulent

frayer /fʀeje/ [**v21**] **A** *vt* **~ un passage à qn à travers la foule** to clear a path for sb through the crowd; **~ le chemin** *or* **la voie à qch** (fig) to pave the way for sth
B se frayer *v refl* (+ *v être*) **se ~ un chemin dans** *or* **à travers** to make one's way through

frayeur /fʀɛjœʀ/ *f* **1** fear
2 fright

fredonner /fʀədɔne/ [**v1**] *vt* to hum

free-lance /fʀilɑ̃s/ *mf* freelance, freelancer; **travailler en ~** to work freelance *or* as a freelancer

freezer /fʀizœʀ/ *m* icebox

frégate /fʀegat/ *f* (Naut) frigate

frein /fʀɛ̃/ *m* brake; **donner un coup de ~** to slam on the brakes; **mettre un ~ à** to curb
IDIOM **ronger son ~** to champ at the bit

freinage /fʀɛnaʒ/ *m* braking

freiner /fʀɛne/ [**v1**] **A** *vt* **1** to slow down ‹*vehicle*›
2 to impede ‹*person*›
3 to curb ‹*inflation*›
B *vi* **1** to brake; **~ à fond** to slam on the brakes
2 (in skiing) to slow down

frelaté, ~e /fʀəlate/ *adj* ‹*alcohol*› adulterated; ‹*taste*› unnatural

frêle /fʀɛl/ *adj* frail

frelon /fʀəlɔ̃/ *m* hornet

frémir /fʀemiʀ/ [**v3**] *vi* **1** ‹*leaf*› to quiver; ‹*water*› to ripple
2 (with emotion) ‹*lip*› to tremble; ‹*person*› to quiver; to shudder
3 (Culin) to start to come to the boil

frémissant, ~e /fʀemisɑ̃, ɑ̃t/ *adj* **faire cuire dans l'eau ~e** simmer gently in water

frémissement /fʀemismɑ̃/ *m* **1** quiver, tremor
2 (of person, hand) quiver, shudder

frêne /fʀɛn/ *m* ash (tree)

frénésie /fʀenezi/ *f* frenzy

frénétique /fʀenetik/ *adj* frenzied; frenetic

frénétiquement /fʀenetikmɑ̃/ *adv* ‹*fight*› frantically; ‹*dance*› frenziedly; ‹*applaud*› wildly

fréquemment /fʀekamɑ̃/ *adv* frequently

fréquence /fʀekɑ̃s/ *f* frequency

fréquent, ~e /fʀekɑ̃, ɑ̃t/ *adj* **1** frequent
2 common

fréquentable /fʀekɑ̃tabl/ *adj* respectable; **ce ne sont pas des gens ~s** they are not the sort of people one should associate with

fréquentation /fʀekɑ̃tasjɔ̃/ *f* **1** company; **avoir de bonnes/mauvaises ~s** to keep good/bad company
2 ~ des théâtres theatre-going (BrE)

fréquenté, ~e /fʀekɑ̃te/ **A** *pp* ▸ **fréquenter**
B *pp adj* popular, busy; **lieu bien ~** place that attracts the right sort of people

fréquenter /fʀekɑ̃te/ [**v1**] **A** *vt* **1** to associate with ‹*person*›; to move in ‹*milieu*›
2 to attend ‹*school*›; to go to ‹*restaurant*›
B se fréquenter *v refl* (+ *v être*) ‹*friends*› to see one another

⚷ **frère** /fʀɛʀ/ *m* brother

fresque /fʀɛsk/ *f* **1** fresco
2 panorama

fret /fʀɛt/ *m* freight

frétiller /fʀetije/ [**v1**] *vi* ‹*fish*› to wriggle; **~ de la queue** ‹*dog*› to wag its tail

freudien, -ienne /fʀødjɛ̃, ɛn/ *adj, mf* Freudian

friable /fʀijabl/ *adj* ‹*rock, biscuit*› crumbly

friand, ~e /fʀijɑ̃, ɑ̃d/ **A** *adj* **être ~ de qch** to be very fond of sth
B *m* (Culin) puff; **~ au fromage** cheese puff

friandise /fʀijɑ̃diz/ *f* sweet (BrE), candy (AmE)

fric /fʀik/ *m* (fam) dough (fam), money

friche /fʀiʃ/ *f* waste land

friction /fʀiksjɔ̃/ *f* **1** (Med) rub
2 friction

frictionner /fʀiksjɔne/ [**v1**] **A** *vt* to give [sb] a rub ‹*person*›; to rub ‹*head, feet*›
B se frictionner *v refl* (+ *v être*) to rub oneself down

frigidaire® /fʀiʒidɛʀ/ *m* refrigerator

frigide /fʀiʒid/ *adj* frigid

frigo /fʀigo/ *m* (fam) fridge (fam)

frigorifique /fʀigɔʀifik/ *adj* refrigerated

frileux, -euse /fʀilø, øz/ *adj* **1** sensitive to the cold
2 ‹*attitude, policy*› cautious

frimas /fʀima/ *mpl* cold weather

frime /fʀim/ *f* (fam) **pour la ~** for show; **c'est de la ~** it's all an act

frimer /fʀime/ [**v1**] *vi* (fam) to show off (fam)

frimousse /fʀimus/ *f* (fam) little face

fringale /fʀɛ̃gal/ *f* (fam) **j'ai la ~** I'm absolutely starving (fam)

fringuer: **se fringuer** /fʀɛ̃ge/ [**v1**] *v refl* (+ *v être*) (fam) to dress

friper /fʀipe/ [**v1**] *vt*, **se friper** *v refl* (+ *v être*) to crease, to crumple

fripon, -onne /fʀipɔ̃, ɔn/ *mf* (fam) rascal

fripouille /fʀipuj/ *f* (fam) crook (fam)

frire /fʀiʀ/ [**v64**] *vt, vi* to fry

frisé, ~e /fʀize/ **A** *pp* ▸ **friser**
B *pp adj* ‹*hair*› curly; ‹*person*› curly-haired

frisée /fʀize/ *f* curly endive

friser /fʀize/ [**v1**] **A** *vt* **1** to curl; **se faire ~** to have one's hair curled
2 to border on; **cela frise les 10%** it's

approaching 10%
B *vi* to curl; ‹*person*› to have curly hair

frisolée /fʀizɔle/ *f* leaf-drop streak; **la ~ de la pomme de terre** potato leaf-drop streak

frisson /fʀisɔ̃/ *m* shiver, shudder; **j'ai des ~s** I keep shivering; **grand ~** great thrill

frissonner /fʀisɔne/ [**v1**] *vi* **1** (with cold) to shiver; (with fear) to shudder
2 ‹*leaves*› to tremble
3 ‹*water, milk*› to simmer

frit /fʀi/ ▶ **frire**

frite /fʀit/ *f* (Culin) chip (BrE), French fry (AmE)

friterie /fʀitʀi/ *f* chip shop (BrE), French fries stall (AmE)

friteuse /fʀitøz/ *f* deep fat fryer, chip pan (BrE)

friture /fʀityʀ/ *f* **1** frying
2 (for frying) fat; oil
3 fried food
4 (fish) **petite ~** ≈ whitebait
5 (on radio) crackling

frivole /fʀivɔl/ *adj* frivolous

⚷ **froid**, **~e** /fʀwa, fʀwad/ **A** *adj* cold; (fig) cold, cool
B *adv* **il fait ~** it's cold
C *m* **1** cold; **coup de ~** chill; **prendre ~** to catch a cold
2 coldness; **ils sont en ~ avec moi** relations between them and me are strained; **jeter un ~** to cast a chill
D à froid *phr* **démarrage à ~** cold start
IDIOMS **il fait un ~ de canard** (fam) it is bitterly cold; **donner ~ dans le dos** to send a shiver down the spine; **ne pas avoir ~ aux yeux** to be fearless

froidement /fʀwadmɑ̃/ *adv* **1** coolly; **abattre ~** to shoot [sb] down in cold blood
2 regarder les choses ~ to look at things with a cool head

froideur /fʀwadœʀ/ *f* (gen) coldness; (of reception) coolness

froissement /fʀwasmɑ̃/ *m* **1** (of paper, fabric) crumpling; (noise) rustling
2 (Med) strain

froisser /fʀwase/ [**v1**] **A** *vt* **1** to crease ‹*fabric*›; to crumple ‹*paper*›
2 to offend ‹*person*›
3 (Med) to strain
B se froisser *v refl* (+ *v être*) **1** to crease
2 to be hurt *or* offended
3 (Med) to strain

frôlement /fʀolmɑ̃/ *m* **1** brushing
2 rustling; fluttering

frôler /fʀole/ [**v1**] **A** *vt* **1** ‹*person*› to brush (against)
2 ‹*bullet, car*› to miss narrowly; **il a frôlé la mort** he came close to dying
B se frôler *v refl* (+ *v être*) ‹*people*› to brush against each other

⚷ **fromage** /fʀɔmaʒ/ *m* cheese; **~ maigre** low-fat cheese; **~ de tête** brawn (BrE), head cheese (AmE)

fromager /fʀɔmaʒe/ *m* **1** cheesemaker
2 cheese seller

fromagerie /fʀɔmaʒʀi/ *f* cheese shop

froment /fʀɔmɑ̃/ *m* wheat

froncement /fʀɔ̃smɑ̃/ *m* **avoir un léger ~ de sourcils** to frown slightly

froncer /fʀɔ̃se/ [**v12**] *vt* **1** to gather ‹*pleats*›
2 ~ les sourcils to frown

fronde /fʀɔ̃d/ *f* **1** (weapon) sling
2 (toy) catapult (BrE), slingshot (AmE)
3 revolt

frondeur, **-euse** /fʀɔ̃dœʀ, øz/ *adj* rebellious

⚷ **front** /fʀɔ̃/ **A** *m* **1** forehead
2 (Mil) front
3 facade
B de front *phr* **ils marchaient à quatre de ~** they were walking four abreast; **mener plusieurs tâches de ~** to have several jobs on the go
IDIOM **avoir le ~ de faire** to have the face *or* effrontery to do

frontal, **~e**, *mpl* **-aux** /fʀɔ̃tal, o/ *adj* ‹*attack*› frontal; ‹*collision*› head-on

frontalier, **-ière** /fʀɔ̃talje, ɛʀ/ **A** *adj* border; **travailleur ~** person who works across the border
B *mf* person living near the border

⚷ **frontière** /fʀɔ̃tjɛʀ/ *f* **1** frontier, border; **~ naturelle** natural boundary
2 ~s entre les disciplines boundaries between disciplines

fronton /fʀɔ̃tɔ̃/ *m* pediment

frottement /fʀɔtmɑ̃/ *m* **1** rubbing
2 friction

frotter /fʀɔte/ [**v1**] **A** *vt* **1** to rub
2 to scrub
B *vi* to rub
C se frotter *v refl* (+ *v être*) **1 se ~ les yeux** to rub one's eyes
2 to scrub oneself
3 se ~ à to take on ‹*person*›
IDIOM **qui s'y frotte s'y pique** if you go looking for trouble, you'll find it

frottis /fʀɔti/ *m inv* (Med) smear

froussard, **~e** /fʀusaʀ, aʀd/ *mf* (fam) chicken (fam), coward

frousse /fʀus/ *f* (fam) fright

fructifier /fʀyktifje/ [**v2**] *vi* ‹*capital*› to yield a profit; ‹*business*› to flourish

fructueux, **-euse** /fʀyktɥø, øz/ *adj* **1** ‹*relationship, meeting*› fruitful; ‹*attempt, career*› successful
2 (financially) profitable

frugal, **~e**, *mpl* **-aux** /fʀygal, o/ *adj* frugal

⚷ **fruit** /fʀɥi/ *m* fruit
■ **~ de la passion** passion fruit; **~ sec** dried fruit; **~s de mer** seafood

fruité, **~e** /fʀɥite/ *adj* ‹*alcohol, aroma*› fruity

fruitier, **-ière** /fʀɥitje, ɛʀ/ **A** *adj* fruit
B *mf* fruiterer (BrE), fruit seller (AmE)

fruste /fʀyst/ *adj* unsophisticated

frustrant, **~e** /fʀystʀɑ̃, ɑ̃t/ *adj* frustrating

f

frustré, **~e** /fʀystʀe/ *adj* frustrated
frustrer /fʀystʀe/ [**v1**] *vt* **1 ~ qn** to thwart sb
2 ~ qn de qch to deprive sb of sth; to cheat sb (out) of sth
3 to frustrate
fuel /fjul/ *m* ▶ **fioul**
fugace /fygas/ *adj* fleeting; ‹*symptom*› elusive
fugitif, **-ive** /fyʒitif, iv/ **A** *adj* **1** ‹*prisoner*› escaped
2 fleeting, elusive
B *mf* fugitive

f

fugue /fyg/ *f* **1 faire une ~** to run away
2 (Mus) fugue
fugueur, **-euse** /fygœʀ, øz/ *mf* runaway (child)
fui, **~e** /fɥi/ ▶ **fuir**
⚷ **fuir** /fɥiʀ/ [**v29**] **A** *vt* **1** to flee ‹*country, oppression*›
2 to avoid ‹*discussion, person*›; to steer clear of ‹*crowd*›; to stay out of ‹*sun*›
B *vi* **1** ‹*person*› to flee; ‹*animal*› to run away; **faire ~** to scare [sb] off ‹*person*›
2 ‹*tap, gas, pen*› to leak
3 ~ devant ses responsabilités not to face up to one's responsibilities
fuite /fɥit/ *f* **1** (gen) flight; (of prisoner) escape; **prendre la ~** to flee; to escape
2 (of information) leak
3 (of liquid, gas) leak
fulgurant, **~e** /fylgyʀɑ̃, ɑ̃t/ *adj* ‹*attack*› lightning; ‹*progression*› dazzling; ‹*imagination*› brilliant
fulminer /fylmine/ [**v1**] *vi* to fulminate
fumé, **~e** /fyme/ **A** *pp* ▶ **fumer**
B *pp adj* **1** (Culin) smoked
2 ‹*lenses*› tinted; ‹*glass*› smoked
⚷ **fumée** /fyme/ *f* **1** smoke; **~s** (from factory) fumes; **partir en ~** (fig) to go up in smoke
2 steam
⚷ **fumer** /fyme/ [**v1**] **A** *vt* to smoke
B *vi* **1** ‹*person, chimney*› to smoke
2 ‹*soup*› to steam; ‹*acid*› to give off fumes
IDIOM **~ comme un pompier** *or* **sapeur** to smoke like a chimney
fûmes /fym/ ▶ **être**[1]
fumet /fymɛ/ *m* (Culin) (of meat) aroma; (of wine) bouquet
fumeur, **-euse** /fymœʀ, øz/ *mf* smoker; **zone non ~s** non-smoking area
fumeux, **-euse** /fymø, øz/ *adj* ‹*theory, ideas*› woolly (BrE), wooly (AmE)
fumier /fymje/ *m* manure
fumigène /fymiʒɛn/ *adj* **grenade ~** smoke grenade
fumiste /fymist/ *mf* (fam) **1** shirker
2 phoney (fam)
fumisterie /fymistəʀi/ *f* **1** (fam) joke; **c'est de la ~** it's a joke
2 chimney engineering; stove fitting

⚷ key word

fumoir /fymwaʀ/ *m* smoking room
funambule /fynɑ̃byl/ *mf* tightrope walker
funèbre /fynɛbʀ/ *adj* **1 cérémonie/service ~** funeral ceremony/service
2 gloomy
funérailles /fyneʀɑj/ *fpl* funeral
funéraire /fyneʀɛʀ/ *adj* ‹*ceremony*› funeral; ‹*monument*› funerary
funeste /fynɛst/ *adj* fatal; fateful
funiculaire /fynikylɛʀ/ *m* funicular
fur: **au fur et à mesure** /ofyʀeaməzyʀ/ *phr* as one goes along; **le chemin se rétrécissait au ~ et à mesure qu'on avançait** the path grew progressively narrower as we went along
furent /fyʀ/ ▶ **être**[1]
furet /fyʀɛ/ *m* ferret
fureter /fyʀte/ [**v18**] *vi* to rummage
fureur /fyʀœʀ/ *f* **1** rage, fury
2 frenzy; **avec ~** frenziedly; **ce sport fait ~ en ce moment** that sport is all the rage at the moment
furibond, **~e** /fyʀibɔ̃, ɔ̃d/ *adj* furious
furie /fyʀi/ *f* rage, fury
furieusement /fyʀjøzmɑ̃/ *adv* **1** furiously, violently
2 (fam) **j'ai ~ envie de dormir** I'm dying to go to sleep
furieux, **-ieuse** /fyʀjø, øz/ *adj* **1** furious, angry
2 (fam) ‹*desire*› terrible
3 ‹*battle*› intense
furoncle /fyʀɔ̃kl/ *m* boil
furtif, **-ive** /fyʀtif, iv/ *adj* **1** furtive; **marcher d'un pas ~** to creep along
2 fleeting
furtivement /fyʀtivmɑ̃/ *adv* furtively
fus /fy/ ▶ **être**[1]
fusain /fyzɛ̃/ *m* charcoal crayon; charcoal drawing
fuseau, *pl* **~x** /fyzo/ *m* **1** spindle; **en ~** tapering
2 ski pants
3 ~ horaire time zone
fusée /fyze/ *f* **1** rocket
2 (Aut) stub axle
fuselage /fyzlaʒ/ *m* fuselage
fuselé, **~e** /fyzle/ *adj* tapering, spindle-shaped
fuser /fyze/ [**v1**] *vi* to ring out; **les rires fusaient** laughter came from all sides
fusible /fyzibl/ *m* fuse
fusil /fyzi/ *m* **1** gun, shotgun; (Mil) rifle
2 sharpening steel
3 gas igniter
fusillade /fyzijad/ *f* **1** gunfire
2 shoot-out
fusiller /fyzije/ [**v1**] *vt* **1** to shoot
2 (fam) to wreck
IDIOM **~ qn du regard** to look daggers at sb

fusil-mitrailleur, *pl* **fusils-mitrailleurs** /fyzimitʀajœʀ/ *m* light machine gun

fusion /fyzjɔ̃/ *f* **1** (of metal, ice) melting; **roche en ~** molten rock
2 (in biology, physics) fusion
3 (of companies, parties) merger; (of systems, cultures) fusion; (of peoples) mixing

fusionner /fyzjɔne/ [**v1**] *vt*, *vi* to merge

fusse /fys/ ▶ **être**[1]

fussent /fys/ ▶ **être**[1]

fusses /fys/ ▶ **être**[1]

fussiez /fysje/ ▶ **être**[1]

fussions /fysjɔ̃/ ▶ **être**[1]

fut /fy/ ▶ **être**[1]

fût[1] /fy/ ▶ **être**[1]

fût[2] /fy/ *m* cask, barrel; drum

futaie /fytɛ/ *f* forest of tall trees

futé, **~e** /fyte/ **A** *adj* wily, crafty; **ce n'est pas très ~** that isn't *or* wasn't very clever
B *mf* **(petit) ~** cunning little devil

fûtes /fyt/ ▶ **être**[1]

futile /fytil/ *adj* trivial; superficial

futilité /fytilite/ **A** *f* superficiality
B futilités *fpl* **1** banalities
2 trifles; trifling activities
3 trivial details

⚷ **futur**, **~e** /fytyʀ/ **A** *adj* future; **mon ~ mari** my husband-to-be
B *m* future

fuyant, **~e** /fɥijɑ̃, ɑ̃t/ *adj* ‹*look*› shifty

fuyard, **~e** /fɥijaʀ, aʀd/ *mf* runaway

Gg

g, **G** /ʒe/ *m inv* **1** (letter) g, G
2 (*written abbr* = **gramme**) **250 g** 250 g

gabarit /gabaʀi/ *m* **1** (of vehicle) size
2 (fam) (of person) calibre (BrE); (physical) build

gabonais, **~e** /gabɔnɛ, ɛz/ *adj* Gabonese

gâcher /gɑʃe/ [**v1**] *vt* **1** to waste ‹*food, talent*›; to throw away ‹*life*›
2 to spoil ‹*party*›

gâchette /gɑʃɛt/ *f* **1** (of gun) tumbler
2 (controversial) trigger
3 (on lock) tumbler

gâchis /gɑʃi/ *m inv* **1** waste
2 mess

gadget /gadʒɛt/ *m* gadget

gadin /gadɛ̃/ *m* (fam) **ramasser** *or* **prendre un ~** to fall flat on one's face

gadoue /gadu/ *f* (fam) mud

gaélique /gaelik/ *adj*, *m* Gaelic

gaffe /gaf/ *f* (fam) **1** blunder; **faire une ~** to make a blunder
2 faire ~ to watch out

gag /gag/ *m* **1** (in film, show) gag
2 joke

gaga /gaga/ *adj inv* (fam) **1** gaga (fam)
2 silly

gage /gaʒ/ **A** *m* **1** security; **mettre qch en ~** to pawn sth; **être le ~ de qch** to be a guarantee of sth
2 (Games) forfeit
3 pledge
B gages (dated) *mpl* wages; **tueur à ~s** hired killer

gager /gaʒe/ [**v13**] *vt* **~ que** to suppose that, to wager that

gageure /gaʒyʀ/ *f* challenge

gagnant, **~e** /gaɲɑ̃, ɑ̃t/ **A** *adj* winning
B *mf* winner; winning horse; winning ticket

gagne-pain /gaɲpɛ̃/ *m inv* livelihood

gagne-petit /gaɲpəti/ *mf inv* low wage earner

⚷ **gagner** /gaɲe/ [**v1**] **A** *vt* **1** to win; **~ d'une longueur** to win by a length; **c'est gagné!** we've done it!; **à tous les coups on gagne!** every one a winner!
2 to earn; **il gagne bien sa vie** he makes a good living
3 to gain ‹*reputation, advantage, time*›; **~ de la vitesse** to gather speed
4 to save ‹*time*›; **~ de la place en faisant** to make more room by doing
5 to win [sb] over
6 to reach ‹*place*›
7 ‹*blaze, disease*› to spread to ‹*place*›
8 ‹*fear*› to overcome
9 to beat [sb]; **~ qn de vitesse** to outstrip sb
B *vi* **1** to win
2 le film gagne à être vu en version originale the film is best seen in the original version
3 to gain
4 y ~ to come off better; **y ~ en** to gain in ‹*comfort*›
5 ‹*sea*› to encroach

gagneur, **-euse** /gaɲœʀ, øz/ *mf* winner

gai, **~e** /gɛ/ *adj* **1** ‹*person*› happy; ‹*smile, expression*› cheerful; ‹*conversation*› light-hearted
2 (ironic) **c'est ~** great!
3 merry, tipsy

gaiement /gɛmɑ̃/ *adv* **1** cheerfully, merrily; gaily
2 (ironic) happily

gaieté /gete/ *f* gaiety, cheerfulness

gaillard, **~e** /gajaʀ, aʀd/ *mf* strapping lad/girl

gain /gɛ̃/ *m* **1** earnings; **mes ~s au jeu** my winnings
2 (on stock exchange) gain
3 saving; **c'est un ~ de temps considérable** it saves a considerable amount of time

gaine /gɛn/ *f* **1** (for dagger) sheath
2 girdle
3 (Tech) sheathing; casing
4 (Bot) sheath

gainer /gene/ [**v1**] *vt* to sheathe

gala /gala/ *m* gala

galamment /galamɑ̃/ *adv* gallantly

galant, **~e** /galɑ̃, ɑ̃t/ *adj* **1** gallant, gentlemanly
2 romantic

galanterie /galɑ̃tʀi/ *f* gallantry

galaxie /galaksi/ *f* galaxy

galbe /galb/ *m* curve

galbé, **~e** /galbe/ *adj* shapely

gale /gal/ *f* **1** scabies
2 (on dog, cat) mange; (on sheep) scab
3 (Bot) scab

galère /galɛʀ/ *f* **1** galley
2 (fam) hell (fam)
IDIOM **être dans la même ~** to be in the same boat

galérer /galeʀe/ [**v14**] *vi* (fam) to have a hard time

galerie /galʀi/ *f* **1** gallery
2 tunnel
■ **~ marchande** shopping arcade; **~ de toit** roof rack; **Galerie des Glaces** hall of mirrors
IDIOMS **amuser la ~** (fam) to play to the gallery; **pour épater la ~** (fam) to impress the crowd

galet /galɛ/ *m* **1** pebble
2 (Tech) roller

galette /galɛt/ *f* **1** round flat biscuit (BrE), cookie (AmE)
2 pancake
■ **~ des Rois** Twelfth Night cake

Galles /gal/ *pr f pl* **le pays de ~** Wales

gallois, **~e** /galwa, az/ **A** *adj* Welsh
B *m* (language) Welsh

Gallois, **~e** /galwa, az/ *mf* Welshman/Welshwoman; **les ~** the Welsh

gallon /galɔ̃/ *m* gallon

galoche /galɔʃ/ *f* clog; **menton en ~** protruding chin

galon /galɔ̃/ *m* **1** (for trimming) braid
2 (Mil) stripe; **prendre du ~** to be promoted

galop /galo/ *m* **1** gallop; **petit ~** canter; **grand ~** full gallop; **au ~!** (fig) hurry up!
2 (Mus) galop
IDIOM **chassez le naturel il revient au ~** (Proverb) what's bred in the bone will come out in the flesh

galopade /galɔpad/ *f* **1** gallop
2 (fam, fig) stampede

galoper /galɔpe/ [**v1**] *vi* **1** to gallop
2 (fam) ‹*child*› to charge (around)

galopin /galɔpɛ̃/ *m* rascal

galvaniser /galvanize/ [**v1**] *vt* to galvanize

gamba /gɑ̃ba/, *pl* /-as/ *f* large (Mediterranean) prawn

gambader /gɑ̃bade/ [**v1**] *vi* to gambol

gamelle /gamɛl/ *f* (of soldier) dixie (BrE), mess kit; (of camper) billycan (BrE), tin dish; (of worker) lunch box; (for pet) dish
IDIOM **prendre une ~** (fam) to fall flat on one's face (fam); (fig) to come a cropper

gamin, **~e** /gamɛ̃, in/ **A** *adj* ‹*air, look*› youthful; ‹*attitude*› childish
B *mf* kid (fam); **~ des rues** street urchin

gaminerie /gaminʀi/ *f* childish behaviour

gamme /gam/ *f* **1** (Mus) scale
2 range; **produit (de) bas de ~** low quality product; cheap product; **~ de produits** product range

gammée /game/ *adj f* **croix ~** swastika

ganglion /gɑ̃glijɔ̃/ *m* ganglion

gangrène /gɑ̃gʀɛn/ *f* **1** (Med) gangrene
2 (fig) canker

gangrener /gɑ̃gʀəne/ [**v16**] **A** *vt* to corrupt
B **se gangrener** *v refl* (+ *v être*) **1** (Med) to become gangrenous
2 (fig) to become corrupt

gangster /gɑ̃gstɛʀ/ *m* **1** gangster
2 swindler

gant /gɑ̃/ *m* glove
■ **~ de boxe** boxing glove; **~ de ménage** rubber glove; **~ de toilette** ≈ (face) flannel (BrE), wash cloth (AmE)
IDIOMS **son tailleur lui va comme un ~** her suit fits her like a glove; **mettre** *or* **prendre des ~s avec qn** to handle sb with kid gloves

⚷ **garage** /gaʀaʒ/ *m* **1** garage
2 garage, filling station
■ **~ à vélos** bicycle shed

garagiste /gaʀaʒist/ *mf* **1** garage owner
2 car mechanic

garant, **~e** /gaʀɑ̃, ɑ̃t/ **A** *adj* **être** *or* **se porter ~ de qn/qch** to vouch for sb/sth
B *mf* guarantor

garanti, **~e** /gaʀɑ̃ti/ **A** *pp* ▶ **garantir**
B *adj* **1** with a guarantee
2 guaranteed

garantie /gaʀɑ̃ti/ *f* **1** (gen), (Law) guarantee
2 (in finance) security; guarantee
3 (in insurance) cover; **montant des ~s** sum insured

⚷ key word

garantir /gaʀɑ̃tiʀ/ [v3] *vt* **1** to guarantee; **~ qch à qn** to guarantee sb sth
2 to safeguard ‹*security*›
3 to guarantee ‹*loan, product*›

garçon /gaʀsɔ̃/ *m* **1** boy
2 young man; **un brave** *or* **gentil ~** a nice chap (BrE) *or* guy (AmE)
3 bachelor
4 ~ (de café) waiter
■ **~ d'écurie** stableboy; **~ d'honneur** best man; **~ manqué** tomboy

garçonnet /gaʀsɔnɛ/ *m* little boy

garçonnière /gaʀsɔnjɛʀ/ *f* bachelor flat (BrE) *or* apartment

garde¹ /gaʀd/ *m* **1** guard
2 (for invalid, patient) carer; (in prison) warder
■ **~ champêtre** ≈ local policeman (*appointed by the municipality*); **~ du corps** bodyguard; **~ forestier** forest warden; **Garde des Sceaux** French Minister of Justice

garde² /gaʀd/ *f* **1** nurse
2 (gen), (Mil, Sport) guard; **la vieille ~** the old guard; **monter la ~** ‹*soldier*› to mount guard; **monter la ~ auprès de qn** to keep watch over sb; to stand guard over sb; **être de ~** ‹*doctor*› to be on call; ‹*soldier*› to be on guard duty
3 mettre qn en ~ to warn sb; **prendre ~** to watch out; to be careful
4 (of sword) hilt
5 (page de) ~ endpaper
■ **~ à vue** (Law) ≈ police custody

garde-à-vous /gaʀdavu/ *m inv* **se mettre au ~** to stand to attention

garde-chasse, *pl* **gardes-chasses** /gaʀdəʃas/ *m* game warden; gamekeeper

garde-côte, *pl* **~s** /gaʀdəkot/ *m* coastguard ship

garde-fou, *pl* **~s** /gaʀdəfu/ *m* **1** parapet
2 safeguard

garde-malade, *pl* **gardes-malades** /gaʀdmalad/ *mf* home nurse

garde-manger /gaʀdmɑ̃ʒe/ *m inv* meat safe

garder /gaʀde/ [v1] **A** *vt* **1** to keep ‹*object*›; to keep on ‹*hat, sweater*›; to keep on ‹*employee*›
2 ‹*soldier*› to guard; ‹*person*› to look after
B se garder *v refl* (+ *v être*) **1 se ~ de faire** to be careful not to do
2 ‹*foodstuff*› to keep

garderie /gaʀdəʀi/ *f* **1** day nursery
2 after-school child-minding facility

garde-robe, *pl* **~s** /gaʀdəʀɔb/ *f* wardrobe

gardien, -ienne /gaʀdjɛ̃, ɛn/ *mf* **1** (in premises) security guard; (in apartment block) caretaker (BrE), janitor (AmE); (in park) keeper; (in prison) warder; (in museum) attendant
2 (Sport) keeper
■ **~ de but** goalkeeper; **~ de nuit** night watchman; **~ de la paix** police officer

gardiennage /gaʀdjɛnaʒ/ *m* (of premises) security; (of apartment block) caretaking

gardienne /gaʀdjɛn/ *f* **1** ▶ **gardien**
2 ~ (d'enfant) childminder (BrE), day-care lady (AmE)

gardon /gaʀdɔ̃/ *m* roach
IDIOM **être frais comme un ~** to be as fresh as a daisy

gare /gaʀ/ **A** *f* (railway) station
B *excl* **~ (à toi)!** (threat) careful!, watch it! (fam)
■ **~ maritime** harbour (BrE) station; **~ de péage** toll plaza; **~ routière** coach station (BrE), bus station (AmE)
IDIOM **sans crier ~** without any warning

garenne /gaʀɛn/ *f* (rabbit) warren

garer /gaʀe/ [v1] **A** *vt* to park
B se garer *v refl* (+ *v être*) **1** to park
2 ‹*vehicle*› to pull over

gargariser: se gargariser /gaʀgaʀize/ [v1] *v refl* (+ *v être*) to gargle

gargarisme /gaʀgaʀism/ *m* **1** gargling
2 mouthwash

gargouille /gaʀguj/ *f* **1** gargoyle
2 waterspout

gargouiller /gaʀguje/ [v1] *vi* ‹*water, fountain*› to gurgle; ‹*stomach*› to rumble

garnement /gaʀnəmɑ̃/ *m* brat (fam)

garni, ~e /gaʀni/ **A** *pp* ▶ **garnir**
B *adj* **bien ~** ‹*wallet*› full; ‹*fridge*› well-stocked; ‹*buffet*› copious

garnir /gaʀniʀ/ [v3] *vt* **1** ‹*objects*› to fill ‹*room*›; ‹*person*› to stock ‹*shelves*›
2 to stuff ‹*cushion*›
3 (Culin) to decorate ‹*cake*›; to garnish ‹*meat*›

garnison /gaʀnizɔ̃/ *f* garrison

garniture /gaʀnityʀ/ *f* **1** (Culin) side dish; (for dessert) decoration; (for meat, fish) garnish
2 (on hat, garment) trimming
■ **~ de cheminée** mantelpiece ornaments

garrigue /gaʀig/ *f* garrigue, scrubland (*in southern France*)

garrot /gaʀo/ *m* **1** (Med) tourniquet
2 (Zool) withers; **le cheval mesure 1,50 m au ~** ≈ the horse is 15 hands

gars /ga/ *m inv* (fam) **1** boy
2 chap (BrE) (fam), guy (AmE) (fam)

Gascogne /gaskɔɲ/ *pr f* Gascony

Gascon, -onne /gaskɔ̃, ɔn/ *mf* Gascon
IDIOM **faire une offre de ~** to raise false hopes

gas-oil /gazwal/ *m* diesel (BrE), fuel oil (AmE)

gaspillage /gaspijaʒ/ *m* **1** wasting; waste
2 squandering

gaspiller /gaspije/ [v1] *vt* **1** to waste ‹*time, food*›
2 to squander ‹*resources, talent*›

gastronome /gastʀɔnɔm/ *mf* gourmet, gastronome

gastronomie /gastʀɔnɔmi/ *f* gastronomy

gastronomique /gastʀɔnɔmik/ *adj* (Culin) gourmet, gastronomic

gâteau, *pl* **~x** /gɑto/ *m* cake; gateau
■ **~ apéritif** cocktail biscuit; **~ de cire** honeycomb; **~ de riz** ≈ rice pudding; **~ sec** biscuit (BrE), cookie (AmE)
IDIOMS **c'est du ~!** (fam) it's a piece of cake! (fam); **c'est pas du ~!** (fam) it's no picnic!

gâter /gɑte/ [**v1**] **A** *vt* to spoil; to ruin ‹*teeth*›
B se gâter *v refl* (+ *v être*) **1** to go bad; to rot
2 to take a turn for the worse

gâterie /gɑtʀi/ *f* little treat

g

gâteux, **-euse** /gɑtø, øz/ *adj* **1** senile
2 il est ~ avec sa fille (fam) he's dotty about his daughter (fam)

gauche¹ /goʃ/ *adj* **1** left
2 ‹*person, manner*› awkward; ‹*style*› clumsy
IDIOM **se lever du pied ~** (fam) to get out of bed on the wrong side (BrE), to get up on the wrong side of the bed (AmE)

gauche² /goʃ/ *f* **1** left; **à ~** ‹*drive*› on the left; ‹*go, look*› to the left; ‹*turn*› left; **de ~** ‹*page*› left-hand
2 Left; **de ~** left-wing
IDIOMS **passer l'arme à ~** (fam) to kick the bucket (fam); **jusqu'à la ~** (fam) completely; **mettre de l'argent à ~** (fam) to put money aside

gauchement /goʃmɑ̃/ *adv* awkwardly

gaucher, **-ère** /goʃe, ɛʀ/ *adj* left-handed

gaucherie /goʃʀi/ *f* awkwardness

gauchiste /goʃist/ *adj*, *mf* leftist

gaufre /gofʀ/ *f* **1** waffle
2 honeycomb

gaufrette /gofʀɛt/ *f* wafer

gaufrier /gofʀije/ *m* waffle iron

Gaule /gol/ *pr f* Gaul

Gaulois, **~e** /golwa, az/ *mf* Gaul

gaver /gave/ [**v1**] **A** *vt* to force-feed ‹*geese*›
B se gaver *v refl* (+ *v être*) **1** to stuff oneself; **ça me gave** (fam) I've had enough of it (fam)
2 se ~ de to devour ‹*novels*›

gay /gɛ/ *adj inv*, *m* gay, homosexual

gaz /gaz/ **A** *m inv* gas
B *mpl* **1** (Aut) air-fuel mixture; **rouler à pleins ~** (fam) to go at full throttle
2 (Med) wind
■ **~ d'échappement** exhaust fumes; **~ à effet de serre** greenhouse gas; **~ de ville** mains gas
IDIOM **il y a de l'eau dans le ~** (fam) there's trouble brewing

gaze /gɑz/ *f* gauze

gazéifier /gazeifje/ [**v2**] *vt* to carbonate ‹*drink*›

gazelle /gazɛl/ *f* gazelle

gazer /gaze/ [**v1**] **A** *vt* to gas
B *vi* (fam) **ça gaze** things are fine

gazette /gazɛt/ *f* newspaper

gazeux, **-euse** /gazø, øz/ *adj* **1** ‹*drink*› fizzy
2 gaseous

gazinière /gazinjɛʀ/ *f* gas cooker (BrE), gas stove

gazoduc /gazɔdyk/ *m* gas pipeline

gazole /gazɔl/ *m* diesel (oil) (BrE), fuel oil (AmE)

gazon /gazɔ̃/ *m* **1** grass, turf
2 lawn

gazouiller /gazuje/ [**v1**] *vi* to twitter; to babble

GDF /ʒedeɛf/ (*abbr* = **Gaz de France**) *French gas board*

géant, **~e** /ʒeɑ̃, ɑ̃t/ **A** *adj* **1** huge
2 giant
B *mf* giant/giantess

geignement /ʒɛɲəmɑ̃/ *m* moan, groan

geindre /ʒɛ̃dʀ/ [**v55**] *vi* (in pain) to moan, to groan; to whimper; (complainingly) to whine

gel /ʒɛl/ *m* **1** frost; **résistant au ~** frost-resistant
2 ~ des prix/salaires price/wage freeze
3 après le ~ du projet after the project had been put on ice
4 gel

gélatine /ʒelatin/ *f* gelatine (BrE), gelatin (AmE)

gelé, **~e** /ʒəle/ **A** *pp* ▶ **geler**
B *adj* **1** ‹*water, ground*› frozen; ‹*toe*› frost-bitten; **j'ai les oreilles ~es** my ears are frozen
2 ‹*prices, negotiations*› frozen

gelée /ʒəle/ *f* **1** (from fruit) jelly; (from meat, fish) gelatinous stock; **œuf en ~** egg in aspic
2 gel
3 frost
■ **~ blanche** hoarfrost

geler /ʒəle/ [**v17**] **A** *vt* **1** to freeze; to nip ‹*plant*›
2 to freeze ‹*salaries*›; to suspend ‹*plan*›
B *vi* ‹*water, ground, finger, foot*› to freeze; ‹*plant*› to be frosted
C *v impers* **il gèle** it's freezing

gélule /ʒelyl/ *f* capsule

Gémeaux /ʒemo/ *pr m pl* Gemini

gémir /ʒemiʀ/ [**v3**] *vi* to moan; to whimper

gémissement /ʒemismɑ̃/ *m* moan

gemme /ʒɛm/ *f* **1** gem, gemstone
2 resin

gênant, **~e** /ʒɛnɑ̃, ɑ̃t/ *adj* **1** ‹*box*› cumbersome; ‹*problem*› annoying
2 embarrassing

gencive /ʒɑ̃siv/ *f* gum

gendarme /ʒɑ̃daʀm/ *m* **1** (Mil) gendarme, French policeman
2 dried sausage
■ **~ couché** road hump

gendarmerie /ʒɑ̃daʀm(ə)ʀi/ *f* **1** ≈ police station

key word

2 ~ (nationale) gendarmerie

gendre /ʒɑ̃dʀ/ *m* son-in-law

gène /ʒɛn/ *m* gene

gêne /ʒɛn/ *f* **1** embarrassment
2 discomfort
3 inconvenience
4 poverty

gêné, **~e** /ʒɛne/ **A** *pp* ▶ **gêner**
B *adj* **1** embarrassed
2 short of money

généalogie /ʒenealɔʒi/ *f* genealogy

généalogique /ʒenealɔʒik/ *adj* genealogical; **arbre ~** family tree

gêner /ʒɛne/ [**v1**] **A** *vt* **1** to disturb, to bother
2 ‹*smoke, noise*› to bother
3 to embarrass
4 ‹*belt*› to restrict ‹*breathing*›
5 ‹*person*› to get in the way of ‹*progress*›
B se gêner *v refl* (+ *v être*) **1** to get in each other's way
2 je vais me ~ (fam) see if I don't; **ne vous gênez pas pour moi** don't mind me

général, **~e** *mpl* **-aux** /ʒeneʀal, o/ **A** *adj* general; **de l'avis ~** in most people's opinion; **en ~**, **de façon ~e** generally, in general; **en règle ~e** as a rule
B *m* general

générale /ʒeneʀal/ *f* **1** dress rehearsal
2 general's wife

généralement /ʒeneʀalmɑ̃/ *adv* generally

généralisation /ʒeneʀalizasjɔ̃/ *f* widespread use; generalization; spread

généralisé, **~e** /ʒeneʀalize/ *adj* ‹*conflict*› widespread; ‹*process*› general; ‹*cancer*› generalized

généraliser /ʒeneʀalize/ [**v1**] **A** *vt* to bring [sth] into general use
B *vi* to generalize
C se généraliser *v refl* (+ *v être*) ‹*technique*› to become standard; ‹*tax*› to become widely applicable; ‹*strike, illness*› to spread

généraliste /ʒeneʀalist/ *adj* non-specialized; **(médecin) ~** GP, general practitioner

généralité /ʒeneʀalite/ *f* generality

générateur, **-trice** /ʒeneʀatœʀ, tʀis/ **A** *adj* **être ~ de** to generate
B *m* generator

génération /ʒeneʀasjɔ̃/ *f* generation

générer /ʒeneʀe/ [**v14**] *vt* to generate

généreusement /ʒeneʀøzmɑ̃/ *adv* generously; liberally

généreux, **-euse** /ʒeneʀø, øz/ *adj* **1** ‹*person, nature*› generous; ‹*idea, gesture*› noble
2 ‹*portion*› generous; **poitrine généreuse** large bust

générique /ʒeneʀik/ **A** *adj* generic
B *m* credits; **le ~ de fin** closing credits

générosité /ʒeneʀɔzite/ *f* generosity

genèse /ʒənɛz/ *f* **1** (of plan) genesis; (of state) birth
2 la Genèse Genesis

genêt /ʒənɛ/ *m* (Bot) broom

généticien, **-ienne** /ʒenetisjɛ̃, ɛn/ *mf* geneticist

génétique /ʒenetik/ **A** *adj* genetic
B *f* genetics

génétiquement /ʒenetikmɑ̃/ *adv* genetically; **~ modifié** genetically modified

Genève /ʒənɛv/ *pr n* Geneva

genévrier /ʒənevʀije/ *m* juniper

génial, **~e**, *mpl* **-iaux** /ʒenjal, o/ *adj*
1 brilliant
2 (fam) great (fam)

génie /ʒeni/ *m* **1** genius; **idée de ~** brainwave
2 spirit; genie
3 engineering

genièvre /ʒənjɛvʀ/ *m* Dutch gin

génisse /ʒenis/ *f* heifer

génital, **~e**, *mpl* **-aux** /ʒenital, o/ *adj* genital

génocide /ʒenɔsid/ *m* genocide

génoise /ʒenwaz/ *f* ≈ sponge cake

genou, *pl* **~x** /ʒ(ə)nu/ **A** *m* knee; **sur les ~x de qn** on sb's lap
B à genoux *phr* **se mettre à ~x** to kneel down; to go down on one's knees
IDIOMS **faire du ~ à qn** (fam) to play footsie with sb (fam); **mettre qn sur les ~x** (fam) to wear sb out

genouillère /ʒənujɛʀ/ *f* (Sport) knee pad; (Med) knee support

genre /ʒɑ̃ʀ/ *m* **1** sort, kind, type; **un peu dans le ~ de ta robe** a bit like your dress
2 pour se donner un ~ (in order) to make oneself look different
3 (in grammar) gender
4 genre
5 (Bot, Zool) genus
■ **le ~ humain** mankind

gens /ʒɑ̃/ *mpl* **1** people
2 servants; retinue
■ **~ d'église** clergymen; **~ de lettres** writers; **~ de maison** servants; **~ du voyage** travelling (BrE) people

gentil, **-ille** /ʒɑ̃ti, ij/ *adj* **1** kind, nice
2 good; **sois ~** be a good boy
3 c'est bien ~ tout ça, mais... that's all very well, but...

gentilhomme, *pl* **gentilshommes** /ʒɑ̃tijɔm, ʒɑ̃tizɔm/ *m* gentleman; **~ campagnard** country gentleman

gentillesse /ʒɑ̃tijɛs/ *f* **1** kindness
2 (ironic) **échanger des ~s** to exchange insults

gentiment /ʒɑ̃timɑ̃/ *adv* **1** kindly
2 quietly

géographie /ʒeɔgʀafi/ *f* geography

geôlier, **-ière** /ʒolje, ɛʀ/ *mf* jailer

géologie /ʒeɔlɔʒi/ *f* geology

géomètre /ʒeɔmɛtʀ/ *mf* land surveyor
géométrie /ʒeɔmetʀi/ *f* geometry; **à ~ variable** ‹*doctrine*› flexible
géométrique /ʒeɔmetʀik/ *adj* geometric
Géorgie /ʒeɔʀʒi/ *pr f* **1** (in US) Georgia **2** (in Europe) Georgia
gérable /ʒeʀabl/ *adj* manageable; **situation difficilement ~** a situation which is hard to handle
gérance /ʒeʀɑ̃s/ *f* management; **mettre en ~** to appoint a manager for ‹*shop, company*›; to appoint a managing agent for ‹*property*›
géranium /ʒeʀanjɔm/ *m* geranium
gérant, ~e /ʒeʀɑ̃, ɑ̃t/ *mf* manager; (of property) (managing) agent
gerbe /ʒɛʀb/ *f* **1** bouquet; wreath **2** (of water) spray **3** (of wheat) sheaf
gercer /ʒɛʀse/ [**v12**] *vi* to become chapped
gerçure /ʒɛʀsyʀ/ *f* (in skin, lips) crack
gérer /ʒeʀe/ [**v14**] *vt* **1** to manage ‹*production, time*›; to run ‹*business*› **2** to handle ‹*situation*›
gériatrie /ʒeʀjatʀi/ *f* geriatrics
germain, ~e /ʒɛʀmɛ̃, ɛn/ *adj* **1 (cousin) ~** first cousin **2** Germanic
germanique /ʒɛʀmanik/ *adj, m* Germanic
germanophone /ʒɛʀmanɔfɔn/ *mf* German speaker
germe /ʒɛʀm/ *m* (of embryo, seed) germ; (of potato) sprout
germer /ʒɛʀme/ [**v1**] *vi* **1** ‹*wheat*› to germinate **2** ‹*idea, suspicion*› to form
gérondif /ʒeʀɔ̃dif/ *m* gerund, gerundive
gésier /ʒezje/ *m* gizzard
gésir /ʒeziʀ/ [**v37**] *vi* (fml) **ci-gît Luc Pichon** here lies Luc Pichon
⚷ **geste** /ʒɛst/ *m* **1** movement; gesture; **joindre le ~ à la parole** to suit the action to the word **2** gesture, act
gesticuler /ʒɛstikyle/ [**v1**] *vt* **1** to gesticulate **2** to fidget
⚷ **gestion** /ʒɛstjɔ̃/ *f* **1** management **2** (of situation) handling **3** (of classroom) management
■ **~ administrative** administration; **~ des déchets** waste management; **~ des stocks** stock (BrE) *or* inventory (AmE) control; **~ de portefeuille** portfolio management; **~ de la production assistée par ordinateur** computer-aided production management
gestionnaire /ʒɛstjɔnɛʀ/ *mf* administrator
■ **~ de fichiers** (Comput) file-management system; **~ de portefeuille** portfolio manager
gestuel, -elle /ʒɛstɥɛl/ *adj* gestural

⚷ key word

gestuelle /ʒɛstɥɛl/ *f* body language
geyser /ʒezɛʀ/ *m* geyser
ghetto /geto/ *m* ghetto
gibecière /ʒibsjɛʀ/ *f* game bag
gibier /ʒibje/ *m* game; **gros ~** big game; (fig) big-time criminals
giboulée /ʒibule/ *f* shower
giclée /ʒikle/ *f* spurt; squirt
gicler /ʒikle/ [**v1**] *vi* to spurt; to squirt
gifle /ʒifl/ *f* slap in the face
gifler /ʒifle/ [**v1**] *vt* to slap [sb] across the face
gigantesque /ʒigɑ̃tɛsk/ *adj* huge, gigantic
gigaoctet /ʒigaɔktɛ/ *m* gigabyte
GIGN /ʒeiʒeɛn/ *m* (*abbr* = **Groupe d'intervention de la gendarmerie nationale**) *branch of the police specialized in cases of armed robbery, terrorism etc*
gigogne /ʒigɔɲ/ *adj* **tables ~s** nest of tables
gigot /ʒigo/ *m* leg of lamb
gigoter /ʒigɔte/ [**v1**] *vi* **1** to wriggle **2** to fidget
gilet /ʒilɛ/ *m* **1** cardigan **2** waistcoat (BrE), vest (AmE)
■ **~ pare-balles** bulletproof vest; **~ de sauvetage** life jacket
gin /dʒin/ *m* gin; **~ tonic** gin and tonic
gingembre /ʒɛ̃ʒɑ̃bʀ/ *m* ginger
girafe /ʒiʀaf/ *f* (Zool) giraffe
giratoire /ʒiʀatwaʀ/ *adj* gyratory
■ **sens ~** roundabout (BrE), traffic circle (AmE)
girls band /gœlzband/ *m* girl band
girofle /ʒiʀɔfl/ *m* **un clou de ~** a clove
girolle /ʒiʀɔl/ *f* chanterelle
girouette /ʒiʀwɛt/ *f* wind vane
gisement /ʒizmɑ̃/ *m* (of oil, minerals) deposit
gît ▸ **gésir**
gitan, ~e /ʒitɑ̃, an/ *mf* gypsy (BrE)
gîte /ʒit/ *m* **1** shelter **2** (of hare) form
■ **~ rural** self-catering cottage
givrant /ʒivʀɑ̃/ *adj m* **brouillard ~** freezing fog
givre /ʒivʀ/ *m* frost; ice
givré, ~e /ʒivʀe/ *adj* **1** frosty; frost-covered; frozen **2** (fam) crazy **3** (Culin) ‹*glass*› frosted
givrer /ʒivʀe/ [**v1**] *vi*, **se givrer** *v refl* (+ *v être*) to frost over
glaçage /glasaʒ/ *m* (Culin) (on dessert) icing
⚷ **glace** /glas/ *f* **1** ice; **de ~** ‹*face*› stony **2** ice cream **3** mirror **4** sheet of glass; (of shop window) glass; (of car) window
IDIOM **rester de ~** to remain unmoved
glacé, ~e /glase/ *adj* **1** ‹*rain*› ice-cold; ‹*hands*› frozen; **thé ~** iced tea **2** ‹*cake*› iced

3 ‹*atmosphere*› frosty; ‹*smile*› chilly
4 ‹*paper*› glossy

glacer /glase/ [**v12**] **A** *vt* **1** to freeze ‹*body*›; to chill [sb] to the bone
2 to intimidate; **~ le sang de qn** to make sb's blood run cold
B se glacer *v refl* (+ *v être*) to freeze

glaciaire /glasjɛʀ/ *adj* glacial

glacial, **~e**, *mpl* **~s** *or* **-iaux** /glasjal, o/ *adj* **1** icy
2 ‹*person, reception*› frosty; ‹*silence*› stony; ‹*look*› icy

glacier /glasje/ *m* **1** glacier
2 ice-cream maker
3 ice-cream parlour (BrE)

glacière /glasjɛʀ/ *f* cool box (BrE), ice chest (AmE)

glaçon /glasɔ̃/ *m* ice cube

glaire /glɛʀ/ *f* **1** mucus
2 albumen

glaise /glɛz/ *f* clay

glaive /glɛv/ *m* double-edged sword

gland /glɑ̃/ *m* **1** acorn
2 (Anat) glans
3 tassel

glande /glɑ̃d/ *f* (Anat) gland

glaner /glane/ [**v1**] *vt* to glean

glapir /glapiʀ/ [**v3**] *vi* **1** ‹*pup*› to yap; ‹*fox*› to bark
2 ‹*person*› to shriek

glas /glɑ/ *m inv* toll, knell

glauque /glok/ *adj* murky; ‹*street*› squalid

glissade /glisad/ *f* slide; skid

glissant, **~e** /glisɑ̃, ɑ̃t/ *adj* slippery

glissement /glismɑ̃/ *m* **1** sliding
2 (in sense) shift; (among voters) swing; (in prices) fall

glisser /glise/ [**v1**] **A** *vt* to slip ‹*object*› (**dans** into); to slip in ‹*remark, criticism*›
B *vi* **1** to be slippery
2 to slip
3 to slide; to glide
4 ~ sur to have no effect on
C se glisser *v refl* (+ *v être*) **se ~ dans** to slip into, to sneak into, to creep into

glissière /glisjɛʀ/ *f* slide; **fermeture à ~** zip (BrE), zipper (AmE)

global, **~e**, *mpl* **-aux** /glɔbal, o/ *adj* ‹*sum*› total; ‹*result, cost*› overall; ‹*agreement, solution*› global; ‹*study*› comprehensive

globalement /glɔbalmɑ̃/ *adv* on the whole

globalisation /glɔbalizasjɔ̃/ *f* globalization

globe /glɔb/ *m* **1 ~ (terrestre)** earth, globe; **parcourir le ~** to globe-trot
2 round glass lampshade; glass case
3 (in architecture) dome
■ **~ oculaire** eyeball

globule /glɔbyl/ *m* globule; blood cell
■ **~ blanc** white cell; **~ rouge** red cell

gloire /glwaʀ/ *f* **1** glory, fame
2 credit; **faire qch pour la ~** to do sth (just) for the sake of it
3 glory, praise
4 tirer ~ de to pride oneself on
5 celebrity; star

glorieux, **-ieuse** /glɔʀjø, øz/ *adj* glorious

glorifier /glɔʀifje/ [**v2**] **A** *vt* to glorify
B se glorifier *v refl* (+ *v être*) to glory (**de** in), to boast (**de** about)

glose /gloz/ *f* gloss; note

gloser /gloze/ [**v1**] *vi* to ramble on (**sur** about)

glossaire /glɔsɛʀ/ *m* glossary

glotte /glɔt/ *f* glottis

gloussement /glusmɑ̃/ *m* (of hen) clucking; (of person) chuckle

glousser /gluse/ [**v1**] *vi* ‹*hen*› to cluck; ‹*person*› to chuckle

glouton, **-onne** /glutɔ̃, ɔn/ *adj* ‹*person*› gluttonous; ‹*appetite*› voracious

glu /gly/ *f* **1** bird lime
2 glue

gluant, **~e** /glyɑ̃, ɑ̃t/ *adj* **1** sticky
2 slimy

glucide /glysid/ *m* carbohydrate

glycémie /glisemi/ *f* **taux de ~** blood sugar level

glycérine /gliseʀin/ *f* glycerine

gnognotte /ɲɔɲɔt/ *f* (fam) **c'est pas de la ~!** it's not your common or garden variety

gnome /gnom/ *m* gnome

gnon /ɲɔ̃/ *m* (fam) dent; bruise; **prendre un ~** to get hit

go: **tout de go** /go/ *phr* ‹*say*› straight out

goal /gol/ *m* (fam) goalkeeper, goalie (fam)

gobelet /gɔblɛ/ *m* cup; tumbler; beaker; **~ en carton** paper cup

gober /gɔbe/ [**v1**] *vt* **1** to suck ‹*egg*›; to swallow [sth] whole
2 (fam) to fall for (fam) ‹*story*›

godasse /gɔdas/ *f* (fam) shoe

godet /gɔdɛ/ *m* **1** goblet
2 pot

goéland /gɔelɑ̃/ *m* gull

goémon /gɔemɔ̃/ *m* wrack

gogo: **à gogo** /gogo/ *phr* (fam) galore; **vin à ~** wine galore

goguette: **en goguette** /ɑ̃gɔgɛt/ *phr* (fam) **partir en ~** to go on a spree

goinfre /gwɛ̃fʀ/ *mf* (fam) greedy pig (fam)

goinfrer: **se goinfrer** /gwɛ̃fʀe/ [**v1**] *v refl* (+ *v être*) (fam) to stuff oneself (fam) (**de** with)

goître /gwatʀ/ *m* goitre (BrE)

golden /gɔldɛn/ *f inv* Golden Delicious (apple)

golf /gɔlf/ *m* **1** golf
2 golf course

golfe /gɔlf/ *m* gulf; bay

gomme /gɔm/ **A** *f* **1** eraser, rubber (BrE)
2 (substance) gum

g

B à la gomme *phr* (fam) ‹*idea*› pathetic, useless; ‹*machine*› useless; ‹*plan*› hopeless

IDIOM **mettre (toute) la ~** (fam) to step on it (fam); to give it full throttle (fam); to turn it up full blast

gommer /gɔme/ [**v1**] *vt* **1** to rub [sth] out
2 to smooth out ‹*wrinkle*›; to erase ‹*past, boundaries*›; to iron out ‹*differences*›

gond /gɔ̃/ *m* hinge; **sortir de ses ~s** to come off its hinges; to fly off the handle (fam)

gondole /gɔ̃dɔl/ *f* **1** gondola
2 sales shelf

gondoler: **se gondoler** /gɔ̃dɔle/ [**v1**] *v refl* (+ *v être*) ‹*paper*› to crinkle; ‹*wood*› to warp

gonflable /gɔ̃flabl/ *adj* inflatable

g

gonflé, **~e** /gɔ̃fle/ **A** *pp* ▶ **gonfler**
B *adj* **1** ‹*tyre, balloon*› inflated; ‹*cheeks*› puffed out
2 swollen; bloated; puffy; **yeux ~s de sommeil** eyes puffy with sleep
3 (fam) **être ~** to have guts (fam); (critical) to have a nerve (fam)

gonfler /gɔ̃fle/ [**v1**] **A** *vt* **1** to blow up, to inflate ‹*balloon, tyre*›; to fill ‹*lungs, sail*›; to puff out ‹*cheeks*›; **être gonflé à bloc** to be fully inflated; to be raring to go (fam)
2 to flex ‹*muscle*›; to make [sth] bulge ‹*pocket, bag*›; to saturate ‹*sponge*›; to make [sth] swollen ‹*river*›; to swell ‹*bud*›
3 il est gonflé d'orgueil he's full of his own importance
4 to increase ‹*profits*›; to push up ‹*prices*›; to inflate ‹*statistics*›
B *vi* (gen) to swell (up); (Culin) to rise

gonfleur /gɔ̃flœʀ/ *m* (air) pump

gong /gɔ̃g/ *m* **1** gong
2 (in boxing) bell

googler /gugle/ *vt* to Google®

goret /gɔʀɛ/ *m* **1** piglet
2 (fam) (child) little pig (fam)

gorge /gɔʀʒ/ *f* **1** throat; **avoir mal à la ~** to have a sore throat; **tenir qn à la ~** to have sb by the throat; (fig) to have a stranglehold over sb; **avoir la ~ serrée** *or* **nouée** to have a lump in one's throat; to have one's heart in one's mouth; **à ~ déployée, à pleine ~** ‹*sing*› at the top of one's voice; ‹*laugh*› uproariously; **ta remarque m'est restée en travers de la ~** I found your comment hard to swallow
2 bosom, breast
3 gorge

IDIOM **faire des ~s chaudes de qn/qch** to laugh at sb/sth; to scorn sb/sth

gorgé, **~e** /gɔʀʒe/ *adj* **~ d'eau** ‹*land*› waterlogged; ‹*sponge*› saturated with water; **fruit ~ de soleil** fruit bursting with sunshine

gorgée /gɔʀʒe/ *f* sip; gulp

gorger: **se gorger** /gɔʀʒe/ [**v13**] *v refl* (+ *v être*) **se ~ de nourriture** to gorge oneself

gorille /gɔʀij/ *m* **1** gorilla
2 (fam) bodyguard

gosier /gozje/ *m* throat, gullet

gosse /gɔs/ *mf* (fam) **1** kid (fam); **sale ~** brat (fam)
2 il est beau ~ he's a good-looking fellow

gothique /gɔtik/ *adj, m* Gothic

gouache /gwaʃ/ *f* gouache, poster paint

gouaille /gwaj/ *f* cheek, cheekiness

goudron /gudʀɔ̃/ *m* tar

goudronner /gudʀɔne/ [**v1**] *vt* to tarmac

gouffre /gufʀ/ *m* chasm, abyss; **le ~ de Padirac** the caves of Padirac

goujat /guʒa/ *m* boor

goujon /guʒɔ̃/ *m* (Zool) gudgeon

goulée /gule/ *f* (fam) gulp

goulet /gulɛ/ *m* **1** narrows
2 gully
■ **~ d'étranglement** bottleneck

goulot /gulo/ *m* (of bottle) neck

goulu, **~e** /guly/ *adj* greedy

goulûment /gulymɑ̃/ *adv* greedily

goupillon /gupijɔ̃/ *m* **1** bottle brush
2 holy water sprinkler

gourd, **~e** /guʀ, guʀd/ *adj* numb

gourde /guʀd/ **A** *adj* (fam) dumb (fam), gormless (BrE) (fam)
B *f* **1** flask; gourd
2 (fam) dope (fam)

gourdin /guʀdɛ̃/ *m* bludgeon, cudgel

gourmand, **~e** /guʀmɑ̃, ɑ̃d/ *adj* fond of good food; **il est ~ (de sucreries)** he has a sweet tooth

gourmandise /guʀmɑ̃diz/ **A** *f* weakness for sweet things; weakness for good food
B gourmandises *fpl* sweets (BrE), candies (AmE)

gourmet /guʀmɛ/ *m* gourmet

gourmette /guʀmɛt/ *f* chain bracelet

gourou /guʀu/ *m* guru

gousse /gus/ *f* pod; **~ d'ail** clove of garlic

gousset /gusɛ/ *m* **1** (pocket) fob
2 gusset

🔑 **goût** /gu/ *m* **1** (gen) taste; palate; **donner du ~ à qch** to give sth flavour (BrE)
2 de bon ~ in good taste; **s'habiller sans ~** to have no dress sense; **avoir le mauvais ~ de faire** to be tactless enough to do
3 liking; **ne pas être du ~ de tout le monde** not to be to everyone's liking; not to be everyone's cup of tea; **chacun ses ~s** each to his own; **être au ~ du jour** to be trendy; **faire qch par ~** to do sth for pleasure

IDIOM **tous les ~s sont dans la nature** (Proverb) it takes all sorts to make a world

🔑 **goûter[1]** /gute/ [**v1**] **A** *vt* **1** to taste, to try
2 to enjoy ‹*peace, solitude*›
B goûter à *v+prep* **1 ~ à** to try ‹*food, drink*›
2 ~ à to have a taste of ‹*freedom, power*›

🔑 key word

goûter² /gute/ *m* **1** snack
2 children's party

goutte /gut/ **A** *f* **1** drop (**de** of); **~ de pluie** raindrop; **à grosses ~s** ‹*rain*› heavily; ‹*perspire*› profusely
2 (Med) gout
B **gouttes** *fpl* (Med) drops
IDIOM **se ressembler comme deux ~s d'eau** to be as alike as two peas in a pod

goutte-à-goutte /gutagut/ *m inv* (Med) drip

gouttelette /gutlɛt/ *f* droplet

goutter /gute/ [**v1**] *vi* to drip

gouttière /gutjɛʀ/ *f* gutter; drainpipe

gouvernail /guvɛʀnaj/ *m* **1** rudder
2 helm

gouvernant, **~e** /guvɛʀnɑ̃, ɑ̃t/ **A** *adj* ruling
B **gouvernants** *mpl* **les ~s** the government

gouvernante /guvɛʀnɑ̃t/ *f* housekeeper

gouverne /guvɛʀn/ *f* **pour votre ~** for your information

gouvernement /guvɛʀnəmɑ̃/ *m* government

gouvernemental, **~e**, *mpl* **-aux** /guvɛʀnəmɑ̃tal, o/ *adj* government; governmental

gouverner /guvɛʀne/ [**v1**] *vt* **1** to govern, to rule
2 ‹*money*› to rule
3 to steer ‹*ship*›

gouverneur /guvɛʀnœʀ/ *m* governor

GPS /ʒepeɛs/ *m* (*abbr* = **Global Positioning System**) GPS

grabataire /gʀabatɛʀ/ *adj* bedridden

grabuge /gʀabyʒ/ *m* (fam) **faire du ~** to raise hell (fam)

grâce /gʀɑs/ **A** *f* **1** (of person, gesture) grace; (of landscape) charm
2 **de bonne ~** with (a) good grace
3 favour (BrE); **faire à qn la ~ d'accepter** to do sb the honour (BrE) of accepting
4 mercy; **~ présidentielle** presidential pardon; **je vous fais ~ des détails** I'll spare you the details
5 **~ à Dieu!** thank God!
B **grâce à** *phr* thanks to

Grâce /gʀɑs/ *f* Grace; **votre ~** your Grace

gracier /gʀasje/ [**v2**] *vt* to pardon, to reprieve

gracieusement /gʀasjøzmɑ̃/ *adv* **1** free of charge
2 gracefully

gracieux, **-ieuse** /gʀasjø, øz/ *adj* **1** graceful
2 gracious

grade /gʀad/ *m* rank; **monter en ~** to be promoted

gradé, **~e** /gʀade/ *mf* non-commissioned officer

gradin /gʀadɛ̃/ *m* (in hall) tier; (in arena) terrace

gradué, **~e** /gʀadɥe/ *adj* **règle ~e** ruler

graduer /gʀadɥe/ [**v1**] *vt* **1** to increase ‹*difficulty*›
2 to graduate ‹*instrument*›

graffiti /gʀafiti/ *mpl* graffiti

graillon /gʀɑjɔ̃/ *m* (fam) **ça sent le ~** it smells of stale fat

grain /gʀɛ̃/ *m* **1** grain; **nourri au ~** corn-fed (BrE) *or* grain-fed
2 grain; **~ de poivre** peppercorn; **~ de café** coffee bean; **~ de moutarde** mustard seed; **~ de raisin** grape
3 speck
4 **le ~** the grain; **à gros ~** coarse grained
■ **~ de beauté** beauty spot, mole
IDIOMS **avoir un ~** (fam) to be loony (fam); **mettre son ~ de sel** (fam) to put one's oar in (fam)

graine /gʀɛn/ *f* seed; birdseed; **monter en ~** ‹*vegetable*› to run to seed; ‹*child*› to shoot up
IDIOM **prends-en de la ~** (fam) let that be an example to you

graisse /gʀɛs/ *f* **1** (gen) fat; (of seal, whale) blubber
2 (Tech) grease

graisser /gʀɛse/ [**v1**] *vt* to grease ‹*pan*›; to lubricate ‹*mechanism*›

graisseux, **-euse** /gʀɛsø, øz/ *adj* (gen) greasy; (Med) fatty

grammaire /gʀamɛʀ/ *f* grammar

grammatical, **~e**, *mpl* **-aux** /gʀamatikal, o/ *adj* grammatical

gramme /gʀam/ *m* gram

grand, **~e** /gʀɑ̃, gʀɑ̃d/ **A** *adj* **1** ‹*person, tree, tower*› tall; ‹*arm, stride, journey*› long; ‹*margin, angle*› wide; ‹*place, object, fire*› big
2 ‹*crowd, family, fortune*› large, big; **pas ~ monde** not many people; **il fait ~ jour** it's broad daylight; **laver à ~e eau** to wash [sth] in plenty of running water; to wash [sth] down
3 ‹*dreamer, collector, friend*› great; ‹*cheat, gambler*› big; ‹*drinker, smoker*› heavy; **c'est un ~ timide** he's very shy
4 ‹*discovery, news, expedition*› great; ‹*date*› important; ‹*role*› major; ‹*problem, decision*› big
5 main
6 ‹*company, brand*› leading; **les ~es industries** the big industries
7 ‹*painter, wine*› great; ‹*heart, spirit*› noble
8 ‹*brother, sister*› elder; ‹*pupil*› senior (BrE), older; **assez ~ pour faire** old enough to do
9 ‹*height, length, value, distance*› great; ‹*size, quantity*› large; ‹*speed*› high
10 ‹*kindness, friendship, danger, interest*› great; ‹*noise*› loud; ‹*cold*› severe; ‹*heat*› intense; ‹*wind*› strong, high; ‹*storm*› big, violent; **à ma ~e surprise** much to my surprise
11 ‹*family, name*› great; **la ~e bourgeoisie** the upper middle class
12 ‹*reception, plan*› grand

g

13 ‹*word*› big; ‹*phrase*› high-sounding; **faire de ~s gestes** to wave one's arms about; **et voilà, tout de suite les ~s mots** there you go, straight off the deep end
B *mf* big boy/girl; (Sch) senior (BrE) *or* older pupil
C *adv* wide; **ouvrir tout ~ les bras** to throw one's arms open; **ouvrir ~ ses oreilles** to prick up one's ears; **voir ~** to think big
D *m* **les ~s de ce monde** the great and the good; the world's leaders
E **en grand** *phr* ‹*open*› wide; **faire les choses en ~** to do things on the grand scale
■ **~s axes** main roads; **~ banditisme** organized crime; **le ~ capital** big money; **~ duc** eagle owl; **~ écart** (Sport) splits; **le ~ écran** the big screen; **~ ensemble** high-density housing complex; **le ~ large** the high seas; **~ magasin** department store; **le ~ monde** high society; **le Grand Nord** the Far North; **Grand Pardon** Day of Atonement; **~ prêtre** high priest; **~ prix** grand prix; **le ~ public** the general public; **produit ~ public** consumer product; **la ~e banlieue** the outer suburbs; **la ~e cuisine** haute cuisine; **la Grande Guerre** the First World War; **la ~e muraille de Chine** the Great Wall of China; **~e personne** grown-up, adult; **~e puissance** superpower; **~e roue** big wheel (BrE), Ferris wheel (AmE); **~e surface** supermarket; **~es eaux** fountains; **dès qu'on la gronde, ce sont les ~es eaux** the minute you tell her off, she turns on the waterworks; **~es lignes** main train routes; **~es marées** spring tides; **~es ondes** long wave; **les ~s blessés** the seriously injured; **~s fauves** big cats

grand-angle, *pl* **grands-angles** /gʀɑ̃tɑ̃gl, gʀɑ̃zɑ̃gl/ *adj* wide-angle; **un (objectif) ~** a wide-angle lens

grand-chose /gʀɑ̃ʃoz/ *pron* **pas ~** not much, not a lot; **il n'y a plus ~ à faire** there isn't much left to do

Grande-Bretagne /gʀɑ̃dbʀətaɲ/ *pr f* Great Britain

grandement /gʀɑ̃dmɑ̃/ *adv* greatly; a great deal; extremely

grandeur /gʀɑ̃dœʀ/ *f* **1** size; **~ nature** ‹*reproduction*› full-scale; ‹*portrait*› life-size
2 scale
3 greatness

Grand-Guignol /gʀɑ̃giɲɔl/ *m* **c'est du ~** it's farcical

grandiloquence /gʀɑ̃dilɔkɑ̃s/ *f* pomposity, grandiloquence

grandiloquent, **~e** /gʀɑ̃dilɔkɑ̃, ɑ̃t/ *adj* pompous, grandiloquent

grandiose /gʀɑ̃djoz/ *adj* ‹*site, decor*› grandiose; ‹*party*› spectacular; ‹*gesture*› grand

grandir /gʀɑ̃diʀ/ [v3] **A** *vt* **1** to magnify
2 to make [sb] look taller
3 to exaggerate
B *vi* **1** to grow; to grow up
2 ‹*company*› to expand; ‹*crowd, anxiety*› to grow
C **se grandir** *v refl* (+ *v être*) to make oneself (look) taller

grandissant, **~e** /gʀɑ̃disɑ̃, ɑ̃t/ *adj* growing

grand-mère, *pl* **grands-mères** /gʀɑ̃mɛʀ/ *f* grandmother

grand-oncle, *pl* **grands-oncles** /gʀɑ̃tɔ̃kl, gʀɑ̃zɔ̃kl/ *m* great-uncle

grand-peine **A** *f* **avoir ~ à faire** to have great difficulty doing
B **à grand-peine** *phr* **à ~** with great difficulty

grand-père, *pl* **grands-pères** /gʀɑ̃pɛʀ/ *m* grandfather

grand-route, *pl* **~s** /gʀɑ̃ʀut/ *f* main road

grand-rue, *pl* **~s** /gʀɑ̃ʀy/ *f* high street

grands-parents /gʀɑ̃paʀɑ̃/ *mpl* grandparents

grand-tante, *pl* **grand(s)-tantes** /gʀɑ̃tɑ̃t/ *f* great-aunt

grand-voile, *pl* **grand(s)-voiles** /gʀɑ̃vwal/ *f* mainsail

grange /gʀɑ̃ʒ/ *f* barn

granit /gʀanit/ *m also* **granite** granite

granité, **~e** /gʀanite/ *adj* grained

granulé /gʀanyle/ *m* granule

graphie /gʀafi/ *f* **1** written form
2 spelling

graphique /gʀafik/ **A** *adj* **1** ‹*work*› graphic
2 ‹*screen*› graphic; ‹*software*› graphics
B *m* graph

graphisme /gʀafism/ *m* **1** style of drawing
2 handwriting
3 graphic design

graphologie /gʀafɔlɔʒi/ *f* graphology

grappe /gʀap/ *f* (of fruit) bunch; (of flowers) cluster

grappiller /gʀapije/ [v1] *vt* to pick up ‹*fruit*›; to glean ‹*information*›

grappin /gʀapɛ̃/ *m* **mettre le ~ sur qn** (fam) to get sb in one's clutches

gras, **grasse** /gʀɑ, gʀɑs/ **A** *adj*
1 ‹*substance*› fatty; ‹*fish*› oily; ‹*paper*› greasy
2 coarse, vulgar
3 (in printing) bold
4 loose, phlegmy
B *adv* **manger ~** to eat fatty foods
C *m* **1** (from meat) fat
2 grease
3 (of arm, calf) **le ~** the fleshy part

grassement /gʀɑsmɑ̃/ *adv* ‹*pay*› handsomely; ‹*feed*› lavishly

grassouillet, **-ette** /gʀasujɛ, ɛt/ *adj* (fam) chubby, plump

graticiel /gʀatisjɛl/ *m* freeware

gratifiant, **~e** /gʀatifjɑ̃, ɑ̃t/ *adj* gratifying

gratification /gʀatifikasjɔ̃/ *f* **1** gratification
2 bonus

key word

gratifier /gʀatifje/ [**v2**] *vt* **~ qn de qch** to give sb sth; **se sentir gratifié** to feel gratified

gratin /gʀatɛ̃/ *m* **1** gratin (*breadcrumbs and cheese*)
2 (fam) **le ~** the upper crust (fam)

gratiné, **~e** /gʀatine/ *adj* **1** (Culin) au gratin
2 (fam) ‹*person*› weird; ‹*problem*› mind-bending (fam)

gratiner /gʀatine/ [**v1**] *vt* **(faire) ~ un plat** to brown a dish

gratis /gʀatis/ **A** *adj inv* free
B *adv* free (BrE), for free

gratitude /gʀatityd/ *f* gratitude; **avoir de la ~ pour qn** to be grateful to sb

gratte-ciel /gʀatsjɛl/ *m inv* skyscraper

gratte-papier /gʀatpapje/ *m inv* (fam) pen pusher

gratter /gʀate/ [**v1**] **A** *vt* **1** to scratch; to scrape (off)
2 to make [sb] itch; **ça me gratte partout** I'm itching all over
B *vi* **~ à la porte** to scratch at the door
C **se gratter** *v refl* (+ *v être*) to scratch; **se ~ la tête** to scratch one's head

grattoir /gʀatwaʀ/ *m* **1** (tool) scraper
2 (on matchbox) striking strip

gratuit, **~e** /gʀatɥi, it/ *adj* **1** ‹*place, service*› free
2 ‹*violence*› gratuitous; ‹*accusation*› spurious; ‹*exercise*› pointless

gratuité /gʀatɥite/ *f* **la ~ de l'enseignement** free education

gratuitement /gʀatɥitmɑ̃/ *adv* **1** free (BrE), for free
2 ‹*work*› for nothing
3 gratuitously

gravats /gʀava/ *mpl* rubble

grave /gʀav/ *adj* **1** ‹*problem, injury*› serious
2 ‹*expression*› grave, solemn
3 ‹*voice*› deep; ‹*note*› low; ‹*sound*› low-pitched
4 (fam) ‹*person*› hopeless

gravement /gʀavmɑ̃/ *adv* **1** gravely, solemnly
2 seriously

graver /gʀave/ [**v1**] *vt* **1** to engrave
2 to burn ‹*CDs etc.*›

graveur, **-euse** /gʀavœʀ, øz/ **A** *mf* engraver; **~ sur bois** wood engraver
B *m* (for CDs etc.) burner

gravier /gʀavje/ *m* **du ~** gravel

gravillon /gʀavijɔ̃/ *m* grit

gravir /gʀaviʀ/ [**v3**] *vt* to climb up

gravitation /gʀavitasjɔ̃/ *f* gravitation; **~ universelle** Newton's law of gravitation

gravité /gʀavite/ *f* **1** seriousness
2 solemnity
3 (in physics) gravity

graviter /gʀavite/ [**v1**] *vi* to orbit

gravure /gʀavyʀ/ *f* **1 la ~** engraving
2 engraving
3 print, reproduction

gré /gʀe/ *m* **1 contre le ~ de qn** against sb's will; **de ~ ou de force** one way or another
2 (fml) **savoir ~ à qn de qch** to be grateful to sb for sth
3 j'ai flâné au ~ de mon humeur I strolled where the mood took me

grec, **grecque** /gʀɛk/ **A** *adj* Greek; Grecian
B *m* (language) Greek

Grec, **Grecque** /gʀɛk/ *mf* Greek

Grèce /gʀɛs/ *pr f* Greece; **~ antique** Ancient Greece

grecque ▸ **grec**

greffe /gʀɛf/ *f* **1** (of organ) transplant; (of skin) graft
2 (in agriculture) grafting; graft

greffer /gʀefe/ [**v1**] **A** *vt* **1** to transplant ‹*organ*›; to graft ‹*tissue*›
2 to graft ‹*tree*›
B **se greffer** *v refl* (+ *v être*) **se ~ sur qch** ‹*problem, event*› to come along on top of sth

greffier, **-ière** /gʀefje, ɛʀ/ *mf* clerk of the court (BrE), court clerk (AmE)

grégaire /gʀegɛʀ/ *adj* gregarious

grège /gʀɛʒ/ *adj*, *m* oatmeal

grêle /gʀɛl/ **A** *adj* **1** skinny; spindly
2 ‹*voice*› reedy; ‹*sound*› thin
B *f* hail

grêlé, **~e** /gʀɛle/ *adj* pockmarked

grêler /gʀɛle/ [**v1**] *v impers* **il grêle** it's hailing

grêlon /gʀɛlɔ̃/ *m* hailstone

grelot /gʀəlo/ *m* small bell

grelotter /gʀəlɔte/ [**v1**] *vi* to shiver

grenade /gʀənad/ *f* **1** grenade
2 pomegranate

Grenade /gʀənad/ **A** *pr n* Granada
B *pr f* **la ~** Grenada

grenadine /gʀənadin/ *f* grenadine

grenaille /gʀənaj/ *f* **1** steel filings
2 lead shot

grenat /gʀəna/ *adj inv* dark red

grenier /gʀənje/ *m* attic, loft; **~ à grain** granary

grenouille /gʀənuj/ *f* frog

grès /gʀɛ/ *m inv* **1** sandstone
2 (piece of) stoneware

grésillement /gʀezijmɑ̃/ *m* **1** crackling
2 sizzling

grésiller /gʀezije/ [**v1**] *vi* **1** ‹*radio*› to crackle
2 ‹*butter, oil*› to sizzle

grève /gʀɛv/ *f* **1** strike; **mouvement de ~** industrial action
2 shore
■ **~ de la faim** hunger strike; **~ sur le tas** sit-down strike; **~ du zèle** work to rule

grever /gʀəve/ [**v16**] *vt* to put a strain on ‹*budget*›; **l'entreprise est grevée de charges** the company has crippling overheads

gréviste /gʀevist/ *mf* striker

gribouillage /gʀibujaʒ/ *m* (fam) scribble

gribouiller /gʀibuje/ [**v1**] *vt* (fam) to scribble
grief /gʀijɛf/ *m* grievance
grièvement /gʀijɛvmɑ̃/ *adv* ‹*injured*› seriously; ‹*burned*› badly; ‹*affected*› severely
griffe /gʀif/ *f* **1** claw; **tomber entre les ∼s de qn** to fall into sb's clutches
2 (on garment) label
3 signature stamp
4 (in jewellery) claw
griffer /gʀife/ [**v1**] **A** *vt* to scratch
B se griffer *v refl* (+ *v être*) to scratch oneself
griffonner /gʀifɔne/ [**v1**] *vt* **1** to scrawl
2 to sketch
griffure /gʀifyʀ/ *f* scratch
grignoter /gʀiɲɔte/ [**v1**] **A** *vt* **1** to nibble
2 to encroach on ‹*territory*›; to conquer ‹*corner of market*›
3 to fritter away ‹*inheritance*›
B *vi* **1** ‹*rodent*› to gnaw
2 ‹*person*› to nibble
gri-gri, *pl* **gris-gris** /gʀigʀi/ *m* lucky charm
gril /gʀil/ *m* grill (BrE), broiler (AmE)
grillage /gʀijaʒ/ *m* wire netting; chicken wire; wire mesh
grille /gʀij/ *f* **1** railings; (iron) gate; (of sink, sewer) drain; (of air vent) grille; (in oven, fridge) shelf; (in fireplace, stove) grate
2 (of crossword) grid
3 (on TV, radio) schedule, listings
4 (for assessing results) model
5 (in administration) scale
grillé, **∼e** /gʀije/ **A** *pp* ▶ **griller**
B *pp adj* **1** ‹*meat*› grilled; ‹*bread*› toasted; ‹*almonds*› roasted
2 crispy, well-browned
3 burned out; **l'ampoule est ∼e** the bulb has blown
4 (fam) ‹*spy*› exposed
grille-pain /gʀijpɛ̃/ *m inv* toaster
griller /gʀije/ [**v1**] **A** *vt* **1** to grill ‹*meat*›; to toast ‹*bread*›; to roast ‹*almonds*›
2 (fam) to jump (fam) ‹*light*›; to ignore ‹*give way sign*›
3 (fam) to give the game away about [sb]
4 (fam) **∼ un adversaire** to manage to get ahead of one's opponent
B *vi* **1** to grill; **faire ∼** to grill; to toast; to roast
2 ‹*bulb*› to blow
grillon /gʀijɔ̃/ *m* cricket
grimaçant, **∼e** /gʀimasɑ̃, ɑ̃t/ *adj* grimacing
grimace /gʀimas/ *f* grimace; funny face
grimacer /gʀimase/ [**v12**] *vi* to grimace
grimer: **se grimer** /gʀime/ [**v1**] *v refl* (+ *v être*) to make oneself up
grimpant, **∼e** /gʀɛ̃pɑ̃, ɑ̃t/ *adj* climbing
grimper /gʀɛ̃pe/ [**v1**] **A** *vt* to climb ‹*stairs*›
B *vi* **1** **∼ aux arbres** to climb (up) trees; **grimpe sur mon dos** get on my back
2 (fam) ‹*road*› to be steep
3 (fam) ‹*prices*› to climb
grimpeur, **-euse** /gʀɛ̃pœʀ, øz/ *mf* rock climber
grinçant, **∼e** /gʀɛ̃sɑ̃, ɑ̃t/ *adj* ‹*tone*› scathing; ‹*joke*› caustic; ‹*laugh*› nasty
grincement /gʀɛ̃smɑ̃/ *m* creak, creaking; squeak, squeaking; screech, screeching
grincer /gʀɛ̃se/ [**v12**] *vi* ‹*door*› to creak; ‹*violin*› to screech; ‹*chalk*› to squeak; **∼ des dents** to grind one's teeth; (fig) to gnash one's teeth
gringalet /gʀɛ̃galɛ/ *m* runt
griotte /gʀijɔt/ *f* morello cherry
grippe /gʀip/ *f* flu
■ **∼ aviaire** bird flu, avian flu; **∼ intestinale** gastric flu (BrE), intestinal flu (AmE)
IDIOM **prendre qn/qch en ∼** (fam) to take a sudden dislike to sb/sth
⚷ **gris**, **∼e** /gʀi, iz/ **A** *adj* **1** grey (BrE), gray (AmE)
2 dreary; dull
3 tipsy
B *m inv* grey (BrE), gray (AmE)
grisaille /gʀizaj/ *f* **1** dullness
2 (of weather) greyness (BrE), grayness (AmE)
grisant, **∼e** /gʀizɑ̃, ɑ̃t/ *adj* **1** ‹*speed*› exhilarating; ‹*success*› intoxicating
2 ‹*perfume*› heady
grisâtre /gʀizɑtʀ/ *adj* ‹*colour, sky*› greyish (BrE), grayish (AmE); ‹*morning*› dull
griser /gʀize/ [**v1**] *vt* ‹*speed*› to exhilarate; ‹*success*› to intoxicate; **se laisser ∼ par le pouvoir** to let power go to one's head
griserie /gʀizʀi/ *f* exhilaration (**de** of)
grisonnant, **∼e** /gʀizɔnɑ̃, ɑ̃t/ *adj* greying
grisonner /gʀizɔne/ [**v1**] *vi* to go grey
grisou /gʀizu/ *m* firedamp
grive /gʀiv/ *f* thrush
grivois, **∼e** /gʀivwa, az/ *adj* bawdy; coarse
grivoiserie /gʀivwazʀi/ *f* suggestive remark
grizzli, **grizzly** /gʀizli/ *m* grizzly bear
grogne /gʀɔɲ/ *f* (fam) discontent
grognement /gʀɔɲəmɑ̃/ *m* grunt; growl
grogner /gʀɔɲe/ [**v1**] *vi* **1** to groan; (fig) to grumble
2 ‹*pig*› to grunt; ‹*dog*› to growl
grognon /gʀɔɲɔ̃/ *adj* grouchy (fam)
groin /gʀwɛ̃/ *m* snout
grommeler /gʀɔmle/ [**v19**] *vi* to grumble
grondement /gʀɔ̃dmɑ̃/ *m* (of torrent, machine) roar; (of crowd) angry murmur
gronder /gʀɔ̃de/ [**v1**] **A** *vt* to tell [sb] off
B *vi* **1** ‹*thunder*› to rumble; ‹*machine, wind*› to roar
2 ‹*rebellion*› to be brewing
groom /gʀum/ *m* bellboy (BrE), bellhop (AmE)

⚷ key word

gros, grosse /gʀo, gʀos/ **A** *adj* **1** big, large
2 thick
3 fat
4 ‹*customer, market*› big; ‹*damage*› considerable
5 ‹*problem*› serious, big; ‹*flaw*› big, major
6 ‹*cold*› bad; ‹*sobs*› loud; ‹*voice*› deep; ‹*rain*› heavy; ‹*smoker*› heavy
B *adv* **1** ‹*write*› big
2 ‹*bet, lose*› a lot of money; (fig) a lot
C *m inv* **1 le ~ de** the majority of ‹*spectators*›; the bulk of ‹*work*›; most of ‹*winter*›
2 wholesale trade
3 la pêche au ~ game fishing
D en ~ *phr* **1** roughly; **en ~ je suis d'accord avec toi** basically, I agree with you
2 wholesale
3 in big letters
■ **~ bonnet** (fam) big shot (fam); **~ lot** first prize; **~ mot** swear word; **~ œuvre** shell (of a building); **~ plan** close-up; **~ sel** cooking salt; **~ titre** headline; **grosse caisse** bass drum; **grosse tête** (fam) brain (fam)
IDIOMS **en avoir ~ sur le cœur** *or* **la patate** (fam) to be very upset; **c'est un peu ~ comme histoire!** that's a bit of a tall story!

groseille /gʀozɛj/ *f* redcurrant; **~ à maquereau** gooseberry

grosse ▸ **gros**

grossesse /gʀosɛs/ *f* pregnancy
■ **~ nerveuse** phantom pregnancy (BrE), false pregnancy

grosseur /gʀosœʀ/ *f* **1** size
2 (of thread) thickness
3 (Med) lump

grossier, -ière /gʀosje, ɛʀ/ *adj* **1** ‹*person, gesture*› rude; ‹*language*› bad
2 ‹*laugh*› coarse
3 ‹*imitation*› crude
4 ‹*sketch, idea*› rough; ‹*work*› crude
5 ‹*error*› glaring

grossièrement /gʀosjɛʀmɑ̃/ *adv*
1 ‹*calculate*› roughly
2 ‹*built*› crudely
3 ‹*speak*› rudely

grossièreté /gʀosjɛʀte/ *f* **1** rudeness
2 dirty word
3 coarseness

grossir /gʀosiʀ/ [v3] **A** *vt* **1** to enlarge ‹*image*›
2 to increase ‹*numbers*›; to boost ‹*profits*›
3 to exaggerate ‹*incident*›
4 to make [sb] look fat
B *vi* **1** to put on weight
2 (gen) to grow; ‹*river*› to swell

grossissant, ~e /gʀosisɑ̃, ɑ̃t/ *adj* magnifying

grossiste /gʀosist/ *mf* wholesaler

grosso modo /gʀosomodo/ *adv* roughly

grotesque /gʀɔtɛsk/ *adj* ridiculous

grotte /gʀɔt/ *f* **1** cave
2 grotto

grouiller /gʀuje/ [v1] **A** *vi* to swarm about; to mill about
B se grouiller *v refl* (+ *v être*) (fam) to get a move on (fam)

groupage /gʀupaʒ/ *m* bulking; **envoi en ~** collective shipment

groupe /gʀup/ *m* **1** (gen), (Econ) group; **par ~s de deux** in pairs, in twos
2 (of objects) group; cluster
■ **~ d'autodéfense** vigilante group; **~ électrogène** (electricity) generator; **~ de pression** pressure group; **~ sanguin** blood group; **~ scolaire** school; **~ des Sept, G7** Group of Seven, G7 countries

groupement /gʀupmɑ̃/ *m* **1** association, group
2 grouping

grouper /gʀupe/ [v1] **A** *vt* to put together
B se grouper *v refl* (+ *v être*) to gather (**autour de** around); to form a group; **se ~ par trois** to form groups of three; **restez groupés** keep together

groupuscule /gʀupyskyl/ *m* small group

gruau, *pl* **~x** /gʀyo/ *m* **1** gruel
2 fine wheat flour

grue /gʀy/ *f* (Tech, Zool) crane
IDIOM **faire le pied de ~** (fam) to hang around

grumeau, *pl* **~x** /gʀymo/ *m* lump

gruyère /gʀyjɛʀ/ *m* Gruyère, Swiss cheese

Guadeloupe /gwadlup/ *pr f* **la ~** Guadeloupe

gué /ge/ *m* ford; **passer un ruisseau à ~** to ford a stream

guenille /gənij/ *f* rag; **en ~s** in rags

guenon /gənɔ̃/ *f* female monkey

guépard /gepaʀ/ *m* cheetah

guêpe /gɛp/ *f* wasp

guêpier /gepje/ *m* **1** wasps' nest
2 tight corner; **dans quel ~ es-tu allé te fourrer?** (fam) what kind of mess have you got (BrE) *or* gotten (AmE) yourself into?

guêpière /gepjɛʀ/ *f* basque, body shaper with suspenders (BrE) *or* garters (AmE)

guère /gɛʀ/ *adv* hardly; **il n'avait ~ le choix** he didn't really have a choice

guéridon /geʀidɔ̃/ *m* pedestal table

guérilla /geʀija/ *f* **1** guerilla warfare
2 guerillas

guérir /geʀiʀ/ [v3] **A** *vt* **1** to cure ‹*person, disease*›
2 ~ qn de to cure sb of ‹*habit*›
B *vi* to recover; to heal; to get better
C se guérir *v refl* (+ *v être*) **se ~ de** to overcome ‹*shyness*›

guérison /geʀizɔ̃/ *f* recovery; healing

guérite /geʀit/ *f* **1** sentry box
2 (on toll road) booth

guerre /gɛʀ/ *f* war; warfare; **les pays en ~** the warring nations
■ **~ chimique** chemical war; chemical warfare; **~ éclair** blitzkrieg, lightning

war; ~ **mondiale** world war; **Première/ Deuxième Guerre mondiale** World War I/II; ~ **nucléaire** nuclear war; nuclear warfare; ~ **de 14** 1914–18 war; ~ **de Sécession** American Civil War; ~ **d'usure** war of attrition; ~ **des prix** price war
IDIOMS **à la ~ comme à la ~** in time of hardship you have to make the best of things; **c'est de bonne ~** it's only fair; **de ~ lasse, elle renonça** realizing that she was fighting a losing battle, she gave up

guerrier, -ière /gɛʀje, ɛʀ/ *mf* warrior

guet /gɛ/ *m* **1** lookout; **faire le ~** to be on the lookout
2 (Mil) watch

guet-apens, *pl* **guets-apens** /gɛtapɑ̃/ *m* ambush; (fig) trap

guêtre /gɛtʀ/ *f* **1** (Sport) leggings
2 gaiter

guetter /gete/ [**v1**] *vt* **1** to watch ‹*prey, criminal, reaction*›; to watch out for ‹*sign*›; to look out for ‹*postman*›
2 to threaten

guetteur, -euse /gɛtœʀ, øz/ *mf* lookout

gueule /gœl/ *f* **1** (pop) face; **il a la ~ de l'emploi** he really looks the part
2 (pop) mouth; **(ferme) ta ~!** shut your face (BrE) *or* mouth!
3 (of animal) mouth
■ ~ **de bois** (fam) hangover
IDIOM **faire la ~** (pop) to be sulking

gueuler /gœle/ (pop) [**v1**] **A** *vt* to yell; to bawl out
B *vi* to yell, to bawl; to kick up a real fuss; ~ **après qn** to have a go at sb (fam)

gui /gi/ *m* mistletoe

guichet /giʃɛ/ *m* window; (in bank) counter; (in museum, station) ticket office; (in theatre, cinema) box office; **la pièce se jouera à ~s fermés** the play is sold out
■ ~ **automatique** automatic teller machine

guichetier, -ière /giʃtje, ɛʀ/ *mf* ticket clerk

guide /gid/ *m* guide

guider /gide/ [**v1**] *vt* **1** (gen) to guide
2 to show [sb] the way

guidon /gidɔ̃/ *m* handlebars

guigne /giɲ/ *f* (fam) bad luck

guignol /giɲɔl/ *m* **1** puppet show; ≈ Punch and Judy show
2 (derog) clown

guillemets /gijmɛ/ *mpl* inverted commas (BrE), quotation marks

guillotine /gijɔtin/ *f* guillotine

guimauve /gimov/ *f* **1** (Bot) (marsh) mallow
2 (confectionery) marshmallow

guimbarde /gɛ̃baʀd/ *f* Jew's harp

guindé, ~e /gɛ̃de/ *adj* formal

guingois: de guingois /degɛ̃gwa/ *phr* **être de ~** to be lopsided

guirlande /giʀlɑ̃d/ *f* garland; tinsel
■ ~ **électrique** set *or* string of fairy lights

guise /giz/ *f* **1 'à votre ~'** 'just as you like *or* please'
2 en ~ de by way of

⚷ **guitare** /gitaʀ/ *f* guitar

guitariste /gitaʀist/ *mf* guitarist

gustatif, -ive /gystatif, iv/ *adj* ‹*organ*› taste

guttural, ~e, *mpl* **-aux** /gytyʀal, o/ *adj* guttural

Guyana /gɥijana/ *pr f* Guyana; **République de ~** Republic of Guyana

Guyane /gɥijan/ *pr f* ~ **(française)** (French) Guyana; ~ **hollandaise** Dutch Guiana

gym /ʒim/ *f* (Sch), (fam) physical education

gymnase /ʒimnɑz/ *m* gymnasium

gymnaste /ʒimnast/ *mf* gymnast

gymnastique /ʒimnastik/ *f* gymnastics; exercises
■ ~ **corrective** ≈ physiotherapy exercises

gynécologie /ʒinekɔlɔʒi/ *f* gynaecology

gyrophare /ʒiʀɔfaʀ/ *m* flashing light, emergency rotating light

Hh

h, H /aʃ/ *m inv* **1** (letter) h, H; **h muet** mute h
2 (*written abbr* = **heure**) **9 h 10** 9.10

ha /'a/ (*written abbr* = **hectare**) ha

habile /abil/ *adj* clever, skilful (BrE)

habilement /abilmɑ̃/ *adv* skilfully (BrE), cleverly

habileté /abilte/ *f* skill; skilfulness (BrE)

habiliter /abilite/ [**v1**] *vt* to authorize

habillé, ~e /abije/ *adj* ‹*dress*› smart; ‹*dinner*› formal

habillement /abijmɑ̃/ *m* clothing

habiller /abije/ [**v1**] **A** *vt* **1** to dress; to dress [sb] up
2 to clothe; to provide [sb] with clothing

⚷ key word

3 to make [sb's] clothes
4 un rien l'habille she looks good in anything
B s'habiller *v refl* (+ *v être*) **1** to get dressed; to dress up; **s'~ long/court** to wear long/short skirts
2 s'~ chez to get one's clothes from

habilleur, **-euse** /abijœʀ, øz/ *mf* dresser

habit /abi/ *m* **1 ~s** clothes
2 outfit, costume
3 (of monk, nun) habit
■ **~ de lumière** matador's costume; **~s du dimanche** Sunday best

habitable /abitabl/ *adj* **1** habitable
2 surface ~ living space

habitacle /abitakl/ *m* **1** (Aviat) cockpit; (of rocket) cabin
2 (Aut) interior
3 (Naut) binnacle

habitant, **~e** /abitɑ̃, ɑ̃t/ *mf* inhabitant; resident; **loger chez l'~** to stay as a paying guest

habitat /abita/ *m* **1** (Bot, Zool) habitat
2 housing

habitation /abitasjɔ̃/ *f* **1** house, dwelling; home
2 living; **immeuble d'~** block of flats (BrE), apartment building (AmE)
■ **~ à loyer modéré, HLM** ≈ (block of) council flats (BrE), low-rent apartment (building) (AmE)

habité, **~e** /abite/ *adj* **1** inhabited
2 ‹*rocket*› manned

habiter /abite/ [**v1**] **A** *vt* to live in
B *vi* to live

habitude /abityd/ **A** *f* **1** habit; **par ~** out of habit; **ils ont l'~ de se coucher tôt** they usually go to bed early; **avoir l'~ de** to be used to
2 custom
B d'habitude *phr* usually

habitué, **~e** /abitɥe/ *mf* regular

habituel, **-elle** /abitɥɛl/ *adj* usual

habituellement /abitɥɛlmɑ̃/ *adv* usually

habituer /abitɥe/ [**v1**] **A** *vt* **1 ~ qn à** to get sb used to
2 to teach
B s'habituer *v refl* (+ *v être*) **s'~ à** to get used to

hache /'aʃ/ *f* axe (BrE), ax (AmE)
IDIOM **enterrer la ~ de guerre** to bury the hatchet

haché, **~e** /'aʃe/ *adj* **1** ‹*meat*› minced
2 ‹*speech*› disjointed

hache-légumes /'aʃlegym/ *m inv* vegetable chopper

hacher /'aʃe/ [**v1**] *vt* to mince; to chop

hachette /'aʃɛt/ *f* hatchet

hachis /'aʃi/ *m inv* mince; **~ de persil** chopped parsley
■ **~ Parmentier** ≈ shepherd's pie

hachisch /'aʃiʃ/ *m* hashish

hachoir /'aʃwaʀ/ *m* **1** mincer
2 chopper

hachurer /'aʃyʀe/ [**v1**] *vt* to hatch

haddock /'adɔk/ *m* smoked haddock

hagard, **~e** /'agaʀ, aʀd/ *adj* ‹*person*› dazed; ‹*eyes*› wild

haï, **~e** /'ai/ ▶ **haïr**

haie /'ɛ/ *f* **1** hedge
2 (Sport) hurdle; fence; **course de ~s** hurdle race; steeple chase
3 line, row; **faire une ~ d'honneur** to form a guard of honour (BrE)

haillon /'ɑjɔ̃/ *m* rag; **en ~s** in rags

haine /'ɛn/ *f* hatred; **s'attirer la ~ de qn** to earn sb's hatred

haineux, **-euse** /'ɛnø, øz/ *adj* full of hatred

haïr /'aiʀ/ [**v25**] *vt* to hate

haïssable /'aisabl/ *adj* detestable, hateful

halage /'alaʒ/ *m* **chemin de ~** towpath

hâle /'ɑl/ *m* (sun)tan

hâlé, **~e** /'ɑle/ *adj* tanned

haleine /alɛn/ *f* breath; breathing; **hors d'~** out of breath; **un travail de longue ~** a long-drawn-out job

haler /'ale/ [**v1**] *vt* to tow ‹*boat*›; to haul in ‹*chain*›

haleter /'alte/ [**v18**] *vi* **1** to gasp for breath; to pant
2 ‹*machine*› to puff; ‹*chest*› to heave

hall /'ol/ *m* entrance hall (BrE), lobby (AmE); **~ (de gare)** concourse

halle /'al/ *f* covered market

hallucination /alysinasjɔ̃/ *f* hallucination; **avoir des ~s** to hallucinate; to be seeing things

halluciné, **~e** /alysine/ *adj* ‹*eyes*› wild

hallucinogène /alysinɔʒɛn/ *adj* hallucinogenic

halo /'alo/ *m* halo; **entouré d'un ~ de mystère** shrouded in mystery

halogène /alɔʒɛn/ *adj* halogen

halte /'alt/ **A** *f* **1** stop
2 stopping place
B *excl* stop!; (Mil) halt!

halte-garderie, *pl* **haltes-garderies** /'altəgaʀdəʀi/ *f* ≈ playgroup

haltère /altɛʀ/ *m* dumb-bell; barbell; **faire des ~s** to do weightlifting

haltérophilie /alteʀɔfili/ *f* weightlifting

hamac /'amak/ *m* hammock

hameau, *pl* **~x** /'amo/ *m* hamlet

hameçon /amsɔ̃/ *m* hook; **mordre à l'~** to take the bait

hanche /'ɑ̃ʃ/ *f* (of person) hip

handicap /'ɑ̃dikap/ *m* handicap

handicapé, **~e** /'ɑ̃dikape/ **A** *adj* **1** disabled
2 être ~ to be at a disadvantage
B *mf* disabled person

handicaper /'ɑ̃dikape/ [**v1**] *vt* to handicap

hangar /'ɑ̃gaʀ/ *m* shed; warehouse; hangar

hanneton /'antɔ̃/ *m* cockchafer (BrE), June bug (AmE)

hanter /'ɑ̃te/ [**v1**] *vt* to haunt

hantise /'ɑ̃tiz/ *f* dread

happer /'ape/ [**v1**] *vt* to catch ‹*insect*›; **happé par** ‹*arm*› caught up in ‹*machine*›; ‹*person*› hit by ‹*train*›; (fig) swallowed up by ‹*crowd*›

haranguer /'aʀɑ̃ge/ [**v1**] *vt* to harangue

haras /'aʀa/ *m inv* stud farm

harassement /'aʀasmɑ̃/ *m* exhaustion

harasser /'aʀase/ [**v1**] *vt* to exhaust

harcèlement /'aʀsɛlmɑ̃/ *m* harassment

harceler /'aʀsəle/ [**v17**] *vt* **1** to pester
2 to harass

hardi, **~e** /'aʀdi/ *adj* bold, daring

hardiesse /'aʀdjɛs/ *f* **1** boldness
2 brazenness

hareng /'aʀɑ̃/ *m* herring

hargne /'aʀɲ/ *f* aggression

hargneux, **-euse** /'aʀɲø, øz/ *adj* aggressive

haricot /'aʀiko/ *m* (Bot) bean; **~ blanc** haricot bean; **~ vert** French bean
IDIOM **c'est la fin des ~s** (fam) we've had it (fam)

harmonica /aʀmɔnika/ *m* mouth organ, harmonica

harmonie /aʀmɔni/ *f* harmony

harmonieux, **-ieuse** /aʀmɔnjø, øz/ *adj* harmonious; ‹*movements*› graceful

harmoniser /aʀmɔnize/ [**v1**] **A** *vt* **1** to coordinate ‹*colours*›
2 to harmonize; to make [sth] consistent; to bring into line
3 (Mus) to harmonize
B **s'harmoniser** *v refl* (+ *v être*) **bien s'~** ‹*colours*› to go together well

harnachement /'aʀnaʃmɑ̃/ *m* **1** (for horse) harness
2 (fam) (clothes) get-up (fam)

harnacher /'aʀnaʃe/ [**v1**] *vt* **1** to harness ‹*horse*›
2 (fam) to rig out (fam) ‹*person*›

harnais /'aʀnɛ/ *m inv* harness

harpe /'aʀp/ *f* harp

harpie /'aʀpi/ *f* harpy

harpon /'aʀpɔ̃/ *m* harpoon

harponner /'aʀpɔne/ [**v1**] *vt* to harpoon

🔑 **hasard** /'azaʀ/ *m* chance; **par ~** by chance; **par un curieux ~** by a curious coincidence; **par un heureux ~** by a stroke of luck; **ce n'est pas un ~ si...** it's no accident that...; **le ~ a voulu que...** as luck would have it,...; **au ~** ‹*choose*› at random; ‹*walk*› aimlessly; ‹*answer*› off the top of one's head; **comme par ~, il a oublié son argent** (ironic) surprise, surprise, he's forgotten his money; **à tout ~** just in case, on the off chance; **les ~s de la vie** the fortunes of life
IDIOM **le ~ fait bien les choses** fate is a great provider

hasarder /'azaʀde/ [**v1**] **A** *vt* **1** to venture ‹*advice*›
2 to risk ‹*life*›
B **se hasarder** *v refl* (+ *v être*) to venture

hasardeux, **-euse** /'azaʀdø, øz/ *adj* risky

hâte /'ɑt/ *f* **1** haste; **à la ~** hastily
2 j'ai ~ de partir/qu'elle parte I can't wait to leave/for her to leave

hâter /'ɑte/ [**v1**] **A** *vt* to hasten; **~ le pas** to quicken one's step
B **se hâter** *v refl* (+ *v être*) to hurry, to rush

hâtif, **-ive** /'ɑtif, iv/ *adj* **1** ‹*judgement*› hasty, hurried
2 ‹*plant*› early

hâtivement /'ɑtivmɑ̃/ *adv* hurriedly, hastily

hausse /'os/ *f* increase, rise; **être en ~** ‹*prices*› to be rising; ‹*goods*› to be going up in price; **en ~ de 10%** up 10%

haussement /'osmɑ̃/ *m* **~ d'épaules** shrug

hausser /'ose/ [**v1**] **A** *vt* to raise; **~ les épaules** to shrug one's shoulders
B **se hausser** *v refl* (+ *v être*) **se ~ sur la pointe des pieds** to stand on tiptoe

🔑 **haut**, **~e** /'o, 'ot/ **A** *adj* **1** high; tall; **l'étagère la plus ~e** the top shelf; **à ~e voix** ‹*speak*› loudly; ‹*read*› aloud, out loud; **à ~ risque** very risky; **au plus ~ point** immensely
2 ‹*rank, society*› high; ‹*person, post*› high-ranking; **~e surveillance** close supervision
3 (in geography) upper; **la ~e Égypte** Upper Egypt
4 le ~ Moyen Âge the early Middle Ages
B *adv* **1** high; **un personnage ~ placé** a high-ranking person; **plus ~ sur la page** higher up on the page; **'voir plus ~'** see above; **de ~** from above
2 (in time) far back
3 loudly; **dire qch tout ~** to say sth aloud; **n'avoir jamais un mot plus ~ que l'autre** never to raise one's voice
C *m* **1** top; **le ~ du corps** the top half of the body; **l'étagère du ~** the top shelf; **les pièces du ~** the upstairs rooms; **parler du ~ d'un balcon** to speak from a balcony
2 faire 50 mètres de ~ to be 50 metres (BrE) high
D **en haut** *phr* upstairs; on an upper floor; **en ~ de** at the top of
■ **~ en couleur** ‹*character*› colourful (BrE); **~ débit** broadband; **~ fait** heroic deed; **~ lieu de** centre (BrE) of *or* for; **en ~ lieu** in high places; **~e mer** open sea; **~es sphères** high social circles
IDIOMS **voir les choses de ~** to have a detached view of things; **tomber de ~** to be dumbfounded; **connaître des ~s et des bas** to have one's ups and downs; **~ les mains!** hands up!; **gagner ~ la main** to win hands down; **prendre qch de ~** to react indignantly

hautain, **~e** /'otɛ̃, ɛn/ *adj* haughty

🔑 key word

hautbois /'obwɑ/ *m inv* **1** oboe
2 oboist

haut-de-forme, *pl* **hauts-de-formes** /'odfɔʀm/ *m* top hat

haute /'ot/ **A** *adj f* ▸ **haut A**
B *f* (fam) **les gens de la ~** the upper crust

haute-fidélité, *pl* **hautes-fidélités** /'otfidelite/ *f* hi-fi, high fidelity

hauteur /'otœʀ/ **A** *f* **1** height; **prendre de la ~** ‹*plane*› to climb; **dans le sens de la ~** upright; **à ~ d'homme** at head height
2 hill; **gagner les ~s** to reach high ground
3 haughtiness
4 (of voice) pitch
B à la hauteur de *phr* **1 arriver à la ~ de** to come up to; to draw level with; **raccourcir une jupe à la ~ des genoux** to shorten a dress to the knee
2 (fig) **être à la ~** to measure up; **être à la ~ de sa tâche** to be equal to one's job
IDIOM **tomber de toute sa ~** to fall headlong

haut-fond, *pl* **hauts-fonds** /'ofɔ̃/ *m* shallows

haut-fourneau, *pl* **hauts-fourneaux** /'ofuʀno/ *m* blast furnace

haut-le-cœur /'olkœʀ/ *m inv* retching, heaving; **avoir un ~** to retch

haut-parleur, *pl* **~s** /'opaʀlœʀ/ *m* loudspeaker

havane /'avan/ **A** *adj inv* tobacco-brown
B *m* **1** Havana tobacco
2 Havana cigar

havre /'ɑvʀ/ *m* haven

Haye /'ɛ/ *pr n* **la ~** the Hague

heaume /'om/ *m* helmet

hebdomadaire /ɛbdomadɛʀ/ *adj, m* weekly

hébergement /ebɛʀʒəmɑ̃/ *m* **1** accommodation
2 housing

héberger /ebɛʀʒe/ [**v13**] *vt* to put [sb] up; to accommodate; to provide shelter for

hébété, **~e** /ebete/ *adj* ‹*look*› stupid

hébraïque /ebʀaik/ *adj* Hebrew

hébreu, *pl* **~x** /ebʀø/ **A** *adj m* Hebrew
B *m* (language) Hebrew
IDIOM **pour moi, c'est de l'~** it's all Greek to me

HEC /aʃəse/ *f* (*abbr* = **Hautes études commerciales**) *major business school*

hécatombe /ekatɔ̃b/ *f* massacre, slaughter

hectare /ɛktaʀ/ *m* hectare

hecto /ɛkto/ **A** *m* (*abbr* = **hectogramme**) hectogram
B hecto(-) (*combining form*) hecto-

hein /'ɛ̃/ *excl* (fam) what (fam)?, sorry?; **ça t'étonne, ~?** that's surprised you, hasn't it?

hélas /'elas/ *excl* alas; **~ non!** unfortunately not!

héler /'ele/ [**v14**] *vt* to hail

hélice /elis/ *f* **1** (screw) propeller
2 helix

hélicoptère /elikɔptɛʀ/ *m* helicopter

héliporté, **~e** /elipɔʀte/ *adj* helicopter-borne

hellène /ellɛn/ *adj* Hellenic

helvétique /ɛlvetik/ *adj* Helvetic, Swiss; **la Confédération ~** Switzerland

helvétisme /ɛlvetism/ *m* Swiss French expression

hématologie /ematɔlɔʒi/ *f* haematology

hématome /ematom/ *m* bruise

hémicycle /emisikl/ *m* semicircular auditorium

hémisphère /emisfɛʀ/ *m* hemisphere

hémoglobine /emɔglɔbin/ *f* haemoglobin

hémophile /emɔfil/ **A** *adj* haemophilic
B *mf* haemophiliac

hémorragie /emɔʀaʒi/ *f* **1** haemorrhage, bleeding
2 (of capital) outflow

hémorroïdes /emɔʀɔid/ *fpl* piles, haemorrhoids

henné /'ene/ *m* henna

hennir /'eniʀ/ [**v3**] *vi* to neigh, to whinny

hépatique /epatik/ **A** *adj* hepatic
B *mf* person with a liver complaint

hépatite /epatit/ *f* hepatitis

heptathlète /ɛptatlɛt/ *mf* heptathlete

héraldique /eʀaldik/ *adj* heraldic

herbacé, **~e** /ɛʀbase/ *adj* herbaceous

herbage /ɛʀbaʒ/ *m* pasture

herbe /ɛʀb/ **A** *f* **1** grass; **mauvaise ~** weed
2 (Culin) herb
B en herbe *phr* **1** ‹*wheat*› in the blade
2 ‹*musician*› budding
IDIOM **couper l'~ sous le pied de qn** to pull the rug from under sb's feet

herbeux, **-euse** /ɛʀbø, øz/ *adj* grassy

herbier /ɛʀbje/ *m* herbarium

herbivore /ɛʀbivɔʀ/ **A** *adj* herbivorous
B *m* herbivore

herboriste /ɛʀbɔʀist/ *mf* herbalist

herboristerie /ɛʀbɔʀistəʀi/ *f* **1** herb trade
2 herbalist's shop (BrE) *or* store (AmE)

héréditaire /eʀeditɛʀ/ *adj* hereditary; (fig) ‹*enemy*› traditional

hérédité /eʀedite/ *f* **1** heredity
2 (of title) hereditary nature

hérésie /eʀezi/ *f* **1** heresy
2 (hum) sacrilege

hérétique /eʀetik/ **A** *adj* heretical
B *mf* heretic

hérissé, **~e** /'eʀise/ *adj* ‹*hair*› bristling, standing up on end; **~ de** spiked with ‹*nails*›

hérisser /'eʀise/ [**v1**] **A** *vt* **1** ‹*bird*› to ruffle (up) ‹*feathers*›
2 ~ qch de to spike sth with
3 (fam) **ça me hérisse** it makes my hackles rise
B se hérisser *v refl* (+ *v être*) ‹*hair*› to stand on end

hérisson /'eʀisɔ̃/ *m* hedgehog

héritage /eʀitaʒ/ *m* **1** inheritance; **laisser qch en ~** to bequeath sth; **recevoir qch en ~** to inherit sth
2 heritage

hériter /eʀite/ [**v1**] **A** *vt* to inherit
B **hériter de** *v+prep* to inherit
C *vi* to inherit; to come into an inheritance; **~ de qn** to receive an inheritance from sb

héritier, **-ière** /eʀitje, ɛʀ/ *mf* heir/heiress

hermétique /ɛʀmetik/ *adj* **1** hermetic; airtight; watertight
2 ‹*milieu*› impenetrable; ‹*poetry, author*› abstruse; ‹*face*› inscrutable

hermétiquement /ɛʀmetikmɑ̃/ *adv*
1 ‹*sealed*› hermetically
2 ‹*speak*› abstrusely

hermine /ɛʀmin/ *f* **1** stoat
2 ermine

hernie /'ɛʀni/ *f* **1** hernia
2 (in tyre) bulge

héroïne /eʀɔin/ *f* **1** heroine
2 heroin

héroïque /eʀɔik/ *adj* heroic; epic

héroïsme /eʀɔism/ *m* heroism

héron /'eʀɔ̃/ *m* heron

⚷ **héros** /'eʀo/ *m inv* hero

herse /'ɛʀs/ *f* **1** harrow
2 portcullis

hertzien, **-ienne** /ɛʀtzjɛ̃, ɛn/ *adj* ‹*wave*› Hertzian; ‹*station*› radio relay

hésitant, **~e** /ezitɑ̃, ɑ̃t/ *adj* **1** hesitant
2 ‹*start*› shaky

hésitation /ezitasjɔ̃/ *f* **1** indecision, hesitancy
2 hesitation

⚷ **hésiter** /ezite/ [**v1**] *vi* to hesitate; **elle hésite encore** she's still undecided; **il n'y a pas à ~** it's got to be done; **j'hésite sur le chemin à prendre** I'm not sure which path to take; **~ à faire** to be hesitant to do

hétéroclite /eteʀɔklit/ *adj* ‹*population, work*› heterogeneous; ‹*objects*› miscellaneous

hétérogène /eteʀɔʒɛn/ *adj* mixed, heterogeneous

hétérosexuel, **-elle** /eteʀɔsɛksɥɛl/ *adj, mf* heterosexual

hêtre /'ɛtʀ/ *m* **1** beech (tree)
2 beechwood

⚷ **heure** /œʀ/ *f* **1** hour; **24 ~s sur 24** 24 hours a day; **dans l'~ qui a suivi** within the hour; **d'~ en ~** ‹*increase*› by the hour; **à trois ~s d'avion de Paris** three hours from Paris by plane; **à trois ~s de marche de Paris** a three-hour walk from Paris; **faire du 60 à l'~** (fam) to do 60 km per hour; **payé à l'~** paid by the hour; **une petite ~** an hour at the most
2 time; **quelle ~ est-il?** what time is it?; **il est 10 ~s** it's 10 (o'clock); **il est 10 ~s 20** it's 20 past 10; **il est 10 ~s moins 20** it's 20 to 10; **mettre sa montre à l'~** to set one's watch; **l'~ tourne** time is passing; **~s d'ouverture** opening times; **être à l'~** to be on time; **à une ~ avancée (de la nuit)** late at night; **de bonne ~** early; **c'est son ~** it's his/her usual time; **à l'~ où je te parle** as we speak; **de la première ~** from the very beginning; **à la première ~** at first light; **ta dernière ~ est arrivée** your time has come; **à l'~ actuelle, pour l'~** at the present time; **l'~ du déjeuner** lunchtime; **l'~ est grave** the situation is serious; **il est peintre à ses ~s** he paints in his spare time; **à la bonne ~!** well done!
3 era, age; **vivre à l'~ des satellites** to live in the satellite era
■ **~ d'affluence** peak hour; **~ d'été** summer time (BrE), daylight saving(s) time; **~ H** (Mil), (fig) zero hour; **~ d'hiver** winter time (BrE), standard time; **~ de pointe** rush hour; **~s supplémentaires** overtime

⚷ **heureusement** /œʀøzmɑ̃/ *adv* fortunately

⚷ **heureux**, **-euse** /œʀø, øz/ *adj* **1** happy; **~ en ménage** happily married; **très ~ de faire votre connaissance** (very) pleased to meet you
2 ‹*ending*› happy; ‹*proportions*› pleasing; ‹*choice*› fortunate; ‹*surprise*› pleasant
3 ‹*winner*› lucky; **'il a réussi!'—'encore ~!'** 'he succeeded!'—'just as well!'
IDIOM **attendre un ~ événement** to be expecting a baby

heurt /'œʀ/ *m* **1** collision
2 (fig) (between people) clash; **sans ~s** ‹*do*› smoothly; ‹*relationship*› smooth

heurter /'œʀte/ [**v1**] **A** *vt* **1** ‹*object*› to hit; ‹*person*› to collide with, to bump into
2 (fig) to go against ‹*convention*›; to hurt ‹*feelings*›
B *vi* **~ contre** to strike
C **se heurter** *v refl* (+ *v être*) to collide; (fig) to clash; **se ~ à** to bump into ‹*table*›; to come up against ‹*refusal, problem*›

hévéa /evea/ *m* rubber tree

hexagonal, **~e**, *mpl* **-aux** /ɛgzagɔnal, o/ *adj* **1** hexagonal
2 (fam) ‹*policy*› inward-looking

hexagone /ɛgzagon/ *m* **1** hexagon
2 (fam) **l'Hexagone** France

hiberner /ibɛʀne/ [**v1**] *vi* to hibernate

hibou, *pl* **~x** /'ibu/ *m* owl

hic /'ik/ *m* (fam) snag; **voilà le ~** there's the snag

hideux, **-euse** /'idø, øz/ *adj* hideous

⚷ **hier** /jɛʀ/ *adv* yesterday; **ça ne date pas d'~** it's nothing new

hiérarchie /'jeʀaʀʃi/ *f* hierarchy

hiérarchique /'jeʀaʀʃik/ *adj* hierarchical; **mon supérieur ~** my immediate superior; **par la voie ~** through the correct channels

⚷ key word

hiérarchiser /'jeʀaʀʃize/ [**v1**] *vt* to organize [sth] into a hierarchy ‹*structure*›

hiératique /jeʀatik/ *adj* hieratic

hiéroglyphe /'jeʀɔglif/ *m* hieroglyph; **les ~s** hieroglyphics

hi-fi /'ifi/ *adj inv*, *f inv* hi-fi

hilarant, **~e** /ilaʀɑ̃, ɑ̃t/ *adj* hilarious; **gaz ~** laughing gas

hilare /ilaʀ/ *adj* **être ~** to be laughing

hilarité /ilaʀite/ *f* mirth, hilarity

hindou, **~e** /ɛ̃du/ *adj*, *mf* Hindu

hindouisme /ɛ̃duism/ *m* Hinduism

hippique /ipik/ *adj* equestrian; **concours ~** showjumping event (BrE), horse show

hippocampe /ipɔkɑ̃p/ *m* sea horse

hippodrome /ipɔdʀom/ *m* racecourse (BrE), racetrack (AmE)

hippopotame /ipɔpɔtam/ *m* hippopotamus

hirondelle /iʀɔ̃dɛl/ *f* swallow

hirsute /'iʀsyt/ *adj* dishevelled (BrE), unkempt

hispanique /ispanik/ *adj*, *mf* Hispanic

hispano-américain, **~e**, *mpl* **~s** /ispanoameʀikɛ̃, ɛn/ *adj* Hispanic-American, Spanish-American

hispanophone /ispanofɔn/ *mf* Spanish speaker

hisse /'is/ *excl* **oh ~!** heave-ho!

hisser /'ise/ [**v1**] **A** *vt* to hoist ‹*flag*›
B se hisser *v refl* (+ *v être*) to heave oneself up

histoire /istwaʀ/ *f* **1** history; **l'~ jugera** posterity will be the judge
2 story; **tout ça, c'est des ~s!** (fam) that's all fiction!; **une ~ à dormir debout** a tall story; **raconter des ~s** to tell fibs
3 matter, business; **~ d'amour** love affair; **~ de famille** family matter; **il m'est arrivé une drôle d'~** a funny thing happened to me
4 fuss; trouble; **elle fait toujours des ~s** she's always making a fuss; **ça va faire des ~s** it will cause trouble; **c'est une femme à ~s** she's a troublemaker; **une vie sans ~s** an uneventful life; **ça a été toute une ~ pour faire** it was a terrible job doing; **au travail, et pas d'~s!** (fam) get on with it, no messing about! (fam)
5 (fam) **~ de rire** just for fun

historien, **-ienne** /istɔʀjɛ̃, ɛn/ *mf* historian

historique /istɔʀik/ **A** *adj* **1** historical
2 historic
3 passé ~ past historic
B *m* (Comput) History (button)

hit-parade, *pl* **~s** /'itpaʀad/ *m* charts

hiver /ivɛʀ/ *m* winter

hivernage /ivɛʀnaʒ/ *m* wintering

hivernal, **~e**, *mpl* **-aux** /ivɛʀnal, o/ *adj* **1** winter
2 wintry

hiverner /ivɛʀne/ [**v1**] *vi* ‹*animals*› to winter

HLM /aʃɛlɛm/ *mf*: *abbr* ▶ **habitation**

hochement /'ɔʃmɑ̃/ *m* nod; shake of the head

hocher /'ɔʃe/ [**v1**] *vt* **~ la tête** to nod; to shake one's head

hochet /'ɔʃɛ/ *m* rattle

hockey /'ɔkɛ/ *m* hockey

holà /'ɔla/ *excl* hey (there)!
IDIOM **mettre le ~ à qch** to put an end *or* a stop to sth

holding /'ɔldiŋ/ *mf* holding company

hold-up, *pl* **~** *or* **~s** /'ɔldœp/ *m* hold-up

hollandais, **~e** /'ɔlɑ̃dɛ, ɛz/ **A** *adj* Dutch
B *m* (language) Dutch

Hollandais, **~e** /'ɔlɑ̃ dɛ, ɛz/ *mf* Dutchman/ Dutchwoman; **les ~** the Dutch

Hollande /'ɔlɑ̃d/ *pr f* Holland

holocauste /ɔlɔkost/ *m* holocaust

homard /'ɔmaʀ/ *m* lobster

homéopathie /ɔmeɔpati/ *f* homeopathy

homéopathique /ɔmeɔpatik/ *adj* homeopathic; **à doses ~s** (fig) in small doses

homicide /ɔmisid/ *m* homicide; manslaughter; murder

hommage /ɔmaʒ/ *m* homage, tribute; **présenter ses ~s** to pay one's respects

hommasse /ɔmas/ *adj* mannish

homme /ɔm/ *m* man; **l'~** man; mankind; **un ~ à la mer!** man overboard!; **comme un seul ~** as one; **leur ~ de confiance** their right-hand man; **il n'est pas ~ à se venger** he's not the type to want revenge
■ **~ d'affaires** businessman; **~ des cavernes** caveman; **~ d'esprit** wit; **~ d'État** statesman; **~ à femmes** womanizer; **~ au foyer** house husband; **~ de main** hired hand; **~ de paille** front man (BrE), straw man (AmE); **~ de terrain** man with practical experience; **~ à tout faire** handyman; **~ de troupe** private; **~s en blanc** surgeons
IDIOM **un ~ averti en vaut deux** (Proverb) forewarned is forearmed

homme-grenouille, *pl* **hommes-grenouilles** /ɔmgʀənuj/ *m* frogman

homme-orchestre, *pl* **hommes-orchestres** /ɔmɔʀkɛstʀ/ *m* one-man band

homogène /ɔmɔʒɛn/ *adj* homogeneous

homogénéité /ɔmoʒeneite/ *f* homogeneity

homologue /ɔmɔlɔg/ **A** *adj* homologous
B *mf* counterpart, opposite number

homologuer /ɔmɔlɔge/ [**v1**] *vt* **1** to approve ‹*product*›
2 (Sport) to recognize officially

homonyme /ɔmɔnim/ *m* **1** homonym
2 namesake

homoparentalité /omɔpaʀɑ̃talite/ *f* gay parenting

homosexualité /omɔsɛksɥalite/ *f* homosexuality

homosexuel, **-elle** /omɔsɛksɥɛl/ *adj, mf* homosexual

Hongrie /'ɔ̃gʀi/ *pr f* Hungary

honnête /ɔnɛt/ *adj* **1** honest
2 decent; respectable
3 fair, reasonable

honnêtement /ɔnɛtmɑ̃/ *adv* **1** ‹*say, manage*› honestly; ‹*reply*› frankly; ‹*behave*› properly; ‹*judge*› fairly
2 fairly, reasonably; **s'acquitter ~ d'une tâche** to do a decent job

honnêteté /ɔnɛtte/ *f* honesty

honneur /ɔnœʀ/ *m* **1** honour (BrE); **à toi l'~!** you do the honours (BrE)!; **j'ai l'~ de vous informer que** I beg to inform you that; **j'ai l'~ de solliciter** I would respectfully request; **d'~** ‹*stairs*› main
2 credit; **c'est tout à leur ~** it's all credit to them
3 mettre qn à l'~ to honour (BrE) sb; **être à l'** *or* **en ~** to be in favour (BrE); **faire ~ à un repas** to do justice to a meal; **faire les ~s de la maison à qn** to show sb around the house; **avoir les ~s de la presse** to be mentioned in the press; **en quel ~?** (fam) (ironic) any particular reason why?
IDIOM **en tout bien tout ~** with no hidden motive

honnir /'ɔniʀ/ [**v3**] *vt* **honni soit qui mal y pense** evil unto him who evil thinks

honorabilité /ɔnɔʀabilite/ *f* integrity

honorable /ɔnɔʀabl/ *adj* **1** honourable (BrE)
2 ‹*score*› creditable; ‹*salary*› decent

honorablement /ɔnɔʀabləmɑ̃/ *adv*
1 honourably (BrE)
2 decently

honoraire /ɔnɔʀɛʀ/ **A** *adj* ‹*member*› honorary
B honoraires *mpl* fee, fees

honorer /ɔnɔʀe/ [**v1**] *vt* **1** to honour (BrE) ‹*god, person, memory*›
2 to honour (BrE) ‹*promise, debt*›
3 to be a credit to ‹*country, profession*›

honorifique /ɔnɔʀifik/ *adj* honorary

honoris causa /ɔnɔʀiskoza/ *phr* **être nommé docteur ~** to be awarded an honorary doctorate

honte /'ɔ̃t/ *f* **1** shame; **avoir ~ de** to be ashamed of; **sans fausse ~** quite openly
2 disgrace; **faire la ~ de** to be a disgrace to; **quelle ~!** what a disgrace!

honteusement /'ɔ̃tøzmɑ̃/ *adv*
1 shamefully
2 shamelessly

honteux, **-euse** /'ɔ̃tø, øz/ *adj* **1** disgraceful
2 ashamed

hôpital, *pl* **-aux** /ɔpital, o/ *m* hospital
IDIOM **c'est l'~ qui se moque de la charité** it's the pot calling the kettle black

hoquet /'ɔkɛ/ *m* **avoir le ~** to have hiccups

hoqueter /'ɔkte/ [**v20**] *vi* ‹*person*› to hiccup

horaire /ɔʀɛʀ/ **A** *adj* per hour, hourly; **tranche** *or* **plage ~** time slot
B *m* timetable, schedule; **les ~s libres** *or* **à la carte** flexitime

horde /'ɔʀd/ *f* horde

horizon /ɔʀizɔ̃/ *m* horizon

horizontal, **~e** *mpl* **-aux** /ɔʀizɔ̃tal, o/ *adj* horizontal

horizontale /ɔʀizɔ̃tal/ *f* horizontal

horloge /ɔʀlɔʒ/ *f* clock

horloger, **-ère** /ɔʀlɔʒe, ɛʀ/ *mf* watchmaker

horlogerie /ɔʀlɔʒʀi/ *f* **1** watchmaking
2 watchmaker's (shop)

hormis /'ɔʀmi/ *prep* (fml) save, except (for)

hormonal, **~e**, *mpl* **-aux** /ɔʀmɔnal, o/ *adj* ‹*problem*› hormonal; ‹*treatment*› hormone

hormone /ɔʀmon/ *f* hormone

horodateur /ɔʀɔdatœʀ/ *m* parking ticket machine

horoscope /ɔʀɔskɔp/ *m* horoscope

horreur /ɔʀœʀ/ *f* **1** horror; **quelle ~!** how horrible!
2 dire des ~s de *or* **sur qn** to say awful things about sb
3 loathing; **avoir ~ de qn/de faire** to loathe sb/doing

horrible /ɔʀibl/ *adj* **1** horrible
2 revolting
3 hideous

horriblement /ɔʀibləmɑ̃/ *adv* ‹*damaged*› horribly; ‹*cold*› terribly

horrifier /ɔʀifje/ [**v2**] *vt* to horrify

horripiler /ɔʀipile/ [**v1**] *vt* to exasperate

hors /'ɔʀ/

> You will find translations for expressions such as *hors série*, *hors d'usage* etc, at the entries **série, usage**, etc.

A *prep* outside; **longueur ~ tout** overall length
B hors de *phr* out of, outside; **~ d'ici!** get out of here!
IDIOM **être ~ de soi** to be beside oneself

hors-bord /'ɔʀbɔʀ/ *m inv* speedboat

hors-d'œuvre /'ɔʀdœvʀ/ *m inv* starter, hors d'oeuvre

hors-jeu /'ɔʀʒø/ *m inv* **(pour) ~** for offside

hors-la-loi /'ɔʀlalwa/ *m inv* outlaw

hors-piste /'ɔʀpist/ *m inv* off-piste skiing

hortensia /ɔʀtɑ̃sja/ *m* hydrangea

horticulteur, **-trice** /ɔʀtikyltœʀ, tʀis/ *mf* horticulturist

hospice /ɔspis/ *m* home; **~ de vieillards** old people's home

hospitalier, **-ière** /ɔspitalje, ɛʀ/ *adj*
1 hospital; **centre ~** hospital
2 hospitable

hospitalisation /ɔspitalizasjɔ̃/ *f* hospitalization; **~ à domicile** home (medical) care

hospitaliser /ɔspitalize/ [**v1**] *vt* to hospitalize

key word

hospitalité /ɔspitalite/ *f* hospitality

hostie /ɔsti/ *f* Host

hostile /ɔstil/ *adj* hostile

hostilité /ɔstilite/ *f* hostility

hôte /ot/ **A** *m* **1** host
2 occupant
B *mf* guest

hôtel /otɛl/ *m* hotel
■ **~ particulier** town house; **~ de passe** hotel used by prostitutes; **~ des ventes** saleroom; **~ de ville** ≈ town hall

hôtelier, **-ière** /otəlje, ɛʀ/ **A** *adj* ‹*industry*› hotel; ‹*school*› hotel management
B *mf* hotelier

hôtellerie /otɛlʀi/ *f* hotel business

hôtesse /otɛs/ *f* (at home, at exhibition) hostess; (in company) receptionist; (in boat) stewardess
■ **~ d'accueil** receptionist; **~ de l'air** air hostess

hotte /'ɔt/ *f* **1** basket
2 hood
■ **~ aspirante** extractor hood (BrE), ventilator (AmE); **la ~ du Père Noël** Santa Claus's sack

houblon /'ublɔ̃/ *m* hop, hops

houille /'uj/ *f* coal

houiller, **-ère** /'uje, ɛʀ/ *adj* ‹*industry*› coal; ‹*area*› coal mining

houle /'ul/ *f* swell

houlette /'ulɛt/ *f* (of shepherd) crook; **sous la ~ de** (fig) under the leadership of

houleux, **-euse** /'ulø, øz/ *adj* **1** ‹*sea*› rough
2 ‹*meeting*› stormy

houppe /'up/ *f* **1** (of hair) tuft; (of threads) tassel
2 powder puff

houppette /'upɛt/ *f* powder puff

hourra /'uʀa/ *m* cheer

houspiller /'uspije/ [**v1**] *vt* to scold

housse /'us/ *f* cover, slipcover; dustcover; garment bag

houx /'u/ *m inv* holly

HT (*written abbr* = **hors taxes**) exclusive of tax

hublot /'yblo/ *m* (in plane) window; (in boat) porthole

huche /'yʃ/ *f* **1** chest
2 ~ à pain bread bin

huer /'ɥe/ [**v1**] *vt* to boo

huile /ɥil/ *f* **1** oil
2 oil painting
■ **~ de coude** (hum) elbow grease; **~ solaire** suntan oil
IDIOMS **tout/ça baigne dans l'~** (fam) everything/it is going smoothly; **jeter** *or* **verser de l'~ sur le feu** to add fuel to the fire

huiler /ɥile/ [**v1**] *vt* to oil

huileux, **-euse** /ɥilø, øz/ *adj* oily

huis /'ɥi/ *m inv* **à ~ clos** (Law) in camera; (fig) behind closed doors

huissier /ɥisje/ *m* **1 ~ (de justice)** bailiff
2 porter; usher

huit /'ɥit/ *but before consonant* /'ɥi/ **A** *adj inv* eight; **mardi en ~** a week on Tuesday
B *pron* eight
C *m inv* **1** eight
2 a figure of eight

huitaine /'ɥitɛn/ *f* **1** about a week; **sous ~** within a week
2 une ~ about eight

huitième /'ɥitjɛm/ **A** *adj* eighth
B *f* (Sch) *fourth year of primary school, age 9–10*

huître /ɥitʀ/ *f* oyster

hululement /'ylylmɑ̃/ *m* hooting

hululer /'ylyle/ [**v1**] *vi* to hoot

humain, **~e** /ymɛ̃, ɛn/ **A** *adj* **1** human; **pertes ~es** loss of life
2 ‹*regime*› humane; ‹*person*› human, understanding
B *m* human (being)

humainement /ymɛnmɑ̃/ *adv* **1** humanly
2 humanely

humaniser /ymanize/ [**v1**] **A** *vt* to humanize
B s'humaniser *v refl* (+ *v être*) to become more human

humanitaire /ymanitɛʀ/ *adj* humanitarian

humanité /ymanite/ *f* humanity

humble /œbl/ *adj* humble

humblement /œbləmɑ̃/ *adv* humbly

humecter /ymɛkte/ [**v1**] *vt* to moisten

humer /'yme/ [**v1**] *vt* to sniff; to smell

humeur /ymœʀ/ *f* **1** mood; **être de bonne/mauvaise ~** to be in a good/bad mood
2 temperament; **être d'~ égale** to be even-tempered; **être d'~ inégale** to be moody; **elle est connue pour sa bonne ~** she's known for her good humour
3 bad temper; **geste d'~** bad-tempered gesture; **avec ~** bad-temperedly

humide /ymid/ *adj* **1** damp
2 ‹*climate*› humid; ‹*season*› rainy; **il fait froid et ~** it's cold and damp; **il fait une chaleur ~** it's muggy

humidifier /ymidifje/ [**v2**] *vt* to humidify

humidité /ymidite/ *f* **1** dampness, damp
2 humidity

humiliant, **~e** /ymiljɑ̃, ɑ̃t/ *adj* humiliating

humiliation /ymiljasjɔ̃/ *f* humiliation

humilier /ymilje/ [**v2**] *vt* to humiliate

humilité /ymilite/ *f* **1** humility
2 (of task) humble nature

humoriste /ymɔʀist/ *mf* **1** humorist
2 joker

humoristique /ymɔʀistik/ *adj* humorous; **dessin ~** cartoon

humour /ymuʀ/ *m* humour (BrE); **avoir de l'~** to have a sense of humour (BrE); **faire de l'~** to make jokes

huppé, **~e** /'ype/ *adj* **1** (fam) ‹*person*› upper crust
2 ‹*bird*› crested

h

hurlement /ˈyʀləmɑ̃/ *m* (of animal) howl, howling; (of person) yell, howl; (of siren) wail, wailing

hurler /ˈyʀle/ [**v1**] **A** *vt* to yell **B** *vi* **1** to yell; (with pain, anger) to howl **2** ‹*siren*› to wail; ‹*wind*› to roar; ‹*radio*› to blare

(IDIOMS) ~ **avec les loups** to follow the crowd; ~ **à la mort** to bay at the moon

hurluberlu, **~e** /yʀlybɛʀly/ *mf* oddball (fam)

hutte /ˈyt/ *f* hut

hybride /ibʀid/ *adj, m* hybrid

hydratant, **~e** /idʀatɑ̃, ɑ̃t/ *adj* moisturizing

hydratation /idʀatasjɔ̃/ *f* **1** hydration **2** moisturizing

hydrate /idʀat/ *m* ~ **de carbone** carbohydrate

hydrater /idʀate/ [**v1**] **A** *vt* **1** to hydrate **2** to moisturize ‹*skin*› **B s'hydrater** *v refl* (+ *v être*) **bien s'~** to take plenty of fluids

hydraulique /idʀolik/ *adj* hydraulic

hydravion /idʀavjɔ̃/ *m* seaplane, hydroplane

hydro /idʀo/ *pref* hydro; **~électrique** hydroelectric

hydrocarbure /idʀɔkaʀbyʀ/ *m* hydrocarbon

hydrocution /idʀɔkysjɔ̃/ *f* immersion hypothermia

hydrofuge /idʀɔfyʒ/ *adj* water-repellent

hydrogène /idʀɔʒɛn/ *m* hydrogen

hydroglisseur /idʀɔglisœʀ/ *m* hydroplane

hydrophile /idʀɔfil/ *adj* absorbent

hydroxyde /idʀɔksid/ *m* hydroxide

hyène /ˈjɛn/ *f* hyena

hygiaphone® /iʒjafɔn/ *m* grill (*perforated communication panel*)

hygiène /iʒjɛn/ *f* hygiene; **bonne ~ alimentaire** healthy diet ■ **~ corporelle** personal hygiene

hygiénique /iʒjenik/ *adj* **1** hygienic **2** ‹*lifestyle*› healthy

hymen /imɛn/ *m* **1** hymen **2** nuptial bond

hymne /imn/ *m* hymn; ~ **national** national anthem

hyperactif, **-ive** /ipɛʀaktif, iv/ *adj* hyperactive

hyperclassique /ipɛʀklasik/ *adj* ‹*reaction*› absolutely classic; **roman** ~ great classic

hypermarché /ipɛʀmaʀʃe/ *m* hypermarket (BrE), large supermarket

hypermétrope /ipɛʀmetʀɔp/ *adj* long-sighted

hypernerveux, **-euse** /ipɛʀnɛʀvø, øz/ *adj* highly strung

hypersensible /ipɛʀsɑ̃sibl/ *adj* hypersensitive

hypersophistiqué, **~e** /ipɛʀsɔfistike/ *adj* very sophisticated

hyperspécialisé, **~e** /ipɛʀspesjalize/ *adj* highly specialized

hypertension /ipɛʀtɑ̃sjɔ̃/ *f* ~ **(artérielle)** high blood pressure

hypertexte /ipɛʀtɛkst/ *m* hypertext

hypertoile /ipɛʀtwal/ *f* World Wide Web

hypertrophie /ipɛʀtʀɔfi/ *f* **1** (Med) enlargement **2** (of town) overdevelopment

hypertrophier: **s'hypertrophier** /ipɛʀtʀɔfje/ [**v2**] *v refl* (+ *v être*) **1** (Med) to hypertrophy **2** ‹*town*› to become overdeveloped

hypnose /ipnoz/ *f* hypnosis

hypnotique /ipnɔtik/ *adj, m* hypnotic

hypnotiser /ipnɔtize/ [**v1**] *vt* to hypnotize; (fig) to mesmerize

hypnotiseur, **-euse** /ipnɔtizœʀ, øz/ *mf* hypnotist

hypocalorique /ipɔkalɔʀik/ *adj* low-calorie

hypocondriaque /ipɔkɔ̃dʀijak/ *adj, mf* hypochondriac

hypocrisie /ipɔkʀizi/ *f* hypocrisy

hypocrite /ipɔkʀit/ **A** *adj* hypocritical **B** *mf* hypocrite

hypodermique /ipɔdɛʀmik/ *adj* hypodermic

hypokhâgne /ipɔkaɲ/ *f*: *first year preparatory class in humanities for entrance to École normale supérieure*

hypotension /ipɔtɑ̃sjɔ̃/ *f* ~ **(artérielle)** low blood pressure

hypothécaire /ipɔtekɛʀ/ *adj* mortgage; **créancier/débiteur** ~ mortgagee/mortgager

hypothèque /ipɔtɛk/ *f* mortgage

hypothéquer /ipɔteke/ [**v14**] *vt* to mortgage

⚷ **hypothèse** /ipɔtɛz/ *f* hypothesis

hypothétique /ipɔtetik/ *adj* hypothetical

hystérie /isteʀi/ *f* hysteria

hystérique /isteʀik/ *adj* hysterical

⚷ key word

Ii

i, **I** /i/ *m inv* i, I
IDIOM **mettre les points sur les i** to make things crystal clear

ibérique /ibeʀik/ *adj* Iberian

iceberg /ajsbɛʀg, isbɛʀg/ *m* iceberg

ici /isi/ *adv* **1** here; **c'est ~ que...** this is where...; **par ~** this way; around here; **les gens d'~** the locals; **je vois ça d'~!** I can just picture it!
2 jusqu'~ until now; until then; **d'~ peu** shortly; **d'~ deux jours** two days from now; **d'~ là** by then; **il l'aime bien, mais d'~ à ce qu'il l'épouse...** he likes her, but as for marrying her...

ici-bas /isibɑ/ *adv* here below

icône /ikon/ *f* icon

id. *written abbr* = **idem**

idéal, **~e**, *mpl* **-aux** /ideal, o/ **A** *adj* ideal
B *m* ideal; **dans l'~** ideally

idéalisme /idealism/ *m* idealism

idée /ide/ *f* idea; thought; **avoir de l'~** to be inventive; **avoir une ~ derrière la tête** to have something in mind; **se faire des ~s** to imagine things; **avoir les ~s larges** to be broad-minded; **changer d'~** to change one's mind; **avoir de la suite dans les ~s** to be single-minded; not to be easily deterred; **avoir dans l'~ de faire** to plan to do; **tu ne m'ôteras pas de l'~ que...** I still think that...; **ça ne m'est pas venu à l'~** it never occurred to me
■ **~ fixe** obsession; **~ de génie** brainwave (fam); **~ noire** dark thought; **~ reçue** received idea

idem /idɛm/ *adv* ditto

identification /idɑ̃tifikasjɔ̃/ *f* identification

identifier /idɑ̃tifje/ [**v2**] **A** *vt* to identify
B s'identifier *v refl* (+ *v être*) **1** to become identified
2 to identify

identique /idɑ̃tik/ *adj* **1** identical
2 unchanged

identité /idɑ̃tite/ *f* **1** identity; **vol d'~** identity theft
2 similarity

idéologie /ideɔlɔʒi/ *f* ideology

idiomatique /idjɔmatik/ *adj* idiomatic

idiome /idjom/ *m* idiom

idiot, **~e** /idjo, ɔt/ **A** *adj* stupid
B *m* idiot; **faire l'~** to behave like an idiot

idiotie /idjɔsi/ *f* **1** stupid thing
2 stupidity

idolâtrer /idɔlɑtʀe/ [**v1**] *vt* to idolize

idole /idɔl/ *f* idol

idylle /idil/ *f* **1** love affair
2 (in literature) idyll

idyllique /idilik/ *adj* idyllic

if /if/ *m* **1** yew (tree)
2 yew (wood)

IFOP /ifɔp/ *m* (*abbr* = **Institut français d'opinion publique**) French institute for opinion polls

ignare /iɲaʀ/ *adj* ignorant

ignifuge /iɲifyʒ/ *adj* fireproofing

ignifuger /iɲifyʒe/ [**v13**] *vt* to fireproof

ignoble /iɲɔbl/ *adj* **1** ‹*person, conduct*› vile
2 ‹*place*› squalid; ‹*food*› revolting

ignominie /iɲɔmini/ *f* **1** ignominy
2 dreadful thing

ignorance /iɲɔʀɑ̃s/ *f* ignorance

ignorant, **~e** /iɲɔʀɑ̃, ɑ̃t/ *adj* ignorant

ignoré, **~e** /iɲɔʀe/ *adj* unknown; ignored

ignorer /iɲɔʀe/ [**v1**] *vt* **1 j'ignore comment/si** I don't know how/whether; **~ tout de qch** to know nothing of *or* about sth; **~ l'existence de** to be unaware of the existence of
2 to ignore ‹*person*›

iguane /igwan/ *m* iguana

il /il/ **A** *pron m* he; it; **~s** they
B *pron impers* it; **~ pleut** it's raining

île /il/ *f* island
■ **l'~ de Beauté** Corsica

illégal, **~e**, *mpl* **-aux** /ilegal, o/ *adj* illegal

illégalité /ilegalite/ *f* illegality; **être dans l'~** to be in breach of the law

illégitime /ileʒitim/ *adj* ‹*child*› illegitimate

illégitimité /ileʒitimite/ *f* (of child) illegitimacy; (of love) illicitness

illettré, **~e** /iletʀe/ *adj*, *mf* illiterate

illicite /ilisit/ *adj* illicit; unlawful

illico /iliko/ *adv* (fam) straightaway

illimité, **~e** /ilimite/ *adj* unlimited

illisible /ilizibl/ *adj* **1** illegible
2 unreadable

illogique /ilɔʒik/ *adj* illogical

illumination /ilyminasjɔ̃/ **A** *f*
1 floodlighting
2 flash of inspiration
B illuminations *fpl* (in town) illuminations

illuminé, **~e** /ilymine/ **A** *adj*
1 ‹*monument*› floodlit
2 ‹*face*› radiant

B *mf* **1** visionary
2 crank

illuminer /ilymine/ [**v1**] **A** *vt* **1** to illuminate; to floodlight
2 ‹*smile*› to light up ‹*face*›
B **s'illuminer** *v refl* (+ *v être*) to light up

✓ **illusion** /ilyzjɔ̃/ *f* illusion; **se faire des ~s** to delude oneself; **il ne fait pas ~** he doesn't fool anyone

illusionner: **s'illusionner** /ilyzjɔne/ *v refl* (+ *v être*) to delude oneself (**sur qch/qn** about sth/sb)

illusionniste /ilyzjɔnist/ *mf* conjurer

illusoire /ilyzwaʀ/ *adj* illusory

illustrateur, **-trice** /ilystʀatœʀ, tʀis/ *mf* illustrator

illustration /ilystʀasjɔ̃/ *f* illustration

illustre /ilystʀ/ *adj* illustrious

illustré /ilystʀe/ *m* comic

illustrer /ilystʀe/ [**v1**] **A** *vt* to illustrate
B **s'illustrer** *v refl* (+ *v être*) to distinguish oneself

îlot /ilo/ *m* **1** islet
2 **~s de végétation** isolated patches of vegetation

ils ▸ **il A**

✓ **image** /imaʒ/ *f* **1** picture
2 (on film) frame
3 reflection, image
4 **à l'~ de ses prédécesseurs...** just like his/her predecessors...
5 image; **les ~s d'un poème** the imagery of a poem
■ **~ d'Épinal** *simplistic print of traditional French life*; (fig) clichéd image; **~ de marque** brand image; corporate image; (public) image

imagé, **~e** /imaʒe/ *adj* ‹*style*› colourful (BrE)

imagerie /imaʒʀi/ *f* **1** imagery
2 print trade
3 imaging

imaginable /imaʒinabl/ *adj* conceivable, imaginable

imaginaire /imaʒinɛʀ/ *adj* imaginary

imaginatif, **-ive** /imaʒinatif, iv/ *adj* imaginative

✓ **imagination** /imaʒinasjɔ̃/ *f* imagination

✓ **imaginer** /imaʒine/ [**v1**] **A** *vt* **1** to imagine, to picture
2 to suppose
3 to devise, to think up
B **s'imaginer** *v refl* (+ *v être*) **1** to imagine, to picture
2 to picture oneself; **s'~ à 60 ans** to picture oneself at 60
3 to think

imbattable /ɛ̃batabl/ *adj* unbeatable

imbécile /ɛ̃besil/ **A** *adj* idiotic
B *mf* fool; **faire l'~** to play the fool

imberbe /ɛ̃bɛʀb/ *adj* beardless

✓ key word

imbiber /ɛ̃bibe/ [**v1**] **A** *vt* to soak
B **s'imbiber** *v refl* (+ *v être*) **s'~ de** to become soaked with

imbriquer: **s'imbriquer** /ɛ̃bʀike/ [**v1**] *v refl* (+ *v être*) **1** ‹*slates*› to overlap
2 ‹*issues*› to be interlinked; ‹*parts*› to interlock

imbu, **~e** /ɛ̃by/ *adj* full; **~ de sa personne** full of oneself

imbuvable /ɛ̃byvabl/ *adj* **1** undrinkable
2 (fam) unbearable

imitateur, **-trice** /imitatœʀ, tʀis/ *mf*
1 impressionist
2 (of painting) imitator

imitation /imitasjɔ̃/ *f* imitation; (of person) impression

imiter /imite/ [**v1**] *vt* **1** to imitate; to forge ‹*signature*›
2 to do an impression of [sb]
3 **il part, je vais l'~** he's leaving and I'm going to do the same

immaculé, **~e** /imakyle/ *adj* immaculate

immangeable /ɛ̃mɑ̃ʒabl/ *adj* inedible

immanquablement /ɛ̃mɑ̃kabləmɑ̃/ *adv* inevitably

immatriculation /imatʀikylasjɔ̃/ *f* registration; **numéro d'~** registration (BrE) *or* license (AmE) number

immatriculer /imatʀikyle/ [**v1**] *vt* to register; to register (BrE) *or* license (AmE) ‹*car*›

immédiat, **~e** /imedja, at/ **A** *adj* immediate
B *m* **dans l'~** for the time being

✓ **immédiatement** /imedjatmɑ̃/ *adv* immediately

✓ **immense** /imɑ̃s/ *adj* (gen) huge; ‹*pain, regret*› immense; ‹*joy, courage*› great

immensité /imɑ̃site/ *f* (of place) immensity; (of knowledge) breadth

immerger /imɛʀʒe/ [**v13**] *vt* to immerse ‹*object*›; to bury [sth] at sea

immersion /imɛʀsjɔ̃/ *f* **1** (of body, object) immersion; (of corpse) burial at sea
2 flooding

immettable /ɛ̃metabl/ *adj* (fam) unwearable

immeuble /imœbl/ *m* **1** building
2 real asset

immigrant, **~e** /imigʀɑ̃, ɑ̃t/ *adj, mf* immigrant

immigration /imigʀasjɔ̃/ *f* immigration

immigré, **~e** /imigʀe/ *adj, mf* immigrant

immigrer /imigʀe/ [**v1**] *vi* to immigrate

imminent, **~e** /iminɑ̃, ɑ̃t/ *adj* imminent

immiscer: **s'immiscer** /imise/ [**v12**] *v refl* (+ *v être*) to interfere

immobile /imɔbil/ *adj* (gen) motionless; ‹*vehicle*› stationary; ‹*stare*› fixed

immobilier /imɔbilje/ *m* **l'~** property (BrE), real estate (AmE)

immobiliser /imɔbilize/ [**v1**] **A** *vt* **1** to bring [sth] to a standstill ‹*vehicle*›; to stop ‹*machine*›
2 to immobilize ‹*person*›
3 to tie up ‹*capital*›
B **s'immobiliser** *v refl* (+ *v être*) to come to a halt; to stop

immobilisme /imɔbilism/ *m* opposition to change

immobilité /imɔbilite/ *f* **1** immobility
2 stillness

immodéré, **~e** /imɔdeʀe/ *adj* **1** excessive
2 immoderate

immoler /imɔle/ [**v1**] *vt* to sacrifice (**à** to)

immonde /imɔ̃d/ *adj* **1** filthy
2 revolting

immondices /imɔ̃dis/ *fpl* refuse (BrE), trash (AmE)

immoral, **~e**, *mpl* **-aux** /imɔʀal, o/ *adj* immoral

immortaliser /imɔʀtalize/ [**v1**] *vt* to immortalize

immortel, **-elle** /imɔʀtɛl/ *adj* immortal

immortelle /imɔʀtɛl/ *f* everlasting (flower)

immuable /imɥabl/ *adj* **1** immutable
2 unchanging
3 perpetual

immuniser /imynize/ [**v1**] *vt* to immunize

immunitaire /imynitɛʀ/ *adj* (Med) immune

immunité /imynite/ *f* immunity

impact /ɛ̃pakt/ *m* impact; mark

impair, **~e** /ɛ̃pɛʀ/ **A** *adj* ‹*number*› odd; ‹*day, year*› odd-numbered
B *m* indiscretion, faux pas

imparable /ɛ̃paʀabl/ *adj* **1** unstoppable
2 unanswerable
3 irrefutable

impardonnable /ɛ̃paʀdɔnabl/ *adj* unforgivable

imparfait, **~e** /ɛ̃paʀfɛ, ɛt/ **A** *adj* imperfect
B *m* **l'~** the imperfect (tense)

impartial, **~e**, *mpl* **-iaux** /ɛ̃paʀsjal, o/ *adj* impartial

impartir /ɛ̃paʀtiʀ/ [**v3**] *vt* to give; **dans les temps impartis** within the given time

impasse /ɛ̃pas/ *f* **1** dead end
2 deadlock

impassible /ɛ̃pasibl/ *adj* impassive

impatience /ɛ̃pasjɑ̃s/ *f* impatience

impatient, **~e** /ɛ̃pasjɑ̃, ɑ̃t/ *adj* impatient

impatienter /ɛ̃pasjɑ̃te/ [**v1**] **A** *vt* to irritate
B **s'impatienter** *v refl* (+ *v être*) to get impatient

impayable /ɛ̃pɛjabl/ *adj* (fam) priceless

impayé, **~e** /ɛ̃peje/ *adj* unpaid

impeccable /ɛ̃pekabl/ *adj* perfect; impeccable; spotless

impénétrable /ɛ̃penetʀabl/ *adj*
1 impenetrable
2 inscrutable

impénitent, **~e** /ɛ̃penitɑ̃, ɑ̃t/ *adj* ‹*drinker*› inveterate; ‹*bachelor*› confirmed

impensable /ɛ̃pɑ̃sabl/ *adj* unthinkable

imper /ɛ̃pɛʀ/ *m* (fam) raincoat, mac (BrE) (fam)

impératif, **-ive** /ɛ̃peʀatif, iv/ **A** *adj* imperative
B *m* **1** (of situation) imperative; (for quality) necessity
2 (in grammar) imperative

impératrice /ɛ̃peʀatʀis/ *f* empress

imperceptible /ɛ̃pɛʀsɛptibl/ *adj* imperceptible

imperfection /ɛ̃pɛʀfɛksjɔ̃/ *f* imperfection

impérial, **~e** *mpl* **-iaux** /ɛ̃peʀjal, o/ *adj* imperial

impériale /ɛ̃peʀjal/ *f* **autobus à ~** double-decker bus

impérialisme /ɛ̃peʀjalism/ *m* imperialism

impérieux, **-ieuse** /ɛ̃peʀjø, øz/ *adj*
1 imperious
2 pressing

impérissable /ɛ̃peʀisabl/ *adj* imperishable

imperméable /ɛ̃pɛʀmeabl/ **A** *adj*
1 ‹*material*› waterproof; ‹*ground*› impermeable
2 impervious
B *m* raincoat

impertinence /ɛ̃pɛʀtinɑ̃s/ *f* **1** impertinence
2 impertinent remark

impertinent, **~e** /ɛ̃pɛʀtinɑ̃, ɑ̃t/ *adj* impertinent

imperturbable /ɛ̃pɛʀtyʀbabl/ *adj* imperturbable; unruffled

imperturbablement /ɛ̃pɛʀtyʀbabləmɑ̃/ *adv* ‹*continue, listen*› unperturbed

impétueux, **-euse** /ɛ̃petɥø, øz/ *adj* (gen) impetuous; ‹*torrent*› raging

impie /ɛ̃pi/ *adj* impious

impitoyable /ɛ̃pitwajabl/ *adj* merciless, pitiless; relentless; ruthless

implacable /ɛ̃plakabl/ *adj* implacable; tough; harsh

implacablement /ɛ̃plakabləmɑ̃/ *adv* relentlessly; ruthlessly

implantation /ɛ̃plɑ̃tasjɔ̃/ *f* establishment; setting up; installation; settlement

implanté, **~e** /ɛ̃plɑ̃te/ *adj* **1** ‹*factory, party*› established; ‹*population*› settled
2 ‹*roots*› established; **dents mal ~es** crooked teeth

implanter /ɛ̃plɑ̃te/ [**v1**] **A** *vt* **1** to establish ‹*factory*›; to build ‹*supermarket*›; to open ‹*agency*›; to introduce ‹*product, fashion*›; to instil (BrE) ‹*ideas*›
2 (Med) to implant
B **s'implanter** *v refl* (+ *v être*) ‹*company, product*› to establish itself; ‹*factory*› to be built; ‹*person*› to settle; ‹*party*› to gain a following

implication /ɛ̃plikasjɔ̃/ *f* **1** involvement

2 implication
3 commitment

implicite /ɛ̃plisit/ *adj* implicit

implicitement /ɛ̃plisitmɑ̃/ *adv* implicitly; (Comput) by default

⚷ **impliquer** /ɛ̃plike/ [**v1**] *vt* **1** to implicate
2 to involve ‹*staff*›
3 to involve (**de faire** doing)
4 to mean

implorer /ɛ̃plɔʀe/ [**v1**] *vt* **1** to beseech, to implore
2 to beg for

imploser /ɛ̃ploze/ [**v1**] *vi* to implode

impoli, **~e** /ɛ̃pɔli/ *adj* rude, impolite

impolitesse /ɛ̃pɔlitɛs/ *f* rudeness

impondérable /ɛ̃pɔ̃deʀabl/ *m* imponderable

impopulaire /ɛ̃pɔpylɛʀ/ *adj* unpopular

⚷ **importance** /ɛ̃pɔʀtɑ̃s/ *f* **1** importance; **quelle ~?** what does it matter?
2 size; (of damage) extent; **prendre de l'~** to increase in size
3 **prendre de l'~** ‹*person*› to become more important

⚷ **important**, **~e** /ɛ̃pɔʀtɑ̃, ɑ̃t/ **A** *adj*
1 important
2 significant; considerable; sizeable; large; lengthy
3 **prendre un air ~** to adopt a self-important manner
B *mf* **jouer les ~s** to act important (fam)

importateur, **-trice** /ɛ̃pɔʀtatœʀ, tʀis/ **A** *adj* importing
B *mf* importer

importation /ɛ̃pɔʀtasjɔ̃/ *f* **1** importation
2 import

⚷ **importer** /ɛ̃pɔʀte/ [**v1**] **A** *vt* to import
B *v impers* **peu importe** *or* **qu'importe que...** it doesn't matter *or* what does it matter if...; **n'importe quel enfant** any child; **n'importe qui** anybody, anyone; **n'importe lequel** any; **n'importe où** anywhere; **prends n'importe quoi** take anything; **elle dit n'importe quoi** she talks nonsense

importun, **~e** /ɛ̃pɔʀtœ̃, yn/ **A** *adj*
1 troublesome; tiresome; **visiteur ~** unwelcome visitor
2 ‹*visit*› ill-timed; ‹*remark*› ill-chosen
B *mf* unwelcome visitor; tiresome individual

importuner /ɛ̃pɔʀtyne/ [**v1**] *vt* **1** to bother
2 to disturb

imposable /ɛ̃pozabl/ *adj* ‹*person*› liable to tax; ‹*income*› taxable

imposant, **~e** /ɛ̃pozɑ̃, ɑ̃t/ *adj* imposing

⚷ **imposer** /ɛ̃poze/ [**v1**] **A** *vt* **1** ‹*person*› to impose ‹*sanctions, deadline*›; to lay down ‹*rule*›; **elle nous a imposé le silence** she made us be quiet
2 to impose ‹*idea, opinion*›; to set ‹*fashion*›
3 to command ‹*respect*›
4 to tax
B **en imposer** *v+prep* **elle en impose à ses élèves** she inspires respect in her pupils
C **s'imposer** *v refl* (+ *v être*) **1** ‹*choice, solution*› to be obvious; ‹*change*› to be called for; **une visite au Louvre s'impose** a visit to the Louvre is a must
2 to impose [sth] on oneself; **s'~ de travailler le soir** to make it a rule to work in the evening
3 to impose (**à qn** on sb)
4 **s'~ comme leader** to establish oneself/itself as the leader; **s'~ sur un marché** to establish itself in a market
5 ‹*person*› to make one's presence felt; ‹*will*› to impose itself

imposition /ɛ̃pozisjɔ̃/ *f* taxation

impossibilité /ɛ̃pɔsibilite/ *f* impossibility; **être dans l'~ de faire** to be unable to do

⚷ **impossible** /ɛ̃pɔsibl/ **A** *adj* impossible
B *m* **l'~** the impossible; **faire** *or* **tenter l'~** to do everything one can

imposteur /ɛ̃pɔstœʀ/ *m* impostor

imposture /ɛ̃pɔstyʀ/ *f* **1** deception
2 fraud

impôt /ɛ̃po/ *m* tax; **après ~** after tax
■ **~ sur le revenu** income tax

impotent, **~e** /ɛ̃pɔtɑ̃, ɑ̃t/ **A** *adj* infirm
B *mf* person with impaired mobility

impraticable /ɛ̃pʀatikabl/ *adj* impassable

imprécis, **~e** /ɛ̃pʀesi, iz/ *adj* ‹*outline, memory*› vague; ‹*concept*› hazy; ‹*aim*› inaccurate; ‹*results*› imprecise; ‹*person*› vague

imprécision /ɛ̃pʀesizjɔ̃/ *f* imprecision; vagueness; inaccuracy

imprégner /ɛ̃pʀeɲe/ [**v14**] **A** *vt* to impregnate
B **s'imprégner** *v refl* (+ *v être*) **s'~ de** to become soaked with ‹*water*›; to immerse oneself in ‹*language*›

imprenable /ɛ̃pʀənabl/ *adj* **avec vue ~** with unobstructed view guaranteed

imprésario /ɛ̃pʀesaʀjo/ *m* agent, impresario

⚷ **impression** /ɛ̃pʀesjɔ̃/ *f* **1** impression; **faire bonne ~** to make a good impression; **j'ai l'~ d'être surveillé** I feel I am being watched
2 printing; **faute d'~** misprint
3 pattern

impressionnant, **~e** /ɛ̃pʀesjɔnɑ̃, ɑ̃t/ *adj*
1 impressive
2 disturbing

impressionner /ɛ̃pʀesjɔne/ [**v1**] *vt* **1** to impress
2 ‹*image*› to disturb
3 to act on ‹*retina*›

impressionnisme /ɛ̃pʀesjɔnism/ *m* Impressionism

impressionniste /ɛ̃pʀesjɔnist/ *mf* Impressionist

⚷ key word

imprévisible /ɛ̃pʀevizibl/ *adj* unpredictable

imprévu, **~e** /ɛ̃pʀevy/ **A** *adj* **1** unforeseen
2 unexpected
B *m* **1** hitch
2 l'~ the unexpected; **plein d'~** ‹*person, film*› quirky; ‹*trip*› with a few surprises
3 unforeseen expense

imprimante /ɛ̃pʀimɑ̃t/ *f* printer
■ **~ à jet d'encre** ink-jet printer; **~ (à) laser** laser printer; **~ à marguerite** daisy-wheel printer; **~ matricielle** dot matrix printer

imprimé, **~e** /ɛ̃pʀime/ **A** *pp* ▸ **imprimer**
B *pp adj* printed (**de** with)
C *m* **1** form
2 printed matter
3 print; **un ~ à fleurs** a floral print

imprimer /ɛ̃pʀime/ [**v1**] *vt* **1** to print ‹*text*›
2 to put ‹*stamp, seal*›
3 to leave an imprint of [sth]

imprimerie /ɛ̃pʀimʀi/ *f* **1** printing; **atelier d'~** printing shop
2 printing works
3 printers, print workers

imprimeur /ɛ̃pʀimœʀ/ *m* printer

improbable /ɛ̃pʀɔbabl/ *adj* unlikely

improductif, **-ive** /ɛ̃pʀɔdyktif, iv/ *adj* unproductive; **capitaux ~s** idle capital

impromptu, **~e** /ɛ̃pʀɔ̃pty/ **A** *adj* impromptu
B *adv* impromptu

impropre /ɛ̃pʀɔpʀ/ *adj* ‹*term, usage*› incorrect; **~ à** unfit for ‹*human consumption*›

improvisation /ɛ̃pʀɔvizasjɔ̃/ *f* improvisation

improvisé, **~e** /ɛ̃pʀɔvize/ *adj* ‹*speech*› improvised; ‹*meal*› impromptu; ‹*means*› makeshift; ‹*solution*› ad hoc; ‹*cook*› stand-in

improviser /ɛ̃pʀɔvize/ [**v1**] **A** *vt* to improvise ‹*meal, speech*›; to concoct ‹*excuse, alibi*›
B *vi* to improvise
C s'improviser *v refl* (+ *v être*) **1 s'~ cuisinier** to act as a cook
2 un camp pour réfugiés ne s'improvise pas you can't create a refugee camp just like that

improviste: **à l'improviste** /alɛ̃pʀɔvist/ *phr* unexpectedly

imprudemment /ɛ̃pʀydamɑ̃/ *adv* ‹*speak*› carelessly; ‹*act*› unwisely

imprudence /ɛ̃pʀydɑ̃s/ *f* **1** carelessness
2 commettre une ~ to do something foolish

imprudent, **~e** /ɛ̃pʀydɑ̃, ɑ̃t/ *adj* ‹*person, words*› careless; ‹*action*› rash

impudence /ɛ̃pydɑ̃s/ *f* impudence

impudent, **~e** /ɛ̃pydɑ̃, ɑ̃t/ *adj* impudent

impudeur /ɛ̃pydœʀ/ *f* immodesty; shamelessness

impuissance /ɛ̃pɥisɑ̃s/ *f* (gen), (Med) impotence; **~ à faire** inability to do

impuissant, **~e** /ɛ̃pɥisɑ̃, ɑ̃t/ *adj*
1 powerless, helpless
2 (Med) impotent

impulsif, **-ive** /ɛ̃pylsif, iv/ *adj* impulsive

impulsion /ɛ̃pylsjɔ̃/ *f* **1** (gen) impulse; (Tech) pulse
2 (fig) impetus

impunément /ɛ̃pynemɑ̃/ *adv* with impunity; **on ne joue pas ~ avec sa santé** you don't play fast and loose with your health and get away with it

impuni, **~e** /ɛ̃pyni/ *adj* unpunished

impunité /ɛ̃pynite/ *f* impunity

impur, **~e** /ɛ̃pyʀ/ *adj* **1** ‹*thoughts*› impure
2 ‹*air*› dirty; ‹*blood*› tainted
3 ‹*ore*› impure

impureté /ɛ̃pyʀte/ *f* impurity

imputable /ɛ̃pytabl/ *adj* **1** attributable (**à** to)
2 chargeable (**sur** to)

imputer /ɛ̃pyte/ [**v1**] *vt* to attribute, to impute

inabordable /inabɔʀdabl/ *adj* **1** ‹*coast*› inaccessible
2 ‹*prices*› prohibitive

inacceptable /inakseptabl/ *adj* unacceptable

inaccessible /inaksesibl/ *adj* **1** inaccessible
2 ‹*person*› unapproachable

inaccoutumé /inakutyme/ *adj* unusual

inachevé, **~e** /inaʃve/ *adj* unfinished

inactif, **-ive** /inaktif, iv/ **A** *adj*, idle; ‹*person*› inactive; ‹*population*› non-working
B *mf* non-worker; **les ~s** the non-working population

inactivité /inaktivite/ *f* inactivity

inadaptation /inadaptasjɔ̃/ *f* **1** (of law, equipment) inappropriateness (**à** for)
2 (emotional, social) maladjustment (**à** to)

inadapté, **~e** /inadapte/ *adj* **1** ‹*child*› maladjusted
2 ‹*means*› inappropriate; ‹*tool*› unsuitable; ‹*law*› ill-adapted

inadéquat, **~e** /inadekwa, at/ *adj* inadequate; unsuitable

inadmissible /inadmisibl/ *adj* **1** intolerable
2 unacceptable

inadvertance: **par inadvertance** /paʀinadvɛʀtɑ̃s/ *phr* inadvertently

inaltérable /inalteʀabl/ *adj* **1** ‹*substance*› unalterable, non-corroding; ‹*colour*› fade-resistant
2 ‹*character*› constant; ‹*principle*› immutable; ‹*hope*› steadfast

inaltéré, **~e** /inalteʀe/ *adj* ‹*substance*› unaltered; ‹*sky, air*› pure

inamovible /inamɔvibl/ *adj* irremovable

inanimé, **~e** /inanime/ *adj* ‹*matter*› inanimate; ‹*person*› unconscious; lifeless

inanition /inanisjɔ̃/ *f* starvation

inaperçu, **~e** /inapɛʀsy/ *adj* **passer ~** to go unnoticed
inapte /inapt/ *adj* unfit
inaptitude /inaptityd/ *f* unfitness
inarticulé, **~e** /inaʀtikyle/ *adj* inarticulate
inassouvi, **~e** /inasuvi/ *adj* ‹*appetite*› insatiable; ‹*person, desire*› unsatisfied
inattaquable /inatakabl/ *adj* **1** (Mil) unassailable
2 irreproachable
3 irrefutable
inattendu, **~e** /inatɑ̃dy/ *adj* unexpected
inattentif, **-ive** /inatɑ̃tif, iv/ *adj*
1 inattentive; distracted
2 heedless
inattention /inatɑ̃sjɔ̃/ *f* inattention; **faute d'~** careless mistake
inaudible /inodibl/ *adj* inaudible
inaugural, **~e**, *mpl* **-aux** /inogyʀal, o/ *adj*
1 ‹*ceremony*› inauguration
2 ‹*flight*› maiden
inauguration /inogyʀasjɔ̃/ *f* (of building) inauguration; (of exhibition) opening
inaugurer /inogyʀe/ [**v1**] *vt* **1** to unveil ‹*statue, plaque*›; to open ‹*motorway, school*›
2 to open ‹*conference*›
3 to mark the start of ‹*period*›
inavouable /inavwabl/ *adj* shameful
inavoué, **~e** /inavwe/ *adj* ‹*crime, vice*› unconfessed; ‹*aim*› undisclosed; ‹*fear*› hidden
incalculable /ɛ̃kalkylabl/ *adj*
1 innumerable
2 incalculable
incandescent, **~e** /ɛ̃kɑ̃dɛsɑ̃, ɑ̃t/ *adj* incandescent; white-hot; glowing
⚷ **incapable** /ɛ̃kapabl/ *adj* **1 ~ de faire** incapable of doing; unable to do
2 incompetent
incapacité /ɛ̃kapasite/ *f* **1** inability; **être dans l'~ de faire** to be unable to do
2 incompetence
3 disability
4 (Law) incapacity
incarcération /ɛ̃kaʀseʀasjɔ̃/ *f* imprisonment
incarcérer /ɛ̃kaʀseʀe/ [**v14**] *vt* to imprison
incarnation /ɛ̃kaʀnasjɔ̃/ *f* incarnation
incarné, **~e** /ɛ̃kaʀne/ *adj* **1 c'est la bêtise ~e** he/she is stupidity itself
2 ‹*nail*› ingrowing
incarner /ɛ̃kaʀne/ [**v1**] **A** *vt* **1** to embody
2 to play, to portray
B s'incarner *v refl* (+ *v être*) to become incarnate
incartade /ɛ̃kaʀtad/ *f* **1** misdemeanour (BrE)
2 (in riding) shy; **faire une ~** to shy
incassable /ɛ̃kasabl/ *adj* unbreakable
incendiaire /ɛ̃sɑ̃djɛʀ/ **A** *adj* **1** ‹*bomb*› incendiary
2 ‹*statement*› inflammatory
B *mf* arsonist
incendie /ɛ̃sɑ̃di/ *m* fire; **~ criminel** arson
incendier /ɛ̃sɑ̃dje/ [**v2**] *vt* **1** to burn (down), to torch
2 (fam) to haul [sb] over the coals
incertain, **~e** /ɛ̃sɛʀtɛ̃, ɛn/ *adj* ‹*person, date, result*› uncertain; ‹*effect*› unknown; ‹*colour*› indeterminate; ‹*smile*› vague; ‹*weather*› unsettle; ‹*step*› hesitant
incertitude /ɛ̃sɛʀtityd/ *f* uncertainty
incessamment /ɛ̃sesamɑ̃/ *adv* very shortly
incessant, **~e** /ɛ̃sɛsɑ̃, ɑ̃t/ *adj* ‹*noise, rain*› incessant; ‹*activity*› unceasing
inceste /ɛ̃sɛst/ *m* incest
incestueux, **-euse** /ɛ̃sɛstɥø, øz/ *adj* incestuous
inchangé, **~e** /ɛ̃ʃɑ̃ʒe/ *adj* unchanged
incidemment /ɛ̃sidamɑ̃/ *adv* **1** in passing
2 by chance
incidence /ɛ̃sidɑ̃s/ *f* **1** impact
2 incidence
incident, **~e** /ɛ̃sidɑ̃, ɑ̃t/ *m* incident; **~ de parcours** hitch; **l'~ est clos** the matter is closed
incinérateur /ɛ̃sineʀatœʀ/ *m* **1** incinerator
2 crematorium (BrE), crematory (AmE)
incinération /ɛ̃sineʀasjɔ̃/ *f* **1** incineration
2 cremation
incinérer /ɛ̃sineʀe/ [**v14**] *vt* **1** to burn; to incinerate
2 to cremate
inciser /ɛ̃size/ [**v1**] *vt* to make an incision in
incisif, **-ive** /ɛ̃sizif, iv/ *adj* ‹*criticism*› incisive; ‹*portrait*› telling; ‹*look*› piercing
incision /ɛ̃sizjɔ̃/ *f* incision
incisive /ɛ̃siziv/ **A** *adj f* ▶ **incisif**
B *f* incisor
incitation /ɛ̃sitasjɔ̃/ *f* **1** incentive
2 (Law) incitement
inciter /ɛ̃site/ [**v1**] *vt* ‹*person, situation*› to encourage; ‹*event, decision*› to prompt; **~ qn à la prudence** to make sb cautious
inclassable /ɛ̃klasabl/ *adj* unclassifiable
inclinable /ɛ̃klinabl/ *adj* adjustable
inclinaison /ɛ̃klinɛzɔ̃/ *f* (of hill) incline; (of wall, seat) angle; (of roof) slope; (of boat) list
inclination /ɛ̃klinasjɔ̃/ *f* inclination
incliné, **~e** /ɛ̃kline/ *adj* **1** ‹*ground*› sloping; ‹*roof*› steep
2 ‹*wall*› leaning
incliner /ɛ̃kline/ [**v1**] **A** *vt* to tilt ‹*sunshade*›; to tip up ‹*bottle*›; **~ le buste** to lean forward
B s'incliner *v refl* (+ *v être*) **1** to lean forward; (politely) to bow
2 s'~ devant qch to bow to sth, to accept sth
3 to give in (fam)
4 s'~ devant le courage de qn to admire sb's courage
inclure /ɛ̃klyʀ/ [**v78**] *vt* **1** to include

⚷ key word

2 to enclose

inclus, **~e** /ɛ̃kly, yz/ **A** *pp* ▶ **inclure**
B *pp adj* **1 jusqu'à jeudi ~** up to and including Thursday (BrE), through Thursday (AmE)
2 enclosed

inclusion /ɛ̃klyzjɔ̃/ *f* inclusion

inclusivement /ɛ̃klyzivmɑ̃/ *adv* **jusqu'au 4 mai ~** till 4 May inclusive

incognito /ɛ̃kɔɲito/ **A** *adv* incognito
B *m* **garder l'~** to remain incognito

incohérence /ɛ̃kɔeʀɑ̃s/ *f* **1** incoherence
2 discrepancy

incohérent, **~e** /ɛ̃kɔeʀɑ̃, ɑ̃t/ *adj* ‹*talk, behaviour*› incoherent; ‹*attitude*› illogical

incollable /ɛ̃kɔlabl/ *adj* **1 elle est ~ en latin** you can't catch her out in Latin
2 riz ~ easy-cook rice

incolore /ɛ̃kɔlɔʀ/ *adj* colourless (BrE); ‹*glass*› clear

incomber /ɛ̃kɔ̃be/ [**v1**] *v+prep* **~ à** ‹*task*› to fall to; ‹*responsibility*› to lie with

incommode /ɛ̃kɔmɔd/ *adj* **1** inconvenient; awkward
2 uncomfortable

incommodé, **~e** /ɛ̃kɔmɔde/ **A** *pp* ▶ **incommoder**
B *pp adj* unwell, indisposed

incommoder /ɛ̃kɔmɔde/ [**v1**] *vt* to bother

incomparable /ɛ̃kɔ̃paʀabl/ *adj* incomparable

incompatible /ɛ̃kɔ̃patibl/ *adj* incompatible

incompétence /ɛ̃kɔ̃petɑ̃s/ *f* (gen) incompetence; (Law) incompetency

incompétent, **~e** /ɛ̃kɔ̃petɑ̃, ɑ̃t/ *adj* incompetent

incomplet, **-ète** /ɛ̃kɔ̃plɛ, ɛt/ *adj* incomplete

incompréhensible /ɛ̃kɔ̃pʀeɑ̃sibl/ *adj* incomprehensible

incompréhension /ɛ̃kɔ̃pʀeɑ̃sjɔ̃/ *f*
1 incomprehension
2 lack of understanding

incompressible /ɛ̃kɔ̃pʀɛsibl/ *adj*
1 incompressible
2 ‹*costs*› fixed

incompris, **~e** /ɛ̃kɔ̃pʀi, iz/ *mf* misunderstood person

inconcevable /ɛ̃kɔ̃svabl/ *adj* inconceivable

inconditionnel, **-elle** /ɛ̃kɔ̃disjɔnɛl/ **A** *adj* unconditional
B *mf* devoted admirer; fan

inconfortable /ɛ̃kɔ̃fɔʀtabl/ *adj*
1 uncomfortable
2 awkward

incongru, **~e** /ɛ̃kɔ̃gʀy/ *adj* ‹*behaviour*› unseemly; ‹*remark*› incongruous

incongruité /ɛ̃kɔ̃gʀɥite/ *f* incongruity

inconnu, **~e** /ɛ̃kɔny/ **A** *adj* unknown; ‹*territories*› unexplored
B *mf* **1** unknown (person)
2 stranger

inconsciemment /ɛ̃kɔ̃sjamɑ̃/ *adv*
1 subconsciously
2 unintentionally, unconsciously

inconscience /ɛ̃kɔ̃sjɑ̃s/ *f* **1** recklessness
2 (Med) unconsciousness

inconscient, **~e** /ɛ̃kɔ̃sjɑ̃, ɑ̃t/ **A** *adj*
1 unthinking; foolhardy
2 (Med) unconscious
3 ‹*act, gesture*› unconscious, automatic
B *mf* **c'est un ~** he's irresponsible
C *m* **l'~** the unconscious

inconséquent, **~e** /ɛ̃kɔ̃sekɑ̃, ɑ̃t/ *adj* ‹*person, behaviour*› inconsistent

inconsidéré, **~e** /ɛ̃kɔ̃sideʀe/ *adj* **1** ‹*remark, act*› ill-considered
2 ‹*consumption*› excessive

inconsidérément /ɛ̃kɔ̃sideʀemɑ̃/ *adv* ‹*drink*› to excess; ‹*spend*› wildly

inconsistant, **~e** /ɛ̃kɔ̃sistɑ̃, ɑ̃t/ *adj* ‹*argument, plot*› flimsy; ‹*programme*› lacking in substance; ‹*person*› characterless

inconstant, **~e** /ɛ̃kɔ̃stɑ̃, ɑ̃t/ *adj* fickle

incontestable /ɛ̃kɔ̃tɛstabl/ *adj* unquestionable, indisputable

incontesté, **~e** /ɛ̃kɔ̃tɛste/ *adj* ‹*victory*› undisputed; ‹*fact*› uncontested

incontinent, **~e** /ɛ̃kɔ̃tinɑ̃, ɑ̃t/ *adj* incontinent

incontournable /ɛ̃kɔ̃tuʀnabl/ *adj* ‹*facts*› that cannot be ignored

incontrôlable /ɛ̃kɔ̃tʀolabl/ *adj*
1 unverifiable
2 uncontrollable

inconvenance /ɛ̃kɔ̃vnɑ̃s/ *f* impropriety

inconvenant, **~e** /ɛ̃kɔ̃vnɑ̃, ɑ̃t/ *adj* unsuitable; improper, unseemly

inconvénient /ɛ̃kɔ̃venjɑ̃/ *m* drawback, disadvantage; **si vous n'y voyez pas d'~** if you have no objection

incorporer /ɛ̃kɔʀpɔʀe/ [**v1**] *vt* **1** (Culin) to blend
2 to incorporate

incorrect, **~e** /ɛ̃kɔʀɛkt/ *adj* **1** incorrect; faulty; inaccurate
2 ‹*behaviour*› improper; ‹*term*› unsuitable; ‹*person*› impolite
3 unfair

incorrection /ɛ̃kɔʀɛksjɔ̃/ *f* (of style, language) incorrectness; (of behaviour) impropriety

incorrigible /ɛ̃kɔʀiʒibl/ *adj* incorrigible

incrédule /ɛ̃kʀedyl/ *adj* incredulous

incrédulité /ɛ̃kʀedylite/ *f* incredulity

incriminer /ɛ̃kʀimine/ [**v1**] *vt* ‹*person*› to accuse; ‹*evidence*› to incriminate; **l'article incriminé** the offending article

incroyable /ɛ̃kʀwajabl/ *adj* incredible, unbelievable; **~ mais vrai** strange but true

incrustation /ɛ̃kʀystasjɔ̃/ *f* **1** inlaying
2 inlay
3 encrustation

incruster /ɛ̃kʀyste/ [**v1**] **A** *vt* **1** to inlay

2 incrusté de diamants encrusted with diamonds
B s'incruster *v refl* (+ *v être*) ‹*pebble, shell*› to become embedded
incubation /ɛ̃kybasjɔ̃/ *f* incubation
incuber /ɛ̃kybe/ [**v1**] *vt* to incubate, to hatch
inculpation /ɛ̃kylpasjɔ̃/ *f* (Law) charge
inculpé, **~e** /ɛ̃kylpe/ *mf* **l'~** ≈ the accused
inculper /ɛ̃kylpe/ [**v1**] *vt* (Law) to charge
inculquer /ɛ̃kylke/ [**v1**] *vt* to inculcate
inculte /ɛ̃kylt/ *adj* uncultivated
incurable /ɛ̃kyʀabl/ *adj*, *mf* incurable
incursion /ɛ̃kyʀsjɔ̃/ *f* incursion, foray
incurver /ɛ̃kyʀve/ [**v1**] *vt*, **s'incurver** *v refl* (+ *v être*) to curve, to bend
Inde /ɛ̃d/ *pr f* India
indécence /ɛ̃desɑ̃s/ *f* (gen) indecency; (of remark) impropriety
indécent, **~e** /ɛ̃desɑ̃, ɑ̃t/ *adj* indecent; ‹*luxury*› obscene
indéchiffrable /ɛ̃deʃifʀabl/ *adj*
1 indecipherable
2 ‹*mystery*› incomprehensible
indécis, **~e** /ɛ̃desi, iz/ **A** *adj* **1 il est encore ~** he hasn't decided yet
2 indecisive
B *mf* **1** indecisive person
2 (in opinion poll) 'don't know'; (in election) floating voter
indécision /ɛ̃desizjɔ̃/ *f* **1** indecision, uncertainty
2 indecisiveness
indécrottable /ɛ̃dekʀɔtabl/ *adj* (fam) hopeless (fam)
indéfini, **~e** /ɛ̃defini/ *adj* **1** ‹*number*› indeterminate
2 ‹*sadness*› undefined; ‹*duration*› indefinite
3 (in grammar) indefinite
indéfiniment /ɛ̃definimɑ̃/ *adv* indefinitely
indéfinissable /ɛ̃definisabl/ *adj* undefinable
indélébile /ɛ̃delebil/ *adj* indelible
indélicatesse /ɛ̃delikatɛs/ *f* **1** indelicacy, tactlessness
2 dishonesty
3 act of dishonesty
indemne /ɛ̃dɛmn/ *adj* unscathed, unharmed
indemnisation /ɛ̃dɛmnizasjɔ̃/ *f*
1 indemnification
2 indemnity, compensation
indemniser /ɛ̃dɛmnize/ [**v1**] *vt* to indemnify
indemnité /ɛ̃dɛmnite/ *f* **1** (Law) indemnity, compensation
2 allowance
■ **~ de chômage** unemployment benefit; **~ journalière** sick pay; **~ de licenciement** severance pay
indéniable /ɛ̃denjabl/ *adj* undeniable
indentation /ɛ̃dɑ̃tasjɔ̃/ *f* indentation

indépendamment /ɛ̃depɑ̃damɑ̃/ **A** *adv* independently
B indépendamment de *phr*
1 regardless of
2 in addition to
indépendance /ɛ̃depɑ̃dɑ̃s/ *f* independence
indépendant, **~e** /ɛ̃depɑ̃dɑ̃, ɑ̃t/ **A** *adj*
1 independent
2 ‹*room*› separate; **maison ~e** detached house
B *mf* freelance, self-employed person
indépendantiste /ɛ̃depɑ̃dɑ̃tist/ **A** *adj* ‹*organization*› (pro-)independence
B *mf* **1** freedom fighter
2 member of an independence movement
indescriptible /ɛ̃dɛskʀiptibl/ *adj* indescribable
indésirable /ɛ̃deziʀabl/ *adj* ‹*person*› undesirable; **effets ~s** (Med) adverse reactions
indéterminé, **~e** /ɛ̃detɛʀmine/ *adj* ‹*form, quantity*› indeterminate; ‹*reason*› unspecified
index /ɛ̃dɛks/ *m inv* **1** index; **mettre qn/qch à l'~** to blacklist sb/sth
2 forefinger
indexer /ɛ̃dɛkse/ [**v1**] *vt* **1** to index-link; **~ qch sur qch** to index sth to sth
2 to index
indicateur, **-trice** /ɛ̃dikatœʀ, tʀis/ **A** *adj* **panneau** *or* **poteau ~** signpost
B *m* **1** informer
2 indicator
3 gauge, indicator
indicatif, **-ive** /ɛ̃dikatif, iv/ **A** *adj* indicative
B *m* **1** (in grammar) indicative
2 ~ (téléphonique) dialling (BrE) code
3 theme tune
indication /ɛ̃dikasjɔ̃/ *f* **1** indication
2 information; **sauf ~ contraire** unless otherwise indicated
3 (for use) instruction
4 indication, clue
indice /ɛ̃dis/ *m* **1** sign, indication
2 (in inquiry) clue
3 (Econ) index; **~ du coût de la vie** cost of living index
4 l'~ d'écoute audience ratings
■ **~ de masse corporel** body mass index
indicible /ɛ̃disibl/ *adj* inexpressible
⚷ **indien**, **-ienne** /ɛ̃djɛ̃, ɛn/ *adj* **1** Indian
2 (North American) Indian
indifféremment /ɛ̃difeʀamɑ̃/ *adv*
1 equally
2 servir ~ de salon ou de bureau to be used either as a living room or a study
indifférence /ɛ̃difeʀɑ̃s/ *f* indifference
indifférent, **~e** /ɛ̃difeʀɑ̃, ɑ̃t/ *adj*
1 indifferent
2 irrelevant
indifférer /ɛ̃difeʀe/ [**v14**] *vt* to leave [sb] indifferent

⚷ key word

indigence /ɛ̃diʒɑ̃s/ *f* destitution, extreme poverty

indigène /ɛ̃diʒɛn/ **A** *adj* **1** ‹*fauna, flora*› indigenous
2 ‹*population, custom*› local; native
B *mf* local; native

indigeste /ɛ̃diʒɛst/ *adj* indigestible

indigestion /ɛ̃diʒɛstjɔ̃/ *f* **1** indigestion
2 avoir une ~ de qch to be fed up with sth (fam)

indignation /ɛ̃diɲasjɔ̃/ *f* indignation

indigne /ɛ̃diɲ/ *adj* **1** ‹*conduct*› disgraceful; ‹*mother, son*› bad
2 ~ de qn unworthy of sb

indigné, **~e** /ɛ̃diɲe/ *adj* indignant

indigner /ɛ̃diɲe/ [**v1**] **A** *vt* to make [sb] indignant, to outrage [sb]
B s'indigner *v refl* (+ *v être*) to be indignant

indignité /ɛ̃diɲite/ *f* **1** despicableness
2 despicable act, disgraceful act

indigo /ɛ̃digo/ *adj inv*, *m* indigo

indiqué, **~e** /ɛ̃dike/ **A** *pp* ▶ **indiquer**
B *pp adj* **1** ‹*treatment*› recommended
2 à l'heure ~e at the specified time; **le village est très mal ~** the village is very badly signposted

indiquer /ɛ̃dike/ [**v1**] *vt* **1** ‹*person*› to point out, to point to; ‹*signpost*› to show the way to; **pouvez-vous m'~ la banque la plus proche?** can you tell me where the nearest bank is?
2 to indicate (**que** that)
3 je peux t'~ un bon médecin I can give you the name of a good doctor
4 to give; **l'heure indiquée sur le programme est fausse** the time given on the programme (BrE) is wrong
5 ‹*meter, map*› to show; **le restaurant n'est pas indiqué** there are no signs to the restaurant

indirect, **~e** /ɛ̃diʀɛkt/ *adj* indirect

indiscipline /ɛ̃disiplin/ *f* lack of discipline

indiscipliné, **~e** /ɛ̃disipline/ *adj* undisciplined, unruly

indiscret, **-ète** /ɛ̃diskʀɛ, ɛt/ *adj* **1** ‹*person*› inquisitive; **à l'abri des regards ~s** away from prying eyes
2 ‹*person, question*› indiscreet; **il est ~** he can't keep a secret

indiscrétion /ɛ̃diskʀesjɔ̃/ *f*
1 inquisitiveness; **sans ~, combien gagnez-vous?** if you don't mind my asking, how much do you earn?
2 lack of discretion
3 indiscreet remark

indiscutable /ɛ̃diskytabl/ *adj* indisputable, unquestionable

indispensable /ɛ̃dispɑ̃sabl/ **A** *adj* essential; **être ~ à qn** to be indispensable to sb
B *m* **l'~** the essentials

indisposé, **~e** /ɛ̃dispoze/ *adj* unwell, indisposed

indisposer /ɛ̃dispoze/ [**v1**] *vt* **1** to annoy
2 to upset [sb], to make [sb] feel ill

indisposition /ɛ̃dispozisjɔ̃/ *f* indisposition

indissociable /ɛ̃disɔsjabl/ *adj* inseparable

indistinct, **~e** /ɛ̃distɛ̃, ɛ̃kt/ *adj* indistinct

individu /ɛ̃dividy/ *m* **1** individual
2 human being, person
3 un sinistre ~ a sinister individual *or* character; **un ~ armé** an armed man
4 (in scientific study) subject

individualiser /ɛ̃dividɥalize/ [**v1**] **A** *vt* **1** to tailor [sth] to individual needs
2 to individualize
B s'individualiser *v refl* (+ *v être*) to become more individual

individualiste /ɛ̃dividɥalist/ *adj* individualistic

individuel, **-elle** /ɛ̃dividɥɛl/ *adj* (gen) individual; ‹*responsibility*› personal; ‹*room*› single; **maison individuelle** (detached) house

indivisible /ɛ̃divizibl/ *adj* indivisible

Indochine /ɛ̃dɔʃin/ *pr f* Indo-China

indo-européen, **-éenne**, *mpl* **~s** /ɛ̃doøʀɔpeɛ̃, ɛn/ *adj* Indo-European

indolence /ɛ̃dɔlɑ̃s/ *f* laziness, indolence

indolent, **~e** /ɛ̃dɔlɑ̃, ɑ̃t/ *adj* lazy, indolent

indolore /ɛ̃dɔlɔʀ/ *adj* painless

indomptable /ɛ̃dɔ̃tabl/ *adj* ‹*person, courage*› indomitable; ‹*anger, passion, person*› uncontrollable; ‹*animal*› untamable; **avec une énergie ~** with tireless energy

Indonésie /ɛ̃dɔnezi/ *pr f* Indonesia

indu, **~e** /ɛ̃dy/ *adj* ‹*hour*› ungodly (fam), unearthly; ‹*remark, reaction*› inappropriate

indubitable /ɛ̃dybitabl/ *adj* indubitable

indubitablement /ɛ̃dybitabləmɑ̃/ *adv* undoubtedly

induction /ɛ̃dyksjɔ̃/ *f* induction

induire /ɛ̃dɥiʀ/ [**v69**] *vt* **1** ‹*event, measures*› to lead to, to bring about
2 to infer, to conclude
3 to induce; **~ qn en erreur** to mislead sb
4 to induce ‹*current*›

indulgence /ɛ̃dylʒɑ̃s/ *f* **1** (of parent, audience) indulgence
2 (of jury) leniency

indulgent, **~e** /ɛ̃dylʒɑ̃, ɑ̃t/ *adj* **1** ‹*parent, audience*› indulgent
2 ‹*jury*› lenient

industrialisation /ɛ̃dystʀializasjɔ̃/ *f* industrialization

industrialiser /ɛ̃dystʀialize/ [**v1**] **A** *vt* to industrialize
B s'industrialiser *v refl* (+ *v être*) to become industrialized

industrie /ɛ̃dystʀi/ *f* **1** industry; **l'~**

hôtelière the hotel trade
2 industrial concern
🔑 **industriel**, **-ielle** /ɛ̃dystʀijɛl/ **A** *adj* industrial; **pain ~** factory-baked bread
B *mf* industrialist, manufacturer
inébranlable /inebʀɑ̃labl/ *adj*
1 unshakeable, unwavering
2 immovable
inédit, **~e** /inedi, it/ *adj* ‹*book*› (previously) unpublished; ‹*situation*› (totally) new
ineffable /inefabl/ *adj* ineffable, unutterable
inefficace /inefikas/ *adj* **1** ineffective
2 inefficient
inefficacité /inefikasite/ *f* **1** ineffectiveness, inefficacy
2 inefficiency
inégal, **~e**, *mpl* **-aux** /inegal, o/ *adj* unequal; uneven; irregular; ‹*mood*› changeable, erratic
inégalable /inegalabl/ *adj* incomparable
inégalé, **~e** /inegale/ *adj* unequalled (BrE), unrivalled (BrE)
inégalement /inegalmɑ̃/ *adv* **1** unequally
2 unevenly
inégalité /inegalite/ *f* **1** disparity
2 inequality
3 (of mood) changeability; (of surface) unevenness
inéluctable /inelyktabl/ *adj*, *m* inevitable
inénarrable /inenaʀabl/ *adj* hilarious
inepte /inɛpt/ *adj* ‹*person*› inept; ‹*judgement*› inane; ‹*remark*› idiotic
ineptie /inɛpsi/ *f* **1** inanity
2 idiotic remark
3 (action) stupid thing
inépuisable /inepɥizabl/ *adj* inexhaustible
inerte /inɛʀt/ *adj* **1** inert
2 apathetic
inertie /inɛʀsi/ *f* **1** inertia
2 apathy, inertia
inespéré, **~e** /inɛspeʀe/ *adj* ‹*victory*› unhoped for; **c'est une occasion ~e de faire** this is a heaven-sent opportunity to do
inestimable /inɛstimabl/ *adj* ‹*value*› inestimable; ‹*help*› invaluable
inévitable /inevitabl/ *adj* inevitable; unavoidable
inexact, **~e** /inegza, akt/ *adj* inaccurate
inexactitude /inegzaktityd/ *f* **1** inaccuracy
2 unpunctuality
inexcusable /inɛkskyzabl/ *adj* inexcusable
inexistant, **~e** /inegzistɑ̃, ɑ̃t/ *adj* ‹*means, help*› non-existent
inexpérience /inɛkspeʀjɑ̃s/ *f* inexperience
inexpérimenté, **~e** /inɛkspeʀimɑ̃te/ *adj* inexperienced
inexplicable /inɛksplikabl/ *adj* inexplicable
inexpressif, **-ive** /inɛkspʀesif, iv/ *adj* inexpressive
inexprimable /inɛkspʀimabl/ *adj* inexpressible
in extremis /inɛkstʀemis/ *phr* at the last minute
infaillible /ɛ̃fajibl/ *adj* infallible
infaisable /ɛ̃fəzabl/ *adj* unfeasible, impossible
infamant, **~e** /ɛ̃famɑ̃, ɑ̃t/ *adj* **1** ‹*remark*› defamatory
2 ‹*act*› infamous
infâme /ɛ̃fɑm/ *adj* **1** ‹*food, smell*› revolting
2 ‹*person*› despicable; ‹*crime*› odious
infamie /ɛ̃fami/ *f* **1** infamy
2 infamous act
3 slanderous remark
infanterie /ɛ̃fɑ̃tʀi/ *f* infantry
infantile /ɛ̃fɑ̃til/ *adj* **1** ‹*illness*› childhood; ‹*mortality*› infant; ‹*psychology*› child
2 ‹*person, behaviour*› infantile, childish
infantilisme /ɛ̃fɑ̃tilism/ *m* childishness
infarctus /ɛ̃faʀktys/ *m inv* heart attack
infatigable /ɛ̃fatigabl/ *adj* tireless
infatué, **~e** /ɛ̃fatɥe/ *adj* **être ~ de sa personne** to be full of oneself
infect, **~e** /ɛ̃fɛkt/ *adj* foul; revolting
infecter /ɛ̃fɛkte/ [**v1**] **A** *vt* **1** (Med) to infect
2 (fig) to poison
B s'infecter *v refl* (+ *v être*) to become infected, to go septic
infectieux, **-ieuse** /ɛ̃fɛksjø, øz/ *adj* infectious
infection /ɛ̃fɛksjɔ̃/ *f* **1** (Med) infection
2 (fig) **c'est une ~!** it stinks to high heaven! (fam)
🔑 **inférieur**, **~e** /ɛ̃feʀjœʀ/ **A** *adj* **1** lower; ‹*size*› smaller; ‹*length*› shorter; **~ à la moyenne** below average; **être en nombre ~** to be fewer in number
2 inferior
3 (in mathematics) **si a est ~ à b** if a is less than b
B *mf* inferior
infériorité /ɛ̃feʀjɔʀite/ *f* inferiority
infernal, **~e**, *mpl* **-aux** /ɛ̃fɛʀnal, o/ *adj* **1** ‹*noise, heat*› infernal; **cycle ~** unstoppable chain of events
2 ‹*situation*› diabolical; **ce gosse est ~** (fam) that child is a monster
infertile /ɛ̃fɛʀtil/ *adj* barren, infertile
infester /ɛ̃fɛste/ [**v1**] *vt* to infest, to overrun; **infesté de puces** flea-ridden
infidèle /ɛ̃fidɛl/ **A** *adj* unfaithful; disloyal
B *mf* infidel
infidélité /ɛ̃fidelite/ *f* **1** infidelity; **faire des ~s à** to be unfaithful to
2 disloyalty
infiltration /ɛ̃filtʀasjɔ̃/ *f* **1 ~s d'eau** water seepage
2 (of spies) infiltration
3 (Med) injection
infiltrer /ɛ̃filtʀe/ [**v1**] **A** *vt* to infiltrate

🔑 key word

B **s'infiltrer** *v refl* (+ *v être*) **1** ‹*liquid*› to seep; ‹*light, cold*› to filter in
2 ‹*person*› **s'~ dans** to infiltrate ‹*group, place*›

infime /ɛ̃fim/ *adj* tiny, minute

infini, **~e** /ɛ̃fini/ **A** *adj* infinite
B *m* **l'~** infinity

infiniment /ɛ̃finimɑ̃/ *adv* immensely; **~ plus** infinitely more

infinité /ɛ̃finite/ *f* **l'~** infinity; **une ~ de** an endless number of

infinitif /ɛ̃finitif/ *m* infinitive

infirme /ɛ̃fiʀm/ **A** *adj* (gen) disabled; (because of age) infirm
B *mf* disabled person; **les ~s** the disabled

infirmer /ɛ̃fiʀme/ [**v1**] *vt* (gen), (Law) to invalidate

infirmerie /ɛ̃fiʀməʀi/ *f* (gen) infirmary; sick room; sick bay

infirmier /ɛ̃fiʀmje/ *m* male nurse

infirmière /ɛ̃fiʀmjɛʀ/ *f* nurse

infirmité /ɛ̃fiʀmite/ *f* (gen) disability; (through old age) infirmity

inflammable /ɛ̃flamabl/ *adj* flammable

inflammation /ɛ̃flamasjɔ̃/ *f* (Med) inflammation

inflammatoire /ɛ̃flamatwaʀ/ *adj* (Med) inflammatory

inflation /ɛ̃flasjɔ̃/ *f* inflation

infléchir /ɛ̃fleʃiʀ/ [**v3**] *vt*, **s'infléchir** *v refl* (+ *v être*) to soften; to deflect

inflexible /ɛ̃flɛksibl/ *adj* inflexible

infliger /ɛ̃fliʒe/ [**v13**] *vt* to impose ‹*fine*›

influençable /ɛ̃flyɑ̃sabl/ *adj* impressionable

influence /ɛ̃flyɑ̃s/ *f* influence

influencer /ɛ̃flyɑ̃se/ [**v12**] *vt* to influence ‹*person*›; to affect ‹*situation*›

influent, **~e** /ɛ̃flyɑ̃, ɑ̃t/ *adj* influential

influer /ɛ̃flye/ [**v1**] *v+prep* **~ sur** to have an influence on

informateur, **-trice** /ɛ̃fɔʀmatœʀ, tʀis/ *mf*
1 (gen) informant
2 (police) informer

informaticien, **-ienne** /ɛ̃fɔʀmatisjɛ̃, ɛn/ *mf* computer scientist

information /ɛ̃fɔʀmasjɔ̃/ *f* **1** information; **une ~** a piece of information
2 (in newspaper, on television) **une ~** a piece of news; **écouter les ~s** to listen to the news; **contrôler l'~** to control the media
3 (Comput) data, information

informatique /ɛ̃fɔʀmatik/ **A** *adj* computer
B *f* computer science, computing

informatisation /ɛ̃fɔʀmatizasjɔ̃/ *f* computerization

informatiser /ɛ̃fɔʀmatize/ [**v1**] **A** *vt* to computerize
B **s'informatiser** *v refl* (+ *v être*) to become computerized

informe /ɛ̃fɔʀm/ *adj* shapeless

informer /ɛ̃fɔʀme/ [**v1**] **A** *vt* to inform
B **s'informer** *v refl* (+ *v être*) **1** to keep oneself informed
2 **s'~ de qch** to enquire about sth
3 **s'~ sur qn** to make enquiries about sb

infortune /ɛ̃fɔʀtyn/ *f* misfortune

infortuné, **~e** **A** *adj* ill-fated
B *mf* unfortunate

infra /ɛ̃fʀa/ *adv* below; **voir ~** see below

infraction /ɛ̃fʀaksjɔ̃/ *f* offence (BrE); **être en ~** to be in breach of the law

infranchissable /ɛ̃fʀɑ̃ʃisabl/ *adj* ‹*obstacle*› insurmountable; ‹*border*› impassable

infrarouge /ɛ̃fʀaʀuʒ/ *adj*, *m* infrared; **missile guidé par ~** heat-seeking missile

infrastructure /ɛ̃fʀastʀyktyʀ/ *f* **1** facilities
2 (Econ) infrastructure

infructueux, **-euse** /ɛ̃fʀyktɥø, øz/ *adj* fruitless

infuser /ɛ̃fyze/ [**v1**] *vi* ‹*tea*› to brew, to infuse

infusion /ɛ̃fyzjɔ̃/ *f* **1** herbal tea
2 infusion

ingénier: **s'ingénier** /ɛ̃ʒenje/ [**v2**] *v refl* (+ *v être*) to do one's utmost (**à faire** to do)

ingénierie /ɛ̃ʒeniʀi/ *f* engineering

ingénieur /ɛ̃ʒenjœʀ/ *m* engineer

ingénieur-conseil, *pl* **ingénieurs-conseils** /ɛ̃ʒenjœʀkɔ̃sɛj/ *m* consulting engineer

ingénieux, **-ieuse** /ɛ̃ʒenjø, øz/ *adj* ingenious

ingéniosité /ɛ̃ʒenjozite/ *f* ingenuity

ingénu, **~e** /ɛ̃ʒeny/ *adj* ingenuous

ingénuité /ɛ̃ʒenɥite/ *f* ingenuousness; **en toute ~** in all innocence

ingérence /ɛ̃ʒeʀɑ̃s/ *f* interference (**dans** in)

ingérer /ɛ̃ʒeʀe/ [**v14**] **A** *vt* to ingest
B **s'ingérer** *v refl* (+ *v être*) to interfere

ingestion /ɛ̃ʒɛstjɔ̃/ *f* ingestion

ingrat, **~e** /ɛ̃gʀa, at/ *adj* **1** ungrateful
2 ‹*face, landscape*› unattractive
3 ‹*task, role*› thankless; ‹*land, soil*› unproductive

ingratitude /ɛ̃gʀatityd/ *f* ingratitude

ingrédient /ɛ̃gʀedjɑ̃/ *m* ingredient

ingurgiter /ɛ̃gyʀʒite/ [**v1**] *vt* to gulp down

inhabitable /inabitabl/ *adj* uninhabitable

inhabité, **~e** /inabite/ *adj* uninhabited

inhabituel, **-elle** /inabitɥɛl/ *adj* unusual

inhalation /inalasjɔ̃/ *f* inhalation

inhaler /inale/ [**v1**] *vt* to inhale

inhérent, **~e** /ineʀɑ̃, ɑ̃t/ *adj* inherent

inhibition /inibisjɔ̃/ *f* inhibition

inhumain, **~e** /inymɛ̃, ɛn/ *adj* inhuman

inhumation /inymasjɔ̃/ *f* **1** burial
2 funeral

inhumer /inyme/ [**v1**] *vt* to bury

inimaginable /inimaʒinabl/ *adj*
1 unimaginable
2 unthinkable

i

inimitable /inimitabl/ *adj* inimitable
ininflammable /inɛ̃flamabl/ *adj* non-flammable
inintéressant, ~**e** /inɛ̃teʀesɑ̃, ɑ̃t/ *adj* uninteresting
ininterrompu, ~**e** /inɛ̃tɛʀɔ̃py/ *adj* **1** ‹*process*› uninterrupted; ‹*drop*› continuous; ‹*traffic*› endless **2** ‹*procession*› unbroken
initial, ~**e** *mpl* **-iaux** /inisjal, o/ *adj* initial
initiale /inisjal/ *f* initial
initiateur, **-trice** /inisjatœʀ, tʀis/ *mf* **1** originator; instigator **2** instructor
initiation /inisjasjɔ̃/ *f* **1** introduction **2** initiation
⚷ **initiative** /inisjativ/ *f* initiative; **avoir l'esprit d'**~ to have initiative
initié, ~**e** /inisje/ **A** *adj* (Comput) ~ **à l'informatique** computer literate **B** *mf* **1** initiate **2** insider trader **3** (Comput) ~ **à l'informatique** computer-literate person
initier /inisje/ [**v2**] **A** *vt* **1** to introduce **2** to initiate **B s'initier** *v refl* (+ *v être*) **s'**~ **à qch** to learn sth
injecter /ɛ̃ʒɛkte/ [**v2**] *vt* to inject
injection /ɛ̃ʒɛksjɔ̃/ *f* injection
injonction /ɛ̃ʒɔ̃ksjɔ̃/ *f* injunction, command
injure /ɛ̃ʒyʀ/ *f* insult, abuse
injurier /ɛ̃ʒyʀje/ [**v1**] *vt* to insult, to swear at
injurieux, **-ieuse** /ɛ̃ʒyʀjø, øz/ *adj* ‹*remark*› abusive; ‹*attitude*› insulting
injuste /ɛ̃ʒyst/ *adj* unfair
injustement /ɛ̃ʒystəmɑ̃/ *adv* unjustly; unfairly
injustice /ɛ̃ʒystis/ *f* injustice; unfairness; **réparer une** ~ to right a wrong
injustifié, ~**e** /ɛ̃ʒystifje/ *adj* unjustified
inlassable /ɛ̃lasabl/ *adj* ‹*person*› tireless; ‹*curiosity*› insatiable; ‹*efforts*› unremitting
inlassablement /ɛ̃lasabləmɑ̃/ *adv* tirelessly
inné, ~**e** /inne/ *adj* innate
innocemment /inɔsamɑ̃/ *adv* innocently; **pas** ~ disingenuously
innocence /inɔsɑ̃s/ *f* innocence
innocent, ~**e** /inɔsɑ̃, ɑ̃t/ *adj* innocent
innocenter /inɔsɑ̃te/ [**v1**] *vt* to prove [sb] innocent
innombrable /innɔ̃bʀabl/ *adj* **1** countless **2** ‹*crowd*› vast
innommable /innɔmabl/ *adj* unspeakable
innovateur, **-trice** /inɔvatœʀ, tʀis/ *mf* innovator
innover /inɔve/ [**v1**] *vi* to innovate
inoculer /inɔkyle/ [**v1**] *vt* to inoculate

⚷ key word

inodore /inɔdɔʀ/ *adj* ‹*substance*› odourless (BrE)
inoffensif, **-ive** /inɔfɑ̃sif, iv/ *adj* harmless
inondation /inɔ̃dasjɔ̃/ *f* **1** flood **2** flooding
inonder /inɔ̃de/ [**v1**] *vt* to flood
inopérant, ~**e** /inɔpeʀɑ̃, ɑ̃t/ *adj* ineffective
inopiné, ~**e** /inɔpine/ *adj* unexpected
inopportun, ~**e** /inɔpɔʀtœ̃, yn/ *adj* **1** inappropriate **2** ill-timed
inoubliable /inublijabl/ *adj* unforgettable
inouï, ~**e** /inwi/ *adj* ‹*event*› unprecedented; ‹*success*› incredible; **c'est** ~ that's unheard of
inox /inɔks/ *m inv* stainless steel
inoxydable /inɔksidabl/ *adj* ‹*metal*› non-oxidizing; **acier** ~ stainless steel
inqualifiable /ɛ̃kalifjabl/ *adj* unspeakable
inquiet, **-iète** /ɛ̃kjɛ, ɛt/ *adj* **1** anxious **2** worried
inquiétant, ~**e** /ɛ̃kjetɑ̃, ɑ̃t/ *adj* **1** worrying **2** frightening
inquiéter /ɛ̃kjete/ [**v14**] **A** *vt* **1** to worry **2 les douaniers ne l'ont pas inquiété** the customs officers didn't bother him **B s'inquiéter** *v refl* (+ *v être*) **1** to worry **2 s'**~ **de qch** to enquire about sth
inquiétude /ɛ̃kjetyd/ *f* **1** anxiety, concern **2** worry; **il n'y a pas d'**~ **à avoir** there's nothing to worry about
inquisiteur, **-trice** /ɛ̃kizitœʀ, tʀis/ **A** *adj* inquisitive **B** *mf* inquisitor
inquisition /ɛ̃kizisjɔ̃/ *f* inquisition
insaisissable /ɛ̃sɛzisabl/ *adj* ‹*person, character*› elusive; ‹*nuance*› imperceptible
insalubre /ɛ̃salybʀ/ *adj* insanitary
insanité /ɛ̃sanite/ *f* **1** rubbish, nonsense **2** insanity
insatiable /ɛ̃sasjabl/ *adj* insatiable
insatisfaction /ɛ̃satisfaksjɔ̃/ *f* dissatisfaction
insatisfait, ~**e** /ɛ̃satisfɛ, ɛt/ *adj* dissatisfied (**de** with); unsatisfied
inscription /ɛ̃skʀipsjɔ̃/ *f* **1** (in school) enrolment (BrE); (at university) registration **2 l'**~ **au club coûte 40 euros** the membership fee for the club is 40 euros; ~ **électorale** registration as a voter **3** inscription; graffiti
⚷ **inscrire** /ɛ̃skʀiʀ/ [**v67**] **A** *vt* **1** to enrol (BrE) ‹*pupil*›; to register ‹*student*› **2** to write down ‹*name, date*› **B s'inscrire** *v refl* (+ *v être*) **1** to enrol (BrE); **s'**~ **au chômage** to register as unemployed; **s'**~ **à un parti** to join a party **2 s'**~ **dans le cadre de** to be in line with **3 s'**~ **en faux contre qch** to dispute the validity of sth
inscrit, ~**e** /ɛ̃skʀi, it/ **A** *pp* ▶ **inscrire** **B** *mf* registered student; registered voter

insecte /ɛ̃sɛkt/ *m* insect
insecticide /ɛ̃sɛktisid/ *m* insecticide
insécurité /ɛ̃sekyʀite/ *f* insecurity
INSEE /inse/ *m* (*abbr* = **Institut National de la Statistique et des Études Économiques**) French national institute of statistics and economic studies
insémination /ɛ̃seminasjɔ̃/ *f* insemination; **~ artificielle** artificial insemination
insensé, **~e** /ɛ̃sɑ̃se/ *adj* **1** insane
2 (fam) ‹*crowd, traffic jam*› phenomenal
insensibiliser /ɛ̃sɑ̃sibilize/ [**v1**] *vt* (Med) to anaesthetize
insensibilité /ɛ̃sɑ̃sibilite/ *f* insensitivity
insensible /ɛ̃sɑ̃sibl/ *adj* **1** impervious
2 insensitive
insensiblement /ɛ̃sɑ̃sibləmɑ̃/ *adv* imperceptibly
inséparable /ɛ̃sepaʀabl/ *adj* inseparable
insérer /ɛ̃seʀe/ [**v14**] **A** *vt* to insert
B **s'insérer** *v refl* (+ *v être*) (gen) to be inserted
insertion /ɛ̃sɛʀsjɔ̃/ *f* **1** insertion
2 integration
insidieux, **-ieuse** /ɛ̃sidjø, øz/ *adj* insidious
insigne /ɛ̃siɲ/ **A** *adj* ‹*honour, favour*› great
B *m* badge
insignifiant, **~e** /ɛ̃siɲifjɑ̃, ɑ̃t/ *adj* insignificant
insinuation /ɛ̃sinɥasjɔ̃/ *f* insinuation
insinuer /ɛ̃sinɥe/ [**v1**] **A** *vt* to insinuate
B **s'insinuer** *v refl* (+ *v être*) **s'~ dans** ‹*person*› to worm one's way into; ‹*liquid*› to seep into
insipide /ɛ̃sipid/ *adj* insipid
insistance /ɛ̃sistɑ̃s/ *f* insistence
insistant, **~e** /ɛ̃sistɑ̃, ɑ̃t/ *adj* insistent
⚷ **insister** /ɛ̃siste/ [**v1**] *vi* **1** to insist; **'ça ne répond pas'—'insiste'** 'there's no reply!'—'keep trying'
2 ~ sur to stress ‹*danger, need*›; to put the emphasis on ‹*spelling*›
3 ~ sur to pay particular attention to ‹*stain*›
insolation /ɛ̃sɔlasjɔ̃/ *f* sunstroke
insolence /ɛ̃sɔlɑ̃s/ *f* **1** insolence
2 insolent remark
insolent, **~e** /ɛ̃sɔlɑ̃, ɑ̃t/ *adj* **1** ‹*child, tone*› insolent
2 ‹*rival, winner*› arrogant
insolite /ɛ̃sɔlit/ *adj*, *m* unusual
insoluble /ɛ̃sɔlybl/ *adj* insoluble
insolvable /ɛ̃sɔlvabl/ *adj* insolvent
insomniaque /ɛ̃sɔmnjak/ *adj*, *mf* insomniac
insomnie /ɛ̃sɔmni/ *f* insomnia
insondable /ɛ̃sɔ̃dabl/ *adj* unfathomable
insonorisation /ɛ̃sɔnɔʀizasjɔ̃/ *f* soundproofing
insonoriser /ɛ̃sɔnɔʀize/ [**v1**] *vt* to soundproof
insouciance /ɛ̃susjɑ̃s/ *f* carefreeness
insouciant, **~e** /ɛ̃susjɑ̃, ɑ̃t/ *adj* carefree
insoumission /ɛ̃sumisjɔ̃/ *f* **1** insubordination
2 (Mil) draft-dodging
insoupçonné, **~e** /ɛ̃supsɔne/ *adj* unsuspected
insoutenable /ɛ̃sutnabl/ *adj* **1** ‹*pain*› unbearable
2 ‹*opinion*› untenable
inspecter /ɛ̃spɛkte/ [**v1**] *vt* to inspect
inspecteur, **-trice** /ɛ̃spɛktœʀ, tʀis/ *mf* inspector
■ **~ de police** ≈ detective constable (BrE); **~ du travail** health and safety inspector
inspection /ɛ̃spɛksjɔ̃/ *f* **1** inspection
2 inspectorate
inspiration /ɛ̃spiʀasjɔ̃/ *f* inspiration
⚷ **inspirer** /ɛ̃spiʀe/ [**v1**] **A** *vt* **1** to inspire ‹*person*›; **être bien/mal inspiré de faire** to be well-/ill-advised to do; **un roman inspiré des vieux contes populaires** a novel based on old folk tales
2 to appeal to; **ça ne m'inspire pas** that doesn't appeal to me
3 ~ la méfiance à qn to inspire distrust in sb
B *vi* to breathe in, to inhale
C **s'inspirer** *v refl* (+ *v être*) **s'~ de** to draw one's inspiration from
instabilité /ɛ̃stabilite/ *f* (gen) instability
instable /ɛ̃stabl/ *adj* (gen) unstable; ‹*weather*› unsettled
installateur, **-trice** /ɛ̃stalatœʀ, tʀis/ *mf* fitter
installation /ɛ̃stalasjɔ̃/ **A** *f* **1** installation, putting in
2 system; **~ électrique** (electric) wiring
3 move; **depuis mon ~ à Paris** since I moved to Paris
B **installations** *fpl* facilities
installé, **~e** /ɛ̃stale/ **A** *pp* ▶ **installer**
B *pp adj* ‹*person*› living (à in); ‹*company*› based; **être bien ~ dans un fauteuil** to be ensconced in an armchair; **ils sont bien ~s dans leur nouvelle maison** they're very snug in their new home; **c'est un homme ~** (fig) he's very nicely set up
⚷ **installer** /ɛ̃stale/ [**v1**] **A** *vt* **1** to install, to put in ‹*central heating, sink*›; to put up ‹*shelves*›; to connect ‹*gas*›
2 to put ‹*guest*› (**dans** in); **~ qn dans un fauteuil** to sit sb in an armchair; **~ qn à un poste** to appoint sb to a post
B **s'installer** *v refl* (+ *v être*) **1** ‹*recession*› to set in; ‹*illness*› to take hold; **le doute commence à s'~ dans leur esprit** they're beginning to have doubts
2 s'~ à son compte to set up one's own business
3 to settle; **partir s'~ à l'étranger** to go and live abroad; **je viendrai te voir quand tu seras installé** I'll come and see you when you're settled in; **s'~ au soleil** to sit in the sun; **s'~ à son bureau** to settle down at one's desk; **installe-toi, j'arrive!** make yourself at home, I'm coming!

i

instamment /ɛ̃stamɑ̃/ *adv* insistently

instance /ɛ̃stɑ̃s/ *f* **1** authority; **les ~s d'un parti politique** the leaders of a political party
2 être en ~ de divorce to be engaged in divorce proceedings

🔑 **instant**, **~e** /ɛ̃stɑ̃, ɑ̃t/ *m* moment, instant; **à tout** *or* **chaque ~** all the time; **par ~s** at times; **pour l'~** for the moment; **il devrait arriver d'un ~ à l'autre** he should arrive any minute now; **à l'~ même où** just when

instantané, **~e** /ɛ̃stɑ̃tane/ **A** *adj* instantaneous; ‹*drink, soup*› instant
B *m* snapshot

instar: **à l'instar de** /alɛ̃staʀdə/ *phr* following the example of

instaurer /ɛ̃stoʀe/ [**v1**] *vt* to establish ‹*regime, dialogue*›; to impose ‹*curfew*›

instigateur, **-trice** /ɛ̃stigatœʀ, tʀis/ *mf* **1** instigator
2 originator

i

instigation /ɛ̃stigasjɔ̃/ *f* **à l'~ de qn** at sb's instigation

instiller /ɛ̃stile/ [**v1**] *vt* to instil (BrE)

instinct /ɛ̃stɛ̃/ *m* instinct; **d'~** instinctively

instinctif, **-ive** /ɛ̃stɛ̃ktif, iv/ *adj* instinctive

instituer /ɛ̃stitɥe/ [**v1**] *vt* to institute

institut /ɛ̃stity/ *m* **1** institute
2 ~ de beauté beauty salon *or* parlour (BrE)
■ **Institut universitaire de formation des maîtres, IUFM** *primary teacher training college*; **Institut universitaire de technologie, IUT** university institute of technology

instituteur, **-trice** /ɛ̃stitytœʀ, tʀis/ *mf* (primary school) teacher

🔑 **institution** /ɛ̃stitysjɔ̃/ *f* **1** institution
2 private school

institutrice ▸ **instituteur**

instructeur /ɛ̃stʀyktœʀ/ *m* (gen), (Mil) instructor

instructif, **-ive** /ɛ̃stʀyktif, iv/ *adj* (gen) instructive; ‹*experience*› enlightening

🔑 **instruction** /ɛ̃stʀyksjɔ̃/ **A** *f* **1** (gen) education; (Mil) training
2 (Law) *preparation of a case for trial*
B instructions *fpl* instructions
■ **~ civique** civics; **~ religieuse** religious instruction

instruire /ɛ̃stʀɥiʀ/ [**v69**] **A** *vt* **1** to teach ‹*child*›; to train ‹*soldiers*›
2 (Law) **~ une affaire** to prepare a case for trial
B s'instruire *v refl* (+ *v être*) to learn

instruit, **~e** /ɛ̃stʀɥi, it/ *adj* educated

🔑 **instrument** /ɛ̃stʀymɑ̃/ *m* (gen), (Mus) instrument; **~ à cordes/à percussion/à vent** string/percussion/wind instrument; **jouer d'un ~** to play an instrument; **être l'~ de qn** to be sb's tool
■ **~s de bord** controls

🔑 key word

insu: **à l'insu de** /alɛ̃sydə/ *phr* **à l'~ de qn** without sb knowing

insubordination /ɛ̃sybɔʀdinasjɔ̃/ *f* insubordination

insubordonné, **~e** /ɛ̃sybɔʀdɔne/ *adj* rebellious; insubordinate

insuffisamment /ɛ̃syfizamɑ̃/ *adv* insufficiently; inadequately

insuffisance /ɛ̃syfizɑ̃s/ *f* **1** insufficiency, shortage
2 poor standard; **l'~ de la production** the shortfall in production
3 (Med) insufficiency

insuffisant, **~e** /ɛ̃syfizɑ̃, ɑ̃t/ *adj* **1** insufficient
2 inadequate

insuffler /ɛ̃syfle/ [**v1**] *vt* to instil (BrE); **~ la vie à qn** to breathe life into sb

insulaire /ɛ̃sylɛʀ/ *adj* ‹*population*› island; ‹*mentality*› insular

insultant, **~e** /ɛ̃syltɑ̃, ɑ̃t/ *adj* insulting

insulte /ɛ̃sylt/ *f* insult

insulter /ɛ̃sylte/ [**v1**] *vt* to insult; to shout abuse at; ‹*attitude*› to be an insult to

insupportable /ɛ̃sypɔʀtabl/ *adj* unbearable

insurgé, **~e** /ɛ̃syʀʒe/ *mf* insurgent, rebel

insurger: **s'insurger** /ɛ̃syʀʒe/ [**v13**] *v refl* (+ *v être*) **1** to rise up
2 to protest

insurmontable /ɛ̃syʀmɔ̃tabl/ *adj* insurmountable; insuperable; unconquerable

insurrection /ɛ̃syʀɛksjɔ̃/ *f* insurrection

intact, **~e** /ɛ̃takt/ *adj* intact

intarissable /ɛ̃taʀisabl/ *adj* ‹*imagination*› inexhaustible; ‹*source*› never-ending

intégral, **~e**, *mpl* **-aux** /ɛ̃tegʀal, o/ *adj* **1** ‹*payment*› full, in full
2 ‹*tan*› all-over
3 ‹*text*› unabridged; **version ~e** uncut version

intégralement /ɛ̃tegʀalmɑ̃/ *adv* ‹*pay*› in full

intégralité /ɛ̃tegʀalite/ *f* **l'~ de leur salaire** their entire salary

intégrante /ɛ̃tegʀɑ̃t/ *adj f* **faire partie ~ de qch** to be an integral part of sth

intégration /ɛ̃tegʀasjɔ̃/ *f* integration

intègre /ɛ̃tɛgʀ/ *adj* ‹*person, life*› honest

intégré /ɛ̃tegʀe/ *adj* **1** included, inserted
2 integrated; ‹*journalist*› embedded

🔑 **intégrer** /ɛ̃tegʀe/ [**v14**] **A** *vt* **1** to insert
2 to integrate ‹*population*›
3 (fam) **il vient d'~ Harvard** he has just got into Harvard
B s'intégrer *v refl* (+ *v être*)
1 ‹*population*› to integrate
2 ‹*building*› to fit in

intégrisme /ɛ̃tegʀism/ *m* fundamentalism

intégriste /ɛ̃tegʀist/ *mf* (religious) fundamentalist

intégrité /ɛ̃tegʀite/ *f* integrity

intellect /ɛ̃telɛkt/ *m* intellect

intellectuel, -elle /ɛ̃telɛktɥɛl/ **A** *adj* ‹*work*› intellectual; ‹*effort*› mental
B *mf* intellectual

intelligence /ɛ̃teliʒɑ̃s/ *f* **1** intelligence
2 agir d'~ avec qn to act in agreement with sb

intelligent, ~e /ɛ̃teliʒɑ̃, ɑ̃t/ *adj* intelligent; clever

intelligible /ɛ̃teliʒibl/ *adj* intelligible

intempéries /ɛ̃tɑ̃peʀi/ *fpl* bad weather

intempestif, -ive /ɛ̃tɑ̃pɛstif, iv/ *adj* untimely; ‹*curiosity, zeal*› misplaced

intemporel, -elle /ɛ̃tɑ̃pɔʀɛl/ *adj* timeless

intenable /ɛ̃t(ə)nabl/ *adj* **1** ‹*situation*› unbearable
2 ‹*child*› difficult

intendance /ɛ̃tɑ̃dɑ̃s/ *f* (Sch) administration

intendant, ~e /ɛ̃tɑ̃dɑ̃, ɑ̃t/ **A** *mf* (Sch) bursar
B *m* (Mil) quartermaster; paymaster

intense /ɛ̃tɑ̃s/ *adj* (gen) intense; ‹*red, green*› vivid; ‹*traffic*› heavy

intensif, -ive /ɛ̃tɑ̃sif, iv/ *adj* intensive

intensification /ɛ̃tɑ̃sifikasjɔ̃/ *f* intensification

intensifier /ɛ̃tɑ̃sifje/ [**v2**] *vt*, **s'intensifier** *v refl* (+ *v être*) to intensify

intensité /ɛ̃tɑ̃site/ *f* intensity

intensivement /ɛ̃tɑ̃sivmɑ̃/ *adv* intensively

intenter /ɛ̃tɑ̃te/ [**v1**] *vt* **~ un procès à qn** to sue sb

intention /ɛ̃tɑ̃sjɔ̃/ *f* intention; **c'est l'~ qui compte** it's the thought that counts; **à l'~ de qn** ‹*remark*› aimed at sb

intentionné, ~e /ɛ̃tɑ̃sjɔne/ *adj* **bien/mal ~** well-/ill-intentioned

intentionnel, -elle /ɛ̃tɑ̃sjɔnɛl/ *adj* intentional

interaction /ɛ̃tɛʀaksjɔ̃/ *f* interaction

interbancaire /ɛ̃tɛʀbɑ̃kɛʀ/ *adj* interbank

intercalaire /ɛ̃tɛʀkalɛʀ/ **A** *adj* **feuille** *or* **feuillet ~** insert
B *m* divider

intercaler /ɛ̃tɛʀkale/ [**v1**] *vt* to insert

intercéder /ɛ̃tɛʀsede/ [**v14**] *vi* to intercede

intercepter /ɛ̃tɛʀsɛpte/ [**v1**] *vt* to intercept

interchangeable /ɛ̃tɛʀʃɑ̃ʒabl/ *adj* interchangeable

interclasse /ɛ̃tɛʀklas/ *m* (Sch) break

interdiction /ɛ̃tɛʀdiksjɔ̃/ *f* **1** banning; **'~ de dépasser'** 'no overtaking' (BrE), 'no passing' (AmE)
2 ban; **lever une ~** to lift a ban
■ **~ de séjour** prohibition on residence

interdire /ɛ̃tɛʀdiʀ/ [**v65**] *vt* to ban; **~ à qn de faire, ~ que qn fasse** to forbid sb to do

interdisciplinaire /ɛ̃tɛʀdisiplinɛʀ/ *adj* (Sch) cross-curricular; (Univ) interdisciplinary

interdit, ~e /ɛ̃tɛʀdi, it/ **A** *pp* ▸ **interdire**
B *pp adj* prohibited, forbidden; **entrée ~e** no entry *or* admittance; **film ~ aux moins de 13 ans** film unsuitable for children under 13
C *adj* dumbfounded
D *m* proscription; taboo

intéressant, ~e /ɛ̃teʀɛsɑ̃, ɑ̃t/ **A** *adj*
1 interesting
2 ‹*prices, conditions*› attractive; **il est plus ~ de payer au comptant qu'à crédit** it's better to pay in cash rather than by credit
B *mf* **faire l'~** *or* **son ~** to show off

intéressé, ~e /ɛ̃teʀese/ **A** *pp* ▸ **intéresser**
B *pp adj* **1** interested
2 attentive
3 les parties ~es those concerned; **les personnes ~es aux bénéfices** people with a share in the profits
4 ‹*person*› self-interested; ‹*action*› motivated by self-interest; **ses conseils étaient ~s** he/she had a selfish motive for giving that advice
C *mf* person concerned

intéressement /ɛ̃teʀɛsmɑ̃/ *m* share in the profits

intéresser /ɛ̃teʀese/ [**v1**] **A** *vt* **1** to interest; **ça ne m'intéresse pas** I'm not interested
2 ‹*problem, decision*› to concern
3 ~ les salariés aux bénéfices to offer a profit-sharing scheme to employees
B s'intéresser *v refl* (+ *v être*) **s'~ à** (gen) to be interested in; to take an interest in

intérêt /ɛ̃teʀɛ/ *m* **1** interest; **recherche digne d'~** worthwhile research; **l'~ supérieur de la nation** the higher good of the country; **je ne vois pas l'~ de cette réforme** I can't see the point of this reform; **par ~** ‹*act*› out of self-interest; ‹*marry*› for money
2 (financial) interest

interface /ɛ̃tɛʀfas/ *f* interface

interférence /ɛ̃tɛʀfeʀɑ̃s/ *f* interference

interférer /ɛ̃tɛʀfeʀe/ [**v14**] *vi* to interfere

intérieur, ~e /ɛ̃teʀjœʀ/ **A** *adj* **1** internal, interior; ‹*sea*› inland; ‹*pocket*› inside; **le côté ~** the inside
2 domestic; **sur le plan ~** on the domestic front
3 ‹*regulations*› internal
B *m* (of box, newspaper) inside; (of car, house) interior; **à l'~** inside; indoors; **à l'~ des terres** inland; **d'~** ‹*game*› indoor; **être fier de son ~** to be proud of one's home

intérim /ɛ̃teʀim/ *m* **1** interim (period); **président par ~** acting president; **assurer l'~ de** to stand in for
2 temporary work; **travailler en ~** to temp (fam)

intérimaire /ɛ̃teʀimɛʀ/ *adj* ‹*committee*› interim; ‹*minister*› acting; ‹*job, staff*› temporary

intérioriser /ɛ̃teʀjɔʀize/ [**v1**] *vt* to internalize

interjection /ɛ̃tɛʀʒɛksjɔ̃/ *f* interjection

interligne /ɛ̃tɛʀliɲ/ *m* line space

interlocuteur, **-trice** /ɛ̃tɛʀlɔkytœʀ, tʀis/ *mf*
1 mon ~ the person I am/was talking to
2 (in negotiations) representative
3 Louis est notre seul ~ Louis is our only contact

interloquer /ɛ̃tɛʀlɔke/ [**v1**] *vt* to take [sb] aback

interlude /ɛ̃tɛʀlyd/ *m* interlude

intermède /ɛ̃tɛʀmɛd/ *m* interlude

intermédiaire /ɛ̃tɛʀmedjɛʀ/ **A** *adj* ‹*rate, stage*› intermediate
B *mf* (in negotiations) go-between; (in industry) middleman
C *phr* **par l'~ de** through

interminable /ɛ̃tɛʀminabl/ *adj*
1 interminable, never-ending
2 endless

intermittence /ɛ̃tɛʀmitɑ̃s/ *f* **par ~** ‹*rain*› on and off; ‹*work*› intermittently

intermittent, **~e** /ɛ̃tɛʀmitɑ̃, ɑ̃t/ *adj* ‹*rain, fever*› intermittent; ‹*noise, efforts*› sporadic

internat /ɛ̃tɛʀna/ *m* boarding school

international, **~e**, *mpl* **-aux** /ɛ̃tɛʀnasjɔnal, o/ *adj* international

interne /ɛ̃tɛʀn/ **A** *adj* (gen) internal; ‹*training*› in-house; ‹*ear*› inner
B *mf* **1** (Sch) boarder
2 ~ (en médecine) houseman (BrE), intern (AmE)

internement /ɛ̃tɛʀnəmɑ̃/ *m* (Med) committal (to a psychiatric institution)

interner /ɛ̃tɛʀne/ [**v1**] *vt* to commit ‹*mental patient*›

Internet /ɛ̃tɛʀnɛt/ *m* Internet; **naviguer sur (l') ~** to surf the Internet

interpellation /ɛ̃tɛʀpelasjɔ̃/ *f* **procéder à des ~s** to take people in for questioning

interpeller /ɛ̃tɛʀpəle/ [**v1**] *vt* **1** to call out to; to shout at
2 to question; (in police station) to take [sb] in for questioning

interphone® /ɛ̃tɛʀfɔn/ *m* **1** intercom
2 entry phone

interposer: **s'interposer** /ɛ̃tɛʀpoze/ [**v1**] *v refl* (+ *v être*) to intervene; **par personne interposée** through an intermediary

interprétariat /ɛ̃tɛʀpʀetaʀja/ *m* interpreting

interprétation /ɛ̃tɛʀpʀetasjɔ̃/ *f* **1** (gen), (Mus) interpretation
2 (profession) interpreting

interprète /ɛ̃tɛʀpʀɛt/ *mf* **1** interpreter
2 performer
3 spokesperson

interpréter /ɛ̃tɛʀpʀete/ [**v14**] *vt* **1** to play ‹*role, sonata*›; to sing ‹*song*›
2 to interpret

interpréteur /ɛ̃tɛʀpʀetœʀ/ *m* (Comput) interpreter

interrogateur, **-trice** /ɛ̃tɛʀɔgatœʀ, tʀis/ *adj* enquiring; **d'un air ~** enquiringly

interrogatif, **-ive** /ɛ̃tɛʀɔgatif, iv/ *adj* interrogative

interrogation /ɛ̃tɛʀɔgasjɔ̃/ *f* **1** (of witness) questioning
2 (in grammar) question
3 (Sch) test; **~ orale** oral test

interrogatoire /ɛ̃tɛʀɔgatwaʀ/ *m* (gen) interrogation; (by police) questioning

interroger /ɛ̃tɛʀɔʒe/ [**v13**] **A** *vt* **1** (gen) to question; to ask; (fig) to examine ‹*conscience*›; **être interrogé comme témoin** (Law) to be called as a witness
2 ~ son répondeur to check one's calls
3 (Sch) to test
B s'interroger *v refl* (+ *v être*) **s'~ sur** to wonder about

interrompre /ɛ̃tɛʀɔ̃pʀ/ [**v53**] **A** *vt* **1** to interrupt; to break off ‹*dialogue*›; ‹*person*› to cease ‹*activity*›; **~ son repas pour faire** to stop eating to do
2 to put an end to ‹*holiday*›; to stop ‹*treatment*›; to terminate ‹*pregnancy*›
B s'interrompre *v refl* (+ *v être*)
1 ‹*person, conversation*› to break off
2 ‹*rain*› to stop

interrupteur /ɛ̃tɛʀyptœʀ/ *m* switch

interruption /ɛ̃tɛʀypsjɔ̃/ *f* **1** break; **sans ~** continuously
2 ending; **l'~ du dialogue entre** the breaking off of the dialogue (BrE) between

intersection /ɛ̃tɛʀsɛksjɔ̃/ *f* intersection

interstice /ɛ̃tɛʀstis/ *m* (in floor) crack; (in shutters, blinds) chink

intervalle /ɛ̃tɛʀval/ *m* **1** space; **à ~s réguliers** at regular intervals
2 interval; **dans l'~** meanwhile, in the meantime

intervenir /ɛ̃tɛʀvəniʀ/ [**v36**] *vi* **1** ‹*changes*› to take place; ‹*agreement*› to be reached
2 ‹*speaker*› to speak
3 (in emergency) ‹*police*› to intervene
4 ~ auprès de qn pour qn to intercede with sb on sb's behalf

intervention /ɛ̃tɛʀvɑ̃sjɔ̃/ *f* **1** intervention
2 speech; lecture
3 (Med) **~ (chirurgicale)** operation

intervertir /ɛ̃tɛʀvɛʀtiʀ/ [**v3**] *vt* to invert

interviewer /ɛ̃tɛʀvjuve/ [**v1**] *vt* to interview

intestin /ɛ̃tɛstɛ̃/ *m* bowel, intestine

intestinal, **~e**, *mpl* **-aux** /ɛ̃tɛstinal, o/ *adj* intestinal

intime /ɛ̃tim/ **A** *adj* **1** ‹*life, diary*› private; ‹*friend, relationship*› intimate; ‹*hygiene*› personal
2 ‹*gathering*› intimate; ‹*conversation*› private; ‹*dinner*› quiet
3 ‹*room*› cosy (BrE), cozy (AmE)
4 ‹*knowledge*› intimate
B *mf* close friend

key word

intimement /ɛ̃timmɑ̃/ *adv* intimately; **je suis ~ convaincu que...** I'm absolutely convinced that...

intimidation /ɛ̃timidasjɔ̃/ *f* intimidation; **d'~** ‹*measures, remarks*› intimidatory

intimider /ɛ̃timide/ [**v1**] *vt* to intimidate

intimité /ɛ̃timite/ *f* **1** intimacy
2 privacy; **dans la plus stricte ~** in the strictest privacy
3 private life
4 (of house, setting) cosiness

intitulé /ɛ̃tityle/ *m* title, heading

intituler /ɛ̃tityle/ [**v1**] **A** *vt* to call
B s'intituler *v refl* (+ *v être*) to be called, to be entitled

intolérable /ɛ̃tɔleʀabl/ *adj* intolerable; deeply shocking

intolérance /ɛ̃tɔleʀɑ̃s/ *f* intolerance

intolérant, **~e** /ɛ̃tɔleʀɑ̃, ɑ̃t/ *adj* intolerant

intonation /ɛ̃tɔnasjɔ̃/ *f* intonation

intoxication /ɛ̃tɔksikasjɔ̃/ *f* **1** (Med) poisoning
2 (fig) disinformation

intoxiquer /ɛ̃tɔksike/ [**v1**] **A** *vt* to poison
B s'intoxiquer *v refl* (+ *v être*) to poison oneself

intraitable /ɛ̃tʀɛtabl/ *adj* inflexible

intra-muros /ɛ̃tʀamyʀos/ *adj inv* **Paris ~** Paris itself

intransigeance /ɛ̃tʀɑ̃ziʒɑ̃s/ *f* intransigence

intransigeant, **~e** /ɛ̃tʀɑ̃ziʒɑ̃, ɑ̃t/ *adj* ‹*attitude*› uncompromising; ‹*person*› intransigent

intraveineuse /ɛ̃tʀavenøz/ *f* intravenous injection

intrépide /ɛ̃tʀepid/ *adj* intrepid, bold

intrépidité /ɛ̃tʀepidite/ *f* boldness

intrigant, **~e** /ɛ̃tʀigɑ̃, ɑ̃t/ *mf* schemer

intrigue /ɛ̃tʀig/ *f* **1** intrigue
2 plot; **une ~ policière** a detective story

intriguer /ɛ̃tʀige/ [**v1**] *vt* to intrigue

intrinsèque /ɛ̃tʀɛ̃sɛk/ *adj* intrinsic

introduction /ɛ̃tʀɔdyksjɔ̃/ *f* **1** (gen) introduction
2 (of key, probe) insertion

introduire /ɛ̃tʀɔdɥiʀ/ [**v69**] **A** *vt* **1** to insert ‹*object*›
2 to usher [sb] in ‹*visitor*›; (surreptitiously) to smuggle [sb] in
3 to introduce ‹*person*›
4 to introduce ‹*product, idea*›
B s'introduire *v refl* (+ *v être*) **s'~ dans** to get into

introduit, **~e** /ɛ̃tʀɔdɥi, it/ ▶ **introduire**

introspection /ɛ̃tʀɔspɛksjɔ̃/ *f* introspection

introverti, **~e** /ɛ̃tʀɔvɛʀti/ *mf* introvert

intrus, **~e** /ɛ̃tʀy, yz/ *mf* intruder

intrusion /ɛ̃tʀyzjɔ̃/ *f* **1** (gen) intrusion
2 interference

intuitif, **-ive** /ɛ̃tɥitif, iv/ *adj* intuitive

intuition /ɛ̃tɥisjɔ̃/ *f* intuition

inusable /inyzabl/ *adj* hard-wearing

inusité, **~e** /inyzite/ *adj* uncommon

inutile /inytil/ *adj* useless; pointless; needless; **(il est) ~ de faire** there's no point in doing; **~ de dire que** needless to say; **sans risques ~s** without unnecessary risks

inutilement /inytilmɑ̃/ *adv* unnecessarily; needlessly; in vain

inutilisable /inytilizabl/ *adj* unusable

inutilité /inytilite/ *f* (of expense, action) pointlessness

invalide /ɛ̃valid/ **A** *adj* disabled
B *mf* disabled person

invalidité /ɛ̃validite/ *f* (Med) disability

invariable /ɛ̃vaʀjabl/ *adj* invariable

invasion /ɛ̃vazjɔ̃/ *f* invasion

invendable /ɛ̃vɑ̃dabl/ *adj* unsaleable

invendu, **~e** /ɛ̃vɑ̃dy/ *adj* unsold

inventaire /ɛ̃vɑ̃tɛʀ/ *m* **1** stocktaking (BrE), inventory (AmE)
2 stocklist (BrE), inventory (AmE)
3 (of wardrobe, suitcase) list of contents

inventer /ɛ̃vɑ̃te/ [**v1**] **A** *vt* to invent; to devise; **je n'invente rien** I'm not making it up
B s'inventer *v refl* (+ *v être*) **ça ne s'invente pas** that has to be true
IDIOM **il n'a pas inventé la poudre** (fam) he is not very bright

inventeur, **-trice** /ɛ̃vɑ̃tœʀ, tʀis/ *mf* inventor

inventif, **-ive** /ɛ̃vɑ̃tif, iv/ *adj* **1** inventive
2 resourceful

invention /ɛ̃vɑ̃sjɔ̃/ *f* **1** invention
2 fabrication; **c'est de l'~ pure** it's a complete fabrication

inventorier /ɛ̃vɑ̃tɔʀje/ [**v2**] *vt* to make out an inventory of

inverse /ɛ̃vɛʀs/ **A** *adj* (gen) opposite; **dans l'ordre ~** (referring to list) in reverse order
B *m* (gen) **l'~** the opposite; **à l'~** conversely; **à l'~ de ce qu'il croyait** contrary to what he thought

inversement /ɛ̃vɛʀsəmɑ̃/ *adv* (gen) conversely

inverser /ɛ̃vɛʀse/ [**v1**] *vt* **1** to invert ‹*position*›; to reverse ‹*roles*›; **image inversée** mirror image
2 to reverse ‹*electric current*›

inversion /ɛ̃vɛʀsjɔ̃/ *f* inversion; reversal

invertébré, **~e** /ɛ̃vɛʀtebʀe/ *adj* invertebrate

invertir /ɛ̃vɛʀtiʀ/ [**v3**] *vt* to reverse; to switch [sth] round ‹*words*›

investigation /ɛ̃vɛstigasjɔ̃/ *f* investigation; **d'~** investigative

investir /ɛ̃vɛstiʀ/ [**v3**] **A** *vt* **1** to invest ‹*capital*›
2 to invest ‹*person, ambassador*›
3 ‹*police*› to go into; ‹*tourists, demonstrators*› to take over
4 ‹*army*› to besiege

B **s'investir** *v refl* (+ *v être*) **s'~ dans** to put a lot of oneself into; to invest emotionally in

investissement /ɛ̃vɛstismɑ̃/ *m* (gen) investment; (Mil) investing

investisseur /ɛ̃vɛstisœʀ/ *m* investor

investiture /ɛ̃vɛstityʀ/ *f* investiture

invétéré, **~e** /ɛ̃veteʀe/ *adj* ‹*drinker, thief*› inveterate; ‹*liar*› compulsive

invincible /ɛ̃vɛ̃sibl/ *adj* ‹*people*› invincible

inviolable /ɛ̃vjɔlabl/ *adj* (gen) inviolable; ‹*door, safe*› impregnable

invisible /ɛ̃vizibl/ *adj* **1** invisible; **la route était ~ depuis la maison** the road could not be seen from the house
2 ‹*danger*› unseen

invitation /ɛ̃vitasjɔ̃/ *f* invitation

invité, **~e** /ɛ̃vite/ *mf* guest

inviter /ɛ̃vite/ [**v1**] *vt* to invite; **ceci invite à penser que...** this suggests that...

invivable /ɛ̃vivabl/ *adj* unbearable

invocation /ɛ̃vɔkasjɔ̃/ *f* invocation

involontaire /ɛ̃vɔlɔ̃tɛʀ/ *adj* ‹*reaction*› involuntary; ‹*mistake*› unintentional

invoquer /ɛ̃vɔke/ [**v1**] *vt* to invoke

invraisemblable /ɛ̃vʀɛsɑ̃blabl/ *adj*
1 ‹*story*› unlikely; ‹*explanation*› implausible
2 (fam) fantastic, incredible

invraisemblance /ɛ̃vʀɛsɑ̃blɑ̃s/ *f*
1 unlikelihood
2 improbability

invulnérable /ɛ̃vylneʀabl/ *adj* invulnerable

iode /jɔd/ *m* iodine

iota /jɔta/ *m inv* iota
(IDIOMS) **ne pas changer d'un ~** not to change one iota; **ne pas bouger d'un ~** not to move an inch

ira /iʀa/ ▶ **aller**[1]

irai /iʀɛ/ ▶ **aller**[1]

iraient /iʀɛ/ ▶ **aller**[1]

irais /iʀɛ/ ▶ **aller**[1]

irait /iʀɛ/ ▶ **aller**[1]

iras /iʀa/ ▶ **aller**[1]

irascible /iʀasibl/ *adj* ‹*person*› quick-tempered

irez /iʀe/ ▶ **aller**[1]

iriez /iʀje/ ▶ **aller**[1]

irions /iʀjɔ̃/ ▶ **aller**[1]

iris /iʀis/ *m inv* **1** (flower) iris
2 (of eye) iris

irisé, **~e** /iʀize/ *adj* iridescent

irlandais, **~e** /iʀlɑ̃dɛ, ɛz/ **A** *adj* Irish
B *m* (language) Irish

Irlandais, **~e** /iʀlɑ̃dɛ, ɛz/ *mf* Irishman/Irishwoman

Irlande /iʀlɑ̃d/ *pr f* Ireland; **la République d'~** the Republic of Ireland; **l'~ du Nord** Northern Ireland

IRM /iɛʀɛm/ *f* (*abbr* = **imagerie par résonance magnétique**) MRI

ironie /iʀɔni/ *f* irony; **faire de l'~** to be ironic

ironique /iʀɔnik/ *adj* ironic

ironiser /iʀɔnize/ [**v1**] *vi* to be ironic (**sur** about)

irons /iʀɔ̃/ ▶ **aller**[1]

iront /iʀɔ̃/ ▶ **aller**[1]

irradier /iʀadje/ [**v2**] **A** *vt* to irradiate
B *vi* to radiate

irrattrapable /iʀatʀapabl/ *adj* irretrievable

irréalisable /iʀealizabl/ *adj* ‹*dream*› impossible; ‹*plan*› unworkable

irrécupérable /iʀekypeʀabl/ *adj*
1 irrecoverable
2 damaged beyond repair
3 ‹*delinquent*› beyond help

irréductible /iʀedyktibl/ *mf* diehard

irréel, **-elle** /iʀeɛl/ *adj* unreal

irréfléchi, **~e** /iʀefleʃi/ *adj* ill-considered

irréfutable /iʀefytabl/ *adj* irrefutable

irrégularité /iʀegylaʀite/ *f* irregularity

irrégulier, **-ière** /iʀegylje, ɛʀ/ *adj*
1 irregular; uneven
2 ‹*procedure*› irregular; **immigré en situation irrégulière** illegal immigrant
3 ‹*athlete*› whose performance is uneven

irrégulièrement /iʀegyljɛʀmɑ̃/ *adv*
1 illegally
2 irregularly; unevenly; erratically

irrémédiable /iʀ(ʀ)emedjabl/ *adj* irreparable

irremplaçable /iʀɑ̃plasabl/ *adj* irreplaceable

irréparable /iʀepaʀabl/ **A** *adj* ‹*car*› beyond repair; ‹*damage, crime*› irreparable
B *m* **commettre l'~** to go beyond the point of no return

irrépressible /iʀepʀesibl/ *adj* (gen) irrepressible; ‹*tears*› uncontrollable

irréprochable /iʀepʀɔʃabl/ *adj* ‹*life, employee*› beyond reproach; ‹*work*› perfect

irrésistible /iʀezistibl/ *adj* irresistible; ‹*person, joke*› hilarious

irrésolu, **~e** /iʀezɔly/ *adj* ‹*person*› indecisive; ‹*problem, mystery*› unsolved

irrespirable /iʀɛspiʀabl/ *adj* ‹*air*› unbreathable; ‹*atmosphere*› stifling

irresponsable /iʀɛspɔ̃sabl/ *adj* irresponsible

irrévérencieux, **-ieuse** /iʀeveʀɑ̃sjø, øz/ *adj* irreverent

irréversible /iʀevɛʀsibl/ *adj* irreversible

irrévocable /iʀevɔkabl/ *adj* irrevocable

irrigation /iʀigasjɔ̃/ *f* **1** (of land) irrigation
2 (Med) supply of blood

irriguer /iʀige/ [**v1**] *vt* to irrigate

irritation /iʀitasjɔ̃/ *f* (gen), (Med) irritation

irriter /iʀite/ [**v1**] **A** *vt* **1** to irritate, to annoy
2 (Med) to irritate
B **s'irriter** *v refl* (+ *v être*) **1** to get angry
2 (Med) to become irritated

key word

irruption /iʀypsjɔ̃/ *f* **faire ~ dans** to burst into ‹*room*›

islam /islam/ *m* **l'~** Islam

islamique /islamik/ *adj* Islamic

islamisme /islamism/ *m* Islam

islamiste **A** *adj* Islamist, Islamic
B *mf* Islamist

Islande /islɑ̃d/ *pr f* Iceland

isolant, **~e** /izɔlɑ̃, ɑ̃t/ *adj* insulating

isolation /izɔlasjɔ̃/ *f* insulation

isolement /izɔlmɑ̃/ *m* **1** (of village) remoteness; (of house) isolated location
2 (of patient, politician) isolation; (of prisoner) solitary confinement

isoler /izɔle/ [**v1**] **A** *vt* **1** to isolate ‹*sick person, dissident*›; to put [sb] in solitary confinement ‹*prisoner*›
2 to isolate ‹*gene, substance*›
3 to soundproof; to insulate
4 to insulate ‹*wire*›
B **s'isoler** *v refl* (+ *v être*) to isolate oneself

isoloir /izɔlwaʀ/ *m* voting *or* polling (BrE) booth

isotherme /izotɛʀm/ *adj* refrigerated; **boîte ~** ice box; **sac ~** cool bag

issu, **~e** /isy/ *adj* **être ~ de** to come from; to result from

issue /isy/ *f* **1** exit; **'sans ~'** 'no exit'
2 solution; **situation sans ~** situation with no solution
3 outcome; **à l'~ de** at the end of; **à l'~ de trois jours de pourparlers** at the close of three days of talks
■ **~ de secours** emergency exit

Italie /itali/ *pr f* Italy

italien, **-ienne** /italjɛ̃, ɛn/ **A** *adj* Italian
B *m* (language) Italian

italique /italik/ *m* italics

itinéraire /itineʀɛʀ/ *m* **1** (gen) route; (detailed) itinerary
2 (fig) career
■ **~ bis** alternative route; **~ de délestage** relief route

itinérance /itineʀɔ̃s/ *adj* (mobile phone) roaming

itinérant, **~e** /itineʀɑ̃, ɑ̃t/ *adj* ‹*exhibition*› touring; ‹*life*› peripatetic; ‹*circus*› travelling (BrE)

IUFM /iyɛfɛm/ *m*: *abbr* ▶ **institut**

IUT /iyte/ *m*: *abbr* ▶ **institut**

ivoire /ivwaʀ/ *adj inv*, *m* ivory

ivoirien, **-ienne** /ivwaʀjɛ̃, ɛn/ *adj* of the Ivory Coast

ivre /ivʀ/ *adj* **1** drunk, intoxicated
2 ~ de rage wild with rage

ivresse /ivʀɛs/ *f* **1** intoxication
2 exhilaration

ivrogne /ivʀɔɲ/ *mf* drunkard

Jj

j, **J** /ʒi/ *m inv* j, J; **le jour J** D-Day

j' ▶ **je**

jabot /ʒabo/ *m* **1** (of bird) crop
2 (of shirt) jabot

jacasser /ʒakase/ [**v1**] *vi* to chatter

jachère /ʒaʃɛʀ/ *f* **(terre en) ~** fallow land

jacinthe /ʒasɛ̃t/ *f* hyacinth

jackpot /(d)ʒakpɔt/ *m* **1** jackpot
2 slot machine

jacquet /ʒakɛ/ *m* backgammon

jacter /ʒakte/ [**v1**] *vi* (pop) to jaw (fam), to talk

jade /ʒad/ *m* jade

jadis /ʒadis/ *adv* formerly, in the past

jaguar /ʒagwaʀ/ *m* jaguar

jaillir /ʒajiʀ/ [**v3**] *vi* ‹*liquid*› to gush out; ‹*tears*› to flow; ‹*flame*› to shoot up; ‹*truth*› to emerge

jais /ʒɛ/ *m inv* **1** jet
2 (noir) de ~ jet-black

jalon /ʒalɔ̃/ *m* **1** marker
2 (fig) **poser les ~s de** to prepare the ground for

jalonner /ʒalɔne/ [**v1**] *vt* **1** ‹*trees*› to line ‹*road*›; ‹*incidents*› to punctuate ‹*career*›
2 to mark out ‹*road*›

jalousement /ʒaluzmɑ̃/ *adv* jealously; enviously

jalouser /ʒaluze/ [**v1**] *vt* to be jealous of

jalousie /ʒaluzi/ *f* **1** jealousy
2 slatted blind

jaloux, **-ouse** /ʒalu, uz/ **A** *adj* jealous
B *mf* jealous man/woman

jamais /ʒamɛ/ *adv* **1** never; **rien n'est ~ certain** nothing is ever certain; **sait-on ~?** you never know; **~ de la vie!** never!
2 ever; **plus belle que ~** prettier than ever; **si ~** if

i
j

3 à tout ~ forever
4 ne... ~ que only; **il ne fait ~ que son devoir** he is only doing his duty

✍ **jambe** /ʒɑ̃b/ *f* leg; **avoir de bonnes ~s** to have strong legs; **courir à toutes ~s** to run as fast as one's legs can carry one; **j'ai les ~s comme du coton** (fam) I feel weak at the knees; **traîner la ~** (fam) to trudge along
IDIOMS **cela me fait une belle ~** (fam) a fat lot of good that does me (fam); **il ne tient plus sur ses ~s** he can hardly stand up; **prendre ses ~s à son cou** to take to one's heels; **tenir la ~ à qn** to keep talking to sb; **par-dessus** *or* **par-dessous la ~** in a slipshod manner

✍ **jambon** /ʒɑ̃bɔ̃/ *m* ham
■ **~ blanc** *or* **de Paris** cooked ham; **~ de pays** cured ham

jambonneau, *pl* **~x** /ʒɑ̃bɔno/ *m* knuckle of ham

jante /ʒɑ̃t/ *f* **1** rim
2 wheel

j

✍ **janvier** /ʒɑ̃vje/ *m* January

Japon /ʒapɔ̃/ *pr m* Japan

japonais, **~e** /ʒapɔnɛ, ɛz/ **A** *adj* Japanese
B *m* (language) Japanese

jappement /ʒapmɑ̃/ *m* yapping

japper /ʒape/ [**v1**] *vi* to yap

jaquette /ʒakɛt/ *f* **1** morning coat
2 dust jacket
3 (on tooth) crown

✍ **jardin** /ʒaʀdɛ̃/ *m* garden (BrE), yard (AmE); **chaise de ~** garden chair (BrE), patio chair (AmE)
■ **~ d'acclimatation** ▶ **jardin zoologique**; **~ d'agrément** ornamental garden; **~ d'enfants** kindergarten; **~ potager** vegetable garden; **~ public** park; **~ zoologique** zoo

jardinage /ʒaʀdinaʒ/ *m* gardening

jardiner /ʒaʀdine/ [**v1**] *vi* to do some gardening

jardinier, **-ière** /ʒaʀdinje, ɛʀ/ **A** *adj* garden
B *mf* gardener

jardinière /ʒaʀdinjɛʀ/ *f* jardinière

jargon /ʒaʀgɔ̃/ *m* **1** jargon; **~ administratif** officialese
2 gibberish

jarre /ʒaʀ/ *f* (earthenware) jar

jarret /ʒaʀɛ/ *m* **1** (of human) ham, hollow of the knee
2 (of animal) hock
3 (Culin) **~ de veau** knuckle of veal

jarretelle /ʒaʀtɛl/ *f* suspender (BrE), garter (AmE)

jars /ʒaʀ/ *m inv* gander

jaser /ʒaze/ [**v1**] *vi* to gossip

jasmin /ʒasmɛ̃/ *m* jasmine

jatte /ʒat/ *f* bowl, basin

jauge /ʒoʒ/ *f* gauge; **~ d'huile** dipstick

✍ key word

jaunâtre /ʒonɑtʀ/ *adj* yellowish

✍ **jaune** /ʒon/ **A** *adj* yellow; **~ d'or** golden yellow; **~ paille** straw-coloured (BrE); **~ poussin** bright yellow; **teint ~** sallow complexion
B *m* **1** yellow
2 ~ (d'œuf) (egg) yolk
3 blackleg (BrE), scab
IDIOM **rire ~** (fam) to give a forced laugh

jaunir /ʒoniʀ/ [**v3**] **A** *vt* to turn [sth] yellow, to make [sth] go yellow
B *vi* to go yellow

jaunisse /ʒonis/ *f* jaundice; **il va en faire une ~!** (fam) that'll put his nose out of joint!

java /ʒava/ *f* **1** popular dance
2 (fam) rave-up (fam)

Javel /ʒavɛl/ *f* **(eau de) ~** ≈ bleach

javelliser /ʒavelize/ [**v1**] *vt* to chlorinate

javelot /ʒavlo/ *m* javelin

J.-C. (*written abbr* = **Jésus-Christ**) **avant ~** BC; **après ~** AD

✍ **je**, **j'** *before vowel or mute h* /ʒ(ə)/ *pron* I

jean /dʒin/ *m* **1** (pair of) jeans
2 denim

jeannette /ʒanɛt/ *f* ≈ Brownie

je-ne-sais-quoi /ʒənsɛkwa/ *m inv* **avoir un ~** to have a certain something

jérémiades /ʒeʀemjad/ *fpl* moaning

jerrican /ʒeʀikan/ *m* jerrycan

jersey /ʒɛʀzɛ/ *m* **1** jersey
2 stocking stitch

jésuite /ʒezɥit/ *adj, m* Jesuit

Jésus /ʒezy/ *pr n* Jesus

jet¹ /ʒɛ/ *m* **1** throwing; throw
2 jet; spurt; burst; **passer au ~** to hose down; **premier ~** (fig) first sketch; **d'un seul ~** ‹*write*› in one go
■ **~ d'eau** fountain; hosepipe

jet² /dʒɛt/ *m* jet (plane)

jetable /ʒətabl/ *adj* disposable

jetée /ʒəte/ *f* pier; jetty

✍ **jeter** /ʒəte/ [**v20**] **A** *vt* **1** to throw; to hurl; to throw away *or* out; **~ qch à qn** to throw sth to sb ‹*ball*›; to throw sth at sb ‹*stone*›; **~ qn dehors** to throw sb out; **~ quelques idées sur le papier** (fig) to jot down a few ideas; **bon à ~** fit for the bin (BrE) *or* the garbage (AmE)
2 to give ‹*cry, light*›; to cast ‹*glance, shadow*›
3 to create ‹*confusion, terror*›; **~ l'émoi dans la ville** to throw the town into turmoil
B se jeter *v refl* (+ *v être*) **1 se ~ du haut d'un pont** to throw oneself off a bridge; **se ~ sur** to fall upon ‹*opponent*›; to pounce on ‹*prey, newspaper*›; **se ~ au cou de qn** to fling oneself around sb's neck; **se ~ à l'eau** to jump into the water; (fig) to take the plunge; **(aller) se ~ contre un arbre** to crash into a tree
2 ‹*river*› to flow

jeton /ʒ(ə)tɔ̃/ *m* (for machine) token; (in board games) counter; (at casino) chip

jeu, *pl* **~x** /ʒø/ *m* **1 le ~** play; **un ~** a game; **faire un ~** to play a game; **par ~** for fun; **entrer en ~** to come into the picture; **se prendre** *or* **se piquer au ~** to get hooked; **mettre en ~** to bring [sth] into play; to stake; **hors ~** offside; **ils ont beau ~ de me critiquer** it's easy for them to criticize me
2 le ~ gambling; **ton avenir est en ~** your future is at stake
3 (in cards) hand; **cacher bien son ~** (fig) to keep it quiet
4 (of cards) deck; **~ d'échecs** chess set
5 (of actor) acting; (of musician) playing; (of sportsman) game
6 (of keys, spanners) set
■ **~ d'argent** game played for money; **~ de construction** construction set; **~ électronique** computer game; **~ de massacre** ≈ coconut shy (BrE); **~ de mots** pun; **~ de l'oie** ≈ snakes and ladders (BrE); **~ de société** board game; party game; **~ télévisé** (TV) game show; **~x Olympiques**, **JO** Olympic Games; **~x Paralympiques** Paralympic Games
IDIOMS **jouer le ~** to play the game; **c'est pas de** *or* **du ~!** (fam) that's not fair!; **faire le ~ de qn** to play into sb's hands

jeu-concours, *pl* **jeux-concours** /ʒøkɔ̃kuʀ/ *m* competition

jeudi /ʒødi/ *m* Thursday
IDIOM **ça aura lieu la semaine des quatre ~s!** (fam) it won't happen, not in a month of Sundays!

jeun: **à jeun** /aʒœ̃/ *phr* **1** on an empty stomach
2 (fam) sober

jeune /ʒœn/ **A** *adj* **1** (gen) young; ‹*industry*› new; ‹*face, hairstyle*› youthful; **nos ~s années** our youth; **le ~ âge** youth; **le ~ marié** the groom; **la ~ mariée** the bride
2 younger; **mon ~ frère** my younger brother
B *mf* young person; **les ~s** young people
C *adv* **s'habiller ~** to wear young styles; **faire ~** to look young
■ **~ femme** young woman; **~ fille** girl; **~ homme** young man; **~ loup** up-and-coming executive; **~ premier** romantic lead

jeûne /ʒøn/ *m* **1** fasting; fast
2 period of fasting

jeûner /ʒøne/ [**v1**] *vi* to fast

jeunesse /ʒœnɛs/ *f* **1** youth; **une seconde ~** a new lease of life; **une erreur de ~** a youthful indiscretion
2 young people
IDIOMS **il faut que ~ se passe** youth will have its fling; **les voyages forment la ~** travel broadens the mind

jf *written abbr* jeune femme *or* jeune fille; ▸ **jeune**

jh *written abbr* jeune homme

JO /ʒio/ *mpl*: *abbr* ▸ **jeu**

joaillerie /ʒɔajʀi/ *f* **1** jeweller's shop (BrE), jewelry store (AmE)
2 jewellery (BrE), jewelry (AmE)

joaillier, **-ière** /ʒɔalje, ɛʀ/ *mf* jeweller (BrE), jeweler (AmE)

Joconde /ʒɔkɔ̃d/ *n pr* **la ~** the Mona Lisa

joggeur, **-euse** /dʒɔgœʀ, øz/ *mf* jogger

joie /ʒwa/ *f* joy; **au comble de la ~** overjoyed; **se faire une ~ de faire** to look forward to doing; to be delighted to do
IDIOM **s'en donner à cœur ~** to enjoy oneself to the full; (fig) to have a field day

joignable /ʒwaɲabl/ *adj* **il n'est pas ~ en ce moment** he's not available at the moment

joindre /ʒwɛ̃dʀ/ [**v56**] **A** *vt* **1** to get hold of ‹*person*›
2 to enclose ‹*cheque*›; to attach ‹*card*›
3 to link ‹*points*›; to put [sth] together ‹*planks, feet*›; **~ l'intelligence à la simplicité** to be intelligent without being pretentious
B se joindre *v refl* (+ *v être*) **1 se ~ à** to join ‹*person, group*›; to join in ‹*conversation*›
2 ‹*lips*› to meet; ‹*hands*› to join
IDIOM **~ les deux bouts** (fam) to make ends meet

joint[1], **~e** /ʒwɛ̃, ɛ̃t/ ▸ **joindre**

joint[2] /ʒwɛ̃/ *m* (in wood) joint; (on pipes) seal

jointure /ʒwɛ̃tyʀ/ *f* joint

jojo **A** *adj inv* **il n'est pas ~ ton chapeau** your hat isn't very nice; **ce n'est pas ~ ce qu'ils lui ont fait** what they did to him/her wasn't very nice
B *m* **un affreux ~** a horrible brat (fam); a weirdo (fam)

joli, **~e** /ʒɔli/ **A** *adj* (gen) nice; ‹*face*› pretty; ‹*sum*› tidy; **faire ~** to look nice
B *m* **c'est du ~!** (ironic) very nice!
■ **~ cœur** smooth talker; **faire le ~ cœur** to play Romeo
IDIOM **être ~ à croquer** *or* **comme un cœur** to be as pretty as a picture

joliment /ʒɔlimɑ̃/ *adv* **1** prettily, nicely
2 (fam) ‹*happy, well*› really; ‹*handle*› nicely

jonc /ʒɔ̃/ *m* rush

joncher /ʒɔ̃ʃe/ [**v1**] *vt* ‹*papers, leaves*› to be strewn over ‹*ground*›

jonction /ʒɔ̃ksjɔ̃/ *f* **1** junction
2 link-up

jongler /ʒɔ̃gle/ [**v1**] *vi* to juggle

jonque /ʒɔ̃k/ *f* junk

jonquille /ʒɔ̃kij/ *f* daffodil

jouable /ʒwabl/ *adj* **1** feasible; **le pari est ~** the gamble might pay off
2 ‹*piece of music*› playable; **une pièce qui n'est pas ~** a play that's impossible to stage

joue /ʒu/ *f* **1** cheek
2 (Mil) **en ~!** aim!; **mettre qn en ~** to take aim at sb

jouer /ʒwe/ [**v1**] **A** *vt* **1** to play ‹*match, music*›
2 to back ‹*horse*›; to stake ‹*money*›; to risk ‹*reputation, life*›; **c'est joué d'avance** it's a foregone conclusion; **tout n'est pas encore joué** the game isn't over yet; **~ le tout pour**

le tout to go for broke (fam)
3 qu'est-ce qu'on joue au théâtre/cinéma? what's on at the theatre/cinema?
4 ~ les imbéciles to play dumb
B jouer à *v+prep* to play ‹*tennis, game*›; to play with ‹*doll*›; **~ à qui perd gagne** to play 'loser takes all'; **~ à la marchande** to play shops
C jouer de *v+prep* **1 ~ de** to play ‹*instrument*›
2 ~ de to use ‹*influence*›
D *vi* **1** to play; **arrête de ~ avec ta bague!** stop fiddling with your ring!; **à toi de ~!** your turn!; (fig) the ball's in your court!; **bien joué!** well played!; (fig) well done!
2 to gamble; **~ avec** to gamble with ‹*life, health*›; **~ aux courses** to bet on the horses; **~ sur** to bank on ‹*credulity*›
3 to act; **il joue bien** he's a good actor
4 ‹*argument, clause*› to apply; ‹*age*› to matter; **faire ~ ses relations** to make use of one's connections
E se jouer *v refl* (+ *v être*) **1** ‹*future, peace*› to be at stake; ‹*drama*› to be played out
2 se ~ de to make light work of ‹*obstacle*›

jouet /ʒwɛ/ *m* **1** toy
2 plaything

🔑 **joueur, -euse** /ʒwœʀ, øz/ **A** *adj* **1** playful
2 être ~/joueuse to be a gambling man/woman
B *mf* **1** player; **être beau/mauvais ~** to be a good/bad loser
2 gambler

joufflu, ~e /ʒufly/ *adj* ‹*person*› chubby-cheeked; ‹*face*› chubby

joug /ʒu/ *m* yoke

🔑 **jouir** /ʒwiʀ/ [**v3**] *v+prep* **~ de** to enjoy; to enjoy the use of ‹*property*›; ‹*place*› to have ‹*view, climate*›

jouissance /ʒwisɑ̃s/ *f* **1** (Law) use
2 pleasure

joujou, *pl* **~x** /ʒuʒu/ *m* (baby talk) toy

🔑 **jour** /ʒuʀ/ *m* **1** day; **quel ~ sommes-nous?** what day is it today?; **un ~ ou l'autre** some day; **~ pour ~** to the day; **à ce ~** to date; **à ~** up to date; **mettre à ~** to bring up to date ‹*work*›; to revise ‹*edition*›; **mise à ~** updating; **de nos ~s** nowadays; **d'un ~ à l'autre** ‹*expected*› any day now; ‹*change*› from one day to the next; **du ~ au lendemain** overnight; **d'un ~** ‹*fashion*› passing; ‹*queen*› for a day; **vivre au ~ le ~** to live one day at a time; **le ~ se lève** it's getting light; **au lever du ~** at daybreak; **le petit ~** the early morning; **de ~** ‹*work*› days; ‹*travel*› in the daytime
2 daylight; light; **en plein ~** in broad daylight; **se faire ~** ‹*truth*› to come to light; **éclairer qch d'un ~ nouveau** to shed new light on sth; **je t'ai vu sous ton vrai ~** I saw you in your true colours (BrE)
3 (fig) **donner le ~ à qn** to bring sb into the world; **voir le ~** ‹*person*› to come into the world; ‹*work of art*› to see the light of day; **mes ~s sont comptés** my days are numbered; **des ~s difficiles** hard times; **les beaux ~s reviennent** spring will soon be here
4 (in wall) gap; **~s** openwork (embroidery)
■ **~ de l'An** New Year's Day; **~ férié** bank holiday (BrE), legal holiday (AmE); **~ de fermeture** closing day; **~ ouvrable** working day

🔑 **journal**, *pl* **-aux** /ʒuʀnal, o/ *m* **1** newspaper
2 magazine
3 news (bulletin)
4 journal
■ **~ de bord** logbook; **~ intime** diary; **Journal officiel** *government publication listing new acts, laws etc*

journalier, -ière /ʒuʀnalje, ɛʀ/ *adj* daily

journalisme /ʒuʀnalism/ *m* journalism

🔑 **journaliste** /ʒuʀnalist/ *mf* journalist

journalistique /ʒuʀnalistik/ *adj* journalistic

🔑 **journée** /ʒuʀne/ *f* day; **~ de repos** day off; **dans la ~** during the day; **la ~ d'hier/de mardi** yesterday/Tuesday; **faire des ~s de huit heures** to work an eight-hour day

joute /ʒut/ *f* **1** (fig) jousting, battle; **~ oratoire** *or* **verbale** sparring match
2 joust

jouvence /ʒuvɑ̃s/ *f* **fontaine de ~** Fountain of Youth

jouxter /ʒukste/ [**v1**] *vt* to adjoin

jovial, ~e, *mpl* **~s** *or* **-iaux** /ʒɔvjal, o/ *adj* jovial

jovialité /ʒɔvjalite/ *f* joviality

joyau, *pl* **~x** /ʒwajo/ *m* jewel, gem

joyeusement /ʒwajøzmɑ̃/ *adv* merrily, cheerfully

🔑 **joyeux, -euse** /ʒwajø, øz/ *adj* merry, cheerful

jubilation /ʒybilasjɔ̃/ *f* joy, jubilation

jubilé /ʒybile/ *m* jubilee

jubiler /ʒybile/ [**v1**] *vi* to be jubilant

jucher /ʒyʃe/ [**v1**] *vt*, **se jucher** *v refl* (+ *v être*) to perch

judaïsme /ʒydaism/ *m* Judaism

judas /ʒyda/ *m inv* peephole

judiciaire /ʒydisjɛʀ/ *adj* judicial

judicieux, -ieuse /ʒydisjø, øz/ *adj* judicious, sensible

judo /ʒydo/ *m* judo

🔑 **juge** /ʒyʒ/ *m* judge; **être à la fois ~ et partie** to be judge and jury
■ **~ d'instruction** examining magistrate; **~ de touche** linesman

jugé: **au jugé** /oʒyʒe/ *phr* ‹*value*› by guesswork; ‹*shoot*› blind

🔑 **jugement** /ʒyʒmɑ̃/ *m* judgement; **passer en ~** ‹*case*› to come to court

jugeote /ʒyʒɔt/ *f* (fam) common sense

🔑 **juger** /ʒyʒe/ [**v13**] **A** *vt* **1** to judge ‹*person,*

🔑 key word

competition›; **mal ~ qn** to misjudge sb
2 to consider; **~ utile de faire** to consider it useful to do
3 (Law) to try ‹*case*›; to judge ‹*case*›
B juger de *v+prep* to assess; **j'en jugerai par moi-même** I'll judge for myself; **à en ~ par** judging by

juguler /ʒygyle/ [**v1**] *vt* to stamp out ‹*epidemic, uprising*›; to curb ‹*inflation*›

juif, **juive** /ʒɥif, ʒɥiv/ **A** *adj* Jewish
B *mf* Jew

juillet /ʒɥijɛ/ *m* July; **le 14 ~** Bastille Day

juin /ʒɥɛ̃/ *m* June

juive ▶ **juif**

jumeau, **-elle** *mpl* **~x** /ʒymo, ɛl/ *adj, mf* twin

jumelage /ʒymlaʒ/ *m* twinning

jumeler /ʒymle/ [**v19**] *vt* to twin

jumelle /ʒymɛl/ *f* **jumelles** *fpl* binoculars; **~s de théâtre** opera glasses

jument /ʒymɑ̃/ *f* mare

jungle /ʒœ̃gl/ *f* jungle

junte /ʒœ̃t/ *f* junta

jupe /ʒyp/ *f* skirt
IDIOM **il est toujours dans les ~s de sa mère** he's tied to his mother's apron strings

jupe-culotte, *pl* **jupes-culottes** /ʒypkylɔt/ *f* culottes, divided skirt

jupette /ʒypɛt/ *f* short skirt

jupon /ʒypɔ̃/ *m* petticoat
IDIOM **courir le ~** to womanize

jurançon /ʒyʀɑ̃sɔ̃/ *m* jurançon wine

juré, **~e** /ʒyʀe/ **A** *pp* ▶ **jurer**
B *pp adj* **1** on oath; sworn-in
2 ‹*enemy*› sworn
C *m* juror; **les ~s** the members of the jury

jurer /ʒyʀe/ [**v1**] **A** *vt* to swear; **on leur a fait ~ le secret** they were sworn to secrecy; **~ de tuer qn** to vow to kill sb; **ah mais je te jure!** (fam) honestly! (fam)
B jurer de *v+prep* to swear to
C *vi* **1** to swear
2 ‹*colours*› to clash
3 ne ~ que par to swear by
D se jurer *v refl* (+ *v être*) **1** to swear [sth] to one another
2 to vow
IDIOM **il ne faut ~ de rien** (Proverb) never say never

juridiction /ʒyʀidiksjɔ̃/ *f* **1** jurisdiction
2 courts

juridique /ʒyʀidik/ *adj* legal; **vide ~** gap in the law

jurisprudence /ʒyʀispʀydɑ̃s/ *f* case law

juriste /ʒyʀist/ *mf* **1** jurist
2 lawyer

juron /ʒyʀɔ̃/ *m* swear word

jury /ʒyʀi/ *m* **1** jury
2 panel of judges
3 board of examiners

jus /ʒy/ *m inv* **1** juice
2 (from meat) juices; gravy
3 electricity; **prendre le ~** to get a shock

jusque, **jusqu'** *before vowel* /ʒysk/ **A** *prep*
1 aller jusqu'à Paris to go as far as Paris; to go all the way to Paris; **courir jusqu'au bout du jardin** to run right down to the bottom of the garden (BrE) *or* the end of the yard (AmE); **suivre qn ~ dans sa chambre** to follow sb right into his/her room; **la nouvelle est arrivée jusqu'à nous** the news has reached us; **jusqu'où comptez-vous aller?** how far do you intend to go?
2 jusqu'à, **jusqu'en** until, till; **jusqu'à présent**, **jusqu'ici** (up) until now
3 monter jusqu'à 20° to go up to 20°
4 to the point of; **aller jusqu'à faire** to go so far as to do
5 even; **des détritus ~ sous la table** rubbish everywhere, even under the table
B jusqu'à ce que *phr* until

jusque-là /ʒyskəla/ *adv* **1** until then, up to then
2 up to here; up to there
IDIOMS **en avoir ~ de qn/qch** (fam) to have had it up to here with sb/sth (fam); **s'en mettre ~** (fam) to stuff one's face (fam)

justaucorps /ʒystokɔʀ/ *m inv* leotard

juste /ʒyst/ **A** *adj* **1** ‹*person*› just, fair
2 ‹*cause*› just; ‹*anger*› righteous; ‹*word, answer*› right, correct
3 ‹*balance, watch*› accurate; **~ milieu** happy medium; **à ~ titre** with good reason; **dire des choses ~s** to make some valid points; **apprécier qn à sa ~ valeur** to get a fair picture of sb
4 (Mus) ‹*piano, voice*› in tune; ‹*note*› true
5 c'est un peu ~ (in width, time) it's a bit tight; (in quantity) it's barely enough
B *adv* **1** ‹*sing*› in tune; ‹*guess*› right; **elle a vu ~** she was right; **viser ~** to aim straight
2 just; **~ à temps** just in time
3 (tout) ~ only just; **j'arrive ~** I've only just arrived; **c'est tout ~ s'il sait lire** he can hardly read
C au juste *phr* exactly
D *m* righteous man; **les ~s** the righteous

justement /ʒystəmɑ̃/ *adv* **1** precisely
2 just
3 correctly
4 justifiably

justesse /ʒystɛs/ **A** *f* **1** correctness; **avec ~** correctly
2 accuracy; **avec ~** accurately
B de justesse *phr* ‹*succeed*› only just

justice /ʒystis/ *f* **1** justice; **rendre la ~** to dispense justice; **il faut leur rendre cette ~ qu'ils sont...** one has to acknowledge that they are...; **ce n'est que ~** it is only fair; **se faire ~** to take the law into one's own hands; to take one's own life
2 la ~ the law; the legal system; the courts; **action en ~** legal action

justicier, **-ière** /ʒystisje, ɛʀ/ *mf* righter of wrongs

j

justificatif, **-ive** /ʒystifikatif, iv/ *m* documentary evidence; ~ **de domicile** proof of domicile; ~ **de frais** receipt

justification /ʒystifikasjɔ̃/ *f* **1** justification **2** explanation; documentary evidence

justifié, **~e** **A** *pp* ▸ **justifier**
B *pp adj* justified; **non** ~ unjustified

✓ **justifier** /ʒystifje/ [**v2**] **A** *vt* to justify ‹*method, absence*›; to vindicate ‹*guilty party*›; to explain ‹*ignorance*›; **les faits ont justifié nos craintes** events proved our fears to have been justified; **tu essaies toujours de la** ~ you are always making excuses for her
B **justifier de** *v+prep* to give proof of
C **se justifier** *v refl* (+ *v être*) **1** to make excuses; (in court) to clear oneself
2 ‹*decision*› to be justified (by)

jute /ʒyt/ *m* jute; **(toile de)** ~ hessian

juteux, **-euse** /ʒytø, øz/ *adj* ‹*fruit*› juicy

juvénile /ʒyvenil/ *adj* youthful; juvenile

juxtaposer /ʒykstapoze/ [**v1**] *vt* to juxtapose

juxtaposition /ʒykstapozisjɔ̃/ *f* juxtaposition

Kk

k, **K** /ka/ *m inv* k, K

kafkaïen, **-ïenne** /kafkajɛ̃, ɛn/ *adj* Kafkaesque

kakatoès /kakatɔɛs/ *m inv* cockatoo

kaki /kaki/ **A** *adj inv* khaki
B *m* **1** persimmon
2 khaki

kaléidoscope /kaleidɔskɔp/ *m* kaleidoscope

kanak ▸ **canaque**

kangourou /kɑ̃guʀu/ **A** *adj inv* **poche** ~ front pocket; **slip** ~ pouch-front briefs
B *m* **1** kangaroo
2 ®baby carrier

karaté /kaʀate/ *m* karate

karité /kaʀite/ *m* shea; **beurre de** ~ shea butter

kart /kaʀt/ *m* go-kart

karting /kaʀtiŋ/ *m* go-karting; **faire du** ~ to go karting

kasher /kaʃɛʀ/ *adj inv* kosher

kayak /kajak/ *m* kayak; **faire du** ~ to go kayaking

képi /kepi/ *m* kepi

kératine /keʀatin/ *f* keratin

kermesse /kɛʀmɛs/ *f* fete

kérosène /keʀɔzɛn/ *m* kerosene

kF *written abbr* ▸ **kilofranc**

kg (*written abbr* = **kilogramme**) kg

kibboutz, *pl* **-tzim** /kibuts, kibutsim/ *m* kibbutz

kick /kik/ *m* kick-start

kidnapper /kidnape/ [**v1**] *vt* to kidnap; **se faire** ~ to be kidnapped

kidnappeur, **-euse** /kidnapœʀ, øz/ *mf* kidnapper

kif-kif /kifkif/ *adj inv* (fam) **c'est** ~ **(bourricot)** it's all the same

kilo¹ /kilo/ *pref* kilo

✓ **kilo²** /kilo/ *m* (*abbr* = **kilogramme**) kilo; **prendre des** ~**s** to put on weight

kilofranc /kilɔfʀɑ̃/ *m* (Hist) 1,000 French francs

kilogramme /kilɔgʀam/ *m* kilogram

kilométrage /kilɔmetʀaʒ/ *m* ≈ mileage

✓ **kilomètre** /kilɔmɛtʀ/ *m* kilometre (BrE)

kilomètre-heure, *pl* **kilomètres-heure** /kilɔmɛtʀœʀ/ *m* kilometre (BrE) per hour

kilométrique /kilɔmetʀik/ *adj* ‹*distance*› in kilometres (BrE); ‹*price*› per kilometre (BrE)

kilo-octet /kilɔɔktɛ/ *m* kilobyte

kilotonne /kilɔtɔn/ *f* kiloton

kilowattheure /kilɔwatœʀ/ *m* kilowatt-hour

kimono /kimɔno/ *m* **1** kimono
2 judo suit

kinésithérapeute /kineziteʀapøt/ *mf* physiotherapist (BrE), physical therapist (AmE)

kinésithérapie /kineziteʀapi/ *f* physiotherapy (BrE), physical therapy (AmE)

kiosque /kjɔsk/ *m* kiosk
■ ~ **à musique** bandstand

kiwi /kiwi/ *m* kiwi

klaxon® /klaksɔn/ *m* (car) horn

klaxonner /klaksɔne/ [**v1**] *vi* to sound one's horn (BrE), to honk the horn

kleptomane /klɛptɔman/ *adj*, *mf* kleptomaniac

knock-out /nɔkaut/ **A** *adj inv* knocked out
B *m* knockout

Ko (*written abbr* = **kilo-octet**) KB

KO /kao/ **A** *adj inv* (*abbr* = **knocked out**) **1** KO'd (fam); **mettre qn** ~ to KO sb (fam)

✓ key word

2 (fam) exhausted
B *m* (*abbr* = **knockout**) KO (fam)

koala /kɔala/ *m* koala (bear)

kopeck /kɔpɛk/ *m* kopeck; **ça ne vaut pas un ~** it's not worth a penny

krach /kʀak/ *m* (on stock exchange) crash

kraft /kʀaft/ *m* **(papier) ~** brown paper

kurde /kyʀd/ *adj*, *m* Kurdish

Kurde /kyʀd/ *mf* Kurd

kW (*written abbr* = **kilowatt**) kW

K-way® /kawe/ *m* windcheater (BrE), windbreaker (AmE)

kyrielle /kiʀjɛl/ *f* **une ~ de** a string of

kyste /kist/ *m* cyst

Ll

l, **L** /ɛl/ *m inv* **1** (letter) l, L
2 (*written abbr* = **litre**) **20 l** 20 l

l' ▸ **le**

la¹ ▸ **le**

la² /la/ *m* (Mus) (note) A; (in sol-fa) lah; **donner le ~** to give an A; (fig) to set the tone

là /la/ *adv* **1** there; here; **viens ~** come here; **~ où je travaille** where I work; **pas par ici, par ~** not this way, that way; **de ~ au village** from there to the village
2 then; **d'ici ~** between now and then; by then; **et ~, le téléphone a sonné** and then the phone rang; **en ce temps-~** in those days; **ce jour-~** that day
3 s'il en est (arrivé) ~, c'est que... if he's got to that point, it's because...; **alors ~ tu exagères!** now you're going too far!; **que vas-tu chercher ~?** what are you thinking of?; **il a fallu en passer par ~** there was no alternative; **qu'entendez-vous par ~?** what do you mean by that?; **si tu vas par ~** if you are saying that; **de ~** hence; from that

là-bas /labɑ/ *adv* over there

labeur /labœʀ/ *m* hard work

labo /labo/ *m* (fam) lab (fam)

laboratoire /labɔʀatwaʀ/ *m* laboratory
■ **~ d'analyses médicales** medical laboratory; **~ de langues** language laboratory; **~ pharmaceutique** pharmaceutical company

laborieusement /labɔʀjøzmɑ̃/ *adv* laboriously

laborieux, **-ieuse** /labɔʀjø, øz/ *adj* **1** ‹*work, process*› arduous; ‹*style*› laboured (BrE)
2 les classes laborieuses the working classes

labour /labuʀ/ *m* ploughing; **cheval de ~** plough horse

labourer /labuʀe/ [**v1**] *vt* to plough (BrE), to plow (AmE)

labyrinthe /labiʀɛ̃t/ *m* maze; labyrinth

lac /lak/ *m* **1** lake
2 reservoir

lacer /lase/ [**v12**] *vt* to lace up ‹*shoes, corset*›

lacérer /laseʀe/ [**v14**] *vt* to lacerate; to slash

lacet /lasɛ/ *m* **1** lace; **chaussures à ~s** lace-up shoes; **nouer ses ~s** to do up one's laces
2 (in road) **une route en ~s** a twisting road

lâche /lɑʃ/ **A** *adj* **1** ‹*person, crime*› cowardly
2 ‹*belt*› loose
3 ‹*regulation*› lax
B *mf* coward

lâchement /lɑʃmɑ̃/ *adv* **ils se sont ~ enfuis** they fled like cowards; **il a été ~ assassiné** he was foully murdered

lâcher¹ /lɑʃe/ [**v1**] **A** *vt* **1** to drop ‹*object*›; to let go of ‹*rope*›; **lâche-moi** let go of me; (fig, fam) give me a break (fam); **~ prise** to lose one's grip
2 to reveal ‹*information*›; to let out ‹*scream*›
3 to let [sb/sth] go ‹*person, animal*›
4 to drop ‹*friend, activity*›; **la peur ne la lâche plus depuis** she's been living in constant terror ever since
B *vi* ‹*rope*› to give way; ‹*brakes*› to fail; **ses nerfs ont lâché** he/she went to pieces

lâcher² /lɑʃe/ *m* (of balloons, birds) release

lâcheté /lɑʃte/ *f* **1** cowardice; **par ~** out of cowardice
2 cowardly act

laconique /lakɔnik/ *adj* laconic; terse

lacrymal, **~e**, *mpl* **-aux** /lakʀimal, o/ *adj* lachrymal

lacrymogène /lakʀimɔʒɛn/ *adj* ‹*grenade, bomb*› tear gas; **gaz ~** tear gas

lacté, **~e** /lakte/ *adj* **1** ‹*product*› milk
2 ‹*liquid*› milky; **la voie ~e** the Milky Way

lacune /lakyn/ *f* (in knowledge, law) gap

là-dedans /lad(ə)dɑ̃/ *adv* in here; in there; **et moi ~ qu'est-ce que je fais?** (fam) and where do I come in?

là-dessous /lad(ə)su/ *adv* under here; under there; **il y a quelque chose de louche ~** (fam) there's something fishy about all this (fam)

là-dessus /lad(ə)sy/ *adv* **1** on here; on there
2 qu'as-tu à dire ~? what have you got to

say about it?
3 ~ **il a raccroché** with that he hung up

ladite ▸ **ledit**

lagon /lagɔ̃/ *m* lagoon

lagune /lagyn/ *f* lagoon

là-haut /lao/ *adv* **1** up here; up there; **tout** ~ (all the) way up there
2 upstairs
3 in heaven

laïc /laik/ *m* layman

laïcité /laisite/ *f* secularism; secularity

laid, **~e** /lɛ, lɛd/ *adj* **1** ugly
2 disgusting

laideur /lɛdœʀ/ *f* ugliness

lainage /lɛnaʒ/ *m* **1** woollen (BrE) material
2 woollen (BrE) garment

laine /lɛn/ *f* wool; **de** *or* **en** ~ woollen (BrE), wool
■ ~ **peignée** worsted; ~ **de verre** glass wool; ~ **vierge** new wool (BrE), virgin wool

laïque /laik/ **A** *adj* ‹*school*› non-denominational (BrE), public (AmE); ‹*state, mind*› secular
B *mf* layman/laywoman; **les ~s** lay people

laisse /lɛs/ *f* (for dog) lead (BrE), leash (AmE)

laissé-pour-compte, **laissée-pour-compte**, *mpl* **laissés-pour-compte** /lesepuʀkɔ̃t/ *mf* **les laissés-pour-compte** (gen) the forgotten people; **les laissés-pour-compte de la révolution technologique** the casualties of the technological revolution

⚷ **laisser** /lese/ [**v1**] **A** *vt* to leave; ~ **la liberté à qn** to let sb go free; **je te laisse** I must go; ~ **le choix à qn** to give sb the choice; **laisse ce jouet à ton frère** let your brother have the toy; **laisse-le, ça lui passera** ignore him, he'll get over it; **cela me laisse sceptique** I'm sceptical (BrE) *or* skeptical (AmE)
B *v aux* ~ **qn/qch faire** to let sb/sth do; **laisse-moi faire** let me do it; leave it to me; **laisse faire!** so what!
C **se laisser** *v refl* (+ *v être*) **se** ~ **bercer par les vagues** to be lulled by the waves; **il se laisse insulter** he puts up with insults; **elle n'est pas du genre à se** ~ **faire** she won't be pushed around; **il ne veut pas se** ~ **faire** he won't let you touch him; **se** ~ **aller** to let oneself go

laisser-aller /leseale/ *m inv* **1** scruffiness
2 sloppiness

laissez-passer /lesepase/ *m inv* pass

⚷ **lait** /lɛ/ *m* milk
■ ~ **de chaux** whitewash; ~ **concentré non sucré** evaporated milk; ~ **demi-écrémé** semi-skimmed milk (BrE), two per cent milk (AmE); ~ **écrémé** skimmed milk (BrE), skim *or* non-fat milk (AmE); ~ **maternel** breast milk; ~ **de poule** eggnog

laitage /lɛtaʒ/ *m* dairy product

laitance /lɛtɑ̃s/ *f* (Culin, Zool) soft roe

laiterie /lɛtʀi/ *f* **1** dairy
2 dairy industry

laiteux, **-euse** /lɛtø, øz/ *adj* ‹*liquid, white*› milky; ‹*complexion*› creamy

laitier, **-ière** /lɛtje, ɛʀ/ **A** *adj* ‹*industry, product*› dairy; ‹*production, cow*› milk
B *mf* milkman/milkwoman

laiton /lɛtɔ̃/ *m* brass

laitue /lɛty/ *f* lettuce

laïus /lajys/ *m inv* (fam) speech

lama /lama/ *m* **1** (animal) llama
2 (religious leader) lama

lambda /lɑ̃bda/ *adj inv* (fam) average

lambeau, *pl* **~x** /lɑ̃bo/ *m* (of cloth) rag; (of paper, hide) strip; (of flesh) bit

lambris /lɑ̃bʀi/ *m inv* panelling (BrE); marble walls; (on ceiling) mouldings (BrE), moldings (AmE)

lambrisser /lɑ̃bʀise/ [**v1**] *vt* to panel

lame /lam/ *f* **1** (of knife, saw) blade
2 knife
3 sword; **une fine** ~ an expert swordsman
4 (of metal, wood) strip; (on blind) slat
■ ~ **de fond** ground swell; (fig) upheaval; ~ **de rasoir** razor blade

lamé /lame/ *m* lamé; **en** ~ lamé

lamelle /lamɛl/ *f* **1** (of wood, metal) small strip
2 (Culin) sliver; **découper en fines ~s** to slice thinly
3 (Bot) (of mushroom) gill

lamentable /lamɑ̃tabl/ *adj* pathetic, awful

lamentablement /lamɑ̃tabləmɑ̃/ *adv* ‹*fail*› miserably; ‹*cry*› piteously

lamentation /lamɑ̃tasjɔ̃/ *f* wailing

lamenter: **se lamenter** /lamɑ̃te/ [**v1**] *v refl* (+ *v être*) to moan; **se** ~ **sur son propre sort** to feel sorry for oneself

lampadaire /lɑ̃padɛʀ/ *m* **1** standard (BrE) *or* floor (AmE) lamp
2 street light

⚷ **lampe** /lɑ̃p/ *f* **1** lamp, light
2 (light) bulb
■ ~ **à bronzer** sun lamp; ~ **de chevet** bedside light; ~ **électrique** torch (BrE), flashlight (AmE); ~ **de poche** pocket torch (BrE), flashlight (AmE); ~ **témoin** indicator light; ~ **tempête** hurricane lamp

lampée /lɑ̃pe/ *f* (fam) gulp

lampion /lɑ̃pjɔ̃/ *m* paper lantern

lance /lɑ̃s/ *f* (gen) spear; (in jousting) lance
■ ~ **d'incendie** fire hose nozzle

lancée /lɑ̃se/ *f* **sur ma** ~ while I was at it; **continuer sur sa** ~ to continue to forge ahead

lancement /lɑ̃smɑ̃/ *m* **1** (of ship, company) launching; (of process) setting up
2 (of product, book) launch; (of loan) floating; (of actor) promotion
3 (of missile) launching; launch

lance-pierres /lɑ̃spjɛʀ/ *m inv* catapult
IDIOM **payer qn avec un** ~ (fam) to pay sb peanuts (fam)

⚷ key word

lancer¹ /lɑ̃se/ [**v12**] **A** *vt* **1** to throw ‹*ball, pebble, javelin*›; **~ le poids** to put the shot
2 to launch ‹*rocket, ship*›; to fire ‹*arrow*›; to drop ‹*bomb*›; to start up ‹*engine*›
3 to throw out ‹*smoke, flames*›; to give ‹*look*›; to put about ‹*rumour*›; to issue ‹*ultimatum*›; to send out ‹*invitation*›
4 to hurl ‹*insult*›; to make ‹*accusation*›; **lança-t-il** he said
B *vi* (fam) to throb; **mon doigt me lance** my finger is throbbing
C **se lancer** *v refl* (+ *v être*) **1 se ~ dans des dépenses** to get involved in expense; **se ~ dans les affaires** to go into business
2 se ~ dans le vide to jump
3 to throw [sth] to each other ‹*ball*›; to exchange ‹*insults*›

lancer² /lɑ̃se/ *m* **1** (Sport) **~ du disque** discus event; **~ du poids** shot put (event)
2 le ~, la pêche au ~ rod and reel fishing

lance-roquettes /lɑ̃sʀɔkɛt/ *m inv* rocket launcher

lancinant, **~e** /lɑ̃sinɑ̃, ɑ̃t/ *adj* ‹*pain*› shooting; ‹*music, rhythm*› insistent

landau /lɑ̃do/ *m* pram (BrE), baby carriage (AmE)

lande /lɑ̃d/ *f* moor

langage /lɑ̃gaʒ/ *m* language
■ **~ administratif** official jargon; **~ des sourds-muets** sign language

lange /lɑ̃ʒ/ *m* **1** swaddling clothes
2 nappy (BrE), diaper (AmE)

langer /lɑ̃ʒe/ [**v13**] *vt* **1** to wrap [sb] in swaddling clothes ‹*baby*›
2 to put a nappy (BrE) *or* diaper (AmE) on ‹*baby*›

langoureux, **-euse** /lɑ̃guʀø, øz/ *adj* languorous

langouste /lɑ̃gust/ *f* spiny lobster

langoustine /lɑ̃gustin/ *f* langoustine

langue /lɑ̃g/ *f* **1** tongue; **tirer la ~** to stick out one's tongue; (for doctor) to put out one's tongue; (fig) to be dying of thirst; to struggle financially
2 language; speech
3 mauvaise ~ malicious gossip
4 ~ de terre spit of land
■ **~ de bois** political cant; **~ maternelle** mother tongue; **~ verte** slang
IDIOMS **avoir la ~ bien pendue** (fam) to be very talkative; **avoir qch sur le bout de la ~** to have sth on the tip of one's tongue

languette /lɑ̃gɛt/ *f* (on shoe) tongue; (on satchel, bag) strap; (of ham) long narrow strip

langueur /lɑ̃gœʀ/ *f* languor

languir /lɑ̃giʀ/ [**v3**] **A** *vi* **1** ‹*conversation*› to languish; ‹*economy*› to be sluggish
2 je languis de vous revoir I'm longing to see you; **faire ~ qn** to keep sb in suspense
B **se languir** *v refl* (+ *v être*) to pine

languissant, **~e** /lɑ̃gisɑ̃, ɑ̃t/ *adj* ‹*economy*› sluggish; ‹*conversation*› desultory

lanière /lanjɛʀ/ *f* (gen) strap; (of whip) lash

lanterne /lɑ̃tɛʀn/ *f* **1** lantern
2 (Aut) sidelight (BrE), parking light (AmE)
IDIOM **éclairer la ~ de qn** to enlighten sb

laper /lape/ [**v1**] *vt* to lap (up) ‹*soup, milk*›

lapider /lapide/ [**v1**] *vt* **1** to stone [sb] to death
2 to throw stones at

lapin /lapɛ̃/ *m* **1** rabbit; **~ de garenne** wild rabbit; **coup du ~** rabbit punch; (in accident) whiplash injury; **cage** *or* **cabane à ~s** rabbit hutch; (fig, fam) tower block
2 rabbit(skin)
IDIOMS **poser un ~ à qn** (fam) to stand sb up; **se faire tirer comme des ~s** (fam) to be picked off like flies; **c'est un chaud ~** (fam) he's a randy devil

lapine /lapin/ *f* doe rabbit

laps /laps/ *m inv* **~ de temps** period of time

lapsus /lapsys/ *m inv* slip

laquais /lakɛ/ *m inv* lackey

laque /lak/ *f* **1** hairspray
2 lacquer; gloss paint (BrE), enamel (AmE)

laqué, **~e** /lake/ *adj* ‹*paint*› gloss

laquelle ▶ **lequel**

laquer /lake/ [**v1**] *vt* to lacquer; to paint [sth] in gloss (BrE) *or* enamel (AmE)

larbin /laʀbɛ̃/ *m* (derog, fam) servant

lard /laʀ/ *m* ≈ fat streaky bacon

larder /laʀde/ [**v1**] *vt* (Culin) to lard; **~ qn de coups de couteau** (fig) to stab sb repeatedly

lardon /laʀdɔ̃/ *m* (Culin) bacon cube

large /laʀʒ/ **A** *adj* **1** ‹*shoulders, hips*› broad; ‹*avenue, bed*› wide; ‹*coat*› loose-fitting; ‹*trousers*› loose; ‹*skirt*› full; ‹*jumper*› big; ‹*smile*› broad; ‹*curve*› long; **~ de trois mètres** three metres (BrE) wide
2 ‹*advance, profit*› substantial; ‹*choice, public*› wide; ‹*majority*› large; **au sens ~** in a broad sense
3 ‹*person*› generous
4 ‹*life*› comfortable
5 avoir les idées ~s, être ~ d'esprit to be broad-minded
B *adv* **1** ‹*plan*› on a generous scale; ‹*calculate, measure*› on the generous side
2 s'habiller ~ to wear loose-fitting clothes
C *m* **1 faire quatre mètres de ~** to be four metres (BrE) wide
2 open sea; **au ~** offshore
■ **~ bande** broadband
IDIOM **ne pas en mener ~** (fam) to be worried sick (fam)

largement /laʀʒəmɑ̃/ *adv* **1** widely
2 largely, to a large extent; **être ~ responsable de qch** to be largely responsible for sth
3 arriver ~ en tête to be a clear winner; **~ en dessous de la limite** well under the limit
4 tu as ~ le temps you've got plenty of time
5 easily; **une chaîne en or vaudrait ~ le double** a gold chain would easily be worth twice as much
6 ‹*contribute*› generously

largesse /laʀʒɛs/ *f* generous gift

largeur /laʀʒœʀ/ *f* **1** width, breadth; **dans le sens de la ~** widthwise
2 ~ d'esprit broad-mindedness

largué, **~e** /laʀge/ *adj* (fam) **1** lost, out of one's depth
2 out of touch

larguer /laʀge/ [**v1**] *vt* **1** (Mil) to drop ‹*bomb, missile*›; to drop ‹*parachutist*›; to release ‹*satellite*›
2 to unfurl ‹*sail*›; **~ les amarres** to cast off; (fig) to set off
3 (fam) to give up ‹*studies*›; to chuck (fam) ‹*boyfriend, girlfriend*›

🔑 **larme** /laʀm/ *f* **1** tear; **elle a ri aux ~s** she laughed till she cried; **avoir la ~ à l'œil** to be a bit weepy
2 (fam) drop

larmoyant, **~e** /laʀmwajɑ̃, ɑ̃t/ *adj* **1** ‹*eyes*› full of tears
2 ‹*voice*› whining; ‹*speech*› maudlin

larmoyer /laʀmwaje/ [**v23**] *vi* **1** ‹*eyes*› to water
2 ‹*person*› to whine

larron /laʀɔ̃/ *m* **1** (hum) scoundrel
2 thief
IDIOM **s'entendre comme ~s en foire** to be as thick as thieves

larvaire /laʀvɛʀ/ *adj* ‹*state*› embryonic

larve /laʀv/ *f* **1** (Zool) larva
2 (person) wimp (fam)

larvé, **~e** /laʀve/ *adj* latent

laryngite /laʀɛ̃ʒit/ *f* laryngitis

larynx /laʀɛ̃ks/ *m inv* larynx

las, **lasse** /lɑ, lɑs/ *adj* weary

lasagnes /lazaɲ/ *fpl* lasagna

lascar /laskaʀ/ *m* (fam) fellow

lascif, **-ive** /lasif, iv/ *adj* ‹*person, look*› lascivious; ‹*temperament*› lustful

laser /lazɛʀ/ *m* laser

lassant, **~e** /lasɑ̃, ɑ̃t/ *adj* **1** ‹*speech*› tedious; ‹*reproaches*› tiresome
2 tiring

lasser /lɑse/ [**v1**] **A** *vt* **1** to bore ‹*person, audience*›
2 to weary ‹*person, audience*›
B se lasser *v refl* (+ *v être*) ‹*person*› to grow tired; **sans se ~** without tiring; patiently

lassitude /lasityd/ *f* weariness

lasso /laso/ *m* lasso; **prendre au ~** to lasso

latence /latɑ̃s/ *f* latency

latent, **~e** /latɑ̃, ɑ̃t/ *adj* ‹*danger, illness*› latent; ‹*anxiety, jealousy*› underlying

latéral, **~e**, *mpl* **-aux** /lateʀal, o/ *adj* ‹*door, exit*› side; ‹*tunnel, aisle*› lateral

latéralement /lateʀalmɑ̃/ *adv* sideways

🔑 **latin**, **~e** /latɛ̃, in/ **A** *adj* **1** ‹*text*› Latin
2 ‹*temperament*› Latin; ‹*culture*› Mediterranean
3 langues ~es Romance languages
B *m* (language) Latin
IDIOM **c'est à y perdre son ~** you can't make head or tail of it

latino-américain, **~e**, *mpl* **~s** /latinoameʀikɛ̃, ɛn/ *adj* Latin American

latitude /latityd/ *f* latitude
IDIOM **avoir toute ~ de faire** to be entirely free to do

latte /lat/ *f* **1** lath; (of floor) board
2 (of bed base) slat

laudatif, **-ive** /lodatif, iv/ *adj* laudatory

lauréat, **~e** /lɔʀea, at/ *mf* **1** (of competition) winner
2 (in exam) successful candidate

laurier /lɔʀje/ **A** *m* **1** (Bot) laurel; **~ commun** bay (tree)
2 (Culin) **feuille de ~** bay leaf
B lauriers *mpl* laurels; **s'endormir sur ses ~s** to rest on one's laurels

laurier-rose, *pl* **lauriers-roses** /lɔʀjeʀoz/ *m* oleander

lavable /lavabl/ *adj* washable

lavabo /lavabo/ *m* washbasin, washbowl

lavage /lavaʒ/ *m* **1** washing; cleaning
2 (washing machine cycle) wash
■ **~ de cerveau** brainwashing; **faire un ~ d'estomac à qn** to pump sb's stomach (out)

lavande /lavɑ̃d/ *adj inv*, *f* lavender

lave /lav/ *f* lava; **coulée de ~** lava flow

lave-glace, *pl* **~s** /lavglas/ *m* windscreen (BrE) *or* windshield (AmE) washer

lave-linge /lavlɛ̃ʒ/ *m inv* washing machine

lavement /lavmɑ̃/ *m* (Med) enema

🔑 **laver** /lave/ [**v1**] **A** *vt* **1** to wash ‹*clothes, child, car*›; **~ son linge** to do one's washing; **~ la vaisselle** to do the dishes; **~ qch à grande eau** to wash sth down
2 to clean ‹*wound*›
3 to clear; **~ qn d'une accusation** to clear sb of an accusation
B se laver *v refl* (+ *v être*) **1** to wash; **se ~ les mains** to wash one's hands; **se ~ les dents** to brush one's teeth
2 to be washable
3 se ~ d'un affront to take revenge for an insult
IDIOM **je m'en lave les mains** I'm washing my hands of it

laverie /lavʀi/ *f* **~ (automatique)** launderette (BrE), laundromat® (AmE)

lave-vaisselle /lavvɛsɛl/ *m inv* dishwasher

lavis /lavi/ *m inv* wash drawing

lavoir /lavwaʀ/ *m* wash house

laxatif /laksatif/ *m* laxative

laxisme /laksism/ *m* laxity

laxiste /laksist/ *adj* lax

layette /lɛjɛt/ *f* baby clothes, layette

🔑 **le**, **la**, **l'** *before vowel or mute h*, *pl* **les** /lə, la, l, le/ **A** *det* **1** the; **la table de la cuisine** the

---
🔑 key word

kitchen table; **les Dupont** the Duponts; **elle aime les chevaux** she likes horses; **arriver sur** *or* **vers les 11 heures** to arrive at about 11 o'clock
2 elle s'est cogné ~ bras she banged her arm
3 a, an; **9 euros ~ kilo** 9 euros a kilo
4 (oh) la jolie robe! what a pretty dress!
B *pron* him; her; it; them; **je ne les comprends pas** I don't understand them
C *pron neutre* **je ~ savais** I knew; I knew it; **je ~ croyais aussi, mais...** I thought so too, but...; **espérons-~!** let's hope so!

lé /le/ *m* (of cloth, wallpaper) width

LEA /ɛləa/ *fpl* (*abbr* = **langues étrangères appliquées**) *university language course with emphasis on business and management*

leadership /lidœʀʃip/ *m* **1** leading role
2 supremacy

lèche-bottes /lɛʃbɔt/ (fam) **A** *mf inv* crawler (BrE) (fam), bootlicker (fam)
B *m* crawling (BrE) (fam), bootlicking (fam)

lécher /leʃe/ [**v1**] **A** *vt* **1** to lick ‹*spoon, plate*›
2 ‹*flames*› to lick; ‹*sea*› to lap against
B se lécher *v refl* (+ *v être*) **se ~ les doigts** to lick one's fingers

lèche-vitrines /lɛʃvitʀin/ *m inv* window-shopping

leçon /ləsɔ̃/ *f* lesson; **~ particulière** private lesson; **cela lui servira de ~** that'll teach him a lesson

lecteur, **-trice** /lɛktœʀ, tʀis/ **A** *mf* **1** reader
2 teaching assistant
B *m* **1** (Comput) reader; **~ optique** optical scanner *or* reader; **~ de disquettes** disk drive; **~ DVD** DVD reader
2 player; **~ laser** CD player

lecture /lɛktyʀ/ *f* **1** (of book, newspaper) reading; **faire la ~ à qn** to read to sb
2 reading, interpretation
3 reading material; **tu as pris de la ~?** have you brought something to read?
4 (of music, X-ray, disk) reading
5 (of cassette, CD) play; playing

ledit, **ladite**, *pl* **lesdits**, **lesdites** /lədi, ladit, ledi, ledit/ *adj* the aforementioned

légal, **~e**, *mpl* **-aux** /legal, o/ *adj* legal; lawful

légalement /legalmɑ̃/ *adv* legally; lawfully

légaliser /legalize/ [**v1**] *vt* to legalize

légalité /legalite/ *f* **1** legality
2 lawfulness

légataire /legatɛʀ/ *mf* legatee

légendaire /leʒɑ̃dɛʀ/ *adj* legendary

légende /leʒɑ̃d/ *f* **1** legend
2 (accompanying picture) caption; (on map) key
3 tall story

léger, **-ère** /leʒe, ɛʀ/ **A** *adj* **1** light; **se sentir plus ~** (fig) to have a great weight off one's mind
2 (Culin) ‹*meal*› light
3 ‹*person*› nimble; ‹*step*› light
4 ‹*laugh*› gentle; ‹*blow, knock*› soft; ‹*error, delay*› slight; ‹*taste, hope*› faint; ‹*wind, rain*› light; ‹*cloud*› thin; ‹*injury*› minor
5 ‹*tea, drink*› weak; ‹*perfume, wine*› light; ‹*tobacco*› mild (BrE), light (AmE)
6 ‹*action*› ill-considered; ‹*remark*› thoughtless; ‹*argument, proof*› weak
7 (fam) **c'est un peu ~** it's a bit skimpy
8 ‹*woman, way of life*› loose; ‹*husband, mood*› fickle
9 (Mil) light
B *adv* ‹*travel*› light; **cuisiner/manger ~** to cook/to eat light meals
C à la légère *phr* (gen) without thinking; ‹*accuse*› rashly; **prendre qch à la légère** not to take sth seriously

légèrement /leʒɛʀmɑ̃/ *adv* **1** ‹*move*› gently; ‹*perfume*› lightly; ‹*tremble, injured*› slightly
2 (Culin) ‹*eat*› lightly
3 ‹*walk, run*› lightly, nimbly
4 ‹*act, speak*› without thinking

légèreté /leʒɛʀte/ *f* **1** lightness; nimbleness
2 thoughtlessness; fickleness; **la ~ de ses mœurs** his/her loose morals

légiférer /leʒifeʀe/ [**v14**] *vi* to legislate

légion /leʒjɔ̃/ *f* **1** (Mil) legion
2 army
■ **la Légion (étrangère)** the Foreign Legion

légionellose /leʒjɔneloz/ *f* Legionnaire's disease

légionnaire /leʒjɔnɛʀ/ *m* (Roman) legionary; (in Foreign Legion) legionnaire

législateur, **-trice** /leʒislatœʀ, tʀis/ *mf* legislator, lawmaker

législatif, **-ive** /leʒislatif, iv/ *adj* legislative; **élections législatives** ≈ general election

législation /leʒislasjɔ̃/ *f* legislation

législature /leʒislatyʀ/ *f* **1** term of office
2 legislature

légiste /leʒist/ *m* jurist

légitime /leʒitim/ *adj* **1** ‹*child, right*› legitimate; ‹*union, heir*› lawful
2 ‹*action*› legitimate; ‹*anger*› justifiable
3 ‹*reward*› just
■ **~ défense** self-defence (BrE)

légitimité /leʒitimite/ *f* **1** legitimacy
2 (of an act) lawfulness

legs /lɛg/ *m inv* (Law), (gen) legacy; (of personal belongings) bequest

léguer /lege/ [**v14**] *vt* **1** (in one's will) to leave
2 to hand down ‹*traditions*›; to pass on ‹*flaw*›

légume /legym/ *m* vegetable; **~s secs** pulses

leitmotiv /lajtmɔtiv/ *m* leitmotiv

Léman /lemɑ̃/ *n pr* **le lac ~** Lake Geneva

lendemain /lɑ̃dəmɛ̃/ **A** *m* **1 le ~, la journée du ~** the following day; **dès le ~** the (very) next day; **le ~ de l'accident** the day after the accident; **du jour au ~** overnight
2 au ~ de (in the period) after; **au ~ de la guerre** just after the war

3 le ~ tomorrow, the future; **sans ~** ‹*happiness, success*› short-lived
B lendemains *mpl* **1** outcome; consequences
2 future; **des ~s difficiles** difficult days ahead

lénifiant, **~e** /lenifjɑ̃, ɑ̃t/ *adj* soothing

lent, **~e** /lɑ̃, ɑ̃t/ *adj* slow; ‹*film, vehicle*› slow-moving; ‹*poison*› slow-acting

lente /lɑ̃t/ *f* (Zool) nit

⚷ **lentement** /lɑ̃t(ə)mɑ̃/ *adv* slowly

lenteur /lɑ̃tœʀ/ *f* slowness; **avec ~** slowly

lentille /lɑ̃tij/ *f* **1** (Bot, Culin) lentil
2 lens; **~s de contact** contact lenses

léopard /leɔpaʀ/ *m* **1** leopard
2 leopard-skin

lèpre /lɛpʀ/ *f* leprosy

lépreux, **-euse** /lepʀø, øz/ *mf* leper

⚷ **lequel** /ləkɛl/, **laquelle** /lakɛl/, *mpl* **lesquels**, *fpl* **lesquelles** /lekɛl/, (*with à*) **auquel**, *mpl* **auxquels**, *fpl* **auxquelles** /okɛl/, (*with de*) **duquel** /dykɛl/, *mpl* **desquels**, *fpl* **desquelles** /dekɛl/ **A lequel**, **laquelle**, **lesquels**, **lesquelles** *adj* who; which; **il m'a présenté son cousin, ~ cousin vit en Grèce** he introduced me to his cousin, who lives in Greece; **auquel cas** in which case
B *rel pron* who; which; **les gens contre lesquels ils luttaient** the people (who) they were fighting against
C *pron* which; **lesquels sont les plus compétents?** which are the most competent?

les ▸ **le**

lesbienne /lɛsbjɛn/ *f* lesbian

lesdites ▸ **ledit**

lesdits ▸ **ledit**

lèse-majesté /lɛzmaʒɛste/ *f inv* lese-majesty

léser /leze/ [**v14**] *vt* to wrong ‹*person*›; to prejudice ‹*interests*›

lésiner /lezine/ [**v1**] *vi* **ne pas ~ sur** to be liberal with ‹*ingredients, money, compliments*›

lésion /lezjɔ̃/ *f* (Med) lesion

lesquels, **lesquelles** ▸ **lequel**

lessive /lesiv/ *f* **1** washing powder; washing liquid
2 washing

lessiver /lesive/ [**v1**] *vt* **1** to wash
2 (fam) **être lessivé** to be washed out (fam)

lessiveuse /lesivøz/ *f* boiler, copper (BrE)

lest /lɛst/ *m* **1** ballast; **jeter** *or* **lâcher du ~** to jettison ballast
2 (on fishing net) weight

leste /lɛste/ *adj* **1** ‹*person, animal*› agile, nimble
2 ‹*joke, remark*› risqué

lestement /lɛstəmɑ̃/ *adv* nimbly

lester /lɛste/ [**v1**] *vt* **1** to ballast
2 (fam) to stuff

létal, **~e**, *mpl* **-aux** /letal, o/ *adj* lethal

léthargie /letaʀʒi/ *f* lethargy

léthargique /letaʀʒik/ *adj* **1** ‹*person*› lethargic; ‹*industry*› sluggish
2 (Med) lethargic

⚷ **lettre** /lɛtʀ/ **A** *f* **1** (of alphabet) letter; **~ majuscule** *or* **capitale** capital letter; **~ d'imprimerie** block letter; **en toutes ~s** in full; **c'est écrit en toutes ~s dans le rapport** it's down in black and white in the report; **les Romains furent des urbanistes avant la ~** the Romans were city planners before the concept was invented; **à la ~**, **au pied de la ~** to the letter; **il prend tout ce qu'on lui dit à la ~** he takes everything you say literally
2 (message) letter; **~ de rupture** letter ending a relationship
B lettres *fpl* **1** (university subject) French; (more general) arts (BrE), humanities (AmE)
2 letters; **femme de ~s** woman of letters; **avoir des ~s** to be well read
■ **~ explicative** covering letter; **~ de recommandation** letter of recommendation; **~ recommandée** registered letter; **~s classiques** French and Latin; **~s modernes** French language and literature
IDIOM **passer comme une ~ à la poste** (fam) ‹*reform*› to go through smoothly; ‹*excuse*› to be accepted without any questions

lettré, **~e** /letʀe/ *mf* man/woman of letters

leu: **à la queue leu leu** /alakøløløl/ *phr* in single file

leucémie /løsemi/ *f* leukaemia

⚷ **leur** /lœʀ/ **A** *pron* them; **il ~ a écrit** he wrote to them; **il ~ a fallu faire** they had to do
B *det* (*pl* **leurs**) their; **un de ~s amis** a friend of theirs; **pendant ~ absence** while they were away
C le leur, **la leur**, **les leurs** *pron* theirs; **c'est le ~** it's theirs; **il est des ~s** he's one of them; **ils m'ont demandé d'être des ~s** they asked me to come along; **ils vivent loin des ~s** they live far away from their families

leurre /lœʀ/ *m* **1** illusion
2 (in fishing, hunting) lure
3 (Mil) decoy

leurrer /lœʀe/ [**v1**] **A** *vt* to delude
B se leurrer *v refl* (+ *v être*) to delude oneself

levain /ləvɛ̃/ *m* (fermenting agent) starter; (for bread) leaven (BrE), sourdough (AmE)

levant /ləvɑ̃/ **A** *adj m* **soleil ~** rising sun
B *m* east; **au ~** in the east; **du ~ au couchant** from east to west

levé, **~e** /ləve/ **A** *pp* ▸ **lever[1]**
B *pp adj* **1 voter à main ~e** to vote by a show of hands
2 up; **elle est toujours la première ~e** she's always the first up

levée /ləve/ *f* **1** (of embargo, sentence, martial law) lifting; (of diplomatic immunity) removal;

I

⚷ key word

(of secrecy, taboo) ending; (of session) close
2 (of mail) collection
3 (embankment) levee
■ **~ de boucliers** outcry

lever¹ /ləve/ [**v16**] **A** *vt* **1** to raise; **~ la main** *or* **le doigt** (for permission to speak) to put up one's hand; **~ la main sur qn** to raise a hand to sb; **~ les bras au ciel** to throw up one's hands; **lève les pieds quand tu marches!** don't drag your feet!; **~ les yeux** *or* **la tête** to look up
2 to lift ‹*object*›; to raise ‹*barrier*›; **~ son verre** to raise one's glass
3 (out of bed) to get [sb] up ‹*child, sick person*›
4 to lift ‹*embargo, restriction*›; to raise ‹*siege*›; to end ‹*taboo, secret*›; to remove ‹*obstacle*›; to close ‹*session*›
5 to levy ‹*tax*›
6 to flush out ‹*game, partridges*›
B *vi* **1** (Culin) ‹*dough*› to rise
2 ‹*seedlings, corn*› to come up
C **se lever** *v refl* (+ *v être*) **1** to get up
2 to stand up; **se ~ de table** to leave the table
3 ‹*person, people*› to rise up
4 ‹*sun*› to rise; **le jour se lève** it's getting light
5 ‹*wind*› to rise
6 ‹*fog, mist*› to clear; ‹*weather*› to clear up

lever² /ləve/ *m* **1 être là au ~ des enfants** to be there when the children get up
2 au ~ du jour at daybreak

lève-tard /lɛvtaʀ/ *mf inv* late riser

lève-tôt /lɛvto/ *mf inv* early riser

levier /ləvje/ *m* lever; **soulever qch avec un ~** to lever sth up
■ **~ de changement de vitesse** (Aut) gear lever (BrE), gear stick (AmE); **~ de commande** control stick

lévitation /levitasjɔ̃/ *f* levitation

lèvre /lɛvʀ/ *f* lip; **avoir le sourire aux ~s** to be smiling; **du bout des ~s** ‹*eat*› half-heartedly; ‹*reply*› grudgingly
IDIOM **être suspendu aux ~s de qn** to hang on sb's every word

lévrier /levʀije/ *m* greyhound

levure /ləvyʀ/ *f* yeast; **~ chimique** baking powder

lexical, **~e**, *mpl* **-aux** /lɛksikal, o/ *adj* lexical

lexique /lɛksik/ *m* **1** glossary; (bilingual) vocabulary (book)
2 lexicon, lexis

lézard /lezaʀ/ *m* **1** lizard
2 lizard skin

lézarde /lezaʀd/ *f* crack

lézarder /lezaʀde/ [**v1**] **A** *vt* to crack
B *vi* (fam) **~ au soleil** to bask in the sun
C **se lézarder** *v refl* (+ *v être*) to crack

liaison /ljɛzɔ̃/ *f* **1** link; **la ~ Calais–Douvres** the Calais–Dover line
2 ~ radio radio contact; **~ satellite** satellite link
3 assurer la ~ entre différents services to liaise between different services
4 (love) affair
5 (between words) liaison

liane /ljan/ *f* creeper, liana

liant, **~e** /ljɑ̃, ɑ̃t/ *adj* sociable

liasse /ljas/ *f* (of banknotes) wad; (of letters, papers, documents) bundle

Liban /libɑ̃/ *pr m* Lebanon

libellé /libɛlle/ *m* wording

libeller /libɛlle/ [**v1**] *vt* **1** to draw up ‹*contract*›
2 to word ‹*article*›
3 to make out ‹*cheque*›

libellule /libɛllyl/ *f* dragonfly

libéral, **~e**, *mpl* **-aux** /libeʀal, o/ *adj*
1 liberal
2 (in politics) Liberal
3 free-market

libéralisation /libeʀalizasjɔ̃/ *f* liberalization; **~ des mœurs** relaxation of moral standards

libéraliser /libeʀalize/ [**v1**] **A** *vt* to liberalize
B **se libéraliser** *v refl* (+ *v être*) ‹*country, attitudes*› to become more liberal

libéralisme /libeʀalism/ *m* liberalism

libéralité /libeʀalite/ *f* liberality

libérateur, **-trice** /libeʀatœʀ, tʀis/ **A** *adj* liberating
B *mf* (of country, person) liberator

libération /libeʀasjɔ̃/ *f* **1** (of prisoner, hostage) release
2 (of country, population) liberation; **~ des femmes** women's liberation
3 relief
4 (of prices) deregulation

Libération /libeʀasjɔ̃/ *f* (of 1944) **la ~** the Liberation

libéré, **~e** /libeʀe/ **A** *pp* ▸ **libérer**
B *pp adj* **1** ‹*man, woman*› liberated
2 ‹*country, area, town*› free
3 ‹*post, premises*› vacant

libérer /libeʀe/ [**v14**] **A** *vt* **1** to liberate ‹*country, town*›; to free ‹*companion, hostage*›
2 to release ‹*prisoner*›; to free ‹*slave, animal*›
3 to allow [sb] to go ‹*employee*›
4 to liberate ‹*person*›; (of post, duties) to relieve ‹*minister*›; **~ qn de l'emprise de qn** to get sb away from sb's influence
5 to release ‹*emotion*›; to give free rein to ‹*imagination*›
6 to relieve ‹*mind, person*›; **~ sa conscience** to unburden oneself
7 to vacate ‹*apartment, office*›; **~ la chambre avant midi** (in hotel) to check out before noon
8 to free ‹*arm, hand*›; to release ‹*spring, catch*›
9 to liberalize ‹*economy, trade*›; to deregulate ‹*prices*›; **~ les loyers** to lift rent controls

10 to release ‹*gas, energy*›
B se libérer *v refl* (+ *v être*) **1** to free oneself/itself; **se ~ d'une dette** to pay a debt
2 j'essaierai de me ~ mercredi I'll try and be free on Wednesday

libertaire /libɛʀtɛʀ/ *adj, mf* libertarian

liberté /libɛʀte/ *f* **1** (gen) freedom; **être en ~** to be free; **élever des animaux en ~** to raise animals in a natural habitat; **espèce vivant en ~** species in the wild; **l'assassin est toujours en ~** the killer is still at large; **prendre la ~ de faire** to take the liberty of doing; **~ de pensée** freedom of thought
2 (Law) **mettre qn en ~ conditionnelle** to release sb on parole; **mise en ~ surveillée** release on probation

liberticide /libɛʀtisid/ *adj* liberty-threatening; **cette loi est-elle ~?** is this law a threat to freedom?

libertin, **~e** /libɛʀtɛ̃, in/ *adj, mf* libertine

libido /libido/ *f* libido

libraire /libʀɛʀ/ *mf* bookseller

librairie /libʀeʀi/ *f* **1** bookshop (BrE), book store
2 bookselling business

librairie-papeterie, *pl* **librairies-papeteries** /libʀeʀipapɛtʀi/ *f* stationer's and bookshop (BrE)

libre /libʀ/ *adj* **1** ‹*person, country*› free; **~ à elle de partir** it's up to her whether she goes or not; **être ~ de ses actes** to do as one wishes
2 ‹*person*› free and easy; ‹*manner*› free; ‹*opinion*› candid; ‹*morality*› easy-going
3 ‹*hand, thumb*› free; ‹*road, way*› clear
4 ‹*person, room*› available; ‹*seat*› free
5 ‹*WC*› vacant; **la ligne n'est pas ~** (on telephone) the number is engaged (BrE) *or* busy (AmE)
■ **~ arbitre** free will; **~ circulation** freedom of movement
IDIOM **être ~ comme l'air** to be as free as a bird

libre-échange /libʀeʃɑ̃ʒ/ *m* free trade

librement /libʀəmɑ̃/ *adv* freely

libre-service, *pl* **libres-services** /libʀəsɛʀvis/ **A** *adj inv* self-service
B *m* **1 le ~** self-service
2 self-service shop (BrE) *or* store (AmE); self-service restaurant
■ **~ bancaire** automatic teller

lice /lis/ *f* **être en ~** to have entered the lists

licence /lisɑ̃s/ *f* **1** (bachelor's) degree; **~ en droit** law degree
2 (Law) licence (BrE); **produit sous ~** licensed product

licencié, **~e** /lisɑ̃sje/ **A** *pp* ▸ **licencier**
B *pp adj* ‹*student*› graduate
C *mf* **1** graduate (BrE), college graduate (AmE)
2 ~ (économique) redundant employee (BrE), laid-off worker

licenciement /lisɑ̃simɑ̃/ *m* dismissal; **~ (économique)** redundancy (BrE), lay-off
~ abusif unfair dismissal; **~ collectif** mass redundancy (BrE); **~ sec** compulsory redundancy (BrE) (*without compensation*)

licencier /lisɑ̃sje/ [**v2**] *vt* **1** to make [sb] redundant (BrE), to lay [sb] off
2 to dismiss (BrE), to let [sb] go

licencieux, **-ieuse** /lisɑ̃sjø, øz/ *adj* licentious

lichen /likɛn/ *m* lichen

licite /lisit/ *adj* lawful

licorne /likɔʀn/ *f* unicorn

lie /li/ *f* **1** dregs, lees
2 (fig) dregs

lie-de-vin /lidvɛ̃/ *adj inv* wine-coloured (BrE)

liège /ljɛʒ/ *m* cork; **bouchon en ~** cork

liégeois, **~e** /ljeʒwa, az/ *adj* of Liège; **café ~** *iced coffee topped with whipped cream*

lien /ljɛ̃/ *m* **1** strap; string
2 connection, link (**entre** between)
3 (gen) link, tie (**avec** with); (emotional) tie, bond; **~s économiques** economic links; **~s de parenté** family ties

lier /lje/ [**v1**] **A** *vt* **1** to tie [sb/sth] up; **il avait les mains liées** his hands were tied
2 to bind; **ils sont très liés** they are very close
3 to link ‹*ideas, events*›
4 ~ amitié avec qn to strike up a friendship with sb
5 (Mus) to slur ‹*notes*›
B se lier *v refl* (+ *v être*) to make friends

lierre /ljɛʀ/ *m* ivy

liesse /ljɛs/ *f* jubilation; **en ~** jubilant

lieu /ljø/ **A** *m* **1** (*pl* **~x**) place; **~ de passage** thoroughfare; **en tous ~x** everywhere; **en ~ et place de qn** ‹*sign, act*› on behalf of sb; **en dernier ~** lastly; **avoir ~** to take place; **tenir ~ de** to serve as ‹*bedroom, study*›; **il y a ~ de s'inquiéter** there is cause for concern; **s'il y a ~** if necessary; **donner ~ à** to cause ‹*scandal*›
2 (*pl* **~s**) coley
B au lieu de *phr* instead of
C lieux *mpl* **1 sur les ~x** at *or* on the scene; on the spot; **repérer les ~x** to have a scout around
2 premises; **visiter les ~x** to visit the premises
■ **~ commun** platitude; **~ public** public place

lieue /ljø/ *f* league; **~ marine** league
IDIOM **j'étais à cent** *or* **mille ~s d'imaginer** I never for a moment imagined

lieutenant /ljøtnɑ̃/ *m* **1** (Mil) (in army) ≈ lieutenant (BrE), ≈ first lieutenant (AmE); (in air force) ≈ flying officer (BrE), ≈ first lieutenant (AmE)
2 (on boat) first officer

lièvre /ljɛvʀ/ *m* (Zool) hare
IDIOM **courir plusieurs ~s à la fois** to try to do too many things at once

key word

lifting /liftiŋ/ *m* face-lift

ligament /ligamɑ̃/ *m* ligament

ligaturer /ligatyʀe/ [**v1**] *vt* (Med) to tie

light /lajt/ *adj inv* low calorie; **des recettes ~** low calorie recipes

lignage /liɲaʒ/ *m* lineage

ligne /liɲ/ *f* **1** (gen) line; **lire les ~s de la main de qn** to read sb's palm; **~ droite** straight line; (driving) straight piece of road; **la dernière ~ droite avant l'arrivée** the home straight; **je vous écris ces quelques ~s pour vous dire...** this is just a quick note to tell you...; **à la ~!** new paragraph!
2 (in public transport) service; route; (of train, underground) line; **~ de chemin de fer** railway line; **~s intérieures** domestic flights
3 cable; **~ aérienne** overhead cable
4 (telephone) line
5 figure; **garder la ~** to stay slim
6 (of body) contours; (of face) shape; (of hills) outline; **la ~ aérodynamique d'une voiture** the aerodynamic lines of a car
7 (of clothes, furniture, style) look
8 outline; **raconter un événement dans ses grandes ~s** to give an outline of events
9 fishing line; **pêche à la ~** angling
10 line; row; **les ~s ennemies** (Mil) the enemy lines
11 (Comput) **en ~** on line
■ **~ de conduite** line of conduct; **se donner comme ~ de conduite de faire** to make it a rule to do; **~ de démarcation** (Mil) demarcation line; **~ de mire** line of sight; **~ de tir** line of fire
IDIOMS **être en première ~** to be in the front line; (fig) to be in the firing line; **entrer en ~ de compte** to be taken into account

lignée /liɲe/ *f* **1** descendants; lineage; **de haute ~** of noble descent
2 tradition

lignite /liɲit/ *m* brown coal, lignite

ligoter /ligɔte/ [**v1**] *vt* to truss [sb] up

ligue /lig/ *f* league

liguer: **se liguer** /lige/ [**v1**] *v refl* (+ *v être*) ‹*people*› to join forces

lilas /lila/ *adj inv*, *m* lilac

lilliputien, **-ienne** /lilipysjɛ̃, ɛn/ *adj*, *mf* Lilliputian

limace /limas/ *f* (Zool) slug

limaçon /limasɔ̃/ *m* snail

limaille /limaj/ *f* filings

limande /limɑ̃d/ *f* (Zool) dab

limande-sole, *pl* **limandes-soles** /limɑ̃dsɔl/ *f* (Zool) lemon sole

lime /lim/ *f* **1** (Tech) file; **~ à ongles** nail file
2 (Bot) lime
3 (Zool) lima

limer /lime/ [**v1**] **A** *vt* **1** to file ‹*nails, metal*›; to file down ‹*key*›
2 to file through ‹*bars of cage*›
B se limer *v refl* (+ *v être*) **se ~ les ongles** to file one's nails

limier /limje/ *m* **1** bloodhound
2 (fam) sleuth

limitatif, **-ive** /limitatif, iv/ *adj* limiting, restrictive

limitation /limitasjɔ̃/ *f* (of power, liberty) limitation, restriction; (of prices, interest rates) control; **~ de vitesse** (Aut) speed limit

limite /limit/ **A** *f* **1** border
2 (of estate, piece of land) boundary; (of sea, forest, village) edge
3 limit; **connaître ses ~s** to know one's (own) limitations; **vraiment, il dépasse les ~s!** he's really going too far!; **à la ~, je préférerais qu'il refuse** I'd almost prefer it if he refused
4 à la ~ de on the verge of; **activités à la ~ de la légalité** activities bordering on the illegal
5 dans une certaine ~ up to a point, to a certain extent; **dans la ~ de, dans les ~s de** within the limits of
B (-)limite (*combining form*) **date(-)~** deadline; **date(-)~ de vente** sell-by date; **vitesse(-)~** maximum speed
■ **~ d'âge** age limit

limiter /limite/ [**v1**] **A** *vt* to limit, to restrict ‹*power, duration, number*›; **cela limite nos possibilités** that rather limits our scope
B se limiter *v refl* (+ *v être*) **1 se ~ à deux verres de bière par jour** to limit oneself to two glasses of beer a day; **je me limiterai à quelques observations** I'll confine myself to a few observations
2 se ~ à to be limited to; **la vie ne se limite pas au travail** there's more to life than work

limitrophe /limitʀɔf/ *adj* ‹*country, region*› adjacent; ‹*city*› border

limoger /limɔʒe/ [**v13**] *vt* to dismiss

limon /limɔ̃/ *m* **1** silt
2 (on horse-drawn carriage) shaft

limonade /limɔnad/ *f* lemonade (BrE), lemon soda (AmE)

limousine /limuzin/ *f* (Aut) limousine

limpide /lɛ̃pid/ *adj* **1** clear, limpid
2 (fig) ‹*explanation, style*› clear, lucid

limpidité /lɛ̃pidite/ *f* clarity

lin /lɛ̃/ *m* **1** flax
2 linen

linceul /lɛ̃sœl/ *m* shroud

linéaire /lineɛʀ/ *adj* linear

linge /lɛ̃ʒ/ *m* **1** linen; **~ sale** dirty linen
2 washing; **corde** *or* **fil à ~** clothes line
3 ~ (de corps) underwear
4 cloth
■ **~ de maison** household linen; **~ de toilette** bathroom linen

lingère /lɛ̃ʒɛʀ/ *f* laundry woman

lingerie /lɛ̃ʒʀi/ *f* **1** linen room
2 lingerie

lingot /lɛ̃go/ *m* ingot

linguiste /lɛ̃gɥist/ *mf* linguist

linguistique /lɛ̃gɥistik/ **A** *adj* linguistic
B *f* linguistics

linotte /linɔt/ *f* linnet

linteau, *pl* **~x** /lɛ̃to/ *m* lintel

lion /ljɔ̃/ *m* lion; **~ de mer** sea lion
IDIOM **avoir mangé du ~** (fam) to be full of beans (BrE) (fam), to be full of pep (AmE) (fam)

Lion /ljɔ̃/ *pr m* Leo

lionceau, *pl* **~x** /ljɔ̃so/ *m* lion cub

lionne /ljɔn/ *f* lioness

lipide /lipid/ *m* lipid

liquéfier /likefje/ [**v2**] *vt*, **se liquéfier** *v refl* (+ *v être*) to liquefy

liquette /likɛt/ *f* (fam) shirt

liqueur /likœʀ/ *f* liqueur

liquidation /likidasjɔ̃/ *f* **1** (Law) (of property) liquidation; (of debts) settlement
2 clearance; **~ totale (du stock)** total clearance

liquide /likid/ **A** *adj* **1** liquid; **miel ~** clear honey
2 argent ~ cash
B *m* **1** liquid
2 cash
■ **~ correcteur** correction fluid, white-out (fluid) (AmE); **~ de frein** brake fluid

liquider /likide/ [**v1**] *vt* **1** to settle ‹*accounts*›; to liquidate ‹*company, business*›
2 to clear ‹*goods, stock*›
3 (fam) to liquidate (fam) ‹*enemy, witness*›
4 (fam) to demolish ‹*meal*›; to empty ‹*glass*›

liquidité /likidite/ *f* **des ~s** liquid assets

⚷ **lire¹** /liʀ/ [**v66**] *vt* to read; **~ qch en diagonale** to skim through sth; **~ sur les lèvres de qn** to lip-read what sb is saying; **~ dans les pensées de qn** to read sb's mind

lire² /liʀ/ *f* lira

lis /lis/ *m inv* lily

liseré /lizʀe/ *m*, **liséré** /lizeʀe/ *m* (on dress) edging; piping

liseron /lizʀɔ̃/ *m* bindweed, convolvulus

liseuse /lizøz/ *f* **1** bed jacket
2 small reading lamp

lisible /lizibl/ *adj* **1** legible
2 readable

lisière /lizjɛʀ/ *f* **1** (of wood, field) edge; (of village) outskirts
2 (on piece of fabric) selvage

lisse /lis/ *adj* ‹*skin, surface*› smooth; ‹*tyre*› worn

lisser /lise/ [**v1**] *vt* to smooth ‹*hair, garment*›; to stroke ‹*beard*›

⚷ **liste** /list/ *f* (gen) list; (at election) list (of candidates) (BrE), ticket (AmE)
■ **~ d'attente** waiting list; **~ électorale** electoral roll; **~ de mariage** wedding list
IDIOM **être sur ~ rouge** to be ex-directory (BrE), to have an unlisted number (AmE)

lister /liste/ [**v1**] *vt* to list

⚷ **lit** /li/ *m* **1** bed; **~ à une place** *or* **d'une personne** single bed; **~ à deux places** *or* **de deux personnes** double bed; **aller** *or* **se mettre au ~** to go to bed; **garder le ~** to stay in bed; **tirer qn du ~** to drag sb out of bed; **au ~!** bedtime!; **~ métallique** iron bedstead; **le ~ n'était pas défait** the bed had not been slept in
2 (Law) marriage
3 (of river) bed; **la rivière est sortie de son ~** the river has overflowed its banks
■ **~ de camp** camp bed (BrE), cot (AmE); **~ pliant** folding bed; **~s superposés** bunk beds

litanie /litani/ *f* litany

literie /litʀi/ *f* bedding

lithographie /litɔgʀafi/ *f* **1** lithography
2 lithograph

litière /litjɛʀ/ *f* **1** (for cattle) litter; (for horses) bedding; (for cats) cat litter
2 (mode of transport) litter

litige /litiʒ/ *m* dispute; **point de ~** bone of contention; point at issue; **les parties en ~** the litigants

litigieux, **-ieuse** /litiʒjø, øz/ *adj* ‹*case, point, argument*› contentious

litre /litʀ/ *m* **1** (measure) litre (BrE)
2 litre (BrE) bottle

⚷ **littéraire** /liteʀɛʀ/ **A** *adj* ‹*work, criticism*› literary; **études ~s** arts studies
B *mf* **1** literary person
2 arts *or* liberal arts (AmE) student

littéral, **~e**, *mpl* **-aux** /liteʀal, o/ *adj* literal

littéralement /liteʀalmɑ̃/ *adv* literally; verbatim

⚷ **littérature** /liteʀatyʀ/ *f* literature

littoral, **~e**, *mpl* **-aux** /litɔʀal, o/ **A** *adj* coastal
B *m* coast

liturgie /lityʀʒi/ *f* liturgy

livide /livid/ *adj* deathly pale

living /liviŋ/ *m* living room

livraison /livʀɛzɔ̃/ *f* delivery; **'~s à domicile'** 'we deliver'; **il est venu prendre ~ de la commande** he came to pick up the order

⚷ **livre¹** /livʀ/ *m* book; **c'est mon ~ de chevet** it's my bedside book; (fig) it's my bible
■ **~ blanc** blue book; **~ de bord** logbook; **~ d'or** visitors' book; **~ de poche®** paperback; **~ scolaire** schoolbook

livre² /livʀ/ *f* **1** pound; **~ sterling** pound sterling; **~ irlandaise** Irish pound, punt
2 (unit of weight) half a kilo; (in UK) pound

livrée /livʀe/ *f* livery

⚷ **livrer** /livʀe/ [**v1**] **A** *vt* **1** to deliver ‹*goods*›; **~ qn** to deliver sb's order
2 to hand [sb] over ‹*criminal*›; to betray ‹*accomplice, secret*›
3 être livré à soi-même to be left to one's own devices
4 il nous livre un peu de lui-même he reveals something of himself
B se livrer *v refl* (+ *v être*) **1 se ~ à**

⚷ key word

un trafic de drogue to engage in drug trafficking
2 se ~ à ‹*criminal*› to give oneself up to
3 se ~ à un ami to confide in a friend

livret /livʀɛ/ *m* **1** booklet
2 libretto
■ **~ de caisse d'épargne** ≈ savings book (BrE), bank book (*for a savings account*) (AmE); **~ de famille** family record book (*of births, marriages and deaths*)

livreur, -euse /livʀœʀ, øz/ *mf* delivery man/woman

lobe /lɔb/ *m* lobe; **~ de l'oreille** ear lobe

local, ~e, *pl* **-aux** /lɔkal, o/ **A** *adj* ‹*newspaper, authorities*› local; ‹*pain, showers*› localized
B *m* **1** place; **les scouts ont besoin d'un ~** the scouts need a place to meet
2 ~ commercial commercial premises; **les locaux du journal** the newspaper offices

localement /lɔkalmɑ̃/ *adv* on a local level; **appliquer la crème ~** apply the cream locally

localisation /lɔkalizasjɔ̃/ *f* **1** location
2 la ~ d'un incendie localizing a fire

localiser /lɔkalize/ [**v1**] *vt* **1** to locate ‹*person, noise*›
2 to confine, to localize ‹*fire*›

localité /lɔkalite/ *f* locality

locataire /lɔkatɛʀ/ *mf* tenant

locatif, -ive /lɔkatif, iv/ *adj* ‹*agreement*› rental

location /lɔkasjɔ̃/ *f* **1** (by owner) renting out; (by tenant) renting; **agence de ~** rental agency
2 rented accommodation
3 rent
4 (of equipment) hire; **~ de voitures** car hire (BrE), car rental; **contrat de ~** rental agreement; **~ de vidéos** video rental
5 (of theatre seats) reservation, booking (BrE)

location-vente, *pl* **locations-ventes** /lɔkasjɔ̃vɑ̃t/ *f* 100% mortgage scheme

locomotion /lɔkɔmɔsjɔ̃/ *f* locomotion

locomotive /lɔkɔmɔtiv/ *f* engine, locomotive; **~ à vapeur** steam engine

locuteur, -trice /lɔkytœʀ, tʀis/ *mf* speaker

locution /lɔkysjɔ̃/ *f* phrase; idiom

logarithme /lɔgaʀitm/ *m* logarithm, log

loge /lɔʒ/ *f* **1** (caretaker's dwelling) lodge
2 (of actor) dressing room; (in theatre) box
3 (in freemasonry) Lodge
4 loggia

logé, ~e /lɔʒe/ **A** *pp* ▸ **loger**
B *pp adj* housed; **être ~, nourri, blanchi** to have bed, board and one's laundry done

logement /lɔʒmɑ̃/ *m* **1** accommodation; **~ individuel** flat (BrE), apartment (AmE)
2 housing; **la crise du ~** the housing crisis

loger /lɔʒe/ [**v13**] **A** *vt* **1** to house ‹*student*›
2 to put [sb] up ‹*friend*›; to provide accommodation for ‹*refugees*›
3 ‹*hotel*› to have accommodation for
4 to put; **je n'ai pas pu ~ tous mes meubles dans le salon** I couldn't fit all my furniture in the living room
5 ~ une balle dans la tête de qn to shoot sb in the head
B *vi* **1** to live
2 to stay; **~ à l'hôtel** to stay at a hotel
C se loger *v refl* (+ *v être*) **1** to find accommodation; **se nourrir et se ~** to pay for food and accommodation
2 se ~ dans qch to get stuck in sth; ‹*dust*› to collect in sth; **la balle est venue se ~ dans le genou** the bullet lodged in his/her knee

logeur, -euse /lɔʒœʀ, øz/ *mf* lodger

loggia /lɔdʒja/ *f* loggia

logiciel /lɔʒisjɛl/ *m* **1** software; **~ de base** system(s) software
2 program
3 (Comput) **~ de navigation** browser

logique /lɔʒik/ **A** *adj* **1** logical; **il n'est pas ~ avec lui-même** he is not consistent
2 (fam) reasonable; **ce serait ~ qu'ils soient en colère** one could understand why they would be angry
B *f* logic; **manquer de ~** to be illogical; **c'est dans la ~ des choses** it's in the nature of things; **en toute ~** logically

logiquement /lɔʒikmɑ̃/ *adv* logically

logis /lɔʒi/ *m inv* home, dwelling

logistique /lɔʒistik/ *f* logistics

logo /lɔgo/ *m* logo

loi /lwa/ *f* **1** law; **voter une ~** to pass a law
2 la ~ the law; **enfreindre la ~** to break the law; **tomber sous le coup de la ~** to be *or* constitute an offence (BrE); **faire la ~** (fig) to lay down the law
3 rule; law; **la ~ du milieu** the law of the underworld; **c'est la ~ des séries** things always happen in a row
■ **~ d'amnistie** *act granting amnesty to some offenders*; **~ communautaire** community law; **~ informatique et libertés** data protection act; **~ de la jungle** law of the jungle

loin /lwɛ̃/ **A** *adv* **1** a long way, far (away); **c'est ~** it's a long way; **c'est trop ~** it's too far; **il habite plus ~** he lives further *or* farther away; **du plus ~ qu'il m'aperçut** as soon as he saw me; **voir plus ~** (in text) see below
2 (in time) **tout cela est bien ~** that was all a long time ago; **aussi ~ que je me souvienne** as far back as I can remember; **l'été n'est plus très ~ maintenant** summer isn't far off now
3 (fig) **de là à dire qu'il est incompétent, il n'y a pas ~** that comes close to saying he's incompetent; **il n'est pas bête, ~ s'en faut!** he's not stupid, far from it!; **ça va beaucoup plus ~** it goes much further
B loin de *phr* **1** (in space) far from; **est-ce encore ~ d'ici?** is it much further *or* farther from here?

l

2 (in time) far from; **cela ne fait pas ~ de quatre ans que je suis ici** I've been here for almost four years now
3 (fig) far from, a long way from; **~ de moi cette idée!** nothing could be further from my mind!; **avec l'imprimante, il faut compter pas ~ de 8 000 euros** if you include the printer, you're talking about 8,000 euros or thereabouts
C **de loin** *phr* from a distance; **je ne vois pas très bien de ~** I can't see very well at a distance; **c'est de ~ ton meilleur roman** it's by far your best novel
D **au loin** *phr* au ~ in the distance
E **de loin en loin** *phr* **1** **on pouvait voir des maisons de ~ en ~** you could see houses scattered here and there
2 every now and then
IDIOM **~ des yeux, ~ du cœur** (Proverb) out of sight, out of mind

🗝 **lointain**, **~e** /lwɛ̃tɛ̃, ɛn/ **A** *adj* **1** ‹*country, past*› distant
2 ‹*link*› remote
3 ‹*person*› distant
B *m* background; **dans le ~** ‹*see, hear*› in the distance

loir /lwaʀ/ *m* (edible) dormouse

loisir /lwaziʀ/ *m* **1** spare time; **(tout) à ~** at (great) leisure
2 **avoir tout ~ de faire** to have plenty of time to do
3 leisure activity

lombaire /lɔ̃bɛʀ/ *f* lumbar vertebra

londonien, **-ienne** /lɔ̃dɔnjɛ̃, ɛn/ *adj* (of) London

Londres /lɔ̃dʀ/ *pr n* London

🗝 **long**, **longue** /lɔ̃, lɔ̃g/ **A** *adj* long; **plus/trop ~ de deux mètres** two metres (BrE) longer/too long; **être ~ (à faire)** ‹*person*› to be slow (to do); **être en longue maladie** to be on extended sick leave; **il guérira, mais ce sera ~** he will get better, but it's going to take a long time; **être ~ à la détente** (fam) to be slow on the uptake (fam)
B *adv* **1** **en dire ~/trop ~/plus ~** to say a lot/too much/more (**sur qn/qch** about sb/sth)
2 **s'habiller ~** to wear longer skirts
C *m* **un câble de six mètres de ~** a cable six metres (BrE) long, a six-metre (BrE) long cable; **en ~** lengthwise; **en ~ et en large** ‹*tell*› in great detail; **marcher de ~ en large** to pace up and down; **en ~, en large et en travers** (fam) ‹*tell*› at great length; **le ~ du mur** along the wall; up *or* down the wall; **tomber de tout son ~** to fall flat (on one's face)
D **à la longue** *phr* in the end, eventually
■ **~ métrage** feature-length film

long-courrier, *pl* **~s** /lɔ̃kuʀje/ *m* **1** ocean-going ship
2 long-haul aircraft

longer /lɔ̃ʒe/ [**v13**] *vt* **1** ‹*person, train*› to go along ‹*coast*›; to follow ‹*river*›
2 ‹*garden, road*› to run alongside ‹*lake, field*›

longévité /lɔ̃ʒevite/ *f* longevity

longiligne /lɔ̃ʒiliɲ/ *adj* lanky, rangy

longitude /lɔ̃ʒityd/ *f* longitude

longitudinal, **~e**, *mpl* **-aux** /lɔ̃ʒitydinal, o/ *adj* longitudinal, lengthwise

🗝 **longtemps** /lɔ̃tɑ̃/ *adv* ‹*wait, sleep*› (for) a long time; **il t'a fallu ~?** did it take you long?; **~ avant/après** long before/after; **je peux le garder plus ~?** can I keep it a bit longer?; **il n'y a pas ~ qu'il travaille ici** he hasn't worked here long; **il y a** *or* **ça fait ~ qu'il n'a pas téléphoné** he hasn't phoned for ages (fam); **il est mort depuis ~** he died a long time ago; **il n'y a pas si ~ c'était encore possible** it was still possible until quite recently

🗝 **longue** ▸ **long A, D**

longuement /lɔ̃gmɑ̃/ *adv* ‹*hesitate, talk*› for a long time; ‹*explain, interview*› at length

🗝 **longueur** /lɔ̃gœʀ/ **A** *f* **1** (in space, time) length; **la maison est tout en ~** the house is long and narrow; **traîner en ~** ‹*film, book*› to go on forever
2 (in race, swimming) length; **avoir une ~ d'avance sur qn** (Sport) to be one length ahead of sb; (fig) to be ahead of sb; **le saut en ~** the long *or* broad (AmE) jump
3 length
B **longueurs** *fpl* (in film, book, speech) overlong passages
C **à longueur de** *phr* **à ~ de journée** all day long; **à ~ d'année** all year round; **à ~ d'émissions** programme (BrE) after programme (BrE)
■ **~ d'onde** wavelength

longue-vue, *pl* **longues-vues** /lɔ̃gvy/ *f* telescope

look /luk/ *m* (fam) look; image

looping /lupiŋ/ *m* loop

lopin /lɔpɛ̃/ *m* **~ (de terre)** patch of land

loquace /lɔkas/ *adj* talkative, loquacious

loque /lɔk/ **A** *f* **~ (humaine)** (human) wreck
B **loques** *fpl* rags

loquet /lɔkɛ/ *m* latch

lorgner /lɔʀɲe/ [**v1**] *vt* (fam) to give [sb] the eye ‹*person*› (fam); to cast longing glances at ‹*jewel, cake*›; to have one's eye on ‹*inheritance, job*›

lorgnette /lɔʀɲɛt/ *f* **1** opera glasses
2 spy-glass

lorgnon /lɔʀɲɔ̃/ *m* **1** lorgnette
2 pince-nez

🗝 **lors**: **lors de** /lɔʀ/ *phr* **1** during
2 at the time of

🗝 **lorsque**, **lorsqu'** *before vowel or mute h* /lɔʀsk(ə)/ *conj* when

losange /lɔzɑ̃ʒ/ *m* (shape) lozenge; **en ~** diamond-shaped

🗝 key word

lot /lo/ *m* **1** (of inheritance) share; (of land) plot
2 (in lottery) prize; **gagner le gros ~** to hit the jackpot
3 (of objects for sale) batch; (at auction) lot
4 (of person) **être au-dessus du ~** to be above the average
5 fate, lot

loterie /lɔtʀi/ *f* raffle; (in fair) tombola (BrE), raffle (AmE); (large scale) lottery

loti, **~e** /lɔti/ *adj* **bien/mal ~** well/badly off

lotion /losjɔ̃/ *f* lotion

lotir /lɔtiʀ/ [**v3**] *vt* **terrain(s) à ~** plots for sale

lotissement /lɔtismɑ̃/ *m* housing estate (BrE), subdivision (AmE)

loto /lɔto/ *m* lotto; **le ~ national** the national lottery

lotte /lɔt/ *f* monkfish; (freshwater) burbot

lotus /lɔtys/ *m inv* lotus

louable /luabl/ *adj* commendable, praiseworthy

louage /luaʒ/ *m* **voiture de ~** hire car (BrE), rental car (AmE)

louange /luɑ̃ʒ/ *f* praise

loubard /lubaʀ/ *m* (fam) hooligan, delinquent youth

louche /luʃ/ **A** *adj* ‹*person, past, affair*› shady; ‹*place*› seedy
B *f* ladle; ladleful

loucher /luʃe/ [**v1**] *vi* to have a squint

louer /lue/ [**v1**] *vt* **1** ‹*owner, landlord*› to let (BrE), to rent out ‹*house*›; to hire out ‹*premises*›; to rent out ‹*equipment*›; **'à ~'** 'for rent', 'to let' (BrE)
2 ‹*tenant*› to rent ‹*house*›; to hire ‹*room*›; to rent ‹*equipment, film*›
3 to hire ‹*staff*›
4 to praise; **Dieu soit loué** thank God

loufoque /lufɔk/ *adj* (fam) crazy (fam)

louis /lwi/ *m inv* **~ d'or** (gold) louis

loukoum /lukum/ *m* Turkish delight

loulou /lulu/ *m* **1** spitz
2 (fam) hooligan, delinquent youth
3 (fam) pet (BrE) (fam), honey (AmE)

loup /lu/ *m* **1** wolf; **le grand méchant ~** the big bad wolf; **à pas de ~** stealthily
2 ~ (de mer) (sea) bass
3 domino, mask
■ **(vieux) ~ de mer** old salt, old tar
IDIOMS **avoir une faim de ~** to be ravenous; **être connu comme le ~ blanc** to be known to everybody; **hurler avec les ~s** to follow the herd *or* crowd; **se jeter dans la gueule du ~** to stick one's head in the lion's mouth; **les ~s ne se mangent pas entre eux** (Proverb) (there is) honour (BrE) among thieves; **quand on parle du ~ (on en voit la queue)** (Proverb) speak of the devil; **l'homme est un ~ pour l'homme** (Proverb) dog eat dog

loupe /lup/ *f* magnifying glass

louper /lupe/ (fam) [**v1**] **A** *vt* **1** to miss ‹*train, opportunity, visitor*›; **il n'en loupe pas une** he's always opening his big mouth
2 to flunk (fam) ‹*exam*›; to screw up (fam) ‹*sauce, piece of work*›
B *vi* **j'avais dit que ça se casserait, ça n'a pas loupé** I said it would break, and sure enough it did; **tu vas tout faire ~** you'll mess everything up

loup-garou, *pl* **loups-garous** /lugaʀu/ *m* werewolf

loupiote /lupjɔt/ *f* (fam) small lamp

lourd, **~e** /luʀ, luʀd/ **A** *adj* **1** ‹*person, object, metal*› heavy
2 ‹*stomach, head, steps*› heavy; ‹*gesture*› clumsy
3 ‹*meal, food*› heavy; ‹*wine*› heady; **~ à digérer** heavy on the stomach
4 ‹*equipment, weapons*› heavy
5 ‹*fine, taxation*› heavy
6 ‹*defeat, responsibility*› heavy; ‹*mistake*› serious
7 ‹*administration, structure*› unwieldy; ‹*staff numbers*› large
8 ‹*person, animal*› ungainly; ‹*body, object, architecture*› heavy; ‹*building*› cumbersome, ponderous
9 ‹*joke*› flat; ‹*style*› clumsy
10 ‹*atmosphere, silence*› heavy; ‹*heat*› sultry
11 être ~ de dangers to be fraught with danger
B *adv* **1 peser ~** to weigh a lot; (fig) to carry a lot of weight
2 (of weather) **il fait ~** it's close
3 (fam) **pas ~** not a lot, not much; **dix personnes, ça ne fait pas ~** ten people, that's not a lot
IDIOMS **avoir la main ~e** to be heavy-handed; **avoir la main ~e avec le sel/le parfum** to overdo the salt/the perfume

lourdement /luʀdəmɑ̃/ *adv* **1** heavily; **se tromper ~** to be gravely mistaken
2 marcher ~ to walk clumsily; **insister ~ sur** to keep going on about

lourdeur /luʀdœʀ/ *f* **1** (of organization) complexity
2 heaviness
3 (of style) clumsiness; (in a text) clumsy expression
4 weight
5 (of person) oafishness; (of joke) poorness; (of architecture) ungainliness
6 (of weather) closeness

loutre /lutʀ/ *f* **1** otter
2 otter skin

louve /luv/ *f* she-wolf

louveteau, *pl* **~x** /luvto/ *m* (Zool) wolf cub

louvoyer /luvwaje/ [**v23**] *vi* **1** ‹*ship*› to tack
2 (fig) to manoeuvre (BrE), to maneuver (AmE)

lover: **se lover** /lɔve/ [**v1**] *v refl* (+ *v être*) ‹*snake*› to coil itself up; ‹*person*› to curl up

loyal, **~e**, *mpl* **-aux** /lwajal, o/ *adj* **1** ‹*friend*› true; ‹*servant*› loyal, faithful
2 ‹*procedure, conduct*› honest; ‹*competition, game*› fair

loyalisme /lwajalism/ *m* loyalty
loyaliste /lwajalist/ *adj*, *mf* loyalist
loyauté /lwajote/ *f* **1** loyalty
2 honesty
loyer /lwaje/ *m* rent
lu, **~e** /ly/ ▶ **lire¹**
lubie /lybi/ *f* whim
lubricité /lybʀisite/ *f* lechery; lewdness
lubrifiant /lybʀifjɑ̃/ *m* lubricant
lubrifier /lybʀifje/ [**v2**] *vt* to lubricate
lubrique /lybʀik/ *adj* ‹*person*› lecherous; ‹*look, dance*› lewd
lucarne /lykaʀn/ *f* (small) window; (in roof) skylight
lucide /lysid/ *adj* clear-headed; lucid
lucidité /lysidite/ *f* lucidity; clear-headedness; clarity; **juger en toute ~** to judge without any illusions
luciole /lysjɔl/ *f* firefly
lucratif, **-ive** /lykʀatif, iv/ *adj* lucrative
ludique /lydik/ *adj* ‹*activity*› play
ludothèque /lydɔtɛk/ *f* toy library
luette /lyɛt/ *f* uvula
lueur /lɥœʀ/ *f* (faint) light; **les ~s de la ville** the city lights; **à la ~ d'une bougie** by candlelight; **à la ~ des événements d'hier** in the light of yesterday's events; **les dernières ~s du soleil couchant** the dying glow of the sunset
luge /lyʒ/ *f* **1** toboggan (BrE), sled (AmE)
2 (Sport) luge
lugubre /lygybʀ/ *adj* gloomy; mournful
✍ **lui¹** /lɥi/ **A** *pron m* **1** he; **elle lit, ~ regarde la télévision** she's reading, he's watching TV; **~ seul a le droit de parler** he alone has the right to talk
2 him; **à cause de ~** because of him; **je les vois plus souvent que ~** I see them more often than he does; I see them more often than I see him; **c'est à ~** it's his, it belongs to him; it's his turn; **c'est à ~ de choisir** it's up to him to choose
B *pron mf* it; **le parti lance un appel, apportez-~ votre soutien** the party is launching an appeal—give it your support; **l'Espagne a signé, le Portugal, ~, n'a pas encore donné son accord** Spain has signed while Portugal hasn't yet agreed
C *pron f* her; **je ~ ai annoncé la nouvelle** I told her the news
lui² /lɥi/ ▶ **luire**
lui-même /lɥimɛm/ *pron* **1** (referring to person) himself; **'M. Greiner?'—'~'** (on phone) 'Mr Greiner?'—'speaking'
2 (referring to object, concept) itself
✍ **luire** /lɥiʀ/ [**v69**] *vi* to shine; to glow; **leur regard luisait de colère** their eyes blazed with anger
luisant, **~e** /lɥizɑ̃, ɑ̃t/ *adj* shining; glistening

✍ key word

lumbago /lœ̃bago/ *m* back pain
✍ **lumière** /lymjɛʀ/ **A** *f* **1** light; **~ naturelle/électrique** natural/electric light; **la ~ du jour** daylight; **il y a une ~ très particulière dans cette région** there's a very special quality to the light in this region; **les ~s de la ville** the city lights; **à la ~ d'une chandelle** by candlelight; **à la ~ des récents événements** in the light of recent events
2 (person) **ce n'est pas une ~** he'll never set the world on fire
B lumières *fpl* **1** (of vehicle) lights
2 (fam) **j'ai besoin de vos ~s** I need to pick your brains
Lumières /lymjɛʀ/ *fpl* **le siècle des ~** the Age of Enlightenment
luminaire /luminɛʀ/ *m* light (fitting)
lumineux, **-euse** /lyminø, øz/ *adj*
1 luminous; **panneau ~** electronic display (board); **enseigne lumineuse** neon sign; **rayon ~** ray of light
2 idée lumineuse brilliant idea
3 ‹*smile, gaze*› radiant
luminosité /lyminozite/ *f* brightness, luminosity
lump /lœ̃p/ *m* **œufs de ~** lumpfish roe
lunaire /lynɛʀ/ *adj* lunar
lunatique /lynatik/ *mf* moody person
lunch /lœʃ/ *m* buffet (lunch); buffet (supper)
✍ **lundi** /lœ̃di/ *m* Monday
✍ **lune** /lyn/ *f* moon; **pleine ~** full moon
■ **~ de miel** honeymoon; **~ rousse** ≈ April moon
IDIOMS **être dans la ~** (fam) to have one's head in the clouds; **avoir l'air de tomber de la ~** to look blank; **demander la ~** (fam) to cry for the moon; **promettre la ~** (fam) to promise the earth; **décrocher la ~** to do the impossible
luné, **~e** /lyne/ *adj* (fam) **mal ~** grumpy
lunette /lynɛt/ **A** *f* lavatory seat
B lunettes *fpl* **1** glasses
2 (protective) goggles; **~s de natation** swimming goggles
■ **~ arrière** (Aut) rear window; **~s noires** dark glasses; **~s de soleil** sunglasses
lunule /lynyl/ *f* (on nail) half-moon
lurette /lyʀɛt/ *f* (fam) **il y a** *or* **cela fait belle ~ que je ne l'ai pas vue** it's been ages since I last saw her (fam)
luron /lyʀɔ̃/ *m* fellow
lustre /lystʀ/ **A** *m* **1** (gen) (decorative) ceiling light; (made of glass) chandelier
2 sheen
3 (of place, institution) prestigious image; **donner un nouveau ~ à** to give fresh appeal to
B lustres *mpl* (fam) **depuis des ~s** for ages (fam)
lustré, **~e** /lystʀe/ *adj* **1** glossy; (through wear) shiny
2 ‹*fabric*› glazed

lustrer /lystʀe/ [**v1**] *vt* to polish ‹*shoes, mirror*›

luth /lyt/ *m* **1** (Mus) lute
2 (Zool) leatherback

luthier /lytjɛ/ *m* stringed instrument maker

lutin /lytɛ̃/ *m* goblin

lutte /lyt/ *f* **1** conflict; struggle; fight; **~ d'influence** power struggle; **la ~ contre le cancer** the fight against cancer
2 (Sport) wrestling
■ **~ armée** armed conflict; **~ de classes** class struggle *or* war; **~ d'intérêts** clash of interests

lutter /lyte/ [**v1**] *vi* to struggle; to fight; **~ contre qn** to fight against sb; **~ contre** to fight ‹*crime, unemployment, illness*›; to fight against ‹*violence*›; to contend with ‹*noise, bad weather*›; **Louis luttait contre le sommeil** Louis was struggling to stay awake

lutteur, **-euse** /lytœʀ, øz/ *mf* (gen) fighter; (Sport) wrestler

luxation /lyksasjɔ̃/ *f* dislocation

luxe /lyks/ *m* luxury; **s'offrir le ~ de faire** to afford the luxury of doing; (fig) to give oneself the satisfaction of doing; **je l'ai nettoyé et ce n'était pas du ~** (fam) I gave it a much needed clean; **avoir des goûts de ~** to have expensive tastes

Luxembourg /lyksɑ̃buʀ/ *pr m* Luxembourg

Luxembourgeois, **~e** /lyksɑ̃buʀʒwa, az/ *mf* **1** native of Luxembourg
2 inhabitant of Luxembourg

luxer: **se luxer** /lykse/ [**v1**] *v refl* (+ *v être*) **se ~ l'épaule** to dislocate one's shoulder

luxueux, **-euse** /lyksɥø, øz/ *adj* luxurious

luxure /lyksyʀ/ *f* lust

luxuriant, **~e** /lyksyʀjɑ̃, ɑ̃t/ *adj* luxuriant

luzerne /lyzɛʀn/ *f* alfalfa, lucerne (BrE)

lycée /lise/ *m* secondary school (*preparing students aged 15–18 for the baccalaureate*)

lycéen, **-éenne** /liseɛ̃, ɛn/ *mf* secondary school student

lymphatique /lɛ̃fatik/ *adj* **1** lethargic
2 lymphatic

lyncher /lɛ̃ʃe/ [**v1**] *vt* to lynch

lynx /lɛ̃ks/ *m inv* lynx
IDIOM **avoir un œil** *or* **des yeux de ~** to have very keen eyesight

lyonnais, **~e** /ljɔnɛ, ɛz/ *adj* of Lyons

lyonnaise /ljɔnɛz/ *f* **1** (Culin) **à la ~** à la lyonnaise
2 *regional game of boules*

lyophiliser /ljɔfilize/ [**v1**] *vt* to freeze-dry

lyre /liʀ/ *f* lyre

lyrique /liʀik/ *adj* **1** (Mus) ‹*song, composer*› operatic; ‹*singer, season*› opera
2 ‹*poetry, poet*› lyric; ‹*content, tone*› lyrical

lyrisme /liʀism/ *m* lyricism

lys /lis/ *m inv* lily

Mm

m, **M** /ɛm/ *m inv* **1** (letter) m, M
2 (*written abbr* = **mètre**) **30 m** 30 m

m' ▶ **me**

M. (*written abbr* = **Monsieur**) Mr

ma ▶ **mon**

macabre /makabʀ/ *adj* macabre

macadam /makadam/ *m* tarmac®

macaque /makak/ *m* macaque

macaron /makaʀɔ̃/ *m* **1** macaroon
2 lapel badge; sticker

macédoine /masedwan/ *f* mixed diced vegetables

macérer /maseʀe/ [**v14**] *vi* ‹*plant, fruit*› to soak, to steep; ‹*meat*› to marinate

mâche /mɑʃ/ *f* corn salad, lamb's lettuce

mâcher /mɑʃe/ [**v1**] *vt* to chew
IDIOMS **~ la besogne** *or* **le travail à qn** to break the back of the work for sb; **il ne mâche pas ses mots** he doesn't mince his words

machette /maʃɛt/ *f* machete

machiavélique /makjavelik/ *adj* Machiavellian

machin /maʃɛ̃/ *m* (fam) **1** thing, thingummy (fam), whatsit (fam)
2 old fogey

Machin, **~e** /maʃɛ̃, in/ *mf* (fam) what's-his-name (fam) /what's-her-name (fam)

machinal, **~e**, *mpl* **-aux** /maʃinal, o/ *adj* ‹*gesture, reaction*› mechanical

machination /maʃinasjɔ̃/ *f* plot

machine /maʃin/ *f* **1** machine; **taper à la ~** to type; **coudre à la ~** to machine-sew; **faire deux~s (de linge)** (fam) to do two loads of washing
2 (Naut) engine; **faire ~ arrière** to go astern; (fig) to back-pedal
■ **~ à calculer** calculating machine; **~ à coudre** sewing machine; **~ à écrire** typewriter; **~ à laver** washing machine; **~ à laver la vaisselle**

dishwasher; ~ **à sous** slot machine, one-armed bandit

machinerie /maʃinʀi/ *f* **1** machinery
2 machine room; (Naut) engine room

machiste /ma(t)ʃist/ *adj, m* male chauvinist

mâchoire /mɑʃwaʀ/ *f* jaw

mâchouiller /mɑʃuje/ [**v1**] *vt* (fam) to chew (on)

maçon /masɔ̃/ *m* bricklayer; builder; mason

maçonnerie /masɔnʀi/ *f* building; bricklaying; masonry work

maculer /makyle/ [**v1**] *vt* to smudge; ~ **qch de sang** to spatter sth with blood

⚷ **madame**, *pl* **mesdames** /madam, medam/ *f*
1 (addressing a woman whose name you do not know) **Madame** (in letter) Dear Madam; **bonsoir ~!** good evening!; **mesdames et messieurs bonsoir** good evening, ladies and gentlemen
2 (addressing a woman whose name you know, for example Bon) Mrs, Ms; (in a letter) **Madame** Dear Ms Bon; **bonjour, ~** good morning, Mrs Bon
3 (polite form of address) madam; **'~ a sonné?'** 'you rang, Madam?'

Madeleine /madlɛn/ *pr n* **pleurer comme une ~** to cry one's eyes out

mademoiselle, *pl* **mesdemoiselles** /madmwazɛl, medmwazɛl/ *f* **1** (addressing a woman whose name you do not know) **Mademoiselle** (in letter) Dear Madam; **bonjour, ~!** good morning!; **mesdames, mesdemoiselles, messieurs** ladies and gentlemen
2 (addressing a woman whose name you know, for example Bon) Miss, Ms; (in a letter) **Mademoiselle** Dear Miss Bon; **bonjour, ~** good morning, Miss Bon
3 (polite form of address) madam; **'~ a sonné?'** 'you rang, Madam?'

madone /madɔn/ *f* madonna

madrier /madʀije/ *m* beam

maestria /maɛstʀija/ *f* brilliance, panache

mafia /mafja/ *f also* **maffia** mafia; **la Mafia** the Mafia

mafieux, **-ieuse** /mafjø, øz/ *adj also* **maffieux** mafia

⚷ **magasin** /magazɛ̃/ *m* **1** shop, store; **grand ~** department store; **faire les ~s** to go shopping
2 avoir en ~ to have in stock

magasinier, **-ière** /magazinje, ɛʀ/ *mf*
1 stock controller
2 warehouse keeper

⚷ **magazine** /magazin/ *m* magazine

mage /maʒ/ *m* magus; **les rois ~s** the (Three) Wise Men

maghrébin, **~e** /magʀebɛ̃, in/ *adj* North African, Maghrebi

magicien, **-ienne** /maʒisjɛ̃, ɛn/ *mf*
1 magician/enchantress
2 conjuror
3 (fig) wizard

magie /maʒi/ *f* **1** magic
2 conjuring

⚷ **magique** /maʒik/ *adj* **1** magic; **formule ~** magic words
2 (fig) magical

magistère /maʒistɛʀ/ *m: high-level University degree*

magistral, **~e**, *mpl* **-aux** /maʒistʀal, o/ *adj*
1 brilliant; **réussir un coup ~** to bring off a master stroke
2 magisterial

magistrat /maʒistʀa/ *m* magistrate

magistrature /maʒistʀatyʀ/ *f* **1** magistracy
2 public office

magma /magma/ *m* **1** magma
2 (fig) jumble

magnanime /maɲanim/ *adj* magnanimous

magnat /maɲa/ *m* magnate, tycoon

magner: **se magner** /maɲe/ [**v1**] *v refl* (+ *v être*) (pop) to get a move on (fam)

magnésie /maɲezi/ *f* magnesia

magnétique /maɲetik/ *adj* magnetic

magnétiser /maɲetize/ [**v1**] *vt* **1** to magnetize
2 to hypnotize, to mesmerize

magnétiseur, **-euse** /maɲetizœʀ, øz/ *mf* healer

magnétisme /maɲetism/ *m* magnetism

magnéto /maɲetɔ(fɔn)/ *m also* **magnéto phone** tape recorder

magnétoscope /maɲetɔskɔp/ *m* VCR, video recorder

magnificence /maɲifisɑ̃s/ *f* magnificence, splendour (BrE)

magnifier /maɲifje/ [**v1**] *vt* **1** to idealize ‹*memory, feeling*›
2 to glorify ‹*heroism, act*›

⚷ **magnifique** /maɲifik/ *adj* gorgeous, magnificent

magot /mago/ *m* (fam) pile (of money) (fam)

magouille /maguj/ *f* (fam) **1** wangling (fam), fiddling (fam)
2 trick; **~s politiques** political skulduggery; **~s électorales** election rigging

magret /magʀɛ/ *m* **~ de canard** duck breast

Mahomet /maɔme/ *pr n* Mohammed

⚷ **mai** /mɛ/ *m* May; **le premier ~** May Day

maigre /mɛgʀ/ **A** *adj* **1** ‹*person*› thin
2 ‹*meat*› lean; ‹*cheese*› low-fat
3 ‹*day*› without meat; **faire** *or* **manger ~** to abstain from meat
4 ‹*talents, savings*› meagre (BrE); ‹*applause*› scant
5 ‹*lawn, hair*› sparse
B *mf* thin man/woman; **c'est une fausse ~** she looks thinner than she is

maigrement /mɛgʀəmɑ̃/ *adv* ‹*paid*› poorly

maigreur /mɛgʀœʀ/ *f* **1** thinness
2 meagreness (BrE)

⚷ key word

maigrichon, -onne /mɛgʀiʃɔ̃, ɔn/ *adj* skinny

maigrir /mɛgʀiʀ/ [**v3**] *vi* to lose weight

mail /maj/ *m* **1** mall
2 (game) pall-mall
3 /mɛl/ email (message)

mailer /mɛle/ *vt* to email

mailing /mɛliŋ/ *m* (controversial) **1** direct mail advertising
2 mail shot
3 mailing pack

maille /maj/ *f* **1** stitch; **une ~ qui file** (in tights) a ladder (BrE), a run (AmE)
2 mesh; **passer à travers les ~s** to slip through the net
3 (in fence) link
IDIOM **avoir ~ à partir avec qn** to have a brush with sb

maillet /majɛ/ *m* mallet

maillon /majɔ̃/ *m* (in chain) link

maillot /majo/ *m* **1 ~ (de corps)** vest (BrE), undershirt (AmE)
2 (of footballer) shirt; (of cyclist) jersey
3 swimsuit
■ **~ de bain** swimsuit; **le ~ jaune** the leader in the Tour de France

main /mɛ̃/ *f* **1** hand; **se donner** *or* **se tenir la ~** to hold hands; **saluer qn de la ~** to wave at sb; **haut les ~s!** hands up!; **demander la ~ de qn** to ask for sb's hand in marriage; **avoir qch bien en ~(s)** to hold sth firmly; (fig) to have sth well in hand; **si tu lèves la ~ sur elle** if you lay a finger on her; **à la ~** ‹*sew*› by hand; ‹*adjust*› manually; **fait ~** handmade; **vol à ~ armée** armed robbery; **donner un coup de ~ à qn** to give sb a hand
2 une ~ secourable a helping hand; **une ~ criminelle** someone with criminal intentions
3 avoir qch sous la ~ to have sth to hand; **cela m'est tombé sous la ~** I just happened to come across it; **mettre la ~ sur qch** to get one's hands on sth; **je n'arrive pas à mettre la ~ dessus** I can't lay my hands on it; **je l'ai eu entre les ~s mais...** I did have it but...; **être entre les ~s de qn** ‹*power*› to be in sb's hands; **prendre qn/qch en ~s** to take sb/sth in hand; **à ne pas mettre entre toutes les ~s** ‹*book*› not for general reading; **tomber entre les ~s de qn** to fall into sb's hands; **les ~s vides** empty-handed; **je le lui ai remis en ~s propres** I gave it to him/her in person; **de la ~ à la ~** ‹*sell*› privately; **être payé de la ~ à la ~** to be paid cash (in hand)
4 écrit de la ~ du président written by the president himself; **de ma plus belle ~** in my best handwriting
5 avoir le coup de ~ to have the knack; **se faire la ~** to practise (BrE)
6 (in cards) hand; deal
7 à ~ droite/gauche on the right/left
■ **~ courante** handrail
IDIOMS **j'en mettrais ma ~ au feu** *or* **à couper** I'd swear to it; **d'une ~ de fer** with an iron rod; **il n'y est pas allé de ~ morte!** (fam) he didn't pull his punches!; **avoir la ~ leste** to be always ready with a slap; **faire ~ basse sur** to help oneself to ‹*goods*›; to take over ‹*market, country*›; **en venir aux ~s** to come to blows; **avoir la ~ heureuse** to be lucky

mainate /mɛnat/ *m* mynah bird

main-d'œuvre, *pl* **mains-d'œuvre** /mɛ̃dœvʀ/ *f* labour (BrE)

main-forte /mɛ̃fɔʀt/ *f inv* **prêter ~ à qn** to come to sb's aid

mainmise /mɛ̃miz/ *f* seizure

maint, **~e** /mɛ̃, mɛ̃t/ *det* many, many a; **à ~es reprises** many times

maintenance /mɛ̃tnɑ̃s/ *f* maintenance

maintenant /mɛ̃t(ə)nɑ̃/ *adv* now; nowadays; **commence dès ~** start straightaway

maintenir /mɛ̃t(ə)niʀ/ [**v36**] **A** *vt* **1** to keep; to maintain; to keep up; **~ qch debout** to keep sth upright
2 to support ‹*wall, ankle*›
3 to stand by ‹*decision*›; **~ que** to maintain that; **~ sa candidature** ‹*politician*› not to withdraw one's candidacy
B se maintenir *v refl* (+ *v être*) ‹*trend*› to persist; ‹*price*› to remain stable; ‹*weather*› to remain fair; ‹*political system*› to remain in force; ‹*currency*› to hold steady

maintien /mɛ̃tjɛ̃/ *m* **1** maintaining; **assurer le ~ de l'ordre** to maintain order
2 support
3 deportment

maire /mɛʀ/ *m* mayor
■ **~ adjoint** deputy mayor

mairie /mɛʀi/ *f* **1** town council (BrE) *or* hall (AmE); **être élu à la ~ de** to be elected mayor of
2 town hall (BrE), city hall (AmE)

mais /mɛ/ *conj* but; **incroyable ~ vrai** strange but true; **il est bête, ~ bête!** (fam) he's so incredibly stupid!; **~, vous pleurez!** good heavens, you're crying!; **~ j'y pense** now that I come to think of it

maïs /mais/ *m inv* **1** maize (BrE), corn (AmE)
2 sweetcorn; **épi de ~** corn on the cob

maison /mɛzɔ̃/ **A** *adj inv* ‹*product*› home-made
B *f* **1** house
2 home
3 family, household; **gens de ~** domestic staff
4 firm; **avoir 15 ans de ~** to have been with the firm for 15 years
■ **~ d'arrêt** prison; **~ bourgeoise** *imposing town house*; **~ de campagne** house in the country; **~ close** brothel; **~ de correction** institution for young offenders; **~ de la culture** ≈ community arts centre (BrE); **~ des jeunes et de la culture, MJC** ≈ youth club; **~ de maître** manor; **~ mère** headquarters; main branch; **~ de passe** brothel; **~ de retraite**

m

old people's *or* retirement home; **~ de santé** nursing home; **la Maison Blanche** the White House

IDIOM **c'est gros comme une ~** (fam) it sticks out a mile

maisonnée /mɛzɔne/ *f* household; family

🔑 **maître, -esse** /mɛtʀ, ɛs/ **A** *adj* **1 être ~ de soi** to have self-control; **être ~ chez soi** to be master/mistress in one's own house; **être ~ de son véhicule** to be in control of one's vehicle
2 main; key; major
B *mf* **1** teacher
2 (of house) master/mistress
3 (of animal) owner
C *m* **1** ruler; **être (le) seul ~ à bord** to be in sole command; **être son propre ~** to be one's own master/mistress; **régner en ~ absolu** to reign supreme
2 master; **être passé ~ dans l'art de qch/de faire** to be a past master of sth/at doing; **en ~** masterfully
3 Me Maître (*form of address given to members of the legal profession*)
■ **~ d'hôtel** maître d'hôtel (BrE), maître d' (AmE); **~ à penser** mentor; **maîtresse femme** strong-minded woman

IDIOM **trouver son ~** to meet one's match

maître-assistant, ~e, *mpl* **maîtres-assistants** /mɛtʀasistɑ̃, ɑ̃t/ *mf* ≈ senior lecturer (BrE), senior instructor (AmE)

m

maître-chanteur, *pl* **maîtres-chanteurs** /mɛtʀəʃɑ̃tœʀ/ *m* blackmailer

maître-nageur, *pl* **maîtres-nageurs** /mɛtʀənaʒœʀ/ *m* **1** swimming instructor
2 pool attendant

maîtresse /mɛtʀɛs/ **A** *adj f* ▸ **maître A**
B *f* **1** ▸ **maître B**
2 mistress

maîtrise /mɛtʀiz/ *f* **1** mastery
2 perfect command
3 ~ (de soi) self-control
4 master's degree

maîtriser /mɛtʀize/ [**v1**] **A** *vt* **1** to control ‹*feelings*›; to bring [sth] under control ‹*fire*›; to overcome ‹*opponent*›
2 to master ‹*language*›
B se maîtriser *v refl* (+ *v être*) to have self-control

maïzena® /maizena/ *f* cornflour

majesté /maʒɛste/ *f* majesty

majestueux, -euse /maʒɛstɥø, øz/ *adj* majestic; stately

🔑 **majeur, ~e** /maʒœʀ/ **A** *adj* **1 être ~** to be over 18 *or* of age
2 main, major; **en ~e partie** for the most part
3 (Mus) major
B *m* middle finger

majoration /maʒɔʀasjɔ̃/ *f* increase

majordome /maʒɔʀdɔm/ *m* butler

majorer /maʒɔʀe/ [**v1**] *vt* to increase

majoritaire /maʒɔʀitɛʀ/ *adj* majority

majoritairement /maʒɔʀitɛʀmɑ̃/ *adv* **1** by a majority (vote)
2 province ~ catholique predominantly Catholic province

🔑 **majorité** /maʒɔʀite/ *f* **1** majority; **ils sont en ~** they are in the majority; **ce sont, en ~, des enfants** they are, for the most part, children
2 la ~ the government, the party in power

majuscule /maʒyskyl/ **A** *adj* capital
B *f* capital (letter)

🔑 **mal,** *mpl* **maux** /mal, mo/ **A** *adj inv*
1 wrong; **qu'a-t-elle fait de ~?** what has she done wrong?
2 bad; **ce ne serait pas ~ de déménager** it wouldn't be a bad idea to move out
3 (fam) **il n'est pas mal** ‹*film*› it's not bad; ‹*man*› he's not bad, he's not bad-looking
B *m* **1** trouble, difficulty; **avoir du ~ à faire** to find it difficult to do; **se donner du ~** to go to a lot of trouble; **ne te donne pas ce ~!** don't bother!
2 pain; **faire ~** to hurt, to be painful; **se faire ~** to hurt oneself; **j'ai ~** it hurts; **avoir ~ partout** to ache all over; **elle avait très ~** she was in pain; **avoir ~ à la tête** to have a headache; **avoir ~ à la gorge** to have a sore throat; **j'ai ~ au genou** my knee hurts; **j'ai ~ au cœur** I feel sick (BrE) *or* nauseous
3 illness, disease
4 être en ~ de to be short of ‹*inspiration*›; to be lacking in ‹*affection*›
5 harm; **faire du ~ à** to harm, to hurt; **une douche ne te ferait pas de ~** (hum) a shower wouldn't do you any harm
6 le ~ evil; **qu'elle parte, est-ce vraiment un ~?** is it really a bad thing that she is leaving?; **sans penser à ~** without meaning any harm; **dire du ~ de qn/qch** to speak ill of sb/sth
C *adv* **1** badly; not properly; **elle travaille ~** her work isn't good; **je t'entends ~** I can't hear you very well
2 with difficulty; **on voit ~ comment** it's difficult to see how
3 ‹*diagnosed, addressed*› wrongly; **j'avais ~ compris** I had misunderstood; **~ informé** ill-informed
4 se trouver ~ to faint; **être ~ (assis** *or* **couché** *or* **installé)** not to be comfortable; **être au plus ~** to be critically ill
D pas mal *phr* **1** ‹*travel, read*› quite a lot
2 il ne s'en est pas ~ tiré (in exam) he coped quite well; (in dangerous situation) he got off lightly
■ **~ de l'air** airsickness; **~ de mer** seasickness; **~ du pays** homesickness; **~ du siècle** world-weariness; **~ des transports** travel sickness

🔑 **malade** /malad/ **A** *adj* ‹*person*› ill, sick; ‹*animal*› sick; ‹*organ, plant*› diseased; **tomber ~** to fall ill *or* sick, to get sick (AmE); **être ~ en voiture/en avion** to get

🔑 key word

carsick/airsick; **j'en suis ~** (fig, fam) it makes me sick; **~ d'inquiétude** worried sick
B *mf* **1** sick man/woman
2 patient
■ **~ imaginaire** hypochondriac; **~ mental** mentally ill person

maladie /maladi/ *f* illness, disease; **il va en faire une ~** (fam) (fig) he'll have a fit (fam)
■ **~ sexuellement transmissible, MST** sexually transmitted disease, STD; **~ du sommeil** sleeping sickness

maladif, -ive /maladif, iv/ *adj* ‹*child*› sickly; ‹*jealousy*› pathological

maladresse /maladʀɛs/ *f* **1** clumsiness, awkwardness
2 tactlessness
3 blunder

maladroit, ~e /maladʀwa, wat/ **A** *adj*
1 clumsy
2 tactless
B *mf* **1** clumsy person
2 tactless person

maladroitement /maladʀwatmɑ̃/ *adv*
1 clumsily, awkwardly
2 tactlessly; ineptly

malaise /malɛz/ *m* **1** dizzy turn; **avoir un ~** to feel faint
2 (fig) uneasiness; unrest
■ **~ cardiaque** mild heart attack

malaxer /malakse/ [**v1**] *vt* **1** to cream ‹*butter*›; to knead ‹*dough*›
2 to mix ‹*cement*›

malchance /malʃɑ̃s/ *f* bad luck, misfortune; **par ~** as ill luck would have it

malchanceux, -euse /malʃɑ̃sø, øz/ *adj* unlucky

maldonne /maldɔn/ *f* misunderstanding

mâle /mɑl/ **A** *adj* **1** male; ‹*elephant*› bull; ‹*antelope, rabbit*› buck; ‹*sparrow*› cock; **cygne ~** cob; **canard ~** drake
2 manly
B *m* **1** male
2 (hum) he-man (fam)

malédiction /malediksjɔ̃/ *f* curse

maléfice /malefis/ *m* evil spell

maléfique /malefik/ *adj* evil

malencontreusement /malɑ̃kɔ̃tʀøzmɑ̃/ *adv* inopportunely; unfortunately

malencontreux, -euse /malɑ̃kɔ̃tʀø, øz/ *adj* unfortunate

malentendant, ~e /malɑ̃tɑ̃dɑ̃, ɑ̃t/ *mf* **les ~s** the hearing-impaired

malentendu /malɑ̃tɑ̃dy/ *m* misunderstanding

malfaçon /malfasɔ̃/ *f* defect

malfaisant, ~e /malfəzɑ̃, ɑ̃t/ *adj* evil; harmful

malfaiteur /malfɛtœʀ/ *m* criminal

malformation /malfɔʀmasjɔ̃/ *f* malformation

malgache /malgaʃ/ *adj, m* Malagasy

malgré /malgʀe/ *prep* in spite of, despite; **~ cela, ~ tout** nevertheless; **~ moi** against my wishes; reluctantly

malhabile /malabil/ *adj* clumsy

malheur /malœʀ/ *m* **1 le ~** misfortune, adversity; **faire le ~ de qn** to bring sb nothing but unhappiness
2 misfortune; accident; **un grand ~** a tragedy; **un ~ est si vite arrivé!** accidents can so easily happen!
3 misfortune; **ceux qui ont le ~ de faire** those who are unfortunate enough to do; **j'ai eu le ~ de le leur dire** I made the mistake of telling them; **par ~** as bad luck would have it; **si par ~ la guerre éclatait** if, God forbid, war should break out; **porter ~** to be bad luck
(IDIOMS) **faire un ~** (fam) to be a sensation; to go wild; **à quelque chose ~ est bon** (Proverb) every cloud has a silver lining

malheureusement /maløʀøzmɑ̃/ *adv* unfortunately

malheureux, -euse /maløʀø, øz/ **A** *adj*
1 ‹*person, life*› unhappy, miserable; ‹*victim, choice, word*› unfortunate; ‹*candidate*› unlucky; **c'est ~ que** it's a pity *or* shame that
2 (fam) ‹*sum*› paltry, pathetic
B *mf* **1** poor wretch; **le ~!** poor man!
2 poor person; **les ~** the poor
(IDIOM) **être ~ comme les pierres** to be as miserable as sin

malhonnête /malɔnɛt/ *adj* dishonest

malhonnêteté /malɔnɛtte/ *f* dishonesty

malice /malis/ *f* **1** mischief
2 (dated) malice; **être sans ~** to be harmless

malicieux, -ieuse /malisjø, øz/ *adj* mischievous

malin, maligne /malɛ̃, maliɲ/ **A** *adj*
1 clever; **j'ai eu l'air ~!** (ironic) I looked like a total fool!
2 malicious
3 (Med) malignant
B *mf* **c'est un ~** he's a crafty one
(IDIOM) **à ~, ~ et demi** (Proverb) there's always someone who will outwit you

malingre /malɛ̃gʀ/ *adj* ‹*person, tree*› sickly

malintentionné, ~e /malɛ̃tɑ̃sjɔne/ *adj* malicious

malle /mal/ *f* trunk

malléabilité /maleabilite/ *f* malleability

mallette /malɛt/ *f* briefcase

malmener /malməne/ [**v16**] *vt* **1** to manhandle
2 to give [sb] a rough ride

malnutrition /malnytʀisjɔ̃/ *f* malnutrition

malodorant, ~e /malɔdɔʀɑ̃, ɑ̃t/ *adj* foul-smelling

malotru, ~e /malɔtʀy/ *mf* boor

Malouines /malwin/ *pr f pl* **les (îles) ~** the Falklands

malpoli, ~e /malpɔli/ *adj* rude

malpropre /malpʀɔpʀ/ **A** *adj* dirty

B *mf* **se faire renvoyer comme un ~** to be chucked out (fam)

malsain, **~e** /malsɛ̃, ɛn/ *adj* unhealthy

Malte /malt/ *pr f* Malta

malthusianisme /maltyzjanism/ *m* Malthusianism

maltraiter /maltʀɛte/ [**v1**] *vt* to mistreat

malus /malys/ *m inv* loaded premium

malveillance /malvɛjɑ̃s/ *f* malice

malveillant, **~e** /malvɛjɑ̃, ɑ̃t/ *adj* malicious

malvenu, **~e** /malvəny/ *adj* out of place

malversation /malvɛʀsasjɔ̃/ *f*
1 malpractice
2 embezzlement

malvoyant, **~e** /malvwajɑ̃, ɑ̃t/ *mf* partially sighted person

🔑 **maman** /mɑmɑ̃/ *f* mum (BrE) (fam), mom (AmE) (fam)

mamelle /mamɛl/ *f* udder; teat

mamelon /mamlɔ̃/ *m* **1** nipple
2 hillock

mamie /mami/ *f* (fam) granny (fam), grandma (fam)

mammifère /mamifɛʀ/ *m* mammal

mammouth /mamut/ *m* mammoth

mamy ▸ **mamie**

manager[1], **manageur** /manaʒœʀ/ *m* manager

manager[2] /manaʒe/ [**v13**] *vt* to manage

manche[1] /mɑ̃ʃ/ *m* **1** (of tool) handle; (of violin) neck
2 (fam) clumsy idiot
■ **~ à balai** broom handle; broomstick; joystick

🔑 **manche[2]** /mɑ̃ʃ/ *f* **1** sleeve; **sans ~s** sleeveless
2 (Sport) round; (in cards) hand; (in bridge) game; (in tennis) set
IDIOMS **avoir qn dans la ~** to have sb in one's pocket; **c'est une autre paire de ~s** (fam) it's a different ball game (fam)

Manche /mɑ̃ʃ/ *pr f* **la ~** the (English) Channel

manchette /mɑ̃ʃɛt/ *f* **1** (double) cuff
2 oversleeve
3 headline

manchot, **-otte** /mɑ̃ʃo, ɔt/ **A** *adj* one-armed; one-handed; **il est ~** he's only got one arm; **ne pas être ~** (fam) to be pretty good with one's hands (fam)
B *m* penguin

mandarine /mɑ̃daʀin/ *f* mandarin orange

mandat /mɑ̃da/ *m* **1 ~ (postal)** money order
2 term of office; **exercer son ~** to be in office
3 mandate
■ **~ d'arrêt** (arrest) warrant; **~ d'expulsion** expulsion order; eviction order; **~ de perquisition** search warrant

mandataire /mɑ̃datɛʀ/ *mf* **1** representative, agent
2 proxy

mandater /mɑ̃date/ [**v1**] *vt* to appoint [sb] as one's representative; to give a mandate to

mandat-lettre, *pl* **mandats-lettres** /mɑ̃dalɛtʀ/ *m* postal order

mandibule /mɑ̃dibyl/ *f* mandible

mandoline /mɑ̃dɔlin/ *f* mandolin

manège /manɛʒ/ *m* **1** merry-go-round
2 riding school
3 (little) trick, (little) game; **j'ai bien observé ton ~** I know what you are up to

manette /manɛt/ *f* **1** lever; joystick
2 (fig) **~s** controls

mangeable /mɑ̃ʒabl/ *adj* edible

mangeoire /mɑ̃ʒwaʀ/ *f* manger; trough; feeding tray

🔑 **manger[1]** /mɑ̃ʒe/ [**v13**] **A** *vt* **1** to eat; **il n'y a rien à ~ dans la maison** there's no food in the house
2 to use up ‹*savings*›; to go through ‹*inheritance*›; to take up ‹*time*›
3 ‹*rust, acid*› to eat away
4 ~ ses mots to mumble
B *vi* to eat; **~ au restaurant** to eat out; **~ à sa faim** to eat one's fill; **donner à ~ à qn** to feed sb; to give sb something to eat; **faire à ~** to cook; **inviter qn à ~** to invite sb for a meal; **~ chinois** to have a Chinese meal; **on mange mal ici** the food is not good here
C se manger *v refl* (+ *v être*) **ça se mange?** can you eat it?; **le gaspacho se mange froid** gazpacho is served cold

manger[2] /mɑ̃ʒe/ *m* food

mangeur, **-euse** /mɑ̃ʒœʀ, øz/ *mf* **bon/gros ~** good/big eater
■ **mangeuse d'hommes** man-eater

mangouste /mɑ̃gust/ *f* **1** mongoose
2 mangosteen

mangue /mɑ̃g/ *f* mango

maniable /manjabl/ *adj* ‹*object, car*› easy to handle; ‹*book*› manageable in size

maniaque /manjak/ **A** *adj* particular, fussy
B *mf* **1** fusspot (BrE), fussbudget (AmE)
2 fanatic; **c'est un ~ de l'ordre** he's obsessive about tidiness
3 maniac
4 (Med) manic

maniaquerie /manjakʀi/ *f* fussiness

manichéen, **-éenne** /manikeɛ̃, ɛn/ *adj* Manichean; dualistic

manie /mani/ *f* **1** habit; **c'est une vraie ~** it's an absolute obsession
2 quirk, idiosyncrasy
3 (Med) mania

maniement /manimɑ̃/ *m* handling; (of machine) operation; (of language) command
■ **~ d'armes** arms drill

manier /manje/ [**v2**] **A** *vt* to handle
B se manier *v refl* (+ *v être*) **se ~ aisément** ‹*tool*› to be easy to handle; ‹*car*›

to handle well
IDIOM ~ **la fourchette avec entrain** (fam, hum) to have a hearty appetite

manière /manjɛʀ/ *f* **1** way; **d'une certaine ~** in a way; **leur ~ de vivre/penser** their way of life/thinking; **de toutes les ~s possibles** in every possible way; **de telle ~ que** in such a way that; **de ~ à faire** so as to do; **de ~ à ce que** so that; **à ma ~** my (own) way; **de quelle ~?** how?; **de toute ~, de toutes ~s** anyway, in any case; **la ~ forte** strong-arm tactics, force
2 style; **à la ~ de qn/qch** in the style of sb/sth
3 manners; **faire des ~s** to stand on ceremony

maniéré, **~e** /manjeʀe/ *adj* affected

manifestant, **~e** /manifɛstɑ̃, ɑ̃t/ *mf* demonstrator

manifestation /manifɛstasjɔ̃/ *f*
1 demonstration
2 event; **~s sportives** sporting events
3 (of phenomenon) appearance
4 (of feeling) expression, manifestation
■ **~ silencieuse** vigil; **~ de soutien** rally

manifeste /manifɛst/ **A** *adj* obvious, manifest
B *m* manifesto

manifester /manifɛste/ [**v1**] **A** *vt* to show ‹*courage*›; to express ‹*desire, fears*›; **~ sa présence** to make one's presence known
B *vi* to demonstrate; **appeler à ~ le 5 juin** to call a demonstration for 5 June
C se manifester *v refl* (+ *v être*)
1 ‹*symptom*› to manifest itself; ‹*phenomenon*› to appear; ‹*worry*› to show itself
2 ‹*witness*› to come forward; ‹*person*› to appear; to get in touch

manigance /manigɑ̃s/ *f* little scheme

manigancer /manigɑ̃se/ [**v12**] *vt* **~ quelque chose** to be up to something; **~ un mauvais coup** to hatch up a scheme

manipulateur, **-trice** /manipylatœʀ, tʀis/ *mf* **1** technician
2 (derog) manipulator

manipulation /manipylasjɔ̃/ *f* **1** (of object) handling
2 manipulation
3 (Sch) experiment

manipuler /manipyle/ [**v1**] *vt* **1** to handle ‹*object*›; to use ‹*words*›
2 to manipulate ‹*person*›

manitou /manitu/ *m* (fam) big noise (fam); **un grand ~ de la finance** a big noise in the financial world

manivelle /manivɛl/ *f* handle
IDIOM **donner le premier tour de ~** to start filming

manne /man/ *f* godsend

mannequin /mankɛ̃/ *m* **1** (fashion) model
2 dummy

manœuvre¹ /manœvʀ/ *m* unskilled worker

manœuvre² /manœvʀ/ *f* manoeuvre (BrE), maneuver (AmE); **champ de ~** military training area; **fausse ~** mistake

manœuvrer /manœvʀe/ [**v1**] **A** *vt* **1** to manoeuvre (BrE), to maneuver (AmE) ‹*vehicle*›
2 to operate ‹*machine*›
3 to manipulate ‹*person*›
B *vi* to manoeuvre (BrE), to maneuver (AmE)

manoir /manwaʀ/ *m* manor (house)

manomètre /manɔmɛtʀ/ *m* pressure gauge

manquant, **~e** /mɑ̃kɑ̃, ɑ̃t/ *adj* missing

manque /mɑ̃k/ **A** *m* **1 ~ de** lack of; shortage of; **~ de chance, il est tombé malade** just his luck, he fell ill
2 gap; **en ~ d'affection** in need of affection; **être en ~** ‹*drug addict*› to be suffering from withdrawal symptoms
B à la manque *phr* (fam) **une idée à la ~** a useless idea

manqué, **~e** /mɑ̃ke/ **A** *pp* ▶ **manquer**
B *pp adj* ‹*attempt*› failed; ‹*opportunity*› missed

manquer /mɑ̃ke/ [**v1**] **A** *vt* **1** to miss; **un film à ne pas ~** a film not to be missed; **tu l'as manquée de cinq minutes** you missed her/it by five minutes
2 ~ son coup (fam) to fail
3 (fam) **la prochaine fois je ne le manquerai pas** next time I won't let him get away with it
B manquer à *v+prep* **1 ~ à qn** to be missed by sb; **ma tante me manque** I miss my aunt
2 ~ à sa parole to break one's word
C manquer de *v+prep* **1 ~ de** to lack; **on ne manque de rien** we don't want for anything; **elle ne manque pas de charme** she's not without charm; **on manque d'air ici** it's stuffy in here
2 je ne manquerai pas de vous le faire savoir I'll be sure to let you know; **et évidemment, ça n'a pas manqué!** (fam) and sure enough that's what happened!
3 il a manqué (de) casser un carreau he almost broke a windowpane
D *vi* **1 les vivres vinrent à ~** the supplies ran out; **le courage leur manqua** their courage failed them; **ce n'est pas l'envie qui m'en manque** it's not that I don't want to
2 ‹*person*› to be absent; to be missing
E *v impers* **il lui manque un doigt** he's got a finger missing; **il nous manque deux joueurs pour former une équipe** we're two players short of a team; **il ne manquerait plus que ça!** (fam) that would be the last straw!
F se manquer *v refl* (+ *v être*) to miss each other

mansarde /mɑ̃saʀd/ *f* attic room

mansardé, **~e** /mɑ̃saʀde/ *adj* ‹*room*› attic

mansuétude /mɑ̃sɥetyd/ *f* indulgence

manteau, *pl* **~x** /mɑ̃to/ *m* coat
■ **~ de cheminée** mantelpiece
IDIOM **sous le ~** illicitly

m

manucure /manykyʀ/ **A** *mf* manicurist
B *f* manicure

manuel, **-elle** /manɥɛl/ **A** *adj* manual
B *m* manual; (Sch) textbook
■ ~ **de conversation** phrase book

manuellement /manɥɛlmɑ̃/ *adv* manually

manufacture /manyfaktyʀ/ *f* **1** factory
2 manufacture

manufacturer /manyfaktyʀe/ [**v1**] *vt* to manufacture

manu militari /manymilitaʀi/ *adv* forcibly

manuscrit, ~**e** /manyskʀi, it/ **A** *adj* handwritten
B *m* manuscript

manutention /manytɑ̃sjɔ̃/ *f* handling

manutentionnaire /manytɑ̃sjɔnɛʀ/ *m* warehouseman

mappemonde /mapmɔ̃d/ *f* **1** map of the world (in two hemispheres)
2 globe

maquereau, *pl* ~**x** /makʀo/ *m* mackerel

maquette /makɛt/ *f* scale model

maquillage /makijaʒ/ *m* **1** making-up
2 make-up

maquiller /makije/ [**v1**] **A** *vt* **1** to make [sb] up
2 to doctor ‹*truth*›; ~ **un crime en accident** to disguise a crime as an accident
B **se maquiller** *v refl* (+ *v être*) **1** to put make-up on
2 to wear make-up

maquilleur, **-euse** /makijœʀ, øz/ *mf* make-up artist

maquis /maki/ *m inv* maquis; **prendre le** ~ to go underground

maquisard, ~**e** /makizaʀ, aʀd/ *mf* member of the Resistance

marabout /maʀabu/ *m* **1** marabou
2 marabout

maraîchage /maʀɛʃaʒ/ *m* market gardening (BrE), truck farming (AmE)

maraîcher, **-ère** /maʀɛʃe, ɛʀ/ **A** *adj* **produits** ~**s** market garden produce (BrE), truck (AmE)
B *mf* market gardener (BrE), truck farmer (AmE)

marais /maʀɛ/ *m inv* marsh; swamp
■ ~ **salant** saltern

marasme /maʀasm/ *m* stagnation

marathon /maʀatɔ̃/ *m* marathon

marathonien, **-ienne** /maʀatɔnjɛ̃, ɛn/ *mf* marathon runner

marâtre /maʀɑtʀ/ *f* cruel mother

maraude /maʀod/ *f* pilfering; **en** ~ ‹*person*› on the prowl

marauder /maʀode/ [**v1**] *vi* **1** to pilfer
2 to prowl around

maraudeur, **-euse** /maʀodœʀ, øz/ *mf* petty thief

marbre /maʀbʀ/ *m* **1** marble
2 marble top
3 marble statue
(IDIOMS) **rester de** ~ to remain stony-faced; **la nouvelle les laissa de** ~ they were completely unmoved by the news

marbrer /maʀbʀe/ [**v1**] *vt* to marble

marbrerie /maʀbʀəʀi/ *f* marble industry; marble masonry

marbrier, **-ière** /maʀbʀije, ɛʀ/ *mf* marble mason

marbrière /maʀbʀijɛʀ/ *f* marble quarry

marbrure /maʀbʀyʀ/ *f* marbling

marc /maʀ/ *m* marc
■ ~ **de café** coffee grounds

marcassin /maʀkasɛ̃/ *m* young wild boar

🔑 **marchand**, ~**e** /maʀʃɑ̃, ɑ̃d/ **A** *adj* ‹*quality*› marketable; ‹*sector*› trade; ‹*value*› market
B *mf* shopkeeper; stallholder; ~ **d'armes/de bestiaux** arms/cattle dealer; ~ **de charbon/vins** coal/wine merchant
■ ~ **ambulant** hawker; ~ **de couleurs** ironmonger (BrE), hardware merchant; ~ **de glaces** ice cream vendor; ~ **en gros** wholesaler; ~ **de journaux** newsagent; news vendor; ~ **des quatre saisons** costermonger (BrE), fruit and vegetable merchant; ~ **de sable** sandman; ~ **de tapis** carpet salesman

marchandage /maʀʃɑ̃daʒ/ *m* haggling

marchander /maʀʃɑ̃de/ [**v1**] *vt* **1** to haggle over
2 (fig) ~ **sa peine** not to put oneself out

marchandise /maʀʃɑ̃diz/ *f* goods, merchandise; **tromper qn sur la** ~ to swindle sb

🔑 **marche** /maʀʃ/ *f* **1** walking; walk; pace, step; **faire de la** ~ to go walking; **à 10 minutes de** ~ 10 minutes' walk away
2 march; **fermer la** ~ to bring up the rear; **ouvrir la** ~ to be at the head of the march
3 (of vehicle) progress; (of events) course; (of time) march; **bus en** ~ moving bus; **dans le sens contraire de la** ~ facing backward(s)
4 (of mechanism) operation; (of organization) running; **en état de** ~ in working order; **mettre en** ~ to start (up) ‹*machine*›; to switch on ‹*TV*›
5 step; **les** ~**s** the stairs
■ ~ **arrière** reverse; **faire** ~ **arrière** to reverse; (fig) to back-pedal; ~ **avant** forward; ~ **à suivre** procedure
(IDIOM) **prendre le train en** ~ to join halfway through; to climb onto the bandwagon

🔑 **marché** /maʀʃe/ *m* **1** market; **faire son** ~ to do one's shopping at the market
2 deal; **conclure un** ~ **avec qn** to strike a deal with sb; ~ **conclu!** it's a deal!; **bon/meilleur** ~ cheap/cheaper; **par-dessus le** ~ (fam) to top it all
■ ~ **de l'emploi** job market; ~ **libre** free market; ~ **noir** black market; ~ **aux puces** flea market; ~ **du travail** labour (BrE) market; **Marché commun** Common Market

🔑 key word

marchepied /maʀʃəpje/ *m* **1** step
2 steps

marcher /maʀʃe/ [**v1**] *vi* **1** to walk; ‹*demonstrators*› to march
2 to tread; **se laisser ~ sur les pieds** (fig) to let oneself be walked over
3 ‹*mechanism, system*› to work; **ma radio marche mal** my radio doesn't work properly; **faire ~ qch** to get sth to work; **~ au gaz** to run on gas; **les bus ne marchent pas le soir** the buses don't run in the evenings
4 (fam) **~ (bien)/~ mal** ‹*work, relationship*› to go well/not to go well; ‹*film, student*› to do well/not to do well; ‹*actor*› to go down well/not to go down well
5 (fam) **c'est trop risqué, je ne marche pas** it's too risky, count me out; **ça marche!** it's a deal!
6 (fam) to fall for it
7 faire ~ qn to pull sb's leg; **faire ~ son monde** (fam) to be good at giving orders
IDIOM **il ne marche pas, il court!** (fam) he's as gullible as they come

marcheur, **-euse** /maʀʃœʀ, øz/ *mf* walker

mardi /maʀdi/ *m* Tuesday

mare /maʀ/ *f* **1** pond
2 ~ de pool of ‹*blood*›

marécage /maʀekaʒ/ *m* marsh, swamp

marécageux, **-euse** /maʀekaʒø, øz/ *adj* ‹*ground*› marshy, swampy; ‹*plant*› marsh

maréchal, *pl* **-aux** /maʀeʃal, o/ *m* ≈ field marshal (BrE), general of the army (AmE)

maréchal-ferrant, *pl* **maréchaux-ferrants** /maʀeʃalfɛʀɑ̃, maʀeʃofeʀɑ̃/ *m* farrier

marée /maʀe/ *f* tide; **la ~ monte/descend** the tide is coming in/is going out; **à ~ haute/basse** at high/low tide
■ **~ noire** oil slick
IDIOM **contre vents et ~s** come hell or high water; against all odds

marelle /maʀɛl/ *f* hopscotch

marémoteur, **-trice** /maʀemɔtœʀ, tʀis/ *adj* tidal; **usine marémotrice** tidal power station

mareyeur, **-euse** /maʀɛjœʀ, øz/ *mf* fish wholesaler

margarine /maʀgaʀin/ *f* margarine

marge /maʀʒ/ **A** *f* **1** margin
2 leeway; **on a 10 minutes de ~** we've got 10 minutes to spare
3 scope; **tu devrais me laisser plus de ~ de décision** you should allow me more scope for making decisions
4 profit margin; mark-up
B en marge de *phr* **vivre en ~ de la loi** to live outside the law; **se sentir en ~** to feel like an outsider
■ **~ bénéficiaire** profit margin; **~ commerciale** gross profit; **~ d'erreur** margin of error; **~ de sécurité** safety margin

marginal, **~e**, *mpl* **-aux** /maʀʒinal, o/ **A** *adj* **1** marginal
2 ‹*artist*› fringe
3 on the margins of society
B *mf* dropout; **les marginaux** the fringe elements of society

marginaliser /maʀʒinalize/ [**v1**] *vt* to marginalize

marguerite /maʀgəʀit/ *f* daisy

mari /maʀi/ *m* husband

mariage /maʀjaʒ/ *m* **1** marriage; **né d'un premier ~** from a previous marriage; **~ de raison** marriage of convenience; **faire un riche ~** to marry into money
2 wedding
3 (fig) (of colours) marriage; (of companies) merger; (of parties) alliance; (of techniques) fusion
■ **~ blanc** marriage in name only; **~ civil** civil wedding; **~ religieux** church wedding

Marianne /maʀjan/ *pr n* Marianne (*female figure personifying the French Republic*)

marié, **~e** /maʀje/ **A** *pp* ▶ **marier**
B *pp adj* married
C *mf* **le (jeune) ~** the (bride)groom; **la (jeune) ~e** the bride; **les ~s** the newly-weds

marier /maʀje/ [**v2**] **A** *vt* to marry
B se marier *v refl* (+ *v être*) **1** to get married
2 ‹*colours*› to blend

marijuana /maʀiʀwana/ *f* marijuana

marin, **~e** /maʀɛ̃, in/ **A** *adj* **1** ‹*life*› marine; ‹*salt*› sea; ‹*drilling*› offshore
2 pull ~ seaman's jersey; **costume ~** sailor suit
B *m* sailor
■ **~ d'eau douce** fair-weather sailor; **~ pêcheur** fisherman
IDIOM **avoir le pied ~** not to get seasick

marine¹ /maʀin/ **A** *adj inv* navy (blue)
B *m* marine

marine² /maʀin/ *f* navy; **de ~** nautical

mariner /maʀine/ [**v1**] *vt, vi* to marinate

marinière /maʀinjɛʀ/ *f* smock

marionnette /maʀjɔnɛt/ *f* **1** puppet
2 ~s puppet show
■ **~ à fils** marionette

marionnettiste /maʀjɔnetist/ *mf* puppeteer

maritalement /maʀitalmɑ̃/ *adv* ‹*live*› as man and wife

maritime /maʀitim/ *adj* ‹*climate, commerce*› maritime; ‹*area*› coastal; ‹*company*› shipping

marivaudage /maʀivodaʒ/ *m* **1** gallant banter
2 refined affectation (*in the style of Marivaux*)

marjolaine /maʀʒɔlɛn/ *f* marjoram

marmaille /maʀmaj/ (fam) *f* rabble of kids (fam)

marmelade /maʀməlad/ *f* stewed fruit

marmite /maʀmit/ *f* **1** (cooking) pot
2 potful

(IDIOM) **faire bouillir la ~** (fam) to bring home the bacon

marmiton /maʀmitɔ̃/ *m* chef's assistant

marmonner /maʀmɔne/ [**v1**] *vt* to mumble, to mutter

marmot /maʀmo/ *m* (fam) kid (fam), brat (fam)

marmotte /maʀmɔt/ *f* **1** marmot **2** (fig) sleepyhead (fam)

maroquinerie /maʀɔkinʀi/ *f* **1** leather shop **2** leather industry; leather trade; **(articles de) ~** leather goods

marotte /maʀɔt/ *f* **1** pet subject, hobby horse; pet *or* favourite (BrE) hobby **2** puppet

marquant, ~e /maʀkɑ̃, ɑ̃t/ *adj* ‹*fact*› memorable; ‹*memory*› lasting

marque /maʀk/ *f* **1** brand, make; **de ~** ‹*product*› branded; ‹*guest*› distinguished; ‹*person*› eminent **2** mark; sign; **~ de doigts** fingermarks; **on voit encore les ~s (de coups)** you can still see the bruises; **~ du pluriel** plural marker; **laisser sa ~** to make one's mark **3** (Sport) score; **à vos ~s, prêts, partez!** on your marks, get set, go!

■ **~ déposée** registered trademark; **~ de fabrication** manufacturer's brand name; **~ de fabrique** trademark

m

marqué, ~e /maʀke/ **A** *pp* ▶ **marquer** **B** *pp adj* **1 il a le corps ~ de traces de coups** he's bruised all over; **elle est restée ~e par la guerre** the war left its mark on her; **visage ~** worn face **2** ‹*difference*› marked

marquer /maʀke/ [**v1**] **A** *vt* **1** to mark ‹*goods*›; to brand ‹*cattle*› **2** to mark, to signal ‹*beginning, end*› **3** to mark ‹*body, object*› **4** (fig) ‹*event, work*› to leave its mark on ‹*person*›; **c'est quelqu'un qui m'a beaucoup marqué** he/she was a strong influence on me **5** to write [sth] down ‹*information*›; to mark ‹*price*›; **qu'est-ce qu'il y a de marqué?** what does it say? **6** to show; **~ la mesure** (Mus) to beat time; **il faut ~ le coup** let's celebrate **7 ~ un temps (d'arrêt)** to pause **8** (Sport) to score ‹*goal*›; to mark ‹*opponent*› **B** *vi* **1** to leave a mark **2** (Sport) to score

marqueur /maʀkœʀ/ *m* marker pen

marquis, ~e /maʀki, iz/ *mf* marquis/ marchioness

marraine /maʀɛn/ *f* **1** godmother **2** sponsor

■ **~ de guerre** *soldier's wartime female penfriend*

marrant, ~e /maʀɑ̃, ɑ̃t/ *adj* (fam) funny

marre /maʀ/ *adv* (fam) **en avoir ~** to be fed up (fam)

marrer: **se marrer** /maʀe/ [**v1**] *v refl* (+ *v être*) (fam) **1** to have a great time **2** to have a good laugh

marron, -onne /maʀɔ̃, ɔn/ **A** *adj* crooked **B** *adj inv* brown; **~ clair/foncé** light/dark brown **C** *m* **1** chestnut **2** brown

■ **~ glacé** marron glacé; **~s chauds** roast chestnuts

marronnier /maʀɔnje/ *m* chestnut (tree)

mars /maʀs/ *m inv* March

(IDIOM) **arriver comme ~ en carême** to come as sure as night follows day

Marseillaise /maʀsɛjɛz/ *f* Marseillaise (*French national anthem*)

marsouin /maʀswɛ̃/ *m* porpoise

marteau, *pl* **~x** /maʀto/ *m* hammer; (of judge) gavel; (on door) knocker

marteler /maʀtəle/ [**v17**] *vt* **1** to hammer, to pound **2** to rap out ‹*words*›

martial, ~e, *mpl* **-iaux** /maʀsjal, o/ *adj* ‹*art, law*› martial; ‹*music, step*› military

martinet /maʀtinɛ/ *m* **1** (Zool) swift **2** whip

martingale /maʀtɛ̃gal/ *f* **1** (on jacket) half belt **2** (for horse) martingale

martre /maʀtʀ/ *f* **1** marten **2** sable

martyr, ~e /maʀtiʀ/ **A** *adj* martyred; **enfant ~** battered child **B** *mf* martyr

martyre /maʀtiʀ/ *m* **1** martyrdom **2** agony; **souffrir le ~** to suffer agony

martyriser /maʀtiʀize/ [**v1**] *vt* **1** to torment ‹*victim, animal*›; to batter ‹*child*› **2** to martyr

marxisme /maʀksism/ *m* Marxism

mas /mɑ/ *m inv* farmhouse (*in Provence*)

mascarade /maskaʀad/ *f* **1** farce; **~ de justice** travesty of justice **2** masked ball

mascotte /maskɔt/ *f* mascot

masculin, ~e /maskylɛ̃, in/ **A** *adj* ‹*population, sex, part*› male; ‹*sport*› man's; ‹*magazine, team*› men's; ‹*face, noun*› masculine **B** *m* masculine

masochisme /mazɔʃism/ *m* masochism

masochiste /mazɔʃist/ *mf* masochist

masque /mask/ *m* **1** mask **2** face pack **3** expression

■ **~ à gaz** gas mask; **~ de plongée** diving mask; **~ de soudeur** face shield

(IDIOM) **jeter le ~** to show one's true colours (BrE)

masqué, ~e /maske/ *adj* **1** ‹*bandit*› masked

2 (fig) concealed

masquer /maske/ [**v1**] **A** *vt* **1** to conceal ‹*defect*›; to mask ‹*problem*›
2 to block ‹*opening, light*›
B **se masquer** *v refl* (+ *v être*) to hide [sth] from oneself ‹*truth*›

massacrante /masakʀɑ̃t/ *adj f* **être d'humeur ~** to be in a foul mood

massacre /masakʀ/ *m* massacre, slaughter

massacrer /masakʀe/ [**v1**] *vt* **1** to massacre, to slaughter
2 (fig, fam) to slaughter (fam) ‹*opponent*›; to massacre ‹*piece of music*›; to botch ‹*job*›; to slate ‹*play, actor*›

massage /masaʒ/ *m* massage

masse /mas/ *f* **1** mass; **~ rocheuse** rocky mass; **une ~ humaine** a mass of humanity
2 **une ~ de** a lot of; **des ~s de** (fam) masses of; **départs en ~** mass exodus
3 **la ~, les ~s** the masses; **culture de ~** mass culture
■ **~ d'armes** mace; **~ monétaire** money supply; **~ salariale** (total) wage bill
IDIOMS **(se laisser) tomber comme une ~** to collapse; **dormir comme une ~** to sleep like a log (fam)

massepain /maspɛ̃/ *m* marzipan cake

masser /mase/ [**v1**] **A** *vt* to massage
B **se masser** *v refl* (+ *v être*) **1** to mass
2 **se ~ les jambes** to massage one's legs

masseur, -euse /masœʀ, øz/ *mf* masseur/masseuse

massicot /masiko/ *m* (for paper) guillotine

massif, -ive /masif, iv/ **A** *adj* **1** ‹*features*› heavy; ‹*silhouette*› massive
2 ‹*dose*› massive; ‹*redundancies*› mass
3 ‹*gold, oak*› solid
B *m* **1** massif
2 (flower) bed

massivement /masivmɑ̃/ *adv* ‹*demonstrate*› in great numbers; ‹*inject*› in massive doses; ‹*approve*› overwhelmingly

mass media /masmedja/ *mpl* mass media

massue /masy/ *f* (gen), (Sport) club, bludgeon

mastic /mastik/ **A** *adj inv* putty-coloured (BrE)
B *m* (for windows) putty; (for holes) filler

mastiquer /mastike/ [**v1**] *vt* to chew

mastoc /mastɔk/ *adj inv* (fam) huge

mastodonte /mastɔdɔ̃t/ *m* **1** mastodon
2 (fig) (person) colossus, hulk (fam); colossus, hulk (fam); (animal) monster

masturber /mastyʀbe/ [**v1**] *vt*, **se masturber** *v refl* (+ *v être*) to masturbate

m'as-tu-vu /matyvy/ *mf inv* (fam) show-off

mat[1], **~e** /mat/ **A** *adj* **1** ‹*paint*› matt (BrE), matte (AmE)
2 ‹*complexion*› olive
3 ‹*sound*› dull
B *m* **(échec et) ~!** checkmate!

mat[2] /mat/ *m* (fam) morning

mât /mɑ/ *m* **1** mast
2 pole; climbing pole; **~ de drapeau** flagpole

matador /matadɔʀ/ *m* matador

match /matʃ/ *m* match; (in team sports) match (BrE), game (AmE) draw (BrE); **~ nul** draw (BrE), tie (AmE); **faire ~ nul** to draw (BrE), to tie (AmE)
■ **~ de classement** league match

matelas /matla/ *m inv* mattress; **~ pneumatique** air bed

matelassé, ~e /matlase/ *adj* ‹*material*› quilted; ‹*door*› padded

matelot /matlo/ *m* **1** sailor
2 ≈ ordinary seaman (BrE), ≈ seaman apprentice (AmE)

mater /mate/ [**v1**] *vt* to bring [sb/sth] into line ‹*rebels*›; to take [sb/sth] in hand ‹*child, horse*›

matérialiser /mateʀjalize/ [**v1**] **A** *vt* **1** to realize ‹*dream*›; to make [sth] happen ‹*plan*›
2 to mark; **'chaussée non matérialisée sur 3 km'** 'no road markings for 3 km'
B **se matérialiser** *v refl* (+ *v être*) to materialize

matérialisme /mateʀjalism/ *m* materialism

matérialiste /mateʀjalist/ *adj* materialistic

matériau, *pl* **~x** /mateʀjo/ *m* material; **~x de construction** building materials

matériel, -ielle /mateʀjɛl/ **A** *adj* ‹*cause, conditions*› material; ‹*means*› practical
B *m* **1** equipment; **~ agricole** farm machinery
2 material
■ **~ informatique** hardware

matériellement /mateʀjɛlmɑ̃/ *adv* **1** **c'est ~ possible** it can be done
2 financially

maternel, -elle /matɛʀnɛl/ *adj* **1** ‹*instinct*› maternal; ‹*love*› motherly
2 ‹*aunt*› maternal; **du côté ~** on the mother's side

maternelle /matɛʀnɛl/ *f* nursery school

maternellement /matɛʀnɛlmɑ̃/ *adv* in a motherly way

materner /matɛʀne/ [**v1**] *vt* **1** to mother
2 to mollycoddle

maternité /matɛʀnite/ *f* **1** motherhood
2 pregnancy; **de ~** ‹*leave*› maternity
3 maternity hospital

mathématicien, -ienne /matematisjɛ̃, ɛn/ *mf* mathematician

mathématiquement /matematikmɑ̃/ *adv* **1** mathematically
2 logically

mathématiques /matematik/ *fpl* mathematics

matheux, -euse /matø, øz/ *mf* (fam) mathematician

maths /mat/ *fpl* (fam) maths (BrE) (fam), math (AmE) (fam)

⚷ **matière** /matjɛʀ/ *f* **1** material; **fournir la ~ d'un roman** to provide the material for a novel
2 matter; **en ~ d'emploi** as far as employment is concerned; **~ à réflexion** food for thought
3 (Sch) subject
■ **~s fécales** faeces; **~s grasses** fat; **~ grise** grey (BrE) *or* gray (AmE) matter; **~ première** raw material

Matignon /matiɲɔ̃/ *pr n: offices of the French Prime Minister*

⚷ **matin** /matɛ̃/ *m* morning; **de bon ~** early in the morning
IDIOM **être du ~** to be a morning person

matinal, **~e**, *mpl* **-aux** /matinal, o/ *adj* ‹*walk*› morning; ‹*hour*› early; **être ~** to be an early riser, to be up early

mâtiné, **~e** /mɑtine/ *adj* **un anglais ~ de français** a mixture of English and French

matinée /matine/ *f* **1** morning
2 matinee
IDIOM **faire la grasse ~** to sleep in

matines /matin/ *fpl* matins

matos /matos/ *m* (fam) equipment, gear; **il vend son ~ de musique** he's selling his music gear

matraquage /matʀakaʒ/ *m* **1** bludgeoning
2 (fig) **~ publicitaire** hype (fam)

matraque /matʀak/ *f* club; truncheon (BrE), billy (AmE); **c'est le coup de ~** (fig, fam) it costs a fortune

matraquer /matʀake/ [**v1**] *vt* **1** to club
2 ‹*media*› to bombard ‹*public*›

matriarcal, **~e**, *mpl* **-aux** /matʀijaʀkal, o/ *adj* matriarchal

matrice /matʀis/ *f* **1** matrix
2 (Tech) die

matricule /matʀikyl/ *m* reference number; (Mil) service number

matrimonial, **~e**, *mpl* **-iaux** /matʀimɔnjal, o/ *adj* marriage, matrimonial

matrone /matʀɔn/ *f* matronly woman

maturation /matyʀasjɔ̃/ *f* ripening; maturing

maturité /matyʀite/ *f* maturity

maudire /modiʀ/ [**v80**] *vt* to curse

maudit, **~e** /modi, it/ **A** *pp* ▶ **maudire**
B *adj* (fam) blasted (fam)
C *mf* damned soul; **les ~s** the damned

maugréer /mogʀee/ [**v11**] *vi* to grumble (**contre** about)

maure /mɔʀ/ *adj* Moorish

maussade /mosad/ *adj* ‹*mood*› sullen; ‹*weather*› dull; ‹*landscape*› bleak

⚷ **mauvais**, **~e** /mɔvɛ, ɛz/ **A** *adj* **1** bad, poor; ‹*lawyer, doctor*› incompetent; ‹*wage*› low; **du ~ tabac** cheap tobacco
2 ‹*address*› wrong
3 ‹*day, moment*› bad; ‹*method*› wrong
4 bad; ‹*surprise*› nasty; ‹*taste, smell*› unpleasant; **par ~ temps** in bad weather; **ça a ~ goût** it tastes horrible
5 ‹*cold, wound*› nasty; ‹*sea*› rough
6 ‹*person, smile*› nasty; ‹*intentions, thoughts*› evil; **préparer un ~ coup** to be up to mischief
B *adv* **sentir ~** to smell; **sentir très ~** to stink; **il fait ~** the weather is bad
C *m* **il n'y a pas que du ~ dans le projet** the project isn't all bad
■ **~ esprit** scoffing person; scoffing attitude; **~ garçon** tough guy; **~ traitements** ill-treatment; **~e herbe** weed; **~es rencontres** bad company
IDIOM **l'avoir ~e** (fam) to be furious

mauve¹ /mov/ *adj*, *m* mauve

mauve² /mov/ *f* mallow

mauviette /movjɛt/ *f* wimp (fam)

maux ▶ **mal**

maxi- /maksi/ *pref* **~-jupe** maxi skirt; **~-bouteille** one and a half litre (BrE) bottle

maxillaire /maksilɛʀ/ *m* jawbone

maxima ▶ **maximum**

maximal, **~e**, *mpl* **-aux** /maksimal, o/ *adj* maximum

maxime /maksim/ *f* maxim

maximum, *pl* **~s** *or* **maxima** /maksimɔm, maksima/ **A** *adj* maximum
B *m* **1** maximum; **10 euros au grand ~** 10 euros at the very most; **au ~** ‹*work*› to the maximum; ‹*reduce*› as much as possible; **obtenir le ~ d'avantages** to get as many advantages as possible; **faire le ~** to do one's utmost
2 (Law) maximum sentence

mayonnaise /majɔnɛz/ *f* mayonnaise

mazagran /mazagʀɑ̃/ *m: thick china goblet for coffee*

mazout /mazut/ *m* (fuel) oil

⚷ **me**, **m'** *before vowel or mute h* /m(ə)/ *pron*
1 me; **tu ne m'as pas fait mal** you didn't hurt me
2 myself; **je ~ lave (les mains)** I wash (my hands)

Me *written abbr* ▶ **maître C3**

méandre /meɑ̃dʀ/ *m* meander; **les ~s de l'administration** the maze of officialdom; **les ~s de ta pensée** the rambling development of your ideas

mec /mɛk/ *m* (fam) guy (fam); **mon ~** my man (fam)

mécanicien, **-ienne** /mekanisjɛ̃, ɛn/ **A** *adj* mechanical
B *mf* mechanic
C *m* (of train) engine driver (BrE), (locomotive) engineer (AmE); (of plane) flight engineer; (of boat) engineer

mécanique /mekanik/ **A** *adj* mechanical; ‹*toy*› clockwork; ‹*razor*› hand
B *f* **1** mechanics; **une merveille de ~** a

⚷ key word

marvel of engineering
2 (fam) machine

mécaniquement /mekanikmɑ̃/ *adv* mechanically; **fabriqué ~** machine-made

mécaniser /mekanize/ [**v1**] *vt*, **se mécaniser** *v refl* (+ *v être*) to mechanize

mécanisme /mekanism/ *m* mechanism

mécano /mekano/ *m* (fam) mechanic

mécénat /mesenɑ/ *m* patronage

mécène /mesɛn/ *m* patron of the arts

méchamment /meʃamɑ̃/ *adv* **1** spitefully, maliciously; viciously; **traiter qn ~** to treat sb badly
2 (fam) ‹*damage*› badly; ‹*good*› terribly

méchanceté /meʃɑ̃ste/ *f* **1** nastiness; **par pure ~** out of pure spite
2 maliciousness, viciousness
3 malicious act; malicious remark

méchant, **~e** /meʃɑ̃, ɑ̃t/ **A** *adj* **1** ‹*person*› nasty, malicious; ‹*animal*› vicious; ‹*flu, business*› nasty, bad
2 (fam) fantastic (fam), terrific (fam)
B *mf* **1** villain, baddie (fam)
2 naughty boy/girl

mèche /mɛʃ/ *f* **1** (of hair) lock
2 (in hair) streak
3 (of candle) wick
4 (Med) packing
5 (of explosive) fuse
6 (drill) bit
IDIOMS **être de ~ avec qn** (fam) to be in cahoots with sb (fam); **vendre la ~** to let the cat out of the bag

méchoui /meʃwi/ *m* North African style barbecue; spit-roast lamb

méconnaissable /mekɔnɛsabl/ *adj* unrecognizable

méconnaissance /mekɔnɛsɑ̃s/ *f*
1 ignorance
2 misreading

méconnaître /mekɔnɛtʀ/ [**v73**] *vt* to misread; to be mistaken about

méconnu, **~e** /mekɔny/ *adj* ‹*artist, work*› neglected; ‹*value*› unrecognized

mécontent, **~e** /mekɔ̃tɑ̃, ɑ̃t/ *adj* dissatisfied; ‹*voter*› discontented; **pas ~** rather pleased

mécontentement /mekɔ̃tɑ̃tmɑ̃/ *m*
1 dissatisfaction
2 discontent
3 annoyance

mécontenter /mekɔ̃tɑ̃te/ [**v1**] *vt* to annoy; to anger

Mecque /mɛk/ *pr n* **la ~** Mecca

médaillable /medajable/ *adj* in medal contention

médaille /medaj/ *f* **1** medal; **~ d'or** gold medal
2 coin
3 medallion

médaillon /medajɔ̃/ *m* **1** locket
2 (in art, architecture) medallion

médecin /mɛdsɛ̃/ *m* doctor; **~ traitant** general practitioner, GP (BrE)
■ **~ de garde** duty doctor, doctor on duty; **~ légiste** forensic surgeon

médecine /mɛdsin/ *f* medicine
■ **~ scolaire** ≈ school health service; **~ du travail** ≈ occupational medicine; **~s douces** *or* **parallèles** alternative medicine

média /medja/ **A** *m* medium
B **médias** *mpl* **les ~s** the media

médias sociaux *mpl* social media

médiateur, **-trice** /medjatœʀ, tʀis/ **A** *adj* mediatory
B *m* mediator; ombudsman

médiathèque /medjatɛk/ *f* multimedia library

médiation /medjasjɔ̃/ *f* mediation

médiatique /medjatik/ *adj* ‹*exploitation*› by the media; ‹*success*› media

médiatisation /medjatizasjɔ̃/ *f* media coverage

médiatiser /medjatize/ [**v1**] *vt* to give [sth] publicity in the media

médical, **~e**, *mpl* **-aux** /medikal, o/ *adj* medical

médicament /medikamɑ̃/ *m* medicine, drug

médication /medikasjɔ̃/ *f* medication

médicinal, **~e**, *mpl* **-aux** /medisinal, o/ *adj* medicinal

médico-légal, **~e**, *mpl* **-aux** /medikolegal, o/ *adj* forensic; **certificat ~** autopsy report

médico-pédagogique, *pl* **~s** /medikopedagɔʒik/ *adj* **institut ~** special school

médiéval, **~e**, *mpl* **-aux** /medjeval, o/ *adj* medieval

médiocre /medjɔkʀ/ *adj* mediocre; ‹*pupil, intelligence*› below average; ‹*soil, light, return, food*› poor; ‹*interest, success*› limited; ‹*income*› meagre (BrE)

médiocrement /medjɔkʀəmɑ̃/ *adv* rather badly

médiocrité /medjɔkʀite/ *f* **1** mediocrity
2 meagreness (BrE)

médire /mediʀ/ [**v65**] *v+prep* **~ de** to speak ill of

médisance /medizɑ̃s/ *f* malicious gossip

médisant, **~e** /medizɑ̃, ɑ̃t/ *adj* malicious

médit /medi/ ▸ **médire**

méditation /meditasjɔ̃/ *f* meditation

méditer /medite/ [**v1**] **A** *vt* to mull over; **longuement médité** ‹*plan*› carefully considered
B *vi* to meditate; **~ sur** to meditate on ‹*existence*›; to ponder on *or* over ‹*problem*›

Méditerranée /mediteʀane/ *pr f* **la (mer) ~** the Mediterranean (Sea)

méditerranéen, **-éenne** /mediteʀaneɛ̃, ɛn/ *adj* Mediterranean

médium /medjɔm/ *m* medium

méduse /medyz/ *f* jellyfish

méduser /medyze/ [**v1**] *vt* to dumbfound
meeting /mitiŋ/ *m* meeting
méfait /mefɛ/ **A** *m* misdemeanour (BrE); crime
B **méfaits** *mpl* detrimental effect
méfiance /mefjɑ̃s/ *f* mistrust, suspicion; **~ de qn envers qn/qch** sb's wariness of sb/sth
méfiant, **~e** /mefjɑ̃, ɑ̃t/ *adj* suspicious; **elle est d'un naturel ~** she's always very wary
méfier: **se méfier** /mefje/ [**v2**] *v refl* (+ *v être*) **1 se ~ de qn/qch** not to trust sb/sth; **sans se ~** quite trustingly
2 se ~ de qch to be wary of sth; **méfie-toi!** be careful!; watch it!
méga /mega/ *pref* mega; **~hertz** megahertz
mégalomane /megalɔman/ *adj*, *mf* megalomaniac
mégaoctet /megaɔktɛ/ *m* megabyte
mégarde: **par mégarde** /paʀmegaʀd/ *phr* inadvertently
mégère /meʒɛʀ/ *f* shrew
mégot /mego/ *m* cigarette butt
meilleur, **~e** /mɛjœʀ/ **A** *adj* **1** better (**que** than)
2 best; **au ~ prix** ‹*buy*› at the lowest price; ‹*sell*› at the highest price
B *mf* **le ~, la ~e** the best one
C *adv* better; **il fait ~ qu'hier** the weather is better than it was yesterday
D *m* **le ~** the best bit; **pour le ~ et pour le pire** for better or for worse
E **meilleure** *f* **ça c'est la ~e!** that's the best one yet!
mél /mel/ *m* (fam) (message) email; (address) email address
mélancolie /melɑ̃kɔli/ *f* (gen) melancholy; (Med) melancholia
mélancolique **A** *adj* melancholy
B *mf* melancholic
mélancoliquement /melɑ̃kɔlikmɑ̃/ *adv* melancholically, in a melancholy fashion
mélange /melɑ̃ʒ/ *m* (of teas, tobaccos) blend; (of products, ideas) combination; (of colours) mixture; **c'est un ~ (coton et synthétique)** it's a mix (of cotton and synthetic fibres (BrE))
mélanger /melɑ̃ʒe/ [**v13**] **A** *vt* **1** to blend ‹*teas, oils, tobaccos*›; to mix ‹*colours, shades*›
2 to put together ‹*styles, people, objects*›
3 to mix up; **~ les cartes** to shuffle (the cards)
B **se mélanger** *v refl* (+ *v être*) **1** ‹*teas, oils, tobaccos*› to blend; ‹*colours, shades*› to mix, to blend together
2 ‹*ideas*› to get muddled
mélangeur /melɑ̃ʒœʀ/ *m* mixer
mélasse /melas/ *f* black treacle (BrE), molasses
mêlée /mele/ *f* **1** melee; **~ générale** free-for-all
2 (Sport) scrum
3 (fig) fray
mêler /mele/ [**v1**] **A** *vt* **1** to mix ‹*products, colours*›; to blend ‹*ingredients, cultures*›; to combine ‹*influences*›
2 être mêlé à un scandale to be involved in a scandal
B **se mêler** *v refl* (+ *v être*) **1** ‹*cultures, religions*› to mix; ‹*smells, voices*› to mingle
2 se ~ à to mingle with ‹*crowd*›; to mix with ‹*people*›; to join in ‹*conversation*›
3 se ~ de to meddle in; **mêle-toi de tes affaires** (fam) mind your own business
méli-mélo, *pl* **mélis-mélos** /melimelo/ *m* jumble, mess
mélo /melo/ *adj* (fam) slushy (fam), schmaltzy (fam)
mélodie /melɔdi/ *f* **1** melody, tune
2 melodiousness
mélodrame /melɔdʀam/ *m* melodrama
mélomane /melɔman/ *mf* music lover
melon /məlɔ̃/ *m* **1** melon
2 bowler (hat) (BrE), derby (hat) (AmE)
membrane /mɑ̃bʀan/ *f* (Anat) membrane
membre /mɑ̃bʀ/ *m* **1** member; **les pays ~s** the member countries
2 limb; **~ postérieur** hind limb
même /mɛm/ **A** *adj* **1** same
2 c'est l'intelligence ~ he's/she's intelligence itself
3 le jour ~ où the very same day that; **c'est cela ~** that's it exactly
B *adv* **1** even; **je ne m'en souviens ~ plus** I can't even remember now
2 very; **c'est ici ~ que je l'ai rencontré** I met him at this very place
C **de même** *phr* **agir** *or* **faire de ~** to do the same; **il en va de ~ pour** the same is true of
D **de même que** *phr* **le prix du café, de ~ que celui du tabac, a augmenté de 10%** the price of coffee, as well as that of tobacco, has risen by 10%
E **même si** *phr* even if
F *pron* **le ~, la ~, les ~s** the same; **ce sac est le ~ que celui de Pierre** this bag is the same as Pierre's
mémé /meme/ *f* (fam) gran (fam), granny (fam)
mémento /memɛ̃to/ *m* guide
mémo /memo/ *m* (fam) note
Mémo-Appel /memoapɛl/ *m* reminder call service
mémoire[1] /memwaʀ/ **A** *m* **1** memo
2 dissertation
B **mémoires** *mpl* memoirs
mémoire[2] /memwaʀ/ *f* **1** memory; **si j'ai bonne ~** if I remember rightly; **ne pas avoir de ~** to have a bad memory; **de ~ d'homme** in living memory; **en ~ de** to the memory of, in memory of; **pour ~** for the record; for reference
2 (Comput) memory; storage; **mettre des données en ~** to input data

key word

■ ~ **centrale** main storage *or* memory; ~ **morte** read-only memory, ROM; ~ **vive** random access memory, RAM

Mémophone /memofɔn/ *m* public voicemail service

mémorable /memɔʀabl/ *adj* memorable

mémorial, ~**e**, *mpl* **-iaux** /memɔʀjal, o/ *m* memorial

mémoriser /memɔʀize/ [**v1**] *vt* to memorize

menaçant, ~**e** /mənasɑ̃, ɑ̃t/ *adj* menacing

menace /mənas/ *f* threat; **sous la** ~ under duress; **sous la** ~ **d'une arme** at gunpoint

menacer /mənase/ [**v12**] *vt* **1** to threaten ‹*person*›
2 to pose a threat to; **être menacé** ‹*stability, economy*› to be in jeopardy; ‹*life*› to be in danger; ‹*population*› to be at risk

ménage /menaʒ/ *m* **1** household; **se mettre en** ~ **avec qn** to set up home with sb; **scènes de** ~ domestic rows; **monter son** ~ to buy the household goods
2 housework; **faire le** ~ to do the cleaning; **faire des** ~**s** to do domestic cleaning work
(IDIOM) **faire bon** ~ to be compatible

ménagement /menaʒmɑ̃/ *m* **avec** ~**s** gently; **sans** ~**s** ‹*say*› bluntly; ‹*push*› roughly

ménager[1] /menaʒe/ [**v13**] **A** *vt* **1** to handle [sb] carefully; to deal carefully with [sb]; to be gentle with [sb]; to be careful with [sth]; ~ **la susceptibilité de qn** to humour (BrE) sb
2 to be careful with ‹*clothes, savings*›; **il ne ménage pas sa peine** he spares no effort
B se ménager *v refl* (+ *v être*) to take it easy

ménager[2], **-ère** /menaʒe, ɛʀ/ *adj* ‹*jobs*› domestic; ‹*equipment*› household; **appareils** ~**s** domestic appliances; **travaux** ~**s** housework

ménagère /menaʒɛʀ/ *f* **1** housewife
2 canteen of cutlery

ménagerie /menaʒʀi/ *f* menagerie

mendiant, ~**e** /mɑ̃djɑ̃, ɑ̃t/ *mf* beggar

mendicité /mɑ̃disite/ *f* begging

mendier /mɑ̃dje/ [**v2**] **A** *vt* to beg for
B *vi* to beg

mener /məne/ [**v16**] **A** *vt* **1** ~ **qn quelque part** to take sb somewhere; to drive sb somewhere
2 to lead ‹*people, country*›; to run ‹*company*›; **il ne se laisse pas** ~ **par sa grande sœur** he won't be bossed about by his sister (fam)
3 ~ **au village** ‹*road*› to go *or* lead to the village
4 ~ **à** to lead to; **cette histoire peut te** ~ **loin** it could be a very nasty business; ~ **à bien** to complete [sth] successfully; to bring [sth] to a successful conclusion; to handle [sth] successfully
5 to carry out ‹*study, reform*›; to run ‹*campaign*›; ~ **une enquête** to hold an investigation; ~ **sa vie comme on l'entend** to live as one pleases
B *vi* (Sport) to be in the lead
(IDIOM) ~ **la danse** *or* **le jeu** to call the tune

ménestrel /menɛstʀɛl/ *m* minstrel

meneur, **-euse** /mənœʀ, øz/ *mf* leader

menhir /meniʀ/ *m* menhir

méninge /menɛ̃ʒ/ **A** *f* (Anat) meninx
B méninges *fpl* (fam) brains (fam)

méningite /menɛ̃ʒit/ *f* meningitis

ménisque /menisk/ *m* meniscus

ménopause /menɔpoz/ *f* menopause

menotte /mənɔt/ **A** *f* tiny hand
B menottes *fpl* handcuffs

mensonge /mɑ̃sɔ̃ʒ/ *m* **1** lie
2 le ~ lying

mensonger, **-ère** /mɑ̃sɔ̃ʒe, ɛʀ/ *adj* ‹*accusations*› false; ‹*advertising*› misleading

mensualité /mɑ̃sɥalite/ *f* monthly instalment (BrE)

mensuel, **-elle** /mɑ̃sɥɛl/ **A** *adj* monthly
B *m* monthly magazine

mensuellement /mɑ̃sɥɛlmɑ̃/ *adv* once a month, monthly

mensurations /mɑ̃syʀasjɔ̃/ *fpl* measurements

mental, ~**e**, *mpl* **-aux** /mɑ̃tal, o/ *adj* mental; **handicapé** ~ person with learning difficulties

mentalité /mɑ̃talite/ *f* mentality

menteur, **-euse** /mɑ̃tœʀ, øz/ **A** *adj* ‹*person*› untruthful; ‹*statement*› full of lies
B *mf* liar

menthe /mɑ̃t/ *f* **1** mint; ~ **poivrée** peppermint; ~ **verte** spearmint
2 mint tea
3 ~ **(à l'eau)** mint cordial

menthol /mɛ̃tɔl/ *m* menthol

mentholé, ~**e** /mɛ̃tɔle/ *adj* mentholated; menthol

mention /mɑ̃sjɔ̃/ *f* **1** mention; **faire** ~ **de qch** to mention sth
2 (Sch) ~ **passable** *pass with 50 to 60%*; ~ **très bien** *pass with 80% upward(s)*
3 note; **rayer la** ~ **inutile** *or* **les** ~**s inutiles** delete as appropriate

mentionner /mɑ̃sjɔne/ [**v1**] *vt* to mention

mentir /mɑ̃tiʀ/ [**v30**] **A** *vi* **1** to lie, to tell lies
2 ‹*figures*› to be misleading
B se mentir *v refl* (+ *v être*) **1** to fool oneself
2 to lie to one another

menton /mɑ̃tɔ̃/ *m* chin

menu, ~**e** /məny/ **A** *adj* **1** ‹*person*› slight; ‹*foot, piece*› tiny; ‹*writing*› small
2 ‹*jobs*› small; ‹*details*› minute
B *adv* ‹*write*› small; ‹*chop*› finely
C *m* menu
D par le menu *phr* in (great) detail
■ ~ **fretin** small fry; ~**e monnaie** small change

menuiserie /mənɥizʀi/ *f* woodwork

m

menuisier /mənɥizje/ *m* joiner (BrE), finish carpenter

méprendre: **se méprendre** /mepʀɑ̃dʀ/ [**v52**] *v refl* (+ *v être*) to be mistaken

mépris /mepʀi/ *m inv* contempt; **au ~ de la loi** regardless of the law

méprisable /mepʀizabl/ *adj* contemptible

méprisant, **~e** /mepʀizɑ̃, ɑ̃t/ *adj* ‹*gesture*› contemptuous; ‹*person*› disdainful

méprise /mepʀiz/ *f* mistake

mépriser /mepʀize/ [**v1**] *vt* to despise ‹*person, wealth*›; to scorn ‹*danger, offer*›

⚷ **mer** /mɛʀ/ *f* **1** sea; **une ~ d'huile** a glassy sea; **en pleine ~** out at sea; **la ~ monte** the tide is coming in
2 seaside
IDIOM **ce n'est pas la ~ à boire** it's not all that difficult

mercantile /mɛʀkɑ̃til/ *adj* mercenary

mercenaire /mɛʀsənɛʀ/ *adj*, *mf* mercenary

mercerie /mɛʀsəʀi/ *f* haberdasher's shop (BrE), notions store (AmE)

⚷ **merci[1]** /mɛʀsi/ *m*, *excl* thank you

merci[2] /mɛʀsi/ *f* mercy; **on est toujours à la ~ d'un accident** there's always the risk of an accident

⚷ **mercredi** /mɛʀkʀədi/ *m* Wednesday

mercure /mɛʀkyʀ/ *m* mercury

mercurochrome® /mɛʀkyʀokʀom/ *m* Mercurochrome®, antiseptic

⚷ **merde** /mɛʀd/ *f*, *excl* (vulg) shit (sl)

⚷ **mère** /mɛʀ/ **A** *f* **1** mother
2 ~ supérieure Mother Superior
B (-)mère (*combining form*) **cellule/maison ~** parent cell/company
■ **~ célibataire** single mother; **~ de famille** mother; housewife; **~ porteuse** surrogate mother; **~ poule** mother hen

merguez /mɛʀgɛz/ *f inv* spicy sausage

méridien /meʀidjɛ̃/ *m* meridian

méridional, **~e**, *mpl* **-aux** /meʀidjɔnal, o/ **A** *adj* southern
B *mf* Southerner

meringue /məʀɛ̃g/ *f* meringue

mérite /meʀit/ *m* merit; credit; **au ~** according to merit; **vanter les ~s de** to sing the praises of

mériter /meʀite/ [**v1**] **A** *vt* to deserve; **~ réflexion** to be worth considering
B se mériter *v refl* (+ *v être*) **ça se mérite** it's something that has to be earned

merlan /mɛʀlɑ̃/ *m* whiting

merle /mɛʀl/ *m* blackbird

mérou /meʀu/ *m* grouper

merveille /mɛʀvɛj/ **A** *f* marvel, wonder
B à merveille *phr* wonderfully

⚷ **merveilleux**, **-euse** /mɛʀvɛjø, øz/ *adj* marvellous (BrE), wonderful

mes ▸ **mon**

⚷ key word

mésaventure /mezavɑ̃tyʀ/ *f* misadventure

mesdames ▸ **madame**

mesdemoiselles ▸ **mademoiselle**

mésentente /mezɑ̃tɑ̃t/ *f* dissension; disagreement

mésestimer /mezɛstime/ [**v1**] *vt* to underrate; to underestimate

mesquin, **~e** /mɛskɛ̃, in/ *adj* **1** petty-minded; petty
2 ‹*person*› mean (BrE), cheap (AmE) (fam)

mesquinerie /mɛskinʀi/ *f* **1** meanness
2 stinginess
3 mean trick; mean remark

⚷ **message** /mesaʒ/ *m* message; **~ publicitaire** commercial

messager, **-ère** /mesaʒe, ɛʀ/ *mf* **1** messenger
2 envoy

messagerie /mesaʒʀi/ *f* freight forwarding
■ **~ électronique** electronic mail service, email; **~ vocale** voice messaging

messe /mɛs/ *f* mass; **~s basses** (fam) whispering

messie /mesi/ *m* messiah

messieurs ▸ **monsieur**

⚷ **mesure** /məzyʀ/ *f* **1** measure; **prendre des ~s** to take measures; to take steps
2 measurement; **c'est du sur ~** it's made to measure; **tu as un emploi sur ~** the job is tailor-made for you; **c'est une adversaire à ta ~** she is a match for you
3 unité de ~ unit of measurement; **instrument de ~** measuring device; **deux ~s de lait pour une ~ d'eau** two parts milk to one of water
4 moderation; **dépasser la ~** to go too far
5 (Mus) bar; **battre la ~** to beat time
6 être en ~ de rembourser to be in a position to reimburse; **dans la ~ du possible** as far as possible; **dans la ~ où** insofar as

⚷ **mesurer** /məzyʀe/ [**v1**] **A** *vt* **1** to measure; **~ le tour de cou de qn** to take sb's neck measurement
2 to measure ‹*productivity, gap*›; to assess ‹*difficulties, risks, effects*›; to consider ‹*consequences*›; **~ ses paroles** to weigh one's words
B *vi* **~ 20 mètres carrés** to be 20 metres (BrE) square; **elle mesure 1,60 m** she's 1.60 m tall
C se mesurer *v refl* (+ *v être*) **1 se ~ en mètres** to be measured in metres (BrE)
2 se ~ à *or* **avec qn** to pit one's strength against sb

métal, *pl* **-aux** /metal, o/ *m* metal; **pièce de** *or* **en ~** metal coin; **~ jaune** gold

métallique /metalik/ *adj* **1** metal; **c'est ~** it's made of metal
2 metallic

métallisé, **~e** /metalize/ *adj* ‹*green, blue*› metallic

métallurgie /metalyʀʒi/ *f* **1** metalworking industry

2 metallurgy

métallurgique /metalyʀʒik/ *adj* metallurgical

métamorphose /metamɔʀfoz/ *f* metamorphosis

métamorphoser /metamɔʀfoze/ [**v1**] **A** *vt* to transform [sb/sth] completely
B **se métamorphoser** *v refl* (+ *v être*) **se ~ en** to metamorphose into

métaphore /metafɔʀ/ *f* metaphor

métayage /metejaʒ/ *m* tenant farming, sharecropping

métayer, **-ère** /meteje, ɛʀ/ *mf* tenant farmer (BrE), sharecropper (AmE)

météo /meteo/ *f* weather forecast

météore /meteɔʀ/ *m* meteor

météorite /meteɔʀit/ *m or f* meteorite

météorologie /meteɔʀɔlɔʒi/ *f* meteorology

météorologique /meteɔʀɔlɔʒik/ *adj* meteorological; **conditions ~s** weather conditions

météorologiste /meteɔʀɔlɔʒist/, **météorologue** /meteɔʀɔlɔg/ *mf* meteorologist

métèque /metɛk/ *m* (offensive) foreigner, dago (offensive)

méthane /metan/ *m* methane

méthode /metɔd/ *f* **1** method
2 (for languages) course book (BrE), textbook (AmE)
3 way; **j'ai ma ~ pour le convaincre** I've got a way of convincing him

méthodique /metɔdik/ *adj* methodical

méthodiquement /metɔdikmɑ̃/ *adv* methodically; **procédons ~** let's take things step by step

méticuleux, **-euse** /metikylø, øz/ *adj* meticulous; painstaking

métier /metje/ *m* **1** job; profession; trade; craft; **avoir 20 ans de ~** to have 20 years' experience; **c'est le ~ qui rentre!** you learn by your mistakes!
2 ~ à tisser weaving loom

métis, **-isse** /metis/ *mf* person of mixed race

métissage /metisaʒ/ *m* (of people) miscegenation; (of plants, animals) crossing

métrage /metʀaʒ/ *m* **1** (of material) length
2 long ~ feature(-length) film

mètre /mɛtʀ/ *m* **1** metre (BrE); **le 60 ~s** the 60 metres (BrE); **piquer un cent ~s** (fam) to break into a run
2 rule (BrE), yardstick (AmE); **~ ruban** *or* **de couturière** tape measure

métrique /metʀik/ *adj* metric

métro /metʀo/ *m* underground (BrE), subway (AmE)
IDIOM **~, boulot, dodo** (fam) the daily grind

métronome /metʀɔnɔm/ *m* metronome

métropole /metʀɔpɔl/ *f* **1** metropolis
2 major city
3 Metropolitan France

métropolitain, **~e** /metʀɔpɔlitɛ̃, ɛn/ *adj* **1** ‹*network*› underground (BrE), subway (AmE)
2 from Metropolitan France

métropolite /metʀɔpɔlit/ *m* metropolitan

mets /mɛ/ *m inv* dish, delicacy

mettable /mɛtabl/ *adj* wearable

metteur /mɛtœʀ/ *m* **~ en scène** director

mettre /mɛtʀ/ [**v60**] **A** *vt* **1** to put; to put in ‹*heating, shower*›; to put up ‹*curtains, shelves*›; **je mets les enfants à la crèche** I send the children to a creche; **mets ton écharpe** put your scarf on; **~ le linge à sécher** to put the washing out to dry; **faire ~ le téléphone** to have a telephone put in
2 to wear
3 ~ qn en colère to make sb angry
4 to put on ‹*radio, TV, heating*›; **mets moins fort!** turn it down!; **~ le réveil** to set the alarm
5 to put up ‹*sign*›; **qu'est-ce que je dois ~?** what shall I put?; **je t'ai mis un mot** I've left you a note; **~ en musique** to set to music; **~ en anglais** to put into English
6 y ~ du sien to put oneself into it; **combien pouvez-vous ~?** how much can you afford?; **elle a mis une heure** it took her an hour (**pour faire** to do)
7 (Sch) **je vous ai mis trois sur vingt** I've given you three out of twenty
8 (fam) **mettons qu'il vienne, qu'est-ce que vous ferez?** supposing he comes, what will you do?
B *vi* **~ bas** ‹*animal*› to give birth; to calve
C **se mettre** *v refl* (+ *v être*) **1 se ~ devant la fenêtre** to stand in front of the window; **se ~ au lit** to go to bed; **se ~ debout** to stand up; **où est-ce que ça se met?** where does this go?
2 to spill [sth] on oneself
3 je ne sais pas quoi me ~ I don't know what to put on
4 se ~ à l'anglais to take up English; **il va se ~ à pleuvoir** it's going to start raining
5 je préfère me ~ bien avec lui I prefer to get on the right side of him; **se ~ à l'aise** to make oneself comfortable

meuble /mœbl/ **A** *adj* ‹*soil*› loose
B *m* **un ~** a piece of furniture
IDIOM **sauver les ~s** to salvage something

meublé /mœble/ *m* furnished apartment

meubler /mœble/ [**v1**] *vt* to furnish; **la plante meuble bien la pièce** the plant makes the room look more cosy (BrE) *or* cozy (AmE)

meugler /møgle/ [**v1**] *vi* to moo

meule /møl/ *f* **1** millstone
2 grindstone
3 ~ de foin haystack

meunier, **-ière** /mønje, ɛʀ/ *mf* miller

meurtre /mœʀtʀ/ *m* murder

meurtrier, **-ière** /mœʀtʀije, ɛʀ/ **A** *adj* ‹*fighting, repression*› bloody; ‹*explosion,*

accident› fatal; ‹*epidemic*› deadly; ‹*arm*› lethal
B *mf* murderer

meurtrir /mœʀtʀiʀ/ [**v3**] *vt* **1** to hurt
2 to bruise
3 to wound ‹*self-esteem*›

meute /møt/ *f* pack of hounds

mexicain, **~e** /mɛksikɛ̃, ɛn/ *adj* Mexican

Mexico /meksiko/ *pr n* Mexico City

Mexique /mɛksik/ *pr m* Mexico

mezzanine /medzanin/ *f* mezzanine

MF /ɛmɛf/ *f* (*abbr* = **modulation de fréquence**) frequency modulation, FM

mi /mi/ *m inv* (Mus) (note) E; (in sol-fa) mi, me

mi- /mi/ *pref* **à la ~-mai/saison** in mid-May/-season; **~-chinois, ~-français** half Chinese, half French

miam-miam /mjammjam/ *excl* (fam) yum-yum! (fam)

miauler /mjole/ [**v1**] *vi* to miaow (BrE), to meow

mi-bas /mibɑ/ *m inv* knee sock, long sock

miche /miʃ/ *f* round loaf

mi-chemin: **à mi-chemin** /amiʃmɛ̃/ *phr* halfway; (fig) halfway through

mi-clos, **~e** /miklo, oz/ *adj* half-closed

micmac /mikmak/ *m* (fam) shady goings-on (fam)

m

mi-côte: **à mi-côte** /amikot/ *phr* halfway up; halfway down

mi-course: **à mi-course** /amikuʀs/ *phr* halfway through the race; (fig) halfway through

micro¹ /mikʀo/ *pref* micro

micro² /mikʀo/ *m* microphone, mike (fam); **~ caché** bug

microbe /mikʀɔb/ *m* germ, microbe

microclimat /mikʀoklima/ *m* microclimate

microcosme /mikʀɔkɔsm/ *m* microcosm

micro-cravate, *pl* **micros-cravates** /mikʀokʀavat/ *m* lapel microphone

micro-édition /mikʀoedisjɔ̃/ *f* desktop publishing

microfilm /mikʀɔfilm/ *m* microfilm

micro-informatique /mikʀoɛ̃fɔʀmatik/ *f* microcomputing

micro-ondes /mikʀoɔ̃d/ *m inv* microwave

micro-ordinateur, *pl* **~s** /mikʀoɔʀdinatœʀ/ *m* microcomputer

microphone /mikʀɔfɔn/ *m* microphone

microprocesseur /mikʀopʀɔsɛsœʀ/ *m* microprocessor

microscope /mikʀɔskɔp/ *m* microscope

microscopique /mikʀɔskɔpik/ *adj* microscopic; (fig) tiny

microsillon /mikʀɔsijɔ̃/ *m* **(disque) ~** microgroove record

mi-cuisse: **à mi-cuisse** /amikɥis/ *phr* above one's knees

✓ **midi** /midi/ *m* **1** twelve o'clock, midday, noon; **je fais mes courses entre ~ et deux** I go shopping in my lunch hour
2 lunchtime
3 le Midi the South of France

midinette /midinɛt/ *f* bimbo (fam)

mi-distance: **à mi-distance** /amidistɑ̃s/ *phr* halfway

mie /mi/ *f* bread without the crusts

miel /mjɛl/ *m* honey
IDIOM **être tout sucre tout ~** to be as nice as pie (fam)

mielleux, **-euse** /mjɛlø, øz/ *adj* ‹*tone*› unctuous, honeyed; ‹*person*› fawning

✓ **mien**, **mienne** /mjɛ̃, mjɛn/ **A** *det* **ces idées, je les ai faites miennes** I adopted these ideas
B le mien, la mienne, les miens, les miennes *pron* mine

miette /mjɛt/ *f* crumb; **réduire en ~s** to smash [sth] to bits ‹*vase*›; to shatter ‹*hopes*›; **elle n'en perd pas une ~** (fam) she's taking it all in

✓ **mieux** /mjø/ **A** *adj inv* better; **le ~, la ~, les ~** the best; the nicest; the most attractive; **ce qu'il y a de ~** the best
B *adv* **1** better; **je ne peux pas te dire ~** that's all I can tell you; **qui dit ~?** any other offers?; any advance on that bid?; **de ~ en ~** better and better; **on la critiquait à qui ~ ~** each person criticized her more harshly than the last
2 le ~, la ~, les ~ the best; (of two) the better
C *m inv* **le ~ est de refuser** the best thing is to refuse; **il y a un/du ~** there is an/some improvement; **je ne demande pas ~ que de rester ici** I'm perfectly happy staying here; **fais pour le ~, fais au ~** do whatever is best; **tout va pour le ~** everything's fine; **elle est au ~ avec sa voisine** she is on very good terms with her neighbour (BrE)

mièvre /mjɛvʀ/ *adj* vapid; soppy

mièvrerie /mjɛvʀəʀi/ *f* vapidity; soppiness

mi-figue /mifig/ *adj inv* **~ mi-raisin** ‹*smile*› half-hearted; ‹*compliment*› ambiguous

mignon, **-onne** /miɲɔ̃, ɔn/ *adj* **1** cute
2 sweet, kind

migraine /migʀɛn/ *f* splitting headache

migration /migʀasjɔ̃/ *f* migration

migratoire /migʀatwaʀ/ *adj* migratory

migrer /migʀe/ [**v1**] *vi* to migrate

mi-hauteur: **à mi-hauteur** /amiotœʀ/ *phr* halfway up; halfway down

mi-jambe: **à mi-jambe** /amiʒɑ̃b/ *phr* (up) to one's knees

mijaurée /miʒoʀe/ *f* **ne fais pas ta ~** don't put on such airs

mijoter /miʒɔte/ [**v1**] **A** *vt* (Culin) to prepare
B *vi* (Culin) to simmer

mijoteuse® /miʒɔtøz/ *f* slow cooker

✓ key word

mikado /mikado/ *m* spillikins
mil /mil/ ▶ **mille A**
milice /milis/ *f* militia; ~ **de quartier** local vigilante group
Milice /milis/ *f* **la** ~ the Milice (*French wartime paramilitary organization which collaborated with the Germans against the Resistance*)
milicien, -ienne /milisjɛ̃, ɛn/ *mf* **1** militiaman/militiawoman **2** member of the Milice
milieu, *pl* ~**x** /miljø/ **A** *m* **1** middle; **au beau** *or* **en plein** ~ right in the middle; **au** ~ **de la nuit** in the middle of the night **2** middle ground **3** environment; **en** ~ **rural** in the country **4** background, milieu; **le** ~ the underworld **B au milieu de** *phr* **1** among; **être au** ~ **de ses amis** to be with one's friends **2** surrounded by; **au** ~ **du désastre** in the midst of disaster
militaire /militɛʀ/ **A** *adj* military; army **B** *m* serviceman
militairement /militɛʀmɑ̃/ *adv* **1** by military means; **zone occupée** ~ military occupied zone **2** with military efficiency; along military lines
militant, ~**e** /militɑ̃, ɑ̃t/ **A** *adj* militant **B** *mf* (of organization) active member, activist; (for cause) campaigner
militantisme /militɑ̃tism/ *m* political activism
militariste /militaʀist/ *adj* militaristic
militer /milite/ [**v1**] *vi* **1** to campaign **2** to be a political activist
mille /mil/ **A** *adj inv* a thousand, one thousand; **deux/trois** ~ two/three thousand **B** *m inv* **1** a thousand, one thousand **2** bull's eye; **taper dans le** ~ to hit the bull's eye; (fig) to hit the nail on the head **C** *m* **1** ~ **(marin** *or* **nautique)** (nautical) mile **2** (air) mile **D pour mille** *phr* per thousand
IDIOM **je vous le donne en** ~ you'll never guess (in a million years)
millénaire /milenɛʀ/ **A** *adj* **1 un arbre** ~ a one thousand year-old tree **2** ‹*tradition*› age-old **B** *m* **1 pendant des** ~**s** for thousands of years **2** millennium, millenary
mille-pattes /milpat/ *m inv* centipede, millipede
millésime /milezim/ *m* vintage, year
milli /mili/ *pref* milli-; ~**mètre** millimetre (BrE)
milliard /miljaʀ/ *m* billion
milliardaire /miljaʀdɛʀ/ *mf* multimillionaire, billionaire
millième /miljɛm/ *adj* thousandth
millier /milje/ *m* **1** thousand **2 un** ~ about a thousand
million /miljɔ̃/ *m* million
millionième /miljɔnjɛm/ *adj* millionth
millionnaire /miljɔnɛʀ/ **A** *adj* **être** ~ ‹*firm*› to be worth millions; ‹*person*› to be a millionaire **B** *mf* millionaire
mime /mim/ *m* mime
mimer /mime/ [**v1**] *vt* **1** to mime **2** to mimic
mimétisme /mimetism/ *m* **1** (Zool) mimicry **2 par** ~ through unconscious imitation
mimique /mimik/ *f* funny face
minable /minabl/ *adj* (fam) **1** ‹*salary, person*› pathetic **2** ‹*place*› crummy (fam); ‹*existence*› miserable **3** (drunk) sloshed (fam)
minage /minaʒ/ *m* mining
minaret /minaʀɛ/ *m* minaret
minauder /minode/ [**v1**] *vi* **1** to mince about **2** to simper
mince /mɛ̃s/ *adj* **1** slim, slender; ‹*face, slice*› thin **2** ‹*consolation*› small; ‹*chance*› slim
minceur /mɛ̃sœʀ/ *f* slimness; slenderness; thinness
mincir /mɛ̃siʀ/ [**v3**] *vi* to lose weight
mine /min/ *f* **1** expression; **faire** ~ **d'accepter** to pretend to accept; **elle nous a dit,** ~ **de rien, que** (fam) she told us, casually, that; **il est doué,** ~ **de rien** (fam) it may not be obvious, but he's very clever **2 avoir bonne** ~ ‹*person*› to look well **3** (in pencil) lead **4** mine; ~ **d'or** gold mine **5** (Mil) mine
IDIOM **ne pas payer de** ~ (fam) not to look anything special (fam)
miner /mine/ [**v1**] *vt* **1** to sap ‹*morale, energy*›; to undermine ‹*health*› **2** (Mil) to mine
minerai /minʀɛ/ *m* ore; ~ **de fer** iron ore
minéral, ~**e**, *mpl* **-aux** /mineʀal, o/ **A** *adj* ‹*water*› mineral; ‹*chemistry*› inorganic **B** *m* mineral
minéralogique /mineʀalɔʒik/ *adj* **plaque** ~ number plate (BrE), license plate (AmE)
minerve /minɛʀv/ *f* (Med) surgical collar (BrE), neck brace (AmE)
minet /minɛ/ *m* **1** pussycat **2** (fam) pretty boy (fam)
minette /minɛt/ *f* **1** pussycat **2** (fam) cool chick (fam)
mineur, ~**e** /minœʀ/ **A** *adj* **1** (Law) under 18 **2** ‹*detail*› minor **3** (Mus) **en ré** ~ in D minor **B** *mf* (Law) person under 18 **C** *m* miner; ~ **de fond** pit worker
mini- /mini/ *pref* mini
miniature /minjatyʀ/ *adj, f* miniature

m

miniaturisation /minjatyʀizasjɔ̃/ *f* miniaturization
minibus /minibys/ *m inv* minibus
minicassette® /minikasɛt/ *f* mini cassette®
minier, **-ière** /minje, ɛʀ/ *adj* mining
mini-informatique /miniɛ̃fɔʀmatik/ *f* minicomputing
mini-jupe, *pl* **~s** /miniʒyp/ *f* mini-skirt
minimal, **~e**, *mpl* **-aux** /minimal, o/ *adj* minimal, minimum
minimalisme /minimalism/ *m* minimalism
minime /minim/ **A** *adj* negligible
B *mf* (Sport) junior (*7 to 13 years old*)
minimiser /minimize/ [**v1**] *vt* to minimize
minimoto /minimoto/ *f* Minimoto, pocket bike
minimum, *pl* **~s** *or* **minima** /minimɔm, minima/ **A** *adj* minimum
B *m* **1** minimum; **un ~ de bon sens** a certain amount of common sense; **il faut au ~ deux heures pour faire le trajet** the journey takes at least two hours
2 (Law) minimum sentence
■ **~ vital** subsistence level
mini-ordinateur, *pl* **~s** /miniɔʀdinatœʀ/ *m* minicomputer
minipilule /minipilyl/ *f* low dose combined pill

m

⚷ **ministère** /ministɛʀ/ *m* ministry; (in UK, US) department
ministériel, **-ielle** /ministeʀjɛl/ *adj* ministerial, cabinet
⚷ **ministre** /ministʀ/ *m* **1** minister; (in UK) Secretary of State; (in US) Secretary
2 (of religion) minister
Minitel® /minitel/ *m* Minitel (*terminal linking phone users to a database*)
minitéler /minitele/ [**v14**] *vt* to contact via Minitel
minitéliste /minitelist/ *n* Minitel user
minivague /minivag/ *f* soft perm
minois /minwɑ/ *m inv* fresh young face
minoration /minɔʀasjɔ̃/ *f*
1 undervaluation; underestimation
2 reduction; **~ des prix** cut in prices
minorer /minɔʀe/ [**v1**] *vt* **1** to reduce (**de** by)
2 to undervalue; to underestimate
minoritaire /minɔʀitɛʀ/ *adj* minority
minorité /minɔʀite/ *f* **1** minority; **être mis en ~** to be defeated
2 (age) minority
■ **~ de blocage** blocking minority
minoterie /minɔtʀi/ *f* **1** flour mill
2 flour milling
minou /minu/ *m* pussycat
minuit /minɥi/ *m* midnight
minuscule /minyskyl/ **A** *adj* ‹*person, thing*› tiny; ‹*quantity*› tiny, minute
B *f* small letter; (in printing) lower-case letter
minutage /minytaʒ/ *m* (precise) timing
⚷ **minute** /minyt/ *f* minute; **la ~ de vérité** the moment of truth
minuter /minyte/ [**v1**] *vt* **1** to time
2 to work out the timing of
minuterie /minytʀi/ *f* **1** time switch
2 automatic lighting
minuteur /minytœʀ/ *m* timer
minutie /minysi/ *f* meticulousness
minutieusement /minysjøzmɑ̃/ *adv* with meticulous care; in great detail
minutieux, **-ieuse** /minysjø, øz/ *adj* meticulous; ‹*description*› detailed
mioche /mjɔʃ/ *mf* (fam) kid (fam)
mirabelle /miʀabɛl/ *f* **1** mirabelle (*small yellow plum*)
2 plum brandy
miracle /miʀɑkl/ **A** *adj inv* **un médicament ~** a wonder drug; **une méthode ~** a magic formula
B *m* **1** miracle; **faire un ~** to work a miracle; (fig) to work miracles; **comme par ~** as if by magic
2 miracle play
miraculeux, **-euse** /miʀakylø, øz/ *adj* miraculous; ‹*product, remedy*› which works wonders
mirador /miʀadɔʀ/ *m* watchtower
mirage /miʀaʒ/ *m* mirage
mi-raisin /miʀezɛ̃/ ▶ **mi-figue**
miraud, **~e** /miʀo, od/ *adj* (fam) short-sighted
mirobolant, **~e** /miʀɔbɔlɑ̃, ɑ̃t/ *adj* (fam) fabulous (fam)
⚷ **miroir** /miʀwaʀ/ *m* mirror
miroitement /miʀwatmɑ̃/ *m* sparkling; shimmering
miroiter /miʀwate/ [**v1**] *vi* to shimmer; **faire ~ qch à qn** to hold out the prospect of sth to sb
mis, **~e** /mi, miz/ ▶ **mettre**
misanthrope /mizɑ̃tʀɔp/ **A** *adj* misanthropic
B *mf* misanthropist, misanthrope
⚷ **mise** /miz/ *f* **une ~ de cinq euros** a five euro bet
■ **~ à jour** update; **~ de fonds** investment; **~ en plis** set
(**IDIOM**) **être de ~** ‹*conduct*› to be proper
miser /mize/ [**v1**] **A** *vt* to bet
B *vi* **1** **~ sur** to bet on, to place a bet on
2 **~ sur qn** to place all one's hopes in sb
misérabilisme /mizeʀabilism/ *m* **1** sordid realism
2 tendency to dwell on the dark side
misérable /mizeʀabl/ **A** *adj* **1** ‹*person*› destitute, poor; ‹*life*› poor
2 ‹*salary*› meagre (BrE)
B *mf* **1** pauper

⚷ key word

2 scoundrel

misère /mizɛʀ/ *f* **1** destitution; **réduire qn à la ~** to reduce sb to poverty
2 misery, wretchedness
3 trouble, woe; **on a tous nos petites ~s** we all have our troubles
4 être payé une ~ to be paid a pittance

miséreux, -euse /mizeʀø, øz/ *mf* destitute person; **les ~** the destitute

miséricorde /mizeʀikɔʀd/ *f, excl* mercy

misogyne /mizɔʒin/ *adj* misogynous

misogynie /mizɔʒini/ *f* misogyny

missel /misɛl/ *m* missal

missile /misil/ *m* missile

mission /misjɔ̃/ *f* mission

missionnaire /misjɔnɛʀ/ *adj, mf* missionary

missive /misiv/ *f* missive

mistral /mistʀal/ *m* mistral

mitaine /mitɛn/ *f* fingerless mitten

mite /mit/ *f* (clothes) moth

mi-temps[1] /mitɑ̃/ *m inv* part-time job

mi-temps[2] /mitɑ̃/ *f inv* (Sport) half-time

miteux, -euse /mitø, øz/ *adj* seedy; shabby

mitigé, ~e /mitiʒe/ *adj* ‹*reception*› lukewarm; ‹*success*› qualified

mitonner /mitɔne/ [**v1**] *vt* to cook [sth] lovingly

mitoyen, -enne /mitwajɛ̃, ɛn/ *adj* ‹*hedge*› dividing; **mur ~** party wall

mitraille /mitʀaj/ *f* hail of bullets

mitrailler /mitʀaje/ [**v1**] *vt* **1** to machine-gun
2 ~ qn de questions to fire questions at sb
3 (fam) to take photo after photo of [sb/sth]

mitraillette /mitʀajɛt/ *f* sub-machine gun

mitrailleuse /mitʀajøz/ *f* machine gun

mi-voix: **à mi-voix** /amivwa/ *phr* in a low voice

mixage /miksaʒ/ *m* sound mixing

mixer[1] /mikse/ [**v1**] *vt* to mix

mixer[2] /miksɛʀ/ ▶ **mixeur**

mixeur /miksœʀ/ *m* **1** mixer
2 blender

mixité /miksite/ *f* (gen) mixing of sexes; (Sch) co-education

mixte /mikst/ *adj* **1** ‹*school*› co-educational; ‹*class*› mixed
2 ‹*couple, marriage*› mixed; ‹*economy*› mixed; **société ~** joint venture

mixture /mikstyʀ/ *f* **1** concoction
2 (in pharmacy) mixture
3 mishmash (fam)

MJC /ɛmʒise/ *f* (*abbr* = **maison des jeunes et de la culture**) ≈ youth club

MLF /ɛmɛlɛf/ *m* (*abbr* = **mouvement de libération des femmes**) ≈ Women's Lib

Mlle (*written abbr* = **Mademoiselle**) Ms, Miss

mm (*written abbr* = **millimètre**) mm

MM. (*written abbr* = **Messieurs**) Messrs

Mme (*written abbr* = **Madame**) Ms, Mrs

mnémotechnique /mnemɔtɛknik/ *adj* mnemonic

Mo (*written abbr* = **mégaoctet**) Mb, MB

mobbing /mɔ̃biŋ/ *m: psychological harassment at work*

mobile /mɔbil/ **A** *adj* (gen) mobile; ‹*leaf*› loose
B *m* **1** motive
2 mobile

mobilier, -ière /mɔbilje, ɛʀ/ **A** *adj* **biens ~s** movable property
B *m* furniture

mobilisation /mɔbilizasjɔ̃/ *f* mobilization

mobiliser /mɔbilize/ [**v1**] **A** *vt* to mobilize ‹*soldier*›; to call up ‹*civilian*›
B se mobiliser *v refl* (+ *v être*) to rally

mobilité /mɔbilite/ *f* mobility

mobylette® /mɔbilɛt/ *f* moped

mocassin /mɔkasɛ̃/ *m* moccasin, loafer

moche /mɔʃ/ *adj* (fam) **1** ‹*person*› ugly; ‹*garment*› ghastly
2 ‹*incident*› dreadful
3 ‹*act*› nasty

modalité /mɔdalite/ **A** *f* modality
B modalités *fpl* terms; practical details

mode[1] /mɔd/ *m* **1** way, mode; **~ de paiement** method of payment
2 (in grammar) mood
■ **~ d'emploi** instructions for use

mode[2] /mɔd/ *f* **1** fashion; **lancer une ~** to start a trend; **à la ~** ‹*garment, club*› fashionable; ‹*singer*› popular
2 fashion industry

modèle /mɔdɛl/ **A** *adj* (gen) model; ‹*conduct*› perfect, exemplary
B *m* **1** (gen) model; **prendre ~ sur qn** to do as sb does/did; **~ à suivre** somebody to look up to; **la tente grand ~** the large size tent; **le ~ au-dessus** the next size up; **~ de signature** specimen signature
2 pattern; **~ déposé** registered pattern
■ **~ réduit** scale model

modeler /mɔdle/ [**v17**] *vt* to model ‹*clay*›; to mould (BrE), to mold (AmE) ‹*character*›

modélisme /mɔdelism/ *m* modelling (BrE)

modération /mɔdeʀasjɔ̃/ *f* **1** moderation
2 (in price, tax) reduction

modéré, ~e /mɔdeʀe/ *adj* ‹*political party, speed, words*› moderate; ‹*price*› reasonable; ‹*temperament*› even; ‹*enthusiasm*› mild

modérément /mɔdeʀemɑ̃/ *adv* **1** relatively
2 slightly

modérer /mɔdeʀe/ [**v14**] *vt* to curb ‹*expenses*›; to moderate ‹*language*›; to reduce ‹*speed*›

moderne /mɔdɛʀn/ *adj* modern

moderniser /mɔdɛʀnize/ [**v1**] *vt* to modernize; to update

modernité /mɔdɛʀnite/ *f* modernity

modeste /mɔdɛst/ *adj* ‹*sum, apartment, person*› modest; ‹*cost*› moderate; ‹*background*› humble

modestement /mɔdɛstəmɑ̃/ *adv* modestly

modestie /mɔdɛsti/ *f* modesty

modification /mɔdifikasjɔ̃/ *f* modification

modifier /mɔdifje/ [**v2**] *vt* to change; to alter, to modify

modique /mɔdik/ *adj* ‹*sum, resources*› modest

modiste /mɔdist/ *f* milliner

modulation /mɔdylasjɔ̃/ *f* modulation
■ ~ **de fréquence, MF** frequency modulation, FM

module /mɔdyl/ *m* (gen), (Sch) module

moduler /mɔdyle/ [**v1**] *vt* **1** to modulate
2 to adjust ‹*price*›; to adapt ‹*policy*›

moelle /mwal/ *f* marrow
■ ~ **épinière** spinal cord

moelleux, **-euse** /mwalø, øz/ *adj* **1** ‹*carpet*› thick; ‹*bed*› soft
2 ‹*wine*› mellow

mœurs /mœʀ(s)/ *fpl* **1** customs; habits; lifestyle; **l'évolution des** ~ the change in attitudes
2 morals; **des** ~ **dissolues** loose morals; **la police des** ~, **les Mœurs** (fam) the vice squad
3 (of animals) behaviour
IDIOM **autres temps, autres** ~ other days, other ways

mohair /mɔɛʀ/ *m* mohair

moi¹ /mwɑ/ *pron* **1** I, me; **c'est** ~ it's me
2 me; **pour** ~ for me; **des amis à** ~ friends of mine; **c'est à** ~ it's mine; it's my turn

moi² /mwɑ/ *m* **le** ~ the self

moignon /mwaɲɔ̃/ *m* stump

moi-même /mwɑmɛm/ *pron* myself

moindre /mwɛ̃dʀ/ *adj* **1** lesser; **à** ~ **prix** more cheaply
2 le ~ the least; **je n'en ai pas la** ~ **idée** I haven't got the slightest idea

moine /mwan/ *m* monk
IDIOM **l'habit ne fait pas le** ~ (Proverb) you can't judge a book by its cover

moineau, *pl* ~**x** /mwano/ *m* sparrow

moins¹ /mwɛ̃/ **A** *prep* **1** minus
2 il est huit heures ~ **dix** it's ten (minutes) to eight; **il était** ~ **une** (fam) it was a close shave (fam)
B *adv* (comparative) less; (superlative) **le** ~ the least; **le** ~ **difficile** the less difficult; the least difficult; **de** ~ **en** ~ less and less; ~ **je sors,** ~ **j'ai envie de sortir** the less I go out, the less I feel like going out; **il n'en est pas** ~ **vrai que** it's nonetheless true that; **il ressemble à son frère en** ~ **gros** he looks like his brother, only thinner; **à tout le** ~, **pour le** ~ to say the least; **il y avait deux fourchettes en** ~ **dans la boîte** there were two forks missing from the box
C moins de *quantif* ~ **de livres** fewer books; ~ **de sucre** less sugar; **les** ~ **de 20 ans** people under 20
D à moins de *phr* unless
E à moins que *phr* unless
F au moins *phr* at least
G du moins *phr* at least

moins² /mwɛ̃/ *m inv* minus
■ ~ **que rien** good-for-nothing, nobody

moiré, ~**e** /mwaʀe/ *adj* moiré; watered

mois /mwa/ *m inv* month

moisi /mwazi/ *m* mould (BrE), mold (AmE)

moisir /mwaziʀ/ [**v3**] *vi* ‹*foodstuff*› to go mouldy (BrE) *or* moldy (AmE); ‹*object, plant*› to become mildewed

moisissure /mwazisyʀ/ *f* **1** mould (BrE), mold (AmE)
2 mildew

moisson /mwasɔ̃/ *f* harvest

moissonner /mwasɔne/ [**v1**] *vt* to harvest

moissonneuse /mwasɔnøz/ *f* reaper

moite /mwat/ *adj* ‹*heat*› muggy; ‹*skin*› sweaty

moiteur /mwatœʀ/ *f* (of air) mugginess; (of skin) sweatiness

moitié /mwatje/ *f* half; **à** ~ **vide** half empty

moitié-moitié /mwatjemwatje/ *adv* half-and-half

moka /mɔka/ *m* **1** mocha
2 mocha cake

molaire /mɔlɛʀ/ *f* molar

molécule /mɔlekyl/ *f* molecule

moleskine /mɔlɛskin/ *f* **1** imitation leather
2 moleskin

molester /mɔlɛste/ [**v1**] *vt* to manhandle

molette /mɔlɛt/ *f* (of spanner) adjusting knob

mollasson, **-onne** /mɔlasɔ̃, ɔn/ *adj* (fam) sluggish

molle ▸ **mou A**

mollement /mɔlmɑ̃/ *adv* **1** idly
2 ‹*work*› without much enthusiasm; ‹*protest*› half-heartedly

mollet /mɔlɛ/ **A** *adj m* **œuf** ~ soft-boiled egg
B *m* (Anat) calf

molleton /mɔltɔ̃/ *m* **1** flannel; flannelette
2 (table) felt
3 (ironing board) cover

molletonner /mɔltɔne/ [**v1**] *vt* to line with fleece

mollir /mɔliʀ/ [**v3**] *vi* **1** ‹*courage*› to fail; ‹*resistance*› to grow weaker; ‹*person*› to soften
2 ‹*knees*› to give way; ‹*arm*› to go weak

mollusque /mɔlysk/ *m* mollusc (BrE), mollusk (AmE)

molosse /mɔlɔs/ *m* huge dog

môme /mom/ *mf* (fam) kid (fam); brat (fam)

moment /mɔmɑ̃/ *m* moment; **le** ~ **venu** when the time comes/came; **il devrait arriver d'un** ~ **à l'autre** he should arrive any

key word

minute now; **à un ~ donné** at some point; at a given moment; **à ce ~-là** at that time; just then; in that case; **au ~ où** at the time (when); **au ~ où il quittait son domicile** as he was leaving his home; **jusqu'au ~ où** until; **du ~ que** as long as, provided; **il arrive toujours au bon** *or* **mauvais ~!** he certainly picks his moment to call!; **un ~!** just a moment!; **ça va prendre un ~** it will take a while; **au bout d'un ~** after a while; **par ~s** at times; **les ~s forts du film** the film's highlights; **dans ses meilleurs ~s, il fait penser à Orson Welles** at his best, he reminds one of Orson Welles; **à mes ~s perdus** in my spare time

momentané, **~e** /mɔmɑ̃tane/ *adj* momentary

momentanément /mɔmɑ̃tanemɑ̃/ *adv* for a moment, momentarily

momie /mɔmi/ *f* mummy

mon, **ma**, *pl* **mes** /mɔ̃, ma, mɛ/ *det* my; **j'ai ~ idée** I have my own ideas about that

monacal, **~e**, *mpl* **-aux** /mɔnakal, o/ *adj* monastic

monarchie /mɔnaʀʃi/ *f* monarchy

monarchiste /mɔnaʀʃist/ *adj, mf* monarchist

monarque /mɔnaʀk/ *m* monarch

monastère /mɔnastɛʀ/ *m* monastery

monceau, *pl* **~x** /mɔ̃so/ *m* (of rubbish) pile

mondain, **~e** /mɔ̃dɛ̃, ɛn/ **A** *adj* ‹*life, ball*› society; ‹*conversation*› polite
B *mf* socialite

monde /mɔ̃d/ *m* **1** world; **pas le moins du ~** not in the least; **aller** *or* **voyager de par le ~** to travel the world; **c'est le bout du ~!** it's in the back of beyond!; **ce n'est pas le bout du ~!** it's not such a big deal!; **à la face du ~** for all the world to see; **en ce bas ~** here below; **elle n'est plus de ce ~** she's no longer with us; **je n'étais pas encore au ~** I wasn't yet born; **le ~ médical** the medical world; **le ~ animal** the animal kingdom; **un ~ nous sépare** we are worlds apart
2 people; **tout le ~** everybody; **tout mon petit ~** my family and friends
3 society; **le beau** *or* **grand ~** high society
IDIOMS **se faire un ~ de qch** to get all worked up about sth; **depuis que le ~ est ~** since the beginning of time; **c'est un ~!** (fam) that's a bit much!

mondial, **~e**, *mpl* **-iaux** /mɔ̃djal, o/ *adj* world; ‹*success*› worldwide; **seconde guerre ~e** Second World War

mondialement /mɔ̃djalmɑ̃/ *adv* **être ~ connu** to be world famous

mondialisation /mɔ̃djalizasjɔ̃/ *f* globalization

mondialiser /mɔ̃djalize/ [**v1**] *vt* to globalize; to cause [sth] to spread worldwide

mondialisme /mɔ̃djalism/ *m* internationalism

mondovision /mɔ̃dɔvizjɔ̃/ *f* satellite broadcasting

monétaire /mɔnetɛʀ/ *adj* ‹*system, stability*› monetary; ‹*market*› money

monétariste /mɔnetaʀist/ *adj, mf* monetarist

monétique /mɔnetik/ *f* electronic banking

monétiser /mɔnetize/ [**v1**] *vt* to monetize

Mongolie /mɔ̃gɔli/ *pr f* Mongolia

mongolien, **-ienne** /mɔ̃gɔljɛ̃, ɛn/ (controversial) *mf* Down's syndrome child

moniteur, **-trice** /mɔnitœʀ, tʀis/ **A** *mf*
1 (Aut, Sport) instructor
2 (in holiday camp) group leader (BrE), counselor (AmE)
B *m* **1** (TV) monitor
2 (Comput) monitor system

monitorat /mɔnitɔʀa/ *m* tutoring; tutorial system

monnaie /mɔnɛ/ *f* **1** currency; **fausse ~** forged *or* counterfeit currency
2 change; **faire de la ~** to get some change
3 coin; **battre ~** to mint *or* strike coins; **l'hôtel de la Monnaie, la Monnaie** the Mint
4 (Econ) money
■ **~ d'échange** trading currency; bargaining chip; **~ de papier** paper money
IDIOMS **rendre à qn la ~ de sa pièce** to pay sb back in his/her own coin; **c'est ~ courante** it's commonplace

monnayable /mɔnɛjabl/ *adj* **1** (in finance) convertible
2 ‹*skill, qualification*› marketable

monnayer /mɔnɛje/ [**v21**] *vt* **1** to convert [sth] into cash
2 to capitalize on ‹*talent, experience*›; **~ qch contre qch** to exchange sth for sth

mono¹ /mono/ *pref* mono; **~chrome** monochrome; **~lingue** monolingual

mono² /mono/ *f* (in hi-fi) mono

monocellulaire /mɔnosɛlylɛʀ/ *adj* **famille ~** nuclear family

monocle /mɔnɔkl/ *m* monocle

monocorde /mɔnɔkɔʀd/ *adj* ‹*voice, speech*› monotonous; ‹*instrument*› single-string

monogame /mɔnɔgam/ *adj* monogamous

monogamie /mɔnɔgami/ *f* monogamy

monoï /mɔnɔj/ *m inv* coconut oil (*used in cosmetics*)

monologue /mɔnɔlɔg/ *m* monologue (BrE)
■ **~ intérieur** stream of consciousness

mononucléose /mɔnonykleoz/ *f* mononucleosis; **~ infectieuse** glandular fever

monoparental, **~e**, *mpl* **-aux** /mɔnopaʀɑ̃tal, o/ *adj* **famille ~e** single-parent family

monopole /mɔnɔpɔl/ *m* monopoly

monopoliser /mɔnɔpɔlize/ [**v1**] *vt* to monopolize

monoprocesseur /mɔnopʀɔsɛsœʀ/ *m* single-chip computer

monoski /mɔnɔski/ *m* **1** monoski
2 monoskiing

monothéiste /mɔnɔteist/ *adj* monotheistic

monotone /mɔnɔtɔn/ *adj* monotonous

monotonie /mɔnɔtɔni/ *f* monotony

monoxyde /mɔnɔksid/ *m* monoxide

Monseigneur, *pl* **Messeigneurs** /mɔ̃sɛɲœʀ, mesɛɲœʀ/ *m* Your Highness; Your Eminence; **~ le duc de Parme** His Grace, the duke of Parma

🔑 **monsieur**, *pl* **messieurs** /məsjø, mesjø/ *m*
1 (addressing a man whose name you do not know) **Monsieur** (in a letter) Dear Sir; **bonjour ~!** good morning!
2 (addressing a man whose name you know, for instance Hallé) **Monsieur** (in a letter) Dear Mr Hallé; **bonjour ~!** good morning, Mr Hallé
3 (polite form of address) **'Monsieur a sonné?'** 'you rang, sir?'
4 man; **le double messieurs** the men's doubles; **c'était un (grand) ~!** he was a (true) gentleman!
■ **~ Tout le Monde** the man in the street

monstre /mɔ̃stʀ/ **A** *adj* (fam) ‹*task, success, publicity*› huge; ‹*nerve*› colossal
B *m* **1** monster
2 freak (of nature)
■ **~ marin** sea monster

monstrueux, -euse /mɔ̃stʀyø, øz/ *adj*
1 ‹*crime, cruelty*› monstrous
2 hideous; **d'une laideur monstrueuse** hideously ugly
3 ‹*error*› colossal

monstruosité /mɔ̃stʀyozite/ *f* **1** (of conduct) monstrousness
2 atrocity
3 monstrosity; **dire des ~s** to say preposterous things

mont /mɔ̃/ *m* mountain
■ **le ~ Blanc** Mont Blanc

montage /mɔ̃taʒ/ *m* **1** set-up
2 (of machine) assembly; (of tent) putting up; **chaîne de ~** assembly line
3 (of film) editing; **salle de ~** cutting room
4 (of gem) setting
■ **~ photo** photomontage; **~ sonore** sound montage

montagnard, **~e** /mɔ̃taɲaʀ, aʀd/ **A** *adj* ‹*people, plant*› mountain; ‹*custom*› highland
B *mf* mountain dweller

🔑 **montagne** /mɔ̃taɲ/ *f* **1** mountain
2 la ~ the mountains; **de ~** ‹*road, animal*› mountain; **il neige en haute ~** it's snowing on the upper slopes
■ **~s russes** big dipper, roller coaster
IDIOM **se faire une ~ de qch** to get really worked up about sth

montagneux, -euse /mɔ̃taɲø, øz/ *adj* mountainous

🔑 key word

montant, **~e** /mɔ̃tɑ̃, ɑ̃t/ **A** *adj* **1** ‹*cabin, group*› going up
2 ‹*road*› uphill
3 ‹*neck*› high; ‹*socks*› long; **chaussures ~es** ankle boots
B *m* **1** sum; **le ~ des pertes** the total losses; **d'un ~ de** ‹*deficit, savings*› amounting to; ‹*cheque*› to the amount of; ‹*goods*› for a total of
2 (of door, window) upright, jamb; transom; (of scaffolding) pole; (of ladder) upright

mont-de-piété, *pl* **monts-de-piété** /mɔ̃dpjete/ *m* pawnshop, pawnbroker's

monte-charge /mɔ̃tʃaʀʒ/ *m inv* goods lift (BrE) *or* elevator (AmE)

montée /mɔ̃te/ *f* **1** (up slope) climb; (of mountain) ascent
2 (of plane) climb
3 rising; rise; **la ~ des eaux** the rise in the water level; **une brusque ~ d'adrénaline** a rush of adrenaline
4 (in prices) rise; (in danger) increase
5 hill; **une légère ~** a slight slope

🔑 **monter** /mɔ̃te/ [**v1**] **A** *vt* (+ *v avoir*) **1** to take [sb/sth] up; to take [sb/sth] upstairs; to bring [sb/sth] up; to bring [sb/sth] upstairs; **impossible de ~ le piano par l'escalier** it's impossible to get the piano up the stairs
2 to put [sth] up; to raise ‹*shelf*›
3 to go up [sth]; **~ la colline à bicyclette** to cycle up the hill
4 to turn up ‹*volume, gas*›
5 ~ les blancs en neige beat *or* whisk the egg whites until stiff
6 ~ qn contre qn to set sb against sb
7 to ride ‹*horse*›
8 (Zool) to mount
9 to assemble ‹*appliance, unit*›; to put up ‹*tent, scaffolding*›; **~ un film** to edit a film
10 to hatch ‹*plot*›; to set up ‹*company*›; to stage ‹*play*›; **monté de toutes pièces** ‹*story*› fabricated from beginning to end
B *vi* (+ *v être*) **1** to go up; to go upstairs; to come up; to come upstairs; ‹*plane*› to climb; ‹*bird*› to fly up; ‹*sun, mist*› to rise; **tu es monté à pied?** did you walk up?; did you come up on foot?; **~ sur** to get onto ‹*footpath*›; to climb onto ‹*stool*›; **~ à l'échelle** to climb (up) the ladder; **faites-les ~** send them up
2 ~ dans une voiture/dans un train to get in a car/on a train; **~ sur** to get on ‹*bike, horse*›
3 ‹*road*› to go uphill, to climb; ‹*ground*› to rise; **~ jusqu'à** ‹*path, wall*› to go up to; **~ en lacets** to wind its way up
4 ‹*garment, water*› to come up (**jusqu'à** to)
5 ‹*temperature, price*› to rise, to go up; ‹*tide*› to come in
6 ~ à *or* **sur Paris** to go up to Paris
7 ~ (à cheval) to ride
8 (Mil) **~ à l'assaut** *or* **l'attaque** to mount an attack
9 ‹*employee*› to rise, to move up; ‹*artist*› to rise

10 ‹*anger, emotion*› to mount; ‹*tears*› to well up; **le ton monta** the discussion became heated
11 **~ à la tête de qn** to go to sb's head
12 (Aut, Tech) **~ à 250 km/h** to go up to 250 km/h
IDIOM **se ~ la tête** (fam) to get worked up (fam)

monteur, **-euse** /mɔ̃tœʀ, øz/ *mf* **1** fitter
2 (in film-making) editor
3 paste-up artist

montgolfière /mɔ̃gɔlfjɛʀ/ *f* hot-air balloon

monticule /mɔ̃tikyl/ *m* **1** hillock
2 mound

montrable /mɔ̃tʀabl/ *adj* ‹*person*› presentable; ‹*images*› suitable for viewing

montre /mɔ̃tʀ/ *f* watch; **trois heures ~ en main** three hours exactly

Montréal /mɔ̃ʀeal/ *pr n* Montreal

montrer /mɔ̃tʀe/ [**v1**] **A** *vt* **1** to show; **~ qch à qn** to show sb sth
2 to show ‹*feelings, knowledge*›
3 ‹*person*› to point out ‹*track, place, object*›; ‹*survey, table*› to show ‹*trend, results*›; **~ qn du doigt** to point at sb; to point the finger at sb
B **se montrer** *v refl* (+ *v être*) **1** to show oneself to be; to prove (to be); **il faut se ~ optimiste** we must try to be optimistic
2 ‹*person*› to show oneself; ‹*sun*› to come out
IDIOMS **~ les dents** to bare one's teeth; **~ le bout de son nez** to show one's face; to peep through

monture /mɔ̃tyʀ/ *f* **1** (for rider) mount
2 (of glasses) frames; (of ring) setting

monument /mɔnymɑ̃/ *m* **1** monument
2 (historic) building; **visiter les ~s de Paris** to see the sights of Paris
3 **un des ~s de la littérature européenne** a masterpiece of European literature
■ **~ historique** ancient monument; **~ aux morts** war memorial

monumental, **~e**, *mpl* **-aux** /mɔnymɑ̃tal, o/ *adj* monumental

moquer: **se moquer** /mɔke/ [**v1**] *v refl* (+ *v être*) **1** **se ~ de** to make fun of
2 **se ~ de** not to care about
3 **se ~ du monde** to take people for fools

moquerie /mɔkʀi/ *f* **1** mocking remark
2 mockery

moquette /mɔkɛt/ *f* wall-to-wall carpet

moqueur, **-euse** /mɔkœʀ, øz/ *adj* mocking

moral, **~e** *mpl* **-aux** /mɔʀal, o/ **A** *adj* **1** moral; **n'avoir aucun sens ~** to have no sense of right and wrong
2 ‹*torture*› mental; ‹*support*› moral
3 ‹*person*› moral; ‹*conduct*› ethical
B *m* **1** morale; **avoir le ~** to be in good spirits; **avoir le ~ à zéro** (fam) to feel very down; **remonter le ~ de qn** to raise sb's spirits
2 mind; **au ~ comme au physique** mentally and physically

morale /mɔʀal/ *f* **1** morality; **leur ~** their moral code
2 moral; **faire la ~ à qn** to give sb a lecture
3 **la ~** moral philosophy, ethics

moralement /mɔʀalmɑ̃/ *adv* **1** morally, ethically
2 psychologically

moralisant, **~e** /mɔʀalizɑ̃, ɑ̃t/ *adj* moralizing

moralisateur, **-trice** /mɔʀalizatœʀ, tʀis/ *adj* moralizing, moralistic

moraliser /mɔʀalize/ [**v1**] *vt* to clean up; to reform

moraliste /mɔʀalist/ *mf* moralist

moralité /mɔʀalite/ *f* **1** morals
2 (of action) morality
3 moral; **~, ne faites confiance à personne** the moral is: don't trust anybody

morbide /mɔʀbid/ *adj* morbid

morbidité /mɔʀbidite/ *f* morbidity

morceau, *pl* **~x** /mɔʀso/ *m* **1** piece, bit; **~ de sucre** sugar lump; **manger un ~** (fam) to have a snack
2 (of meat) cut; **bas ~** cheap cut
3 (Mus) piece; **~ de piano** piano piece
4 (from book) extract
IDIOM **recoller les ~x** to patch things up

morceler /mɔʀsəle/ [**v19**] *vt* to divide [sth] up

mordant, **~e** /mɔʀdɑ̃, ɑ̃t/ **A** *adj* **1** caustic, scathing
2 ‹*cold*› biting
B *m* **1** sarcasm
2 (fam) (of person, team) zip (fam)

mordiller /mɔʀdije/ [**v1**] *vt* to nibble at

mordoré, **~e** /mɔʀdɔʀe/ *adj* golden brown

mordre /mɔʀdʀ/ [**v6**] **A** *vt* to bite
B **mordre à** *v+prep* **~ à l'appât** *or* **l'hameçon** to take the bait
C *vi* **1** **~ dans une pomme** to bite into an apple
2 **~ sur** to go over ‹*white line*›; to encroach on ‹*territory*›
3 (fam) to fall for it (fam)
D **se mordre** *v refl* (+ *v être*) **se ~ la langue** to bite one's tongue
IDIOM **je m'en suis mordu les doigts** I could have kicked myself

mordu, **~e** /mɔʀdy/ **A** *adj* (fam) **1** **être ~ de qch** to be mad about sth (fam)
2 smitten
B *mf* (fam) fan; **les ~s du ski** skiing fans

morfondre: **se morfondre** /mɔʀfɔ̃dʀ/ [**v6**] *v refl* (+ *v être*) **1** **se ~ à attendre** *or* **en attendant** to wait dejectedly
2 to pine

morgue /mɔʀg/ *f* **1** morgue; (hospital) mortuary
2 arrogance

moribond, **~e** /mɔʀibɔ̃, ɔ̃d/ **A** *adj* ‹*person*› dying; ‹*civilization*› moribund
B *mf* dying man/woman

morille /mɔʀij/ *f* morel (mushroom)
morne /mɔʀn/ *adj* **1** gloomy; ‹*face*› glum
2 ‹*landscape, life*› dreary
morose /mɔʀoz/ *adj* morose; gloomy
morosité /mɔʀozite/ *f* gloom
morphine /mɔʀfin/ *f* morphine
morphologie /mɔʀfɔlɔʒi/ *f* morphology
morpion /mɔʀpjɔ̃/ *m* noughts and crosses (BrE), tick-tack-toe (AmE)
mors /mɔʀ/ *m inv* bit; **prendre le ~ aux dents** to take the bit between its/one's teeth
morse /mɔʀs/ *m* **1** walrus
2 (code) ~ Morse code
morsure /mɔʀsyʀ/ *f* **1** bite; **~ de chien** dog bite
2 la ~ du froid the biting cold
⚷ **mort¹** /mɔʀ/ *f* death; **mourir de sa belle ~** to die peacefully in old age; **il n'y a pas eu ~ d'homme** there were no fatalities; **trouver la ~** to die; **mise à ~** (of condemned) killing; (of bull) dispatch; **à ~** ‹*fight*› to the death; ‹*war*› ruthless; ‹*brake, squeeze*› like mad (fam)
■ **~ cérébrale** brain death
IDIOM **la ~ dans l'âme** with a heavy heart
⚷ **mort²**, **~e** /mɔʀ, mɔʀt/ **A** *pp* ▶ **mourir**
B *pp adj* **1** dead
2 je suis ~ de froid I'm freezing to death; **je suis ~** (fam) I'm dead tired
3 ‹*district*› dead; ‹*season*› slack
4 ‹*civilization*› dead; ‹*city*› lost
C *mf* dead person, dead man/woman
D *m* **1** fatality; **il y a eu 12 ~s** there were 12 dead
2 body; **faire le ~** to play dead; to lie low
IDIOM **ne pas y aller de main ~e** (fam) not to pull any punches
mortalité /mɔʀtalite/ *f* mortality
mort-aux-rats /mɔʀɔʀa/ *f inv* rat poison
mortel, **-elle** /mɔʀtɛl/ **A** *adj* **1** ‹*blow, illness*› fatal; ‹*poison*› lethal; ‹*venom*› deadly
2 ‹*cold*› deathly
3 ‹*enemy*› mortal
4 ‹*person, meeting*› deadly boring
5 ‹*being*› mortal
B *mf* mortal
mortellement /mɔʀtɛlmɑ̃/ *adv* **1** ‹*injured*› fatally
2 ‹*boring*› deadly
mortier /mɔʀtje/ *m* mortar
mort-né, **~e**, *mpl* **~s** /mɔʀne/ *adj*
1 stillborn
2 ‹*plan*› abortive
mortuaire /mɔʀtɥɛʀ/ *adj* **cérémonie ~** funeral ceremony; **veillée ~** wake
morue /mɔʀy/ *f* cod
morve /mɔʀv/ *f* nasal mucus, snot (sl)
mosaïque /mɔzaik/ *f* mosaic
Moscou /mɔsku/ *pr n* Moscow

⚷ key word

mosquée /mɔske/ *f* mosque
⚷ **mot** /mo/ *m* **1** word; **à ~s couverts** in veiled terms; **au bas ~** at least; **il est bête et le ~ est faible!** he's stupid and that's putting it mildly!; **dire un ~ à qn** to have a word with sb; **il ne dit jamais un ~ plus haut que l'autre** he never raises his voice; **avoir son ~ à dire** to be entitled to one's say
2 note; **je t'ai laissé un ~** I left you a note
■ **~ d'esprit** witticism; **~ d'ordre** watchword; **~ d'ordre de grève** strike call; **~ de passe** password; **~s croisés** crossword; **~s doux** sweet nothings
IDIOMS **ne pas avoir peur des ~s** to call a spade a spade; **manger ses ~s** to mumble; **se donner le ~** to pass the word around
motard, **~e** /mɔtaʀ, aʀd/ **A** *mf* (fam) biker (fam)
B *m* police motorcyclist
mot-clé, *pl* **mots-clés** /mokle/ *m* key word
⚷ **moteur**, **-trice** /mɔtœʀ, tʀis/ **A** *adj* **1** ‹*force, principle*› driving; **la voiture a quatre roues motrices** the car has four-wheel drive
2 (Med) **troubles ~s** motor problems
B *m* **1** motor
2 engine
3 être le ~ de qch to be the driving force behind sth
■ **~ éolien** wind turbine
⚷ **motif** /mɔtif/ *m* **1** grounds; **des ~s d'espérer** grounds for hope
2 reason
3 motive
4 pattern; **à ~ floral** with a floral pattern
motion /mɔsjɔ̃/ *f* motion
motivant, **~e** /mɔtivɑ̃, ɑ̃t/ *adj* ‹*salary*› attractive; ‹*work*› rewarding
motivation /mɔtivasjɔ̃/ *f* **1** motivation
2 motive; **~s profondes** deeper motives
motivé, **~e** /mɔtive/ *adj* **1** motivated
2 ‹*complaint*› justifiable
motiver /mɔtive/ [**v1**] *vt* **1** to motivate
2 to lead to ‹*decision, action*›; **motivé par** caused by
moto /moto/ *f* **1** (motor)bike
2 motorcycling
motocyclette /motosiklɛt/ *f* motorcycle
motocyclisme /motosiklism/ *m* motorcycle racing
motocycliste /motosiklist/ **A** *adj* motorcycle
B *mf* motorcyclist
motoneige /motonɛʒ/ *f* snowmobile
motoriser /mɔtɔʀize/ [**v1**] *vt* to motorize; **être motorisé** (fam) to have transport (BrE) *or* transportation (AmE)
motrice ▶ **moteur A**
motte /mɔt/ *f* **~ (de terre)** clod (of earth); **~ de gazon** sod, piece of turf; **~ (de beurre)** slab of butter
motus /mɔtys/ *excl* (fam) **~ (et bouche cousue)!** keep it under your hat!

mou, **mol** *before vowel or mute h*, **molle** /mu, mɔl/ **A** *adj* **1** ‹*substance, cushion*› soft; ‹*blow*› dull
2 ‹*stomach*› flabby
3 ‹*person*› listless; ‹*growth*› sluggish
4 ‹*parent*› soft
5 ‹*speech*› feeble
B *m* **1** wimp (fam)
2 (in butchery) lights (BrE), lungs (AmE)
3 (in rope) slack; **donner du ~ à qn** (fam) to give sb a bit of leeway

mouchard, **~e** /muʃaʀ, aʀd/ **A** *mf* (fam)
1 grass (BrE) (fam), informer
2 sneak (fam)
B *m* **1** tachograph
2 spyhole

moucharder /muʃaʀde/ [**v1**] *vt* (fam) **1 ~ qn** to inform on sb; to squeal (fam) on sb
2 to sneak (fam)

mouche /muʃ/ *f* **1** fly
2 patch, beauty spot
3 bull's eye; **faire ~** to hit the bull's eye; (fig) to be right on target
4 (Sport) (on foil) button
■ **~ verte** greenbottle; **~ du vinaigre** fruit fly
IDIOMS **quelle ~ les a piqués?** (fam) what's got (BrE) *or* gotten (AmE) into them?; **prendre la ~** to fly off the handle

moucher /muʃe/ [**v1**] **A** *vt* **~ qn** to blow sb's nose; (fig, fam) to put sb in their place
B **se moucher** *v refl* (+ *v être*) to blow one's nose
IDIOM **il ne se mouche pas du pied** *or* **du coude** (fam) he's full of airs and graces

moucheron /muʃʀɔ̃/ *m* midge

moucheté, **~e** /muʃte/ *adj* **1** ‹*material*› flecked; ‹*plumage, fish*› speckled; ‹*coat*› spotted
2 (Sport) ‹*foil*› buttoned

mouchoir /muʃwaʀ/ *m* handkerchief; tissue

moudre /mudʀ/ [**v77**] *vt* to grind

moue /mu/ *f* pout; **faire la ~** to pout; (doubtfully) to pull a face

mouette /mwɛt/ *f* (sea)gull

moufle /mufl/ *f* mitten

mouiller /muje/ [**v1**] **A** *vt* **1** to wet; to get [sth] wet
2 to drop ‹*anchor*›; to lay ‹*mine*›
B *vi* to anchor, to drop anchor
C **se mouiller** *v refl* (+ *v être*) to get wet

mouillette /mujɛt/ *f* (fam) soldier (fam), finger of bread (*eaten with a boiled egg*)

moulage /mulaʒ/ *m* **1** casting; **faire un ~ de qch** to take a cast of sth
2 (of grain) milling

moulant, **~e** /mulɑ̃, ɑ̃t/ *adj* tight-fitting

moule¹ /mul/ *m* **1** mould (BrE), mold (AmE)
2 tin, pan (AmE); **~ à gaufre** waffle iron

moule² /mul/ *f* mussel

mouler /mule/ [**v1**] *vt* **1** to mould (BrE), to mold (AmE) ‹*substance*›; to cast ‹*bronze*›; to mint ‹*medal*›
2 to take a cast of
3 ‹*garment*› to hug

moulin /mulɛ̃/ *m* mill
■ **~ à paroles** (fam) chatterbox; **~ à vent** windmill
IDIOMS **apporter de l'eau au ~ de qn** to fuel sb's arguments; **on ne peut être à la fois au four et au ~** one can't be in two places at once; **on y entre comme dans un ~** (fam) one can just slip in

mouliner /muline/ [**v1**] *vt* to grind, to mill

moulinet /mulinɛ/ *m* **faire des ~s avec les bras** to wave one's arms about

moulu, **~e** /muly/ **A** *pp* ▶ **moudre**
B *pp adj* ‹*coffee, pepper*› ground
C *adj* (fam) **~ (de fatigue)** worn out

moumoute /mumut/ *f* (fam) **1** toupee
2 sheepskin jacket

mourant, **~e** /muʀɑ̃, ɑ̃t/ *adj* ‹*person, animal*› dying; ‹*light*› fading; ‹*voice*› faint

mourir /muʀiʀ/ [**v34**] *vi* (+ *v être*) to die; **~ de froid** to die of exposure; to die of cold; **je meurs de soif/de froid** I'm dying of thirst/freezing to death; **c'était à ~ (de rire)!** it was hilarious!; **~ debout** to be active to the end
IDIOMS **partir c'est ~ un peu** to say goodbye is to die a little; **je ne veux pas ~ idiot** (fam) I want to know

mouroir /muʀwaʀ/ *m* (derog) old people's home, twilight home

mousquetaire /muskətɛʀ/ *m* musketeer

mousqueton /muskətɔ̃/ *m* snap clasp

moussant, **~e** /musɑ̃, ɑ̃t/ *adj* ‹*gel*› foaming

mousse¹ /mus/ *m* ship's apprentice

mousse² /mus/ *f* **1** moss
2 foam; (from soap) lather; (on milk) froth; (on beer) head
3 ~ au chocolat chocolate mousse
4 foam rubber
■ **~ carbonique** fire foam; **~ à raser** shaving foam

mousseline /muslin/ *f* **1** muslin
2 chiffon

mousser /muse/ [**v1**] *vi* to foam; to lather
IDIOM **se faire ~** (fam) to blow one's own trumpet

mousseux, **-euse** /musø, øz/ *adj* **1** ‹*wine*› sparkling; ‹*beer*› fizzy
2 ‹*lace*› frothy

mousson /musɔ̃/ *f* monsoon

moustache /mustaʃ/ **A** *f* moustache (BrE), mustache (AmE)
B **moustaches** *fpl* (Zool) whiskers

moustachu, **~e** /mustaʃy/ *adj* ‹*person*› with a moustache (BrE) *or* mustache (AmE)

moustiquaire /mustikɛʀ/ *f* mosquito net

moustique /mustik/ *m* mosquito

moutarde /mutaʀd/ *adj inv*, *f* mustard
IDIOM **la ~ me monte au nez!** (fam) I'm beginning to see red!

mouton /mutɔ̃/ **A** *m* **1** sheep

2 mutton
3 sheepskin
4 (derog) sheep
B **moutons** *mpl* **1** small fleecy clouds
2 whitecaps
3 fluff
■ ~ **à cinq pattes** rare bird
IDIOM **revenons à nos ~s** (fam) let's get back to the point

mouture /mutyʀ/ *f* **1** (of coffee) grind
2 première/nouvelle ~ first/new version

mouvant, **~e** /muvɑ̃, ɑ̃t/ *adj* **1** ‹*ground*› unstable
2 ‹*group*› shifting
3 ‹*opinion*› changing

✓ **mouvement** /muvmɑ̃/ *m* **1** (gen) movement; **faire un ~** to move; **~ perpétuel** perpetual motion; **accélérer le ~** to speed up
2 bustle; **suivre le ~** (fig) to follow the crowd
3 impulse, reaction; **un ~ de colère** a surge of anger
4 **le ~ étudiant** the student protest movement; **~ de grève** strike, industrial action
5 **le ~ des idées** the evolution of ideas; **un milieu en ~** a changing environment
6 (Econ) **le ~ du marché** market fluctuations; **~ de hausse** upward trend

mouvementé, **~e** /muvmɑ̃te/ *adj* **1** ‹*life, week, trip*› eventful, hectic
2 ‹*terrain*› rough

mouvoir: **se mouvoir** /muvwaʀ/ [**v43**] *v refl* (+ *v être*) to move

✓ **moyen**, **-enne** /mwajɛ̃, ɛn/ **A** *adj*
1 medium; medium-sized
2 ‹*income*› middle; ‹*level*› intermediate
3 average, mean; **le Français ~** the average Frenchman
B *m* **1** means, way (**de faire** of doing); **employer les grands ~s** to resort to drastic measures; **(il n'y a) pas ~ de lui faire comprendre qu'il a tort** it's impossible to make him realize he's wrong
2 (of expression, production) means; (of investigation, payment) method
C **au moyen de** *phr* by means of
D **par le moyen de** *phr* by means of
E **moyens** *mpl* **1** means; **faute de ~s** through lack of money; **avoir de petits ~s** not to be very well off
2 resources; **donner à qn les ~s de faire** to give sb the means to do
3 ability; **perdre ses ~s** to go to pieces
■ ~ **de locomotion** *or* **transport** means of transport (BrE) *or* transportation (AmE); **Moyen Âge** Middle Ages

moyenâgeux, **-euse** /mwajɛnɑʒø, øz/ *adj*
1 medieval
2 antiquated

moyen-courrier, *pl* **~s** /mwajɛ̃kuʀje/ *m* medium-haul airliner

✓ key word

moyennant /mwajɛnɑ̃/ *prep* **~ finances** for a fee; **~ quoi** in view of which; in return for which

moyenne /mwajɛn/ **A** *adj f* ▶ **moyen**
B *f* **1** average; **la ~ d'âge** the average age; **en ~** on average
2 half marks (BrE), 50%
3 (Aut) average speed

moyennement /mwajɛnmɑ̃/ *adv* ‹*intelligent, wealthy*› moderately; ‹*like*› to a certain extent

Moyen-Orient /mwajɛnɔʀjɑ̃/ *pr m* Middle East

moyeu, *pl* **~x** /mwajø/ *m* hub

MST /ɛmɛste/ *f*: *abbr* ▶ **maladie**

mû, **mue** /my/ ▶ **mouvoir**

mucoviscidose /mykovisidoz/ *f* cystic fibrosis

mucus /mykys/ *m inv* mucus

mue /my/ *f* **1** (of insect) metamorphosis; (of reptile) sloughing of the skin; (of bird, mammal) moulting (BrE), molting (AmE); (of stag) casting
2 (of snake, insect) slough, sloughed skin
3 breaking (BrE) *or* changing (AmE) of voice

muer /mɥe/ [**v1**] **A** *vi* **1** ‹*insect*› to metamorphose; ‹*snake*› to slough its skin; ‹*bird, mammal*› to moult (BrE), to molt (AmE)
2 sa voix mue, il mue his voice is breaking (BrE) *or* changing (AmE)
B **se muer** *v refl* (+ *v être*) **1** to be transformed
2 to transform oneself

muet, **-ette** /mɥɛ, ɛt/ **A** *adj* **1** dumb; speechless
2 ‹*witness*› silent
3 ‹*vowel, consonant*› mute
4 ‹*film*› silent; ‹*role*› non-speaking
B *mf* mute

mufle /myfl/ **A** *adj* boorish, loutish
B *m* **1** (Zool) muffle; muzzle
2 boor, lout

muflerie /myfləʀi/ *f* boorishness

mugir /myʒiʀ/ [**v3**] *vi* **1** to low; to bellow
2 ‹*wind*› to howl; ‹*siren*› to wail; ‹*torrent*› to roar

mugissement /myʒismɑ̃/ *m* **1** (of cow) lowing; (of bull, ox) bellowing
2 (of wind) howling; (of waves) roar

muguet /mygɛ/ *m* lily of the valley

mulâtre /mylɑtʀ/ *adj* mulatto

mule /myl/ *f* **1** female mule
2 (slipper) mule

mulet /mylɛ/ *m* (male) mule

mulot /mylo/ *m* field mouse

multi /mylti/ *pref* multi-; **~colore** multicoloured (BrE); **~media** multimedia; **~programmation** multiple programming

multicarte /myltikaʀt/ *adj inv* **représentant ~** representative for several firms

multifonction /myltifɔ̃ksjɔ̃/ *adj inv* multipurpose; (Comput) multifunction

multipare /myltipaʀ/ *adj* multiparous

multiple /myltipl/ **A** *adj* **1** ‹*reasons, occasions*› numerous, many; ‹*births*› multiple; **à choix ~** multiple-choice
2 ‹*causes, facets*› many, various
3 (in science) multiple
B *m* multiple

multipliable /myltiplijabl/ *adj* multiplicable

multiplication /myltiplikasjɔ̃/ *f* **1 ~ de** increase in the number of
2 (in mathematics, science) multiplication

multiplicité /myltiplisite/ *f* multiplicity

multiplier /myltiplije/ [**v2**] **A** *vt* **1** to multiply
2 to increase ‹*risks, fortune*›; to increase the number of ‹*trains, accidents*›
B se multiplier *v refl* (+ *v être*)
1 ‹*branches, villas*› to grow in number; ‹*incidents*› to be on the increase; ‹*difficulties*› to increase
2 ‹*animals, germs*› to multiply

multipropriété /myltipʀɔpʀijete/ *f* timesharing

multirisque /myltiʀisk/ *adj* **assurance ~** comprehensive insurance

multisalle /myltisal/ *adj inv* **cinéma ~** cinema complex, multiplex

multitude /myltityd/ *f* **1 une ~ de** a mass of ‹*tourists, objects*›; a lot of ‹*reasons, ideas*›
2 multitude, throng

municipal, **~e**, *mpl* **-aux** /mynisipal, o/ *adj* ‹*council*› local, town; city; ‹*park, pool*› municipal; **arrêté ~** bylaw

municipales /mynisipal/ *fpl* local elections

municipalité /mynisipalite/ *f*
1 municipality
2 town council; city council

munir /myniʀ/ [**v3**] **A** *vt* to provide; **~ un bâtiment d'un escalier de secours** to put a fire escape on a building; **muni de** fitted with
B se munir *v refl* (+ *v être*) **se ~ de** to bring; to take

munitions /mynisjɔ̃/ *fpl* ammunition

muqueuse /mykøz/ *f* mucous membrane

mur /myʀ/ **A** *m* wall; **faire les pieds au ~** to do a handstand against the wall; (fig) to tie oneself up in knots
B murs *mpl* (of business) premises; (of palace, embassy) confines; **être dans ses ~s** to own one's own house
■ **~ portant** *or* **porteur** load-bearing wall; **~ du son** sound barrier; **Mur des lamentations** Wailing Wall
IDIOMS **faire le ~** to go over the wall; **mettre qn au pied du ~** to call sb's bluff; **être au pied du ~** to be up against the wall

mûr, **~e** /myʀ/ *adj* **1** ripe
2 mature; **l'âge ~** middle age; **après ~e réflexion** after careful consideration
3 ready; **il est ~ pour des aveux** he's ready to confess
4 ‹*situation*› at a decisive stage
IDIOM **en voir des vertes et des pas ~es** (fam) to go through a lot

muraille /myʀɑj/ *f* great wall

mural, **~e**, *mpl* **-aux** /myʀal, o/ *adj* ‹*covering, map*› wall; ‹*plant*› climbing

mûre /myʀ/ **A** *adj f* ▶ **mûr**
B *f* blackberry

mûrement /myʀmɑ̃/ *adv* **~ réfléchi** carefully thought through

murer /myʀe/ [**v1**] *vt* to build a wall around [sth]; to brick [sth] up; to block [sth] off

muret /myʀɛ/ *m* low wall

mûrier /myʀje/ *m* mulberry tree

mûrir /myʀiʀ/ [**v3**] **A** *vt* **1** to ripen ‹*fruit*›
2 to mature ‹*person*›; to develop ‹*plan*›
B *vi* **1** ‹*fruit*› to ripen
2 ‹*person, talent*› to mature; ‹*plan, idea*› to evolve; ‹*passion*› to develop
3 ‹*abscess*› to come to a head

murmure /myʀmyʀ/ *m* **1** murmur
2 ~s mutterings
3 (of wind) whisper

murmurer /myʀmyʀe/ [**v1**] **A** *vt* **1** to murmur
2 to say; **on murmure qu'il est riche** he is rumoured (BrE) to be rich
B *vi* ‹*person*› to murmur; ‹*wind*› to whisper

musaraigne /myzaʀɛɲ/ *f* (Zool) shrew

musc /mysk/ *m* musk

muscade /myskad/ *f* nutmeg

muscle /myskl/ *m* muscle

musclé, **~e** /myskle/ *adj* **1** muscular
2 ‹*music, speech*› powerful; ‹*reaction*› strong; ‹*intervention*› tough
3 (Econ) competitive

muscler /myskle/ [**v1**] **A** *vt* **1 ~ les bras** to develop the arm muscles
2 to strengthen
B se muscler *v refl* (+ *v être*) to develop one's muscles

musculaire /myskylɛʀ/ *adj* muscle; muscular

musculation /myskylasjɔ̃/ *f* **(exercices de) ~** (gen) bodybuilding; (Med) exercises to strengthen the muscles; **salle de ~** weights room

musculature /myskylatyʀ/ *f* musculature

muse /myz/ *f* **1** Muse
2 (fig) muse

museau, *pl* **~x** /myzo/ *m* **1** muzzle; snout; nose
2 (fam) face

musée /myze/ *m* museum; art gallery (BrE), art museum (AmE); **une ville ~** a city of great historical and artistic importance

museler /myzəle/ [**v19**] *vt* to muzzle

muselière /myzəljɛʀ/ *f* muzzle

musette[1] /myzɛt/ *m* accordion music

musette[2] /myzɛt/ *f* **1** haversack
2 lunch bag

m

muséum /myzeɔm/ *m* ~ **(d'histoire naturelle)** natural history museum

musical, **~e**, *mpl* **-aux** /myzikal, o/ *adj* ‹*event*› musical; ‹*critic*› music; ‹*choice*› of music

music-hall, *pl* **~s** /mysikol/ *m* music hall

musicien, **-ienne** /myzisjɛ̃, ɛn/ **A** *adj* musical
B *mf* musician

🔑 **musique** /myzik/ *f* music; **travailler en ~** to work with music in the background; **mettre en ~** to set [sth] to music; **faire de la ~** to play an instrument; **une ~ de film** a film score
(IDIOMS) **connaître la ~** (fam) to know the score (fam); **je ne peux pas aller plus vite que la ~** (fam) I can't go any faster than I'm already going; **être réglé comme du papier à ~** (fam) ‹*person*› to be as regular as clockwork; ‹*conference, project*› to go very smoothly

🔑 **musulman**, **~e** /myzylmɑ̃, an/ *adj*, *mf* Muslim

mutabilité /mytabilite/ *f* mutability

mutant, **~e** /mytɑ̃, ɑ̃t/ *adj*, *mf* mutant

mutation /mytasjɔ̃/ *f* **1** transfer
2 transformation; **en pleine ~** undergoing radical transformation
3 mutation

muter /myte/ [**v1**] *vt* to transfer ‹*official*›

mutilation /mytilasjɔ̃/ *f* mutilation

mutilé, **~e** /mytile/ *mf* disabled person; **~ de guerre** disabled war veteran

mutiler /mytile/ [**v1**] *vt* to mutilate

mutin, **~e** /mytɛ̃, in/ **A** *adj* mischievous
B *m* mutineer; rioter

mutiner: **se mutiner** /mytine/ [**v1**] *v refl* (+ *v être*) to mutiny; to riot

mutinerie /mytinʀi/ *f* mutiny; riot

mutisme /mytism/ *m* silence

mutuel, **-elle** /mytɥɛl/ *adj* mutual

mutuelle /mytɥɛl/ *f* mutual insurance company

mutuellement /mytɥɛlmɑ̃/ *adv* mutually; **s'aider ~** to help each other

myopathe /mjɔpat/ *mf* myopathy patient

myopathie /mjɔpati/ *f* myopathy

myope /mjɔp/ *adj* short-sighted (BrE), near-sighted (AmE)

myopie /mjɔpi/ *f* short-sightedness (BrE), near-sightedness (AmE)

myosotis /mjɔzɔtis/ *m inv* forget-me-not

myriade /miʀjad/ *f* myriad (**de** of)

myrrhe /miʀ/ *f* myrrh

myrtille /miʀtij/ *f* bilberry, blueberry

🔑 **mystère** /mistɛʀ/ *m* **1** mystery
2 secrecy
3 rite

mystérieusement /misteʀjøzmɑ̃/ *adv* mysteriously

mystérieux, **-ieuse** /misteʀjø, øz/ *adj* mysterious

mysticisme /mistisism/ *m* mysticism

mystification /mistifikasjɔ̃/ *f* **1** hoax
2 myth

mystique /mistik/ **A** *adj* mystical
B *f* **1** mysticism
2 mystique
3 blind belief

mythe /mit/ *m* myth

mythique /mitik/ *adj* mythical

mythologie /mitɔlɔʒi/ *f* mythology

mythologique /mitɔlɔʒik/ *adj* mythological

mythomane /mitɔman/ *adj*, *mf* mythomaniac

Nn

n, **N** /ɛn/ **A** *m inv* **1** (letter) n, N
2 **n°** (*written abbr* = **numéro**) no
B **N** *f* (*abbr* = **nationale**) **la N7** the N7

n' ▸ **ne**

nabot, **~e** /nabo, ɔt/ *mf* (offensive) dwarf

NAC *mpl* (*abbr* = **nouveaux animaux de compagnie**) exotic pets

nacelle /nasɛl/ *f* **1** (of hot-air balloon) gondola
2 carrycot (BrE), carrier (AmE)
3 (of worker) cradle

nacre /nakʀ/ *f* mother-of-pearl

nacré, **~e** /nakʀe/ *adj* pearly

nage /naʒ/ *f* **1** swimming; **200 mètres quatre ~s** 200 metres (BrE) medley; **traverser à la ~** to swim across
2 **être en ~** to be in a sweat
■ **~ indienne** sidestroke; **~ libre** freestyle

nageoire /naʒwaʀ/ *f* **1** (of fish) fin
2 (of seal) flipper

nager /naʒe/ [**v13**] **A** *vt* to swim
B *vi* **1** to swim
2 (fig) **~ dans le bonheur** to bask in

🔑 key word

contentment; **elle nage dans sa robe** her dress is far too big for her
3 (fam) to be absolutely lost
IDIOM **~ entre deux eaux** to run with the hare and hunt with the hounds

nageur, **-euse** /naʒœʀ, øz/ *mf* swimmer

naguère /nagɛʀ/ *adv* **1** quite recently
2 formerly

naïf, **naïve** /naif, iv/ *adj* naïve

nain, **~e** /nɛ̃, nɛn/ **A** *adj* ‹*tree*› dwarf; ‹*dog*› miniature
B *mf* dwarf

naissance /nɛsɑ̃s/ *f* **1** (gen) birth; (of rumour) start; **de ~** ‹*Italian, French*› by birth; ‹*deaf*› from birth; **à ma ~** when I was born
2 à la ~ du cou at the base of the neck

naissant, **~e** /nɛsɑ̃, ɑ̃t/ *adj* new

naître /nɛtʀ/ [**v74**] *vi* (+ *v être*) **1** to be born; **elle est née le 5 juin** she was born on 5 June; **le bébé doit ~ à la fin du mois** the baby is due at the end of the month; **l'enfant à ~** the unborn baby *or* child; **je l'ai vu ~** (fig) I have known him since he was a baby
2 (fig) ‹*idea*› to be born; ‹*company*› to come into existence; ‹*love*› to spring up; ‹*day*› to break; **faire ~** to give rise to ‹*hope*›; **voir ~** to see the birth of ‹*newspaper, century*›

naïve ▸ **naïf**

naïvement /naivmɑ̃/ *adv* naively; artlessly

naïveté /naivte/ *f* naivety

nanisme /nanism/ *m* dwarfism

nantir /nɑ̃tiʀ/ [**v3**] *vt* **~ qn de** to provide sb with; to award [sth] to sb

nantis /nɑ̃ti/ *mpl* **les ~** the well-off

naphtaline /naftalin/ *f* mothballs

nappe /nap/ *f* **1** tablecloth
2 (of oil, gas) layer; (of water, fire) sheet; (of fog) blanket

napper /nape/ [**v1**] *vt* (Culin) to coat; to glaze

napperon /napʀɔ̃/ *m* mat

narcisse /naʀsis/ *m* (flower) narcissus

narcissisme /naʀsisism/ *m* narcissism

narco /naʀko/ *pref also* **narco-** drug; **~-dollars/-trafiquant** drug money/trafficker

narcotique /naʀkɔtik/ *adj, m* narcotic

narguer /naʀge/ [**v1**] *vt* to taunt ‹*person*›

narine /naʀin/ *f* nostril

narquois, **~e** /naʀkwa, az/ *adj* mocking

narrateur, **-trice** /naʀatœʀ, tʀis/ *mf* narrator

narratif, **-ive** /naʀatif, iv/ *adj* narrative

narration /naʀasjɔ̃/ *f* narration

narrer /naʀe/ [**v1**] *vt* to relate

nasal, **~e**, *mpl* **-aux** /nazal, o/ *adj* nasal; **hémorragie ~e** heavy nosebleed

naseau, *pl* **~x** /nazo/ *m* nostril

nasillard, **~e** /nazijaʀ, aʀd/ *adj* ‹*voice*› nasal; ‹*instrument*› tinny

nasillement /nazijmɑ̃/ *m* nasal twang

nasiller /nazije/ [**v1**] *vi* **1** to speak with a nasal voice
2 ‹*duck*› to quack

nasse /nas/ *f* **1** keepnet
2 (fig) net

natal, **~e**, *mpl* **~s** /natal/ *adj* native

nataliste /natalist/ *adj* ‹*policy*› pro birth

natalité /natalite/ *f* **(taux de) ~** birth rate

natation /natasjɔ̃/ *f* swimming

natif, **-ive** /natif, iv/ *adj* **~ de** native of

nation /nasjɔ̃/ *f* nation
■ **les Nations unies** the United Nations

national, **~e** *mpl* **-aux** /nasjɔnal, o/ *adj* national

nationale /nasjɔnal/ *f* ≈ A road (BrE), highway (AmE)

nationalisation /nasjɔnalizasjɔ̃/ *f* nationalization

nationaliser /nasjɔnalize/ [**v1**] *vt* to nationalize

nationalisme /nasjɔnalism/ *m* nationalism

nationalité /nasjɔnalite/ *f* nationality

nativité /nativite/ *f* nativity

natte /nat/ *f* **1** plait (BrE), braid (AmE)
2 mat

natter /nate/ [**v1**] *vt* to plait

naturalisation /natyʀalizasjɔ̃/ *f* naturalization

naturalisé, **~e** /natyʀalize/ *adj* naturalized

naturaliser /natyʀalize/ [**v1**] *vt* to naturalize ‹*foreigner, species*›; to assimilate ‹*word, custom*›

naturalisme /natyʀalism/ *m* naturalism

nature /natyʀ/ **A** *adj inv* **1** ‹*yoghurt*› plain; ‹*tea*› black
2 (fam) ‹*person*› natural
B *f* **1** nature; **protection de la ~** protection of the environment; **en pleine ~** in the heart of the countryside; **lâcher qn dans la ~** to leave sb in the middle of nowhere; (fig) to let sb loose
2 de ~ à faire likely to do; **des offres de toute ~** offers of all kinds
3 peindre d'après ~ to paint from life; **plus vrai que ~** larger than life
4 en ~ ‹*pay*› in kind
■ **~ humaine** human nature; **~ morte** still life; ▸ **petit**

naturel, **-elle** /natyʀɛl/ **A** *adj* natural
B *m* **1** nature, disposition; **être d'un ~ craintif** to be timid by nature
2 il manque de ~ he's not very natural
3 au ~ ‹*rice*› plain; ‹*tuna*› in brine

naturellement /natyʀɛlmɑ/ *adv* **1** (by nature) naturally
2 (obviously) of course

naturisme /natyʀism/ *m* nudism

naturiste /natyʀist/ *mf* naturist (BrE), nudist

naufrage /nofʀaʒ/ *m* shipwreck, sinking; **faire ~** ‹*ship*› to be wrecked; ‹*sailor*› to be shipwrecked; ‹*company*› to collapse

naufragé, **~e** /nofʀaʒe/ **A** *adj* shipwrecked

B *mf* survivor (of a shipwreck); castaway
nauséabond, **~e** /nozeabɔ̃, ɔ̃d/ *adj* sickening, nauseating
nausée /noze/ *f* nausea
nautique /notik/ *adj* ‹*science*› nautical; ‹*sports*› water
nautisme /notism/ *m* water sports
naval, **~e**, *mpl* **~s** /naval/ *adj* **1** ‹*industry*› shipbuilding
2 (Mil) naval
navet /navɛ/ *m* **1** turnip
2 rubbishy film (BrE), turkey (AmE) (fam)
navette /navɛt/ *f* shuttle; shuttle service; **faire la ~** (to work) to commute
■ **~ spatiale** space shuttle
navigable /navigabl/ *adj* navigable
navigant, **~e** /navigɑ̃, ɑ̃t/ *adj* **personnel ~** (on plane) flight personnel; (Naut) seagoing personnel; **mécanicien ~** flight engineer
navigateur, **-trice** /navigatœʀ, tʀis/ *mf*
1 navigator
2 sailor
3 (Comput) browser
navigation /navigasjɔ̃/ *f* navigation
■ **~ de plaisance** boating; yachting
naviguer /navige/ [**v1**] *vi* **1** ‹*ship, sailor*› to sail; ‹*pilot, plane*› to fly; **en état de ~** ‹*ship*› seaworthy
2 to navigate
3 (Comput) to browse; **~ sur l'Internet** to surf the Internet
n ✓ **navire** /naviʀ/ **A** *m* ship
B **navire-** (*combining form*) **~-école/-usine** training/factory ship; **~s-citernes** tankers
■ **~ amiral** flagship; **~ de guerre** warship
navrant, **~e** /navʀɑ̃, ɑ̃t/ *adj* **1** depressing
2 distressing
navré, **~e** /navʀe/ *adj* **je suis vraiment ~** I am terribly sorry; **avoir l'air ~** to look sad
nazi, **~e** /nazi/ *adj*, *mf* Nazi
nazisme /nazism/ *m* Nazism
✓ **ne** /nə/, **n'** *before vowel or mute h adv*

> In cases where *ne* is used with *pas, jamais, guère, rien, plus, aucun, personne* etc, one should consult the corresponding entry.
> *ne + verb + que* is treated in the entry below.

je n'ai que 20 euros I've only got 20 euros; **il n'y a que lui pour être aussi désagréable** only he can be so unpleasant; **tu n'es qu'un raté** you're nothing but a loser (fam); **je n'ai que faire de tes conseils** you can keep your advice
né, **~e** /ne/ **A** *pp* ▸ **naître**
B *pp adj* **bien ~** high-born; **Madame Masson ~e Roux** Mrs Masson née Roux
C **(-)né** (*combining form*) **musicien(-)/écrivain(-)~** born musician/writer

✓ key word

✓ **néanmoins** /neɑ̃mwɛ̃/ *adv* nevertheless
néant /neɑ̃/ *m* **1 le ~** nothingness; **réduire à ~** to destroy ‹*argument, hopes*›
2 'revenus: ~' 'income: nil'
nébuleux, **-euse** /nebylø, øz/ *adj* **1** ‹*sky*› cloudy
2 ‹*idea*› vague, nebulous
✓ **nécessaire** /nesesɛʀ/ **A** *adj* necessary (à for); **plus qu'il n'est ~** more than is necessary; **les voix ~s pour renverser le gouvernement** the votes needed in order to overthrow the government
B *m* **1 faire le ~** to do what is necessary
2 essentials; **le strict ~** the bare essentials
■ **~ de couture** sewing kit; **~ à ongles** manicure set; **~ de toilette** toiletries
nécessairement /nesesɛʀmɑ̃/ *adv* necessarily; **passe-t-on ~ par Oslo?** do you have to go via Oslo?
✓ **nécessité** /nesesite/ *f* **1** necessity; **~ urgente** urgent need; **~ de qch/de faire/d'être** need for sth/to do/to be; **de première ~** vital; **par ~** out of necessity; **être dans la ~ de faire** to have no choice but to do
2 need; **être dans la ~** to be in need
IDIOM **~ fait loi** (Proverb) necessity knows no law
nécessiter /nesesite/ [**v1**] *vt* to require
nécessiteux, **-euse** /nesesitø, øz/ *mf* needy person; **les ~** the needy
nec plus ultra /nɛkplyzyltʀa/ *m inv* **le ~** the last word (**de** in)
nécrologie /nekʀɔlɔʒi/ *f* deaths column
nécrologique /nekʀɔlɔʒik/ *adj* obituary
nectar /nɛktaʀ/ *m* nectar
néerlandais, **~e** /neɛʀlɑ̃dɛ, ɛz/ **A** *adj* Dutch
B *m* (language) Dutch
Néerlandais, **~e** /neɛʀlɑ̃dɛ, ɛz/ *mf* Dutchman/Dutchwoman; **les ~** the Dutch
nef /nɛf/ *f* nave; **~ latérale** side aisle
néfaste /nefast/ *adj* harmful
✓ **négatif**, **-ive** /negatif, iv/ **A** *adj* negative
B *m* negative
négation /negasjɔ̃/ *f* **1** negation
2 (in grammar) negative
négative /negativ/ **A** *adj f* ▸ **négatif A**
B *f* **répondre par la ~** to reply in the negative
négativement /negativmɑ̃/ *adv* negatively
négligé, **~e** /negliʒe/ **A** *adj* ‹*person*› sloppy; ‹*house*› neglected; ‹*injury*› untreated
B *m* negligee
négligeable /negliʒabl/ *adj* ‹*amount*› negligible; ‹*person*› insignificant
négligemment /negliʒamɑ̃/ *adv*
1 nonchalantly
2 carelessly
négligence /negliʒɑ̃s/ *f* **1** negligence
2 oversight

négligent, **~e** /neglizɑ̃, ɑ̃t/ *adj* ‹*employee*› negligent, careless; ‹*glance*› casual

négliger /neglize/ [**v13**] **A** *vt* (gen) to neglect; to leave untreated ‹*cold*›; to ignore ‹*rule*›; **une offre qui n'est pas à ~** an offer that's worth considering; **~ de faire** to fail to do
B **se négliger** *v refl* (+ *v être*) **1** not to take care over one's appearance
2 not to look after oneself

négoce /negɔs/ *m* trade (**avec** with)

négociable /negɔsjabl/ *adj* negotiable

négociant, **~e** /negɔsjɑ̃, ɑ̃t/ *mf* merchant; wholesaler

négociateur, **-trice** /negɔsjatœʀ, tʀis/ *mf* negotiator

négociation /negɔsjasjɔ̃/ *f* negotiation

négocier /negɔsje/ [**v2**] *vt*, *vi* to negotiate

nègre /nɛgʀ/ *m* **1** (offensive) Negro
2 ghostwriter

négresse /negʀɛs/ *f* (offensive) Negress

négritude /negʀityd/ *f* black identity, Negritude

négroïde /negʀɔid/ *adj* Negroid

neige /nɛʒ/ *f* snow; **~ fondue** slush; sleet; **aller à la ~** to go skiing; **blancs battus en ~** stiffly beaten egg whites
IDIOM **être blanc comme ~** to be completely innocent

neiger /neʒe/ [**v13**] *v impers* to snow

nénuphar /nenyfaʀ/ *m* water lily

néo /neo/ *pref* neo-

néologisme /neɔlɔʒism/ *m* neologism

néon /neɔ̃/ *m* **1** neon
2 neon light

néo-zélandais, **~e** /neozelɑ̃dɛ, ɛz/ *adj* New Zealand

Néo-Zélandais, **~e** /neozelɑ̃dɛ, ɛz/ *mf* New Zealander

népotisme /nepɔtism/ *m* nepotism

nerf /nɛʀ/ **1** nerve; **être malade des ~s** to suffer from nerves
2 spirit, go (fam); **redonner du ~ à qn** to put new heart into sb
IDIOMS **jouer avec les ~s de qn** to be deliberately annoying; **ses ~s ont lâché** he/she went to pieces; **avoir les ~s à fleur de peau** to have frayed nerves; **avoir les ~s en pelote** (fam) *or* **en boule** (fam) *or* **à vif** to be really wound up; **être sur les ~s, avoir ses ~s** (fam) to be on edge; **taper** (fam) *or* **porter sur les ~s de qn** to get on sb's nerves; **être à bout de ~s** to be at the end of one's tether *or* rope (AmE); **passer ses ~s sur** (fam) **qn/qch** to take it out on sb/sth; **l'argent est le ~ de la guerre** money is the sinews of war

nerveusement /nɛʀvøzmɑ̃/ *adv* **1** ‹*wait*› nervously
2 **être épuisé ~** to be suffering from nervous exhaustion

nerveux, **-euse** /nɛʀvø, øz/ **A** *adj* **1** ‹*person*› tense
2 ‹*engine*› responsive; ‹*horse*› vigorous
3 (Anat) ‹*cell*› nerve; ‹*system*› nervous
B *mf* nervous person

nervosité /nɛʀvozite/ *f* **1** nervousness
2 excitability
3 (of engine) responsiveness

nervure /nɛʀvyʀ/ *f* (of leaf) nervure

n'est-ce pas /nɛspa/ *adv* **c'est joli, ~?** it's pretty, isn't it?; **~ qu'il est gentil?** isn't he nice?

net, **nette** /nɛt/ **A** *adj* **1** ‹*price, weight*› net
2 ‹*change*› marked; ‹*tendency*› distinct
3 ‹*victory, memory*› clear; ‹*situation*› clear-cut; ‹*handwriting*› neat; ‹*break*› clean; **en avoir le cœur ~** to be clear in one's mind about it
4 ‹*house, hands*› clean; (fig) ‹*conscience*› clear; **faire place nette** to clear everything away
B *adv* ‹*stop*› dead; ‹*kill*› outright; ‹*refuse*› flatly; **la corde a cassé ~** the rope snapped

Net /nɛt/ *m* **le ~** the Net

netiquette /netikɛt/ *f* netiquette

nettement /nɛtmɑ̃/ *adv* **1** ‹*increase, deteriorate*› markedly; ‹*dominate*› clearly; ‹*prefer*› definitely
2 ‹*see, say*› clearly; ‹*refuse*› flatly; ‹*remember*› distinctly

netteté /nɛtte/ *f* **1** (of image, features) sharpness; (of result, statement) definite nature
2 (of place) cleanness; (of work) neatness

nettoyage /netwajaʒ/ *m* **1** clean(up); **~ de printemps** spring-cleaning
2 cleaning; (of skin) cleansing; **~ à sec** dry-cleaning
3 **opération de ~** (fam) (by army, police) mopping-up operation

nettoyant /nɛtwajɑ̃/ *m* cleaning agent

nettoyer /netwaje/ [**v23**] *vt* **1** (gen) to clean; to clean up ‹*garden*›; to clean out ‹*river*›; to clean off ‹*stain*›
2 (fig) ‹*police*› to clean up ‹*town*›

neuf[1] /nœf/ *adj inv*, *pron*, *m inv* nine

neuf[2], **neuve** /nœf, nœv/ **A** *adj* new; **tout ~** brand new; **'état ~'** 'as new'
B *m inv* new; **quoi de ~?** what's new?; **habillé de ~** dressed in new clothes; **faire du ~ avec du vieux** to revamp things
IDIOM **faire peau neuve** to undergo a transformation

neurasthénie /nøʀasteni/ *f* depression

neurasthénique /nøʀastenik/ *mf* depressive

neuro /nøʀo/ *pref* neuro-

neurone /nøʀɔn/ *m* neurone

neutralisation /nøtʀalizasjɔ̃/ *f* neutralization

neutraliser /nøtʀalize/ [**v1**] *vt* to neutralize

neutralité /nøtʀalite/ *f* neutrality

neutre /nøtʀ/ *adj* neutral; neuter; **~ en carbone** carbon neutral

neutron /nøtʀɔ̃/ *m* neutron

neuvième /nœvjɛm/ **A** *adj* ninth
B *f* (Sch) *third year of primary school, age 8–9*

neveu, *pl* **~x** /n(ə)vø/ *m* nephew

névralgie /nevʀalʒi/ *f* neuralgia

névralgique /nevʀalʒik/ *adj* **1** neuralgic
2 point ~ key point

névrose /nevʀoz/ *f* neurosis

névrosé, **~e** /nevʀoze/ *adj, mf* neurotic

New York /njujɔʀk/ *pr n* **1** New York City
2 l'État de ~ New York (State)

✓ **nez** /ne/ *m* nose; **~ en trompette** turned-up nose; **ça sent le parfum à plein ~** (fam) there's a strong smell of perfume; **je n'ai pas mis le ~ dehors** (fam) I didn't set foot outside; **mettre le ~ à la fenêtre** (fam) to show one's face at the window; **lever le ~** to look up; **tu as le ~ dessus** (fam) it's staring you in the face; **avoir du ~, avoir le ~ fin** (fig) to be shrewd
IDIOMS **mener qn par le bout du ~** (fam) to have sb under one's thumb; **avoir qn dans le ~** (fam) to have it in for sb; **avoir un coup** *or* **verre dans le ~** (fam) to have had one too many (fam); **au ~ (et à la barbe) de qn** right under sb's nose; **filer** *or* **passer sous le ~ de qn** to slip through sb's fingers; **se casser le ~** (fam) to fail

NF /ɛnɛf/ *adj, f* (*abbr* = **norme française**) French manufacturing standard

✓ **ni** /ni/ *conj* nor, or; **elle ne veut ~ ne peut changer** she doesn't want to change, nor can she; **elle ne veut pas le voir ~ lui parler** she doesn't want to see him or talk to him; **~... ~** neither... nor; **~ l'un ~ l'autre** neither of them; **il ne m'a dit ~ oui ~ non** he didn't say yes or no
IDIOMS **~ vu ~ connu** (fam) on the sly (fam); **c'est ~ fait ~ à faire** (fam) it's a botched job (fam); **il n'a fait ~ une ~ deux** (fam) he didn't have a second's hesitation

niais, **~e** /njɛ, njɛz/ *adj* stupid

niaiserie /njɛzʀi/ *f* **1** stupidity
2 stupid *or* inane remark

nicaraguayen, **-enne** /nikaʀagwajɛ̃, ɛn/ *adj* Nicaraguan

niche /niʃ/ *f* **1** kennel, doghouse (AmE)
2 recess; (for statue) niche
3 (fam) trick

nichée /niʃe/ *f* (of birds) brood; (of mice) litter

nicher /niʃe/ [**v1**] **A** *vi* **1** ‹*bird*› to nest
2 (fam) ‹*person*› to live
B se nicher *v refl* (+ *v être*) **1** ‹*bird*› to nest
2 ‹*person, cottage*› to nestle

nickel /nikɛl/ **A** *adj* (fam) spotless
B *m* nickel

nicotine /nikɔtin/ *f* nicotine

nid /ni/ *m* nest
■ **~ d'aigle** eyrie; **~ d'ange** snuggle suit; **~ à poussière** dust trap; **~ de résistance** pocket of resistance

nid-d'abeilles, *pl* **nids-d'abeilles** /nidabɛj/ *m* honeycomb weave

nid-de-poule, *pl* **nids-de-poule** /nidpul/ *m* pothole

nièce /njɛs/ *f* niece

nième /ɛnjɛm/ ▶ **énième**

nier /nje/ [**v2**] *vt* to deny ‹*fact, existence*›

nigaud, **~e** /nigo, od/ *adj* silly

nigérian, **~e** /niʒeʀjɑ̃, an/ *adj* Nigerian

nigérien, **-ienne** /niʒeʀjɛ̃, ɛn/ *adj* of Niger

nihiliste /niilist/ *adj, mf* nihilist

nîmois, **~e** /nimwa, az/ *adj* of Nîmes

nipper: **se nipper** /nipe/ [**v1**] *v refl* (+ *v être*) (fam) to get rigged out in one's Sunday best (fam)

nippes /nip/ *fpl* (fam) rags (fam), old clothes

nippon, **-onne** /nipɔ̃, ɔn/ *adj* Japanese

✓ **niveau**, *pl* **~x** /nivo/ *m* (gen) level; (of knowledge, education) standard; **au ~ du sol** at ground level; **être de ~** to be level; **arrivé au ~ du bus, il...** when he drew level with the bus he...; **bâtiment sur deux ~x** two-storey (BrE) *or* two-story (AmE) building; **'~ bac + 3'** baccalaureate or equivalent plus 3 years' higher education; **de haut ~** ‹*athlete*› top; ‹*candidate*› high-calibre (BrE); **au plus haut ~** ‹*discussion*› top-level
■ **~ de langue** register; **~ social** social status; **~ sonore** sound level; **~ de vie** standard of living

nivelage /nivlaʒ/ *m* standardization

niveler /nivle/ [**v19**] *vt* **1** to level ‹*ground*›
2 to bring [sth] to the same level ‹*salaries*›; **~ par le bas/haut** to level down/up

nobiliaire /nɔbiljɛʀ/ *adj* nobiliary

✓ **noble** /nɔbl/ **A** *adj* (gen) noble; ‹*family*› aristocratic; ‹*person*› of noble birth
B *mf* nobleman/noblewoman

noblement /nɔbləmɑ̃/ *adv* **1** nobly
2 handsomely

noblesse /nɔblɛs/ *f* nobility; **la petite ~** the gentry

noce /nɔs/ *f* **1** (fam) party; **faire la ~** (fig, fam) to live it up (fam), to party (fam)
2 wedding party
3 ~s wedding

noceur, **-euse** /nɔsœʀ, øz/ *mf* (fam) party animal (fam)

nocif, **-ive** /nɔsif, iv/ *adj* noxious, harmful

noctambule /nɔktɑ̃byl/ *mf* night owl

nocturne[1] /nɔktyʀn/ *adj* ‹*attack*› night; ‹*animal*› nocturnal; **la vie ~ à Londres** nightlife in London

nocturne[2] /nɔktyʀn/ *f* **1** (in sport) evening fixture
2 (of shop) late-night opening

Noël /nɔɛl/ *m* Christmas; **'Joyeux ~'** 'Merry Christmas'; **de ~** ‹*tree, gift*› Christmas

✓ key word

nœud /nø/ *m* **1** (gen) knot; **faire un ~ de cravate** to tie a tie
2 (of matter) crux; (of play) core
■ **~ coulant** slip knot; **~ papillon** bow tie; **~ de vipères** nest of vipers

noir, **~e** /nwaʀ/ **A** *adj* **1** (gen) black; ‹*eyes*› dark; ‹*person, race*› black; **être ~ de coups** to be black and blue; **être ~ de monde** to be swarming with people
2 ‹*street*› dark; **il fait ~** it's dark
3 ‹*year*› bad, bleak; ‹*poverty*› dire; ‹*idea*› gloomy, dark
4 ‹*look*› black; ‹*plot, design*› evil, dark; **se mettre dans une colère ~e** to fly into a towering rage
B *m* **1** (colour) black
2 avoir du ~ sur le visage to have a black mark on one's face
3 darkness
4 au ~ ‹*sell*› on the black market; **travailler au ~** to work without declaring one's earnings; to moonlight (fam)
5 (fam) **un (petit) ~** an espresso
IDIOM **voir tout en ~** to look on the black side (of things)

Noir, **~e** /nwaʀ/ *mf* black man/woman

noirâtre /nwaʀɑtʀ/ *adj* blackish

noiraud, **~e** /nwaʀo, od/ *adj* swarthy

noirceur /nwaʀsœʀ/ *f* (gen) blackness; (of hair, night, eyes) darkness

noircir /nwaʀsiʀ/ [v3] **A** *vt* **1** ‹*coal*› to make [sth] dirty; ‹*smoke*› to blacken
2 (fig) **~ du papier** to scribble away; **~ la situation** to paint a black picture of the situation
B *vi* ‹*banana*› to go black; ‹*wall*› to get dirty; ‹*metal*› to tarnish; ‹*person*› to get brown
C se noircir *v refl* (+ *v être*) ‹*sky*› to darken; **se ~ le visage** to blacken one's face

noire /nwaʀ/ **A** *adj f* ▸ **noir A**
B *f* (Mus) crotchet (BrE), quarter note (AmE)

noise /nwaz/ *f* **chercher ~** *or* **des ~s à qn** to pick a quarrel with sb

noisetier /nwaztje/ *m* hazel (tree)

noisette /nwazɛt/ *f* **1** hazelnut
2 ~ de beurre small knob of butter

noix /nwa/ *f inv* **1** walnut (BrE), English walnut (AmE)
2 ~ de beurre knob of butter
■ **~ de cajou** cashew nut; **~ de coco** coconut; **~ (de) muscade** nutmeg

nom /nɔ̃/ **A** *m* **1** name; **petit ~** first name; **~ et prénom** full name; **donner un ~ à** to name; **sans ~** unspeakable; **George Sand, de son vrai ~ Aurore Dupin** George Sand, whose real name was Aurore Dupin; **parler en son propre ~** to speak for oneself
2 noun
B au nom de *phr* **1** in the name of
2 on behalf of
■ **~ de baptême** Christian name; **~ d'emprunt** pseudonym; **~ de famille** surname; **~ de jeune fille** maiden name
IDIOMS **traiter qn de tous les ~s** (fam) to call sb all the names under the sun; **appeler les choses par leur ~** to call a spade a spade

nomade /nɔmad/ *mf* nomad

nombre /nɔ̃bʀ/ *m* number; **un ~ à deux chiffres** a two-digit number; **un certain ~ de** some; **être en ~ inférieur** ‹*players*› to be fewer in number; ‹*group*› to be smaller; **ils étaient au ~ de 30** there were 30 of them; **écrasé sous le ~** (of people) overcome by sheer weight of numbers; (of letters) overwhelmed by the sheer volume; **bon ~ de** a good many; **~ de fois** many times

nombreux, **-euse** /nɔ̃bʀø, øz/ *adj* ‹*population, collection*› large; ‹*people, objects*› numerous, many; **ils étaient peu ~** there weren't many of them; **ils ont répondu ~ à l'appel** a great many people responded to the appeal; **les touristes deviennent trop ~** the number of tourists is becoming excessive

nombril /nɔ̃bʀil/ *m* navel; **elle se prend pour le ~ du monde** (fam) she thinks she's God's gift to mankind

nombrilisme /nɔ̃bʀilism/ *m* (fam) navel-gazing (fam)

nombriliste /nɔ̃bʀilist/ *adj* (fam) egocentric

nomenclature /nɔmɑ̃klatyʀ/ *f* nomenclature; (in dictionary) word list

nominal, **~e**, *mpl* **-aux** /nɔminal, o/ *adj* (gen) nominal; ‹*list*› of names

nominatif, **-ive** /nɔminatif, iv/ **A** *adj* ‹*list*› of names; ‹*invitation*› personal; ‹*share*› registered
B *m* nominative

nomination /nɔminasjɔ̃/ *f* **1** appointment
2 letter of appointment
3 (controversial) nomination

nominativement /nɔminativmɑ̃/ *adv* by name

nominer /nɔmine/ [v1] *vt* to nominate

nommément /nɔmemɑ̃/ *adv* specifically, by name

nommer /nɔme/ [v1] **A** *vt* **1** to appoint; **être nommé à Paris** to be posted to Paris
2 to name ‹*person*›; to call ‹*thing*›; **pour ne ~ personne** to mention no names
B se nommer *v refl* (+ *v être*) **1** to be called
2 to give one's name

non /nɔ̃/ **A** *adv* **1** no; **'tu y vas?'—'~'** 'are you going?'—'no, I'm not'; **ah, ça ~!** definitely not!; **faire ~ de la tête** to shake one's head; **je pense que ~** I don't think so; **je te dis que ~** no, I tell you; **il paraît que ~** apparently not; **tu trouves ça drôle? moi ~** do you think that's funny? I don't; **~ sans raison** not without reason; **~ moins difficile** just as difficult; **qu'il soit d'accord ou ~** whether he agrees or not; **tu viens, oui ou ~?** are you coming or not?; **sois un peu plus poli, ~ mais!** (fam) be a bit more polite, for

heaven's sake!
2 non; ~ **alcoolisé** nonalcoholic; ~ **négligeable** considerable
B *m inv* **1** no
2 'no' vote
C non plus *phr* **je ne suis pas d'accord ~ plus** I don't agree either; **il n'a pas aimé le film, moi ~ plus** he didn't like the film and neither did I
D non(-) /nɔn/ *before vowel or mute h* (*combining form*) **~-fumeur** nonsmoker; **~-syndiqué** non union member

nonagénaire /nɔnaʒenɛʀ/ *adj* **être ~** to be in one's nineties

non-aligné, **~e**, *mpl* **~s** /nɔnaliɲe/ *mf* nonaligned country

nonante /nɔnɑ̃t/ *adj inv*, *pron* ninety

non-assistance /nɔnasistɑ̃s/ *f* **~ à personne en danger** failure to render assistance

nonchalance /nɔ̃ʃalɑ̃s/ *f* nonchalance

nonchalant, **~e** /nɔ̃ʃalɑ̃, ɑ̃t/ *adj* nonchalant

non-dit /nɔ̃di/ *m inv* **le ~** what is left unsaid

non-figuratif, **-ive**, *mpl* **~s** /nɔ̃figyʀatif, iv/ *adj* abstract

non-fonctionnement /nɔ̃fɔ̃ksjɔnmɑ̃/ *m* failure to operate

non-initié, **~e**, *mpl* **~s** /nɔninisje/ *mf* layman, lay person

non-inscrit, **~e**, *mpl* **~s** /nɔnɛ̃skʀi, it/ *mf* independent

n

non-lieu, *pl* **~x** /nɔ̃ljø/ *m* (Law) dismissal (of a charge); **il y a eu ~** the case was dismissed

nonne /nɔn/ *f* nun

nonnette /nɔnɛt/ *f* small iced gingerbread

non-recevoir /nɔ̃ʀəsəvwaʀ/ *m* **fin de ~** flat refusal

non-reconduction, *pl* **~s** /nɔ̃ʀəkɔ̃dyksjɔ̃/ *f* (of contract) non-renewal

non-respect /nɔ̃ʀɛspɛ/ *m* **~ de** failure to comply with ‹*clause*›; failure to respect ‹*person*›

non-sens /nɔ̃sɑ̃s/ *m inv* nonsense

non-spécialiste, *pl* **~s** /nɔ̃spesjalist/ *mf* layman, lay person

non-violent, **~e**, *mpl* **~s** /nɔ̃vjɔlɑ̃, ɑ̃t/ *mf* advocate of nonviolence

non-voyant, **~e**, *mpl* **~s** /nɔ̃vwajɑ̃, ɑ̃t/ *mf* visually impaired person

⚷ **nord** /nɔʀ/ **A** *adj inv* north; northern
B *m* **1** north; **le vent du ~** the north wind; **le ~ de l'Europe** northern Europe
2 le Nord the North; **la Corée du Nord** North Korea
IDIOM **il ne perd pas le ~!** (fam) he's got his head screwed on! (fam)

nord-africain, **~e**, *mpl* **~s** /nɔʀafʀikɛ̃, ɛn/ *adj* North African

nord-américain, **~e**, *mpl* **~s** /nɔʀameʀikɛ̃, ɛn/ *adj* North American

nord-est /nɔʀ(d)ɛst/ **A** *adj inv* northeast; northeastern
B *m* northeast

nordique /nɔʀdik/ *adj* Nordic

nord-ouest /nɔʀ(d)wɛst/ **A** *adj inv* northwest; northwestern
B *m* northwest

Nord-Sud /nɔʀsyd/ *adj inv* North-South

⚷ **normal**, **~e** *mpl* **-aux** /nɔʀmal, o/ *adj* normal; **il est ~ que** it is natural that; **il n'est pas ~ que** it is not right that

normale /nɔʀmal/ *f* **1** average
2 norm; **retour à la ~** return to normal

normalement /nɔʀmalmɑ̃/ *adv* normally

normalisation /nɔʀmalizasjɔ̃/ *f*
1 normalization
2 standardization

normaliser /nɔʀmalize/ [**v1**] *vt* **1** to normalize ‹*relations*›
2 to standardize ‹*sizes*›

normalité /nɔʀmalite/ *f* normality

normand, **~e** /nɔʀmɑ̃, ɑ̃d/ **A** *adj*
1 ‹*conquest*› Norman
2 ‹*coast*› Normandy; ‹*team*› from Normandy
B *m* Norman (French)

Normand, **~e** /nɔʀmɑ̃, ɑ̃d/ *mf* Norman
IDIOM **une réponse de ~** a noncommittal reply

normatif, **-ive** /nɔʀmatif, iv/ *adj* normative

⚷ **norme** /nɔʀm/ *f* (gen) norm; (Tech) standard

Norvège /nɔʀvɛʒ/ *pr f* Norway

norvégien, **-ienne** /nɔʀveʒjɛ̃, ɛn/ **A** *adj* Norwegian
B *m* (language) Norwegian

nos ▸ **notre**

nostalgie /nɔstalʒi/ *f* nostalgia

nostalgique /nɔstalʒik/ *adj* nostalgic

notable /nɔtabl/ **A** *adj* ‹*fact*› notable; ‹*progress*› significant
B *m* notable

notaire /nɔtɛʀ/ *m* notary public

⚷ **notamment** /nɔtamɑ̃/ *adv* **1** notably
2 in particular

notation /nɔtasjɔ̃/ *f* **1** notation
2 (of pupil) marking (BrE), grading (AmE); (of staff) grading

⚷ **note** /nɔt/ *f* **1** bill (BrE), check (AmE); **faire la ~ de qn** to write out sb's bill (BrE) *or* check (AmE)
2 (Mus) note; **forcer la ~** to overdo it
3 mark (BrE), grade (AmE); **~ éliminatoire** fail mark (BrE) *or* grade (AmE)
4 (written) note; **prendre qch en ~** to make a note of sth; **prendre (bonne) ~ de qch** (fig) to take (due) note of sth
■ **~ de frais** expense account; **~ d'honoraires** bill; **~ de service** memorandum

⚷ **noter** /nɔte/ [**v1**] *vt* **1** to write down ‹*idea*,

⚷ key word

address›
2 to notice ‹*change*›; **notez (bien) que je n'ai rien à lui reprocher** mind you I haven't got anything particular against him; **il faut quand même ~** it has to be said
3 to mark (BrE), to grade (AmE) ‹*exercise*›; to give a mark (BrE) *or* grade (AmE) to; to grade ‹*employee*›

notice /nɔtis/ *f* **1** note
2 instructions

notifier /nɔtifje/ [**v2**] *vt* **~ qch à qn** (gen) to notify sb of sth; (Law) to give sb notice of sth

notion /nɔsjɔ̃/ *f* **1** notion; **perdre la ~ de** to lose all sense of
2 ~s basic knowledge

notoire /nɔtwaʀ/ *adj* ‹*fact, position*› well-known; ‹*swindler, stupidity*› notorious

notoirement /nɔtwaʀmɑ̃/ *adv* manifestly; notoriously

notoriété /nɔtɔʀjete/ *f* **1** fame; (of product) reputation; **il est de ~ (publique) que** it's common knowledge that
2 (person) celebrity

notre, *pl* **nos** /nɔtʀ, no/ *det* our; **à nos âges** at our age; **c'était ~ avis à tous** we all felt the same; **nos enfants à nous** (fam) our children

nôtre /notʀ/ **A** *det* **nous avons fait ~s ces idées** we've adopted these ideas
B le nôtre, **la nôtre**, **les nôtres** *pron* ours; **soyez des ~s!** won't you join us?; **les ~s** our own people; (team, group) our side

nouer /nwe/ [**v1**] **A** *vt* **1** (gen) to tie; to knot ‹*tie*›; to tie up ‹*parcel*›; **avoir la gorge nouée** to have a lump in one's throat
2 to establish ‹*relations*›; to engage in ‹*dialogue*›
B se nouer *v refl* (+ *v être*) **1** ‹*plot*› to take shape
2 ‹*diplomatic relations*› to be established; ‹*dialogue, friendship*› to begin

nougat /nuga/ *m* nougat

nouilles /nuj/ *fpl* noodles, pasta

nounou /nunu/ *f* (fam) nanny (BrE), nurse

nounours /nunuʀs/ *m inv* (fam) teddy bear

nourrice /nuʀis/ *f* **1** childminder (BrE), babysitter (AmE)
2 wet nurse

nourrir /nuʀiʀ/ [**v3**] **A** *vt* **1** to feed ‹*person, animal*›; to nourish ‹*skin, leather*›; **bien nourri** well-fed; **~ au sein/au biberon** to breastfeed/bottle-feed; **mon travail ne me nourrit pas** I don't make enough to live on
2 (fig) to harbour (BrE) ‹*hopes*›; to feed ‹*fire*›; to fuel ‹*passion*›
B se nourrir *v refl* (+ *v être*) ‹*animal*› to feed; ‹*person*› to eat; **se ~ de** to live on ‹*vegetables*›; to feed on ‹*illusions*›

nourrissant, **~e** /nuʀisɑ̃, ɑ̃t/ *adj* nourishing

nourrisson /nuʀisɔ̃/ *m* infant

nourriture /nuʀityʀ/ *f* **1** food
2 diet

nous /nu/ *pron* **1** (subject) we; (object) us; **~ sommes en avance** we're early; **donne-~ l'adresse** give us the address; **entre ~, il n'est pas très intelligent** between you and me, he isn't very intelligent; **une maison à ~** a house of our own; **pensons à ~** let's think of ourselves
2 (with reflexive verb) **~ ~ soignons** we look after ourselves; **~ ~ aimons** we love each other

nous-même, *pl* **nous-mêmes** /numɛm/ *pron* **1** (in plural) ourselves
2 (the royal or modest we) **~ sommes convaincu de...** we are convinced of...

nouveau, **nouvel** *before vowel or mute h* **nouvelle** *mpl* **~x** /nuvo, nuvɛl/ **A** *adj* (gen) new; ‹*attempt, attack*› fresh; **tout ~** brand new; **se faire faire un ~ costume** to have a new suit made; to have another suit made; **une nouvelle fois** once again; **les ~x élus** the newly elected members; **les ~x mariés** the newlyweds
B *mf* (in school) new boy/girl; (in company) new employee; (in army) new recruit
C *m* **téléphone-moi s'il y a du ~** give me a call if there is anything new to report; **j'ai du ~ pour toi** I've got some news for you
D à nouveau, **de nouveau** *phr* (once) again

nouveau-né, **~e**, *mpl* **~s** /nuvone/ *mf* newborn baby

nouveauté /nuvote/ *f* **1** novelty; **ce n'est pas une ~!** that's nothing new!
2 (gen) new thing; (book) new publication; (record) new release; (car, machine) new model

nouvel ▶ **nouveau A**

nouvelle /nuvɛl/ **A** *adj f* ▶ **nouveau A**
B *f* **1** ▶ **nouveau B**
2 news; **une ~** a piece of news; **tu connais la ~?** have you heard the news?; **recevoir des ~s de qn** to hear from sb; (through somebody else) to hear news of sb; **il m'a demandé de tes ~s** he asked after you; **aux dernières ~s, il se porte bien** (fam) the last I heard he was doing fine; **il aura de mes ~s!** (fam) he'll be hearing from me!; **goûte ce petit vin, tu m'en diras des ~s** (fam) have a taste of this wine, it's really good!
3 short story

nouvellement /nuvɛlmɑ̃/ *adv* recently

Nouvelle-Zélande /nuvɛlzelɑ̃d/ *pr f* New Zealand

nouvelliste /nuvelist/ *mf* short story writer

novateur, **-trice** /nɔvatœʀ, tʀis/ **A** *adj* innovative
B *mf* innovator, pioneer

novembre /nɔvɑ̃bʀ/ *m* November

novice /nɔvis/ **A** *adj* inexperienced, green
B *mf* novice

noyade /nwajad/ *f* drowning

n

noyau, *pl* **~x** /nwajo/ *m* **1** stone (BrE), pit (AmE)
2 small group; **~x de résistance** pockets of resistance
3 nucleus

noyauter /nwajote/ [**v1**] *vt* to infiltrate

noyé, **~e** /nwaje/ *mf* drowned person

noyer[1] /nwaje/ [**v23**] **A** *vt* (gen) to drown; to flood ‹*village, engine*›; **~ qn sous un flot de paroles** to talk sb's head off (fam)
B se noyer *v refl* (+ *v être*) to drown; (suicide) to drown oneself; **mourir noyé** to drown
IDIOM **se ~ dans un verre d'eau** to make a mountain out of a molehill

noyer[2] /nwaje/ *m* walnut (tree)

🔑 **nu**, **~e** /ny/ **A** *adj* ‹*person*› naked; ‹*wall, tree, coastline*› bare; ‹*truth*› plain; **pieds ~s** barefoot; **torse ~** stripped to the waist
B *m* (in art) nude
C à nu *phr* **être à ~** to be exposed; **mettre son cœur à ~** to open one's heart

🔑 **nuage** /nyaʒ/ *m* cloud; **sans ~s** ‹*sky*› cloudless; ‹*happiness*› unclouded; **~ de lait** dash of milk
IDIOM **descendre de son ~** to come back to earth

nuageux, **-euse** /nyaʒø, øz/ *adj* ‹*sky*› cloudy

nuance /nyɑ̃s/ *f* **1** (of colour) shade
2 (of meaning) nuance; **sans ~** ‹*commentary*› clear-cut; ‹*personality*› straightforward
3 slight difference; **à cette ~ près que** with the small reservation that
4 (Mus) nuance

nuancer /nyɑ̃se/ [**v12**] *vt* **1** to qualify ‹*opinion*›; to modify ‹*view of situation*›; **peu nuancé** unsubtle
2 to moderate ‹*remarks, statements*›

nucléaire /nykleɛʀ/ **A** *adj* nuclear
B *m* **le ~** nuclear energy; nuclear technology

nudité /nydite/ *f* **1** nakedness, nudity
2 (of place, wall) bareness

nuée /nye/ *f* (of insects) swarm; (of people) horde

nues /ny/ *fpl* **tomber des ~** (fam) to be flabbergasted (fam); **porter qn aux ~** to praise sb to the skies

nui /nɥi/ ▶ **nuire**

nuire /nɥiʀ/ [**v69**] **A nuire à** *v+prep* to harm ‹*person*›; to be harmful to ‹*health, interests, reputation*›; to damage ‹*crops*›
B se nuire *v refl* (+ *v être*) **1** to do each other a lot of harm
2 to do oneself a lot of harm

nuisance /nɥizɑ̃s/ *f* nuisance

nuisible /nɥizibl/ *adj* ‹*substance, waste*› dangerous; ‹*influence*› harmful; **insecte ~** (insect) pest; **~ à** detrimental to

🔑 **nuit** /nɥi/ *f* night; **cette ~** last night; tonight; **voyager de ~** to travel by night; **avant la ~** before dark; **à la tombée de la ~** at nightfall; **il fait ~** it's dark; **il faisait ~ noire** it was pitch dark; **ça se perd dans la ~ des temps** it is lost in the mists of time
■ **~ blanche** sleepless night; **~ bleue** *night of terrorist bomb attacks*
IDIOMS **c'est le jour et la ~** they're as different as chalk and cheese; **attends demain pour donner ta réponse: la ~ porte conseil** wait till tomorrow to give your answer: sleep on it first

nuitée /nɥite/ *f* (in a hotel) overnight stay

🔑 **nul**, **nulle** /nyl/ **A** *adj* **1** (fam) ‹*person*› hopeless; ‹*piece of work*› worthless; ‹*film*› trashy (fam)
2 (Law) ‹*contract*› void; ‹*will*› invalid; ‹*elections*› null and void; ‹*vote*› spoiled
3 (Sport) **match ~** tie, draw (BrE); nil-all draw (BrE)
4 ‹*difference*› nil
5 ~ homme/pays no man/country; **~ autre que vous** no one else but you
B *mf* (fam) idiot (fam); **c'est un ~** he's a dead loss (fam)
C *pron* no one
D nulle part *phr* nowhere

nullement /nylmɑ̃/ *adv* not at all

nullité /nylite/ *f* **1** (Law) nullity; **frapper de ~** to render void
2 (of argument) invalidity; (of book, film) (fam) worthlessness
3 (fam) (person) idiot (fam)

numéraire /nymeʀɛʀ/ *m* cash

numéral, **~e**, *mpl* **-aux** /nymeʀal, o/ **A** *adj* numeral
B *m* numeral

numération /nymeʀasjɔ̃/ *f* (Math) numeration
■ **~ globulaire** blood count

numérique /nymeʀik/ *adj* (gen) numerical; ‹*display*› digital; **clavier ~** keypad

numériser /nymeʀize/ *vt* to digitize

🔑 **numéro** /nymeʀo/ *m* **1** number; **~ de téléphone** telephone number
2 (magazine) issue; **suite au prochain ~** to be continued
3 (in show) act
4 (fam) **quel ~!** what a character!
■ **~ d'abonné** customer's number; **~ d'appel gratuit** Freefone number (BrE), toll-free number (AmE); **~ vert** ▶ **numéro d'appel gratuit**
IDIOM **tirer le bon ~** to be lucky

numérotation /nymeʀɔtasjɔ̃/ *f* numbering

numéroter /nymeʀɔte/ [**v1**] *vt* to number

numerus clausus /nymeʀysklozys/ *m inv* quota

nunuche /nynyʃ/ *adj* (fam) bird-brained (fam), silly

nu-pied, *pl* **~s** /nypje/ *m* sandal

nuptial, **~e**, *mpl* **-iaux** /nypsjal, o/ *adj* ‹*mass*› nuptial; ‹*room*› bridal; **cérémonie**

🔑 key word

~e wedding
nuque /nyk/ *f* nape (of the neck)
nurse /nœʀs/ *f* nanny (BrE), nurse
nutritif, **-ive** /nytʀitif, iv/ *adj* ‹*skin cream*› nourishing; ‹*value*› nutritive
nutrition /nytʀisjɔ̃/ *f* nutrition
nymphe /nɛ̃f/ *f* nymph
nymphéa /nɛ̃fea/ *m* water lily
nymphomane /nɛ̃fɔman/ *adj*, *f* nymphomaniac

Oo

✓ **o**, **O** /o/ *m inv* o, O
oasis /ɔazis/ *f inv* oasis
✓ **obéir** /ɔbeiʀ/ **[v3]** *v+prep* **1** to obey; **~ à** to obey ‹*order*›
2 ‹*brakes, vehicle*› to respond
obéissance /ɔbeisɑ̃s/ *f* obedience
obéissant, **~e** /ɔbeisɑ̃, ɑ̃t/ *adj* obedient
obélisque /ɔbelisk/ *m* obelisk
obèse /ɔbɛz/ *adj* obese
objecter /ɔbʒɛkte/ **[v1]** *vt* **1** (suggest) to put forward ‹*argument, idea*›
2 (excuse) **~ un mal de tête pour refuser une invitation** to give a headache as an excuse for refusing an invitation
✓ **objectif**, **-ive** /ɔbʒɛktif, iv/ **A** *adj* objective
B *m* **1** objective
2 lens
3 target
objection /ɔbʒɛksjɔ̃/ *f* objection
objectivité /ɔbʒɛktivite/ *f* objectivity
✓ **objet** /ɔbʒɛ/ **A** *m* **1** object; **~ fragile** fragile item; **~s personnels** personal possessions
2 (of debate, research) subject; (of hatred, desire) object; **faire l'~ de** to be the subject of ‹*inquiry, research*›; to be subjected to ‹*surveillance*›; to be the object of ‹*desire, hatred*›
3 purpose, object; **'~: réponse à votre lettre du...'** 're: your letter of...'
4 (Law) **~ d'un litige** matter at issue
B -objet (*combining form*) as an object; **femme-~** woman as an object
■ **~s trouvés** lost property; **~ volant non identifié, ovni** unidentified flying object, UFO
obligataire /ɔbligatɛʀ/ (Fin) *adj* ‹*market, issue*› bond; **emprunt ~** bond issue
✓ **obligation** /ɔbligasjɔ̃/ *f* **1** obligation, responsibility; duty
2 necessity; **se voir** *or* **se trouver dans l'~ de faire** to be forced to do
3 (Econ) bond
4 (Law) obligation
■ **~s militaires, OM** military service
obligatoire /ɔbligatwaʀ/ *adj* **1** compulsory
2 (fam) inevitable
obligatoirement /ɔbligatwaʀmɑ̃/ *adv* inevitably, necessarily
obligé, **~e** **A** *pp* ▶ **obliger**
B *pp adj* **1** (constrained) **se voir ~ de faire** to be forced to do
2 (indebted) **être ~ à qn de** to be obliged *or* grateful to sb for
3 (necessary) essential; **un passage ~ (pour)** (fig) a prerequisite (for)
C *mf* **1 être l'~ de qn** to be obliged *or* indebted to sb
2 (in law) obligor
obligeamment /ɔbliʒamɑ̃/ *adv* obligingly
obligeance /ɔbliʒɑ̃s/ *f* **avoir l'~ de** to be kind enough to
obligeant, **~e** /ɔbliʒɑ̃, ɑ̃t/ *adj* obliging; kind
✓ **obliger** /ɔbliʒe/ **[v13]** **A** *vt* **1 ~ qn à faire** to force sb to do; ‹*rules*› to make it compulsory for sb to do; ‹*duty*› to compel sb to do; **je suis obligé de partir** I have to go
2 ~ qn to oblige sb
B s'obliger *v refl* (+ *v être*) **s'~ à faire** to force oneself to do
oblique /ɔblik/ *adj* slanting; sidelong; oblique
obliquement /ɔblikmɑ̃/ *adv* at an angle; diagonally
oblitération /ɔbliteʀasjɔ̃/ *f* (of stamp) cancelling (BrE); **(cachet d')~** postmark
oblitérer /ɔbliteʀe/ **[v14]** *vt* to cancel, to obliterate ‹*stamp*›
oblong, **-ongue** /ɔblɔ̃, ɔ̃g/ *adj* oblong
obnubiler /ɔbnybile/ **[v1]** *vt* to obsess
obscène /ɔpsɛn/ *adj* obscene
obscur, **~e** /ɔpskyʀ/ *adj* **1** dark
2 obscure
3 lowly
4 vague
obscurcir /ɔpskyʀsiʀ/ **[v3]** **A** *vt* **1** to make [sth] dark ‹*place*›
2 to obscure ‹*view*›
B s'obscurcir *v refl* (+ *v être*) **1** ‹*sky, place*› to darken

2 ‹*situation*› to become confused

obscurément /ɔpskyʀemɑ̃/ *adv* **1** ‹*feel*› vaguely
2 ‹*live*› in obscurity

obscurité /ɔpskyʀite/ *f* darkness

obsédant, **~e** /ɔpsedɑ̃, ɑ̃t/ *adj* ‹*memory, dream, music*› haunting; ‹*rhythm*› insistent

obsédé, **~e** /ɔpsede/ *mf* **~ (sexuel)** sex maniac

obséder /ɔpsede/ [**v14**] *vt* ‹*memory, dream*› to haunt; ‹*idea, problem*› to obsess

obsèques /ɔpsɛk/ *fpl* funeral

obséquieux, **-ieuse** /ɔpsekjø, øz/ *adj* obsequious

observateur, **-trice** /ɔpsɛʀvatœʀ, tʀis/
A *adj* observant
B *mf* observer; (Comput) **~ passif** lurker

🔑 **observation** /ɔpsɛʀvasjɔ̃/ *f* **1** observation
2 observation, remark; comment
3 reproach

observatoire /ɔpsɛʀvatwaʀ/ *m*
1 observatory
2 look-out post

🔑 **observer** /ɔpsɛʀve/ [**v1**] **A** *vt* **1** to watch, to observe
2 to notice, to observe ‹*phenomenon, reaction*›
3 to observe ‹*rules, treaty*›; to keep to ‹*diet*›; to maintain ‹*strategy*›; **~ le silence** to keep quiet
B **s'observer** *v refl* (+ *v être*) **1** to watch each other
2 to keep a check on oneself

obsession /ɔpsɛsjɔ̃/ *f* obsession

obsolescence programmée *f* planned obsolescence

obsolète /ɔpsɔlɛt/ *adj* obsolete

obstacle /ɔpstakl/ *m* **1** obstacle
2 (in horse riding) fence

obstétricien, **-ienne** /ɔpstetʀisjɛ̃, ɛn/ *mf* obstetrician

obstétrique /ɔpstetʀik/ *f* obstetrics

obstination /ɔpstinasjɔ̃/ *f* obstinacy

obstiné, **~e** /ɔpstine/ **A** *pp* ▸ **obstiner**
B *pp adj* **1** stubborn
2 dogged

obstinément /ɔpstinemɑ̃/ *adv* obstinately

obstiner: **s'obstiner** /ɔpstine/ [**v1**] *v refl* (+ *v être*) to persist

obstruction /ɔpstʀyksjɔ̃/ *f* obstruction

obstruer /ɔpstʀye/ [**v1**] **A** *vt* to obstruct
B **s'obstruer** *v refl* (+ *v être*) to get blocked

obtempérer /ɔptɑ̃peʀe/ [**v14**] *v+prep* to comply; **~ à** to comply with ‹*order*›

🔑 **obtenir** /ɔptəniʀ/ [**v36**] *vt* to get, to obtain

obtention /ɔptɑ̃sjɔ̃/ *f* getting, obtaining

obturation /ɔptyʀasjɔ̃/ *f* **1** blocking (up)
2 **vitesse d'~** shutter speed

🔑 key word

obturer /ɔptyʀe/ [**v1**] *vt* to block up

obtus, **~e** /ɔpty, yz/ *adj* obtuse

obus /oby/ *m inv* shell

🔑 **occasion** /ɔkazjɔ̃/ *f* **1** occasion; **à l'~** some time; **à** *or* **en plusieurs ~s** on several occasions; **les grandes ~s** special occasions
2 opportunity, chance; **être l'~ de qch** to give rise to sth
3 second-hand buy
4 bargain

occasionnel, **-elle** /ɔkazjɔnɛl/ *adj* occasional

occasionner /ɔkazjɔne/ [**v1**] *vt* to cause

occident /ɔksidɑ̃/ *m* **1** west
2 **l'Occident** the West

🔑 **occidental**, **~e**, *mpl* **-aux** /ɔksidɑ̃tal, o/ *adj* western

Occidental, **~e**, *mpl* **-aux** /ɔksidɑ̃tal, o/ *mf* Westerner

occitan /ɔksitɑ̃/ *m* langue d'oc

occulte /ɔkylt/ *adj* **1** occult
2 secret

occulter /ɔkylte/ [**v1**] *vt* **1** to eclipse
2 to obscure ‹*issue*›; to conceal ‹*truth*›

occultisme /ɔkyltism/ *m* occultism

occupant, **~e** /ɔkypɑ̃, ɑ̃t/ **A** *adj* occupying
B *mf* (of house) occupier; (of vehicle) occupant

occupation /ɔkypasjɔ̃/ *f* **1** (pastime) occupation
2 occupation, job
3 occupancy
4 (of country, factory) occupation

occupé, **~e** /ɔkype/ **A** *pp* ▸ **occuper**
B *pp adj* **1** ‹*person, life*› busy
2 ‹*seat*› taken; ‹*phone*› engaged (BrE), busy; ‹*toilet*› engaged
3 (Mil) ‹*country*› occupied

🔑 **occuper** /ɔkype/ [**v1**] **A** *vt* **1** to live in, to occupy ‹*flat, house*›; to be in ‹*shower, cell*›; to sit in ‹*seat*›
2 to take up ‹*space, time*›
3 to occupy ‹*person, mind*›; **ça m'occupe!** it keeps me busy!; **le sujet qui nous occupe** the matter which we are dealing with
4 to have ‹*employment*›; to hold ‹*job, office*›
5 ‹*strikers, army*› to occupy ‹*place*›; **~ les locaux** to stage a sit-in
B **s'occuper** *v refl* (+ *v être*) **1** to keep oneself busy *or* occupied
2 **s'~ de** to see to, to take care of ‹*dinner, tickets*›; to be dealing with ‹*file, matter*›; to take care of ‹*child, animal, plant*›; to attend to ‹*customer*›; to be in charge of ‹*finance, library*›; **occupe-toi de tes affaires** (fam) *or* **de ce qui te regarde!** (fam) mind your own business! (fam)

occurrence /ɔkyʀɑ̃s/ *f* **1** case, instance; **en l'~** in this case
2 occurrence

OCDE /osedeə/ *f* (*abbr* = **Organisation de coopération et de développement**

économiques) OECD
océan /ɔseɑ̃/ *m* ocean
océanique /ɔseanik/ *adj* oceanic
océanographe /ɔseanɔgʀaf/ *mf* oceanographer
ocre /ɔkʀ/ *adj inv*, *m* ochre (BrE)
octante /ɔktɑ̃t/ *adj inv*, *pron* (in Belgian, Canadian, Swiss, French) eighty
octave /ɔktav/ *f* octave
octet /ɔktɛt/ *m* **1** (Comput) byte
2 (in physics) octet
octobre /ɔktɔbʀ/ *m* October
octogénaire /ɔktɔʒenɛʀ/ *mf* octogenarian
octogonal, **~e**, *mpl* **-aux** /ɔktɔgɔnal, o/ *adj* octagonal
octroi /ɔktʀwa/ *m* **1** granting
2 octroi
octroyer /ɔktʀwaje/ [**v23**] *vt* **~ à qn** to grant sb ‹*pardon, favour*›; to allocate sb [sth] ‹*budget*›
oculaire /ɔkylɛʀ/ *adj* **troubles ~s** eye trouble; **témoin ~** eyewitness
oculiste /ɔkylist/ *mf* oculist, ophthalmologist
ode /ɔd/ *f* ode
odeur /ɔdœʀ/ *f* smell
odieux, **-ieuse** /ɔdjø, øz/ *adj* horrible
odorant, **~e** /ɔdɔʀɑ̃, ɑ̃t/ *adj* which has a smell
odorat /ɔdɔʀa/ *m* sense of smell
OECE /oəseə/ *f* (*abbr* = **Organisation européenne de coopération économique**) OEEC
œdème /edɛm/ *m* (Med) oedema
œdipe /edip/ *m* Oedipus complex
œil, *pl* **yeux** /œj, jø/ *m* eye; **ouvrir l'~** to keep one's eyes open; **fermer les yeux sur qch** to turn a blind eye to sth; **acheter qch les yeux fermés** to buy sth with complete confidence; **avoir l'~ à tout** to be vigilant; **jeter un ~ à** *or* **sur qch** to have a quick look at sth; **aux yeux de tous** openly; **jeter un coup d'~ à qch** to glance at sth; **avoir le coup d'~** to have a good eye; **regarder qch d'un ~ neuf** to see sth in a new light; **voir qch d'un mauvais ~** to take a dim view of sth; **à mes yeux** in my opinion
■ **~ de verre** glass eye
(IDIOMS) **mon ~!** (fam) my eye! (fam), my foot! (fam); **à l'~** (fam) for nothing, for free (fam); **faire les gros yeux à qn** to glare at sb; **dévorer qn/qch des yeux** to gaze longingly at sb/sth; **faire les yeux doux à qn** to make eyes at sb; **tourner de l'~** (fam) to faint; **cela me sort par les yeux** (fam) I've had it up to here (fam); **avoir bon pied bon ~** to be as fit as a fiddle; **sauter aux yeux** to be obvious
œillade /œjad/ *f* **1** wink
2 glance
œillère /œjɛʀ/ *f* blinker
œillet /œjɛ/ *m* **1** carnation
2 (in shoe, tarpaulin) eyelet; (in belt) hole; (made of metal) grommet
œilleton /œjtɔ̃/ *m* (in door) peephole
œnologie /enɔlɔʒi/ *f* oenology
œsophage /ezɔfaʒ/ *m* oesophagus
œstrogène /ɛstʀɔʒɛn/ *m* oestrogen
œuf /œf/, *pl* /ø/ *m* egg; **~s de cabillaud** cod's roe
■ **~ à la coque** boiled egg; **~ dur** hard-boiled egg; **~ sur le plat** fried egg; **~s brouillés** scrambled eggs
œuvre /œvʀ/ *f* **1** (artistic, literary) work; **~s complètes** complete works
2 être à l'~ to be at work; **voir qn à l'~** to see sb in action; **mettre en ~** to implement ‹*reform*›; to display ‹*ingenuity*›; **tout mettre en ~ pour faire** to make every effort to do
■ **~ d'art** work of art; **~ de bienfaisance** *or* **de charité** charity
off /ɔf/ *adj inv* (fam) **voix ~** voice-over
offensant, **~e** /ɔfɑ̃sɑ̃, ɑ̃t/ *adj* offensive (**pour** to)
offense /ɔfɑ̃s/ *f* insult
offenser /ɔfɑ̃se/ [**v1**] **A** *vt* to offend
B s'offenser *v refl* (+ *v être*) to take offence (BrE)
offensif, **-ive** /ɔfɑ̃sif, iv/ *adj* (Mil) offensive
offensive /ɔfɑ̃siv/ *f* (Mil), (fig) offensive
offert, **-e** /ɔfɛʀ, ɛʀt/ ▶ **offrir**
office /ɔfis/ **A** *m* **1 faire ~ de table** to serve as a table
2 ~ religieux service
3 (butler's) pantry
B d'office *phr* **d'~** without consultation; **nos propositions ont été rejetées d'~** our proposals were dismissed out of hand; **commis d'~** ‹*lawyer*› appointed by the court
■ **~ du tourisme** tourist information office
officiel, **-ielle** /ɔfisjɛl/ **A** *adj* official; **être en visite officielle** to be on a state visit
B *m* official
officier¹ /ɔfisje/ [**v2**] *vi* to officiate
officier² /ɔfisje/ *m* officer
officieusement /ɔfisjøzmɑ̃/ *adv* unofficially
officieux, **-ieuse** /ɔfisjø, øz/ *adj* unofficial
officine /ɔfisin/ *f* dispensary; pharmacy
offrande /ɔfʀɑ̃d/ *f* offering
offrant /ɔfʀɑ̃/ **A** *pres p* ▶ **offrir**
B *m* **vendre qch au plus ~** to sell sth to the highest bidder
offre /ɔfʀ/ *f* **1** offer; **répondre à une ~ d'emploi** to reply to a job advertisement
2 (Econ) supply
■ **~ d'achat** bid; **~ publique d'achat, OPA** takeover bid
offrir /ɔfʀiʀ/ [**v4**] **A** *vt* **1 ~ qch à qn** to give sth to sb
2 to buy (**à qn** for sb)
3 to offer ‹*choice*›; to offer ‹*resignation*›; to present ‹*problems*›
B s'offrir *v refl* (+ *v être*) **1 s'~** to buy

oneself ‹*flowers*›; **ils ne peuvent pas s'~ le théâtre** they can't afford to go to the theatre (BrE); **s'~ un jour de vacances** to give oneself a day off
2 ‹*solution*› to present itself; **s'~ en spectacle** to make an exhibition of oneself

offshore /ɔfʃɔʀ/ **A** *m* **faire de l'~** offshoring
B *adj* offshore

offusquer /ɔfyske/ [**v1**] **A** *vt* to offend
B s'offusquer *v refl* (+ *v être*) to be offended

ogive /ɔʒiv/ *f* (Archit) rib

ogre /ɔgʀ/ *m* ogre

🔑 **oh** /o/ *excl* oh!; **~ hisse!** heave-ho!

oie /wa/ *f* goose; **~ blanche** naïve young girl

oignon /ɔɲɔ̃/ *m* **1** onion
2 (of flower) bulb
IDIOM **occupe-toi de tes ~s** (fam) mind your own business (fam)

🔑 **oiseau**, *pl* **~x** /wazo/ *m* bird; **un (drôle d')~** an oddball (fam)
IDIOM **trouver l'~ rare** (fam) to find the one person in a million

oiseau-mouche, *pl* **oiseaux-mouches** /wazomuʃ/ *m* hummingbird

oiseleur /wazlœʀ/ *m* bird catcher

oisellerie /wazɛlʀi/ *f* bird shop

oisif, **-ive** /wazif, iv/ **A** *adj* idle
B *mf* idler; **les ~s** the idle rich

oisillon /wazijɔ̃/ *m* fledgling

oisiveté /wazivte/ *f* idleness
IDIOM **l'~ est mère de tous les vices** (Proverb) the devil makes work for idle hands

olé: **olé olé** /ɔleɔle/ *phr* (fam) ‹*joke*› naughty

oléagineux, **-euse** /ɔleaʒinø, -øz/ **A** *adj* oleaginous
B *m inv* oleaginous plant

oléiculture /ɔleikyltyʀ/ *f* olive-growing

oléoduc /ɔleɔdyk/ *m* (oil) pipeline

olfactif, **-ive** /ɔlfaktif, iv/ *adj* olfactory

oligo-élément, *pl* **~s** /ɔligoelemɑ̃/ *m* trace element

olivâtre /ɔlivɑtʀ/ *adj* olive green; sallow

olive /ɔliv/ *f* olive

oliveraie /ɔlivʀɛ/ *f* olive grove

olivier /ɔlivje/ *m* **1** olive tree
2 olive wood

olympiade /ɔlɛ̃pjad/ **A** *f* Olympiad
B olympiades *fpl* Olympics

olympique /ɔlɛ̃pik/ *adj* Olympic

ombilic /ɔ̃bilik/ *m* umbilicus, navel

ombrage /ɔ̃bʀaʒ/ *m* shade
IDIOMS **porter ~ à qn** to offend sb; **prendre ~ de qch** to take umbrage at sth

ombrager /ɔ̃bʀaʒe/ [**v13**] *vt* to shade

ombrageux, **-euse** /ɔ̃bʀaʒø, øz/ *adj* tetchy

🔑 **ombre** /ɔ̃bʀ/ *f* **1** shade; **tu leur fais de l'~** you're (standing) in their light; (fig) you put them in the shade; **rester dans l'~ de qn** to be in sb's shadow
2 shadow
3 darkness
4 laisser certains détails dans l'~ to be deliberately vague about certain details
5 hint; **une ~ de tristesse passa dans son regard** a look of sadness crossed his/her face
■ **~ chinoise** shadow puppet; **~ à paupières** eye shadow
IDIOM **jeter une ~ au tableau** to spoil the picture

ombrelle /ɔ̃bʀɛl/ *f* parasol, sunshade

OMC /oɛmse/ *f* (*abbr* = **Organisation Mondiale du Commerce**) WTO, World Trade Organization

omelette /ɔmlɛt/ *f* omelette

omettre /ɔmɛtʀ/ [**v60**] *vt* to leave out, to omit

omission /ɔmisjɔ̃/ *f* omission

omnibus /ɔmnibys/ *m inv* slow *or* local train

omniprésent, **~e** /ɔmnipʀezɑ̃, ɑ̃t/ *adj* omnipresent

omnisports /ɔmnispɔʀ/ *adj inv* **salle ~** sports hall; **club ~** (multi-)sports club

omnivore /ɔmnivɔʀ/ *mf* omnivore

omoplate /ɔmɔplat/ *f* shoulder blade

OMS /oɛmɛs/ *f* (*abbr* = **Organisation mondiale de la santé**) WHO, World Health Organization

🔑 **on** /ɔ̃/ *pron* **1 ~ a refait la route** the road was resurfaced; **~ a prétendu que** it was claimed that; **il pleut des cordes, comme ~ dit** it's raining cats and dogs, as they say
2 we; **mon copain et moi, ~ va en Afrique** my boyfriend and I are going to Africa
3 you; **alors, ~ se promène?** so you're taking a stroll then?
4 ~ fait ce qu'~ peut! one does what one can!; **toi, ~ ne t'a rien demandé** nobody asked you for your opinion; **~ ne m'a pas demandé mon avis** they didn't ask me for my opinion

once /ɔ̃s/ *f* ounce

🔑 **oncle** /ɔ̃kl/ *m* uncle

onctueux, **-euse** /ɔ̃ktɥø, øz/ *adj* **1** smooth, creamy
2 unctuous

onde /ɔ̃d/ *f* wave; **grandes ~s** long wave; **sur les ~s** on the air

ondée /ɔ̃de/ *f* shower

on-dit /ɔ̃di/ *m inv* **les ~** hearsay

ondoyant, **~e** /ɔ̃dwajɑ̃, ɑ̃t/ *adj* rippling; lithe; swaying

ondoyer /ɔ̃dwaje/ [**v23**] *vi* to undulate; to sway

ondulant, **~e** /ɔ̃dylɑ̃, ɑ̃t/ *adj* swaying; undulating

ondulation /ɔ̃dylasjɔ̃/ *f* **1** undulation; swaying
2 curves; wave

ondulé, **~e** /ɔ̃dyle/ *adj* ‹*hair, shape*› wavy; ‹*cardboard*› corrugated

onéreux, **-euse** /ɔneʀø, øz/ *adj* expensive

ONG /oɛnʒe/ *f* (*abbr* = **organisation non gouvernementale**) NGO

ongle /ɔ̃gl/ *m* nail
IDIOM **jusqu'au bout des ~s** through and through

onglet /ɔ̃glɛ/ *m* **1** tab; **avec ~s** with thumb index
2 (Culin) *prime cut of beef*

onirique /ɔniʀik/ *adj* dream-like

onomatopée /ɔnɔmatɔpe/ *f* onomatopoeia

ont /ɔ̃/ ▸ **avoir**[1]

ONU /ɔny, oɛny/ *f* (*abbr* = **Organisation des Nations unies**) UN, UNO

onyx /ɔniks/ *m inv* onyx

onze /ɔ̃z/ **A** *adj inv, pron, m inv* eleven
B *m* football team; **le ~ lyonnais** the Lyons football team

onzième /ɔ̃zjɛm/ **A** *adj* eleventh
B *f* (Sch) *first year of primary school, age 6–7*

OPA /opea/ *f* (*abbr* = **offre publique d'achat**) takeover bid

opaque /ɔpak/ *adj* **1** opaque
2 (fig) ‹*text*› opaque; ‹*night*› dark; ‹*wood, fog*› impenetrable

OPEP /ɔpɛp/ *f* (*abbr* = **Organisation des pays producteurs de pétrole**) OPEC

opéra /ɔpeʀa/ *m* **1** opera
2 opera house

opérateur, **-trice** /ɔpeʀatœʀ, tʀis/ *mf* operator; **~ de saisie** keyboarder

opération /ɔpeʀasjɔ̃/ *f* **1 ~ (chirurgicale)** operation, surgery
2 calculation
3 (Tech) operation
4 process
5 transaction
■ **~ escargot** convoy protest

opératoire /ɔpeʀatwaʀ/ *adj* **1** ‹*technique*› surgical; ‹*risk*› in operating
2 operative

opercule /ɔpɛʀkyl/ *m* **1** (Bot, Zool) operculum
2 lid

opéré, **~e** /ɔpeʀe/ *mf* person who has had an operation

opérer /ɔpeʀe/ [**v14**] **A** *vt* **1** to operate on; **~ qn de l'appendicite** to remove sb's appendix; **se faire ~** to have an operation, to have surgery
2 to bring about ‹*change*›
B *vi* **1** (Med) to operate
2 ‹*cure, charm*› to work
3 to proceed
4 ‹*thief*› to operate

opérette /ɔpeʀɛt/ *f* operetta, light opera

ophtalmologiste /ɔftalmɔlɔʒist/ *mf* ophthalmologist

opiner /ɔpine/ [**v1**] *vi* **~ du bonnet** *or* **de la tête** to nod in agreement

opiniâtre /ɔpinjɑtʀ/ *adj* ‹*resistance*› dogged; ‹*work*› relentless; ‹*person*› tenacious

opinion /ɔpinjɔ̃/ *f* **1** opinion; **mon ~ est faite** my mind is made up
2 l'~ (publique) public opinion

opium /ɔpjɔm/ *m* opium

opportun, **~e** /ɔpɔʀtœ̃, yn/ *adj* appropriate

opportuniste /ɔpɔʀtynist/ *mf* opportunist

opportunité /ɔpɔʀtynite/ *f*
1 appropriateness
2 opportunity

opposant, **~e** /ɔpozɑ̃, ɑ̃t/ *mf* opponent

opposé, **~e** /ɔpoze/ **A** *adj* **1** ‹*direction*› opposite
2 ‹*opinion*› opposite; ‹*parties, sides*› opposing; ‹*interests*› conflicting
3 opposed
B à l'opposé *phr* **1 à l'~ de mes frères** in contrast to my brothers
2 il est parti à l'~ he went off in the opposite direction

opposer /ɔpoze/ [**v1**] **A** *vt* **1** to put up ‹*resistance, argument*›
2 ~ à to match *or* pit [sb] against ‹*person, team*›
3 ‹*problem*› to divide ‹*people*›
4 to compare
B s'opposer *v refl* (+ *v être*) **1 s'~ à qch** to be opposed to sth
2 s'~ à to stand in the way of ‹*change*›
3 to contrast
4 ‹*ideas, opinions*› to conflict; ‹*people*› to disagree
5 ‹*teams*› to confront each other

opposition /ɔpozisjɔ̃/ *f* **1** opposition; **par ~ à** in contrast with *or* to
2 faire ~ à un chèque to stop a cheque (BrE) *or* check (AmE)

oppressant, **~e** /ɔpʀesɑ̃, ɑ̃t/ *adj* oppressive

oppresser /ɔpʀese/ [**v1**] *vt* to oppress; **se sentir oppressé** to feel breathless

oppression /ɔpʀesjɔ̃/ *f* oppression

opprimer /ɔpʀime/ [**v1**] *vt* to oppress ‹*people*›

opter /ɔpte/ [**v1**] *vi* to opt

opticien, **-ienne** /ɔptisjɛ̃, ɛn/ *mf* optician

optimal, **~e**, *mpl* **-aux** /ɔptimal, o/ *adj* optimum

optimiser /ɔptimize/ [**v1**] *vt* to optimize

optimisme /ɔptimism/ *m* optimism

optimiste /ɔptimist/ *adj* optimistic

option /ɔpsjɔ̃/ *f* option; **en ~** optional

optique /ɔptik/ **A** *adj* **1** (Anat) optic
2 optical
B *f* **1** optics
2 perspective

opulence /ɔpylɑ̃s/ *f* opulence

or[1] /ɔʀ/ *conj* and yet; **~, ce jour-là, il…** now, on that particular day, he…

or[2] /ɔʀ/ **A** *adj inv* gold; ‹*hair*› golden
B *m* **1** gold; **en ~** gold; ‹*husband*› marvellous (BrE); ‹*opportunity*› golden
2 gilding

oracle /ɔʀakl/ *m* oracle
orage /ɔʀaʒ/ *m* storm
orageux, **-euse** /ɔʀaʒø, øz/ *adj* stormy
oraison /ɔʀɛzɔ̃/ *f* prayer; **~ funèbre** funeral oration
oral, **~e**, *mpl* **-aux** /ɔʀal, o/ **A** *adj* **1** oral
2 (Med) **par voie ~e** orally
B *m* (Sch) oral (examination)
oralement /ɔʀalmɑ̃/ *adv* **1** (Med) orally
2 verbally
orange¹ /ɔʀɑ̃ʒ/ *adj inv* orange; ‹*light*› amber (BrE), yellow (AmE)
orange² /ɔʀɑ̃ʒ/ *f* orange
orangeade /ɔʀɑ̃ʒad/ *f* orangeade
oranger /ɔʀɑ̃ʒe/ *m* orange tree
orangerie /ɔʀɑ̃ʒʀi/ *f* orangery
orateur, **-trice** /ɔʀatœʀ, tʀis/ *mf* **1** speaker
2 orator
orbite /ɔʀbit/ *f* **1** orbit
2 eye socket
orchestral, **~e**, *mpl* **-aux** /ɔʀkɛstʀal, o/ *adj* orchestral
orchestration /ɔʀkɛstʀasjɔ̃/ *f* orchestration
orchestre /ɔʀkɛstʀ/ *m* **1** orchestra
2 band
3 orchestra stalls (BrE), orchestra (AmE)
orchestrer /ɔʀkɛstʀe/ [**v1**] *vt* to orchestrate
orchidée /ɔʀkide/ *f* orchid
ordinaire /ɔʀdinɛʀ/ **A** *adj* **1** ordinary; ‹*quality*› standard; ‹*reader, tourist*› average; **journée peu ~** unusual day
2 très ~ ‹*meal, wine*› very average; ‹*person*› very ordinary
B *m* **sortir de l'~** to be out of the ordinary
C à l'ordinaire, **d'ordinaire** *phr* usually
ordinal, **~e**, *mpl* **-aux** /ɔʀdinal, o/ *adj* ordinal
ordinateur /ɔʀdinatœʀ/ *m* computer
ordination /ɔʀdinasjɔ̃/ *f* ordination
ordiphone /ɔʀdifɔn/ *m* smartphone
ordonnance /ɔʀdɔnɑ̃s/ *f* prescription
ordonner /ɔʀdɔne/ [**v1**] *vt* **1** to order
2 to put [sth] in order
3 to ordain
ordre /ɔʀdʀ/ *m* **1** (command) order; **j'ai des ~s** I'm acting under orders; **à vos ~s!** (Mil) yes, sir!; **jusqu'à nouvel ~** until further notice
2 (sequence) order; **par ~ alphabétique** in alphabetical order
3 tidiness, orderliness
4 (orderly state) order; **rappeler qn à l'~** to reprimand sb; **tout est rentré dans l'~** everything is back to normal; **rétablir l'~ (public)** to restore law and order
5 nature; **c'est dans l'~ des choses** it's in the nature of things; **de l'~ de 30%** in the order of 30% (BrE), on the order of 30% (AmE); **de premier ~** first-rate
6 (in religion) order; **entrer dans les ~s** to take (holy) orders
7 libellez le chèque à l'~ de X make the cheque (BrE) *or* check (AmE) payable to X
■ **~ du jour** agenda
ordure /ɔʀdyʀ/ **A** *f* filth
B ordures *fpl* refuse (BrE), garbage (AmE)
ordurier, **-ière** /ɔʀdyʀje, ɛʀ/ *adj* filthy
orée /ɔʀe/ *f* **1** edge
2 (fig) start
oreille /ɔʀɛj/ *f* **1** ear; **n'écouter que d'une ~** to half listen; **ouvre-bien les ~s!** listen carefully
2 hearing; **avoir l'~ fine** to have keen hearing
3 à l'abri des ~s indiscrètes where no one can hear
IDIOM **tirer les ~s à qn** to tell sb off
oreiller /ɔʀɛje/ *m* pillow
oreillons /ɔʀɛjɔ̃/ *mpl* mumps
ores: **d'ores et déjà** /dɔʀzedeʒa/ *phr* already
orfèvre /ɔʀfɛvʀ/ *mf* goldsmith; **être ~ en la matière** to be an expert in the field
orfèvrerie /ɔʀfɛvʀəʀi/ *f* **1** goldsmith's art
2 goldsmith's and silversmith's
organe /ɔʀgan/ *m* organ
organigramme /ɔʀganigʀam/ *m* organization chart
organique /ɔʀganik/ *adj* organic
organisation /ɔʀganizasjɔ̃/ *f* organization
organiser /ɔʀganize/ [**v1**] **A** *vt* to organize
B s'organiser *v refl* (+ *v être*)
1 ‹*opposition*› to get organized
2 to organize oneself
3 ‹*fight, help*› to be organized
organisme /ɔʀganism/ *m* **1** body
2 organism
3 organization, body
orgasme /ɔʀgasm/ *m* orgasm
orge /ɔʀʒ/ *f* barley
orgie /ɔʀʒi/ *f* orgy
orgue /ɔʀg/ *m* (Mus) organ
orgueil /ɔʀgœj/ *m* pride
orgueilleux, **-euse** /ɔʀgœjø, øz/ *adj* overly proud
orient /ɔʀjɑ̃/ *m* **1** east
2 l'Orient the East
oriental, **~e**, *mpl* **-aux** /ɔʀjɑ̃tal, o/ *adj* eastern; oriental
Oriental, **~e**, *mpl* **-aux** /ɔʀjɑ̃tal, o/ *mf* Asian; **les Orientaux** Asians
orientation /ɔʀjɑ̃tasjɔ̃/ *f* **1** (of house) aspect; (of aerial) angle
2 (of inquiry) direction
3 (Sch) **changer d'~** to change courses
orienter /ɔʀjɑ̃te/ [**v1**] **A** *vt* **1** to adjust ‹*aerial, lamp*›
2 ~ la conversation sur to bring the conversation around to
3 to direct ‹*person*›
4 (Sch) to give [sb] career advice
B s'orienter *v refl* (+ *v être*) **1** to get *or* find one's bearings

key word

O

2 s'∼ vers ‹*person*› to turn toward(s); **s'∼ vers les carrières scientifiques** to go in for a career in science

orifice /ɔʀifis/ *m* **1** orifice
2 (of pipe) mouth; (of tube) neck

originaire /ɔʀiʒinɛʀ/ *adj* ‹*plant, animal*› native; **famille ∼ d'Asie** Asian family

original, **∼e**, *mpl* **-aux** /ɔʀiʒinal, o/ **A** *adj*
1 original
2 eccentric
B *m* original

originalité /ɔʀiʒinalite/ *f* originality

origine /ɔʀiʒin/ *f* origin; **être d'∼ modeste** to come from a modest background; **dès l'∼** right from the start; **à l'∼** originally

originel, **-elle** /ɔʀiʒinɛl/ *adj* original

orme /ɔʀm/ *m* **1** elm (tree)
2 elm (wood)

ornement /ɔʀnəmɑ̃/ *m* **1** ornament
2 decorative detail

orner /ɔʀne/ [**v1**] *vt* to decorate

ornière /ɔʀnjɛʀ/ *f* rut

ornithologie /ɔʀnitɔlɔʒi/ *f* ornithology

ornithorynque /ɔʀnitɔʀɛ̃k/ *m* (duck-billed) platypus, duckbill (AmE)

orphelin, **∼e** /ɔʀfəlɛ̃, in/ *mf* orphan

orphelinat /ɔʀfəlina/ *m* orphanage

orque /ɔʀk/ *mf* killer whale

orteil /ɔʀtɛj/ *m* toe; **gros ∼** big toe

orthodoxe /ɔʀtɔdɔks/ *adj*, *mf* Orthodox

orthographe /ɔʀtɔgʀaf/ *f* spelling

orthographier /ɔʀtɔgʀafje/ [**v2**] *vt* to spell

orthopédie /ɔʀtɔpedi/ *f* orthopedics

orthophoniste /ɔʀtɔfɔnist/ *mf* speech therapist

ortie /ɔʀti/ *f* (stinging) nettle

orvet /ɔʀvɛ/ *m* slow-worm, blindworm

os /ɔs/, *pl* /o/ *m inv* bone; **en chair et en ∼** in the flesh
IDIOMS **il y a un ∼** (fam) there's a hitch; **tomber sur un ∼** (fam) to come across a snag; **être trempé jusqu'aux ∼** (fam) to be soaked to the skin (fam)

osciller /ɔsile/ [**v1**] *vi* **1** ‹*pendulum*› to swing; ‹*boat*› to rock; ‹*head*› to roll from side to side
2 ‹*currency*› to fluctuate
3 to vacillate

osé, **∼e** /oze/ *adj* **1** risqué
2 ‹*behaviour*› daring; ‹*words*› outspoken

oseille /ozɛj/ *f* **1** sorrel
2 (fam) dough (fam), money

oser /oze/ [**v1**] *vt* to dare; **si j'ose dire** if I may say so

osier /ozje/ *m* **1** (tree) osier
2 wicker, osier

osmose /ɔsmoz/ *f* osmosis

ossature /ɔsatyʀ/ *f* skeleton; **∼ du visage** bone structure

ossements /ɔsmɑ̃/ *mpl* remains

osseux, **-euse** /ɔsø, øz/ *adj* **1** bony
2 ‹*disease*› bone

ostentatoire /ɔstɑ̃tatwaʀ/ *adj* ostentatious

ostéopathe /ɔsteɔpat/ *mf* osteopath

ostracisme /ɔstʀasism/ *m* ostracism

ostréiculture /ɔstʀeikyltyʀ/ *f* oyster farming

otage /ɔtaʒ/ *m* hostage

OTAN /ɔtɑ̃/ *f* (*abbr* = **Organisation du traité de l'Atlantique Nord**) NATO

otarie /ɔtaʀi/ *f* eared seal

ôter /ote/ [**v1**] **A** *vt* **1** to take off ‹*clothes, glasses*›; to remove ‹*bones, stain*›
2 ∼ qch à qn to take sth away from sb
3 (in mathematics) **4 ôté de 9, il reste 5** 9 minus *or* take away 4 leaves 5
B s'ôter *v refl* (+ *v être*) **s'∼ qch de l'esprit** to get sth out of one's mind *or* head

otite /ɔtit/ *f* inflammation of the ear

oto-rhino-laryngologiste, *pl* **∼s** /otoʀinolaʀɛ̃gɔlɔʒist/ *mf* ENT specialist

ou /u/ *conj* or; **∼ (bien)... ∼ (bien)...** either... or...

où /u/ **A** *adv* where; **je l'ai perdu je ne sais ∼** I've lost it somewhere or other; **par ∼ êtes-vous passés pour venir?** which way did you come?; **∼ en êtes-vous?** where have you got to?; **∼ allons-nous?** what are things coming to!
B *rel pron* **1** where; **le quartier ∼ nous habitons** the area we live in; **d'∼ s'élevait de la fumée** out of which smoke was rising; **∼ qu'ils aillent** wherever they go
2 la misère ∼ elle se trouvait the poverty in which she was living; **au train** *or* **à l'allure ∼ vont les choses** (at) the rate things are going; **le travail s'est accumulé, d'∼ ce retard** there is a backlog of work, hence the delay
3 when; **le matin ∼ je l'ai rencontré** the morning I met him

ouate /wat/ *f* **1** cotton wool (BrE), cotton (AmE)
2 wadding

oubli /ubli/ *m* **1 l'∼ de qch** forgetting sth; (of duty) neglect of sth
2 omission
3 oblivion; **tomber dans l'∼** to be completely forgotten

oublier /ublije/ [**v2**] **A** *vt* **1** to forget ‹*name, date, fact*›; to forget about ‹*worries, incident*›; **se faire ∼** to keep a low profile
2 to leave out ‹*person, detail*›
3 to neglect ‹*duty, friend*›
B s'oublier *v refl* (+ *v être*) **1** to be forgotten
2 to leave oneself out

oubliettes /ublijɛt/ *fpl* oubliette

oued /wɛd/ *m* wadi

ouest /wɛst/ **A** *adj inv* west; western
B *m* **1** west
2 l'Ouest the West

ouf /uf/ **A** *m* **faire ∼** to breathe a sigh of relief
B *excl* phew!

O

✓ **oui** /wi/ **A** *adv* yes; **alors c'est ~?** so the answer is yes?; **découvrir si ~ ou non** to discover whether or not; **dire ~ à qch** to welcome sth; to agree to sth; **faire ~ de la tête** to nod; **lui, prudent? un lâche, ~!** him, cautious? a coward, more like! (fam); **je crois que ~** I think so
B *m inv* **1** yes
2 'yes' vote; **le ~ l'a emporté** the ayes have it
IDIOM **pour un ~ (ou) pour un non** ‹*get angry*› for the slightest thing; ‹*change one's mind*› at the drop of a hat

ouï, **~e** /wi/ ▶ **ouïr**

ouï-dire /widiʀ/ *m inv* **par ~** by hearsay

ouïe /wi/ *f* **1** hearing; **être tout ~** to be all ears
2 (of fish) gill

ouïr /wiʀ/ [**v38**] *vt* (dated) to hear; **j'ai ouï dire que** word has reached me that

ouistiti /wistiti/ *m* marmoset

ouragan /uʀagɑ̃/ *m* hurricane

ourler /uʀle/ [**v1**] *vt* to hem

ourlet /uʀlɛ/ *m* hem

ours /uʀs/ *m inv* **1** bear
2 il est un peu ~ he's a bit surly
■ **~ blanc** polar bear; **~ en peluche** teddy bear; **~ polaire** ▶ **ours blanc**
IDIOM **vendre la peau de l'~ avant de l'avoir tué** (Proverb) to count one's chickens before they're hatched

ourse /uʀs/ *f* she-bear

oursin /uʀsɛ̃/ *m* (sea) urchin

ourson /uʀsɔ̃/ *m* bear cub

✓ **outil** /uti/ *m* tool; **~ de travail** work tool

outrage /utʀaʒ/ *m* insult
■ **~ à agent** *verbal assault of a policeman*

outrager /utʀaʒe/ [**v13**] *vt* to offend

outrance /utʀɑ̃s/ *f* **à ~** excessively

outrancier, **-ière** /utʀɑ̃sje, ɛʀ/ *adj* extreme

outre /utʀ/ **A** *prep* in addition to
B *adv* **passer ~** to pay no heed
C **outre mesure** *phr* unduly
D **en outre** *phr* in addition

outre-Atlantique /utʀatlɑ̃tik/ *adv* across the Atlantic; **d'~** American

outre-Manche /utʀəmɑ̃ʃ/ *adv* across the Channel; **d'~** British

outremer /utʀəmɛʀ/ *adj inv*, *m* ultramarine

outre-mer /utʀəmɛʀ/ *adv* overseas

outrer /utʀe/ [**v1**] *vt* **1** to outrage
2 to exaggerate

outre-tombe /utʀətɔ̃b/ *adv* **une voix d'~** a voice from beyond the grave

✓ **ouvert**, **~e** /uvɛʀ, ɛʀt/ **A** *pp* ▶ **ouvrir**
B *pp adj* **1** open; **grand ~** wide open; **être ~ aux idées nouvelles** to be open to new ideas
2 ‹*gas*› on; ‹*tap*› running
3 ‹*question*› open-ended

ouvertement /uvɛʀtəmɑ̃/ *adv* openly; blatantly

✓ key word

✓ **ouverture** /uvɛʀtyʀ/ *f* **1** opening; **heures d'~** opening hours
2 openness; **~ d'esprit** open-mindedness; **~ à l'Ouest** opening up to the West
3 (Mus) overture

ouvrable /uvʀabl/ *adj* ‹*day*› working; ‹*hours*› business

✓ **ouvrage** /uvʀaʒ/ *m* **1** work
2 book, work
3 piece of work; **~ de broderie** piece of embroidery
IDIOM **avoir du cœur à l'~** to work with a will

ouvragé, **~e** /uvʀaʒe/ *adj* finely wrought

ouvrant, **~e** /uvʀɑ̃, ɑ̃t/ *adj* **toit ~** sunroof

ouvré, **~e** /uvʀe/ *adj* **jour ~** working day

ouvre-boîtes /uvʀəbwat/ *m inv* can opener

ouvreur, **-euse** /uvʀœʀ, øz/ *mf* usher/usherette

✓ **ouvrier**, **-ière** /uvʀije, ɛʀ/ **A** *adj* of the workers; **classe ouvrière** working class
B *mf* worker; workman

✓ **ouvrir** /uvʀiʀ/ [**v32**] **A** *vt* (gen) to open; to undo ‹*collar, shirt, zip*›; to initiate ‹*dialogue*›; to open up ‹*possibilities, market*›; **ne pas ~ la bouche** not to say a word; **~ les bras à qn** to welcome sb with open arms; **~ l'esprit à qn** to open sb's mind
B *vi* **1** to open the door; **ouvre-moi!** let me in!
2 to open
3 to be opened
C **s'ouvrir** *v refl* (+ *v être*) (gen) to open; ‹*shirt, dress*› to come undone; ‹*dialogue, process*› to be initiated; ‹*country, economy*› to open up; ‹*ground, scar*› to open up; ‹*person*› to cut open ‹*head*›; **s'~ les veines** to slash one's wrists; **s'~ à qn** to open one's heart to sb

ovaire /ɔvɛʀ/ *m* ovary

ovale /ɔval/ *adj*, *m* oval

ovation /ɔvasjɔ̃/ *f* **1** ovation
2 accolade

ovationner /ɔvasjɔne/ [**v1**] *vt* to greet [sb/sth] with wild applause

ovni /ɔvni/ *m* (*abbr* = **objet volant non identifié**) unidentified flying object, UFO

ovulation /ɔvylasjɔ̃/ *f* ovulation

ovule /ɔvyl/ *m* **1** (Anat) ovum
2 (Bot) ovule

oxyde /ɔksid/ *m* oxide; **~ de carbone** carbon monoxide

oxyder /ɔkside/ [**v1**] *vt*, **s'oxyder** *v refl* (+ *v être*) to oxidize

oxygène /ɔksiʒɛn/ *m* **1** oxygen
2 air

oxygéner /ɔksiʒene/ [**v14**] **A** *vt* to oxygenate
B **s'oxygéner** *v refl* (+ *v être*) ‹*person*› to get some fresh air

ozone /ozon/ *f* ozone; **la couche d'~** the ozone layer

Pp

p, **P** /pe/ *m inv* p, P

PAC *f* (*abbr* = **politique agricole commune**) CAP

pacha /paʃa/ *m* pasha

pachyderme /paʃidɛʀm/ *m* (Zool) pachyderm; **de ~** (fig) heavy

pacifier /pasifje/ [**v1**] *vt* to establish peace in

pacifique /pasifik/ **A** *adj* peaceful **B** *mf* peace-loving person

Pacifique /pasifik/ *pr m* **le ~** the Pacific

pacifiste /pasifist/ *adj*, *mf* pacifist

pacotille /pakɔtij/ *f* **de la ~** cheap rubbish

PACS /paks/ *m* (*abbr* = **pacte civil de solidarité**) contract of civil union

pacsé, **-e** /pakse/ *mf* civil partner

pacser: **se pacser** /pakse/ [**v1**] *v refl* (+ *v être*) to sign a PACS

pacte /pakt/ *m* pact

PAF /paf/ **A** *m: abbr* ▶ **paysage** **B** *f: abbr* ▶ **police**

pagaie /pagɛ/ *f* (Naut) paddle

pagaille **A** *f* mess; **semer la ~** to cause chaos **B** **en pagaille** *phr* in a mess

paganisme /paganism/ *m* paganism

pagayer /pageje/ [**v21**] *vi* to paddle

page¹ /paʒ/ *m* page (boy)

page² /paʒ/ *f* page; **en première ~** on the front page; **tourner la ~** (fig) to turn over a new leaf
■ **~ d'accueil** (Comput) home page; **~ de publicité** commercial break
IDIOM **être à la ~** to be up to date

pagination /paʒinasjɔ̃/ *f* pagination

paginer /paʒine/ [**v1**] *vt* to paginate

pagne /paɲ/ *m* **1** loincloth **2** grass skirt

pagode /pagɔd/ *f* pagoda

paie /pɛ/ *f* pay; **bulletin** *or* **fiche de ~** payslip
IDIOM **ça fait une ~ que je ne l'ai pas vu** (fam) it's ages since I saw him (fam)

paiement /pɛmɑ̃/ *m* payment

païen, **-ïenne** /pajɛ̃, ɛn/ *adj*, *mf* pagan

paillard, **~e** /pajaʀ, aʀd/ *adj* bawdy

paillasse /pajas/ *f* **1** straw mattress **2** lab bench **3** draining board

paillasson /pajasɔ̃/ *m* doormat

paille /pɑj/ **A** *adj inv* **jaune ~** straw yellow **B** *f* straw; **~ de fer** steel wool
IDIOMS **être sur la ~** (fam) to be penniless; **tirer à la courte ~** to draw lots

paillette /pajɛt/ *f* **1** sequin, spangle (AmE); **robe à ~s** sequined *or* spangled (AmE) dress **2** glitter **3** **savon en ~s** soap flakes

pain /pɛ̃/ *m* **1** bread; **des miettes de ~** breadcrumbs **2** loaf; **un petit ~** a (bread) roll **3** **~ de viande** meat loaf **4** (of soap) bar
■ **~ blanc** white bread; **~ de campagne** farmhouse bread; **~ complet** wholemeal bread (BrE), wholewheat bread (AmE); **~ d'épices** gingerbread; **~ grillé** toast; **~ au lait** milk roll; **~ de mie** sandwich loaf; **~ de seigle** rye bread; **~ de son** bran loaf
IDIOMS **se vendre comme des petits ~s** to sell like hot cakes; **ça ne mange pas de ~** (fam) it doesn't cost anything; **je ne mange pas de ce ~-là** (fam) I won't have anything to do with it

pair, **~e** /pɛʀ/ **A** *adj* ‹*number*› even **B** *m* **1** peer; **c'est une cuisinière hors ~** she's an excellent cook **2** **aller** *or* **marcher de ~ avec qch** to go hand in hand with sth **C** **au pair** *phr* **travailler au ~** to work as an au pair

paire /pɛʀ/ *f* pair; **donner une ~ de gifles à qn** to box sb's ears
IDIOM **les deux font la ~!** they're two of a kind!

paisible /pɛzibl/ *adj* peaceful, quiet, calm

paisiblement /pɛzibləmɑ̃/ *adv* peacefully

paître /pɛtʀ/ [**v74**] *vi* to graze
IDIOM **envoyer ~ qn** (fam) to send sb packing (fam)

paix /pɛ/ *f inv* peace; **avoir la ~** to get some peace; **laisser qn en ~** to leave sb alone; **la ~!** (fam) be quiet!

pakistanais, **~e** /pakistanɛ, ɛz/ *adj* Pakistani

palabrer /palabʀe/ [**v1**] *vi* to discuss endlessly

palace /palas/ *m* luxury hotel

palais /palɛ/ *m inv* **1** palate **2** palace **3** (Law) **~ (de justice)** law courts
■ **~ des sports** sports centre (BrE)

palan /palɑ̃/ *m* hoist

pale /pal/ *f* (of propeller, oar) blade

pâle /pɑl/ *adj* pale; **vert ~** pale green
IDIOM **faire ~ figure à côté de** to pale into insignificance beside

palefrenier, -ière /palfʀənje, ɛʀ/ *mf* groom
paléolithique /paleɔlitik/ *adj, m* Palaeolithic
paléontologie /paleɔ̃tɔlɔʒi/ *f* palaeontology
palet /palɛ/ *m* **1** (in ice hockey) puck
2 quoit
paletot /palto/ *m* jacket
IDIOM **tomber sur le ~ de qn** (fam) to lay into sb (fam)
palette /palɛt/ *f* **1** palette
2 range; **une ~ d'activités** a range of activities
3 (of pork, mutton) ≈ shoulder
pâleur /pɑlœʀ/ *f* paleness; pallor
palier /palje/ *m* **1** landing; **mon voisin de ~** my neighbour (BrE) on the same floor
2 level; plateau
3 (in diving) **~ (de décompression)** (decompression) stage
palière /paljɛʀ/ *adj f* **porte ~** entry door
pâlir /pɑliʀ/ [**v3**] *vi* **1** to fade
2 to grow pale
palissade /palisad/ *f* fence
palliatif /paljatif/ *m* palliative
pallier /palje/ [**v2**] *vt* to compensate for
palmarès /palmaʀɛs/ *m inv* **1** honours (BrE) list; list of (award) winners
2 record of achievements
3 hit parade
4 bestsellers list
palme /palm/ *f* **1** palm leaf
2 palm (tree)
3 (for diver) flipper
4 (Mil) ≈ bar
5 prize
palmé, ~e /palme/ *adj* **1** ‹*feet*› webbed
2 ‹*leaf*› palmate
palmier /palmje/ *m* palm (tree)
palombe /palɔ̃b/ *f* wood pigeon
palourde /paluʀd/ *f* clam
palpable /palpabl/ *adj* palpable; tangible
palper /palpe/ [**v1**] *vt* **1** (Med) to palpate
2 to feel
palpitant, ~e /palpitɑ̃, ɑ̃t/ *adj* thrilling
palpitation /palpitasjɔ̃/ *f* **1** (Med) palpitation
2 twitching
palpiter /palpite/ [**v1**] *vi* ‹*heart*› to beat; to flutter; ‹*vein*› to pulse
paludisme /palydism/ *m* malaria
pâmer: se pâmer /pɑme/ [**v1**] *v refl* (+ *v être*) (liter) **se ~ devant qch** to swoon over sth
pamphlet /pɑ̃flɛ/ *m* satirical tract
pamphlétaire /pɑ̃fletɛʀ/ *mf* pamphleteer
pamplemousse /pɑ̃pləmus/ *m* grapefruit
pan /pɑ̃/ **A** *m* **1** (of cliff, house) section; (of life) part
2 (of tower) side; **~s d'un manteau** coat-tails
B *excl also onomatopoeic* bang!; thump!; whack!

pan- /pɑ̃, pan/ *pref* Pan; **~-russe** Pan-Russian; **~-européen** Pan-European
panacée /panase/ *f* panacea
panache /panaʃ/ *m* **1** panache
2 plume
panaché, ~e /panaʃe/ **A** *adj* ‹*bouquet, salad*› mixed; ‹*tulip, ivy*› variegated
B *m* shandy (BrE), shandygaff (AmE)
panacher /panaʃe/ [**v1**] *vt* to mix
panama /panama/ *m* panama (hat)
panaris /panaʀi/ *m inv* whitlow
pancarte /pɑ̃kaʀt/ *f* **1** notice (BrE), sign (AmE)
2 placard (BrE), sign (AmE)
pancréas /pɑ̃kʀeas/ *m inv* pancreas
panda /pɑ̃da/ *m* panda
pandémie /pɑ̃demi/ *f* pandemic
paner /pane/ [**v1**] *vt* to coat with breadcrumbs
panier /panje/ *m* **1** basket
2 (in dishwasher) rack
3 (Sport) basket
■ **~ à linge** linen basket; **~ à salade** salad shaker; Black Maria (BrE), paddy wagon (AmE)
IDIOMS **être un ~ percé** (fam) to spend money like water; **ils sont tous à mettre dans le même ~** (fam) they are all about the same; **le dessus du ~** (fam) the pick of the bunch; **mettre au ~** to throw [sth] out; to get rid of [sth]
panique /panik/ *f* panic; **semer** *or* **jeter la ~** to spread panic; **être pris de ~** to be panic-stricken
paniquer /panike/ [**v1**] *vi* (fam) to panic
panne /pan/ *f* (of vehicle, machine) breakdown; (of engine) failure; **~ de courant** power failure; **tomber en ~ sèche** *or* **d'essence** to run out of petrol (BrE) *or* gas (AmE); **être en ~ de** (fam) to be out of ‹*coffee*›; to have run out of ‹*ideas*›
panneau, *pl* **~x** /pano/ *m* **1** sign; board
2 notice board (BrE), bulletin board (AmE)
3 panel
■ **~ de configuration** (Comput) control panel; **~ indicateur** signpost; **~ publicitaire** hoarding (BrE), billboard; **~ de signalisation routière** road sign; **~ solaire** solar panel
IDIOM **tomber dans le ~** (fam) to fall for it (fam)
panonceau, *pl* **~x** /panɔ̃so/ *m* sign; board
panoplie /panɔpli/ *f* **1** outfit
2 display of weapons
panorama /panɔʀama/ *m* **1** panorama
2 (of art, culture) survey
panoramique /panɔʀamik/ *adj* **1** ‹*view, visit*› panoramic
2 ‹*windscreen*› wrap-around
3 ‹*screen*› wide
panse /pɑ̃s/ *f* **1** (of cow) paunch
2 (fam) belly (fam)
3 (of jug) belly

key word

pansement /pɑ̃smɑ̃/ *m* dressing; ~ **(adhésif)** plaster (BrE), Band-Aid®

panser /pɑ̃se/ [**v1**] *vt* to dress ‹*wound*›; to put a dressing on ‹*arm, leg*›

pantalon /pɑ̃talɔ̃/ *m* trousers (BrE), pants (AmE); ~ **de pyjama** pyjama (BrE) *or* pajama (AmE) bottoms

panthère /pɑ̃tɛʀ/ *f* panther

pantin /pɑ̃tɛ̃/ *m* puppet

pantois, **~e** /pɑ̃twa, az/ *adj* flabbergasted

pantomime /pɑ̃tɔmim/ *f* **1** mime
2 mime show

pantouflard, **~e** /pɑ̃tuflaʀ, aʀd/ *adj* (fam) **qu'est-ce que tu es ~!** what a stay-at-home you are!

pantoufle /pɑ̃tufl/ *f* slipper

panure /panyʀ/ *f* breadcrumbs

PAO /peao/ *f* **1** *abbr* ▸ **production**
2 *abbr* ▸ **publication**

paon /pɑ̃/ *m* peacock

paonne /pan/ *f* peahen

papa /papa/ *m* dad (fam), daddy (fam), father; **fils/fille à ~** spoiled little rich kid (fam)

pape /pap/ *m* **1** pope
2 (fig) high priest

paperasse /papʀas/ *f* (fam) **1** bumph (BrE) (fam), documents
2 paperwork

papeterie /papɛtʀi/ *f* **1** stationer's (shop), stationery shop (BrE) *or* store (AmE)
2 stationery
3 papermaking industry
4 paper mill

papi /papi/ *m* (fam) granddad (fam), grandpa (fam)

papier /papje/ *m* **1** paper
2 ~s (d'identité) (identity) papers *or* documents
3 (fam) (newspaper) article, piece (fam)
■ **~ alu** (fam) **~ (d')aluminium** aluminium (BrE) *or* aluminum (AmE) foil, kitchen foil; **~ brouillon** rough paper (BrE), scrap paper; **~ cadeau** gift wrap; **~ d'emballage** wrapping paper; **~ hygiénique** toilet paper; **~ journal** newsprint; **~ à lettres** writing paper; **~ peint** wallpaper; **~ de verre** sandpaper; **~s gras** litter
IDIOM **être dans les petits ~s de qn** (fam) to be in sb's good books; ▸ **musique**

papier-calque, *pl* **papiers-calque** /papjekalk/ *m* tracing paper

papillon /papijɔ̃/ *m* **1** butterfly; **~ de nuit** moth
2 (brasse) ~ butterfly (stroke)

papillonner /papijɔne/ [**v1**] *vi* **1** to flit about
2 to flirt incessantly

papillote /papijɔt/ *f* **1** (Culin) foil parcel
2 (for hair) curl paper

papoter /papɔte/ [**v1**] *vi* (fam) to chatter

paprika /papʀika/ *m* paprika

papy ▸ **papi**

Pâque /pɑk/ *f* **la ~ juive** Passover

paquebot /pakbo/ *m* liner

pâquerette /pɑkʀɛt/ *f* daisy
IDIOM **être au ras des ~s** (fam) to be very basic

Pâques /pɑk/ *m, fpl* Easter

paquet /pakɛ/ *m* **1** packet (BrE), package (AmE); (of cigarettes, coffee) packet (BrE), pack (AmE)
2 parcel
3 (of clothes) bundle
4 (fam) masses
5 (fam) packet (BrE) (fam), bundle (AmE) (fam)
■ **~ de muscles** (fam) muscleman
IDIOM **mettre le ~** (fam) to pull out all the stops

paquet-cadeau, *pl* **paquets-cadeaux** /pakɛkado/ *m* gift-wrapped present

par /paʀ/ **A** *prep* **1 elle est arrivée ~ la droite** she came from the right; **le peintre a terminé** *or* **fini ~ la cuisine** the painter did the kitchen last
2 ~ le passé in the past; **~ une belle journée d'été** on a beautiful summer's day; **ils sortent même ~ moins 40°** they go outdoors even when it's minus 40°
3 per; **~ jour/an** a day/year; **~ personne** per person
4 by; **payer ~ carte de crédit** to pay by credit card; **être pris ~ son travail** to be taken up with one's work; **deux ~ deux** ‹*work*› in twos; ‹*walk*› two by two
5 in; **~ étapes** in stages; **~ endroits** in places
6 l'accident est arrivé ~ sa faute it was his/her fault that the accident happened; **~ jalousie** out of jealousy
7 through; **tu peux me faire passer le livre ~ ta sœur** you can get the book to me via your sister; **entre ~ le garage** come in through the garage
B de par *phr* (fml) **1 voyager de ~ le monde** to travel all over the world
2 de ~ leurs origines by virtue of their origins

parabole /paʀabɔl/ *f* **1** parable
2 parabola

parachever /paʀaʃve/ [**v16**] *vt* **1** to complete
2 to put the finishing touches to

parachutage /paʀaʃytaʒ/ *m* airdrop

parachute /paʀaʃyt/ *m* parachute

parachuter /paʀaʃyte/ [**v1**] *vt* to parachute

parachutisme /paʀaʃytism/ *m* parachuting

parachutiste /paʀaʃytist/ *mf* **1** parachutist
2 paratrooper

parade /paʀad/ *f* **1** (Mil) parade
2 (in fencing) parry
3 (by animal) display

parader /paʀade/ [**v1**] *vi* to strut about

paradis /paʀadi/ *m inv* **1** heaven
2 paradise
■ **~ terrestre** Garden of Eden
IDIOM **tu ne l'emporteras pas au ~** (fam) you'll live to regret it

paradisiaque /paʀadizjak/ *adj* heavenly

paradoxal, **~e**, *mpl* **-aux** /paʀadɔksal, o/ *adj* paradoxical

paradoxe /paʀadɔks/ *m* paradox

paraffine /paʀafin/ *f* **1** paraffin (BrE), kerosene (AmE)
2 paraffin wax

parages /paʀaʒ/ *mpl* neighbourhood (BrE); **elle est dans les ~** she is around somewhere

paragraphe /paʀagʀaf/ *m* paragraph

🔑 **paraître** /paʀɛtʀ/ [**v73**] **A** *vi* **1** to come out, to be published; **'à ~'** 'forthcoming titles'
2 to appear, to seem, to look
3 to appear; to show; **elle ne laisse rien ~ de ses sentiments** she doesn't let her feelings show at all; **~ en public** to appear in public; **~ à son avantage** to look one's best
B *v impers* **il paraît qu'il a menti** apparently he lied; **oui, il paraît** so I hear

parallèle¹ /paʀalɛl/ **A** *adj* **1** parallel
2 ‹*market*› unofficial; ‹*medicine*› alternative
B *m* parallel

parallèle² /paʀalɛl/ *f* parallel line

parallèlement /paʀalɛlmɑ̃/ *adv* **1 ~ à** parallel to
2 at the same time

paralyser /paʀalize/ [**v1**] *vt* **1** (Med) to paralyse (BrE)
2 to paralyse (BrE) [sth]; to bring [sth] to a halt

paralysie /paʀalizi/ *f* paralysis

paralytique /paʀalitik/ *adj*, *mf* paralytic

paramédical, **~e**, *mpl* **-aux** /paʀamedikal, o/ *adj* paramedical

paramètre /paʀamɛtʀ/ *m* parameter; **~s** (Comput) settings

paranoïaque /paʀanɔjak/ *adj*, *mf* paranoiac

paranormal, **~e**, *mpl* **-aux** /paʀanɔʀmal, o/ *adj* paranormal

parapente /paʀapɑ̃t/ *m* **1** paraglider
2 paragliding

parapharmacie /paʀafaʀmasi/ *f* toiletries and vitamins

paraphe /paʀaf/ *m* **1** initials
2 signature

paraphrase /paʀafʀɑz/ *f* paraphrase

paraplégique /paʀapleʒik/ *adj*, *mf* paraplegic

parapluie /paʀaplɥi/ *m* umbrella

parascolaire /paʀaskɔlɛʀ/ *adj* extracurricular

parasitaire /paʀazitɛʀ/ *adj* parasitic(al)

parasite /paʀazit/ **A** *adj* ‹*organism*› parasitic(al); ‹*idea*› intrusive
B *m* **1** parasite
2 (on TV, radio) **~s** interference

parasol /paʀasɔl/ *m* beach umbrella; sun umbrella

paratonnerre /paʀatɔnɛʀ/ *m* lightning rod

paravent /paʀavɑ̃/ *m* screen

🔑 **parc** /paʀk/ *m* **1** park
2 playpen
3 (for animals) pen
4 (of facilities) (total) number; (of capital goods) stock; **~ automobile** fleet of cars; (nationwide) number of cars (on the road); **~ immobilier** housing stock
■ **~ d'attractions** amusement *or* theme park; **~ de loisirs** theme park; **~ national** national park; **~ naturel** nature park

🔑 **parce**: **parce que** /paʀs(ə)k(ə)/ *phr* because

parcelle /paʀsɛl/ *f* **1** plot (of land)
2 une ~ de bonheur a bit of happiness

parchemin /paʀʃəmɛ̃/ *m* parchment

par-ci /paʀsi/ *adv* **~ par-là** here and there

parcimonie /paʀsimɔni/ *f* parsimony

parcmètre /paʀkmɛtʀ/ *m* parking meter

🔑 **parcourir** /paʀkuʀiʀ/ [**v26**] *vt* **1** to travel all over ‹*country*›; **~ la ville** to go all over town
2 to cover ‹*distance*›
3 to glance through ‹*letter*›; to scan ‹*horizon*›

parcours /paʀkuʀ/ *m inv* **1** (of bus, traveller) route; (of river) course; **~ fléché** waymarked trail
2 (Sport) course; **~ de golf** round of golf
3 career; **son ~** (of artist) the development of his/her art; **incident de ~** hitch

par-delà /paʀdəla/ *prep* beyond

par-derrière /paʀdɛʀjɛʀ/ *adv* **1 passer ~** to go round (BrE) *or* to the back; **ils m'ont attaqué ~** they attacked me from behind
2 critiquer qn ~ to criticize sb behind his/her back

par-dessous /paʀdəsu/ *prep*, *adv* underneath

pardessus /paʀdəsy/ *m inv* overcoat

par-dessus /paʀdəsy/ **A** *adv* **1 pose ton sac dans un coin et mets ton manteau ~** put your bag in a corner and put your coat on top of it
2 le mur n'est pas haut, passe ~ the wall isn't high, climb over it
B *prep* **1 saute ~ le ruisseau** jump over the stream
2 ce que j'aime ~ tout what I like best of all

par-devant /paʀdəvɑ̃/ *adv* **1 passer ~** to come round by the front
2 il te fait des sourires ~ mais dit du mal de toi dans ton dos he's all smiles to your face but says nasty things about you behind your back

pardon /paʀdɔ̃/ *m* **1** forgiveness; pardon; **je te demande ~** I'm sorry
2 ~! sorry!; **~ madame/monsieur, je cherche...** excuse me please, I'm looking for...

🔑 key word

pardonnable /paʀdɔnabl/ *adj* forgivable; **ils ne sont pas ~s** it's unforgivable of them

pardonner /paʀdɔne/ [**v1**] **A** *vt* to forgive; **pardonnez-moi, mais...** excuse me, but... **B** *vi* **ne pas ~** ‹*illness, error*› to be fatal

pare-balles /paʀbal/ *adj inv* bulletproof

pare-brise /paʀbʀiz/ *m inv* windscreen (BrE), windshield (AmE)

pare-chocs /paʀʃɔk/ *m inv* bumper (BrE), fender (AmE)

pare-feu, *pl* **~** *or* **pare-feux** /paʀfø/ *m* **1** (outdoor) firebreak **2** (Comput) firewall

pareil, **-eille** /paʀɛj/ **A** *adj* **1** similar; **c'est toujours ~ avec toi** it's always the same with you; **à nul autre ~** without equal **2** such; **je n'ai jamais dit une chose pareille** I never said any such thing **B** *mf* equal; **d'un dynamisme sans ~** incredibly dynamic; **pour moi c'est du ~ au même** (fam) it makes no difference to me **C** *adv* (fam) **faire ~** to do the same

parent, **~e** /paʀɑ̃, ɑ̃t/ **A** *adj* ‹*languages*› similar; **~ avec** ‹*person*› related to **B** *mf* **1** relative, relation **2** (Zool) parent **C** *m* **1** parent **2** **~s** forebears ■ **~ pauvre** poor relation

parental, **~e**, *mpl* **-aux** /paʀɑ̃tal, o/ *adj* parental

parenté /paʀɑ̃te/ *f* **1** (between people) blood relationship **2** (between stories) connection

parenthèse /paʀɑ̃tɛz/ *f* **1** bracket; **ouvrir une ~** (fig) to digress; **entre ~s** (fig) incidentally **2** interlude

parer /paʀe/ [**v1**] **A** *vt* **1** to ward off **2** to protect **3** to adorn **4** **~ qn/qch de qch** to attribute sth to sb/sth **B** **parer à** *v+prep* **~ à toute éventualité** to be prepared for all contingencies; **~ au plus pressé** to deal with the most urgent matters first

pare-soleil /paʀsɔlɛj/ *m inv* visor

paresse /paʀɛs/ *f* laziness

paresser /paʀɛse/ [**v1**] *vi* to laze (around)

paresseux, **-euse** /paʀɛsø, øz/ **A** *adj* lazy **B** *mf* lazy person **C** *m* (Zool) sloth

parfaire /paʀfɛʀ/ [**v10**] *vt* to complete ‹*education, works*›; to perfect ‹*technique*›

parfait, **~e** /paʀfɛ, ɛt/ **A** *adj* **1** perfect **2** ‹*likeness*› exact; ‹*discretion*› absolute **3** ‹*tourist*› archetypal; ‹*example*› classic **B** *m* (in grammar) perfect

parfaitement /paʀfɛtmɑ̃/ *adv* ‹*happy, capable*› perfectly; ‹*tolerate, accept*› fully

parfois /paʀfwa/ *adv* sometimes

parfum /paʀfœ̃/ *m* **1** perfume **2** (of flower, fruit) scent; (of bath salts) fragrance; (of wine) bouquet; (of coffee) aroma **3** flavour (BrE)

IDIOM **mettre qn au ~** (fam) to put sb in the picture

parfumé, **~e** /paʀfyme/ **A** *pp* ▸ **parfumer** **B** *pp adj* **1** ‹*flower*› sweet-scented; ‹*fruit, air*› fragrant **2** ‹*handkerchief*› scented **3** **glace ~e au café** coffee-flavoured (BrE) ice cream

parfumer /paʀfyme/ [**v1**] **A** *vt* **1** **les fleurs parfument la pièce** the room is fragrant with flowers **2** to put scent on ‹*handkerchief*›; to put scent in ‹*bath*› **3** to flavour (BrE) **B** **se parfumer** *v refl* (+ *v être*) **1** to wear perfume **2** to put perfume on

parfumerie /paʀfymʀi/ *f* perfumery

pari /paʀi/ *m* **1** bet **2** betting **3** gamble

parier /paʀje/ [**v2**] *vt* to bet; **il y a fort** *or* **gros à ~ que** it's a safe bet that; **je l'aurais parié!** I knew it!

Paris /paʀi/ *pr n* Paris

parisien, **-ienne** /paʀizjɛ̃, ɛn/ *adj* Parisian, Paris

parité /paʀite/ *f* parity; **à ~** at parity

parjure /paʀʒyʀ/ *m* perjury

parking /paʀkiŋ/ *m* car park (BrE), parking lot (AmE)

par-là /paʀla/ *adv* **par-ci ~** here and there

parlant, **~e** /paʀlɑ̃, ɑ̃t/ *adj* **1** ‹*gesture*› eloquent; ‹*evidence, figure*› which speaks for itself **2** **le cinéma ~** the talkies (fam); **un film ~** a talking picture

Parlement /paʀləmɑ̃/ *m* Parliament

parlementaire /paʀləmɑ̃tɛʀ/ **A** *adj* parliamentary **B** *mf* **1** Member of Parliament **2** negotiator

parlementer /paʀləmɑ̃te/ [**v1**] *vi* to negotiate

parler /paʀle/ [**v1**] **A** *vt* **1** to speak; **~ (l')italien** to speak Italian **2** **~ affaires/politique** to talk (about) business/politics **B** **parler à** *v+prep* **~ à qn** to talk *or* speak to sb **C** **parler de** *v+prep* **1** **~ de qn/qch** to talk about sb/sth; to mention sb/sth; **~ de tout et de rien, ~ de choses et d'autres** to talk about this and that; **les journaux en ont parlé** it was in the papers; **faire ~ de soi** to get oneself talked about; to make the news; **qui parle de vous expulser?** who said anything about throwing you out?; **ta promesse, parlons-en!** some promise!; **n'en parlons plus!** let's drop it; that's the end of

it; **on m'a beaucoup parlé de vous** I've heard a lot about you
2 ∼ **de** ‹*book, film*› to be about
D *vi* to talk, to speak; **parle plus fort** speak up, speak louder; ∼ **en connaissance de cause** to know what one is talking about; **une prime? tu parles!** (fam) a bonus? you must be joking! (fam); **il s'écoute** ∼ he loves the sound of his own voice
E se parler *v refl* (+ *v être*) **1** to talk *or* speak (to each other)
2 to be on speaking terms
3 ‹*language, dialect*› to be spoken
IDIOM **trouver à qui** ∼ to meet one's match

parloir /paʀlwaʀ/ *m* (in school) visitors' room; (in prison) visiting room; (in convent) parlour (BrE)

parme /paʀm/ *adj inv*, *m* mauve

Parmentier /paʀmɑ̃tje/ *pr n* **hachis** ∼ cottage pie, shepherd's pie

🔑 **parmi** /paʀmi/ *prep* **1** among, amongst
2 demain il sera ∼ **nous** he'll be with us tomorrow
3 choisir ∼ **huit destinations** to choose from eight destinations

parodie /paʀɔdi/ *f* **1** parody
2 mockery

parodier /paʀɔdje/ [**v2**] *vt* to parody

paroi /paʀwa/ *f* **1** (of tunnel) side; (of cave) wall; (of tube, pipe) inner surface
2 (of house) wall
3 ∼ **rocheuse** rock face
4 (Anat) wall

paroisse /paʀwas/ *f* parish

paroissial, ∼**e**, *mpl* **-iaux** /paʀwasjal, o/ *adj* parish

P

🔑 **parole** /paʀɔl/ *f* **1** speech; **avoir la** ∼ **facile** to have the gift of the gab (fam)
2 laisser la ∼ **à qn** to let sb speak; **temps de** ∼ speaking time
3 word; ∼**s en l'air** empty words; **une** ∼ **blessante** a hurtful remark
4 (promise) word; **donner sa** ∼ to give one's word; ∼ **d'honneur!** cross my heart!, I promise!; **ma** ∼**!** (upon) my word!
5 words; **c'est** ∼ **d'évangile** it's gospel truth; ∼**s** words, lyrics; **film sans** ∼**s** silent film

parolier, **-ière** /paʀɔlje, ɛʀ/ *mf* **1** lyric writer
2 librettist

paroxysme /paʀɔksism/ *m* (of pleasure) paroxysm; (of battle) climax; (of ridiculousness) height

parpaing /paʀpɛ̃/ *m* breeze-block, cinder block

parquer /paʀke/ [**v1**] *vt* **1** to pen ‹*cattle*›
2 to coop up ‹*people*›
3 to park ‹*car*›

parquet /paʀkɛ/ *m* **1** parquet (floor)
2 (Law) **le** ∼ ≈ the prosecution

parrain /paʀɛ̃/ *m* **1** godfather
2 (of candidate) sponsor; (of organization) patron

parrainer /paʀene/ [**v1**] *vt* **1** to be patron of ‹*organization*›
2 to sponsor ‹*programme, race*›

parricide /paʀisid/ *m* parricide

parsemer /paʀsəme/ [**v16**] *vt* **une pelouse parsemée de fleurs** a lawn dotted with flowers

🔑 **part** /paʀ/ **A** *f* **1** (of cake) slice; (of meat, rice) helping; (of market, legacy) share; **avoir sa** ∼ **de misères** to have one's (fair) share of misfortunes
2 proportion; **une grande** ∼ **de** a high proportion *or* large part of; **pour une bonne** ∼ to a large *or* great extent; **à** ∼ **entière** ‹*member*› full; ‹*science*› in its own right
3 share; **faire sa** ∼ **de travail** to do one's share of the work; **prendre** ∼ **à** to take part in; **il m'a fait** ∼ **de ses projets** he told me about his plans
4 de toute(s) ∼**(s)** from all sides; **de** ∼ **et d'autre** on both sides, on either side; **de** ∼ **en** ∼ ‹*pierce*› right *or* straight through
5 pour ma/notre ∼ for my/our part; **d'une** ∼**..., d'autre** ∼**...** on (the) one hand... on the other hand...; **prendre qch en mauvaise** ∼ to take sth badly
B à part *phr* **1** ‹*file*› separately; **mettre qch à** ∼ to put sth to one side; **prendre qn à** ∼ to take sb aside; **une salle à** ∼ a separate room; **blague à** ∼ joking aside
2 être un peu à ∼ ‹*person*› to be out of the ordinary; **un cas à** ∼ a special case
3 apart from; **à** ∼ **ça** apart from that
C de la part de *phr* **1 de la** ∼ **de** ‹*write, act*› on behalf of
2 de la ∼ **de qn** from sb; **donne-leur le bonjour de ma** ∼ say hello to them for me; **de leur** ∼**, rien ne m'étonne** nothing they do surprises me
IDIOM **faire la** ∼ **des choses** to put things in perspective

partage /paʀtaʒ/ *m* **1** dividing, sharing; **recevoir qch en** ∼ to be left sth (in a will)
2 distribution
3 sharing, division; **régner sans** ∼ to reign absolutely; **une victoire sans** ∼ a total victory
4 division, partition

partagé, ∼**e** /paʀtaʒe/ **A** *pp* ▶ **partager**
B *pp adj* **1** ‹*opinion, unions*› divided
2 ‹*reactions, feelings*› mixed
3 être ∼ to be torn
4 ‹*grief*› shared; **les torts sont** ∼**s** they are both to blame
5 ‹*affection*› mutual

🔑 **partager** /paʀtaʒe/ [**v13**] **A** *vt* **1** to share; **faire** ∼ **qch à qn** to let sb share in sth; **il sait nous faire** ∼ **ses émotions** he knows how to get his feelings across
2 to divide ‹*country, room*›
3 to divide [sth] (up), to split ‹*inheritance, work*›

🔑 key word

B **se partager** *v refl* (+ *v être*) **1** to share ‹*money, work, responsibility*›
2 to be divided, to be split
3 ‹*costs, responsibility*› to be shared; ‹*cake*› to be cut (up)

partance /paʀtɑ̃s/ *f* **en ~** about to take off; about to sail; about to leave; **être en ~ pour** *or* **vers** to be bound for

partenaire /paʀtənɛʀ/ *mf* partner; **qui était le ~ d'Arletty?** who played opposite Arletty?
■ **~ civil, -e** civil partner; **~s sociaux** ≈ unions and management

partenariat /paʀtənaʀja/ *m* partnership

parterre /paʀtɛʀ/ *m* **1** (in garden) bed
2 stalls (BrE), orchestra (AmE)

✓ **parti**, **~e** /paʀti/ **A** *adj* (fam) **être ~** to be tight (fam)
B *m* **1** group; party; **les ~s de l'opposition** the opposition parties
2 option; **prendre ~** to commit oneself; **prendre le ~ de qn** to side with sb
3 (dated) **bon ~** suitable match
■ **~ pris** bias
IDIOMS **prendre son ~ de qch** to come to terms with sth; **tirer ~ de** to take advantage of [sth]; to turn [sth] to good account

partial, **~e**, *mpl* **-iaux** /paʀsjal, o/ *adj* biased (BrE)

partialité /paʀsjalite/ *f* bias

participant, **~e** /paʀtisipɑ̃, ɑ̃t/ *mf* participant

participation /paʀtisipasjɔ̃/ *f*
1 participation; involvement
2 contribution; **~ aux frais** (financial) contribution
3 (Fin) stake, holding

participe /paʀtisip/ *m* participle; **~ passé** past participle

✓ **participer** /paʀtisipe/ [**v1**] *v+prep* **1 ~ à** to participate in, to take part in; to be involved in
2 ~ à to contribute to

particularisme /paʀtikylaʀism/ *m* distinctive identity

particularité /paʀtikylaʀite/ *f* **1** special feature
2 (of disease, situation) particular nature

particule /paʀtikyl/ *f* particle; **nom à ~** aristocratic name

✓ **particulier**, **-ière** /paʀtikylje, ɛʀ/ **A** *adj*
1 particular
2 ‹*rights, privileges, role*› special; ‹*example, objective*› specific
3 ‹*car, secretary*› private
4 ‹*case, situation*› unusual; ‹*talent, effort*› special; ‹*habits*› odd; ‹*accent, style*› distinctive, unusual; **c'est quelqu'un de très ~** he's/she's somebody out of the ordinary; he's/she's weird
B **en particulier** *phr* **1** in private
2 individually
3 in particular, particularly
C *m* **(simple) ~** private individual

✓ **particulièrement** /paʀtikyljɛʀmɑ̃/ *adv*
1 particularly, exceptionally
2 in particular

✓ **partie** /paʀti/ **A** *adj f* ▶ **parti A**
B *f* **1** part; (of amount, salary) proportion, part; **~ de corps** body part; **la majeure ~ des gens** most people; **en ~** partly, in part; **faire ~ des premiers** to be among the first; **cela fait ~ de leurs avantages** that's one of their advantages
2 line (of work); **il est de la ~** it's in his line (of work)
3 game; **faire une ~** to have a game; **gagner la ~** to win the game; (fig) to win the day; **j'espère que tu seras de la ~** I hope you can come; **ce n'est que ~ remise** maybe next time
4 (in contract, negotiations) party; **les ~s en présence** the parties involved; **être ~ prenante dans** to be actively involved in
5 (Mus) part
■ **~ civile** plaintiff; **~ de pêche** fishing trip; **~ de plaisir** fun
IDIOMS **avoir affaire à forte ~** to have a tough opponent; **prendre qn à ~** to take sb to task

partiel, **-ielle** /paʀsjɛl/ *adj* ‹*payment*› part; ‹*destruction, agreement*› partial

✓ **partir** /paʀtiʀ/ [**v30**] **A** *vi* (+ *v être*) **1** to leave, to go; **~ à pied** to leave on foot; **~ en courant** to run off; **~ sans laisser d'adresse** to disappear without trace; **~ loin/à Paris** to go far away/to Paris; **~ en week-end** to go away for the weekend; **~ à la pêche** to go fishing; **~ en tournée** to set off on tour (BrE) *or* on a tour; **~ en retraite** to retire
2 ‹*vehicle, train*› to leave; ‹*plane*› to take off; ‹*motor*› to start; **les coureurs sont partis** the runners are off; **à vos marques, prêts, partez!** on your marks, get set, go!
3 ‹*bullet*› to be fired; ‹*cork*› to shoot out; ‹*capsule*› to shoot off; ‹*retort*› to slip out; **le coup de feu est parti** the gun went off; **il était tellement énervé que la gifle est partie toute seule** he was so angry that he slapped him/her before he could stop himself
4 ‹*path, road*› to start; **~ favori** to start favourite (BrE); **~ battu d'avance** to be doomed from the start; **~ de rien** to start from nothing; **c'est parti!** go!; **et voilà, c'est parti, il pleut!** (fam) here we go, it's raining!; **être bien parti** to have got (BrE) *or* gotten (AmE) off to a good start; **être bien parti pour gagner** to seem all set to win; **c'est mal parti** (fam) things don't look too good
5 ~ de to start from ‹*idea*›; **~ du principe que** to work on the assumption that; **~ d'une bonne intention** to be well-meant
6 ‹*stain*› to come out; ‹*smell*› to go; ‹*enamel, button*› to come off
7 ‹*parcel, application*› to be sent (off)
8 quand il est parti on ne l'arrête plus (fam) once he starts *or* gets going there's no

p

stopping him
B **à partir de** *phr* from; **à ~ de 16 heures/de 2 000 euros** from 4 o'clock onwards/2,000 euros; **à ~ du moment où** as soon as; as long as; **fabriqué à ~ d'un alliage** made from an alloy

partisan, **~e** /paʀtizɑ̃, an/ **A** *adj* **1** partisan
2 ~ de qch/de faire in favour (BrE) of sth/of doing; **être ~ du moindre effort** (fam) to be lazy
B *mf* (gen) supporter, partisan; (Mil) partisan

partition /paʀtisjɔ̃/ *f* (Mus) score

🔑 **partout** /paʀtu/ *adv* **1** everywhere; **avoir mal ~** to ache all over; **un peu ~ dans le monde** more or less all over the world; **~ où je vais** wherever I go
2 (Sport) **trois (points** *or* **buts) ~** three all
IDIOM **fourrer son nez ~** (fam) to stick one's nose into everything (fam)

parure /paʀyʀ/ *f* **1** finery
2 set of jewels

parution /paʀysjɔ̃/ *f* publication

🔑 **parvenir** /paʀvəniʀ/ [**v36**] *v+prep* (+ *v être*)
1 ~ à to reach ‹*place, person*›; **faire ~ qch à qn** to send sth to sb; to get sth to sb
2 ~ à to reach ‹*agreement*›; to achieve ‹*balance*›
3 ~ à faire to manage to do

parvenu, **~e** /paʀvəny/ *mf* upstart

parvis /paʀvi/ *m inv* (of church) square

🔑 **pas¹** /pa/ *adv* **1 je ne prends ~ de sucre** I don't take sugar; **ils n'ont ~ le téléphone** they haven't got a phone; **je ne pense ~** I don't think so; **elle a aimé le film, mais lui ~** she liked the film but he didn't
2 (in expressions, exclamations) **~ du tout** not at all; **~ le moins du monde** not in the least; **~ tant que ça**, **~ plus que ça** not all that much; **~ d'histoires!** I don't want any arguments *or* fuss!; **~ de chance!** hard luck!; **~ possible!** I can't believe it!; **~ vrai?** (fam) isn't that so?

pas² /pa/ *m inv* **1** step; **marcher à ~ feutrés** to walk softly; **faire ses premiers ~** to take one's first steps; **faire le premier ~** to make the first move; **suivre qn ~ à ~** to follow sb everywhere; **de là à dire qu'il s'en fiche** (fam), **il n'y a qu'un ~** there's only a fine line between that and saying he doesn't care; **j'habite à deux ~ (d'ici)** I live very near here; **l'hiver arrive à grands ~** winter is fast approaching; **apprendre les ~ du tango** to learn how to tango
2 pace; **marcher d'un bon ~** to walk at a brisk pace; **marcher au ~** to march; (on horseback) to walk; **'roulez au ~'** 'dead slow' (BrE), '(very) slow' (AmE); **mettre qn au ~** to bring sb to heel; **partir au ~ de course** to rush off; **j'y vais de ce ~** I'm on my way now
3 footstep
4 footprint; **revenir sur ses ~** to retrace one's steps
IDIOMS **se tirer d'un mauvais ~** to get out of a tight corner; **sauter le ~** to take the plunge; **prendre le ~ sur qch** to overtake sth

pascal, **~e**, *mpl* **~s** *or* **-aux** /paskal, o/ *adj* ‹*weekend*› Easter; ‹*candle, lamb*› paschal

pas-de-porte /padpɔʀt/ *m inv* key money

passable /pasabl/ *adj* **1** ‹*film*› fairly good; ‹*results*› reasonable
2 (Sch) fair

passablement /pasabləmɑ̃/ *adv* ‹*drunk, annoyed*› rather; ‹*drink, worry*› quite a lot

passade /pasad/ *f* fad

🔑 **passage** /pasaʒ/ *m* **1** traffic; **interdire le ~ des camions dans la ville** to ban lorries from (driving through) the town
2 stay; **ton ~ dans la ville a été bref** your stay in the town was brief
3 attendre le ~ du boulanger to wait for the baker's van to come; **je peux te prendre au ~** I can pick you up on the way; **des hôtes de ~** short-stay guests; **se servir au ~** to help oneself; (fig) to take a cut (of the profits); to pocket some of the profits
4 '~ interdit, voie privée' 'no entry, private road'; **pour céder le ~ à l'ambulance** in order to let the ambulance go past
5 chaque ~ de votre chanson à la radio every time your song is played on the radio
6 way, path; **prévoir le ~ de câbles** to plan the route of cables
7 ~ (de qch) à qch transition (from sth) to sth
8 alley; passageway
9 (in novel) passage; (in film) sequence
■ **~ à l'acte** acting out; **~ à niveau** level crossing (BrE), grade crossing (AmE); **~ pour piétons** pedestrian crossing; **~ à tabac** beating; **~ à vide** bad patch; unproductive period

passager, **-ère** /pasaʒe, ɛʀ/ **A** *adj* ‹*situation, crisis*› temporary; ‹*feeling*› passing; ‹*shower*› brief; ‹*unease*› slight, short-lived
B *mf* passenger; **~ clandestin** stowaway

passant, **~e** /pasɑ̃, ɑ̃t/ **A** *adj* ‹*street*› busy
B *mf* passer-by
C *m* (on belt, watch strap) loop

passation /pasasjɔ̃/ *f* **~ des pouvoirs** transfer of power

passe¹ /pɑs/ *m* (fam) **1** master key
2 pass

passe² /pɑs/ *f* **1** (Sport) pass
2 être dans une ~ difficile to be going through a difficult patch; **être en ~ de faire** to be (well) on the way to doing

🔑 **passé**, **~e** /pɑse/ **A** *pp* ▸ **passer**
B *pp adj* **1** ‹*years, experiences*› past; **~ de mode** dated
2 l'année passée last year
3 ‹*colour, material*› faded
C *m* **1** past

🔑 key word

p

2 past (tense)
D *prep* after; **~ 8 heures il s'endort dans son fauteuil** come eight o'clock he goes to sleep in his armchair
■ **~ antérieur** past anterior; **~ composé** present perfect; **~ simple** past historic

passéisme /paseism/ *m* attachment to the past

passe-montagne, *pl* **~s** /pasmɔ̃taɲ/ *m* balaclava

passe-partout /paspaʀtu/ *adj inv* ‹*expression*› catch-all; ‹*garment*› for all occasions

passe-passe /paspas/ *m inv* **tour de ~** conjuring trick; (fig) sleight of hand

passeport /paspɔʀ/ *m* passport

✓ **passer** /pɑse/ [**v1**] **A** *vt* **1** to cross ‹*river, border*›; to go through ‹*door, customs*›; to get over ‹*hedge, obstacle*›; **il m'a fait ~ la frontière** he got me across the border; **~ qch à la douane** to get sth through customs
2 to go past, to pass; **quand vous aurez passé le feu, tournez à droite** turn right after the lights; **le malade ne passera pas la nuit** the patient won't last the night
3 ~ le doigt sur la table to run one's finger over the table-top; **~ la tête à la fenêtre** to stick one's head out of the window
4 to pass ‹*object*›; to pass [sth] on ‹*instructions, disease*›; **~ sa colère sur ses collègues** to take one's anger out on one's colleagues
5 to lend; to give
6 (on phone) **tu peux me ~ Chris?** can you put Chris on?; **je vous le passe** I'm putting you through
7 to take, to sit (BrE) ‹*examination*›; to have ‹*interview*›; **faire ~ un test à qn** to give sb a test
8 to spend ‹*time*›; **dépêche-toi, on ne va pas y ~ la nuit!** (fam) hurry up, or we'll be here all night!
9 elle leur passe tout she lets them get away with murder
10 to skip ‹*page, paragraph*›; **je vous passe les détails** I'll spare you the details
11 ~ l'aspirateur to vacuum
12 to filter ‹*coffee*›; to strain ‹*fruit juice, sauce*›; to purée ‹*vegetables*›
13 to slip [sth] on ‹*garment, ring*›; to slip into ‹*dress*›
14 to play ‹*record, cassette*›; to show ‹*film, slides*›; to place ‹*ad*›
15 to enter into ‹*agreement*›; to place ‹*order*›
16 (Aut) **~ la troisième** to go into third gear
17 (Games) **~ son tour** to pass
B *vi* (+ *v être*) **1** to go past *or* by, to pass; **~ sur un pont** to go over a bridge; **le facteur n'est pas encore passé** the postman (BrE) *or* mailman (AmE) hasn't been yet; **~ à côté de** ‹*person*› to pass; ‹*road*› to run alongside; **~ à pied/à bicyclette** to walk/cycle past
2 je ne fais que ~ I've just popped in (BrE) *or* dropped by for a minute; **~ dans la matinée** ‹*plumber*› to come by in the morning; **~ prendre qn/qch** to pick sb/sth up
3 to go; **passons au salon** let's go into the lounge; **les contrebandiers sont passés en Espagne** the smugglers have crossed into Spain
4 to get through; **tu ne passeras pas, c'est trop étroit** you'll never get through, it's too narrow; **il m'a fait signe de ~** he waved me on; **vas-y, ça passe!** go on, there's plenty of room!; **~ par-dessus bord** to fall overboard; **il est passé par la fenêtre** he fell out of the window; he got in through the window
5 ~ par to go through; **~ par le standard** to go through the switchboard; **je ne sais jamais ce qui te passe par la tête** I never know what's going on in your head
6 (fam) **il accuse le patron, ses collègues, bref, tout le monde y passe** he's accusing the boss, his colleagues—basically, everyone in sight; **que ça te plaise ou non, il va falloir y ~** whether you like it or not, there's no alternative; **on ne peut pas faire autrement que d'en ~ par là** there is no other way around it
7 ~ sur to pass over ‹*question, mistake*›; **~ à côté d'une question** to miss the point; **laisser ~ une occasion** to miss an opportunity
8 soit dit en passant incidentally
9 ‹*comments, speech*› to go down well; ‹*law, measure, candidate*› to get through; ‹*attitude, doctrine*› to be accepted; **j'ai mangé quelque chose qui n'est pas passé** I ate something which didn't agree with me; **que je sois critiqué, passe encore, mais calomnié, non!** criticism is one thing, but I draw the line at slander; **~ au premier tour** to be elected in the first round; **~ dans la classe supérieure** to move up to the year above; **(ça) passe pour cette fois** (fam) I'll let it go this time
10 ~ à l'ennemi to go over to the enemy; **~ de main en main** to be passed around; **~ constamment d'un sujet à l'autre** to flit from one subject to another; **~ à un taux supérieur** to go up to a higher rate
11 ~ pour un imbécile to look a fool; **~ pour un génie** to pass as a genius; **il passe pour l'inventeur de l'ordinateur** he's supposed to have invented computers; **il se fait ~ pour mon frère** he passes himself off as my brother
12 ‹*pain, crisis*› to pass; **quand l'orage sera** *or* **aura passé** when the storm is over; **ça passera** ‹*bad mood*› it'll pass; ‹*hurt*› you'll get over it; **~ de mode** to go out of fashion; **faire ~ à qn l'envie de faire** to cure sb of the desire to do; **ce médicament fait ~ les maux d'estomac** this medicine relieves stomach ache
13 ‹*performer, group*› (on stage) to be appearing; (on TV, radio) to be on; ‹*show, film*›

P

to be on; ‹*music*› to be playing
14 ~ avant/après to come before/after; **il fait ~ sa famille avant ses amis** he puts his family before his friends
15 (fam) **où étais-tu passé?** where did you get to?; **où est passé mon livre?** where has my book got to?
16 ‹*time*› to pass, to go by; **je ne vois pas le temps ~** I don't know where the time goes
17 ~ de père en fils to be handed down from father to son; **l'expression est passée dans la langue** the expression has become part of the language
18 to be promoted to; **elle est passée maître dans l'art de mentir** she's an accomplished liar
19 (fam) **y ~** to die
20 ‹*colour, material*› to fade
21 ‹*coffee*› to filter
22 ~ en marche arrière to go into reverse; **la troisième passe mal** third gear is a bit stiff
23 (in bridge, poker) to pass
24 passer à to turn to; **~ à l'étape suivante** to move on to the next stage; **nous allons ~ au vote** let's vote now
25 passer en *or* **y** ‹*money, amount*› to go on *or* into; ‹*product, material*› to go into
C se passer *v refl* (+ *v être*) **1** to happen; **tout s'est passé très vite** it all happened very fast; **tout se passe comme si le yen avait été dévalué** it's as if the yen had been devalued
2 to take place; **la scène se passe au Viêt Nam** the scene is set in Vietnam
3 ‹*examination, negotiations*› to go; **ça ne se passera pas comme ça!** I won't leave it at that!
4 ‹*period*› to go by, to pass; **deux ans se sont passés depuis** that was two years ago
5 se ~ de to do without ‹*object, activity, person*›; to go without ‹*meal, sleep*›; **se ~ de commentaires** to speak for itself
6 se ~ la langue sur les lèvres to run one's tongue over one's lips; **se ~ la main sur le front** to put a hand to one's forehead
7 ils se sont passé des documents they exchanged some documents
IDIOM **qu'est-ce qu'elle nous a passé!** (fam) she really went for us! (fam)

passerelle /pasʀɛl/ *f* **1** footbridge
2 link
3 (to boat) gangway; (to plane) steps

passe-temps /pastɑ̃/ *m inv* pastime, hobby

passeur, -euse /pasœʀ, øz/ *mf* **1** ferryman/ferrywoman
2 smuggler; (for drugs) courier

passible /pasibl/ *adj* (Law) **~ de** ‹*crime*› punishable by; ‹*person*› liable to

passif, -ive /pasif, iv/ **A** *adj* passive
B *m* **1** passive (voice)
2 debit; **mettre qch au ~ de qn** to count sth amongst sb's failures

✓ **passion** /pasjɔ̃/ *f* passion

passionnant, ~e /pasjɔnɑ̃, ɑ̃t/ *adj* exciting, fascinating, riveting

passionné, ~e /pasjɔne/ **A** *adj* ‹*love*› passionate; ‹*debate, argument*› impassioned; **être ~ de** *or* **pour qch** to have a passion for sth
B *mf* enthusiast

passionnel, -elle /pasjɔnɛl/ *adj* ‹*debate*› impassioned; ‹*crime*› of passion

passionner /pasjɔne/ [**v1**] **A** *vt* **1** to fascinate; **la botanique le passionne** he has a passion for botany
2 to inflame ‹*debate*›
B se passionner *v refl* (+ *v être*) to have a passion (**pour** for)

passivité /pasivite/ *f* passivity

passoire /paswaʀ/ *f* **1** colander
2 strainer

pastel /pastɛl/ **A** *adj inv* ‹*shade*› pastel
B *m* pastel

pastèque /pastɛk/ *f* watermelon

pasteur /pastœʀ/ *m* **1** minister, pastor
2 priest
3 shepherd

pasteuriser /pastœʀize/ [**v1**] *vt* to pasteurize

pastiche /pastiʃ/ *m* pastiche

pastille /pastij/ *f* **1** pastille, lozenge; **~ contre la toux** cough drop
2 ~ de menthe peppermint
3 spot
4 (of cloth, rubber) patch; (of plastic) disc

pastoral, ~e *mpl* **-aux** /pastɔʀal, o/ *adj* pastoral

pastorale /pastɔʀal/ *f* (Mus) pastoral

patachon /pataʃɔ̃/ *m* (fam) **mener une vie de ~** to live in the fast lane

patata /patata/ *excl* (fam) ▸ **patati**

patate /patat/ *f* (fam) **1** spud (fam); **~ douce** sweet potato
2 blockhead (fam), idiot

patati /patati/ *excl* (fam) **~, patata** and so on and so forth

pataud, ~e /pato, od/ *adj* clumsy

patauger /patoʒe/ [**v13**] *vi* **1** to splash about; to paddle
2 to flounder

pâte /pɑt/ **A** *f* **1** pastry; dough; batter
2 paste
B pâtes *fpl* **~s (alimentaires)** pasta
■ **~ d'amandes** marzipan; **~s de fruit(s)** fruit jellies; **~ à modeler** Plasticine®; **~ à tartiner** spread
IDIOM **mettre la main à la ~** to pitch in

pâté /pɑte/ *m* **1** pâté
2 pie; **~ en croûte** ≈ pie
3 ~ de maisons block (of houses)
4 (ink)blot
5 sandcastle

pâtée /pɑte/ *f* dog food; cat food; swill

✓ key word

patelin /patlɛ̃/ *m* (fam) small village
patente /patɑ̃t/ *f: licence* (BrE) *to exercise a trade or profession*
patère /patɛʀ/ *f* peg, hook
paternalisme /patɛʀnalism/ *m* paternalism
paternaliste /patɛʀnalist/ *adj* paternalistic
paternel, -elle /patɛʀnɛl/ *adj* **1** paternal
2 fatherly
paternité /patɛʀnite/ *f* **1** fatherhood; (Law) paternity
2 authorship
pâteux, -euse /pɑtø, øz/ *adj* **1** ‹*substance*› doughy; ‹*gruel*› mushy
2 ‹*voice*› thick
pathétique /patetik/ *adj* moving
pathologique /patɔlɔʒik/ *adj* pathological
patiemment /pasjamɑ̃/ *adv* patiently
patience /pasjɑ̃s/ *f* patience
IDIOM **prendre son mal en ~** to resign oneself to one's fate
patient, ~e /pasjɑ̃, ɑ̃t/ *adj, mf* patient
patienter /pasjɑ̃te/ [**v1**] *vi* to wait
patin /patɛ̃/ *m* **1** skate
2 (Tech) (on helicopter) skid; (on sledge) runner
■ **~ à glace** ice skate; ice-skating; **~ à roulettes** roller skate; roller-skating
patinage /patinaʒ/ *m* skating
patine /patin/ *f* patina; finish, sheen
patiner /patine/ [**v1**] **A** *vt* to apply a finish to
B *vi* **1** to skate
2 (Aut) ‹*wheel*› to spin; ‹*clutch*› to slip; **faire ~ l'embrayage** to slip the clutch
C se patiner *v refl* (+ *v être*) to acquire a patina
patineur, -euse /patinœʀ, øz/ *mf* skater
patinoire /patinwaʀ/ *f* ice rink
pâtir /pɑtiʀ/ [**v3**] *vi* **~ de** to suffer as a result of
pâtisserie /pɑtisʀi/ *f* **1** cake shop, patisserie
2 pastry, cake
pâtissier, -ière /pɑtisje, ɛʀ/ *mf* confectioner, pastry cook
patois /patwa/ *m inv* patois, dialect
patraque /patʀak/ *adj* (fam) **être ~** to be under the weather (fam)
patriarche /patʀijaʀʃ/ *m* patriarch
patrie /patʀi/ *f* homeland, country
patrimoine /patʀimwan/ *m* **1** (of person, family) patrimony; (of firm) capital
2 heritage
■ **~ génétique** gene pool
patriote /patʀijɔt/ **A** *adj* patriotic
B *mf* patriot; **en ~** patriotically
patriotisme /patʀijɔtism/ *m* patriotism
patron, -onne /patʀɔ̃, ɔn/ **A** *mf* boss (fam)
B *m* (sewing) pattern
■ **~ de pêche** skipper, master
patronal, ~e, *mpl* **-aux** /patʀɔnal, o/ *adj* ‹*organization*› employers'
patronat /patʀɔna/ *m* employers
patronne ▸ **patron A**
patronner /patʀɔne/ [**v1**] *vt* to sponsor
patronyme /patʀɔnim/ *m* patronymic
patrouille /patʀuj/ *f* patrol
patrouiller /patʀuje/ [**v1**] *vi* to be on patrol
patte /pat/ *f* **1** leg; paw; foot; **donner la ~** to give its paw; **retomber sur ses ~s** to fall on its feet
2 (fam) leg, foot; **tu es toujours dans mes ~s** you are always getting under my feet; **marcher à quatre ~s** to walk on all fours; to crawl; **traîner la ~** to limp
3 (fam) hand; **bas les~s!** (fam) keep your hands to yourself!; hands off! (fam)
4 tab; (on shelving unit) lug; (on garment) flap
5 sideburn
■ **~s d'éléphant** flares; **~ folle** (fam) gammy leg (BrE), game leg (AmE); **~s de mouche** spidery scrawl
IDIOMS **faire ~ de velours** ‹*cat*› to draw in its claws; ‹*person*› to switch on the charm; **montrer ~ blanche** to prove one is acceptable; **se tirer dans les ~s** to pull dirty tricks on each other
patte-d'oie, *pl* **pattes-d'oie** /patdwɑ/ *f* **1** crow's foot
2 junction
pâturage /pɑtyʀaʒ/ *m* pasture
pâture /pɑtyʀ/ *f* **1** feed; **être jeté en ~** (fig) to be thrown to the lions
2 pasture
paume /pom/ *f* palm (of the hand)
paumé, ~e /pome/ *adj* (fam) **1** ‹*person*› mixed up (BrE), out of it (AmE) (fam)
2 ‹*place*› godforsaken
paumer /pome/ [**v1**] (fam) **A** *vt, vi* to lose
B se paumer *v refl* (+ *v être*) to get lost
paupière /popjɛʀ/ *f* eyelid
paupiette /popjɛt/ *f* **~ de veau** stuffed escalope of veal
pause /poz/ *f* **1** break; **faire une ~** to take a break
2 (in process) pause
3 (Mus) rest
pauvre /povʀ/ **A** *adj* **1** poor
2 sparse; **~ en sucre** low in sugar; lacking sugar
3 un ~ type (fam) a poor guy; a dead loss (fam)
B *mf* (fam) **le/la ~!** poor thing!, poor man/woman!
C *m* **un ~** a poor man; **~ d'esprit** half-wit
pauvrement /povʀəmɑ̃/ *adv* poorly
pauvresse /povʀɛs/ *f* poor wretch, pauper
pauvreté /povʀəte/ *f* **1** poverty
2 shabbiness
pavage /pavaʒ/ *m* paving
pavaner: se pavaner /pavane/ [**v1**] *v refl* (+ *v être*) to strut (about)
pavé /pave/ *m* cobblestone; **se retrouver sur le ~** to find oneself out on the street
IDIOMS **lancer un ~ dans la mare** to set the

cat among the pigeons; **tenir le haut du ~** to head the field

paver /pave/ [**v1**] *vt* to lay [sth] with cobblestones

pavillon /pavijɔ̃/ *m* **1** (detached) house
2 (for exhibition) pavilion; (of hospital) wing
3 (of ear) auricle
4 (of loudspeaker) horn
5 (Naut) flag

pavillonnaire /pavijɔnɛʀ/ *adj* **zone ~** residential area; **banlieue ~** suburb consisting of houses (*as opposed to high-rise buildings*)

pavoiser /pavwaze/ [**v1**] *vi* (fam) to crow

pavot /pavo/ *m* poppy

payable /pɛjabl/ *adj* payable; **~ à la commande** cash with order

payant, **~e** /pɛjɑ̃, ɑ̃t/ *adj* **1** ‹*person*› paying
2 ‹*show*› not free
3 (fam) lucrative, profitable

paye /pɛj/ ▶ **paie**

payement /pɛjmɑ̃/ ▶ **paiement**

⚷ **payer** /peje/ [**v21**] **A** *vt* **1** to pay; to pay for; **il est payé pour le savoir!** he knows that to his cost!; **faire ~ qch à qn** to charge sb for sth; **~ qch à qn** (fam) to buy sb sth
2 to pay for ‹*mistake, carelessness*›
B *vi* **1** ‹*efforts, sacrifice*› to pay off; ‹*profession, activity*› to pay
2 (fam) to be funny
C **se payer** *v refl* (+ *v être*) **1** ‹*service, goods*› to have to be paid for
2 (fam) to treat oneself to ‹*holiday*›; to get ‹*cold, bad mark*›; to get landed with ‹*job*›; **se ~ un arbre** to crash into a tree
IDIOMS **se ~ du bon temps** (fam) to have a good time; **se ~ la tête de qn** (fam) to take the mickey out of sb (BrE) (fam), to razz sb (AmE) (fam)

p

⚷ **pays** /pei/ *m* **1** country
2 la Bourgogne est le ~ du bon vin Burgundy is the home of good wine; **gens du ~** local people
IDIOM **voir du ~** to do some travelling (BrE)

⚷ **paysage** /peizaʒ/ *m* landscape, scenery
■ **~ audiovisuel français, PAF** French radio and TV scene

paysager, **-ère** /peizaʒe, ɛʀ/ *adj* **1** environmental
2 ‹*garden*› landscaped

paysagiste /peizaʒist/ *mf* **(jardinier) ~** landscape gardener

⚷ **paysan**, **-anne** /peizɑ̃, an/ **A** *adj* ‹*life*› rural; ‹*ways*› peasant; ‹*soup, bread*› country
B *mf* **1** ≈ small farmer
2 (derog) peasant

paysannerie /peizanʀi/ *f* small farmers; peasantry

Pays-Bas /peibɑ/ *pr m pl* **les ~** The Netherlands

⚷ key word

PC /pese/ *m* **1** (Pol) (*abbr* = **parti communiste**) CP, Communist Party
2 (*abbr* = **personal computer**) PC

PCF /peseɛf/ *m* (*abbr* = **parti communiste français**) French Communist Party

PCV /peseve/ *m* (*abbr* = **paiement contre vérification**) reverse charge call (BrE), collect call (AmE)

PDG /pedeʒe/ *m* (*abbr* = **président-directeur général**) CEO, chief executive officer

péage /peaʒ/ *m* **1** toll
2 tollbooth

⚷ **peau**, *pl* **~x** /po/ *f* **1** skin; **n'avoir que la ~ sur les os** to be all skin and bone
2 leather; **gants de ~** leather gloves
3 peel
4 (fam) life; **risquer sa ~** to risk one's life; **faire la ~ à qn** to kill sb; **vouloir la ~ de qn** to want sb dead
IDIOMS **être bien dans sa ~** (fam) to feel good about oneself; **avoir qn dans la ~** (fam) to be crazy about sb (fam); **prendre une balle dans la ~** (fam) to be shot

peaufiner /pofine/ [**v1**] *vt* to put the finishing touches to ‹*work, text*›

Peau-Rouge, *pl* **Peaux-Rouges** /poʀuʒ/ *mf* Red Indian

⚷ **pêche** /pɛʃ/ *f* **1** peach
2 fishing; **aller à la ~** to go fishing
3 (fam) clout (fam)
4 (fam) **avoir la ~** to be feeling great
■ **~ à la ligne** angling

péché /peʃe/ *m* sin; **ce serait un ~ de rater ça** (fam) it would be a crime to miss that; **le chocolat, c'est mon ~ mignon** I've got a weakness for chocolate

pécher /peʃe/ [**v14**] *vi* to sin; **~ par excès de confiance** to be overconfident; **le roman pèche sur un point** the novel has one shortcoming

pêcher¹ /pɛʃe/ [**v1**] **A** *vt* to go fishing for
B *vi* to fish; **~ à la mouche** to fly-fish; **~ à la ligne** to angle

pêcher² /pɛʃe/ *m* peach tree

pécheresse /peʃʀɛs/ *f* sinner

pêcherie /pɛʃʀi/ *f* **1** fish factory
2 fishing ground

pécheur /peʃœʀ/ *m* sinner

pêcheur /pɛʃœʀ/ *m* fisherman

pectoral, *pl* **-aux** /pɛktɔʀal, o/ *m* pectoral muscle

pécule /pekyl/ *m* savings, nest egg (fam)

pécuniaire /pekynjɛʀ/ *adj* financial

pédagogie /pedagɔʒi/ *f* **1** education, pedagogy
2 teaching skills
3 teaching method

pédagogique /pedagɔʒik/ *adj* ‹*activity*› educational; ‹*system*› education; ‹*method*› teaching

pédagogue /pedagɔg/ *mf* educationalist

pédale /pedal/ *f* pedal
(IDIOM) **perdre les ~s** (fam) to lose one's grip
pédaler /pedale/ [**v1**] *vi* to pedal
pédalier /pedalje/ *m* (of bicycle) chain transmission; (of piano) pedals
pédalo® /pedalo/ *m* pedalo (BrE), pedal boat
pédant, **~e** /pedɑ̃, ɑ̃t/ *adj* pedantic
pédérastie /pedeʀasti/ *f* **1** pederasty
2 homosexuality
pédestre /pedɛstʀ/ *adj* **randonnée ~** ramble
pédiatre /pedjatʀ/ *mf* paediatrician
pédiatrie /pedjatʀi/ *f* paediatrics
pédicure /pedikyʀ/ *mf* chiropodist (BrE), podiatrist (AmE)
pedigree /pedigʀe/ *m* pedigree
pédologue /pedɔlɔg/ *mf* pedologist
pédophilie /pedɔfili/ *f* paedophilia
pédopornographie /pedopɔʀnɔgʀafi/ *f* child pornography
pègre /pɛgʀ/ *f* underworld
peigne /pɛɲ/ *m* comb
peigner /peɲe/ [**v1**] **A** *vt* to comb ‹*hair, wool*›
B **se peigner** *v refl* (+ *v être*) to comb one's hair
peignoir /pɛɲwaʀ/ *m* dressing gown (BrE), robe (AmE); **~ de bain** bathrobe
peinard, **~e** /penaʀ, aʀd/ *adj* (fam) ‹*job*› cushy (fam); ‹*place*› snug
peindre /pɛ̃dʀ/ [**v55**] **A** *vt* **1** to paint
2 to depict
B *vi* to paint
peine /pɛn/ **A** *f* **1** sorrow, grief; **avoir de la ~** to feel sad; **faire de la ~ à qn** ‹*person*› to hurt sb; ‹*event, remark*› to upset sb
2 effort, trouble; **c'est ~ perdue** it's a waste of effort; **il n'est pas au bout de ses ~s** his troubles are far from over; he's still got a long way to go; **ce n'est pas la ~ de crier** there's no need to shout; **pour ta ~** for your trouble
3 difficulty; **sans ~** easily; **avec ~** with difficulty
4 (Law) penalty, sentence; **~ de prison** prison sentence; **'défense de fumer sous ~ d'amende'** 'no smoking, offenders will be fined'
B **à peine** *phr* hardly; **il était à ~ arrivé qu'il pensait déjà à repartir** no sooner had he arrived than he was thinking of leaving again
■ **~ capitale** capital punishment; **~ de cœur** heartache; **~ de mort** death penalty
peiner /pene/ [**v1**] **A** *vt* to sadden, to upset
B *vi* ‹*person*› to struggle; ‹*car*› to labour (BrE)
peint, **~e** /pɛ̃, ɛ̃t/ ▸ **peindre**
peintre /pɛ̃tʀ/ *m* painter
peinture /pɛ̃tyʀ/ *f* **1** paint
2 paintwork
3 painting; **je ne peux pas le voir en ~** (fam) I can't stand the sight of him
4 portrayal
peinturlurer /pɛ̃tyʀlyʀe/ [**v1**] *vt* to daub
péjoratif, **-ive** /peʒɔʀatif, iv/ *adj* pejorative
Pékin /pekɛ̃/ *pr n* Beijing, Peking
PEL /peəɛl/ *m*: *abbr* ▸ **plan**
pelage /pəlaʒ/ *m* coat, fur
pelé, **~e** /pəle/ *adj* ‹*animal*› mangy; ‹*hill*› bare
pêle-mêle /pɛlmɛl/ *adv* higgledy-piggledy
peler /pəle/ [**v17**] **A** *vt* to peel
B *vi* **1** ‹*skin, nose*› to peel
2 (fam) **~ (de froid)** to freeze
pèlerin /pɛlʀɛ̃/ *m* pilgrim
pèlerinage /pɛlʀinaʒ/ *m* pilgrimage
pélican /pelikɑ̃/ *m* pelican
pelisse /pəlis/ *f* fur-trimmed coat, pelisse
pelle /pɛl/ *f* shovel; spade; **à la ~** (fam) by the dozen
■ **~ à tarte** cake slice
pelleteuse /pɛltøz/ *f* mechanical digger
pellicule /pelikyl/ **A** *f* film
B **pellicules** *fpl* dandruff
pelote /p(ə)lɔt/ *f* (of wool) ball
peloton /p(ə)lɔtɔ̃/ *m* **1** platoon; **~ d'exécution** firing squad
2 (in cycling) pack; **dans le ~ de tête** in the leading pack
pelotonner: **se pelotonner** /p(ə)lɔtɔne/ [**v1**] *v refl* (+ *v être*) **1** to snuggle up
2 to huddle up
pelouse /p(ə)luz/ *f* lawn; **'~ interdite'** 'keep off the grass'
peluche /p(ə)lyʃ/ *f* **1** plush; **jouet en ~** cuddly toy (BrE), stuffed animal (AmE)
2 fluff
pelucher /p(ə)lyʃe/ [**v1**] *vi* to become fluffy
pelure /p(ə)lyʀ/ *f* (of vegetable, fruit) peel; (of onion) skin
pelvis /pɛlvis/ *m inv* pelvis
pénal, **~e**, *mpl* **-aux** /penal, o/ *adj* criminal
pénaliser /penalize/ [**v1**] *vt* to penalize
pénalité /penalite/ *f* penalty
penaud, **~e** /pəno, od/ *adj* sheepish
penchant /pɑ̃ʃɑ̃/ *m* **1** fondness
2 weakness
3 tendency
penché, **~e** /pɑ̃ʃe/ **A** *pp* ▸ **pencher**
B *pp adj* ‹*tree*› leaning; ‹*writing*› slanting
pencher /pɑ̃ʃe/ [**v1**] **A** *vt* to tilt; to tip [sth] up; **~ la tête en avant** to bend one's head forward(s)
B *vi* **1** ‹*tower, tree*› to lean; ‹*boat*› to list; ‹*picture*› to slant
2 **~ pour** to incline toward(s) ‹*theory*›; to be in favour (BrE) of ‹*solution*›
C **se pencher** *v refl* (+ *v être*) **1** to lean
2 to bend down
3 **se ~ sur** to look into ‹*problem*›
pendable /pɑ̃dabl/ *adj* **jouer un tour ~ à qn** to play a rotten trick on sb

pendaison /pɑ̃dɛzɔ̃/ *f* hanging

🔑 **pendant** /pɑ̃dɑ̃/ **A** *prep* for; **je t'ai attendu ~ des heures** I waited for you for hours; **~ combien de temps avez-vous vécu à Versailles?** how long did you live in Versailles?; **il a été malade ~ tout le trajet** he was sick throughout the journey; **~ ce temps(-là)** meanwhile
B **pendant que** *phr* while

pendeloque /pɑ̃dlɔk/ *f* pendant, drop (*on earring*)

pendentif /pɑ̃dɑ̃tif/ *m* pendant

penderie /pɑ̃dʀi/ *f* **1** wardrobe
2 walk-in cupboard (BrE) *or* closet

pendouiller /pɑ̃duje/ [**v1**] *vi* (fam) to dangle down

pendre /pɑ̃dʀ/ [**v6**] **A** *vt* **1** to hang ‹*person*›
2 to hang ‹*picture, curtains*›; to hang up ‹*clothes*›
B *vi* **1** ‹*object, clothes*› to hang; ‹*arms, legs*› to dangle
2 ‹*strips, lock of hair*› to hang down; ‹*cheek, breasts*› to sag
C **se pendre** *v refl* (+ *v être*) **1** to hang oneself
2 **se ~ à** to hang from ‹*branch*›; **se ~ au cou de qn** to throw one's arms around sb's neck
IDIOM **ça te pend au nez** (fam) you've got it coming to you

pendu, **~e** /pɑ̃dy/ **A** *pp* ▸ **pendre**
B *pp adj* **1** ‹*person*› hanged
2 ‹*object*› hung, hanging; **être ~ aux lèvres de qn** to hang on sb's every word; **être toujours ~ au téléphone** to spend all one's time on the telephone
C *mf* hanged man/woman

pendulaire /pɑ̃dylɛʀ/ *adj* pendular

pendule¹ /pɑ̃dyl/ *m* pendulum

pendule² /pɑ̃dyl/ *f* clock
IDIOM **remettre les ~s à l'heure** to set the record straight

pénétrant, **~e** /penetʀɑ̃, ɑ̃t/ *adj* ‹*wind*› penetrating; ‹*cold*› piercing; ‹*comment*› shrewd; ‹*mind, look*› penetrating

pénétration /penetʀasjɔ̃/ *f* penetration

pénétré, **~e** /penetʀe/ **A** *pp* ▸ **pénétrer**
B *pp adj* earnest, intense; **être ~ de** to be imbued with ‹*feeling*›

🔑 **pénétrer** /penetʀe/ [**v14**] **A** *vt* **1** ‹*rain*› to soak *or* seep into ‹*ground*›; ‹*sun*› to penetrate ‹*foliage*›
2 to fathom ‹*secret, thoughts*›
3 to penetrate
4 ‹*idea, fashion*› to reach ‹*group*›
B *vi* **~ dans** to enter, to get into; to penetrate; **faire ~ la pommade en massant doucement** rub the ointment into your skin

pénible /penibl/ *adj* ‹*effort*› painful; ‹*work*› hard; ‹*journey*› difficult; ‹*person*› tiresome

péniblement /penibləmɑ̃/ *adv* ‹*walk*› with difficulty; ‹*reach*› barely

🔑 key word

péniche /peniʃ/ *f* barge

pénicilline /penisilin/ *f* penicillin

péninsulaire /penɛ̃sylɛʀ/ *adj* peninsular

péninsule /penɛ̃syl/ *f* peninsula

pénis /penis/ *m inv* penis

pénitence /penitɑ̃s/ *f* **1** penance
2 punishment

pénitencier /penitɑ̃sje/ *m* prison

pénitentiaire /penitɑ̃sjɛʀ/ *adj* ‹*institution*› penal; ‹*regime*› prison

pénombre /penɔ̃bʀ/ *f* half-light

pensable /pɑ̃sabl/ *adj* thinkable; **ce n'est pas ~** it's unthinkable

pense-bête, *pl* **pense-bêtes** /pɑ̃sbɛt/ *m* reminder

🔑 **pensée** /pɑ̃se/ *f* **1** thought; **être perdu dans ses ~s** to be lost in thought
2 mind; **nous serons avec vous par la ~** we'll be with you in spirit
3 thinking
4 (Bot) pansy

🔑 **penser** /pɑ̃se/ [**v1**] **A** *vt* **1** to think; **~ du bien de qn** to think well of sb; **je n'en pense rien** I have no opinion about it; **c'est bien ce que je pensais!** I thought as much!; **tu penses vraiment ce que tu dis?** do you really mean what you're saying?; **tout porte à ~ que** there's every indication that; **vous pensez si j'étais content!** you can imagine how pleased I was!; **'il s'est excusé?'—'penses-tu!'** 'did he apologize?'—'you must be joking!'
2 **ça me fait ~ qu'il faut que je leur écrive** that reminds me that I must write to them
3 **~ faire** to be thinking of doing, to intend to do
4 to think [sth] up ‹*plan, device*›
B **penser à** *v+prep* **1** **~ à** to think of, to think about; **ne pensez plus à rien** empty your mind; **sans ~ à mal** without meaning any harm; **tu n'y penses pas!** you can't be serious!; **n'y pensons plus!** let's forget about it!
2 **~ à** to remember; **il me fait ~ à mon père** he reminds me of my father
3 **~ à faire** to be thinking of doing
C *vi* to think; **je lui ai dit ma façon de ~!** I gave him/her a piece of my mind!; **~ tout haut** to think out loud

penseur /pɑ̃sœʀ/ *m* thinker

pensif, **-ive** /pɑ̃sif, iv/ *adj* pensive, thoughtful

pension /pɑ̃sjɔ̃/ *f* **1** pension
2 boarding house
3 boarding school
■ **~ alimentaire** alimony; **~ complète** full board; **~ de famille** family hotel

pensionnaire /pɑ̃sjɔnɛʀ/ *mf* **1** (in hotel) resident
2 (in prison) inmate
3 (Sch) boarder

pensionnat /pɑ̃sjɔna/ *m* boarding school

pensionné, **~e** /pɑ̃sjɔne/ *mf* pensioner
pensivement /pɑ̃sivmɑ̃/ *adv* pensively
pentagone /pɛ̃tagɔn/ *m* pentagon
pente /pɑ̃t/ *f* slope; **toit en ~** sloping roof
IDIOMS **être sur la mauvaise ~** ‹*person*› to be going astray; ‹*company*› to be going downhill; **remonter la ~** to get back on one's feet
Pentecôte /pɑ̃tkot/ *f* Pentecost; **à la ~** at Whitsun
pénurie /penyʀi/ *f* shortage
pépé /pepe/ *m* (fam) **1** grandpa (fam)
2 old man
pépère /pepɛʀ/ *adj* (fam) ‹*life*› cushy (fam); ‹*place*› nice
pépin /pepɛ̃/ *m* **1** pip; **sans ~s** seedless
2 (fam) slight problem
3 (fam) umbrella
pépinière /pepinjɛʀ/ *f* (for trees, plants) nursery
pépite /pepit/ *f* nugget
péquenaud, **~e** /pɛkno, od/ *mf* (fam) country bumpkin (fam)
perçant, **~e** /pɛʀsɑ̃, ɑ̃t/ *adj* **1** ‹*cry, voice*› shrill; ‹*gaze*› piercing
2 ‹*vision*› sharp
percée /pɛʀse/ *f* **1** opening
2 breakthrough
perce-neige /pɛʀsənɛʒ/ *m inv or f inv* snowdrop
perce-oreille, *pl* **~s** /pɛʀsɔʀɛj/ *m* earwig
percepteur /pɛʀsɛptœʀ/ *m* tax inspector
perceptible /pɛʀsɛptibl/ *adj* **1** ‹*sound*› perceptible
2 ‹*tax*› payable
perception /pɛʀsɛpsjɔ̃/ *f* **1** tax office
2 perception
percer /pɛʀse/ **[v12]** **A** *vt* **1** to pierce ‹*body, surface*›; to burst ‹*abscess, eardrum*›
2 to make ‹*door*›; to bore ‹*tunnel*›; to build ‹*road*›; **~ un trou dans** to make a hole in
3 to pierce ‹*silence, air*›; to break through ‹*clouds*›
4 to penetrate ‹*secret*›; **~ qn à jour** to see through sb
5 ~ ses dents to be teething
B *vi* **1** ‹*sun*› to break through; ‹*plant*› to come up; ‹*tooth*› to come through
2 (Mil, Sport) to break through
3 ‹*actor*› to become known
perceuse /pɛʀsøz/ *f* drill
percevable /pɛʀsəvabl/ *adj* ‹*tax*› payable
⚷ **percevoir** /pɛʀsəvwaʀ/ **[v5]** *vt* **1** to collect ‹*tax*›; to receive ‹*rent*›
2 to perceive ‹*change*›; to feel ‹*vibration*›; **être perçu comme** to be seen as
perche /pɛʀʃ/ *f* **1** (gen) pole; (of ski tow) T-bar; (for microphone) boom
2 (fam) **(grande) ~** beanpole (fam)
3 (Zool) perch
IDIOM **tendre la ~ à qn** to throw sb a line
perché, **~e** /pɛʀʃe/ *pp adj* perched; **voix haut ~e** high-pitched voice; **ma valise est ~e en haut de l'armoire** my suitcase is on top of the wardrobe
percher /pɛʀʃe/ **[v1]** **A** *vt* **~ qch sur une étagère** to stick sth up on a shelf
B *vi* to perch; to roost
C **se percher** *v refl* (+ *v être*) to perch
perchoir /pɛʀʃwaʀ/ *m* **1** perch
2 (Pol), (fam) Speaker's Chair
perclus, **~e** /pɛʀkly, yz/ *adj* crippled (offensive)
percolateur /pɛʀkɔlatœʀ/ *m* (espresso) coffee machine
percussions /pɛʀkysjɔ̃/ *fpl* **les ~** percussion instruments; percussion section; drums
percutant, **~e** /pɛʀkytɑ̃, ɑ̃t/ *adj* ‹*criticism*› hard-hitting; ‹*slogan*› punchy (fam)
percuter /pɛʀkyte/ **[v1]** **A** *vt* ‹*car, driver*› to hit
B *vi* **~ contre** ‹*vehicle*› to crash into; ‹*shell*› to explode against
C **se percuter** *v refl* (+ *v être*) to collide
perdant, **~e** /pɛʀdɑ̃, ɑ̃t/ **A** *adj* losing; **être ~** to have lost out
B *mf* loser
perdition /pɛʀdisjɔ̃/ *f* **1** **lieu de ~** den of iniquity
2 **en ~** ‹*ship*› in distress
⚷ **perdre** /pɛʀdʀ/ **[v6]** **A** *vt* **1** to lose; **~ de vue** to lose sight of; **leurs actions ont perdu 9%** their shares have dropped 9%
2 to shed ‹*leaves, flowers*›
3 to miss ‹*chance*›
4 to waste ‹*day, years*›; **perdre son temps** to waste one's time
5 **je perds mes chaussures** my shoes are too big; **je perds mon pantalon** my trousers are falling down
6 to bring [sb] down; **cet homme te perdra** that man will be your undoing
B *vi* to lose; **j'y perds** I lose out
C **se perdre** *v refl* (+ *v être*) **1** to get lost; **se ~ dans ses pensées** to be lost in thought
2 ‹*tradition*› to die out
IDIOM **~ la raison** *or* **l'esprit** to go out of one's mind
perdrix /pɛʀdʀi/ *f inv* partridge
perdu, **~e** /pɛʀdy/ **A** *pp* ▸ **perdre**
B *pp adj* **1** lost; **chien ~** stray dog; **balle ~e** stray bullet; **c'est ~ d'avance** it's hopeless
2 ‹*day, opportunity*› wasted; **c'est du temps ~** it's a waste of time
3 ‹*harvest*› ruined; **il est ~** there's no hope for him
4 ‹*person*› lost
C *adj* remote, isolated
IDIOMS **se lancer à corps ~ dans** to throw oneself headlong into; **ce n'est pas ~ pour tout le monde** somebody will do all right out of it
⚷ **père** /pɛʀ/ *m* father; **Dupont ~** Dupont senior; **le ~ Dupont** (fam) old Dupont (fam)
■ **le ~ Noël** Santa Claus

p

pérégriner /peʀegʀine/ *vi* travel

péremption /peʀɑ̃psjɔ̃/ *f* **date de ~** use-by date

péremptoire /peʀɑ̃ptwaʀ/ *adj* peremptory

pérenne /peʀɛn/ *adj* perennial

perfection /pɛʀfɛksjɔ̃/ *f* perfection

perfectionnement /pɛʀfɛksjɔnmɑ̃/ *m* improvement

perfectionner /pɛʀfɛksjɔne/ [**v1**] **A** *vt* to perfect ‹*technique*›; to refine ‹*art*›
B se perfectionner *v refl* (+ *v être*) to improve

perfectionniste /pɛʀfɛksjɔnist/ *adj, mf* perfectionist

perfide /pɛʀfid/ *adj* perfidious, treacherous

perfidie /pɛʀfidi/ *f* perfidy, treachery

perforation /pɛʀfɔʀasjɔ̃/ *f* perforation

perforer /pɛʀfɔʀe/ [**v1**] *vt* **1** to pierce; to perforate
2 to punch; **carte perforée** punch card

performance /pɛʀfɔʀmɑ̃s/ *f* **1** result, performance
2 achievement

performant, **~e** /pɛʀfɔʀmɑ̃, ɑ̃t/ *adj* ‹*car, equipment*› high-performance; ‹*person, technique*› efficient; ‹*company*› competitive

perfusion /pɛʀfyzjɔ̃/ *f* (Med) drip (BrE), IV (AmE)

péricliter /peʀiklite/ [**v1**] *vi* to be going downhill

péridurale /peʀidyʀal/ *f* epidural

péril /peʀil/ *m* peril, danger; **à ses risques et ~s** at his/her own risk; **il n'y a pas ~ en la demeure** what's the hurry?

périlleux, **-euse** /peʀijø, øz/ *adj* perilous

périmé, **~e** /peʀime/ *adj* **1** out-of-date; **son passeport est ~** his/her passport has expired
2 ‹*idea, custom*› outdated

périmètre /peʀimɛtʀ/ *m* **1** perimeter
2 area

périnée /peʀine/ *m* perineum

🔑 **période** /peʀjɔd/ *f* period; era

périodique /peʀjɔdik/ **A** *adj* **1** ‹*fever*› recurring
2 serviette ~ sanitary towel (BrE), sanitary napkin (AmE)
B *m* periodical

péripétie /peʀipesi/ *f* **1** incident
2 event
3 adventure
4 les ~s d'une intrigue the twists and turns of a plot

périphérie /peʀifeʀi/ *f* periphery

périphérique /peʀifeʀik/ **A** *adj* (gen) peripheral; ‹*area*› outlying; **radio ~** *broadcasting station situated outside the territory to which it transmits*
B *m* ring road (BrE), beltway (AmE)

périphrase /peʀifʀɑz/ *f* circumlocution

périple /peʀipl/ *m* journey; voyage

périr /peʀiʀ/ [**v3**] *vi* to die, to perish

périscolaire /peʀiskɔlɛʀ/ *adj* extracurricular

périscope /peʀiskɔp/ *m* periscope

périssable /peʀisabl/ *adj* perishable

Péritel® /peʀitɛl/ *f* **prise ~** Scart socket; Scart plug

perle /pɛʀl/ *f* **1** pearl; **~ fine** real pearl
2 (fig) gem; **~ rare** real treasure
3 (fam) howler (fam)

perler /pɛʀle/ [**v1**] *vi* ‹*drop, tear*› to appear

permanence /pɛʀmanɑ̃s/ **A** *f*
1 permanence
2 persistence
3 ~ téléphonique manned line; **assurer** *or* **tenir une ~** to be on duty; to hold a surgery (BrE), to have office hours (AmE)
4 permanently manned office
5 (Sch) (private) study room (BrE), study hall (AmE)
B en permanence *phr* **1** permanently
2 constantly

🔑 **permanent**, **~e** /pɛʀmanɑ̃, ɑ̃t/ *adj* **1** ‹*staff, exhibition*› permanent; ‹*committee*› standing
2 ‹*tension, danger*› constant; ‹*show*› continuous

permanente /pɛʀmanɑ̃t/ *f* perm

perméable /pɛʀmeabl/ *adj* permeable

🔑 **permettre** /pɛʀmɛtʀ/ [**v60**] **A** *vt* **1 ~ à qn de faire** to allow sb to do, to give sb permission to do; **(vous) permettez! j'étais là avant!** excuse me! I was here first!; **il est menteur comme c'est pas permis** (fam) he's an incredible liar
2 ~ à qn de faire to allow *or* enable sb to do, to give sb the opportunity to do; **leurs moyens ne le leur permettent pas** they can't afford it; **autant qu'il est permis d'en juger** as far as one can tell
B se permettre *v refl* (+ *v être*) **1 je peux me ~ ce genre de plaisanterie avec lui** I can get away with telling him that kind of joke; **se ~ de faire** to take the liberty of doing
2 je ne peux pas me ~ d'acheter une nouvelle voiture I can't afford to buy a new car

permis, **~e** /pɛʀmi, iz/ **A** *pp* ▶ **permettre**
B *pp adj* permitted
C *m inv* permit, licence (BrE)
■ **~ de conduire** driving licence (BrE), driver's license (AmE); **~ de séjour** residence permit; **~ de travail** work permit

permission /pɛʀmisjɔ̃/ *f* **1** permission
2 (Mil) leave; **partir en ~** to go on leave

permutable /pɛʀmytabl/ *adj* interchangeable

permuter /pɛʀmyte/ [**v1**] *vt* to switch [sth] around ‹*letters, labels*›

🔑 key word

pernicieux, -ieuse /pɛʀnisjø, øz/ *adj* pernicious

Pérou /peʀu/ *pr m* Peru
IDIOM **ce n'est pas le ~** it's not a fortune

perpendiculaire /pɛʀpɑ̃dikylɛʀ/ *adj, f* perpendicular

perpète /pɛʀpɛt/ *f* (fam) **être condamné à ~** (sl) to get life (fam); **habiter à ~** to live miles away

perpétrer /pɛʀpetʀe/ [**v14**] *vt* to perpetrate

perpétuel, -elle /pɛʀpetɥɛl/ *adj* perpetual

perpétuellement /pɛʀpetɥɛlmɑ̃/ *adv* constantly, perpetually

perpétuer /pɛʀpetɥe/ [**v1**] *vt* to perpetuate

perpétuité /pɛʀpetɥite/ *f* perpetuity; **à ~** (Law) ‹*imprisonment*› life; ‹*imprisonment*› life

perplexe /pɛʀplɛks/ *adj* perplexed, baffled

perplexité /pɛʀplɛksite/ *f* perplexity

perquisition /pɛʀkizisjɔ̃/ *f* search

perquisitionner /pɛʀkizisjɔne/ [**v1**] *vt* to search ‹*house*›

perron /peʀɔ̃/ *m* flight of steps

perroquet /peʀɔkɛ/ *m* parrot

perruche /peʀyʃ/ *f* budgerigar (BrE), parakeet (AmE)

perruque /peʀyk/ *f* wig

persan, ~e /pɛʀsɑ̃, an/ *adj* Persian

perse /pɛʀs/ *adj* Persian

persécuter /pɛʀsekyte/ [**v1**] *vt* to persecute

persécution /pɛʀsekysjɔ̃/ *f* persecution

persévérance /pɛʀseveʀɑ̃s/ *f* perseverance

persévérer /pɛʀseveʀe/ [**v14**] *vi* **1** to persevere
2 to persist

persienne /pɛʀsjɛn/ *f* (louvred (BrE)) shutter

persiflage /pɛʀsiflaʒ/ *m* mockery

persifleur, -euse /pɛʀsiflœʀ, øz/ *adj* ‹*tone, comment*› mocking

persil /pɛʀsi(l)/ *m* parsley

persistance /pɛʀsistɑ̃s/ *f* persistence

persistant, ~e /pɛʀsistɑ̃, ɑ̃t/ *adj* ‹*heat, problem*› continuing; ‹*smell, snow*› lingering; ‹*cough, symptom*› persistent

persister /pɛʀsiste/ [**v1**] *vi* ‹*symptom, pain*› to persist; ‹*inflation*› to continue; **je persiste à croire que** I still think that

perso /pɛʀso/ *adj* (fam) personal

personnage /pɛʀsɔnaʒ/ *m* **1** character
2 figure; **un ~ public** a public figure

personnaliser /pɛʀsɔnalize/ [**v1**] *vt* to add a personal touch to

personnalité /pɛʀsɔnalite/ *f* **1** personality
2 important person

personne[1] /pɛʀsɔn/ *pron* anyone, anybody; no one, nobody; **~ n'est parfait** nobody's perfect

personne[2] /pɛʀsɔn/ *f* person; **dix ~s** ten people; **les ~s âgées** the elderly; **bien fait de sa ~** good-looking; **le respect de la ~** respect for the individual; **il s'en occupe en ~** he's dealing with it personally; **c'est la cupidité en ~** he/she is greed personified
■ **~ à charge** dependant; **~ civile** *or* **morale** artificial person, legal entity

personnel, -elle /pɛʀsɔnɛl/ **A** *adj* **1** ‹*friend, effects*› personal; ‹*papers*› private
2 individual
3 selfish
4 ‹*pronoun*› personal
B *m* staff; workforce; employees, personnel

personnellement /pɛʀsɔnɛlmɑ̃/ *adv* personally

personnifier /pɛʀsɔnifje/ [**v2**] *vt* to personify

perspective /pɛʀspɛktiv/ *f* **1** (in art) perspective
2 view
3 perspective, angle
4 prospect

perspicace /pɛʀspikas/ *adj* perceptive

perspicacité /pɛʀspikasite/ *f* insight, perspicacity

persuader /pɛʀsɥade/ [**v1**] *vt* to persuade

persuasif, -ive /pɛʀsɥazif, iv/ *adj* persuasive

persuasion /pɛʀsɥazjɔ̃/ *f* persuasion

perte /pɛʀt/ *f* **1** loss; **à ~ de vue** as far as the eye can see
2 waste
3 ruin; **courir** *or* **aller à sa ~** to be heading for a fall

pertinemment /pɛʀtinamɑ̃/ *adv*
1 perfectly well
2 pertinently

pertinence /pɛʀtinɑ̃s/ *f* pertinence

pertinent, ~e /pɛʀtinɑ̃, ɑ̃t/ *adj* pertinent

perturbant, ~e /pɛʀtyʀbɑ̃, ɑ̃t/ *adj* disturbing

perturbation /pɛʀtyʀbasjɔ̃/ *f* **1** disruption
2 disturbance
3 upheaval

perturber /pɛʀtyʀbe/ [**v1**] *vt* to disrupt ‹*traffic, market, meeting*›; to interfere with ‹*development*›; to disturb ‹*sleep*›

pervenche /pɛʀvɑ̃ʃ/ *f* **1** periwinkle
2 (fam) (female) traffic warden (BrE), meter maid (AmE) (fam)

pervers, ~e /pɛʀvɛʀ, ɛʀs/ **A** *adj* **1** wicked
2 perverted
3 ‹*effect*› pernicious
B *mf* pervert

perversion /pɛʀvɛʀsjɔ̃/ *f* perversion

perversité /pɛʀvɛʀsite/ *f* perversity

pervertir /pɛʀvɛʀtiʀ/ [**v3**] *vt* to corrupt

pesant, ~e /pəzɑ̃, ɑ̃t/ *adj* **1** heavy
2 cumbersome
3 ‹*atmosphere, silence*› oppressive
IDIOM **valoir son ~ d'or** to be worth its weight in gold

pesanteur /pəzɑ̃tœʀ/ *f* **1** (of style) heaviness; (of bureaucracy) inertia
2 gravity

pèse-personne, *pl* **~s** /pɛzpɛʀsɔn/ *m* bathroom scales

⚷ **peser** /pəze/ [**v16**] **A** *vt* **1** to weigh
2 to weigh up; **~ ses mots** to choose one's words carefully; **tout bien pesé** all things considered
B *vi* **1** to weigh; **je pèse 70 kg** I weigh 70 kg; **~ lourd** to weigh a lot
2 to carry weight; **~ dans/sur une décision** to have a decisive influence in/on a decision
3 ~ sur ‹*suspicion*› to hang over ‹*person*›
4 ‹*tax, debts*› to weigh [sb/sth] down ‹*person, country*›
5 ‹*person, decision*› to influence (greatly) ‹*policy*›

peseta /pezeta/ *f* peseta

pessimisme /pesimism/ *m* pessimism

pessimiste /pesimist/ **A** *adj* pessimistic
B *mf* pessimist

peste /pɛst/ *f* **1** plague
2 (fam) pest (fam)
IDIOM **je me méfie de lui comme de la ~** (fam) I don't trust him an inch

pester /pɛste/ [**v1**] *vi* **~ contre qn/qch** to curse sb/sth

pesticide /pɛstisid/ *m* pesticide

pet /pɛ/ *m* (fam) fart (fam)

pétale /petal/ *m* petal

pétanque /petɑ̃k/ *f* pétanque

pétarader /petaʀade/ [**v1**] *vi* to backfire

pétard /petaʀ/ *m* banger (BrE), firecracker (AmE); **les cheveux en ~** spiky hair, bed hair; **être en ~** (fam) to be hopping mad (BrE) (fam), to be real mad (AmE) (fam)

péter /pete/ [**v14**] *vi* **1** (pop) to fart (fam)
2 (fam) ‹*balloon*› to burst; ‹*situation*› to blow up; ‹*thread*› to snap

pétillant, **~e** /petijɑ̃, ɑ̃t/ *adj* sparkling

pétiller /petije/ [**v1**] *vi* ‹*drink*› to fizz; ‹*firewood*› to crackle; ‹*eyes*› to sparkle

⚷ **petit**, **~e** /p(ə)ti, it/ **A** *adj* **1** small, little; short; **une toute ~e pièce** a tiny room; **se faire tout ~** (fig) to try to make oneself inconspicuous
2 ‹*walk, distance*› short
3 young, little; **c'est notre ~ dernier** he's our youngest
4 ‹*eater*› light; ‹*wage*› low; ‹*cry, worry*› little; ‹*hope*› slight; ‹*detail, defect*› minor; ‹*job*› modest
5 une ~e trentaine de personnes under thirty people
B *adv* **tailler ~** to be small-fitting; **~ à ~** little by little
■ **~ ami** boyfriend; **~ bois** kindling; **~ coin** (fam, euph) loo (BrE) (fam), bathroom (AmE); **~ déjeuner** breakfast; **~ noir** (fam) coffee; **~ nom** (fam) first name; **~ pois** (garden) pea, petit pois; **~ pot** jar of baby food; **~ rat (de l'Opéra)** *pupil at Paris Opéra's ballet school*; **~ salé** streaky salted pork; **~e amie** girlfriend; **~e annonce** classified advertisement; **~e nature** weakling; **~e reine** cycling; **~e voiture** toy car; **~s chevaux** ≈ ludo

petit-beurre, *pl* **petits-beurre** /p(ə)tibœʀ/ *m* petit beurre biscuit

petit-cousin, **petite-cousine**, *mpl* **petits-cousins** /p(ə)tikuzɛ̃, p(ə)titkuzin/ *mf* second cousin

petite-fille, *pl* **petites-filles** /p(ə)titfij/ *f* granddaughter

petitesse /p(ə)titɛs/ *f* **1** pettiness
2 small size

petit-fils, *pl* **petits-fils** /p(ə)tifis/ *m* grandson

pétition /petisjɔ̃/ *f* petition

petit-lait /p(ə)tilɛ/ *m* **ça se boit comme du ~!** (fam) it slips down nicely!

petit-nègre /p(ə)tinɛgʀ/ *m inv* (fam) pidgin French

petits-enfants /p(ə)tizɑ̃fɑ̃/ *mpl* grandchildren

pétrifiant, **~e** /petʀifjɑ̃, ɑ̃t/ *adj* petrifying

pétrifier /petʀifje/ [**v2**] *vt* **1** to petrify
2 (fig) to transfix

pétrin /petʀɛ̃/ *m* dough trough
IDIOM **être dans le ~** to be in a fix (fam)

pétrir /petʀiʀ/ [**v3**] *vt* **1** to knead ‹*dough*›
2 to mould (BrE), to mold (AmE) ‹*personality*›

pétrole /petʀɔl/ *m* oil, petroleum

pétrolette /petʀɔlɛt/ *f* (fam) moped

pétrolier, **-ière** /petʀɔlje, ɛʀ/ **A** *adj* oil
B *m* oil tanker

pétulant, **~e** /petylɑ̃, ɑ̃t/ *adj* exuberant

⚷ **peu** /pø/

> See the entries *avant, depuis, d'ici* and *sous* for the use of *peu* with these words.

A *adv* **1** not much; **il parle ~** he doesn't talk much; **elle gagne très ~** she earns very little; **deux semaines c'est trop ~** two weeks isn't long enough; **si ~ que ce soit** however little; **très ~ pour moi!** (fam) thanks, but no thanks!
2 not very; **assez ~ connu** little-known; **elle n'est pas ~ fière** she's more than a little proud
B *pron* few, not many
C de peu *phr* only just
D peu de *quantif* **~ de mots** few words; **~ de temps** little time
E *m* **le ~ de** the little ‹*trust, freedom*›; the few ‹*books, friends*›; the lack of ‹*interest*›
F un peu *phr* **1** a little, a bit; **reste encore un ~** stay a little longer; **parle un ~ plus fort** speak a little louder; **un ~ plus de** a few more ‹*books*›; a little more ‹*time*›; **un ~ beaucoup** more than a bit

P

⚷ key word

2 just; **répète un ~ pour voir!** (fam) you just try saying that again!; **pour un ~ ils se seraient battus** they very nearly had a fight
G **peu à peu** *phr* gradually, little by little
H **pour peu que** *phr* if; **pour ~ qu'il ait bu, il va nous raconter sa vie** one drink, and he'll tell us his life story

peuplade /pœplad/ *f* small tribe

peuple /pœpl/ *m* people

peuplement /pœpləmɑ̃/ *m* population

peupler /pœple/ [**v1**] **A** *vt* **1** to populate ‹*country*›; to stock ‹*forest, pond*›
2 ‹*animals, plants*› to colonize ‹*region*›; ‹*students*› to fill ‹*street*›
B **se peupler** *v refl* (+ *v être*) to fill up

peuplier /pøplije/ *m* poplar

peur /pœʀ/ *f* fear; fright, scare; **être mort** *or* **vert** (fam) **de ~** to be scared to death; **une ~ panique s'empara de lui** he was panic-stricken; **avoir ~** to be afraid; **j'en ai bien ~** I'm afraid so; **faire ~ à qn** to frighten sb; **maigre à faire ~** terribly thin

peureusement /pœʀøzmɑ̃/ *adv* fearfully

peureux, -euse /pœʀø, øz/ *adj* fearful

peut-être /pøtɛtʀ/ *adv* perhaps, maybe

phalange /falɑ̃ʒ/ *f* phalanx

phallocrate /falɔkʀat/ *m* male chauvinist

phalloïde /falɔid/ *adj* **amanite ~** death cap

phallus /falys/ *m inv* phallus

pharaon /faʀaɔ̃/ *m* pharaoh

phare /faʀ/ *m* **1** headlight
2 lighthouse

pharmacie /faʀmasi/ *f* **1** chemist's (shop) (BrE), drugstore (AmE), pharmacy
2 medicine cabinet
3 (science) pharmacy

pharmacien, -ienne /faʀmasjɛ̃, ɛn/ *mf* (dispensing) chemist (BrE), pharmacist

pharyngite /faʀɛ̃ʒit/ *f* pharyngitis

pharynx /faʀɛ̃ks/ *m inv* pharynx

phase /fɑz/ *f* **1** stage
2 phase

phénoménal, ~e, *mpl* **-aux** /fenɔmenal, o/ *adj* phenomenal

phénomène /fenɔmɛn/ *m* **1** phenomenon
2 (fam) **c'est un ~** he/she's quite a character

philanthropie /filɑ̃tʀɔpi/ *f* philanthropy

philatélie /filateli/ *f* stamp collecting

philatéliste /filatelist/ *mf* philatelist

philosophe /filɔzɔf/ *mf* philosopher

philosophie /filɔzɔfi/ *f* philosophy

philosophique /filɔzɔfik/ *adj* philosophical

phobie /fɔbi/ *f* phobia

phonétique /fɔnetik/ **A** *adj* phonetic
B *f* phonetics

phonographe /fɔnɔgʀaf/ *m* gramophone (BrE), phonograph (AmE)

phoque /fɔk/ *m* **1** seal
2 sealskin

phosphate /fɔsfat/ *m* phosphate

phosphore /fɔsfɔʀ/ *m* phosphorus

phosphorescent, ~e /fɔsfɔʀesɑ̃, ɑ̃t/ *adj* phosphorescent

photo /fɔto/ *f* **1** photography
2 photo
■ **~ d'identité** passport photo

photocomposition /fɔtokɔ̃pozisjɔ̃/ *f* filmsetting (BrE), photocomposition (AmE)

photocopie /fɔtokɔpi/ *f* photocopy

photocopier /fɔtokɔpje/ [**v2**] *vt* to photocopy

photocopieur /fɔtokɔpjœʀ/ *m* photocopier

photocopieuse /fɔtokɔpjøz/ *f* photocopier

photogénique /fɔtoʒenik/ *adj* photogenic

photographe /fɔtogʀaf/ *mf* photographer

photographie /fɔtogʀafi/ *f* **1** photography
2 photograph, picture

photographier /fɔtogʀafje/ [**v2**] *vt* to photograph, to take a photo of

photographique /fɔtogʀafik/ *adj* photographic

photomaton® /fɔtomatɔ̃/ *m* photo booth

photosynthèse /fɔtosɛ̃tɛz/ *f* photosynthesis

photothèque /fɔtotɛk/ *f* picture library

phrase /fʀɑz/ *f* **1** sentence
2 phrase; **avoir une ~ malheureuse** to say the wrong thing; **~ toute faite** stock phrase
3 (Mus) phrase

phréatique /fʀeatik/ *adj* **nappe ~** ground water

physicien, -ienne /fizisjɛ̃, ɛn/ *mf* physicist

physiologie /fizjɔlɔʒi/ *f* physiology

physiologique /fizjɔlɔʒik/ *adj* physiological

physionomie /fizjɔnɔmi/ *f* **1** face
2 (fig) (of country) face; (of area) appearance, look

physiothérapie /fizjɔteʀapi/ *f* physiotherapy (BrE), physical therapy (AmE)

physique[1] /fizik/ **A** *adj* physical
B *m* **1** physical appearance
2 physique; **avoir un ~ séduisant** to look attractive
IDIOM **avoir le ~ de l'emploi** to look the part

physique[2] /fizik/ *f* physics

piaf /pjaf/ *m* (fam) little bird

piaffer /pjafe/ [**v1**] *vi* **1** ‹*horse*› to paw the ground
2 ‹*person*› to be impatient; **~ d'impatience** to be champing at the bit

piailler /pjɑje/ [**v1**] *vi* ‹*bird*› to chirp

pianiste /pjanist/ *mf* pianist

piano /pjano/ **A** *m* piano; **jouer qch au ~** to play sth on the piano
B *adv* (Mus) piano
■ **~ à queue** grand piano

pianoter /pjanɔte/ [**v1**] *vi* to tinkle on the piano

PIB /peibe/ *m*: *abbr* ▶ **produit**
pic /pik/ **A** *m* **1** peak
2 pick
3 woodpecker
B **à pic** *phr* ‹*cliff*› sheer; ‹*ravine*› very steep
IDIOM **tomber à ~** to come just at the right time
pichenette /piʃnɛt/ *f* flick
pichet /piʃɛ/ *m* jug (BrE), pitcher
pick-up /pikœp/ *m inv* (fam) record player
picorer /pikɔʀe/ [**v1**] *vi* ‹*bird*› to peck about
picotement /pikɔtmɑ̃/ *m* tingling; tickling
picoter /pikɔte/ [**v1**] **A** *vt* to sting ‹*eyes, nose, skin*›; to tickle ‹*throat*›
B *vi* ‹*throat*› to tickle; ‹*eyes*› to sting
pie /pi/ *f* **1** magpie
2 (fam) chatterbox (fam)
pièce /pjɛs/ **A** *f* **1** room
2 coin; **~ de monnaie** coin
3 play; **~ de théâtre** play
4 bit, piece; **en ~s** in bits; **mettre qn/qch en ~s** to pull sb/sth to pieces
5 part; **~ de rechange** spare part
6 patch
7 document; **juger sur ~s** to judge on the actual evidence; **c'est inventé de toutes ~s** (fig) it's a complete fabrication
8 piece, item; (in chess set, puzzle) piece; **~ de collection** collector's item; **on n'est pas aux ~s** (fam) we're not in a sweat shop
B **-pièces** (*combining form*) **1** **un trois-~s cuisine** a three-roomed apartment with kitchen
2 **un deux-~s** a two-piece swimsuit
■ **~ à conviction** exhibit; **~ détachée** spare part; **en ~s détachées** in kit form; dismantled; **~ d'identité** identity papers; **~ maîtresse** showpiece; key element; **~ montée** layer cake
piécette /pjesɛt/ *f* small coin
pied /pje/ *m* **1** foot; **être ~s nus** to be barefoot; **sauter à ~s joints** to jump with one's feet together; (fig) to jump in with both feet; **coup de ~** kick; **à ~** on foot; **promenade à ~** walk; **taper du ~** to stamp one's foot; to tap one's foot; **de la tête aux ~s** from head to foot; **portrait en ~** full-length portrait; **avoir conscience de là où on met les ~s** (fam) to know what one is letting oneself in for; **sur un ~ d'égalité** on an equal footing
2 (of hill, stairs) foot, bottom; (of glass) stem; (of lamp) base; (of camera) stand
3 (of celery, lettuce) head; **~ de vigne** vine
4 (measurement) foot
■ **~ à coulisse** calliper rule
IDIOMS **être sur ~** ‹*person*› to be up and about; ‹*business*› to be up and running; **mettre sur ~** to set up; **j'ai ~** I can touch the bottom; **perdre ~** to go out of one's depth; to lose ground; **être à ~ d'œuvre** to be ready to get down to work; **elle joue au tennis comme un ~** (fam) she's hopeless at tennis; **faire un ~ de nez à qn** to thumb one's nose at sb; **faire du ~ à qn** to play footsie with sb (fam); **faire des ~s et des mains** (fam) **pour obtenir** to work really hard at getting; **ça lui fera les ~s** (fam) that will teach him a lesson; **c'est le ~** (fam) that's terrific (fam); **mettre à ~** to suspend; **lever le ~** (fam) to slow down
pied-à-terre /pjetatɛʀ/ *m inv* pied-à-terre
pied-bot, *pl* **pieds-bots** /pjebo/ *m* person with a club foot
piédestal, *pl* **-aux** /pjedɛstal, o/ *m* pedestal
pied-noir, *pl* **pieds-noirs** /pjenwaʀ/ *mf* (fam) *French colonial born in Algeria*
piège /pjɛʒ/ *m* **1** trap; **il s'est laissé prendre au ~** he walked into the trap
2 pitfall
■ **~ du surendettement** debt trap
piéger /pjeʒe/ [**v15**] *vt* **1** to trap ‹*animal, criminal*›
2 to trick, to trap ‹*person*›
3 to booby-trap ‹*letter, parcel, car*›
piercing /piʀsiŋ/ *m* **le ~** body piercing; **elle a un ~ au nombril** she has a pierced navel
pierre /pjɛʀ/ *f* stone; rock; **poser la première ~** to lay the foundation stone
IDIOMS **jeter la ~ à qn** to accuse sb; **faire d'une ~ deux coups** to kill two birds with one stone
pierreries /pjɛʀʀi/ *fpl* gems
pierreux, **-euse** /pjɛʀø, øz/ *adj* stony
piété /pjete/ *f* piety; **de ~** devotional
piétiner /pjetine/ [**v1**] **A** *vt* **1** to trample [sth] underfoot
2 to trample on
B *vi* **1** **~ d'impatience** to hop up and down with impatience
2 to shuffle along; to trudge along
3 to make no headway
piéton, **-onne** /pjetɔ̃, ɔn/ **A** *adj* pedestrianized
B *mf* pedestrian
piétonnier, **-ière** /pjetɔnje, ɛʀ/ *adj* pedestrianized
piètre /pjɛtʀ/ *adj* ‹*actor, writer*› very mediocre; ‹*health, results*› very poor; **c'est une ~ consolation** that's small comfort
pieu, *pl* **~x** /pjø/ *m* stake
pieuvre /pjœvʀ/ *f* octopus
pieux, **pieuse** /pjø, øz/ *adj* **1** pious, religious
2 ‹*affection, silence*› reverent
■ **~ mensonge** white lie
pif /pif/ *m* (fam) **1** nose, conk (BrE) (fam), schnozz (AmE) (fam)
2 intuition; **j'ai eu du ~** I had a hunch (fam); **au ~** ‹*measure*› roughly; ‹*decide*› just like that
pige /piʒ/ *f* **travailler à la ~**, **faire des ~s** to do freelance work
pigeon /piʒɔ̃/ *m* **1** pigeon

key word

2 (fam) sucker (fam)
■ **~ voyageur** carrier pigeon
pigeonnier /piʒɔnje/ *m* pigeon house; pigeon loft; dovecote
piger /piʒe/ [**v13**] *vt* (fam) to understand
pigiste /piʒist/ *mf* freelance
pigment /pigmɑ̃/ *m* pigment
pigmenter /pigmɑ̃te/ [**v1**] *vt* to alter the pigmentation of
pignon /piɲɔ̃/ *m* **1** gable
2 gearwheel
3 pine kernel
IDIOM **avoir ~ sur rue** to be well-established
pilaf /pilaf/ *m* pilau; **riz ~** pilau rice
pile¹ /pil/ *adv* (fam) **1 s'arrêter ~** to stop dead
2 exactly; **à 10 heures et demie ~** at ten thirty sharp; **~ à l'heure** right on time; **tu tombes ~** you're just the person I wanted to see
pile² /pil/ *f* **1** pile; stack
2 ~ (électrique) battery; **à ~s** battery-operated
3 pier
4 (of coin) **le côté ~** the reverse side; **jouer à ~ ou face** to play heads or tails
■ **~ bouton** button battery; **~ solaire** solar cell
piler /pile/ [**v1**] **A** *vt* to grind; to crush
B *vi* (fam) ‹*car*› to pull up short; ‹*driver*› to slam on the brakes
pileux, -euse /pilø, øz/ *adj* **système ~** hair
pilier /pilje/ *m* **1** pillar
2 (fig) mainstay
3 (in rugby) prop forward
pillage /pijaʒ/ *m* pillage, plundering; looting
pillard, ~e /pijaʀ, aʀd/ *mf* looter; pillager
piller /pije/ [**v1**] *vt* to pillage ‹*town*›; to loot ‹*shop*›; to plunder ‹*temple*›
pilleur, -euse /pijœʀ, øz/ *mf* looter; plunderer
pilon /pilɔ̃/ *m* **1** pestle
2 (of poultry) drumstick
pilonnage /pilɔnaʒ/ *m* (Mil) bombardment
pilotage /pilɔtaʒ/ *m* piloting
pilote /pilɔt/ **A** *m* pilot
B (-)pilote (*combining form*) **projet(-)~** pilot project; **hôpital(-)~** experimental hospital
■ **~ automobile** racing driver
piloter /pilɔte/ [**v1**] *vt* to pilot ‹*plane, ship*›; to drive ‹*car*›
pilotis /pilɔti/ *m inv* stilts
pilule /pilyl/ *f* pill
IDIOMS **avaler la ~** (fam) to grin and bear it; **faire passer la ~** (fam) to sweeten the pill
pilule du lendemain /pilyl dy lɑ̃dəmɛ̃/ *f* morning-after pill
pimbêche /pɛ̃bɛʃ/ *f* stuck-up madam (fam)
piment /pimɑ̃/ *m* **1** hot pepper
2 spice
■ **~ rouge** hot red pepper, chilli; **~ vert** green chilli pepper
pimpant, ~e /pɛ̃pɑ̃, ɑ̃t/ *adj* spruce, smart
pin /pɛ̃/ *m* pine (tree); **pomme de ~** pine cone
pinailler /pinɑje/ [**v1**] *vi* (pop) to split hairs
pince /pɛ̃s/ *f* **1** (pair of) pliers; (pair of) tongs
2 (in garment) dart; **un pantalon à ~s** pleat front trousers (BrE) *or* pants (AmE)
3 (of crab) pincer, claw
■ **~ à cheveux** hair grip; **~ coupante** wire cutters; **~ à dessin** bulldog clip; **~ à épiler** tweezers; **~ à linge** clothes peg (BrE), clothespin(AmE); **~ à sucre** sugar tongs; **~ à vélo** bicycle clip
pincé, ~e /pɛ̃se/ *adj* ‹*smile*› tight-lipped; **prendre un air ~** to become stiff *or* starchy
pinceau, *pl* **~x** /pɛ̃so/ *m* (paint) brush
pincée /pɛ̃se/ **A** *adj f* ▶ **pincé**
B *f* (of pepper, salt) pinch
pincement /pɛ̃smɑ̃/ *m* pinch; **avoir un ~ de cœur** to feel a twinge of sadness
pince-monseigneur, *pl* **pinces-monseigneur** /pɛ̃smɔ̃sɛɲœʀ/ *f* jemmy, slim jim
pince-nez /pɛ̃sne/ *m inv* pince-nez
pincer /pɛ̃se/ [**v12**] **A** *vt* **1** ‹*person*› to pinch; ‹*crab*› to nip
2 (fam) to nab (fam), to catch ‹*thief*›
3 ~ les lèvres to purse one's lips
4 to pluck ‹*string*›
5 ‹*wind, cold*› to sting ‹*face*›
B se pincer *v refl* (+ *v être*) to pinch oneself; **se ~ le nez** to hold one's nose; **elle s'est pincée en refermant le tiroir** she caught her fingers closing the drawer
IDIOM **en ~ pour qn** (fam) to be stuck on sb (fam)
pince-sans-rire /pɛ̃ssɑ̃ʀiʀ/ *mf inv* **c'est un ~** he has a deadpan sense of humour (BrE)
pincettes /pɛ̃sɛt/ *fpl* **il n'est pas à prendre avec des ~** (fam) he's like a bear with a sore head (fam)
pinède /pinɛd/ *f* pine forest
pingouin /pɛ̃gwɛ̃/ *m* **1** auk
2 penguin
ping-pong®, *pl* **~s** /piŋpɔ̃ŋ/ *m* table tennis, ping-pong®
pingre /pɛ̃gʀ/ *adj* stingy, niggardly
pingrerie /pɛ̃gʀəʀi/ *f* stinginess
pin-pon /pɛ̃pɔ̃/ *m: sound of a two-tone siren*
pin's /pins/ *m inv* lapel badge
pintade /pɛ̃tad/ *f* guinea fowl
pintadeau, *pl* **~x** /pɛ̃tado/ *m* young guinea fowl
pinte /pɛ̃t/ *f* **1** pint (BrE) (= 0,57 litre)
2 ≈ quart (AmE) (= 0,94 litre)
3 pot, tankard
pinter: **se pinter** /pɛ̃te/ [**v1**] *v refl* (+ *v être*) (fam) to get plastered (fam) *or* drunk
pin-up /pinœp/ *f inv* (fam) glamour (BrE) girl

pioche /pjɔʃ/ *f* **1** mattock; pickaxe (BrE), pickax (AmE)
2 (Games) stack

piocher /pjɔʃe/ [**v1**] *vt* **1** to dig [sth] over ‹*soil*›
2 (Games) to take [sth] from the stack ‹*card*›

piolet /pjɔlɛ/ *m* ice axe (BrE), ice pick (AmE)

pion, pionne /pjɔ̃, pjɔn/ **A** *mf* (Sch), (fam) *student paid to supervise pupils*
B *m* **1** (in games) counter; (in chess) pawn; (in draughts) draught (BrE), checker (AmE)
2 (fig) pawn

pionnier, -ière /pjɔnje, ɛʀ/ *adj, mf* pioneer

pipe /pip/ *f* pipe
IDIOM **casser sa ~** (fam) to kick the bucket (fam)

pipeau, *pl* **~x** /pipo/ *m* (reed) pipe
IDIOMS **c'est du ~** (fam) it's no great shakes (fam); **c'est pas du ~** (fam) it's for real (fam)

pipelette /piplɛt/ *f* (fam) gossip, gossipmonger

piper /pipe/ [**v1**] *vt* **1** (fam) **ne pas ~ (mot)** not to say a word
2 to load ‹*dice*›

pipi /pipi/ *m* (fam) pee (fam); wee-wee (fam)

pipole /pipɔl/ *mf* (fam) celeb (fam)

piquant, ~e /pikɑ̃, ɑ̃t/ **A** *adj* **1** ‹*stem, thistle*› prickly; ‹*nail*› sharp
2 ‹*mustard, sauce*› hot; ‹*cheese*› sharp
B *m* **1** (of stem, thistle) prickle; (of hedgehog, cactus) spine; (of barbed wire) spike, barb
2 (of story) spiciness; (of situation) piquancy

pique¹ /pik/ *m* (Games) spades

pique² /pik/ *f* **1** cutting remark
2 pike; (of picador) lance

piqué, ~e /pike/ *adj* ‹*wood*› worm-eaten; ‹*linen, mirror, fruit*› spotted; ‹*paper*› foxed

pique-assiette /pikasjɛt/ *mf inv* (fam) sponger (fam)

pique-nique, *pl* **~s** /piknik/ *m* picnic

piquer /pike/ [**v1**] **A** *vt* **1** to sting; to bite; to prick
2 (fam) to give [sb] an injection; **faire ~ un animal** to have an animal put down
3 ‹*mildew, rust*› to spot ‹*linen, mirror*›; to fox ‹*paper, book*›
4 ses yeux la piquaient her eyes were stinging; **ça me pique partout** I'm itchy all over
5 (fam) to pinch (BrE) (fam), to steal ‹*book, idea*›; to borrow ‹*pencil, pullover*›
6 to catch; **ils se sont fait ~ à tricher pendant l'examen** they got caught cheating in the exam
7 ~ qn au vif to cut sb to the quick
8 to arouse ‹*curiosity*›
9 (fam) **~ un fou rire** to have a fit of the giggles; **~ une crise de nerfs** to throw a fit (fam); **~ un cent mètres** to break into a run
10 ~ une tête to dive
B *vi* **1** ‹*beard*› to be bristly; ‹*wool*› to be scratchy; ‹*throat, eyes*› to sting
2 ‹*bird*› to swoop down; ‹*plane*› to dive; **~ du nez** ‹*person*› to nod off; ‹*plane*› to go into a nosedive
3 (fam) **arrête de ~ dans le plat** stop picking (things out of the dish)
C se piquer *v refl* (+ *v être*) **1** to prick oneself; **se ~ aux orties** to get stung by nettles
2 to inject oneself
3 se ~ de pouvoir réussir seul to claim that one can manage on one's own
IDIOMS **quelle mouche t'a piqué?** (fam) what's got into you? (fam); **son article n'était pas piqué des hannetons** (fam) his/her article didn't pull any punches

piquet /pikɛ/ *m* **1** stake
2 peg
3 (in skiing) gate pole
4 (of sunshade) pole
5 picket; **~ de grève** (strike) picket, picket line

piquette /pikɛt/ *f* (fam) plonk (BrE) (fam), cheap wine

piqûre /pikyʀ/ *f* **1** injection, shot
2 (of thorn, pin) prick; (of nettle, bee) sting; (of mosquito) bite
3 stitch; stitching

piratage de téléphone *m* phone hacking

pirate /piʀat/ *m* pirate
■ **~ de l'air** hijacker, skyjacker

pirater /piʀate/ [**v1**] *vt* to pirate

piraterie /piʀatʀi/ *f* piracy
■ **~ aérienne** hijacking, skyjacking; **~ informatique** computer hacking

⚷ **pire** /piʀ/ **A** *adj* **1** worse (**que** than)
2 worst; **les ~s mensonges** the most wicked lies
B *m* **le ~** the worst; **au ~** at the very worst

pirogue /piʀɔg/ *f* dugout canoe

pirouette /piʀwɛt/ *f* pirouette; **s'en tirer par une ~** to dodge the question skilfully (BrE)

pis /pi/ **A** *adj inv* worse
B *adv* worse; **tant ~** too bad
C *m inv* (of cow) udder

pis-aller /pizale/ *m inv* makeshift solution

pisciculteur, -trice /pisikyltœʀ, tʀis/ *mf* fish farmer

pisciculture /pisikyltyʀ/ *f* fish farming

piscine /pisin/ *f* swimming pool

piscine panoramique *f* infinity pool

pisse /pis/ *f* (pop) piss (sl)

pissenlit /pisɑ̃li/ *m* dandelion
IDIOM **manger les ~s par la racine** (pop) to be pushing up the daisies (fam)

pisser /pise/ (pop) [**v1**] **A** *vt* **~ le sang** ‹*person, nose, injury*› to pour with blood
B *vi* to pee (fam), to piss (sl)
IDIOMS **il pleut comme vache qui pisse** it's pissing down (sl); **laisse ~!** forget it!

pissotière /pisɔtjɛʀ/ *f* (fam) street urinal

⚷ key word

pistache /pistaʃ/ *f* pistachio

piste /pist/ *f* **1** trail; **être sur une fausse ~** to be on the wrong track
2 (in police investigation) lead
3 (in stadium) track; (in horse racing) racecourse (BrE), racetrack (AmE); (in motor racing) racetrack; (in circus) ring; (in skiing) slope; (in cross-country skiing) trail; **~ de danse** dance floor; **entrer en ~** (at circus) to come into the ring; (fig) to enter the fray
4 track, path; (in desert) trail
5 (in airport) runway
6 (on record, cassette) track
■ **~ cyclable** cycle lane; cycle path

pister /piste/ [**v1**] *vt* to trail, to track

pistil /pistil/ *m* pistil

pistolet /pistɔlɛ/ *m* **1** pistol, gun; **tirer au ~** to fire a pistol
2 (Tech) gun; **~ à peinture** spray gun

pistolet-mitrailleur, *pl* **pistolets-mitrailleurs** /pistɔlɛmitʀajœʀ/ *m* submachine gun

piston /pistɔ̃/ *m* **1** (Tech) piston
2 (fam) contacts; **avoir du ~** to have connections in the right places

pistonner /pistɔne/ [**v1**] *vt* (fam) to pull strings for

pitance /pitɑ̃s/ *f* fare

piteusement /pitøzmɑ̃/ *adv* pitifully, pathetically

piteux, -euse /pitø, øz/ *adj* **1** ‹*results*› poor, pitiful
2 ‹*air*› crestfallen

pitié /pitje/ *f* pity; mercy; **prendre qn en ~** to take pity on sb; **il fait ~** he's a pitiful sight; **par ~, tais-toi!** for pity's sake, be quiet!

piton /pitɔ̃/ *m* **1** hook
2 (in climbing) piton
3 (of mountain) peak

pitoyable /pitwajabl/ *adv* **1** pitiful
2 pathetic

pitoyablement /pitwajabləmɑ̃/ *adv* **1** pitifully
2 ‹*fail*› miserably; ‹*sing*› pathetically

pitre /pitʀ/ *m* clown, buffoon

pitrerie /pitʀəʀi/ *f* clowning

pittoresque /pitɔʀɛsk/ *adj* picturesque; colourful (BrE)

pivert /pivɛʀ/ *m* green woodpecker

pivoine /pivwan/ *f* peony

pivot /pivo/ *m* **1** (Tech) pivot
2 (of economy, strategy, group) linchpin; (of plot) kingpin
3 (Sport) (player) pivot, post
4 (of tooth) post and core

pivotant, ~e /pivɔtɑ̃, ɑ̃t/ *adj* ‹*chair*› swivel; ‹*sign*› pivoting; ‹*door*› revolving

pivoter /pivɔte/ [**v1**] *vi* ‹*person, animal, panel*› to pivot; ‹*door*› to revolve; ‹*chair*› to swivel

PJ /peʒi/ *f* **1** (*abbr* = **police judiciaire**) *detective division of the French police force*
2 (*abbr* = **pièce(s) jointe(s)**) encl.

PL (*written abbr* = **poids lourd**) HGV (BrE), heavy truck (AmE)

placard /plakaʀ/ *m* **1** cupboard; **mettre au ~** (fig) to put [sth] on ice ‹*plan*›; to shunt [sb] aside ‹*person*›
2 poster, bill

placarder /plakaʀde/ [**v1**] *vt* **1** to post, to stick
2 to cover [sth] with posters

place /plas/ *f* **1** room, space
2 (in theatre, cinema, bus) seat; **payer sa ~** (in cinema, theatre) to pay for one's ticket; (on train) to pay one's fare
3 place; **remettre qch à sa ~** to put sth back in its place; **être en bonne ~ pour gagner** to be well-placed *or* in a good position to win; **la ~ d'un mot dans une phrase** the position of a word in a sentence; **sur ~** to/on the scene; on the spot; **il faut savoir rester à sa ~** you must know your place; **tenir une grande ~ dans la vie de qn** to play a large part in sb's life
4 à la ~ de instead of, in place of; **(si j'étais) à ta ~** if I were in your position
5 en ~ ‹*system, structure*› in place; ‹*troops*› in position; ‹*leader, party, regime*› ruling; **ne plus tenir en ~** to be restless; **mettre en ~** to put [sth] in place ‹*programme*›; to put [sth] in position ‹*team*›; to establish, to set up ‹*network, institution*›
6 (in town) square; **la ~ du village** the village square
7 (Econ) market; **~ financière** financial market
8 job; **perdre sa ~** to lose one's job
9 être dans la ~ to be on the inside; **avoir un pied dans la ~** to have a foot in the door

placé, ~e /plase/ **A** *pp* ▶ **placer**
B *pp adj* **1** (located) **être ~** ‹*object, tap, window*› to be; ‹*chair, table, statue*› to be placed; ‹*person*› (gen) to be; (at the theatre, cinema) to be sitting; **être bien/mal ~** ‹*building, shop*› to be well/badly situated; ‹*person*› (at table, at a function) to have a good/bad place
2 (in a hierarchy) **être bien ~ sur une liste** to have a good position on the list; **il est bien ~ pour le poste** he's a likely candidate for the job; **avoir des amis haut ~s** to have friends in high places
3 être bien/mal ~ pour faire (to succeed) to be well/badly placed to do; (to know, judge) to be in a (good)/in no position to do

placebo /plasebo/ *m* placebo

placement /plasmɑ̃/ *m* **1** investment
2 assurer le ~ des diplômés to ensure that graduates find employment
3 (of child) fostering

placenta /plasɛ̃ta/ *m* placenta

placer /plase/ [**v12**] **A** *vt* **1** to put, to place ‹*object*›; to seat ‹*person*›; **~ sa confiance en qn** to put one's trust in sb; **~ ses espoirs en qn** to pin one's hopes on sb; **mal placé**

‹*pride*› misplaced
2 to place, to find a job for ‹*person*›
3 to invest ‹*money*›
4 to slip in ‹*remark, anecdote*›; **je n'arrive pas à en ~ une** (fam) **avec elle!** I can't get a word in edgeways (BrE) *or* edgewise (AmE) with her!
5 to place [sb] in care ‹*child*›
B **se placer** *v refl* (+ *v être*) **1 se ~ près de** to sit next to
2 se ~ premier to come first

placeur, -euse /plasœʀ, øz/ *mf* usher/ usherette

placide /plasid/ *adj* placid, calm

placier, -ière /plasje, ɛʀ/ *mf* **1** sales representative
2 market superintendent

plafond /plafɔ̃/ *m* **1** ceiling; (of tent, vehicle, tunnel) roof
2 ceiling, limit

plafonnement /plafɔnmɑ̃/ *m* **1** setting a ceiling on ‹*pay*›; setting a limit on ‹*spending*›
2 (on pay) ceiling (**de** on); (on spending) limitation (**de** of)

plafonnier /plafɔnje/ *m* (gen) flush-fitting ceiling light; (in car) interior light

plage /plaʒ/ *f* beach
■ **~ arrière** rear window shelf; **~ horaire** time slot

plagiaire /plaʒjɛʀ/ *mf* plagiarist

plagiat /plaʒja/ *m* plagiarism

plagier /plaʒje/ [**v2**] *vt* to plagiarize

plaid /plɛd/ *m* tartan rug (BrE), plaid blanket (AmE)

plaidant, ~e /plɛdɑ̃, ɑ̃t/ *adj* litigant

plaider /plede/ [**v1**] **A** *vt* to plead ‹*case*›
B *vi* **1** to plead
2 ~ en faveur de qn ‹*circumstances*› to speak in favour (BrE) of sb

plaidoirie /plɛdwaʀi/ *f* plea

plaidoyer /plɛdwaje/ *m* **1** speech for the defence (BrE)
2 plea

plaie /plɛ/ *f* **1** wound; sore; cut
2 (fam) **cet enfant, quelle ~!** (fam) that child is such a pain! (fam)

plaignant, ~e /plɛɲɑ̃, ɑ̃t/ *mf* plaintiff

⚷ **plaindre** /plɛ̃dʀ/ [**v54**] **A** *vt* to pity
B **se plaindre** *v refl* (+ *v être*) **1** to complain
2 ‹*injured person*› to moan

plaine /plɛn/ *f* plain

plain-pied: **de plain-pied** /dəplɛ̃pje/ *phr* **une maison de ~** a single-storey (BrE) *or* single-story (AmE) house

plainte /plɛ̃t/ *f* **1** (gen), (Law) complaint
2 moan, groan

plaintif, -ive /plɛ̃tif, iv/ *adj* plaintive

plaintivement /plɛ̃tivmɑ̃/ *adv* plaintively, dolefully

⚷ **plaire** /plɛʀ/ [**v59**] **A** **plaire à** *v+prep* **1 elle plaît aux hommes** men find her attractive; **elle m'a plu tout de suite** I liked her straight away
2 mon travail me plaît I like my job; **un modèle qui plaît beaucoup** a very popular model
B **se plaire** *v refl* (+ *v être*) **1** ‹*people, couple*› to like each other
2 ils se plaisent ici they like it here
3 il se plaît à dire qu'il est issu du peuple he likes to say that he's a son of the people
C *v impers* **s'il te plaît, s'il vous plaît** please

plaisamment /plɛzamɑ̃/ *adv* **1** agreeably
2 amusingly

plaisance /plɛzɑ̃s/ *f* **la navigation de ~** boating; **bateau de ~** pleasure boat

plaisancier, -ière /plɛzɑ̃sje, ɛʀ/ *mf* amateur sailor

plaisant, ~e /plɛzɑ̃, ɑ̃t/ *adj* **1** pleasant
2 amusing, funny

plaisanter /plɛzɑ̃te/ [**v1**] *vi* to joke

plaisanterie /plɛzɑ̃tʀi/ *f* joke

⚷ **plaisir** /plɛziʀ/ *m* pleasure; **prendre un malin ~ à faire** to take a wicked delight in doing; **faire ~ à qn** to please sb; **faites-moi le ~ de vous taire!** would you please shut up! (fam); **faire durer le ~** to make the pleasure last; (ironic) to prolong the agony

⚷ **plan** /plɑ̃/ *m* **1** (of town, underground) map; (in building) plan, map
2 (for building) plan; **tirer des ~s** to draw up plans
3 (of machine) blueprint
4 (of essay, book) outline, framework
5 (in cinematography) shot; **premier ~** foreground
6 level; **au premier ~ de l'actualité** at the forefront of the news; **sur le ~ politique** from a political point of view
7 plan; **c'est le bon ~** (fam) it's a good idea
■ **~ d'eau** artificial lake; **~ d'épargne** savings plan; **~ d'épargne-logement, PEL** *savings scheme entitling depositor to a cheap mortgage*
IDIOMS **laisser qn en ~** (fam) to leave sb in the lurch; **laisser qch en ~** (fam) to leave sth unfinished

⚷ **planche** /plɑ̃ʃ/ *f* **1** (gen) plank; (for kneading dough) board; **faire la ~** to float on one's back
2 plate
■ **~ à roulettes** (Sport) skateboard; **~ de salut** lifeline; **~ à voile** windsurfing board
IDIOMS **monter sur les ~s** to go on the stage; **avoir du pain sur la ~** (fam) to have one's work cut out

plancher[1] /plɑ̃ʃe/ [**v1**] *vi* (sl) to work

plancher[2] /plɑ̃ʃe/ *m* **1** floor
2 (Econ) floor; **atteindre un ~** to bottom out

planchiste /plɑ̃ʃist/ *mf* windsurfer

plancton /plɑ̃ktɔ̃/ *m* plankton

plané /plane/ *adj m* **vol ~** glide; **faire un vol ~** (fig) to go flying

⚷ key word

planer /plane/ [**v1**] *vi* **1** ‹*plane, bird*› to glide
2 laisser ~ le doute to allow uncertainty to persist
3 (fam) to have one's head in the clouds

planétaire /planetɛʀ/ *adj* planetary; (fig) global

planète /planɛt/ *f* planet

planeur /planœʀ/ *m* **1** glider
2 gliding

planifier /planifje/ [**v2**] *vt* to plan

planning /planiŋ/ *m* (controversial, fam) schedule
■ **~ familial** family planning service

planque /plɑ̃k/ *f* (fam) (for person) hideout

planquer /plɑ̃ke/ [**v1**] (fam) **A** *vt* to hide ‹*person*›; to hide [sth] away ‹*object*›
B se planquer *v refl* (+ *v être*) to hide

plan-séquence, *pl* **plans-séquences** /plɑ̃sekɑ̃s/ *m* sequence shot

plant /plɑ̃/ *m* young plant

plantaire /plɑ̃tɛʀ/ *adj* (Anat) plantar; **voûte ~** arch of the foot

plantation /plɑ̃tasjɔ̃/ *f* **1** plantation
2 (of flowers) bed; (of vegetables) patch

plante /plɑ̃t/ *f* **1** plant; **~ verte** house plant; **~ grasse** succulent
2 ~ (des pieds) sole (of the foot)

planter /plɑ̃te/ [**v1**] **A** *vt* **1** to plant ‹*flowers, shrub*›
2 to drive in ‹*stake*›; to knock in ‹*nail*›; **~ un couteau dans** to stick a knife into
3 to pitch ‹*tent*›; **~ le décor** to set the scene
4 ~ (là) to drop ‹*tool*›; to abandon ‹*car*›
B se planter *v refl* (+ *v être*) **1** (fam) **aller se ~ devant qch** to go and stand in front of sth
2 (fam) to crash
3 (fam) to get it wrong; **il s'est planté en histoire** he made a mess of the history exam

plantureux, **-euse** /plɑ̃tyʀø, øz/ *adj* ‹*bosom*› ample; ‹*woman*› buxom

plaque /plak/ *f* (of ice) patch; (on skin) blotch; (of glass) plate; (of marble) slab; (on door of surgery) brass plate; (of policeman) badge
■ **~ d'égout** manhole cover; **~ d'immatriculation** number plate (BrE), license plate (AmE)
(IDIOM) **être à côté de la ~** (fam) to be completely mistaken

plaqué, **~e** /plake/ *adj* **~ or** gold-plated

plaquer /plake/ [**v1**] **A** *vt* **1 ~ qn contre qch** to pin sb against sth
2 (fam) to leave ‹*job, spouse*›
B se plaquer *v refl* (+ *v être*) **se ~ contre un mur** to flatten oneself against a wall

plaquette /plakɛt/ *f* **1** (of butter) packet
2 (of pills) ≈ blister strip
■ **~ de frein** brake shoe

plastic /plastik/ *m* plastic explosive

plasticage /plastikaʒ/ *m* bomb attack (**de** on)

plastifier /plastifje/ [**v2**] *vt* to coat [sth] with plastic

plastique¹ /plastik/ *m* plastic

plastique² /plastik/ *f* (of object, statue) formal beauty; (of person) physique

plastiquer /plastike/ [**v1**] *vt* to carry out a bomb attack on

plastron /plastʀɔ̃/ *m* shirt front

plat, **~e** /pla, plat/ **A** *adj* **1** flat
2 ‹*boat*› flat-bottomed; ‹*watch, lighter*› slimline; ‹*hair*› limp
3 ‹*style, description*› lifeless
B *m* **1** dish
2 course
C à plat *phr* **1 poser qch à ~** to lay sth down flat; **à ~ ventre** flat on one's stomach; **tomber à ~** ‹*joke*› to fall flat
2 ‹*tyre*› flat; ‹*battery*› flat (BrE), dead
3 (fam) **être à ~** ‹*person*› to be run down
■ **~ de résistance** main course
(IDIOMS) **mettre les pieds dans le ~** (fam) to put one's foot in it; **faire tout un ~ de qch** (fam) to make a big deal about sth

platane /platan/ *m* plane tree

plateau, *pl* **~x** /plato/ *m* **1** tray
2 ~ de tournage film set
3 (in geography) plateau
4 (of weighing scales) pan

plate-bande, *pl* **plates-bandes** /platbɑ̃d/ *f* border, flower bed

platée /plate/ *f* (fam) plateful (**de** of)

plate-forme, *pl* **plates-formes** /platfɔʀm/ *f* platform; **~ pétrolière** oil rig

platine¹ /platin/ *adj inv*, *m* platinum

platine² /platin/ *f* (record player) turntable

platitude /platityd/ *f* platitude

platonique /platɔnik/ *adj* platonic

plâtre /plɑtʀ/ *m* **1** plaster
2 (Med) plaster cast
(IDIOM) **essuyer les ~s** to put up with the initial problems

plâtrer /plɑtʀe/ [**v1**] *vt* **1** to plaster ‹*wall*›
2 (Med) **~ le bras de qn** to put sb's arm in plaster

plâtreux, **-euse** /plɑtʀø, øz/ *adj* chalky

plâtrier, **-ière** /plɑtʀije, ɛʀ/ *mf* plasterer

plausible /plozibl/ *adj* plausible

playback /plɛbak/ *m inv* miming, lip syncing; **chanter en ~** to lip-sync (a song)

plébiscite /plebisit/ *m* plebiscite

plébisciter /plebisite/ [**v1**] *vt* **1** to elect [sb] with a huge majority
2 to vote overwhelmingly in favour (BrE) of

pléiade /plejad/ *f* galaxy, pleiad

plein, **~e** /plɛ̃, plɛn/ **A** *adj* **1** full
2 un ~ panier a basketful; **prendre à ~es mains** to pick up a handful of ‹*earth, sand, coins*›
3 ‹*brick, wall*› solid; ‹*cheeks, face*› plump; ‹*shape*› rounded
4 ‹*power, effect*› full; ‹*satisfaction, confidence*› complete
5 ‹*day, month*› whole, full; ‹*moon*› full
6 en ~e poitrine/réunion/forêt (right) in

P

the middle of the chest/meeting/forest; **en ~ jour** in broad daylight; **en ~ été** at the height of summer
7 (Zool) **pleine** ‹*animal*› pregnant; ‹*cow*› in calf
8 (fam) sloshed (fam), drunk
9 veste ~e peau jacket made out of full skins
B *adv* **1 avoir des billes ~ les poches** to have one's pockets full of marbles; **il a des idées ~ la tête** he's full of ideas
2 être orienté ~ sud to face due south
C *m* **faire le ~ de** to fill up with ‹*water, petrol*›; **le ~, s'il vous plaît** fill it up, please
D plein de (fam) *quantif* **~ de** lots of, loads (fam) of
E à plein *phr* fully
F tout plein *phr* (fam) really
IDIOM **en avoir ~ le dos** (fam) to be fed up

plein-air /plɛnɛʀ/ *m inv* (Sch) (outdoor) games

pleinement /plɛnmɑ̃/ *adv* fully

plein-emploi /plɛnɑ̃plwɑ/ *m inv* full employment

plein-temps, *pl* **pleins-temps** /plɛ̃tɑ̃/ *m* full-time job

plénier, -ière /plenje, ɛʀ/ *adj* plenary

pléonasme /pleɔnasm/ *m* pleonasm

⚷ **pleurer** /plœʀe/ [**v1**] **A** *vt* to mourn ‹*friend*›
B *vi* **1** to cry, to weep
2 ‹*eyes*› to water
3 ~ sur qn/qch to shed tears over sb/sth; **arrête de ~ sur ton sort!** stop feeling sorry for yourself!
4 (fam) ‹*person*› to whine
IDIOM **elle n'a plus que ses yeux pour ~** all she can do is cry

P

pleureur /plœʀœʀ/ *adj m* **saule ~** weeping willow

pleureuse /plœʀøz/ *f* (hired) mourner

pleurnicher /plœʀniʃe/ [**v1**] *vi* (fam) to snivel

pleurnicheur, -euse /plœʀniʃœʀ, øz/ *mf* (fam) sniveller

pleurs /plœʀ/ *mpl* tears; **en ~** in tears

pleuvoir /pløvwaʀ/ [**v39**] **A** *v impers* to rain; **il pleut** it's raining; **il pleut à torrents** it's pouring with rain
B *vi* ‹*blows, bombs*› to rain down

pli /pli/ *m* **1** (gen) fold; (in trousers) crease; (in skirt) pleat
2 (Games) trick
3 letter; **sous ~ cacheté** in a sealed envelope
IDIOMS **ça ne fait pas un ~** (fam) there's no doubt about it; **c'est un ~ à prendre** it's something you've got to get used to

pliage /plijaʒ/ *m* folding

pliant, ~e /plijɑ̃, ɑ̃t/ **A** *adj* folding
B *m* folding stool, camp stool

plier /plije/ [**v2**] **A** *vt* **1** to fold; to fold up
2 to bend ‹*stem, arm*›
3 to submit
B *vi* **1** ‹*tree, branch, joint*› to bend; ‹*plank, floor*› to sag
2 to give in
C se plier *v refl* (+ *v être*) **1** to fold
2 se ~ à to submit to
IDIOM **être plié (en deux** *or* **quatre)** (fam) to be doubled up with laughter

plinthe /plɛ̃t/ *f* skirting board (BrE), baseboard (AmE)

plisser /plise/ [**v1**] **A** *vt* **1** to pleat ‹*cloth*›
2 to crease ‹*garment*›
3 ~ le front to knit one's brows; **~ les yeux** to screw up one's eyes
B *vi* ‹*stocking*› to wrinkle; ‹*skirt*› to be creased

pliure /plijyʀ/ *f* fold; **la ~ du genou** the back of the knee

plomb /plɔ̃/ *m* **1** lead; **sans ~** ‹*petrol*› unleaded; **soleil de ~** burning sun; **ciel de ~** leaden sky
2 (in hunting) **un ~** a lead pellet; **du ~** lead shot
3 fuse
IDIOMS **avoir du ~ dans l'aile** (fam) to be in a bad way (fam); **cela va leur mettre du ~ dans la cervelle** (fam) that will knock some sense into them

plombage /plɔ̃baʒ/ *m* (in dentistry) filling

plomber /plɔ̃be/ [**v1**] *vt* to fill ‹*tooth*›

plombier /plɔ̃bje/ *m* plumber

plonge /plɔ̃ʒ/ *f* (fam) washing up (BrE), dishwashing (AmE)

plongée /plɔ̃ʒe/ *f* **1** (skin) diving
2 scuba diving
3 snorkelling (BrE); **~ sous-marine** deep-sea diving; **faire de la ~** to go diving

plongeoir /plɔ̃ʒwaʀ/ *m* **1** diving board
2 springboard

plongeon /plɔ̃ʒɔ̃/ *m* **1** dive
2 fall

⚷ **plonger** /plɔ̃ʒe/ [**v13**] **A** *vt* to plunge
B *vi* **1** to dive
2 ‹*bird*› to swoop down
C se plonger *v refl* (+ *v être*) **1** to plunge
2 to bury oneself

plongeur, -euse /plɔ̃ʒœʀ, øz/ *mf* **1** diver
2 dishwasher

plot /plo/ *m* **1** (electrical) contact
2 (of wood) block

plouc /pluk/ *m* (fam) country bumpkin (fam)

plouf /pluf/ **A** *m inv* splash; **faire un ~** to go splash
B *excl* splash!

ployer /plwaje/ [**v23**] *vi* ‹*branch, person*› to bend; **~ sous un fardeau** to be weighed down by a burden

plu /ply/ ▶ **plaire, pleuvoir**

⚷ **pluie** /plɥi/ *f* **1** rain; **sous une ~ battante** in driving rain
2 (of missiles, insults) hail; (of sparks, compliments) shower

⚷ key word

■ **~s acides** acid rain
IDIOMS **il n'est pas né de la dernière ~** (fam) he wasn't born yesterday (fam); **faire la ~ et le beau temps** to call the shots (fam)

plume /plym/ *f* **1** (Zool) feather
2 (pen) nib; **écrire au fil de la ~** to write as the thoughts come into one's head
IDIOM **voler dans les ~s de qn** (fam) to fly at sb

plumeau, *pl* **~x** /plymo/ *m* **1** feather duster
2 tuft

plumer /plyme/ [**v1**] *vt* to pluck ‹*bird*›

plumier /plymje/ *m* pencil box

plupart, **la plupart** /laplypaʀ/ *f inv* **la ~ des gens** most people; **la ~ du temps** most of the time, mostly

pluridisciplinaire /plyʀidisiplinɛʀ/ *adj* multidisciplinary

pluriel, **-elle** /plyʀjɛl/ **A** *adj* plural
B *m* plural

plus¹ /ply, plys, plyz/ **A** *prep* plus
B *adv* **1** (comparative) more; (superlative) **le ~** the most; **il travaille ~ (que moi)** he works more (than I do); **~ j'y pense, moins je comprends** the more I think about it, the less I understand; **~ ça va** as time goes on; **qui ~ est** furthermore; **de ~ en ~** more and more; **~ petit** smaller; **le ~ petit** the smallest; **trois heures ~ tôt** three hours earlier; **deux fois ~ cher** twice as expensive; **il est on ne peut ~ désagréable** he's as unpleasant as can be; **il est ~ ou moins artiste** he's an artist of sorts; **il a été ~ ou moins poli** he wasn't particularly polite
2 (in negative constructions) **elle ne fume ~** she doesn't smoke any more; **il n'y a ~ d'œufs** there are no more eggs; **~ jamais ça!** never again!; **~ que trois jours avant Noël!** only three days to go until Christmas!
C **plus de** *quantif* **deux fois ~ de livres que** twice as many books as; **il a gagné le ~ d'argent** he won the most money; **les gens de ~ de 60 ans** people over 60
D **au plus** *phr* at the most
E **de plus** *phr* **1** furthermore, what's more
2 donnez-moi deux pommes de ~ give me two more apples; **une fois de ~** once more
F **en plus** *phr* **en ~ (de cela)** on top of that; **les taxes en ~** plus tax

plus² /plys/ *m inv* **1 le signe ~** the plus sign
2 (fam) plus (fam)

plusieurs /plyzjœʀ/ **A** *adj* several; **une ou ~ personnes** one or more people
B *pron* **~ ont déjà signé** several people have already signed

plus-value, *pl* **~s** /plyvaly/ *f* **1** (of property) increase in value; (sales profit) capital gain
2 surcharge
3 (Econ) surplus value

plutôt /plyto/ *adv* rather; instead; **passe ~ le matin** call round (BrE) *or* come by (AmE) in the morning preferably; **~ mourir!** I'd rather die!; **demande ~ à Corinne** ask Corinne instead; **dis ~ que tu n'as pas envie de le faire** why don't you just say that you don't want to do it?; **la nouvelle a été ~ bien accueillie** the news went down rather well

pluvieux, **-ieuse** /plyvjø, øz/ *adj* wet, rainy

PME /peɛmə/ *fpl* (*abbr* = **petites et moyennes entreprises**) small and medium-sized enterprises, SMEs

PMI /peɛmi/ *fpl* (*abbr* = **petites et moyennes industries**) small and medium-sized industries

PMU /peɛmy/ *m* (*abbr* = **Pari mutuel urbain**) *French state-controlled betting system*

PNB /peɛnbe/ *m* (*abbr* = **produit national brut**) gross national product, GNP

pneu /pnø/ *m* tyre (BrE), tire (AmE)

pneumatique /pnømatik/ *adj* inflatable

pneumonie /pnømɔni/ *f* pneumonia
■ **~ atypique** SARS

poche¹ /pɔʃ/ *m* **(livre de) ~** paperback

poche² /pɔʃ/ *f* **1** (in garment, bag) pocket; **en ~** in one's pocket; **il avait 200 euros en ~** he had 200 euros on him; **s'en mettre plein** *or* **se remplir les ~s** (fam) to line one's pockets; **faire les ~s de qn** to pick sb's pocket
2 ~ de gaz/d'air gas/air pocket
3 avoir des ~s sous les yeux to have bags under one's eyes
4 (Zool) (of kangaroo) pouch
■ **~ revolver** hip pocket
IDIOMS **c'est dans la ~** (fam) it's in the bag (fam); **en être de sa ~** (fam) to be out of pocket; **ne pas avoir les yeux dans sa ~** (fam) not to miss a thing (fam); **connaître un endroit comme sa ~** (fam) to know a place like the back of one's hand

pocher /pɔʃe/ [**v1**] *vt* (Culin) to poach

pochette /pɔʃɛt/ *f* **1** (for pencils) case; (for credit cards) wallet; (for make-up, glasses) pouch; (for document) folder; (for record) sleeve
2 (of matches) book
3 clutch bag

pochoir /pɔʃwaʀ/ *m* stencil

podcaster /pɔdkaste/ *vi* to podcast

podium /pɔdjɔm/ *m* podium

poêle¹ /pwal/ *m* **1** stove
2 (on coffin) pall

poêle² /pwal/ *f* frying pan

poème /pɔɛm/ *m* poem; **c'est tout un ~** (fam) it's quite something

poésie /pɔezi/ *f* **1** poetry
2 poem

poète /pɔɛt/ *m* **1** poet
2 dreamer

poétique /pɔetik/ *adj* poetic

poids /pwɑ/ *m inv* **1** weight; **peser son ~** to be very heavy; **adversaire de ~** opponent to be reckoned with
2 burden; **être un ~ pour qn** to be a burden

P

on sb; **avoir un ~ sur la conscience** to have a guilty conscience
3 influence
4 des ~ en laiton brass weights
5 (in athletics) shot; **lancer le ~** to put the shot
■ **~ et haltères** weightlifting; **~ lourd** (Sport) heavyweight; heavy truck
(IDIOM) **avoir** *or* **faire deux ~ deux mesures** to have double standards

poignant, **~e** /pwaɲɑ̃, ɑ̃t/ *adj* **1** poignant
2 heart-rending, harrowing

poignard /pwaɲaʀ/ *m* dagger; **coup de ~** stab

poignarder /pwaɲaʀde/ [**v1**] *vt* to stab

poigne /pwaɲ/ *f* **avoir de la ~** to have a strong grip; **homme à ~** strong man

poignée /pwaɲe/ *f* **1** handful
2 (of door, drawer, bag) handle; (of sword) hilt
■ **~ de main** handshake

poignet /pwaɲɛ/ *m* **1** wrist
2 (of shirt) cuff

poil /pwal/ *m* **1** (on body, animal) hair; **à ~** (pop) stark naked; **caresser dans le sens du ~** to stroke [sth] the way the fur lies; to butter [sb] up (fam); **ça marche au ~** (fam) it works like a dream
2 (fam) (of irony) touch; (of common sense) shred; **à un ~ près** by a whisker
3 (of cloth) nap; (of brush) bristle
■ **~ à gratter** itching powder
(IDIOMS) **être de bon/mauvais ~** (fam) to be in a good/bad mood; **hérisser le ~ de qn** (fam) to put sb's back up (fam); **avoir un ~ dans la main** (fam) to be bone idle

poilu, **~e** /pwaly/ *adj* hairy

poinçon /pwɛ̃sɔ̃/ *m* **1** (tool) punch
2 (on gold) die, stamp; hallmark

poinçonner /pwɛ̃sɔne/ [**v1**] *vt* **1** to punch, to clip
2 to hallmark

poinçonneur, **-euse** /pwɛ̃sɔnœʀ, øz/ *mf* ticket puncher

poindre /pwɛ̃dʀ/ [**v56**] *vi* ‹*day*› to break

poing /pwɛ̃/ *m* fist; **coup de ~** punch; **montrer le ~** to shake one's fist; **être pieds et ~s liés** (fig) to have one's hands tied
(IDIOM) **dormir à ~s fermés** to sleep like a log

⚷ **point** /pwɛ̃/ **A** *m* **1** point; **un ~ de rencontre** a meeting point; **~ de vente** (sales) outlet
2 (at sea) position; **faire le ~** to take bearings; (fig) to take stock of the situation
3 être sur le ~ de faire to be just about to do; **au ~ où j'en suis, ça n'a pas d'importance!** I'm past caring!
4 il m'agace au plus haut ~ he annoys me intensely; **je ne le pensais pas bête à ce ~** I didn't think he was that stupid; **à tel ~ que** to such an extent that; **douloureux au ~ que** so painful that
5 (on agenda) item, point; **un ~ de détail** a minor point; **en tout ~**, **en tous ~s** in every respect *or* way
6 dot; **un ~ de colle** a spot of glue; **un ~ de rouille** a speck of rust; **~ d'intersection** point of intersection
7 (Games, Sport) point; **compter les ~s** to keep (the) score
8 (Sch) mark (BrE), point (AmE); **être un bon ~ pour** to be a plus point for
9 full stop (BrE), period (AmE); **mettre un ~ final à qch** (fig) to put a stop to sth; **tu vas te coucher un ~ c'est tout!** (fam) you're going to bed and that's final!
10 (Med) pain; **avoir un ~ à la poitrine** to have a pain in one's chest
11 (in sewing, knitting) stitch
B à point *phr* **1 à ~ nommé** just at the right moment
2 à ~ ‹*meat*› medium rare
C au point *phr* **être au ~** ‹*system, machine*› to be well designed; ‹*show*› to be well put together; **mettre au ~** to perfect ‹*system, method*›; to develop ‹*vaccine, machine*›; **faire la mise au ~** (in photography) to focus; **faire une mise au ~** (fig) to set the record straight
■ **~ argent** cash point; **~ chaud** trouble *or* hot spot; **~ de côté** (pain) stitch; **~ de départ** starting point; **nous revoilà à notre ~ de départ** (fig) we're back to square one; **~ d'eau** water tap (BrE) *or* faucet (AmE); **~ d'exclamation** exclamation mark (BrE) *or* point (AmE); **~ faible** weak point; **~ fort** strong point; **~ d'interrogation** question mark; **~ de mire** (Mil) target; (fig) focal point; **~ mort** neutral; **être au ~ mort** (in car) to be in neutral; ‹*business, trade*› to be at a standstill; **~ noir** (Med) blackhead; (of situation) problem; **~ de repère** landmark; point of reference; **~ de suture** (Med) stitch; **~ de vue** point of view; viewpoint; **du ~ de vue du sens** as far as meaning is concerned; **~s de suspension** suspension points; **~ zéro** ground zero
(IDIOM) **être mal en ~** to be in a bad way

pointage /pwɛ̃taʒ/ *m* **1** (on list) ticking off (BrE), checking off (AmE)
2 (of employee) clocking in

pointe /pwɛ̃t/ **A** *f* **1** (of knife) point; (of shoe) toe; (of hair) end; (of railing) spike; (of spear) tip; **en ~** pointed
2 de ~ ‹*technology*› advanced, state-of-the-art; ‹*sector, industry*› high-tech; **à la ~ du progrès** state-of-the-art
3 high; **une vitesse de ~ de 200 km/h** a maximum *or* top speed of 200 km/h; **heure de ~** rush hour; **aux heures de ~** at peak time
4 (of garlic) touch; (of accent) hint
5 blocked shoe
B pointes *fpl* **faire des ~s** to dance on points
■ **~ du pied** tiptoe

⚷ key word

p

pointer /pwɛ̃te/ [**v1**] **A** *vt* **1** to tick off (BrE), to check off (AmE) ‹*names, figures*›; to check ‹*list*›
2 to point ‹*weapon*›; ~ **le doigt vers** to point at; ~ **son nez** (fam) to show one's face
B *vi* **1** ‹*employee*› to clock in; ~ **à l'agence pour l'emploi** to sign on at the jobcentre (BrE) *or* unemployment office
2 ‹*sun, plant*› to come up; ‹*day*› to break
C se pointer *v refl* (+ *v être*) (fam) to turn up

pointillé, ~**e** /pwɛ̃tije/ **A** *adj* dotted
B *m* dotted line

pointilleux, **-euse** /pwɛ̃tijø, øz/ *adj* ‹*person*› fussy, pernickety

pointu, ~**e** /pwɛ̃ty/ *adj* **1** (gen) pointed; ‹*scissors*› with a sharp point
2 ‹*check*› close, thorough
3 ‹*question, approach*› precise

pointure /pwɛ̃tyʀ/ *f* (of glove, shoe) size

point-virgule, *pl* **points-virgules** /pwɛ̃viʀgyl/ *m* semicolon

poire /pwaʀ/ *f* **1** pear
2 (fam) sucker (fam)
IDIOMS **couper la ~ en deux** to split the difference; **garder une ~ pour la soif** to save something for a rainy day

poireau, *pl* ~**x** /pwaʀo/ *m* leek

poirier /pwaʀje/ *m* **1** pear (tree)
2 faire le ~ to do a headstand

pois /pwa/ *m inv* **1** (Bot, Culin) pea; **petit ~** (garden) pea, petit pois
2 dot; **à ~** polka dot, spotted
■ ~ **cassé** split pea; ~ **chiche** chickpea

poison /pwazɔ̃/ *m* poison

poisse /pwas/ *f* (fam) **1** rotten luck (fam)
2 drag (fam)

poisseux, **-euse** /pwasø, øz/ *adj* ‹*hands, table*› sticky; ‹*atmosphere*› muggy; ‹*restaurant*› greasy

poisson /pwasɔ̃/ *m* fish; **les ~s d'eau douce/de mer** freshwater/saltwater fish
■ ~ **rouge** goldfish
IDIOM **être comme un ~ dans l'eau** to be in one's element

poissonnerie /pwasɔnʀi/ *f* fishmonger's (shop) (BrE), fish shop (AmE)

poissonnier, **-ière** /pwasɔnje, ɛʀ/ *mf* fishmonger (BrE), fish vendor (AmE)

Poissons /pwasɔ̃/ *pr m pl* Pisces

poitrail /pwatʀɑj/ *m* breast

poitrine /pwatʀin/ *f* **1** chest; **tour de ~** chest size
2 breasts; **tour de ~** bust size
■ ~ **fumée** ≈ smoked streaky bacon

poivre /pwavʀ/ *m* pepper

poivré, ~**e** /pwavʀe/ *adj* ‹*sauce*› peppery

poivrer /pwavʀe/ [**v1**] *vt* to add pepper to

poivron /pwavʀɔ̃/ *m* sweet pepper, capsicum

poivrot, ~**e** /pwavʀo, ɔt/ *mf* (fam) drunk

poker /pɔkɛʀ/ *m* poker; **coup de ~** gamble

polaire /pɔlɛʀ/ *adj* polar; arctic

polar /pɔlaʀ/ *m* (fam) detective novel

polariser /pɔlaʀize/ [**v1**] *vt*, **se polariser** *v refl* (+ *v être*) **1** to polarize
2 to focus

pôle /pol/ *m* **1** pole
2 centre (BrE)

polémique /pɔlemik/ *f* debate

poli, ~**e** /pɔli/ **A** *pp* ▶ **polir**
B *pp adj* ‹*metal, style*› polished
C *adj* polite
D *m* shine

police /pɔlis/ *f* **1** police; police force
2 security service
3 faire la ~ to keep order
4 (in insurance) policy
■ ~ **judiciaire**, **PJ** *detective division of the French police force*; ~ **de l'air et des frontières**, **PAF** border police; ~ **des mœurs** *or* **mondaine** vice squad; ~ **secours** ≈ emergency services

policier, **-ière** /pɔlisje, ɛʀ/ **A** *adj* (gen) police; ‹*novel*› detective
B *m* policeman; **femme ~** policewoman

poliment /pɔlimɑ̃/ *adv* politely

polir /pɔliʀ/ [**v3**] *vt* to polish ‹*stone, metal*›

polisson, **-onne** /pɔlisɔ̃, ɔn/ *mf* naughty child

politesse /pɔlitɛs/ *f* politeness; **rendre la ~ à qn** to return the compliment

politicien, **-ienne** /pɔlitisjɛ̃, ɛn/ *mf* politician

politique[1] /pɔlitik/ *adj* (gen) political; ‹*behaviour, act*› calculating

politique[2] /pɔlitik/ *f* **1** politics; **faire de la ~** ‹*militant*› to be involved in politics
2 policy; **notre ~ des prix** our pricing policy
IDIOMS **pratiquer la ~ de l'autruche** to stick one's head in the sand; **pratiquer la ~ du pire** to envisage the worst-case scenario

politiser /pɔlitize/ [**v1**] *vt* to politicize

pollen /pɔl(l)ɛn/ *m* pollen

polluant, ~**e** /pɔl(l)yɑ̃, ɑ̃t/ **A** *adj* polluting
B *m* pollutant

polluer /pɔl(l)ɥe/ [**v1**] *vt* to pollute

pollution /pɔl(l)ysjɔ̃/ *f* pollution

polo /pɔlo/ *m* **1** polo shirt
2 (Sport) polo

polochon /pɔlɔʃɔ̃/ *m* (fam) bolster; **bataille de ~s** pillow fight

Pologne /pɔlɔɲ/ *pr f* Poland

polonais, ~**e** /pɔlɔnɛ, ɛz/ **A** *adj* Polish
B *m* (language) Polish

Polonais, ~**e** /pɔlɔnɛ, ɛz/ *mf* Pole

poltronnerie /pɔltʀɔnʀi/ *f* cowardice

polycopier /pɔlikɔpje/ [**v2**] *vt* to duplicate

polyculture /pɔlikyltyʀ/ *f* mixed farming

polygame /pɔligam/ *adj* polygamous

polyglotte /pɔliglɔt/ *adj*, *mf* polyglot

Polytechnique /pɔlitɛknik/ *f*: *Grande École of Science and Technology*

polyvalence /pɔlivalɑ̃s/ *f* **1** versatility
2 (of employee) flexibility

polyvalent, **~e** /pɔlivalɑ̃, ɑ̃t/ *adj* ‹*equipment*› multipurpose; ‹*employee*› who does several jobs

pommade /pɔmad/ *f* (Med) ointment
IDIOM **passer de la ~ à qn** (fam) to butter sb up (fam)

✓ **pomme** /pɔm/ *f* **1** apple
2 (of watering can) rose; (of shower) shower head; (of walking stick) pommel, knob
3 (fam) mug (BrE) (fam), sucker (fam); **ça va encore être pour ma ~** I'm in for it again (fam)
■ **~ d'Adam** Adam's apple; **~ de pin** pine cone; **~ de terre** potato; **~s frites** chips (BrE), (French) fries
IDIOM **tomber dans les ~s** (fam) to faint

pommeau, *pl* **~x** /pɔmo/ *m* knob; pommel

pommette /pɔmɛt/ *f* cheekbone

pommier /pɔmje/ *m* apple tree

pompe /pɔ̃p/ *f* **1** pump
2 (pop) shoe
3 pomp
4 (Sport), (fam) press-up (BrE), push-up
■ **~ à essence** petrol pump (BrE), gas pump (AmE); **~s funèbres** undertaker's (BrE), funeral director's (BrE), funeral parlor (AmE)
IDIOM **avoir un coup de ~** (fam) to be knackered (BrE) (sl) *or* pooped (fam)

pomper /pɔ̃pe/ [**v1**] *vt* **1** to pump ‹*liquid, air*›
2 (sl) to copy
IDIOM **~ l'air à qn** (fam) to get on sb's nerves

pompette /pɔ̃pɛt/ *adj* (fam) tipsy (fam), drunk

P

pompeux, **-euse** /pɔ̃pø, øz/ *adj* pompous

pompier, **-ière** /pɔ̃pje, ɛʀ/ **A** *adj* pompous
B *m* fireman, firefighter; **appeler les ~s** to call the fire brigade (BrE) *or* department (AmE)

pompiste /pɔ̃pist/ *mf* petrol (BrE) *or* gas (AmE) pump attendant

pompon /pɔ̃pɔ̃/ *m* (on hat) pompom, bobble; (on slipper) pompom
IDIOM **décrocher le ~** (fam) to win first prize

pomponner: **se pomponner** /pɔ̃pɔne/ [**v1**] *v refl* (+ *v être*) to get dolled up

ponce /pɔ̃s/ *f* **pierre ~** pumice stone

poncer /pɔ̃se/ [**v12**] *vt* **1** (Tech) to sand
2 to pumice

ponceuse /pɔ̃søz/ *f* sander

ponction /pɔ̃ksjɔ̃/ *f* **1** (Med) puncture
2 levy

ponctualité /pɔ̃ktɥalite/ *f* punctuality

ponctuation /pɔ̃ktɥasjɔ̃/ *f* punctuation

ponctuel, **-elle** /pɔ̃ktɥɛl/ *adj* **1** ‹*person*› punctual
2 ‹*action*› limited; ‹*problem*› isolated

ponctuer /pɔ̃ktɥe/ [**v1**] *vt* to punctuate

pondéré, **~e** /pɔ̃deʀe/ *adj* **1** ‹*person*› level-headed
2 ‹*factor*› weighted

pondre /pɔ̃dʀ/ [**v6**] *vt* **1** to lay ‹*egg*›
2 (fam) to churn out (fam) ‹*poetry, articles*›

poney /pɔnɛ/ *m* pony

✓ **pont** /pɔ̃/ **A** *m* **1** bridge
2 link, tie; **couper les ~s** to break off all contact
3 extended weekend (*including days between a public holiday and a weekend*)
4 deck
B **ponts** *mpl* **~s (et chaussées)** highways department
■ **~ aérien** airlift; **~ à péage** toll bridge
IDIOMS **coucher sous les ~s** to sleep rough, to be a tramp; **il coulera beaucoup d'eau sous les ~s avant que...** it will be a long time before...; **faire un ~ d'or à qn** to offer sb a large sum to accept a job

pontife /pɔ̃tif/ *m* **1** pontiff; **le souverain ~** the pope
2 (fam) pundit (fam)

pontificat /pɔ̃tifika/ *m* pontificate

pontifier /pɔ̃tifje/ [**v2**] *vi* to pontificate

pont-levis, *pl* **ponts-levis** /pɔ̃ləvi/ *m* drawbridge

ponton /pɔ̃tɔ̃/ *m* **1** landing stage
2 pontoon

pope /pɔp/ *m* pope, orthodox priest

popote /pɔpɔt/ *f* (fam) cooking

populace /pɔpylas/ *f* **la ~** the masses

✓ **populaire** /pɔpylɛʀ/ *adj* **1** ‹*suburb*› working-class; ‹*art, novel*› popular; ‹*edition*› cheap; ‹*restaurant*› basic; **classe ~** working class
2 ‹*tradition*› folk; **culture ~** folklore
3 popular
4 ‹*revolt*› popular; ‹*will*› of the people
5 ‹*expression, term*› vulgar
6 **République ~** People's Republic

popularité /pɔpylaʀite/ *f* popularity

✓ **population** /pɔpylasjɔ̃/ *f* population

populeux, **-euse** /pɔpylø, øz/ *adj* densely populated, populous

popup /pɔpəp/ **A** *m* (Comput) pop-up advertisement
B *adj* (Comput) pop-up

porc /pɔʀ/ *m* **1** pig, hog (AmE)
2 pork
3 pigskin

porcelaine /pɔʀsəlɛn/ *f* porcelain, china

porcelet /pɔʀsəlɛ/ *m* piglet

porc-épic, *pl* **~s** /pɔʀkepik/ *m* porcupine

porche /pɔʀʃ/ *m* porch

porcherie /pɔʀʃəʀi/ *f* pigsty

porcin, **~e** /pɔʀsɛ̃, in/ *adj* porcine

pore /pɔʀ/ *m* pore

poreux, **-euse** /pɔʀø, øz/ *adj* porous

porno /pɔʀno/ *adj*, *m* (fam) porn (fam)

✓ key word

pornographique /pɔʀnɔgʀafik/ *adj* pornographic

port /pɔʀ/ *m* **1** harbour (BrE)
2 haven
3 wearing; carrying
4 bearing
5 (transport) carriage; postage
■ **~ d'attache** port of registry; home base; **~ de pêche** fishing harbour (BrE); **~ de plaisance** marina
IDIOM **arriver à bon ~** to arrive safe and sound

portable /pɔʀtabl/ **A** *adj* portable; **ordinateur ~** laptop computer
B *m* mobile (phone) (BrE); cellular phone, cell phone (AmE)

portail /pɔʀtaj/ *m* (of park) gate; (of church) great door

portant, **~e** /pɔʀtɑ̃, ɑ̃t/ *adj* **1** ‹*wall*› load-bearing
2 bien ~ in good health
IDIOM **à bout ~** at point-blank range

portatif, **-ive** /pɔʀtatif, iv/ *adj* portable

porte /pɔʀt/ *f* **1** door; gate; **devant la ~ de l'hôpital** outside the hospital; **aux ~s du désert** at the edge of the desert; **ouvrir sa ~ à qn** to let sb in; **c'est la ~ ouverte à la criminalité** it's an open invitation to crime; **mettre à la ~** to expel; to fire; **ce n'est pas la ~ à côté** (fam) it's quite far
2 gateway; **la victoire leur ouvre la ~ de la finale** the victory clears the way to the final for them
3 (in airport) gate
4 (car) door
■ **~ battante** swing door; **~ d'écluse** lock gate; **~ d'entrée** front door; main entrance; **~ de service** service entrance; **~ de sortie** exit; escape route
IDIOMS **prendre la ~** to leave; **entrer par la petite/grande ~** to start at the bottom/top

porté, **~e** /pɔʀte/ *adj* **être ~ sur qch** to be keen on sth

porte-à-faux /pɔʀtafo/ *m inv* **être en ~** ‹*wall*› to be out of plumb; ‹*construction*› to be cantilevered; ‹*person*› to be in an awkward position

porte-à-porte /pɔʀtapɔʀt/ *m inv* **1** door-to-door selling
2 door-to-door canvassing

porte-avions /pɔʀtavjɔ̃/ *m inv* aircraft carrier

porte-bagages /pɔʀt(ə)bagaʒ/ *m inv* carrier; luggage rack; roof rack

porte-bébé /pɔʀt(ə)bebe/ *m inv* baby carrier

porte-bonheur /pɔʀt(ə)bɔnœʀ/ *m inv* lucky charm

porte-clés, **porte-clefs** /pɔʀt(ə)kle/ *m inv* key ring

porte-documents /pɔʀt(ə)dɔkymɑ̃/ *m inv* briefcase, attaché case

portée /pɔʀte/ **A** *adj f* ▸ **porté**
B *f* **1** range; **être à ~ de main** *or* **à la ~ de la main** to be within reach; to be to hand
2 c'est à la ~ de n'importe qui anybody can do it; anybody can understand it; **se mettre à la ~ de qn** to come down to sb's level
3 impact
4 (of kittens) litter
5 (Mus) staff, stave (BrE)

porte-fenêtre, *pl* **portes-fenêtres** /pɔʀt(ə)fənɛtʀ/ *f* French window

portefeuille /pɔʀt(ə)fœj/ **A** *adj* **jupe ~** wrap-over skirt
B *m* **1** wallet (BrE), billfold (AmE)
2 portfolio

porte-jarretelles /pɔʀt(ə)ʒaʀtɛl/ *m inv* suspender belt (BrE), garter belt (AmE)

portemanteau, *pl* **~x** /pɔʀt(ə)mɑ̃to/ *m*
1 coat rack
2 coat stand
3 coat hanger

portemine /pɔʀt(ə)min/ *m* propelling (BrE) *or* mechanical (AmE) pencil

porte-monnaie /pɔʀt(ə)mɔnɛ/ *m inv* purse (BrE), coin purse (AmE)

porte-parapluies /pɔʀt(ə)paʀaplɥi/ *m inv* umbrella stand

porte-parole /pɔʀt(ə)paʀɔl/ *m inv* spokesperson, spokesman/spokeswoman

porte-plume /pɔʀt(ə)plym/ *m inv* pen holder

porter /pɔʀte/ [v1] **A** *vt* **1** to carry
2 ~ qch quelque part to take sth somewhere; **~ qch à qn** to take sb sth
3 ‹*wall, chair*› to carry, to bear ‹*weight*›
4 to wear ‹*dress, contact lenses*›; to have ‹*moustache*›
5 to have ‹*initials, date, name*›; to bear ‹*seal*›; **il porte bien son nom** the name suits him
6 to bear ‹*flowers*›
7 ~ qch à to bring sth up to, to put sth up to ‹*rate, number*›; **~ la température de l'eau à 80°C** to heat the water to 80°C
8 ~ son regard vers to look at; **si tu portes la main sur elle** if you lay a finger on her; **~ un jugement sur qch** to pass judgement on sth
9 ~ qch sur un registre to enter sth on a register; **se faire ~ malade** to report sick; **~ plainte** to lodge a complaint
10 tout nous porte à croire que... everything leads us to believe that...
11 ~ bonheur *or* **chance** to be lucky
B porter sur *v+prep* ‹*debate*› to be about; ‹*measure*› to concern; ‹*ban*› to apply to
C *vi* **une voix qui porte** a voice that carries; **le coup a porté** the blow hit home
D se porter *v refl* (+ *v être*) **1 se ~ bien/mal** ‹*person*› to be well/ill; ‹*business*› to be going well/badly
2 se ~ sur ‹*suspicion*› to fall on; ‹*infection*› to spread to

porte-savon /pɔʀt(ə)savɔ̃/ *m inv* soap dish

P

porte-serviettes /pɔʀt(ə)sɛʀvjɛt/ *m inv* towel rail

porteur, **-euse** /pɔʀtœʀ, øz/ **A** *adj* **1** **être ~ d'un virus** to carry a virus
2 **mur ~** load-bearing wall
3 ‹*market, sector*› expanding
4 ‹*current, wave, frequency*› carrier
B *mf* holder, bearer
C *m* **1** porter; messenger
2 (of cheque) bearer; **~ d'actions** shareholder
■ **~ sain** (Med) symptom-free carrier

porte-voix /pɔʀt(ə)vwɑ/ *m inv* megaphone

portier /pɔʀtje/ *m* porter

portière /pɔʀtjɛʀ/ *f* (of car) door

portillon /pɔʀtijɔ̃/ *m* gate

portion /pɔʀsjɔ̃/ *f* **1** (Culin) portion; helping
2 part, portion; (of road) stretch
(IDIOM) **réduire qn à la ~ congrue** to give sb the strict minimum

portique /pɔʀtik/ *m* **1** portico
2 (in gym) frame
3 swing frame

porto /pɔʀto/ *m* port

portoricain, **~e** /pɔʀtoʀikɛ̃, ɛn/ *adj* Puerto Rican

portrait /pɔʀtʀɛ/ *m* **1** portrait
2 description, picture
3 **tu es tout le ~ de ton père** you're the spitting image of your father
4 (fam) face; **se faire tirer le ~** to have one's photo taken

portrait-robot, *pl* **portraits-robots** /pɔʀtʀɛʀɔbo/ *m* photofit®, identikit®

portuaire /pɔʀtɥɛʀ/ *adj* port

portugais, **~e** /pɔʀtygɛ, ɛz/ **A** *adj* Portuguese
B *m* (language) Portuguese

Portugal /pɔʀtygal/ *pr m* Portugal

pose /poz/ *f* **1** (of window) putting in; (of cupboard) fitting; (of carpet) laying
2 pose; **prendre une ~** to strike a pose
3 (in photography) exposure

posé, **~e** /poze/ *adj* ‹*air, person*› composed; ‹*gesture, voice*› controlled

posément /pozemɑ̃/ *adv* calmly, carefully

⚷ **poser** /poze/ [**v1**] **A** *vt* **1** to put down ‹*book, glass*›
2 to put in ‹*window*›; to install ‹*radiator*›; to fit ‹*lock*›; to lay ‹*tiling, cable*›; to plant ‹*bomb*›; to put up ‹*wallpaper, curtains*›
3 to assert ‹*theory*›; **~ sa candidature à un poste** to apply for a job; **~ une addition** to write a sum down
4 to ask ‹*question*›; to set ‹*riddle*›; **ça ne pose aucun problème** that's no problem at all
5 (Mus) to place ‹*voice*›
B *vi* **1** to pose
2 to put on airs
C **se poser** *v refl* (+ *v être*) **1** ‹*bird, insect*› to settle
2 ‹*plane*› to land
3 ‹*eyes*› to fall
4 **se ~ en** to claim to be; to present oneself as
5 **se ~ des questions** to ask oneself questions
6 ‹*problem, case*› to arise; **la question ne se pose pas** there's no question of it; it goes without saying

poseur, **-euse** /pozœʀ, øz/ *mf* poser (fam)
■ **~ de bombes** bomber; **~ de moquette** carpet fitter

⚷ **positif**, **-ive** /pozitif, iv/ *adj* **1** ‹*reply*› affirmative
2 ‹*interview*› constructive; ‹*outcome*› positive
3 ‹*reaction*› favourable (BrE)
4 ‹*person, attitude*› positive
5 ‹*number*› positive

⚷ **position** /pozisjɔ̃/ *f* **1** position; **en ~ horizontale** horizontally; **placer qn dans une ~ difficile** to put sb in a difficult *or* an awkward position
2 (in ranking) place, position
3 position, stance; **prendre ~ sur un problème** to take a stand on an issue; **camper sur ses ~s** to stand one's ground
4 (bank) balance

positivement /pozitivmɑ̃/ *adv* ‹*answer*› positively; ‹*react, judge*› favourably (BrE)

posologie /pɔzɔlɔʒi/ *f* dosage

possédant, **~e** /pɔsedɑ̃, ɑ̃t/ *mf* **les ~s** the rich, the wealthy

possédé, **~e** /pɔsede/ *mf* **les ~s** the possessed

⚷ **posséder** /pɔsede/ [**v14**] *vt* **1** to own, to possess ‹*property, army*›; to hold ‹*responsibility*›
2 to have ‹*skill, quality*›
3 to speak [sth] fluently; to have a thorough knowledge of [sth]
4 ‹*anger, pain*› to overwhelm
5 (fam) **il nous a bien possédés** he really had us there (fam)

possesseur /pɔsɛsœʀ/ *m* (of property) owner; (of diploma) holder; (of passport) bearer

possessif, **-ive** /pɔsesif, iv/ *adj* possessive

possession /pɔsesjɔ̃/ *f* possession

⚷ **possibilité** /pɔsibilite/ **A** *f* **1** possibility
2 opportunity; **~ d'embauche** job opportunity
B **possibilités** *fpl* **1** (of person) abilities; (of device) potential uses
2 resources

⚷ **possible** /pɔsibl/ **A** *adj* **1** possible; **dès que ~** as soon as possible; **tout le courage ~** the utmost courage; **tous les cas ~s et imaginables** every conceivable case; **le plus cher ~** ‹*sell*› at the highest possible price; **autant que ~** as much as possible; **il n'y a pas d'erreur ~, c'est lui** it's him, without a shadow of a doubt; **tout est ~** anything is possible; **pas ~!** (fam) I don't believe it!; **'tu vas acheter une voiture?'—'~'** 'are you

⚷ key word

going to buy a car?'—'maybe'
2 (fam) **il a une chance pas ~** he's incredibly lucky
B *m* **faire (tout) son ~** to do one's best

post /pɔst/ *pref also* **post-** post, post-

postal, **~e**, *mpl* **-aux** /pɔstal, o/ *adj* ‹*van*› post office (BrE), mail (AmE); ‹*services*› postal

poste¹ /pɔst/ *m* **1** position, job; post; **~s vacants** *or* **à pourvoir** vacancies
2 (Sport) position
3 post; **~ (de travail)** work station; **il est toujours fidèle au ~** you can always rely on him
4 ~ de police police station
5 ~ de radio radio set
6 (tele)phone; extension
7 shift
8 (in accountancy) item
■ **~ d'aiguillage** signal box; **~ de douane** customs post; **~ de pilotage** flight deck; **~ de secours** first-aid station

poste² /pɔst/ *f* post office; **envoyer par la ~** to send [sth] by post (BrE), to mail (AmE)
■ **~ aérienne** airmail; **~ restante** poste restante (BrE), general delivery (AmE)

poster¹ /pɔste/ [**v1**] **A** *vt* **1** to post (BrE), to mail (AmE)
2 to post ‹*guard*›; to put [sb] in place ‹*spy*›
B se poster *v refl* (+ *v être*) **se ~ devant** to station oneself in front of

poster² /pɔstɛʀ/ *m* poster

postérieur, **~e** /pɔsteʀjœʀ/ *adj* **1** ‹*date*› later; ‹*event*› subsequent; **un écrivain ~ à Flaubert** a writer who came after Flaubert
2 ‹*part, section*› posterior; ‹*legs*› hind

postérité /pɔsteʀite/ *f* posterity; **passer à la ~** ‹*person*› to go down in history; ‹*work*› to become part of the cultural heritage

posthume /pɔstym/ *adj* posthumous

postiche /pɔstiʃ/ **A** *adj* ‹*beard*› false
B *m* **1** hairpiece; toupee; wig
2 false moustache (BrE) *or* mustache (AmE)
3 false beard

postier, **-ière** /pɔstje, ɛʀ/ *mf* postal worker

postillon /pɔstijɔ̃/ *m* (fam) drop of saliva

postillonner /pɔstijɔne/ [**v1**] *vi* (fam) to spit (saliva)

post-scriptum /pɔstskʀiptɔm/ *m inv* postscript

postsynchroniser /pɔstsɛ̃kʀɔnize/ [**v1**] *vt* to dub, to add the soundtrack to

postulant, **~e** /pɔstylɑ̃, ɑ̃t/ *mf* candidate

postulat /pɔstyla/ *m* premise; postulate

postuler /pɔstyle/ [**v1**] *vi* to apply

posture /pɔstyʀ/ *f* **1** posture
2 position

pot /po/ *m* **1** container; jar; carton, tub; (earthenware) pot; jug; **un ~ de peinture** a tin of paint
2 (chamber) pot
3 (fam) drink
4 (fam) do (BrE) (fam), drinks party
5 avoir du ~ to be lucky
■ **~ catalytique** catalytic converter; **~ d'échappement** (Aut) silencer (BrE), muffler (AmE); exhaust
IDIOMS **payer les ~s cassés** to pick up the pieces; **tourner autour du ~** (fam) to beat about the bush

potable /pɔtabl/ *adj* **1 eau ~** drinking water
2 (fam) decent

potage /pɔtaʒ/ *m* soup

potager /pɔtaʒe/ *m* kitchen garden

pot-au-feu /pɔtofø/ *m inv* **1** boiled beef (*with vegetables*)
2 boiling beef

pot-aux-roses, *pl* **pots-aux-roses** /pɔtoʀoz/ *m* (fig) skeleton in the closet

pot-de-vin, *pl* **pots-de-vin** /podvɛ̃/ *m* bribe, backhander (BrE) (fam)

pote /pɔt/ *m* (fam) mate (BrE) (fam), pal (AmE) (fam)

poteau, *pl* **~x** /pɔto/ *m* post; goalpost
■ **~ électrique** electricity pole (*supplying domestic power lines*)

potelé, **~e** /pɔtle/ *adj* chubby

potence /pɔtɑ̃s/ *f* gallows

potentiel, **-ielle** /pɔtɑ̃sjɛl/ **A** *adj* potential
B *m* potential

poterie /pɔtʀi/ *f* **1** pottery
2 piece of pottery

potiche /pɔtiʃ/ *f* vase

potier, **-ière** /pɔtje, ɛʀ/ *mf* potter

potin /pɔtɛ̃/ *m* (fam) **1** gossip
2 din (fam)

potion /posjɔ̃/ *f* potion

potiron /pɔtiʀɔ̃/ *m* pumpkin (BrE), winter squash (AmE)

pot-pourri, *pl* **pots-pourris** /popuʀi/ *m* **1** (Mus) medley
2 potpourri

pou, *pl* **~x** /pu/ *m* louse
IDIOMS **chercher des ~x** (fam) to nitpick (fam); **être laid comme un ~** (fam) to be as ugly as sin

poubelle /pubɛl/ *f* (inside) bin (BrE), trash can (AmE); (outside) dustbin (BrE), garbage can (AmE)

pouce /pus/ *m* **1** thumb
2 big toe
3 inch; **ne pas bouger d'un ~** not to budge an inch
IDIOMS **se tourner** *or* **rouler les ~s** (fam) to twiddle one's thumbs; **manger sur le ~** to have a quick bite to eat; **donner un coup de ~ à qn** to help sb get started

poudre /pudʀ/ *f* (gen) powder; **~ (à canon)** gunpowder; **~ à récurer** scouring powder
IDIOMS **mettre le feu aux ~s** to bring things to a head; **jeter de la ~ aux yeux** to try to impress

poudrer /pudʀe/ [**v1**] *vt* to powder

poudreux, **-euse** /pudʀø, øz/ *adj* powdery

poudrier /pudʀije/ *m* powder compact

poudrière /pudʀijɛʀ/ *f* **1** powder magazine
2 (fig) time bomb

pouf /puf/ *m* **1** pouffe
2 faire ~ to fall with a soft thud

pouffer /pufe/ [**v1**] *vi* **~ (de rire)** to burst out laughing

pouilleux, **-euse** /pujø, øz/ *adj* **1** (fam) seedy
2 flea-ridden

poulailler /pulɑje/ *m* **1** henhouse; hen run
2 hens
3 (fam) (in theatre) **le ~** the Gods (BrE), the gallery

poulain /pulɛ̃/ *m* **1** colt; foal
2 protégé

poularde /pulaʀd/ *f* fattened chicken

poule /pul/ *f* **1** hen
2 boiling fowl
3 (fam) **ma ~** my pet (BrE) (fam), honey (AmE) (fam)
■ **~ d'eau** moorhen; **~ faisane** hen pheasant; **~ mouillée** (fam) wimp (fam); **~ naine** bantam; **~ au pot** boiled chicken
IDIOMS **quand les ~s auront des dents** (fam) pigs might fly; **tuer la ~ aux œufs d'or** to kill the goose that lays the golden egg

🔑 **poulet** /pulɛ/ *m* chicken
■ **~ d'élevage** ≈ battery chicken; **~ fermier** ≈ free-range chicken

pouliche /puliʃ/ *f* filly

poulie /puli/ *f* pulley

poulpe /pulp/ *m* octopus

pouls /pu/ *m inv* pulse

poumon /pumɔ̃/ *m* lung; **~ d'acier** *or* **artificiel** iron lung; **à pleins ~s** ‹*shout*› at the top of one's voice; ‹*breathe*› deeply

poupe /pup/ *f* stern; **avoir le vent en ~** to sail *or* run before the wind; (fig) to have the wind in one's sails

poupée /pupe/ *f* doll

poupon /pupɔ̃/ *m* **1** tiny baby
2 baby doll

pouponner /pupɔne/ [**v1**] *vi* (fam) to play the doting father/mother

🔑 **pour¹** /puʀ/ *prep* **1** (in order) to; **~ faire** to do; in order to do; **~ ne pas faire** so as not to do; **c'était ~ rire** *or* **plaisanter** it was a joke; **~ que** so that; **~ ainsi dire** so to speak
2 for; **le train ~ Paris** the train for Paris *or* to Paris; **ce sera prêt ~ vendredi?** will it be ready by Friday?; **~ toujours** forever; **le bébé c'est ~ quand?** when is the baby due?; **se battre ~ une femme** to fight over a woman; **c'est fait** *or* **étudié ~!** (fam) that's what it's for; **je suis ~** (fam) I'm in favour (BrE)
3 about; as regards; **se renseigner ~** to find out about; **~ l'argent** as regards the money, as for the money; **~ moi, il a tort** as far as I am concerned, he's wrong
4 elle a ~ ambition d'être pilote her ambition is to be a pilot
5 elle avait ~ elle de savoir écouter she had the merit of being a good listener
6 ~ autant que je sache as far as I know; **~ être intelligente, ça elle l'est!** she really is intelligent!
7 j'ai mis ~ 40 euros d'essence I've put in 40 euros' worth of petrol (BrE) *or* gas (AmE); **merci ~ tout** thank you for everything; **je n'y suis ~ rien** I had nothing to do with it; **je n'en ai pas ~ longtemps** it won't take long
8 dix ~ cent ten per cent; **une cuillère de vinaigre ~ quatre d'huile** one spoonful of vinegar to four of oil; **~ une large part** to a large extent

pour² /puʀ/ *m* **le ~ et le contre** the pros and the cons

pourboire /puʀbwaʀ/ *m* tip

pourcentage /puʀsɑ̃taʒ/ *m* **1** percentage
2 commission
3 cut (fam)

pourchasser /puʀʃase/ [**v1**] *vt* **1** to hunt ‹*animal, criminal*›
2 to pursue ‹*person*›

pourparlers /puʀpaʀle/ *mpl* talks; **être en ~** ‹*people*› to be engaged in talks

pourpre /puʀpʀ/ *adj*, *m* crimson

🔑 **pourquoi** /puʀkwa/ **A** *adv*, *conj* why; **~ donc?** but why?; **~ pas** *or* **non?** why not?; **~ pas un week-end à Paris?** what *or* how about a weekend in Paris?; **va donc savoir ~!** God knows why!
B *m inv* **le ~ et le comment** the why and the wherefore

pourri, **~e** /puʀi/ **A** *pp* ▶ **pourrir**
B *pp adj* **1** (gen) rotten; ‹*vegetation*› rotting
2 (fam) ‹*weather, car*› rotten (fam); ‹*person*› crooked (fam)
C *m* rotten part; **ça sent le ~** it smells rotten

pourrir /puʀiʀ/ [**v3**] **A** *vt* **1** to rot ‹*wood*›
2 to spoil ‹*person*›
3 (fam) to spoil [sb] rotten (fam)
B *vi* **1** ‹*food*› to go bad
2 ‹*wood*› to rot
3 ‹*person*› to rot; ‹*situation*› to deteriorate

pourriture /puʀityʀ/ *f* **1** rot, decay
2 corruption, rottenness

poursuite /puʀsɥit/ *f* **1** pursuit; **être à la ~ de** to be in pursuit of
2 chase
3 continuation
4 ~ (judiciaire) (judicial) proceedings

🔑 **poursuivre** /puʀsɥivʀ/ [**v62**] **A** *vt* **1** to chase
2 ‹*person*› to hound; ‹*nightmare*› to haunt; **~ qn de ses assiduités** to force one's attentions on sb
3 to seek (after) ‹*honours, truth*›; to pursue ‹*goal*›

🔑 key word

p

4 to continue ‹*journey, studies*›; to pursue ‹*talks*›
5 (Law) ~ **qn (en justice** *or* **devant les tribunaux)** to sue sb
B *vi* to continue; ~ **sur un sujet** to continue talking on a subject
C se poursuivre *v refl* (+ *v être*) ‹*talks, conflict, journey*› to continue

pourtant /puʀtɑ̃/ *adv* though; **et** ~ and yet; **techniquement** ~**, le film est parfait** technically, however, the film is perfect

pourtour /puʀtuʀ/ *m* **1** perimeter; circumference
2 surrounding area

pourvoir /puʀvwaʀ/ [**v40**] **A** *vt* **1** to fill ‹*post*›
2 ~ **qn de** to endow sb with
B pourvoir à *v+prep* to provide for
C se pourvoir *v refl* (+ *v être*) **se** ~ **de** to provide oneself with ‹*currency*›; to equip oneself with ‹*boots*›

pourvoyeur, **-euse** /puʀvwajœʀ, øz/ *mf* ~ **de** source of ‹*jobs, funding*›

pourvu, ~**e** /puʀvy/ **A** *pp* ▸ **pourvoir**
B pourvu que *phr* **1** provided (that), as long as
2 let's hope; ~ **que ça dure!** let's hope it lasts!

pousse /pus/ *f* **1** (Bot) shoot
2 growth

poussé, ~**e** /puse/ **A** *pp* ▸ **pousser**
B *pp adj* ‹*inquiry*› thorough; ‹*studies*› advanced

poussée /puse/ *f* **1** (of water, crowd) pressure; (of wind) force
2 thrust
3 (Med) attack; ~ **de fièvre** sudden high temperature
4 (in price) (sharp) rise; (in racism, violence) upsurge

pousser /puse/ [**v1**] **A** *vt* **1** to push ‹*wheelbarrow, person*›; to move *or* shift [sth] (out of the way), to push [sth] aside; ~ **une porte** to push a door to; to push a door open; ~ **qn du coude** to give sb a dig *or* to nudge sb with one's elbow
2 ~ **qn à faire** to encourage sb to do; to urge sb to do; ‹*hunger, despair*› to drive sb to do; ~ **à la consommation** to encourage people to buy more; to encourage people to drink more
3 to push ‹*pupil*›; to keep [sb] at it ‹*employee*›; to drive [sth] hard ‹*car*›
4 to push ‹*product, protégé*›
5 to pursue ‹*studies, research*›; **c'est** ~ **un peu loin la plaisanterie** that's taking the joke a bit far
6 to let out ‹*cry*›; to heave ‹*sigh*›
B *vi* **1** ‹*child*› to grow; ‹*plant*› to grow; to sprout; ‹*tooth*› to come through; ‹*buildings*› to spring up; **je fais** ~ **des légumes** I grow vegetables; **se laisser** ~ **les cheveux** to grow one's hair
2 ~ **plus loin** to go on further
3 (fam) to overdo it, to go too far
C se pousser *v refl* (+ *v être*) to move over

IDIOM **à la va comme je te pousse** (fam) any old how

poussette /pusɛt/ *f* pushchair (BrE), stroller (AmE)

poussière /pusjɛʀ/ *f* **1** dust; **tomber en** ~ to crumble away; to fall to bits
2 speck of dust

IDIOM **10 euros/20 ans et des** ~**s** (fam) just over 10 euros/20 years

poussiéreux, **-euse** /pusjeʀø, øz/ *adj*
1 dusty
2 outdated, fossilized

poussin /pusɛ̃/ *m* chick

poussoir /puswaʀ/ *m* (push) button

poutre /putʀ/ *f* **1** beam
2 girder

pouvoir[1] /puvwaʀ/ [**v49**] **A** *v aux* **1** to be able to; **peux-tu soulever cette boîte?** can you lift this box?; **dès que je pourrai** as soon as I can; **je n'en peux plus** I've had it (fam); **tout peut arriver** anything could happen; **il ne peut pas ne pas gagner** he's bound to win; **on peut toujours espérer** there's no harm in wishing; **qu'est-ce que cela peut (bien) te faire?** (fam) what business is it of yours?
2 to be allowed to; **est-ce que je peux me servir de ta voiture?** can I use your car?; **on peut dire que** it can be said that; **on peut ne pas faire l'accord** the agreement is optional
3 pouvez-vous/pourriez-vous me tenir la porte s'il vous plaît? can you/could you hold the door (open) for me please?
4 puisse cette nouvelle année exaucer vos vœux les plus chers may the new year bring you everything you could wish for; **s'il croit que je vais payer il peut toujours attendre** if he thinks I'm going to pay he's got another think coming; **ce qu'il peut être grand!** how tall he is!
B *vt* **que puis-je pour vous?** what can I do for you?; **je fais ce que je peux** I'm doing my best
C *v impers* **il peut faire très froid en janvier** it can get very cold in January; **ce qu'il a pu pleuvoir!** you wouldn't believe how much it rained!
D il se peut *v impers* **il se peut que les prix augmentent en juin** prices may *or* might rise in June; **cela se pourrait qu'il soit fâché** he might be angry
E on ne peut plus *phr* **il est on ne peut plus timide** he is as shy as can be
F on ne peut mieux *phr* **ils s'entendent on ne peut mieux** they get on extremely well

IDIOM **autant que faire se peut** as far as possible

pouvoir[2] /puvwaʀ/ *m* **1** (gen) power; ~ **d'achat** purchasing power; **avoir le** ~ **de faire** to be able to do, to have the power to

p

do; **je n'ai pas le ~ de décider** it's not up to me to decide
2 (Pol) power; **avoir tous ~s** to have *or* exercise full powers; **le ~ en place** the government in power
■ **le ~ judiciaire** the judiciary; **~ législatif** legislative power; **~s publics** authorities

pragmatisme /pʀagmatism/ *m* pragmatism

praire /pʀɛʀ/ *f* clam

prairie /pʀeʀi/ *f* meadow

praline /pʀalin/ *f* sugared (BrE) *or* sugar-coated (AmE) almond

praliné, **~e** /pʀaline/ **A** *adj* praline
B *m* praline

praticable /pʀatikabl/ *adj* ‹*road*› passable

praticien, **-ienne** /pʀatisjɛ̃, ɛn/ *mf*
1 general practitioner, GP
2 practitioner

pratiquant, **~e** /pʀatikɑ̃, ɑ̃t/ *adj* practising (BrE); **être très ~** to be very devout

⚷ **pratique** /pʀatik/ **A** *adj* practical; ‹*device*› handy; ‹*place, route*› convenient
B *f* **1 la ~ des arts martiaux est très répandue** many people practise (BrE) martial arts; **cela nécessite de longues heures de ~** it takes hours of practice; **avoir une bonne ~ de l'anglais** to have a good working knowledge of English
2 practical experience
3 practice; **mettre qch en ~** to put sth into practice
4 les ~s religieuses religious practices

pratiquement /pʀatikmɑ̃/ *adv* **1** in practice
2 practically, virtually; **~ jamais** hardly ever

⚷ **pratiquer** /pʀatike/ [**v1**] **A** *vt* **1** to play ‹*tennis*›; to do ‹*yoga*›; to take part in ‹*activity*›; to practise (BrE) ‹*language*›; **il est croyant mais ne pratique pas** he believes in God but doesn't practise (BrE) his religion
2 to use ‹*method, blackmail*›; to pursue ‹*policy*›; to charge ‹*rate of interest*›
3 to carry out ‹*examination, graft*›
B se pratiquer *v refl* (+ *v être*) ‹*sport*› to be played; ‹*technique, policy, strategy*› to be used; ‹*price, tariff*› to be charged

pré /pʀe/ *m* meadow

pré- /pʀe/ *pref* pre, pre-; **~-accord** preliminary agreement

pré-affranchi /pʀeafʀɑ̃ʃi/ *adj* postage paid

préalable /pʀealabl/ **A** *adj* ‹*notice*› prior; ‹*study*› preliminary
B *m* precondition; preliminary
C au préalable *phr* first, beforehand

préalablement /pʀealabləmɑ̃/ *adv* beforehand

préambule /pʀeɑ̃byl/ *m* **1** preamble
2 forewarning

préau, *pl* **~x** /pʀeo/ *m* (of school) covered playground; (of prison) exercise yard

⚷ key word

préavis /pʀeavi/ *m inv* notice

précaire /pʀekɛʀ/ *adj* ‹*existence*› precarious; ‹*job*› insecure; ‹*construction*› flimsy

précariat /pʀekaʀja/ *m* (Socio, Econ) precariat (*social group suffering multiple forms of insecurity*)

précariser /pʀekaʀize/ [**v1**] *vt* **~ l'emploi** to casualize labour (BrE)

précarité /pʀekaʀite/ *f* precariousness; **la ~ de l'emploi** job insecurity

précaution /pʀekosjɔ̃/ *f* precaution; caution; **par ~** as a precaution

précédemment /pʀesedamɑ̃/ *adv* previously

⚷ **précédent**, **~e** /pʀesedɑ̃, ɑ̃t/ **A** *adj* previous
B *mf* **le ~, la ~e** the previous one
C *m* precedent; **sans ~** unprecedented

précéder /pʀesede/ [**v14**] *vt* **1** ‹*person*› to go in front of, to precede; ‹*vehicle*› to be in front of
2 il m'avait précédé de cinq minutes he'd got there five minutes ahead of me
3 ‹*paragraph, crisis*› to precede; **la semaine qui a précédé votre départ** the week before you left

précepte /pʀesɛpt/ *m* precept

précepteur, **-trice** /pʀesɛptœʀ, tʀis/ *mf* (private) tutor

prêcher /pʀeʃe/ [**v1**] **A** *vt* **1** to preach
2 to advocate
B *vi* to preach
IDIOM **~ le faux pour savoir le vrai** to tell a lie in order to get at the truth

précieusement /pʀesjøzmɑ̃/ *adv* carefully

⚷ **précieux**, **-ieuse** /pʀesjø, øz/ *adj* **1** ‹*stone, book*› precious; ‹*piece of furniture*› valuable
2 ‹*information*› very useful; ‹*collaborator*› valued
3 ‹*friendship, right*› precious; ‹*friend*› very dear
4 ‹*style, language*› precious

précipice /pʀesipis/ *m* precipice

précipitamment /pʀesipitamɑ̃/ *adv* hurriedly

précipitation /pʀesipitasjɔ̃/ **A** *f* haste
B précipitations *fpl* rainfall, precipitation

précipité, **~e** /pʀesipite/ *adj* **1** rapid
2 hasty, precipitate

précipiter /pʀesipite/ [**v1**] **A** *vt* **1 ~ qn dans le vide** (from roof) to push sb off; (out of window) to push sb out
2 to hasten ‹*departure, decision*›; to precipitate ‹*event*›; **~ les choses** to rush things
B se précipiter *v refl* (+ *v être*) **1 il s'est précipité dans le vide** he jumped off
2 to rush; **se ~ au secours de qn** to rush to sb's aid; **se ~ sur** to rush at ‹*person*›; to

rush for ‹*object*›
3 to rush
4 ‹*action*› to move faster

précis, **~e** /pResi, iz/ **A** *adj* **1** ‹*programme, criterion*› specific; ‹*idea, date*› definite; ‹*moment*› particular
2 ‹*person, gesture*› precise; ‹*figure, data*› accurate; ‹*place*› exact
B *m inv* handbook

précisément /pResizemɑ̃/ *adv* precisely

préciser /pResize/ [**v1**] **A** *vt* **1** to add; **faut-il le** *or* **est-il besoin de ~** needless to say
2 to state; **~ ses intentions** to state one's intentions
3 to specify; **pouvez-vous ~?** could you be more specific?
4 to clarify ‹*ideas*›
B se préciser *v refl* (+ *v être*) **1** ‹*danger, future*› to become clearer; ‹*plan, trip*› to take shape
2 ‹*shape, reality*› to become clear

précision /pResizjɔ̃/ *f* **1** precision
2 accuracy; **localiser avec ~** to pinpoint; **instrument de ~** precision instrument
3 detail

précité, **~e** /pResite/ *adj* aforementioned

précoce /pRekɔs/ *adj* **1** precocious
2 ‹*season*› early
3 ‹*senility*› premature

précompte /pRekɔ̃t/ *m* deduction; **~ de l'impôt** deduction of tax at source

préconçu, **~e** /pRekɔ̃sy/ *adj* preconceived

préconiser /pRekɔnize/ [**v1**] *vt* to recommend

précuit, **~e** /pRekɥi, it/ *adj* pre-cooked

précurseur /pRekyRsœR/ **A** *adj m* precursory; **signes ~s de l'orage** signs that herald a storm
B *m* pioneer; **~ de** precursor of

prédateur /pRedatœR/ *m* **1** predator
2 hunter-gatherer

prédécesseur /pRedesesœR/ *m* predecessor

prédestiner /pRedɛstine/ [**v1**] *vt* to predestine

prédicateur, **-trice** /pRedikatœR, tRis/ *mf* preacher

prédiction /pRediksjɔ̃/ *f* prediction

prédilection /pRedilɛksjɔ̃/ *f* predilection, liking; **de ~** favourite (BrE)

prédire /pRediR/ [**v65**] *vt* to predict

prédisposer /pRedispoze/ [**v1**] *vt* to predispose

prédominant, **~e** /pRedɔminɑ̃, ɑ̃t/ *adj* predominant

prédominer /pRedɔmine/ [**v1**] *vi* to predominate

préétablir /pReetabliR/ [**v3**] *vt* to pre-establish

préexister /pReɛgziste/ [**v1**] *vi* to pre-exist

préfabriqué /pRefabRike/ *m*
1 prefabricated material
2 prefab (fam)

préface /pRefas/ *f* preface

préfacer /pRefase/ [**v12**] *vt* to write a *or* the preface to

préfectoral, **~e**, *mpl* **-aux** /pRefɛktɔRal, o/ *adj* ‹*level, authorization*› prefectorial; ‹*administration, building*› prefectural

préfecture /pRefɛktyR/ *f* **1** prefecture
2 *main city of a French department*
■ **~ de police** police headquarters (*in some large French cities*)

préférable /pRefeRabl/ *adj* preferable

préféré, **~e** /pRefeRe/ *adj*, *mf* favourite (BrE)

préférence /pRefeRɑ̃s/ *f* preference; **achète cette marque de ~** if you can, buy this brand

préférentiel, **-ielle** /pRefeRɑ̃sjɛl/ *adj* preferential

préférer /pRefeRe/ [**v14**] *vt* to prefer; **j'aurais préféré ne jamais l'apprendre** I wish I'd never found out

préfet /pRefɛ/ *m* prefect

préfigurer /pRefigyRe/ [**v1**] *vt* to prefigure

préfixe /pRefiks/ *m* prefix

préhistoire /pReistwaR/ *f* prehistory

préjudice /pReʒydis/ *m* harm, damage; **~ moral** moral wrong; **porter ~ à qn** to harm sb; **au ~ de qn** to the detriment of sb

préjugé /pReʒyʒe/ *m* prejudice; **~(s) en faveur de qn** bias in favour (BrE) of sb

préjuger /pReʒyʒe/ [**v13**] *vt*, **préjuger de** *v+prep* to prejudge

prélasser: **se prélasser** /pRelase/ [**v1**] *v refl* (+ *v être*) to lounge

prélat /pRela/ *m* prelate

prélavage /pRelavaʒ/ *m* pre-wash

prêle /pRɛl/ *f* (Bot) horsetail

prélèvement /pRelɛvmɑ̃/ *m* **1** sampling; sample; **faire un ~ de sang** to take a blood sample
2 faire un ~ bancaire de 100 euros to make a debit of 100 euros
■ **~ automatique** direct debit; **~ à la source** deduction at source

prélever /pRelve/ [**v16**] *vt* **1** to take a sample of ‹*blood, water*›; to remove ‹*organ*›
2 to debit
3 to deduct ‹*tax*›
4 to take ‹*percentage*›

préliminaire /pRelimineR/ **A** *adj* preliminary
B préliminaires *mpl* preliminaries

prélude /pRelyd/ *m* prelude

préluder /pRelyde/ [**v1**] *v+prep* **~ à** to be a prelude to

prématuré, **~e** /pRematyRe/ **A** *adj* premature
B *mf* premature baby

préméditation /pRemeditasjɔ̃/ *f* premeditation

préméditer /pRemedite/ [**v1**] *vt* to premeditate

p

🔑 **premier**, **-ière** /pʀəmje, ɛʀ/ **A** *adj* **1** first; **(dans) les ~s temps** at first
2 ‹*artist, power*› leading; ‹*student*› top; **être ~** to be top; to be first; **c'est le ~ prix** it's the cheapest
3 ‹*impression*› first, initial
4 ‹*quality*› prime; ‹*objective*› primary
B *mf* first; **je préfère le ~** I prefer the first one; **arriver le ~** to come first; **être le ~ de la classe** to be top of the class
C *m* **1** first floor (BrE), second floor (AmE)
2 first; **le ~ de l'an** New Year's Day
3 first arrondissement
D **en premier** *phr* first
■ **~ âge** ‹*clothes*› for babies up to six months; **~ de cordée** (Sport) leader; **~ ministre** prime minister; **le ~ venu** just anybody; the first person to come along; **~s secours** first aid

première /pʀəmjɛʀ/ **A** ▶ **premier A, B**
B *f* **1** first; **~ mondiale** world first
2 premiere
3 (Sch) *sixth year of secondary school, age 16–17*
4 (Aut) first (gear)
5 (fam) first class
C **de première** *phr* (fam) first-rate

premièrement /pʀəmjɛʀmɑ̃/ *adv* **1** firstly, first
2 for a start, for one thing

prémisse /pʀemis/ *f* premise, premiss (BrE)

prémolaire /pʀemɔlɛʀ/ *f* premolar

prémonition /pʀemɔnisjɔ̃/ *f* premonition

prémonitoire /pʀemɔnitwaʀ/ *adj* premonitory

prémunir /pʀemyniʀ/ [v3] **A** *vt* to protect
B **se prémunir** *v refl* (+ *v être*) to protect oneself

prenant, **~e** /pʀənɑ̃, ɑ̃t/ *adj* ‹*film*› fascinating; ‹*voice*› captivating; ‹*work*› absorbing

🔑 **prendre** /pʀɑ̃dʀ/ [v52]

> *Prendre* is very often translated by *to take* but see the entry below for a wide variety of usages.
> For translations of certain fixed phrases such as *prendre froid*, *prendre soin de*, *prendre parti* etc, refer to the entries **froid**, **soin**, **parti**.

A *vt* **1** to take; **~ un vase dans le placard** to take a vase out of the cupboard; **prenez donc une chaise** take a seat; **~ un congé** to take time off; **~ le train/l'avion** to take the train/plane; **on m'a pris tous mes bijoux** I had all my jewellery (BrE) *or* jewelry (AmE) stolen; **la guerre leur a pris deux fils** they lost two sons in the war; **~ les mensurations de qn** to take sb's measurements; **~ les choses comme elles sont** to take things as they come; **ne le prends pas mal** don't take it the wrong way; **je vous ai pris pour quelqu'un d'autre** I thought you were someone else
2 **~ un accent** to pick up an accent; to put on an accent
3 to bring; **n'oublie pas de ~ des bottes** don't forget to bring a pair of boots
4 to get ‹*food, petrol*›; **~ de l'argent au distributeur** to get some money out of the cash dispenser
5 to have ‹*drink, meal*›; to take ‹*medicine*›; **aller ~ une bière** to go for a beer
6 to choose ‹*topic, question*›
7 to charge; **il prend 15% au passage** (fam) he takes a cut of 15%
8 to take up ‹*space, time*›
9 to take [sb] on; to engage [sb]
10 to pick [sb/sth] up; **~ les enfants à l'école** to collect the children from school
11 to catch; **elle s'est fait ~ en train de voler** she got caught stealing
12 (fam) **qu'est-ce qui te prend?** what's the matter with you?; **ça te/leur prend souvent?** are you/they often like this?
13 to involve ‹*spectator, reader*›; **être pris par un livre/film** to get involved in a book/film
14 to get ‹*slap, sunburn*›; to catch ‹*cold*›
15 **il est très gentil quand on sait le ~** he's very nice when you know how to handle him
16 to take [sth] down ‹*address*›
17 **où a-t-il pris qu'ils allaient divorcer?** where did he get the idea they were going to get divorced?
18 to take over ‹*management, power*›; to assume ‹*control*›; **je prends ça sur moi** I'll see to it; **elle a pris sur elle de leur parler** she took it upon herself to talk to them
19 to put on ‹*weight*›; to gain ‹*lead*›
20 to take on ‹*lease*›; to take ‹*job*›
21 to take on ‹*rival*›
22 to take, to seize ‹*town*›; to capture ‹*ship, tank*›; to take ‹*chess piece, card*›
B *vi* **1** **~ à gauche/vers le nord** to go left/north
2 ‹*wood*› to catch; ‹*fire*› to break out
3 ‹*jelly, glue*› to set; ‹*mayonnaise*› to thicken
4 ‹*strike, innovation*› to be a success; ‹*idea, fashion*› to catch on; ‹*dye, cutting*› to take
5 **~ sur son temps libre pour traduire un roman** to translate a novel in one's spare time
6 **~ sur soi** to take a hold on oneself, to get a grip on oneself
7 (fam) **ça ne prend pas!** it won't work!
8 (fam) **c'est toujours moi qui prends!** I'm always the one who gets it in the neck! (fam); **il en a pris pour 20 ans** he got 20 years
C **se prendre** *v refl* (+ *v être*) **1** **en Chine le thé se prend sans sucre** in China they don't put sugar in their tea
2 **les mauvaises habitudes se prennent vite** bad habits are easily picked up
3 **se ~ par la taille** to hold each other around the waist

🔑 key word

4 se ~ les doigts dans la porte to catch one's fingers in the door
5 (fam) **il s'est pris une gifle** he got a slap in the face
6 se ~ à faire to find oneself doing; **se ~ de sympathie pour qn** to take to sb
7 pour qui est-ce que tu te prends? who do you think you are?
8 s'en ~ à to attack ‹*person, press*›; to take it out on [sb]; to go for [sb]
9 savoir s'y ~ avec to have a way with ‹*children*›
10 il faut s'y ~ à l'avance pour avoir des places you have to book ahead to get seats; **tu t'y es pris trop tard** you left it too late; **il s'y est pris à plusieurs fois** he tried several times; **elle s'y prend mal** she goes about it the wrong way
IDIOM **c'est à ~ ou à laisser** take it or leave it

preneur, **-euse** /pʀənœʀ, øz/ *mf* **il n'y a pas ~** there are no takers; **trouver ~** to attract a buyer; to find a buyer

prénom /pʀenɔ̃/ *m* first name, forename

prénommer /pʀenɔme/ [**v1**] **A** *vt* to name, to call
B se prénommer *v refl* (+ *v être*) to be called

prénuptial, **~e**, *pl* **-iaux** /pʀenypsjal, o/ *adj* prenuptial; prior to marriage

préoccupant, **~e** /pʀeɔkypɑ̃, ɑ̃t/ *adj* worrying

préoccupation /pʀeɔkypasjɔ̃/ *f* worry

préoccuper /pʀeɔkype/ [**v1**] **A** *vt* **1** to worry; **avoir l'air préoccupé** to look worried
2 to preoccupy
3 to concern
B se préoccuper *v refl* (+ *v être*) **se ~ de** to be concerned about ‹*situation*›; to think about ‹*future*›

préparateur, **-trice** /pʀepaʀatœʀ, tʀis/ *mf* **~ en pharmacie** pharmacist's assistant

préparatifs /pʀepaʀatif/ *mpl* preparations

préparation /pʀepaʀasjɔ̃/ *f* **1** preparation
2 training

préparatoire /pʀepaʀatwaʀ/ *adj* preliminary

préparer /pʀepaʀe/ [**v1**] **A** *vt* **1** (gen) to prepare; to make ‹*meal*›; to get [sth] ready ‹*clothes, file*›; to plan ‹*holidays, future*›; to draw up ‹*plan*›; to hatch ‹*plot*›; **il est en train de ~ le dîner** he's getting dinner ready; **des plats préparés** ready meals
2 ~ qn à qch (gen) to prepare sb for sth; to coach sb for sth ‹*race, examination*›; **essaie de la ~ avant de lui annoncer la nouvelle** try and break the news to her gently
B se préparer *v refl* (+ *v être*) **1** to get ready
2 to prepare
3 ‹*storm, trouble*› to be brewing; ‹*changes*› to be in the offing; **un coup d'État se prépare dans le pays** a coup d'état is imminent in the country
4 se ~ une tasse de thé to make (BrE) *or* fix (AmE) oneself a cup of tea

prépondérance /pʀepɔ̃deʀɑ̃s/ *f* predominance

prépondérant, **~e** /pʀepɔ̃deʀɑ̃, ɑ̃t/ *adj* predominant

préposé, **~e** /pʀepoze/ *mf* **1** official; **~ des douanes** customs official; **~ au vestiaire** cloakroom attendant
2 postman/postwoman, mailman/mailwoman (AmE)

préposition /pʀepozisjɔ̃/ *f* preposition

prépuce /pʀepys/ *m* foreskin

préretraite /pʀeʀətʀɛt/ *f* early retirement

prérogative /pʀeʀɔgativ/ *f* prerogative; **~ de qn/qch sur** primacy of sb/sth over

près /pʀɛ/ **A** *adv* **1** close; **ce n'est pas tout ~** it's quite a way; **se raser de ~** to have a close shave
2 ça pèse 10 kg, à quelques grammes ~ it weighs 10 kg, give or take a few grams; **à ceci** *or* **cela ~ que** except that; **il m'a remboursé au centime ~** he paid me back to the very last penny; **gagner à deux voix ~** to win by two votes; **à une exception ~** with only one exception
B près de *phr* **1** near; **être ~ du but** to be close to achieving one's goal; **j'aimerais être ~ de toi** I'd like to be with you
2 near, nearly; **je ne suis pas ~ de recommencer** I'm not about to do that again; **le problème n'est pas ~ d'être résolu** the problem is nowhere near solved
3 close; **ils sont très ~ l'un de l'autre** they are very close
4 nearly, almost; **cela coûte ~ de 1 000 euros** it costs nearly 1,000 euros
C de près *phr* closely; **se suivre de ~** ‹*competitors*› to be close together; ‹*siblings*› to be close in age
D à peu près *phr* **à peu ~ vide** practically empty; **à peu ~ 200 euros** about 200 euros; **à peu ~ de la même façon** in much the same way

présage /pʀezaʒ/ *m* **1** omen
2 harbinger
3 prediction

présager /pʀezaʒe/ [**v13**] *vt* ‹*event*› to presage; ‹*person*› to predict; **laisser ~** to suggest

presbyte /pʀɛsbit/ *adj* long-sighted (BrE), far-sighted (AmE)

presbytère /pʀɛsbitɛʀ/ *m* presbytery

presbytie /pʀɛsbisi/ *f* long-sightedness (BrE), far-sightedness (AmE)

préscolaire /pʀeskɔlɛʀ/ *adj* preschool

prescription /pʀɛskʀipsjɔ̃/ *f* prescription; **'se conformer aux ~s du médecin'** 'to be taken in accordance with doctor's instructions'

prescrire /pʀɛskʀiʀ/ [**v67**] *vt* **1** (Med) to prescribe
2 to stipulate

présélection /pʀeselɛksjɔ̃/ *f* **1** shortlisting
2 (Tech) presetting

présélectionner /pʀeselɛksjɔne/ [**v1**] *vt*
1 to shortlist
2 to preselect; to preset

⚷ **présence** /pʀezɑ̃s/ *f* (gen) presence; (at work) attendance; **il fait de la ~, c'est tout** he's present and not much else; **les forces en ~ dans le conflit** the forces involved in the conflict; **il a besoin d'une ~** he needs company; **avoir beaucoup de ~ (sur scène)** to have great stage presence
■ **~ d'esprit** presence of mind

⚷ **présent**, **~e** /pʀezɑ̃, ɑ̃t/ **A** *adj* **1** present; **M. Maquanne, ici ~** Mr Maquanne, who is here with us; **avoir qch ~ à l'esprit** to have sth in mind ‹*advice*›; to have sth fresh in one's mind ‹*memory*›
2 actively involved; **un chanteur très ~ sur scène** a singer with a strong stage presence
B *mf* **la liste des ~s** the list of those present
C *m* **1 le ~** the present
2 (in grammar) present (tense)
3 gift, present
D à présent *phr* at present; now

présentable /pʀezɑ̃tabl/ *adj* presentable

présentateur, **-trice** /pʀezɑ̃tatœʀ, tʀis/ *mf* presenter; newsreader (BrE), newscaster (AmE)

⚷ **présentation** /pʀezɑ̃tasjɔ̃/ *f* **1** introduction; **faire les ~s** to make the introductions
2 appearance
3 (of dish, letter) presentation; (of products) display
4 show, showing; **~ de mode** fashion show
5 (of programme) presentation
6 (of card, ticket) production; (of cheque) presentation
7 presentation, exposé

présente /pʀezɑ̃t/ **A** *adj f* ▶ **présent A**
B *f* **1 par la ~** hereby
2 ▶ **présent B**

⚷ **présenter** /pʀezɑ̃te/ [**v1**] **A** *vt* **1** to introduce; to present
2 to show ‹*ticket, card, menu*›
3 to present ‹*programme, show, collection*›; to display ‹*goods*›
4 to present ‹*receipt, bill*›; to submit ‹*estimate, report*›; to introduce ‹*proposal, bill*›; **~ une liste pour les élections** to put forward a list (of candidates) for the elections
5 to present ‹*situation, budget, theory*›; to set out ‹*objections, point of view*›; **~ qn comme (étant) un monstre** to portray sb as a monster
6 to offer ‹*condolences*›; **~ des excuses** to apologize
7 to involve ‹*risk, difficulty*›; to show ‹*differences*›; to offer ‹*advantage*›; to have ‹*aspect, feature*›
B *vi* **~ bien** to have a smart appearance
C se présenter *v refl* (+ *v être*) **1 il faut se ~ à la réception** you must go to reception; **présentez-vous à 10 heures** come at 10 o'clock
2 to introduce oneself
3 se ~ à to take ‹*examination*›; to stand for ‹*election*›
4 ‹*opportunity*› to arise; ‹*solution*› to emerge
5 se ~ en, se ~ sous forme de ‹*product*› to come in the form of
6 l'affaire se présente bien things are looking good

présentoir /pʀezɑ̃twaʀ/ *m* **1** display stand *or* unit
2 display shelf

préservatif /pʀezɛʀvatif/ *m* condom

préservation /pʀezɛʀvasjɔ̃/ *f* protection; preservation

préserver /pʀezɛʀve/ [**v1**] *vt* **1** to preserve
2 to protect

présidence /pʀezidɑ̃s/ *f* **1** presidency; chairmanship
2 presidential palace

⚷ **président** /pʀezidɑ̃/ *m* president; chairman
■ **~ de la République** President of the Republic

président-directeur, *pl* **présidents-directeurs** /pʀezidɑ̃diʀɛktœʀ/ *m* **~ général** chairman and managing director (BrE), chief executive officer

présidente /pʀezidɑ̃t/ *f* **1** president; chairwoman, chairperson; chairman
2 First Lady

présidentiel, **-ielle** /pʀezidɑ̃sjɛl/ *adj* presidential

présidentielles /pʀezidɑ̃sjɛl/ *fpl* presidential election

présider /pʀezide/ [**v1**] *vt* **1** to chair
2 to be the president of; to be the chairman/chairwoman of; to preside over

présomption /pʀezɔ̃psjɔ̃/ *f* **1** (Law) presumption
2 assumption
3 plein de ~ presumptuous

présomptueux, **-euse** /pʀezɔ̃ptɥø, øz/ *adj* arrogant; presumptuous

⚷ **presque** /pʀɛsk/ *adv* almost, nearly; **il y a trois ans ~ jour pour jour** it's nearly three years to the day; **c'était le bonheur ou ~** it was as close to happiness as one can get; **il ne reste ~ rien** there's hardly anything left

presqu'île /pʀɛskil/ *f* peninsula

pressant, **~e** /pʀɛsɑ̃, ɑ̃t/ *adj* ‹*need*› pressing; ‹*appeal*› urgent; ‹*salesman*› insistent

⚷ **presse** /pʀɛs/ *f* **1** press; newspapers; **avoir bonne ~** to be well thought of
2 (gen) press; (printing) press; **mettre sous ~** to send [sth] to press; **'sous ~'** 'in preparation'

pressé, **~e** /pʀese/ *adj* **1** ‹*person*› in a hurry; ‹*steps*› hurried

⚷ key word

2 ~ de faire keen to do
3 ‹*business*› urgent; **parer au plus ~** to do the most urgent thing(s) first

presse-ail /pʀɛsaj/ *m inv* garlic press

presse-citron /pʀɛssitʀɔ̃/ *m inv* lemon squeezer

pressentiment /pʀesɑ̃timɑ̃/ *m* premonition

pressentir /pʀesɑ̃tiʀ/ **[v30]** *vt* to have a premonition about

presse-papiers /pʀɛspapje/ *m inv* paperweight

presser /pʀese/ **[v1]** **A** *vt* **1 ~ qn de faire** to urge sb to do
2 to press ‹*debtor*›; to harry ‹*enemy*›
3 ‹*hunger, necessity*› to drive [sb] on
4 to increase ‹*rhythm*›; **~ le pas** *or* **mouvement** to hurry
5 to press ‹*button*›
6 to squeeze ‹*hand, object*›
7 to squeeze ‹*orange, sponge*›; to press ‹*grapes*›
8 to press ‹*record*›
B *vi* ‹*matter*› to be pressing; ‹*work*› to be urgent; **le temps presse** time is running out
C se presser *v refl* (+ *v être*) **1 se ~ autour de qn/qch** to press around sb/sth
2 to hurry up
3 to flock

pressing /pʀesiŋ/ *m* dry-cleaner's

pression /pʀɛsjɔ̃/ *f* **1** (gen) pressure; **~ artérielle** blood pressure; **sous ~** under pressure; pressurized; **faire ~ sur** to press on ‹*surface*›; to put pressure on ‹*person*›
2 snap (fastener)

pressoir /pʀeswaʀ/ *m* **1** pressing shed
2 press; **~ à pommes** cider press

pressurer /pʀesyʀe/ **[v1]** *vt* **1** to press ‹*fruit, seeds*›
2 (fam) (exploiter) to milk (fam)

pressuriser /pʀesyʀize/ **[v1]** *vt* to pressurize

prestance /pʀɛstɑ̃s/ *f* **avoir de la ~** to have great presence

prestataire /pʀɛstatɛʀ/ *m* **1 ~ de service** (service) contractor, service provider
2 recipient (*of a state benefit*)

prestation /pʀɛstasjɔ̃/ *f* **1** benefit
2 provision; **~ de service** (provision of a) service
3 service
4 performance; **~ télévisée** televised appearance

prestidigitation /pʀɛstidiʒitasjɔ̃/ *f* conjuring

prestige /pʀɛstiʒ/ *m* prestige; **le ~ de l'uniforme** the glamour (BrE) of a uniform

prestigieux, -ieuse /pʀɛstiʒjø, øz/ *adj* prestigious

présumé, ~e /pʀezyme/ *adj* alleged

présumer /pʀezyme/ **[v1]** **A** *vt* to presume; **le présumé terroriste** the alleged terrorist
B présumer de *v+prep* **(trop) ~ de ses forces** to overestimate one's strength

présupposer /pʀesypoze/ **[v1]** *vt* to presuppose

prêt, ~e /pʀɛ, pʀɛt/ **A** *adj* ready; **être fin ~** to be all set; **il est ~ à tout** he will stop at nothing
B *m* **1 le service de ~ de la bibliothèque** the library loans service
2 loan
■ **~ immobilier** property loan; **~ personnalisé** personal loan

prêt-à-porter /pʀɛtapɔʀte/ *m* ready-to-wear

prétendant, ~e /pʀetɑ̃dɑ̃, ɑ̃t/ **A** *mf*
1 candidate
2 pretender
B *m* suitor

prétendre /pʀetɑ̃dʀ/ **[v6]** **A** *vt* to claim; **à ce qu'il prétend** according to him; **on le prétend très spirituel** he is said to be very witty
B prétendre à *v+prep* to claim ‹*damages*›; to aspire to ‹*job*›
C se prétendre *v refl* (+ *v être*) **il se prétend artiste** he makes out *or* claims he is an artist

prétendu, ~e /pʀetɑ̃dy/ *adj* ‹*culprit*› alleged; ‹*doctor*› would-be

prétendument /pʀetɑ̃dymɑ̃/ *adv* supposedly

prête-nom, *pl* **~s** /pʀɛtnɔ̃/ *m* frontman, man of straw; **société ~** dummy (AmE) company

prétentieux, -ieuse /pʀetɑ̃sjø, øz/ **A** *adj* pretentious
B *mf* pretentious person

prétention /pʀetɑ̃sjɔ̃/ **A** *f* **1** pretentiousness; **être sans ~** to be unpretentious
2 avoir la ~ de faire to claim to do
B prétentions *fpl* **quelles sont vos ~s?** what salary are you asking for?

prêter /pʀete/ **[v1]** **A** *vt* **1** to lend ‹*money, object*›; **~ sur gages** to loan against security
2 ~ attention à to pay attention to; **~ la main à qn** to lend sb a hand; **~ l'oreille** to listen; **~ serment** to take an oath
3 ~ à qn to attribute [sth] to sb
B prêter à *v+prep* to give rise to ‹*confusion*›; **son attitude prête à rire** his/her attitude is ridiculous; **tout prête à croire** *or* **penser que...** all the indications would suggest that...
C se prêter *v refl* (+ *v être*) **1 se ~ à** to take part in
2 roman qui se prête à une adaptation cinématographique novel which lends itself to a film adaptation

prétérit /pʀeteʀit/ *m* preterite

prêteur, -euse /pʀɛtœʀ, øz/ **A** *adj* **il n'est pas ~** he's very possessive about his belongings
B *mf* **~ sur gages** pawnbroker

prétexte /pʀetɛkst/ *m* excuse, pretext; **donner qch comme ~, prendre ~ de qch**

to use sth as an excuse; **sous aucun ~** on no account

prétexter /pʀetɛkste/ [**v1**] **A** *vt* to use [sth] as an excuse, to plead
B prétexter de *v+prep* **~ de qch pour faire** to use sth as an excuse for doing

prêtre /pʀɛtʀ/ *m* priest

prêtresse /pʀɛtʀɛs/ *f* priestess

preuve /pʀœv/ *f* **1** proof; **une ~** a piece of evidence; **apporter la ~ de/que** to offer proof of/that; **la ~ est faite de/que** now there is proof of/that; **~ en main** with concrete proof; **faire ses ~s** to prove oneself
2 demonstration; **faire ~ de** to show; **~ de bonne volonté** gesture of goodwill

prévaloir /pʀevalwaʀ/ [**v45**] **A** *vi* to prevail
B se prévaloir *v refl* (+ *v être*) **se ~ de son ancienneté** to claim seniority

prévenance /pʀevnɑ̃s/ *f* consideration

prévenant, **~e** /pʀevnɑ̃, ɑ̃t/ *adj* considerate

prévenir /pʀevniʀ/ [**v36**] *vt* **1** to tell
2 to call ‹*doctor, police*›
3 to warn
4 to prevent ‹*disaster*›
5 to anticipate ‹*wishes*›
IDIOM **mieux vaut ~ que guérir** (Proverb) prevention is better than cure

préventif, **-ive** /pʀevɑ̃tif, iv/ *adj* preventive

prévention /pʀevɑ̃sjɔ̃/ *f* prevention; **faire de la ~** to take preventive action

prévenu, **~e** /pʀevny/ *mf* (Law) defendant

prévisible /pʀevizibl/ *adj* predictable

prévision /pʀevizjɔ̃/ *f* **1** forecasting; **en ~ de** in anticipation of
2 prediction; forecast; **~s météorologiques** weather forecast

P

prévisionnel, **-elle** /pʀevizjɔnɛl/ *adj* projected

prévisionniste /pʀevizjɔnist/ *mf* forecaster

prévoir /pʀevwaʀ/ [**v42**] *vt* **1** to predict ‹*change*›; to foresee ‹*event, victory*›; to anticipate ‹*reaction*›; to forecast ‹*result, weather*›; **c'était à ~!** that was predictable!
2 to plan ‹*meeting, journey, building*›; to set the date for ‹*return, move*›; (Law) to make provision for ‹*case, eventuality*›; **ce n'était pas prévu!** that wasn't meant to happen!; **remplissez le formulaire prévu à cet effet** fill in the appropriate form; **tout a été prévu** all the arrangements have been made
3 to make sure one takes ‹*coat, umbrella*›
4 to expect ‹*visitor, shortage, strike*›
5 to allow ‹*sum of money, time*›

prévoyance /pʀevwajɑ̃s/ *f* foresight

prévoyant, **~e** /pʀevwajɑ̃, ɑ̃t/ *adj* far-sighted

prévu, **~e** /pʀevy/ ▸ **prévoir**

prier /pʀije/ [**v2**] **A** *vt* **1 ~ qn de faire** to ask sb to do; **je vous prie d'excuser mon retard** I'm so sorry I'm late; **je vous prie de vous taire** will you kindly be quiet; **elle ne s'est pas fait ~** she didn't have to be asked twice
2 to pray to ‹*god*›; **~ que** to pray that
B *vi* to pray

prière /pʀijɛʀ/ *f* **1** prayer; **faire sa ~** to say one's prayers
2 request; plea, entreaty; **~ de ne pas fumer** no smoking please

prieuré /pʀijœʀe/ *m* **1** priory
2 priory church

primaire /pʀimɛʀ/ **A** *adj* **1** primary
2 ‹*person*› limited; ‹*reasoning*› simplistic
B *m* **1** (Sch) **le ~** primary education
2 (Econ) **le ~** the primary sector
3 le ~ the Palaeozoic era

primate /pʀimat/ *m* primate

primauté /pʀimote/ *f* primacy

prime /pʀim/ **A** *adj* **1 de ~ abord** at first, initially
2 A ~ A prime
B *f* **1** bonus; free gift
2 allowance
3 subsidy
4 (in insurance) premium
■ **~ d'ancienneté** seniority bonus; **~ de risque** danger money

primer /pʀime/ [**v1**] **A** *vt* **1** to take precedence over, to prevail over
2 to award a prize to
B primer sur *v+prep* (controversial) ▸ **A1**
C *vi* **pour moi, c'est la qualité qui prime** what counts for me is quality

primeur /pʀimœʀ/ **A** *f* **avoir la ~ de l'information** to be the first to hear sth
B primeurs *fpl* early fruit and vegetables

primevère /pʀimvɛʀ/ *f* primrose

primitif, **-ive** /pʀimitif, iv/ *adj* (gen) primitive; ‹*budget*› initial; ‹*project, state*› original

primoaccédant /pʀimoaksedɑ̃/ *mf* first-time buyer

primordial, **~e**, *mpl* **-iaux** /pʀimɔʀdjal, o/ *adj* essential, vital

prince /pʀɛ̃s/ *m* prince
IDIOM **être bon ~** to be magnanimous

princesse /pʀɛ̃sɛs/ *f* princess
IDIOM **aux frais de la ~** (fam) at the company's expense; at sb's expense

princier, **-ière** /pʀɛ̃sje, ɛʀ/ *adj* ‹*title, tastes, sum*› princely; ‹*luxury*› dazzling

principal, **~e**, *mpl* **-aux** /pʀɛ̃sipal, o/ **A** *adj* **1** ‹*factor*› main; ‹*task*› principal
2 ‹*country, role*› leading
3 ‹*inspector*› chief
B *m* **1 le ~** the main thing
2 (Sch) principal

principalement /pʀɛ̃sipalmɑ̃/ *adv* mainly

principauté /pʀɛ̃sipote/ *f* principality

principe /pʀɛ̃sip/ **A** *m* **1** principle; **par ~** on principle
2 assumption

3 (concept) principle; **quel est le ~ de la machine à vapeur?** how does a steam engine work?
B en principe *phr* **1** as a rule
2 in theory

printanier, **-ière** /pʀɛ̃tanje, ɛʀ/ *adj* ‹*sun*› spring; ‹*weather*› spring-like

printemps /pʀɛ̃tɑ̃/ *m inv* **1** spring
2 (fam) **mes 60 ~** my 60 summers

printemps arabe *m* Arab spring

prion /pʀijɔ̃/ *m* prion

priori ▶ **a priori**

prioritaire /pʀijɔʀitɛʀ/ *adj* ‹*file, project*› priority; **être ~** to have priority

priorité /pʀijɔʀite/ *f* priority; **avoir la ~** to have right (BrE) *or* the right (AmE) of way

pris, **~e** /pʀi, pʀiz/ **A** *pp* ▶ **prendre**
B *pp adj* **1** busy; **j'ai les mains ~es** I've got my hands full; **les places sont toutes ~es** all the seats are taken
2 ‹*nose*› stuffed up; ‹*lungs*› congested
3 ~ de overcome with; **~ de panique** panic-stricken

prise /pʀiz/ *f* **1** storming; **la ~ de la Bastille** the storming of the Bastille
2 catching; **une belle ~** a fine catch
3 (in judo, wrestling) hold
4 n'offrir aucune ~ to have no handholds; to have no footholds; **avoir ~ sur qn** to have a hold over sb; **donner ~ à** to lay oneself open to
5 socket (BrE), outlet (AmE); **~ multiple** (multi-plug) adaptor; trailing socket
■ **~ de bec** (fam) row, argument; **~ en charge** (of expenses) payment; **~ de conscience** realization; **~ de contact** initial contact; **~ de courant** socket (BrE), outlet (AmE); **~ d'eau** water supply point; **~ de sang** blood test; **~ de vue** shooting; shot
IDIOM **être aux ~s avec des difficultés** to be grappling with difficulties

priser /pʀize/ [**v1**] *vt* **1** to hold [sth] in esteem
2 ~ (du tabac) to take snuff

prisme /pʀism/ *m* prism

prison /pʀizɔ̃/ *f* prison; **condamné à trois ans de ~** sentenced to three years' imprisonment

prisonnier, **-ière** /pʀizɔnje, ɛʀ/ **A** *adj* **il est ~** he is a prisoner
B *mf* prisoner

privatif, **-ive** /pʀivatif, iv/ *adj* private

privation /pʀivasjɔ̃/ *f* **1** (of rights) deprivation
2 want; **s'imposer des ~s** to make sacrifices

privatisation /pʀivatizasjɔ̃/ *f* privatization

privatiser /pʀivatize/ [**v1**] *vt* to privatize

privé, **~e** /pʀive/ **A** *pp* ▶ **priver**
B *pp adj* **~ de** deprived of; **tu seras ~ de dessert!** you'll go without dessert!
C *adj* (gen) private; ‹*interview*› unofficial
D *m* **1** (Econ) private sector
2 (Sch) **le ~** private schools
3 en ~ in private

priver /pʀive/ [**v1**] **A** *vt* **~ qn/qch de** to deprive sb/sth of; **~ qn de sorties** to forbid sb to go out
B se priver *v refl* (+ *v être*) **pourquoi se ~?** why deprive ourselves?; **se ~ de qch/de faire** to go *or* do without sth/doing

privilège /pʀivilɛʒ/ *m* privilege

privilégié, **~e** /pʀivileʒje/ **A** *pp* ▶ **privilégier**
B *pp adj* **1** privileged
2 fortunate
3 ‹*moment, links*› special; ‹*treatment*› preferential

privilégier /pʀivileʒje/ [**v2**] *vt* **1** to favour (BrE)
2 to give priority to

prix /pʀi/ *m inv* **1** price; **à** *or* **au ~ coûtant** at cost price; **acheter qch à ~ d'or** to pay a small fortune for sth; **il faut être prêt à y mettre le ~** you have to be prepared to pay for it; **mettre qch à ~ à 50 euros** to start the bidding for sth at 50 euros
2 (fig) price; **à tout ~** at all costs; **attacher beaucoup de ~ à** to value [sth] highly ‹*friendship*›
3 prize

pro /pʀo/ *pref also* **pro-** pro, pro-

probabilité /pʀɔbabilite/ *f* **1** probability, likelihood
2 les ~s probability theory

probable /pʀɔbabl/ *adj* probable, likely

probablement /pʀɔbabləmɑ̃/ *adv* probably

probant, **~e** /pʀɔbɑ̃, ɑ̃t/ *adj* ‹*argument, demonstration*› convincing; ‹*force, proof*› conclusive

probatoire /pʀɔbatwaʀ/ *adj* **examen ~** assessment test; **épreuve ~** aptitude test

probité /pʀɔbite/ *f* integrity, probity

problématique /pʀɔblematik/ *adj* ‹*situation*› problematic; ‹*outcome*› uncertain

problème /pʀɔblɛm/ *m* problem

procédé /pʀɔsede/ *m* **1** process
2 practice (BrE); **échange de bons ~s** exchange of courtesies

procéder /pʀɔsede/ [**v14**] **A procéder à** *v+prep* to carry out ‹*check, survey*›; to undertake ‹*reform*›; **~ à un tirage au sort/un vote** to hold a draw/a vote
B procéder de *v+prep* to be a product of
C *vi* to go about things; **~ par élimination** to use a process of elimination

procédure /pʀɔsedyʀ/ *f* **1** proceedings
2 procedure

procès /pʀɔsɛ/ *m inv* **1** trial
2 lawsuit, case; **intenter un ~ à qn** to sue sb
3 indictment; **faire le ~ de qn/qch** to put sb/sth in the dock
IDIOM **sans autre forme de ~** without further ado

processeur /pʀɔsesœʀ/ *m* processor

procession /pʀɔsesjɔ̃/ *f* procession

p

processus /pʀɔsesys/ *m inv* **1** process
2 (Med) evolution

procès-verbal, *pl* **-aux** /pʀɔsɛvɛʀbal, o/ *m*
1 (of meeting) minutes
2 statement of offence (BrE)

prochain, **~e** /pʀɔʃɛ̃, ɛn/ **A** *adj* **1** next; **en juin ~** next June; **à la ~e!** (fam) see you! (fam)
2 ‹*meeting*› coming, forthcoming; ‹*departure, war*› imminent; **un jour ~** one day soon
B *m* fellow man; **aime ton ~** love thy neighbour (BrE)

prochainement /pʀɔʃɛnmɑ̃/ *adv* soon

proche /pʀɔʃ/ **A** *adj* **1** nearby; **~ de** close to, near
2 ‹*departure*› imminent; **la victoire est ~** victory is at hand; **la fin est ~** the end is (drawing) near
3 ‹*event*› recent; ‹*memory*› real, vivid
4 similar; **~ de** ‹*figure, language*› close to; ‹*attitude*› verging on
5 ‹*people*› close; (on form) **(plus) ~ parent** next of kin
B *m* **1** close relative
2 close friend

Proche-Orient /pʀɔʃɔʀjɑ̃/ *pr m* **le ~** the Near East

proclamation /pʀɔklamasjɔ̃/ *f* proclamation

proclamer /pʀɔklame/ [**v1**] *vt* **1** to proclaim
2 to declare

procréer /pʀɔkʀee/ [**v11**] *vi* to procreate

procuration /pʀɔkyʀasjɔ̃/ *f* **1** power of attorney
2 proxy; proxy form

procurer /pʀɔkyʀe/ [**v1**] **A** *vt* to bring; to give
B **se procurer** *v refl* (+ *v être*) **1** to obtain
2 to buy

procureur /pʀɔkyʀœʀ/ *m* prosecutor

prodige /pʀɔdiʒ/ *m* **1** prodigy
2 feat; **faire des ~s** to work wonders; **~ technique** technical miracle

prodigieux, **-ieuse** /pʀɔdiʒjø, øz/ *adj* ‹*quantity*› prodigious; ‹*person*› wonderful

prodigue /pʀɔdig/ *adj* **1** extravagant
2 être ~ de to be lavish with

prodiguer /pʀɔdige/ [**v1**] *vt* **1** to give lots of ‹*advice*›
2 to give ‹*treatment, first aid*›

producteur, **-trice** /pʀɔdyktœʀ, tʀis/ **A** *adj* **pays ~ de pétrole** oil-producing country
B *mf* producer

productif, **-ive** /pʀɔdyktif, iv/ *adj* ‹*work*› productive; ‹*investment*› profitable

production /pʀɔdyksjɔ̃/ *f* **1** (gen) production; (of energy) generation
2 (gen) products, goods
■ **~ assistée par ordinateur**, **PAO** computer aided manufacturing, CAM

P

productivité /pʀɔdyktivite/ *f* productivity

produire /pʀɔdɥiʀ/ [**v69**] **A** *vt* **1** (gen) to produce; **cette usine produit peu** this factory has a low output; **un artiste/écrivain qui produit beaucoup** a prolific artist/writer
2 to bring in ‹*money, wealth*›; to yield ‹*interest*›
3 to produce, to have ‹*effect, result*›; to create, to make ‹*impression*›; to cause ‹*sensation, emotion*›
B **se produire** *v refl* (+ *v être*) **1** ‹*event*› to occur, to happen
2 ‹*singer*› to perform

produit /pʀɔdɥi/ *m* **1** product; **des ~s** goods, products; **~s alimentaires** foodstuffs; **~s agricoles** agricultural produce
2 income; yield, return; profit; **vivre du ~ de sa terre** to live off the land; **le ~ de la vente** the proceeds of the sale
3 (of research) result; (of activity) product
■ **~ chimique** chemical; **~ d'entretien** cleaning product, household product; **~ intérieur brut**, **PIB** gross domestic product, GDP; **~ national brut**, **PNB** gross national product, GNP

proéminent, **~e** /pʀɔeminɑ̃, ɑ̃t/ *adj* prominent

profanateur, **-trice** /pʀɔfanatœʀ, tʀis/ *mf* profaner

profanation /pʀɔfanasjɔ̃/ *f* desecration; defilement; debasement

profane /pʀɔfan/ **A** *adj* secular
B *mf* **1** layman/laywoman
2 non-believer
C *m* **le ~ et le sacré** the sacred and the profane

profaner /pʀɔfane/ [**v1**] *vt* to desecrate ‹*temple*›; to defile ‹*memory*›; to debase ‹*institution*›

proférer /pʀɔfeʀe/ [**v14**] *vt* to hurl ‹*insults*›; to make ‹*threats*›; to utter ‹*words*›

professer /pʀɔfese/ [**v1**] *vt* to profess

professeur /pʀɔfesœʀ/ *m* (in school) teacher; (in higher education) lecturer (BrE), professor (AmE); (holding university chair) professor; **~ des écoles** primary school teacher

profession /pʀɔfesjɔ̃/ *f* **1** occupation; profession; **exercer la ~ d'infirmière** to be a nurse by profession; **être sans ~** to have no occupation
2 declaration, profession
■ **~ libérale** profession

professionnalisme /pʀɔfesjɔnalism/ *m* professionalism

professionnel, **-elle** /pʀɔfesjɔnɛl/
A *adj* **1** ‹*qualifications*› professional; ‹*life, environment*› working; ‹*disease*› occupational; ‹*training*› vocational
2 ‹*player*› professional
B *mf* professional; **le salon est réservé aux ~s** the fair is restricted to people in the trade

key word

professionnellement /pRɔfesjɔnɛlmɑ̃/ *adv* professionally

professoral, **~e**, *mpl* **-aux** /pRɔfesɔRal, o/ *adj* professorial

profil /pRɔfil/ *m* profile; **être de ~** to be in profile; **se mettre de ~** to turn sideways

profiler /pRɔfile/ [**v1**] **A** *vt* **la tour profile sa silhouette dans le ciel** the tower is silhouetted *or* outlined against the sky
B se profiler *v refl* (+ *v être*) ‹*shape*› to stand out; ‹*problem*› to emerge; ‹*events*› to approach

profit /pRɔfi/ *m* **1** benefit, advantage; **au ~ des handicapés** in aid of the disabled; **mettre à ~** to make the most of ‹*free time, course*›; to turn [sth] to good account ‹*situation*›; to make good use of ‹*idea*›
2 profit; **être une source de ~ pour** to be a source of wealth for

profitable /pRɔfitabl/ *adj* **1** beneficial
2 profitable

profiter /pRɔfite/ [**v1**] **A profiter à** *v+prep* **~ à qn** to benefit sb
B profiter de *v+prep* to use ‹*advantage*›; to make the most of ‹*holiday, situation*›; to take advantage of ‹*visit, weakness, person*›
C *vi* (fam) ‹*person*› to grow; ‹*plant*› to thrive

profiteur, **-euse** /pRɔfitœR, øz/ *mf* profiteer

profond, **~e** /pRɔfɔ̃, ɔ̃d/ **A** *adj* **1** deep; **peu ~** shallow
2 ‹*boredom*› acute; ‹*sigh*› heavy; ‹*feeling, sleep, colour*› deep
3 ‹*change, ignorance*› profound
4 ‹*mind, remark*› profound; ‹*gaze*› penetrating
5 la France ~e provincial France; **l'Amérique ~e** small-town America
B *adv* deeply, deep down

profondément /pRɔfɔ̃demɑ̃/ *adv* **1** ‹*dig*› deep
2 deeply; greatly; profoundly; **détester ~** to loathe

profondeur /pRɔfɔ̃dœR/ *f* **1** depth; **avoir une ~ de 3 mètres** to be 3 metres (BrE) deep
2 (of feeling) depth; (of remark, work) profundity; **en ~** ‹*analysis*› in-depth; ‹*work*› thorough

profusion /pRɔfyzjɔ̃/ *f* profusion; abundance

progéniture /pRɔʒenityR/ *f* progeny

progiciel /pRɔʒisjɛl/ *m* software package

programmateur, **-trice** /pRɔgRamatœR, tRis/ **A** *mf* programme (BrE) planner
B *m* timer

programmation /pRɔgRamasjɔ̃/ *f* programming

programme /pRɔgRam/ *m* **1** programme (BrE)
2 (of action) plan; (of work) programme (BrE); **c'est tout un ~!** (hum) that'll take some doing!
3 (Sch) syllabus
4 (Comput) program

programmer /pRɔgRame/ [**v1**] *vt* **1** to schedule ‹*broadcast*›; to plan ‹*work*›
2 (Comput) to program

programmeur, **-euse** /pRɔgRamœR, øz/ *mf* (computer) programmer

progrès /pRɔgRɛ/ *m inv* **1** progress; **les ~ de la médecine** advances in medicine; **être en ~** ‹*person*› to be making progress; ‹*results*› to be improving
2 increase; **être en ~ de 10%** to be up by 10%
3 (of illness) progression

progresser /pRɔgRese/ [**v1**] *vi* **1** to rise; to increase; **~ de 3%** ‹*rate*› to rise by 3%; ‹*party*› to gain 3%
2 ‹*politician*› to make gains; ‹*illness*› to spread; ‹*crime*› to be on the increase
3 ‹*pupil, inquiry, country*› to make progress; ‹*relations*› to improve; ‹*technology*› to progress
4 ‹*climber*› to make progress; ‹*army*› to advance

progressif, **-ive** /pRɔgResif, iv/ *adj* progressive

progression /pRɔgResjɔ̃/ *f* **1** progress; advance; spread; increase
2 (in mathematics, music) progression

progressiste /pRɔgResist/ *adj* progressive

prohibé, **~e** /pRɔibe/ *adj* ‹*goods, substance, weapon*› prohibited; ‹*trade, action*› illegal; **port d'arme ~** illegal possession of a firearm

prohiber /pRɔibe/ [**v1**] *vt* to prohibit

prohibitif, **-ive** /pRɔibitif, iv/ *adj* **1** ‹*price*› prohibitive
2 ‹*law*› prohibition

prohibition /pRɔibisjɔ̃/ *f* prohibition

proie /pRwa/ *f* prey; **être en ~ à l'angoisse** to be racked by anxiety; **pays en ~ à la guerre civile** country in the grip of civil war

projecteur /pRɔʒɛktœR/ *m* **1** searchlight; floodlight; **être sous les ~s** to be in the spotlight
2 projector

projectile /pRɔʒɛktil/ *m* missile; projectile

projection /pRɔʒɛksjɔ̃/ *f* **1 l'éruption commença par une ~ de cendres** the eruption began with a discharge of ashes
2 le cuisinier a reçu des ~s d'huile bouillante the cook got spattered with scalding oil
3 projection; showing; **salle de ~** screening room

projectionniste /pRɔʒɛksjɔnist/ *mf* projectionist

projet /pRɔʒɛ/ *m* **1** plan; **en ~, à l'état de ~** at the planning stage
2 project
3 (rough) draft
4 (in architecture) execution plan
■ **~ de loi** (government) bill

projeter /pRɔʒte/ [**v20**] *vt* **1** to throw; **le choc l'a projeté par terre** the shock sent him

p

hurtling to the ground
2 to cast ‹*shadow*›
3 to show ‹*film*›
4 to plan (**de faire** to do)

prolétaire /pʀɔletɛʀ/ *adj, mf* proletarian

prolétariat /pʀɔletaʀja/ *m* proletariat

proliférer /pʀɔlifeʀe/ [**v14**] *vi* to proliferate

prolifique /pʀɔlifik/ *adj* prolific

prolixe /pʀɔliks/ *adj* verbose, prolix

prologue /pʀɔlɔg/ *m* prologue

prolongation /pʀɔlɔ̃gasjɔ̃/ *f* continuation; extension; (Sport) extra time

prolongé, **~e** /pʀɔlɔ̃ʒe/ *adj* ‹*effort*› sustained; ‹*stay*› extended; ‹*exhibition*› prolonged

prolongement /pʀɔlɔ̃ʒmɑ̃/ *m* **1** (of road, stay) extension
2 la rue Berthollet se trouve dans le ~ de la rue de la Glacière Rue de la Glacière becomes Rue Berthollet

prolonger /pʀɔlɔ̃ʒe/ [**v13**] **A** *vt* to extend ‹*stay*›; to prolong ‹*meeting, life*›
B se prolonger *v refl* (+ *v être*) **1** to persist; to go on
2 ‹*street*› **se ~ jusqu'à** to go as far as

promenade /pʀɔmnad/ *f* **1** walk; ride; drive
2 walkway; promenade

promener /pʀɔmne/ [**v16**] **A** *vt* **1** to take [sb] out ‹*person*›; to take [sth] out for a walk ‹*animal*›; **ça te promènera** (fam) it'll get you out
2 to carry ‹*object*›
3 to show [sb] around
B se promener *v refl* (+ *v être*) to go for a walk/drive/ride

promeneur, **-euse** /pʀɔmnœʀ, øz/ *mf* walker

promesse /pʀɔmɛs/ *f* **1** promise; **avoir la ~ de qn** to have sb's word; **tenir ses ~s** to keep one's promises
2 ~ de vente agreement to sell
■ **~ en l'air** *or* **de Gascon** *or* **d'ivrogne** empty *or* idle promise

prometteur, **-euse** /pʀɔmɛtœʀ, øz/ *adj* promising

promettre /pʀɔmɛtʀ/ [**v60**] **A** *vt* **1 ~ qch à qn** to promise sb sth; **je te promets qu'il le regrettera** he'll regret it, I guarantee you
2 une soirée qui promet bien des surprises an evening that holds a few surprises in store
B *vi* **1** ‹*pupil*› to show promise; **un film qui promet** a film which sounds interesting
2 (fam) **cet enfant promet!** that child is going to be a handful!; **ça promet!** that promises to be fun!
C se promettre *v refl* (+ *v être*) **1** to promise oneself
2 se ~ de faire to resolve to do

promiscuité /pʀɔmiskɥite/ *f* lack of privacy

promontoire /pʀɔmɔ̃twaʀ/ *m* promontory

promoteur, **-trice** /pʀɔmɔtœʀ, tʀis/ *mf* **~ (immobilier)** property developer

promotion /pʀɔmɔsjɔ̃/ *f* **1** promotion
2 (special) offer; **en ~** on (special) offer

promotionnel, **-elle** /pʀɔmɔsjɔnɛl/ *adj* promotional

promouvoir /pʀɔmuvwaʀ/ [**v43**] *vt* to promote

prompt, **~e** /pʀɔ̃, pʀɔ̃t/ *adj* ‹*reaction*› prompt; ‹*gesture, glance*› swift; ‹*return*› sudden

promulguer /pʀɔmylge/ [**v1**] *vt* to promulgate

prôner /pʀone/ [**v1**] *vt* to advocate

pronom /pʀɔnɔ̃/ *m* pronoun

pronominal, **~e**, *mpl* **-aux** /pʀɔnɔminal, o/ *adj* pronominal

prononcé, **~e** /pʀɔnɔ̃se/ *adj* ‹*accent, taste*› strong; ‹*wrinkles*› deep; **avoir un goût ~ pour** to be particularly fond of

prononcer /pʀɔnɔ̃se/ [**v12**] **A** *vt* **1** to pronounce ‹*word*›
2 to mention ‹*name*›; to say ‹*phrase*›
3 to deliver ‹*speech*›
4 to pronounce ‹*death penalty*›; **~ le divorce** to grant a divorce
B se prononcer *v refl* (+ *v être*) **1** to be pronounced
2 se ~ contre/en faveur de qch to declare oneself against/in favour (BrE) of sth; **se ~ sur qch** to give one's opinion on sth

prononciation /pʀɔnɔ̃sjasjɔ̃/ *f* pronunciation

pronostic /pʀɔnɔstik/ *m* **1** forecast
2 prediction
3 (medical) prognosis

pronostiquer /pʀɔnɔstike/ [**v1**] *vt* (in sport) to forecast ‹*result*›; to herald ‹*defeat, victory*›

propagande /pʀɔpagɑ̃d/ *f* propaganda

propagateur, **-trice** /pʀɔpagatœʀ, tʀis/ *mf* proponent

propagation /pʀɔpagasjɔ̃/ *f* spread; propagation

propager /pʀɔpaʒe/ [**v13**] **A** *vt* to spread ‹*rumour, disease*›; to propagate ‹*species, sound*›
B se propager *v refl* (+ *v être*) to spread; to propagate

propane /pʀɔpan/ *m* propane

propension /pʀɔpɑ̃sjɔ̃/ *f* propensity

prophète /pʀɔfɛt/ *m* prophet

prophétie /pʀɔfesi/ *f* prophecy

prophétiser /pʀɔfetize/ [**v1**] *vt* to prophesy

propice /pʀɔpis/ *adj* favourable (BrE); **trouver le moment ~** to find the right moment

proportion /pʀɔpɔʀsjɔ̃/ *f* proportion; **en ~, ils sont mieux payés** they are proportionately better paid; **être sans ~ avec** to be out of (all) proportion to; **toutes**

key word

~s gardées relatively speaking

proportionnel, -elle /pʀɔpɔʀsjɔnɛl/ *adj* proportional

proportionnelle /pʀɔpɔʀsjɔnɛl/ *f* proportional representation

proportionner /pʀɔpɔʀsjɔne/ [**v1**] *vt* **~ qch à qch** to make sth proportional to sth; **proportionné à** proportional to

propos /pʀɔpo/ **A** *m inv* **1 à ~, je...** by the way, I...; **à ~ de** about; **à ~ de qui?** about who?; **à ce ~, je voudrais...** in this connection, I would like...
2 à ~ at the right moment; **mal à ~** at (just) the wrong moment
B *mpl* comments; **'~ recueillis par J. Brun'** 'interview by J. Brun'

proposer /pʀɔpoze/ [**v1**] **A** *vt* **1** to suggest
2 to offer ‹*drink, dish*›
3 to put forward ‹*solution*›; to propose ‹*strategy*›
B se proposer *v refl* (+ *v être*) **1 se ~ pour faire** to offer to do
2 se ~ de faire to intend to do

proposition /pʀɔpozisjɔ̃/ *f* **1** suggestion
2 proposal
3 clause
■ **~ de loi** ≈ bill

propre /pʀɔpʀ/ **A** *adj* **1** clean; **nous voilà ~s!** (fig) we're in a fine mess now!
2 tidy, neat
3 ‹*person, life*› decent; **des affaires pas très ~s** unsavoury (BrE) business
4 own; **ma ~ voiture** my own car; **ce sont tes ~s paroles** you said so yourself; those were your very words
5 of one's own; **chaque pays a des lois qui lui sont ~s** each country has its own particular laws
6 ‹*baby*› toilet-trained; ‹*animal*› house-trained (BrE), housebroken (AmE)
B propre à *phr* **1 ~ à** peculiar to
2 ~ à faire likely to do; liable to do
3 ~ à appropriate for; **produit déclaré ~ à la consommation** product fit for consumption
C *m* **1 mettre qch au ~** to make a fair copy of sth
2 c'est du ~! (ironic) that's very nice!
3 le ~ de cette nouvelle technologie est de faire what is peculiar to this new technology is that it does; **~ à rien** good-for-nothing

proprement /pʀɔpʀəmɑ̃/ *adv* **1** purely; **à ~ parler** strictly speaking
2 absolutely
3 really
4 literally; **l'air est devenu ~ irrespirable** the air has become literally unbreathable
5 specifically
6 well and truly; **le professeur l'a ~ remis à sa place** he was well and truly put in his place by the teacher
7 neatly
8 ‹*earn living*› honestly; ‹*live*› decently

propreté /pʀɔpʀəte/ *f* **1** cleanliness; **d'une ~ douteuse** not very clean
2 honesty

propriétaire /pʀɔpʀijetɛʀ/ *mf* **1** owner; **un petit ~** a small-scale property owner; **ils sont ~s de leur maison** they own their own house; **faire le tour du ~** to look round (BrE) *or* around the house
2 landlord/landlady

propriété /pʀɔpʀijete/ *f* **1** ownership
2 property; **~ privée** private property
3 (of substance) property
4 (of term) aptness
■ **~ artistique et littéraire** copyright

propulser /pʀɔpylse/ [**v1**] *vt* to propel

propulseur /pʀɔpylsœʀ/ **A** *adj m* propellant
B *m* engine; **~ (de fusée)** (rocket) engine
■ **~ à hélice** propeller

propulsion /pʀɔpylsjɔ̃/ *f* propulsion; **à ~ nucléaire** nuclear-powered

prorata /pʀɔʀata/ *m inv* proportion

proroger /pʀɔʀɔʒe/ [**v13**] *vt* **1** to defer ‹*date*›; to renew ‹*passport*›
2 to adjourn ‹*meeting*›

prosaïque /pʀɔzaik/ *adj* prosaic

proscription /pʀɔskʀipsjɔ̃/ *f* **1** proscription
2 banishment; **frapper qn de ~** to banish sb

proscrire /pʀɔskʀiʀ/ [**v67**] *vt* to ban; to banish

proscrit, ~e /pʀɔskʀi, it/ *mf* outcast

prose /pʀoz/ *f* **1** prose; **poème en ~** prose poem
2 (hum) distinctive prose

prosélytisme /pʀɔzelitism/ *m* proselytizing

prospecter /pʀɔspɛkte/ [**v1**] *vt* **1** to canvass
2 to prospect

prospecteur, -trice /pʀɔspɛktœʀ, tʀis/ *mf* **1** canvasser
2 prospector

prospectif, -ive /pʀɔspɛktif, iv/ *adj* long-term

prospection /pʀɔspɛksjɔ̃/ *f* **1** canvassing
2 prospecting

prospectus /pʀɔspɛktys/ *m inv* leaflet

prospère /pʀɔspɛʀ/ *adj* thriving; prosperous

prospérer /pʀɔspeʀe/ [**v14**] *vi* to thrive; to prosper

prospérité /pʀɔspeʀite/ *f* prosperity

prostate /pʀɔstat/ *f* prostate (gland)

prosternation /pʀɔstɛʀnasjɔ̃/ *f* **1** prostration
2 (fig) self-abasement

prosternement /pʀɔstɛʀnəmɑ̃/ *m* **1** prostrate position
2 prostration

prosterner: se prosterner /pʀɔstɛʀne/ [**v1**] *v refl* (+ *v être*) **1** to prostrate oneself
2 (fig) to grovel

prostitué /pʀɔstitɥe/ *m* (male) prostitute
prostituée /pʀɔstitɥe/ *f* prostitute
prostituer: se prostituer /pʀɔstitɥe/ [**v1**] *v refl* (+ *v être*) to prostitute oneself
prostitution /pʀɔstitysjɔ̃/ *f* prostitution
prostration /pʀɔstʀasjɔ̃/ *f* prostration
protagoniste /pʀɔtagɔnist/ *mf* protagonist
protecteur, -trice /pʀɔtɛktœʀ, tʀis/ **A** *adj* **1** protective
2 patronizing
B *mf* protector
⚷ **protection** /pʀɔtɛksjɔ̃/ *f* **1** protection; **être sous haute ∼** to be under tight security; **de ∼** ‹*screen, measures*› protective; ‹*zone, system*› protection
2 protective device
■ **∼ sociale** social welfare system
protectionnisme /pʀɔtɛksjɔnism/ *m* protectionism
protectionniste /pʀɔtɛksjɔnist/ *adj, mf* protectionist
protégé, ∼e /pʀɔteʒe/ *mf* protégé
⚷ **protéger** /pʀɔteʒe/ [**v15**] **A** *vt* to protect
B se protéger *v refl* (+ *v être*) to protect oneself
protège-slip, *pl* **∼s** /pʀɔtɛʒslip/ *m* panty-liner
protège-tibia, *pl* **∼s** /pʀɔtɛʒtibja/ *m* shin pad
protéine /pʀɔtein/ *f* protein
protestant, ∼e /pʀɔtɛstɑ̃, ɑ̃t/ *adj, mf* Protestant
protestantisme /pʀɔtɛstɑ̃tism/ *m* Protestantism
protestataire /pʀɔtɛstatɛʀ/ *mf* protester
protestation /pʀɔtɛstasjɔ̃/ *f* protest
protester /pʀɔtɛste/ [**v1**] **A protester de** *v+prep* **∼ de son innocence** to protest one's innocence
B *vi* to protest
prothèse /pʀɔtɛz/ *f* prosthesis; artificial limb; dentures; **∼ auditive** hearing aid
prothésiste /pʀɔtezist/ *mf* prosthetist
protocolaire /pʀɔtɔkɔlɛʀ/ *adj* formal; official; **question ∼** question of protocol
protocole /pʀɔtɔkɔl/ *m* **1** formalities; protocol
2 ∼ d'accord draft agreement
prototype /pʀɔtɔtip/ *m* prototype
protubérance /pʀɔtybeʀɑ̃s/ *f* protuberance
protubérant, ∼e /pʀɔtybeʀɑ̃, ɑ̃t/ *adj* protruding
prou /pʀu/ *adv* **peu ou ∼** more or less
proue /pʀu/ *f* prow, bow(s)
prouesse /pʀuɛs/ *f* feat; (ironic) exploit
⚷ **prouver** /pʀuve/ [**v1**] **A** *vt* **1** to prove
2 to show
3 to demonstrate

B se prouver *v refl* (+ *v être*) **1** to prove to oneself
2 ils se sont prouvé qu'ils s'aimaient they proved their love for each other
(IDIOM) **n'avoir plus rien à ∼** to have proved oneself
provenance /pʀɔvnɑ̃s/ *f* origin; **en ∼ de** from
provençal, ∼e, *mpl* **-aux** /pʀɔvɑ̃sal, o/ *adj* Provençal; **à la ∼e** (Culin) (à la) provençale
provenir /pʀɔvniʀ/ [**v36**] *vi* **1** to come (**de** from); **provenant de** from
2 to stem (**de** from)
proverbe /pʀɔvɛʀb/ *m* proverb
proverbial, ∼e, *mpl* **-iaux** /pʀɔvɛʀbjal, o/ *adj* proverbial
providence /pʀɔvidɑ̃s/ **A** *f* **1** salvation
2 providence
B (-)providence (*combining form*) **État(-)∼** welfare state
providentiel, -ielle /pʀɔvidɑ̃sjɛl/ *adj* providential
⚷ **province** /pʀɔvɛ̃s/ *f* **1** province
2 la ∼ the provinces; **ville de ∼** provincial town
provincial, ∼e, *mpl* **-iaux** /pʀɔvɛ̃sjal, o/ *adj, mf* provincial
proviseur /pʀɔvizœʀ/ *m* head teacher (BrE) *or* principal (AmE) (*of a lycée*)
provision /pʀɔvizjɔ̃/ **A** *f* **1** stock; supply
2 deposit; credit (balance)
B provisions *fpl* food shopping
provisoire /pʀɔvizwaʀ/ *adj* provisional; temporary
provisoirement /pʀɔvizwaʀmɑ̃/ *adv* provisionally
provocant, ∼e /pʀɔvɔkɑ̃, ɑ̃t/ *adj* provocative
provocateur, -trice /pʀɔvɔkatœʀ, tʀis/ *mf* agitator
provocation /pʀɔvɔkasjɔ̃/ *f* provocation
⚷ **provoquer** /pʀɔvɔke/ [**v1**] *vt* **1** to cause ‹*accident*›; to provoke ‹*reaction, anger*›; **∼ l'accouchement** to induce labour (BrE)
2 to provoke; **∼ qn en duel** to challenge sb to a duel
3 (sexually) to arouse
proxénète /pʀɔksenɛt/ *m* procurer, pimp
proxénétisme /pʀɔksenetism/ *m* procuring
proximité /pʀɔksimite/ *f* **1** nearness, proximity; **à ∼** nearby; **à ∼ de** near
2 imminence; **à cause de la ∼ de Noël** because it is/was so close to Christmas
prude /pʀyd/ *adj* prudish
prudemment /pʀydamɑ̃/ *adv* **1** carefully
2 cautiously
prudence /pʀydɑ̃s/ *f* caution; **avec ∼** cautiously; with caution; **par ∼** as a precaution; **redoubler de ∼** to be doubly careful
prudent, ∼e /pʀydɑ̃, ɑ̃t/ *adj* **1** careful; **ce n'est pas ∼ de faire** it isn't safe to do

⚷ key word

2 cautious
3 wise
prud'homme /pʀydɔm/ *m* **Conseil des ~s** ≈ industrial tribunal (BrE), labor relations board (AmE)
prune /pʀyn/ *f* **1** plum
2 plum brandy
IDIOM **pour des ~s** (fam) for nothing
pruneau, *pl* **~x** /pʀyno/ *m* prune
prunelle /pʀynɛl/ *f* **1** sloe; ≈ sloe gin
2 (of eye) pupil
prunier /pʀynje/ *m* plum tree
Prusse /pʀys/ *pr f* Prussia
PS /pees/ *m* (*abbr* = **post-scriptum**) PS
psalmodier /psalmɔdje/ [**v2**] *vi* to chant psalms
psaume /psom/ *m* psalm
pseudo- /psødo/ *pref* pseudo; **~-équilibre** so-called balance; **~-savant** self-styled scientist
pseudonyme /psødɔnim/ *m* pseudonym
psy /psi/ *mf* (fam) shrink (fam), therapist
psychanalyse /psikanaliz/ *f* psychoanalysis
psychanalyser /psikanalize/ [**v1**] *vt* to psychoanalyse (BrE)
psyché /psiʃe/ *f* **1** cheval glass
2 psyche
psychiatrie /psikjatʀi/ *f* psychiatry
psychiatrique /psikjatʀik/ *adj* psychiatric
psychique /psiʃik/ *adj* mental
psychisme /psiʃism/ *m* psyche
psychologie /psikɔlɔʒi/ *f* **1** psychology
2 (psychological) insight
psychologique /psikɔlɔʒik/ *adj* psychological
psychologue /psikɔlɔg/ **A** *adj* **être ~** to understand people very well
B *mf* psychologist
psychopathe /psikɔpat/ *mf* psychopath
psychose /psikoz/ *f* **1** psychosis
2 ~ de la guerre obsessive fear of war
psychosomatique /psikosɔmatik/ *adj* psychosomatic
psychothérapeute /psikoteʀapøt/ *mf* psychotherapist
psychothérapie /psikoteʀapi/ *f* psychotherapy
PTT /petete/ *fpl* (*abbr* = **Administration des postes et télécommunications et de la télédiffusion**) *former French postal and telecommunications service*
pu /py/ ▶ **pouvoir**[1]
puant, **~e** /pɥɑ̃, ɑ̃t/ *adj* **1** stinking; smelly
2 (fam) **un type ~** an incredibly arrogant guy (fam)
puanteur /pɥɑ̃tœʀ/ *f* stench
pub /pyb/ (fam) *abbr* ▶ **publicité**
pubère /pybɛʀ/ *adj* pubescent
puberté /pybɛʀte/ *f* puberty
pubis /pybis/ *m inv* pubes; pubis

public, **-ique** /pyblik/ **A** *adj* public; ‹*education*› state (BrE), public (AmE); ‹*company*› state-owned; **la dette publique** the national debt
B *m* **1** public; **'interdit au ~'** 'no admittance'; **'avis au ~'** 'public notice'
2 audience; spectators; **tous ~s** for all ages
3 readership
4 avoir un ~ to have a following
5 le ~ the public sector
publication /pyblikasjɔ̃/ *f* publication
■ **~ assistée par ordinateur, PAO** desktop publishing, DTP
publicitaire /pyblisitɛʀ/ **A** *adj* ‹*campaign*› advertising; ‹*gift*› promotional
B *mf* **il/elle est ~** he/she's in advertising
C *m* advertising agency
publicité /pyblisite/ *f* **1** advertising; **faire de la ~ pour** to advertise
2 (*also* **pub** (fam)) advertisement, advert (BrE), ad (fam)
3 publicity; **faire une mauvaise ~ à qn/qch** to give sb/sth a bad press
■ **~ comparative** knocking copy (fam); **~ mensongère** misleading advertising
publier /pyblije/ [**v2**] *vt* to publish
publiquement /pyblikmɑ̃/ *adv* publicly
puce /pys/ *f* **1** flea
2 (silicon) chip; **~ à mémoire** memory chip
IDIOMS **ça m'a mis la ~ à l'oreille** that set me thinking; **secouer les ~s à qn** (fam) to bawl sb out (fam)
puceau, *pl* **~x** /pyso/ *adj m* (fam) **il est encore ~** he's still a virgin
pucelle /pysɛl/ *adj f* (fam) **être ~** to be a virgin
puceron /pysʀɔ̃/ *m* aphid
pudeur /pydœʀ/ *f* **1** sense of modesty; **sans ~** shamelessly
2 decency; sense of propriety
pudibond, **~e** /pydibɔ̃, ɔ̃d/ *adj* prudish
pudique /pydik/ *adj* **1** modest
2 discreet
pudiquement /pydikmɑ̃/ *adv* **1** modestly
2 discreetly
puer /pɥe/ [**v1**] **A** *vt* to stink of
B *vi* to stink; **il puait des pieds** his feet stank
puéricultrice /pɥeʀikyltʀis/ *f* paediatric nurse
puériculture /pɥeʀikyltyʀ/ *f* childcare
puéril, **~e** /pɥeʀil/ *adj* childish; puerile
puis /pɥi/ *adv* **1** then; **des poires et ~ des pêches** pears and peaches; **et ~ quoi encore!** (fam) what next?
2 il va être en colère? et ~ (après)? (fam) so what if he's angry!
puisard /pɥizaʀ/ *m* soakaway (BrE), sink hole (AmE)
puiser /pɥize/ [**v1**] *vt* **~ qch dans qch** to draw sth from sth
puisque, **puisqu'** *before vowel or mute h* /pɥisk(ə)/ *conj* since; **~ c'est comme ça, je**

P

m'en vais if that's how it is, I'm off

⚷ **puissance** /pɥisɑ̃s/ *f* **1** power; **la ~ militaire** military strength *or* might
2 (country) power; **une grande ~** a superpower
3 (of light) intensity; (of sound) volume
4 (in algebra) power; **dix ~ trois** ten to the power (of) three

⚷ **puissant**, **~e** /pɥisɑ̃, ɑ̃t/ **A** *adj* powerful; strong
B puissants *mpl* **les ~s** the powerful

puits /pɥi/ *m* **1** well; **~ de pétrole** oil well
2 shaft
■ **~ de science** fount of knowledge

⚷ **pull** /pyl/ *m* (fam) sweater

pull-over, *pl* **~s** /pylɔvɛʀ/ *m* sweater

pullulement /pylylmɑ̃/ *m* **1** proliferation
2 multitude

pulluler /pylyle/ [**v1**] *vi* **1** to proliferate
2 les touristes pullulent dans la région the area is swarming with tourists

pulmonaire /pylmɔnɛʀ/ *adj* ‹*disease*› lung; ‹*artery*› pulmonary

pulpe /pylp/ *f* (of fruit) pulp; (of potato) flesh

pulpeux, **-euse** /pylpø, øz/ *adj* ‹*body, lips*› luscious; ‹*fruit*› fleshy

pulsation /pylsasjɔ̃/ *f* beat; **~s cardiaques** heartbeat; heartbeats

pulsion /pylsjɔ̃/ *f* impulse, urge

pulvérisation /pylveʀizasjɔ̃/ *f* **1** (liquid) spraying
2 (of solid) pulverization (BrE)

pulvériser /pylveʀize/ [**v1**] *vt* **1** to spray
2 to pulverize
3 to shatter (fam) ‹*record*›

puma /pyma/ *m* puma

punaise /pynɛz/ *f* **1** drawing pin (BrE), thumbtack (AmE)
2 (Zool) bug

punaiser /pynɛze/ [**v1**] *vt* (fam) to pin *or* tack (AmE) [sth] up

punch¹ /pɔ̃ʃ/ *m* (drink) punch

punch² /pœnʃ/ *m* **1** punch
2 energy; **avoir du ~** ‹*slogan*› to be punchy (fam); ‹*person*› to have drive

punching-ball, *pl* **~s** /pœnʃiŋbol/ *m* punchball (BrE), punching bag (AmE)

punir /pyniʀ/ [**v3**] *vt* to punish

punitif, **-ive** /pynitif, iv/ *adj* punitive

punition /pynisjɔ̃/ *f* **1** punishment
2 il n'a pas fait sa ~ he hasn't done the task he was given as punishment

pupille¹ /pypij/ *mf* ward; **~ de l'État** child in care; **~ de la Nation** war orphan

pupille² /pypij/ *f* (of eye) pupil

pupitre /pypitʀ/ *m* **1** control panel; console
2 music stand; music rest
3 desk
4 lectern

pupitreur, **-euse** /pypitʀœʀ, øz/ *mf* computer operator

⚷ **pur**, **~e** /pyʀ/ **A** *adj* **1** (gen) pure; ‹*diamond*› flawless; ‹*voice, sky*› clear
2 ‹*truth*› pure; ‹*coincidence, madness*› sheer; **en ~e perte** to no avail; **c'est de la paresse ~e et simple** it's laziness, pure and simple; **~ et dur** hard-line
3 ‹*tradition*› true; **un ~ produit de** a typical product of; **à l'état ~** ‹*genius*› sheer
B *mf* virtuous person

purée /pyʀe/ *f* purée; **~ (de pommes de terre)** mashed potatoes
■ **~ de pois** pea souper (BrE), fog

purement /pyʀmɑ̃/ *adv* purely

pureté /pyʀte/ *f* purity

purgatif, **-ive** /pyʀgatif, iv/ *adj* purgative

purgatoire /pyʀgatwaʀ/ *m* **le ~** purgatory

purge /pyʀʒ/ *f* **1** purgative
2 purge

purger /pyʀʒe/ [**v13**] *vt* **1** (Med) to purge
2 to bleed ‹*radiator*›; to drain ‹*pipe*›; to purify ‹*metal*›
3 (Law) to serve ‹*sentence*›

purificateur /pyʀifikatœʀ/ *m* **~ d'atmosphère** *or* **d'air** air purifier

purification /pyʀifikasjɔ̃/ *f* purification

purifier /pyʀifje/ [**v2**] *vt* to purify; to cleanse

purin /pyʀɛ̃/ *m* slurry

puriste /pyʀist/ *mf* purist

puritain, **~e** /pyʀitɛ̃, ɛn/ **A** *adj* puritanical; Puritan
B *mf* puritan; Puritan

pur-sang /pyʀsɑ̃/ *m inv* thoroughbred

pus /py/ *m inv* pus

pustule /pystyl/ *f* pustule

putois /pytwa/ *m inv* **1** polecat
2 skunk (fur)

putréfaction /pytʀefaksjɔ̃/ *f* putrefaction; **en état de ~** decomposing

putsch /putʃ/ *m* putsch

putt /pœt/ *m* putt

putter /pœte/ [**v1**] *vt* to putt

puzzle /pœzl, pyzl/ *m* jigsaw puzzle

PV /peve/ *m* (fam) (*abbr* = **procès-verbal**) fine; parking ticket; speeding ticket

PVC /pevese/ *m* (*abbr* = **chlorure de polyvinyle**) PVC

pygmée /pigme/ *mf* pygmy

pyjama /piʒama/ *m* (pair of) pyjamas (BrE), (pair of) pajamas (AmE)

pylône /pilon/ *m* pylon; (for radio, TV transmitter) mast; (of bridge) tower

pyramide /piʀamid/ *f* pyramid

pyrénéen, **-éenne** /piʀeneɛ̃, ɛn/ *adj* Pyrenean

pyrex® /piʀɛks/ *m inv* Pyrex®

pyrogravure /piʀogʀavyʀ/ *f* pokerwork

pyromane /piʀɔman/ *mf* pyromaniac; (Law) arsonist

python /pitɔ̃/ *m* python

⚷ key word

Qq

q, **Q** /ky/ *m inv* q, Q

qcm /kyseɛm/ *m* (*abbr* = **questionnaire à choix multiple**) multiple-choice questionnaire, mcq

QG /kyʒe/ *m*: *abbr* ▶ **quartier**

QI /kyi/ *m*: *abbr* ▶ **quotient**

qu' ▶ **que**

quadragénaire /kwadʀaʒenɛʀ/ *mf* forty year-old

quadrature /kwadʀatyʀ/ *f* quadrature; **c'est la ~ du cercle** it's like squaring the circle

quadriennal, **~e**, *mpl* **-aux** /kwadʀijenal, o/ *adj* **1** ‹*plan*› four-year
2 quadrennial

quadrillage /kadʀijaʒ/ *m* cross-ruling

quadrillé, **~e** /kadʀije/ *adj* ‹*paper*› squared

quadriller /kadʀije/ [**v1**] *vt* **1** ‹*police*› to spread one's net over
2 to cross-rule ‹*paper*›

quadrimoteur /k(w)adʀimɔtœʀ/ *m* four-engined plane

quadrupède /k(w)adʀypɛd/ *adj*, *m* quadruped

quadruple /k(w)adʀypl/ *m* **le ~ de cette quantité** four times this amount

quadruplé, **~e** /k(w)adʀyple/ *mf* quadruplet, quad

quai /kɛ/ *m* **1** quay; **le navire est à ~** the ship has docked
2 (of river) bank
3 (station) platform
■ **~ d'embarquement** loading dock; **Quai des Orfèvres** *criminal investigation department of the French police force*; **Quai d'Orsay** French Foreign Office

qualificatif, **-ive** /kalifikatif, iv/ **A** *adj* qualifying
B *m* **1** (in grammar) qualifier
2 term, word

qualification /kalifikasjɔ̃/ *f* **1** qualification
2 skills; **sans ~** unskilled

qualifié, **~e** /kalifje/ *adj* ‹*staff, labour*› skilled; qualified

qualifier /kalifje/ [**v2**] **A** *vt* **1** to describe
2 to qualify
B se qualifier *v refl* (+ *v être*) (Sport) to qualify

qualitatif, **-ive** /kalitatif, iv/ *adj* qualitative

🔑 **qualité** /kalite/ *f* **1** quality; **de première ~** of the highest quality; **avoir beaucoup de ~s** to have many qualities
2 en (sa) ~ de représentant in his/her capacity as a representative; **nom, prénom et ~** surname, first name and occupation

🔑 **quand** /kɑ̃, kɑ̃t/ **A** *conj* **1** when; **~ il arrivera, vous lui annoncerez la nouvelle** when he gets here, you can tell him the news; **~ je pense que ma fille va avoir dix ans!** to think that my daughter's almost ten!; **~ je vous le disais!** I told you so!
2 whenever; **~ il pleut plus de trois jours la cave est inondée** whenever it rains for more than three days, the cellar floods
3 even if; **~ (bien même) la terre s'écroulerait, il continuerait à dormir** he'd sleep through an earthquake
B *adv* when; **de ~ date votre dernière réunion?** when was your last meeting?; **depuis ~ habitez-vous ici?** how long have you been living here?; **à ~ la semaine de 30 heures?** (fam) when will we get a 30-hour working week?
C quand même *phr* still; **ils ne veulent pas de moi, mais j'irai ~ même!** they don't want me, but I'm still going!; **~ même, tu exagères!** (fam) come on, that's going too far!

🔑 **quant**: **quant à** /kɑ̃ta/ *phr* **1** as for; **la France, ~ à elle,...** as for France, it...
2 about, concerning

quantifier /kɑ̃tifje/ [**v2**] *vt* to quantify

quantitatif, **-ive** /kɑ̃titatif, iv/ *adj* quantitative

🔑 **quantité** /kɑ̃tite/ *f* **1** quantity, amount
2 des ~s de scores of ‹*people*›; a lot of ‹*things*›; **du pain/vin en ~** plenty of bread/wine

quarantaine /kaʀɑ̃tɛn/ *f* **1 une ~** about forty
2 être en ~ to be in quarantine; to be ostracized

quarante /kaʀɑ̃t/ *adj inv*, *pron*, *m inv* forty

quarante-cinq /kaʀɑ̃tsɛ̃k/ *adj inv*, *pron*, *m inv* forty-five
■ **~ tours** single

quarantième /kaʀɑ̃tjɛm/ *adj* fortieth

🔑 **quart** /kaʀ/ *m* **1** quarter; **un ~ d'heure** a quarter of an hour; **les trois ~s du temps** (fam) most of the time
2 quarter-litre (BrE) bottle; quarter-litre (BrE) pitcher
3 (Naut) **être de ~** to be on watch
■ **~ de cercle** quadrant; **~ de tour** 90° turn; **faire qch au ~ de tour** (fam) to do sth immediately

⚷ **quartier** /kaʀtje/ *m* **1** area, district; **de ~** ‹*cinema, grocer*› local
2 quarter; **un ~ de pommes** a slice of apple; **un ~ d'orange** an orange segment
3 (of moon) quarter
4 (Mil) **~s** quarters; **avoir ~ libre** to be off duty; to have time off
■ **~ général, QG** headquarters, HQ
IDIOM **ne pas faire de ~** to show no mercy

quart-monde /kaʀmɔ̃d/ *m inv* underclass

quartz /kwaʀts/ *m* quartz

quasi /kazi/ **A** *adv* almost
B quasi- (*combining form*) **~-indifférence** virtual indifference; **la ~-totalité de** almost all of; **à la ~-unanimité** almost unanimously

quasiment /kazimɑ̃/ *adv* (fam) practically

quaternaire /kwatɛʀnɛʀ/ *adj, m* Quaternary

quatorze /katɔʀz/ *adj inv, pron, m inv* fourteen
IDIOM **chercher midi à ~ heures** (fam) to complicate matters

quatorzième /katɔʀzjɛm/ *adj* fourteenth

quatrain /katʀɛ̃/ *m* quatrain

⚷ **quatre** /katʀ/ *adj inv, pron, m inv* four
IDIOMS **faire les ~ volontés de qn** to give in to sb's every whim; **être tiré à ~ épingles** to be dressed up to the nines (fam); **ne pas y aller par ~ chemins** not to beat about the bush; **je vais leur parler entre ~ yeux** I'm going to talk to them face to face; **monter un escalier ~ à ~** to go up the stairs four at a time; **être entre ~ planches** (fam) to be six feet under

quatre-heures /katʀœʀ/ *m inv* afternoon snack (*for children*)

quatre-quarts /kat(ʀə)kaʀ/ *m inv* pound cake

q

quatre-vingt /katʀəvɛ̃/ *adj, pron, m also* **quatre-vingts** eighty

quatre-vingt-dix /katʀəvɛ̃dis/ *adj inv, pron, m inv* ninety

quatre-vingt-dixième /katʀəvɛ̃dizjɛm/ *adj* ninetieth

quatre-vingtième /katʀəvɛ̃tjɛm/ *adj* eightieth

quatrième /katʀijɛm/ **A** *adj* fourth
B *f* **1** (Sch) *third year of secondary school, age 13–14*
2 (Aut) fourth (gear)
■ **le ~ âge** very old people
IDIOM **en ~ vitesse** (fam) in double quick time (fam)

quatuor /kwatɥɔʀ/ *m* quartet

⚷ **que, qu'** *before vowel or mute h* /k(ə)/
A *conj* **1** that; **je pense qu'il a raison** I think he's right; **je veux ~ tu m'accompagnes** I want you to come with me
2 so (that); **approche, ~ je te regarde** come closer so I can look at you
3 whether; **~ cela vous plaise ou non** whether you like it or not
4 si vous venez et ~ vous ayez le temps if you come and (if you) have the time
5 il n'était pas sitôt parti qu'elle appela la police no sooner had he left than she called the police
6 ~ tout le monde sorte! everyone must leave!; **~ ceux qui n'ont pas compris le disent** let anyone who hasn't understood say so; **qu'il crève!** (pop) let him rot! (fam)
7 than; as; **plus gros ~ moi** fatter than me; **aussi grand ~ mon frère** as tall as my brother
B *pron* what; **~ dire?** what can you say?; **je ne sais pas ce qu'il a dit** I don't know what he said; **qu'est-ce que c'est que ça?** what's that?
C *rel pron* that; who(m); which; **je n'aime pas la voiture ~ tu as achetée** I don't like the car (that) you've bought
D *adv* **~ c'est joli** it's so pretty; **~ de monde** what a lot of people

Québec /kebɛk/ **A** *pr m* **le ~** Quebec
B *pr n* Quebec

québécois, ~e /kebekwa, az/ *adj* of Quebec

Québécois, ~e /kebekwa, az/ *mf* Quebecois, Quebecker

⚷ **quel, quelle** /kɛl/ **A** *det* who; what; which; **je me demande quelle est la meilleure solution** I wonder what the best solution is; **de ces deux médicaments, ~ est le plus efficace?** which of these two medicines is more effective?
B *adj* **1** what; which; **quelle heure est-il?** what time is it?; **dans ~ tiroir l'as-tu mis?** which drawer did you put it in?; **~ âge as-tu?** how old are you?
2 what; how; **quelle coïncidence!** what a coincidence!
3 quelle que soit la route que l'on prenne whatever *or* whichever road we take; **~ que soit le vainqueur** whoever the winner may be

quelconque /kɛlkɔ̃k/ **A** *adj* ‹*person*› ordinary; ordinary-looking; ‹*novel, actor*› poor; ‹*restaurant*› second-rate; ‹*place*› characterless
B *adj* any; **si pour une raison ~** if for some reason or other; **si le livre avait un intérêt ~** if the book was in any way interesting

quelle ▸ **quel**

⚷ **quelque** /kɛlk/ **A** *quantif* some; a few; any; **depuis ~ temps** for some time; **je voudrais ajouter ~s mots** I'd like to add a few words; **ça dure trois heures et ~s** it lasts over three hours; **si pour ~ raison que ce soit** if for whatever reason
B *adv* **1 les ~ deux mille spectateurs** the two thousand odd spectators
2 however; **~ admirable que soit son attitude** however admirable his/her attitude may be
C quelque chose *pron* something;

⚷ key word

anything; **il y a ~ chose qui ne va pas** something's wrong; **si ~ chose leur arrive** if anything should happen to them; **il a ~ chose de son grand-père** he's got a look of his grandfather about him; **ça me dit ~ chose** it rings a bell

D quelque part *phr* somewhere; anywhere

E quelque peu *phr* somewhat

quelquefois /kɛlkəfwa/ *adv* sometimes

quelques-uns, **quelques-unes** /kɛlkəzœ̃, yn/ *pron* some, a few

quelqu'un /kɛlkœ̃/ *pron* someone, somebody; anyone, anybody; **~ d'autre** someone else; **c'est ~ de compétent** he/she is competent

quémander /kemɑ̃de/ [**v1**] *vt* to beg

qu'en-dira-t-on /kɑ̃diʀatɔ̃/ *m inv* gossip

quenelle /kənɛl/ *f: dumpling made of flour and egg, flavoured with meat or fish*

quenotte /kənɔt/ *f* (fam) toothy peg (fam), tooth

quenouille /kənuj/ *f* distaff

querelle /kəʀɛl/ *f* **1** quarrel; **chercher ~ à qn** to pick a quarrel with sb

2 dispute

quereller: **se quereller** /kəʀɛle/ [**v1**] *v refl* (+ *v être*) to quarrel

question /kɛstjɔ̃/ *f* **1** question; **je ne me suis jamais posé la ~** I've never really thought about it; **pose-leur la ~** ask them

2 matter, question; issue; **~ d'habitude!** it's a matter of habit; **en ~** in question; at issue; **(re)mettre en ~** to reappraise; to reassess; **se remettre en ~** to take a new look at oneself; **la ~ n'est pas là** that's not the point; **il est ~ d'elle dans l'article** she's mentioned in the article; **il n'est pas ~ que tu partes** you can't possibly leave; **pas ~!** no way! (fam)

3 (fam) **~ santé, ça va** where health is concerned, things are OK

questionnaire /kɛstjɔnɛʀ/ *m* questionnaire

questionner /kɛstjɔne/ [**v1**] *vt* to question

quête /kɛt/ *f* **1** collection; **faire la ~** to take the collection; to pass the hat round; to collect for charity

2 search; **la ~ du Graal** the quest for the Holy Grail

quêter /kete/ [**v1**] *vi* to take the collection; **~ pour une œuvre** to collect for a charity

quetsche /kwɛtʃ/ *f* (sweet purple) plum

queue /kø/ *f* **1** tail

2 (of flower) stem; (of apple) stalk (BrE), stem (AmE)

3 (of pot) handle

4 (Sport) cue

5 (of procession) tail(-end); (of train) rear, back; **ils arrivent en ~ (de peloton) des grandes entreprises** they come at the bottom of the league table of companies

6 faire la ~ to queue up (BrE), to stand in a queue (BrE), to stand in line (AmE)

IDIOMS **une histoire sans ~ ni tête** (fam) a cock and bull story; **la ~ basse** with one's tail between one's legs; **il n'y en avait pas la ~ d'un(e)** (fam) there were none to be seen; **faire une ~ de poisson à qn** to cut in front of sb; **finir en ~ de poisson** to fizzle out

queue-de-cheval, *pl* **queues-de-cheval** /kødʃəval/ *f* ponytail

queue-de-pie, *pl* **queues-de-pie** /kødpi/ *f* (fam) tails, tailcoat

queux /kø/ *m inv* (dated) **maître ~** chef

qui /ki/ **A** *pron* who; whom; **~ veut-elle voir?** who does she want to speak to?

B *rel pron* **1** who; that; which; **est-ce vous ~ venez d'appeler?** was it you who called just now?; **ce ~ me plaît chez lui** what I like about him

2 ~ que vous soyez whoever you are; **je n'ai jamais frappé ~ que ce soit** I've never hit anybody

quiche /kiʃ/ *f* quiche, flan

quiconque /kikɔ̃k/ **A** *rel pron* whoever, anyone who

B *pron* anyone, anybody

quiétude /kjetyd/ *f* tranquillity

quignon /kiɲɔ̃/ *m* crusty end (of a loaf)

quille /kij/ *f* **1** skittle

2 (Naut) keel

IDIOM **être reçu comme un chien dans un jeu de ~s** (fam) to be given a very unfriendly welcome

quincaillerie /kɛ̃kajʀi/ *f* **1** hardware shop (BrE) *or* store (AmE)

2 hardware

3 hardware business

quinconce /kɛ̃kɔ̃s/ *m* **en ~** in staggered rows

quinquagénaire /kɛ̃kaʒenɛʀ/ *mf* fifty year-old

quinquennal, **~e**, *mpl* **-aux** /kɛ̃kenal, o/ *adj* **1** ‹*plan*› five-year

2 five-yearly

quintal, *pl* **-aux** /kɛ̃tal, o/ *m* quintal

quinte /kɛ̃t/ *f* **1** (Mus) fifth

2 une ~ (de toux) a coughing fit

quintette /kɛ̃tɛt/ *m* quintet

quintuple /kɛ̃typl/ *m* **le ~ de cette quantité** five times the amount

quintuplé, **~e** /kɛ̃typle/ *mf* quintuplet, quin (BrE), quint (AmE)

quinzaine /kɛ̃zɛn/ *f* **1** fortnight (BrE), two weeks; **sous ~** within 2 weeks

2 une ~ about fifteen

quinze /kɛ̃z/ *adj inv, pron, m inv* fifteen

quinzième /kɛ̃zjɛm/ *adj* fifteenth

quiproquo /kipʀɔko/ *m* misunderstanding

quittance /kitɑ̃s/ *f* **1** receipt

2 bill

quitte /kit/ **A** *adj* **1 nous sommes ~s, je suis ~ avec lui** we're quits

2 en être ~ pour la peur/un rhume to get off

q

with a fright/a cold
B quitte à *phr* ~ **à aller à Londres, autant que ce soit pour quelques jours** if you're going to London anyway, you might as well go for a few days
■ ~ **ou double** double or quits

🗝 **quitter** /kite/ [**v1**] **A** *vt* **1** to leave ‹*place, person, road*›
2 to leave ‹*job, organization*›; ~ **la scène** to give up acting; **il ne l'a pas quittée des yeux de tout le repas** he didn't take his eyes off her throughout the meal; **ne quittez pas** hold the line
3 ‹*company*› to move from ‹*street*›; to move out of ‹*building*›
4 un grand homme nous a quittés a great man has passed away
5 to take off ‹*garment, hat*›
B se quitter *v refl* (+ *v être*) to part; **ils ne se quittent plus** they're inseparable now

qui-vive /kiviv/ *m inv* **être sur le** ~ to be on the alert

🗝 **quoi** /kwɑ/ **A** *pron* **1** what; **à** ~ **penses-tu?** what are you thinking about?; **à** ~ **bon recommencer?** what's the point of starting again?
2 ~ **qu'elle puisse en dire** whatever she may say; ~ **qu'il en soit** be that as it may
B *rel pron* **il n'y a rien sur** ~ **vous puissiez fonder vos accusations** there's nothing on which to base your accusations; **à** ~ **il a répondu** to which he replied; **après** ~ **ils sont partis** after which they left; **(il n'y a) pas de** ~**!** my pleasure; **il n'y a pas de** ~ **se fâcher** there's no reason to get angry; **il n'a (même) pas de** ~ **s'acheter un livre** he hasn't (even) got enough money to buy a book

🗝 **quoique**, **quoiqu'** *before vowel or mute h* /kwak(ə)/ *conj* although, though; **nous sommes mieux ici qu'à Paris,** ~ we're better off here than in Paris, but then (again)

quota /kɔta/ *m* quota (**sur** on)

quote-part, *pl* **quotes-parts** /kɔtpaʀ/ *f* share

🗝 **quotidien**, **-ienne** /kɔtidjɛ̃, ɛn/ **A** *adj*
1 daily
2 everyday
B *m* **1** daily (paper)
2 everyday life

quotidiennement /kɔtidjɛnmɑ̃/ *adv* every day, daily

quotient /kɔsjɑ̃/ *m* quotient
■ ~ **intellectuel, QI** intelligence quotient, IQ

Rr

r, **R** /ɛʀ/ *m inv* r, R

rab /ʀab/ *m* (fam) **1** extra; **faire du** ~ to do extra hours
2 demander du ~ to ask for seconds

rabâcher /ʀabɑʃe/ [**v1**] **A** *vt* to keep repeating
B *vi* to keep harping on

rabais /ʀabɛ/ *m inv* discount

rabaisser /ʀabese/ [**v1**] **A** *vt* to belittle
B se rabaisser *v refl* (+ *v être*) to demean oneself

rabat /ʀaba/ *m* (of bag, table, pocket) flap

rabat-joie /ʀabaʒwɑ/ *adj inv* **être** ~ to be a killjoy

rabattre /ʀabatʀ/ [**v61**] **A** *vt* **1** ‹*person*› to shut ‹*lid*›; to put *or* fold up ‹*foldaway seat, tray*›
2 to turn [sth] down ‹*collar, sheet*›
3 ‹*player*› to smash ‹*ball*›
4 ~ **le gibier** to beat the undergrowth for game
B se rabattre *v refl* (+ *v être*) **1** ‹*lid*› to shut; ‹*leaf of table*› to fold up
2 ‹*driver, vehicle*› to pull back in
3 se ~ **sur** to make do with

rabbin /ʀabɛ̃/ *m* rabbi; **grand** ~ chief rabbi

râblé, ~**e** /ʀɑble/ *adj* **1** ‹*animal*› sturdy
2 ‹*person*› stocky

rabot /ʀabo/ *m* (tool) plane

raboter /ʀabɔte/ [**v1**] *vt* to plane

rabougri, ~**e** /ʀabugʀi/ *adj* ‹*tree*› stunted

rabrouer /ʀabʀue/ [**v1**] *vt* to snub

racaille /ʀakaj/ *f* scum

raccommoder /ʀakɔmɔde/ [**v1**] *vt* **1** to darn ‹*socks*›
2 (fam) to reconcile ‹*people*›

raccompagner /ʀakɔ̃paɲe/ [**v1**] *vt* ~ **qn chez lui** to walk/to drive sb (back) home

raccord /ʀakɔʀ/ *m* **1** (in wallpaper) join
2 (in painting) touch-up
3 (in film) link shot

raccordement /ʀakɔʀdəmɑ̃/ *m* link road

raccorder /ʀakɔʀde/ [**v1**] *vt* to connect

raccourci /ʀakuʀsi/ *m* (road) shortcut

raccourcir /ʀakuʀsiʀ/ [**v3**] **A** *vt* **1** (gen) to shorten

---
🗝 key word

2 to cut ‹*text, speech*›
B *vi* ‹*days*› to get shorter, to draw in
IDIOM **tomber sur qn à bras raccourcis** (fam) to lay into sb

raccrocher /ʀakʀɔʃe/ [**v1**] **A** *vt* to hang [sth] back up
B *vi* to hang up
C **se raccrocher** *v refl* (+ *v être*) **se ~ à** to grab hold of ‹*rail*›; (fig) to cling to ‹*person, excuse*›

race /ʀas/ *f* **1** race
2 (Zool) breed; **chien de ~** pedigree (dog)

racheter /ʀaʃte/ [**v18**] **A** *vt* **1** to buy [sth] back
2 to buy some more ‹*wine*›
3 to buy new ‹*sheets*›
4 to buy out ‹*company, factory*›; **je rachète votre voiture 1 000 euros** I'll buy your car off you for 1,000 euros
5 to redeem ‹*sinner*›
B **se racheter** *v refl* (+ *v être*) to redeem oneself

rachitique /ʀaʃitik/ *adj* ‹*animal, plant, person*› scrawny

rachitisme /ʀaʃitism/ *m* rickets

racial, **~e**, *mpl* **-iaux** /ʀasjal, o/ *adj* racial; **émeutes ~es** race riots

racine /ʀasin/ *f* root

racisme /ʀasism/ *m* racism

raciste /ʀasist/ *adj, mf* racist

racket /ʀakɛt/ *m* extortion racket; racketeering

raclée /ʀɑkle/ *f* (fam) hiding (fam)

racler /ʀɑkle/ [**v1**] **A** *vt* **1** to scrape [sth] clean ‹*plate*›
2 to scrape off ‹*rust*›
3 to scrape against
B **se racler** *v refl* (+ *v être*) **se ~ la gorge** to clear one's throat

raclette /ʀɑklɛt/ *f* **1** raclette (*Swiss cheese dish*)
2 scraper

racolage /ʀakɔlaʒ/ *m* touting (**de** for); soliciting (**de** for)

racoler /ʀakɔle/ [**v1**] *vt* ‹*prostitute*› to solicit

racontar /ʀakɔ̃taʀ/ *m* (fam) **des ~s** idle gossip

raconter /ʀakɔ̃te/ [**v1**] *vt* to tell ‹*story*›; to describe ‹*incident*›; **~ qch à qn** to tell sb sth; **qu'est-ce que tu racontes?** what are you talking about?

racornir /ʀakɔʀniʀ/ [**v3**] *vt*, **se racornir** *v refl* (+ *v être*) **1** to harden
2 to shrivel (up)

radar /ʀadaʀ/ *m* radar; **~ automatique** speed camera

rade /ʀad/ *f* harbour (BrE); **rester en ~** (fam) ‹*person*› to be left stranded

radeau, *pl* **~x** /ʀado/ *m* raft

radiateur /ʀadjatœʀ/ *m* radiator; **~ électrique** electric heater

radiation /ʀadjasjɔ̃/ *f* radiation

radical, **~e**, *mpl* **-aux** /ʀadikal, o/ *adj, mf* radical

radicalement /ʀadikalmɑ̃/ *adv* radically; completely

radier /ʀadje/ [**v2**] *vt* **~ un médecin** to strike off a doctor (BrE), to take away a doctor's license (AmE); **~ un avocat** to disbar a lawyer

radieux, **-ieuse** /ʀadjø, øz/ *adj* **1** ‹*sun*› dazzling
2 ‹*weather*› glorious
3 ‹*face, smile*› radiant; ‹*person*› radiant with joy

radin, **~e** /ʀadɛ̃, in/ *adj* (fam) stingy (fam)

radinerie /ʀadinʀi/ *f* (fam) stinginess (fam)

radio¹ /ʀadjo/ **A** *adj inv* ‹*contact, signal*› radio
B *m* radio operator

radio² /ʀadjo/ *f* **1** radio
2 X-ray

radioactivité /ʀadjoaktivite/ *f* radioactivity

radiocassette /ʀadjokasɛt/ *m* radio cassette player

radio-crochet /ʀadjokʀɔʃɛ/ *m*: *singing competition on the radio*

radiodiffuser /ʀadjodifyze/ [**v1**] *vt* to broadcast

radiographie /ʀadjɔgʀafi/ *f* **1** radiography
2 X-ray (photograph)

radiologue /ʀadjɔlɔg/ *mf* radiologist

radiophonique /ʀadjofɔnik/ *adj* radio

radio-réveil, *pl* **radios-réveils** /ʀadjoʀevɛj/ *m* clock radio

radioscopie /ʀadjɔskɔpi/ *f* fluoroscopy

radiothérapie /ʀadjoteʀapi/ *f* radiotherapy

radis /ʀadi/ *m inv* radish; **je n'ai plus un ~** (fam) I haven't got a penny

radoter /ʀadɔte/ [**v1**] *vi* **1** to talk nonsense
2 to repeat oneself

radoucir: **se radoucir** /ʀadusiʀ/ [**v3**] *v refl* (+ *v être*) ‹*person*› to soften up; ‹*weather*› to turn milder

radoucissement /ʀadusismɑ̃/ *m* **la météo annonce un ~** the forecast is for milder weather

rafale /ʀafal/ *f* **1** (of wind, rain) gust; (of snow) flurry
2 (of gunfire) burst

raffermir /ʀafɛʀmiʀ/ [**v3**] *vt* **1** to tone ‹*skin*›; to tone up ‹*muscles*›
2 to strengthen ‹*position*›; to steady ‹*market*›

raffinage /ʀafinaʒ/ *m* refining

raffiné, **~e** /ʀafine/ *adj* refined; ‹*food*› sophisticated

raffinement /ʀafinmɑ̃/ *m* **1** refinement
2 elegance

raffiner /ʀafine/ [**v1**] *vt* to refine

raffinerie /ʀafinʀi/ *f* refinery; **~ de pétrole** oil refinery

r

raffoler /ʀafɔle/ [**v1**] *v+prep* ~ **de** to be crazy about (fam)

raffut /ʀafy/ *m* (fam) **1** racket (fam)
2 stink (fam), row

rafiot /ʀafjo/ *m* (fam) boat, (old) tub (fam)

rafistoler /ʀafistɔle/ [**v1**] *vt* (fam) to patch up

rafle /ʀɑfl/ *f* **1** raid
2 round-up

rafler /ʀɑfle/ [**v1**] *vt* (fam) **1** to make off with, to swipe (fam)
2 to walk off with ‹*medal, reward*›

rafraîchir /ʀafʀɛʃiʀ/ [**v3**] **A** *vt* ‹*rain*› to cool ‹*atmosphere*›; **le thé glacé te rafraîchira** the iced tea will cool you down
B se rafraîchir *v refl* (+ *v être*) ‹*weather*› to get cooler; ‹*person*› to refresh oneself
(IDIOM) ~ **la mémoire de qn** (fam) to refresh sb's memory

rafraîchissant, ~**e** /ʀafʀɛʃisɑ̃, ɑ̃t/ *adj* refreshing

rafraîchissement /ʀafʀɛʃismɑ̃/ *m* refreshment

ragaillardir /ʀagajaʀdiʀ/ [**v3**] *vt* to cheer [sb] up

rage /ʀaʒ/ *f* **1** rabies
2 rage; **être fou de** ~ to be in a mad rage; **faire** ~ ‹*disease*› to be rife; ‹*epidemic, fire*› to rage
■ ~ **de dents** raging toothache

rageant, ~**e** /ʀaʒɑ̃, ɑ̃t/ *adj* (fam) infuriating

rageusement /ʀaʒøzmɑ̃/ *adv* furiously; angrily

ragot /ʀago/ *m* (fam) malicious gossip

ragoût /ʀagu/ *m* stew, ragout

rai /ʀɛ/ *m* ~ **de lumière** ray of light

raï /ʀaj/ *m: music from the Maghreb with Western influences*

raid /ʀɛd/ *m* **1** (Mil) raid
2 (Sport) trek

raide /ʀɛd/ *adj* **1** (gen) stiff; ‹*hair*› straight; ‹*rope*› taut
2 steep
3 (fam) **je trouve ça un peu** ~ that's a bit steep
(IDIOMS) **être** ~ **comme un piquet** to be stiff as a ramrod; **tomber** ~ to be flabbergasted

raideur /ʀɛdœʀ/ *f* **1** stiffness
2 steepness

raidir /ʀɛdiʀ/ [**v3**] **A** *vt* to tense ‹*arm, body*›
B se raidir *v refl* (+ *v être*) ‹*body*› to tense up; **se** ~ **contre la douleur** to brace oneself against pain

raie /ʀɛ/ *f* **1** (in hair) parting (BrE), part (AmE)
2 scratch
3 (Zool) skate

rail /ʀɑj/ *m* rail, track
■ ~ **de sécurité** crash barrier

raillerie /ʀɑjʀi/ *f* mockery

rainette /ʀɛnɛt/ *f* tree frog

rainure /ʀenyʀ/ *f* groove

raisin /ʀɛzɛ̃/ *m* grapes; ~**s secs** raisins

⚷ **raison** /ʀɛzɔ̃/ *f* **1** reason; ~ **d'agir** reason for action; **en** ~ **d'une panne** owing to a breakdown; **à plus forte** ~ even more so, especially; **avec** ~ justifiably; **comme de** ~ as one might expect
2 avoir ~ to be right; **donner** ~ **à qn** to agree with sb
3 reason; **se rendre à la** ~ to see reason; **ramener qn à la** ~ to bring sb to his/her senses; **se faire une** ~ **de qch** to resign oneself to sth; **plus que de** ~ more than is sensible; **avoir** ~ **de qn/qch** to get the better of sb/sth; **à** ~ **de** at the rate of

raisonnable /ʀɛzɔnabl/ *adj* reasonable; moderate; sensible

raisonné, ~**e** /ʀɛzɔne/ **A** *pp* ▶ **raisonner**
B *pp adj* **1** ‹*attitude*› cautious; ‹*decision*› carefully thought out
2 ‹*enthusiasm*› measured

raisonnement /ʀɛzɔnmɑ̃/ *m* reasoning; **selon le même** ~ by the same token; **il tient le** ~ **suivant** his argument is as follows; **je ne tiens pas le même** ~ I look at it differently

raisonner /ʀɛzɔne/ [**v1**] **A** *vt* to reason with
B *vi* to think
C se raisonner *v refl* (+ *v être*) ‹*person*› to be more sensible, to pull oneself together

rajeunir /ʀaʒœniʀ/ [**v3**] **A** *vt* **1** to make [sb] look/feel younger
2 ~ **qn** to make sb out to be younger
3 to bring *or* inject new blood into
B *vi* to look/to feel younger

rajeunissement /ʀaʒœnismɑ̃/ *m* **1 nous avons enregistré un** ~ **de la population** we see that the population is getting younger
2 modernization
3 updating
4 rejuvenation

rajouter /ʀaʒute/ [**v1**] *vt* to add; **en** ~ (fam) to exaggerate

rajuster /ʀaʒyste/ [**v1**] *vt* to straighten ‹*clothing*›

râle /ʀɑl/ *m* **1** rale
2 groan
3 death rattle

ralenti, ~**e** /ʀalɑ̃ti/ **A** *pp* ▶ **ralentir**
B *pp adj* ‹*gesture, rhythm, growth*› slower
C *m* slow motion

ralentir /ʀalɑ̃tiʀ/ [**v3**] *vt*, *vi*, **se ralentir** *v refl* (+ *v être*) to slow down

ralentissement /ʀalɑ̃tismɑ̃/ *m* **1** slowing down
2 tailback

ralentisseur /ʀalɑ̃tisœʀ/ *m* speed ramp

râler /ʀɑle/ [**v1**] *vi* **1** (fam) to moan (fam); **ça me fait** ~ it annoys me
2 to groan

râleur, **-euse** /ʀɑlœʀ, øz/ *mf* (fam) moaner (fam)

ralliement /ʀalimɑ̃/ *m* rallying

⚷ key word

rallier /ʀalje/ [**v2**] **A** *vt* **~ qn à sa cause** to win sb over
B se rallier *v refl* (+ *v être*) **se ~ à** to rally to ‹*republicans*›; to come round to ‹*opinion*›

rallonge /ʀalɔ̃ʒ/ *f* **1** extension cord, extension lead (BrE)
2 (of table) leaf

rallonger /ʀalɔ̃ʒe/ [**v13**] **A** *vt* to extend; to lengthen
B *vi* **les jours rallongent** the days are drawing out

rallye /ʀali/ *m* (car) rally

ramadan /ʀamadɑ̃/ *m* Ramadan; **faire le ~** to keep Ramadan

ramage /ʀamaʒ/ **A** *m* (of bird) song
B ramages *mpl* foliage pattern

ramassage /ʀamasaʒ/ *m* **car de ~** (for employees) works *or* company bus; (for pupils) school bus

ramassé, **~e** /ʀamase/ **A** *pp* ▶ **ramasser**
B *pp adj* **1** stocky, squat
2 être ~ sur soi-même to be hunched up

ramasser /ʀamase/ [**v1**] **A** *vt* to collect; to pick up; to dig up ‹*potatoes*›; **se faire ~ dans une rafle** (fam) to get picked up in a (police) raid
B se ramasser *v refl* (+ *v être*) **1** to huddle up
2 (fam) to come a cropper (fam); **se faire ~ à un examen** to fail an exam

ramassis /ʀamasi/ *m inv* (derog) (of people) bunch; (of ideas, objects) jumble

rambarde /ʀɑ̃baʀd/ *f* guard rail

rame /ʀam/ *f* **1** oar
2 (of paper) ream
3 une ~ de métro a metro train

rameau, *pl* **~x** /ʀamo/ *m* (Bot) branch

ramener /ʀamne/ [**v16**] **A** *vt* **1 ~ l'inflation à 5%** to reduce inflation to 5 per cent
2 to restore ‹*order*›; **~ qn à la réalité** to bring sb back to reality; **~ qn à la vie** to bring sb round; **~ toujours tout à soi** always to relate everything to oneself
3 to take [sb/sth] back
4 to bring back; to return
B se ramener *v refl* (+ *v être*) **se ~ à** to come down to, to boil down to

ramequin /ʀamkɛ̃/ *m* ramekin

ramer /ʀame/ [**v1**] *vi* to row

rameur, **-euse** /ʀamœʀ, øz/ *mf* rower

rameuter /ʀamøte/ [**v1**] *vt* to round up

ramification /ʀamifikasjɔ̃/ *f* **1** network
2 ramification

ramifier: **se ramifier** /ʀamifje/ [**v2**] *v refl* (+ *v être*) ‹*stem, nerve*› to branch; ‹*branch*› to divide

ramollir /ʀamɔliʀ/ [**v3**] **A** *vt* to soften
B se ramollir *v refl* (+ *v être*) **1** to become soft
2 (fam) ‹*person*› to get soft

ramollissement /ʀamɔlismɑ̃/ *m* softening

ramoner /ʀamɔne/ [**v1**] *vt* to sweep ‹*chimney*›

ramoneur /ʀamɔnœʀ/ *m* chimney sweep

rampant, **~e** /ʀɑ̃pɑ̃, ɑ̃t/ *adj* **1** ‹*animal*› crawling; ‹*plant*› creeping
2 ‹*inflation*› creeping

rampe /ʀɑ̃p/ *f* **1** banister; hand rail
2 (in theatre) **la ~** the footlights
■ **~ d'accès** (for motorway) slip road (BrE), entrance ramp (AmE); (of building) ramp

ramper /ʀɑ̃pe/ [**v1**] *vi* **1** to crawl
2 to creep

ramure /ʀamyʀ/ *f* **1** (of tree) branches
2 antlers

rancard /ʀɑ̃kaʀ/ *m* (pop) **1** (rendezvous) date
2 (information) tip

rancart /ʀɑ̃kaʀ/ *m* (fam) **mettre au ~** to shunt [sb] aside

rance /ʀɑ̃s/ *adj* rancid

rancœur /ʀɑ̃kœʀ/ *f* resentment

rançon /ʀɑ̃sɔ̃/ *f* **1** ransom
2 la ~ de la gloire the price of fame

rancune /ʀɑ̃kyn/ *f* **1** resentment
2 grudge; **sans ~!** no hard feelings

rancunier, **-ière** /ʀɑ̃kynje, ɛʀ/ *adj* **être ~** to be a person who holds grudges

randonnée /ʀɑ̃dɔne/ *f* hiking

randonneur, **-euse** /ʀɑ̃dɔnœʀ, øz/ *mf* hiker, rambler

rang /ʀɑ̃/ *m* **1** row; (in necklace) strand; **se mettre en ~s** ‹*children*› to get into (a) line
2 (Mil), (fig) rank; **sortir du ~** to rise *or* come up through the ranks; **serrer les ~s** to close ranks
3 (in a hierarchy) rank; **être au 5ᵉ ~ mondial des exportateurs** to be the 5th largest exporter in the world; **acteur de second ~** second-rate actor; **des personnes de son ~** people of one's own station

rangé, **~e** /ʀɑ̃ʒe/ **A** *pp* ▶ **ranger**[1]
B *pp adj* ‹*life*› orderly; ‹*person*› well-behaved

rangée /ʀɑ̃ʒe/ *f* row

rangement /ʀɑ̃ʒmɑ̃/ *m* **1 c'est un maniaque du ~** he's obsessively tidy
2 storage space

ranger[1] /ʀɑ̃ʒe/ [**v13**] **A** *vt* **1** to put away; **où ranges-tu tes verres?** where do you keep the glasses?
2 to arrange, to put into order; **~ un animal dans les mammifères** to class an animal as a mammal
3 to tidy
B se ranger *v refl* (+ *v être*) **1** to line up
2 ‹*vehicle, driver*› to pull over
3 se ~ à l'avis de qn to go along with sb
4 to settle down

ranger[2] /ʀɑ̃dʒɛʀ/ *m* **1** ranger
2 heavy-duty boot

ranimer /ʀanime/ [**v1**] *vt* **1** to revive ‹*person*›
2 to rekindle ‹*fire, hope*›; to stir up ‹*quarrel*›

rapace /ʀapas/ **A** *adj* ‹*person*› rapacious
B *m* bird of prey

rapacité /ʀapasite/ *f* **1** (of animal) ferocity
2 (of trader) greed

rapatrié, **~e** /ʀapatʀije/ *mf* repatriate (**de** from)

rapatrier /ʀapatʀije/ [**v2**] *vt* to repatriate

râpe /ʀɑp/ *f* (Culin) grater

râper /ʀɑpe/ [**v1**] *vt* to grate ‹*cheese, carrot*›; **c'est râpé** (fig, fam) it's off (fam)

rapetisser /ʀap(ə)tise/ [**v1**] *vi* to shrink

râpeux, **-euse** /ʀɑpø, øz/ *adj* rough

raphia /ʀafja/ *m* raffia

🔑 **rapide** /ʀapid/ **A** *adj* quick, rapid; fast
B *m* **1** rapids; **descendre un ~** to shoot the rapids
2 (train) express

🔑 **rapidement** /ʀapidmɑ̃/ *adv* quickly; fast

rapidité /ʀapidite/ *f* speed

rapiécer /ʀapjese/ [**v14**] *vt* to patch

rappel /ʀapɛl/ *m* **1** reminder; **~ à l'ordre** call to order
2 (lettre de) ~ reminder
3 back pay
4 (of ambassador) recall; (of actors) curtain call
5 (Med) booster

🔑 **rappeler** /ʀaple/ [**v19**] **A** *vt* **1 ~ qch à qn** to remind sb of sth; **rappelons-le** let's not forget; **~ qn à l'ordre** to call sb to order
2 to call [sb] back
3 (on phone) to call *or* to ring [sb] back
B se rappeler *v refl* (+ *v être*) to remember

rappliquer /ʀaplike/ [**v1**] *vi* (fam) **1** to turn up (fam)
2 to come back

🔑 **rapport** /ʀapɔʀ/ **A** *m* **1** connection, link; **être sans ~ avec, n'avoir aucun ~ avec** to have nothing to do with
2 ~s relations; **avoir** *or* **entretenir de bons ~s avec qn** to be on good terms with sb
3 être en ~ avec qn to be in touch with sb
4 sous tous les ~s in every respect
5 report
6 return, yield; **immeuble de ~** block of flats (BrE) *or* apartment block (AmE) that is rented out
7 ratio; **bon ~ qualité prix** good value for money
B par rapport à *phr* **1** compared with; **par ~ au dollar** against the dollar
2 le nombre de voitures par ~ au nombre d'habitants the number of cars per head of the population
3 with regard to, toward(s); **l'attitude de la population par ~ à l'immigration** people's attitudes to immigration
■ **~ de force** power struggle; **~s sexuels** sexual relations

🔑 **rapporter** /ʀapɔʀte/ [**v1**] **A** *vt* **1** to bring back; to take back
2 to bring in ‹*income*›; **~ 10%** to yield *or* to return 10%
3 to report; **on m'a rapporté que** I was told that
B *vi* **1** to bring in money
2 (fam) to tell tales
C se rapporter *v refl* (+ *v être*) **se ~ à** to relate to, to bear a relation to

rapproché, **~e** /ʀapʀɔʃe/ **A** *pp* ▸ **rapprocher**
B *pp adj* close together

rapprochement /ʀapʀɔʃmɑ̃/ *m*
1 rapprochement
2 connection

🔑 **rapprocher** /ʀapʀɔʃe/ [**v1**] **A** *vt* **1** to move [sth] closer
2 to bring [sth] forward(s) ‹*date*›
3 to bring [sb] (closer) together ‹*people*›
4 to compare
B se rapprocher *v refl* (+ *v être*) to get closer, to get nearer; **leurs peintures se rapprochent des fresques antiques** their paintings are similar to classical frescoes

rapt /ʀapt/ *m* kidnapping (BrE), abduction

raquette /ʀakɛt/ *f* **1** (for tennis) racket; (for table tennis) bat (BrE), paddle (AmE)
2 snowshoe

🔑 **rare** /ʀɑʀ/ *adj* **1** (not common) (gen) rare; ‹*job*› unusual; ‹*intelligence*› exceptional; **il est ~ qu'il vienne en train** it's unusual for him to come by train
2 (not numerous) few, rare; ‹*visits*› infrequent; (not abundant) (gen) scarce; ‹*hair*› thin; ‹*vegetation*› sparse; **se faire ~** ‹*product*› to become scarce; **vous vous faites ~ ces temps-ci** you are not around much these days

raréfier /ʀɑʀefje/ [**v2**] **A** *vt* **1** to rarefy ‹*air, gas*›
2 to make [sth] rare
B se raréfier *v refl* (+ *v être*) ‹*air*› to become thinner; ‹*gas*› to rarefy; ‹*food, money*› to become scarce; ‹*species*› to become rare

rarement /ʀɑʀmɑ̃/ *adv* rarely, seldom

rareté /ʀɑʀte/ *f* shortage, scarcity; rarity

rarissime /ʀɑʀisim/ *adj* extremely rare

ras, **~e** /ʀɑ, ʀɑz/ **A** *adj* ‹*hair*› close-cropped; ‹*fur*› short; **à poil ~** ‹*animal*› short-haired; ‹*carpet*› short-piled; **en ~e campagne** in (the) open country; **une cuillère à café ~e** a level teaspoonful; **à ~ bord** to the brim
B *adv* short; **couper (à) ~** to cut [sth] very short ‹*hair, lawn*›
C au ras de *phr* **au ~ du sol** at ground level
IDIOM **faire table ~e de** to make a clean sweep of

RAS /ɛʀaɛs/ (*abbr* = **rien à signaler**) nothing to report

rasade /ʀɑzad/ *f* **1** glassful
2 swig (fam)

rasage /ʀɑzaʒ/ *m* **1** (action) shaving
2 (result) shave

ras-de-cou /ʀɑdku/ *m inv* **1** crew-neck sweater
2 choker

🔑 key word

rase-mottes /ʀɑzmɔt/ *m inv* **faire du ~, voler en ~** to fly low

raser /ʀɑze/ [**v1**] **A** *vt* **1** to shave; to shave off; **~ de près** to give [sb] a close shave
2 to demolish; to raze [sth] to the ground
3 ‹*bullet*› to graze; ‹*plane, bird*› to skim
B se raser *v refl* (+ *v être*) to shave
IDIOM **~ les murs** to hug the walls

ras-le-bol /ʀɑlbɔl/ *m inv* (fam) discontent

rasoir /ʀɑzwaʀ/ **A** *adj inv* (fam) boring
B *m* **~ mécanique** razor; **~ électrique** electric shaver

rassasier /ʀasazje/ [**v2**] **A** *vt* ‹*food*› to fill [sb] up
B se rassasier *v refl* (+ *v être*) to eat one's fill

rassemblement /ʀasɑ̃bləmɑ̃/ *m* **1** rally
2 gathering
3 meeting

rassembler /ʀasɑ̃ble/ [**v1**] **A** *vt* to gather [sb/sth] together ‹*people*›; to round up ‹*sheep, herd*›; to unite ‹*citizens, nation*›; to gather ‹*information, proof*›; **~ ses forces** to summon up one's strength
B se rassembler *v refl* (+ *v être*) **1** to gather
2 to assemble

rasseoir: **se rasseoir** /ʀaswaʀ/ [**v41**] *v refl* (+ *v être*) to sit down (again)

rasséréner /ʀaseʀene/ [**v14**] *vt* to calm [sb] down ‹*person*›

rassis, **~e** /ʀasi, iz/ *adj* ‹*bread*› stale

rassurant, **~e** /ʀasyʀɑ̃, ɑ̃t/ *adj* reassuring

rassurer /ʀasyʀe/ [**v1**] **A** *vt* to reassure
B se rassurer *v refl* (+ *v être*) to reassure oneself; **rassure-toi** don't worry; **je suis rassuré** I'm relieved

rat /ʀa/ *m* **1** rat
2 skinflint, cheapskate (fam)

ratatiner: **se ratatiner** /ʀatatine/ [**v1**] *v refl* (+ *v être*) **1** ‹*fruit*› to shrivel
2 ‹*face, person*› to become wizened

ratatouille /ʀatatuj/ *f* ratatouille

rate /ʀat/ *f* **1** (Zool) female rat
2 (Anat) spleen

raté, **~e** /ʀate/ **A** *pp* ▸ **rater**
B *pp adj* **1** ‹*actor, painter*› failed; **une vie ~e** a wasted life
2 ‹*opportunity*› missed
C *mf* (person) failure
D ratés *mpl* (in negotiations, system) hiccups

râteau, *pl* **~x** /ʀɑto/ *m* rake

râtelier /ʀɑtəlje/ *m* hay rack
IDIOM **manger à tous les ~s** to run with the hare and hunt with the hounds

rater /ʀate/ [**v1**] **A** *vt* **1** to fail ‹*exam*›; to spoil ‹*sauce*›; **elle a raté son coup** (fam) she has failed
2 to miss ‹*train, target*›
B *vi* ‹*plan*› to fail; **il dit toujours des bêtises, ça ne rate jamais** (fam) he can always be relied upon to say something stupid

ratifier /ʀatifje/ [**v2**] *vt* **1** to ratify ‹*treaty, contract*›
2 to confirm ‹*plan, proposal*›

ration /ʀasjɔ̃/ *f* **1** ration
2 share

rationaliser /ʀasjɔnalize/ [**v1**] *vt* to rationalize

rationnel, **-elle** /ʀasjɔnɛl/ *adj* rational

rationnement /ʀasjɔnmɑ̃/ *m* rationing

rationner /ʀasjɔne/ [**v1**] **A** *vt* to ration ‹*petrol*›; to impose rationing on ‹*population*›
B se rationner *v refl* (+ *v être*) to cut down

ratisser /ʀatise/ [**v1**] *vt* **1** to rake over; to rake up
2 to comb ‹*area*›

raton /ʀatɔ̃/ *m* young rat
■ **~ laveur** racoon

rattachement /ʀataʃmɑ̃/ *m* **1** (of country) unification
2 (of person) **demander son ~ à** to ask to be posted to

rattacher /ʀataʃe/ [**v1**] *vt* **1** to attach ‹*region*›; to post ‹*employee*›
2 to retie; to fasten [sth] again
3 plus rien ne la rattache à Lyon she no longer has any ties with Lyons

rattrapage /ʀatʀapaʒ/ *m* **1** (Econ) adjustment
2 catching up; **cours de ~** remedial lesson

rattraper /ʀatʀape/ [**v1**] **A** *vt* **1** to catch up with ‹*competitor*›
2 to catch ‹*fugitive*›
3 to make up for ‹*lost time, deficit*›; to make up ‹*points, distance*›; **~ son retard** to catch up
4 to put right ‹*error*›; to smooth over ‹*blunder*›; to save ‹*situation*›
5 to catch ‹*object*›
B se rattraper *v refl* (+ *v être*) **1** to redeem oneself
2 to make up for it
3 (Sch) to catch up
4 to make up one's losses
5 se ~ de justesse to stop oneself just in time; **se ~ à une branche** to save oneself by catching hold of a branch

rature /ʀatyʀ/ *f* crossing out; deletion

raturer /ʀatyʀe/ [**v1**] *vt* to cross out

rauque /ʀok/ *adj* **1** husky
2 hoarse

ravage /ʀavaʒ/ *m* **les ~s de la guerre** the ravages of war; **faire des ~s** to wreak havoc; ‹*epidemic*› to take a terrible toll; **tu vas faire des ~s avec ta mini-jupe** (hum) you'll knock them dead in that mini-skirt

ravagé, **~e** /ʀavaʒe/ *adj* (fam) crazy

ravager /ʀavaʒe/ [**v13**] *vt* **1** ‹*fire, war*› to devastate, to ravage
2 ‹*disease*› to ravage ‹*face*›; ‹*grief*› to tear [sb] apart

ravalement /ʀavalmɑ̃/ *m* **1** cleaning
2 refacing
3 (fig) facelift

ravaler /ʀavale/ [**v1**] *vt* **1** to clean; to reface; to renovate ‹*building*›
2 to revamp ‹*image*›
3 to suppress ‹*anger*›; ~ **ses larmes** to hold back one's tears

ravier /ʀavje/ *m* small dish (*for hors d'œuvre*)

ravigoter /ʀavigɔte/ [**v1**] *vt* (fam) ‹*fresh air*› to invigorate; ‹*drink*› to perk [sb] up

ravin /ʀavɛ̃/ *m* ravine

ravir /ʀaviʀ/ [**v3**] *vt* **1** to delight; **ça te va à** ~ it really suits you
2 to steal

raviser: **se raviser** /ʀavize/ [**v1**] *v refl* (+ *v être*) to change one's mind

ravissant, **~e** /ʀavisɑ̃, ɑ̃t/ *adj* beautiful

ravisseur, **-euse** /ʀavisœʀ, øz/ *mf* kidnapper (BrE), abductor

ravitaillement /ʀavitajmɑ̃/ *m* supplies

ravitailler /ʀavitaje/ [**v1**] **A** *vt* **1** to provide [sb] with fresh supplies ‹*town*›
2 to refuel
B **se ravitailler** *v refl* (+ *v être*) to obtain fresh supplies

raviver /ʀavive/ [**v1**] *vt* to rekindle; to revive

rayé, **~e** /ʀeje/ **A** *pp* ▶ **rayer**
B *pp adj* **1** ‹*fabric*› striped
2 ‹*record*› scratched

rayer /ʀeje/ [**v21**] *vt* **1** to cross [sth] out; **'~ la mention inutile'** 'delete whichever does not apply'
2 **la ville a été rayée de la carte** the town was wiped off the map
3 to scratch

✓ **rayon** /ʀɛjɔ̃/ *m* **1** radius; **dans un ~ de 10 km** within a 10 km radius; **~ d'action** range; (fig) sphere of activity
2 ray; beam; **les ~s X** X-rays; **être soigné aux ~s** to undergo radiation treatment
3 (of wheel) spoke
4 shelf; **~ de bibliothèque** (book)shelf
5 (in big store) department; (in small shop) section; **tous nos modèles sont en ~** all our styles are on display
6 (fam) **c'est mon ~** that's my department (fam); **il en connaît un ~ à ce sujet** he knows a lot about it

rayonnage /ʀɛjɔnaʒ/ *m* shelves

rayonnant, **~e** /ʀɛjɔnɑ̃, ɑ̃t/ *adj* radiant

rayonne /ʀɛjɔn/ *f* rayon

rayonnement /ʀɛjɔnmɑ̃/ *m* **1** radiation
2 radiance
3 (of country) influence

rayonner /ʀɛjɔne/ [**v1**] *vi* **1** ‹*light, heat*› to radiate
2 ‹*star*› to shine
3 ‹*person*› to glow
4 ‹*city*› to exert its influence
5 ‹*soldiers*› to patrol; ‹*tourists*› to tour around
6 ‹*streets*› to radiate

rayure /ʀɛjyʀ/ *f* **1** stripe
2 scratch

raz-de-marée /ʀadmaʀe/ *m inv* tidal wave

razzia /ʀazja/ *f* raid

ré /ʀe/ *m inv* (Mus) (note) D; (in sol-fa) re

réabonner /ʀeabɔne/ [**v1**] *vt* **~ qn** to renew sb's subscription (**à** to)

réaccoutumer /ʀeakutyme/ [**v1**] *vt* **~ qn à qch** to get sb used to sth again

réacheminer /ʀeaʃ(ə)mine/ *vt* to redirect

réacteur /ʀeaktœʀ/ *m* **1** **~ (nucléaire)** (nuclear) reactor
2 jet engine

✓ **réaction** /ʀeaksjɔ̃/ *f* **1** reaction; response
2 **avion à ~** jet aircraft

réactionnaire /ʀeaksjɔnɛʀ/ *adj, mf* reactionary

réactualiser /ʀeaktɥalize/ [**v1**] *vt* (gen) to update; to relaunch ‹*debate*›

réadapter: **se réadapter** /ʀeadapte/ [**v1**] *v refl* (+ *v être*) to readjust (**à qch** to sth)

réaffirmer /ʀeafiʀme/ [**v1**] *vt* to reaffirm, to reassert

réagir /ʀeaʒiʀ/ [**v3**] *vi* to react; to respond

réalisable /ʀealizabl/ *adj* feasible; workable

réalisateur, **-trice** /ʀealizatœʀ, tʀis/ *mf* director

✓ **réalisation** /ʀealizasjɔ̃/ *f* **1** (of dream) fulfilment (BrE)
2 (of study) carrying out
3 achievement
4 (of film) production

✓ **réaliser** /ʀealize/ [**v1**] **A** *vt* **1** to fulfil (BrE) ‹*ambition*›; to achieve ‹*ideal, feat*›
2 to make ‹*model*›; to carry out ‹*survey, study*›
3 to direct ‹*film*›
4 to realize
B **se réaliser** *v refl* (+ *v être*) **1** ‹*dream*› to come true; ‹*predictions*› to be fulfilled
2 **se ~ (dans qch)** to find fulfilment (BrE) (in sth)

réalisme /ʀealism/ *m* realism

réaliste /ʀealist/ *adj* (gen) realistic; (in art) realist

✓ **réalité** /ʀealite/ *f* **la ~** reality; **en ~** in reality; **tenir compte des ~s** to take the facts into consideration

réanimation /ʀeanimasjɔ̃/ *f* **1** **(service de) ~** intensive care (unit)
2 resuscitation

réapparaître /ʀeapaʀɛtʀ/ [**v73**] *vi* ‹*sun*› to come out again; ‹*illness*› to recur

réapprovisionner /ʀeapʀɔvizjɔne/ [**v1**] *vt* to restock ‹*shop*›

réarmer /ʀeaʀme/ [**v1**] *vt* **1** to rearm
2 to reload ‹*gun*›

✓ key word

réassortir /ʀeasɔʀtiʀ/ [**v3**] *vt* to replenish

rébarbatif, **-ive** /ʀebaʀbatif, iv/ *adj* off-putting; forbidding

rebâtir /ʀ(ə)bɑtiʀ/ [**v3**] *vt* to rebuild

rebattre /ʀ(ə)batʀ/ [**v61**] *vt* **~ les oreilles de qn avec une histoire** to go on (and on) about something

rebattu, **~e** /ʀ(ə)baty/ **A** *pp* ▶ **rebattre**
B *pp adj* ‹*joke, story*› hackneyed

rebelle /ʀəbɛl/ **A** *adj* **1** rebel
2 rebellious
3 ‹*curl, lock of hair*› stray; ‹*stain*› stubborn
B *mf* rebel

rebeller: **se rebeller** /ʀəbele/ [**v1**] *v refl* (+ *v être*) to rebel

rébellion /ʀebɛljɔ̃/ *f* rebellion

rebiffer: **se rebiffer** /ʀ(ə)bife/ [**v1**] *v refl* (+ *v être*) (fam) to rebel

rebiquer /ʀ(ə)bike/ [**v1**] *vi* (fam) to stick up

reboiser /ʀ(ə)bwaze/ [**v1**] *vt* to reafforest

rebond /ʀ(ə)bɔ̃/ *m* **1** bounce
2 recovery

rebondi, **~e** /ʀ(ə)bɔ̃di/ *adj* **1** ‹*shape*› round, rounded; ‹*cheek*› chubby; ‹*stomach*› fat; ‹*buttocks*› rounded
2 (fig) ‹*wallet*› bulging

rebondir /ʀ(ə)bɔ̃diʀ/ [**v3**] *vi* **1** to bounce
2 to start up again; to take a new turn

rebondissement /ʀ(ə)bɔ̃dismɑ̃/ *m* (of controversy) sudden revival; (in trial) new development

rebord /ʀ(ə)bɔʀ/ *m* **1** ledge; **~ de fenêtre** window sill
2 rim
3 edge

rebours: **à rebours** /aʀ(ə)buʀ/ *phr* ‹*count, walk*› backward(s)

rebouteux, **-euse** /ʀ(ə)butø, øz/ *mf* (fam) bonesetter

rebrousse-poil: **à rebrousse-poil** /aʀ(ə)bʀuspwal/ *phr* the wrong way

rebrousser /ʀ(ə)bʀuse/ [**v1**] *vt* **~ chemin** to turn back

rébus /ʀebys/ *m inv* rebus

rebut /ʀ(ə)by/ *m* rubbish; **mettre qch au ~** to throw sth on the scrapheap

rebuter /ʀ(ə)byte/ [**v1**] *vt* **1** to disgust; to repel
2 to put [sb] off

récalcitrant, **~e** /ʀekalsitʀɑ̃, ɑ̃t/ *adj* recalcitrant

recaler /ʀ(ə)kale/ [**v1**] *vt* (fam) to fail ‹*candidate*›

récapitulatif /ʀekapitylatif/ *m* summary of the main points

récapituler /ʀekapityle/ [**v1**] *vt* to sum up

receler /ʀəs(ə)le, ʀsəle/ [**v17**] *vt* **1 ~ des marchandises** to possess stolen goods
2 to contain

receleur, **-euse** /ʀ(ə)s(ə)lœʀ, ʀsəlœʀ, øz/ *mf* possessor of stolen goods

récemment /ʀesamɑ̃/ *adv* recently

recensement /ʀ(ə)sɑ̃smɑ̃/ *m* **1** census
2 inventory

recenser /ʀ(ə)sɑ̃se/ [**v1**] *vt* **1** to take a census of ‹*population*›
2 to list ‹*objects*›

🔑 **récent**, **~e** /ʀesɑ̃, ɑ̃t/ *adj* recent; ‹*house*› new

recentrer /ʀəsɑ̃tʀe/ [**v1**] *vt*, **se recentrer** *v refl* (+ *v être*) to refocus

récépissé /ʀesepise/ *m* receipt

réceptacle /ʀesɛptakl/ *m* container; **~ à verre** bottle bank

récepteur /ʀesɛptœʀ/ *m* receiver

réceptif, **-ive** /ʀesɛptif, iv/ *adj* receptive

réception /ʀesɛpsjɔ̃/ *f* **1** reception
2 welcome
3 s'occuper de la ~ des marchandises to take delivery of the goods

réceptionner /ʀesɛpsjɔne/ [**v1**] *vt* **1** to take delivery of ‹*goods*›
2 to catch ‹*ball*›

réceptionniste /ʀesɛpsjɔnist/ *mf* receptionist

récession /ʀesesjɔ̃/ *f* recession

recette /ʀ(ə)sɛt/ *f* **1 ~ (de cuisine)** recipe
2 formula, recipe
3 takings; **faire ~** to bring in money; (fig) to be a success; **les ~s et (les) dépenses** receipts and expenses

receveur, **-euse** /ʀəs(ə)vœʀ, øz/ *mf* (on bus) conductor
■ **~ des postes** postmaster

🔑 **recevoir** /ʀəsvwaʀ, ʀ(ə)səvwaʀ/ [**v5**] *vt* **1** to receive, to get; **il a reçu une tuile sur la tête** he got hit on the head by a tile; **je n'ai d'ordre à ~ de personne** I don't take orders from anyone
2 to welcome ‹*guests*›; **être bien reçu** to be well received; to get a good reception; **ils reçoivent beaucoup** they do a lot of entertaining; **Laval reçoit Caen** (Sport) Laval is playing host to Caen
3 to see ‹*patients*›
4 to receive ‹*radio signal*›
5 (Sch) to pass ‹*candidate*›; **être reçu à un examen** to pass an exam

rechange: **de rechange** /dəʀ(ə)ʃɑ̃ʒ/ *phr* ‹*part*› spare; ‹*solution*› alternative

réchapper /ʀeʃape/ [**v1**] *v+prep* **~ de** to come through ‹*illness, accident*›

recharge /ʀ(ə)ʃaʀʒ/ *f* refill; reload

rechargeable /ʀ(ə)ʃaʀʒabl/ *adj* ‹*lighter, pen*› refillable; ‹*battery, appliance*› rechargeable

recharger /ʀ(ə)ʃaʀʒe/ [**v13**] *vt* to reload; to refill; to recharge ‹*battery*›

réchaud /ʀeʃo/ *m* stove; **~ électrique** electric ring (BrE), hotplate

réchauffé, **~e** /ʀeʃofe/ **A** *pp* ▶ **réchauffer**
B *pp adj* ‹*joke, story*› hackneyed
C *m* **c'est du ~** there's nothing new about it

réchauffement /ʀeʃofmɑ̃/ *m* warming (up); **le ~ de la planète** global warming

r

réchauffer /ʀeʃofe/ [**v1**] **A** *vt* **1** (Culin) to reheat, to heat [sth] up
2 to warm up ‹*person, hands, room*›
B se réchauffer *v refl* (+ *v être*) to warm up

rêche /ʀɛʃ/ *adj* ‹*hands, fabric*› rough

recherche /ʀ(ə)ʃɛʀʃ/ *f* **1** research
2 search; **être à la ~ de** to be looking for
3 ~ de pursuit of ‹*happiness*›
4 sans ~ without affectation
■ **~ d'emploi** job-hunting

recherché, **~e** /ʀ(ə)ʃɛʀʃe/ **A** *pp* ▶ **rechercher**
B *pp adj* **1** sought-after
2 in demand
3 ‹*dress*› meticulous; ‹*style*› original
4 ‹*aim*› intended

rechercher /ʀ(ə)ʃɛʀʃe/ [**v1**] *vt* **1** to look for; **il est recherché par la police** he's wanted by the police; **'recherchons vendeuse qualifiée'** 'qualified sales assistant (BrE) *or* clerk (AmE) required'
2 to seek ‹*security*›; to fish for ‹*compliments*›

rechigner /ʀ(ə)ʃiɲe/ [**v1**] **A** *v+prep* **~ à faire** to balk at doing
B *vi* to grumble

rechute /ʀəʃyt/ *f* relapse

rechuter /ʀ(ə)ʃyte/ [**v1**] *vi* **1** (Med) to have a relapse
2 (Econ) ‹*price, currency*› to fall again

récidive /ʀesidiv/ *f* **1** (Law) second offence (BrE)
2 (fig) repetition
3 (Med) recurrence

récidiver /ʀesidive/ [**v1**] *vi* (Law) to reoffend

récidiviste /ʀesidivist/ *mf* second offender, recidivist; habitual offender

récif /ʀesif/ *m* reef

récipient /ʀesipjɑ̃/ *m* container

réciprocité /ʀesipʀɔsite/ *f* reciprocity

réciproque /ʀesipʀɔk/ **A** *adj* reciprocal
B *f* reverse; **la ~ est vraie** the reverse is true

réciproquement /ʀesipʀɔkmɑ̃/ *adv* **et ~** and vice versa

récit /ʀesi/ *m* **1** story
2 narrative

récital /ʀesital/ *m* recital

récitation /ʀesitasjɔ̃/ *f* **apprendre une ~** to learn a text (off) by heart

réciter /ʀesite/ [**v1**] *vt* to recite

réclamation /ʀeklamasjɔ̃/ *f* **1** complaint
2 claim; **sur ~** on request

réclame /ʀeklam/ *f* **1** publicity
2 advertisement
3 'en ~' 'on offer' (BrE), 'on sale'

réclamer /ʀeklame/ [**v1**] **A** *vt* to ask for ‹*person, thing, money*›; to call for ‹*reform, inquiry*›; to claim ‹*compensation*›; **travail qui réclame de l'attention** work that requires attention
B se réclamer *v refl* (+ *v être*) **se ~ de** ‹*person, group*› to claim to be representative of

reclasser /ʀəklase/ [**v1**] *vt* **1** to reclassify ‹*documents*›
2 to redeploy

reclus, **~e** /ʀəkly, yz/ *adj* reclusive; **vivre ~** to live as a recluse

réclusion /ʀeklyzjɔ̃/ *f* **1** (Law) imprisonment
2 reclusion

recoin /ʀəkwɛ̃/ *m* corner; (fig) recess

récolte /ʀekɔlt/ *f* harvest; crop

récolter /ʀekɔlte/ [**v1**] *vt* **1** to harvest ‹*corn*›; to dig up ‹*potatoes*›
2 ‹*bee*› to collect ‹*pollen*›; ‹*person*› to win ‹*points*›; to collect ‹*information*›

recommandable /ʀəkɔmɑ̃dabl/ *adj* **un individu peu ~** a disreputable individual

recommandation /ʀəkɔmɑ̃dasjɔ̃/ *f* recommendation

recommandé, **~e** /ʀəkɔmɑ̃de/ **A** *pp* ▶ **recommander**
B *pp adj* ‹*letter*› registered

recommander /ʀəkɔmɑ̃de/ [**v1**] **A** *vt* **1** to advise
2 to recommend
B se recommander *v refl* (+ *v être*) **se ~ de qn** to give sb's name as a reference

recommencement /ʀəkɔmɑ̃smɑ̃/ *m* **l'histoire est un éternel ~** history is constantly repeating itself

recommencer /ʀəkɔmɑ̃se/ [**v12**] *vt* **1** to start [sth] again
2 to do [sth] again

récompense /ʀekɔ̃pɑ̃s/ *f* **1** reward
2 award

récompenser /ʀekɔ̃pɑ̃se/ [**v1**] *vt* to reward

réconciliation /ʀekɔ̃siljasjɔ̃/ *f* reconciliation

réconcilier /ʀekɔ̃silje/ [**v2**] **A** *vt* **~ Pierre avec Paul** to bring Pierre and Paul back together; **~ morale et politique** to reconcile morality with politics
B se réconcilier *v refl* (+ *v être*) ‹*friends*› to make up; ‹*nations*› to be reconciled

reconduction /ʀ(ə)kɔ̃dyksjɔ̃/ *f* renewal

reconduire /ʀ(ə)kɔ̃dɥiʀ/ [**v69**] *vt* **1** to see [sb] out; **~ qn chez lui** to take sb home
2 to extend ‹*strike, ceasefire*›; to renew ‹*mandate*›

réconfort /ʀekɔ̃fɔʀ/ *m* comfort

réconfortant, **~e** /ʀekɔ̃fɔʀtɑ̃, ɑ̃t/ *adj*
1 comforting
2 cheering
3 fortifying

réconforter /ʀekɔ̃fɔʀte/ [**v1**] *vt* **1** to comfort; to console
2 ~ qn to cheer sb up
3 to fortify

reconnaissance /ʀ(ə)kɔnɛsɑ̃s/ *f*
1 gratitude; **en ~ de** in appreciation of
2 recognition
3 (of wrongs) admission, admitting; (of qualities)

key word

recognition, recognizing
4 (Mil) reconnaissance

reconnaissant, **~e** /ʀ(ə)kɔnɛsɑ̃, ɑ̃t/ *adj* grateful

reconnaître /ʀ(ə)kɔnɛtʀ/ [**v73**] **A** *vt* **1** to recognize ‹*person*›
2 to identify; **je reconnais bien là leur générosité** it's just like them to be so generous
3 to admit ‹*facts, errors*›
4 to recognize ‹*trade union, regime*›; **~ un enfant** to recognize a child legally
5 to acknowledge
B se reconnaître *v refl* (+ *v être*) **se ~ à qch** to be recognizable by sth

reconnu, **~e** /ʀ(ə)kɔny/ **A** *pp* ▶ **reconnaître**
B *pp adj* ‹*fact*› recognized

reconquérir /ʀ(ə)kɔ̃keʀiʀ/ [**v35**] *vt* to reconquer, to recover ‹*territory*›; (fig) to regain ‹*esteem*›; to win back ‹*person, right*›

reconstituer /ʀ(ə)kɔ̃stitɥe/ [**v1**] *vt* to re-form ‹*association*›; to reconstruct ‹*crime*›; to recreate ‹*era, decor*›; to piece [sth] together again ‹*broken object*›; to build up again ‹*reserves*›

reconstitution /ʀ(ə)kɔ̃stitysjɔ̃/ *f* (of crime, event) reconstruction

reconstruire /ʀ(ə)kɔ̃stʀɥiʀ/ [**v69**] *vt* **1** to reconstruct
2 to rebuild

reconversion /ʀ(ə)kɔ̃vɛʀsjɔ̃/ *f* (of worker) redeployment; (of region) redevelopment; (of economy) restructuring; (of factory) conversion

reconvertir /ʀ(ə)kɔ̃vɛʀtiʀ/ [**v3**] **A** *vt* to redeploy ‹*staff*›; to convert ‹*factory*›; to adapt ‹*equipment*›
B se reconvertir *v refl* (+ *v être*) ‹*staff*› to switch to a new type of employment; ‹*company*› to switch to a new type of production

recopier /ʀ(ə)kɔpje/ [**v2**] *vt* **1** to copy out
2 to write up ‹*notes*›

record /ʀ(ə)kɔʀ/ **A** *adj inv* record
B *m* (Sport), (fig) record

recoudre /ʀ(ə)kudʀ/ [**v76**] *vt* **1** to sew [sth] back on ‹*button*›
2 (Med) to stitch up ‹*wound*›

recoupement /ʀ(ə)kupmɑ̃/ *m* cross-check

recouper /ʀ(ə)kupe/ [**v1**] **A** *vt* to cut [sth] again ‹*hair, hedge*›; to recut ‹*garment*›
B se recouper *v refl* (+ *v être*)
1 ‹*versions*› to tally; ‹*results*› to add up
2 ‹*lines*› to intersect

recourbé, **~e** /ʀ(ə)kuʀbe/ *adj* (gen) curved; ‹*nose, beak*› hooked

recourir /ʀ(ə)kuʀiʀ/ [**v26**] *v+prep* **~ à** to use ‹*remedy*›; to resort to ‹*strategy*›

recours /ʀ(ə)kuʀ/ *m inv* **1** recourse; resort; **sans autre ~ que** with no other way out but; **avoir ~ à** to have recourse to ‹*remedy*›; to resort to ‹*strategy*›; to go to ‹*expert*›
2 (Law) appeal

recouvrement /ʀ(ə)kuvʀəmɑ̃/ *m* (of tax, contributions) collection; (of sum, debt) recovery

recouvrer /ʀ(ə)kuvʀe/ [**v1**] *vt* to recover; to collect ‹*tax*›

recouvrir /ʀ(ə)kuvʀiʀ/ [**v32**] *vt* **1** to cover
2 to re-cover
3 to hide, to conceal

recracher /ʀ(ə)kʀaʃe/ [**v1**] *vt* to spit out

récréation /ʀekʀeasjɔ̃/ *f* **1** playtime (BrE), break (BrE), recess (AmE)
2 recreation

recréer /ʀ(ə)kʀee/ [**v11**] *vt* to recreate

récrier: **se récrier** /ʀekʀije/ [**v2**] *v refl* (+ *v être*) to exclaim

récrimination /ʀekʀiminasjɔ̃/ *f* recrimination

récriminer /ʀekʀimine/ [**v1**] *vi* to rail

recroqueviller: **se recroqueviller** /ʀ(ə)kʀɔkvije/ [**v1**] *v refl* (+ *v être*) **1** ‹*person*› to huddle up
2 ‹*leaf, petal*› to shrivel up

recrudescence /ʀ(ə)kʀydesɑ̃s/ *f* (of violence, interest) fresh upsurge; (of bombing, demands) new wave; (of fire) renewed outbreak

recrudescent, **~e** /ʀ(ə)kʀydesɑ̃, ɑ̃t/ *adj* **être ~** to be on the increase

recrue /ʀəkʀy/ *f* recruit

recrutement /ʀ(ə)kʀytmɑ̃/ *m* recruitment

recruter /ʀ(ə)kʀyte/ [**v1**] *vt* to recruit

rectangle /ʀɛktɑ̃gl/ *m* rectangle

rectangulaire /ʀɛktɑ̃gylɛʀ/ *adj* rectangular

recteur /ʀɛktœʀ/ *m* (Sch, Univ) chief education officer

rectificatif, **-ive** /ʀɛktifikatif, iv/ *m* **1** (in newspaper) correction
2 (to law) amendment

rectification /ʀɛktifikasjɔ̃/ *f* correction; rectification; adjustment

rectifier /ʀɛktifje/ [**v2**] *vt* to correct, to rectify; to adjust

rectiligne /ʀɛktiliɲ/ *adj* straight

recto /ʀɛkto/ *m* front; **~ verso** on both sides

rectorat /ʀɛktɔʀa/ *m* ≈ local education authority (BrE), ≈ board of education (AmE)

rectum /ʀɛktɔm/ *m* rectum

reçu, **~e** /ʀ(ə)sy/ **A** *pp* ▶ **recevoir**
B *pp adj* ‹*candidate*› successful
C *m* receipt

recueil /ʀ(ə)kœj/ *m* collection; anthology

recueillement /ʀəkœjmɑ̃/ *m*
1 contemplation
2 reverence

recueilli, **~e** /ʀəkœji/ **A** *pp* ▶ **recueillir**
B *pp adj* ‹*air*› rapt; ‹*person*› rapt in prayer; ‹*crowd, silence*› reverential

recueillir /ʀəkœjiʀ/ [**v27**] **A** *vt* **1** to collect ‹*donations, anecdotes*›; to gather ‹*evidence, testimonies*›
2 to get ‹*votes, news*›; to gain ‹*consensus*›; to win ‹*praise*›
3 to collect ‹*water, resin*›; to gather ‹*honey*›

4 to take in ‹*orphan*›
5 to record ‹*impressions, opinions*›
B **se recueillir** *v refl* (+ *v être*) to engage in private prayer

recul /ʀ(ə)kyl/ *m* **1** detachment; **avec le ~** with hindsight, in retrospect; **prendre du ~** to stand back
2 (in production) drop, fall; (of doctrine) decline
3 (of army) pulling back; (of tide, floodwaters) recession; **avoir un mouvement de ~** to recoil; **feu de ~** reversing light

reculé, **~e** /ʀəkyle/ *adj* remote

reculer /ʀ(ə)kyle/ [**v1**] **A** *vt* **1** to move back ‹*object*›
2 (in car) to reverse (BrE), to back up
3 to put off ‹*event, decision*›; to put back ‹*date*›
B *vi* **1** ‹*person*› to move back; to stand back; ‹*driver, car*› to reverse (BrE), to back up
2 ‹*army*› to pull *or* to draw back
3 ‹*forest*› to be gradually disappearing; ‹*river*› to go down; ‹*sea*› to recede
4 ‹*currency, exports*› to fall; ‹*doctrine*› to decline; **faire ~ le chômage** to reduce unemployment
5 to back down; **ne ~ devant rien** to stop at nothing
C **se reculer** *v refl* (+ *v être*) (gen) to move back; to stand back

reculons: **à reculons** /aʀ(ə)kylɔ̃/ *phr* **aller à ~** to go backward(s)

récupérable /ʀekypeʀabl/ *adj* **1** ‹*material*› reusable
2 ‹*object*› which can be made good again
3 ‹*delinquent*› who can be rehabilitated

récupération /ʀekypeʀasjɔ̃/ *f* **1** salvage; recycling
2 recovery
3 appropriation

récupérer /ʀekypeʀe/ [**v14**] **A** *vt* **1** to get back ‹*money, strength*›
2 to retrieve
3 to salvage ‹*scrap iron*›; to reclaim ‹*rags*›
4 to save ‹*boxes*›
5 to make up ‹*days*›
6 to appropriate ‹*ideas*›
B *vi* to recover

récurer /ʀekyʀe/ [**v1**] *vt* to scour; to scrub

récurrent, **~e** /ʀekyʀɑ̃, ɑ̃t/ *adj* recurrent

récuser /ʀekyze/ [**v1**] **A** *vt* to challenge ‹*jury*›
B **se récuser** *v refl* (+ *v être*) ‹*judge*› to decline to act in a case

recyclable /ʀ(ə)siklabl/ *adj* recyclable

recyclage /ʀ(ə)siklaʒ/ *m* **1** recycling
2 retraining

recycler /ʀ(ə)sikle/ [**v1**] **A** *vt* **1** to recycle ‹*material*›
2 **~ le personnel** to retrain the staff
B **se recycler** *v refl* (+ *v être*) **1** to retrain
2 to change jobs

rédacteur, **-trice** /ʀedaktœʀ, tʀis/ *mf*
1 author, writer
2 editor

rédaction /ʀedaksjɔ̃/ *f* **1** writing
2 editing
3 editorial offices
4 editorial staff
5 (Sch) essay (BrE), theme (AmE)

reddition /ʀɛdisjɔ̃/ *f* surrender

rédemption /ʀedɑ̃psjɔ̃/ *f* redemption

redescendre /ʀədɛsɑ̃dʀ/ [**v6**] **A** *vt* (gen) to take [sb/sth] back down; ‹*person*› to go/come back down ‹*stairs*›
B *vi* (+ *v être*) to go (back) down; to go down again

redevable /ʀədvabl, ʀ(ə)dəvabl/ *adj* **être ~ de qch à qn** to owe sth to sb; **être ~ de l'impôt** to be liable for tax

redevance /ʀədvɑ̃s, ʀ(ə)dəvɑ̃s/ *f* **1** (gen) charge; (for television) licence (BrE) fee; (for telephone) rental charge
2 royalty

rédhibitoire /ʀedibitwaʀ/ *adj* ‹*cost*› prohibitive; ‹*obstacle*› insurmountable

rediffuser /ʀ(ə)difyze/ [**v1**] *vt* to repeat, to rerun ‹*programme*›

🔑 **rédiger** /ʀediʒe/ [**v13**] *vt* to write ‹*article*›; to write up ‹*notes*›; to draft ‹*contract*›

redingote /ʀ(ə)dɛ̃gɔt/ *f* (for man) frock coat; (for woman) fitted coat

redire /ʀədiʀ/ [**v65**] *vt* to repeat; **trouver quelque chose à ~ à qch** to find fault with sth

redite /ʀ(ə)dit/ *f* (needless) repetition

redondance /ʀ(ə)dɔ̃dɑ̃s/ *f* redundancy

redondant, **~e** /ʀ(ə)dɔ̃dɑ̃, ɑ̃t/ *adj*
1 superfluous
2 redundant

redonner /ʀ(ə)dɔne/ [**v1**] *vt* **~ qch à qn** to give sb sth again

redorer /ʀ(ə)dɔʀe/ [**v1**] *vt* to regild; **~ son blason** ‹*person*› to restore one's image

redoublant, **~e** /ʀ(ə)dublɑ̃, ɑ̃t/ *mf* student repeating a year

redoublement /ʀ(ə)dubləmɑ̃/ *m* intensification

redoubler /ʀ(ə)duble/ [**v1**] **A** *vt* (Sch) **~ une classe** to repeat a year
B **redoubler de** *v+prep* **~ de prudence** to be twice as careful; **la tempête a redoublé de violence** the storm has become even fiercer
C *vi* **1** to repeat a year
2 to intensify

redoutable /ʀ(ə)dutabl/ *adj* ‹*weapon, exam*› formidable; ‹*disease*› dreadful

redouter /ʀ(ə)dute/ [**v1**] *vt* to fear

redressement /ʀədʀɛsmɑ̃/ *m* **maison de ~** reformatory

redresser /ʀ(ə)dʀese/ [**v1**] **A** *vt* **1** to straighten (up); to put [sth] up again; **~ la tête** to lift one's head up

🔑 key word

2 to put [sth] back on its feet ‹*economy*›; to turn [sth] around ‹*company*›; to aid the recovery of ‹*currency*›
3 to straighten up ‹*glider, steering wheel*›; **~ la barre** to right the helm; (fig) to put things back on an even keel
4 to rectify ‹*error*›
B se redresser *v refl* (+ *v être*) **1** to stand up; to sit up; to stand up straight; to sit up straight
2 ‹*economy, plant*› to recover; ‹*country*› to get back on its feet

redresseur /ʀədʀɛsœʀ/ *m* **~ de torts** righter of wrongs

réductible /ʀedyktibl/ *adj* ‹*costs*› which can be reduced *or* cut

réduction /ʀedyksjɔ̃/ *f* **1** discount, reduction; **~ étudiants** concession for students
2 cutting, reducing
3 reduction, cut; **~s d'effectifs** staff cuts
4 (of statue) small replica

réduire /ʀedɥiʀ/ [**v68**] **A** *vt* **1** to reduce; to cut ‹*tax*›; to cut down on ‹*staff, spending*›
2 to reduce ‹*photograph*›; to scale down ‹*drawing*›; to cut ‹*text*›
3 ~ qch en poudre to crush sth to powder; **être réduit en cendres** ‹*city*› to be reduced to ashes; ‹*dreams*› to turn to ashes
4 ~ à to reduce to; **voilà à quoi j'en suis réduit!** this is what I've been reduced to!
5 to reduce ‹*sauce*›
B *vi* ‹*sauce*› to reduce; ‹*spinach*› to shrink
C se réduire *v refl* (+ *v être*) **1** ‹*costs*› to be reduced; ‹*imports*› to be cut
2 cela se réduit à bien peu de chose it doesn't amount to very much

réduit, **~e** /ʀedɥi, it/ **A** *pp* ▶ **réduire**
B *pp adj* **1** ‹*rate, speed*› reduced, lower; ‹*time*› shorter; ‹*activity*› reduced; ‹*group*› smaller; **visibilité ~e** restricted visibility
2 ‹*means, choice*› limited; ‹*group*› small
3 ‹*size*› small
C *m* cubbyhole

rééditer /ʀeedite/ [**v1**] *vt* to reprint ‹*book*›

rééducation /ʀeedykasjɔ̃/ *f*
1 physiotherapy; **~ de la parole** speech therapy
2 rehabilitation

rééduquer /ʀeedyke/ [**v1**] *vt* to restore normal functioning to ‹*limb*›; to rehabilitate

réel, **réelle** /ʀeɛl/ **A** *adj* (gen) real; ‹*fact*› true
B *m* **le ~** the real

réellement /ʀeɛlmɑ̃/ *adv* really

réembaucher /ʀeɑ̃boʃe/ [**v1**] *vt* to take [sb] on again

réemployer /ʀeɑ̃plwaje/ [**v23**] *vt* to reinvest ‹*funds*›; to re-employ ‹*staff*›

rééquilibrer /ʀeekilibʀe/ [**v1**] *vt* **1** (Aut) to balance ‹*wheels*›
2 to balance ‹*budget*›

réévaluer /ʀeevalɥe/ [**v1**] *vt* **1** to revalue ‹*currency*›; to revise ‹*tax*›
2 to reappraise

réexpédier /ʀeɛkspedje/ [**v2**] *vt* **1** to forward, to redirect
2 to send [sth] back

réf (*written abbr* = **référence**) ref

refaire /ʀəfɛʀ/ [**v10**] **A** *vt* **1** to do [sth] again ‹*exercise*›; to make [sth] again ‹*journey, mistake*›; **~ le même chemin** to go back the same way; **~ un numéro de téléphone** to redial a number
2 je vais ~ de la soupe I'll make some more soup
3 vouloir ~ le monde to want to change the world; **se faire ~ le nez** to have one's nose remodelled (BrE); **~ sa vie** to start all over again
4 to redo ‹*roof*›; to redecorate ‹*room*›; to resurface ‹*road*›
B se refaire *v refl* (+ *v être*) **1 se ~ une santé** to recuperate; **se ~ une beauté** to redo one's make-up
2 se ~ à to get used to [sth] again
3 on ne se refait pas a person can't change

réfection /ʀefɛksjɔ̃/ *f* repairing

réfectoire /ʀefɛktwaʀ/ *m* refectory; (Mil) mess

référence /ʀefeʀɑ̃s/ **A** *f* **1** reference; **en** *or* **par ~ à** in reference to; **faire ~ à** to refer to; **lui? ce n'est pas une ~!** who, him? well, he's not much of an example!
2 reference number
B références *fpl* references

référendum /ʀefeʀɛ̃dɔm/ *m* referendum

référer /ʀefeʀe/ [**v14**] **A référer à** *v+prep* **en ~ à** to consult
B se référer *v refl* (+ *v être*) **1 se ~ à** to refer to
2 se ~ à to consult

refermer /ʀ(ə)fɛʀme/ [**v1**] **A** *vt* **1** to close
2 to close [sth] again
B se refermer *v refl* (+ *v être*) ‹*door*› to close; ‹*wound*› to close up

refiscalisation /ʀəfiskalizasjɔ̃/ *f* (Fin) new taxation; **la ~ des heures supplémentaires** revised taxation of overtime

réfléchi, **~e** /ʀefleʃi/ *adj* **1** ‹*person*› reflective, thoughtful
2 ‹*decision*› considered; ‹*action*› well-considered; **c'est tout ~** my mind is made up
3 ‹*image*› reflected
4 ‹*verb*› reflexive

réfléchir /ʀefleʃiʀ/ [**v3**] **A** *vt* to reflect ‹*heat*›
B réfléchir à *v+prep* to think about
C *vi* to think; **mais réfléchis donc un peu!** use your brain!
D se réfléchir *v refl* (+ *v être*) to be reflected

réflecteur /ʀeflɛktœʀ/ *m* reflector

reflet /ʀ(ə)flɛ/ *m* **1** reflection

2 glint; shimmer; sheen; **cheveux châtains aux ~s roux** brown hair with auburn highlights

refléter /ʀ(ə)flete/ [**v14**] **A** *vt* to reflect; **son visage reflétait son émotion** his/her emotion showed in his/her face
B se refléter *v refl* (+ *v être*) to be reflected

réflexe /ʀeflɛks/ **A** *adj* reflex
B *m* **1** reflex
2 reaction; **manquer de ~** to be slow to react; **par ~** automatically
■ **~ conditionné** conditioned reflex

🔑 **réflexion** /ʀeflɛksjɔ̃/ *f* **1** thought, reflection
2 thinking, reflection; **~ faite** *or* **à la ~, je n'irai pas** on second thoughts, I won't go; **donner matière à ~** to be food for thought
3 remark, comment; **s'attirer des ~s** to attract criticism
4 study; **document de ~** discussion paper
5 (of image) reflection

refluer /ʀ(ə)flɥe/ [**v1**] *vi* ‹*liquid*› to flow back

reflux /ʀ(ə)fly/ *m inv* ebb tide

refonte /ʀ(ə)fɔ̃t/ *f* **1** overhaul
2 (of contract) rewriting

reforestation /ʀ(ə)fɔʀɛstasjɔ̃/ *f* reafforestation

réformateur, **-trice** /ʀefɔʀmatœʀ, tʀis/ *mf* reformer

🔑 **réforme** /ʀefɔʀm/ *f* **1** reform
2 (Mil) discharge
3 la Réforme the Reformation

réformé, **~e** /ʀefɔʀme/ *mf* Calvinist

reformer /ʀ(ə)fɔʀme/ [**v1**] *vt* to re-form

réformer /ʀefɔʀme/ [**v1**] *vt* **1** to reform
2 (Mil) to declare [sb] unfit for service ‹*conscript*›; to discharge ‹*soldier*›

refoulé, **~e** /ʀ(ə)fule/ *mf* repressed *or* inhibited person

refoulement /ʀ(ə)fulmɑ̃/ *m* **1** (of impulse) repression
2 pushing back; turning back; driving back; forcing back

refouler /ʀ(ə)fule/ [**v1**] *vt* **1** to suppress ‹*memory*›; to repress ‹*tendency*›; to hold back ‹*tears*›
2 to force [sth] back ‹*liquid*›; to push back ‹*enemy*›; to turn back ‹*immigrant*›

réfractaire /ʀefʀaktɛʀ/ *adj* **1 ~ à** resistant to ‹*influence*›; impervious to ‹*music*›
2 refractory

réfracter /ʀefʀakte/ [**v1**] *vt* to refract

réfraction /ʀefʀaksjɔ̃/ *f* refraction

refrain /ʀ(ə)fʀɛ̃/ *m* **1** chorus
2 (old) refrain

refréner /ʀ(ə)fʀene/, **réfréner** /ʀefʀene/ [**v14**] *vt* to curb

réfrigérant, **~e** /ʀefʀiʒeʀɑ̃, ɑ̃t/ *adj* cooling

réfrigérateur /ʀefʀiʒeʀatœʀ/ *m* refrigerator

🔑 key word

réfrigérer /ʀefʀiʒeʀe/ [**v14**] *vt* to refrigerate ‹*food*›; to cool ‹*place*›

refroidir /ʀəfʀwadiʀ/ [**v3**] **A** *vt* **1** to cool down; to cool
2 ~ qn to dampen sb's spirits
B *vi* **1** to cool down
2 to get cold
C se refroidir *v refl* (+ *v être*) ‹*weather*› to get colder; ‹*joint*› to stiffen up; ‹*person*› to get cold

refroidissement /ʀəfʀwadismɑ̃/ *m* **1** drop in temperature
2 cooling
3 (Med) chill

refuge /ʀ(ə)fyʒ/ *m* **1** refuge
2 (mountain) refuge
3 (for animals) sanctuary
4 traffic island

réfugié, **~e** /ʀefyʒje/ *mf* refugee; **~ économique** economic refugee

réfugier: **se réfugier** /ʀefyʒje/ [**v2**] *v refl* (+ *v être*) to take refuge

refus /ʀ(ə)fy/ *m inv* refusal; **ce n'est pas de ~** (fam) I wouldn't say no (fam)
■ **~ de priorité** failure to give way

🔑 **refuser** /ʀ(ə)fyze/ [**v1**] **A** *vt* **1** (gen) to refuse; to turn down ‹*offer*›; **~ de faire** to refuse to do
2 to reject ‹*budget, manuscript, racism*›; to refuse to accept ‹*fact*›; to turn away ‹*spectator*›
B se refuser *v refl* (+ *v être*) **1 ça ne se refuse pas** it's too good to pass up (fam); I wouldn't say no (fam)
2 to deny oneself ‹*pleasure*›; **on ne se refuse rien!** (fam) you're certainly not stinting yourself!
3 se ~ à to refuse to accept ‹*evidence*›; to refuse to adopt ‹*solution*›

réfuter /ʀefyte/ [**v1**] *vt* to refute

regagner /ʀ(ə)gaɲe/ [**v1**] *vt* **1** to get back to ‹*place*›
2 to regain ‹*esteem*›

regain /ʀ(ə)gɛ̃/ *m* **~ de** rise in ‹*inflation*›; revival of ‹*interest*›; resurgence of ‹*violence*›

régal /ʀegal/ *m* **1** culinary delight; **c'est un ~!** it's delicious!
2 (fig) delight; **un ~ pour les yeux** a feast for the eyes

régalade /ʀegalad/ *f* **boire à la ~** *to drink without letting one's lips touch the bottle*

régaler: **se régaler** /ʀegale/ [**v1**] *v refl* (+ *v être*) **1 je me régale** it's delicious; **les enfants se sont régalés avec ton dessert** the children really enjoyed your dessert
2 (fig) **se ~ avec** to enjoy [sth] thoroughly ‹*film*›; **se ~ de** to love ‹*anecdote*›

🔑 **regard** /ʀ(ə)gaʀ/ **A** *m* **1** look; **porter son ~ sur qch** to look at sth; **détourner le ~** to look away; **j'ai croisé son ~** our eyes met; **à l'abri des ~s indiscrets** far from prying eyes
2 expression; **son ~ triste** his/her sad

expression; **sous le ~ amusé de qn** under the amused eye of sb; **jeter un ~ noir à qn** to give sb a black look
3 le ~ des autres other people's opinion; **porter un ~ nouveau sur qch** to take a fresh look at sth
B au regard de *phr* (fml) **au ~ de la loi** in the eyes of the law
C en regard *phr* **avec une carte en ~** with a map on the opposite page

regardant, **~e** /ʀəgaʀdɑ̃, ɑ̃t/ *adj* **ne pas être très ~** not to be very particular *or* fussy

regarder /ʀ(ə)gaʀde/ [**v1**] **A** *vt* **1** to look at ‹*person, scene, landscape*›; **~ qch méchamment/fixement/longuement** to glare/stare/gaze at sth; **~ qn en face** to look sb in the face; **~ la réalité** *or* **les choses en face** to face facts; **~ qn de haut** to look down one's nose at sb
2 to watch ‹*film, TV*›; **regarde bien comment je fais** watch what I do carefully
3 to look at ‹*watch, map*›; to have a look at ‹*tyres, oil*›; **~ qch dans** to look sth up in ‹*dictionary*›; **~ si** to have a look and see if
4 to look at ‹*situation*›; **~ pourquoi/si/qui** to see why/if/who
5 (fam) to concern ‹*person*›; **ça ne vous regarde pas** it's none of your business
6 elle ne regarde que ses intérêts she thinks only of her own interests
B regarder à *v+prep* to think about; **ne pas ~ à la dépense** to spare no expense; **à y ~ de plus près** on closer examination
C *vi* to look; **~ en l'air/par terre** to look up/down; **regarde où tu mets les pieds** watch where you put your feet
D se regarder *v refl* (+ *v être*) **1** to look at oneself
2 to look at one another

régate /ʀegat/ *f* regatta

régence /ʀeʒɑ̃s/ *f* **1** regency
2 la Régence the Regency

régénérer /ʀeʒeneʀe/ [**v14**] **A** *vt* **1** to regenerate
2 to reactivate
B se régénérer *v refl* (+ *v être*) **1** ‹*cells*› to regenerate
2 (fig) to regain one's strength

régent, **~e** /ʀeʒɑ̃, ɑ̃t/ *mf* regent

régenter /ʀeʒɑ̃te/ [**v1**] *vt* **1** to rule
2 to regulate

régie /ʀeʒi/ *f* **1** state control; local government control
2 ~ d'État state-owned company
3 stage management; production department
4 central control room

regimber /ʀ(ə)ʒɛ̃be/ [**v1**] *vi* **1** ‹*person*› to balk (**contre** at)
2 ‹*horse*› to jib

régime /ʀeʒim/ *m* **1** diet; **être au ~** to be on a diet
2 (Pol) system (of government); government; regime
3 (in administration) system, regime; **~ de faveur** preferential treatment
4 (Law) **~ matrimonial** marriage settlement
5 (of engine) (running) speed; **tourner à plein ~** ‹*engine*› to run at top speed; ‹*factory*› to work at full capacity
6 (of bananas) bunch

régiment /ʀeʒimɑ̃/ *m* regiment

région /ʀeʒjɔ̃/ *f* region; area

régional, **~e**, *mpl* **-aux** /ʀeʒjɔnal, o/ *adj* regional

régionalisme /ʀeʒjɔnalism/ *m* regionalism

régir /ʀeʒiʀ/ [**v3**] *vt* to govern

régisseur /ʀeʒisœʀ/ *m* **1** (of estate) steward, manager
2 stage manager

registre /ʀ(ə)ʒistʀ/ *m* **1** register; **les ~s de la police** police records
2 (of novel) style
3 (of language, voice) register; **cet acteur a un ~ limité** this actor has a limited range

réglable /ʀeglabl/ *adj* **1** adjustable
2 payable

réglage /ʀeglaʒ/ *m* regulating; setting; adjustment

règle /ʀɛgl/ **A** *f* **1** ruler
2 rule; **~s de sécurité** safety regulations; **respecter les ~s du jeu** to play by the rules; **dans les ~s de l'art** by the rule book; **en ~ générale** as a rule
B règles *fpl* period
C en règle *phr* ‹*request*› formal; ‹*papers, accounts*› in order; **subir un interrogatoire en ~** to be given a grilling; **pour passer la frontière, il faut être en ~** to cross the border, your papers must be in order

réglé, **~e** /ʀegle/ *adj* **1** ruled, lined
2 ‹*life*› well-ordered
3 l'affaire est ~e the matter is settled

règlement /ʀɛgləmɑ̃/ *m* **1** regulations, rules
2 payment
3 settlement
■ **~ de comptes** settling of scores

réglementaire /ʀɛgləmɑ̃tɛʀ/ *adj* ‹*uniform*› regulation; ‹*format*› prescribed; ‹*procedure*› statutory

réglementation /ʀɛgləmɑ̃tasjɔ̃/ *f* **1** rules, regulations
2 regulation, control

réglementer /ʀɛgləmɑ̃te/ [**v1**] *vt* to regulate

régler /ʀegle/ [**v14**] *vt* **1** to settle ‹*debt*›; to pay ‹*bill*›; to pay for ‹*purchase, work*›; **avoir des comptes à ~ avec qn** (fig) to have a score to settle with sb; **~ son compte à qn** (fam) to sort sb out
2 to settle, to sort out ‹*problem*›
3 to settle ‹*details, terms*›
4 to adjust ‹*height*›; to regulate ‹*speed*›; to tune ‹*engine*›; to set ‹*pressure*›
5 ~ sa conduite sur celle de qn to model one's behaviour (BrE) on sb's
6 to rule (lines on) ‹*paper*›

réglisse /ʀeglis/ *f* liquorice (BrE), licorice (AmE)

régnant, **~e** /ʀeɲɑ̃, ɑ̃t/ *adj* ‹*dynasty*› reigning; ‹*ideology*› prevailing

règne /ʀɛɲ/ *m* **1** reign; rule
2 (fig) reign
3 (in biology) kingdom

régner /ʀeɲe/ [**v14**] *vi* **1** ‹*sovereign*› to reign, to rule
2 ‹*boss*› to be in control; **~ en maître sur** to reign supreme over
3 ‹*confusion, fear*› to reign; ‹*smell*› to prevail; **la confiance règne!** (ironic) there's trust for you!; **faire ~** to give rise to ‹*insecurity*›; to impose ‹*order*›

regonfler /ʀ(ə)gɔ̃fle/ [**v1**] *vt* **1** to reinflate ‹*tyre*›; to blow [sth] up again ‹*balloon*›
2 (fam) to increase ‹*staff*›; to boost ‹*sales, profits*›

regorger /ʀ(ə)gɔʀʒe/ [**v13**] *vi* **~ de** ‹*shop*› to be packed with; ‹*region*› to have an abundance of

régresser /ʀegʀese/ [**v1**] *vi* **1** ‹*waters*› to recede; ‹*unemployment*› to go down
2 ‹*industry*› to be in decline
3 ‹*epidemic*› to die out

régressif, **-ive** /ʀegʀesif, iv/ *adj* regressive

régression /ʀegʀesjɔ̃/ *f* **1** decline
2 regression

regret /ʀəgʀɛ/ *m* regret; **j'apprends avec ~ que** I'm sorry to hear that; **j'ai le ~ de vous annoncer** I regret to inform you

regrettable /ʀəgʀɛtabl/ *adj* regrettable

⚷ **regretter** /ʀəgʀete/ [**v1**] *vt* **1** to be sorry about, to regret ‹*situation, action*›; **je regrette de ne pas pouvoir t'aider** I'm sorry I can't help you
2 to regret ‹*decision*›; **~ d'avoir fait** to regret doing; **je ne regrette rien** I have no regrets
3 to miss ‹*person, place*›; **notre regretté collègue** (fml) our late colleague

r

regroupement /ʀ(ə)gʀupmɑ̃/ *m*
1 grouping; pooling; bringing together
2 merger
3 getting [sb/sth] back together; rounding up

regrouper /ʀ(ə)gʀupe/ [**v1**] **A** *vt* **1** to group [sth] together; to bring [sth] together; to pool ‹*interests*›; **~ deux chapitres en un seul** to merge two chapters into one
2 to reassemble ‹*pupils*›; to round up ‹*animals*›
B se regrouper *v refl* (+ *v être*)
1 ‹*companies*› to group together; ‹*malcontents*› to gather
2 ‹*runners*› to bunch together again

régularisation /ʀegylaʀizasjɔ̃/ *f* **1** (of situation) sorting out, regularization
2 (of watercourse) regulation

régulariser /ʀegylaʀize/ [**v1**] *vt* **1** to sort out, to regularize ‹*position, situation*›
2 to regulate ‹*flow*›; to stabilize ‹*price, market*›

régularité /ʀegylaʀite/ *f* **1** regularity
2 (of rhythm, production, progress) steadiness; (of features) regularity; (of writing) neatness; (of surface) evenness; (of quantity) consistency
3 legality

régulateur, **-trice** /ʀegylatœʀ, tʀis/ **A** *adj* regulating
B *m* regulator

régulation /ʀegylasjɔ̃/ *f* regulation, control

régulier, **-ière** /ʀegylje, ɛʀ/ *adj* **1** (gen) regular; ‹*flow, rise, effort*› steady; ‹*quality*› consistent; ‹*thickness*› even; ‹*writing*› neat; ‹*life*› well-ordered; **vol ~** scheduled flight
2 ‹*person*› honest; ‹*papers, ballot*› in order; ‹*government*› legitimate
3 ‹*verb*› regular

régulièrement /ʀegyljɛʀmɑ̃/ *adv* **1** regularly
2 steadily
3 evenly
4 normally

régurgiter /ʀegyʀʒite/ [**v1**] *vt* to regurgitate

réhabiliter /ʀeabilite/ [**v1**] **A** *vt* **1** to rehabilitate
2 to renovate
B se réhabiliter *v refl* (+ *v être*) to redeem oneself

réhabituer /ʀeabitɥe/ [**v1**] *vt* to reaccustom (**qn à qch** sb to sth, **qn à faire** sb to doing)

rehausser /ʀəose/ [**v1**] *vt* **1** to raise
2 to enhance ‹*prestige*›
3 to set off ‹*pattern*›

réimplanter /ʀeɛ̃plɑ̃te/ [**v1**] *vt* to re-establish ‹*factory, industry*›

réimprimer /ʀeɛ̃pʀime/ [**v1**] *vt* to reprint

rein /ʀɛ̃/ **A** *m* kidney; **~ artificiel** kidney machine
B reins *mpl* **les ~s** the small of the back; **une serviette autour des ~s** a towel around one's waist

réincarner: **se réincarner** /ʀeɛ̃kaʀne/ [**v1**] *v refl* (+ *v être*) to be reincarnated

reine /ʀɛn/ *f* **1** queen
2 (fig) **être la ~ des imbéciles** (fam) to be a prize idiot

reine-claude, *pl* **reines-claudes** /ʀɛnklod/ *f* greengage

reinette /ʀɛnɛt/ *f* rennet apple

réinscrire: **se réinscrire** /ʀeɛ̃skʀiʀ/ [**v67**] *v refl* (+ *v être*) to re-enrol (BrE)

réinsérer /ʀeɛ̃seʀe/ [**v14**] *vt* **1** to reintegrate
2 to reinsert

réinstaller /ʀeɛ̃stale/ [**v1**] **A** *vt* to put [sth] back
B se réinstaller *v refl* (+ *v être*) **se ~ dans un fauteuil** to settle (oneself) back into an armchair

réintégrer /ʀeɛ̃tegʀe/ [**v14**] *vt* **1** to return to ‹*place, group, system*›
2 ~ qn (dans ses fonctions) to reinstate sb

réitérer /ʀeiteʀe/ [**v14**] *vt* to repeat

⚷ key word

rejaillir /ʀ(ə)ʒajiʀ/ [**v3**] *vi* **1** ‹*liquid*› to splash back; to spurt back
2 ~ sur qn ‹*success*› to reflect on sb; ‹*scandal*› to affect sb adversely

rejaillissement /ʀ(ə)ʒajismɑ̃/ *m* (of scandal) adverse effect; (of success) reflection

rejet /ʀ(ə)ʒɛ/ *m* **1** (gen) rejection; (of complaint) dismissal; (of motion) defeat; (of request) denial
2 (of waste) discharge; disposal; **~s** waste

rejeter /ʀəʒte, ʀʒəte/ [**v20**] **A** *vt* **1** to reject ‹*advice, candidacy, outsider*›; to turn down ‹*offer*›; to deny ‹*request*›; to set aside ‹*decision*›
2 ~ qch sur qn to shift sth onto sb ‹*blame*›
3 ‹*factory*› to discharge ‹*waste*›; to eject ‹*smoke*›
4 ‹*person, company*› to dispose of ‹*waste*›; ‹*sea*› to wash up ‹*body, debris*›
5 ~ [qch] en arrière to throw back ‹*head, hair*›
B se rejeter *v refl* (+ *v être*) **se ~ la faute** to blame each other

rejeton /ʀəʒ(ə)tɔ̃, ʀʒətɔ̃/ *m* **1** offshoot
2 (fam) offspring

rejoindre /ʀ(ə)ʒwɛ̃dʀ/ [**v56**] **A** *vt* **1** to meet up with
2 to catch up with
3 to join; to rejoin
4 to get to; to get back to, to return to
5 ~ qn sur qch to concur with sb on sth
B se rejoindre *v refl* (+ *v être*) ‹*people*› to meet up; ‹*roads*› to meet

rejouer /ʀ(ə)ʒwe/ [**v1**] *vt* (gen) to play [sth] again; to replay ‹*match, point*›

réjoui, **~e** /ʀejwi/ *adj* cheerful

réjouir /ʀeʒwiʀ/ [**v3**] **A** *vt* **1** to delight ‹*person*›; to gladden ‹*heart*›
2 to amuse
B se réjouir *v refl* (+ *v être*) to rejoice; **se ~ de** to be delighted at ‹*news*›; to be delighted with ‹*success*›

réjouissance /ʀeʒwisɑ̃s/ **A** *f* rejoicing
B réjouissances *fpl* celebrations; **quel est le programme des ~s?** (fam) what delights are in store for us?

réjouissant, **~e** /ʀeʒwisɑ̃, ɑ̃t/ *adj*
1 heartening, delightful
2 amusing

relâche /ʀ(ə)lɑʃ/ *f* **1** (of theatre, cinema) closure; **faire ~** to be closed
2 break, rest; **sans ~** relentlessly

relâchement /ʀ(ə)lɑʃmɑ̃/ *m* **1** (of discipline, effort) slackening; (of morals) loosening
2 (of muscle) slackening

relâcher /ʀ(ə)lɑʃe/ [**v1**] **A** *vt* **1** to loosen ‹*hold*›
2 to release ‹*captive*›
3 to relax ‹*discipline*›; **~ son attention** to let one's attention wander; **~ ses efforts** to let up
B se relâcher *v refl* (+ *v être*) **1** ‹*hold, tie*› to loosen; ‹*muscle*› to relax
2 ‹*effort*› to slacken; ‹*zeal*› to flag; ‹*pupil*› to grow slack

relais /ʀ(ə)lɛ/ *m inv* **1** intermediary; **prendre le ~ (de qn/qch)** to take over (from sb/sth)
2 (Sport) relay
3 restaurant; hotel
4 (Tech) relay; **~ hertzien** radio relay station

relance /ʀ(ə)lɑ̃s/ *f* (of industry, idea) revival; (of economy) reflation; (in inflation) rise; **mesures de ~** reflationary measures

relancer /ʀ(ə)lɑ̃se/ [**v12**] *vt* **1** to throw [sth] again ‹*ball*›; to throw [sth] back (again) ‹*ball*›
2 to restart ‹*engine*›; to relaunch ‹*company*›; to revive ‹*idea*›; to reopen ‹*debate*›; to boost ‹*investment*›; to reflate ‹*economy*›
3 ‹*creditor*› to chase [sb] up; ‹*person*› to pester

relater /ʀ(ə)late/ [**v1**] *vt* (fml) to recount

relatif, **-ive** /ʀ(ə)latif, iv/ **A** *adj* relative; **le risque est très ~** there is relatively little risk
B *m* relative (pronoun)

relation /ʀ(ə)lasjɔ̃/ **A** *f* **1** connection
2 acquaintance; **~s d'affaires** business acquaintances
3 relationship; **avoir de bonnes ~s avec qn** to have a good relationship with sb; **entrer en ~ avec qn** to get in touch with sb
B relations *fpl* relations
■ **~s extérieures** foreign affairs; **~s publiques** public relations

relative /ʀ(ə)lativ/ **A** *adj f* ▶ **relatif A**
B *f* relative (clause)

relativement /ʀ(ə)lativmɑ̃/ **A** *adv* relatively
B relativement à *phr* in relation to

relativiser /ʀ(ə)lativize/ [**v1**] *vt* to put [sth] into perspective

relativité /ʀ(ə)lativite/ *f* relativity

relax /ʀəlaks/ *adj inv* (fam) ‹*person*› laid-back (fam); ‹*clothes*› casual; ‹*party*› informal

relaxant, **~e** /ʀəlaksɑ̃, ɑ̃t/ *adj* relaxing

relaxation /ʀəlaksasjɔ̃/ *f* relaxation

relaxer /ʀəlakse/ [**v1**] **A** *vt* **1** to discharge ‹*defendant*›
2 to relax ‹*muscle, person*›
B se relaxer *v refl* (+ *v être*) to relax

relayer /ʀ(ə)leje/ [**v21**] **A** *vt* **1** to take over from, to relieve
2 to relay ‹*broadcast*›
B se relayer *v refl* (+ *v être*) **1** to take turns
2 to take over from each other

reléguer /ʀ(ə)lege/ [**v14**] *vt* (gen) to relegate; to consign ‹*object*›; **~ qn/qch au second plan** to push sb/sth into the background

relent /ʀ(ə)lɑ̃/ *m* **1** lingering odour (BrE)
2 (fig) whiff

relève /ʀ(ə)lɛv/ *f* **1 la ~ s'effectue à 20 heures** the changeover takes place at 8 pm; **la ~ de**

r

la garde the changing of the guard; **prendre la ~** to take over
2 relief; relief team

relevé, **~e** /Rəlve, Rləve/ **A** *adj* spicy
B *m* **1** noting down; **faire le ~ de** to list ‹*mistakes*›; to make a note of ‹*expenses*›; to read ‹*meter*›
2 ~ bancaire bank statement; **~ d'identité bancaire, RIB** *bank account details for direct debits*

⚷ **relever** /Rəlve, Rləve/ [**v16**] **A** *vt* **1** to pick up ‹*person, stool*›; to put [sth] back up (again)
2 to raise ‹*lever*›
3 ~ la tête to raise one's head; to look up; (fig) to refuse to accept defeat
4 to turn up ‹*collar*›; to lift ‹*skirt*›; to wind up ‹*car window*›; to raise ‹*sail, blind*›; **~ ses cheveux** to put one's hair up
5 to note, to notice; to point out; **~ la moindre inexactitude** to seize on the slightest inaccuracy
6 to take down ‹*date, name*›; to take ‹*prints*›; **~ le compteur** to read the meter
7 to take in ‹*exam papers*›
8 to react to ‹*remark*›; **~ le défi/un pari** to take up the challenge/a bet
9 to rebuild ‹*wall*›; to put [sth] back on its feet ‹*country, economy*›
10 to raise ‹*standard, price*›; to increase ‹*productivity*›
11 to relieve ‹*team*›; **~ la garde** to change the guard
12 to spice up ‹*dish, story*›
13 ~ qn de ses fonctions to relieve sb of their duties
B relever de *v+prep* **1 ~ de** ‹*department*› to come under ‹*Ministry*›; **cela ne relève pas de mes fonctions** that's not part of my duties
2 cela relève de la gageure this comes close to being impossible
C se relever *v refl* (+ *v être*) **1** to pick oneself up; to get up again
2 se ~ automatiquement to be raised automatically
3 ‹*blind*› to be raised
4 se ~ de to recover from

relief /Rəljɛf/ *m* **1** relief; (on medal, coin) raised pattern; **en ~** ‹*globe of the world*› in relief; ‹*letters*› raised; **cinéma en ~** three-dimensional cinema; **mettre qch en ~** to accentuate sth; **un ~ accidenté** a hilly landscape
2 depth; **l'effet de ~** the effect of depth

relier /Rəlje/ [**v2**] *vt* **1** to link; to link up; to link together; to join up; to connect
2 to bind ‹*book*›; **relié cuir** leather-bound

religieuse /Rəliʒjøz/ **A** *adj f* ▶ **religieux A**
B *f* **1** nun
2 (Culin) religieuse

religieusement /Rəliʒjøzmɑ̃/ *adv*
1 religiously
2 ‹*listen*› with rapt attention
3 ‹*get married*› in church

⚷ **religieux**, **-ieuse** /Rəliʒjø, øz/ **A** *adj*
1 religious; ‹*school, wedding*› church; ‹*music*› sacred
2 ‹*silence*› reverent
B *m* monk

⚷ **religion** /R(ə)liʒjɔ̃/ *f* **1** religion
2 faith
3 entrer en ~ to enter the Church

reliquaire /R(ə)likɛR/ *m* reliquary

reliquat /R(ə)lika/ *m* (of sum) remainder; (of account) balance

relique /R(ə)lik/ *f* relic

relire /R(ə)liR/ [**v66**] *vt* to reread; to read [sth] over

reliure /RəljyR/ *f* **1** binding
2 bookbinding

reloger /R(ə)lɔʒe/ [**v13**] *vt* to rehouse

relooking /Rəlukiŋ/ *m* makeover

reluire /R(ə)lɥiR/ [**v69**] *vi* to shine; to glisten
IDIOM **il sait passer la brosse à ~** he's a real flatterer

reluisant, **~e** /R(ə)lɥizɑ̃, ɑ̃t/ *adj* shiny; glistening; **peu ~** (fig) far from brilliant

remâcher /R(ə)mɑʃe/ [**v1**] *vt* **1** to chew [sth] again
2 (fam) to ruminate over ‹*problem, past*›

remaniement /R(ə)manimɑ̃/ *m* modification; revision; reorganization

remanier /R(ə)manje/ [**v2**] *vt* to modify; to redraft; to reorganize; to reshuffle

remarier: **se remarier** /R(ə)maRje/ [**v2**] *v refl* (+ *v être*) to remarry

remarquable /R(ə)maRkabl/ *adj*
1 remarkable
2 striking
3 noteworthy

remarquablement /R(ə)maRkabləmɑ̃/ *adv* remarkably

⚷ **remarque** /R(ə)maRk/ *f* **1** remark; **faire des ~s** to comment
2 (written) comment
3 critical remark, criticism

remarqué, **~e** /R(ə)maRke/ *adj* ‹*initiative*› noteworthy; ‹*increase*› noticeable

⚷ **remarquer** /R(ə)maRke/ [**v1**] **A** *vt* **1** to point out
2 to observe
3 to notice; **remarque, ce n'est pas très important** mind you, it's not very important; **se faire ~** to draw attention to oneself
4 ~ un visage dans la foule to spot a face in the crowd
B se remarquer *v refl* (+ *v être*) **1** to attract attention
2 to show

remballer /Rɑ̃bale/ [**v1**] *vt* to pack [sth] up again

rembarrer /Rɑ̃baRe/ [**v1**] *vt* (fam) to send [sb] packing (fam)

⚷ key word

r

remblai /ʀɑ̃blɛ/ *m* **1** embankment; **route en ~** raised road
2 filling in; banking up
3 (terre de) ~ (for railway, road) ballast; (for ditch) fill; (for excavation) backfill

rembobiner /ʀɑ̃bɔbine/ [**v1**] *vt* to rewind

rembourrer /ʀɑ̃buʀe/ [**v1**] *vt* to stuff ‹*chair*›; to pad ‹*shoulders*›

remboursable /ʀɑ̃buʀsabl/ *adj* ‹*loan, debt*› repayable; ‹*ticket, medicine, treatment*› refundable

remboursement /ʀɑ̃buʀsəmɑ̃/ *m*
1 repayment
2 refund
3 reimbursement

rembourser /ʀɑ̃buʀse/ [**v1**] *vt* **1** to pay off, to repay ‹*loan, debt*›
2 to give a refund to ‹*customer*›; to refund the price of ‹*item*›
3 to reimburse ‹*expenses, employee*›; **~ un ami** to pay a friend back

rembrunir: **se rembrunir** /ʀɑ̃bʀyniʀ/ [**v3**] *v refl* (+ *v être*) ‹*face*› to darken, to cloud over

remède /ʀ(ə)mɛd/ *m* medicine; remedy, cure
■ **~ de bonne femme** folk remedy; **~ de cheval** strong medicine
IDIOM **aux grands maux les grands ~s** desperate times call for desperate measures

remédier /ʀ(ə)medje/ [**v2**] *v+prep* **~ à** to remedy

remembrement /ʀ(ə)mɑ̃bʀəmɑ̃/ *m* regrouping of lands

remémorer: **se remémorer** /ʀ(ə)memɔʀe/ [**v1**] *v refl* (+ *v être*) to recall, to recollect

remerciement /ʀ(ə)mɛʀsimɑ̃/ *m* thanks; **je n'ai pas eu un seul ~** I didn't get a word of thanks; **lettre de ~** thank-you letter

remercier /ʀ(ə)mɛʀsje/ [**v2**] *vt* **1** to thank; **je vous remercie** thank you
2 (ironic) to dismiss

remettre /ʀ(ə)mɛtʀ/ [**v60**] **A** *vt* **1 ~ qch dans/sur** to put sth back in/on; **~ qch en mémoire à qn** to remind sb of sth
2 ~ à qn to hand [sth] over to sb ‹*keys*›; to hand [sth] in to sb ‹*letter*›; to present [sth] to sb ‹*reward*›
3 ~ qch droit *or* **d'aplomb** to put sth straight again
4 to postpone ‹*visit*›
5 to put [sth] on again ‹*heating*›; to play [sth] again ‹*record*›
6 ~ une vis to put a new screw in
7 to add some more ‹*salt*›; to add another ‹*nail*›
8 to put [sth] back on ‹*coat*›
9 (Med) to put [sth] back in place ‹*joint*›
10 ‹*medicine*› to make [sb] feel better
11 ~ qn/le visage de qn to remember sb/sb's face
12 (fam) **~ ça** to start again; **on s'est bien amusé, quand est-ce qu'on remet ça?** that was fun, when are we going to do it again?
B se remettre *v refl* (+ *v être*) **1 se ~ à un endroit** to go *or* get back to a place
2 se ~ au travail to go back to work; **se ~ au dessin** to start drawing again
3 se ~ en jean to wear jeans again
4 se ~ de to recover from ‹*illness*›; to get over ‹*shock*›
5 s'en ~ à qn to leave it to sb; **s'en ~ à la décision de qn** to accept sb's decision
6 se ~ avec qn to get back together with sb

réminiscence /ʀeminisɑ̃s/ *f* **1** reminiscence
2 recollection

remise /ʀ(ə)miz/ *f* **1 attendre la ~ des clés** to wait for the keys to be handed over; **~ des prix** prize-giving; **~ des médailles** medals ceremony
2 discount
3 une ~ de peine a remission
4 ~ de fonds remittance of funds
5 (at a bank) paying in slip
6 shed

remiser /ʀ(ə)mize/ [**v1**] *vt* to put [sth] away (**dans** in)

rémission /ʀemisjɔ̃/ *f* remission; **sans ~** ‹*punish*› mercilessly; ‹*rain*› without stopping

remmener /ʀɑ̃mne/ [**v16**] *vt* to take [sb] back

remodeler /ʀəmɔdle/ [**v17**] *vt* to restructure; to reshape; to replan

remontant /ʀ(ə)mɔ̃tɑ̃/ *m* pick-me-up (fam), tonic

remontée /ʀ(ə)mɔ̃te/ *f* **1** climb up; **la ~ de la Saône en péniche** going up the Saône by barge
2 (in price) rise; (in violence) increase
■ **~ mécanique** (Sport) ski lift

remonte-pente, *pl* **~s** /ʀ(ə)mɔ̃tpɑ̃t/ *m* ski tow

remonter /ʀəmɔ̃te/ [**v1**] **A** *vt* (+ *v avoir*)
1 ~ qch to take sth back up/upstairs; to bring sth back up/upstairs
2 to put [sth] back up; **~ un seau d'un puits** to pull a bucket up from a well
3 to raise ‹*shelf, blind*›; to wind [sth] back up ‹*car window*›; to roll up ‹*sleeves*›; to turn up ‹*collar*›; to pull up ‹*socks*›
4 to go/to come back up; to climb back up; to drive back up
5 to sail up ‹*river*›; to go up ‹*road*›; **~ une filière** *or* **piste** to follow a trail
6 ~ qn *or* **le moral de qn** to cheer sb up
7 to put [sth] back together again; to put [sth] back ‹*wheel*›
8 to wind [sth] up; **être remonté à bloc** (fam) to be full of energy
9 to revive ‹*play, show*›
B *vi* (+ *v être*) **1** ‹*person*› to go/to come back up; ‹*tide*› to come in again; ‹*price, temperature*› to rise again; **~ sur** to step back onto ‹*pavement*›; to climb back onto

r

‹*wall*›; ~ **à la surface** ‹*diver*› to surface; ‹*oil, object*› to rise to the surface; ~ **dans les sondages** to move up in the opinion polls
2 ~ **dans le temps** to go back in time; ~ **à** ‹*historian*› to go back to; ‹*event*› to date back to; **faire** ~ to trace (back) ‹*origins*›
3 ‹*skirt*› to ride up
4 les odeurs d'égout remontent dans la maison the smell from the drains reaches our house
C se remonter *v refl* (+ *v être*) **se ~ le moral** to cheer oneself up; to cheer each other up

remontoir /R(ə)mɔ̃twaR/ *m* winder

remontrance /Rəmɔ̃tRɑ̃s/ *f* reprimand

remontrer /Rəmɔ̃tRe/ [**v1**] *vi* **en ~ à qn** to teach sb a thing or two

remords /RəmɔR/ *m inv* remorse

remorquage /RəmɔRkaʒ/ *m* towing

remorque /RəmɔRk/ *f* **1** tow rope; **prendre en ~** to tow ‹*car*›
2 trailer

remorquer /RəmɔRke/ [**v1**] *vt* to tow ‹*vehicle*›

remorqueur /RəmɔRkœR/ *m* tug

remous /R(ə)mu/ *m inv* **1** eddy
2 backwash; wash
3 (of ideas) turmoil; (in crowd) stir

rempailler /Rɑ̃pɑje/ [**v1**] *vt* to reseat ‹*chair*›

rempart /Rɑ̃paR/ *m* **1** rampart; battlements; **les ~s de la ville** the city walls
2 defence (BrE)

remplaçable /Rɑ̃plasabl/ *adj* replaceable

remplaçant, **~e** /Rɑ̃plasɑ̃, ɑ̃t/ *mf* **1** (gen) substitute; (at school) supply (BrE) *or* substitute (AmE) teacher; (actor) stand-in
2 successor

remplacement /Rɑ̃plasmɑ̃/ *m* replacement; **faire des ~s** ‹*teacher*› to do supply (BrE) *or* substitute (AmE) teaching; ‹*temp*› to do temporary work; **produit de ~** substitute

r

🗝 **remplacer** /Rɑ̃plase/ [**v12**] *vt* **1** to stand in for, to cover for ‹*colleague*›
2 to replace; **on peut ~ le vinaigre par du jus de citron** you can use lemon juice instead of vinegar

🗝 **remplir** /Rɑ̃pliR/ [**v3**] *vt* **1** to fill (up) ‹*container*›; to fill in ‹*form*›; **~ qch à moitié** to half fill sth; **~ qn de joie** to fill sb with joy; **une vie bien remplie** a full life
2 to carry out ‹*role, mission*›; to fulfil (BrE) ‹*duty, role*›

remplissage /Rɑ̃plisaʒ/ *m* **1** filling
2 (derog) **faire du ~** to pad out one's work

remplumer: **se remplumer** /Rɑ̃plyme/ [**v1**] *v refl* (+ *v être*) (fam) (financially) to get back on one's feet; (physically) to put some weight back on

rempocher /Rɑ̃pɔʃe/ [**v1**] *vt* to put [sth] back in one's pocket

🗝 key word

remporter /Rɑ̃pɔRte/ [**v1**] *vt* to win ‹*seat, title, victory*›; **~ un vif succès** to be a great success

rempoter /Rɑ̃pɔte/ [**v1**] *vt* to repot

remuant, **~e** /R(ə)mɥɑ̃, ɑ̃t/ *adj* **1** rowdy
2 boisterous; energetic

remue-ménage /R(ə)mymenaʒ/ *m inv*
1 commotion
2 bustle

remuer /R(ə)mɥe/ [**v1**] **A** *vt* **1** to move ‹*hand, head*›; to wiggle ‹*toe, hips*›; to wag ‹*tail*›
2 to shake ‹*object*›
3 to move ‹*object*›
4 to stir ‹*soup*›; to toss ‹*salad*›
5 to turn over ‹*earth*›; to poke ‹*ashes*›
6 (fig) to rake up ‹*past*›; to stir up ‹*memories*›
7 to upset ‹*person*›
B *vi* ‹*person*› to move; ‹*leaves*› to flutter; ‹*boat*› to bob up and down
C se remuer *v refl* (+ *v être*) (fam) **1** to get a move on (fam)
2 se ~ pour obtenir to make an effort to get

rémunérateur, **-trice** /RemyneRatœR, tRis/ *adj* lucrative

rémunération /RemyneRasjɔ̃/ *f* pay; payment

rémunérer /RemyneRe/ [**v14**] *vt* to pay ‹*person*›; to pay for ‹*work*›

renâcler /R(ə)nɑkle/ [**v1**] *vi* **1** ‹*person*› to show reluctance
2 ‹*animal*› to snort

renaissance /R(ə)nɛsɑ̃s/ *f* rebirth; revival

Renaissance /R(ə)nɛsɑ̃s/ *f* Renaissance

renaître /R(ə)nɛtR/ [**v74**] *vi* (+ *v être*) **1** to come back to life
2 ‹*hope, desire*› to return; **faire ~ l'espoir** to bring new hope

rénal, **~e**, *mpl* **-aux** /Renal, o/ *adj* ‹*artery*› renal; ‹*infection*› kidney

renard /R(ə)naR/ *m* **1** fox
2 wily old fox

renarde /R(ə)naRd/ *f* vixen

renardeau, *pl* **~x** /R(ə)naRdo/ *m* fox cub

renchérir /Rɑ̃ʃeRiR/ [**v3**] *vi* **1** to add; **~ sur ce que dit qn** to add something to what sb says
2 to go one step further
3 to raise the bidding

🗝 **rencontre** /Rɑ̃kɔ̃tR/ *f* **1** meeting; encounter; **faire la ~ de qn** to meet sb
2 (Sport) match (BrE), game (AmE); **~ d'athlétisme** athletics meeting (BrE), track meet (AmE)
■ **~ en ligne** online dating; **~ au sommet** summit meeting

🗝 **rencontrer** /Rɑ̃kɔ̃tRe/ [**v1**] **A** *vt* **1** to meet ‹*person*›; **~ qn sur son chemin** to come across sb
2 to encounter, to meet with ‹*problem, opposition*›
3 to come across ‹*object, word*›
4 to meet ‹*player, team*›

B **se rencontrer** *v refl* (+ *v être*) **1** to meet
2 ‹*quality, object, person*› to be found

rendant /ʀɑ̃dɑ̃/ ▶ **rendre**

rendement /ʀɑ̃dmɑ̃/ *m* **1** (from land, investment) yield; (of machine, worker) output
2 (of factory) productivity; (of machine, worker) efficiency
3 (of sportsman, pupil) performance

rendez-vous /ʀɑ̃devu/ *m inv* **1** appointment; date; **sur ~** by appointment; **j'ai ~ avec un ami** I'm meeting a friend; **le soleil n'était pas au ~** the sun didn't shine
2 meeting
3 gathering; meeting place

rendormir: **se rendormir** /ʀɑ̃dɔʀmiʀ/ [**v30**] *v refl* (+ *v être*) to go back to sleep

rendre /ʀɑ̃dʀ/ [**v6**] **A** *vt* **1** (gen) to give back, to return; to repay, to pay back ‹*loan*›; to return ‹*greeting, invitation, goods*›; **~ la pareille à qn** to pay sb back; **il la déteste mais elle le lui rend bien** he hates her and she feels the same about him
2 ~ la santé/vue à qn to restore sb's health/sight
3 ~ qch possible to make sth possible; **~ qn fou** to drive sb mad
4 to hand in ‹*homework*›
5 ‹*land*› to yield ‹*crop, quantity*›
6 to convey ‹*atmosphere, nuance*›; **ça ne rendra rien en couleurs** it won't come out in colour (BrE)
7 (fam) to bring up ‹*food, bile*›
8 to pronounce ‹*sentence*›; to return ‹*verdict*›
9 les tomates rendent de l'eau (à la cuisson) tomatoes give out water during cooking
B *vi* **1** ‹*land*› to be productive; ‹*plant*› to produce a good crop
2 (fam) to throw up (fam)
C **se rendre** *v refl* (+ *v être*) **1 se ~ à Rome/en ville** to go to Rome/to town
2 se ~ indispensable/malade to make oneself indispensable/ill
3 to give oneself up; to surrender
4 se ~ à qch to bow to ‹*argument*›
IDIOM **~ l'âme** *or* **l'esprit** to pass away

rendu, **-e** /ʀɑ̃dy/ ▶ **rendre**

rêne /ʀɛn/ *f* rein

renfermé, **~e** /ʀɑ̃fɛʀme/ **A** *pp* ▶ **renfermer**
B *pp adj* ‹*person*› withdrawn; ‹*feeling*› hidden
C *m* **odeur de ~** musty smell

renfermer /ʀɑ̃fɛʀme/ [**v1**] **A** *vt* to contain
B **se renfermer** *v refl* (+ *v être*) to become withdrawn

renflé, **~e** /ʀɑ̃fle/ *adj* ‹*vase*› rounded; ‹*dome*› bulbous; ‹*stomach*› bulging

renflement /ʀɑ̃fləmɑ̃/ *m* bulge

renflouer /ʀɑ̃flue/ [**v1**] *vt* **1** to raise ‹*ship*›
2 to bail out ‹*person, company*›

renfoncement /ʀɑ̃fɔ̃smɑ̃/ *m* recess; **~ de porte** doorway

renforcer /ʀɑ̃fɔʀse/ [**v12**] **A** *vt* to reinforce; to strengthen
B **se renforcer** *v refl* (+ *v être*) ‹*power*› to increase; ‹*control*› to become tighter; ‹*team, numbers*› to grow; ‹*sector*› to grow stronger

renfort /ʀɑ̃fɔʀ/ *m* **1** (Mil) reinforcement
2 support; **annoncé à grand ~ de publicité** well publicized
3 (Sport) substitute

renfrogné, **~e** /ʀɑ̃fʀɔɲe/ *adj* sullen

renfrogner: **se renfrogner** /ʀɑ̃fʀɔɲe/ [**v1**] *v refl* (+ *v être*) to become sullen

rengaine /ʀɑ̃gɛn/ *f* **c'est toujours la même ~** (fig) it's the same old thing every time

rengainer /ʀɑ̃gɛne/ [**v1**] *vt* to sheathe ‹*sword*›; to put [sth] back in its holster ‹*pistol*›

rengorger: **se rengorger** /ʀɑ̃gɔʀʒe/ [**v13**] *v refl* (+ *v être*) ‹*bird*› to puff out its breast; ‹*person*› to swell with conceit

reniement /ʀ(ə)nimɑ̃/ *m* disavowal

renier /ʀənje/ [**v2**] **A** *vt* to renounce ‹*religion, opinion*›; to disown ‹*child, work, friend*›
B **se renier** *v refl* (+ *v être*) to go back on what one has said *or* promised

reniflement /ʀ(ə)nifləmɑ̃/ *m* **1** sniffing
2 sniff

renifler /ʀ(ə)nifle/ [**v1**] *vt*, *vi* to sniff

renne /ʀɛn/ *m* reindeer

renom /ʀənɔ̃/ *m* **1** fame
2 reputation

renommé, **~e** /ʀənɔme/ *adj* famous

renommée /ʀənɔme/ *f* **1** reputation
2 fame

renoncement /ʀ(ə)nɔ̃smɑ̃/ *m* renunciation

renoncer /ʀ(ə)nɔ̃se/ [**v12**] *v+prep* to give up; **~ à** to give up; to abandon; to renounce; **~ à faire** to abandon the idea of doing

renonciation /ʀ(ə)nɔ̃sjasjɔ̃/ *f* giving up

renouer /ʀənwe/ [**v1**] **A** *vt* **1** to retie ‹*laces*›
2 to pick up the thread of ‹*conversation*›
B **~ avec** *v+prep* to get back in touch with ‹*person*›; to revive ‹*tradition*›; to go back to ‹*past*›

renouveau, *pl* **~x** /ʀənuvo/ *m* revival

renouveler /ʀənuvle/ [**v19**] **A** *vt* **1** (gen) to renew; to repeat ‹*suggestion, experience*›; to replace ‹*equipment, team*›; to change ‹*water*›
2 to revitalize ‹*genre, style*›
B **se renouveler** *v refl* (+ *v être*) **1 une pièce où l'air ne se renouvelle pas** a room which isn't aired
2 ‹*artist*› to try out new ideas
3 ‹*experience*› to be repeated

renouvellement /ʀənuvɛlmɑ̃/ *m*
1 renewal
2 replacement
3 revitalization

rénovateur, **-trice** /ʀenɔvatœʀ, tʀis/ *mf* reformer

rénovation /ʀenɔvasjɔ̃/ *f* renovation

rénover /ʀenɔve/ [**v1**] *vt* **1** to renovate ‹*area, house*›; to restore ‹*furniture*›
2 to reform ‹*institution, policy*›; to revamp ‹*project*›

🔑 **renseignement** /ʀɑ̃sɛɲmɑ̃/ **A** *m*
1 information; **est-ce que je peux vous demander un ~?** can I ask you something?; **~s pris** upon investigation; **'pour tous ~s, s'adresser à...'** 'all enquiries to...'
2 (Mil) intelligence
B renseignements *mpl* **1** information
2 directory enquiries (BrE) *or* assistance (AmE)

renseigner /ʀɑ̃seɲe/ [**v1**] **A** *vt* **~ qn** to give information to sb
B se renseigner *v refl* (+ *v être*) to find out, to enquire; to make enquiries

rentabilisation /ʀɑ̃tabilizasjɔ̃/ *f* **la ~ de l'entreprise est notre premier objectif** our primary aim is to make the company profitable

rentabiliser /ʀɑ̃tabilize/ [**v1**] *vt* to secure a return on ‹*investment*›; to make a profit on ‹*product*›; to make [sth] profitable ‹*business*›

rentabilité /ʀɑ̃tabilite/ *f* **1** profitability
2 return

rentable /ʀɑ̃tabl/ *adj* profitable

rente /ʀɑ̃t/ *f* **1** private income
2 annuity; **~ viagère** life annuity
3 government stock

rentrée /ʀɑ̃tʀe/ *f* **1** (general) return to work (*after the slack period of the summer break in France*); **~ (des classes** *or* **scolaire)** start of the (new) school year; **mon livre sera publié à la ~** my book will be published in the autumn (BrE) *or* fall (AmE)
2 return (to work)
3 comeback; **~ politique** political comeback
4 receipts; **~ (d'argent)** income; takings
■ **~ parlementaire** reassembly of Parliament

🔑 **rentrer** /ʀɑ̃tʀe/ [**v1**] **A** *vt* **1** to bring [sth] in; to take [sth] in
2 to raise ‹*landing gear*›; to draw in ‹*claws*›; **rentrez le ventre!** hold your stomach in!
3 to tuck ‹*shirt*› (**dans** into)
B *vi* (+ *v être*) **1** to go in; to get in; to fit; **~ dans un arbre** (fam) to hit a tree
2 ~ dans to go back into; to come back into
3 ~ (chez soi) to get (*or* go *or* come) back (home); to return (home)
4 ~ dans ses frais to recoup one's money
5 ‹*money*› to come in
6 faire ~ qch dans la tête de qn to get sth into sb's head
IDIOM **il m'est rentré dedans** (pop) he bumped *or* ran into me; he crashed into me

renversant, **~e** /ʀɑ̃vɛʀsɑ̃, ɑ̃t/ *adj* astounding, astonishing

renverse /ʀɑ̃vɛʀs/ *f* **tomber à la ~** to fall flat on one's back

renversement /ʀɑ̃vɛʀsəmɑ̃/ *m* **1** reversal
2 overthrow; removal from office

renverser /ʀɑ̃vɛʀse/ [**v1**] **A** *vt* **1** to knock over; to knock down
2 to spill
3 to turn [sth] upside down
4 to reverse
5 to overthrow; to vote [sb/sth] out of office
B se renverser *v refl* (+ *v être*) ‹*boat*› to capsize; ‹*bottle*› to fall over; ‹*liquid*› to spill

renvoi /ʀɑ̃vwɑ/ *m* **1** expulsion; dismissal
2 return; **~ d'un colis** return of a parcel
3 postponement
4 cross-reference
5 belch, burp (fam)

🔑 **renvoyer** /ʀɑ̃vwaje/ [**v24**] *vt* **1** to throw [sth] back ‹*ball*›; to reflect ‹*light, heat*›; to echo ‹*sound*›
2 to return ‹*mail*›
3 to send [sb] back; **~ qn chez lui** to send sb home
4 to expel; to dismiss
5 to postpone ‹*debate*›; to adjourn ‹*case*›
6 ~ à to refer to

réorganisation /ʀeɔʀganizasjɔ̃/ *f* reorganization

réorienter /ʀeɔʀjɑ̃te/ [**v1**] *vt* to reorientate ‹*pupil, student*› (**vers** toward(s)); to reshape ‹*policy*›

réouverture /ʀeuvɛʀtyʀ/ *f* reopening

repaire /ʀ(ə)pɛʀ/ *m* den; hideout

🔑 **répandre** /ʀepɑ̃dʀ/ [**v6**] **A** *vt* **1** to spread ‹*substance*›; to pour ‹*liquid*›; to spill ‹*liquid*›
2 to scatter ‹*seeds, rubbish*›
3 to spread ‹*news, religion*›; to give off ‹*heat, smoke, smell*›
B se répandre *v refl* (+ *v être*) to spread

répandu, **~e** /ʀepɑ̃dy/ *adj* widespread

réparable /ʀepaʀabl/ *adj* **1** ‹*object*› repairable
2 ‹*mistake*› which can be put right

reparaître /ʀ(ə)paʀɛtʀ/ [**v73**] *vi*
1 ▶ **réapparaître**
2 ‹*magazine*› to be back in print

réparateur, **-trice** /ʀepaʀatœʀ, tʀis/ **A** *adj* refreshing
B *mf* engineer (BrE), fixer (AmE)

réparation /ʀepaʀasjɔ̃/ *f* **1** repairing, mending; repair
2 compensation
3 redress

réparer /ʀepaʀe/ [**v1**] *vt* **1** to repair, to mend, to fix
2 to put [sth] right ‹*error*›; to make up for ‹*oversight*›
3 to compensate for ‹*damage*›

reparler /ʀ(ə)paʀle/ [**v1**] *vt* **1 ~ de** to discuss [sth] again (**à qn, avec qn** with sb)
2 ~ à qn to be back on speaking terms with sb

repartie /ʀepaʀti/ *f* rejoinder; **elle a de la ~** she always has a ready reply

🔑 key word

repartir /ʀ(ə)paʀtiʀ/ [**v30**] *vi* (+ *v être*) **1** to leave (again); to go back
2 ‹*person*› to set off again; ‹*machine*› to start again; ‹*sector*› to pick up again
3 ~ **à zéro** to start again from scratch

répartir /ʀepaʀtiʀ/ [**v3**] **A** *vt* **1** to share [sth] out; to split ‹*profits, expenses*›; to distribute ‹*weight*›
2 to spread ‹*payments*›
B se répartir *v refl* (+ *v être*) **1** to share out, to split
2 ‹*work, votes*› to be split; **se ~ en** ‹*people, objects*› to divide (up) into

répartition /ʀepaʀtisjɔ̃/ *f* **1** sharing out; dividing up
2 distribution

repas /ʀ(ə)pɑ/ *m inv* meal

repassage /ʀ(ə)pasaʒ/ *m* ironing

repasser /ʀ(ə)pase/ [**v1**] **A** *vt* **1** to iron
2 to cross [sth] again ‹*river, border*›
3 to take [sth] again ‹*exam*›
4 to pass [sth] again ‹*tool, salt*›; **je te repasse Jean** (on phone) I'll put you back on to Jean
5 (fam) ~ **qch à qn** to give sb sth ‹*cold*›
B *vi* (+ *v être*) **1** to go past again; **si tu repasses à Lyon, viens me voir** if you're ever back in Lyons, come and see me
2 ‹*film*› to be showing again
3 quand elle fait la vaisselle, je dois ~ derrière elle I always have to do the dishes again after she's done them

repêchage /ʀ(ə)pɛʃaʒ/ *m* **1** recovery (*from water*)
2 épreuve de ~ resit (BrE), retest (AmE)

repêcher /ʀ(ə)peʃe/ [**v1**] *vt* to recover; to fish out

repeindre /ʀ(ə)pɛ̃dʀ/ [**v55**] *vt* to repaint

repenser /ʀ(ə)pɑ̃se/ [**v1**] **A** *vt* to rethink
B repenser à *v+prep* to think back to ‹*childhood*›; to think again about ‹*anecdote*›

repenti, **~e** /ʀ(ə)pɑ̃ti/ *adj* repentant

repentir[1]**: se repentir** /ʀ(ə)pɑ̃tiʀ/ [**v30**] *v refl* (+ *v être*) **1** to regret
2 to repent

repentir[2] /ʀ(ə)pɑ̃tiʀ/ *m* repentance

repérable /ʀ(ə)peʀabl/ *adj* that can be spotted

repérage /ʀ(ə)peʀaʒ/ *m* (Mil) location (**de** of)

répercussion /ʀepɛʀkysjɔ̃/ *f* repercussion

répercuter /ʀepɛʀkyte/ [**v1**] **A** *vt* **1** to pass [sth] on ‹*increase*›
2 to send back ‹*sound*›
B se répercuter *v refl* (+ *v être*) ‹*sound*› to echo; ‹*increase*› to be reflected (**sur** in)

repère /ʀ(ə)pɛʀ/ *m* **1** marker; (reference) mark
2 (event) landmark; (date) reference point

repérer /ʀ(ə)peʀe/ [**v14**] **A** *vt* **1** (fam) to spot; **~ les lieux** to check out a place
2 to locate ‹*target*›
B se repérer *v refl* (+ *v être*) to get one's bearings

répertoire /ʀepɛʀtwaʀ/ *m* **1** notebook with thumb index
2 ~ téléphonique telephone book
3 repertoire

répertorier /ʀepɛʀtɔʀje/ [**v2**] *vt* **1** to list; to index
2 to identify

répéter /ʀepete/ [**v14**] **A** *vt* **1** to repeat; **~ qch à qn** to say sth to sb again; **je te répète que tu as tort** I'm telling you, you're wrong
2 to rehearse ‹*play*›; to rehearse for ‹*concert*›
B se répéter *v refl* (+ *v être*) **1** to repeat oneself
2 j'ai beau me ~ que... no matter how often I tell myself that...
3 ‹*incident*› to be repeated

répétitif, **-ive** /ʀepetitif, iv/ *adj* repetitive

répétition /ʀepetisjɔ̃/ *f* **1** repetition
2 rehearsal; **~ générale** dress rehearsal

repeupler /ʀ(ə)pœple/ [**v1**] *vt* **1** to repopulate
2 to restock
3 to reforest

repiquer /ʀ(ə)pike/ [**v1**] *vt* to transplant ‹*rice*›; to prick out ‹*seedlings*›

répit /ʀepi/ *m* respite

replacer /ʀ(ə)plase/ [**v12**] *vt* **~ qch dans son contexte** to set sth back in context

replanter /ʀ(ə)plɑ̃te/ [**v1**] *vt* **1** to transplant
2 to replant

replâtrer /ʀ(ə)plɑtʀe/ [**v1**] *vt* **1** to replaster
2 to patch up ‹*group*›

replet, **-ète** /ʀəplɛ, ɛt/ *adj* plump, chubby

repli /ʀ(ə)pli/ *m* **1** double fold
2 fold
3 (Mil) withdrawal
4 ~ sur soi(-même) withdrawal

replier /ʀ(ə)plije/ [**v2**] **A** *vt* **1** to fold up ‹*map*›
2 to fold [sth] back ‹*sheet*›
3 to fold up ‹*deckchair, fan*›; to close ‹*umbrella, penknife*›
4 elle replia ses jambes she tucked her legs under her; **~ ses ailes** ‹*bird*› to fold its wings
B se replier *v refl* (+ *v être*) **1** ‹*blade*› to fold up
2 ‹*army*› to withdraw
3 se ~ sur soi-même ‹*person*› to become withdrawn

réplique /ʀeplik/ *f* **1** retort, rejoinder; **il a la ~ facile** he's always ready with an answer
2 line; **donner la ~ à qn** to play opposite sb
3 replica; **elle est la ~ de sa mère** she is the image of her mother

répliquer /ʀeplike/ [**v1**] **A** *vt* to retort
B répliquer à *v+prep* to argue with ‹*person*›; to respond to ‹*criticism*›
C *vi* **1** to answer back
2 to retaliate, to respond

répondant, **~e** /Repɔ̃dɑ̃, ɑ̃t/ *mf* referee; (Law) surety, guarantor

répondeur /Repɔ̃dœR/ *m* **~ (téléphonique)** (telephone) answering machine

🔑 **répondre** /Repɔ̃dR/ **[v6]** **A** *vt* to answer, to reply; **il m'a été répondu que...** I was told that...; **qu'as-tu à ~?** what's your answer?
B **répondre à** *v+prep* **1** **~ à** to reply to, to answer ‹*person, question, letter*›; to answer ‹*phone*›
2 **~ à** to talk back to
3 **~ à** to answer, to meet ‹*needs*›; to fulfil (BrE) ‹*wishes*›; to fit ‹*description*›; to come up to ‹*expectations*›
4 **~ à** to respond to ‹*appeal, criticism*›; to return ‹*greeting*›; **~ à un sourire** to smile back; **les freins ne répondent plus** the brakes have failed
C **répondre de** *v+prep* **~ de qn** to vouch for sb; **~ de ses actes** to answer for one's actions

🔑 **réponse** /Repɔ̃s/ *f* **1** answer, reply
2 response

report /RəpɔR/ *m* **1** adjournment; postponement; deferment
2 transfer

reportage /R(ə)pɔRtaʒ/ *m* **1** report
2 reporting

reporter¹ /R(ə)pɔRte/ **[v1]** **A** *vt* **1** to put back ‹*date*›; to postpone ‹*event*›; to defer ‹*judgement*›
2 to carry forward ‹*result*›; to copy out ‹*name*›
3 to take [sth] back ‹*goods*›
4 to transfer ‹*affection*›; **~ son agressivité sur qn** to take one's aggression out on sb
B **se reporter** *v refl* (+ *v être*) **se ~ à** to refer to; to think back to

reporter² /RəpɔRtɛR/ *m* reporter

🔑 **repos** /Rəpo/ *m inv* rest; **mon jour de ~** my day off

reposant, **~e** /Rəpozɑ̃, ɑ̃t/ *adj* peaceful, restful; soothing; relaxing

repose-pieds /R(ə)pozpje/ *m inv* footrest

🔑 **reposer** /Rəpoze/ **[v1]** **A** *vt* **1** to rest; **avoir le visage reposé** to look rested; **lire qch à tête reposée** to read sth at one's leisure
2 to put [sth] down ‹*phone*›; to put [sth] down again
3 to ask [sth] again ‹*question*›
B *vi* **1** to rest; **'ici repose le Dr Grunard'** 'here lies Dr Grunard'; **laisser ~ la terre** to rest the land; **'laisser ~ la pâte'** 'let the dough stand'
2 **~ sur** to be based on; **la poutre repose sur...** the beam is supported by...
C **se reposer** *v refl* (+ *v être*) **1** to have a rest, to rest
2 **se ~ sur qn** to rely on sb

repose-tête /Rəpoztɛt/ *m inv* head rest

repoussant, **~e** /Rəpusɑ̃, ɑ̃t/ *adj* hideous

repousser /R(ə)puse/ **[v1]** **A** *vt* **1** to push [sth] to ‹*door*›; to push back ‹*object*›
2 to push away ‹*object*›; to push back ‹*lock of hair*›
3 to push *or* drive back ‹*crowd, animal*›; (Mil) to repel ‹*attack*›
4 to dismiss ‹*objection*›; to decline ‹*help*›; to turn down ‹*request*›
5 to revolt
6 to postpone ‹*event*›; to move [sth] back ‹*date*›
B *vi* to grow again; to grow back

répréhensible /Repreɑ̃sibl/ *adj* reprehensible

🔑 **reprendre** /R(ə)pRɑ̃dR/ **[v52]** **A** *vt* **1** **~ du pain/vin** to have some more bread/wine; **j'en ai repris deux fois** I had three helpings
2 to pick [sth] up again ‹*object, tool*›; to take [sth] back ‹*present*›; to collect ‹*person, car*›
3 to take [sb] on again ‹*employee*›; ‹*shop*› to take [sth] back ‹*item*›; **si on me reprend ma vieille voiture** if I can trade in my old car
4 to resume ‹*walk, story*›; to take up [sth] again ‹*studies*›; to revive ‹*play, tradition*›; **~ le travail** to go back to work; **tu reprends le train à quelle heure?** what time is your train back?; **~ une histoire au début** to go back to the beginning of a story
5 to take over ‹*business, shop*›
6 **on ne me reprendra plus à lui rendre service!** you won't catch me doing him/her any favours (BrE) again!
7 **~ confiance** to regain one's confidence
8 to alter ‹*clothes*›
9 to take up ‹*idea, thesis, policy*›
10 to repeat ‹*argument*›; to take up ‹*slogan, news*›
11 to correct ‹*pupil*›; **~ le travail de qn** to correct sb's work
12 **mon mal de dents m'a repris** my toothache has come back
B *vi* **1** ‹*business*› to pick up again; ‹*plant*› to recover
2 to start again
3 **'c'est étrange,' reprit-il** 'it's strange,' he continued
C **se reprendre** *v refl* (+ *v être*) **1** to correct oneself
2 to pull oneself together
3 **s'y ~ à trois fois pour faire** to make three attempts to do *or* at doing

représailles /R(ə)pRezaj/ *fpl* reprisals; retaliation

🔑 **représentant**, **~e** /R(ə)pRezɑ̃tɑ̃, ɑ̃t/ *mf* **1** representative
2 **~ (de commerce)** sales representative

représentatif, **-ive** /RəpRezɑ̃tatif, iv/ *adj* representative

🔑 **représentation** /RəpRezɑ̃tasjɔ̃/ *f* **1** representation
2 performance
3 commercial travelling (BrE); **~ exclusive** sole agency

🔑 **représenter** /RəpRezɑ̃te/ **[v1]** **A** *vt* **1** (in

🔑 key word

painting) to depict; to portray
2 to represent; to mean; **les enfants représentent les deux tiers de la population** children make up two thirds of the population
3 to represent ‹*person, company*›
4 to perform ‹*play*›
B se représenter *v refl* (+ *v être*) **1** to imagine ‹*scene*›
2 ‹*opportunity*› to arise again
3 se ~ à un examen to retake an examination

répressif, **-ive** /ʀepʀesif, iv/ *adj* repressive

répression /ʀepʀesjɔ̃/ *f* suppression

réprimande /ʀepʀimɑ̃d/ *f* reprimand

réprimander /ʀepʀimɑ̃de/ [**v1**] *vt* to reprimand

réprimer /ʀepʀime/ [**v1**] *vt* to suppress; to repress ‹*desire*›

repris /ʀ(ə)pʀi/ *m inv* **~ de justice** ex-convict

reprise /ʀəpʀiz/ *f* **1** (of work, negotiations) resumption; (of play, film) rerun; **à plusieurs** *or* **maintes ~s** on several occasions, repeatedly
2 (of demand, production) increase; (of business) revival; (of economy) upturn
3 (of goods) return, taking back; trade-in; (of company) takeover
4 key money
5 (Aut) acceleration
6 mend; darn
7 (in boxing) round; (in football) start of the second half

repriser /ʀəpʀize/ [**v1**] *vt* to mend; to darn

réprobation /ʀepʀɔbasjɔ̃/ *f* disapproval

reproche /ʀ(ə)pʀɔʃ/ *m* reproach; **j'ai un ou deux ~s à vous faire** I've one or two criticisms to make; **sans ~** beyond reproach

reprocher /ʀəpʀɔʃe/ [**v1**] **A** *vt* **1 ~ qch à qn** to criticize *or* reproach sb for sth; **on ne peut rien lui ~** he's/she's beyond reproach; **elle me reproche de ne jamais lui écrire** she complains that I never write to her
2 les faits qui lui sont reprochés the charges against him/her
B se reprocher *v refl* (+ *v être*) **se ~ qch** to blame *or* reproach oneself for sth

reproducteur, **-trice** /ʀəpʀɔdyktœʀ, tʀis/ *adj* **1** reproductive
2 ‹*animal*› breeding

reproduction /ʀ(ə)pʀɔdyksjɔ̃/ *f*
1 reproduction
2 reproduction, copy; **droit de ~** copyright

reproduire /ʀ(ə)pʀɔdɥiʀ/ [**v69**] **A** *vt* (gen) to reproduce; to recreate ‹*conditions*›
B se reproduire *v refl* (+ *v être*)
1 ‹*humans, plants*› to reproduce
2 ‹*situation*› to recur

réprouver /ʀepʀuve/ [**v1**] *vt* to condemn

reptile /ʀɛptil/ *m* reptile

repu, **~e** /ʀəpy/ *adj* full

républicain, **~e** /ʀepyblikɛ̃, ɛn/ *adj*, *mf* republican

✓ **république** /ʀepyblik/ *f* republic; **on est en ~** it's a free country

répudier /ʀepydje/ [**v2**] *vt* **1** to repudiate ‹*spouse*›
2 to renounce ‹*right, faith*›

répugnance /ʀepyɲɑ̃s/ *f* **1** revulsion
2 reluctance; **avec ~** reluctantly

répugnant, **~e** /ʀepyɲɑ̃, ɑ̃t/ *adj* **1** revolting
2 disgusting
3 loathsome

répugner /ʀepyɲe/ [**v1**] *v+prep* **1 ~ à** ‹*food*› to disgust ‹*person*›
2 ~ à ‹*person*› to be averse to ‹*work*›; **~ à faire** to be reluctant to do

répulsion /ʀepylsjɔ̃/ *f* repulsion

réputation /ʀepytasjɔ̃/ *f* reputation; **se faire une ~** to make a name for oneself

réputé, **~e** /ʀepyte/ *adj* **1** ‹*company*› reputable; ‹*writer*› of repute; ‹*product*› well-known; **~ pour qch** renowned for sth; **l'avocat le plus ~ de Paris** the best lawyer in Paris
2 ~ cher reputed to be expensive

requérir /ʀəkeʀiʀ/ [**v35**] *vt* **1** to request
2 to require

requête /ʀəkɛt/ *f* **1** request
2 (Law) petition

requiem /ʀekwijɛm/ *m inv* requiem

requin /ʀ(ə)kɛ̃/ *m* (Zool), (fig) shark

requis, **~e** /ʀəki, iz/ **A** *pp* ▸ **requérir**
B *pp adj* ‹*patience*› necessary; ‹*age*› required

réquisition /ʀekizisjɔ̃/ *f* requisitioning

réquisitionner /ʀekizisjɔne/ [**v1**] *vt* **1** to requisition
2 to commandeer ‹*premises*›; to conscript ‹*workers*›

réquisitoire /ʀekizitwaʀ/ *m* closing speech for the prosecution

RER /ɛʀəɛʀ/ *m* (*abbr* = **réseau express régional**) *rapid transit rail system in the Paris region*

rescapé, **~e** /ʀɛskape/ **A** *adj* surviving
B *mf* survivor

rescousse: **à la rescousse** /alaʀɛskus/ *phr* **aller à la ~ de qn** to go to sb's rescue

✓ **réseau**, *pl* **~x** /ʀezo/ *m* network

réseau social *m* (Comput) social network

réseautage /ʀezotaʒ/ *m* networking; **~ social** social networking

réseautique /ʀezotik/ *f* computer network technology

réservation /ʀezɛʀvasjɔ̃/ *f* reservation, booking (BrE)

✓ **réserve** /ʀezɛʀv/ *f* **1** reservation; **sous ~ de changement** subject to alteration; **'sous (toute) ~'** (in a programme) 'to be confirmed'
2 stock; **des ~s de sucre** a stock of sugar; **~(s) d'argent** money in reserve

3 (Econ) **~s de charbon** coal reserves; **~s d'eau** water supply
4 (of person, manner) reserve
5 stockroom
6 (in museum) storeroom
7 **~ naturelle** nature reserve
8 **~ indienne** Indian reservation
9 (Mil) **officier de ~** reserve officer

réservé, **~e** /ʀezɛʀve/ **A** *pp* ▸ **réserver**
B *pp adj* **1** ‹*fishing*› private
2 **~ à la clientèle** for patrons only; **voie ~e aux autobus** bus lane; **'tous droits ~s'** 'all rights reserved'
3 ‹*person*› reserved

réserver /ʀezɛʀve/ [**v1**] **A** *vt* **1** to reserve, to book (BrE) ‹*seat, ticket*›
2 to put aside ‹*goods*›
3 to set aside ‹*money, time*›
4 **~ un bon accueil à qn** to give sb a warm welcome; **sans savoir ce que l'avenir nous réserve** without knowing what the future has in store for us
5 **~ son jugement** to reserve judgement
B **se réserver** *v refl* (+ *v être*) **se ~ les meilleurs morceaux** to save the best bits for oneself; **se ~ le droit de faire** to reserve the right to do; **il se réserve pour la candidature à la présidence** he's saving himself for the presidential race

réserviste /ʀezɛʀvist/ *mf* reservist

réservoir /ʀezɛʀvwaʀ/ *m* **1** tank
2 reservoir

résidant, **~e** /ʀezidɑ̃, ɑ̃t/ *adj* resident

résidence /ʀezidɑ̃s/ *f* **1** residence
2 place of residence; **assigné à ~** under house arrest
■ **~ principale/secondaire** main/second home; **~ universitaire** (university) hall of residence (BrE), residence hall (AmE)

résident, **~e** /ʀezidɑ̃, ɑ̃t/ *mf* resident

résidentiel, **-ielle** /ʀezidɑ̃sjɛl/ *adj* residential

résider /ʀezide/ [**v1**] *vi* **1** to live
2 **~ dans qch** to lie in sth

résidu /ʀezidy/ *m* **1** residue
2 remnant
3 waste

résignation /ʀeziɲasjɔ̃/ *f* resignation (**à** to)

résigner: **se résigner** /ʀeziɲe/ [**v1**] *v refl* (+ *v être*) to resign oneself

résiliation /ʀeziljasjɔ̃/ *f* (of contract) termination

résilier /ʀezilje/ [**v2**] *vt* to terminate ‹*contract*›

résine /ʀezin/ *f* resin

résineux /ʀezinø/ *m* conifer

résistance /ʀezistɑ̃s/ *f* **1** resistance; **manquer de ~** ‹*person*› to lack stamina
2 (in electricity) (gen) resistance; (of household appliance) element

résistant, **~e** /ʀezistɑ̃, ɑ̃t/ **A** *adj* **1** ‹*person*› tough, resilient; ‹*plant*› hardy
2 ‹*metal*› resistant; ‹*fabric, garment*› hard-wearing
B *mf* Resistance fighter

résister /ʀeziste/ [**v1**] *v+prep* (gen) to resist; **~ à** to resist ‹*offer*›; to stand ‹*strain*›; to withstand ‹*pressure*›; to get through ‹*ordeal*›; **le mur n'a pas résisté** the wall collapsed; **~ à l'épreuve du temps** to stand the test of time; **il ne supporte pas qu'on lui résiste** he doesn't like it when people stand up to him

résolu, **~e** /ʀezɔly/ **A** *pp* ▸ **résoudre**
B *pp adj* resolute, determined

résolument /ʀezɔlymɑ̃/ *adv* resolutely

résolution /ʀezɔlysjɔ̃/ *f* **1** (gen), (Pol) resolution
2 resolve
3 solution

résonance /ʀezɔnɑ̃s/ *f* (gen) resonance

résonner /ʀezɔne/ [**v1**] *vi* **1** ‹*step, laughter*› to ring out; ‹*cry, echo*› to resound; ‹*cymbals*› to clash
2 ‹*room*› to echo; **~ de** to resound with

résorber /ʀezɔʀbe/ [**v1**] **A** *vt* to absorb ‹*deficit, surplus*›; to reduce ‹*inflation*›
B **se résorber** *v refl* (+ *v être*) **1** ‹*deficit*› to be reduced
2 (Med) to be resorbed

résorption /ʀezɔʀpsjɔ̃/ *f* (of unemployment, inflation) reduction (**de** of)

résoudre /ʀezudʀ/ [**v75**] **A** *vt* to solve ‹*equation, problem*›; to resolve ‹*crisis*›
B **se résoudre** *v refl* (+ *v être*) **se ~ à faire** to resolve *or* make up one's mind to do; **être résolu à faire** to be determined to do

respect /ʀɛspɛ/ *m* (gen) respect; **manquer de ~ à qn** to be disrespectful to sb; **le ~ de soi** self-respect
IDIOMS **sauf votre ~** with all due respect; **tenir qn en ~** to keep sb at bay

respectabilité /ʀɛspɛktabilite/ *f* respectability

respectable /ʀɛspɛktabl/ *adj* respectable

respecter /ʀɛspɛkte/ [**v1**] **A** *vt* (gen) to respect; to treat [sth] with respect; to honour (BrE) ‹*commitment*›; **faire ~ l'ordre/la loi** to enforce order/the law
B **se respecter** *v refl* (+ *v être*) to respect oneself; **tout homme qui se respecte** any self-respecting man

respectif, **-ive** /ʀɛspɛktif, iv/ *adj* respective

respectueux, **-euse** /ʀɛspɛktɥø, øz/ *adj* respectful; **~ de la loi** law-abiding; **salutations respectueuses** yours faithfully

respirable /ʀɛspiʀabl/ *adj* **1** breathable
2 ‹*atmosphere, mood*› bearable

respiration /ʀɛspiʀasjɔ̃/ *f* **1** breathing; **avoir une ~ difficile** to have breathing difficulties
2 breath; **retenir sa ~** to hold one's breath

respiratoire /ʀɛspiʀatwaʀ/ *adj* respiratory

key word

respirer /ʀɛspiʀe/ [**v1**] **A** *vt* **1** to breathe in ‹*air, dust*›
2 to smell ‹*perfume*›
3 ‹*person, place*› to exude
B *vi* **1** to breathe
2 (fig) to catch one's breath; **laisse-moi ~** let me get my breath back

resplendir /ʀɛsplɑ̃diʀ/ [**v3**] *vi* **1** ‹*light*› to shine brightly; ‹*snow*› to sparkle
2 ~ de santé to be glowing with health

resplendissant, **~e** /ʀɛsplɑ̃disɑ̃, ɑ̃t/ *adj*
1 ‹*light*› brilliant
2 ‹*beauty*› radiant

responsabiliser /ʀɛspɔ̃sabilize/ [**v1**] *vt* to give [sb] a sense of responsibility

responsabilité /ʀɛspɔ̃sabilite/ *f* (gen) responsibility; (Law) liability; **avoir la ~ de** to be responsible for; **engageant la ~ de la société** for which the company is liable
■ **~ civile** (in insurance) personal liability

responsable /ʀɛspɔ̃sabl/ **A** *adj* **1** ‹*person, error*› responsible
2 accountable; (Law) liable
3 être ~ de qn/qch to be in charge of sb/sth
4 ‹*person, attitude, act*› responsible
B *mf* **1** (gen) person in charge; (of shop, project) manager; (of party) leader; (of department) head
2 les ~s de la catastrophe the people responsible for the catastrophe
3 le grand ~ c'est le tabac smoking is the main cause

resquiller /ʀɛskije/ [**v1**] *vi* (fam) (on train) not to pay the fare; (at show) to sneak in (fam)

resquilleur, **-euse** /ʀɛskijœʀ, øz/ *mf* (fam) fare dodger

ressac /ʀəsak/ *m* backwash

ressaisir: **se ressaisir** /ʀ(ə)seziʀ/ [**v3**] *v refl* (+ *v être*) to pull oneself together

ressasser /ʀ(ə)sase/ [**v1**] *vt* to brood over ‹*failure*›; to dwell on ‹*misfortunes*›

ressemblance /ʀ(ə)sɑ̃blɑ̃s/ *f*
1 resemblance, likeness
2 (between things) similarity

ressemblant, **~e** /ʀ(ə)sɑ̃blɑ̃, ɑ̃t/ *adj* **un portrait ~** a portrait which is a good likeness

ressembler /ʀ(ə)sɑ̃ble/ [**v1**] **A** **ressembler à** *v+prep* to look like, to resemble; to be like
B **se ressembler** *v refl* (+ *v être*) **1** to look alike
2 to be alike

ressemeler /ʀ(ə)səmle/ [**v19**] *vt* to resole

ressentiment /ʀ(ə)sɑ̃timɑ̃/ *m* resentment

ressentir /ʀ(ə)sɑ̃tiʀ/ [**v30**] **A** *vt* to feel
B **se ressentir** *v refl* (+ *v être*) **se ~ de** to feel the effects of; to suffer from

resserrer /ʀ(ə)seʀe/ [**v1**] **A** *vt* **1** to tighten ‹*knot, screw, grip*›
2 resserrez les rangs! close up a bit!
3 to tighten up on ‹*discipline, supervision*›
B **se resserrer** *v refl* (+ *v être*) **1** ‹*road*› to narrow
2 ‹*friendship*› to become stronger
3 ‹*link, knot, grip*› to tighten
4 ‹*gap*› to close
5 ‹*group of people*› to draw closer together
6 ‹*discipline*› to become stricter

resservir /ʀ(ə)sɛʀviʀ/ [**v30**] **A** *vt* **1** to serve [sth] (up) again
2 to give [sb] another helping
B **se resservir** *v refl* (+ *v être*) to take another helping

ressort /ʀ(ə)sɔʀ/ *m* **1** (Tech) spring
2 avoir du ~ to have resilience
3 être du ~ de qn to be within sb's province; (Law) to fall within the jurisdiction of ‹*court*›; **en premier ~** in the first resort

ressortir /ʀ(ə)sɔʀtiʀ/ [**v30**] **A** *vt* **1** to take [sth] out again
2 to bring [sth] out again; to dig out (fam) ‹*affair, scandal*›
B *vi* (+ *v être*) **1** ‹*person*› to go out again
2 ‹*bullet*› to come out
3 to stand out; **voici ce qui ressort de l'étude** the results of the study are as follows; **faire ~** to bring to light ‹*contradiction*›; ‹*make-up*› to accentuate ‹*eyes*›
4 ‹*film, record*› to be re-released
C *v impers* (+ *v être*) **il ressort que** it emerges that

ressortissant, **~e** /ʀ(ə)sɔʀtisɑ̃, ɑ̃t/ *mf* national

ressouder /ʀ(ə)sude/ [**v1**] *vt* to solder [sth] again

ressource /ʀ(ə)suʀs/ *f* **1** resource; **les ~s énergétiques** energy resources
2 option; **en dernière ~** as a last resort
3 avoir de la ~ (fam) to be resourceful
4 ~s means; **être sans ~s** to have no means of support

ressourcer: **se ressourcer** /ʀ(ə)suʀse/ [**v12**] *v refl* (+ *v être*) to recharge one's batteries

ressusciter /ʀesysite/ [**v1**] **A** *vt* **1** to revive ‹*tradition*›; to resurrect ‹*past*›
2 to raise [sb] from the dead; (fig) to bring [sb] back to life
B *vi* ‹*dead person*› to rise from the dead

restant, **~e** /ʀɛstɑ̃, ɑ̃t/ **A** *adj* remaining
B *m* **1 le ~** the remainder; the rest
2 un ~ de poulet some left-over chicken

restaurant /ʀɛstɔʀɑ̃/ *m* restaurant
■ **~ universitaire**, **RU** university canteen (BrE), cafeteria

restaurateur, **-trice** /ʀɛstɔʀatœʀ, tʀis/ *mf*
1 restaurant owner
2 restorer

restauration /ʀɛstɔʀasjɔ̃/ *f* **1** catering; **~ rapide** fast-food industry
2 restoration

restaurer /ʀɛstɔʀe/ [**v1**] **A** *vt* **1** to feed
2 to restore
B **se restaurer** *v refl* (+ *v être*) to have something to eat

r

⚷ **reste** /rɛst/ **A** *m* **le ~** the rest; the remainder; **un ~ de tissu** some left-over material; **au ~, du ~** besides
B restes *mpl* **1** remains
2 leftovers
IDIOMS **sans demander son ~** without further ado; **être en ~ avec qn** to feel indebted to sb; **pour ne pas être en ~** so as not to be outdone

⚷ **rester** /rɛste/ [**v1**] (+ *v être*) **A** *vi* **1** to stay, to remain; **que ça reste entre nous!** this is strictly between you and me!
2 to remain; **restez assis!** remain seated!; don't get up!; **~ sans manger** to go without food; **~ paralysé** to be left paralysed; **~ les bras croisés** (fig) to stand idly by
3 to be left, to remain
4 ‹*memory, work of art*› to live on
5 ~ sur une bonne impression to be left with a good impression
6 en ~ à to go no further than; **je compte bien ne pas en ~ là** I won't let the matter rest there; **restons-en là pour le moment** let's leave it at that for now
B *v impers* **il reste une minute** there is one minute left; **il ne me reste plus que lui** he's all I've got left; **il reste que, il n'en reste pas moins que** the fact remains that

restituer /rɛstitɥe/ [**v1**] *vt* **1** to restore
2 to reconstruct ‹*text*›; to reproduce ‹*sound*›

restitution /rɛstitysjɔ̃/ *f* **1** return; restoration
2 reproduction

restreindre /rɛstrɛ̃dr/ [**v55**] **A** *vt* to curb, to cut back on; to limit; to restrict
B se restreindre *v refl* (+ *v être*)
1 ‹*possibilities*› to become restricted; ‹*influence*› to wane
2 se ~ (dans ses dépenses) to cut back (on one's expenses)

restreint, ~e /rɛstrɛ̃, ɛ̃t/ *adj* ‹*public, vocabulary*› limited; ‹*team*› small

restrictif, -ive /rɛstriktif, iv/ *adj* restrictive

restriction /rɛstriksjɔ̃/ *f* **1** restriction; **~s salariales** wage restraints; **sans ~** freely
2 sans ~ ‹*approve*› without reservations; ‹*support*› unreservedly

restructurer /rəstryktyre/ [**v1**] *vt* to restructure; to redevelop ‹*area*›

⚷ **résultat** /rezylta/ *m* (gen) result; (of research) results, findings; (of negotiations, inquiry) result, outcome; **sans ~** without success

résulter /rezylte/ [**v1**] **A résulter de** *v+prep* to be the result of, to result from
B *v impers* **il résulte de ce que vous venez de dire que...** it follows from what you have just said that...; **il en résulte que...** as a result...

résumé /rezyme/ *m* summary, résumé; **en ~** to sum up; **faire un ~ de qch (à qn)** to give (sb) a rundown of *or* on sth

⚷ key word

résumer /rezyme/ [**v1**] **A** *vt* **1** to summarize ‹*text*›
2 to sum up ‹*news*›
B se résumer *v refl* (+ *v être*) **1** to sum up
2 se ~ à to come down to

résurgence /rezyrʒɑ̃s/ *f* resurgence; revival

resurgir /r(ə)syrʒir/ [**v3**] *vi* to reappear

résurrection /rezyrɛksjɔ̃/ *f* **1** resurrection
2 revival
3 rebirth

rétablir /retablir/ [**v3**] **A** *vt* **1** to restore; **~ la circulation** to get the traffic moving again
2 to re-establish ‹*truth, facts*›
3 ~ qn dans ses fonctions to reinstate sb in his/her job
B se rétablir *v refl* (+ *v être*) **1** to recover
2 ‹*calm*› to return; ‹*situation*› to return to normal

rétablissement /retablismɑ̃/ *m*
1 restoration
2 re-establishment
3 recovery

rétamer /retame/ [**v1**] (fam) **A** *vt* (tire) to wear [sb] out; (beat) to hammer (fam)
B se rétamer *v refl* (+ *v être*) to fall, to come a cropper (fam)

retape /r(ə)tap/ *f* (pop) **faire de la ~ pour qch** to beat the drum for sth

retaper /r(ə)tape/ [**v1**] *vt* (fam) **1** to do up ‹*house*›
2 to put [sb] on his/her feet again

retard /r(ə)tar/ *m* **1** lateness
2 delay; **avoir du ~** to be late; **nous sommes en ~ sur l'emploi du temps** we're behind schedule; **prendre du ~** to fall *or* get behind; **avoir du courrier en ~** to have a backlog of mail; **sans ~** without delay
3 backwardness; **il a deux ans de ~** (Sch) he's two years behind at school

retardataire /r(ə)tardatɛr/ *mf* latecomer

retardé, ~e /rətarde/ *adj* ‹*person*› backward

retardement: à retardement /ar(ə)tardəmɑ̃/ *phr* ‹*mechanism, device*› delayed-action; **bombe à ~** time bomb; ‹*act, get angry*› after the event

retarder /r(ə)tarde/ [**v1**] **A** *vt* **1** to make [sb] late; **être retardé** ‹*train*› to be delayed
2 to hold [sb] up
3 to put off, to postpone ‹*departure, operation*›
4 to put back ‹*clock*›
B *vi* ‹*clock*› to be slow

⚷ **retenir** /rət(ə)nir, rtənir/ [**v36**] **A** *vt* **1** to keep ‹*person*›; **~ qn prisonnier** to hold sb captive; **~ qn à dîner** to ask sb to stay for dinner
2 to hold [sb] up, to detain ‹*person*›
3 to hold ‹*object, attention*›; to hold back ‹*hair, dog, crowd*›; to stop ‹*person*›; **~ sa langue** to hold one's tongue; **~ qn par la manche** to catch hold of sb's sleeve; **votre**

réclamation a retenu toute notre attention your complaint is receiving our full attention
4 to hold back ‹*tears*›; to hold ‹*breath*›; to stifle ‹*scream, yawn*›; to contain, to suppress ‹*anger*›
5 to retain ‹*heat, water, odour*›
6 to reserve, to book (BrE) ‹*table, room*›; to set ‹*date*›
7 to deduct ‹*sum*›
8 to remember; **toi, je te retiens!** (fam) I won't forget this!
9 to accept ‹*argument, plan*›; (Law) to uphold ‹*charge*›
10 (in mathematics) **je pose 5 et je retiens 2** I put down 5 and carry 2
B **se retenir** *v refl* (+ *v être*) **1** to stop oneself; **se ~ à qch** to hang on to sth
2 se ~ de pleurer to hold back the tears
3 (fam) to control oneself

rétention /ʀetɑ̃sjɔ̃/ *f* **1** (Med) retention
2 withholding

retentir /ʀ(ə)tɑ̃tiʀ/ [**v3**] *vi* to ring out; to resound

retentissant, **~e** /ʀ(ə)tɑ̃tisɑ̃, ɑ̃t/ *adj* **1** ‹*failure*› resounding; ‹*trial, film*› sensational
2 ‹*cry, noise*› ringing; resounding

retentissement /ʀ(ə)tɑ̃tismɑ̃/ *m* (gen) effect; (of book, artist) impact

retenue /ʀət(ə)ny/ *f* **1** restraint; **perdre toute ~** to lose one's inhibitions; **boire sans ~** to drink to excess
2 deduction
3 (Sch) detention
4 tu as oublié la ~ des dizaines you forgot to carry over from the tens column

réticence /ʀetisɑ̃s/ *f* **1** reluctance
2 ses ~s en ce qui concerne le passé his/her reticence about the past

réticent, **~e** /ʀetisɑ̃, ɑ̃t/ *adj* **1** hesitant
2 reluctant

rétif, **-ive** /ʀetif, iv/ *adj* restive; rebellious

rétine /ʀetin/ *f* retina

retiré, **~e** /ʀətiʀe/ *adj* **1** ‹*life*› secluded
2 ‹*place*› remote

retirer /ʀətiʀe/ [**v1**] **A** *vt* **1** to take off ‹*garment, piece of jewellery*›
2 to take out, to remove; **~ ses troupes d'un pays** to withdraw one's troops from a country
3 to withdraw ‹*foot, hand*›; **retire ta main** move your hand away
4 to withdraw ‹*permission, privilege*›; to take away ‹*right, property*›; **~ un produit de la vente** to recall a product; **~ une pièce de l'affiche** to close a play
5 to withdraw ‹*complaint, offer, support*›; **je retire ce que j'ai dit** I take back what I said
6 to collect, to pick up ‹*ticket, luggage*›; to withdraw ‹*money*›
7 to get, to derive ‹*profit*›; **il en retire 2 000 euros par an** he gets 2,000 euros a year out of it
B **se retirer** *v refl* (+ *v être*) **1** to withdraw, to leave
2 la mer se retire the tide is going out

retombées /ʀətɔ̃be/ *fpl* **1 ~ radioactives** radioactive fallout
2 effects, consequences
3 (of invention) spin-offs

retomber /ʀətɔ̃be/ [**v1**] *vi* (+ *v être*) **1** to fall again; **~ en enfance** to regress to childhood
2 ‹*person, cat, projectile*› to land; ‹*ball, curtain*› to come down; ‹*fog*› to set in again; **ça va te ~ sur le nez** (fig, fam) it'll come down on your head
3 ‹*anger*› to subside; ‹*interest*› to wane
4 ‹*currency, temperature*› to fall
5 ~ sur qn ‹*responsibility*› to fall on sb; **faire ~ la responsabilité sur qn** to pass the buck to sb (fam)

retordre /ʀ(ə)tɔʀdʀ/ [**v6**] *vt* **donner du fil à ~ à qn** to give sb a hard time

rétorquer /ʀetɔʀke/ [**v1**] *vt* to retort

retors, **~e** /ʀətɔʀ, ɔʀs/ *adj* ‹*person*› crafty; ‹*argument*› devious

rétorsion /ʀetɔʀsjɔ̃/ *f* retaliation

retouche /ʀ(ə)tuʃ/ *f* alteration; (of photograph, picture) retouching

retoucher /ʀ(ə)tuʃe/ [**v1**] *vt* to make alterations to; to touch up

retour /ʀ(ə)tuʀ/ *m* return; **(billet de) ~** return (ticket) (BrE), round trip (ticket) (AmE); **au ~** on the way back; **être de ~ (à la maison)** to be back (home); **on attend le ~ au calme** people are waiting for things to calm down; **il connaît maintenant le succès et c'est un juste ~ des choses** he's successful now, and deservedly so; **elle s'engage, en ~, à payer la facture** she undertakes for her part to pay the bill; **'sans ~ ni consigne'** 'no deposit or return'; **par ~ du courrier** by return of post (BrE), by the next mail (AmE)
■ **~ d'âge** change of life; **~ en arrière** flashback; **~ de bâton** (fam) backlash
IDIOM **être sur le ~** (fam) to be over the hill (fam)

retournement /ʀ(ə)tuʀnəmɑ̃/ *m* reversal; **un ~ de l'opinion publique** a turnaround in public opinion

retourner /ʀ(ə)tuʀne/ [**v1**] **A** *vt* (+ *v avoir*)
1 to turn [sth] over; to turn ‹*mattress*›
2 to turn [sth] inside out
3 to turn over ‹*earth*›; to toss ‹*salad*›
4 to return ‹*compliment, criticism*›; **~ la situation** to reverse the situation
5 to turn [sth] upside down ‹*room*›; ‹*news, film*› to shake ‹*person*›
6 to send [sth] back, to return
B *vi* (+ *v être*) to go back, to return
C **se retourner** *v refl* (+ *v être*) **1** to turn around
2 to turn over; **il n'a pas arrêté de se ~ (dans son lit)** he kept tossing and turning

3 (fam) to get organized
4 se ~ contre qn ‹*person*› to turn against sb; ‹*arguments*› to backfire on sb
5 elle s'est retourné le doigt she bent back her finger
6 s'en ~ (chez soi) to go back (home)
D *v impers* **j'aime savoir de quoi il retourne** I like to know what's going on
IDIOM **~ qn comme une crêpe** (fam) to make sb change their mind completely

retracer /Rətrase/ [**v12**] *vt* **1** to redraw ‹*line*›
2 to recount ‹*event*›

rétractable /Retraktabl/ *adj* retractable

rétracter /Retrakte/ [**v1**] *vt*, **se rétracter** *v refl* (+ *v être*) to retract

retrait /R(ə)trɛ/ **A** *m* (gen) withdrawal; (of suitcase, packet) collection; **~ du permis (de conduire)** disqualification from driving
B en retrait *phr* **maison en ~ de** house set back from ‹*road*›; **se tenir en ~** to stand back; **rester en ~** to stay in the background

🔑 **retraite** /R(ə)trɛt/ *f* **1** retirement; **prendre sa ~** to retire
2 pension
3 (Mil) retreat
4 (place) retreat; (of bandits) hiding place
■ **~ par capitalisation** loan-back pension; **~ complémentaire** private pension

retraité, **~e** /Rətrete/ *mf* retired person

retraiter /Rətrete/ [**v1**] *vt* to reprocess ‹*plutonium*›

retranché, **~e** /R(ə)trɑ̃ʃe/ *adj* entrenched

retranchement /R(ə)trɑ̃ʃmɑ̃/ *m* entrenchment; **pousser qn dans ses derniers ~s** to drive sb into a corner

retrancher /R(ə)trɑ̃ʃe/ [**v1**] **A** *vt* **1** to cut out ‹*word*›
2 to subtract ‹*amount*›; to deduct ‹*costs*›
B se retrancher *v refl* (+ *v être*) (Mil), (gen) to take up position; to entrench oneself

r

retransmettre /Rətrɑ̃smɛtR/ [**v60**] *vt* **1** to broadcast; **retransmis par satellite** relayed by satellite
2 to retransmit

retransmission /Rətrɑ̃smisjɔ̃/ *f* **1** broadcast
2 relay
3 retransmission

rétrécir /RetResiR/ [**v3**] *vi*, **se rétrécir** *v refl* (+ *v être*) **1** to narrow
2 to shrink

rétrécissement /RetResismɑ̃/ *m*
1 shrinkage
2 narrowing
3 contraction

rétribuer /RetRibɥe/ [**v1**] *vt* to remunerate

rétribution /RetRibysjɔ̃/ *f* remuneration

rétro /RetRo/ *m* **1** nostalgic style
2 retro fashions

rétroactif, **-ive** /RetRoaktif, iv/ *adj* (Law), (gen) retroactive

rétrograde /RetRogRad/ *adj* ‹*person*› reactionary; ‹*policy, measure*› retrograde

rétrograder /RetRogRade/ [**v1**] **A** *vt* **1** to demote
2 (Sport) to relegate
B *vi* (Aut) to change down (BrE), to downshift (AmE)

rétrospectif, **-ive** /RetRɔspɛktif, iv/ *adj* retrospective

rétrospective /RetRɔspɛktiv/ *f* (gen) retrospective; (of films) festival

rétrospectivement /RetRɔspɛktivmɑ̃/ *adv* in retrospect; looking back

retroussé, **~e** /R(ə)tRuse/ *adj* ‹*nose*› turned up; ‹*lip*› curling

retrousser /R(ə)tRuse/ [**v1**] *vt* to hitch up (BrE), to hike up (AmE) ‹*skirt*›; to roll up ‹*sleeves*›

retrouvailles /RətRuvɑj/ *fpl* **1** reunion
2 reconciliation

🔑 **retrouver** /RətRuve/ [**v1**] **A** *vt* **1** to find ‹*lost object*›
2 to find [sth] again ‹*work, object*›
3 to regain ‹*strength, health*›
4 to remember ‹*name, tune*›
5 to be back in ‹*place*›
6 to recognize ‹*person, style*›; **je retrouve sa mère en elle** I can see her mother in her
7 to join, to meet ‹*person*›
B se retrouver *v refl* (+ *v être*) **1** to meet (again); **on s'est retrouvé en famille** the family got together; **comme on se retrouve!** fancy seeing you here!
2 se ~ enceinte to find oneself pregnant; **se ~ sans argent** to be left penniless
3 se *or* **s'y ~ dans** to find one's way around in ‹*place, mess*›; to follow, to understand ‹*explanation*›; **il y a trop de changements, on ne s'y retrouve plus** there are too many changes, we don't know if we're coming or going
4 (fam) **s'y ~** to break even; (making profit) to do well
5 ‹*quality*› to be found; ‹*problem*› to occur
6 se ~ dans qn/qch to see *or* recognize oneself in sb/sth

rétroviseur /RetRovizœR/ *m* **1** rear-view mirror
2 wing mirror (BrE), outside rear-view mirror (AmE)

réunification /Reynifikasjɔ̃/ *f* reunification

réunifier /Reynifje/ [**v2**] **A** *vt* to reunify
B se réunifier *v refl* (+ *v être*) to be reunified

🔑 **réunion** /Reynjɔ̃/ *f* **1** meeting; **être en ~** ‹*person*› to be at a meeting
2 gathering
3 reunion
4 (of different talents) combination; (of poems) collection
5 union

🔑 **réunir** /ReyniR/ [**v3**] **A** *vt* **1** ‹*conference*› to bring together ‹*participants*›; ‹*organizer*›

🔑 key word

to get [sb] together ‹*participants*›
2 to call [sb] together ‹*delegates*›; to convene ‹*assembly*›
3 to have [sb] round (BrE) *or* over
4 to join ‹*edges*›
5 to unite ‹*provinces*›
6 **~ les conditions nécessaires** to fulfil (BrE) all the necessary conditions
7 to raise ‹*funds*›
8 to assemble ‹*elements, evidence*›; to gather [sth] together ‹*documents*›
9 ‹*road, canal*› to connect
B **se réunir** *v refl* (+ *v être*) to meet; to get together

réussir /ʀeysiʀ/ [**v3**] **A** *vt* to achieve ‹*unification*›; to carry out [sth] successfully ‹*operation*›; to make a success of ‹*life*›
B **réussir à** *v+prep* **1** **~ à faire** to succeed in doing; **~ à un examen** to pass an exam
2 **~ à qn** ‹*life, method*› to turn out well for sb; ‹*rest*› to do sb good
C *vi* **1** to succeed
2 ‹*attempt*› to be successful
3 ‹*person*› to do well

réussite /ʀeysit/ *f* (gen) success

revaloir /ʀ(ə)valwaʀ/ [**v45**] *vt* **je te revaudrai ça** (vengefully) I'll get even with you for that; (in gratitude) I'll return the favour (BrE)

revalorisation /ʀ(ə)valɔʀizasjɔ̃/ *f* **1** (increase) **une ~ des salaires de 3%** a 3% wage increase
2 (renewed esteem) **la ~ des enseignants** the enhanced prestige of teachers

revaloriser /ʀ(ə)valɔʀize/ [**v1**] *vt* **1** to increase ‹*salary*›; to revalue ‹*currency*›
2 to reassert the value of ‹*traditions*›
3 to renovate ‹*area*›

revanche /ʀ(ə)vɑ̃ʃ/ **A** *f* **1** revenge
2 (Sport) return match (BrE) *or* game (AmE)
B **en revanche** *phr* on the other hand

rêvasser /ʀɛvase/ [**v1**] *vi* to daydream

rêve /ʀɛv/ *m* **1** dreaming
2 dream; **fais de beaux ~s!** sweet dreams!
3 ideal; **une maison de ~** a dream house; **c'est le ~** this is just perfect

rêvé, **~e** /ʀeve/ *adj* ideal, perfect

revêche /ʀəvɛʃ/ *adj* ‹*manner, tone*› sour; ‹*person*› crabby

réveil /ʀevɛj/ *m* **1** waking (up)
2 (after anaesthetic) **j'ai eu des nausées au ~** I felt nauseous when I regained consciousness
3 (of movement) resurgence; (of pain) return; (of volcano) return to activity
4 (Mil) reveille
5 alarm clock

réveille-matin /ʀevɛjmatɛ̃/ *m inv* alarm clock

réveiller /ʀeveje/ [**v1**] **A** *vt* **1** to wake [sb] up, to wake
2 to revive ‹*person*›; to awaken ‹*feeling*›; to arouse ‹*curiosity*›; to stir up ‹*memory*›
B **se réveiller** *v refl* (+ *v être*) **1** to wake up; to awaken
2 to regain consciousness
3 ‹*volcano*› to become active again
4 ‹*pain, appetite*› to come back; ‹*memory*› to be reawakened

réveillon /ʀevɛjɔ̃/ *m* **~ du Nouvel An** New Year's Eve party

réveillonner /ʀevɛjɔne/ [**v1**] *vi* to celebrate Christmas Eve; to see the New Year in

révélateur, **-trice** /ʀevelatœʀ, tʀis/ **A** *adj* ‹*detail, fact*› revealing, telling
B *m* (in photography) developer

révélation /ʀevelasjɔ̃/ *f* revelation

révéler /ʀevele/ [**v14**] **A** *vt* **1** to reveal; to give away ‹*secret*›
2 to show
3 to discover ‹*artist*›
4 (in photography) to develop
B **se révéler** *v refl* (+ *v être*) **se ~ faux** to turn out to be wrong

revenant, **~e** /ʀəv(ə)nɑ̃, ɑ̃t/ *mf* ghost

revendeur, **-euse** /ʀ(ə)vɑ̃dœʀ, øz/ *mf*
1 stockist
2 **un ~ de drogue** a drug dealer
3 seller (of stolen goods)

revendicatif, **-ive** /ʀ(ə)vɑ̃dikatif, iv/ *adj* protest; **journée revendicative** day of protest

revendication /ʀ(ə)vɑ̃dikasjɔ̃/ *f* (of workers) demand; (of country) claim

revendiquer /ʀ(ə)vɑ̃dike/ [**v1**] *vt* **1** to demand ‹*pay rise*›; to claim ‹*territory*›
2 to claim responsibility for ‹*attack*›
3 to proclaim ‹*origins*›

revendre /ʀ(ə)vɑ̃dʀ/ [**v6**] *vt* **1** to sell [sth] retail, to retail
2 to resell ‹*car, house*›; to sell on ‹*stolen object*›; **avoir de l'énergie à ~** to have energy to spare

revenir /ʀəvniʀ, ʀvəniʀ/ [**v36**] **A** *vi* **1** to come back; to come again
2 ‹*person, animal, vehicle*› to come back, to return; **~ de loin** (fig) to have had a close shave; **mon chèque m'est revenu** my cheque (BrE) *or* check (AmE) was returned
3 **~ à** to return to, to come back to ‹*method, story*›
4 ‹*appetite, memory*› to come back; ‹*sun*› to come out again; ‹*season*› to return; ‹*idea, theme*› to recur; **~ à la mémoire** *or* **l'esprit de qn** to come back to sb; **ça me revient!** now I remember!
5 **~ à 100 euros** to come to 100 euros; **ça revient cher** it works out expensive
6 **~ sur** to go back over ‹*question, past*›; to go back on ‹*decision, promise*›; to retract ‹*confession*›
7 **~ de** to get over ‹*illness, surprise*›; to lose ‹*illusion*›; **la vie à la campagne, j'en suis revenu** as for life in the country, I've seen it for what it is; **je n'en reviens pas des progrès que tu as faits** (fam) I'm amazed at the progress you've made

r

8 ~ aux oreilles de qn ‹*remark*› to reach sb's ears

9 ~ à qn ‹*property*› to go to sb; ‹*honour*› to fall to sb; **ça leur revient de droit** it's theirs by right; **la décision revient au rédacteur** it is the editor's decision

10 (Culin) **faire ~** to brown

B *v impers* **c'est à vous qu'il revient de trancher** it is for you to decide

IDIOM **il a une tête qui ne me revient pas** I don't like the look of him

⚷ **revenu** /Rəv(ə)ny, Rvəny/ *m* income; (of state) revenue

■ **~ minimum d'insertion, RMI** *minimum benefit paid to those with no other source of income*

⚷ **rêver** /Reve/ [**v1**] **A** *vt* **1** to dream

2 to dream of ‹*success, revenge*›

B *vi* to dream

réverbération /ReveRbeRasjɔ̃/ *f* **1** glare

2 reflection

3 reverberation

réverbère /ReveRbeR/ *m* street lamp *or* light

réverbérer /ReveRbeRe/ [**v14**] **A** *vt* to reflect

B se réverbérer *v refl* (+ *v être*) ‹*light, heat*› to be reflected; ‹*sound*› to reverberate

révérence /ReveRɑ̃s/ *f* **1** curtsey; bow

2 reverence

IDIOM **tirer sa ~** (fam) to take one's leave

révérencieux, -ieuse /ReveRɑ̃sjø, øz/ *adj* deferential (**envers** to); **attitude peu révérencieuse** irreverent attitude

révérend, ~e /ReveRɑ̃, ɑ̃d/ *mf* **1** Father/Mother Superior

2 reverend

révérer /ReveRe/ [**v14**] *vt* to revere

rêverie /RɛvRi/ *f* **1** daydreaming

2 daydream

revers /R(ə)vɛR/ *m inv* **1** (of hand) back; (of cloth) wrong side; (of coin) reverse; **le ~ de la médaille** (fig) the downside (fam)

2 (on jacket) lapel; (of trousers) turn-up (BrE), cuff (AmE)

3 (in tennis) backhand (stroke)

4 setback

réversibilité /ReveRsibilite/ *f* reversibility; (in law) reversion

réversible /ReveRsibl/ *adj* (gen) reversible

revêtement /R(ə)vɛtmɑ̃/ *m* **1** (of road) surface

2 coating; covering

revêtir /R(ə)vetiR/ [**v33**] **A** *vt* **1** to assume ‹*gravity, solemnity*›; to have ‹*disadvantage*›; to take on ‹*significance*›; **~ la forme de** to take the form of

2 to put on ‹*garment*›

3 ~ qch de to cover sth with ‹*carpet, tiles*›

B se revêtir *v refl* (+ *v être*) **se ~ de** to put on ‹*cloak*›; to become covered with ‹*snow*›

rêveur, -euse /RɛvœR, øz/ **A** *adj* dreamy

B *mf* dreamer

revient /R(ə)vjɛ̃/ *m* **prix de ~** cost price

revigorer /R(ə)vigɔRe/ [**v1**] *vt* to revive

revirement /R(ə)viRmɑ̃/ *m* turnaround

réviser /Revize/ [**v1**] *vt* **1** to revise ‹*position, prices*›; to review ‹*constitution*›

2 to overhaul ‹*car, boiler*›; to revise ‹*manuscript*›

3 (Sch) to revise (BrE), to review (AmE)

révision /Revizjɔ̃/ *f* **1** revision; review

2 (of car) service; (of manuscript) revision; (of accounts) audit

3 (Sch) revision (BrE), review (AmE)

revitaliser /R(ə)vitalize/ [**v1**] *vt* to revitalize

revivifier /R(ə)vivifje/ [**v2**] *vt* to revive; to revivify

revivre /R(ə)vivR/ [**v63**] **A** *vt* **1** to go over, to relive ‹*event, past*›; **faire ~ qch à qn** to bring back memories of sth to sb

2 to live through [sth] again ‹*war*›

B *vi* **1** to come alive again

2 to be able to breathe again

3 faire ~ to revive ‹*tradition*›

révocation /Revɔkasjɔ̃/ *f* (of will) revocation; (of person) dismissal

revoici /R(ə)vwasi/ *prep* (fam) **~ Marianne!** here's Marianne again!

revoilà /R(ə)vwala/ ▶ **revoici**

revoir¹ /R(ə)vwaR/ [**v46**] *vt* **1** to see [sb/sth] again

2 to go over ‹*exercise, lesson*›; to review ‹*method*›; to check through ‹*accounts*›

⚷ **revoir²**: **au revoir** /ɔR(ə)vwaR/ *phr* goodbye

révoltant, ~e /Revɔltɑ̃, ɑ̃t/ *adj* appalling

révolte /Revɔlt/ *f* **1** revolt

2 rebellion

révolté, ~e /Revɔlte/ *adj* **1** (insubordinate) rebellious

2 (shocked) appalled

révolter /Revɔlte/ [**v1**] **A** *vt* to appal (BrE)

B se révolter *v refl* (+ *v être*) **1** to rebel

2 to be appalled

révolu, ~e /Revɔly/ *adj* **1 ce temps est ~** those days are over *or* past

2 avoir 12 ans ~s to be over 12 years of age

⚷ **révolution** /Revɔlysjɔ̃/ *f* **1** revolution

2 turmoil

3 (of planet) revolution

révolutionnaire /RevɔlysjɔnɛR/ *adj, mf* revolutionary

révolutionner /Revɔlysjɔne/ [**v1**] *vt* to revolutionize

revolver /RevɔlvɛR/ *m* **1** revolver

2 handgun; **coup de ~** gunshot

révoquer /Revɔke/ [**v1**] *vt* **1** to revoke ‹*will*›

2 to dismiss ‹*person*›

⚷ **revue** /R(ə)vy/ *f* **1** (gen) magazine; (academic) journal

2 (Mil) parade; **passer en ~** to review

⚷ key word

‹*troops*›; to inspect ‹*equipment*›
3 revue
4 examination; **passer qch en ~** to go over sth
■ **~ de presse** review of the papers

révulser /Revylse/ [**v1**] **A** *vt* to appal (BrE)
B se révulser *v refl* (+ *v être*) ‹*eyes*› to roll (upward(s)); ‹*face*› to contort

révulsion /Revylsjɔ̃/ *f* (Med), (gen) revulsion

rez-de-chaussée /Redʃose/ *m inv* ground floor (BrE), first floor (AmE)

RF (*written abbr* = **République française**) French Republic

rhabiller: **se rhabiller** /Rabije/ [**v1**] *v refl* (+ *v être*) to get dressed again
IDIOM **il peut aller se ~!** (pop) he can go back where he came from!

rhapsodie /Rapsɔdi/ *f* rhapsody

rhésus /Rezys/ *m inv* **1 facteur ~** rhesus factor
2 rhesus monkey

rhétorique /RetɔRik/ **A** *adj* rhetorical
B *f* rhetoric

Rhin /Rɛ̃/ *pr m* **le ~** the Rhine

rhinocéros /RinɔseRɔs/ *m inv* rhinoceros

rhubarbe /RybaRb/ *f* rhubarb

rhum /Rɔm/ *m* rum

rhumatisme /Rymatism/ *m* rheumatism

rhume /Rym/ *m* cold; **~ des foins** hay fever

ri /Ri/ ▸ **rire**[1]

ribambelle /Ribɑ̃bɛl/ *f* (fam) (of children) flock; (of friends) host; (of names) whole string

Ricain, **~e** /Rikɛ̃, ɛn/ (fam, offensive or hum) *mf* Yank (fam)

ricaner /Rikane/ [**v1**] *vi* **1** to snigger
2 to giggle

riche /Riʃ/ **A** *adj* (gen) rich; ‹*person*› rich, wealthy; ‹*library*› well-stocked; ‹*decor*› elaborate; **une ~ idée** an excellent idea
B *mf* rich man/woman; **les ~s** the rich

richement /Riʃmɑ̃/ *adv* richly, lavishly ‹*furnished, decorated*›

richesse /Riʃɛs/ **A** *f* **1** wealth; **c'est toute notre ~** it's all we have
2 (of jewellery) magnificence; (of garment) richness
3 (of foodstuff) richness
4 (of fauna, vocabulary) richness; (of documentation) wealth
B richesses *fpl* wealth; **~s naturelles** natural resources

richissime /Riʃisim/ *adj* (fam) fabulously rich

ricin /Risɛ̃/ *m* **huile de ~** castor oil

ricocher /Rikɔʃe/ [**v1**] *vi* ‹*bullet*› to ricochet (**sur** off); (off an obstacle) to rebound (**sur** off)

ricochet /Rikɔʃɛ/ *m* (of bullet) ricochet; (of stone) bounce; **faire des ~s** to skim stones

rictus /Riktys/ *m inv* (fixed) grin, rictus

ride /Rid/ *f* (on face, fruit) wrinkle; (on lake) ripple

rideau, *pl* **~x** /Rido/ *m* **1** curtain
2 (of shop) roller shutter
3 (of flames) wall
■ **~ de fumée** blanket of smoke

rider /Ride/ [**v1**] **A** *vt* **1** to wrinkle ‹*face, skin*›
2 to ripple ‹*surface, lake*›
B se rider *v refl* (+ *v être*) **1** ‹*skin*› to wrinkle
2 ‹*lake*› to ripple

ridicule /Ridikyl/ **A** *adj* **1** ridiculous
2 ‹*wage*› ridiculously low, pathetic
B *m* **1** ridicule
2 (of situation) absurdity

ridiculiser /Ridikylize/ [**v1**] **A** *vt* to ridicule; to wipe the floor with ‹*competitor*›
B se ridiculiser *v refl* (+ *v être*) ‹*person*› to make a fool of oneself

ridule /Ridyl/ *f* fine wrinkle

rien[1] /Rjɛ̃/ **A** *pron* **1** nothing; **il n'y a plus ~** there's nothing left; **~ n'y fait!** nothing's any good!; **~ d'autre** nothing else; **'pourquoi?'—'pour ~'** 'why?'—'no reason'; **'merci'—'de ~'** 'thank you'—'you're welcome' *or* 'not at all'; **en moins de ~** in no time at all; **ça ou ~, c'est pareil** it makes no odds; **c'est trois fois ~** (fam) it's next to nothing
2 ~ que la bouteille pèse deux kilos the bottle alone weighs two kilos; **elle voudrait un bureau ~ qu'à elle** (fam) she would like an office all to herself; **~ que ça?** (fam) is that all?; **ils habitent un château, ~ que ça!** (ironic) they live in a castle, no less! *or* if you please!
3 anything; **sans que j'en sache ~** without my knowing anything about it
4 (Sport), (gen) nil; (in tennis) love
B de rien (du tout) *phr* **un petit bleu de ~ (du tout)** a tiny bruise
C en rien *phr* at all, in any way
IDIOMS **~ à faire!** it's no good *or* use!; **ce n'est pas ~!** (exploit) it's quite something!; (task) it's no joke!; (sum of money) it's not exactly peanuts! (fam)

rien[2] /Rjɛ̃/ **A** *m* **un ~ le fâche** the slightest thing annoys him; **se disputer pour un ~** to quarrel over nothing; **les petits ~s qui rendent la vie agréable** the little things which make life pleasant; **un/une ~ du tout** a worthless person
B un rien *phr* (fam) a (tiny) bit

rieur, **rieuse** /RijœR, øz/ *adj* ‹*person, tone*› cheerful; ‹*face, eyes*› laughing

rigide /Riʒid/ *adj* **1** rigid
2 stiff

rigidité /Riʒidite/ *f* rigidity

rigolade /Rigɔlad/ *f* (fam) **1 quelle ~!** what a laugh! (fam)
2 joke
3 réparer ça, c'est de la ~! repairing this is a piece of cake (fam)

rigole /Rigɔl/ *f* **1** channel
2 rivulet

r

rigoler /ʀigɔle/ [**v1**] *vi* (fam) **1** to laugh
2 to have fun
3 to joke, to kid (fam)

rigolo, **-ote** /ʀigɔlo, ɔt/ **A** *adj* **1** funny
2 odd
B *mf* **1** joker
2 c'est un petit ~ he's quite a little comedian

rigoriste /ʀigɔʀist/ *adj* ‹*attitude*› unbending; ‹*morals*› strict

rigoureusement /ʀiguʀøzmɑ̃/ *adv* completely; carefully

rigoureux, **-euse** /ʀiguʀø, øz/ *adj*
1 ‹*discipline, person*› strict
2 ‹*climate, working conditions*› harsh, severe
3 ‹*research, demonstration*› meticulous; ‹*analysis*› rigorous

rigueur /ʀigœʀ/ **A** *f* **1** strictness
2 harshness
3 rigour (BrE)
4 (Econ) austerity
B de rigueur *phr* obligatory
C à la rigueur *phr* **à la ~ je peux te prêter 50 euros** at a pinch (BrE) *or* in a pinch (AmE) I can lend you 50 euros
IDIOM **tenir ~ à qn de qch** to bear sb a grudge for sth

rillettes /ʀijɛt/ *fpl* ≈ potted meat

rime /ʀim/ *f* rhyme

rimer /ʀime/ [**v1**] *vi* **1** to rhyme
2 cela ne rime à rien it makes no sense

rimmel® /ʀimɛl/ *m* mascara

rinçage /ʀɛ̃saʒ/ *m* **1** rinsing
2 rinse

rince-doigts /ʀɛ̃sdwa/ *m inv* **1** finger bowl
2 finger wipe

rincer /ʀɛ̃se/ [**v12**] **A** *vt* **1** to rinse
2 to rinse [sth] out
B se rincer *v refl* (+ *v être*) **se ~ les mains/les cheveux** to rinse one's hands/hair

ring /ʀiŋ/ *m* (boxing) ring

ringard, **~e** /ʀɛ̃gaʀ, aʀd/ *adj* (fam) out of date

riper /ʀipe/ [**v1**] *vi* ‹*foot*› to slip; ‹*bicycle*› to skid

riposte /ʀipɔst/ *f* **1** reply, riposte
2 response
3 (Sport) (in fencing) riposte; (in boxing) counter

riposter /ʀipɔste/ [**v1**] **A** *vt* to retort
B *vi* **1** to retort; **~ à qn/qch par** to counter sb/sth with
2 to respond
3 (Mil) to return fire, to shoot back
4 (in sport) to riposte

ripou, *pl* **~x** /ʀipu/ *adj* (pop) crooked (fam), bent (fam)

riquiqui /ʀikiki/ *adj inv* (fam) ‹*room, car*› poky (fam); ‹*portion*› measly (fam)

🔑 key word

🔑 **rire¹** /ʀiʀ/ [**v68**] **A** *vi* **1** to laugh; **tu nous feras toujours ~!** you're a real scream! (fam)
2 to have fun; **il faut bien ~ un peu** you need a bit of fun now and again; **fini de ~** the fun's over; **c'était pour ~** it was a joke; **sans ~** (fam) seriously; **laisse-moi ~** (fam), **ne me fais pas ~** (fam) don't make me laugh
3 ~ de qn/qch to laugh at sb/sth
B se rire *v refl* (+ *v être*) **se ~ de qn** (fml) to laugh at sb; **se ~ des difficultés** (fml) to make light of difficulties
IDIOMS **rira bien qui rira le dernier** (Proverb) he who laughs last laughs longest; **être mort de ~** (fam) to be doubled up (with laughter)

rire² /ʀiʀ/ *m* laughter; **un ~** a laugh; **il a eu un petit ~** he chuckled
■ **~s préenregistrés** canned laughter

ris /ʀi/ *m inv* **1** (Culin) **~ (de veau)** calf's sweetbread
2 (Naut) reef

risée /ʀize/ *f* **être la ~ de** to be the laughing stock of

risette /ʀizɛt/ *f* (fam) smile

risible /ʀizibl/ *adj* ridiculous, laughable

🔑 **risque** /ʀisk/ *m* risk; **c'est sans ~** it's safe; **à ~s** ‹*group, loan*› high-risk
■ **les ~s du métier** occupational hazards

risqué, **~e** /ʀiske/ *adj* **1** risky; ‹*investment*› high-risk
2 ‹*joke*› risqué; ‹*hypothesis*› daring

🔑 **risquer** /ʀiske/ [**v1**] **A** *vt* **1** to face ‹*accusation, condemnation*›
2 to risk ‹*death, criticism*›; **vas-y, tu ne risques rien** go ahead, you're safe; (fig) go ahead, you've got nothing to lose; **~ gros** to take a major risk
3 to risk ‹*life, reputation, job*›
4 to venture ‹*look, question*›; to attempt ‹*operation*›; **~ un œil** to venture a glance; **~ le coup** (fam) to risk it
B risquer de *v+prep* **1 tu risques de te brûler** you might burn yourself
2 il ne veut pas ~ de perdre son travail he doesn't want to risk losing his job
C se risquer *v refl* (+ *v être*) **1** to venture; **je ne m'y risquerais pas!** I wouldn't risk it
2 se ~ à dire to dare to say
D *v impers* **il risque de pleuvoir** it might rain; **il risque d'y avoir du monde** there may well be a lot of people there
IDIOM **~ le tout pour le tout** to stake *or* risk one's all

risque-tout /ʀiskətu/ *adj inv* daredevil

rissoler /ʀisɔle/ [**v1**] *vt*, *vi* (Culin) to brown

ristourne /ʀistuʀn/ *f* discount, rebate

rite /ʀit/ *m* rite

rituel, **-elle** /ʀitɥɛl/ *adj*, *m* ritual

rivage /ʀivaʒ/ *m* shore

rival, **~e**, *mpl* **-aux** /ʀival, o/ *adj*, *mf* rival

rivaliser /ʀivalize/ [**v1**] *vi* **~ avec** to compete with; **~ avec qch** to rival sth

rivalité /ʀivalite/ *f* rivalry

rive /ʀiv/ *f* **1** (of river) bank
2 (of sea, lake) shore

river /ʀive/ [**v1**] *vt* to clinch ‹*nail, rivet*›; **être rivé à** (fig) to be tied to ‹*one's work*›; **avoir les yeux rivés sur** to have one's eyes riveted on

riverain, **~e** /ʀivʀɛ̃, ɛn/ *mf* (of street) resident; (beside river) riverside resident

rivet /ʀivɛ/ *m* rivet

rivière /ʀivjɛʀ/ *f* river
■ **~ de diamants** diamond necklace

rixe /ʀiks/ *f* brawl

riz /ʀi/ *m* rice

rizière /ʀizjɛʀ/ *f* paddy field

RMI /ɛʀɛmi/ *m* (*abbr* = **revenu minimum d'insertion**) *minimum benefit paid to those with no other source of income*

RN /ɛʀɛn/ *f* (*abbr* = **route nationale**) ≈ A road (BrE), highway (AmE)

robe /ʀɔb/ *f* **1** (gen) dress
2 (of lawyer) gown
3 (of horse) coat; (of wine) colour (BrE)
■ **~ de chambre** dressing gown, robe (AmE)

robinet /ʀɔbinɛ/ *m* (for water) tap (BrE), faucet (AmE); (for gas) tap (BrE), valve (AmE)

robot /ʀɔbo/ *m* robot; **~ ménager** food processor

robotique /ʀɔbɔtik/ *f* robotics

robotisation /ʀɔbɔtizasjɔ̃/ *f* automation

robotiser /ʀɔbɔtize/ [**v1**] *vt* to automate

robuste /ʀɔbyst/ *adj* robust, sturdy; ‹*appetite*› healthy; ‹*faith*› strong

robustesse /ʀɔbystɛs/ *f* **1** robustness, sturdiness
2 soundness

roc /ʀɔk/ *m* rock

rocade /ʀɔkad/ *f* bypass; ring road (BrE)

rocaille /ʀɔkaj/ *f* **1** loose stones
2 rock garden

rocailleux, **-euse** /ʀɔkajø, øz/ *adj* **1** ‹*terrain*› rocky, stony
2 ‹*voice*› harsh, grating

rocambolesque /ʀɔkɑ̃bɔlɛsk/ *adj* fantastic, incredible

roche /ʀɔʃ/ *f* rock

rocher /ʀɔʃe/ *m* rock

rocheux, **-euse** /ʀɔʃø, øz/ *adj* rocky

rock /ʀɔk/ *m* **1** rock (music)
2 jive

rockeur, **-euse** /ʀɔkœʀ, øz/ *mf* **1** rock musician
2 rock fan

rococo /ʀɔkoko/ *adj inv* ‹*art, style*› rococo

rodage /ʀɔdaʒ/ *m* (of vehicle, engine) running in (BrE), breaking in (AmE)

rodéo /ʀɔdeo/ *m* rodeo

roder /ʀɔde/ [**v1**] *vt* **1** to run in (BrE), to break in (AmE) ‹*engine*›
2 to polish up ‹*show*›; **être (bien) rodé** ‹*department*› to be running smoothly

rôder /ʀode/ [**v1**] *vi* to prowl; **~ autour de qn** to hang around sb

rôdeur, **-euse** /ʀodœʀ, øz/ *mf* prowler

rogne /ʀɔɲ/ *f* (fam) **se mettre en ~** to get mad (fam)

rogner /ʀɔɲe/ [**v1**] *vt* **1** to trim ‹*angle*›; to clip ‹*nails*›
2 ~ sur to cut down on ‹*budget*›

rognon /ʀɔɲɔ̃/ *m* (Culin) kidney

roi /ʀwa/ *m* king
■ **les ~s mages** the (Three) Wise Men
IDIOM **tirer les Rois** to eat Twelfth Night cake

roitelet /ʀwatlɛ/ *m* **1** wren
2 kinglet

rôle /ʀol/ *m* **1** (for actor) part, role; **premier ~** lead, leading role
2 (gen) role; (of heart, part of body) function, role; **à tour de ~** in turn
IDIOM **avoir le beau ~** (fam) to have the easy job

roller /ʀolɛʀ/ *m* (skate) rollerblade; (activity) rollerblading

romain, **~e** /ʀɔmɛ̃, ɛn/ *adj* **1** Roman
2 l'Église ~e the Roman Catholic Church
3 caractères ~s roman typeface

romaine /ʀɔmɛn/ *f* cos lettuce

roman, **~e** /ʀɔmɑ̃, an/ **A** *adj* **1** ‹*church, style*› Romanesque; (in England) Norman
2 ‹*language*› Romance
B *m* **1** novel; **~ courtois** courtly romance
2 (style) **le ~** the Romanesque
■ **~ policier** detective story

romance /ʀɔmɑ̃s/ *f* **1** love song
2 (Literature) romance

romancer /ʀɔmɑ̃se/ [**v12**] *vt* **1** to romanticize
2 to fictionalize

romanche /ʀɔmɑ̃ʃ/ *m*, *adj* Romans(c)h

romancier, **-ière** /ʀɔmɑ̃sje, ɛʀ/ *mf* novelist

romand, **~e** /ʀɔmɑ̃, ɑ̃d/ *adj* ‹*Swiss person*› French-speaking

romanesque /ʀɔmanɛsk/ **A** *adj* **1** ‹*person*› romantic
2 ‹*narrative, story*› fictional
B *m* **1 le ~** fiction
2 le ~ d'une situation the fantastical aspect of a situation

roman-feuilleton, *pl* **romans-feuilletons** /ʀɔmɑ̃fœjtɔ̃/ *m* serial

roman-fleuve, *pl* **romans-fleuves** /ʀɔmɑ̃flœv/ *m* roman-fleuve, saga

roman-photo, *pl* **romans-photos** /ʀɔmɑ̃foto/ *m* photo-story

romantique /ʀɔmɑ̃tik/ *adj*, *mf* romantic

romantisme /ʀɔmɑ̃tism/ *m* romanticism

romarin /ʀɔmaʀɛ̃/ *m* rosemary

rombière /ʀɔ̃bjɛʀ/ *f* (pop) **une ~** an old bag (fam)

rompre /ʀɔ̃pʀ/ [**v53**] **A** *vt* (gen) to break, to break off ‹*relationship*›; to upset ‹*equilibrium*›; to disrupt ‹*harmony*›; to end ‹*isolation*›

B *vi* ~ **avec** to break with ‹*habit, tradition*›; to make a break from ‹*past*›; to break away from ‹*background*›; to break up with ‹*fiancé*›
C **se rompre** *v refl* (+ *v être*) to break

rompu, **~e** /ʀɔ̃py/ **A** *pp* ▸ **rompre**
B *pp adj* ~ **(de fatigue)** worn-out

romsteck /ʀɔmstɛk/ *m* rump steak

ronce /ʀɔ̃s/ *f* bramble

ronchon, **-onne** /ʀɔ̃ʃɔ̃, ɔn/ *adj* (fam) grumpy (fam)

ronchonner /ʀɔ̃ʃɔne/ [**v1**] *vi* (fam) to grumble

🔑 **rond**, **~e** /ʀɔ̃, ʀɔ̃d/ **A** *adj* **1** ‹*object, hole*› round
2 ‹*writing*› rounded; ‹*face*› round; ‹*person*› plump
3 ‹*number*› round
4 (fam) drunk
B *m* circle; **faire des ~s dans l'eau** to make ripples in the water
■ ~ **de serviette** napkin ring
IDIOM **ouvrir des yeux ~s** to be wide-eyed with astonishment

ronde /ʀɔ̃d/ **A** *adj f* ▸ **rond A**
B *f* **1** round dance; **entrer dans la ~** to join the dance
2 (of policeman) patrol; (of soldiers) watch
3 (Mus) semibreve (BrE), whole note (AmE)
C **à la ronde** *phr* around

rondelle /ʀɔ̃dɛl/ *f* **1** slice
2 (Tech) washer

rondement /ʀɔ̃dmɑ̃/ *adv* promptly

rondeur /ʀɔ̃dœʀ/ *f* **1** roundness
2 curve

rondin /ʀɔ̃dɛ̃/ *m* log

rondouillard, **~e** /ʀɔ̃dujaʀ, aʀd/ *adj* (fam) tubby (fam)

rond-point, *pl* **ronds-points** /ʀɔ̃pwɛ̃/ *m* roundabout (BrE), traffic circle (AmE)

ronflant, **~e** /ʀɔ̃flɑ̃, ɑ̃t/ *adj* **1** ‹*stove*› roaring
2 ‹*style*› high-flown

r

ronflement /ʀɔ̃fləmɑ̃/ *m* **1** snore
2 (of engine) purr

ronfler /ʀɔ̃fle/ [**v1**] *vi* **1** ‹*sleeper*› to snore; ‹*engine*› to purr
2 (fam) to be fast asleep

ronger /ʀɔ̃ʒe/ [**v13**] **A** *vt* **1** ‹*mouse, dog*› to gnaw; ‹*worms*› to eat into; ‹*caterpillar*› to eat away
2 ‹*acid, rust*› to erode
3 ‹*disease*› to wear down
B **se ronger** *v refl* (+ *v être*) **se ~ les ongles** to bite one's nails
IDIOM **se ~ les sangs** (fam) to worry oneself sick

rongeur /ʀɔ̃ʒœʀ/ *m* rodent

ronronnement /ʀɔ̃ʀɔnmɑ̃/ *m* (of cat, engine) purring

ronronner /ʀɔ̃ʀɔne/ [**v1**] *vi* to purr

roquet /ʀɔkɛ/ *m* **1** yappy little dog
2 (fam) bad-tempered little runt (fam)

roquette /ʀɔkɛt/ *f* (Mil) rocket

rosace /ʀozas/ *f* **1** rosette
2 rose window
3 (decorative motif) rose

rosaire /ʀozɛʀ/ *m* rosary

rosâtre /ʀozɑtʀ/ *adj* pinkish

rosbif /ʀɔsbif/ *m* joint of beef (BrE), roast of beef (AmE); (meal) roast beef

🔑 **rose¹** /ʀoz/ *adj* (gen) pink; ‹*cheeks*› rosy
IDIOM **la vie n'est pas ~** life isn't a bed of roses

rose² /ʀoz/ *f* (Bot) rose
■ ~ **des sables** gypsum flower; ~ **trémière** hollyhock
IDIOMS **envoyer qn sur les ~s** (fam) to send sb packing (fam); **découvrir le pot aux ~s** (fam) to find out what is going on

rosé /ʀoze/ *m* rosé

roseau, *pl* **~x** /ʀozo/ *m* (Bot) reed

rosée /ʀoze/ *f* dew

roseraie /ʀozʀɛ/ *f* rose garden

rosier /ʀozje/ *m* (Bot) rose bush, rose

rosir /ʀoziʀ/ [**v3**] *vi* ‹*sky*› to turn pink; ‹*face*› to go pink

rosse /ʀɔs/ **A** *adj* (fam) nasty, mean
B *f* **1** nag (fam)
2 meanie (fam), nasty person

rosser /ʀɔse/ [**v1**] *vt* (fam) to give [sb] a good thrashing; to beat ‹*animal*›

rosserie /ʀɔsʀi/ *f* **1** nasty remark; mean trick
2 meanness; nastiness

rossignol /ʀɔsiɲɔl/ *m* nightingale

rot /ʀo/ *m* (fam) burp (fam); **faire un ~** to burp (fam)

rotation /ʀɔtasjɔ̃/ *f* **1** (movement) rotation
2 (Mil) turnaround
3 (of crops, staff, shift) rotation

roter /ʀɔte/ [**v1**] *vt* (fam) to burp (fam), to belch

🔑 **rôti** /ʀɔti/ *m* **1** joint
2 roast

rotin /ʀɔtɛ̃/ *m* rattan

rôtir /ʀɔtiʀ/ [**v3**] *vt* to roast ‹*meat*›; to toast, to grill ‹*bread*›

rôtisseur, **-euse** /ʀɔtisœʀ, øz/ *mf* seller of roast meat

rôtissoire /ʀɔtiswaʀ/ *f* rotisserie, roasting spit

rotonde /ʀɔtɔ̃d/ *f* (building) rotunda

rotondité /ʀɔtɔ̃dite/ *f* roundness

rotule /ʀɔtyl/ *f* (Anat) kneecap
IDIOM **être sur les ~s** (fam) to be on one's last legs

roturier, **-ière** /ʀɔtyʀje, ɛʀ/ *mf* commoner

rouage /ʀwaʒ/ *m* **1** (of machine) (cog)wheel; **les ~s** the parts *or* works
2 (of administration) machinery; **les ~s bureaucratiques** the wheels of bureaucracy

roublard, **~e** /ʀublaʀ, aʀd/ *adj* (fam) crafty, cunning

🔑 key word

roublardise /ʀublaʀdiz/ *f* (fam) craftiness, cunning

rouble /ʀubl/ *m* rouble

roucouler /ʀukule/ [**v1**] *vi* **1** ‹*bird*› to coo
2 ‹*lovers*› to bill and coo

roue /ʀu/ *f* wheel; **~ dentée** cogwheel
■ **~ motrice** driving wheel; **~ de secours** spare wheel *or* tyre (BrE), spare tire (AmE)
IDIOMS **être la cinquième ~ du carrosse** to feel unwanted; **pousser qn à la ~** to be behind sb; **faire la ~** ‹*peacock*› to spread its tail, to display; ‹*person*› to strut around; (in gymnastics) to do a cartwheel

rouer /ʀwe/ [**v1**] *vt* **~ qn de coups** to beat sb up

rouerie /ʀuʀi/ *f* **1** cunning
2 cunning trick

rouet /ʀwɛ/ *m* spinning wheel

rouge /ʀuʒ/ **A** *adj* **1** (gen) red; ‹*person, face*› flushed
2 ‹*beard, hair, fur*› ginger
3 red-hot
B *mf* (communist) Red
C *m* **1** red; **le ~ lui monta au visage** he/she went red in the face
2 ~ à joues blusher, rouge; **~ à lèvres** lipstick
3 le feu est au ~ the (traffic) lights are red; **passer au ~** to jump the lights (BrE) *or* a red light
4 (fam) red (wine); **gros ~** (fam) cheap red wine; **un coup de ~** (fam) a glass of red wine
IDIOM **être ~ comme une tomate** *or* **une écrevisse** (from embarrassment) to be as red as a beetroot (BrE) *or* a beet (AmE); (from running) to be red in the face

rougeâtre /ʀuʒɑtʀ/ *adj* reddish

rougeaud, **~e** /ʀuʒo, od/ *adj* ‹*person*› ruddy-faced; ‹*face, complexion*› ruddy

rouge-gorge, *pl* **rouges-gorges** /ʀuʒgɔʀʒ/ *m* robin (redbreast)

rougeoiement /ʀuʒwamɑ̃/ *m* red glow

rougeole /ʀuʒɔl/ *f* measles

rougeoyer /ʀuʒwaje/ [**v23**] *vi* ‹*sun*› to glow fiery red; ‹*fire*› to glow red

rouget /ʀuʒɛ/ *m* red mullet, goatfish (AmE)

rougeur /ʀuʒœʀ/ *f* **1** redness
2 redness; flushing
3 red blotch

rougir /ʀuʒiʀ/ [**v3**] **A** *vt* to redden
B *vi* **1** to blush; to flush; to go red; **ne ~ de rien** to have no shame
2 ‹*fruit, sky*› to turn red
3 ‹*metal*› to become red hot

rougissant, **~e** /ʀuʒisɑ̃, ɑ̃t/ *adj* ‹*person*› blushing; ‹*sky*› reddening

rouille /ʀuj/ **A** *adj inv* red-brown
B *f* rust

rouiller /ʀuje/ [**v1**] **A** *vt* to rust
B *vi* to rust, to go rusty
C se rouiller *v refl* (+ *v être*) to get rusty

roulade /ʀulad/ *f* (Sport) roll

roulant, **~e** /ʀulɑ̃, ɑ̃t/ *adj* **table ~e** trolley; **personnel ~** train crew

roulé /ʀule/ *m* (Culin) roll

rouleau, *pl* **~x** /ʀulo/ *m* **1** roll
2 breaker, roller
3 (Tech) roller
4 roller, curler
■ **~ compresseur** steamroller; **~ à pâtisserie** rolling pin

roulement /ʀulmɑ̃/ *m* **1** (of thunder) rumble; (of drum) roll
2 (of capital) circulation
3 rotation; **travailler par ~** to work (in) shifts
4 (Tech) **~ à billes** ball bearing

rouler /ʀule/ [**v1**] **A** *vt* **1** to roll ‹*barrel, tyre*›; to wheel ‹*cart*›
2 to roll up ‹*carpet, sleeve, paper*›; to roll ‹*cigarette*›
3 ~ les épaules to roll one's shoulders
4 (fam) **~ qn** to cheat sb
B *vi* **1** ‹*ball, person*› to roll
2 ‹*vehicle*› to go; **~ à gauche** to drive on the left; **les bus ne roulent pas le dimanche** the buses don't run on Sundays
C se rouler *v refl* (+ *v être*) **se ~ dans** to roll in ‹*grass, mud*›

roulette /ʀulɛt/ *f* **1** caster
2 roulette
3 (dentist's) drill
IDIOM **marcher comme sur des ~s** (fam) to go smoothly *or* like a dream

roulis /ʀuli/ *m* (of boat) rolling; (of car, train) swaying

roulotte /ʀulɔt/ *f* (horse-drawn) caravan (BrE), trailer (AmE)

Roumanie /ʀumani/ *pr f* Romania

roupie /ʀupi/ *f* rupee

roupiller /ʀupije/ [**v1**] *vi* (fam) to sleep

roupillon /ʀupijɔ̃/ *m* (fam) snooze (fam), nap

rouquin, **~e** /ʀukɛ̃, in/ *mf* (fam) redhead

rouspéter /ʀuspete/ [**v14**] *vi* (fam) to grumble

rousse /ʀus/ ▶ **roux**

rousseur /ʀusœʀ/ *f* (of hair, foliage) redness; (of shade) russet colour (BrE)

roussi /ʀusi/ *m* **ça sent le ~** there's a smell of burning; (fig) there's trouble brewing

roussir /ʀusiʀ/ [**v3**] **A** *vt* to turn [sth] brown
B *vi* **1** to go brown
2 (Culin) **faire ~** to brown

routage /ʀutaʒ/ *m* sorting and mailing

routard, **~e** /ʀutaʀ, aʀd/ *mf* (fam) backpacker

route /ʀut/ *f* **1** road, highway (AmE); **tenir la ~** ‹*car*› to hold the road; (fig, fam) ‹*argument*› to hold water; ‹*equipment*› to be well-made
2 road; **il y a six heures de ~** it's a six-hour drive; **faire de la ~** (fam) to do a lot of mileage

r

3 route; **~s maritimes** sea routes
4 way; **la ~ sera longue** it will be a long journey; **j'ai changé d'avis en cours de ~** I changed my mind along the way; **être en ~** ‹*person*› to be on one's way; ‹*dish*› to be cooking; **être en ~ pour** to be en route to; **faire fausse ~** to go off course; (fig) to be mistaken; **se mettre en ~** to set off; **en ~!** let's go!; **mettre en ~** to start ‹*machine, car*›; to get [sth] going ‹*project*›
■ **~ départementale** secondary road; **~ nationale** trunk road (BrE), ≈ A road (BrE), national highway (AmE)

routeur /ʀutœʀ/ *m* router

routier, -ière /ʀutje, ɛʀ/ **A** *adj* road
B *m* **1** lorry driver (BrE), truck driver
2 transport cafe (BrE), truck stop (AmE)

routine /ʀutin/ *f* routine

routinier, -ière /ʀutinje, ɛʀ/ *adj* ‹*person*› set in one's ways; ‹*work, life*› routine

rouvrir: **se rouvrir** /ʀuvʀiʀ/ **[v32]** *v refl* (+ *v être*) ‹*door*› to open (again); ‹*wound*› to open up (again)

roux, **rousse** /ʀu, ʀus/ **A** *adj* ‹*leaves*› russet; ‹*hair*› red; ‹*person*› red-haired; ‹*fur*› ginger
B *mf* red-haired person, redhead

royal, **~e**, *mpl* **-aux** /ʀwajal, o/ *adj* **1** royal
2 ‹*present*› fit for a king; ‹*tip, salary*› princely
3 ‹*indifference*› supreme; ‹*peace*› blissful

royalement /ʀwajalmɑ̃/ *adv* **1** royally; **être payé ~** to be paid handsomely
2 (fam) **il se moque ~ de son travail** he really couldn't care less about his work

royaliste /ʀwajalist/ *adj, mf* royalist
IDIOM **être plus ~ que le roi** to be more Catholic than the pope

✓ **royaume** /ʀwajom/ *m* kingdom

Royaume-Uni /ʀwajomyni/ *pr m* **le ~** the United Kingdom

royauté /ʀwajote/ *f* **1** kingship
2 monarchy

RSA *m* (*abbr* = **Revenu de solidarité active**) *additional top-up benefit given to those in low-paid employment*

RSVP (*written abbr* = **répondez s'il vous plaît**) RSVP

ruade /ʀyad/ *f* **1** (by horse) buck
2 (by person, party) attack

Ruanda /ʀwɑ̃da/ *pr m* Rwanda

ruban /ʀybɑ̃/ *m* ribbon; **~ adhésif** adhesive tape, sticky tape (BrE)

rubéole /ʀybeɔl/ *f* German measles

rubis /ʀybi/ *m inv* **1** ruby
2 ruby (red)

rubrique /ʀybʀik/ *f* **1** (of newspaper) section; **~ mondaine** social column
2 category

ruche /ʀyʃ/ *f* **1** beehive
2 hive of activity

rude /ʀyd/ *adj* **1** ‹*job, day*› hard, tough; ‹*winter*› harsh; ‹*ordeal*› severe
2 ‹*material, beard*› rough
3 ‹*features*› coarse
4 **c'est un ~ gaillard** he's a strapping fellow
5 ‹*opponent*› tough

rudement /ʀydmɑ̃/ *adv* **1** roughly
2 (fam) really

rudesse /ʀydɛs/ *f* **1** harshness, severity
2 coarseness

rudimentaire /ʀydimɑ̃tɛʀ/ *adj* **1** basic
2 (Anat) rudimentary

rudiments /ʀydimɑ̃/ *mpl* **avoir quelques ~ de** to have a rudimentary knowledge of

rudoyer /ʀydwaje/ **[v23]** *vt* to bully

✓ **rue** /ʀy/ *f* street
IDIOMS **ça ne court pas les ~s** (fam) it's pretty thin on the ground; **descendre dans la ~** to take to the street

ruée /ʀɥe/ *f* rush; **~ vers l'or** gold rush

ruelle /ʀɥɛl/ *f* alleyway, back street

ruer /ʀɥe/ **[v1]** **A** *vi* ‹*horse*› to buck
B **se ruer** *v refl* (+ *v être*) to rush
IDIOM **~ dans les brancards** to rebel

✓ **rugby** /ʀygbi/ *m* rugby; **~ à treize** rugby league; **~ à quinze** rugby union

rugbyman, *pl* **rugbymen** /ʀygbiman, mɛn/ *m* rugby player

rugir /ʀyʒiʀ/ **[v3]** **A** *vt* to bellow (out), to growl
B *vi* ‹*animal, engine*› to roar; ‹*wind*› to howl

rugissement /ʀyʒismɑ̃/ *m* (of animal, person) roar; (of wind) howling

rugosité /ʀygozite/ *f* roughness

rugueux, -euse /ʀygø, øz/ *adj* rough

ruine /ʀɥin/ *f* **1** (of building, person, reputation, company) ruin; (of civilization) collapse; (of hope) death; **en ~(s)** ruined; **ce n'est pas la ~** (fam) it's not that expensive
2 ruin
3 wreck

ruiner /ʀɥine/ **[v1]** **A** *vt* **1** to ruin ‹*person, economy*›; **~ qn** to be a drain on sb's resources
2 to destroy ‹*health, happiness*›
3 to ruin ‹*life*›; to shatter ‹*hopes*›
B **se ruiner** *v refl* (+ *v être*) to be ruined, to lose everything; to ruin oneself

ruineux, -euse /ʀɥinø, øz/ *adj* very expensive

ruisseau, *pl* **~x** /ʀɥiso/ *m* **1** stream, brook
2 **~ de larmes** stream of tears

ruisseler /ʀɥisle/ **[v19]** *vi* **1** ‹*water*› to stream; ‹*grease*› to drip
2 to be streaming; **~ de sueur** to be dripping with sweat

ruissellement /ʀɥisɛlmɑ̃/ *m* (of rain) streaming; (of grease) dripping

rumeur /ʀymœʀ/ *f* **1** rumour (BrE)
2 (of voices, wind) murmur

ruminant /ʀyminɑ̃/ *m* ruminant
ruminer /ʀymine/ [**v1**] **A** *vt* **1** to ruminate
2 to brood on ‹*misery*›; to chew over (fam) ‹*idea, plan*›
B *vi* **1** to ruminate
2 ‹*person*› to brood
rumsteck /ʀɔmstɛk/ *m* rump steak
rupestre /ʀypɛstʀ/ *adj* **1** ‹*plants*› rock
2 ‹*paintings*› cave, rock
rupture /ʀyptyʀ/ *f* **1** (of relations) breaking-off
2 breakdown
3 break-up; **lettre de ~** letter ending a relationship
4 (of dam, dyke) breaking; (of pipe) fracture
rural, **~e**, *mpl* **-aux** /ʀyʀal, o/ *adj* ‹*exodus, environment*› rural; ‹*road, life*› country
rurbain, **~e** /ʀyʀbɛ̃, ɛn/ **A** *adj* from the rural outer suburbs
B *mf* inhabitant of the rural outer suburbs
rurbanisation /ʀyʀbanizasjɔ̃/ *f* *urbanisation of formerly rural areas on the fringes of towns or cities*
ruse /ʀyz/ *f* **1** trick, ruse; **~ de guerre** (hum) cunning stratagem
2 cunning, craftiness
rusé, **~e** /ʀyze/ *adj* cunning, crafty
ruser /ʀyze/ [**v1**] *vi* **1** to be crafty
2 ~ avec to trick ‹*enemy, police*›
rush, *pl* **rushes** /ʀœʃ/ **A** *m* (in race) final burst
B rushes *mpl* (of film) rushes
russe /ʀys/ *adj, m* Russian
Russie /ʀysi/ *pr f* Russia
rustaud, **~e** /ʀysto, od/ *adj* rustic
rusticité /ʀystisite/ *f* rustic character
rustine® /ʀystin/ *f* (puncture repair) patch
rustique /ʀystik/ *adj* rustic, country
rustre /ʀystʀ/ **A** *adj* uncouth
B *m* lout
rut /ʀyt/ *m* rutting season
rutilant, **~e** /ʀytilɑ̃, ɑ̃t/ *adj* sparkling; gleaming
rythme /ʀitm/ *m* **1** rhythm; **marquer le ~** to beat time
2 (of growth) rate; (of life) pace
■ **~ cardiaque** heart rate
rythmer /ʀitme/ [**v1**] *vt* **1** to give rhythm to
2 to regulate ‹*life, work*›
rythmique /ʀitmik/ *adj* rhythmic

Ss

s, **S** /ɛs/ *m inv* s, S
s' 1 ▶ **se**
2 ▶ **si[1] B**
sa ▶ **son[1]**
sabbat /saba/ *m* **1** Sabbath
2 witches' Sabbath
sabbatique /sabatik/ *adj* (Univ) sabbatical
sable /sɑbl/ *m* sand; **~s mouvants** quicksands
sablé, **~e** /sable/ **A** *adj* **pâte ~e** shortcrust pastry
B *m* shortbread biscuit (BrE) *or* cookie (AmE)
sabler /sable/ [**v1**] *vt* to grit] ‹*roadway*›
IDIOM **~ le champagne** to crack open some champagne
sablier /sablije/ *m* hourglass; egg timer
sablonneux, **-euse** /sablɔnø, øz/ *adj* sandy
sabot /sabo/ *m* **1** clog
2 (Zool) hoof
sabotage /sabɔtaʒ/ *m* sabotage
saboter /sabɔte/ [**v1**] *vt* to sabotage
saboteur, **-euse** /sabɔtœʀ, øz/ *mf* (of equipment) saboteur
sabre /sɑbʀ/ *m* **1** sword
2 sabre (BrE)
sabrer /sɑbʀe/ [**v1**] *vt* (fam) to cut chunks out of ‹*article*›
sac /sak/ *m* **1** (gen) bag
2 sack
3 bag(ful), sack(ful)
4 mettre à ~ to sack ‹*city, region*›; to ransack ‹*shop, house*›
■ **~ de couchage** sleeping bag; **~ à dos** rucksack, backpack; **~ à main** handbag (BrE), purse (AmE); **~ postal** mail sack; **~ à provisions** shopping bag, carry-all (AmE)
IDIOMS **l'affaire est dans le ~** (fam) it's in the bag (fam); **avoir plus d'un tour dans son ~** to have more than one trick up one's sleeve; **vider son ~** (fam) to get it off one's chest; **se faire prendre la main dans le ~** to be caught red-handed; **mettre dans le même ~** (fam) to lump together
saccade /sakad/ *f* jerk
saccadé, **~e** /sakade/ *adj* ‹*movement*› jerky; ‹*rhythm*› staccato; ‹*voice*› clipped
saccager /sakaʒe/ [**v13**] *vt* **1** to wreck, to devastate ‹*region*›; to vandalize ‹*building*›
2 to sack
saccharine /sakaʀin/ *f* saccharin

r
s

SACEM /sasɛm/ *f* (*abbr* = **Société des auteurs, compositeurs et éditeurs de musique**) *association of composers and music publishers to protect copyright and royalties*

sacerdoce /sasɛʀdɔs/ *m* priesthood

sachet /saʃɛ/ *m* (of powder) packet; (of herbs, spices) sachet; **~ de thé** tea bag

sacoche /sakɔʃ/ *f* **1** bag
2 (on bicycle) pannier (BrE), saddlebag (AmE)

sacquer /sake/ [**v1**] *vt* (fam) **1** to sack (BrE) (fam), to fire (fam)
2 ‹*teacher*› to mark [sb] strictly
3 je ne peux pas le ~ I can't stand the sight of him

sacre /sakʀ/ *m* (of king) coronation; (of bishop) consecration

sacré, **~e** /sakʀe/ *adj* **1** ‹*art, object, place*› sacred; ‹*cause*› holy
2 ‹*rule, right*› sacred
3 (fam) **être un ~ menteur** to be a hell of a liar (fam)
4 (fam) **~ Paul, va!** Paul, you old devil!
IDIOM **avoir le feu ~** to be full of zeal

sacrement /sakʀəmɑ̃/ *m* sacrament; **les derniers ~s** the last rites

sacrément /sakʀemɑ̃/ *adv* (fam) incredibly (fam)

sacrer /sakʀe/ [**v1**] *vt* to crown ‹*king*›; to consecrate ‹*bishop*›

sacrifice /sakʀifis/ *m* sacrifice

sacrifier /sakʀifje/ [**v1**] **A** *vt* to sacrifice
B sacrifier à *v+prep* to conform to ‹*fashion*›
C se sacrifier *v refl* (+ *v être*) **1** to sacrifice oneself
2 (fam) to make sacrifices

sacrilège /sakʀilɛʒ/ *m* sacrilege

sacristie /sakʀisti/ *f* (of Catholic church) sacristy; (of Protestant church) vestry

sacro-saint, **~e**, *mpl* **~s** /sakʀosɛ̃, ɛ̃t/ *adj* sacrosanct

sadique /sadik/ **A** *adj* sadistic
B *mf* sadist

S

sadisme /sadism/ *m* sadism

sadomasochisme /sadomazɔʃism/ *m* sadomasochism

safari /safaʀi/ *m* safari

safran /safʀɑ̃/ *adj inv*, *m* saffron

saga /saga/ *f* saga

sagacité /sagasite/ *f* sagacity, shrewdness

sage /saʒ/ **A** *adj* **1** wise, sensible
2 good, well-behaved
3 ‹*tastes, fashion*› sober
B *m* **1** wise man, sage
2 expert

sage-femme, *pl* **sages-femmes** /saʒfam/ *f* midwife

sagement /saʒmɑ̃/ *adv* **1** wisely
2 ‹*sit, listen*› quietly
3 ‹*dress*› soberly

sagesse /saʒɛs/ *f* **1** wisdom, common sense; (of advice) soundness; **la voix de la ~** the voice of reason
2 good behaviour (BrE)

Sagittaire /saʒitɛʀ/ *pr m* Sagittarius

Sahara /saaʀa/ *pr m* Sahara

saignant, **~e** /sɛɲɑ̃, ɑ̃t/ *adj* **1** ‹*meat*› rare
2 (fig, fam) ‹*criticism*› savage

saignée /sɛɲe/ *f* **1** (Med) bloodletting, bleeding
2 (in budget) hole
3 (in tree) cut

saignement /sɛɲ(ə)mɑ̃/ *m* bleeding

saigner /sɛɲe/ [**v1**] **A** *vt* **1** (Med) to bleed
2 to kill ‹*animal*› *by slitting its throat*; **~ un cochon** to stick a pig
B *vi* to bleed; **~ du nez** to have a nosebleed
IDIOMS **~ qn à blanc** to bleed sb dry; **se ~ (aux quatre veines) pour qn** to make big sacrifices for sb

saillant, **~e** /sajɑ̃, ɑ̃t/ *adj* **1** ‹*jaw*› prominent; ‹*muscle, eyes*› bulging; ‹*angle*› salient
2 ‹*fact, episode*› salient

saillie /saji/ *f* **1** projection; **le balcon est en ~** the balcony juts out
2 (Zool) covering

saillir /sajiʀ/ [**v28**] *vi* **1** to jut out
2 ‹*ribs, muscles*› to bulge

sain, **~e** /sɛ̃, sɛn/ *adj* (gen) healthy, sound; ‹*wound*› clean; **~ d'esprit** sane; **~ de corps et d'esprit** sound in body and mind; **~ et sauf** ‹*return*› safe and sound

saindoux /sɛ̃du/ *m inv* lard

sainement /sɛnmɑ̃/ *adv* **1** ‹*live*› healthily
2 ‹*reason*› soundly

saint, **~e** /sɛ̃, sɛ̃t/ **A** *adj* **1** holy; **vendredi ~** Good Friday
2 ~ Paul Saint Paul
B *mf* saint
■ **~e nitouche** goody-goody (fam); **la Sainte Vierge** the Virgin Mary

Saint-Barthélémy /sɛ̃baʀtelemi/ *f* **la ~** the St Bartholomew's Day massacre

saint-bernard /sɛ̃bɛʀnaʀ/ *m inv* St Bernard

Saint-Esprit /sɛ̃tɛspʀi/ *pr m* Holy Spirit

sainteté /sɛ̃tte/ *f* saintliness

saint-glinglin: **à la saint-glinglin** /alasɛ̃glɛ̃glɛ̃/ *phr* (fam) probably never; **rester/attendre jusqu'à la ~** to stay/to wait till the cows come home (fam)

saint-honoré /sɛ̃tɔnɔʀe/ *m inv: cream-filled tart topped with choux and caramel*

Saint-Jacques /sɛ̃ʒak/ *pr n* **coquille ~** scallop

Saint-Jean /sɛ̃ʒɑ̃/ *f* **la ~** Midsummer Day

Saint-Sylvestre /sɛ̃silvɛstʀ/ *f* **la ~** New Year's Eve

saisie /sezi/ *f* **1** (gen), (Law) seizure
2 keyboarding; **~ de données** data capture

saisir /seziʀ/ [**v3**] **A** *vt* **1** to grab; to seize; **~ au vol** to catch ‹*ball*›; **'affaire à ~'** 'amazing

key word

bargain'
2 to understand
3 to catch ‹*name, bits of conversation*›
4 ‹*emotion, cold*› to grip ‹*person*›
5 to strike, to impress ‹*person*›
6 (Law) to seize ‹*property*›; **~ la justice d'une affaire** to refer a matter to a court
7 (Comput) to capture ‹*data*›; to key ‹*text*›
B **se saisir** *v refl* (+ *v être*) **se ~ de** to catch *or* grab hold of ‹*object*›

saisissant, **~e** /sezisɑ̃, ɑ̃t/ *adj* **1** ‹*cold*› piercing
2 ‹*effect, resemblance*› striking

saison /sɛzɔ̃/ *f* (gen) season; **en cette ~** at this time of year; **en toute ~** all (the) year round; **la haute/morte ~** the high/slack season; **prix hors ~** off-season prices

saisonnier, **-ière** /sɛzɔnje, ɛʀ/ **A** *adj* seasonal
B *mf* (worker) seasonal worker

salace /salas/ *adj* salacious

salade /salad/ *f* **1** lettuce
2 salad
3 (fam) muddle; **raconter des ~s** to spin yarns (fam)

saladier /saladje/ *m* salad bowl

salaire /salɛʀ/ *m* salary; wages

salaison /salɛzɔ̃/ *f* salt meat

salamandre /salamɑ̃dʀ/ *f* salamander

salant /salɑ̃/ *adj m* **marais ~** saltern

salarial, **~e**, *mpl* **-iaux** /salaʀjal, o/ *adj*
1 ‹*policy, rise*› wage
2 cotisation ~e employee's contribution

salarié, **~e** /salaʀje/ **A** *adj* ‹*worker*› wage-earning; ‹*job*› salaried
B *mf* **1** wage earner
2 salaried employee

salaud /salo/ *m* (offensive, pop) bastard (sl)

sale /sal/ **A** *adj* **1** (*after n*) dirty
2 (*before n*) (fam) ‹*person*› horrible; ‹*animal, illness, habit*› nasty; ‹*weather*› foul, horrible; ‹*work, place*› rotten; **~ menteur!** you dirty liar!; **il a une ~ tête** he looks dreadful; **faire une ~ tête** to look annoyed; **un ~ coup** a very nasty blow; **un ~ caractère** a foul temper
B *m* **mettre qch au ~** to put sth in the wash

salé, **~e** /sale/ *adj* **1** salt, salty
2 salted; ‹*snack*› savoury (BrE)
3 (fam) ‹*bill*› steep

salement /salmɑ̃/ *adv* **1 manger ~** to be a messy eater
2 (fam) badly, seriously

saler /sale/ [**v1**] *vt* **1** to salt ‹*food*›; **~ et poivrer** to add salt and pepper to
2 to grit (BrE), to salt (AmE) ‹*road*›

saleté /salte/ *f* **1** dirtiness; dirt; filth; **ramasser les ~s** to pick up the rubbish (BrE) *or* trash (AmE); **faire des ~s** to make a mess
2 (fam) **c'est de la ~** ‹*gadget, goods*› it's rubbish; **c'est une vraie ~ ce virus!** it's a rotten bug!

salière /saljɛʀ/ *f* salt cellar, salt shaker (AmE)

salir /saliʀ/ [**v3**] **A** *vt* **1** to dirty; to soil
2 to sully ‹*reputation*›
B *vi* ‹*industry, coal*› to pollute
C **se salir** *v refl* (+ *v être*) to get dirty, to dirty oneself

salissant, **~e** /salisɑ̃, ɑ̃t/ *adj* **1** ‹*colour*› which shows the dirt
2 ‹*work*› dirty

salive /saliv/ *f* saliva

saliver /salive/ [**v1**] *vi* to salivate; **~ devant qch** to drool over sth

salle /sal/ *f* **1** (gen) room; hall; (in restaurant) (dining) room; (in hospital) ward; (in theatre) auditorium; **faire ~ comble** ‹*show*› to be packed; **en ~** ‹*sport*› indoor
2 audience
■ **~ d'attente** waiting room; **~ de bains** bathroom; **~ de cinéma** cinema (BrE), movie theater (AmE); **~ de classe** classroom; **~ de concert** concert hall; **~ d'eau** shower room; **~ d'embarquement** departure lounge; **~ des fêtes** village hall; community centre (BrE); **~ de garde** (in hospital) staff room; **~ de gymnastique** gymnasium; **~ de jeu(x)** (in casino) gaming room; (for children) playroom; **~ à manger** dining room; dining room suite; **~ de séjour** living room; **~ des ventes** auction room

salon /salɔ̃/ *m* **1** (gen) lounge; drawing room
2 sitting room suite; **~ de jardin** garden furniture
3 (trade) show; fair; exhibition; **~ du livre** book fair
4 (of intellectuals) salon
5 (Comput) chatroom
■ **~ de beauté** beauty salon; **~ de coiffure** hairdressing salon; **~ d'essayage** fitting room; **~ de thé** tearoom

salopette /salɔpɛt/ *f* overalls

salpêtre /salpɛtʀ/ *m* saltpetre (BrE)

salsifis /salsifi/ *m inv* salsify

saltimbanque /saltɛ̃bɑ̃k/ *mf* **1** street acrobat
2 entertainer

salubre /salybʀ/ *adj* ‹*lodgings*› salubrious

salubrité /salybʀite/ *f* (of air, climate) healthiness; (of dwelling) salubrity
■ **~ publique** public health

saluer /salɥe/ [**v1**] *vt* **1** to greet ‹*person*›; **~ qn de la tête** to nod to sb
2 to say goodbye to ‹*person*›
3 (Mil) to salute
4 to welcome ‹*decision, news*›
5 to pay tribute to ‹*memory*›

salut /saly/ *m* **1** greeting; **~!** hello!, hi!; **~ de la tête** nod
2 salute
3 salvation

salutaire /salytɛʀ/ *adj* ‹*experience*› salutary; ‹*effect*› beneficial; ‹*air*› healthy

salutation /salytasjɔ̃/ *f* greeting

salvateur, **-trice** /salvatœʀ, tʀis/ *adj* saving

S

salve /salv/ *f* **1** salvo; **tirer une ~ d'honneur** to fire a salute
2 ~ d'applaudissements burst of applause

♂ **samedi** /samdi/ *m* Saturday

SAMU /samy/ *m* (*abbr* = **Service d'assistance médicale d'urgence**) ≈ mobile accident unit (BrE), emergency medical service, EMS (AmE)

sanatorium /sanatɔʀjɔm/ *m* sanatorium (BrE), sanitarium (AmE)

sanctifier /sɑ̃ktifje/ [**v1**] *vt* to sanctify

sanction /sɑ̃ksjɔ̃/ *f* (Law) penalty, sanction; disciplinary measure; (Sch) punishment

sanctionner /sɑ̃ksjɔne/ [**v1**] *vt* **1** to punish
2 to give official recognition to ‹*training*›

sanctuaire /sɑ̃ktɥɛʀ/ *m* **1** shrine
2 sanctuary

sandale /sɑ̃dal/ *f* sandal

sandwich, *pl* **~s** *or* **~es** /sɑ̃dwitʃ/ *m* sandwich; **(pris) en ~** sandwiched

♂ **sang** /sɑ̃/ *m* **1** blood; **être en ~** to be covered with blood; **se terminer dans le ~** to end in bloodshed
2 de ~ ‹*brother, ties*› blood; **être du même ~** to be kin
(IDIOMS) **il a ça dans le ~** it's in his blood; **mettre qch à feu et à ~** to put sth to fire and sword; **mon ~ n'a fait qu'un tour** my heart missed a beat; I saw red; **se faire du mauvais ~** (fam) to worry; **bon ~!** for God's sake! (fam)

sang-froid /sɑ̃fʀwɑ/ *m inv* composure; **garde ton ~!** keep calm!; **de ~** in cold blood

sanglant, **~e** /sɑ̃glɑ̃, ɑ̃t/ *adj* bloody

sangle /sɑ̃gl/ *f* **1** (gen) strap
2 (of saddle) girth
3 (of seat, bed) webbing

sangler /sɑ̃gle/ [**v1**] *vt* to girth ‹*horse*›

sanglier /sɑ̃glije/ *m* wild boar

sanglot /sɑ̃glo/ *m* sob

sangloter /sɑ̃glɔte/ [**v1**] *vi* to sob

sangsue /sɑ̃sy/ *f* leech

sanguin, **~e** /sɑ̃gɛ̃, in/ *adj* blood

S

sanguinaire /sɑ̃ginɛʀ/ *adj* ‹*crime*› bloody; ‹*person*› bloodthirsty

sanguine /sɑ̃gin/ **A** *adj f* ▸ **sanguin**
B *f* **1** blood orange
2 red chalk drawing

sanguinolent, **~e** /sɑ̃ginɔlɑ̃, ɑ̃t/ *adj* blood-stained

sanisette® /sanizɛt/ *f* automatic public toilet

sanitaire /sanitɛʀ/ **A** *adj* ‹*regulations*› health; ‹*conditions*› sanitary
B sanitaires *mpl* **les ~s** (in house) the bathroom; (in campsite) the toilet block

♂ **sans** /sɑ̃/ **A** *adv* without
B *prep* **1** without; **un couple ~ enfant** a childless couple; **~ cela** otherwise
2 il est resté trois mois ~ téléphoner he didn't call for three months; **il est poli, ~ plus** he's polite, but that's as far as it goes
3 on sera dix ~ les enfants there'll be ten of us not counting the children; **500 euros ~ l'hôtel** 500 euros not including accommodation
C sans que *phr* without; **pars ~ qu'on te voie** leave without anyone seeing you
■ **~ domicile fixe, SDF** of no fixed abode, NFA

sans-abri /sɑ̃zabʀi/ *mf inv* **un ~** a homeless person; **les ~** the homeless

sans-emploi /sɑ̃zɑ̃plwɑ/ *mf inv* unemployed person

sans-faute /sɑ̃fot/ *m inv* faultless performance

sans-gêne /sɑ̃ʒɛn/ *adj inv* bad-mannered

sans-papiers /sɑ̃papje/ *m* illegal immigrant

santal /sɑ̃tal/ *m* sandalwood

♂ **santé** /sɑ̃te/ *f* health; **avoir la ~** to enjoy good health; **se refaire une ~** to build up one's strength; **avoir une petite ~** to be frail; **à votre ~!** cheers!; **à la ~ de Janet!** here's to Janet!

santon /sɑ̃tɔ̃/ *m* Christmas crib figure

saoul, **~e** ▸ **soûl**

saper /sape/ [**v1**] **A** *vt* to undermine
B se saper *v refl* (+ *v être*) (fam) to dress

sapeur /sapœʀ/ *m* sapper
(IDIOM) **fumer comme un ~** to smoke like a chimney

sapeur-pompier, *pl* **sapeurs-pompiers** /sapœʀpɔ̃pje/ *m* fireman

saphir /safiʀ/ *m* **1** sapphire
2 (on record player) stylus

sapin /sapɛ̃/ *m* **1** fir tree; **~ de Noël** Christmas tree
2 deal

saquer /sake/ [**v1**] (fam) ▸ **sacquer**

sarbacane /saʀbakan/ *f* blowpipe

sarcasme /saʀkasm/ *m* **1** sarcasm
2 sarcastic remark

sarcastique /saʀkastik/ *adj* sarcastic

sarcophage /saʀkɔfaʒ/ *m* sarcophagus

sardine /saʀdin/ *f* **1** (Zool) sardine
2 (fam) tent peg

sarment /saʀmɑ̃/ *m* vine shoot

sarrasin /saʀazɛ̃/ *m* buckwheat

sarrau /saʀo/ *m* smock

sas /sɑs/ *m inv* **1** airlock
2 (on canal) lock
3 (in bank) security double door system

satanique /satanik/ *adj* **1** ‹*smile, ruse*› fiendish
2 ‹*cult*› Satanic

satellite /satɛlit/ *m* satellite

satiété /sasjete/ **A** *f* satiation, satiety
B à satiété *phr* **1 manger à ~** to eat one's fill
2 ‹*say, repeat*› ad nauseam

satin /satɛ̃/ *m* satin

♂ key word

satiné, **~e** /satine/ *adj* ‹*fabric, cloth*› satiny; ‹*paint*› satin finish

satire /satiʀ/ *f* satire

satirique /satiʀik/ *adj* satirical

satisfaction /satisfaksjɔ̃/ *f* satisfaction; **la ~ de nos besoins** the fulfilment (BrE) of our needs

satisfaire /satisfɛʀ/ [**v10**] **A** *vt* (gen) to satisfy; to fulfil (BrE) ‹*aspiration, requirement*›
B **satisfaire à** *v+prep* to fulfil (BrE) ‹*obligation*›; to meet ‹*norm, standard*›
C **se satisfaire** *v refl* (+ *v être*) **se ~ de** to be satisfied with ‹*explanation*›; to be content with ‹*low salary*›

satisfaisant, **~e** /satisfəzɑ̃, ɑ̃t/ *adj*
1 satisfactory
2 satisfying

satisfait, **~e** /satisfɛ, ɛt/ *adj* ‹*customer, need, smile*› satisfied; ‹*desire*› gratified; ‹*person*› happy

saturation /satyʀasjɔ̃/ *f* (of market) saturation; (in trains, hotels) overcrowding; (of network) overloading; **arriver à ~** ‹*market, network*› to reach saturation point; ‹*person*› to have had as much as one can take

saturé, **~e** /satyʀe/ *adj* ‹*market*› saturated; ‹*profession*› overcrowded

saturer /satyʀe/ [**v1**] *vt* to saturate

satyre /satiʀ/ *m* **1** satyr
2 lecher

sauce /sos/ *f* (Culin) sauce; **(r)allonger la ~** (fig, fam) to spin things out
IDIOM **mettre qch à toutes les ~s** to adapt sth to any purpose

saucière /sosjɛʀ/ *f* sauce boat

saucisse /sosis/ *f* sausage; **chair à ~** sausage meat
■ **~ de Francfort** frankfurter

saucisson /sosisɔ̃/ *m* (slicing) sausage; **~ à l'ail** garlic sausage; **~ sec** ≈ salami

sauf¹ /sof/ **A** *prep* **1** except, but
2 ~ contrordre failing an order to the contrary; **~ avis contraire** unless otherwise stated; **~ erreur de ma part** if I'm not mistaken
B **sauf si** *phr* unless
C **sauf que** *phr* except that

sauf², **sauve** /sof, sov/ *adj* **1** safe; **laisser la vie sauve à qn** to spare sb's life
2 ‹*honour, reputation*› intact

sauf-conduit, *pl* **~s** /sofkɔ̃dɥi/ *m* safe conduct

sauge /soʒ/ *f* sage

saugrenu, **~e** /sogʀəny/ *adj* crazy, potty (BrE) (fam)

saule /sol/ *m* willow

saumâtre /somɑtʀ/ *adj* ‹*water*› brackish; ‹*taste*› bitter and salty

saumon /somɔ̃/ *m* salmon

saumure /somyʀ/ *f* brine

sauna /sona/ *m* sauna

saupoudrer /sopudʀe/ [**v1**] *vt* **1** to sprinkle
2 (fig) to give [sth] sparingly

saur /sɔʀ/ *adj m* **hareng ~** kippered herring

saut /so/ *m* **1** jump; **faire un petit ~** to skip; **au ~ du lit** first thing in the morning
2 (Sport) **le ~** jumping
3 (fam) **faire un ~ chez qn** to pop in and see sb
■ **~ à la corde** skipping; **~ à l'élastique** bungee jumping; **~ en hauteur** high jump; **~ à la perche** pole vault; **~ périlleux** mid-air somersault

saute /sot/ *f* **~ de température** sudden change in temperature; **~ d'humeur** mood swing

sauté, **~e** /sote/ **A** *adj* (Culin) sautéed
B *m* (Culin) **~ d'agneau** sautéed lamb

saute-mouton /sotmutɔ̃/ *m inv* leapfrog

sauter /sote/ [**v1**] **A** *vt* **1** to jump ‹*distance, height*›; to jump over ‹*stream*›
2 to skip ‹*meal, paragraph*›; to leave out ‹*details*›; (Sch) **~ une classe** to skip a year
3 to miss ‹*word, turn*›
B *vi* **1** to jump; **~ à pieds joints** to jump with one's feet together; **~ à la corde** to skip, to jump rope (AmE); **faire ~ un enfant sur ses genoux** to dandle a child on one's knee; **~ sur qn** to pounce on sb; **~ à la gorge de qn** to go for sb's throat; **~ au cou de qn** to greet sb with a kiss
2 ~ dans un taxi to jump *or* hop into a taxi
3 ~ d'un sujet à l'autre to skip from one subject to another
4 (fam) **faire ~ une réunion** to cancel a meeting; **faire ~ une contravention** to get out of paying a parking ticket
5 ‹*bicycle chain, fan belt*› to come off
6 faire ~ une serrure to force a lock; **faire ~ les boutons** to burst one's buttons
7 ‹*bridge, building*› to be blown up, to go up; **faire ~ les plombs** to blow the fuses
8 (Culin) **faire ~** to sauté ‹*onions*›
IDIOMS **~ aux yeux** to be blindingly obvious; **et que ça saute!** (fam) make it snappy! (fam); **~ au plafond** (fam) to jump for joy; to hit the roof (fam); to be staggered

sauterelle /sotʀɛl/ *f* grasshopper

sauterie /sotʀi/ *f* party

sautillant, **~e** /sotijɑ̃, ɑ̃t/ *adj* ‹*rhythm, gait*› bouncy; ‹*bird*› hopping

sautiller /sotije/ [**v1**] *vi* **1** ‹*bird*› to hop
2 ‹*child*› to skip along; to jump up and down

sauvage /sovaʒ/ **A** *adj* **1** ‹*animal, plant*› wild; ‹*tribe*› primitive
2 ‹*behaviour*› savage, wild; ‹*struggle*› fierce
3 unsociable
4 illegal
B *mf* **1** savage
2 unsociable person, loner

sauvagement /sovaʒmɑ̃/ *adv* savagely

sauvageon, **-onne** /sovaʒɔ̃, ɔn/ *mf* wild child

S

sauvagerie /sovaʒʀi/ *f* savagery

sauve ▸ **sauf²**

sauvegarde /sovgaʀd/ *f* (of heritage, peace, values) maintenance; (of rights) protection

sauvegarder /sovgaʀde/ [**v1**] *vt* **1** to safeguard
2 (Comput) to save; to back [sth] up ‹*file*›

sauve-qui-peut /sovkipø/ *m inv* stampede

sauver /sove/ [**v1**] **A** *vt* **1** (gen) to save; **~ la vie à qn** to save sb's life; **elle est sauvée** ‹*ill person*› she has pulled through (fam)
2 to salvage ‹*goods*›
3 ce qui le sauve à mes yeux, c'est sa générosité his redeeming feature for me is his generosity
B se sauver *v refl* (+ *v être*) **1** to escape; to run away; (from danger) to run
2 (fam) **il faut que je me sauve** I've got to rush off now
IDIOMS **~ la situation** to save the day; **sauve qui peut!** run for your life!

sauvetage /sovtaʒ/ *m* rescue; **cours de ~** life-saving training

sauveteur /sovtœʀ/ *m* rescuer

sauvette: **à la sauvette** /alasovɛt/ *phr*
1 ‹*prepare, sign*› in a rush
2 ‹*film, record*› on the sly

sauveur /sovœʀ/ *m* saviour (BrE)

savamment /savamɑ̃/ *adv* **1** learnedly, eruditely
2 skilfully (BrE)

savane /savan/ *f* savannah

savant, **~e** /savɑ̃, ɑ̃t/ **A** *adj* **1** ‹*person*› learned, erudite
2 ‹*study*› scholarly; ‹*calculation*› complicated
3 ‹*manoeuvre*› clever; ‹*direction*› skilful (BrE)
4 ‹*animal*› performing
B *mf* scholar
C *m* scientist

savate /savat/ *f* (fam) **1** old slipper
2 old shoe

saveur /savœʀ/ *f* flavour (BrE); **sans ~** tasteless

savoir¹ /savwaʀ/ [**v47**] **A** *vt* **1** to know ‹*truth, answer*›; **vous n'êtes pas sans ~ que...** you are no doubt aware that...; **va** *or* **allez ~!** who knows!; **est-ce que je sais, moi!** how should I know!; **pour autant que je sache** as far as I know; **comment l'as-tu su?** how did you find out?; **je l'ai su par elle** she told me about it; **ne ~ que faire pour...** to be at a loss as to how to...; **sachant que** knowing that; given that; **qui vous savez** you-know-who; **je ne sais qui** somebody or other; **tu en sais des choses!** you really know a thing or two!
2 ~ faire to know how to do; **je sais conduire** I can drive; **~ écouter** to be a good listener; **elle sait y faire avec les hommes** she knows how to handle men
B se savoir *v refl* (+ *v être*) **ça se saurait** people would know about it
C à savoir *phr* that is to say
IDIOM **ne pas ~ où donner de la tête** not to know whether one is coming or going

savoir² /savwaʀ/ *m* **1** learning
2 knowledge
3 body of knowledge

savoir-faire /savwaʀfɛʀ/ *m inv* know-how

savoir-vivre /savwaʀvivʀ/ *m inv* manners

savon /savɔ̃/ *m* **1** soap; **~ de Marseille** household soap
2 (bar of) soap
IDIOM **passer un ~ à qn** (fam) to give sb a telling-off

savonner /savɔne/ [**v1**] *vt* to soap

savonnette /savɔnɛt/ *f* small cake of soap

savourer /savuʀe/ [**v1**] *vt* to savour (BrE)

savoureux, **-euse** /savuʀø, øz/ *adj* ‹*dish*› tasty; ‹*anecdote*› juicy

saxophone /saksɔfɔn/ *m* saxophone

saxophoniste /saksɔfɔnist/ *mf* saxophonist

scabreux, **-euse** /skabʀø, øz/ *adj* obscene

scalp /skalp/ *m* **1** scalp
2 scalping

scalpel /skalpɛl/ *m* scalpel

scalper /skalpe/ [**v1**] *vt* to scalp

scandale /skɑ̃dal/ *m* scandal; **faire (un** *or* **du) ~** (gen) to cause a scandal; ‹*person*› to cause a fuss; **la presse à ~** the gutter press; **c'est un ~!** it's scandalous!

scandaleux, **-euse** /skɑ̃dalø, øz/ *adj* scandalous, outrageous

scandaliser /skɑ̃dalize/ [**v1**] **A** *vt* to outrage
B se scandaliser *v refl* (+ *v être*) to be shocked

scander /skɑ̃de/ [**v1**] *vt* **1** to scan
2 to chant ‹*slogan, name*›

scandinave /skɑ̃dinav/ *adj* Scandinavian

scanneur /skanœʀ/ *m* scanner

scaphandre /skafɑ̃dʀ/ *m* **1** deep-sea diving suit
2 spacesuit

scaphandrier /skafɑ̃dʀije/ *m* deep-sea diver

scarabée /skaʀabe/ *m* **1** beetle
2 scarab

scarlatine /skaʀlatin/ *f* scarlet fever

scatologie /skatɔlɔʒi/ *f* scatology

sceau, *pl* **~x** /so/ *m* **1** seal; **sous le ~ du secret** in strictest secrecy
2 stamp, hallmark

scélérat, **~e** /seleʀa, at/ *mf* villain

scellé /sele/ *m* seal; **apposer les ~s** to affix seals

sceller /sele/ [**v1**] *vt* **1** to seal
2 to fix [sth] securely ‹*shelf, bar*›

scénario /senaʀjo/ *m* **1** screenplay, script
2 scenario; **~ catastrophe** nightmare scenario

scénariste /senaʀist/ *mf* scriptwriter

key word

scène /sɛn/ *f* **1** (in theatre) stage; **entrer en ~** to come on
2 scene; **la ~ se passe à Paris** the scene is set in Paris
3 quitter la ~ to give up the stage; **mettre en ~** to stage ‹*play*›; to direct ‹*film*›
4 scene; **occuper le devant de la ~** (fig) to be in the news
5 faire une ~ to throw a fit (fam)
6 scene; **~s de panique** scenes of panic
■ **~ de ménage** domestic dispute

scepticisme /sɛptisism/ *m* scepticism (BrE), skepticism (AmE)

sceptique /sɛptik/ **A** *adj* sceptical (BrE), skeptical (AmE); **laisser qn ~** to leave sb unconvinced
B *mf* sceptic (BrE), skeptic (AmE)

sceptre /sɛptʀ/ *m* sceptre (BrE)

schéma /ʃema/ *m* **1** diagram
2 outline
3 pattern

schématique /ʃematik/ *adj* **1** ‹*vision, argument*› simplistic
2 schematic

schématiser /ʃematize/ [**v1**] *vt* to simplify

schizophrénie /skizɔfʀeni/ *f* schizophrenia

sciatique /sjatik/ **A** *adj* **nerf ~** sciatic nerve
B *f* **avoir une ~** to have sciatica

scie /si/ *f* saw; **~ sauteuse** jigsaw

sciemment /sjamɑ̃/ *adv* knowingly

science /sjɑ̃s/ *f* **1** science
2 knowledge
■ **~s naturelles** ≈ biology (*sg*); **~s occultes** black arts; **Sciences Po** (fam) *Institute of Political Science*

science-fiction /sjɑ̃sfiksjɔ̃/ *f* science fiction

scientifique /sjɑ̃tifik/ **A** *adj* scientific
B *mf* scientist

scier /sje/ [**v2**] *vt* **1** to saw
2 (fam) to stun

scierie /siʀi/ *f* sawmill

scinder /sɛ̃de/ [**v1**] **A** *vt* to split ‹*group*›
B se scinder *v refl* (+ *v être*) to split up

scintillant, **~e** /sɛ̃tijɑ̃, ɑ̃t/ *adj* twinkling

scintiller /sɛ̃tije/ [**v1**] *vi* ‹*diamond*› to sparkle; ‹*star*› to twinkle; ‹*water*› to glisten

scission /sisjɔ̃/ *f* **1** split, schism
2 fission

sciure /sjyʀ/ *f* **~ (de bois)** sawdust

sclérose /skleʀoz/ *f* **1** (Med) sclerosis
2 fossilization, ossification
■ **~ en plaques** multiple sclerosis, MS

scléroser /skleʀoze/ [**v1**] **A** *vt* (Med) to sclerose
B se scléroser *v refl* (+ *v être*)
1 ‹*institution, person*› to become fossilized
2 (Med) ‹*tissue*› to become hardened

scolaire /skɔlɛʀ/ *adj* ‹*holidays, book*› school; ‹*reform, publication*› educational; ‹*failure*› academic; **établissement ~** school

scolarisation /skɔlaʀizasjɔ̃/ *f* schooling

scolariser /skɔlaʀize/ [**v1**] *vt* to send [sb] to school

scolarité /skɔlaʀite/ *f* **1** schooling; **durant ma ~** when I was at school; **la ~ obligatoire** compulsory education
2 (in university) registrar's office

scoliose /skɔljoz/ *f* scoliosis

scooter /skutœʀ/ *m* (motor) scooter

score /skɔʀ/ *m* **1** (Sch, Sport) score; **~ nul** draw (BrE), tie (AmE)
2 results

scorie /skɔʀi/ *f* **1** scoria
2 slag

scorpion /skɔʀpjɔ̃/ *m* (Zool) scorpion

Scorpion /skɔʀpjɔ̃/ *pr m* Scorpio

scotch, *pl* **~es** /skɔtʃ/ *m* **1** Scotch (whisky)
2 ® Sellotape® (BrE), Scotch® tape (AmE)

scotcher /skɔtʃe/ [**v1**] *vt* to Sellotape® (BrE), to Scotch-tape® (AmE)

scout, **~e** /skut/ **A** *adj* scout
B *mf* boy scout/girl scout

scribe /skʀib/ *m* scribe

scribouillard, **~e** /skʀibujaʀ, aʀd/ *mf* (fam) pen pusher (BrE) (fam), pencil pusher (AmE)

script /skʀipt/ *m* **1 écrire en ~** to print
2 script

scripte /skʀipt/ *mf* continuity man/girl

scrupule /skʀypyl/ *m* scruple

scrupuleusement /skʀypyløzmɑ̃/ *adv* scrupulously

scrupuleux, **-euse** /skʀypylø, øz/ *adj* scrupulous; **peu ~** unscrupulous

scrutateur, **-trice** /skʀytatœʀ, tʀis/ *adj* searching

scruter /skʀyte/ [**v1**] *vt* to scan ‹*horizon*›; to scrutinize ‹*object*›; to examine ‹*ground, person*›

scrutin /skʀytɛ̃/ *m* **1** ballot; **dépouiller le ~** to count the votes
2 polls; **jour du ~** polling day; **mode de ~** electoral system
■ **~ majoritaire** election by majority vote

sculpter /skylte/ [**v1**] *vt* to sculpt, to carve

sculpteur /skyltœʀ/ *m* sculptor

sculptural, **~e**, *mpl* **-aux** /skyltyʀal, o/ *adj* ‹*art*› sculptural; ‹*shape, beauty*› statuesque

sculpture /skyltyʀ/ *f* sculpture; **la ~ sur bois** woodcarving

SDF /ɛsdeɛf/ ▶ **sans**

se, **s'** *before vowel or mute h* /sə, s/ *pron*
1 oneself; himself; herself; itself; **il ~ regarde** he's looking at himself
2 each other; **ils ~ regardaient** they were looking at each other
3 ~ ronger les ongles to bite one's nails; **il ~ lave les pieds** he's washing his feet
4 elle ~ comporte honorablement she behaves honourably (BrE); **l'écart ~ creuse** the gap is widening
5 les exemples ~ comptent sur les doigts de la main the examples can be counted on the

S

fingers of one hand
6 comment ~ fait-il que...? how come...?, how is it that...?

séance /seɑ̃s/ *f* **1** (of court, parliament) session; (of committee) meeting; **~ tenante** immediately
2 (in cinema) show
■ **~ de spiritisme** séance

seau, *pl* **~x** /so/ *m* bucket, pail

sébile /sebil/ *f* begging bowl

sec, **sèche** /sɛk, sɛʃ/ **A** *adj* **1** ‹*weather, hair*› dry; ‹*fruit*› dried
2 ‹*wine, cider*› dry; **boire son gin ~** to like one's gin straight
3 ‹*person, statement*› terse; ‹*letter*› curt
4 ‹*noise*› sharp
B *m* **être à ~** ‹*river*› to have dried up; (fig) ‹*person*› to have no money
C *adv* **1 se briser ~** to snap
2 (fam) ‹*rain, drink*› a lot
IDIOM **aussi ~** (fam) immediately

sécateur /sekatœʀ/ *m* clippers

sécession /sesesjɔ̃/ *f* secession

sèche /sɛʃ/ ▶ **sec A**

sèche-cheveux /sɛʃʃəvø/ *m inv* hairdrier (BrE), blow-dryer

sèche-linge /sɛʃlɛ̃ʒ/ *m inv* tumble drier (BrE), tumble dryer

sèchement /sɛʃmɑ̃/ *adv* drily, coldly

sécher /seʃe/ [**v1**] **A** *vt* **1** (gen) to dry
2 (fam) to skip ‹*class*›
B *vi* ‹*hair, clothes*› to dry; ‹*mud*› to dry up; **fleur séchée** dried flower; **mettre des vêtements à ~** to hang clothes up to dry

sécheresse /seʃʀɛs/ *f* **1** drought
2 dryness
3 curt manner

séchoir /seʃwaʀ/ *m* **1** clothes airer, clothes horse
2 tumble drier (BrE), tumble dryer

second, **~e** /səgɔ̃, ɔ̃d/ **A** *adj* **1** (in sequence, series) second; **chapitre ~** chapter two; **en ~ lieu** secondly; **dans un ~ temps...** subsequently...; **c'est à prendre au ~ degré** it is not to be taken literally
2 (in hierarchy) second; **de ~ ordre** second-rate; **politicien de ~ plan** minor politician; **jouer un ~ rôle** (in theatre) to play a supporting role; **jouer les ~s rôles** (fig) to play second fiddle
B *mf* second one
C *m* **1** second-in-command
2 second floor (BrE), third floor (AmE)
D en second *phr* ‹*arrive, leave*› second

secondaire /səgɔ̃dɛʀ/ **A** *adj* **1** secondary
2 minor
3 (Sch) **école ~** secondary school (BrE), high school (AmE)
4 effets ~s side effects
B *m* (Sch) secondary school (BrE) *or* high school (AmE) education

seconde /səgɔ̃d/ **A** *adj f* ▶ **second A**
B *f* **1** ▶ **second B**
2 second; **en une fraction de ~** in a split second
3 (Sch) *fifth year of secondary school, age 15–16*
4 billet de ~ second-class ticket
5 (Aut) second (gear)

seconder /səgɔ̃de/ [**v1**] *vt* ‹*person*› to assist

secouer /səkwe/ [**v1**] **A** *vt* **1** to shake ‹*bottle, branch, person*›; to shake out ‹*rug, umbrella*›; **~ la tête** to shake one's head; **être un peu secoué** (in car, plane) to have rather a bumpy ride
2 to shake off ‹*dust, snow, yoke*›
3 ‹*crisis*› to shake ‹*person, country*›
4 (fam) to get [sb] going (fam)
B se secouer *v refl* (+ *v être*) **1** to give oneself a shake
2 (fam) to pull oneself together
3 (fam) to wake up, to get moving (fam)

secourable /səkuʀabl/ *adj* ‹*person*› helpful

secourir /səkuʀiʀ/ [**v26**] *vt* **1** to help
2 to rescue
3 to give first aid to

secourisme /səkuʀism/ *m* first aid

secouriste /səkuʀist/ *mf* first-aid worker

secours /səkuʀ/ **A** *m inv* help; **au ~!** help!; **appeler** *or* **crier au ~** to shout for help; **porter ~ à qn** to help sb; **le ~ en mer** sea rescue operations; **de ~** ‹*wheel*› spare; ‹*exit*› emergency; ‹*kit*› first-aid; ‹*team*› rescue; ‹*battery*› back-up
B *mpl* **1** rescuers; reinforcements
2 relief supplies; supplies; **premiers ~** first aid

secousse /səkus/ *f* jolt; **~ (sismique)** (earth) tremor

secret, **-ète** /səkʀɛ, ɛt/ **A** *adj* **1** secret
2 ‹*person*› secretive
B *m* **1** secret; **ne pas avoir de ~s pour qn** to have no secrets from sb; **il n'en fait pas un ~** he makes no secret of it
2 secrecy; **mettre qn dans le ~** to let sb in on the secret; **en ~** in secret; **encore une de ces gaffes dont il a le ~** another of those blunders that only he knows how to make
3 solitary confinement
■ **~ bancaire** bank confidentiality; **~ de fabrication** industrial secret; **~ de Polichinelle** open secret; **~ professionnel** professional confidentiality

secrétaire /s(ə)kʀetɛʀ/ **A** *mf* secretary
B *m* (piece of furniture) secretaire (BrE), secretary (AmE)
■ **~ de direction** personal assistant; **~ d'État** (in France) minister; (in Great Britain, America) Secretary of State; **~ de rédaction** sub-editor (BrE), copy editor

secrétariat /s(ə)kʀetaʀja/ *m* **1** secretarial work
2 secretariat

secrète ▶ **secret A**

S

key word

secrètement /səkʀɛtmɑ̃/ *adv* secretly
sécréter /sekʀete/ [**v14**] *vt* **1** to secrete ‹*sap, bile*›
2 to exude ‹*liquid*›
sécrétion /sekʀesjɔ̃/ *f* secretion
sectaire /sɛktɛʀ/ *adj, mf* sectarian
secte /sɛkt/ *f* sect; faction
secteur /sɛktœʀ/ *m* **1** (Econ) sector; **~ tertiaire** service sector; **~ d'activité** sector
2 area, territory; (Mil) sector
3 (electrical) **le ~** the mains; **appareil fonctionnant sur ~** mains-operated appliance; **panne de ~** power failure
section /sɛksjɔ̃/ *f* **1** section; (of party, trade union) branch; (of book) part
2 (Sch) stream (BrE), track (AmE)
■ **~ d'autobus** fare stage
sectionner /sɛksjɔne/ [**v1**] *vt* **1** to sever
2 to divide up ‹*organization*›
sectoriel, **-ielle** /sɛktɔʀjɛl/ *adj* sectoral
sectorisation /sɛktɔʀizasjɔ̃/ *f* division
sectoriser /sɛktɔʀize/ [**v1**] *vt* to divide [sth] into sectors
Sécu /seky/ *f* National Health Service
séculaire /sekylɛʀ/ *adj* **1** ‹*tradition*› ancient
2 ‹*house, tree*› hundred year-old
séculier, **-ière** /sekylje, ɛʀ/ *adj* secular
secundo /səgɔ̃do/ *adv* secondly
sécurisé, **~e** /sekyʀize/ **A** *pp* ▶ **sécuriser**
B *pp adj* secure; (Comput) **une ligne ~e** a secure line
sécuriser /sekyʀize/ [**v1**] *vt* **1** to reassure
2 to make [sb] feel secure
sécurité /sekyʀite/ *f* **1** security; **~ de l'emploi** job security; **de ~** ‹*system*› security; ‹*reasons*› of security
2 safety; **se sentir en ~** to feel secure *or* safe
■ **~ routière** road safety; **~ sociale** *French national health and pensions organization*
sédatif /sedatif/ *m* sedative
sédentaire /sedɑ̃tɛʀ/ *adj* sedentary
sédentariser /sedɑ̃taʀize/ [**v1**] *vt* to settle
sédentarité /sedɑ̃taʀite/ *f* (of population) settled way of life; (of job) sedentary nature
sédiment /sedimɑ̃/ *m* sediment
sédimentation /sedimɑ̃tasjɔ̃/ *f* sedimentation
séducteur, **-trice** /sedyktœʀ, tʀis/ **A** *adj* seductive, attractive
B *mf* **1** charmer
2 seducer/seductress
séduction /sedyksjɔ̃/ *f* **1** charm
2 seduction; **pouvoir de ~** (of person) power of seduction; (of money) lure; (of words) seductive power
séduire /sedɥiʀ/ [**v1**] *vt* **1** ‹*person*› to captivate, to charm
2 to appeal to ‹*person*›
3 ‹*person*› to win over
4 to seduce
séduisant, **~e** /sedɥizɑ̃, ɑ̃t/ *adj* ‹*person*› attractive; ‹*idea*› appealing
segment /sɛgmɑ̃/ *m* segment
segmenter /sɛgmɑ̃te/ [**v1**] *vt*, **se segmenter** *v refl* (+ *v être*) to segment
ségrégation /segʀegasjɔ̃/ *f* segregation
seiche /sɛʃ/ *f* cuttlefish
seigle /sɛgl/ *m* rye; **pain de ~** rye bread
seigneur /sɛɲœʀ/ *m* lord; **être grand ~** to be full of largesse
■ **~ de la guerre** warlord
IDIOM **à tout ~ tout honneur** (Proverb) credit where credit is due
Seigneur /sɛɲœʀ/ *m* Lord; **~!** Good Lord!
seigneurial, **~e**, *mpl* **-iaux** /sɛɲœʀjal, o/ *adj* ‹*home*› stately; ‹*manner*› lordly
sein /sɛ̃/ *m* **1** (Anat) breast; **les ~s nus** topless; **nourrir (son enfant) au ~** to breast-feed (one's baby)
2 au ~ de within
séisme /seism/ *m* earthquake, seism
seize /sɛz/ *adj inv, pron, m inv* sixteen
seizième /sɛzjɛm/ *adj* sixteenth
séjour /seʒuʀ/ *m* **1** stay; **~s à l'étranger** (on CV) time spent abroad
2 (salle de) ~ living room
3 un ~ champêtre a rural retreat
■ **~ linguistique** language study vacation
séjourner /seʒuʀne/ [**v1**] *vi* **1** ‹*person*› to stay
2 ‹*liquid*› to remain; ‹*snow*› to lie
sel /sɛl/ *m* **1** salt; **gros ~** coarse salt
2 (fig) **la situation ne manque pas de ~** the situation has a certain piquancy
■ **~s de bain** bath salts
sélect, **~e** /selɛkt/ *adj* (fam) ‹*club, bar*› exclusive; ‹*clientele*› select
sélecteur, **-trice** /selɛktœʀ, tʀis/ **A** *adj* selective
B *m* **1** (Comput) selector
2 (Aut) gear lever, gear shift (AmE)
sélectif, **-ive** /selɛktif, iv/ *adj* selective
sélection /selɛksjɔ̃/ *f* (gen) selection; (for a job) selection process; **~ à l'entrée** selective entry
sélectionner /selɛksjɔne/ [**v1**] *vt* to select
self-service, *pl* **~s** /sɛlfsɛʀvis/ *m* self-service restaurant
selle /sɛl/ **A** *f* saddle; **remis en ~** ‹*player, regime*› firmly (re)established
B selles *fpl* (Med) stools
seller /sele/ [**v1**] *vt* to saddle
sellette /selɛt/ *f* **être sur la ~** to be in the hot seat
selon /səlɔ̃/ *prep* **1** according to; **~ moi, il va pleuvoir** in my opinion, it's going to rain; **~ les termes du président** in the President's words; **l'idée ~ laquelle** the idea that
2 depending on ‹*time, circumstances*›; **la situation varie ~ les régions** the situation varies from region to region; **c'est ~** (fam) it all depends

S

semailles /səmɑj/ *fpl* **1** sowing season
2 seeds
3 faire les ~ to sow

✍ **semaine** /s(ə)mɛn/ *f* **1** week
2 week's wages
IDIOM **vivre à la petite ~** to live from day to day

sémantique /semɑ̃tik/ **A** *adj* semantic
B *f* semantics

✍ **semblable** /sɑ̃blabl/ **A** *adj* **1** similar
2 identical
B *mf* fellow creature; **eux et leurs ~s** they and their kind

semblant /sɑ̃blɑ̃/ *m* **un ~ de légalité** a semblance of legality; **faire ~ d'être triste** to pretend to be sad

✍ **sembler** /sɑ̃ble/ [**v1**] **A** *vi* to seem
B *v impers* **il semble bon de faire** it seems appropriate to do; **le problème est réglé à ce qu'il me semble** the problem has been solved, or so it seems to me; **faites comme bon vous semble** do whatever you think best; **elle a, semble-t-il, refusé** apparently, she refused

semelle /s(ə)mɛl/ *f* sole
■ **~ compensée** wedge heel; **~ intérieure** insole
IDIOM **être dur comme de la ~** (fam) to be as tough as old boots (BrE) *or* leather (AmE) (fam)

semence /s(ə)mɑ̃s/ *f* seed

semer /s(ə)me/ [**v16**] *vt* **1** to sow ‹*seeds*›
2 to sow ‹*discord, doubt*›; to spread ‹*confusion, panic*›
3 to scatter ‹*objects*›; **semé de difficultés** plagued with difficulties; **ciel semé d'étoiles** star-spangled sky; **on récolte ce qu'on a semé** as you sow so shall you reap
4 (fam) to drop ‹*purse, keys*›
5 (fam) to shake off ‹*pursuer*›

semestre /s(ə)mɛstʀ/ *m* (Sch) semester

semestriel, **-ielle** /səmɛstʀijɛl/ *adj* **1** twice-yearly; half-yearly
2 (at university) ‹*exam*› end-of-semester (BrE), final (AmE); ‹*class*› one-semester

S

semeur, **-euse** /səmœʀ, øz/ *mf* sower; **~ de troubles** troublemaker

semi /səmi/ *pref* **~-automatic** semi-automatic; **~-liberté** relative freedom; **~-remorque** articulated lorry (BrE), tractor-trailer (AmE)

semi-échec, *pl* **~s** /səmieʃɛk/ *m* partial failure

sémillant, **~e** /semijɑ̃, ɑ̃t/ *adj* spirited

séminaire /seminɛʀ/ *m* **1** seminar
2 seminary

séminariste /seminaʀist/ *m* seminarist

sémiologie /semjɔlɔʒi/ *f* semiology

sémiotique /semjɔtik/ **A** *adj* semiotic
B *f* semiotics

semis /s(ə)mi/ *m inv* **1** sowing
2 seedling
3 seedbed

semonce /səmɔ̃s/ *f* reprimand; **coup de ~** warning shot

semoule /səmul/ *f* semolina; **sucre ~** caster sugar

sempiternel, **-elle** /sɑ̃pitɛʀnɛl/ *adj* perpetual

sénat /sena/ *m* senate

sénateur /senatœʀ/ *m* senator

sénile /senil/ *adj* senile

sénilité /senilite/ *f* senility

✍ **sens** /sɑ̃s/ **A** *m inv* **1** direction, way; **dans le ~ de la largeur** widthways, across; **être dans le bon ~** to be the right way up; **retourner un problème dans tous les ~** to consider a problem from every angle; **courir dans tous les ~** to run all over the place; **~ dessus dessous** upside down; (fig) very upset; **aller dans le bon ~** ‹*reforms*› to be a step in the right direction; **le ~ de l'histoire** the tide of history; **nous travaillons dans ce ~** that's what we are working toward(s)
2 meaning; **le ~ figuré d'un mot** the figurative sense of a word; **employer un mot au ~ propre** to use a word literally; **cela n'a pas de ~** it doesn't make sense; it's absurd
3 sense; **retrouver l'usage de ses ~** to regain consciousness; **avoir le ~ pratique** to be practical; **ne pas avoir le ~ du ridicule** not to realize when one looks silly; **avoir le ~ des affaires** to have a flair for business; **n'avoir aucun ~ des réalités** to live in a dream world
B *mpl* senses; **plaisirs des ~** sensual pleasures
■ **~ giratoire** roundabout (BrE), traffic circle (AmE); **~ interdit** no-entry sign; one-way street; **~ obligatoire** one-way sign; **~ unique** one-way sign; one-way street

✍ **sensation** /sɑ̃sasjɔ̃/ *f* feeling, sensation; **aimer les ~s fortes** to like one's thrills; **la décision a fait ~** the decision caused a sensation; **un journal à ~** a tabloid

sensationnel, **-elle** /sɑ̃sasjɔnɛl/ *adj* **1** (fam) fantastic (fam)
2 sensational, astonishing

sensé, **~e** /sɑ̃se/ *adj* sensible

sensément /sɑ̃semɑ̃/ *adv* sensibly

sensibilisation /sɑ̃sibilizasjɔ̃/ *f* **1 campagne de ~** awareness campaign
2 (Med) sensitizing

sensibiliser /sɑ̃sibilize/ [**v1**] *vt* **1 ~ le public à un problème** to increase public awareness of an issue
2 (Med) to sensitize

sensibilité /sɑ̃sibilite/ *f* **1** sensibility
2 (in photography) sensitivity

✍ **sensible** /sɑ̃sibl/ *adj* **1** (gen) sensitive; **être ~ aux compliments** to like compliments; **je suis ~ au fait que** I am aware that; **un être ~** a sentient being; **je suis très ~ au froid**

✍ key word

I really feel the cold
2 ‹*skin*› sensitive; (because of injury) tender; ‹*limb*› sore; **j'ai la gorge ~** I often get a sore throat
3 ‹*rise, difference*› appreciable; ‹*effort*› real; **la différence est à peine ~** the difference is hardly noticeable

sensiblement /sɑ̃sibləmɑ̃/ *adv* **1** ‹*reduce, increase*› appreciably, noticeably; ‹*different*› perceptibly
2 ‹*alike*› roughly

sensiblerie /sɑ̃sibləʀi/ *f* sentimentality

sensitif, **-ive** /sɑ̃sitif, iv/ *adj* sensory

sensoriel, **-ielle** /sɑ̃sɔʀjɛl/ *adj* sensory; **organe ~** sense organ

sensualité /sɑ̃sɥalite/ *f* sensuality

sensuel, **-elle** /sɑ̃sɥɛl/ *adj* sensual

sentence /sɑ̃tɑ̃s/ *f* **1** sentence
2 maxim

sentencieux, **-ieuse** /sɑ̃tɑ̃sjø, øz/ *adj* sententious

senteur /sɑ̃tœʀ/ *f* scent

senti, **~e** /sɑ̃ti/ *adj* **bien ~** ‹*words*› well-chosen; ‹*answer*› blunt; ‹*speech*› forthright

sentier /sɑ̃tje/ *m* path, track; **hors des ~s battus** off the beaten track

sentiment /sɑ̃timɑ̃/ *m* feeling; **il est incapable de ~** he's incapable of emotion; **faire du ~** to sentimentalize; **prendre qn par les ~s** to appeal to sb's better nature; **les beaux** *or* **bons ~s** fine sentiments; **être animé de mauvais ~s** to have bad intentions; **~s affectueux** *or* **amicaux** best wishes

sentimental, **~e**, *mpl* **-aux** /sɑ̃timɑ̃tal, o/ *adj* sentimental; romantic; **vie ~e** love life

sentinelle /sɑ̃tinɛl/ *f* sentry

sentir /sɑ̃tiʀ/ [**v30**] **A** *vt* **1** to smell
2 to feel; **je ne sens rien** I can't feel anything; **je ne sens plus mes pieds** my feet are numb
3 to be conscious of ‹*importance*›; to feel ‹*beauty, force*›; to appreciate ‹*difficulties*›; to sense ‹*danger, disapproval*›; **je sens qu'il est sincère** I feel that he's sincere; **je te sens inquiet** I can tell you're worried; **se faire ~** ‹*need*› to be felt
B *vi* **1** to smell; **ça sent l'ail** it smells of garlic
2 le poisson commence à ~ the fish is beginning to smell
3 to smack of; **ciel nuageux qui sent l'orage** cloudy sky that heralds a storm
C se sentir *v refl* (+ *v être*) **1** to feel; **se ~ mieux** to feel better
2 ‹*effect*› to be felt
IDIOM **je ne peux pas le ~** I can't stand him

seoir /swaʀ/ [**v41**] (dated) **A seoir à** *vt* ‹*dress*› to suit
B *v impers* **il sied de faire** it is appropriate to do

sépale /sepal/ *m* sepal

séparable /sepaʀabl/ *adj* separable

séparation /sepaʀasjɔ̃/ *f* **1** (gen), (Law) separation
2 (between gardens) boundary; (fig) boundary, dividing line
■ **~ de biens** (Law) matrimonial division of property; **~ de corps** (Law) judicial separation

séparatisme /sepaʀatism/ *m* separatism

séparé, **~e** /sepaʀe/ *adj* **1 vivre ~** to live apart
2 separate

séparément /sepaʀemɑ̃/ *adv* separately

séparer /sepaʀe/ [**v1**] **A** *vt* **1** (gen) to separate; to pull [sb] apart ‹*fighters*›; **c'est un malentendu qui les a séparés** they parted because of a misunderstanding
2 to distinguish between ‹*concepts, areas*›
3 to divide; **tout les sépare** they are worlds apart
B se séparer *v refl* (+ *v être*) **1** ‹*guests*› to part; ‹*partners, lovers*› to split up
2 se ~ de to leave ‹*friend, group*›; to split up with; (Law) to separate from ‹*husband, wife*›
3 se ~ de to let [sb] go ‹*employee*›; to part with ‹*personal possession*›
4 to divide; **la route se sépare (en deux)** the road forks

sépia /sepja/ *adj inv* sepia

sept /sɛt/ *adj inv, pron, m inv* seven
■ **les ~ Familles** (Games) Happy Families
IDIOM **tourne ~ fois ta langue dans ta bouche avant de parler** think before you speak

septante /sɛptɑ̃t/ *adj inv, pron* seventy

septembre /sɛptɑ̃bʀ/ *m* September

septennat /sɛptena/ *m* seven-year term (of office)

septentrional, **~e**, *mpl* **-aux** /sɛptɑ̃tʀijɔnal, o/ *adj* northern

septicémie /sɛptisemi/ *f* blood poisoning

septième /sɛtjɛm/ **A** *adj* seventh
B *f* (Sch) *fifth year of primary school, age 10–11*
■ **le ~ art** cinematography

septuagénaire /sɛptɥaʒenɛʀ/ *adj* **être ~** to be in one's seventies

septuor /sɛptɥɔʀ/ *m* septet

sépulture /sepyltyʀ/ *f* **1** grave
2 burial

séquelle /sekɛl/ *f* **1** after-effect
2 repercussion
3 consequence

séquence /sekɑ̃s/ *f* sequence

séquestrer /sekɛstʀe/ [**v1**] *vt* (gen) to hold ‹*hostage*›; (Law) to confine [sb] illegally

sera /səʀa/ ▶ **être**[1]

serai /səʀɛ/ ▶ **être**[1]

seraient /səʀɛ/ ▶ **être**[1]

sérail /seʀaj/ *m* **1** seraglio
2 innermost circle

serais /səʀɛ/ ▶ **être**[1]

S

serait /səʀɛ/ ▶ **être¹**

seras /səʀa/ ▶ **être¹**

serein, **~e** /səʀɛ̃, ɛn/ *adj* ‹*sky*› clear; ‹*person, face*› serene; ‹*criticism*› objective

sereinement /səʀɛnmɑ̃/ *adv* ‹*look*› serenely; ‹*speak*› calmly; ‹*judge*› dispassionately

sérénade /seʀenad/ *f* **1** serenade
2 (fam) racket (fam), din

sérénité /seʀenite/ *f* **1** (of face, mind) serenity; (of person) equanimity
2 (of judge, verdict) impartiality
3 (of sky, weather) calmness

serez /səʀe/ ▶ **être¹**

serf, **serve** /sɛʀ, sɛʀv/ *mf* serf

sergent /sɛʀʒɑ̃/ *m* (Mil) (in army) ≈ sergeant

série /seʀi/ *f* **1** series; **catastrophes en ~** a series of catastrophes
2 numéro de ~ serial number; **~ limitée** limited edition; **modèle de ~** (gen) mass-produced model; (car) production model; **numéro hors ~** special issue
3 set, collection
4 (on television) series
5 (Sport) division
■ **~ noire** series of disasters

sérieusement /seʀjøzmɑ̃/ *adv* seriously; considerably

sérieux, **-ieuse** /seʀjø, øz/ **A** *adj* **1** serious; **être ~ dans son travail** to be serious about one's work; **avoir des lectures sérieuses** to read serious books
2 ‹*situation, threat*› serious; ‹*clue, lead*› important; ‹*offer*› genuine; **'pas ~ s'abstenir'** 'genuine enquiries only'
3 reliable
4 responsible; **cela ne fait pas très ~** that doesn't make a very good impression
5 ‹*effort, need*› real; ‹*progress*› considerable; ‹*handicap*› serious
B *m* seriousness; **garder son ~** to keep a straight face; **perdre son ~** to start to laugh; **se prendre au ~** to take oneself seriously

seriez /səʀje/ ▶ **être¹**

sérigraphie /seʀigʀafi/ *f* **1** silk-screen printing
2 silk-screen print

serin /səʀɛ̃/ *m* (Zool) canary

seriner /səʀine/ [**v1**] *vt* (fam) **~ qch à qn** to drum sth into sb

seringue /səʀɛ̃g/ *f* syringe

serions /səʀjɔ̃/ ▶ **être¹**

serment /sɛʀmɑ̃/ *m* **1** oath; **prêter ~** to take the oath
2 vow
■ **un ~ d'ivrogne** an empty promise

sermon /sɛʀmɔ̃/ *m* **1** sermon
2 lecture

sermonner /sɛʀmɔne/ [**v1**] *vt* to lecture, to give [sb] a talking-to

séronégatif, **-ive** /seʀonegatif, iv/ *adj* HIV negative

serons /səʀɔ̃/ ▶ **être¹**

seront /səʀɔ̃/ ▶ **être¹**

séropositif, **-ive** /seʀopozitif, iv/ *adj* **1** (gen) seropositive
2 HIV positive

séropositivité /seʀopozitivite/ *f* (HIV antibody) seropositivity

serpe /sɛʀp/ *f* billhook

serpent /sɛʀpɑ̃/ *m* (Zool) snake; **~ à sonnette** rattlesnake

serpenter /sɛʀpɑ̃te/ [**v1**] *vi* ‹*road, river*› to wind

serpentin /sɛʀpɑ̃tɛ̃/ *m* streamer

serpillière /sɛʀpijɛʀ/ *f* floorcloth

serre /sɛʀ/ *f* **1** greenhouse
2 talon, claw

serré, **~e** /seʀe/ **A** *adj* **1** ‹*screw, nut*› tight; ‹*skirt, trousers*› tight; **trop serré** too tight
2 ‹*grass*› thick; ‹*writing*› cramped
3 ‹*deadline, budget*› tight; ‹*bend*› sharp; ‹*control*› strict; ‹*struggle*› hard; ‹*debate*› heated; ‹*match*› close
4 ‹*coffee*› very strong
B *adv* ‹*write*› in a cramped hand; ‹*knit*› tightly; **il va falloir jouer ~ si...** we can't take any chances if...

serre-livres /sɛʀlivʀ/ *m inv* book end

serrement /sɛʀmɑ̃/ *m* **1 ~ de main** handshake
2 avoir *or* **ressentir un ~ de cœur** to feel a pang

serrer /seʀe/ [**v1**] **A** *vt* **1** to grip ‹*steering wheel, rope*›; **~ qn/qch dans ses bras** to hug sb/sth; **~ la main de qn** to shake hands with sb; **~ les poings** to clench one's fists; **ça me serre le cœur de voir ça** it wrings my heart to see that
2 to tighten ‹*knot, screw*›; to turn [sth] off tightly ‹*tap*›; **sans ~** ‹*attach, screw*› loosely
3 ‹*shoes, clothes*› to be too tight
4 ~ à droite to get *or* stay in the right-hand lane; **~ qn de près** to be hot on sb's tail
5 to push [sth] closer together ‹*objects, tables*›; to squeeze ‹*person*›; **être serrés** to be packed together
6 to cut ‹*expenses, prices*›
B se serrer *v refl* (+ *v être*) **1** to squeeze up; **ils se sont serrés les uns contre les autres** they huddled together
2 se ~ dans une jupe to squeeze oneself into a skirt; **nous nous sommes serré la main** we shook hands
3 avoir la gorge qui se serre to have a lump in one's throat

serrure /seʀyʀ/ *f* lock; **trou de ~** keyhole

serrurerie /seʀyʀʀi/ *f* locksmith's

serrurier /seʀyʀje/ *m* locksmith

sertir /sɛʀtiʀ/ [**v3**] *vt* to set ‹*stone*›

sérum /seʀɔm/ *m* serum; **~ de vérité** truth drug

key word

S

servage /sɛʀvaʒ/ *m* serfdom

servante /sɛʀvɑ̃t/ *f* maidservant

serve ▶ **serf**

serveur, **-euse** /sɛʀvœʀ, øz/ *mf* waiter/waitress

servi, **~e** /sɛʀvi/ **A** *pp* ▶ **servir**
B *pp adj* **1 'prends de la viande'—'merci je suis déjà ~'** 'have some meat'—'I already have some, thank you'
2 (fam) **nous voulions du soleil, nous sommes ~s** we wanted some sunshine and we've certainly got it

serviable /sɛʀvjabl/ *adj* obliging, helpful

✓ **service** /sɛʀvis/ **A** *m* **1** favour (BrE); **rendre un ~ à qn** to do sb a favour (BrE)
2 (in transport) service; **~ de bus** bus service
3 être en ~ ‹*lift*› to be in working order; ‹*motorway*› to be open; ‹*bus*› to be running
4 rendre ~ à qn ‹*machine*› to be a help to sb; ‹*shop*› to be convenient (for sb)
5 service; **être au ~ de son pays** to serve one's country; **travailler au ~ de la paix** to work for peace; **'à votre ~!'** 'don't mention it!', 'not at all!'; **avoir 20 ans de ~ dans une entreprise** to have been with a firm 20 years; **être de** *or* **en ~** to be on duty; **état de ~(s)** record of service; **pharmacie de ~** duty chemist
6 (at table) service; **faire le ~** to serve; to act as waiter
7 (domestic) service; **entrer au ~ de qn** to go to work for sb; **prendre qn à son ~** to take sb on; **escalier de ~** backstairs
8 department; **~ du personnel** personnel department; **~ des urgences** casualty department (BrE), emergency room (AmE); **les ~s de sécurité** the security services; **chef de ~** (in administration) section head; (in hospital) senior consultant
9 (Mil) **~ (militaire)** military *or* national service
10 set; **un ~ à thé** a tea set; **~ de table** dinner service
11 (in church) service
12 (Sport) service, serve; **être au ~** to serve
B services *mpl* services; **se passer des ~s de qn** to dispense with sb's services
■ **~ après-vente** after-sales service; **~ d'ordre** stewards; **~ de presse** press office; press and publicity department; **~ public** public service

serviette /sɛʀvjɛt/ *f* **1 ~ (de toilette)** towel; **~ (de table)** (table) napkin
2 briefcase
■ **~ de bain** bath towel; **~ hygiénique** sanitary towel (BrE), sanitary napkin (AmE)

serviette-éponge, *pl* **serviettes-éponges** /sɛʀvjɛtepɔ̃ʒ/ *f* terry towel

servile /sɛʀvil/ *adj* servile; slavish

servilement /sɛʀvilmɑ̃/ *adv* ‹*obey, imitate*› slavishly; ‹*flatter*› obsequiously

servilité /sɛʀvilite/ *f* servility

✓ **servir** /sɛʀviʀ/ [v30] **A** *vt* **1** to serve; **qu'est-ce que je vous sers (à boire)?** what would you like to drink?; **tu es mal servi** you haven't got much; **'Madame est servie'** 'dinner is served, Madam'; **au moment de ~** before serving
2 ‹*situation*› to help ‹*person, cause*›; to serve ‹*interests*›; ‹*person*› to further ‹*ambition*›
3 to deal ‹*cards*›
B servir à *v+prep* **1 ~ à qn** to be used by sb; **~ à qch** to be used for sth; **les exercices m'ont servi à comprendre la règle** the exercises helped me to understand the rule
2 to come in useful; **cela ne sert à rien de faire** there's no point in doing
C servir de *v+prep* **~ d'intermédiaire à qn** to act as an intermediary for sb; **~ d'arme** to be used as a weapon
D *vi* **1** (Mil) **~ dans** to serve in
2 (Sport) to serve
3 il a servi dix ans chez nous he was in our service for ten years
4 ‹*object*› to be used
E se servir *v refl* (+ *v être*) **1** (at table) to help oneself; **se ~ un verre de vin** to pour oneself a glass of wine
2 (in shop) to serve oneself
3 se ~ de qn/qch to use sb/sth; **se ~ d'une situation** to make use of a situation
4 (Culin) to be served

serviteur /sɛʀvitœʀ/ *m* servant

servitude /sɛʀvityd/ *f* **1** servitude
2 (fig) constraint

ses ▶ **son**[1]

sésame /sezam/ *m* sesame

session /sɛsjɔ̃/ *f* **1** session
2 examination session; **~ de rattrapage** retakes
3 course

set /sɛt/ *m* (Sport) set
■ **~ de table** place mat

seuil /sœj/ *m* **~ (de la porte)** doorstep; doorway, threshold

✓ **seul**, **~e** /sœl/ **A** *adj* **1** alone, on one's own; **vous êtes ~ dans la vie?** are you single?; **elle veut vous parler ~ à ~** *or* **~e à ~(e)** she wants to speak to you in private; **parler tout ~** to talk to oneself
2 by oneself, on one's own; **il a mangé un poulet à lui tout ~** he ate a whole chicken all by himself; **ça va tout ~** it's really easy; things are running smoothly
3 only; **la ~e et unique personne** the one and only person; **pas un ~ client** not a single customer; **l'espion et l'ambassadeur sont une ~e et même personne** the spy and the ambassador are one and the same person; **d'une ~e pièce** in one piece; **à la ~e idée de faire** at the very idea of doing; **ils ont parlé d'une ~e voix** they were unanimous; **elle ~e pourrait vous le dire** only she could tell you
4 lonely; **c'est un homme ~** he's a lonely man

S

B *mf* **le ~, la ~e** the only one; **les ~s, les ~es** the only ones; **ils sont les ~s à croire que...** they're alone in thinking that...

⚷ **seulement** /sœlmɑ̃/ *adv* **1** only; **nous étions ~ deux** there were only the two of us; **'nous étions dix'—'~?'** 'there were ten of us'—'is that all?'; **elle revient ~ demain** she's not coming back until tomorrow
2 c'est possible, ~ je veux y réfléchir it's possible, only *or* but I'd like to think about it
3 si ~ if only

sève /sɛv/ *f* **1** sap
2 (fig) vigour (BrE)

sévère /sevɛʀ/ *adj* ‹*look, tone, punishment*› severe; ‹*person, upbringing*› strict; ‹*selection*› rigorous; ‹*judgement*› harsh; ‹*losses*› heavy

sévèrement /sevɛʀmɑ̃/ *adv* severely; harshly; strictly

sévérité /seveʀite/ *f* **1** strictness, harshness
2 sternness, severity

sévices /sevis/ *mpl* physical abuse

sévir /seviʀ/ [**v3**] *vi* **1** to clamp down
2 ‹*storm, war*› to rage; ‹*poverty*› to be rife
3 (fig) ‹*doctrine*› to hold sway; ‹*phenomenon*› to be rife

sevrage /səvʀaʒ/ *m* weaning

sevrer /səvʀe/ [**v16**] *vt* to wean

sexagénaire /sɛksaʒenɛʀ/ *mf* sixty year-old

⚷ **sexe** /sɛks/ *m* **1** sex; **indépendamment du ~, de l'ethnie, de l'âge** irrespective of gender, race or age; **un bébé de ~ féminin** a female baby
2 genitals

sexiste /sɛksist/ *adj, mf* sexist

sexologue /sɛksɔlɔg/ *mf* sex therapist

sextuor /sɛkstɥɔʀ/ *m* sextet

sextuplé, ~e /sɛkstyple/ *mf* sextuplet

sexualité /sɛksɥalite/ *f* sexuality

sexué, ~e /sɛksɥe/ *adj* sexed; sexual

⚷ **sexuel, -elle** /sɛksɥɛl/ *adj* (gen) sexual; ‹*education, gland*› sex

seyant, ~e /sɛjɑ̃, ɑ̃t/ *adj* becoming

SF /ɛsɛf/ *f* (*abbr* = **science-fiction**) sci-fi

SFP /ɛsɛfpe/ *f* (*abbr* = **Société française de production et de création audiovisuelles**) *French TV and video production company*

shaker /ʃekœʀ/ *m* cocktail shaker

shampooing /ʃɑ̃pwɛ̃/ *m* shampoo

shampouiner /ʃɑ̃pwine/ [**v1**] *vt* to shampoo

shampouineur, -euse /ʃɑ̃pwinœʀ, øz/ *mf: trainee hairdresser (who washes hair)*

shérif /ʃeʀif/ *m* sheriff

shetland /ʃɛtlɑ̃d/ *m* **1** Shetland wool
2 Shetland pony

shoot /ʃut/ *m* **1** (Sport) shot
2 (fam) (of drug) fix (fam)

⚷ key word

shooter /ʃute/ [**v1**] **A** *vi* to shoot
B se shooter *v refl* (+ *v être*) (fam) to shoot up (fam)

short /ʃɔʀt/ *m* shorts

⚷ **si¹** /si/ **A** *adv* **1** yes; **'tu ne le veux pas?'—'~!'** 'don't you want it?'—'yes I do!'; **il n'ira pas, moi ~** he won't go, but I will
2 so; **c'est un homme ~ agréable** he's such a pleasant man; **~ bien que** so; so much so that; **rien n'est ~ beau qu'un coucher de soleil** there's nothing so beautiful as a sunset; **est-elle ~ bête qu'on le dit?** is she as stupid as people say (she is)?
B *conj* (**s'** *before il or ils*) **1** if; **~ j'étais riche** if I were rich; **~ j'avais su!** if only I'd known!; **vous pensez ~ j'étais content!** you can imagine how happy I was!; **~ ce n'est (pas) toi, qui est-ce?** if it wasn't you, who was it?; **il n'a rien pris avec lui ~ ce n'est un livre** he didn't take anything with him apart from a book; **à quoi servent ces réunions ~ ce n'est à nous faire perdre notre temps?** what purpose do these meetings serve other than to waste our time?; **~ tant est qu'une telle distinction ait un sens** if such a distinction makes any sense
2 ~ tu venais avec moi? how about coming with me?
3 whereas

si² /si/ *m inv* (Mus) (note) B; (in sol-fa) ti

siamois, ~e /sjamwa, az/ **A** *adj* **1** ‹*cat*› Siamese
2 des frères ~ male Siamese twins
B *m inv* **1** (language) Siamese
2 Siamese cat

sibylle /sibil/ *f* sibyl

SICAV /sikav/ *f* (*abbr* = **société d'investissement à capital variable**) unit trust, mutual fund

sida /sida/ *m* (*abbr* = **syndrome immunodéficitaire acquis**) Aids

side-car, *pl* **~s** /sidkaʀ/ *m* **1** sidecar
2 motorcycle combination

sidéral, ~e, *mpl* **-aux** /sideʀal, o/ *adj* sidereal

sidérer /sideʀe/ [**v14**] *vt* (fam) (astonish) to stagger (fam)

sidérurgie /sideʀyʀʒi/ *f* steel industry

sidérurgique /sideʀyʀʒik/ *adj* steel

⚷ **siècle** /sjɛkl/ *m* **1** century; **au Vᵉ ~ après J.-C.** in the 5th century AD; **d'ici la fin du ~** by the turn of the century; **il y a des ~s** (fam) **que je ne suis venu ici** I haven't been here for ages
2 age; **le ~ de Louis XIV** the age of Louis XIV

sied ▸ **seoir**

⚷ **siège** /sjɛʒ/ *m* **1** seat
2 ~ (social) (of company) head office; (of organization) headquarters
3 (of MP) seat
4 (Mil) siege
5 (Anat) seat

siéger /sjeʒe/ [**v15**] *vi* **1** to sit

2 to be in session
3 to have its headquarters

sien, **sienne** /sjɛ̃, sjɛn/ **A** *det* **cette maison est sienne à présent** the house is now his/hers
B le sien, la sienne, les siens, les siennes *pron* his/hers; **être de retour parmi les ~s** to be back with one's family; to be back among one's own friends; **faire des siennes** ‹*person*› to be up to mischief; ‹*computer*› to act up

sieste /sjɛst/ *f* nap, siesta

sifflant, **~e** /siflɑ̃, ɑ̃t/ *adj* **1** hissing; wheezing
2 sibilant

sifflement /sifləmɑ̃/ *m* (of person, train) whistle; (of kettle, wind) whistling; (of bird, insect) chirping; (of snake) hissing

siffler /sifle/ [**v1**] **A** *vt* **1** to whistle ‹*tune*›; to whistle for ‹*dog*›; to whistle at ‹*person*›
2 ‹*referee*› to blow one's whistle for ‹*foul*›
3 to hiss, to boo
B *vi* **1** (gen) to whistle; ‹*projectile*› to whistle through the air; ‹*bird*› to chirp; ‹*snake*› to hiss
2 to blow one's whistle

sifflet /siflɛ/ *m* **1** whistle; **coup de ~** whistle
2 (of train) whistle; (of kettle) whistling
3 hiss, boo
IDIOM **couper le ~ à qn** (fam) to shut sb up (fam)

sifflotement /siflɔtmɑ̃/ *m* whistling

siffloter /siflɔte/ [**v1**] *vi* to whistle away to oneself

sigle /sigl/ *m* (set of) initials; abbreviation

signal, *pl* **-aux** /siɲal, o/ *m* signal
■ **~ d'alarme** alarm signal; **~ sonore** (on answerphone) tone

signalement /siɲalmɑ̃/ *m* description

signaler /siɲale/ [**v1**] **A** *vt* **1 ~ qch à qn** to point sth out to sb; to inform sb of sth
2 ~ à qn que to remind sb that
3 to indicate ‹*roadworks, danger*›
4 to report ‹*fact*›
B se signaler *v refl* (+ *v être*) **se ~ par qch** to distinguish oneself by sth

signalétique /siɲaletik/ *adj* descriptive; **fiche ~** specification sheet

signalisation /siɲalizasjɔ̃/ *f* **1** signalling (BrE)
2 signals
■ **~ routière** road signs and markings

signaliser /siɲalize/ [**v1**] *vt* to signpost ‹*road*›; to mark out and light ‹*runway*›

signataire /siɲatɛʀ/ *mf* signatory

signature /siɲatyʀ/ *f* **1** signature
2 signing

signe /siɲ/ *m* sign; **~ astral** star sign; **~ précurseur** omen; **~ distinctif** *or* **particulier** distinguishing feature; **c'était un ~ du destin** it was fate; **~s de ponctuation** punctuation marks; **faire ~ à qn** to wave to sb; (fig) to get in touch with sb; **d'un ~ de la main/tête, elle m'a montré la cuisine** she pointed to/nodded her head in the direction of the kitchen; **faire ~ que oui** to indicate agreement
IDIOM **il n'a pas donné ~ de vie depuis six mois** there's been no sign of him for six months

signer /siɲe/ [**v1**] **A** *vt* to sign; **il signe son troisième roman** he's written his third novel
B se signer *v refl* (+ *v être*) to cross oneself

signet /siɲɛ/ *m* (Comput) bookmark; **créer un ~ sur** to bookmark ‹*site*›

signifiant, **~e** /siɲifjɑ̃, ɑ̃t/ *adj* significant

significatif, **-ive** /siɲifikatif, iv/ *adj* significant

signification /siɲifikasjɔ̃/ *f* **1** meaning
2 importance

signifié /siɲifje/ *m* signified

signifier /siɲifje/ [**v1**] *vt* **1** to mean
2 ~ qch à qn to inform sb of sth

silence /silɑ̃s/ *m* **1** silence; **'un peu de ~ s'il vous plaît'** 'quiet please'; **passer qch sous ~** to say nothing about sth
2 (Mus) rest

silencieusement /silɑ̃sjøzmɑ̃/ *adv* silently

silencieux, **-ieuse** /silɑ̃sjø, øz/ **A** *adj* silent; quiet
B *m* **1** (on gun) silencer
2 (on exhaust) silencer (BrE), muffler (AmE)

silex /silɛks/ *m inv* flint; **en** *or* **de ~** flint

silhouette /silwɛt/ *f* **1** silhouette; outline
2 figure; shape

silice /silis/ *f* silica

silicium /silisjɔm/ *m* silicon

silicone /silikon/ *f* silicone

sillage /sijaʒ/ *m* **1** (of ship) wake; (of plane) vapour (BrE) trail; slipstream
2 (of person) wake

sillon /sijɔ̃/ *m* **1** furrow
2 line
3 fissure
4 groove

sillonner /sijɔne/ [**v1**] *vt* **1** ‹*roads*› to criss-cross; ‹*police*› to patrol; **~ la France en voiture** to drive all over France
2 to furrow

silo /silo/ *m* silo

simagrée /simagʀe/ *f* play-acting

simiesque /simjɛsk/ *adj* ape-like

similaire /similɛʀ/ *adj* similar

similarité /similaʀite/ *f* similarity

similicuir /similikɥiʀ/ *m* imitation leather

similitude /similityd/ *f* similarity

simple /sɛ̃pl/ **A** *adj* **1** (gen) simple; **c'est (bien) ~, il ne fait plus rien** he simply doesn't do anything any more
2 ‹*decor*› plain; ‹*person, air*› unaffected
3 ‹*origins*› modest
4 ‹*worker*› ordinary; **c'est un ~ avertissement** it's just a warning; **le ~ fait de poser la question** the mere fact of asking

the question; **par ~ curiosité** out of pure curiosity; **sur ~ présentation du passeport** on presentation of one's passport
5 ‹*ice-cream cone, knot*› single
B *m* **1 le prix varie du ~ au double** the price can turn out to be twice as high
2 (Sport) **~ dames/messieurs** ladies'/men's singles
■ **~ d'esprit** simple-minded (offensive)

simplement /sɛ̃pləmɑ̃/ *adv* **1** simply, merely, just; **vas-y, ~ fais attention** you can go, only be careful
2 ‹*dress, live*› simply
3 easily

simplet, -ette /sɛ̃plɛ, ɛt/ *adj* simple

simplicité /sɛ̃plisite/ *f* **1** simplicity; **c'est d'une ~ enfantine** it's so easy a child could do it
2 (of person) unpretentiousness; (of thing) simplicity; **avec ~** simply

simplification /sɛ̃plifikasjɔ̃/ *f* simplification

simplifier /sɛ̃plifje/ [**v2**] **A** *vt* to simplify
B se simplifier *v refl* (+ *v être*) **se ~ la vie** to make life easier for oneself

simpliste /sɛ̃plist/ *adj* simplistic

simulacre /simylakʀ/ *m* **1** pretence (BrE); **~ de procès** mock trial
2 sham; **~ de justice** travesty of justice

simulateur, -trice /simylatœʀ, tʀis/ **A** *mf* **1** shammer, faker
2 malingerer
B *m* (Tech) simulator

simulation /simylasjɔ̃/ *f* **1** simulation
2 malingering

simuler /simyle/ [**v1**] *vt* to feign; to simulate

simultané, ~e /simyltane/ *adj* simultaneous

sincère /sɛ̃sɛʀ/ *adj* (gen) sincere; ‹*friend*› true; ‹*emotion, offer*› genuine; ‹*opinion*› honest

sincèrement /sɛ̃sɛʀmɑ̃/ *adv* **1** ‹*think*› really; ‹*regret, thank, speak*› sincerely
2 frankly

sincérité /sɛ̃seʀite/ *f* sincerity; honesty; genuineness

sinécure /sinekyʀ/ *f* sinecure

sine qua non /sinekwanɔn/ *phr* **condition ~** sine qua non

singe /sɛ̃ʒ/ *m* **1** monkey; ape; **les grands ~s** the apes
2 mimic; **faire le ~** to clown around

singer /sɛ̃ʒe/ [**v13**] *vt* to ape; to feign

singeries /sɛ̃ʒʀi/ *fpl* antics; **faire des ~** to monkey around; to pull funny faces

singulariser: se singulariser /sɛ̃gylaʀize/ [**v1**] *v refl* (+ *v être*) to draw attention to oneself

singularité /sɛ̃gylaʀite/ *f* **1** peculiarity, singularity
2 uniqueness

singulier, -ière /sɛ̃gylje, ɛʀ/ **A** *adj* **1** peculiar, unusual
2 combat ~ single combat
B *m* **1** singular
2 singularity

singulièrement /sɛ̃gyljɛʀmɑ̃/ *adv* **1** oddly
2 radically

sinistre /sinistʀ/ **A** *adj* sinister; ‹*place, future*› bleak; ‹*evening*› dreary
B *m* disaster; accident; blaze

sinistré, ~e /sinistʀe/ **A** *adj* stricken; **région ~e** disaster area
B *mf* disaster victim

sinon /sinɔ̃/ **A** *conj* **1** otherwise, or else
2 except, apart from
3 not to say; **c'est devenu difficile ~ impossible** it has become difficult if not impossible
B sinon que *phr* except that, other than that

sinueux, -euse /sinɥø, øz/ *adj* sinuous; winding; tortuous

sinus /sinys/ *m inv* sinus

sinusite /sinyzit/ *f* sinusitis

siphon /sifɔ̃/ *m* **1** (gen) siphon
2 U-bend

siphonné, ~e /sifɔne/ *adj* (fam) nuts (fam), crazy (fam)

sire /siʀ/ *m* Sire

sirène /siʀɛn/ *f* **1** (gen) siren; (of boat) foghorn
2 mermaid, siren
■ **~ d'alarme** fire alarm

sirop /siʀo/ *m* **1** syrup (BrE), sirup (AmE), cordial
2 (medicine) syrup (BrE), sirup (AmE), mixture; **~ pectoral** cough mixture

siroter /siʀɔte/ [**v1**] *vt* (fam) to sip

sirupeux, -euse /siʀypø, øz/ *adj* syrupy (BrE), sirupy (AmE)

sis, ~e /si, siz/ *adj* located

sismique /sismik/ *adj* seismic

sismographie /sismɔgʀafi/ *f* seismography

site /sit/ *m* **1** area; **~ touristique** place of interest; **~ archéologique** archaeological site
2 site
■ **~ de bavardage** (Comput) chat room; **~ de réseau social** social networking site; **~ vierge** green-field site; **~ Web** Web site

sitôt /sito/ **A** *adv* **~ rentrés** as soon as we/they get back; as soon as we/they got back; **je n'y retournerai pas de ~** I won't go back there in a hurry (fam)
B *conj* **~ que** as soon as
IDIOM **~ dit, ~ fait** no sooner said than done

situation /sitɥasjɔ̃/ *f* **1** situation
2 job, position
3 location
■ **~ de famille** marital status

situer /sitɥe/ [**v1**] **A** *vt* **1** (in space and time) to

S

place; **l'hôtel est bien situé** the hotel is in a good location
2 ~ **une histoire en 2001/à Palerme** to set a story in 2001/in Palermo
B se situer *v refl* (+ *v être*) **1 se** ~ **à Paris en 1900** to be set in Paris in 1900
2 politiquement, je me situe plutôt à gauche politically, I'm more to the left

six /sis/ *but before consonant* /si/ *and before vowel or mute h* /siz/ *adj inv, pron, m inv* six

sixième /sizjɛm/ **A** *adj* sixth
B *f* (Sch) *first year of secondary school, age 11–12*

skaï® /skaj/ *m* imitation leather

skate-board, *pl* ~**s** /skɛtbɔʀd/ *m* **1** skateboard
2 skateboarding

sketch, *pl* ~**es** /skɛtʃ/ *m* sketch

ski /ski/ *m* **1** ski
2 le ~ skiing
■ ~ **de fond** cross-country skiing; ~ **nautique** water skiing; ~ **de piste** downhill skiing

skier /skje/ [**v2**] *vi* to ski

skieur, -ieuse /skjœʀ, øz/ *mf* skier

slalom /slalɔm/ *m* slalom

slalomer /slalɔme/ [**v1**] *vi* **1** (Sport) to slalom
2 (fig) to zigzag

slave /slav/ *adj* Slavonic

Slave /slav/ *mf* Slav

slip /slip/ *m* **1** underpants
2 slipway

slogan /slɔgɑ̃/ *m* slogan

slow /slo/ *m* slow dance

smala /smala/ *f* (fam) tribe (fam)

SME /ɛsɛmə/ *m*: *abbr* ▶ **système**

SMIC /smik/ *m* (*abbr* = **salaire minimum interprofessionel de croissance**) guaranteed minimum wage

smicard, ~**e** /smikaʀ, -aʀd/ *mf*: *person on the minimum wage*

smoking /smɔkiŋ/ *m* dinner jacket (BrE), tuxedo

SNCF /ɛsɛnseɛf/ *f* (*abbr* = **Société nationale des chemins de fer français**) *French national railway company*

snob /snɔb/ **A** *adj* ‹*person*› stuck-up (fam); ‹*restaurant*› posh
B *mf* snob; **c'est un** ~ he's a snob

snober /snɔbe/ [**v1**] *vt* to snub

snobisme /snɔbism/ *m* snobbery

sobre /sɔbʀ/ *adj* **1** ‹*person*› abstemious; sober; temperate; ‹*life*› simple
2 ‹*style*› plain, sober

sobrement /sɔbʀəmɑ̃/ *adv* soberly; in moderation; ‹*live*› frugally

sobriété /sɔbʀijete/ *f* sobriety, temperance; restraint; moderation

sobriquet /sɔbʀikɛ/ *m* nickname

soc /sɔk/ *m* ploughshare (BrE), plowshare (AmE)

sociabilité /sɔsjabilite/ *f* sociability

sociable /sɔsjabl/ *adj* **1** sociable
2 social

social, ~**e**, *mpl* **-iaux** /sɔsjal, o/ **A** *adj* **1** social; **le milieu** ~ **de qn** sb's social background
2 conflit ~ industrial dispute
B *m* **le** ~ social issues

socialement /sɔsjalmɑ̃/ *adv* socially; **être** ~ **pris en charge** to be in the care of the social services

socialiser /sɔsjalize/ [**v1**] *vt* **1** to socialize
2 to collectivize

socialisme /sɔsjalism/ *m* socialism

socialiste /sɔsjalist/ *adj, mf* socialist

sociétaire /sɔsjetɛʀ/ *mf* member

société /sɔsjete/ *f* **1** society; **la haute** ~ high society
2 company; ~ **de nettoyage** cleaning company
3 (fml) **rechercher la** ~ **de qn** to seek sb's company

socioculturel, -elle /sɔsjokyltyʀɛl/ *adj* sociocultural; **centre** ~ recreation centre (BrE)

socio-démocrate, *pl* ~**s** **A** *adj* social democratic
B *mf* social democrat

socio-éducatif, **-ive**, *mpl* ~**s** /sɔsjoedykatif, iv/ *adj* socio-educational

sociologie /sɔsjɔlɔʒi/ *f* sociology

sociologue /sɔsjɔlɔg/ *mf* sociologist

socioprofessionnel, -elle /sɔsjopʀɔfɛsjɔnɛl/ *adj* social and occupational

socle /sɔkl/ *m* pedestal, plinth; base; stand

socque /sɔk/ *m* clog

socquette /sɔkɛt/ *f* ankle sock, anklet (AmE)

soda /sɔda/ *m* fizzy drink (BrE), soda (AmE)

sodium /sɔdjɔm/ *m* sodium

sodomiser /sɔdɔmize/ [**v1**] *vt* to sodomize, to bugger

sœur /sœʀ/ *f* sister; ~ **jumelle** twin sister

sofa /sɔfa/ *m* sofa

soi /swa/ *pron* **1 autour de** ~ around one; **laisser la porte se refermer derrière** ~ to let the door shut behind one; **trouver en** ~ **les ressources nécessaires** to find the necessary inner resources; **garder qch pour** ~ to keep sth to oneself
2 la logique n'est pas un objectif en ~ logic is not an end in itself; **cela va de** ~ it goes without saying

soi-disant /swadizɑ̃/ **A** *adj inv* **1** self-styled
2 (controversial) so-called
B *adv* supposedly; **elle a** ~ **la migraine** she has a migraine, or so she says

soie /swɑ/ *f* **1** silk
2 bristle

soient /swa/ ▶ **être**[1]

soierie /swaʀi/ *f* **1** silk
2 silk industry

soif /swaf/ *f* **1** thirst; **avoir** ~ to be thirsty

S

2 ~ de thirst for; hunger for; lust for; **avoir ~ d'affection** to crave affection

soignant, **~e** /swaɲɑ̃, ɑ̃t/ *adj* medical; **médecin ~** doctor, GP

soigné, **~e** /swaɲe/ **A** *pp* ▶ **soigner**
B *pp adj* **1** ‹*nails*› well manicured; ‹*hair, clothes*› immaculate
2 ‹*publication*› carefully produced; ‹*work*› meticulous; **peu ~** ‹*work*› careless

soigner /swaɲe/ [**v1**] **A** *vt* **1** ‹*doctor*› to treat
2 to look after ‹*person, customer*›
3 to take care over ‹*appearance*›; to look after ‹*hands*›
B se soigner *v refl* (+ *v être*) **1** to treat oneself; to look after oneself
2 ‹*illness*› to be treatable
3 to take care over one's appearance

soigneusement /swaɲøzmɑ̃/ *adv* carefully; meticulously; neatly

soigneux, **-euse** /swaɲø, øz/ *adj* **1** ‹*work*› conscientious; ‹*examination*› careful
2 ‹*person*› neat, tidy

soi-même /swamɛm/ *pron* oneself

✓ **soin** /swɛ̃/ **A** *m* **1** care; **prendre ~ de qch** to take care of sth; **prendre ~ de qn/sa santé** to look after sb/one's health; **prendre ~ de sa petite personne** to coddle oneself; **laisser à qn le ~ de faire** to leave it to sb to do
2 product; **~ antipelliculaire** dandruff treatment
B soins *mpl* **1** (Med) treatment; care; **recevoir des ~s** to receive treatment; **~s dentaires** dental care; **les premiers ~s à donner aux brûlés** first-aid treatment for burns; **~s à domicile** home care
2 care; **~s corporels** *or* **du corps** body care
3 'aux bons ~s de' 'care of', 'c/o'
(IDIOM) **être aux petits ~s pour qn** to attend to sb's every need

✓ **soir** /swaʀ/ *m* evening; night; **le ~ du 3, le 3 au ~** on the evening of the 3rd; **il sort tous les samedis ~** he goes out every Saturday night; **6 heures du ~** 6 pm; **à ce ~!** see you tonight!

✓ **soirée** /swaʀe/ *f* **1** evening; **dans** *or* **pendant la ~, en ~** in the evening
2 party; **aller dans une ~** to go to a party
3 evening performance *or* show

sois /swa/ ▶ **être**[1]

✓ **soit**[1] /swa/ **A** ▶ **être**[1]
B *conj* **1 ~, ~** either, or; **~ du fromage, ~ un gâteau** either cheese, or a cake
2 that is, ie; **toutes mes économies, ~ 200 euros** all my savings, ie *or* that is, 200 euros
3 (in mathematics) **~ un triangle ABC** let ABC be a triangle

soit[2] /swat/ *adv* very well; **je me suis trompé, ~, mais là n'est pas la question** all right, so I was wrong, but that's not the point

soixantaine /swasɑ̃tɛn/ *f* **1 une ~** about sixty
2 avoir la ~ to be about sixty

soixante /swasɑ̃t/ *adj inv, pron, m inv* sixty

soixante-dix /swasɑ̃tdis/ *adj inv, pron, m inv* seventy

soixante-dixième /swasɑ̃tdizjɛm/ *adj* seventieth

soixantième /swasɑ̃tjɛm/ *adj* sixtieth

soja /sɔʒa/ *m* soya bean (BrE), soybean (AmE); **sauce de ~** soy sauce

✓ **sol** /sɔl/ *m* **1** ground; floor
2 soil
3 (Mus) (note) G; (in sol-fa) soh

solaire /sɔlɛʀ/ *adj* ‹*energy*› solar; ‹*engine*› solar-powered; ‹*cream*› sun

✓ **soldat** /sɔlda/ *m* soldier, serviceman

solde[1] /sɔld/ **A** *m* balance; **faire le ~ d'un compte** to settle an account
B en solde *phr* **acheter une veste en ~** to buy a jacket in a sale
C soldes *mpl* sales; sale

solde[2] /sɔld/ *f* (Mil) pay; **avoir qn à sa ~** (fig) to have sb in one's pay

solder /sɔlde/ [**v1**] **A** *vt* **1** to sell off ‹*merchandise*›
2 to settle the balance of ‹*account*›
B se solder *v refl* (+ *v être*) **se ~ par qch** to end in sth

solderie /sɔldəʀi/ *f* discount shop

sole /sɔl/ *f* (Zool) sole

✓ **soleil** /sɔlɛj/ *m* sun; **~ de minuit** midnight sun; **en plein ~** ‹*sit*› in (the) hot sun; ‹*leave something*› in direct sunlight; **quand il y a du ~** when it's sunny; **attraper un coup** *or* **des coups de ~** to get sunburned

solennel, **-elle** /sɔlanɛl/ *adj* (gen) solemn; ‹*appeal, declaration*› formal

solennité /sɔlanite/ *f* solemnity

solfège /sɔlfɛʒ/ *m* **1** music theory; **~ chanté** sol-fa
2 music theory book

solidaire /sɔlidɛʀ/ *adj* **1** ‹*team, group*› united
2 (Tech) ‹*parts*› interdependent

solidariser: **se solidariser** /sɔlidaʀize/ [**v1**] *v refl* (+ *v être*) **se ~ avec qn/qch** to stand by sb/sth

solidarité /sɔlidaʀite/ *f* solidarity

✓ **solide** /sɔlid/ **A** *adj* **1** ‹*food, matter*› solid
2 ‹*house, friendship*› solid; ‹*shoes, bag*› sturdy; ‹*link, fastening, blade*› strong; ‹*position, base*› firm
3 ‹*person, constitution, heart*› strong; **avoir la tête ~** (fig) to have one's head screwed on (right)
4 ‹*business, experience, reason*› sound; ‹*guarantee*› firm
B *m* **1** solid; **manger du ~** to eat solids
2 ce qu'il te dit, c'est du ~ what he says is sound
3 les meubles anciens, c'est du ~ antique furniture is solidly built

✓ key word

solidement /sɔlidmɑ̃/ *adv* ‹*attach, establish*› firmly; ‹*barricaded*› securely; **un rapport ~ documenté** a well-documented report

solidifier /sɔlidifje/ [**v2**] *vt*, **se solidifier** *v refl* (+ *v être*) to solidify

solidité /sɔlidite/ *f* **1** (of construction) solidity; (of machine) strength; (of link) firmness; (of clothes) hard-wearing quality; **d'une grande ~** well-built; sturdy; strong; hard-wearing
2 (of argument) soundness

soliloque /sɔlilɔk/ *m* soliloquy

soliste /sɔlist/ *mf* soloist

solitaire /sɔlitɛʀ/ **A** *adj* **1** ‹*person, life*› solitary; ‹*old age, childhood*› lonely; **navigateur ~** single-handed yachtsman
2 ‹*house*› isolated
B *mf* solitary person, loner; **en ~** ‹*live*› alone; ‹*sail*› single-handed
C *m* **1** (diamond) solitaire
2 rogue boar
3 (Games) solitaire

solitude /sɔlityd/ *f* **1** solitude
2 loneliness

solliciter /sɔlisite/ [**v1**] *vt* **1** (fml) to seek ‹*interview, post, advice*›
2 to approach ‹*person, organization*›; to canvass ‹*customer, voter*›; **être très sollicité** to be assailed by requests; to be very much in demand

sollicitude /sɔlisityd/ *f* concern, solicitude

solstice /sɔlstis/ *m* solstice

soluble /sɔlybl/ *adj* soluble

solution /sɔlysjɔ̃/ *f* **1** solution, solving; resolution
2 solution; **une ~ de facilité** an easy way out
3 (in chemistry) solution

solutionner /sɔlysjɔne/ [**v1**] *vt* to solve

solvabilité /sɔlvabilite/ *f* **1** solvency
2 creditworthiness

solvable /sɔlvabl/ *adj* solvent; creditworthy

solvant /sɔlvɑ̃/ *m* solvent

somatiser /sɔmatize/ [**v1**] *vt* to have a psychosomatic reaction to

sombre /sɔ̃bʀ/ *adj* **1** dark; **il fait ~** it's dark
2 ‹*thought, future*› dark, black; ‹*conclusion*› depressing; ‹*air, person*› solemn
3 (*before n*) (fam) ‹*idiot*› absolute; ‹*affair*› murky

sombrer /sɔ̃bʀe/ [**v1**] *vi* **1** ‹*ship*› to sink
2 ~ dans ‹*person*› to sink into ‹*despair, alcoholism*›

sommaire /sɔmmɛʀ/ **A** *adj* ‹*explanation*› cursory; ‹*description*› rough; ‹*installation, meal*› rough and ready; ‹*execution*› summary
B *m* **1** contents; **au ~ de notre numéro de juillet** featured in our July issue
2 (fam) **au ~: un débat sur le chômage** a debate on unemployment is on the programme (BrE)

sommairement /sɔmmɛʀmɑ̃/ *adv* summarily

sommation /sɔmmasjɔ̃/ *f* (from police) warning; (from guard) challenge

somme[1] /sɔm/ *m* nap, snooze (fam)

somme[2] /sɔm/ *f* **1** sum, amount
2 sum total; **la ~ de nos connaissances** the sum total of our knowledge; **il a fourni une grosse ~ de travail** he did a great deal of work; **en ~, ~ toute** all in all

sommeil /sɔmɛj/ *m* sleep; **avoir le ~ agité** to sleep fitfully; **avoir le ~ léger** to be a light sleeper

sommeiller /sɔmeje/ [**v1**] *vi* **1** to doze
2 to lie dormant

sommelier, -ière /sɔməlje, ɛʀ/ *mf* wine waiter, sommelier

sommer /sɔmme/ [**v1**] *vt* **~ qn de faire** to command sb to do

sommes /sɔm/ ▶ **être[1]**

sommet /sɔmmɛ/ *m* **1** (of mountain) peak; summit
2 (gen) top; (of wave) crest; (of curve, career) peak
3 (of glory, stupidity) height; **atteindre des ~s** ‹*prices, sales*› to peak
4 summit; **conférence au ~** summit meeting
5 (of triangle, angle) apex; (of cone) vertex

sommier /sɔmje/ *m* (bed) base

somnambule /sɔmnɑ̃byl/ **A** *adj* **être ~** to sleepwalk
B *mf* sleepwalker

somnifère /sɔmnifɛʀ/ **A** *adj* soporific
B *m* **1** soporific
2 sleeping pill

somnolence /sɔmnɔlɑ̃s/ *f* drowsiness

somnolent, ~e /sɔmnɔlɑ̃, ɑ̃t/ *adj* **1** drowsy
2 ‹*town*› sleepy; ‹*industry, country*› lethargic

somnoler /sɔmnɔle/ [**v1**] *vi* **1** to drowse
2 ‹*town*› to be sleepy; ‹*industry, country*› to be lethargic

somptueux, -euse /sɔ̃ptɥø, øz/ *adj* sumptuous

somptuosité /sɔ̃ptɥozite/ *f* sumptuousness

son[1], sa, *pl* **ses** /sɔ̃, sa, sɛ/ *det* his/her/its; **ses enfants** his/her children; **ses pattes** its paws; **elle a ~ lundi** she's off on Monday; she gets Mondays off; **~ étourdie de sœur** (fam) his/her absent-minded sister

son[2] /sɔ̃/ *m* **1** sound; **ingénieur du ~** sound engineer
2 volume; **baisser le ~** to turn the volume down
3 bran; **pain au ~** bran loaf
■ **~ et lumière** son et lumière

sonar /sɔnaʀ/ *m* sonar

sonate /sɔnat/ *f* sonata

sondage /sɔ̃daʒ/ *m* **1** poll; survey
2 (Med) catheterization; probe
3 (Naut) sounding

sonde /sɔ̃d/ *f* **1** (Med) catheter; probe
2 sounding lead; sounding line
3 drill
4 taster

sonder /sɔ̃de/ [**v1**] *vt* **1** to poll; to survey; to sound out
2 to probe
3 (Med) to catheterize; to probe
4 (Naut) to sound

songe /sɔ̃ʒ/ *m* dream

songer /sɔ̃ʒe/ [**v13**] *v+prep* **~ à qch/à faire** to think of sth/of doing; **tu n'y songes pas!** you can't be serious!

songeur, **-euse** /sɔ̃ʒœʀ, øz/ *adj* pensive

sonnant, **~e** /sɔnɑ̃, ɑ̃t/ *adj* **à trois heures ~es** on the stroke of three

sonné, **~e** /sɔne/ **A** *pp* ▶ **sonner**
B *pp adj* **1** groggy; shattered
2 elle a quarante ans bien ~s (fam) she's well into her forties

sonner /sɔne/ [**v1**] **A** *vt* **1** to ring ‹*bell*›
2 ‹*clock*› to strike ‹*hour*›; ‹*person*› to sound ‹*retreat, alarm*›; to ring out ‹*vespers*›
3 to ring for; **on ne t'a pas sonné!** (fam) did anyone ask you?
4 (fam) ‹*blow*› to make [sb] dizzy; ‹*news*› to stagger
B sonner de *v+prep* to sound ‹*horn*›; to play ‹*bagpipes*›
C *vi* **1** ‹*bell, phone*› to ring; ‹*hour*› to strike; ‹*alarm clock*› to go off; ‹*alarm, trumpet*› to sound; **leur dernière heure a sonné** their last hour has come
2 ‹*word, expression*› to sound

sonnerie /sɔnʀi/ *f* **1** ringing; chimes; **système qui déclenche une ~** system that sets off an alarm
2 (of horn) sounding
3 (of mobile phone) ringtone

sonnet /sɔnɛ/ *m* sonnet

sonnette /sɔnɛt/ *f* bell; doorbell; **tirer la ~ d'alarme** to pull the emergency cord; (fig) to sound the alarm

sonore /sɔnɔʀ/ *adj* **1** ‹*laugh, kiss, slap*› resounding
2 resonant; echoing; hollow-sounding
3 ‹*vibrations*› sound; **le volume ~ est tel que...** the noise level is so high that...; **effets ~s** sound effects; **un document ~** a recording
4 ‹*consonant*› voiced

sonorisation /sɔnɔʀizasjɔ̃/ *f* public address system, PA system

sonorité /sɔnɔʀite/ *f* **1** (of instrument, voice) tone; **les ~s de l'italien** the sound of Italian
2 (of hi-fi) sound quality
3 resonance

sont /sɔ̃/ ▶ **être**[1]

sophistication /sɔfistikasjɔ̃/ *f* sophistication

sophistiqué, **~e** /sɔfistike/ *adj*
1 sophisticated
2 artificial, mannered

sophrologie /sɔfʀɔlɔʒi/ *f* relaxation therapy

soporifique /sɔpɔʀifik/ *adj*, *m* soporific

soprano /sɔpʀano/ *mf* soprano

sorbet /sɔʀbɛ/ *m* sorbet

sorcellerie /sɔʀsɛlʀi/ *f* witchcraft; sorcery

sorcier /sɔʀsje/ **A** *adj m* (fam) **ce n'est (pourtant) pas ~!** (but) it's dead easy (fam)
B *m* **1** wizard; sorcerer
2 witch doctor

sorcière /sɔʀsjɛʀ/ *f* witch; sorceress

sordide /sɔʀdid/ *adj* squalid; sordid

sornettes /sɔʀnɛt/ *fpl* tall stories

sort /sɔʀ/ *m* **1** lot; **être satisfait de son ~** to be satisfied with one's lot
2 fate; **le ~ est contre moi** I'm ill-fated; **tirer qch au ~** to draw lots for sth
3 curse, spell; **jeter un ~ à qn** to put a curse on sb; **le ~ en est jeté** the die is cast

sortable /sɔʀtabl/ *adj* **mon mari n'est pas ~** I can't take my husband anywhere

sorte /sɔʀt/ **A** *f* sort, kind
B de la sorte *phr* in this way
C de sorte que *phr* **1** so that
2 la toile est peinte de ~ que... the canvas is painted in such a way that...
3 de ~ que je n'ai pas pu venir with the result that I couldn't come
D en quelque sorte *phr* in a way
E en sorte de *phr* **fais en ~ d'être à l'heure** try to be on time
F en sorte que *phr* **fais en ~ que tout soit en ordre** make sure everything is tidy

sortie /sɔʀti/ *f* **1** exit; **je t'attendrai à la ~** I'll wait for you outside (the building); **à la ~ de la ville** on the outskirts of the town; on the edge of the town
2 à ma ~ du tribunal when I left the court; **se retrouver à la ~ de l'école** to meet after school; **à la ~ de l'hiver** at the end of winter
3 faire une ~ fracassante to make a dramatic exit; **la ~ de la récession/crise** the end of the recession/crisis
4 outing; **faire une ~ avec l'école** to go on a school outing; **ce soir, c'est mon soir de ~** tonight is my night out; **priver qn de ~** to keep sb in, to ground sb (fam)
5 (of new product) launching; (of film) release; (of book) publication; (of fashion collection) showing
6 (Tech) output; **faire une ~ sur imprimante** to print
■ **~ des artistes** stage door; **~ d'autoroute** motorway exit, highway exit (AmE); **~ de bain** bathrobe

sortilège /sɔʀtilɛʒ/ *m* spell

sortir[1] /sɔʀtiʀ/ [**v30**] **A** *vt* **1** to take [sb/sth] out ‹*person, dog*›
2 to get [sb/sth] out; **~ les mains de ses poches** to take one's hands out of one's pockets; **~ la poubelle** to put the bin *or* the garbage (AmE) *or* the trash (AmE) out; **~ sa langue** to stick one's tongue out
3 (fam) to chuck (fam) [sb] out ‹*person*›; to send [sb] out ‹*pupil*›

S

4 ~ qn de to get sb out of ‹*situation*›
5 to bring out ‹*book*›; to release ‹*film*›; to show ‹*collection*›
6 to turn out ‹*book, record, film, product*›
7 to bring [sth] out ‹*newspaper*›
8 (fam) to come out with (fam) ‹*remarks*›; **~ une blague** to crack a joke
B *vi* (+ *v être*) **1** to go out; to come out; **~ déjeuner** to go out for lunch; **être sorti** to be out; **~ en courant** to run out; **faire ~ qn** to get sb outside; **laisser ~ qn** to allow sb out
2 to go out; **~ avec qn** to go out with sb; **inviter qn à ~** to ask sb out
3 ~ de to leave; **~ de chez qn** to leave sb's house; **sortez d'ici!** get out of here!; **~ de son lit** to get out of bed; **~ tout chaud du four** to be hot from the oven; **~ de chez le médecin** to come out of the doctor's
4 ~ d'un rêve to wake up from a dream; **~ de la récession** to pull out of the recession; **~ de l'hiver** to reach the end of winter
5 ~ à peine de l'enfance to be just emerging from childhood; **~ d'une guerre** to emerge from a war
6 ‹*water, smoke, cork*› to come out; **faire ~** to squeeze [sth] out ‹*juice*›; to eject ‹*cassette*›
7 ‹*bud, insect*› to come out; ‹*tooth*› to come through
8 to stick out
9 ‹*film, book, new model*› to come out; **~ tous les jours/tous les mois** ‹*paper*› to be published daily/monthly
10 ~ de ‹*person, product*› to come from; **~ de Berkeley** to have graduated from Berkeley; **d'où sors-tu à cette heure?** (fam) where have you been?
11 ~ du sujet ‹*remark*› to be beside the point; **cela sort de mes fonctions** that's not within my authority
12 ‹*number*› to come up
13 (Comput) to exit
C se sortir *v refl* (+ *v être*) **1 se ~ de la pauvreté** to escape from poverty; **s'en ~** to get out of it; to get over it; **s'en ~ vivant** to escape with one's life
2 s'en ~ to pull through; to cope; to manage; **s'en ~ à peine** to scrape a living

sortir² /sɔʀtiʀ/ *m* **au ~ de** at the end of

SOS /ɛsoɛs/ *m* **1** SOS
2 emergency service; **~ médecins** emergency medical service
3 helpline; **~ enfants battus** child abuse helpline

sosie /sɔzi/ *m* double; **c'est ton ~!** he/she's the spitting image of you!

sot, sotte /so, sɔt/ **A** *adj* silly
B *mf* silly thing; **petit ~!** you silly thing!

sottement /sɔtmɑ̃/ *adv* foolishly, stupidly

sottise /sɔtiz/ *f* **1** silliness, foolishness
2 silly remark; **dire des ~s** to talk rubbish
3 faire des ~s ‹*children*› to be naughty

⚷ **sou** /su/ *m* **1** (fam) penny (BrE), cent (AmE); **il est près de ses ~s** he's a penny-pincher; **c'est une affaire de gros ~s** there's big money involved
2 (fam) **il n'a pas un ~ de bon sens** he hasn't got a scrap of common sense
3 (former unit of French currency) sou

soubassement /subasmɑ̃/ *m* **1** (of building, pillar) base
2 bedrock

soubresaut /subʀəso/ *m* start; jolt

soubrette /subʀɛt/ *f* maid

souche /suʃ/ *f* **1** (tree) stump; (vine) stock
2 stock; **de ~ paysanne** of peasant stock
3 (of chequebook) stub
IDIOM **dormir comme une ~** to sleep like a log

⚷ **souci** /susi/ *m* **1 se faire du ~** to worry
2 problem; **j'ai d'autres ~s (en tête)** I've got other things to worry about
3 (fml) **avoir le ~ de qch** to care about sth; **avoir le ~ de faire** to be anxious to do; **dans le seul ~ de faire plaisir** with the sole intention of pleasing
4 marigold

soucier: **se soucier** /susje/ [**v2**] *v refl* (+ *v être*) to care (**de** about); **sans se ~ de qch/faire** without concerning oneself with sth/doing

soucieux, -ieuse /susjø, øz/ *adj* worried

soucoupe /sukup/ *f* saucer
■ **~ volante** flying saucer

⚷ **soudain, ~e** /sudɛ̃, ɛn/ **A** *adj* sudden
B *adv* suddenly, all of a sudden

soudainement /sudɛnmɑ̃/ *adv* suddenly

soude /sud/ *f* **~ caustique** caustic soda

souder /sude/ [**v1**] **A** *vt* **1** to weld
2 to join ‹*edges*›; to bind [sb] together ‹*people*›
B se souder *v refl* (+ *v être*) ‹*vertebrae*› to fuse; ‹*bone*› to knit together

soudoyer /sudwaje/ [**v23**] *vt* to bribe

soudure /sudyʀ/ *f* weld, join; welding

soufflant, ~e /suflɑ̃, ɑ̃t/ *adj* **1 machine ~e** blowing apparatus
2 (fam) stunning

⚷ **souffle** /sufl/ *m* **1** breath; **couper le ~ à qn** to wind sb; (fig) to take sb's breath away; **(en) avoir le ~ coupé** to be winded; (fig) to be speechless; **être à bout de ~** ‹*person*› to be out of breath; ‹*country, economy*› to be running out of steam; **donner un second** *or* **nouveau ~ à qn/qch** to put new life into sb/sth; **avoir du ~** ‹*saxophonist*› to have good lungs; ‹*singer*› to have a powerful voice; ‹*sportsman*› to be fit; (fig) ‹*person*› to have staying power
2 breathing
3 breeze; **pas un ~ d'air** not a breath of air
4 spirit; **~ révolutionnaire** revolutionary spirit
5 inspiration
6 (from fan, explosion) blast
7 (Med) **~ au cœur** heart murmur

S

soufflé, **~e** /sufle/ **A** *adj* (fam) flabbergasted
B *m* (Culin) soufflé

souffler /sufle/ [**v1**] **A** *vt* **1** to blow out ‹*candle*›
2 to blow ‹*air, smoke, dust*›
3 to whisper ‹*words*›; **~ qch à l'oreille de qn** to whisper sth in sb's ear; **~ la réplique à un acteur** to prompt an actor
4 to suggest ‹*idea*›
5 to blow ‹*glass*›; to blast ‹*metal*›
6 ‹*explosion*› to blow out ‹*window*›; to blow up ‹*building*›
7 (fam) to flabbergast
B *vi* **1** ‹*wind*› to blow; **le vent souffle fort** there's a strong wind
2 ‹*person*› to get one's breath back; ‹*horse*› to get its wind back
3 to puff; **suant et soufflant** huffing and puffing
4 ‹*person, animal*› to blow; **~ dans une trompette** to blow into a trumpet
5 to tell sb the answer; **on ne souffle pas!** no prompting!
IDIOM **~ comme un bœuf** *or* **un phoque** *or* **une locomotive** to puff and pant

soufflerie /suflәʀi/ *f* **1** blower; blower house
2 glass blower; glass blowing company

soufflet /suflɛ/ *m* **1** bellows
2 gusset

souffleur, **-euse** /suflœʀ, øz/ *mf*
1 prompter
2 ~ (de verre) glass blower

⚷ **souffrance** /sufʀɑ̃s/ *f* suffering

souffrant, **~e** /sufʀɑ̃, ɑ̃t/ *adj* unwell

souffre-douleur /sufʀәdulœʀ/ *m inv* punchbag (BrE), punching bag (AmE)

⚷ **souffrir** /sufʀiʀ/ [**v4**] **A** *vt* **1 ~ tout de qn** to put up with anything from sb; **il ne souffre pas la critique** he can't take criticism
2 cette affaire ne peut ~ aucun retard this matter brooks no delay
B *vi* **1** ‹*person*› to suffer; **~ de** to suffer from; **ma cheville me fait ~** my ankle hurts; **est-ce qu'il souffre?** is he in pain?; **faire ~** ‹*person*› to make [sb] suffer; ‹*situation*› to upset; **~ du racisme** to be a victim of racism
2 ‹*crops, economy*› to be badly affected; ‹*country, city*› to suffer

soufre /sufʀ/ *m* sulphur (BrE), sulfur (AmE)

souhait /swɛ/ *m* wish
IDIOM **à vos ~s!** bless you!

souhaitable /swɛtabl/ *adj* desirable

⚷ **souhaiter** /swete/ [**v1**] *vt* **1** to hope for
2 ~ qch à qn to wish sb sth; **~ la bienvenue à qn** to welcome sb; **je vous souhaite d'obtenir très bientôt votre diplôme** I hope you get your degree very soon
3 il souhaite se rendre là-bas en voiture he would like to go by car

⚷ key word

souiller /suje/ [**v1**] *vt* **1** to soil, to make [sth] dirty; **être souillé de** to be stained with
2 to defile ‹*place, person*›; to sully ‹*memory*›

souillon /sujɔ̃/ *f* slattern

souillure /sujyʀ/ *f* stain

souk /suk/ *m* **1** souk
2 (fam) mess; racket (fam)

soûl, **~e** /su, sul/ **A** *adj* drunk
B tout son soûl *phr* ‹*drink, eat*› one's fill

soulagement /sulaʒmɑ̃/ *m* relief

soulager /sulaʒe/ [**v13**] *vt* (gen) to relieve; to ease ‹*conscience*›; **le comprimé m'a soulagé** the tablet made me feel better; **tu m'as soulagé d'un grand poids** you've taken a great weight off my shoulders

soûlant, **~e** /sulɑ̃, ɑ̃t/ *adj* (fam) **elle est ~e!** she makes my head spin!

soûler /sule/ [**v1**] **A** *vt* **1** ‹*person*› to get [sb] drunk; ‹*alcohol*› to make [sb] drunk
2 ‹*perfume*› to intoxicate
3 (fam) **tu me soûles avec tes histoires** you're making my head spin!
B se soûler *v refl* (+ *v être*) to get drunk

soulèvement /sulɛvmɑ̃/ *m* uprising

⚷ **soulever** /sulve/ [**v16**] **A** *vt* **1** to lift ‹*object*›; to raise ‹*dust*›; **~ qn/qch de terre** to pick sb/sth up
2 to arouse ‹*enthusiasm, anger*›; to stir up ‹*crowd*›; to raise ‹*problems*›
B se soulever *v refl* (+ *v être*) **1** to raise oneself up
2 to rise up
IDIOM **ça me soulève le cœur** it turns my stomach; it makes me sick

soulier /sulje/ *m* shoe
IDIOM **être dans ses petits ~s** to feel uncomfortable

⚷ **souligner** /suliɲe/ [**v1**] *vt* **1** to underline ‹*word*›; to outline ‹*eyes*›
2 to emphasize

⚷ **soumettre** /sumɛtʀ/ [**v60**] **A** *vt* **1** to bring [sb/sth] to heel ‹*person, group, region*›; to subdue ‹*rebels*›
2 ~ qn/qch à to subject sb/sth to
3 to submit
4 ~ un produit à une température élevée to subject a product to a high temperature
B se soumettre *v refl* (+ *v être*) **1** to submit
2 se ~ à to accept ‹*rule*›

soumis, **~e** /sumi, iz/ **A** *pp* ▶ **soumettre**
B *pp adj* submissive

soumission /sumisjɔ̃/ *f* submission

soupape /supap/ *f* valve

soupçon /supsɔ̃/ *m* **1** suspicion
2 (fam) (of milk, wine) drop; (of salt) pinch; (of flavour) hint

soupçonner /supsɔne/ [**v1**] *vt* to suspect

soupçonneux, **-euse** /supsɔnø, øz/ *adj* suspicious, mistrustful

soupe /sup/ *f* **1** soup; **à la ~!** (fam) (hum) grub's up! (fam)

2 (fam) slush
■ **~ populaire** soup kitchen
IDIOMS **être ~ au lait** (fam) to be quick-tempered; **cracher dans la ~** (fam) to look a gift horse in the mouth

soupente /supɑ̃t/ *f* **1** loft, garret
2 cupboard under the stairs

souper¹ /supe/ [**v1**] *vi* to have late dinner

souper² /supe/ *m* late dinner, supper

soupeser /supəze/ [**v16**] *vt* **1** to feel the weight of
2 to weigh up ‹*arguments*›

soupière /supjɛʀ/ *f* soup tureen

soupir /supiʀ/ *m* sigh

soupirail, *pl* **-aux** /supiʀaj, o/ *m* cellar window

soupirer /supiʀe/ [**v1**] *vi* to sigh

souple /supl/ *adj* **1** ‹*body*› supple; ‹*stalk*› flexible; ‹*hair*› soft
2 ‹*step, style*› flowing; ‹*shape*› smooth
3 ‹*rule*› flexible

souplesse /suplɛs/ *f* **1** (of stalk) flexibility; (of hair) softness; (of body) suppleness
2 (of step) litheness; (of gesture) grace; (of car) smoothness; (of style) fluidity
3 (of rule) flexibility

source /suʀs/ *f* **1** spring
2 source; **prendre sa ~ dans** *or* **à** ‹*river*› to rise in *or* at; **citer ses ~s** to give one's sources
IDIOMS **ça coule de ~** it's obvious; **retour aux ~s** return to basics

sourcil /suʀsi/ *m* eyebrow

sourciller /suʀsije/ [**v1**] *vi* to raise one's eyebrows; **sans ~** without batting an eyelid (BrE) *or* eyelash (AmE)

sourd, **~e** /suʀ, suʀd/ **A** *adj* **1** deaf; **~ à** deaf to ‹*pleas*›
2 ‹*noise*› dull; ‹*voice*› muffled
3 ‹*pain*› dull
4 ‹*consonant*› voiceless, surd
B *mf* deaf person; **les ~s** the deaf
IDIOMS **faire la ~e oreille** to turn a deaf ear; **comme un ~** ‹*shout*› at the top of one's voice; ‹*hit, strike*› like one possessed; **ce n'est pas tombé dans l'oreille d'un ~** it didn't go unheard

sourdine /suʀdin/ *f* (Mus) mute; (on piano) soft pedal; **écouter la radio en ~** to have the radio on quietly

sourd-muet, **sourde-muette**, *pl* **sourds-muets**, **sourdes-muettes** /suʀmɥɛ, suʀdmɥɛt/ **A** *adj* deaf and dumb
B *mf* deaf-mute

souriant, **~e** /suʀjɑ̃, ɑ̃t/ *adj* smiling

souriceau, *pl* **~x** /suʀiso/ *m* young mouse

souricière /suʀisjɛʀ/ *f* **1** mousetrap
2 trap

sourire¹ /suʀiʀ/ [**v68**] *vi* **1** to smile; **~ jusqu'aux oreilles** to grin from ear to ear
2 ~ à qn ‹*fate, fortune*› to smile on sb

sourire² /suʀiʀ/ *m* smile; **le ~ aux lèvres** with a smile on one's face

souris /suʀi/ *f inv* mouse

sournois, **~e** /suʀnwa, az/ *adj* ‹*person, look*› sly; ‹*behaviour*› underhand; ‹*pain*› insidious

sous /su/ *prep* **1** under, underneath; **un journal ~ le bras** a newspaper under one's arm; **~ la pluie** in the rain
2 under; **~ le numéro 4757** under number 4757
3 during; **~ la présidence de Mitterrand** during Mitterrand's presidency
4 within; **~ peu** before long
5 ~ traitement undergoing treatment; **~ antibiotiques** on antibiotics; **travailler ~ Windows®** (Comput) to work in Windows®

sous-alimenté, **~e**, *mpl* **~s** /suzalimɑ̃te/ *adj* undernourished

sous-bois /subwɑ/ *m inv* undergrowth

sous-catégorie, *pl* **~s** /sukategɔʀi/ *f* subcategory

sous-chef, *pl* **~s** /suʃɛf/ *m* second-in-command

souscripteur, **-trice** /suskʀiptœʀ, tʀis/ *mf* subscriber (**de** to)

souscription /suskʀipsjɔ̃/ *f* **1** subscription
2 ~ d'un contrat d'assurances taking out an insurance policy

souscrire /suskʀiʀ/ [**v67**] **A** *vt* to take out ‹*insurance*›; to sign ‹*contract*›; to subscribe ‹*sum of money*›
B souscrire à *v+prep* to subscribe to

souscrit, **~e A** *pp* ▸ **souscrire**
B *pp adj* **1** subscribed
2 subscript

sous-cutané, **~e**, *mpl* **~s** /sukytane/ *adj* subcutaneous

sous-développé, **~e**, *mpl* **~s** /sudevlɔpe/ *adj* underdeveloped

sous-directeur, **-trice**, *mpl* **~s** /sudiʀɛktœʀ, tʀis/ *mf* assistant manager

sous-direction, *pl* **~s** /sudiʀɛksjɔ̃/ *f* division; **~ des affaires économiques et financières** economic and financial affairs division

sous-effectif, *pl* **~s** /suzefɛktif/ *m* understaffing; **ils sont en ~** they're understaffed

sous-employer /suzɑ̃plwaje/ [**v23**] *vt* to underemploy

sous-entendre /suzɑ̃tɑ̃dʀ/ [**v6**] *vt* to imply

sous-entendu, **~e**, *mpl* **~s** /suzɑ̃tɑ̃dy/
A *pp* ▸ **sous-entendre**
B *pp adj* understood
C *m* innuendo

sous-équipé, **~e**, *mpl* **~s** /suzekipe/ *adj* underequipped

sous-estimer /suzestime/ [**v1**] *vt* to underestimate

sous-évaluer /suzevalɥe/ [**v1**] *vt* to underestimate; to undervalue

sous-fifre, *pl* **~s** /sufifʀ/ *m* (fam) underling

S

sous-jacent, **~e**, *mpl* **~s** /suʒasɑ̃, ɑ̃t/ *adj*
1 ‹*idea, problem, tension*› underlying
2 subjacent

sous-lieutenant, *pl* **~s** /suljøtnɑ̃/ *m* (in the army) ≈ second lieutenant; (in the air force) ≈ pilot officer

sous-louer /sulwe/ [**v1**] *vt* to sublet; to sublease

sous-main /sumɛ̃/ **A** *m inv* desk blotter
B **en sous-main** *phr* secretly

sous-marin, **~e**, *mpl* **~s** /sumaʀɛ̃, in/
A *adj* submarine, underwater; deep-sea
B *m* **1** submarine
2 (fam) spy

sous-marque, *pl* **~s** /sumaʀk/ *f* sub-brand

sous-officier, *pl* **~s** /suzɔfisje/ *m* non-commissioned officer

sous-ordre, *pl* **~s** /suzɔʀdʀ/ *m* suborder

sous-payer /supeje/ [**v21**] *vt* to underpay

sous-préfecture, *pl* **~s** /supʀefɛktyʀ/ *nf: administrative subdivision of a department in France*

sous-produit, *pl* **~s** /supʀɔdɥi/ *m* **1** by-product
2 second-rate product

sous-prolétariat, *pl* **~s** /supʀɔletaʀja/ *m* underclass

sous-pull, *pl* **~s** /supyl/ *m* thin polo-neck jumper

soussigné, **~e** /susiɲe/ *adj, mf* undersigned

sous-sol, *pl* **~s** /susɔl/ *m* **1** basement
2 subsoil

sous-tasse, *pl* **~s** /sutas/ *f* saucer

sous-titrage, *pl* **~s** /sutitʀaʒ/ *m* subtitling

sous-titre, *pl* **~s** /sutitʀ/ *m* subtitle

sous-titrer /sutitʀe/ [**v1**] *vt* to subtitle

soustraction /sustʀaksjɔ̃/ *f* subtraction

soustraire /sustʀɛʀ/ [**v58**] **A** *vt* **1** to subtract
2 to steal
3 to take away ‹*person*›; **~ qn/qch à la vue de qn** to hide sb/sth from sb
4 to shield ‹*person*›; **~ qn à la mort** to save sb's life
B **se soustraire** *v refl* (+ *v être*) **1 se ~ à** to escape from
2 se ~ à la justice to escape justice

S

sous-traitance, *pl* **~s** /sutʀetɑ̃s/ *f* subcontracting; **travail donné en ~** work contracted out

sous-traiter /sutʀete/ [**v1**] *vt* to subcontract

sous-verre /suvɛʀ/ *m inv* **1** clip frame
2 coaster

sous-vêtement, *pl* **~s** /suvetmɑ̃/ *m* underwear

soutane /sutan/ *f* cassock

soute /sut/ *f* hold; **~ à bagages** baggage hold

soutenable /sutnabl/ *adj* **1** bearable; **pas ~** unbearable
2 tenable

soutenance /sutnɑ̃s/ *f* viva (voce) (BrE), orals (AmE)

soutènement /sutɛnmɑ̃/ *m* retaining structure; (in mine) props

souteneur /sutnœʀ/ *m* pimp (fam), procurer

⚷ **soutenir** /sutniʀ/ [**v36**] **A** *vt* **1** (gen) to support ‹*person, team, currency*›; **~ à bout de bras** to keep [sb/sth] afloat ‹*person, project*›; **~ qn contre qn** to side with sb against sb; **~ le moral de qn** to keep sb's spirits up
2 to maintain ‹*contrary*›; to defend ‹*paradox*›; to uphold ‹*opinion*›
3 to keep [sb] going
4 to keep [sth] going ‹*conversation*›; to keep up ‹*effort, pace*›
5 to withstand ‹*shock, attack, stares*›; to bear ‹*comparison*›
6 ~ sa thèse to have one's viva (voce) (BrE) *or* defense (AmE)
B **se soutenir** *v refl* (+ *v être*) to support each other

soutenu, **~e** /sutny/ **A** *pp* ▶ **soutenir**
B *pp adj* ‹*effort, activity*› sustained; ‹*attention*› close; ‹*rhythm*› steady
C *adj* **1** ‹*market*› firm; ‹*colour*› deep; ‹*language*› formal
2 (Mus) ‹*note*› sustained

souterrain, **~e** /sutɛʀɛ̃, ɛn/ **A** *adj*
1 underground
2 économie ~e black economy
B *m* underground passage, tunnel

⚷ **soutien** /sutjɛ̃/ *m* support

soutien-gorge, *pl* **soutiens-gorge** /sutjɛ̃gɔʀʒ/ *m* bra

soutirer /sutiʀe/ [**v1**] *vt* **~ qch à qn** to squeeze sth out of sb ‹*money*›; to extract sth from sb ‹*confession*›

souvenance /suvnɑ̃s/ *f* **à ma ~** as far as I recall; **avoir ~ de qch** to remember sth

souvenir[1]: **se souvenir** /suvniʀ/ [**v36**] *v refl* (+ *v être*) **se ~ de qn/qch** to remember sb/sth

⚷ **souvenir**[2] /suvniʀ/ *m* **1** memory; **garder un bon ~ de qch** to have happy memories of sth; **ne pas avoir ~ de** to have no recollection of
2 memory; **s'effacer du ~ de qn** to fade from sb's memory
3 souvenir; memento; **en ~** as a souvenir; as a memento; as a keepsake; **boutique de ~s** souvenir shop (BrE) *or* store (AmE)
4 mon bon ~ à remember me to

⚷ **souvent** /suvɑ̃/ *adv* often

souverain, **~e** /suvʀɛ̃, ɛn/ **A** *adj* **1** ‹*state*› sovereign; ‹*authority*› supreme
2 ‹*happiness, scorn*› supreme
3 ‹*remedy*› sovereign; ‹*advice, virtue*› sterling
4 ‹*person*› haughty

⚷ key word

B *mf* sovereign, monarch

souverainement /suvʀɛnmɑ̃/ *adv* **votre attitude me déplaît ~** I dislike your attitude intensely

souveraineté /suvʀɛnte/ *f* sovereignty

soviet /sɔvjɛt/ *m* soviet; **Soviet suprême** Supreme Soviet

soviétique /sɔvjetik/ *adj* Soviet

soyeux, **-euse** /swajø, øz/ *adj* silky

soyez /swaje/ ▶ **être**[1]

soyons /swajɔ̃/ ▶ **être**[1]

SPA /ɛspea/ *f* (*abbr* = **Société protectrice des animaux**) society for the prevention of cruelty to animals

spacieux, **-ieuse** /spasjø, øz/ *adj* spacious

spaghetti /spageti/ *m inv* **des ~** spaghetti

sparadrap /spaʀadʀa/ *m* **1** surgical *or* adhesive tape
2 (sticking) plaster (BrE), Band-aid®

spartiate /spaʀsjat/ *adj*, *mf* Spartan

spasme /spasm/ *m* spasm

spasmophilie /spasmɔfili/ *f* spasmophilia

spatial, **~e**, *mpl* **-iaux** /spasjal, o/ *adj*
1 spatial
2 space; **vaisseau ~** spaceship

spatule /spatyl/ *f* **1** spatula
2 filling knife

speaker /spikœʀ/, **speakerine** /spikʀin/ *mf* announcer

spécial, **~e**, *mpl* **-iaux** /spesjal, o/ *adj*
1 special
2 odd

spécialement /spesjalmɑ̃/ *adv* **1** specially
2 especially; **pas ~** not especially

spécialiser: **se spécialiser** /spesjalize/ [**v1**] *v refl* (+ *v être*) to specialize

spécialiste /spesjalist/ *mf* specialist

spécialité /spesjalite/ *f* speciality (BrE), specialty (AmE)

spécificité /spesifisite/ *f* **1** specificity
2 characteristic
3 uniqueness

spécifier /spesifje/ [**v2**] *vt* to specify

spécifique /spesifik/ *adj* specific

spécimen /spesimɛn/ *m* **1** specimen
2 (free) sample
3 (fam) odd specimen (fam)

spectacle /spɛktakl/ *m* **1** sight; **se donner** *or* **s'offrir en ~** to make an exhibition of oneself
2 show; **~ de danse** dance show; **'~s'** 'entertainment'; **film à grand ~** spectacular
3 show business

spectaculaire /spɛktakylɛʀ/ *adj* spectacular

spectateur, **-trice** /spɛktatœʀ, tʀis/ *mf*
1 member of the audience
2 spectator

spectre /spɛktʀ/ *m* **1** ghost
2 spectre (BrE)
3 ~ lumineux spectrum of light

spéculateur, **-trice** /spekylatœʀ, tʀis/ *mf* speculator

spéculatif, **-ive** /spekylatif, iv/ *adj* speculative

spéculation /spekylasjɔ̃/ *f* **1** (Econ) speculation; **~ sur** speculation in
2 (gen) speculation (**sur** on, about)

spéculer /spekyle/ [**v1**] *vi* to speculate; **~ à la hausse/baisse** to bull/bear

spéléologie /speleɔlɔʒi/ *f* **1** caving, potholing (BrE), spelunking (AmE)
2 speleology

spermatozoïde /spɛʀmatɔzɔid/ *m* spermatozoon

sperme /spɛʀm/ *m* sperm

sphère /sfɛʀ/ *f* sphere

sphérique /sfeʀik/ *adj* spherical

sphincter /sfɛ̃ktɛʀ/ *m* sphincter

sphinx /sfɛ̃ks/ *m inv* **1** Sphinx
2 hawkmoth

spirale /spiʀal/ *f* spiral

spiritisme /spiʀitism/ *m* spiritualism

spiritualité /spiʀitɥalite/ *f* spirituality

spirituel, **-elle** /spiʀitɥɛl/ *adj* **1** spiritual
2 witty

spiritueux, **-euse** /spiʀitɥø, øz/ *m inv* spirit

splendeur /splɑ̃dœʀ/ *f* (of scenery, site) splendour (BrE); (of era, reign) glory

splendide /splɑ̃did/ *adj* splendid; stunning

spolier /spɔlje/ [**v2**] *vt* to despoil (**de** of)

spongieux, **-ieuse** /spɔ̃ʒjø, øz/ *adj* spongy

sponsoriser /spɔ̃sɔʀize/ [**v1**] *vt* to sponsor

spontané, **~e** /spɔ̃tane/ *adj* spontaneous

spontanéité /spɔ̃taneite/ *f* spontaneity

sporadique /spɔʀadik/ *adj* sporadic

spore /spɔʀ/ *f* spore

sport /spɔʀ/ *m* sport; sports; **aller aux ~s d'hiver** to go on a winter sports holiday (BrE) *or* vacation (AmE)

sportif, **-ive** /spɔʀtif, iv/ **A** *adj* **1** ‹*event*› sports; **je ne suis pas ~** I'm not the sporty type
2 ‹*appearance*› athletic, sporty (fam)
B *mf* sportsman/sportswoman; **c'est un ~** he's athletic

spot /spɔt/ *m* **1** spotlight
2 ~ (publicitaire) commercial

squale /skwal/ *m* shark

square /skwaʀ/ *m* small public garden

squash /skwaʃ/ *m* squash

squatter[1] /skwate/ [**v1**] *vt* to squat in

squatter[2] /skwatœʀ/ *m* squatter

squelette /skəlɛt/ *m* **1** skeleton
2 (fam) bag of bones (fam)
3 framework

squelettique /skəlɛtik/ *adj* ‹*person, legs*› scrawny; ‹*tree*› skeletal; ‹*report*› sketchy

SRAS /ɛsɛʀaɛs/ *m* (*abbr* = **syndrome respiratoire aigu sévère**) SARS

S

stabiliser /stabilize/ [**v1**] **A** *vt* to stabilize; to consolidate
B se stabiliser *v refl* (+ *v être*) ‹*unemployment*› to stabilize; ‹*person*› to become stable
stabilité /stabilite/ *f* stability
stable /stabl/ *adj* stable
stade /stad/ *m* **1** (Sport) stadium
2 stage; **à ce ~** at this stage
stage /staʒ/ *m* **1** professional training
2 work experience; **~ pratique** period of work experience
3 course; **suivre un ~ de formation** to go on a training course
stagiaire /staʒjɛʀ/ *mf* **1** trainee
2 student teacher
stagnation /stagnasjɔ̃/ *f* stagnation
stagner /stagne/ [**v1**] *vi* to stagnate
stalactite /stalaktit/ *f* stalactite
stalagmite /stalagmit/ *f* stalagmite
stalle /stal/ *f* stall
stand /stɑ̃d/ *m* stand; stall
■ **~ de tir** shooting range; shooting gallery
standard /stɑ̃daʀ/ **A** *adj inv* standard
B *m* switchboard
standardisation /stɑ̃daʀdizasjɔ̃/ *f* standardization
standardiste /stɑ̃daʀdist/ *mf* switchboard operator
standing /stɑ̃diŋ/ *m* **1 de ~** ‹*apartment*› luxury
2 standard of living
star /staʀ/ *f* star
starter /staʀtɛʀ/ *m* (Aut) choke
station /stasjɔ̃/ *f* **1** station; taxi rank (BrE), taxi stand; **c'est à deux ~s d'ici** it's two stops from here
2 ~ (de radio) (radio) station
3 ~ balnéaire seaside resort; **~ thermale** spa
4 ~ debout *or* **verticale** upright posture *or* position
5 stop, pause
stationnaire /stasjɔnɛʀ/ *adj* **1** stationary
2 stable
stationnement /stasjɔnmɑ̃/ *m* parking
stationner /stasjɔne/ [**v1**] *vi* to park
station-service, *pl* **stations-service** /stasjɔ̃sɛʀvis/ *f* service *or* filling station
statique /statik/ *adj* static
statistique /statistik/ *f* **1** statistics
2 statistic
statue /staty/ *f* statue
statuer /statɥe/ [**v1**] *vi* to give a ruling
statuette /statɥɛt/ *f* statuette
statu quo /statykwo/ *m inv* status quo
stature /statyʀ/ *f* **1** stature
2 height
✍ **statut** /staty/ *m* **1** statute
2 status

✍ key word

statutaire /statytɛʀ/ *adj* statutory
steak /stɛk/ *m* steak; **un ~ haché** a hamburger
sténodactylo /stenodaktilo/ **A** *mf* shorthand typist (BrE), stenographer (AmE)
B *f* shorthand typing (BrE), stenography (AmE)
sténographier /stenɔgʀafje/ [**v2**] *vt* to take [sth] down in shorthand
sténotypiste /stenɔtipist/ *mf* stenotypist
steppe /stɛp/ *f* steppe
stéréo /steʀeo/ *adj inv*, *f* stereo
stéréophonique /steʀeɔfɔnik/ *adj* stereophonic
stéréotype /steʀeɔtip/ *m* **1** stereotype
2 cliché
stérile /steʀil/ *adj* (gen) sterile; ‹*land*› barren; ‹*discussion*› fruitless
stérilet /steʀilɛ/ *m* coil, IUD
stériliser /steʀilize/ [**v1**] *vt* to sterilize
stérilité /steʀilite/ *f* **1** sterility; barrenness
2 fruitlessness
sterling /stɛʀliŋ/ *adj inv* sterling; **livre ~** pound sterling
sternum /stɛʀnɔm/ *m* breastbone, sternum
stéthoscope /stetɔskɔp/ *m* stethoscope
stigmate /stigmat/ *m* **1** scar
2 mark
stimulant, **~e** /stimylɑ̃, ɑ̃t/ *adj* invigorating; bracing; stimulating
stimulation /stimylasjɔ̃/ *f* stimulation
stimuler /stimyle/ [**v1**] **A** *vt* **1** to stimulate ‹*organ, function*›
2 to spur [sb] on
B *vi* **1** to be bracing
2 (fam) to act as a spur
stimulus, *pl* **stimuli** /stimylys, stimyli/ *m* stimulus
stipuler /stipyle/ [**v1**] *vt* to stipulate
stock /stɔk/ *m* stock; **avoir qch en ~** to have sth in stock
stockage /stɔkaʒ/ *m* **1** stocking; stockpiling
2 (Comput) storage
stocker /stɔke/ [**v1**] *vt* **1** to stock
2 to stockpile
3 to store ‹*data*›
stoïque /stɔik/ *adj* stoical
stop /stɔp/ *m* **1** stop sign
2 (fam) hitch-hiking (fam); **prendre qn en ~** to give sb a lift (BrE) *or* ride (AmE)
stopper /stɔpe/ [**v1**] **A** *vt* **1** to stop; to halt ‹*development*›
2 to mend
B *vi* to stop
store /stɔʀ/ *m* **1** blind
2 awning
strabisme /stʀabism/ *m* squint
strapontin /stʀapɔ̃tɛ̃/ *m* foldaway seat
stratagème /stʀataʒɛm/ *m* stratagem
strate /stʀat/ *f* stratum

stratégie /stʀateʒi/ *f* strategy
stratégique /stʀateʒik/ *adj* strategic
stratifié, **~e** /stʀatifje/ *adj* **1** stratified
2 laminated
stratosphère /stʀatɔsfɛʀ/ *f* stratosphere
streaming /stʀimiŋ/ *m* streaming; **visionner des films en ~** to watch streaming videos
stress /stʀɛs/ *m inv* stress
stressant, **~e** /stʀɛsɑ̃, ɑ̃t/ *adj* stressful
stresser /stʀese/ [**v1**] *vt* to put [sb] on edge; to put [sb] under stress
strict, **~e** /stʀikt/ *adj* **1** (gen) strict; **au sens ~** in the strict sense of the word
2 ‹*hairstyle, outfit*› severe
strident, **~e** /stʀidɑ̃, ɑ̃t/ *adj* ‹*noise*› piercing; ‹*voice*› strident
strie /stʀi/ *f* **1** streak
2 groove
3 (in geology) **des ~s** striation
strip-tease /stʀiptiz/ *m* striptease
strophe /stʀɔf/ *f* stanza, verse
structure /stʀyktyʀ/ *f* **1** structure
2 organization; **~ d'accueil** shelter, refuge
structurer /stʀyktyʀe/ [**v1**] *vt* to structure
stuc /styk/ *m* stucco
studieux, **-ieuse** /stydjø, øz/ *adj* ‹*pupil*› studious; ‹*holiday*› study
studio /stydjo/ *m* **1** studio flat (BrE), studio apartment (AmE)
2 studio
stupéfaction /stypefaksjɔ̃/ *f* stupefaction
stupéfait, **~e** /stypefɛ, ɛt/ *adj* astounded
stupéfiant, **~e** /stypefjɑ̃, ɑ̃t/ **A** *adj* stunning **B** *m* drug, narcotic
stupéfier /stypefje/ [**v2**] *vt* to astound
stupeur /stypœʀ/ *f* **1** astonishment
2 (Med) stupor
stupide /stypid/ *adj* stupid
stupidité /stypidite/ *f* stupidity
style /stil/ *m* **1** style; **~ de vie** lifestyle; **c'est bien ton ~ de faire** it's just like you to do
2 meubles de ~ (reproduction) period furniture
3 speech form; **~ indirect** indirect *or* reported speech
stylé, **~e** /stile/ *adj* well trained
styliser /stilize/ [**v1**] *vt* to stylize
styliste /stilist/ *mf* fashion designer
stylo /stilo/ *m* (fountain) pen; **~ bille** ball-point pen; **~ feutre** felt-tip pen
su[1], **~e** /sy/ ▶ **savoir**[1]
su[2] /sy/ *m* **au vu et au ~ de tous** openly
suaire /sɥɛʀ/ *m* shroud
suant, **~e** /sɥɑ̃, ɑ̃t/ *adj* **1** sweaty
2 (fam) deadly dull
suave /sɥav/ *adj* ‹*perfume, music, smile*› sweet; ‹*voice*› mellifluous; ‹*person, manner*› suave
subalterne /sybaltɛʀn/ *mf* subordinate; (Mil) low-ranking officer, subaltern
subconscient /sybkɔ̃sjɑ̃/ *m* subconscious
subdiviser /sybdivize/ [**v1**] *vt* to subdivide
subir /sybiʀ/ [**v3**] *vt* **1** to be subjected to ‹*violence, pressure*›; to suffer ‹*defeat, damage*›
2 to take ‹*examination*›; to have ‹*operation, test*›; **~ l'influence de qn** to be under sb's influence
3 to put up with
4 to undergo
subit, **~e** /sybi, it/ *adj* sudden
subitement /sybitmɑ̃/ *adv* suddenly
subjectif, **-ive** /sybʒɛktif, iv/ *adj* subjective
subjectivité /sybʒɛktivite/ *f* subjectivity
subjonctif /sybʒɔ̃ktif/ *m* subjunctive
subjuguer /sybʒyge/ [**v1**] *vt* **1** to captivate, to enthral (BrE)
2 to subjugate
sublime /syblim/ *adj* sublime
sublimer /syblime/ [**v1**] *vt, vi* to sublimate
submerger /sybmɛʀʒe/ [**v13**] *vt* **1** to submerge
2 to flood ‹*market, switchboard*›
3 ‹*crowd, emotion*› to overwhelm
4 ~ qn de travail to inundate sb with work
subodorer /sybɔdɔʀe/ [**v1**] *vt* to detect
subordination /sybɔʀdinasjɔ̃/ *f* subordination
subordonné, **~e** /sybɔʀdɔne/ *mf* subordinate
subordonnée /sybɔʀdɔne/ *f* subordinate clause; **~ relative** relative clause
subordonner /sybɔʀdɔne/ [**v1**] *vt* **1 être subordonné à qn** to be subordinate to sb
2 être subordonné à qch to be subject to sth
suborner /sybɔʀne/ [**v1**] *vt* to bribe ‹*witness*›
subreptice /sybʀɛptis/ *adj* surreptitious
subside /sybsid/ *m* **1** grant
2 allowance
subsidiaire /sybzidjɛʀ/ *adj* subsidiary; **question ~** tiebreaker
subsistance /sybzistɑ̃s/ *f* subsistence; **(moyens de) ~** means of support
subsister /sybziste/ [**v1**] *vi* **1** to remain
2 ‹*custom*› to survive
3 ça leur suffit à peine pour ~ it's barely enough for them to live on
substance /sypstɑ̃s/ *f* substance
substantif /sypstɑ̃tif/ *m* noun, substantive
substituer /sypstitɥe/ [**v1**] **A** *vt* to substitute **B se substituer** *v refl* (+ *v être*) **se ~ à** to take the place of
substitut /sypstity/ *m* substitute
substitution /sypstitysjɔ̃/ *f* substitution; **produit de ~ du sucre** sugar substitute
subterfuge /sypteʀfyʒ/ *m* ploy, subterfuge
subtil, **~e** /syptil/ *adj* subtle; skilful (BrE)
subtiliser /syptilize/ [**v1**] *vt* **~ qch à qn** to steal sth from sb
subtilité /syptilite/ *f* subtlety

subvenir /sybvəniʀ/ [**v36**] *v+prep* **~ à** to meet ‹*expenses, needs*›; **~ aux besoins de sa famille** to provide for one's family

subvention /sybvɑ̃sjɔ̃/ *f* **1** grant
2 subsidy

subventionner /sybvɑ̃sjɔne/ [**v1**] *vt* to subsidize

subversif, **-ive** /sybvɛʀsif, iv/ *adj* subversive

subversion /sybvɛʀsjɔ̃/ *f* subversion

suc /syk/ *m* (of fruit) juice; (of plant) sap; **~s digestifs** *or* **gastriques** gastric juices

succédané /syksedane/ *m* substitute, ersatz

succéder /syksede/ [**v14**] **A** **succéder à** *v+prep* **1 ~ à** to succeed ‹*person*›
2 ~ à to follow
B **se succéder** *v refl* (+ *v être*) to succeed *or* follow one another

succès /syksɛ/ *m inv* success; **avoir du ~, être un ~** to be a success; ‹*record*› to be a hit; **à ~** ‹*actor, film*› successful

successeur /syksesœʀ/ *m* successor

successif, **-ive** /syksesif, iv/ *adj* successive

succession /syksesjɔ̃/ *f* **1** series, succession
2 (Law) succession; **prendre la ~ de** to succeed
3 inheritance, estate

succinct, **~e** /syksɛ̃, ɛ̃t/ *adj* ‹*essay*› succinct; ‹*speech*› brief; ‹*meal*› frugal

succomber /sykɔ̃be/ [**v1**] *vi* **1** to die
2 to give way, to yield; **~ sous le poids** to collapse under the weight
3 ~ à to succumb to ‹*charm, despair*›; to give in to ‹*temptation*›

succulent, **~e** /sykylɑ̃, ɑ̃t/ *adj* delicious

succursale /sykyʀsal/ *f* branch, outlet

sucer /syse/ [**v12**] *vt* to suck

sucette /sysɛt/ *f* lollipop, lolly (BrE) (fam)

suçoter /sysɔte/ [**v1**] *vt* to suck

sucre /sykʀ/ *m* **1** sugar
2 sugar lump
■ **~ cristallisé** granulated sugar; **~ glace** icing sugar (BrE), powdered sugar (AmE); **~ en poudre** caster sugar (BrE), superfine sugar (AmE); **~ roux** brown sugar
IDIOM **casser du ~ sur le dos de qn** to run sb down, to bad-mouth sb (fam)

sucré, **~e** /sykʀe/ *adj* sweet; sweetened

sucrer /sykʀe/ [**v1**] *vt* to put sugar in; to sweeten

sucrerie /sykʀəʀi/ *f* **1** sugar refinery
2 ~s sweets (BrE), candy (AmE)

sucrier /sykʀije/ *m* sugar bowl

sud /syd/ **A** *adj inv* south; southern
B *m* **1** south; **exposé au ~** south-facing
2 le Sud the South

sudation /sydasjɔ̃/ *f* sweating

sud-est /sydɛst/ **A** *adj inv* south-east; south-eastern
B *m* south-east; **le Sud-Est asiatique** South East Asia

sudiste /sydist/ *adj*, *mf* Confederate

sud-ouest /sydwɛst/ **A** *adj inv* south-west; south-western
B *m* south-west

Suède /sɥɛd/ *pr f* Sweden

suédois, **~e** /sɥedwa, az/ **A** *adj* Swedish
B *m* (language) Swedish

Suédois, **~e** /sɥedwa, az/ *mf* Swede

suer /sɥe/ [**v1**] **A** *vt* to sweat; **~ sang et eau** to sweat blood and tears
B *vi* to sweat; **faire ~ qn** (fam) to bore sb stiff (fam)

sueur /sɥœʀ/ *f* sweat; **j'en avais des ~s froides** I was in a cold sweat about it

suffi /syfi/ ▶ **suffire**

suffire /syfiʀ/ [**v64**] **A** *vi* to be enough; **un rien suffit à le mettre en colère** it only takes the slightest thing to make him lose his temper
B **se suffire** *v refl* (+ *v être*) **se ~ (à soi-même)** to be self-sufficient
C *v impers* **il suffit de me téléphoner** all you have to do is phone me; **il suffit d'une lampe pour éclairer la pièce** one lamp is enough to light the room; **il suffit que je sorte sans parapluie pour qu'il pleuve!** every time I go out without my umbrella, it's guaranteed to rain; **ça suffit (comme ça)!** that's enough!

suffisamment /syfizamɑ̃/ *adv* enough

suffisance /syfizɑ̃s/ *f* self-importance

suffisant, **~e** /syfizɑ̃, ɑ̃t/ *adj* **1** sufficient
2 self-important

suffixe /syfiks/ *m* suffix

suffocant, **~e** /syfɔkɑ̃, ɑ̃t/ *adj* **1** suffocating
2 staggering

suffocation /syfɔkasjɔ̃/ *f* suffocation; choking

suffoquer /syfɔke/ [**v1**] **A** *vt* to suffocate
B *vi* **1** to suffocate
2 to choke

suffrage /syfʀaʒ/ *m* suffrage; **~s exprimés** recorded votes

suggérer /sygʒeʀe/ [**v14**] *vt* to suggest

suggestif, **-ive** /sygʒɛstif, iv/ *adj* ‹*music*› evocative; ‹*pose*› suggestive; ‹*dress*› provocative

suggestion /sygʒɛstjɔ̃/ *f* suggestion

suicidaire /sɥisidɛʀ/ *adj* suicidal

suicide /sɥisid/ *m* suicide

suicider: **se suicider** /sɥiside/ [**v1**] *v refl* (+ *v être*) to commit suicide

suie /sɥi/ *f* soot

suinter /sɥɛ̃te/ [**v1**] *vi* **1** ‹*liquid*› to seep; to ooze
2 ‹*walls*› to sweat; ‹*wound*› to weep

suis /sɥi/ ▶ **être**[1]

suisse /sɥis/ **A** *adj* Swiss
B *m* **1** Swiss Guard
2 verger

S

key word

Suisse /sɥis/ *pr f* Switzerland
suite /sɥit/ **A** *f* **1** rest; **la ~ des événements** what happens next
2 (of story) continuation; (of series) next instalment (BrE); (of meal) next course
3 sequel
4 result; **les ~s** (of action) the consequences; (of incident) the repercussions; (of illness) the after-effects
5 donner ~ à to follow up ‹*complaint*›; to deal with ‹*order*›; **rester sans ~** ‹*plan*› to be dropped
6 faire ~ à to follow upon ‹*incident*›; **prendre la ~ de qn** to take over from sb
7 avoir de la ~ dans les idées to be single-minded
8 (of incidents) series; (of successes) run
9 (hotel) suite
10 (of monarch) suite
11 (Mus) suite
B de suite *phr* in succession, in a row; **et ainsi de ~** and so on
C par la suite *phr* **1** afterwards
2 later
D par suite de *phr* due to
E à la suite de *phr* **1** following
2 behind
F suite à *phr* **~ à votre lettre** with reference to your letter
suivant¹ /sɥivɑ̃/ *prep* **1** in accordance with ‹*tradition*›; **~ leur habitude** as they usually do
2 depending on
3 according to
suivant², **~e** /sɥivɑ̃, ɑ̃t/ **A** *adj* **1** following
2 next
B *mf* **le ~** the following one; the next one
C le suivant, **la suivante** *phr* as follows
suivi, **~e** /sɥivi/ **A** *pp* ▶ **suivre**
B *pp adj* **1** ‹*work*› steady; ‹*effort*› sustained; ‹*correspondence*› regular
2 ‹*policy*› coherent
C *m* **1** monitoring
2 follow-up; **~ des malades** follow-up care for patients
suivre /sɥivʀ/ [**v62**] **A** *vt* **1** to follow ‹*person, car*›; **suivez le guide!** this way, please!
2 to follow, to come after ‹*period, incident*›; **'à ~'** 'to be continued'
3 to follow ‹*route, coast*›; ‹*road*› to run alongside ‹*railway line*›; **~ le droit chemin** to keep to the straight and narrow
4 to follow ‹*example*›; to obey ‹*impulse*›
5 to follow ‹*lesson, match*›; to follow the progress of ‹*pupil, patient*›; **~ l'actualité** to keep up with the news
6 to do ‹*course*›
7 to follow ‹*explanation, logic*›; **je vous suis** I'm with you
8 to keep pace with [sb/sth]
B *vi* **faire ~ son courrier** to have one's mail forwarded; **faire ~** please forward
C se suivre *v refl* (+ *v être*) **1** ‹*numbers, pages*› to be in order; ‹*cards*› to be consecutive
2 to happen one after the other
D *v impers* **comme suit** as follows
sujet, **-ette** /syʒɛ, ɛt/ **A** *adj* **être ~ à** to be prone to ‹*migraine*›
B *m* **1** subject; **un ~ d'actualité** a topical issue; **c'est à quel ~?** what is it about?; **au ~ de** about
2 (Sch) question; **~ libre** topic of one's own choice; **hors ~** off the subject
3 cause; **c'est un ~ d'étonnement** it is amazing
4 c'est un brillant ~ he's a brilliant student
5 (of kingdom) subject
sulfate /sylfat/ *m* sulphate (BrE), sulfate (AmE)
sulfureux, **-euse** /sylfyʀø, øz/ *adj* ‹*vapour*› sulphurous (BrE), sulfurous (AmE); ‹*bath*› sulphur (BrE), sulfur (AmE)
sultan /syltɑ̃/ *m* sultan
sultane /syltan/ *f* sultana
summum /sɔm(m)ɔm/ *m* height
sumo /sumo, symo/ *m inv* sumo wrestling
sunnisme /syn(n)ism/ *m* Sunnism
sunnite /syn(n)it/ *adj, nmf* Sunni
super¹ /sypɛʀ/ *pref* super
super² /sypɛʀ/ **A** *adj inv* (fam) great (fam)
B *m* four-star (petrol) (BrE), super
superbe /sypɛʀb/ *adj* superb, magnificent
superbement /sypɛʀbəmɑ̃/ *adv* **1** superbly
2 haughtily
supercarburant /sypɛʀkaʀbyʀɑ̃/ *m* four-star petrol (BrE), super
supercherie /sypɛʀʃəʀi/ *f* **1** deception
2 hoax
supérette /sypeʀɛt/ *f* minimarket
superficie /sypɛʀfisi/ *f* area
superficiel, **-ielle** /sypɛʀfisjɛl/ *adj* (gen) superficial; ‹*layer*› surface
superflu, **~e** /sypɛʀfly/ *adj* **1** superfluous
2 unnecessary
supérieur, **~e** /sypeʀjœʀ/ **A** *adj* **1** ‹*jaw, lip, floor*› upper
2 ‹*ranks, classes*› upper
3 higher (**à** than); ‹*size*› bigger (**à** than); ‹*length*› longer (**à** than)
4 ‹*work, quality*› superior (**à** to)
5 ‹*air, tone*› superior
B *mf* **1** superior; **~ hiérarchique** immediate superior
2 (in monastery, convent) Superior
C *m* higher education
supérieurement /sypeʀjœʀmɑ̃/ *adv* exceptionally
supériorité /sypeʀjɔʀite/ *f* superiority
superlatif, **-ive** /sypɛʀlatif, iv/ **A** *adj* superlative
B *m* superlative
supermarché /sypɛʀmaʀʃe/ *m* supermarket
superposer /sypɛʀpoze/ [**v1**] *vt* **1** to stack [sth] (up); **lits superposés** bunk beds
2 to superimpose ‹*drawings*›

S

superposition /sypɛʀpozisjɔ̃/ *f* superposition

superproduction /sypɛʀpʀɔdyksjɔ̃/ *f* blockbuster (fam)

superpuissance /sypɛʀpɥisɑ̃s/ *f* superpower

superstitieux, **-ieuse** /sypɛʀstisjø, øz/ *adj* superstitious

superstition /sypɛʀstisjɔ̃/ *f* superstition

superviser /sypɛʀvize/ [**v1**] *vt* to supervise

supplanter /syplɑ̃te/ [**v1**] *vt* to supplant

suppléant, **~e** /sypleɑ̃, ɑ̃t/ *mf* replacement; (for judge) deputy; (for teacher) supply (BrE) *or* substitute (AmE) teacher; (for doctor) locum

suppléer /syplee/ [**v11**] *v+prep* **~ à** to make up for, to compensate for

supplément /syplemɑ̃/ *m* **1** extra charge; supplement; **le vin est en ~** the wine is extra
2 ~ d'informations additional information
3 (newspaper) supplement

supplémentaire /syplemɑ̃tɛʀ/ *adj* additional, extra; **train ~** relief train

suppliant, **~e** /syplijɑ̃, ɑ̃t/ *adj* ‹*voice*› pleading; ‹*look*› imploring

supplice /syplis/ *m* torture

supplicier /syplisje/ [**v2**] *vt* **1** to torture
2 to execute

supplier /syplije/ [**v2**] *vt* to beg, to beseech

support /sypɔʀ/ *m* **1** support; **servir de ~ à qch** to serve as a support for sth
2 (for ornaments) stand
3 back-up; **~ audiovisuel** audio-visual aid

supportable /sypɔʀtabl/ *adj* bearable

🔑 **supporter¹** /sypɔʀte/ [**v1**] **A** *vt* **1** to support, to bear the weight of ‹*structure*›
2 to bear ‹*costs*›
3 to put up with ‹*misery, behaviour, person*›; to bear ‹*suffering*›; ‹*plant*› to withstand ‹*cold*›; **elle ne supporte pas d'attendre** she can't stand waiting
B se supporter *v refl* (+ *v être*) **ils ne peuvent plus se ~** they can't stand each other any more

supporter² /sypɔʀtœʀ/ *mf* supporter

supporteur, **-trice** /sypɔʀtœʀ, -tʀis/ *mf* supporter

🔑 **supposer** /sypoze/ [**v1**] *vt* **1** to suppose
2 to assume
3 to presuppose

supposition /sypozisjɔ̃/ *f* supposition

suppositoire /sypozitwaʀ/ *m* suppository

suppôt /sypo/ *m* **~ de Satan** fiend

suppression /sypʀesjɔ̃/ *f* removal; abolition; withdrawal; suppression; elimination; breaking, ending; deletion; **~s d'emplois** job cuts

supprimer /sypʀime/ [**v1**] *vt* **1** to cut ‹*job*›; to stop ‹*aid, vibration*›; to abolish ‹*tax, law*›; to remove ‹*effect, obstacle*›; to do away with ‹*class*›; to withdraw ‹*licence*›; to break ‹*monopoly*›; to suppress ‹*evidence*›; to cut out ‹*sugar, salt*›; to delete ‹*word*›; **~ un train** to cancel a train
2 to eliminate ‹*person*›

suppurer /sypyʀe/ [**v1**] *vi* to suppurate

supputer /sypyte/ [**v1**] *vt* to calculate, to work out

supranational, **~e**, *mpl* **-aux** /sypʀanasjɔnal, o/ *adj* supranational

suprématie /sypʀemasi/ *f* supremacy

suprême /sypʀɛm/ *adj* supreme

🔑 **sur¹** /syʀ/ *prep* **1** on; **~ la table** on the table; **prends un verre ~ la table** take a glass from the table; **appliquer la lotion ~ vos cheveux** apply the lotion to your hair; **la clé est ~ la porte** the key is in the door; **écrire ~ du papier** to write on paper; **elle est ~ la photo** she's in the photograph
2 over; **un pont ~ la rivière** a bridge across *or* over the river
3 une table d'un mètre ~ deux a table that measures one metre (BrE) by two; **~ 150 hectares** over an area of 150 hectares
4 se diriger ~ Valence to head for Valence
5 ‹*debate, essay, thesis*› on; ‹*poem*› about
6 être ~ une affaire to be involved in a business deal
7 une personne ~ dix one person out of *or* in ten; **un mardi ~ deux** every other Tuesday
8 faire proposition ~ proposition to make one offer after another
9 ils se sont quittés ~ ces mots with these words, they parted; **~ le moment** at the time; **~ ce, je vous laisse** with that, I must leave you

sur², **~e** /syʀ/ *adj* (slightly) sour

🔑 **sûr**, **~e** /syʀ/ **A** *adj* **1** ‹*information, service, person*› reliable; ‹*opinion, investment*› sound; **d'une main ~e** with a steady hand
2 safe
3 certain; **c'est ~ et certain** it's definite; **à coup ~** definitely
4 sure; **j'en suis ~ et certain** I'm positive; **il est ~ de lui** he's self-confident; **j'en étais ~!** I knew it!
B *adv* **bien ~ (que oui)** of course
IDIOM **être ~ de son coup** (fam) to be confident of success

surabondance /syʀabɔ̃dɑ̃s/ *f* overabundance

surabonder /syʀabɔ̃de/ [**v1**] *vi* to abound

surajouter: **se surajouter** /syʀaʒute/ [**v1**] *v refl* (+ *v être*) to be added on (**à** to)

suranné, **~e** /syʀane/ *adj* ‹*ideas*› outmoded; ‹*style*› outdated

surcharge /syʀʃaʀʒ/ *f* excess load, overload; **une ~ de travail** extra work

surchargé, **~e** /syʀʃaʀʒe/ *adj* ‹*day*› overloaded; ‹*class*› overcrowded

surcharger /syʀʃaʀʒe/ [**v13**] *vt* to overload; **~ qn de travail** to overburden sb with work

surchauffer /syʀʃofe/ [**v1**] *vt* to overheat

🔑 key word

surclasser /syrklase/ [**v1**] *vt* to outclass
surconsommation /syrkõsɔmasjõ/ *f* (Econ) overconsumption; ~ **de médicaments** excessive drug consumption
surcroît /syrkrwa/ *m* increase; **un ~ de travail** extra work; **de ~** moreover
surdité /syrdite/ *f* deafness
surdoué, **~e** /syrdwe/ *adj* (exceptionally) gifted
sureau, *pl* **~x** /syro/ *m* elder (tree)
sureffectif /syrefɛktif/ *m* excess staff
surélever /syrelve/ [**v16**] *vt* to raise the height of ‹*house, road*›
sûrement /syrmɑ̃/ *adv* **1** most probably
2 ~ pas certainly not
3 safely
surenchère /syrɑ̃ʃɛr/ *f* **1** higher bid
2 faire de la ~ to try to go one better
surenchérir /syrɑ̃ʃerir/ [**v3**] *vi* **1** to make a higher bid
2 to chime in
surendetté, **~e** /syrɑ̃dete/ *adj* deeply in debt; overextended
surendettement /syrɑ̃dɛtmɑ̃/ *m* excessive debt
surestimer /syrɛstime/ [**v1**] **A** *vt* to overvalue ‹*property*›; to overrate ‹*qualities*›
B se surestimer *v refl* (+ *v être*) to rate oneself too highly
sûreté /syrte/ *f* **1** (of place, person) safety; (of country) security
2 (of judgement) soundness; (of gesture) steadiness
3 (on gun) safety catch; (on door) safety lock
surévaluer /syrevalɥe/ [**v1**] *vt* to overvalue ‹*currency*›; to overestimate ‹*cost*›
surexciter /syrɛksite/ [**v1**] *vt* to overexcite
surf /sœrf/ *m* surfing
surface /syrfas/ *f* **1** surface; **de ~** ‹*installations*› above ground; ‹*friendliness*› superficial; **faire ~** to surface
2 surface area; **en ~** in area
surfait, **~e** /syrfɛ, ɛt/ *adj* overrated
surfer /sœrfe/ [**v1**] *vi* **1** to go surfing
2 (Comput) **~ sur l'Internet** to surf the Internet
surfiler /syrfile/ [**v1**] *vt* to oversew
surgelé, **~e** /syrʒəle/ *adj* deep-frozen; **les produits ~s** frozen food
surgeler /syrʒəle/ [**v17**] *vt* to deep-freeze
surgénérateur /syrʒeneratœr/ *m* fast-breeder reactor
surgir /syrʒir/ [**v3**] *vi* ‹*person*› to appear suddenly; ‹*difficulty*› to crop up; **faire ~ la vérité** to bring the truth to light
surhomme /syrɔm/ *m* superman
surhumain, **~e** /syrymɛ̃, ɛn/ *adj* superhuman
surimpression /syrɛ̃presjõ/ *f* double exposure; **en ~** superimposed
surinformation /syrɛ̃fɔrmasjõ/ *f* surfeit of information
sur-le-champ /syrləʃɑ̃/ *adv* right away
surlendemain /syrlɑ̃d(ə)mɛ̃/ *m* **le ~** two days later
surligner /syrliɲe/ [**v1**] *vt* to highlight
surligneur /syrliɲœr/ *m* highlighter (pen)
surmenage /syrmənaʒ/ *m* overwork
surmener /syrmene/ [**v16**] **A** *vt* to overwork
B se surmener *v refl* (+ *v être*) to push oneself too hard
surmontable /syrmõtabl/ *adj* surmountable
surmonter /syrmõte/ [**v1**] *vt* to overcome
surmultiplié, **~e** /syrmyltiplije/ *adj* **vitesse ~e** overdrive
surnager /syrnaʒe/ [**v13**] *vi* to float
surnaturel, **-elle** /syrnatyrɛl/ *adj*
1 supernatural
2 eerie
surnom /syrnõ/ *m* nickname
surnombre /syrnõbr/ *m* **en ~** ‹*objects*› surplus; ‹*staff*› excess; ‹*passenger*› extra
surnommer /syrnɔme/ [**v1**] *vt* to nickname
surnuméraire /syrnymerɛr/ *adj, mf* supernumerary
surpasser /syrpase/ [**v1**] **A** *vt* to surpass
B se surpasser *v refl* (+ *v être*) to surpass oneself, to excel oneself
surpêche /syrpɛʃ/ *f* overfishing
surpeuplé, **~e** /syrpœple/ *adj*
1 overpopulated
2 overcrowded
surplace /syrplas/ *m inv* **faire du ~** (in traffic jam) to be stuck; (in work, inquiry) to be getting nowhere; (in cycling) to do a track stand
surplomb /syrplõ/ *m* **en ~** overhanging
surplomber /syrplõbe/ [**v1**] *vt* to overhang
surplus /syrply/ *m inv* (of goods) surplus
surpopulation /syrpɔpylasjõ/ *f* overpopulation
surprenant, **~e** /syrprənɑ̃, ɑ̃t/ *adj* surprising; amazing
surprendre /syrprɑ̃dr/ [**v52**] **A** *vt* **1** to surprise
2 to take [sb] by surprise; **se laisser ~ par la pluie** to get caught in the rain
3 to catch ‹*thief*›
4 to overhear ‹*conversation*›; to intercept ‹*smile*›
B *vi* ‹*behaviour*› to be surprising; ‹*show*› to surprise; ‹*person*› to surprise people
surprise /syrpriz/ *f* surprise; **créer la ~** to cause a stir; **il m'a fait la ~ de venir me voir** he came to see me as a surprise; **avoir la bonne ~ d'apprendre que** to be pleasantly surprised to hear that; **voyage sans ~** uneventful trip; **gagner sans ~** to win as expected

S

surproduction /syʀpʀɔdyksjɔ̃/ *f* overproduction
surqualifié, **~e** /syʀkalifje/ *adj* overqualified
surréalisme /suʀ(ʀ)ealism/ *m* surrealism
surréaliste /suʀ(ʀ)ealist/ **A** *adj* **1** surrealist
2 ‹*landscape, vision*› surreal
B *mf* surrealist
surrégénérateur /syʀʀeʒeneʀatœʀ/ *m* fast-breeder reactor
sursaut /syʀso/ *m* **1** start; **en ~** with a start
2 (of energy, enthusiasm) sudden burst; (of pride, indignation) flash; **dans un dernier ~** in a final spurt of effort
sursauter /syʀsote/ [**v1**] *vi* to jump, to start
sursis /syʀsi/ *m inv* **1** respite
2 (Law) suspended sentence
3 (Mil) deferment of military service
surtaxe /syʀtaks/ *f* surcharge
surtaxer /syʀtakse/ [**v1**] *vt* to surcharge
surtout /syʀtu/ *adv* above all; **~ quand/que** especially when/as; **~ pas!** certainly not!
surveillance /syʀvɛjɑ̃s/ *f* **1** watch; (police) surveillance; **déjouer la ~ de qn** to escape detection by sb
2 supervision; **sous ~ médicale** under medical supervision
surveillant, **~e** /syʀvɛjɑ̃, ɑ̃t/ *mf* **1** (Sch) supervisor
2 ~ de prison prison warder (BrE) *or* guard
3 store detective
surveiller /syʀveje/ [**v1**] **A** *vt* **1** (gen) to watch; to keep watch on ‹*building*›
2 to supervise ‹*work, pupils*›; to monitor ‹*progress*›
3 ~ sa santé to take care of one's health
B se surveiller *v refl* (+ *v être*) to watch oneself
survenir /syʀvəniʀ/ [**v36**] *vi* (+ *v être*) ‹*death, storm*› to occur; ‹*difficulty, conflict*› to arise
survêtement /syʀvɛtmɑ̃/ *m* tracksuit
survie /syʀvi/ *f* survival
survivant, **~e** /syʀvivɑ̃, ɑ̃t/ *mf* survivor
survivre /syʀvivʀ/ [**v63**] **A survivre à** *v+prep* ‹*person*› to survive ‹*event, injuries*›; to outlive ‹*person*›; ‹*work, influence*› to outlast ‹*person*›
B *vi* to survive
survol /syʀvɔl/ *m* **1** flying over
2 synopsis
survoler /syʀvɔle/ [**v1**] *vt* **1** to fly over ‹*place*›
2 to do a quick review of ‹*problem*›
survolté, **~e** /syʀvɔlte/ *adj* (fam) overexcited
sus: **en sus** /ɑ̃sys/ *phr* **être en ~** to be extra; **en ~ de** on top of; in addition to
susceptibilité /sysɛptibilite/ *f* touchiness
susceptible /sysɛptibl/ *adj* **1** touchy
2 ~ de faire likely to do
susciter /sysite/ [**v1**] *vt* **1** to spark off ‹*reaction, debate*›; to create ‹*problem*›
2 to arouse ‹*enthusiasm, interest*›; to give rise to ‹*fear*›
susmentionné, **~e** /sysmɑ̃sjɔne/ *adj* aforementioned
suspect, **~e** /syspɛ, ɛkt/ **A** *adj* suspicious; ‹*information, logic*› dubious; ‹*foodstuff, honesty*› suspect; ‹*person*› suspicious-looking
B *mf* suspect
suspecter /syspɛkte/ [**v1**] *vt* to suspect
suspendre /syspɑ̃dʀ/ [**v6**] **A** *vt* **1** to hang up; **être suspendu aux lèvres de qn** to be hanging on sb's every word
2 to suspend ‹*programme, payment*›; to end ‹*strike*›; to adjourn ‹*session, inquiry*›
3 to suspend ‹*official, athlete*›
B se suspendre *v refl* (+ *v être*) to hang; **se ~ à une corde** to hang from a rope
suspens: **en suspens** /ɑ̃syspɑ̃/ *phr*
1 laisser qch en ~ to leave sth unresolved ‹*question*›; to leave sth unfinished ‹*work*›
2 tenir qn en ~ to keep sb in suspense
suspense /syspɛns/ *m* suspense; **film/roman à ~** thriller
suspension /syspɑ̃sjɔ̃/ *f* **1** (gen), (Tech) suspension
2 (of aid, work) suspension; (of session, trial) adjournment
3 en ~ ‹*particles*› in suspension
4 pendant, ceiling light
suspicieux, **-ieuse** /syspisjø, øz/ *adj* suspicious
suspicion /syspisjɔ̃/ *f* suspicion
sustenter: **se sustenter** /systɑ̃te/ [**v1**] *v refl* (+ *v être*) to have a little snack
susurrer /sysyʀe/ [**v1**] *vt*, *vi* to whisper
suture /sytyʀ/ *f* suture; **point de ~** stitch
suzerain, **~e** /syzʀɛ̃, ɛn/ *mf* suzerain
svelte /svɛlt/ *adj* slender
sveltesse /svɛltɛs/ *f* slenderness
SVP (*written abbr* = **s'il vous plaît**) please
syllabe /sil(l)ab/ *f* syllable
sylviculture /silvikyltyʀ/ *f* forestry
symbiose /sɛ̃bjoz/ *f* symbiosis
symbole /sɛ̃bɔl/ *m* **1** symbol
2 creed
symbolique /sɛ̃bɔlik/ *adj* **1** symbolic
2 ‹*gesture*› token; ‹*price*› nominal
symboliser /sɛ̃bɔlize/ [**v1**] *vt* to symbolize
symétrie /simetʀi/ *f* symmetry
symétrique /simetʀik/ *adj* **1** ‹*design, face*› symmetrical
2 ‹*relation*› symmetric
sympa /sɛ̃pa/ *adj inv* (fam) nice
sympathie /sɛ̃pati/ *f* **1 avoir de la ~ pour qn** to like sb
2 sympathy; **croyez à toute ma ~** you have my deepest sympathy
sympathique /sɛ̃patik/ *adj* nice; pleasant
sympathisant, **~e** /sɛ̃patizɑ̃, ɑ̃t/ *mf* sympathizer
sympathiser /sɛ̃patize/ [**v1**] *vi* to get on well
symphonie /sɛ̃fɔni/ *f* symphony
symphonique /sɛ̃fɔnik/ *adj* symphonic

key word

symptomatique /sɛ̃ptɔmatik/ *adj* symptomatic
symptôme /sɛ̃ptom/ *m* symptom
synagogue /sinagɔg/ *f* synagogue
synchronique /sɛ̃kʀɔnik/ *adj* synchronic
synchronisation /sɛ̃kʀɔnizasjɔ̃/ *f* synchronization
synchroniser /sɛ̃kʀɔnize/ [**v1**] *vt* to synchronize
syncope /sɛ̃kɔp/ *f* **1** fainting fit; **tomber en ~** to faint
2 (Mus) syncopation
syndic /sɛ̃dik/ *m* property manager
syndical, **~e**, *mpl* **-aux** /sɛ̃dikal, o/ *adj* (trade) union
syndicalisme /sɛ̃dikalism/ *m* **1** trade unionism
2 union activities
syndicaliste /sɛ̃dikalist/ *mf* union activist
syndicat /sɛ̃dika/ *m* **1** trade union (BrE), labor union (AmE)
2 (employers') association
■ **~ d'initiative** tourist information office
syndiqué, **~e** /sɛ̃dike/ *adj* **être ~** to be a union member
syndrome /sɛ̃dʀom/ *m* syndrome
■ **~ de la classe économique** economy class syndrome; **~ immunodéficitaire acquis** acquired immunodeficiency syndrome
synergie /sinɛʀʒi/ *f* synergy (**entre** between)
synonyme /sinɔnim/ **A** *adj* synonymous
B *m* synonym; **dictionnaire de ~s** ≈ thesaurus
syntaxe /sɛ̃taks/ *f* syntax
synthèse /sɛ̃tɛz/ *f* **1** synthesis
2 produit de ~ synthetic product
3 images de ~ computer-generated images
synthétique /sɛ̃tetik/ *adj* **1** synthetic
2 ‹*vision*› global
synthétiseur /sɛ̃tetizœʀ/ *m* synthesizer
syphilis /sifilis/ *f inv* syphilis
systématique /sistematik/ *adj* systematic
⚷ **système** /sistɛm/ *m* **1** system; **~ de canaux** canal system *or* network
2 ~ pileux hair
■ **le ~ D** (fam) resourcefulness; **~ monétaire européen, SME** European Monetary System, EMS
IDIOM **taper sur le ~ de qn** (fam) to get on sb's nerves

Tt

t, **T** /te/ *m inv* t, T; **en (forme de) T** T-shaped
t' ▶ **te**
ta ▶ **ton**[1]
tabac /taba/ *m* **1** tobacco
2 tobacconist's (BrE), smoke shop (AmE)
3 (fam) big hit
■ **~ blond** Virginia tobacco; **~ brun** dark tobacco; **~ à priser** snuff
IDIOM **passer qn à ~** (fam) to beat sb up
tabagie /tabaʒi/ *f* **c'est une vraie ~ ici!** it's really smoky in here!
tabagisme /tabaʒism/ *m* tobacco addiction
■ **~ passif** passive smoking
tabernacle /tabɛʀnakl/ *m* tabernacle
⚷ **table** /tabl/ *f* **1** table; **mettre** *or* **dresser la ~** to set *or* lay the table; **nous étions toujours à ~ quand...** we were still eating when...; **passer** *or* **se mettre à ~** to sit down at the table; (fig, fam) to spill the beans (fam)
2 ~ des négociations negotiating table
3 ~ de logarithmes log table
■ **~ basse** coffee table; **~ de chevet** bedside table (BrE), night stand (AmE); **~ d'écoute** wiretapping set; **être mis sur ~ d'écoute** to have one's phone tapped; **~ des matières** (table of) contents; **~ de mixage** mixing desk; **~ de nuit** ▶ **table de chevet**; **~ ronde** round table
IDIOM **mettre les pieds sous la ~** to let others wait on you
⚷ **tableau**, *pl* **~x** /tablo/ *m* **1** picture; painting
2 (description) picture; **en plus, il était ivre, tu vois un peu le ~!** (fam) on top of that he was drunk, you can just imagine!
3 table, chart
4 (Sch) blackboard
5 (displaying information) (gen) board; (for trains) indicator board; **~ horaire** timetable
6 (in play) short scene
■ **~ d'affichage** notice board; **~ de bord** (in car) dashboard; (on plane, train) instrument panel; **~ de chasse** (in hunting) total number of kills; (fig) list of conquests
IDIOM **jouer sur les deux ~x** to hedge one's bets
tablée /table/ *f* table; **une grande ~** a large party
tabler /table/ [**v1**] *vi* **~ sur** to bank on (fam)
tablette /tablɛt/ *f* **1** (of chocolate) bar; (of chewing gum) stick
2 shelf

tablier /tablije/ *m* **1** apron
2 roadway
IDIOM **rendre son ~** to give in (BrE) *or* give (AmE) one's notice

tabloïd /tablɔid/ *adj, m* tabloid

tabou /tabu/ **A** *adj* **1** taboo
2 sacred
B *m* taboo

tabouret /tabuʀɛ/ *m* stool

tac /tak/ *m* **répondre du ~ au ~** to answer as quick as a flash

tache /taʃ/ *f* **1** stain; **~ d'humidité** damp patch
2 (fig) stain, blot; **sans ~** ‹*reputation*› spotless
3 (on fruit) mark; (on skin) blotch, mark
4 (of colour) spot; patch
■ **~s de rousseur** freckles
IDIOM **faire ~ d'huile** to spread like wildfire

🔑 **tâche** /tɑʃ/ *f* task, job; **tu ne me facilites pas la ~!** you're not making my job any easier!; **les ~s ménagères** household chores

tacher /taʃe/ [**v1**] **A** *vt* **1** ‹*substance*› to stain; ‹*person*› to get a stain on ‹*garment*›
2 to tarnish, to stain ‹*reputation*›
B *vi* to stain; **ça ne tache pas** it doesn't stain

tâcher /tɑʃe/ [**v1**] *v+prep* **~ de faire** to try to do

tacheté /taʃte/ *adj* ‹*fur*› speckled

tacite /tasit/ *adj* tacit

taciturne /tasityʀn/ *adj* taciturn

tacler /takle/ *vt* (Sport) to tackle

tact /takt/ *m* tact; **avec ~** tactfully

tactile /taktil/ *adj* ‹*sense*› tactile

tactique /taktik/ **A** *adj* (gen), (Mil) tactical
B *f* tactic; **la ~** tactics

taggeur, **-euse** /tagœʀ, øz/ *mf* **tagueur**

taie /tɛ/ *f* **~ (d'oreiller)** pillowcase; **~ (de traversin)** bolster case

taillader /tajade/ [**v1**] *vt* to slash

🔑 **taille** /taj/ *f* **1** waist, waistline
2 size; **de grande/petite ~** large/small; **de ~** ‹*problem, ambition*› considerable; ‹*event, question*› very important; **être de ~ à faire** to be up to *or* capable of doing
3 (of garment) size; **'~ unique'** 'one size'; **essaie la ~ au-dessus** try the next size up
4 height; **être de grande/petite ~** to be tall/short
5 (of tree, shrub) pruning; (of hedge) clipping, trimming; (of diamond, glass) cutting

taillé, **~e** **A** *pp* ▸ **tailler**
B *pp adj* **1 ~ en athlète** built like an athlete
2 être ~ pour faire to be cut out to do
3 cristal ~ cut glass

taille-crayons /tajkʀɛjɔ̃/ *m inv* pencil sharpener

tailler /taje/ [**v1**] **A** *vt* **1** to cut ‹*glass, marble*›; to sharpen ‹*pencil*›; to prune ‹*tree, shrub*›; to trim ‹*hair, beard*›
2 to cut ‹*steak*›; to carve ‹*sculpture*›; to cut out ‹*garment*›; **taillé sur mesure** ‹*garment*› custom-made; (fig) ‹*role*› tailor-made; ‹*role*› tailor-made
B *vi* **~ grand/petit** ‹*garment*› to be cut on the large/small side
C se tailler *v refl* (+ *v être*) **1** to carve out [sth] for oneself ‹*career, empire*›; to make [sth] for oneself ‹*reputation*›
2 (pop) to beat it (fam)

tailleur /tajœʀ/ *m* **1** (woman's) suit
2 tailor; **s'asseoir en ~** to sit down cross-legged
■ **~ de pierre** stone-cutter

taillis /taji/ *m inv* **1** undergrowth
2 coppice

tain /tɛ̃/ *m* **miroir sans ~** two-way mirror

🔑 **taire** /tɛʀ/ [**v59**] **A** *vt* **1** not to reveal ‹*name, secret*›; to hush up ‹*truth*›
2 to keep [sth] to oneself ‹*sadness, resentment*›
B *vi* **faire ~** to make [sb] be quiet ‹*pupils*› to silence ‹*opponent, media*›; to put a stop to ‹*rumours*›
C se taire *v refl* (+ *v être*) **1** ‹*person*› to be silent
2 ‹*person*› to stop talking; ‹*bird, journalist*› to fall silent; **tais-toi!** be quiet!
3 ‹*noise*› to stop; ‹*orchestra*› to fall silent

talc /talk/ *m* talc, talcum powder

🔑 **talent** /talɑ̃/ *m* talent; **de ~** talented

talentueux, **-euse** /talɑ̃tɥø, øz/ *adj* talented

talisman /talismɑ̃/ *m* talisman

talkie-walkie, *pl* **talkies-walkies** /tokiwoki/ *m* walkie-talkie

taloche /talɔʃ/ *f* (fam) clout (fam)

talon /talɔ̃/ *m* **1** (of foot, shoe) heel
2 (of cheque, ticket) stub
3 (in cards) pile
■ **~ aiguille** stiletto heel
IDIOM **être sur les ~s de qn** to be hard *or* hot on sb's heels

talonner /talɔne/ [**v1**] *vt* **1 ~ qn** to be hot on sb's heels
2 ‹*person*› to badger ‹*person*›; ‹*hunger, anxiety*› to torment ‹*person*›

talonnette /talɔnɛt/ *f* lift (in a shoe)

talus /taly/ *m inv* **1** embankment
2 bank, slope

tamanoir /tamanwaʀ/ *m* anteater

tambouille /tɑ̃buj/ *f* (fam) grub (fam)

tambour /tɑ̃buʀ/ *m* drum; **mener qch ~ battant** to deal with sth briskly

tambourin /tɑ̃buʀɛ̃/ *m* tambourine

tambouriner /tɑ̃buʀine/ [**v1**] *vi* **~ à la porte de qn** to hammer on sb's door

tamis /tami/ *m inv* sieve

Tamise /tamiz/ *pr f* **la ~** the Thames

🔑 key word

tamiser /tamize/ [**v1**] *vt* to sieve, to sift ‹*sand, flour*›; to filter ‹*light, colours*›

tampon /tɑ̃pɔ̃/ *m* **1** (in office) stamp; **~ (encreur)** (ink) pad
2 (for sponging) (gen) pad; (Med) swab; **~ à récurer** scouring pad
3 ~ hygiénique tampon

tamponner /tɑ̃pɔne/ [**v1**] *vt* **1** to swab ‹*wound, cut*›; to mop ‹*forehead*›
2 to stamp ‹*document*›
3 to crash into ‹*vehicle*›

tamponneuse /tɑ̃pɔnøz/ *adj f* **auto ~** bumper car, dodgem (BrE)

tam-tam, *pl* **~s** /tamtam/ *m* tom-tom

tanche /tɑ̃ʃ/ *f* tench

tandem /tɑ̃dɛm/ *m* **1** tandem
2 (fig) duo

tandis: **tandis que** /tɑ̃di(s)k(ə)/ *phr* while

tangent, **~e** /tɑ̃ʒɑ̃, ɑ̃t/ *adj* **1** tangent, tangential
2 (fam) **elle a été reçue, mais c'était ~** she got through, but only by the skin of her teeth (fam)

tangente /tɑ̃ʒɑ̃t/ *f* tangent

tangible /tɑ̃ʒibl/ *adj* tangible

tanguer /tɑ̃ge/ [**v1**] *vi* ‹*ship, plane*› to pitch

tanière /tanjɛʀ/ *f* **1** den
2 lair

tank /tɑ̃k/ *m* tank

tanner /tane/ [**v1**] *vt* **1** to tan ‹*leather, hides*›
2 ‹*sun*› to make [sth] leathery ‹*face, skin*›

tannerie /tanʀi/ *f* **1** tannery
2 tanning

tant /tɑ̃/ **A** *adv* **1** (so) much; **il a ~ insisté que...** he was so insistent that...; **vous m'en direz ~!** (fam) you don't say!; **le moment ~ attendu** the long-awaited moment
2 n'aimer rien ~ que... to like nothing so much as...; **~ bien que mal** ‹*repair, lead*› after a fashion; ‹*manage*› more or less; **essayer ~ bien que mal de s'adapter** to be struggling to adapt
3 ~ que as long as; **je ne partirai pas ~ qu'il ne m'aura pas accordé un rendez-vous** I won't leave until he's given me an appointment; **traite-moi de menteur ~ que tu y es!** (fam) go ahead and call me a liar!
4 (replacing number) **gagner ~ par mois** to earn so much a month
B tant de *quantif* **Loulou, Pivachon et ~ d'autres** Loulou, Pivachon and so many others; **~ de travail** so much work
C (in phrases) **~ pis** too bad; **~ mieux** so much the better; **~ mieux pour toi** good for you; **~ et plus** a great deal; a great many; **~ et si bien que** so much so that; **s'il avait un ~ soit peu de bon sens** if he had the slightest bit of common sense; **~ qu'à faire, autant repeindre toute la pièce** we may as well repaint the whole room while we're at it; **en ~ que** as; **en ~ que tel** as such; **si ~ est qu'il puisse y aller** that is if he can go at all; **je ne l'aime pas ~ que ça** I don't like him/her all that much

tante /tɑ̃t/ *f* aunt

tantôt /tɑ̃to/ *adv* sometimes

taon /tɑ̃/ *m* horsefly

tapage /tapaʒ/ *m* **1** din, racket (fam)
2 furore (BrE), furor (AmE)
3 hype; **~ médiatique** media hype
■ **~ nocturne** disturbance of the peace at night

tapageur, **-euse** /tapaʒœʀ, øz/ *adj*
1 ‹*person*› rowdy
2 ‹*luxury*› showy; ‹*campaign*› hyped up

tapant, **~e** /tapɑ̃, ɑ̃t/ *adj* **à trois heures ~es** at three o'clock sharp *or* on the dot

tape /tap/ *f* pat; slap

tape-à-l'œil /tapalœj/ *adj inv* (fam) ‹*colour*› loud; ‹*jewellery, decor*› garish

taper /tape/ [**v1**] **A** *vt* **1** to hit ‹*person, dog*›
2 to type ‹*letter*›
B taper sur *v+prep* to hit; **~ sur l'épaule de qn** to tap sb on the shoulder
C *vi* **1 ~ des mains** to clap one's hands; **~ à la porte** to knock at the door; **le soleil tape aujourd'hui** (fam) the sun is beating down today
2 ~ (à la machine) to type
D se taper *v refl* (+ *v être*) **1** (fam) **se ~ dessus** to knock each other about
2 c'est à se ~ la tête contre les murs (fig) it's enough to drive you up the wall
3 (fam) to get stuck with (fam) ‹*chore, person*›
IDIOM **elle m'a tapé dans l'œil** (fam) I thought she was striking

tapette /tapɛt/ *f* **1** carpet beater
2 fly swatter
3 mousetrap

tapeur, **-euse** /tapœʀ, øz/ *mf* (fam) scrounger (fam)

tapioca /tapjɔka/ *m* tapioca

tapir[1]: **se tapir** /tapiʀ/ [**v3**] *v refl* (+ *v être*)
1 ‹*person, animal*› to hide
2 to crouch

tapir[2] /tapiʀ/ *m* (Zool) tapir

tapis /tapi/ *m inv* rug; carpet; mat; **mettre qch sur le ~** (fig) to bring sth up; **mettre** *or* **envoyer qn au ~** to throw sb
■ **~ de bain(s)** bath mat; **~ roulant** moving walkway; (for luggage) carousel; (in factory, supermarket) conveyor belt

tapisser /tapise/ [**v1**] *vt* **1** to wallpaper; to decorate ‹*room*›; to cover ‹*armchair*›
2 ‹*snow*› to carpet ‹*ground*›; ‹*residue*› to line ‹*bottom of container*›

tapisserie /tapisʀi/ *f* **1** tapestry
2 wallpaper
3 tapestry work
IDIOM **faire ~** to be a wallflower

tapissier, **-ière** /tapisje, ɛʀ/ *mf* **1** upholsterer
2 tapestry maker

tapoter /tapɔte/ [**v1**] *vt* to tap ‹*table, object*›; to pat ‹*cheeks, back*›

taquin, **~e** /takɛ̃, in/ *adj* ‹*person*› teasing

taquiner /takine/ [**v1**] *vt* ‹*person*› to tease
tarabiscoté, **~e** /taʀabiskɔte/ *adj* ‹*design*› over-ornate; ‹*reasoning*› convoluted
tarama /taʀama/ *m* taramasalata
taratata /taʀatata/ *excl* (fam) nonsense!, rubbish! (fam)
tard /taʀ/ **A** *adv* late; **plus ~** later; **bien plus ~** much later (on); **au plus ~** at the latest; **pas plus ~ qu'hier** only yesterday
B **sur le tard** *phr* ‹*marry*› late in life
tarder /taʀde/ [**v1**] **A** *vi* **1 ~ à faire** to take a long time doing; to put off *or* delay doing
2 ‹*reaction*› to be a long time coming; **les enfants ne vont pas ~** the children won't be long
B *v impers* **il me tarde de la revoir** I'm longing to see her again
tardif, **-ive** /taʀdif, iv/ *adj* late; belated
tardivement /taʀdivmɑ̃/ *adv* ‹*arrive*› late; ‹*react*› rather belatedly
tare /taʀ/ *f* **1** tare
2 defect
taré, **~e** /taʀe/ *adj* (fam) crazy (fam)
targette /taʀʒɛt/ *f* bolt
targuer: **se targuer** /taʀge/ [**v1**] *v refl* (+ *v être*) to claim, to boast
tarif /taʀif/ *m* **1** (gen) rate; (on bus, train) fare; (for consultation) fee; **payer plein ~** to pay full price; to pay full fare; **~ de nuit** night-time rate
2 price list
■ **~ douanier** customs tariff
tarification /taʀifikasjɔ̃/ *f* price setting; tariff
tarir /taʀiʀ/ [**v23**] **A** *vt* to dry up ‹*source, well*›; to sap ‹*strength*›
B *vi* **ne pas ~ d'éloges sur qn/qch** to be full of praise for sb/sth
C **se tarir** *v refl* (+ *v être*) to dry up
tarot /taʀo/ *m* tarot (*card game*)
tartare /taʀtaʀ/ *adj* **1** Tartar
2 (Culin) **sauce ~** tartare sauce
tarte /taʀt/ *f* **1** (Culin) tart
2 (pop) wallop (fam)
IDIOM **c'est pas de la ~** (fam) it's no picnic (fam)
tartelette /taʀtəlɛt/ *f* (small) tart
tartine /taʀtin/ *f* **1** slice of bread and butter
2 (fam) **il en a écrit une ~** he wrote reams about it
tartiner /taʀtine/ [**v1**] *vt* to spread
tartre /taʀtʀ/ *m* (in kettle) scale; (on teeth) tartar
tartufe /taʀtyf/ *m* hypocrite
tas /tɑ/ **A** *m inv* **1** heap, pile; **en ~** ‹*put, place*› in a heap *or* pile; **~ de ferraille** scrap heap; (fig, fam) wreck
2 (fam) **un ~**, **des ~** loads (fam)
B **dans le tas** *phr* (fam) **tirer dans le ~** to fire into the crowd
C **sur le tas** *phr* **apprendre sur le ~** to learn on the job; **grève sur le ~** sit-down strike
tasse /tɑs/ *f* cup; **~ à thé** teacup
IDIOM **boire la ~** (fam) to swallow a mouthful of water (when swimming)
tassement /tɑsmɑ̃/ *m* contraction; **~ de vertèbres** compression of the vertebrae
tasser /tɑse/ [**v1**] **A** *vt* to press down ‹*earth*›; to pack down ‹*hay*›; to pack ‹*clothes, people*› (**dans** into); **il a la cinquantaine bien tassée** (fam) he's well over fifty
B **se tasser** *v refl* (+ *v être*) **1** (with age) to shrink
2 (in train, car) ‹*people*› to squash up
3 (fam) ‹*rumour, conflict*› to die down
tata /tata/ *f* (fam) auntie
tâter /tɑte/ [**v1**] **A** *vt* to feel; **~ le sol du pied** to test the ground
B **se tâter** *v refl* (+ *v être*) (fam) **je me tâte** I'm thinking about it
IDIOM **~ le terrain** to put out feelers
tatillon, **-onne** /tatijɔ̃, ɔn/ *adj* nit-picking
tâtonnement /tɑtɔnmɑ̃/ *m* **~s dans l'obscurité** groping around in the dark; **les ~s des chercheurs** tentative research; **après dix années de ~s** after ten years of trial and error
tâtonner /tɑtɔne/ [**v1**] *vi* to grope about *or* around
tâtons: **à tâtons** /atɑtɔ̃/ *phr* **avancer à ~** to feel one's way along
tatouage /tatwaʒ/ *m* tattoo
tatouer /tatwe/ [**v1**] *vt* to tattoo
tatoueur, **-euse** /tatwœʀ, øz/ *mf* tattooist
taudis /todi/ *m inv* **1** hovel
2 pigsty
taule /tol/ *f* (pop) prison
taupe /top/ *f* **1** (Zool) mole
2 moleskin
taupinière /topinjɛʀ/ *f* **1** molehill
2 (mole) tunnels
taureau, *pl* **~x** /tɔʀo/ *m* (Zool) bull
IDIOM **prendre le ~ par les cornes** to take the bull by the horns
Taureau /tɔʀo/ *pr m* Taurus
tauromachie /tɔʀɔmaʃi/ *f* bullfighting
taux /to/ *m inv* **1** (gen) rate; **~ de chômage** unemployment rate
2 (Med) (of alcohol, albumen, sugar) level; (of bacteria, sperm) count
taxation /taksasjɔ̃/ *f* **1** taxation
2 assessment
taxe /taks/ *f* tax; **boutique hors ~s** duty-free shop (BrE) *or* store (AmE); **1 000 euros toutes ~s comprises** 1,000 euros inclusive of tax
■ **~ de douane** customs duty; **~ foncière** property tax; **~ d'habitation** ≈ council tax (BrE) (*paid by residents to cover local services*); **~ à la valeur ajoutée** value added tax
taxer /takse/ [**v1**] *vt* **1** (Econ) to tax

key word

t

2 ~ **qn de laxisme** to accuse sb of being lax
taxi /taksi/ *m* taxi, cab (AmE)
taxidermiste /taksidɛʀmist/ *mf* taxidermist
Tchad /tʃad/ *pr m* Chad
tchador /tʃadɔʀ/ *m* chador
tchao /tʃao/ *excl* (fam) bye! (fam), see you! (fam)
tchat vidéo /tʃat video/ *m* video chat
tchater /tʃate/ *vi* to chat (online)
tchèque /tʃɛk/ **A** *adj* Czech; **République** ~ Czech Republic
B *m* (Ling) Czech
tchin /tʃin/ *excl also* **tchin-tchin** /tʃintʃin/ (fam) cheers!
TD /tede/ *m pl* (fam) (*abbr* = **travaux dirigés**) (Sch) practical
te, **t'** *before vowel or mute h* /t(ə)/ *pron*
1 (direct or indirect object) you
2 (reflexive pronoun) yourself; **va** ~ **laver les mains** go and wash your hands
té /te/ *m* T-square; **en** ~ T-shaped
technicien, **-ienne** /tɛknisjɛ̃, ɛn/ *mf*
1 technician
2 technical expert
3 engineer
■ ~ **de surface** cleaner
technique¹ /tɛknik/ **A** *adj* technical
B *m* technical subjects
technique² /tɛknik/ *f* **1** technique
2 technology
technocrate /tɛknɔkʀat/ *mf* technocrat
technologie /tɛknɔlɔʒi/ *f* technology
teck /tɛk/ *m* teak; **en** ~ teak
teckel /tekɛl/ *m* dachshund
tee-shirt, *pl* ~**s** /tiʃœʀt/ *m* T-shirt
teigne /tɛɲ/ *f* **1** (Med) ringworm
2 moth
3 (fam) **être méchant comme une** ~ to be a nasty (BrE) *or* real (AmE) piece of work
teigneux, **-euse** /tɛɲø, øz/ *adj* (fam) cantankerous
teindre /tɛ̃dʀ/ [**v73**] **A** *vt* to dye; to stain
B se teindre *v refl* (+ *v être*) to dye one's hair
teint, ~**e** /tɛ̃, tɛ̃t/ **A** *pp* ▶ **teindre**
B *pp adj* dyed; stained
C *m* complexion; **avoir le** ~ **rose** *or* **frais** to have a healthy glow to one's cheeks
teinte /tɛ̃t/ *f* **1** shade
2 colour (BrE)
teinter /tɛ̃te/ [**v1**] **A** *vt* **1** to tint; to stain; to dye
2 ~ **qch de** to tinge sth with
B se teinter *v refl* (+ *v être*) **se** ~ **de** to become tinged with
teinture /tɛ̃tyʀ/ *f* dye; (for wood) stain
teinturerie /tɛ̃tyʀʀi/ *f* (dry) cleaner's
teinturier, **-ière** /tɛ̃tyʀje, ɛʀ/ *mf* **1** dry-cleaner
2 dyer
tel, **telle** /tɛl/ *adj* **1** such; **une telle conduite** such behaviour (BrE)
2 like; ~ **père**, ~ **fils** like father like son
3 **telle est la vérité** that is the truth; **comme** ~, **en tant que** ~ as such; **ses affaires étaient restées telles quelles** his/her things were left as they were
4 **avec un** ~ **enthousiasme** with such enthusiasm; **de telle sorte** *or* **façon** *or* **manière que** in such a way that; so that
5 **admettons qu'il arrive** ~ **jour, à telle heure** suppose that he arrives on such and such a day, at such and such a time
télé /tele/ *adj inv*, *f* (fam) TV
■ ~ **réalité** reality TV
télé-achat /teleaʃa/ *m* teleshopping
téléchargeable /teleʃaʀʒabl/ *adj* (Comput) downloadable; uploadable
téléchargement /teleʃaʀʒəmɑ̃/ *m* (Comput) download; upload
télécharger /teleʃaʀʒe/ *vt* (Comput) to download; to upload
télécommande /telekɔmɑ̃d/ *f* remote control
télécommander /telekɔmɑ̃de/ [**v1**] *vt* **1** to operate [sth] by remote control; **voiture télécommandée** remote-controlled car
2 (fig) to mastermind
télécommunication /telekɔmynikasjɔ̃/ *f* telecommunications
téléconférence /telekɔ̃feʀɑ̃s/ *f*
1 conference call
2 teleconference
télécopie /telekɔpi/ *f* fax
télécopier /telekɔpje/ [**v2**] *vt* to fax
télécopieur /telekɔpjœʀ/ *m* fax machine, fax
télé-crochet /telekʀɔʃɛ/ *m: singing competition on the television*
télédiffuser /teledifyze/ [**v1**] *vt* to broadcast
télé-enseignement, *pl* ~**s** /teleɑ̃sɛɲəmɑ̃/ *m* distance learning
téléfilm /telefilm/ *m* TV film, TV movie
télégramme /telegʀam/ *m* telegram
télégraphier /telegʀafje/ [**v1**] *vt* to telegraph
télégraphique /telegʀafik/ *adj* ‹*pole, message*› telegraph; ‹*style*› telegraphic
téléguidage /telegidaʒ/ *m* radio control
téléguider /telegide/ [**v1**] *vt* **1** to control [sth] by radio
2 (fig) to mastermind
télématique /telematik/ **A** *adj* ‹*service, network*› viewdata (BrE), videotex®
B *f* telematics
téléobjectif /teleɔbʒɛktif/ *m* telephoto lens
télépathie /telepati/ *f* telepathy
téléphérique /telefeʀik/ *m* cable car
téléphone /telefɔn/ *m* phone
■ ~ **arabe** (fam) grapevine, bush telegraph; ~ **intelligent** smartphone; ~ **portable** mobile phone (BrE), cellphone (AmE); ~ **portatif** pocket car phone; **le** ~ **rouge** the

hotline; ~ **satellite** satphone, satellite phone

téléphoner /telefɔne/ [**v1**] *vi* to phone; to make a phone call; ~ **à qn** to phone sb

téléphonique /telefɔnik/ *adj* (tele)phone

télescope /telɛskɔp/ *m* telescope

télescoper /telɛskɔpe/ [**v1**] **A** *vt* ‹*truck, juggernaut*› to crush ‹*car*›
B se télescoper *v refl* (+ *v être*)
1 ‹*vehicles*› to collide
2 ‹*notions, tendencies*› to overlap

télescopique /telɛskɔpik/ *adj* telescopic

téléscripteur /teleskʀiptœʀ/ *m* teleprinter, teletypewriter

télésiège /telesjɛʒ/ *m* chair lift

téléski /teleski/ *m* ski tow

téléspectateur, **-trice** /telespɛktatœʀ, tʀis/ *mf* viewer

télésurveillance /telesyʀvɛjɑ̃s/ *f* electronic surveillance

télétransmission /teletʀɑ̃smisjɔ̃/ *f* transmission

télétravail /teletʀavaj/ *m* teleworking

télévente /televɑ̃t/ *f* telesales

télévisé, **~e** /televize/ *adj* television; televised

téléviseur /televizœʀ/ *m* television (set)

🔑 **télévision** /televizjɔ̃/ *f* television, TV
■ ~ **numérique** digital television; ~ **numérique terrestre, TNT** digital terrestrial television, DTT

télex /telɛks/ *m inv* telex; **par** ~ by telex

télexer /telɛkse/ [**v1**] *vt* to telex

🔑 **tellement** /tɛlmɑ̃/ **A** *adv* (modifying an adjective or adverb) so; (modifying a verb or comparative) so much; **pas** ~ not much; **il n'aime pas** ~ **lire** he doesn't like reading much; **j'ai de la peine à suivre** ~ **c'est compliqué** it's so complicated that I find it hard to follow
B tellement de *quantif* (fam) **il y a** ~ **de choses à voir** there's so much to see; **il a eu** ~ **de chance** he was so lucky; **il y en a** ~ **qui aimeraient le faire** so many people would like to do it

t

téméraire /temeʀɛʀ/ *adj* ‹*person, plan*› reckless; ‹*judgement*› rash; **courageux mais pas** ~ brave but not foolhardy

témérité /temeʀite/ *f* recklessness; rashness; **avoir la** ~ **de faire** to have the temerity to do

🔑 **témoignage** /temwaɲaʒ/ *m* **1** story
2 account; ~**s recueillis auprès de** accounts given by
3 evidence; testimony; **des** ~**s contradictoires/qui concordent** conflicting/corroborating evidence
4 ~ **d'amitié** (gift) token of friendship; **les** ~**s de sympathie** expressions of sympathy

🔑 **témoigner** /temwaɲe/ [**v1**] **A** *vt* **1** **'il était toujours poli', témoignent les voisins** neighbours (BrE) say he was always polite; (Law) ~ **que** to testify that
2 ~ **de l'affection** to show affection
B témoigner de *v+prep* **1** ~ **de** to show
2 ~ **du courage de qn** to vouch for sb's courage
C *vi* (Law) to give evidence

🔑 **témoin** /temwɛ̃/ *m* **1** (gen), (Law) witness; ~ **oculaire** eyewitness
2 (at duel) second
3 (Tech) indicator *or* warning light

tempe /tɑ̃p/ *f* temple

tempérament /tɑ̃peʀamɑ̃/ *m* disposition; **avoir du** ~ to have a strong character

tempérance /tɑ̃peʀɑ̃s/ *f* temperance

température /tɑ̃peʀatyʀ/ *f* temperature

tempéré, **~e** /tɑ̃peʀe/ *adj* temperate

tempérer /tɑ̃peʀe/ [**v14**] *vt* to temper; to moderate ‹*argument*›

tempête /tɑ̃pɛt/ *f* **1** gale; storm
2 uproar; **déclencher une** ~ **de protestations** to trigger a wave of protest

tempêter /tɑ̃pete/ [**v1**] *vi* to rage

🔑 **temple** /tɑ̃pl/ *m* **1** (gen) temple; (Protestant) church
2 (fig) temple

tempo /tɛmpo/ *m* (Mus) tempo

temporaire /tɑ̃pɔʀɛʀ/ *adj* temporary

temporel, **-elle** /tɑ̃pɔʀɛl/ *adj* (gen) temporal

temporisateur, **-trice** **A** *adj* temporizing
B *mf* temporizer

temporiser /tɑ̃pɔʀize/ [**v1**] *vi* to stall

🔑 **temps** /tɑ̃/ *m inv* **1** weather; **un beau** ~ fine weather; **le** ~ **est à la pluie** it looks like rain; **quel** ~ **fait-il?** what's the weather like?; **par tous les** ~ in all weathers
2 time; **le** ~ **arrangera les choses** time will take care of everything; **peu de** ~ **avant** shortly before; **en peu de** ~ in a short time; **dans peu de** ~ shortly; **dans quelque** ~ before long; **pendant ce** ~**(-là)** meanwhile; **qu'as-tu fait tout ce** ~**(-là)?** what have you been doing all this time?; **en un rien de** ~ in no time at all; **les trois quarts du** ~ most of the time; **le** ~ **de ranger mes affaires et j'arrive** just let me put my things away and I'll be with you; **on a (tout) le** ~ we've got (plenty of) time; **avoir dix** *or* **cent fois le** ~ to have all the time in the world; **laisser à qn le** ~ **de faire** to give sb time to do; **mettre** *or* **prendre du** ~ to take time; **beaucoup de** ~ a long time; **tu y as mis le** ~**!, tu en as mis du** ~**!** you (certainly) took your time!; **le** ~ **passe vite** time flies; **faire passer le** ~ to while away the time; **avoir du** ~ **à perdre** to have time on one's hands; **c'est du** ~ **perdu, c'est une perte de** ~ it's a waste of time; **le** ~ **presse!** time is short!; **j'ai trouvé le** ~ **long** (the) time seemed to drag; **finir dans les** ~ to finish in time; **à** ~

‹*leave, finish*› in time; **juste à ~** just in time; **de ~ en ~, de ~ à autre** from time to time; **il était ~!** (impatiently) (and) about time too!; (with relief) just in the nick of time!; **en ~ utile** in time; **en ~ voulu** in due course; at the right time; **ne durer qu'un ~** to be short-lived
3 au *or* **du ~ des Grecs** in the time of the Greeks; **au** *or* **du ~ où** in the days when; **le bon vieux ~** the good old days; **ces derniers ~** recently; **ces ~-ci** lately; **de mon ~** in my day; **dans le ~** in those days; **en ~ normal** usually; **en d'autres ~** at any other time
4 stage; **en deux ~** in two stages; **dans un premier ~** first; **dans un deuxième ~** subsequently; **dans un dernier ~** finally
5 (of verb) tense
6 avoir un travail à ~ partiel/plein to have a part-/full-time job
7 (Sport) time; **il a réalisé le meilleur ~** he got the best time; **améliorer son ~ d'une seconde** to knock a second off one's time
8 (of engine) stroke
9 (Mus) time; **mesure à deux ~** two-four time
■ **~ d'antenne** airtime; **~ fort** (Mus) forte; (fig) high point; **~ mort** slack period; **~ universel** Greenwich Mean Time, GMT
IDIOMS **au ~ pour moi!** my mistake!; **par les ~ qui courent** with things as they are; **se payer du bon ~** (fam) to have a whale of a time

tenable /tənabl/ *adj* **1** bearable; **la situation n'est pas ~** the situation is unbearable
2 (defendable) tenable
3 les élèves ne sont pas ~s aujourd'hui the pupils are being impossible today

tenace /tənas/ *adj* **1** ‹*stain, headache*› stubborn; ‹*perfume*› long-lasting; ‹*fog, cough, memory*› persistent
2 ‹*person*› tenacious; persistent; ‹*will*› tenacious

ténacité /tenasite/ *f* tenacity; persistence

tenaille /tənɑj/ *f* pincers

tenailler /tənɑje/ [v1] *vt* **il était tenaillé par le remords** he was racked with remorse

tenancier, **-ière** /tənɑ̃sje, ɛʀ/ *mf* (of cafe) landlord/landlady; (of hotel, casino) manager/manageress

tenant, **~e** /tənɑ̃, ɑ̃t/ **A** *mf* (Sport) **~ du titre** title-holder
B *m* **d'un seul ~** all in one piece
IDIOM **les ~s et les aboutissants de qch** the ins and outs of sth

tendance /tɑ̃dɑ̃s/ *f* **1** tendency
2 (in politics) tendency; **toutes ~s politiques confondues** across party lines
3 trend

tendancieux, **-ieuse** /tɑ̃dɑ̃sjø, øz/ *adj* biased (BrE), tendentious

tendeur /tɑ̃dœʀ/ *m* **1** (of tent) guy rope
2 (for roof rack) elastic strap

tendon /tɑ̃dɔ̃/ *m* tendon

tendre[1] /tɑ̃dʀ/ [v6] **A** *vt* **1** to tighten ‹*rope, cable*›; to stretch ‹*elastic, skin*›; to extend ‹*spring*›; **~ le bras** to reach out; **~ les bras à qn** to greet sb with open arms; **~ la main** to reach out; to hold out one's hand; **~ la main à qn** to hold one's hand out to sb; (fig) to lend sb a helping hand
2 to spread ‹*cloth, sheet*›
3 to set ‹*trap*›; to put up ‹*clothes line*›
4 ~ qch à qn to hold sth out to sb
B tendre à *v+prep* **~ à faire** to tend to do
C *vi* **1 ~ vers** to strive for
2 ~ vers to approach ‹*value*›; to tend to ‹*zero*›
D se tendre *v refl* (+ *v être*) **1** to tighten
2 to become strained

tendre[2] /tɑ̃dʀ/ **A** *adj* **1** ‹*wood, fibre*› soft; ‹*skin, vegetables*› tender
2 ‹*shoot, grass*› new; **~ enfance** earliest childhood
3 ‹*pink, green*› soft
4 ‹*person*› loving; ‹*love, smile, words*› tender; ‹*temperament*› gentle; **ne pas être ~ avec qn/qch** to be hard on sb/sth
5 ‹*husband, wife*› dear
B *mf* soft-hearted person

tendrement /tɑ̃dʀəmɑ̃/ *adv* tenderly

tendresse /tɑ̃dʀɛs/ *f* **1** tenderness
2 affection

tendu, **~e** /tɑ̃dy/ **A** *pp* ▸ **tendre[1]**
B *pp adj* ‹*rope*› tight
C *adj* ‹*person, meeting*› tense

ténèbres /tenɛbʀ/ *fpl* **les ~** darkness

ténébreux, **-euse** /tenebʀø, øz/ *adj* **1** dark
2 obscure

teneur /tənœʀ/ *f* **1** (of solid) content; (of gas, liquid) level
2 (of report) import

ténia /tenja/ *m* tapeworm

tenir /təniʀ/ [v36] **A** *vt* **1** to hold; **~ qn par la main** to hold sb's hand; **tiens!** (giving sth to sb) here you are!; **tiens, regarde!** hey, look!; **si je le tenais!** if I could get my hands on him!
2 to keep [sb] under control; **il nous tient** he's got a hold on us
3 (Mil) to hold ‹*hill, bridge, city*›
4 to hold ‹*captive, animal*›; **je te tiens!** I've caught you!
5 to have ‹*information*›
6 to hold ‹*job*›; to run ‹*shop, house, business*›; to be in charge of ‹*switchboard, reception*›
7 to keep; **'~ hors de portée des enfants'** 'keep out of reach of children'
8 ~ sa tête droite to hold one's head upright; **~ les yeux baissés** to keep one's eyes lowered
9 to hold down ‹*load, cargo*›; to hold up ‹*trousers, socks*›
10 to keep to ‹*itinerary*›
11 ~ la mer ‹*ship*› to be seaworthy; **~ le coup** to hold out; **~ le choc** ‹*person*› to stand the strain
12 ‹*object*› to take up ‹*room*›; ‹*person*› to hold ‹*role, position*›

13 ~ qn/qch pour responsable to hold sb/ sth responsible; **~ qn pour mort** to give sb up for dead

B tenir à *v+prep* **1 ~ à** to be fond of, to like; **~ à la vie** to value one's life

2 j'y tiens I insist; **~ à ce que qn fasse** to insist that sb should do

C tenir de *v+prep* **~ de qn** to take after sb

D *vi* **1** ‹*rope, shelf, dam*› to hold; ‹*stamp, glue*› to stick; ‹*bandage, structure*› to stay in place; ‹*hairstyle*› to stay tidy

2 ~ (bon) (gen) to hang on; (Mil) to hold out

3 la neige tient the snow is settling; **les fleurs n'ont pas tenu** the flowers didn't last long

4 ‹*theory*› to hold good; ‹*alibi*› to stand up

5 ‹*people, objects*› to fit; **~ à six dans une voiture** to fit six into a car; **mon article tient en trois pages** my article takes up only three pages

E se tenir *v refl* (+ *v être*) **1 se ~ la tête à deux mains** to hold one's head in one's hands

2 se ~ par le bras to be arm in arm; **se ~ par la main** to hold hands

3 se ~ à qch to hold onto sth; **tiens-toi** *or* **tenez-vous bien** (fig, fam) prepare yourself for a shock

4 se ~ accroupi to be squatting; **se ~ au milieu** to be standing in the middle; **se ~ prêt** to be ready

5 to behave; **se ~ bien/mal** to behave well/ badly

6 se ~ bien/mal to have (a) good posture/ (a) bad posture; **tiens-toi droit!** stand up straight!

7 ‹*demonstration, exhibition*› to be held

8 ‹*argument, book*› to hold together; **ça se tient** it makes sense

9 tenez-vous le pour dit! (fam) I don't want to have to tell you again!

10 s'en ~ à to keep to; **s'en ~ aux ordres** to stick to orders; **ne pas savoir à quoi s'en ~** not to know what to make of it

F *v impers* **il ne tient qu'à toi de partir** it's up to you to decide whether to leave; **qu'à cela ne tienne!** never mind!

tennis /tenis/ **A** *m inv* tennis; **~ de table** table tennis

B *m inv or f inv* tennis shoe

tennisman, *pl* **tennismen** /tenisman, mɛn/ *m* (male) tennis player

ténor /tenɔʀ/ *m* tenor

tension /tɑ̃sjɔ̃/ *f* **1** (of cable, muscle) tension

2 (Med) **~ (artérielle)** blood pressure; **être sous ~** to be under stress

3 (in electricity) tension; **basse ~** low voltage; **sous ~** ‹*wire*› live; ‹*machine*› switched on

4 (between people) tension

tentacule /tɑ̃takyl/ *m* tentacle

tentateur, **-trice** /tɑ̃tatœʀ, tʀis/ *mf* tempter/temptress

tentation /tɑ̃tasjɔ̃/ *f* temptation

tentative /tɑ̃tativ/ *f* attempt; **~ de meurtre** (gen) murder attempt; (Law) attempted murder

tente /tɑ̃t/ *f* tent

tenter /tɑ̃te/ [**v1**] *vt* **1** to attempt; **~ sa chance** to try one's luck; **~ le tout pour le tout** to risk one's all

2 to tempt; **cela ne la tente guère** that doesn't appeal to her very much; **laisse-toi ~!** be a devil!; **~ le diable** to court disaster

tenture /tɑ̃tyʀ/ *f* **1** curtain; **~s** draperies

2 fabric wall covering

tenu, **~e** /təny/ **A** *pp* ▶ **tenir**

B *pp adj* **1 bien/mal ~** ‹*child*› well/badly cared for; ‹*house*› well/badly kept

2 ~ de faire required to do; **~ à** bound by

tenue /təny/ *f* **1 ~ (vestimentaire)** dress, clothes; **être en ~ légère** to be scantily dressed; **en ~** (Mil) uniformed

2 avoir de la ~ to have good manners; **un peu de ~!** mind your manners!

3 posture

ter /tɛʀ/ *adv* **1** (in address) ter; **15 ~ rue du Rocher** 15 ter rue du Rocher

2 three times

térébenthine /teʀebɑ̃tin/ *f* turpentine

tergal® /tɛʀgal/ *m* Terylene®

tergiversation /tɛʀʒivɛʀsasjɔ̃/ *f* equivocation

tergiverser /tɛʀʒivɛʀse/ [**v1**] *vi* **1** to dither

2 to shilly-shally

terme /tɛʀm/ **A** *m* **1** term, word

2 end; **mettre un ~ à qch** to put an end to sth; **toucher à son ~** to come to an end; **arriver à ~** ‹*period, contract*› to expire; **accoucher avant ~** to give birth prematurely

3 passé ce ~ vous paierez des intérêts after this date, you will pay interest; **à moyen ~** ‹*loan*› medium term

4 trouver un moyen ~ to find a compromise

B termes *mpl* terms; **~s de l'échange** terms of trade; **en bons ~s** on good terms

terminaison /tɛʀminɛzɔ̃/ *f* ending

terminal, **~e** *mpl* **-aux** /tɛʀminal, o/

A *adj* ‹*year*› final; **phase ~e** (of operation) concluding phase; (of illness) terminal phase

B *m* terminal

terminale /tɛʀminal/ *f* (Sch) final year (*of secondary school*)

terminer /tɛʀmine/ [**v1**] **A** *vt* to finish; to end; **être terminé** to be over

B *vi* to finish; **en ~ avec** to be through with; **pour ~** in conclusion

C se terminer *v refl* (+ *v être*) **1** to end

2 se ~ par ‹*word, number, object*› to end in

terminologie /tɛʀminɔlɔʒi/ *f* terminology

terminus /tɛʀminys/ *m inv* (of train) end of the line; (of bus) terminus

termite /tɛʀmit/ *m* termite

ternaire /tɛʀnɛʀ/ *adj* (in maths, physics) ternary; (Mus) compound

key word

terne /tɛʀn/ *adj* ‹*hair, life*› dull; ‹*colour*› drab; ‹*eyes, expression*› lifeless

ternir /tɛʀniʀ/ [**v3**] **A** *vt* **1** to tarnish ‹*metal*›; to fade ‹*fabric*›
2 to tarnish ‹*image, reputation*›
B se ternir *v refl* (+ *v être*) to tarnish

terrain /tɛʀɛ̃/ *m* **1** (gen) ground; (Mil) field
2 plot of land
3 land
4 (for football, rugby, cricket) pitch (BrE), field; ground; (for volleyball, handball, tennis) court; (in golf) course
5 (fig) **nous ne vous suivrons pas sur ce ~** we won't go along with you there; **un ~ d'entente** common ground; **travailler sur le ~** to do fieldwork; **~ favorable** (Med) predisposing factors; (in sociology) favourable (BrE) environment; **déblayer le ~** to clear the ground; **préparer le ~** to pave the way; **tâter le ~** to put out feelers
■ **~ d'atterrissage** landing strip; **~ d'aviation** airfield; **~ de camping** campsite; **~ de jeu(x)** playground; **~ de sport(s)** sports ground; **~ vague** wasteland

terrasse /tɛʀas/ *f* **1** terrace; **s'installer à la ~ d'un café** to sit at a table outside a cafe
2 flat roof
3 large balcony

terrassement /tɛʀasmɑ̃/ *m* excavation; **faire des travaux de ~** to carry out excavation work

terrasser /tɛʀase/ [**v1**] *vt* ‹*illness*› to strike down; **terrassé par** (by heat, grief) prostrated by

terrassier /tɛʀasje/ *m* building labourer (BrE)

terre /tɛʀ/ **A** *f* **1** ground; **sous ~** underground
2 earth; soil; **sortir de ~** ‹*plant*› to come up
3 land; **le retour à la ~** the movement back to the land; **aller à ~** to go ashore; **s'enfoncer à l'intérieur des ~s** to go deep inland
4 earth; **il croit que la ~ entière est contre lui** he thinks the whole world is against him; **redescends sur ~!** come back to earth!
5 de la ~ (glaise) clay; **un pot en ~** an earthenware pot
6 (in electricity) earth (BrE), ground (AmE)
B terre à terre *phr* ‹*question*› basic; ‹*conversation, person*› pedestrian
C par terre *phr* on the ground; on the floor; **c'est à se rouler par ~** (fam) it's hilarious; **ça a fichu tous nos projets par ~** (fam) it messed up all our plans (fam)
■ **~ d'asile** country of refuge; **~ battue** trodden earth; **sur ~ battue** on a clay court
IDIOM **avoir les pieds sur ~** (fam) to have one's feet firmly planted on the ground

Terre /tɛʀ/ *f* Earth; **sur la ~** on Earth

terreau, *pl* **~x** /tɛʀo/ *m* compost; **~ de feuilles** leaf mould (BrE), leaf mold (AmE)

terre-plein, *pl* **terres-pleins** /tɛʀplɛ̃/ *m* (of road) central reservation (BrE), median strip (AmE)

terrer: se terrer /tɛʀe/ [**v1**] *v refl* (+ *v être*)
1 ‹*rabbit*› to disappear into its burrow; ‹*fox*› to go to earth
2 ‹*fugitive*› to hide

terrestre /tɛʀɛstʀ/ *adj* **1** ‹*surface, diameter*› of the Earth
2 ‹*animals*› land
3 ‹*war, transport*› land; **la vie/le paradis ~** life/heaven on earth

terreur /tɛʀœʀ/ *f* terror; **c'est ma grande ~** it's my greatest fear

terrible /tɛʀibl/ *adj* **1** (gen) terrible; ‹*thirst, desire*› tremendous; **il est ~, il ne veut jamais avoir tort** (fam) it's terrible the way he never wants to admit that he's wrong
2 (fam) terrific (fam)

terriblement /tɛʀibləmɑ̃/ *adv* terribly; **il a ~ grandi** he's grown an awful lot

terrien, **-ienne** /tɛʀjɛ̃, ɛn/ *adj* **propriétaire ~** landowner

terrier /tɛʀje/ *m* **1** (gen) hole; **un ~ de renard** a fox's earth
2 (Zool) terrier

terrifiant, **~e** /tɛʀifjɑ̃, ɑ̃t/ *adj* terrifying

terrifier /tɛʀifje/ [**v2**] *vt* to terrify

terrine /tɛʀin/ *f* (gen) terrine; (round) earthenware bowl

territoire /tɛʀitwaʀ/ *m* territory
■ **~ d'outre-mer, TOM** French overseas (administrative) territory

territorial, **~e**, *mpl* **-iaux** /tɛʀitɔʀjal, o/ *adj*
1 ‹*waters, integrity*› territorial
2 ‹*administration*› divisional; regional

terroir /tɛʀwaʀ/ *m* land; **vin du ~** local wine

terroriser /tɛʀɔʀize/ [**v1**] *vt* **1** to terrorize
2 to terrify

terrorisme /tɛʀɔʀism/ *m* terrorism

terroriste /tɛʀɔʀist/ *adj, mf* terrorist

tertiaire /tɛʀsjɛʀ/ *adj* **1** (Econ) ‹*sector, industry*› service
2 (in geology) Tertiary

tertio /tɛʀsjo/ *adv* thirdly

tes ▸ **ton**[1]

tesson /tesɔ̃/ *m* shard, fragment

test /tɛst/ *m* test; **~ (de dépistage) du sida** Aids test; **faire passer des ~s à qn** (gen) to give sb tests; (Med) to carry out tests on sb

testament /tɛstamɑ̃/ *m* (Law) will; (fig) legacy

testamentaire /tɛstamɑ̃tɛʀ/ *adj* of a will

tester /tɛste/ [**v1**] *vt* to test

testicule /tɛstikyl/ *m* testicle

tétanos /tetanos/ *m inv* tetanus

têtard /tɛtaʀ/ *m* (Zool) tadpole

tête /tɛt/ *f* **1** head; **en pleine ~** (right) in the head; **~ baissée** ‹*rush*› headlong; **la ~ en bas** ‹*hang*› upside down; **se laver la ~** to wash one's hair; **au-dessus de nos ~s** overhead; **être tombé sur la ~** (fig, fam) to have gone off one's rocker (fam); **ma ~ est mise à prix** there's a price on my head;

vouloir la ~ de qn to want sb's head; to be after sb's head; **risquer sa ~** to risk one's neck (fam); **des ~s vont tomber** (fig) heads will roll
2 face; **une bonne/sale ~** a nice/nasty face; **tu en fais une ~!** what a face!; **quelle ~ va-t-il faire?** how's he going to react?; **il (me) fait la ~** he's sulking; **il a une ~ à tricher** he looks like a cheat; **tu as une ~ à faire peur, aujourd'hui!** you look dreadful today!
3 de ~ ‹*quote, recite*› from memory; ‹*calculate*› in one's head; **tu n'as pas de ~!** you have a mind like a sieve!; **avoir qch en ~** to have sth in mind; **où avais-je la ~?** whatever was I thinking of?; **ça (ne) va pas, la ~?** (fam) are you out of your mind or what?; **mets-lui ça dans la ~** drum it into him/her; **passer par la ~ de qn** ‹*idea*› to cross sb's mind; **monter la ~ à Pierre contre Paul** to turn Pierre against Paul; **j'ai la ~ qui tourne** my head's spinning; **monter à la ~ de qn** ‹*alcohol, success*› to go to sb's head; **il a encore toute sa ~ (à lui)** he's still got all his faculties; **n'en faire qu'à sa ~** to go one's own way; **tenir ~ à qn** to stand up to sb
4 (person) **avoir ses ~s** to have one's favourites (BrE); **un dîner en ~ à ~** an intimate dinner for two; **par ~** (gen) a head, each; (in statistics) per capita
5 (measurement) head; **avoir une ~ d'avance sur qn** to be a short length in front of sb
6 il a été nommé à la ~ du groupe he was appointed head of the group; **prendre la ~ des opérations** to take charge of operations; **être à la ~ d'une immense fortune** to be the possessor of a huge fortune
7 top; **être en ~** (of list, category) to be at the top; (in election, race, survey) to be in the lead; **en ~ de phrase** at the beginning of a sentence
8 (of train) front; (of convoy) head; (of tree, mast) top; (of screw, nail) head; **en ~ de file** first in line
9 (Sport) (in football) **faire une ~** to head the ball
10 (Mil) (of missile) warhead
11 ~ de lecture (in tape recorder, video recorder) head
■ **~ en l'air** scatterbrain; **~ brûlée** daredevil; **~ à claques** (fam) pain (fam); **~ de linotte** ▸ **tête en l'air**; **~ de mort** skull; death's head; skull and crossbones; **~ de mule** (fam) mule; **être une vraie ~ de mule** (fam) to be as stubborn as a mule; **~ de Turc** (fam) whipping boy
IDIOMS **j'en mettrais ma ~ à couper** I'd swear to it; **en avoir par-dessus la ~** (fam) to be fed up to the back teeth (fam); **ça me prend la ~** (fam) it's a real drag (fam)

tête-à-queue /tɛtakø/ *m inv* **faire un ~** to slew round *or* around

tête-à-tête /tɛtatɛt/ *m inv* **1** tête-à-tête
2 private meeting

tête-bêche /tɛtbɛʃ/ *adv* **1** top to tail
2 head to tail

tétée /tete/ *f* **1** feeding
2 feed

téter /tete/ [**v14**] **A** *vt* to suck at ‹*breast*›; to feed from ‹*bottle*›; to suck ‹*milk*›
B *vi* to suckle; **donner à ~ à** to feed ‹*baby*›

tétine /tetin/ *f* **1** teat (BrE), nipple (AmE)
2 dummy (BrE), pacifier (AmE)
3 (of animal) teat

têtu, ~e /tety/ *adj* stubborn

⚷ **texte** /tɛkst/ *m* **1** text; **'~ intégral'** 'unabridged'
2 (Law) **~ de loi** bill; law

textile /tɛkstil/ **A** *adj* textile
B *m* **1** textile industry
2 ~s synthétiques synthetic fibres (BrE)

texto /tɛksto/ **A** (fam) ▸ **textuellement**
B *m* text message

textphone /tɛkstfɔn/ *m* textphone

textuellement /tɛkstɥɛlmɑ̃/ *adv* ‹*recount*› word for word

texture /tɛkstyʀ/ *f* **1** (of fabric, material) texture
2 (of novel) structure

TGV /teʒeve/ *m* (*abbr* = **train à grande vitesse**) TGV, high-speed train

thé /te/ *m* **1** tea
2 tea party

théâtral, ~e, *mpl* **-aux** /teɑtʀal, o/ *adj*
1 ‹*performance*› stage; ‹*season, company*› theatre (BrE); ‹*production, technique*› theatrical; **l'œuvre ~e de Racine** the plays of Racine
2 ‹*gesture*› histrionic; ‹*tone*› melodramatic

⚷ **théâtre** /teɑtʀ/ *m* theatre (BrE); **le ~ antique** Greek classical drama; **de ~** ‹*actor, director, ticket*› theatre (BrE); ‹*decor, costume*› stage; **coup de ~** coup de théâtre; (fig) dramatic turn of events; **faire du ~** (as profession) to be an actor; (at school) to do drama; **être le ~ d'affrontements** (fig) to be the scene of fighting
■ **~ de Boulevard** farce

théière /tejɛʀ/ *f* teapot

théine /tein/ *f* theine

thématique /tematik/ **A** *adj* thematic
B *f* themes

⚷ **thème** /tɛm/ *m* **1** topic, subject; (of film) theme
2 (translation) prose
3 (Mus) theme
■ **~ astral** birth chart

théologie /teɔlɔʒi/ *f* theology

théorème /teɔʀɛm/ *m* theorem

théoricien, -ienne /teɔʀisjɛ̃, ɛn/ *mf* theoretician

⚷ **théorie** /teɔʀi/ *f* theory; **en ~** in theory

théorique /teɔʀik/ *adj* theoretical

thérapeute /teʀapøt/ *mf* therapist

thérapeutique /teʀapøtik/ *adj* ‹*effect*› therapeutic; **choix ~** choice of treatment

⚷ key word

t

thérapie /teʀapi/ *f* **1** (Med) treatment
2 (in psychology) therapy

thermal, **~e**, *mpl* **-aux** /tɛʀmal, o/ *adj* ‹*spring*› thermal; **station ~e** spa

thermalisme /tɛʀmalism/ *m* **1** balneology
2 hydrotherapy industry

thermes /tɛʀm/ *mpl* **1** (Roman) thermae
2 thermal baths

thermique /tɛʀmik/ *adj* thermal

thermo /tɛʀmo/ *pref* thermo; **~nucléaire** thermonuclear

thermomètre /tɛʀmɔmɛtʀ/ *m* thermometer

thermostat /tɛʀmɔsta/ *m* thermostat

thèse /tɛz/ *f* **1** (for doctorate) thesis (BrE), dissertation (AmE)
2 thesis, argument
3 avancer la ~ de l'accident to put forward the theory that it was an accident

thon /tɔ̃/ *m* tuna

thonier /tɔnje/ *m* tuna boat

thoracique /tɔʀasik/ *adj* **cage ~** ribcage

thorax /tɔʀaks/ *m inv* thorax

thym /tɛ̃/ *m* thyme

thyroïde /tiʀɔid/ *adj*, *f* thyroid

tibia /tibja/ *m* shin bone, tibia

tic /tik/ *m* **1** tic; **être plein de ~s** to be constantly twitching
2 ~ de langage verbal tic

ticket /tikɛ/ *m* (for train, platform) ticket; **~ de caisse** till receipt (BrE), sales slip (AmE); **~ modérateur** *patient's contribution towards the cost of medical treatment*

ticket-restaurant®, *pl* **tickets-restaurant** /tikeʀɛstɔʀɑ̃/ *m* luncheon voucher, meal ticket

tic-tac /tiktak/ *m inv* **faire ~** to tick

tiède /tjɛd/ *adj* **1** lukewarm; warm; mild
2 (fig) lukewarm

tièdement /tjɛdmɑ̃/ *adv* half-heartedly

tiédeur /tjedœʀ/ *f* **1** (of season) mildness; (of air, room) warmth
2 (fig) half-heartedness

tiédir /tjediʀ/ [**v3**] *vi* **1 faire ~** to warm *or* heat (up); **laisser ~** to allow [sth] to cool
2 ‹*feelings*› to cool; ‹*enthusiasm*› to wane

tien, **tienne** /tjɛ̃, tjɛn/ **le tien**, **la tienne**, **les tiens**, **les tiennes** *pron* yours; **un métier comme le ~** a job like yours; **à la tienne!** cheers!; (ironic) good luck to you!

tiens ▸ **tenir**

tierce /tjɛʀs/ ▸ **tiers A**

tiercé /tjɛʀse/ *m* (Games) **jouer au ~** to bet on the horses

tiers, **tierce** /tjɛʀ, tjɛʀs/ **A** *adj* third; **un pays ~** (gen) another country; a non-member country; **une tierce personne** a third party
B *m inv* **1** third; **le ~/les deux ~ du travail** one third/two thirds of the work
2 (person) outsider; (Law) third party
■ **le Tiers État** the Third Estate

tiers-monde /tjɛʀmɔ̃d/ *m* Third World

tiers-mondisme /tjɛʀmɔ̃dism/ *m* support for the Third World

tiers-mondiste /tjɛʀmɔ̃dist/ **A** *adj* in support of the Third World
B *mf* supporter of the Third World

tige /tiʒ/ *f* (of plant) (gen) stem, stalk

tigre /tigʀ/ *m* (Zool) tiger

tigré, **~e** /tigʀe/ *adj* **1** striped
2 spotted

tigresse /tigʀɛs/ *f* (Zool), (fig) tigress

tilleul /tijœl/ *m* **1** lime tree
2 lime wood
3 lime blossom tea

tilt /tilt/ *m* (fam) **ça a fait ~ (dans mon esprit)** (fam) the penny dropped (fam)

timbale /tɛ̃bal/ *f* **1** (metal) tumbler
2 (Mus) kettledrum; **~s** timpani
3 (Culin) timbale

timbre /tɛ̃bʀ/ *m* **1** stamp
2 postmark
3 (of voice) tone, timbre
4 (Med) patch

timbre-poste, *pl* **timbres-poste** /tɛ̃bʀəpɔst/ *m* postage stamp

timbrer /tɛ̃bʀe/ [**v1**] *vt* to stamp

timide /timid/ *adj* ‹*person*› shy, timid; ‹*criticism*› timid; ‹*success*› limited

timidement /timidmɑ̃/ *adv* shyly; timidly; (without conviction) half-heartedly

timidité /timidite/ *f* shyness

timoré, **~e** /timɔʀe/ *adj* timorous

tintamarre /tɛ̃tamaʀ/ *m* din; **faire du ~** to make a din

tintement /tɛ̃tmɑ̃/ *m* chiming; tinkling

tinter /tɛ̃te/ [**v1**] *vi* ‹*bells*› to chime; ‹*doorbell*› to ring; ‹*small bell*› to tinkle; ‹*glass, coins*› to clink; ‹*keys*› to jingle; (Mus) ‹*triangle*› to ring

tintinnabuler /tɛ̃tinabyle/ [**v1**] *vi* to tinkle

tipi /tipi/ *m* te(e)pee

tique /tik/ *f* (Zool) tick

tiquer /tike/ [**v1**] *vi* (fam) to wince; **sans ~** without batting an eyelid (BrE) *or* eyelash (AmE)

tir /tiʀ/ *m* **1** (Mil) fire; **déclencher le ~** to open fire
2 (Sport) shooting
3 ~ de grenades grenade firing
4 (in games, sports) (with ball) shot
5 shooting

tirade /tiʀad/ *f* **1** declamation
2 tirade

tirage /tiʀaʒ/ *m* **1 ~ (au sort)** draw; **désigner par ~ (au sort)** to draw ‹*name, winner*›
2 impression
3 edition; **~ limité** limited edition
4 (of book) run; (of newspaper) circulation

tiraillement /tiʀajmɑ̃/ *m* **1** pulling, tugging
2 nagging pain; **~s d'estomac** hunger pangs
3 friction

tirailler /tiʀaje/ [**v1**] *vt* to tug (at), to pull (at) ‹*rope, sleeve*›; **être tiraillé entre son travail et sa famille** to be torn between one's work and one's family

tire-au-flanc /tiʀoflɑ̃/ *m inv* (fam) shirker, skiver (fam)

tire-bouchon, *pl* **∼s** /tiʀbuʃɔ̃/ *m* corkscrew; **en ∼** ‹*tail*› curly

tire-d'aile: **à tire-d'aile** /atiʀdɛl/ *phr* in a flurry of wings; (fig) hurriedly

tirelire /tiʀliʀ/ *f* piggy bank

⚷ **tirer** /tiʀe/ [**v1**] **A** *vt* **1** to pull ‹*vehicle*›; to pull up ‹*chair, armchair*›; to pull away ‹*rug*›
2 to pull ‹*hair*›; to pull on ‹*rope*›; to tug at ‹*sleeve*›; **∼ qn par le bras** to pull sb's arm
3 ∼ ses cheveux en arrière to pull back one's hair; **avoir les traits tirés** to look drawn
4 to draw ‹*bolt, curtain*›; to pull down ‹*blind*›; to close ‹*door, shutter*›
5 to fire off ‹*bullet, grenade*›; to fire ‹*missile*›; to shoot ‹*arrow*›
6 (Sport) **∼ un penalty** to take a penalty
7 ∼ (au sort) to draw ‹*card, name, winner*›; to draw for ‹*partner*›
8 (in astrology) **∼ les cartes à qn** to tell the cards for sb
9 to draw ‹*wine*›; to withdraw ‹*money*›; **∼ qch de sa poche** to pull sth out of one's pocket
10 ∼ le pays de la récession to get the country out of recession; **tire-moi de là!** get me out of this!
11 ∼ qch de qn to get sth from sb ‹*information, confession*›; **∼ qch de qch** to draw sth from sth ‹*strength, resources*›; to derive sth from sth ‹*pride, satisfaction*›; to make sth out of sth ‹*money*›
12 ∼ de qch to base [sth] on sth ‹*story, film*›; to get [sth] from sth ‹*name*›
13 to print ‹*book, negative*›; to run off ‹*proofs, copies*›
14 to draw ‹*line*›
15 (fam) **plus qu'une semaine à ∼** only one more week to go
16 ∼ un chèque to draw a cheque (BrE) *or* check (AmE)
B *vi* **1** to pull; **∼ sur qch** to pull on sth; to tug at sth
2 (with firearm) to shoot; to fire
3 (in football) to shoot; (in handball, basketball) to take a shot
4 ∼ (au sort) to draw lots
5 la cheminée tire bien the chimney draws well
6 ∼ à mille exemplaires ‹*periodical*› to have a circulation of one thousand
7 ∼ sur le jaune/l'orangé ‹*colour*› to be yellowish/orangy
C se tirer *v refl* (+ *v être*) **1 se ∼ de** to come through ‹*situation, difficulties*›
2 se ∼ une balle to shoot oneself; **se ∼ dessus** to shoot at one another
3 (fam) **s'en ∼** to cope; (from accident) to escape; (from illness) to pull through; **s'en ∼ à bon prix** to get off lightly

tiret /tiʀɛ/ *m* dash

tirette /tiʀɛt/ *f* pull tab; cord

tireur, -euse /tiʀœʀ, øz/ *mf* **1** (Mil, Sport) marksman/markswoman
2 gunman

tiroir /tiʀwaʀ/ *m* (in piece of furniture) drawer; **à ∼s** (fig) ‹*novel, play*› episodic
IDIOM **racler les fonds de ∼** to scrape some money together

tiroir-caisse, *pl* **tiroirs-caisses** /tiʀwaʀkɛs/ *m* cash register

tisane /tizan/ *f* herbal tea, tisane

tison /tizɔ̃/ *m* (fire) brand

tisonnier /tizɔnje/ *m* poker

tissage /tisaʒ/ *m* **1** weaving
2 weave

tisser /tise/ [**v1**] *vt* **1** ‹*person, machine*› to weave
2 ‹*spider*› to spin ‹*web*›

tisserand, **∼e** /tisʀɑ̃, ɑ̃d/ *mf* weaver

tissu /tisy/ *m* **1** material, fabric
2 (Anat) **∼ osseux** bone tissue
3 (of intrigue) web; (of lies) pack; (of insults) string; **∼ social** social fabric

titan /titɑ̃/ *m* titan; **de ∼** titanic

titane /titan/ *m* titanium

titiller /titije/ [**v1**] *vt* to titillate

⚷ **titre** /titʀ/ *m* **1** (of book, film, chapter) title; (in newspaper) headline; **avoir pour ∼** to be entitled; **les ∼s de l'actualité** the headlines
2 (rank) title; **∼ mondial** world title; **∼ nobiliaire** *or* **de noblesse** title; **le ∼ d'ingénieur** the status of qualified engineer; **en ∼** ‹*professor, director*› titular; ‹*supplier*› appointed; ‹*mistress, rival*› official; **∼s universitaires** university qualifications
3 à juste ∼ quite rightly; **à ∼ d'exemple** as an example; **à ∼ définitif** on a permanent basis; **à ∼ privé** in a private capacity; **à ∼ gracieux** free; **à ∼ indicatif** as a rough guide; **à quel ∼ a-t-il été invité?** why was he invited?
4 (Law) deed; **∼ de propriété** title deed
5 (on stock exchange) security
6 (Econ) item; **∼ budgétaire** budgetary item
7 (of solution) titre (BrE); (of wines, spirits) strength; (of precious metal) fineness
■ **∼ de gloire** claim to fame; **∼ interbancaire de paiement, TIP** *bank account details to make a payment by direct debit*; **∼ de séjour** residence permit; **∼ de transport** ticket

titré, **∼e** /titʀe/ *adj* titled; **être ∼** to be titled

tituber /titybe/ [**v1**] *vi* to stagger

titulaire /tityIɛʀ/ **A** *adj* (gen) permanent; ‹*lecturer*› tenured
B *mf* **1** (gen) permanent staff member; tenured lecturer (BrE) *or* professor (AmE)

⚷ key word

t

2 holder; **être ~ de** to hold ‹*degree, post*›; to have ‹*bank account*›

titularisation /titylaʀizasjɔ̃/ *f* confirmation in a post; (Univ) granting of tenure

titulariser /titylaʀize/ [**v1**] *vt* to give permanent status to ‹*staff*›; to grant tenure to ‹*professor*›

toast /tost/ *m* toast

toboggan /tɔbɔɡɑ̃/ *m* **1** slide
2 ® flyover (BrE), overpass (AmE)
3 (Tech) (for rubble) chute

toc /tɔk/ **A** *m* (fam) **c'est du ~** it's fake
B *excl* **~! ~!** knock! knock!

tocsin /tɔksɛ̃/ *m* alarm (bell), tocsin

toge /tɔʒ/ *f* **1** (of academic) gown; (of judge) robe
2 toga

toi /twɑ/ *pron* **1** you; **~, ne dis rien** don't say anything; **elle est plus âgée que ~** she's older than you; **à ~** (in game) your turn; **c'est à ~** it's yours; **c'est à ~ de choisir** it's your turn to choose; it's up to you to choose
2 yourself; **reprends-~** pull yourself together

toile /twal/ *f* **1** cloth; **~ de lin** linen (cloth); **de la grosse ~** canvas
2 (in art) canvas; painting; **~ de maître** master painting
3 (Naut) canvas
4 (Comput) (World Wide) Web
■ **~ d'araignée** spider's web; cobweb; **~ cirée** oilcloth; **~ de jute** hessian; **~ de tente** canvas; tent

toilettage /twalɛtaʒ/ *m* (of animal) grooming

toilette /twalɛt/ **A** *f* **1 faire sa ~** ‹*person*› to have a wash; ‹*animal*› to wash itself; **faire la ~ d'un mort** to lay out a corpse
2 outfit; **en grande ~** all dressed up
B toilettes *fpl* toilet (BrE), bathroom (AmE)

toiletter /twalete/ [**v1**] *vt* to groom ‹*dog*›

toi-même /twamɛm/ *pron* yourself

toise /twaz/ *f* height gauge

toiser /twaze/ [**v1**] *vt* to look [sb] up and down

toit /twɑ/ *m* roof
■ **le ~ du Monde** the roof of the world; **~ ouvrant** sunroof
IDIOM **crier qch sur (tous) les ~s** to shout sth from the rooftops

toiture /twatyʀ/ *f* **1** roof
2 roofing

tôle /tol/ *f* **1** sheet metal
2 metal sheet *or* plate
3 (pop) ▶ **taule**

tolérable /tɔleʀabl/ *adj* bearable; tolerable

tolérance /tɔleʀɑ̃s/ *f* **1** tolerance; indulgence
2 ce n'est pas un droit, c'est une ~ it isn't legal but it is tolerated
3 (of medicine, noise) tolerance

tolérant, **~e** /tɔleʀɑ̃, ɑ̃t/ *adj* tolerant

tolérer /tɔleʀe/ [**v14**] *vt* to tolerate

tôlerie /tolʀi/ *f* sheet metal working; sheet metal trade; sheet metal works

tollé /tɔle/ *m* outcry, hue and cry

TOM /tɔm/ *m*: *abbr* ▶ **territoire**

tomate /tɔmat/ *f* **1** tomato
2 tomato plant
3 *pastis with a dash of grenadine*

tombal, **~e**, *mpl* **-aux** /tɔ̃bal, o/ *adj* **inscription ~e** gravestone inscription

tombant, **~e** /tɔ̃bɑ̃, ɑ̃t/ *adj* ‹*shoulders*› sloping; ‹*moustache, eyelids*› drooping; ‹*ears*› floppy

tombe /tɔ̃b/ *f* **1** grave
2 gravestone

tombeau, *pl* **~x** /tɔ̃bo/ *m* **1** tomb; **mettre qn au ~** to lay sb in their grave
2 c'est un ~ ‹*person*› he/she will keep quiet

tombée /tɔ̃be/ *f* **à la ~ du jour** at close of day; **la ~ de la nuit** nightfall

tomber[1] /tɔ̃be/ [**v1**] **A** *vi* (+ *v être*) **1** (gen) to fall; ‹*person, chair*› to fall over; ‹*tree, wall*› to fall down; (from height) ‹*person, vase*› to fall off; ‹*hair, teeth*› to fall out; ‹*plaster, covering*› to come off; ‹*clothes*› to take off; **~ du lit/de ma poche** to fall out of bed/out of my pocket; **le vent a fait ~ une tuile du toit** the wind blew a tile off the roof; **se laisser ~ dans un fauteuil** to flop into an armchair; **laisser ~ un gâteau sur le tapis** to drop a cake on the carpet
2 ‹*rain, snow, theatre curtain*› to fall; ‹*fog*› to come down; **qu'est-ce que ça tombe!** (fam) it's pouring down!; **la foudre est tombée sur un arbre** the lightning struck a tree
3 ‹*price, temperature*› to fall; ‹*anger*› to subside; ‹*fever*› to come down; ‹*wind*› to drop; ‹*day*› to draw to a close; ‹*conversation*› to die down; **faire ~** to bring down ‹*price, temperature*›; to dampen ‹*enthusiasm*›; **je tombe de sommeil** I can't keep my eyes open
4 ‹*dictator, regime, city*› to fall; ‹*obstacle*› to vanish; **faire ~** to bring down ‹*regime, dictator*›; (fig) to break down ‹*barriers*›
5 ‹*belly*› to sag; ‹*shoulders*› to slope
6 ‹*lock of hair*› to fall; **~ bien/mal** ‹*garment, curtain*› to hang well/badly
7 ~ dans un piège (fig) to fall into a trap; **~ sous le coup d'une loi** to fall within the provisions of a law; **~ aux mains** *or* **entre les mains de qn** ‹*document, power*› to fall into sb's hand; **~ malade/amoureux** to fall ill/in love
8 ‹*decision, verdict*› to be announced; ‹*news*› to break; ‹*reply*› to be given
9 ~ sur to come across ‹*stranger, object*›; to run into ‹*friend*›; **~ sur la bonne page** to hit on the right page; **si tu prends cette rue, tu tomberas sur la place** if you follow that street, you'll come to the square
10 c'est tombé juste au bon moment it came just at the right time; **tu ne pouvais pas mieux ~!** you couldn't have come at

t

a better time!; you couldn't have done better!; **tu tombes mal, j'allais partir** you're unlucky, I was just about to leave; **il faut toujours que ça tombe sur moi!** (fam) (decision, choice) why does it always have to be me?; (misfortune) why does it always have to happen to me?
11 ‹*birthday*› to fall on ‹*day*›
12 laisser ~ to give up ‹*job, activity*›; to drop ‹*plan, habit*›; **laisse ~!** forget it!; **laisser ~ qn** to drop sb; to let sb down
13 ~ sur qn ‹*soldiers, thugs*› to fall on sb; ‹*raiders, police*› to descend on sb
B *vt* to take off ‹*clothes*›

tomber² /tɔ̃be/ *m* hang; **ce velours a un beau ~** this velvet hangs well

tombeur /tɔ̃bœʀ/ *m* (fam) lady-killer

tombola /tɔ̃bɔla/ *f* tombola (BrE), lottery

tome¹ /tom/ *m* **1** volume
2 part, book

tome² /tɔm/ ▶ **tomme**

tomme /tɔm/ *f* tomme *or* tome (cheese)

tommette /tɔmɛt/ *f* hexagonal floor tile

✐ **ton¹**, **ta**, *pl* **tes** /tɔ̃, ta, te/ *det* your; **un de tes amis** a friend of yours

ton² /tɔ̃/ *m* **1** pitch; tone; **~ grave/aigu** low/high pitch; **d'un ~ dédaigneux** scornfully; **baisser le ~** to lower one's voice; (fig) to moderate one's tone; **eh bien, si tu le prends sur ce ~** well, if you're going to take it like that
2 (in linguistics) tone; **langue à ~s** tone language
3 donner le ~ to set the tone; to set the fashion; **de bon ~** in good taste
4 (Mus) pitch; key; tone; (instrument) pitch pipe
5 (of colour) shade; **~ sur ~** in matching tones

tonalité /tɔnalite/ *f* **1** (Mus) key; tonality
2 (of vowel) tone
3 (of voice) tone
4 (of colours) tonality
5 dialling tone (BrE), dial tone (AmE)

tondeuse /tɔ̃døz/ *f* **1** (for sheep) shears
2 (for cutting hair) clippers
3 ~ (à gazon) lawnmower

t

tondre /tɔ̃dʀ/ [**v6**] *vt* to shear ‹*sheep*›; to clip ‹*dog*›; to mow ‹*lawn*›; **~ qn** to shave sb's head

tongs /tɔ̃g/ *fpl* flip-flops, thongs (AmE)

tonicité /tɔnisite/ *f* **1** bracing effect
2 tone

tonifiant, **~e** /tɔnifjɑ̃, ɑ̃t/ *adj* **1** ‹*climate, air*› bracing
2 ‹*exercise, lotion*› toning

tonifier /tɔnifje/ [**v2**] *vt* to tone up

tonique¹ /tɔnik/ *adj* **1** ‹*drink*› tonic; (fig) ‹*air*› bracing; ‹*book*› stimulating
2 lotion ~ toning lotion
3 ‹*accent*› tonic

tonique² /tɔnik/ *f* (Mus) tonic

tonitruant, **~e** /tɔnitʀyɑ̃, ɑ̃t/ *adj* booming

tonitruer /tɔnitʀye/ [**v1**] *vi* to thunder

tonnage /tɔnaʒ/ *m* tonnage

tonnant, **~e** /tɔnɑ̃, ɑ̃t/ *adj* booming; thunderous

tonne /tɔn/ *f* (1,000 kg) tonne, metric ton; **des ~s de choses à faire** (fam) loads of things to do (fam)

tonneau, *pl* **~x** /tɔno/ *m* **1** barrel
2 (of car) somersault
3 (of plane) barrel roll
4 (Naut) ton
IDIOM **du même ~** (fam) of the same kind

tonnelle /tɔnɛl/ *f* arbour (BrE)

tonner /tɔne/ [**v1**] *vi, v impers* to thunder

tonnerre /tɔnɛʀ/ *m* **1** thunder; **un coup de ~** a clap of thunder; (fig) a thunderbolt
2 (of cannons, artillery) thundering; **un ~ d'applaudissements** thunderous applause
3 (fam) **ça marche du ~** it's going fantastically well

tonsure /tɔ̃syʀ/ *f* (of monk) tonsure

tonte /tɔ̃t/ *f* **1 ~ (des moutons)** shearing
2 fleece

tonton /tɔ̃tɔ̃/ *m* (fam) uncle; **~ Pierre** Uncle Pierre

tonus /tɔnys/ *m inv* **1** (of person) energy, dynamism
2 (of muscle) tone, tonus

top /tɔp/ *m* pip, beep; **donner le ~ de départ** to give the starting signal

topaze /tɔpaz/ *f* topaz

toper /tɔpe/ [**v1**] *vi* **topons là!** let's shake on it!

topo /tɔpo/ *m* (fam) short talk; short piece; **c'est toujours le même ~** it's always the same old story (fam)

topographie /tɔpɔgʀafi/ *f* topography

toquade /tɔkad/ *f* (fam) **1** (for thing) passion
2 (on person) crush (fam)

toque /tɔk/ *f* **1** (of woman) toque; (of chef) chef's hat; (of judge) hat; **~ en fourrure** fur cap
2 (of jockey) cap

toqué, **~e** /tɔke/ *adj* (fam) crazy (fam)

torche /tɔʀʃ/ *f* torch
■ **~ électrique** torch (BrE), flashlight

torcher /tɔʀʃe/ [**v1**] *vt* (fam) **1** to wipe
2 to dash off (fam) ‹*article, report*›; to cobble [sth] together

torchis /tɔʀʃi/ *m inv* cob (*for walls*)

torchon /tɔʀʃɔ̃/ *m* **1** (gen) cloth; **~ (de cuisine)** tea towel (BrE), dish towel (AmE)
2 (newspaper) (derog) rag (fam)
3 (fam) messy piece of work
IDIOM **le ~ brûle** (fam) it's war

tordant, **~e** /tɔʀdɑ̃, ɑ̃t/ *adj* (fam) hilarious

tordre /tɔʀdʀ/ [**v6**] **A** *vt* **1** to twist ‹*arm, wrist*›; to wring ‹*neck*›
2 to bend ‹*nail, bar, bumper*›
3 to wring out ‹*washing*›

✐ key word

B se tordre *v refl* (+ *v être*) **1** ‹*person*› **se ~ la cheville** to twist one's ankle; **se ~ de douleur** to writhe in pain
2 ‹*bumper*› to bend

tordu, ~e /tɔʀdy/ *adj* **1** ‹*nose, legs*› crooked; ‹*branches, trunk, iron bar*› twisted
2 (fig) ‹*idea*› weird, strange; ‹*logic, reasoning*› twisted

tornade /tɔʀnad/ *f* tornado

torpeur /tɔʀpœʀ/ *f* torpor

torpille /tɔʀpij/ *f* torpedo

torpiller /tɔʀpije/ [**v1**] *vt* to torpedo

torréfier /tɔʀefje/ [**v2**] *vt* to roast

torrent /tɔʀɑ̃/ *m* torrent; **pleuvoir à ~s** to rain very heavily

torrentiel, -ielle /tɔʀɑ̃sjɛl/ *adj* torrential

torride /tɔʀid/ *adj* torrid; ‹*sun*› scorching

tors, torse /tɔʀ, tɔʀs/ *adj* (gen) twisted

torsade /tɔʀsad/ *f* **1** twist, coil
2 cable stitch
3 (in architecture) cable moulding (BrE), cable molding (AmE)

torsader /tɔʀsade/ [**v1**] *vt* to twist; **une colonne torsadée** a cable column

torse /tɔʀs/ *m* **1** (gen) chest; **se mettre ~ nu** to strip to the waist
2 (Anat) torso

torsion /tɔʀsjɔ̃/ *f* **1** twisting
2 torsion

tort /tɔʀ/ **A** *m* **1 avoir ~** to be wrong; **j'aurais bien ~ de m'inquiéter!** it would be silly of me to worry!; **être en ~** to be in the wrong; **donner ~ à qn** ‹*referee, judge*› to blame sb; ‹*facts*› to prove sb wrong
2 fault; **les ~s sont partagés** there are faults on both sides; **avoir des ~s envers qn** to have wronged sb
3 mistake; **j'ai eu le ~ de le croire** I made the mistake of believing him
4 faire du ~ à qn/qch to harm sb/sth
B à tort *phr* ‹*accuse*› wrongly; **à ~ et à travers** ‹*spend*› wildly; **parler à ~ et à travers** to talk a lot of nonsense

torticolis /tɔʀtikɔli/ *m inv* stiff neck

tortillard /tɔʀtijaʀ/ *m* (fam) small local train

tortiller /tɔʀtije/ [**v1**] **A** *vt* to twist ‹*fibres, strands*›; to twiddle ‹*handkerchief*›
B se tortiller *v refl* (+ *v être*) to wriggle

tortionnaire /tɔʀsjɔnɛʀ/ *mf* torturer

tortue /tɔʀty/ *f* **1** (sea) turtle
2 tortoise (BrE), turtle (AmE)
3 (butterfly) tortoiseshell

tortueux, -euse /tɔʀtɥø, øz/ *adj* **1** ‹*road, staircase*› winding
2 (fig) ‹*behaviour*› devious; ‹*mind, reasoning*› tortuous

torture /tɔʀtyʀ/ *f* torture

torturer /tɔʀtyʀe/ [**v1**] **A** *vt* **1** to torture ‹*person*›
2 ‹*thought, feeling*› to torment
3 to distort ‹*text*›; **style torturé** tortured style
B se torturer *v refl* (+ *v être*) to torment oneself; **se ~ l'esprit** to rack one's brains

torve /tɔʀv/ *adj* ‹*look*› menacing, baleful

tôt /to/ *adv* **1** ‹*start*› early; **~ le matin** early in the morning
2 soon, early; **le plus ~ serait le mieux** the sooner the better; **~ ou tard** sooner or later; **on ne m'y reprendra pas de si ~** I won't do that again in a hurry

total, ~e, *mpl* **-aux** /tɔtal, o/ **A** *adj* complete, total
B *m* total
C au total *phr* **au ~ cela fait 350 euros** altogether that comes to 350 euros

totalement /tɔtalmɑ̃/ *adv* totally, completely

totaliser /tɔtalize/ [**v1**] *vt* **1** to total ‹*profits*›
2 to have a total of ‹*points, votes*›

totalitaire /tɔtalitɛʀ/ *adj* **1** ‹*regime, state*› totalitarian
2 ‹*doctrine*› all-embracing

totalitarisme /tɔtalitaʀism/ *m* totalitarianism

totalité /tɔtalite/ *f* **la ~ du personnel** all the staff; **la ~ des dépenses** the total expenditure; **nous vous rembourserons en ~** we will refund you in full

totem /tɔtɛm/ *m* **1** totem
2 totem pole

toubib /tubib/ *m* (fam) doctor, quack (fam)

toucan /tukɑ̃/ *m* toucan

touchant, ~e /tuʃɑ̃, ɑ̃t/ *adj* moving; touching

touche /tuʃ/ *f* **1** (gen) button; (on keyboard) key; (on stringed instrument) fret
2 (of paintbrush) stroke; (of paint) dash; (of artist) touch
3 (Sport) sideline, touchline; **mettre qn sur la ~** (fig) to push sb aside
4 (in fencing) hit
5 (in fishing) bite
■ **~ dièse** hash key; **~ étoile** star key

touche-à-tout /tuʃatu/ *adj inv* **être ~** to be into everything; to be a jack of all trades

toucher¹ /tuʃe/ [**v1**] **A** *vt* **1 ~ (de la main)** to touch ‹*object, surface, person*›; **~ du bois** (superstitiously) to touch wood; **~ le front de qn** to feel sb's forehead
2 to be touching ‹*wall, ceiling, bottom of sth*›; **~ le sol** to land
3 to hit ‹*opponent, car, kerb*›
4 to touch, to move ‹*person*›; **ça me touche beaucoup** I am very touched
5 ‹*event, crisis*› to affect ‹*person, country*›; ‹*storm*› to hit ‹*region, city*›
6 ‹*country, house*› to be next to
7 ‹*person*› to get ‹*money*›; to cash ‹*cheque*›
B toucher à *v+prep* **1 ~ à** to touch ‹*object*›; **~ à tout** to be into everything; (fig) to be a jack of all trades; **avec son air de ne pas y ~, c'est un malin** (fam) he looks as if butter wouldn't melt in his mouth, but he's a sly one

t

2 ~ à to concern ‹*activity, issue*›
3 ~ à to infringe on ‹*right, freedom*›
4 ~ à to get on to ‹*problem*›
C se toucher *v refl* (+ *v être*) ‹*houses, gardens*› to be next to each other

toucher² /tuʃe/ *m* **1 le ~** touch, the sense of touch
2 (of pianist) touch

touche-touche: **à touche-touche** /atuʃtuʃ/ *phr* (fam) **être à ~** ‹*cars*› to be bumper to bumper; ‹*people*› to be on top of each other (fam)

touffe /tuf/ *f* (of hair, grass) tuft

touffu, ~e /tufy/ *adj* **1** ‹*eyebrows, beard*› bushy; ‹*vegetation*› dense; ‹*bush*› thick; **au poil ~** with thick fur
2 ‹*text*› dense

touiller /tuje/ [**v1**] *vt* (fam) to stir ‹*sauce*›

toujours /tuʒuʀ/ *adv* **1** always; **comme ~** as always; **de ~** ‹*friend*› very old; ‹*friendship*› long-standing; **~ plus vite** faster and faster
2 still; **il n'est ~ pas levé?** is he still not up?
3 anyway; **on peut ~ essayer** we can always try; **c'est ~ ça de pris** *or* **de gagné** that's something at least; **~ est-il que** the fact remains that

toupet /tupɛ/ *m* **1** (fam) cheek (fam), nerve (fam)
2 (of hair) tuft; quiff (BrE), forelock (AmE)

toupie /tupi/ *f* top; **faire tourner une ~** to spin a top

tour¹ /tuʀ/ *m* **1** (gen) turn; (around axis) revolution; **donner un ~ de clé** to turn the key; **faire un ~ de manège** to have a go on the merry-go-round; **faire un ~ sur soi-même** ‹*dancer*› to spin around; ‹*planet*› to rotate; **fermer qch à double ~** to double-lock sth; **à ~ de bras** (fam) ‹*invest, buy up*› left, right and centre (BrE) (fam), left and right (AmE) (fam)
2 faire le ~ de qch (gen) to go around sth; to drive around sth; **la nouvelle a vite fait le ~ du village** the news spread rapidly through the village
3 (of pond) edges; (of pipe, tree trunk) circumference; (of head, hips) measurement; (standard measurement) size
4 walk, stroll; (on bicycle) ride; (in car) drive, spin; **je suis allé faire un ~ à Paris** I went to Paris
5 look; **faire le ~ d'un problème** to have a look at a problem; **faire le ~ de ses relations** to go through one's acquaintances; **ce roman, on en a vite fait le ~** (fam) there's not much to this novel
6 (gen) turn; (in competition) round; **à qui le ~?** whose turn is it?; **chacun son ~** each one in his turn; **il perd plus souvent qu'à son ~** he loses more often than he would like; he loses more often than he should; **~ à ~** by turns; in turn
7 ~ de scrutin ballot, round of voting
8 trick; **jouer un ~ à qn** to play a trick on sb; **ça te jouera des ~s** it's going to get you into trouble one of these days
9 trick; **~ de cartes** card trick; **~ d'adresse** feat of skill
10 (in situation) turn; **donner un ~ nouveau à qch** to give a new twist to sth
11 (Tech) lathe
■ **~ de chant** song recital; **~ de garde** turn of duty; **~ de potier** potter's wheel; **~ de rein(s)** back strain

tour² /tuʀ/ *f* **1** tower
2 tower block (BrE), high rise (AmE)
3 (in chess) rook, castle
4 siege tower

tourbe /tuʀb/ *f* peat

tourbière /tuʀbjɛʀ/ *f* peat bog

tourbillon /tuʀbijɔ̃/ *m* **1** whirlwind; whirlpool; **~ de poussière** whirl of dust
2 (of memories) swirl; (of reforms) whirlwind

tourbillonner /tuʀbijɔne/ [**v1**] *vi* ‹*snow, leaves*› to swirl, to whirl; ‹*dancers*› to twirl

tourelle /tuʀɛl/ *f* (of building, tank) turret; (of submarine) conning tower

tourisme /tuʀism/ *m* tourism
■ **~ culturel** heritage tourism; **~ vert** countryside holidays

touriste /tuʀist/ *mf* tourist

touristique /tuʀistik/ *adj* ‹*brochure, menu, season*› tourist; ‹*influx*› of tourists; ‹*town, area*› which attracts tourists

tourment /tuʀmɑ̃/ *m* torment

tourmente /tuʀmɑ̃t/ *f* **1** storm
2 turmoil

tourmenté, ~e /tuʀmɑ̃te/ *adj* **1** ‹*person, face*› tormented; ‹*soul*› tortured
2 ‹*era, life*› turbulent
3 ‹*landscape*› rugged

tourmenter /tuʀmɑ̃te/ [**v1**] **A** *vt* **1** to worry
2 to torment
3 ‹*creditors*› to harass
B se tourmenter *v refl* (+ *v être*) to worry

tournage /tuʀnaʒ/ *m* **1** shooting, filming
2 film set

tournant, ~e /tuʀnɑ̃, ɑ̃t/ **A** *adj* **1** ‹*seat*› swivel; ‹*sprinkler*› rotating; ‹*door*› revolving
2 ‹*presidency*› rotating; ‹*strike*› staggered
B *m* **1** (in road) bend
2 turning point
3 turn; **au ~ du siècle** at the turn of the century
4 change of direction

tourné, ~e /tuʀne/ *adj* **1 ~ vers** ‹*eyes, look, person*› turned toward(s); ‹*activity, policy*› oriented toward(s); **~ vers le passé/l'avenir** backward-/forward-looking; **porte ~e vers la mer** gate facing the sea
2 bien ~ ‹*compliment, letter*› nicely phrased
3 ‹*milk*› off

tourne-disque, *pl* **~s** /tuʀnədisk/ *m* record player

key word

tournée /tuʀne/ *f* **1** (of postman) round
2 (of team, singer) tour
3 (fam) (of drinks) round

tournemain: **en un tournemain** /ɑ̃nɛ̃tuʀnəmɛ̃/ *phr* in no time

tourner /tuʀne/ [**v1**] **A** *vt* **1** to turn; **~ la tête vers** to turn to look at; **~ les yeux vers** to look at
2 to shoot ‹*film*›
3 to get around ‹*difficulty, law*›
4 to phrase ‹*letter, criticism*›
5 ~ qn/qch en dérision to deride sb/sth
6 ~ et retourner qch dans son esprit to mull sth over
7 to stir ‹*sauce*›; to toss ‹*salad*›
B *vi* **1** (gen) to turn; ‹*planet*› to rotate; ‹*rotating door*› to revolve; ‹*dancer*› to spin; **faire ~** to turn; to spin; **faire ~ les tables** (in spiritualism) to do table-turning
2 ~ autour de (gen) to turn around; ‹*planet*› to revolve around; ‹*plane*› to circle
3 ~ (en rond) ‹*person*› to go round and round; ‹*driver*› to drive round and round; **~ en rond** (fig) ‹*discussion*› to go round in circles
4 ~ autour de ‹*sum of money*› to be (somewhere) in the region of
5 ‹*engine, factory*› to run; **~ rond** ‹*engine*› to run smoothly; ‹*business*› to be doing well; **faire ~** to run ‹*business, company*›; **mon frère ne tourne pas rond depuis quelque temps** (fam) my brother has been acting strangely for some time
6 les choses ont bien/mal tourné pour lui things turned out well/badly for him
7 ‹*director*› to shoot; **~ (dans un film)** ‹*actor*› to make a film (BrE) *or* movie (AmE)
8 ‹*milk, meat*› to go off
9 ~ autour de qn to hang around sb
C se tourner *v refl* (+ *v être*) **1 se ~ vers qn/qch** to turn to sb/sth
2 se ~ vers qn/qch to turn toward(s) sb/sth
3 to turn around

tournesol /tuʀnəsɔl/ *m* sunflower

tournevis /tuʀnəvis/ *m inv* screwdriver

tourniquet /tuʀnikɛ/ *m* **1** turnstile
2 revolving stand
3 sprinkler

tournoi /tuʀnwɑ/ *m* tournament

tournoyer /tuʀnwaje/ [**v23**] *vi* **1** ‹*leaves, papers*› to swirl around; ‹*vultures*› to wheel; ‹*flies*› to fly around in circles
2 ‹*dancers*› to whirl; **faire ~** to twirl ‹*stick, skirt*›

tournure /tuʀnyʀ/ *f* **1** turn; **prendre ~** ‹*plan*› to take shape
2 ~ (de phrase) turn of phrase
■ **~ d'esprit** frame of mind

tourte /tuʀt/ *f* pie; **~ à la viande** meat pie

tourteau, *pl* **~x** /tuʀto/ *m* (Culin, Zool) crab

tourtereau, *pl* **~x** /tuʀtəʀo/ **A** *m* (Zool) young turtle dove
B tourtereaux *mpl* (hum) lovebirds

tourterelle /tuʀtəʀɛl/ *f* turtle dove

tous ▸ tout

Toussaint /tusɛ̃/ *f* **la ~** All Saints' Day

tousser /tuse/ [**v1**] *vi* ‹*person*› to cough

toussotement /tusɔtmɑ̃/ *m* cough; splutter

toussoter /tusɔte/ [**v1**] *vi* ‹*person*› to have a slight cough; ‹*engine*› to splutter

tout /tu/, **~e** /tut/, *mpl* **tous** /tu/ *adj*, /tus/ *pron*; *fpl* **toutes** /tut/

> You will find translations for expressions such as *à tout hasard, tout compte fait, tout neuf* etc, at the entries **hasard, compte, neuf**[2] etc.

A *pron* **1 tout** everything; all; anything; **~ est prétexte à querelle(s)** any pretext will do to start a quarrel; **~ n'est pas perdu** all is not lost; **en ~** in all; in every respect; **en ~ et pour ~** all told; **~ bien compté** *or* **pesé** *or* **considéré** all in all
2 tous /tus/ **toutes** all; all of them/us/you; **tous ensemble** all together; **est-ce que ça conviendra à tous?** will it suit everybody?
B *adj* **1 bois ~ ton lait** drink all your milk; **~ le reste** everything else; **~ le monde** everybody; **manger ~ un pain** to eat a whole loaf; **il a plu ~e la journée** it rained all day (long)
2 c'est ~ un travail it's quite a job
3 all; everything; anything; **~ ce qui compte** all that matters; **~ ce qu'il dit n'est pas vrai** not all of what he says is true; **être ~ ce qu'il y a de plus serviable** to be most obliging
4 any; **à ~ moment** at any time; constantly; **~ autre que lui/toi aurait abandonné** anybody else would have given up
5 en ~e franchise in all honesty; **il aurait ~ intérêt à placer cet argent** it would be in his best interests to invest this money
6 il a souri pour ~e réponse his only reply was a smile
7 tous, toutes all, every; **j'ai ~es les raisons de me plaindre** I have every reason to complain; **nous irons tous les deux** we'll both go; **je les prends tous les trois** I'm taking all three
8 tous/toutes les every; **tous les deux jours** every other day; **tous les combien?** how often?
C *adv* **1** very, quite; all; **être ~ étonné** to be very surprised; **~ seul** all by oneself; **~ en haut** right at the top; **la colline est ~ en fleurs** the hill is a mass of flowers; **veste ~ cuir** all leather jacket
2 ~ prêt ready-made
3 while; although; **il lisait ~ en marchant** he was reading as he walked; **elle le défendait ~ en le sachant coupable** she defended him although she knew he was guilty
4 ~ malin/roi qu'il est, il... he may be clever/a king, but he...
D du tout *phr* **(pas) du ~** not at all

E *m* whole; **le ~** the (whole) lot; the main thing; **former un ~** to make up *or* form a whole
F Tout- (*combining form*) **le Tout-Paris/-Londres** the Paris/London smart set
■ **~ à coup** suddenly; **~ d'un coup** suddenly; all at once; **~ à fait** quite, absolutely; **~ à l'heure** in a moment; a little while ago, just now; **à ~ à l'heure!** see you later!; **~ de même** all the same, even so; **~ de même!** really!; **~ de suite** at once
IDIOM **être ~ yeux ~ oreilles** to be very attentive

tout-à-l'égout /tutalegu/ *m inv* main drainage, main sewer

✐ **toutefois** /tutfwɑ/ *adv* however

toute-puissance /tutpɥisɑ̃s/ *f* omnipotence; supremacy

toutou /tutu/ *m* (fam) doggie (fam), dog

tout-petit, *pl* **~s** /tup(ə)ti/ *m* **1** baby
2 toddler

Tout-Puissant /tupɥisɑ̃/ *m* **le ~** the Almighty, God Almighty

tout-venant /tuv(ə)nɑ̃/ *m inv* all and sundry

toux /tu/ *f inv* cough

toxicité /tɔksisite/ *f* toxicity

toxicodépendance /tɔksikodepɑ̃dɑ̃s/ *f* drug dependency

toxicologie /tɔksikɔlɔʒi/ *f* toxicology

toxicomane /tɔksikɔman/ *mf* drug addict

toxicomanie /tɔksikɔmani/ *f* drug addiction

toxine /tɔksin/ *f* toxin

toxique /tɔksik/ *adj* toxic, poisonous

TP /tepe/ *mpl*: *abbr* ▶ **travail**

trac /tʀak/ *m* (fam) (of actor) stage fright; (before exam, conference) nerves; **avoir le ~** (gen) to feel nervous; ‹*actor, performer*› to have stage fright

traçage /tʀasaʒ/ *m* **1** marking out; laying out
2 (Comput) tracing

tracas /tʀaka/ *m inv* **1** trouble
2 problems; **~ quotidiens** everyday problems
3 worries; **se faire du ~ pour qn/qch** to worry about sb/sth

t

tracasser /tʀakase/ [**v1**] **A** *vt* to bother ‹*person*›
B se tracasser *v refl* (+ *v être*) to worry

tracasserie /tʀakasʀi/ *f* **1** hassle (fam)
2 harassment

✐ **trace** /tʀas/ *f* **1** trail; **suivre qn à la ~** to track sb; (fig) to follow sb's trail
2 ~s tracks; **~s d'ours/de ski** bear's/ski tracks; **~s de pas** footprints; **sur les ~s de Van Gogh** in the footsteps of Van Gogh
3 (of burn) mark; (of wound) scar; (of paint) mark; (of blood, dampness) trace; **~s de doigts** fingermarks; **~s de coups** bruises
4 (of activity) sign; (of presence) trace; **des ~s d'effraction** signs of a break-in

tracé /tʀase/ *m* **1** (of town) layout; (of road) plan
2 (of road, railway) route; (of river) course; (of border, coast) line
3 (on graph, in sketch) line

tracer /tʀase/ [**v12**] *vt* **1** to draw ‹*line, map, portrait*›; (on graph) to plot ‹*curve*›; to write ‹*word, letters*›
2 à 15 ans son avenir était déjà tout tracé at 15, his/her future was already mapped out
3 ~ le chemin à qn (fig) to show sb the way

trachée /tʀaʃe/ *f* windpipe

trachée-artère, *pl* **trachées-artères** /tʀaʃeaʀtɛʀ/ *f* windpipe, trachea

trachéite /tʀakeit/ *f* tracheitis

tract /tʀakt/ *m* pamphlet, tract

tractation /tʀaktasjɔ̃/ *f* negotiation

tracter /tʀakte/ [**v1**] *vt* ‹*vehicle*› to tow ‹*trailer*›; ‹*cable*› to pull up ‹*cable car*›

tracteur /tʀaktœʀ/ *m* tractor

traction /tʀaksjɔ̃/ *f* **1** traction; **à ~ mécanique** mechanically drawn
2 (Tech) tension
■ **~ arrière** (Aut) rear-wheel drive; **~ avant** (Aut) front-wheel drive

✐ **tradition** /tʀadisjɔ̃/ *f* **1** tradition
2 legend; **la ~ veut que...** legend has it that...

traditionaliste /tʀadisjɔnalist/ *adj, mf* traditionalist

✐ **traditionnel**, **-elle** /tʀadisjɔnɛl/ *adj* traditional

traducteur, **-trice** /tʀadyktœʀ, tʀis/ *mf* translator

✐ **traduction** /tʀadyksjɔ̃/ *f* translation; **faire des ~s** to do translation work

✐ **traduire** /tʀadɥiʀ/ [**v69**] **A** *vt* **1** to translate
2 ‹*word, artist, book*› to convey; ‹*rebellion, violence*› to be the expression of; ‹*price rise*› to be the result of
3 (Law) **~ qn en justice** to bring sb to justice
B se traduire *v refl* (+ *v être*) **1** ‹*joy, fear*› to show
2 ‹*crisis, instability*› to result; **se ~ par un échec** to result in failure

traduisible /tʀadɥizibl/ *adj* translatable

trafic /tʀafik/ *m* **1** traffic; **~ d'armes** arms dealing; **~ de drogue** drug trafficking
2 ~ (routier) (road) traffic; **~ aérien** air traffic

trafiquant, **~e** /tʀafikɑ̃, ɑ̃t/ *mf* trafficker, dealer; **~ de drogue** drugs dealer

trafiquer /tʀafike/ [**v1**] *vt* **1** to fiddle with ‹*car, meter*›
2 (fam) **je me demande ce qu'il trafique** I wonder what he's up to

tragédie /tʀaʒedi/ *f* tragedy

tragédien, **-ienne** /tʀaʒedjɛ̃, ɛn/ *mf* tragic actor

tragique /tʀaʒik/ **A** *adj* tragic
B *m* tragedy

✐ key word

trahir /tʀaiʀ/ [v3] **A** *vt* **1** to betray; to break ‹*promise*›
2 ‹*writing, words*› to betray ‹*thoughts*›
3 ‹*translator, words*› to misrepresent
4 ‹*strength, legs*› to fail ‹*person*›
B **se trahir** *v refl* (+ *v être*) to give oneself away, to betray oneself

trahison /tʀaizɔ̃/ *f* **1** treachery; **~ de qn/qch** betrayal of sb/sth
2 treason

train /tʀɛ̃/ **A** *m* **1** train; **par le** *or* **en ~** ‹*travel*› by train
2 (convoy) train; **~ de péniches** train of barges
3 series (**de** of)
4 pace; **aller bon ~** to walk briskly; (fig) ‹*rumours*› to be flying around; ‹*sales*› to be going well; ‹*conversation*› to flow easily; **au ~ où vont les choses** (at) the rate things are going; **à fond de ~** (fam) at top speed
5 (Zool) **~ de derrière** hindquarters; **~ de devant** forequarters
B **en train** *phr* **1 être en ~** to be full of energy
2 mettre en ~ to get [sth] started ‹*process*›
3 être en ~ de faire to be (busy) doing; **j'étais en ~ de dormir** I was sleeping
■ **~ d'atterrissage** undercarriage; **~ électrique** (toy) train set; **~ de vie** lifestyle

traînant, **~e** /tʀɛnɑ̃, ɑ̃t/ *adj* shuffling; **voix ~e** drawl

traînard, **~e** /tʀɛnaʀ, aʀd/ *mf* (fam) slowcoach, slowpoke; straggler

traînasser /tʀenase/ [**v1**] (fam) *vi* **1** to loaf about (fam)
2 to take ages

traîne /tʀɛn/ *f* **1** (of dress) train
2 seine (net)
IDIOM **être à la ~** to lag behind

traîneau, *pl* **~x** /tʀeno/ *m* **1** sleigh
2 (of vacuum cleaner) cylinder

traînée /tʀene/ *f* **1** streak; **~ de sang** streak of blood
2 trail

traîner /tʀene/ [**v1**] **A** *vt* **1** to drag [sb/sth] (along) ‹*person, suitcase*›; to drag [sth] across the floor ‹*chair*›
2 (fam) to lug [sth] around (fam) ‹*object*›; to drag [sth] around ‹*object*›
3 ~ qn chez le médecin to drag sb off to the doctor's
4 il traîne un rhume depuis deux semaines for two weeks now he's had a cold that he can't shake off; **~ les pieds** to drag one's feet
B *vi* **1 ~ dans les rues** to hang around on the streets; **j'ai traîné au lit** I slept in
2 to take forever; **ne traîne pas, on doit terminer à 4 heures** get a move on (fam), we've got to finish at four
3 to dawdle
4 ‹*building work, illness*› to drag on
5 ~ par terre ‹*skirt*› to trail on the ground; ‹*curtains*› to trail on the floor
6 ~ derrière qch to be trailing behind sth
7 ‹*clothes, toys*› to be lying about *or* around; **laisser ~ qch** to leave sth lying about *or* around
C **se traîner** *v refl* (+ *v être*) **1** ‹*injured person*› **se ~ par terre** to drag oneself along the ground
2 se ~ jusqu'à la cuisine to drag oneself through to the kitchen
3 ‹*train*› to crawl along; ‹*negotiations*› to drag on
IDIOMS **~ la jambe** *or* **la patte** (fam) to limp; **~ ses guêtres** (fam) *or* **ses bottes** (fam) to knock around (fam)

train-train /tʀɛ̃tʀɛ̃/ *m inv* (derog, fam) daily routine

traire /tʀɛʀ/ [**v58**] *vt* to milk ‹*cow, goat*›

trait¹, **~e** /tʀɛ, ɛt/ ▶ **traire**

trait² /tʀɛ/ **A** *m* **1** line; stroke; **souligner un mot d'un ~ rouge** to underline a word in red; **~ pour ~** ‹*replica*› line for line; ‹*reproduce*› line by line
2 (of style, book) feature; (of person) trait; **~ caractéristique** characteristic; **~ de caractère** trait, characteristic
3 ~ d'humour *or* **d'esprit** witticism; **~ de génie** stroke of genius
4 avoir ~ à to relate to
5 d'un (seul) ~ (gen) in one go
6 de ~ ‹*animal*› draught (BrE), draft (AmE)
B **traits** *mpl* features
■ **~ d'union** hyphen; (fig) link
IDIOM **tirer un ~ sur qch** to put sth firmly behind one

traitant /tʀɛtɑ̃/ *adj m* **médecin ~** doctor, GP

traite /tʀɛt/ **A** *f* **1** (Econ) draft, bill
2 la ~ des Blanches the white slave trade
3 milking; **la ~ des vaches** milking cows
B **d'une traite** *phr* **d'une (seule) ~** ‹*recite*› in one breath; ‹*drink*› in one go

traité /tʀete/ *m* **1** (Law) treaty; **~ commercial** trade agreement
2 treatise

traitement /tʀɛtmɑ̃/ *m* **1** (Med) treatment
2 salary
3 handling; **il faut accélérer le ~ des demandes** applications must be dealt with more quickly
4 (of data) processing
5 (Tech) (of water, waste) processing; (of wood) treatment
■ **~ de faveur** preferential treatment; **~ de texte** word-processing (package)

traiter /tʀete/ [**v1**] **A** *vt* **1** to treat ‹*person, animal, object*›
2 (Med) to treat ‹*sick person, infection*›
3 to deal with ‹*question, problem*›
4 to treat ‹*wood, textile*›; to process ‹*waste*›
5 to process ‹*data*›
6 ~ qn de qch to call sb sth
B **traiter de** *v+prep* to deal with
C *vi* to negotiate, to do (BrE) *or* make a deal
D **se traiter** *v refl* (+ *v être*) **ils se sont traités de tous les noms** they called each other all sorts of names

traiteur /tʀɛtœʀ/ *m* caterer
traître, **traîtresse** /tʀɛtʀ, tʀɛtʀɛs/ *mf* traitor; **en ~** by surprise
traîtrise /tʀɛtʀiz/ *f* **1** act of treachery
2 (of person) treachery
trajectoire /tʀaʒɛktwaʀ/ *f* **1** (of bullet, missile) trajectory
2 (of planet, satellite) path
3 career
trajet /tʀaʒɛ/ *m* **1** journey, trip; (by sea) crossing
2 route
trame /tʀam/ *f* **1** (of fabric) weft
2 (of story) framework
tramer: **se tramer** /tʀame/ [**v1**] *v refl* (+ *v être*) ‹*plot*› to be hatched
trampoline /tʀɑ̃pɔlin/ *m* trampoline
tramway /tʀamwɛ/ *m* **1** tram (BrE), streetcar (AmE)
2 tramway (BrE), streetcar line (AmE)
tranchant, **~e** /tʀɑ̃ʃɑ̃, ɑ̃t/ **A** *adj* **1** sharp
2 ‹*person*› forthright; ‹*tone*› curt
B *m* (of blade) sharp edge, cutting edge
tranche /tʀɑ̃ʃ/ *f* **1** (of bread, meat, cheese) slice; (of lard, bacon) rasher
2 (of operation) phase; (in timetable) period, time slot
3 (of book, coin) edge
■ **~ d'âge** age bracket
tranché, **~e** /tʀɑ̃ʃe/ **A** *pp* ▶ **trancher**
B *pp adj* ‹*salmon*› pre-sliced
C *adj* **1** ‹*opinion, position, reply*› cut and dried; ‹*inequalities*› marked
2 ‹*colours*› bold
tranchée /tʀɑ̃ʃe/ *f* **1** (Mil) trench
2 (of road) cutting
trancher /tʀɑ̃ʃe/ [**v1**] **A** *vt* to slice, to cut ‹*bread, meat*›; to cut through ‹*rope*›; to cut [sth] off ‹*head*›; to slit ‹*throat*›
B *vi* **1** ‹*colour, outline*› to stand out
2 to come to a decision
✔ **tranquille** /tʀɑ̃kil/ *adj* **1** quiet; calm; peaceful; **tiens-toi ~!** keep still!; be quiet!; **il s'est tenu ~ pendant quelques mois** he behaved himself for a few months
2 être ~ to be *or* feel easy in one's mind; **sa mère n'est pas ~ quand il sort** his mother worries when he goes out
3 avoir la conscience ~ to have a clear conscience
tranquillement /tʀɑ̃kilmɑ̃/ *adv* **1 elle dort ~** she's sleeping peacefully; **j'aimerais pouvoir travailler ~** I wish I could work in peace
2 quietly
3 nous avons marché ~ we walked along at a leisurely pace
4 nous étions ~ en train de discuter we were chatting away happily
tranquillisant, **~e** /tʀɑ̃kilizɑ̃, ɑ̃t/ **A** *adj* reassuring, comforting
B *m* tranquillizer (BrE)
tranquilliser /tʀɑ̃kilize/ [**v1**] *vt* to reassure
tranquillité /tʀɑ̃kilite/ *f* **1** calmness; calm
2 ~ (d'esprit) peace of mind
transaction /tʀɑ̃zaksjɔ̃/ *f* transaction
transalpin, **~e** /tʀɑ̃zalpɛ̃, in/ *adj*
1 transalpine
2 Italian
transat¹ /tʀɑ̃zat/ *m* (fam) **1** deckchair
2 baby chair
transat² /tʀɑ̃zat/ *f* (Sport) transatlantic race
transatlantique /tʀɑ̃zatlɑ̃tik/ *adj* transatlantic
transborder /tʀɑ̃sbɔʀde/ [**v1**] *vt* to tranship ‹*goods*›; to transfer ‹*passengers*›
transbordeur /tʀɑ̃sbɔʀdœʀ/ *m*
1 transporter bridge
2 traverser
3 ferry
transcendant, **~e** /tʀɑ̃sɑ̃dɑ̃, ɑ̃t/ *adj* **1** (in philosophy) transcendent
2 (fam) wonderful
transcender /tʀɑ̃sɑ̃de/ [**v1**] *vt* to transcend
transcription /tʀɑ̃skʀipsjɔ̃/ *f* transcription
transcrire /tʀɑ̃skʀiʀ/ [**v67**] *vt* to transcribe
transe /tʀɑ̃s/ *f* trance
transférer /tʀɑ̃sfeʀe/ [**v14**] *vt* **1** (gen) to transfer; to relocate ‹*offices*›
2 (Law) to transfer, to convey ‹*property*›
transfert /tʀɑ̃sfɛʀ/ *m* **1** (of person, data, money, property) transfer; (of offices) relocation
2 (psychological) transference
transfert de technologie *m* technology transfer
transfigurer /tʀɑ̃sfigyʀe/ [**v1**] *vt* to transform
transformable /tʀɑ̃sfɔʀmabl/ *adj* convertible
transformateur /tʀɑ̃sfɔʀmatœʀ/ *m* transformer
transformation /tʀɑ̃sfɔʀmasjɔ̃/ *f* transformation; (of mineral, energy) conversion
✔ **transformer** /tʀɑ̃sfɔʀme/ [**v1**] **A** *vt* **1** to alter ‹*garment, facade*›; to change ‹*person, landscape*›
2 ~ qn/qch en (gen) to turn sb/sth into; to transform sb/sth into; **~ un garage en bureau** to convert a garage into an office
B se transformer *v refl* (+ *v être*)
1 ‹*person*› to transform oneself; to be transformed
2 se ~ en ‹*embryo, larva, bud*› to turn into
transfrontalier, **-ière** /tʀɑ̃sfʀɔ̃talje, ɛʀ/ *adj* cross-border
transfuge /tʀɑ̃sfyʒ/ **A** *mf* defector
B *m* (Mil) deserter
transfusé, **~e** /tʀɑ̃sfyze/ **A** *pp* ▶ **transfuser**
B *pp adj* ‹*blood*› transfused; ‹*person*› who has been given a blood transfusion
transfuser /tʀɑ̃sfyze/ [**v1**] *vt* to give a blood transfusion to

✔ key word

t

transfusion /tʀɑ̃sfyzjɔ̃/ *f* transfusion

transgresser /tʀɑ̃sgʀese/ [**v1**] *vt* to break ‹*law, rule, taboo*›; to defy ‹*ban*›

transhumance /tʀɑ̃zymɑ̃s/ *f* transhumance, seasonal migration of livestock to summer pastures

transi, **~e** /tʀɑ̃zi/ **A** *pp* ▶ **transir**
B *pp adj* chilled; **~ de peur** paralysed (BrE) with fear; **un amoureux ~** a bashful lover

transiger /tʀɑ̃ziʒe/ [**v13**] *vi* to compromise

transir /tʀɑ̃ziʀ/ [**v3**] *vt* to chill; to paralyse (BrE)

transistor /tʀɑ̃zistɔʀ/ *m* transistor

transit /tʀɑ̃zit/ *m* transit; **en ~** in transit

transitaire /tʀɑ̃zitɛʀ/ **A** *adj* transit; **pays ~** transit point
B *mf* forwarding agent

transiter /tʀɑ̃zite/ [**v1**] *vi* **~ par** ‹*goods, passengers*› to pass through, to go via

transitif, **-ive** /tʀɑ̃zitif, iv/ *adj* transitive

transition /tʀɑ̃zisjɔ̃/ *f* transition

transitoire /tʀɑ̃zitwaʀ/ *adj* transitional

translucide /tʀɑ̃slysid/ *adj* translucent

transmanche /tʀɑ̃smɑ̃ʃ/ *adj inv* cross-Channel

transmetteur /tʀɑ̃smɛtœʀ/ *m* transmitter

transmettre /tʀɑ̃smɛtʀ/ [**v60**] **A** *vt* **1** to pass [sth] on, to convey ‹*information, order, news*›; to pass [sth] on ‹*story, knowledge*›; to pass [sth] down ‹*culture, fortune*›; **transmets-leur mes félicitations** give them my congratulations
2 to transmit ‹*image, signal, data*›
3 to broadcast ‹*news, programme*›
4 to hand [sth] on ‹*property, land*›; to hand over ‹*power*›
5 (Med) to transmit ‹*virus, illness*›
B **se transmettre** *v refl* (+ *v être*) **1** to pass [sth] on to each other ‹*message, data*›
2 ‹*signals, data*› to be transmitted
3 ‹*tradition, culture*› to be handed down; ‹*story*› to be passed on
4 ‹*virus, illness*› to be transmitted

transmissible /tʀɑ̃smisibl/ *adj* transmissible, transmittable

transmission /tʀɑ̃smisjɔ̃/ *f* **1** transmission, passing on; **la ~ des connaissances** the communication of knowledge
2 (of data, signals) transmission
3 (of programme) broadcasting
4 (of tradition, secret, culture) handing down; (of fortune, property) transfer
5 (Aut, Med) transmission
■ **~ de pensées** thought transference

transparaître /tʀɑ̃spaʀɛtʀ/ [**v73**] *vi* to show through; **laisser ~** ‹*face, words*› to betray; ‹*person*› to let [sth] show ‹*emotions*›

transparence /tʀɑ̃spaʀɑ̃s/ *f* **1** (of glass, fabric) transparency; (of water) clearness; **on voyait ses jambes en ~ (à travers sa jupe)** you could see her legs through her skirt
2 (of skin) translucency; (of colour) limpidity
3 (of person) transparency; (of policy) openness

transparent, **~e** /tʀɑ̃spaʀɑ̃, ɑ̃t/ **A** *adj*
1 transparent; ‹*water*› clear
2 ‹*complexion*› translucent
3 ‹*person*› transparent
B *m* (for overhead projector) transparency

transpercer /tʀɑ̃spɛʀse/ [**v12**] *vt* **1** ‹*sword, arrow*› to pierce ‹*body*›; ‹*bullet*› to go through
2 ‹*rain*› to go through
3 ‹*pain*› to shoot through

transpiration /tʀɑ̃spiʀasjɔ̃/ *f* **1** sweating, perspiration
2 sweat
3 (Bot) transpiration

transpirer /tʀɑ̃spiʀe/ [**v1**] *vi* **1** to sweat, to perspire
2 ‹*secret*› to leak out

transplantation /tʀɑ̃splɑ̃tasjɔ̃/ *f*
1 transplant; **~ d'organes** organ transplants
2 transplantation

transplanter /tʀɑ̃splɑ̃te/ [**v1**] *vt* to transplant

transport /tʀɑ̃spɔʀ/ **A** *m* transport, transportation (AmE)
B **transports** *mpl* **~s en commun** public transport *or* transportation (AmE)

transportable /tʀɑ̃spɔʀtabl/ *adj* transportable; **il n'est pas ~** (injured person) he cannot be moved

transporter /tʀɑ̃spɔʀte/ [**v1**] *vt* **1** to carry ‹*person, object*›; to transport ‹*passengers, goods*›; **être transporté à l'hôpital** to be taken to hospital
2 to carry ‹*pollen, virus, disease*›
3 **être transporté dans un monde féerique** to be transported to a magical world

transporteur /tʀɑ̃spɔʀtœʀ/ *m* carrier; **~ aérien** air carrier; **~ routier** road haulier (BrE), road haulage contractor (BrE), trucking company (AmE)

transposer /tʀɑ̃spoze/ [**v1**] *vt* to transpose

transsexuel, **-elle** /tʀɑ̃ssɛksɥɛl/ *adj, mf* transsexual

transsibérien, **-ienne** /tʀɑ̃ssibeʀjɛ̃, ɛn/
A *adj* trans-Siberian
B *m* **le Transsibérien** the Trans-Siberian Railway

transvaser /tʀɑ̃svaze/ [**v1**] *vt* to decant ‹*liquid*›

transversal, **~e**, *mpl* **-aux** /tʀɑ̃svɛʀsal, o/ *adj* transverse; **rue ~e** side street

trapèze /tʀapɛz/ *m* **1** (Sport) trapeze
2 (in geometry) trapezium (BrE), trapezoid (AmE)

trapéziste /tʀapezist/ *mf* trapeze artist

trappe /tʀap/ *f* (gen) trap door

trappeur /tʀapœʀ/ *m* trapper

trapu, **~e** /tʀapy/ *adj* ‹*man, outline*› stocky

traquenard /tʀaknaʀ/ *m* trap

traquer /tʀake/ [**v1**] *vt* (gen) to track down; ‹*photographer*› to hound ‹*film star*›

traumatisant, **~e** /tʀomatizɑ̃, ɑ̃t/ *adj* traumatic

traumatiser /tʀomatize/ [**v1**] *vt* to traumatize

traumatisme /tʀomatism/ *m* **1** (Med) traumatism
2 (psychological) trauma

travail, *pl* **-aux** /tʀavaj, o/ **A** *m* **1** (gen) work; job; **se mettre au ~** to get down to work; **avoir du ~** to have work to do; **les gros travaux** the heavy work; **(félicitations) c'est du beau ~!** you've done a great job on that!; **qu'est-ce que c'est que ce ~?** what do you call this?; **ne me téléphone pas à mon ~** don't call me at work; **chercher du/un ~** to look for work/a job; **être sans ~** to be out of work; **le ~ temporaire** temporary work; **le ~ de nuit** night work
2 (Econ) labour (BrE); **entrer dans le monde du ~** to enter the world of work
3 le ~ musculaire muscular effort
4 le ~ de working with *or* in ‹*metal, wood, stone*›
5 workmanship; **un ~ superbe** a superb piece of workmanship
6 (of water, erosion) action
7 (of wine) fermentation; (of wood) warping
8 (of woman in childbirth) labour (BrE)
B travaux *mpl* **1** (gen) work; (on road) roadworks (BrE), roadwork (AmE); **faire faire des travaux dans sa maison** to have work done in one's house
2 (of researcher) work
3 (of commission) deliberations
4 les travaux agricoles agricultural work; **travaux de couture** needlework
■ **~ à la chaîne** assembly-line work; **~ à domicile** working at *or* from home; **~ au noir** (gen) *work for which no earnings are declared*; (holding two jobs) moonlighting; **travaux manuels** handicrafts; **travaux pratiques, TP** practical work; lab work; **travaux publics, TP** civil engineering

travaillé, **~e** /tʀavaje/ **A** *pp* ▶ **travailler**
B *pp adj* ‹*jewel*› finely worked; ‹*carving*› elaborate; ‹*gold, silver*› wrought; ‹*style*› polished

travailler /tʀavaje/ [**v1**] **A** *vt* **1** to work on ‹*style, school subject, voice, muscles*›; to practise (BrE) ‹*sport, instrument*›
2 to work ‹*wood, metal*›; (Culin) to knead ‹*dough*›; to cultivate ‹*land*›
3 ~ qn ‹*idea, affair*› to be on sb's mind; ‹*jealousy, pain*› to plague sb; **un doute me travaillait** I had a nagging doubt
B travailler à *v+prep* to work on ‹*project, essay*›; to work toward(s) ‹*objective*›
C *vi* **1** ‹*person, machine, muscles*› to work; **faire ~ son cerveau** to apply one's mind; **~ en équipes** to work shifts
2 ‹*shop, hotel, shopkeeper*› to do business; **~ à perte** ‹*company, business*› to run at a loss
3 nous voulons la paix et c'est dans ce sens que nous travaillons we want peace and we are working toward(s) it
4 ‹*athlete*› to train; ‹*musician*› to practise (BrE)
5 ‹*wood*› to warp

travailleur, **-euse** /tʀavajœʀ, øz/ **A** *adj* **1** ‹*pupil*› hard-working
2 ‹*classes*› working
B *mf* worker

travailliste /tʀavajist/ **A** *adj* Labour
B *mf* Labour MP

travée /tʀave/ *f* **1** row
2 (Tech) span

travelling /tʀavliŋ/ *m* (in cinema) tracking; tracking shot

travers /tʀavɛʀ/ **A** *m inv* **1** foible, quirk
2 (Naut) beam
3 (Culin) **~ de porc** spare rib
B à travers *phr* **1** ‹*see, look*› through
2 ‹*walk*› across; **voyager à ~ le monde** to travel all over the world
3 voyager à ~ le temps to travel through time
4 through; **à ~ ces informations** through this information
C au travers *phr* through; **passer au ~ de** (fig) to escape ‹*inspection*›
D de travers *phr* **1** askew; **ta veste est boutonnée de ~** your jacket is buttoned up wrongly; **il a le nez de ~** he has a twisted nose; **j'ai avalé de ~** it went down the wrong way; **regarder qn de ~** to give sb filthy looks
2 wrong; **comprendre de ~** to misunderstand
E en travers *phr* across; **un bus était en ~ de la route** a bus was stuck across the road; **se mettre en ~ de la route** ‹*people*› to stand in the middle of the road; **rester en ~ de la gorge de qn** (fam) to be hard to swallow

traverse /tʀavɛʀs/ *f* (on railway line) sleeper (BrE), tie (AmE)

traversée /tʀavɛʀse/ *f* **1** crossing; **la ~ du désert** crossing the desert; (fig) (of company) a difficult period
2 (of city) **évitez la ~ de Paris** avoid going through Paris

traverser /tʀavɛʀse/ [**v1**] *vt* **1** to cross ‹*road, bridge, border, town, ocean, room*›; to go through ‹*town, forest, tunnel*›; to make one's way through ‹*group, crowd*›; **il traversa le jardin en courant** he ran across the garden (BrE) *or* yard (AmE)
2 ‹*river*› to run through ‹*region*›; ‹*road*› to go through ‹*region*›; ‹*bridge, river*› to cross ‹*railway line, town*›
3 ‹*rain*› to soak through ‹*clothes*›; **la balle lui a traversé le bras** the bullet went right through his/her arm
4 to go through ‹*crisis*›; to live through ‹*war*›
5 ~ l'esprit de qn to cross sb's mind

traversin /tʀavɛʀsɛ̃/ *m* bolster

---
key word

travesti, **~e** /tʀavɛsti/ **A** *pp* ▶ **travestir**
B *pp adj* in disguise; **rôle ~** role played by a member of the opposite sex
C *m* **1** transvestite
2 (actor) actor playing a female role; (in cabaret) drag artist (fam)

travestir /tʀavɛstiʀ/ [**v3**] **A** *vt* **1** to dress [sb] up ‹*person*›
2 to distort ‹*truth*›
B se travestir *v refl* (+ *v être*) **1** to dress up
2 to cross-dress

trébucher /tʀebyʃe/ [**v1**] *vi* to stumble

trèfle /tʀɛfl/ *m* **1** clover
2 (Games) (card) club; (suit) clubs
3 shamrock

tréfonds /tʀefɔ̃/ *m inv* **le ~ de** the very depths of

treillage /tʀɛjaʒ/ *m* **1** trellis
2 lattice fence

treille /tʀɛj/ *f* **1** (vine) arbour (BrE)
2 climbing vine

treillis /tʀeji/ *m inv* **1** (Mil) fatigues
2 canvas
3 trellis; **~ métallique** wire grille

treize /tʀɛz/ *adj inv, pron, m inv* thirteen

treizième /tʀɛzjɛm/ *adj* thirteenth

tréma /tʀema/ *m* diaeresis; **i ~** i diaeresis

tremblant, **~e** /tʀɑ̃blɑ̃, ɑ̃t/ *adj* **1** ‹*person, hands*› shaking
2 ‹*voice*› trembling
3 ‹*image, light*› flickering; ‹*sound*› tremulous

tremble /tʀɑ̃bl/ *m* aspen

tremblement /tʀɑ̃bləmɑ̃/ *m* **1** (of person, hands) shaking, trembling; (of lips) trembling
2 (of voice) trembling
3 (of leaves) quivering
■ **~ de terre** earthquake

trembler /tʀɑ̃ble/ [**v1**] *vi* **1** ‹*person, legs*› to shake, to tremble
2 ‹*voice*› to tremble; ‹*sound, note*› to waver
3 ‹*building, floor*› to shake
4 (be afraid) to tremble; **~ pour qn** to fear for sb
5 ‹*light, image*› to flicker
6 ‹*leaves*› to quiver

trembloter /tʀɑ̃blɔte/ [**v1**] *vi* **1** ‹*person, hands*› to tremble slightly
2 ‹*voice*› to tremble

trémolo /tʀemɔlo/ *m* **1** (of voice) quaver
2 (of instrument) tremolo

trémousser: **se trémousser** /tʀemuse/ [**v1**] *v refl* (+ *v être*) **1** to fidget
2 to wiggle around

trempe /tʀɑ̃p/ *f* **avoir la ~ d'un dirigeant** to have the makings of a leader

trempé, **~e** /tʀɑ̃pe/ **A** *pp* ▶ **tremper**
B *pp adj* **1** ‹*person, garments*› soaked (through); ‹*grass*› sodden
2 (Tech) ‹*steel*› tempered; ‹*glass*› toughened

tremper /tʀɑ̃pe/ [**v1**] **A** *vt* **1** ‹*rain, person*› to soak ‹*person, garment*›
2 to dip; **j'ai juste trempé mes lèvres** I just had a sip
3 to soak ‹*hands*›
4 (Tech) to temper
B *vi* **1** ‹*clothes, vegetables*› to soak; **faire ~ qch** to soak sth
2 (fam) **~ dans qch** to be mixed up in sth

tremplin /tʀɑ̃plɛ̃/ *m* **1** springboard
2 ski jump; water-ski jump

trentaine /tʀɑ̃tɛn/ *f* **1 une ~** about thirty
2 avoir la ~ to be about thirty

trente /tʀɑ̃t/ *adj inv, pron, m inv* thirty

trente-et-un /tʀɑ̃teœ̃/ *m* **être sur son ~** (fam) to be dressed up to the nines

trentenaire /tʀɑ̃tənɛʀ/ *adj* ‹*person*› in his/her thirties; ‹*tree, building*› around thirty years old

trente-six /tʀɑ̃tsis/ *adj inv, pron, m inv* thirty six
IDIOM **voir ~ chandelles** (fam) to see stars

trente-trois /tʀɑ̃ttʀwa/ *adj inv, pron, m inv* thirty three
■ **~ tours** LP

trentième /tʀɑ̃tjɛm/ *adj* thirtieth

trépas /tʀepɑ/ *m* (dated) demise

trépidant, **~e** /tʀepidɑ̃, ɑ̃t/ *adj* ‹*rhythm, speed*› pulsating; ‹*life*› hectic; ‹*story*› exciting

trépied /tʀepje/ *m* (gen) tripod

trépigner /tʀepiɲe/ [**v1**] *vi* (with anger, impatience) to stamp one's feet

très /tʀɛ/ *adv* very; **~ connu** very well-known; **être ~ amoureux** to be very much in love; **~ en avance** very early; **~ volontiers** gladly; **'tu vas bien?'—'non, pas ~'** 'are you well?'—'no, not terribly'; **elle a ~ envie de partir** she's dying to leave (fam)

trésor /tʀezɔʀ/ *m* **1** treasure
2 déployer des ~s d'inventivité to show infinite inventiveness
3 (person) **mon ~** precious

trésorerie /tʀezɔʀʀi/ *f* **1** funds; cash
2 (of company) accounts
3 government finance

trésorier, **-ière** /tʀezɔʀje, ɛʀ/ *mf* treasurer

tressaillement /tʀesajmɑ̃/ *m* **1** (from surprise, fear) start; (of hope, pleasure) quiver; (from pain) wince
2 (of person, muscle, animal) twitch; (of machine, ground) vibration

tressaillir /tʀesajiʀ/ [**v28**] *vi* **1** (with surprise) to start; (with pleasure) to quiver
2 ‹*person, muscle*› to twitch

tresse /tʀɛs/ *f* **1** plait, braid (AmE)
2 (of thread) braid

tresser /tʀese/ [**v1**] *vt* to plait, to braid (AmE) ‹*hair, threads*›; to weave ‹*straw, string*›

tréteau, *pl* **~x** /tʀeto/ *m* trestle

treuil /tʀœj/ *m* winch

trêve /tʀɛv/ *f* **1** (Mil) truce
2 respite; **~ de plaisanteries!** that's enough joking!

tri /tʀi/ *m* sorting; sorting out; **centre de ~ (postal)** sorting office; **faire le ~ de** to sort ‹*mail*›; to sort out ‹*documents, clothes*›; **faire un ~ parmi des choses** to select among things

triage /tʀijaʒ/ *m* **gare de ~** marshalling (BrE) yard

triangle /tʀijɑ̃gl/ *m* triangle
■ **~ des Bermudes** Bermuda Triangle

triangulaire /tʀijɑ̃gylɛʀ/ *adj* **1** triangular
2 ‹*agreement, partnership*› three-way

triathlon /tʀiatlɔ̃/ *m* triathlon

tribal, **~e**, *mpl* **-aux** /tʀibal, o/ *adj* tribal

tribord /tʀibɔʀ/ *m* starboard

tribu /tʀiby/ *f* tribe

tribulations /tʀibylasjɔ̃/ *fpl* tribulations

tribun /tʀibœ̃/ *m* **1** tribune
2 great orator

⚷ **tribunal**, *pl* **-aux** /tʀibynal, o/ *m* (Law) court; **traîner qn devant les tribunaux** to take sb to court

tribune /tʀibyn/ *f* **1** (in stadium) stand; (in court) gallery
2 (of speaker) platform, rostrum
3 (in newspaper) comments column

tribut /tʀiby/ *m* tribute

tributaire /tʀibytɛʀ/ *adj* **être ~ de** ‹*country, person*› to depend on

tricentenaire /tʀisɑ̃tnɛʀ/ *adj* three hundred year-old

triche /tʀiʃ/ *f* (fam) **c'est de la ~** that's cheating

tricher /tʀiʃe/ [**v1**] *vi* to cheat; **~ sur son âge** to lie about one's age

tricherie /tʀiʃʀi/ *f* cheating

tricheur, **-euse** /tʀiʃœʀ, øz/ *mf* cheat

tricolore /tʀikɔlɔʀ/ *adj* **1** three-coloured (BrE); **feux ~s** traffic lights
2 (fam) French; **l'équipe ~** the French team

tricot /tʀiko/ *m* **1** knitting; **faire du ~** to knit
2 knitwear; **en ~** knitted

tricoter /tʀikɔte/ [**v1**] *vt* to knit; **tricoté (à la) main** hand knitted

tricycle /tʀisikl/ *m* tricycle

trident /tʀidɑ̃/ *m* trident

tridimensionnel, **-elle** /tʀidimɑ̃sjɔnɛl/ *adj* three-dimensional

triennal, **~e**, *mpl* **-aux** /tʀijenal, o/ *adj*
1 ‹*mandate*› three-year
2 ‹*vote*› three-yearly

trier /tʀije/ [**v2**] *vt* **1** to sort ‹*mail*›
2 to sort [sth] out ‹*information*›; to select ‹*clients*›
(IDIOM) **~ sur le volet** to hand-pick

trifouiller /tʀifuje/ [**v1**] *vi* (fam) **~ dans** to rummage through; to tinker with

trilingue /tʀilɛ̃g/ *adj* trilingual

trilogie /tʀilɔʒi/ *f* trilogy

trimbaler /tʀɛ̃bale/ [**v1**] *vt also* **trimballer** (fam) to lug [sth] around; to drag [sb] around

⚷ key word

trimer /tʀime/ [**v1**] *vi* (fam) to slave away

trimestre /tʀimɛstʀ/ *m* **1** (period) quarter; (Sch) term
2 quarterly income; quarterly payment

trimestriel, **-ielle** /tʀimɛstʀijɛl/ *adj* (gen) quarterly; ‹*exam*› end-of-term

trimoteur /tʀimɔtœʀ/ *m* three-engined plane

tringle /tʀɛ̃gl/ *f* **1** (gen) rail
2 (Tech) rod

trinité /tʀinite/ *f* trinity

trinquer /tʀɛ̃ke/ [**v1**] *vi* to clink glasses; **~ à qch** to drink to sth

trio /tʀi(j)o/ *m* trio

triomphal, **~e**, *mpl* **-aux** /tʀijɔ̃fal, o/ *adj* triumphant

triomphalisme /tʀijɔ̃falism/ *m* triumphalism

triomphant, **~e** /tʀijɔ̃fɑ̃, ɑ̃t/ *adj* triumphant

triomphateur, **-trice** /tʀijɔ̃fatœʀ, tʀis/ *adj* triumphant

triomphe /tʀijɔ̃f/ *m* triumph; **faire un ~ à qn** to give sb a triumphal reception

triompher /tʀijɔ̃fe/ [**v1**] **A** **triompher de** *v+prep* to triumph over ‹*enemy*›; to overcome ‹*resistance*›
B *vi* **1** ‹*fighter*› to triumph; ‹*truth*› to prevail
2 to be triumphant

tripartisme /tʀipaʀtism/ *m* tripartite *or* three-party system

tripatouiller /tʀipatuje/ [**v1**] *vt* (fam) to fiddle with (fam) ‹*object*›; to paw (fam) ‹*person*›

triperie /tʀipʀi/ *f* **1** tripe shop
2 tripe trade

tripes /tʀip/ *fpl* **1** (Culin) tripe
2 (fam) guts, innards

triplace /tʀiplas/ *adj* three-seater

triple /tʀipl/ **A** *adj* triple; **l'avantage est ~** the advantages are threefold; **en ~ exemplaire** in triplicate; **~ idiot!** (fam) prize idiot! (fam)
B *m* **coûter le ~** to cost three times as much

triplé, **~e** /tʀiple/ *mf* triplet

triplement /tʀipləmɑ̃/ *adv* **1** in three respects
2 trebly

tripler /tʀiple/ [**v1**] **A** *vt* to treble ‹*quantity, price*›
B *vi* to treble (**de** in)

triporteur /tʀipɔʀtœʀ/ *m* delivery tricycle

tripot /tʀipo/ *m* **1** gambling joint (fam)
2 dive (fam)

tripotée /tʀipɔte/ *f* (fam) **1** (good) hiding (fam)
2 une ~ de hordes of

tripoter /tʀipɔte/ [**v1**] *vt* (fam) to fiddle with ‹*object*›

trique /tʀik/ *f* cudgel; **battre à coups de ~** to cudgel
IDIOM **être maigre** *or* **sec comme un coup de ~** to be as thin as a rake

trisaïeul, **~e** /tʀizajœl/ *mf* great-great-grandfather/grandmother

trisannuel, **-elle** /tʀizanɥɛl/ *adj* triennial

trisomie /tʀizɔmi/ *f* trisomy; **~ 21** Down's Syndrome

trisomique /tʀizɔmik/ *adj* **enfant ~** Down's Syndrome child

triste /tʀist/ *adj* **1** (gen) sad; ‹*town, existence*› dreary; ‹*weather, day*› gloomy; ‹*colour*› drab
2 ‹*end, business, reputation*› dreadful; ‹*show, state*› sorry; ‹*character*› unsavoury (BrE); **c'est la ~ vérité** unfortunately, that's the truth of the matter; **faire la ~ expérience de qch** to learn about sth to one's cost

tristement /tʀistəmɑ̃/ *adv* sadly

tristesse /tʀistɛs/ *f* (gen) sadness; (of place, evening) dreariness; (of weather, day) gloominess

triton /tʀitɔ̃/ *m* (Zool) **1** (mollusc) triton
2 newt

triturer /tʀityʀe/ [**v1**] *vt* to fiddle with ‹*button*›; to knead] ‹*dough*›
IDIOM **se ~ la cervelle** (fam) *or* **les méninges** (fam) to rack one's brains (fam)

trivial, **~e**, *mpl* **-iaux** /tʀivjal, o/ *adj*
1 coarse
2 ordinary, everyday; ‹*style*› mundane

trivialité /tʀivjalite/ *f* **1** coarseness
2 triteness, triviality
3 platitude

troc /tʀɔk/ *m* barter; **faire du ~** to barter

troène /tʀɔɛn/ *m* privet

troglodyte /tʀɔglɔdit/ *m* cave-dweller

trogne /tʀɔɲ/ *f* (fam) mug (fam), face

trognon /tʀɔɲɔ̃/ *m* (of apple) core

trois /tʀwɑ/ *adj inv*, *pron*, *m inv* three
IDIOMS **être haut comme ~ pommes** to be knee-high to a grasshopper; **jamais deux sans ~** bad luck comes in threes

trois-huit /tʀwaɥit/ *mpl* system of three eight-hour shifts

troisième /tʀwazjɛm/ **A** *adj* third
B *f* **1** (Sch) *fourth year of secondary school, age 14–15*
2 (Aut) third (gear)
■ **le ~ âge** the elderly

troisièmement /tʀwazjɛmmɑ̃/ *adv* thirdly

trois-mâts /tʀwamɑ/ *m inv* three-master

trois-quarts /tʀwakaʀ/ **A** *m inv* **1** three-quarter-length coat
2 (rugby player) three-quarter
B **de trois-quarts** *phr* ‹*portrait*› three-quarter-length

trombe /tʀɔ̃b/ *f* **1** (caused by whirlwind) waterspout; **partir en ~** to go hurtling off
2 **~s d'eau** masses of water; torrential rain

trombone /tʀɔ̃bɔn/ *m* **1** trombone
2 trombonist
3 paper clip

trompe /tʀɔ̃p/ *f* **1** (Zool) (of elephant) trunk; (of insect) proboscis
2 (Mus) horn

trompe-la-mort /tʀɔ̃plamɔʀ/ *mf inv* daredevil

trompe-l'œil /tʀɔ̃plœj/ *m inv* **1** (painting) trompe l'œil
2 (fig) smokescreen

tromper /tʀɔ̃pe/ [**v1**] **A** *vt* **1** (gen) to deceive; to be unfaithful to ‹*husband, wife*›; **~ les électeurs** to mislead the voters
2 **~ la vigilance de qn** to slip past sb's guard
3 **pour ~ l'attente** to while away the time
B **se tromper** *v refl* (+ *v être*) **1** to be mistaken; **se ~ sur qn** to be wrong about sb; **il ne faut pas s'y ~, qu'on ne s'y trompe pas** make no mistake about it
2 to make a mistake; **se ~ de bus** to take the wrong bus

tromperie /tʀɔ̃pʀi/ *f* deceit

trompette[1] /tʀɔ̃pɛt/ *m* (in army) bugler

trompette[2] /tʀɔ̃pɛt/ *f* trumpet

trompettiste /tʀɔ̃petist/ *mf* trumpet (player)

trompeur, **-euse** /tʀɔ̃pœʀ, øz/ *adj* ‹*promise*› misleading; ‹*appearance*› deceptive

tronc /tʀɔ̃/ *m* **1** (of tree, body) trunk; (of column) shaft
2 collection box
■ **~ commun** (of species) common origin; (of disciplines) (common) core curriculum

tronche /tʀɔ̃ʃ/ *f* (pop) mug (fam), face

tronçon /tʀɔ̃sɔ̃/ *m* section

tronçonneuse /tʀɔ̃sɔnøz/ *f* chain saw

trône /tʀon/ *m* throne

trôner /tʀone/ [**v1**] *vi* **le professeur trônait au milieu de ses étudiants** the professor was holding court among his students; **~ sur** ‹*photograph*› to have pride of place on

tronquer /tʀɔ̃ke/ [**v1**] *vt* to truncate

trop /tʀo/ **A** *adv* too; too much; **beaucoup** *or* **bien ~ lourd** far *or* much too heavy; **j'ai ~ mangé** I've had too much to eat; **j'ai ~ dormi** I've slept too long; **nous sommes ~ peu nombreux** there are too few of us; **12 francs c'est ~ peu** 12 francs is too little; **ce serait ~ beau!** one should be so lucky!; **c'est ~ bête!** how stupid!; **~ enthousiaste** overenthusiastic; **~ c'est ~!** enough is enough!; **c'était ~ drôle** it was so funny
B **trop de** *quantif* **~ de pression/meubles** too much pressure/furniture; **~ de livres/monde** too many books/people
C **de trop**, **en trop** *phr* **il y a une assiette en ~** there's one plate too many; **il y a 12 euros de ~** there's 12 euros too much; **ta remarque était de ~** your remark was uncalled for; **se sentir de ~** to feel one is in the way

trophée /tʀɔfe/ *m* trophy

tropical, **~e**, *mpl* **-aux** /tʀɔpikal, o/ *adj* tropical

tropique /tʀɔpik/ *m* tropic

trop-perçu, *pl* **~s** /tʀopɛʀsy/ *m* **1** excess payment
2 overpayment of tax; **remboursement d'un ~** tax refund

trop-plein, *pl* **~s** /tʀoplɛ̃/ *m* **1** (of energy) excess
2 (Tech) (from bath) overflow

troquer /tʀɔke/ [**v1**] *vt* (gen) **~ qch contre qch** to swap sth for sth, to barter sth for sth

troquet /tʀɔke/ *m* (fam) bar

trot /tʀo/ *m* trot

trotte /tʀɔt/ *f* (fam) **ça fait une ~** it's a fair walk

trotter /tʀɔte/ [**v1**] *vi* **1** ‹*horse, rider*› to trot
2 ‹*person, mouse*› to scurry (about)
3 (fig) **~ dans la tête** ‹*thought*› to go through one's mind; ‹*music*› to go through one's head

trotteur /tʀɔtœʀ/ *m* **1** trotter
2 *shoe with a low, broad heel*

trotteuse /tʀɔtøz/ *f* (on watch) second hand

trottiner /tʀɔtine/ [**v1**] *vi* **1** ‹*horse*› to jog
2 ‹*person, mouse*› to scurry along

trottinette /tʀɔtinɛt/ *f* scooter

🔑 **trottoir** /tʀɔtwaʀ/ *m* pavement (BrE), sidewalk (AmE); **le bord du ~** the kerb (BrE) *or* curb (AmE)

🔑 **trou** /tʀu/ *m* **1** hole
2 (in timetable) (gen) gap; (in budget) deficit; (in savings) hole
3 (fam) **~ (perdu)** dump (fam)
■ **~ d'aération** air hole; **~ d'air** air pocket; **~ de mémoire** memory lapse; **~ normand** *glass of spirits between courses to aid digestion*; **~ de serrure** keyhole

troublant, **~e** /tʀublɑ̃, ɑ̃t/ *adj* **1** disturbing; disconcerting
2 (sexually) unsettling

🔑 **trouble** /tʀubl/ **A** *adj* **1** ‹*liquid*› cloudy; ‹*glasses*› smudgy
2 ‹*picture, outline*› blurred
3 ‹*feeling*› confused; ‹*business, milieu*› shady
B *adv* **je vois ~** my eyes are blurred
C *m* **1** unrest; **~s ethniques** ethnic unrest
2 trouble; **jeter le ~** to stir up trouble
3 confusion; embarrassment
4 emotion; **ressentir un ~** to feel a thrill of emotion
5 (Med) **~s** disorders
■ **~ obsessionnel compulsif**, **TOC** (Med) obsessive compulsive disorder, OCD

trouble-fête /tʀubləfɛt/ *mf inv* spoilsport

troubler /tʀuble/ [**v1**] **A** *vt* **1** to make [sth] cloudy ‹*liquid*›; to blur ‹*sight, picture*›
2 to disturb ‹*sleep, person*›; to disrupt ‹*plans*›; **en ces temps troublés** in these troubled times
3 to disconcert ‹*person*›
B se troubler *v refl* (+ *v être*) **1** ‹*person*› to become flustered
2 ‹*liquid*› to become cloudy; **ma vue se troubla** my eyes became blurred

trouée /tʀue/ *f* **1** gap
2 (Mil) breach

trouer /tʀue/ [**v1**] *vt* to make a hole (*or* holes) in; to wear a hole (*or* holes) in; **semelle trouée** sole with a hole (*or* holes) in it

troufion /tʀufjɔ̃/ *m* (pop) soldier

trouillard, **~e** /tʀujaʀ, ʀd/ (pop) **A** *adj* cowardly
B *mf* chicken (fam), coward

trouille /tʀuj/ *f* (pop) **avoir la ~** to be scared

🔑 **troupe** /tʀup/ *f* **1** (Mil) troops
2 (of actors) company; (on tour) troupe
3 (of deer) herd; (of birds) flock; (of tourists) troop; (of children) band

troupeau, *pl* **~x** /tʀupo/ *m* (of buffalo, cattle) herd; (of sheep) flock; (of geese) gaggle

trousse /tʀus/ *f* **1** (little) case
2 kit
■ **~ d'écolier** pencil case; **~ de médecin** doctor's bag; **~ de secours** first-aid kit; **~ de toilette** toilet bag
IDIOM **être aux ~s de qn** to be hot on sb's heels

trousseau, *pl* **~x** /tʀuso/ *m* **1** (of keys) bunch
2 (of bride) trousseau; (of baby) clothes

trouvaille /tʀuvɑj/ *f* **1** (object) find
2 bright idea, brainwave

trouvé, **~e** /tʀuve/ **A** *pp* ▶ **trouver**
B *pp adj* **réplique bien ~e** neat riposte; **tout ~** ‹*solution*› ready-made; ‹*culprit*› obvious

🔑 **trouver** /tʀuve/ [**v1**] **A** *vt* **1** (gen) to find; **~ qch par hasard** to come across sth; **~ un intérêt à qch** to find sth interesting; **~ à redire** to find fault; **~ le moyen de faire** to manage to do; **j'ai trouvé!** I've got it!; **tu as trouvé ça tout seul?** (ironic) did you work that out all by yourself?; **si tu continues tu vas me ~!** (fam) don't push your luck! (fam); **~ du plaisir à faire** to get pleasure out of doing; **aller ~ qn** to go and see sb
2 je trouve ça drôle I think it's funny; **j'ai trouvé bon de vous prévenir** I thought it right to warn you; **je me demande ce qu'elle te trouve!** I wonder what she sees in you!; **je te trouve bien calme, qu'est-ce que tu as?** you're very quiet, what's the matter?
B se trouver *v refl* (+ *v être*) **1** to be; **se ~ à Rome** to be in Rome; **se ~ dans l'impossibilité de faire** to be unable to do
2 to feel; **j'ai failli me ~ mal** I nearly passed out
3 il se trouve beau he thinks he's good-looking
4 to find ‹*excuse*›
C *v impers* **il se trouve qu'elle ne leur avait**

🔑 key word

t

rien dit as it happened, she hadn't told them anything; **si ça se trouve ça te plaira** (fam) you might like it

truand /tʀɥɑ̃/ *m* **1** gangster
2 crook

trublion /tʀyblijɔ̃/ *m* troublemaker

truc /tʀyk/ *m* **1** (fam) knack; trick; **avoir un ~ pour gagner de l'argent** to know a good way of making money; **un ~ du métier** a trick of the trade
2 thing; **il y a un tas de ~s à faire dans la maison** there are loads of things to do in the house (fam); **il y a un ~ qui ne va pas** there's something wrong
3 (fam) thingummy (fam), whatsit (fam)
4 (person) what's-his-name/what's-her-name, thingy (fam)

trucage /tʀykaʒ/ *m* (in cinema) special effect

truchement /tʀyʃmɑ̃/ *m* **par le ~ de qch** through sth; **par le ~ de qn** through the intervention of sb

truculent, **~e** /tʀykylɑ̃, ɑ̃t/ *adj* earthy

truelle /tʀyɛl/ *f* trowel

truffe /tʀyf/ *f* **1** (Culin) truffle
2 (of dog) nose

truffer /tʀyfe/ [**v1**] *vt* **ta lettre est truffée de fautes** your letter is riddled with mistakes

truie /tʀɥi/ *f* sow

truite /tʀɥit/ *f* trout

truquage ▸ **trucage**

truquer /tʀyke/ [**v1**] *vt* **1** to fiddle (fam) ‹*accounts*›
2 to mark ‹*cards*›
3 to fix ‹*elections, match*›

trust /tʀœst/ *m* trust

tsar /tsaʀ/ *m* tsar

tsé-tsé /tsetse/ *f inv* **(mouche) ~** tsetse (fly)

tsigane ▸ **tzigane**

TTC (*abbr* = **toutes taxes comprises**) inclusive of tax

tu /ty/ *pron* you
IDIOM **être à ~ et à toi avec qn** to be on familiar terms with sb

tuant, **~e** /tɥɑ̃, ɑ̃t/ *adj* (fam) exhausting

tuba /tyba/ *m* **1** (Mus) tuba
2 (of swimmer) snorkel

tube /tyb/ **A** *m* **1** tube; pipe
2 (fam) (song) hit
B **à pleins tubes** *phr* (fam) **mettre le son à pleins ~s** to turn the sound right up (fam)
■ **~ cathodique** cathode ray tube; **~ digestif** digestive tract; **~ à essai** test tube

tubercule /tybɛʀkyl/ *m* **1** (Bot) tuber
2 (Anat) tuberosity

tuberculeux, **-euse** /tybɛʀkylø, øz/ *adj* tubercular; **être ~** to have TB

tuberculose /tybɛʀkyloz/ *f* tuberculosis, TB

tubulaire /tybylɛʀ/ *adj* tubular

TUC /tyk/ *mpl* (*abbr* = **travaux d'utilité collective**) paid community service (*for the young unemployed*)

tué /tɥe/ *m* person killed; **sept ~s, cinq blessés** seven people killed, five injured

tuer /tɥe/ [**v1**] **A** *vt* **1** (gen) to kill
2 (fam) to wear [sb] out
B **se tuer** *v refl* (+ *v être*) **1** (accidentally) to be killed
2 to kill oneself
3 se ~ au travail to work oneself to death

tuerie /tyʀi/ *f* killings

tue-tête: **à tue-tête** /atytɛt/ *phr* at the top of one's voice

tueur, **-euse** /tɥœʀ, øz/ *mf* **1** killer
2 slaughterer
■ **~ à gages** hired *or* professional killer

tuile /tɥil/ *f* **1** tile
2 (fam) blow; **quelle ~!** what a blow!
3 (Culin) *thin almond biscuit*

tulipe /tylip/ *f* tulip

tuméfier /tymefje/ [**v2**] *vt* to make [sth] swell up

tumeur /tymœʀ/ *f* tumour (BrE)

tumulte /tymylt/ *m* **1** uproar
2 turmoil

tumultueux, **-euse** /tymyltɥø, øz/ *adj* turbulent; tempestuous; stormy

tungstène /tœ̃gstɛn/ *m* tungsten

tunique /tynik/ *f* tunic

tunisien, **-ienne** /tynizjɛ̃, ɛn/ *adj* Tunisian

tunnel /tynɛl/ *m* tunnel; **le ~ sous la Manche** the Channel Tunnel
IDIOM **voir le bout du ~** to see light at the end of the tunnel

turban /tyʀbɑ̃/ *m* turban

turbin /tyʀbɛ̃/ *m* (pop) daily grind (fam), work

turbine /tyʀbin/ *f* turbine

turboréacteur /tyʀboʀeaktœʀ/ *m* turbojet (engine)

turbot /tyʀbo/ *m* turbot

turbulence /tyʀbylɑ̃s/ *f* **1** turbulence
2 unruliness
3 unrest

turbulent, **~e** /tyʀbylɑ̃, ɑ̃t/ *adj* ‹*child*› unruly; ‹*class*› rowdy; ‹*teenager*› rebellious; **être ~ en classe** to be disruptive in class

turc, **turque** /tyʀk/ **A** *adj* Turkish
B *m* (language) Turkish

Turc, **Turque** /tyʀk/ *mf* Turk

turfiste /tœʀfist/ *mf* racegoer, punter (fam)

turlupiner /tyʀlypine/ [**v1**] *vt* (fam) to bother

turpitude /tyʀpityd/ *f* **1** turpitude, depravity
2 base act; low remark

turque ▸ **turc A**

Turquie /tyʀki/ *pr f* Turkey

turquoise /tyʀkwaz/ *adj inv*, *f* turquoise

tutelle /tytɛl/ *f* guardianship

tuteur, **-trice** /tytœʀ, tʀis/ **A** *mf* **1** (Law) guardian
2 tutor
B *m* (Bot) stake

tutoiement /tytwamɑ̃/ *m* using the 'tu' form

tutoyer /tytwaje/ [**v23**] *vt* to address [sb] using the 'tu' form

tutu /tyty/ *m* tutu

tuyau, *pl* **~x** /tɥijo/ *m* **1** (Tech) pipe
2 (fam) tip (fam)
■ **~ d'arrosage** hose; **~ d'échappement** exhaust

tuyauterie /tɥijotʀi/ *f* (Tech) piping

TVA /tevea/ *f* (*abbr* = **taxe à la valeur ajoutée**) VAT

tweeter /twite/ *vi* (Comp) to tweet, to write a tweet

twiter /twite/ *vi* (Comp) ▶ **tweeter**

tympan /tɛ̃pɑ̃/ *m* eardrum

✓ **type** /tip/ **A** *m* **1** type, kind; **plusieurs accidents de ce ~** several accidents of this kind
2 (classic) example; **elle est le ~ même de la femme d'affaires** she's the classic example of a business woman
3 (physical) type
4 (fam) guy (fam); **sale ~!** swine! (fam); **brave ~** nice chap (fam)
B (-)type (*combining form*) typical, classic

typer /tipe/ [**v1**] *vt* to portray [sb] as a type; to play [sb] as a type

typhoïde /tifɔid/ *adj*, *f* typhoid

typhon /tifɔ̃/ *m* typhoon

typique /tipik/ *adj* typical

typiquement /tipikmɑ̃/ *adv* typically; **une famille ~ américaine** a typically American family

typographie /tipɔgʀafi/ *f* typography

typographique /tipɔgʀafik/ *adj* typographical

tyran /tiʀɑ̃/ *m* tyrant

tyrannie /tiʀani/ *f* tyranny

tyrannique /tiʀanik/ *adj* tyrannical

tyranniser /tiʀanize/ [**v1**] *vt* to tyrannize

tzigane /dzigan, tsigan/ **A** *adj*, *mf* gypsy
B *m* (language) Romany

Uu

u, U /y/ *m inv* u, U; **en (forme de) U** U-shaped

ubac /ybak/ *m* north-facing side

ubiquité /ybikɥite/ *f* ubiquity; **je n'ai pas le don d'~!** I can't be everywhere at once!

ubuesque /ybyɛsk/ *adj* grotesque

ulcère /ylsɛʀ/ *m* ulcer

ulcérer /ylseʀe/ [**v14**] *vt* **1** to sicken, to revolt
2 (Med) to ulcerate

ulcéreux, **-euse** /ylseʀø, øz/ *adj* ‹*wound*› ulcerated

ULM /yɛlɛm/ *m inv* (*abbr* = **ultraléger motorisé**) microlight; microlighting; **faire de l'~** to go microlighting

ultérieur, **~e** /ylteʀjœʀ/ *adj* subsequent; **une date ~e** a later date

ultérieurement /ylteʀjœʀmɑ̃/ *adv*
1 subsequently
2 later

ultimatum /yltimatɔm/ *m* ultimatum

ultime /yltim/ *adj* **1** final
2 ultimate

ultra /yltʀa/ *adj*, *mf* extremist

ultraconfidentiel, **-ielle** /yltʀakɔ̃fidɑ̃sjɛl/ *adj* top secret

ultrafin, **~e** /yltʀafɛ̃, in/ *adj* ‹*slice*› wafer-thin; ‹*stocking*› sheer; ‹*fibre*› ultra-fine

ultraléger, **-ère** /yltʀaleʒe, ɛʀ/ *adj* ‹*material, cigarette*› ultra light; ‹*clothing, fabric, equipment*› very light

ultramoderne /yltʀamɔdɛʀn/ *adj* (gen) ultra-modern; ‹*system, technology*› state-of-the-art

ultrarapide /yltʀaʀapid/ *adj* high-speed

ultrasecret, **-ète** /yltʀasəkʀɛ, ɛt/ *adj* top secret

ultrasensible /yltʀasɑ̃sibl/ *adj* ‹*person*› hypersensitive; ‹*film*› ultra-sensitive; ‹*issue*› highly sensitive

ultrason /yltʀasɔ̃/ *m* ultrasound

ultraviolet, **-ette** /yltʀavjɔlɛ, ɛt/ **A** *adj* ultraviolet
B *m* ultraviolet ray; **séance d'~s** session on a sunbed

ululer /ylyle/ [**v1**] *vi* to hoot

✓ **un**, **une** /œ̃(n), yn/ **A** *det* (*pl* **des**) **1** a, an; one; **un homme** a man; **une femme** a woman; **avec ~ sang-froid remarquable** with remarkable self-control; **il n'y avait pas ~ arbre** there wasn't a single tree; **~ accident est vite arrivé** accidents soon happen
2 il y avait des roses et des lis there were roses and lilies; **il y a des gens qui trichent** there are some people who cheat
3 il fait ~ froid *or* **~ de ces froids!** it's so

✓ key word

cold!; **elle m'a donné une de ces gifles!** she gave me such a slap!; **il y a ~ monde aujourd'hui!** there are so many people today!
B *pron* (*pl* **uns, unes**) one; **(l')~ de** *or* **d'entre nous** one of us; **les ~s pensent que...** some think that...
C *adj* one, a, an; **trente et une personnes** thirty one people; **~ jour sur deux** every other day
D *mf* one; **~ par personne** one each; **les deux villes n'en font plus qu'une** the two cities have merged into one; **~ à** *or* **par ~** one by one
E *m* one; **page ~** page one
IDIOMS **fière comme pas une** extremely proud; **il est menteur comme pas ~** he's the biggest liar; **~ pour tous et tous pour ~** all for one and one for all

unanime /ynanim/ *adj* unanimous

unanimement /ynanimmɑ̃/ *adv*
1 ‹*adopted, elected*› unanimously
2 (fig) ‹*admired*› universally

unanimité /ynanimite/ *f* unanimity; **à l'~** ‹*elected*› unanimously; **à l'~ moins deux voix** with only two votes against; **faire l'~** to have unanimous support *or* backing

une /yn/ **A** *det, pron, adj* ▸ **un A, B, C, D**
B *f* **la ~** the front page; **être à la ~** to be in the headlines

uni, ~e /yni/ **A** *pp* ▸ **unir**
B *pp adj* **1** ‹*family*› close-knit; ‹*couple*› close; ‹*people, rebels*› united
2 ‹*fabric, colour*› plain
3 ‹*surface*› smooth, even

unicité /ynisite/ *f* uniqueness

unidirectionnel, -elle /ynidiʀɛksjɔnɛl/ *adj* ‹*transmitter*› unidirectional; ‹*receiver*› one-way

unième /ynjɛm/ *adj* first; **vingt et ~** twenty first

unification /ynifikasjɔ̃/ *f* unification

unifier /ynifje/ [**v2**] **A** *vt* **1** to unify ‹*country, market*›
2 to standardize ‹*procedure, system*›
B s'unifier *v refl* (+ *v être*) ‹*countries, groups*› to unite

uniforme /ynifɔʀm/ **A** *adj* (gen) uniform; ‹*buildings, streets, existence*› monotonous; ‹*regulation*› across-the-board
B *m* uniform; **en ~** uniformed

uniformément /ynifɔʀmemɑ̃/ *adv* uniformly

uniformiser /ynifɔʀmize/ [**v1**] *vt* to standardize ‹*rate*›; to make [sth] uniform ‹*colour*›

uniformité /ynifɔʀmite/ *f* (of tastes) uniformity; (of life, buildings) monotony

unijambiste /ynizɑ̃bist/ **A** *adj* **être ~** to have only one leg
B *mf* one-legged person

unilatéral, ~e, *mpl* **-aux** /ynilateʀal, o/ *adj* unilateral; ‹*parking*› on one side only

unilingue /ynilɛ̃g/ *adj* unilingual, monolingual

uninominal, ~e, *mpl* **-aux** /yninɔminal, o/ *adj* (Pol) ‹*ballot*› for a single candidate

union /ynjɔ̃/ *f* **1** union
2 association; **~ de consommateurs** consumers' association
3 marriage
■ **~ libre** cohabitation; **~ sportive, US** sports club; **Union européenne** European Union
IDIOM **l'~ fait la force** (Proverb) united we stand, divided we fall

unique /ynik/ *adj* **1** only; **il est l'~ témoin** he's the only witness; **être fille** *or* **fils ~** to be an only child
2 single; **parti ~** single party; **système à parti ~** one-party system; **'prix ~'** 'all at one price'
3 unique; **une occasion ~** a unique opportunity; **~ en son genre** ‹*person, object*› one of a kind; ‹*event*› one-off (BrE), one-shot (AmE)
4 (fam) **ce type est ~!** that guy's priceless! (fam)

uniquement /ynikmɑ̃/ *adv* (gen) only; **en vente ~ par correspondance** available by mail order only; **c'était ~ pour te taquiner** it was only to tease you; **il pense ~ à s'amuser** all he thinks about is having fun; **~ dans un but commercial** purely for commercial ends

unir /yniʀ/ [**v3**] **A** *vt* **1** to unite ‹*people, country*›; **des hommes unis par les mêmes idées** men brought together by the same ideas
2 to combine ‹*qualities, resources*›
3 to join [sb] in matrimony
B s'unir *v refl* (+ *v être*) **1** to unite
2 to marry

unisexe /yniseks/ *adj* unisex

unisson /ynisɔ̃/ *m* unison; **à l'~** (Mus) in unison; (fig) in accord

unitaire /ynitɛʀ/ *adj* ‹*cost*› unit

unité /ynite/ *f* **1** unity; **film qui manque d'~** film lacking in cohesion; **il y a ~ de vues entre eux** they share the same viewpoint
2 unit; **~ monétaire** unit of currency; **20 euros l'~** 20 euros each; **vendre qch à l'~** to sell sth singly
■ **~ centrale (de traitement)** (Comput) central processing unit, CPU; **~ de disque** (Comput) disk drive

univers /univɛʀ/ *m inv* **1** universe
2 whole world
3 world; **l'~ de Kafka** Kafka's world

universaliser /yniveʀsalize/ [**v1**] *vt* to universalize

universalité /yniveʀsalite/ *f* universality

universel, -elle /yniveʀsɛl/ *adj* ‹*language, theme*› universal; ‹*history*› world; ‹*remedy*› all-purpose

universitaire /yniveʀsitɛʀ/ **A** *adj* ‹*town*› university; ‹*work*› academic
B *mf* academic

u

✓ **université** /ynivɛʀsite/ *f* university (BrE), college (AmE)
■ **~ d'été** summer school

uns ▶ **un B**

Untel, **Unetelle** /œ̃tɛl, yntɛl/ *mf* **Monsieur ~** Mr so-and-so; **Madame Unetelle** Mrs so-and-so

urbain, **~e** /yʀbɛ̃, ɛn/ *adj* **1** urban; **vie ~e** city life
2 (fml) urbane

urbanisation /yʀbanizasjɔ̃/ *f* urbanization

urbaniser /yʀbanize/ [**v1**] *vt* to urbanize ‹*region*›; **zone urbanisée** built-up area

urbanisme /yʀbanism/ *m* town planning (BrE), city planning (AmE)

urbaniste /yʀbanist/ *mf* town planner (BrE), city planner (AmE)

urée /yʀe/ *f* urea

urètre /yʀɛtʀ/ *m* urethra

urgence /yʀʒɑ̃s/ *f* **1** urgency; **il y a ~** it's urgent, it's a matter of urgency; **d'~** ‹*act*› immediately; ‹*summon*› urgently; ‹*measures, treatment*› emergency; **de toute** *or* **d'extrême ~** as a matter of great urgency; **transporter qn d'~ à l'hôpital** to rush sb to hospital (BrE) *or* to the hospital (AmE); **en ~** as a matter of urgency
2 (Med) **une ~** an emergency; **le service des ~s, les ~s** the casualty department

urgent, **~e** /yʀʒɑ̃, ɑ̃t/ *adj* urgent

urinaire /yʀinɛʀ/ *adj* urinary; **appareil ~** urinary tract

urinal, *pl* **-aux** /yʀinal, o/ *m* urinal

urine /yʀin/ *f* urine

uriner /yʀine/ [**v1**] *vi* to urinate

urinoir /yʀinwaʀ/ *m* urinal

urne /yʀn/ *f* **1 ~ (électorale)** ballot box; **se rendre aux ~s** to go to the polls
2 urn

urologie /yʀɔlɔʒi/ *f* urology

urologue /yʀɔlɔg/ *mf* urologist

URSS /yɛʀɛsɛs, yʀs/ *pr f* (*abbr* = **Union des Républiques socialistes soviétiques**) USSR

urticaire /yʀtikɛʀ/ *f* hives

uruguayen, **-enne** /yʀygwejɛ̃, ɛn/ *adj* Uruguayan

us /ys/ *mpl* **les ~ et coutumes** the ways and customs

US /yɛs/ *f* (*abbr* = **union sportive**) sports club

USA /yɛsa/ *mpl* (*abbr* = **United States of America**) USA

✓ **usage** /yzaʒ/ *m* **1** use; **à l'~, par l'~** with use; **en ~** in use; **faire ~ de** to use ‹*product*›; to exercise ‹*authority*›; **faire bon/mauvais ~ de qch** to put sth to good/bad use; **faire de l'~** ‹*garment*› to last; **à ~ privé** for private use; **à ~s multiples** ‹*appliance*› multipurpose; **il a perdu l'~ d'un œil/l'~ de la parole** he's lost the use of one eye/the power of speech; **hors d'~** ‹*garment*› unwearable; ‹*machine*› out of order
2 (in a language) usage; **en ~** in usage
3 custom; **l'~ est de faire** the custom is to do; it's usual practice to do; **entrer dans l'~** ‹*word*› to come into common use; ‹*behaviour*› to become common practice; **d'~** ‹*politeness*› customary; ‹*precautions*› usual
■ **~ de faux** (Law) use of false documents; **faux et ~ de faux** forgery and use of false documents

usagé, **~e** /yzaʒe/ *adj* **1** ‹*garment*› well-worn; ‹*tyre*› worn
2 ‹*syringe*› used

usager /yzaʒe/ *m* (of service) user; (of language) speaker; **~ de la route** road user

usant, **~e** /yzɑ̃, ɑ̃t/ *adj* exhausting, wearing

usé, **~e** /yze/ **A** *pp* ▶ **user**
B *pp adj* ‹*object*› worn; ‹*person*› worn-down; ‹*heart, eyes*› worn-out; ‹*joke*› hackneyed; **~ jusqu'à la corde** ‹*carpet*› threadbare; ‹*tyre*› worn down to the tread; (fig) ‹*joke*› hackneyed

✓ **user** /yze/ [**v1**] **A** *vt* to wear out ‹*shoes*›; to wear down ‹*person*›; **les piles sont usées** the batteries have run down *or* out; **~ ses vêtements jusqu'à la corde** to wear one's clothes out; **~ sa santé** to ruin one's health
B user de *v+prep* (gen) to use; to exercise ‹*right*›; to take ‹*precautions*›; **~ de diplomatie** to be diplomatic
C s'user *v refl* (+ *v être*) **1** ‹*shoes*› to wear out
2 ‹*person*› **s'~ à la tâche** *or* **au travail** to wear oneself out with overwork; **s'~ la santé** to ruin one's health

usinage /yzinaʒ/ *m* **1** (with a machine tool) machining
2 (industrial production) manufacture

usine /yzin/ *f* factory, plant
■ **~ de traitement** recycling plant; **~ métallurgique** ironworks; **~ sidérurgique** steelworks

usiner /yzine/ [**v1**] *vt* **1** to machine
2 to manufacture

usité, **~e** /yzite/ *adj* commonly used

ustensile /ystɑ̃sil/ *m* utensil

usuel, **-elle** /yzɥɛl/ *adj* ‹*object*› everyday; ‹*word*› common

usufruit /yzyfʀɥi/ *m* (Law) usufruct

usufruitier, **-ière** /yzyfʀɥitje, ɛʀ/ *mf* tenant for life

usure /yzyʀ/ *f* **1** (of clothes) wear and tear; (of tyre, machine) wear; **résister à l'~** to wear well
2 (of energy, enemy) wearing down
3 ~ du temps wearing effect of time
4 usury

usurier, **-ière** /yzyʀje, ɛʀ/ *mf* usurer

usurpateur, **-trice** /yzyʀpatœʀ, tʀis/ *mf* usurper

✓ key word

usurpation /yzyʀpasjɔ̃/ *f* usurpation
usurper /yzyʀpe/ [**v1**] *vt* to usurp
ut /yt/ *m* (Mus) C
utérus /yteʀys/ *m inv* womb
utile /ytil/ **A** *adj* (gen) useful; **être ~** ‹*person, book*› to be helpful; ‹*umbrella*› to come in handy; **il est ~ de signaler** it's worth pointing out; **il n'a pas jugé ~ de me prévenir** he didn't think it necessary to let me know; **en quoi puis-je vous être ~?** how can I help you?
B *m* **joindre l'~ à l'agréable** to mix business with pleasure
utilement /ytilmɑ̃/ *adv* ‹*intervene*› effectively; ‹*occupy oneself*› usefully
utilisable /ytilizabl/ *adj* usable
utilisateur, **-trice** /ytilizatœʀ, tʀis/ *mf* user
utilisation /ytilizasjɔ̃/ *f* use
utiliser /ytilize/ [**v1**] *vt* (gen) to use; to make use of ‹*resources*›
utilitaire /ytilitɛʀ/ *adj* ‹*role*› practical; ‹*object*› functional, utilitarian; ‹*vehicle*› commercial
utilité /ytilite/ *f* **1** usefulness; **d'une grande ~** ‹*book, machine*› very useful; ‹*person*› very helpful; **d'aucune ~** of no use
2 use; **je n'en ai pas l'~** I have no use for it
utopie /ytɔpi/ *f* **1** Utopia
2 wishful thinking
utopique /ytɔpik/ *adj* utopian
UV /yve/ *mpl* (*abbr* = **ultraviolets**) ultraviolet rays; **séance d'~** session on a sunbed
uvule /yvyl/ *f* uvula

Vv

v, **V** /ve/ *m inv* v, V; **en (forme de) V** V-shaped; **pull en V** V-necked sweater
va /va/ ▶ **aller**[1]
vacance /vakɑ̃s/ **A** *f* vacancy
B vacances *fpl* holiday (BrE), vacation (AmE); **être en ~s** to be on holiday (BrE) *or* vacation (AmE)
■ **~s scolaires** (Sch) school holidays (BrE) *or* vacation (AmE)
vacancier, **-ière** /vakɑ̃sje, ɛʀ/ *mf* holidaymaker (BrE), vacationer (AmE)
vacant, **~e** /vakɑ̃, ɑ̃t/ *adj* vacant
vacarme /vakaʀm/ *m* din, racket (fam)
vacataire /vakatɛʀ/ *mf* **1** temporary employee
2 supply teacher (BrE), substitute teacher (AmE)
vaccin /vaksɛ̃/ *m* (Med) vaccine
vaccination /vaksinasjɔ̃/ *f* vaccination
vacciner /vaksine/ [**v1**] *vt* **1** to vaccinate
2 (hum) **je suis vacciné!** (fam) I've learned my lesson!
vache /vaʃ/ **A** *adj* (fam) mean, nasty
B *f* **1** cow
2 cowhide
■ **~ à eau** water bottle; **~ à lait** (fig) money-spinner (fam); **années de ~s maigres** lean years
IDIOM **parler français comme une ~ espagnole** (fam) to speak very bad French
vachement /vaʃmɑ̃/ *adv* (fam) really
vacherie /vaʃʀi/ *f* (fam) **1** meanness
2 bitchy remark (fam)
3 dirty trick
4 c'est une vraie ~ ce virus this virus is a damned nuisance (fam)
vachette /vaʃɛt/ *f* **1** young cow
2 calfskin
vacillant, **~e** /vasijɑ̃, ɑ̃t/ *adj* **1** ‹*legs*› unsteady; ‹*person*› unsteady on one's legs; ‹*light, flame*› flickering
2 ‹*power, majority*› shaky
vaciller /vasije/ [**v1**] *vi* **1** ‹*person*› to be unsteady on one's legs; ‹*legs*› to be unsteady
2 ‹*person, object*› to sway; ‹*light, flame*› to flicker
3 ‹*health*› to fail; ‹*majority*› to weaken
vadrouille /vadʀuj/ *f* (fam) stroll; **être en ~** to be wandering about
vadrouiller /vadʀuje/ [**v1**] *vi* (fam) to wander around
va-et-vient /vaevjɛ̃/ *m inv* **1** comings and goings; **faire le ~** to go to and fro; to go back and forth
2 two-way switch
vagabond, **~e** /vagabɔ̃, ɔ̃d/ **A** *adj* ‹*dog*› stray; ‹*mood*› ever-changing
B *mf* vagrant
vagabondage /vagabɔ̃daʒ/ *m* **1** wandering
2 (Law) vagrancy
vagabonder /vagabɔ̃de/ [**v1**] *vi* to wander
vagin /vaʒɛ̃/ *m* vagina
vagissement /vaʒismɑ̃/ *m* wail
vague[1] /vag/ **A** *adj* vague; **ce sont de ~s parents** they're distant relatives

B *m* **1 il regardait dans le ~** he was staring into space
2 avoir du ~ à l'âme to feel melancholic

⚷ **vague²** /vag/ *f* wave; **faire des ~s** ‹*wind*› to make ripples; (fig) ‹*scandal*› to cause a stir
■ **~ de chaleur** heatwave; **~ de froid** cold spell
(IDIOM) **être au creux de la ~** to be at a low ebb

vaguement /vagmɑ̃/ *adv* vaguely

vaillamment /vajamɑ̃/ *adv* courageously, valiantly

vaillance /vajɑ̃s/ *f* courage; **avec ~** courageously

vaillant, **~e** /vajɑ̃, ɑ̃t/ *adj* **1** courageous
2 strong

⚷ **vain**, **~e** /vɛ̃, vɛn/ **A** *adj* **1** futile; **mes efforts ont été ~s** my efforts were in vain
2 ‹*promises*› empty; ‹*hopes*› vain
3 ‹*person*› vain
B en vain *phr* in vain

⚷ **vaincre** /vɛ̃kʀ/ **[v57]** **A** *vt* **1** to defeat ‹*opponent*›
2 to overcome ‹*prejudices, complex*›; to beat ‹*unemployment, illness*›
B *vi* to win

vaincu, **~e** /vɛ̃ky/ ▶ **vaincre**

vainement /vɛnmɑ̃/ *adv* in vain

vainqueur /vɛ̃kœʀ/ **A** *adj m* victorious
B *m* victor; winner; prizewinner; conqueror

vais /vɛ/ ▶ **aller¹**

⚷ **vaisseau**, *pl* **~x** /vɛso/ *m* **1** (Anat, Bot) vessel
2 (Naut) vessel; warship
■ **~ spatial** spaceship

vaisselier /vɛsəlje/ *m* dresser

vaisselle /vɛsɛl/ *f* **1** crockery, dishes
2 dishes; **faire la ~** to do the dishes

val, *pl* **~s** *or* **vaux** /val, vo/ *m* valley
(IDIOM) **être toujours par monts et par vaux** to be always on the move

valable /valabl/ *adj* **1** ‹*explanation*› valid; ‹*solution*› viable
2 ‹*document*› valid
3 (fam) ‹*work, project*› worthwhile

valdinguer /valdɛ̃ge/ **[v1]** *vi* (fam) to go flying (fam)

valet /valɛ/ *m* **1** manservant
2 (in cards) jack
■ **~ de chambre** valet; **~ de ferme** farm hand; **~ de nuit** rack, valet (AmE)

⚷ **valeur** /valœʀ/ *f* **1** value; **prendre de la ~** to go up in value; **les objets de ~** valuables
2 (of person, artist) worth; (of work) value, merit; (of method, discovery) value; **attacher de la ~ à qch** to value sth; **mettre qch en ~** to emphasize ‹*fact, talent*›; to set off ‹*eyes, painting*›; **se mettre en ~** to make the best of oneself; to show oneself to best advantage
3 validity
4 value; **nous n'avons pas les mêmes ~s** we don't share the same values
5 (on stock exchange) security; **~s** securities, stock, stocks and shares
■ **~ sûre** gilt-edged security (BrE), blue chip; (fig) safe bet; **~s mobilières** securities

valeureux, **-euse** /valøʀø, øz/ *adj* valorous (dated)

validation /validasjɔ̃/ *f* **1** validation
2 stamping

valide /valid/ *adj* **1** valid
2 able-bodied; fit

valider /valide/ **[v1]** *vt* to stamp ‹*ticket*›; **faire ~** to have [sth] recognized ‹*diploma*›

validité /validite/ *f* validity

valise /valiz/ *f* suitcase; **faire ses ~s** to pack
(IDIOM) **avoir des ~s sous les yeux** (fam) to have bags under one's eyes

vallée /vale/ *f* valley

vallon /valɔ̃/ *m* dale, small valley

vallonné, **~e** /valɔne/ *adj* ‹*landscape*› undulating; ‹*country*› hilly

⚷ **valoir** /valwaʀ/ **[v45]** **A** *vt* **~ qch à qn** to earn sb sth ‹*praise, criticism*›; to win sb sth ‹*friendship*›; to bring sb sth ‹*problems*›
B *vi* **1 ~ une fortune/cher** to be worth a fortune/a lot; **ça vaut combien?** how much is it worth?; **~ de l'or** (fig) to be very valuable
2 que vaut ce film/vin? what's that film/wine like?; **il ne vaut pas mieux que son frère** he's no better than his brother; **ne rien ~** to be rubbish; to be useless; to be worthless; **la chaleur ne me vaut rien** the heat doesn't suit me; **ça ne me dit rien qui vaille** I don't like the sound of it
3 to be as good as; **ton travail vaut bien/largement le leur** your work is just as good/every bit as good as theirs; **rien ne vaut la soie** nothing beats silk
4 to be worth; **le musée vaut le détour** the museum is worth a detour; **ça vaut la peine** *or* **le coup** (fam) it's worth it
5 ‹*rule, criticism*› to apply
6 faire ~ to put [sth] to work ‹*money*›; to point out ‹*necessity*›; to emphasize ‹*quality*›; to assert ‹*right*›; **faire ~ que** to point out that; **se faire ~** to push oneself forward
C se valoir *v refl* (+ *v être*) to be the same
D *v impers* **il vaut mieux faire, mieux vaut faire** it's better to do; **il vaut mieux que tu y ailles** you'd better go

valorisation /valɔʀizasjɔ̃/ *f* **1** (of product) promotion
2 (of region, resources) development

valoriser /valɔʀize/ **[v1]** *vt* **1** to promote ‹*product*›; to make [sth] attractive ‹*profession, course*›
2 to develop ‹*region, resources*›

valse /vals/ *f* waltz

valse-hésitation, *pl* **valses-hésitations** /valsezitasjɔ̃/ *f* shilly-shallying (fam)

valser /valse/ **[v1]** *vi* to waltz

V

⚷ key word

valseur, **-euse** /valsœʀ, øz/ *mf* waltzer
valu, **~e** /valy/ ▶ **valoir**
valve /valv/ *f* valve
vamp /vɑ̃p/ *f* (fam) vamp
vampire /vɑ̃piʀ/ *m* **1** vampire
2 (fig) bloodsucker
3 (Zool) vampire bat
vampiriser /vɑ̃piʀize/ [**v1**] *vt* (fig) to cannibalize
van /vɑ̃/ *m* **1** horsebox (BrE), horse-car (AmE)
2 van
vandale /vɑ̃dal/ *mf* vandal
vandalisme /vɑ̃dalism/ *m* vandalism
vanille /vanij/ *f* vanilla; **une gousse de ~** a vanilla pod
vanité /vanite/ *f* **1** vanity; **tirer ~ de qch** to pride oneself on sth
2 (of efforts) futility; (of promise) emptiness; (of undertaking) uselessness
vaniteux, **-euse** /vanitø, øz/ *adj* vain
vanne /van/ *f* **1** gate; sluice gate; floodgate
2 (fam) dig (fam)
IDIOM **fermer les ~s** (fam) to cut funding
vanner /vane/ [**v1**] *vt* (fam) to tire [sb] out
vannerie /vanʀi/ *f* basket-making; **objets en ~** wickerwork
vantardise /vɑ̃taʀdiz/ *f* **1** boastfulness
2 boast
vanter /vɑ̃te/ [**v1**] **A** *vt* to praise, to extol
B **se vanter** *v refl* (+ *v être*) **1** to boast
2 se ~ de faire to pride oneself on doing
va-nu-pieds /vanypje/ *mf inv* tramp, bum (AmE) (fam)
vapeur /vapœʀ/ **A** *f* steam; **bateau à ~** steamboat; **renverser la ~** (fig) to back-pedal; **faire cuire qch à la ~** to steam sth
B **vapeurs** *fpl* fumes
vaporeux, **-euse** /vapɔʀø, øz/ *adj* diaphanous
vaporisateur /vapɔʀizatœʀ/ *m* spray
vaporisation /vapɔʀizasjɔ̃/ *f* spraying
vaporiser /vapɔʀize/ [**v1**] *vt* to spray
vaquer /vake/ [**v1**] *v+prep* **~ à ses occupations** to attend to one's business
varappe /vaʀap/ *f* rock-climbing
varappeur, **-euse** /vaʀapœʀ, øz/ *mf* rock climber
varech /vaʀɛk/ *m* kelp
vareuse /vaʀøz/ *f* **1** jersey
2 (Mil) uniform jacket
variable /vaʀjabl/ **A** *adj* **1** variable
2 ‹*weather*› changeable; ‹*mood*› unpredictable
B *f* variable
variante /vaʀjɑ̃t/ *f* variant
variation /vaʀjasjɔ̃/ *f* variation; **connaître de fortes ~s** to fluctuate considerably
varice /vaʀis/ *f* varicose vein
varicelle /vaʀisɛl/ *f* chicken pox
varié, **~e** /vaʀje/ *adj* **1** varied
2 various
varier /vaʀje/ [**v2**] **A** *vt* to vary; **pour ~ les plaisirs** just for a (pleasant) change
B *vi* to vary; **l'inflation varie de 4% à 6%** inflation fluctuates between 4% and 6%
variété /vaʀjete/ **A** *f* **1** variety; **une grande ~ d'articles** a wide range of items
2 (Bot) variety
3 sort
B **variétés** *fpl* **spectacle de ~s** variety show; **les ~s françaises** French popular music
variole /vaʀjɔl/ *f* smallpox
Varsovie /vaʀsɔvi/ *pr n* Warsaw
vas /va/ ▶ **aller**[1]
vase[1] /vɑz/ *m* vase
IDIOM **c'est la goutte d'eau qui fait déborder le ~** it's the last straw
vase[2] /vɑz/ *f* silt, sludge
vasectomie /vazɛktɔmi/ *f* vasectomy
vaseux, **-euse** /vazø, øz/ *adj* **1** muddy
2 (fam) **je me sens plutôt ~** I'm not really with it (fam)
3 (fam) ‹*speech, explanation*› woolly
vasistas /vazistas/ *m inv* louvre (BrE) window
vasque /vask/ *f* **1** (of fountain) basin
2 bowl
vassal, **~e**, *mpl* **-aux** /vasal, o/ *mf* vassal
⚷ **vaste** /vast/ *adj* **1** ‹*estate, sector*› vast; ‹*market*› huge
2 ‹*audience, choice*› large
3 ‹*fraud*› massive; ‹*campaign*› extensive; ‹*movement, attack*› large-scale; ‹*work*› wide-ranging
va-t-en-guerre /vatɑ̃gɛʀ/ *m inv* warmonger
va-tout /vatu/ *m inv* **jouer/tenter son ~** to stake/to risk everything
vaudeville /vodvil/ *m* light comedy; **tourner au ~** to turn into a farce
vaudou /vodu/ *adj inv*, *m* voodoo
vaurien, **-ienne** /voʀjɛ̃, ɛn/ *mf* **1** rascal
2 lout, yobbo (BrE) (fam), hoodlum (fam)
vautour /votuʀ/ *m* vulture
vautrer: **se vautrer** /votʀe/ [**v1**] *v refl* (+ *v être*) **1 se ~ sur** to sprawl on
2 se ~ dans un fauteuil to loll in an armchair
va-vite: **à la va-vite** /alavavit/ *phr* in a rush
veau, *pl* **~x** /vo/ *m* **1** calf
2 (Culin) veal
3 calfskin
vecteur /vɛktœʀ/ *m* **1** vector
2 (fig) vehicle
3 (of disease) carrier
vécu, **~e** /veky/ **A** *pp* ▶ **vivre**
B *pp adj* ‹*drama, story*› real-life
C *m* personal experiences
vedette /vədɛt/ *f* **1** star; **avoir la ~** to have top billing
2 (Naut) launch

végétal, **~e**, *mpl* **-aux** /veʒetal, o/ **A** *adj* vegetable
B *m* vegetable

végétalien, **-ienne** /veʒetaljɛ̃, ɛn/ *adj*, *mf* vegan

végétarien, **-ienne** /veʒetaʀjɛ̃, ɛn/ *adj*, *mf* vegetarian

végétatif, **-ive** /veʒetatif, iv/ *adj* vegetative

végétation /veʒetasjɔ̃/ **A** *f* vegetation
B **végétations** *fpl* (Med) adenoids

végéter /veʒete/ [**v14**] *vi* ‹*person*› to vegetate; ‹*project*› to stagnate

véhémence /veemɑ̃s/ *f* vehemence

⚷ **véhicule** /veikyl/ *m* vehicle
■ **~ propre** zero-emission vehicle; **~ utilitaire** commercial vehicle

véhiculer /veikyle/ [**v1**] *vt* to carry ‹*people, goods, substance*›; **~ une image** to promote an image

⚷ **veille** /vɛj/ *f* **1** **la ~** the day before; **la ~ au soir** the night before; **à la ~ de** on the eve of
2 **être en état de ~** to be awake
3 vigil

veillée /veje/ *f* **1** evening; **à la ~** in the evening
2 vigil; **~ funèbre** wake

⚷ **veiller** /veje/ [**v1**] **A** *vt* to watch over ‹*ill person*›; to keep watch over ‹*dead person*›
B **veiller à** *v+prep* to look after ‹*health*›; **~ à ce que** to see to it that, to make sure that
C **veiller sur** *v+prep* to watch over ‹*child*›
D *vi* **1** to stay up
2 to be on watch
3 to be watchful
(IDIOM) **~ au grain** to be on one's guard

veilleur /vɛjœʀ/ *mf* **~ de nuit** night watchman

veilleuse /vɛjøz/ *f* **1** night light
2 pilot light
3 side light (BrE), parking light (AmE)

veinard, **~e** /venaʀ, aʀd/ *mf* (fam) lucky devil (fam)

veine /vɛn/ *f* **1** vein
2 (in wood) grain
3 (of coal) seam
4 inspiration; **dans la même ~** in the same vein; **en ~ de générosité** in a generous mood
5 (fam) luck; **il a de la ~** he's lucky

veiné, **~e** /vene/ *adj* ‹*skin, hand, marble*› veined; ‹*wood*› grained

veinure /venyʀ/ *f* (in wood) grain; (in marble) veining

vêler /vɛle/ [**v1**] *vi* ‹*cow*› to calve

velléité /vɛlleite/ *f* **1** vague desire
2 vague attempt

⚷ **vélo** /velo/ *m* (fam) bike; **faire du ~** to cycle
■ **~ d'appartement** exercise bike; **~ tout terrain**, **VTT** mountain bike

vélo-cross /velokʀɔs/ *m inv* **1** cyclo-cross
2 cyclo-cross bike

vélomoteur /velomɔtœʀ/ *m* moped

velours /vəluʀ/ *m inv* **1** velvet
2 corduroy
(IDIOMS) **une main de fer dans un gant de ~** an iron fist in a velvet glove; **faire patte de ~** to switch on the charm

velouté, **~e** /vəlute/ **A** *adj* ‹*skin, voice*› velvety; ‹*wine*› smooth
B *m* **1** (Culin) **~ de champignons** cream of mushroom soup
2 softness; smoothness

velu, **~e** /vəly/ *adj* **1** hairy
2 (Bot) villous

vénal, **~e**, *mpl* **-aux** /venal, o/ *adj* ‹*person*› venal; ‹*behaviour*› mercenary

vendable /vɑ̃dabl/ *adj* saleable (BrE)

vendange /vɑ̃dɑ̃ʒ/ *f* grape harvest

vendanger /vɑ̃dɑ̃ʒe/ [**v13**] **A** *vt* to harvest ‹*grapes*›; to pick the grapes from ‹*vine*›
B *vi* to harvest the grapes

vendeur, **-euse** /vɑ̃dœʀ, øz/ *mf* **1** shop assistant, sales clerk (AmE)
2 salesman/saleswoman
■ **~ ambulant** pedlar (BrE), peddler (AmE); **~ de journaux** news vendor

⚷ **vendre** /vɑ̃dʀ/ [**v6**] **A** *vt* **1** to sell; **~ à crédit** to sell on credit; **~ en gros** to wholesale; **~ au détail** to retail; **'à ~'** 'for sale'
2 to betray ‹*person*›; to sell ‹*secrets*›
B **se vendre** *v refl* (+ *v être*) **1** to be sold
2 **se ~ bien** to sell well
3 to sell oneself; **se ~ à l'ennemi** to sell out to the enemy

⚷ **vendredi** /vɑ̃dʀədi/ *m* Friday; **~ saint** Good Friday

vendu, **~e** /vɑ̃dy/ **A** *pp* ▸ **vendre**
B *pp adj* bribed
C *mf* traitor

vénéneux, **-euse** /venenø, øz/ *adj* poisonous

vénérable /veneʀabl/ *adj* ‹*person*› venerable; ‹*tree, object*› ancient

vénération /veneʀasjɔ̃/ *f* veneration

vénérer /veneʀe/ [**v14**] *vt* to venerate; to revere

vénérien, **-ienne** /veneʀjɛ̃, ɛn/ *adj* venereal

vengeance /vɑ̃ʒɑ̃s/ *f* revenge

venger /vɑ̃ʒe/ [**v13**] **A** *vt* to avenge
B **se venger** *v refl* (+ *v être*) to get one's revenge; **se ~ sur qn/qch** to take it out on sb/sth

vengeur, **vengeresse** /vɑ̃ʒœʀ, vɑ̃ʒʀɛs/ *adj* vengeful; avenging; vindictive

véniel, **-ielle** /venjɛl/ *adj* ‹*sin*› venial

venimeux, **-euse** /vənimø, øz/ *adj* venomous

venin /vənɛ̃/ *m* venom

⚷ **venir** /vəniʀ/ [**v36**] **A** *v aux* **1** **~ de faire** to have just done; **elle vient de partir** she's just

V

⚷ key word

left; **'vient de paraître'** (of book) 'new!'
2 ~ aggraver la situation to make the situation worse
3 le ballon est venu rouler sous mes pieds the ball rolled up to my feet
4 s'il venait à pleuvoir if it should rain
B *vi* (+ *v être*) **1** to come; **~ de** to come from; **~ après/avant** to come after/before; **allez, viens!** come on!; **viens voir** come and see; **j'en viens** I've just been there; **je viens de sa part** he/she sent me to see you; **faire ~ qn** to send for sb; to get sb to come; **faire ~ le médecin** to call the doctor; **ça ne m'est jamais venu à l'idée** it never crossed my mind; **dans les jours à ~** in the next few days
2 en ~ à to come to; **en ~ aux mains** to come to blows

vent /vɑ̃/ *m* **1** wind; **~ d'est** east wind; **~ du large** seaward wind; **grand ~** gale, strong wind; **il fait** *or* **il y a du ~** it's windy; **en plein ~** exposed to the wind; in the open; **passer en coup de ~** (fig) to rush through; **faire du ~** (with fan) to create a breeze; **~ favorable, bon ~** favourable (BrE) wind; **avoir le ~ en poupe** to sail *or* run before the wind; (fig) to have the wind in one's sails; **coup de ~** fresh gale
2 un ~ de liberté a wind of freedom; **un ~ de folie** a wave of madness
3 (euph) wind
IDIOMS **c'est du ~!** it's just hot air!; **du ~!** (fam) get lost! (fam); **quel bon ~ vous amène?** to what do I owe the pleasure (of your visit)?; **être dans le ~** to be trendy; **avoir ~ de qch** to get wind of sth; **contre ~s et marées** come hell or high water; against all odds

vente /vɑ̃t/ *f* sale; **en ~ libre** (gen) freely available; ‹*medicines*› available over the counter; **mettre qch en ~** to put [sth] up for sale
■ **~ par correspondance** mail order selling; **~ au détail** retailing; **~ aux enchères** auction (sale); **~ en gros** wholesaling

ventilateur /vɑ̃tilatœʀ/ *m* fan; ventilator

ventilation /vɑ̃tilasjɔ̃/ *f* ventilation (system)

ventiler /vɑ̃tile/ [**v1**] *vt* **1** to ventilate
2 to break down ‹*expenses, profits*›
3 to assign ‹*staff*›; to allocate ‹*tasks, equipment*›

ventouse /vɑ̃tuz/ *f* **1** suction pad (BrE), suction cup (AmE); **faire ~** to stick
2 plunger
3 (Med) cupping glass

ventral, **~e**, *mpl* **-aux** /vɑ̃tʀal, o/ *adj* ventral; **parachute ~** lap-pack parachute

ventre /vɑ̃tʀ/ *m* **1** stomach; **avoir mal au ~** to have stomach ache; **ça me donne mal au ~ de voir ça** (fig, fam) it makes me sick to see that sort of thing
2 (of animal) (under)belly
3 ne rien avoir dans le ~ (fam) to have no guts (fam); **avoir la peur au ~** to feel sick with fear
4 (of pot, boat, plane) belly
IDIOM **courir ~ à terre** to run flat out

ventricule /vɑ̃tʀikyl/ *m* ventricle

ventriloque /vɑ̃tʀilɔk/ *mf* ventriloquist

ventripotent, **~e** /vɑ̃tʀipɔtɑ̃, ɑ̃t/ *adj* (fam) portly, fat-bellied

ventru, **~e** /vɑ̃tʀy/ *adj* ‹*man*› paunchy, pot-bellied; ‹*pot, piece of furniture*› rounded; ‹*wall*› bulging

venu, **~e** /vəny/ **A** *pp* ▶ **venir**
B *pp adj* **bien ~** apt; **mal ~** badly timed; **il serait mal ~ de le leur dire** it wouldn't be a good idea to tell them
C *mf* **nouveau ~** newcomer

venue /vəny/ *f* visit; **~ au monde** birth

vêpres /vɛpʀ/ *fpl* vespers

ver /vɛʀ/ *m* worm; woodworm; maggot
■ **~ à soie** silkworm; **~ solitaire** tapeworm; **~ de terre** earthworm
IDIOM **tirer les ~s du nez à qn** (fam) to worm information out of sb

véracité /veʀasite/ *f* truthfulness

véranda /veʀɑ̃da/ *f* veranda

verbal, **~e**, *mpl* **-aux** /vɛʀbal, o/ *adj* verbal; verb

verbaliser /vɛʀbalize/ [**v1**] *vi* to record an offence (BrE)

verbe /vɛʀb/ *m* **1** verb
2 language; **avoir le ~ haut** to be arrogant in one's speech

verdâtre /vɛʀdɑtʀ/ *adj* greenish

verdeur /vɛʀdœʀ/ *f* sprightliness

verdict /vɛʀdikt/ *m* verdict

verdir /vɛʀdiʀ/ [**v3**] *vi* **1** (gen) to turn green; ‹*copper*› to tarnish
2 to turn pale

verdoyant, **~e** /vɛʀdwajɑ̃, ɑ̃t/ *adj* green

verdure /vɛʀdyʀ/ *f* **1** greenery
2 green vegetables

véreux, **-euse** /veʀø, øz/ *adj* **1** ‹*fruit*› worm-eaten
2 ‹*politician, lawyer*› bent (fam), crooked

verge /vɛʀʒ/ *f* **1** penis
2 switch, birch

vergé /vɛʀʒe/ *m* laid paper

verger /vɛʀʒe/ *m* orchard

vergeture /vɛʀʒətyʀ/ *f* stretch mark

verglacé, **~e** /vɛʀglase/ *adj* icy

verglas /vɛʀgla/ *m inv* black ice

vergogne: **sans vergogne** /sɑ̃vɛʀgɔɲ/ *phr* shamelessly

véridique /veʀidik/ *adj* true

vérifiable /veʀifjabl/ *adj* **être facilement ~** to be easy to check *or* verify

vérification /veʀifikasjɔ̃/ *f* (on equipment, identity) check; (of alibi, fact) verification

vérifier /veʀifje/ [**v2**] **A** *vt* to check; to verify
B se vérifier *v refl* (+ *v être*) ‹*hypothesis, theory*› to be borne out

✔ **véritable** /veritabl/ *adj* real; true; genuine
véritablement /veritabləmɑ̃/ *adv* really
✔ **vérité** /verite/ *f* **1** truth; **l'épreuve de ~** the acid test; **à la ~** to tell the truth
2 énoncer des ~s premières to state the obvious
3 sincerity
verlan /vɛrlɑ̃/ *m: French slang formed by inverting the syllables*
vermeil, -eille /vɛrmɛj/ **A** *adj* **1** bright red
2 ‹*wine*› ruby
B *m* vermeil
vermicelle /vɛrmisɛl/ *m* **du ~, des ~s** vermicelli
vermifuge /vɛrmifyʒ/ *m* wormer
vermillon /vɛrmijɔ̃/ *adj inv* bright red
vermine /vɛrmin/ *f* **1** vermin
2 (fig) scum
vermoulu, ~e /vɛrmuly/ *adj* worm-eaten
verni, ~e /vɛrni/ **A** *pp* ▶ **vernir**
B *pp adj* varnished; patent-leather; glazed
C *adj* (fam) lucky; **il n'est pas ~** he's unlucky
vernir /vɛrnir/ [**v3**] **A** *vt* to varnish; to glaze
B se vernir *v refl* (+ *v être*) **se ~ les ongles** to paint one's nails
vernis /vɛrni/ *m inv* **1** varnish; glaze
2 (fig) veneer; **si on gratte le ~, on voit que...** if you scratch the surface, you'll see that...
■ **~ à ongles** nail varnish (BrE) *or* polish
vernissage /vɛrnisaʒ/ *m* **1** (of art exhibition) preview, private view
2 varnishing; glazing
vernissé, ~e /vɛrnise/ *adj* **1** glazed
2 glossy
✔ **verre** /vɛr/ *m* **1** glass; **de** *or* **en ~** glass; **un ~ à eau/vin** a water/wine glass; **~s et couverts** glassware and cutlery; **lever son ~ à la santé de qn** to raise one's glass to sb
2 glass, glassful; **un ~ d'eau/de vin** a glass of water/wine
3 drink
4 lens; **~ grossissant** magnifying glass
■ **~ de contact** contact lens; **~ à pied** stemmed glass
verrerie /vɛrri/ *f* **1** glassmaking
2 glassworks, glass factory
verrière /vɛrjɛr/ *f* **1** glass roof
2 glass wall
verroterie /vɛrɔtri/ *f* glass jewellery (BrE) *or* jewelry (AmE)
verrou /vɛru/ *m* bolt
IDIOM **être sous les ~s** to be behind bars
verrouillage /vɛrujaʒ/ *m* bolting; locking; locking mechanism
■ **~ central** *or* **centralisé (des portes)** central locking
verrouiller /vɛruje/ [**v1**] *vt* to bolt ‹*window, door*›; to lock ‹*car door, gun*›

✔ key word

verrue /vɛry/ *f* wart; **~ plantaire** verruca
✔ **vers**[1] /vɛr/ *prep*

> When *vers* is part of an expression such as *se tourner vers, tendre vers* etc, you will find the translation at the entries **tourner, tendre**[1] C etc.
> See below for other uses of *vers*.

1 toward(s); **se déplacer de la gauche ~ la droite** to move from left to right
2 near, around; about; toward(s); **~ cinq heures** at about five o'clock; **~ le soir** toward(s) evening
vers[2] /vɛr/ *m inv* line (of verse)
versant /vɛrsɑ̃/ *m* side
versatile /vɛrsatil/ *adj* unpredictable, volatile
verse: **à verse** /avɛrs/ *phr* **il pleut à ~** it's pouring down
Verseau /vɛrso/ *pr m* Aquarius
versement /vɛrsəmɑ̃/ *m* **1** payment; **~ comptant** cash payment
2 instalment (BrE)
3 deposit; **faire un ~ sur son compte** to pay money into one's account
✔ **verser** /vɛrse/ [**v1**] **A** *vt* **1** to pour
2 to pay ‹*sum, pension*›
3 to shed ‹*tear, blood*›
4 ~ une pièce à un dossier to add a document to a file
B *vi* **1** to overturn
2 to lapse
3 ‹*jug*› to pour
verset /vɛrsɛ/ *m* (in Bible, Koran) verse
verseur, -euse /vɛrsœr, øz/ *adj* pouring; **flacon ~** bottle with a pouring spout
versifier /vɛrsifje/ [**v2**] *vt* to put [sth] into verse
✔ **version** /vɛrsjɔ̃/ *f* **1** translation (*into one's own language*)
2 version
■ **~ originale, vo** (of film) original version
verso /vɛrso/ *m* back; **voir au ~** see over(leaf)
✔ **vert, ~e** /vɛr, vɛrt/ **A** *adj* **1** green; **être ~ de peur** to be white with fear
2 ‹*fruit*› green, unripe; ‹*wine*› immature
3 sprightly
4 (*before n*) ‹*reprimand*› sharp, stiff
B *m* green
C verts *mpl* **les ~s** the Greens
IDIOM **avoir la main ~e** to have green fingers (BrE) *or* a green thumb (AmE)
vert-de-gris /vɛrdəgri/ **A** *adj inv* blue-green
B *m inv* verdigris
vertébral, ~e, *mpl* **-aux** /vɛrtebral, o/ *adj* vertebral
vertèbre /vɛrtɛbr/ *f* vertebra
vertébré /vɛrtebre/ *m* vertebrate
vertement /vɛrtəmɑ̃/ *adv* sharply
vertical, ~e *mpl* **-aux** /vɛrtikal, o/ *adj* vertical; upright

verticale /vɛʀtikal/ *f* vertical
verticalement /vɛʀtikalmɑ̃/ *adv*
1 vertically
2 (in crossword) down
vertige /vɛʀtiʒ/ *m* **1** dizziness; vertigo; **avoir le ~** to suffer from vertigo; to feel dizzy
2 avoir des ~s to have dizzy *or* giddy spells
vertigineux, **-euse** /vɛʀtiʒinø, øz/ *adj* dizzy, giddy; breathtaking; staggering
vertu /vɛʀty/ **A** *f* **1** virtue; **de petite ~** of easy virtue
2 (of plant, remedy) property
B en vertu de *phr* by virtue of ‹*law*›; in accordance with ‹*agreement*›
vertueux, **-euse** /vɛʀtɥø, øz/ *adj* virtuous
verve /vɛʀv/ *f* eloquence
verveine /vɛʀvɛn/ *f* verbena (tea)
vésicule /vezikyl/ *f* vesicle; **~ biliaire** gall bladder
vespéral, **~e**, *mpl* **-aux** /vɛspeʀal, o/ *adj* evening
vessie /vesi/ *f* bladder
IDIOM **prendre des ~s pour des lanternes** (fam) to think the moon is made of green cheese
veste /vɛst/ *f* jacket; **~ de survêtement** tracksuit top
IDIOM **retourner sa ~** (fam) to change sides
vestiaire /vɛstjɛʀ/ *m* (in gym) changing room (BrE), locker room; (in theatre) cloakroom; **laisser sa fierté au ~** to forget one's pride
vestibule /vɛstibyl/ *m* hall; foyer (BrE), lobby
vestige /vɛstiʒ/ *m* **1** relic; **des ~s archéologiques** archaeological remains
2 vestige
vestimentaire /vɛstimɑ̃tɛʀ/ *adj* **tenue ~** way of dressing; **mode ~** fashion
veston /vɛstɔ̃/ *m* (man's) jacket
vêtement /vɛtmɑ̃/ *m* piece of clothing; **des ~s** clothes; **'~s pour hommes'** 'menswear'; **~s de sport** sportswear
vétéran /veteʀɑ̃/ *m* veteran
vétérinaire /veteʀinɛʀ/ **A** *adj* veterinary
B *mf* veterinary surgeon (BrE), veterinarian (AmE)
vétille /vetij/ *f* trifle
vêtir /vetiʀ/ [**v33**] **A** *vt* to dress ‹*person, doll*›
B se vêtir *v refl* (+ *v être*) to dress (oneself)
veto /veto/ *m* veto; **mettre** *or* **opposer son ~ à qch** to veto sth
vêtu, **~e** /vety/ ▶ **vêtir**
vétuste /vetyst/ *adj* **1** dilapidated
2 outdated
vétusté /vetyste/ *f* dilapidation (**de** of), run-down state (**de** of); outdated state (**de** of)
veuf, **veuve** /vœf, vœv/ **A** *adj* widowed
B *mf* widower/widow
veule /vøl/ *adj* weak, spineless
veuvage /vœvaʒ/ *m* widowhood
veuve ▶ **veuf**
vexant, **~e** /vɛksɑ̃, ɑ̃t/ *adj* **1** hurtful
2 tiresome, vexing
vexation /vɛksasjɔ̃/ *f* humiliation
vexer /vekse/ [**v1**] **A** *vt* **1** to offend
2 to annoy
B se vexer *v refl* (+ *v être*) to take offence (BrE)
via /vja/ *prep* via; through
viabilité /vjabilite/ *f* **1** viability
2 (of road) suitability for vehicles
viable /vjabl/ *adj* **1** viable
2 ‹*project*› feasible; ‹*situation*› bearable, tolerable
viaduc /vjadyk/ *m* viaduct
viager /vjaʒe/ *m* life annuity
viande /vjɑ̃d/ *f* meat; **~ de bœuf/mouton** beef/mutton
■ **~ des Grisons** dried beef
vibrant, **~e** /vibʀɑ̃, ɑ̃t/ *adj* **1** vibrating
2 ‹*voice*› resonant; ‹*speech*› vibrant; ‹*praise*› glowing; ‹*plea*› impassioned; ‹*crowd*› excited
vibration /vibʀasjɔ̃/ *f* vibration; **traitement par ~s** vibra-massage
vibrer /vibʀe/ [**v1**] *vi* **1** to vibrate
2 ‹*voice*› to quiver; ‹*heart*› to thrill
vibromasseur /vibʀomasœʀ/ *m* vibrator
vicaire /vikɛʀ/ *m* curate
vice /vis/ *m* **1** vice; **vivre dans le ~** to lead a dissolute life
2 vice; **mon ~, c'est le tabac** my vice is smoking
3 fault, defect; **~ de fabrication** manufacturing defect
vice versa /visvɛʀsa/ *adv also* **vice-versa** vice versa
vice-président, **~e**, *mpl* **~s** /vispʀezidɑ̃, ɑ̃t/ *mf* (of state) vice-president; (of committee, company) vice-chair(man), vice-president (AmE)
vice-roi, *pl* **~s** /visʀwa/ *m* viceroy
vichy /viʃi/ *m* **1** gingham
2 Vichy water
vicier /visje/ [**v2**] *vt* to pollute ‹*air*›; to contaminate ‹*blood*›
vicieux, **-ieuse** /visjø, øz/ *adj* **1** lecherous; **il faut être ~ pour aimer ça** you've got to be perverted to like that
2 ‹*person*› sly; ‹*attack*› well disguised; ‹*question*› trick; ‹*argument*› deceitful
3 un cercle ~ a vicious circle
vicinal, **~e**, *mpl* **-aux** /visinal, o/ *adj* **chemin ~** byroad
vicomte /vikɔ̃t/ *m* viscount
vicomtesse /vikɔ̃tɛs/ *f* viscountess
victime /viktim/ *f* **1** victim, casualty; **être ~ d'un infarctus** to suffer a heart attack
2 sacrificial victim
victoire /viktwaʀ/ *f* (gen) victory; (Sport) win
victorien, **-ienne** /viktɔʀjɛ̃, ɛn/ *adj* Victorian

victorieux, **-ieuse** /viktɔʀjø, øz/ *adj* ‹*army*› victorious; ‹*athlete*› winning; ‹*smile*› of victory

victuailles /viktɥɑj/ *fpl* provisions, victuals

vidange /vidɑ̃ʒ/ *f* **1** emptying
2 oil change; **huile de ~** waste oil
3 (of washing machine) waste pipe

vidanger /vidɑ̃ʒe/ [**v13**] **A** *vt* **1** to empty, to drain ‹*tank, ditch*›
2 to drain off ‹*liquid*›
B *vi* ‹*washing machine*› to empty

⚷ **vide** /vid/ **A** *adj* **1** empty; ‹*tape, page*› blank; ‹*flat*› vacant; **tu l'as loué ~ ou meublé?** are you renting it unfurnished or furnished?
2 ‹*mind, day*› empty; ‹*look*› vacant
B *m* **1** space; **sauter** *or* **se jeter dans le ~** to jump; (fig) to leap into the unknown; **parler dans le ~** to talk to oneself; to talk at random
2 vacuum; void; **emballé sous ~** vacuum-packed; **faire le ~ autour de soi** to drive everybody away; **j'ai besoin de faire le ~ dans ma tête** I need to forget about everything
3 emptiness; **le ~ de l'existence** the emptiness of life
4 gap; **combler un** *or* **le ~** to fill in a gap; (fig) to fill a gap
C **à vide** *phr* **1** empty
2 with no result

vidéaste /videast/ *mf* video director

vide-greniers /vidgʀənje/ *m inv* bric-a-brac sale

vidéo /video/ **A** *adj inv* video
B *f* video; **tourner un film en ~** to make a video

vidéocassette /videokasɛt/ *f* videotape

vidéoclip /videoklip/ *m* (music) video

vidéoclub /videoklœb/ *m* video store

vidéoconférence /videokɔ̃feʀɑ̃s/ *f*
1 videoconference
2 videoconferencing

vidéodisque /videodisk/ *m* videodisc

vidéoludique /videolydik/ *adj* **l'industrie ~** the video games industry

vide-ordures /vidɔʀdyʀ/ *m inv* rubbish (BrE) *or* garbage (AmE) chute

vidéothèque /videɔtɛk/ *f* **1** video library
2 video collection

vide-poches /vidpɔʃ/ *m inv* tidy

V

vider /vide/ [**v1**] **A** *vt* **1** to empty; to drain ‹*tank, pond*›
2 to empty [sth] (out) ‹*water, rubbish*›
3 (fam) to throw [sb] out (fam)
4 (Culin) to gut ‹*fish*›; to draw ‹*game*›
5 (fam) to wear [sb] out; to drain
B **se vider** *v refl* (+ *v être*) to empty; **en été, Paris se vide de ses habitants** in the summer all Parisians leave town

videur, **-euse** /vidœʀ, øz/ *mf* (fam) bouncer

⚷ **vie** /vi/ *f* (gen) life; **être en ~** to be alive; **il y a laissé sa ~** that was how he lost his life; **donner la ~ à qn** to bring sb into the world; **la ~ est chère** the cost of living is high; **mode de ~** lifestyle; **notre ~ de couple** our relationship; **donner de la ~ à une fête** to liven up a party; **sans ~** lifeless
■ **~ active** working life
IDIOMS **c'est la belle ~!** this is the life!; **avoir la ~ dure** ‹*prejudices*› to be ingrained; **mener la ~ dure à qn** to make life hard for sb; **faire la ~** (fam) to have a wild time; to live it up (fam); **à la ~, à la mort!** till death us do part!

vieil ▸ **vieux**

vieillard, **~e** /vjɛjaʀ, aʀd/ *mf* old man/woman; **les ~s** old people

vieille ▸ **vieux**

vieillesse /vjɛjɛs/ *f* (of person) old age; (of building, tree) great age

vieilli, **~e** /vjɛji/ **A** *pp* ▸ **vieillir**
B *pp adj* **1** old-looking
2 ‹*equipment*› outdated; ‹*expression*› dated
3 **vin ~ en fût** wine matured in the cask

vieillir /vjɛjiʀ/ [**v3**] **A** *vt* **1** ‹*hairstyle*› to make [sb] look older
2 ‹*illness*› to age ‹*person*›
B *vi* **1** to get older; **je vieillis** I'm getting old; **j'ai vieilli** I'm older; **notre population vieillit** we have an ageing population
2 ‹*body, building*› to show signs of age; ‹*person*› to age; **il vieillit mal** he's losing his looks
3 ‹*wine*› to mature
4 ‹*work*› to become outdated
C **se vieillir** *v refl* (+ *v être*) **1** to make oneself look older
2 to make oneself out to be older

vieillissant, **~e** /vjɛjisɑ̃, ɑ̃t/ *adj* ageing

vieillissement /vjɛjismɑ̃/ *m* ageing

vieillot, **-otte** /vjɛjo, ɔt/ *adj* quaint; old-fashioned

viennois, **~e** /vjɛnwa, az/ *adj* **1** (in Austria) Viennese; (in France) of Vienne
2 (Culin) ‹*chocolate, coffee*› Viennese

viennoiserie /vjɛnwazʀi/ *f* Viennese pastry

⚷ **vierge** /vjɛʀʒ/ **A** *adj* **1** virgin
2 blank; unused; clean
3 ‹*wool*› new; ‹*olive oil*› virgin
B *f* virgin

Vierge /vjɛʀʒ/ **A** *f* **1** **la (Sainte) ~** the (Blessed) Virgin
2 madonna
B *pr f* Virgo

Viêt Nam /viɛtnam/ *pr m* Vietnam

vietnamien, **-ienne** /vjɛtnamjɛ̃, ɛn/ **A** *adj* Vietnamese
B *m* (language) Vietnamese

⚷ **vieux**, **vieil** *before vowel or mute h*, **vieille**, *mpl* **vieux** /vjø, vjɛj/ **A** *adj* old; **être ~ avant l'âge** to be old before one's time; **une institution vieille de 100 ans** a 100 year-old institution; **il est très vieille France** he's a

gentleman of the old school
B *mf* **1** old person; **un petit ~** a little old man; **les ~** old people; **mes ~** (fam) my parents
2 (fam) **mon pauvre ~** you poor old thing
C *adv* **vivre ~** to live to a ripe old age; **il s'habille ~** he dresses like an old man
D *m* **prendre un coup de ~** to age; **faire du neuf avec du ~** to revamp things
■ **vieille fille** old maid; **~ beau** ageing Romeo; **~ garçon** old bachelor; **~ jeu** old-fashioned; **~ rose** dusty pink
IDIOM **~ comme le monde, ~ comme Hérode** as old as the hills

vif, vive /vif, viv/ **A** *adj* **1** ‹*colour, light*› bright
2 ‹*person*› lively, vivacious; ‹*imagination*› vivid
3 ‹*protests*› heated; ‹*opposition*› fierce; **sa réaction a été un peu vive** he/she reacted rather strongly
4 ‹*contrast*› sharp; ‹*interest, desire*› keen; ‹*pain*› acute; ‹*success*› notable
5 ‹*pace, movement*› brisk; **à vive allure** ‹*drive*› at high speed; **avoir l'esprit ~** to be very quick
6 ‹*cold, wind*› biting; ‹*edge*› sharp; **air ~** fresh air; **cuire à feu ~** to cook over a high heat
7 de vive voix in person
B *m* **à ~** ‹*flesh*› bared; ‹*knee*› raw; ‹*wire*› exposed; **avoir les nerfs à ~** to be on edge; **la plaie est à ~** it's an open wound; **piquer qn au ~** to cut sb to the quick

vigie /viʒi/ *f* (Naut) **1** lookout
2 crow's nest

vigilance /viʒilɑ̃s/ *f* vigilance; **échapper à la ~ de qn** to escape sb's attention

vigilant, ~e /viʒilɑ̃, ɑ̃t/ *adj* ‹*person*› vigilant; ‹*eye*› watchful

vigile /viʒil/ *m* **1** night watchman
2 security guard

Vigipirate /viʒipiʀat/ *m: government public security measures*

vigne /viɲ/ *f* **1** vine
2 vineyard
■ **~ vierge** Virginia creeper

vigneron, -onne /viɲ(ə)ʀɔ̃, ɔn/ *mf* winegrower

vignette /viɲɛt/ *f*: **1** *detachable label on medicines for reimbursement by social security*
2 tax disc (BrE)
3 label
4 vignette

vignoble /viɲɔbl/ *m* vineyard

vigoureux, -euse /viguʀø, øz/ *adj*
1 ‹*person, handshake*› vigorous; ‹*athlete, body*› strong; ‹*plant*› sturdy
2 ‹*resistance, style*› vigorous

vigueur /vigœʀ/ **A** *f* **1** vigour (BrE)
2 strength
B en vigueur *phr* ‹*law, system*› in force; ‹*regime, conditions*› current; **entrer en ~** to come into force

VIH /veiaʃ/ *m* (*abbr* = **virus immunodéficitaire humain**) HIV

viking /vikiŋ/ *adj* Viking

vil, ~e /vil/ *adj* ‹*person*› base; ‹*deed*› vile, base

vilain, ~e /vilɛ̃, ɛn/ **A** *adj* **1** ugly
2 (fam) ‹*germ, creature*› nasty; ‹*child*› naughty
3 ‹*fault*› bad; ‹*word*› dirty
B *mf* naughty boy/girl

vilenie /vileni/ *f* **1** baseness (**de** of)
2 vile *or* base act

villa /villa/ *f* **1** ≈ detached house
2 villa

village /vilaʒ/ *m* village

villageois, ~e /vilaʒwa, az/ *mf* villager

ville /vil/ *f* **1** town; city; **la vieille ~** the old town; **aller en ~** to go into town
2 town *or* city council
■ **~ d'eau(x)** spa town; **~ franche** free city; **~ nouvelle** new town

ville-dortoir, *pl* **villes-dortoirs** /vildɔʀtwaʀ/ *f* dormitory town (BrE)

villégiature /vileʒjatyʀ/ *f* holiday (BrE), vacation (AmE)

vin /vɛ̃/ *m* wine; **~ blanc/rouge** white/red wine; **~ de pays** *or* **de terroir** quality wine produced in a specific region; **couper son ~** to add water to one's wine
■ **~ d'appellation d'origine contrôlée** appellation contrôlée wine (*with a guarantee of origin*); **~ cuit** *wine which has undergone heating during maturation*; **~ d'honneur** reception
IDIOMS **avoir le ~ gai/triste** to get happy/maudlin after one has had a few drinks; **mettre de l'eau dans son ~** to mellow; **quand le ~ est tiré, il faut le boire** (Proverb) once you have started something, you have to see it through

vinaigre /vinɛgʀ/ *m* vinegar
IDIOM **tourner au ~** to turn sour

vinaigrette /vinɛgʀɛt/ *f* French dressing

vinasse /vinas/ *f* (fam) plonk (BrE) (fam), cheap wine

vindicatif, -ive /vɛ̃dikatif, iv/ *adj* vindictive

vingt /vɛ̃, vɛ̃t/ **A** *adj inv* twenty
B *pron* twenty; (Sch) **j'ai eu ~ sur ~** ≈ I got full marks (BrE) *or* full credit (AmE)
C *m inv* twenty

vingtaine /vɛ̃tɛn/ *f* **une ~** about twenty

vingtième /vɛ̃tjɛm/ *adj* twentieth

vinicole /vinikɔl/ *adj* ‹*sector, region*› wine-producing; ‹*cellar, trade*› wine

vinyle /vinil/ *m* vinyl

viol /vjɔl/ *m* **1** rape
2 (of law, temple) violation

violacé, ~e /vjɔlase/ *adj* purplish

violation /vjɔlasjɔ̃/ *f* **1** (of law, territory) violation

V

2 (of agreement, confidentiality) breach
■ **~ de domicile** forcible entry (*into a person's home*)
violemment /vjɔlamɑ̃/ *adv* violently
🔑 **violence** /vjɔlɑ̃s/ *f* **1** violence; **~ verbale** verbal abuse; **par la ~** through violence; with violence; **se faire ~** to force oneself
2 act of violence; **~s à l'enfant** child abuse
■ **~ conjugale** domestic violence
🔑 **violent**, **~e** /vjɔlɑ̃, ɑ̃t/ *adj* violent; ‹*colour*› harsh
violenter /vjɔlɑ̃te/ [**v1**] *vt* to assault sexually
violer /vjɔle/ [**v1**] *vt* **1** to rape; **se faire ~** to be raped
2 to desecrate ‹*tomb*›; **~ l'intimité de qn** to invade sb's privacy
3 to infringe ‹*law*›
violet, **-ette** /vjɔlɛ, ɛt/ **A** *adj* purple
B *m* purple
violette /vjɔlɛt/ *f* violet
violeur /vjɔlœʀ/ *m* rapist
violon /vjɔlɔ̃/ *m* violin
■ **~ d'Ingres** hobby
IDIOM **accorder ses ~s** to agree on which line to take
violoncelle /vjɔlɔ̃sɛl/ *m* cello
violoncelliste /vjɔlɔ̃sɛlist/ *mf* cellist
violoniste /vjɔlɔnist/ *mf* violinist
vipère /vipɛʀ/ *f* viper; **avoir une langue de ~** to have a wicked tongue
virage /viʀaʒ/ *m* **1** bend
2 change of direction
3 (in skiing) turn
virago /viʀago/ *f* virago
viral, **~e**, *mpl* **-aux** /viʀal, o/ *adj* viral
virement /viʀmɑ̃/ *m* transfer; **faire un ~** to make a transfer
■ **~ automatique** standing order
virer /viʀe/ [**v1**] **A** *vt* **1** to transfer ‹*money*›
2 (fam) to fire ‹*employee*›; **se faire ~** to get fired
B virer à *v+prep* **~ au rouge** to turn red
C *vi* **1** ‹*vehicle*› to turn; **~ de bord** (fig) to do a U-turn, to do a flip-flop (AmE)
2 to change colour (BrE); ‹*colour*› to change
virevolter /viʀvɔlte/ [**v1**] *vi* to twirl
virginité /viʀʒinite/ *f* virginity
virgule /viʀgyl/ *f* **1** comma; **à la ~ près** down to the last comma
2 (decimal) point
V **viril**, **~e** /viʀil/ *adj* manly, virile; masculine
virilité /viʀilite/ *f* virility
virtualité /viʀtɥalite/ *f* **1** virtuality
2 potentiality
virtuel, **-elle** /viʀtɥɛl/ *adj* **1** potential
2 (in science) virtual
virtuellement /viʀtɥɛlmɑ̃/ *adv* **1** virtually
2 potentially
virtuose /viʀtɥoz/ **A** *adj* virtuoso
B *mf* **1** (Mus) virtuoso
2 master
virtuosité /viʀtɥozite/ *f* **1** (Mus) virtuosity
2 brilliance
virulence /viʀylɑ̃s/ *f* virulence
virulent, **~e** /viʀylɑ̃, ɑ̃t/ *adj* virulent
virus /viʀys/ *m inv* **1** (Med, Comput) virus
2 bug (fam), craze
vis /vis/ *f inv* screw
IDIOM **serrer la ~ à qn** to tighten the screws on sb
visa /viza/ *m* visa
■ **~ de censure** (censor's) certificate
🔑 **visage** /vizaʒ/ *m* face; **à ~ découvert** openly
vis-à-vis /vizavi/ **A** *m inv* **1 maison sans ~** house with an open outlook
2 assis en ~ sitting opposite each other
3 (Sport) opponent
4 meeting, encounter
B vis-à-vis de *phr* **1 ~ de qch** in relation to sth; **~ de qn** toward(s) sb
2 beside
viscéral, **~e**, *mpl* **-aux** /viseʀal, o/ *adj*
1 réaction ~e gut reaction
2 visceral
viscéralement /viseʀalmɑ̃/ *adv* violently, virulently
viscère /visɛʀ/ *m* **1** internal organ
2 les ~s viscera
viscosité /viskozite/ *f* viscosity
visée /vize/ *f* **1** aim
2 design
3 sighting; aiming
🔑 **viser** /vize/ [**v1**] **A** *vt* **1** to aim at ‹*target*›; to aim for ‹*heart, middle*›
2 to aim for ‹*job, results*›; to aim at ‹*market*›
3 ‹*law, campaign*› to be aimed at; ‹*remark, allusion*› to be meant for
B viser à *v+prep* **~ à qch/à faire** to aim at sth/to do
C *vi* to aim; **~ (trop) haut** (fig) to set one's sights (too) high
viseur /vizœʀ/ *m* **1** viewfinder
2 (of gun) sight
visibilité /vizibilite/ *f* visibility
🔑 **visible** /vizibl/ *adj* **1** visible
2 obvious
visiblement /viziblәmɑ̃/ *adv* visibly
visière /vizjɛʀ/ *f* **1** (of cap) peak
2 eyeshade
🔑 **vision** /vizjɔ̃/ *f* **1** eyesight, vision
2 view; **~ globale** global view
3 sight
4 avoir des ~s to see things, to have visions
visionnaire /vizjɔnɛʀ/ *adj*, *mf* visionary
visionner /vizjɔne/ [**v1**] *vt* to view ‹*film, slides*›
visionneuse /vizjɔnøz/ *f* viewer
🔑 **visite** /vizit/ *f* visit; call; **rendre ~ à qn** to pay sb a call; **avoir de la ~** to have visitors
■ **~ de contrôle** (Med) follow-up visit; **~**

🔑 key word

médicale medical (examination)

visiter /vizite/ [**v1**] *vt* **1** to visit ‹*museum, town*›
2 to view ‹*apartment*›
3 to visit ‹*patient*›

visiteur, **-euse** /vizitœʀ, øz/ *mf* visitor

vison /vizɔ̃/ *m* **1** mink
2 mink (coat)

visqueux, **-euse** /viskø, øz/ *adj* **1** viscous, viscid
2 sticky, gooey (fam)

visser /vise/ [**v1**] *vt* **1** to screw [sth] on
2 être vissé sur sa chaise to be glued to one's chair

visualisation /vizɥalizasjɔ̃/ *f* visualization; (Comput) display

visualiser /vizɥalize/ [**v1**] *vt* to visualize

visuel, **-elle** /vizɥɛl/ *adj* visual

vital, **~e**, *mpl* **-aux** /vital, o/ *adj* vital

vitalité /vitalite/ *f* vitality; energy

vitamine /vitamin/ *f* vitamin

vitaminé, **~e** /vitamine/ *adj* with added vitamins

vite /vit/ *adv* **1** quickly; **~!** quick!; **ça ira ~** it'll soon be over; it won't take long; **on a pris un verre ~ fait** (fam) we had a quick drink
2 j'ai parlé trop ~ I spoke too hastily; I spoke too soon; **c'est ~ dit!** that's easy to say!

vitesse /vitɛs/ *f* **1** speed; **partir à toute ~** to rush away; **à deux ~s** ‹*system*› two-tier; **faire de la ~** to drive fast; **prendre qn de ~** to outstrip sb; **en ~** quickly; in a rush
2 gear
IDIOM **à la ~ grand V, en quatrième ~** at top speed

viticole /vitikɔl/ *adj* wine; wine-producing

viticulteur, **-trice** /vitikyltœʀ, tʀis/ *mf* winegrower

viticulture /vitikyltyʀ/ *f* wine-growing

vitrage /vitʀaʒ/ *m* windows; **double ~** double glazing

vitrail, *pl* **-aux** /vitʀaj, o/ *m* stained glass window

vitre /vitʀ/ *f* **1** windowpane
2 pane of glass
3 (of car, train) window

vitrerie /vitʀəʀi/ **1** glazier's
2 glass work

vitrier /vitʀije/ *m* glazier

vitrifier /vitʀifje/ [**v2**] *vt* **1** to varnish ‹*floor*›
2 (Tech) to vitrify

vitrine /vitʀin/ *f* **1** (shop (*or* store (AmE))) window; **faire les ~s** to go window-shopping
2 display cabinet (BrE), curio cabinet (AmE)
3 (show)case

vitriol /vitʀijɔl/ *m* vitriol

vitupérer /vitypeʀe/ [**v14**] *vi* to rail

vivable /vivabl/ *adj* bearable; **ce n'est pas ~ ici** it is impossible to live here

vivace /vivas/ *adj* enduring

vivacité /vivasite/ *f* **1** (of person) vivacity; (of feeling) intensity
2 (of intelligence) keenness; (of reaction, movement) swiftness; **avec ~** ‹*move, react*› swiftly
3 (of memory, colour, impression) vividness; (in eyes) spark; (of light) brightness

vivant, **~e** /vivɑ̃, ɑ̃t/ **A** *adj* **1** living; **il est ~** he is alive; **un homard ~** a live lobster
2 ‹*person, style*› lively; ‹*description*› vivid
3 être encore ~ ‹*custom*› to be still alive
B *m* **1** living being; **les ~s** the living
2 du ~ de mon père while my father was alive

vive /viv/ **A** *adj f* ▶ **vif A**
B *f* weever

vivement /vivmɑ̃/ *adv* ‹*encourage, react*› strongly; ‹*contrast, speak*› sharply; ‹*move, feel, regret*› deeply; ‹*rise*› swiftly

vivier /vivje/ *m* **1** fish pond
2 fish tank

vivifiant, **~e** /vivifjɑ̃, ɑ̃t/ *adj* **1** invigorating
2 stimulating

vivifier /vivifje/ [**v2**] *vt* to invigorate

vivisection /vivisɛksjɔ̃/ *f* vivisection

vivoter /vivɔte/ [**v1**] *vi* to struggle along

vivre /vivʀ/ [**v63**] **A** *vt* **1** to live through ‹*era*›; to go through ‹*difficult times*›; to experience ‹*love*›
2 to cope with ‹*divorce, failure, change*›
B *vi* **1** to live; **~ vieux** to live to a great age; **vive la révolution!** long live the revolution!; **~ à la campagne** to live in the country; **être facile à ~** to be easy to live with; to be easy to get on with; **~ avec son temps** to move with the times; **se laisser ~** to take things easy; **apprendre à ~ à qn** (fam) to teach sb some manners (fam); **~ aux dépens de qn** to live off sb
2 ‹*fashion*› to last; **avoir vécu** ‹*person*› to have seen a great deal of life; (hum) ‹*object*› to have had its day
3 ‹*town*› to be full of life
IDIOM **qui vivra verra** what will be will be

vivres /vivʀ/ *mpl* **1** food, supplies
2 couper les ~ à qn to cut off sb's allowance

vizir /viziʀ/ *m* vizier; **le Grand ~** the Grand Vizier

vo /veo/ *f*: *abbr* ▶ **version**

vocable /vɔkabl/ *m* term

vocabulaire /vɔkabylɛʀ/ *m* vocabulary

vocal, **~e**, *mpl* **-aux** /vɔkal, o/ *adj* vocal

vocalement /vɔkalmɑ̃/ *adv* vocally

vocalise /vɔkaliz/ *f* singing exercise

vocation /vɔkasjɔ̃/ *f* **1** vocation, calling
2 purpose; **région à ~ agricole** farming area

vociférer /vɔsifeʀe/ [**v14**] *vt*, *vi* to shout

vodka /vɔdka/ *f* vodka

vœu, *pl* **~x** /vø/ *m* **1** wish; **faire un ~** to make a wish
2 New Year's greetings; **adresser ses ~x à**

qn to wish sb a happy New Year
3 vow; **faire ~ de pauvreté** to take a vow of poverty

vogue /vɔg/ *f* fashion, vogue

voguer /vɔge/ [**v1**] *vi* ‹*ship*› to sail
IDIOM **et vogue la galère!** come what may!

🗝 **voici** /vwasi/ **A** *prep* here is, this is; here are, these are; **~ mes clés** here are my keys; **~ un mois** a month ago; **~ bientôt deux mois qu'elle travaille chez nous** she's been working with us for nearly two months
B voici que *phr* all of a sudden

🗝 **voie** /vwa/ *f* **1** way; **montrer la ~ à qn** to show sb the way; **ouvrir la ~ à** to pave the way for; **être sur la bonne ~** ‹*person*› to be on the right track; **les travaux sont en bonne ~** the work is progressing; **par ~ de conséquence** consequently; **espèce en ~ de disparition** endangered species
2 channels; **par des ~ détournées** by roundabout means
3 lane; **route à trois ~s** three-lane road
4 (of railway) track; **le train entre en gare ~ 2** the train is arriving at platform 2
5 par ~ buccale *or* **orale** orally
■ **~ aérienne** air route; **~ ferrée** railway track (BrE), railroad track (AmE); **~ de garage** siding; **mettre qn sur une ~ de garage** (fig) to shunt sb onto the sidelines; **Voie lactée** Milky Way; **~ privée** private road; **~ publique** public highway; **~ rapide** expressway; **~ sans issue** dead end; no through road; **~s respiratoires** respiratory tract

🗝 **voilà** /vwala/ **A** *prep* here is, this is; here are, these are; **voici mon fils et ~ ma fille** this is my son and this is my daughter; **me ~!** I'm coming!; **le ~ qui se remet à rire!** there he goes again laughing!; **~ tout** that's all; **~ un mois** a month ago
B en voilà *phr* **tu veux des fraises? en ~** you'd like some strawberries? here you are
C voilà que *phr* (fam) **et ~ qu'une voiture arrive** and the next thing you know, a car pulls up
D *excl* **~! j'arrive!** (I'm) coming!; **(et) ~! il remet ça!** there he goes again!
IDIOM **il a de l'argent, en veux-tu en ~!** he has as much money as he could wish for!

voilage /vwalaʒ/ *m* net curtain (BrE), sheer curtain (AmE)

voile[1] /vwal/ *m* **1** veil; **lever le ~ sur qch** to bring sth out in the open
2 voile
■ **~ islamique** yashmak; **~ du palais** soft palate, velum

🗝 **voile**[2] /vwal/ *f* (Naut) **1** sail; **faire ~ vers** to sail toward(s)
2 sailing

voilé, ~e /vwale/ *adj* **1** ‹*person, object*› veiled
2 ‹*sun, sky*› hazy; ‹*eyes*› misty; ‹*voice*› with a catch in it; ‹*photo*› fogged
3 ‹*threat, criticism*› veiled
4 ‹*wheel*› buckled

voiler /vwale/ [**v1**] **A** *vt* **1** to veil ‹*landscape, sun*›; ‹*person, fact*› to conceal ‹*event, fact*›
2 to buckle ‹*wheel*›
3 to mist ‹*eyes*›
4 to cover ‹*face, nudity*›; to veil ‹*statue*›
B se voiler *v refl* (+ *v être*) **1** ‹*sky*› to cloud over; ‹*sun*› to become hazy; ‹*eyes*› to become misty
2 ‹*person*› to wear a veil
IDIOM **se ~ la face** to look the other way

voilette /vwalɛt/ *f* veil

voilier /vwalje/ *m* **1** sailing boat (BrE), sailboat (AmE)
2 yacht, sailing ship

voilure /vwalyʀ/ *f* sails; **une ~ de $500m^2$** $500m^2$ of sail

🗝 **voir** /vwaʀ/ [**v46**] **A** *vt* **1** to see; **faire ~ qch à qn** to show sb sth; **laisser ~ qch** to show sth; **~ si/pourquoi** to find out *or* to see if/why; **on l'a vue entrer** she was seen going in; **je le vois** *or* **verrais bien enseignant** I can just see him as a teacher; **aller ~ qn** to go to see sb; **le film est à ~** the film is worth seeing; **~ du pays** to see the world; **on voit bien qu'elle n'a jamais travaillé!** you can tell she's never worked!; **on n'a jamais vu ça!** it's unheard of!
2 avoir quelque chose à ~ avec to have something to do with
B voir à *v+prep* to see to; **voyez à ce que tout soit prêt** see to it that everything is ready
C *vi* **1 ~, y ~** to be able to see; **~ double** to see double
2 ~ clair dans qch to have a clear understanding of sth; **il faut ~** we'll have to see
D se voir *v refl* (+ *v être*) **1** to see oneself
2 ‹*stain*› to show; **la tour se voit de loin** the tower can be seen from far away; **ça ne s'est jamais vu!** it's unheard of!
3 se ~ obligé *or* **dans l'obligation de faire** to find oneself forced to do
4 to see each other; **ils ne peuvent pas se ~ (en peinture)** (fam) they can't stand each other
IDIOMS **ne pas ~ plus loin que le bout de son nez** to see no further than the end of one's nose; **j'en ai vu d'autres** I've seen worse; **en faire ~ à qn** to give sb a hard time

🗝 **voire** /vwaʀ/ *adv* or even, not to say

voirie /vwaʀi/ *f* road, rail and waterways network

🗝 **voisin, ~e** /vwazɛ̃, in/ **A** *adj* **1** ‹*house, town*› neighbouring (BrE); ‹*lake, forest*› nearby; ‹*room*› next; **les régions ~es de la Manche** the regions bordering the English Channel
2 ‹*date, result*› close **(de** to)
3 ‹*feelings, ideas*› similar; ‹*species*› (closely) related

🗝 key word

B *mf* neighbour (BrE); **ma ~e de palier** the woman across the landing; **mon ~ de table** the man next to me at table

voisinage /vwazinaʒ/ *m* **1** neighbourhood (BrE); **entretenir des rapports de bon ~** to maintain neighbourly (BrE) relations
2 proximity; **vivre dans le ~ d'une usine** to live close to a factory

voiture /vwatyʀ/ *f* **1** car, automobile (AmE)
2 carriage (BrE), car (AmE); **en ~!** all aboard!
■ **~ à bras** hand-drawn cart; **~ de tourisme** saloon (car) (BrE), sedan (AmE)

voiture-balai, *pl* **voitures-balais** /vwatyʀbalɛ/ *f* support vehicle

voiture-lit, *pl* **voitures-lits** /vwatyʀli/ *f* sleeper, sleeping car (AmE)

voix /vwa/ *f inv* **1** (gen) voice; **élever la ~** to raise one's voice; **à ~ haute** out loud; **rester sans ~** to be speechless; **à portée de ~** within earshot; **faire entendre sa ~** (fig) to make oneself heard
2 vote
3 à la ~ active/passive in the active/passive voice

vol /vɔl/ **A** *m* **1** (of bird, plane) flight; **prendre son ~** to fly off; **à ~ d'oiseau** as the crow flies; **il y a trois heures de ~** it's a three-hour flight; **de ~** ‹*conditions*› flying; ‹*plan*› flight
2 un ~ de a flock of ‹*birds*›; a cloud of ‹*insects*›; **de haut ~** (fig) ‹*diplomat*› high-flying; ‹*burglar*› big-time
3 theft, robbery
B au vol *phr* **attraper une balle au ~** to catch a ball in mid-air; **saisir des bribes de conversation au ~** to catch snatches of conversation
■ **~ à l'arraché** bag snatching; **~ avec effraction** burglary; **~ à l'étalage** shoplifting; **~ à la tire** pickpocketing

volage /vɔlaʒ/ *adj* fickle

volaille /vɔlɑj/ *f* **1** poultry
2 fowl

volant, **~e** /vɔlɑ̃, ɑ̃t/ **A** *adj* flying
B *m* **1** steering wheel; **être au ~** to be at the wheel; **un brusque coup de ~** a sharp turn of the wheel; **un as du ~** an ace driver; **la sécurité au ~** safe driving
2 flounce; **à ~s** flounced
3 shuttlecock

volatil, **~e** /vɔlatil/ *adj* volatile

volatile /vɔlatil/ *m* **1** fowl
2 bird

volatiliser: **se volatiliser** /vɔlatilize/ [**v1**] *v refl* (+ *v être*) **1** to volatilize
2 (hum) to vanish into thin air

volcan /vɔlkɑ̃/ *m* volcano

volcanique /vɔlkanik/ *adj* **1** ‹*region*› volcanic
2 ‹*temperament*› explosive

volée /vɔle/ **A** *f* **1** (of birds) flock, flight
2 (of blows, stones) volley; **donner une ~ à qn** to give sb a good thrashing
3 flight (of stairs)
4 (Sport) volley
B à toute volée *phr* **les cloches sonnaient à toute ~** the bells were pealing out

voler /vɔle/ [**v1**] **A** *vt* **1 ~ qch à qn** to steal sth from sb; **tu ne l'as pas volé!** (fig) it serves you right!
2 ~ qn to rob sb; **~ le client** to rip the customer off (fam)
B *vi* **1** to fly; **~ au secours de qn** to rush to sb's aid
2 ~ en éclats ‹*window*› to shatter

volet /vɔlɛ/ *m* **1** shutter
2 (of leaflet, brochure) (folding) section; (of plan) part, component
3 (of film, series) instalment (BrE)

voleter /vɔlte/ [**v20**] *vi* to flutter

voleur, **-euse** /vɔlœʀ, øz/ **A** *adj* **être ~** ‹*child*› to be a thief; ‹*shopkeeper*› to be dishonest
B *mf* thief; swindler
IDIOM **se sauver comme un ~** to slip away like a thief in the night

volière /vɔljɛʀ/ *f* aviary

volley /vɔlɛ/ *m also* **volley-ball** /vɔlɛbol/ volleyball

volontaire /vɔlɔ̃tɛʀ/ **A** *adj* **1** ‹*work*› voluntary; ‹*omission*› deliberate
2 ‹*person, air*› determined; ‹*child*› self-willed
B *mf* volunteer; **se porter ~** to volunteer

volonté /vɔlɔ̃te/ **A** *f* **1** will; **bonne ~** goodwill; **aller contre la ~ de qn** to go against sb's wishes; **manifester la ~ de faire** to show one's willingness to do
2 willpower; **avoir une ~ de fer** to have an iron will
B à volonté *phr* **1 'vin/pain à ~'** 'unlimited wine/bread'
2 ‹*modifiable*› as required

volontiers /vɔlɔ̃tje/ *adv* **1** gladly; **j'irais ~ à Paris** I'd love to go to Paris; **'tu me le prêtes?'—'~'** 'will you lend it to me?'—'certainly'
2 ‹*admit*› readily

volt /vɔlt/ *m* volt

voltage /vɔltaʒ/ *m* voltage

volte-face /vɔlt(ə)fas/ *f inv* **1 faire ~** to turn around
2 (fig) volte-face, U-turn

voltige /vɔltiʒ/ *f* **(haute) ~** acrobatics

voltiger /vɔltiʒe/ [**v13**] *vi* **1** to flutter
2 to go flying

volubilité /vɔlybilite/ *f* volubility

volume /vɔlym/ *m* (gen) volume; **donner du ~ à ses cheveux** to give one's hair body; **~ sonore** sound level

volumineux, **-euse** /vɔlyminø, øz/ *adj* voluminous, bulky

volupté /vɔlypte/ *f* voluptuousness

voluptueux, **-euse** /vɔlyptɥø, øz/ *adj* voluptuous

V

volute /vɔlyt/ *f* (on pillar, column) volute; (of violin) scroll; (of smoke) curl

vomi /vɔmi/ *m* (fam) vomit

vomir /vɔmiʀ/ [v3] **A** *vt* to bring up ‹*meal*›; to vomit ‹*bile*›
B *vi* ‹*person*› to be sick

vomissement /vɔmismɑ̃/ *m* vomiting

vont /vɔ̃/ ▸ **aller**[1]

vorace /vɔʀas/ *adj* voracious

voracité /vɔʀasite/ *f* voracity, voraciousness

vos ▸ **votre**

votant, **~e** /vɔtɑ̃, ɑ̃t/ *mf* voter

vote /vɔt/ *m* **1** voting; (of law) passing
2 vote

vote préférentiel *m* alternative vote

voter /vɔte/ [v1] **A** *vt* to vote ‹*budget*›; to pass ‹*parliamentary bill*›; to vote for ‹*amnesty*›
B *vi* to vote; **~ blanc** to cast a blank vote

votre, *pl* **vos** /vɔtʀ, vo/ *det* your; **c'est pour ~ bien** it's for your own good; **à ~ arrivée** when you arrive; when you arrived

vôtre /votʀ/ **A** *det* **mes biens sont ~s** all Ihave is yours; **'amicalement ~'** 'best wishes'
B le vôtre, la vôtre, les vôtres *pron* yours; **à la ~!** (fam) cheers!

vouer /vwe/ [v1] **A** *vt* **1 ~ une reconnaissance éternelle à qn** to be eternally grateful to sb; **~ un véritable culte à qn** to worship sb
2 to doom; **film voué à l'échec** film doomed to failure
3 ~ sa vie à qch to devote one's life to sth
B se vouer *v refl* (+ *v être*) **1 se ~ à qch** to devote oneself to sth
2 ils se vouent une haine féroce they hate each other intensely

vouloir[1] /vulwaʀ/ [v48] **A** *vt* **1** (gen) to want; **qu'est-ce qu'ils nous veulent encore?** (fam) what do they want now?; **il en veut 2 000 euros** he wants 2,000 euros for it; **comme le veut la loi** as the law requires; **que veux-tu boire?** what do you want to drink?; **je voudrais un kilo de poires** I'd like a kilo of pears; **je comprends très bien que tu ne veuilles pas répondre** I can quite understand that you may not wish to reply; **sans le ~** ‹*knock over, reveal*› by accident; ‹*annoy*› without meaning to; **que tu le veuilles ou non** whether you like it or not; **elle fait ce qu'elle veut de son mari** she twists her husband around her little finger; **je ne vous veux aucun mal** I don't wish you any harm; **tu ne voudrais pas me faire croire que...** you're not trying to tell me that...; **tu voudrais que je leur fasse confiance?** do you expect me to trust them?; **comment veux-tu que je le sache?** how should I know?; **j'aurais voulu t'y voir!** (fam) I'd like to have seen you in the same position!; **tu l'auras voulu!** it'll be all your own fault!
2 voulez-vous fermer la fenêtre? would you mind closing the window?; **voudriez-vous avoir l'obligeance de faire** (fml) would you be so kind as to do; **veuillez patienter** (on phone) please hold the line; **si vous voulez bien me suivre** if you'd like to follow me; **veux-tu te taire!** will you be quiet!; **ils ont bien voulu nous prêter leur voiture** they were kind enough to lend us their car; **je veux bien te croire** I'm quite prepared to believe you; **je veux bien qu'il soit malade mais...** I know he's ill, but...; **'ce n'est pas cher'—'si on veut!'** 'it's not expensive'—'or so you say!'
3 ~ dire to mean; **qu'est-ce que ça veut dire?** what does that mean?; what's all this about?
4 comme le veut la tradition as tradition has it
B en vouloir *v+prep* **1 en ~ à qn** to bear a grudge against sb; **je leur en veux de m'avoir trompé** I hold it against them for not being honest with me; **ne m'en veux pas** please forgive me
2 en ~ à qch to be after sth
C se vouloir *v refl* (+ *v être*) **1** ‹*person*› to like to think of oneself as; ‹*book, method*› to be meant to be
2 s'en ~ to be cross (BrE) *or* mad (AmE) with oneself; **s'en ~ de** to regret; **je m'en serais voulu de ne pas vous avoir prévenu** I would never have forgiven myself if I hadn't warned you
IDIOM **~ c'est pouvoir** (Proverb) where there's a will there's a way

vouloir[2] /vulwaʀ/ *m* will

voulu, **~e** /vuly/ **A** *pp* ▸ **vouloir**[1]
B *pp adj* **1** required; **on n'obtient jamais les renseignements ~s** you never get the information you want; **en temps ~** in time; **au moment ~** at the right time
2 ‹*omission*› deliberate; ‹*meeting*› planned

vous /vu/ *pron* **1** you; **je sais que ce n'est pas ~** I know it wasn't you; **c'est ~ qui avez gagné** you have won; **~ aussi, ~ avez l'air malade** you don't look very well either; **ce sont des amis à ~?** are they friends of yours?; **c'est à ~** it's yours, it belongs to you; it's your turn
2 yourself; yourselves; **allez ~ laver les mains** go and wash your hands; **pensez à ~ deux** think of yourselves

vous-même, *pl* **vous-mêmes** /vumɛm/ *pron* **1** yourself; **vous me l'avez dit ~** you told me yourself
2 allez-y ~s go yourselves; **vous verrez par ~s** you'll see for yourselves

voûte /vut/ *f* (gen) vault; (of porch) archway; (of tunnel) roof; (fig) (of leaves, branches) arch
■ **la ~ céleste** the sky; the heavens; **~ du palais** roof of the mouth; **~ plantaire** arch of the foot

voûté, **~e** /vute/ *adj* **1** ‹*cellar*› vaulted

key word

2 ‹*back*› bent; **il est ~** he has a stoop

voûter /vute/ [**v1**] **A** *vt* **1** (in architecture) to vault ‹*room*›
2 to give [sb] a stoop
B se voûter *v refl* (+ *v être*) ‹*person*› to develop a stoop; ‹*back*› to become bent

vouvoiement /vuvwamɑ̃/ *m* using the 'vous' *or* polite form

vouvoyer /vuvwaje/ [**v23**] *vt* to address [sb] using the 'vous' form

voyage /vwajaʒ/ *m* trip; journey; **partir en ~** to go on a trip; **le ~ aller** the outward journey; **aimer les ~s** to love travelling (BrE)
■ **~ d'affaires** business trip; **être en ~ d'affaires** to be on a business trip; **~ d'études** study trip; **~ de noces** honeymoon; **~ organisé** package tour (BrE)

voyager /vwajaʒe/ [**v13**] *vi* to travel

voyageur, **-euse** /vwajaʒœʀ, øz/ *mf*
1 passenger; **'réservé aux ~s munis de billets'** 'ticket-holders only'
2 traveller (BrE)
■ **~ de commerce** travelling (BrE) salesman

voyagiste /vwajaʒist/ *mf* tour operator

voyance /vwajɑ̃s/ *f* clairvoyance

voyant, **~e** /vwajɑ̃, ɑ̃t/ **A** *adj* ‹*colour*› loud
B *mf* **1** clairvoyant
2 sighted person
C *m* light; **~ d'huile** (Aut) oil warning light

voyelle /vwajɛl/ *f* vowel

voyeur, **-euse** /vwajœʀ, øz/ *mf* voyeur

voyeurisme /vwajœʀism/ *m* voyeurism

voyou /vwaju/ *m* lout

vrac: **en vrac** /ɑ̃vʀak/ *phr* **1** loose, unpackaged
2 in bulk
3 jeter ses idées en ~ sur le papier to jot down one's ideas as they come

vrai, **~e** /vʀɛ/ **A** *adj* true; real, genuine; **il n'y a rien de ~ dans ses déclarations** there's no truth in his statements; **la ~e raison de mon départ** the real reason for my leaving; **des ~s jumeaux** identical twins; **plus ~ que nature** ‹*picture, scene*› larger than life
B *m* truth; **il y a du ~ dans ce que tu dis** there's some truth in what you say; **être dans le ~** to be in the right; **pour de ~** for real; **à ~ dire, à dire ~** to tell the truth
C *adv* **faire ~** to look real; **son discours sonne ~** his speech has the ring of truth

vraiment /vʀɛmɑ̃/ *adv* really

vraisemblable /vʀɛsɑ̃blabl/ *adj* ‹*excuse*› convincing; ‹*scenario*› plausible; ‹*hypothesis*› likely; **il est ~ que** it is likely that

vraisemblablement /vʀɛsɑ̃blabləmɑ̃/ *adv* probably

vraisemblance /vʀɛsɑ̃blɑ̃s/ *f* (of hypothesis) likelihood; (of situation, explanation) plausibility

vrille /vʀij/ *f* **1** spiral; (of airplane) tailspin; **descendre en ~** ‹*airplane*› to go into a spiral dive
2 (Bot) tendril
3 (Tech) gimlet

vrombir /vʀɔ̃biʀ/ [**v3**] *vi* ‹*engine*› to roar; **faire ~ un moteur** to rev up an engine

VRP /veɛʀpe/ *m* (*abbr* = **voyageur représentant placier**) representative, rep (fam)

VTC /vetese/ *m* (*abbr* = **vélo tous chemins**) hybrid bike

VTT /vetete/ ▶ **vélo**

vu, **~e** /vy/ **A** *pp* ▶ **voir**
B *pp adj* **1 être bien/mal ~** ‹*person*› to be/not to be well thought of; **c'est bien ~ de faire cela** it's good form to do that; **ce serait plutôt mal ~** it wouldn't go down well
2 bien ~! good point!; **c'est tout ~** my mind is made up
3 ~? got it? (fam)
C *prep* in view of
D vu que *phr* in view of the fact that

vue /vy/ *f* **1** sight; **avoir une bonne ~** to have good eyesight; **don de double ~** gift of second sight; **perdre qn de ~** (fig) to lose touch with sb; **à ~** ‹*shoot*› on sight; ‹*fly plane*› without instruments; ‹*payable*› on demand
2 view; **à ma ~, il s'enfuit** he took to his heels when he saw me; **avoir ~ sur le lac** to look out onto the lake
3 (opinion) view; **~s** views; **~ optimiste des choses** optimistic view of things
4 avoir des ~s sur qn/qch to have designs on sb/sth
5 en ~ in sight; ‹*person*› prominent; **mettre une photo bien en ~** to display a photo prominently; **c'est quelqu'un de très en ~** he's/she's very much in the public eye; **j'ai un terrain en ~** I have a plot of land in mind; I've got my eye on a piece of land; **en ~ de faire** with a view to doing
■ **~ d'ensemble** overall view
IDIOMS **à ~ d'œil** *or* **de nez** (fam) at a rough guess; **vouloir en mettre plein la ~ à qn** to try to dazzle sb

vulcanologue /vylkanɔlɔg/ *mf* volcanologist

vulgaire /vylgɛʀ/ *adj* **1** vulgar, coarse
2 common, ordinary; **c'est un ~ employé** he's just a lowly employee

vulgairement /vylgɛʀmɑ̃/ *adv* **1** ‹*speak*› coarsely
2 commonly

vulgarisation /vylgaʀizasjɔ̃/ *f* popularization; **revue de ~ scientifique** scientific magazine for the general public

vulgariser /vylgaʀize/ [**v1**] **A** *vt* to popularize; to bring [sth] into general use
B se vulgariser *v refl* (+ *v être*) ‹*technology*› to become generally accessible; ‹*expression*› to come into general use

vulgarité /vylgaʀite/ *f* vulgarity, coarseness

vulnérable /vylneʀabl/ *adj* vulnerable

vulve /vylv/ *f* vulva

Ww

w, **W** /dublǝve/ *m inv* **1** (letter) w, W **2 W** (*written abbr* = **watt**) **60 W** 60 W

wagon /vagɔ̃/ *m* **1** wagon (BrE), car (AmE); (for passengers) carriage (BrE), car (AmE) **2** wagonload (BrE), carload (AmE)
■ **~ à bestiaux** cattle truck (BrE), cattle car (AmE); **~ de marchandises** goods wagon (BrE), freight car (AmE)

wagon-bar, *pl* **wagons-bars** /vagɔ̃baʀ/ *m* buffet car

wagon-citerne, *pl* **wagons-citernes** /vagɔ̃sitɛʀn/ *m* tanker

wagon-lit, *pl* **wagons-lits** /vagɔ̃li/ *m* sleeper, sleeping car (AmE)

wagonnet /vagɔnɛ/ *m* trolley (BrE), cart (AmE)

wagon-restaurant, *pl* **wagons-restaurants** /vagɔ̃ʀɛstɔʀɑ̃/ *m* restaurant car (BrE), dining car (AmE)

wallon, **-onne** /walɔ̃, ɔn/ **A** *adj* Walloon **B** *m* (language) Walloon

Wallonie /walɔni/ *pr f* Walloon area of Belgium

waters /watɛʀ/ *mpl* (fam) toilets

watt-heure, *pl* **watts-heures** /watœʀ/ *m* watt-hour

WC /(dublǝ)vese/ *mpl* toilet; **aller aux ~** to go to the toilet

webmestre /wɛbmɛstʀ/ *mf* webmaster

winchester /winʃɛstɛʀ/ *f* Winchester® rifle

wishbone /wiʃbon/ *m* (Naut, Sport) wishbone boom

Xx

x, **X** /iks/ *m inv* x, X; **il y a x temps que c'est fini** it's been over for ages; **porter plainte contre X** (Law) to take an action against person or persons unknown; **film classé X** X-rated film (BrE) *or* movie (AmE)

xénophobe /gzenɔfɔb/ **A** *adj* xenophobic **B** *mf* xenophobe

xénophobie /gzenɔfɔbi/ *f* xenophobia

xérès /kseʀɛs/ *m inv* sherry

xylographe /ksilɔgʀaf/ *m* xylographer

xylophène® /ksilɔfɛn/ *m* wood preservative

w

x

y

y[1], **Y** /igʀɛk/ *m inv* y, Y

✓ **y**[2] /i/ *pron* **1** it; **tu t'~ attendais?** were you expecting it?; **il n'~ connaît rien** he knows nothing about it; **j'~ pense parfois** I sometimes think about it; **elle n'~ peut rien** there's nothing she can do about it; **j'~ viens** I'm coming to that; **rien n'~ fait** it's no use; **je n'~ comprends rien** I don't understand a thing; **tu ~ as gagné** you got the best deal; **plus difficile qu'il n'~ paraît** harder than it seems **2** there; **j'~ ai mangé une fois** I ate there

✓ key word

once; **n'~ va pas** don't go
3 il ~ a there is/are; **du vin? il n'~ en a plus** wine? there's none left; **il n'~ a qu'à téléphoner** just phone
IDIOM **~ mettre du sien** to work at it

yak /'jak/ *m also* **yack** yak
yaourt /'jauʀ(t)/ *m* yoghurt
yaourtière /'jauʀtjɛʀ/ *f* yoghurt maker
yéménite /'jemenit/ *adj* Yemeni
yen /'jɛn/ *m* yen
yéti /'jeti/ *m* yeti
yeux ▶ **œil**
yoga /'jɔga/ *m* yoga
yole /'jɔl/ *f* skiff
yougoslave /'jugɔslav/ *adj* Yugoslavian
youpi /'jupi/ *excl* (fam) yippee!
youyou /'juju/ *m* **1** ululation
2 dinghy

Zz

z, Z /zɛd/ *m inv* z, Z
zaïrois, ~e /zaiʀwa, az/ *adj* Zairean
zambien, -ienne /zɑ̃bjɛ̃, ɛn/ *adj* Zambian
zapper /zape/ [**v1**] *vi* to flick through the TV channels
zèbre /zɛbʀ/ *m* **1** zebra
2 (fig, fam) bloke (BrE) (fam), guy (fam)
zébré, ~e /zebʀe/ *adj* ‹*fabric*› zebra-striped; **~ de** streaked with
zébrure /zebʀyʀ/ *f* stripe
zébu /zeby/ *m* zebu
zèle /zɛl/ *m* zeal, enthusiasm; **faire du ~** *or* **de l'excès de ~** to be overzealous
zélé, ~e /zele/ *adj* enthusiastic, zealous
zénith /zenit/ *m* zenith; **à son ~** ‹*career*› at its height
zéphyr /zefiʀ/ *m* zephyr
zéro /zeʀo/ **A** *adj* **~ heure** midnight, twenty-four hundred (hours); **il sera exactement ~ heure vingt minutes dix secondes** the time will be twelve twenty and ten seconds precisely; **j'ai eu ~ faute dans ma dictée** I didn't make a single mistake in my dictation; **niveau/croissance ~** zero level/growth
B *m* **1** zero, nought (BrE); **avoir un ~ en latin** to get zero *or* nought in Latin; **remettre un compteur à ~** to reset a counter to zero; **avoir le moral à ~** (fig) to be down in the dumps (fam); **c'est beau à regarder mais question goût c'est ~** (fam) it's nice to look at, but no marks for flavour (BrE)
2 (in sport) (gen) nil (BrE), zero; (in tennis) love; **trois (buts) à ~** three nil
■ **~ de conduite** (Sch) bad mark for behaviour (BrE)
IDIOMS **partir de ~** to start from scratch; **tout reprendre à ~** to start all over again
zeste /zɛst/ *m* **un ~ de citron** the zest of a lemon
zézayer /zezeje/ [**v21**] *vi* to lisp
zibeline /ziblin/ *f* sable
zieuter /zjøte/ [**v1**] *vt* (fam) to get a load of (fam), to take a look at
zigoto /zigɔto/ *m* (fam) guy (fam); **faire le ~** to clown around
zigue /zig/ *m* (fam) guy (fam)
zigzag /zigzag/ *m* zigzag; **route en ~** winding road; **faire des ~s** to zigzag (**parmi** through); **partir en ~** to zigzag off
zinc /zɛ̃g/ *m* **1** zinc; **toiture de** *or* **en ~** tin roofing
2 (fam) counter, bar
zingueur /zɛ̃gœʀ/ *m* roofer
zinzin **A** *adj inv* (crazy) cracked (fam)
B *m* thingamajig (fam)
zip /zip/ *m* zip (BrE), zipper (AmE)
zippé, ~e /zipe/ *adj* zip-up
zipper /zipe/ [**v1**] *vt* (Comput) to zip
zizanie /zizani/ *f* ill feeling, discord
zizi /zizi/ *m* (fam) willy (BrE) (fam), penis
zodiac® /zɔdjak/ *m* inflatable dinghy
zodiaque /zɔdjak/ *m* zodiac
zona /zona/ *m* shingles
zonage /zonaʒ/ *m* zoning
zonard, ~e /zonaʀ, aʀd/ *mf* (fam) dropout (fam)
zone /zon/ *f* **1** zone, area; **~ interdite** off-limits area; (on signpost) no entry
2 la ~ (fam) the slum belt; **de seconde ~** second-rate
■ **~ d'activités** business park; **~ artisanale** small industrial estate (BrE) *or* park; **~ bleue** restricted parking zone; **~ industrielle** industrial estate (BrE) *or* park; **~ de saisie** (Comput) input box
zoner /zone/ [**v1**] *vi* (fam) to hang about (fam)
zoo /zo/ *m* zoo
zoologie /zɔɔlɔʒi/ *f* zoology

zoom /zum/ *m* **1** zoom lens
2 zoom

zouave /zwav/ *m* **1** (fam) clown, comedian; **faire le ~** to clown around (fam)
2 (soldier) Zouave

zoulou, **~e** /zulu/ *adj* Zulu

zozo /zozo/ *m* (fam) ninny (BrE) (fam), jerk (fam)

zozoter /zɔzɔte/ [**v1**] *vi* to lisp

zut /zyt/ *excl* (fam) damn! (fam)

Contents

French traditions, festivals, and holidays

1 January

le jour de l'an (New Year's Day) is a public holiday and a day of family celebration, with a large lunch, traditionally featuring seafood.

6 January

la Fête des Rois (Epiphany or Twelfth night). Around this time, most families have a *galette des Rois*, a puff pastry cake filled with *frangipane* (almond paste). The cake contains a *fève*, literally a bean, as this is what was originally used. Nowadays the *fève* takes the form of a tiny plastic or ceramic figure. The person who gets the *fève* in their portion becomes the king or queen and puts on the cardboard crown which comes with the cake.

2 February

la Chandeleur (Candlemas) is celebrated in the Church but is not a public holiday. However, it is traditional to eat *crêpes* (pancakes) on this day.

14 February

la Saint Valentin (St Valentine's Day). As in many other countries, people celebrate a romantic relationship with gifts of flowers or chocolates.

1 April

le premier avril (April Fool's Day). The French take advantage of this occasion to play tricks on one another, calling out *poisson d'avril!* (literally 'April fish').

1 May

La Fête du Travail (International Labour Day) is a public holiday.

8 May

le 8 mai or **la Fête de la Victoire** is a public holiday commemorating Victory in Europe (VE day) on 8 May 1945.

24 June

la Saint-Jean (Midsummer's Day). In many areas, bonfires (*les feux de la Saint-Jean*) are lit on Midsummer's Night. People are supposed to jump over these, re-enacting a pagan custom intended to ward off the cold of winter.

14 July

la Fête Nationale (le 14 juillet) is usually called Bastille Day in English and is a public holiday in France. It commemorates the taking of the Bastille prison in Paris and the liberation of its prisoners by the people of Paris in 1789, one of the first events of the Revolution. All over France there are parades on the day of the 14th and firework displays and *bals* (local dances) either on the night of the 13th or of the 14th.

15 August

l'Assomption (Feast of the Assumption) is a Catholic festival and a public holiday. Many people in France are either setting off on holiday around the 15th or else returning home, so this is traditionally a very busy time on the roads.

1 November

la Toussaint (All Saints' Day) is a public holiday and the day when people remember their dead relatives and friends, although properly speaking it is All Souls' Day the following day that is set aside for this in the Church. People take flowers to the cemetery, particularly chrysanthemums, as these are in bloom at this time. Because of this association, it is best to avoid taking chrysanthemums as a gift for someone. Schoolchildren have a two-week holiday around this time.

11 November

L'Armistice; le 11 novembre is a public holiday to commemorate the end of World War I in 1918, and a day of remembrance for those who died in the two world wars and in subsequent conflicts. All towns and villages hold parades in which war veterans accompany local officials and a brass band to lay wreaths on the war memorial. In Paris, the President lays a wreath on the tomb of the unknown soldier beneath the Arc de Triomphe on the Champs-Élysées.

8 December

la Fête de l'Immaculée Conception (Feast of the Immaculate Conception). In the city of Lyons, this is celebrated as **la Fête de la Lumière** (Festival of Light) said to commemorate the Virgin Mary's intervention to prevent the plague reaching Lyons in the Middle Ages. People put rows of candles in coloured glass jars on the outsides of their windowsills, so that all the buildings in the centre of the city are illuminated.

24 December

la veille de Noël (Christmas Eve) is the time when most people exchange presents. Traditionally, the evening is the time for *le réveillon de Noël*, a large meal often starting with seafood, oysters being particularly popular. Turkey is generally eaten as a main course, sometimes with chestnut stuffing. A variety of cheeses will be followed by *la bûche de Noël*, a delicious rolled sponge in the form of a snow-covered log, filled with chocolate, coffee or even Grand Marnier flavoured buttercream. Many people go to church to celebrate *la messe de minuit* (Midnight Mass).

25 December

Noël (Christmas) is a public holiday and a day of eating and drinking, often with relatives. French people do not usually send Christmas cards, the custom being to send wishes for the coming year to more distant friends and relatives during the month of January.

26 December

There is no particular name in French for the day after Christmas Day and it is not a public holiday.

31 December

la Saint-Sylvestre (New Year's Eve). Many people have parties to celebrate *le réveillon de la Saint-Sylvestre* (New Year's Eve Party). Once again, food plays a major part and, as at Christmas, this is a time to splash out on luxury foods such as *foie gras*. There will often be dancing and the New Year will be welcomed in with champagne.

Movable feasts

Mardi gras Shrove Tuesday, the last day of carnival before the beginning of Lent on Ash Wednesday. Traditionally, *crêpes* (pancakes) are eaten for supper. In many areas of France, sugared fritters are eaten between *la fête des Rois* and *mardi gras*. These are called *bugnes* in and around Lyons and *oreillettes* farther south.

le vendredi saint Good Friday is celebrated in the Church, but is not a public holiday.

Pâques An important Christian festival, Easter is celebrated throughout France; *le lundi de Pâques* (Easter Monday) is a public holiday. Easter Sunday, *le dimanche de Pâques*, is for many people the occasion for a big family lunch. Easter hunts are organised for children, with chocolate eggs, rabbits, hens, or fish traditionally hidden in the family garden.

l'Ascension The celebration of Ascension Day takes place (usually on a Thursday) 40 days after Easter. It is a Catholic festival and a public holiday in France.

la Pentecôte The Catholic feast is celebrated seven weeks after Easter, with the following Monday traditionally a public holiday in France. Between 2004 and 2007 **le lundi de Pentecôte** reverted to a normal working day for economic reasons, but the public holiday was reinstated for certain members of society (for example, schoolchildren and teachers) in 2008.

la Fête des Mères (Mother's Day) is the Sunday after *Pentecôte*. This is another occasion for a big family meal, with presents for the mother. **La Fête des Pères** (Father's Day) is celebrated in similar fashion two weeks later.

A–Z of French life and culture

Académie française A learned body, founded by Cardinal Richelieu in 1635, whose main role nowadays is to monitor new developments in the French language. It is not always taken entirely seriously by the public at large. Its 40 members are elected for life on the basis of their contribution to scholarship or literature, and are known as '*les Immortels*'.

Agence France Presse ▸ PRESSE

agrégation This qualification, attained through competitive examination or CONCOURS, entitles the holder to teach at the highest level in secondary and tertiary education.

Air France Created in 1933, the French national airline merged in 2004 with KLM Royal Dutch Airlines to become the world's largest airline group by turnover. The French state no longer holds a majority stake in the group. The company once operated five supersonic Concorde jets, but the last ever Air France Concorde passenger flight was from New York to Paris on 31 May 2003.

Alliance Française A private organization that aims to spread awareness of French language and culture. It has centres in cities throughout the world, providing language classes and a variety of cultural activities.

Allocations familiales Known colloquially as *les allocs*, *les allocations familiales* (family allowances) are paid to any French family with two or more children. A range of other *allocations* (benefits) are also available: for single parents, to help with childcare, to pay towards housing, etc.

Alps, The A mountain range that runs north to south along the border between France, Switzerland, and Italy. It is 350 km (219 miles) long and 50–60 km (31–37.5 miles) wide. The highest peak in western Europe, Mont Blanc (4,810 m [15,776 ft]) lies in the Alps, straddling the French/Italian border. The Alpine region is home to many popular ski resorts.

Alsace Lying on the frontier of Germany and Switzerland in the northeast of France, Alsace has long been the object of territorial disputes between Germany and France. French during the RÉVOLUTION, German after the Franco-German war (1871), French in 1918, German in 1940, the region has been French again since 1945. Since 1949, Strasbourg, the capital of Alsace, has been the seat of the CONSEIL DE L'EUROPE. Alsatian white wines are highly regarded, as is its traditional cabbage dish, *choucroute* (*sauerkraut*).

année scolaire School holidays are fixed nationally, and each *académie* (local education authority or school district) falls into one of three zones, so that the starts and ends of holidays are staggered. The year lasts from early September to late June, and main breaks occur in early November (*la Toussaint*), at Christmas and New Year, in February and in Spring.

ANPE (*Agence Nationale pour l'emploi*) The national agency providing services for the unemployed as well as for employers seeking workers. In order to qualify for unemployment benefits (*allocations chômage*), job hunters must have been unemployed for at least six months. Benefits, paid by the ASSEDIC (*Association pour l'emploi dans l'industrie et le commerce*), are calculated according to the last salary earned by the job seeker and the duration of his/her period of unemployment. In the initial period of unemployment, a job seeker receives a high percentage of his/her last salary. This figure is gradually reduced to the point where the job seeker no longer qualifies for benefits and is known as a *chômeur/-euse en fin de droits*. In December 2008, ANPE and ASSEDIC merged to create a single organization, called *Pôle Emploi*.

antisémitisme ▸ RACISME

Arc de Triomphe This Paris monument stands at the centre of the radiating spokes formed by 12 avenues including the CHAMPS-ÉLYSÉES. It was commissioned by NAPOLÉON to commemorate his victories, and completed in 1836. In 1921 it became a war memorial, and the site of the tomb of the 'unknown soldier'; a flame is lit there every evening in memory of those who have fallen in battle.

architecture Since the 1970s, the French state has promoted several major architectural projects, particularly in Paris, including the 1977 Pompidou Centre (also known as BEAUBOURG), the glass pyramid of the Louvre designed by American architect I. M. Pei and built in 1989, the Grande Arche de la Défense in western Paris, and the Institut du Monde Arabe, designed by Jean Nouvel. In 2004 the Millau viaduct, the tallest in the world, was opened by the French president, Jacques Chirac. Designed by English architect Lord Norman Foster, the 2.5 km (1.6 mile) long, 340 m (1,122 ft) high structure was dubbed 'the bridge in the clouds'.

Ariane The name of the European Space Agency's rockets, produced and operated by the private company Arianespace and launched from Kourou in French Guiana (Guyane française). The Ariane rockets have been used to put commercial satellites into space, but have met with mixed fortunes. Ariane 5-ECA, whose maiden flight ended in an explosion, successfully launched Superbird 7 in August 2008.

Armistice ▸ FRENCH TRADITIONS, FESTIVALS, AND HOLIDAYS

arrondissement A subdivision of a département. Each *arrondissement* has a *sous-préfet* representing the state administration at local level. In Paris, Lyons, and Marseilles, an arrondissement is a subdivision of the COMMUNE, and has its own *maire* and local council.

ARTE A TV channel, run jointly by France and Germany, which provides a high standard of cultural programmes.

Assemblée Nationale The lower house of the French parliament, in which 577 DÉPUTÉS are elected for a five-year term. A member, who must be at least 23 years old, has to be elected by at least 50 per cent of the votes cast and, if necessary, a second round of voting is held to ensure this. Party affiliation is indicated by a *député*'s allocation to a seat within a left–right gradation in the semi-circular chamber. The Assemblée Nationale passes laws, votes on the budget, and questions MINISTRES (who cannot be *députés*).

Astérix ▸ BANDE DESSINÉE

autoroutes France has an extensive motorway system, which is largely financed by tolls calculated according to the distance travelled and the vehicle type. Tickets are obtained and tolls paid at *péages* (tollgates). The speed limit for standard vehicles is 130 km/h (approx. 80 mph) and 110 km/h (approx. 70 mph) in wet weather.

Avignon Historic town in the southeast of France. Surrounded by 17th-century city walls, the centre of Avignon is dominated by the 14th-century Pope's Palace (the Popes lived here from 1309 to 1403). The 12th-century Saint-Bénezet Bridge, which spans the River RHÔNE here and which has mostly collapsed, is familiar from the song, '*Sur le pont d'Avignon*', but the town is now probably best known for its annual theatre festival, held since 1947, and one of the main cultural events of the year.

baccalauréat Known informally as *le bac*, this is an examination sat in the final year of the LYCÉE (*la terminale*), so usually at age 17 or 18. Students sit exams in a fairly broad range of subjects in a particular category: the '*bac S*' places the emphasis on the sciences, for example, whilst the '*bac L*' has a literary bias. Some categories cater for students specializing in more job-based subjects such as agriculture. The final result is given as a single overall mark or grade out of 20, although the scores for individual subjects are also given. It is common to use *le bac* as a point of reference in job adverts, so that *bac + 4* would mean a person who had completed four years of full-time study after the bac, with appropriate diplomas to show for it.

bachelier Holder of the BACCALAURÉAT, entitled to enrol for university courses.

bande dessinée plays a significant cultural role in France. More than a comic book or entertainment for youth, it is a form of popular literature known as the *neuvième art* (the 'ninth art', films being the 'seventh' and TV the 'eighth') and celebrated annually at the *Festival d'Angoulême*. Cartoon characters such as Astérix, Lucky Luke, and TINTIN are household names, and older comic books are often collectors' items.

banlieue The *banlieue* are the suburbs around main cities, and particularly the poorer residential areas around city centres, which have expanded dramatically in recent decades. The term often has a pejorative connotation, and evokes images of concrete tower blocks ('*grands ensembles*'), urban decay, and crime. The *cités* (deprived estates) are often difficult areas to live in. The government – along with the *banlieusards* (those who live there) – is trying to find ways to rehabilitate the *banlieue*.

Basque A people that has – since prehistoric times – inhabited le Pays Basque (the Basque region), an area that borders the coast of the Bay of Biscay and lies on the slopes of the Pyrenees mountains, encompassing parts of both France and Spain. Around 2.1 million Basques live in the region, the majority in Spain. The town of Bayonne is the largest city in the French Basque region (le Pays Basque français); every year a carnival (*une feria*) is held there, featuring bullfights and swordstick dancing. The Basque language, Euskara, is said to be the earliest European language; the Basque name for their country is Euzkadi. *Les Basques* have long sought autonomy from France and Spain; in Spain the region now has some autonomy, with responsibility for education, health care, policing, and taxation. In France, however, the region does not have any autonomous status, nor is Basque recognized as an official language, though it is taught in some schools.

bateaux-mouches The *bateaux-mouches* are large riverboats that transport (mainly) tourists along the River SEINE on sightseeing tours. Some also have restaurants on board. The boats were first introduced on the River Saône in Lyons in 1863; they were built in 'the flies' quarter' and the name stuck (*une mouche* is a fly). The boats' pointed noses and two large windows at the front also make them look like flies.

BCBG An abbreviation, which is a term in its own right, for '*bon chic bon genre*'. It describes a social type and the associated lifestyle, dress code, and linguistic mannerisms: someone who is essentially conventionally *bourgeois* or upper middle-class in their values and tastes. It is not necessarily intended as a compliment.

BCD *La Bibliothèque et Centre de Documentation* is a library and resource centre that exists in all French secondary schools, and is where pupils prepare school work. *Documentalistes* are the people responsible for the centres; they work in partnership with the schoolteachers.

Beaubourg Designed by the English architect Richard Rogers and the Italian Renzo Piano, the Centre National d'Art et de Culture Georges Pompidou (named after the former president of France) took its name from the district where it stands, though it is more often known as the Pompidou Centre. With its colourful ventilation pipes, and escalators in clear tubes (all on the exterior of the building), the centre was controversial when it was opened in 1977. Nowadays, as host to contemporary art exhibitions – and 800,000 visitors a year – it is an accepted addition to the Parisian scene. The terrace in front of the building is popular with street entertainers, and there are superb views of MONTMARTRE and Sacré-Cœur from the top of the building.

Bercy Though it's the name of a district in southeastern Paris, Bercy is primarily associated, if not synonymous, with the Ministry of Finance which is located there. Bercy is also home to a large stadium and concert complex, the Palais Omnisports Paris Bercy or POPB, and to a multiplex cinema and shopping area known as Bercy Village.

Beur (fem. Beurette) A term in VERLAN derived from the French word *Arabe,* which refers to the French-born children of North African immigrants (primarily Algerian but also Tunisian and Moroccan). The *jeunes Beurs* have been at the heart of anti-racist activity in recent years, but equally at the centre of ethnic tensions in the suburbs (BANLIEUE) of major French cities. Educated within the French school system, many Beurs feel set apart from both French and Arabic culture. Beur artists express this sense of 'in-between-ness' through music, cinema, and literature in works such as *La Haine* (Hate; 1995), a film by Mathieu Kassovitz, which looks at the alienation felt by a Jew, an Arab, and a black African living in a housing project in Paris, and Leïla Houari's *Zeida de nulle part* (Zeida from Nowhere, 1985), a book that explores the hopes and dreams of a young *Maghrébine*. The term is not used so frequently now as it has been in the past. *See also* MAGHRÉBINS.

Bison Futé Symbolized by a little Native American, *Bison Futé* is a creation of the *Centre National d'Information Routière*, the French traffic information service, which reports on travel conditions nationwide, particularly during holiday periods when traffic is heaviest, and recommends alternative routes (*les itinéraires 'bis'*) for travellers keen to avoid traffic jams. The *Bison Futé* traffic tips are broadcast across the full range of media (radio, TV, the national press, the internet, and MINITEL) and appear at regular intervals on the road system itself. Information is updated constantly to reflect actual traffic conditions, enabling motorists to choose the best time to travel. Allied to *Bison Futé* is a colour-coding system to mark the relative intensity of traffic at any time (green, red, yellow, and black), which is a key factor in staggering holiday traffic on the roads.

Bleus, Les The French national football team, who wear a blue strip, are known as *Les Bleus*. Supporters shout, '*Allez les Bleus*' ('Come on, Blues !') to urge them on. The team entered footballing legend in 1998 when they won the World Cup at home, beating Brazil in the final. Zinedine Zidane (known as Zizou), who captained the team and scored two goals in their 3–0 victory, achieved iconic status in France. The French rugby union team is also known as *Les Bleus*.

Bordeaux A region in the southwest of France that borders the Atlantic Ocean. Its historical capital of the same name is also one of the main commercial centres in the southwest of France. Bordeaux is probably best known for its world-famous wines.

boules A type of bowls, also known as *pétanque*, played all over France using metal balls and a jack known as a *cochonnet*. *Terrains de boules* (playing areas) are set aside for the game in many towns and villages, though one of the beauties of the game is that it can be played virtually anywhere. So a family lunch in the summer will often end in a game of *boules* (*une partie de boules*). There are some regional variations, notably in the size and form of the playing area and the size of the bowls.

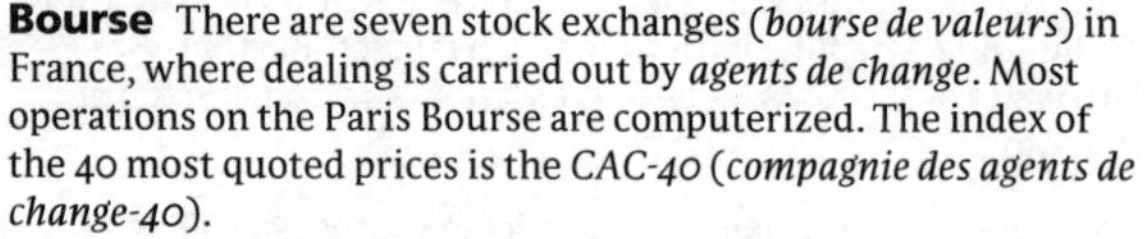

Bourse There are seven stock exchanges (*bourse de valeurs*) in France, where dealing is carried out by *agents de change*. Most operations on the Paris Bourse are computerized. The index of the 40 most quoted prices is the *CAC-40* (*compagnie des agents de change-40*).

brasserie The original meaning of *brasserie* is 'brewery', and although the word is still used in this sense, it has also come to mean a type of bar-restaurant, usually serving simple, traditional French food at reasonable prices. Most brasseries offer a set-price menu (*prix fixe*), especially at lunchtime.

Bretagne Known in English as Brittany, this northwestern peninsula is lapped by the English Channel and the Atlantic Ocean. Prehistoric chambers and standing stones bear witness to the presence of peoples who later resisted the Romans. In the fifth and sixth centuries, the Celtic Bretons (from what is now Great Britain) sought refuge here, and it was only in the 16th century that Brittany was unified with France. Rennes, Brest, and Lorient are the main cities; agriculture, fishing, and tourism the main economic activities. Folklore is still very important, as is the use of the BRETON language.

Breton The ancient Celtic language of Brittany (BRETAGNE). It is related to Welsh, Irish, Scottish Gaelic, and Cornish. Recent decades have seen a revival of interest in the language going hand in hand with the assertion of a regional cultural identity and a movement for independence from France. Breton is fairly widely spoken and is taught in secondary schools in the region, although it is not recognized as an official language in France. *See also* LANGUES.

brevet This usually designates a type of vocational qualification such as the *brevet d'études professionnelles*, or *BEP*, which is awarded after two years of practically oriented coursework at a LYCÉE *professionnel*, or the *brevet de technicien supérieur*, or *BTS*, taken after the BACCALAURÉAT and representing two years of study in a specific vocational field. The *brevet des collèges* is a general educational qualification taken at around the age of 15 at the end of study in a COLLÈGE.

bureau de tabac Tobacconists can be individual shops or be found in a *bar-tabac* or *café-tabac*. They are also often combined with a newsagent's (*marchand de journaux*). They are licensed to sell tobacco and cigarettes, and also have a state licence to sell stamps, LOTO and other game tickets, and certain official documents. The red cigar-shaped sign that marks the *tabac* is known as a '*carotte*'.

café Since 1910 the number of traditional cafés or bistros in France has dropped from 510,000 to 57,000, and Paris has even been invaded by branches of Starbucks and McDonalds. In Paris the Café de Flore (which played host to famous French writers and philosophers such as Jean-Paul Sartre and Simone de Beauvoir), Les Deux Magots (a favourite of Pablo Picasso's) and Café de la Gare (opened by Coluche and Depardieu as a theatre) are among many famous cafés with a long history. Parisian waiters often still dress in traditional style, with black waistcoats and long white aprons.

Camargue The Camargue lies at the delta of the RHÔNE, near the Mediterranean, in the far south of France. Around 85,000 hectares (209,950 acres) have been designated as a nature reserve. Its protected species include the famous black bulls, white horses, and pink flamingoes. In the southeast corner of the Camargue are salt marshes, which have been worked since ancient times. Every year Gypsies make a May pilgrimage to Saintes-Maries de la Mer, a little port in the middle of the Camargue, to meet and attend religious ceremonies.

Canal Plus A privately owned French television channel. Viewers pay a subscription to view. One of its most popular programmes is *Les Guignols de l'Info*, which uses puppets to satirize French politicians and other well-known public figures.

Cannes film festival The first Cannes film festival (*Association Française du Festival International du Film*) took place in 1946 at the glamorous Côte d'Azur resort. Now many in the film industry travel from around the world to see and be seen at the May festival, which showcases films 'showing talent deserving encouragement'. The *Palme d'Or* (Golden Palm) is awarded for the best feature film.

canton An administrative unit of French local government which contains several communes. It elects a member of the CONSEIL GÉNÉRAL. Also, a state in the Swiss federation. Each of the 26 Swiss cantons has its own constitution, elected assemblies, and courts.

CAPES is a teaching qualification, awarded by competitive examination or CONCOURS, which is normally required to teach in a COLLÈGE or LYCÉE. Those who gain the qualification are known as *capésiens* and are committed to at least five years' service in a state school.

carnet de notes is a pupil's school report book, in which teachers enter test and exam results and write notes for parents to summarize students' progress. This is also where all communication passing between parents and the school is archived, as well as any detentions.

carte bancaire There are more than 30 million credit cards in France. The '*Carte bleue*' (blue card) was the first credit card to be introduced in France, in 1967, and used to be the most ubiquitous, but nowadays Mastercard, Eurocard, and Visa are also commonly used.

carte grise; certificat d'immatriculation The registration document for a motor vehicle. It is an offence not to carry it when driving the vehicle, and police checks are frequent. Up to 15 April 2009 vehicles were registered in the DÉPARTEMENT in which the owner lived, so numbers had to be changed if the owner moved to a different area.

carte nationale d'identité Although not obligatory, most French citizens possess a national identity card, obtained from their local MAIRIE, PRÉFECTURE, or police station. It is accepted as a travel document by all EU countries and is valid for 10 years.

cassoulet This meat and bean dish from the southwest of France (especially Toulouse) is named after the earthenware pot in which it is served. It consists of white beans baked slowly in goose or duck fat, along with meat such as duck or goose confit, lamb, and Toulouse sausages.

Catalan The language spoken by 25 per cent of people in Spain and by some people in the Perpignan area of southwest France. It is taught in schools in the area but is not recognized as an official language in France. *See also* LANGUES.

CE *Cycle* or *cours élémentaire* (*CE*) is the programme for the two years of primary school for children aged 7 to 9 (*CE1* and *CE2*).

Césars Prizes awarded annually for achievements in the film industry; the French equivalent of the Oscars.

Chambre des députés ▸ ASSEMBLÉE NATIONALE

champagne An alcoholic drink inextricably linked with indulgence and celebration, champagne is the produce of a particular region of northeast France, comprising the DÉPARTEMENTS of Aube, Marne, Ardennes, and Haute-Marne.Wine production in the region dates back to Roman times, but it was not until the 17th century that sparkling wine was deliberately produced in Champagne (the monk, Dom Pérignon, was one of the first to develop the process). Champagne is now a protected brand: only sparkling wine produced in this region can bear the name. In the 19th century, 6,000 hectares (14,830 acres) of vines destroyed by the phylloxera aphid had to be replaced with American vinestocks; World War II also wreaked havoc in the region. The industry has since boomed, however, and around 300 million bottles of champagne are now sold each year.

champignons Refers to any mushroom-like fungi, whether edible or not. Hunting for edible mushrooms is a popular leisure activity and many varieties are highly prized. Advice on whether they are edible or not can usually be obtained from a PHARMACIE.

Champs-Elysées The world-famous avenue in central Paris, known for its luxury shops, hotels, and clubs. At one end stands the ARC DE TRIOMPHE, the scene of the remembrance ceremony each year for the Armistice of 1918.

Chandeleur ▸ FRENCH TRADITIONS, FESTIVALS AND HOLIDAYS

chanson à textes ▸ CHANSON FRANÇAISE

chanson française Often referred to as '*chanson à textes*', *la chanson française* is characterized by two main features: the lyrics must be meaningful and the song must be sung in French. The genre was popularized by singers such as Maurice Chevalier and Joséphine Baker during World War II, Edith Piaf and Juliette Gréco in the 1950s and 1960s, and Johnny Hallyday from the 1970s onward. In the 1960s, the lyrics of singer-poets such as Georges Brassens and Jacques Brel reinvigorated the genre; their texts are often studied in schools today. *La chanson française* was taken through the 1980s and beyond by singers such as Patricia Kaas and Alain Souchon, and today MC Solaar, the rap singer, and Corneille (soul) have brought it into the 21st century.

charcuterie A shop or supermarket counter selling a wide variety of pork products. As well as cuts of pork, *charcutiers* usually sell sausages and various types of raw and cooked ham, pâtés, and a selection of *saucissons*. Most *charcuteries* also offer a variety of salads, savoury pastries, and dishes that can be reheated at home or on the premises. *Charcuteries* offering a catering service usually advertise themselves as *charcutier-traiteur (traiteur* means 'caterer'). *La charcuterie* is also used to refer to pork products such as ham and *saucisson*.

chasse *La chasse* (hunting) is a widely practised sport in France, particularly among older people. Legislation as to the rights of hunters to hunt over privately owned land varies according to the region and the amount of land concerned. During the hunting season, it is advisable not to stray from public footpaths in the countryside on the days of the week when hunting is permitted. *CPNT* (*Chasse, Pêche, Nature et Traditions*) [Hunting, Fishing, Nature, and Traditions] is a single-issue party representing the interests of hunters in the ASSEMBLÉE NATIONALE.

châteaux A distinctive feature of the French countryside are the châteaux: the castles, palaces, mansions, and stately homes that can be seen throughout the region. Many are old castles dating from the Middle Ages and called '*châteaux forts*'. Later, unfortified palaces were built: the most famous are the '*châteaux de la Loire*', such as Amboise and Chenonceau, which were built in the Renaissance period. One of the largest châteaux in France is Versailles. Rebuilt for Louis XIV in the 17th century, today it has 3 million visitors each year. Two other châteaux – the Grand and Petit Trianon – stand in its grounds, as does Marie-Antoinette's hamlet, built in the style of Normandy cottages.

chômage ▸ANPE

CHU *Centre Hospitalier Universitaire* is a teaching hospital attached to the medical faculty of a university.

CIDJ (*Centre d'Informations et de Documentation pour la Jeunesse*) is where pupils and students often go in order to find information related to youth issues as well as information about careers and studies in general.

cinéma Cinema has always been a popular medium in France; it was in Paris in December 1895 that the Lumière brothers first demonstrated their *cinématographe*, showing moving pictures to a paying audience. In the 1920s, French filmmakers such as Louis Delluc and Jean Cocteau experimented with avant-garde cinema, while in the 1930s Jean Renoir produced masterpieces such as *La Grande Illusion*. Marcel Carné's epic tale, *Les Enfants du Paradis*, followed in 1945. In 1959, Jean-Luc Godard's *À Bout de Souffle* established him at the forefront of the *nouvelle vague*, the 'new wave', along with François Truffaut. *Cinéma Beur* (from the slang word meaning second-generation North Africans) arrived in the 1980s with Rachid Bouchareb, and has since coexisted with *cinéma du look*. Visually impressive, with non-naturalistic photography, intense colours, and romantic stories filmed in the studio, the best-known example of the genre is *Le Fabuleux destin d'Amélie Poulain* (2001), which grossed more than $33 million at the box office.

Cinquième Republique ▸ RÉPUBLIQUE

classe de neige A period, generally a week, that a school class, usually of under-twelves, spends in a mountain area. Ski tuition is integrated with normal schoolwork.

Code Napoléon A civil code introduced by the French emperor NAPOLÉON BONAPARTE in 1804 and named Code Napoléon in 1807. It still underpins the legal systems of France and many other European countries. The code attempted to unify the customs of northern and southern France, and was a combination of rational and traditional principles. It includes key concepts such as equality for all in the eyes of the law, and no recognition of privilege. The code was adopted in most of continental Europe, and survived Napoleon's downfall in 1815.

cohabitation is when a president and a prime minister from opposing political parties (PARTIS POLITIQUES) rule the country together. This can happen because there are separate elections for the National Assembly and the presidency. It last occurred from 1997 to 2002, when the socialists won a majority of seats in the National Assembly, so socialist Lionel Jospin was appointed prime minister in the government of the right-wing president, Jacques Chirac.

collège A state school for pupils between the ages of 11 and 15, between the ÉCOLE PRIMAIRE and LYCÉE. The organization of the school and the curriculum followed are laid down at national level.

colonie de vacances A holiday village or summer camp for children. Originally a means of giving poor city children a break in the country, these are still largely state-subsidized. They are known informally as '*colo*'.

Comédie Française The oldest national theatre company, this society of French actors was founded in 1680. Its repertoire is mainly classical. Molière's plays have been performed more than 30,000 times by the Comédie; Shakespeare is one of the few foreign authors who is also regularly performed. Every 15 January, on the anniversary of Molière's birth in 1622, a bust of him is brought on stage so that actors can pay homage to the writer.

commune The smallest administrative unit of French local government. Each has its own MAIRIE and CONSEIL MUNICIPAL, and with other communes forms a CANTON.

concours A competitive examination that is used to determine entry into many areas of the public services, including teaching, as well as to the most prestigious institutes of higher education.

conduite accompagnée Learner drivers who are 16 years old and have passed the theory (*code de la route*) part of the driving test in a state-approved driving school are allowed to practise driving a vehicle accompanied by a qualified driver aged 28 or over who has a clean driving licence. Such drivers can only drive at a maximum of 110 km/h (69 mph) on AUTOROUTES and must have a white sticker with a red A (for *apprenant*, or 'learner') affixed to the car.

conseil de classe A committee representing each class in a COLLÈGE or LYCÉE consisting of the class teachers, two elected parent members, and two elected class members. It is chaired by the head teacher. The *conseil de classe* meets regularly to discuss the progress of the class and any problems that may have arisen.

Conseil de l'Europe The Council of Europe was founded in 1949. Its headquarters are in Strasbourg, the capital of ALSACE, and it has 45 member states, all of whom are committed to democracy and human rights. The Council's main purpose is to draft treaties and legislation; these are sent to member countries for ratification by individual national legislatures. The 1950 Convention for the Protection of Human Rights and Fundamental Freedoms set up the European Court of Human Rights, which hears cases brought by individuals. Member states must adhere to the court's rulings or face expulsion from the Council.

conseil général The body of representatives elected every six years to implement public policy in each DÉPARTEMENT.

conseil municipal The *conseil municipal* is the local council elected for a six-year term by the inhabitants of a COMMUNE. The *conseil municipal* then elects the mayor (*le maire*). It is responsible for the management of local public services and amenities.

conseil régional Each member of a *conseil régional* is elected for a term of six years to represent a DÉPARTEMENT. The *conseillers régionaux* then appoint a president and an executive team.

conservatoires Many towns play host to these academies, which dispense specialist teaching in music and drama. There are 20 in Paris alone. Prizes are given to the best pupils.

Corse, La Island situated off the southeast of mainland France in the Mediterranean. Italian for many centuries, the island was sold to France in 1767. Ajaccio in the south and Bastia in the north are the main towns of the two DÉPARTEMENTS making up La Corse. The economic activities are agriculture, fishing, and tourism. Corsica enjoys special status and has an assembly with additional powers, though since the late 1970s there have been sometimes violent protests against the French government by those wanting complete independence from France.

Côte d'Azur The Côte d'Azur (literally 'Azure Coast') is the name for the French Riviera, the coastal region in the south of France that borders the Mediterranean and extends from south of Marseilles to the border with Italy. It became very famous in the 1920s as many foreigners – English aristocrats in particular – fell in love with its wild coastline. The towns of Nice, Cannes, and Monte Carlo are well known for attracting rich and famous holidaymakers.

couscous A North African dish introduced into France by the MAGHRÉBINS. The name comes from the granulated wheat-flour, or couscous, that forms the basis for the dish; this is served with a vegetable stew and various accompaniments, such as *merguez* (spicy sausages), chicken, mutton, or fish.

CP The *cycle préparatoire* or *cours préparatoire* is the first year of primary school, starting a child's formal education off at the statutory age of six. Most children will already have attended an ÉCOLE MATERNELLE.

CRS *Compagnies républicaines de sécurité* are special police units trained in public order techniques and riot control. They also police the AUTOROUTES and support mountain rescue and lifeguard work. *See also* MAI 1968.

décentralisation The tendency for the government in Paris to order the affairs of the rest of the country has been questioned for decades. A 1982 bill covering the rights and freedoms of COMMUNES, DÉPARTEMENTS, and RÉGIONS gave them much more autonomy. There is a slow movement to increase the decentralization of power; advocates of this are called *décentralisateurs*.

Déclaration des Droits de l'Homme et du Citoyen In August 1789 the French Assembly produced the 'Declaration of the Rights of Man and of the Citizen', which was adopted and signed under pressure by Louis XVI. It established the importance of recognizing human rights in all circumstances. The first article states: 'Men are born and remain free and equal in rights.' These principles have informed many conventions since.

de Gaulle, Charles One of the key figures in recent French political history, General Charles de Gaulle's striking profile is instantly recognizable. Having served in the army during World War I, de Gaulle's attempt to modernize it met with little success. When France fell to German forces in June 1940, de Gaulle travelled to Britain. From there he rallied his 'Free French' volunteers and resistance fighters within France; he entered Paris with the liberating forces in 1944. Politically sidelined for some years, he came back to power during the Algerian War and became the first president of the Cinquième RÉPUBLIQUE (Fifth Republic) from 1958 to 1969. The increased presidential powers he instituted at that time are still in force.

département An administrative unit of government in France. Each *département* has a number and this appears as the first two digits in postcodes for addresses within the area, and as the two-digit number at the end of the registration plates of vehicles registered before 15 April 2009.

député An elected member of the ASSEMBLÉE NATIONALE.

Disneyland Resort Paris (was EuroDisney) opened near Paris in 1992 amid great controversy, with many people fearing that French culture would be undermined by this American intruder. However, the many visitors do not seem to share this concern; after a slow start, the theme park now attracts more than 12 million people a year to the 'lands', studios, and costumed parades familiar from its counterparts in the United States.

DOM-TOM Acronym for *Département d'outre-mer* and *Territoire d'outre-mer*, the French overseas territories. The DÉPARTEMENTS have the status of a RÉGION. At present there are four: Guadeloupe, Guyane, Martinique, and Réunion. The *territoires*, which include Nouvelle-Calédonie (New Caledonia) and Tahiti, are constitutionally part of the French republic, and citizens have French nationality.

école libre Private sector school education, provided predominantly by the Catholic Church.

école maternelle A school providing free nursery education from age two to six. Many children start at two and virtually all children attend between the ages of four and six, which is the statutory school starting age and the time at which children move into the ÉCOLE PRIMAIRE.

école primaire A primary school for children between the ages of six, the statutory minimum age for starting school, and 11.

école secondaire Secondary education in France consists of two phases: COLLÈGE (11 to 15 years) and LYCÉE (15/16 to 17/18 years).

EDF-GDF *Électricité de France-Gaz de France* was the utility combining electricity generation and distribution of gas and electricity. It was split into two entities in January 2008: *ErDF* owned by *EDF*, and *GrDF* owned by *GDF Suez*, now a private gobal company.

Eiffel Tower Built by Gustave Eiffel for the Paris World Exhibition in 1889, La Tour Eiffel was the highest in the world until 1930. The tower has three lifts and 1,665 steps and – with 6 million visitors per year – is one of the biggest attractions in Paris.

Élysée ▸ PALAIS DE L'ÉLYSÉE

Emmaüs A charitable organization founded in 1954 by Abbé Pierre, a Catholic priest and well-known public figure who died in 2007. The organization, which has wide public support, aims to help the underprivileged. It has centres throughout France, run by volunteers, who collect and sell secondhand furniture, clothes, and bric-à-brac.

énergie nucléaire Nearly 80 per cent of French electricity is produced by nuclear power; only the United States produces more. There are more nuclear sites in France than in any other European country. Defenders of nuclear power argue that, because of its policy, France creates much less CO_2 than most industrialized countries. However, disposal of nuclear waste remains a problem.

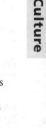

Entente Cordiale A colonial-era agreement signed by the British and French on 8 April 1904, which aimed to settle long-standing disputes between the UK and France in countries such as Morocco, Egypt, Siam, Madagascar, the New Hebrides, West and Central Africa, and Newfoundland. But it also represented a shift from a history overshadowed by conflict and rivalry to a sustained era of *rapprochement* and alliance. In 2004 many Franco-British events were held to celebrate the 100th anniversary of its signing.

L'Équipe ▸ PRESSE

EuroDisney ▸ DISNEYLAND RESORT PARIS

faculté More usually known as *la fac*, this is how students describe their university, in particular the location. So 'to go to university' would be '*aller à la fac*.'

festivals All year round there are theatre, music, dance, contemporary art, circus, and street festivals, but the majority take place in the summer months between June and September. The most popular are: Vienne for Jazz, La Rochelle for Francofolies (featuring CHANSONS FRANÇAISES), Orange and Aix-en-Provence for opera, Avignon for theatre, Chalon-sur-Saône for street performances, Arles for photography and dance, La Côte-St-André for Berlioz, Lyons for advertising and contemporary art. In Brittany the Festival Interceltique is becoming more and more popular. *See also* FÊTE DE LA MUSIQUE.

Fête de la Musique, created in 1982, is celebrated each year on the summer solstice, 21 June. It is now a major musical event all over France. In Paris amateur and professional musicians alike dust off their instruments and set up in any spare spot, from courtyards to châteaux, parks to doorways. The night echoes to every imaginable style of music as musicians play to large crowds.

Fête Nationale ▸ FRENCH TRADITIONS, FESTIVALS, AND HOLIDAYS

Figaro, Le ▶ PRESSE

FNAC A large chain of bookshops that also sells music, software, phones, and photographic equipment. They also run a booking system – in-store and via the internet – for all cultural events in France.

France 2 (FR2) is the main publicly owned television channel, which aims to provide a wide range of quality programmes.

France 3 (FR3), a state-owned TV channel, is regionally based and required to promote regional diversity and cover a wide range of beliefs and opinions.

France Télécom Orange is one of the world's leading telecommunications companies, providing mobile telephony and internet broadband services amongst other high-tech products.

Francophonie Invented by a French geographer in 1880, the word describes the French-speaking world – that is, countries where French is spoken as the official language or a language of culture. In 2005 this comprised 51 countries plus five associated ones. Five hundred million people live in Francophone countries, but only 120 million are actually Francophones (French-speaking).

Franglais can mean either French characterized by excessive use of English words, or the mixing of French and English (either intentionally, for fun, or unintentionally). There has been a long battle in France since World War II to preserve the national language from corruption by foreign words, particularly Americanisms. This has been only partially successful. The government's support of French cinema and the dubbing industry has gone some way to protecting the language. The use of French is officially monitored and regulated by the ACADÉMIE FRANÇAISE.

Front National ▶ PARTIS POLITIQUES

gastronomie The art or science of good eating is an enduring passion in France. It can be traced through the long history of some Parisian restaurants – *L'Auberge de la Mère Poulard* dates from 1888, Maxim's dates from 1893; through its tradition of great French chefs from Marie-Antoine Carême (1784–1833) to Paul Bocuse (1926–); through its world-famous culinary academy, *Le Cordon Bleu*, established in 1895; and through the great variety of its regional dishes, from *bouillabaisse* to *pâté de foie gras*. As in the rest of Europe, chefs strive to gain 'chefs' hats' (the mark of excellence from the *Gault Millau Guide*), and stars (the supreme accolade being three) from the *Michelin Guide*.

Gaule, La The region that now comprises modern France was once occupied by a Celtic tribe known as the Gauls. Between 57 and 52 BC, Julius Caesar and the Roman army conquered La Gaule. The Gauls saw many changes in their way of life: Roman buildings such as Le Pont du Gard and the amphitheatre at Nîmes were erected; wine was drunk in preference to beer; their own gods were replaced by Roman ones. In 486 AD the Romans were expelled from Gaul by Clovis (465–511), ruler of the Franks, and the country was renamed 'France' after its new occupiers.

gendarmerie nationale A section of the military which provides police services outside the major towns.

gîte rural A farmhouse or other building in the country that has been turned into a holiday cottage. Houses displaying the official *gîtes de France* sign must conform to certain standards.

GR or *grandes randonnées* are long-distance footpaths, maintained by the *Fédération française de randonnée pédestre. GR* (major hiking routes) are marked by white and red or yellow and red signs; *PR* (*petites randonnées*) are marked by yellow signs. GR20 is a famous route across Corsica.

grande école A prestigious higher education establishment admitting students on the results of a CONCOURS. They have different areas of specialization, and competition for entry is fierce, as they are widely believed to offer the highest level of education available and thus a guarantee of subsequent career success.

grottes There are many prehistoric *grottes*, or caves, in France, relics of the cave-dwelling peoples who settled in the south of France nearly a million years ago. La grotte Chauvet, in the Ardèche in southeastern France, was discovered by amateur speleologists. It is famous for its more than 300 animal paintings and engravings dating back to the Paleolithic era, between 32,000 and 30,000 years ago. The cave is closed to the public, but a reproduction is being built for visitors at La Mathe. La grotte de Lourdes is a place of pilgrimage; in 1858 a young girl claimed to have seen the Virgin Mary here.

Guyane ▸DOM-TOM

Harki From the Arab *harka*, meaning movement, this is the name given to Algerian soldiers who fought on the French side against those Algerians seeking independence from 1954 to 1962. Around 50,000–70,000 *Harkis* were killed in Algeria. Since the 1990s there has been a greater recognition of the role they played on behalf of France.

haute couture The *Chambre Syndicale de la Couture Parisienne* was founded in 1868 by Charles Worth (1825–95), who was actually born in England but became a highly successful Parisian designer. This association of *haute-couture* ('high-tailoring') houses defined the art of *couture*. Nowadays *haute couture* is a term regulated by the government. Each year the *Chambre Syndicale de la Haute Couture* decides which houses qualify to carry the *haute-couture* label; they have to meet strict criteria in terms of design, production, and presentation of fashion shows. *Haute-couture* clothes are the product of many hours of work, and are therefore extremely expensive. Famous French designers include Christian Dior (1905–57), Yves St Laurent (1936–), and Jean-Paul Gaultier (1952–).

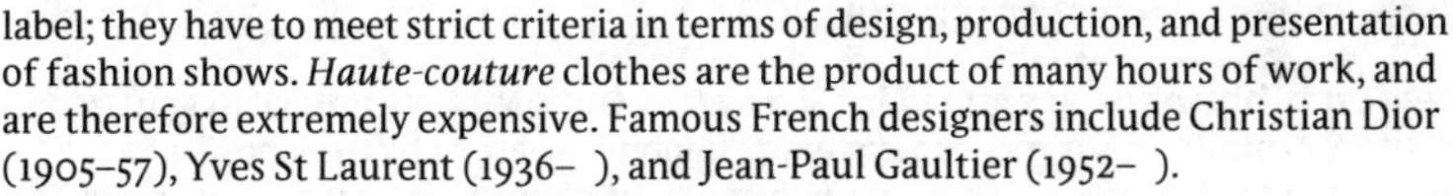

l'Hexagone Because of the shape of the map of France, which resembles a six-sided figure, France is often referred to as 'the Hexagon'. *L'Hexagone* refers to mainland France, excluding its islands and other dependencies. *See also* DOM-TOM.

HLM An abbreviation of *habitation à loyer modéré*. A type of public housing, usually an apartment in an estate, available for a relatively low rent with an option to buy as long as the property is retained for a minimum of five years. *HLMs* are built and managed either by public bodies, by the private sector supported by state loans, or by cooperatives. About 13 million people live in *HLMs*.

hôtel de ville ▸MAIRIE

immatriculation ▸PLAQUE D'IMMATRICULATION

immigration Of the 63 million people who live in France, about 5 million (around 7 per cent) are immigrants (*les immigrés*). Immigration used to be dominated by Europeans (54 per cent of those entering France in 1975 were from Europe), but today most immigrants are Algerians, Moroccans, Tunisians, people from the African colonies, Turks, and Asians (from the former colonies of Vietnam, Laos, and Cambodia). To work in France, incomers have to obtain *une carte de séjour* from the authorities. This is not always easy, particularly for non-EU citizens. People in illegal situations are called '*sans papiers*' (literally, 'without papers'). There are believed to be about 1 million '*sans papiers*' in the country. *See also* RACISME.

Islam ▸ RELIGION

justice The French Minister of Justice is called *Le Garde des Sceaux* (*un sceau* is a stamp, or seal). Barristers, or *avocats*, plead at the bar (*le barreau*). Solicitors, known as *notaires*, are very involved in local life, as they deal with property. You may sometimes need to go to see the *notaire*, even when you are just looking for a place to rent.

laïcité The concept of *laïcité* has been a fundamental principle in French society since the RÉVOLUTION, which separated religion from the functions of government – though the Church and State were only formally separated in 1905. *Laïcité* literally means secularism, but implies a free expression of religion, although religion is not accorded any special status. The issue has been hotly debated recently in France, after a Muslim girl was expelled from her school for wearing a *hijab*, or veil. In 2004, a law was passed forbidding the wearing of notable religious symbols in a move designed to protect the secular state.

langues French is the official language of France, though regional languages are now also taught in some schools. Since 1951 it has been possible to take some part of the BACCALAURÉAT in BRETON, CATALAN, or OCCITAN, and since 1974 in Corsican. There are six principal regional languages spoken in France: Breton (Britanny), Alsatian (ALSACE), Occitan (or *langue d'Oc*, spoken in 32 French DÉPARTEMENTS in the south); Catalan (south); and Corsican (French Riviera and Corsica). Up to 76 languages are spoken in France and the DOM-TOM, 29 in Nouvelle-Calédonie (New Caledonia) alone.

Latin Quarter ▸ QUARTIER LATIN

Légion d'honneur Instituted in 1802 by NAPOLÉON BONAPARTE to honour military exploits, this is now the system of honours awarded by the state for meritorious achievement. There are five grades of distinction, of which the basic rank is *chevalier* and the highest is *grand-croix*. The award is in the gift of the president, who is the *grand maître*.

Libération ▸ PRESSE

Liberté, Egalité, Fraternité This rousing cry for 'liberty, equality, and fraternity' was first invoked during the RÉVOLUTION of 1789. It summarizes the driving principles behind French society. The motto can be seen on objects such as stamps or coins. It is also frequently emblazoned on the façades of town halls and schools.

licence The first level of university degree, awarded after a three-year course. *See* UNIVERSITÉ.

livret de famille An official family record book, recording births, marriages, and deaths, which is given to married and unmarried parents alike and is often used to verify family links.

Loire The Loire is the name of a DÉPARTEMENT in Rhône-Alpes around St-Étienne; it is also the longest river in France, running for 1,020 km (637.5 miles) from the Cévennes region to the Atlantic Ocean. In the 15th century, the river was an ideal way to transport goods; in addition the beautiful forests, ideal for hunting, encouraged kings and nobles to build castles nearby (*les* CHÂTEAUX *de la Loire*).

LOTO The French national lottery, played using special machines that can be found in BUREAUX DE TABAC throughout France.

Louvre Originally a medieval fortress, then the palace of the kings of France, the Louvre became a museum after the French RÉVOLUTION. In 1989 the architect I. M. Pei added the glass pyramid to create an underground entrance. The *Mona Lisa* (*La Joconde*) by Leonardo da Vinci is probably the most famous of some 3,150 paintings displayed in the museum. It also houses around 350,000 Egyptian, Greek and Roman antiquities, as well as many other exhibits dating from classical times to the early 19th century. More than 8 million people visit the Louvre each year.

Luxembourg ▸ PALAIS DU LUXEMBOURG

lycée A school providing the last three years of secondary education after the COLLÈGE. The first year is *la seconde* at the age of 15/16, going through *la première*, and ending with *la terminale* at age 17/18, when students sit the BACCALAURÉAT. As well as those *lycées* that provide a conventional education, there are a number of different types of *lycée* offering a more vocationally based education.

M6 A popular, privately owned commercial TV company.

magasins Opening and closing times of shops (*les magasins*) vary according to the type of shop and the location. Department stores (*les grands magasins*) are generally open all day from 9 a.m. to 7 p.m. In larger towns, most other shops, with the exception of small food shops, are also open all day. Privately owned food shops such as butchers and fishmongers generally open at 8 a.m. and do not close in the evening until 7 or 7.30 p.m. They usually close, however, between midday and 2 or 3 p.m. In small towns, all the shops generally close for two or three hours in the middle of the day. In both small and large towns, all types of food shops tend to be open on Sunday mornings until midday. In smaller towns many shops are closed on Mondays.

Maghrébins About 1.3 million people of Maghreb origin (from France's ex-colonial territories of Morocco, Algeria, and Tunisia) live and work in France. They came to work in France during the '*trente glorieuses*', the three decades of postwar boom (1945–75). Many worked in car factories. Their children are known as BEURS in VERLAN.

Mai 1968: les événements Following disputes with university authorities and the police, students all over France went on strike. The government's attempts to suppress dissent using the CRS riot police made the situation much worse; street battles followed, and the students ripped cobbles up from the roads to form barricades. Ten million French workers joined the students in their protest and the country was paralysed for nearly two weeks. In response, President Charles DE GAULLE dissolved the ASSEMBLÉE NATIONALE and called new elections. The revolutionary fervour of the protesters subsided and de Gaulle was re-elected, though in return he promised major reforms in education.

mairie Administrative headquarters of the CONSEIL MUNICIPAL and the office of the *maire*, who is the local representative of state authority, officiating at marriages and supervising local elections. The *maire*'s powers can be quite extensive, especially in the larger towns, while the position can also be held on a part-time basis. The *maire*'s office is also known as the *hôtel de ville* (town hall) in larger towns.

Mans, Le town midway between Paris and the Atlantic coast, Le Mans is renowned for its 24-hour endurance motor car race, held every year.

marchés All towns in France have a weekly market with stalls selling a variety of produce, and some areas in big cities have a market every day. Many stalls are run by local people selling their own produce. Despite having access to supermarkets, many people still do much of their shopping *au marché*.

mariage Church weddings are not legally recognized in France, Belgium, or Switzerland (although they are in Quebec), so all couples must be married legally in a civil ceremony, whether or not they want a church wedding (which usually takes place afterwards but can be up to several weeks later). In France, the civil ceremony is a relatively short affair held in the *mairie* (town hall), and conducted by the mayor or his/her deputy. The couple vow to be responsible for the moral instruction and education of their future family, and are presented with a LIVRET DE FAMILLE. If the couple are holding a church ceremony then that is often the 'public' wedding, with the civil marriage usually a private family affair. Guests are often invited to the *vin d'honneur*, which begins the reception, where they can simply toast the newlyweds with a glass of champagne without staying on for a meal. For those who do stay, celebrations can continue for days, particularly in rural areas. The traditional wedding cake is the *pièce montée* or *croquembouche*, a magnificent tower of custard-filled choux buns coated in caramel. The legal age for getting married in France is 18 for men and 15 for women; in Belgium, Switzerland, and Quebec it is 18 for both parties (although it is possible to marry younger with parental consent). Since 2003 same-sex marriage has been legally possible in Belgium. It became legal in Quebec the following year.

Marianne The symbolic female figure often used to represent the French Republic (la RÉPUBLIQUE française). There are statues of her in public places all over France, frequently in town halls, and she also appears on the standard French stamp. She is often depicted wearing a Phrygian bonnet, a pointed cap which became one of the symbols of liberty of the 1789 RÉVOLUTION. Actresses Brigitte Bardot, Catherine Deneuve, and Laetitia Casta are among the well-known figures who have been used to represent the modern-day Marianne.

Marseillaise, La The popular name for the French national anthem, composed by Claude-Joseph Rouget de Lisle in 1792. It was adopted as a marching song by a group of republican volunteers from Marseilles, and it marked their entry into Paris. Many rock and jazz adaptations exist; there is even a reggae version, written in 1979 by Serge Gainsbourg.

Matignon L'Hôtel Matignon in the rue de Varenne in Paris is the official residence and office of the prime minister (PREMIER MINISTRE). (Hôtel is used here in the sense of a large private town house, which would have been its original use in the 18th century.) *Matignon* is effectively a synonym for the prime ministerial office, like 'Downing Street' in the UK.

Médecins du monde A charitable organization that provides medical and humanitarian aid in areas stricken by war, famine, or natural disaster.

Médecins sans frontières A charitable organization that sends medical teams anywhere in the world (hence their title) in order to cope with the effects on people of war and natural disasters.

MEDEF Known until 1998 as *le CNPF* (*Conseil national du patronat français*), *le MEDEF* (*Mouvement des entreprises de France*) is an umbrella organization representing the majority of employers' interest groups, large and small.

Métro (Chemin de fer métropolitain) The first line (Line 1) on the Parisian *métro* was completed in 1900. Now there are 16 lines (1–14 and 3b and 7b) in this underground rail system. It is run by RATP. The RER, a rapid-transit rail network, is linked to the *métro*. Many of the distinctive and charming Art Nouveau entrances to the underground, created by the architect Hector Guimard (1867–1942) in the early 1900s, still survive. Other main cities in France such as Lyons, Marseilles, and Lille also have underground railway systems. Rennes is the smallest town in the world to have its own métro system.

ministre Appointed by the PRÉSIDENT DE LA RÉPUBLIQUE on the advice of the PREMIER MINISTRE, a *ministre* heads a department of state and becomes a member of the *conseil des ministres*. The title *ministre d'État* is a recognition that the ministry is of greater than normal significance. In the *Cinquième* RÉPUBLIQUE, a DÉPUTÉ has to resign his or her seat in order to take office as a *ministre*.

MJC (Maison des jeunes et de la culture) Founded in 1944, these youth clubs are established in most towns. They offer cultural, scientific, social, and sporting activities. They are subsidized partly by the COMMUNE or by associations, and partly by the State.

Monaco Situated on the southern coast of France, near the border with Italy, Monaco is just 1.95 sq km in area. A principality under the protection of France, it was ruled by Prince Rainier III of the Grimaldi family from 1949 until his death in 2005, when he was succeeded by his son Albert II. Monaco is a tax haven, famous for its Casino, its expensive yacht-filled marina, and many very chic boutiques.

Monde, Le ▸PRESSE

Montmartre The 18th ARRONDISSEMENT of Paris, Montmartre is the highest point of the city. Its 130 m (426 ft) summit is topped by the basilica of Sacré Cœur. Montmartre has a strong association with artists: Renoir, Monet, and Van Gogh were among those who frequented the area in the early 20th century. Today it is a busy tourist attraction that still retains its village-like atmosphere.

Moulin Rouge Created in 1889, the Moulin Rouge cabaret became famous for the can-can dance performed by its beautiful stars, and was immortalized in the paintings of artist Toulouse-Lautrec. Edith Piaf and Joséphine Baker are among the many famous names who have sung there. The 2001 film, *Moulin Rouge*, starring Nicole Kidman and Ewan McGregor, vividly recreated its early *demi-monde* atmosphere.

Musée national A museum directly under the control of the MINISTRE *de la Culture*, for example the LOUVRE or Musée d'Orsay in Paris. These museums are generally closed on Tuesdays.

Napoléon Bonaparte French politician and military leader, Napoléon (1769–1821) was emperor of France from 1804 to 1815. As a general, he waged wars throughout Europe and North Africa; as a politician he instituted a number of important political and social changes, including reorganizing the Treasury, setting up the Bank of France, creating LYCÉES, and establishing the CODE NAPOLÉON. He married and divorced Joséphine de Beauharnais; his marriage to Marie Louise, daughter of the Emperor Francis I, resulted in the birth of a son (Napoléon) in 1811. His failure in the Peninsular War and a disastrous campaign in Russia signalled a reversal in his military fortunes, which was compounded by his defeat at Waterloo in 1815. He died in exile on the island of St Helena.

Notre Dame The Gothic cathedral of Notre Dame was built between 1163 and 1345 and stands on the Île de la Cité in the centre of the River SEINE. With its dramatic gargoyles, flying buttresses and stunning stained-glass rose windows, it is one of Paris's main tourist attractions. *Notre-Dame de Paris* (also known as *The Hunchback of Notre Dame*), by the French Romantic writer Victor Hugo (1802–85), is set around the cathedral and tells the story of the deformed bell-ringer Quasimodo and his love for the beautiful Esméralda.

Occitan The old language of the southern half of France (*langue d'Oc*). It is still spoken in a number of different dialects by an estimated four million people, and recent years have seen an immense revival of interest in promoting its survival. It can now be learned in many schools in the south, although it has no status as an official language in France. *See also* LANGUES.

OGM Only some very specific varieties of *organismes génétiquement modifiés* or genetically modified foods can be sold and consumed in France. The French Ministry of Agriculture is closely monitoring the use and consumption of genetically modified foods (*la biovigilance*) in order to assess the possible side effects.

Ouest-France ▸ PRESSE

PACS *Le pacte civil de solidarité* (contract of civil union), established in November 1999, is designed to safeguard the common interests of partners living together either in mixed or same-sex couples. The PACS does not apply to under-18s, to couples who are blood relatives, or those already in another marriage or relationship. It entails certain obligations on the part of the couple who sign the 'pact', such as a commitment to mutual support and maintenance and shared responsibility for joint expenses. In return, couples are given certain rights, for example over joint property, accommodation, etc.

Palais Bourbon A large 18th-century residence on the Left Bank of the River SEINE that is now the seat of the ASSEMBLÉE NATIONALE.

Palais de l'Élysée The official residence and office of the French president, situated just off the CHAMPS-ÉLYSÉES in Paris.

Palais des Congrès A huge conference centre. Several large cities have one of these, notably Paris and Lyons. As well as supplying luxury conference facilities, they have a large amount of exhibition space, and auditoriums where concerts and performances are held.

Palais du Luxembourg A 17th-century palace in the Jardin du Luxembourg in Paris. It is now the seat of the SÉNAT.

Pâques ▸ FRENCH TRADITIONS, FESTIVALS, AND HOLIDAYS

Partis politiques In general, French political parties reflect a basic left/right divide. On the left, the main parties are the *Parti Socialiste* (*PS*) and the *Parti*

Communiste Française (*PCF*), while the principal party on the right is the *Union pour un Mouvement Populaire* (*UMP*), with the *Mouvement Démocrate* (*MoDem*) for the centre. There are in addition more extreme groups at both ends of the political spectrum; such as the extreme right *Front National* (*FN*). Beyond the general left/ right divide, the ecological movement is represented by *Europe Ecologie Les Verts* (*EELV*) and *Génération Écologie*.

Pei, I. M. ▸ARCHITECTURE, LOUVRE

pelote The most popular sport in the Basque region, there are several variations on pelota, or *la pelote basque*. The European version is thought to derive from 'real' tennis. It can be played just using the hand, with rackets, with a wooden bat (*pala*) or with a wicker basket that propels the ball (*cesta*). It can be played against a wall or between two teams separated by a net, and the ball can reach speeds of around 160 km/h (100 mph).

périphérique *Le périphérique* (*le périph*) is the ring road or beltway that runs round the central area of Paris. It is often blocked with traffic jams. Other major cities in France have ring roads which are also often congested, particularly during the rush hour, '*l'heure de pointe*'.

permis de conduire A driving licence can be issued to a person over the age of 18 who has passed both parts of the driving test, the theory and the practical. The first part is the theory test (*code de la route*) and consists of 40 questions about the highway code. This can be sat from the age of 16 upwards and gives the right to the CONDUITE ACCOMPAGNÉE. The practical driving test has to be taken within two years of the theory test. It is compulsory to carry your driving licence when driving a vehicle.

pétanque ▸ BOULES

pharmacie Pharmacies in France used to sell only medicines and closely related products such as toiletries and some brands of perfume. However, these days they often sell a wider range of goods. Pharmacists generally play an active paramedical role, and people will often consult a pharmacist rather than a doctor in the case of minor ailments, or accidents such as snake bites. Pharmacies are easily spotted by the green cross, lit up when the pharmacy is open. A *pharmacie de garde* (duty chemist) can dispense medicines outside normal opening hours as part of a local rota.

plaque d'immatriculation A vehicle's registration plate for vehicles registered before 15 April 2009. The last two figures indicate the number of the DÉPARTEMENT in which the owner lives.

PMU The PMU (*pari mutuel urbain*) sign can be seen outside many BUREAUX DE TABAC. It indicates a state-regulated horse-race betting outlet. The most popular form of betting is the *tiercé*, in which punters have to predict the first three places in a given race.

Pole Emploi ▸ANPE

police There are three principal police forces: the *police municipale*, responsible for routine local policing such as traffic offences, who are locally organized and not armed; the *police nationale*, who are nationally organized and generally armed; and the GENDARMERIE NATIONALE, which is a branch of the military.

Pompidou Centre ▸ BEAUBOURG

pompiers There are around 240,000 '*sapeurs-pompiers*', or firemen, in France, of whom more than 200,000 are volunteer non-professionals. *Les sapeurs-pompiers* play a unique role in modern France. They deal with fires, but also have teams of highly trained paramedics who are constantly on call to deal with all manner of emergencies, including traffic accidents. Unless there is a crime involved, in emergencies people tend to call *les pompiers* by dialling 18.

Poste, La is in charge of all mail and parcel deliveries. *Les facteurs* and *les factrices* (postmen and -women) deliver the mail. In 2006 *La Banque Postale* was created as a bank subsidiary of *La Poste*. It now has nearly 30 million customers.

préfecture The administrative headquarters of a DÉPARTEMENT. *Le préfet* is the most senior official responsible for representing the state within the *département*.

premier ministre The chief minister of the government, appointed by the PRÉSIDENT DE LA RÉPUBLIQUE and responsible for the overall management of government affairs.

président de la République The president is head of state and is elected for a term of five years. Under the terms of the constitution of the *Cinquième* RÉPUBLIQUE, the president plays a strong executive role in the governing of the country.

Presse Also referred to as *le quatrième pouvoir*, the press plays a central role in French cultural life. The best-known and most respected French newspaper is *Le Monde*, which provides in-depth coverage of national and international news. In its new format, it publishes more photographs than in the past. National newspapers reflect the main political trends in public life (*Le Figaro* is associated with the right, while *Libération* is a left-wing publication, and so on). There are also several large-circulation regional newspapers (e.g. *Ouest-France*), as well as specialist publications like *L'Équipe*, the sports daily. France publishes more than 15,000 weekly and monthly magazines. The main French press agency is *l'Agence France Presse* (*AFP*).

Prix Goncourt A literary prize awarded every November for a novel published in that year. The event attracts considerable media coverage and speculation.

Quai d'Orsay The *ministère des Affaires étrangères* (Ministry of Foreign Affairs) is situated here, so journalists often use Quai d'Orsay to mean the ministry.

Quartier Latin As the location of France's oldest university, the Sorbonne, the Latin Quarter still bustles with students. Situated on the Left Bank of the SEINE, it is a lively district, full of a range of new and second-hand bookshops (*librairies*), ethnic restaurants, and markets. Many of the cafés and bistros have played host to major literary and artistic figures of the 20th century, such as Jean-Paul Sartre and Pablo Picasso, and the legacy of its past lives on. Other attractions include the remains of Gallo-Roman baths, and the Panthéon, in which many of France's great and good have been laid to rest.

Québec was founded in 1608 by the French explorer, Samuel de Champlain. It is Canada's largest province and Quebec City is its capital. Montreal is the largest city in the province. Eighty per cent of the inhabitants of Quebec – *un(e) Québécois(e)* – speak French. In 1995, a referendum on independence from Canada was held: those living in Quebec voted 50.6 per cent against independence and 49.4 per cent in favour. *Les Québécois* speak French with a recognizable accent, and certain words are unique to the province.

racisme As in many other countries, racism has remained an issue in France into the 21st century. In the 2002 elections, *Le Front National* made strong gains before being defeated in the second round of voting; the party leader, Jean-Marie Le Pen, has been widely criticized for his xenophobic and anti-Semitic pronouncements. Since the 1980s, rising racial tensions, particularly but not exclusively in LA BANLIEUE, have aided the party's growing influence. Debates about immigration, integration, assimilation, and the right to difference have dominated the news in recent years. Anti-racist movements such as SOS RACISME aim to reverse the trend towards extremism.

radio There are three types of radio station in France: public stations run by the state-owned RADIO FRANCE; commercial stations such as *Europe 1*, *RTL*, *Radio Monte Carlo*, which are financed by advertising and which broadcast from border areas; and privately owned local stations (originally known as *radios libres*), which began to develop following a change in broadcasting laws in 1982.

Radio France The state-owned radio broadcasting company runs stations covering a range of interests, including *France Info*, which features 24-hour news, *France Culture*, which covers cultural and social topics, and *France Musique*, featuring classical, jazz, and world music.

RATP The Paris public transport authority, with a monopoly over the provision of bus, métro, and tram services. It is jointly responsible with the SNCF for running the RER (the *Réseau Express Régional*; *see* MÉTRO).

région The largest administrative unit in France, consisting of a number of DÉPARTEMENTS. Each has its own CONSEIL RÉGIONAL (regional council), which has responsibilities in education and economic planning.

religion Historically and culturally, France is a Catholic country, but the Catholic Church is no longer so influential as it once was. In 1970, 75 per cent of babies were baptised, but by 2000 the figure had dropped to 20 per cent. With 5 million Muslims, more than any other European country, Islam is the second religion in France.

rentrée The week at the beginning of September when the new school year starts and around which much of French administrative life revolves. The preceding weeks see intensive advertising of associated merchandise, from books and stationery to clothes and sports equipment. Many stores and supermarkets have a range of special purchases at bargain prices. *La rentrée littéraire* marks the start of the literary year and *la rentrée parlementaire* signals the return of members of parliament after the recess.

repas Traditionally the midday meal was the big meal of the day, and for people who live in country areas this is still largely the case. Even in big cities many people continue to eat a big meal in the middle of the day, either in a family restaurant near their place of work, or by buying a freshly cooked hot dish from a CHARCUTERIE. However, people living and working in the larger cities are tending more and more to have a snack lunch and to eat their main meal in the evening. In either case, the main meal virtually always consists of a number of courses, typically a starter such as pâté, *saucisson*, or *crudités*, then meat or fish with a vegetable dish, followed by cheese and dessert. Cheese is virtually always eaten, as one might expect in a country that boasts such a huge variety and number of cheeses, and is always served before the dessert. In town and country alike, Sunday is the day for a big family meal in the middle of the day, and the pâtisseries are usually crowded on Sunday mornings as people queue up to buy a large tart or gâteau for dessert.

République France is a republic; the first republic was declared in 1792 after the French Revolution. Its new constitution was based on the DÉCLARATION DES DROITS DE L'HOMME ET DU CITOYEN. The *Cinquième République* (Fifth Republic) is now in force; it was established by DE GAULLE in 1958 after 80 per cent of French people voted in favour of a new constitution.

Résistance The Resistance movement fought military occupation by German forces in France (1940–44). After France signed an armistice with Germany in June 1940, acts of resistance were organized by students and miners; armed resistance came from communists and socialists who had been forced into hiding, and from Belgian, Polish, Dutch, and Spanish fighters. These men and women formed themselves into '*maquis*' units. Despite the terrible risks involved, there were many resistance groups. They carried out ambushes and acts of sabotage, such as derailing trains, attacking German garrisons, and blowing up bridges. During the D-day landings in June 1944, they helped Allied troops liberate their country. Many memorials recall the courage and determination of these fighters.

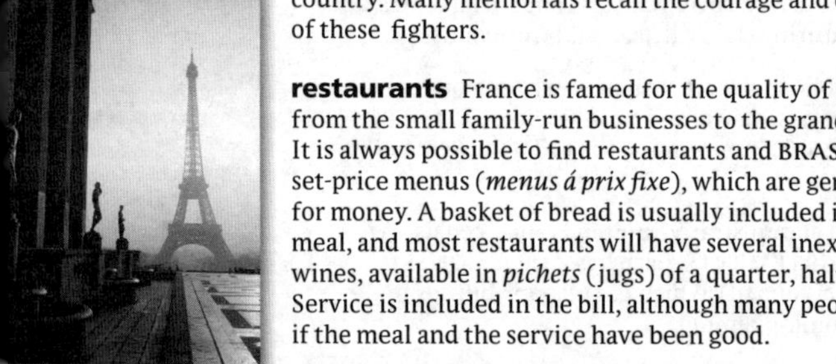

restaurants France is famed for the quality of its restaurants, from the small family-run businesses to the grand establishments. It is always possible to find restaurants and BRASSERIES offering set-price menus (*menus á prix fixe*), which are generally good value for money. A basket of bread is usually included in the price of the meal, and most restaurants will have several inexpensive house wines, available in *pichets* (jugs) of a quarter, half, and one litre. Service is included in the bill, although many people do leave a tip if the meal and the service have been good.

restos du cœur A charitable organization, *les restos* (*restaurants*) *du cœur* are widely publicized by virtue of having been set up by a much-loved humourist called Coluche. He died in a motorcycle accident in 1986. *Les restos du cœur* serve meals to the poor and homeless, particularly in winter.

Révolution (française); Révolution de 1789 By 1789 administrative and revenue reforms were long overdue in France; the 'third estate' (middle-classes) set up a National Assembly demanding change. Louis XVI's indecisive response led to the storming of the Bastille prison on 14 July, and the DÉCLARATION DES DROITS DE L'HOMME ET DU CITOYEN. By the following year a new constitution had been set up, and in 1792 the National Convention, which had replaced the National Assembly, abolished the monarchy. Louis XVI was executed on 21 January 1793. The Revolution's major legacies were the establishment of individual rights and a nationalist pride: the right to vote, civil equality, the Constitution, the TRICOLORE, and the MARSEILLAISE were some of its many products.

Rhône Department of France around Lyons, and a major French river. The Rhône is 812 km (507.5 miles) long and flows from Switzerland through the mountains of the Jura and down to Lyons. There it is joined by the Saône, its main tributary. It then continues south to its delta in the CAMARGUE. The world-famous Côtes du Rhone vineyards line the valley from Vienne, south of Lyons, to AVIGNON, producing wines such as Crozes-Hermitage and Châteauneuf du Pape.

RMI (*Revenue minimum d'insertion*) Introduced in 1988, the *RMI* is an allowance designed to support the poorest members of society by bringing them above the poverty line and allowing them access to various social security benefits.

roller *Le roller*, or rollerblading, is a very popular sport in France, with an estimated five million practitioners. In Paris on Friday evenings rollerbladers stream through the streets; up to 12,000 people can take part in these impressive displays.

route départementale These are signalled on French road maps as 'D' followed by a number, and are marked in yellow. They are roads maintained by the DÉPARTEMENT and are secondary roads, not intended for fast travel. Many of them have stretches marked in green on maps to highlight areas or views of particular interest.

route nationale A *route nationale* forms part of the state-maintained road network, outside the AUTOROUTES but providing fast roads for travel between towns and cities. They are signalled by 'N' followed by the road number and are marked in red on French road maps.

SAMU A 24-hour service coordinated by each DÉPARTEMENT to send mobile medical services and staff to accident scenes and emergencies. SAMU stands for *le Service d'Aide Médicale d'Urgence*.

sans papiers ▸ IMMIGRATION

SARL Acronym for *société à responsabilité limité*. A private limited company. All such companies are officially registered at the Chamber of Commerce. In situations where such a company goes bankrupt, the director is not personally liable for debts unless he has committed fraud.

SDF Abbreviation of *sans domicile fixe* ('of no fixed abode'), describing those living on the streets, below the poverty line. In winter the authorities in Paris and other major cities provide dormitories where people can sleep, but space is limited. *SDFs* often sleep in MÉTRO stations. There are estimated to be about 50,000 homeless people in Paris alone. See also RESTOS DU CŒUR.

Sécu An abbreviation of *Sécurité sociale*, the national system for provision of sickness, maternity, child, unemployment, old-age, and housing benefits. All workers make contributions. However, the social-security budget deficit in France is large and the government is trying to find ways to reduce it (for instance, by getting people to see their GP before consulting a specialist).

Seine The river that flows through the centre of Paris. Its source is northwest of Dijon, and it flows into the sea between Le Havre and Honfleur. It is an important commercial route, carrying cargo from Paris to the coast, and a major tourist attraction. The banks of the river in Paris became a UNESCO World Heritage Site in 1991. Since 2002, for two months in the summer, two miles of the Right Bank have been transformed from dual carriageway into a 'beach' – '*Paris Plage*' – complete with tons of sand, palm trees, sunbeds, and parasols.

Sénat The upper house of parliament which meets in the PALAIS DU LUXEMBOURG. It consists of 343 elected *sénateurs*. It votes on laws and the state budget.

SIDA The *Syndrome Immunodéficitaire Acquis*, or AIDS. The first case occurred in France in 1981. Nowadays death from AIDS has decreased enormously in France due to effective treatment and prevention, helped by campaign groups such as SIDACTION.

SMIC *Salaire Minimum Interprofessionnel de Croissance*: the basic minimum legal wage fixed annually by decree. People earning the SMIC are known as *smicards*. Those under the age of 18 can be paid less than the minimum wage.

SNCF *La Société Nationale des Chemins de Fer Français*. The state-owned rail company, founded in 1937, which also has access to private finance. Its remit covers the full range of rail transport services from small local trains to the high-speed TGV.

Solaar MC ▸ CHANSON FRANÇAISE

Sorbonne ▸ QUARTIER LATIN

syndicats Although it plays a less central role than it did in the first half of the 20th century, with only 10 per cent of employees unionized, the trade union movement is still a significant actor in French public life and has considerable power and influence. Major unions include the *CGC (Confédération générale des cadres)* and the *CGT (Confédération générale du travail)*. There is also an employers' association, the MEDEF.

tabac ▸ BUREAU DE TABAC

télécarte A phone card for use in telephone kiosks, widely available from FRANCE TÉLÉCOM, *bureaux de poste*, BUREAUX DE TABAC, and *marchands de journaux*.

télé réalité *La télé réalité* (reality TV), imported from abroad, has enjoyed great success recently in France. The first reality TV show, *Loft Story*, known as 'Big Brother' in other countries, was shown on the French channel M6 in 2001. To the horror of the cultural élite, the show attracted record numbers of viewers. TF1 responded by launching a whole series of similar reality shows, the most successful being *Star Academy* (creating a pop star, rights now owned by NRJ12) and *Koh-Lanta*, where players are stranded on a desert island. Many others have followed.

TF1 *Télévision Française 1* was originally a state-controlled television station, but is now privately owned. *TF1* has an obligation to ensure that 50 per cent of its programmes are of French origin.

TGV *Le train à grande vitesse* is a high-speed electric train operated by the SNCF. In March 2007 the new TGV broke the world rail speed record hitting 574 km/h (356 mph).

Tintin A comic-book character invented by the Belgian cartoonist Hergé in 1929. Tintin's adventures with the irrepressible Captain Haddock are still bestsellers and have been translated into more than 40 languages. *See also* BANDE DESSINÉE.

TOM (territoires d'outre mer) ▸ DOM-TOM

Tour de France Probably the most famous cycle race in the world, the Tour de France takes place over a different route each year but always ends around 14 July on the CHAMPS-ÉLYSÉES. The race was inaugurated in 1903 by Henri Desgrange, editor of the sports newspaper *L'Auto*, in order to boost circulation above that of a rival publication.

travail (work) People cannot officially work below the age of 16. In 2000, the working week was reduced to 35 hours (in companies with more than 20 employees), which is now the shortest in Europe. French workers get five weeks' paid holiday per year. Retirement is fixed at the age of 60, but people can take early retirement, known as '*préretraite*'. Those who have children under the age of three can choose to take *un congé parental d'éducation* (parental child-rearing leave). Many French women and men work *à mi-temps* (part-time) or *à temps partiel* (partial time, generally four days a week). One quarter of the workforce is employed by the French state. Unemployment, at around 10 per cent, is among the highest in Europe.

(le drapeau) tricolore The name of the French flag, so called because it is made up of three colours: blue, white, and red, arranged in vertical stripes. The flag was adopted during the RÉVOLUTION. It was intended to represent the ideals of the Revolution: LIBERTÉ, EGALITÉ, FRATERNITÉ.

troisième âge Nowadays called *les séniors*, *le troisième âge* (the elderly) refers to people who are retired (generally over 60). The '*université du troisième âge*', created in 1973, offers over-60s the chance to study a wide range of subjects for a minimal fee.

Tuileries These central Parisian gardens originally housed a palace begun in 1564. Later Louis XV lived there while Versailles was being built. The palace was eventually destroyed during the period of the Commune in 1871. The site takes its name from the tile kilns that used to stand here (*une tuilerie* is a tile factory). The gardens were designed in 1664 by Le Nôtre, who also designed the gardens at Versailles. The Tuileries now host the Orangerie and Jeu de Paume art galleries.

UDF *Union pour la Démocratie Française*, or *UDF*, was a political grouping that allows various centre-right parties to work together at times of elections. In 2007 it was fully integrated within the *Mouvement Démocrate (le MoDem)*.

UMP *Union pour un Mouvement Populaire* (*UMP*) is a French political party of the centre right. Renamed after the 2002 election, it was formed from the *Rassemblement pour la République* or *RPR* (Jacques Chirac's party), and Chirac supporters from the *Démocratie Libérale (DL)*, and *L'Union pour la Démocratie Française (UDF)*.

Union Européenne The European Union, previously known as the European Community, was founded on 1 November 1993. Its aim is to further political, economic, and social cooperation between members. There are now 27 countries in the union. Twelve member countries, including France, have undergone monetary union and adopted a common currency, the euro. They were joined by Slovenia in 2007, and Malta and Cyprus in 2008.

Université There are 90 universities in France. The State subsidises the French universities but there are also independent establishments, mainly Catholic universities, in Lyons, Paris, Toulouse, Angers, and Lille. The university system now has three levels: LICENCE (BACCALAURÉAT +3), *master* (*Bac* +5), and *doctorat* (*Bac* +8). Some universities have a special reputation for certain subjects (historically the most renowned is the Sorbonne). To enter university students have to have the *baccalauréat*. Fees for the year are minimal, except for private education. The most popular course is humanities, followed by sciences, medicine, and sport.

Variété française ▸ CHANSON FRANÇAISE

vendanges The grape harvests (*les vendanges*) are traditionally held in September, though the harvest can often begin at the end of August and finish in October, depending on the maturity of the grapes, the region, and the weather. *Les vendanges tardives* (late harvests) make sweet wines such as Sauternes. Now widely mechanized, harvesting is still done by hand in Beaujolais and CHAMPAGNE.

verlan A form of French slang that reverses the order of syllables in many common words, rendering them more or less incomprehensible to the uninitiated. For example, the term itself is derived from the word *l'envers*, the syllables of which are reversed to create *vers-l'en*, which in turn becomes *verlan*. Single syllable words are also converted, so *femme* becomes *meuf*, *mec* becomes *keum*, etc. A recent coinage for *énervé* ('irritated') is *vénère*. Originally used as an anti-authoritarian weapon by French youth and others, *verlan* is now commonly heard in everyday speech in France. Some words have been through the process twice: *beur*, for example, has now been reversed back to '*reub*' or '*reubeu*'.

Verts, Les ▸ PARTIS POLITIQUES

Vichy After the German invasion of France in June 1940, Vice-Premier Marshal Henri Pétain signed an armistice with Hitler, which divided France into occupied and unoccupied sectors, and allowed Pétain to set up a government in the spa town of Vichy, central France. The Vichy government became a German tool, deporting French Jews to Germany and substituting the motto *Travail, Famille, Patrie* (Work, Family, Country) for *Liberté, Egalité, Fraternité*. In response, the British cut off diplomatic relations with Vichy France and allowed General DE GAULLE to rally his Free French forces from London. When the Allies invaded North Africa in November 1942, Hitler annulled the armistice of 1940 and invaded Vichy France anyway. After the war, many members of the Vichy government were arrested and some executed. Pétain was sentenced to life imprisonment.

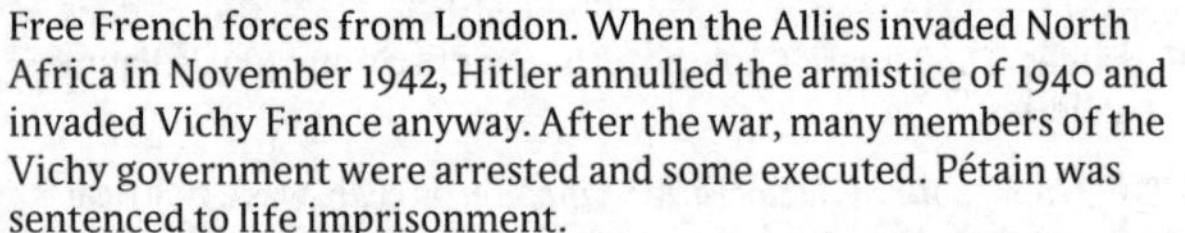

Vigipirate An emergency plan to reinforce police and military security, bringing an increased uniformed presence to public places at times of potential disorder, such as terrorist attacks, etc.

Villette, La In the heart of Paris's 19th ARRONDISSEMENT is the Parc La Villette, the largest green space in the city. It is home to the Cité des Sciences et de l'Industrie, a modern science museum, the Cité de la Musique, which stages concerts and exhibitions, and the Conservatoire National Supérieur de Musique et de Danse de Paris. La Grande Halle, on the southern edge of the park, is used for exhibitions and the Villette Jazz Festival. The park also contains theme gardens, the Zenith rock venue, and the Theâtre Paris Villette.

VTT *Vélo tout terrain* or *VTT* is the French for mountain bike. Mountain biking is a popular French sport, particularly among younger people. The signposted tracks are called Parcours *VTT*.

Zidane ▸ BLEUS, LES

Letter-writing in French and using the Internet

Invitation (informal)

Invitations to parties are usually by word of mouth, but for more formal events such as weddings, invitations are sent out.

❶ *Note the use of the informal form* tu *betweeen good friends.*

Paris, le 28/04/13

Cher Denis,

Que fais-tu ❶ cet été? Pascal et moi avons décidé d'inviter tous les copains d'Orléans à nous rejoindre dans notre maison de Dordogne pour le weekend du 16 juillet. Il y aura fête au village avec bal populaire et feu d'artifice. Le petit vin du pays n'est pas mal non plus!

Nous comptons sur toi pour venir trinquer avec nous,

Bises,

Martine

■ *Endings (informal):* Bises *(= lots of love) is very informal and is appropriate for very good friends and family. Alternatives for close friends and family include* Bien à toi, Bons baisers *or affectionately* Je t'embrasse. *If the letter is addressed to more than one person use* Bien à vous *or* Je vous embrasse.

Invitation (formal)

Christine et Félix Prévost
81 rue Esque moise
59000 Lille

Lille, le 28 avril 2013

Chers amis,

Nous avons l'immense plaisir de vous annoncer le mariage de notre fils Victor et de mademoiselle Stéphanie Heusdens.

La cérémonie aura lieu à l'Hôtel de Ville à 15 heures le samedi 11 juin. Vous recevrez bientôt un faire-part et une invitation à dîner mais nous tenions à vous prévenir suffisamment tôt pour que vous puissiez arranger votre voyage. Nous espérons qu'il vous sera possible de vous joindre à nous.

Amicalement, ❶

Christine et Félix

- In a more formal letter, especially where a reply is generally required, the sender's address is written on the left-hand side of the page. An alternative is in the centre of the page, particularly on printed stationery.

❶ *Endings: Alternatives could be* Amitiés, Bien amicalement.

Sending an email

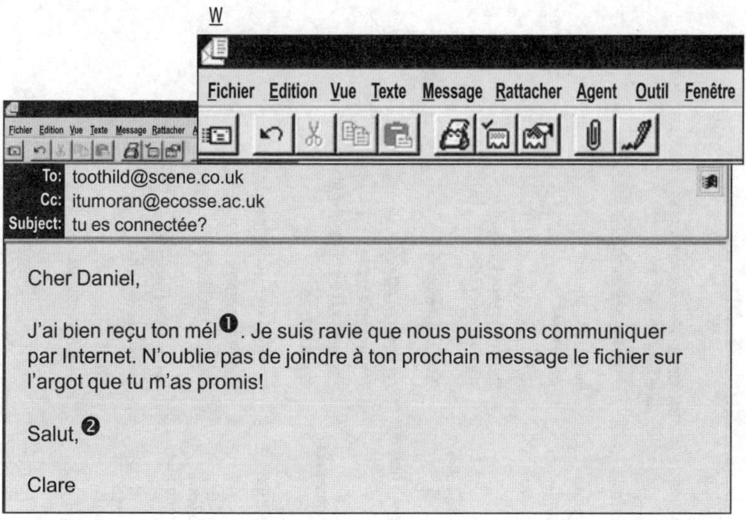

Cher Daniel,

J'ai bien reçu ton mél❶. Je suis ravie que nous puissons communiquer par Internet. N'oublie pas de joindre à ton prochain message le fichier sur l'argot que tu m'as promis!

Salut,❷

Clare

❶ *Note that* mél *is an abbreviated form of* message électronique. *To send an attachment* = joindre un fichier.

❷ *Endings (informal): An alternative could be* A bientôt *or simply* Bises *to a close friend in an informal context.*

Buying train tickets online

Achetez vos billets en ligne avec **Europtrains**

Billets | Horaires | Plans, destinations & itineraries

De
Sélectionnez une gare ▼ **voir toutes les gares**

À
Sélectionnez une gare ▼ **voir toutes les gares**

Date de départ
Jun ▼ 17 ▼ 2013 ▼
calendrier

Heure
Toutes les heures ▼

Date de retour
(à ignorer en cas d'aller simple)
Jun ▼ 18 ▼ 2013 ▼
calendrier

Heure
Toutes les heures ▼

Dates flexibles? ☐

Nombre de passagers **Adultes** ▼ **Enfants** ▼ **Etudiants** ▼ **Seniors** ▼

1e classe ☐
2e classe ☐

RECHERCHE

Offre Spéciale

Economisez 25%
en réservant en ligne
à partir du 1er juillet 2009

•

Aller simple Londres–Bruxelles: moitié prix

Cliquez ici pour en savoir plus

•

Aller-retour Londres–Paris à partir de 50€ seulement

Cliquez ici pour plus de détails

•

Etudiants: achetez votre abonnement rail et économisez à chaque voyage

Pour plus de détails, veuillez téléphoner.

Offre soumise à conditions

Mon compte

Nom de utilisateur
Mot de passe

Retenir mon mot de passe ☐
Mot de passe oublié?
Inscrivez-vous ici

Autres options

Voyageurs d'affaires
Voyages en groupe
Voyager avec un fauteuil roulant
Voyager à vélo

Modifier une réservation
Annuler une réservation
Recevoir vos billets

Autres offres spéciales
Abonnements rail
Hôtels
Assurance voyage

plan du site | à propos de nous | FAQ | contactez-nous

SMS (electronic text messaging)

The basic principles governing French SMS abbreviations are similar to those governing English SMS. Certain words or syllables can be represented by letters or numbers that sound the same but take up less space. Also, points, accents and other diacritics are generally omitted altogether. For example, the syllables '-pé' and '-té' can be replaced by the letters P and T, the word 'sans' by '100', and the conjunction 'que' by 'ke'. Another way of shortening words is simply to omit certain letters, especially vowels. For example, 'bonjour' becomes 'bjr' and 'quand' becomes 'qd'.

As in English, 'emoticons' are very popular, and some of the more established ones are included in the table below.

Glossary of French SMS abbreviations

Abbreviation	*Full word*
1mn	juste une minute
100	sans
5pa	sympa
6né	cinéma
@+	à plus tard
@2m1	à demain
ap	après
aprM, AM	après-midi
bi1to	bientôt
bjr	bonjour
bsr	bonsoir
C	c'est
cad	c'est à dire
dak	d'accord
d1ngue	dingue
dzolé	désolé
entouK	en tout cas
fet	fête
frR	frère
G	j'ai
IR	hier
jamé	jamais
jenémar	j'en ai marre
je t'M	je t'aime
ke	que
kekina	qu'est-ce qu'il ya?

Abbreviation	*Full word*
kfé	café
ki	qui
koi29	quoi de neuf
l8	lui
L	elle
mat1	matin
MDR	mort de rire
MSG	message
pb	problème
pk	pourquoi
pr	pour
qd	quand
ri1	rien
rstp	réponds s'il te plaît
seur	sœur
slt cv?	salut ça va?
strC	stressé
svp	s'il vous plaît
tjr	toujours
TOK	t'es OK?
TOQP	t'es occupé?
Vlo	vélo
vs	vous
we	week-end

<table>
<tr><th>Emoticons*</th><th></th></tr>
<tr><td>:-)</td><td>sourire</td></tr>
<tr><td>;-)</td><td>clin d'œil</td></tr>
<tr><td>:-(</td><td>pas content, déçu</td></tr>
<tr><td>:-D</td><td>je rigole</td></tr>
<tr><td>:-X</td><td>motus et bouche cousue</td></tr>
<tr><td>:-|</td><td>indifférent</td></tr>
<tr><td>:'(</td><td>je pleure</td></tr>
<tr><td>|I</td><td>endormi</td></tr>
<tr><td>:|</td><td>hmmm...</td></tr>
<tr><td>:-o</td><td>oh!</td></tr>
<tr><td>:-@</td><td>hurlant</td></tr>
<tr><td>:-P</td><td>lapsus (ma langue a fourché)</td></tr>
<tr><td>0:-)</td><td>un ange</td></tr>
<tr><td>:-*</td><td>bisou</td></tr>
<tr><td>:[</td><td>abattu</td></tr>
<tr><td>@-`-,—</td><td>une rose</td></tr>
</table>

*NB: the '-' which depicts the nose is often omitted or replaced by an 'o' eg. :) or :o)

▶36

Phrasefinder

Key phrases / Phrases-clés

yes, please	oui, s'il vous plaît
no, thank you	non, merci
sorry!	désolé/-e!
you're welcome	de rien
Meeting people	**Rencontres**
hello/goodbye	bonjour/au revoir
how are you?	comment allez-vous?
nice to meet you!	enchanté/-e!
Asking questions	**Poser des questions**
do you speak English/French?	parlez-vous anglais/français?
what's your name?	comment vous appelez-vous?
where are you from?	d'où venez-vous?
how much is it?	combien ça coûte?
is it far?	c'est loin d'ici?
where is...?	où est...?
can I have...?	est-ce que je peux avoir...?
would you like...?	voulez-vous...?
About you	**Parler de soi**
my name is...	je m'appelle...
I'm English/French/American	je suis anglais/-e/français/-e/américain/-e
I don't speak French/English very well	je ne parle pas très bien français/anglais
I'm here on holiday	je suis en vacances ici

I live near Sheffield/Bordeaux	j'habite près de Sheffield/Bordeaux
I'm a student	je suis étudiant/-e

Emergencies	**Urgences**
can you help me?	pouvez-vous m'aider?
I'm lost	je me suis perdu/-e
I'm ill	je suis malade
call an ambulance	appelez une ambulance
watch out!	attention!

Reading signs	**Les pancartes**
no entry	défense d'entrer
no smoking	défense de fumer
fire exit	sortie de secours
for sale	à vendre
push	pousser
pull	tirer
press	appuyer

Going Places / Se déplacer

By rail and underground	En train et en métro
where can I buy a ticket?	où est-ce que je peux acheter un billet?
what time is the next train to Paris/New York?	à quelle heure est le prochain train pour Paris/New York?
do I have to change?	est-ce qu'il y a un changement?
can I take my bike on the train?	est-ce que je peux prendre mon vélo dans le train?
which platform for the train to Marseilles/Bath?	de quel quai part le train pour Marseille/Bath?
a single/return, (*Amer*) round trip to Baltimore/Nice, please	un aller/aller-retour pour Baltimore/ Nice, s'il vous plaît
I'd like an all-day ticket	je voudrais un billet valable toute la journée
I'd like to reserve a seat	je voudrais réserver une place
is there a student/senior citizen discount?	est-ce qu'il y a une réduction pour les étudiants/les personnes âgées?
is this the train for Lyons/Manchester?	est-ce que c'est bien le train pour Lyon/Manchester?
what time does the train arrive in Paris/London?	à quelle heure le train arrive-t-il à Paris/Londres?
have I missed the train?	est-ce que j'ai raté le train?
which line do I need to take for the Eiffel Tower/London Eye?	quelle ligne dois-je prendre pour aller à la tour Eiffel/au London Eye?

YOU WILL HEAR:	VOUS ENTENDREZ:
le train entre en gare au quai numéro 2	the train is arriving at platform 2
il y a un train pour Paris à 10 heures	there's a train to Paris at 10 o'clock
le train est en retard/à l'heure	the train is delayed/on time
prochain arrêt : ...	the next stop is...
votre ticket n'est pas valable	your ticket isn't valid

MORE USEFUL WORDS:	D'AUTRES MOTS UTILES:
underground station, (*Amer*) subway station	la station de métro
timetable	l'horaire
connection	la correspondance, le changement
express train	le train express
local train	le train régional
high-speed train	le TGV

DID YOU KNOW...?	LE SAVIEZ-VOUS...?
In a French train station, before you get on the train you must *composter* your ticket, i.e. have it stamped in the special machine positioned at the entrance of the platform to make it valid for your journey. You risk a fine if you forget to do this.	En Angleterre, l'aéroport de Londres–Heathrow est relié au centre de la capitale par le train Heathrow Express qui met moins de vingt minutes à parcourir ce trajet.

At the airport — En avion

when's the next flight to Paris/Rome?	quand part le prochain vol pour Paris/Rome?
what time do I have to check in?	à quelle heure est-ce que je dois me présenter à l'enregistrement?
where do I check in?	où est le comptoir d'enregistrement?
I'd like to confirm my flight	je voudrais confirmer mon vol
I'd like a window seat/an aisle seat	je voudrais une place côté fenêtre/ côté couloir
I want to change/cancel my reservation	je voudrais modifier/annuler ma réservation
can I carry this in my hand, (*Amer*) carry-on luggage?	puis-je prendre ce sac en bagage à main?
my luggage hasn't arrived	mes bagages ne sont pas arrivés

YOU WILL HEAR:	VOUS ENTENDREZ:
le vol BA7057 est retardé/annulé	flight BA7057 is delayed/cancelled
veuillez vous rendre à la porte d'embarquement numéro 29	please go to gate 29
votre carte d'embarquement, s'il vous plaît	your boarding card, please

MORE USEFUL WORDS:	D'AUTRES MOTS UTILES:
arrivals	arrivées
departures	départs
baggage claim	réception des bagages

Asking how to get there — Trouver son chemin

how do I get to the airport?	comment est-ce que je fais pour aller à l'aéroport?
how long will it take to get there?	combien de temps est-ce qu'il faut pour y arriver?
how far is it from here?	combien y a-t-il d'ici?
which bus do I take for the cathedral?	quel bus est-ce que je dois prendre pour aller à la cathédrale?
where does this bus go?	où va ce bus?
does this bus/train go to...?	est-ce que ce bus/train va à ...?
where do I get off?	pouvez-vous me dire où je dois descendre?
how much is it to the town centre?	quel est le prix d'un billet pour le centre-ville?...?
what time is the last bus?	à quelle heure est le dernier bus?
where's the nearest underground station, (*Amer*) subway station?	où est la station de métro la plus proche?
is this the turning for...?	est-ce que c'est là qu'il faut tourner pour aller à ...?
can you call me a taxi?	pouvez-vous m'appeler un taxi, s'il vous plaît?

YOU WILL HEAR:	VOUS ENTENDREZ:
prenez la première rue à droite	take the first turning on the right
prenez à gauche aux feux/juste après l'église	turn left at the traffic lights/just past the church

Disabled travellers | Les voyageurs handicapés

I'm disabled	je suis handicapé/-e
is there wheelchair access?	y a-t-il un accès pour les fauteuils roulants?
are guide dogs permitted?	les chiens d'aveugle sont-ils autorisés?

On the road | Par la route

where's the nearest petrol station, (*Amer*) gas station?	où se trouve la station d'essence la plus proche?
what's the best way to get there?	quel est le meilleur chemin pour y aller?
I've got a puncture, (*Amer*) flat tire	j'ai crevé
I'd like to hire, (*Amer*) rent a bike/car	je voudrais louer un vélo/une voiture
where can I park around here?	où peut-on se garer par ici?
there's been an accident	il y a eu un accident
my car's broken down	ma voiture est en panne
the car won't start	la voiture ne démarre pas
where's the nearest garage?	où se trouve le garage le plus proche?
pump number six, please	la pompe numéro 6, s'il vous plaît
fill it up, please	le plein, s'il vous plaît
can I get my car washed here?	est-ce que je peux utiliser le lavage automatique?
can I park here?	puis-je me garer ici?
there's a problem with the brakes/lights	il y a un problème de freins/phares
the clutch/gearstick isn't working	l'embrayage/le levier de vitesse ne fonctionne pas
take the third exit off the roundabout, (*Amer*) traffic circle	prenez la troisième sortie au rond-point
turn right at the next junction	tournez à droite au prochain carrefour
slow down	ralentissez
I can't drink – I'm driving	je ne peux pas boire d'alcool, je conduis
can I buy a road map here?	est-ce que vous vendez des cartes routières?

YOU WILL HEAR:	**VOUS ENTENDREZ:**
votre permis de conduire, s'il vous plaît?	**can I see your driving licence?**
vous devez remplir un constat d'accident	**you need to fill out an accident report**
c'est un sens unique	**this road is one-way**
il est interdit de se garer ici	**you can't park here**

MORE USEFUL WORDS:	D'AUTRES MOTS UTILES:
diesel	le diesel, le gazole
unleaded	sans plomb
motorway, (*Amer*) expressway	l'autoroute
toll	le péage
satnav, (*Amer*) GPS	le GPS
speed camera	le radar
roundabout	le rond-point
crossroads	l'intersection, le carrefour
dual carriageway, (*Amer*) divided highway	la route à quatre voies
traffic lights	les feux de circulation
driver	le conducteur/la conductrice

DID YOU KNOW...?	LE SAVIEZ-VOUS...?
The speed limits on French roads are as follows: motorway 130 km/h (80 m/h), 110 km/h (74 m/h) when it rains, open roads 90 km/h (56 m/h), towns and villages 50 km/h (31 mph).	Pour circuler dans le centre de Londres, les motoristes doivent payer une taxe appelée *congestion charge*.

COMMON FRENCH ROAD SIGNS

Aire de Lavallière : 2000 m	Lavallière rest area in two kilometres
Allumez vos feux	Switch on dipped headlights
Chaussée déformée	Uneven road surface
Circulation alternée, circulation à sens alterné	Contraflow
Déviation	Diverted traffic, Diversion
Halte péage/douanes/gendarmerie	Stop: Toll/ Customs/ Police
Interdiction de tourner à droite/ gauche	No right/left turn
Interdit sauf de 19h à 9h	No entry except between 7pm and 9am
Prochaine sortie : gendarmerie	Next exit: Police
Sauf riverains	Local residents only
Sens interdit	No entry
SOS (*on motorway*)	Emergency stopping area
Travaux sur 15 kms	Roadworks for 15 kms

Phrasefinder

PANNEAUX DE SIGNALISATION EN PAYS ANGLOPHONES

Cattle	Bétail
Contraflow	Circulation à sens alterné, circulation alternée
Ford	Passage à gué
Get in lane	Mettez-vous dans la bonne file
Give way	Cédez le passage
Keep clear	Arrêt et stationnement interdits
No overtaking, (*Amer*) Do not pass	Interdiction de dépasser
Pedestrians crossing	Passage pour piétons
Red route – no stopping	Axe rouge – arrêt et stationnement interdits
Reduce speed now	Ralentir
Stop	Stop

Keeping in touch / Rester en contact

On the phone — Au téléphone

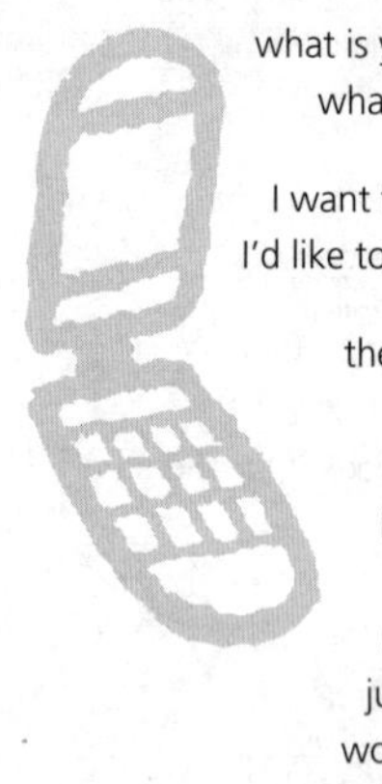

where can I buy a phone card?	où est-ce que je peux acheter une carte de téléphone?
may I use your phone?	est-ce que je peux utiliser votre téléphone?
do you have a mobile, (*Amer*) cell phone?	avez-vous un portable?
what is your phone number?	quel est votre numéro de téléphone?
what is the area code for Lyons/St Albans?	quel est l'indicatif pour Lyon/St Albans?
I want to make a phone call	je veux téléphoner
I'd like to reverse the charges, (*Amer*) call collect	je voudrais appeler en PCV
the line's engaged/busy	la ligne est occupée
there's no answer	ça ne répond pas
hello, this is Natalie	allô, c'est Natalie
is Jean there, please?	est-ce que Jean est là, s'il vous plaît?
who's calling?	qui est à l'appareil?
sorry, wrong number	désolé/-e, vous faites erreur
just a moment, please	un instant, s'il vous plaît
would you like to hold?	vous patientez?
it's a business/personal call	c'est un appel professionnel/privé
I'll put you through to him/her	je vous le/la passe
s/he cannot come to the phone at the moment	il/elle n'est pas disponible pour l'instant
please tell him/her I called	pourriez-vous lui dire que j'ai appelé?

I'd like to leave a message for him/her	j'aimerais lui laisser un message
I'll try again later	je réessaierai plus tard
please tell him/her that Marie called	pourriez-vous lui dire que Marie a appelé, s'il vous plaît
can he/she ring me back?	est-ce qu'il/elle peut me rappeler?
my home number is…	mon numéro personnel est...
my business number is…	mon numéro professionnel est...
my fax number is…	mon numéro de télécopie est...
we were cut off	on a été coupé
I'll call you later	je vous rappelle plus tard
I need to top up my phone	j'ai besoin de recharger mon portable
the battery's run out	il n'y a plus de batterie
I'm running low on credit	je n'ai presque plus de crédit sur mon portable
send me a text	envoie-moi un texto/message
there's no signal here	il n'y a pas de réception ici
you're breaking up	la ligne est mauvaise
could you speak a little louder?	pouvez-vous parler un peu plus fort?

YOU WILL HEAR:	**VOUS ENTENDREZ:**
allô	**hello**
appelez-moi sur mon portable	**call me on my mobile, (*Amer*) cell phone**
vous voulez laisser un message?	**would you like to leave a message?**

MORE USEFUL WORDS:	**D'AUTRES MOTS UTILES:**
text message	**le texto, le message**
top-up card	**la carte de recharge, la carte prépayée**
phone box, (*Amer*) phone booth	**la cabine téléphonique**
dial 3615	**composez le 3615**
directory enquiries	**les renseignements**

Writing — Écrire

what's your address?	quelle est votre adresse?
where is the nearest post office?	où est le bureau de poste le plus roche?
could I have a stamp for France/Italy, please?	je voudrais un timbre pour la France/l'Italie, s'il vous plaît
I'd like to send a parcel	je voudrais envoyer un paquet
where is the nearest postbox, (*Amer*) mailbox?	où se trouve la boîte aux lettres la plus proche?
dear Isabelle/Fred	Chère Isabelle/Cher Fred
dear Sir or Madam	Monsieur/Madame

yours sincerely	veuillez agréer, Monsieur/Madame, mes/nos sincères salutations
yours faithfully	veuillez agréer, Monsieur/Madame, mes/nos sincères salutations
best wishes	(*letter*) meilleurs vœux; (*e-mail*) bien amicalement

YOU WILL HEAR:	VOUS ENTENDREZ:
vous voulez l'envoyer en tarif normal?	would you like to send it first class?
c'est un objet de valeur?	is it valuable?

MORE USEFUL WORDS:	D'AUTRES MOTS UTILES:
letter	la lettre
postcode, (*Amer*) ZIP code	le code postal
airmail	par avion
fragile	fragile
urgent	urgent
registered post, (*Amer*) mail	le courrier recommandé

On line — En ligne

are you on the Internet?	êtes-vous sur Internet?
what's your e-mail address?	quelle est votre adresse électronique?
I'll e-mail it to you on Tuesday	je vous l'enverrai par courrier électronique mardi
I looked it up on the Internet	j'ai vérifié sur Internet
the information is on their website	l'information se trouve sur leur site Internet
my e-mail address is jane dot smith at new99 dot com	mon adresse électronique est jane point smith arobase new99 point com
can I check my e-mail here?	puis-je vérifier mon courrier électronique ici?
I have broadband/dial-up	j'ai une connexion Internet haut-débit/par ligne téléphonique
do you have wireless Internet access?	avez-vous un accès sans fil à Internet?
I'll send you the file as an attachment	je vous enverrai le fichier en pièce jointe

YOU WILL SEE:	VOUS VERREZ:
rechercher	search
double-cliquer sur l'icône	double-click on the icon
ouvrir l'application	open (up) the application
télécharger le fichier	download file

MORE USEFUL WORDS:	D'AUTRES MOTS UTILES:
subject (of an email)	le sujet
password	le mot de passe
social networking site	le site de réseau social
search engine	le moteur de recherche
mouse	la souris
keyboard	le clavier

Meeting up — Se retrouver

what shall we do this evening?	qu'est-ce qu'on fait ce soir?
do you want to go out tonight?	tu veux sortir ce soir?
where shall we meet?	où est-ce qu'on se retrouve?
I'll see you outside the café at 6 o'clock	on se retrouve à 6 heures devant le café
see you later	à tout à l'heure
I can't today, I'm busy	je ne peux pas aujourd'hui, je suis occupé/-e
I'm sorry, I've got something planned	je suis désolé/-e, j'ai déjà quelque chose de prévu
let's meet for a coffee in town	allons prendre un café en ville
would you like to see a show/film, (*Amer*) movie?	est-ce que tu voudrais aller voir un spectacle/un film?
what about next week instead?	la semaine prochaine alors?
shall we go for something to eat?	si on allait manger quelque part?

YOU WILL HEAR:	VOUS ENTENDREZ
enchanté/-e (de faire votre connaissance)	nice to meet you
puis-je vous offrir un verre?	can I buy you a drink?

MORE USEFUL WORDS:	D'AUTRES MOTS UTILES:
bar	le bar
bar (*serving counter in a bar/pub*)	le comptoir, le bar
meal	le repas
snack	le repas léger, le casse-croûte
date	le rendez-vous
cigarette	la cigarette

Phrasefinder

Food and Drink / Boire et manger

Booking a table / Réserver une table

can you recommend a good restaurant?	pouvez-vous me recommander un bon restaurant?
I'd like to reserve a table for four	je voudrais réserver une table pour quatre personnes
a reservation for tomorrow evening at eight o'clock	une réservation pour demain soir à huit heures
I booked a table for two	j'ai réservé une table pour deux

Ordering / Passer commande

could we see the menu/wine list, please?	est-ce qu'on pourrait voir la carte/ la carte des vins?
do you have a vegetarian/ children's menu?	est-ce que vous avez un menu végétarien/enfant?
what would you recommend?	que (nous) conseillez-vous?
I'd like a white/black coffee	J'aimerais un café/un café noir
... an espresso	… un express
... a decaffeinated coffee	… un café décaféiné
... a tea/a herbal tea	… un thé/une infusion
the bill, (*Amer*) check, please	l'addition, s'il vous plaît
we'd like to pay separately	on voudrait payer séparément

YOU WILL HEAR:	**ON VOUS DIRA:**
Désirez-vous un apéritif?	Would you like an aperitif?
Souhaitez-vous commander?	Are you ready to order?
Désirez-vous une entrée?	Would you like a starter?
Quel plat avez-vous choisi?	What will you have for the main course?
Je (vous) conseille le/la…	I can recommend the …
Souhaitez-vous prendre un dessert?	Would you like a dessert?
Désirez-vous un café/un digestif?	Would you like coffee?/a liqueur?
Désirez-vous autre chose?	Anything else?
Bon appétit	Enjoy your meal!

The menu Le menu

starters	entrées
hors d'oeuvres	hors d'œuvres
omelette	omelette
soup	soupe

fish	poisson
bass	perche
cod	cabillaud
eel	anguille
hake	colin
herring	hareng
monkfish	lotte
mullet	mulet
mussels	moules
oysters	huîtres
prawns	crevettes roses
salmon	saumon
sardines	sardines
shrimps	crevettes grises
sole	sole
squid	cal(a)mar
trout	truite
tuna	thon
turbot	turbot

meat	viande
beef	bœuf
chicken	poulet
duck	canard
goose	oie
guinea fowl	pintade
hare	lièvre
kidneys	rognons
lamb	agneau
liver	foie
pork	porc
rabbit	lapin
steak	bifteck
veal	veau
wild boar	sanglier

entrées	starters
hors d'œuvres	hors d'oeuvres
omelette	omelette
soupe	soup

poisson	fish
anguille	eel
cabillaud	cod
cal(a)mar	squid
crevettes grises	shrimps
crevettes roses	prawns
colin	hake
hareng	herring
huîtres	oysters
lotte	monkfish
moules	mussels
mulet	mullet
perche	bass
sardines	sardines
saumon	salmon
sole	sole
thon	tuna
truite	trout
turbot	turbot

viande	meat
agneau	lamb
bifteck	steak
bœuf	beef
canard	duck
foie	liver
lapin	rabbit
lièvre	hare
oie	goose
poulet	chicken
pintade	guinea fowl
porc	pork
rognons	kidneys
sanglier	wild boar
veau	veal

vegetables	légumes
artichokes	artichaut
asparagus	asperges
aubergine	aubergine
cabbage	chou
carrots	carrottes
cauliflower	chou-fleur
celery	céleri
courgettes	courgettes
endive	endives
green beans	haricots verts
mushrooms	champignons
onions	oignons
peas	petits pois
peppers	poivron
potatoes	pommes de terre
spinach	épinards

the way it's cooked	la cuisson
fried	poêlé
grilled	grillé
medium rare	à point
puréed	mixé
rare	saignant
roast	rôti
steamed	à la vapeur
stewed	cuit à l'étouffée
very rare	bleu
well done	bien cuit

desserts	fromages et desserts
cheeseboard	plateau de fromages
fruit	fruit
ice cream	glace
pie	tarte (recouverte de pâte)
sorbet	sorbet
tart	tarte

légumes	vegetables
artichaut	artichokes
asperges	asparagus
aubergine	aubergine
carrottes	carrots
céleri	celery
champignons	mushrooms
chou	cabbage
chou-fleur	cauliflower
courgettes	courgettes
endives	endive
épinards	spinach
haricots verts	green beans
oignons	onions
petits pois	peas
poivron	peppers
pommes de terre	potatoes

la cuisson	the way it's cooked
à la vapeur	steamed
à point	medium rare
bien cuit	well done
bleu	very rare
cuit à l'étouffée	stewed
grillé	grilled
mixé	puréed
poêlé	fried
rôti	roast
saignant	rare

fromages et desserts	desserts
fruit	fruit
glace	ice cream
plateau de fromages	cheeseboard
sorbet	sorbet
tarte	tart
tarte (recouverte de pâte)	pie

sundries	divers
bread	pain
butter	beurre
green salad	salade verte
herbs	herbes
mayonnaise	mayonnaise
mustard	moutarde
olive oil	huile d'olive
pepper	poivre
salt	sel
sauce	sauce
seasoning	assaisonnement
vinegar	vinaigre

divers	sundries
assaisonnement	seasoning
beurre	butter
herbes	herbs
huile d'olive	olive oil
mayonnaise	mayonnaise
moutarde	mustard
pain	bread
poivre	pepper
salade verte	green salad
sauce	sauce
sel	salt
vinaigre	vinegar

drinks	boissons
beer	bière
bottle	bouteille
carbonated	gazeux
half-bottle	demi-bouteille
liqueur	digestif
mineral water	eau minérale
red wine	vin rouge
rosé	rosé
soft drinks	boissons non alcoolisées
still	plat, non gazeux
table wine	vin de table
white wine	vin blanc
wine	vin

boissons	drinks
bière	beer
boissons non alcoolisées	soft drinks
bouteille	bottle
demi-bouteille	half-bottle
digestif	liqueur
eau minérale	mineral water
gazeux	carbonated
plat	still
rosé	rosé
vin	wine
vin blanc	white wine
vin de table	table wine
vin rouge	red wine

Places to stay / Où dormir

Camping	Camper
can we pitch our tent here?	est-ce qu'on peut planter notre tente ici?
can we park our caravan here?	est-ce qu'on peut mettre notre caravane ici?
what are the facilities like?	le camping est-il bien équipé?
how much is it per night?	c'est combien par nuit?
where do we park the car?	où est-ce qu'on peut garer la voiture?
we're looking for a campsite	on cherche un camping
this is a list of local campsites	c'est une liste des campings de la région
we go on a camping holiday every year	nous partons camper chaque année pour les vacances

At the hotel | À l'hôtel

I'd like a double/single room with bath	je voudrais une chambre double/simple avec bain
we have a reservation in the name of Milne	nous avons une réservation au nom de Milne
we'll be staying three nights, from Friday to Sunday	nous resterons trois nuits, de vendredi à dimanche
how much does the room cost?	combien coûte la chambre?
I'd like to see the room, please	je voudrais voir la chambre, s'il vous plaît
what time is breakfast?	à quelle heure est le petit déjeuner?
bed and breakfast	chambres d'hôtes
we'd like to stay another night	on voudrait rester une nuit de plus
please call me at 7:30	réveillez-moi à 7h30
are there any messages for me?	est-ce qu'il y a des messages pour moi?

Hostels | Auberges de jeunesse

could you tell me where the youth hostel is?	pourriez-vous me dire où se trouve l'auberge de jeunesse?
what time does the hostel close?	à quelle heure ferme l'auberge de jeunesse?
I'm staying in a hostel	je loge à l'auberge de jeunesse
I know a really good hostel in Dublin	je connais une très bonne auberge de jeunesse à Dublin
I'd like to go backpacking in Australia	j'aimerais bien aller faire de la randonnée en Australie

Rooms to let | Locations

I'm looking for a room with a reasonable rent	je cherche une chambre à louer avec un loyer raisonnable
I'd like to rent an apartment for a few weeks	je voudrais louer un appartement pendant quelques semaines
where do I find out about rooms to let?	où est-ce que je peux me renseigner sur des chambres à louer?
what's the weekly rent?	quel est le montant du loyer pour la semaine?
I'm staying with friends at the moment	je loge chez des amis pour le moment
I rent an apartment on the outskirts of town	je loue un appartement en banlieue
the room's fine – I'll take it	la chambre est bien – je la prends
the deposit is one month's rent in advance	l'acompte correspond à un mois de loyer payable d'avance

Shopping / Achats

At the bank / À la banque

At the bank	À la banque
I'd like to change some money	je voudrais changer de l'argent
I want to change some euros into pounds	je veux changer des euros en livres
do you take Eurocheques?	acceptez-vous les Eurochèques?
what's the exchange rate today?	quel est le taux de change aujourd'hui?
I prefer traveller's cheques, (*Amer*) traveler's checks to cash	je préfère les chèques de voyage à l'argent liquide
I'd like to transfer some money from my account	je voudrais retirer de l'argent sur mon compte
I'll get some money from the cash machine	je vais retirer de l'argent au distributeur
I usually pay by direct debit	d'habitude, je paye par prélèvement automatique

Finding the right shop / Trouver le bon magasin

Finding the right shop	Trouver le bon magasin
where's the main shopping district?	où se trouve le principal quartier commerçant?
where's a good place to buy sunglasses?	quel est le meilleur endroit pour acheter des lunettes de soleil?
where can I buy batteries/postcards?	où est-ce que je peux acheter des piles/cartes postales?
where's the nearest chemist/bookshop?	où est la pharmacie/librairie la plus proche?
is there a good food shop around here?	est-ce qu'il y a une bonne épicerie près d'ici?
what time do the shops open/close?	à quelle heure ouvrent/ferment les magasins?
where did you get those?	où les avez-vous trouvés?
I'm looking for presents for my family	je cherche des cadeaux pour ma famille
we'll do all our shopping on Saturday	nous ferons toutes nos courses samedi

Are you being served? / On s'occupe de vous?

Are you being served?	On s'occupe de vous?
how much does that cost?	combien ça coûte?
can I try it on?	est-ce que je peux l'essayer?
can you keep it for me?	pouvez-vous me le/la garder?
do you have this in another colour, (*Amer*) color?	est-ce que vous avez ce modèle-ci dans une autre couleur?
I'm just looking	je regarde
I'll think about it	je vais réfléchir
I need a bigger/smaller size	il me faut une taille au-dessus/au-dessous

I take a size 10/a medium	je fais du 38/il me faut une taille moyenne
it doesn't suit me	ça ne me va pas
could you wrap it for me, please?	pourriez-vous l'emballer, s'il vous plaît?
do you take credit cards?	est-ce que vous acceptez les cartes de crédit?
can I pay by cheque, (*Amer*) check?	est-ce que je peux payer par chèque?
I'm sorry, I don't have any change	je suis désolé/-e mais je n'ai pas de monnaie
I'd like a receipt, please	je voudrais un reçu, s'il vous plaît

Changing things — Faire un échange

can I have a refund?	j'aimerais être remboursé/-e
can you mend it for me?	est-ce que vous pouvez me le/la réparer?
can I speak to the manager?	je voudrais parler au responsable
it doesn't work	ça ne marche pas
I'd like to change it, please	je voudrais l'échanger, s'il vous plaît
I bought this here yesterday	je l'ai acheté/-e ici hier

Leisure time / Temps libre

Movies/theatres/clubs — Aller au cinéma/théâtre/en boîte

what's on?	qu'est-ce qu'il y a au programme?
when does the box office open/close?	à quelle heure ouvre/ferme le guichet?
what time does the concert/performance start?	à quelle heure commence le concert/la représentation?
when does it finish?	à quelle heure ça finit?
are there any seats left for tonight?	est-ce qu'il y a encore des places pour ce soir?
how much are the tickets?	combien coûtent les billets?
where can I get a programme, (*Amer*) program?	où est-ce que je peux me procurer un programme?
I want to book tickets for tonight's performance	je veux réserver des places pour la représentation de ce soir
I'll book seats in the circle	je vais réserver des places au balcon
I'd rather have seats in the stalls, (*Amer*) orchestra	je préfère avoir des places à l'orchestre
somewhere in the middle, but not too far back	au milieu, mais pas trop loin de la scène
four, please	quatre, s'il vous plaît
we'd like to go to a club	on voudrait aller en boîte

Hobbies / Passe-temps

what do you do at, (*Amer*) on weekends?	que faites-vous les week-ends?
I like reading/listening to music/going out	j'aime lire/écouter de la musique/sortir
do you like watching TV/shopping/ travelling, (*Amer*) traveling?	est-ce que tu aimes regarder la télé/faire du shopping/voyager?
I read a lot	je lis beaucoup
I collect comic books	je collectionne les bandes dessinées

Good timing / En temps et en heure

Telling the time / Exprimer l'heure

could you tell me the time?	pourriez-vous me dire l'heure?
what time is it?	quelle heure est-il?
it's 2 o'clock	il est 2 heures
at about 8 o'clock	vers 8 heures
at 9 o'clock tomorrow	à 9 heures demain
from 10 o'clock onwards	à partir de 10 heures
it starts at 8 p.m.	ça commence à 20 heures
at 5 o'clock in the morning/afternoon	à 5 heures du matin/de l'après-midi
it's five past/quarter past/half past one	il est une heure cinq/et quart/et demie
it's twenty-five to/quarter to/five to one	il est une heure moins vingt-cinq/ le quart/cinq
a quarter of an hour	un quart d'heure

Days and dates / Jours et dates

Sunday, Monday, Tuesday, Wednesday,	dimanche, lundi, mardi, mercredi,
Thursday, Friday, Saturday	jeudi, vendredi, samedi
January, February, March,	janvier, février, mars,
April, May, June, July,	avril, mai, juin, juillet,
August, September, October,	août, septembre, octobre,
November, December	novembre, décembre
what's the date today?	on est le combien aujourd'hui?
it's the second of June	on est le deux juin
what day is it? it's Monday	on est quel jour? on est lundi
we meet up every Monday	on se réunit tous les lundis
she comes on Tuesdays	elle vient le mardi
we're going away in August	nous partons en août
on November 8th	le 8 novembre

Public holidays and special days	Jours fériés
Bank holiday	jour férié
long weekend	week-end prolongé
New Year's Day (1 Jan)	le Jour de l'an
St Valentine's Day (14 Feb)	la Saint-Valentin
Shrove Tuesday/Pancake Day	Mardi gras
Ash Wednesday	le mercredi des Cendres
Mother's Day	la fête des Mères
Palm Sunday	le dimanche des Rameaux
Good Friday	vendredi saint
Easter Day	Pâques
Easter Monday	le lundi de Pâques
Ascension Day	l'Ascension
Pentecost/Whitsun	la Pentecôte
Whit Monday	le lundi de Pentecôte
Father's Day	la fête des Pères
St John the Baptist's Day (24 Jun)	la Saint-Jean
Independence day (4 Jul)	la fête de l'Indépendance (aux États-Unis)
Bastille day (14 July)	le 14 juillet
Halloween (31 Oct)	Halloween (soir des fantômes et des sorcières)
All Saints' Day (1 Nov)	la Toussaint
Guy Fawkes Day/Bonfire Night (5 Nov)	fête de la Conspiration des Poudres avec feux de joie et feux d'artifice
Remembrance Sunday	le jour du Souvenir
Thanksgiving	le jour d'Action de grâces
Christmas Day (25 Dec)	Noël
Boxing Day (26 Dec)	le lendemain de Noël
New Year's Eve (31 Dec)	la Saint-Sylvestre

Aa

a¹, **A** /eɪ/ *n* **1** (letter) a, A *m*
2 A (Mus) la *m*

a², **an** /eɪ, ə/ *det* un/une

> The determiner or indefinite article *a* or *an* is translated by *un* + *masculine noun* and by *une* + *feminine noun*: *a tree* = un arbre; *a chair* = une chaise. There are, however, some cases where the article is not translated:
> with professions and trades: *her mother is a teacher* = sa mère est professeur;
> with other nouns used in apposition: *he's a widower* = il est veuf;
> with *what a*: *what a pretty house* = quelle jolie maison.
> When expressing prices in relation to weight, the definite article *le*/*la* is used in French: *ten euros a kilo* = dix euros le kilo. In other expressions where *a*/*an* means *per* the French translation is *par*: *twice a day* = deux fois par jour; but: *50 kilometres an hour* = 50 kilomètres/heure.

A2 level /ˌeɪˈtuː ˌlevl/ *n* (BrE) *seconde moitié des épreuves pour les A levels*

aback /əˈbæk/ *adv* **to be taken ~** être déconcerté/-e

abandon /əˈbændən/ *vt* abandonner ‹*person, hope*›; renoncer à ‹*activity, attempt*›

abbey /ˈæbɪ/ *n* abbaye *f*

abbreviate /əˈbriːvɪeɪt/ *vt* abréger (**to** en)

abbreviation /əˌbriːvɪˈeɪʃn/ *n* abréviation *f*

abdomen /ˈæbdəmən/ *n* abdomen *m*

abduct /əbˈdʌkt/ *vt* enlever

abide /əˈbaɪd/ *vi* (*prét, pp* **abode**, **~d**) **to ~ by** respecter ‹*rule, decision*›

ability /əˈbɪlətɪ/ *n* **1** (capability) capacité *f*; **to the best of one's ~** de son mieux
2 (talent) talent *m*

able /ˈeɪbl/ *adj*

> *to be able to* meaning *can* is usually translated by the verb *pouvoir*: *I was not able to help him* = je ne pouvais pas l'aider.
> When *to be able to* implies the acquiring of skill, *savoir* is used: *he's nine and he's still not able to read* = il a neuf ans et il ne sait toujours pas lire.

1 to be ~ to do pouvoir faire; **she was ~ to play the piano at the age of four** elle savait jouer du piano à quatre ans **2** ‹*lawyer, teacher*› compétent/-e; ‹*child*› doué/-e

able-bodied *adj* robuste, fort/-e

abnormal /æbˈnɔːml/ *adj* anormal/-e

abnormality /ˌæbnɔːˈmælətɪ/ *n* anomalie *f*

aboard /əˈbɔːd/ **A** *adv* à bord
B *prep* à bord de ‹*plane*›; dans ‹*train*›; **~ ship** à bord

abolish /əˈbɒlɪʃ/ *vt* abolir ‹*law, right*›; supprimer ‹*service, allowance*›

abolition /ˌæbəˈlɪʃn/ *n* (of law, right) abolition *f*; (of service) suppression *f*

abominable /əˈbɒmɪnəbl/ *adj* abominable

aborigine /ˌæbəˈrɪdʒənɪ/ *n* aborigène *mf*

abort /əˈbɔːt/ *vt* faire avorter ‹*foetus*›; abandonner ‹*computer program*›

abortion /əˈbɔːʃn/ *n* avortement *m*; **to have an ~** se faire avorter

abortive /əˈbɔːtɪv/ *adj* ‹*attempt, project*› avorté/-e; ‹*coup, raid*› manqué/-e

about /əˈbaʊt/ **A** *adj* **to be ~ to do** être sur le point de faire
B *adv* **1** environ, à peu près; **~ an hour** environ une heure; **it's ~ the same** c'est à peu près pareil; **at ~ 6 pm** vers 18 h; **it's just ~ ready** c'est presque prêt
2 there was no one ~ il n'y avait personne; **there is a lot of flu ~** il y a beaucoup de grippes en ce moment; **he's somewhere ~** il est dans les parages
C *prep* **1** (concerning) **a book ~ France** un livre sur la France; **what's it ~?** (of book, film) ça parle de quoi?; **may I ask what it's ~?** pourriez-vous me dire de quoi il s'agit?; **it's ~ my son** c'est au sujet de mon fils
2 there's something odd ~ him il a quelque chose de bizarre; **what I like ~ her is her honesty** ce que j'aime chez elle c'est sa franchise
3 (around) **to wander ~ the streets** errer dans les rues
4 how *or* **what ~ some tea?** et si on prenait un thé?; **how ~ going into town?** et si on allait en ville?
5 what ~ the legal costs? et les frais de justice?; **what ~ you?** et toi?
IDIOMS **it's ~ time (that) somebody made an effort** il serait temps que quelqu'un fasse un effort; **~ time too!** ce n'est pas trop tôt! (fam)

about-face *n* volte-face *f inv*

above /əˈbʌv/ **A** *prep* au-dessus de; **~ the painting** au-dessus du tableau; **~ it** au-dessus; **children ~ the age of 12** les enfants âgés de plus de 12 ans; **~ all else** par-dessus tout; **to hear sth ~ the shouting** entendre qch au milieu des cris
B *adj* **the ~ items** les articles susmentionnés *or* figurant ci-dessus

C *adv* **1** au-dessus; **a desk with a shelf ~** un bureau avec une étagère au-dessus; **the apartment ~** l'appartement du dessus
2 (in text) **see ~** voir ci-dessus
3 (more) plus; **children of 12 and ~** les enfants âgés de 12 ans et plus
D **above all** *phr* surtout

above-mentioned *adj* susmentionné/-e

abrasive /ə'breɪsɪv/ *adj* ‹*person, manner*› mordant/-e

abreast /ə'brest/ *adv* **to walk three ~** marcher à trois de front; **to keep ~ of** se tenir au courant de

abroad /ə'brɔ:d/ *adv* à l'étranger; **from ~** de l'étranger

abrupt /ə'brʌpt/ *adj* brusque

ABS *n* (*abbr* = **anti-lock braking system**) ABS; **~ brakes** freins *mpl* ABS

abscess /'æbses/ *n* abcès *m*

abseiling /'æbseɪlɪŋ/ *n* (BrE) descente *f* en rappel

🔑 **absence** /'æbsəns/ *n* absence *f*

absent /'æbsənt/ *adj* absent/-e (**from** de)

absentee /,æbsən'ti:/ *n* absent/-e *m/f*

absentee ballot *n* bulletin de vote *m* d'un (électeur) absent

absent-minded *adj* distrait/-e

absolute /'æbsəlu:t/ *adj* absolu/-e

🔑 **absolutely** /'æbsəlu:tlɪ/ *adv* absolument

absorb /əb'zɔ:b/ *vt* absorber; **~ed in one's work** plongé/-e dans son travail

absorbent /əb'zɔ:bənt/ *adj* absorbant/-e

abstain /əb'steɪn/ *vi* s'abstenir (**from** de)

abstract /'æbstrækt/ *adj* abstrait/-e

absurd /əb'sɜ:d/ *adj* absurde, ridicule

abundant /ə'bʌndənt/ *adj* abondant/-e

🔑 **abuse** **A** /ə'bju:s/ *n* **1** (maltreatment) mauvais traitement *m*; (sexual) sévices *mpl* (sexuels)
2 (of alcohol, power) abus *m*; **drug ~** usage *m* des stupéfiants
3 (insults) injures *fpl*
B /ə'bju:z/ *vt* **1** (hurt) maltraiter; (sexually) abuser de ‹*woman*›; exercer des sévices sexuels sur ‹*child*›
2 abuser de ‹*position, power, trust*›
3 (insult) injurier

abusive /ə'bju:sɪv/ *adj* ‹*person*› grossier/-ière; ‹*words*› injurieux/-ieuse

abyss /ə'bɪs/ *n* abîme *m*

🔑 **academic** /,ækə'demɪk/ **A** *n* universitaire *mf*
B *adj* **1** ‹*career, book*› universitaire; ‹*year*› académique
2 (theoretical) théorique

academy /ə'kædəmɪ/ *n* (school) école *f*; (learned society) académie *f*

accelerate /ək'seləreɪt/ *vi* accélérer

accelerator /ək'seləreɪtə(r)/ *n* accélérateur *m*

accent /'æksent, -sənt/ *n* accent *m*

accentuate /æk'sentʃʊeɪt/ *vt* souligner

🔑 **accept** /ək'sept/ *vt* (gen) accepter; (tolerate) admettre

acceptable /ək'septəbl/ *adj* acceptable

acceptance /ək'septəns/ *n* acceptation *f*

🔑 **access** /'ækses/ **A** *n* accès *m*; **to have ~ to** avoir accès à ‹*information, funds, place*›
B *vt* accéder à ‹*database, information*›

accessible /ək'sesəbl/ *adj* accessible (**to** à)

accessory /ək'sesərɪ/ *n* accessoire *m*; (on car) extra *m*

🔑 **accident** /'æksɪdənt/ *n* accident *m*; **car/road ~** accident de voiture/de la route; **by ~** accidentellement; (by chance) par hasard

accidental /,æksɪ'dentl/ *adj* **1** ‹*death*› accidentel/-elle
2 ‹*mistake*› fortuit/-e

accidentally /,æksɪ'dentəlɪ/ *adv* **1** (by accident) accidentellement
2 (by chance) par hasard

accident-prone /,æksɪdənt'prəʊn/ *adj* sujet/-ette aux accidents

accommodate /ə'kɒmədeɪt/ *vt* **1** (put up) loger
2 (hold, provide space for) contenir
3 (adapt to) s'adapter à ‹*change, view*›
4 (satisfy) satisfaire ‹*need*›

accommodating /ə'kɒmədeɪtɪŋ/ *adj* accommodant/-e (**to** envers)

accommodation /ə,kɒmə'deɪʃn/ *n* (*also* **~s** (AmE)) logement *m*

accommodation officer *n* responsable *mf* de l'hébergement

🔑 **accompany** /ə'kʌmpənɪ/ *vt* accompagner

accomplice /ə'kʌmplɪs, (AmE) ə'kɒm-/ *n* complice *mf*

accomplish /ə'kʌmplɪʃ, (AmE) ə'kɒm-/ *vt* accomplir ‹*task, mission*›; réaliser ‹*objective*›

accomplishment /ə'kʌmplɪʃmənt, (AmE) ə'kɒm-/ *n* réussite *f*

accord /ə'kɔ:d/ *n* accord *m*; **of my own ~** de moi-même

accordance: **in accordance with** /ə'kɔ:dəns/ *phr* ‹*act*› conformément à ‹*rules, instructions*›; ‹*be*› conforme à ‹*law, agreement*›

according: **according to** /ə'kɔ:dɪŋ/ *phr* **1** ‹*act*› selon ‹*law, principles*›; **~ to plan** comme prévu
2 d'après ‹*newspaper, person*›

accordingly /ə'kɔ:dɪŋlɪ/ *adv* en conséquence

accordion /ə'kɔ:dɪən/ *n* accordéon *m*

accost /ə'kɒst/ *vt* (approach) aborder; (sexually) accoster

🔑 **account** /ə'kaʊnt/ **A** *n* **1** (in bank, post office, shop) compte *m* (**at, with** à); **in my ~** sur mon compte
2 to take sth into ~, to take ~ of sth tenir compte de qch

🔑 mot clé

3 (description) compte-rendu *m*
4 on ~ of à cause de; **on no ~** sous aucun prétexte; **on my ~** à cause de moi
B accounts *npl* **1** (records) comptabilité *f*, comptes *mpl*
2 (department) (service *m*) comptabilité *f*
▪ **account for 1** (explain) expliquer ‹*fact, behaviour*›; justifier ‹*expense*›
2 (represent) représenter ‹*proportion, percentage*›

accountable /ə'kaʊntəbl/ *adj* responsable (**to** devant, **for** de)

accountancy /ə'kaʊntənsɪ/ *n* comptabilité *f*

accountant /ə'kaʊntənt/ *n* comptable *mf*

account holder *n* titulaire *mf*

account manager *n* responsable *mf* de clientèle

account number *n* numéro *m* de compte

accumulate /ə'kjuːmjʊleɪt/ **A** *vt* accumuler **B** *vi* s'accumuler

accuracy /'ækjərəsɪ/ *n* (of figures, watch) justesse *f*; (of map, aim) précision *f*; (of forecast) exactitude *f*

accurate /'ækjərət/ *adj* ‹*figures, watch, information*› juste; ‹*report, map, forecast*› exact/-e

accurately /'ækjərətlɪ/ *adv* ‹*calculate*› exactement; ‹*report*› avec exactitude; ‹*assess*› précisément

accusation /ˌækjuː'zeɪʃn/ *n* accusation *f*

accuse /ə'kjuːz/ *vt* accuser (**of** de)

accused /ə'kjuːzd/ *n* **the ~** l'accusé/-e *m/f*

accuser /ə'kjuːzə(r)/ *n* accusateur/-trice *m/f*

accustomed /ə'kʌstəmd/ *adj* **1 to be ~ to sth/to doing** avoir l'habitude de qch/de faire
2 (usual) habituel/-elle

ace /eɪs/ *n* as *m*

ache /eɪk/ **A** *n* douleur *f* (**in** à)
B *vi* ‹*person*› avoir mal; **my back ~s** j'ai mal au dos

achieve /ə'tʃiːv/ *vt* atteindre ‹*aim*›; atteindre à ‹*perfection*›; obtenir ‹*result*›; réaliser ‹*ambition*›

achievement /ə'tʃiːvmənt/ *n* réussite *f*

aching /'eɪkɪŋ/ *adj* ‹*body, limbs*› douloureux/-euse

acid /'æsɪd/ *n, adj* acide *m*

acid rain *n* pluies *fpl* acides

acknowledge /ək'nɒlɪdʒ/ *vt* admettre ‹*fact*›; reconnaître ‹*error, problem, authority*›; accuser réception de ‹*letter*›

acknowledgement /ək'nɒlɪdʒmənt/ **A** *n*
1 (of error, guilt) aveu *m*
2 (confirmation of receipt) accusé *m* de réception
B acknowledgements *npl* (in book) remerciements *mpl*

acne /'æknɪ/ *n* acné *f*

acorn /'eɪkɔːn/ *n* gland *m*

acoustic /ə'kuːstɪk/ *adj* acoustique

acoustic guitar *n* guitare *f* sèche

acoustics /ə'kuːstɪks/ *npl* **the ~ are good** l'acoustique *f* est bonne

acquaintance /ə'kweɪntəns/ *n* connaissance *f* (**with** de)

acquainted *adj* **to be ~** se connaître; **to get** *or* **become ~ with sb** faire la connaissance de qn; **to get** *or* **become ~ with sth** découvrir qch

acquiesce /ˌækwɪ'es/ *vi* accepter; **to ~ in sth** donner son accord tacite à qch

acquire /ə'kwaɪə(r)/ *vt* acquérir ‹*expertise*›; obtenir ‹*information*›; faire l'acquisition de ‹*possessions*›; acheter ‹*company*›

acquit /ə'kwɪt/ *vt* (*p prés etc* **-tt-**) (Law) acquitter; **to be ~ted** être disculpé/-e (**of** de)

acre /'eɪkə(r)/ *n* acre *f*, ≈ demi-hectare *m*

acrobat /'ækrəbæt/ *n* acrobate *mf*

acrobatics /ˌækrə'bætɪks/ *npl* acrobaties *fpl*

across /ə'krɒs/ **A** *prep* **1 a journey ~ the desert** un voyage à travers le désert; **the bridge ~ the river** le pont qui traverse la rivière; **to go** *or* **travel ~ sth** traverser qch; **she leaned ~ the table** elle s'est penchée au-dessus de la table
2 (on the other side of) de l'autre côté de; **~ the street (from me)** de l'autre côté de la rue
B *adv* **to help sb ~** aider qn à traverser; **to go ~ to sb** aller vers qn; **to look ~ at sb** regarder dans la direction de qn
C across from *phr* en face de

acrylic /ə'krɪlɪk/ *n* acrylique *m*

act /ækt/ **A** *n* **1** acte *m*; **an ~ of kindness** un acte de bonté
2 (Law) loi *f*; **Act of Parliament** loi votée par le Parlement
3 (in show) numéro *m*
4 to put on an ~ jouer la comédie
B *vt* jouer ‹*part, role*›
C *vi* **1** (take action) agir
2 (behave) agir, se comporter
3 ‹*actor*› jouer, faire du théâtre
4 (pretend) jouer la comédie, faire semblant
5 (take effect) ‹*drug*› agir
6 to ~ as ‹*person, object*› servir de
▪ **act out** jouer ‹*role, part*›; réaliser ‹*fantasy*›

acting /'æktɪŋ/ **A** *n* (performance) jeu *m*, interprétation *f*; (occupation) métier *m* d'acteur; **I've done some ~** j'ai fait du théâtre
B *adj* ‹*director, manager*› intérimaire

action /'ækʃn/ *n* **1** (gen) action *f*; (steps) mesures *fpl*; **to take ~** agir, prendre des mesures (**against** contre); **to put a plan into ~** mettre un projet à exécution
2 (fighting) action *f*, combat *m*; **killed in ~** tué/-e au combat
3 (in filming) action *f*; **~!** moteur!

action film *n* film *m* d'action

action group *n* groupe *m* de pression

action-packed *adj* ‹*film*› plein/-e d'action; ‹*holiday*› bien rempli/-e

action replay *n* (BrE) répétition *f* d'une séquence

activate /'æktɪveɪt/ *vt* faire démarrer ‹*system*›; actionner ‹*switch*›; déclencher ‹*alarm*›

🔑 **active** /'æktɪv/ *adj* ‹*person, life*› actif/-ive; ‹*volcano*› en activité

activist /'æktɪvɪst/ *n* activiste *mf*

🔑 **activity** /æk'tɪvətɪ/ *n* activité *f*

activity holiday *n* (BrE) ≈ vacances *fpl* sportives

🔑 **actor** /'æktə(r)/ *n* acteur *m*, comédien *m*

actress /'æktrɪs/ *n* actrice *f*, comédienne *f*

🔑 **actual** /'æktʃʊəl/ *adj* ‹*circumstances*› réel/réelle; ‹*words*› exact/-e; **in ~ fact** en fait; **the ~ problem** le problème lui-même

🔑 **actually** /'æktʃʊəlɪ/ *adv* **1** (in fact) en fait; **their profits have ~ risen** en fait, leurs bénéfices ont augmenté; **~, I don't feel like it** à vrai dire je n'en ai pas envie
2 (really) vraiment; **yes, it ~ happened!** mais oui, c'est vraiment arrivé!

acupuncture /'ækjʊpʌŋktʃə(r)/ *n* acupuncture *f*

acute /ə'kju:t/ *adj* **1** ‹*anxiety, pain*› vif/vive; ‹*boredom*› profond/-e
2 ‹*illness*› aigu/aiguë
3 ‹*mind*› pénétrant/-e
4 ‹*accent, angle*› aigu/aiguë

🔑 **ad** /æd/ *n* (*abbr* = **advertisement**) **1 (small) ~** (petite) annonce *f* (**for** pour)
2 (on radio, TV) pub *f* (fam) (**for** pour)

AD (*abbr* = **Anno Domini**) ap J.-C.

adamant /'ædəmənt/ *adj* catégorique (**about** sur); **he is ~ that** il maintient que

adapt /ə'dæpt/ **A** *vt* adapter (**to** à, **for** pour, **from** de)
B *vi* ‹*person*› s'adapter (**to** à)

adaptable /ə'dæptəbl/ *adj* souple

adapter, **adaptor** /ə'dæptə(r)/ *n* adaptateur *m*

🔑 **add** /æd/ *vt* **1** ajouter, rajouter (**onto, to** à)
2 (*also* **~ together**) additionner ‹*numbers*›; **to ~ sth to** ajouter qch à ‹*figure, total*›
▪ **add up**: **A** *vi* **~ up** ‹*facts, figures*› s'accorder; **to ~ up to** s'élever à ‹*total*›
B *vt* **~ up [sth]** additionner ‹*cost, numbers*›

adder /'ædə(r)/ *n* (snake) vipère *f*

addict /'ædɪkt/ *n* **1** (drug-user) toxicomane *mf*
2 (of TV, coffee) accro *mf* (fam) (**of** de)

addicted /ə'dɪktɪd/ *adj* **to be ~** (to alcohol, drugs) avoir une dépendance (**to** à); (to TV, coffee) être accro (fam) (**to** de)

addiction /ə'dɪkʃn/ *n* dépendance *f* (**to** à)

addictive /ə'dɪktɪv/ *adj* ‹*drug, substance*› qui crée une dépendance; **to be ~** ‹*chocolate, power*› être comme une drogue

🔑 **addition** /ə'dɪʃn/ **A** *n* **1** (to list, house) ajout *m*
2 (in mathematics) addition *f*
B **in addition** *phr* en plus

🔑 **additional** /ə'dɪʃənl/ *adj* supplémentaire

additive /'ædɪtɪv/ *n* additif *m*

add-on /'ædɒn/ *adj* supplémentaire

🔑 **address** /ə'dres, (AmE) 'ædres/ **A** *n* adresse *f*; **to change (one's) ~** changer d'adresse
B *vt* **1** mettre l'adresse sur ‹*parcel, letter*›; **to ~ sth to sb** adresser qch à qn
2 (speak to) s'adresser à ‹*group*›
3 (aim) adresser ‹*remark, complaint*› (**to** à)

address book *n* carnet *m* d'adresses

adenoids /'ædɪnɔɪdz, (AmE) -dən-/ *npl* végétations *fpl* (adénoïdes)

adept /ə'dept/ *adj* expert/-e (**at** en)

adequate /'ædɪkwət/ *adj* **1** (sufficient) suffisant/-e
2 (satisfactory) satisfaisant/-e

adhere /əd'hɪə(r)/ *vi* adhérer (**to** à)

adhesive /əd'hi:sɪv/ **A** *n* colle *f*, adhésif *m*
B *adj* collant/-e; **~ tape** papier *m* collant, Scotch® *m*

adjacent /ə'dʒeɪsnt/ *adj* contigu/contiguë; **~ to sth** attenant à qch

adjective /'ædʒɪktɪv/ *n* adjectif *m*

adjourn /ə'dʒɜ:n/ *vt* ajourner ‹*trial*› (**for** pour, **until** à)

adjudicate /ə'dʒu:dɪkeɪt/ *vt* juger ‹*contest*›; examiner ‹*case, claim*›

adjust /ə'dʒʌst/ **A** *vt* régler ‹*component, level, position, speed*›; ajuster ‹*price, rate*›; rajuster ‹*clothing*›; modifier ‹*figures*›
B *vi* ‹*person*› s'adapter (**to** à)

adjustable /ə'dʒʌstəbl/ *adj* réglable

adjustment /ə'dʒʌstmənt/ *n* **1** (of rates) rajustement *m* (**of** de); (of controls, machine) réglage *m* (**of** de)
2 (mental) adaptation *f* (**to** à)
3 (modification) modification *f*; **to make ~s to** apporter des modifications à ‹*system, machine*›

ad-lib /ˌæd 'lɪb/ *vt, vi* (*p prés etc* **-bb-**) improviser

administer /əd'mɪnɪstə(r)/ *vt* (*also* **administrate**) gérer ‹*company, affairs, estate*›; gouverner ‹*territory*›

🔑 **administration** /ədˌmɪnɪ'streɪʃn/ *n* (gen) administration *f*; (paperwork) travail *m* administratif

administrative /əd'mɪnɪstrətɪv, (AmE) -streɪtɪv/ *adj* administratif/-ive

administrator /əd'mɪnɪstreɪtə(r)/ *n* administrateur/-trice *m/f*

admirable /'ædmərəbl/ *adj* admirable

admiral /'ædmərəl/ *n* amiral *m*

admiration /ˌædmə'reɪʃn/ *n* admiration *f* (**for** pour)

admire /əd'maɪə(r)/ *vt* admirer

admirer /əd'maɪərə(r)/ *n* admirateur/-trice *m/f*

admission /əd'mɪʃn/ *n* **1** (entry) entrée *f*, admission *f* (**to** dans); **'no ~'** 'entrée

🔑 mot clé

interdite’
2 (fee) (droit *m* d’)entrée *f*
3 (confession) aveu *m*; **an ~ of guilt** un aveu de culpabilité

admissions office *n* (Univ) service *m* d’inscriptions

admit /əd'mɪt/ *vt* (*p prés etc* **-tt-**)
1 reconnaître, admettre ‹*mistake, fact*›; **to ~ that...** reconnaître que...; **to ~ to** reconnaître, admettre ‹*mistake, fact*›
2 (confess) reconnaître ‹*guilt*›; **to ~ to sth/doing** avouer qch/avoir fait
3 (let in) laisser entrer ‹*person*› (**into** dans); **to be ~ted to hospital** être hospitalisé/-e

admittance /əd'mɪtns/ *n* accès *m*, entrée *f*; **‘no ~’** ‘accès interdit au public’

admittedly /əd'mɪtɪdlɪ/ *adv* il est vrai, il faut en convenir

adolescent /ˌædə'lesnt/ **A** *n* adolescent/-e *m/f*
B *adj* **1** (gen) adolescent/-e; ‹*crisis, rebellion*› d’adolescent; ‹*problem*› des adolescents
2 (childish) puéril/-e

adopt /ə'dɒpt/ *vt* adopter

adopted /ə'dɒptɪd/ *adj* ‹*child*› adopté/-e; ‹*son, daughter*› adoptif/-ive

adoption /ə'dɒpʃn/ *n* adoption *f*

adorable /ə'dɔːrəbl/ *adj* adorable

adore /ə'dɔː(r)/ *vt* adorer (**doing** faire)

adoring /ə'dɔːrɪŋ/ *adj* ‹*husband*› épris/-e; ‹*fan*› passionné/-e

adrenalin /ə'drenəlɪn/ *n* (*also* **adrenaline**) adrénaline *f*

Adriatic /ˌeɪdrɪ'ætɪk/ *pr n* (*also* **Adriatic Sea**) **the ~** la mer Adriatique, l’Adriatique *f*

adrift /ə'drɪft/ *adj, adv* ‹*person, boat*› à la dérive; **to come ~** se détacher (**of, from** de)

ADSL *n* (*abbr* = **asymmetrical digital subscriber line**) ADSL *f*

adult /'ædʌlt, ə'dʌlt/ **A** *n* adulte *mf*
B *adj* (gen) adulte; ‹*life*› d’adulte; ‹*film, magazine*› pour adultes

adultery /ə'dʌltərɪ/ *n* adultère *m* (**with** avec)

adulthood /'ædʌlthʊd/ *n* âge *m* adulte

advance /əd'vɑːns, (AmE) -'væns/ **A** *n*
1 (forward movement) avance *f*; (progress) progrès *m*
2 (sum of money) avance *f*, acompte *m* (**on** sur)
3 to make ~s to sb (gen) faire des démarches auprès de qn; (sexually) faire des avances à qn
B *vt* **1** avancer ‹*sum of money*›
2 faire avancer ‹*career, research*›; servir ‹*cause, interests*›
C *vi* **1** (move forward) ‹*person*› avancer, s’avancer (**on, towards** vers); (Mil) ‹*army*› avancer (**on** sur)
2 (progress) progresser, faire des progrès
D in advance *phr* à l’avance

advanced /əd'vɑːnst, (AmE) -'vænst/ *adj* ‹*course, class*› supérieur/-e; ‹*student, stage*› avancé/-e; ‹*equipment, technology*› de pointe, perfectionné/-e

advance warning *n* préavis *m*

advantage /əd'vɑːntɪdʒ, (AmE) -'vænt-/ *n*
1 avantage *m*; **it is to our ~ to do** il est dans notre intérêt de faire
2 (asset) atout *m*
3 to take ~ of utiliser, profiter de ‹*situation, offer, service*›; exploiter ‹*person*›

advantageous /ˌædvən'teɪdʒəs/ *adj* avantageux/-euse

advent /'ædvent/ *n* (gen) apparition *f* (**of** de); **Advent** (prior to Christmas) l’Avent *m*

adventure /əd'ventʃə(r)/ *n* aventure *f*

adventure holiday *n* vacances *fpl* ‘aventure’

adventurous /əd'ventʃərəs/ *adj* aventureux/-euse

adverb /'ædvɜːb/ *n* adverbe *m*

adverse /'ædvɜːs/ *adj* ‹*reaction, conditions, publicity*› défavorable; ‹*effect, consequences*› négatif/-ive

advert /'ædvɜːt/ *n* (BrE) (fam) (in paper) annonce *f*; (small ad) petite annonce *f*; (on TV, radio) pub *f* (fam), spot *m* publicitaire

advertise /'ædvətaɪz/ **A** *vt* faire de la publicité pour ‹*product, event, service*›; mettre *or* passer une annonce pour ‹*car, house, job*›
B *vi* **1** (for publicity) faire de la publicité
2 (in small ads) passer une annonce

advertisement /əd'vɜːtɪsmənt, (AmE) ˌædvər'taɪzmənt/ *n* **1** (for product, event) publicité *f* (**for** pour); **a good/bad ~ for** une bonne/mauvaise publicité pour
2 (to sell house, get job) annonce *f*; (in small ads) petite annonce *f*

advertising /'ædvətaɪzɪŋ/ *n* publicité *f*

advertising agency *n* agence *f* de publicité

advertising campaign *n* campagne *f* publicitaire

advice /əd'vaɪs/ *n* conseils *mpl* (**on** sur, **about** à propos de); **a piece of ~** un conseil; **it was good ~** c’était un bon conseil

advisable /əd'vaɪzəbl/ *adj* **it is ~ to do** il est recommandé de faire

advise /əd'vaɪz/ *vt* **1** conseiller, donner des conseils à (**about** sur); **to ~ sb to do** conseiller à qn de faire; **to ~ sb against doing** déconseiller à qn de faire
2 recommander ‹*rest, course of action*›
3 (inform) **to ~ sb (of)** aviser qn (de)

adviser, **advisor** /əd'vaɪzə(r)/ *n* conseiller/-ère *m/f* (**to** auprès de)

advisory service *n* service *m* d’aide et de conseil

Aegean *pr n* (*also* **Aegean Sea**) **the ~** la mer Égée

a

aerial /'eərɪəl/ **A** *n* antenne *f* **B** *adj* aérien/-ienne

aerobics /eə'rəʊbɪks/ *n* aérobic *m*

aeroplane /'eərəpleɪn/ *n* (BrE) avion *m*

aerosol /'eərəsɒl, (AmE) -sɔːl/ *n* bombe *f* aérosol

aesthetic, **esthetic** (AmE) /iːs'θetɪk/ *adj* esthétique

⚷ **affair** /ə'feə(r)/ *n* **1** affaire *f*; **state of ~s** situation *f*
2 (relationship) liaison *f* (**with** avec)

⚷ **affect** /ə'fekt/ *vt* **1** (have effect on) avoir une incidence sur ‹*price*›; affecter, avoir des conséquences pour ‹*career, environment*›; affecter, toucher ‹*region, population*›; influer sur ‹*decision, outcome*›
2 (emotionally) émouvoir
3 (Med) atteindre ‹*person*›; affecter ‹*health, heart*›

affection /ə'fekʃn/ *n* affection *f* (**for sb** pour qn)

affectionate /ə'fekʃənət/ *adj* affectueux/-euse

affinity /ə'fɪnətɪ/ *n* **1** (attraction) attirance *f* (**with, for** pour)
2 (resemblance) ressemblance *f*

affinity card *n* carte *f* de fidélité

affluence /'æflʊəns/ *n* richesse *f*

⚷ **afford** /ə'fɔːd/ *vt* **1** (financially) **to be able to ~ sth** avoir les moyens d'acheter qch; **if I can ~ it** si j'ai les moyens; **I can't ~ to pay the rent** je n'ai pas les moyens de payer le loyer
2 (spare) **to be able to ~** disposer de ‹*time*›
3 (risk) **to be able to ~ sth/to do** se permettre qch/de faire; **he can't ~ to wait** il ne peut pas se permettre d'attendre

affordable /ə'fɔːdəbl/ *adj* ‹*price*› abordable

afield /ə'fiːld/ *adv* **far ~** loin; **further ~** plus loin

afloat /ə'fləʊt/ *adj, adv* **to stay ~** ‹*person, object*› rester à la surface (de l'eau); ‹*boat*› rester à flot

⚷ **afraid** /ə'freɪd/ *adj* **1** (scared) **to be ~** avoir peur (**of** de, **to do, of doing** de faire)
2 (anxious) **she was ~ (that) there would be an accident** elle craignait un accident; **I'm ~ it might rain** je crains qu'il (ne) pleuve
3 I'm ~ I can't come je suis désolé mais je ne peux pas venir; **I'm ~ so/not** je crains que oui/non

afresh /ə'freʃ/ *adv* à nouveau

Africa /'æfrɪkə/ *pr n* Afrique *f*; **to ~** en Afrique

⚷ **African** /'æfrɪkən/ **A** *n* Africain/-e *m/f* **B** *adj* africain/-e; ‹*elephant*› d'Afrique

African-American *n* Afro-américain/-e *m/f*

Afro-Caribbean /ˌæfrəʊˌkærɪ'biːən/ *adj* antillais/-e

⚷ **after** /'ɑːftə(r), (AmE) 'æftər/ **A** *adv* après; **soon** *or* **not long ~** peu après; **the year ~** l'année suivante *or* d'après; **the day ~** le lendemain
B *prep* **1** après; **shortly ~ the strike** peu après la grève; **~ that** après (cela); **the day ~ tomorrow** après-demain; **to tidy up ~ sb** ranger derrière qn; **to ask ~ sb** demander des nouvelles de qn; **~ you!** après vous!
2 that's the house they're ~ c'est la maison qu'ils veulent acheter; **the police are ~ him** il est recherché par la police
3 year ~ year tous les ans; **it was one disaster ~ another** on a eu catastrophe sur catastrophe
4 we called her Kate ~ my mother nous l'avons appelée Kate comme ma mère
5 (AmE) **it's twenty ~ eleven** il est onze heures vingt
C *conj* **1** (in the past) après avoir *or* être (+ *pp*), après que (+ *indicative*); **~ he had consulted Bill, he left** après avoir consulté Bill, il est parti; **~ he had changed she brought him to the office** après qu'il se fut changé, elle le conduisit au bureau; **~ we married/he left** après notre mariage/son départ
2 (in the future) quand, une fois que
3 why did he do that ~ we'd warned him? pourquoi a-t-il fait ça alors que nous l'avions prévenu?
D after all *phr* après tout

after-effect *n* (Med) contrecoup *m*; (fig) répercussion *f*

aftermath /'ɑːftəmæθ, -mɑːθ, (AmE) 'æf-/ *n* conséquences *fpl*; **in the ~ of** à la suite de ‹*war, scandal, election*›

afternoon /ˌɑːftə'nuːn, (AmE) ˌæf-/ *n* après-midi *m or f inv*; **in the ~** (dans) l'après-midi; **on Friday ~(s)** le vendredi après-midi; **good ~!** bonjour!

after-sales service *n* service *m* après-vente

after-shave *n* après-rasage *m*

aftershock *n* secousse *f* secondaire

after-sun *adj* après-soleil *inv*

aftertaste *n* arrière-goût *m*

afterthought /'ɑːftəθɔːt, (AmE) 'æf-/ *n* pensée *f* après coup

afterwards, **afterward** (AmE) /'ɑːftəwədz, (AmE) 'æf-/ *adv* **1** (after) après; **straight ~** tout de suite après
2 (later) plus tard

⚷ **again** /ə'geɪn, ə'gen/ *adv* encore

> When used with a verb, *again* is often translated by adding the prefix *re* to the verb in French: *to start again* = recommencer; *to marry again* = se remarier; *I'd like to read that book again* = j'aimerais relire ce livre; *she never saw them again* = elle ne les a jamais revus. You can check *re+* verbs by consulting the French side of the dictionary.
> For other uses of *again*, see below.

⚷ mot clé

sing it ~! chante-le encore!; **once ~** encore une fois; **yet ~ he refused** il a encore refusé; **when you are well ~** quand tu seras rétabli; **I'll never go there ~** je n'y retournerai jamais; **~ and ~** à plusieurs reprises

against /ə'geɪnst, ə'genst/ *prep* contre; **~ the wall** contre le mur; **I'm ~ it** je suis contre; **to be ~ doing** être contre l'idée de faire; **the pound fell ~ the dollar** la livre a baissé par rapport au dollar; **~ a background of** sur un fond de; **~ the light** à contre-jour

age /eɪdʒ/ **A** *n* **1** âge *m*; **to come of ~** atteindre la majorité; **to be under ~** (Law) être mineur/-e
2 (era) ère *f*, époque *f* (**of** de); **the video ~** l'ère de la vidéo; **in this day and ~** à notre époque
3 (fam) **it's ~s since I've played golf** ça fait une éternité que je n'ai pas joué au golf; **I've been waiting for ~s** j'attends depuis des heures
B *vt*, *vi* vieillir

aged *adj* **1** /eɪdʒd/ **~ between 20 and 25** âgé/-e de 20 à 25 ans; **a boy ~ 12** un garçon de 12 ans
2 /'eɪdʒɪd/ (old) âgé/-e

age group *n* tranche *f* d'âge

ageism /'eɪdʒɪzəm/ *n* discrimination *f* en raison de l'âge

agency /'eɪdʒənsɪ/ *n* agence *f*

agenda /ə'dʒendə/ *n* ordre *m* du jour

agent /'eɪdʒənt/ *n* agent *m* (**for sb** de qn)

aggravate /'ægrəveɪt/ *vt* (make worse) aggraver; (annoy) exaspérer

aggression /ə'greʃn/ *n* (gen) agression *f*; (of person) agressivité *f*

aggressive /ə'gresɪv/ *adj* agressif/-ive

aggro /'ægrəʊ/ *n* (fam) (violence) violence *f*; (hostility) hostilité *f*

agile /'ædʒaɪl, (AmE) 'ædʒl/ *adj* agile

agitate /'ædʒɪteɪt/ *vi* faire campagne (**for** pour)

agitated /'ædʒɪteɪtɪd/ *adj* agité/-e, inquiet/-iète

AGM *n* (*abbr* = **annual general meeting**) assemblée *f* générale annuelle

agnostic /æg'nɒstɪk/ *n*, *adj* agnostique *mf*

ago /ə'gəʊ/ *adv* **three weeks ~** il y a trois semaines; **long ~** il y a longtemps; **how long ~?** il y a combien de temps?; **not long ~** il y a peu de temps

agonize /'ægənaɪz/ *vi* se tourmenter (**over, about** à propos de)

agonizing /'ægənaɪzɪŋ/ *adj* ‹*pain, death*› atroce; ‹*choice*› déchirant/-e

agony /'ægənɪ/ *n* (physical) douleur *f* atroce; (mental) angoisse *f*

agony aunt *n* journaliste *mf* responsable du courrier du cœur

agony column *n* courrier *m* du cœur

agree /ə'griː/ **A** *vt* (*prét*, *pp* **agreed**)
1 (concur) être d'accord (**that** sur le fait que)
2 (admit) convenir (**that** que)
3 (consent) **to ~ to do** accepter de faire; **she ~d to speak to me** elle a accepté de me parler
4 (settle on, arrange) se mettre d'accord sur ‹*date, price*›; **to ~ to do** convenir de faire
B *vi* (*prét*, *pp* **agreed**) **1** (hold same opinion) être d'accord (**with** avec, **about, on** sur, **about doing** pour faire); **'I ~!'** 'je suis bien d'accord!'
2 (reach mutual understanding) se mettre d'accord (**about, on** sur)
3 (consent) accepter; **to ~ to** consentir à ‹*suggestion, terms*›
4 (hold with, approve) **to ~ with** approuver ‹*belief, idea, practice*›
5 (tally) ‹*stories, statements, figures*› concorder (**with** avec)
6 (suit) **to ~ with sb** ‹*climate*› être bon/bonne pour qn; ‹*food*› réussir à qn
7 (in grammar) s'accorder (**with** avec, **in** en)
C agreed *pp adj* convenu/-e; **is that ~d?** c'est entendu?

agreeable /ə'griːəbl/ *adj* agréable

agreement /ə'griːmənt/ *n* **1** accord *m* (**to do** pour faire); **to reach an ~** parvenir à un accord
2 (undertaking) engagement *m*
3 (contract) contrat *m*
4 (in grammar) accord *m*

agricultural /ˌægrɪ'kʌltʃərəl/ *adj* agricole

agriculture /'ægrɪkʌltʃə(r)/ *n* agriculture *f*

aground /ə'graʊnd/ *adv* **to run ~** s'échouer

ahead /ə'hed/ **A** *adv* **1** ‹*run*› en avant; **to send sb on ~** envoyer qn en éclaireur; **to send one's luggage on ~** faire envoyer ses bagages; **a few kilometres ~** à quelques kilomètres
2 (in time) **in the months ~** pendant les mois à venir
3 (in leading position) **to be ~ in the polls** être en tête des sondages; **to be 30 points ~** avoir 30 points d'avance
B ahead of *phr* **1** (in front of) devant ‹*person, vehicle*›; **to be three metres ~ of sb** avoir trois mètres d'avance sur qn
2 to be ~ of sb (in polls, ratings) avoir un avantage sur qn; **to be ~ of the others** ‹*pupil*› être plus avancé/-e que les autres

aid /eɪd/ **A** *n* aide *f* (**from** de, **to, for** à); **in ~ of** au profit de ‹*charity*›
B *adj* ‹*organization*› d'entraide
C *vt* aider ‹*person*› (**to do** à faire); faciliter ‹*digestion, recovery*›

aid agency *n* organisation *f* humanitaire

aide /eɪd/ *n* aide *mf*, assistant/-e *m/f*

Aids /eɪdz/ *n* (*abbr* = **Acquired Immune Deficiency Syndrome**) sida *m*

Aids awareness *n* sensibilisation *f* au problème du sida

Aids sufferer *n* sidéen/-éenne *m/f*

Aids virus *n* virus *m* du sida

aid worker *n* travailleur *m* humanitaire

🔑 **aim** /eɪm/ **A** *n* **1** (purpose) but *m*
2 (with weapon) **to take ∼ at sb/sth** viser qn/qch
B *vt* **1 to be ∼ed at sb** ‹*campaign, product, remark*› viser qn
2 braquer ‹*gun, camera*› (**at** sur); lancer ‹*ball, stone*› (**at** sur)
C *vi* **to ∼ for sth, to ∼ at sth** viser qch; **to ∼ at doing, to ∼ to do** avoir l'intention de faire

🔑 **air** /eə(r)/ **A** *n* **1** air *m*; **in the open ∼** en plein air, au grand air; **to let the ∼ out of sth** dégonfler qch; **he threw the ball up into the ∼** il a jeté le ballon en l'air
2 to travel by ∼ voyager par avion
3 (on radio, TV) **to be/go on the ∼** être/passer à l'antenne
B *vt* **1** aérer ‹*garment, room, bed*›
2 exprimer ‹*opinion, view*›; **to ∼ one's grievances** exposer ses griefs
IDIOMS **to put on ∼s** se donner de grands airs; **to vanish into thin ∼** se volatiliser

air ambulance *n* avion *m* sanitaire

airbag *n* airbag *m*

air bed *n* (BrE) matelas *m* pneumatique

air-conditioned *adj* climatisé/-e

air conditioning *n* climatisation *f*, air *m* conditionné

🔑 **aircraft** *n* (*pl* ∼) avion *m*, aéronef *m*

aircrew *n* équipage *m* d'un avion

airfare *n* tarif *m* d'avion

airfield *n* aérodrome *m*, terrain *m* d'aviation

air force *n* armée *f* de l'air, forces *fpl* aériennes

air freshener *n* désodorisant *m* d'atmosphère

air gun *n* fusil *m* à air comprimé

airhead *n* (fam) évaporé/-e *m/f*

air hostess *n* hôtesse *f* de l'air

airline /'eəlaɪn/ *n* compagnie *f* aérienne

airmail /'eəmeɪl/ *n* poste *f* aérienne; **by ∼** par avion

airplane *n* (AmE) avion *m*

🔑 **airport** /'eəpɔːt/ *n* aéroport *m*

air raid *n* attaque *f* aérienne, raid *m* (aérien)

air strike *n* frappe *f* aérienne

air terminal *n* (at airport) aérogare *f*; (in town) terminal *m*

airtight *adj* étanche à l'air

air traffic controller *n* contrôleur/-euse *m/f* aérien/-ienne, aiguilleur *m* du ciel

air travel *n* voyages *mpl* aériens

airwaves /'eəweɪvz/ *npl* ondes *fpl*

airy /'eərɪ/ *adj* **1** ‹*room*› clair/-e et spacieux/-ieuse
2 ‹*manner*› désinvolte, insouciant/-e

aisle /aɪl/ *n* **1** (in church) (side passage) bas-côté *m*; (centre passage) allée *f* centrale
2 (in train, plane) couloir *m*; (in cinema, shop) allée *f*

ajar /ə'dʒɑː(r)/ *adj, adv* entrouvert/-e, entrebaillé/-e

alarm /ə'lɑːm/ **A** *n* **1** (warning) alarme *f*; **smoke ∼** détecteur *m* de fumée
2 (fear) frayeur *f*; (concern) inquiétude *f*
B *vt* inquiéter ‹*person*›

alarm clock *n* réveille-matin *m*, réveil *m*

alarmed /ə'lɑːmd/ *adj* **1** (afraid) effrayé/-e
2 (equipped with warning device) ‹*door*› équipé/-e d'un système d'alarme

🔑 **album** /'ælbəm/ *n* album *m*

🔑 **alcohol** /'ælkəhɒl, (AmE) -hɔːl/ *n* alcool *m*; **∼-free** sans alcool; **∼ content** teneur *f* en alcool

alcoholic /ˌælkə'hɒlɪk, (AmE) -hɔːl-/ **A** *n* alcoolique *mf*
B *adj* ‹*drink*› alcoolisé/-e; ‹*stupor*› alcoolique

alcoholism /'ælkəhɒlɪzəm, (AmE) -hɔːl-/ *n* alcoolisme *m*

alcopop /'ælkəʊpɒp/ *n* soda *m* alcoolisé

alcove /'ælkəʊv/ *n* renfoncement *m*

ale /eɪl/ *n* bière *f*

alert /ə'lɜːt/ **A** *n* alerte *f*
B *adj* **1** (lively) ‹*child*› éveillé/-e; ‹*adult*› alerte
2 (attentive) vigilant/-e
C *vt* **1** alerter ‹*authorities*›
2 to ∼ sb to mettre qn en garde contre ‹*danger*›; attirer l'attention de qn sur ‹*fact, situation*›

A levels *npl* (BrE) (Sch) ≈ baccalauréat *m*

algebra /'ældʒɪbrə/ *n* algèbre *f*

Algeria /æl'dʒɪərɪə/ *pr n* Algérie *f*

alias /'eɪlɪəs/ **A** *n* (Comput) alias *m*
B *adv* alias

alibi /'ælɪbaɪ/ *n* **1** (Law) alibi *m*
2 (excuse) excuse *f*

alien /'eɪlɪən/ *n* **1** (gen), (Law) étranger/-ère *m/f* (**to** à)
2 (from space) extraterrestre *mf*

alienate /'eɪlɪəneɪt/ *vt* éloigner ‹*supporters, colleagues*›

alight /ə'laɪt/ **A** *adj* **to set sth ∼** mettre le feu à qch
B *vi* ‹*passenger*› descendre (**from** de)

alike /ə'laɪk/ **A** *adj* (identical) pareil/-eille; (similar) semblable; **to look ∼** se ressembler
B *adv* ‹*dress, think*› de la même façon

alimony /'ælɪmənɪ, (AmE) -məʊnɪ/ *n* pension *f* alimentaire

🔑 **alive** /ə'laɪv/ *adj* **1** vivant/-e, en vie; **to be burnt ∼** être brûlé/-e vif/vive
2 to come ∼ ‹*party, place*› s'animer; ‹*history*› prendre vie
3 to be ∼ ‹*tradition*› être vivant/-e; ‹*interest*› être vif/vive
4 ∼ with grouillant/-e de ‹*insects*›

🔑 mot clé

alkaline /ˈælkəlaɪn/ *adj* alcalin/-e

all /ɔːl/

> When *all* is used as a pronoun, it is generally translated by *tout*.
>
> When *all* is followed by a *that* clause, *all that* is translated by *tout ce que*: *after all (that) we've done* = après tout ce que nous avons fait.
>
> When referring to a specified group of people or objects, the translation of *all* reflects the number and gender of the people or objects referred to; *tous* is used for a group of people or objects of masculine or mixed or unspecified gender and *toutes* for a group of feminine gender: *we were all delighted* = nous étions tous ravis; *'where are the cups?'—'they're all in the kitchen'* = 'où sont les tasses?'—'elles sont toutes dans la cuisine'. ▶ A
>
> In French, determiners agree in gender and number with the noun that follows: *all the time* = tout le temps; *all the family* = toute la famille; *all men* = tous les hommes; *all the books* = tous les livres; *all women* = toutes les femmes; *all the chairs* = toutes les chaises. ▶ B
>
> As an adverb meaning *completely*, *all* is generally translated by *tout*: *he was all alone* = il était tout seul; *the girls were all excited* = les filles étaient tout excitées.
>
> However, when the adjective that follows is in the feminine and begins with a consonant the translation is *toute/toutes*: *she was all alone* = elle était toute seule; *the girls were all alone* = les filles étaient toutes seules. ▶ C1
>
> For more examples and particular usages see the entry below.

A *pron* tout; **that's ~ I want** c'est tout ce que je veux; **I spent it ~, I spent ~ of it** j'ai tout dépensé; **~ of our things** toutes nos affaires

B *det* tout/toute (+ *sg*); tous/toutes (+ *pl*); **~ those who came** (men, mixed group) tous ceux qui sont venus; (women) toutes celles qui sont venues; **~ his life** toute sa vie; **~ the time** tout le temps

C *adv* **1** tout; **she's ~ wet** elle est toute mouillée; **~ in white** tout en blanc; **~ along the canal** tout le long du canal; **to be ~ for sth** être tout à fait pour qch; **tell me ~ about it!** raconte-moi tout!

2 (Sport) **(they are) six ~** (il y a) six partout

D **all along** *phr* ‹*know*› depuis le début, toujours

E **all the** *phr* **~ the more difficult** d'autant plus difficile; **~ the better!** tant mieux!

F **all too** *phr* ‹*easy, often*› bien trop

G **at all** *phr* **not at ~!** (acknowledging thanks) de rien!; (answering query) pas du tout!; **it is not at ~ certain** ce n'est pas du tout certain; **nothing at ~** rien du tout

H **of all** *phr* **the easiest of ~** le plus facile; **first of ~** pour commencer

all clear *n* **to give sb the ~** donner le feu vert à qn (**to do** pour faire); ‹*doctor*› déclarer qn guéri/-e

allegation /ˌælɪˈgeɪʃn/ *n* allégation *f*

allege /əˈledʒ/ *vt* **to ~ that** (claim) prétendre que (+ *conditional*); (publicly) déclarer que (+ *conditional*); **it was ~d that** il a été dit que

alleged *adj* présumé/e

allegedly /əˈledʒɪdlɪ/ *adv* prétendument

allegiance /əˈliːdʒəns/ *n* allégeance *f*

allergic /əˈlɜːdʒɪk/ *adj* allergique (**to** à)

allergist /ˈælədʒɪst/ *n* allergologue *mf*

allergy /ˈælədʒɪ/ *n* allergie *f* (**to** à)

alleviate /əˈliːvɪeɪt/ *vt* soulager ‹*boredom, pain*›; réduire ‹*overcrowding, stress*›

alley /ˈælɪ/ *n* (walkway) allée *f*; (for vehicles) ruelle *f*

alliance /əˈlaɪəns/ *n* alliance *f*

allied /ˈælaɪd/ *adj* ‹*group*› allié/-e

all-important *adj* essentiel/-ielle

all-inclusive *adj* ‹*fee, price*› tout compris

all-in-one *adj* ‹*garment*› d'une seule pièce

all-night *adj* ‹*party, meeting*› qui dure toute la nuit; ‹*service*› ouvert/-e toute la nuit; ‹*radio station*› qui émet 24 heures sur 24

allocate /ˈæləkeɪt/ *vt* affecter ‹*funds*› (**for, to** à); accorder ‹*time*› (**to** à); assigner ‹*tasks*› (**to** à)

allot /əˈlɒt/ *vt* (*p prés etc* **-tt-**) attribuer ‹*money*› (**to** à); **in the ~ted time** dans le temps imparti

allotment /əˈlɒtmənt/ *n* (BrE) parcelle *f* de terre

all-out /ˈɔːlaʊt/ *adj* ‹*strike*› total/-e; ‹*attack*› en règle; ‹*effort*› acharné/-e

all over /ˌɔːlˈəʊvə(r)/ **A** *adj* fini/-e; **when it's ~** quand tout sera fini

B *adv* (everywhere) partout; **to be trembling ~** trembler de partout

C *prep* partout dans ‹*room, town*›; **~ China** partout en Chine

allow /əˈlaʊ/ *vt* **1** (authorize) permettre à, autoriser ‹*person, organization*› (**to do** à faire); **it isn't ~ed** c'est interdit; **she isn't ~ed to go out** elle n'a pas le droit de sortir

2 (let) laisser; **he ~ed the situation to get worse** il a laissé la situation s'aggraver

3 (enable) **to ~ sb/sth to do** permettre à qn/qch de faire; **it would ~ the company to expand** cela permettrait à la société de s'agrandir

4 (allocate) prévoir; **to ~ two days for the job** prévoir deux jours pour faire le travail

5 ‹*referee*› accorder ‹*goal*›; ‹*insurer*› agréer ‹*claim*›

6 (condone) tolérer ‹*rudeness, swearing*›

■ **allow for** tenir compte de

allowance /əˈlaʊəns/ *n* **1** (gen) allocation *f*; (from employer) indemnité *f*

2 (tax) ~ abattement *m* fiscal
3 (spending money) (for child) argent *m* de poche; (for student) argent *m* (pour vivre); (from trust, guardian) rente *f*
4 your baggage ~ is 40 kg vous avez droit à 40 kg de bagages
5 to make ~(s) for sth tenir compte de qch; **to make ~(s) for sb** essayer de comprendre qn

alloy wheel *n* jante *f* en alliage léger

all right, alright /ˌɔːlˈraɪt/ **A** *adj ‹film, garment, place›* pas mal (fam); **is my hair ~?** ça va mes cheveux?; **are you ~?** ça va?; **I'm ~ thanks** ça va merci; **is it ~ if...?** est-ce que ça va si...?
B *adv* **1** (giving agreement) d'accord
2 *‹work›* comme il faut; *‹see, hear›* bien

all-round (BrE), **all-around** (AmE) /ˌɔːlˈraʊnd/ *adj ‹athlete›* complet/-ète; *‹improvement›* général/-e

all-rounder /ˌɔːlˈraʊndə(r)/ *n* **to be a good ~** être bon/bonne en tout

all-time /ˈɔːltaɪm/ *adj ‹record›* absolu/-e; **the ~ greats** (people) les grands *mpl*; **~ high** record *m* absolu

all told *adv* en tout

allusion /əˈluːʒn/ *n* allusion *f* **(to** à)

ally /ˈælaɪ/ **A** *n* (*pl* **-ies**) allié/-e *m/f*
B /əˈlaɪ/ *v refl* **to ~ oneself with** s'allier avec

almond /ˈɑːmənd/ *n* **1** (nut) amande *f*
2 (*also* **~ tree**) amandier *m*

🔑 **almost** /ˈɔːlməʊst/ *adv* **1** (practically) presque; **we're ~ there** nous sommes presque arrivés; **it's ~ dark** il fait presque nuit
2 he ~ died/forgot il a failli mourir/oublier

🔑 **alone** /əˈləʊn/ **A** *adj* seul/-e; **all ~** tout seul/ toute seule; **to leave sb ~** laisser qn seul/-e; (in peace) laisser qn tranquille; **leave that bike ~!** ne touche pas à ce vélo!
B *adv* **1** *‹work, live, travel›* seul/-e
2 for this reason ~ rien que pour cette raison
IDIOM **to go it ~** (fam) faire cavalier seul

🔑 **along** /əˈlɒŋ, (AmE) əˈlɔːŋ/

> When *along* is used as a preposition meaning *all along,* it can usually be translated by *le long de*: *there were trees along the road* = il y avait des arbres le long de la route. For particular usages see the entry below.
> *Along* is often used after verbs of movement. If the addition of *along* does not change the meaning of the verb, *along* will not be translated: *as he walked along* = tout en marchant.

A *adv* **to push sth ~** pousser qch; **to be running ~** courir; **I'll be ~ in a second** j'arrive tout de suite
B *prep* **1** (all along) le long de; **there were chairs ~ the wall** il y avait des chaises contre le mur
2 to walk ~ the beach marcher sur la plage; **to look ~ the shelves** chercher dans les rayons; **halfway ~ the path** à mi-chemin
C along with *phr* (accompanied by) accompagné/-e de; (at same time as) en même temps que

alongside /əˈlɒŋsaɪd, (AmE) əlɔːŋˈsaɪd/ **A** *prep*
1 (all along) le long de
2 to draw up ~ sb *‹vehicle›* s'arrêter à la hauteur de qn
B *adv* à côté

aloud /əˈlaʊd/ *adv ‹read›* à haute voix; *‹think›* tout haut

alphabet /ˈælfəbet/ *n* alphabet *m*

alphabetically /ˌælfəˈbetɪklɪ/ *adv* par ordre alphabétique

alpine /ˈælpaɪn/ *adj* (*also* **Alpine**) alpin/-e

Alps /ælps/ *pr n pl* **the ~** les Alpes *fpl*

🔑 **already** /ɔːlˈredɪ/ *adv* déjà; **it's 10 o'clock ~** il est déjà 10 heures; **he's ~ left** il est déjà parti

alright = **all right**

Alsatian /ælˈseɪʃn/ *n* (BrE) (dog) berger *m* allemand

🔑 **also** /ˈɔːlsəʊ/ *adv* aussi

alter /ˈɔːltə(r)/ **A** *vt* **1** changer *‹person›*; (radically) transformer *‹person›*; changer *‹opinion, rule, timetable›*; modifier *‹amount, document›*; affecter *‹value, climate›*
2 retoucher *‹dress, shirt›*
B *vi* changer

alteration /ˌɔːltəˈreɪʃn/ **A** *n* modification *f* **(to, in** de)
B alterations *npl* (building work) travaux *mpl*

alternate **A** /ɔːlˈtɜːnət/ *adj* **1** (successive) *‹chapters, layers›* en alternance
2 (every other) **on ~ days** un jour sur deux
3 (AmE) (other) autre
B /ˈɔːltəneɪt/ *vt* **to ~ sth and** *or* **with sth** alterner qch et qch
C /ˈɔːltəneɪt/ *vi ‹people›* se relayer; *‹colours, patterns, seasons›* alterner (**with** avec)

alternately /ɔːlˈtɜːnətlɪ/ *adv* alternativement

🔑 **alternative** /ɔːlˈtɜːnətɪv/ **A** *n* (from two) alternative *f*, autre possibilité *f*; (from several) possibilité *f*; **to have no ~** ne pas avoir le choix
B *adj* **1** *‹date, flight, plan›* autre; *‹accommodation, product›* de remplacement; *‹solution›* de rechange
2 (unconventional) alternatif/-ive

alternative energy *n* énergie *f* de substitution

alternatively /ɔːlˈtɜːnətɪvlɪ/ *adv* sinon; **~, you can book by phone** vous avez aussi la possibilité de réserver par téléphone

alternative medicine *n* médecines *fpl* parallèles *or* douces

---

🔑 mot clé

alternative technology *n* technologie *f* alternative

alternative vote *n* vote *m* préférentiel, vote *m* alternatif

although /ɔ:lˈðəʊ/ *conj* bien que (+ *subjunctive*); ~ **he is shy** bien qu'il soit timide

altitude /ˈæltɪtju:d, (AmE) -tu:d/ *n* altitude *f*

alto /ˈæltəʊ/ *n* (*pl* **-tos**) (voice) (of female) contralto *m*; (of male) haute-contre *f*

altogether /ˌɔ:ltəˈgeðə(r)/ *adv* **1** (completely) complètement; **not ~ true** pas complètement vrai
2 (in total) en tout; **how much is that ~?** ça fait combien en tout?

aluminium /ˌæljʊˈmɪnɪəm/ (BrE), **aluminum** /əˈlu:mɪnəm/ (AmE) *n* aluminium *m*

aluminium foil *n* papier *m* aluminium

always /ˈɔ:lweɪz/ *adv* toujours; **he's ~ complaining** il n'arrête pas de se plaindre

Alzheimer's disease /ˈæltshaɪməz/ *n* maladie *f* d'Alzheimer

am *adv* (*abbr* = **ante meridiem**) **three ~** trois heures (du matin)

amalgamate /əˈmælgəmeɪt/ **A** *vt* (merge) fusionner ‹*companies, schools*› (**with** avec, **into** en)
B *vi* ‹*company, union*› fusionner (**with** avec)

amateur /ˈæmətə(r)/ **A** *n* amateur *m*
B *adj* ‹*sportsperson, musician*› amateur; ‹*sport*› en amateur

amaze /əˈmeɪz/ *vt* surprendre; (stronger) stupéfier

amazed /əˈmeɪzd/ *adj* stupéfait/-e; **I'm ~ (that)** ça m'étonne que (+ *subjunctive*)

amazement /əˈmeɪzmənt/ *n* stupéfaction *f*

amazing /əˈmeɪzɪŋ/ *adj* extraordinaire

Amazon /ˈæməzən, (AmE) -zɒn/ *pr n* Amazone *m*

ambassador /æmˈbæsədə(r)/ *n* ambassadeur *m*

amber /ˈæmbə(r)/ *n* **1** (resin, colour) ambre *m*
2 (BrE) (traffic signal) orange *m*

ambiguous /æmˈbɪgjʊəs/ *adj* ambigu/ambiguë

ambition /æmˈbɪʃn/ *n* ambition *f* (**to do** de faire)

ambitious /æmˈbɪʃəs/ *adj* ambitieux/-ieuse

ambulance /ˈæmbjʊləns/ *n* ambulance *f*; **~ crew** équipe *f* d'ambulanciers/-ières

ambush /ˈæmbʊʃ/ **A** *n* embuscade *f*
B *vt* tendre une embuscade à

amenable /əˈmi:nəbl/ *adj* **~ to** ‹*person*› sensible à ‹*reason, advice*›

amend /əˈmend/ *vt* amender ‹*law*›; modifier ‹*document*›

amendment /əˈmendmənt/ *n* (to law) amendement *m* (**to** à); (to contract) modification *f* (**to** à)

amends /əˈmendz/ *npl* **to make ~** se racheter; **to make ~ for** réparer ‹*damage*›; **to make ~ to sb** (financially) dédommager qn

amenities *npl* (of hotel) équipements *mpl*; (of house, sports club) installations *fpl*

America /əˈmerɪkə/ *pr n* Amérique *f*

American /əˈmerɪkən/ **A** *n* **1** (person) Américain/-e *m/f*
2 (*also* **~ English**) américain *m*
B *adj* américain/-e; ‹*embassy*› des États-Unis

American Indian *n* Indien/-ienne *m/f* d'Amerique du Nord

amiable /ˈeɪmɪəbl/ *adj* aimable (**to** avec)

amicable /ˈæmɪkəbl/ *adj* (friendly) amical/-e; **an ~ settlement** un arrangement à l'amiable

amiss /əˈmɪs/ **A** *adj* **there is something ~** il y a quelque chose qui ne va pas
B *adv* **to take sth ~** prendre qch de travers

ammunition /ˌæmjʊˈnɪʃn/ *n* munitions *fpl*

amnesty /ˈæmnəstɪ/ *n* amnistie *f*

among, amongst /əˈmʌŋ/ *prep* **1** (amidst) parmi; **~ the crowd** parmi la foule; **to be ~ friends** être entre amis
2 (one of) **~ the world's poorest countries** un des pays les plus pauvres du monde; **she was ~ those who survived** elle faisait partie des survivants; **to be ~ the first** être dans les premiers
3 (between) entre

amount /əˈmaʊnt/ *n* (of goods, food) quantité *f*; (of people, objects) nombre *m*; (of money) somme *f*; **a large ~ of** beaucoup de; **the full ~** le montant total
■ **amount to 1** s'élever à ‹*total*›
2 (be equivalent to) revenir à ‹*confession, betrayal*›; **it ~s to the same thing** cela revient au même

amp /æmp/ *n* **1** (*abbr* = **ampere**) ampère *m*
2 (fam) (*abbr* = **amplifier**) ampli *m* (fam)

amphetamine /æmˈfetəmi:n/ *n* amphétamine *f*

ample /ˈæmpl/ *adj* **1** ‹*provisions, resources*› largement suffisant/-e (**for** pour); **there's ~ room** il y a largement la place
2 ‹*proportions, bust*› généreux/-euse

amplifier /ˈæmplɪfaɪə(r)/ *n* amplificateur *m*

amputate /ˈæmpjʊteɪt/ *vt* amputer; **to ~ sb's leg** amputer qn de la jambe

amuse /əˈmju:z/ **A** *vt* **1** (cause laughter) amuser; **to be ~d at** *or* **by** s'amuser de
2 (entertain) ‹*game, story*› distraire
3 (occupy) ‹*activity, hobby*› occuper
B *v refl* **to ~ oneself 1** (entertain) se distraire
2 (occupy) s'occuper

amusement /əˈmju:zmənt/ *n* **1** (mirth) amusement *m* (**at** face à)
2 (diversion) distraction *f*

amusement arcade *n* (BrE) salle *f* de jeux électroniques

amusement park *n* parc *m* d'attractions

a

amusing /əˈmjuːzɪŋ/ *adj* amusant/-e
an /æn, ən/ ▶ **a²**
anachronism /əˈnækrənɪzəm/ *n* anachronisme *m*
anaemic /əˈniːmɪk/ *adj* (Med) anémique
anaesthetic (BrE), **anesthetic** (AmE) /ˌænɪsˈθetɪk/ *n, adj* anesthésique *m*
anaesthetize (BrE), **anesthetize** (AmE) /əˈniːsθətaɪz/ *vt* anesthésier
analogy /əˈnælədʒɪ/ *n* analogie *f*
⚷ **analyse** (BrE), **analyze** (AmE) /ˈænəlaɪz/ *vt* analyser
⚷ **analysis** /əˈnælɪsɪs/ *n* analyse *f*
analytic (*also* **analytical**) /ˌænəˈlɪtɪk(l)/ *adj* analytique
anarchist /ˈænəkɪst/ *n, adj* anarchiste *mf*
anarchy /ˈænəkɪ/ *n* anarchie *f*
anatomy /əˈnætəmɪ/ *n* anatomie *f*
ancestor /ˈænsestə(r)/ *n* ancêtre *mf*
anchor /ˈæŋkə(r)/ *n* ancre *f*; **to drop ∼** jeter l'ancre
anchovy /ˈæntʃəvɪ, (AmE) ˈæntʃəʊvɪ/ *n* anchois *m*
⚷ **ancient** /ˈeɪnʃənt/ *adj* (dating from BC) antique; (very old) ancien/-ienne; **∼ Greek** grec ancien; **∼ Greece** la Grèce antique; **∼ monument** monument *m* historique
⚷ **and** /ænd, ənd, ən, n/ *conj* et; **cups ∼ plates** des tasses et des assiettes; **he stood up ∼ went out** il s'est levé et il est sorti; **come ∼ see** viens voir; **two hundred ∼ sixty-two** deux cent soixante-deux; **faster ∼ faster** de plus en plus vite
Andorra /ænˈdɔːrə/ *pr n* Andorre *f*
angel /ˈeɪndʒl/ *n* ange *m*
⚷ **anger** /ˈæŋgə(r)/ **A** *n* colère *f* (**at** devant, **towards** contre)
B *vt* mettre [qn] en colère ‹*person*›
angle /ˈæŋgl/ **A** *n* angle *m*
B *vi* **1** (fish) pêcher (à la ligne)
2 (fam) **to ∼ for sth** chercher à obtenir qch
Anglo-French /ˌæŋgləʊˈfrentʃ/ *adj* anglo-français/-e, franco-britannique
angrily /ˈæŋgrɪlɪ/ *adv* ‹*react, speak*› avec colère
⚷ **angry** /ˈæŋgrɪ/ *adj* ‹*person, expression*› furieux/-ieuse; ‹*scene, words*› de colère; **to be ∼ (at *or* with sb)** être en colère (contre qn); **to get ∼** se fâcher; **to make sb ∼** mettre qn en colère
⚷ **animal** /ˈænɪml/ **A** *n* animal *m*, bête *f*
B *adj* animal/-e
animal activist *n* militant/-e *m/f* pour les droits des animaux
animal experiment *n* expérience *f* sur les animaux
animal rights *npl* droits *mpl* des animaux
animal testing *n* expérimentation *f* animale

⚷ mot clé

animated /ˈænɪmeɪtɪd/ *adj* animé/-e
animator /ˈænɪmeɪtə(r)/ *n* (cartoonist) animateur/-trice *m/f*
ankle /ˈæŋkl/ *n* cheville *f*
ankle chain *n* chaîne *f* de cheville
ankle sock *n* socquette *f*
annex **A** /ˈæneks/ *n* (*also* **annexe** (BrE)) annexe *f*
B /əˈneks/ *vt* annexer ‹*territory, land, country*› (**to** à)
annihilate /əˈnaɪəleɪt/ *vt* anéantir
anniversary /ˌænɪˈvɜːsərɪ/ *n* anniversaire *m* (**of** de)
annotate /ˈænəteɪt/ *vt* annoter
⚷ **announce** /əˈnaʊns/ *vt* annoncer (**that** que)
announcement /əˈnaʊnsmənt/ *n* **1** (spoken) annonce *f*
2 (written) avis *m*; (of birth, death) faire-part *m inv*
announcer /əˈnaʊnsə(r)/ *n* (on TV) speaker/-erine *m/f*; **radio ∼** présentateur/-trice *m/f* de radio
annoy /əˈnɔɪ/ *vt* ‹*person*› (by behaviour) agacer; (by opposing wishes) contrarier; ‹*noise*› gêner
annoyance /əˈnɔɪəns/ *n* agacement *m* (**at** devant), contrariété *f* (**at** à cause de)
annoyed /əˈnɔɪd/ *adj* contrarié/-e (**at, by** par); (stronger) agacé/-e, fâché/-e (**at, by** par); **∼ with sb** fâché/-e contre qn
annoying /əˈnɔɪɪŋ/ *adj* agaçant/-e (**to do** de faire)
⚷ **annual** /ˈænjʊəl/ **A** *n* **1** (book) album *m* (annuel)
2 (plant) plante *f* annuelle
B *adj* annuel/-elle
annually /ˈænjʊəlɪ/ *adv* ‹*earn, produce*› par an; ‹*do, inspect*› tous les ans
anomaly /əˈnɒməlɪ/ *n* anomalie *f*
anonymous /əˈnɒnɪməs/ *adj* anonyme
anorak /ˈænəræk/ *n* anorak *m*
anorexia *n* (*also* **anorexia nervosa**) anorexie *f* mentale
⚷ **another** /əˈnʌðə(r)/

> *Another* is translated by *un autre* or *une autre* according to the gender of the noun it refers to: *another book* = un autre livre; *another chair* = une autre chaise.
> Note that *en* is always used with *un/une autre* in French to represent a noun that is understood: *that cake was delicious, can I have another (one)?* = ce gâteau était délicieux, est-ce que je peux en prendre un autre? For more examples and particular usages, see the entry below.

A *det* **1** (an additional) un/-e autre, encore un/-e; **would you like ∼ drink?** est-ce que tu veux un autre verre?; **I've broken ∼ plate** j'ai encore cassé une assiette; **that will cost you ∼ £5** cela vous coûtera 5 livres sterling de plus; **in ∼ five weeks** dans cinq semaines

2 (a different) un/-e autre; **~ time** une autre fois; **he has ~ job now** il a un nouveau travail maintenant
B *pron* un/-e autre; **she had ~** elle en a pris un/-e autre; **one after ~** l'un/l'une après l'autre; **in one way or ~** d'une façon ou d'une autre

answer /ˈɑːnsə(r), (AmE) ˈænsər/ **A** *n* (gen) réponse *f* (**to** à); (to problem, puzzle) solution *f* (**to** à); **there's no ~** (to door) il n'y a personne; (on phone) ça ne répond pas; **the right/wrong ~** la bonne/mauvaise réponse
B *vt* répondre à; **to ~ the door** aller *or* venir ouvrir la porte; **to ~ the phone** répondre au téléphone
C *vi* **1** répondre; **to ~ to** répondre *or* correspondre à
2 (be accountable) **to ~ to sb** être responsable devant qn
■ **answer back** répondre
■ **answer for** répondre de ‹*action, person*›; **they have a lot to ~ for!** ils ont beaucoup de comptes à rendre!

answerable /ˈɑːnsərəbl, (AmE) ˈæns-/ *adj* responsable (**to sb** devant qn, **for sth** de qch)

answering machine, **answerphone** *n* répondeur *m* (téléphonique)

ant /ænt/ *n* fourmi *f*

antagonize /ænˈtæɡənaɪz/ *vt* (annoy) contrarier; (stronger) éveiller l'hostilité de

Antarctic /ænˈtɑːktɪk/ **A** *pr n* **the ~** l'Antarctique *m*
B *adj* antarctique

antelope /ˈæntɪləʊp/ *n* antilope *f*

antenatal /ˌæntɪˈneɪtl/ *adj* prénatal/-e

antenatal class *n* (BrE) cours *m* de préparation à l'accouchement

antenna /ænˈtenə/ *n* (*pl* **-ae** *ou* **-as**) antenne *f*

anthropology /ˌænθrəˈpɒlədʒɪ/ *n* anthropologie *f*

anti /ˈæntɪ/ **A** *prep* contre
B **anti(-)** *pref* anti(-)

antibacterial /ˈæntɪbækˈtɪərɪəl/ *adj* antibactérien/-ienne

antibiotic /ˌæntɪbaɪˈɒtɪk/ *n* antibiotique *m*; **on ~s** sous antibiotiques

anticipate /ænˈtɪsɪpeɪt/ *vt* **1** (foresee) prévoir, s'attendre à ‹*problem, delay*›; **as ~d** comme prévu
2 (guess in advance) anticiper ‹*needs, result*›
3 (pre-empt) devancer ‹*person, act*›

anticipation /ænˌtɪsɪˈpeɪʃn/ *n* **1** (excitement) excitation *f*; (pleasure in advance) plaisir *m* anticipé
2 (expectation) prévision *f* (**of** de)

anticlimax /ˌæntɪˈklaɪmæks/ *n* déception *f*

anticlockwise /ˌæntɪˈklɒkwaɪz/ *adj, adv* (BrE) dans le sens inverse des aiguilles d'une montre

antidepressant /ˌæntɪdɪˈpresnt/ *n* antidépresseur *m*

antidote /ˈæntɪdəʊt/ *n* antidote *m* (**to, for** contre, à)

anti-globalization *n* antimondialisme *m*

antihistamine /ˌæntɪˈhɪstəmɪn/ *n* antihistaminique *m*

antique /ænˈtiːk/ **A** *n* (object) objet *m* ancien *or* d'époque; (furniture) meuble *m* ancien *or* d'époque
B *adj* ancien/-ienne

antique shop *n* magasin *m* d'antiquités

anti-Semitism /ˌæntɪˈsemɪtɪzəm/ *n* antisémitisme *m*

antiseptic /ˌæntɪˈseptɪk/ *n, adj* antiseptique *m*

antisocial /ˌæntɪˈsəʊʃl/ *adj* **1 ~ behaviour** comportement *m* incorrect; (criminal behaviour) comportement *m* délinquant
2 (reclusive) sauvage

antiterrorism /ˌæntiˈterərɪzəm/ *n* antiterrorisme *m*; **~ measures** mesures *fpl* antiterrorisme; **~ legislation** législation *f* antiterroriste

anti-terrorist *adj* antiterroriste

anti-theft /ˌæntɪˈθeft/ *adj* ‹*lock, device*› antivol *inv*

anti-virus software *n* logiciel *m* antivirus

anti-war /ˌæntiˈwɔː(r)/ /ˌæntiˈwɔː(r)/ *adj* anti-guerre

antlers /ˈæntləz/ *npl* bois *mpl* de cerf

anxiety /æŋˈzaɪətɪ/ *n* **1** (worry) grandes inquiétudes *fpl* (**about** à propos de, **for** pour); **to be in a state of ~** être angoissé/-e
2 (eagerness) désir *m* ardent (**to do** de faire)
3 (in psychology) anxiété *f*

anxiety attack *n* crise *f* d'angoisse

anxious /ˈæŋkʃəs/ *adj* **1** (worried) très inquiet/-iète (**about** à propos de, **for** pour); **to be ~ about doing** s'inquiéter de faire
2 ‹*moment, time*› angoissant/-e
3 (eager) très désireux/-euse (**to do** de faire)

anxiously /ˈæŋkʃəslɪ/ *adv* **1** (worriedly) avec inquiétude
2 (eagerly) avec impatience

any /ˈenɪ/

When *any* is used as a determiner in questions and conditional sentences it is translated by *du, de l', de la* or *des* according to the gender and number of the noun that follows: *is there any soap?* = y a-t-il du savon?; *is there any flour?* = y a-t-il de la farine?; *are there any questions?* = est-ce qu'il y a des questions?

In negative sentences *any* is translated by *de* or *d'* (before a vowel or mute 'h'): *we don't have any money* = nous n'avons pas d'argent.

When *any* is used as a pronoun in negative sentences and in questions it is translated by *en*: *we don't have any* = nous n'en avons pas; *have you got any?* = est-ce que vous en avez?

For more examples and other uses see the entry below.

A *det* **1** (in questions, conditional sentences) du/de l'/de la/des; **is there ~ tea?** est-ce qu'il y a du thé?; **if you have ~ money** si vous avez de l'argent
2 (with negative) de, d'; **I don't need ~ advice** je n'ai pas besoin de conseils
3 (no matter which) n'importe quel/quelle, tout; **~ pen will do** n'importe quel stylo fera l'affaire; **you can have ~ cup you like** vous pouvez prendre n'importe quelle tasse; **I'm ready to help in ~ way I can** je suis prêt à faire tout ce que je peux pour aider; **come round and see me ~ time** passe me voir quand tu veux
B *pron, quantif* **1** (in questions, conditional sentences) **have you got ~?** est-ce que vous en avez?; **have ~ of you got a car?** est-ce que l'un/-e d'entre vous a une voiture?
2 (with negative) en; **he hasn't got ~** il n'en a pas; **there is hardly ~ left** il n'en reste presque pas; **she doesn't like ~ of them** (people) elle n'aime aucun/-e d'entre eux/elles; (things) elle n'en aime aucun/-e
3 (no matter which) n'importe lequel/laquelle; **'which colour would you like?'—'~'** 'quelle couleur veux-tu?'—'n'importe laquelle'; **~ of those pens** n'importe lequel de ces stylos; **~ of them could do it** n'importe qui d'entre eux/elles pourrait le faire
C *adv* **have you got ~ more of these?** est-ce que vous en avez d'autres?; **do you want ~ more wine?** voulez-vous encore du vin?; **he doesn't live here ~ more** il n'habite plus ici

anybody /ˈenɪbɒdɪ/ *pron* (*also* **anyone**)
1 (in questions, conditional sentences) quelqu'un; **is there ~ in the house?** est-ce qu'il y a quelqu'un dans la maison?; **if ~ asks, tell them I've gone out** si quelqu'un me cherche, dis que je suis sorti
2 (with negative) personne; **there wasn't ~ in the house** il n'y avait personne dans la maison; **I didn't have ~ to talk to** il n'y avait personne avec qui j'aurais pu parler
3 (no matter who) n'importe qui; **~ could do it** n'importe qui pourrait le faire; **~ who wants to, can go** tous ceux qui le veulent, peuvent y aller; **~ can make a mistake** ça arrive à tout le monde de faire une erreur; **~ would think you were deaf** c'est à croire que tu es sourd

anyhow /ˈenɪhaʊ/ *adv* **1** = **anyway 1**
2 (carelessly) n'importe comment

✓ **anyone** /ˈenɪwʌn/ = **anybody**

✓ **anything** /ˈenɪθɪŋ/ *pron* **1** (in questions, conditional sentences) quelque chose; **is there ~ to be done?** peut-on faire quelque chose?
2 (with negative) rien; **she didn't say ~** elle n'a rien dit; **he didn't have ~ to do** il n'avait rien à faire; **don't believe ~ he says** ne crois pas un mot de ce qu'il dit
3 (no matter what) tout; **~ is possible** tout est possible; **she'll eat ~** elle mange tout; **he was ~ but happy** il n'était pas du tout heureux

anytime /ˈenɪtaɪm/ *adv* (*also* **any time**) n'importe quand; **~ after 2 pm** n'importe quand à partir de 14 heures; **~ you like** quand tu veux; **he could arrive ~ now** il pourrait arriver d'un moment à l'autre

✓ **anyway** /ˈenɪweɪ/ *adv* **1** (*also* **anyhow**) (in any case) de toute façon
2 (all the same) quand même; **I don't really like hats, but I'll try it on ~** je n'aime pas vraiment les chapeaux, mais je vais quand même l'essayer; **thanks ~** merci quand même
3 (at any rate) en tout cas; **we can't go out, not yet ~** nous ne pouvons pas sortir, pas pour l'instant en tout cas
4 (well) **'~, we arrived at the station...'** 'bref, nous sommes arrivés à la gare...'

✓ **anywhere** /ˈenɪweə(r), (AmE) -hweər/ *adv*
1 (in questions, conditional sentences) quelque part; **we're going to Spain, if ~** si on va quelque part, ce sera en Espagne
2 (with negative) nulle part; **you can't go ~** tu ne peux aller nulle part; **there isn't ~ to sit** il n'y a pas de place pour s'asseoir; **you won't get ~ if you don't pass your exams** tu n'arriveras à rien si tu ne réussis pas tes examens; **crying isn't going to get you ~** ça ne t'avancera à rien de pleurer
3 (no matter where) n'importe où; **~ you like** où tu veux; **~ in England** partout en Angleterre

✓ **apart** /əˈpɑːt/ **A** *adj, adv* **1 trees planted 10 metres ~** des arbres plantés à 10 mètres d'intervalle
2 (separated) séparé/-e; **we hate being ~** nous détestons être séparés; **they need to be kept ~** il faut les garder séparés
3 (to one side) **he stood ~ (from the group)** il se tenait à l'écart (du groupe)
B apart from *phr* **1** (separate from) à l'écart de; **it stands ~ from the other houses** elle est à l'écart des autres maisons; **he lives ~ from his wife** il vit séparé de sa femme
2 (leaving aside) en dehors de, à part; **~ from being illegal, it's also dangerous** (mis) à part que c'est illégal, c'est aussi dangereux

apartheid /əˈpɑːtheɪt, -aɪt/ *n* apartheid *m*

✓ **apartment** /əˈpɑːtmənt/ *n* appartement *m*

apartment block *n* immeuble *m*

apartment house *n* (AmE) résidence *f*

apathetic /ˌæpəˈθetɪk/ *adj* (by nature) amorphe; (from illness, depression) apathique

apex /ˈeɪpeks/ *n* (*pl* **-exes**, **-ices**) sommet *m*

APEX /ˈeɪpeks/ *n* (*abbr* = **Advance Purchase Excursion**) APEX *m*

apologetic /əˌpɒləˈdʒetɪk/ *adj* ‹*gesture, letter*› d'excuse; **to be ~ (about)** s'excuser (de)

apologize /əˈpɒlədʒaɪz/ *vi* s'excuser (**to sb** auprès de qn, **for sth** de qch, **for doing** d'avoir fait)

✓ mot clé

apology /əˈpɒlədʒɪ/ *n* excuses *fpl* (**for sth** pour qch, **for doing** pour avoir fait); **to make an ~** s'excuser

apostrophe /əˈpɒstrəfɪ/ *n* apostrophe *f*

app /ap/ *n* (Comput) application *f*

appal (BrE), **appall** (AmE) /əˈpɔːl/ *vt* ((BrE) *p prés etc* **-ll-**) (shock) scandaliser; (horrify, dismay) horrifier

appalling /əˈpɔːlɪŋ/ *adj* **1** ‹*crime, conditions*› épouvantable
2 ‹*manners, joke, taste*› exécrable; ‹*noise, weather*› épouvantable

apparatus /ˌæpəˈreɪtəs, (AmE) -ˈrætəs/ *n* (gen) appareil *m*; (in gym) agrès *mpl*

apparent /əˈpærənt/ *adj* **1** (seeming) ‹*contradiction, willingness*› apparent/-e
2 (clear) évident/-e; **for no ~ reason** sans raison apparente

apparently /əˈpærəntlɪ/ *adv* apparemment

appeal /əˈpiːl/ **A** *n* **1** (gen), (Law) appel *m* (**for** à, **on behalf of** en faveur de)
2 (attraction) charme *m*; (interest) intérêt *m*
B *vi* **1** (Law) faire appel (**against** de)
2 (Sport) **to ~ to** demander l'arbitrage de ‹*referee*›; **to ~ against** contester ‹*decision*›
3 to ~ for lancer un appel à ‹*order, tolerance*›; faire appel à ‹*witnesses*›; **to ~ for help** demander de l'aide
4 (attract) **to ~ to sb** ‹*idea*› tenter qn; ‹*person*› plaire à qn; ‹*place*› attirer qn

appeal fund *n* fonds *m* d'aide

appealing /əˈpiːlɪŋ/ *adj* **1** (attractive) ‹*child*› attachant/-e; ‹*idea*› séduisant/-e; ‹*modesty*› charmant/-e
2 ‹*look*› suppliant/-e

appear /əˈpɪə(r)/ *vi* **1** (become visible) apparaître
2 (turn up) arriver
3 (seem) **to ~ to be/to do** ‹*person*› avoir l'air d'être/de faire; **to ~ depressed** avoir l'air déprimé; **it ~s that** il semble que
4 ‹*book, article, name*› paraître
5 to ~ on stage paraître en scène; **to ~ on TV** passer à la télévision
6 (Law) **to ~ in court** comparaître devant le tribunal

appearance /əˈpɪərəns/ *n* **1** (arrival) (of person, vehicle) arrivée *f*; (of development, invention) apparition *f*; **to put in an ~** faire une apparition
2 (on TV, in play, film) passage *m*
3 (look) (of person) apparence *f*; (of district, object) aspect *m*; **to judge** *or* **go by ~s** se fier aux apparences

appendicitis /əˌpendɪˈsaɪtɪs/ *n* appendicite *f*

appendix /əˈpendɪks/ *n* (*pl* **-ixes**, **-ices**) appendice *m*; **to have one's ~ removed** se faire opérer de l'appendicite

appetite /ˈæpɪtaɪt/ *n* appétit *m*

appetite suppressant *n* anorexigène *m*

appetizer /ˈæpɪtaɪzə(r)/ *n* (biscuit, olive etc) amuse-gueule *m inv*; (starter) hors-d'œuvre *m*

appetizing /ˈæpɪtaɪzɪŋ/ *adj* appétissant/-e

applaud /əˈplɔːd/ *vt*, *vi* applaudir

applause /əˈplɔːz/ *n* applaudissements *mpl*; **there was a burst of ~** les applaudissements ont éclaté

apple /ˈæpl/ *n* pomme *f*

apple core *n* trognon *m* de pomme

applet /ˈæplɪt/ *n* (Comput) applet *m*, applette *f*

apple tree *n* pommier *m*

appliance /əˈplaɪəns/ *n* appareil *m*; **household ~** appareil électroménager

applicant /ˈæplɪkənt/ *n* (for job, membership) candidat/-e *m/f* (**for** à); (for passport, benefit, loan) demandeur/-euse *m/f* (**for** de); (for citizenship) postulant/-e *m/f* (**for** à)

application /ˌæplɪˈkeɪʃn/ *n* **1** (for job) candidature *f* (**for** à); (for membership, passport, loan) demande *f* (**for** de)
2 (of ointment) application *f* (**to** à)
3 (of law, penalty, rule) application *f*

application form *n* (gen) formulaire *m* de demande; (for job) formulaire *m* de candidature; (for membership) demande *f* d'inscription

apply /əˈplaɪ/ **A** *vt* (gen) appliquer; exercer ‹*pressure*› (**to** sur)
B *vi* **1 to ~ (for)** faire une demande (de) ‹*passport, loan, visa, permit*›; poser sa candidature (à) ‹*job*›; **to ~ to** faire une demande d'inscription à ‹*college*›
2 (be valid) ‹*definition, term*› s'appliquer (**to** à); ‹*ban, rule, penalty*› être en vigueur
C *v refl* **to ~ oneself** s'appliquer

appoint /əˈpɔɪnt/ *vt* nommer ‹*person*› (**to sth** à qch, **to do** pour faire, **as** comme); fixer ‹*date, place*›

appointment /əˈpɔɪntmənt/ *n* **1** (meeting) rendez-vous *m* (**at** chez, **with** avec, **to do** pour faire); **business ~** rendez-vous *m* d'affaires; **to make an ~** prendre rendez-vous
2 (to post) nomination *f*

appraisal /əˈpreɪzl/ *n* évaluation *f*

appreciate /əˈpriːʃɪeɪt/ **A** *vt* **1** apprécier ‹*help, effort*›; être sensible à ‹*favour*›; être reconnaissant/-e de ‹*kindness, sympathy*›; **I'd ~ it if you could reply soon** je vous serais reconnaissant de répondre sans tarder
2 (realize) se rendre (bien) compte de, être conscient/-e de
3 (enjoy) apprécier ‹*music, art, food*›
B *vi* ‹*object*› prendre de la valeur; ‹*value*› monter

appreciation /əˌpriːʃɪˈeɪʃn/ *n* **1** (gratitude) remerciement *m* (**for** pour)
2 (enjoyment) appréciation *f* (**of** de)
3 (increase) hausse *f* (**of**, **in** de)

appreciative /əˈpriːʃətɪv/ *adj* **1** (grateful) reconnaissant/-e (**of** de)
2 (admiring) admiratif/-ive

apprehensive /ˌæprɪˈhensɪv/ *adj* inquiet/-iète; **to be ~ about sth/doing**

appréhender qch/de faire

apprentice /ə'prentɪs/ *n* apprenti/-e *m/f* (**to** de)

apprenticeship /ə'prentɪsʃɪp/ *n* apprentissage *m*

🔑 **approach** /ə'prəʊtʃ/ **A** *n* **1** (route of access) voie *f* d'accès
2 (arrival) approche *f*
3 (to problem) approche *f*
4 to make ~es to sb faire des démarches auprès de qn
B *vt* **1** (draw near to) s'approcher de ‹*person, place*›; (verge on) approcher de
2 (deal with) aborder ‹*problem, subject*›
3 to ~ sb (about sth) s'adresser à qn (au sujet de qch); (more formally) faire des démarches auprès de qn (pour qch)
C *vi* ‹*person, car*› (s')approcher; ‹*event, season*› approcher

approachable /ə'prəʊtʃəbl/ *adj* abordable, d'un abord facile

🔑 **appropriate** **A** /ə'prəʊprɪət/ *adj*
1 ‹*behaviour, choice, place*› approprié/-e (**for** pour); ‹*dress, gift*› qui convient *after n* (**for** à); ‹*punishment*› juste (**for** à); ‹*name*› bien choisi/-e
2 (relevant) ‹*authority*› compétent/-e
B /ə'prəʊprɪeɪt/ *vt* s'approprier ‹*property, document*›; affecter ‹*funds, land*› (**for** à)

appropriately /ə'prəʊprɪətlɪ/ *adv*
1 ‹*behave, speak*› avec à-propos; ‹*dress*› convenablement
2 ‹*designed, chosen, sited*› judicieusement

approval /ə'pru:vl/ *n* approbation *f* (**of** de, **to do** pour faire); **on ~** à l'essai

🔑 **approve** /ə'pru:v/ **A** *vt* approuver ‹*product, plan*›; accepter ‹*person*›
B *vi* **to ~ of sb/sth** apprécier qn/qch; **he doesn't ~ of drinking** il est contre l'alcool

approving /ə'pru:vɪŋ/ *adj* approbateur/-trice

approximate /ə'prɒksɪmət/ *adj* approximatif/-ive

🔑 **approximately** /ə'prɒksɪmətlɪ/ *adv*
1 (about) environ; **at ~ four o'clock** vers quatre heures
2 ‹*equal, correct*› à peu près

apricot /'eɪprɪkɒt/ *n* (fruit) abricot *m*

🔑 **April** /'eɪprɪl/ *n* avril *m*

April Fools' Day *n* le premier avril

apron /'eɪprən/ *n* tablier *m*

apt *adj* ‹*choice, description*› heureux/-euse; ‹*title, style*› approprié/-e (**to, for** à)

aptitude /'æptɪtju:d, (AmE) -tu:d/ *n* aptitude *f*

aquarium /ə'kweərɪəm/ *n* (*pl* **-iums, -ia**) aquarium *m*

Aquarius /ə'kweərɪəs/ *n* Verseau *m*

aquarobics /ˌækwə'rɒbɪks/ *n* aquagym *f*

aquatic /ə'kwætɪk/ *adj* (gen) aquatique; ‹*sport*› nautique

aqueduct /'ækwɪdʌkt/ *n* aqueduc *m*

Arab /'ærəb/ **A** *n* (person) Arabe *mf*
B *adj* arabe

Arabic /'ærəbɪk/ **A** *n* (language) arabe *m*
B *adj* arabe; ‹*lesson, teacher*› d'arabe

Arab-Israeli *adj* israélo-arabe

Arab Spring *n* (Pol) printemps *m* arabe

arbitrary /'ɑ:bɪtrərɪ, (AmE) 'ɑ:rbɪtrerɪ/ *adj* arbitraire

arbitration /ˌɑ:bɪ'treɪʃn/ *n* arbitrage *m*; **to go to ~** ≈ aller aux prud'hommes

arcade /ɑ:'keɪd/ *n* arcade *f*; **shopping ~** galerie *f* marchande

arch /ɑ:tʃ/ **A** *n* arche *f*
B *vt* arquer; **to ~ one's back** ‹*person*› cambrer le dos; ‹*cat*› faire le dos rond
C **arch(-)** *pref* par excellence; **~-enemy** ennemi/-e *m/f* juré/-e; **~-rival** grand rival

archaeologist (BrE), **archeologist** (AmE) /ˌɑ:kɪ'ɒlədʒɪst/ *n* archéologue *mf*

archaeology (BrE), **archeology** (AmE) /ˌɑ:kɪ'ɒlədʒɪ/ *n* archéologie *f*

archery /'ɑ:tʃərɪ/ *n* tir *m* à l'arc

architect /'ɑ:kɪtekt/ *n* architecte *mf*

architecture /'ɑ:kɪtektʃə(r)/ *n* architecture *f*

archive /'ɑ:kaɪv/ *n* archive *f*

Arctic /'ɑ:ktɪk/ **A** *pr n* **the ~** l'Arctique *m*
B *adj* arctique

ardent /'ɑ:dnt/ *adj* ‹*defence, opposition, lover*› passionné/-e; ‹*supporter*› fervent/-e

🔑 **area** /'eərɪə/ *n* **1** (region) région *f*; (of city) zone *f*; (district) quartier *m*; **in the London ~** dans la région de Londres; **residential ~** zone *f* résidentielle
2 (in building) **dining ~** coin *m* salle-à-manger; **no smoking ~** zone *f* non-fumeurs; **waiting ~** salle *f* d'attente
3 (of knowledge) domaine *m*; (of business) secteur *m*
4 (in geometry) aire *f*; (of land) superficie *f*

area code *n* indicatif *m* de zone

arena /ə'ri:nə/ *n* arène *f*

Argentina /ˌɑ:dʒən'ti:nə/ *pr n* Argentine *f*

🔑 **argue** /'ɑ:gju:/ **A** *vt* (debate) discuter (de), débattre (de); **to ~ that** (maintain) soutenir que
B *vi* **1** (quarrel) se disputer (**with** avec, **about, over** sur, pour)
2 (debate) discuter (**about** de)
3 (put one's case) argumenter (**for** en faveur de, **against** contre)

🔑 **argument** /'ɑ:gjʊmənt/ *n* **1** (quarrel) dispute *f* (**about** à propos de); **to have an ~** se disputer
2 (discussion) débat *m*, discussion *f*
3 (case) argument *m* (**for** en faveur de, **against** contre)

argumentative /ˌɑ:gjʊ'mentətɪv/ *adj* ergoteur/-euse

Aries /'eəri:z/ *n* Bélier *m*

🔑 **arise** /ə'raɪz/ *vi* (*prét* **arose**, *pp* **arisen**)

1 ‹*problem*› survenir; ‹*question*› se poser; **if the need ~s** si le besoin se fait sentir
2 (be the result of) résulter (**from** de)

aristocrat /ærɪstəkræt, (AmE) ə'rɪst-/ *n* aristocrate *mf*

arithmetic /ə'rɪθmətɪk/ *n* arithmétique *f*

arm /ɑːm/ **A** *n* bras *m*; (of chair) accoudoir *m*; **~ in ~** bras dessus bras dessous; **to have sth over/under one's ~** avoir qch sur/sous le bras; **to fold one's ~s** croiser les bras
B arms *npl* (weapons) armes *fpl*
C *vt* (Mil) armer
IDIOM **to keep sb at ~'s length** tenir qn à distance

armaments *npl* armements *mpl*

armband /ɑːmbænd/ *n* (for swimmer) bracelet *m* de natation; (for mourner) crêpe *m* de deuil

armchair /ɑːmtʃeə(r)/ *n* fauteuil *m*

armed /ɑːmd/ *adj* armé/-e (**with** de); ‹*raid, robbery*› à main armée

armed forces, **armed services** *npl* forces *fpl* armées

armour (BrE), **armor** (AmE) /'ɑːmə(r)/ *n* armure *f*

armoured (BrE), **armored** (AmE) /'ɑːməd/ *adj* blindé/-e

armour-plated (BrE), **armor-plated** (AmE) *adj* ‹*vehicle*› blindé/-e; ‹*ship*› cuirassé/-e

armpit *n* aisselle *f*

arms control *n* contrôle *m* des armements

arms race *n* course *f* aux armements

arms treaty *n* traité *m* sur le contrôle des armements

army /'ɑːmɪ/ **A** *n* armée *f*; **to join the ~** s'engager
B *adj* militaire

aroma /ə'rəʊmə/ *n* arôme *m*

aromatherapist /əˌrəʊmə'θerəpɪst/ *n* aromathérapeute *mf*

aromatherapy /əˌrəʊmə'θerəpɪ/ *n* aromathérapie *f*

around /ə'raʊnd/ **A** *adv* **1** (approximately) environ, à peu près; **at ~ 3 pm** vers 15 heures
2 (in the vicinity) **to be (somewhere) ~** être dans les parages; **are they ~?** est-ce qu'ils sont là?
3 (in circulation) **CDs have been ~ for years** ça fait des années que les CD existent; **one of the most gifted musicians ~** un des musiciens les plus doués du moment
4 all ~ tout autour; **the only garage for miles ~** le seul garage à des kilomètres à la ronde; **to ask sb (to come) ~** dire à qn de passer
B *prep* **1** autour de ‹*fire, table*›; **the villages ~ Dublin** les villages des environs de Dublin; **clothes scattered ~ the room** des vêtements éparpillés partout dans la pièce; **(all) ~ the world** partout dans le monde; **to walk ~ the town** se promener dans la ville; **the people ~ here** les gens d'ici
2 (at) vers; **~ midnight** vers minuit

arouse /ə'raʊz/ *vt* éveiller ‹*interest, suspicion*›; exciter ‹*anger, jealousy*›; **to be ~d** ‹*person*› être excité/-e

arrange /ə'reɪndʒ/ **A** *vt* **1** disposer ‹*chairs, ornaments*›; arranger ‹*room, hair, clothes*›; arranger, disposer ‹*flowers*›
2 (organize) organiser ‹*party, meeting, holiday*›; fixer ‹*date, appointment*›; **to ~ to do** s'arranger pour faire
3 convenir de ‹*loan*›
B *vi* **to ~ for sth** prendre des dispositions pour qch; **to ~ for sb to do** prendre des dispositions pour que qn fasse

arrangement /ə'reɪndʒmənt/ *n* **1** (of objects, chairs) disposition *f*; (of flowers) composition *f*
2 (agreement) entente *f*, accord *m*; **to come to an ~** s'arranger
3 (preparations) **~s** préparatifs *mpl*; **to make ~s to do** s'arranger pour faire

array /ə'reɪ/ *n* gamme *f*

arrears /ə'rɪəz/ *npl* arriéré *m*; **I am in ~ with my payments** j'ai du retard dans mes paiements

arrest /ə'rest/ **A** *n* arrestation *f*; **to be under ~** être en état d'arrestation
B *vt* arrêter

arrival /ə'raɪvl/ *n* arrivée *f*; **on sb's ~** à l'arrivée de qn

arrival(s) lounge *n* salon *m* d'arrivée

arrivals board *n* tableau *m* d'arrivée

arrival time *n* heure *f* d'arrivée

arrive /ə'raɪv/ *vi* **1** arriver (**at** à, **from** de)
2 to ~ at parvenir à ‹*decision, solution*›

arrogant /'ærəgənt/ *adj* arrogant/-e

arrow /'ærəʊ/ *n* flèche *f*

arse /ɑːs/ *n* (BrE) (sl) cul *m*

arson /'ɑːsn/ *n* incendie *m* criminel

arsonist /'ɑːsənɪst/ *n* pyromane *mf*

art /ɑːt/ *n* art *m*; **I'm bad at ~** je suis mauvais en dessin

artefact /'ɑːtɪfækt/ *n* objet *m* (fabriqué)

artery /'ɑːtərɪ/ *n* artère *f*

art exhibition *n* (paintings) exposition *f* de tableaux; (sculpture) exposition *f* de sculpture

art gallery *n* (museum) musée *m* d'art; (commercial) galerie *f* d'art

arthritis /ɑː'θraɪtɪs/ *n* arthrite *f*

artichoke /'ɑːtɪtʃəʊk/ *n* artichaut *m*

article /'ɑːtɪkl/ *n* article *m* (**about, on** sur)

artificial /ˌɑːtɪ'fɪʃl/ *adj* artificiel/-ielle

artificial limb *n* prothèse *f*, membre *m* artificiel

artificial respiration *n* respiration *f* artificielle

artillery /ɑː'tɪlərɪ/ *n* artillerie *f*

artisan /ˌɑːtɪ'zæn, (AmE) 'ɑːrtɪzn/ *n* artisan *m*

a

artist /ˈɑːtɪst/ *n* artiste *mf*

artistic /ɑːˈtɪstɪk/ *adj* ‹*talent*› artistique; ‹*temperament, person*› artiste

arts *npl* **1** (culture) **the ~** les arts *mpl*
2 (Univ) lettres *fpl*
3 ~ and crafts artisanat *m*

art school *n* école *f* des beaux-arts

arts student *n* étudiant/-e *m/f* en lettres

art student *n* étudiant/-e *m/f* des beaux-arts

as /æz, əz/ **A** *conj* **1** comme; **~ you know** comme vous le savez; **~ usual** comme d'habitude; **do ~ I say** fais ce que je te dis; **leave it ~ it is** laisse-le tel quel; **~ she was coming down the stairs** comme elle descendait l'escalier; **~ she grew older** au fur et à mesure qu'elle vieillissait; **~ a child, he...** (quand il était) enfant, il...
2 (because, since) comme, puisque; **~ you were out, I left a note** comme *or* puisque tu étais sorti, j'ai laissé un petit mot
3 (although) **strange ~ it may seem** aussi curieux que cela puisse paraître; **try ~ he might, he could not forget it** il avait beau essayer, il ne pouvait pas oublier
4 the same...~ le/la même...que; **I've got a jacket the same ~ yours** j'ai la même veste que toi
5 so ~ to do pour faire, afin de faire
B *prep* comme, en; **dressed ~ a sailor** habillé/-e en marin; **he works ~ a pilot** il travaille comme pilote; **a job ~ a teacher** un poste d'enseignant/-e; **to treat sb ~ an equal** traiter qn en égal
C *adv* (in comparisons) **he is ~ intelligent ~ you** il est aussi intelligent que toi; **~ fast ~ you can** aussi vite que possible; **he's twice ~ strong ~ me** il est deux fois plus fort que moi; **I have ~ much** *or* **~ many ~ she has** j'en ai autant qu'elle; **~ much ~ possible** autant que possible; **~ little ~ possible** le moins possible; **~ soon ~ possible** dès que possible; **he has a house in Nice ~ well ~ an apartment in Paris** il a une maison à Nice ainsi qu'un appartement à Paris
D as for *phr* quant à, pour ce qui est de
E as of *phr* à partir de
F as if *phr* comme (si); **it looks ~ if we've lost** on dirait que nous avons perdu
G as long as *phr* du moment que (+ *indicative*), pourvu que (+ *subjunctive*)
H as such *phr* en tant que tel

asbestos /æzˈbestɒs, æs-/ *n* amiante *m*

ASBO /ˈæzbəʊ/ *n* (BrE) (*abbr* = **anti-social behaviour order**) ordre *m* sur le comportement antisocial

ascend /əˈsend/ *vt* gravir ‹*steps, hill*›

ascent /əˈsent/ *n* ascension *f*

ascertain /ˌæsəˈteɪn/ *vt* établir (**that** que)

ash /æʃ/ *n* **1** cendre *f*
2 (*also* **~ tree**) frêne *m*

ashamed /əˈʃeɪmd/ *adj* honteux/-euse; **to be ~** avoir honte (**of** de, **to do** de faire, **that** que (+ *subjunctive*))

ashen /ˈæʃn/ *adj* ‹*complexion*› terreux/-euse

ashore /əˈʃɔː(r)/ *adv* **to go ~** débarquer; **washed ~** rejeté/-e sur le rivage

ashtray *n* cendrier *m*

Asia /ˈeɪʃə, (AmE) ˈeɪʒə/ *pr n* Asie *f*

Asian /ˈeɪʃn, (AmE) ˈeɪʒn/ **A** *n* (from Far East) Asiatique *mf*; (in UK) personne *f* originaire du sous-continent indien
B *adj* asiatique

aside /əˈsaɪd/ **A** *n* **to say sth in an ~** dire qch en aparté
B *adv* **to stand ~** s'écarter; **to put sth ~** (save) mettre qch de côté; (in shop) réserver qch; **to take sb ~** prendre qn à part
C aside from *phr* à part

ask /ɑːsk, (AmE) æsk/ **A** *vt* **1** demander; **to ~ a question** poser une question; **to ~ sb sth** demander qch à qn; **to ~ sb to do** demander à qn de faire
2 (invite) inviter ‹*person*› (**to** à); **to ~ sb to dinner** inviter qn à dîner
B *vi* **1** (request) demander
2 (make enquiries) se renseigner; **to ~ about sb** s'informer au sujet de qn
C *v refl* **to ~ oneself** se demander

■ **ask after** demander des nouvelles de ‹*person*›

■ **ask for**: **A ~ for [sth]** demander ‹*drink, money, help*›
B ~ for [sb] demander à voir; (on phone) demander à parler à

askance /əˈskæns/ *adv* **to look ~ at sb/sth** considérer qn/qch avec méfiance

askew /əˈskjuː/ *adj, adv* de travers

asking price *n* prix *m* demandé

asleep /əˈsliːp/ *adj* **to be ~** dormir; **to fall ~** s'endormir; **to be sound** *or* **fast ~** dormir à poings fermés

asparagus /əˈspærəgəs/ *n* asperge *f*

aspect /ˈæspekt/ *n* **1** aspect *m*
2 (of house) orientation *f*

asphalt /ˈæsfælt, (AmE) -fɔːlt/ *n* bitume *m*

aspic /ˈæspɪk/ *n* aspic *m*

aspiration /ˌæspɪˈreɪʃn/ *n* aspiration *f* (**to** à)

aspire /əˈspaɪə(r)/ *vi* aspirer (**to** à, **to do** à faire)

aspirin /ˈæsprɪn/ *n* aspirine® *f*

ass /æs/ *n* **1** (donkey) âne *m*
2 (fam) (fool) idiot/-e *m/f*
3 (AmE) (sl) cul *m*

assassin /əˈsæsɪn, (AmE) -sn/ *n* assassin *m*

assassinate /əˈsæsɪneɪt, (AmE) -sən-/ *vt* assassiner

assassination /əˌsæsɪˈneɪʃn, (AmE) -səˈneɪʃn/ *n* assassinat *m*

assault /əˈsɔːlt/ **A** *n* **1** (Law) agression *f* (**on** sur)
2 (Mil) assaut *m* (**on** de)
B *vt* **1** (Law) agresser; **to be indecently ~ed**

---

mot clé

être victime d'une agression sexuelle
2 (Mil) assaillir

assemble /ə'sembl/ **A** *vt* **1** (gather) rassembler
2 (construct) assembler; **easy to ~** facile à monter
B *vi* ‹*passengers, marchers*› se rassembler; ‹*parliament, team, family*› se réunir

assembly /ə'semblɪ/ *n* **1** (gen) assemblée *f*
2 (Sch) rassemblement *m*
3 (of components, machines) assemblage *m*

assembly line *n* chaîne *f* de montage

assent /ə'sent/ **A** *n* assentiment *m* (**to** à)
B *vi* donner son assentiment (**to** à)

assert /ə'sɜːt/ *vt* **1** (state) affirmer (**that** que); **to ~ oneself** s'affirmer
2 revendiquer ‹*right, claim*›

assertion /ə'sɜːʃn/ *n* déclaration *f* (**that** selon laquelle)

assertive /ə'sɜːtɪv/ *adj* assuré/-e

assess /ə'ses/ *vt* **1** évaluer ‹*person, problem*›; estimer ‹*damage, value*›
2 fixer ‹*tax*›
3 (Sch) contrôler ‹*pupil*›

assessment /ə'sesmənt/ *n* **1** (evaluation) appréciation *f* (**of** de); (of damage, value) estimation *f* (**of** de)
2 (for tax) imposition *f*
3 (Sch) contrôle *m*

asset /'æset/ *n* atout *m*; **~s** (private) avoir *m*; (of company) actif *m*

assign /ə'saɪn/ *vt* **1** assigner ‹*resources*› (**to** à)
2 to ~ a task to sb confier une tâche à qn
3 (attribute) attribuer (**to** à)
4 (appoint) nommer (**to** à)

assignment /ə'saɪnmənt/ *n* **1** (specific duty) mission *f*
2 (academic) devoir *m*

assimilate /ə'sɪmɪleɪt/ **A** *vt* assimiler
B *vi* s'assimiler (**into** dans)

assist /ə'sɪst/ **A** *vt* **1** (help) aider; (in organization) assister (**to do, in doing** à faire)
2 (facilitate) faciliter ‹*development, process*›
B *vi* aider (**in doing** à faire); **to ~ in** prendre part à ‹*operation, rescue*›

assistance /ə'sɪstəns/ *n* aide *f* (**to** à); (more formal) assistance *f* (**to** à)

assistant /ə'sɪstənt/ **A** *n* **1** (helper) assistant/-e *m/f*; (in hierarchy) adjoint/-e *m/f*
2 (*also* **shop ~**) vendeur/-euse *m/f*
3 (BrE) **(foreign language) ~** (in school) assistant/-e *m/f*; (in university) lecteur/-trice *m/f*
B *adj* ‹*editor, manager*› adjoint/-e

associate **A** /ə'səʊʃɪət/ *n* associé/-e *m/f*
B /ə'səʊʃɪeɪt/ *vt* **1** associer ‹*idea, memory*› (**with** à)
2 to be ~d with ‹*person*› faire partie de ‹*movement, group*›; être mêlé/-e à ‹*shady deal*›
C /ə'səʊʃɪeɪt/ *vi* **to ~ with sb** fréquenter qn

association /əˌsəʊsɪ'eɪʃn/ *n* association *f*

assorted /ə'sɔːtɪd/ *adj* ‹*objects, colours*› varié/-e; ‹*foodstuffs*› assorti/-e

assortment /ə'sɔːtmənt/ *n* (of objects, colours) assortiment *m* (**of** de); (of people) mélange *m* (**of** de)

assume /ə'sjuːm, (AmE) ə'suːm/ *vt* **1** (suppose) supposer (**that** que)
2 prendre ‹*control, identity, office*›; assumer ‹*responsibility*›; affecter ‹*expression, indifference*›; **under an ~d name** sous un nom d'emprunt

assumption /ə'sʌmpʃn/ *n* supposition *f*

assurance /ə'ʃɔːrəns, (AmE) ə'ʃʊərəns/ *n* assurance *f*

assure /ə'ʃɔː(r), (AmE) ə'ʃʊər/ *vt* assurer; **to ~ sb that** assurer à qn que

asterisk /'æstərɪsk/ *n* astérisque *m*

asthma /'æsmə, (AmE) 'æzmə/ *n* asthme *m*

asthmatic /æs'mætɪk/ *n, adj* asthmatique *mf*

astonish /ə'stɒnɪʃ/ *vt* surprendre, étonner

astonished /ə'stɒnɪʃt/ *adj* étonné/-e (**by, at** par, **to do** de faire)

astonishing /ə'stɒnɪʃɪŋ/ *adj* étonnant/-e

astonishment /ə'stɒnɪʃmənt/ *n* étonnement *m*

astound /ə'staʊnd/ *vt* stupéfier

astounding /ə'staʊndɪŋ/ *adj* incroyable

astray /ə'streɪ/ *adv* **1 to go ~** (go missing) se perdre
2 to lead sb ~ (confuse) induire qn en erreur; (corrupt) détourner qn du droit chemin

astride /ə'straɪd/ **A** *adv* à califourchon
B *prep* à califourchon sur

astrologer, **astrologist** /ə'strɒlədʒə(r)/ *n* astrologue *mf*

astrology /ə'strɒlədʒɪ/ *n* astrologie *f*

astronaut /'æstrənɔːt/ *n* astronaute *mf*

astronomer /ə'strɒnəmə(r)/ *n* astronome *mf*

astronomic, **astronomical** *adj* astronomique

astronomy /ə'strɒnəmɪ/ *n* astronomie *f*

astute /ə'stjuːt, (AmE) ə'stuːt/ *adj* astucieux/-ieuse

asylee /əˌsaɪliː/ *n* bénéficiaire *mf* du droit d'asile

asylum /ə'saɪləm/ *n* asile *m*; **lunatic ~** asile de fous

asylum seeker *n* demandeur/-euse *m/f* d'asile

at /æt, ət/ *prep*

At is often translated by *à*: *at the airport* = à l'aéroport; *at midnight* = à minuit; *at the age of 50* = à l'âge de 50 ans.
Remember that *à* + *le always* becomes *au* and *à* + *les always* becomes *aux* (*au bureau, aux bureaux*).

a

> When *at* means *at the house, shop* etc *of*, it is translated by *chez*: *at Amanda's* = chez Amanda; *at the hairdresser's* = chez le coiffeur.
> For examples and other usages, see the entry below.
> *At* is used with many verbs, adjectives and nouns (*look at, good at, at last*) etc. For translations consult the appropriate verb, adjective or noun entry.

1 à; ~ **school** à l'école; ~ **4 o'clock** à quatre heures; ~ **Easter** à Pâques; ~ **night** la nuit; ~ **the moment** en ce moment **2** chez; ~ **my house** chez moi; ~ **home** à la maison, chez soi

atheist /'eɪθɪɪst/ *n, adj* athée *mf*

Athens /'æθɪnz/ *pr n* Athènes

athlete /'æθli:t/ *n* athlète *mf*

athlete's foot /ˌæθli:ts 'fʊt/ *n* mycose *f*

athletic /æθ'letɪk/ *adj* athlétique

athletics /æθ'letɪks/ *n* (BrE) athlétisme *m*; (AmE) sports *mpl*

Atlantic /ət'læntɪk/ **A** *pr n* **the** ~ l'Atlantique *m*
B *adj* ‹*coast*› atlantique

atlas /'ætləs/ *n* atlas *m*

ATM *n* (*abbr* = **automated teller machine**) guichet *m* automatique

atmosphere /'ætməsfɪə(r)/ *n* **1** (air) atmosphère *f*
2 (mood) ambiance *f*; (bad) atmosphère *f*

atom /'ætəm/ *n* atome *m*

atom bomb *n* bombe *f* atomique

atomic /ə'tɒmɪk/ *adj* atomique, nucléaire

atrocious /ə'trəʊʃəs/ *adj* atroce

atrocity /ə'trɒsətɪ/ *n* atrocité *f*

at sign /'æt saɪn/ *n* (Comput) arobase *m*

🔑 **attach** /ə'tætʃ/ *vt* attacher (**to** à)

attaché /ə'tæʃeɪ, (AmE) ˌætə'ʃeɪ/ *n* attaché/-e *m/f*

attaché case *n* attaché-case *m*

attached /ə'tætʃt/ *adj* **1** (fond) **to be** ~ **to** être attaché/-e à
2 ‹*document*› ci-joint/-e

attachment /ə'tætʃmənt/ *n* **1** (affection) attachement *m*
2 (device) accessoire *m*
3 (in email) pièce-jointe *f*

🔑 **attack** /ə'tæk/ **A** *n* **1** (gen) attaque *f* (**on** contre); (criminal) agression *f* (**against, on** contre); (terrorist) attentat *m*
2 (of illness) crise *f* (**of** de)
B *vt* **1** (gen) attaquer; (criminally) agresser ‹*victim*›
2 s'attaquer à ‹*task, problem*›

attacker /ə'tækə(r)/ *n* (gen) agresseur *m*; (Mil, Sport) attaquant/-e *m/f*

🔑 **attempt** /ə'tempt/ **A** *n* **1** tentative *f* (**to do** de faire); **to make an** ~ **to do** *or* **at doing** tenter de faire
2 to make an ~ **on sb's life** attenter à la vie de qn
B *vt* tenter (**to do** de faire); ~**ed murder** tentative *f* de meurtre

🔑 **attend** /ə'tend/ **A** *vt* assister à ‹*ceremony, meeting*›; aller à ‹*church, school*›; suivre ‹*class, course*›
B *vi* être présent/-e
■ **attend to** s'occuper de ‹*person, problem*›

attendance /ə'tendəns/ *n* présence *f* (**at** à)

attendant /ə'tendənt/ *n* (in cloakroom, museum, car park) gardien/-ienne *m/f*; (at petrol station) pompiste *mf*; (at pool) surveillant/-e *m/f*

attendee /ˌæten'di:/ *n* participant/-e *m/f*

🔑 **attention** /ə'tenʃn/ *n* **1** attention *f*; **to draw** ~ **to sth** attirer l'attention sur qch
2 (Mil) **to stand to** *or* **at** ~ être au garde-à-vous; ~! garde-à-vous!

attention deficit disorder *n* troubles *mpl* chroniques de l'attention

attentive /ə'tentɪv/ *adj* (alert) attentif/-ive; (solicitous) attentionné/-e (**to** à)

attic /'ætɪk/ *n* grenier *m*; **the toys are in the** ~ les jouets sont au grenier

attic room *n* mansarde *f*

🔑 **attitude** /'ætɪtju:d, (AmE) -tu:d/ *n* attitude *f* (**to, towards** (BrE) à l'égard de)

attorney /ə'tɜ:nɪ/ *n* (AmE) avocat *m*

🔑 **attract** /ə'trækt/ *vt* attirer

attraction /ə'trækʃn/ *n* **1** (favourable feature) attrait *m* (**of** de, **for** pour)
2 (entertainment, sight) attraction *f*
3 (sexual) attirance *f* (**to** pour)

attractive /ə'træktɪv/ *adj* ‹*person, offer*› séduisant/-e; ‹*child*› charmant/-e; ‹*place*› attrayant/-e

attribute **A** /'ætrɪbju:t/ *n* attribut *m*
B /ə'trɪbju:t/ *vt* attribuer (**to** à)

aubergine /'əʊbəʒi:n/ *n* (BrE) aubergine *f*

auburn /'ɔ:bən/ *adj* auburn *inv*

auction /'ɔ:kʃn/ **A** *n* enchères *fpl*
B *vt* (*also* ~ **off**) vendre [qch] aux enchères

auctioneer /ˌɔ:kʃə'nɪə(r)/ *n* commissaire-priseur *m*

auction house *n* société *f* de commissaires-priseurs

audacity /ɔ:'dæsətɪ/ *n* audace *f*

audible /'ɔ:dəbl/ *adj* audible

🔑 **audience** /'ɔ:dɪəns/ *n* (in cinema, concert, theatre) public *m*, salle *f*; (of radio programme) auditeurs *mpl*; (of TV programme) téléspectateurs *mpl*

audience ratings *npl* indice *m* d'écoute

audio /'ɔ:dɪəʊ/ *adj* audio *inv*

audiobook *n* livre-cassette *m*

audiovisual, **AV** /ˌɔ:dɪəʊ'vɪʒʊəl/ *adj* audiovisuel/-elle

🔑 mot clé

audit /'ɔ:dɪt/ **A** *n* audit *m*
B *vt* auditer, vérifier

audition /ɔ:'dɪʃn/ **A** *n* audition *f* (**for** pour)
B *vt, vi* auditionner (**for** pour)

auditor /'ɔ:dɪtə(r)/ *n* **1** commissaire *m* aux comptes
2 (AmE) (student) auditeur/-trice *m/f*

auditorium /ˌɔ:dɪ'tɔ:rɪəm/ *n* (*pl* **-iums** *ou* **-ia**) salle *f*

augur /'ɔ:gə(r)/ *vi* **to ~ well** être de bon augure

August /'ɔ:gəst/ *n* août *m*

aunt /ɑ:nt, (AmE) ænt/ *n* tante *f*

au pair /ˌəʊ 'peə(r)/ *n* (jeune) fille *f* au pair

aura /'ɔ:rə/ *n* (*pl* **-ras** *ou* **-rae**) (of place) atmosphère *f*; (of person) aura *f*

aural /'ɔ:rəl, aʊrəl/ *adj* **1** (gen) auditif/-ive
2 (Sch) ‹*comprehension, test*› oral/-e

auspicious /ɔ:'spɪʃəs/ *adj* prometteur/-euse

austere /ɒ'stɪə(r), ɔ:'stɪə(r)/ *adj* austère

austerity /ɒ'sterətɪ, ɔ:'sterətɪ/ *n* austérité *f*

Australia /ɒ'streɪlɪə, ɔ:'s-/ *pr n* Australie *f*

Australian /ɒ'streɪlɪən, ɔ:'s-/ **A** *n* Australien/-ienne *m/f*
B *adj* australien/-ienne; ‹*embassy*› d'Australie

Austria /'ɒstrɪə, 'ɔ:strɪə/ *pr n* Autriche *f*

Austrian /'ɒstrɪən, 'ɔ:strɪən/ **A** *n* Autrichien/-ienne *m/f*
B *adj* autrichien/-ienne; ‹*embassy*› d'Autriche

authentic /ɔ:'θentɪk/ *adj* authentique

author /'ɔ:θə(r)/ *n* auteur *m*

authoritarian /ɔ:ˌθɒrɪ'teərɪən/ *adj* autoritaire

authoritative /ɔ:'θɒrətətɪv, (AmE) -teɪtɪv/ *adj* **1** (forceful) autoritaire
2 (reliable) ‹*work*› qui fait autorité; ‹*source*› bien informé/-e

authority /ɔ:'θɒrətɪ/ *n* **1** autorité *f*; **the authorities** les autorités
2 (permission) autorisation *f*

authorization /ˌɔ:θəraɪ'zeɪʃn/ *n* autorisation *f*

authorize /'ɔ:θəraɪz/ *vt* autoriser (**to do** à faire)

autism /'ɔ:tɪzəm/ *n* autisme *m*

autobiographical /ˌɔ:təʊbaɪə'græfɪkl/ *adj* autobiographique

autobiography /ˌɔ:təʊbaɪ'ɒgrəfɪ/ *n* autobiographie *f*

Autocue® *n* prompteur *m*

autograph /'ɔ:təgrɑ:f, (AmE) -græf/ **A** *n* autographe *m*
B *vt* dédicacer

automatic /ˌɔ:tə'mætɪk/ **A** *n* **1** (washing machine) machine *f* à laver automatique
2 (car) voiture *f* (à changement de vitesse) automatique
3 (gun) automatique *m*
B *adj* automatique

automatically /ˌɔ:tə'mætɪklɪ/ *adv* automatiquement

automatic pilot *n* (device) pilote *m* automatique

automation /ˌɔ:tə'meɪʃn/ *n* automatisation *f*

automobile /'ɔ:təməbi:l, ˌɔ:təmə'bi:l/ *n* (AmE) automobile *f*

autonomy /ɔ:'tɒnəmɪ/ *n* autonomie *f*

autopsy /'ɔ:tɒpsɪ/ *n* autopsie *f*

autumn /'ɔ:təm/ *n* automne *m*; **in ~** en automne

auxiliary /ɔ:g'zɪlɪərɪ/ *n, adj* auxiliaire *mf*

availability /əˌveɪlə'bɪlətɪ/ *n* (of option, service) existence *f*; **subject to ~** (of holidays, rooms, theatre seats) dans la limite des places disponibles

available /ə'veɪləbl/ *adj* disponible (**for** pour, **to** à)

avalanche /'ævəlɑ:nʃ, (AmE) -læntʃ/ *n* avalanche *f*

avarice /'ævərɪs/ *n* cupidité *f*

avenge /ə'vendʒ/ *vt* venger

avenue /'ævənju:, (AmE) -nu:/ *n* **1** (street, road) avenue *f*
2 (path, driveway) allée *f*

average /'ævərɪdʒ/ **A** *n* moyenne *f* (**of** de); **on (the) ~** en moyenne; **above/below (the) ~** au-dessus de/au-dessous de la moyenne
B *adj* moyen/-enne
C *vt* faire en moyenne

averse /ə'vɜ:s/ *adj* opposé/-e (**to** à); **to be ~ to doing** répugner à faire

aversion /ə'vɜ:ʃn, (AmE) ə'vɜ:rʒn/ *n* aversion *f* (**to** pour)

avert /ə'vɜ:t/ *vt* éviter; **to ~ one's eyes from sth** détourner les yeux de qch

avian flu /eɪvɪən 'flu:/ *n* grippe *f* aviaire

aviary /'eɪvɪərɪ, (AmE) -vɪerɪ/ *n* volière *f*

aviation /ˌeɪvɪ'eɪʃn/ *n* aviation *f*

avid /'ævɪd/ *adj* ‹*collector, reader*› passionné/-e; **to be ~ for sth** être avide de qch

avocado /ˌævə'kɑ:dəʊ/ *n* (*also* **~ pear**) avocat *m*

avoid /ə'vɔɪd/ *vt* (gen) éviter; esquiver ‹*issue, question*›; **to ~ doing** éviter de faire

await /ə'weɪt/ *vt* attendre

awake /ə'weɪk/ **A** *adj* (not yet asleep) éveillé/-e; **wide ~** bien réveillé/-e; **the noise kept me ~** le bruit m'a empêché de dormir
B *vt* (*prét* **awoke**, *pp* **awoken**) réveiller ‹*person*›
C *vi* (*prét* **awoke**, *pp* **awoken**) ‹*person*› se réveiller

award /ə'wɔ:d/ **A** *n* (prize) prix *m* (**for** de)
B *vt* décerner ‹*prize*›; attribuer ‹*grant*›; accorder ‹*points, penalty*›

award ceremony *n* cérémonie *f* de remise de prix

award-winning /ə'wɔːdwɪnɪŋ/ *adj* ‹*book, film*› primé/-e; ‹*writer*› lauréat/-e

aware /ə'weə(r)/ *adj* (conscious) conscient/-e (**of** de); (informed) au courant (**of** de)

awareness /ə'weənɪs/ *n* conscience *f* (**of** de, **that** que)

away /ə'weɪ/

> *away* often appears after a verb in English to show that an action is continuous or intense. If *away* does not change the basic meaning of the verb, only the verb is translated: *he was snoring away* = il ronflait.

A *adj* (Sport) ‹*goal, match, win*› à l'extérieur; **the ~ team** les visiteurs *mpl*
B *adv* **1 to be ~** être absent/-e (**from** de); **to be ~ on business** être en voyage d'affaires; **to be ~ from home** ne pas être chez soi, être absent/-e de chez soi; **she's ~ in Paris** elle est à Paris; **to crawl ~** partir en rampant; **3 km ~** à 3 km; **London is two hours ~** Londres est à deux heures d'ici; **my birthday is two months ~** mon anniversaire est dans deux mois
2 (Sport) ‹*play*› à l'extérieur

awe /ɔː/ *n* crainte *f* mêlée d'admiration; **to listen in ~** écouter impressionné/-e; **to be in ~ of sb** avoir peur de qn

awe-inspiring /'ɔːɪnspaɪərɪŋ/ *adj* impressionnant/-e

awful /'ɔːfl/ *adj* **1** affreux/-euse, atroce; (in quality) exécrable
2 I feel ~ (ill) je ne me sens pas bien du tout; (guilty) je culpabilise
3 (fam) **an ~ lot (of)** énormément (de)

awfully /'ɔːflɪ/ *adv* extrêmement

awkward /'ɔːkwəd/ *adj* **1** ‹*tool*› peu commode; ‹*shape, design*› difficile
2 (clumsy) ‹*person, gesture*› maladroit/-e
3 ‹*issue, choice*› difficile; **at an ~ time** au mauvais moment
4 (embarrassing) ‹*question*› embarrassant/-e; ‹*situation*› délicat/-e; ‹*silence*› gêné/-e
5 (uncooperative) ‹*person*› difficile (**about** à propos de)

awning /'ɔːnɪŋ/ *n* (on shop) banne *f*, auvent *m*; (on tent, house) auvent *m*; (on market stall) bâche *f*

awry /ə'raɪ/ **A** *adj* de travers *inv*
B *adv* **to go ~** mal tourner

axe, ax (AmE) /æks/ **A** *n* hache *f*
B *vt* virer (fam) ‹*employee*›; supprimer ‹*jobs*›; abandonner ‹*plan*›

axis /'æksɪs/ *n* (*pl* **axes**) axe *m*

axle /'æksl/ *n* essieu *m*

Bb

b, B /biː/ *n* **1** (letter) b, B *m*
2 B (Mus) si *m*

BA *n* (*abbr* = **Bachelor of Arts**) (degree) diplôme *m* universitaire de lettres

babe /beɪb/ *n* (fam) super nana *f* (fam)

baby /'beɪbɪ/ **A** *n* bébé *m*
B *adj* ‹*clothes, food*› pour bébés; ‹*brother, sister*› petit/-e *before n*; **~ seal** bébé phoque

babysit *vi* faire du babysitting

babysitter *n* baby-sitter *mf*

babysitting *n* baby-sitting *m*

baccalaureate /ˌbækə'lɔːrɪət/ *n* **European/International Baccalaureate** baccalauréat *m* européen/international

bachelor /'bætʃələ(r)/ *n* célibataire *m*

Bachelor of Arts *n* (person) licencié/-e *m/f* ès lettres

back /bæk/ **A** *n* **1** (of person, animal) dos *m*; **to turn one's ~ on sb/sth** tourner le dos à qn/qch; **behind sb's ~** dans le dos de qn
2 (of page, cheque, hand, envelope, coat) dos *m*; (of vehicle, plane, building, head) arrière *m*; (of chair, sofa) dossier *m*; (of cupboard, drawer, fridge, bus) fond *m*; **the ones at the ~ couldn't see** ceux qui étaient derrière ne pouvaient pas voir; **the steps at the ~ of the building** l'escalier à l'arrière de l'immeuble; **at the ~ of the drawer** au fond du tiroir; **at the ~ of the plane/bus** à l'arrière de l'avion/au fond du bus; **in the ~ (of the car)** à l'arrière
3 (Sport) arrière *m*; **left ~** arrière gauche
B *adj* ‹*paw, wheel*› arrière; ‹*bedroom*› du fond; ‹*page*› dernier/-ière *before n*; ‹*garden, gate*› de derrière
C *adv* **1 to be ~** être de retour; **I'll be ~ in five minutes** je reviens dans cinq minutes; **to come ~** rentrer (**from** de); **to come ~ home** rentrer chez soi
2 to give/put sth ~ rendre/remettre qch; **to phone ~** rappeler; **I'll write ~ (to him)** je lui répondrai
3 ‹*look, jump, lean*› en arrière
4 ~ in 1964/April en 1964/avril
5 to travel to London and ~ faire un aller-retour à Londres

---
mot clé

D *vt* **1** (support) soutenir ‹*candidate, bill*›; apporter son soutien à ‹*project*›; justifier ‹*claim*› (**with** à l'aide de); financer ‹*venture*›
2 to ~ the car into the garage rentrer la voiture au garage en marche arrière
3 (bet on) parier sur ‹*favourite, winner*›
E back and forth *phr* **to go** *or* **travel ~ and forth** (commute) faire la navette (**between** entre); **to go** *or* **walk ~ and forth** faire des allées et venues (**between** entre); **to sway ~ and forth** se balancer

- **back away** reculer; **to ~ away from** s'éloigner de ‹*person*›; chercher à éviter ‹*confrontation*›
- **back down** céder
- **back out A ~ out 1** ‹*car, driver*› sortir en marche arrière
2 ‹*person*› se désister; **to ~ out of** annuler ‹*deal*›
B ~ [sth] out to ~ the car out of the garage faire sortir la voiture du garage en marche arrière
- **back up** confirmer ‹*claim, theory*›; soutenir ‹*person*›; (Comput) sauvegarder

backache /'bækeɪk/ *n* **to have ~** avoir mal au dos

backbencher /bæk'bentʃə(r)/ *n* (BrE) (Pol) député *m* (sans portefeuille ministériel)

backbone /'bækbəʊn/ *n* colonne *f* vertébrale

back button *n* (Comput) bouton *m* retour

back cover *n* dos *m*

backdate /'bækdeɪt/ *vt* antidater ‹*cheque, letter*›

back door *n* (of car) portière *f* arrière; (of building) porte *f* de derrière

backdrop /'bækdrɒp/ *n* toile *f* de fond

backer /'bækə(r)/ *n* **1** (supporter) allié/-e *m/f*
2 (of project) commanditaire *m*; (of business) bailleur *m* de fonds

backfire /'bækfaɪə(r)/ *vi* **1** ‹*scheme*› avoir l'effet inverse; **to ~ on sb** se retourner contre qn
2 ‹*car*› pétarader

backgammon *n* jaquet *m*

background /'bækgraʊnd/ **A** *n* **1** (of person) (social) milieu *m*; (family) origines *fpl*; (professional) formation *f*
2 (of events, situation) contexte *m*; **against a ~ of violence** dans un climat de violence; **to remain in the ~** rester au second plan; **voices in the ~** des voix en bruit de fond
3 (of painting, photo, scene) arrière-plan *m*; **in the ~** à l'arrière-plan
B *adj* **1** ‹*information*› sur les origines de la situation; **~ reading** lectures *fpl* complémentaires
2 ‹*music, lighting*› d'ambiance; ‹*noise*› de fond

backhand /'bækhænd/ *n* (Sport) revers *m*

backhander /'bækhændə(r)/ *n* (fam) (bribe) pot-de-vin *m*

backing /'bækɪŋ/ *n* **1** (support) soutien *m*
2 (reverse layer) revêtement *m* intérieur

backing singer *n* chanteur/-euse *m/f* d'accompagnement

backing vocals *npl* chœurs *mpl*

backlash /'bæklæʃ/ *n* réaction *f* violente (**against** contre)

backlog /'bæklɒg/ *n* retard *m*; **I've got a huge ~ (of work)** j'ai plein de travail en retard

back number *n* ancien numéro *m*

backpack /'bækpæk/ **A** *n* sac *m* à dos
B *vi* **to go ~ing** partir en voyage avec son sac à dos

backpacker /'bækpækə(r)/ *n* routard/-e *m/f*

back pay *n* rappel *m* de salaire

back-pedal /ˌbæk'pedl/ *vi* (*p prés etc* **-ll-** (BrE), **-l-** (AmE)) (fig) faire marche arrière

back rest *n* dossier *m*

back seat *n* siège *m* arrière; **to take a ~** (fig) s'effacer

backside /'bæksaɪd/ *n* (fam) derrière *m* (fam)

backstage /'bæksteɪdʒ/ *adv* dans les coulisses

backstreet /'bækstri:t/ **A** *n* petite rue *f*
B *adj* ‹*loan shark, abortionist*› clandestin/-e

backstroke *n* dos *m* crawlé

back to back *adv* **to stand ~** ‹*two people*› se mettre dos à dos

back to front *adj, adv* à l'envers

backtrack /'bæktræk/ *vi* rebrousser chemin; (fig) faire marche arrière

backup /'bækʌp/ **A** *n* (gen) soutien *m*; (Mil) renforts *mpl*; (Comput) sauvegarde *f*
B *adj* ‹*copy, disk, file*› de sauvegarde

backward /'bækwəd/ **A** *adj* **1** ‹*look, step*› en arrière
2 ‹*nation*› arriéré/-e
3 ‹*person*› arriéré/-e
B *adv* (*also* **backwards**) **1** ‹*walk*› à reculons; ‹*lean, step, fall*› en arrière; **to move ~** reculer; **to walk ~ and forward** faire des allées et venues
2 ‹*count*› à rebours; ‹*play*› à l'envers

backwards /'bækwədz/ = **backward B**

backwater /'bækwɔ:tə(r)/ *n* village *m* tranquille, trou *m* (fam)

backyard /ˌbæk'jɑ:d/ *n* **1** (BrE) (courtyard) arrière-cour *f*
2 (AmE) (back garden) jardin *m* de derrière

bacon /'beɪkən/ *n* bacon *m*, ≈ lard *m*; **~ and egg(s)** des œufs au bacon

bacteria /bæk'tɪərɪə/ *npl* bactéries *fpl*

bad /bæd/ **A** *n* **the good and the ~** le bon et le mauvais; **there is good and ~ in everyone** il y a du bon et du mauvais dans chacun
B *adj* (*comp* **worse**, *superl* **worst**)
1 (gen) mauvais/-e *before n*; ‹*joke*› stupide; ‹*language*› grossier/-ière; **to be ~ at** être mauvais/-e en ‹*subject*›; **not ~** (fam) pas mal

b

(fam); **too ~!** (sympathetic) pas de chance!; (hard luck) tant pis!; **it will look ~** cela fera mauvais effet; **to feel ~** avoir mauvaise conscience (**about** à propos de)
2 (serious) ‹*accident, injury, mistake*› grave; **a ~ cold** un gros rhume
3 it's ~ for you *or* **your health** c'est mauvais pour la santé
4 to have a ~ back souffrir du dos; **to have a ~ chest** être malade des poumons; **to be in a ~ way** (fam) aller très mal
5 ‹*fruit*› pourri/-e; **to go ~** pourrir

badge /bædʒ/ *n* (gen) badge *m*; (official) insigne *m*

badly /ˈbædlɪ/ *adv* (*comp* **worse**, *superl* **worst**) **1** ‹*begin, behave, sleep*› mal; ‹*made, worded*› mal; **to go ~** ‹*exam, interview*› mal se passer; **to do ~** ‹*candidate, company*› obtenir de mauvais résultats; **to take sth ~** mal prendre qch
2 ‹*suffer*› beaucoup; ‹*affect*› sérieusement; ‹*hurt, damaged*› gravement
3 to want/need sth ~ avoir très envie de/grand besoin de qch

badly behaved *adj* désobéissant/-e

badly off *adj* pauvre

bad-mannered /ˌbædˈmænəd/ *adj* ‹*person*› mal élevé/-e

badminton /ˈbædmɪntn/ *n* badminton *m*

bad-tempered /ˌbædˈtempəd/ *adj* (temporarily) irrité/-e; (habitually) irritable

baffle /ˈbæfl/ *vt* rendre [qn] perplexe, confondre

baffled /ˈbæfld/ *adj* perplexe (**by** devant)

⚷ **bag** /bæg/ **A** *n* sac *m* (**of** de)
B bags *npl* bagages *mpl*; **to pack one's ~s** faire ses bagages; (fig) faire ses valises
IDIOM **to have ~s under one's eyes** avoir des valises sous les yeux (fam)

baggage /ˈbægɪdʒ/ *n* bagages *mpl*

baggage allowance *n* franchise *f* de bagages

baggage reclaim *n* réception *f* des bagages

baggy /ˈbægɪ/ *adj* large, ample

bagpipes *n* cornemuse *f*

bail /beɪl/ *n* caution *f*; **to be (out) on ~** être libéré/-e sous caution
■ **bail out**: **A ~ out** (of plane) sauter
B ~ [sb] out (gen) tirer [qn] d'affaire ‹*person*›; (Law) payer la caution pour ‹*person*›

bailiff /ˈbeɪlɪf/ *n* huissier *m*

bailout /ˈbeɪlaʊt/ *n* (Fin) renflouement *m*, financier sauvetage *m*

bait /beɪt/ *n* appât *m*

bake /beɪk/ **A** *vt* faire cuire [qch] au four ‹*dish, vegetable*›; faire ‹*bread, cake*›
B *vi* **1** (make bread) faire du pain; (make cakes) faire de la pâtisserie
2 (cook) ‹*food*› cuire

baked beans *npl* haricots *mpl* blancs à la sauce tomate

baked potato *n* pomme *f* de terre en robe des champs (au four)

baker /ˈbeɪkə(r)/ *n* boulanger/-ère *m/f*

bakery /ˈbeɪkərɪ/ *n* boulangerie *f*

⚷ **balance** /ˈbæləns/ **A** *n* **1** équilibre *m* (**between** entre); **to lose one's ~** perdre l'équilibre; **the right ~** le juste milieu
2 (scales) balance *f*; **to hang in the ~** être en jeu
3 (of account) solde *m*; **to pay the ~** verser le surplus
B *vt* **1** mettre [qch] en équilibre ‹*ball, plate*› (**on** sur)
2 (*also* **~ out**) (compensate for) compenser, équilibrer
3 (counterbalance) contrebalancer ‹*weights*›
4 (adjust) équilibrer ‹*diet, budget*›; **to ~ the books** dresser le bilan
C *vi* **1** ‹*person*› se tenir en équilibre (**on** sur); ‹*object*› tenir en équilibre (**on** sur)
2 (*also* **~ out**) s'equilibrer
3 ‹*books, figures*› être en équilibre
D balanced *pp adj* ‹*person, view, diet*› équilibré/-e; ‹*article, report*› objectif/-ive

balance of payments *n* balance *f* des paiements

balance of power *n* équilibre *m* des forces

balance of trade *n* balance *f* du commerce extérieur

balance sheet *n* bilan *m*

balcony /ˈbælkənɪ/ *n* **1** (in house, hotel) balcon *m*
2 (in theatre) deuxième balcon *m*

bald /bɔːld/ *adj* **1** ‹*man, head*› chauve
2 ‹*tyre*› lisse

Bali /ˈbɑːlɪ/ *pr n* Bali *f*; **in ~** à Bali

Balkan /ˈbɔːlkən/ **A Balkans** *pr n pl* **the ~s** les Balkans *mpl*
B *adj* balkanique

⚷ **ball** /bɔːl/ **A** *n* **1** (gen) balle *f*; (in football, rugby) ballon *m*; (in billiards) bille *f*
2 (of dough, clay) boule *f* (**of** de); (of wool, string) pelote *f* (**of** de)
3 (dance) bal *m*
B balls *npl* (sl) **1** (testicles) couilles *fpl* (pop)
2 (rubbish) conneries *fpl* (pop)

ballet /ˈbæleɪ/ *n* ballet *m*

ball gown *n* robe *f* de bal

balloon /bəˈluːn/ *n* **1** ballon *m*
2 (*also* **hot air ~**) montgolfière *f*

ballot /ˈbælət/ **A** *n* **1** scrutin *m*
2 (*also* **~ paper**) bulletin *m* de vote
B *vt* consulter [qn] (par vote) (**on** sur)

ballot box *n* urne *f* (électorale)

ballpark figure *n* (fam) chiffre *m* approximatif

ballpoint *n* (*also* **ballpoint pen**) stylo *m* (à) bille

ballroom *n* salle *f* de danse

⚷ mot clé

ballroom dancing *n* danse *f* de salon

Baltic /'bɔːltɪk/ *adj* **the ~ Sea** la mer Baltique

ban /bæn/ **A** *n* interdiction *f* (**on** de)
B *vt* (*p prés etc* **-nn-**) (gen) interdire; suspendre ‹*athlete*›; **to ~ sb from doing** interdire à qn de faire

banal /bə'nɑːl/ *adj* banal/-e

banana /bə'nɑːnə/ *n* banane *f*

band /bænd/ *n* **1** (of people) groupe *m* (**of** de); (of musicians) (rock) groupe (de rock); (municipal) fanfare *f*; **jazz ~** orchestre *m* de jazz
2 (strip) bande *f*
3 (BrE) (of age, income tax) tranche *f*
4 (around arm) brassard *m*; **(hair) ~** bandeau *m*
■ **band together** se réunir (**to do** pour faire)

bandage /'bændɪdʒ/ **A** *n* bandage *m*
B *vt* bander ‹*head, limb, wound*›

bandit /'bændɪt/ *n* bandit *m*

bandwagon /'bændwægən/ *n*
IDIOM **to jump** *or* **climb on the ~** prendre le train en marche

bang /bæŋ/ **A** *n* **1** (of explosion) détonation *f*, boum *m*; (of door, window) claquement *m*
2 (knock) coup *m*
B *adv* **~ in the middle** en plein centre
C *vt* **1** taper sur ‹*drum, saucepan*›; **to ~ sth down on the table** poser bruyamment qch sur la table; **to ~ one's head** se cogner la tête (**on** contre); **to ~ one's fist on the table** taper du poing sur la table
2 (slam) claquer ‹*door, window*›
D *vi* ‹*door, shutter*› claquer
IDIOM **~ goes** (fam) **my holiday/my promotion** je peux dire adieu à mes vacances/mon avancement
■ **bang into**: **~ into [sb/sth]** heurter

bangle /'bæŋgl/ *n* bracelet *m*

banish /'bænɪʃ/ *vt* bannir (**from** de)

banister, **bannister** (BrE) /'bænɪstə(r)/ *n* rampe *f* (d'escalier)

bank /bæŋk/ **A** *n* **1** banque *f*
2 (of river, lake) rive *f*; (of major river) bord *m*; (of canal) berge *f*
3 (mound) talus *m*; (of snow) congère *f*; (of flowers) massif *m*; (of fog, mist) banc *m*
B *vi* **to ~ with the National** avoir un compte (bancaire) à la Nationale
■ **bank on** compter sur ‹*person*› (**to do** pour faire); **to ~ on doing** escompter faire

bank account *n* compte *m* bancaire

bank card *n* carte *f* bancaire

bank charges *npl* frais *mpl* bancaires

bank clerk *n* employé/-e *m/f* de banque

banker /'bæŋkə(r)/ *n* banquier/-ière *m/f*

banker's draft *n* traite *f* bancaire

banker's order *n* virement *m* bancaire

bank holiday *n* (BrE) jour *m* férié; (AmE) jour *m* de fermeture des banques

banking /'bæŋkɪŋ/ *n* **1** (business) opérations *fpl* bancaires
2 (profession) la banque

banking hours *npl* heures *fpl* d'ouverture des banques

bank manager *n* directeur/-trice *m/f* d'agence bancaire

banknote *n* billet *m* de banque

bank robber *n* cambrioleur/-euse *m/f* de banque

bank robbery *n* cambriolage *m* de banque

bankroll /'bæŋkrəʊl/ *vt* (fam) financer

bankrupt /'bæŋkrʌpt/ *adj* ‹*person*› ruiné/-e; ‹*economy*› en faillite; **to go ~** faire faillite

bankruptcy /'bæŋkrʌpsɪ/ *n* faillite *f*

bank statement *n* relevé *m* de compte

banner /'bænə(r)/ *n* banderole *f*

baptism /'bæptɪzəm/ *n* baptême *m*

baptize /bæp'taɪz/ *vt* baptiser

bar /bɑː(r)/ **A** *n* **1** (of metal, wood) barre *f*; (on cage, window) barreau *m*
2 (pub) bar *m*; (counter) comptoir *m*
3 ~ of soap savonnette *f*; **~ of chocolate** tablette *f* de chocolat
4 (Law) (profession) **the ~** le barreau
5 (Sport) barre *f*
6 (Mus) mesure *f*
B *prep* sauf; **all ~ one** tous sauf un seul/une seule
C *vt* (*p prés etc* **-rr-**) **1** barrer ‹*way, path*›; **to ~ sb's way** barrer le passage à qn
2 (ban) exclure ‹*person*› (**from sth** de qch); **to ~ sb from doing** interdire à qn de faire

barbaric /bɑː'bærɪk/ *adj* barbare

barbecue /'bɑːbɪkjuː/ *n* barbecue *m*

barbed wire, **barbwire** (AmE) *n* (fil *m* de fer) barbelé *m*

barber /'bɑːbə(r)/ *n* coiffeur *m* (pour hommes)

Barcelona /ˌbɑːsɪ'ləʊnə/ *pr n* Barcelone *f*

bar chart *n* histogramme *m*

bar code *n* code *m* à barres

bare /beə(r)/ **A** *adj* (gen) nu/-e; ‹*cupboard, room*› vide; **with one's ~ hands** à mains nues; **the ~ minimum** le strict nécessaire
B *vt* **to ~ one's teeth** montrer les dents

bareback *adv* ‹*ride*› à cru

barefoot /'beəfʊt/ **A** *adj* **to be ~** être nu-pieds
B *adv* ‹*run, walk*› pieds nus

barely /'beəlɪ/ *adv* à peine

bargain /'bɑːgɪn/ **A** *n* **1** (deal) marché *m* (**between** entre)
2 (good buy) affaire *f*
B *vi* **1** (for deal) négocier (**with** avec)
2 (over price) marchander (**with** avec)
■ **bargain for**, **bargain on** s'attendre à

bargaining /'bɑːgɪnɪŋ/ **A** *n* négociations *fpl*
B *adj* ‹*position, power*› de négociation

barge /bɑːdʒ/ **A** *n* péniche *f*; (for freight) chaland *m*
B *vi* **to ~ past sb** passer devant qn en le bousculant

b

■ **barge in** (enter noisily) faire irruption; (interrupt) interrompre brutalement

bark /bɑːk/ **A** *n* **1** (of tree) écorce *f*
2 (of dog) aboiement *m*
B *vi* aboyer (**at sb/sth** après qn/qch)

barley /ˈbɑːlɪ/ *n* orge *f*

barmaid *n* serveuse *f* de bar

barman *n* (*pl* **~men**) barman *m*

barn /bɑːn/ *n* (for crops) grange *f*; (for cattle) étable *f*

baron /ˈbærən/ *n* baron *m*

barracks *n* caserne *f*

barrage /ˈbærɑːʒ, (AmE) bəˈrɑːʒ/ *n* (gen) barrage *m*; (Mil) tir *m* de barrage

barrel /ˈbærəl/ *n* **1** (for beer, wine) tonneau *m*, fût *m*; (for oil) baril *m*
2 (of gun) canon *m*

barricade /ˌbærɪˈkeɪd/ *n* barricade *f*

barrier /ˈbærɪə(r)/ *n* barrière *f*

barrier cream *n* crème *f* protectrice

barring /ˈbɑːrɪŋ/ *prep* à moins de

barrister /ˈbærɪstə(r)/ *n* (BrE) avocat/-e *m/f*

barter /ˈbɑːtə(r)/ *vi* (exchange) faire du troc; (haggle) marchander

🔑 **base** /beɪs/ **A** *n* (gen), (Mil) base *f*; (of tree, lamp) pied *m*
B *adj* ignoble
C *vt* fonder (**on** sur); **the film is ~d on a true story** le film est tiré d'une histoire vraie; **to be ~d in Paris** ‹*person, company*› être basé/-e à Paris

baseball *n* base-ball *m*

basement /ˈbeɪsmənt/ *n* sous-sol *m*; **in the ~** au sous-sol

bash /bæʃ/ **A** *n* (fam) (*pl* **-es**) **1** (blow) coup *m*
2 (attempt) tentative *f*; **to have a ~ at sth, to give sth a ~** s'essayer à qch
3 (party) grande fête *f*
B *vt* cogner ‹*person*›; rentrer dans ‹*tree, wall, kerb*›

■ **bash into**: **~ into [sth]** rentrer dans

bashful /ˈbæʃfl/ *adj* timide

🔑 **basic** /ˈbeɪsɪk/ *adj* **1** (gen) essentiel/-ielle; ‹*problem, principle*› fondamental/-e
2 (elementary) ‹*knowledge, skill*› élémentaire; ‹*wage, training*› de base

🔑 **basically** /ˈbeɪsɪklɪ/ *adv* fondamentalement

basics *npl* essentiel *m*; **to get down to ~** aborder l'essentiel

basil /ˈbæzl/ *n* basilic *m*

basin /ˈbeɪsn/ *n* **1** (bowl) bol *m*
2 (in bathroom) lavabo *m*; (portable) cuvette *f*

🔑 **basis** /ˈbeɪsɪs/ *n* (*pl* **-ses**) base *f* (**for, of** de); **on a regular/temporary ~** régulièrement/à titre provisoire

basket /ˈbɑːskɪt, (AmE) ˈbæskɪt/ *n* panier *m*

basketball /ˈbɑːskɪtbɔːl, (AmE) ˈbæsk-/ *n* (game) basket(-ball) *m*; (ball) ballon *m* de basket

bass *n* basse *f*

bass drum *n* grosse caisse *f*

bass guitar *n* basse *f*

bastard /ˈbɑːstəd, (AmE) ˈbæs-/ *n* (sl)
1 (illegitimate child) bâtard/-e *m/f*
2 (unpleasant man) salaud *m* (pop)

baste /beɪst/ *vt* (Culin) arroser

bastion /ˈbæstɪən/ *n* bastion *m*

bat /bæt/ **A** *n* **1** (in cricket, baseball) batte *f*; (in table tennis) raquette *f*
2 (Zool) chauve-souris *f*
B *vi* (*p prés etc* **-tt-**) (be batsman) être le batteur; (handle a bat) manier la batte

batch /bætʃ/ *n* (of loaves) fournée *f*; (of goods) lot *m*

bated /ˈbeɪtɪd/ *adj* **with ~ breath** en retenant son souffle

bath /bɑːθ, (AmE) bæθ/ **A** *n* bain *m*; (BrE) (tub) baignoire *f*; **to have a ~** prendre un bain
B baths *npl* **1** (for swimming) piscine *f*
2 (in spa) thermes *mpl*
C *vt* (BrE) baigner

bathe /beɪð/ **A** *vt* laver ‹*wound*› (**in** dans, **with** à)
B *vi* **1** (swim) se baigner
2 (AmE) (take bath) prendre un bain
3 to be ~d in ruisseler de ‹*sweat*›; être inondé/-e de ‹*light*›

bather /ˈbeɪðə(r)/ *n* baigneur/-euse *m/f*

bathing /ˈbeɪðɪŋ/ *n* baignade *f*

bathing cap *n* bonnet *m* de bain

bathing costume *n* costume *m* de bain

bath mat *n* tapis *m* de bain

bathrobe *n* sortie *f* de bain

bathroom /ˈbɑːθruːm, -rʊm/ *n* **1** salle *f* de bains
2 (AmE) (lavatory) toilettes *fpl*

bathroom cabinet *n* armoire *f* de toilette

bathroom scales *npl* pèse-personne *m*

bath towel *n* serviette *f* de bain

bathtub *n* baignoire *f*

baton /ˈbætn, ˈbætɒn, (AmE) bəˈtɒn/ *n* (BrE) (policeman's) matraque *f*; (traffic policeman's) bâton *m*; (Mus) baguette *f*; (in relay race) témoin *m*

batsman /ˈbætsmən/ *n* batteur *m*

batter /ˈbætə(r)/ **A** *n* pâte *f*
B *vt* battre

battered /ˈbætəd/ *adj* **1** ‹*kettle, hat*› cabossé/-e; ‹*suitcase*› très abîmé/-e
2 ‹*wife*› battu/-e

battery /ˈbætərɪ/ *n* pile *f*; (in car) batterie *f*

battery charger *n* chargeur *m* de batteries

battery farming *n* élevage *m* en batterie

battery powered *adj* à piles

🔑 **battle** /ˈbætl/ **A** *n* bataille *f*; (fig) lutte *f*
B *vi* (gen), (Mil) combattre (**with sb** contre qn); **to ~ for sth/to do** lutter pour qch/pour faire

🔑 mot clé

battlefield *n* champ *m* de bataille

battleship *n* cuirassé *m*

bawdy /'bɔːdɪ/ *adj* ‹*song*› grivois/-e; ‹*person*› paillard/-e

bawl /bɔːl/ *vi* (weep) brailler; (shout) hurler

bay /beɪ/ **A** *n* **1** (on coast) baie *f*
2 (*also* ~ **tree**) (Bot) laurier(-sauce) *m*
3 loading/parking ~ aire *f* de chargement/stationnement
B *vi* ‹*dog*› aboyer (**at** contre, après)
IDIOM **to hold sb/sth at** ~ tenir qn/qch à distance

bay leaf *n* feuille *f* de laurier

bayonet /'beɪənɪt/ *n* baïonnette *f*

BC (*abbr* = **Before Christ**) av. J.-C.

Bcc *n* (*abbr* = **Blind carbon copy**) copie *f* invisible

be /biː, bɪ/

For translations of *there is, there are, here is* and *here are*, see the entries **there** and **here**.

A *vi* (*p prés* **being**, 3e *pers sg prés* **is**, *prét* **was**, *pp* **been**) **1** être; **she is French** elle est française; **we are late** nous sommes en retard; **he is a doctor/widower** il est médecin/veuf; **it is Monday** c'est lundi; **it's me!** c'est moi!; ~ **good!** sois sage!
2 (physical and mental states) avoir; **I am cold/hot** j'ai froid/chaud; **are you hungry/thirsty?** as-tu faim/soif?; **his hands were cold** il avait froid aux mains
3 (weather) faire; **it is cold/windy** il fait froid/du vent; **it is 40°** il fait 40°
4 (health) aller; **how are you?** (polite) comment allez-vous?; (more informally) comment vas-tu?; (very informally) ça va?; **how is your son?** comment va votre fils?; ▶ **well**[1], **fine, better**
5 (visit) **I've never been to Sweden** je ne suis jamais allé en Suède; **have you ever been to Africa?** tu es déjà allé en Afrique?; **has the postman been?** est-ce que le facteur est passé?
6 (age) avoir; **how old are you?** quel âge as-tu?; **I am 23** j'ai 23 ans
7 (in mathematics) faire; **2 plus 2 is 4** 2 et 2 font 4
8 (cost) coûter; **how much is it?** combien ça coûte?
9 (phrases) **so** ~ **it** d'accord; **if I were you** à ta place
B *v aux* **1** (in passives) être; **the doors have been repainted** les portes ont été repeintes, on a repeint les portes; **it is said that...** on dit que...
2 (in continuous tenses) **we are going to London tomorrow** nous allons à Londres demain; **it is raining** il pleut; **he is reading** il lit, il est en train de lire; ▶ **for, since**
3 (with infinitive) devoir; **you are to do it at once** tu dois le faire tout de suite; **they are to** ~ **married** ils vont se marier; **it was to** ~ **expected** il fallait s'y attendre; **it was nowhere to** ~ **found** il était introuvable
4 (in tag questions) **it's a lovely house, isn't it?** c'est une très belle maison, n'est-ce pas?; **they're not in the garden, are they?** ils ne sont pas dans le jardin, par hasard?; **today is Tuesday, isn't it?** c'est bien mardi aujourd'hui?
5 (in short answers) **'you are not going out'—'yes I am!'** 'tu ne sors pas'—'si!'; **'are you English?'—'yes, I am'** 'vous êtes anglais?'—'oui, je suis anglais'

beach /biːtʃ/ *n* plage *f*

beach ball *n* ballon *m* de plage

beach buggy *n* buggy *m*

beacon /'biːkən/ *n* **1** (on runway) balise *f*
2 (lighthouse) phare *m*
3 (*also* **radio** ~) radiobalise *f*

bead /biːd/ *n* **1** perle *f*; **(string of)** ~**s** collier *m*
2 (of sweat, dew) goutte *f*

beak /biːk/ *n* bec *m*

beam /biːm/ **A** *n* **1** (of light, torch) rayon *m*; (of car lights, lighthouse) faisceau *m*
2 (wooden) poutre *f*
B *vt* transmettre ‹*signal*›
C *vi* rayonner

bean /biːn/ *n* haricot *m*

bean sprout *n* germe *m* de soja

bear /beə(r)/ **A** *n* ours *m*
B *vt* (*prét* **bore**, *pp* **borne**) **1** (carry) porter; **to** ~ **a resemblance to** ressembler à; **to** ~ **no relation to** n'avoir aucun rapport avec; **to** ~ **sth in mind** tenir compte de qch
2 (endure) supporter; **I can't** ~ **to watch** je ne veux pas voir ça
3 (stand up to) résister à ‹*scrutiny, inspection*›
4 (yield) donner ‹*fruit, crop*›; ‹*investment*› rapporter ‹*interest*›
C *vi* (*prét* **bore**, *pp* **borne**) **1 to** ~ **left/right** ‹*person*› prendre à gauche/à droite
2 to bring pressure to ~ **on sb** exercer une pression sur qn
■ **bear out** confirmer ‹*claim, story*›; appuyer ‹*person*›
■ **bear up** ‹*person*› tenir le coup; ‹*structure*› résister
■ **bear with**: ~ **with [sb]** être indulgent/-e avec; ~ **with me for a minute** pardonnez-moi un instant

bearable /'beərəbl/ *adj* supportable

beard /'bɪəd/ *n* barbe *f*

bearded /'bɪədɪd/ *adj* barbu/-e

bearer /'beərə(r)/ *n* (of news, gift, letter) porteur/-euse *m/f*; (of passport) titulaire *mf*

bearing /'beərɪŋ/ *n* **1** (of person) allure *f*
2 to have no/little ~ **on sth** n'avoir aucun rapport/avoir peu de rapport avec qch
3 to take a compass ~ faire un relevé au compas

bearings *npl* **to get one's** ~ se repérer

beast /biːst/ *n* **1** (animal) bête *f*
2 (fam) (person) brute *f*

b

⚷ **beat** /biːt/ **A** *n* **1** (of drum, heart) battement *m*
2 (rhythm) rythme *m*
3 (of policeman) ronde *f*
B *vt* (*prét* **beat**, *pp* **beaten**) **1** battre; **to ~ sb with a stick** donner des coups de bâton à qn; **to ~ sb at tennis** battre qn au tennis; **to ~ time** (Mus) battre la mesure; **she beat me to it** elle a été plus rapide que moi
2 it ~s walking c'est mieux que marcher; **you can't ~ Italian shoes** rien ne vaut les chaussures italiennes
C *vi* (*prét* **beat**, *pp* **beaten**) ‹*waves, rain*› battre (**against** contre); ‹*person*› cogner (**at, on** à); ‹*heart, drum, wings*› battre
■ **beat back** repousser ‹*group, flames*›
■ **beat down** ‹*rain*› tomber à verse (**on** sur); ‹*sun*› taper (**on** sur)
■ **beat off** repousser ‹*attacker*›
■ **beat up** tabasser (fam) ‹*person*›

beating /ˈbiːtɪŋ/ *n* **1** (punishment) raclée *f* (fam), correction *f*
2 (of drum, heart, wings) battement *m*

beautician /bjuːˈtɪʃn/ *n* esthéticien/-ienne *m/f*

⚷ **beautiful** /ˈbjuːtɪfl/ *adj* beau/belle *before n*; ‹*weather, shot*› superbe; **a ~ place** un bel endroit

> The irregular form *bel* of the adjective *beau, belle* is used before masculine nouns beginning with a vowel or a mute 'h'.

beautifully /ˈbjuːtɪfəlɪ/ *adv* **1** ‹*play, write*› admirablement
2 ‹*furnished*› magnifiquement; **~ dressed** habillé/-e avec beaucoup de goût

⚷ **beauty** /ˈbjuːtɪ/ *n* beauté *f*

beauty parlour (BrE), **beauty parlor** (AmE) *n* salon *m* de beauté

beauty queen *n* reine *f* de beauté

beauty salon *n* salon *m* de beauté

beauty spot *n* **1** (on skin) grain *m* de beauté; (fake) mouche *f*
2 (place) beau site *m or* coin *m*

beaver /ˈbiːvə(r)/ *n* castor *m*

⚷ **because** /bɪˈkɒz, (AmE) *also*-kɔːz/ **A** *conj* parce que
B because of *phr* à cause de

beckon /ˈbekən/ **A** *vt* faire signe à; **to ~ sb in** faire signe à qn d'entrer
B *vi* faire signe; **to ~ to sb to do** faire signe à qn de faire

⚷ **become** /bɪˈkʌm/ **A** *vi* (*prét* **became** *pp* **become**) devenir; **to ~ ill** tomber malade
B *v impers* (*prét* **became** *pp* **become**) **what has ~ of your brother?** qu'est-ce que ton frère est devenu?

becoming /bɪˈkʌmɪŋ/ *adj* ‹*behaviour*› convenable; ‹*garment, haircut*› seyant/-e

⚷ **bed** /bed/ *n* **1** lit *m*; **to go to ~** aller au lit
2 (of flowers) parterre *m*
3 (of sea) fond *m*; (of river) lit *m*

bed and breakfast, **B and B** /ˌbed ən ˈbrekfəst/ *n* chambre *f* avec petit déjeuner, ≈ chambre *f* d'hôte

bedclothes *npl* couvertures *fpl*

bedraggled /bɪˈdræɡld/ *adj* dépenaillé/-e

bedridden *adj* alité/-e, cloué/-e au lit

bedroom /ˈbedruːm, -rʊm/ *n* chambre *f* (à coucher)

bedside /ˈbedsaɪd/ *n* chevet *m*

bedsit, **bedsitter** *n* (BrE) chambre *f* meublée

bedspread *n* dessus *m* de lit

bedtime /ˈbedtaɪm/ *n* **it's ~** c'est l'heure d'aller se coucher

bee /biː/ *n* abeille *f*

beech /biːtʃ/ *n* hêtre *m*

beef /biːf/ *n* bœuf *m*; **roast ~** rôti *m* de bœuf

beefburger *n* hamburger *m*

beehive /ˈbiːhaɪv/ *n* ruche *f*

beeline /ˈbiːlaɪn/ *n*
IDIOM **to make a ~ for** se diriger tout droit vers

beep /biːp/ **A** *n* (of electronic device) bip *m*; (of car) coup *m* de klaxon®
B *vi* ‹*device*› faire bip *or* bip-bip; ‹*car*› klaxonner

beer /bɪə(r)/ *n* bière *f*

bee sting *n* piqûre *f* d'abeille

beet /biːt/ *n* betterave *f*

beetle /ˈbiːtl/ *n* scarabée *m*

beetroot /ˈbiːtruːt/ *n* (BrE) betterave *f*

⚷ **before** /bɪˈfɔː(r)/ **A** *prep* **1** avant; **the day ~ yesterday** avant-hier; **the day ~ the exam** la veille de l'examen
2 (in front of) devant
3 (AmE) (in telling time) **ten ~ six** six heures moins dix
B *adj* précédent/-e, d'avant; **the day ~** la veille; **the week ~** la semaine précédente
C *adv* **1** (beforehand) avant; **long ~** bien avant; (previously) auparavant; **two months ~** deux mois auparavant
2 (already) déjà; **have you been to India ~?** est-ce que tu es déjà allé en Inde?; **I've never seen him ~ in my life** c'est la première fois que je le vois; **you never told me ~** tu ne m'as jamais dit ça
D *conj* avant de (+ *infinitive*), avant que (+ *subj*); **~ I go, I would like to say that…** avant de partir, je voudrais dire que…; **~ he goes, I must remind him that…** avant qu'il parte, il faut que je lui rappelle que…

beforehand /bɪˈfɔːhænd/ *adv* (ahead of time) à l'avance; (earlier) auparavant, avant

befriend /bɪˈfrend/ *vt* (look after) prendre [qn] sous son aile; (make friends with) se lier d'amitié avec

beg /beɡ/ **A** *vt* (*p prés etc* **-gg-**) demander (**from** à); **to ~ sb for sth** demander qch à qn; **I ~ your pardon** je vous demande pardon
B *vi* (*p prés etc* **-gg-**) ‹*person*› mendier (**from** à); ‹*dog*› faire le beau; **to ~ for help**

⚷ mot clé

demander de l'aide

beggar /ˈbegə(r)/ *n* mendiant/-e *m/f*

begin /bɪˈɡɪn/ **A** *vt* (*p prés* **-nn-**, *prét* **began**, *pp* **begun**) commencer ‹*journey, meeting, meal, game*› (**with** par, avec); provoquer ‹*debate, dispute*›; lancer ‹*campaign, trend*›; déclencher ‹*war*›; **to ~ doing** commencer à faire
B *vi* (*p prés* **-nn-**, *prét* **began**, *pp* **begun**) commencer; **to ~ with sth** commencer par qch; **to ~ again** recommencer
C to begin with *phr* (at first) au début, au départ; (firstly) d'abord, premièrement

beginner /bɪˈɡɪnə(r)/ *n* débutant/-e *m/f*

beginning /bɪˈɡɪnɪŋ/ *n* début *m*, commencement *m*; **in** *or* **at the ~** au départ, au début; **to go back to the ~** reprendre au début

beginnings *npl* (of person, business) débuts *mpl*; (of movement) origines *fpl*

behalf: /bɪˈhɑːf, (AmE) -ˈhæf/ **on ~ of** (BrE), **in ~ of** (AmE) *phr* ‹*act, speak*› au nom de, pour; ‹*phone, write*› de la part de; ‹*negotiate*› pour le compte de

behave /bɪˈheɪv/ **A** *vi* se comporter, se conduire (**towards** envers)
B *v refl* **to ~ oneself** bien se comporter; **~ yourself!** tiens-toi bien!

behaviour (BrE), **behavior** (AmE) /bɪˈheɪvjə(r)/ *n* (gen) comportement *m* (**towards** envers); (Sch) conduite *f*; **to be on one's best ~** bien se tenir

behead /bɪˈhed/ *vt* décapiter

behind /bɪˈhaɪnd/ **A** *n* (fam) derrière *m* (fam)
B *adj* **to be ~ with** avoir du retard dans ‹*work*›; **to be too far ~** avoir trop de retard
C *adv* ‹*follow on*› derrière; ‹*look, glance*› en arrière; **the car ~** la voiture de derrière
D *prep* **1** derrière; **~ my back** derrière le dos; (fig) derrière mon dos; **~ the scenes** en coulisses
2 (supporting) **to be (solidly) ~ sb** soutenir qn (à fond)

beige /beɪʒ/ *n, adj* beige *m*

Beijing /beɪˈdʒɪŋ/ *pr n* Pékin, Bei-jing

being /ˈbiːɪŋ/ *n* **1 (human) ~** être *m* (humain)
2 to come into ~ prendre naissance

Beirut /ˈbeɪruːt, ˌbeɪˈruːt/ *pr n* Beyrouth

Belarus /ˌbjeləʊˈrus/ *pr n* Bélarus *f*

belch /beltʃ/ **A** *n* renvoi *m*, rot *m*
B *vt* (*also* **~ out**) vomir, cracher ‹*smoke, fire*›
C *vi* avoir un renvoi

belfry /ˈbelfrɪ/ *n* beffroi *m*, clocher *m*

Belgian /ˈbeldʒən/ **A** *n* Belge *mf*
B *adj* belge; ‹*embassy*› de Belgique

Belgium /ˈbeldʒəm/ *pr n* Belgique *f*

belie /bɪˈlaɪ/ *vt* démentir

belief /bɪˈliːf/ *n* **1** (opinion) conviction *f* (**about** sur, à propos de)
2 (confidence) confiance *f*, foi *f* (**in** dans)
3 (religious faith) foi *f*

believable /bɪˈliːvəbl/ *adj* crédible

believe /bɪˈliːv/ **A** *vt* croire; **I don't ~ you!** ce n'est pas vrai!
B *vi* **to ~ in** croire à ‹*promises, ghosts*›; croire en ‹*God*›

believer /bɪˈliːvə(r)/ *n* (in God) croyant/-e *m/f*; (in progress, liberty) adepte *mf* (**in** de)

belittle /bɪˈlɪtl/ *vt* rabaisser

bell /bel/ *n* (in church) cloche *f*; (handbell) clochette *f*; (on toy, cat) grelot *m*; (on bicycle) sonnette *f*; **door ~** sonnette *f*
IDIOM **that name rings a ~** ce nom me dit quelque chose

belligerent /bɪˈlɪdʒərənt/ **A** *n* belligérant *m*
B *adj* ‹*person*› agressif/-ive; ‹*country*› belligérant/-e

bellow /ˈbeləʊ/ *vi* ‹*bull*› mugir; ‹*person*› hurler (**with** de)

bellows /ˈbeləʊz/ *npl* soufflet *m*

belly /ˈbelɪ/ *n* ventre *m*

bellyache /ˈbelɪeɪk/ *n* (fam) mal *m* au ventre

belly button *n* (fam) nombril *m*

belong /bɪˈlɒŋ, (AmE) -lɔːŋ/ *vi* **to ~ to** ‹*property*› appartenir à ‹*person*›; ‹*person*› faire partie de ‹*club, society, set*›; **where do these books ~?** où vont ces livres?

belongings /bɪˈlɒŋɪŋz, (AmE) -ˈlɔːŋ-/ *npl* affaires *fpl*; **personal ~** effets *mpl* personnels

beloved /bɪˈlʌvɪd/ *n, adj* bien-aimé/-e *m/f*

below /bɪˈləʊ/ **A** *prep* au-dessous de; **~ freezing** au-dessous de zéro; **~ the surface** sous la surface
B *adv* **the apartment ~** l'appartement du dessous; **the people (in the street) ~** les gens en bas (dans la rue); **the village ~** le village en contrebas; **100 metres ~** 100 mètres plus bas; **see ~** (on page) voir ci-dessous

belt /belt/ **A** *n* (gen) ceinture *f*; (Tech) courroie *f*
B *vt* (fam) (hit) flanquer une beigne à (fam) ‹*person*›
IDIOMS **to tighten one's ~** se serrer la ceinture; **that was below the ~** c'était un coup bas

- **belt out**: **~ out [sth]**, **~ [sth] out** chanter [qch] à pleins poumons ‹*song*›
- **belt up 1** (fam) (shut up) la fermer (fam), se taire
2 (Aut) attacher sa ceinture de sécurité

bemused /bɪˈmjuːzd/ *adj* perplexe

bench /bentʃ/ *n* **1** (gen) banc *m*; (workbench) établi *m*
2 (*also* **Bench**) (Law) (judges collectively) magistrature *f* (assise); (judges hearing a case) Cour *f*

benchmark /ˈbentʃmɑːk/ **A** *n* **1** (gen) point *m* de référence
2 (Comput) test *m* de performance
B *vt* évaluer les performances de ‹*computer system*›

b

bend /bend/ **A** *n* (in road) tournant *m*, virage *m*; (in river) courbe *f*
B *vt* (*prét*, *pp* **bent**) plier ‹*arm, leg*›; pencher ‹*head*›; tordre ‹*pipe, nail, wire*›
C *vi* (*prét*, *pp* **bent**) **1** ‹*road, path*› tourner; ‹*branch*› ployer
2 ‹*person*› se pencher; **to ~ forward** se pencher en avant
■ **bend down**, **bend over** se pencher

beneath /bɪ'ni:θ/ **A** *prep* **1** sous; **~ the calm exterior** sous des apparences calmes
2 it is ~ you to do c'est indigne de toi de faire
B *adv* en dessous; **the apartment ~** l'appartement en dessous

benefactor /'benɪfæktə(r)/ *n* bienfaiteur *m*

beneficial /ˌbenɪ'fɪʃl/ *adj* ‹*effect, influence*› bénéfique; ‹*change*› salutaire

beneficiary /ˌbenɪ'fɪʃərɪ, (AmE) -fɪʃierɪ/ *n* bénéficiaire *mf*

⚷ **benefit** /'benɪfɪt/ **A** *n* **1** (advantage) avantage *m* (**from** de)
2 (financial aid) allocation *f*; **to be on ~(s)** (BrE) toucher les allocations
B *adj* ‹*concert, match*› de bienfaisance
C *vt* (*p prés etc* **-t-**) profiter à ‹*person*›; être avantageux/-euse pour ‹*group, nation*›
D *vi* (*p prés etc* **-t-**) profiter; **to ~ from** tirer profit de; **to ~ from doing** gagner à faire
IDIOM **to give sb the ~ of the doubt** accorder à qn le bénéfice du doute

benevolent /bɪ'nevələnt/ *adj* bienveillant/-e

benign /bɪ'naɪn/ *adj* **1** ‹*person, smile*› bienveillant/-e
2 (Med) bénin/-igne

bent /bent/ *adj* **1** ‹*nail, wire, stick*› tordu/-e; ‹*person*› (stooped) courbé/-e
2 to be ~ on doing vouloir à tout prix faire

bereaved /bɪ'ri:vd/ *adj* endeuillé/-e, en deuil

bereavement /bɪ'ri:vmənt/ *n* deuil *m*

berry /'berɪ/ *n* baie *f*

berserk /bə'sɜ:k/ *adj* **to go ~** être pris/-e de folie furieuse

berth /bɜ:θ/ **A** *n* **1** (bunk) couchette *f*
2 (at dock) mouillage *m*
B *vt* faire mouiller ‹*ship*›
C *vi* ‹*ship*› venir à quai
IDIOM **to give sb/sth a wide ~** (fam) éviter qn/qch

beset /bɪ'set/ *adj* **a country ~ by strikes** un pays en proie aux grèves

⚷ **beside** /bɪ'saɪd/ *prep* **1** (next to) à côté de; **~ the sea** au bord de la mer
2 (in comparison with) par rapport à
IDIOM **to be ~ oneself (with anger)** être hors de soi; **to be ~ oneself (with joy)** être fou/folle de joie

⚷ mot clé

besides /bɪ'saɪdz/ **A** *adv* **1** (moreover) d'ailleurs
2 (in addition) en plus, aussi
B *prep* en plus de

besiege /bɪ'si:dʒ/ *vt* (Mil) assiéger; (fig) assaillir

besotted /bɪ'sɒtɪd/ *adj* follement épris/-e (**with** de)

best /best/ **A** *n* **the ~** le meilleur/la meilleure *m/f*; **the ~ of friends** les meilleurs amis/meilleures amies du monde; **at ~** au mieux; **to make the ~ of sth** s'accommoder de qch; **to do one's ~ to do** faire de son mieux *or* faire (tout) son possible pour faire; **all the ~!** (good luck) bonne chance!; (cheers) à ta santé!
B *adj* (*superlative of* **good**) meilleur/-e; **the ~ book I've ever read** le meilleur livre que j'aie jamais lu; **my ~ dress** ma plus belle robe
C *adv* (*superlative of* **well**) le mieux; **~ of all** mieux que tout

best friend *n* meilleur ami/meilleure amie *m/f*

best man *n* témoin *m*

bestow /bɪ'stəʊ/ *vt* accorder ‹*honour*› (**on** à); conférer ‹*title*› (**on** à)

bestseller /ˌbest'selə(r)/ *n* bestseller *m*

best-selling /ˌbest'selɪŋ/ *adj* ‹*product*› le/la plus vendu/-e; **the ~ novelist of 1999** le romancier qui s'est vendu le plus en 1999

bet /bet/ **A** *n* pari *m*; (in casino) mise *f*
B *vt* (*p prés etc* **-tt-**, *prét*, *pp* **bet** *ou* **~ted**) parier (**on** sur)
C *vi* (*p prés etc* **-tt-**, *prét*, *pp* **bet** *ou* **~ted**) parier (**on** sur); (in casino) miser

betray /bɪ'treɪ/ *vt* trahir

betrayal /bɪ'treɪəl/ *n* trahison *f*

better

> When *better* is used as an adjective, it is translated by *meilleur* or *mieux* depending on the context (see 2 below, and note that *meilleur* is the comparative form of *bon*, *mieux* the comparative form of *bien*).

A *n* **the ~ of the two** le meilleur/la meilleure *or* le/la mieux des deux; **so much the ~** tant mieux
B *adj* (*comparative of* **good**) meilleur/-e; **this wine is ~** ce vin est meilleur; **to get ~** ‹*situation, weather*› s'améliorer; ‹*ill person*› aller mieux; **things are getting ~** ça va mieux; **to be ~** ‹*patient, cold*› aller mieux; **to be a ~ swimmer than sb** nager mieux que qn; **to be ~ at** être meilleur/-e en ‹*subject, sport*›; **it's ~ than nothing** c'est mieux que rien; **the bigger/sooner the ~** le plus grand/vite possible; **the less said about that the ~** mieux vaut ne pas parler de ça
C *adv* (*comparative of* **well**) mieux; **you had ~ do, you'd ~ do** (advising) tu ferais mieux de faire; (warning) tu as intérêt à faire; **we'd ~ leave** on ferait mieux de partir
D *vt* améliorer

IDIOMS **for ~ (or) for worse** advienne que pourra; (in wedding vow) pour le meilleur et pour le pire; **to get the ~ of** triompher de ‹*opponent*›; **his curiosity got the ~ of him** sa curiosité a pris le dessus; **to go one ~** faire encore mieux (**than** que); **to think ~ of it** changer d'avis

better off /ˌbetər'ɒf/ *adj* **1** (more wealthy) plus riche (**than** que)
2 (in better situation) mieux

betting /'betɪŋ/ *n* paris *mpl*

betting shop *n* (BrE) bureau *m* de PMU

✓ **between** /bɪ'twiːn/ **A** *prep* **1** entre; **~ you and me, ~ ourselves** entre nous; **~ now and next year** d'ici l'année prochaine
2 they drank the whole bottle ~ (the two of) them ils ont bu toute la bouteille à eux deux
B *adv* (*also* **in ~**) (in space) au milieu, entre les deux; (in time) entre-temps; **the two main roads and the streets (in) ~** les deux rues principales et les petites rues situées entre elles; **neither red nor orange, but somewhere in ~** ni rouge ni orange mais entre les deux

beverage /'bevərɪdʒ/ *n* boisson *f*, breuvage *m*

beware /bɪ'weə(r)/ **A** *excl* prenez garde!, attention!
B *vi* se méfier (**of** de); **~ of…** attention à…

bewildered /bɪ'wɪldəd/ *adj* ‹*person*› déconcerté/-e (**at, by** par); ‹*look*› perplexe

bewildering /bɪ'wɪldərɪŋ/ *adj* déconcertant/-e

bewitch /bɪ'wɪtʃ/ *vt* ensorceler

✓ **beyond** /bɪ'jɒnd/ **A** *prep* **1** (in space and time) au-delà de
2 ~ one's means au-dessus de ses moyens; **~ all hope** au-delà de toute espérance; **~ one's control** hors de son contrôle; **he is ~ help** on ne peut rien faire pour lui; **it's ~ me** ça me dépasse
3 (other than) en dehors de, à part
B *adv* au-delà
C *conj* à part (+ *infinitive*)

IDIOM **to be in the back of ~** être au bout du monde

bias /'baɪəs/ **A** *n* (*pl* **-es**) **1** (prejudice) parti *m* pris
2 (tendency) tendance *f*
B *vt* (*p prés etc* **-s-** *ou* **-ss-**) **to ~ sb against/in favour of** prévenir qn contre/en faveur de

biased, biassed /'baɪəst/ *adj* ‹*person*› partial/-e; ‹*report*› manquant d'objectivité; **to be ~** ‹*person*› avoir des partis pris; **to be ~ against** avoir un préjugé défavorable envers

bib /bɪb/ *n* (baby's) bavoir *m*; (of apron, dungarees) bavette *f*

Bible /'baɪbl/ *n* Bible *f*

biblical /'bɪblɪkl/ *adj* biblique

bibliography /ˌbɪblɪ'ɒgrəfɪ/ *n* bibliographie *f*

bicarbonate of soda *n* bicarbonate *m* de soude

bicentenary, /ˌbaɪsen'tiːnərɪ, (AmE) -'sentənerɪ/, **bicentennial** *n* bicentenaire *m*

biceps /'baɪseps/ *n* (*pl* **~**) biceps *m*

bicker /'bɪkə(r)/ *vi* se chamailler (**about** au sujet de)

bickering /'bɪkərɪŋ/ *n* chamailleries *fpl*

bicycle /'baɪsɪkl/ **A** *n* bicyclette *f*, vélo *m*; **on a/by ~** à bicyclette
B *adj* ‹*pump*› à bicyclette; ‹*bell, lamp*› de bicyclette; ‹*race*› cycliste

bicycle clip *n* pince *f* à vélo

bicycle lane *n* piste *f* cyclable

✓ **bid** /bɪd/ **A** *n* **1** (at auction) enchère *f* (**for** sur, **of** de)
2 (for contract) soumission *f*
3 (attempt) tentative *f* (**to do** pour faire)
B *vt* (*p prés* **-dd-**, *prét* **bade** *ou* **bid**, *pp* **bidden** *ou* **bid**) **1** offrir ‹*money*› (**for** pour)
2 (say) **to ~ sb good morning** dire bonjour à qn
C *vi* (*p prés* **-dd-**, *prét* **bade** *ou* **bid**, *pp* **bidden** *ou* **bid**) (at auction) enchérir (**for** sur); (for contract) soumissionner (**for** pour)

bidder /'bɪdə(r)/ *n* (at auction) enchérisseur/-euse *m/f*; **to go to the highest ~** être adjugé/-e au plus offrant/-e

bidding /'bɪdɪŋ/ *n* (at auction) enchères *fpl*

bide /baɪd/ *vi*

IDIOM **to ~ one's time** attendre le bon moment

bidet /'biːdeɪ, (AmE) biː'deɪ/ *n* bidet *m*

bifocals /baɪ'fəʊklz/ *npl* verres *mpl* à double foyer

✓ **big** /bɪg/ *adj* (gen) grand/-e *before n*; (bulky, fat) gros/grosse *before n*; ‹*meal*› copieux/-ieuse; **to get ~(ger)** (taller) grandir; (fatter) grossir; **a ~ book** (thick) un gros livre; (large-format) un grand livre; **his ~ brother** son grand frère, son frère aîné; **a ~ mistake** une grave erreur; **to be in ~ trouble** être dans le pétrin (fam); **to have ~ ideas, to think ~** voir grand

bigamy /'bɪgəmɪ/ *n* bigamie *f*

big business *n* **1** les grandes entreprises *fpl*
2 to be ~ rapporter gros

big dipper *n* (BrE) (at fair) montagnes *fpl* russes

big game *n* gros gibier *m*

big-headed *adj* (fam) prétentieux/-ieuse

bigmouth /'bɪgmaʊθ/ *n* (fam) **he's such a ~!** il ne sait pas tenir sa langue!

big name *n* (in music, art) grand nom *m*; (in film, sport) star *f*; **to be a ~** être connu/-e (**in** dans le monde de)

bigoted /'bɪgətɪd/ *adj* intolérant/-e, sectaire

bigotry /'bɪgətrɪ/ *n* intolérance *f*, sectarisme *m*

big screen *n* grand écran *m*

big shot *n* (fam) gros bonnet *m* (fam)

big toe *n* gros orteil *m*

b

big top *n* (tent) grand chapiteau *m*
bike /baɪk/ *n* (cycle) vélo *m*; (motorbike) moto *f*
biker /ˈbaɪkə(r)/ *n* (fam) motard *m* (fam)
bikini /bɪˈkiːnɪ/ *n* bikini® *m*
bilingual /ˌbaɪˈlɪŋgwəl/ *adj* bilingue
⚷ **bill** /bɪl/ **A** *n* **1** (in restaurant) addition *f*; (for services, electricity) facture *f*; (from hotel, doctor, dentist) note *f*
2 (Pol) projet *m* de loi
3 (poster) affiche *f*
4 (AmE) **dollar ~** billet *m* d'un dollar
5 (beak) bec *m*
B *vt* **to ~ sb for sth** facturer qch à qn
IDIOM **to fit** *or* **fill the ~** faire l'affaire
billboard *n* panneau *m* d'affichage
billet /ˈbɪlɪt/ *vt* cantonner (**on, with** chez)
billiards *n* billard *m*
⚷ **billion** /ˈbɪlɪən/ *n* (a thousand million) milliard *m*; (BrE) (a million million) billion *m*
billionaire /ˌbɪlɪəˈneə(r)/ *n* milliardaire *mf*
billow /ˈbɪləʊ/ *vi* ‹*clouds, smoke*› s'élever en tourbillons
▪ **billow out** ‹*skirt, sail*› se gonfler; ‹*steam*› s'élever
billy goat *n* bouc *m*
bimbo /ˈbɪmbəʊ/ *n* (fam) ravissante idiote *f* (derog)
bin /bɪn/ *n* (BrE) (for rubbish) poubelle *f*
bind /baɪnd/ *vt* (*prét*, *pp* **bound**) **1** (tie up) attacher (**to** à)
2 to be bound by être tenu/-e par ‹*law, oath*›
3 (*also* **~ together**) unir ‹*people, community*›
4 relier ‹*book*›
binder /ˈbaɪndə(r)/ *n* (for papers, lecture notes) classeur *m*
binding /ˈbaɪndɪŋ/ **A** *n* reliure *f*
B *adj* ‹*agreement, contract*› qui engage
binge /bɪndʒ/ *n* (fam) **to go on a ~** faire la noce
binge-drinking /ˌbɪndʒˈdrɪŋkɪŋ/ /ˌbɪndʒˈdrɪŋkɪŋ/ *n: habitude de consommer une quantité excessive de boissons alcooliques en un temps très court*
bingo /ˈbɪŋgəʊ/ *n* bingo *m*
bin liner *n* (BrE) sac *m* poubelle
binoculars /bɪˈnɒkjʊləz/ *npl* jumelles *fpl*
biochemist /ˌbaɪəʊˈkemɪst/ *n* biochimiste *mf*
biochemistry /ˌbaɪəʊˈkemɪstrɪ/ *n* biochimie *f*
biodegradable /ˌbaɪəʊdɪˈgreɪdəbl/ *adj* biodégradable
biodiesel /baɪəʊˌdiːzl/ *n* biodiesel *m*
biodiversity /ˌbaɪəʊdɪˈvɜːsətɪ/ *n* diversité *f* biologique
bioengineering /ˌbaɪəʊˌendʒɪˈnɪərɪŋ/ *n* génie *m* biologique
biographical /ˌbaɪəˈgræfɪkl/ *adj* biographique
biography /baɪˈɒgrəfɪ/ *n* biographie *f*

⚷ mot clé

biological /ˌbaɪəˈlɒdʒɪkl/ *adj* biologique
biological clock *n* horloge *f* biologique
biological warfare *n* guerre *f* biologique
biologist /baɪˈɒlədʒɪst/ *n* biologiste *mf*
biology /baɪˈɒlədʒɪ/ *n* biologie *f*
biometric /ˌbaɪəʊˈmetrɪk/ *adj* biométrique
biopsy /ˈbaɪɒpsɪ/ *n* biopsie *f*
biotechnology /ˌbaɪəʊtekˈnɒlədʒɪ/ *n* biotechnologie *f*
birch /bɜːtʃ/ *n* bouleau *m*
⚷ **bird** /bɜːd/ *n* **1** (Zool) oiseau *m*
2 (BrE) (fam) (girl) nana *f* (fam)
IDIOM **to kill two ~s with one stone** faire d'une pierre deux coups
bird flu *n* grippe *f* aviaire
bird of prey *n* oiseau *m* de proie
bird's eye view *n* vue *f* d'ensemble
birdsong *n* chant *m* des oiseaux
bird-watching /ˈbɜːdwɒtʃɪŋ/ *n* **to go ~** observer les oiseaux
biro® /ˈbaɪərəʊ/ *n* (BrE) (*pl* **~s**) stylo-bille *m*, bic® *m*
⚷ **birth** /bɜːθ/ *n* naissance *f* (**of** de)
birth certificate *n* certificat *m* de naissance
birth control *n* (in society) contrôle *m* des naissances; (by couple) contraception *f*
⚷ **birthday** /ˈbɜːθdeɪ/ *n* anniversaire *m*; **Happy Birthday!** Bon *or* Joyeux Anniversaire!
birthday party *n* (for child) goûter *m* d'anniversaire; (for adult) soirée *f* d'anniversaire
birthing pool *n* piscine *f* d'accouchement
birthmark *n* tache *f* de naissance
birth mother *n* mère *f* biologique
birthplace *n* lieu *m* de naissance
birth rate *n* taux *m* de natalité
birth sign *n* signe *m* du zodiaque
biscuit /ˈbɪskɪt/ *n* **1** (BrE) biscuit *m*, petit gâteau *m*
2 (AmE) pain *m* au lait
bisexual /baɪˈsekʃʊəl/ *n*, *adj* bisexuel/-elle *m/f*
bishop /ˈbɪʃəp/ *n* **1** évêque *m*
2 (in chess) fou *m*
⚷ **bit** /bɪt/ **A** *n* **1** (gen) morceau *m* (**of** de); (of paper, string, land) bout *m* (**of** de); (of book, film) passage *m*
2 (fam) **a ~ (of)** un peu (de); **a little ~** un petit peu
3 (of horse) mors *m*
B a bit *phr* (fam) un peu; **a ~ early** un peu trop tôt; **she isn't a ~ like me** elle ne me ressemble pas du tout
IDIOMS **~ by ~** petit à petit; **~s and pieces** (fragments) morceaux *mpl*; (belongings) affaires *fpl*
bitch /bɪtʃ/ *n* **1** (dog) chienne *f*
2 (colloq derog) garce *f* (fam)

bite /baɪt/ **A** *n* **1** morsure *f*; (from insect) piqûre *f*
2 (mouthful) bouchée *f*; **to have a ~ to eat** manger un morceau
B *vt* (*prét* **bit**, *pp* **bitten**) ‹*animal, person*› mordre; ‹*insect*› piquer; **to ~ one's nails** se ronger les ongles
C *vi* (*prét* **bit**, *pp* **bitten**) ‹*fish*› mordre
■ **bite off**: **~ off [sth], ~ [sth] off** arracher [qch] d'un coup de dent

biting /ˈbaɪtɪŋ/ *adj* **1** ‹*wind*› cinglant/-e
2 ‹*comment*› mordant/-e

bitter /ˈbɪtə(r)/ *adj* (gen) amer/-ère; ‹*wind*› glacial/-e; ‹*disappointment, truth*› cruel/-elle
IDIOM **to the ~ end** jusqu'au bout

bitterly /ˈbɪtəlɪ/ *adv* ‹*complain, speak*› amèrement; ‹*regret*› profondément; **it's ~ cold** il fait un froid terrible

bitterness /ˈbɪtənɪs/ *n* amertume *f*

bizarre /bɪˈzɑː(r)/ *adj* bizarre

black /blæk/ **A** *n* **1** (colour) noir *m*
2 (*also* **Black**) (person) Noir/-e *m/f*
3 to be in the ~ être créditeur/-trice
B *adj* **1** (gen) noir/-e; ‹*night*› obscur/-e; ‹*tea*› nature; **to turn ~** noircir
2 (*also* **Black**) ‹*community, culture*› noir/-e
■ **black out** ‹*person*› s'évanouir

black and white **A** *n* noir et blanc *m*
B *adj* ‹*TV, camera film*› noir et blanc *inv*; ‹*movie, photography*› (en) noir et blanc *inv*

blackberry /ˈblækbrɪ, -berɪ/ *n* mûre *f*

blackbird *n* merle *m*

blackboard /ˈblækbɔːd/ *n* tableau *m* (noir); **on the ~** au tableau

black box *n* boîte *f* noire

blackcurrant /ˌblækˈkʌrənt/ *n* cassis *m*

blacken /ˈblækən/ *vt* noircir

black eye /ˌblækˈaɪ/ *n* œil *m* poché

blackhead *n* point *m* noir

black ice *n* verglas *m*

blacklist /ˈblæklɪst/ **A** *n* liste *f* noire
B *vt* mettre [qn] à l'index

blackmail /ˈblækmeɪl/ **A** *n* chantage *m*
B *vt* faire chanter ‹*victim*›

blackmailer /ˈblækmeɪlə(r)/ *n* maître-chanteur *m*

black market *n* **on the ~** au marché noir

blackout /ˈblækaʊt/ *n* **1** (power cut) panne *f* de courant; (in wartime) black-out *m*
2 (faint) étourdissement *m*

Black Sea *pr n* mer *f* Noire

black sheep *n* brebis *f* galeuse

blacksmith *n* forgeron *m*

black tie *n* (on invitation) **'~'** 'tenue *f* de soirée'

bladder /ˈblædə(r)/ *n* vessie *f*

blade /bleɪd/ *n* (of knife, sword, axe) lame *f*; (of fan, propeller, oar) pale *f*; (of grass) brin *m*

blame /bleɪm/ **A** *n* responsabilité *f* (**for** de)
B *vt* **I ~ you** c'est ta faute; **to ~ sb for sth** reprocher qch à qn; **to ~ sth on sb** tenir qn responsable de qch; **to be to ~ for sth** être responsable de qch
C *v refl* **to ~ oneself for sth** se sentir responsable de qch

blameless /ˈbleɪmlɪs/ *adj* irréprochable

blancmange /bləˈmɒnʒ/ *n* blanc-manger *m*

bland /blænd/ *adj* ‹*food, flavour*› fade; ‹*person*› terne

blank /blæŋk/ **A** *n* **1** (empty space) blanc *m*; **my mind's a ~** j'ai la tête vide
2 (cartridge) cartouche *f* à blanc
B *adj* **1** ‹*paper, page*› blanc/blanche; ‹*screen*› vide; ‹*cassette*› vierge
2 ‹*expression*› ébahi/-e; **my mind went ~** j'ai eu un trou de mémoire
■ **blank out**: **~ [sth] out, ~ out [sth]** rayer [qch] de sa mémoire

blank cheque (BrE), **blank check** (AmE) *n* chèque *m* en blanc; (fig) carte *f* blanche

blanket /ˈblæŋkɪt/ *n* **1** couverture *f*
2 (of snow) couche *f*; (of cloud, fog) nappe *f*

blare /bleə(r)/
■ **blare out**: **A ~ out** ‹*music, radio*› jouer à plein volume
B ~ out [sth] déverser ‹*music*›

blasphemous /ˈblæsfəməs/ *adj* ‹*person*› blasphémateur/-trice; ‹*statement*› blasphématoire

blasphemy /ˈblæsfəmɪ/ *n* blasphème *m*

blast /blɑːst, (AmE) blæst/ **A** *n* **1** (explosion) explosion *f*
2 (of air) souffle *m*
3 at full ~ ‹*play music*› à plein volume
B *vt* (blow up) faire sauter; **to ~ a hole in the wall** percer un mur à l'explosif
■ **blast off** ‹*rocket*› décoller

blast-off /ˈblɑːstɒf, (AmE) ˈblæst-/ *n* lancement *m*

blatant /ˈbleɪtnt/ *adj* ‹*lie, disregard*› éhonté/-e; ‹*abuse*› flagrant/-e

blatantly /ˈbleɪtntlɪ/ *adv* ouvertement; **to be ~ obvious** sauter aux yeux

blaze /bleɪz/ **A** *n* (fire) incendie *m*; (in hearth) feu *m*, flambée *f*; **in a ~ of publicity** sous les feux des médias
B *vt* **to ~ a trail** faire œuvre de pionnier
C *vi* (*also* **~ away**) **1** ‹*fire, house*› brûler
2 ‹*lights*› briller

blazer /ˈbleɪzə(r)/ *n* blazer *m*

blazing *adj* (violent) ‹*argument*› violent/-e; ‹*fire*› ronflant/-e; ‹*building, car*› embrasé/-e

bleach /bliːtʃ/ **A** *n* **1** (disinfectant) eau *f* de javel
2 (for hair) décolorant *m*
B *vt* décolorer ‹*hair*›; blanchir ‹*linen*›

bleak /bliːk/ *adj* ‹*landscape*› désolé/-e; ‹*weather*› maussade; ‹*outlook, future*› sombre

bleary /ˈblɪərɪ/ *adj* ‹*eyes*› bouffi/-e; **to be ~-eyed** avoir les yeux bouffis

bleat /bliːt/ *vi* ‹*sheep, goat*› bêler

bleed /bli:d/ **A** *vt* (*prét*, *pp* **bled**) **to ~ sb dry** saigner qn à blanc
B *vi* (*prét*, *pp* **bled**) saigner; **my finger's ~ing** j'ai le doigt qui saigne

bleep /bli:p/ **A** *n* (signal) bip *m*, bip-bip *m*
B *vt* **to ~ sb** appeler qn (au bip), biper qn

bleeper /'bli:pə(r)/ *n* (BrE) bip *m*

blemish /'blemɪʃ/ *n* (gen) imperfection *f*; (on fruit) tache *f*; (pimple) bouton *m*

blend /blend/ **A** *n* mélange *m* (**of** de)
B *vt* mélanger ‹*ingredients, colours, styles*›
C *vi* **to ~ (together)** ‹*colours, tastes, styles*› se fondre; **to ~ with** ‹*colours, tastes, sounds*› se marier à; ‹*smells*› se mêler à

■ **blend in**: **A** **~ in** s'harmoniser (**with** avec)
B **~ [sth] in** incorporer ‹*ingredient*›

blender /'blendə(r)/ *n* mixeur *m*, mixer *m*

bless /bles/ *vt* bénir; **~ you!** (after sneeze) à vos souhaits!; **to be ~ed with** jouir de ‹*health, beauty*›

blessing /'blesɪŋ/ *n* **1** bénédiction *f*
2 (good thing) bienfait *m*; **a ~ in disguise** un bienfait caché

blight /blaɪt/ *n* (on society) plaie *f* (**on** de); **urban ~** délabrement *m* urbain

blind /blaɪnd/ **A** *n* **1** **the ~** les aveugles *mpl*
2 (on window) store *m*
B *adj* ‹*person*› aveugle; **to go ~** perdre la vue; **~ in one eye** borgne
C *vt* **1** ‹*injury, accident*› rendre aveugle
2 ‹*sun, light*› éblouir
3 ‹*pride, love*› aveugler
(IDIOM) **to turn a ~ eye** fermer les yeux (**to** sur)

blind alley *n* voie *f* sans issue

blind date *n* rendez-vous *m* avec un/-e inconnu/-e

blindfold /'blaɪndfəʊld/ **A** *n* bandeau *m*
B *adj* (*also* **~ed**) aux yeux bandés
C *adv* les yeux bandés
D *vt* bander les yeux à ‹*person*›

blinding /'blaɪndɪŋ/ *adj* ‹*light*› aveuglant/-e; ‹*headache*› atroce

blindly /'blaɪndlɪ/ *adv* ‹*obey, follow*› aveuglément

blindness /'blaɪndnɪs/ *n* cécité *f*; (fig) aveuglement *m*

blind spot *n* **1** (in eye) point *m* aveugle
2 (in car, on hill) angle *m* mort

blink /blɪŋk/ *vi* ‹*person*› cligner des yeux; ‹*light*› clignoter

blinker /'blɪŋkə(r)/ *n* **1** (Aut) clignotant *m*
2 **~s** œillères *fpl*

blinkered *adj* ‹*attitude, approach*› borné/-e

blip /blɪp/ *n* (on screen) spot *m*; (on graph) accident *m* (d'une courbe)

bliss /blɪs/ *n* bonheur *m* parfait

blissfully /'blɪsfəlɪ/ *adv* **~ happy** au comble du bonheur; **~ ignorant** dans la plus parfaite ignorance

blister /'blɪstə(r)/ **A** *n* (on skin) ampoule *f*
B *vi* ‹*skin, paint*› cloquer

blister pack *n* blister *m*, habillage *m* transparent

blithely /'blaɪðlɪ/ *adv* (nonchalantly) avec insouciance; (cheerfully) allègrement

blitz /blɪts/ **A** *n* bombardement *m* aérien
B *vt* bombarder

blizzard /'blɪzəd/ *n* tempête *f* de neige; (in Arctic regions) blizzard *m*

bloated /'bləʊtɪd/ *adj* ‹*face, body*› bouffi/-e; ‹*stomach*› ballonné/-e

blob /blɒb/ *n* **1** (drop) grosse goutte *f*
2 (shape) forme *f* floue

⚷ **block** /blɒk/ **A** *n* **1** (slab) bloc *m*
2 **~ of flats** immeuble *m* (d'habitation); **office ~** immeuble de bureaux
3 (of houses) pâté *m* de maisons
4 (for butcher, executioner) billot *m*
B *vt* bloquer ‹*exit, road, ball*›; boucher ‹*drain, hole, artery, view*›; **to have a ~ed nose** avoir le nez bouché

■ **block out**: **~ out [sth]**, **~ [sth] out** **1** (hide) boucher ‹*view*›; cacher ‹*light, sun*›
2 (suppress) refouler ‹*memory, problem*›

blockade /blɒ'keɪd/ **A** *n* blocus *m*
B *vt* bloquer, faire le blocus de ‹*port*›

blockage /'blɒkɪdʒ/ *n* obstruction *f*

block-book *vt* louer [qch] en groupe ‹*seats*›

blockbuster /'blɒkbʌstə(r)/ *n* (fam) **1** (book) livre *m* à succès, bestseller *m*
2 (film) superproduction *f*

block capitals, **block letters** *npl* **in ~** (on form) en caractères *mpl or* capitales *fpl* d'imprimerie

blog /blɒg/ **A** *n* blog *m*
B *vi* bloguer

blogger /'blɒgə(r)/ *n* blogger *m*

bloke /bləʊk/ *n* (fam) type *m* (fam), mec *m* (fam)

blonde /blɒnd/ **A** *n* blonde *f*
B *adj* blond/-e

⚷ **blood** /blʌd/ *n* sang *m*
(IDIOM) **in cold ~** de sang-froid

blood bank *n* banque *f* du sang

blood-curdling /'blʌdkɜ:dlɪŋ/ *adj* à vous figer le sang dans les veines

blood donor *n* donneur/-euse *m/f* de sang

blood group *n* groupe *m* sanguin

blood pressure *n* tension *f* artérielle; **high ~** hypertension *f*

blood relation *n* parent/-e *m/f* par le sang

bloodshed *n* effusion *f* de sang

bloodshot *adj* injecté/-e de sang

blood sport *n* sport *m* sanguinaire

bloodstained *adj* taché/-e de sang

bloodstream *n* sang *m*

blood test *n* analyse *f* de sang

bloodthirsty /'blʌdθɜ:stɪ/ *adj* sanguinaire

blood type *n* groupe *m* sanguin

⚷ mot clé

bloody /ˈblʌdɪ/ **A** *adj* **1** ‹*hand, body*› ensanglanté/-e; ‹*battle*› sanglant/-e
2 (BrE) (fam) sacré/-e *before n*; **~ fool!** espèce d'idiot!
B *adv* (BrE) (sl) sacrément (fam)

bloom /bluːm/ **A** *n* (flower) fleur *f*; **in ~** en fleur
B *vi* **1** (be in flower) être fleuri/-e; (come into flower) fleurir
2 to be ~ing with health être resplendissant/-e de santé

blossom /ˈblɒsəm/ **A** *n* (flower) fleur *f*; (flowers) fleurs *fpl*
B *vi* fleurir; (fig) s'épanouir

blot /blɒt/ **A** *n* (gen) tache *f*; (of ink) pâté *m*; (fig) ombre *f*
B *vt* (*p prés etc* **-tt-**) **1** (dry) sécher [qch] au buvard ‹*ink*›
2 (stain) tacher
■ **blot out** effacer ‹*memories*›; masquer ‹*view*›

blotch /blɒtʃ/ *n* (on skin) plaque *f* rouge; (of ink, colour) tache *f*

blotchy /ˈblɒtʃɪ/ *adj* ‹*complexion*› marbré/-e

blotting paper *n* papier *m* buvard

blouse /blaʊz, (AmE) blaʊs/ *n* chemisier *m*

blow /bləʊ/ **A** *n* coup *m*
B *vt* (*prét* **blew**, *pp* **blown**) **1 the wind blew the door shut** un coup de vent a fermé la porte; **to be blown off course** ‹*ship*› être dévié/-e par le vent
2 ‹*person*› faire ‹*bubble, smoke ring*›; souffler ‹*glass*›; **to ~ one's nose** se moucher; **to ~ one's whistle** donner un coup de sifflet
3 ‹*explosion*› faire ‹*hole*› (**in** dans); **to be blown to pieces** *or* **bits by** être réduit/-e en poussière par
4 faire sauter ‹*fuse*›; griller ‹*light bulb*›
C *vi* (*prét* **blew**, *pp* **blown**) **1** ‹*wind*› souffler; ‹*person*› souffler (**into** dans, **on** sur)
2 to ~ in the wind ‹*flag, clothes*› voler au vent
3 ‹*fuse*› sauter; ‹*bulb*› griller; ‹*tyre*› éclater
■ **blow away**: **A ~ away** s'envoler
B ~ [sth] away, ~ away [sth] ‹*wind*› emporter ‹*object*›
■ **blow down** ‹*wind*› faire tomber ‹*tree*›
■ **blow off**: **A ~ off** ‹*hat*› s'envoler
B ~ [sth] off ‹*wind*› emporter ‹*hat*›; ‹*explosion*› emporter ‹*roof*›
■ **blow out** souffler ‹*candle*›; éteindre ‹*flames*›
■ **blow over** ‹*storm*› s'apaiser; ‹*affair*› être oublié/-e
■ **blow up**: **A ~ up** ‹*building*› sauter; ‹*bomb*› exploser
B ~ [sb/sth] up 1 faire sauter ‹*building, person*›; faire exploser ‹*bomb*›
2 gonfler ‹*tyre*›
3 agrandir ‹*photograph*›

blow-dry /ˈbləʊdraɪ/ **A** *n* brushing *m*
B *vt* **to ~ sb's hair** faire un brushing à qn

blowout /ˈbləʊaʊt/ *n* **1** (electrical) court-circuit *m*
2 (of tyre) crevaison *f*
3 (fam) (meal) gueuleton *m* (fam)

blowtorch *n* lampe *f* à souder

blubber /ˈblʌbə(r)/ **A** *n* (of whale) graisse *f* de baleine
B *vi* (AmE) (cry) (fam) pleurer comme un veau

bludgeon /ˈblʌdʒən/ *vt* **to ~ sb to death** tuer qn à coups de matraque

blue /bluː/ **A** *n* bleu *m*
B *adj* **1** bleu/-e
2 (fam) ‹*movie*› porno (fam); ‹*joke*› cochon/-onne (fam)
IDIOM **to appear/happen out of the ~** apparaître/se passer à l'improviste

bluebell /ˈbluːbel/ *n* jacinthe *f* des bois

blueberry *n* (AmE) myrtille *f*

blue cheese *n* (fromage *m*) bleu *m*

blue chip *adj* ‹*company, share*› de premier ordre

blue collar worker *n* ouvrier *m*, col *m* bleu

blue jeans *npl* jean *m*

blueprint /ˈbluːprɪnt/ *n* bleu *m*; (fig) projet *m* (**for** pour, **for doing** pour faire)

blues *npl* **1** (Mus) **the ~** le blues *m*
2 (fam) **to have the ~** avoir le cafard (fam)

bluff /blʌf/ *vt, vi* bluffer (fam)
IDIOM **to call sb's ~** prendre qn au mot

blunder /ˈblʌndə(r)/ **A** *n* bourde *f*
B *vi* **1** (make mistake) faire une bourde
2 (move clumsily) **to ~ into sth** se cogner à qch

blunt /blʌnt/ **A** *adj* **1** ‹*knife, scissors*› émoussé/-e; ‹*pencil*› mal taillé/-e; ‹*instrument*› contondant/-e
2 ‹*person, manner*› abrupt/-e; ‹*criticism*› direct/-e
B *vt* émousser ‹*knife*›

bluntly /ˈblʌntlɪ/ *adv* franchement

blur /blɜː(r)/ **A** *n* image *f* floue
B *vt* (*p prés etc* **-rr-**) brouiller

blurb /blɜːb/ *n* (on book cover) texte *m* de présentation; (derog) baratin *m*

blurred /blɜːd/ *adj* indistinct/-e; ‹*image, idea*› flou/-e; ‹*memory*› confus/-e; **to have ~ vision** avoir des troubles de la vue

blurt /blɜːt/
■ **blurt out** laisser échapper ‹*truth, secret*›

blush /blʌʃ/ *vi* rougir (**at** devant, **with** de)

blusher /ˈblʌʃə(r)/ *n* fard *m* à joues

blustery /ˈblʌstərɪ/ *adj* **~ wind** bourrasque *f*

Blu-tack® /ˈbluːtæk/ *n* patafix® *m*

BMI *n* (*abbr* = **body mass index**) IMC *m*

BO *n* (fam) (*abbr* = **body odour**) odeur *f* corporelle; **he's got ~** il sent mauvais

boar /bɔː(r)/ *n* (*also* **wild ~**) sanglier *m*

board /bɔːd/ **A** *n* **1** (plank) planche *f*; **bare ~s** plancher *m* nu
2 (committee) conseil *m*; **~ of directors**

conseil d'administration
3 (for chess, draughts) tableau *m*
4 (in classroom) tableau *m* (noir)
5 (notice board) panneau *m* d'affichage; (to advertise) panneau *m*
6 (Comput) plaquette *f*
7 (accommodation) **full ~** pension *f* complète; **half ~** demi-pension *f*; **~ and lodging** le gîte et le couvert
B *vt* monter à bord de ‹*plane, ship*›; monter dans ‹*bus, train*›; ‹*pirates*› aborder ‹*vessel*›
C **on board** *phr* à bord
IDIOMS **above ~** légal/-e; **across the ~** à tous les niveaux
▪ **board up** boucher [qch] avec des planches ‹*window*›; barricader [qch] avec des planches ‹*house*›

boarder /'bɔːdə(r)/ *n* **1** (lodger) pensionnaire *m* **2** (school pupil) interne *mf*

board game *n* jeu *m* de société (à damier)

boarding /'bɔːdɪŋ/ *n* embarquement *m*

boarding card *n* carte *f* d'embarquement

boarding school *n* école *f* privée avec internat

board meeting *n* réunion *f* du conseil d'administration

boardroom /'bɔːdruːm, -rʊm/ *n* salle *f* du conseil

boast /bəʊst/ **A** *n* vantardise *f*
B *vt* s'enorgueillir de
C *vi* se vanter (**about** de)

boastful /'bəʊstfl/ *adj* vantard/-e

boat /bəʊt/ *n* (gen) bateau *m*; (sailing) voilier *m*; (rowing) barque *f*; (liner) paquebot *m*
IDIOM **to be in the same ~** (fam) être tous/toutes dans la même galère

boater /'bəʊtə(r)/ *n* (hat) canotier *m*

boathouse *n* abri *m* à bateaux

boating /'bəʊtɪŋ/ **A** *n* navigation *f* de plaisance
B *adj* ‹*accident, enthusiast*› de bateau; ‹*trip*› en bateau

boatyard *n* chantier *m* de construction de bateaux

bob /bɒb/ **A** *n* (haircut) coupe *f* au carré
B *vi* (*p prés etc* **-bb-**) (*also* **~ up and down**) ‹*boat, float*› danser

bobsled, **bobsleigh** /'bɒbsled/ *n* bobsleigh *m*

bode /bəʊd/ *vi* **to ~ well/ill** être de bon/mauvais augure

bodily /'bɒdɪlɪ/ *adj* ‹*function*› physiologique; ‹*fluid*› organique

body /'bɒdɪ/ *n* **1** (of person, animal) corps *m*
2 (corpse) corps *m*, cadavre *m*
3 (of car) carrosserie *f*
4 (of water) étendue *f*
5 (organization) organisme *m*
6 (of wine) corps *m*; (of hair) volume *m*

mot clé

bodybuilder /'bɒdɪbɪldə(r)/ *n* culturiste *mf*

body-building /'bɒdɪbɪldɪŋ/ *n* culturisme *m*

bodyguard /'bɒdɪgɑːd/ *n* garde *m* du corps

body language *n* langage *m* corporel

body mass index *n* indice *m* de masse corporelle

body part *n* partie *f* de corps

body piercing *n* piercing *m*

body warmer *n* gilet *m* matelassé

bodywork *n* carrosserie *f*

bog /bɒg/ *n* **1** (marshy ground) marais *m*
2 (*also* **peat ~**) tourbière *f*
IDIOM **to get ~ged down in sth** s'enliser dans qch

boggle /'bɒgl/ *vi* **the mind ~s!** c'est époustouflant!

bog-standard /bɒg,stændəd/ *adj* (fam) ordinaire

bogus /'bəʊgəs/ *adj* ‹*doctor, document*› faux/fausse *before n*; ‹*claim*› bidon *inv*; ‹*company*› factice

bohemian /bəʊ'hiːmɪən/ *adj* ‹*lifestyle*› de bohème; ‹*person*› bohème

boil /bɔɪl/ **A** *n* **1 to bring sth to the ~** porter qch à ébullition
2 (on skin) furoncle *m*
B *vt* faire bouillir; **to ~ an egg** faire cuire un œuf
C *vi* bouillir; **the kettle is ~ing** l'eau bout (dans la bouilloire); **to make sb's blood ~** faire sortir qn de ses gonds
▪ **boil down to** (fig) se ramener à
▪ **boil over** déborder

boiled egg *n* œuf *m* à la coque

boiled potatoes *npl* pommes *fpl* de terre à l'anglaise

boiler /'bɔɪlə(r)/ *n* chaudière *f*

boiler suit *n* (BrE) bleu *m* de travail

boiling /'bɔɪlɪŋ/ *adj* ‹*liquid*› bouillant/-e; **it's ~!** (fam) il fait une chaleur infernale!

boiling point *n* point *m* d'ébullition; (fig) point *m* limite

boisterous /'bɔɪstərəs/ *adj* ‹*adult, game*› bruyant/-e; ‹*child*› turbulent/-e

bold /bəʊld/ *adj* **1** (daring) ‹*person*› intrépide; ‹*attempt, plan*› audacieux/-ieuse
2 (cheeky) ‹*person*› effronté/-e
3 ‹*colour*› vif/vive; ‹*design*› voyant/-e; **~ print** caractères *mpl* gras

bollard /'bɒlɑːd/ *n* balise *f*

bolster /'bəʊlstə(r)/ **A** *n* traversin *m*
B *vt* (*also* **~ up**) soutenir

bolt /bəʊlt/ **A** *n* **1** (lock) verrou *m*
2 ~ of lightning coup *m* de foudre
B *vt* **1** (lock) verrouiller
2 (*also* **~ down**) engloutir ‹*food*›
C *vi* ‹*horse*› s'emballer; ‹*person*› détaler (fam)
D **bolt upright** *phr* droit/-e comme un i
IDIOM **a ~ out of the blue** un coup de tonnerre

⚷ **bomb** /bɒm/ **A** *n* bombe *f*
B *vt* bombarder ‹*town, house*›

bombard /bɒm'bɑːd/ *vt* bombarder (**with** de)

bomb blast *n* explosion *f*

bomb disposal unit *n* équipe *f* de déminage *m*

bomber /'bɒmə(r)/ *n* **1** (plane) bombardier *m*
2 (terrorist) poseur/-euse *m/f* de bombes

bomber jacket *n* blouson *m* d'aviateur

bombing /'bɒmɪŋ/ *n* bombardement *m*; (by terrorists) attentat *m* à la bombe

bomb scare *n* alerte *f* à la bombe

bombshell /'bɒmʃel/ *n* obus *m*; (fig) bombe *f*

bomb site /'bɒmsaɪt/ *n* zone *f* touchée par une explosion

Bomb Squad *n* brigade *f* antiterroriste

bona fide /ˌbəʊnə 'faɪdɪ/ *adj* ‹*attempt*› sincère; ‹*member*› vrai/-e *before n*; ‹*contract*› de bonne foi

bond /bɒnd/ **A** *n* **1** (link) liens *mpl* (**of** de, **between** entre)
2 (in finance) obligation *f*; **savings ~** bon *m* d'épargne
B *vt* (stick) faire adhérer
C *vi* ‹*person*› s'attacher (**with** à)

⚷ **bone** /bəʊn/ **A** *n* os *m*; (of fish) arête *f*
B *vt* désosser ‹*joint, chicken*›; enlever les arêtes de ‹*fish*›
IDIOMS **~ of contention** sujet *m* de dispute; **to have a ~ to pick with sb** avoir un compte à régler avec qn

bone china *n* porcelaine *f* tendre *or* à l'os

bone dry *adj* complètement sec/sèche

bone idle *adj* flemmard/-e

bone marrow transplant *n* greffe *f* de moelle osseuse

bonfire /'bɒnfaɪə(r)/ *n* (of rubbish) feu *m* de jardin; (for celebration) feu *m* de joie

Bonfire Night *n* (BrE) la soirée du 5 novembre (*fêtée avec feux de joie et feux d'artifice*)

bonnet /'bɒnɪt/ *n* **1** (hat) bonnet *m*
2 (BrE) (Aut) capot *m*

bonus /'bəʊnəs/ *n* **1** (payment) prime *f*
2 (advantage) avantage *m*

bony /'bəʊnɪ/ *adj* ‹*person, body*› anguleux/-euse; ‹*finger, arm*› osseux/-euse

boo /buː/ **A** *n* huée *f*
B *excl* (to give sb a fright) hou!; (to jeer) hou! hou!
C *vt* (3ᵉ *pers sg prés* **boos**, *prét, pp* **booed**) huer ‹*actor, speaker*›
D *vi* (3ᵉ *pers sg prés* **boos**, *prét, pp* **booed**) pousser des huées

booby trap **A** *n* **1** mécanisme *m* piégé
2 (practical joke) traquenard *m*
B *vt* (*p prés etc* **-pp-**) piéger

booing /'buːɪŋ/ *n* huées *fpl*

⚷ **book** /bʊk/ **A** *n* **1** livre *m* (**about** sur, **of** de); **history ~** livre d'histoire
2 (exercise book) cahier *m*
3 (of cheques, tickets, stamps) carnet *m*; **~ of matches** pochette *f* d'allumettes
B **books** *npl* (accounts) livres *mpl* de comptes
C *vt* **1** réserver ‹*table, room, taxi, ticket*›; faire les réservations pour ‹*holiday*›; **to be fully ~ed** être complet/-ète
2 ‹*policeman*› dresser un procès-verbal *or* un P.V. (fam) à ‹*motorist, offender*›; (AmE) (arrest) arrêter ‹*suspect*›
3 ‹*referee*› donner un carton jaune à ‹*player*›
D *vi* réserver
IDIOMS **to be in sb's good ~s** être dans les petits papiers de qn (fam); **to be in sb's bad ~s** ne pas avoir la cote avec qn

bookcase *n* bibliothèque *f*

book club *n* club *m* du livre

booking /'bʊkɪŋ/ *n* (BrE) réservation *f*

booking form *n* bon *m* de réservation

booking office *n* (BrE) bureau *m* de location

bookkeeping *n* comptabilité *f*

booklet /'bʊklɪt/ *n* brochure *f*

book list *n* liste *f* de livres

bookmaker *n* bookmaker *m*

bookmark /'bʊkmɑːk/ **A** *n* (for page) marque-pages *m*, signet *m*; (Comput) signet *m*
B *vt* créer un signet sur ‹*website*›

bookseller *n* libraire *mf*

bookshelf *n* (*pl* **-shelves**) (single) étagère *f*; (in bookcase) rayon *m*

bookshop, **book store** (AmE) *n* librairie *f*

book token *n* (BrE) chèque-livre *m*

bookworm /'bʊkwɜːm/ *n* mordu/-e *m/f* (fam) de la lecture

boom /buːm/ **A** *n* **1** (of cannon, thunder) grondement *m*; (of drum) boum *m*; (of explosion) détonation *f*; **~!** badaboum!
2 (Econ) boom *m*; (in prices, sales) explosion *f* (**in** de)
B *vi* **1** ‹*cannon, thunder*› gronder; ‹*voice*› retentir
2 ‹*economy*› prospérer; ‹*exports, sales*› monter en flèche; **business is ~ing** les affaires vont bien

boon /buːn/ *n* **1** (asset) aide *f* précieuse (**to** à)
2 (stroke of luck) aubaine *f* (**for** pour)

boost /buːst/ **A** *n* **to give sb/sth a ~** encourager qn/stimuler qch
B *vt* stimuler ‹*economy, sales*›; encourager ‹*investment*›; augmenter ‹*profit*›; **to ~ sb's confidence** redonner confiance à qn; **to ~ morale** remonter le moral

booster /'buːstə(r)/ *n* (Med) vaccin *m* de rappel

boot /buːt/ *n* **1** botte *f*; (of climber, hiker) chaussure *f*; (for workman, soldier) brodequin *m*; **football ~** (BrE) chaussure *f* de football

b

2 (BrE) (of car) coffre *m*
▪ **boot up**: ~ **[sth] up**, ~ **up [sth]** amorcer ‹*computer*›
boot camp *n* **1** (Mil) camp *m* d'entraînement militaire *pour nouvelles recrues*
2 (intensive training) stage *m* intensif; **maths ~** stage intensif de maths; **fitness ~** camp *m* de remise en forme
booth /buːð, (AmE) buːθ/ *n* (in language lab) cabine *f*; (at fair) baraque *f*; **polling ~** isoloir *m*; **telephone ~** cabine *f* (téléphonique)
bootlace *n* lacet *m* (de chaussure)
booze /buːz/ *n* (fam) bibine *f* (fam); (wine only) pinard *m* (fam)
🗝 **border** /'bɔːdə(r)/ **A** *n* **1** (frontier) frontière *f*; **to cross the ~** passer la frontière
2 (edge) bord *m*
3 (flower bed) plate-bande *f*
B *vt* **1** ‹*road, land*› longer ‹*lake, forest*›; ‹*country*› border ‹*ocean*›; avoir une frontière commune avec ‹*country*›
2 (surround) border
C *adj* frontalier/-ière
▪ **border on** ~ **on [sth]** **1** ‹*country*› être limitrophe de; ‹*garden, land*› toucher
2 (verge on) friser ‹*rudeness, madness*›
border dispute *n* différend *m* frontalier
borderline /'bɔːdəlaɪn/ *n* frontière *f*, limite *f* (**between** entre); **a ~ case** un cas limite
bore /bɔː(r)/ **A** *n* **1** (person) raseur/-euse *m/f* (fam)
2 (situation) **what a ~!** quelle barbe!
3 (of gun) calibre *m*
B *vt* **1** ennuyer ‹*person*›
2 (drill) percer ‹*hole*›; creuser ‹*well, tunnel*›
bored /bɔːd/ *adj* ‹*expression*› ennuyé/-e; **to be** *or* **get ~** s'ennuyer (**with** de)
(IDIOM) **to be ~ stiff** *or* **~ to tears** s'ennuyer à mourir
boredom /'bɔːdəm/ *n* ennui *m*
boring /'bɔːrɪŋ/ *adj* ennuyeux/-euse
🗝 **born** /bɔːn/ *adj* né/-e; **to be ~** naître; **she was ~ in May** elle est née en mai
born-again /ˌbɔːnə'geɪn/ *adj* né/-e de nouveau
borough /'bʌrə, (AmE) -rəʊ/ *n* arrondissement *m* urbain
borrow /'bɒrəʊ/ *vt* emprunter (**from** à)
borrower /'bɒrəʊə(r)/ *n* emprunteur/-euse *m/f*
borrowing /'bɒrəʊɪŋ/ *n* emprunt *m*
Bosnia *pr n* Bosnie *f*
Bosnian /'bɒznɪən/ *adj* bosniaque, bosnien/-ienne; **~ Serb/Muslim** Serbe/ Musulman de Bosnie
bosom /'bʊzəm/ *n* poitrine *f*; **in the ~ of one's family** au sein de sa famille; **~ friend** ami/-e *m/f* intime
🗝 **boss** /bɒs/ *n* (fam) patron/-onne *m/f*, chef *m*
▪ **boss about** (fam) **boss around** (fam) mener [qn] par le bout du nez ‹*person*›
bossy /'bɒsɪ/ *adj* (fam) autoritaire
botanic /bə'tænɪk(l)/ *adj* (*also* **botanical**) botanique; **~ gardens** jardin *m* botanique
botany /'bɒtənɪ/ *n* botanique *f*
botch /bɒtʃ/ *vt* (fam) bâcler
🗝 **both** /bəʊθ/ **A** *det* **~ sides of the road** les deux côtés de la rue; **~ children came** les enfants sont venus tous les deux; **~ her parents** ses deux parents
B *conj* **~ here and abroad** ici comme à l'étranger
C *pron, quantif* (of things) les deux; **let's take ~ of them** prenons les deux; **~ of you are wrong** vous avez tort tous les deux
🗝 **bother** /'bɒðə(r)/ **A** *n* **1** (inconvenience) ennui *m*, embêtement *m* (fam); **without any ~** sans aucune difficulté
2 (BrE) (fam) (trouble) ennuis *mpl*; **to be in a spot of ~** avoir des ennuis
B *vt* **1** (worry) tracasser; **don't let it ~ you** ne te tracasse pas avec ça
2 (disturb) déranger; **I'm sorry to ~ you** je suis désolé de vous déranger
C *vi* **1** (take trouble) **please don't ~** s'il te plaît, ne te dérange pas; **don't ~ doing** ce n'est pas la peine de faire
2 (worry) **it's not worth ~ing about** ça ne vaut pas la peine qu'on s'en occupe
🗝 **bottle** /'bɒtl/ **A** *n* (gen) bouteille *f*; (for perfume, medicine) flacon *m*; (for baby) biberon *m*
B *vt* **1** embouteiller ‹*milk, wine*›
2 (BrE) mettre [qch] en conserve ‹*fruit*›
C **bottled** *pp adj* ‹*beer, gas*› en bouteille; **~d water** eau *f* minérale
▪ **bottle up** étouffer ‹*anger, grief*›
bottle bank *n* réceptacle *m* à verre
bottle feed *vt* nourrir [qn] au biberon
bottleneck /'bɒtlnek/ *n* **1** (traffic jam) embouteillage *m*
2 (narrow part of road) rétrécissement *m* de la chaussée
bottle opener *n* décapsuleur *m*
bottle top *n* capsule *f* (de bouteille)
🗝 **bottom** /'bɒtəm/ **A** *n* **1** (of hill, steps, wall) pied *m*; (of page, list) bas *m*; (of bag, bottle, hole, river, sea, garden) fond *m*; (of boat) carène *f*; (of vase, box) dessous *m*; (of league) dernière place *f*; **at the ~ of the pile** sous le tas; **to be ~ of the class** être dernier/-ière de la classe
2 (fam) (buttocks) derrière *m* (fam)
B *adj* ‹*layer, shelf*› du bas; ‹*sheet*› de dessous; ‹*bunk*› inférieur/-e; ‹*division, half*› dernier/-ière *before n*
C (fam) **bottoms** *npl* **pyjama ~s** pantalon *m* de pyjama; **bikini ~s** bas *m* de maillot de bain
(IDIOM) **to get to the ~ of a matter** découvrir le fin fond d'une affaire
bottom line *n* (decisive factor) **the ~ is that...** la vérité c'est que...; **that's the ~** ça c'est le vrai problème
boulder /'bəʊldə(r)/ *n* rocher *m*

bounce /baʊns/ **A** *n* **1** (of ball) rebond *m*
2 (of mattress, material) élasticité *f*; (of hair) souplesse *f*
B *vt* faire rebondir ‹*ball*›
C *vi* **1** ‹*ball, object*› rebondir (**off** sur, **over** au dessus de); **to ~ up and down on sth** ‹*person*› sauter sur qch
2 (fam) ‹*cheque*› être sans provision
■ **bounce back** (after illness) se remettre; (in career) faire un retour en force

bouncer /ˈbaʊnsə(r)/ *n* (fam) videur *m*

bound /baʊnd/ **A** **bounds** *npl* limites *fpl*; **to be out of ~s** être interdit/-e d'accès
B *adj* **1 to be ~ to do sth** aller sûrement faire qch; **it was ~ to happen** cela devait arriver
2 (obliged) (by promise, rules, terms) tenu/-e (**by** par, **to do** de faire)
3 ~ for ‹*person, bus, train*› en route pour; ‹*aeroplane*› à destination de
C *vi* bondir; **to ~ into the room** entrer dans la pièce en coup de vent

boundary /ˈbaʊndrɪ/ *n* (gen) limite *f* (**between** entre); (of sports field) limites *fpl* du terrain

bouquet /bʊˈkeɪ/ *n* bouquet *m*

bourgeois /ˈbɔːʒwɑː, (AmE) ˌbʊərˈʒwɑː/ *adj* bourgeois/-e

bout /baʊt/ *n* **1** (of fever, malaria) accès *m*; (of insomnia) crise *f*; **drinking ~** soûlerie *f*
2 (in boxing) combat *m*
3 (period of activity) période *f*

boutique /buːˈtiːk/ *n* boutique *f*

bow¹ /bəʊ/ *n* **1** (weapon) arc *m*
2 (for violin) archet *m*
3 (knot) nœud *m*

bow² /baʊ/ **A** *n* **1** (movement) salut *m*; **to take a ~** saluer
2 (of ship) avant *m*, proue *f*
B *vt* baisser ‹*head*›; courber ‹*branch*›; incliner ‹*tree*›
C *vi* **1** saluer; **to ~ to sb** saluer qn
2 to ~ to pressure céder à la pression

bowel /ˈbaʊəl/ *n* intestin *m*; **the ~s of the earth** les entrailles *fpl* de la terre

bowl /bəʊl/ **A** *n* (for food) bol *m*; (for salad) saladier *m*; (for soup) assiette *f* creuse; (for washing) cuvette *f*; (of lavatory) cuvette *f*
B *vt* lancer ‹*ball*›
C *vi* **1** lancer; **to ~ to sb** lancer la balle à qn
2 (AmE) (go bowling) aller au bowling
■ **bowl over 1** (knock down) renverser ‹*person*›
2 to be ~ed over (by news) être stupéfait/-e; (by beauty, generosity) être bouleversé/-e

bow-legged /ˌbəʊˈlegɪd/ *adj* ‹*person*› aux jambes arquées

bowler /ˈbəʊlə(r)/ *n* **1** (in cricket) lanceur *m*
2 (*also* **~ hat**) chapeau *m* melon

bowling /ˈbəʊlɪŋ/ *n* (*also* **tenpin ~**) bowling *m*

bowling alley *n* bowling *m*

bowling green *n* terrain *m* de boules (sur gazon)

bowls /bəʊlz/ *n* jeu *m* de boules (sur gazon)

bow tie *n* nœud-papillon *m*

box /bɒks/ **A** *n* **1** (cardboard) boîte *f*; (crate) caisse *f*; **~ of matches** boîte d'allumettes
2 (on page, form) case *f*
3 (in theatre) loge *f*; (in stadium) tribune *f*
4 (*also* **PO Box**) boîte *f* postale
B *vt* **1** (pack) mettre [qch] en caisse
2 to ~ sb's ears gifler qn
C *vi* (Sport) boxer

boxer /ˈbɒksə(r)/ *n* **1** (fighter) boxeur *m*
2 (dog) boxer *m*

boxer shorts *npl* caleçon *m* (court)

boxing /ˈbɒksɪŋ/ *n* boxe *f*

Boxing Day /ˈbɒksɪŋ deɪ/ *n* (BrE) lendemain *m* de Noël

box number *n* numéro *m* de boîte postale

box office *n* guichet *m*

boy /bɔɪ/ *n* garçon *m*

boy band *n* boys band *m*

boycott /ˈbɔɪkɒt/ **A** *n* boycottage *m* (**against, of, on** de)
B *vt* boycotter

boyfriend *n* (petit) copain *m* *or* ami *m*

bra /brɑː/ *n* soutien-gorge *m*

brace /breɪs/ **A** *n* **1** (for teeth) appareil *m* dentaire
2 (for broken limb) attelle *f*
B **braces** *npl* (BrE) bretelles *fpl*
C *vt* ‹*person*› arc-bouter ‹*body, back*› (**against** contre)
D *v refl* **to ~ oneself** (physically) s'arc-bouter; (mentally) se préparer (**for** à, **to do** à faire)

bracelet /ˈbreɪslɪt/ *n* bracelet *m*

bracing /ˈbreɪsɪŋ/ *adj* vivifiant/-e, tonifiant/-e

bracken /ˈbrækən/ *n* fougère *f*

bracket /ˈbrækɪt/ **A** *n* **1** (round) parenthèse *f*; (square) crochet *m*; **in ~s** entre parenthèses *or* crochets
2 (for shelf) équerre *f*; (for lamp) applique *f*
3 (category) **age ~** tranche *f* d'âge
B *vt* **1** (put in brackets) (round) mettre [qch] entre parenthèses; (square) mettre [qch] entre crochets
2 (*also* **~ together**) mettre [qn] dans le même groupe ‹*people*›

brag /bræg/ *vi* (*p prés etc* **-gg-**) se vanter (**to** auprès de, **about** de)

braid /breɪd/ *n* **1** (of hair) tresse *f*, natte *f*
2 (trimming) galon *m*

brain /breɪn/ *n* cerveau *m*; **~s** cervelle *f*

brainchild *n* grande idée *f*

brain damage *n* lésions *fpl* cérébrales

brain dead /ˈbreɪnded/ *adj* dans un coma dépassé

brain drain *n* fuite *f* des cerveaux

brain surgery *n* neurochirurgie *f*

brain teaser *n* (fam) casse-tête *m inv*

brainwash /ˈbreɪnwɒʃ/ *vt* faire subir un lavage de cerveau à

b

brainwashing *n* (of prisoners) lavage *m* de cerveau; (of public) bourrage *m* (fam) de crâne

brainwave /ˈbreɪnweɪv/ *n* idée *f* géniale, illumination *f*

brainy /ˈbreɪnɪ/ *adj* (fam) doué/-e

braise /breɪz/ *vt* braiser

brake /breɪk/ **A** *n* frein *m*
B *vi* freiner

brake pad *n* plaquette *f* de frein

bramble /ˈbræmbl/ *n* **1** ronce *f*
2 (BrE) (berry) mûre *f*

bran /bræn/ *n* son *m*

⚷ **branch** /brɑːntʃ, (AmE) bræntʃ/ *n* **1** (of tree) branche *f*; (of road, railway) embranchement *m*
2 (of shop) succursale *f*; (of bank) agence *f*; (of company) filiale *f*
▪ **branch off** bifurquer
▪ **branch out** se diversifier

⚷ **brand** /brænd/ **A** *n* marque *f*
B *vt* **1** marquer (au fer) ‹*animal*›
2 to ~ sb as sth désigner qn comme qch

branded /ˈbrændɪd/ *adj* ‹*goods*› de marque *inv*

brandish /ˈbrændɪʃ/ *vt* brandir

brand leader *n* leader *m* du marché

brand name *n* marque *f* déposée

brand new *adj* tout neuf/toute neuve

brandy /ˈbrændɪ/ *n* eau-de-vie *f*; (cognac) cognac *m*

brash /bræʃ/ *adj* ‹*person, manner*› bravache

brass /brɑːs, (AmE) bræs/ *n* **1** (metal) laiton *m*, cuivre *m* jaune
2 (*also* **~ section**) (Mus) cuivres *mpl*

brass band *n* fanfare *f*

brat /bræt/ *n* (fam) marmot *m* (fam), môme *mf* (fam)

bravado /brəˈvɑːdəʊ/ *n* bravade *f*

brave /breɪv/ **A** *n* (Indian) brave *m*
B *adj* (gen) courageux/-euse; ‹*smile*› brave; **to put on a ~ face** faire bonne contenance
C *vt* braver

bravely /ˈbreɪvlɪ/ *adv* courageusement

bravery /ˈbreɪvərɪ/ *n* courage *m*, bravoure *f*

brawl /brɔːl/ **A** *n* bagarre *f*
B *vi* se bagarrer (**with** avec)

bray /breɪ/ *vi* ‹*donkey*› braire; ‹*person*› brailler

brazen /ˈbreɪzn/ *adj* éhonté/-e
▪ **brazen out**: **~ it out** payer d'audace

Brazil /brəˈzɪl/ *pr n* Brésil *m*

breach /briːtʃ/ **A** *n* **1** (of rule) infraction *f* (**of** à); (of discipline, duty) manquement *m* (**of** à); (of copyright) violation *f*; **to be in ~ of** enfreindre ‹*law*›; violer ‹*agreement*›
2 (gap) brèche *f*
B *vt* faire une brèche dans ‹*defence*›

breach of contract *n* rupture *f* de contrat

breach of the peace *n* atteinte *f* à l'ordre public

bread /bred/ *n* pain *m*

bread and butter *n* tartine *f* de pain beurré; (fig) gagne-pain *m*

bread bin *n* (BrE) boîte *f or* huche *f* à pain

breadboard *n* planche *f* à pain

breadcrumbs *npl* miettes *fpl* de pain; (Culin) chapelure *f*

breadline /ˈbredlaɪn/ *n* **to be on the ~** être au seuil de l'indigence

bread roll *n* petit pain *m*

breadth /bretθ/ *n* largeur *f*; (fig) (of experience, knowledge) étendue *f*

breadwinner *n* soutien *m* de famille

⚷ **break** /breɪk/ **A** *n* **1** (gap) (in wall) brèche *f*; (in row, line) espace *m*; (in circuit) rupture *f*
2 (pause) (gen) pause *f*; (at school) récréation *f*; **to take a ~** faire une pause; **the Christmas ~** les vacances de Noël; **to have a ~ from work** arrêter de travailler; **a ~ with the past** une rupture avec le passé
3 (*also* **commercial ~**) page *f* de publicité
4 a lucky ~ un coup de veine (fam)
B *vt* (*prét* **broke**, *pp* **broken**) **1** (gen) casser; briser ‹*seal*›; rompre ‹*silence, monotony, spell*›; **to ~ one's leg** se casser la jambe
2 enfreindre ‹*law*›; **to ~ one's promise** manquer à sa promesse
3 dépasser ‹*speed limit*›; battre ‹*record*›
4 ‹*branches*› freiner ‹*fall*›; ‹*hay*› amortir ‹*fall*›
5 débourrer ‹*horse*›
6 (in tennis) **to ~ sb's serve** faire le break
7 to ~ the news to sb apprendre la nouvelle à qn
C *vi* (*prét* **broke**, *pp* **broken**) **1** (gen) se casser; ‹*arm, bone, leg*› se fracturer; ‹*bag*› se déchirer; **to ~ in two** se casser en deux
2 ‹*waves*› se briser
3 ‹*good weather*› se gâter; ‹*heatwave*› cesser
4 ‹*storm, scandal, story*› éclater
5 to ~ with sb rompre les relations avec qn; **to ~ with tradition** rompre avec la tradition
6 ‹*boy's voice*› muer
▪ **break away 1** se détacher (**from** de)
2 (escape) échapper
▪ **break down A ~ down 1** ‹*car, machine*› tomber en panne
2 ‹*person*› s'effondrer, craquer (fam); **to ~ down in tears** fondre en larmes
B ~ [sth] down 1 enfoncer ‹*door*›; (fig) faire tomber ‹*barriers*›; vaincre ‹*resistance*›
2 (analyse) ventiler ‹*cost, statistics*›; décomposer ‹*data, findings*› (**into** par)
▪ **break even** rentrer dans ses frais
▪ **break free** s'échapper
▪ **break in A ~ in 1** ‹*thief*› entrer (par effraction); ‹*police*› entrer de force
2 (interrupt) interrompre

⚷ mot clé

B ~ **[sth] in** débourrer ‹*horse*›; assouplir ‹*shoe*›
- **break into 1** entrer dans [qch] (par effraction) ‹*building*›; forcer ‹*safe*›
  2 entamer ‹*new packet, savings*›
  3 to ~ into song/into a run se mettre à chanter/courir
- **break off A** ~ **off 1** ‹*end*› se casser; ‹*handle, piece*› se détacher
  2 ‹*speaker*› s'interrompre
  B ~ **[sth] off 1** casser ‹*branch, piece*›
  2 rompre ‹*engagement*›; interrompre ‹*conversation*›
- **break out 1** ‹*epidemic, fire*› se déclarer; ‹*fight, riot, storm*› éclater; **to ~ out in a rash** avoir une éruption de boutons
  2 ‹*prisoner*› s'échapper (**of** de)
- **break up A** ~ **up 1** ‹*couple*› se séparer
  2 ‹*crowd, cloud*› se disperser; ‹*meeting*› se terminer
  3 (BrE) (Sch) **schools ~ up on Friday** les cours finissent vendredi
  B ~ **[sth] up** démanteler ‹*drugs ring*›; séparer ‹*couple*›; désunir ‹*family*›; briser ‹*marriage*›; mettre fin à ‹*demonstration*›

breakaway /ˈbreɪkəweɪ/ *n* ‹*faction, group, state*› séparatiste

breakdown /ˈbreɪkdaʊn/ *n* **1** (of vehicle, machine) panne *f*
2 (of communications, negotiations) rupture *f*; (of discipline, order) effondrement *m*
3 to have a (nervous) ~ faire une dépression (nerveuse)
4 (of figures, statistics) ventilation *f*

breakfast /ˈbrekfəst/ *n* petit déjeuner *m*

breakfast television *n* télévision *f* à l'heure du petit déjeuner

break-in *n* cambriolage *m*

breaking point *n* (fig) **to be at ~** être à bout

breakneck *adj* ‹*pace, speed*› fou/folle, insensé/-e

breakthrough /ˈbreɪkθruː/ *n* (gen) percée *f*; (in negotiations, investigation) progrès *m*

break-up /ˈbreɪkʌp/ *n* (of alliance, relationship) rupture *f*; (of political party, family, group) éclatement *m*; (of marriage) échec *m*

breakwater *n* brise-lames *m inv*

breast /brest/ *n* **1** (woman's) sein *m*; (chest) poitrine *f*
2 (Culin) (of poultry) blanc *m*, filet *m*

breast-feed /ˈbrestfiːd/ *vt*, *vi* (*prét*, *pp* **-fed**) allaiter

breast stroke *n* brasse *f*

breath /breθ/ *n* **1** souffle *m*; **out of ~** à bout de souffle; **to hold one's ~** retenir sa respiration; (fig) retenir son souffle
2 (from mouth) haleine *f*; (visible) respiration *f*; **to have bad ~** avoir (une) mauvaise haleine
IDIOM to take sb's ~ away couper le souffle à qn

breathalyse (BrE), **breathalyze** (AmE) /ˈbreθəlaɪz/ *vt* faire subir un alcootest à ‹*driver*›

breathalyzer (BrE), **Breathalyzer®** (AmE) /ˈbreθəlaɪzə(r)/ *n* alcootest *m*

breathe /briːð/ **A** *vt* **1** respirer ‹*oxygen*›
2 souffler ‹*germs*› (**on** sur)
3 don't ~ a word! pas un mot!
B *vi* **1** ‹*person, animal*› respirer; **to ~ heavily** souffler fort, haleter
2 ‹*wine*› s'aérer
- **breathe in**: **A** ~ **in** inspirer
  B ~ **[sth] in** inhaler
- **breathe out**: **A** ~ **out** expirer
  B ~ **out**, ~ **[sth] out** exhaler

breather /ˈbriːðə(r)/ *n* pause *f*; **take a ~** faire une pause

breathing /ˈbriːðɪŋ/ *n* respiration *f*

breathing space *n* **1** (respite) répit *m*
2 (postponement) délai *m*

breathless /ˈbreθlɪs/ *adj* ‹*runner*› hors d'haleine; ‹*asthmatic*› haletant/-e

breathtaking *adj* ‹*feat, skill*› stupéfiant/-e; ‹*scenery*› à vous couper le souffle

breath test A *n* alcootest *m*
B *vt* faire subir un alcootest à ‹*driver*›

breed /briːd/ **A** *n* race *f*
B *vt* (*prét*, *pp* **bred**) élever ‹*animals*›; (fig) engendrer
C *vi* (*prét*, *pp* **bred**) se reproduire
D bred *pp adj* **ill-/well-~** mal/bien élevé/-e

breeder /ˈbriːdə(r)/ *n* (of animals) éleveur *m*

breeding /ˈbriːdɪŋ/ *n* **1** (of animals) reproduction *f*
2 (good manners) bonnes manières *fpl*

breeding ground *n* (fig) foyer *m* (**for** de)

breeze /briːz/ **A** *n* brise *f*
B *vi* **to ~ in/out** entrer/sortir d'un air dégagé; **to ~ through an exam** réussir un examen sans difficulté

brevity /ˈbrevətɪ/ *n* brièveté *f*

brew /bruː/ **A** *vt* brasser ‹*beer*›; préparer ‹*tea*›; **freshly ~ed coffee** du café fraîchement passé
B *vi* **1** ‹*beer*› fermenter; ‹*tea*› infuser
2 ‹*storm, crisis*› se préparer

brewer /ˈbruːə(r)/ *n* brasseur *m*

brewery /ˈbruːərɪ/ *n* brasserie *f*

bribe /braɪb/ **A** *n* pot-de-vin *m*
B *vt* soudoyer ‹*police*›; suborner ‹*witness*›; acheter ‹*servant, voter*›

bribery /ˈbraɪbərɪ/ *n* corruption *f*

bric-a-brac sale *n* vide-greniers *m inv*

brick /brɪk/ *n* brique *f*

bricklayer *n* maçon *m*

bridal /ˈbraɪdl/ *adj* ‹*gown*› de mariée; ‹*car*› des mariés; ‹*suite*› nuptial/-e

bride /braɪd/ *n* (jeune) mariée *f*; **the ~ and groom** les (jeunes) mariés *mpl*

b

bridegroom /ˈbraɪdgruːm, -grʊm/ *n* jeune marié *m*

bridesmaid /ˈbraɪdzmeɪd/ *n* demoiselle *f* d'honneur

bridge /brɪdʒ/ **A** *n* **1** pont *m* (**over** sur, **across** au-dessus de); (fig) (link) rapprochement *m*
2 (on ship) passerelle *f*
3 (of nose) arête *f*; (of spectacles) arcade *f*
4 (on guitar, violin) chevalet *m*
5 (for teeth) bridge *m*
6 (game) bridge *m*
B *vt* **1 to ~ a gap in [sth]** combler un vide dans ‹*conversation*›; combler un trou dans ‹*budget*›
2 (span) enjamber ‹*two eras*›

bridle /ˈbraɪdl/ **A** *n* bride *f*
B *vt* brider
C *vi* se cabrer (**at** contre, **with** sous l'effet de)

bridle path *n* piste *f* cavalière

⚷ **brief** /briːf/ **A** *n* **1** (BrE) (remit) attributions *fpl*; (role) tâche *f*
2 (Law) dossier *m*
B briefs *npl* slip *m*
C *adj* bref/brève; **in ~** en bref
D *vt* (inform) informer (**on** de); (instruct) donner des instructions à (**on** sur)

briefcase /ˈbriːfkeɪs/ *n* serviette *f*; (without handle) porte-documents *m inv*

briefing /ˈbriːfɪŋ/ *n* briefing *m* (**on** sur)

briefly /ˈbriːflɪ/ *adv* **1** (gen) brièvement; ‹*look, pause*› un bref instant
2 (in short) en bref

brigade /brɪˈgeɪd/ *n* brigade *f*

⚷ **bright** /braɪt/ *adj* **1** ‹*colour*› vif/vive; ‹*garment*› aux couleurs vives; ‹*sunshine*› éclatant/-e; ‹*room, day*› clair/-e; ‹*star, eye, metal*› brillant/-e
2 (clever) intelligent/-e; **a ~ idea** une idée lumineuse
3 to look on the ~ side voir le bon côté des choses

brighten /ˈbraɪtn/
■ **brighten up A ~ up 1** ‹*person*› s'égayer (**at** à); ‹*face*› s'éclairer (**at** à)
2 ‹*weather*› s'éclaircir
B ~ [sth] up égayer ‹*room, decor*›

brightly /ˈbraɪtlɪ/ *adv* **1** ‹*dressed*› de couleurs vives
2 ‹*shine, burn*› d'un vif éclat

brightness /ˈbraɪtnɪs/ *n* **1** (of colour, light, smile) éclat *m*
2 (of room) clarté *f*

bright spark *n* (BrE) (fam) petit/-e futé/-e *m/f* (fam)

brilliance /ˈbrɪlɪəns/ *n* éclat *m*

brilliant /ˈbrɪlɪənt/ *adj* **1** ‹*student, career, success*› brillant/-e
2 (bright) éclatant/-e
3 (BrE) (fam) (fantastic) super (fam), génial/-e (fam); **to be ~ at sth** être doué/-e en qch

brilliantly /ˈbrɪlɪəntlɪ/ *adv* **1** (very well) brillamment
2 (very brightly) ‹*shine*› avec éclat

brim /brɪm/ *n* bord *m*

brine /braɪn/ *n* **1** (sea water) eau *f* de mer
2 (for pickling) saumure *f*

⚷ **bring** /brɪŋ/ *vt* (*prét, pp* **brought**)
1 apporter ‹*present, object, message*›; amener ‹*person, animal, car*›; **to ~ sth with one** apporter qch; **to ~ sb/sth into the room** faire entrer qn/qch dans la pièce
2 apporter ‹*happiness, rain, change, hope*›; **to ~ a smile to sb's face** faire sourire qn

■ **bring about** provoquer ‹*change, disaster*›; entraîner ‹*success, defeat*›

■ **bring along** apporter ‹*object*›; amener, venir avec ‹*friend, partner*›

■ **bring back 1** rapporter ‹*souvenir*› (**from** de); **to ~ back memories** ranimer des souvenirs
2 rétablir ‹*custom*›; restaurer ‹*monarchy*›

■ **bring down 1** renverser ‹*government*›
2 réduire ‹*inflation, expenditure*›; faire baisser ‹*price, temperature*›
3 (shoot down) abattre

■ **bring forward** avancer ‹*date*›

■ **bring in** rapporter ‹*money, interest*›; introduire ‹*legislation, measure*›; rentrer ‹*harvest*›; faire appel à ‹*expert, army*›

■ **bring off** réussir ‹*feat*›; conclure ‹*deal*›

■ **bring on 1** provoquer ‹*attack, migraine*›
2 faire entrer ‹*substitute player*›

■ **bring out 1** sortir ‹*edition, new model*›
2 (highlight) faire ressortir ‹*flavour, meaning*›

■ **bring round 1** (revive) faire revenir [qn] à soi
2 (convince) convaincre

■ **bring up 1** aborder, parler de ‹*subject*›
2 vomir, rendre ‹*food*›
3 élever ‹*child*›; **well brought up** bien élevé/-e

brink /brɪŋk/ *n* bord *m*

brisk /brɪsk/ *adj* **1** (efficient) ‹*manner, tone*› vif/vive; ‹*person*› efficace
2 (energetic) ‹*trot*› rapide; **at a ~ pace** à vive allure
3 ‹*business, trade*› florissant/-e; **business was ~** les affaires marchaient bien
4 ‹*air*› vivifiant/-e; ‹*wind*› vif/vive

bristle /ˈbrɪsl/ **A** *n* (gen) poil *m*; (on pig) soie *f*
B *vi* **1** ‹*hairs*› se dresser
2 ‹*person*› se hérisser (**at** à, **with** de)

Britain /ˈbrɪtn/ *pr n* (*also* **Great ~**) Grande-Bretagne *f*

⚷ **British** /ˈbrɪtɪʃ/ **A** *npl* **the ~** les Britanniques *mpl*
B *adj* britannique; **the ~ embassy** l'ambassade *f* de Grande-Bretagne

British Isles *pr n pl* îles *fpl* Britanniques

Briton /ˈbrɪtn/ *n* Britannique *mf*

⚷ mot clé

Brittany /'brɪtənɪ/ *pr n* Bretagne *f*

brittle /'brɪtl/ *adj* ‹*twig*› cassant/-e; ‹*nails, hair*› fragile

broach /brəʊtʃ/ *vt* aborder ‹*subject*›

broad /brɔːd/ *adj* **1** (wide) large; **to have ~ shoulders** être large d'épaules
2 ‹*meaning*› large; ‹*outline*› général/-e
3 ‹*accent*› fort/-e *before n*; **in ~ daylight** en plein jour

broadband /brɔːdbænd/ *adj* à haut débit

broad-based /ˌbrɔːd'beɪst/ *adj* ‹*approach, campaign*› global/-e; ‹*education*› généralisé/-e

broad bean *n* fève *f*

broadcast /'brɔːdkɑːst, (AmE) -kæst/ **A** *n* émission *f*
B *vt* (*prét, pp* **~** *ou* **~ed**) diffuser ‹*programme*› (**to** à)
C *vi* (*prét, pp* **~** *ou* **~ed**) ‹*station, channel*› émettre (**on** sur)

broadcaster /'brɔːdkɑːstə(r), (AmE) -kæst-/ *n* animateur/-trice *m/f*

broadcasting /brɔːdkɑːstɪŋ, (AmE) -kæst-/ *n* (field) communication *f* audiovisuelle; (action) diffusion *f*; **to work in ~** travailler dans l'audiovisuel

broaden /'brɔːdn/ **A** *vt* étendre ‹*appeal, scope*›; élargir ‹*horizons, knowledge*›; **travel ~s the mind** les voyages ouvrent l'esprit
B *vi* s'élargir

broad-minded *adj* ‹*person*› large d'esprit; ‹*attitude*› libéral/-e

broadsheet *n* journal *m* de grand format

brocade /brə'keɪd/ *n* brocart *m*

broccoli /'brɒkəlɪ/ *n* (Bot) brocoli *m*; (Culin) brocolis *mpl*

brochure /'brəʊʃə(r), (AmE) brəʊ'ʃʊər/ *n* (booklet) brochure *f*; (leaflet) dépliant *m*; (for hotel) prospectus *m*

broil /brɔɪl/ *vt* (AmE) faire griller ‹*meat*›

broke /brəʊk/ *adj* (fam) ‹*person*› fauché/-e (fam)

broken /'brəʊkən/ *adj* **1** (gen) cassé/-e; ‹*glass, window, line*› brisé/-e; ‹*radio, machine*› détraqué/-e
2 ‹*man, woman*› brisé/-e
3 ‹*French*› mauvais/-e *before n*

broken-down /ˌbrəʊkən'daʊn/ *adj* ‹*machine*› en panne

broken-hearted /ˌbrəʊkən'hɑːtɪd/ *adj* **to be ~** avoir le cœur brisé

broken home *n* famille *f* désunie

broken marriage *n* foyer *m* désuni

broker /'brəʊkə(r)/ *n* courtier *m*; **insurance ~** courtier d'assurance; **real estate ~** (AmE) agent *m* immobilier

brolly /'brɒlɪ/ *n* (BrE) (fam) parapluie *m*

bronchitis /brɒŋ'kaɪtɪs/ *n* bronchite *f*

bronze /brɒnz/ *n* bronze *m*

brooch /brəʊtʃ/ *n* broche *f*

brood /bruːd/ **A** *n* (of birds) couvée *f*; (of mammals) nichée *f*
B *vi* **1** (ponder) broyer du noir; **to ~ about** ressasser, ruminer ‹*problem*›
2 ‹*bird*› couver

brook /brʊk/ *n* ruisseau *m*

broom /bruːm, brʊm/ *n* balai *m*

broth /brɒθ, (AmE) brɔːθ/ *n* bouillon *m*

brothel /'brɒθl/ *n* maison *f* close

brother /'brʌðə(r)/ *n* frère *m*

brother-in-law *n* beau-frère *m*

brotherly /'brʌðəlɪ/ *adj* fraternel/-elle

brow /braʊ/ *n* **1** (forehead) front *m*; (eyebrow) sourcil *m*
2 (of hill) sommet *m*

brown /braʊn/ **A** *n* (of object) marron *m*; (of hair, skin, eyes) brun *m*
B *adj* **1** ‹*shoes, leaves, paint, eyes*› marron *inv*; ‹*hair*› châtain *inv*; **light/dark ~** marron clair/foncé
2 (tanned) bronzé/-e; **to go ~** bronzer
C *vt* faire roussir ‹*sauce*›; faire dorer ‹*meat, onions*›
D *vi* ‹*meat, potatoes*› dorer

brown bread *n* pain *m* complet

brown envelope *n* enveloppe *f* kraft

Brownie *n* jeannette *f*

brown paper *n* papier *m* kraft

brown rice *n* riz *m* complet

brown sugar *n* sucre *m* brun, cassonade *f*

browse /braʊz/ *vi* **1** (in shop) regarder
2 (graze) brouter
▪ **browse through** feuilleter ‹*book*›

browser /'braʊzə(r)/ *n* (Comput) navigateur *m*

bruise /bruːz/ **A** *n* (on skin) bleu *m*, ecchymose *f* (**on** sur); (on fruit) tache *f* (**on** sur)
B *vt* meurtrir ‹*person*›; taler, abîmer ‹*fruit*›; **to ~ one's arm** se faire un bleu sur le bras

brunette /bruː'net/ *n* brune *f*

brunt /brʌnt/ *n* **to bear the ~ of** être le plus touché/la plus touchée par ‹*disaster*›; subir tout le poids de ‹*anger*›

brush /brʌʃ/ **A** *n* **1** (for hair, clothes, shoes) brosse *f*; (small, for sweeping up) balayette *f*; (broom) balai *m*; (for paint) pinceau *m*
2 to have a ~ with death frôler la mort; **to have a ~ with the law** avoir des démêlés avec la justice
B *vt* brosser ‹*carpet, clothes*›; **to ~ one's hair/teeth** se brosser les cheveux/les dents
C *vi* **to ~ against** frôler; **to ~ past sb** frôler qn en passant
▪ **brush aside** repousser ‹*criticism, person*›
▪ **brush up (on)** se remettre à ‹*subject*›

brushwood /'brʌʃwʊd/ *n* (firewood) brindilles *fpl*; (brush) broussailles *fpl*

brusque /bruːsk, (AmE) brʌsk/ *adj* brusque (**with** avec)

Brussels /'brʌslz/ *pr n* Bruxelles

Brussels sprout *n* chou *m* de Bruxelles
brutal /ˈbruːtl/ *adj* brutal/-e
brutality /bruːˈtælətɪ/ *n* brutalité *f* (**of** de)
brute /bruːt/ **A** *n* **1** (man) brute *f*
2 (animal) bête *f*
B *adj* ‹*strength*› simple *before n*; **by ~ force** par la force
BSc *n* (BrE) (Univ) (*abbr* = **Bachelor of Science**) diplôme *m* universitaire en sciences
BSE *n* (*abbr* = **Bovine Spongiform Encephalopathy**) ESB *f*, encéphalopathie *f* spongiforme bovine
bubble /ˈbʌbl/ **A** *n* bulle *f* (**in** dans); **to blow ~s** faire des bulles
B *vi* ‹*fizzy drink*› pétiller; ‹*boiling liquid*› bouillonner; **to ~ (over) with** déborder de ‹*enthusiasm, ideas*›
bubble bath *n* bain *m* moussant
bubble wrap *n* bulle-pack® *m*
buck /bʌk/ **A** *n* **1** (AmE) (fam) dollar *m*
2 (male animal) mâle *m*
B *vi* ‹*horse*› ruer
IDIOM **to pass the ~** refiler (fam) la responsabilité à quelqu'un d'autre
bucket /ˈbʌkɪt/ *n* seau *m* (**of** de)
buckle /ˈbʌkl/ **A** *n* boucle *f*
B *vt* **1** attacher, boucler ‹*belt, shoe*›
2 (damage) gondoler
C *vi* **1** ‹*metal, surface*› se gondoler; ‹*wheel*› se voiler
2 ‹*belt, shoe*› s'attacher, se boucler
3 ‹*knees, legs*› céder
bud /bʌd/ **A** *n* (of leaf) bourgeon *m*; (of flower) bouton *m*
B *vi* (*p prés etc* **-dd-**) **1** (develop leaf buds) bourgeonner; (develop flower buds) boutonner
2 ‹*flower, breast*› pointer
Buddha /ˈbʊdə/ *pr n* Bouddha *m*
Buddhism /ˈbʊdɪzəm/ *n* bouddhisme *m*
Buddhist /ˈbʊdɪst/ *n, adj* bouddhiste *mf*
budding /ˈbʌdɪŋ/ *adj* ‹*athlete, champion*› en herbe; ‹*talent, career, romance*› naissant/-e
buddy /ˈbʌdɪ/ *n* (fam) copain *m*, pote *m* (fam)
budge /bʌdʒ/ **A** *vt* **1** (move) bouger
2 (persuade) faire changer d'avis à
B *vi* **1** (move) bouger (**from, off** de)
2 (give way) changer d'avis (**on** sur)
■ **budge over** (fam) **budge up** (fam) se pousser
budgerigar /ˈbʌdʒərɪgɑː(r)/ *n* perruche *f*
budget /ˈbʌdʒɪt/ **A** *n* budget *m* (**for** pour)
B *vi* **to ~ for** budgétiser ses dépenses en fonction de ‹*increase, needs*›
buff /bʌf/ *n* **1** (fam) (enthusiast) mordu/-e *m/f*
2 (colour) chamois *m*
buffalo /ˈbʌfələʊ/ *n* (*pl* **-oes** *or collect* ~) (BrE) buffle *m*; (AmE) bison *m*
buffer /ˈbʌfə(r)/ *n* tampon *m*
buffet¹ /ˈbʊfeɪ, (AmE) bəˈfeɪ/ *n* buffet *m*
buffet² /ˈbʌfɪt/ *vt* ‹*wind*› ballotter ‹*ship*›; battre ‹*coast*›
buffoon /bəˈfuːn/ *n* bouffon/-onne *m/f*
bug /bʌg/ **A** *n* **1** (fam) (insect) (gen) bestiole *f*; (bedbug) punaise *f*
2 (*also* **stomach ~**) (fam) ennuis *mpl* gastriques
3 (germ) microbe *m*
4 (fault) (gen) défaut *m*; (Comput) bogue *f or m*, bug *m*
5 (hidden microphone) micro *m* caché
B *vt* (*p prés etc* **-gg-**) **1** poser des micros dans ‹*room, building*›; **the room is ~ged** il y a un micro (caché) dans la pièce
2 (fam) (annoy) embêter ‹*person*›
buggy /ˈbʌgɪ/ *n* **1** (BrE) (pushchair) poussette *f*
2 (AmE) (pram) landau *m*
3 (carriage) boghei *m*
bugle /ˈbjuːgl/ *n* clairon *m*
build /bɪld/ **A** *n* (of person) carrure *f*
B *vt* (*prét, pp* **built**) (gen) construire; édifier ‹*church, monument*›; bâtir ‹*career, future*›; fonder ‹*empire*›; créer ‹*software, interface*›; **to be well built** ‹*person*› être bien bâti/-e
C *vi* (*prét, pp* **built**) construire; **to ~ on** tirer parti de ‹*popularity, success*›
■ **build up**: **A ~ up** ‹*gas, deposits*› s'accumuler; ‹*traffic*› s'intensifier; ‹*business, trade*› se développer; ‹*tension, excitement*› monter
B ~ [sth] up accumuler ‹*wealth*›; établir ‹*trust*›; constituer ‹*collection*›; créer ‹*business*›; établir ‹*picture, profile*›; se faire ‹*reputation*›; affermir ‹*muscles*›; **to ~ oneself up, to ~ up one's strength** prendre des forces
builder /ˈbɪldə(r)/ *n* (contractor) entrepreneur *m* en bâtiment; (worker) ouvrier/-ière *m/f* du bâtiment
building /ˈbɪldɪŋ/ *n* (gen) bâtiment *m*; (with offices, apartments) immeuble *m*; (palace, church) édifice *m*
building contractor *n* entrepreneur *m* en bâtiment
building site *n* chantier *m* (de construction)
building society *n* (BrE) société *f* d'investissement et de crédit immobilier
build-up /ˈbɪldʌp/ *n* **1** (in traffic, pressure) intensification *f* (**of** de); (in weapons, stocks) accumulation *f* (**of** de); (in tension) accroissement *m* (**of** de)
2 (publicity) **the ~ to sth** les préparatifs de qch
built-in /ˌbɪltˈɪn/ *adj* ‹*wardrobe*› encastré/-e; (fig) intégré/-e
built-up /ˌbɪltˈʌp/ *adj* ‹*region*› urbanisé/-e; **~ area** agglomération *f*
bulb /bʌlb/ *n* **1** (electric) ampoule *f* (électrique)
2 (of plant) bulbe *m*
Bulgaria /bʌlˈgeərɪə/ *pr n* Bulgarie *f*

mot clé

Bulgarian /bʌl'geərɪən/ **A** *n* **1** (person) Bulgare *mf*
2 (language) bulgare *m*
B *adj* bulgare

bulge /bʌldʒ/ **A** *n* (in clothing, carpet) bosse *f*; (in pipe, tube) renflement *m*; (in tyre) hernie *f*; (in wall) bombement *m*; (in cheek) gonflement *m*
B *vi* ‹*bag, pocket, cheeks*› être gonflé/-e; ‹*wallet*› être bourré/-e; ‹*surface*› se boursoufler; ‹*stomach*› ballonner; **his eyes were bulging** les yeux lui sortaient de la tête

bulimia /bju:ˌlɪmɪə/ *n* (*also* **bulimia nervosa**) boulimie *f*

bulimic /bju:'lɪmɪk/ *n, adj* boulimique *mf*

bulk /bʌlk/ *n* **1** (of package, correspondence) volume *m*; (of building, vehicle) masse *f*; **the ~ of** la majeure partie de
2 in ~ ‹*buy, sell*› en gros; ‹*transport*› en vrac

bulk-buying *n* achat *m* en gros

bulky /'bʌlkɪ/ *adj* ‹*person*› corpulent/-e; ‹*package*› volumineux/-euse; ‹*book*› épais/-aisse

bull /bʊl/ *n* (ox) taureau *m*; (elephant, whale) mâle *m*

bull bar *n* pare-buffle(s) *m*

bulldog /'bʊldɒg/ *n* bouledogue *m*

bulldozer /'bʊldəʊzə(r)/ *n* bulldozer *m*, bouteur *m*

bullet /'bʊlɪt/ *n* balle *f*

bulletin /'bʊlətɪn/ *n* bulletin *m*; **news ~** bulletin d'informations

bulletin board *n* (gen) tableau *m* d'affichage; (Comput) messagerie *f* électronique

bulletproof /'bʊlɪtpru:f/ *adj* ‹*glass, vehicle, door*› blindé/-e

bulletproof vest *n* gilet *m* pare-balles *inv*

bullfight *n* corrida *f*

bullfighter *n* torero *m*

bullfighting *n* (gen) corridas *fpl*; (art) tauromachie *f*

bullion /'bʊlɪən/ *n* lingots *mpl*

bullock /'bʊlək/ *n* bœuf *m*

bullring *n* arène *f*

bull's eye /'bʊlzaɪ/ *n* mille *m*

bully /'bʊlɪ/ **A** *n* (child) petite brute *f*; (adult) tyran *m*
B *vt* intimider; (stronger) tyranniser

bum /bʌm/ *n* (fam) **1** (BrE) (buttocks) derrière *m* (fam)
2 (AmE) (vagrant) clochard *m*

bumbag *n* (sacoche *f*) banane *f*

bumblebee /'bʌmblbi:/ *n* bourdon *m*

bumf, **bumph** /'bʌmf/ *n* (BrE) (fam) paperasserie *f* (fam)

bump /bʌmp/ **A** *n* **1** (lump) (on body) bosse *f* (**on** à); (on road) bosse *f* (**on, in** sur)
2 (jolt) secousse *f*
3 (sound) bruit *m* sourd
B *vt* cogner (**against, on** contre); **to ~ one's head** se cogner la tête
■ **bump into A** rentrer dans ‹*person, object*›
B (meet) tomber sur (fam) ‹*person*›

bumper /'bʌmpə(r)/ **A** *n* pare-chocs *m inv*
B *adj* ‹*crop, sales, year*› record *after n*; ‹*edition*› exceptionnel/-elle

bumper car *n* auto *f* tamponneuse

bumpkin /'bʌmpkɪn/ *n* (fam) (*also* **country ~**) péquenaud/-e *m/f* (fam)

bumpy /'bʌmpɪ/ *adj* ‹*road*› accidenté/-e; ‹*wall*› irrégulier/-ière; ‹*landing*› agité/-e

bun /bʌn/ *n* **1** (cake) petit pain *m* sucré
2 (hairstyle) chignon *m*

bunch /bʌntʃ/ *n* (of flowers) bouquet *m*; (of vegetables) botte *f*; (of grapes) grappe *f*; (of bananas) régime *m*; (of keys) trousseau *m*; (of people) groupe *m*

bundle /'bʌndl/ **A** *n* (of clothes) ballot *m*; (of papers, notes) liasse *f*; (of books) paquet *m*; (of straw) botte *f*; **~ of sticks** fagot *m* de bois; **~ of nerves** boule *f* de nerfs
B *vt* **to ~ sb/sth into** fourrer (fam) qn/qch dans

bundled software /ˌbʌndld 'sɒftweə(r), (AmE) 'sɔ:ft-/ *n* ensemble *m* de logiciels complémentaires (*livré avec un ordinateur*)

bungalow /'bʌŋgələʊ/ *n* pavillon *m* (sans étage)

bungee jumping /'bʌndʒi: dʒʌmpɪŋ/ *n* saut *m* à l'élastique

bungle /'bʌŋgl/ *vt* rater (fam) ‹*attempt, burglary*›

bunion /'bʌnjən/ *n* oignon *m*

bunk /bʌŋk/ *n* **1** (on ship, train) couchette *f*
2 (*also* **~ bed**) lits *mpl* superposés
■ **bunk off** (fam): **to ~ off school** sécher l'école

bunker /'bʌŋkə(r)/ *n* **1** (Mil) bunker *m*
2 (in golf) bunker *m*
3 (for coal) soute *f*

bunny /'bʌnɪ/ *n* **1** (*also* **~ rabbit**) (Jeannot) lapin *m*
2 (*also* **~ girl**) hôtesse *f*

bunting /'bʌntɪŋ/ *n* guirlandes *fpl*

buoy /bɔɪ/ **A** *n* (gen) bouée *f*; (for marking) balise *f* (flottante)
B *vt* (*also* **~ up**) **1** revigorer ‹*person, morale*›
2 stimuler ‹*prices, economy*›
3 (keep afloat) maintenir à flot

buoyant /'bɔɪənt/ *adj* **1** ‹*object*› qui flotte
2 ‹*person*› vif/vive; ‹*mood, spirits*› enjoué/-e; ‹*step*› allègre
3 ‹*market, prices*› ferme; ‹*economy*› en expansion

burden /'bɜ:dn/ **A** *n* fardeau *m* (**to sb** pour qn)
B *vt* **1** (*also* **~ down**) encombrer (**with** de)
2 (fig) (with work, taxes) accabler (**with** de); **I don't want to ~ you with my problems**

b

je ne veux pas vous ennuyer avec mes problèmes

bureau /'bjʊərəʊ, (AmE) -'rəʊ/ *n* (*pl* **~s** *ou* **~x**) **1** (office) bureau *m*
2 (AmE) (government department) service *m*
3 (BrE) (desk) secrétaire *m*
4 (AmE) (chest of drawers) commode *f*

bureaucracy /bjʊə'rɒkrəsɪ/ *n* bureaucratie *f*

bureaucrat /'bjʊərəkræt/ *n* bureaucrate *mf*

bureaucratic /ˌbjʊərə'krætɪk/ *adj* bureaucratique

burgeoning /'bɜːdʒənɪŋ/ *adj* ‹*talent, love, industry, crime*› croissant/-e; ‹*population, industries*› en plein essor

burger /'bɜːgə(r)/ *n* hamburger *m*

burger bar *n* fast-food *m*

burglar /'bɜːglə(r)/ *n* cambrioleur/-euse *m/f*

burglar alarm *n* sonnerie *f* d'alarme

burglary /'bɜːglərɪ/ *n* (gen) cambriolage *m*; (Law) vol *m* avec effraction

burgle /'bɜːgl/ *vt* cambrioler

burgundy **A** **Burgundy** *pr n* Bourgogne *f*
B *n* **1** (*also* **Burgundy**) (wine) bourgogne *m*
2 (colour) (couleur *f*) bordeaux *m*

burial /'berɪəl/ *n* enterrement *m*

burka /bʊəkə/ *n* burqa *f*

burly /'bɜːlɪ/ *adj* ‹*person*› solidement charpenté/-e

Burma /'bɜːmə/ *pr n* Birmanie *f*

⚷ **burn** /bɜːn/ **A** *n* brûlure *f*
B *vt* (*prét, pp* **burned** *ou* **burnt** (BrE)) (gen) brûler; laisser brûler ‹*food*›
C *vi* (*prét, pp* **burned** *ou* **burnt** (BrE)) brûler

■ **burn down**: **A** **~ down** ‹*house*› être détruit/-e par le feu
B **~ [sth] down** réduire [qch] en cendres ‹*house*›

■ **burn up** brûler ‹*calories*›; dépenser ‹*energy*›

burner /'bɜːnə(r)/ *n* (on cooker) brûleur *m*; (for CDs etc) graveur *m*
IDIOM **to put sth on the back ~** mettre qch en veilleuse

burning /'bɜːnɪŋ/ **A** *n* **there's a smell of ~** ça sent le brûlé
B *adj* **1** (on fire) en flammes, en feu; (alight) ‹*candle, lamp, fire*› allumé/-e
2 ‹*desire*› brûlant/-e; ‹*passion*› ardent/-e

burnt-out *adj* ‹*building, car*› calciné/-e; ‹*person*› usé/-e (par le travail)

burp /bɜːp/ (fam) **A** *n* rot *m* (fam), renvoi *m*
B *vi* ‹*person*› roter (fam); ‹*baby*› faire son rot (fam)

burrow /'bʌrəʊ/ **A** *n* terrier *m*
B *vi* ‹*animal*› creuser un terrier; **to ~ into/ under sth** creuser dans/sous qch

bursary /'bɜːsərɪ/ *n* (BrE) (grant) bourse *f* (d'études)

burst /bɜːst/ **A** *n* (of flame) jaillissement *m*; (of gunfire) rafale *f*; (of activity, enthusiasm) accès *m*; **a ~ of laughter** un éclat de rire; **a ~ of applause** un tonnerre d'applaudissements
B *vt* (*prét, pp* **burst**) (gen) crever; rompre ‹*blood vessel*›; **to ~ its banks** ‹*river*› déborder
C *vi* (*prét, pp* **burst**) (gen) crever; ‹*pipe*› éclater; ‹*dam*› rompre; **to be ~ing with health/pride** déborder de santé/fierté

■ **burst into** **1** faire irruption dans ‹*room*›
2 **to ~ into flames** s'enflammer; **to ~ into tears** fondre en larmes

■ **burst out**: **to ~ out laughing** éclater de rire; **to ~ out crying** fondre en larmes

■ **burst through** rompre ‹*barricade*›; **to ~ through the door** entrer violemment

bury /'berɪ/ *vt* enterrer

⚷ **bus** /bʌs/ *n* (*pl* **buses**) autobus *m*, bus *m*; (long-distance) autocar *m*, car *m*; **by ~** en (auto)bus, par le bus; **on the ~** dans le bus

bus conductor *n* receveur *m* d'autobus

bus driver *n* conducteur/-trice *m/f* d'autobus

bush /bʊʃ/ *n* **1** buisson *m*
2 (bushland) **the ~** la brousse *f*
IDIOM **don't beat about the ~** cessez de tourner autour du pot

bush fire *n* feu *m* de brousse

bushy /'bʊʃɪ/ *adj* ‹*hair, tail*› touffu/-e; ‹*beard*› épais/-aisse; ‹*eyebrows*› broussailleux/-euse

⚷ **business** /'bɪznɪs/ **A** *n* **1** (commerce) affaires *fpl*; **to go into ~** se lancer dans les affaires; **she's gone to Brussels on ~** elle est allée à Bruxelles en voyage d'affaires; **to mix ~ with pleasure** joindre l'utile à l'agréable; **he's in the insurance ~** il travaille dans les assurances
2 (company, firm) affaire *f*, entreprise *f*; (shop) commerce *m*, boutique *f*; **small ~es** les petites entreprises
3 **let's get down to ~** passons aux choses sérieuses; **to go about one's ~** vaquer à ses occupations
4 (concern) **that's her ~** ça la regarde; **it's none of your ~!** ça ne te regarde pas!; **mind your own ~!** (fam) occupe-toi de tes affaires! (fam)
B *adj* ‹*address, letter, transaction*› commercial/-e; ‹*meeting*› d'affaires
IDIOMS **she means ~!** elle ne plaisante pas!; **to work like nobody's ~** (fam) travailler d'arrache-pied

business associate *n* associé/-e *m/f*

business card *n* carte *f* de visite

business class *n* (on plane) classe *f* affaires

business hours *npl* (in office) heures *fpl* de bureau; (of shop) heures *fpl* d'ouverture

businesslike /'bɪznɪslaɪk/ *adj* sérieux/-ieuse

businessman /'bɪznɪsmən/ *n* (*pl* **-men**) homme *m* d'affaires

business park *n* parc *m* d'affaires *or* d'activités

⚷ mot clé

business plan *n* projet *m* commercial

business school *n* école *f* de commerce

business studies *npl* études *fpl* de commerce

business trip *n* voyage *m* d'affaires

businesswoman *n* (*pl* **women**) femme *f* d'affaires

busker /ˈbʌskə(r)/ *n* (BrE) musicien/-ienne *m/f* ambulant/-e

bus lane *n* couloir *m* d'autobus

bus pass *n* carte *f* de bus

bus shelter *n* abribus® *m*

bus station *n* gare *f* routière

bus stop *n* arrêt *m* de bus

bust /bʌst/ **A** *n* **1** (breasts) poitrine *f*
2 (statue) buste *m*
B *adj* (fam) **1** (broken) fichu/-e (fam)
2 (bankrupt) **to go ~** faire faillite

bustle /ˈbʌsl/ **A** *n* (activity) affairement *m* (of de); **hustle and ~** grande animation *f*
B *vi* ‹*person, crowd*› s'affairer; **to ~ in/out** entrer/sortir d'un air affairé

bustling /ˈbʌslɪŋ/ *adj* ‹*street, shop, town*› animé/-e

busy /ˈbɪzɪ/ **A** *adj* **1** ‹*person*› occupé/-e (**with** avec, **doing** à faire)
2 ‹*shop*› où il y a beaucoup de monde; ‹*junction, airport*› où le trafic est intense; ‹*road*› très fréquenté/-e; ‹*street, town*› animé/-e; ‹*day, week*› chargé/-e
3 (engaged) ‹*line*› occupé/-e
B *v refl* **to ~ oneself doing** s'occuper à faire

busybody *n* (fam) **he's a real ~** il se mêle de tout

but /bʌt, bət/ **A** *conj* mais
B *prep* sauf; **anybody ~ him** n'importe qui sauf lui; **nobody ~ me knows how to do it** il n'y a que moi qui sache le faire; **he's nothing ~ a coward** ce n'est qu'un lâche; **the last ~ one** l'avant-dernier
C *adv* **one can't help ~ admire her** on ne peut pas s'empêcher de l'admirer
D **but for** *phr* **~ for you, I would have died** sans toi je serais mort; **he would have gone ~ for me** si je n'avais pas été là il serait parti

butane /ˈbjuːteɪn/ *n* butane *m*

butcher /ˈbʊtʃə(r)/ **A** *n* boucher *m*; **~'s (shop)** boucherie *f*
B *vt* abattre ‹*animal*›; massacrer ‹*people*›

butchery /ˈbʊtʃərɪ/ *n* **1** (trade) boucherie *f*
2 (slaughter) massacre *m*

butler /ˈbʌtlə(r)/ *n* maître *m* d'hôtel, majordome *m*

butt /bʌt/ **A** *n* **1** (of rifle) crosse *f*; (of cigarette) mégot *m* (fam)
2 (AmE) (buttocks) derrière *m* (fam)
3 **to be the ~ of sb's jokes** être la cible des blagues de qn
B *vt* ‹*person*› donner un coup de tête à; ‹*animal*› donner un coup de corne à
■ **butt in** interrompre

butter /ˈbʌtə(r)/ **A** *n* beurre *m*
B *vt* beurrer ‹*bread*›
■ **butter up** (fam): **~ [sb] up, ~ up [sb]** passer de la pommade à (fam)

buttercup *n* bouton d'or *m*

butterfingers *n* empoté/-e *m/f*

butterfly /ˈbʌtəflaɪ/ *n* papillon *m*
(IDIOM) **to have butterflies (in one's stomach)** avoir le trac (fam)

butterfly stroke *n* brasse *f* papillon

buttock /ˈbʌtək/ *n* fesse *f*

button /ˈbʌtn/ **A** *n* **1** (on coat, switch) bouton *m*
2 (AmE) (badge) badge *m*
3 (Comput) bouton *m*
B *vi* ‹*dress*› se boutonner
■ **button up** boutonner ‹*garment*›

buttonhole /ˈbʌtnhəʊl/ **A** *n* **1** (on garment) boutonnière *f*
2 (BrE) (flower) (fleur *f* de) boutonnière *f*
B *vt* (fam) accrocher (fam) ‹*person*›

buttress /ˈbʌtrɪs/ *n* **1** contrefort *m*; (fig) soutien *m*
2 (*also* **flying ~**) arc-boutant *m*

buxom /ˈbʌksəm/ *adj* ‹*woman*› à la poitrine généreuse

buy /baɪ/ **A** *n* **a good ~** une bonne affaire
B *vt* (*prét, pp* **bought**) acheter (**from sb** à qn); **to ~ sth from the supermarket/from the baker's** acheter qch au supermarché/ chez le boulanger; **to ~ sb sth** acheter qch à qn; **to ~ some time** gagner du temps
■ **buy off** acheter ‹*person, witness*›
■ **buy out** racheter la part de ‹*co-owner*›
■ **buy up** acheter systématiquement ‹*shares, property*›

buyer /ˈbaɪə(r)/ *n* acheteur/-euse *m/f*

buyout *n* rachat *m* d'entreprise

buzz /bʌz/ **A** *n* **1** (of insect) bourdonnement *m*
2 (fam) (phone call) **to give sb a ~** passer un coup de fil à qn
3 (fam) (thrill) **it gives me a ~** (from alcohol) ça me fait planer (fam); **to get a ~ out of doing** prendre son pied (fam) en faisant
B *vt* **to ~ sb** appeler qn au bip, biper qn
C *vi* ‹*bee, fly*› bourdonner; ‹*buzzer*› sonner

buzzard /ˈbʌzəd/ *n* buse *f*

buzzer /ˈbʌzə(r)/ *n* (gen) sonnerie *f*; (on pocket) bip *m*

buzzword *n* (fam) mot *m* à la mode

by /baɪ/ **A** *prep* **1** (with passive verbs) par; **he was bitten ~ a snake** il a été mordu par un serpent
2 (with present participle) en; **~ working extra hours** en faisant des heures supplémentaires; **to learn French ~ listening to the radio** apprendre le français en écoutant la radio; **to begin ~ doing** commencer par faire
3 (by means of) par; **to pay ~ cheque** payer par chèque; **~ mistake/accident** par erreur/ accident; **to travel to Rome ~ Venice** aller à Rome en passant par Venise; **to travel ~ bus/train** voyager en bus/train; **~ bicycle** à

bicyclette, en vélo; ~ **candlelight** ‹*dine*› aux chandelles; ‹*read*› à la bougie
4 (from) à; **I could tell ~ the look on her face that** rien qu'à la regarder je savais que
5 (near) à côté de, près de; **~ the window** à côté de la fenêtre; **~ the sea** au bord de la mer
6 (showing authorship) de; **a film ~ Claude Chabrol** un film de Claude Chabrol; **who is it ~?** c'est de qui?
7 (in time expressions) avant; **~ midnight** avant minuit; **~ this time next week** d'ici la semaine prochaine; **~ the time she had got downstairs he was gone** le temps qu'elle descende, il était parti; **he should be here ~ now** il devrait être déjà là
8 (according to) selon; **to play ~ the rules** jouer selon les règles; **~ my watch** à ma montre
9 (showing amount) de; **prices have risen ~ 20%** les prix ont augmenté de 20%; **he's taller than me ~ two centimetres** il fait deux centimètres de plus que moi
10 (in measurements) sur; **20 metres ~ 10 metres** 20 mètres sur 10
11 (showing rate, quantity) à; **paid ~ the hour** payé à l'heure
12 little ~ little peu à peu; **day ~ day** jour après jour; **one ~ one** un par un, une par une; **~ oneself** tout seul/toute seule; **to go** *or* **pass ~ sb/sth** passer devant qn/qch
13 (in compass directions) quart; **south ~ south-west** sud quart sud-ouest
B *adv* **1** (past) **to go ~** passer; **the people walking ~** les gens qui passent/passaient, les passants; **as time goes ~** avec le temps
2 (near) près; **he lives close ~** il habite tout près
3 (aside) **to put money ~** mettre de l'argent de côté

bye /baɪ/ *excl* (fam) (*also* **~ bye**) au revoir!

by-election *n* (*also* **bye-election**) (BrE) élection *f* partielle

bygone /'baɪgɒn/ *adj* ‹*days, years, scene*› d'antan; **a ~ era** une époque révolue
IDIOM **to let ~s be ~s** enterrer le passé

by-law /'baɪlɔː/ *n* (*also* **bye-law**) arrêté *m* municipal

bypass /'baɪpɑːs/ **A** *n* **1** (road) rocade *f*
2 (pipe, channel) by-pass *m inv*
3 (in electricity) dérivation *f*
4 (*also* **~ operation**) (Med) pontage *m*
B *vt* contourner ‹*town, city*›

by-product *n* dérivé *m*; (fig) effet *m* secondaire

bystander *n* spectateur/-trice *m/f*

byte /baɪt/ *n* (Comput) octet *m*

byword /'baɪwɜːd/ *n* **to be a ~ for** être synonyme de

Cc

c, C /siː/ *n* **1** (letter) c, C *m*
2 C (Mus) do *m*

cab /kæb/ *n* **1** (taxi) taxi *m*
2 (for driver) cabine *f*

cabbage /'kæbɪdʒ/ *n* chou *m*

cab driver /'kæbdraɪvə(r)/ *n* chauffeur *m* de taxi

cabin /'kæbɪn/ *n* **1** (hut) cabane *f*; (in holiday camp) chalet *m*
2 (in boat, plane) cabine *f*

cabin crew *n* personnel *m* de bord

cabinet /'kæbɪnɪt/ *n* **1** (cupboard) petit placard *m*; **display ~** vitrine *f*; **cocktail ~** meuble *m* bar
2 (BrE) (Pol) cabinet *m*

cabinet minister *n* (BrE) ministre *m*

cable /'keɪbl/ **A** *n* câble *m*
B *adj* ‹*channel, network*› câblé/-e

cable car *n* téléphérique *m*

cable TV *n* télévision *f* par câble

cab rank, cab stand *n* station *f* de taxis

cackle /'kækl/ *vi* ‹*hen*› caqueter; ‹*person*› (talk) caqueter; (laugh) ricaner

CAD *n* (*abbr* = **computer-aided design**) CAO *f*

CADCAM /'kædkæm/ *n* (*abbr* = **computer-aided design and computer-aided manufacture**) CFAO *f*

caddy /'kædɪ/ *n* caddie *m*

cadet /kə'det/ *n* (Mil) élève *mf* officier

cadge /kædʒ/ *vt* (fam) **to ~ sth off** *or* **from sb** taper (fam) qch à qn ‹*cigarette, money*›; **to ~ a meal/a lift** se faire inviter/emmener en voiture

Caesarean, Caesarian /sɪ'zeərɪən/ *n* (*also* **~ section**) césarienne *f*

cafe /'kæfeɪ, (AmE) kæ'feɪ/ *n* **1** ≈ snack bar *m*
2 (AmE) bistro *m*

mot clé

cafeteria /ˌkæfəˈtɪərɪə/ *n* (gen) cafétéria *f*; (Sch) cantine *f*; (Univ) restaurant *m* universitaire

caffeine /ˈkæfiːn/ *n* caféine *f*; **~-free** décaféiné/-e

cage /keɪdʒ/ **A** *n* cage *f*
B *vt* mettre [qch] en cage ‹*animal*›; **a ~d animal** un animal en cage

cagoule /kəˈguːl/ *n* (BrE) K-way® *m*

cahoots /kəˈhuːts/ *npl* (fam) **to be in ~** être de mèche (fam) (**with** avec)

Cairo /ˈkaɪərəʊ/ *pr n* Le Caire

cajole /kəˈdʒəʊl/ *vt* cajoler

cake /keɪk/ *n* **1** (Culin) gâteau *m*; (sponge) génoise *f*
2 (of soap, wax) pain *m*
IDIOM **it's a piece of ~** (fam) c'est du gâteau (fam)

cake shop *n* ≈ pâtisserie *f*

calcium /ˈkælsɪəm/ *n* calcium *m*

calculate /ˈkælkjʊleɪt/ *vt* **1** calculer ‹*cost, distance, price*›
2 évaluer ‹*effect, probability*›
3 to be ~d to do avoir été conçu/-e pour faire

calculated /ˈkælkjʊleɪtɪd/ *adj* ‹*crime*› prémédité/-e; ‹*attempt, insult*› délibéré/-e; ‹*risk*› calculé/-e

calculating /ˈkælkjʊleɪtɪŋ/ *adj* ‹*manner, person*› calculateur/-trice

calculation /ˌkælkjʊˈleɪʃn/ *n* calcul *m*

calculator /ˈkælkjʊleɪtə(r)/ *n* calculatrice *f*, calculette *f*

calendar /ˈkælɪndə(r)/ *n* calendrier *m*

calf /kɑːf, (AmE) kæf/ *n* (*pl* **calves**) **1** (Zool) veau *m*
2 (*also* **~skin**) vachette *f*
3 (Anat) mollet *m*

calibre (BrE), **caliber** (AmE) /ˈkælɪbə(r)/ *n* calibre *m*

California /ˌkælɪˈfɔːnɪə/ *pr n* Californie *f*

call /kɔːl/ **A** *n* **1** (*also* **phone ~**) appel *m* (téléphonique) (**from** de); **to make a ~** appeler, téléphoner
2 (cry) (human) appel *m* (**for** à); (animal) cri *m*
3 (summons) appel *m*
4 (visit) visite *f*
5 (demand) demande *f* (**for** de)
6 (need) **there's no ~ for sth** il n'y a pas de raison pour qch
7 (Sport) décision *f*
8 to be on ~ ‹*doctor*› être de garde; ‹*engineer*› être de service
B *vt* **1** (gen) appeler; **what is he ~ed?** comment s'appelle-t-il?; **the boss ~ed me into his office** le chef m'a fait venir dans son bureau
2 organiser ‹*strike*›; convoquer ‹*meeting*›; fixer ‹*election*›
3 (waken) réveiller ‹*person*›
4 (describe as) **to ~ sb stupid** traiter qn d'imbécile; **I wouldn't ~ it spacious** je ne dirais pas que c'est spacieux
C *vi* **1** (gen) appeler; **who's ~ing?** qui est à l'appareil?
2 (visit) passer; **to ~ at** passer chez ‹*person, shop*›; passer à ‹*bank, library*›; ‹*train*› s'arrêter à ‹*town, station*›

■ **call back**: **A ~ back** (on phone) rappeler
B ~ [sb] back rappeler ‹*person*›

■ **call for ~ for [sth] 1** (shout) appeler ‹*ambulance, doctor*›; **to ~ for help** appeler à l'aide
2 (demand) réclamer
3 (require) exiger ‹*treatment, skill*›; nécessiter ‹*change*›

■ **call in**: **A ~ in** (visit) passer
B ~ [sb] in faire entrer ‹*client, patient*›; faire appel à ‹*expert*›

■ **call off** abandonner ‹*investigation*›; annuler ‹*deal, wedding*›; rompre ‹*engagement*›

■ **call on 1** (visit) rendre visite à ‹*relative, friend*›; visiter ‹*patient, client*›
2 to ~ on sb to do demander à qn de faire

■ **call out**: **A ~ out** appeler; (louder) crier
B ~ [sb] out 1 appeler ‹*doctor, troops*›
2 ‹*union*› lancer un ordre de grève à ‹*members*›
C ~ [sth] out appeler ‹*name, number*›

■ **call up**: **A ~ up** appeler
B ~ [sb/sth] up 1 (on phone) appeler
2 (Mil) appeler [qn] sous les drapeaux ‹*soldier*›

call box *n* (BrE) cabine *f* téléphonique; (AmE) poste *m* téléphonique

call centre *n* centre *m* d'appels

caller /ˈkɔːlə(r)/ *n* **1** (on phone) personne *f* qui appelle
2 (visitor) visiteur/-euse *m/f*

callous /ˈkæləs/ *adj* inhumain/-e

call-out charge *n* frais *mpl* de déplacement

calm /kɑːm, (AmE) *also* kɑːlm/ **A** *n* calme *m*; (in adversity) sang-froid *m*
B *adj* calme; **keep ~!** du calme!
C *vt* calmer

■ **calm down**: **A ~ down** se calmer
B ~ [sb/sth] down calmer

calmly /ˈkɑːmlɪ, (AmE) *also* ˈkɑːlmlɪ/ *adv* ‹*act, speak*› calmement; ‹*sleep, smoke*› tranquillement

Calor gas® /ˈkælə gæs/ *n* (BrE) butane *m*

calorie /ˈkælərɪ/ *n* calorie *f*

camcorder /ˈkæmkɔːdə(r)/ *n* caméscope® *m*

camel /ˈkæml/ *n* chameau *m*

camera /ˈkæmərə/ *n* **1** (for photos) appareil *m* photo
2 (for movies) caméra *f*

camera crew *n* équipe *f* de télévision

cameraman *n* (*pl* **-men**) cadreur *m*, cameraman *m*

camisole /ˈkæmɪsəʊl/ *n* caraco *m*

camouflage /ˈkæməflɑːʒ/ **A** *n* camouflage *m*
B *vt* camoufler (**with** avec)

⚷ **camp** /kæmp/ **A** *n* camp *m*
B *vi* camper; **to go ~ing** faire du camping

⚷ **campaign** /kæm'peɪn/ **A** *n* campagne *f*
B *vi* faire campagne (**for** pour, **against** contre)

campaigner /kæm'peɪnə(r)/ *n* militant/-e *m/f* (**for** pour, **against** contre); (Pol) candidat/-e *m/f* en campagne (électorale)

camp bed *n* lit *m* de camp

camper /'kæmpə(r)/ *n* **1** (person) campeur/-euse *m/f*
2 (*also* **~ van**) camping-car *m*

campfire *n* feu *m* de camp

camping /'kæmpɪŋ/ *n* camping *m*; **to go ~** faire du camping

campsite *n* terrain *m* de camping, camping *m*

campus /'kæmpəs/ *n* (*pl* **-puses** /'kæmpəsɪz/) campus *m*

⚷ **can**[1] /kæn, kən/ *modal aux* (*prét, cond* **could**, *nég au prés* **cannot, can't**) **1** (be able to) pouvoir; **~ you come?** est-ce que tu peux venir?, peux-tu venir?; **we will do all we ~** nous ferons tout ce que nous pouvons *or* tout notre possible
2 (know how to) savoir; **she ~ swim** elle sait nager; **I can't drive** je ne sais pas conduire; **he ~ speak French** il parle français
3 (permission, requests, offers, suggestions) pouvoir; **~ we park here?** est-ce que nous pouvons nous garer ici?; **you can't turn right** vous ne pouvez pas *or* vous n'avez pas le droit de tourner à droite; **~ you do me a favour?** peux-tu *or* est-ce que tu peux me rendre un service?
4 (with verbs of perception) **~ they see us?** est-ce qu'ils nous voient?; **I can't feel a thing** je ne sens rien; **she can't understand English** elle ne comprend pas l'anglais
5 (in expressions) **you can't be hungry!** tu ne peux pas avoir faim!; **you can't be serious!** tu veux rire!; **this can't be right** il doit y avoir une erreur; **~ you believe it!** tu te rends compte?; **what ~ she want from me?** qu'est-ce qu'elle peut bien me vouloir?

can[2] /kæn/ **A** *n* (of food) boîte *f*; (of drink) cannette *f*; (aerosol) bombe *f*; (for petrol) bidon *m*; (of paint) pot *m*
B *vt* (*p prés etc* **-nn-**) mettre [qch] en conserve

Canada /'kænədə/ *pr n* Canada *m*

Canadian /kə'neɪdɪən/ **A** *n* Canadien/-ienne *m/f*
B *adj* canadien/-ienne; ‹*embassy*› du Canada

canal /kə'næl/ *n* canal *m*

canal boat, **canal barge** *n* péniche *f*

Canaries /kə'neərɪz/ *pr n pl* (*also* **Canary Islands**) **the ~** les Canaries *fpl*

cancel /'kænsl/ *vt* (gen) annuler; mettre une opposition à ‹*cheque*›

cancellation /ˌkænsə'leɪʃn/ *n* annulation *f*

⚷ **cancer** /'kænsə(r)/ *n* cancer *m*; **to have ~** avoir un cancer; **lung ~** cancer du poumon

Cancer /'kænsə(r)/ *n* Cancer *m*

cancer patient *n* cancéreux/-euse *m/f*

cancer research *n* cancérologie *f*

candid /'kændɪd/ *adj* franc/franche

⚷ **candidate** /'kændɪdət, (AmE) -deɪt/ *n* candidat/-e *m/f*

candle /'kændl/ *n* bougie *f*; (in church) cierge *m*

candlelight /'kændllaɪt/ *n* lueur *f* de bougie

candlelit dinner *n* dîner *m* aux chandelles

candlestick *n* bougeoir *m*; (ornate) chandelier *m*

candy /'kændɪ/ *n* (AmE) (sweets) bonbons *mpl*; (sweet) bonbon *m*

candyfloss *n* (BrE) barbe *f* à papa

cane /keɪn/ *n* **1** (material) rotin *m*; **~ furniture** meubles *mpl* en rotin
2 (of sugar, bamboo) canne *f*
3 (for walking) canne *f*; (for plant) tuteur *m*; (BrE) (for punishment) badine *f*

canine /'keɪnaɪn/ *n* canine *f*

canister /'kænɪstə(r)/ *n* boîte *f* métallique; **a tear gas ~** une bombe lacrymogène

cannabis /'kænəbɪs/ *n* cannabis *m*

canned *adj* **1** ‹*food*› en boîte
2 (fam) ‹*laughter*› enregistré/-e

cannibal /'kænɪbl/ *n* cannibale *mf*

cannon /'kænən/ *n* (*pl* **cannon** *ou* **cannons**) canon *m*

canoe /kə'nuː/ **A** *n* (gen) canoë *m*; (dugout) pirogue *f*; (Sport) canoë-kayac *m*
B *vi* faire du canoë

canoeing /kə'nuːɪŋ/ *n* **to go ~** faire du canoë-kayac

can opener *n* ouvre-boîtes *m inv*

cantankerous /kæn'tæŋkərəs/ *adj* acariâtre

canteen /kæn'tiːn/ *n* **1** (BrE) (dining room) cantine *f*
2 (Mil) (flask) bidon *m*; (mess tin) gamelle *f*
3 a ~ of cutlery une ménagère

canter /'kæntə(r)/ *vi* ‹*rider*› faire un petit galop; ‹*horse*› galoper

canvas /'kænvəs/ *n* toile *f*

canvass /'kænvəs/ *vt* **1 to ~ voters** faire du démarchage électoral auprès des électeurs
2 to ~ opinion on sth sonder l'opinion au sujet de qch
3 (for business) prospecter ‹*area*›

canvasser /'kænvəsə(r)/ *n* agent *m* électoral

canyon /'kænjən/ *n* cañon *m*

canyoning /'kænjənɪŋ/ *n* canyoning *m*

cap /kæp/ **A** *n* **1** casquette *f*; **baseball ~** casquette de baseball
2 (of pen) capuchon *m*; (of bottle) capsule *f*
3 (for tooth) couronne *f*
B *vt* (*p prés etc* **-pp-**) **1** (limit) imposer une limite budgétaire à ‹*local authority*›; plafonner ‹*budget*›

⚷ mot clé

2 (cover) couronner (**with** de)
IDIOM **to ~ it all** pour couronner le tout

capability /ˌkeɪpəˈbɪlətɪ/ *n* **1** (capacity) capacité *f* (**to do** de faire)
2 (aptitude) aptitude *f*; **outside my capabilities** au-delà de mes compétences

capable /ˈkeɪpəbl/ *adj* **1** (competent) compétent/-e
2 (able) capable (**of** de)

capacity /kəˈpæsətɪ/ *n* **1** (of box, bottle) contenance *f*; (of building) capacité *f* d'accueil; **full to ~** comble
2 (of factory) capacité *f* de production
3 (role) **in my ~ as a doctor** en ma qualité de médecin
4 (ability) **to have a ~ for** avoir des facilités pour ‹*learning, mathematics*›; **a ~ for doing** une aptitude à faire

cape /keɪp/ *n* **1** (cloak) cape *f*
2 (on coast) cap *m*

caper /ˈkeɪpə(r)/ *n* **1** (Culin) câpre *f*
2 (fam) (scheme) combine *f*
3 (fam) (antic) pitrerie *f*

Cape Town *pr n* Le Cap

capital /ˈkæpɪtl/ **A** *n* **1** (letter) majuscule *f*
2 (*also* **~ city**) capitale *f*
3 (money) capital *m*
B *adj* **1** ‹*letter*› majuscule; **~ A** A majuscule
2 (Law) ‹*offence*› capital/-e

capital expenditure *n* dépenses *fpl* d'investissement

capital investment *n* dépenses *fpl* d'investissement

capitalism /ˈkæpɪtəlɪzəm/ *n* capitalisme *m*

capitalist /ˈkæpɪtəlɪst/ *n*, *adj* capitaliste *mf*

capitalize /ˈkæpɪtəlaɪz/ *vi* **to ~ on** tirer parti de ‹*situation, advantage*›

capital punishment *n* peine *f* capitale

capitulate /kəˈpɪtʃʊleɪt/ *vi* capituler (**to** devant)

Capricorn /ˈkæprɪkɔːn/ *n* Capricorne *m*

capsize /kæpˈsaɪz, (AmE) ˈkæpsaɪz/ *vi* chavirer

captain /ˈkæptɪn/ **A** *n* capitaine *m*
B *vt* être le capitaine de ‹*team*›; commander ‹*ship, platoon*›

caption /ˈkæpʃn/ *n* légende *f*

captivate /ˈkæptɪveɪt/ *vt* captiver, fasciner

captive /ˈkæptɪv/ *n* captif/-ive *m/f*

captivity /kæpˈtɪvətɪ/ *n* captivité *f*

captor /ˈkæptə(r)/ *n* (of person) geôlier/-ière *m/f*

capture /ˈkæptʃə(r)/ **A** *n* (of person, animal) capture *f*; (of stronghold) prise *f*
B *vt* **1** capturer ‹*person, animal*›; prendre ‹*stronghold*›
2 saisir ‹*likeness*›; rendre ‹*feeling*›

car /kɑː(r)/ **A** *n* **1** (Aut) voiture *f*
2 (on train) wagon *m*; **restaurant ~** wagon-restaurant *m*
B *adj* ‹*industry, insurance*› automobile; ‹*journey, chase*› en voiture; ‹*accident*› de voiture

caramel /ˈkærəmel/ *n* caramel *m*

carat /ˈkærət/ *n* carat *m*; **18 ~ gold** or 18 carats

caravan /ˈkærəvæn/ **A** *n* caravane *f*; (horse-drawn) roulotte *f*
B *vi* (*p prés etc* **-nn-**) **to go ~ning** (BrE) faire du caravanage

caravan site *n* camping *m* pour caravanes

carbohydrate /ˌkɑːbəˈhaɪdreɪt/ *n* hydrate *m* de carbone

car bomb *n* bombe *f* dissimulée dans une voiture

carbon /ˈkɑːbən/ *n* carbone *m*

carbon copy *n* copie *f* carbone; (fig) réplique *f* exacte

carbon dating *n* datation *f* au carbone 14

carbon dioxide *n* dioxyde *m* de carbone

carbon fibre (BrE), **carbon fiber** (AmE) *n* fibre *f* de carbone

carbon footprint *n* empreinte *f* écologique

carbon monoxide /ˌkɑːbən mənˈɒksaɪd/ *n* monoxyde *m* de carbone

carbon neutral /ˌkɑːbən ˈnjuːtrəl/ (AmE) ˈnuː-/ *adj* neutre en carbone

carbon offsetting /ˌkɑːbən ˈɒfsetɪŋ/ *n* compensation *f* carbone

carbon trading *n* commerce *m* de droits d'émission de gaz à effet de serre

car boot sale *n* (BrE) brocante *f* (*d'objets apportés dans le coffre de sa voiture*)

carburettor (BrE), **carburetor** (AmE) /ˌkɑːbəˈretə(r)/ *n* carburateur *m*

card /kɑːd/ *n* carte *f*
IDIOM **to play one's ~s right** bien jouer son jeu (fam)

cardboard /ˈkɑːdbɔːd/ *n* carton *m*

cardboard box *n* (boîte *f* en) carton *m*

cardboard city *n: zone urbaine où les sans-abri logent dans des cartons*

card game *n* partie *f* de cartes

cardiac /ˈkɑːdɪæk/ *adj* cardiaque

cardiac arrest *n* arrêt *m* du cœur

cardigan /ˈkɑːdɪgən/ *n* cardigan *m*

card key *n* carte *f* magnétique

cardphone *n* téléphone *m* à carte

card trick *n* tour *m* de cartes

care /keə(r)/ **A** *n* **1** (attention) attention *f*, soin *m*; **to take ~ to do** prendre soin de faire; **'take ~!'** (be careful) 'fais attention!'; (goodbye) 'à bientôt!'; **'handle with ~'** 'fragile'
2 (looking after) (of person, animal) soins *mpl*; (of car, plant, clothes) entretien *m* (**of** de); **to take ~ of** (deal with) s'occuper de ‹*child, client, garden, details*›; (be careful with) prendre soin de ‹*machine, car*›; (keep in good condition) entretenir ‹*car, teeth*›; (look after) garder ‹*shop, watch*›; **to take ~ of oneself** (look after oneself) prendre soin de soi; (cope) se débrouiller tout seul/toute seule; (defend

C

oneself) se défendre
3 (Med) soins *mpl*
4 (BrE) **to be in ~** ‹*child*› être (placé/-e) en garde
5 (worry) souci *m*
B *vi* **1** (be concerned) **to ~ about** s'intéresser à ‹*art, environment*›; se soucier du bien-être de ‹*pupils, the elderly*›; **I don't ~!** ça m'est égal!; **she couldn't ~ less about...** elle se moque *or* se fiche (fam) complètement de...; **I'm past caring** je m'en moque
2 (love) **to ~ about sb** aimer qn

■ **care for A ~ for [sth] 1** (like) aimer; **would you ~ for a drink?** voulez-vous boire quelque chose?
2 (maintain) entretenir ‹*car, garden*›; prendre soin de ‹*skin, plant*›
B ~ for [sb/sth] s'occuper de ‹*child, animal*›; soigner ‹*patient*›

care assistant *n* aide-soignant/-e *m/f*

✓ **career** /kəˈrɪə(r)/ *n* carrière *f*

career break *n* interruption *f* de carrière

careers adviser, **careers officer** *n* conseiller/-ère *m/f* d'orientation

careers office *n* service *m* d'orientation professionnelle

carefree *adj* insouciant/-e

careful /ˈkeəfl/ *adj* ‹*person, driving*› prudent/-e; ‹*planning, preparation*› minutieux/-ieuse; ‹*research, examination*› méticuleux/-euse; **to be ~ to do** *or* **about doing** prendre soin de faire; **to be ~ with sth** faire attention à qch; **be ~!** (fais) attention!

✓ **carefully** /ˈkeəfəlɪ/ *adv* ‹*walk, open, handle*› prudemment; ‹*write*› soigneusement; ‹*listen, read, look*› attentivement

caregiver *n* (AmE) *personne ayant un parent handicapé ou malade à charge*

careless /ˈkeəlɪs/ *adj* ‹*person*› négligent/-e, imprudent/-e; ‹*work*› bâclé/-e; ‹*writing*› négligé/-e; ‹*driving*› négligent/-e; **~ mistake** faute *f* d'étourderie; **it was ~ of me to do** ça a été de la négligence de ma part de faire

carelessness /ˈkeəlɪsnɪs/ *n* négligence *f*

carer /ˈkeərə(r)/ *n* (BrE) (relative) *personne ayant un parent handicapé ou malade à charge*; (professional) aide *f* familiale, aidant/-e *m/f*

caress /kəˈres/ *vt* caresser

caretaker /ˈkeəteɪkə(r)/ *n* concierge *mf*

care worker *n* assistant/-e *m/f* social/-e

car ferry *n* ferry *m*

cargo /ˈkɑːgəʊ/ *n* (*pl* **~es** *ou* **~s**) chargement *m*

cargo ship *n* cargo *m*

car hire *n* location *f* de voitures

car hire company *n* société *f* de location de voitures

Caribbean /ˌkærɪˈbiːən/ *pr n* **the ~ (Sea)** la mer des Antilles *or* des Caraïbes

caricature /ˈkærɪkətʃʊə(r)/ *n* caricature *f*

caring /ˈkeərɪŋ/ *adj* **1** (loving) ‹*parent*› affectueux/-euse
2 (compassionate) ‹*person, attitude*› compréhensif/-ive; ‹*society*› humain/-e

carjacking /ˈkɑːdʒækɪŋ/ *n* vol *m* de voiture (avec agression du conducteur)

carnage /ˈkɑːnɪdʒ/ *n* carnage *m*

carnation /kɑːˈneɪʃn/ *n* œillet *m*

carnival /ˈkɑːnɪvl/ *n* **1** carnaval *m*
2 (AmE) (funfair) fête *f* foraine

carol /ˈkærəl/ *n* chant *m* de Noël

carousel /ˌkærəˈsel/ *n* **1** (merry-go-round) manège *m*
2 (for luggage, slides) carrousel *m*

car park /ˈkɑːpɑːk/ *n* (BrE) parc *m* de stationnement

carpenter /ˈkɑːpəntə(r)/ *n* menuisier *m*

carpentry /ˈkɑːpəntrɪ/ *n* menuiserie *f*

carpet /ˈkɑːpɪt/ *n* (fitted) moquette *f*; (loose) tapis *m*

carpet sweeper *n* balai *m* mécanique

car phone *n* téléphone *m* de voiture

car radio *n* autoradio *m*

carriage /ˈkærɪdʒ/ *n* **1** (ceremonial) carrosse *m*
2 (of train) wagon *m*, voiture *f*
3 (of goods) transport *m*; **~ paid** port *m* payé
4 (of typewriter) chariot *m*

carriageway *n* chaussée *f*

carrier /ˈkærɪə(r)/ *n* **1** (transport company) transporteur *m*; (airline) compagnie *f* aérienne
2 (of disease) porteur/-euse *m/f*
3 (*also* **~ bag**) (BrE) sac *m* (en plastique)

carrot /ˈkærət/ *n* carotte *f*

✓ **carry** /ˈkærɪ/ **A** *vt* **1** ‹*person*› porter; **to ~ sth in/out** apporter/emporter qch
2 ‹*vehicle, pipe, vein*› transporter; ‹*tide, current*› emporter
3 comporter ‹*warning*›
4 comporter ‹*risk, responsibility*›; être passible de ‹*penalty*›
5 ‹*bridge, road*› supporter ‹*load, traffic*›
6 faire voter ‹*bill*›; **the motion was carried by 20 votes to 13** la motion l'a emporté par 20 votes contre 13
7 (Med) être porteur/-euse de ‹*disease, virus*›
8 (in mathematics) retenir
9 (hold) porter ‹*head*›
B *vi* ‹*sound, voice*› porter

IDIOM **to get carried away** (fam) s'emballer (fam), se laisser emporter

■ **carry forward** reporter ‹*balance, total*›

■ **carry off** (gen) emporter; remporter ‹*prize*›

■ **carry on A ~ on 1** (continue) continuer (doing à faire)
2 (behave) se conduire
B ~ on [sth] maintenir ‹*tradition*›;

✓ mot clé

poursuivre ‹*activity, discussion*›
■ **carry out** réaliser ‹*study*›; effectuer ‹*experiment, reform, attack, repairs*›; exécuter ‹*plan, orders*›; mener ‹*investigation, campaign*›; accomplir ‹*mission*›; remplir ‹*duties*›; mettre [qch] à exécution ‹*threat*›; tenir ‹*promise*›
carryall *n* (AmE) fourre-tout *m inv*
carrycot *n* (BrE) porte-bébé *m*
carry-on *n* (fam) cirque *m* (fam)
carry-out /ˈkærɪaʊt/ *n* repas *m* à emporter
car seat *n* siège-auto *m*
carsick /ˈkɑːsɪk/ *adj* **to be ∼** avoir le mal de la route
cart /kɑːt/ **A** *n* charrette *f*
B *vt* (fam) (*also* **∼ around**, **∼ about** (fam)) trimballer (fam) ‹*bags*›
cartel /kɑːˈtel/ *n* cartel *m*; **drug ∼** cartel *m* de la drogue
car theft *n* vol *m* de voitures
carton /ˈkɑːtn/ *n* (of juice, milk) carton *m*, brique *f*; (of yoghurt, cream) pot *m*; (of cigarettes) cartouche *f*; (AmE) (for house removals) carton *m*
cartoon /kɑːˈtuːn/ *n* **1** (film) dessin *m* animé
2 (drawing) dessin *m* humoristique; (comic strip) bande *f* dessinée
cartridge /ˈkɑːtrɪdʒ/ *n* (for pen, gun, video) cartouche *f*; (for camera) chargeur *m*
cartwheel /ˈkɑːtwiːl, (AmE) -hwiːl/ *n* **to do a ∼** faire la roue
carve /kɑːv/ **A** *vt* **1** tailler, sculpter ‹*wood, stone, figure*› (**out of** dans)
2 graver ‹*letters, name*› (**onto** sur)
3 découper ‹*meat*›
B *vi* découper
■ **carve out 1** se faire ‹*niche, name*›; se tailler ‹*reputation, market*›
2 creuser ‹*gorge, channel*›
■ **carve up**: **∼ up [sth]**, **∼ [sth] up** partager ‹*proceeds*›; morceler ‹*estate, territory*›
carving /ˈkɑːvɪŋ/ *n* sculpture *f*
carving knife *n* couteau *m* à découper
car wash *n* lavage *m* automatique
case¹ /keɪs/ **A** *n* **1** (gen) cas *m*; **in that ∼** en ce cas, dans ce cas-là; **in 7 out of 10 ∼s** 7 fois sur 10, dans 7 cas sur 10; **a ∼ in point** un cas d'espèce, un exemple typique
2 (Law) affaire *f*; procès *m*; **the ∼ for the Crown** (BrE), **the ∼ for the State** (AmE) l'accusation *f*; **the ∼ for the defence** la défense
3 (argument) arguments *mpl*
B in any case *phr* **1** (besides, anyway) de toute façon
2 (at any rate) en tout cas
C in case *phr* au cas où (+ *conditional*); **just in ∼** au cas où
D in case of *phr* en cas de ‹*fire, accident*›
case² /keɪs/ *n* **1** (suitcase) valise *f*; (crate, chest) caisse *f*
2 (display cabinet) vitrine *f*
3 (for spectacles, binoculars, weapon) étui *m*; (for camera, watch) boîtier *m*
CASE /keɪs/ *n* (*abbr* = **computer-aided software engineering**) CPAO *f*
case study *n* étude *f* de cas
cash /kæʃ/ **A** *n* **1** (notes and coin) espèces *fpl*, argent *m* liquide; **to pay in ∼** payer en espèces; **I haven't got any ∼ on me** je n'ai pas d'argent liquide
2 (money in general) argent *m*
3 (payment) comptant *m*; **discount for ∼** remise *f* pour paiement comptant
B *vt* encaisser ‹*cheque*›
■ **cash in**: **A to ∼ in on** tirer profit de, profiter de
B ∼ [sth] in se faire rembourser, réaliser ‹*bond, policy*›; (AmE) encaisser ‹*check*›
cash-and-carry /ˌkæʃənˈkærɪ/ *n* libre-service *m* de vente en gros
cash card *n* carte *f* de retrait
cash desk *n* caisse *f*
cash dispenser *n* (*also* **cashpoint**) distributeur *m* automatique de billets de banque, billetterie *f*
cashew nut *n* cajou *m*
cash flow *n* marge *f* brute d'autofinancement, MBA *f*
cashier /kæˈʃɪə(r)/ *n* caissier/-ière *m/f*
cashless /ˈkæʃlɪs/ *adj* ‹*society*› sans argent liquide
cashmere /ˌkæʃˈmɪə(r)/ *n* (lainage *m* en) cachemire *m*
cash on delivery, **COD** *n* envoi *m* contre remboursement
cashpoint = **cash dispenser**
cash register *n* caisse *f* enregistreuse
casino /kəˈsiːnəʊ/ *n* casino *m*
cask /kɑːsk, (AmE) kæsk/ *n* fût *m*, tonneau *m*
casserole /ˈkæsərəʊl/ *n* **1** (container) daubière *f*, cocotte *f*
2 (BrE) (food) ragoût *m* cuit au four
cassette /kəˈset/ *n* cassette *f*
cassette deck *n* platine *f* à cassettes
cassette player *n* lecteur *m* de cassettes
cast /kɑːst, (AmE) kæst/ **A** *n* **1** (list of actors) distribution *f*; (actors) acteurs *mpl*
2 (*also* **plaster ∼**) (Med) plâtre *m*
3 (mould) moule *m*
B *vt* (*prét*, *pp* **cast**) **1** jeter, lancer ‹*stone, fishing line*›; projeter ‹*shadow*›; **to ∼ doubt on** émettre des doutes sur; **to ∼ light on** éclairer; **to ∼ a spell on** jeter un sort à
2 jeter ‹*glance*› (**at** sur)
3 distribuer les rôles de ‹*play, film*›; **she was cast as Blanche** elle a joué Blanche
4 couler ‹*plaster, metal*›
5 to ∼ one's vote voter
castaway *n* naufragé/-e *m/f*
caste /kɑːst/ *n* caste *f*
caster sugar *n* (BrE) sucre *m* en poudre
casting /ˈkɑːstɪŋ, (AmE) ˈkæst-/ *n* distribution *f*
casting vote *n* voix *f* prépondérante

C

cast iron *n* fonte *f*; **a cast-iron alibi** un alibi en béton (fam)

castle /'kɑːsl, (AmE) 'kæsl/ *n* **1** château *m* **2** (in chess) tour *f*

cast-offs *npl* vêtements *mpl* dont on n'a plus besoin, vieux vêtements

castrate /kæ'streɪt, (AmE) 'kæstreɪt/ *vt* castrer

casual /'kæʒʊəl/ *adj* **1** (informal) ‹*clothes, person*› décontracté/-e **2** ‹*acquaintance, relationship*› de passage; **~ sex** relations *fpl* sexuelles non suivies **3** ‹*attitude, gesture, remark*› désinvolte **4** ‹*glance*› superficiel/-ielle **5** ‹*work*› (temporary) temporaire; (occasional) occasionnel/-elle

casualize *vt* **to ~ labour** précariser l'emploi

casually /'kæʒʊəlɪ/ *adv* **1** ‹*enquire, remark*› d'un air détaché **2** ‹*dressed*› simplement

casualty /'kæʒʊəltɪ/ **A** *n* **1** (person) victime *f* **2** (hospital ward) urgences *fpl*; **in ~** aux urgences **B casualties** *npl* (soldiers) pertes *fpl*; (civilians) victimes *fpl*

casual wear *n* vêtements *mpl* sport

⚷ **cat** /kæt/ *n* (domestic) chat *m*; (female) chatte *f*; **the big ~s** les grands félins *mpl*
IDIOMS **to let the ~ out of the bag** vendre la mèche; **to rain ~s and dogs** pleuvoir des cordes

catalogue, catalog (AmE) /'kætəlɒg, (AmE) -lɔːg/ *n* catalogue *m*

catalyst /'kætəlɪst/ *n* catalyseur *m*

catalytic converter *n* pot *m* catalytique

catapult /'kætəpʌlt/ *n* (hand-held) lance-pierres *m inv*

catarrh /kə'tɑː(r)/ *n* catarrhe *m*

catastrophe /kə'tæstrəfɪ/ *n* catastrophe *f*

⚷ **catch** /kætʃ/ **A** *n* **1** (on purse, door) fermeture *f* **2** (drawback) piège *m* **3** (act of catching) prise *f*; **to play ~** jouer à la balle **4** (in fishing) pêche *f*; (one fish) prise *f*
B *vt* (*prét, pp* **caught**) **1** ‹*person*› attraper ‹*ball, fish, person*›; **to ~ hold of sth** attraper qch; **to ~ sb's attention** *or* **eye** attirer l'attention de qn; **to ~ sight of sb/sth** apercevoir qn/qch **2** (take by surprise) prendre, attraper; **to ~ sb doing** surprendre qn en train de faire; **we got caught in the rain** nous avons été surpris par la pluie **3** prendre ‹*bus, plane*› **4** (grasp) prendre ‹*hand, arm*›; agripper ‹*branch, rope*›; captiver, éveiller ‹*interest*› **5** (hear) saisir (fam), comprendre **6 to ~ one's fingers in** se prendre les doigts dans ‹*drawer, door*›; **to get one's shirt caught on** accrocher sa chemise à ‹*nail*›; **to get caught in** se prendre dans ‹*barbed wire, thorns*› **7** attraper ‹*cold, disease, flu*› **8 to ~ fire** prendre feu, s'enflammer
C *vi* (*prét, pp* **caught**) **1 to ~ on** ‹*shirt*› s'accrocher à ‹*nail*›; ‹*wheel*› frotter contre ‹*frame*› **2** ‹*wood, fire*› prendre

■ **catch on 1** (become popular) devenir populaire (**with** auprès de) **2** (understand) comprendre, saisir

■ **catch out 1** (take by surprise) prendre [qn] de court; (doing something wrong) prendre [qn] sur le fait **2** (trick) attraper, jouer un tour à

■ **catch up**: **A ~ up** (in race) regagner du terrain; **to ~ up on** rattraper ‹*work, sleep*›; se remettre au courant de ‹*news*›
B ~ [sb/sth] up rattraper

catch-22 situation *n* situation *f* inextricable

catching /'kætʃɪŋ/ *adj* contagieux/-ieuse

catchphrase *n* formule *f* favorite, rengaine *f*

catchy /'kætʃɪ/ *adj* ‹*tune*› entraînant/-e; ‹*slogan*› accrocheur/-euse

categorical /ˌkætə'gɒrɪkl, (AmE) -'gɔːr-/ *adj* catégorique

categorize /'kætəgəraɪz/ *vt* classer (**by** d'après)

⚷ **category** /'kætəgərɪ, (AmE) -gɔːrɪ/ *n* catégorie *f*

cater /'keɪtə(r)/ *vi* **1** ‹*caterer*› organiser des réceptions **2 to ~ for** (BrE) *or* **to** (AmE) accueillir ‹*children, guests*›; pourvoir à ‹*needs*›; ‹*programme*› s'adresser à ‹*audience*›

caterer /'keɪtərə(r)/ *n* traiteur *m*

catering /'keɪtərɪŋ/ *n* (provision) approvisionnement *m*; (trade, industry, career) restauration *f*

caterpillar /'kætəpɪlə(r)/ *n* chenille *f*

cathedral /kə'θiːdrəl/ *n* cathédrale *f*

Catholic /'kæθəlɪk/ *n, adj* catholique *mf*

Catholicism /kə'θɒlɪsɪzəm/ *n* catholicisme *m*

catnap /'kætnæp/ *vi* (*p prés etc* **-pp-**) faire un somme, sommeiller

Catseye® *n* (BrE) plot *m* rétroréfléchissant

cattle /'kætl/ *n* bétail *m*

catwalk /'kætwɔːk/ *n* podium *m*; **~ show** défilé *m* de mode

cauliflower /'kɒlɪflaʊə(r), (AmE) 'kɔːlɪ-/ *n* chou-fleur *m*

⚷ **cause** /kɔːz/ **A** *n* cause *f* (**of** de); **there is ~ for concern** il y a des raisons de s'inquiéter; **to have ~ to do** avoir des raisons de faire; **with good ~** à juste titre
B *vt* causer, occasionner ‹*damage, grief, problem*›; provoquer ‹*chaos, disease, controversy*›; entraîner ‹*suffering*›; amener ‹*confusion*›; **to ~ sb problems** causer des problèmes à qn; **to ~ trouble** créer des problèmes

⚷ mot clé

caustic /ˈkɔːstɪk/ *adj* caustique

caution /ˈkɔːʃn/ **A** *n* **1** (care) prudence *f*
2 (wariness) circonspection *f*
3 (warning) avertissement *m*
B *vt* **1** (warn) avertir (**that** que)
2 (Sport) donner un avertissement à ‹*player*›
IDIOM **to throw** *or* **cast ~ to the wind(s)** oublier toute prudence

cautionary /ˈkɔːʃənərɪ, (AmE) -nerɪ/ *adj* ‹*look, gesture*› d'avertissement; **a ~ tale** un conte moral

cautious /ˈkɔːʃəs/ *adj* **1** (careful) prudent/-e
2 (wary) ‹*person, reception, response*› réservé/-e; ‹*optimism*› prudent/-e

cave /keɪv/ *n* grotte *f*
■ **cave in 1** ‹*tunnel, roof*› s'effondrer
2 ‹*person*› céder

caveman /ˈkeɪvmæn/ *n* (*pl* **-men**) homme *m* des cavernes

caviar /ˈkævɪɑː(r), ˌkævɪˈɑː(r)/ *n* (*also* **caviare**) caviar *m*

caving /ˈkeɪvɪŋ/ *n* spéléologie *f*; **to go ~** faire de la spéléologie

cavity /ˈkævətɪ/ *n* cavité *f*

cavort /kəˈvɔːt/ *vi* faire des cabrioles

caw /kɔː/ *vi* croasser

cc *n* (*abbr* = **cubic centimetre**) cm^3

CCTV *n* (*abbr* = **closed-circuit television**) télévision *f* en circuit fermé

CD *n* (*abbr* = **compact disc**) CD *m*

CD player, **CD system** *n* platine *f* laser

CD-ROM /ˌsiːdiːˈrɒm/ *n* CD-ROM *m*, disque *m* optique compact

cease /siːs/ *vt, vi* cesser

cease-fire /ˈsiːsfaɪə(r)/ *n* cessez-le-feu *m inv*

cedar /ˈsiːdə(r)/ *n* cèdre *m*

cede /siːd/ *vt, vi* céder (**to** à)

cedilla /sɪˈdɪlə/ *n* cédille *f*

ceiling /ˈsiːlɪŋ/ *n* plafond *m*

celebrate /ˈselɪbreɪt/ **A** *vt* fêter; (more formally) célébrer
B *vi* faire la fête

celebrated /ˈselɪbreɪtɪd/ *adj* célèbre (**for** pour)

celebration /ˌselɪˈbreɪʃn/ *n* **1** (celebrating) célébration *f*
2 (party) fête *f*
3 (public festivities) **~s** cérémonies *fpl*

celebrity /sɪˈlebrətɪ/ **A** *n* célébrité *f*
B *adj* ‹*guest*› célèbre; ‹*panel*› de célébrités

celery /ˈselərɪ/ *n* céleri *m*

celibate /ˈselɪbət/ *adj* (chaste) chaste

cell /sel/ *n* cellule *f*

cellar /ˈselə(r)/ *n* cave *f*

cello /ˈtʃeləʊ/ *n* violoncelle *m*

cell phone, **cellular phone** *n*
1 radiotéléphone *m*
2 téléphone *m* portable

cellulite /ˈseljʊlaɪt/ *n* cellulite *f*

Celsius /ˈselsɪəs/ *adj* Celsius *inv*

Celt /kelt, (AmE) selt/ *n* Celte *mf*

Celtic /ˈkeltɪk, (AmE) ˈseltɪk/ *adj* celtique, celte

cement /sɪˈment/ *n* ciment *m*

cement mixer *n* bétonnière *f*

cemetery /ˈsemətrɪ, (AmE) -terɪ/ *n* cimetière *m*

censor /ˈsensə(r)/ **A** *n* censeur *mf*
B *vt* censurer

censorship /ˈsensəʃɪp/ *n* censure *f* (**of** de)

censure /ˈsenʃə(r)/ **A** *n* censure *f*
B *vt* critiquer

census /ˈsensəs/ *n* recensement *m*

cent /sent/ *n* (of dollar) cent *m*; (of euro) cent *m*, centime *m* [d'euro]

centenary /senˈtiːnərɪ/ *n* centenaire *m*

center (AmE) = **centre**

centigrade /ˈsentɪɡreɪd/ *adj* **in degrees ~** en degrés Celsius

centimetre (BrE), **centimeter** (AmE) /ˈsentɪmiːtə(r)/ *n* centimètre *m*

central /ˈsentrəl/ *adj* **1** central/-e; **~ London** le centre de Londres
2 (in the town centre) situé/-e en centre-ville
3 (key) principal/-e

Central America *pr n* Amérique *f* centrale

central heating *n* chauffage *m* central

centralize /ˈsentrəlaɪz/ *vt* centraliser

central locking *n* verrouillage *m* central *or* centralisé

central reservation *n* (BrE) (Aut) terre-plein *m* central

centre (BrE), **center** (AmE) /ˈsentə(r)/
A *n* centre *m*; **in the ~** au centre; **town ~, city ~** centre-ville *m*; **the ~ of attention** le centre de l'attention; **the ~ of power** le siège du pouvoir; **shopping/sports ~** centre commercial/sportif
B *vt, vi* centrer
■ **centre around**, **centre on** ‹*activities, person*› se concentrer sur; ‹*people, industry*› se situer autour de ‹*town*›; ‹*life, thoughts*› être centré/-e sur ‹*person, work*›

centre forward *n* (Sport) avant-centre *m*

centre ground *n* centre *m*; **to occupy the ~** être au centre

centre half *n* (Sport) demi-centre *m*

centrepiece (BrE), **centerpiece** (AmE) *n* (of table) décoration *f* centrale; (of exhibition) clou *m*

centre stage to take/occupy ~ devenir/être le point de mire

century /ˈsentʃərɪ/ *n* siècle *m*; **in the 20th ~** au XXᵉ siècle; **at the turn of the ~** au début du siècle

ceramic /sɪˈræmɪk/ *adj* en céramique

ceramics /sɪˈræmɪks/ *n* céramiques *fpl*

cereal /ˈsɪərɪəl/ *n* céréale *f*; **breakfast ~** céréales pour le petit déjeuner

cerebral palsy *n* paralysie *f* motrice centrale

ceremony /ˈserɪmənɪ, (AmE) -məʊnɪ/ *n* cérémonie *f*; **to stand on ~** faire des cérémonies

cert /sɜːt/ *n* (fam) **it's a (dead) ~!** ça ne fait pas un pli! (fam)

⚷ **certain** /ˈsɜːtn/ *adj* **1** (sure) certain/-e, sûr/-e (**about, of** de); **I'm ~ (of it)** j'en suis certain *or* sûr; **absolutely ~** sûr et certain; **I'm ~ that I checked** je suis sûr d'avoir vérifié; **I'm ~ that he refused** je suis sûr qu'il a refusé
2 (specific) ‹*amount, number, conditions*› certain/-e *before n*; **~ people** certains *mpl*; **to a ~ extent** dans une certaine mesure

⚷ **certainly** /ˈsɜːtnlɪ/ *adv* certainement

certainty /ˈsɜːtntɪ/ *n* certitude *f*

certificate /səˈtɪfɪkət/ *n* (gen) certificat *m*; (of birth, death, marriage) acte *m*; **18-~ film** film *m* interdit aux moins de 18 ans

certified *adj* certifié/-e

certified mail *n* (AmE) **to send by ~** envoyer en recommandé

certified public accountant *n* (AmE) expert-comptable *m*

certify /ˈsɜːtɪfaɪ/ *vt* **1** (confirm) certifier
2 (authenticate) authentifier

cervical cancer *n* cancer *m* du col de l'utérus

cervical smear *n* frottis *m* vaginal

CFC *n* (*abbr* = **chlorofluorocarbon**) CFC *m*

chafe /tʃeɪf/ *vi* frotter (**on, against** sur)

⚷ **chain** /tʃeɪn/ **A** *n* **1** (metal links) chaîne *f*
2 (on lavatory) chasse *f* (d'eau)
3 (on door) chaîne *f* de sûreté
4 (of shops, hotels) chaîne *f* (**of** de)
5 (of events) série *f*; (of ideas) enchaînement *m*
B *vt* enchaîner ‹*person, animal*›; **to ~ a bicycle to sth** attacher une bicyclette à qch avec une chaîne

chain reaction *n* réaction *f* en chaîne

chain saw *n* tronçonneuse *f*

chain-smoke /ˈtʃeɪnsməʊk/ *vi* (fam) fumer comme un sapeur (fam), fumer sans arrêt

chain-smoker *n* gros fumeur/grosse fumeuse *m/f*

chain store *n* (single shop) magasin *m* faisant partie d'une chaîne; (retail group) magasin *m* à succursales multiples

⚷ **chair** /tʃeə(r)/ **A** *n* **1** chaise *f*; (armchair) fauteuil *m*
2 (chairperson) président/-e *m/f*
3 (Univ) chaire *f* (**of, in** de)
B *vt* présider ‹*meeting*›

chair lift *n* télésiège *m*

⚷ **chairman** /ˈtʃeəmən/ *n* président/-e *m/f*; **Mr Chairman** monsieur le Président; **Madam Chairman** madame la Présidente

chairperson /ˈtʃeəpɜːsn/ *n* président/-e *m/f*

chalet /ˈʃæleɪ/ *n* (mountain) chalet *m*; (in holiday camp) bungalow *m*

chalk /tʃɔːk/ *n* craie *f*

⚷ **challenge** /ˈtʃælɪndʒ/ **A** *n* **1** défi *m*; **to take up a ~** relever un défi
2 (challenging task) challenge *m*; **to rise to the ~** relever le challenge
B *vt* **1** défier ‹*person*› (**to** à, **to do** de faire)
2 débattre ‹*ideas*›; contester ‹*statement, authority*›

challenger /ˈtʃælɪndʒə(r)/ *n* challenger *m* (**for** de)

challenging /ˈtʃælɪndʒɪŋ/ *adj* **1** ‹*work*› stimulant/-e
2 ‹*look*› provocateur/-trice

chamber /ˈtʃeɪmbə(r)/ **A** *n* chambre *f*
B chambers *npl* (Law) cabinet *m*; (BrE) (Pol); **the upper/lower ~** la Chambre des lords/des communes

chambermaid *n* femme *f* de chambre

chamber music *n* musique *f* de chambre

Chamber of Commerce *n* chambre *f* de commerce et d'industrie

chameleon /kəˈmiːlɪən/ *n* caméléon *m*

champagne /ʃæmˈpeɪn/ *n, adj* champagne *m inv*

⚷ **champion** /ˈtʃæmpɪən/ *n* champion/-ionne *m/f*

championship /ˈtʃæmpɪənʃɪp/ *n* championnat *m*

⚷ **chance** /tʃɑːns, (AmE) tʃæns/ **A** *n*
1 (opportunity) occasion *f*; **to have** *or* **get the ~ to do** avoir l'occasion de faire; **you've missed your ~** tu as laissé passer l'occasion
2 (likelihood) chance *f*; **there is a ~ that she'll get a job in Paris** il y a des chances qu'elle trouve un travail à Paris; **she has a good ~** elle a de bonnes chances
3 (luck) hasard *m*; **by ~** par hasard
4 (risk) risque *m*; **to take a ~** prendre un risque
5 (possibility) chance *f*; **not to stand a ~** n'avoir aucune chance; **by any ~** par hasard
B *vt* **to ~ doing** courir le risque de faire; **to ~ it** tenter sa chance
IDIOM **no ~!** (fam) pas question! (fam)

chancellor /ˈtʃɑːnsələ(r), (AmE) ˈtʃæns-/ *n* (head of government) chancelier/-ière *m/f*; (Univ) président *m*

Chancellor of the Exchequer *n* (BrE) Chancelier *m* de l'Échiquier

chandelier /ʃændəˈlɪə(r)/ *n* lustre *m*

⚷ **change** /tʃeɪndʒ/ **A** *n* **1** (gen) changement *m*; (adjustment) modification *f*; **the ~ in the schedule** la modification du programme; **~ of plan** changement de programme; **a ~ of clothes** des vêtements de rechange; **a ~ for the better** un changement en mieux; **that makes a nice ~** ça change agréablement; **she needs a ~** elle a besoin de se changer les idées; **to need a ~ of air** avoir besoin de changer d'air; **for a ~** pour changer
2 (cash) monnaie *f*; **small ~** petite monnaie; **she gave me 10 euros ~** elle m'a rendu 10 euros; **have you got ~ for 50 euros?**

⚷ mot clé

pouvez-vous me changer un billet de 50 euros?
B *vt* **1** (alter) changer; (in part) modifier; **to ~ sb/sth into** transformer qn/qch en; **to ~ one's mind** changer d'avis; **to ~ one's mind about doing** abandonner l'idée de faire; **to ~ colour** changer de couleur
2 changer de ‹*clothes, name, car, job, TV channel*›; (in shop) échanger ‹*item*› (**for** pour); **to ~ places** (seats) changer de place (**with** avec)
3 changer ‹*battery, tyre*›; **to ~ a bed** changer les draps
4 changer ‹*cheque, currency*› (**into, for** en)
C *vi* **1** ‹*situation, person*› changer; ‹*wind*› tourner; **the lights ~d from red to amber** les feux sont passés du rouge à l'orange
2 (into different clothes) se changer; **to ~ into** passer ‹*garment*›; **to ~ out of** ôter, enlever ‹*garment*›
3 (from bus, train) changer
D changed *pp adj* ‹*man, woman*› autre *before n*
▪ **change round** déplacer ‹*large objects*›; changer [qn/qch] de place ‹*workers, objects, words*›

changeable /'tʃeɪndʒəbl/ *adj* ‹*condition, weather*› changeant/-e; ‹*price*› variable

changeover /'tʃeɪndʒəʊvə(r)/ *n* passage *m* (**to** à)

changing /'tʃeɪndʒɪŋ/ *adj* ‹*colours, environment*› changeant/-e; ‹*attitude, world*› en évolution

changing room *n* (at sports centre) vestiaire *m*; (AmE) (in shop) cabine *f* d'essayage

🔑 **channel** /'tʃænl/ **A** *n* **1** (TV station) chaîne *f*; (radio band) canal *m*
2 (groove) rainure *f*
3 (in sea, river) chenal *m*
4 through the proper ~s par la voie normale; **to go through official ~s** passer par la voie officielle
B *vt* (*p prés etc* **-ll-** (BrE), **-l-** (AmE)) canaliser (**to, into** dans)

Channel /'tʃænl/ *pr n* **the (English) ~** la Manche

channel ferry *n* ferry *m* trans-Manche

channel-hop *vi* (*p prés etc* **-pp-**) zapper (fam)

Channel Islands *pr n pl* îles *fpl* Anglo-Normandes

Channel Tunnel *pr n* tunnel *m* sous la Manche

chant /tʃɑːnt, (AmE) tʃænt/ **A** *n* **1** (of crowd) chant *m* scandé
2 (of devotees) mélopée *f*
B *vi* ‹*crowd*› scander des slogans; ‹*choir, monks*› psalmodier

chaos /'keɪɒs/ *n* (gen) pagaille *f* (fam); (economic, cosmic) chaos *m*; **in a state of ~** ‹*house*› sens dessus dessous; ‹*country*› en plein chaos

chaotic /keɪ'ɒtɪk/ *adj* désordonné/-e

chap /tʃæp/ **A** *n* (BrE) (fam) type *m* (fam)
B *vt* (*p prés etc* **-pp-**) gercer; **~ped lips** lèvres *fpl* gercées

chapel /'tʃæpl/ *n* chapelle *f*

chaperone /'ʃæpərəʊn/ **A** *n* chaperon *m*
B *vt* chaperonner

chaplain /'tʃæplɪn/ *n* aumônier *m*

🔑 **chapter** /'tʃæptə(r)/ *n* chapitre *m*; **in ~ 3** au chapitre 3

🔑 **character** /'kærəktə(r)/ *n* **1** (gen) caractère *m*
2 (in book, play, film) personnage *m* (**from** de)
3 a real ~ un sacré numéro (fam); **a local ~** une figure locale

characteristic /ˌkærəktə'rɪstɪk/ **A** *n* (gen) caractéristique *f*; (of person) trait *m* de caractère
B *adj* caractéristique (**of** de)

characterize /'kærəktəraɪz/ *vt* **1** (depict) dépeindre (**as** comme)
2 (typify) caractériser; **to be ~d by** se caractériser par

character reference *n* références *fpl*

charade /ʃə'rɑːd, (AmE) ʃə'reɪd/ *n* comédie *f*

charades *npl* (game) charades *fpl*

charcoal /'tʃɑːkəʊl/ **A** *n* **1** (fuel) charbon *m* de bois
2 (for drawing) fusain *m*
B *adj* (*also* **~ grey**) (gris) anthracite *inv*

🔑 **charge** /tʃɑːdʒ/ **A** *n* **1** (fee) frais *mpl*; **additional** *or* **extra ~** supplément *m*; **to reverse the ~s** (on phone) appeler en PCV
2 (accusation) accusation *f* (**of** de); (Law) inculpation *f*; **murder ~** inculpation d'assassinat; **to press ~s against sb** engager des poursuites contre qch
3 (attack) charge *f* (**against** contre)
4 to be in ~ (gen) être responsable (**of** de); (Mil) commander; **the person in ~** le/la responsable; **to take ~** prendre les choses en main
5 (child) enfant *mf* dont on s'occupe; (pupil) élève *mf*; (patient) malade *mf*
6 (explosive, electrical) charge *f*
B *vt* **1** prélever ‹*commission*›; percevoir ‹*interest*› (**on** sur); **to ~ sb for sth** faire payer qch à qn; **how much do you ~?** vous prenez combien?; **I ~ £20 an hour** je prends 20 livres sterling de l'heure
2 to ~ sth to mettre qch sur ‹*account*›
3 ‹*police*› inculper ‹*suspect*› (**with** de)
4 (rush at) charger ‹*enemy*›; ‹*bull*› foncer sur ‹*person*›
5 charger ‹*battery*›
C *vi* **to ~ into/out of** se précipiter dans/de ‹*room*›

charge account *n* (AmE) compte-client *m*

charge card *n* (credit card) carte *f* de crédit; (store card) carte *f* d'achat

char-grilled *adj* ‹*steak*› grillé/-e au charbon de bois

charisma /kə'rɪzmə/ *n* charisme *m*

charismatic /ˌkærɪz'mætɪk/ *adj* charismatique

C

charitable /'tʃærɪtəbl/ *adj ‹person, act, explanation›* charitable (**to** envers); *‹organization›* caritatif/-ive

charity /'tʃærətɪ/ *n* **1** (virtue) charité *f*
2 (organization) organisation *f* caritative; **to give to/collect money for ~** donner à/collecter des fonds pour des œuvres de bienfaisance

charity shop *n* magasin *m* d'articles d'occasion (*vendus au profit d'une œuvre de bienfaisance*)

charity work *n* travail *m* bénévole (*au profit d'une œuvre de bienfaisance*)

charm /tʃɑːm/ *n* **1** charme *m*
2 lucky ~ porte-bonheur *m inv*

charming /'tʃɑːmɪŋ/ *adj ‹person, place›* charmant/-e; *‹child, animal›* adorable

charred *adj* carbonisé/-e

chart /tʃɑːt/ **A** *n* **1** (graph) graphique *m*
2 (table) tableau *m*
3 (map) carte *f*
4 the ~s le hit-parade
B *vt* **1** (on map) tracer *‹route›*
2 enregistrer *‹progress›*

charter /'tʃɑːtə(r)/ **A** *n* charte *f*
B *vt* affréter *‹plane›*

chartered accountant, CA *n* (BrE) ≈ expert-comptable *m*

charter flight *n* (BrE) vol *m* charter

chase /tʃeɪs/ **A** *n* poursuite *f* (**after** de)
B *vt* **1** pourchasser *‹person, animal›*; **to ~ sb/sth up** *or* **down the street** courir après qn/qch dans la rue
2 (*also* **~ after**) courir après *‹woman, man, success›*
▪ **chase away, chase off** chasser *‹person, animal›*

chassis /'ʃæsɪ/ *n* (*pl* **~**) châssis *m*

chastity /'tʃæstətɪ/ *n* chasteté *f*

chat /tʃæt/ **A** *n* conversation *f*; **to have a ~** bavarder (**with** avec, **about** sur)
B *vi* (*p prés etc* **-tt-**) bavarder (**with, to** avec)
▪ **chat up** (BrE) (fam) draguer (fam)

chatline *n* réseau *m* téléphonique; (sexual) ≈ téléphone *m* rose

chat room *n* site *m* de bavardage, salon *m* virtuel

chat show *n* (BrE) talk-show *m*

chatter /'tʃætə(r)/ **A** *n* (of person) bavardage *m*; (of birds) gazouillis *m*
B *vi ‹person›* bavarder; *‹birds›* gazouiller; **her teeth were ~ing** elle claquait des dents

chatterbox *n* moulin *m* à paroles (fam)

chatty /'tʃætɪ/ *adj ‹person›* ouvert/-e; *‹letter›* vivant/-e

chauffeur /'ʃəʊfə(r), (AmE) ʃəʊ'fɜːr/ **A** *n* chauffeur *m*; **a ~-driven car** une voiture avec chauffeur
B *vt* conduire

chauvinist /'ʃəʊvɪnɪst/ *n, adj* **1** (gen) chauvin/-e *m/f*
2 (*also* **male ~**) macho *m* (fam)

⚷ **cheap** /tʃiːp/ *adj* **1** bon marché *inv*; **to be ~** être bon marché, ne pas coûter cher *inv*; **~er** moins cher/-ère
2 (shoddy) de mauvaise qualité
3 *‹joke›* facile; *‹trick›* sale *before n*

cheapen /'tʃiːpən/ *vt* rabaisser

cheaply /'tʃiːplɪ/ *adv ‹produce, sell›* à bas prix; **to eat ~** manger pour pas cher

cheap rate *adj, adv* à tarif réduit

cheat /tʃiːt/ **A** *n* tricheur/-euse *m/f*
B *vt* tromper; **to feel ~ed** se sentir lésé/-e; **to ~ sb (out) of** dépouiller qn de
C *vi* tricher (**in** à); **to ~ at cards** tricher aux cartes; **to ~ on sb** tromper qn

Chechnya /ˌtʃetʃ'njɑː/ *pr n* Tchétchénie *f*

⚷ **check** /tʃek/ **A** *n* **1** (for quality, security) contrôle *m* (**on** sur)
2 (medical) examen *m*
3 (restraint) frein *m* (**on** à)
4 (in chess) **~!** échec au roi!; **in ~** en échec
5 (*also* **~ fabric**) tissu *m* à carreaux (*also* **~ pattern**) carreaux *mpl*
6 (AmE) (cheque) chèque *m*
7 (AmE) (bill) addition *f*
8 (AmE) (receipt) ticket *m*
9 (AmE) (tick) croix *f*
B *adj ‹shirt, skirt›* à carreaux
C *vt* **1** (gen) vérifier; contrôler *‹ticket, area, work›*; prendre *‹temperature›*; examiner *‹watch, map, pocket›*
2 (curb) contrôler *‹prices, inflation›*; freiner *‹growth›*; maîtriser *‹emotions›*
D *vi* **1** vérifier; **to ~ with sb** demander à qn; **to ~ for** dépister *‹problems›*; chercher *‹leaks, flaws›*
2 to ~ into arriver à *‹hotel›*
▪ **check in**: **A ~ in** (at airport) enregistrer; (at hotel) arriver (**at** à)
B ~ [sb/sth] in enregistrer *‹baggage, passengers›*
▪ **check off** cocher *‹items›*
▪ **check out**: **A ~ out** (leave) partir; **to ~ out of** quitter *‹hotel›*
B ~ [sth] out vérifier *‹information›*; examiner *‹package, building›*; se renseigner sur *‹club, scheme›*
▪ **check up on** faire une enquête sur *‹person›*; vérifier *‹story, details›*

checkbook *n* (AmE) = **chequebook**

checkered (AmE) = **chequered**

checkers (AmE) = **chequers**

check-in /'tʃekɪn/ *n* enregistrement *m*

checking account *n* (AmE) compte *m* courant

checklist *n* liste *f* de contrôle

checkmate /'tʃekmeɪt/ *n* échec *m* et mat

checkout /'tʃekaʊt/ *n* caisse *f*

checkout assistant *n* caissier/-ière *m/f*

⚷ mot clé

checkpoint /'tʃekpɔɪnt/ *n* poste *m* de contrôle

checkroom /'tʃekru:m, -rʊm/ *n* (AmE) (cloakroom) vestiaire *m*; (for baggage) consigne *f*

check-up /'tʃekʌp/ *n* **1** (at doctor's) examen *m* médical, bilan *m* de santé; **to have a ~** passer *or* se faire faire un examen médical
2 (at dentist's) visite *f* de routine

cheek /tʃi:k/ *n* **1** (of face) joue *f*; **~ to ~** joue contre joue
2 culot *m* (fam); **what a ~!** quel culot!

cheekbone *n* pommette *f*

cheeky /'tʃi:kɪ/ *adj* ‹*person*› effronté/-e, insolent/-e; ‹*question*› impoli/-e; ‹*grin*› espiègle, coquin/-e

cheer /tʃɪə(r)/ **A** *n* acclamation *f*; **to get a ~** être acclamé/-e
B **cheers** *excl* **1** (toast) à la vôtre! (fam); (to close friend) à la tienne! (fam)
2 (BrE) (fam) (thanks) merci!
3 (BrE) (fam) (goodbye) salut!
C *vt, vi* applaudir

■ **cheer up**: **A** **~ up** reprendre courage; **~ up!** courage!
B **~ [sb] up** remonter le moral à ‹*person*›
C **~ [sth] up** égayer ‹*room*›

cheerful /'tʃɪəfl/ *adj* ‹*person, mood, music*› joyeux/-euse; ‹*tone*› enjoué/-e; ‹*colour*› gai/-e

cheerleader *n* majorette *f*

cheese /tʃi:z/ *n* fromage *m*; **~ sandwich** sandwich *m* au fromage

cheeseboard *n* (object) plateau *m* à fromage; (selection) plateau *m* de fromages

cheetah /'tʃi:tə/ *n* guépard *m*

chef /ʃef/ *n* chef *m* cuisinier

chemical /'kemɪkl/ **A** *n* produit *m* chimique
B *adj* chimique

chemist /'kemɪst/ *n* **1** (BrE) pharmacien/-ienne *m/f*; **~'s (shop)** pharmacie *f*
2 (scientist) chimiste *mf*

chemistry /'kemɪstrɪ/ *n* chimie *f*

chemotherapy /ˌki:məʊ'θerəpɪ/ *n* chimiothérapie *f*

cheque (BrE), **check** (AmE) /tʃek/ *n* chèque *m*; **to make out** *or* **write a ~ for £20** faire un chèque de 20 livres sterling

chequebook (BrE), **checkbook** (AmE) *n* chéquier *m*, carnet *m* de chèques

cheque card *n* (BrE) carte *f* de garantie bancaire

chequered (BrE), **checkered** (AmE) /'tʃekəd/ *adj* **1** ‹*cloth*› à damiers
2 ‹*career, history*› en dents de scie

chequers (BrE), **checkers** (AmE) /'tʃekəz/ *n* jeu *m* de dames

cherish /'tʃerɪʃ/ *vt* caresser ‹*hope*›; chérir ‹*memory, person*›

cherry /'tʃerɪ/ **A** *n* **1** (fruit) cerise *f*
2 (*also* **~ tree**) cerisier *m*
B *adj* (*also* **~-red**) rouge cerise *inv*

chess /tʃes/ *n* échecs *mpl*; **a game of ~** une partie d'échecs

chessboard *n* échiquier *m*

chess set *n* jeu *m* d'échecs

chest /tʃest/ *n* **1** (of person) poitrine *f*; **~ measurement** tour *m* de poitrine
2 (furniture) coffre *m*; **~ of drawers** commode *f*
3 (crate) caisse *f*
IDIOM **to get something off one's ~** (fam) vider son sac (fam)

chestnut /'tʃesnʌt/ **A** *n* **1** (nut) marron *m*, châtaigne *f*
2 (*also* **~ tree**) (horse ~) marronnier *m* (d'Inde); (sweet ~) châtaignier *m*
B *adj* ‹*hair*› châtain *inv*; **a ~ horse** un (cheval) alezan

chew /tʃu:/ *vt* mâcher ‹*food, gum*›; mordiller ‹*pencil*›; ronger ‹*bone*›

chewing gum *n* chewing-gum *m*

chewy /'tʃu:ɪ/ *adj* difficile à mâcher

chick /tʃɪk/ *n* (fledgling) oisillon *m*; (of fowl) poussin *m*

chicken /'tʃɪkɪn/ *n* **1** (fowl) poulet *m*, poule *f*
2 (meat) poulet *m*
3 (fam) (coward) poule *f* mouillée

■ **chicken out** (fam) se dégonfler (fam)

chicken pox *n* varicelle *f*

chicken wire *n* grillage *m* (à mailles fines)

chickpea *n* pois *m* chiche

chicory /'tʃɪkərɪ/ *n* **1** (vegetable) endive *f*
2 (in coffee) chicorée *f*

chief /tʃi:f/ **A** *n* chef *m*
B *adj* **1** ‹*reason*› principal/-e
2 ‹*editor*› en chef

chief executive *n* directeur *m* général

chiefly /'tʃi:flɪ/ *adv* notamment, surtout

chief of police *n* ≈ préfet *m* de police

Chief of Staff *n* (Mil) chef *m* d'état-major; (of White House) secrétaire *m* général

chiffon /'ʃɪfɒn, (AmE) ʃɪ'fɒn/ *n* mousseline *f*

chilblain /'tʃɪlbleɪn/ *n* engelure *f*

child /tʃaɪld/ *n* (*pl* **children**) enfant *mf*; **when I was a ~** quand j'étais enfant

child abuse *n* mauvais traitements *mpl* infligés à un enfant; (sexual) sévices *mpl* sexuels exercés sur l'enfant

childbirth /'tʃaɪldbɜ:θ/ *n* accouchement *m*

childcare *n* (nurseries etc) structures *fpl* d'accueil pour les enfants d'âge préscolaire; (bringing up children) éducation *f* des enfants

childcare facilities *npl* crèche *f*

childhood /'tʃaɪldhʊd/ **A** *n* enfance *f*; **in (his) early ~** dans sa prime enfance
B *adj* ‹*friend, memory*› d'enfance; ‹*illness*› infantile

childish /'tʃaɪldɪʃ/ *adj* puéril/-e

childless /'tʃaɪldlɪs/ *adj* sans enfants

childlike /'tʃaɪldlaɪk/ *adj* enfantin/-e

childminder *n* (BrE) nourrice *f*

C

child pornography *n* pédopornographie *f*
children's home *n* maison *f* d'enfants
Chile /'tʃɪlɪ/ *pr n* Chili *m*
chill /tʃɪl/ **A** *n* **1** (coldness) fraîcheur *f*; **there is a ~ in the air** le fond de l'air est frais; **to send a ~ down sb's spine** donner des frissons à qn
2 (illness) coup *m* de froid
B *adj* **1** ‹*wind*› frais/fraîche
2 ‹*reminder, words*› brutal/-e
C *vt* **1** mettre [qch] à refroidir ‹*dessert, soup*›; rafraîchir ‹*wine*›
2 (make cold) faire frissonner ‹*person*›; **to ~ sb's** *or* **the blood** glacer le sang à qn
D *vi* ‹*dessert*› refroidir; ‹*wine*› rafraîchir
■ **chill out** (fam) décompresser (fam); **~ out!** laisse faire!
chilled /tʃɪld/ *adj* **1** (of food or drink) frais/fraîche; **a glass of ~ white wine** un verre de vin blanc servi bien frais
2 (fam) (very relaxed) décontracté, relax (fam); **by Sunday evening I'm usually feeling pretty ~** d'habitude, quand vient le dimanche soir, je me sens plutôt relax
chilli, chili /'tʃɪlɪ/ *n* **1** (*also* **~ pepper**) piment *m* rouge
2 (*also* **~ powder**) chili *m*
3 (*also* **~ con carne**) chili *m* con carne
chilly /'tʃɪlɪ/ *adj* froid/-e; **it's ~** il fait froid
chime /tʃaɪm/ *n* carillon *m*
chimney /'tʃɪmnɪ/ *n* (*pl* **-neys**) cheminée *f*
chimpanzee /ˌtʃɪmpən'ziː, ˌtʃɪmpæn'ziː/ *n* chimpanzé *m*
chin /tʃɪn/ *n* menton *m*
china /'tʃaɪnə/ **A** *n* porcelaine *f*
B *adj* ‹*cup, plate*› en porcelaine
China /'tʃaɪnə/ *pr n* Chine *f*
⚷ **Chinese** /tʃaɪ'niːz/ **A** *n* **1** (person) Chinois/-oise *m/f*
2 (language) chinois *m*
B *adj* chinois/-oise; ‹*embassy*› de Chine
chink /tʃɪŋk/ *n* **1** (in wall) fente *f*; (in curtain) entrebâillement *m*
2 (sound) tintement *m*
chip /tʃɪp/ **A** *n* **1** (fragment) fragment *m* (**of** de); (of wood) copeau *m*; (of glass) éclat *m*
2 (in wood, china) ébréchure *f*
3 (microchip) puce *f* (électronique)
B chips *npl* **1** (BrE) (fried potatoes) frites *fpl*
2 (AmE) (crisps) chips *fpl*
C *vt* (*p prés etc* **-pp-**) ébrécher ‹*glass, plate*›; écailler ‹*paint*›; **to ~ a tooth** se casser une dent
(**IDIOM**) **to have a ~ on one's shoulder** être amer/-ère
■ **chip in** (BrE) (fam) (financially) donner un peu d'argent
chipboard *n* aggloméré *m*
chip shop *n* marchand *m* de frites
chiropodist /kɪ'rɒpədɪst/ *n* pédicure *mf*

⚷ mot clé

chiropractor /'kaɪərəʊpræktə(r)/ *n* chiropraticien/-ienne *m/f*, chiropracteur *m*
chirp /tʃɜːp/ *vi* ‹*bird*› pépier
chisel /'tʃɪzl/ **A** *n* ciseau *m*
B *vt* (*p prés etc* **-ll-** (BrE), **-l-** (AmE)) ciseler
chitchat /'tʃɪttʃæt/ *n* (fam) bavardage *m*
chivalry /'ʃɪvəlrɪ/ *n* **1** chevalerie *f*
2 (courtesy) galanterie *f*
chive /tʃaɪv/ *n* ciboulette *f*
chlorine /'klɔːriːn/ *n* chlore *m*
choc ice *n* (BrE) esquimau *m*
chock-a-block /ˌtʃɒkə'blɒk/ *adj* plein/-e à craquer
chocolate /'tʃɒklət/ **A** *n* chocolat *m*
B *adj* ‹*sweets*› en chocolat; ‹*biscuit, cake, ice cream*› au chocolat
⚷ **choice** /tʃɔɪs/ *n* choix *m* (**between, of** entre); **to make a ~** faire un choix, choisir; **to be spoilt for ~** avoir l'embarras du choix; **out of** *or* **from ~** par choix
choir /'kwaɪə(r)/ *n* (of church, school) chorale *f*; (professional) chœur *m*
choirboy *n* petit chanteur *m*, jeune choriste *m*
choke /tʃəʊk/ **A** *n* (Aut) starter *m*
B *vt* **1** (throttle) étrangler ‹*person*›
2 ‹*fumes, smoke*› étouffer
C *vi* s'étouffer
■ **choke back** étouffer ‹*cough, sob*›; **to ~ back one's tears** retenir ses larmes
cholera /'kɒlərə/ *n* choléra *m*
cholesterol /kə'lestərɒl/ *n* cholestérol *m*
⚷ **choose** /tʃuːz/ **A** *vt* (*prét* **chose**, *pp* **chosen**) **1** (select) choisir (**from** parmi)
2 (decide) décider (**to do** de faire)
B *vi* (*prét* **chose**, *pp* **chosen**) **1** (select) choisir (**between** entre)
2 (prefer) **to ~ to do** préférer faire
choosy /'tʃuːzɪ/ *adj* difficile (**about** en ce qui concerne)
chop /tʃɒp/ **A** *n* (Culin) côtelette *f*; **pork ~** côtelette de porc
B *vt* (*p prés etc* **-pp-**) **1** (*also* **~ up**) couper ‹*wood*›; couper, émincer ‹*vegetable, meat*›; hacher ‹*parsley, onion*›; **to ~ sth finely** hacher qch
2 réduire ‹*service, deficit*›
(**IDIOM**) **to ~ and change** ‹*person*› changer d'avis comme de chemise
■ **chop down** abattre ‹*tree*›
■ **chop off** couper ‹*branch, end*›; trancher ‹*head, hand, finger*›
chopping board *n* planche *f* à découper
chopping knife *n* couteau *m* de cuisine
choppy /'tʃɒpɪ/ *adj* ‹*sea, water*› agité/-e
chopstick *n* baguette *f* (chinoise)
chord /kɔːd/ *n* accord *m*
chore /tʃɔː(r)/ *n* tâche *f*; **to do the ~s** faire le ménage
choreograph /'kɒrɪəgrɑːf, -græf, (AmE) -græf/ *vt* chorégraphier

chorus /ˈkɔːrəs/ *n* **1** (singers) chœur *m*
2 (piece of music) chœur *m*
3 (refrain) refrain *m*

Christ /kraɪst/ *pr n* le Christ, Jésus-Christ

christen /ˈkrɪsn/ *vt* baptiser

christening /ˈkrɪsnɪŋ/ *n* baptême *m*

Christian /ˈkrɪstʃən/ **A** *n* chrétien/-ienne *m/f*
B *adj* chrétien/-ienne; ‹*attitude*› charitable

Christianity /ˌkrɪstɪˈænətɪ/ *n* christianisme *m*

Christian name *n* nom *m* de baptême

Christmas /ˈkrɪsməs/ *n* ~ **(day)** (jour *m* de) Noël; **at ~** à Noël; **Merry ~!, Happy ~!** Joyeux Noël!

Christmas card *n* carte *f* de Noël

Christmas eve *n* veille *f* de Noël

Christmas tree *n* sapin *m* de Noël

chrome /krəʊm/ *n* chrome *m*

chronic /ˈkrɒnɪk/ *adj* **1** ‹*illness*› chronique
2 ‹*liar*› invétéré/-e; ‹*problem, shortage*› chronique

chronicle /ˈkrɒnɪkl/ *n* chronique *f*

chronological /ˌkrɒnəˈlɒdʒɪkl/ *adj* chronologique

chubby /ˈtʃʌbɪ/ *adj* ‹*child, finger*› potelé/-e; ‹*cheek*› rebondi/-e; ‹*face*› joufflu/-e; ‹*adult*› rondelet/-ette

chuck /tʃʌk/ *vt* (fam) **1** (*also* ~ **away**) balancer (fam), jeter
2 larguer (fam) ‹*boyfriend, girlfriend*›

chuckle /ˈtʃʌkl/ *vi* glousser; **to ~ at sth** rire de qch

chuffed /tʃʌft/ *adj* (BrE) (fam) vachement (fam) content/-e (**about, at, with** de)

chum /tʃʌm/ *n* (fam) copain/copine *m/f* (fam), pote *m* (fam)

chunk /tʃʌŋk/ *n* **1** (of meat, fruit) morceau *m*; (of wood) tronçon *m*; (of bread) quignon *m*; **pineapple ~s** ananas *m* en morceaux
2 (of population, text, day) partie *f* (**of** de)

church /tʃɜːtʃ/ **A** *n* (*pl* **~es**) (Catholic, Anglican) église *f*; (Protestant) temple *m*
B *adj* ‹*bell, choir, steeple*› d'église; ‹*fête*› paroissial/-e; ‹*wedding*› religieux/-ieuse

churchgoer *n* pratiquant/-e *m/f*

church hall *n* salle *f* paroissiale

churchyard *n* cimetière *m*

churn /tʃɜːn/ **A** *n* **1** (for butter) baratte *f*
2 (BrE) (for milk) bidon *m*
B *vt* **to ~ butter** baratter
■ **churn out** pondre [qch] en série ‹*novels*›; produire [qch] en série ‹*goods*›
■ **churn up** faire des remous dans ‹*water*›

chute /ʃuːt/ *n* **1** (slide) toboggan *m*
2 (for rubbish) vide-ordures *m inv*
3 (for toboggan) piste *f* de toboggan

cicada /sɪˈkɑːdə, (AmE) -ˈkeɪdə/ *n* cigale *f*

cider /ˈsaɪdə(r)/ *n* cidre *m*

cigar /sɪˈgɑː(r)/ *n* cigare *m*

cigarette /ˌsɪgəˈret, (AmE) ˈsɪgərət/ **A** *n* cigarette *f*
B *adj* ‹*ash, smoke*› de cigarette; ‹*case, paper*› à cigarettes

cigarette lighter *n* (portable) briquet *m*; (in car) allume-cigares *m inv*

cinder /ˈsɪndə(r)/ *n* (glowing) braise *f*; (ash) cendre *f*

Cinderella /ˌsɪndəˈrelə/ *pr n* Cendrillon

cine camera *n* caméra *f* (d'amateur)

cine film *n* pellicule *f* cinématographique

cinema /ˈsɪnəmɑː, ˈsɪnəmə/ *n* cinéma *m*

cinemagoer *n* (regular) cinéphile *mf*, amateur *m* de cinéma; (spectator) spectacteur/-trice *m/f*

cinnamon /ˈsɪnəmən/ *n* cannelle *f*

circle /ˈsɜːkl/ **A** *n* **1** (gen) cercle *m*; **to go round in ~s** tourner en rond; **to have ~s under one's eyes** avoir les yeux cernés
2 (in theatre) balcon *m*; **in the ~** au balcon
B *vt* **1** ‹*plane*› tourner autour de ‹*airport*›; ‹*person, animal, vehicle*› faire le tour de ‹*building*›; tourner autour de ‹*person, animal*›
2 (surround) encercler
C *vi* tourner en rond (**around** autour de)

circuit /ˈsɜːkɪt/ *n* **1** (gen) circuit *m*
2 (lap) tour *m*

circuit breaker *n* disjoncteur *m*

circular /ˈsɜːkjʊlə(r)/ **A** *n* (newsletter) circulaire *f*; (advertisement) prospectus *m*
B *adj* ‹*object*› rond/-e; ‹*argument*› circulaire

circulate /ˈsɜːkjʊleɪt/ **A** *vt* faire circuler
B *vi* **1** (gen) circuler
2 (at party) **let's ~** on va aller faire connaissance

circulation /ˌsɜːkjʊˈleɪʃn/ *n* **1** (gen) circulation *f*
2 (of newspaper) tirage *m*

circulation figures *npl* chiffres *mpl* de tirage

circumcision /ˌsɜːkəmˈsɪʒn/ *n* (of boy) circoncision *f*; (of girl) excision *f*

circumference /səˈkʌmfərəns/ *n* circonférence *f*

circumflex /ˈsɜːkəmfleks/ *n* accent *m* circonflexe

circumstances *npl* **1** circonstances *fpl*; **in** *or* **under the ~** dans ces circonstances; **under no ~** en aucun cas
2 (financial position) situation *f*

circumstantial /ˌsɜːkəmˈstænʃl/ *adj* ‹*evidence*› indirect/-e

circus /ˈsɜːkəs/ *n* cirque *m*

CIS *pr n* (*abbr* = **Commonwealth of Independent States**) CEI *f*

cistern /ˈsɪstən/ *n* (of lavatory) réservoir *m* de chasse d'eau; (in loft or underground) citerne *f*

citizen /ˈsɪtɪzn/ *n* **1** (of state) citoyen/-enne *m/f*; (when abroad) ressortissant/-e *m/f*
2 (of town) habitant/-e *m/f*

citizenship /ˈsɪtɪznʃɪp/ *n* nationalité *f*

C

citrus fruit *n* agrume *m*

🔑 **city** /'sɪtɪ/ *n* (grande) ville *f*; **the City** (BrE) la City

city centre (BrE), **city center** (AmE) *n* centre-ville *m*

civic /'sɪvɪk/ *adj* ‹*administration, official*› municipal/-e; ‹*pride, responsibility*› civique

civic centre (BrE), **civic center** (AmE) *n* centre *m* municipal (culturel et administratif)

🔑 **civil** /'sɪvl/ *adj* **1** ‹*case, court, offence*› civil/-e **2** (polite) courtois/-e

civil engineering *n* génie *m* civil

civilian /sɪ'vɪlɪən/ *n* civil/-e *m/f*

civilization /ˌsɪvəlaɪ'zeɪʃn, (AmE) -əlɪ'z-/ *n* civilisation *f*

civilized /'sɪvəlaɪzd/ *adj* civilisé/-e

civil law *n* droit *m* civil

civil liberty *n* libertés *fpl* individuelles

civil partner *n* partenaire *mf* civil/-e, pacsé/-e *mf*

civil partnership *n* union *f* civile (*entre partenaires de même sexe*)

civil rights *npl* droits *mpl* civils

civil servant *n* fonctionnaire *mf*

civil service *n* fonction *f* publique

civil war *n* guerre *f* civile

🔑 **claim** /kleɪm/ **A** *n* **1** (demand) revendication *f*
2 (in insurance) (against a person) réclamation *f*; (for fire, theft) demande *f* d'indemnisation
3 (for welfare benefit) demande *f* d'allocation
4 (assertion) affirmation *f*
B *vt* **1** (maintain) prétendre
2 revendiquer ‹*money, property, responsibility, right*›
3 faire une demande de ‹*benefit*›; faire une demande de remboursement de ‹*expenses*›
C *vi* **1 to ∼ for damages** faire une demande pour dommages et intérêts
2 (apply for benefit) faire une demande d'allocation

claimant /'kleɪmənt/ *n* **1** (for benefit, compensation) demandeur/-euse *m/f* (**to** à)
2 (to title, estate) prétendant/-e *m/f* (**to** à)

claim form *n* déclaration *f* de sinistre

clairvoyant /kleə'vɔɪənt/ *n* voyant/-e *m/f*, extralucide *mf*

clam /klæm/ *n* palourde *f*

■ **clam up** ne plus piper mot (**on sb** à qn)

clammy /'klæmɪ/ *adj* moite

clamour (BrE), **clamor** (AmE) /'klæmə(r)/
A *n* (shouting) clameur *f*
B *vi* **1** (demand) **to ∼ for sth** réclamer qch; **to ∼ for sb to do** réclamer à qn de faire
2 (rush, fight) se bousculer (**for** pour avoir, **to do** pour faire)

clamp /klæmp/ **A** *n* **1** (on bench) valet *m*
2 (*also* **wheel∼**) sabot *m* de Denver
B *vt* **1** cramponner ‹*two parts*›; (at bench) fixer [qch] à l'aide d'un valet (**onto** à)
2 serrer ‹*jaw, teeth*›
3 (*also* **wheel∼**) mettre un sabot de Denver à ‹*car*›

■ **clamp down**: **∼ down on** faire de la répression contre ‹*crime*›; mettre un frein à ‹*extravagance*›

clampdown *n* mesures *fpl* de répression (**on sb** contre qn, **on sth** de qch)

clan /klæn/ *n* clan *m*

clandestine /klæn'destɪn/ *adj* clandestin/-e

clang /'klæŋ/ **A** *n* fracas *m*, bruit *m* métallique
B *vi* ‹*gate*› claquer avec un son métallique; ‹*bell*› retentir

clap /klæp/ **A** *n* **to give sb a ∼** applaudir qn; **a ∼ of thunder** un coup de tonnerre
B *vt* (*p prés etc* **-pp-**) **to ∼ one's hands** battre *or* taper des mains, frapper dans ses mains
C *vi* (*p prés etc* **-pp-**) applaudir

clapping /'klæpɪŋ/ *n* applaudissements *mpl*

claret /'klærət/ *n* **1** (wine) bordeaux *m* (rouge)
2 (colour) bordeaux *m*

clarification /ˌklærɪfɪ'keɪʃn/ *n* éclaircissement *m*, clarification *f*

clarify /'klærɪfaɪ/ *vt* éclaircir, clarifier

clarinet /ˌklærə'net/ *n* clarinette *f*

clarity /'klærətɪ/ *n* clarté *f*

clash /klæʃ/ **A** *n* **1** (confrontation) affrontement *m*
2 (of cultures, interests, personalities) conflit *m*
3 a ∼ of cymbals un coup de cymbales
B *vt* entrechoquer ‹*bin lids*›; frapper ‹*cymbals*›
C *vi* **1** (fight, disagree) s'affronter; **to ∼ with sb** (fight) se heurter à qn; (disagree) se quereller avec qn (**on, over** au sujet de)
2 (be in conflict) ‹*interests, beliefs*› être incompatibles
3 (coincide) ‹*meetings*› avoir lieu en même temps (**with** que)
4 ‹*colours*› jurer

clasp /klɑːsp, (AmE) klæsp/ *n* (on bracelet, bag, purse) fermoir *m*; (on belt) boucle *f*

🔑 **class** /klɑːs, (AmE) klæs/ **A** *n* (gen) classe *f*; (lesson) cours *m* (**in** de); **to be in a ∼ of one's own** être hors catégorie; **to travel first/second ∼** voyager en première/deuxième classe **first/second ∼ degree** ≈ licence *f* avec mention très bien/bien
B *vt* classer

class conscious *adj* soucieux/-ieuse des distinctions sociales

classic /'klæsɪk/ *n*, *adj* classique *m*

classical /'klæsɪkl/ *adj* classique

classics /'klæsɪks/ *n* lettres *fpl* classiques

classification /ˌklæsɪfɪ'keɪʃn/ *n* **1** (category) classification *f*, catégorie *f*
2 (categorization) classement *m*

classified /'klæsɪfaɪd/ **A** *n* (*also* **∼ ad**) petite annonce *f*

🔑 mot clé

B *adj* (secret) confidentiel/-ielle

classify /ˈklæsɪfaɪ/ *vt* **1** (file) classer
2 (declare secret) classer [qch] confidentiel/-ielle

classmate *n* camarade *mf* de classe

classroom *n* salle *f* de classe

classroom assistant *n* aide-éducateur/-trice *m/f*

class system *n* système *m* de classes

classy /ˈklɑːsɪ, (AmE) ˈklæsɪ/ *adj* (fam) ‹*person, dress*› qui a de la classe; ‹*car, hotel*› de luxe; ‹*actor, performance*› de grande classe

clatter /ˈklætə(r)/ **A** *n* cliquetis *m*; (loud) fracas *m*
B *vi* ‹*typewriter*› cliqueter; ‹*dishes*› s'entrechoquer

clause /klɔːz/ *n* **1** (in grammar) proposition *f*
2 (in contract, treaty) clause *f*; (in will, act of Parliament) disposition *f*

claustrophobia /ˌklɔːstrəˈfəʊbɪə/ *n* claustrophobie *f*

claw /klɔː/ *n* **1** (gen) griffe *f*; (of bird of prey) serre *f*; (of crab, lobster) pince *f*
2 (on hammer) arrache-clou *m*, pied-de-biche *m*

clay /kleɪ/ *n* argile *f*

clean /kliːn/ **A** *adj* **1** (gen) propre; ‹*air, water*› pur/-e; **my hands are ~** j'ai les mains propres; **~ and tidy** d'une propreté irréprochable; **a ~ sheet of paper** une feuille blanche
2 ‹*joke*› anodin/-e
3 ‹*reputation*› sans tache; ‹*record, licence*› vierge
4 (Sport) ‹*tackle*› sans faute; ‹*hit*› précis/-e
5 (neat) ‹*lines, profile*› pur/-e
B *vt* nettoyer; **to ~ one's teeth** se brosser les dents

■ **clean out** nettoyer [qch] à fond ‹*cupboard, room*›

■ **clean up** **A** **~ up 1** tout nettoyer
2 (wash oneself) se débarbouiller
B **~ [sth] up** nettoyer

clean-cut *adj* ‹*image, person*› soigné/-e

cleaner /ˈkliːnə(r)/ *n* **1** (woman) femme *f* de ménage; (man) agent *m* de nettoyage
2 (detergent) produit *m* de nettoyage
3 (shop) **cleaner's** pressing *m*

cleaning /ˈkliːnɪŋ/ *n* (domestic) ménage *m*; (commercial) nettoyage *m*, entretien *m*

cleaning product *n* produit *m* d'entretien

cleanliness /ˈklenlɪnɪs/ *n* propreté *f*

cleanse /klenz/ *vt* nettoyer ‹*skin, wound*›

cleanser /ˈklenzə(r)/ *n* **1** (for face) démaquillant *m*
2 (household) produit *m* d'entretien

clean-shaven /ˌkliːnˈʃeɪvn/ *adj* **he's ~** il n'a ni barbe ni moustache

clear /klɪə(r)/ **A** *adj* **1** (transparent) ‹*glass, liquid*› transparent/-e; ‹*blue*› limpide; ‹*lens, varnish*› incolore; ‹*honey*› liquide; **~ soup** consommé *m*
2 (distinct) ‹*image, outline*› net/nette; ‹*sound, voice*› clair/-e
3 (comprehensible) ‹*description, instruction*› clair/-e; **to make sth ~ to sb** faire comprendre qch à qn; **is that ~?** est-ce que c'est clair?
4 (obvious) ‹*need, sign*› évident/-e; ‹*advantage*› net/nette *before n*; ‹*majority*› large *before n*; **it is ~ that** il est clair que
5 (not confused) ‹*idea, memory*› clair/-e; ‹*plan*› précis/-e; **to keep a ~ head** garder les idées claires
6 (empty) ‹*view*› dégagé/-e; ‹*table*› débarrassé/-e; ‹*space*› libre
7 ‹*conscience*› tranquille
8 ‹*skin*› net/nette; ‹*sky*› sans nuage; ‹*day, night*› clair/-e; **on a ~ day** par temps clair/-e
B *adv* **to jump ~ of sth** éviter qch en sautant sur le côté; **to pull sb ~ of** extraire qn de ‹*wreckage*›; **to stay** *or* **steer ~ of** éviter ‹*town centre, troublemakers*›
C *vt* **1** enlever ‹*rubbish, papers, mines*›; dégager ‹*snow*› (**from, off** de)
2 déboucher ‹*drains*›; débarrasser ‹*table, room*›; vider ‹*desk*›; évacuer ‹*area, building*›; effacer ‹*screen*›; défricher ‹*land*›; **to ~ one's throat** se racler la gorge; **to ~ a path through sth** se frayer un chemin à travers qch
3 dissiper ‹*fog, smoke*›; disperser ‹*crowd*›
4 s'acquitter de ‹*debt*›
5 ‹*bank*› compenser ‹*cheque*›
6 innocenter ‹*accused*› (**of** de); **to ~ one's name** blanchir son nom
7 approuver ‹*request*›; **to ~ sth with sb** obtenir l'accord de qn pour qch
8 franchir ‹*hurdle, wall*›
9 **to ~ customs** passer à la douane
D *vi* **1** ‹*liquid, sky*› s'éclaircir
2 ‹*smoke, fog, cloud*› se dissiper
3 ‹*air*› se purifier
4 ‹*rash*› disparaître
5 ‹*cheque*› être compensé/-e

■ **clear away**: **A** **~ away** débarrasser
B **~ [sth] away** balayer ‹*leaves*›; enlever ‹*rubbish*›; ranger ‹*papers, toys*›

■ **clear up** **A** **~ up 1** (tidy up) faire du rangement
2 ‹*weather*› s'éclaircir; ‹*infection*› disparaître
B **~ [sth] up 1** ranger ‹*mess, room, toys*›; ramasser ‹*litter*›
2 résoudre ‹*problem*›; dissiper ‹*misunderstanding*›

clearance /ˈklɪərəns/ *n* **1** (of rubbish) enlèvement *m*; **land ~** défrichement *m* du terrain
2 (permission) autorisation *f*
3 (*also* **~ sale**) liquidation *f*

clear-cut /ˌklɪəˈkʌt/ *adj* ‹*plan, division*› précis/-e; ‹*difference*› net/nette *before n*; ‹*problem, rule*› clair/-e

clear-headed *adj* lucide

clearing /ˈklɪərɪŋ/ *n* (glade) clairière *f*

C

⚷ **clearly** /ˈklɪəlɪ/ *adv* **1** ‹*speak, hear, think, write*› clairement; ‹*see*› bien; ‹*visible*› bien; ‹*labelled*› clairement
2 (obviously) manifestement

clear-out /ˈklɪəraʊt/ *n* (fam) **to have a ~** faire du rangement

cleavage /ˈkliːvɪdʒ/ *n* décolleté *m*

cleaver /ˈkliːvə(r)/ *n* fendoir *m*

clef /klef/ *n* clef *f*; **in the treble ~** en clef de fa

cleft /kleft/ *adj* ‹*chin*› marqué/-e d'un sillon; ‹*palate*› fendu/-e

clench /klentʃ/ *vt* serrer

clergy /ˈklɜːdʒɪ/ *n* clergé *m*

clergyman /ˈklɜːdʒɪmən/ *n* (*pl* **-men**) ecclésiastique *m*

clerical /ˈklerɪkl/ *adj* **1** (of clergy) clérical/-e
2 ‹*staff*› de bureau; **~ work** travail *m* de bureau

clerk /klɑːk, (AmE) klɜːrk/ *n* **1** (in office, bank) employé/-e *m/f*
2 (BrE) (to lawyer) ≈ clerc *m*; (in court) greffier/-ière *m/f*
3 (AmE) (in hotel) réceptionniste *mf*; (in shop) vendeur/-euse *m/f*

clever /ˈklevə(r)/ *adj* **1** (intelligent) intelligent/-e
2 (ingenious) ‹*solution, gadget, person*› astucieux/-ieuse, futé/-e
3 (skilful) habile, adroit/-e

cliché /ˈkliːʃeɪ, (AmE) kliːˈʃeɪ/ *n* cliché *m*, lieu *m* commun

clichéd /ˈkliːʃeɪd, (AmE) kliːˈʃeɪd/ *adj* ‹*expression*› rebattu/-e; ‹*idea, technique*› éculé/-e; ‹*art, music*› bourré/-e (fam) de clichés

click /klɪk/ **A** *n* **1** (of machine, lock) déclic *m*
2 (of fingers, heels, tongue) claquement *m*
3 (Comput) clic *m*
B *vt* **to ~ one's fingers** faire claquer ses doigts; **to ~ one's heels** claquer des talons
C *vi* ‹*camera, lock*› faire un déclic; ‹*door*› faire un petit bruit sec; **to ~ on** cliquer sur ‹*icon*›

⚷ **client** /ˈklaɪənt/ *n* client/-e *m/f*

clientele /ˌkliːɒnˈtel, (AmE) ˌklaɪənˈtel/ *n* clientèle *f*

cliff /klɪf/ *n* (by sea) falaise *f*; (inland) escarpement *m*

climate /ˈklaɪmɪt/ *n* climat *m*

climate change *n* changement *m* climatique

climatologist /ˌklaɪməˈtɒlədʒɪst/ *n* climatologue *mf*

climatology /ˌklaɪməˈtɒlədʒɪ/ *n* climatologie *f*

climax /ˈklaɪmæks/ *n* (of war, conflict) paroxysme *m*; (of plot, speech, play) point *m* culminant; (of career) apogée *m*

⚷ **climb** /klaɪm/ **A** *n* (up hill) escalade *f*; (up tower) montée *f*; (up mountain) ascension *f*
B *vt* grimper ‹*hill*›; faire l'ascension de ‹*mountain*›; escalader ‹*lamp post, wall*›; grimper à ‹*ladder, tree*›; monter ‹*staircase*›
C *vi* **1** ‹*person*› grimper; **to ~ down** descendre ‹*rock face*›; **to ~ over** enjamber ‹*stile*›; passer par-dessus ‹*fence, wall*›; escalader ‹*debris, rocks*›; **to ~ up** grimper à ‹*ladder, tree*›; monter ‹*steps*›
2 ‹*aircraft*› monter
3 ‹*road*› monter
4 (increase) monter
▪ **climb down** revenir sur sa décision

climber /ˈklaɪmə(r)/ *n* grimpeur/-euse *m/f*, alpiniste *mf*

climbing /ˈklaɪmɪŋ/ *n* escalade *f*

clinch /klɪntʃ/ *vt* **1 to ~ a deal** conclure une affaire
2 décider de ‹*argument*›

cling /klɪŋ/ *vi* (*prét, pp* **clung**) **1 to ~ (on) to sb/sth** se cramponner à qn/qch; **to ~ together** se cramponner l'un à l'autre
2 ‹*clothes*› coller (**to** à)
3 ‹*smell*› résister

cling film /ˈklɪŋfɪlm/ *n* (BrE) scellofrais® *m*

clinic /ˈklɪnɪk/ *n* centre *m* médical

⚷ **clinical** /ˈklɪnɪkl/ *adj* **1** ‹*medicine*› clinique; ‹*approach*› objectif/-ive
2 (unfeeling) froid/-e

clink /klɪŋk/ **A** *vt* faire tinter ‹*glass, keys*›; **to ~ glasses with** trinquer avec
B *vi* ‹*glass, keys*› tinter

clip /klɪp/ **A** *n* **1** (on earring) clip *m*; (for hair) barrette *f*
2 (from film) extrait *m*
B *vt* (*p prés etc* **-pp-**) **1** tailler ‹*hedge*›; couper ‹*nails, moustache*›; tondre ‹*dog, sheep*›
2 accrocher ‹*microphone*› (**to** à); fixer ‹*brooch*› (**to** à)
IDIOM **to ~ sb's wings** rogner les ailes à qn

clip art *n* clip-art *m*

clipboard *n* (gen) porte-bloc *m inv* à pince; (Comput) presse-papiers *m inv*

clip frame *n* sous-verre *m inv*

clip-ons *npl* clips *mpl*

clippers *npl* (for nails) coupe-ongles *m inv*; (for hair, hedge) tondeuse *f*

clipping /ˈklɪpɪŋ/ *n* (from paper) coupure *f* de presse

cloak /kləʊk/ **A** *n* cape *f*
B *vt* **1 ~ed in** enveloppé/-e dans ‹*darkness*›; enveloppé/-e de ‹*secrecy*›
2 (disguise) masquer

cloakroom /ˈkləʊkrʊm/ *n* **1** (for coats) vestiaire *m*
2 (BrE) (lavatory) toilettes *fpl*

clock /klɒk/ *n* (large) horloge *f*; (small) pendule *f*; (Sport) chronomètre *m*; **to put the ~s forward/back one hour** avancer/reculer les pendules d'une heure; **to work around the ~** travailler 24 heures sur 24
▪ **clock off** (BrE) pointer (à la sortie)

⚷ mot clé

■ **clock on** (BrE) pointer

clock radio *n* radio-réveil *m*

clock tower *n* beffroi *m*

clockwise /'klɒkwaɪz/ *adj, adv* dans le sens des aiguilles d'une montre

clockwork /'klɒkwɜːk/ *adj* ‹*toy*› mécanique
IDIOM **to go like ~** aller comme sur des roulettes

clog /klɒg/ *n* sabot *m*

cloister /'klɔɪstə(r)/ *n* cloître *m*

clone /kləʊn/ **A** *n* clone *m*
B *vt* cloner

cloning /'kləʊnɪŋ/ *n* clonage *m*

close¹ /kləʊs/ **A** *adj* **1** (near) proche (**to** de), voisin/-e (**to** de)
2 ‹*relative, friend*› proche; ‹*resemblance*› frappant/-e
3 ‹*contest, result*› serré/-e
4 ‹*scrutiny*› minutieux/-ieuse; ‹*supervision*› étroit/-e; **to pay ~ attention to sth** faire une attention toute particulière à qch; **to keep a ~ watch** *or* **eye on sb/sth** surveiller étroitement qn/qch
5 ‹*print, formation*› serré/-e
6 ‹*weather*› lourd/-e; **it's ~** il fait lourd
B *adv* **to live quite ~ (by)** habiter tout près; **to move sth ~r** approcher qch; **to follow ~ behind** suivre de près; **to hold sb ~** serrer qn; **~ together** serrés les uns contre les autres; **Christmas is ~** Noël approche
C **close by** *phr* près de ‹*wall, bridge*›; **the ambulance is ~ by** l'ambulance n'est pas loin
D **close to** *phr* **1** (near) près de
2 (on point of) au bord de ‹*tears, hysteria*›; **to be ~ to doing** être sur le point de faire
3 (almost) près de; **to come ~ to doing** faillir faire
IDIOM **it was a ~ call** (fam) *or* **shave** (fam) *or* **thing** je l'ai/tu l'as *etc* échappé belle

close² /kləʊz/ **A** *n* fin *f*
B *vt* **1** fermer ‹*door, book*›
2 fermer ‹*border, port*›; barrer ‹*road*›; interdire l'accès à ‹*area*›
3 mettre fin à ‹*meeting*›; fermer ‹*account*›
4 to ~ the gap réduire l'écart
5 conclure ‹*deal*›
C *vi* **1** ‹*airport, polls, shop*› fermer; ‹*door, container, eyes, mouth*› se fermer
2 (cease to operate) fermer définitivement
3 ‹*meeting, play*› prendre fin; **to ~ with** se terminer par ‹*song*›
4 ‹*currency, index*› clôturer (**at** à)
5 ‹*gap*› se réduire
D **closed** *pp adj* fermé/-e; **behind ~d doors** à huis clos

■ **close down**: **A** **~ down** fermer définitivement
B **~ [sth] down** fermer [qch] définitivement

■ **close up** **A** **~ up 1** ‹*flower, wound*› se refermer; ‹*group*› se serrer
2 ‹*shopkeeper*› fermer
B **~ [sth] up 1** fermer ‹*shop*›
2 boucher ‹*hole*›

closed-circuit television, **CCTV** /kləʊzd/ *n* télévision *f* en circuit fermé

close-fitting *adj* ‹*garment*› ajusté/-e, près du corps

close-knit /ˌkləʊs'nɪt/ *adj* ‹*family, group*› très uni/-e

closely /'kləʊslɪ/ *adv* ‹*follow, watch*› de près; ‹*resemble*› beaucoup; **to be ~ related** ‹*people*› être proches parents

close-run *adj* très serré/-e

closet /'klɒzɪt/ **A** *n* (AmE) (cupboard) placard *m*; (for clothes) penderie *f*
B *adj* ‹*alcoholic, fascist*› inavoué/-e

close-up **A** /'kləʊsʌp/ *n* gros plan *m*; **in ~** en gros plan
B **close up** *adv* **(from) ~** de près

closing /'kləʊzɪŋ/ **A** *n* fermeture *f*
B *adj* ‹*minutes, words*› dernier/-ière *before n*; ‹*scene, stage*› final/-e; ‹*speech*› de clôture

closing date *n* date *f* limite (**for** de)

closing down sale, **closing out sale** (AmE) *n* liquidation *f*

closing time *n* heure *f* de fermeture

closure /'kləʊʒə(r)/ *n* fermeture *f*

clot /klɒt/ **A** *n* caillot *m*
B *vt, vi* (*p prés etc* **-tt-**) coaguler, cailler

cloth /klɒθ, (AmE) klɔːθ/ *n* **1** (fabric) tissu *m*
2 (for polishing, dusting) chiffon *m*; (for floor) serpillière *f*; (for drying dishes) torchon *m*; (for table) nappe *f*

clothes /kləʊðz, (AmE) kləʊz/ *npl* vêtements *mpl*; **to put on/take off one's ~** s'habiller/se déshabiller

clothes brush *n* brosse *f* à habits

clothes hanger *n* cintre *m*

clothes line *n* corde *f* à linge

clothes peg *n* pince *f* à linge

clothes shop *n* magasin *m* de vêtements

clothing /'kləʊðɪŋ/ *n* vêtements *mpl*; **an item** *or* **article of ~** un vêtement

cloud /klaʊd/ **A** *n* nuage *m*; **to cast a ~ over sth** jeter une ombre sur qch
B *vt* **1** ‹*steam, breath*› embuer ‹*mirror*›; ‹*tears*› brouiller ‹*vision*›
2 obscurcir ‹*judgement*›; brouiller ‹*memory*›; **to ~ the issue** brouiller les cartes
IDIOM **to be living in ~ cuckoo land** croire au père Noël

■ **cloud over** ‹*sky*› se couvrir (de nuages); ‹*face*› s'assombrir

cloudy /'klaʊdɪ/ *adj* **1** ‹*weather*› couvert/-e
2 ‹*liquid*› trouble

clout /klaʊt/ *n* **1** (blow) claque *f*, coup *m*
2 (influence) influence *f* (**with** auprès de, sur)

clove /kləʊv/ *n* **1** (spice) clou *m* de girofle
2 (of garlic) gousse *f*

clover /'kləʊvə(r)/ *n* trèfle *m*

clown /klaʊn/ *n* clown *m*

■ **clown around** (BrE) faire le clown *or* le pitre

⚷ **club** /klʌb/ *n* **1** (association) club *m*
2 (fam) (nightclub) boîte *f* de nuit
3 (in cards) trèfle *m*
4 (for golf) club *m*
5 (weapon) massue *f*
■ **club together** cotiser

club car *n* (AmE) wagon-bar *m* de première classe

club class *n* classe *f* club *or* affaires

cluck /klʌk/ *vi* ‹*hen*› glousser

clue /klu:/ *n* indication *f* (**to, as to** quant à); (in police investigation) indice *m* (**to** quant à); (in crossword) définition *f*

clued-up /ˌklu:dˈʌp/ *adj* (fam) calé/-e (fam) (**about** sur)

clueless /ˈklu:lɪs/ *adj* (fam) nul/nulle (fam) (**about** en)

clump /klʌmp/ *n* (of flowers, grass) touffe *f*; (of trees) massif *m*; (of earth) motte *f*

clumsiness /ˈklʌmzɪnɪs/ *n* (carelessness) maladresse *f*; (awkwardness) gaucherie *f*; (of system) côté *m* peu pratique

clumsy /ˈklʌmzɪ/ *adj* ‹*person, attempt*› maladroit/-e; ‹*object*› grossier/-ière; ‹*animal*› pataud/-e; ‹*tool*› peu maniable; ‹*style*› lourd/-e

cluster /ˈklʌstə(r)/ **A** *n* (of flowers, berries) grappe *f*; (of people, islands, trees) groupe *m*; (of houses) ensemble *m*; (of diamonds) entourage *m*; (of stars) amas *m*
B *vi* ‹*people*› se rassembler (**around** autour de)

clutch /klʌtʃ/ **A** *n* (Aut) embrayage *m*
B *vt* tenir fermement
■ **clutch at** tenter d'attraper ‹*branch, rail, person*›; saisir ‹*arm*›

clutch bag *n* pochette *f*

clutches *npl* **to fall into the ~ of** tomber sous les griffes *or* la patte (fam) de

clutter /ˈklʌtə(r)/ **A** *n* désordre *m*
B *vt* (*also* **~ up**) encombrer

Co *n* (*abbr* = **company**) Cie

c/o *prep* (*abbr* = **care of**) chez

⚷ **coach** /kəʊtʃ/ **A** *n* **1** (bus) (auto)car *m*
2 (BrE) (of train) wagon *m*
3 (Sport) entraîneur/-euse *m/f*
4 (for drama, voice) répétiteur/-trice *m/f*
5 (horse-drawn) carrosse *m*
B *vt* **1** (Sport) entraîner ‹*team*›
2 (teach) **to ~ sb** donner des leçons particulières à qn (**in** en)

coach station *n* gare *f* routière

coach trip *n* excursion *f* en autocar

coal /kəʊl/ *n* charbon *m*
IDIOM **to haul sb over the ~s** (fam) passer un savon à qn (fam)

coalfield *n* bassin *m* houiller

coal fire *n* cheminée *f* (*où brûle un feu de charbon*)

coalition /ˌkəʊəˈlɪʃn/ *n* coalition *f*

coal mine *n* mine *f* de charbon

coal miner *n* mineur *m*

coarse /kɔ:s/ *adj* **1** ‹*texture*› grossier/-ière; ‹*skin*› épais/-aisse; ‹*sand, salt*› gros/grosse *before n*
2 ‹*manners*› grossier/-ière; ‹*language, joke*› cru/-e

coast /kəʊst/ **A** *n* côte *f*; **off the ~** près de la côte
B *vi* ‹*car, bicycle*› descendre en roue libre

coastal /ˈkəʊstl/ *adj* côtier/-ière

coaster /ˈkəʊstə(r)/ *n* (mat) dessous-de-verre *m inv*

coastguard /ˈkəʊstgɑ:d/ *n* **1** (person) garde-côte *m*
2 (organization) gendarmerie *f* maritime

coastline *n* littoral *m*

coat /kəʊt/ **A** *n* **1** (garment) manteau *m*
2 (of dog, cat) pelage *m*; (of horse, leopard) robe *f*
3 (layer) couche *f*
B *vt* **to ~ sth with** enduire qch de ‹*paint, adhesive*›; couvrir qch de ‹*dust, oil*›; enrober qch de ‹*breadcrumbs, chocolate, sauce*›

coat hanger *n* cintre *m*

coat of arms *n* blason *m*, armoiries *fpl*

coat rack *n* portemanteau *m*

coax /kəʊks/ *vt* cajoler; **to ~ sb into doing** persuader qn (gentiment) de faire

cobbler /ˈkɒblə(r)/ *n* cordonnier *m*

cobblestones /ˈkɒblstəʊnz/ *npl* pavés *mpl*

cobweb /ˈkɒbweb/ *n* toile *f* d'araignée

cocaine /kəʊˈkeɪn/ *n* cocaïne *f*

cock /kɒk/ **A** *n* **1** (rooster) coq *m*
2 (male bird) (oiseau *m*) mâle *m*
B *vt* **1 to ~ an eyebrow** hausser les sourcils; **to ~ a leg** ‹*dog*› lever la patte; **to ~ an ear** dresser l'oreille
2 (tilt) pencher
3 (Mil) armer ‹*gun*›

cock and bull story *n* histoire *f* abracadabrante *or* à dormir debout

cockatoo /ˌkɒkəˈtu:/ *n* cacatoès *m*

cockerel /ˈkɒkərəl/ *n* jeune coq *m*

cockle /ˈkɒkl/ *n* coque *f*

cockpit *n* cockpit *m*, poste *m* de pilotage

cockroach *n* cafard *m*

cocktail /ˈkɒkteɪl/ *n* cocktail *m*

cocktail bar *n* bar *m*

cocky /ˈkɒkɪ/ *adj* impudent/-e

cocoa /ˈkəʊkəʊ/ *n* cacao *m*; (drink) chocolat *m*

coconut /ˈkəʊkənʌt/ *n* noix *f* de coco

cocoon /kəˈku:n/ *n* cocon *m*

cod /ˈkɒd/ *n* (*pl* **~**) morue *f*

COD *n* (*abbr* = **cash on delivery**) envoi *m* contre remboursement

⚷ **code** /kəʊd/ **A** *n* **1** (gen) code *m*
2 (*also* **dialling ~**) indicatif *m*
B *vt* coder

⚷ mot clé

codeine /'kəʊdiːn/ *n* codéine *f*

code name *n* nom *m* de code

code word *n* (password) mot *m* de passe

co-educational /ˌkəʊedʒuː'keɪʃənl/ *adj* mixte

coeliac /'siːlɪæk/ *adj* cœliaque

coerce /kəʊ'ɜːs/ *vt* exercer des pressions sur; **to ~ sb into doing** contraindre qn à faire

coexist /ˌkəʊɪg'zɪst/ *vi* coexister (**with** avec)

coffee /'kɒfɪ, (AmE) 'kɔːfɪ/ **A** *n* café *m*; **a black/white ~** un café (noir)/au lait
B *adj* ‹*dessert*› au café; ‹*cup, filter, spoon*› à café

coffee break *n* pause(-)café *f*

coffee pot *n* cafetière *f*

coffee table *n* table *f* basse

coffin /'kɒfɪn/ *n* cercueil *m*

cog /kɒg/ *n* (tooth) dent *f* d'engrenage; (wheel) pignon *m*

cohabit /kəʊ'hæbɪt/ *vi* cohabiter (**with** avec)

coherent /kəʊ'hɪərənt/ *adj* cohérent/-e

coil /kɔɪl/ **A** *n* **1** (of rope, barbed wire) rouleau *m*; (of electric wire) bobine *f*; (of hair) boucle *f*; (of snake) anneau *m*
2 (contraceptive) stérilet *m*
B *vt* (*also* **~ up**) enrouler ‹*hair, rope, wire*›
C *vi* s'enrouler (**round** autour de)

coin /kɔɪn/ **A** *n* pièce *f* (de monnaie); **a pound ~** une pièce d'une livre
B *vt* forger ‹*term*›

coin box *n* (pay phone) cabine *f* (téléphonique) à pièces

coincide /ˌkəʊɪn'saɪd/ *vi* coïncider (**with** avec)

coincidence /kəʊ'ɪnsɪdəns/ *n* coïncidence *f*, hasard *m*; **it is a ~ that** c'est par coïncidence que; **by ~** par hasard

coincidental /kəʊˌɪnsɪ'dentl/ *adj* fortuit/-e

coin operated *adj* qui marche avec des pièces

coke /kəʊk/ *n* **1** (fuel) coke *m*
2 (fam) (cocaine) coke *f* (fam)

Coke® /kəʊk/ *n* coca *m*

colander /'kʌləndə(r)/ *n* passoire *f*

cold /kəʊld/ **A** *n* **1** (chilliness) froid *m*; **to feel the ~** être sensible au froid, être frileux/-euse
2 (Med) rhume *m*; **to have a ~** être enrhumé/-e, avoir un rhume
B *adj* **1** (chilly) froid; **to be** *or* **feel ~** ‹*person*› avoir froid; **the room was ~** il faisait froid dans la pièce; **it's** *or* **the weather's ~** il fait froid; **to go ~** ‹*food, water*› se refroidir
2 ‹*manner*› froid/-e; **to be ~ to** *or* **towards sb** être froid/-e avec qn
IDIOMS **in ~ blood** de sang-froid; **to be out ~** être sans connaissance

cold-blooded /ˌkəʊld'blʌdɪd/ *adj* ‹*animal*› à sang froid; ‹*killer*› sans pitié

cold calling *n* démarchage *m* par téléphone

coldness /'kəʊldnɪs/ *n* froideur *f*

cold shoulder *n* **to give sb the ~** snober qn, battre froid à qn

cold sore *n* bouton *m* de fièvre

cold sweat *n* **to bring sb out in a ~** donner des sueurs froides à qn

cold turkey *n* (fam) (treatment) sevrage *m*; (reaction) réaction *f* de manque; **to be ~** être en manque

Cold War *n* guerre *f* froide

coleslaw /'kəʊlslɔː/ *n* salade *f* à base de chou cru

colic /'kɒlɪk/ *n* coliques *fpl*

collaborate /kə'læbəreɪt/ *vi* collaborer (**on, in** à, **with** avec)

collaboration /kəˌlæbə'reɪʃn/ *n* collaboration *f*

collaborator /kə'læbəreɪtə(r)/ *n* collaborateur/-trice *m/f*

collapse /kə'læps/ **A** *n* **1** (of regime, economy) effondrement *m* (**of, in** de)
2 (of deal, talks) échec *m*
3 (of company) faillite *f* (**of** de)
4 (of person) (physical) écroulement *m*; (mental) effondrement *m*
5 (of building, bridge) effondrement *m*; (of tunnel, wall) écroulement *m*
6 (Med) (of lung) collapsus *m*
B *vi* **1** ‹*regime, economy*› s'effondrer; ‹*deal, talks*› échouer
2 ‹*company*› faire faillite
3 ‹*person*› s'écrouler
4 ‹*building, bridge*› s'effondrer; ‹*tunnel, wall*› s'écrouler; ‹*chair*› s'affaisser (**under** sous)
5 (Med) ‹*lung*› se dégonfler
6 (fold) ‹*bike, pushchair*› se plier

collapsible /kə'læpsəbl/ *adj* pliant/-e

collar /'kɒlə(r)/ *n* **1** (on garment) col *m*
2 (for animal) collier *m*
IDIOM **to get hot under the ~** se mettre en rogne (fam)

collarbone *n* clavicule *f*

collar size *n* encolure *f*

collate /kə'leɪt/ *vt* collationner

colleague /'kɒliːg/ *n* collègue *mf*

collect /kə'lekt/ **A** *adv* (AmE) **to call sb ~** appeler qn en PCV
B *vt* **1** ramasser ‹*wood, litter, rubbish*›; rassembler ‹*information*›; recueillir ‹*signatures*›
2 (as hobby) collectionner, faire collection de ‹*stamps, coins*›
3 ‹*objects*› prendre, ramasser ‹*dust*›
4 percevoir ‹*rent*›; encaisser ‹*fares, money*›; recouvrer ‹*debt*›; toucher ‹*pension*›; percevoir ‹*tax, fine*›
5 faire la levée de ‹*mail, post*›
6 (pick up) aller chercher ‹*person*›; récupérer ‹*keys, book*›

C

C *vi* **1** ‹*dust, leaves*› s'accumuler; ‹*people*› se rassembler
2 to ~ for charity faire la quête pour des bonnes œuvres
D collected *pp adj* **1** ‹*person*› calme
2 (assembled) **the ~ed works of Dickens** les œuvres complètes de Dickens

collection /kə'lekʃn/ *n* **1** (of coins, records) collection *f*; (anthology) recueil *m*; **art ~** collection (de tableaux)
2 (money) collecte *f* (**for** pour); (in church) quête *f*
3 (of mail) levée *f*

collective /kə'lektɪv/ *adj* collectif/-ive

collective ownership *n* copropriété *f*

collector /kə'lektə(r)/ *n* **1** (of coins, stamps) collectionneur/-euse *m/f*
2 (of taxes) percepteur *m*; (of rent, debts) encaisseur *m*

collector's item *n* pièce *f* de collection

college /'kɒlɪdʒ/ *n* établissement *m* d'enseignement supérieur; (school, part of university) collège *m*; (AmE) (Univ) faculté *f*; **to go to ~, to be at** *or* **in** (AmE) **~** faire des études supérieures

college of further education, CFE *n* (BrE) *école ouverte aux adultes et aux jeunes pour terminer un cycle d'études secondaires*

collide /kə'laɪd/ *vi* ‹*vehicle, plane*› entrer en collision (**with** avec)

collie /'kɒlɪ/ *n* (dog) colley *m*

colliery /'kɒlɪərɪ/ *n* houillère *f*

collision /kə'lɪʒn/ *n* collision *f*

colloquial /kə'ləʊkwɪəl/ *adj* familier/-ière

colon /'kəʊlən/ *n* **1** (Anat) côlon *m*
2 (punctuation) deux points *mpl*

colonel /'kɜːnl/ *n* colonel *m*

colonialist /kə'ləʊnɪəlɪst/ *n, adj* colonialiste *mf*

colonization /ˌkɒlənaɪ'zeɪʃn, (AmE) -nɪ'z-/ *n* colonisation *f*

colonize /'kɒlənaɪz/ *vt* coloniser

colonizer /'kɒlənaɪzə(r)/ *n* colon *m*

colony /'kɒlənɪ/ *n* colonie *f*

colour (BrE), **color** (AmE) /'kʌlə(r)/ **A** *n*
1 couleur *f*; **what ~ is it?** de quelle couleur est-il/elle?; **to put ~ into sb's cheeks** redonner des couleurs à qn
2 (dye) (for food) colorant *m*; (for hair) teinture *f*
B *vt* **1** (with paints, crayons) colorier; (with food dye) colorer
2 (prejudice) fausser ‹*judgement*›
C *vi* ‹*person*› rougir
IDIOMS **to be off ~** ne pas être en forme; **to show one's true ~s** se montrer sous son vrai jour

colour blind *adj* daltonien/-ienne

coloured (BrE), **colored** (AmE) /'kʌləd/ *adj* ‹*pen, paper, bead*› de couleur; ‹*picture*› en couleur; ‹*light, glass*› coloré/-e

colour film *n* (for camera) pellicule *f* couleur

colourful (BrE), **colorful** (AmE) /'kʌləfl/ *adj*
1 ‹*dress, shirt*› aux couleurs vives
2 ‹*story, life*› haut en couleur; ‹*character*› pittoresque

colouring (BrE), **coloring** (AmE) /'kʌlərɪŋ/ *n* **1** (of animal) couleurs *fpl*; (of person) teint *m*
2 (for food) colorant *m*

colour scheme *n* couleurs *fpl*, coloris *m*

colour supplement *n* supplément *m* illustré

colour television *n* télévision *f* (en) couleur

colt /kəʊlt/ *n* poulain *m*

column /'kɒləm/ *n* **1** (pillar) colonne *f*
2 (on page, list) colonne *f*
3 (newspaper article) rubrique *f*; **sports ~** rubrique sportive

columnist /'kɒləmnɪst/ *n* journaliste *mf*

coma /'kəʊmə/ *n* coma *m*; **in a ~** dans le coma

comatose /'kəʊmətəʊs/ *adj* (Med) comateux/-euse; (fig) abruti/-e

comb /kəʊm/ **A** *n* peigne *m*
B *vt* **to ~ sb's hair** peigner qn; **to ~ one's hair** se peigner

combat /'kɒmbæt/ **A** *n* combat *m*
B *vt* (*p prés etc* **-tt-**) lutter contre, combattre

combat jacket *n* veste *f* de treillis

combination /ˌkɒmbɪ'neɪʃn/ *n* combinaison *f*

combine **A** /'kɒmbaɪn/ *n* groupe *m*
B /kəm'baɪn/ *vt* **1** combiner ‹*activities, colours, items*› (**with** avec); associer ‹*ideas, aims*› (**with** à); **to ~ forces** (merge) s'allier; (cooperate) collaborer
2 (Culin) mélanger (**with** avec)
C /kəm'baɪn/ *vi* **1** ‹*activities, colours, elements*› se combiner
2 ‹*people, groups*› s'associer; ‹*firms*› fusionner

combined /kəm'baɪnd/ *adj* **1** (joint) **~ operation** collaboration *f*; **a ~ effort** une collaboration
2 (total) ‹*salary, age*› total/-e
3 ‹*effects*› combiné/-e

combine harvester *n* moissonneuse-batteuse *f*

come /kʌm/ *vi* (*prét* **came**, *pp* **come**)
1 ‹*person, day*› venir; ‹*bus, news, winter, war*› arriver; ‹*dustman, postman*› passer; **to ~ down** descendre ‹*stairs, street*›; **to ~ up** monter ‹*stairs, street*›; **to ~ into** entrer dans ‹*house, room*›; **when the time ~s** lorsque le moment sera venu; **(I'm) coming!** j'arrive!; **to ~ to sb for** venir demander [qch] à qn ‹*money, advice*›; **don't ~ any closer** ne vous approchez pas (plus); **to ~ as a shock/surprise** être un choc/une surprise
2 (reach) **to ~ up/down to** ‹*water*› venir jusqu'à; ‹*dress, curtain*› arriver à

mot clé

3 (happen) **how ~?** comment ça se fait?; **to take things as they ~** prendre les choses comme elles viennent; **~ what may** advienne que pourra
4 (begin) **to ~ to do** finir par faire
5 to ~ from ‹*person*› être originaire de, venir de ‹*city, country*›; ‹*word, legend*› venir de ‹*language, country*›; ‹*stamps, painting*› provenir de ‹*place*›; ‹*smell, sound*› venir de ‹*place*›
6 (in order) **to ~ after** suivre, venir après; **to ~ before** (in time, list, queue) précéder; (in importance) passer avant; **to ~ first/last** (in race) arriver premier/dernier
7 when it ~s to sth/to doing lorsqu'il s'agit de qch/de faire
8 to ~ true se réaliser; **to ~ undone** se défaire

■ **come across**: **A** **~ across** ‹*meaning, message*› passer; ‹*feelings*› transparaître; **~ across as** donner l'impression d'être ‹*liar, expert*›; paraître ‹*honest*›
B **~ across [sth]** tomber sur ‹*article*›

■ **come along 1** ‹*bus, person*› arriver; ‹*opportunity*› se présenter
2 (hurry up) **~ along!** dépêche-toi!
3 (attend) venir (**to** à)
4 (progress) ‹*pupil*› faire des progrès; ‹*book, work, project*› avancer; ‹*painting, tennis*› progresser

■ **come apart 1** (accidentally) ‹*book, box*› se déchirer; ‹*toy, camera*› se casser
2 (intentionally) ‹*components*› se séparer; ‹*machine*› se démonter

■ **come around** (AmE) = **come round**

■ **come away** partir

■ **come back 1** (return) revenir (**from** de, **to** à); (to one's house) rentrer
2 ‹*law, system*› être rétabli/-e; ‹*trend*› revenir à la mode

■ **come down 1** ‹*person, lift, blind*› descendre; ‹*curtain*› tomber
2 ‹*price, inflation, temperature*› baisser; ‹*cost*› diminuer
3 ‹*snow, rain*› tomber
4 ‹*ceiling, wall*› s'écrouler; ‹*hem*› se défaire
5 to ~ down with attraper ‹*flu*›

■ **come forward 1** (step forward) s'avancer
2 (volunteer) se présenter

■ **come in 1** (enter) entrer (**through** par)
2 ‹*tide*› monter
3 to ~ in useful être utile
4 to ~ in for criticism ‹*person*› être critiqué/-e; ‹*plan*› faire l'objet de nombreuses critiques

■ **come into 1** hériter de ‹*money*›; entrer en possession de ‹*inheritance*›
2 luck doesn't ~ into it ce n'est pas une question de hasard

■ **come off 1** ‹*button, handle*› se détacher; ‹*lid*› s'enlever; ‹*paint*› s'écailler
2 ‹*ink*› s'effacer; ‹*stain*› partir
3 ‹*plan, trick*› réussir

■ **come on 1 ~ on!** allez!
2 ‹*person, patient*› faire des progrès; ‹*bridge, novel*› avancer; ‹*plant*› pousser
3 ‹*light*› s'allumer; ‹*heating, fan*› se mettre en route
4 ‹*actor*› entrer en scène

■ **come out 1** ‹*person, animal, vehicle*› sortir (**of** de); ‹*star*› apparaître; ‹*sun, moon*› se montrer
2 (strike) faire la grève; **to ~ out on strike** faire la grève
3 ‹*contact lens, tooth*› tomber; ‹*contents*› sortir; ‹*cork*› s'enlever
4 ‹*water, smoke*› sortir (**through** par)
5 ‹*stain*› s'en aller, partir
6 ‹*magazine, novel*› paraître; ‹*album, film, product*› sortir
7 ‹*details, facts*› être révélé/-e; ‹*results*› être connu/-e
8 ‹*photo, photocopy*› être réussi/-e
9 to ~ out with sortir ‹*excuse*›; raconter ‹*nonsense*›; **to ~ straight out with it** le dire franchement
10 ‹*homosexual*› déclarer publiquement son homosexualité

■ **come over**: **~ over** venir (**to do** faire); **what's ~ over you?** qu'est-ce qui te prend?

■ **come round** (BrE), **come around** (AmE)
1 (regain consciousness) reprendre connaissance
2 (visit) venir
3 (change mind) changer d'avis

■ **come through** **A** **~ through 1** (survive) s'en tirer
2 ‹*heat, ink*› traverser; ‹*light*› passer
B **~ through [sth]** se tirer de ‹*crisis*›; survivre à ‹*operation, ordeal*›

■ **come to**: **A** **~ to** reprendre connaissance
B **~ to [sth]** ‹*shopping*› revenir à; ‹*bill, total*› s'élever à; **that ~s to £40** cela fait 40 livres sterling; **it may not ~ to that** nous n'en arriverons peut-être pas là

■ **come under**: **1 to ~ under threat** être menacé/-e
2 (be classified under) être classé/-e dans le rayon ‹*reference, history*›

■ **come up 1** ‹*problem, issue*› être soulevé/-e; ‹*name*› être mentionné/-e
2 ‹*opportunity*› se présenter; **something urgent has ~ up** j'ai quelque chose d'urgent à faire
3 ‹*sun, moon*› sortir; ‹*daffodils*› sortir
4 (in law) ‹*case*› passer au tribunal
5 to ~ up against se heurter à ‹*problem*›
6 to ~ up with trouver ‹*answer, idea*›

comeback /ˈkʌmbæk/ *n* come-back *m*; **to make a ~** ‹*person*› faire un come-back; ‹*trend*› revenir à la mode

comedian /kəˈmiːdɪən/ *n* (male) comique *m*

comedienne /kəˌmiːdɪˈen/ *n* actrice *f* comique

comedy /ˈkɒmədɪ/ *n* comédie *f*

comet /ˈkɒmɪt/ *n* comète *f*

comeuppance /kʌmˈʌpəns/ *n* (fam) **to get one's ~** avoir ce qu'on mérite

comfort /ˈkʌmfət/ **A** *n* **1** confort *m*; **to live in ~** vivre dans l'aisance; **home ~s** le confort du foyer

C

2 (consolation) réconfort *m*, consolation *f*
B *vt* consoler; (stronger) réconforter

🔑 **comfortable** /ˈkʌmftəbl, (AmE) -fərt-/ *adj*
1 ‹*chair, clothes, journey*› confortable; ‹*temperature*› agréable
2 ‹*person*› à l'aise

comfortably /ˈkʌmftəblɪ, (AmE) -fərt-/ *adv* (gen) confortablement; (easily) facilement, aisément; **to be ~ off** être à l'aise

comforting /ˈkʌmfətɪŋ/ *adj* réconfortant/-e

comic /ˈkɒmɪk/ **A** *n* **1** = **comedian**
2 (magazine) bande *f* dessinée
B *adj* comique

comical /ˈkɒmɪkl/ *adj* cocasse, comique

comic strip *n* bande *f* dessinée

coming /ˈkʌmɪŋ/ **A** *n* arrivée *f*; **~s and goings** allées et venues *fpl*
B *adj* ‹*election, event*› prochain/-e *before n*; ‹*months, weeks*› à venir

comma /ˈkɒmə/ *n* virgule *f*

🔑 **command** /kəˈmɑːnd, (AmE) -ˈmænd/ **A** *n*
1 (order) ordre *m*
2 (military control) commandement *m*; **to be in ~** commander
3 (of language) maîtrise *f*; **to be in ~ of the situation** avoir la situation en main
4 (Comput) commande *f*
B *vt* **1** ordonner à ‹*person*› (**to do** de faire)
2 inspirer ‹*affection, respect*›
3 (Mil) commander ‹*regiment*›

commander /kəˈmɑːndə(r), (AmE) -mæn-/ *n* (gen) chef *m*; (Mil) commandant *m*

commanding /kəˈmɑːndɪŋ, (AmE) -ˈmæn-/ *adj* ‹*manner, voice*› impérieux/-ieuse; ‹*presence*› imposant/-e

commanding officer, **CO** *n* commandant *m*

commando /kəˈmɑːndəʊ, (AmE) -ˈmæn-/ *n* (*pl* **-os**) commando *m*

commemorate /kəˈmeməreɪt/ *vt* commémorer

commence /kəˈmens/ *vt*, *vi* commencer

commend /kəˈmend/ *vt* louer (**on** pour)

🔑 **comment** /ˈkɒment/ **A** *n* **1** (public) commentaire *m* (**on** sur); (in conversation) remarque *f* (**on** sur); (written) annotation *f*
2 to be a ~ on en dire long sur
B *vi* faire des commentaires (**on** sur)

commentary /ˈkɒməntrɪ, (AmE) -terɪ/ *n* commentaire *m* (**on** de)

commentator /ˈkɒmənteɪtə(r)/ *n* (sports) commentateur/-trice *m/f*; (current affairs) journaliste *mf*

commerce /ˈkɒmɜːs/ *n* commerce *m*

🔑 **commercial** /kəˈmɜːʃl/ **A** *n* annonce *f* publicitaire
B *adj* commercial/-e

commercial break *n* publicité *f*

commercial traveller *n* voyageur *m* de commerce

commiserate /kəˈmɪzəreɪt/ *vi* compatir (**with** avec, **about, over** à propos de)

🔑 **commission** /kəˈmɪʃn/ **A** *n* **1** (fee) commission *f*
2 (order) commande *f* (**for** de)
3 (committee) commission *f* (**on** sur)
B *vt* **1** commander ‹*work*› (**from** à); **to ~ sb to do** charger qn de faire
2 (Mil) **to be ~ed (as) an officer** être nommé/-e officier

commissioner /kəˈmɪʃənə(r)/ *n* **1** (gen) membre *m* d'une commission
2 (BrE) (in police) ≈ préfet *m* de police
3 (in the EC) membre *m* de la Commission européenne

🔑 **commit** /kəˈmɪt/ *vt* (*p prés etc* **-tt-**)
1 commettre ‹*crime, error, sin*›; **to ~ suicide** se suicider
2 to ~ oneself s'engager (**to** à)
3 consacrer ‹*money, time*› (**to** à)

🔑 **commitment** /kəˈmɪtmənt/ *n* **1** (obligation) engagement *m* (**to do** à faire)
2 (sense of duty) attachement *m* (**to** à)

committed /kəˈmɪtɪd/ *adj* **1** (devoted) ‹*parent, teacher*› dévoué/-e; ‹*Christian, Socialist*› fervent/-e; **to be ~ to/to doing** se consacrer à/à faire
2 (with commitments) pris/-e

🔑 **committee** /kəˈmɪtɪ/ *n* comité *m*; (to investigate, report) commission *f*

commodity /kəˈmɒdətɪ/ *n* article *m*; (food) denrée *f*

🔑 **common** /ˈkɒmən/ **A** *n* terrain *m* communal
B Commons *npl* (BrE) (Pol) **the Commons** les Communes *fpl*
C *adj* **1** (frequent) courant/-e, fréquent/-e; **in ~ use** d'un usage courant
2 (shared) commun/-e (**to** à); **in ~** en commun; **it is ~ knowledge** c'est de notoriété publique
3 the ~ people le peuple; **a ~ criminal** un criminel ordinaire
4 (low-class) commun/-e; **it looks/sounds ~** ça fait commun

common-law husband *n* concubin *m*

common-law marriage *n* concubinage *m*

common-law wife *n* concubine *f*

commonly /ˈkɒmənlɪ/ *adv* communément

Common Market *n* Marché *m* commun

commonplace /ˈkɒmənpleɪs/ *adj* (common) commun/-e; (trite) banal/-e

common room *n* salle *f* de détente

common sense *n* bon sens *m*, sens *m* commun

Commonwealth /ˈkɒmənwelθ/ *n* **the ~** le Commonwealth

Commonwealth of Independent States *pr n* Communauté *f* des États indépendants

commotion /kəˈməʊʃn/ *n* **1** (noise) vacarme *m*, brouhaha *m*

🔑 mot clé

2 (disturbance) émoi *m*, agitation *f*

communal /ˈkɒmjʊnl, kəˈmjuːnl/ *adj* ‹*property, area, showers*› commun/-e; ‹*garden*› collectif/-ive; ‹*life*› communautaire

commune /ˈkɒmjuːn/ *n* communauté *f*

communicate /kəˈmjuːnɪkeɪt/ **A** *vt* communiquer ‹*ideas, feelings*› (**to** à); transmettre ‹*information*› (**to** à)
B *vi* communiquer

communication /kəˌmjuːnɪˈkeɪʃn/ *n* communication *f*

communication cord *n* (BrE) sonnette *f* d'alarme

communications *npl* (BrE) communications *fpl*, liaison *f*

communications company *n* société *f* de communications

communication studies *npl* études *fpl* en communication

communion /kəˈmjuːnɪən/ *n* communion *f*

communism *n* communisme *m*

communist *n, adj* communiste *mf*

community /kəˈmjuːnətɪ/ *n* communauté *f*

community care *n* soins *mpl* en dehors du milieu hospitalier

community centre (BrE), **community center** (AmE) *n* maison *f* de quartier

community service *n* travail *m* d'intérêt public

commute /kəˈmjuːt/ *vi* **to ~ between Oxford and London** faire le trajet entre Oxford et Londres tous les jours

commuter /kəˈmjuːtə(r)/ *n* navetteur/-euse *m/f*, migrant/-e *m/f* journalier/-ière

compact **A** /ˈkɒmpækt/ *n* poudrier *m*
B /kəmˈpækt/ *adj* compact/-e

compact disc *n* disque *m* compact

companion /kəmˈpænɪən/ *n* compagnon/compagne *m/f*

companionship /kəmˈpænɪənʃɪp/ *n* compagnie *f*

company /ˈkʌmpənɪ/ *n* **1** (firm) société *f*; **airline ~** compagnie *f* aérienne
2 theatre ~ troupe *f* de théâtre, compagnie *f* théâtrale
3 (Mil) compagnie *f*
4 (companionship) compagnie *f*; **to keep sb ~** tenir compagnie à qn
5 (visitors) visiteurs *mpl*

company car *n* voiture *f* de fonction

company director *n* directeur/-trice *m/f* général/-e

company pension scheme *n* régime *m* de retraite de l'enterprise

company secretary *n* secrétaire *mf* général/-e

comparable /ˈkɒmpərəbl/ *adj* comparable (**to, with** à)

comparative /kəmˈpærətɪv/ *adj* **1** (in grammar) comparatif/-ive
2 (relative) relatif/-ive; **in ~ terms** en termes relatifs
3 ‹*study*› comparatif/-ive

comparatively /kəmˈpærətɪvlɪ/ *adv* relativement

compare /kəmˈpeə(r)/ **A** *vt* comparer (**with, to** avec, à)
B *vi* être comparable (**with** à)
C compared with *prep phr* **~d with sb/sth** par rapport à qn/qch
D *v refl* **to ~ oneself with** *or* **to** se comparer à

comparison /kəmˈpærɪsn/ *n* comparaison *f*; **in** *or* **by ~ with** par rapport à

compartment /kəmˈpɑːtmənt/ *n* compartiment *m*

compass /ˈkʌmpəs/ *n* boussole *f* (*also* **ship's ~**) compas *m*; **the points of the ~** les points *mpl* cardinaux

compasses *npl* **(a pair of) ~** un compas

compassion /kəmˈpæʃn/ *n* compassion *f* (**for** pour)

compassionate /kəmˈpæʃənət/ *adj* compatissant/-e; **on ~ grounds** pour raisons personnelles

compatible /kəmˈpætəbl/ *adj* compatible (**with** avec)

compel /kəmˈpel/ *vt* (*p prés etc* **-ll-**) contraindre (**to do** à faire), obliger (**to do** de faire)

compelling /kəmˈpelɪŋ/ *adj* ‹*reason, argument*› convaincant/-e; ‹*speaker*› fascinant/-e

compensate /ˈkɒmpenseɪt/ **A** *vt* dédommager, indemniser
B *vi* **to ~ for** compenser

compensation /ˌkɒmpenˈseɪʃn/ *n* **1** (gen) compensation *f* (**for** de)
2 (financial) indemnisation *f*

compete /kəmˈpiːt/ **A** *vi* **1** (gen) rivaliser; **to ~ against** *or* **with** rivaliser avec (**for** pour obtenir)
2 (commercially) ‹*companies*› se faire concurrence; **to ~ with** faire concurrence à (**for** pour obtenir)
3 (in sport) être en compétition (**against, with** avec); **to ~ in** participer à ‹*Olympics, race*›
B competing *pres p adj* rival/-e

competence /ˈkɒmpɪtəns/ *n* **1** (ability) compétence *f*
2 (skill) compétences *fpl*

competent /ˈkɒmpɪtənt/ *adj* compétent/-e, capable

competition /ˌkɒmpəˈtɪʃn/ *n* **1** (gen) concurrence *f*
2 (contest) concours *m*; (race) compétition *f*
3 (competitors) concurrence *f*

competitive /kəmˈpetɪtɪv/ *adj*
1 ‹*person*› qui a l'esprit de compétition; ‹*environment*› compétitif/-ive
2 ‹*price, product*› compétitif/-ive

C

3 ‹*sport*› de compétition

competitor /kəm'petɪtə(r)/ *n* concurrent/-e *m/f*

compilation /ˌkɒmpɪ'leɪʃn/ *n* **1** (collection) compilation *f*
2 (act of compiling) (of reference book) rédaction *f*; (of dossier) constitution *f*

compile /kəm'paɪl/ *vt* **1** dresser ‹*list, catalogue*›; établir ‹*report*›
2 (Comput) compiler

complacent /kəm'pleɪsnt/ *adj* suffisant/-e; **to be ~ about** être trop confiant/-e de ‹*success, future*›

🔑 **complain** /kəm'pleɪn/ *vi* se plaindre (**to** à, **about** de, **of** de); (officially) se plaindre (**to** auprès de)

🔑 **complaint** /kəm'pleɪnt/ *n* plainte *f*; (official) réclamation *f*; **there have been ~s about the noise** on s'est plaint du bruit; **to have grounds** *or* **cause for ~** avoir lieu de se plaindre

complement /'kɒmplɪmənt/ **A** *n* complément *m*
B *vt* compléter

complementary /ˌkɒmplɪ'mentrɪ/ *adj* complémentaire (**to** de)

complementary medicine *n* médecine *f* parallèle

🔑 **complete** /kəm'pliːt/ **A** *adj* **1** complet/-ète
2 (finished) achevé/-e
B *vt* **1** (finish) terminer ‹*building, course, exercise*›; achever ‹*task, journey*›
2 compléter ‹*collection, phrase*›
3 remplir ‹*form*›

🔑 **completely** /kəm'pliːtlɪ/ *adv* complètement

completion /kəm'pliːʃn/ *n* achèvement *m*

🔑 **complex** /'kɒmpleks/ **A** *n* complexe *m*; **sports ~** complexe sportif; **he's got a ~ about his weight** son poids le complexe
B *adj* (AmE) kəm'pleks/ complexe

complexion /kəm'plekʃn/ *n* teint *m*

complexity /kəm'pleksətɪ/ *n* complexité *f*

compliance /kəm'plaɪəns/ *n* conformité (**with** à)

compliant /kəm'plaɪənt/ *adj* conciliant/-e

complicate /'kɒmplɪkeɪt/ *vt* compliquer

complicated /'kɒmplɪkeɪtɪd/ *adj* compliqué/-e

complication /ˌkɒmplɪ'keɪʃn/ *n* **1** (problem) inconvénient *m*, problème *m*
2 (Med) complication *f*

compliment /'kɒmplɪmənt/ **A** *n* compliment *m*; **to pay sb a ~** faire un compliment à qn
B *vt* complimenter, faire des compliments à

complimentary /ˌkɒmplɪ'mentrɪ/ *adj*
1 ‹*remark*› flatteur/-euse
2 (free) gratuit/-e

compliments *npl* compliments *mpl* (**to** à)

comply /kəm'plaɪ/ *vi* **to ~ with** se conformer à ‹*orders*›; respecter, observer ‹*rules*›

🔑 **component** /kəm'pəʊnənt/ *n* (gen) composante *f*; (in car, machine) pièce *f*; (electrical) composant *m*

compose /kəm'pəʊz/ *vt* **1** (gen) composer; **~d of** composé/-e de
2 to ~ oneself se ressaisir

composed /kəm'pəʊzd/ *adj* calme

composer /kəm'pəʊzə(r)/ *n* compositeur/-trice *m/f*

composition /ˌkɒmpə'zɪʃn/ *n* **1** (gen) composition *f*
2 (essay) rédaction *f* (**about, on** sur)

compost /'kɒmpɒst/ *n* compost *m*

composure /kəm'pəʊʒə(r)/ *n* calme *m*

compound **A** /'kɒmpaʊnd/ *n* **1** (enclosure) enceinte *f*
2 (in chemistry) composé *m* (**of** de)
3 (word) mot *m* composé
B *adj* **1** (gen) composé/-e
2 (Med) ‹*fracture*› multiple

comprehend /ˌkɒmprɪ'hend/ *vt* comprendre

comprehensible /ˌkɒmprɪ'hensəbl/ *adj* compréhensible, intelligible

comprehension /ˌkɒmprɪ'henʃn/ *n* compréhension *f*

comprehensive /ˌkɒmprɪ'hensɪv/ **A** *n* (*also* **~ school**) (BrE) (Sch) école *f* (publique) secondaire
B *adj* ‹*report, list*› complet/-ète, détaillé/-e; ‹*knowledge*› étendu/-e; **~ insurance policy** assurance *f* tous risques

compress **A** /'kɒmpres/ *n* compresse *f*
B /kəm'pres/ *vt* comprimer

comprise /kəm'praɪz/ *vt* comprendre; **to be ~d of** être composé/-e de

compromise /'kɒmprəmaɪz/ **A** *n* compromis *m*
B *vt* compromettre
C *vi* transiger, arriver à un compromis; **to ~ on sth** trouver un compromis sur qch

compromising /'kɒmprəmaɪzɪŋ/ *adj* compromettant/-e

compulsive /kəm'pʌlsɪv/ *adj* **1** (inveterate) invétéré/-e; (psychologically) compulsif/-ive
2 (fascinating) fascinant/-e

compulsory /kəm'pʌlsərɪ/ *adj* obligatoire

🔑 **computer** /kəm'pjuːtə(r)/ *n* ordinateur *m*

computer-aided design, **CAD** *n* conception *f* assistée par ordinateur, CAO *f*

computer-aided learning, **CAL** *n* enseignement *m* assisté par ordinateur

computer crime *n* piratage *m* informatique

computer dating *n* organisation *f* de rencontres (en utilisant un ordinateur)

computer game *n* jeu *m* informatique

computer graphics *n* infographie *f*

🔑 mot clé

computer hacker *n* pirate *m* informatique

computerize /kəm'pjuːtəraɪz/ *vt* mettre [qch] sur ordinateur ‹*accounts*›; informatiser ‹*list*›

computer literate *adj* **to be ~** avoir des notions d'informatique

computer program *n* programme *m* informatique

computer programmer *n* programmeur/-euse *m/f*

computer science *n* informatique *f*

computer scientist *n* informaticien/-ienne *m/f*

computing /kəm'pjuːtɪŋ/ *n* informatique *f*

comrade /'kɒmreɪd, (AmE) -ræd/ *n* camarade *mf*

comradeship /'kɒmreɪdʃɪp, (AmE) -ræd-/ *n* camaraderie *f*

con /kɒn/ (fam) **A** *n* escroquerie *f*, arnaque *f* (pop)
B *vt* (*p prés etc* **-nn-**) tromper, rouler (fam), arnaquer (pop)

conceal /kən'siːl/ *vt* dissimuler (**from** à)

concede /kən'siːd/ **A** *vt* concéder
B *vi* céder

conceit /kən'siːt/ *n* suffisance *f*

conceited /kən'siːtɪd/ *adj* ‹*person*› vaniteux/-euse; ‹*remark*› suffisant/-e

conceive /kən'siːv/ *vt*, *vi* concevoir

concentrate /'kɒnsntreɪt/ **A** *vt* concentrer ‹*effort*›; employer ‹*resources*›; centrer ‹*attention*›
B *vi* **1** ‹*person*› se concentrer (**on** sur); **to ~ on doing** s'appliquer à faire
2 to ~ on ‹*film, journalist*› s'intéresser surtout à

concentration /ˌkɒnsn'treɪʃn/ *n* concentration *f* (**on** sur); **to lose one's ~** se déconcentrer

concentration camp *n* camp *m* de concentration

concept /'kɒnsept/ *n* concept *m*

conception /kən'sepʃn/ *n* conception *f*

concern /kən'sɜːn/ **A** *n* **1** (worry) inquiétude *f* (**about** à propos de); **to cause ~** être inquiétant/-e
2 (preoccupation) préoccupation *f*; **environmental ~s** des préoccupations écologiques
3 (company) entreprise *f*; **a going ~** une affaire rentable
B *vt* **1** (worry) inquiéter
2 (affect, interest) concerner, intéresser; **to whom it may ~** à qui de droit; (in letter) Monsieur; **as far as the pay is ~ed** en ce qui concerne le salaire
3 (be about) ‹*book, programme*› traiter de; ‹*fax, letter*› concerner

concerned /kən'sɜːnd/ *adj* **1** (anxious) inquiet/-ète (**about** à propos de); **to be ~ for sb** se faire du souci pour qn
2 (involved) concerné/-e; **all (those) ~** toutes les personnes concernées

concerning /kən'sɜːnɪŋ/ *prep* concernant

concert /'kɒnsət/ *n* concert *m*

concerted /kən'sɜːtɪd/ *adj* ‹*action, campaign*› concerté/-e; **to make a ~ effort to do** faire un sérieux effort pour faire

concert hall *n* salle *f* de concert

concertina /ˌkɒnsə'tiːnə/ **A** *n* concertina *m*
B *vi* se plier en accordéon

concerto /kən'tʃeətəʊ, -'tʃɜːt-/ *n* (*pl* **-tos** *ou* **-tia**) concerto *m*

concession /kən'seʃn/ *n* **1** (compromise) concession *f* (**on** sur, **to** à)
2 (discount) réduction *f*; **'~s'** 'tarif réduit'

conciliatory /kən'sɪlɪətərɪ, (AmE) -tɔːrɪ/ *adj* ‹*gesture, terms*› conciliant/-e; ‹*measures*› conciliatoire

concise /kən'saɪs/ *adj* concis/-e

conclude /kən'kluːd/ **A** *vt* conclure
B *vi* ‹*story, event*› se terminer (**with** par, sur); ‹*speaker*› conclure (**with** par)

concluding /kən'kluːdɪŋ/ *adj* final/-e

conclusion /kən'kluːʒn/ *n* **1** (end) fin *f*
2 (opinion, resolution) conclusion *f*

conclusive /kən'kluːsɪv/ *adj* concluant/-e

concoct /kən'kɒkt/ *vt* concocter

concrete /'kɒŋkriːt/ **A** *n* béton *m*
B *adj* **1** ‹*block*› de béton; ‹*base*› en béton
2 (real) concret/-ète

concuss /kən'kʌs/ *vt* **to be ~ed** être commotionné/-e

concussion /kən'kʌʃn/ *n* commotion *f* cérébrale

condemn /kən'dem/ **A** *vt* **1** (gen) condamner
2 déclarer [qch] inhabitable ‹*building*›
B condemned *pp adj* ‹*cell*› des condamnés à mort; **~ed man/woman** condamné/-e *m/f* à mort

condensation /ˌkɒnden'seɪʃn/ *n* (on walls) condensation *f*; (on windows) buée *f*

condense /kən'dens/ **A** *vt* condenser
B *vi* se condenser

condensed milk *n* lait *m* concentré sucré

condescend /ˌkɒndɪ'send/ *vt* **to ~ to do** condescendre à faire

condescending /ˌkɒndɪ'sendɪŋ/ *adj* condescendant/-e

condition /kən'dɪʃn/ *n* **1** (gen) condition *f*; **on ~ that you come** à condition que tu viennes
2 (state) état *m*, condition *f*; **to be in good/bad ~** ‹*house, car*› être en bon/mauvais état
3 (disease) maladie *f*

conditional /kən'dɪʃənl/ *adj* conditionnel/-elle

conditioner /kən'dɪʃənə(r)/ *n* après-shampooing *m*, démêlant *m*

condolences *npl* condoléances *fpl*

C

condom /'kɒndɒm/ *n* préservatif *m*

condominium /ˌkɒndə'mɪnɪəm/ *n* (*also* ~ **unit**) (AmE) appartement *m* (dans une copropriété)

condone /kən'dəʊn/ *vt* tolérer

conducive /kən'dju:sɪv, (AmE) -'du:-/ *adj* ~ to favorable à

🔑 **conduct** **A** /'kɒndʌkt/ *n* conduite *f* (**towards** envers)
B /kən'dʌkt/ *vt* **1** mener ‹*business, campaign*›
2 mener ‹*experiment, inquiry*›; célébrer ‹*ceremony*›
3 (Mus) diriger ‹*orchestra*›
4 conduire ‹*electricity, heat*›

conductor /kən'dʌktə(r)/ *n* **1** (Mus) chef *m* d'orchestre
2 (on bus) receveur *m*; (on train) chef *m* de train

conductress /kən'dʌktrɪs/ *n* receveuse *f*

cone /kəʊn/ *n* **1** (shape) cône *m*
2 (*also* **ice-cream** ~) cornet *m*
3 (for traffic) balise *f*

confectioner /kən'fekʃənə(r)/ *n* (of sweets) confiseur/-euse *m/f*; (of cakes) pâtissier-confiseur *m*; **~'s (shop)** pâtisserie-confiserie *f*

confectionery /kən'fekʃənərɪ, (AmE) -ʃənerɪ/ *n* (sweets) confiserie *f*; (cakes) pâtisserie *f*

confer /kən'fɜ:(r)/ **A** *vt* (*p prés etc* **-rr-**) conférer (**on** à)
B *vi* (*p prés etc* **-rr-**) conférer (**about** de, **with** avec)

🔑 **conference** /'kɒnfərəns/ *n* (academic, business) conférence *f*; (political) congrès *m*

confess /kən'fes/ **A** *vt* **1** avouer (**that** que)
2 confesser ‹*sins*›
B *vi* avouer; **to ~ to a crime** avouer (avoir commis) un crime

confession /kən'feʃn/ *n* **1** (gen), (Law) aveu *m* (**of** de)
2 (in religion) confession *f*; **to go to ~** se confesser

confetti /kən'fetɪ/ *n* confettis *mpl*

confide /kən'faɪd/ *vi* **to ~ in** se confier à ‹*person*›

🔑 **confidence** /'kɒnfɪdəns/ *n* **1** (faith) confiance *f* (**in** en); **to have (every) ~ in sb/sth** avoir (pleine) confiance en qn/qch
2 (in politics) **vote of ~** vote *m* de confiance; **motion of no ~** motion *f* de censure
3 (self-assurance) assurance *f*, confiance *f* en soi
4 to tell sb sth in ~ dire qch à qn confidentiellement

confidence trick *n* escroquerie *f*

confident /'kɒnfɪdənt/ *adj* **1** (sure) sûr/-e, confiant/-e
2 (self-assured) assuré/-e, sûr/-e de soi

confidential /ˌkɒnfɪ'denʃl/ *adj* confidentiel/-ielle

configure /kən'fɪgə(r)/ *vt* configurer

confine /kən'faɪn/ *vt* **1** confiner ‹*person*› (**in, to** dans); enfermer ‹*animal*› (**in** dans)
2 (limit) limiter (**to** à)

confined /kən'faɪnd/ *adj* (gen) confiné/-e; ‹*space*› restreint/-e

confinement /kən'faɪnmənt/ *n* (in prison) détention *f*

🔑 **confirm** /kən'fɜ:m/ *vt* confirmer; **to ~ receipt of sth** accuser réception de qch

confirmation /ˌkɒnfə'meɪʃn/ *n* confirmation *f*

confirmed /kən'fɜ:md/ *adj* ‹*smoker, liar*› invétéré/-e; ‹*bachelor, sinner*› endurci/-e

confiscate /'kɒnfɪskeɪt/ *vt* confisquer (**from** à)

🔑 **conflict** **A** /'kɒnflɪkt/ *n* conflit *m*
B /kən'flɪkt/ *vi* être en contradiction (**with** avec)

conflicting /kən'flɪktɪŋ/ *adj* contradictoire

conform /kən'fɔ:m/ **A** *vt* conformer (**to** à)
B *vi* ‹*person*› se conformer (**with, to** à)

conformist /kən'fɔ:mɪst/ *n, adj* conformiste *mf*

confront /kən'frʌnt/ *vt* affronter ‹*danger, enemy*›; faire face à ‹*problem*›

confrontation /ˌkɒnfrʌn'teɪʃn/ *n* affrontement *m*

confrontational /ˌkɒnfrən'teɪʃənəl/ *adj* provocateur/-trice

🔑 **confuse** /kən'fju:z/ *vt* **1** (bewilder) troubler ‹*person*›
2 (mistake) confondre (**with** avec)
3 (complicate) compliquer ‹*argument*›; **to ~ the issue** compliquer les choses

confused /kən'fju:zd/ *adj* ‹*person*› troublé/-e; ‹*account, thoughts, mind*› confus/-e; **to get ~** s'embrouiller

confusing /kən'fju:zɪŋ/ *adj* déroutant/-e, peu clair/-e

confusion /kən'fju:ʒn/ *n* confusion *f*

congeal /kən'dʒi:l/ *vi* ‹*fat*› se figer; ‹*blood*› se coaguler

congenial /kən'dʒi:nɪəl/ *adj* agréable

congenital /kən'dʒenɪtl/ *adj* congénital/-e

congested /kən'dʒestɪd/ *adj* **1** ‹*road*› embouteillé/-e; ‹*district*› surpeuplé/-e
2 ‹*lungs*› congestionné/-e

congestion /kən'dʒestʃn/ *n* **1 traffic ~** embouteillages *mpl*
2 (of lungs) congestion *f*

congestion charge *n* péage *m* urbain

conglomerate /kən'glɒmərət/ *n* conglomérat *m*

congratulate /kən'grætʃʊleɪt/ *vt* féliciter (**on** de)

congratulations *npl* félicitations *fpl*; **~ on the birth of your new baby** félicitations à l'occasion de la naissance de votre bébé

congregate /'kɒŋgrɪgeɪt/ *vi* se rassembler

🔑 mot clé

congregation /ˌkɒŋgrɪˈgeɪʃn/ *n* assemblée *f* des fidèles

congress /ˈkɒŋgres, (AmE) ˈkɒŋgrəs/ *n* congrès *m* (**on** sur)

Congress /ˈkɒŋgres, (AmE) ˈkɒŋgrəs/ *n* (AmE) Congrès *m*

Congressional /kənˈgreʃənl/ *adj* (AmE) ‹*candidate*› au Congrès; ‹*committee*› du Congrès

congressman *n* (*pl* **-men**) (AmE) membre *m* du Congrès

conifer /ˈkɒnɪfə(r), ˈkəʊn-/ *n* conifère *m*

conjugal /ˈkɒndʒʊgl/ *adj* conjugal/-e

conjugate /ˈkɒndʒʊgeɪt/ **A** *vt* conjuguer **B** *vi* ‹*verb*› se conjuguer

conjunctivitis /kənˌdʒʌŋktɪˈvaɪtɪs/ *n* conjonctivite *f*

conjure /ˈkʌndʒə(r)/ *vi* faire des tours de prestidigitation

■ **conjure up** évoquer ‹*image*›

conjurer /ˈkʌndʒərə(r)/ *n* prestidigitateur/-trice *m/f*

con man *n* arnaqueur *m* (pop), escroc *m*

connect /kəˈnekt/ *vt* **1** raccorder ‹*end, hose*› (**to** à); accrocher ‹*coach*› (**to** à)
2 ‹*road, railway*› relier ‹*place, road*› (**to, with** à)
3 brancher ‹*appliance*› (**to** à)
4 raccorder ‹*phone, subscriber*›

connected /kəˈnektɪd/ *adj* **1** ‹*idea, event*› lié/-e (**to, with** à); **everything ~ with music** tout ce qui se rapporte à la musique
2 (in family) apparenté/-e (**to** à)

connecting /kəˈnektɪŋ/ *adj* **1** ‹*flight*› de correspondance
2 ‹*room*› attenant/-e

connection /kəˈnekʃn/ *n* **1** (link) (between events) rapport *m*; (of person) lien *m* (**between** entre, **with** avec); **in ~ with** au sujet de, à propos de
2 (contact) relation *f*; **to have useful ~s** avoir des relations
3 (to mains) branchement *m*
4 (to telephone network) raccordement *m*; (to number) mise *f* en communication (**to** avec); **bad ~** mauvaise communication *f*
5 (in travel) correspondance *f*
6 (Comput) connexion *f*; **Internet ~** connexion Internet

connive /kəˈnaɪv/ *vi* **to ~ at** contribuer délibérément à; **to ~ (with sb) to do** être de connivence *or* de mèche (fam) (avec qn) pour faire

connoisseur /ˌkɒnəˈsɜː(r)/ *n* connaisseur/-euse *m/f*

connotation /ˌkɒnəˈteɪʃn/ *n* connotation *f* (**of** de)

conquer /ˈkɒŋkə(r)/ *vt* conquérir ‹*territory, people*›; vaincre ‹*enemy, unemployment*›

conqueror /ˈkɒŋkərə(r)/ *n* conquérant/-e *m/f*

conquest /ˈkɒŋkwest/ *n* conquête *f*

conscience /ˈkɒnʃəns/ *n* conscience *f*; **they have no ~** ils n'ont aucun sens moral; **to have a guilty ~** avoir mauvaise conscience; **to have a clear ~** avoir la conscience tranquille

conscientious /ˌkɒnʃɪˈenʃəs/ *adj* consciencieux/-ieuse

conscientious objector, CO *n* objecteur *m* de conscience

conscious /ˈkɒnʃəs/ *adj* **1** (aware) conscient/-e (**of** de, **that** du fait que)
2 (deliberate) ‹*decision*› réfléchi/-e; ‹*effort*› consciencieux/-ieuse
3 (awake) réveillé/-e

consciousness /ˈkɒnʃəsnɪs/ *n* **to lose/regain ~** perdre/reprendre connaissance

conscript /ˈkɒnskrɪpt/ *n* appelé *m*

conscription /kənˈskrɪpʃn/ *n* (system) conscription *f*

consecrate /ˈkɒnsɪkreɪt/ *vt* consacrer

consecutive /kənˈsekjʊtɪv/ *adj* consécutif/-ive

consensus /kənˈsensəs/ *n* consensus *m* (**among** au sein de, **about** quant à, **on** sur)

consent /kənˈsent/ **A** *n* consentement *m*; **age of ~** âge *m* légal; **by common** *or* **mutual ~** d'un commun accord
B *vi* consentir (**to** à); **to ~ to sb doing** consentir à ce que qn fasse

consequence /ˈkɒnsɪkwəns, (AmE) -kwens/ *n* **1** conséquence *f*; **as a ~ of** du fait de ‹*change, process*›; à la suite de ‹*event*›
2 (importance) importance *f*

consequently /ˈkɒnsɪkwentlɪ/ *adv* par conséquent

conservation /ˌkɒnsəˈveɪʃn/ *n* **1** (of nature) protection *f* (**of** de); **energy ~** maîtrise *f* de l'énergie
2 (of heritage) conservation *f*

conservation area *n* zone *f* protégée

conservationist /ˌkɒnsəˈveɪʃənɪst/ *n* défenseur *m* des ressources naturelles

conservative /kənˈsɜːvətɪv/ **A** *n* conservateur/-trice *m/f*
B *adj* **1** ‹*party*› conservateur/-trice
2 ‹*taste, style*› classique

Conservative Party *n* (BrE) parti *m* conservateur

conservatory /kənˈsɜːvətrɪ, (AmE) -tɔːrɪ/ *n* **1** (for plants) jardin *m* d'hiver
2 (academy) conservatoire *m*

conserve /kənˈsɜːv/ **A** *n* confiture *f*
B *vt* **1** protéger ‹*forest*›; sauvegarder ‹*wildlife*›; conserver ‹*remains, ruins*›
2 économiser ‹*resources*›; ménager ‹*energy*›

consider /kənˈsɪdə(r)/ *vt* **1** (give thought to) considérer ‹*options, facts*›; examiner ‹*evidence, problem*›; étudier ‹*offer*›
2 (take into account) prendre [qch] en considération ‹*risk, cost*›; songer à ‹*person*›; faire attention à ‹*person's feelings*›

C

3 (envisage) **to ~ doing** envisager de faire; **to ~ sb/sth as sth** penser à qn/qch comme qch
4 (regard) **to ~ that** considérer *or* estimer que; **to ~ oneself (to be) a genius** se considérer comme un génie

considerable /kən'sɪdərəbl/ *adj* considérable

considerate /kən'sɪdərət/ *adj* ‹*person*› attentionné/-e; ‹*behaviour*› courtois/-e; **to be ~ towards sb** avoir des égards pour qn

🔑 **consideration** /kən,sɪdə'reɪʃn/ *n*
1 considération *f* (**for** envers); **to give sth careful ~** réfléchir longuement à qch; **to take sth into ~** prendre qch en considération; **out of ~** par considération
2 (fee) **for a ~** moyennant finance

considering /kən'sɪdərɪŋ/ *prep, conj* étant donné, compte tenu de

consign /kən'saɪn/ *vt* expédier ‹*goods*› (**to** à)

consignment /kən'saɪnmənt/ *n* (sending) expédition *f*; (goods) lot *m*, livraison *f*

🔑 **consist** /kən'sɪst/ *vi* **to ~ of** se composer de; **to ~ in** résider dans; **to ~ in doing** consister à faire

consistency /kən'sɪstənsɪ/ *n* **1** (texture) consistance *f*
2 (of view, policy) cohérence *f*

🔑 **consistent** /kən'sɪstənt/ *adj* **1** ‹*growth, level, quality*› régulier/-ière
2 ‹*attempts, demands*› répété/-e
3 ‹*argument*› cohérent/-e; **~ with** en accord avec ‹*account, belief*›

consistently /kən'sɪstəntlɪ/ *adv* (invariably) systématiquement; (repeatedly) à maintes reprises

consolation /,kɒnsə'leɪʃn/ *n* consolation *f* (**to** pour)

console **A** /'kɒnsəʊl/ *n* **1** (control panel) console *f*
2 (for hi-fi) meuble *m* hi-fi; (for video) meuble *m* vidéo
B /kən'səʊl/ *vt* consoler (**for, on** de, **with** avec)

consolidate /kən'sɒlɪdeɪt/ *vt* **1** consolider ‹*position*›
2 réunir ‹*resources*›; fusionner ‹*companies*›

consonant /'kɒnsənənt/ *n* consonne *f*

consortium /kən'sɔ:tɪəm/ *n* (*pl* **-tiums** *ou* **-tia**) consortium *m*

conspicuous /kən'spɪkjʊəs/ *adj* ‹*feature, sign*› visible; ‹*garment*› voyant/-e; **to be ~** se remarquer

conspiracy /kən'spɪrəsɪ/ *n* conspiration *f*

conspirator /kən'spɪrətə(r)/ *n* conspirateur/-trice *m/f*

conspire /kən'spaɪə(r)/ *vi* conspirer; **to ~ to do** ‹*people*› conspirer en vue de faire; ‹*events*› conspirer à faire

constable /'kʌnstəbl, (AmE) 'kɒn-/ *n* (BrE) agent *m* de police

🔑 **constant** /'kɒnstənt/ *adj* ‹*problem, reminder, threat*› permanent/-e; ‹*care, temperature*› constant/-e; ‹*disputes, questions*› incessant/-e; ‹*attempts*› répété/-e; ‹*companion*› éternel/-elle

constantly /'kɒnstəntlɪ/ *adv* constamment

constellation /,kɒnstə'leɪʃn/ *n* constellation *f*

constipated /'kɒnstɪpeɪtɪd/ *adj* constipé/-e

constipation /,kɒnstɪ'peɪʃn/ *n* constipation *f*

constituency /kən'stɪtjʊənsɪ/ *n* (district) circonscription *f* électorale; (voters) électeurs *mpl*

constituent /kən'stɪtjʊənt/ *n* **1** (Pol) électeur/-trice *m/f*
2 (of character) trait *m*; (of event, work of art) élément *m*

constitute /'kɒnstɪtju:t/ *vt* constituer

constitution /,kɒnstɪ'tju:ʃn, (AmE) -'tu:ʃn/ *n* constitution *f*

constitutional /,kɒnstɪ'tju:ʃənl, (AmE) -'tu:-/ *adj* constitutionnel/-elle

constraint /kən'streɪnt/ *n* contrainte *f*

constrict /kən'strɪkt/ *vt* comprimer ‹*flow, blood vessel*›; gêner ‹*breathing, movement*›

🔑 **construct** /kən'strʌkt/ *vt* construire (**of** avec, **in** en)

🔑 **construction** /kən'strʌkʃn/ *n* construction *f*

construction site *n* chantier *m*

construction worker *n* ouvrier/-ière *m/f* du bâtiment

constructive /kən'strʌktɪv/ *adj* constructif/-ive

consul /'kɒnsl/ *n* consul *m*

consulate /'kɒnsjʊlət, (AmE) -səl-/ *n* consulat *m*

consult /kən'sʌlt/ **A** *vt* consulter (**about** sur)
B *vi* s'entretenir (**about** sur, **with** avec)

consultancy /kən'sʌltənsɪ/ *n* (*also* **~ firm**) cabinet-conseil *m*

consultant /kən'sʌltənt/ *n* **1** (expert) consultant/-e *m/f*, conseiller/-ère *m/f* (**on, in** en)
2 (BrE) (doctor) spécialiste *mf*

consultation /,kɒnsl'teɪʃn/ *n* (for advice) consultation *f* (**about** sur); (for discussion) entretien *m* (**about** sur); **after ~ with** après avoir consulté

consumables /kən'sju:məblz, (AmE) -'su:m-/ *npl* consommables *mpl*

consume /kən'sju:m, (AmE) -'su:m-/ *vt* **1** (use up) consommer ‹*fuel, food, drink*›
2 to be ~d by *or* **with** être dévoré/-e par ‹*envy*›; brûler de ‹*desire*›; être rongé/-e par ‹*guilt*›

🔑 **consumer** /kən'sju:mə(r), (AmE) -'su:m-/ *n* consommateur/-trice *m/f*; (of electricity, gas) abonné/-e *m/f*

consumer advice *n* conseils *mpl* au consommateurs

🔑 mot clé

consumer goods *npl* biens *mpl* de consommation

consumer protection *n* défense *f* du consommateur

consumer society *n* société *f* de consommation

consummate /ˈkɒnsəmeɪt/ *vt* consommer ‹*marriage*›

consumption /kənˈsʌmpʃn/ *n* consommation *f*

contact **A** /ˈkɒntækt/ *n* **1** (gen) contact *m* (**between** entre, **with** avec); **to be in/make ~** être en/se mettre en contact
2 (acquaintance) connaissance *f*; (professional) contact *m*
B /kənˈtækt, ˈkɒntækt/ *vt* contacter, se mettre en rapport avec

contact lens *n* lentille *f* *or* verre *m* de contact

contactless /ˈkɒntæktləs/ *adj* ‹*card*› sans contacts

contagious /kənˈteɪdʒəs/ *adj* contagieux/-ieuse

contain /kənˈteɪn/ *vt* **1** contenir ‹*amount, ingredients*›; contenir, comporter ‹*information, mistakes*›
2 (curb) maîtriser ‹*blaze*›; enrayer ‹*epidemic*›; limiter ‹*costs, problem*›; retenir ‹*flood*›

container /kənˈteɪnə(r)/ *n* (for food, liquids) récipient *m*; (for plants) bac *m*; (for waste, for transporting) conteneur *m*

contaminate /kənˈtæmɪneɪt/ *vt* contaminer

contamination /kənˌtæmɪˈneɪʃn/ *n* contamination *f*

contemplate /ˈkɒntəmpleɪt/ *vt* **1** (consider) envisager (**doing** de faire)
2 (look at) contempler

contemporary /kənˈtemprərɪ, (AmE) -pərerɪ/ **A** *n* contemporain/-e *m/f*
B *adj* (present-day) contemporain/-e; (up-to-date) moderne; (of same period) de l'époque

contempt /kənˈtempt/ *n* mépris *m* (**for** de); **to hold sb/sth in ~** mépriser qn/qch; **~ of court** (Law) outrage *m* à magistrat

contemptible /kənˈtemptəbl/ *adj* méprisable

contemptuous /kənˈtemptjʊəs/ *adj* méprisant/-e

contend /kənˈtend/ **A** *vt* soutenir (**that** que)
B *vi* **1** (deal with) **to ~ with** affronter
2 (compete) **to ~ with sb for sth** disputer qch à qn

contender /kənˈtendə(r)/ *n* **1** (in competition) concurrent/-e *m/f*
2 (for post) candidat/-e *m/f* (**for** à)

content **A** *n* **1** (quantity) teneur *f*
2 (of book, essay) fond *m*
B /kənˈtent/ *adj* satisfait/-e (**with** de)

contented /kənˈtentɪd/ *adj* ‹*person*› content/-e (**with** de); ‹*feeling*› de bien-être

contention /kənˈtenʃn/ *n* **1** (opinion) assertion *f*
2 (dispute) dispute *f*

contentment /kənˈtentmənt/ *n* contentement *m*

contents *npl* (gen) contenu *m*; (of house, for insurance) biens *mpl* mobiliers; **list** *or* **table of ~** table *f* des matières

contest **A** /ˈkɒntest/ *n* **1** (competition) concours *m*
2 (struggle) lutte *f*
B /kənˈtest/ *vt* **1** contester ‹*decision, will*›
2 (compete for) disputer ‹*match*›

contestant /kənˈtestənt/ *n* (in competition, game) concurrent/-e *m/f*; (in fight) adversaire *mf*; (for job, in election) candidat/-e *m/f*

context /ˈkɒntekst/ *n* contexte *m*

continent /ˈkɒntɪnənt/ *n* **1** continent *m*
2 the Continent (BrE) l'Europe *f* continentale

continental /ˌkɒntɪˈnentl/ *adj*
1 continental/-e
2 (BrE) ‹*holiday*› en Europe continentale

continental breakfast *n* petit déjeuner *m* (*avec café, pain, beurre et confiture*)

continental quilt *n* (BrE) couette *f*

contingency /kənˈtɪndʒənsɪ/ *n* imprévu *m*

contingency fund *n* fonds *m* de secours

contingency plan *n* plan *m* de réserve

continual /kənˈtɪnjʊəl/ *adj* continuel/-elle

continually /kənˈtɪnjʊəlɪ/ *adv* continuellement

continuation /kənˌtɪnjʊˈeɪʃn/ *n* **1** (gen) continuation *f*
2 (of story) suite *f*; (of route) prolongement *m*

continue /kənˈtɪnjuː/ **A** *vt* continuer
B *vi* ‹*person*› continuer (**doing, to do** à *or* de faire); ‹*noise, debate, strike*› se poursuivre; **to ~ with** continuer, poursuivre ‹*task, treatment*›

continuity /ˌkɒntɪˈnjuːɪtɪ/ *n* continuité *f*

continuous /kənˈtɪnjʊəs/ *adj* **1** ‹*growth, decline, noise*› continu/-e; ‹*care*› constant/-e; ‹*line*› ininterrompu/-e; **~ assessment** (BrE) contrôle *m* continu
2 ‹*tense*› progressif/-ive

continuously /kənˈtɪnjʊəslɪ/ *adv* (without a break) sans interruption; (repeatedly) continuellement

contort /kənˈtɔːt/ *vt* tordre

contortion /kənˈtɔːʃn/ *n* contorsion *f*

contour /ˈkɒntʊə(r)/ *n* **1** (outline) contour *m*
2 (*also* **~ line**) courbe *f* hypsométrique *or* de niveau

contraband /ˈkɒntrəbænd/ *n* contrebande *f*

contraception /ˌkɒntrəˈsepʃn/ *n* contraception *f*

contraceptive /ˌkɒntrəˈseptɪv/ **A** *n* contraceptif *m*
B *adj* contraceptif/-ive

C

🔑 **contract** **A** /ˈkɒntrækt/ *n* contrat *m*
B /kənˈtrækt/ *vt* **1** (gen) contracter
2 to be ~ed to do être tenu/-e par contrat de faire
C /kənˈtrækt/ *vi* **1 to ~ to do** s'engager par contrat à faire
2 ‹*muscle, wood*› se contracter

contraction /kənˈtrækʃn/ *n* contraction *f*

contract killer *n* tueur/-euse *m/f* à gages

contractor /kənˈtræktə(r)/ *n* **1** (business) entrepreneur/-euse *m/f*
2 (worker) contractuel/-elle *m/f*

contradict /ˌkɒntrəˈdɪkt/ *vt, vi* contredire

contradiction /ˌkɒntrəˈdɪkʃn/ *n* contradiction *f*

contradictory /ˌkɒntrəˈdɪktərɪ/ *adj* contradictoire (**to** à)

contraflow /ˈkɒntrəfləʊ/ *n* (BrE) circulation *f* à sens alterné

contraindication /ˌkɒntrəɪndɪˈkeɪʃn/ *n* contre-indication *f*

contrary /ˈkɒntrərɪ, (AmE) -trerɪ/ **A** *n* contraire *m*; **on the ~** (bien) au contraire; **unless you hear anything to the ~** sauf contrordre
B *adj* **1** ‹*idea, view*› contraire
2 ‹*person*› contrariant/-e
C contrary to *phr* contrairement à

🔑 **contrast** **A** /ˈkɒntrɑːst, (AmE) -træst/ *n* contraste *m*; **in ~ to sth, by ~ with sth** par contraste avec qch; **in ~ to sb** à la différence de qn; **by** *or* **in ~** par contre
B /kənˈtrɑːst, (AmE) -ˈtræst/ *vt* **to ~ X with Y** faire ressortir le contraste (qui existe) entre X et Y
C *vi* contraster (**with** avec)

contrasting *adj* ‹*examples*› opposé/-e; ‹*colour*› contrasté/-e; ‹*views*› très different/-e

🔑 **contribute** /kənˈtrɪbjuːt/ **A** *vt* **1** verser ‹*sum*› (**to** à); **to ~ £5m** contribuer pour 5 millions de livres sterling
2 (to gift, charity) donner (**to** à, **towards** pour)
3 apporter ‹*ideas*› (**to** à); écrire ‹*article*› (**to** pour)
B *vi* **1 to ~ to** *or* **towards** contribuer à ‹*change, decline*›
2 (to community life, research) participer (**to** à); (to programme, magazine) collaborer (**to** à)
3 to ~ to cotiser à ‹*pension fund*›
4 (to charity) donner (**to** à)

🔑 **contribution** /ˌkɒntrɪˈbjuːʃn/ *n* **1** (to tax, pension, profits, cost) contribution *f* (**towards** à)
2 (to charity, campaign) don *m*; **to make a ~** faire un don (**to** à)
3 sb's ~ to le rôle que qn a joué dans ‹*success, undertaking*›; ce que qn a apporté à ‹*science, sport*›
4 (to programme) participation *f*; (to magazine) article *m*

contributor /kənˈtrɪbjʊtə(r)/ *n* (to charity) donateur/-trice *m/f*; (in discussion) participant/-e *m/f*; (to magazine, book) collaborateur/-trice *m/f*

con trick *n* (fam) escroquerie *f*, duperie *f*

contrive /kənˈtraɪv/ *vt* (arrange) organiser; **to ~ to do** parvenir à faire

contrived /kənˈtraɪvd/ *adj* **1** ‹*incident, meeting*› non fortuit/-e
2 ‹*plot*› tiré/-e par les cheveux; ‹*style, effect*› étudié/-e

🔑 **control** /kənˈtrəʊl/ **A** *n* **1** (gen) contrôle *m* (**of** de); (of operation, project) direction *f* (**of** de); (of life, emotion, self) maîtrise *f* (**of, over** de); **to be in ~ of** contrôler ‹*territory*›; diriger ‹*operation, organization*›; maîtriser ‹*problem*›; avoir le contrôle de ‹*ball, vehicle*›; **to be in ~ (of oneself)** se maîtriser; **to bring** *or* **keep [sth] under ~** maîtriser; **to lose ~ (of sth)** perdre le contrôle (de qch)
2 (on vehicle, equipment) commande *f*; (on TV) bouton *m* de réglage; **to be at the ~s** être aux commandes
B *vt* (*p prés etc* **-ll-**) **1** dominer ‹*organization, situation*›; contrôler ‹*territory*›; diriger ‹*traffic, project*›; être majoritaire dans ‹*company*›
2 maîtriser ‹*person, animal, inflation, fire*›; endiguer ‹*epidemic*›; dominer ‹*emotion*›; retenir ‹*laughter*›; **to ~ oneself** se contrôler
3 commander ‹*machine*›; manœuvrer ‹*boat, vehicle*›; piloter ‹*plane*›; contrôler ‹*ball*›
4 régler ‹*speed, temperature*›; contrôler ‹*immigration, prices*›

control panel *n* (on plane) tableau *m* de bord; (on machine) tableau *m* de contrôle; (on TV) (panneau *m* de) commandes *fpl*; (on computer) panneau *m* de configuration

control room *n* poste *m* de commande; (TV) (salle *f* de) régie *f*

control tower *n* tour *f* de contrôle

controversial /ˌkɒntrəˈvɜːʃl/ *adj* (gen) controversé/-e; (open to criticism) qui prête à controverse

controversy /ˈkɒntrəvɜːsɪ, kənˈtrɒvəsɪ/ *n* controverse *f*

conundrum /kəˈnʌndrəm/ *n* énigme *f*

convalesce /ˌkɒnvəˈles/ *vi* se remettre

convene /kənˈviːn/ *vt* organiser ‹*meeting*›; convoquer ‹*group*›

convenience /kənˈviːnɪəns/ *n* avantage *m* (**of doing** de faire); (of device, food, shop) commodité *f*; **for (the sake of) ~** pour raisons de commodité; **at your ~** quand cela vous conviendra

convenience foods *npl* plats *mpl* (tout) préparés

convenient /kənˈviːnɪənt/ *adj* **1** ‹*place, time*› pratique; **to be ~ for sb** convenir à qn
2 (useful, practical) pratique, commode
3 ‹*shops*› situé/-e tout près; ‹*chair*› à portée de main

convent /ˈkɒnvənt, (AmE) -vent/ *n* couvent *m*

🔑 mot clé

convention /kən'venʃn/ *n* **1** (gen) convention *f*
2 (social norms) convenances *fpl*, conventions *fpl*

conventional /kən'venʃənl/ *adj* (gen) conventionnel/-elle; ‹*person*› conformiste; ‹*medicine*› traditionnel/-elle

converge /kən'vɜːdʒ/ *vi* converger

conversant /kən'vɜːsnt/ *adj* **to be ~ with** être versé/-e dans

conversation /ˌkɒnvə'seɪʃn/ *n* conversation *f*

converse /kən'vɜːs/ *vi* converser (**with** avec, **in** en)

conversion /kən'vɜːʃn, (AmE) kən'vɜːrʒn/ *n* (of currency, measurement) conversion *f* (**from** de, **into** en); (of building) aménagement *m* (**to, into** en); (to new beliefs) conversion *f* (**from** de, **to** à); (in rugby) transformation *f*

conversion rate *n* taux *m* de change

convert **A** /'kɒnvɜːt/ *n* converti/-e *m/f* (**to** à)
B /kən'vɜːt/ *vt* **1** (change into sth else) transformer; (modify) adapter
2 convertir ‹*currency, measurement*› (**from** de, **to, into** en)
3 aménager ‹*building, loft*› (**to, into** en)
4 (to new beliefs) convertir (**to** à, **from** de)
5 (in rugby) transformer ‹*try*›
C /kən'vɜːt/ *vi* **1** ‹*sofa, device*› être convertible (**into** en)
2 ‹*person*› se convertir (**to** à, **from** de)

convertible /kən'vɜːtəbl/ *n* décapotable *f*

convex /'kɒnveks/ *adj* convexe

convey /kən'veɪ/ *vt* **1** ‹*person*› transmettre ‹*information*› (**to** à); exprimer ‹*condolences, feeling, idea*› (**to** à)
2 ‹*words, images*› traduire ‹*mood, impression*›
3 ‹*vehicle*› transporter; ‹*pipes*› amener

conveyancing /kən'veɪənsɪŋ/ *n* rédaction *f* des actes de propriété

conveyor belt *n* (in factory) transporteur *m* à bande *or* à courroie; (for luggage) tapis *m* roulant

convict **A** /'kɒnvɪkt/ *n* (imprisoned criminal) détenu/-e *m/f*; (deported criminal) bagnard *m*
B /kən'vɪkt/ *vt* reconnaître *or* déclarer [qn] coupable (**of** de, **of doing** d'avoir fait)

conviction /kən'vɪkʃn/ *n* **1** (Law) condamnation *f* (**for** pour)
2 (belief) conviction *f* (**that** que)

convince /kən'vɪns/ *vt* convaincre ‹*person*› (**to do** de faire)

convincing /kən'vɪnsɪŋ/ *adj* ‹*account, evidence*› convaincant/-e; ‹*victory, lead*› indiscutable

convoy /'kɒnvɔɪ/ *n* convoi *m*

convulsion /kən'vʌlʃn/ *n* convulsion *f*

coo /kuː/ *vi* roucouler

cook /kʊk/ **A** *n* cuisinier/-ière *m/f*
B *vt* faire cuire ‹*vegetables, pasta, eggs*›; préparer ‹*meal*› (**for** pour)
C *vi* ‹*person*› cuisiner, faire la cuisine; ‹*vegetable, meat, meal*› cuire

cook-chill foods *npl* plats *mpl* préparés, plats *mpl* cuisinés

cooker /'kʊkə(r)/ *n* (BrE) cuisinière *f*

cookery book *n* (BrE) livre de cuisine

cookie /'kʊkɪ/ *n* **1** (biscuit) gateau *m* sec, biscuit *m*
2 (Comput) cookie *m*

cooking /'kʊkɪŋ/ *n* cuisine *f*

cooking apple *n* pomme *f* à cuire

cooking chocolate *n* chocolat *m* pâtissier

cool /kuːl/ **A** *n* **1** (coldness) fraîcheur *f*
2 (fam) (calm) sang-froid *m*; **to keep one's ~** (not get angry) ne pas s'énerver; (stay calm) garder son sang-froid; **to lose one's ~** (get angry) s'énerver; (panic) perdre son sang-froid
B *adj* **1** ‹*day, drink, water, weather*› frais/fraîche; ‹*dress*› léger/-ère; ‹*colour*› froid/-e
2 (calm) calme
3 (unfriendly) froid/-e
4 (casual) décontracté/-e, cool *inv* (fam)
5 (fam) (trendy) branché/-e (fam)
C *vt* **1** refroidir ‹*soup*›; rafraîchir ‹*wine, room*›
2 calmer ‹*anger, ardour*›
D *vi* **1** (get colder) refroidir
2 ‹*enthusiasm*› faiblir; ‹*friendship*› se dégrader

■ **cool down** ‹*engine, water*› refroidir; ‹*person, situation*› se calmer

cool bag *n* sac *m* isotherme

cool box *n* (BrE) glacière *f*

cooling-off period *n* (in industrial relations) délai *m* de conciliation; (in contract) délai *m* de réflexion

coop /kuːp/ *n* poulailler *m*

■ **coop up**: **~ [sb/sth] up** enfermer, cloîtrer

cooperate /kəʊ'ɒpəreɪt/ *vi* coopérer (**with** avec, **in** à, **in doing** pour faire)

cooperation /kəʊˌɒpə'reɪʃn/ *n* coopération *f* (**on** à)

cooperative /kəʊ'ɒpərətɪv/ **A** *n*
1 (organization) coopérative *f*
2 (AmE) (apartment house) immeuble *m* en copropriété
B *adj* coopératif/-ive

coordinate **A** /ˌkəʊ'ɔːdɪnət/ *n* (on map, graph) coordonnée *f*
B /ˌkəʊ'ɔːdɪneɪt/ *vt* coordonner (**with** avec)

coordinates *npl* (clothes) ensemble *m*

coordination /ˌkəʊˌɔːdɪ'neɪʃn/ *n* coordination *f*

coordinator /ˌkəʊ'ɔːdɪneɪtə(r)/ *n* coordinateur/-trice *m/f*

cope /kəʊp/ *vi* s'en sortir (fam), se débrouiller; **to ~ with** s'occuper de ‹*person, work*›; faire face à ‹*demand, disaster, problem*›; supporter ‹*death, depression, difficult person*›

Copenhagen /ˌkəʊpn'heɪgən/ *pr n* Copenhague

copious /'kəʊpɪəs/ *adj* **1** (plentiful) ‹*supply*› abondant/-e
2 (generous) ‹*quantity, serving*› copieux/-ieuse

cop-out *n* (fam) (excuse) excuse *f* bidon (fam)

copper /'kɒpə(r)/ *n* **1** (metal) cuivre *m*
2 (BrE) (fam) (coin) petite monnaie *f*
3 (BrE) (fam) (policeman) flic *m* (fam)
4 (colour) couleur *f* cuivre

⚷ **copy** /'kɒpɪ/ **A** *n* **1** (gen) copie *f*
2 (of book, newspaper, report) exemplaire *m*
B *vt* copier (**from** sur)
C *vi* copier
■ **copy down**, **copy out** recopier ‹*quote, address*›

copyright /'kɒpɪraɪt/ *n* copyright *m*, droit *m* d'auteur

coral /'kɒrəl, (AmE) 'kɔːrəl/ *n* corail *m*

cord /kɔːd/ **A** *n* cordon *m*
B **cords** *npl* (fam) (*also* **corduroys**) pantalon *m* en velours (côtelé)

cordial /'kɔːdɪəl, (AmE) 'kɔːrdʒəl/ **A** *n* **1** (fruit drink) sirop *m* de fruits
2 (AmE) (liqueur) liqueur *m*
B *adj* cordial/-e (**to, with** avec)

cordless /'kɔːdlɪs/ *adj* ‹*telephone, kettle*› sans fil

cordon /'kɔːdn/ *n* cordon *m*
■ **cordon off** boucler ‹*street, area*›; contenir ‹*crowd*›

corduroy /'kɔːdərɔɪ/ *n* velours *m* côtelé

⚷ **core** /kɔː(r)/ *n* **1** (of apple) trognon *m*
2 (of problem) cœur *m*
3 **rotten to the ∼** pourri/-e jusqu'à l'os; **English to the ∼** anglais/-e jusqu'au bout des ongles
4 (of nuclear reactor) cœur *m*
5 (small group) noyau *m*; **hard ∼** noyau dur

core curriculum *n* tronc *m* commun

Corfu /kɔː'fuː/ *pr n* Corfou *f*

cork /kɔːk/ *n* **1** (substance) liège *m*
2 (object) bouchon *m*

corkscrew *n* tire-bouchon *m*

corn /kɔːn/ *n* **1** (BrE) (wheat) blé *m*
2 (AmE) (maize) maïs *m*
3 (on foot) cor *m*

cornea /'kɔːnɪə/ *n* (*pl* **∼s** *ou* **-neae**) cornée *f*

⚷ **corner** /'kɔːnə(r)/ **A** *n* **1** (gen) coin *m*; **the house on the ∼** la maison qui fait l'angle; **at the ∼ of the street** au coin de la rue; **to go round the ∼** tourner au coin de la rue; **just around the ∼** (nearby) tout près; (around the bend) juste après le coin; **out of the ∼ of one's eye** du coin de l'œil
2 (bend) virage *m*
3 (in boxing) coin *m* (de repos); (in football, hockey) corner *m*
B *vt* **1** acculer ‹*animal, enemy*›; coincer (fam) ‹*person*›
2 accaparer ‹*market*›
IDIOMS **in a tight ∼** dans une impasse; **to cut ∼s** (financially) faire des économies

corner shop *n* petite épicerie *f*

cornerstone *n* pierre *f* angulaire

cornflour *n* farine *f* de maïs

cornflower *n* bleuet *m*, barbeau *m*

corn on the cob *n* maïs *m* en épi

Cornwall /'kɔːnwɔːl/ *pr n* (comté *m* de) Cornouailles *f*

corny /'kɔːnɪ/ *adj* (fam) ‹*joke*› (old) éculé/-e; (feeble) faiblard/-e (fam); ‹*film, story*› à la guimauve

coronary /'kɒrənrɪ, (AmE) 'kɔːrənerɪ/ *n* infarctus *m*

coronation /ˌkɒrə'neɪʃn, (AmE) ˌkɔːr-/ *n* couronnement *m*

coroner /'kɒrənə(r), (AmE) 'kɔːr-/ *n* coroner *m*

corporal /'kɔːpərəl/ *n* (gen) caporal *m*; (in artillery) brigadier *m*

corporal punishment *n* châtiment *m* corporel

⚷ **corporate** /'kɔːpərət/ *adj* **1** ‹*accounts, funds*› appartenant/-e à une société; ‹*clients, employees*› d'une société (*or* de sociétés)
2 ‹*action*› commun/-e; ‹*decision*› collectif/-ive

corporate identity, **corporate image** *n* image *f* de marque (d'une société)

corporate raider *n* raider *m* (*organisateur d'OPA*)

corporation /ˌkɔːpə'reɪʃn/ *n* (grande) société *f*

corps /kɔː(r)/ *n* corps *m*

corpse /kɔːps/ *n* cadavre *m*

⚷ **correct** /kə'rekt/ **A** *adj* **1** ‹*amount, answer, decision*› correct/-e; ‹*figure, time*› exact/-e
2 ‹*behaviour*› correct/-e, convenable
B *vt* corriger

correcting fluid *n* liquide *m* correcteur

correction /kə'rekʃn/ *n* correction *f*

correspond /ˌkɒrɪ'spɒnd, (AmE) ˌkɔːr-/ *vi* **1** (match) concorder, correspondre (**with** à)
2 (be equivalent) être équivalent/-e (**to** à)
3 (exchange letters) correspondre (**with** avec, **about** au sujet de)

correspondence /ˌkɒrɪ'spɒndəns, (AmE) ˌkɔːr-/ *n* correspondance *f*

correspondence course *n* cours *m* par correspondance

correspondent /ˌkɒrɪ'spɒndənt, (AmE) ˌkɔːr-/ *n* **1** (journalist) journaliste *mf*; (abroad) correspondant/-e *m/f*
2 (letter writer) correspondant/-e *m/f*

corresponding /ˌkɒrɪ'spɒndɪŋ, (AmE) ˌkɔːr-/ *adj* (matching) correspondant/-e; (similar) équivalent/-e

⚷ mot clé

corridor /ˈkɒrɪdɔː(r), (AmE) ˈkɔːr-/ *n* **1** couloir *m*
2 (of land) corridor *m*
corroborate /kəˈrɒbəreɪt/ *vt* corroborer
corrode /kəˈrəʊd/ **A** *vt* corroder
B *vi* se corroder
corrosion /kəˈrəʊʒn/ *n* corrosion *f*
corrugated /ˈkɒrəgeitɪd, (AmE) ˈkɔːr-/ *adj* ondulé/-e
corrugated iron *n* tôle *f* ondulée
corrupt /kəˈrʌpt/ **A** *adj* corrompu/-e
B *vt* corrompre
corruption /kəˈrʌpʃn/ *n* corruption *f*
Corsica /ˈkɔːsɪkə/ *pr n* Corse *f*
cosh /kɒʃ/ *n* (BrE) matraque *f*
cosmetic /kɒzˈmetɪk/ **A** *n* produit *m* de beauté
B *adj* (fig) superficiel/-ielle
cosmetic surgery *n* chirurgie *f* esthétique
cosmonaut /ˈkɒzmənɔːt/ *n* cosmonaute *mf*
cosmopolitan /ˌkɒzməˈpɒlɪtn/ *n, adj* cosmopolite *mf*
cost /kɒst, (AmE) kɔːst/ **A** *n* **1** (price) coût *m*, prix *m* (**of** de); (expense incurred) frais *mpl*; **at ~** au prix coûtant
2 (fig) prix *m*; **at all ~s** à tout prix; **he knows to his ~ that** il a appris à ses dépens que
B *vt* **1** (*prét, pp* **cost**) coûter; **how much does it ~?** combien ça coûte?; **the TV will ~ £100 to repair** la réparation de la télé coûtera 100 livres sterling
2 (*prét, pp* **costed**) (estimate price of) calculer le prix de revient de ‹*product*›; calculer le coût de ‹*project, work*›
co-star /ˈkəʊstɑː(r)/ **A** *n* co-vedette *f*
B *vt* **a film ~ring X and Y** un film avec X et Y
cost-cutting /ˈkɒstkʌtɪŋ, (AmE) ˈkɔːst-/ *n* réduction *f* des frais
cost-effective *adj* rentable
costly /ˈkɒstlɪ, (AmE) ˈkɔːstlɪ/ *adj* coûteux/-euse
cost of living *n* coût *m* de la vie
cost price *n* (for producer) prix *m* de revient; (for consumer) prix *m* coûtant
costume /ˈkɒstjuːm, (AmE) -tuːm/ *n*
1 (clothes) costume *m*
2 (*also* **swimming ~**) (BrE) maillot *m* de bain
costume jewellery (BrE), **costume jewelry** (AmE) *n* bijoux *mpl* fantaisie
cosy (BrE), **cozy** (AmE) /ˈkəʊzɪ/ *adj* (comfortable) douillet/-ette; (intimate) intime; **it's ~ here** on est bien ici
cot /kɒt/ *n* **1** (BrE) (for baby) lit *m* de bébé
2 (AmE) (bed) lit *m* de camp
cot death *n* (BrE) mort *f* subite du nourrisson
cottage /ˈkɒtɪdʒ/ *n* maisonnette *f*; (thatched) chaumière *f*
cottage cheese *n* fromage *m* blanc à gros grains
cotton /ˈkɒtn/ *n* **1** (plant, material) coton *m*
2 (thread) fil *m* de coton
cotton bud *n* Coton-Tige® *m*
cotton wool *n* ouate *f* (de coton)
couch /kaʊtʃ/ *n* **1** (sofa) canapé *m*
2 (doctor's) lit *m*; (psychoanalyst's) divan *m*
couch potato *n* (fam) pantouflard/-e *m/f* (fam) (*qui passe son temps devant la télé*)
cough /kɒf, (AmE) kɔːf/ **A** *n* toux *f*; **to have a ~** tousser
B *vi* tousser
cough mixture *n* (sirop *m*) antitussif *m*
could /kʊd, kəd/ *modal aux* **1** (be able to) pouvoir; **I couldn't move** je ne pouvais pas bouger; **she couldn't come yesterday** elle n'a pas pu venir hier
2 (know how to) savoir; **he couldn't swim** il ne savait pas nager; **she ~ speak four languages** elle parlait quatre langues
3 (permission, requests, suggestions) pouvoir; **we ~ only go out at weekends** nous ne pouvions sortir *or* nous n'avions le droit de sortir que le week-end; **~ I speak to Annie?** est-ce que je pourrais parler à Annie?; **~ you help me?** pourrais-tu m'aider?
4 (with verbs of perception) **I couldn't see a thing** je n'y voyais rien; **they couldn't understand me** ils ne me comprenaient pas; **we ~ hear them laughing** on les entendait rire
5 you ~ have died tu aurais pu mourir; **they ~ have warned us** ils auraient pu nous prévenir; **I ~ be wrong** je me trompe peut-être; **if only I ~ start again** si seulement je pouvais tout recommencer
council /ˈkaʊnsl/ *n* conseil *m*; **the town ~** le conseil municipal; **the Council of Europe** le Conseil de l'Europe
council estate *n* lotissement *m* de logements sociaux
council house *n* habitation *f* à loyer modéré
council housing *n* logements *mpl* sociaux
councillor, **councilor** (BrE) /ˈkaʊnsələ(r)/ *n* conseiller/-ère *m/f*
council scheme *n* (Scotland) ▶ **council estate**
council tax *n* (BrE) ≈ impôts *mpl* locaux
counsel /ˈkaʊnsl/ **A** *n* (lawyer) avocat/-e *m/f*
B *vt* conseiller ‹*person*› (**about, on** sur)
counselling (BrE), **counseling** (AmE) /ˈkaʊnsəlɪŋ/ *n* (advice) assistance *f*; (psychological) aide *f* psychosociale; **debt ~** assistance aux personnes endettées; **bereavement ~** aide psychosociale aux personnes endeuillées
counsellor, **counselor** (BrE) /ˈkaʊnsələ(r)/ *n* conseiller/-ère *m/f*
count /kaʊnt/ **A** *n* **1** (numerical record) décompte *m*; (at election) dépouillement *m*; **at the last ~** au dernier décompte; **to keep (a) ~ of** tenir compte de; **to lose ~** ne plus savoir où on en est dans ses calculs; **to be**

out for the ~ (fam) être KO (fam)
2 (level) taux *m*; **cholesterol ~** taux de cholestérol
3 (figure) chiffre *m*
4 (Law) chef *m* d'accusation; **on three ~s** pour trois chefs d'accusation
5 (nobleman) comte *m*
B *vt* **1** compter ‹*points, people, objects*›; énumérer ‹*reasons, causes*›; **~ing the children** en comptant les enfants; **not ~ing my sister** sans compter ma sœur
2 (consider) **to ~ sb as sth** considérer qn comme qch
C *vi* compter; **it's the thought that ~s** c'est l'intention qui compte

▪ **count against** jouer contre ‹*person*›
▪ **count on** compter sur ‹*person, event*›; **don't ~ on it!** ne comptez pas dessus!
▪ **count up** calculer ‹*cost, hours*›; compter ‹*money, boxes*›

countdown /ˈkaʊntdaʊn/ *n* compte *m* à rebours (**to** avant)

counter /ˈkaʊntə(r)/ **A** *n* **1** (in shop, snack bar) comptoir *m*; (in bank, post office) guichet *m*; (in pub, bar) bar *m*
2 (in game) jeton *m*
B *vt* répondre à ‹*threat*›; neutraliser ‹*effet*›; parer ‹*blow*›; enrayer ‹*inflation*›
C *vi* riposter (**with sth** par qch)
D **counter to** *phr* (gen) contrairement à; ‹*be, go, run*› à l'encontre de

counteract /ˌkaʊntəˈrækt/ *vt* contrebalancer ‹*influence*›; contrecarrer ‹*negative effects*›

counter-attack /ˈkaʊntərətæk/ *n* contre-attaque *f* (**against** sur)

counter-clockwise /ˌkaʊntəˈklɒkwaɪz/ *adj, adv* (AmE) dans le sens inverse des aiguilles d'une montre

counterfeit /ˈkaʊntəfɪt/ **A** *adj* ‹*signature, note*› contrefait/-e; **~ money** fausse monnaie *f*
B *vt* contrefaire

counterfoil /ˈkaʊntəfɔɪl/ *n* talon *m*, souche *f*

counterpart /ˈkaʊntəpɑːt/ *n* (of person) homologue *mf*; (of company, institution) équivalent *m*

counter-productive /ˌkaʊntəprəˈdʌktɪv/ *adj* contre-productif/-ive

countersign /ˈkaʊntəsaɪn/ *vt* contresigner

countertop *n* (AmE) plan *m* de travail

countess /ˈkaʊntɪs/ *n* comtesse *f*

countless /ˈkaʊntlɪs/ *adj* **~ letters** un nombre incalculable de lettres; **on ~ occasions** je ne sais combien de fois

🔑 **country** /ˈkʌntrɪ/ *n* **1** pays *m*; **developing/third world ~** pays en voie de développement/du tiers monde; **~ of birth** pays natal
2 (countryside) campagne *f*; **in the ~** à la campagne; **open ~** rase campagne; **across ~** à travers la campagne

country club *n* club *m* de loisirs

country dancing *n* danse *f* folklorique

country house *n* manoir *m*

country music *n* country music *f*

countryside /ˈkʌntrɪsaɪd/ *n* campagne *f*

🔑 **county** /ˈkaʊntɪ/ *n* comté *m*

county council *n* (BrE) ≈ conseil *m* régional

coup /kuː/ *n* **1** (*also* ~ **d'état**) coup *m* d'État
2 **to pull off a ~** réussir un beau coup

🔑 **couple** /ˈkʌpl/ *n* **1** couple *m*
2 **a ~ (of)** (two) deux; (a few) deux ou trois; **a ~ of times** deux ou trois fois

coupon /ˈkuːpɒn/ *n* **1** (voucher) bon *m*; **petrol ~** (BrE) bon d'essence
2 (in ad) coupon *m*; **reply ~** coupon-réponse *m*

courage /ˈkʌrɪdʒ/ *n* courage *m*

courageous /kəˈreɪdʒəs/ *adj* courageux/-euse

courgette /kɔːˈʒet/ *n* courgette *f*

courier /ˈkʊrɪə(r)/ *n* **1** (*also* **travel ~**) accompagnateur/-trice *m/f*
2 (for parcels, documents) coursier *m*; (for drugs) transporteur *m*

🔑 **course** /kɔːs/ **A** *n* **1** (gen) cours *m* (**of** de); **in the ~ of** au cours de; **in the ~ of time** avec le temps; **in due ~** en temps utile; **~ of action** moyen *m* d'action, parti *m*
2 (route) cours *m*; (of boat, plane) cap *m*; **to be on ~** ‹*boat, plane*› tenir le cap; **to go off ~** ‹*ship*› dévier de son cap; **to change ~** (gen) changer de direction; ‹*boat, plane*› changer de cap
3 (classes) cours *m* (**in** en, **of** de)
4 (Med) **a ~ of treatment** un traitement
5 (Sport) (in golf) terrain *m* de golf; (in racing) champ *m* de courses
6 (part of meal) plat *m*; **the main ~** le plat principal; **five-~ meal** repas *m* de cinq plats
B **of course** *phr* bien sûr, évidemment

course book *n* méthode *f*

coursework *n* devoirs *mpl* (de contrôle continu)

🔑 **court** /kɔːt/ **A** *n* **1** (Law) cour *f*, tribunal *m*; **to go to ~** aller devant les tribunaux (**over** pour); **to take sb to ~** poursuivre qn en justice
2 (for tennis, squash) court *m*; (for basketball) terrain *m*
3 (of sovereign) cour *f*
4 (courtyard) cour *f*
B *vt* courtiser ‹*woman, voters*›

court case *n* procès *m*, affaire *f*

courteous /ˈkɜːtɪəs/ *adj* courtois/-e (**to** envers)

courtesy /ˈkɜːtəsɪ/ *n* courtoisie *f*

courthouse /ˈkɔːthaʊs/ *n* (Law) palais *m* de justice

court-martial /ˌkɔːtˈmɑːʃl/ *vt* (*p prés etc* **-ll-**) faire passer [qn] en cour martiale

🔑 mot clé

courtroom *n* salle *f* d'audience

courtyard *n* cour *f*

cousin /ˈkʌzn/ *n* cousin/-e *m/f*

cove /kəʊv/ *n* (bay) anse *f*

cover /ˈkʌvə(r)/ **A** *n* **1** (lid) couvercle *m*; (for duvet, typewriter, cushion, furniture) housse *f*; (of record) pochette *f*; (blanket) couverture *f*
2 (shelter) abri *m*; **to take ~** se mettre à l'abri; **under ~** à l'abri
3 (for teacher, doctor) remplacement *m*
4 (insurance) assurance *f* (**for** pour, **against** contre)
B *vt* **1** (gen) couvrir (**with** avec); recouvrir ‹*cushion, sofa, surface, person, cake*› (**with** de)
2 (deal with) ‹*article, speaker*› traiter; ‹*journalist*› couvrir
3 (insure) assurer, couvrir (**for, against** contre, **for doing** pour faire)
■ **cover for** remplacer ‹*employee*›
■ **cover up**: **A** **to ~ up for** couvrir ‹*friend*›
B **~ [sth] up** recouvrir ‹*object*›; dissimuler ‹*mistake, truth*›; étouffer ‹*scandal*›

coverage /ˈkʌvərɪdʒ/ *n* (gen) couverture *f*; **newspaper ~** couverture par les journaux; **live ~** reportage *m* en direct

cover charge *n* prix *m* de couvert

covering /ˈkʌvərɪŋ/ *n* **1** (for wall, floor) revêtement *m*
2 (layer of snow, moss) couche *f*

covering letter *n* lettre *f* d'accompagnement

cover note *n* (from insurance company) attestation *f* d'assurance

covert /ˈkʌvət, (AmE) ˈkəʊvɜːrt/ *adj* ‹*operation*› secret/-ète; ‹*glance*› furtif/-ive; ‹*threat*› voilé/-e

cover-up *n* opération *f* de camouflage

cover version *n* version *f*

covetous /ˈkʌvɪtəs/ *adj* cupide

cow /kaʊ/ *n* vache *f*

coward /ˈkaʊəd/ *n* lâche *mf*

cowardice /ˈkaʊədɪs/ *n* lâcheté *f*

cowardly /ˈkaʊədlɪ/ *adj* lâche

cowboy /ˈkaʊbɔɪ/ *n* **1** (AmE) cowboy *m*
2 (incompetent worker) fumiste *m*

cower /ˈkaʊə(r)/ *vi* se recroqueviller

cox /kɒks/ **A** *n* barreur *m*
B *vt, vi* barrer

coy /kɔɪ/ *adj* **1** ‹*smile, look*› de fausse modestie
2 (reticent) réservé/-e (**about** à propos de)

cozy (AmE) = **cosy**

crab /kræb/ *n* crabe *m*

crack /kræk/ **A** *n* **1** (in rock) fissure *f*; (in varnish, ground) craquelure *f*; (in wall, cup, bone) fêlure *f*
2 (in door) entrebâillement *m*; (in curtains) fente *f*
3 (*also* **~ cocaine**) crack *m*
4 (noise) craquement *m*
5 (fam) (attempt) essai *m*, tentative *f*; **to have a ~ at doing** essayer de faire
B *adj* ‹*player*› de première; ‹*troops, shot*› d'élite
C *vt* **1** fêler ‹*bone, wall, cup*›
2 casser ‹*nut, egg*›; **to ~ a safe** fracturer un coffre-fort; **to ~ sth open** ouvrir qch; **to ~ one's head open** se fendre le crâne
3 déchiffrer ‹*code*›
4 faire claquer ‹*whip*›; faire craquer ‹*knuckles, joints*›
D *vi* **1** ‹*bone, cup, wall, ice*› se fêler; ‹*varnish*› se craqueler; ‹*skin*› se crevasser; ‹*ground*› se fendre
2 ‹*person*› craquer (fam)
3 ‹*knuckles, twig*› craquer; ‹*whip*› claquer
4 ‹*voice*› se casser
■ **crack down** prendre des mesures énergiques, sévir (**on** contre)

crackdown /ˈkrækdaʊn/ *n* mesure *f* sévère (**on** contre); **the ~ on drugs** l'action *f* antidrogue

cracker /ˈkrækə(r)/ *n* **1** (biscuit) cracker *m*, biscuit *m* salé
2 (for Christmas) diablotin *m*

crackle /ˈkrækl/ **A** *n* crépitement *m*
B *vi* ‹*fire, radio*› crépiter; ‹*hot fat*› grésiller

cradle /ˈkreɪdl/ **A** *n* berceau *m*
B *vt* bercer ‹*baby*›; tenir [qch] délicatement ‹*object*›

craft /krɑːft, (AmE) kræft/ *n* **1** (skill) métier *m*
2 (craftwork) artisanat *m*; **arts and ~s** artisanat (d'art)
3 (boat) embarcation *f*

craftsman *n* artisan *m*

crafty /ˈkrɑːftɪ, (AmE) ˈkræftɪ/ *adj* astucieux/-ieuse

crag /kræg/ *n* rocher *m* escarpé

cram /kræm/ **A** *vt* (*p prés etc* **-mm-**) **to ~ sth into** enfoncer *or* fourrer (fam) qch dans ‹*bag, car*›; **~med full** plein à craquer
B *vi* (*p prés etc* **-mm-**) ‹*student*› bachoter (**for** pour)

cramp /kræmp/ **A** *n* crampe *f*
B *vt* gêner

cramped /kræmpt/ *adj* ‹*house, office*› exigu/-uë

cranberry /ˈkrænbərɪ, (AmE) -berɪ/ *n* canneberge *f*

crane /kreɪn/ *n* grue *f*

crank /kræŋk/ *n* **1** (fam) (freak) fanatique *mf*, fana *mf* (fam)
2 (handle) manivelle *f*

crash /kræʃ/ **A** *n* **1** (noise) fracas *m*
2 (accident) accident *m*; **car ~** accident de voiture; **train ~** catastrophe *f* ferroviaire
3 (of stock market) krach *m*
B *vt* **to ~ one's car** avoir un accident de voiture
C *vi* **1** ‹*car, plane*› s'écraser; ‹*vehicles, planes*› se rentrer dedans, se percuter; **to ~ into sth** rentrer dans *or* percuter qch
2 ‹*share prices*› s'effondrer
■ **crash out** (fam) (go to sleep) pioncer (pop);

(collapse) s'écrouler (fam)
crash course *n* cours *m* intensif
crash diet *n* régime *m* d'amaigrissement intensif
crash helmet *n* casque *m*
crash landing *n* atterrissage *m* en catastrophe
crass /kræs/ *adj* grossier/-ière; **~ ignorance** ignorance *f* crasse
crate /kreɪt/ *n* (for bottles, china) caisse *f*; (for fruit, vegetables) cageot *m*
crater /ˈkreɪtə(r)/ *n* (of volcano) cratère *m*; (caused by explosion) entonnoir *m*
cravat /krəˈvæt/ *n* foulard *m* (pour homme)
crave /kreɪv/ *vt* (*also* **~ for**) avoir un besoin maladif de ‹*drug*›; avoir soif de ‹*affection*›; avoir envie de ‹*food*›
crawl /krɔːl/ **A** *n* **1** (in swimming) crawl *m*
2 at a ~ au pas; **to go at a ~** ‹*vehicle*› rouler au pas
B *vi* **1** ‹*insect, snake, person*› ramper
2 ‹*baby*› marcher à quatre pattes
3 ‹*vehicle*› rouler au pas
4 ‹*time*› se traîner
5 to be ~ing with fourmiller de ‹*insects, tourists*›
6 (fam) (flatter) faire du lèche-bottes (fam) (**to** à)
crayfish /ˈkreɪfɪʃ/ *n* **1** (freshwater) écrevisse *f*
2 (spiny lobster) langouste *f*
crayon /ˈkreɪən/ *n* (wax) craie *f* grasse; (pencil) crayon *m* de couleur
craze /kreɪz/ *n* vogue *f*; **to be the latest ~** faire fureur
crazy /ˈkreɪzɪ/ *adj* (fam) (gen) fou/folle; ‹*idea*› insensé/-e; **~ about** fou/folle de ‹*person*›; passionné/-e de ‹*activity*›
crazy golf *n* (BrE) mini-golf *m*
creak /kriːk/ *vi* ‹*hinge*› grincer; ‹*floorboard*› craquer
cream /kriːm/ **A** *n* crème *f*; **strawberries and ~** fraises *fpl* à la crème
B *adj* **1** (couleur) crème *inv*
2 ‹*cake, bun*› à la crème
▪ **cream off**: **~ off [sth], ~ [sth] off** prélever ‹*best pupils*›; ramasser ‹*profits*›
cream cheese *n* fromage *m* à tartiner
cream soda *n* soda *m* parfumé à la vanille
crease /kriːs/ **A** *n* (intentional) pli *m*; (accidental) faux pli *m*
B *vt* froisser ‹*paper, cloth*›
C *vi* ‹*cloth*› se froisser
⚷ **create** /kriːˈeɪt/ *vt* (gen) créer; provoquer ‹*interest*›; poser ‹*problem*›; faire ‹*good impression*›
⚷ **creation** /kriːˈeɪʃn/ *n* création *f*
⚷ **creative** /kriːˈeɪtɪv/ *adj* **1** ‹*person*› créatif/-ive
2 ‹*process, imagination*› créateur/-trice

⚷ mot clé

creator /kriːˈeɪtə(r)/ *n* créateur/-trice *m/f* (**of** de)
creature /ˈkriːtʃə(r)/ *n* **1** (living being) créature *f*
2 (animal) animal *m*
crèche /kreʃ, kreɪʃ/ *n* (BrE) (nursery) crèche *f*; (in shopping centre) halte-garderie *f*; **workplace ~** crèche d'entreprise
credentials /krɪˈdenʃlz/ *npl* **1** (reputation) qualifications *fpl*
2 (reference) pièce *f* d'identité
credibility /ˌkredəˈbɪlətɪ/ *n* crédibilité *f*
credible /ˈkredəbl/ *adj* crédible
⚷ **credit** /ˈkredɪt/ **A** *n* **1** (merit) mérite *m* (**for** de); **to get/take the ~** se voir attribuer/s'attribuer le mérite (**for** de); **to be a ~ to sb/sth** faire honneur à qn/qch
2 (in business) crédit *m*; **to buy sth on ~** acheter qch à crédit; **to be in ~** être créditeur/-trice
B *vt* **1 to ~ sb with** attribuer à qn ‹*achievement*›
2 créditer ‹*account*› (**with** de)
credit card *n* carte *f* de crédit
credit crunch *n* crise *f* du crédit
credit facilities *npl* facilités *fpl* de crédit
credit note *n* avoir *m*
creditor /ˈkredɪtə(r)/ *n* créancier/-ière *m/f*
credits *npl* générique *m*
creditworthy /ˈkredɪtwɜːðɪ/ *adj* solvable
credulous /ˈkredjʊləs, (AmE) -dʒə-/ *adj* crédule, naïf/naïve
creed /kriːd/ *n* (religious persuasion) croyance *f*; (opinions) principes *mpl*, credo *m*
creek /kriːk, (AmE) *also* krɪk/ *n* **1** (BrE) crique *f*
2 (AmE) (stream) ruisseau *m*
creep /kriːp/ *vi* (*prét, pp* **crept**) **1 to ~ in/out** ‹*person*› entrer/sortir à pas de loup; **to ~ under sth** se glisser sous qch; **to ~ along** ‹*vehicle*› avancer lentement; ‹*insect, cat*› ramper
2 ‹*plant*› grimper
creeper /ˈkriːpə(r)/ *n* (in jungle) liane *f*; (climbing plant) plante *f* grimpante
creepy /ˈkriːpɪ/ *adj* (fam) qui donne la chair de poule
creepy-crawly *n* (fam) bestiole *f* (fam)
cremate /krɪˈmeɪt/ *vt* incinérer
cremation /krɪˈmeɪʃn/ *n* **1** (ceremony) crémation *f*
2 (practice) incinération *f*
crematorium /ˌkreməˈtɔːrɪəm/ *n* (*pl* **-oria** *ou* **-oriums**) (BrE) crématorium *m*
crepe, **crêpe** /kreɪp/ *n* crêpe *m*
crescent /ˈkresnt/ *n* croissant *m*
crescent moon *n* croissant *m* de (la) lune
cress /kres/ *n* cresson *m*
crest /krest/ *n* **1** (ridge) crête *f*
2 (coat of arms) armoiries *fpl*
Crete /kriːt/ *pr n* Crète *f*

Creutzfeldt-Jacob disease, **CJD** *n* maladie *f* de Creutzfeldt-Jacob

crevice /'krevɪs/ *n* fissure *f*

crew /kruː/ *n* **1** (on ship, plane) équipage *m*
2 (on film, radio) équipe *f*

crew cut *n* coupe *f* (de cheveux) en brosse

crew neck sweater *n* pull *m* ras du cou

crib /krɪb/ **A** *n* (cot) lit *m* d'enfant
B *vi* (*p prés etc* **-bb-**) copier (**from** sur)

crick /krɪk/ *n* **a ~ in one's neck** un torticolis

cricket /'krɪkɪt/ *n* **1** (insect) grillon *m*
2 (game) cricket *m*

cricketer /'krɪkɪtə(r)/ *n* joueur *m* de cricket

crime /kraɪm/ *n* **1** (minor) délit *m*; (serious) crime *m* (**against** contre)
2 (phenomenon) criminalité *f*

criminal /'krɪmɪnl/ *n, adj* criminel/-elle *m/f*

criminal record *n* casier *m* judiciaire; **to have a/no ~** avoir un casier judiciaire chargé/vierge

crimson /'krɪmzn/ **A** *n* cramoisi *m*
B *adj* pourpre

cringe /krɪndʒ/ *vi* **1** (in fear) avoir un mouvement de recul
2 (with embarrassment) avoir envie de rentrer sous terre

cripple /'krɪpl/ (offensive) **A** *n* impotent/-e *m/f*
B *vt* **1** estropier; **~d for life** infirme à vie
2 paralyser ‹*country, industry*›

crisis /'kraɪsɪs/ *n* (*pl* **-ses**) crise *f* (**in** dans, **over** à cause de)

crisp /krɪsp/ *adj* ‹*biscuit*› croustillant/-e; ‹*fruit*› croquant/-e; ‹*garment*› frais/fraîche; ‹*banknote, snow*› craquant/-e; ‹*air*› vif/vive; ‹*manner*› brusque

crispbread *n* pain *m* grillé suédois

crisps *npl* (*also* **potato ~** (BrE)) chips *fpl*

criss-cross /'krɪskrɒs, (AmE) -krɔːs/ **A** *adj* ‹*pattern*› en croisillons
B *vi* s'entrecroiser

criterion /kraɪ'tɪərɪən/ *n* (*pl* **-ia**) critère *m* (**for** de)

critic /'krɪtɪk/ *n* **1** (reviewer) critique *m*
2 (opponent) détracteur/-trice *m/f*

critical /'krɪtɪkl/ *adj* ‹*point, condition, remark*› critique; ‹*stage*› crucial/-e; ‹*moment*› décisif/-ive; **to be ~ of sb/sth** critiquer qn/qch

critically /'krɪtɪklɪ/ *adv* **1** ‹*examine*› d'un œil critique
2 ‹*ill*› très gravement

criticism /'krɪtɪsɪzəm/ *n* critique *f*

criticize /'krɪtɪsaɪz/ *vt, vi* critiquer

croak /krəʊk/ *vi* ‹*frog*› coasser

Croatia /krəʊ'eɪʃə/ *pr n* Croatie *f*

crochet /'krəʊʃeɪ, (AmE) krəʊ'ʃeɪ/ *vt* faire [qch] au crochet; **a ~(ed) sweater** un pull au crochet

crockery /'krɒkərɪ/ *n* vaisselle *f*

crocodile /'krɒkədaɪl/ *n* crocodile *m*

croissant *n* croissant *m*

crony /'krəʊnɪ/ *n* (petit/-e) copain/copine *m/f*

crook /krʊk/ *n* **1** (person) escroc *m*
2 (shepherd's) houlette *f*
3 (of arm) creux *m*
IDIOM **by hook or by ~** coûte que coûte

crooked /'krʊkɪd/ *adj* **1** ‹*line*› brisé/-e; ‹*picture, teeth, beam*› de travers
2 (fam) (dishonest) malhonnête

crop /krɒp/ *n* **1** (produce) culture *f*; (harvest) récolte *f*
2 (whip) cravache *f*
■ **crop up** ‹*matter, problem*› surgir; ‹*name*› être mentionné/-e; ‹*opportunity*› se présenter

cross /krɒs, (AmE) krɔːs/ **A** *n* **1** croix *f*; **to put a ~ against** cocher ‹*name, item*›
2 (hybrid) croisement *m*
B *adj* (angry) fâché/-e (**with** contre); **to get ~** se fâcher
C *vt* **1** (gen) traverser; franchir ‹*border, line*›; **it ~ed his mind that** il lui est venu à l'esprit *or* l'idée que; **to ~ one's legs** croiser les jambes
2 (intersect) couper
3 barrer ‹*cheque*›
D *vi* se croiser
■ **cross off**, **cross out** barrer, rayer ‹*name, item*›

cross-border *adj* trans-frontalier/-ière

cross-Channel *adj* trans-Manche

cross-check /ˌkrɒs'tʃek, (AmE) ˌkrɔːs-/ *vt, vi* revérifier

cross-country /ˌkrɒs'kʌntrɪ, (AmE) ˌkrɔːs-/ *n* **1** (running) cross *m*
2 (skiing) ski *m* de fond

cross-cultural *adj* inter-culturel/-elle

cross-examine /ˌkrɒsɪg'zæmɪn, (AmE) ˌkrɔːs-/ *vt* (gen) interroger; (Law) faire subir un contre-interrogatoire à

cross-eyed /'krɒsaɪd, (AmE) 'krɔːs-/ *adj* ‹*person*› atteint/-e de strabisme; **to be ~** loucher, avoir un strabisme

crossfire /'krɒsfaɪə(r), (AmE) 'krɔːs-/ *n* feux *mpl* croisés; **to get caught in the ~** être pris/-e entre deux feux

crossing /'krɒsɪŋ, (AmE) 'krɔːsɪŋ/ *n* **1** (journey) traversée *f*
2 (on road) passage *m* clouté; (level crossing) passage *m* à niveau

cross-legged /ˌkrɒs'legɪd, (AmE) ˌkrɔːs-/ *adv* ‹*sit*› en tailleur

cross purposes /ˌkrɒs'pɜːpəsɪz, (AmE) ˌkrɔːs-/ *npl* **we are at ~** il y a un malentendu; (disagreement) nous sommes en désaccord

cross-reference /ˌkrɒs'refrəns, (AmE) ˌkrɔːs-/ *n* renvoi *m* (**to** à)

crossroads /'krɒsrəʊdz, (AmE) 'krɔːs-/ *n* (*pl* **~**) carrefour *m*

C

C

cross-section /ˌkrɒsˈsekʃn, (AmE) ˌkrɔːs-/ *n* échantillon *m* (**of** de)

crosswalk *n* (AmE) passage *m* (pour) piétons

crossword /ˈkrɒswɜːd, (AmE) ˈkrɔːs-/ *n* (*also* **~ puzzle**) mots *mpl* croisés

crotch /krɒtʃ/ *n* **1** (of body) entrecuisse *m*
2 (in trousers) entrejambe *m*

crotchet /ˈkrɒtʃɪt/ *n* (BrE) noire *f*

crouch /kraʊtʃ/ *vi* (*also* **~ down**) s'accroupir; (to spring) ‹*animal*› se ramasser

crow /krəʊ/ **A** *n* corbeau *m*
B *vi* **1** (exult) exulter
2 (**~ed** *or* **crew**) ‹*cock*› chanter
IDIOM **as the ~ flies** à vol d'oiseau

crowbar *n* pince-monseigneur *f*

⚷ **crowd** /kraʊd/ **A** *n* foule *f*; (watching sport, play) spectateurs *mpl*
B *vt* **1** entasser ‹*people, furniture*› (**into** dans)
2 encombrer ‹*room, house*› (**with** de)
C *vi* **to ~ into** s'entasser dans ‹*room, lift, vehicle*›

crowded /ˈkraʊdɪd/ *adj* **1** ‹*place*› plein/-e de monde; (jam-packed) bondé/-e; **to be ~ with** être plein/-e de
2 ‹*schedule*› chargé/-e

crowd-puller *n* (event) grosse attraction *f*

crown /kraʊn/ **A** *n* **1** (of monarch) couronne *f*
2 (of hill) crête *f*; (of head) crâne *m*
3 (on tooth) couronne *f*
B *vt* couronner

Crown court *n* (BrE) ≈ cour *f* d'assises

crown jewels *npl* joyaux *mpl* de la Couronne

crown prince *n* prince *m* héritier

crow's nest *n* nid *m* de pie

⚷ **crucial** /ˈkruːʃl/ *adj* crucial/-e

crucifix /ˈkruːsɪfɪks/ *n* crucifix *m*

crude /kruːd/ *adj* **1** ‹*method*› rudimentaire; ‹*estimate*› approximatif/-ive
2 ‹*joke*› grossier/-ière; ‹*person*› vulgaire
3 (unprocessed) brut/-e; **~ oil** pétrole *m* brut

cruel /ˈkrʊəl/ *adj* cruel/-elle

cruelty /ˈkrʊəltɪ/ *n* cruauté *f* (**to** envers)

cruise /kruːz/ **A** *n* croisière *f*; **to go on a ~** faire une croisière
B *vt* ‹*driver, taxi*› parcourir ‹*street, city*›
C *vi* ‹*ship*› croiser; ‹*plane*› voler

cruise missile *n* missile *m* de croisière

cruiser /ˈkruːzə(r)/ *n* **1** (cabin cruiser) petit bateau *m* de croisière
2 (Mil) croiseur *m*

crumb /krʌm/ *n* miette *f*

crumble /ˈkrʌmbl/ **A** *vt* émietter ‹*bread*›
B *vi* **1** ‹*rock*› s'effriter; ‹*building*› se délabrer
2 ‹*relationship, economy*› se désagréger; ‹*opposition*› s'effondrer

crummy /ˈkrʌmɪ/ *adj* (fam) **1** (substandard) minable (fam)
2 (unwell) **to feel ~** se sentir patraque (fam)

crumple /ˈkrʌmpl/ *vt* froisser ‹*paper*›; **to ~ sth into a ball** rouler qch en boule

crunch /krʌntʃ/ *vt* croquer ‹*apple, biscuit*›
IDIOM **when** *or* **if it comes to the ~** au moment crucial

crunchy /ˈkrʌntʃɪ/ *adj* croquant/-e

crusade /kruːˈseɪd/ *n* croisade *f*

crush /krʌʃ/ **A** *n* bousculade *f*
B *vt* **1** écraser ‹*can, fruit, person, vehicle*› (**against** contre); broyer ‹*arm, leg*›; piler ‹*ice*›
2 écraser ‹*enemy, uprising*›; étouffer ‹*protest*›
3 chiffonner ‹*garment, fabric*›

crushing /ˈkrʌʃɪŋ/ *adj* ‹*defeat, weight*› écrasant/-e; ‹*blow*› percutant/-e; **a ~ setback** un revers cuisant

crust /krʌst/ *n* (gen) croûte *f*; **the earth's ~** l'écorce *f* terrestre

crutch /krʌtʃ/ *n* béquille *f*

crux /krʌks/ *n* **the ~ of the matter** le point crucial

⚷ **cry** /kraɪ/ **A** *n* cri *m*
B *vi* pleurer (**about** à cause de); **to ~ with laughter** rire aux larmes
■ **cry out 1** (with pain, grief) pousser un cri *or* des cris
2 (call) crier, s'écrier
■ **cry off** (cancel) se décommander

cryogenics /ˌkraɪəˈdʒenɪks/ *n* cryogénie *f*

crypt /krɪpt/ *n* crypte *f*

cryptic /ˈkrɪptɪk/ *adj* ‹*remark*› énigmatique; ‹*crossword*› crypté/-e

crystal /ˈkrɪstl/ *n* cristal *m*

crystal ball *n* boule *f* de cristal

crystal clear *adj* **1** ‹*water*› cristallin/-e
2 (obvious) clair/-e comme de l'eau de roche

CS gas *n* gaz *m* lacrymogène

cub /kʌb/ *n* (Zool) petit *m*

Cuba /ˈkjuːbə/ *pr n* Cuba *f*

cubby-hole /ˈkʌbɪhəʊl/ *n* (fam) cagibi *m* (fam)

cube /kjuːb/ **A** *n* (gen) cube *m*; **ice ~** glaçon *m*
B *vt* couper [qch] en cubes ‹*meat*›

cubic /ˈkjuːbɪk/ *adj* **1** cubique
2 ‹*metre, centimetre*› cube

cubicle /ˈkjuːbɪkl/ *n* (in changing room) cabine *f*; (in public toilets) cabinet *m*

cuckoo /ˈkʊkuː/ *n* coucou *m*

cucumber /ˈkjuːkʌmbə(r)/ *n* concombre *m*

cuddle /ˈkʌdl/ **A** *n* câlin *m*; **to give sb a ~** faire un câlin à qn
B *vt* câliner

cuddly toy *n* (BrE) peluche *f*

cue /kjuː/ *n* **1** (line) réplique *f*; (action) signal *m*
2 (Sport) queue *f* de billard

cuff /kʌf/ *n* **1** poignet *m*
2 (AmE) (on trousers) revers *m*
IDIOM **off the ~** au pied levé

⚷ mot clé

cuff link *n* bouton *m* de manchette

cul-de-sac /ˈkʌldəsæk/ *n* impasse *f*, cul-de-sac *m*

culinary /ˈkʌlɪnərɪ, (AmE) -nerɪ/ *adj* culinaire

cull /kʌl/ **A** *n* massacre *m*
B *vt* massacrer ‹*seals, whales*›

culminate /ˈkʌlmɪneɪt/ *vt* aboutir (**in** à)

culottes /kjuːˈlɒts/ *npl* jupe-culotte *f*

culprit /ˈkʌlprɪt/ *n* coupable *mf*

cult /kʌlt/ **A** *n* culte *m*; (contemporary religion) secte *f*
B *adj* **a ~ film** un film-culte; **to be a ~ figure** faire l'objet d'un culte

cultivate /ˈkʌltɪveɪt/ *vt* cultiver

cultural /ˈkʌltʃərəl/ *adj* culturel/-elle

cultural attaché *n* attaché/-e *m/f* culturel/-elle

culture /ˈkʌltʃə(r)/ *n* culture *f*

cultured /ˈkʌltʃəd/ *adj* cultivé/-e

culture shock *n* choc *m* culturel

culture vulture *n* (fam) fana *mf* de culture (fam)

cumbersome /ˈkʌmbəsəm/ *adj* encombrant/-e

cumulative /ˈkjuːmjʊlətɪv, (AmE) -leɪtɪv/ *adj* cumulatif/-ive

cunning /ˈkʌnɪŋ/ **A** *n* (of person) ruse *f*; (nastier) fourberie *f*
B *adj* **1** ‹*person*› rusé/-e; (nastier) fourbe
2 ‹*trick*› habile; ‹*device*› astucieux/-ieuse

cup /kʌp/ **A** *n* **1** tasse *f*
2 (trophy) coupe *f*
B *vt* (*p prés etc* **-pp-**) **to ~ sth in one's hands** prendre qch dans le creux de ses mains

cupboard /ˈkʌbəd/ *n* placard *m*

curable /ˈkjʊərəbl/ *adj* guérissable

curate /ˈkjʊərət/ *n* vicaire *m*

curator /kjʊəˈreɪtə(r), (AmE) *also* ˈkjʊərətər/ *n* conservateur/-trice *m/f*

curb /kɜːb/ **A** *n* **1** restriction *f* (**on** à)
2 (AmE) (sidewalk) bord *m* du trottoir
B *vt* refréner ‹*desires*›; limiter ‹*powers*›; juguler ‹*spending*›; restreindre ‹*consumption*›

curdle /ˈkɜːdl/ *vi* ‹*milk*› se cailler; ‹*sauce*› tourner

cure /kjʊə(r)/ **A** *n* remède *m* (**for** à)
B *vt* **1** (gen) guérir (**of** de)
2 (Culin) (dry) sécher; (salt) saler; (smoke) fumer

cure-all *n* panacée *f* (**for** contre)

curfew /ˈkɜːfjuː/ *n* couvre-feu *m*; **ten o'clock ~** couvre-feu à partir de dix heures

curio /ˈkjʊərɪəʊ/ *n* curiosité *f*, objet *m* rare

curiosity /ˌkjʊərɪˈɒsətɪ/ *n* curiosité *f* (**about** sur, au sujet de); **out of ~** par curiosité

curious /ˈkjʊərɪəs/ *adj* curieux/-ieuse

curiously /ˈkjʊərɪəslɪ/ *adv* ‹*silent, detached*› étrangement; **~ enough** chose assez curieuse

curl /kɜːl/ **A** *n* boucle *f*
B *vt* friser ‹*hair*›
C *vi* **1** ‹*hair*› friser
2 (*also* **~ up**) ‹*paper*› (se) gondoler; ‹*edges, leaf*› se racornir
■ **curl up** ‹*person*› se pelotonner; ‹*cat*› se mettre en rond; **to ~ up in bed** se blottir dans son lit

curler /ˈkɜːlə(r)/ *n* bigoudi *m*

curly /ˈkɜːlɪ/ *adj* ‹*hair*› (tight curls) frisé/-e; (loose curls) bouclé/-e; ‹*tail, eyelashes*› recourbé/-e

currant /ˈkʌrənt/ *n* raisin *m* de Corinthe

currency /ˈkʌrənsɪ/ *n* monnaie *f*, devise *f*

current /ˈkʌrənt/ **A** *n* courant *m*
B *adj* ‹*leader, situation, policy*› actuel/-elle; ‹*year, research*› en cours

current account *n* (BrE) compte *m* courant

current affairs *n* actualité *f*

currently /ˈkʌrəntlɪ/ *adv* actuellement, en ce moment

curriculum /kəˈrɪkjʊləm/ *n* (*pl* **-lums** *ou* **-la**) programme *m*; **in the ~** au programme

curriculum vitae *n* curriculum vitae *m*

curry /ˈkʌrɪ/ **A** *n* curry *m*; **chicken ~** curry de poulet
B *vt* **to ~ favour** chercher à se faire bien voir (**with sb** de qn)

curse /kɜːs/ **A** *n* **1** (scourge) fléau *m*
2 (swearword) juron *m*
3 (spell) malédiction *f*
B *vt* maudire
C *vi* jurer (**at** après)

cursor /ˈkɜːsə(r)/ *n* curseur *m*

curt /kɜːt/ *adj* sec/sèche

curtail /kɜːˈteɪl/ *vt* (restrict) mettre une entrave à; (cut back) réduire

curtain /ˈkɜːtn/ *n* rideau *m*

curtsey /ˈkɜːtsɪ/ **A** *n* (*pl* **-seys** *ou* **-sies**) révérence *f*
B *vi* (*prét, pp* **-seyed** *ou* **-sied**) faire la révérence (**to** à)

curve /kɜːv/ **A** *n* courbe *f*
B *vi* ‹*line, wall*› s'incurver; ‹*road, railway*› faire une courbe

cushion /ˈkʊʃn/ **A** *n* coussin *m*
B *vt* amortir

cushy /ˈkʊʃɪ/ *adj* (fam) peinard/-e (fam)

custard /ˈkʌstəd/ *n* (BrE) (creamy) ≈ crème *f* anglaise

custodial sentence *n* peine *f* de prison

custodian /kʌˈstəʊdɪən/ *n* (of collection) gardien/-ienne *m/f*; (in museum) conservateur/-trice *m/f*

custody /ˈkʌstədɪ/ *n* **1** (detention) détention *f*; **to take sb into ~** arrêter qn
2 (of child) garde *f*

custom /ˈkʌstəm/ *n* **1** coutume *f*, usage *m*
2 (customers) clientèle *f*

customary /ˈkʌstəmərɪ, (AmE) -merɪ/ *adj* habituel/-elle; (more formal) coutumier/-ière

⚷ **customer** /ˈkʌstəmə(r)/ *n* client/-e *m/f*
customer services *n* service *m* clientèle
customize /ˈkʌstəmaɪz/ *vt* fabriquer [qch] sur commande ‹*car*›
custom-made *adj* ‹*clothes*› fait/-e sur mesure
customs /ˈkʌstəmz/ *n* douane *f*; **to go through ~** passer à la douane
customs duties *npl* droits *mpl* de douane
customs hall *n* douane *f*
customs officer, **customs official** *n* douanier/-ière *m/f*
⚷ **cut** /kʌt/ **A** *n* **1** (incision) entaille *f*; (in surgery) incision *f*
2 (wound) coupure *f*
3 (hairstyle) coupe *f*
4 (fam) (share) part *f*
5 (reduction) réduction *f* (**in** de); **job ~s** suppression *f* d'emplois; **a ~ in salary** une baisse de salaire
B *vt* (*p prés* **-tt-**, *prét*, *pp* **cut**) **1** (gen) couper; **to ~ oneself** se couper; **to ~ one's finger** se couper le doigt; **to have one's hair cut** se faire couper les cheveux
2 tailler ‹*gem, suit, marble*›; ‹*locksmith*› faire ‹*key*›
3 (edit) couper ‹*article, film*›; supprimer ‹*scene*›
4 (reduce) réduire ‹*cost, inflation, list*› (**by** de); baisser ‹*price*›
5 to ~ a tooth percer une dent
6 (record) faire, graver ‹*album*›
7 (Comput) couper ‹*text*›
C *vi* (*p prés* **-tt-**, *prét*, *pp* **cut**) **1** (with knife, scissors) couper; **to ~ into** entamer ‹*cake*›; couper ‹*fabric, paper*›; inciser ‹*flesh*›
2 to ~ down a sidestreet couper par une petite rue
IDIOM **to ~ sb dead** ignorer complètement qn
■ **cut back A ~ back** faire des économies
B ~ [sth] back 1 (reduce) réduire (**to** à)
2 (prune) tailler
■ **cut down**: **A ~ down** réduire sa consommation; **to ~ down on smoking** fumer moins
B ~ [sth] down 1 (chop down) abattre
2 (reduce) réduire
■ **cut off 1** couper ‹*hair, piece, corner*›; enlever ‹*excess, crusts*›; amputer ‹*limb*›
2 (disconnect) couper ‹*mains service*›
3 to ~ off sb's allowance couper les vivres à qn
4 to ~ sb off (on phone) couper qn; (interrupt) interrompre qn
5 to feel ~ off se sentir isolé/-e
■ **cut out**: **A ~ out** ‹*engine, fan*› s'arrêter
B ~ [sth] out 1 découper ‹*article, picture*› (**from** dans)
2 (fam) **~ it out!** ça suffit!
■ **cut short** abréger ‹*holiday, discussion*›

⚷ mot clé

■ **cut up** couper
cut and paste *n* couper-coller *m*
cutback /ˈkʌtbæk/ *n* réduction *f*; **~s in** réductions dans le budget de ‹*defence, health*›; **government ~s** réductions budgétaires du gouvernement
cute /kjuːt/ *adj* (fam) **1** mignon/-onne
2 (AmE) (clever) malin/-igne
cutlery /ˈkʌtlərɪ/ *n* couverts *mpl*
cutlet /ˈkʌtlɪt/ *n* côtelette *f*
cut-off /ˈkʌtɒf/ **A** *n* (upper limit) limite *f*
B cut-offs *npl* jean *m* coupé
cut-price (BrE), **cut-rate** (AmE) /ˌkʌtˈpraɪs/ *adj* à prix réduit
cut-throat /ˈkʌtθrəʊt/ *adj* ‹*competition*› acharné/-e; **a ~ business** un milieu très dur
cutting /ˈkʌtɪŋ/ **A** *n* **1** (from newspaper) coupure *f* (**from** de)
2 (in film-making) montage *m*
B *adj* ‹*tone*› cassant/-e; ‹*remark*› désobligeant/-e
cutting edge *n* **to be at the ~ of** être à l'avant-garde de
CV, cv *n* (*abbr* = **curriculum vitae**) cv, CV *m*
cyanide /ˈsaɪənaɪd/ *n* cyanure *m*
cyber attack /ˈsaɪbər əˌtæk/ *n* cyberattaque *f*
cyberbullying /ˈsaɪbəˌbʊlɪɪŋ/ *n* cyber-harcèlement *m*
cybercafe *n* cybercafé *m*
cyberculture /ˈsaɪbəkʌltʃə(r)/ *n* cyberculture *f*
cyberspace /ˈsaɪbəspeɪs/ *n* cyberespace *m*
⚷ **cycle** /ˈsaɪkl/ **A** *n* **1** cycle *m*
2 (bicycle) vélo *m*
B *vi* faire du vélo
cycle lane *n* piste *f* cyclable
cycle race *n* course *f* cycliste
cycling /ˈsaɪklɪŋ/ *n* cyclisme *m*
cycling shorts *npl* cuissard *m*
cyclist /ˈsaɪklɪst/ *n* (gen) cycliste *mf*; (Sport) coureur/-euse *m/f* cycliste
cyclone /ˈsaɪkləʊn/ *n* cyclone *m*
cygnet /ˈsɪgnɪt/ *n* jeune cygne *m*
cylinder /ˈsɪlɪndə(r)/ *n* **1** (in engine) cylindre *m*
2 (of gas) bouteille *f*
3 (*also* **hot water ~**) (BrE) ballon *m* d'eau chaude
cynic /ˈsɪnɪk/ *n* cynique *mf*
cynical /ˈsɪnɪkl/ *adj* cynique
cynicism /ˈsɪnɪsɪzəm/ *n* cynisme *m*
Cyprus /ˈsaɪprəs/ *pr n* Chypre *f*
cyst /sɪst/ *n* kyste *m*
Czech /tʃek/ **A** *n* **1** (person) Tchèque *mf*
2 (language) tchèque *m*
B *adj* tchèque
Czech Republic *pr n* République *f* tchèque

Dd

d, **D** /diː/ *n* **1** (letter) d, D *m*
2 **D** (Mus) ré *m*

dab /dæb/ **A** *n* (of paint) touche *f*; (of butter) petit morceau *m*
B *vt* tamponner ‹*stain*› (**with** de); **to ∼ one's eyes** se tamponner les yeux

dabble /ˈdæbl/ *v*
■ **dabble in** faire [qch] en amateur ‹*painting, politics*›

dachshund /ˈdækshʊnd/ *n* teckel *m*

dad, **Dad** /dæd/ *n* (fam) papa *m* (fam); père *m*

daddy, **Daddy** /ˈdædɪ/ *n* (fam) papa *m* (fam)

daffodil /ˈdæfədɪl/ *n* jonquille *f*

daft /dɑːft, (AmE) dæft/ *adj* (fam) bête

dagger /ˈdægə(r)/ *n* poignard *m*
IDIOM **to look ∼s at sb** fusiller qn du regard

daily /ˈdeɪlɪ/ **A** *n* (*pl* **dailies**) (newspaper) quotidien *m*
B *adj* **1** ‹*visit, routine*› quotidien/-ienne; **on a ∼ basis** tous les jours
2 ‹*wage, rate*› journalier/-ière
C *adv* quotidiennement; **twice ∼** deux fois par jour

dainty /ˈdeɪntɪ/ *adj* ‹*porcelain, handkerchief*› délicat/-e; ‹*shoe, hand, foot*› mignon/-onne

dairy /ˈdeərɪ/ **A** *n* **1** (on farm) laiterie *f*; (shop) crémerie *f*
2 (company) société *f* laitière
B *adj* ‹*butter*› fermier/-ière; ‹*cow, farm, product, cream*› laitier/-ière

daisy /ˈdeɪzɪ/ *n* (common) pâquerette *f*; (garden) marguerite *f*
IDIOM **to be as fresh as a ∼** être frais/fraîche comme un gardon

dam /dæm/ *n* barrage *m*

damage /ˈdæmɪdʒ/ **A** *n* **1** (gen) dégâts *mpl* (**to** causés à)
2 (Med) **brain ∼** lésions *fpl* cérébrales
3 (fig) **to do ∼ to** porter atteinte à; **the ∼ is done** le mal est fait
B *vt* **1** endommager ‹*building*›; nuire à ‹*environment, health*›; **to ∼ one's eyesight** s'abîmer les yeux
2 porter atteinte à ‹*reputation*›

damages *npl* (Law) dommages-interêts *mpl*

damaging /ˈdæmɪdʒɪŋ/ *adj* (to reputation, person) préjudiciable (**to** à, pour); ‹*effect*› préjudiciable; (to health, environment) nuisible (**to** pour)

damn /dæm/ (fam) **A** *n* **not to give a ∼ about sb/sth** se ficher (fam) éperdument de qn/qch
B *adj* (*also* **damned**) ‹*key, car*› fichu/-e (fam) *before n*
C *excl* merde! (fam), zut! (fam)

damp /dæmp/ **A** *n* humidité *f*
B *adj* ‹*clothes, house*› humide; ‹*skin*› moite

dampen /ˈdæmpən/ *vt* **1** humecter ‹*cloth*›
2 refroidir ‹*enthusiasm*›

damson /ˈdæmzn/ *n* prune *f* (de Damas)

dance /dɑːns, (AmE) dæns/ **A** *n* (gen) danse *f*; (social occasion) soirée *f* dansante
B *vi* **1** ‹*person*› danser (**with** avec)
2 ‹*eyes*› briller (**with** de)
■ **dance about**, **dance up and down** sautiller sur place

dancer /ˈdɑːnsə(r), (AmE) ˈdænsər/ *n* danseur/-euse *m/f*

dancing /ˈdɑːnsɪŋ, (AmE) ˈdænsɪŋ/ *n* danse *f*

dandruff /ˈdændrʌf/ *n* pellicules *fpl*

danger /ˈdeɪndʒə(r)/ *n* danger *m* (**of** de, **to** pour); **to be in ∼** être en danger; **to be in ∼ of doing** risquer de faire

danger list *n* **on the ∼** dans un état critique

dangerous /ˈdeɪndʒərəs/ *adj* dangereux/-euse (**for** pour, **to do** de faire)
IDIOM **to be on ∼ ground** avancer en terrain miné

dangerously /ˈdeɪndʒərəslɪ/ *adv* (gen) dangereusement; ‹*ill*› gravement; **to live ∼** prendre des risques

danger signal *n* signal *m* de danger

dangle /ˈdæŋgl/ **A** *vt* balancer ‹*puppet, keys*›; laisser pendre ‹*legs*›
B *vi* ‹*puppet, keys*› se balancer (**from** à); ‹*earrings*› pendiller; ‹*legs*› pendre

Danish /ˈdeɪnɪʃ/ **A** *n* (language) danois *m*
B *adj* (gen) danois/-e; ‹*embassy*› du Danemark

dare /deə(r)/ **A** *n* défi *m*
B *modal aux* oser; **to ∼ (to) do** oser faire; **I ∼ say** c'est bien possible
C *vt* **to ∼ sb to do** défier qn de faire; **I ∼ you!** chiche que tu ne le fais pas! (fam)

daredevil /ˈdeədevl/ *n*, *adj* casse-cou *mf inv*

daring /ˈdeərɪŋ/ *adj* **1** (courageous, novel) audacieux/-ieuse
2 ‹*suggestion, dress*› osé/-e

dark /dɑːk/ **A** *n* **in the ∼** dans le noir *or* l'obscurité; **before ∼** avant la (tombée de la) nuit; **after ∼** après la tombée de la nuit
B *adj* **1** ‹*room, alley, day, sky*› sombre; **it is getting ∼** il commence à faire noir *or* nuit; **it's ∼** il fait noir *or* nuit
2 ‹*colour, suit*› sombre; **a ∼ blue dress** une

robe bleu foncé
3 ‹*hair, complexion*› brun/-e
4 ‹*secret, thought*› noir/-e *before n*
IDIOMS **to be in the ~** être dans le noir; **to leave sb in the ~** laisser qn dans l'ignorance; **to keep sb in the ~ about sth** cacher qch à qn

darken /ˈdɑːkən/ **A** *vt* **1** obscurcir ‹*sky, landscape*›; assombrir ‹*house*›
2 foncer ‹*colour*›
B *vi* **1** ‹*sky, room*› s'obscurcir
2 (in colour) foncer; ‹*skin*› brunir

dark glasses *npl* lunettes *fpl* noires

darkness /ˈdɑːknɪs/ *n* obscurité *f*; **in ~** dans l'obscurité

darkroom *n* chambre *f* noire

dark skinned *adj* basané/-e

darling /ˈdɑːlɪŋ/ *n* **1** **(my) ~** (to loved one) chéri/-e *m/f*; (to child) mon chou (fam); (to acquaintance) mon cher/ma chère *m/f*
2 (kind, lovable person) amour *m*, ange *m*

darn /dɑːn/ *vt* repriser

dart /dɑːt/ *n* fléchette *f*; **to play ~s** jouer aux fléchettes

dartboard *n* cible *f*

dash /dæʃ/ **A** *n* **1** (rush) course *f* folle; **it was a mad ~** on a dû se presser
2 (small amount) (of liquid) goutte *f*; (of powder) pincée *f*; (of colour) touche *f*
3 (punctuation) tiret *m*
B *vt* **1** **to ~ sb/sth against** projeter qn/qch contre ‹*rocks*›
2 anéantir ‹*hopes*›
C *vi* se précipiter (**into** dans); **to ~ out of** sortir en courant de ‹*shop, room*›
■ **dash off**: **A** **~ off** se sauver
B **~ [sth] off** écrire [qch] en vitesse

dashboard /ˈdæʃbɔːd/ *n* tableau *m* de bord

⚷ **data** /ˈdeɪtə/ *npl* données *fpl*

database *n* base *f* de données

data entry *n* introduction *f* de données

data processing *n* (procedure) traitement *m* des données; (career) informatique *f*; (department) service *m* informatique

data protection *n* protection *f* de l'information

data security *n* sécurité *f* des données

data storage device *n* périphérique *m* de stockage

⚷ **date** /deɪt/ **A** *n* **1** date *f*; **~ of birth** date de naissance; **what's the ~ today?** on est le combien aujourd'hui?; **at a later ~, at some future ~** plus tard
2 (on coin) millésime *m*
3 (meeting) rendez-vous *m*; **to have a lunch ~** être pris/-e à déjeuner
4 **who's your ~ for tonight?** avec qui sors-tu ce soir?
5 (fruit) datte *f*
B *vt* **1** (gen) dater
2 sortir avec ‹*person*›
C *vi* **to ~ from** *or* **back to** ‹*building*› dater de; ‹*problem, friendship*› remonter à
D **to date** *phr* à ce jour, jusqu'ici

dated /ˈdeɪtɪd/ *adj* ‹*clothes, style*› démodé/-e; ‹*idea, custom*› dépassé/-e; ‹*language*› vieilli/-e; **the film seems ~ now** le film a mal vieilli

date night *n* sortie *f* en amoureux (*en parlant d'un couple marié*)

date rape *n* viol *m* (*au cours d'une sortie en tête à tête*)

dating agency *n* club *m* de rencontres

⚷ **daughter** /ˈdɔːtə(r)/ *n* fille *f*

daughter-in-law *n* (*pl* **daughters-in-law**) belle-fille *f*, bru *f*

daunting /ˈdɔːntɪŋ/ *adj* ‹*task, prospect*› décourageant/-e; ‹*person*› intimidant/-e

dawdle /ˈdɔːdl/ *vi* (fam) flâner, traînasser (fam)

dawn /dɔːn/ **A** *n* aube *f*; **at ~** à l'aube; **at the crack of ~** à l'aube
B *vi* **1** ‹*day*› se lever
2 **it ~ed on me that** je me suis rendu compte que; **it suddenly ~ed on her why** elle a soudain compris pourquoi

dawn raid *n* descente *f* de police très tôt le matin

⚷ **day** /deɪ/ *n* **1** jour *m*; **what ~ is it today?** quel jour sommes-nous aujourd'hui?; **every ~** tous les jours; **every other ~** tous les deux jours; **from ~ to ~** ‹*live*› au jour le jour; ‹*change*› d'un jour à l'autre; **the ~ when** *or* **that** le jour où; **the ~ after** le lendemain; **the ~ before** la veille; **the ~ before yesterday** avant-hier; **the ~ after tomorrow** après-demain
2 (with emphasis on duration) journée *f*; **all ~** toute la journée; **during the ~** pendant la journée
3 (age, period) époque *f*; **in those ~s** à cette époque; **these ~s** ces temps-ci
IDIOMS **those were the ~s** c'était le bon temps; **that'll be the ~!** je voudrais voir ça!; **to call it a ~** s'arrêter là; **to save the ~** sauver la situation

daybreak *n* aube *f*

day-care /ˌdeɪˈkeə(r)/ *n* (for children) service *m* de garderie

daydream /ˈdeɪdriːm/ **A** *n* rêves *mpl*
B *vi* rêvasser

daylight /ˈdeɪlaɪt/ *n* **1** (light) jour *m*, lumière *f* du jour; **it was still ~** il faisait encore jour
2 (dawn) lever *m* du jour, point *m* du jour

daylight robbery *n* (fam) **it's ~!** c'est de l'arnaque! (fam)

day nursery *n* garderie *f*

day release *n* formation *f* permanente

day return *n* (BrE) aller-retour *m* valable une journée

daytime /ˈdeɪtaɪm/ *n* journée *f*

day-to-day /ˌdeɪtəˈdeɪ/ *adj* quotidien/-ienne

day trip *n* excursion *f* pour la journée

⚷ mot clé

daze /deɪz/ *n* **in a ~** (from news) ahuri/-e; (from blow) étourdi/-e; (from drugs) hébété/-e

dazed /deɪzd/ *adj* (by news) ahuri/-e; (by blow) étourdi/-e

dazzle /ˈdæzl/ *vt* éblouir; **to ~ sb with** éblouir qn par ‹*beauty, knowledge*›

dazzling /ˈdæzlɪŋ/ *adj* éblouissant/-e

D-Day /ˈdiː deɪ/ *n* **1** (important day) jour *m* J **2** (Mil) le 6 juin 1944 (*jour du débarquement des Alliés en Normandie*)

dead /ded/ **A** *n* **1 the ~** les morts *mpl* **2 at ~ of night** en pleine nuit; **in the ~ of winter** en plein hiver **B** *adj* mort/-e; **the ~ man/woman** le mort/la morte; **a ~ body** un cadavre; **to drop (down) ~** tomber raide mort/-e; **the phone went ~** la ligne a été coupée **C** *adv* (BrE) ‹*certain, straight*› absolument; **~ on time** pile (fam) à l'heure; **~ easy** (fam) simple comme bonjour (fam); **they were ~ lucky!** (fam) ils ont eu du pot! (fam); **~ tired** (fam) crevé/-e (fam), claqué/-e (fam); **to be ~ set on doing** être tout à fait décidé/-e à faire; **to stop ~** s'arrêter net

deaden /ˈdedn/ *vt* calmer ‹*pain*›; amortir ‹*blow*›; assourdir ‹*sound*›

dead end /ˌdedˈend/ **A** *n* impasse *f* **B dead-end** *adj* ‹*job*› sans perspectives

dead heat *n* (in athletics) arrivée *f* ex-aequo; (in horseracing) dead-heat *m inv*

deadline /ˈdedlaɪn/ *n* date *f or* heure *f* limite, délai *m*; **to meet a ~** respecter un délai

deadlock /ˈdedlɒk/ *n* impasse *f*; **to reach (a) ~** aboutir à une impasse

dead loss *n* (fam) **to be a ~** être nul/nulle (fam)

deadly /ˈdedlɪ/ **A** *adj* **1** ‹*poison, enemy*› mortel/-elle **2 in ~ earnest** avec le plus grand sérieux **B** *adv* ‹*dull, boring*› terriblement

deadpan /ˈdedpæn/ *adj* ‹*humour*› pince-sans-rire *inv*

deaf /def/ **A** *n* **the ~** les sourds *mpl*, les malentendants *mpl* **B** *adj* **1** sourd/-e; **to go ~** devenir sourd/-e **2 to turn a ~ ear to** faire la sourde oreille à, rester sourd/-e à

deaf aid *n* (BrE) prothèse *f* auditive

deafening /ˈdefnɪŋ/ *adj* assourdissant/-e

deaf without speech *adj* sourd-muet/sourde-muette

deal /diːl/ **A** *n* **1** (agreement) accord *m*; (in business) affaire *f*; (with friend) marché *m*; **it's a ~!** marché conclu! **2 a great** *or* **good ~** beaucoup (**of** de) **B** *vt* (*prét, pp* **dealt**) **1** porter ‹*blow*› (**to** à) **2** distribuer ‹*cards*›; donner ‹*hand*› **C** *vi* (*prét, pp* **dealt**) **to ~ in** être dans le commerce de ‹*commodity, shares*›

■ **deal with 1** s'occuper de ‹*problem, request*› **2** traiter de ‹*topic*›

dealer /ˈdiːlə(r)/ *n* **1** (in business) marchand/-e *m/f*; (large-scale) négociant/-e *m/f* **2** (on stock exchange) opérateur/-trice *m/f* **3** (in drugs) revendeur/-euse *m/f* de drogue, dealer *m* (fam) **4** (in cards) donneur/-euse *m/f*

dealing /ˈdiːlɪŋ/ **A** *n* **1** (trading) vente *f*; **foreign exchange ~** opérations *fpl* de change; **share ~** transactions *fpl* boursières **2** (trafficking) trafic *m*; **drug ~** le trafic de drogue **B dealings** *npl* relations *fpl* (**with** avec)

dear /dɪə(r)/ **A** *n* **(my) ~** mon chéri/ma chérie *m/f*; (more formal) mon cher/ma chère *m/f* **B** *adj* **1** (gen) cher/chère; **he's my ~est friend** c'est mon meilleur ami; **to hold sb/sth ~** être attaché/-e à qn/qch, chérir qn/qch **2** (in letter) cher/chère; **Dear Sir/Madam** Monsieur, Madame; **Dear Sirs** Messieurs; **Dear Mr Jones** Cher Monsieur; **Dear Mr and Mrs Jones** Cher Monsieur, Chère Madame; **Dear Anne and Paul** Chers Anne et Paul **C** *excl* **oh ~!** (dismay, surprise) oh mon Dieu!; (less serious) aïe!, oh là là!

death /deθ/ *n* mort *f*; (more formally) décès *m*; **to drink/to work oneself to ~** se tuer en buvant/au travail

IDIOMS **to be at ~'s door** être à l'article de la mort; **to frighten sb to ~** faire une peur bleue à qn (fam); **to be bored to ~** (fam) s'ennuyer à mourir; **I'm sick to ~ of this!** (fam) j'en ai par-dessus la tête!

death camp *n* camp *m* de la mort

death penalty *n* peine *f* de mort

death row *n* quartier *m* des condamnés à mort

death sentence *n* condamnation *f* à mort

death threat *n* menaces *fpl* de mort

death toll *n* nombre *m* de morts

death trap *n* **to be a ~** être très dangereux/-euse

debar /dɪˈbɑː(r)/ *vt* (*p prés etc* **-rr-**) **to be ~red from doing** ne pas avoir le droit de faire

debatable /dɪˈbeɪtəbl/ *adj* discutable

debate /dɪˈbeɪt/ *n* débat *m* (**on, about** sur); (informal discussion) discussion *f* (**about** à propos de); **to hold a ~ on** débattre de ‹*issue*›

debauchery /dɪˈbɔːtʃərɪ/ *n* débauche *f*

debit /ˈdebɪt/ **A** *n* débit *m* **B** *vt* débiter ‹*account*› (**with** de)

debit card *n* carte *f* bancaire (*sans paiement différé*)

debrief /ˌdiːˈbriːf/ *vt* interroger; **to be ~ed** ‹*diplomat, agent*› rendre compte (oralement) d'une mission; ‹*defector, freed hostage*› être interrogé/-e

debris /ˈdeɪbriː, ˈde-, (AmE) dəˈbriː/ *n* (of plane) débris *mpl*; (of building) décombres *mpl*; (rubbish) déchets *mpl*

🔑 **debt** /det/ *n* dette *f* (**to** envers); **to get into ~** s'endetter
debt collector *n* agent *m* de recouvrement
debtor /'detə(r)/ *n* débiteur/-trice *m/f*
debt trap *n* piège *m* du surendettement
debug /ˌdiː'bʌg/ *vt* (*p prés etc* **-gg-**) déboguer ‹*software*›

d

debut /'deɪbjuː, (AmE) dɪ'bjuː/ *n* débuts *mpl*
🔑 **decade** /'dekeɪd, dɪ'keɪd, (AmE) dɪ'keɪd/ *n* décennie *f*
decadent /'dekədənt/ *adj* décadent/-e
decaffeinated /ˌdiː'kæfɪneɪtɪd/ *adj* décaféiné/-e
decanter /dɪ'kæntə(r)/ *n* (for wine, port) carafe *f* (à décanter); (for whisky) flacon *m* à whisky
decathlon /dɪ'kæθlɒn/ *n* décathlon *m*
decay /dɪ'keɪ/ **A** *n* **1** (of vegetation, body) pourriture *f*; (of building) délabrement *m*
2 tooth ~ carie *f* dentaire
3 (of society) décadence *f*
B *vi* ‹*timber, vegetation*› pourrir; ‹*tooth*› se carier; ‹*building*› se détériorer
deceased /dɪ'siːst/ **A** *n* **the ~** le défunt/la défunte
B *adj* décédé/-e, défunt/-e
deceit /dɪ'siːt/ *n* malhonnêteté *f*
deceitful /dɪ'siːtfl/ *adj* malhonnête
deceive /dɪ'siːv/ **A** *vt* **1** tromper, duper ‹*friend*›; **to be ~d** être dupe
2 tromper ‹*spouse, lover*›
B *v refl* **to ~ oneself** se faire des illusions
🔑 **December** /dɪ'sembə(r)/ *n* décembre *m*
decency /'diːsnsɪ/ *n* **1** (good manners) politesse *f*
2 (propriety) convenances *fpl*
decent /'diːsnt/ *adj* **1** ‹*family, man, woman*› comme il faut, bien *inv* (fam); **it's ~ of him** c'est très gentil à lui
2 (adequate) convenable
3 (good) ‹*camera, education, result*› bon/bonne *before n*; ‹*profit*› appréciable; **to make a ~ living** bien gagner sa vie
4 ‹*behaviour, clothes, language*› décent/-e, correct/-e
decentralize /diː'sentrəlaɪz/ *vt* décentraliser
deception /dɪ'sepʃn/ *n* duplicité *f*
deceptive /dɪ'septɪv/ *adj* trompeur/-euse
🔑 **decide** /dɪ'saɪd/ **A** *vt* **1 to ~ to do** décider de faire; (after much hesitation) se décider à faire
2 (settle) régler ‹*matter*›; décider de ‹*fate, outcome*›
B *vi* décider; **to ~ against** écarter ‹*plan, idea*›; **to ~ between** choisir, faire un choix entre ‹*applicants, books*›
■ **decide on 1** se décider pour ‹*hat, wallpaper*›; fixer ‹*date*›
2 décider de ‹*course of action, size, budget*›

deciduous /dɪ'sɪdjʊəs, dɪ'sɪdʒʊəs/ *adj* ‹*tree*› à feuilles caduques
decimal /'desɪml/ *adj* ‹*system, currency*› décimal/-e; **~ point** virgule *f*
decipher /dɪ'saɪfə(r)/ *vt* déchiffrer
🔑 **decision** /dɪ'sɪʒn/ *n* décision *f*; **to make** *or* **take a ~** prendre une décision
decision-maker *n* décideur/-euse *m/f*
decision-making *n* **to be good/bad at ~** savoir/ne pas savoir prendre des décisions
decisive /dɪ'saɪsɪv/ *adj* **1** ‹*manner, tone*› ferme
2 ‹*battle, factor*› décisif/-ive; ‹*argument*› concluant/-e
deck /dek/ *n* **1** (on ship) pont *m*; **on ~** sur le pont; **below ~(s)** sur le pont inférieur
2 (AmE) (terrace) terrasse *f*
3 ~ of cards jeu *m* de cartes
IDIOM **to clear the ~s** déblayer le terrain
deckchair *n* chaise *f* longue, transat *m*
declaration /ˌdeklə'reɪʃn/ *n* déclaration *f*
🔑 **declare** /dɪ'kleə(r)/ *vt* **1** déclarer annoncer (**that** que); annoncer ‹*intention, support*›
2 déclarer ‹*war*› (**on** à); proclamer ‹*independence*›
3 déclarer ‹*income*›
🔑 **decline** /dɪ'klaɪn/ **A** *n* **1** (waning) déclin *m* (**of** de); **to be in ~** être sur le déclin
2 (drop) baisse *f* (**in, of** de); **to be on the** *or* **in ~** être en baisse
B *vi* **1** (drop) ‹*demand, quality*› baisser (**by** de); ‹*support*› être en baisse
2 (wane) être sur le déclin
3 (refuse) refuser
decode /ˌdiː'kəʊd/ *vt* décoder ‹*code, message, signal*›
decompose /ˌdiːkəm'pəʊz/ *vi* se décomposer
decompress /ˌdiːkəm'pres/ *vt* décomprimer, décompresser
decor /'deɪkɔː(r), (AmE) deɪ'kɔːr/ *n* décoration *f*; (in theatre) décor *m*
decorate /'dekəreɪt/ **A** *vt* **1** décorer ‹*cake, tree*› (**with** de, avec)
2 to ~ a room (paint) peindre une pièce; (paper) tapisser une pièce
B *vi* faire des travaux de décoration
decoration /ˌdekə'reɪʃn/ *n* décoration *f*
decorative /'dekərətɪv, (AmE) 'dekəreɪtɪv/ *adj* décoratif/-ive
decorator /'dekəreɪtə(r)/ *n* peintre *m*, décorateur/-trice *m/f*
decoy **A** /'diːkɔɪ/ *n* leurre *m*
B /dɪ'kɔɪ/ *vt* attirer [qn] dans un piège
🔑 **decrease** **A** /'diːkriːs/ *n* diminution *f* (**in** de); (in price) baisse *f* (**in** de)
B /dɪ'kriːs/ *vi* ‹*population*› diminuer; ‹*price, popularity, rate*› baisser, diminuer
decreasing /dɪ'kriːsɪŋ/ *adj* décroissant/-e
decree /dɪ'kriː/ *n* **1** (order) décret *m*
2 (judgment) jugement *m*, arrêt *m*

🔑 mot clé

decrepit /dɪ'krepɪt/ *adj* ‹*building*› délabré/-e; ‹*horse, old person*› décrépit/-e

decriminalize /dɪ'krɪmɪnəlaɪz/ *vt* décriminaliser, légaliser

dedicate /'dedɪkeɪt/ *vt* dédier ‹*book*› (**to** à); consacrer ‹*life*› (**to** à)

dedicated /'dedɪkeɪtɪd/ *adj* ‹*teacher, mother, fan*› dévoué/-e; ‹*worker*› zélé/-e

dedication /ˌdedɪ'keɪʃn/ *n* **1** (devotion) dévouement *m* (**to** à); **~ to duty** dévouement
2 (in a book, on music programme) dédicace *f*

deduce /dɪ'djuːs, (AmE) -'dus/ *vt* déduire (**that** que)

deduct /dɪ'dʌkt/ *vt* prélever ‹*subscription, tax*› (**from** sur); déduire ‹*sum*› (**from** de)

deduction /dɪ'dʌkʃn/ *n* **1** (from wages) retenue *f* (**from** sur); (of tax) prélèvement *m*
2 (conclusion) déduction *f*, conclusion *f*

deed /diːd/ *n* **1** (action) action *f*; **to do one's good ~ for the day** faire sa bonne action *or* sa BA (fam)
2 (for property) acte *m* de propriété

deep /diːp/ **A** *adj* **1** (gen) profond/-e; ‹*snow*› épais/épaisse; **a ~-pile carpet** une moquette de haute laine; **how ~ is the lake?** quelle est la profondeur du lac?; **the lake is 13 m ~** le lac fait 13 m de profondeur
2 (dark) ‹*colour*› intense; ‹*tan*› prononcé/-e; **~ blue eyes** des yeux d'un bleu profond
3 to be ~ in thought être plongé/-e dans ses pensées; **to be ~ in conversation** être en grande conversation
B *adv* **1** ‹*dig, bury, cut*› profondément
2 ~ down *or* **inside she was frightened** dans son for intérieur elle avait peur

deepen /'diːpən/ **A** *vt* **1** creuser ‹*channel*›
2 approfondir ‹*knowledge, understanding*›
B *vi* **1** ‹*concern, love*› augmenter; ‹*knowledge*› s'approfondir; ‹*crisis*› s'aggraver; ‹*mystery*› s'épaissir; ‹*silence*› se faire plus profond
2 ‹*voice*› devenir plus grave
3 ‹*colour*› foncer
C deepening *pres p adj* ‹*mystery, need, rift*› croissant/-e; ‹*crisis*› de plus en plus grave; ‹*confusion*› de plus en plus grand/-e

deep fat fryer *n* friteuse *f*

deep-freeze /ˌdiːp'friːz/ *n* congélateur *m*

deep-fry *vt* faire frire

deeply /'diːplɪ/ *adv* profondément

deep-rooted *adj* ‹*anxiety, prejudice*› profondément enraciné/-e

deep-sea *adj* ‹*diver, diving*› sous-marin/-e; ‹*fisherman, fishing*› hauturier/-ière

deep-vein thrombosis *n* thrombose *f* veineuse profonde, phlébite *f*

deer /dɪə(r)/ *n* (*pl* **~**) (red) cerf *m*; (roe) chevreuil *m*; (fallow) daim *m*; (doe) biche *f*

de-escalate /ˌdiː'eskəleɪt/ *vt* faire baisser ‹*tension, violence*›; désamorcer ‹*crisis*›

deface /dɪ'feɪs/ *vt* abîmer ‹*wall*›; couvrir [qch] d'inscriptions, dégrader ‹*monument*›

default /dɪ'fɔːlt/ **A** *vi* ne pas régler ses échéances
B by default *phr* par défaut; **to win by ~** gagner par forfait

defeat /dɪ'fiːt/ **A** *n* défaite *f*; **to admit ~** ‹*team, troops*› concéder la défaite; ‹*person*› avouer son échec
B *vt* **1** vaincre ‹*enemy*›; battre ‹*team, opposition, candidate*›; **the government was ~ed** le gouvernement a été mis en échec
2 rejeter ‹*bill, proposal*›
3 it ~s me ça me dépasse

defeatist /dɪ'fiːtɪst/ *n, adj* défaitiste *mf*

defect **A** /'diːfekt/ *n* (flaw) défaut *m*; (minor) imperfection *f*; **a speech ~** un défaut d'élocution
B /dɪ'fekt/ *vi* faire défection; **to ~ to the West** passer à l'Ouest

defective /dɪ'fektɪv/ *adj* défectueux/-euse

defector /dɪ'fektə(r)/ *n* transfuge *mf* (**from** de)

defence (BrE), **defense** (AmE) /dɪ'fens/ *n* (gen), (Law, Sport) défense *f*; **in her ~** à sa décharge

defenceless (BrE), **defenseless** (AmE) /dɪ'fenslɪs/ *adj* ‹*person, animal*› sans défense; ‹*town, country*› sans défenses

defend /dɪ'fend/ *vt* défendre ‹*fort, freedom, interests, title*›; justifier ‹*behaviour, decision*›

defendant /dɪ'fendənt/ *n* accusé/-e *m/f*

defender /dɪ'fendə(r)/ *n* défenseur *m*

defensive /dɪ'fensɪv/ *adj* ‹*reaction, behaviour*› de défense; **to be (very) ~** être sur la défensive

defer /dɪ'fɜː(r)/ **A** *vt* (*p prés etc* **-rr-**) reporter ‹*meeting, decision*› (**until** à); remettre [qch] à plus tard ‹*departure*›; différer ‹*payment*›
B *vi* (*p prés etc* **-rr-**) **to ~ to sb** s'incliner devant qn

deference /'defərəns/ *n* déférence *f*; **in ~ to** par déférence pour

defiance /dɪ'faɪəns/ *n* attitude *f* de défi

defiant /dɪ'faɪənt/ *adj* ‹*person*› rebelle; ‹*behaviour*› provocant/-e

deficiency /dɪ'fɪʃənsɪ/ *n* **1** (shortage) insuffisance *f* (**of, in** de); (of vitamins) carence *f* (**of** en)
2 (weakness) faiblesse *f*

deficient /dɪ'fɪʃnt/ *adj* déficient/-e (**in** en)

deficit /'defɪsɪt/ *n* déficit *m*

define /dɪ'faɪn/ *vt* définir

definite /'defɪnɪt/ *adj* ‹*plan, amount*› précis/-e; ‹*feeling, improvement, increase*› net/nette; ‹*decision, agreement*› ferme; **a ~ answer** une réponse claire et nette; **nothing is ~ yet** rien n'est encore sûr; **to be ~** (sure) être certain/-e (**about** de); (unyielding) être formel/-elle (**about** sur)

d

🔑 **definitely** /ˈdefɪnɪtlɪ/ *adv* sans aucun doute; **he ~ said he wasn't coming** il a bien dit qu'il ne viendrait pas

🔑 **definition** /ˌdefɪˈnɪʃn/ *n* définition *f*

definitive /dɪˈfɪnətɪv/ *adj* définitif/-ive

deflate /dɪˈfleɪt/ *vt* dégonfler

deflationary /ˌdiːˈfleɪʃənərɪ, (AmE) -nerɪ/ *adj* déflationniste

deflect /dɪˈflekt/ *vt* **1** défléchir, dévier ‹*missile*›
2 détourner ‹*blame, criticism, attention*›

deformed *adj* déformé/-e; (from birth) difforme

defraud /dɪˈfrɔːd/ *vt* escroquer ‹*client, employer*›; frauder ‹*tax office*›

defrost /ˌdiːˈfrɒst/ **A** *vt* décongeler ‹*food*›; dégivrer ‹*refrigerator*›
B *vi* ‹*refrigerator*› dégivrer; ‹*food*› décongeler

deft /deft/ *adj* adroit/-e de ses mains, habile

defunct /dɪˈfʌŋkt/ *adj* défunt/-e

defuse /ˌdiːˈfjuːz/ *vt* désamorcer

defy /dɪˈfaɪ/ *vt* **1** défier ‹*authority, person*›
2 to ~ sb to do mettre qn au défi de faire
3 défier ‹*description*›; résister à ‹*efforts*›

degenerate **A** /dɪˈdʒenərət/ *adj* dégénéré/-e
B /dɪˈdʒənəreɪt/ *vi* dégénérer

degrade /dɪˈgreɪd/ *vt* humilier ‹*person*›

degrading /dɪˈgreɪdɪŋ/ *adj* ‹*conditions, film*› dégradant/-e; ‹*job*› avilissant/-e; ‹*treatment*› humiliant/-e

🔑 **degree** /dɪˈgriː/ *n* **1** (measurement) degré *m*
2 (from university) diplôme *m* universitaire; **first** *or* **bachelor's ~** ≈ licence *f*
3 to such a ~ that à tel point que; **to a ~, to some ~** dans une certaine mesure; **by ~s** petit à petit
4 (AmE) **first ~ murder** homicide *m* volontaire avec préméditation

degree ceremony *n* (BrE) (Univ) cérémonie *f* de remise des diplômes

degree course *n* (BrE) (Univ) programme *m* d'études universitaires

dehydrated /ˌdiːˈhaɪdreɪtɪd/ *adj* déshydraté/-e; ‹*milk*› en poudre; **to become ~** se déshydrater

de-icer /ˌdiːˈaɪsə(r)/ *n* dégivrant *m*

deign /deɪn/ *vt* **to ~ to do** condescendre à faire, daigner faire

deity /ˈdiːətɪ/ *n* divinité *f*

dejected /dɪˈdʒektɪd/ *adj* découragé/-e

delay /dɪˈleɪ/ **A** *n* (gen) retard *m* (**of** de, **to, on** sur); **a few minutes' ~** un délai de quelques minutes; **without (further) ~** sans (plus) tarder
B *vt* **1** différer ‹*decision, publication*›; **to ~ doing** attendre pour faire
2 retarder ‹*train, arrival, post*›

delayed *adj* **to be ~** être retardé/-e

delegate **A** /ˈdelɪgət/ *n* délégué/-e *m/f*
B /ˈdelɪgeɪt/ *vt* déléguer ‹*responsibility, task*› (**to** à)

delegation /ˌdelɪˈgeɪʃn/ *n* délégation *f*

delete /dɪˈliːt/ *vt* supprimer (**from** de); (with pen) barrer; (on computer) effacer

delete key *n* touche *f* effacement

deli /ˈdelɪ/ *n* (fam) **delicatessen**

deliberate /dɪˈlɪbərət/ *adj* **1** (intentional) délibéré/-e; **it was ~** il/elle l'a fait *etc* exprès
2 (measured) ‹*movement*› mesuré/-e

deliberately /dɪˈlɪbərətlɪ/ *adv* ‹*do, say*› exprès; ‹*sarcastic, provocative*› délibérément

delicacy /ˈdelɪkəsɪ/ *n* **1** (of object, situation) délicatesse *f*; (of mechanism) sensibilité *f*
2 (food) (savoury) mets *m* raffiné; (sweet) friandise *f*

delicate /ˈdelɪkət/ *adj* (gen) délicat/-e; ‹*features*› fin/-e

delicatessen /ˌdelɪkəˈtesn/ *n* **1** (shop) épicerie *f* fine
2 (AmE) (eating-place) restaurant-traiteur *m*

delicious /dɪˈlɪʃəs/ *adj* délicieux/-ieuse

delight /dɪˈlaɪt/ **A** *n* joie *f*, plaisir *m*; **to take ~ in sth/in doing** prendre plaisir à qch/à faire
B *vt* ravir ‹*person*› (**with** par)

delighted /dɪˈlaɪtɪd/ *adj* ravi/-e (**at, by, with** de, **to do** de faire); **~ to meet you** enchanté

delightful /dɪˈlaɪtfl/ *adj* charmant/-e

delinquency /dɪˈlɪŋkwənsɪ/ *n* délinquance *f*

delinquent /dɪˈlɪŋkwənt/ *n, adj* délinquant/-e *m/f*

delirious /dɪˈlɪrɪəs/ *adj* **to be ~** délirer

🔑 **deliver** /dɪˈlɪvə(r)/ **A** *vt* **1** livrer ‹*goods, groceries*› (**to** à); distribuer ‹*mail*› (**to** à); remettre ‹*note*› (**to** à)
2 mettre au monde ‹*baby*›; délivrer ‹*baby animal*›
3 faire ‹*speech*›; donner ‹*ultimatum*›; rendre ‹*verdict*›
B *vi* ‹*tradesman*› livrer; ‹*postman*› distribuer le courrier

🔑 **delivery** /dɪˈlɪvərɪ/ *n* **1** (of goods, milk) livraison *f*; (of mail) distribution *f*; **on ~** à la livraison
2 (of baby) accouchement *m*

delude /dɪˈluːd/ *vt* tromper; **to ~ oneself** se faire des illusions

deluge /ˈdeljuːdʒ/ *n* déluge *m*

delusion /dɪˈluːʒn/ *n* illusion *f*

🔑 **demand** /dɪˈmɑːnd, (AmE) dɪˈmænd/ **A** *n* **1** (gen) demande *f* (**for** de); **on ~** (gen) à la demande; ‹*payable*› à vue; **to be in ~** être très demandé/-e
2 (pressure) exigence *f*
B *vt* **1** (request) demander ‹*reform*›; (forcefully) exiger ‹*ransom*›; réclamer ‹*inquiry*›
2 (require) demander ‹*skill, time, patience*›

🔑 mot clé

(of sb de qn); (more imperatively) exiger

demanding /dɪˈmɑːndɪŋ, (AmE) -ˈmænd-/ *adj* **1** ‹*person*› exigeant/-e
2 ‹*work, course*› ardu/-e; ‹*schedule*› chargé/-e

demean /dɪˈmiːn/ *v refl* **to ~ oneself** s'abaisser

demeaning /dɪˈmiːnɪŋ/ *adj* humiliant/-e

demented /dɪˈmentɪd/ *adj* fou/folle

dementia /dɪˈmenʃə/ *n* démence *f*

demerara /ˌdeməˈreərə/ *n* (*also* **demerara sugar**) sucre *m* roux cristallisé

demilitarize /ˌdiːˈmɪlɪtəraɪz/ *vt* démilitariser

demister /ˌdiːˈmɪstə(r)/ *n* (BrE) dispositif *m* antibuée

demo /ˈdeməʊ/ *n* (fam) (*pl* **-mos**) **1** (protest) manif *f* (fam)
2 (sample version) démo *f* (fam), version *f* de démonstration

demobilize /diːˈməʊbɪlaɪz/ *vt* démobiliser

democracy /dɪˈmɒkrəsɪ/ *n* démocratie *f*

democrat /ˈdeməkræt/ *n* démocrate *mf*

democratic /ˌdeməˈkrætɪk/ *adj* démocratique

demolish /dɪˈmɒlɪʃ/ *vt* démolir

demolition /ˌdeməˈlɪʃn/ *n* démolition *f*

demon /ˈdiːmən/ *n* démon *m*

demonstrate /ˈdemənstreɪt/ **A** *vt*
1 démontrer ‹*theory, truth*›
2 manifester ‹*concern, support*›; montrer ‹*skill*›
3 faire la démonstration de ‹*machine, product*›; **to ~ how to do** montrer comment faire
B *vi* manifester (**for** en faveur de, **against** contre)

demonstration /ˌdemənˈstreɪʃn/ *n* **1** (march) manifestation *f* (**against** contre, **for** en faveur de)
2 (of machine, theory) démonstration *f*

demonstrative /dɪˈmɒnstrətɪv/ *adj* démonstratif/-ive

demonstrator /ˈdemənstreɪtə(r)/ *n* manifestant/-e *m/f*

demoralize /dɪˈmɒrəlaɪz, (AmE) -ˈmɔːr-/ *vt* démoraliser

demote /ˌdiːˈməʊt/ *vt* rétrograder

den /den/ *n* **1** (of lion) antre *m*; (of fox) tanière *f*
2 (room) tanière *f*

denial /dɪˈnaɪəl/ *n* (of accusation, rumour) démenti *m*; (of guilt, rights, freedom) négation *f*; **to be in ~** refuser d'admettre qch

denim /ˈdenɪm/ **A** *n* jean *m*; **~s** jean *m*
B *adj* ‹*jacket, skirt*› en jean; **~ jeans** jean *m*

Denmark /ˈdenmɑːk/ *pr n* Danemark *m*

denomination /dɪˌnɒmɪˈneɪʃn/ *n* **1** (name) dénomination *f*
2 (faith) confession *f*
3 (value) valeur *f*

denounce /dɪˈnaʊns/ *vt* **1** (inform on, criticize) dénoncer
2 (accuse) accuser

dense /dens/ *adj* dense

density /ˈdensətɪ/ *n* densité *f*

dent /dent/ **A** *n* (in metal) bosse *f*
B *vt* cabosser ‹*car*›

dental /ˈdentl/ *adj* dentaire

dental floss *n* fil *m* dentaire

dental surgeon *n* chirurgien-dentiste *m*

dental surgery *n* (BrE) (premises) cabinet *m* dentaire

dentist /ˈdentɪst/ *n* dentiste *mf*

dentistry /ˈdentɪstrɪ/ *n* médecine *f* dentaire

dentures *npl* dentier *m*

deny /dɪˈnaɪ/ *vt* **1** démentir ‹*rumour*›; nier ‹*accusation*›; **to ~ doing** *or* **having done** nier avoir fait
2 to ~ sb sth refuser qch à qn

deodorant /diːˈəʊdərənt/ *n* (personal) déodorant *m*; (for room) déodorisant *m*

depart /dɪˈpɑːt/ *vi* **1** partir (**from** de, **for** pour)
2 (deviate) **to ~ from** s'éloigner de

department /dɪˈpɑːtmənt/ *n* **1** (of company) service *m*
2 (governmental) ministère *m*; (administrative) service *m*; **social services ~** services sociaux
3 (in store) rayon *m*; **toy ~** rayon jouets
4 (in hospital) service *m*
5 (in university) département *m*
6 (in school) section *f*

departmental /ˌdiːpɑːtˈmentl/ *adj* ‹*head, meeting*› de service

department store *n* grand magasin *m*

departure /dɪˈpɑːtʃə(r)/ *n* (of person, train) départ *m*; (from truth, regulation) entorse *f* (**from** à); (from policy, tradition) rupture *f* (**from** par rapport à)

departure gate *n* porte *f* de départ

departures board *n* tableau *m* des départs

departure time *n* heure *f* de départ

depend /dɪˈpend/ *vi* **to ~ on** dépendre de, compter sur (**for** pour); **to ~ on sb/sth to do** compter sur qn/qch pour faire; **that ~s** cela dépend; **~ing on the season** suivant la saison

dependable /dɪˈpendəbl/ *adj* ‹*person*› digne de confiance; ‹*machine*› fiable

dependant /dɪˈpendənt/ *n* personne *f* à charge

dependence /dɪˈpendəns/ *n* **1** (reliance) dépendance *f* (**on** vis-à-vis de)
2 (addiction) dépendance *f* (**on** à)

dependent /dɪˈpendənt/ *adj* ‹*relative*› à charge; **to be ~ (up)on** (gen) dépendre de; (financially) vivre à la charge de

depict /dɪˈpɪkt/ *vt* (visually) représenter; (in writing) dépeindre (**as** comme)

depiction /dɪ'pɪkʃn/ *n* peinture *f*, représentation *f*

deplete /dɪ'pliːt/ *vt* réduire

deplorable /dɪ'plɔːrəbl/ *adj* déplorable

deplore /dɪ'plɔː(r)/ *vt* déplorer

deploy /dɪ'plɔɪ/ *vt* déployer

depopulation /diːˌpɒpjʊ'leɪʃn/ *n* dépeuplement *m*

deport /dɪ'pɔːt/ *vt* expulser (**to** vers)

deportation /ˌdiːpɔː'teɪʃn/ *n* expulsion *f*

depose /dɪ'pəʊz/ *vt* déposer

deposit /dɪ'pɒzɪt/ **A** *n* **1** (to bank account) dépôt *m*; **on ~** en dépôt
2 (on house, hire purchase goods) versement *m* initial (**on** sur); (on holiday, goods) acompte *m*, arrhes *fpl*
3 (against damage, breakages) caution *f*
4 (on bottle) consigne *f*
5 (of silt, mud) dépôt *m*; (of coal, mineral) gisement *m*
B *vt* déposer ‹*money*›; **to ~ sth with sb** confier qch à qn

deposit account *n* (BrE) compte *m* de dépôt

depot /'depəʊ, (AmE) 'diːpəʊ/ *n* **1** (gen) dépôt *m*
2 (AmE) (station) (bus) gare *f* routière; (rail) gare *f* ferroviaire

depress /dɪ'pres/ *vt* **1** déprimer ‹*person*›
2 appuyer sur ‹*button*›
3 faire baisser ‹*prices*›; affaiblir ‹*trading*›

depressed /dɪ'prest/ *adj* **1** ‹*person*› déprimé/-e
2 ‹*region, industry*› en déclin

depressing /dɪ'presɪŋ/ *adj* déprimant/-e

depression /dɪ'preʃn/ *n* dépression *f*; **to suffer from ~** être dépressif/-ive

deprivation /ˌdeprɪ'veɪʃn/ *n* (poverty) privations *fpl*

deprive /dɪ'praɪv/ *vt* priver (**of** de)

deprived *adj* ‹*area, family*› démuni/-e; ‹*childhood*› malheureux/-euse

depth /depθ/ **A** *n* **1** (of hole, water) profondeur *f*; (of layer) épaisseur *f*; **to be out of one's ~** (in water) ne plus avoir pied; (in situation) être complètement perdu/-e
2 (of colour, emotion) intensité *f*; (of crisis) gravité *f*
3 (of knowledge) étendue *f*; (of analysis, novel) profondeur *f*; **to examine sth in ~** examiner qch en détail
B depths *npl* (of sea) profondeurs *fpl*; **in the ~s of winter** au plus profond de l'hiver; **to be in the ~s of despair** toucher le fond du désespoir

deputize /'depjʊtaɪz/ *vi* **to ~ for sb** remplacer qn

deputy /'depjʊtɪ/ **A** *n* **1** (aide) adjoint/-e *m/f*; (replacement) remplaçant/-e *m/f*
2 (politician) député *m*
B *adj* adjoint/-e

deputy chairman *n* vice-président *m*

deputy president *n* vice-président *m*

derail /dɪ'reɪl/ *vt* faire dérailler

deranged *adj* dérangé/-e

deregulate /ˌdiː'regjʊleɪt/ *vt* libérer ‹*prices*›; déréguler ‹*market*›

derelict /'derəlɪkt/ *adj* ‹*building*› délabré/-e

derision /dɪ'rɪʒn/ *n* moqueries *fpl*

derive /dɪ'raɪv/ *vt* tirer ‹*benefit, income*› (**from** de)

derogatory /dɪ'rɒgətrɪ, (AmE) -tɔːrɪ/ *adj* désobligeant/-e (**about** envers); ‹*term*› péjoratif/-ive

descend /dɪ'send/ **A** *vt* descendre ‹*steps, slope, path*›
B *vi* **1** ‹*person, plane*› descendre (**from** de)
2 ‹*rain, darkness, mist*› tomber (**on, over** sur)
3 to ~ on sb débarquer chez qn (fam)
4 to be ~ed from descendre de

descendant /dɪ'sendənt/ *n* descendant/-e *m/f* (**of** de)

descent /dɪ'sent/ *n* **1** descente *f* (**on, upon** sur)
2 (extraction) descendance *f*

✔ **describe** /dɪ'skraɪb/ *vt* décrire

✔ **description** /dɪ'skrɪpʃn/ *n* description *f* (**of** de); (for police) signalement *m* (**of** de)

descriptive /dɪ'skrɪptɪv/ *adj* descriptif/-ive

desecrate /'desɪkreɪt/ *vt* profaner ‹*altar, shrine*›

desert A /'dezət/ *n* désert *m*
B /dɪ'zɜːt/ *vt* abandonner ‹*person*› (**for** pour); déserter ‹*cause*›; abandonner ‹*post*›
C /dɪ'zɜːt/ *vi* ‹*soldier*› déserter
IDIOM **to get one's just ~s** avoir ce qu'on mérite

desert boot *n* bottine *f* en croûte de cuir, clarks® *f inv*

deserted /dɪ'zɜːtɪd/ *adj* désert/-e

deserter /dɪ'zɜːtə(r)/ *n* déserteur *m* (**from** de)

desert island *n* île *f* déserte

✔ **deserve** /dɪ'zɜːv/ *vt* mériter (**to do** de faire)

deserving /dɪ'zɜːvɪŋ/ *adj* ‹*winner*› méritant/-e; ‹*cause*› louable

✔ **design** /dɪ'zaɪn/ **A** *n* **1** (development) (of object, appliance) conception *f*; (of building, room) agencement *m*; (of clothing) création *f*
2 (drawing, plan) plan *m* (**for** de)
3 (art of designing) design *m*; (fashion) stylisme *m*
4 (pattern) motif *m*; **a leaf ~** un motif de feuilles
5 (subject of study) arts *mpl* appliqués
B *vt* **1** concevoir ‹*building, appliance*›; **to be ~ed for sth/to do** être conçu/-e pour qch/pour faire
2 ‹*designer*› créer ‹*costume, garment*›; dessiner ‹*building, appliance*›

✔ mot clé

designate /ˈdezɪgneɪt/ *vt* **to ~ sb (as) sth** désigner qn (comme) qch; **to ~ sth (as) sth** classer qch (comme) qch; **to ~ sth for** destiner qch à

designer /dɪˈzaɪnə(r)/ **A** *n* (gen) concepteur/-trice *m/f*; (of furniture, in fashion) créateur/-trice *m/f*; (of sets) décorateur/-trice *m/f*; **costume ~** costumier/-ière *m/f*
B *adj* **~ clothes**, **~ labels** vêtements *mpl* griffés; **~ label** griffe *f*

design fault *n* faute *f* de conception

desirable /dɪˈzaɪərəbl/ *adj* **1** ‹*outcome, solution*› souhaitable; ‹*area, position*› convoité/-e; ‹*job, gift*› séduisant/-e
2 (sexually) désirable

desire /dɪˈzaɪə(r)/ **A** *n* désir *m* (**for** de); **to have no ~ to do** n'avoir aucune envie de faire
B *vt* désirer; **it leaves a lot to be ~d** cela laisse beaucoup à désirer

desk /desk/ *n* **1** bureau *m*; **writing ~** secrétaire *m*
2 (in classroom) (pupil's) table *f*; (teacher's) bureau *m*
3 reception ~ réception *f*; **information ~** bureau *m* de renseignements; **cash ~** caisse *f*

desktop /ˈdesktɒp/ *n* (*also* **~ computer**) ordinateur *m* de bureau

desktop publishing, **DTP** *n* micro-édition *f*, PAO *f*

desolate /ˈdesələt/ *adj* désolé/-e

despair /dɪˈspeə(r)/ **A** *n* désespoir *m*; **in** *or* **out of ~** de désespoir
B *vi* désespérer (**of** de, **of doing** de faire)

desperate /ˈdespərət/ *adj* ‹*person, plea, situation*› désespéré/-e; ‹*criminal*› prêt/-e à tout; **to be ~ for** avoir désespérément besoin de ‹*affection, help*›; attendre désespérément ‹*news*›

desperately /ˈdespərətlɪ/ *adv* **1** ‹*plead, look, fight*› désespérément; **to need sth ~** avoir très besoin de qch
2 ‹*poor*› terriblement; ‹*ill*› très gravement

desperation /ˌdespəˈreɪʃn/ *n* désespoir *m*

despicable /dɪˈspɪkəbl, ˈdespɪkəbl/ *adj* méprisable

despise /dɪˈspaɪz/ *vt* mépriser

despite /dɪˈspaɪt/ *prep* malgré

despondent /dɪˈspɒndənt/ *adj* abattu/-e, découragé/-e

despot /ˈdespɒt/ *n* despote *m*

dessert /dɪˈzɜːt/ *n* dessert *m*

dessertspoon *n* cuillère *f* à dessert

dessert wine *n* vin *m* doux

destabilize /ˌdiːˈsteɪbəlaɪz/ *vt* déstabiliser

destination /ˌdestɪˈneɪʃn/ *n* destination *f*

destined /ˈdestɪnd/ *adj* **1** destiné/-e (**for, to** à, **to do** à faire)
2 (bound for) **~ for Paris** à destination de Paris

destiny /ˈdestɪnɪ/ *n* destin *m*, destinée *f*

destitute /ˈdestɪtjuːt, (AmE) -tuːt/ *adj* sans ressources

destroy /dɪˈstrɔɪ/ *vt* **1** détruire ‹*building, evidence*›; briser ‹*career, person*›
2 (kill) abattre ‹*animal*›; détruire, anéantir ‹*population, enemy*›

destruction /dɪˈstrʌkʃn/ *n* destruction *f*

destructive /dɪˈstrʌktɪv/ *adj* destructeur/-trice

detach /dɪˈtætʃ/ *vt* détacher (**from** de)

detachable /dɪˈtætʃəbl/ *adj* ‹*coupon, section, strap*› détachable; ‹*lever, collar*› amovible

detached /dɪˈtætʃt/ *adj* détaché/-e

detached house *n* maison *f* (individuelle)

detachment /dɪˈtætʃmənt/ *n* détachement *m*

detail /ˈdiːteɪl, (AmE) dɪˈteɪl/ **A** *n* détail *m*; **in (more) ~** (plus) en détail; **to go into ~s** entrer dans les détails; **to have an eye for ~** prêter attention aux détails
B *vt* exposer [qch] en détail ‹*plans*›; énumérer ‹*items*›

detain /dɪˈteɪn/ *vt* **1** (delay) retenir
2 (keep in custody) placer [qn] en détention

detainee /ˌdiːteɪˈniː/ *n* détenu/-e *m/f*

detect /dɪˈtekt/ *vt* déceler ‹*error, traces*›; détecter ‹*crime, leak, sound*›; sentir ‹*mood*›

detectable /dɪˈtektəbl/ *adj* discernable

detection /dɪˈtekʃn/ *n* (of disease, error) détection *f*; **crime ~** la lutte contre la criminalité; **to escape ~** ‹*criminal*› ne pas être découvert/-e; ‹*error*› ne pas être décelé/-e

detective /dɪˈtektɪv/ *n* ≈ inspecteur/-trice *m/f* (de police); **private ~** détective *m*

detective story *n* roman *m* policier

detector /dɪˈtektə(r)/ *n* détecteur *m*

detention /dɪˈtenʃn/ *n* **1** (confinement) détention *f*
2 (in school) retenue *f*, colle *f* (fam)

detention centre *n* centre *m* de détention pour mineurs

deter /dɪˈtɜː(r)/ *vt* (*p prés etc* **-rr-**) dissuader (**from doing** de faire)

detergent /dɪˈtɜːdʒənt/ *n* détergent *m*

deteriorate /dɪˈtɪərɪəreɪt/ *vi* se détériorer

determination /dɪˌtɜːmɪˈneɪʃn/ *n* détermination *f*

determine /dɪˈtɜːmɪn/ *vt* déterminer; **to ~ how** établir comment

determined /dɪˈtɜːmɪnd/ *adj* ‹*person*› fermement décidé/-e (**to do** à faire); ‹*air*› résolu/-e

deterrent /dɪˈterənt, (AmE) -ˈtɜː-/ *n* (gen) moyen *m* de dissuasion; (Mil) force *f* de dissuasion

detest /dɪˈtest/ *vt* détester (**doing** faire)

detonate /ˈdetəneɪt/ *vt* faire exploser ‹*bomb*›

detour /ˈdiːtʊə(r), (AmE) dɪˈtʊər/ *n* détour *m*

detox /ˌdiːˈtɒks/ (fam) **A** *n* **to be in ~** être en cure de désintoxication
B *adj* ‹*centre, treatment*› de désintoxication

detract /dɪˈtrækt/ *vi* **to ~ from** porter atteinte à ‹*success, value*›; nuire à ‹*image*›; diminuer ‹*pleasure*›

detriment /ˈdetrɪmənt/ *n* **to the ~ of** au détriment de

detrimental /ˌdetrɪˈmentl/ *adj* nuisible (**to** à)

deuce /djuːs, (AmE) duːs/ *n* (in tennis) **~!** égalité!

devaluation /ˌdiːvæljʊˈeɪʃn/ *n* (of currency) dévaluation *f*

devastated *adj* ‹*land, region*› ravagé/-e; ‹*person*› anéanti/-e

devastation /ˌdevəˈsteɪʃn/ *n* dévastation *f*

develop /dɪˈveləp/ **A** *vt* **1** attraper ‹*illness*›; prendre ‹*habit*›; présenter ‹*symptom*›
2 élaborer ‹*plan*›; mettre au point ‹*technique*›; développer ‹*argument*›
3 développer ‹*mind, business, market*›
4 mettre en valeur ‹*land, site*›; aménager ‹*city centre*›
5 (in photography) développer
B *vi* **1** (evolve) ‹*child, society, country, plot*› se développer; ‹*skills*› s'améliorer; **to ~ into** devenir
2 (come into being) ‹*friendship, difficulty*› naître; ‹*crack*› se former; ‹*illness*› se déclarer
3 (progress, advance) ‹*friendship*› se développer; ‹*difficulty, illness*› s'aggraver; ‹*crack, fault*› s'accentuer; ‹*game, story*› se dérouler
4 (in size) ‹*town, business*› se développer

developer /dɪˈveləpə(r)/ *n* (*also* **property ~**) promoteur *m* (immobilier)

developing country *n* pays *m* en voie de développement

development /dɪˈveləpmənt/ *n* **1** (gen) développement *m*
2 (of product) mise *f* au point; (of housing, industry) création *f*
3 (of land) mise *f* en valeur; (of site, city centre) aménagement *m*
4 (innovation) progrès *m*; **major ~s** des découvertes *fpl* majeures (**in** dans le domaine de)
5 (event) changement *m*; **recent ~s in Europe** les derniers événements en Europe

deviate /ˈdiːvɪeɪt/ *vi* **1** (from norm) s'écarter (**from** de)
2 (from course) dévier (**from** de)

device /dɪˈvaɪs/ *n* **1** (household) appareil *m*
2 (Tech) dispositif *m*
3 (*also* **explosive ~, incendiary ~**) engin *m* explosif
4 (means) moyen *m* (**for doing, to do** de *or* pour faire)

IDIOM **to be left to one's own ~s** être laissé/-e à soi-même

devil /ˈdevl/ *n* **1** (*also* **Devil**) **the ~** le Diable
2 (evil spirit) démon *m*

IDIOM **speak of the ~!** quand on parle du loup (on en voit la queue)! (fam)

devil's advocate *n* avocat *m* du diable

devious /ˈdiːvɪəs/ *adj* retors/-e

devise /dɪˈvaɪz/ *vt* concevoir ‹*scheme, course*›; inventer ‹*product, machine*›

devoid /dɪˈvɔɪd/ *adj* **~ of** dépourvu/-e de

devolution /ˌdiːvəˈluːʃn, (AmE) ˌdev-/ *n* **1** (of powers) transfert *m* (**from** de, **to** à)
2 (policy) régionalisation *f*

devote /dɪˈvəʊt/ *vt* consacrer (**to** à, **to doing** à faire); **to ~ oneself** se consacrer (**to** à)

devoted /dɪˈvəʊtɪd/ *adj* ‹*person, animal*› dévoué/-e (**to** à); ‹*fan*› fervent/-e

devotion /dɪˈvəʊʃn/ *n* (to person, work) dévouement *m* (**to** à); (to cause) attachement *m* (**to** à); (to God) dévotion *f* (**to** à)

devour /dɪˈvaʊə(r)/ *vt* dévorer

devout /dɪˈvaʊt/ *adj* ‹*Catholic, prayer*› fervent/-e; ‹*person*› pieux/pieuse

dew /djuː, (AmE) duː/ *n* rosée *f*

diabetes /ˌdaɪəˈbiːtiːz/ *n* diabète *m*

diabetic /ˌdaɪəˈbetɪk/ *n, adj* diabétique *mf*

diagnose /ˈdaɪəgnəʊz, (AmE) ˌdaɪəgˈnəʊs/ *vt* diagnostiquer

diagnosis /ˌdaɪəgˈnəʊsɪs/ *n* (*pl* **-ses**) diagnostic *m*

diagonal /daɪˈægənl/ **A** *n* diagonale *f*
B *adj* diagonal/-e

diagonally /daɪˈægənəlɪ/ *adv* en diagonale

diagram /ˈdaɪəgræm/ *n* schéma *m*; (in mathematics) figure *f*

dial /ˈdaɪəl/ **A** *n* cadran *m*
B *vt* (*p prés etc* **-ll-** (BrE), **-l-** (AmE)) faire, composer ‹*number*›; appeler ‹*person*›; **to ~ 999** (for police, ambulance) ≈ appeler police secours; (for fire brigade) ≈ appeler les pompiers

dialect /ˈdaɪəlekt/ *n* dialecte *m*

dialling code *n* (BrE) indicatif *m*

dialling tone (BrE), **dial tone** (AmE) *n* tonalité *f*

dialogue /ˈdaɪəlɒg, (AmE) -lɔːg/ *n* dialogue *m*

dialogue box *n* boîte *f* de dialogue

dialysis /ˌdaɪˈæləsɪs/ *n* (*pl* **-lyses**) dialyse *f*

diameter /daɪˈæmɪtə(r)/ *n* diamètre *m*

diamond /ˈdaɪəmənd/ *n* **1** (gem) diamant *m*
2 (shape) losange *m*
3 (in cards) carreau *m*

diaper /ˈdaɪəpə(r), (AmE) ˈdaɪpər/ *n* (AmE) couche *f* (de bébé)

diaphragm /ˈdaɪəfræm/ *n* diaphragme *m*

diarrhoea (BrE), **diarrhea** (AmE) /ˌdaɪəˈrɪə/ *n* diarrhée *f*

mot clé

diary /'daɪərɪ/ *n* **1** (for appointments) agenda *m*; **to put sth in one's ~** noter qch dans son agenda
2 (journal) journal *m* intime

dice /daɪs/ **A** *n* (*pl* ~) (object) dé *m*; (game) dés *mpl*
B *vt* couper [qch] en cubes ‹*vegetable, meat*›

dictate /dɪk'teɪt, (AmE) 'dɪkteɪt/ **A** *vt* **1** dicter ‹*letter*›
2 imposer ‹*terms*› (**to** à); déterminer ‹*outcome*›
B **1** **to ~ to one's secretary** dicter une lettre (*or* un texte) à sa secrétaire
2 **to ~ to sb** imposer sa volonté à qn

dictation /dɪk'teɪʃn/ *n* dictée *f*

dictator /dɪk'teɪtə(r), (AmE) 'dɪkteɪtər/ *n* dictateur *m*

dictatorship /dɪk'teɪtəʃɪp, (AmE) 'dɪkt-/ *n* dictature *f*

dictionary /'dɪkʃənrɪ, (AmE) -nerɪ/ *n* dictionnaire *m*

die /daɪ/ *vi* (*p prés* **dying**, *prét*, *pp* **died**) mourir (**of, from** de); **to be dying** être mourant/-e, se mourir; **to be dying to do** mourir d'envie de faire; **to be dying for** avoir une envie folle de

■ **die down** ‹*emotion, row*› s'apaiser; ‹*fighting*› s'achever; ‹*storm*› se calmer; ‹*laughter*› diminuer; ‹*applause*› se calmer

■ **die out** ‹*species*› disparaître

diesel /'di:zl/ *n* **1** (*also* **~ fuel, ~ oil**) gazole *m*
2 (*also* **~ car**) diesel *m*

diesel engine *n* (moteur *m*) diesel *m*

diet /'daɪət/ *n* **1** (normal food) alimentation *f* (**of** à base de)
2 (slimming food) régime *m*; **to go on a ~** se mettre au régime

dietician /ˌdaɪə'tɪʃn/ *n* diététicien/-ienne *m/f*

differ /'dɪfə(r)/ *vi* **1** (be different) différer (**from** de, **in** par)
2 (disagree) différer (**on** sur, **from sb** de qn)

difference /'dɪfrəns/ *n* **1** différence *f* (**in, of** de); **to tell the ~ between** faire la différence entre; **it won't make any ~** ça ne changera rien; **it makes no ~ to me** cela m'est égal
2 (disagreement) différend *m* (**over** à propos de, **with** avec); **a ~ of opinion** une divergence d'opinion

different /'dɪfrənt/ *adj* différent/-e (**from, to** (BrE), **than** (AmE)) de

differentiate /ˌdɪfə'renʃɪeɪt/ **A** *vt* différencier (**from** de)
B *vi* **1** (tell the difference) faire la différence (**between** entre)
2 (show the difference) faire la distinction (**between** entre)

differently /'dɪfrəntlɪ/ *adv* (in another way) autrement (**from** que); (in different ways) différemment (**from** de)

difficult /'dɪfɪkəlt/ *adj* difficile; **to find it ~ to do** avoir du mal à faire; **to be ~ to get on with** être difficile à vivre

difficulty /'dɪfɪkəltɪ/ *n* difficulté *f*; **to have ~ (in) doing** avoir du mal à faire

diffident /'dɪfɪdənt/ *adj* ‹*person*› qui manque d'assurance; ‹*smile, gesture*› timide

dig /dɪg/ **A** *n* **1** (with elbow) coup *m* de coude (**in** dans)
2 (fam) (jibe) **to take a ~ at sb** lancer une pique (fam) à qn
3 (in archaeology) fouilles *fpl*; **to go on a ~** aller faire des fouilles
B **digs** *npl* (BrE) chambre *f* (meublée)
C *vt* (*p prés* **-gg-**, *pp* **dug**) **1** creuser ‹*hole, tunnel, grave*› (**in** dans)
2 bêcher ‹*garden*›; fouiller ‹*site*›
3 extraire ‹*coal*› (**out of** de)
D *vi* (*p prés* **-gg-**, *pp* **dug**) ‹*miner*› creuser; ‹*archaeologist*› fouiller; ‹*gardener*› bêcher

■ **dig up 1** déterrer ‹*body, treasure, scandal*›; arracher ‹*roots, weeds*›; excaver ‹*road*›
2 bêcher ‹*garden*›

digest /daɪ'dʒest, dɪ-/ *vt* digérer ‹*food*›; assimiler ‹*facts*›

digestion /daɪ'dʒestʃn, dɪ-/ *n* digestion *f*

digit /'dɪdʒɪt/ *n* **1** (number) chiffre *m*
2 (finger) doigt *m*; (toe) orteil *m*

digital /'dɪdʒɪtl/ *adj* ‹*display, recording*› numérique; ‹*watch*› à affichage numérique; ‹*camera, TV*› numérique

digital television *n* télévision *f* numérique

digitize /'dɪdʒɪtaɪz/ *vt* numériser

dignified /'dɪgnɪfaɪd/ *adj* ‹*person*› digne; ‹*manner*› empreint/-e de dignité

dignity /'dɪgnətɪ/ *n* dignité *f*

digress /daɪ'gres/ *vi* faire une digression; **to ~ from** s'écarter de

dilapidated /dɪ'læpɪdeɪtɪd/ *adj* délabré/-e

dilate /daɪ'leɪt/ **A** *vt* dilater
B *vi* se dilater

dilemma /daɪ'lemə, dɪ-/ *n* dilemme *m* (**about** à propos de); **to be in a ~** être pris/-e dans un dilemme

diligent /'dɪlɪdʒənt/ *adj* appliqué/-e

dilute /daɪ'lju:t, (AmE) -'lu:t/ *vt* diluer (**with** avec)

dim /dɪm/ **A** *adj* **1** ‹*room*› sombre
2 ‹*light*› faible; **to grow ~** baisser
3 ‹*outline*› vague
4 ‹*memory*› vague *before n*
5 (fam) (stupid) bouché/-e (fam)
B *vt* (*p prés etc* **-mm-**) baisser ‹*light, headlights*›; mettre [qch] en veilleuse ‹*lamp*›

dime /daɪm/ *n* (AmE) (pièce *f* de) dix cents *mpl*
IDIOM **they're a ~ a dozen** (fam) on en trouve à la pelle (fam)

d

dimension /dɪ'menʃn/ *n* dimension *f*

-dimensional /-dɪmenʃənl/ *combining form* **three~** à trois dimensions

dime store *n* (AmE) bazar *m*

diminish /dɪ'mɪnɪʃ/ *vt*, *vi* diminuer

dimple /'dɪmpl/ *n* fossette *f*

din /dɪn/ *n* vacarme *m*

dine /daɪn/ *vi* dîner

diner /'daɪnə(r)/ *n* **1** (person) dîneur/-euse *m/f*
2 (AmE) (restaurant) café-restaurant *m*

dinghy /'dɪŋgɪ/ *n* **1** (*also* **sailing ~**) dériveur *m*
2 (inflatable) canot *m*

dingy /'dɪndʒɪ/ *adj* ‹*colour*› défraîchi/-e; ‹*place*› minable

dining car *n* wagon-restaurant *m*

dining room *n* (in house) salle *f* à manger; (in hotel) salle *f* de restaurant

⚷ **dinner** /'dɪnə(r)/ *n* **1** dîner *m*; **to go out to ~** dîner dehors; **to have ~** dîner
2 (banquet) dîner *m* (**for** en l'honneur de)

dinner hour *n* (BrE) (Sch) heure *f* du déjeuner

dinner jacket, **DJ** *n* smoking *m*

dinner party *n* dîner *m*

dinner time *n* heure *f* du dîner

dinosaur /'daɪnəsɔ:(r)/ *n* dinosaure *m*

dip /dɪp/ **A** *n* **1** (in ground, road) creux *m*
2 (bathe) baignade *f*
3 (in prices, rate, sales) (mouvement *m* de) baisse *f* (**in** dans)
4 (Culin) sauce *f*
B *vt* (*p prés etc* **-pp-**) **1** tremper (**in, into** dans)
2 (BrE) (Aut) baisser ‹*headlights*›; **~ped headlights** codes *mpl*
C *vi* (*p prés etc* **-pp-**) **1** ‹*bird, plane*› piquer
2 ‹*land, road*› être en pente
3 to ~ into puiser dans ‹*savings*›; parcourir ‹*novel*›

diploma /dɪ'pləʊmə/ *n* diplôme *m* (**in** en)

diplomacy /dɪp'ləʊməsɪ/ *n* diplomatie *f*

diplomat /'dɪpləmæt/ *n* diplomate *mf*

diplomatic /ˌdɪplə'mætɪk/ *adj* diplomatique; **to be ~** avoir du tact

dipstick /'dɪpstɪk/ *n* jauge *f* de niveau d'huile

⚷ **direct** /daɪ'rekt, dɪ-/ **A** *adj* (gen) direct/-e; ‹*person*› franc/franche
B *adv* directement; **to fly ~** prendre un vol direct
C *vt* **1** (address, aim) adresser ‹*appeal, criticism*› (**at** à, **against** contre); cibler ‹*campaign*› (**at** sur); orienter ‹*effort, resource*› (**to, towards** vers)
2 (control) diriger ‹*company, project*›; régler ‹*traffic*›
3 diriger ‹*attack, light*› (**at** vers)
4 réaliser ‹*film, programme*›; mettre [qch] en scène ‹*play*›; diriger ‹*actor, opera*›
5 (show route) **to ~ sb to sth** indiquer le chemin de qch à qn
D *vi* (in cinema, radio, TV) faire de la réalisation; (in theatre) faire de la mise en scène

direct debit *n* prélèvement *m* automatique

⚷ **direction** /daɪ'rekʃn, dɪ-/ **A** *n* direction *f*; **in the right/wrong ~** dans la bonne/mauvaise direction; **to go in the opposite ~** aller en sens inverse; **from all ~s** de tous les côtés
B directions *npl* **1** (for route) indications *fpl*; **to ask for ~s** demander son chemin (**from** à)
2 (for use) instructions *fpl* (**as to, about** sur); **~s for use** mode *m* d'emploi

⚷ **directly** /daɪ'rektlɪ, dɪ-/ *adv* **1** ‹*connect, challenge, go*› directement; ‹*point*› droit; ‹*above*› juste
2 (at once) **~ after** aussitôt après; **~ before** juste avant
3 (very soon) d'ici peu
4 (frankly) ‹*speak*› franchement

direct mail *n* mailing *m*, publipostage *m*

⚷ **director** /daɪ'rektə(r), dɪ-/ *n* **1** (of company) (sole) directeur/-trice *m/f*; (on board) administrateur/-trice *m/f*
2 (of play, film) metteur *m* en scène; (of orchestra) chef *m* d'orchestre; (of choir) chef *m* des chœurs

directory /daɪ'rektərɪ, dɪ-/ *n* **1** (*also* **telephone ~**) annuaire *m*
2 (for business use) répertoire *m* d'adresses; **street ~** répertoire *m* des rues
3 (Comput) répertoire *m*

directory enquiries (BrE), **directory assistance** (AmE) *npl* (service *m* des) renseignements *mpl*

direct speech *n* style *m* direct

dirt /dɜ:t/ *n* **1** (on clothing, in room) saleté *f*; (on body, cooker) crasse *f*; (in carpet, engine, filter) saletés *fpl*
2 (soil) terre *f*; (mud) boue *f*

dirt track *n* chemin *m* de terre battue

dirty /dɜ:tɪ/ **A** *adj* **1** ‹*face, clothing, street*› sale; ‹*work*› salissant/-e; **to get ~** se salir; **to get sth ~** salir qch
2 ‹*needle*› qui a déjà servi; ‹*wound*› infecté/-e
3 (fam) ‹*book, joke*› cochon/-onne (fam); ‹*mind*› mal tourné/-e
4 (fam) ‹*trick*› sale *before n*
B *vt* salir
IDIOM **to give sb a ~ look** regarder qn d'un sale œil

disability /ˌdɪsə'bɪlətɪ/ *n* infirmité *f*; **mental/physical ~** handicap *m* mental/physique

disable /dɪs'eɪbl/ *vt* **1** ‹*accident*› rendre [qn] infirme
2 immobiliser ‹*machine*›
3 (Comput) désactiver

disabled /dɪs'eɪbld/ **A** *n* **the ~** les handicapés *mpl*

⚷ mot clé

B *adj* handicapé/-e

disabled access *n* voie *f* d'accès pour handicapés

disadvantage /ˌdɪsəd'vɑːntɪdʒ, (AmE) -'væn-/ *n* inconvénient *m*; **to be at a ~** être désavantagé/-e

disadvantaged /ˌdɪsəd'vɑːntɪdʒd, (AmE) -'væn-/ *adj* défavorisé/-e

disagree /ˌdɪsə'griː/ *vi* **1** ne pas être d'accord (**with** avec, **on, about** sur); **we often ~** nous avons souvent des avis différents
2 ‹*facts, accounts, result*› être en désaccord (**with** avec)
3 to ~ with sb ‹*food*› ne pas réussir à qn

disagreeable /ˌdɪsə'griːəbl/ *adj* désagréable

disagreement /ˌdɪsə'griːmənt/ *n* **1** (difference of opinion) désaccord *m* (**about, on** sur)
2 (argument) différend *m* (**about, over** sur)

disallow /ˌdɪsə'laʊ/ *vt* **1** (Sport) refuser ‹*goal*›
2 (gen), (Law) rejeter ‹*claim, decision*›

disappear /ˌdɪsə'pɪə(r)/ *vi* disparaître

disappearance /ˌdɪsə'pɪərəns/ *n* disparition *f* (**of** de)

disappoint /ˌdɪsə'pɔɪnt/ *vt* décevoir

disappointed /ˌdɪsə'pɔɪntɪd/ *adj* déçu/-e (**about, with sth** par qch)

disappointing /ˌdɪsə'pɔɪntɪŋ/ *adj* décevant/-e

disappointment /ˌdɪsə'pɔɪntmənt/ *n* déception *f*; **to be a ~ to sb** décevoir qn

disapproval /ˌdɪsə'pruːvl/ *n* désapprobation *f* (**of** de)

disapprove /ˌdɪsə'pruːv/ *vi* **to ~ of** désapprouver ‹*person, lifestyle*›; être contre ‹*smoking*›

disapproving /ˌdɪsə'pruːvɪŋ/ *adj* désapprobateur/-trice

disarm /dɪs'ɑːm/ *vt, vi* désarmer

disarmament /dɪs'ɑːməmənt/ *n* désarmement *m*

disaster /dɪ'zɑːstə(r), (AmE) -zæs-/ *n* catastrophe *f*; (long-term) désastre *m*

disaster area *n* région *f* sinistrée; (fig) catastrophe *f*

disaster fund *n* fonds *m* de soutien

disaster movie *n* film *m* catastrophe

disaster victim *n* sinistré/-e *m/f*

disastrous /dɪ'zɑːstrəs, (AmE) -zæs-/ *adj* désastreux/-euse

disbelief /ˌdɪsbɪ'liːf/ *n* incrédulité *f*

disc, disk (AmE) /dɪsk/ *n* **1** (gen), (Mus) disque *m*
2 identity ~ plaque *f* d'identité; **tax ~** vignette *f* (automobile)

discard /dɪs'kɑːd/ *vt* **1** (get rid of) se débarrasser de ‹*possessions*›; mettre [qch] au rebut ‹*furniture*›
2 (drop) abandonner ‹*plan, policy*›; laisser tomber ‹*person*›

discerning /dɪ'sɜːnɪŋ/ *adj* perspicace

discharge **A** /'dɪstʃɑːdʒ/ *n* **1** (of patient) renvoi *m* au foyer
2 (of gas, smoke) émission *f*; (of liquid) écoulement *m*; (of waste) déversement *m*
3 (from eye, wound) sécrétions *fpl*
B /dɪs'tʃɑːdʒ/ *vt* **1** renvoyer ‹*patient*›; décharger ‹*accused*›; **to be ~d from hospital** être autorisé/-e à quitter l'hôpital; **to be ~d from the army** être libéré/-e de l'armée
2 renvoyer ‹*employee*›
3 émettre ‹*gas*›; déverser ‹*sewage*›
4 (Med) **to ~ pus** suppurer

discipline /'dɪsɪplɪn/ **A** *n* discipline *f*
B *vt* **1** (control) discipliner
2 (punish) punir

disciplined /'dɪsɪplɪnd/ *adj* discipliné/-e

disclaim /dɪs'kleɪm/ *vt* nier

disclaimer /dɪs'kleɪmə(r)/ *n* démenti *m*

disclose /dɪs'kləʊz/ *vt* révéler ‹*information*›

disclosure /dɪs'kləʊʒə(r)/ *n* révélation *f* (**of** de)

disco /'dɪskəʊ/ *n* discothèque *f*

discomfort /dɪs'kʌmfət/ *n* **1** (physical) sensation *f* pénible
2 (embarrassment) sentiment *m* de gêne

disconcerting /ˌdɪskən'sɜːtɪŋ/ *adj* (worrying) troublant/-e; (unnerving) déconcertant/-e

disconnect /ˌdɪskə'nekt/ *vt* débrancher ‹*pipe, fridge*›; couper ‹*telephone*›; décrocher ‹*carriage*›

discontent /ˌdɪskən'tent/ *n* mécontentement *m*

discontented /ˌdɪskən'tentɪd/ *adj* mécontent/-e

discontinue /ˌdɪskən'tɪnjuː/ *vt* supprimer ‹*service*›; arrêter ‹*production*›; cesser ‹*visits*›

discount **A** /'dɪskaʊnt/ *n* remise *f* (**on** sur); **to give sb a ~** faire une remise à qn
B /dɪs'kaʊnt, (AmE) 'dɪskaʊnt/ *vt* écarter ‹*idea, possibility*›; ne pas tenir compte de ‹*advice, report*›

discount store *n* solderie *f*

discourage /dɪ'skʌrɪdʒ/ *vt* décourager

discover /dɪs'kʌvə(r)/ *vt* découvrir (**that** que)

discovery /dɪ'skʌvərɪ/ *n* découverte *f*

discredit /dɪs'kredɪt/ *vt* discréditer ‹*person, organization*›; mettre en doute ‹*report, theory*›

discreet /dɪ'skriːt/ *adj* discret/-ète

discrepancy /dɪs'krepənsɪ/ *n* divergence *f*

discretion /dɪ'skreʃn/ *n* discrétion *f*; **to use one's ~** agir à sa discrétion

discriminate /dɪ'skrɪmɪneɪt/ *vi* **1** (act with bias) établir une discrimination (**against** envers, **in favour of** en faveur de)
2 (distinguish) **to ~ between** faire une *or* la distinction entre

discrimination /dɪˌskrɪmɪ'neɪʃn/ *n* discrimination *f*

discus /'dɪskəs/ *n* disque *m*

⚷ **discuss** /dɪ'skʌs/ *vt* (talk about) discuter de; (in writing) examiner

⚷ **discussion** /dɪ'skʌʃn/ *n* discussion *f*; (in public) débat *m*

discussion board *n* (Comput) forum m de discussion

d

disdainful /dɪs'deɪnfl/ *adj* dédaigneux/-euse

⚷ **disease** /dɪ'zi:z/ *n* maladie *f*

disembark /ˌdɪsɪm'bɑ:k/ *vt, vi* débarquer

disenchanted /ˌdɪsɪn'tʃɑ:ntɪd, (AmE) -'tʃænt-/ *adj* désabusé/-e

disengage /ˌdɪsɪn'geɪdʒ/ *vt* dégager (**from** de)

disfigure /dɪs'fɪgə(r), (AmE) dɪs'fɪgjər/ *vt* défigurer

disgrace /dɪs'greɪs/ **A** *n* honte *f*; **to be in ~** (officially) être en disgrâce
B *vt* déshonorer ‹*team, family*›

disgraceful /dɪs'greɪsfl/ *adj* scandaleux/-euse

disguise /dɪs'gaɪz/ **A** *n* déguisement *m*; **in ~** déguisé/-e
B *vt* déguiser ‹*person, voice*›; camoufler ‹*blemish*›; cacher ‹*emotion, fact*›

disgust /dɪs'gʌst/ **A** *n* (physical) dégoût *m*; (moral) écœurement *m* (**at** devant)
B *vt* (physically) dégoûter; (morally) écœurer

disgusting /dɪs'gʌstɪŋ/ *adj* (physically) répugnant/-e; (morally) écœurant/-e

dish /dɪʃ/ *n* **1** plat *m*; **to do the ~es** faire la vaisselle
2 (*also* **satellite ~**) antenne *f* parabolique

■ **dish out** distribuer ‹*advice, compliments, money*›; servir ‹*food*›

dishcloth *n* (for washing) lavette *f*; (for drying) torchon *m* (à vaisselle)

dishevelled /dɪ'ʃevld/ *adj* ‹*person*› débraillé/-e; ‹*hair*› décoiffé/-e; ‹*clothes*› en désordre

dishonest /dɪs'ɒnɪst/ *adj* malhonnête

dishonesty /dɪs'ɒnɪstɪ/ *n* (financial) malhonnêteté *f*; (moral) mauvaise foi *f*

dishonour (BrE), **dishonor** (AmE) /dɪs'ɒnə(r)/ *n* déshonneur *m*

dish towel *n* torchon *m* (à vaisselle)

dishwasher *n* (machine) lave-vaisselle *m inv*; (person) plongeur/-euse *m/f*

disillusioned /ˌdɪsɪ'lu:ʒnd/ *adj* désabusé/-e; **to be ~ with** perdre ses illusions sur

disinfect /ˌdɪsɪn'fekt/ *vt* désinfecter

disinfectant /ˌdɪsɪn'fektənt/ *n* désinfectant *m*

disintegrate /dɪs'ɪntɪgreɪt/ *vi* se désagréger

disinterested /dɪs'ɪntrəstɪd/ *adj* impartial/-e

disk /dɪsk/ *n* **1** (Comput) disque *m*
2 (AmE) = **disc**

disk drive *n* (*also* **disk drive unit**) unité *f* de disques

dislike /dɪs'laɪk/ **A** *n* aversion *f* (**for** pour); **to take a ~ to sb** prendre qn en aversion
B *vt* ne pas aimer (**doing** faire)

dislocate /'dɪsləkeɪt, (AmE) 'dɪsləʊkeɪt/ *vt* **to ~ one's shoulder** se démettre l'épaule

dislodge /dɪs'lɒdʒ/ *vt* déplacer ‹*rock, tile, obstacle*›

disloyal /dɪs'lɔɪəl/ *adj* déloyal/-e (**to** envers)

dismal /'dɪzməl/ *adj* **1** ‹*place, sight*› lugubre
2 (fam) ‹*failure, attempt*› lamentable

dismantle /dɪs'mæntl/ *vt* **1** démonter ‹*construction*›
2 démanteler ‹*organization*›

dismay /dɪs'meɪ/ *n* consternation *f* (**at** devant)

⚷ **dismiss** /dɪs'mɪs/ *vt* **1** écarter ‹*idea, suggestion*›; exclure ‹*possibility*›
2 chasser ‹*thought, worry*›
3 licencier ‹*employee*›; démettre [qn] de ses fonctions ‹*director, official*›
4 (end interview with) congédier ‹*person*›; (send out) ‹*teacher*› laisser sortir ‹*class*›
5 (Law) **the case was ~ed** il y a eu non-lieu

dismissal /dɪs'mɪsl/ *n* (of employee) licenciement *m*; (of manager, minister) destitution *f*

dismissive /dɪs'mɪsɪv/ *adj* dédaigneux/-euse

disobedient /ˌdɪsə'bi:dɪənt/ *adj* désobéissant/-e

disobey /ˌdɪsə'beɪ/ **A** *vt* désobéir à ‹*person*›; enfreindre ‹*law*›
B *vi* ‹*person*› désobéir

disorder /dɪs'ɔ:də(r)/ *n* **1** (lack of order) désordre *m*
2 (disturbances) émeutes *fpl*
3 (Med) (malfunction) troubles *mpl*; (disease) maladie *f*

disorganized /dɪs'ɔ:gənaɪzd/ *adj* désorganisé/-e

disorientate /dɪs'ɔ:rɪənteɪt/ *vt* désorienter

disown /dɪs'əʊn/ *vt* renier ‹*person*›; désavouer ‹*document*›

dispassionate /dɪ'spæʃənət/ *adj* (impartial) objectif/-ive (**about** au sujet de)

dispatch /dɪ'spætʃ/ **A** *n* (report) dépêche *f*
B *vt* envoyer ‹*person*› (**to** à); expédier ‹*letter, parcel*› (**to** à)

dispel /dɪ'spel/ *vt* (*p prés etc* **-ll-**) dissiper ‹*doubt, fear, myth*›

dispensary /dɪ'spensərɪ/ *n* (BrE) (in hospital) pharmacie *f*; (in chemist's) officine *f*

dispense /dɪ'spens/ *vt* **1** ‹*machine*› distribuer ‹*drinks, money*›
2 ‹*chemist*› préparer ‹*medicine, prescription*›
3 (exempt) dispenser (**from sth** de qch, **from doing** de faire)

■ **dispense with 1** se passer de ‹*services, formalities*›
2 abandonner ‹*policy*›
3 (make unnecessary) rendre inutile

dispenser /dɪ'spensə(r)/ *n* distributeur *m*

⚷ mot clé

disperse /dɪ'spɜːs/ **A** *vt* disperser ‹*crowd, fumes*›
B *vi* **1** ‹*crowd*› se disperser
2 ‹*mist*› se dissiper

displaced person *n* personne *f* déplacée

display /dɪ'spleɪ/ **A** *n* **1** (in shop) étalage *m*; (of furniture, vehicles) exposition *f*; **window ~** vitrine *f*; **to be on ~** être exposé/-e
2 (demonstration) (of art, craft) démonstration *f*; (of dance, sport) exhibition *f*; **air ~** fête *f* aéronautique
3 (of emotion) démonstration *f*; (of strength) déploiement *m*; (of wealth) étalage *m*
4 (Aut, Comput) écran *m*
B *vt* **1** (show, set out) afficher ‹*information, poster*›; exposer ‹*object*›
2 (reveal) faire preuve de ‹*intelligence, interest, skill*›; révéler ‹*emotion, vice, virtue*›
3 (flaunt) faire étalage de ‹*beauty, knowledge, wealth*›; exhiber ‹*legs, chest*›

displeased /dɪs'pliːzd/ *adj* mécontent/-e (**with, at** de)

disposable /dɪ'spəʊzəbl/ *adj* **1** (throwaway) jetable
2 (available) disponible

disposal /dɪ'spəʊzl/ *n* **1** (of waste product) élimination *f*; **for ~** à jeter
2 (of company, property) vente *f*
3 to be at sb's ~ être à la disposition de qn

dispose /dɪ'spəʊz/ *v*
▪ **dispose of 1** se débarrasser de ‹*body, rubbish*›; détruire ‹*evidence*›; désarmer ‹*bomb*›
2 écouler ‹*stock*›; vendre ‹*car, shares*›

disproportionate /ˌdɪsprə'pɔːʃənət/ *adj* disproportionné/-e (**to** par rapport à)

disprove /dɪs'pruːv/ *vt* réfuter

dispute /dɪ'spjuːt/ **A** *n* **1** (quarrel) (between individuals) dispute *f*; (between groups) conflit *m* (**over, about** à propos de)
2 (controversy) controverse *f* (**over, about** sur)
B *vt* **1** contester ‹*claim, figures*›
2 se disputer ‹*property, title*›

disqualify /dɪs'kwɒlɪfaɪ/ *vt* **1** (gen) exclure; **to ~ sb from doing** interdire à qn de faire
2 (Sport) disqualifier
3 (BrE) (Aut) **to ~ sb from driving** retirer le permis de conduire à qn

disregard /ˌdɪsrɪ'gɑːd/ **A** *n* (for problem, person) indifférence *f* (**for sth** à qch, **for sb** envers qn); (for danger, life, law) mépris *m* (**for** de)
B *vt* **1** ne pas tenir compte de ‹*problem, evidence, remark*›; fermer les yeux sur ‹*fault*›; mépriser ‹*danger*›
2 ne pas respecter ‹*law, instruction*›

disrepair /ˌdɪsrɪ'peə(r)/ *n* délabrement *m*; **to fall into ~** se délabrer

disreputable /dɪs'repjʊtəbl/ *adj* ‹*person*› peu recommandable; ‹*place*› mal famé/-e

disrespect /ˌdɪsrɪ'spekt/ *n* manque *m* de respect (**for** envers)

disrespectful /ˌdɪsrɪ'spektfl/ *adj* ‹*person*› irrespectueux/-euse (**to, towards** envers)

disrupt /dɪs'rʌpt/ *vt* perturber ‹*traffic, trade, meeting*›; bouleverser ‹*lifestyle, schedule, routine*›; interrompre ‹*power supply*›

disruption /dɪs'rʌpʃn/ *n* (disorder) perturbations *fpl*; (of schedule) bouleversement *m*

disruptive /dɪs'rʌptɪv/ *adj* perturbateur/-trice

dissatisfaction /dɪˌsætɪs'fækʃn/ *n* mécontentement *m*

dissatisfied /dɪ'sætɪsfaɪd/ *adj* mécontent/-e (**with** de)

dissect /dɪ'sekt/ *vt* disséquer

dissertation /ˌdɪsə'teɪʃn/ *n* (BrE) (Univ) mémoire *m* (**on** sur)

dissident /'dɪsɪdənt/ *n*, *adj* dissident/-e *m/f*

dissimilar /dɪ'sɪmɪlə(r)/ *adj* dissemblable; **~ to** différent/-e de

dissolve /dɪ'zɒlv/ **A** *vt* **1** ‹*acid, water*› dissoudre ‹*solid, grease*›
2 faire dissoudre ‹*tablet, powder*› (**in** dans)
3 dissoudre ‹*assembly, parliament, partnership*›
B *vi* **1** ‹*tablet*› se dissoudre (**in** dans, **into** en)
2 ‹*hope*› s'évanouir; ‹*outline, image*› disparaître
3 to ~ into tears fondre en larmes

dissuade /dɪ'sweɪd/ *vt* dissuader (**from doing** de faire)

distance /'dɪstəns/ *n* distance *f* (**between** entre, **from** de, **to** à); **to keep one's ~** garder ses distances (**from** avec); **in the ~** au loin; **it's within walking ~** on peut y aller à pied

distance learning *n* enseignement *m* à distance

distant /'dɪstənt/ *adj* **1** (remote) éloigné/-e
2 (faint) ‹*memory, prospect*› lointain/-e
3 (cool) ‹*person*› distant/-e

distaste /dɪs'teɪst/ *n* dégoût *m*

distinct /dɪ'stɪŋkt/ *adj* (gen) distinct/-e (**from** de); ‹*resemblance, preference, progress*› net/nette *before n*; ‹*advantage*› indéniable

distinction /dɪ'stɪŋkʃn/ *n* **1** (gen) distinction *f*
2 (Univ) mention *f* très bien

distinctive /dɪ'stɪŋktɪv/ *adj* caractéristique (**of** de)

distinguish /dɪ'stɪŋgwɪʃ/ *vt* distinguer (**from** de); **to be ~ed by** se caractériser par

distinguished /dɪ'stɪŋgwɪʃt/ *adj* **1** (elegant) distingué/-e
2 (famous) éminent/-e

distinguishing *adj* distinctif/-ive

distort /dɪ'stɔːt/ *vt* déformer

distract /dɪ'strækt/ *vt* distraire; **to ~ sb from doing** empêcher qn de faire

distracting /dɪ'stræktɪŋ/ *adj* gênant/-e

distraction /dɪˈstrækʃn/ *n* **1** (from concentration) distraction *f*
2 (diversion) diversion *f*

distraught /dɪˈstrɔːt/ *adj* éperdu/-e

distress /dɪˈstres/ **A** *n* **1** (emotional) désarroi *m*; **to cause sb ~** faire de la peine à qn
2 (physical) souffrance *f*
3 ‹*ship*› **in ~** en détresse
B *vt* faire de la peine à ‹*person*›; (stronger) bouleverser ‹*person*› (**to do** de faire)

distressed /dɪˈstrest/ *adj* (upset) peiné/-e (**at, by** par); (stronger) bouleversé/-e (**at, by** par)

distressing /dɪˈstresɪŋ/ *adj* ‹*case, event, idea*› pénible; ‹*news*› navrant/-e; ‹*sight*› affligeant/-e

distribute /dɪˈstrɪbjuːt/ *vt* **1** (share out) distribuer ‹*films, supplies, money*› (**to** à, **among** entre)
2 (spread out) répartir ‹*load, tax burden*›

🔑 **distribution** /ˌdɪstrɪˈbjuːʃn/ *n* distribution *f*

distributor /dɪˈstrɪbjʊtə(r)/ *n* distributeur *m* (**for sth** de qch)

🔑 **district** /ˈdɪstrɪkt/ *n* (in country) région *f*; (in city) quartier *m*; (administrative) district *m*

district attorney *n* (AmE) représentant *m* du ministère public

distrust /dɪsˈtrʌst/ *vt* se méfier de

disturb /dɪˈstɜːb/ *vt* **1** (interrupt) déranger ‹*person*›; troubler ‹*silence, sleep*›
2 (upset) troubler ‹*person*›; (concern) inquiéter ‹*person*›

disturbance /dɪˈstɜːbəns/ *n* **1** (interruption, inconvenience) dérangement *m*
2 (riot) troubles *mpl*; (fight) altercation *f*

disturbed /dɪˈstɜːbd/ *adj* **1** ‹*sleep*› agité/-e
2 ‹*child*› perturbé/-e

disturbing /dɪˈstɜːbɪŋ/ *adj* ‹*portrayal*› troublant/-e; ‹*book, film*› perturbant/-e; ‹*report, increase*› inquiétant/-e

disused /dɪsˈjuːzd/ *adj* désaffecté/-e

ditch /dɪtʃ/ **A** *n* fossé *m*
B *vt* laisser tomber ‹*friend*›; abandonner ‹*idea, vehicle*›; plaquer (fam) ‹*girlfriend, boyfriend*›

dither /ˈdɪðə(r)/ *vi* tergiverser (**about, over** sur)

ditto /ˈdɪtəʊ/ *adv* idem

dive /daɪv/ **A** *n* **1** (by swimmer) plongeon *m*
2 (of plane, bird) piqué *m*
B *vi* (*prét* **~d** (BrE), **dove** (AmE))
1 ‹*person*› plonger (**off, from** de, **down to** jusqu'à)
2 (as hobby) faire de la plongée

diver /ˈdaɪvə(r)/ *n* plongeur/-euse *m/f*; (deep-sea) scaphandrier *m*

diverge /daɪˈvɜːdʒ/ *vi* diverger; **to ~ from** s'écarter de

diverse /daɪˈvɜːs/ *adj* (varied) divers/-e; (different) différent/-e

diversify /daɪˈvɜːsɪfaɪ/ *vi* se diversifier

diversion /daɪˈvɜːʃn, (AmE) -ˈvɜːrʒn/ *n*
1 (distraction) diversion *f* (**from** à)
2 (of river, money) détournement *m*
3 (of traffic) déviation *f*

diversity /daɪˈvɜːsətɪ/ *n* diversité *f*

divert /daɪˈvɜːt/ *vt* **1** détourner ‹*water*›; dévier ‹*traffic*›; dérouter ‹*flight*› (**to** sur); détourner ‹*funds*› (**to** au profit de)
2 (distract) détourner

🔑 **divide** /dɪˈvaɪd/ **A** *vt* **1** (*also* **~ up**) partager ‹*food, money, time, work*›
2 (separate) séparer (**from** de)
3 (split) diviser ‹*friends, group*›
4 (in mathematics) diviser (**by** par)
B *vi* ‹*road*› bifurquer; ‹*river, train*› se séparer en deux; ‹*group*› (into two) se séparer en deux; ‹*cell, organism*› se diviser

dividend /ˈdɪvɪdend/ *n* dividende *m*

dividing line *n* ligne *f* de démarcation

diving /ˈdaɪvɪŋ/ *n* (from board) plongeon *m*; (under sea) plongée *f* sous-marine

diving board *n* plongeoir *m*

diving suit *n* scaphandre *m*

🔑 **division** /dɪˈvɪʒn/ *n* (gen) division *f*

divisive /dɪˈvaɪsɪv/ *adj* ‹*policy*› qui sème la discorde; **to be socially ~** créer des inégalités sociales

divorce /dɪˈvɔːs/ **A** *n* divorce *m*
B *vt* **to ~ sb** divorcer de *or* d'avec qn; **they're ~d** ils ont divorcé; **she's ~d** elle est divorcée

divorcee /dɪˌvɔːˈsiː/ *n* divorcé/-e *m/f*

DIY *n* (BrE) (*abbr* = **do-it-yourself**) bricolage *m*

dizzy /ˈdɪzɪ/ *adj* ‹*height*› vertigineux/-euse; **to make sb ~** donner le vertige à qn; **to feel ~** avoir la tête qui tourne

DJ *n* (*abbr* = **disc jockey**) DJ *mf*

DNA *n* (*abbr* = **deoxyribonucleic acid**) ADN *m*

🔑 **do** **A** *v aux* (*3ᵉ pers sg prés* **does**, *prét* **did**, *pp* **done**) **1** (gen) **~ you like Mozart?** est-ce que tu aimes Mozart?, aimes-tu Mozart?; **I don't smoke** je ne fume pas; **don't shut the door** ne ferme pas la porte; **~ sit down** asseyez-vous; **I ~ like your dress** j'aime beaucoup ta robe; **he lives in London, doesn't he?** il habite à Londres, n'est-ce pas?; **Lola didn't phone, ~ she?** Lola n'a pas téléphoné par hasard?; **don't ~ that!** ne fais pas ça!; **he said he'd tell her and he did** il a dit qu'il le lui dirait et il l'a fait; **so/neither does he** lui aussi/non plus
2 (in short answers) **'I love peaches'—'so ~ I'** 'j'adore les pêches'—'moi aussi'; **'who wrote it?'—'I did'** 'qui l'a écrit?'—'moi'; **'shall I tell him?'—'no don't'** 'est-ce que je le lui dis?'—'non'; **'he knows the President'—'does he?'** 'il connaît le Président'—'vraiment?'; **'Tim didn't say that' — 'yes he did'** 'Tim n'a pas dit ça' — 'si'
B *vt* (*3ᵉ pers sg prés* **does**, *prét* **did**, *pp* **done**) **1** (gen) faire; **to ~ the cooking/one's**

🔑 mot clé

homework faire la cuisine/ses devoirs; **to ~ sth again** refaire qch; **to ~ sb's hair** coiffer qn; **to ~ one's teeth** se brosser les dents; **what have you done to your hair?** qu'est-ce que vous avez fait à vos cheveux?; **what has he done with the newspaper?** qu'est-ce qu'il a fait du journal?; **to ~ 60** ‹*car, driver*› faire du 60 à l'heure
2 (fam) (cheat) **we've been done** on s'est fait avoir; **to ~ sb out of £5** refaire (fam) qn de 5 livres sterling
C *vi* (*3e pers sg prés* **does**, *prét* **did**, *pp* **done**) **1** (behave) faire; **~ as you're told** (by me) fais ce que je te dis; (by others) fais ce qu'on te dit
2 (serve purpose) faire l'affaire; **that box will ~** cette boîte fera l'affaire
3 (be acceptable) **this really won't ~!** (of situation, attitude) ça ne peut pas continuer comme ça!; (of work) c'est franchement mauvais!
4 (be enough) ‹*amount of money*› suffire
5 (get on) ‹*person*› s'en sortir; ‹*business*› marcher
6 (in health) **mother and baby are both ~ing well** la mère et l'enfant se portent bien; **the patient is ~ing well** le malade est en bonne voie
IDIOMS **how ~ you do** enchanté; **well done!** bravo!; **it doesn't ~ to be** ce n'est pas une bonne chose d'être; **it was all I could ~ not to laugh** je me suis retenu pour ne pas rire; **she does nothing but moan** elle ne fait que se plaindre
■ **do away with** se débarrasser de
■ **do up 1** (fasten) nouer ‹*laces*›; remonter ‹*zip*›; **~ up your buttons** boutonne-toi
2 (wrap) faire ‹*parcel*›
3 (renovate) restaurer ‹*house*›
■ **do with 1 what's it (got) to ~ with you?** en quoi est-ce que ça te regarde?; **it has nothing to ~ with you** cela ne vous concerne pas
2 (tolerate) supporter
3 (need) **I could ~ with a holiday** j'aurais bien besoin de partir en vacances
4 (finish) **it's all over and done with** c'est bien fini
■ **do without** se passer de ‹*person, advice*›

dock /dɒk/ **A** *n* **1** (in port) dock *m*; (for repairing ship) cale *f*
2 (AmE) (wharf) appontement *m*
3 (BrE) (Law) banc *m* des accusés
B *vi* arriver au port

dock worker *n* docker *m*

dockyard *n* chantier *m* naval

doctor /ˈdɒktə(r)/ **A** *n* **1** (Med) médecin *m*, docteur *m*
2 (Univ) docteur *m*
B *vt* frelater ‹*food, wine*›; falsifier ‹*figures*›; altérer ‹*document*›

doctorate /ˈdɒktərət/ *n* doctorat *m*

docudrama /ˈdɒkjʊdrɑːmə/ *n* docudrame *m*

document /ˈdɒkjʊmənt/ *n* document *m*

documentary /ˌdɒkjʊˈmentrɪ, (AmE) -terɪ/ *n* documentaire *m* (**about, on** sur)

dodge /dɒdʒ/ **A** *n* (BrE) (fam) (trick) combine *f* (fam)
B *vt* esquiver ‹*bullet, blow, question*›

dodgem /ˈdɒdʒəm/ *n* (*also* **dodgem car**) (BrE) auto *f* tamponneuse

dodgy /ˈdɒdʒɪ/ *adj* (fam) (untrustworthy) louche (fam); (risky) ‹*decision, plan*› risqué/-e; ‹*situation, moment*› délicat/-e

dog /dɒg, (AmE) dɔːg/ *n* **1** chien *m*; (female) chienne *f*
2 (male fox, wolf) mâle *m*
IDIOM **to go to the ~s** ‹*company, country*› aller à vau-l'eau

dog collar *n* **1** collier *m* de chien
2 (clerical) col *m* romain

dog-eared *adj* écorné/-e

dogged /ˈdɒgɪd, (AmE) ˈdɔːgɪd/ *adj* ‹*attempt*› obstiné/-e; ‹*person, refusal*› tenace; ‹*resistance*› opiniâtre

doghouse /ˈdɒghaʊs, (AmE) ˈdɔːg-/ *n* (AmE) niche *f* (à chien)
IDIOM **to be in the ~** être tombé/-e en disgrâce

dogmatic /dɒgˈmætɪk, (AmE) dɔːg-/ *adj* dogmatique (**about** sur)

dog paddle (AmE) *n* nage *f* à la manière d'un chien

dogsbody *n* (BrE) (fam) bonne *f* à tout faire

doh /dəʊ/ *n* (Mus) do *m*, ut *m*

doing /ˈduːɪŋ/ *n* **this is her ~** c'est son ouvrage; **it takes some ~!** ce n'est pas facile du tout!

dole /dəʊl/ *n* (BrE) allocation *f* de chômage; **on the ~** au chômage
■ **dole out** (fam) distribuer

doll /dɒl, (AmE) dɔːl/ *n* poupée *f*

dollar /ˈdɒlə(r)/ *n* dollar *m*

dollar bill *n* billet *m* d'un dollar

dolphin /ˈdɒlfɪn/ *n* dauphin *m*

domain /dəʊˈmeɪn/ *n* domaine *m* (**of** de)

dome /dəʊm/ *n* dôme *m*

domestic /dəˈmestɪk/ *adj* **1** ‹*market, flight*› intérieur/-e; ‹*crisis, issue*› de politique intérieure
2 ‹*life, harmony*› familial/-e; ‹*dispute*› conjugal/-e

domestic appliance *n* appareil *m* électroménager

domesticate /dəˈmestɪkeɪt/ *vt* domestiquer

domestic violence *n* violence *f* conjugale

dominant /ˈdɒmɪnənt/ *adj* dominant/-e

dominate /ˈdɒmɪneɪt/ *vt, vi* dominer

domineering /ˌdɒmɪˈnɪərɪŋ/ *adj* autoritaire

domino /ˈdɒmɪnəʊ/ *n* domino *m*; **to play ~es** jouer aux dominos

donate /dəʊˈneɪt, (AmE) ˈdəʊneɪt/ *vt* faire don de (**to** à)

donation /dəʊˈneɪʃn/ *n* don *m* (**of** de, **to** à)

done /dʌn/ **A** *adj* ‹*food*› cuit/-e; **well ~** bien cuit/-e

d

B *excl* (deal) marché conclu!
IDIOM **it's not the ~ thing** ça ne se fait pas
donkey /ˈdɒŋkɪ/ *n* âne *m*
donor /ˈdəʊnə(r)/ *n* **1** (of organ) donneur/-euse *m/f*
2 (of money) donateur/-trice *m/f*
donor card *n* carte *f* de donneur d'organes
doodle /ˈduːdl/ *vi* gribouiller
doom /duːm/ *n* (of person) perte *f*; (of country) catastrophe *f*
doomed *adj* condamné/-e; **to be ~ to failure** être voué/-e à l'échec
⚷ **door** /dɔː(r)/ *n* (in building) porte *f* (**to** de); (in car, train) porte *f*, portière *f*; **behind closed ~s** à huis clos
doorbell *n* sonnette *f*
doorman *n* portier *m*
doormat *n* paillasson *m*
doorstep /ˈdɔːstep/ *n* pas *m* de porte
door-to-door /ˌdɔːtəˈdɔː/ *adj* ‹*canvassing*› à domicile; **~ selling** porte à porte *m inv*
doorway /ˈdɔːweɪ/ *n* **1** (frame) embrasure *f*
2 (entrance) porte *f*, entrée *f*
dope /dəʊp/ **A** *n* (fam) **1** cannabis *m*
2 (fool) imbécile *mf* (fam)
B *vt* (Sport) doper ‹*horse, athlete*›; (gen) droguer ‹*person*›
dope test *n* (Sport) contrôle *m* antidopage
dormant /ˈdɔːmənt/ *adj* **1** ‹*emotion, talent*› latent/-e
2 ‹*volcano*› au repos
dormitory /ˈdɔːmɪtrɪ, (AmE) -tɔːrɪ/ *n* **1** (BrE) dortoir *m*
2 (AmE) (Univ) résidence *f*, foyer *m*
dormitory town *n* ville *f* dortoir
dormouse /ˈdɔːmaʊs/ *n* (*pl* **dormice**) muscardin *m*
dose /dəʊs/ *n* dose *f* (**of** de); **a ~ of flu** une bonne grippe
IDIOM **he's all right in small ~s** il est supportable à doses homéopathiques
dot /dɒt/ *n* (gen) point *m*; (on fabric) pois *m*
IDIOM **at ten on the ~** à dix heures pile
dot-com /dɒtˈkɒm/ **A** *n* (*also* **~ company**) société *f* Internet *or* virtuelle, société *f* dot-com
B *adj* ‹*shares*› des sociétés Internet *or* virtuelles; ‹*millionaire*› du commerce électronique
dot-com bubble *n* bulle *f* Internet
dote /dəʊt/ *vi* **to ~ on sb/sth** adorer qn/qch
dotted line *n* pointillé *m*
⚷ **double** /ˈdʌbl/ **A** *n* **1** (drink) double *m*
2 (of person) sosie *m*; (in film, play) doublure *f*
B doubles *npl* double *m*; **mixed ~s** double mixte
C *adj* double; **with a ~ 'n'** avec deux 'n'; **two ~ four (244)** deux cent quarante-quatre
D *adv* **1 ~ the amount** deux fois plus
2 to see ~ voir double
3 ‹*fold, bend*› en deux
E *vt* doubler ‹*amount, dose*›; multiplier [qch] par deux ‹*number*›
F *vi* **1** ‹*sales, prices, salaries*› doubler
2 to ~ for sb (actor) doubler qn
3 the sofa ~s as a bed le canapé fait aussi lit
IDIOM **on** *or* **at the ~** au plus vite
▪ **double back** rebrousser chemin
double act *n* duo *m*
double-barrelled name *n* (BrE) ≈ nom *m* à particule
double bass *n* contrebasse *f*
double bed *n* lit *m* double, grand lit *m*
double-breasted *adj* ‹*jacket*› croisé/-e
double-check *vt* vérifier [qch] à nouveau
double chin *n* double menton *m*
double-click /dʌblˈklɪk/ *vi* double-cliquer
double cream *n* (BrE) ≈ crème *f* fraîche
double-cross /ˌdʌblˈkrɒs/ *vt* (fam) doubler, trahir ‹*person*›
double-decker *n* (BrE) (bus) autobus *m* à impériale *or* à deux étages; (sandwich) sandwich *m* double
double-dip *adj* (Econ) à double creux, en W; **~ recession** récession *f* à double creux, récession *f* en W
double door *n* porte *f* à deux battants
double Dutch *n* (fam) baragouinage *m* (fam)
double glazing *n* double vitrage *m*
double-park *vi* se garer en double file
double room *n* chambre *f* pour deux personnes
double standard *n* **to have ~s** faire deux poids deux mesures
double take *n* **to do a ~** avoir une réaction à retardement
double vision *n* **to have ~** voir double
double yellow line(s) *n (pl)* (BrE) (Aut) *marquage au sol interdisant le stationnement*
⚷ **doubt** /daʊt/ **A** *n* doute *m*; **there is no ~ (that)** il ne fait aucun doute que; **to have no ~ (that)** être certain/-e que; **to be in ~** ‹*person*› être dans le doute; ‹*outcome*› être incertain/-e; **if** *or* **when in ~** dans le doute; **without (a) ~** sans aucun doute
B *vt* douter de ‹*fact, ability, honesty, person*›; **I ~ it!** j'en doute!; **I ~ if he'll come** je doute qu'il vienne
doubtful /ˈdaʊtfl/ *adj* **1** (unsure) incertain/-e
2 ‹*character, activity, taste*› douteux/-euse
dough /dəʊ/ *n* (Culin) pâte *f*
doughnut, **donut** (AmE) /ˈdəʊnʌt/ *n* beignet *m*
douse, **dowse** /daʊs/ *vt* éteindre ‹*fire*›; tremper ‹*person*›; **to ~ sth with petrol** arroser qch d'essence
dove /dʌv/ *n* colombe *f*

⚷ mot clé

Dover /'dəʊvə(r)/ *pr n* Douvres
dowdy /'daʊdɪ/ *adj* ‹*person*› mal fagoté/-e; ‹*clothes*› sans chic
down¹ /daʊn/

> When used to indicate vague direction, *down* often has no explicit translation in French: *to go down to London* = aller à Londres; *down in Brighton* = à Brighton.
> For examples and further usages, see the entry below.

A *adv* **1 to go** *or* **come ~** descendre; **to fall ~** tomber; **to sit ~ on the floor** s'asseoir par terre; **to pull ~ a blind** baisser un store; **~ below** en bas; **the telephone lines are ~** les lignes téléphoniques sont coupées; **face ~** ‹*fall*› face contre terre; ‹*lie*› à plat ventre; (in water) le visage dans l'eau
2 (lower) **profits are well ~ on last year's** les bénéfices sont nettement inférieurs à ceux de l'année dernière; **to get one's weight ~** maigrir; **I'm ~ to my last cigarette** il ne me reste plus qu'une cigarette
3 (Sport) **to be two sets ~** ‹*tennis player*› perdre par deux sets
4 (as deposit) **to pay £40 ~** payer 40 livres sterling comptant
B *prep* **to go ~ the street** descendre la rue; **to run ~ the hill** descendre la colline en courant; **to go ~ town** aller en ville; **they live ~ the road** ils habitent un peu plus loin dans la rue
C *adj* **1** (fam) **to feel ~** être déprimé/-e
2 ‹*escalator*› qui descend
3 ‹*computer*› en panne
IDIOMS **it's ~ to you to do it** c'est à toi de le faire; **~ with tyrants!** à bas les tyrans!
down² /daʊn/ *n* duvet *m*
down-and-out /ˌdaʊnən'aʊt/ *n* clochard/-e *m/f*
downbeat /'daʊnbiːt/ *adj* **1** (pessimistic) pessimiste
2 (laidback) décontracté/-e
downfall /'daʊnfɔːl/ *n* chute *f*; **drink proved to be his ~** c'est la boisson qui a causé sa perte
downhearted /ˌdaʊn'hɑːtɪd/ *adj* abattu/-e
downhill /ˌdaʊn'hɪl/ *adv* **to go ~** ‹*person, vehicle*› descendre; **he's going ~** (declining) il est sur le déclin
downhill skiing *n* ski *m* de piste
download *vt* (Comput) télécharger
downmarket *adj* ‹*products*› bas de gamme *inv*; ‹*area*› populaire; ‹*newspaper, programme*› grand public *inv*
down payment *n* acompte *m*
downplay *vt* minimiser l'importance de
downpour *n* averse *f*
downright /'daʊnraɪt/ **A** *adj* ‹*insult*› véritable *before n*; ‹*refusal*› catégorique; ‹*liar*› fieffé/-e *before n*
B *adv* ‹*stupid, rude*› carrément
downsize *vi* réduire les effectifs
Down's syndrome /'daʊnz sɪndrəʊm/ *n* trisomie *f* 21
downstairs /ˌdaʊn'steəz/ **A** *adj* ‹*room*› en bas; **the ~ flat** (BrE) *or* **apartment** (AmE) l'appartement du rez-de-chaussée
B *adv* en bas; **to go** *or* **come ~** descendre (l'escalier)
downstream /'daʊnstriːm/ *adj, adv* en aval (**of** de); **to go ~** descendre le courant
down-to-earth /'daʊntə'ɜːθ/ *adj* pratique; **she's very ~** (practical) elle a les pieds sur terre; (unpretentious) elle est très simple
downtown /'daʊntaʊn/ *adj* (AmE) ‹*store, hotel*› du centre ville
downtrodden *adj* tyrannisé/-e
downturn *n* (in economy, career) déclin *m* (**in** de); (in demand, profits) chute *f* (**in** de)
down under *adv* (fam) en Australie
downward /'daʊnwəd/ **A** *adj* ‹*movement*› vers le bas; **~ trend** (Econ) tendance *f* à la baisse
B *adv* = **downwards**
downwards /'daʊnwədz/ *adv* (*also* **downward**) vers le bas; **to slope ~** descendre en pente (**to** vers)
doze /dəʊz/ *vi* somnoler
■ **doze off** (momentarily) s'assoupir; (to sleep) s'endormir
dozen /'dʌzn/ *n* **1** (twelve) douzaine *f*; **a ~ eggs** une douzaine d'œufs; **£1 a ~** une livre sterling la douzaine
2 (several) **~s of** des dizaines de ‹*people, things, times*›
drab /dræb/ *adj* terne
draft /drɑːft, (AmE) dræft/ **A** *n* **1** (of letter, speech) brouillon *m*; (of novel, play) ébauche *f*; (of contract, law) avant-projet *m*
2 (on bank) traite *f* (**on** sur)
3 (AmE) (conscription) service *m* militaire
4 (AmE) = **draught**
B *vt* **1** faire le brouillon de ‹*letter, speech*›; rédiger ‹*contract, law*›
2 (AmE) (conscript) incorporer (**into** dans)
3 (BrE) (transfer) détacher (**to** auprès de, **from** de)
■ **draft in** faire venir, amener ‹*police, troops*›
draft dodger *n* (AmE) (Mil) insoumis *m*
draftsman (AmE) = **draughtsman**
drag /dræg/ **A** *n* **1** (fam) **what a ~!** quelle barbe! (fam)
2 ‹*person*› **in ~** en travesti
B *adj* **1** ‹*artist*› de spectacle de travestis
2 ‹*racing*› de dragsters
C *vt* (*p prés etc* **-gg-**) **1** (trail) traîner; (pull) tirer ‹*boat, sledge*›; **to ~ sth along the ground** traîner qch par terre; **to ~ one's feet** traîner les pieds; (fig) faire preuve de mauvaise volonté (**on** quant à); **don't ~ my mother into this** ne mêle pas ma mère à ça
2 draguer ‹*river, lake*›
3 (Comput) glisser
D *vi* (*p prés etc* **-gg-**) **1** ‹*hours, days*› traîner; ‹*story, plot*› traîner en longueur

2 (trail) **to ~ in** ‹*hem, belt*› traîner dans ‹*mud*›
3 to ~ on tirer une bouffée de ‹*cigarette*›

■ **drag on** traîner en longueur

drag and drop *n* glisser-lâcher *m*

drain /dreɪn/ **A** *n* **1** (in street) canalisation *f*; (in building) canalisation *f* d'évacuation; (pipe) descente *f* d'eau; (ditch) fossé *m* d'écoulement
2 (of people, skills, money) hémorragie *f*; **to be a ~ on sb's resources** épuiser les ressources de qn
B *vt* **1** drainer ‹*land*›
2 épuiser ‹*resources*›
3 vider ‹*glass*›
4 (Culin) égoutter ‹*pasta, vegetables*›
C *vi* **1** ‹*liquid*› s'écouler (**out of, from** de, **into** dans)
2 ‹*dishes, food*› s'égoutter

drainage /ˈdreɪnɪdʒ/ *n* (of land) drainage *m*; (system) tout-à-l'égout *m inv*

draining board *n* égouttoir *m*

drainpipe /ˈdreɪnpaɪp/ *n* descente *f*

drake /dreɪk/ *n* canard *m* (mâle)

drama /ˈdrɑːmə/ *n* (genre) théâtre *m*; (acting, directing) art *m* dramatique; (play, dramatic event) drame *m*; **TV/radio ~** dramatique *f*; **to make a ~ out of sth** faire tout un drame de qch

dramatic /drəˈmætɪk/ *adj* ‹*art, effect, event*› dramatique; ‹*change, landscape*› spectaculaire; ‹*entrance*› théâtral/-e

dramatist /ˈdræmətɪst/ *n* auteur *m* dramatique

dramatize /ˈdræmətaɪz/ *vt* **1** (for stage) adapter [qch] à la scène; (for screen) adapter [qch] à l'écran; (for radio) adapter [qch] pour la radio
2 (make dramatic) donner un caractère dramatique à; (excessively) dramatiser

drape /dreɪp/ **A** *n* (AmE) rideau *m*
B *vt* draper (**in, with** de)

drastic /ˈdræstɪk/ *adj* ‹*policy, measure*› draconien/-ienne; ‹*reduction, remedy*› drastique; ‹*effect*› catastrophique; ‹*change*› radical/-e

drastically /ˈdræstɪklɪ/ *adv* ‹*change, reduce*› radicalement; ‹*reduce, limit*› sévèrement

draught (BrE), **draft** (AmE) /drɑːft, (AmE) dræft/ *n* **1** (cold air) courant *m* d'air
2 on ~ ‹*beer*› à la pression

draughts /drɑːfts, (AmE) dræfts/ *n* (BrE) jeu *m* de dames; **to play ~** jouer aux dames

draughtsman (BrE), **draftsman** (AmE) /ˈdrɑːftsmən, (AmE) ˈdræft-/ *n* dessinateur/-trice *m/f*

draughty (BrE), **drafty** (AmE) /ˈdrɑːftɪ, (AmE) ˈdræftɪ/ *adj* plein/-e de courants d'air

🔑 **draw** /drɔː/ **A** *n* **1** (in lottery) tirage *m* (au sort)
2 (Sport) match *m* nul; **it was a ~** (in race) ils sont arrivés ex aequo
B *vt* (*prét* **drew**, *pp* **drawn**) **1** faire ‹*picture, plan*›; dessiner ‹*person, object*›; tracer ‹*line*›
2 (pull) ‹*animal, engine*› tirer
3 tirer ‹*conclusion*› (**from** de)
4 (attract) attirer ‹*crowd*› (**to** vers); susciter ‹*reaction*›; **to ~ sb into** mêler qn à ‹*conversation*›; entraîner qn dans ‹*argument, battle*›
5 retirer ‹*money*› (**from** de); tirer ‹*cheque*› (**on** sur); toucher ‹*wages, pension*›
6 (in lottery) tirer [qch] au sort ‹*ticket*›
7 sortir ‹*sword, knife*›; **to ~ a gun on sb** sortir un pistolet et le braquer sur qn
C *vi* (*prét* **drew**, *pp* **drawn**) **1** (make picture) dessiner
2 to ~ ahead (of sb/sth) (in race) gagner du terrain (sur qn/qch); (in contest, election) prendre de l'avance (sur qn/qch); **to ~ alongside** ‹*boat*› accoster; **to ~ near** ‹*time*› approcher; **to ~ level** se retrouver au même niveau
3 (BrE) (in match) faire match nul
IDIOMS **to ~ the line** fixer des limites; **to ~ the line at doing** se refuser à faire

■ **draw away** (move off) s'éloigner (**from** de); (move ahead) prendre de l'avance (**from** sur)

■ **draw in A ~ in 1** ‹*days, nights*› raccourcir
2 ‹*bus*› arriver; ‹*train*› entrer en gare
B ~ [sth] in rentrer ‹*stomach, claws*›

■ **draw out**: **A ~ out** ‹*train, bus*› partir; **the train drew out of the station** le train a quitté la gare
B ~ [sth] out 1 (remove) tirer ‹*purse, knife*› (**of** de); retirer ‹*nail, cork*› (**of** de)
2 (withdraw) retirer ‹*money*›
3 (prolong) faire durer
C ~ [sb] out faire sortir [qn] de sa coquille

■ **draw up 1** établir ‹*contract*›; dresser, établir ‹*list, report*›
2 approcher ‹*chair*› (**to** de)

drawback /ˈdrɔːbæk/ *n* inconvénient *m*

drawer /ˈdrɔː(r)/ *n* tiroir *m*

drawing /ˈdrɔːɪŋ/ *n* dessin *m*

drawing board *n* planche *f* à dessin

drawing pin *n* punaise *f*

drawing room *n* salon *m*

drawl /drɔːl/ *n* voix *f* traînante

drawn /drɔːn/ *adj* **1 to look ~** avoir les traits tirés
2 (BrE) ‹*game, match*› nul/nulle

dread /dred/ *vt* appréhender (**doing** de faire); (stronger) redouter (**doing** de faire)

dreadful /ˈdredfl/ *adj* épouvantable, affreux/-euse

dreadfully /ˈdredfəlɪ/ *adv* ‹*disappointed*› terriblement; ‹*suffer*› affreusement; ‹*behave*› abominablement; **I'm ~ sorry** je suis navré

🔑 **dream** /driːm/ **A** *n* rêve *m*
B *adj* ‹*house, car, holiday*› de rêve
C *vt* (*prét*, *pp* **dreamt** /dremt/, **~ed**) rêver (**that** que)

🔑 mot clé

D *vi* (*prét, pp* **dreamt** /dremt/, **~ed**) rêver; **he dreamt about** *or* **of sth/doing** il a rêvé de qch/qu'il faisait; **I wouldn't ~ of selling the house** il ne me viendrait jamais à l'esprit de vendre la maison

■ **dream up** concevoir ‹*idea*›; imaginer ‹*character, plot*›

dreamer /ˈdri:mə(r)/ *n* **1** (inattentive person) rêveur/-euse *m/f*
2 (idealist) idéaliste *mf*

dreary /ˈdrɪərɪ/ *adj* ‹*weather, landscape, life*› morne; ‹*person*› ennuyeux/-euse

dredge /dredʒ/ *vt* draguer ‹*river*›

dregs /dregz/ *npl* (of wine) lie *f*; (of coffee) marc *m*

drench /drentʃ/ *vt* (in rain, sweat) tremper (**in** de)

dress /dres/ **A** *n* **1** (garment) robe *f*
2 (clothes) tenue *f*; **formal ~** tenue habillée
B *vt* **1** habiller ‹*person*›; **to get ~ed** s'habiller; **to be ~ed in** être vêtu/-e de
2 assaisonner ‹*salad*›; préparer ‹*meat, fish*›
3 panser ‹*wound*›

■ **dress up** (smartly) s'habiller; (in fancy dress) se déguiser (**as** en)

dress circle *n* premier balcon *m*

dresser /ˈdresə(r)/ *n* **1 to be a stylish ~** s'habiller avec chic
2 (for dishes) buffet *m*
3 (AmE) (for clothes) commode-coiffeuse *f*

dressing /ˈdresɪŋ/ *n* **1** (Med) pansement *m*
2 (sauce) assaisonnement *m*
3 (AmE) (stuffing) farce *f*

dressing gown *n* (BrE) robe *f* de chambre

dressing room *n* loge *f*

dressing table *n* coiffeuse *f*

dressmaker *n* couturière *f*

dress rehearsal *n* (répétition *f*) générale *f*

dress sense *n* **to have ~** s'habiller avec goût

dribble /ˈdrɪbl/ **A** *n* (of liquid) filet *m*; (of saliva) bave *f*
B *vi* **1** ‹*liquid*› dégouliner (**on, onto** sur, **from** de); ‹*person*› baver
2 (Sport) dribler

dried /draɪd/ *adj* ‹*fruit, herb*› sec/sèche; ‹*flower, vegetable*› séché/-e; ‹*milk, egg*› en poudre

drier /ˈdraɪə(r)/ *n* séchoir *m*

drift /drɪft/ **A** *n* **1 the ~ of the current** le sens du courant
2 (of snow) congère *f*; (of leaves) tas *m*
3 (meaning) sens *m* (général)
B *vi* **1** ‹*boat*› dériver; ‹*balloon*› voler à la dérive; ‹*smoke, fog*› flotter
2 ‹*snow*› former des congères *fpl*; ‹*leaves*› s'amonceler
3 to ~ through life errer sans but dans la vie

■ **drift apart** ‹*friends*› se perdre de vue; ‹*lovers*› se détacher progressivement l'un de l'autre

driftwood *n* bois *m* flotté

drill /drɪl/ **A** *n* **1** (for wood, masonry) perceuse *f*; (for oil) trépan *m*; (for mining) foreuse *f*; (for teeth) roulette *f*
2 (Mil) exercice *m*
3 fire ~ exercice *m* d'évacuation en cas d'incendie
B *vt* **1** percer ‹*hole, metal*›; passer la roulette à ‹*tooth*›
2 (Mil) entraîner ‹*soldiers*›
C *vi* **1** (in wood, masonry) percer un trou (**into** dans); **to ~ for sth** faire des forages pour trouver qch
2 (Mil) ‹*soldiers*› faire de l'exercice

drink /drɪŋk/ **A** *n* boisson *f*; **to have a ~** boire quelque chose; (alcoholic) prendre un verre
B *vt* (*prét* **drank**, *pp* **drunk**) boire (**from** dans)
C *vi* (*prét* **drank**, *pp* **drunk**) boire (**from** dans); **don't ~ and drive** ne conduisez pas si vous avez bu

drinkable /ˈdrɪŋkəbl/ *adj* (safe) potable; (nice) buvable

drink-driving /ˌdrɪŋkˈdraɪvɪŋ/ *n* (BrE) conduite *f* en état d'ivresse

drinking water *n* eau *f* potable

drip /drɪp/ **A** *n* **1** (drop) goutte *f* (qui tombe)
2 (BrE) (Med) **to be on a ~** être sous perfusion
B *vi* (*p prés etc* **-pp-**) **1** ‹*liquid*› tomber goutte à goutte; **to ~ from** *or* **off** dégouliner de
2 ‹*tap, branches*› goutter; ‹*washing*› s'égoutter

drive /draɪv/ **A** *n* **1 to go for a ~** aller faire un tour (en voiture); **it's a 40 km ~** il y a 40 km de route
2 (campaign) campagne *f* (**against** contre, **for, towards** pour, **to do** pour faire)
3 (motivation) dynamisme *m*
4 (Comput) entraînement *m* de disques
5 (Aut) transmission *f*
6 (*also* **~way**) allée *f*
7 (Sport) drive *m*
B *vt* (*prét* **drove**, *pp* **driven**) **1** conduire ‹*vehicle, passenger*›; piloter ‹*racing car*›; **I ~ 15 km every day** je fais 15 km en voiture chaque jour; **to ~ sth into** rentrer qch dans ‹*garage, space*›
2 (compel) pousser ‹*person*› (**to do** à faire)
3 (power, propel) actionner ‹*engine, pump*›
4 to ~ a nail through sth enfoncer un clou dans qch
C *vi* (*prét* **drove**, *pp* **driven**) conduire; **to ~ along** rouler; **to ~ to work** aller au travail en voiture; **to ~ into** entrer dans ‹*car park*›; rentrer dans ‹*tree*›

■ **drive back 1** repousser ‹*people, animals*›
2 ramener ‹*passenger*›

drive-by shooting *n* attaque *f* criminelle (*exécutée d'une voiture en marche*)

driver /ˈdraɪvə(r)/ *n* **1** conducteur/-trice *m/f*;

~s (motorists) automobilistes *mfpl*
2 (of taxi) chauffeur *m*

driver's license *n* (AmE) permis *m* de conduire

driving /ˈdraɪvɪŋ/ **A** *n* conduite *f*
B *adj* ‹*rain*› battant/-e; ‹*wind, hail*› cinglant/-e

driving force *n* (person) force *f* agissante (**behind** de); (money, ambition) moteur *m* (**behind** de)

d

driving instructor *n* moniteur/-trice *m/f* d'auto-école

driving lesson *n* leçon *f* de conduite

driving licence *n* (BrE) permis *m* de conduire

driving school *n* auto-école *f*

driving seat *n* place *f* du conducteur
IDIOM **to be in the ~** être aux commandes

driving test *n* examen *m* du permis de conduire; **to take/pass one's ~** passer/réussir son permis (de conduire)

drizzle /ˈdrɪzl/ **A** *n* bruine *f*
B *vi* bruiner

drone /drəʊn/ *n* **1** (of engine) ronronnement *m*; (of insects) bourdonnement *m*
2 (Zool) faux bourdon *m*

drool /druːl/ *vi* baver; **to ~ over sb/sth** s'extasier sur qn/qch

droop /druːp/ *vi* ‹*eyelids, head, shoulders*› tomber; ‹*plant*› commencer à se faner

⚷ **drop** /drɒp/ **A** *n* **1** (of liquid) goutte *f*
2 (decrease) baisse *f* (**in** de); **a 5% ~ in sth** une baisse de 5% de qch
3 (fall) **there's a ~ of 100 m** il y a un dénivelé de 100 m; **a steep ~ on either side** une pente abrupte de chaque côté; **a sheer ~** un à-pic
4 (delivery) (from aircraft) largage *m*
B *vt* (*p prés etc* **-pp-**) **1** (by accident) laisser tomber; (on purpose) lâcher
2 ‹*aircraft*› parachuter ‹*person, supplies*›; larguer ‹*bomb*›
3 (*also* **~ off**) déposer ‹*person, object*›
4 (lower) baisser ‹*eyes, voice, level, price*›
5 to ~ a hint about sth faire allusion à qch; **to ~ sb a line** envoyer un mot à qn
6 laisser tomber ‹*friend, school subject*›; renoncer à ‹*habit, idea*›
C *vi* (*p prés etc* **-pp-**) **1** (fall) ‹*object*› tomber; ‹*person*› (deliberately) se laisser tomber; **the plane ~ped to an altitude of 1,000 m** l'avion est descendu à une altitude de 1 000 m
2 the cliff ~s into the sea la falaise tombe dans la mer
3 (decrease) baisser; **to ~ (from sth) to sth** tomber (de qch) à qch
IDIOM **a ~ in the ocean** une goutte d'eau dans la mer
■ **drop in** passer; **to ~ in on sb** passer voir qn
■ **drop off 1** (fall off) tomber
2 ~ off (to sleep) s'endormir
3 (decrease) diminuer
■ **drop out 1** (fall out) tomber (**of** de)
2 (from race) se désister; (from project) se retirer; (from school, university) abandonner ses études; (from society) se marginaliser

drop-dead /ˈdrɒpded/ *adv* (fam) **~ gorgeous** super beau/belle (fam)

drop-down menu *n* menu *m* déroulant

dropout /ˈdrɒpaʊt/ *n* marginal/-e *m/f*

droppings /ˈdrɒpɪŋz/ *npl* (of mouse, sheep) crottes *fpl*; (of horse) crottin *m*; (of bird) fiente *f*

drop shot *n* (Sport) amorti *m*

drought /draʊt/ *n* sécheresse *f*

drown /draʊn/ **A** *vt* **1** noyer ‹*person, animal*›
2 (*also* **~ out**) couvrir ‹*sound*›
B *vi* se noyer
IDIOM **to ~ one's sorrows** noyer son chagrin dans l'alcool

drowning /ˈdraʊnɪŋ/ *n* noyade *f*

drowsy /ˈdraʊzɪ/ *adj* à moitié endormi/-e; **to feel ~** avoir envie de dormir

⚷ **drug** /drʌg/ **A** *n* **1** (Med) médicament *m*; **to be on ~s** prendre des médicaments
2 (narcotic) drogue *f*; **to be on** *or* **to take ~s** (gen) se droguer; ‹*athlete*› se doper
B *vt* (*p prés etc* **-gg-**) administrer des somnifères à ‹*person*›

drug abuse *n* consommation *f* de stupéfiants

drug addict *n* toxicomane *mf*

drug addiction *n* toxicomanie *f*

drug-driving *n* drogue *f* au volant

drugged /drʌgd/ *adj* ‹*person*› drogué/-e; ‹*drink*› additionné/-e d'un narcotique

drug habit *n* accoutumance *f* à la drogue

drug mule *n* mule *f*

drugs raid *n* opération *f* antidrogue

drugstore *n* (AmE) drugstore *m*

drug-taking *n* usage *m* de stupéfiants; (in sport) dopage *m*

drug test *n* (Sport) contrôle *m* antidopage

drug user *n* toxicomane *mf*

drum /drʌm/ **A** *n* **1** (Mus) tambour *m*
2 (barrel) bidon *m*; (larger) baril *m*
B drums *npl* batterie *f*; **to play ~s** jouer de la batterie
C *vt* (*p prés etc* **-mm-**) **to ~ one's fingers** tambouriner des doigts (**on** sur); **to ~ sth into sb** enfoncer qch dans le crâne de qn (fam)
■ **drum up** trouver ‹*business*›; racoler ‹*customers*›

drummer /ˈdrʌmə(r)/ *n* (in army) tambour *m*; (jazz or pop) batteur *m*; (classical) percussionniste *mf*

drumstick /ˈdrʌmstɪk/ *n* **1** (Mus) baguette *f* de tambour
2 (of chicken, turkey) pilon *m*

⚷ mot clé

drunk /drʌŋk/ **A** *n* (*also* **drunkard**) ivrogne *m*
B *adj* ivre; **to get ~** s'enivrer (**on** de)

drunken /'drʌŋkən/ *adj* ‹*person*› ivre; ‹*party*› bien arrosé/-e; ‹*sleep*› éthylique; ‹*state*› d'ivresse

dry /draɪ/ **A** *adj* **1** sec/sèche; **to keep sth ~** tenir qch au sec; **on ~ land** sur la terre ferme; **a ~ day** un jour sans pluie
2 ‹*wit, person, remark*› pince-sans-rire *inv*; ‹*book*› aride
B *vt* faire sécher ‹*clothes, washing*›; sécher ‹*meat, produce*›; **to ~ the dishes** essuyer la vaisselle; **to ~ one's hands** se sécher les mains
C *vi* ‹*clothes, washing*› sécher

■ **dry out 1** ‹*cloth*› sécher; ‹*plant*› se dessécher
2 (fam) ‹*alcoholic*› se faire désintoxiquer

■ **dry up A ~ up 1** ‹*river, well*› s'assécher
2 (run out) se tarir
3 (dry the dishes) essuyer la vaisselle
B ~ [sth] up essuyer ‹*dishes*›

dry-clean /ˌdraɪ'kliːn/ *vt* **to have sth ~ed** faire nettoyer qch (chez le teinturier)

dry-cleaner's *n* teinturerie *f*

dryer /'draɪə(r)/ *n* séchoir *m*

DTP *n* (*abbr* = **desktop publishing**) PAO *f*

dual /'djuːəl, (AmE) 'duːəl/ *adj* double

dual carriageway *n* (BrE) route *f* à quatre voies

dual nationality *n* double nationalité *f*

dub /dʌb/ *vt* (*p prés etc* **-bb-**) (into foreign language) doubler (**into** en); **~bed film** film *m* doublé

dubious /'djuːbɪəs, (AmE) 'duː-/ *adj* ‹*reputation, answer*› douteux/-euse; ‹*claim*› suspect/-e

duchess /'dʌtʃɪs/ *n* duchesse *f*

duck /dʌk/ **A** *n* (*pl* **~s**, *collect* **~**) canard *m*
B *vt* **1 to ~ one's head** baisser vivement la tête
2 (dodge) esquiver ‹*blow*›
3 se dérober de ‹*responsibility*›
C *vi* baisser vivement la tête; ‹*boxer*› esquiver un coup; **to ~ behind** se cacher derrière

duckling /'dʌklɪŋ/ *n* caneton *m*

duct /'dʌkt/ *n* **1** (for air, water) conduit *m*; (for wiring) canalisation *f*
2 (Anat, Med) conduit *m*

dud /dʌd/ *adj* (fam) ‹*banknote*› faux/fausse *before n*; ‹*cheque*› en bois (fam); ‹*book, movie*› nul/nulle (fam)

due /djuː, (AmE) duː/ **A** *n* dû *m*; **I must give her her ~, she...** il faut lui rendre cette justice, elle...
B *adj* **1** (payable) **to be/fall ~** arriver/venir à échéance; **the rent is ~ on the 6th** le loyer doit être payé le 6; **the balance ~** le solde dû
2 (owed) **the respect ~ to him** le respect auquel il a droit, le respect qu'on lui doit
3 we are ~ (for) a wage increase soon nos salaires doivent bientôt être augmentés
4 after ~ consideration après mûre réflexion; **in ~ course** (at the proper time) en temps voulu; (later) plus tard
5 to be ~ to do devoir faire; **to be ~ (in)** ‹*train, bus*› être attendu/-e; ‹*person*› devoir arriver
C *adv* **to face ~ north** ‹*building*› être orienté/-e plein nord; **to go ~ south** aller droit vers le sud
D due to *phr* en raison de; **to be ~ to** ‹*delay, cancellation*› être dû/due à; **~ to unforeseen circumstances** pour des raisons indépendantes de notre volonté

dues *npl* (for membership) cotisation *f*; (for import, taxes) droits *mpl*

duet /djuː'et, (AmE) duː-/ *n* duo *m*

duffel bag *n* sac *m* (de) marin

duffel coat *n* duffle-coat *m*

duke /djuːk, (AmE) duːk/ *n* duc *m*

dull /dʌl/ **A** *adj* **1** ‹*person, book*› ennuyeux/-euse; ‹*life, journey*› monotone; ‹*appearance*› triste; ‹*weather*› maussade
2 ‹*eye, colour, complexion*› terne
B *vt* ternir ‹*shine*›; émousser ‹*blade, pain*›

duly /'djuːlɪ, (AmE) 'duː-/ *adv* (in proper fashion) dûment; (as expected, as arranged) comme prévu

dumb /dʌm/ *adj* **1** muet/muette; **to be struck ~** rester muet/muette (**with** de)
2 (fam) (stupid) ‹*person*› bête; ‹*question, idea*› idiot/-e

dumb down *vt* abaisser le niveau intellectuel de ‹*course, programme*›

dumbfounded /dʌm'faʊndɪd/ *adj* abasourdi/-e

dummy /'dʌmɪ/ **A** *n* **1** (model) mannequin *m*
2 (BrE) (for baby) tétine *f*
B *adj* faux/fausse

dummy run *n* (trial) essai *m*

dump /dʌmp/ **A** *n* **1** (for rubbish) décharge *f* publique
2 (Mil) **arms ~** dépôt *m* d'armes
3 (fam) (town, village) trou *m* (fam); (house) baraque *f* (fam) minable
B *vt* **1** jeter ‹*refuse*›; ensevelir ‹*nuclear waste*›; déverser ‹*sewage*›
2 (fam) plaquer (fam) ‹*boyfriend*›; se débarrasser de ‹*car*›

IDIOM **to be down in the ~s** (fam) avoir le cafard (fam)

dumper, **dump truck** *n* (*also* **dumper truck**) tombereau *m*

dunce /dʌns/ *n* cancre *m* (**at, in** en)

dune /djuːn, (AmE) duːn/ *n* dune *f*

dung /dʌŋ/ *n* (for manure) fumier *m*

dungarees /ˌdʌŋgə'riːz/ *npl* (fashionwear) salopette *f*; (workwear) bleu *m* de travail

Dunkirk /dʌn'kɜːk/ *pr n* Dunkerque

duo /'djuːəʊ, (AmE) 'duːəʊ/ *n* (*pl* **~s**) duo *m*

duplicate **A** /ˈdjuːplɪkət, (AmE) ˈduːpləkət/ *n* (of document) double *m* (**of** de); (of painting, cassette) copie *f*
B /ˈdjuːplɪkət, (AmE) ˈduːpləkət/ *adj* **1** ‹*cheque, receipt*› en duplicata; **a ~ key** un double de clé
2 (in two parts) ‹*form, invoice*› en deux exemplaires
C /ˈdjuːplɪkeɪt, (AmE) ˈduːpləkeɪt/ *vt* **1** (copy) faire un double de ‹*document*›; copier ‹*painting, cassette*›
2 (photocopy) photocopier

d

e

durable /ˈdjʊərəbl, (AmE) ˈdʊərəbl/ *adj* ‹*material*› résistant/-e; ‹*equipment*› solide; ‹*friendship, tradition*› durable

duration /djʊˈreɪʃn, (AmE) dʊˈreɪʃn/ *n* durée *f*

duress /djʊˈres, (AmE) dʊˈres/ *n* **under ~** sous la contrainte

✓ **during** /ˈdjʊərɪŋ/ *prep* pendant, au cours de

dusk /dʌsk/ *n* nuit *f* tombante, crépuscule *m*; **at ~** à la nuit tombante

dust /dʌst/ **A** *n* poussière *f*
B *vt* épousseter ‹*furniture*›; saupoudrer ‹*cake*› (**with** de, avec)

dustbin *n* (BrE) poubelle *f*

dust cover *n* (on book) jaquette *f*; (on furniture) housse *f* (de protection)

duster /ˈdʌstə(r)/ *n* chiffon *m* (à poussière)

dustman *n* (BrE) éboueur *m*

dustpan /ˈdʌstpæn/ *n* pelle *f* (à poussière)

dusty /ˈdʌstɪ/ *adj* poussiéreux/-euse

Dutch /dʌtʃ/ **A** *n* **1** (people) **the ~** les Néerlandais *mpl*
2 (language) néerlandais *m*
B *adj* (gen) néerlandais/-e; ‹*ambassador, embassy*› des Pays-Bas
IDIOMS **to go ~** (fam) payer chacun sa part; **to go ~ with sb** (fam) faire fifty-fifty avec qn (fam)

✓ **duty** /ˈdjuːtɪ, (AmE) ˈduːtɪ/ *n* **1** (obligation) devoir *m* (**to** envers); **in the course of ~** (Mil) en service; (gen) dans l'exercice de ses fonctions
2 (task) fonction *f*; **to take up one's duties** prendre ses fonctions
3 (work) service *m*; **to be on/off ~** (Mil, Med) être/ne pas être de service; (Sch) être/ne pas être de surveillance
4 (tax) taxe *f*; **customs duties** droits *mpl* de douane

duty-free /ˌdjuːtɪˈfriː, (AmE) ˌduː-/ *adj, adv* hors taxe(s)

duvet /ˈduːveɪ/ *n* (BrE) couette *f*

duvet cover *n* housse *f* de couette

DVD *n* (*abbr* = **digital video disc**) DVD *m*

DVT *n* (*abbr* = **deep-vein thrombosis**) TVP *f*

dwarf /dwɔːf/ *n, adj* nain/naine *m/f*

dwell /dwel/
■ **dwell on** (talk about) s'étendre sur; (think about) s'attarder sur

dwindle /ˈdwɪndl/ *vi* diminuer

dye /daɪ/ **A** *n* teinture *f*
B *vt* teindre; **to ~ sth red** teindre qch en rouge; **to ~ one's hair** se teindre les cheveux

dying /ˈdaɪɪŋ/ *adj* ‹*person, animal*› mourant/-e; ‹*art*› en voie de disparition

dyke /daɪk/ *n* **1** (on coast) digue *f*; (beside ditch) remblai *m*
2 (BrE) (ditch) fossé *m*

dynamic /daɪˈnæmɪk/ *adj* dynamique

dynamite /ˈdaɪnəmaɪt/ *n* dynamite *f*

dynamo /ˈdaɪnəməʊ/ *n* **1** dynamo *f*
2 (fam) **he's a real ~** il déborde d'énergie

dysentery /ˈdɪsəntrɪ, (AmE) -terɪ/ *n* dysenterie *f*

dysfunctional /dɪsˈfʌŋkʃənl/ *adj* dysfonctionnel/-elle

dyslexia /dɪsˈleksɪə, (AmE) dɪsˈlekʃə/ *n* dyslexie *f*

dyslexic /dɪsˈleksɪk/ *n, adj* dyslexique *mf*

Ee

e, E /iː/ *n* **1** (letter) e, E *m*
2 E (Mus) mi *m*
3 E (drug) ecstasy *m*

✓ **each** /iːtʃ/ **A** *det* ‹*person, group, object*› chaque *inv*; **~ morning** chaque matin, tous les matins; **~ one** chacun/-e
B *pron* chacun/-e *m/f*; **~ of you** chacun/-e de vous, chacun/-e d'entre vous; **oranges at 30p ~** des oranges à 30 pence (la) pièce

✓ **each other** /ˌiːtʃˈʌðə(r)/ *pron*

each other is very often translated by using a reflexive pronoun (*nous, vous, se, s'*).

(*also* **one another**) **they know ~** ils se connaissent; **to help ~** s'entraider; **kept apart from ~** séparés l'un de l'autre

eager /ˈiːgə(r)/ *adj* ‹*person, acceptance*› enthousiaste; ‹*face*› où se lit l'enthousiasme;

‹*student*› plein d'enthousiasme; **~ to do** (keen) désireux/-euse de faire; (impatient) pressé/-e de faire; **~ for sth** avide de qch; **to be ~ to please** chercher à faire plaisir

eagle /ˈiːɡl/ *n* aigle *m*

ear /ɪə(r)/ *n* **1** oreille *f*
2 (of wheat, corn) épi *m*
IDIOM **to play it by ~** improviser

earache /ˈɪəreɪk/ *n* **to have ~** (BrE) *or* **an ~** avoir une otite

eardrum *n* tympan *m*

earl /ɜːl/ *n* comte *m*

early /ˈɜːlɪ/ **A** *adj* **1** (one of the first) ‹*years, novels*› premier/-ière *before n*; **~ man** les premiers hommes
2 ‹*delivery*› rapide; ‹*vegetable, fruit*› précoce; **to have an ~ lunch/night** déjeuner/se coucher tôt; **in ~ childhood** dans la petite *or* première enfance; **at an ~ age** à un très jeune âge; **to be in one's ~ thirties** avoir entre 30 et 35 ans; **at the earliest** au plus tôt; **in the ~ spring** au début du printemps; **in the ~ afternoon** en début d'après-midi
B *adv* **1** tôt; **to get up ~** se lever tôt *or* de bonne heure; **it's too ~** il est trop tôt; **as I said earlier** comme je l'ai déjà dit
2 (sooner than expected) en avance; **I'm a bit ~** je suis un peu en avance

early retirement *n* retraite *f* anticipée

earmark /ˈɪəmɑːk/ *vt* désigner ‹*person, money, site*›

earn /ɜːn/ *vt* **1** ‹*person*› gagner ‹*money*›; ‹*investment*› rapporter ‹*interest*›; **to ~ a** *or* **one's living** gagner sa vie
2 to ~ sb's respect se faire respecter de qn

earner /ˈɜːnə(r)/ *n* salarié/-e *m/f*

earnest /ˈɜːnɪst/ **A** *n* **in ~** ‹*speak*› sérieusement; ‹*begin*› vraiment, pour de bon
B *adj* ‹*person*› sérieux/-ieuse; ‹*wish*› sincère

earning power *n* capacité *f* de gain

earnings /ˈɜːnɪŋz/ *npl* (of person) salaire *m*, revenu *m* (**from** de); (of company) gains *mpl* (**from** de); (from shares) (taux *m* de) rendement *m*

earphones *npl* (over ears) casque *m*; (in ears) écouteurs *mpl*

earring *n* boucle *f* d'oreille

earth /ɜːθ/ **A** *n* **1** terre *f*
2 (fam) **how/where/who on ~...?** comment/où/qui donc *or* diable (fam) ...?; **nothing on ~ would persuade me to come** je ne viendrais pour rien au monde
B *vt* (BrE) mettre [qch] à la terre

earthenware /ˈɜːθnweə(r)/ *n* faïence *f*

earthquake *n* tremblement *m* de terre

earth tremor *n* secousse *f* sismique

earwig *n* perce-oreille *m*

ease /iːz/ **A** *n* **1** (lack of difficulty) facilité *f*
2 to feel/to be at ~ se sentir/être à l'aise; **to put sb's mind at ~** rassurer qn (**about** à propos de)
B *vt* **1** atténuer ‹*pain, tension, pressure*›; réduire ‹*congestion*›; diminuer ‹*burden*›
2 faciliter ‹*communication, transition*›
3 to ~ sth into introduire qch délicatement dans
C *vi* ‹*tension, pain, pressure*› s'atténuer; ‹*rain*› diminuer

■ **ease off** ‹*business*› ralentir; ‹*demand*› se réduire; ‹*traffic, rain*› diminuer; ‹*person*› relâcher son effort

■ **ease up** ‹*tense person, storm*› se calmer; ‹*authorities*› relâcher la discipline; **to ~ up on sb/on sth** être moins sévère envers qn/pour qch

easel /ˈiːzl/ *n* chevalet *m*

easily /ˈiːzɪlɪ/ *adv* facilement; **it's ~ the best** c'est de loin le meilleur; **she could ~ die** elle pourrait bien mourir

east /iːst/ **A** *n* **1** (compass direction) est *m*
2 the East (Orient) l'Orient *m*; (part of country) l'Est *m*
B *adj* (gen) est *inv*; ‹*wind*› d'est
C *adv* ‹*move*› vers l'est; ‹*live, lie*› à l'est (**of** de)

Easter /ˈiːstə(r)/ **A** *n* Pâques *m*; **at ~** à Pâques; **Happy ~** Joyeuses Pâques
B *adj* ‹*Sunday, egg*› de Pâques

eastern /ˈiːstən/ *adj* **1** ‹*coast*› est *inv*; ‹*town, accent*› de l'est; **Eastern Europe** l'Europe *f* de l'Est; **~ France** l'est *m* de la France
2 (*also* **Eastern**) (oriental) oriental/-e

East Timor /iːst ˈtiːmɔː(r)/ *pr n* Timor *m* oriental

easy /ˈiːzɪ/ **A** *adj* **1** ‹*job, question, life, victim*› facile; **it's ~ to do** c'est facile à faire; **it's ~ to make a mistake** il est facile de se tromper; **it isn't ~ to do** ce n'est pas facile à faire; **it isn't ~ to park** il n'est pas facile de se garer; **to make it** *or* **things easier** faciliter les choses (**for** pour)
2 (relaxed) ‹*smile, grace*› décontracté/-e; ‹*style*› plein/-e d'aisance; **at an ~ pace** d'un pas tranquille
3 (fam) **I'm ~** ça m'est égal
B *adv* **1 to take it** *or* **things ~** ne pas s'en faire
2 (fam) **to go ~ on** *or* **with** y aller doucement avec

easy-going *adj* ‹*person*› accommodant/-e; ‹*manner, attitude*› souple

easy terms *npl* facilités *fpl* de paiement

eat /iːt/ **A** *vt* (*prét* **ate**, *pp* **eaten**) manger ‹*food*›; prendre ‹*meal*›
B *vi* (*prét* **ate**, *pp* **eaten**) manger

■ **eat out** aller au restaurant

eating disorder *n* trouble *m* du comportement alimentaire

eating habits *npl* habitudes *fpl* alimentaires

eavesdrop /ˈiːvzdrɒp/ *vi* (*p prés etc* **-pp-**) écouter aux portes

e

e-banking /ˈiːˌbæŋkɪŋ/ *n* e-banking *m*, banque *f* en ligne

ebb /eb/ **A** *n* reflux *m*
B *vi* ‹*tide*› descendre; ‹*enthusiasm*› décliner

ebony /ˈebənɪ/ *n* **1** (wood) ébène *f*
2 (colour) noir *m* d'ébène

e-book /iːbʊk/ *n* e-book *m*

EC *n* (*abbr* = **European Commission**) CE *f*

e-cash /ˈiːkæʃ/ *n* argent *m* électronique, argent *m* virtuel

eccentric /ɪkˈsentrɪk/ *n, adj* excentrique *mf*

ECG *n* (*abbr* = **electrocardiogram**) ECG *m*

echo /ˈekəʊ/ **A** *n* (*pl* **~es**) écho *m*
B *vt* **1** répercuter ‹*sound*›
2 reprendre ‹*ideas, opinions*›
C *vi* retentir, résonner

e-cigarette *n* cigarette *f* électronique, e-cigarette *f*

eclipse /ɪˈklɪps/ **A** *n* éclipse *f* (**of** de)
B *vt* éclipser

eco-friendly *adj* qui ne nuit pas à l'environnement

eco-labelling /ˈiːkəʊleɪblɪŋ/ *n* étiquetage *m* écologique

ecological /ˌiːkəˈlɒdʒɪkl/ *adj* écologique

ecological footprint *n* empreinte *f* écologique

ecologist /iːˈkɒlədʒɪst/ *n, adj* écologiste *mf*

ecology /ɪˈkɒlədʒɪ/ *n* écologie *f*

e-commerce /ˈiːkɒmɜːs/ *n* commerce *m* électronique

✓ **economic** /ˌiːkəˈnɒmɪk, ˌek-/ *adj* (gen) économique; (profitable) rentable

economical /ˌiːkəˈnɒmɪkl, ˌek-/ *adj* ‹*person*› économe; ‹*machine, method*› économique

economic refugee *n* réfugié/-e *mf* économique

economics /ˌiːkəˈnɒmɪks, ˌek-/ *n* (science) économie *f*; (subject of study) sciences *fpl* économiques; (financial aspects) aspects *mpl* économiques (**of** de)

economist /ɪˈkɒnəmɪst, ˌek-/ *n* économiste *mf*

economize /ɪˈkɒnəmaɪz/ *vt, vi* économiser

✓ **economy** /ɪˈkɒnəmɪ/ *n* économie *f*

economy class *n* classe *f* économique

economy class syndrome *n* syndrome *m* de la classe économique

economy drive *n* campagne *f* de restriction

ecosphere /ˈiːkəʊsfɪə(r)/ *n* écosphère *f*

ecotourism /ˈiːkəʊtʊərɪzəm, -tɔːr-/ *n* tourisme *m* vert, écotourisme *m*

ecotourist /ˌiːkəʊˈtʊərɪst/ *n* écotouriste *mf*

eco-warrior /ˈiːkəʊwɒrɪə(r), (AmE) -wɔːr-/ *n* éco-guerrier/-ière *m/f*

ecstasy /ˈekstəsɪ/ *n* **1** extase *f*
2 (drug) ecstasy *m*

eczema /ˈeksɪmə, (AmE) ɪgˈziːmə/ *n* eczéma *m*

Eden /ˈiːdn/ *pr n* Éden *m*, paradis *m* terrestre

✓ **edge** /edʒ/ **A** *n* **1** (outer limit) bord *m*; (of wood, clearing) lisière *f*; **the film had us on the ~ of our seats** le film nous a tenus en haleine
2 (of blade) tranchant *m*
3 (of book, plank) tranche *f*
4 to be on ~ ‹*person*› être énervé/-e
B *vi* **to ~ forward** avancer doucement; **to ~ towards** s'approcher à petits pas de

edgeways, **edgewise** /ˈedʒweɪz/ *adv* ‹*move*› latéralement; ‹*lay, put*› sur le côté
IDIOM **I can't get a word in ~** je n'arrive pas à placer un mot

edible /ˈedɪbl/ *adj* comestible

Edinburgh /ˈedɪnbərə/ *pr n* Édimbourg

edit /ˈedɪt/ *vt* **1** (in publishing) éditer
2 (cut) couper ‹*text, version*›
3 monter ‹*film, programme*›

edition /ɪˈdɪʃn/ *n* édition *f*

✓ **editor** /ˈedɪtə(r)/ *n* (of newspaper) rédacteur/-trice *m/f* en chef (**of** de); (of book, manuscript) correcteur/-trice *m/f*; (of writer, works, anthology) éditeur/-trice *m/f*; (of film) monteur/-euse *m/f*

editorial /ˌedɪˈtɔːrɪəl/ **A** *n* éditorial *m* (**on** sur)
B *adj* **1** (in journalism) de la rédaction, rédactionnel/-elle
2 (in publishing) éditorial/-e

educate /ˈedʒʊkeɪt/ *vt* **1** ‹*teacher*› instruire; ‹*parent*› assurer l'instruction de; **to be ~d in Paris** faire ses études à Paris
2 informer ‹*public*› (**about, in** sur)

educated /ˈedʒʊkeɪtɪd/ *adj* ‹*person, classes*› instruit/-e; ‹*accent*› élégant/-e

✓ **education** /ˌedʒʊˈkeɪʃn/ *n* **1** éducation *f*, instruction *f*; **health ~** hygiène *f*
2 (formal schooling) études *fpl*; **to have had a university** *or* **college ~** avoir fait des études supérieures
3 (national system) enseignement *m*

educational /ˌedʒʊˈkeɪʃənl/ *adj*
1 ‹*establishment*› d'enseignement
2 ‹*game, programme*› éducatif/-ive; ‹*talk*› instructif/-ive

EEC *n* (*abbr* = **European Economic Community**) CEE *f*

eel /iːl/ *n* anguille *f*

eerie /ˈɪərɪ/ *adj* ‹*silence, place*› étrange et inquiétant/-e

✓ **effect** /ɪˈfekt/ **A** *n* **1** effet *m* (**of** de, **on** sur); **to take ~** ‹*price increases*› prendre effet; ‹*pills, anaesthetic*› commencer à agir; **to come into ~** ‹*law, rate*› entrer en vigueur; **she dresses like that for ~** elle s'habille comme ça pour faire de l'effet
2 (repercussions) répercussions *fpl* (**of** de, **on** sur)
B effects *npl* effets *mpl*
C *vt* effectuer ‹*repair, sale, change*›
D in effect *phr* en fait, en réalité

✓ mot clé

effective /ɪ'fektɪv/ *adj* efficace

effectively /ɪ'fektɪvlɪ/ *adv* **1** (efficiently) efficacement
2 (in effect) en fait, en réalité

effeminate /ɪ'femɪnət/ *adj* efféminé/-e

efficiency /ɪ'fɪʃnsɪ/ *n* (of person, method, organization) efficacité *f* (**in doing** à faire); (of machine) rendement *m*

efficient /ɪ'fɪʃnt/ *adj* **1** ‹*person, management*› efficace (**at doing** pour ce qui est de faire)
2 ‹*machine*› économique

effort /'efət/ *n* effort *m*; **to make the ~** faire l'effort; **to spare no ~** ne pas ménager ses efforts; **to be worth the ~** en valoir la peine; **it is an ~ to do** il est pénible de faire

EFL *n* (*abbr* = **English as a Foreign Language**) anglais *m* langue étrangère

eg (*abbr* = **exempli gratia**) par ex

egalitarian /ɪˌgælɪ'teərɪən/ *adj* égalitaire

egg /eg/ *n* œuf *m*
■ **egg on** pousser ‹*person*›

egg cup *n* coquetier *m*

eggplant *n* (AmE) aubergine *f*

egg white *n* blanc *m* d'œuf

egg yolk *n* jaune *m* d'œuf

ego /'egəʊ, 'iːgəʊ, (AmE) 'iːgəʊ/ *n* **1** amour-propre *m*; **it boosted his ~** ça lui a redonné confiance en lui-même
2 (in psychology) moi *m*, ego *m*

egoism /'egəʊɪzəm, 'iːg-, (AmE) 'iːg-/ *n* égoïsme *m*

egoist /'egəʊɪst, 'iːg-, (AmE) 'iːg-/ *n* égoïste *mf*

egotist /'egəʊtɪst, 'iːg-, (AmE) 'iːg-/ *n* égotiste *mf*

Egypt /'iːdʒɪpt/ *pr n* Égypte *f*

EHIC *n* (*abbr* = **European Health Insurance Card**) CEAM *f*

Eid al-Adha /ˌiːd ʊl'ɑːdə/ *pr n* Aïd el-Kebir

eiderdown /'aɪdədaʊn/ *n* édredon *m*

Eid-ul-Fitr /ˌiːdʊl'fɪtrə/ *pr n* Aïd el-Fitr

eight /eɪt/ *n, pron, det* huit *m inv*

eighteen /eɪ'tiːn/ *n, pron, det* dix-huit *m inv*

eighteenth /eɪ'tiːnθ/ **A** *n* **1** (in order) dix-huitième *mf*
2 (of month) dix-huit *m inv*
3 (fraction) dix-huitième *m*
B *adj, adv* dix-huitième

eighth /eɪtθ/ **A** *n* **1** (in order) huitième *mf*
2 (of month) huit *m inv*
3 (fraction) huitième *m*
B *adj, adv* huitième

eighties *npl* **1** (era) **the ~** les années *fpl* quatre-vingt
2 (age) **to be in one's ~** avoir entre quatre-vingts et quatre-vingt-dix ans

eightieth /'eɪtɪəθ/ *n, adj, adv* quatre-vingtième *mf*

eighty /'eɪtɪ/ *n, pron, det* quatre-vingts *m*

eighty-one *n, pron, det* quatre-vingt-un *m*

Éire /'eərə/ *pr n* Éire *f*, République *f* d'Irlande

either /'aɪðər, (AmE) 'iːðər/ **A** *pron, quantif* **1** (one or other) l'un/-e ou l'autre; **take ~ (of them)** prends l'un/-e ou l'autre; **I don't like ~ (of them)** je n'aime ni l'un/-e ni l'autre; **'which book do you want?'—'~'** 'quel livre veux-tu?'—'n'importe'
2 (both) **~ of the two is possible** les deux sont possibles
B *det* **1** (one or the other) n'importe lequel/laquelle; **take ~ road** prenez n'importe laquelle des deux routes; **I can't see ~ child** je ne vois aucun des deux enfants
2 (both) **in ~ case** dans un cas comme dans l'autre; **~ way, it will be difficult** de toute manière, ce sera difficile
C *adv* non plus; **I can't do it ~** je ne peux pas le faire non plus
D *conj* **1** (as alternatives) **~...or...** soit...soit..., (ou)...ou...
2 (in the negative) **I wouldn't believe ~ Patrick or Emily** je ne croirais ni Patrick ni Emily

eject /ɪ'dʒekt/ **A** *vt* **1** ‹*machine, system*› rejeter ‹*waste*›; ‹*volcano*› cracher ‹*lava*›
2 faire sortir ‹*cassette*›
3 expulser ‹*troublemaker*›
B *vi* ‹*pilot*› s'éjecter

eject button *n* touche *f* d'éjection

eke /iːk/
■ **eke out** faire durer ‹*income, supplies*› (**by** à force de, **by doing** en faisant); **to ~ out a living** essayer de joindre les deux bouts

elaborate **A** /ɪ'læbərət/ *adj* ‹*excuse*› compliqué/-e; ‹*network, plan*› complexe; ‹*design*› travaillé/-e; ‹*painting, sculpture*› ouvragé/-e
B /ɪ'læbəreɪt/ *vt* élaborer ‹*theory*›
C /ɪ'læbəreɪt/ *vi* entrer dans les détails; **to ~ on** s'étendre sur ‹*proposal*›; développer ‹*remark*›

elapse /ɪ'læps/ *vi* s'écouler

elastic /ɪ'læstɪk/ *n, adj* élastique *m*

elasticated /ɪ'læstɪkeɪtɪd/ *adj* élastique

elastic band *n* élastique *m*

elated /ɪ'leɪtɪd/ *adj* transporté/-e de joie

elbow /'elbəʊ/ *n* coude *m*

elbow grease *n* huile *f* de coude (fam)

elbow room /'elbəʊruːm/ *n* (room to move) espace *m* vital; (fig) marge *f* de manœuvre

elder /'eldə(r)/ **A** *n* **1** (older person) aîné/-e *m/f*; (of tribe, group) ancien *m*
2 (tree) sureau *m*
B *adj* aîné/-e; **the ~ girl** l'aînée *f*, la fille aînée

elderly /'eldəlɪ/ **A** *n* **the ~** les personnes *fpl* âgées
B *adj* ‹*person, population*› âgé/-e

eldest /'eldɪst/ **A** *n* aîné/-e *m/f*
B *adj* aîné/-e; **the ~ child** l'aîné/-e

e-learning *n* formation *f* en ligne, e-learning *m*; **~ software** logiciel *m* de formation en ligne

🔑 **elect** /ɪ'lekt/ *vt* **1** (by vote) élire (**from, from among** parmi)
2 (choose) choisir (**to do** de faire)

🔑 **election** /ɪ'lekʃn/ *n* élection *f*, scrutin *m*; **to win an ~** gagner aux élections

election campaign *n* campagne *f* électorale

electoral /ɪ'lektərəl/ *adj* électoral/-e

electorate /ɪ'lektərət/ *n* électorat *m*, électeurs *mpl*

electric /ɪ'lektrɪk/ *adj* électrique

electrical /ɪ'lektrɪkl/ *adj* électrique

electric blanket *n* couverture *f* chauffante

electrician /ˌɪlek'trɪʃn/ *n* électricien/-ienne *m/f*

electricity /ˌɪlek'trɪsətɪ/ *n* électricité *f*; **to turn off/on the ~** couper/rétablir le courant (électrique)

electric shock *n* décharge *f* électrique

electrify /ɪ'lektrɪfaɪ/ *vt* **1** électrifier ‹*railway*›
2 électriser ‹*audience*›

electrocute /ɪ'lektrəkjuːt/ *vt* électrocuter

electromagnetic /ɪˌlektrəʊmæg'netɪk/ *adj* électromagnétique

electronic /ˌɪlek'trɒnɪk/ *adj* électronique

electronic cigarette *n* = **e-cigarette**

electronic engineer *n* électronicien/-ienne *m/f*

electronic organizer *n* ordinateur *m* de poche

electronic publishing *n* éditique *f*

electronics /ˌɪlek'trɒnɪks/ *n* électronique *f*

electronic tagging *n* marquage *m* électronique (des criminels)

elegant /'elɪgənt/ *adj* ‹*person, clothes, gesture*› élégant/-e; ‹*manners*› distingué/-e; ‹*restaurant*› chic

🔑 **element** /'elɪmənt/ *n* **1** élément *m*; **an ~ of luck** une part de chance
2 (in heater, kettle) résistance *f*

elementary /ˌelɪ'mentrɪ/ *adj* **1** (basic) élémentaire
2 ‹*school*› primaire; ‹*teacher*› de primaire

elephant /'elɪfənt/ *n* éléphant *m*

elevate /'elɪveɪt/ *vt* élever (**to** au rang de)

elevated /'elɪveɪtɪd/ *adj* ‹*language, rank, site*› élevé/-e; ‹*railway, canal*› surélevé/-e

elevator /'elɪveɪtə(r)/ *n* **1** (AmE) (lift) ascenseur *m*
2 (hoist) élévateur *m*

eleven /ɪ'levn/ *n, pron, det* onze *m inv*

eleventh /ɪ'levnθ/ **A** *n* **1** (in order) onzième *mf*
2 (of month) onze *m inv*
3 (fraction) onzième *m*
B *adj, adv* onzième

elf /elf/ *n* (*pl* **elves**) lutin *m*

eligible /'elɪdʒəbl/ *adj* **to be ~ for** avoir droit à ‹*allowance, benefit, membership*›; **to be ~ to do** être en droit de faire

🔑 **eliminate** /ɪ'lɪmɪneɪt/ *vt* (gen) éliminer; écarter ‹*suspect*›

elimination /ɪˌlɪmɪ'neɪʃn/ *n* élimination *f*; **by a process of ~** en procédant par élimination

elite /eɪ'liːt/ **A** *n* élite *f*
B *adj* ‹*group, minority*› élitaire; ‹*restaurant, club*› réservé/-e à l'élite; ‹*squad*› d'élite

elm /elm/ *n* orme *m*

elongated /'iːlɒŋgeɪtɪd, (AmE) ɪ'lɔːŋ-/ *adj* allongé/-e

elope /ɪ'ləʊp/ *vi* s'enfuir (**with** avec)

eloquent /'eləkwənt/ *adj* éloquent/-e

🔑 **else** /els/ **A** *adv* d'autre; **somebody/nothing ~** quelqu'un/rien d'autre; **something ~** autre chose; **somewhere** *or* **someplace** (AmE) **~** ailleurs; **how ~ can we do it?** comment le faire autrement?; **what ~ would you like?** qu'est-ce que tu voudrais d'autre?
B or else *phr* sinon

🔑 **elsewhere** /ˌels'weə(r), (AmE) ˌels'hweər/ *adv* ailleurs

elusive /ɪ'luːsɪv/ *adj* ‹*person, animal, happiness*› insaisissable; ‹*prize, victory*› hors d'atteinte

emaciated /ɪ'meɪʃɪeɪtɪd/ *adj* ‹*person, feature*› émacié/-e; ‹*limb, body*› décharné/-e; ‹*animal*› étique

🔑 **email**, **e-mail** **A** *n* (medium) e-mail *m*, courrier *m* électronique, courriel *m*; (item of mail) e-mail *m*, message *m* électronique
B *vt* envoyer un e-mail à ‹*person*›; envoyer [qch] par e-mail ‹*document*›

email address *n* adresse *f* électronique

emancipate /ɪ'mænsɪpeɪt/ *vt* émanciper

emancipation /ɪˌmænsɪ'peɪʃn/ *n* émancipation *f*

embalm /ɪm'bɑːm, (AmE) -bɑːlm/ *vt* embaumer

embankment /ɪm'bæŋkmənt/ *n* **1** (for railway, road) remblai *m*
2 (by river) quai *m*, digue *f*

embargo /ɪm'bɑːgəʊ/ *n* embargo *m*

embark /ɪm'bɑːk/ *vi* **1** (on ship) s'embarquer (**for** pour)
2 to ~ on entreprendre ‹*journey*›; se lancer dans ‹*career, process, project*›

embarkation /ˌembɑː'keɪʃn/ *n* embarquement *m*

embarrass /ɪm'bærəs/ *vt* plonger [qn] dans l'embarras; **to be/to feel ~ed** être/se sentir gêné/-e

embarrassing /ɪm'bærəsɪŋ/ *adj* embarrassant/-e

embarrassment /ɪm'bærəsmənt/ *n* confusion *f*, gêne *f*; **to my ~** à ma grande confusion

embassy /'embəsɪ/ *n* ambassade *f*

🔑 mot clé

embedded /ɪm'bedɪd/ *adj* **1** ‹*software*› embarqué/-e
2 ‹*journalist*› intégré/-e

embers *npl* braises *fpl*

embezzle /ɪm'bezl/ *vt* détourner ‹*funds*› (**from** de)

emblem /'embləm/ *n* emblème *m*

embody /ɪm'bɒdɪ/ *vt* incarner ‹*virtue, evil, ideal*›

embrace /ɪm'breɪs/ **A** *n* étreinte *f*
B *vt* **1** (hug) étreindre
2 (include) comprendre
C *vi* s'étreindre

embroider /ɪm'brɔɪdə(r)/ **A** *vt* **1** broder (**with** de)
2 embellir ‹*story, truth*›
B *vi* broder, faire de la broderie

embroidery /ɪm'brɔɪdərɪ/ *n* broderie *f*

embryo /'embrɪəʊ/ *n* embryon *m*

emerald /'emərəld/ *n* **1** (stone) émeraude *f*
2 (colour) émeraude *m*

emerge /ɪ'mɜːdʒ/ *vi* **1** ‹*person, animal*› sortir (**from** de)
2 ‹*problem, result*› se faire jour; ‹*pattern*› se dégager; ‹*truth*› apparaître

emergency /ɪ'mɜːdʒənsɪ/ **A** *n* (gen) cas *m* d'urgence; (Med) urgence *f*; **in an ~, in case of ~** en cas d'urgence; **it's an ~** c'est urgent
B *adj* ‹*plan, repairs, call, stop*› d'urgence; ‹*brakes, vehicle*› de secours

emergency exit *n* sortie *f* de secours

emergency landing *n* atterrissage *m* d'urgence

emergency services *npl* (police) ≈ police *f* secours; (ambulance) service *m* d'aide médicale d'urgence; (fire brigade) (sapeurs-)pompiers *mpl*

emergency worker *n* secouriste *mf*

emigrant /'emɪgrənt/ *n* (about to leave) émigrant/-e *m/f*; (settled elsewhere) émigré/-e *m/f*

emigrate /'emɪgreɪt/ *vi* émigrer

emission /ɪ'mɪʃn/ *n* émission *f* (**from** provenant de)

emit /ɪ'mɪt/ *vt* émettre

emoticon /ɪ'məʊtɪkɒn, -'mɒtɪ-/ *n* (Comput) émoticône *f*, smiley *m* (fam)

emotion /ɪ'məʊʃn/ *n* émotion *f*

emotional /ɪ'məʊʃənl/ *adj* ‹*problem*› émotif/-ive; ‹*reaction*› émotionnel/-elle; ‹*tie, response*› affectif/-ive; ‹*speech*› passionné/-e; **to feel ~** être ému/-e (**about** par); **she's rather ~** elle est assez émotive

emotionally /ɪ'məʊʃənəlɪ/ *adv* ‹*speak, react*› avec émotion; **~ deprived** privé/-e d'affection; **~ disturbed** caractériel/-ielle

emotive /ɪ'məʊtɪv/ *adj* ‹*issue*› qui soulève les passions; ‹*word*› chargé/-e de connotations

empathize /'empəθaɪz/ *vi* **to ~ with** s'identifier à ‹*person*›

emperor /'empərə(r)/ *n* empereur *m*

emphasis /'emfəsɪs/ *n* (*pl* **-ses**) accent *m*; **to lay** *or* **put the ~ on sth** mettre l'accent sur qch

emphasize /'emfəsaɪz/ *vt* mettre l'accent sur ‹*policy, need*›; mettre [qch] en valeur ‹*eyes*›

emphatic /ɪm'fætɪk/ *adj* ‹*statement*› catégorique; ‹*voice, manner*› énergique; **to be ~ about** insister sur

empire /'empaɪə(r)/ *n* empire *m*

employ /ɪm'plɔɪ/ *vt* **1** employer ‹*person, company*› (**as** en qualité de); **to be ~ed** avoir un emploi
2 (use) utiliser ‹*machine, tool*›; employer ‹*tactics, technique*›; recourir à ‹*measures*›

employable /ɪm'plɔɪəbl/ *adj* capable de faire un travail

employee /ˌemplɔɪ'iː, ɪm'plɔɪiː/ *n* salarié/-e *m/f*

employer /ɪm'plɔɪə(r)/ *n* employeur/-euse *m/f*

employment /ɪm'plɔɪmənt/ *n* travail *m*, emploi *m*

employment agency *n* bureau *m* de recrutement

empower /ɪm'paʊə(r)/ *vt* (legally) **to ~ sb to do** autoriser qn à faire; (politically) donner à qn le pouvoir de faire

empress /'emprɪs/ *n* impératrice *f*

empty /'emptɪ/ **A** *adj* **1** ‹*street*› désert/-e; ‹*desk*› libre; ‹*container*› vide; ‹*page*› vierge
2 ‹*promise, threat*› en l'air; ‹*gesture*› vide de sens; ‹*life*› vide
B *vt, vi* = **empty out**

■ **empty out**: **A ~ out** ‹*building, container*› se vider; ‹*contents*› se répandre
B ~ [sth] out vider ‹*container, drawer*›; verser ‹*liquid*›

empty-handed /ˌemptɪ'hændɪd/ *adj* ‹*arrive, leave*› les mains vides; ‹*return*› bredouille *inv*

emulate /'emjʊleɪt/ *vt* imiter

emulsion /ɪ'mʌlʃn/ *n* émulsion *f*

enable /ɪ'neɪbl/ *vt* **1 to ~ sb to do** permettre à qn de faire
2 faciliter ‹*growth*›; favoriser ‹*learning*›

enamel /ɪ'næml/ *n* émail *m*

enchant /ɪn'tʃɑːnt, (AmE) -tʃænt/ *vt* enchanter

enchanting /ɪn'tʃɑːntɪŋ, (AmE) -tʃænt-/ *adj* enchanteur/-eresse

encircle /ɪn'sɜːkl/ *vt* ‹*troops, police*› encercler; ‹*fence, wall*› entourer; ‹*belt, bracelet*› enserrer

enclose /ɪn'kləʊz/ *vt* **1** (gen) entourer (**with, by** de); (with fence, wall) clôturer (**with, by** avec)
2 (in letter) joindre (**with, in** à); **please find ~d a cheque for £10** veuillez trouver ci-joint un chèque de dix livres sterling

e

enclosure /ɪn'kləʊʒə(r)/ *n* **1** (for animals) enclos *m*; (for racehorses) paddock *m*; (for officials) enceinte *f*
2 (fence) clôture *f*

encompass /ɪn'kʌmpəs/ *vt* inclure, comprendre

encore /'ɒŋkɔː(r)/ **A** *n* bis *m*; **to play an ~** jouer un bis
B *excl* **~!** bis!

encounter /ɪn'kaʊntə(r)/ **A** *n* (gen) rencontre *f* (**with** avec); (Mil) affrontement *m*
B *vt* rencontrer ‹*opponent, resistance, problem*›; essuyer ‹*setback*›; croiser ‹*person*›

encourage /ɪn'kʌrɪdʒ/ *vt* **1** encourager (**to do** à faire)
2 stimuler ‹*investment*›; favoriser ‹*growth*›

encouragement /ɪn'kʌrɪdʒmənt/ *n* encouragement *m*

encouraging /ɪn'kʌrɪdʒɪŋ/ *adj* encourageant/-e

encroach /ɪn'krəʊtʃ/ *vi* **to ~ on** ‹*person*› empiéter sur; ‹*sea, vegetation*› gagner du terrain sur ‹*land*›

encrypt /en'krɪpt/ *vt* crypter

encyclopedia /ɪnˌsaɪklə'piːdɪə/ *n* (*also* **encyclopaedia**) encyclopédie *f*

end /end/ **A** *n* **1** (final part) fin *f*; **'The End'** 'Fin'; **to put an ~ to sth** mettre fin à qch; **to come to an ~** se terminer; **in the ~ I went home** finalement je suis rentré chez moi; **for days on ~** pendant des jours et des jours
2 (extremity) bout *m*, extrémité *f*; **at the ~ of, on the ~ of** au bout de; **at the ~ of the garden** au fond du jardin; **the third from the ~** le/la troisième avant la fin; **to stand sth on (its) ~** mettre qch debout
3 (aim) but *m*; **to this ~** dans ce but; **a means to an ~** un moyen d'arriver à ses fins
4 (Sport) **to change ~s** changer de côté
B *vt* mettre fin à; **to ~ sth with** terminer qch par; **to ~ it all** en finir avec la vie
C *vi* ‹*day, book*› se terminer (**in, with** par); ‹*contract, agreement*› expirer
■ **end up** finir par devenir ‹*president*›; finir par être ‹*rich*›; **to ~ up doing** finir par faire

endanger /ɪn'deɪndʒə(r)/ *vt* mettre [qch] en danger ‹*health, life*›; compromettre ‹*career, prospects*›

endangered species *n* espèce *f* menacée

endearing /ɪn'dɪərɪŋ/ *adj* ‹*person, habit*› attachant/-e; ‹*smile*› engageant/-e

endeavour (BrE), **endeavor** (AmE) /ɪn'devə(r)/ **A** *n* tentative *f* (**to do** de faire)
B *vt* **to ~ to do** (do one's best) faire tout son possible pour faire; (find a means) trouver un moyen de faire

ending /'endɪŋ/ *n* fin *f*, dénouement *m*

endive /'endɪv, (AmE) -daɪv/ *n* (BrE) chicorée *f*; (AmE) endive *f*

endless /'endlɪs/ *adj* ‹*patience, choice*› infini/-e; ‹*supply*› inépuisable; ‹*list, search, meeting*› interminable

endorse /ɪn'dɔːs/ *vt* donner son aval à ‹*policy*›; appuyer ‹*decision*›; approuver ‹*product*›; endosser ‹*cheque*›

endow /ɪn'daʊ/ *vt* doter (**with** de)

end result *n* résultat *m* final

endurance /ɪn'djʊərəns, (AmE) -dʊə-/ *n* endurance *f*

endure /ɪn'djʊə(r), (AmE) -'dʊər/ **A** *vt* endurer ‹*hardship*›; supporter ‹*behaviour, person*›; subir ‹*attack, defeat*›
B *vi* durer

enemy /'enəmɪ/ **A** *n* (*pl* **-mies**) ennemi/-e *m/f*
B *adj* ‹*forces, aircraft, territory*› ennemi/-e; ‹*agent*› de l'ennemi

energetic /ˌenə'dʒetɪk/ *adj* énergique

energy /'enədʒɪ/ *n* énergie *f*

energy drink *n* boisson *f* énergétique, boisson *f* énergisante

energy policy *n* politique *f* énergétique

energy-saving *adj* qui permet de faire des économies d'énergie

enforce /ɪn'fɔːs/ *vt* appliquer ‹*rule, policy*›; faire respecter ‹*law, court order*›

engage /ɪn'geɪdʒ/ **A** *vt* **1 to be ~d in** se livrer à ‹*activity*›; **to ~ sb in conversation** engager la conversation avec qn
2 passer ‹*gear*›; **to ~ the clutch** embrayer
B *vi* **to ~ in** se livrer à ‹*activity*›; se lancer dans ‹*research*›

engaged /ɪn'geɪdʒd/ *adj* **1 to be ~** être fiancé/-e (**to** à); **to get ~** se fiancer (**to** à)
2 ‹*WC, phone*› occupé/-e

engaged tone *n* (BrE) tonalité *f* 'occupé'

engagement /ɪn'geɪdʒmənt/ *n*
1 (appointment) rendez-vous *m inv*
2 (before marriage) fiançailles *fpl*

engagement ring *n* bague *f* de fiançailles

engine /'endʒɪn/ *n* **1** (gen) moteur *m*; (in ship) machines *fpl*
2 locomotive *f*; **steam ~** locomotive à vapeur

engine driver *n* mécanicien *m*

engineer /ˌendʒɪ'nɪə(r)/ **A** *n* (graduate) ingénieur *m*; (in factory) mécanicien *m* monteur; (repairer) technicien *m*; (on ship) mécanicien *m*
B *vt* **1** (plot) manigancer
2 (build) construire

engineering /ˌendʒɪ'nɪərɪŋ/ *n* ingénierie *f*; **civil ~** génie *m* civil

England /'ɪŋglənd/ *pr n* Angleterre *f*

English /'ɪŋglɪʃ/ **A** *n* **1** (people) **the ~** les Anglais
2 (language) anglais *m*
B *adj* ‹*language, food*› anglais/-e; ‹*lesson, teacher*› d'anglais; ‹*team*› d'Angleterre

English breakfast *n* petit déjeuner *m* anglais
English Channel *pr n* **the ~** la Manche
Englishman /ˈɪŋglɪʃmən/ *n* (*pl* **-men**) Anglais *m*
English-speaking *adj* anglophone
Englishwoman *n* (*pl* **-women**) Anglaise *f*
engrave /ɪnˈgreɪv/ *vt* graver
engraving /ɪnˈgreɪvɪŋ/ *n* gravure *f*
engrossed *adj* **to be ~ in** être absorbé/-e par, être plongé/-e dans
engulf /ɪnˈgʌlf/ *vt* engloutir
enhance /ɪnˈhɑːns, (AmE) -hæns/ *vt* améliorer ‹*prospects, status*›; mettre [qch] en valeur ‹*appearance, qualities*›
enigma /ɪˈnɪgmə/ *n* énigme *f*
enigmatic /ˌenɪgˈmætɪk/ *adj* énigmatique
enjoy /ɪnˈdʒɔɪ/ **A** *vt* **1** aimer (**doing** faire); **I didn't ~ the party** je ne me suis pas amusé à la soirée
2 (have) jouir de ‹*good health, popularity*›
B *v refl* **to ~ oneself** s'amuser
enjoyable /ɪnˈdʒɔɪəbl/ *adj* agréable
enjoyment /ɪnˈdʒɔɪmənt/ *n* plaisir *m*
enlarge /ɪnˈlɑːdʒ/ **A** *vt* agrandir
B *vi* **1** ‹*pupil, pores*› se dilater; ‹*tonsils*› enfler
2 to ~ on s'étendre sur ‹*subject*›; développer ‹*idea*›
enlighten /ɪnˈlaɪtn/ *vt* éclairer (**on** sur)
enlightening /ɪnˈlaɪtnɪŋ/ *adj* instructif/-ive
enlightenment /ɪnˈlaɪtnmənt/ *n* (edification) instruction *f*; (clarification) éclaircissement *m*; **the (Age of) Enlightenment** le Siècle des lumières
enlist /ɪnˈlɪst/ **A** *vt* recruter; **to ~ sb's help** s'assurer l'aide de qn
B *vi* s'enrôler, s'engager
enmity /ˈenmətɪ/ *n* inimitié *f* (**towards** envers)
enormity /ɪˈnɔːmətɪ/ *n* énormité *f*
enormous /ɪˈnɔːməs/ *adj* (gen) énorme; ‹*effort*› prodigieux/-ieuse
enough /ɪˈnʌf/

> When *enough* is used as a pronoun and if the sentence does not specify what it is enough of, the pronoun *en*, meaning *of it/of them*, must be added before the verb in French: *will there be enough?* = est-ce qu'il y en aura assez?

A *pron, quantif* assez; **have you had ~ to eat?** avez-vous assez mangé?; **more than ~** largement assez; **is that ~?** ça suffit?; **I've had ~ of him** j'en ai assez de lui
B *adv* assez; **curiously ~,...** aussi bizarre que cela puisse paraître...
C *det* assez de; **have you got ~ chairs?** avez-vous assez de chaises?
enquire **A** *vt* demander
B *vi* se renseigner (**about** sur); **to ~ after sb** demander des nouvelles de qn
enquiring *adj* ‹*look, voice*› interrogateur/-trice; ‹*mind*› curieux/-ieuse
enquiry *n* demande *f* de renseignements; **to make enquiries** demander des renseignements (**about** sur); ▶ **inquiry**
enrage /ɪnˈreɪdʒ/ *vt* rendre [qn] furieux/-ieuse
enrich /ɪnˈrɪtʃ/ *vt* enrichir
enrol, enroll (AmE) /ɪnˈrəʊl/ **A** *vt* (*p prés etc* **-ll-**) (gen) inscrire; (Mil) enrôler
B *vi* (*p prés etc* **-ll-**) (gen) s'inscrire (**in, on** à); (Mil) s'engager (**in** dans)
enrolment, enrollment (AmE) /ɪnˈrəʊlmənt/ *n* (gen) inscription *f* (**in, on** à); (Mil) enrôlement *m*
ensuing /ɪnˈsjuːɪŋ, (AmE) -ˈsuː-/ *adj* ‹*period*› qui suivit; ‹*event*› qui s'ensuivit
en suite /ˌɒn ˈswiːt/ *adj* attenant/-e
ensure /ɪnˈʃɔː(r), (AmE) ɪnˈʃʊər/ *vt* garantir; **to ~ that...** s'assurer que...
entail /ɪnˈteɪl/ *vt* impliquer ‹*travel, work*›; entraîner ‹*expense*›; nécessiter ‹*effort*›
enter /ˈentə(r)/ **A** *vt* **1** entrer dans ‹*room, house, phase, period, profession, army*›; participer à ‹*race, competition*›; entrer à ‹*parliament*›; **to ~ sb's mind** *or* **head** venir à l'idée *or* à l'esprit de qn
2 engager ‹*horse*› (**for** dans); présenter ‹*poem, picture*› (**for** à)
3 inscrire ‹*figure, fact*› (**in** dans); (in diary) noter ‹*appointment*› (**in** dans); (in computer) entrer ‹*data*›
B *vi* **1** (come in) entrer
2 to ~ for s'inscrire à ‹*exam*›; s'inscrire pour ‹*race*›
■ **enter into** entrer en ‹*conversation*›; entamer ‹*negotiations*›; passer ‹*contract*›
enterprise /ˈentəpraɪz/ *n* **1** (gen) entreprise *f*
2 (initiative) esprit *m* d'initiative
enterprising /ˈentəpraɪzɪŋ/ *adj* ‹*person*› entreprenant/-e; ‹*plan*› audacieux/-ieuse
entertain /ˌentəˈteɪn/ **A** *vt* **1** (keep amused) divertir; (make laugh) amuser; (keep occupied) distraire, occuper
2 (play host to) recevoir ‹*guests*›
3 entretenir ‹*idea*›; nourrir ‹*doubt, ambition, illusion*›
B *vi* recevoir
entertainer /ˌentəˈteɪnə(r)/ *n* (comic) comique *mf*; (performer, raconteur) amuseur/-euse *m/f*
entertaining /ˌentəˈteɪnɪŋ/ **A** *adj* divertissant/-e
B *n* **they do a lot of ~** ils reçoivent beaucoup
entertainment /ˌentəˈteɪnmənt/ *n*
1 divertissement *m*, distractions *fpl*
2 (event) spectacle *m*
entertainment industry *n* industrie *f* du spectacle
enthusiasm /ɪnˈθjuːzɪæzəm, (AmE) -ˈθuːz-/ *n* enthousiasme *m* (**for** pour)

enthusiast /ɪn'θju:zɪæst, (AmE) -'θu:z-/ *n* (of sport, DIY) passionné/-e *m/f*; (for music, composer) fervent/-e *m/f*

enthusiastic /ɪn,θju:zɪ'æstɪk, (AmE) -,θu:z-/ *adj* (gen) enthousiaste; ‹*discussion*› exalté/-e; ‹*worker, gardener*› passionné/-e

entice /ɪn'taɪs/ *vt* (with offer, charms, prospects) attirer; (with food, money) appâter

⚷ **entire** /ɪn'taɪə(r)/ *adj* entier/-ière; **the ~ family** toute la famille, la famille entière

⚷ **entirely** /ɪn'taɪəlɪ/ *adv* ‹*destroy, escape*› entièrement; ‹*different, unnecessary*› complètement

entirety /ɪn'taɪərətɪ/ *n* ensemble *m*, totalité *f*

⚷ **entitle** /ɪn'taɪtl/ *vt* **to ~ sb to sth** donner droit à qch à qn; **to be ~d to sth** avoir droit à qch; **to be ~d to do** avoir le droit de faire

entitlement /ɪn'taɪtlmənt/ *n* droit *m*

entity /'entətɪ/ *n* entité *f*

entrance **A** /'entrəns/ *n* (gen) entrée *f*; **to gain ~ to** être admis/-e à *or* dans ‹*club, university*›
B /ɪn'trɑ:ns, (AmE) -'træns/ *vt* transporter, ravir

entrance examination *n* (BrE) (Sch, Univ) examen *m* d'entrée; (for civil service) concours *m* d'entrée

entrance fee *n* droit *m* d'entrée

entrance hall *n* (in house) vestibule *m*; (in public building) hall *m*

entrance requirements *npl* diplômes *mpl* requis

entrant /'entrənt/ *n* (in competition) participant/-e *m/f*; (in exam) candidat/-e *m/f*

entreat /ɪn'tri:t/ *vt* implorer, supplier (**to do** de faire)

entreaty /ɪn'tri:tɪ/ *n* prière *f*, supplication *f*

entrepreneur /,ɒntrəprə'nɜ:(r)/ *n* entrepreneur/-euse *m/f*

entrust /ɪn'trʌst/ *vt* confier; **to ~ sb with sth, to ~ sth to sb** confier qch à qn

⚷ **entry** /'entrɪ/ *n* **1** (gen) entrée *f*; **to gain ~ to** *or* **into** s'introduire dans ‹*building*›; accéder à ‹*computer file*›; **'no ~'** (on door) 'défense d'entrer'; (in one way street) 'sens interdit'
2 (in diary) note *f*; (in ledger) écriture *f*
3 (for competition) œuvre *f* présentée à un concours

entry form *n* (for membership) fiche *f* d'inscription; (for competition) bulletin *m* de participation

entryphone *n* interphone *m*

envelope /'envələʊp, 'ɒn-/ *n* enveloppe *f*

environmentalist /ɪn,vaɪərən'mentəlɪst/ *n* (Pol, Ecol) écologiste *mf*

envious /'envɪəs/ *adj* envieux/-ieuse; **to be ~ of sb/sth** envier qn/qch

⚷ **environment** /ɪn'vaɪərənmənt/ *n* (physical, cultural) environnement *m*; (social) milieu *m*

⚷ **environmental** /ɪn,vaɪərən'mentl/ *adj* ‹*conditions, changes*› du milieu; ‹*concern, issue*› lié/-e à l'environnement, écologique; ‹*protection, pollution*› de l'environnement; **~ disaster** catastrophe *f* écologique

environmental health *n* hygiène *f* publique

environmentally /ɪn,vaɪərən'mentəlɪ/ *adv* **~ safe, ~ sound** qui ne nuit pas à l'environnement; **~ friendly product** produit *m* qui respecte l'environnement

environmental studies *npl* (BrE) (Sch) études *fpl* géographiques et biologiques de l'environnement

envisage /ɪn'vɪzɪdʒ/ *vt* (anticipate) prévoir (**doing** de faire); (visualize) envisager (**doing** de faire)

envoy /'envɔɪ/ *n* envoyé/-e *m/f*

envy /'envɪ/ **A** *n* envie *f*; (long-term) jalousie *f*
B *vt* **to ~ sb sth** envier qch à qn

enzyme /'enzaɪm/ *n* enzyme *f*

epic /'epɪk/ **A** *n* (gen) épopée *f*; (film) film *m* à grand spectacle; (novel) roman-fleuve *m*
B *adj* épique

epidemic /,epɪ'demɪk/ **A** *n* épidémie *f*
B *adj* épidémique

epidural /,epɪ'djʊərəl/ *n* péridurale *f*

epilepsy /'epɪlepsɪ/ *n* épilepsie *f*

epileptic /,epɪ'leptɪk/ *n, adj* épileptique *mf*

⚷ **episode** /'epɪsəʊd/ *n* épisode *m*

epitome /ɪ'pɪtəmɪ/ *n* épitomé *m*; **the ~ of kindness** la bonté incarnée

epitomize /ɪ'pɪtəmaɪz/ *vt* personnifier, incarner

epoch /'i:pɒk, (AmE) 'epək/ *n* époque *f*

⚷ **equal** /'i:kwəl/ **A** *n* égal/-e *m/f*
B *adj* **1** égal/-e (**to** à); **~ opportunities/rights** égalité *f* des chances/des droits
2 to be ~ to être à la hauteur de ‹*task*›
C *adv* ‹*finish*› à égalité
D *vt* égaler

equality /ɪ'kwɒlətɪ/ *n* égalité *f*; **~ of opportunity** égalité des chances

equalize /'i:kwəlaɪz/ *vi* égaliser

⚷ **equally** /'i:kwəlɪ/ *adv* ‹*divide, share*› en parts égales; **~ difficult** tout aussi difficile; **~, we might say that...** de même, on pourrait dire que...

equate /ɪ'kweɪt/ *vt* (identify) assimiler (**with, to** à); (compare) comparer (**with, to** à)

equation /ɪ'kweɪʒn/ *n* équation *f*

equator /ɪ'kweɪtə(r)/ *n* équateur *m*

equilibrium /,i:kwɪ'lɪbrɪəm/ *n* (*pl* **-riums** *ou* **-ria**) équilibre *m*

equip /ɪ'kwɪp/ *vt* (*p prés etc* **-pp-**) équiper (**for** pour, **with** de)

⚷ **equipment** /ɪ'kwɪpmənt/ *n* (gen) équipement *m*; (office, electrical, photographic) matériel *m*; **a piece** *or* **item of ~** un article

equivalent /ɪ'kwɪvələnt/ **A** *n* équivalent *m*

⚷ mot clé

B *adj* équivalent/-e

era /ˈɪərə/ *n* (in history, geology) ère *f*; (in politics, fashion) époque *f*

eradicate /ɪˈrædɪkeɪt/ *vt* éliminer ‹*poverty, crime*›; éradiquer ‹*disease*›

erase /ɪˈreɪz, (AmE) ɪˈreɪs/ *vt* effacer

eraser /ɪˈreɪzə(r), (AmE) -sər/ *n* (rubber) gomme *f*; (for blackboard) brosse *f* feutrée

erect /ɪˈrekt/ **A** *adj* ‹*posture*› droit/-e; ‹*tail, ears*› dressé/-e
B *vt* ériger ‹*building*›; monter ‹*scaffolding, tent, screen*›

erection /ɪˈrekʃn/ *n* (gen) érection *f*; (of building) construction *f*; (edifice) édifice *m*

ermine /ˈɜːmɪn/ *n* hermine *f*

erode /ɪˈrəʊd/ *vt* éroder ‹*rock, metal*›; saper ‹*confidence*›

erosion /ɪˈrəʊʒn/ *n* érosion *f*

erotic /ɪˈrɒtɪk/ *adj* érotique

err /ɜː(r)/ *vi* **1** (make mistake) faire erreur
2 to ~ on the side of caution pécher par excès de prudence

errand /ˈerənd/ *n* commission *f*, course *f*; **to run an ~ for sb** aller faire une commission pour qn

erratic /ɪˈrætɪk/ *adj* ‹*behaviour, person, driver*› imprévisible; ‹*moods*› changeant/-e

error /ˈerə(r)/ *n* (in spelling, grammar, typing) faute *f*; (in calculation, on computer) erreur *f*

erupt /ɪˈrʌpt/ *vi* **1** ‹*volcano*› entrer en éruption
2 ‹*violence*› éclater

eruption /ɪˈrʌpʃn/ *n* (of volcano) éruption *f*; (of violence, anger) explosion *f*

escalate /ˈeskəleɪt/ *vi* ‹*conflict, violence*› s'intensifier; ‹*prices*› monter en flèche; ‹*unemployment*› augmenter rapidement

escalator /ˈeskəleɪtə(r)/ *n* escalier *m* mécanique, escalator® *m*

escapade /ˈeskəpeɪd, ˌeskəˈpeɪd/ *n* frasque *f*

escape /ɪˈskeɪp/ **A** *n* fuite *f*, évasion *f* (**from** de, **to** vers); **to have a narrow** *or* **lucky ~** l'échapper belle
B *vt* échapper à
C *vi* **1** ‹*person*› s'enfuir, s'évader (**from** de); ‹*animal*› s'échapper (**from** de); (fig) s'évader; **to ~ with one's life** s'en sortir vivant
2 (leak) fuir

escape clause *n* clause *f* dérogatoire

escape key *n* touche *f* d'échappement

escape route *n* (in case of fire etc) plan *m* d'évacuation; (for fugitives) itinéraire *m* d'évasion

escapism /ɪˈskeɪpɪzəm/ *n* évasion *f* (du réel)

escort **A** /ˈeskɔːt/ *n* **1** (for security) escorte *f*; **police ~** escorte de police
2 (companion) compagnon/compagne *m/f*
3 (in agency) hôtesse *f*; **~ agency** agence *f* d'hôtesses
B /ɪˈskɔːt/ *vt* **1** (for security) escorter; **to ~ sb in/out** faire entrer/sortir qn sous escorte
2 (to a function) accompagner; (home) raccompagner

especially /ɪˈspeʃəlɪ/ *adv* **1** (above all) surtout, en particulier; **him ~** lui en particulier; **~ as it's so hot** d'autant plus qu'il fait si chaud
2 (on purpose) exprès, spécialement
3 (unusually) particulièrement

espresso /eˈspresəʊ/ *n* (*pl* **~s**) express *m inv*

essay /ˈeseɪ/ *n* **1** (Sch) rédaction *f* (**on, about** sur); (extended) dissertation *f* (**on** sur)
2 (literary) essai *m* (**on** sur)

essence /ˈesns/ *n* essence *f*

essential /ɪˈsenʃl/ **A** *n* **a car is not an ~** une voiture n'est pas indispensable; **the ~s** l'essentiel *m*
B *adj* ‹*role, feature, element*› essentiel/-ielle; ‹*ingredient, reading*› indispensable; ‹*difference*› fondamental/-e; **it is ~ that we agree** il est indispensable que nous soyons d'accord

essentially /ɪˈsenʃəlɪ/ *adv* essentiellement

essential oil *n* huile *f* essentielle

establish /ɪˈstæblɪʃ/ *vt* (gen) établir; fonder ‹*company*›

establishment /ɪˈstæblɪʃmənt/ *n* **1** (gen) établissement *m*
2 (shop, business) maison *f*
3 the Establishment l'ordre *m* établi

estate /ɪˈsteɪt/ *n* **1** (stately home and park) domaine *m*, propriété *f*
2 = **housing estate**
3 (assets) biens *mpl*
4 (*also* **~ car**) (BrE) break *m*

estate agency *n* (BrE) agence *f* immobilière

estate agent *n* (BrE) agent *m* immobilier

esteem /ɪˈstiːm/ *n* estime *f*

estimate **A** /ˈestɪmət/ *n* **1** estimation *f*
2 (quote for client) devis *m*
B /ˈestɪmeɪt/ *vt* évaluer ‹*value, size, distance*›; **to ~ that** estimer que
C estimated *pp adj* ‹*cost, figure*› approximatif/-ive; **an ~d 300 people** environ 300 personnes

estimator /ˈestɪmeɪtə(r)/ *n* (AmE) métreur *m*

Estonia /ɪˈstəʊnɪə/ *pr n* Estonie *f*

estranged *adj* **~ from sb** séparé/-e de qn; **her ~ husband** son mari dont elle est séparée

etc. *adv* (*written abbr* = **et cetera**) etc

etching /ˈetʃɪŋ/ *n* eau-forte *f*

eternal /ɪˈtɜːnl/ *adj* ‹*life*› éternel/-elle; ‹*chatter, optimist*› perpétuel/-elle

ethical /ˈeθɪkl/ *adj* ‹*problem, objection*› moral/-e; ‹*investment, theory*› éthique

ethics /ˈeθɪks/ *n* (code) moralité *f*; **professional ~** déontologie *f*

ethnic /ˈeθnɪk/ *adj* ethnique

ethnic cleansing *n* purification *f* ethnique

e

ethnic minority *n* minorité *f* ethnique
e-ticket /'iːtɪkɪt/ *n* e-billet *m*
etiquette /'etɪket, -kət/ *n* **1** (social) bienséance *f*, étiquette *f*
2 (professional, diplomatic) protocole *m*
euphemism /'juːfəmɪzəm/ *n* euphémisme *m*
euphoria /juː'fɔːrɪə/ *n* euphorie *f*
euro /'jʊərəʊ/ *n* euro *m*
Euro- *pref* euro-
Eurocheque /'jʊərəʊtʃek/ *n* Eurochèque *m*
Eurocrat /'jʊərəʊkræt/ *n* eurocrate *mf*
Euro-MP /ˌjʊərəʊem'piː/ *n* député *m* européen
Europe /'jʊərəp/ *pr n* Europe *f*
⚷ **European** /ˌjʊərə'pɪən/ **A** *n* Européen/-éenne *m/f*
B *adj* européen/-éenne
European Commission *n* Commission *f* européenne
European Monetary System, EMS *n* système *m* monétaire européen, SME *m*
European Monetary Union, EMU *n* Union *f* monétaire européenne
European Union, EU *n* Union *f* européenne, UE *f*
Eurosceptic /'jʊərəʊskeptɪk/ *n* eurosceptique *mf*
Eurozone *n* Eurozone *f*
euthanasia /ˌjuːθə'neɪzɪə, (AmE) -'neɪʒə/ *n* euthanasie *f*
evacuate /ɪ'vækjʊeɪt/ *vt* évacuer
evacuee /ɪˌvækjuː'iː/ *n* évacué/-e *m/f*
evade /ɪ'veɪd/ *vt* esquiver ‹*blow*›; éluder ‹*problem*›
evaluate /ɪ'væljʊeɪt/ *vt* évaluer
evaluation /ɪˌvæljʊ'eɪʃn/ *n* évaluation *f*
evaporate /ɪ'væpəreɪt/ *vi* ‹*liquid*› s'évaporer
evaporated milk *n* lait *m* condensé non sucré
evasion /ɪ'veɪʒn/ *n* (of responsibility) dérobade *f* (**of** à); **tax ∼** évasion *f* fiscale
evasive /ɪ'veɪsɪv/ *adj* ‹*answer*› évasif/-ive; ‹*look*› fuyant/-e
eve /iːv/ *n* veille *f*; **on the ∼ of** à la veille de
⚷ **even¹** /'iːvn/ **A** *adv* **1** (gen) même; **he didn't ∼ try** il n'a même pas essayé; **don't tell anyone, not ∼ Bob** ne dis rien à personne, pas même à Bob; **∼ if/when** même si/quand
2 (with comparative) encore; **∼ colder** encore plus froid
B even so *phr* quand même
C even though *phr* bien que (+ *subjunctive*)
even² /'iːvn/ *adj* ‹*surface, voice, temper*› égal/-e; ‹*teeth, hemline*› régulier/-ière; ‹*temperature*› constant/-e; ‹*number*› pair/-e; **to get ∼ with sb** rendre à qn la monnaie de sa pièce

⚷ **evening** /'iːvnɪŋ/ *n* soir *m*; (with emphasis on duration) soirée *f*; **in the ∼** le soir; **all ∼** toute la soirée; **every ∼** tous les soirs
evening class *n* cours *m* du soir
evening dress *n* (formal clothes) tenue *f* de soirée
⚷ **event** /ɪ'vent/ *n* **1** événement *m*
2 (eventuality) cas *m*; **in the ∼ of a fire** en cas d'incendie; **in any ∼** de toute façon
3 (in athletics) épreuve *f*
eventful /ɪ'ventfl/ *adj* mouvementé/-e
⚷ **eventually** /ɪ'ventʃʊəlɪ/ *adv* finalement; **to do sth ∼** finir par faire qch
⚷ **ever** /'evə(r)/ **A** *adv* **1** jamais; **no one will ∼ forget** personne n'oubliera jamais; **hardly ∼** rarement, presque jamais; **has he ∼ lived abroad?** est-ce qu'il a déjà vécu à l'étranger?; **do you ∼ make mistakes?** est-ce qu'il t'arrive de te tromper?; **he's happier than he's ∼ been** il n'a jamais été aussi heureux; **more beautiful than ∼** plus beau/belle que jamais
2 (always) toujours; **as cheerful as ∼** toujours aussi gai; **the same as ∼** toujours le même; **they lived happily ∼ after** ils vécurent toujours heureux
B ever since *phr* depuis; **∼ since we arrived** depuis notre arrivée
evergreen /'evəgriːn/ *n* arbre *m* à feuilles persistantes
everlasting /ˌevə'lɑːstɪŋ, (AmE) -'læst-/ *adj* éternel/-elle
⚷ **every** /'evrɪ/ **A** *det* **1** (each) chaque; **∼ time** chaque fois; **∼ house in the street** toutes les maisons de la rue; **I've read ∼ one of her books** j'ai lu tous ses livres
2 (emphatic) **there is ∼ chance that you'll have a place** il y a toutes les chances que tu aies une place; **to have ∼ right to complain** avoir tous les droits de se plaindre
3 (indicating frequency) **∼ day** tous les jours; **∼ Thursday** tous les jeudis; **once ∼ few days** tous les deux ou trois jours
B every other *phr* **∼ other day** tous les deux jours; **∼ other Sunday** un dimanche sur deux
IDIOM **∼ now and then, ∼ so often** de temps en temps
⚷ **everybody** /'evrɪbɒdɪ/ *pron* (*also* **everyone**) tout le monde
everyday /'evrɪdeɪ/ *adj* ‹*life*› quotidien/-ienne; ‹*clothes*› de tous les jours; **in ∼ use** d'usage courant
⚷ **everyone** /'evrɪwʌn/ = **everybody**
⚷ **everything** /'evrɪθɪŋ/ *pron* tout
⚷ **everywhere** /'evrɪweə(r), (AmE) -hweər/ *adv* partout
evict /ɪ'vɪkt/ *vt* expulser (**from** de)
eviction /ɪ'vɪkʃn/ *n* expulsion *f*
⚷ **evidence** /'evɪdəns/ *n* **1** (proof) preuves *fpl* (**that** que, **of, for** de, **against** contre)
2 (testimony) témoignage *m* (**from** de); **to give ∼** témoigner, déposer (**for sb** en

⚷ mot clé

faveur de qn, **against sb** contre qn)
3 (trace) trace *f* (**of** de)

evident /ˈevɪdənt/ *adj* manifeste

evidently /ˈevɪdəntlɪ/ *adv* **1** (apparently) apparemment
2 (patently) manifestement

evil /ˈiːvl/ **A** *n* mal *m*
B *adj* ‹*person, forces*› malfaisant/-e; ‹*act*› diabolique; ‹*spirit*› maléfique; ‹*smell*› nauséabond/-e

evolution /ˌiːvəˈluːʃn/ *n* évolution *f* (**from** à partir de)

evolve /ɪˈvɒlv/ *vi* évoluer

ewe /juː/ *n* brebis *f*

ex- *pref* ex-, ancien/-ienne *before n*

exact /ɪgˈzækt/ *adj* exact/-e; **to be (more) ~** plus précisément

exactly /ɪgˈzæktlɪ/ *adv* exactement

exaggerate /ɪgˈzædʒəreɪt/ *vt, vi* exagérer

exaggeration /ɪgˌzædʒəˈreɪʃn/ *n* exagération *f*

exam /ɪgˈzæm/ *n* examen *m*

examination /ɪgˌzæmɪˈneɪʃn/ *n* examen *m* (in de); **French ~** examen de français; **to take/pass an ~** passer/réussir un examen; **to have an ~** (Med) passer un examen médical

examination paper *n* sujets *mpl* d'examen

examine /ɪgˈzæmɪn/ *vt* examiner

examiner /ɪgˈzæmɪnə(r)/ *n* examinateur/-trice *m/f*

example /ɪgˈzɑːmpl, (AmE) -ˈzæmpl/ *n* exemple *m*; **for ~** par exemple; **to set a good ~** donner l'exemple; **to make an ~ of sb** punir qn pour l'exemple

excavate /ˈekskəveɪt/ **A** *vt* fouiller ‹*site*›; creuser ‹*tunnel*›
B *vi* faire des fouilles

exceed /ɪkˈsiːd/ *vt* dépasser (**by** de)

excel /ɪkˈsel/ *vi* exceller (**at, in** en, **at** *ou* **in doing** à faire)

excellent /ˈeksələnt/ *adj* excellent/-e

except /ɪkˈsept/ **A** *prep* sauf; **everybody ~ Lisa** tout le monde sauf Lisa, tout le monde à l'exception de *or* excepté Lisa; **who could have done it ~ him?** qui aurait pu le faire sinon lui?
B except for *phr* à part, à l'exception de

exception /ɪkˈsepʃn/ *n* **1** exception *f* (**for** pour); **with the ~ of** à l'exception de
2 to take ~ to prendre [qch] comme une insulte

exceptional /ɪkˈsepʃənl/ *adj* exceptionnel/-elle

excess /ɪkˈses/ **A** *n* excès *m* (**of** de)
B *adj* **~ weight** excès *m* de poids; **~ baggage** excédent *m* de bagages

excessive /ɪkˈsesɪv/ *adj* excessif/-ive

exchange /ɪksˈtʃeɪndʒ/ **A** *n* **1** échange *m*; **in ~** en échange (**for** de); **~ visit** voyage *m* d'échange
2 (in banking) change *m*; **the ~ rate** le taux de change
3 (*also* **telephone ~**) central *m* (téléphonique)
B *vt* échanger (**for** contre, **with** avec)

exchange control *n* contrôle *m* des changes

Exchange Rate Mechanism, ERM *n* système *m* monétaire européen

Exchequer *pr n* (BrE) **the ~** l'Échiquier *m*, le ministère des finances

excite /ɪkˈsaɪt/ *vt* exciter

excited /ɪkˈsaɪtɪd/ *adj* (gen) excité/-e; ‹*voice, conversation*› animé/-e

excitement /ɪkˈsaɪtmənt/ *n* excitation *f*

exciting /ɪkˈsaɪtɪŋ/ *adj* passionnant/-e

exclaim /ɪkˈskleɪm/ *vt* s'exclamer

exclamation mark, exclamation point (AmE) *n* point *m* d'exclamation

exclude /ɪkˈskluːd/ *vt* exclure (**from** de)

excluding /ɪkˈskluːdɪŋ/ *prep* à l'exclusion de; **~ VAT** TVA non comprise

exclusion zone *n* zone *f* interdite

exclusive /ɪkˈskluːsɪv/ **A** *n* (report) exclusivité *f*
B *adj* **1** ‹*club*› fermé/-e; ‹*hotel*› de luxe; ‹*district*› huppé/-e
2 ‹*story, rights*› exclusif/-ive; ‹*interview*› en exclusivité; **~ of meals** les repas non compris

excruciating /ɪkˈskruːʃɪeɪtɪŋ/ *adj* ‹*pain*› atroce

excursion /ɪkˈskɜːʃn/ *n* (organized) excursion *f*

excuse A /ɪkˈskjuːs/ *n* excuse *f* (**for sth** à qch, **for doing** pour faire, **to do** pour faire); **to make ~s** trouver des excuses; **an ~ to leave early** un bon prétexte pour partir tôt; **there's no ~ for such behaviour** ce genre de conduite est inexcusable
B /ɪkˈskjuːz/ *vt* **1** excuser ‹*person*› (**for doing** de faire, d'avoir fait); **~ me!** (apology) excusez-moi!, pardon!; (beginning an enquiry) excusez-moi; (pardon) pardon?
2 (exempt) dispenser (**from sth** de qch, **from doing** de faire)

ex-directory /ˌeksdaɪˈrektərɪ, -dɪ-/ *adj* sur la liste rouge

execute /ˈeksɪkjuːt/ *vt* exécuter

execution /ˌeksɪˈkjuːʃn/ *n* exécution *f*

executioner /ˌeksɪˈkjuːʃənə(r)/ *n* bourreau *m*

executive /ɪgˈzekjʊtɪv/ **A** *n* **1** cadre *m*; **sales ~** cadre commercial
2 (committee) exécutif *m*, comité *m* exécutif; **party ~** bureau *m* du parti
B *adj* **1** ‹*post*› de cadre
2 ‹*power*› exécutif/-ive

exemplify /ɪgˈzemplɪfaɪ/ *vt* illustrer, exemplifier

exempt /ɪgˈzempt/ **A** *adj* exempt/-e (**from** de)
B *vt* exempter (**from** de)

e

exemption /ɪg'zempʃn/ *n* exemption *f*; (from exam) dispense *f*

⚷ **exercise** /'eksəsaɪz/ **A** *n* exercice *m*
B *vt* **1** exercer ‹*body*›; faire travailler ‹*limb, muscles*›
2 faire preuve de ‹*control, restraint*›; exercer ‹*power, right*›
C *vi* faire de l'exercice

exercise bike *n* (at home) vélo *m* d'appartement; (in gym) vélo *m* d'entraînement

exercise book *n* cahier *m*

exert /ɪg'zɜːt/ *vt* exercer ‹*pressure, influence*› (**on** sur); **to ~ oneself** se fatiguer

exfoliator /eks,fəʊlieɪtə(r)/ *n* (Cosmet) exfoliant *m*

exhale /eks'heɪl/ *vi* ‹*person*› expirer

exhaust /ɪg'zɔːst/ **A** *n* **1** (*also* **~ pipe**) pot *m* d'échappement
2 (*also* **~ fumes**) gaz *mpl* d'échappement
B *vt* épuiser; **~ed** épuisé/-e

exhaustion /ɪg'zɔːstʃn/ *n* épuisement *m*

exhibit /ɪg'zɪbɪt/ **A** *n* **1** œuvre *f* exposée
2 (AmE) (exhibition) exposition *f*
B *vt* exposer ‹*work of art*›; manifester ‹*preference, sign*›

⚷ **exhibition** /,eksɪ'bɪʃn/ *n* exposition *f*; **art ~** exposition; **to make an ~ of oneself** se donner en spectacle

exhibition centre (BrE), **exhibition center** (AmE) *n* palais *m* des expositions

exhilarating /ɪg'zɪləreɪtɪŋ/ *adj* ‹*game*› stimulant/-e; ‹*experience*› exaltant/-e; ‹*speed*› enivrant/-e

exile /'eksaɪl/ **A** *n* **1** (person) exilé/-e *m/f*
2 (expulsion) exil *m* (**from** de); **in ~** en exil
B *vt* exiler (**de** from)

⚷ **exist** /ɪg'zɪst/ *vi* exister

⚷ **existence** /ɪg'zɪstəns/ *n* existence *f* (**of** de)

existing /ɪg'zɪstɪŋ/ *adj* ‹*laws, order*› existant/-e; ‹*policy, management*› actuel/-elle

exit /'eksɪt/ **A** *n* sortie *f*; **'no ~'** 'interdit'
B *vi* sortir

exodus /'eksədəs/ *n* exode *m*

exotic /ɪg'zɒtɪk/ *adj* exotique

⚷ **expand** /ɪk'spænd/ **A** *vt* développer ‹*business, network, range*›; élargir ‹*horizon, knowledge*›; étendre ‹*empire*›; gonfler ‹*lungs*›
B *vi* ‹*business, sector, town*› se développer; ‹*economy*› être en expansion; ‹*metal*› se dilater

expanse /ɪk'spæns/ *n* étendue *f*

expansion /ɪk'spænʃn/ *n* développement *m* (**in** de, **into** dans); (of economy) expansion *f*; (of population) accroissement *m*

expatriate /,eks'pætrɪət/ *n*, *adj* expatrié/-e *m/f*

⚷ **expect** /ɪk'spekt/ **A** *vt* **1** s'attendre à ‹*event, victory, defeat, trouble*›; **to ~ the worst** s'attendre au pire; **to ~ sb to do** s'attendre à ce que qn fasse; **I ~ (that) I'll lose** je m'attends à perdre; **more than ~ed** plus que prévu
2 s'attendre à ‹*sympathy, help*› (**from** de la part de)
3 attendre ‹*baby, guest*›
4 (require) demander, attendre ‹*hard work*› (**from** de); **I ~ you to be punctual** je vous demande d'être ponctuel
5 (BrE) (suppose) **I ~ so** je pense que oui; **I ~ he's tired** il doit être fatigué
B *vi* **1 to ~ to do** s'attendre à faire
2 (require) **I ~ to see you there** je compte bien vous y voir
3 (be pregnant) **to be ~ing** attendre un enfant

expectant /ɪk'spektənt/ *adj* **1** ‹*look*› plein d'attente
2 ‹*mother*› futur/-e *before n*

⚷ **expectation** /,ekspek'teɪʃn/ *n* **1** (prediction) prévision *f*; **against all ~(s)** à l'encontre des prévisions générales
2 (hope) aspiration *f*, attente *f*; **to live up to sb's ~s** répondre à l'attente de qn

expedient /ɪk'spiːdɪənt/ *adj* **1** (appropriate) opportun/-e
2 (advantageous) politique

expedition /,ekspɪ'dɪʃn/ *n* expédition *f*; **to go on an ~** partir en expédition

expel /ɪk'spel/ *vt* (*p prés etc* **-ll-**) (gen) expulser; renvoyer ‹*pupil*›

expenditure /ɪk'spendɪtʃə(r)/ *n* dépense *f*

⚷ **expense** /ɪk'spens/ **A** *n* **1** (cost) frais *mpl*; (money spent) dépense *f*; **at one's own ~** à ses propres frais; **to go to great ~** dépenser beaucoup d'argent (**to do** pour faire); **to spare no ~** ne pas regarder à la dépense
2 at the ~ of au détriment de ‹*health, public, safety*›; **at sb's ~** ‹*laugh, joke*› aux dépens de qn
B expenses *npl* frais *mpl*

expense account *n* frais *mpl* de représentation

⚷ **expensive** /ɪk'spensɪv/ *adj* (gen) cher/chère; ‹*holiday, mistake*› coûteux/-euse; ‹*taste*› de luxe

⚷ **experience** /ɪk'spɪərɪəns/ **A** *n* expérience *f*
B *vt* connaître ‹*loss, problem*›; éprouver ‹*emotion*›

experienced /ɪk'spɪərɪənst/ *adj* (gen) expérimenté/-e; ‹*eye*› entraîné/-e

⚷ **experiment** /ɪk'sperɪmənt/ **A** *n* expérience *f* (**in** en, **on** sur)
B *vi* expérimenter, faire des essais

experimental /ɪk,sperɪ'mentl/ *adj* expérimental/-e

experimentation /ɪk,sperɪmen'teɪʃn/ *n* expériences *fpl*

⚷ **expert** /'ekspɜːt/ **A** *n* spécialiste *mf* (**in** en, de), expert *m* (**in** en)
B *adj* ‹*opinion, advice*› autorisé/-e;

⚷ mot clé

‹*witness*› expert/-e; ‹*eye*› exercé/-e; **an ~ cook** un cordon bleu

expertise /ˌekspɜːˈtiːz/ *n* compétences *fpl*; (very specialized) expertise *f* (**in** dans le domaine de)

expire /ɪkˈspaɪə(r)/ *vi* ‹*deadline, offer*› expirer; ‹*period*› arriver à terme; **my passport has ~d** mon passeport est périmé

expiry date *n* (of credit card, permit) date *f* d'expiration

⚷ **explain** /ɪkˈspleɪn/ *vt* expliquer (**that** que, **to** à)

⚷ **explanation** /ˌekspləˈneɪʃn/ *n* explication *f* (**of** de, **for** à)

explicit /ɪkˈsplɪsɪt/ *adj* explicite

explode /ɪkˈspləʊd/ **A** *vt* **1** faire exploser ‹*bomb*›
2 pulvériser ‹*theory, rumour, myth*›
B *vi* (gen) exploser; ‹*boiler, building, ship*› sauter

exploit **A** /ˈeksplɔɪt/ *n* exploit *m*
B /ɪkˈsplɔɪt/ *vt* exploiter

exploitation /ˌeksplɔɪˈteɪʃn/ *n* exploitation *f*

⚷ **explore** /ɪkˈsplɔː(r)/ **A** *vt* explorer
B *vi* **to go exploring** partir en exploration

explorer /ɪkˈsplɔːrə(r)/ *n* explorateur/-trice *m/f*

explosion /ɪkˈspləʊʒn/ *n* explosion *f*

explosive /ɪkˈspləʊsɪv/ **A** *n* explosif *m*
B *adj* ‹*device, force*› explosif/-ive; ‹*substance*› explosible

export **A** /ˈekspɔːt/ *n* (process) exportation *f* (**of** de); (product) produit *m* d'exportation
B /ɪkˈspɔːt/ *vt*, *vi* exporter

exporter /ɪkˈspɔːtə(r)/ *n* exportateur/-trice *m/f* (**of** de)

⚷ **expose** /ɪkˈspəʊz/ *vt* **1** exposer (**to** à)
2 (make public) révéler ‹*identity*›; dénoncer ‹*person, scandal*›
3 to ~ oneself commettre un outrage à la pudeur

⚷ **exposure** /ɪkˈspəʊʒə(r)/ *n* **1** (of secret, crime) révélation *f*
2 (to light, sun, radiation) exposition *f* (**to** à)
3 to die of ~ mourir de froid
4 (*also* **~ time**) temps *m* de pose
5 (picture) pose *f*

⚷ **express** /ɪkˈspres/ **A** *n* rapide *m*
B *adj* ‹*letter, parcel*› exprès; ‹*delivery, train*› rapide
C *adv* **to send sth ~** envoyer qch en exprès
D *vt* exprimer; **to ~ oneself** s'exprimer

⚷ **expression** /ɪkˈspreʃn/ *n* expression *f*

expressive /ɪkˈspresɪv/ *adj* expressif/-ive

exquisite /ˈekskwɪzɪt, ɪkˈskwɪzɪt/ *adj* exquis/-e

⚷ **extend** /ɪkˈstend/ **A** *vt* **1** agrandir ‹*house*›; prolonger ‹*runway*›; élargir ‹*range*›; **~ed family** famille *f* étendue
2 prolonger ‹*visit, visa*›
3 étendre ‹*arm, leg*›; tendre ‹*hand*›
B *vi* s'étendre (**as far as** jusqu'à, **from** de)

extension /ɪkˈstenʃn/ *n* **1** (on cable, table) rallonge *f*; (to house) addition *f*
2 (phone) poste *m* supplémentaire; **~ (number)** (numéro *m* de) poste *m*
3 (of deadline) délai *m* supplémentaire

extension lead *n* rallonge *f*

extensive /ɪkˈstensɪv/ *adj* **1** ‹*network*› vaste *before n*; ‹*list*› long/longue *before n*; ‹*tests*› approfondi/-e; ‹*changes*› important/-e
2 ‹*damage, loss*› grave, considérable; ‹*burns*› grave

⚷ **extent** /ɪkˈstent/ *n* **1** (of area, problem, power) étendue *f*; (of damage) ampleur *f*
2 (degree) mesure *f*; **to a certain/great ~** dans une certaine/large mesure

exterior /ɪkˈstɪərɪə(r)/ **A** *n* extérieur *m* (**of** de)
B *adj* extérieur/-e (**to** à)

exterminate /ɪkˈstɜːmɪneɪt/ *vt* éliminer ‹*vermin*›; exterminer ‹*people, race*›

external /ɪkˈstɜːnl/ *adj* (gen) extérieur/-e (**to** à); ‹*surface, injury, examiner*› externe

extinct /ɪkˈstɪŋkt/ *adj* ‹*species*› disparu/-e; ‹*volcano*› éteint/-e; **to become ~** ‹*species, animal, plant*› disparaître

extinguish /ɪkˈstɪŋgwɪʃ/ *vt* éteindre ‹*fire, cigarette*›

extinguisher /ɪkˈstɪŋgwɪʃə(r)/ *n* extincteur *m*

⚷ **extra** /ˈekstrə/ **A** *n* **1** (feature) option *f*; **the sunroof is an ~** le toit ouvrant est en option
2 (actor) figurant/-e *m/f*
B *adj* supplémentaire; **an ~ £1,000** 1 000 livres sterling de plus
C *adv* **~ careful** encore plus prudent (que d'habitude); **you have to pay ~** il faut payer un supplément

extra charge *n* supplément *m*

extract **A** /ˈekstrækt/ *n* extrait *m* (**from** de)
B /ɪkˈstrækt/ *vt* **1** extraire (**from** de)
2 arracher ‹*promise*› (**from** à)

extra-curricular /ˌekstrəkəˈrɪkjʊlə(r)/ *adj* parascolaire

extraordinary /ɪkˈstrɔːdnrɪ, (AmE) -dənerɪ/ *adj* extraordinaire

extraterrestrial /ˌekstrətəˈrestrɪəl/ *n*, *adj* extraterrestre *mf*

extra time *n* (BrE) (in sport) prolongation *f*; **to go into ~** jouer les prolongations

extravagance /ɪkˈstrævəgəns/ *n* **1** (trait) prodigalité *f*
2 (luxury) luxe *m*

extravagant /ɪkˈstrævəgənt/ *adj* **1** ‹*person*› dépensier/-ière; ‹*way of life*› dispendieux/-ieuse; **to be ~ with sth** gaspiller qch
2 (luxurious) luxueux/-euse

extra virgin olive oil *n* huile *f* d'olive extra vierge

extreme /ɪkˈstriːm/ **A** *n* extrême *m*; **to go to ~s** pousser les choses à l'extrême
B *adj* (gen) extrême; ‹*view, measure, reaction*› extrémiste

✓ **extremely** /ɪk'stri:mlɪ/ *adv* extrêmement
extreme sports *npl* sports *mpl* extrêmes
extremism /ɪk'stri:mɪzəm/ *n* extrémisme *m*
extrovert /'ekstrəvɜ:t/ *n, adj* extraverti/-e *m/f*
✓ **eye** /aɪ/ **A** *n* **1** œil *m*; **with blue ~s** aux yeux bleus; **in front of** *or* **before your (very) ~s** sous vos yeux; **to keep an ~ on sb/sth** surveiller qn/qch; **to have one's ~ on** (watch) surveiller ‹*person*›; (want) avoir envie de ‹*house*›; viser ‹*job*›; **to catch sb's ~** attirer l'attention de qn; **as far as the ~ can see** à perte de vue; **to have an ~ for** avoir le sens de ‹*detail*›
2 (of needle) chas *m*
B *vt* regarder
IDIOMS **an ~ for an ~** œil pour œil; **to make ~s at sb** faire les yeux doux à qn; **to see ~ to ~ with sb (about sth)** partager le point de vue de qn (au sujet de qch)
eyeball /'aɪbɔ:l/ *n* globe *m* oculaire
eyebrow /'aɪbraʊ/ *n* sourcil *m*
eyebrow pencil *n* crayon *m* à sourcils
eye-catching *adj* ‹*design, poster*› attrayant/-e; ‹*advertisement, headline*› accrocheur/-euse
eye drops *npl* gouttes *fpl* pour les yeux
eyelash *n* cil *m*
eyelid *n* paupière *f*
eye liner *n* eye-liner *m*
eye shadow *n* fard *m* à paupières
eyesight /'aɪsaɪt/ *n* vue *f*
eye test *n* examen *m* de la vue
eyewitness /'aɪwɪtnɪs/ *n* témoin *m* oculaire
e-zine /'i:zi:n/ *n* magazine *m* électronique, e-zine *m*

Ff

f, F /ef/ *n* **1** (letter) f, F *m*
2 F (Mus) fa *m*
fable /'feɪbl/ *n* fable *f*
fabric /'fæbrɪk/ *n* **1** (cloth) tissu *m*
2 (of building) structure *f*; **the ~ of society** le tissu social
fabricate /'fæbrɪkeɪt/ *vt* **1** inventer [qch] de toutes pièces ‹*story, evidence*›
2 fabriquer ‹*document*›
fabric softener *n* assouplissant *m*
fabulous /'fæbjʊləs/ *adj* **1** fabuleux/-euse
2 (fam) (wonderful) sensationnel/-elle (fam)
facade /fə'sɑ:d/ *n* façade *f* (**of** de)
✓ **face** /feɪs/ **A** *n* **1** (of person) visage *m*, figure *f*; (of animal) face *f*; **to slam the door/laugh in sb's ~** claquer la porte/rire au nez de qn; **to pull** *or* **make a ~** faire une grimace; (in disgust) faire la grimace
2 to lose ~ perdre la face; **to save ~** sauver la face
3 (of clock, watch) cadran *m*; (of coin) côté *m*; (of planet) surface *f*; (of cliff, mountain) face *f*; (of playing card) face *f*; **~ up/down** à l'endroit/l'envers
B *vt* **1** (look towards) ‹*person*› faire face à; ‹*building, room*› donner sur; **to ~ south** ‹*person*› regarder au sud; ‹*building*› être orienté/-e au sud
2 se trouver face à ‹*challenge, crisis*›; se trouver menacé/-e de ‹*defeat, redundancy*›; affronter ‹*rival, team*›; **to be ~d with** se trouver confronté/-e à ‹*problem, decision*›
3 (acknowledge) **~ the facts, you're finished!** regarde la réalité en face, tu es fini!; **let's ~ it, nobody's perfect** admettons-le, personne n'est parfait
4 (tolerate prospect) **I can't ~ doing** je n'ai pas le courage de faire; **he couldn't ~ the thought of eating** l'idée de manger lui était insupportable
5 revêtir ‹*facade, wall*› (**with** de)
C in the face of *phr* **1** en dépit de ‹*difficulties*›
2 face à, devant ‹*opposition, enemy, danger*›
D face to face *adv* ‹*be seated*› face à face; **to come ~ to ~ with** se retrouver face à; **to talk to sb ~ to ~** parler à qn en personne
▪ **face up to** faire face à ‹*problem, responsibilities*›
faceless /'feɪslɪs/ *adj* anonyme
facelift /'feɪslɪft/ *n* lifting *m*; **to have a ~** se faire faire un lifting; **to give [sth] a ~** rénover ‹*building*›; réaménager ‹*town centre*›
face mask /'feɪs mɑ:sk/ (AmE) -mæsk/ *n* masque *m* de beauté
facet /'fæsɪt/ *n* facette *f*
facetious /fə'si:ʃəs/ *adj* ‹*remark*› facétieux/-ieuse; ‹*person*› farceur/-euse
face-to-face /ˌfeɪstə'feɪs/ **A** *adj* **a ~ discussion, a ~ meeting** un face-à-face *inv*

✓ mot clé

B face to face *adv* = **face D**

face value *n* (of coin) valeur *f* nominale; **to take [sth] at ~** prendre [qch] au pied de la lettre; **to take sb at ~** juger qn sur les apparences

facilitate /fəˈsɪlɪteɪt/ *vt* faciliter ‹*progress, talks*›; favoriser ‹*development*›

facility /fəˈsɪlətɪ/ **A** *n* **1** (building) complexe *m*, installation *f*
2 (ease) facilité *f*
3 (feature) fonction *f*
B facilities *npl* (equipment) équipement *m*; (infrastructure) infrastructure *f*; **facilities for the disabled** installations *fpl* pour les handicapés; **parking facilities** parking *m*

facsimile /fækˈsɪməlɪ/ *n* (gen) fac-similé *m*; (sculpture) reproduction *f*

fact /fækt/ *n* fait *m*; **~s and figures** les faits et les chiffres; **to know for a ~ that** savoir de source sûre que; **due to the ~ that** étant donné que; **in ~, as a matter of ~** en fait; **to be based on ~** être fondé/-e sur des faits réels
(**IDIOMS**) **to know the ~s of life** savoir comment les enfants viennent au monde; **the (hard) ~s of life** les réalités de la vie

fact-finding /ˈfæktfaɪndɪŋ/ *adj* ‹*mission, tour*› d'information

faction /ˈfækʃn/ *n* (group) faction *f*

factor /ˈfæktə(r)/ *n* facteur *m*; **common ~** point *m* commun; (in mathematics) facteur commun; **protection ~** indice *m* de protection

factory /ˈfæktərɪ/ *n* usine *f*

factory farming *n* élevage *m* industriel

factory shop *n* magasin *m* d'usine

factory worker *n* ouvrier/-ière *m/f* (d'usine)

fact sheet *n* bulletin *m* d'informations

factual /ˈfæktʃʊəl/ *adj* ‹*evidence*› factuel/-elle; ‹*account, description*› basé/-e sur les faits; **~ programme** reportage *m*

faculty /ˈfækltɪ/ *n* (*pl* **-ties**) **1** (ability) faculté *f* (**for** de)
2 (BrE) (Univ) faculté *f*
3 (AmE) (Univ, Sch) (staff) corps *m* enseignant

fad /fæd/ *n* **1** (craze) engouement *m* (**for** pour)
2 (whim) (petite) manie *f*

fade /feɪd/ **A** *vt* décolorer
B *vi* ‹*fabric*› se décolorer, se défraîchir; ‹*colour*› passer; ‹*lettering, smile, memory*› s'effacer; ‹*flowers*› se faner; ‹*image*› s'estomper; ‹*sound*› s'affaiblir; ‹*interest, excitement*› s'évanouir; ‹*hearing, light*› baisser
■ **fade away** ‹*sound*› s'éteindre; ‹*sick person*› dépérir

faded /ˈfeɪdɪd/ *adj* ‹*clothing*› décoloré/-e; ‹*jeans*› délavé/-e; ‹*photo*› jauni/-e; ‹*flower*› fané/-e

faeces (BrE), **feces** (AmE) /ˈfiːsiːz/ *npl* matières *fpl* fécales

fail /feɪl/ **A** *n* (in exam) échec *m*
B *vt* **1** échouer à ‹*exam, driving test*›; échouer en ‹*subject*›; coller (fam) ‹*candidate, pupil*›
2 (omit) **to ~ to do** manquer de faire; **to ~ to mention that...** omettre de signaler que...
3 (be unable) **to ~ to do** ne pas réussir à faire
4 ‹*person*› laisser tomber ‹*friend*›; ‹*courage*› manquer à ‹*person*›; ‹*memory*› faire défaut à ‹*person*›
C *vi* **1** (not succeed) ne pas réussir; ‹*exam candidate, attempt, plan*› échouer; ‹*crop*› être mauvais/-e; **if all else ~s** en dernier recours
2 ‹*eyesight, hearing, light*› baisser; ‹*health*› décliner
3 ‹*brakes*› lâcher; ‹*power*› être coupé/-e; ‹*heart*› lâcher
D without fail *phr* ‹*arrive, do*› sans faute; ‹*happen*› à coup sûr

failing /ˈfeɪlɪŋ/ **A** *n* défaut *m*
B *prep* **~ that, ~ this** sinon

failure /ˈfeɪljə(r)/ *n* **1** (lack of success) échec *m* (**in** à)
2 (person) raté/-e *m/f* (fam); (venture or event) échec *m*
3 (of engine, machine) panne *f*
4 (Med) défaillance *f*
5 (omission) **~ to comply with the rules** non-respect *m* de la réglementation; **~ to pay** non-paiement *m*

faint /feɪnt/ **A** *adj* **1** ‹*smell, accent, breeze*› léger/-ère; ‹*sound, voice, protest*› faible; ‹*markings*› à peine visible; ‹*recollection*› vague; **I haven't the ~est idea** je n'en ai pas la moindre idée
2 to feel ~ se sentir mal, défaillir
B *vi* s'évanouir (**from** sous l'effet de)

faint-hearted /ˌfeɪntˈhɑːtɪd/ *n* **the ~** (cowardly) les timorés *mpl*; (over-sensitive) les natures *fpl* sensibles

fair /feə(r)/ **A** *n* (funfair, market) foire *f*; (for charity) kermesse *f*; **trade ~** foire commerciale
B *adj* **1** (just) ‹*arrangement, person, trial, wage*› équitable (**to** pour); ‹*comment, decision, point*› juste; **it's only ~ that she should be first** ce n'est que justice qu'elle soit la première; **it isn't ~** ce n'est pas juste
2 (quite good) assez bon/bonne
3 a ~ number of un bon nombre de; **the house was a ~ size** la maison était de bonne taille
4 ‹*weather*› beau/belle *before n*; ‹*wind*› favorable
5 ‹*hair*› blond/-e; ‹*complexion*› clair/-e
6 with her own ~ hands de ses blanches mains; **the ~ sex** le beau sexe
C *adv* ‹*play*› franc jeu
(**IDIOM**) **to win ~ and square** remporter une victoire indiscutable

fairground *n* champ *m* de foire

fair-haired *adj* blond/-e

fairly /ˈfeəlɪ/ *adv* **1** (quite, rather) assez; ‹*sure*› pratiquement
2 (justly) ‹*obtain, win*› honnêtement

fair-minded *adj* impartial/-e

fairness /ˈfeənɪs/ *n* **1** (of person) équité *f*; (of judgment) impartialité *f*; **in all ~** en toute justice
2 (of complexion) blancheur *f*; (of hair) blondeur *f*

fair play *n* **to have a sense of ~** jouer franc jeu, être fair-play; **to ensure ~** faire respecter les règles du jeu

fairy /ˈfeərɪ/ *n* fée *f*

fairy story, **fairy tale** *n* conte *m* de fées

faith /feɪθ/ *n* **1** (confidence) confiance *f*; **I have no ~ in her** elle ne m'inspire pas confiance; **in good ~** en toute bonne foi
2 (belief) foi *f* (**in** en); **the Muslim ~** la foi musulmane

faithful /ˈfeɪθfl/ **A** *n* **the ~** les fidèles *mpl*
B *adj* fidèle (**to** à)

faithfully /ˈfeɪθfəlɪ/ *adv* fidèlement; **yours ~** (in letter) veuillez agréer, Monsieur/Madame, mes/nos salutations distinguées

faith healer *n* guérisseur *m*

faith healing *n* guérison *f* par la foi

fake /feɪk/ **A** *n* **1** (jewel, work of art, note) faux *m*
2 (person) imposteur *m*
B *adj* faux/fausse *before n*
C *vt* contrefaire ‹*signature, document*›; falsifier ‹*results*›; feindre ‹*emotion, illness*›
D *vi* faire semblant

falcon /ˈfɔːlkən, (AmE) ˈfælkən/ *n* faucon *m*

Falklands /ˈfɔːkləndz/ *pr n pl* (*also* **Falkland Islands**) **the ~** les îles *fpl* Malouines

fall /fɔːl/ **A** *n* **1** (gen) chute *f* (**from** de); (in wrestling) tombé *m*
2 (decrease) baisse *f* (**in** de); (more drastic) chute *f* (**in** de)
3 (in pitch) descente *f*
4 (of government) chute *f*; (of monarchy) renversement *m*
5 (AmE) (autumn) automne *m*
B **falls** *npl* chutes *fpl*
C *vi* (*prét* **fell**, *pp* **fallen**) **1** (gen) tomber (**from, off, out of** de, **into** dans); **to ~ 10 metres** tomber de 10 mètres; **to ~ down** tomber dans ‹*hole, stairs*›; **to ~ on** *or* **to the floor** *or* **the ground** tomber par terre; **to ~ at sb's feet** se jeter aux pieds de qn; **to ~ from power** tomber
2 ‹*quality, standard, level*› diminuer; ‹*temperature, price, production, number*› baisser (**by** de); **to ~ to/from** descendre à/de

■ **fall apart 1** ‹*bike, table*› être délabré/-e; ‹*shoes*› être usé/-e; ‹*car, house*› tomber en ruine
2 ‹*country*› se désagréger; ‹*person*› craquer (fam)

■ **fall back** reculer; (Mil) se replier

■ **fall back on** avoir recours à ‹*savings, parents*›

■ **fall behind** prendre du retard; **to ~ behind with** (BrE) *or* **in** (AmE) prendre du retard dans ‹*work, project*›; être en retard pour ‹*payments, rent*›

■ **fall down 1** ‹*person, poster*› tomber; ‹*tent, scaffolding*› s'effondrer
2 (BrE) ‹*argument, comparison*› faiblir

■ **fall for**: **A** **~ for [sth]** se laisser prendre à ‹*trick, story*›
B **~ for [sb]** tomber amoureux/-euse de

■ **fall in 1** ‹*walls, roof*› s'écrouler, s'effondrer
2 ‹*soldiers*› former les rangs

■ **fall off 1** ‹*person, hat, label*› tomber
2 ‹*attendance, sales, output*› diminuer; ‹*quality*› baisser; ‹*support*› retomber

■ **fall open** ‹*book*› tomber ouvert/-e; ‹*robe*› s'entrebâiller

■ **fall out 1** tomber; **his hair is ~ing out** il perd ses cheveux
2 (quarrel) se brouiller (**over** à propos de, **with** avec)

■ **fall over**: **A** **~ over** ‹*person*› tomber (par terre); ‹*object*› se renverser
B **~ over [sth]** trébucher sur ‹*object*›

■ **fall through** ‹*plans, deal*› échouer

fallacy /ˈfæləsɪ/ *n* erreur *f*

fallible /ˈfæləbl/ *adj* faillible

fallout *n* retombées *fpl*

false /fɔːls/ *adj* faux/fausse

false alarm *n* fausse alerte *f*

false bottom *n* (in bag, box) double fond *m*

falsely /ˈfɔːlslɪ/ *adv* **1** (wrongly) faussement; (mistakenly) à tort
2 ‹*smile, laugh*› avec affectation

false pretences *npl* **on** *or* **under ~** en utilisant un subterfuge; (by an action) par des moyens frauduleux

false start *n* faux départ *m*

false teeth *npl* dentier *m*

falsify /ˈfɔːlsɪfaɪ/ *vt* falsifier

falsity /ˈfɔːlsətɪ/ *n* fausseté *f*

falter /ˈfɔːltə(r)/ *vi* **1** ‹*person, courage*› faiblir
2 (when speaking) ‹*person*› bafouiller; ‹*voice*› trembloter
3 (when walking) ‹*person*› chanceler; ‹*footstep*› hésiter

faltering /ˈfɔːltərɪŋ/ *adj* ‹*economy, demand*› en déclin; ‹*voice*› hésitant/-e

fame /feɪm/ *n* renommée *f* (**as** en tant que); **~ and fortune** la gloire et la fortune

familiar /fəˈmɪlɪə(r)/ *adj* familier/-ière (**to** à); **her face looked ~ to me** son visage m'était familier; **that name sounds ~** ce nom me dit quelque chose; **it's a ~ story** c'est un scénario connu; **to be ~ with sth** connaître qch

familiarity /fəˌmɪlɪˈærətɪ/ *n* familiarité *f* (**with** avec)

mot clé

familiarize /fə'mɪlɪəraɪz/ **A** *vt* **to ~ sb with** familiariser qn avec
B *v refl* **to ~ oneself with** se familiariser avec ‹*system, work*›; s'habituer à ‹*person, place*›

family /'fæməlɪ/ *n* famille *f*; **this must run in the ~** ça doit être de famille

family name *n* nom *m* de famille

family planning *n* planning *m* familial

family tree *n* arbre *m* généalogique

family unit *n* cellule *f* familiale

famine /'fæmɪn/ *n* famine *f*

famished /'fæmɪʃt/ *adj* (fam) **I'm ~** je meurs de faim

famous /'feɪməs/ *adj* (gen) célèbre (**for** pour); ‹*school, university*› réputé/-e (**for** pour)

fan /fæn/ **A** *n* **1** (of jazz) mordu/-e *m/f* (fam); (of star, actor) fan *mf* (fam); (Sport) supporter *m*
2 (for cooling) (mechanical) ventilateur *m*; (hand-held) éventail *m*
B *vt* (*p prés etc* **-nn-**) attiser ‹*fire*›; **to ~ one's face** s'éventer le visage
■ **fan out**: **A ~ out** ‹*police, troops*› se déployer (en éventail)
B ~ [sth] out ouvrir [qch] en éventail ‹*cards, papers*›

fanatic /fə'nætɪk/ *n* fanatique *mf*

fanaticism /fə'nætɪsɪzəm/ *n* fanatisme *m*

fan belt *n* courroie *f* de ventilateur

fancy /'fænsɪ/ **A** *n* **1** (liking) **to take sb's ~** ‹*object*› faire envie à qn; **to take a ~ to sb** s'attacher à qn; (sexually) (BrE) s'enticher de qn
2 (whim) caprice *m*; **as the ~ takes me** comme ça me prend
3 (fantasy) imagination *f*; **a flight of ~** une lubie
B *adj* ‹*equipment*› sophistiqué/-e; ‹*food, hotel, restaurant*› de luxe; ‹*paper, box*› fantaisie *inv*; ‹*clothes*› chic
C *vt* **1** (fam) (want) avoir (bien) envie de ‹*food, drink, object*›; **what do you ~ for lunch?** qu'est-ce qui te plairait pour le déjeuner?
2 (BrE) (fam) **she fancies him** elle s'est entichée de lui
3 ~ seeing you here! (fam) tiens donc, toi ici?
4 (Sport) voir [qn/qch] gagnant ‹*athlete, horse*›

fancy dress *n* (BrE) déguisement *m*; **in ~** déguisé/-e

fancy dress party *n* (BrE) bal *m* costumé

fang /fæŋ/ *n* (of dog, wolf) croc *m*; (of snake) crochet *m* (à venin)

fan mail *n* lettres *fpl* envoyées par des admirateurs

fantasize /'fæntəsaɪz/ *vi* fantasmer (**about** sur); **to ~ about doing** rêver de faire

fantastic /fæn'tæstɪk/ *adj* **1** (fam) (wonderful) merveilleux/-euse, super *inv* (fam)
2 (unrealistic) ‹*story*› invraisemblable
3 (fam) (huge) ‹*profit*› fabuleux/-euse; ‹*speed, increase*› vertigineux/-euse
4 (magical) fantastique

fantasy /'fæntəsɪ/ *n* **1** (dream) rêve *m*; (in psychology) fantasme *m*
2 (fiction) fantastique *m*

fanzine /'fænziːn/ *n* magazine *m* des fans, fanzine *m*

FAQ *n* (*abbr* = **frequently asked questions**) FAQ *f*, foire *f* aux questions

far /fɑː(r)/ **A** *adv* **1** (in space) loin; **~ off, ~ away** au loin; **is it ~ to York?** est-ce que York est loin d'ici?; **how ~ is it to Leeds?** combien y a-t-il (de kilomètres) jusqu'à Leeds?; **how ~ is Glasgow from London?** Glasgow est à quelle distance de Londres?; **as ~ as** jusqu'à
2 (in time) **as ~ back as 1965** déjà en 1965; **as ~ back as he can remember** d'aussi loin qu'il s'en souvienne; **the holidays are not ~ off** c'est bientôt les vacances
3 (very much) bien; **~ better** bien mieux; **~ too fast** bien trop vite
4 how ~ have they got? où en sont-ils?; **as ~ as possible** autant que possible, dans la mesure du possible; **as ~ as we know** pour autant que nous le sachions; **as ~ as I am concerned** quant à moi
5 to go too ~ aller trop loin; **to push sb too ~** pousser qn à bout
B *adj* **1 the ~ north/south (of)** l'extrême nord/sud (de); **the ~ east/west (of)** tout à fait à l'est/l'ouest (de)
2 autre; **at the ~ end of the room** à l'autre bout de la pièce; **on the ~ side of the wall** de l'autre côté du mur
3 (of party) **the ~ right/left** l'extrême droite/gauche
C by far *phr* de loin
D far from *phr* loin de; **~ from satisfied** loin d'être satisfait/-e
E so far *phr* **1** (up till now) jusqu'ici, jusqu'à présent; **so ~, so good** pour l'instant tout va bien
2 (up to a point) **you can only trust him so ~** tu ne peux pas lui faire entièrement confiance
IDIOMS **not to be ~ off** *or* **out** *or* **wrong** ne pas être loin du compte; **~ and wide** partout; **to be a ~ cry from** être bien loin de; **she will go ~** elle ira loin; **this wine won't go very ~** on ne va pas aller loin avec ce vin

faraway *adj* lointain/-e

farce /fɑːs/ *n* farce *f*

farcical /'fɑːsɪkl/ *adj* ridicule

fare /feə(r)/ *n* (on bus, underground) prix *m* du ticket; **half/full ~** demi-/plein tarif *m*

Far East *pr n* Extrême-Orient *m*

farewell /ˌfeə'wel/ *n* adieu *m*

far-fetched *adj* tiré/-e par les cheveux (fam)

✎ **farm** /fɑːm/ **A** *n* ferme *f*
B *vt* cultiver, exploiter ‹*land*›
■ **farm out**: **~ out [sth]** sous-traiter ‹*work*› (**to** à)

✎ **farmer** /ˈfɑːmə(r)/ *n* (gen) fermier *m*; (in official terminology) agriculteur *m*; (arable) cultivateur *m*; **pig ~** éleveur *m* de porcs

farmers' market *n* marché *m* de producteurs

farming /ˈfɑːmɪŋ/ *n* (profession) agriculture *f*; (of land) exploitation *f*; **sheep ~** élevage *m* de moutons

farmyard /ˈfɑːmjɑːd/ *n* cour *f* de ferme

far off *adj* lointain/-e

far-reaching /ˌfɑːˈriːtʃɪŋ/ *adj* ‹*effect*› considérable; ‹*change, reform*› radical/-e; ‹*plan, proposal*› d'une portée considérable

far-sighted /ˌfɑːˈsaɪtɪd/ *adj* **1** (prudent) ‹*person, policy*› prévoyant/-e
2 (AmE) ‹*person*› presbyte

farther /ˈfɑːðə(r)/ *adj*, *adv* (*comparative of* **far**) = **further A1, A2, B2**

farthest /ˈfɑːðɪst/ = **furthest**

fascinate /ˈfæsɪneɪt/ *vt* (interest) passionner; (stronger) fasciner

fascinating /ˈfæsɪneɪtɪŋ/ *adj* ‹*book, discussion*› passionnant/-e; ‹*person*› fascinant/-e

fascination /ˌfæsɪˈneɪʃn/ *n* passion *f* (**with, for** pour)

fascism /ˈfæʃɪzəm/ *n* fascisme *m*

fascist /ˈfæʃɪst/ *n*, *adj* fasciste *mf*

✎ **fashion** /ˈfæʃn/ **A** *n* **1** mode *f* (**for** de); **in ~** à la mode; **to go out of ~** se démoder, passer de mode; **to be all the ~** faire fureur
2 (manner) façon *f*, manière *f*; **after a ~** plus ou moins bien
B *vt* façonner ‹*clay, wood*› (**into** en); fabriquer ‹*object*› (**out of, from** de)

fashionable /ˈfæʃnəbl/ *adj* ‹*clothes*› à la mode (**among, with** parmi); ‹*resort, restaurant*› chic (**among, with** parmi)

fashion designer *n* modéliste *mf*; (world-famous) grand couturier *m*

fashion house *n* maison *f* de couture

fashion model *n* mannequin *m*

fashion show *n* présentation *f* de collection

✎ **fast** /fɑːst, (AmE) fæst/ **A** *n* jeûne *m*
B *adj* **1** rapide; **to be a ~ reader/runner** lire/courir vite
2 (ahead of time) **my watch is ~** ma montre avance; **you're five minutes ~** ta montre avance de cinq minutes
C *adv* **1** vite, rapidement; **how ~ can you run?** est-ce que tu cours vite?
2 ‹*hold*› ferme; ‹*stuck*› bel et bien; ‹*shut*› bien; **to be ~ asleep** dormir à poings fermés

fasten /ˈfɑːsn, (AmE) ˈfæsn/ **A** *vt* **1** fermer ‹*lid, case*›; attacher ‹*belt, necklace*›; boutonner ‹*coat*›
2 fixer ‹*notice, shelf*› (**to** à, **onto** sur); attacher ‹*lead, rope*› (**to** à)
B *vi* ‹*box*› se fermer; ‹*necklace, skirt*› s'attacher

fastener /ˈfɑːsnə(r), (AmE) ˈfæsnə(r)/ *n* (gen) attache *f*; (hook) agrafe *f*; (clasp) fermoir *m*

fast food /ˌfɑːstˈfuːd, (AmE) ˌfæst-/ *n* restauration *f* rapide

fast food restaurant *n* fast-food *m*, restovite *m*

fast-forward /ˌfɑːstˈfɔːwəd, (AmE) ˌfæst-/ **A** *n* avance *f* rapide
B *vt* faire avancer rapidement ‹*tape*›

fast-growing *adj* en pleine expansion

fast lane /ˈfɑːstleɪn, (AmE) ˈfæst-/ *n* voie *f* de dépassement

fast track **A** *n* promotion *f* accélérée
B **fast-track** *vt* former [qn] de façon accélérée

fat /fæt/ **A** *n* **1** (in diet) matières *fpl* grasses; **animal ~s** graisses *fpl* animales
2 (on meat) gras *m*
3 (for cooking) matière *f* grasse
4 (in body) graisse *f*
B *adj* **1** ‹*person, animal, body, bottom*› gros/grosse *before n*; **to get ~** grossir
2 ‹*wallet*› rebondi/-e; ‹*envelope, file, magazine*› épais/épaisse
3 ‹*profit, cheque*› gros/grosse *before n*

fatal /ˈfeɪtl/ *adj* ‹*accident, injury*› mortel/-elle (**to** pour); ‹*flaw, mistake*› fatal/-e; ‹*decision*› funeste; ‹*day, hour*› fatidique

fatalist /ˈfeɪtəlɪst/ *n* fataliste *mf*

fatality /fəˈtælətɪ/ *n* (person killed) mort *m*

fatally /ˈfeɪtəlɪ/ *adv* **1** ‹*wounded*› mortellement
2 ‹*flawed*› irrémédiablement

fate /feɪt/ *n* sort *m*

fateful /ˈfeɪtfl/ *adj* ‹*decision*› fatal/-e; ‹*day*› fatidique

fat-free *adj* sans matières grasses

✎ **father** /ˈfɑːðə(r)/ **A** *n* père *m*
B *vt* engendrer ‹*child*›

Father Christmas *n* (BrE) le père Noël

father-in-law *n* (*pl* **~s-in-law**) beau-père *m*

fatherly /ˈfɑːðəlɪ/ *adj* paternel/-elle

fathom /ˈfæðəm/ **A** *n* brasse *f* anglaise (= *1.83 m*)
B *vt* (*also* **~ out** (BrE)) comprendre

fatigue /fəˈtiːg/ *n* **1** (of person) épuisement *m*
2 metal ~ fatigue *f* du métal
3 (AmE) (Mil) corvée *f*

fatten /ˈfætn/ *vt* (*also* **~ up**) engraisser ‹*animal*›; faire grossir ‹*person*›

fattening /ˈfætnɪŋ/ *adj* ‹*food, drink*› qui fait grossir

fatty /ˈfætɪ/ *adj* ‹*tissue, deposit*› graisseux/-euse; ‹*food, meat*› gras/grasse

fatuous /ˈfætʃʊəs/ *adj* stupide

✎ mot clé

faucet /'fɔːsɪt/ *n* (AmE) robinet *m*

fault /fɔːlt/ **A** *n* **1** (flaw) défaut *m* (**in** dans); **he's always finding ~** il trouve toujours quelque chose à redire
2 (responsibility) faute *f*; **to be sb's ~** être (de) la faute de qn; **it's my own ~** c'est de ma faute
3 (in tennis) **~!** faute!
4 (in earth) faille *f*
B *vt* prendre [qn/qch] en défaut; **it cannot be ~ed** c'est irréprochable

faultless /'fɔːltlɪs/ *adj* ‹*performance, manners*› impeccable; ‹*taste*› irréprochable

faulty /'fɔːltɪ/ *adj* ‹*wiring, machine*› défectueux/-euse

fauna /'fɔːnə/ *n* (*pl* **~s** *ou* **-ae**) faune *f*

faux pas /ˌfəʊ 'pɑː/ *n* (*pl* **~**) impair *m*

favour (BrE), **favor** (AmE) /'feɪvə(r)/ **A** *n*
1 (kindness) service *m*; **to do sb a ~** rendre service à qn; **to return a** *or* **the ~** rendre la pareille
2 to be in sb's ~ ‹*situation*› être avantageux/-euse pour qn; ‹*financial rates, wind*› être favorable à qn
3 to win/lose ~ with sb s'attirer/perdre les bonnes grâces de qn
B *vt* **1** (prefer) être pour ‹*method, solution*›; être partisan de ‹*political party*›
2 (benefit) ‹*circumstances*› favoriser ‹*person*›; ‹*law*› privilégier ‹*person*›
C in favour of *phr* **1** (on the side of) en faveur de; **to be in ~ of sb/sth** être pour qn/qch
2 (to the advantage of) **to work in sb's ~** avantager qn; **to decide in sb's ~** (Law) donner gain de cause à qn
3 (out of preference for) ‹*reject*› au profit de

favourable (BrE), **favorable** (AmE) /'feɪvərəbl/ *adj* ‹*conditions, impression, reply*› favorable (**to** à); ‹*result, sign*› bon/bonne *before n*

favourably (BrE), **favorably** (AmE) /'feɪvərəblɪ/ *adv* ‹*speak, write*› en termes favorables; ‹*look on*› d'un œil favorable; **to compare ~ with sth** soutenir la comparaison avec qch

favourite (BrE), **favorite** (AmE) /'feɪvərɪt/
A *n* (gen) préféré/-e *m/f*; (Sport) favori/-ite *m/f*
B *adj* préféré/-e, favori/-ite

favouritism (BrE), **favoritism** (AmE) /'feɪvərɪtɪzəm/ *n* favoritisme *m*

fawn /fɔːn/ **A** *n* (Zool) faon *m*
B *vi* **to ~ on sb** flagorner qn

fax /fæks/ **A** *n* (*pl* **~es**) **1** (*also* **~ message**) télécopie *f*, fax *m*
2 (*also* **~ machine**) télécopieur *m*, fax *m*
B *vt* télécopier, faxer ‹*document*›; envoyer une télécopie *or* un fax à ‹*person*›

fax number *n* numéro *m* de télécopie *or* de fax

faze /feɪz/ *vt* (fam) dérouter

fear /fɪə(r)/ **A** *n* **1** (fright) peur *f*
2 (apprehension) crainte *f* (**for** pour)
3 (possibility) **there's no ~ of him** *or* **his being late** il n'y a pas de danger qu'il soit en retard
B *vt* craindre; **to ~ the worst** craindre le pire, s'attendre au pire
C *vi* **to ~ for sb/sth** craindre pour qn/qch

fearless /'fɪəlɪs/ *adj* sans peur, intrépide

feasible /'fiːzəbl/ *adj* **1** ‹*project*› réalisable
2 ‹*excuse, explanation*› plausible

feast /fiːst/ **A** *n* (meal) festin *m*; (religious) fête *f*
B *vi* se régaler (**on** de)

feat /fiːt/ *n* exploit *m*; **it was no mean ~** cela n'a pas été une mince affaire; **a ~ of engineering** une prouesse technologique

feather /'feðə(r)/ *n* plume *f*

feature /'fiːtʃə(r)/ **A** *n* **1** (distinctive characteristic) trait *m*, caractéristique *f*
2 (aspect) aspect *m*, côté *m*
3 (of face) trait *m*
4 (of car, computer, product) accessoire *m*
5 (report) (in paper) article *m* de fond (**on** sur); (on TV, radio) reportage *m* (**on** sur)
B *vt* ‹*film, magazine*› présenter ‹*story, star*›; ‹*advert, poster*› représenter ‹*person*›
C *vi* **1** (figure) figurer
2 ‹*performer*› jouer (**in** dans)

feature film *n* long métrage *m*

February /'februərɪ, (AmE) -ʊerɪ/ *n* février *m*

federal /'fedərəl/ *adj* fédéral/-e

federation /ˌfedə'reɪʃn/ *n* fédération *f*

fed up /ˌfed 'ʌp/ *adj* (fam) **to be ~** en avoir marre (fam) (**of** de)

fee /fiː/ *n* **1** (for service) honoraires *mpl*; **school ~s** frais *mpl* de scolarité
2 (for admission) droit *m* d'entrée; (for membership) cotisation *f*

feeble /'fiːbl/ *adj* (gen) faible; ‹*excuse*› peu convaincant/-e; ‹*joke, attempt*› médiocre

feed /fiːd/ **A** *n* (for animals) ration *f* de nourriture; (for baby) (breast) tétée *f*; (bottle) biberon *m*
B *vt* (*prét, pp* **fed**) **1** nourrir ‹*animal, plant, person*› (**on** de); donner à manger à ‹*pet*›; ravitailler ‹*army*›
2 (supply) alimenter ‹*machine*›; mettre des pièces dans ‹*meter*›; faire passer ‹*ball*› (**to** à); **to ~ sth into** mettre *or* introduire qch dans

feedback /'fiːdbæk/ *n* **1** (from people) remarques *fpl* (**on** sur, **from** de la part de)
2 (on hi-fi) réaction *f* parasite

feeding bottle *n* biberon *m*

feel /fiːl/ **A** *n* **1** (atmosphere) atmosphère *f*
2 (sensation) sensation *f*
3 to get the ~ of se faire à ‹*controls, system*›; **to have a ~ for language** bien savoir manier la langue
B *vt* (*prét, pp* **felt**) **1** éprouver ‹*affection, desire, pride*›; ressentir ‹*hostility, obligation, effects*›

2 (believe) **to ~ (that)** estimer que
3 sentir ‹*blow, draught, heat*›; ressentir ‹*ache, stiffness, effects*›
4 (touch) tâter ‹*washing, cloth*›; palper ‹*patient, shoulder, parcel*›; **to ~ one's way** avancer à tâtons; (fig) tâter le terrain
5 avoir conscience de ‹*presence, tension*›
C *vi* (*prét*, *pp* **felt**) **1** se sentir ‹*sad, happy, nervous, safe, ill, tired*›; être ‹*sure, surprised*›; avoir l'impression d'être ‹*trapped, betrayed*›; **to ~ afraid/ashamed** avoir peur/honte; **to ~ hot/thirsty** avoir chaud/soif; **to ~ as if** *or* **as though** avoir l'impression que; **she isn't ~ing herself today** elle n'est pas dans son assiette aujourd'hui (fam)
2 (seem) être ‹*cold, smooth*›; avoir l'air ‹*eerie*›; **it ~s odd** ça fait drôle; **it ~s like (a) Sunday** on se croirait un dimanche
3 (want) **to ~ like sth** avoir envie de qch; **I ~ like a drink** je prendrais bien un verre
4 to ~ (around *or* **about) in** fouiller dans ‹*bag, pocket, drawer*›; **to ~ along** tâtonner le long de ‹*edge, wall*›

■ **feel for**: **A** **~ (around) for [sth]** chercher [qch] à tâtons
B **~ for [sb]** plaindre

■ **feel up to**: **~ up to (doing) sth** se sentir d'attaque (fam) *or* assez bien pour (faire) qch

feel-good /fi:lgʊd/ *adj* optimiste; **to play on the ~ factor** essayer de créer un sentiment de bien-être

⚷ **feeling** /ˈfi:lɪŋ/ *n* **1** (emotion) sentiment *m*; **to hurt sb's ~s** blesser qn
2 (opinion, belief) sentiment *m*; **~s are running high** les esprits s'échauffent
3 (sensitivity) sensibilité *f*; **to speak with great ~** parler avec beaucoup de passion
4 (impression) impression *f*; **I had a ~ you'd say that** je sentais que tu allais dire ça; **I've got a bad ~ about this** j'ai le pressentiment que cela va mal se passer
5 (physical sensation) sensation *f*; **a dizzy ~** une sensation de vertige

fee-paying /ˈfi:peɪɪŋ/ *adj* ‹*school*› payant/-e

feign /feɪn/ *vt* feindre ‹*innocence, surprise*›; simuler ‹*illness, sleep*›

fell /fel/ **A** *n* montagne *f*
B *vt* abattre ‹*tree*›; assommer ‹*person*›
IDIOM **in one ~ swoop** d'un seul coup

⚷ **fellow** /ˈfeləʊ/ **A** *n* **1** (fam) (man) type *m* (fam), homme *m*
2 (of society, association) membre *m* (**of** de)
3 (BrE) (lecturer) membre *m* (du corps enseignant) d'un collège universitaire
4 (AmE) (researcher) universitaire *mf* titulaire d'une bourse de recherche
B *adj* **her ~ teachers** ses collègues professeurs; **a ~ Englishman** un compatriote anglais

fellowship /ˈfeləʊʃɪp/ *n* **1** (companionship) camaraderie *f*
2 (association) association *f*

felony /ˈfelənɪ/ *n* crime *m*

felt /felt/ *n* feutre *m*

felt-tip pen, **felt-tip** *n* feutre *m*

⚷ **female** /ˈfi:meɪl/ **A** *n* **1** (Bot, Zool) femelle *f*
2 (woman) femme *f*
B *adj* **1** (Bot, Zool) femelle; **~ rabbit** lapine *f*
2 ‹*population, role*› féminin/-e; ‹*voice*› de femme; **~ student** étudiante *f*
3 ‹*plug, socket*› femelle

feminine /ˈfemənɪn/ **A** *n* féminin *m*
B *adj* féminin/-e

feminist /ˈfemɪnɪst/ *n, adj* féministe *mf*

fence /fens/ **A** *n* **1** clôture *f*
2 (in showjumping) obstacle *m*; (in horseracing) haie *f*
B *vt* clôturer ‹*area, garden*›
IDIOM **to sit on the ~** ne pas prendre position

fencing /ˈfensɪŋ/ *n* escrime *f*

fend /fend/ *vi* **to ~ for oneself** se débrouiller (tout seul/toute seule)

■ **fend off** repousser ‹*attacker*›; parer ‹*blow*›; écarter ‹*question*›

fender /ˈfendə(r)/ *n* **1** (for fire) garde-cendre *m*
2 (AmE) (Aut) aile *f*

fennel /ˈfenl/ *n* fenouil *m*

fern /fɜ:n/ *n* fougère *f*

ferocious /fəˈrəʊʃəs/ *adj* ‹*animal*› féroce; ‹*attack*› sauvage; ‹*heat*› accablant/-e

ferret /ˈferɪt/ *n* furet *m*

■ **ferret about** fureter, fouiller (**in** dans)

ferry /ˈferɪ/ **A** *n* (long-distance) ferry *m*; (over short distances) bac *m*
B *vt* transporter ‹*passenger, goods*›

fertile /ˈfɜ:taɪl, (AmE) ˈfɜ:rtl/ *adj* ‹*land, imagination*› fertile; ‹*human, animal, egg*› fécond/-e

fertility treatment *n* traitement *m* contre la stérilité

fertilize /ˈfɜ:tɪlaɪz/ *vt* fertiliser ‹*land*›; féconder ‹*animal, plant, egg*›

fertilizer /ˈfɜ:tɪlaɪzə(r)/ *n* engrais *m*

fervent /ˈfɜ:vənt/ *adj* ‹*admirer*› fervent/-e

fester /ˈfestə(r)/ *vi* ‹*wound, sore*› suppurer

⚷ **festival** /ˈfestɪvl/ *n* (gen) fête *f*; (arts event) festival *m*

festivity /feˈstɪvətɪ/ *n* réjouissance *f*

fetch /fetʃ/ *vt* **1** aller chercher; **~!** (to dog) rapporte!
2 ‹*goods*› rapporter; **to ~ a good price** rapporter un bon prix; **these vases can ~ up to £600** le prix de ces vases peut atteindre 600 livres sterling

fetching /ˈfetʃɪŋ/ *adj* ravissant/-e

fête *n* (church, village) kermesse *f* (paroissiale)

fetus (AmE) = **foetus**

feud /fju:d/ **A** *n* querelle *f*
B *vi* se quereller

feudal /ˈfju:dl/ *adj* féodal/-e

⚷ mot clé

fever /ˈfiːvə(r)/ *n* fièvre *f*; **to have a ~** avoir de la fièvre; **gold ~** la fièvre de l'or

feverish /ˈfiːvərɪʃ/ *adj* ‹*person, eyes*› fiévreux/-euse; ‹*dreams*› délirant/-e; ‹*excitement, activity*› fébrile

fever pitch *n* **to bring a crowd to ~** déchaîner une foule; **our excitement had reached ~** notre excitation était à son comble

few /fjuː/

> When **a few** is used as a pronoun and if the sentence does not specify what it refers to, the pronoun *en* (= *of them*) must be added before the verb in French: *there were only a few* = il n'y en avait que quelques-uns/quelques-unes.

A *det* **1** (not many) peu de; **~ visitors/letters** peu de visiteurs/lettres
2 (couple of) **every ~ days** tous les deux ou trois jours; **the first ~ weeks** les premières semaines
B *pron, quantif* peu; **~ of us succeeded** peu d'entre nous ont réussi
C a few *det, quantif, pron* **1** (as determiner, quantifier) quelques; **a ~ people** quelques personnes; **quite a ~ people** pas mal (fam) de gens, un bon nombre de personnes; **a ~ of the soldiers** quelques soldats; **a ~ of us** un certain nombre d'entre nous
2 (as pronoun) quelques-uns/quelques-unes; **I would like a ~ more** j'en voudrais quelques-uns/quelques-unes de plus; **I only need a ~** il ne m'en faut que quelques-uns/quelques-unes
IDIOM **they are ~ and far between** ils sont rarissimes

fewer /ˈfjuːə(r)/ **A** *det* moins de; **~ and ~ pupils** de moins en moins d'élèves
B *pron* (*comparative of* **few**) moins; **~ than 50 people** moins de 50 personnes; **no ~ than** pas moins de

fewest /ˈfjuːɪst/ *det* le moins de

fiancé /fɪˈɒnseɪ, (AmE) ˌfiːɑːnˈseɪ/ *n* fiancé *m*

fiancée /fɪˈɒnseɪ, (AmE) ˌfiːɑːnˈseɪ/ *n* fiancée *f*

fibre (BrE), **fiber** (AmE) /ˈfaɪbə(r)/ *n* **1** (gen) fibre *f*
2 (in diet) fibres *fpl*

fibreglass (BrE), **fiberglass** (AmE) /ˈfaɪbəglɑːs/ *n* fibres *fpl* de verre

fibre optic (BrE), **fiber optic** (AmE) *adj* ‹*cable*› à fibres optiques; ‹*link*› par fibres optiques

fickle /ˈfɪkl/ *adj* ‹*lover, friend*› inconstant/-e; ‹*fate, public opinion*› changeant/-e; ‹*weather*› capricieux/-ieuse

fiction /ˈfɪkʃn/ *n* **1** (genre) le roman
2 (invention) fiction *f*

fictional /ˈfɪkʃənl/ *adj* ‹*character, event*› imaginaire

fictionalize /ˈfɪkʃənəlaɪz/ *vt* romancer

fictitious /fɪkˈtɪʃəs/ *adj* **1** (false) ‹*name, address*› fictif/-ive
2 (imaginary) imaginaire

fiddle /ˈfɪdl/ **A** *vt* (fam) falsifier ‹*tax return, figures*›
B *vi* **1** (fidget) **to ~ with sth** tripoter qch
2 (adjust) **to ~ with** tourner ‹*knobs, controls*›

fidelity /fɪˈdelətɪ/ *n* fidélité *f* (**of** de, **to** à)

fidget /ˈfɪdʒɪt/ *vi* ne pas tenir en place

field /fiːld/ **A** *n* **1** (gen) champ *m* (**of** de); (sports ground) terrain *m*; **football ~** terrain de football
2 (of knowledge) domaine *m* (**of** de)
B *adj* **1** ‹*hospital*› de campagne
2 ‹*test, study*› sur le terrain; ‹*work*› de terrain

field day *n* **1** (school trip) sortie *f* (éducative)
2 (AmE) (sports day) journée *f* sportive
IDIOM **to have a ~** (gen) s'amuser comme un fou/une folle; ‹*press, critics*› jubiler; (make money) ‹*shopkeepers*› faire d'excellentes affaires

field trip *n* (one day) sortie *f* éducative; (longer) voyage *m* d'études

fieldwork *n* travail *m* de terrain

fierce /fɪəs/ *adj* ‹*animal, expression, person*› féroce; ‹*battle, storm*› violent/-e; ‹*competition*› acharné/-e; ‹*flames, heat*› intense

fiercely /ˈfɪəslɪ/ *adv* ‹*oppose*› avec acharnement; ‹*fight*› sauvagement; ‹*shout*› violemment; ‹*burn*› avec intensité; ‹*competitive, critical*› extrêmement; ‹*determined, loyal*› farouchement

fifteen /ˌfɪfˈtiːn/ *n, pron, det* quinze *m inv*

fifteenth /ˌfɪfˈtiːnθ/ **A** *n* **1** (in order) quinzième *mf*
2 (of month) quinze *m inv*
3 (fraction) quinzième *m*
B *adj, adv* quinzième

fifth /fɪfθ/ **A** *n* **1** (in order) cinquième *mf*
2 (of month) cinq *m*
3 (fraction) cinquième *m*
B *adj, adv* cinquième

fifties *npl* **1** (era) **the ~** les années *fpl* cinquante
2 (age) **to be in one's ~** avoir entre cinquante et soixante ans

fiftieth /ˈfɪftɪəθ/ *n, adj, adv* cinquantième *mf*

fifty /ˈfɪftɪ/ *n, pron, det* cinquante *m inv*

fifty-fifty /ˌfɪftɪˈfɪftɪ/ **A** *adj* **to have a ~ chance** avoir une chance sur deux (**of doing** de faire)
B *adv* **to share sth ~** partager qch moitié-moitié; **to go ~** faire moitié-moitié

fig /fɪg/ *n* figue *f*

fight /faɪt/ **A** *n* **1** (gen) bagarre *f* (**between** entre, **over** pour); (Mil) bataille *f* (**between** entre, **for** pour); (in boxing) combat *m* (**between** entre)
2 (struggle) lutte *f* (**against** contre, **for** pour, **to do** pour faire)
3 (argument) dispute *f* (**over** au sujet de, **with** avec)

B *vt* (*prét*, *pp* **fought**) **1** se battre contre ‹*person*›
2 lutter contre ‹*disease, opponent, emotion, proposal*›; combattre ‹*fire*›; mener ‹*campaign, war*› (**against** contre); **to ~ one's way through** se frayer un passage dans ‹*crowd*›
C *vi* (*prét*, *pp* **fought**) **1** (gen), (Mil) se battre
2 (campaign) lutter
3 (argue) se quereller (**over** à propos de)
▪ **fight back**: **A** **~ back** se défendre
B **~ back [sth]** refréner ‹*tears, fear, anger*›
▪ **fight off**: **A** **~ off [sth]**, **~ [sth] off** se libérer de ‹*attacker*›; repousser ‹*attack*›
B **~ off [sth]** lutter contre ‹*illness*›; rejeter ‹*criticism, proposal*›

fighter /ˈfaɪtə(r)/ *n* **1** (Sport) boxeur *m*
2 (determined person) lutteur/-euse *m/f*
3 (*also* **~ plane**) avion *m* de chasse

fighting /ˈfaɪtɪŋ/ **A** *n* (gen) bagarre *f*; (Mil) combat *m*
B *adj* **1** ‹*unit, force*› de combat
2 ‹*talk*› agressif/-ive

fighting chance *n* **to have a ~** avoir de bonnes chances

fighting fit *adj* **to be ~** être en pleine forme

figment /ˈfɪgmənt/ *n* **a ~ of your imagination** un produit de ton imagination

figurative /ˈfɪgərətɪv/ *adj* figuré/-e

⚷ **figure** /ˈfɪgə(r), (AmE) ˈfɪgjər/ **A** *n* **1** chiffre *m*; **a four-~ number** un nombre de quatre chiffres; **in double ~s** à deux chiffres
2 (person) personnage *m*; **well-known ~** personnalité *f* célèbre; **father ~** image *f* du père
3 (body shape) ligne *f*; **to lose one's ~** prendre de l'embonpoint
4 (diagram, shape) figure *f*
B *vi* (appear) figurer (**in** dans)
▪ **figure out** trouver ‹*answer, reason*›; **to ~ out who/why** arriver à comprendre qui/pourquoi

figurehead /ˈfɪgəhed, (AmE) ˈfɪgjər-/ *n* (symbolic leader) représentant/-e *m/f* nominal/-e; (of ship) figure *f* de proue

figure of speech /ˌfɪgə əv ˈspiːtʃ, (AmE) ˌfɪgjər-/ *n* figure *f* de rhétorique

figure skating *n* patinage *m* artistique

⚷ **file** /faɪl/ **A** *n* **1** (for papers) (gen) dossier *m*; (cardboard) chemise *f*; (binder) classeur *m*
2 (record) dossier *m* (**on** sur)
3 (Comput) fichier *m*
4 (tool) lime *f*
5 in single ~ en file indienne
B *vt* **1** classer ‹*invoice, letter, record*› (**under** sous)
2 déposer ‹*application, complaint*› (**with** auprès de); **to ~ a lawsuit (against sb)** intenter *or* faire un procès (à qn)
3 limer ‹*wood, metal*›; **to ~ one's nails** se limer les ongles
C *vi* **they ~d into/out of the classroom** ils sont entrés dans/sortis de la salle l'un après l'autre

file cabinet (AmE), **filing cabinet** *n* classeur *m* à tiroirs

file-sharing *n* partage *m* de fichiers

⚷ **fill** /fɪl/ **A** *vt* **1** remplir ‹*container, page*› (**with** de); garnir ‹*cushion, pie, sandwich*› (**with** de); ‹*dentist*› plomber ‹*tooth, cavity*›
2 ‹*crowd, sound*› remplir ‹*room, street*›; ‹*smoke, protesters*› envahir ‹*building, room*›; occuper ‹*time, day, hours*›; ‹*emotion, thought*› remplir ‹*mind, person*›
3 boucher ‹*crack, hole, void*› (**with** avec)
4 répondre à ‹*need*›
5 ‹*company, university*› pourvoir ‹*post, vacancy*›
6 ‹*applicant*› occuper ‹*post, vacancy*›
7 ‹*wind*› gonfler ‹*sail*›
B *vi* se remplir (**with** de)
▪ **fill in**: **A** **to ~ in for sb** remplacer qn
B **~ [sth] in** remplir ‹*form*›; donner ‹*detail, name, date*›
C **~ [sb] in** mettre [qn] au courant (**on** de)
▪ **fill out**: **A** **~ out** ‹*person*› prendre du poids; ‹*face*› s'arrondir
B **~ [sth] out** remplir ‹*form*›; faire ‹*prescription*›
▪ **fill up**: **A** **~ up** ‹*bath, theatre, bus*› se remplir (**with** de)
B **~ [sth] up** remplir ‹*kettle, box, room*› (**with** de)

filler /ˈfɪlə(r)/ *n* **1** (for car body) mastic *m*; (for wall) reboucheur *m*
2 (TV show) bouche-trou *m*

fillet /ˈfɪlɪt/ **A** *n* filet *m*; **~ steak** filet de bœuf
B *vt* enlever les arêtes de, fileter ‹*fish*›

filling /ˈfɪlɪŋ/ **A** *n* **1** (of sandwich, baked potato) garniture *f*; (for peppers, meat) farce *f*
2 (for tooth) plombage *m*
B *adj* ‹*food, dish*› bourratif/-ive (fam)

filling station *n* station-service *f*

⚷ **film** /fɪlm/ **A** *n* **1** (movie) film *m*
2 (for camera) pellicule *f*
3 (layer) pellicule *f*
B *vt* filmer
C *vi* tourner

film fan *n* cinéphile *mf*

film festival *n* festival *m* de cinéma

film industry *n* industrie *f* cinématographique

filming /ˈfɪlmɪŋ/ *n* tournage *m*

film set *n* plateau *m* de tournage

film star *n* vedette *f* de cinéma

film studio *n* studio *m* de cinéma

filter /ˈfɪltə(r)/ **A** *n* filtre *m*
B *vt* filtrer ‹*liquid, gas*›; faire passer ‹*coffee*›
C *vi* **to ~ into** ‹*light, sound, water*› pénétrer dans ‹*area*›

⚷ mot clé

filth /fɪlθ/ *n* **1** (dirt) crasse *f*
2 (vulgarity) obscénités *fpl*; (swearing) grossièretés *fpl*

filthy /'fɪlθɪ/ *adj* **1** (dirty) crasseux/-euse; (revolting) répugnant/-e
2 ‹*language*› ordurier/-ière; ‹*mind*› mal tourné/-e
3 (BrE) ‹*look*› noir/-e

fin /fɪn/ *n* (of fish, seal) nageoire *f*; (of shark) aileron *m*

🔑 **final** /'faɪnl/ **A** *n* (Sport) finale *f*
B *adj* **1** (last) dernier/-ière
2 ‹*decision*› définitif/-ive; ‹*result*› final/-e

finale /fɪ'nɑːlɪ, (AmE) -nælɪ/ *n* finale *f*

finalist /'faɪnəlɪst/ *n* finaliste *mf*

finalize /'faɪnəlaɪz/ *vt* conclure ‹*contract*›; arrêter ‹*plan, details*›; faire la dernière mise au point de ‹*article*›; fixer ‹*timetable, route*›

🔑 **finally** /'faɪnəlɪ/ *adv* **1** (eventually) finalement, enfin
2 (lastly) finalement, pour finir
3 (definitively) définitivement

finals /'faɪnlz/ *npl* (BrE) (Univ) examens *mpl* de fin d'études; (AmE) (Univ) examens *mpl* de fin de semestre

finance /'faɪnæns, fɪ'næns/ **A** *n* **1** (gen) finance *f*
2 (funds) fonds *mpl* (**for** pour, **from** auprès de)
B *vt* financer ‹*project*›

finance company *n* société *f* de financement

finances *npl* situation *f* financière

🔑 **financial** /faɪ'nænʃl, fɪ-/ *adj* financier/-ière

financial year *n* (BrE) exercice *m*, année *f* budgétaire

🔑 **find** /faɪnd/ **A** *n* **1** (gen) découverte *f*
2 (good buy) trouvaille *f*
B *vt* (*prét, pp* **found**) **1** trouver; **I can't ~ my keys** je ne trouve pas mes clés; **I couldn't ~ the time** je n'ai pas eu le temps
2 (experience) éprouver ‹*pleasure, satisfaction*› (**in** dans)
3 (Law) **to ~ that** conclure que; **to ~ sb guilty** déclarer qn coupable

▪ **find out**: **A** **~ out** se renseigner; **if he ever ~s out** si jamais il l'apprend
B **~ [sth] out** découvrir ‹*fact, answer, name, cause, truth*›
C **~ out who/why/where** trouver qui/pourquoi/où
D **~ out about [sth]** **1** (learn by chance) découvrir ‹*plan, affair, breakage*›
2 (research) faire des recherches sur ‹*subject*›

🔑 **findings** *npl* conclusions *fpl*

🔑 **fine** /faɪn/ **A** *n* (gen) amende *f*; (for traffic offence) contravention *f*
B *adj* **1** (very good) excellent/-e
2 (satisfactory) bon/bonne *before n*; **that's ~** très bien; **'~, thanks'** 'très bien, merci'
3 (nice) ‹*weather, day*› beau/belle *before n*
4 (delicate) fin/-e
5 (subtle) ‹*adjustment, detail, distinction*› subtil/-e
6 (refined) ‹*lady, clothes*› beau/belle *before n*
7 (commendable) ‹*person*› merveilleux/-euse
C *adv* ‹*get along, come along, do*› très bien
D *vt* (gen) condamner [qn] à une amende; (for traffic offence) donner une contravention à

fine art *n* beaux-arts *mpl*
IDIOM **she's got cheating down to a ~** elle est passée maître dans l'art de tricher

fine-tune *vt* ajuster

🔑 **finger** /'fɪŋɡə(r)/ **A** *n* doigt *m*
B *vt* toucher ‹*fruit, goods*›; tripoter (fam) ‹*necklace*›
IDIOM **to keep one's ~s crossed** croiser les doigts (**for sb** pour qn)

fingernail *n* ongle *m*

fingerprint /'fɪŋɡəprɪnt/ *n* empreinte *f* digitale

fingertip /'fɪŋɡətɪp/ *n* bout *m* du doigt

finicky /'fɪnɪkɪ/ *adj* ‹*person*› difficile (**about** pour); ‹*job, task*› minutieux/-ieuse

🔑 **finish** /'fɪnɪʃ/ **A** *n* (*pl* **~es**) **1** (end) fin *f*
2 (Sport) arrivée *f*
3 (of wood, car) finition *f*; (of fabric, leather) apprêt *m*
B *vt* **1** finir, terminer ‹*chapter, sentence, task*›; terminer, achever ‹*building, novel*›; **to ~ doing** finir de faire
2 (leave) finir ‹*work, school*›
3 (consume) finir ‹*cigarette, drink, meal*›
4 (put an end to) briser ‹*career*›
C *vi* (gen) finir; ‹*speaker*› finir de parler; ‹*conference, programme, term*› finir, se terminer; ‹*holidays*› se terminer

▪ **finish off** finir, terminer ‹*letter, meal, task*›

▪ **finish up**: **A** **~ up** finir
B **~ [sth] up** finir ‹*milk, paint, cake*›

finishing line (BrE), **finish line** (AmE) *n* ligne *f* d'arrivée

finishing touch *n* **to put the ~(es) to sth** mettre la dernière main à qch

finite /'faɪnaɪt/ *adj* (gen) fini/-e; ‹*resources*› limité/-e

Finland /'fɪnlənd/ *pr n* Finlande *f*

Finn /fɪn/ *n* Finlandais/-e *m/f*

Finnish /'fɪnɪʃ/ **A** *n* (language) finnois *m*
B *adj* **1** ‹*culture, food, politics*› finlandais/-e; ‹*ambassador, embassy*› de Finlande
2 ‹*grammar*› finnois/-e; ‹*teacher, lesson*› de finnois

fir /fɜː(r)/ *n* (*also* **~ tree**) sapin *m*

🔑 **fire** /'faɪə(r)/ **A** *n* **1** feu *m*; **to set ~ to sth** mettre le feu à qch; **to be on ~** être en feu; **to catch ~** prendre feu; **to sit by the ~** s'asseoir près du feu *or* au coin du feu
2 (blaze) incendie *m*; **to start a ~** provoquer un incendie
3 to open ~ on sb ouvrir le feu sur qn
B *excl* **1** (raising alarm) au feu!
2 (Mil) feu!
C *vt* **1** décharger ‹*gun, weapon*›; tirer

‹*shot*›; lancer ‹*arrow, missile*›; **to ~ questions at sb** bombarder qn de questions
2 (dismiss) renvoyer, virer (fam) ‹*person*›
D *vi* tirer (**at, on** sur)

fire alarm *n* alarme *f* incendie

firearm *n* arme *f* à feu

firebomb /ˈfaɪəbɒm/ **A** *n* bombe *f* incendiaire
B *vt* incendier ‹*building*›

fire brigade *n* pompiers *mpl*

fire engine *n* voiture *f* de pompiers

fire escape *n* escalier *m* de secours

fire exit *n* sortie *f* de secours

fire extinguisher *n* extincteur *m*

firefighter *n* pompier *m*

fireguard *n* pare-étincelles *m inv*

fireman *n* pompier *m*

fireplace *n* cheminée *f*

fireproof /ˈfaɪəpruːf/ *adj* ‹*door, clothing*› ignifugé/-e

fire service *n* (sapeurs-)pompiers *mpl*

fire station *n* caserne *f* de pompiers

firewall /ˈfaɪəwɔːl/ *n* (Comput) pare-feu *m*, barrière *f* de sécurité

firewood *n* bois *m* à brûler

firework /ˈfaɪəwɜːk/ *n* feu *m* d'artifice

firing /ˈfaɪərɪŋ/ *n* (of guns) tir *m*

firing line *n* **to be in the ~** (Mil) être dans la ligne de tir; (under attack) faire l'objet de violentes critiques

firing squad *n* peloton *m* d'exécution

🔑 **firm** /fɜːm/ **A** *n* entreprise *f*, société *f*
B *adj* **1** ‹*mattress, fruit, handshake*› ferme
2 ‹*basis, grasp*› solide
3 ‹*offer, intention, refusal*› ferme; ‹*evidence*› concret/-ète
4 ‹*person, leadership*› ferme (**with sb** avec qn)
C *adv* **to stand ~** tenir bon

🔑 **first** /fɜːst/ **A** *n* **1** (gen) premier/-ière *m/f* (**to do** à faire)
2 (of month) premier *m inv*; **the ~ of May** le premier mai
3 (*also* **~-class honours degree**) (BrE) (Univ) ≈ licence *f* avec mention très bien
B *adj* premier/-ière *before n*; **the ~ three pages** les trois premières pages; **at ~ glance** *or* **sight** à première vue; **I'll ring ~ thing in the morning** je vous appellerai en tout début de matinée
C *adv* **1** ‹*arrive, leave*› le premier/la première; **women and children ~** les femmes et les enfants d'abord; **to come ~** ‹*contestant*› terminer premier/première (**in** à); ‹*career, family*› passer avant tout
2 (to begin with) d'abord; **~ of all** tout d'abord
3 (for the first time) pour la première fois; **I ~ met him in Paris** je l'ai rencontré pour la première fois à Paris
D **at first** *phr* au début
(IDIOM) **~ things ~** chaque chose en son temps

first aid *n* **1** (treatment) premiers soins *mpl*
2 (as skill) secourisme *m*

first-aid kit *n* trousse *f* de secours

first-class *adj* **1** ‹*hotel, ticket*› de première (classe)
2 ‹*stamp, mail*› (au) tarif rapide
3 (BrE) ‹*degree*› avec mention très bien
4 (excellent) excellent/-e

first cousin *n* (male) cousin *m* germain; (female) cousine *f* germaine

first floor *n* (BrE) premier étage *m*; (AmE) rez-de-chaussée *m*

first form *n* (BrE) (Sch) (classe *f* de) sixième *f*

first grade *n* (AmE) (Sch) cours *m* préparatoire

first-hand /ˌfɜːstˈhænd/ *adj, adv* de première main

firstly /ˈfɜːstlɪ/ *adv* premièrement

first name *n* prénom *m*

first night *n* première *f*

first-rate *adj* excellent/-e

first-time buyer *n* personne *f* qui achète sa première maison

🔑 **fish** /fɪʃ/ **A** *n* (*pl* **~, ~es**) poisson *m*
B *vi* pêcher; **to ~ for trout** pêcher la truite; **to ~ for compliments** rechercher les compliments
■ **fish out ~ out [sth] 1** (from bag, pocket) sortir
2 (from water) repêcher

fish and chips *n* poisson *m* frit avec des frites

fish and chip shop *n* (BrE) friterie *f*

fishbowl *n* bocal *m* (à poissons)

fisherman *n* pêcheur *m*

fish finger *n* (BrE) bâtonnet *m* de poisson

fishing /ˈfɪʃɪŋ/ *n* pêche *f*; **to go ~** aller à la pêche

fishing boat *n* bateau *m* de pêche

fishing rod *n* canne *f* à pêche

fish market *n* halle *f* aux poissons

fishmonger /ˈfɪʃmʌŋgə(r)/ *n* (BrE) poissonnier/-ière *m/f*; **~'s (shop)** poissonnerie *f*

fishnet *adj* ‹*stockings*› à résille

fish stick *n* (AmE) bâtonnet *m* de poisson

fish tank *n* aquarium *m*

fishy /ˈfɪʃɪ/ *adj* **1** ‹*smell, taste*› de poisson
2 (fam) (suspect) louche (fam)

fist /fɪst/ *n* poing *m*

🔑 **fit** /fɪt/ **A** *n* **1** (Med) crise *f*, attaque *f*
2 (of anger, passion, panic) accès *m*; **~ of coughing** quinte *f* de toux; **to have sb in ~s** (fam) donner le fou rire à qn
3 (of garment) **to be a good ~** être à la bonne taille; **to be a tight ~** être juste
B *adj* **1** ‹*person*› (in trim) en forme; **to get ~** retrouver la forme

2 to be ~ for (worthy of) être digne de ‹*person, hero, king*›; (capable of) être capable de faire ‹*job*›; **not ~ for human consumption** impropre à la consommation; **to see** *or* **think ~ to do** juger bon de faire; **to be in no ~ state to do** ne pas être en état de faire
C *vt* (*prét* **fitted**, **fit** (AmE), *pp* **fitted**)
1 ‹*garment*› être à la taille de; ‹*shoe*› être à la pointure de; ‹*key*› aller dans ‹*lock*›; aller dans ‹*envelope, space*›
2 to ~ sth in *or* **into** trouver de la place pour qch dans ‹*room, house, car*›
3 (install) mettre [qch] en place ‹*lock, door, kitchen, shower*›
4 correspondre à ‹*description, requirements*›
D *vi* (*prét* **fitted**, **fit** (AmE), *pp* **fitted**)
1 ‹*garment*› être à ma/ta/sa taille, aller; ‹*shoes*› être à ma/ta/sa pointure, aller; ‹*key, lid, sheet*› aller
2 ‹*toys, books*› tenir (**into** dans); **will the table ~ in that corner?** y a-t-il de la place pour la table dans ce coin?
3 to ~ with correspondre à ‹*story, facts*›
IDIOM **in ~s and starts** par à-coups
■ **fit in A ~ in 1** ‹*key, object*› aller; **will you all ~ in?** (into car, room) est-ce qu'il y a de la place pour vous tous?
2 (fig) ‹*person*› s'intégrer (**with** à); **I'll ~ in with your plans** j'accorderai mes projets avec les vôtres
B ~ [sb/sth] in caser ‹*objects*›; caser ‹*game, meeting*›; trouver le temps pour voir ‹*patient, colleague*›

fitness /'fɪtnɪs/ *n* (physical) forme *f*

fitted /'fɪtɪd/ *adj* ‹*wardrobe*› encastré/-e; ‹*kitchen*› intégré/-e

fitted carpet *n* moquette *f*

fitting /'fɪtɪŋ/ **A** *n* **1** (part) installation *f*
2 (for clothes, hearing aid) essayage *m*
B *adj* ‹*description*› adéquat/-e; ‹*memorial, testament*› qui convient

fitting room *n* salon *m* d'essayage

five /faɪv/ *n, pron, det* cinq *m inv*

five-a-side /ˌfaɪvə'saɪd/ *n* (*also* **~ football**) football *m* à cinq (joueurs)

fix /fɪks/ **A** *n* **1** (difficulty) **to be in a ~** être dans le pétrin (fam)
2 (fam) (dose of drugs) shoot *m* (fam)
B *vt* **1** fixer ‹*date, venue, price, limit*›; déterminer ‹*position*›
2 arranger ‹*meeting, visit*›; préparer ‹*drink, meal*›; **to ~ one's hair** se donner un coup de peigne; **how are we ~ed for time/money?** qu'est-ce qu'on a comme temps/argent? (fam)
3 (mend) réparer
4 fixer ‹*handle, shelf*› (**on** sur, **to** à)
5 fixer ‹*attention*› (**on** sur); tourner ‹*thoughts*› (**on** vers)
6 (fam) truquer ‹*contest, election*›
C fixed *pp adj* ‹*gaze, income, price*› fixe; ‹*expression*› figé/-e; ‹*menu*› à prix fixe
■ **fix up** organiser ‹*holiday, meeting*›; décider de ‹*date*›

fixed-term contract *n* contrat *m* à durée déterminée

fixture /'fɪkstʃə(r)/ *n* **1** installation *f*; **~s and fittings** équipements *mpl*
2 (Sport) rencontre *f*

fizzle /'fɪzl/
■ **fizzle out** ‹*interest, romance*› s'éteindre; ‹*campaign, project*› faire fiasco; ‹*story*› se terminer en queue de poisson

fizzy /'fɪzɪ/ *adj* gazeux/-euse

flabby /'flæbɪ/ *adj* ‹*skin, muscle*› flasque; ‹*person*› aux chairs flasques

flag /flæg/ **A** *n* drapeau *m*
B *vi* (*p prés etc* **-gg-**) ‹*interest*› faiblir; ‹*strength*› baisser; ‹*conversation*› languir; ‹*athlete*› flancher (fam)
■ **flag down** faire signe de s'arrêter à ‹*person*›; héler ‹*taxi*›

flagpole /'flægpəʊl/ *n* mât *m*

flagrant /'fleɪgrənt/ *adj* flagrant/-e

flagstone *n* dalle *f*

flair /'fleə(r)/ *n* **1** (talent) don *m*; **to have a ~ for** être doué/-e pour ‹*languages*›
2 (style) classe *f*

flake /fleɪk/ **A** *n* (of snow) flocon *m*
B *vi* (*also* **~ off**) ‹*plaster, stone*› s'effriter; ‹*skin*› peler

flamboyant /flæm'bɔɪənt/ *adj* ‹*person*› haut/-e en couleur; ‹*lifestyle*› exubérant/-e; ‹*colour, clothes*› voyant/-e; ‹*gesture*› extravagant/-e

flame /fleɪm/ *n* flamme *f*; **in ~s** en flammes; **to go up in ~s** s'enflammer; **to burst into ~s** s'embraser

flamer /'fleɪmə(r)/ *n* (Internet) auteur *m* d'un message injurieux

flaming /'fleɪmɪŋ/ **A** *n* (Internet) envoi *m* de messages injurieux
B *adj* **1** ‹*vehicle, building*› en flammes
2 ‹*row*› violent/-e

flamingo /flə'mɪŋgəʊ/ *n* (*pl* **~s** *ou* **-oes**) flamant *m* (rose)

flammable /'flæməbl/ *adj* inflammable

flan /flæn/ *n* (savoury) quiche *f*, tarte *f*; (sweet) tarte *f*

flank /flæŋk/ **A** *n* flanc *m*
B *vt* **to be ~ed by** ‹*person*› être flanqué/-e par; ‹*place*› être bordé/-e par

flannel /'flænl/ *n* **1** (wool) flanelle *f*; (cotton) pilou *m*
2 (*also* **face ~**) (BrE) ≈ gant *m* de toilette

flap /flæp/ **A** *n* **1** (on pocket, envelope, tent) rabat *m*; (on table) abattant *m*
2 (of wings) battement *m*
B *vt* (*p prés etc* **-pp-**) **the bird ~ped its wings** l'oiseau battait des ailes
C *vi* (*p prés etc* **-pp-**) ‹*wing*› battre; ‹*sail, flag*› claquer; ‹*clothes*› voleter

flare /fleə(r)/ **A** *n* **1** (on runway) balise *f* lumineuse; (distress signal) fusée *f* (de

détresse); (Mil) (on target) fusée *f* éclairante
2 (of match, lighter) lueur *f*
B *vi* **1** ‹*firework, match*› jeter une brève lueur
2 ‹*skirt*› s'évaser; ‹*nostrils*› se dilater
■ **flare up 1** ‹*fire*› s'embraser
2 ‹*violence*› éclater; ‹*person*› s'emporter
3 ‹*illness*› réapparaître; ‹*pain*› se réveiller

flares *npl* pantalon *m* à pattes d'éléphant

flash /flæʃ/ **A** *n* **1** (of torch, headlights) lueur *f* soudaine; (of jewels, metal) éclat *m*; **a ~ of lightning** un éclair
2 in *or* **like a ~** en un clin d'œil
3 (on camera) flash *m*
B *vt* **1 to ~ one's headlights (at)** faire un appel de phares (à)
2 lancer ‹*look, smile*› **(at** à)
3 (transmit) faire apparaître ‹*message*›
4 (fam) (show) ‹*person*› montrer [qch] rapidement ‹*card, money*›
5 (*also* **~ about**, **~ around**) exhiber ‹*credit card*›; étaler ‹*money*›
C *vi* ‹*light*› clignoter; ‹*eyes*› lancer des éclairs; **to ~ on and off** clignoter
■ **flash by**, **flash past** ‹*person, bird*› passer comme un éclair; ‹*landscape*› défiler

flashback /ˈflæʃbæk/ *n* **1** (in film) flash-back *m* **(to** à)
2 (memory) souvenir *m*

flashing /ˈflæʃɪŋ/ *adj* ‹*light, sign*› clignotant/-e

flashlight (AmE) *n* lampe *f* de poche

flashy /ˈflæʃɪ/ *adj* (fam) ‹*car, dress, tie*› tape-à-l'œil *inv*; ‹*jewellery*› clinquant/-e

flask /flɑːsk, (AmE) flæsk/ *n* thermos® *f or m inv*; **(hip) ~** flasque *f*

flat /flæt/ **A** *n* **1** (BrE) appartement *m*; **one-bedroom ~** deux pièces *m inv*
2 the ~ of le plat de ‹*hand, sword*›
B *adj* **1** (gen) plat/-e; ‹*nose, face*› aplati/-e
2 ‹*tyre, ball*› dégonflé/-e; **to have a ~ tyre** avoir un pneu à plat
3 ‹*refusal, denial*› catégorique
4 ‹*fare, fee*› forfaitaire; ‹*charge, rate*› fixe
5 ‹*beer*› éventé/-e
6 (BrE) ‹*car battery*› à plat; ‹*battery*› usé/-e
7 (Mus) ‹*note*› bémol *inv*; ‹*voice, instrument*› faux/fausse
C *adv* **1** ‹*lay, lie*› à plat; **~ on one's back** sur le dos
2 in 10 minutes ~ en 10 minutes pile
3 ‹*sing*› faux
IDIOM **to fall ~** ‹*joke*› tomber à plat; ‹*party*› tourner court; ‹*plan*› tomber à l'eau

flatmate *n* (BrE) colocataire *mf*

flat out /ˌflætˈaʊt/ *adv* (fam) ‹*drive*› à fond de train; ‹*work*› d'arrache-pied

flat rate /ˌflætˈreɪt/ **A** *n* taux *m* fixe
B flat-rate *adj* ‹*fee, tax*› forfaitaire

flatten /ˈflætn/ **A** *vt* **1** ‹*rain*› coucher ‹*crops, grass*›; abattre ‹*fence*›; ‹*bombing*› raser ‹*building*›
2 (smooth out) aplanir ‹*surface*›; aplatir ‹*metal*›
3 (crush) écraser ‹*fruit, object*›
B *v refl* **to ~ oneself** s'aplatir **(against** contre)

flatter /ˈflætə(r)/ *vt* flatter **(on** sur)

flattering /ˈflætərɪŋ/ *adj* flatteur/-euse

flattery /ˈflætərɪ/ *n* flatterie *f*

flaunt /flɔːnt/ *vt* étaler ‹*wealth*›; faire étalage de ‹*charms, knowledge*›

flavour (BrE), **flavor** (AmE) /ˈfleɪvə(r)/
A *n* goût *m*; (subtler) saveur *f*; **full of ~** savoureux/-euse
B *vt* (gen) donner du goût à; (add specific taste) parfumer **(with** à)

flavouring (BrE), **flavoring** (AmE) /ˈfleɪvərɪŋ/ *n* (for sweet taste) parfum *m*; (for meat, fish) assaisonnement *m*

flaw /flɔː/ *n* défaut *m*

flawed /ˈflɔːd/ *adj* défectueux/-euse

flea /fliː/ *n* puce *f*

flea market *n* marché *m* aux puces

fleck /flek/ **A** *n* (of colour, light) tache *f*; (of foam) flocon *m*; (of blood, paint) petite tache *f*; (of dust) particule *f*
B *vt* **~ed with** ‹*fabric*› moucheté/-e de ‹*colour*›

fledgling /ˈfledʒlɪŋ/ *n* (*also* **fledgeling**) oisillon *m*

flee /fliː/ *vt*, *vi* (*prét*, *pp* **fled**) fuir

fleece /fliːs/ *n* toison *f*; **~-lined** fourré/-e

fleet /fliːt/ *n* **1** (of ships) flotte *f*; (of small vessels) flottille *f*
2 (of vehicles) (on road) convoi *m*

fleeting /ˈfliːtɪŋ/ *adj* ‹*memory, pleasure*› fugace; ‹*moment*› bref/brève *before n*; ‹*glance*› rapide

Flemish /ˈflemɪʃ/ **A** *n* **1 the ~** les Flamands *mpl*
2 (language) flamand *m*
B *adj* flamand/-e

flesh /fleʃ/ *n* chair *f*

fleshy /ˈfleʃɪ/ *adj* charnu/-e

flex /fleks/ **A** *n* (BrE) fil *m*
B *vt* faire jouer ‹*muscle*›; fléchir ‹*limb*›

flexibility /ˌfleksəˈbɪlətɪ/ *n* souplesse *f*, flexibilité *f*

flexible /ˈfleksəbl/ *adj* **1** ‹*arrangement, plan*› flexible
2 ‹*person*› souple (**about** en ce qui concerne)

flexitime (BrE), **flextime** (AmE) /ˈfleks(ɪ)taɪm/ *n* horaire *m* flexible *or* souple

flick /flɪk/ **A** *n* (with finger) chiquenaude *f*; (with whip, cloth) petit coup *m*
B *vt* **1** (with finger) donner une chiquenaude à; (with tail, cloth) donner un petit coup à; **he ~ed his ash on the floor** il a fait tomber sa cendre par terre
2 appuyer sur ‹*switch*›

flicker /'flɪkə(r)/ *vi* ‹*fire, light*› vaciller, trembloter; ‹*image*› clignoter; ‹*eye, eyelid*› cligner
■ **flick through** feuilleter ‹*book*›

flick knife *n* (BrE) couteau *m* à cran d'arrêt

flight /flaɪt/ *n* **1** (gen) vol *m* (**to** vers, **from** de); **we took the next ~ (out)** nous avons pris l'avion suivant
2 (escape) fuite *f* (**from** devant); **to take ~** prendre la fuite
3 a ~ of steps une volée de marches; **six ~s (of stairs)** six étages
4 a ~ of fancy une invention

flight attendant *n* (male) steward *m*; (female) hôtesse *f* de l'air

flight bag *n* bagage *m* à main

flight path *n* route *f* de vol

flimsy /'flɪmzɪ/ *adj* ‹*fabric*› léger/-ère; ‹*structure*› peu solide; ‹*excuse*› piètre *before n*; ‹*evidence*› mince

flinch /flɪntʃ/ *vi* tressaillir; **without ~ing** sans broncher; **to ~ from doing** hésiter à faire

fling /flɪŋ/ **A** *n* **1** (fam) (spree) bon temps *m*
2 (affair) aventure *f*
B *vt* (*prét, pp* **flung**) lancer
C *v refl* **to ~ oneself** se jeter (**across** en travers de, **over** par dessus)
■ **fling away**: **~ [sth] away** jeter
■ **fling open** ouvrir [qch] brusquement ‹*door*›; ouvrir [qch] tout grand ‹*window*›

flint /flɪnt/ *n* **1** (rock) silex *m*
2 (in lighter) pierre *f* à briquet

flip /flɪp/ **A** *n* (somersault) tour *m*
B *vt* (*p prés etc* **-pp-**) **1** lancer ‹*coin*›; faire sauter ‹*pancake*›
2 basculer ‹*switch*›
■ **flip through** feuilleter ‹*book*›

flip chart *n* tableau *m* de conférence, paperboard *m*

flip-flop /'flɪpflɒp/ *n* **1** (sandal) tong *f*
2 (AmE) (about-face) volte-face *f inv*

flippant /'flɪpənt/ *adj* ‹*remark, person*› désinvolte; ‹*tone, attitude*› cavalier/-ière

flipper /'flɪpə(r)/ *n* **1** (Zool) nageoire *f*
2 (for swimmer) palme *f*

flirt /flɜːt/ **A** *n* flirteur/-euse *m/f*
B *vi* flirter; **to ~ with** flirter avec ‹*person*›; jouer avec ‹*danger*›; caresser ‹*idea*›

flirtatious /ˌflɜː'teɪʃəs/ *adj* charmeur/-euse, dragueur/-euse (fam derog)

flit /flɪt/ *vi* (*p prés etc* **-tt-**) **1** (*also* **~ about**) ‹*bird, moth*› voleter; ‹*person*› aller d'un pas léger
2 a look of panic ~ted across his face une expression de panique lui traversa le visage

float /fləʊt/ **A** *n* **1** (on net) flotteur *m*; (on line) bouchon *m*
2 (BrE) (swimmer's aid) planche *f*; (AmE) (life jacket) gilet *m* de sauvetage
3 (carnival vehicle) char *m*
B *vt* **1** ‹*person*› faire flotter ‹*boat, logs*›
2 émettre ‹*shares, loan*›; lancer [qch] en Bourse ‹*company*›; laisser flotter ‹*currency*›
C *vi* **1** flotter; **to ~ on one's back** ‹*swimmer*› faire la planche; **the boat was ~ing out to sea** le bateau voguait vers le large; **to ~ up into the air** s'envoler
2 ‹*currency*› flotter
■ **float off** ‹*boat*› dériver; ‹*balloon*› s'envoler

floating /'fləʊtɪŋ/ *adj* **1** ‹*bridge*› flottant/-e
2 ‹*population*› instable

floating voter *n* électeur *m* indécis

flock /flɒk/ **A** *n* (of sheep, goats) troupeau *m*; (of birds) volée *f*
B *vi* ‹*animals, people*› affluer (**around** autour de, **into** dans); **to ~ together** ‹*people*› s'assembler; ‹*animals*› se rassembler

flog /flɒg/ *vt* (*p prés etc* **-gg-**) (beat) flageller

flood /flʌd/ **A** *n* **1** inondation *f*
2 a ~ of un flot de ‹*people, memories*›; un déluge de ‹*letters, complaints*›; **to be in ~s of tears** verser des torrents de larmes
B *vt* **1** inonder ‹*area*›; faire déborder ‹*river*›
2 ‹*light*› inonder
3 inonder ‹*market*› (**with** de)
4 (Aut) noyer ‹*engine*›
C *vi* **1** ‹*river*› déborder
2 to ~ into sth ‹*light*› inonder qch; ‹*people*› envahir qch; **to ~ over sb** ‹*emotion*› envahir qn

floodgate /'flʌdgeɪt/ *n* vanne *f*

floodlight /'flʌdlaɪt/ **A** *n* projecteur *m*; **under ~s** (Sport) en nocturne
B *vt* (*prét, pp* **floodlit**) illuminer ‹*building*›; éclairer ‹*stage*›

floor /flɔː(r)/ **A** *n* **1** (of room) (wooden) plancher *m*, parquet *m*; (stone) sol *m*; (of car, lift) plancher *m*; **dance ~** piste *f* de danse; **on the ~** par terre
2 (of stock exchange) parquet *m*; (of debating chamber) auditoire *m*; (of factory) atelier *m*
3 (storey) étage *m*; **on the first ~** au premier étage (BrE); au rez-de-chaussée (AmE)
B *vt* **1** terrasser ‹*attacker, boxer*›
2 ‹*question*› décontenancer ‹*candidate*›
IDIOM **to wipe the ~ with sb** battre qn à plates coutures

floorboard *n* latte *f*, planche *f*

floor cloth *n* serpillière *f*

floor show *n* spectacle *m* (*de cabaret*)

flop /flɒp/ **A** *n* (failure) fiasco *m* (fam)
B *vi* (*p prés etc* **-pp-**) **1 to ~ (down)** s'effondrer
2 (fam) ‹*play, film*› faire un four (fam); ‹*project, venture*› être un fiasco (fam)

floppy /'flɒpɪ/ *adj* ‹*ears*› pendant/-e; ‹*hat*› à bords tombants

floppy disk *n* disquette *f*

flora /'flɔːrə/ *n* flore *f*

floral /'flɔːrəl/ *adj* ‹*design, fabric*› à fleurs; ‹*arrangement*› floral/-e

Florida /'flɒrɪdə/ *pr n* Floride *f*

florist /'flɒrɪst, (AmE) 'flɔːrɪst/ *n* (person) fleuriste *mf*; (shop) fleuriste *m*

floss /flɒs, (AmE) flɔːs/ *n* fil *m* dentaire

flotsam /'flɒtsəm/ *n* **~ and jetsam** épaves *fpl*

flounce /flaʊns/ **A** *n* (frill) volant *m*
B *vi* **to ~ in/off** entrer/partir dans un mouvement d'indignation

flounder /'flaʊndə(r)/ *vi* **1** ‹*animal, person*› se débattre (**in** dans)
2 (falter) ‹*speaker*› bredouiller; ‹*economy*› stagner; ‹*career, company*› piétiner

flour /'flaʊə(r)/ *n* farine *f*

flourish /'flʌrɪʃ/ **A** *n* **1** (gesture) geste *m* théâtral; **with a ~** ‹*do*› de façon théâtrale
2 (in style) fioriture *f*
B *vt* brandir ‹*ticket, document*›
C *vi* prospérer

flourishing /'flʌrɪʃɪŋ/ *adj* ‹*garden, industry*› florissant/-e; ‹*business, town*› prospère

flout /flaʊt/ *vt* se moquer de ‹*convention, rules*›

flow /fləʊ/ **A** *n* **1** (of liquid) écoulement *m*; (of blood, electricity, water) circulation *f*; (of refugees, words) flot *m*; (of information) circulation *f*; **in full ~** ‹*speaker*› en plein discours; **traffic ~** circulation *f*
2 (of tide) flux *m*
B *vi* **1** ‹*liquid*› couler (**into** dans); **the river ~s into the sea** le fleuve se jette dans la mer
2 ‹*conversation, words*› couler; ‹*wine, beer*› couler à flots
3 ‹*blood, electricity*› circuler (**through, round** dans)
4 ‹*hair, dress*› flotter

flow chart *n* organigramme *m*

flower /'flaʊə(r)/ **A** *n* fleur *f*; **to be in ~** être en fleur
B *vi* **1** ‹*flower, tree*› fleurir
2 ‹*love, person*› s'épanouir

flower arranging *n* décoration *f* florale

flower bed *n* parterre *m* de fleurs

flowering /'flaʊərɪŋ/ **A** *n* floraison *f* (**of** de)
B *adj* (producing blooms) à fleurs; (in bloom) en fleurs

flower pot *n* pot *m* de fleurs

flower shop *n* fleuriste *m*

flowery /'flaʊərɪ/ *adj* ‹*design*› à fleurs; ‹*language, speech*› fleuri/-e

flu /fluː/ *n* grippe *f*

fluctuate /'flʌktjʊeɪt/ *vi* fluctuer (**between** entre)

flue /fluː/ *n* (of chimney) conduit *m*; (of stove, boiler) tuyau *m*

fluency /'fluːənsɪ/ *n* aisance *f*

fluent /'fluːənt/ *adj* **1 her French is ~** elle parle couramment français; **in ~ English** dans un anglais parfait
2 ‹*speech*› éloquent/-e; ‹*style*› coulant/-e

fluently /'fluːəntlɪ/ *adv* couramment

mot clé

fluff /flʌf/ **A** *n* (on clothes) peluche *f*; (on carpet) poussière *f*; (under furniture) mouton *m*, flocon *m* de poussière
B *vt* **1** (*also* **~ up**) hérisser ‹*feathers*›; faire bouffer ‹*hair*›
2 (fam) rater ‹*cue, exam*›

fluffy /'flʌfɪ/ *adj* **1** ‹*toy*› en peluche; ‹*hair*› bouffant/-e
2 (light) ‹*mixture*› léger/-ère; ‹*egg white, rice*› moelleux/-euse

fluid /'fluːɪd/ *n, adj* fluide *m*

fluid ounce *n* once *f* liquide ((BrE) = *0.028 l*; (AmE) = *0.030 l*)

fluke /fluːk/ *n* coup *m* de veine (fam); **by a (sheer) ~** (tout à fait) par hasard

fluorescent /flɔː'resənt, (AmE) flʊə'r-/ *adj* fluorescent/-e

fluoride /'flɔːraɪd, (AmE) 'flʊəraɪd/ *n* fluorure *m*

flurry /'flʌrɪ/ *n* **1** (gust) rafale *f*
2 (bustle) agitation *f* soudaine; **a ~ of activity** un tourbillon d'activité
3 (of complaints, enquiries) vague *f*

flush /flʌʃ/ **A** *n* **1** (blush) rougeur *f*
2 (surge) **a ~ of** un élan de ‹*pleasure, pride*›; un accès de ‹*anger, shame*›
3 (of toilet) chasse *f* d'eau
B *vt* **to ~ the toilet** tirer la chasse (d'eau); **to ~ sth down the toilet** faire partir qch dans les toilettes
C *vi* **1** (redden) rougir (**with** de)
2 the toilet doesn't ~ la chasse d'eau ne fonctionne pas
■ **flush out** débusquer ‹*sniper, spy*›; **to ~ sb/sth out of** faire sortir qn/qch de ‹*shelter*›

flushed /flʌʃt/ *adj* **1** ‹*cheeks*› rouge (**with** de); **to be ~** avoir les joues rouges
2 ~ with rayonnant/-e de ‹*pride*›

fluster /'flʌstə(r)/ **A** *n* agitation *f*
B *vt* énerver; **to look ~ed** avoir l'air énervé

flute /fluːt/ *n* flûte *f*

flutter /'flʌtə(r)/ **A** *n* (of wings, lashes) battement *m*
B *vt* **1 the bird ~ed its wings** l'oiseau battait des ailes
2 agiter ‹*fan, handkerchief*›; **to ~ one's eyelashes** battre des cils
C *vi* **1 the bird's wings ~ed** l'oiseau battit des ailes
2 ‹*flag*› flotter; ‹*clothes, curtains*› s'agiter; ‹*eyelids, lashes*› battre
3 (*also* **~ down**) ‹*leaves*› tomber en voltigeant
4 ‹*heart*› palpiter (**with** de); ‹*pulse*› battre faiblement

flux /flʌks/ *n* **in (a state of) ~** dans un état de perpétuel changement

fly /flaɪ/ **A** *n* mouche *f*
B flies *npl* (BrE) (of trousers) braguette *f*
C *vt* (*prét* **flew**, *pp* **flown**) **1** piloter ‹*aircraft, balloon*›; faire voler ‹*kite*›
2 (transport) emmener [qn] par avion ‹*person*›

3 ‹*bird, aircraft*› parcourir ‹*distance*›
4 ‹*ship*› arborer ‹*flag*›
D *vi* (*prét* **flew**, *pp* **flown**) **1** ‹*bird, insect, aircraft, kite*› voler; **to ~ over** *or* **across sth** survoler qch
2 ‹*passenger*› voyager en avion, prendre l'avion; ‹*pilot*› piloter, voler; **to ~ from Rome to Athens** aller de Rome à Athènes en avion
3 ‹*sparks, insults*› voler; **to ~ open** s'ouvrir brusquement; **to go ~ing** (fam) ‹*person*› faire un vol plané; ‹*object*› valdinguer (fam); **to ~ into a rage** se mettre en colère
4 (*also* **~ past**, **~ by**) ‹*time, holidays*› passer très vite, filer (fam)
5 ‹*flag, scarf, hair*› flotter; **to ~ in the wind** flotter au vent
■ **fly away** s'envoler

fly-by-night /ˈflaɪbaɪnaɪt/ *adj* ‹*company*› douteux/-euse; ‹*person*› irresponsable

fly-drive *adj* avec formule avion plus voiture

flying /ˈflaɪɪŋ/ **A** *n* **to be afraid of ~** avoir peur de l'avion
B *adj* **1** ‹*insect, machine*› volant/-e; ‹*object, broken glass*› qui vole; **to take a ~ leap** sauter avec élan
2 ‹*visit*› éclair *inv*
IDIOMS **with ~ colours** ‹*pass*› haut la main; **to get off to a ~ start** prendre un très bon départ

fly-on-the-wall /ˌflaɪɒnðəˈwɔːl/ *adj* ‹*film*› pris/-e sur le vif

flyover /ˈflaɪəʊvə(r)/ *n* **1** (BrE) pont *m* routier
2 (AmE) (aerial display) défilé *m* aérien

fly spray *n* bombe *f* insecticide

FM *n* (*abbr* = **frequency modulation**) FM *f*

foal /fəʊl/ *n* poulain *m*

foam /fəʊm/ **A** *n* **1** (on sea, from mouth) écume *f*; (on drinks) mousse *f*
2 (chemical) mousse *f*
3 (*also* **~ rubber**) mousse *f*
B *vi* **1** (*also* **~ up**) ‹*beer*› mousser; ‹*sea*› se couvrir d'écume; **to ~ at the mouth** écumer; (fig) écumer de rage
2 ‹*horse*› suer

foam bath *n* bain *m* moussant

fob /fɒb/ *n* (pocket) gousset *m*; (chain) chaîne *f*
■ **fob off** se débarrasser de ‹*enquirer, customer*›; rejeter ‹*enquiry*›

focal point *n* **1** (in optics) foyer *m*
2 (of village, building) point *m* de convergence (**of** de, **for** pour)
3 (main concern) point *m* central

focus /ˈfəʊkəs/ **A** *n* (*pl* **~es**, **foci**) **1** (focal point) foyer *m*; **in ~** au point; **to go out of ~** ‹*device*› se dérégler; ‹*image*› devenir flou
2 (device on lens) mise *f* au point
3 (of attention, interest) centre *m*
4 (emphasis) accent *m*
B *vt* (*p prés etc* **-s-** *ou* **-ss-**) **1** concentrer ‹*ray*› (**on** sur); fixer ‹*eyes*› (**on** sur)
2 mettre [qch] au point, régler ‹*lens, camera*›
C *vi* (*p prés etc* **-s-** *ou* **-ss-**) **to ~ on** ‹*photographer*› cadrer sur; ‹*eyes, attention*› se fixer sur; ‹*report*› se concentrer sur
D **focused** *pp adj* ‹*person*› déterminé/-e

fodder /ˈfɒdə(r)/ *n* fourrage *m*

foe /fəʊ/ *n* ennemi/-e *m/f*

foetus (BrE), **fetus** (AmE) /ˈfiːtəs/ *n* fœtus *m*

fog /fɒg/ **A** *n* brouillard *m*
B *vt* (*p prés etc* **-gg-**) (*also* **~ up**) ‹*steam*› embuer ‹*glass*›; ‹*light*› voiler ‹*film*›

foggy /ˈfɒgɪ/ *adj* ‹*day, weather*› brumeux/-euse; **it's ~** il y a du brouillard

foghorn /ˈfɒghɔːn/ *n* corne *f* de brume

foible /ˈfɔɪbl/ *n* petite manie *f*

foil /fɔɪl/ **A** *n* papier *m* d'aluminium; **silver ~** papier argenté
B *vt* contrecarrer ‹*person*›; déjouer ‹*attempt*›

foist /fɔɪst/ *vt* **to ~ sth on sb** repasser qch à qn

fold /fəʊld/ **A** *n* **1** (in fabric, paper, skin) pli *m*
2 (for sheep) parc *m*
B *vt* **1** plier ‹*paper, shirt, chair*›; replier ‹*wings*›
2 croiser ‹*arms*›; joindre ‹*hands*›
C *vi* **1** ‹*chair*› se plier
2 (fail) ‹*play*› quitter l'affiche; ‹*company*› fermer
IDIOM **to return to the ~** rentrer au bercail
■ **fold back** rabattre ‹*shutters, sheet, sleeve*›
■ **fold in** incorporer ‹*sugar, flour*›
■ **fold up** plier ‹*newspaper, chair*›

folder /ˈfəʊldə(r)/ *n* **1** (for papers) chemise *f*
2 (for artwork) carton *m*

folding /ˈfəʊldɪŋ/ *adj* ‹*bed, table, chair*› pliant/-e; ‹*door*› en accordéon

foliage /ˈfəʊlɪɪdʒ/ *n* feuillage *m*

folk /fəʊk/ **A** *n* (people) gens *mpl*
B *adj* **1** (traditional) ‹*tale, song*› folklorique
2 (modern) ‹*music*› folk *inv*
3 ‹*hero*› populaire

folklore *n* folklore *m*

follow /ˈfɒləʊ/ **A** *vt* (gen) suivre; poursuivre ‹*career*›; **~ed by** suivi/-e de
B *vi* **1** suivre; **to ~ in sb's footsteps** suivre les traces de qn; **there's ice cream to ~** ensuite il y a de la glace; **the results were as ~s** les résultats ont été les suivants
2 (understand) suivre; **I don't ~** je ne suis pas
3 **it ~s that** il s'ensuit que
■ **follow through** mener [qch] à terme ‹*project*›; aller jusqu'au bout de ‹*idea*›
■ **follow up** donner suite à ‹*letter, threat, offer*› (**with** par); suivre ‹*story, lead*›

follower /ˈfɒləʊwə(r)/ *n* **1** (of thinker, artist) disciple *m*; (of political leader) partisan/-e *m/f*
2 (of team) supporter *m*

following /ˈfɒləʊwɪŋ/ **A** *n* (of religion, cult) adeptes *mfpl*; (of party, political figure) partisans/-anes *mpl/fpl*; (of soap opera, show)

public *m*; (of sports team) supporters *mpl*
B *adj* suivant/-e
C *prep* suite à, à la suite de

follow-up /ˈfɒləʊʌp/ **A** *n* **1** (film, record, single, programme) suite *f* (**to** à)
2 (of patient, social work case) suivi *m*
B *adj* **1** (supplementary) ‹*work*› de suivi; ‹*check*› de contrôle; ‹*discussion, article*› complémentaire; ‹*letter*› de rappel
2 (of patient, ex-inmate) ‹*visit*› de contrôle

folly /ˈfɒlɪ/ *n* folie *f*

fond /fɒnd/ *adj* **1** ‹*embrace, farewell*› affectueux/-euse; ‹*eyes, smile*› tendre; **~ memories** de très bons souvenirs
2 ‹*wish, ambition*› cher/chère
3 to be ~ of sb aimer beaucoup qn; **to be ~ of sth** aimer qch

fondle /ˈfɒndl/ *vt* caresser

food /fuːd/ *n* nourriture *f*, alimentation *f*; **frozen ~** aliments *mpl* surgelés; **Chinese ~** la cuisine chinoise; **that's ~ for thought** ça donne à réfléchir

food aid *n* aide *f* alimentaire

foodie /ˈfuːdɪ/ *n* (fam) amateur *m* de bonne bouffe (fam)

food poisoning *n* intoxication *f* alimentaire

food processor *n* robot *m* ménager

food security *n* sécurité *f* alimentaire

foodstuff *n* denrée *f* alimentaire

fool /fuːl/ **A** *n* **1** idiot/-e *m/f* (**to do** de faire); **you stupid ~!** (fam) espèce d'idiot/-e!; **to make sb look a ~** faire passer qn pour un/-e idiot/-e; **to act the ~** faire l'imbécile
2 (jester) fou *m*
B *vt* tromper, duper

foolhardy /ˈfuːlhɑːdɪ/ *adj* téméraire

foolish /ˈfuːlɪʃ/ *adj* **1** ‹*person*› bête (**to do** de faire)
2 ‹*grin, expression*› stupide; **to feel ~** se sentir ridicule
3 ‹*decision, question, remark*› idiot/-e

foolproof /ˈfuːlpruːf/ *adj* **1** ‹*method, plan*› infaillible
2 ‹*machine*› d'utilisation très simple

foot /fʊt/ **A** *n* (*pl* **feet**) **1** (of person) pied *m*; (of animal) patte *f*; (of sock, chair) pied *m*; **on ~** à pied; **from head to ~** de la tête aux pieds; **to put one's ~ down** faire acte d'autorité; (Aut) accélérer
2 (measurement) pied *m* (= *0.3048 m*)
3 (of mountain) pied *m* (**of** de); **at the ~ of** au pied de ‹*bed*›; à la fin de ‹*list, letter*›; en bas de ‹*page, stairs*›
B *vt* **to ~ the bill** payer la facture (**for** de, pour)
IDIOMS **to be under sb's feet** être dans les jambes de qn; **rushed off one's feet** débordé/-e; **to put one's ~ in it** (fam) faire une gaffe; **to stand on one's own two feet** se débrouiller tout seul/toute seule

footage /ˈfʊtɪdʒ/ *n* film *m*, pellicule *f*; **some ~ of** des images de

foot and mouth *n* (*also* **foot and mouth disease**) fièvre *f* aphteuse

football /ˈfʊtbɔːl/ *n* **1** (game) (BrE) football *m*; (AmE) football *m* américain
2 (ball) ballon *m* de football

footballer /ˈfʊtbɔːlə(r)/ *n* (BrE) joueur/-euse *m/f* de football

foot brake *n* (Aut) frein *m* (à pied)

footbridge *n* passerelle *f*

foothold /ˈfʊthəʊld/ *n* prise *f* (de pied); **to gain a ~** ‹*company*› prendre pied; ‹*ideology*› s'imposer

footing /ˈfʊtɪŋ/ *n* **1** (basis) **on a firm ~** sur une base solide; **to be on an equal ~ with sb** être sur un pied d'égalité avec qn
2 (grip for feet) **to lose one's ~** perdre pied

footlights /ˈfʊtlaɪts/ *npl* rampe *f*

footloose /ˈfʊtluːs/ *adj* libre comme l'air

footnote *n* note *f* de bas de page

foot passenger *n* passager *m* sans véhicule

footpath *n* (in countryside) sentier *m*; (in town) trottoir *m*

footprint *n* empreinte *f* (de pied)

footstep /ˈfʊtstep/ *n* pas *m*

footstool *n* repose-pied *m*

footwear *n* chaussures *fpl*

for /fɔː(r), fə(r)/ *prep* **1** (gen) pour; **~ sb** pour qn; **he cooked dinner ~ us** il nous a préparé à manger; **what's it ~?** c'est pour quoi faire?, ça sert à quoi?; **to go ~ a swim** aller nager; **that's ~ us to decide** c'est à nous de décider; **she's the person ~ the job** elle est la personne qu'il faut pour le travail; **the reason ~ doing** la raison pour laquelle on fait; **if it weren't ~ her...** sans elle...; **'~ sale'** 'à vendre'; **it is impossible ~ me to stay** il m'est impossible de rester
2 ‹*work, play*› pour; ‹*MP*› de; **the minister ~ education** le ministre de l'éducation
3 (on behalf of) pour; **to be pleased ~ sb** être content/e pour qn; **say hello to him ~ me** dis-lui bonjour de ma part
4 (in time expressions) (with a completed action in the past) pendant; (with an incomplete action started in the past) depuis; **I waited ~ two hours** j'ai attendu pendant deux heures; **I have/had been waiting ~ an hour** j'attends/j'attendais depuis une heure; **I'm going to Tokyo ~ five weeks** je vais à Tokyo pour cinq semaines; **the best show I've seen ~ years** le meilleur spectacle que j'aie vu depuis des années; **we've been together ~ two years** ça fait deux ans que nous sommes ensemble; **she's off to Paris ~ the weekend** elle va à Paris pour le week-end; **to stay ~ a year** rester un an; **to be away ~ a year** être absent/-e pendant un an; **I was in Paris ~ two weeks** j'ai passé deux semaines à Paris; **the car won't be ready ~ another six weeks** la voiture ne sera pas

prête avant six semaines; **it's time ~ bed** c'est l'heure d'aller au lit
5 (indicating distance) pendant; **to drive ~ miles** rouler pendant des kilomètres; **the last shop ~ 30 miles** le dernier magasin avant 50 kilomètres
6 (indicating cost, value) pour; **it was sold ~ £100** ça s'est vendu (pour) 100 livres sterling; **a cheque ~ £20** un chèque de 20 livres sterling
7 (in favour of) **to be ~** être pour ‹*peace, divorce*›; **the argument ~ recycling** l'argument en faveur du recyclage
8 T ~ Tom T comme Tom; **what's the French ~ 'boot'?** comment dit-on 'boot' en français?
9 ~ one thing... and ~ another... premièrement... et deuxièmement...; **I, ~ one, agree with her** en tout cas moi, je suis d'accord avec elle

forbid /fə'bɪd/ *vt* (*p prés* **-dd-**, *prét* **forbad(e)**, *pp* **forbidden**) défendre, interdire; **to ~ sb to do** défendre *or* interdire à qn de faire; **to ~ sb sth** défendre *or* interdire qch à qn; **God ~!** Dieu m'en/l'en *etc* garde!

forbidden /fə'bɪdn/ *adj* ‹*subject, fruit*› défendu/-e; ‹*place*› interdit/-e; **smoking is ~** il est interdit de fumer

forbidding /fə'bɪdɪŋ/ *adj* ‹*building*› intimidant/-e; ‹*landscape*› inhospitalier/-ière; ‹*expression*› rébarbatif/-ive

force /fɔːs/ **A** *n* force *f*; **by ~** par la force; **the police ~** la police; **a ~ 10 gale** un vent de force 10
B forces *npl* (*also* **armed ~s**) **the ~s** les forces *fpl* armées
C *vt* forcer (**to do** à faire)
D in force *phr* **1** (in large numbers) en force
2 ‹*law, prices, ban*› en vigueur
■ **force on**: **~ [sth] on sb** imposer [qch] à qn, forcer qn à accepter [qch]

forced /fɔːst/ *adj* ‹*smile, landing*› forcé/-e; ‹*conversation*› peu naturel/-elle

force-feed /'fɔːsfiːd/ *vt* (*prét, pp* **-fed**) gaver ‹*animal, bird*›; alimenter [qn] de force ‹*person*›

forceful /'fɔːsfl/ *adj* ‹*person, behaviour*› énergique; ‹*attack, speech*› vigoureux/-euse

ford /fɔːd/ **A** *n* gué *m*
B *vt* **to ~ a river** passer une rivière à gué

fore /fɔː(r)/ *n* **to the ~** en vue, en avant; **to come to the ~** ‹*person, issue*› s'imposer à l'attention; ‹*quality*› ressortir

forearm /'fɔːrɑːm/ *n* avant-bras *m inv*

foreboding /fɔː'bəʊdɪŋ/ *n* pressentiment *m*

forecast /'fɔːkɑːst, (AmE) -kæst/ **A** *n* **1** (*also* **weather ~**) météo *f* (fam), bulletin *m* météorologique
2 (outlook) (gen) pronostics *mpl*; (Econ) prévisions *fpl*
B *vt* (*prét, pp* **-cast**) prévoir (**that** que)

forecaster /'fɔːkɑːstə(r), (AmE) -kæst-/ *n* **1** (of weather) spécialiste *mf* de la météorologie
2 (economic) conjoncturiste *mf*

forecourt /'fɔːkɔːt/ *n* (of shop) parking *m*; (of garage) aire *f* de stationnement; (of station) cour *f* de la gare

forefinger /'fɔːfɪŋgə(r)/ *n* index *m*

forefront /'fɔːfrʌnt/ *n* **at** *or* **in the ~ of** à la pointe de ‹*change, research, debate*›; au premier plan de ‹*campaign, struggle*›

foregone /'fɔːgɒn, (AmE) -'gɔːn/ *adj* **it is a ~ conclusion** c'est couru d'avance

foreground /'fɔːgraʊnd/ *n* premier plan *m*

forehand /'fɔːhænd/ *n* (Sport) coup *m* droit

forehead /'fɒrɪd, 'fɔːhed, (AmE) 'fɔːrɪd/ *n* front *m*

foreign /'fɒrən, (AmE) 'fɔːr-/ *adj* **1** ‹*country, imports, policy*› étranger/-ère; ‹*market*› extérieur/-e; ‹*trade, travel*› à l'étranger
2 (alien) ‹*concept*› étranger/-ère (**to** à)

foreign affairs *npl* affaires *fpl* étrangères

foreign body *n* corps *m* étranger

foreign correspondent *n* correspondant/-e *m/f* à l'étranger

foreigner /'fɒrənə(r)/ *n* étranger/-ère *m/f*

foreign exchange *n* devises *fpl*

foreign exchange market *n* marché *m* des changes

foreign minister, **foreign secretary** (BrE) *n* ministre *m* des Affaires étrangères

foreign national *n* ressortissant/-e *m/f* étranger/-ère; **most of the students affected were said to be ~s** la plupart des étudiants concernés seraient étrangers

Foreign Office, **FO** *n* (BrE) ministère *m* des Affaires étrangères

foreman /'fɔːmən/ *n* **1** (supervisor) contremaître *m*
2 (Law) président *m* (d'un jury)

foremost /'fɔːməʊst/ **A** *adj* premier/-ière *before n*, plus grand
B *adv* **first and ~** avant tout

forename /'fɔːneɪm/ *n* prénom *m*

forensic evidence *n* résultats *mpl* des expertises médico-légales

forensic science *n* médecine *f* légale

forensic scientist *n* médecin *m* légiste

forensic tests *npl* expertises *fpl* médico-légales

forerunner /'fɔːrʌnə(r)/ *n* (person) précurseur *m*; (institution, invention, model) ancêtre *m*

foresee /fɔː'siː/ *vt* (*prét* **foresaw**, *pp* **foreseen**) prévoir

foreseeable /fɔː'siːəbl/ *adj* prévisible

foreshadow /fɔː'ʃædəʊ/ *vt* annoncer

foresight /'fɔːsaɪt/ *n* prévoyance *f* (**to do** de faire)

foreskin /'fɔːskɪn/ *n* prépuce *m*

forest /'fɒrɪst, (AmE) 'fɔːr-/ *n* forêt *f*

forester /'fɒrɪstə(r), (AmE) 'fɔːr-/ *n* forestier/-ière *m/f*

f

forest fire *n* incendie *m* de forêt
forestry /ˈfɒrɪstrɪ, (AmE) ˈfɔːr-/ *n* (science) sylviculture *f*
foretaste /ˈfɔːteɪst/ *n* avant-goût *m* (**of** de)
foretell /fɔːˈtel/ *vt* (*prét*, *pp* **foretold**) prédire
⚷ **forever** /fəˈrevə(r)/ *adv* pour toujours; **to go on ~** ‹*pain, noise, journey*› durer une éternité; **the desert seemed to go on ~** le désert semblait ne pas avoir de limites; **she is ~ complaining** elle est toujours en train de se plaindre
foreword /ˈfɔːwɜːd/ *n* avant-propos *m inv*
forfeit /ˈfɔːfɪt/ **A** *n* gage *m*
B *vt* perdre ‹*right, liberty*›
forge /fɔːdʒ/ **A** *n* forge *f*
B *vt* **1** forger ‹*metal*›
2 contrefaire ‹*banknotes, signature*›; **a ~d passport** un faux passeport
3 forger ‹*alliance*›; établir ‹*identity, link*›
C *vi* **to ~ ahead** accélérer; **to ~ ahead with** aller de l'avant dans ‹*plan*›
forger /ˈfɔːdʒə(r)/ *n* (of documents) faussaire *m*; (of artefacts) contrefacteur/-trice *m/f*; (of money) faux-monnayeur *m*
forgery /ˈfɔːdʒərɪ/ *n* contrefaçon *f*
⚷ **forget** /fəˈget/ **A** *vt* (*prét* **-got**, *pp* **-gotten**) oublier (**that** que, **to do** de faire)
B *vi* (*prét* **-got**, *pp* **-gotten**) oublier
■ **forget about** oublier
forgetful /fəˈgetfl/ *adj* distrait/-e
forget-me-not *n* myosotis *m*
forgive /fəˈgɪv/ *vt* (*prét* **-gave**, *pp* **-given**) pardonner à ‹*person*›; pardonner ‹*act, remark*›; **to ~ sb sth** pardonner qch à qn; **to ~ sb for doing** pardonner à qn d'avoir fait
forgiveness /fəˈgɪvnɪs/ *n* pardon *m*
forgo /fɔːˈgəʊ/ *vt* (*prét* **-went**, *pp* **-gone**) renoncer à
fork /fɔːk/ **A** *n* **1** (for eating) fourchette *f*
2 (tool) fourche *f*
3 (in river, on bicycle) fourche *f*; (in railway) embranchement *m*; (in road) bifurcation *f*
B *vi* (*also* **~ off**) bifurquer
■ **fork out** (fam) casquer (fam) (**for** pour)
forked lightning *n* éclair *m* ramifié
forklift truck (BrE) (*also* **forklift** (AmE)) *n* chariot *m* élévateur à fourche
forlorn /fəˈlɔːn/ *adj* **1** (sad) ‹*appearance*› malheureux/-euse
2 (desperate) ‹*attempt*› désespéré/-e
⚷ **form** /fɔːm/ **A** *n* **1** (gen) forme *f*; **in the ~ of** sous forme de; **to be in good ~** être en bonne *or* pleine forme; **it is bad ~ (to do)** cela ne se fait pas (de faire); **as a matter of ~** pour la forme
2 (document) formulaire *m*; **blank ~** formulaire vierge
3 (BrE) (Sch) classe *f*; **in the first ~** ≈ en sixième
B *vt* **1** former ‹*queue, circle, barrier*› (**from** avec); nouer ‹*friendship, relationship*›; **to ~ part of** faire partie de
2 se faire ‹*impression, opinion*›
3 former ‹*personality, tastes, ideas, attitudes*›
C *vi* se former
formal /ˈfɔːml/ *adj* **1** (official) ‹*agreement, complaint, invitation*› officiel/-ielle
2 (not casual) ‹*language*› soutenu/-e; ‹*occasion*› solennel/-elle; ‹*manner*› cérémonieux/-ieuse; ‹*clothing*› habillé/-e
3 ‹*training*› professionnel/-elle; ‹*qualification*› reconnu/-e
formal dress *n* tenue *f* de soirée
formality /fɔːˈmælətɪ/ *n* **1** (legal or social convention) formalité *f*
2 (of occasion, manner) solennité *f*; (of language) caractère *m* soutenu
formally /ˈfɔːməlɪ/ *adv* **1** (officially) officiellement
2 (not casually) cérémonieusement
format /ˈfɔːmæt/ **A** *n* format *m*
B *vt* (*p prés etc* **-tt-**) (Comput) formater
⚷ **formation** /fɔːˈmeɪʃn/ *n* formation *f*
⚷ **former** /ˈfɔːmə(r)/ **A** *n* **the ~** (singular noun) celui-là/celle-là *m/f*; (plural noun) ceux-là/celles-là *mpl/fpl*
B *adj* **1** ‹*era, life*› antérieur/-e; ‹*size, state*› initial/-e, original/-e; **he's a shadow of his ~ self** il n'est plus que l'ombre de lui-même
2 ‹*leader, husband, champion*› ancien/-ienne *before n*
3 (first of two) premier/-ière *before n*
formerly /ˈfɔːməlɪ/ *adv* autrefois
formidable /ˈfɔːmɪdəbl, fɔːˈmɪd-/ *adj*
1 (intimidating) redoutable
2 (awe-inspiring) impressionnant/-e
formula /ˈfɔːmjʊlə/ *n* (*pl* **-lae** *ou* **~s**)
1 formule *f* (**for** de, **for doing** pour faire)
2 (baby milk) lait *m* en poudre
fort /fɔːt/ *n* fort *m*
forte /ˈfɔːteɪ, (*also* AmE) fɔːrt/ *n* **to be sb's ~** être le fort de qn
forth /fɔːθ/ *adv* **from this day ~** à partir d'aujourd'hui; **from that day ~** à dater de ce jour; ▶ **back, so**
forthcoming /ˌfɔːθˈkʌmɪŋ/ *adj* **1** ‹*event, book*› prochain/-e *before n*
2 she wasn't very ~ about it elle était peu disposée à en parler
forthright /ˈfɔːθraɪt/ *adj* direct/-e
forties *npl* **1** (era) **the ~** les années *fpl* quarante
2 (age) **to be in one's ~** avoir entre quarante et cinquante ans
fortieth /ˈfɔːtɪɪθ/ *n, adj, adv* quarantième *mf*
fortified *adj* ‹*place*› fortifié/-e; **~ wine** vin *m* doux; **~ with vitamins** vitaminé/-e
fortify /ˈfɔːtɪfaɪ/ *vt* fortifier
fortnight /ˈfɔːtnaɪt/ *n* (BrE) quinze jours *mpl*; **the first ~ in August** la première

⚷ mot clé

quinzaine d'août

fortnightly /ˈfɔːtnaɪtlɪ/ *adj* ‹*meeting, visit*› qui a lieu toutes les deux semaines; ‹*magazine*› publié/-e toutes les deux semaines

fortunate /ˈfɔːtʃənət/ *adj* heureux/-euse

fortunately /ˈfɔːtʃənətlɪ/ *adv* heureusement

fortune /ˈfɔːtʃuːn/ *n* **1** fortune *f*; **to make a ∼** faire fortune
2 to have the good ∼ to do avoir la chance *or* le bonheur de faire
3 to tell sb's ∼ dire la bonne aventure à qn

fortune-teller *n* diseur/-euse *m/f* de bonne aventure

forty /ˈfɔːtɪ/ *n, pron, det* quarante *m inv*

forward /ˈfɔːwəd/ **A** *n* (Sport) avant *m*
B *adj* **1** (bold) effronté/-e
2 (towards the front) ‹*movement*› en avant; **to be too far ∼** ‹*seat*› être trop en avant
3 (advanced) avancé/-e; **he's no further ∼** il n'est pas plus avancé
C *adv* (*also* **forwards**) **to step ∼** faire un pas en avant; **to fall ∼** tomber en avant; **to go** *or* **walk ∼** avancer; **to move sth ∼** avancer qch; **a way ∼** une solution
D *vt* **1** expédier ‹*goods*›; envoyer ‹*parcel*›
2 (send on) faire suivre, réexpédier ‹*mail*›

forwarding address *n* nouvelle adresse *f* (pour faire suivre le courrier)

forward-looking *adj* ‹*company, person*› tourné/-e vers l'avenir

forward planning *n* planification *f* à long terme

forwards /ˈfɔːwədz/ = **forward C**

fossil /ˈfɒsl/ *n* fossile *m*

fossil fuel *n* combustible *m* fossile

foster /ˈfɒstə(r)/ **A** *adj* ‹*child, parent*› adoptif/-ive
B *vt* **1** (encourage) encourager ‹*attitude*›; promouvoir ‹*activity*›
2 prendre [qn] en placement ‹*child*›

foster family *n* famille *f* de placement

foster home *n* foyer *m* de placement

foul /faʊl/ **A** *n* (Sport) faute *f* (**by** de, **on** sur)
B *adj* **1** ‹*smell, air*› fétide; ‹*taste*› infect/-e
2 ‹*weather, day*› épouvantable; **to be in a ∼ mood** être d'une humeur massacrante (fam); **to have a ∼ temper** avoir un sale caractère; **to taste ∼** avoir un goût infect
3 ‹*language*› ordurier/-ière
C *vt* **1** polluer ‹*environment*›; souiller ‹*pavement*›
2 (Sport) commettre une faute contre ‹*player*›

foul-mouthed *adj* grossier/-ière

foul play /ˌfaʊlˈpleɪ/ *n* acte *m* criminel; (in sport) jeu *m* irrégulier

foul-up *n* (fam) cafouillage *m* (fam)

found /faʊnd/ *vt* fonder (**on** sur)

foundation /ˌfaʊnˈdeɪʃn/ *n* **1** (founding) fondation *f*
2 ∼s (of building) fondations *fpl*
3 (*also* **∼ cream**) fond *m* de teint

foundation course *n* (BrE) (Univ) année *f* de préparation à des études supérieures

founder /ˈfaʊndə(r)/ *n* fondateur/-trice *m/f*

foundry /ˈfaʊndrɪ/ *n* fonderie *f*

fountain /ˈfaʊntɪn, (AmE) -tn/ *n* fontaine *f*

fountain pen *n* stylo *m* (à encre)

four /fɔː(r)/ *n, pron, det* quatre *m inv*
IDIOM **on all ∼s** à quatre pattes

four-by-four /ˌfɔːbaɪˈfɔː(r)/ *n* quatre-quatre *m inv*

four-letter word *n* mot *m* grossier

four-star /ˈfɔːstɑː(r)/ **A** *n* (*also* **∼ petrol**) (BrE) super(carburant) *m*
B *adj* ‹*hotel, restaurant*› quatre étoiles

fourteen /ˌfɔːˈtiːn/ *n, pron, det* quatorze *m inv*

fourteenth /ˌfɔːˈtiːnθ/ **A** *n* **1** (in order) quatorzième *mf*
2 (of month) quatorze *m inv*
3 (fraction) quatorzième *m*
B *adj, adv* quatorzième

fourth /fɔːθ/ **A** *n* **1** (in order) quatrième *mf*
2 (of month) quatre *m inv*
3 (fraction) quatrième *m*
4 (*also* **∼ gear**) (Aut) quatrième *f*
B *adj, adv* quatrième

four-wheel drive *n* (*also* **four-wheel drive vehicle**) quatre-quatre *m inv*

fowl /faʊl/ *n* volaille *f*

fox /fɒks/ *n* renard *m*

foxhound *n* fox-hound *m*

fox hunting *n* chasse *f* au renard

fracking /ˈfrækɪŋ/ *n* fracturation *f* hydraulique, fracking *m*

fraction /ˈfrækʃn/ *n* fraction *f* (**of** de)

fracture /ˈfræktʃə(r)/ **A** *n* fracture *f*
B *vt* fracturer ‹*bone, rock*›
C *vi* ‹*bone*› se fracturer

fragile /ˈfrædʒaɪl, (AmE) -dʒl/ *adj* fragile

fragment /ˈfrægmənt/ *n* (of rock, manuscript) fragment *m*; (of glass, china) morceau *m*

fragrance /ˈfreɪgrəns/ *n* parfum *m*

fragrant /ˈfreɪgrənt/ *adj* odorant/-e

frail /freɪl/ *adj* ‹*person*› frêle; ‹*health, hope*› précaire

frame /freɪm/ **A** *n* **1** (of building, boat, roof) charpente *f*; (of car) châssis *m*; (of bicycle, racquet) cadre *m*; (of bed) sommier *m*; (of tent) armature *f*
2 (of picture, window) cadre *m*; (of door) encadrement *m*
3 (body) corps *m*
B frames *npl* (of spectacles) monture *f*
C *vt* **1** encadrer ‹*picture, face*›
2 formuler ‹*question*›

frame of mind *n* état *m* d'esprit; **to be in the right/wrong ∼ for doing** être/ne pas être d'humeur à faire

framework /'freɪmwɜ:k/ *n* structure *f*; (fig) cadre *m*

franc /fræŋk/ *n* franc *m*

France /frɑ:ns/ *pr n* France *f*

franchise /'fræntʃaɪz/ *n* **1** (right to vote) droit *m* de vote
2 (commercial) franchise *f*

Francophile /'fræŋkəʊfaɪl/ *n, adj* francophile *mf*

frank /fræŋk/ *adj* franc/franche

Frankfurt /'fræŋkfət/ *pr n* Francfort

f

frankly /'fræŋklɪ/ *adv* franchement

frantic /'fræntɪk/ *adj* **1** ‹*activity*› frénétique
2 ‹*effort, search*› désespéré/-e; **to be ~ with worry** être fou/folle d'inquiétude

frantically /'fræntɪklɪ/ *adv* **1** (wildly) frénétiquement
2 (desperately) désespérément

fraternal /frə'tɜ:nl/ *adj* fraternel/-elle

fraternity /frə'tɜ:nətɪ/ *n* fraternité *f*

fraud /frɔ:d/ *n* fraude *f*

fraudulent /'frɔ:djʊlənt, (AmE) -dʒʊ-/ *adj* ‹*practice, use*› frauduleux/-euse; ‹*signature, cheque*› falsifié/-e; ‹*earnings*› illicite

fraught /frɔ:t/ *adj* ‹*situation, atmosphere*› tendu/-e; ‹*person*› accablé/-e (**with** de); **to be ~ with** être lourd/-e de ‹*danger, difficulty*›

fray /freɪ/ *vi* ‹*material, rope*› s'effilocher

frayed *adj* ‹*nerves*› à bout; **tempers were ~** les gens s'énervaient

frazzle /'fræzl/ *n* (fam) **to burn sth to a ~** calciner qch; **to be worn to a ~** être lessivé/-e (fam)

freak /fri:k/ **A** *n* **1** (strange person) original/-e *m/f*
2 (at circus) phénomène *m*; **~ show** exhibition *f* de monstres
3 (unusual occurrence) aberration *f*; **a ~ of nature** une bizarrerie de la nature
4 (fam) (enthusiast) mordu/-e *m/f* (fam), fana *mf* (fam)
B *adj* ‹*accident, storm*› exceptionnel/-elle
■ **freak out** (fam) (get angry) piquer une crise (fam); (go mad) flipper (fam)

freckle /'frekl/ *n* tache *f* de rousseur

⚷ **free** /fri:/ **A** *adj* **1** (gen) libre; **to be ~ to do** être libre de faire; **to set [sb/sth] ~** libérer ‹*person*›; rendre la liberté à ‹*animal*›
2 (*also* **~ of charge**) gratuit/-e; **'admission ~'** 'entrée gratuite'
3 to be ~ with être prodigue de ‹*advice*›; **to be very ~ with money** dépenser sans compter
B *adv* **1** ‹*run, roam*› librement, en toute liberté; **to go ~** ‹*hostage*› être libéré/-e; ‹*criminal*› circuler en toute liberté
2 (without paying) gratuitement
C *vt* **1** (gen) libérer; (from wreckage) dégager
2 débloquer ‹*money, resources*›
D -free *combining form* **smoke/sugar-~** sans fumée/sucre; **interest-~** sans intérêt
E for free *phr* gratuitement
IDIOMS **to have a ~ hand** avoir carte blanche (**in** pour); **to be a ~ agent** pouvoir agir à sa guise; **~ and easy** décontracté/-e

freebie, **freebee** *n* (fam) (free gift) cadeau *m*; (newspaper) journal *m* gratuit; (trip) voyage *m* gratuit

⚷ **freedom** /'fri:dəm/ *n* liberté *f* (**to do** de faire); **~ of the press** liberté de la presse; **~ of information** libre accès *m* à l'information

freedom fighter *n* combattant *m* de la liberté

free fall /'fri:fɔ:l/ *n* chute *f* libre

Freefone® /'fri:fəʊn/ (*also* **Freephone**®) *n* numéro *m* vert d'appel gratuit

free-for-all *n* mêlée *f* générale

free gift *n* cadeau *m*

free kick *n* coup *m* franc

freelance /'fri:lɑ:ns, (AmE) -læns/ **A** *n* (*also* **freelancer**) free-lance *mf*
B *adv* ‹*work*› en free-lance

freely /'fri:lɪ/ *adv* (gen) librement; ‹*spend, give*› sans compter; ‹*admit*› volontiers

free market *n* (*also* **~ economy**) économie *f* de marché

Freephone® = **Freefone**

Freepost /'fri:pəʊst/ *n* (BrE) port *m* payé

free-range *adj* ‹*chicken*› élevé/-e en plein air; ‹*eggs*› de poules élevées en plein air

free speech *n* liberté *f* d'expression

freestyle /'fri:staɪl/ *n* (in swimming) nage *f* libre; (in skiing) figures *fpl* libres; (in wrestling) lutte *f* libre

free-to-air *adj* gratuit/-e

free trade *n* libre-échange *m*

freeware *n* freeware *m*, graticiel *m*

freeway *n* (AmE) autoroute *f*

free will *n* libre arbitre *m*; **of one's (own) ~** de plein gré

freeze /fri:z/ **A** *n* **1** (in weather) gelées *fpl*
2 (Econ) gel *m* (**on** de)
B *vt* (*prét* **froze**, *pp* **frozen**) **1** congeler ‹*food*›; ‹*cold weather*› geler ‹*liquid, pipes*›
2 (Econ) bloquer, geler ‹*prices, wages, assets*›
3 (anaesthetize) insensibiliser ‹*gum, skin*›
C *vi* (*prét* **froze**, *pp* **frozen**) **1** ‹*water, pipes*› geler; ‹*food*› se congeler
2 (feel cold) geler; **to be freezing to death** mourir de froid
3 (not move) ‹*person, blood, smile*› se figer
D *v impers* geler

freeze-dried *adj* lyophilisé/-e

freeze frame *n* arrêt *m* sur image

freezer /'fri:zə(r)/ *n* congélateur *m*

freezer compartment *n* freezer *m*

freezing /'fri:zɪŋ/ **A** *n* zéro *m*; **below ~** en-dessous de zéro

B *adj* **I'm ~** je suis gelé; **it's ~ in here** on gèle ici

freezing cold *adj* ‹*room, wind*› glacial/-e; ‹*water*› glacé/-e

freight /ˈfreɪt/ *n* **1** (goods) fret *m*, marchandises *fpl*
2 (transport system) transport *m*
3 (cost) (frais *mpl* de) port *m*

freighter /ˈfreɪtə(r)/ *n* **1** (ship) cargo *m*
2 (plane) avion-cargo *m*

French /frentʃ/ **A** *n* **1** (people) **the ~** les Français *mpl*
2 (language) français *m*
B *adj* ‹*culture, food, politics*› français/-e; ‹*teacher, lesson*› de français; ‹*ambassador, embassy*› de France

French fries *npl* frites *fpl*

Frenchman *n* (*pl* **-men**) Français *m*

French-speaking *adj* francophone

French toast *n* pain *m* perdu

French window *n* porte-fenêtre *f*

Frenchwoman *n* (*pl* **-women**) Française *f*

frenetic /frəˈnetɪk/ *adj* ‹*activity*› frénétique; ‹*lifestyle*› trépidant/-e

frenzied /ˈfrenzɪd/ *adj* ‹*activity*› frénétique; ‹*attempt*› désespéré/-e

frenzy /ˈfrenzɪ/ *n* frénésie *f*, délire *m*

frequency /ˈfriːkwənsɪ/ *n* fréquence *f* (**of** de)

frequent /ˈfriːkwənt/ *adj* **1** (common) ‹*expression*› courant/-e
2 (happening often) fréquent/-e; **to make ~ use of sth** se servir souvent *or* fréquemment de qch

frequently /ˈfriːkwəntlɪ/ *adv* souvent, fréquemment

fresco /ˈfreskəʊ/ *n* (*pl* **-oes**) fresque *f*

fresh /freʃ/ *adj* **1** frais/fraîche; **to smell ~** avoir une odeur fraîche; **~ orange juice** jus *m* d'orange pressée; **while it is still ~ in your mind** tant que tu l'as tout frais à l'esprit
2 ‹*evidence, attempt*› nouveau/-elle *before n*; ‹*linen*› propre; **to make a ~ start** prendre un nouveau départ
3 ‹*approach, outlook*› (tout) nouveau/(toute) nouvelle *before n*
4 to feel *or* **be ~** ‹*person*› être plein/-e d'entrain
5 (fam) (cheeky) impertinent/-e; **to be ~ with sb** être un peu familier/-ière avec qn

fresh air *n* air *m* frais; **to get some ~** prendre l'air, s'oxygéner

freshen /ˈfreʃn/
▪ **freshen up** faire un brin de toilette

freshly /ˈfreʃlɪ/ *adv* fraîchement; **~ ironed/washed** qui vient d'être repassé/lavé

fresh water *n* eau *f* douce

fret /fret/ *vi* (*p prés etc* **-tt-**) **1** (be anxious) s'inquiéter (**over, about** pour, au sujet de)
2 (cry) pleurer

Freudian slip *n* lapsus *m*

friction /ˈfrɪkʃn/ *n* **1** (rubbing) frottement *m*
2 (conflict) conflits *mpl* (**between** entre); **to cause ~** être cause de friction

Friday /ˈfraɪdɪ/ *n* vendredi *m*

fridge /frɪdʒ/ *n* (BrE) frigo *m* (fam), réfrigérateur *m*

fridge-freezer /ˌfrɪdʒˈfriːzə(r)/ *n* réfrigérateur-congélateur *m*

friend /frend/ *n* ami/-e *m/f* (**of** de); **to make ~s** se faire des amis; **to make ~s with sb** devenir ami/-e avec qn

friendly /ˈfrendlɪ/ **A** *adj* ‹*person, attitude, argument, match*› amical/-e; ‹*animal*› affectueux/-euse; ‹*government, nation*› ami *after n*; **to be ~ with sb** être ami/-e *m/f* avec qn
B **-friendly** *combining form* **environment-~** qui ne nuit pas à l'environnement; **user-~** d'utilisation facile, convivial/-e

friendly fire *n* (Mil) feu *m* allié

friendship /ˈfrendʃɪp/ *n* amitié *f*

fries /fraɪz/ *npl* (AmE) (fam) frites *fpl*

fright /fraɪt/ *n* peur *f*; **to take ~** prendre peur, s'effrayer; **to give sb a ~** faire peur à qn, effrayer qn

frighten /ˈfraɪtn/ *vt* faire peur à, effrayer

frightened /ˈfraɪtnd/ *adj* **to be ~** avoir peur (**of** de, **to do** de faire)

frightening /ˈfraɪtnɪŋ/ *adj* effrayant/-e

frightful /ˈfraɪtfl/ *adj* **1** (inducing horror) abominable, épouvantable
2 (fam) (bad) ‹*prospect, mistake*› terrible; ‹*headache*› affreux/-euse

frill /frɪl/ *n* (on dress) volant *m*; (on shirt) jabot *m*

fringe /frɪndʒ/ *n* **1** frange *f*; **on the ~s of society** en marge de la societé
2 (in theatre) **the ~** théâtre *m* alternatif

fringe benefits *npl* avantages *mpl* sociaux *or* en nature

frisk /frɪsk/ *vt* fouiller ‹*person*›

fritter /ˈfrɪtə(r)/ *n* beignet *m*
▪ **fritter away** gaspiller ‹*time, money*›

frivolous /ˈfrɪvələs/ *adj* frivole

frizzy /ˈfrɪzɪ/ *adj* ‹*hair*› crépu/-e

frog /frɒg, (AmE) frɔːg/ *n* grenouille *f*
IDIOM **to have a ~ in one's throat** avoir un chat dans la gorge

frogman *n* homme-grenouille *m*

frogs' legs *npl* cuisses *fpl* de grenouille

from /frɒm, frəm/ *prep*

> *from* is often translated by *de*: *from Rome* = de Rome; *from the sea* = de la mer.
> Remember that *de* + *le* always becomes *du* (*from the office* = du bureau), and *de* + *les* always becomes *des* (*from the United States* = des États-Unis).
> For examples and particular usages, see the entry below.

1 de; **where is he ~?** d'où est-il?, d'où vient-il?; **she comes ~ Oxford** elle vient d'Oxford; **paper ~ Denmark** du papier provenant du Danemark; **a flight ~ Nice** un vol en

provenance de Nice; **a friend ~ Chicago** un ami (qui vient) de Chicago; **a colleague ~ Japan** un collègue japonais; **a man ~ the council** un homme qui travaille pour le conseil municipal; **a letter ~ Tim** une lettre (de la part) de Tim; **who is it ~?** c'est de la part de qui?; **alcohol can be made ~ a wide range of products** on peut faire de l'alcool à partir de produits très variés; **10 km ~ the sea** à 10 km de la mer; **15 years ~ now** dans 15 ans, d'ici 15 ans
2 ~ ... to... de ... à...; **the journey ~ A to B** le voyage de A à B; **the road ~ A to B** la route qui va de A à B; **open ~ 2 pm to 5 pm** ouvert de 14 à 17 heures; **~ June to August** du mois de juin au mois d'août; **to rise ~ 10 to 17%** passer de 10 à 17%; **~ start to finish** du début à la fin; **everything ~ paper clips to wigs** tout, des trombones aux perruques; **~ day to day** de jour en jour
3 (starting from) à partir de; **~ today/May** à partir d'aujourd'hui/du mois de mai; **wine ~ £5 a bottle** du vin à partir de 5 livres sterling la bouteille; **~ then on** dès lors; **~ the age of 8** depuis l'âge de 8 ans
4 (based on) **~ a short story** d'après un conte; **to speak ~ experience** parler d'expérience
5 (among) **to choose** *or* **pick ~** choisir parmi
6 (in mathematics) **10 ~ 27 leaves 17** 27 moins 10 égale 17
7 (because of) **I know her ~ work** je la connais car on travaille ensemble; **~ what I saw/he said** d'après ce que j'ai vu/ce qu'il a dit

⚷ **front** /frʌnt/ **A** *n* **1** (of house) façade *f*; (of shop) devanture *f*; (of cupboard, box, sweater, building) devant *m*; (of book) couverture *f*; (of card, coin, banknote) recto *m*; (of car, boat) avant *m*; (of fabric) endroit *m*; **to button at the ~** se boutonner sur le devant; **on the ~ of the envelope** au recto de l'enveloppe
2 (of train, queue) tête *f*; (of auditorium) premier rang *m*; **at the ~ of the line** en tête de la file; **to sit at the ~ of the class** s'asseoir au premier rang de la classe; **I'll sit in the ~** je vais m'asseoir devant; **at the ~ of the coach** à l'avant du car
3 (BrE) (promenade) front *m* de mer, bord *m* de mer; **on the sea ~** au bord de la mer
4 (Mil) front *m*
5 (in weather) front *m*
6 (façade) façade *f*; **it's just a ~** ce n'est qu'une façade
B *adj* ‹*entrance*› côté rue; ‹*garden, window*› de devant; ‹*bedroom*› qui donne sur la rue; ‹*wheel*› avant; ‹*seat*› (in cinema) au premier rang; (in vehicle) de devant; ‹*leg, paw, tooth*› de devant; ‹*view*› de face
C *vt* **1** (fam) être à la tête de ‹*band*›
2 présenter ‹*TV show*›
D *vi* **to ~ on to** (BrE) *or* **on** (AmE) donner sur
E in front *phr* ‹*walk*› devant; **the car in ~** la voiture de devant; **the people in ~** les gens qui sont devant; **to be in ~** (in race) être en tête; **I'm 30 points in ~** j'ai 30 points d'avance
F in front of *phr* devant

front bench /ˌfrʌntˈbentʃ/ *n* (BrE) (Pol) (seats) rangs *mpl* du gouvernement

front door *n* porte *f* d'entrée

frontier /ˈfrʌntɪə(r), (AmE) frʌnˈtɪər/ *n* frontière *f*

front line /ˈfrʌntlaɪn/ *n* **1** (Mil) front *m*
2 (exposed position) **to be in the ~** être en première ligne

front page A *n* première page *f*
B front-page *adj* ‹*picture, story*› à la une (fam); **the ~ headlines** les gros titres, la manchette

frost /frɒst/ *n* gel *m*

frostbite /ˈfrɒstbaɪt/ *n* gelures *fpl*

frosted *adj* ‹*nail varnish*› nacré/-e; ‹*glass*› dépoli/-e, opaque

frosty /ˈfrɒstɪ/ *adj* **1** ‹*morning*› glacial/-e; ‹*windscreen*› couvert/-e de givre; **it was a ~ night** il gelait cette nuit-là
2 (unfriendly) glacial/-e

froth /frɒθ, (AmE) frɔːθ/ *n* (on beer, champagne) mousse *f*; (on water) écume *f*; (around mouth) écume *f*

frown /fraʊn/ *vi* froncer les sourcils; **to ~ at sb** regarder qn en fronçant les sourcils
■ **frown on, frown upon** désapprouver, critiquer

frozen /ˈfrəʊzn/ *adj* **1** ‹*food*› congelé/-e
2 ‹*lake, pipe, ground*› gelé/-e; **I'm ~** je suis gelé; **to be ~ stiff** être transi/-e de froid

⚷ **fruit** /fruːt/ *n* (*pl for collective* ~) fruit *m*; **a piece of ~** un fruit

fruit cake *n* cake *m*

fruition /fruːˈɪʃn/ *n* **to come to ~** se réaliser; **to bring sth to ~** réaliser qch

fruit juice *n* jus *m* de fruits

fruit machine *n* machine *f* à sous

fruit salad *n* salade *f* de fruits

fruity /ˈfruːtɪ/ *adj* ‹*wine, fragrance*› fruité/-e

frustrate /frʌˈstreɪt, (AmE) ˈfrʌstreɪt/ *vt* frustrer ‹*person*›; réduire [qch] à néant ‹*effort*›; contrarier ‹*plan*›; entraver ‹*attempt*›

frustrated /frʌˈstreɪtɪd, (AmE) ˈfrʌst-/ *adj* frustré/-e

frustrating /frʌˈstreɪtɪŋ, (AmE) ˈfrʌst-/ *adj*
1 (irritating) énervant/-e
2 (unsatisfactory) frustrant/-e

frustration /frʌˈstreɪʃn/ *n* frustration *f* (**at, with** quant à)

fry /fraɪ/ **A** *vt* (*prét, pp* **fried**) faire frire
B fried *pp adj* **fried fish** poisson *m* frit; **fried food** friture *f*; **fried eggs** œufs *mpl* au plat; **fried potatoes** pommes *fpl* de terre sautées

frying pan *n* (BrE) poêle *f* (à frire)

⚷ **fuel** /ˈfjuːəl/ **A** *n* (for heating) combustible *m*; (for car, plane) carburant *m*
B *vt* (*p prés etc* **-ll-** (BrE), **-l-** (AmE))

f

1 alimenter *‹engine›*
2 ravitailler *‹plane›*
3 aggraver *‹tension›*; attiser *‹hatred›*

fuel tank *n* (of car) réservoir *m*

fugitive /'fjuːdʒətɪv/ *n* fugitif/-ive *m/f*, fuyard/-e *m/f*

fulfil (BrE), **fulfill** (AmE) /fʊl'fɪl/ *vt* (*p prés etc* **-ll-**) **1** réaliser *‹ambition›*; répondre à *‹desire, need›*; **to feel ~led** se sentir comblé/-e
2 remplir *‹duty, conditions, contract›*

fulfilment (BrE), **fulfillment** (AmE) /fʊl'fɪlmənt/ *n* **1** (satisfaction) épanouissement *m*
2 the ~ of la réalisation de *‹ambition, need›*

full /fʊl/ **A** *adj* **1** (gen) plein/-e (**of** de); *‹hotel, flight, car park›* complet/-ète; *‹theatre›* comble; **I'm ~ (up)** je n'en peux plus
2 (busy) *‹day, week›* chargé/-e, bien rempli/-e; **a very ~ life** une vie très remplie
3 (complete) *‹name, breakfast, story›* complet/-ète; *‹price, control›* total/-e; *‹responsibility›* entier/-ière; *‹support›* inconditionnel/-elle
4 *‹member›* à part entière
5 *‹employment, bloom›* plein/-e *before n*; **at ~ volume** à plein volume; **at ~ speed** à toute vitesse; **to get ~ marks** (BrE) obtenir la note maximale
6 (for emphasis) *‹hour, kilo, month›* bon/bonne *before n*
7 (rounded) *‹cheeks›* rond/-e; *‹figure›* fort/-e; *‹skirt, sleeve›* ample
B *adv* **to know ~ well that** savoir fort bien que; **with the heating up ~** avec le chauffage à fond
C in full *phr ‹pay›* intégralement; **to write sth in ~** écrire qch en toutes lettres

full blast /ˌfʊl'blɑːst/ *adv* (fam) **the TV was on (at) ~** la télé marchait à pleins tubes (fam)

full-blown /ˌfʊl'bləʊn/ *adj* **1** *‹disease›* déclaré/-e; *‹epidemic›* extensif/-ive
2 *‹crisis, war›* à grande échelle

full board *n* (in hotel) pension *f* complète

full-cream milk *n* (BrE) lait *m* entier

full-length /ˌfʊl'leŋθ/ *adj ‹coat, curtain›* long/longue; *‹mirror›* en pied; **a ~ film** un long métrage

full moon *n* pleine lune *f*

full name *n* nom *m* et prénom *m*

full price *adj, adv* au prix fort

full-scale /ˌfʊl'skeɪl/ *adj* **1** *‹drawing›* grandeur *f* nature
2 *‹investigation›* approfondi/-e
3 *‹alert›* général/-e; *‹crisis›* généralisé/-e

full-size (*also* **full-sized**) /ˌfʊl'saɪz(d)/ *adj* grand format *inv*

full stop *n* (BrE) point *m*

full time **A** *n* (Sport) fin *m* du match
B full-time *adj* **1** (Sport) *‹score›* final/-e
2 *‹job, student›* à plein temps
C *adv ‹study, work›* à plein temps

fully /'fʊlɪ/ *adv* **1** *‹understand›* très bien; *‹recover›* complètement; *‹dressed›* entièrement; *‹awake, developed›* complètement; **to be ~ qualified** avoir obtenu tous ses diplômes
2 *‹open›* à fond; **~ booked** complet/-ète

fully-fledged /ˌfʊlɪ'fledʒd/ *adj ‹member›* à part entière; *‹lawyer›* diplômé/-e

fumble /'fʌmbl/ *vt* mal attraper *‹ball›*
■ **fumble about** (in dark) tâtonner (**to do** pour faire); **to ~ about in** fouiller dans *‹bag›*

fume /fjuːm/ *vi* **1** *‹chemical, mixture›* fumer
2 (fam) **to be fuming** être furibond/-e (fam)

fumes /fjuːmz/ *npl* émanations *fpl*; **petrol ~** (BrE), **gas ~** (AmE) vapeurs *fpl* d'essence

fun /fʌn/ *n* plaisir *m*, amusement *m*; **to have ~** s'amuser (**doing** en faisant, **with** avec); **windsurfing is ~** c'est amusant de faire de la planche à voile; **for ~** pour s'amuser; **she is great ~ to be with** on s'amuse beaucoup avec elle
IDIOM **to make ~ of** *or* **poke ~ at sb/sth** se moquer de qn/qch

function /'fʌŋkʃn/ **A** *n* **1** (gen) fonction *f*
2 (reception) réception *f*; (ceremony) cérémonie *f* (officielle)
B *vi* **1** (work properly) fonctionner
2 to ~ as *‹object›* faire fonction de, servir de; *‹person›* jouer le rôle de

functional /'fʌŋkʃənl/ *adj* **1** (in working order) opérationnel/-elle
2 *‹furniture, design›* fonctionnel/-elle

function key *n* touche *f* de fonction

fund /fʌnd/ **A** *n* fonds *m*; **relief ~** caisse *f* de secours; **disaster ~** collecte *f* en faveur des sinistrés
B funds *npl* fonds *mpl*, capitaux *mpl*; **to be in ~s** avoir de l'argent
C *vt* financer *‹company, project›*

fundamental /ˌfʌndə'mentl/ *adj ‹issue›* fondamental/-e; *‹error, importance›* capital/-e; *‹concern›* principal/-e

fundamentalist /ˌfʌndə'mentəlɪst/ *n, adj* (gen) fondamentaliste *mf*; (religious) intégriste *mf*

funding /'fʌndɪŋ/ *n* financement *m*

fund-raising /'fʌndreɪzɪŋ/ *n* collecte *f* de fonds

funeral /'fjuːnərəl/ *n* enterrement *m*, obsèques *fpl*

funeral home, **funeral parlour** *n* entreprise *f* de pompes funèbres

fun fair *n* fête *f* foraine

fungus /'fʌŋgəs/ *n* (*pl* **-gi**) **1** (mushroom) champignon *m*
2 (mould) moisissure *f*

fun-loving /'fʌnlʌvɪŋ/ *adj ‹person›* qui aime s'amuser

funnel /'fʌnl/ *n* **1** (for liquids) entonnoir *m*
2 (on ship) cheminée *f*

funny /'fʌnɪ/ *adj* (amusing) drôle, amusant/-e;

(odd) bizarre; **to feel ~** (fam) se sentir tout/-e chose (fam)

fur /fɜ:(r)/ **A** *n* (of animal) poils *mpl*; (for garment) fourrure *f*
B *adj* ‹*collar, coat*› de fourrure

furious /'fjʊərɪəs/ *adj* **1** furieux/-ieuse (**with, at** contre); **he's ~ about it** cela l'a rendu furieux
2 ‹*debate, struggle*› acharné/-e; ‹*storm*› déchaîné/-e; **at a ~ rate** à un rythme effréné

furnace /'fɜ:nɪs/ *n* (boiler) chaudière *f*; (in foundry) fourneau *m*; (for forging) four *m*

furnish /'fɜ:nɪʃ/ *vt* meubler ‹*room, apartment*›

furnishings *npl* ameublement *m*

furniture /'fɜ:nɪtʃə(r)/ *n* mobilier *m*, meubles *mpl*; **a piece of ~** un meuble

furry /'fɜ:rɪ/ *adj* ‹*toy*› en peluche; ‹*kitten*› au poil touffu

⚷ **further** /'fɜ:ðə(r)/ **A** *adv* (*comparative of* **far**) **1** (*also* **farther**) (gen) plus loin (**than** que); **how much ~ is it?** c'est encore loin?; **~ back/forward** plus en arrière/en avant; **~ away** *or* **off** plus loin; **~ on** encore plus loin
2 (*also* **farther**) (in time) **~ back than 1964** avant 1964; **we must look ~ ahead** nous devons regarder plus vers l'avenir
3 I haven't read ~ than page twenty je n'ai pas lu au-delà de la page vingt; **prices fell (even) ~** les prix ont baissé encore plus
B *adj* (*comparative of* **far**) **1** (additional) **a ~ 500 people** 500 personnes de plus; **~ changes** d'autres changements; **without ~ delay** sans plus attendre
2 (*also* **farther**) ‹*side, end*› autre
C *vt* augmenter ‹*chances*›; faire avancer ‹*career, plan*›; servir ‹*cause*›

further education *n* (BrE) (Univ) ≈ enseignement *m* professionnel

furthest /'fɜ:ðɪst/ **A** *adj* (*superlative of* **far**) le plus éloigné/la plus éloignée
B *adv* (*also* **the ~**) le plus loin

furtive /'fɜ:tɪv/ *adj* ‹*glance, movement*› furtif/-ive; ‹*behaviour*› suspect/-e

fury /'fjʊərɪ/ *n* fureur *f*; **to be in a ~** être en fureur

fuse, fuze (AmE) /fju:z/ **A** *n* fusible *m*; **to blow a ~** faire sauter un fusible; (get angry) piquer une crise (fam)
B *vt* **1** (BrE) **to ~ the lights** faire sauter les plombs
2 (join) fondre [qch] ensemble ‹*metals*›

fuse box *n* boîte *f* à fusibles

fuselage /'fju:zəlɑ:ʒ, -lɪdʒ/ *n* fuselage *m*

fuse wire *n* fusible *m*

fuss /fʌs/ **A** *n* **1** (agitation) remue-ménage *m inv*; **to make a ~** faire des histoires; **to make a ~ about sth** faire toute une histoire à propos de qch
2 to kick up a ~ about sth (fam) piquer une crise à propos de qch (fam)
3 (attention) **to make a ~ of** être aux petits soins avec *or* pour ‹*person*›; caresser ‹*animal*›
B *vi* **1** (worry) se faire du souci (**about** pour)
2 (show attention) **to ~ over sb** (fam) être aux petits soins avec *or* pour qn

fussy /'fʌsɪ/ *adj* **to be ~ about one's food/about details** être maniaque sur la nourriture/sur les détails

futile /'fju:taɪl, (AmE) -tl/ *adj* **1** (vain) vain/-e
2 (inane) futile

⚷ **future** /'fju:tʃə(r)/ **A** *n* **1** avenir *m*; **in the ~** dans l'avenir; **in ~** à l'avenir
2 (*also* **~ tense**) futur *m*
B *adj* ‹*generation, developments, investment, earnings*› futur/-e; ‹*prospects*› d'avenir; ‹*queen, king*› futur/-e *before n*; **at some ~ date** à une date ultérieure

fuze (AmE) = **fuse**

fuzzy /'fʌzɪ/ *adj* **1** ‹*hair, beard*› crépu/-e
2 ‹*image*› flou/-e; ‹*idea, mind*› confus/-e

Gg

g, G /dʒi:/ *n* **1** (letter) g, G *m*
2 G (Mus) sol *m*
3 g (*written abbr* = **gram**) g

gab /gæb/ *n* (fam)
IDIOM **to have the gift of the ~** (fam) avoir du bagou(t) (fam)

gadget /'gædʒɪt/ *n* gadget *m*

gaffe /gæf/ *n* bévue *f*

gag /gæg/ **A** *n* **1** (on mouth) bâillon *m*
2 (fam) (joke) blague *f* (fam)
B *vt* (*p prés etc* **-gg-**) bâillonner ‹*person*›
C *vi* (*p prés etc* **-gg-**) avoir un haut-le-cœur

gage /geɪdʒ/ (AmE) = **gauge**

⚷ mot clé

gain /geɪn/ **A** *n* **1** (financial) gain *m*, profit *m*
2 (increase) augmentation *f* (**in** de)
3 (advantage) gain *m*; (advances) progrès *m* (**in** de)
B *vt* **1** (gen) gagner; acquérir ‹*experience*› (**from** de); obtenir ‹*advantage*› (**from** grâce à); **we have nothing to ~** nous n'avons rien à gagner
2 to ~ speed prendre de la vitesse *or* de l'élan; **to ~ weight** prendre du poids
C *vi* **1** (increase) **to ~ in popularity** gagner en popularité; **to ~ in value** prendre de la valeur
2 (profit) **she hasn't ~ed by it** cela ne lui a rien rapporté
■ **gain on** rattraper ‹*person, vehicle*›

galaxy /'gæləksɪ/ *n* galaxie *f*

gale /geɪl/ *n* vent *m* violent

gallery /'gælərɪ/ *n* **1** (gen) galerie *f*
2 (art) ~ musée *m* (d'art)
3 (in theatre) dernier balcon *m*

Gallic /'gælɪk/ *adj* (French) français/-e

galling /'gɔːlɪŋ/ *adj* vexant/-e

gallon /'gælən/ *n* gallon *m* ((BrE) = *4.546 l*; (AmE) = *3.785 l*)

gallop /'gæləp/ **A** *n* galop *m*
B *vi* galoper

galore /gə'lɔː(r)/ *adv* ‹*prizes, bargains*› à profusion; ‹*drinks, sandwiches*› à volonté, à gogo (fam)

galvanize /'gælvənaɪz/ *vt* galvaniser ‹*group, community*›; relancer ‹*campaign*›; **to ~ sb into doing** pousser qn à faire

gambit /'gæmbɪt/ *n* **1** tactique *f*
2 (in chess) gambit *m*

gamble /'gæmbl/ **A** *n* pari *m*; **it's a ~** c'est risqué
B *vt* **1** jouer ‹*money*›
2 (fig) miser (**on** sur)
C *vi* (at cards, on shares) jouer; (on horses) parier; (fig) miser (**on** sur)

gambler /'gæmblə(r)/ *n* joueur/-euse *m/f*

gambling /'gæmblɪŋ/ *n* jeu *m* (d'argent)

game /geɪm/ **A** *n* **1** jeu *m*; **to play a ~** jouer à un jeu; **to have a ~ of** faire une partie de
2 (match) match *m* (**of** de); (in tennis) jeu *m*
3 (Culin) gibier *m*
B games *npl* **1** (BrE) (Sch) sport *m*
2 (*also* **Games**) (sporting event) Jeux *mpl*
IDIOM **to give the ~ away** vendre la mèche

gamekeeper *n* garde-chasse *m*

game plan *n* stratégie *f*

game reserve *n* (for hunting) réserve *f* de chasse; (for protection) réserve *f* naturelle

games console *n* console *f* de jeux vidéo

game show *n* jeu *m* télévisé

games room *n* salle *f* de jeux

games software *n* logiciel *m* de jeux, ludiciel *m*

gaming /'geɪmɪŋ/ *n* **on-line ~** jeux *mpl* en ligne

gaming zone *n* (on Internet) salle *f* de jeux en ligne

gammon /'gæmən/ *n* jambon *m*

gang /gæŋ/ *n* **1** (of criminals) gang *m*; (of youths, friends) bande *f*
2 (of workmen, prisoners) équipe *f*
■ **gang up** se coaliser (**on, against** contre)

gangland /'gæŋlænd/ *n* ≈ le Milieu

gang leader *n* chef *m* de bande

gangmaster *n* gangmaster *m*, chef *m* d'équipe (d'ouvriers saisonniers)

gang-rape *n* viol *m* collectif

gangster /'gæŋstə(r)/ *n* gangster *m*

gangway /'gæŋweɪ/ *n* **1** (to ship) passerelle *f*
2 (BrE) (in bus, cinema) allée *f*

gap /gæp/ *n* **1** (gen) trou *m* (**in** dans); (between planks, curtains) interstice *m* (**in** entre); (between cars) espace *m* (**in** entre); (in cloud) trouée *f* (**in** dans)
2 (of time) intervalle *m*; (in conversation) silence *m*
3 (discrepancy) écart *m* (**between** entre); **a 15-year age ~** une différence d'âge de 15 ans
4 (in knowledge) lacune *f* (**in** dans)
5 (in market) créneau *m*

gape /geɪp/ *vi* **1** (stare) rester bouche bée; **to ~ at sb/sth** regarder qn/qch bouche bée
2 to ~ open ‹*chasm*› s'ouvrir tout grand; ‹*wound*› être béant/-e; ‹*garment*› bâiller

gaping /'geɪpɪŋ/ *adj* ‹*person*› bouche bée; ‹*wound, hole*› béant/-e

gap year *n: année d'interruption des études entre le lycée et l'université*

garage /'gærɑːʒ, 'gærɪdʒ, (AmE) gə'rɑːʒ/ *n* garage *m*

garbage /'gɑːbɪdʒ/ *n* **1** (AmE) (refuse) ordures *fpl*
2 (nonsense) âneries *fpl*, bêtises *fpl*

garbage can *n* (AmE) poubelle *f*

garbage truck *n* (AmE) camion *m* des éboueurs

garbled /'gɑːbld/ *adj* ‹*account, instructions*› confus/-e

garden /'gɑːdn/ **A** *n* jardin *m*
B *vi* jardiner, faire du jardinage

garden centre (BrE), **garden center** (AmE) *n* jardinerie *f*

gardener /'gɑːdnə(r)/ *n* jardinier/-ière *m/f*

gardening /'gɑːdnɪŋ/ *n* jardinage *m*

gargle /'gɑːgl/ *vi* se gargariser (**with** avec)

garish /'geərɪʃ/ *adj* tape-à-l'œil *inv*

garland /'gɑːlənd/ *n* guirlande *f*

garlic /'gɑːlɪk/ *n* ail *m*

garment /'gɑːmənt/ *n* vêtement *m*

garnish /'gɑːnɪʃ/ **A** *n* garniture *f*
B *vt* garnir (**with** de)

garter /'gɑːtə(r)/ *n* **1** (for stocking) jarretière *f*; (for socks) fixe-chaussette *m*
2 (AmE) (suspender) jarretelle *f*

gas /gæs/ **A** *n* **1** (fuel) gaz *m*
2 (anaesthetic) anesthésie *f*

g

3 (AmE) (petrol) essence *f*
B *vt* (*p prés etc* **-ss-**) gazer

gas chamber *n* chambre *f* à gaz

gas cooker *n* cuisinière *f* à gaz

gas fire *n* (appareil *m* de) chauffage *m* à gaz

gash /gæʃ/ **A** *n* entaille *f*
B *vt* entailler

gas mask *n* masque *m* à gaz

gasoline /ˈgæsəliːn/ *n* (AmE) essence *f*

gas oven *n* four *m* à gaz

gasp /gɑːsp/ **A** *n* halètement *m*
B *vi* **1** (for air) haleter
2 to ~ (in amazement) avoir le souffle coupé (par la surprise)

gas pedal *n* (AmE) accélérateur *m*

gas station *n* (AmE) station-service *f*

gastroenteritis /ˌgæstrəʊˌentəˈraɪtɪs/ *n* gastro-entérite *f*

gate /geɪt/ *n* (of field, level crossing) barrière *f*; (in town, prison, airport, garden) porte *f*; (of courtyard, palace) portail *m*; **at the ~** à l'entrée

gatecrash /ˈgeɪtkræʃ/ *vt* (fam) (without paying) resquiller (fam) à; (without invitation) se pointer (fam) sans invitation à

gatecrasher /ˈgeɪtkræʃə(r)/ *n* (fam) (at concert) resquilleur/-euse *m/f*; (at party) intrus/-e *m/f*

⚷ **gather** /ˈgæðə(r)/ **A** *n* (in garment) fronce *f*
B *vt* **1** cueillir ‹*fruit, flowers*›; ramasser ‹*fallen fruit, wood*›; recueillir ‹*information*›; rassembler ‹*courage, strength*›; **to ~ speed** prendre de la vitesse
2 to ~ that... déduire que...; **I ~ (that) he was there** d'après ce que j'ai compris il était là
3 (in sewing) faire des fronces à
C *vi* ‹*people, crowd*› se rassembler; ‹*family*› se réunir; ‹*clouds*› s'amonceler

gathering /ˈgæðərɪŋ/ *n* réunion *f*; **social/family ~** réunion entre amis/de famille

gaudy /ˈgɔːdɪ/ *adj* tape-à-l'œil *inv*

gauge, **gage** (AmE) /geɪdʒ/ **A** *n* **1** (of gun, screw) calibre *m*; (of metal, wire) épaisseur *f*
2 (of railway) écartement *m* (des voies)
3 (measuring instrument) jauge *f*; **fuel ~** jauge d'essence
B *vt* **1** mesurer ‹*diameter*›; jauger ‹*distance, quantity*›; calibrer ‹*gun*›
2 évaluer ‹*mood, reaction*›

gaunt /gɔːnt/ *adj* décharné/-e

gauze /gɔːz/ *n* (fabric) gaze *f*; (wire) grillage *m*

⚷ **gay** /geɪ/ **A** *n* homosexuel/-elle *m/f*, gay *mf*
B *adj* **1** homosexuel/-elle
2 (happy) gai/-e; ‹*laughter*› joyeux/-euse

gay marriage *n* mariage homosexuel *nm*

Gaza strip /ˌgɑːzə ˈstrɪp/ *pr n* bande *f* de Gaza

gaze /geɪz/ **A** *n* regard *m*
B *vi* **to ~ at sb/sth** regarder qn/qch; (in wonder) contempler qn/qch

⚷ mot clé

GCSE *n* (BrE) (*pl* **~s**) (*abbr* = **General Certificate of Secondary Education**) certificat *m* d'études secondaires

gear /gɪə(r)/ *n* **1** (equipment) matériel *m*
2 (clothes) fringues *fpl* (fam); **football ~** tenue *f* de football
3 (Aut) vitesse *f*; **to be in third ~** être en troisième; **to put a car in ~** passer la vitesse; **you're not in ~** tu es au point mort
■ **gear up** se préparer; **to be ~ed up** être prêt/-e (**for** pour)

gearbox *n* boîte *f* de vitesses

gearstick (BrE), **gearshift** (AmE) *n* levier *m* de vitesses

gear wheel *n* pignon *m*

gel /dʒel/ **A** *n* gel *m*
B *vi* (*p prés etc* **-ll-**) **1** (Culin) prendre
2 (fig) prendre forme

gelateria /dʒəlætəˈriːə/ *n* glacier *m*

gem /dʒem/ *n* (jewel) pierre *f* précieuse

Gemini /ˈdʒemɪnaɪ, -niː/ *n* Gémeaux *mpl*

gender /ˈdʒendə(r)/ *n* **1** (of word) genre *m*
2 (of person, animal) sexe *m*

gender-neutral *adj* non sexiste, unisexe; **~-neutral games and toys** des jeux *mpl* et des jouets *mpl* unisexes

gene /dʒiːn/ *n* gène *m*

genealogy /ˌdʒiːnɪˈælədʒɪ/ *n* généalogie *f*

gene library *n* génothèque *f*

gene pool *n* patrimoine *m* héréditaire

⚷ **general** /ˈdʒenrəl/ **A** *n* général *m*
B *adj* général/-e
C **in general** *phr* (usually) en général; (overall) dans l'ensemble

general election *n* élections *fpl* législatives

generalization /ˌdʒenrəlaɪˈzeɪʃn, (AmE) -lɪˈz-/ *n* généralisation *f* (**about** sur)

generalize /ˈdʒenrəlaɪz/ *vt*, *vi* généraliser (**about** à propos de)

general knowledge *n* culture *f* générale

⚷ **generally** /ˈdʒenrəlɪ/ *adv* **1** (usually) en général, généralement; **~ speaking...** en règle générale...
2 (overall) **the quality is ~ good** dans l'ensemble la qualité est bonne
3 ‹*talk*› d'une manière générale

general practitioner, **GP** *n* (médecin *m*) généraliste *mf*

general public *n* (grand) public *m*

general-purpose *adj* à usages multiples

general strike *n* grève *f* générale

⚷ **generate** /ˈdʒenəreɪt/ *vt* produire ‹*power, heat, income, waste*›; créer ‹*employment*›; susciter ‹*interest, tension, ideas*›; entraîner ‹*profit, publicity*›

⚷ **generation** /ˌdʒenəˈreɪʃn/ *n* **1** génération *f*; **the younger/older ~** la jeune/l'ancienne génération
2 (of electricity, data) production *f*

generation gap *n* fossé *m* des générations

generator /ˈdʒenəreɪtə(r)/ *n* (of electricity) générateur *m*; (in hospital, on farm) groupe *m* électrogène

generosity /ˌdʒenəˈrɒsətɪ/ *n* générosité *f*

generous /ˈdʒenərəs/ *adj* (gen) généreux/-euse; ‹*size*› grand/-e *before n*; ‹*hem*› bon/bonne *before n*

gene therapy *n* thérapie *f* génique

genetic /dʒɪˈnetɪk/ *adj* génétique

genetically modified, **GM** *adj* génétiquement modifié/-e

genetic engineering *n* génie *m* génétique

genetic fingerprinting *n* empreintes *fpl* génétiques

genetics /dʒɪˈnetɪks/ *n* génétique *f*

genetic testing *n* tests *mpl* de dépistage génétique

Geneva /dʒɪˈniːvə/ *pr n* Genève

genial /ˈdʒiːnɪəl/ *adj* cordial/-e

genitals /ˈdʒenɪtlz/ *npl* organes *mpl* génitaux

genius /ˈdʒiːnɪəs/ *n* (*pl* **~es** *or* **-ii** (literary)) génie *m*

genome /ˈdʒiːnəʊm/ *n* génome *m*

gentle /ˈdʒentl/ *adj* (gen) doux/douce; ‹*hint, reminder*› discret/-ète; ‹*pressure, touch, breeze*› léger/-ère; ‹*exercise*› modéré/-e

gentleman /ˈdʒentlmən/ *n* (*pl* **-men**)
1 (man) monsieur *m*
2 (well-bred) gentleman *m*

gently /ˈdʒentlɪ/ *adv* (gen) doucement; ‹*treat, cleanse*› avec douceur; ‹*cook*› à feu doux; ‹*speak*› gentiment; **to break the news ~** annoncer la nouvelle avec ménagement

gents *npl* (toilets) toilettes *fpl*; (on sign) 'Messieurs'

genuine /ˈdʒenjʊɪn/ *adj* ‹*reason, motive*› vrai/-e *before n*; ‹*work of art*› authentique; ‹*jewel, substance*› véritable; ‹*person, effort, interest*› sincère; ‹*buyer*› sérieux/-ieuse

genuinely /ˈdʒenjʊɪnlɪ/ *adv* (really and truly) vraiment; (in reality) réellement

geoengineering /ˌdʒiəʊˌendʒɪˈnɪərɪŋ/ *n* géoingénierie *f*

geography /dʒɪˈɒgrəfɪ/ *n* géographie *f*

geology /dʒɪˈɒlədʒɪ/ *n* géologie *f*

geometry /dʒɪˈɒmətrɪ/ *n* géométrie *f*

geothermal /ˌdʒiːəʊˈθɜːml/ *adj* géothermique

gerbil /ˈdʒɜːbɪl/ *n* gerbille *f*

geriatric /ˌdʒerɪˈætrɪk/ *adj* ‹*hospital, ward*› gériatrique

germ /dʒɜːm/ *n* **1** (microbe) microbe *m*
2 (seed) germe *m*

German /ˈdʒɜːmən/ **A** *n* **1** (person) Allemand/-e *m/f*
2 (language) allemand *m*
B *adj* ‹*custom, food*› allemand/-e; ‹*ambassador, embassy*› d'Allemagne; ‹*teacher, course*› d'allemand

German measles *n* rubéole *f*

Germany /ˈdʒɜːmənɪ/ *pr n* Allemagne *f*

germinate /ˈdʒɜːmɪneɪt/ **A** *vt* faire germer **B** *vi* germer

germ warfare *n* guerre *f* bactériologique

gesticulate /dʒeˈstɪkjʊleɪt/ *vi* gesticuler

gesture /ˈdʒestʃə(r)/ **A** *n* geste *m* (**of** de)
B *vi* faire un geste; **to ~ at** *or* **towards sth** désigner qch d'un geste; **to ~ to sb** faire signe à qn

get /get/

> This much-used verb has no multi-purpose equivalent in French and therefore is very often translated by choosing a synonym: *to get lunch* = *to prepare lunch* = préparer le déjeuner.
>
> When *get* is used to express the idea that a job is done not by you but by somebody else (*to get a room painted*), *faire* is used in French followed by an infinitive (*faire repeindre une pièce*).
>
> When *get* has the meaning of *become* and is followed by an adjective (*to get rich*), *devenir* is sometimes useful but check the appropriate entry (**rich**) as a single verb often suffices (*s'enrichir*).
>
> The phrasal verbs (*get around, get down, get on etc*) are listed separately at the end of the entry *GET*.
>
> For examples and further uses of *get* see the entry below.

A *vt* (*p prés* **-tt-**, *prét* **got**, *pp* **got**, **gotten** (AmE)) **1** (receive) recevoir ‹*letter, grant*›; recevoir, percevoir ‹*salary, pension*›; capter ‹*channel*›
2 (inherit) **to ~ sth from sb** hériter qch de qn ‹*article, money*›; tenir qch de qn ‹*trait*›
3 (obtain) obtenir ‹*permission, divorce*›; trouver ‹*job*›
4 (buy) acheter ‹*item, newspaper*› (**from** chez); avoir ‹*ticket*›; **to ~ sb sth, to ~ sth for sb** (as gift) acheter qch à qn
5 (acquire) se faire ‹*reputation*›
6 (achieve) obtenir ‹*grade*›
7 (fetch) chercher ‹*person, help*›; **to ~ sb sth, to ~ sth for sb** aller chercher qch pour qn
8 (move) **to ~ sb/sth downstairs** faire descendre qn/qch
9 (help progress) **this is ~ting us nowhere** ça ne nous avance à rien; **where will that ~ you?** à quoi ça t'avancera?
10 (deal with) **I'll ~ it** (of phone) je réponds; (of doorbell) j'y vais
11 (prepare) préparer ‹*breakfast, lunch*›
12 (take hold of) attraper ‹*person*› (**by** par)
13 (fam) (oblige to give) **to ~ sth out of sb** faire sortir qch à qn ‹*money*›; obtenir qch de qn ‹*truth*›
14 (contract) attraper ‹*cold, disease*›; **he got measles from his sister** sa sœur lui a passé la rougeole

15 (catch) prendre ‹*bus, train*›
16 (have) **to have got** avoir ‹*object, money, friend*›; **I've got a headache** j'ai mal à la tête; **to ~ the idea that** se mettre dans la tête que
17 to ~ a surprise être surpris/-e; **to ~ a shock** avoir un choc; **to ~ a bang on the head** recevoir un coup sur la tête
18 (as punishment) prendre ‹*five years*›; avoir ‹*fine*›
19 (understand, hear) comprendre
20 (fam) (annoy) **what ~s me is...** ce qui m'agace c'est que...
21 to ~ to like sb finir par apprécier qn; **how did you ~ to hear of…?** comment avez-vous entendu parler de...?; **we got to know them last year** on a fait leur connaissance l'année dernière
22 (have opportunity) **to ~ to do** avoir l'occasion de faire, pouvoir faire
23 (must) **to have got to do** devoir faire ‹*homework, chore*›; **it's got to be done** il faut le faire; **you've got to realize that…** il faut que tu te rendes compte que...
24 (make) **to ~ sb to pay** faire payer qn; **to ~ sb to tell the truth** faire dire la vérité à qn
25 (ask) **to ~ sb to wash the dishes** demander à qn de faire la vaisselle
26 to ~ the car repaired faire réparer la voiture; **to ~ one's hair cut** se faire couper les cheveux; **to ~ the car going** faire démarrer la voiture; **to ~ one's socks wet** mouiller ses chaussettes; **to ~ one's finger trapped** se coincer le doigt; **to ~ a dress made** se faire faire une robe
B *vi* (*p prés* **-tt-**, *prét* **got**, *pp* **got**, **gotten** (AmE)) **1** (become) devenir ‹*suspicious, old*›; **it's ~ting late** il se fait tard
2 (forming passive) **to ~ killed** se faire tuer; **to ~ hurt** être blessé/-e
3 (become involved in) **to ~ into** (fam) se mettre à ‹*hobby*›; commencer dans ‹*profession*›; **to ~ into a fight** se battre
4 (arrive) **to ~ there** arriver; **to ~ to the airport** arriver à l'aéroport; **how did you ~ here?** comment est-ce que tu es venu?; **where did you ~ to?** où est-ce que tu étais passé?
5 (progress) **I'm ~ting nowhere with this essay** je n'avance pas dans cette dissertation; **now we're ~ting somewhere** il y a du progrès
6 (put on) **to ~ into** mettre, enfiler ‹*pyjamas*›
■ **get about 1** (move) se déplacer
2 (travel) voyager
■ **get across 1** traverser ‹*river, road*›
2 faire passer ‹*message*› (**to** à)
■ **get ahead** (make progress) progresser
■ **get along**: **1 how are you ~ting along?** (in job, school) comment ça se passe?
2 ‹*people*› bien s'entendre (**with** avec)
■ **get around A ~ around 1** = **get about**
2 (manage to do) **she'll ~ around to visiting us eventually** elle va bien finir par venir nous voir; **I haven't got around to it yet** je n'ai pas encore eu le temps de m'en occuper
B ~ around [sth] contourner ‹*problem, law*›
■ **get at** (fam) **1** (reach) atteindre ‹*object*›; découvrir ‹*truth*›
2 (criticize) être après ‹*person*›
3 (insinuate) **what are you ~ting at?** où est-ce que tu veux en venir?
■ **get away 1** (leave) partir
2 (escape) s'échapper
3 to ~ away with a crime échapper à la justice; **you won't ~ away with it!** tu ne vas pas t'en tirer comme ça!
■ **get away from 1** quitter ‹*place*›; échapper à ‹*person*›
2 there's no ~ting away from it on ne peut pas le nier
■ **get back A ~ back 1** (return) rentrer; (after short time) revenir
2 (move backwards) reculer
B ~ back to [sth] 1 (return to) rentrer à ‹*house, city*›; revenir à ‹*office, point*›; **when we ~ back to London** à notre retour à Londres; **to ~ back to sleep** se rendormir; **to ~ back to normal** redevenir normal
2 (return to earlier stage) revenir à ‹*main topic, former point*›
C ~ back to [sb] revenir à; **I'll ~ back to you** (on phone) je vous rappelle
D ~ [sth] back (regain) récupérer ‹*lost object*›; reprendre ‹*strength*›; **she got her money back** elle a été remboursée
■ **get by 1** (pass) passer
2 (survive) s'en sortir (**on, with** avec)
■ **get down A ~ down 1** (descend) descendre (**from, out of** de)
2 (on floor) se coucher; (crouch) se baisser; **to ~ down on one's knees** s'agenouiller
3 to ~ down to se mettre à ‹*work*›; **to ~ down to doing** se mettre à faire
B ~ down [sth] descendre ‹*slope*›
C ~ [sth] down (from height) descendre
D ~ [sb] down (depress) déprimer
■ **get in A ~ in 1** (to building) entrer; (to vehicle) monter
2 (return home) rentrer
3 (arrive) arriver
4 (penetrate) pénétrer
5 ‹*party*› passer; ‹*candidate*› être élu/-e
6 (Sch, Univ) ‹*applicant*› être admis/-e
B ~ [sth] in (buy) acheter
■ **get into 1** (enter) entrer dans ‹*building*›; monter dans ‹*vehicle*›
2 (as member) devenir membre de; (as student) être admis/-e à
3 (squeeze into) rentrer dans ‹*garment, size*›
■ **get off A ~ off 1** (from bus) descendre (**at** à)
2 (start on journey) partir
3 (leave work) finir
4 (fam) (escape punishment) s'en tirer (**with** avec)
5 to ~ off to a good start prendre un bon

🔑 mot clé

départ; **to ~ off to sleep** s'endormir
B **~ off [sth] 1** descendre de ‹*wall, bus*›
2 s'écarter de ‹*subject*›
C **~ [sth] off 1** (send off) envoyer ‹*letter*›
2 (remove) enlever

■ **get on** **A** **~ on 1** (climb aboard) monter
2 (BrE) (like each other) bien s'entendre
3 (fare) **how did you ~ on?** comment est-ce que ça s'est passé?; **how are you ~ting on?** comment est-ce que tu t'en sors?
4 (BrE) (approach) **he's ~ting on for 40** il approche des quarante ans; **it's ~ting on for midnight** il est presque minuit
B **~ on [sth]** monter dans ‹*vehicle*›
C **~ [sth] on** mettre ‹*garment, lid*›; monter ‹*tyre*›

■ **get on with**: **A** **to ~ on with one's work** continuer à travailler
B **to ~ on with [sb]** (BrE) s'entendre avec ‹*person*›

■ **get out** **A** **~ out 1** (exit) sortir (**through, by** par); **~ out!** va-t'en!
2 (alight) descendre
3 ‹*prisoner*› être libéré/-e
4 ‹*news*› être révélé/-e
B **~ [sth] out 1** (take out) sortir (**of** de)
2 retirer ‹*cork*›
3 enlever ‹*stain*›
4 emprunter ‹*library book*›

■ **get out of 1** sortir de ‹*building*›; descendre de ‹*vehicle*›; être libéré/-e de ‹*prison*›; quitter ‹*profession*›
2 **to ~ out of doing** s'arranger pour ne pas faire; **I'll try to ~ out of it** j'essaierai de me libérer
3 perdre ‹*habit*›
4 **what do you ~ out of your job?** qu'est-ce que ton travail t'apporte?; **what will you ~ out of it?** qu'est-ce que vous en retirerez?

■ **get over 1** traverser ‹*stream, bridge*›; passer au-dessus de ‹*wall*›
2 se remettre de ‹*illness, shock*›; **I can't ~ over it** (amazed) je n'en reviens pas
3 surmonter ‹*problem*›; **to ~ sth over with** en finir avec qch

■ **get round** (BrE): **A** **~ round = get around**
B **~ round [sb]** (fam) persuader [qn]

■ **get through** **A** **1** (squeeze through) passer
2 **to ~ through to sb** (on phone) avoir qn au téléphone; (make oneself understood) se faire comprendre
3 ‹*news, supplies*› arriver
4 ‹*examinee*› réussir
B **~ through [sth] 1** terminer ‹*book*›; finir ‹*meal, task*›; réussir à ‹*exam*›
2 (use) manger ‹*food*›; dépenser ‹*money*›

■ **get together**: **A** **~ together** se réunir (**about, over** pour discuter de)
B **~ [sb/sth] together** réunir ‹*people*›; former ‹*company*›

■ **get up** **A** **~ up 1** (from bed, chair) se lever (**from** de)
2 (on ledge, wall) monter
3 ‹*storm*› se préparer; ‹*wind*› se lever
4 **what did you ~ up to?** (enjoyment) qu'est-ce que tu as fait de beau?; (mischief) qu'est-ce que tu as fabriqué? (fam)
B **~ up [sth] 1** arriver en haut de ‹*hill, ladder*›
2 augmenter ‹*speed*›

get-together /ˈgettəgeðə(r)/ *n* réunion *f* (entre amis)

ghastly /ˈgɑːstlɪ, (AmE) ˈgæstlɪ/ *adj* horrible

gherkin /ˈgɜːkɪn/ *n* cornichon *m*

ghetto /ˈgetəʊ/ *n* (*pl* **~s** *ou* **~es**) ghetto *m*

ghetto blaster *n* (fam) (gros) radiocassette *m* portable

ghost /gəʊst/ *n* fantôme *m*

giant /ˈdʒaɪənt/ **A** *n* géant *m*
B *adj* géant/-e

gibberish /ˈdʒɪbərɪʃ/ *n* charabia *m*

giddy /ˈgɪdɪ/ *adj* **1** **to feel ~** avoir la tête qui tourne
2 ‹*height, speed*› vertigineux/-euse

⚷ **gift** /gɪft/ *n* **1** (present) cadeau *m* (**to** à); **to give sb a ~** faire *or* offrir un cadeau à qn
2 (donation) don *m*
3 (talent) don *m*; **to have a ~ for doing** avoir le don de faire; **to have the ~ of the gab** avoir du bagou(t) (fam)

gifted /ˈgɪftɪd/ *adj* doué/-e

gift shop *n* magasin *m* de cadeaux

gift token, **gift voucher** *n* (BrE) chèque-cadeau *m*

gift wrap /ˈgɪftræp/ *n* papier *m* cadeau

gig /gɪg/ *n* (fam) concert *m* de rock

gigantic /dʒaɪˈgæntɪk/ *adj* gigantesque

giggle /ˈgɪgl/ **A** *n* petit rire *m*; **to get the ~s** attraper le fou rire
B *vi* rire

gilt /gɪlt/ **A** *n* dorure
B *adj* ‹*frame, paint*› doré/-e

gimmick /ˈgɪmɪk/ *n* (scheme) truc *m* (fam); (object) gadget *m*

gin /dʒɪn/ *n* gin *m*; **~ and tonic** gin tonic *m*

ginger /ˈdʒɪndʒə(r)/ *n* **1** (Bot, Culin) gingembre *m*
2 (colour) roux *m*

ginger-haired *adj* roux/rousse

⚷ **girl** /gɜːl/ *n* **1** (child) fille *f*; (teenager) jeune fille; **baby ~** petite fille, bébé *m*; **little ~** petite fille, fillette *f*
2 (daughter) fille *f*

girl band *n* girls band *m*

girlfriend *n* (female friend) amie *f*; (sweetheart) (petite) amie *f*

girl guide (BrE), **girl scout** (AmE) *n* éclaireuse *f*

giro /ˈdʒaɪrəʊ/ *n* (BrE) (system) système *m* de virement bancaire; (cheque) mandat *m*

gist /dʒɪst/ *n* essentiel *m* (**of** de)

⚷ **give** /gɪv/ **A** *n* élasticité *f*
B *vt* (*prét* **gave**, *pp* **given**) (gen) donner (**to** à); transmettre ‹*message*› (**to** à); transmettre, passer ‹*illness*› (**to** à); laisser

‹*seat*› (**to** à); accorder ‹*grant*› (**to** à); faire ‹*injection, massage*› (**to** à); faire ‹*speech*›; **to ~ sb sth** donner qch à qn; (politely, as a gift) offrir qch à qn; **to ~ sb pleasure** faire plaisir à qn; **~ him my best (wishes)** transmets-lui mes amitiés; **she gave him a drink** elle lui a donné à boire; **to ~ sb enough room** laisser suffisamment de place à qn
C *vi* (*prét* **gave**, *pp* **given**) ‹*mattress, sofa*› s'affaisser; ‹*shelf, floorboard*› fléchir; ‹*branch*› ployer
IDIOMS **~ or take an inch (or two)** à quelques centimètres près; **to ~ and take** faire des concessions; **to ~ as good as one gets** rendre coup pour coup; **to ~ it all one's got** (fam) (y) mettre le paquet

■ **give away** **A** **~ [sth] away 1** donner ‹*item, sample*›
2 révéler ‹*secret*›
3 laisser échapper ‹*match, goal, advantage*› (**to** au bénéfice de)
B **~ [sb] away 1** (betray) ‹*expression, fingerprints*› trahir; ‹*person*› dénoncer (**to** à); **to ~ oneself away** se trahir
2 (in marriage) conduire [qn] à l'autel

■ **give back** rendre (**to** à)

■ **give in** **A** **~ in 1** (yield) céder (**to** à)
2 (stop trying) abandonner; **I ~ in—tell me!** je donne ma langue au chat (fam)—dis-le-moi!
B **~ [sth] in** rendre ‹*work*›; remettre ‹*ticket, key*›

■ **give off** émettre ‹*signal, radiation, light*›; dégager ‹*heat, fumes*›

■ **give out**: **A** **~ out** ‹*strength*› s'épuiser; ‹*engine*› tomber en panne
B **~ [sth] out** (distribute) distribuer (**to** à)

■ **give up**: **A** **~ up** abandonner; **to ~ up on** laisser tomber ‹*diet, crossword, pupil, patient*›; ne plus compter sur ‹*friend, partner*›
B **~ up [sth] 1** renoncer à ‹*habit, title, claim*›; sacrifier ‹*free time*›; quitter ‹*job*›; **to ~ up smoking/drinking** cesser de fumer/de boire
2 abandonner ‹*search, hope, struggle*›; renoncer à ‹*idea*›
3 céder ‹*seat, territory*›
C **~ [sb] up 1** (hand over) livrer (**to** à); **to ~ oneself up** se livrer (**to** à)
2 laisser tomber ‹*lover*›

■ **give way 1** (collapse) s'effondrer; ‹*fence, cable*› céder; **his legs gave way** ses jambes se sont dérobées sous lui
2 (BrE) (when driving) céder le passage (**to** à)
3 (yield) céder; **to ~ way to** faire place à

give and take *n* concessions *fpl* mutuelles

giveaway /'gɪvəweɪ/ *n* **to be a ~** être révélateur/-trice

given /'gɪvn/ **A** *adj* **1** ‹*point, level, number*› donné/-e; ‹*volume, length*› déterminé/-e; **at any ~ moment** à n'importe quel moment
2 to be ~ to sth/to doing avoir tendance à qch/à faire; **I am not ~ to doing** je n'ai pas l'habitude de faire
B *prep* **1** (in view of) **~ (the fact) that** étant donné que
2 (with) avec ‹*training, proper care*›

given name *n* prénom *m*

⚷ **glad** /glæd/ *adj* content/-e, heureux/-euse (**about** de, **that** que, **to do** de faire); **he was only too ~ to help me** il ne demandait qu'à m'aider

gladly /'glædlɪ/ *adv* (willingly) volontiers; (with pleasure) avec plaisir

glamorize /'glæməraɪz/ *vt* peindre [qn/qch] sous de belles couleurs

glamorous /'glæmərəs/ *adj* ‹*person, image, look*› séduisant/-e; ‹*older person*› élégant/-e; ‹*dress*› splendide; ‹*occasion*› brillant/-e; ‹*job*› prestigieux/-ieuse

glamour, **glamor** (AmE) /'glæmə(r)/ *n* (of person) séduction *f*; (of job) prestige *m*; (of travel, cars) fascination *f*

⚷ **glance** /glɑːns, (AmE) glæns/ **A** *n* coup *m* d'œil
B *vi* **to ~ at** jeter un coup d'œil à; **to ~ around the room** parcourir la pièce du regard

■ **glance off** ‹*bullet, stone*› ricocher sur *or* contre

glancing /'glɑːnsɪŋ, (AmE) 'glænsɪŋ/ *adj* ‹*blow, kick*› oblique

gland /glænd/ *n* glande *f*; **to have swollen ~s** avoir des ganglions

glandular fever *n* mononucléose *f* infectieuse

glare /gleə(r)/ **A** *n* **1** (angry look) regard *m* furieux
2 (from lights) lumière *f* éblouissante
B *vi* ‹*person*› lancer un regard furieux (**at** à)

glaring /'gleərɪŋ/ *adj* **1** ‹*mistake, injustice*› flagrant/-e
2 ‹*light*› éblouissant/-e

⚷ **glass** /glɑːs, (AmE) glæs/ **A** *n* **1** verre *m*; **wine ~** verre à vin; **a ~ of wine** un verre de vin
2 (mirror) miroir *m*
B *adj* ‹*bottle, shelf*› en verre; ‹*door*› vitré/-e
C **glasses** *npl* lunettes *fpl*

glass ceiling *n: niveau professionnel que la discrimination empêche certains groupes sociaux de dépasser*

glassy-eyed *adj* (from drink, illness) aux yeux vitreux; (hostile) au regard glacial

glaze /gleɪz/ **A** *n* **1** (on pottery) vernis *m*
2 (Culin) nappage *m*; (icing) glaçage *m*
B *vt* **1** vernisser ‹*pottery*›
2 (Culin) glacer

glazed /gleɪzd/ *adj* ‹*door*› vitré/-e; **to have a ~ look in one's eyes** avoir les yeux vitreux

gleam /gliːm/ **A** *n* (of light) lueur *f*; (of sunshine) rayon *m*; (of gold, polished surface) reflet *m*
B *vi* ‹*light*› luire; ‹*knife, leather, surface*›

reluire; ‹*eyes*› briller

gleaming /'gliːmɪŋ/ *adj* **1** ‹*eyes, light*› brillant/-e; ‹*leather, surface*› reluisant/-e **2** (clean) étincelant/-e (de propreté)

glide /glaɪd/ *vi* ‹*skater, boat*› glisser (**on, over** sur); (in air) planer

glider /'glaɪdə(r)/ *n* planeur *m*

gliding /'glaɪdɪŋ/ *n* vol *m* à voile

glimpse /glɪmps/ **A** *n* **1** vision *f* fugitive (**of** de); **to catch a ∼ of sth** entrevoir qch **2** (insight) aperçu *m* (**of, at** de)
B *vt* entrevoir

glisten /'glɪsn/ *vi* ‹*eyes, hair, surface*› luire; ‹*water*› scintiller

glitch /glɪtʃ/ *n* (fam) (gen) pépin *m* (fam); (Comput) problème *m* technique

glitter /'glɪtə(r)/ **A** *n* **1** (substance) paillettes *fpl*
2 (sparkle) éclat *m*
B *vi* scintiller

gloat /gləʊt/ *vi* jubiler (**at, over** à l'idée de)

global /'gləʊbl/ *adj* **1** (world-wide) mondial/-e **2** (comprehensive) global/-e

global warming *n* réchauffement *m* de la planète

globe /gləʊb/ *n* **1 the ∼** le globe
2 (model) globe *m* terrestre

gloom /gluːm/ *n* **1** (darkness) obscurité *f*
2 (despondency) morosité *f* (**about, over** à propos de)

gloomy /'gluːmɪ/ *adj* **1** (dark) sombre
2 ‹*expression, person, voice*› lugubre; ‹*weather*› morose; ‹*news, outlook*› déprimant/-e

glorify /'glɔːrɪfaɪ/ *vt*, glorifier

glorious /'glɔːrɪəs/ *adj* **1** ‹*view, weather*› magnifique; ‹*holiday*› merveilleux/-euse
2 (illustrious) glorieux/-ieuse

glory /'glɔːrɪ/ **A** *n* **1** (honour) gloire *f*
2 (splendour) splendeur *f*
B *vi* **to ∼ in** être très fier/fière de

gloss /glɒs/ *n* **1** (shine) lustre *m*
2 (paint) laque *f*
■ **gloss over** (pass rapidly over) glisser sur; (hide) dissimuler

glossary /'glɒsərɪ/ *n* glossaire *m*

glossy /'glɒsɪ/ *adj* ‹*hair, material*› luisant/-e; ‹*photograph*› brillant/-e; ‹*brochure*› luxueux/-euse

glossy magazine *n* magazine *m* illustré (de luxe)

glove /glʌv/ *n* gant *m*

glove compartment *n* boîte *f* à gants

glow /gləʊ/ **A** *n* **1** (from fire) rougeoiement *m*; (of candle) lueur *f*
2 (of complexion) éclat *m*
B *vi* **1** ‹*metal, embers*› rougeoyer; ‹*lamp, cigarette*› luire
2 to ∼ with health resplendir de santé; **to ∼ with pride** rayonner de fierté

glower /'glaʊə(r)/ *vi* lancer des regards noirs (**at** à)

glowing /'gləʊɪŋ/ *adj* **1** ‹*ember*› rougeoyant/-e; ‹*face, cheeks*› (from exercise) rouge; (from pleasure) radieux/-ieuse
2 ‹*account, terms*› élogieux/-ieuse

glue /gluː/ **A** *n* colle *f*
B *vt* coller; **to ∼ sth on** *or* **down** coller qch
C glued (fam) *pp adj* **to be ∼d to the TV** être collé/-e devant la télé (fam); **to be ∼d to the spot** être cloué/-e sur place

glue sniffer *n* sniffeur/-euse *m/f* (fam) de colle

glue-sniffing *n* inhalation *f* de colle

glut /glʌt/ *n* surabondance *f*, excès *m*

glutton /'glʌtn/ *n* glouton/-onne *m/f*

glycerin (*also* **glycerine**) /'glɪsəriːn, (AmE) -rɪn/ *n* glycérine *f*

GMT *n* (*abbr* = **Greenwich Mean Time**) TU

gnash /næʃ/ *vt* **to ∼ one's teeth** grincer des dents

gnaw /nɔː/ **A** *vt* ronger ‹*bone, wood*›
B *vi* **1 to ∼ at** *or* **on sth** ronger qch
2 to ∼ at sb ‹*hunger, remorse, pain*› tenailler qn

GNP *n* (= **gross national product**) PNB *m*

GNVQ *n* (*abbr* = **General National Vocational Qualification**) ≈ baccalauréat *m* professionnel

go /gəʊ/

> *As an intransitive verb*
> *Go* as a simple intransitive verb is translated by *aller*: *where are you going?* = où vas-tu?; *Sasha went to London last week* = Sasha est allé à Londres la semaine dernière.
> Note that *aller* conjugates with *être* in compound tenses. For the conjugation of *aller*, see the French verb tables.
> The verb *go* produces a great many phrasal verbs (*go up, go down, go out, go back* etc). Many of these are translated by a single verb in French (*monter, descendre, sortir, retourner* etc).
> The phrasal verbs are listed separately at the end of the entry GO.
> *As an auxiliary verb*
> When *go* is used as an auxiliary to show intention, it is also translated by *aller*: *I'm going to buy a car* = je vais acheter une voiture; *I was going to talk to you about it* = j'allais t'en parler.

A *vi* (*3ᵉ pers sg prés* **goes**, *prét* **went**, *pp* **gone**) **1** aller (**from** de, **to** à, en); **to ∼ to Paris/to California** aller à Paris/en Californie; **to ∼ to town/to the country** aller en ville/à la campagne; **they went home** ils sont rentrés chez eux; **to ∼ on holiday** partir en vacances; **to ∼ for a drink** aller prendre un verre; **∼ and ask her** va lui demander; **to ∼ to school/work** aller à l'école/au travail; **to ∼ to the doctor's** aller chez le médecin; **let's ∼, let's get ∼ing** allons-y
2 (leave) partir; **I'm ∼ing** je m'en vais

g

3 (become) **to ~ red** rougir; **to ~ white** blanchir; **to ~ mad** devenir fou/folle
4 to ~ unnoticed passer inaperçu/-e; **the question went unanswered** la question est restée sans réponse; **to ~ free** être libéré/-e
5 (become impaired) **his memory is going** il perd la mémoire; **my voice is going** je n'ai plus de voix; **the battery is going** la pile est presque à plat
6 (of time) passer, s'écouler
7 (operate, function) ‹*vehicle, machine, clock*› marcher, fonctionner; **to get [sth] going** mettre [qch] en marche; **to keep going** ‹*business*› se maintenir; ‹*machine*› continuer à marcher; ‹*person*› continuer
8 (belong, be placed) aller; **where do these plates ~?** où vont ces assiettes?; **it won't ~ into the box** ça ne rentre pas dans la boîte; **five into four won't ~** quatre n'est pas divisible par cinq
9 (be about to) **to be going to do** aller faire; **it's going to snow** il va neiger
10 (turn out) passer; **how did the party ~?** comment s'est passée la soirée?; **it went well/badly** ça s'est bien/mal passé
11 (make sound, perform action or movement) (gen) faire; ‹*bell, alarm*› sonner; **she went like this with her fingers** elle a fait comme ça avec ses doigts
12 (take one's turn) **you ~ next** c'est ton tour après, c'est à toi après; **you ~ first** après vous
13 (match) **those two colours don't ~ together** ces deux couleurs ne vont pas ensemble
B *vt* (*3ᵉ pers sg prés* **goes**, *prét* **went**, *pp* **gone**) faire ‹*distance, number of miles*›
C *n* (*pl* **goes**) (BrE) (turn) tour *m*; (try) essai *m*; **whose ~ is it?** à qui le tour?; (in game) à qui de jouer?
D to go *phr* **there are three days/pages to ~** il reste encore trois jours/pages

IDIOMS **to make a ~ of sth** réussir qch; **she's always on the ~** elle n'arrête jamais; **in one ~** d'un seul coup; **it goes without saying that** il va sans dire que; **as the saying goes** comme dit le proverbe; **anything goes** tout est permis

■ **go about** s'attaquer à ‹*task*›; **to ~ about one's business** vaquer à ses occupations
■ **go ahead** ‹*event*› avoir lieu; **~ ahead!** vas-y!; **they are going ahead with the project** ils ont décidé de mettre le projet en route
■ **go along** aller; **to make sth up as one goes along** inventer qch au fur et à mesure
■ **go along with** être d'accord avec ‹*person, view*›; accepter ‹*plan*›
■ **go around 1** se promener, circuler; **they ~ around everywhere together** ils vont partout ensemble
2 ‹*rumour*› courir
■ **go away** partir; **~ away!** va-t-en!
■ **go back 1** (return) retourner; (turn back) rebrousser chemin; **to ~ back to sleep** se rendormir; **to ~ back to work** se remettre au travail
2 (date back) remonter (**to** à)
3 (revert) revenir (**to** à)
■ **go back on** revenir sur ‹*promise, decision*›
■ **go by**: **A ~ by** ‹*person*› passer; **as time goes by** avec le temps
B ~ by [sth] juger d'après ‹*appearances*›; **to ~ by the rules** suivre le règlement
■ **go down A ~ down 1** (descend) (gen) descendre; ‹*sun*› se coucher; **to ~ down on one's knees** se mettre à genoux
2 to ~ down well/badly être bien/mal reçu/-e
3 ‹*price, temperature, standard*› baisser
4 ‹*swelling*› désenfler; ‹*tyre*› se dégonfler
5 (Comput) tomber en panne
B ~ down [sth] descendre ‹*hill*›
■ **go for A ~ for [sb/sth]** (fam) **1** (be keen on) aimer
2 (apply to) **the same goes for him!** c'est valable pour lui aussi!
B ~ for [sb] 1 (attack) attaquer
2 he has a lot going for him il a beaucoup de choses pour lui
C ~ for [sth] 1 essayer d'obtenir ‹*honour, victory*›; **she's going for the world record** elle vise le record mondial; **~ for it!** (fam) vas-y, fonce! (fam)
2 (choose) choisir, prendre
■ **go in 1** (enter) entrer; (go back in) rentrer
2 ‹*troops*› attaquer
3 ‹*sun*› se cacher
■ **go in for 1** (be keen on) aimer
2 s'inscrire à ‹*exam, competition*›
■ **go into 1** (enter) entrer dans ‹*building*›; se lancer dans ‹*business, profession*›
2 (examine) étudier ‹*question*›
3 a lot of work went into this project beaucoup de travail a été investi dans ce projet
■ **go off A ~ off 1** ‹*bomb*› exploser
2 ‹*alarm clock*› sonner; ‹*fire alarm*› se déclencher
3 ‹*person*› partir, s'en aller
4 (BrE) ‹*milk, cream*› tourner; ‹*meat*› s'avarier; ‹*butter*› rancir; ‹*performer, athlete*› perdre sa forme
5 ‹*lights, heating*› s'éteindre
6 (happen, take place) **the concert went off very well** le concert s'est très bien passé
B ~ off [sb/sth] (BrE) ne plus aimer
■ **go on A ~ on 1** (happen) se passer; **how long has this been going on?** depuis combien de temps est-ce que ça dure?
2 (continue on one's way) poursuivre son chemin
3 (continue) continuer; **the list goes on and on** la liste est infinie
4 (of time) (elapse) **as time went on, they...** avec le temps, ils...; **as the evening went on** au fur et à mesure que la soirée avançait
5 to ~ on about sth ne pas arrêter de parler de qch

6 (proceed) passer; **let's ~ on to the next item** passons au point suivant; **he went on to say that...** puis il a dit que...
7 ‹*heating, lights*› s'allumer
8 ‹*actor*› entrer en scène
B **~ on [sth]** se fonder sur ‹*evidence, information*›; **that's all we've got to ~ on** c'est tout ce que nous savons avec certitude

■ **go on at** s'en prendre à ‹*person*›

■ **go out 1** (leave, depart) sortir; **to ~ out for a drink** aller prendre un verre
2 to ~ out with sb sortir avec qn
3 ‹*tide*› descendre
4 ‹*fire, light*› s'éteindre

■ **go over**: **A** **~ over** (cross over) aller (**to** vers)
B **~ over [sth] 1** passer [qch] en revue ‹*details, facts*›; vérifier ‹*accounts, figures*›; relire ‹*article*›
2 (exceed) dépasser ‹*limit, sum*›

■ **go round** (BrE) **A** **~ round 1** ‹*wheel*› tourner
2 to ~ round to see sb aller voir qn
3 ‹*rumour*› circuler
4 (make detour) faire un détour
B **~ round [sth]** faire le tour de ‹*shops, house, museum*›

■ **go through**: **A** **~ through** ‹*law*› passer; ‹*business deal*› être conclu/-e
B **~ through [sth] 1** endurer, subir ‹*experience*›; passer par ‹*stage, phase*›; **she's gone through a lot** elle a beaucoup souffert
2 (check) examiner
3 (search) fouiller ‹*belongings*›
4 (perform) remplir ‹*formalities*›
5 (use up) dépenser ‹*money*›; consommer ‹*food, drink*›

■ **go through with** réaliser ‹*plan*›; **I can't ~ through with it** je ne peux pas le faire

■ **go under** couler

■ **go up** **A** **~ up 1** (ascend) monter; **to ~ up to bed** monter se coucher
2 ‹*price, temperature*› monter; ‹*figures*› augmenter; ‹*curtain*› se lever (**on** sur)
B **~ up [sth]** monter, gravir ‹*hill*›

■ **go without**: **A** **~ without** s'en passer
B **~ without [sth]** se passer de

go-ahead /ˈgəʊəhed/ *n* (fam) **to give sb the ~** donner le feu vert à qn; **to get the ~** recevoir le feu vert

goal /gəʊl/ *n* but *m*

goalkeeper *n* gardien *m* de but

goalpost /ˈgəʊlpəʊst/ *n* poteau *m* de but

goat /gəʊt/ *n* chèvre *f*

gobble /ˈgɒbl/ **A** *vt* (*also* **~ down**, **~ up**) engloutir
B *vi* ‹*turkey*› glouglouter

gobbledygook /ˈgɒbldɪguːk/ *n* (fam) charabia *m* (fam)

go-between *n* intermédiaire *mf*

gobsmacked /ˈgɒbsmækt/ *adj* (BrE) (fam) estomaqué/-e (fam)

god /gɒd/ *n* dieu *m*; **God** Dieu *m*

godchild *n* filleul/-e *m/f*

god-daughter *n* filleule *f*

goddess /ˈgɒdɪs/ *n* déesse *f*

godfather *n* parrain *m*

godmother *n* marraine *f*

godparent /ˈgɒdpeərənt/ *n* parrain/marraine *m/f*; **the ~s** le parrain et la marraine

godsend *n* aubaine *f*

godson *n* filleul *m*

goggles /ˈgɒglz/ *npl* lunettes *fpl*; (for swimming) lunettes *fpl* de plongée

going /ˈgəʊɪŋ/ **A** *n* **1** (departure) départ *m*
2 (progress) **that's good ~!** c'est rapide!; **it was slow ~** (on journey) ça a été long; (at work) ça n'avançait pas vite; **to be heavy ~** ‹*book*› être difficile à lire; ‹*work, conversation*› être laborieux/-ieuse
3 when the ~ gets tough quand les choses vont mal; **she finds her new job hard ~** elle trouve que son nouveau travail est difficile; **they got out while the ~ was good** ils s'en sont tirés (fam) avant qu'il ne soit trop tard
B *adj* **1** ‹*price*› actuel/-elle, en cours; **the ~ rate** le tarif en vigueur
2 ~ concern affaire *f* qui marche
3 it's the best model ~ c'est le meilleur modèle sur le marché

goings-on /ˌgəʊɪŋzˈɒn/ *npl* (fam) (events) événements *mpl*; (activities) activités *fpl*; (behaviour) conduite *f*

go-kart *n* kart *m*

gold /gəʊld/ **A** *n* or *m*
B *adj* ‹*jewellery, tooth*› en or; ‹*coin, ingot, ore, wire*› d'or
IDIOMS **as good as ~** sage comme une image; **to be worth one's weight in ~** valoir son pesant d'or

gold dust *n* poudre *f* d'or; **to be like ~** être une denrée rare

golden /ˈgəʊldən/ *adj* **1** (made of gold) en or, d'or
2 (gold coloured) doré/-e, d'or; **~ hair** cheveux *mpl* blonds dorés
3 ‹*age, days*› d'or; **a ~ opportunity** une occasion en or

golden handshake *n* prime *f* de départ

golden rule *n* règle *f* d'or

goldfish *n* (*pl* **-fish** *ou* **-fishes**) poisson *m* rouge

gold medal *n* médaille *f* d'or

gold mine *n* mine *f* d'or

gold-plated *adj* plaqué/-e or

gold rush *n* ruée *f* vers l'or

goldsmith *n* orfèvre *m*

golf /gɒlf/ *n* golf *m*; **to play ~** faire du golf

golf club *n* (place) club *m* de golf; (stick) crosse *f* de golf

golf course *n* (terrain *m* de) golf *m*

golfer /ˈgɒlfə(r)/ *n* joueur/-euse *m/f* de golf, golfeur/-euse *m/f*

gone /gɒn/ *adj* **1** (departed) parti/-e; (dead) disparu/-e
2 (past) **it's ~ six o'clock** il est six heures passées

gong /gɒŋ/ *n* gong *m*

⚷ **good** /gʊd/ **A** *n* **1** (virtue) bien *m*; **~ and evil** le bien et le mal; **to be up to no ~** mijoter qch (fam); **to come to no ~** mal tourner
2 (benefit) bien *m*; **it'll do you ~** ça te fera du bien; **it didn't do my migraine any ~** ça n'a pas arrangé ma migraine
3 (use) **it's no ~ crying** ça ne sert à rien de pleurer; **what ~ would it do me?** à quoi cela me servirait-il?
B *adj* (*comp* **better**, *superl* **best**) **1** (gen) bon/bonne *before n*; **it's a ~ film** c'est un bon film; **it was a ~ party** c'était une soirée réussie; **the ~ weather** le beau temps; **she's a ~ swimmer** elle nage bien; **to be ~ at** être bon/bonne en ‹*Latin, physics*›; être bon/bonne à ‹*badminton, chess*›; **to be ~ with** savoir comment s'y prendre avec ‹*children, animals*›; aimer ‹*figures*›; **to have a ~ time** bien s'amuser; **it's ~ to see you again** je suis content de vous revoir; **I don't feel too ~** je ne me sens pas très bien; **the ~ thing is that...** ce qui est bien c'est que...; **to taste ~** avoir bon goût; **to smell ~** sentir bon; **we had a ~ laugh** on a bien ri; **to wait/walk for a ~ hour** attendre/marcher une bonne heure
2 (well-behaved) ‹*child, dog*› sage; **be ~!** sois sage!
3 (high quality) ‹*hotel*› bon/bonne *before n*; ‹*coat, china*› beau/belle *before n*; ‹*degree*› avec mention
4 (kind) ‹*person*› gentil/-ille; (virtuous) ‹*man, life*› vertueux/-euse; **to do sb a ~ turn** rendre service à qn; **would you be ~ enough to do** auriez-vous la gentillesse de faire
5 (beneficial) **to be ~ for** faire du bien à ‹*person, plant*›; être bon/bonne pour ‹*health, business, morale*›
6 (fortunate) **it's a ~ job** *or* **thing (that)...** heureusement que...; **it's a ~ job** *or* **thing too!** tant mieux!; ▶ **better, best**
C *excl* (expressing pleasure, satisfaction) c'est bien!; (with relief) tant mieux!; (to encourage, approve) très bien!
D as good as *phr* quasiment; **to be as ~ as new** être comme neuf/neuve
E for good *phr* pour toujours
(IDIOMS) **~ for you!** bravo!; **it's too ~ to be true** c'est trop beau pour être vrai

good afternoon *phr* bonjour

goodbye /ˌgʊd'baɪ/ *phr* au revoir

good evening *phr* bonsoir

good-for-nothing /'gʊdfənʌθɪŋ/ *n* bon/bonne *m/f* à rien

good-humoured (BrE), **good-humored** (AmE) /ˌgʊd'hjuːməd/ *adj* ‹*crowd, discussion*› détendu/-e; ‹*rivalry*› amical/-e; ‹*remark, smile*› plaisant/-e; **to be ~** ‹*person*› avoir bon caractère

good-looking *adj* beau/belle *before n*

good morning *phr* bonjour

good-natured /ˌgʊd'neɪtʃəd/ *adj* ‹*person*› agréable; ‹*animal*› placide

goodness /'gʊdnɪs/ **A** *n* **1** (quality, virtue) bonté *f*
2 (nourishment) **to be full of ~** être plein/-e de bonnes choses
B *excl* (*also* **~ gracious!**) mon Dieu!
(IDIOM) **for ~' sake!** pour l'amour de Dieu!

goodnight /ˌgʊd'naɪt/ *phr* bonne nuit

goods *npl* articles *mpl*, marchandise *f*

goods train *n* (BrE) train *m* de marchandises

goodwill /ˌgʊd'wɪl/ *n* **1** (kindness) bonne volonté *f*
2 (of business) clientèle *f*

google® /guːgl/ **A** *vt* googler
B *vi* chercher sur (le moteur de recherche) Google®

goose /guːs/ *n* (*pl* **geese**) oie *f*

gooseberry /'gʊzbərɪ, (AmE) 'guːsberɪ/ *n* groseille *f* à maquereau
(IDIOM) **to be a** *or* **play ~** tenir la chandelle

goose pimples /'guːspɪmplz/ *npl* chair *f* de poule

gorge /gɔːdʒ/ **A** *n* gorge *f*
B *v refl* **to ~ oneself** se gaver (**on** de)

gorgeous /'gɔːdʒəs/ *adj* **1** (fam) ‹*food, scenery*› formidable (fam); ‹*kitten, baby*› adorable; ‹*weather, day, person*› splendide
2 (sumptuous) somptueux/-euse

gorilla /gə'rɪlə/ *n* gorille *m*

gorse /'gɔːs/ *n* ajoncs *mpl*

gory /'gɔːrɪ/ *adj* sanglant/-e

gosh /gɒʃ/ *excl* (fam) ça alors! (fam)

go-slow /ˌgəʊ'sləʊ/ *n* (BrE) grève *f* perlée

gospel /'gɒspl/ *n* Évangile *m*

gospel music *n* gospel *m*

gossip /'gɒsɪp/ **A** *n* **1** (malicious) commérages *mpl* (**about** sur); (not malicious) nouvelles *fpl* (**about** sur)
2 (person) commère *f*
B *vi* bavarder; (more maliciously) faire des commérages (**about** sur)

gossip column *n* échos *mpl*

got: **to have got** /gɒt/ *phr* **1 to have ~** avoir
2 I've ~ to go il faut que j'y aille

gouge A *n* rainure *f*
B *vt* **1** (dig) creuser ‹*hole*› (**in** dans)
2 (AmE) (fam) (overcharge) estamper (fam)
■ **gouge out ~ out [sth], ~ [sth] out** creuser ‹*pattern*›; enlever ‹*bad bit*›; **to ~ sb's eyes out** arracher les yeux à qn

gourd /gʊəd/ *n* **1** (container) gourde *f*
2 (fruit) calebasse *f*

gout /gaʊt/ *n* goutte *f*

⚷ mot clé

govern /'gʌvn/ **A** *vt* **1** gouverner ‹*country, state, city*›; administrer ‹*colony, province*›
2 (control) régir ‹*use, conduct, treatment*›
3 (determine) déterminer ‹*decision*›; régler ‹*flow, speed*›
B *vi* ‹*parliament, president*› gouverner

governess /'gʌvənɪs/ *n* (*pl* **~es**) gouvernante *f*

governing /'gʌvənɪŋ/ *adj* ‹*party*› au pouvoir; ‹*class*› dirigeant/-e; **the ~ principle** l'idée directrice

government /'gʌvənmənt/ **A** *n* gouvernement *m*; (the state) l'État *m*; **in ~** au pouvoir
B *adj* ‹*minister, plan*› du gouvernement; ‹*department, majority, policy*› gouvernemental/-e; ‹*expenditure, borrowing*› de l'État; ‹*funds*› public/-ique

governmental /ˌgʌvən'mentl/ *adj* gouvernemental/-e

governor /'gʌvənə(r)/ *n* (of state, colony, bank) gouverneur *m*; (of prison) (BrE) directeur *m*; (of school) (BrE) membre *m* du conseil d'établissement

gown /gaʊn/ *n* (dress) robe *f*; (of judge, academic) toge *f*; (of surgeon) blouse *f*

GP *n* (*abbr* = **general practitioner**) (médecin *m*) généraliste *mf*

GPS *n* (*abbr* = **global positioning system**) GPS

grab /græb/ **A** *vt* (*p prés etc* **-bb-**) empoigner ‹*money, object*›; saisir ‹*arm, person, opportunity*›; **to ~ hold of** se saisir de
B *vi* (*p prés etc* **-bb-**) **to ~ at** se jeter sur

grace /greɪs/ *n* **1** (gen) grâce *f*; **sb's saving ~** ce qui sauve qn
2 to give sb two days' ~ accorder un délai de deux jours à qn
3 (prayer) (before meal) bénédicité *m*; (after meal) grâces *fpl*
IDIOM **to be full of airs and ~s** prendre des airs

graceful /'greɪsfl/ *adj* ‹*dancer, movement*› gracieux/-ieuse; ‹*person*› élégant/-e

grade /greɪd/ **A** *n* **1** (quality) qualité *f*; **high-/low-~** de qualité supérieure/inférieure
2 (mark) note *f* (**in** en)
3 (rank) échelon *m*
4 (AmE) (class) classe *f*
B *vt* (by quality) classer (**according to** selon); (by size) calibrer (**according to** selon)

grade school *n* (AmE) école *f* primaire

gradient /'greɪdɪənt/ *n* pente *f*, inclinaison *f*

gradual /'grædʒʊəl/ *adj* **1** ‹*change, increase*› progressif/-ive
2 ‹*slope*› doux/douce

gradually /'grædʒʊlɪ/ *adv* (slowly) peu à peu; (by degrees) progressivement

graduate **A** /'grædʒʊət/ *n* diplômé/-e *m/f*
B /'grædjʊeɪt/ *vi* **1** terminer ses études (**at, from** à); (AmE) (Sch) ≈ finir le lycée
2 (progress) **to ~ (from sth) to** passer (de qch) à

graduate training scheme *n* programme *m* de formation professionnelle pour étudiants diplômés

graduation /ˌgrædʒʊ'eɪʃn/ *n* (*also* **~ ceremony**) (cérémonie *f* de) remise *f* des diplômes

graffiti /grə'fiːtɪ/ *n* graffiti *mpl*

graffiti artist *n* tagger *m*

graft /grɑːft, (AmE) græft/ **A** *n* greffe *f*; **skin ~** greffe de la peau
B *vt* greffer (**onto** sur)

grain /greɪn/ *n* **1** (of rice, wheat, sand, salt) grain *m*
2 (crops) céréales *fpl*
3 (fig) (of truth, comfort) brin *m*
4 (in wood, stone) veines *fpl*; (in leather, paper, fabric) grain *m*
IDIOM **it goes against the ~** c'est contre tous mes/nos/leurs principes

gram /græm/ *n* (*also* **gramme**) gramme *m*

grammar /'græmə(r)/ *n* grammaire *f*

grammar school *n* (BrE) ≈ lycée *m* (à recrutement sélectif)

grammatical /grə'mætɪkl/ *adj* **1** ‹*error*› de grammaire
2 (correct) grammaticalement correct

granary /'grænərɪ/ *n* grenier *m*

granary bread *n* pain *m* aux céréales

grand /grænd/ *adj* ‹*building, ceremony*› grandiose; **on a ~ scale** à très grande échelle; **the Grand Canyon** le Grand Cañon; **to play the ~ lady** jouer à la grande dame

grandchild /'græntʃaɪld/ *n* (girl) petite-fille *f*; (boy) petit-fils *m*; **his grandchildren** ses petits-enfants *mpl*

granddaughter *n* petite-fille *f*

grandeur /'grændʒə(r)/ *n* (of scenery) majesté *f*; (of building) caractère *m* grandiose

grandfather *n* grand-père *m*

grandfather clock *n* horloge *f* comtoise

grandma /'grænmɑː/ *n* (fam) mémé *f* (fam), mamy *f* (fam), mamie *f* (fam)

grandmother /'grænmʌðə(r)/ *n* grand-mère *f*

grandpa *n* (fam) pépé *m* (fam), papy *m* (fam), papi *m* (fam)

grandparents *npl* grands-parents *mpl*

grand piano *n* piano *m* à queue

grand slam® /ˌgrænd'slæm/ *n* grand chelem *m*

grandson *n* petit-fils *m*

grandstand /'grænstænd/ *n* tribune *f*

grand total *n* total *m*

granite /'grænɪt/ *n* granit(e) *m*

granny /'grænɪ/ *n* (fam) mémé *f* (fam)

grant /grɑːnt, (AmE) grænt/ **A** *n* (gen) subvention *f*; (for study) bourse *f*
B *vt* **1** accorder ‹*permission*›; accéder à ‹*request*›
2 to ~ sb [sth] accorder [qch] à qn

g

‹interview, leave, visa›; concéder [qch] à qn *‹citizenship›*
3 to ~ that reconnaître que
IDIOMS **to take sth for ~ed** considérer qch comme allant de soi; **he takes his mother for ~ed** il croit que sa mère est à son service

granulated *adj ‹sugar›* cristallisé/-e

granule /ˈgrænjuːl/ *n* (of sugar, salt) grain *m*; (of coffee) granulé *m*

grape /greɪp/ *n* grain *m* de raisin; **a bunch of ~s** une grappe de raisin

grapefruit /ˈgreɪpfruːt/ *n* pamplemousse *m*

grapeseed oil *n* huile *f* de pépins de raisin

grapevine /ˈgreɪpvaɪn/ *n* (in vineyard) pied *m* de vigne; (in greenhouse, garden) vigne *f*
IDIOM **to hear sth on the ~** apprendre qch par le téléphone arabe

graph /grɑːf, (AmE) græf/ *n* graphique *m*

graphic /ˈgræfɪk/ *adj* **1** *‹art, display, technique›* graphique
2 *‹account›* (pleasantly described) vivant/-e; (gory) cru/-e

graphic design *n* graphisme *m*

graphic designer *n* graphiste *mf*

graphics *npl* **1** (on screen) visualisation *f* graphique
2 computer ~ infographie *f*
3 (in film, TV) images *fpl*; (in book) illustrations *fpl*

graphics card *n* carte *f* graphique

graphics interface *n* interface *f* graphique

graph paper *n* papier *m* millimétré

grasp /grɑːsp, (AmE) græsp/ **A** *n* **1** (hold, grip) prise *f*
2 (understanding) maîtrise *f*
B *vt* **1** empoigner *‹rope, hand›*; saisir *‹opportunity›*
2 (comprehend) saisir, comprendre
C *vi* **to ~ at** tenter de saisir

grasping /ˈgrɑːspɪŋ, (AmE) ˈgræspɪŋ/ *adj* cupide

grass /grɑːs, (AmE) græs/ *n* herbe *f*; (lawn) pelouse *f*
IDIOM **the ~ is greener (on the other side of the fence)** on croit toujours que c'est mieux ailleurs

grass court *n* court *m* en gazon

grasshopper /ˈgrɑːshɒpə(r), (AmE) ˈgræs-/ *n* sauterelle *f*

grassroots /ˌgrɑːsˈruːts, (AmE) ˌgræs-/ **A** *npl* **the ~** le peuple
B *adj ‹movement›* populaire; *‹support›* de base

grate /greɪt/ **A** *n* grille *f* de foyer
B *vt* râper *‹carrot, cheese›*
C *vi* **1** *‹metal object›* grincer (**on** sur)
2 (annoy) agacer; **that ~s** ça m'agace

grateful /ˈgreɪtfl/ *adj* reconnaissant/-e (**to** à, **for** de)

grater /ˈgreɪtə(r)/ *n* râpe *f*

gratify /ˈgrætɪfaɪ/ *vt* faire plaisir à *‹person›*; satisfaire *‹desire›*; **to be gratified** être satisfait/-e

grating /ˈgreɪtɪŋ/ **A** *n* (bars) grille *f*
B *adj ‹noise›* grinçant/-e; *‹voice›* désagréable

gratitude /ˈgrætɪtjuːd, (AmE) -tuːd/ *n* reconnaissance *f* (**to, towards** envers, **for** de)

gratuitous /grəˈtjuːɪtəs, (AmE) -ˈtuː-/ *adj* gratuit/-e

grave **A** *n* tombe *f*
B *adj* **1** *‹illness›* grave; *‹risk›* sérieux/-ieuse; *‹danger›* grand/-e *before n*
2 (solemn) sérieux/-ieuse

gravel /ˈgrævl/ *n* (coarse) graviers *mpl*; (fine) gravillons *mpl*

gravestone /ˈgreɪvstəʊn/ *n* pierre *f* tombale

graveyard /ˈgreɪvjɑːd/ *n* cimetière *m*

gravitate /ˈgrævɪteɪt/ *vi* **to ~ to(wards)** graviter vers

gravity /ˈgrævətɪ/ *n* **1** pesanteur *f*; **centre of ~** centre *m* de gravité
2 (of situation) gravité *f*

gravy /ˈgreɪvɪ/ *n* sauce *f* (au jus de rôti)

gravy boat *n* saucière *f*

gray (AmE) = **grey**

graze /greɪz/ **A** *n* écorchure *f*
B *vt* **1 to ~ one's knee** s'écorcher le genou (**on, against** sur)
2 (touch lightly) frôler
C *vi ‹sheep›* brouter; *‹cow›* paître

grease /griːs/ **A** *n* graisse *f*
B *vt* graisser

greasy /ˈgriːsɪ/ *adj ‹hair, skin, food›* gras/grasse; *‹overalls›* graisseux/-euse

great /greɪt/ *adj* **1** (gen) grand/-e *before n*; *‹number, increase›* important/-e; *‹heat›* fort/-e *before n*; **a ~ deal (of)** beaucoup (de); **with ~ difficulty** avec beaucoup de mal
2 (fam) *‹book, party, weather›* génial/-e (fam), formidable (fam); *‹opportunity›* formidable (fam); **to feel ~** se sentir en pleine forme; **~!** génial!

great aunt *n* grand-tante *f*

great big *adj* (très) grand/-e *before n*, énorme

Great Britain *pr n* Grande-Bretagne *f*

great grandchild *n* (girl) arrière-petite-fille *f*; (garçon) arrière-petit-fils *m*

great grandfather *n* arrière-grand-père *m*

great grandmother *n* arrière-grand-mère *f*

great-great grandchild *n* (girl) arrière-arrière-petite-fille *f*; (boy) arrière-arrière-petit-fils *m*

greatly /ˈgreɪtlɪ/ *adv ‹admire, regret›* beaucoup, énormément; *‹surprised,*

mot clé

distressed› très, extrêmement; ‹*improved, changed*› considérablement

greatness /'greɪtnɪs/ *n* (of achievement) importance *f*; (of person) grandeur *f*

great uncle *n* grand-oncle *m*

Greece /gri:s/ *pr n* Grèce *f*

greed /gri:d/ *n* **1** (for money, power) avidité *f* (**for** de)
2 (*also* **greediness**) (for food) gourmandise *f*

greedy /'gri:dɪ/ *adj* **1** (for food) gourmand/-e; (stronger) goulu/-e; ‹*look*› avide; **a ~ pig** (fam) un goinfre (fam)
2 (for money, power) avide (**for** de)

Greek /gri:k/ **A** *n* **1** (person) Grec/Grecque *m/f*
2 (language) grec *m*
B *adj* ‹*government, island*› grec/grecque; ‹*ambassador, embassy*› de Grèce
IDIOM **it's all ~ to me** c'est du chinois pour moi

green /gri:n/ **A** *n* **1** (colour) vert *m*
2 village ~ terrain *m* communal
3 (in bowling) boulingrin *m*; (in golf) green *m*
4 (person) écologiste *mf*; **the Greens** les Verts *mpl*
B greens *npl* (BrE) légumes *mpl* verts
C *adj* **1** (in colour) vert/-e
2 ‹*countryside*› verdoyant/-e
3 (fam) (naïve) naïf/naïve
4 (inexperienced) novice
5 ‹*policies, candidate, issues*› écologiste; ‹*product*› écologique

green card *n* **1** (driving insurance) carte *f* verte (internationale)
2 (AmE) (residence and work permit) carte *f* de séjour

greenery /'gri:nərɪ/ *n* verdure *f*

greenfield site *n* terrain *m* vert

greengrocer /'gri:ngrəʊsə(r)/ *n* marchand *m* de fruits et légumes

greenhouse *n* serre *f*

greenhouse effect *n* effet *m* de serre

greenhouse gas *n* gaz *m* à effet de serre

Greenland /'gri:nlənd/ *pr n* Groenland *m*

greet /gri:t/ *vt* **1** (say hello to) saluer
2 to be ~ed with *or* **by** provoquer ‹*dismay, amusement*›

greeting /'gri:tɪŋ/ **A** *n* salutation *f*
B greetings *npl* **Christmas ~s** vœux *mpl* de Noël; **Season's ~s** meilleurs vœux

greetings card (BrE), **greeting card** (AmE) *n* carte *f* de vœux

grey (BrE), **gray** (AmE) /greɪ/ **A** *n* gris *m*
B *adj* **1** (in colour) gris/-e
2 (grey-haired) **to go** *or* **turn ~** grisonner
3 (dull) ‹*existence, day*› morne; ‹*person, town*› terne
▪ **grey out**: **to be ~ed out** (Comput) être en grisé

grey area *n* zone *f* floue

grey-haired *adj* aux cheveux gris

greyhound *n* lévrier *m*

grid /grɪd/ *n* **1** grille *f*
2 (BrE) (network) réseau *m*

gridlock /'grɪdlɒk/ *n* embouteillage *m*, bouchon *m*

grief /gri:f/ *n* chagrin *m*
IDIOM **to come to ~** ‹*person*› (have an accident) avoir un accident; (fail) échouer; ‹*business*› péricliter; **good ~!** mon Dieu!

grief-stricken *adj* accablé/-e de douleur

grievance /'gri:vns/ *n* griefs *mpl* (**against** contre)

grieve /gri:v/ *vi* **to ~ for** *or* **over** pleurer ‹*person*›

grievous bodily harm, **GBH** *n* (Law) coups *mpl* et blessures *fpl*

grill /grɪl/ **A** *n* gril *m*
B *vt* **1** faire griller ‹*meat, fish*›
2 (fam) (interrogate) mettre [qn] sur la sellette (fam)

grille /grɪl/ *n* (gen) grille *f*; (on car) calandre *f*

grim /grɪm/ *adj* **1** ‹*news, town, future*› sinistre; ‹*sight, conditions*› effroyable; ‹*reality*› dur/-e
2 ‹*struggle*› acharné/-e; ‹*resolve*› terrible
3 ‹*face*› grave

grimace /'grɪməs/ **A** *n* grimace *f* (**of** de)
B *vi* (involuntary) faire une grimace (**with, in** de); (pull a face) faire la grimace

grime /graɪm/ *n* (of city) saleté *f*; (on object, person) crasse *f*

grimy /'graɪmɪ/ *adj* ‹*city*› noir/-e; ‹*hands, window*› crasseux/-euse

grin /grɪn/ **A** *n* sourire *m*
B *vi* (*p prés etc* **-nn-**) sourire (**at** à, **with** de)

grind /graɪnd/ **A** *n* (fam) boulot *m* (fam) *or* travail *m* monotone
B *vt* (*prét, pp* **ground**) moudre ‹*corn, coffee beans*›; écraser ‹*grain*›; hacher ‹*meat*›; **to ~ one's teeth** grincer des dents
C *vi* (*prét, pp* **ground**) ‹*machine*› grincer; **to ~ to a halt** ‹*machine*› s'arrêter; ‹*vehicle*› s'arrêter avec un grincement de freins; ‹*factory, production*› s'immobiliser

grindstone /'graɪndstəʊn/ *n* meule *f or* pierre *f* à aiguiser
IDIOM **to keep** *or* **have one's nose to the ~** travailler sans relâche

grip /grɪp/ **A** *n* **1** prise *f* (**on** sur)
2 to lose one's ~ on reality perdre contact avec la réalité; **to come to ~s with sth** en venir aux prises avec qch; **get a ~ on yourself!** ressaisis-toi!
3 (of tyre) adhérence *f*
B *vt* (*p prés etc* **-pp-**) **1** (grab) agripper; (hold) serrer
2 ‹*tyres*› adhérer à ‹*road*›; ‹*shoes*› accrocher à ‹*ground*›
3 (captivate) captiver

gripping /'grɪpɪŋ/ *adj* captivant/-e

grisly /'grɪzlɪ/ *adj* ‹*story, sight*› horrible; ‹*remains*› macabre

gristle /'grɪsl/ *n* cartilage *m*

g

grit /grɪt/ **A** *n* **1** (on lens) grains *mpl* de poussière; (sandy dirt) grains *mpl* de sable
2 (BrE) (for roads) sable *m*
B *vt* (*p prés etc* **-tt-**) (BrE) sabler ‹*road*›
IDIOM **to ~ one's teeth** serrer les dents

grizzly /'grɪzlɪ/ *n* (*also* **~ bear**) grizzli *m*

groan /grəʊn/ **A** *n* (of pain, despair) gémissement *m*; (of disgust, protest) grognement *m*
B *vi* (in pain) gémir; (in disgust, protest) grogner

grocer /'grəʊsə(r)/ *n* (person) épicier/-ière *m/f*; **~'s (shop)** (BrE) épicerie *f*

groceries /'grəʊsərɪz/ *npl* provisions *fpl*

grocery /'grəʊsərɪ/ *n* (*also* **~ shop** (BrE), **~ store** (AmE)) épicerie *f*

groggy /'grɒgɪ/ *adj* groggy; **to feel ~** avoir les jambes en coton (fam)

groin /grɔɪn/ *n* aine *f*

groom /gruːm/ **A** *n* **1** (bridegroom) **the ~** le jeune marié
2 (for horse) palefrenier/-ière *m/f*
B *vt* **1** panser ‹*horse*›
2 to ~ sb for préparer à qn ‹*exam, career*›

groove /gruːv/ *n* (gen) rainure *f*; (on record) sillon *m*; (on screw) fente *f*

grope /grəʊp/ **A** *vt* (sexually) tripoter (fam)
B *vi* **to ~ for sth** chercher qch à tâtons

gross /grəʊs/ **A** *n* (*pl* **~**) grosse *f*
B *adj* **1** ‹*income, profit*› brut/-e
2 ‹*error, exaggeration*› grossier/-ière; ‹*abuse, inequality*› choquant/-e; ‹*injustice*› flagrant/-e
3 ‹*behaviour*› vulgaire; ‹*language*› cru/-e
4 (fam) (revolting) dégoûtant/-e
5 (fam) (obese) obèse
C *vt* ‹*business, company*› faire un bénéfice brut de

grossly /'grəʊslɪ/ *adv* ‹*misleading, irresponsible*› extrêmement; ‹*underpaid*› scandaleusement; **~ overweight** obèse

gross national product, **GNP** *n* produit *m* national brut, PNB *m*

grotesque /grəʊ'tesk/ *n*, *adj* grotesque *m*

grotto /'grɒtəʊ/ *n* (*pl* **~s** *ou* **~es**) grotte *f*

grotty /'grɒtɪ/ *adj* (fam) minable (fam); **to feel ~** se sentir tout chose (fam)

⚷ **ground** /graʊnd/ **A** *n* **1** sol *m*, terre *f*; **on the ~** par terre; **above ~** en surface; **below ~** sous terre
2 (area, territory) terrain *m*; **a piece of ~** un terrain
3 (sportsground) terrain *m*
B grounds *npl* **1** (garden) parc *m* (**of** de)
2 (reasons) **~s for sth** motifs *mpl* de qch; **~s for doing** motifs pour faire; **on the ~s that** en raison du fait que
C *pp adj* ‹*coffee, pepper*› moulu/-e
D *vt* **1** immobiliser ‹*aircraft*›
2 ‹*ship*› **to be ~ed** s'échouer
IDIOMS **to gain ~** gagner du terrain (**on, over** sur); **to hold one's ~** tenir bon; **to go to ~** se terrer; **that suits me down to the ~** ça me convient parfaitement

ground floor *n* rez-de-chaussée *m inv*; **on the ~** au rez-de-chaussée

grounding /'graʊndɪŋ/ *n* bases *fpl* (**in** en, de)

groundnut oil *n* huile *f* d'arachide

ground rules *npl* grands principes *mpl*; **to change the ~** modifier les règles du jeu

groundsheet *n* tapis *m* de sol

ground troops *npl* troupes *fpl* terrestres

groundwork /'graʊndwɜːk/ *n* travail *m* préparatoire (**for** à)

ground zero *n* (New York) point *m* zéro

⚷ **group** /gruːp/ **A** *n* groupe *m*; **in ~s** en groupes
B *vt* grouper
C *vi* **~ together** ‹*people*› se grouper

group booking *n* réservation *f* de groupe

group therapy *n* thérapie *f* de groupe

group work *n* travail *m* en groupes

grouse /graʊs/ *n* (*pl* **~**) tétras *m*

grove /grəʊv/ *n* bosquet *m*; **lemon ~** verger *m* de citronniers

grovel /'grɒvl/ *vi* (*p prés etc* **-ll-** (BrE), **-l-** (AmE)) ramper (**to, before** devant)

⚷ **grow** /grəʊ/ **A** *vt* (*prét* **grew**, *pp* **grown**)
1 cultiver ‹*plant, crop*›
2 laisser pousser ‹*beard, nails*›; **to ~ 5 cm** ‹*person*› grandir de 5 cm; ‹*plant*› pousser de 5 cm
B *vi* (*prét* **grew**, *pp* **grown**) **1** ‹*person*› grandir (**by** de); ‹*plant, hair*› pousser (**by** de)
2 ‹*population, tension*› augmenter (**by** de); ‹*company, economy*› se développer; ‹*opposition, support, problem*› devenir plus important; ‹*crisis*› s'aggraver
3 devenir ‹*hotter, stronger*›; **to ~ old** vieillir; **to ~ impatient** s'impatienter; **I grew to like him** j'ai appris à l'aimer
■ **grow apart** s'éloigner l'un de l'autre
■ **grow on**: **it ~s on you** on finit par l'aimer; **he's ~ing on me** je commence à le trouver plus sympathique
■ **grow out of**: **1 he's grown out of his suit** son costume est devenu trop petit pour lui
2 he'll ~ out of it (of habit) ça lui passera
■ **grow up** (gen) grandir; **when I ~ up** quand je serai grand

grower /'grəʊə(r)/ *n* (of fruit) producteur/-trice *m/f*; (of crops) cultivateur/-trice *m/f*

growl /graʊl/ **A** *n* grondement *m*
B *vi* ‹*dog*› gronder

grown-up **A** /'grəʊnʌp/ *n* adulte *mf*, grande personne *f*
B /ˌgrəʊn'ʌp/ *adj* adulte

⚷ **growth** /grəʊθ/ *n* **1** (gen) croissance *f* (**in, of** de); (of hair, nails) pousse *f*; (of economy) expansion *f* (**in, of** de); (in numbers, productivity) augmentation *f* (**in** de)
2 (tumour) grosseur *f*, tumeur *f*

⚷ mot clé

growth area *n* secteur *m* en expansion
growth industry *n* industrie *f* en expansion
growth rate *n* taux *m* de croissance
grubby /'grʌbɪ/ *adj* malpropre
grudge /grʌdʒ/ **A** *n* **to bear sb a ~** en vouloir à qn
B *vt* **to ~ sb their success** en vouloir à qn de sa réussite; **to ~ doing** rechigner à faire
grudgingly /'grʌdʒɪŋlɪ/ *adv* ‹*admit*› avec réticence
gruelling (BrE), **grueling** (AmE) /'gruːəlɪŋ/ *adj* exténuant/-e
gruesome /'gruːsəm/ *adj* horrible
gruff /grʌf/ *adj* bourru/-e
grumble /'grʌmbl/ *vi* ‹*person*› ronchonner (**at sb** après qn, **to** auprès de); **to ~ about** se plaindre de
grumpy /'grʌmpɪ/ *adj* grincheux/-euse
grunge /'grʌndʒ/ *n* (fam) (dirt) crasse *f*; (style) grunge *m*
grunt /grʌnt/ **A** *n* grognement *m*
B *vi* grogner
G-string *n* (garment) string *m*
guarantee /ˌgærən'tiː/ **A** *n* garantie *f*
B *vt* garantir
⚷ **guard** /gɑːd/ **A** *n* **1** (for person) surveillant/-e *m/f*; (for place, object, at prison) gardien/-ienne *m/f*; (soldier) garde *m*
2 (military duty) garde *f*, surveillance *f*; **to be on ~** être de garde
3 to catch sb off ~ prendre qn au dépourvu
4 (BrE) (on train) chef *m* de train
B *vt* **1** (protect) surveiller ‹*place, object*›; protéger ‹*person*›
2 surveiller ‹*hostage, prisoner*›
3 garder ‹*secret*›
guard dog *n* chien *m* de garde
guarded /'gɑːdɪd/ *adj* circonspect/-e (**about** à propos de)
guardian /'gɑːdɪən/ *n* **1** (gen) gardien/-ienne *m/f* (**of** de)
2 (of child) tuteur/-trice *m/f*
guardian angel *n* ange *m* gardien
Guernsey /'gɜːnzɪ/ *pr n* Guernesey *f*
guerrilla /gə'rɪlə/ *n* guérillero *m*
guerrilla war *n* guérilla *f*
⚷ **guess** /ges/ **A** *n* supposition *f*, conjecture *f*; **at a (rough) ~ I would say that...** au hasard je dirais que...; **it's anybody's ~!** les paris sont ouverts!
B *vt* **1** deviner; **~ what!** tu sais quoi! (fam)
2 (suppose) supposer
C *vi* deviner; **to keep sb ~ing** ne pas satisfaire la curiosité de qn
guesswork /'geswɜːk/ *n* conjecture *f*
⚷ **guest** /gest/ *n* (in one's home) invité/-e *m/f*; (at hotel) client/-e *m/f*; **be my ~!** je vous en prie!
guest house *n* pension *f* de famille
guest room *n* chambre *f* d'amis
guest worker *n* travailleur immigré/travailleuse immigrée *m/f*
guidance /'gaɪdns/ *n* conseils *mpl* (**from** de)
guide /gaɪd/ **A** *n* **1** (person, book) guide *m* (**to** de)
2 (idea) indication *f*; **as a rough ~** à titre d'indication
3 (*also* **Girl Guide**) guide *f*
B *vt* guider (**to** vers)
guide book *n* guide *m*
guide dog *n* chien *m* d'aveugle
guided tour *n* visite *f* guidée
guideline /'gaɪdlaɪn/ *n* (rough guide) indication *f*; (in political context) directive *f*; (advice) conseils *mpl*
guild /gɪld/ *n* (medieval) guilde *f*; (modern) association *f*
guillotine /'gɪlətiːn/ *n* **1** guillotine *f*
2 (for paper) massicot *m*
guilt /gɪlt/ *n* culpabilité *f*
⚷ **guilty** /'gɪltɪ/ *adj* coupable; **to feel ~** culpabiliser; **to feel ~ about** se sentir coupable vis-à-vis de
guinea pig /'gɪnɪpɪg/ *n* **1** (Zool) cochon *m* d'Inde
2 (in experiment) cobaye *m*
guitar /gɪ'tɑː(r)/ *n* guitare *f*
guitarist /gɪ'tɑːrɪst/ *n* guitariste *mf*
gulch /gʌltʃ/ *n* (AmE) ravin *m*
gulf /gʌlf/ *n* **1** golfe *m*; **the Gulf** la région du Golfe
2 (fig) fossé *m* (**between** qui sépare)
Gulf States *pr n pl* **the ~** (in Middle East) les États *mpl* du Golfe
Gulf War *pr n* guerre *f* du Golfe
gull /gʌl/ *n* mouette *f*
gullible /'gʌləbl/ *adj* crédule
gully /'gʌlɪ/ *n* ravin *m*
gulp /gʌlp/ **A** *n* (of liquid) gorgée *f*; (of air) bouffée *f*, goulée *f*; (of food) bouchée *f*
B *vt* (*also* **~ down**) engloutir ‹*food, drink*›
C *vi* avoir la gorge serrée
gum /gʌm/ *n* **1** (in mouth) gencive *f*
2 (*also* **chewing ~**) chewing-gum *m*
3 (adhesive) colle *f*; (resin) gomme *f*
⚷ **gun** /gʌn/ *n* (weapon) arme *f* à feu; (revolver) revolver *m*; (rifle) fusil *m*; (cannon) canon *m*; **to fire a ~** tirer
IDIOMS **to jump the ~** agir prématurément; **to stick to one's ~s** (fam) s'accrocher (fam)
▪ **gun down** abattre, descendre
gunfire /'gʌnfaɪə(r)/ *n* (from hand-held gun) coups *mpl* de feu; (from artillery) fusillade *f*
gun laws *npl* législation *f* sur les armes à feu
gun licence *n* (BrE) permis *m* de port d'armes
gunman *n* homme *m* armé
gunpoint /'gʌnpɔɪnt/ *n* **to hold sb up at ~** tenir qn sous la menace d'une arme
gunpowder *n* poudre *f*

gunshot /ˈɡʌnʃɒt/ *n* coup *m* de feu

gunshot wound *n* blessure *f* par balle

gurgle /ˈɡɜːɡl/ **A** *n* (of water) gargouillement *m*; (of baby) gazouillis *m*
B *vi* ‹*water*› gargouiller; ‹*baby*› gazouiller

guru /ˈɡʊruː, (AmE) ɡəˈruː/ *n* gourou *m*

gush /ɡʌʃ/ *vi* jaillir

gust /ɡʌst/ *n* rafale *f*

gusto /ˈɡʌstəʊ/ *n* **with ~** avec enthousiasme

gut /ɡʌt/ **A** *n* (fam) bide *m* (fam)
B *adj* ‹*feeling, reaction*› viscéral/-e, instinctif/-ive
C *vt* (*p prés etc* **-tt-**) ‹*fire*› ravager ‹*building*›

guts *npl* (fam) **1** (of human) tripes *fpl* (fam); (of animal) entrailles *fpl*
2 (courage) cran *m* (fam)

gutsy /ˈɡʌtsɪ/ *adj* (fam) (spirited) fougueux/-euse; (brave) courageux/-euse

gutter /ˈɡʌtə(r)/ *n* (on roof) gouttière *f*; (in street) caniveau *m*

gutter press *n* presse *f* à sensation

⚷ **guy** /ɡaɪ/ *n* (fam) type *m* (fam); **a good/bad ~** (in films) un bon/méchant

Guy Fawkes Day *n* (BrE) le 5 novembre (*anniversaire de la Conspiration des Poudres*)

guzzle /ˈɡʌzl/ *vt* (fam) engloutir

gym /dʒɪm/ *n* **1** (*abbr* = **gymnasium**) salle *f* de gym (fam), gymnase *m*
2 (*abbr* = **gymnastics**) gym *f* (fam)

gymnasium /dʒɪmˈneɪzɪəm/ *n* (*pl* **~s** *ou* **-ia**) gymnase *m*

gymnast /ˈdʒɪmnæst/ *n* gymnaste *mf*

gymnastics /dʒɪmˈnæstɪks/ *npl* gymnastique *f*

gym shoe *n* tennis *f*

gynaecologist (BrE), **gynecologist** (AmE) /ˌɡaɪnəˈkɒlədʒɪst/ *n* gynécologue *mf*

gypsy /ˈdʒɪpsɪ/ *n* (gen) bohémien/-ienne *m/f*; (Central European) tzigane *mf*; (Spanish) gitan/-e *m/f*

Hh

h, H /eɪtʃ/ *n* h, H *m*

habit /ˈhæbɪt/ *n* **1** habitude *f*; **to get into/out of the ~ of doing** prendre/perdre l'habitude de faire; **out of ~** par habitude
2 (addiction) accoutumance *f*
3 (of monk, nun) habit *m*

habitable /ˈhæbɪtəbl/ *adj* habitable

habitat /ˈhæbɪtæt/ *n* habitat *m*

habit-forming /ˈhæbɪtfɔːmɪŋ/ *adj* **to be ~** créer une accoutumance

habitual /həˈbɪtʃʊəl/ *adj* ‹*behaviour, reaction*› habituel/-elle; ‹*drinker, smoker, liar*› invétéré/-e

habitual offender *n* récidiviste *mf*

hack /hæk/ **A** *n* (fam) (writer) écrivaillon *m*; (journalist) journaliste *m/f* qui fait la rubrique des chiens écrasés
B *vt* tailler dans ‹*bushes*› (**with** à coups de); **to ~ sb/sth to pieces** tailler qn/qch en pièces
C *vi* **1 to ~ through sth** tailler dans qch
2 (Comput) (fam) pirater (fam); **to ~ into** s'introduire dans ‹*system*›

hacker /ˈhækə(r)/ *n* **(computer) ~** pirate *m* informatique

hacking /ˈhækɪŋ/ *n* (Comput) piratage *m* (fam) informatique

hackles *npl* (on dog) poils *mpl* du cou; **the dog's ~ began to rise** le chien se hérissait

hackneyed /ˈhæknɪd/ *adj* ‹*joke*› éculé/-e; ‹*subject*› rebattu/-e; **~ phrase** cliché *m*

haddock /ˈhædək/ *n* (*pl* **~s** *ou* **~**) églefin *m*

haemophilia (BrE), **hemophilia** (AmE) /ˌhiːməˈfɪlɪə/ *n* hémophilie *f*

haemophiliac (BrE), **hemophiliac** (AmE) /ˌhiːməˈfɪlɪæk/ *n, adj* hémophile *mf*

haemorrhage (BrE), **hemorrhage** (AmE) /ˈhemərɪdʒ/ **A** *n* hémorragie *f*
B *vi* faire une hémorragie

haemorrhoids (BrE), **hemorrhoids** (AmE) /ˈhemərɔɪdz/ *npl* hémorroïdes *fpl*

haggard /ˈhæɡəd/ *adj* ‹*appearance, person*› exténué/-e; ‹*face, expression*› défait/-e

haggle /ˈhæɡl/ *vi* marchander; **to ~ over sth** discuter du prix de qch

Hague /heɪɡ/ *pr n* **The ~** La Haye

hail /heɪl/ **A** *n* grêle *f*
B *vt* **1** héler ‹*person, taxi, ship*›
2 (praise) **to ~ sb as** acclamer qn comme; **to ~ sth as sth** saluer qch comme qch
C *v impers* grêler

hailstone *n* grêlon *m*

hailstorm *n* averse *f* de grêle

⚷ **hair** /heə(r)/ *n* **1** (on head) cheveux *mpl*; (on body) poils *mpl*; (of animal) poil *m*; **to have**

⚷ mot clé

one's ~ done se faire coiffer; **long-~ed** ‹*person*› aux cheveux longs; ‹*animal*› à poil long
2 (individually) (on head) cheveu *m*; (on body) poil *m*
IDIOM **to split ~s** couper les cheveux en quatre
hairband *n* bandeau *m*
hairbrush *n* brosse *f* à cheveux
haircut /'heəkʌt/ *n* coupe *f* (de cheveux)
hairdo *n* (fam) coiffure *f*
hairdresser /'heədresə(r)/ *n* coiffeur/-euse *m/f*
hairdrier *n* (hand-held) sèche-cheveux *m inv*; (hood) casque *m*
hair gel *n* gel *m* coiffant
hairgrip *n* (BrE) pince *f* à cheveux
hairpin bend *n* virage *m* en épingle à cheveux
hair-raising *adj* ‹*adventure, tale*› à vous faire dresser les cheveux sur la tête
hair remover *n* crème *f* dépilatoire
hair slide *n* (BrE) barrette *f*
hairspray *n* laque *f*
hair straighteners *npl* fer *m* à défriser
hairstyle *n* coiffure *f*
hairy /'heərɪ/ *adj* (gen) poilu/-e
halal /hɑː'lɑːl/ *adj* ‹*meat*› hallal *inv*
half /hɑːf, (AmE) hæf/ **A** *n* (*pl* **halves**)
1 moitié *f*; **to cut sth in ~** couper qch en deux
2 (fraction) demi *m*; **four and a ~** quatre et demi
3 (BrE) (half pint) demi-pinte *f*
B *adj* **~ an hour** une demi-heure; **a ~-litre, ~ a litre** un demi-litre; **two and a ~ cups** deux tasses et demie; **it's ~ the price** c'est moitié moins cher
C *pron* **1** la moitié *f*; **~ of the students** la moitié des étudiants
2 (in time) demi/-e *m/f*; **an hour and a ~** une heure et demie; **~ past two** (BrE) deux heures et demie
D *adv* à moitié; **to ~ close sth** fermer qch à moitié; **I ~ expected it** je m'y attendais plus ou moins
IDIOM **to go halves with sb** partager avec qn
halfback *n* (Sport) demi *m*
half board *n* demi-pension *f*
half-brother *n* demi-frère *m*
half day *n* demi-journée *f*
half fare *n* demi-tarif *m*
half-hearted *adj* peu enthousiaste
half-heartedly *adv* sans conviction
half hour /ˌhɑːf'aʊə(r), (AmE) ˌhæf-/ *n* demi-heure *f*; **on the ~** à la demie
half-mast /ˌhɑːfmɑːst, (AmE) ˌhæf-/ *n* **at ~** en berne
half-moon /ˌhɑːfmuːn, (AmE) ˌhæf-/ *n*
1 demi-lune *f*
2 (of fingernail) lunule *f*
half price *adv, adj* à moitié prix
half-sister *n* demi-sœur *f*
half term *n* (BrE) (Sch) vacances *fpl* de la mi-trimestre
half-time /ˌhɑːf'taɪm, (AmE) ˌhæf-/ *n* (Sport) mi-temps *f*; **at ~** à la mi-temps
halfway /ˌhɑːf'weɪ, (AmE) ˌhæf-/ *adv* **1** à mi-chemin (**between** entre, **to** de); **~ up** *or* **down** à mi-hauteur de ‹*stairs, tree*›; **~ down the page** à mi-page
2 (in time) **~ through** au milieu
halfway house *n* (rehabilitation centre) centre *m* de réadaptation
hall /hɔːl/ *n* **1** (in house) entrée *f*; (in hotel, airport) hall *m*; (for public events) (grande) salle *f*
2 (country house) manoir *m*
hallelujah /ˌhælɪ'luːjə/ *excl* alléluia!
hallmark /'hɔːlmɑːk/ **A** *n* **1** (BrE) (on metal) poinçon *m*
2 (typical feature) caractéristique *f*
B *vt* poinçonner; **to be ~ed** porter un poinçon
hall of residence *n* résidence *f* universitaire
Halloween /ˌhæləʊ'iːn/ *n*: *la veille de la Toussaint*
hallucinate /hə'luːsɪneɪt/ *vi* avoir des hallucinations
hallucination /həˌluːsɪ'neɪʃn/ *n* hallucination *f*
hallway *n* entrée *f*
halo /'heɪləʊ/ *n* (*pl* **~s** *ou* **~es**) **1** auréole *f*
2 (in astronomy) halo *m*
halt /hɔːlt/ **A** *n* (stop) arrêt *m*; **to come to a ~** ‹*vehicle, troops*› s'arrêter; ‹*work*› être interrompu/-e; **to call a ~ to sth** mettre fin à qch
B *vt* arrêter
C *vi* s'arrêter
halter-neck *n, adj* dos *m inv* nu
halve /hɑːv, (AmE) hæv/ **A** *vt* réduire [qch] de moitié ‹*number, rate*›; couper [qch] en deux ‹*carrot, cake*›
B *vi* ‹*number, rate, time*› diminuer de moitié
ham /hæm/ *n* jambon *m*
hamburger /'hæmbɜːgə(r)/ *n* **1** (burger) hamburger *m*
2 (AmE) (ground beef) pâté *m* de viande
hammer /'hæmə(r)/ **A** *n* marteau *m*
B *vt* **1** marteler ‹*metal, table*›; **to ~ sth into** enfoncer qch dans ‹*wall, fence*›
2 to ~ sth into sb faire entrer qch dans la tête de qn; **to ~ home a message** bien faire comprendre un message
3 (fam) (defeat) battre [qn] à plates coutures
C *vi* (pound) tambouriner (**on, at** contre)
■ **hammer out**: **~ out [sth], ~ [sth] out** (negotiate) parvenir à [qch] après maintes discussions ‹*agreement, policy, formula*›

hamper /'hæmpə(r)/ **A** *n* panier *m* à pique-nique
B *vt* entraver ‹*movement, career, progress*›

hamster /'hæmstə(r)/ *n* hamster *m*

hamstring /'hæmstrɪŋ/ *n* tendon *m* du jarret

⚷ **hand** /hænd/ **A** *n* **1** main *f*; **he had a pencil in his ~** il avait un crayon à la main; **to hold sb's ~** tenir qn par la main; **to make sth by ~** faire qch à la main; **the letter was delivered by ~** la lettre a été remise en mains propres; **to give sb a (helping) ~** donner un coup de main à qn; **to have sth to ~** avoir qch sous la main; **to be on ~** ‹*person*› être disponible; **to get out of ~** devenir incontrôlable; **to take sb/sth in ~** prendre qn/qch en main ‹*situation, person*›
2 (cards) jeu *m*
3 (worker) ouvrier/-ière *m/f*; (crew member) membre *m* de l'équipage
4 (on clock, dial) aiguille *f*
5 on the one ~..., on the other ~... d'une part..., d'autre part...
B *vt* **to ~ sth to sb** donner qch à qn
C **hand in hand** *phr* ‹*run, walk*› la main dans la main; **to go ~ in ~** aller de pair (**with** avec)
D **out of hand** *phr* ‹*reject*› d'emblée
IDIOMS **to have one's ~s full** avoir assez à faire; **to try one's ~ at sth** s'essayer de faire qch; **to know sth like the back of one's ~** connaître qch comme sa poche
■ **hand down** passer ‹*object, clothes*› (**to sb** à qn); transmettre ‹*property*›
■ **hand in** remettre ‹*form*› (**to** à); rendre ‹*homework, keys*›
■ **hand out** distribuer ‹*food, leaflets*›
■ **hand over**: **A** **~ over to [sb]** passer l'antenne à ‹*reporter*›; passer la main à ‹*deputy, successor*›
B **~ [sth] over** rendre ‹*weapon*›; céder ‹*business*›; remettre ‹*keys, money*›
C **~ [sb] over** livrer ‹*prisoner*›

handbag *n* sac *m* à main

hand baggage *n* bagages *mpl* à main

handball /'hændbɔːl/ *n* (Sport) handball *m*

handbook /'hændbʊk/ *n* manuel *m*; (technical) livret *m* technique

handbrake *n* frein *m* à main

handcuffs *npl* menottes *fpl*

handful /'hændfʊl/ *n* **1** (fistful) poignée *f*
2 (of people) poignée *f*; (of buildings, objects) petit nombre *m*
3 (fam) **to be a ~** être épuisant/-e

handgun *n* arme *f* de poing

handheld /ˌhænd'held/ *adj* ‹*camera*› de reportage; ‹*tool*› à main; ‹*device*› portatif/-ive; ‹*computer*› de poche

handheld device *n* (Comput) terminal *m* mobile de poche

handicap /'hændɪkæp/ **A** *n* (dated or offensive) handicap *m*
B *vt* (*p prés etc* **-pp-**) handicaper

handicapped /'hændɪkæpt/ *adj* ‹*person*› handicapé/-e; **mentally/physically ~ children** des enfants handicapés mentaux/physiques

handicrafts *npl* (Sch) travaux *mpl* manuels

handiwork /'hændɪwɜːk/ *n* ouvrage *m*

handkerchief /'hæŋkətʃɪf, -tʃiːf/ *n* mouchoir *m*

⚷ **handle** /'hændl/ **A** *n* (on door, drawer, bag) poignée *f*; (on bucket, cup, basket) anse *f*; (on frying pan) queue *f*; (on saucepan, cutlery, hammer, spade) manche *m*; (on wheelbarrow, pump) bras *m*
B *vt* **1** manipuler ‹*explosives, food*›; manier ‹*gun*›; **'~ with care'** 'fragile'
2 (manage) manier ‹*horse*›; manœuvrer ‹*car*›; **to know how to ~ children** savoir s'y prendre avec les enfants
3 (deal with) faire face à ‹*crisis*›; supporter ‹*stress*›; ‹*department, lawyer*› s'occuper de ‹*enquiries, case*›

handlebars *npl* guidon *m*

handling /'hændlɪŋ/ *n* **1** (holding, touching) (of food, waste) manipulation *f*; (of tool, weapon) maniement *m*
2 (way of dealing) **her ~ of the theme** sa façon de traiter le thème; **their ~ of the economy** leur gestion de l'économie

handling charge *n* **1** (for goods) frais *mpl* de manutention
2 (administrative) frais *mpl* administratifs

hand luggage *n* bagages *mpl* à main

handmade *adj* fait/-e à la main

handout /'hændaʊt/ *n* **1** (charitable) don *m*
2 (leaflet) prospectus *m*

hand-pick *vt* **1** cueillir [qch] à la main ‹*grapes*›
2 trier [qn] sur le volet ‹*staff*›

handshake *n* poignée *f* de main

handsome /'hænsəm/ *adj* beau/belle *before n*

hands-on *adj* ‹*experience, manager*› de terrain; ‹*control*› direct/-e; ‹*approach*› pragmatique

handstand /'hændstænd/ *n* (Sport) équilibre *m*

handwriting /'hændraɪtɪŋ/ *n* écriture *f*

handwritten *adj* manuscrit/-e

handy /'hændɪ/ *adj* ‹*book, skill*› utile; ‹*tool, pocket, size*› pratique; ‹*shop*› bien situé/-e; **to keep/have sth ~** garder/avoir qch sous la main ‹*keys, passport*›

handyman *n* bricoleur *m*

⚷ **hang** /hæŋ/ **A** *n* **to get the ~ of sth** (fam) piger qch (fam)
B *vt* (*prét, pp* **hung**) **1** (from hook, coat hanger) accrocher (**from** à, **by** par, **on** à); (from string, rope) suspendre (**from** à); (peg up) étendre ‹*washing*› (**on** sur)
2 poser ‹*wallpaper*›

⚷ mot clé

3 pendre ‹*criminal, victim*›
C *vi* (*prét, pp* **hung**) **1** (on hook) être accroché/-e; (from height) être suspendu/-e; (on washing line) être étendu/-e
2 ‹*arm, leg*› pendre
3 ‹*curtain, garment*› tomber
4 ‹*person*› être pendu/-e (**for** pour)
D *v refl* (*prét, pp* **hanged**) **to ~ oneself** se pendre (**from** à)
▪ **hang around** (fam) **1** (*also* **~ about**) (wait) attendre; (aimlessly) traîner
2 to ~ around with sb passer son temps avec qn
▪ **hang back** (in fear) rester derrière; (fig) être réticent/-e
▪ **hang down** (gen) pendre; ‹*hem*› être défait/-e
▪ **hang on A ~ on 1** (hold on) **to ~ on (to sth)** s'accrocher (à qch)
2 (wait) attendre
3 (fam) (survive) tenir (fam); **~ on in there!** (fam) tiens bon!
B ~ on [sth] (depend on) dépendre de
▪ **hang out A ~ out 1** (protrude) dépasser
2 (fam) (live) crécher (fam)
3 (fam) (sit around) traîner (fam)
B ~ [sth] out étendre ‹*washing*›; sortir ‹*flag*›
▪ **hang up**: **A ~ up** (on phone) raccrocher; **to ~ up on sb** raccrocher au nez de qn
B ~ [sth] up (on hook) accrocher; (on hanger) suspendre; (on line) étendre

hangar /'hæŋə(r)/ *n* hangar *m*

hanger-on *n* (fam) parasite *m*

hang-glider *n* deltaplane *m*

hanging /'hæŋɪŋ/ *n* **1** (of person) pendaison *f*
2 (curtain) rideau *m*; (on wall) tenture *f*

hangover /'hæŋəʊvə(r)/ *n* (from drink) gueule *f* de bois (fam)

hang-up /'hæŋʌp/ *n* (fam) complexe *m*, problème *m*

hanker /'hæŋkə(r)/ *vi* **to ~ after** *or* **for sth** rêver de qch

hanky, hankie (fam) /'hæŋkɪ/ *n* mouchoir *m*

haphazard /hæp'hæzəd/ *adj* peu méthodique

happen /'hæpən/ *vi* **1** (occur) arriver, se passer, se produire; **what's ~ing?** qu'est-ce qui se passe?; **to ~ again** se reproduire; **whatever ~s** quoi qu'il arrive
2 (occur by chance) **if you ~ to see her, say hello** si par hasard tu la vois, salue-la de ma part; **as it ~ed, the weather that day was bad** il s'est trouvé qu'il faisait mauvais ce jour-là

happily /'hæpɪlɪ/ *adv* **1** (cheerfully) joyeusement; **a ~ married man** un mari heureux; **they all lived ~ ever after** ils vécurent heureux jusqu'à la fin de leurs jours
2 (willingly) ‹*admit*› volontiers
3 (luckily) heureusement

happiness /'hæpɪnɪs/ *n* bonheur *m*

happy /'hæpɪ/ *adj* **1** heureux/-euse (**about** de, **that** que (+ *subjunctive*)); **to be ~ with sth** être satisfait/-e de qch; **to keep a child ~** amuser un enfant; **to be ~ to do** être heureux/-euse de faire
2 (in greetings) **Happy Birthday!** Bon anniversaire!; **Happy Christmas!** Joyeux Noël!; **Happy New Year!** Bonne année!

happy ending *n* heureux dénouement *m*

happy medium *n* juste milieu *m*

harangue /hə'ræŋ/ *vt* (*p prés* **haranguing**) (about politics) haranguer; (moralize) sermonner

harass /'hærəs, (AmE) hə'ræs/ **A** *vt* harceler
B harassed *pp adj* excédé/-e

harassment /'hærəsmənt, (AmE) hə'ræsmənt/ *n* (general) harcèlement *m*; (in the workplace) mobbing *m*

harbour (BrE), **harbor** (AmE) /'hɑːbə(r)/
A *n* port *m*
B *vt* nourrir ‹*suspicion, illusion*›; receler ‹*criminal*›

hard /hɑːd/ **A** *adj* **1** (firm) dur/-e; **to go ~** durcir
2 (difficult) ‹*problem, question, task*› dur/-e, difficile; ‹*choice, decision, life*› difficile; **it's ~ to do** c'est dur *or* difficile à faire; **to find it ~ to do** avoir du mal à faire; **it was ~ work** ça a été dur *or* difficile; **to be a ~ worker** être travailleur/-euse
3 (severe) ‹*person, look, words*› dur/-e, sévère; ‹*blow*› dur/-e, terrible; ‹*winter*› rude; **to be ~ on sb** ‹*person*› être dur/-e envers qn; **~ luck!** pas de chance!; **no ~ feelings!** sans rancune!
4 ‹*evidence, fact*› solide
5 ‹*liquor*› fort/-e; ‹*drug*› dur/-e
6 ‹*water*› dur/-e, calcaire
B *adv* ‹*push, hit, cry*› fort; ‹*work*› dur; ‹*study, think*› sérieusement; ‹*look, listen*› attentivement; **to try ~** (mentally) faire beaucoup d'efforts; (physically) essayer de toutes ses forces

hard and fast *adj* ‹*rule, distinction*› absolu/-e

hardback *n* (*also* **hardback book**) livre *m* relié

hardboard /'hɑːdbɔːd/ *n* aggloméré *m*

hard-boiled egg *n* œuf *m* dur

hard copy *n* (Comput) tirage *m*

hard core A *n* (group, demonstrators) noyau *m* dur
B hard-core *adj* **1** (established) ‹*supporter, opponent, protest*› irréductible
2 (extreme) ‹*pornography, video*› hard *inv* (fam)

hard court *n* court *m* en dur

hard disk *n* disque *m* dur

hard-earned *adj* ‹*cash*› durement gagné/-e

harden /'hɑːdn/ **A** *vt* **1** (faire) durcir ‹*glue, wax*›
2 endurcir ‹*person*› (**to** à); durcir ‹*attitude*›;

to ~ one's heart s'endurcir (**to** à)
B *vi* **1** ‹*glue, wax, skin*› durcir
2 ‹*voice, stance*› se durcir

hardened /'hɑːdnd/ *adj* ‹*criminal*› endurci/-e; ‹*drinker*› invétéré/-e

hard hat *n* (helmet) casque *m*; (for riding) bombe *f*

hard-hearted /ˌhɑːd'hɑːtɪd/ *adj* insensible

hard-hitting *adj* ‹*speech, criticism*› musclé/-e; ‹*report*› très critique

hard labour (BrE), **hard labor** (AmE) *n* travaux *mpl* forcés

hardliner *n* jusqu'au-boutiste *mf*; (political) partisan/-e *m/f* de la ligne dure

🔑 **hardly** /'hɑːdlɪ/ *adv* **1** (barely) ‹*begin, know, see*› à peine; **~ had they set off when** à peine étaient-ils partis que
2 (not really) **one can ~ expect that** on ne peut guère s'attendre à ce que; **it's ~ likely** c'est peu probable; **it's ~ surprising** ce n'est guère étonnant; **I can ~ believe it!** j'ai peine à le croire!
3 ~ any/ever/anybody presque pas/jamais/personne; **he ~ ever writes** il n'écrit presque jamais

hard of hearing *adj* **to be ~** entendre mal

hard-pressed, **hard-pushed** /ˌhɑːd'prest/ *adj* en difficulté; (for time) pressé/-e; **to be ~ to do** avoir du mal à faire

hardship /'hɑːdʃɪp/ *n* **1** (difficulty) détresse *f*; (poverty) privations *fpl*
2 (ordeal) épreuve *f*

hard shoulder *n* (BrE) bande *f* d'arrêt d'urgence

hard up /ˌhɑːd'ʌp/ *adj* (fam) fauché/-e (fam)

hardware /'hɑːdweə(r)/ *n* **1** (gen) articles *mpl* de quincaillerie
2 (Comput) matériel *m* (informatique)
3 (Mil) équipement *m*

hardware shop, **hardware store** *n* quincaillerie *f*

hard-working *adj* travailleur/-euse

hardy /'hɑːdɪ/ *adj* ‹*person*› robuste; ‹*plant*› résistant/-e

hare /heə(r)/ *n* lièvre *m*

haricot /'hærɪkəʊ/ *n* (BrE) (*also* **~ bean**) (dried) haricot *m* blanc; (fresh) haricot *m* vert

harm /hɑːm/ **A** *n* mal *m*; **to do sb ~** faire du mal à qn; **to do ~ to sth** endommager qch; **out of ~'s way** en sûreté
B *vt* faire du mal à ‹*person*›; endommager ‹*crops, lungs*›; nuire à ‹*population*›

harmful /'hɑːmfl/ *adj* ‹*chemical, ray*› nocif/-ive; ‹*behaviour, gossip*› nuisible (**to** pour)

harmless /'hɑːmlɪs/ *adj* **1** ‹*chemical, virus*› inoffensif/-ive (**to** pour); ‹*growth*› bénin/bénigne
2 ‹*person*› inoffensif/-ive; ‹*fun, joke*› innocent/-e

harmonica /hɑː'mɒnɪkə/ *n* harmonica *m*

harmonious /hɑː'məʊnɪəs/ *adj* harmonieux/-ieuse

harmonize /'hɑːmənaɪz/ **A** *vt* harmoniser
B *vi* jouer en harmonie (**with** avec)

harmony /'hɑːmənɪ/ *n* harmonie *f*

harness /'hɑːnɪs/ **A** *n* harnais *m*
B *vt* **1** harnacher ‹*horse*›
2 (attach) atteler ‹*animal*› (**to** à)
3 exploiter ‹*power, energy*›

harp /hɑːp/ *n* harpe *f*
■ **harp on** (fam) rabâcher (fam) toujours la même chose sur ‹*issue, event*›

harpoon /hɑː'puːn/ *n* harpon *m*

harrowing /'hærəʊɪŋ/ *adj* ‹*experience*› atroce; ‹*film, image*› déchirant/-e

harsh /hɑːʃ/ *adj* **1** ‹*punishment, measures*› sévère; ‹*tone, regime, person*› dur/-e; ‹*conditions*› difficile
2 ‹*light, colour*› cru/-e; ‹*sound*› rude, dur/-e à l'oreille

harshly /'hɑːʃlɪ/ *adv* ‹*treat, speak*› durement; ‹*punish*› sévèrement

harvest /'hɑːvɪst/ **A** *n* (of wheat, fruit) récolte *f*; (of grapes) vendange *f*
B *vt* moissonner ‹*corn*›; récolter ‹*vegetables*›; cueillir ‹*fruit*›; vendanger ‹*grapes*›

has-been /'hæzbiːn/ *n* (fam) homme fini/femme finie *m/f*

hashtag /'hæʃtæg/ *n* hashtag *m*, mot-clic *m*

hassle /'hæsl/ (fam) **A** *n* complications *fpl*; **it was a real ~** c'était enquiquinant (fam)
B *vt* talonner (**about** à propos de)

haste /heɪst/ *n* hâte *f*; **to act in ~** agir à la hâte

hasten /'heɪsn/ **A** *vt* accélérer ‹*destruction*›; précipiter ‹*departure, death, decline*›
B *vi* se hâter; **to ~ to do** s'empresser de faire

hasty /'heɪstɪ/ *adj* ‹*talks, marriage, departure*› précipité/-e; ‹*meal*› rapide; ‹*note*› écrit/-e à la hâte; ‹*decision*› inconsidéré/-e; ‹*conclusion*› hâtif/-ive

hat /hæt/ *n* chapeau *m*

hatch /hætʃ/ **A** *n* **1** (on aircraft) panneau *m* mobile; (in boat) écoutille *f*; (in car) portière *f*
2 (*also* **serving ~**) passe-plats *m inv*
B *vt* **1** faire éclore ‹*eggs*›
2 tramer ‹*plot, scheme*›
C *vi* ‹*chicks, fish eggs*› éclore

hatchback *n* voiture *f* avec hayon

hatchet /'hætʃɪt/ *n* hachette *f*

🔑 **hate** /heɪt/ **A** *n* haine *f*
B *vt* **1** (dislike) détester; (violently) haïr
2 (not enjoy) avoir horreur de ‹*sport, food*›; **to ~ doing** avoir horreur de faire
3 (in apology) **to ~ to do** être désolé/-e de faire

hate mail *n* lettres *fpl* d'injures

hatred /'heɪtrɪd/ *n* haine *f* (**of** de, **for** pour)

hat trick *n* triplé *m*

🔑 mot clé

haughty /'hɔːtɪ/ *adj* ‹*person*› hautain/-e; ‹*manner*› altier/-ière

haul /hɔːl/ **A** *n* **1** (taken by criminals) butin *m*
2 (found by police, customs) saisie *f*; **arms ~** saisie d'armes
3 it's a long ~ la route est longue
4 (of fish) pêche *f*
B *vt* (drag) tirer

haulage /'hɔːlɪdʒ/ *n* **1** (transport) transport *m* routier
2 (cost) frais *mpl* de transport

haunch /hɔːntʃ/ *n* hanche *f*

haunt /hɔːnt/ **A** *n* lieu *m* de prédilection
B *vt* hanter

haunted /'hɔːntɪd/ *adj* ‹*house*› hanté/-e; ‹*face, look*› tourmenté/-e

haunting /'hɔːntɪŋ/ *adj* (gen) lancinant/-e; ‹*memory*› obsédant/-e

have /hæv, həv/ **A** *vt* **1** (possess) avoir; **she has (got) a dog** elle a un chien; **I haven't (got) enough time** je n'ai pas assez de temps
2 (with noun object) **to ~ a wash** se laver; **to ~ a sandwich** manger un sandwich; **to ~ a whisky** boire un whisky; **to ~ a cigarette** fumer une cigarette; **to ~ breakfast** prendre le petit déjeuner; **to ~ lunch** déjeuner; **I had some more cake** j'ai repris du gâteau
3 (receive, get) recevoir ‹*letter*›; **I've had no news from him** je n'ai pas eu de nouvelles de lui; **to let sb ~ sth** donner qch à qn
4 (hold) faire ‹*party*›; tenir ‹*meeting*›; organiser ‹*competition, exhibition*›; avoir ‹*conversation*›
5 (exert, exhibit) avoir ‹*effect, influence*›; avoir ‹*courage, courtesy*› (**to do** de faire)
6 (spend) passer; **to ~ a nice day** passer une journée agréable; **to ~ a good time** bien s'amuser; **to ~ a hard time** traverser une période difficile; **to ~ a good holiday** (BrE) *or* **vacation** (AmE) passer de bonnes vacances
7 (*also* **~ got**) **I've got letters to write** j'ai du courrier à faire; **I've got a lot of work to do** j'ai beaucoup de travail
8 (suffer) avoir; **to ~ (the) flu/a heart attack** avoir la grippe/une crise cardiaque; **to ~ toothache** avoir mal aux dents; **he had his car stolen** il s'est fait voler sa voiture; **she has had her windows broken** on lui a cassé ses vitres
9 (cause to be done) **to ~ the car fixed** faire réparer la voiture; **to ~ the house painted** faire peindre la maison; **to ~ one's hair cut** se faire couper les cheveux; **to ~ an injection** se faire faire une piqûre
10 (cause to become) **she had them completely baffled** elle les a complètement déroutés; **I had it finished by 5 o'clock** je l'avais fini avant 5 heures
11 (allow) tolérer; **I won't ~ this kind of behaviour!** je ne tolérerai pas ce comportement!
12 (give birth to) ‹*woman*› avoir ‹*child*›; ‹*animal*› mettre bas, avoir ‹*young*›
B *modal aux* (must) **I ~ to leave** il faut que je parte, je dois partir; **something has (got) to be done** il faut faire quelque chose; **you don't ~ to leave so early** tu n'as pas besoin de *or* tu n'es pas obligé de partir si tôt
C *v aux* **1** avoir; (with movement and reflexive verbs) être; **she has lost her bag** elle a perdu son sac; **she has already left** elle est déjà partie; **he has hurt himself** il s'est blessé; **having finished his breakfast, he went out** après avoir fini son petit déjeuner, il est sorti
2 (in tags, short answers) **you've seen the film, haven't you?** tu as vu le film, n'est-ce pas?; **you haven't seen the film, ~ you?** tu n'as pas vu le film?; **you haven't seen my bag, ~ you?** tu n'as pas vu mon sac, par hasard?; **'~ you seen him?'—'yes, I ~'** 'est-ce que tu l'as vu?'—'oui'; **'you've never met him'—'yes I ~!'** 'tu ne l'as jamais rencontré'—'mais si!'
3 (if) **had I known, I wouldn't have bought it** si j'avais su, je ne l'aurais pas acheté

IDIOMS **I've had it (up to here) with...** (fam) j'en ai marre de... (fam); **to ~ it in for sb** (fam) avoir qn dans le collimateur (fam); **she doesn't ~ it in her to do** elle est incapable de faire; **to ~ it out with sb** s'expliquer avec qn; **the ~s and the ~-nots** les riches et les pauvres

■ **have on 1** porter ‹*coat, skirt*›; **he had (got) nothing on** il n'avait rien sur lui
2 to ~ sth on (be busy) avoir qch de prévu
3 to ~ sb on (fam) faire marcher qn (fam)

haven /'heɪvn/ *n* **1** (safe place) refuge *m* (**for** pour)
2 (harbour) port *m*

havoc /'hævək/ *n* dévastation *f*; **to wreak ~** provoquer des dégâts; (fig) tout mettre sens dessus dessous

Hawaii /hə'waɪɪ/ *pr n* Hawaï *m*

hawk /hɔːk/ *n* faucon *m*

hawthorn /'hɔːθɔːn/ *n* aubépine *f*

hay /heɪ/ *n* foin *m*

hay fever *n* rhume *m* des foins

haystack /'heɪstæk/ *n* meule *f* de foin
IDIOM **it is/was like looking for a needle in a ~** autant chercher une aiguille dans une botte de foin

haywire /'heɪwaɪə(r)/ *adj* (fam) **1** (faulty) **to go ~** ‹*plan*› dérailler; ‹*machinery*› se détraquer
2 (crazy) détraqué/-e (fam)

hazard /'hæzəd/ **A** *n* risque *m* (**to** pour); **a health ~** un risque pour la santé
B *vt* hasarder ‹*opinion, guess*›

hazardous /'hæzədəs/ *adj* dangereux/-euse

haze /heɪz/ *n* (mist) brume *f*; (of smoke, dust) nuage *m*

hazel /'heɪzl/ **A** *n* noisetier *m*
B *adj* ‹*eyes*› (couleur de) noisette *inv*

hazelnut /'heɪzlnʌt/ *n* noisette *f*

hazy /ˈheɪzɪ/ *adj* ‹*weather, morning*› brumeux/-euse; ‹*sunshine*› voilé/-e; ‹*idea, memory*› vague *before n*

HD (= **high-definition**) *n* haute définition *f*

🔑 **he** /hiː, hɪ/ *pron* il; **~'s seen us** il nous a vus; **there ~ is** le voilà; **she lives in Oxford but ~ doesn't** elle habite Oxford mais lui non; **~'s a genius** c'est un génie; **~ and I** lui et moi

🔑 **head** /hed/ **A** *n* **1** (gen) tête *f*; **from ~ to foot** *or* **toe** de la tête aux pieds; **to stand on one's ~** faire le poirier; **£10 a ~** *or* **per ~** 10 livres sterling par personne
2 (of family, church) chef *m*; (of organization) responsable *mf*, directeur/-trice *m/f*; **~ of State** chef d'État
B heads *npl* (of coin) face *f*; **'~s or tails?'** 'pile ou face?'
C *adj* **1** ‹*injury*› à la tête
2 (chief) ‹*cashier, cook, gardener*› en chef
D *vt* **1** être en tête de ‹*list, queue*›; être à la tête de ‹*firm, team*›; mener ‹*expedition, inquiry*›
2 ~ed writing paper papier *m* à lettres à en-tête
3 (steer) diriger ‹*vehicle*› (**towards** vers)
4 (Sport) **to ~ the ball** faire une tête
E *vi* **where was the train ~ed** *or* **~ing?** où allait le train?; **to ~ home** rentrer; **he's ~ing this way!** il vient par ici!
IDIOMS **to go to sb's ~** monter à la tête de qn; **to keep/lose one's ~** garder/perdre son sang-froid; **off the top of one's ~** ‹*say, answer*› sans réfléchir
■ **head for 1** se diriger vers ‹*place*›
2 courir à ‹*defeat*›; courir vers ‹*trouble*›

headache /ˈhedeɪk/ *n* mal *m* de tête; **to have a ~** avoir mal à la tête

headband *n* bandeau *m*

headbutt *vt* donner un coup de tête à

head cold *n* rhume *m* de cerveau

headdress /ˈheddres/ *n* (of feathers) coiffure *f*; (of lace) coiffe *f*

header /ˈhedə(r)/ *n* **1** (fam) (dive) **to take a ~** piquer une tête (fam)
2 (in sport) tête *f*

head first /ˌhed ˈfɜːst/ *adv* ‹*fall, plunge*› la tête la première; ‹*rush into*› tête baissée

head-hunt /ˈhedhʌnt/ *vt* (seek to recruit) (chercher à) recruter

head-hunter /ˈhedhʌntə(r)/ *n* chasseur *m* de têtes

heading /ˈhedɪŋ/ *n* (of article, column) titre *m*; (of subject area, topic) rubrique *f*; (on notepaper, letter) en-tête *m*

headlamp, headlight /ˈhedlæmp/ *n* (of car) phare *m*

headline /ˈhedlaɪn/ *n* (in paper) gros titre *m*; **to hit the ~s** faire la une (fam); **the front-page ~** la manchette; **the news ~s** les grands titres (de l'actualité)

headlong /ˈhedlɒŋ/ **A** *adj* **a ~ dash** une ruée
B *adv* ‹*fall*› la tête la première; ‹*run*› à toute vitesse

head office *n* siège *m* social

head-on /ˌhedˈɒn/ *adj* ‹*crash, collision*› de front

headphones /ˈhedfəʊnz/ *npl* casque *m*

headquarters /ˌhedˈkwɔːtəz/ *npl* (gen) siège *m* social; (Mil) quartier *m* général

head rest *n* (gen) appui-tête *m*; (Aut) repose-tête *m inv*

head start *n* **to have a ~** avoir une longueur d'avance (**over** sur)

headstone *n* pierre *f* tombale

headstrong /ˈhedstrɒŋ/ *adj* ‹*person*› têtu/-e; ‹*attitude*› obstiné/-e

head teacher *n* directeur/-trice *m/f*

headway /ˈhedweɪ/ *n* **to make ~** avancer, faire des progrès

heady /ˈhedɪ/ *adj* ‹*wine, mixture*› capiteux/-euse; ‹*perfume*› entêtant/-e; ‹*experience*› grisant/-e

heal /hiːl/ **A** *vt* guérir ‹*person, injury*›
B *vi* ‹*wound, cut*› se cicatriser; **the fracture has ~ed** l'os s'est ressoudé

healer /ˈhiːlə(r)/ *n* guérisseur/-euse *m/f*

healing /ˈhiːlɪŋ/ **A** *n* guérison *f*
B *adj* ‹*power*› curatif/-ive; ‹*effect*› salutaire; **the ~ process** le rétablissement

🔑 **health** /helθ/ *n* santé *f*; **in good/bad ~** en bonne/mauvaise santé; **here's to your ~!** à votre santé!

health club *n* club *m* de remise en forme

health farm *n*: *établissement pour cures d'amaigrissement, de rajeunissement*

health food *n* aliments *mpl* naturels, aliments *mpl* diététiques

healthily /ˈhelθɪlɪ/ *adv* sainement

health insurance *n* assurance *f* maladie

Health Service *n* **1** (BrE) (for public) services *mpl* de santé
2 (AmE) (Univ) infirmerie *f*

🔑 **healthy** /ˈhelθɪ/ *adj* ‹*person, dog*› en bonne santé; ‹*livestock, plant, lifestyle, diet*› sain/-e; ‹*air*› salutaire; ‹*appetite*› robuste; ‹*economy*› sain/-e; ‹*profit*› excellent/-e

heap /hiːp/ **A** *n* **1** (pile) tas *m*
2 (fam) **~s of** plein de
B *vt* **1** (pile) entasser
2 to ~ sth on sb couvrir qn de qch ‹*praise*›; accabler qn de qch ‹*scorn*›

heaped /hiːpt/ *adj* **a ~ spoonful** une bonne cuillerée

🔑 **hear** /hɪə(r)/ **A** *vt* (*prét*, *pp* **heard**) **1** (gen) entendre; **to make oneself heard** se faire entendre; (fig) faire entendre sa voix
2 apprendre ‹*news, rumour*›
3 (listen to) écouter ‹*lecture, broadcast*›; ‹*judge*› entendre ‹*case, evidence*›
B *vi* (*prét*, *pp* **heard**) entendre; **to ~**

🔑 mot clé

about entendre parler de
IDIOM ~! ~! bravo!
▪ **hear from** avoir des nouvelles de ‹*person*›
▪ **hear of** entendre parler de; **I won't ~ of it!** il n'en est pas question!

hearing /ˈhɪərɪŋ/ *n* **1** (sense) ouïe *f*, audition *f*; **his ~ is not very good** il n'a pas l'oreille très fine
2 (before court) audience *f*

hearing aid *n* prothèse *f* auditive

hearing-impaired *adj* malentendant/-e

hearsay /ˈhɪəseɪ/ *n* ouï-dire *m inv*, on-dit *m inv*

hearse /hɜːs/ *n* corbillard *m*

heart /hɑːt/ *n* **1** (gen) cœur *m*; **by ~** ‹*learn, know*› par cœur; **to take sth to ~** prendre qch à cœur; **right in the ~ of London** en plein cœur de Londres; **the ~ of the matter** le fond du problème
2 (in cards) **~(s)** cœur *m*
IDIOMS **to have one's ~ set on sth** vouloir qch à tout prix; **to take/lose ~** prendre/perdre courage

heartache *n* chagrin *m*

heart attack *n* crise *f* cardiaque, infarctus *m*

heartbeat /ˈhɑːtbiːt/ *n* battement *m* de cœur

heartbreaking /ˈhɑːtbreɪkɪŋ/ *adj* ‹*sight, story*› navrant/-e; ‹*cry, appeal*› déchirant/-e

heartbroken /ˈhɑːtbrəʊkn/ *adj* **to be ~** avoir le cœur brisé

heart disease *n* maladies *fpl* cardiaques

heartening /ˈhɑːtnɪŋ/ *adj* encourageant/-e

heart failure *n* arrêt *m* du cœur

heartfelt /ˈhɑːtfelt/ *adj* sincère

hearth /hɑːθ/ *n* foyer *m*; **~ rug** petit tapis *m*

heartless /ˈhɑːtlɪs/ *adj* ‹*person*› sans cœur; ‹*attitude, treatment*› cruel/-elle

heart-throb *n* (fam) idole *f*

heart-to-heart /ˌhɑːttəˈhɑːt/ *n* **to have a ~ (with sb)** parler à cœur ouvert (avec qn)

heart transplant *n* greffe *f* du cœur

hearty /ˈhɑːtɪ/ *adj* ‹*welcome, greeting*› cordial/-e; ‹*person*› jovial/-e; ‹*laugh*› franc/franche; ‹*appetite*› solide; ‹*approval*› chaleureux/-euse

heat /hiːt/ **A** *n* **1** chaleur *f*; **in this ~** par cette chaleur; **in the ~ of the moment** dans le feu de l'action
2 (Sport) (round) épreuve *f* éliminatoire; (in athletics) série *f*
3 (Zool) **to be on** (BrE) *or* **in** (AmE) **~** être en chaleur
B *vt* chauffer ‹*house, pool*›; faire chauffer ‹*food, oven*›
▪ **heat up** faire chauffer ‹*food*›; (reheat) faire réchauffer

heated /ˈhiːtɪd/ *adj* **1** ‹*water, pool*› chauffé/-e
2 ‹*debate, argument*› animé/-e

heater /ˈhiːtə(r)/ *n* appareil *m* de chauffage

heathen /ˈhiːðn/ *n*, *adj* (irreligious) païen/-ïenne *m/f*; (uncivilized) barbare *mf*

heather /ˈheðə(r)/ *n* bruyère *f*

heating /ˈhiːtɪŋ/ *n* chauffage *m*

heat stroke *n* coup *m* de chaleur (*avec collapsus*)

heatwave *n* vague *f* de chaleur

heave /hiːv/ **A** *vt* (*prét, pp* **heaved**; (Naut) **hove**) (lift) hisser; (pull) traîner péniblement; (throw) lancer (**at** sur); **to ~ a sigh** pousser un soupir
B *vi* (*prét, pp* **heaved**; (Naut) **hove**)
1 ‹*sea, ground*› se soulever et s'abaisser
2 (pull) tirer de toutes ses forces
3 (retch) avoir un haut-le-cœur; (vomit) vomir

heaven /ˈhevn/ *n* ciel *m*, paradis *m*; **thank ~(s)!** Dieu soit loué!; **good ~s!** grands dieux!

heavenly /ˈhevənlɪ/ *adj* **1** ‹*choir, body*› céleste; ‹*peace*› divin/-e
2 (fam) (wonderful) divin/-e

heavily /ˈhevɪlɪ/ *adv* **1** ‹*lean, fall*› lourdement; ‹*sleep, sigh*› profondément; ‹*breathe*› (noisily) bruyamment; (with difficulty) péniblement; **~ underlined** souligné/-e d'un gros trait
2 ‹*rain*› très fort; ‹*snow, invest, smoke, drink, rely*› beaucoup; ‹*bleed*› abondamment; ‹*taxed, armed*› fortement

heavy /ˈhevɪ/ *adj* (gen) lourd/-e; ‹*shoes, frame*› gros/grosse *before n*; ‹*line, features*› épais/épaisse; ‹*blow, fighting*› violent/-e; ‹*rain, frost, perfume, accent*› fort/-e; ‹*snow*› abondant/-e; ‹*traffic*› dense; ‹*gunfire*› nourri/-e; ‹*bleeding*› abondant/-e; ‹*sentence, fine*› sévère; ‹*cold*› gros/grosse *before n*; **with a ~ heart** le cœur gros; **to be a ~ sleeper** avoir le sommeil lourd; **to be a ~ drinker** boire beaucoup

heavy-handed /ˌhevɪˈhændɪd/ *adj* maladroit/-e

heavy metal *n* hard rock *m*

heavyweight /ˈhevɪweɪt/ *n* **1** (boxer) poids *m* lourd
2 (fig, fam) grosse légume *f* (fam)

Hebrew /ˈhiːbruː/ **A** *n* **1** (person) Hébreu *m*
2 (language) hébreu *m*
B *adj* ‹*language*› hébraïque; ‹*person*› hébreu/hébraïque

heckle /ˈhekl/ **A** *vt* interpeller
B *vi* chahuter

hectic /ˈhektɪk/ *adj* ‹*activity*› intense; ‹*day, life, schedule*› mouvementé/-e

hedge /hedʒ/ **A** *n* haie *f*
B *vi* se dérober
IDIOM **to ~ one's bets** se couvrir

hedge fund *n* fonds *m* spéculatif

hedgehog *n* hérisson *m*

hedgerow *n* haie *f*

heed /hiːd/ **A** *n* **to take ~ of sb** tenir compte de ce que dit qn; **to take ~ of sth** tenir compte de qch
B *vt* tenir compte de ‹*warning, advice*›

heel /hiːl/ *n* talon *m*
(IDIOMS) **to fall head over ∼s in love with sb** tomber éperdument amoureux de qn; **to be hot on sb's ∼s** talonner qn
heel bar *n* talon-minute *m*
hefty /ˈheftɪ/ *adj* ‹*person*› costaud (fam); ‹*object*› pesant/-e; ‹*blow*› puissant/-e; ‹*sum*› considérable
heifer /ˈhefə(r)/ *n* génisse *f*
height /haɪt/ *n* **1** (of person) taille *f*; (of table, tower, tree) hauteur *f*
2 (of plane) altitude *f*; **to be scared of ∼s** avoir le vertige
3 (peak) **at the ∼ of the season** en pleine saison; **at the ∼ of** au plus fort de ‹*storm, crisis*›; **the ∼ of** le comble de ‹*luxury, stupidity, cheek*›; **to be the ∼ of fashion** être le dernier cri

h

heighten /ˈhaɪtn/ **A** *vt* intensifier ‹*emotion*›; augmenter ‹*tension, suspense*›; accentuer ‹*effect*›
B *vi* ‹*tension*› monter
heir /eə(r)/ *n* héritier/-ière *m/f* (**to** de)
heiress /ˈeərɪs/ *n* héritière *f*
heirloom /ˈeəluːm/ *n* héritage *m*; **a family ∼** un objet de famille
helicopter /ˈhelɪkɒptə(r)/ *n* hélicoptère *m*
hell /hel/ *n* **1** enfer *m*; **to make sb's life ∼** rendre la vie infernale à qn
2 (fam) **a ∼ of a shock** un choc terrible; **a ∼ of a lot worse** nettement pire; **oh, what the ∼!** tant pis!; **why the ∼...?** pourquoi..., bon Dieu? (fam); **what the ∼ is he doing?** qu'est-ce qu'il fait, bon Dieu? (fam)
(IDIOMS) **for the ∼ of it** (fam) par plaisir; **to raise ∼** (fam) faire une scène (**with sb** à qn)
hello /həˈləʊ/ *excl* **1** (greeting) bonjour!; (on the phone) allô!
2 (in surprise) tiens!
helm /helm/ *n* barre *f*; **at the ∼** à la barre
helmet /ˈhelmɪt/ *n* casque *m*
⚷ **help** /help/ **A** *n* aide *f*; (in emergency) secours *m*; **with the ∼ of** à l'aide de ‹*stick, knife*›; avec l'aide de ‹*person*›; **it's/she's a (great) ∼** ça/elle aide beaucoup; **to cry for ∼** appeler au secours
B *excl* au secours!
C *vt* **1** aider (**to do** à faire); **to ∼ each other** s'entraider; **to ∼ sb across** aider qn à traverser
2 (serve) **to ∼ sb to** servir [qch] à qn ‹*food, wine*›; **to ∼ oneself** se servir
3 (prevent) **I couldn't ∼ laughing** je n'ai pas pu m'empêcher de rire; **it can't be ∼ed!** on n'y peut rien!; **he can't ∼ being stupid!** ce n'est pas de sa faute s'il est stupide!
D *vi* aider; **he never ∼s with the housework** il n'aide jamais à faire le ménage; **this map doesn't ∼ much** cette carte n'est pas d'un grand secours
■ **help out**: **A** **∼ out** aider, donner un coup de main (fam)
B **∼ [sb] out** aider, donner un coup de main à (fam); (financially) dépanner (fam)
help desk *n* service *m* d'assistance technique téléphonique
helper /ˈhelpə(r)/ *n* aide *mf*, assistant/-e *m/f*; (for disabled person) aide *f* sociale
helpful /ˈhelpfl/ *adj* ‹*person*› serviable; ‹*advice, suggestion*› utile
helping /ˈhelpɪŋ/ *n* portion *f*
helpless /ˈhelplɪs/ *adj* **1** (powerless) ‹*person*› impuissant/-e; (because of infirmity, disability) impotent/-e
2 (defenceless) ‹*person*› sans défense
helpline *n* service *m* d'assistance (téléphonique)
hem /hem/ *n* ourlet *m*
■ **hem in** cerner ‹*person*›
hemisphere /ˈhemɪsfɪə(r)/ *n* hémisphère *m*
hemp /hemp/ *n* chanvre *m*
hen /hen/ *n* (chicken) poule *f*; (female bird) femelle *f*
hence /hens/ *adv* **1** (for this reason) d'où (*before n*); donc (*before adj*)
2 (from now) d'ici
henchman /ˈhentʃmən/ *n* acolyte *m*
henna /ˈhenə/ *n* henné *m*
hen night *n* soirée *f* passée entre femmes (*avant le mariage de l'une d'elles*)
henpecked /ˈhenpekt/ *adj* **∼ husband** mari *m* mené par le bout du nez
hepatitis /ˌhepəˈtaɪtɪs/ *n* hépatite *f*
heptathlete /hepˈtæθliːt/ *n* heptathlonien/-ne *mf*, heptathlète *mf*
heptathlon /hepˈtæθlən, -lɒn/ *n* heptathlon *m*
⚷ **her** /hɜː(r), hə(r)/

> In French, determiners agree in gender and number with the noun that follows. So *her*, when used as a determiner, is translated by *son* + masculine singular noun (son chien), by *sa* + feminine singular noun (sa maison) BUT by *son* + feminine noun beginning with a vowel or mute 'h' (son assiette) and by *ses* + plural noun (ses enfants).
> When *her* is stressed, *à elle* is added after the noun: *HER house* = sa maison à elle.

A *pron* **1** (direct object) la, l'; **I saw ∼** je l'ai vue; **he gave ∼ the book** il lui a donné le livre; **catch ∼!** attrape-la!; **give it to ∼** donne-le-lui
2 (after preposition, to be) elle; **it's for ∼** c'est pour elle; **it's ∼** c'est elle
B *det* son/sa/ses
herald /ˈherəld/ **A** *n* héraut *m*
B *vt* (*also* **∼ in**) annoncer
heraldry /ˈherəldrɪ/ *n* héraldique *f*
herb /hɜːb, (AmE) ɜːrb/ *n* herbe *f*; **mixed ∼s** ≈ herbes de Provence
herbal tea *n* tisane *f*, infusion *f*
herd /hɜːd/ **A** *n* troupeau *m*

⚷ mot clé

B *vt* rassembler <*animals*>; **to ~ people into a room** conduire des gens dans une pièce

IDIOM **to follow the ~** être un mouton de Panurge

here /hɪə(r)/ *adv*

When *here* is used to indicate the location of an object, a point etc close to the speaker, it is generally translated by *ici*: *come and sit here* = viens t'asseoir ici.

When the location is not so clearly defined, *là* is the usual translation: *he's not here at the moment* = il n'est pas là pour l'instant.

Voici is used to translate *here is* and *here are* when the speaker is drawing attention to an object, a place, a person etc physically close to him or her.

For examples and particular usages, see the entry below.

1 ici; **near ~** près d'ici; **come over ~** venez par ici; **~ and there** par endroits; **~ they are/she comes!** les/la voici!; **~ are my keys** voici mes clés; **~ you are** tiens, tenez
2 (indicating presence, arrival) **she's not ~ right now** elle n'est pas là pour le moment; **~ we are at last** nous voilà enfin; **we get off ~** c'est là qu'on descend; **now that summer's ~** maintenant que c'est l'été; **~'s our chance** voilà notre chance

IDIOMS **~'s to our success!** à notre succès!; **~'s to you!** à la tienne!

hereabouts (BrE), **hereabout** (AmE) *adv* par ici

hereafter /hɪər'ɑːftə(r)/ **A** *n* **the ~** l'au-delà *m*
B *adv* (Law) ci-après

here and now *n* **the ~** (present) le présent

hereby /hɪə'baɪ/ *adv* par la présente

hereditary /hɪ'redɪtrɪ, (AmE) -terɪ/ *adj* héréditaire

heresy /'herəsɪ/ *n* hérésie *f*

heritage /'herɪtɪdʒ/ *n* patrimoine *m*; **~ tourism** tourisme *m* culturel

hermit /'hɜːmɪt/ *n* ermite *m*

hernia /'hɜːnɪə/ *n* (*pl* **~s** *ou* **~e**) hernie *f*

hero /'hɪərəʊ/ *n* (*pl* **~es**) héros *m*

heroic /hɪ'rəʊɪk/ *adj* héroïque

heroin /'herəʊɪn/ *n* héroïne *f*

heroin addict *n* héroïnomane *mf*

heroine /'herəʊɪn/ *n* héroïne *f*

heroism /'herəʊɪzəm/ *n* héroïsme *m*

heron /'herən/ *n* héron *m*

hero-worship /'hɪərəʊwɜːʃɪp/ **A** *n* culte *m* du héros, adulation *f*
B *vt* (*p prés etc* **-pp-** (BrE), **-p-** (AmE)) aduler

herring /'herɪŋ/ *n* hareng *m*

hers /hɜːz/ *pron*

In French, possessive pronouns reflect the gender and number of the noun they are standing for; *hers* is translated by *le sien*, *la sienne*, *les siens*, *les siennes*, according to what is being referred to.

my car is red but ~ is blue ma voiture est rouge mais la sienne est bleue; **the green pen is ~** le stylo vert est à elle; **which house is ~?** laquelle est sa maison?; **I'm a friend of ~** c'est une amie à moi; **it's not ~** ce n'est pas à elle

herself /hə'self/ *pron* **1** (reflexive) se, s'; **she's hurt ~** elle s'est blessée
2 (after preposition) elle, elle-même; **for ~** pour elle, pour elle-même; **(all) by ~** toute seule
3 (emphatic) elle-même; **she made it ~** elle l'a fait elle-même
4 she's not ~ today elle n'est pas dans son assiette aujourd'hui

hesitant /'hezɪtənt/ *adj* hésitant/-e; **to be ~ about doing** hésiter à faire

hesitate /'hezɪteɪt/ *vi* hésiter (**over** sur, **to do** à faire)

hesitation /ˌhezɪ'teɪʃn/ *n* hésitation *f*

heterosexual /ˌhetərə'sekʃʊəl/ *n, adj* hétérosexuel/-elle *m/f*

hexagon /'heksəgən, (AmE) -gɒn/ *n* hexagone *m*

hey /heɪ/ *excl* (fam) (call for attention) hé!, eh!; (in protest) dis donc!

heyday /'heɪdeɪ/ *n* (gen) âge *m* d'or; (of person) beaux jours *mpl*

HGV *n* (BrE) (*abbr* = **heavy goods vehicle**) PL *m*, poids *m* lourd

hi /haɪ/ *excl* (fam) salut! (fam)

hibernate /'haɪbəneɪt/ *vi* hiberner

hiccup, **hiccough** /'hɪkʌp/ *n* **1** hoquet *m*; **to have (the) ~s** avoir le hoquet
2 (setback) anicroche *f*

hidden /'hɪdn/ *adj* caché/-e

hide /haɪd/ **A** *n* (skin) peau *f*; (leather) cuir *m*
B *vt* (*prét* **hid**, *pp* **hidden**) cacher <*object, person*> (**from** à); dissimuler <*feeling*> (**from** à)
C *vi* (*prét* **hid**, *pp* **hidden**) se cacher

hide and seek (BrE), **hide and go seek** (AmE) *n* cache-cache *m inv*

hideaway *n* retraite *f*

hideous /'hɪdɪəs/ *adj* <*person, monster, object*> hideux/-euse; <*noise*> affreux/-euse

hiding /'haɪdɪŋ/ *n* **1 to go into ~** se cacher; **to come out of ~** sortir de sa cachette
2 (beating) correction *f*

hiding place *n* cachette *f*

hierarchy /'haɪərɑːkɪ/ *n* hiérarchie *f*

hieroglyph, **hieroglyphic** /'haɪərəglɪf/ *n* hiéroglyphe *m*

hi-fi /'haɪfaɪ/ *n* **1** (set of equipment) chaîne *f* hi-fi *inv*
2 (*abbr* = **high fidelity**) hi-fi *f inv*

high /haɪ/ **A** *n* **1 to reach a new ~** atteindre son niveau le plus élevé
2 (fam) **to be on a ~** être en pleine euphorie

h

B *adj* **1** (gen) haut/-e; **how ~ is the cliff?** quelle est la hauteur de la falaise?; **it is 50 m ~** ça fait 50 m de haut
2 ‹*number, price, volume*› élevé/-e; ‹*wind*› violent/-e; ‹*hope*› grand/-e *before n*; **at ~ speed** à grande vitesse; **to have a ~ temperature** avoir de la fièvre; **~ in** riche en ‹*fat, iron*›
3 ‹*quality, standard, rank*› supérieur/-e; **friends in ~ places** des amis haut placés
4 ‹*ideal, principle*› noble
5 ‹*pitch, voice*› aigu/aiguë; ‹*note*› haut/-e
6 (fam) (on drug) défoncé/-e (fam); (happy) ivre de joie
C *adv* haut

highbrow *n, adj* intellectuel/-elle *m/f*

high chair *n* chaise *f* de bébé

high-class *adj* ‹*hotel, shop, car*› de luxe; ‹*goods*› de première qualité; ‹*area*› de grand standing

high court *n* cour *f* suprême

high-definition TV, **HDTV** *n* télévision *f* à haute définition

higher education *n* enseignement *m* supérieur

high fashion *n* haute couture *f*

high-flier *n* jeune loup *m*

high-handed *adj* despotique

high heels *npl* hauts talons *mpl*

high jump *n* (Sport) saut *m* en hauteur

Highlands *pr n pl* Highlands *mpl*, Hautes-Terres *fpl* (d'Écosse)

⚷ **highlight** /'haɪlaɪt/ **A** *n* **1** (in hair) (natural) reflet *m*; (artificial) mèche *f*
2 (of match, event) point *m* culminant; (of year, evening) point *m* fort
B highlights *npl* (on radio, TV) résumé *m*
C *vt* (*prét, pp* **-lighted**) **1** (with pen) surligner
2 (emphasize) mettre l'accent sur

highlighter /'haɪlaɪtə(r)/ *n* (pen) surligneur *m*

⚷ **highly** /'haɪlɪ/ *adv* ‹*dangerous, intelligent*› extrêmement; **~ unlikely** fort peu probable; **to think ~ of sb** penser beaucoup de bien de qn

highly paid *adj* très bien payé/-e

highly strung *adj* très tendu/-e

Highness /'haɪnɪs/ *n* **His** *or* **Her (Royal) ~** Son Altesse *f*

high-pitched /ˌhaɪ'pɪtʃt/ *adj* ‹*voice, sound*› aigu/aiguë

high point *n* point *m* culminant

high-powered /ˌhaɪ'paʊəd/ *adj* ‹*car, engine*› de grande puissance; ‹*person*› dynamique; ‹*job*› de haute responsabilité

high-profile /ˌhaɪ'prəʊfaɪl/ *adj* ‹*politician, group*› bien en vue; ‹*visit*› qui fait beaucoup de bruit

high-ranking *adj* de haut rang

high rise *n* (*also* **high rise building**) tour *f* (d'habitation)

high school *n* (AmE) (Sch) ≈ lycée *m*; (BrE) (Sch) établissement *m* secondaire

high-speed *adj* ‹*train*› à grande vitesse

high street *n* (BrE) (*also* **High Street**) (in town) rue *f* principale; (in village) grand-rue *f*

high-street shop *n* (BrE) boutique *f* appartenant à une chaîne

high street spending *n* dépenses *fpl* de consommation courante

high-tech *adj* ‹*industry*› de pointe; ‹*equipment, car*› ultramoderne

high tide *n* marée *f* haute

highway /'haɪweɪ/ *n* (BrE) route *f* nationale; (AmE) autoroute *f*

Highway Code *n* (BrE) Code *m* de la Route

hijack /'haɪdʒæk/ *vt* détourner ‹*plane*›

hijacker /'haɪdʒækə(r)/ *n* (of plane) pirate *m* (de l'air); (of bus, truck) pirate *m* (de la route)

hijacking /'haɪdʒækɪŋ/ *n* détournement *m*

hike /haɪk/ **A** *n* randonnée *f*; **to go on a ~** faire une randonnée
B *vt* (*also* **~ up**) augmenter ‹*rate, price*›

hiker /'haɪkə(r)/ *n* randonneur/-euse *m/f*

hiking /'haɪkɪŋ/ *n* randonnée *f*

hilarious /hɪ'leərɪəs/ *adj* désopilant/-e, hilarant/-e

hill /hɪl/ *n* colline *f*; (hillside) coteau *m*; (incline) pente *f*, côte *f*

hillside /'hɪlsaɪd/ *n* **on the ~** à flanc de coteau

hilltop /'hɪltɒp/ *n* sommet *m* de colline

hilly /'hɪlɪ/ *adj* vallonné/-e

⚷ **him** /hɪm/ *pron* **1** (direct object) le, l'; **I know ~** je le connais; **catch ~!** attrape-le!; **I gave ~ the book** je lui ai donné le livre; **phone ~!** téléphone-lui!
2 (after preposition, to be) lui; **it's for ~** c'est pour lui; **it's ~** c'est lui

Himalayas /ˌhɪmə'leɪəz/ *pr n pl* **the ~** (les montagnes *fpl* de) l'Himalaya *m*

⚷ **himself** /hɪm'self/ *pron* **1** (reflexive) se, s'; (indirect object) lui; **he's hurt ~** il s'est blessé
2 (after preposition) lui, lui-même; **for ~** pour lui, pour lui-même; **(all) by ~** tout seul
3 (emphatic) lui-même; **he made it ~** il l'a fait lui-même
4 he's not ~ today il n'est pas dans son assiette aujourd'hui

hinder /'hɪndə(r)/ *vt* entraver ‹*development, career*›; freiner ‹*progress, efforts*›

hind legs *npl* pattes *fpl* de derrière

hindrance /'hɪndrəns/ *n* entrave *f*; **to be a ~ to sb/sth** gêner qn/qch

hindsight /'haɪndsaɪt/ *n* **with (the benefit of) ~** avec le recul, rétrospectivement

Hindu /ˌhɪn'duː, (AmE) 'hɪnduː/ **A** *n* Hindou/-e *m/f*
B *adj* hindou/-e

hinge /hɪndʒ/ **A** *n* charnière *f*; (lift-off) gond *m*

B *vi* (*p prés* **hingeing**) **to ~ on** dépendre de

hint /hɪnt/ **A** *n* **1** (remark) allusion *f* (**about** à); **to drop ~s** faire des allusions
2 (clue) indication *f*; (piece of advice) conseil *m*
3 (of spice, accent) pointe *f*; (of colour) touche *f*; (of smile) ébauche *f*; (of irony) soupçon *m*
B *vt* **to ~ that** laisser entendre que (**to** à)
C *vi* faire des allusions; **to ~ at** faire allusion à

hip /hɪp/ **A** *n* hanche *f*
B *adj* (fam) ‹*person*› branché/-e
C *excl* **~ ~ hurrah!** hip hip hip hourra!

hippie, **hippy** /ˈhɪpɪ/ *n*, *adj* hippie *mf*

hippopotamus, **hippo** /ˌhɪpəˈpɒtəməs/ *n* (*pl* **-muses** *ou* **-mi**) hippopotame *m*

hire /ˈhaɪə(r)/ **A** *n* location *f*; **for ~** ‹*boat, skis*› à louer; ‹*taxi*› libre
B *vt* louer ‹*equipment, vehicle*›; engager ‹*person*›

hire purchase, **HP** *n* achat *m* à crédit; **on ~** à crédit

his /hɪz/

> In French, determiners agree in gender and number with the noun that follows. So *his*, when used as a determiner, is translated by *son* + masculine singular noun (son chien), by *sa* + feminine singular noun (sa maison) BUT by *son* + feminine noun beginning with a vowel or mute 'h' (son assiette) and by *ses* + plural noun (ses enfants).
> When *his* is stressed, *à lui* is added after the noun: *HIS house* = sa maison à lui.
> In French, possessive pronouns reflect the gender and number of the noun they are standing for. When used as a possessive pronoun, *his* is translated by *le sien*, *la sienne*, *les siens* or *les siennes* according to what is being referred to.

A *det* son/sa/ses
B *pron* **all the drawings were good but ~ was the best** tous les dessins étaient bons mais le sien était le meilleur; **the blue car is ~** la voiture bleue est à lui; **it's not ~** ce n'est pas à lui; **which house is ~?** laquelle est sa maison?; **I'm a colleague of ~** je suis un/-e de ses collègues

hiss /hɪs/ **A** *n* sifflement *m*
B *vi* ‹*person, steam, snake*› siffler; ‹*cat*› cracher; ‹*fat*› grésiller

historian /hɪˈstɔːrɪən/ *n* historien/-ienne *m/f*

historic /hɪˈstɒrɪk, (AmE) -ˈstɔːr-/ *adj* (*also* **historical**) historique

history /ˈhɪstrɪ/ *n* **1** histoire *f*; **to make ~** entrer dans l'histoire
2 (past experience) antécédents *mpl*; **to have a ~ of violence** avoir un passé violent

hit /hɪt/ **A** *n* **1** (blow, stroke) coup *m*
2 (success) (play, film) succès *m*; (record) tube *m* (fam); **to be a big ~** avoir un succès fou
3 (Comput) (visit to Website) hit *m* (fam), visite *f* (à un site Web); (occurence in search) occurence *f*
B *vt* (*p prés* **-tt-**, *prét*, *pp* **hit**) **1** (strike) frapper ‹*person, ball*›; **to ~ one's head on sth** se cogner la tête contre qch
2 atteindre ‹*target, enemy*›
3 (collide with) heurter ‹*wall*›; ‹*vehicle*› renverser ‹*person*›
4 (affect adversely) affecter, toucher
5 (reach) arriver à ‹*motorway*›; rencontrer ‹*traffic, bad weather*›; ‹*figures, weight*› atteindre ‹*level*›
IDIOM **to ~ it off with sb** bien s'entendre avec qn
■ **hit back**: **A** **~ [sb] back** rendre un coup à
B **~ [sth] back** renvoyer ‹*ball*›

hit-and-run *adj* ‹*accident*› où le chauffeur a pris la fuite

hitch /hɪtʃ/ **A** *n* problème *m*, pépin *m* (fam)
B *vt* **1** attacher ‹*trailer*› (**to** à)
2 (fam) **to ~ a lift** faire du stop (fam)
C *vi* (fam) faire du stop (fam)

hitch-hike /ˈhɪtʃhaɪk/ *vi* faire du stop (fam); **to ~ to Paris** aller à Paris en stop (fam)

hitch-hiker *n* auto-stoppeur/-euse *m/f*

hitch-hiking *n* auto-stop *m*

hit man *n* tueur *m* à gages

hit parade *n* palmarès *m*, hit-parade *m*

hit single *n* tube *m* (fam)

HIV *n* (*abbr* = **human immunodeficiency virus**) (virus *m*) VIH *m*; **~ positive** séropositif/-ive; **~ negative** séronégatif/-ive

hive /haɪv/ *n* ruche *f*; **a ~ of activity** une vraie ruche

hoard /hɔːd/ **A** *n* (of treasure) trésor *m*; (of provisions) provisions *fpl*; (of miser) magot *m* (fam)
B *vt* amasser ‹*objects, money, food*›

hoarding /ˈhɔːdɪŋ/ *n* (BrE) **1** (billboard) panneau *m* publicitaire
2 (fence) palissade *f*

hoarse /hɔːs/ *adj* ‹*voice*› rauque; **to be ~** être enroué/-e

hoax /həʊks/ **A** *n* canular *m*
B *adj* ‹*call, warning*› bidon *inv* (fam)

hob /hɒb/ *n* (BrE) (on cooker) table *f* de cuisson

hobble /ˈhɒbl/ *vi* boitiller

hobby /ˈhɒbɪ/ *n* passe-temps *m inv*

hockey /ˈhɒkɪ/ *n* (BrE) hockey *m*; (AmE) hockey *m* sur glace; **~ stick** crosse *f* de hockey

hoe /həʊ/ **A** *n* houe *f*, binette *f*
B *vt* biner ‹*ground*›; sarcler ‹*flower beds*›

hog /hɒg/ **A** *n* (AmE) (pig) porc *m*, verrat *m*
B *vt* (fam) (*prét*, *pp* **-gg-**) monopoliser
IDIOM **to go the whole ~** (fam) (be extravagant) faire les choses en grand; (go to extremes) aller jusqu'au bout

hoist /hɔɪst/ *vt* hisser ‹*flag, sail, heavy object*›

hold /həʊld/ **A** *n* **1** (grasp) prise *f*; **to get ~ of** attraper ‹*rope, handle*›
2 to get ~ of se procurer ‹*book, ticket*›;

découvrir ‹*information*›
3 to get ~ of sb (contact) joindre qn; (find) trouver qn
4 (control) emprise *f* (**on, over** sur); **to have a ~ on** *or* **over sb** avoir de l'emprise sur qn; **to get a ~ of oneself** se reprendre
5 to put a call on ~ mettre un appel en attente
6 (in plane) soute *f*; (on boat) cale *f*
B *vt* (*prét, pp* **held**) **1** tenir; **to ~ sth in one's hand** tenir qch à la main ‹*brush, pencil*›; (enclosed) tenir qch dans la main ‹*coin, sweet*›; **to ~ sb (in one's arms)** serrer qn dans ses bras; **to ~ sth in place** maintenir qch en place
2 organiser ‹*meeting, competition, reception*›; célébrer ‹*church service*›; mener ‹*inquiry*›; faire passer ‹*interview*›
3 (contain) ‹*drawer, box, case*› contenir ‹*objects, possessions*›
4 avoir ‹*opinion, belief*›
5 (keep against will) détenir ‹*person*›; **to ~ sb hostage** garder qn en otage
6 détenir, avoir ‹*power, record*›; être titulaire de ‹*degree*›
7 to ~ sb's attention retenir l'attention de qn; **to ~ sb responsible** tenir qn pour responsable
8 (defend successfully) tenir ‹*territory, city*›; conserver ‹*title, seat*›; **to ~ one's own** bien se défendre
9 (on phone) **can you ~ the line please?** ne quittez pas s'il vous plaît
C *vi* (*prét, pp* **held**) **1** ‹*bridge, dam, rope*› tenir
2 ‹*weather*› se maintenir; ‹*luck*› durer
3 (on phone) patienter
4 ~ still! tiens-toi tranquille!

▪ **hold against**: **to ~ sth against sb** reprocher qch à qn

▪ **hold back**: **A ~ back** se retenir (**from doing** de faire)
B ~ [sb/sth] back 1 contenir ‹*water, crowd, anger*›; retenir ‹*tears, person*›
2 entraver ‹*development*›

▪ **hold down 1** tenir, maîtriser ‹*person*›
2 garder ‹*job*›

▪ **hold on 1** (wait) attendre; **'~ on...'** (on phone) 'ne quittez pas...'
2 (grip) s'accrocher; **'~ on (tight)!'** 'tiens-toi (bien)!'

▪ **hold on to** s'agripper à ‹*branch, rope, person*›; (to prevent from falling) retenir ‹*person*›; serrer ‹*object, purse*›

▪ **hold out**: **A ~ out** tenir bon; **to ~ out against** tenir bon devant ‹*threat, changes*›
B ~ [sth] out tendre ‹*hand*› (**to** à)

▪ **hold to**: **~ sb to [sth]** faire tenir [qch] à qn ‹*promise*›

▪ **hold up 1** soutenir ‹*shelf*›; tenir ‹*trousers*›
2 (raise) lever; **to ~ one's hand up** lever la main
3 (delay) retarder ‹*person, flight*›; ralentir ‹*production, traffic*›
4 (rob) attaquer

holdall *n* fourre-tout *m*, sac *m*

holder /ˈhəʊldə(r)/ *n* (of passport, degree, post, account) titulaire *mf*; (of ticket, record) détenteur/-trice *m/f*; (of title) tenant/-e *m/f*

holding /ˈhəʊldɪŋ/ *n* (share) participation *f*

hold-up /ˈhəʊldʌp/ *n* **1** (delay) retard *m*; (on road) embouteillage *m*, bouchon *m*
2 (robbery) hold-up *m*

🔑 **hole** /həʊl/ *n* **1** (gen) trou *m*
2 (BrE) (in tooth) cavité *f*
3 (of fox, rabbit) terrier *m*

hole in the wall *n* (fam) distributeur *m* automatique de billets de banque

🔑 **holiday** /ˈhɒlədeɪ/ *n* **1** (BrE) (vacation) vacances *fpl*; **to go on ~** partir en vacances
2 (BrE) (time off work) congé *m*
3 (public, bank) jour *m* férié

holiday home *n* résidence *f* secondaire

holiday job *n* (in summer) job *m* (fam) d'été

holidaymaker *n* (BrE) vacancier/-ière *m/f*

holiday resort *n* lieu *m* de villégiature

Holland /ˈhɒlənd/ *pr n* Hollande *f*, Pays-Bas *mpl*

hollow /ˈhɒləʊ/ **A** *n* creux *m*
B *adj* ‹*object, cheeks*› creux/creuse; ‹*words*› faux/fausse, vain/-e; **a ~ laugh** un rire forcé; **to sound ~** sonner faux

holly /ˈhɒlɪ/ *n* houx *m*

holocaust /ˈhɒləkɔːst/ *n* holocauste *m*; **the Holocaust** l'Holocauste

hologram /ˈhɒləɡræm/ *n* hologramme *m*

holster /ˈhəʊlstə(r)/ *n* étui *m* de revolver

holy /ˈhəʊlɪ/ *adj* (gen) saint/-e; ‹*water*› bénit/-e

Holy Bible *n* Sainte Bible *f*

Holy Land *pr n* Terre *f* Sainte

Holy Spirit *n* Saint-Esprit *m*

homage /ˈhɒmɪdʒ/ *n* hommage *m*; **to pay ~ to** rendre hommage à

🔑 **home** /həʊm/ **A** *n* **1** (house) maison *f*; (country) pays *m* natal; **broken ~** foyer *m* désuni; **to leave ~** quitter la maison
2 (institution) maison *f*; **to put sb in a ~** mettre qn dans un établissement spécialisé
3 (Sport) **to play at ~** jouer à domicile
B *adj* **1** ‹*life*› de famille; ‹*comforts*› du foyer
2 ‹*market, affairs*› intérieur/-e; ‹*news*› national/-e
3 (Sport) ‹*match, win*› à domicile; ‹*team*› qui reçoit
C *adv* **1** ‹*come, go*› (to house) à la maison, chez soi; (to country) dans son pays
2 to bring sth ~ to sb faire comprendre *or* voir qch à qn; **to strike ~** toucher juste
D at home *phr* **1** ‹*be, work, stay*› à la maison, chez soi
2 (Sport) ‹*play*› à domicile
3 (at ease) ‹*feel*› à l'aise (**with** avec); **make yourself at ~** fais comme chez toi

🔑 mot clé

home address *n* adresse *f* personnelle
home cooking *n* bonne cuisine *f* familiale
home economics *n* (Sch) cours *m* d'économie domestique
home help *n* (BrE) aide *f* familiale
homeland *n* pays *m* d'origine, patrie *f*
homeland security *n* (AmE) sécurité *f* des frontières
homeless /'həʊmlɪs/ *n* **the ~** les sans-abri *mpl*
homely /'həʊmlɪ/ *adj* **1** (BrE) (cosy, welcoming) accueillant/-e
2 (BrE) (unpretentious) simple
3 (AmE) (plain) ‹*person*› sans attraits
home-made *adj* fait/-e maison, maison *inv*
Home Office *n* (BrE) ministère *m* de l'Intérieur
homeopathic /ˌhəʊmɪə'pæθɪk/ *adj* homéopathique
home owner *n* propriétaire *mf*
home page *n* page *f* d'accueil
home rule *n* gouvernement *m* autonome
Home Secretary *n* (BrE) Ministre *m* de l'Intérieur
home shopping *n* téléachat *m*
homesick /'həʊmsɪk/ *adj* **to be ~** (for country) avoir le mal du pays
home town *n* ville *f* natale
home video *n* vidéo *f* d'amateur
homeward /'həʊmwəd/ *adv* **to travel ~(s)** rentrer; **to be ~ bound** être sur le chemin de retour
homework /'həʊmwɜːk/ *n* **1** (Sch) devoirs *mpl*
2 (research) **to do some ~ on** faire quelques recherches au sujet de
homeworker *n* travailleur/-euse *m/f* à domicile
home working *n* travail *m* à domicile
homicidal /ˌhɒmɪ'saɪdl/ *adj* homicide
homicide /'hɒmɪsaɪd/ *n* **1** (murder) homicide *m*
2 (person) meurtrier/-ière *m/f*
homogenous /hə'mɒdʒɪnəs/ *adj* homogène
homosexual /ˌhɒmə'sekʃʊəl/ *n, adj* homosexuel/-elle *m/f*
homosexuality /ˌhɒməˌsekʃʊ'ælətɪ/ *n* homosexualité *f*
honest /'ɒnɪst/ *adj* ‹*answer, account*› sincère; ‹*person*› (truthful, trustworthy) honnête; **to be ~ with sb** être franc/franche avec qn; **to be ~, I don't care** à dire vrai, ça m'est égal
honestly /'ɒnɪstlɪ/ *adv* **1** (truthfully) honnêtement
2 (really) vraiment
3 (sincerely) franchement
honesty /'ɒnɪstɪ/ *n* honnêteté *f*
honey /'hʌnɪ/ *n* **1** miel *m*
2 (fam) (dear) chéri/-e *m/f*
honeycomb /'hʌnɪkəʊm/ *n* (in hive) rayon *m* de miel; (for sale) gâteau *m* de miel
honeymoon /'hʌnɪmuːn/ *n* lune *f* de miel; **to go on ~** partir en voyage de noces
honeysuckle *n* chèvrefeuille *m*
Hong Kong /ˌhɒŋ 'kɒŋ/ *pr n* Hongkong *m*
honk /hɒŋk/ *vt* **to ~ one's horn** donner un coup de klaxon®
honor (AmE) = **honour**
honorable (AmE) = **honourable**
honorary /'ɒnərərɪ, (AmE) 'ɒnərerɪ/ *adj* honoraire
honour (BrE), **honor** (AmE) /'ɒnə(r)/ **A** *n* **1** honneur *m*; **in ~ of** en l'honneur de
2 (in titles) **Your Honour** Votre Honneur
B *vt* honorer ‹*person, cheque, contract*›; tenir ‹*promise, commitment*›
honourable (BrE), **honorable** (AmE) /'ɒnərəbl/ *adj* (gen) honorable; ‹*person, intention*› honnête
honours degree *n: licence réservée aux meilleurs étudiants*
hood /hʊd/ *n* **1** (of coat) capuchon *m*; (balaclava) cagoule *f*
2 (on cooker) hotte *f*
3 (BrE) (on car, pram) capote *f*
4 (AmE) (Aut) (bonnet) capot *m*
5 (AmE) (fam) (gangster) truand *m*
hoof /huːf/ *n* (*pl* **~s** *ou* **hooves**) sabot *m*
hook /hʊk/ **A** *n* **1** (on wall, for picture) crochet *m*
2 (on fishing line) hameçon *m*
3 (fastener) agrafe *f*; **~s and eyes** agrafes *fpl*
4 to take the phone off the ~ décrocher le téléphone
5 (in boxing) crochet *m*; **left ~** crochet du gauche
B *vt* accrocher (**on, onto** à)
IDIOM **to get sb off the ~** tirer qn d'affaire
hooked /hʊkt/ *adj* **1** ‹*nose, beak*› crochu/-e
2 to be ~ on se camer (fam) à ‹*drugs*›; être mordu/-e (fam) de ‹*films, computer games*›
hooligan /'huːlɪgən/ *n* vandale *m*, voyou *m*; **soccer ~** hooligan *m*
hoop /huːp/ *n* (ring) cerceau *m*; (in croquet) arceau *m*
hooray /hʊ'reɪ/ *excl* hourra!
hoot /huːt/ **A** *n* (of owl) (h)ululement *m*; (of car) coup *m* de klaxon®
B *vt* **to ~ one's horn** donner un coup de klaxon®
C *vi* ‹*owl*› (h)ululer; ‹*car*› klaxonner; ‹*person, crowd*› (derisively) huer; **to ~ with laughter** éclater de rire
hoover /'huːvə(r)/ *vt* (BrE) **to ~ a room** passer l'aspirateur dans une pièce
Hoover® /'huːvə(r)/ *n* (BrE) aspirateur *m*
hop /hɒp/ **A** *n* (of frog, rabbit, child) bond *m*; (of bird) sautillement *m*
B hops *npl* houblon *m*
C *vi* (*p prés etc* **-pp-**) ‹*person*› sauter; (on one leg) sauter à cloche-pied; ‹*bird*› sautiller; **to ~ into bed/off a bus** sauter

dans son lit/d'un bus

hope /həʊp/ **A** *n* espoir *m* (**of** de); **to raise sb's ~s** faire naître l'espoir chez qn; **to give up ~** abandonner tout espoir; **to have no ~ of sth** n'avoir aucune chance de qch
B *vt* espérer (**that** que); **to ~ to do** espérer faire; **I (do) ~ so/not** j'espère (bien) que oui/que non
C *vi* espérer; **to ~ for a reward** espérer avoir une récompense; **let's ~ for the best** espérons que tout se passera bien

hopeful /ˈhəʊpfl/ *adj* ‹*person, expression*› plein/-e d'espoir; ‹*attitude, mood*› optimiste; ‹*sign, situation*› encourageant/-e

hopefully /ˈhəʊpfəlɪ/ *adv* **1** (with luck) avec un peu de chance
2 (with hope) ‹*say*› avec optimisme

hopeless /ˈhəʊplɪs/ *adj* **1** ‹*attempt, case, struggle*› désespéré/-e; **it's ~!** inutile!
2 (fam) (incompetent) nul/nulle (fam)

hopelessness /ˈhəʊplɪsnɪs/ *n* **1** (despair) désespoir *m*
2 (futility) futilité *f* (**of doing** de faire)

hopscotch *n* marelle *f*

horizon /həˈraɪzn/ *n* horizon *m*; **on the ~** à l'horizon; (fig) en vue

horizontal /ˌhɒrɪˈzɒntl, (AmE) ˌhɔːr-/ *adj* horizontal/-e

hormone *n* hormone *f*

hormone replacement therapy, **HRT** *n* hormonothérapie *f* substitutive

horn /hɔːn/ *n* **1** (of animal, snail) corne *f*
2 (Mus) cor *m*
3 (of car) klaxon® *m*; (of ship) sirène *f*

hornet /ˈhɔːnɪt/ *n* frelon *m*

horoscope /ˈhɒrəskəʊp, (AmE) ˈhɔːr-/ *n* horoscope *m*

horrendous /hɒˈrendəs/ *adj* épouvantable

horrible /ˈhɒrɪbl, (AmE) ˈhɔːr-/ *adj*
1 (unpleasant) ‹*place, clothes, smell*› affreux/-euse; ‹*weather, food, person*› épouvantable; **to be ~ to sb** être méchant/-e avec qn
2 (shocking) ‹*death, crime*› horrible

horrid /ˈhɒrɪd, (AmE) ˈhɔːrɪd/ *adj* affreux/-euse

horrific /həˈrɪfɪk/ *adj* atroce

horrify /ˈhɒrɪfaɪ, (AmE) ˈhɔːr-/ *vt* horrifier

horrifying /ˈhɒrɪfaɪɪŋ, (AmE) ˈhɔːr-/ *adj* ‹*experience, sight*› horrifiant/-e; ‹*behaviour*› effroyable

horror /ˈhɒrə(r), (AmE) ˈhɔːr-/ *n* horreur *f* (**at** devant); **to have a ~ of sth/of doing** avoir horreur de qch/de faire

horror film *n* film *m* d'épouvante

horror story *n* histoire *f* d'épouvante

horse /hɔːs/ *n* cheval *m*
IDIOM **from the ~'s mouth** de source sûre
■ **horse about**, **horse around** chahuter

horseback /ˈhɔːsbæk/ *n* **on ~** à cheval

horseback riding *n* (AmE) équitation *f*

horse chestnut *n* (tree) marronnier *m* (d'Inde); (fruit) marron *m* (d'Inde)

horsefly *n* taon *m*

horsepower /ˈhɔːspaʊə(r)/ *n* puissance *f* (en chevaux)

horse race *n* course *f* de chevaux

horse racing *n* courses *fpl* de chevaux, courses *fpl* hippiques

horseradish sauce *n* sauce *f* au raifort

horse riding *n* équitation *f*

horseshoe *n* fer *m* à cheval

horse show *n* concours *m* hippique

horticulture /ˈhɔːtɪkʌltʃə(r)/ *n* horticulture *f*

hose, **hosepipe** (BrE) /həʊz(paɪp)/ *n* (gen) tuyau *m*; (for garden) tuyau *m* d'arrosage; **(fire) ~** lance *f* à incendie

hosepipe ban *n* (BrE) interdiction *f* d'utiliser les tuyaux d'arrosage

hospice /ˈhɒspɪs/ *n* établissement *m* de soins palliatifs

hospitable /hɒˈspɪtəbl/ *adj* hospitalier/-ière (**to** envers)

hospital /ˈhɒspɪtl/ *n* hôpital *m*; **to be taken to ~** être hospitalisé/-e; **in ~** à l'hôpital

hospitality /ˌhɒspɪˈtælətɪ/ *n* hospitalité *f*

hospitalize /ˈhɒspɪtəlaɪz/ *vt* hospitaliser

host /həʊst/ **A** *n* **1** (gen) hôte *m*
2 (on radio, TV) animateur/-trice *m/f*
3 (multitude) foule *f* (**of** de)
B *vt* organiser ‹*party*›; animer ‹*show*›

hostage /ˈhɒstɪdʒ/ *n* otage *m*; **to hold sb ~** garder qn en otage

host country *n* pays *m* hôte *or* d'accueil

hostel /ˈhɒstl/ *n* (for workers, refugees) foyer *m*; **(youth) ~** auberge *f* de jeunesse

hostess /ˈhəʊstɪs/ *n* hôtesse *f*

hostile /ˈhɒstaɪl, (AmE) -tl/ *adj* hostile (**to** à)

hostility /hɒˈstɪlətɪ/ *n* hostilité *f* (**towards** à l'égard de)

hot /hɒt/ *adj* **1** (gen) chaud/-e; **it's ~ here** il fait chaud ici; **to be *or* feel ~** ‹*person*› avoir chaud; **to go ~ and cold** (with fever) être fiévreux/-euse; (with fear) avoir des sueurs froides
2 (Culin) ‹*mustard, spice*› fort/-e; ‹*sauce, dish*› épicé/-e
3 to be ~ on sb's trail être sur les talons de qn

hot air balloon *n* montgolfière *f*

hotbed *n* foyer *m* (**of** de)

hot dog *n* hot dog *m*

hotel /həʊˈtel/ *n* hôtel *m*

hotelier /həʊˈtelɪə(r)/ *n* (BrE) hôtelier/-ière *m/f*

hot-headed /ˌhɒtˈhedɪd/ *adj* ‹*person*› impétueux/-euse

hotline /ˈhɒtlaɪn/ *n* **1** (for orders, tickets) ligne *f* ouverte, permanence *f* téléphonique
2 (Mil, Pol) téléphone *m* rouge

mot clé

hotplate *n* plaque *f* de cuisson

hot seat *n*
IDIOM **to be in the ~** être sur la sellette

hotshot /ˈhɒtʃɒt/ *n* gros bonnet *m* (fam)

hot spot *n* (fam) **1** (trouble spot) point *m* chaud
2 (sunny country) pays *m* chaud

hot-tempered *adj* colérique

hot water bottle *n* bouillotte *f*

hound /haʊnd/ **A** *n* chien *m* de chasse
B *vt* harceler, traquer ‹*person*›
■ **hound out** chasser (of de)

hour /aʊə(r)/ *n* heure *f*; **£10 per ~** 10 livres sterling (de) l'heure; **to be paid by the ~** être payé/-e à l'heure; **60 km an hour** 60 km à l'heure; **in the early ~s** au petit matin

hourly /ˈaʊəlɪ/ **A** *adj* horaire
B *adv* ‹*arrive, phone*› toutes les heures

house **A** /haʊs *pl* haʊzɪz/ *n* **1** (gen) maison *f*; **at my/his ~** chez moi/lui; **to go to sb's ~** aller chez qn; **on the ~** aux frais de la maison
2 (in theatre) (audience) assistance *f*; (auditorium) salle *f*; (performance) séance *f*
3 (music) house music *f*
B /haʊz/ *vt* loger ‹*person*›; abriter ‹*collection*›

houseboat /ˈhaʊsbəʊt/ *n* péniche *f* aménagée

housebound /ˈhaʊsbaʊnd/ *adj* confiné/-e chez soi

house call *n* visite *f* à domicile

household /ˈhaʊshəʊld/ **A** *n* maison *f*; (in survey) ménage *m*; **head of the ~** chef *m* de famille
B *adj* ‹*expenses*› du ménage; ‹*chore*› ménager/-ère

household appliance *n* appareil *m* électroménager

householder /ˈhaʊshəʊldə(r)/ *n* **1** (occupier) occupant/-e *m/f*
2 (owner) propriétaire *mf*

household name *n* **he's a ~** il est célèbre

house husband *n* homme *m* au foyer

housekeeper /ˈhaʊskiːpə(r)/ *n* gouvernante *f*

housekeeping /ˈhaʊskiːpɪŋ/ *n* (money) argent *m* du ménage

House of Commons *n* (BrE) Chambre *f* des communes

House of Lords *n* (BrE) Chambre *f* des lords, Chambre *f* haute

House of Representatives *n* (AmE) Chambre *f* des représentants

house plant *n* plante *f* d'intérieur

house-proud *adj* fier/fière de son intérieur

Houses of Parliament *npl* (BrE) Parlement *m* Britannique

house-to-house *adj* ‹*search*› de maison en maison

house-trained *adj* (BrE) propre

house-warming *n* (*also* **house-warming party**) pendaison *f* de crémaillère

housewife /ˈhaʊswaɪf/ *n* (*pl* **-wives** /-waɪvz/) femme *f* au foyer; ménagère *f*

housework /ˈhaʊswɜːk/ *n* travaux *mpl* ménagers; **to do the ~** faire le ménage

housing /ˈhaʊzɪŋ/ *n* logements *mpl*

housing estate *n* (BrE) cité *f*

hover /ˈhɒvə(r)/ *vi* ‹*eagle*› planer; ‹*helicopter*› faire du surplace; **to ~ around sb/sth** tourner autour de qn/qch

hovercraft *n* (*pl* ~) aéroglisseur *m*

how /haʊ/ **A** *adv* **1** (gen) comment; **~ are you?** comment allez-vous?; **~'s your brother?** comment va ton frère?; **~ are things?** comment ça va?; **~ do you do?** enchanté!; **to know ~ to do** savoir faire
2 (in number, quantity questions) **~ much is this?** combien ça coûte?; **~ much do you weigh?** combien pèses-tu?; **~ many people?** combien de personnes?; **~ many times?** combien de fois?; **~ long will it take?** combien de temps cela va-t-il prendre?; **~ tall are you?** combien mesures-tu?; **~ far is it?** c'est à quelle distance?; **~ old is she?** quel âge a-t-elle?; **~ soon can you get here?** dans combien de temps peux-tu être ici?
3 (in exclamations) **~ wonderful/awful!** c'est fantastique/affreux!; **~ clever of you!** comme c'est intelligent de ta part!
B **how come** *phr* (fam) **~ come?** pourquoi?; **~ come you always get the best place?** comment ça se fait que tu aies toujours la meilleure place?

however /haʊˈevə(r)/ **A** *conj* (nevertheless) toutefois, cependant
B *adv* (no matter how) **~ hard I try, I can't** j'ai beau essayer, je n'y arrive pas; **~ difficult the task is** aussi difficile que soit la tâche; **~ small she may be** si petite soit-elle; **~ much it costs** quel qu'en soit le prix; **~ long it takes** quel que soit le temps que ça prendra; **~ you like** comme tu veux

howl /haʊl/ **A** *n* hurlement *m*
B *vi* hurler

HQ *n* (Mil) (*abbr* = **headquarters**) QG *m*

HTML *n* (*abbr* = **HyperText Markup Language**) HTML *m*

hub /hʌb/ *n* (of wheel) moyeu *m*; (fig) centre *m*

hubcap /ˈhʌbkæp/ *n* enjoliveur *m*

huddle /ˈhʌdl/ *vi* **to ~ around** se presser autour de ‹*fire, radio*›; **to ~ together** se serrer les uns contre les autres

hue /hjuː/ *n* **1** (colour) couleur *f*, teinte *f*
2 **~ and cry** tollé *m*

huff /hʌf/ (fam) **A** *n* **in a ~** vexé/-e
B *vi* souffler

hug /hʌg/ **A** *n* étreinte *f*; **to give sb a ~** serrer qn dans ses bras

B *vt* (*p prés etc* **-gg-**) **1** (embrace) serrer [qn] dans ses bras
2 to ~ the coast/kerb serrer la côte/le trottoir

🔑 **huge** /hju:dʒ/ *adj* ‹*object, garden, city, country*› immense; ‹*person, animal*› gigantesque; ‹*appetite, success*› énorme; ‹*debts, sum*› gros/grosse *before n*

hugely /'hju:dʒlɪ/ *adv* **1** (emphatic) extrêmement
2 ‹*increase, vary*› considérablement; ‹*enjoy*› énormément

hull /hʌl/ *n* (of ship, plane) coque *f*; (of tank) carcasse *f*

hum /hʌm/ **A** *n* (of insect, traffic, voices) bourdonnement *m*; (of machinery) ronronnement *m*
B *vi* (*p prés etc* **-mm-**) ‹*person*› fredonner; ‹*insect, aircraft*› bourdonner; ‹*machine*› ronronner

h

🔑 **human** /'hju:mən/ **A** *n* humain *m*
B *adj* ‹*body, behaviour*› humain/-e; ‹*characteristic, rights*› de l'homme

human being *n* être *m* humain

humane /hju:'meɪn/ *adj* ‹*person*› humain/-e; ‹*act*› d'humanité

human interest story *n* histoire *f* vécue

humanitarian /hju:ˌmænɪ'teərɪən/ *adj* humanitaire

humanity /hju:'mænətɪ/ *n* humanité *f*

human nature *n* nature *f* humaine

human resources manager *n* responsable *mf* de la gestion des ressources humaines

human shield *n* bouclier *m* humain

humble /'hʌmbl/ *adj* (gen) modeste; ‹*person*› humble

humid /'hju:mɪd/ *adj* ‹*climate*› humide; ‹*weather*› lourd/-e

humidity /hju:'mɪdətɪ/ *n* humidité *f*

humiliate /hju:'mɪlɪeɪt/ *vt* humilier

humiliating /hju:'mɪlɪeɪtɪŋ/ *adj* humiliant/-e

humiliation /hju:ˌmɪlɪ'eɪʃn/ *n* humiliation *f*

humorous /'hju:mərəs/ *adj* **1** ‹*story, book*› humoristique
2 ‹*person, look*› plein/-e d'humour

humour (BrE), **humor** (AmE) /'hju:mə(r)/
A *n* **1** (wit) humour *m*; **a good sense of ~** le sens de l'humour
2 (mood) humeur *f*; **to be in good/bad ~** être de bonne/mauvaise humeur
B *vt* amadouer ‹*person*›

hump /hʌmp/ *n* bosse *f*

hunch /hʌntʃ/ **A** *n* intuition *f*
B *vt* **to ~ one's shoulders** rentrer les épaules

hunched /hʌntʃt/ *adj* ‹*back, figure*› voûté/-e; ‹*shoulders*› rentré/-e

🔑 **hundred** /'hʌndrəd/ **A** *n* cent *m*; **two ~** deux cents; **two ~ and one** deux cent un; **in nineteen ~** en mille neuf cents; **in nineteen ~ and three** en mille neuf cent trois; **~s of times** des centaines de fois
B *pron, det* cent; **two ~ euros** deux cents euros; **two ~ and five euros** deux cent cinq euros; **about a ~ people** une centaine de personnes

hundredth /'hʌndrətθ/ *n, adj, adv* centième *mf*

hundredweight *n* (BrE) = *50.80 kg*; (AmE) = *45.36 kg*

Hungarian /hʌŋ'geərɪən/ **A** *n* **1** (person) Hongrois/-e *m/f*
2 (language) hongrois *m*
B *adj* hongrois/-e

Hungary /'hʌŋgərɪ/ *pr n* Hongrie *f*

hunger /'hʌŋgə(r)/ *n* faim *f*

hunger strike *n* grève *f* de la faim

hung-over /ˌhʌŋ'əʊvə(r)/ *adj* (fam) **to be ~** avoir la gueule de bois (fam)

hungry /'hʌŋgrɪ/ *adj* **to be ~** avoir faim; **to make sb ~** donner faim à qn; **~ for** assoiffé/-e de ‹*success, power*›

hunk /hʌŋk/ *n* **1** (of bread, cheese) gros morceau *m*
2 (fam) (man) beau mec *m* (fam)

hunt /hʌnt/ **A** *n* **1** (for animals) chasse *f* (**for** à)
2 (search) recherche *f* (**for** de)
B *vt* rechercher ‹*person*›; chasser ‹*animal*›
C *vi* **1** (for prey) chasser
2 (search) **to ~ for sth** chercher [qch] partout ‹*object, person*›

hunter /'hʌntə(r)/ *n* (person) chasseur/-euse *m/f*

hunting /'hʌntɪŋ/ *n* chasse *f* (**of** à); **to go ~** aller à la chasse

hunt saboteur *n* opposant/-e *m/f* à la chasse au renard

hurdle /'hɜ:dl/ *n* **1** (Sport) haie *f*
2 (obstacle) obstacle *m*

hurl /hɜ:l/ *vt* **1** (throw) lancer (**at** sur)
2 (shout) **to ~ insults at sb** accabler qn d'injures

hurrah, **hurray** /hʊ'rɑ:/ *n, excl* hourra *m*

hurricane /'hʌrɪkən, (AmE) -keɪn/ *n* ouragan *m*

hurry /'hʌrɪ/ **A** *n* hâte *f*, empressement *m*; **to be in a ~** être pressé/-e (**to do** de faire); **to leave in a ~** partir à la hâte
B *vt* terminer [qch] à la hâte ‹*meal, task*›; bousculer ‹*person*›
C *vi* se dépêcher (**over doing** de faire); **to ~ out** sortir précipitamment
■ **hurry up** se dépêcher; **~ up!** dépêche-toi!

🔑 **hurt** /hɜ:t/ **A** *adj* (gen) blessé/-e; **to feel ~** être peiné/-e
B *vt* (*prét, pp* **hurt**) **1** (injure) **to ~ oneself** se blesser, se faire mal; **to ~ one's back** se blesser *or* se faire mal au dos
2 (cause pain to) faire mal à; **you're ~ing my arm** vous me faites mal au bras
3 (emotionally) blesser; (offend) froisser; **to ~ sb's feelings** blesser quelqu'un

🔑 mot clé

C *vi* (*prét*, *pp* **hurt**) **1** (be painful) faire mal; **my throat ~s** j'ai mal à la gorge **2** (emotionally) blesser

hurtful /ˈhɜːtfl/ *adj* blessant/-e

hurtle /ˈhɜːtl/ *vi* **to ~ down sth** dévaler qch; **to ~ along a road** foncer sur une route

husband /ˈhʌzbənd/ *n* mari *m*; (on form) époux *m*

hush /hʌʃ/ **A** *n* silence *m*
B *excl* chut!
■ **hush up**: **A** **~ [sth] up** étouffer ‹*affair*›
B **~ [sb] up** faire taire ‹*person*›

hush-hush /ˌhʌʃˈhʌʃ/ *adj* (fam) très confidentiel/-ielle

hustle /ˈhʌsl/ **A** *n* **~ (and bustle)** (lively) effervescence *f*; (tiring) agitation *f*
B *vt* pousser, bousculer ‹*person*›

hut /hʌt/ *n* (gen) cabane *f*; (dwelling) hutte *f*; (on beach) cabine *f* (de plage)

hutch /hʌtʃ/ *n* (for rabbits) clapier *m*

hybrid bike *n* vélo *m* tous chemins, VTC *m*

hydrant /ˈhaɪdrənt/ *n* (*also* **fire ~**) bouche *f* d'incendie

hydraulic /haɪˈdrɔːlɪk/ *adj* hydraulique

hydroelectricity /ˌhaɪdrəʊɪlekˈtrɪsətɪ/ *n* hydroélectricité *f*

hydrofoil /ˈhaɪdrəfɔɪl/ *n* **1** (craft) hydroptère *m* **2** (foil) aile *f* portante

hydrogen /ˈhaɪdrədʒən/ *n* hydrogène *m*

hyena /haɪˈiːnə/ *n* hyène *f*

hygiene /ˈhaɪdʒiːn/ *n* hygiène *f*

hygienic /haɪˈdʒiːnɪk/ *adj* hygiénique

hymn /hɪm/ *n* cantique *m*

hype /haɪp/ *n* (fam) battage *m* publicitaire
■ **hype up** faire du battage pour ‹*film, star, book*›; gonfler ‹*story*›

hyper /ˈhaɪpə(r)/ *adj* (fam) surexcité/-e

hyperactive /ˌhaɪpərˈæktɪv/ *adj* hyperactif/-ive

hyperlink /ˈhaɪpəlɪŋk/ *n* lien *m* (hypertext)

hypermarket /ˈhaɪpəmɑːkɪt/ *n* (BrE) hypermarché *m*

hypertext /ˈhaɪpətekst/ *n* hypertext *m*

hyperventilate /ˌhaɪpəˈventɪleɪt/ *vi* être en hyperventilation

hyphen /ˈhaɪfn/ *n* trait *m* d'union

hypnosis /hɪpˈnəʊsɪs/ *n* hypnose *f*

hypnotherapy /ˌhɪpnəˈθerəpɪ/ *n* hypnothérapie *f*

hypnotist /ˈhɪpnətɪst/ *n* hypnotiseur *m*

hypnotize /ˈhɪpnətaɪz/ *vt* hypnotiser

hypoallergenic /ˌhaɪpəʊæləˈdʒenɪk/ *adj* hypoallergénique

hypocrisy /hɪˈpɒkrəsɪ/ *n* hypocrisie *f*

hypocrite /ˈhɪpəkrɪt/ *n* hypocrite *mf*

hypocritical /ˌhɪpəˈkrɪtɪkl/ *adj* hypocrite

hypodermic /ˌhaɪpəˈdɜːmɪk/ *adj* hypodermique

hypothermia /ˌhaɪpəʊˈθɜːmɪə/ *n* hypothermie *f*

hypothesis /haɪˈpɒθəsɪs/ *n* (*pl* **-theses**) hypothèse *f*

hysteria /hɪˈstɪərɪə/ *n* hystérie *f*

hysterical /hɪˈsterɪkl/ *adj* **1** ‹*person, behaviour*› hystérique **2** (fam) (funny) délirant/-e

hysterics /hɪˈsterɪks/ *n* **1** (fit) crise *f* de nerfs; **to have ~** avoir une crise de nerfs **2** (laughter) **to be in ~** rire aux larmes

Ii

i, **I** *n* i, I *m*

I *pron* je, j'; **I am called Frances** je m'appelle Frances; **I closed the door** j'ai fermé la porte; **he's a student but I'm not** il est étudiant mais moi pas; **he and I went to the cinema** lui et moi sommes allés au cinéma

IBAN *n* (*abbr* = **International Bank Account Number**) IBAN *m*

ice /aɪs/ **A** *n* glace *f*; (on roads) verglas *m*; (in drink) glaçons *mpl*
B *vt* glacer ‹*cake*›
C **iced** *pp adj* ‹*water*› avec des glaçons; **~d tea** thé *m* glacé
■ **ice over** ‹*windscreen, river*› se couvrir de glace

iceberg /ˈaɪsbɜːg/ *n* iceberg *m*

icebox /ˈaɪsbɒks/ *n* **1** (BrE) (freezer compartment) freezer *m* **2** (AmE) (fridge) réfrigérateur *m*

ice-cold *adj* glacé/-e

ice cream *n* glace *f*

ice-cube *n* glaçon *m*

ice hockey *n* hockey *m* sur glace

Iceland /ˈaɪslənd/ *pr n* Islande *f*

Icelandic /aɪsˈlændɪk/ **A** *n* (language) islandais *m*
B *adj* ‹*people, customs*› islandais/-e

ice rink *n* patinoire *f*

ice-skate **A** *n* patin *m* à glace

B *vi* faire du patin *m* à glace

ice-skating *n* patinage *m* sur glace

icicle /ˈaɪsɪkl/ *n* stalactite *f* (de glace)

icing /ˈaɪsɪŋ/ *n* glaçage *m*

icing sugar *n* (BrE) sucre *m* glace

icon /ˈaɪkɒn/ *n* icône *f*

iconize *vt* (Comput) iconiser

icy /ˈaɪsɪ/ *adj* **1** ‹*road*› verglacé/-e
2 ‹*wind*› glacial/-e; ‹*hands*› glacé/-e
3 ‹*look, reception*› glacial/-e

ID *n* pièce *f* d'identité

ID card *n* carte *f* d'identité

🔑 **idea** /aɪˈdɪə/ *n* idée *f* (**about, on** sur); **I have no ~** je n'ai aucune idée; **to have no ~ why/how** ne pas savoir pourquoi/comment; **I've an ~ that he might be lying** j'ai dans l'idée qu'il ment

ideal /aɪˈdiːəl/ **A** *n* idéal *m*
B *adj* idéal/-e

idealism /aɪˈdɪəlɪzəm/ *n* idéalisme *m*

idealist /aɪˈdɪəlɪst/ *n* idéaliste *mf*

idealistic /ˌaɪdɪəˈlɪstɪk/ *adj* idéaliste

idealize /aɪˈdɪəlaɪz/ *vt* idéaliser

ideally /aɪˈdɪəlɪ/ *adv* **1** (preferably) **~, the tests should be free** l'idéal serait que les examens soient gratuits; **~, we'd like to stay** l'idéal pour nous, ce serait de rester
2 (perfectly) **~ situated** idéalement situé/-e

identical /aɪˈdentɪkl/ *adj* identique (**to, with** à)

identical twin *n* vrai jumeau/vraie jumelle *m/f*

identification /aɪˌdentɪfɪˈkeɪʃn/ *n*
1 identification *f* (**with** à)
2 (proof of identity) pièce *f* d'identité

identify /aɪˈdentɪfaɪ/ **A** *vt* identifier (**as** comme étant, **to** à); **to ~ sb/sth with sb/sth** identifier qn/qch à qn/qch
B *vi* **to ~ with** s'identifier à

identikit /aɪˈdentɪkɪt/ *n* (*also* **Identikit®**) portrait-robot *m*

🔑 **identity** /aɪˈdentətɪ/ *n* identité *f*

identity bracelet *n* gourmette *f*

identity card *n* carte *f* d'identité

identity parade *n* (BrE) séance *f* d'identification

identity theft *n* vol *m* d'identité

ideological /ˌaɪdɪəˈlɒdʒɪkl/ *adj* idéologique

ideology /ˌaɪdɪˈɒlədʒɪ/ *n* idéologie *f*

idiom /ˈɪdɪəm/ *n* **1** (phrase) idiome *m*
2 (language) (of speakers) parler *m*; (of theatre, sport) langue *f*; (of music) style *m*

idiomatic /ˌɪdɪəˈmætɪk/ *adj* idiomatique

idiosyncrasy /ˌɪdɪəˈsɪŋkrəsɪ/ *n* particularité *f*

idiosyncratic /ˌɪdɪəsɪŋˈkrætɪk/ *adj* particulier/-ière

idiot /ˈɪdɪət/ *n* idiot/-e *m/f*

idiotic /ˌɪdɪˈɒtɪk/ *adj* bête

🔑 mot clé

idle /ˈaɪdl/ **A** *adj* **1** (lazy) ‹*person*› paresseux/-euse
2 ‹*boast, threat*› vain/-e; ‹*curiosity*› oiseux/-euse; ‹*chatter*› inutile
3 (without occupation) ‹*person*› oisif/-ive; ‹*day, hour, moment*› de loisir
4 ‹*dock, mine*› à l'arrêt; ‹*machine*› arrêté/-e
B *vi* ‹*engine*› tourner au ralenti

■ **idle away** passer [qch] à ne rien faire ‹*day, time*›

idol /ˈaɪdl/ *n* idole *f*

idolize /ˈaɪdəlaɪz/ *vt* adorer ‹*friend, parent*›; idolâtrer ‹*star*›

idyllic /ɪˈdɪlɪk, (AmE) aɪˈd-/ *adj* idyllique

🔑 **ie** (*abbr* = **that is**) c-à-d

🔑 **if** /ɪf/ **A** *conj* **1** si; **~ I won a lot of money, I would travel** si je gagnais beaucoup d'argent, je voyagerais; **~ I had known, I would have told you** si j'avais su, je te l'aurais dit; **~ I were you, I...** (moi) à ta place, je...; **~ not** sinon; **I wonder ~ they will come** je me demande s'ils vont venir; **do you mind ~ I smoke?** cela vous dérange si je fume?; **what ~ he died?** et s'il mourait?
2 (although) bien que; **it's a good shop, ~ a little expensive** c'est un bon magasin, bien qu'un peu cher
B **if only** *phr* **1** (I wish) si seulement; **~ only I had known!** si (seulement) j'avais su!
2 **~ only because (of)** ne serait-ce qu'à cause de; **~ only for a moment** ne serait-ce que pour un instant

iffy /ˈɪfɪ/ *adj* (fam) (dubious) suspect/-e

igloo /ˈɪgluː/ *n* igloo *m*, iglou *m*

ignite /ɪgˈnaɪt/ **A** *vt* faire exploser ‹*fuel*›; enflammer ‹*material*›
B *vi* ‹*petrol, gas*› s'enflammer; ‹*rubbish, timber*› prendre feu

ignition /ɪgˈnɪʃn/ *n* **1** (system) allumage *m*
2 (*also* **~ switch**) contact *m*

ignition key *n* clé *f* de contact

ignorance /ˈɪgnərəns/ *n* ignorance *f*

ignorant /ˈɪgnərənt/ *adj* (of a subject) ignorant/-e; **to be ~ about** tout ignorer de ‹*subject*›; **to be ~ of** ignorer ‹*possibilities*›

🔑 **ignore** /ɪgˈnɔː(r)/ *vt* ignorer ‹*person*›; ne pas relever ‹*mistake, remark*›; ne pas tenir compte de ‹*feeling, fact*›; ne pas suivre ‹*advice*›; se désintéresser complètement de ‹*problem*›

ill /ɪl/ **A** *n* mal *m*; **to wish sb ~** souhaiter du mal à qn
B *adj* malade; **I feel ~** je ne me sens pas bien; **to be taken ~, to fall ~** tomber malade
C *adv* **he is ~ suited to the post** il n'est guère fait pour ce poste; **to speak ~ of sb** dire du mal de qn

ill at ease *adj* gêné/-e, mal à l'aise

🔑 **illegal** /ɪˈliːgl/ **A** *n* (AmE) immigrant/-e *m/f* clandestin/-e
B *adj* (gen) illégal/-e; ‹*parking*› illicite; ‹*immigrant*› clandestin/-e; (Sport)

irrégulier/-ière

illegally /ɪ'li:gəlɪ/ *adv* illégalement

illegible /ɪ'ledʒəbl/ *adj* illisible

illegitimate /ˌɪlɪ'dʒɪtɪmət/ *adj* illégitime

ill-equipped *adj* mal équipé/-e

ill-fitting *adj* ‹*garment, shoe*› qui va mal

ill health *n* mauvaise santé *f*

illicit /ɪ'lɪsɪt/ *adj* illicite

ill-informed *adj* mal informé/-e

illiterate /ɪ'lɪtərət/ *n, adj* analphabète *mf*

illness /'ɪlnɪs/ *n* maladie *f*

illogical /ɪ'lɒdʒɪkl/ *adj* illogique

ill-treatment *n* mauvais traitements *mpl*

illuminate /ɪ'lu:mɪneɪt/ *vt* éclairer

illuminated /ɪ'lu:mɪneɪtɪd/ *adj* ‹*sign*› lumineux/-euse

illumination /ɪˌlu:mɪ'neɪʃn/ *n* (lighting) éclairage *m*

illuminations *npl* (BrE) illuminations *fpl*

illusion /ɪ'lu:ʒn/ *n* illusion *f*; **to have no ~s about sth** ne pas se faire d'illusions sur qch; **to be** *or* **to labour under the ~ that** s'imaginer que

illustrate /'ɪləstreɪt/ *vt* illustrer

illustration /ˌɪlə'streɪʃn/ *n* illustration *f*

illustrator /'ɪləstreɪtə(r)/ *n* illustrateur/-trice *m/f*

ill will *n* rancune *f*

image /'ɪmɪdʒ/ *n* (gen) image *f*; (of company, personality) image *f* de marque; **he is the (spitting) ~ of you** c'est toi tout craché

image-conscious *adj* conscient/-e de son image de marque

image maker *n* professionnel/-elle *m/f* de l'image de marque

image processing *n* traitement *m* de l'image

imagery /'ɪmɪdʒərɪ/ *n* images *fpl*

imaginary /ɪ'mædʒɪnərɪ, (AmE) -ənerɪ/ *adj* imaginaire

imagination /ɪˌmædʒɪ'neɪʃn/ *n* imagination *f*

imaginative /ɪ'mædʒɪnətɪv, (AmE) -əneɪtɪv/ *adj* ‹*person, performance*› plein d'imagination; ‹*mind*› imaginatif/-ive; ‹*solution, device*› ingénieux/-ieuse

imagine /ɪ'mædʒɪn/ *vt* **1** (visualize, picture) (s')imaginer; **to ~ being rich/king** s'imaginer riche/roi; **you must have ~d it** ce doit être un effet de ton imagination
2 (suppose) supposer, imaginer (**that** que)

imbalance /ˌɪm'bæləns/ *n* déséquilibre *m*

imbecile /'ɪmbəsi:l, (AmE) -sl/ *n, adj* imbécile *mf*

imitate /'ɪmɪteɪt/ *vt* imiter

imitation /ˌɪmɪ'teɪʃn/ **A** *n* imitation *f*
B *adj* ‹*snow*› artificiel/-ielle; **~ fur** imitation *f* fourrure; **~ jewel** faux bijou *m*; **~ leather** similicuir *m*

imitator /'ɪmɪteɪtə(r)/ *n* imitateur/-trice *m/f*

immaculate /ɪ'mækjʊlət/ *adj* ‹*dress, manners*› impeccable; ‹*performance*› parfait/-e

immaterial /ˌɪmə'tɪərɪəl/ *adj* **1** (unimportant) sans importance
2 (intangible) immatériel/-ielle

immature /ˌɪmə'tjʊə(r), (AmE) -tʊər/ *adj* **1** ‹*plant*› qui n'est pas arrivé à maturité
2 (childish) immature; **don't be so ~!** ne te conduis pas comme un enfant!

immediate /ɪ'mi:dɪət/ *adj* **1** ‹*effect, reaction*› immédiat/-e; ‹*thought*› premier/-ière *before n*
2 ‹*concern, goal*› premier/-ière *before n*; ‹*problem, crisis*› urgent/-e
3 ‹*vicinity*› immédiat/-e; **his ~ family** ses proches; **in the ~ future** dans l'avenir proche

immediately /ɪ'mi:dɪətlɪ/ *adv* immédiatement; **~ after/before** juste après/avant

immense /ɪ'mens/ *adj* immense

immerse /ɪ'mɜ:s/ *vt* plonger (**in** dans)

immersion course *n* (BrE) cours *m* avec immersion linguistique

immigrant /'ɪmɪgrənt/ *n, adj* (recent) immigrant/-e *m/f*; (established) immigré/-e *m/f*

immigration /ˌɪmɪ'greɪʃn/ *n* immigration *f*

immigration control *n* (system) contrôle *m* de l'immigration

imminent /'ɪmɪnənt/ *adj* imminent/-e

immobile /ɪ'məʊbaɪl, (AmE) -bl/ *adj* immobile

immobilize /ɪ'məʊbɪlaɪz/ *vt* paralyser ‹*traffic, organization*›; immobiliser ‹*engine, patient, limb*›

immobilizer /ɪ'məʊbɪlaɪzə(r)/ *n* système *m* antidémarrage

immoral /ɪ'mɒrəl, (AmE) ɪ'mɔ:rəl/ *adj* immoral/-e

immorality /ˌɪmə'rælətɪ/ *n* immoralité *f*

immortal /ɪ'mɔ:tl/ *n, adj* immortel/-elle *m/f*

immortality /ˌɪmɔ:'tælətɪ/ *n* immortalité *f*

immortalize /ɪ'mɔ:təlaɪz/ *vt* immortaliser

immune /ɪ'mju:n/ *adj* **1** (Med) ‹*person*› immunisé/-e (**to** contre); ‹*reaction, system*› immunitaire
2 (oblivious) **~ to** insensible à
3 to be ~ from être à l'abri de ‹*attack, arrest*›; être exempté/-e de ‹*tax*›

immunity /ɪ'mju:nətɪ/ *n* immunité *f* (**to, against** contre)

immunize /'ɪmju:naɪz/ *vt* immuniser

impact /'ɪmpækt/ *n* **1** (effect) impact *m* (**on** sur); **to make an ~** faire de l'effet
2 (of hammer, vehicle) choc *m*; (of bomb, bullet) impact *m*; **on ~** au moment de l'impact

impair /ɪm'peə(r)/ *vt* affecter ‹*performance*›; diminuer ‹*ability*›; affaiblir ‹*hearing, vision*›; détériorer ‹*health*›

impaired /ɪm'peəd/ *adj* ‹*hearing, vision*› affaibli/-e; **his speech is ~** il a des problèmes d'élocution

impart /ɪm'pɑːt/ *vt* **1** transmettre ‹*knowledge, enthusiasm*› (**to** à); communiquer ‹*information*› (**to** à)
2 donner ‹*atmosphere*›

impartial /ɪm'pɑːʃl/ *adj* ‹*advice, judge*› impartial/-e; ‹*account*› objectif/-ive

impassable /ɪm'pɑːsəbl, (AmE) -'pæs-/ *adj* ‹*obstacle*› infranchissable; ‹*road*› impraticable

impassive /ɪm'pæsɪv/ *adj* impassible

impatience /ɪm'peɪʃns/ *n* **1** (eagerness) impatience *f* (**to do** de faire)
2 (irritation) agacement *m* (**with** à l'égard de, **at** devant)

impatient /ɪm'peɪʃnt/ *adj* **1** (eager) ‹*person*› impatient/-e; ‹*gesture, tone*› d'impatience; **to be ~ to do** être impatient/-e *or* avoir hâte de faire
2 (irritable) agacé/-e (**at** par); **to be/get ~ with sb** s'impatienter contre qn

impeach /ɪm'piːtʃ/ *vt* mettre [qn] en accusation

impeccable /ɪm'pekəbl/ *adj* ‹*behaviour*› irréprochable; ‹*appearance*› impeccable

impede /ɪm'piːd/ *vt* entraver

impending /ɪm'pendɪŋ/ *adj* imminent/-e

impenetrable /ɪm'penɪtrəbl/ *adj* impénétrable

imperative /ɪm'perətɪv/ **A** *n* impératif *m*
B *adj* ‹*need*› urgent/-e; ‹*tone*› impérieux/-ieuse

imperceptible /ˌɪmpə'septəbl/ *adj* imperceptible

imperfect /ɪm'pɜːfɪkt/ **A** *n* imparfait *m*
B *adj* ‹*goods*› défectueux/-euse; ‹*logic, knowledge*› imparfait/-e; **the ~ tense** l'imparfait *m*

imperial /ɪm'pɪərɪəl/ *adj* **1** (gen) impérial/-e
2 (BrE) ‹*measure*› conforme aux normes britanniques

imperious /ɪm'pɪərɪəs/ *adj* impérieux/-ieuse

impersonal /ɪm'pɜːsənl/ *adj* impersonnel/-elle

impersonate /ɪm'pɜːsəneɪt/ *vt* (imitate) imiter; (pretend to be) se faire passer pour ‹*police officer*›

impersonator /ɪm'pɜːsəneɪtə(r)/ *n* imitateur/-trice *m/f*

impertinent /ɪm'pɜːtɪnənt/ *adj* impertinent/-e (**to** envers)

impervious /ɪm'pɜːvɪəs/ *adj* (to charm, suffering) indifférent/-e (**to** à); (to demands) imperméable (**to** à)

impetuous /ɪm'petʃʊəs/ *adj* ‹*person*› impétueux/-euse; ‹*action*› impulsif/-ive

impetus /'ɪmpɪtəs/ *n* **1** impulsion *f* (**to** à)
2 (momentum) élan *m*; **to gain/lose ~** prendre/perdre de l'élan

impinge /ɪm'pɪndʒ/ *vi* **to ~ on** (restrict) empiéter sur; (affect) affecter

implacable /ɪm'plækəbl/ *adj* implacable

implant **A** /'ɪmplɑːnt, (AmE) -plænt/ *n* implant *m*
B /ɪm'plɑːnt, (AmE) -'plænt/ *vt* implanter (**in** dans)

implausible /ɪm'plɔːzəbl/ *adj* peu plausible

⚷ **implement** **A** /'ɪmplɪmənt/ *n* (gen) instrument *m*; (tool) outil *m*; **farm ~s** outillage *m* agricole
B /'ɪmplɪment/ *vt* exécuter ‹*contract, decision, idea*›; mettre [qch] en application ‹*law*›

implementation /ˌɪmplɪmen'teɪʃn/ *n* (of contract, idea) exécution *f*; (of law, policy) mise *f* en application; (Comput) implémentation *f*

implicate /'ɪmplɪkeɪt/ *vt* impliquer (**in** dans)

implication /ˌɪmplɪ'keɪʃn/ *n* **1** (possible consequence) implication *f*
2 (suggestion) insinuation *f*

implicit /ɪm'plɪsɪt/ *adj* **1** (implied) implicite (**in** dans)
2 ‹*faith, trust*› absolu/-e

imply /ɪm'plaɪ/ *vt* **1** ‹*person*› (insinuate) insinuer (**that** que); (make known) laisser entendre (**that** que)
2 (mean) ‹*argument*› impliquer; ‹*term, word*› laisser supposer (**that** que)

impolite /ˌɪmpə'laɪt/ *adj* impoli/-e (**to** envers)

import **A** /'ɪmpɔːt/ *n* importation *f*
B /ɪm'pɔːt/ *vt* importer (**from** de, **to** en)

⚷ **importance** /ɪm'pɔːtns/ *n* importance *f*

⚷ **important** /ɪm'pɔːtnt/ *adj* important/-e; **it is ~ that** il est important que (+ *subjunctive*); **his children are very ~ to him** ses enfants comptent beaucoup pour lui

importer /ɪm'pɔːtə(r)/ *n* importateur/-trice *m/f*

⚷ **impose** /ɪm'pəʊz/ **A** *vt* imposer ‹*embargo, rule*› (**on sb** à qn, **on sth** sur qch); infliger ‹*sanction*› (**on** à); **to ~ a fine on sb** frapper qn d'une amende; **to ~ a tax on tobacco** imposer le tabac
B *vi* s'imposer; **to ~ on sb's kindness** abuser de la bonté de qn

imposing /ɪm'pəʊzɪŋ/ *adj* ‹*person*› imposant/-e; ‹*sight*› impressionnant/-e

⚷ **impossible** /ɪm'pɒsəbl/ **A** *n* **the ~** l'impossible *m*
B *adj* impossible; **to make it ~ for sb to do** mettre qn dans l'impossibilité de faire

impotent /'ɪmpətənt/ *adj* impuissant/-e

impound /ɪm'paʊnd/ *vt* emmener [qch] à la fourrière ‹*vehicle*›; confisquer ‹*goods*›

impractical /ɪm'præktɪkl/ *adj* ‹*suggestion, idea*› peu réaliste; **to be ~** ‹*person*› manquer d'esprit pratique

imprecise /ˌɪmprɪ'saɪs/ *adj* imprécis/-e

⚷ mot clé

impress /ɪm'pres/ **A** *vt* **1** impressionner ‹*person*› (**with** par, **by doing** en faisant); **they were ~ed** ça leur a fait bonne impression
2 to ~ sth (up)on sb faire bien comprendre qch à qn
B *vi* faire bonne impression

impression /ɪm'preʃn/ *n* **1** (gen) impression *f*; **to be under** *or* **have the ~ that** avoir l'impression que; **to make a good/bad ~** faire bonne/mauvaise impression (**on** sur)
2 (imitation) imitation *f*; **to do ~s** faire des imitations

impressionable /ɪm'preʃənəbl/ *adj* influençable

✓ **impressive** /ɪm'presɪv/ *adj* (gen) impressionnant/-e; ‹*building, sight*› imposant/-e

imprint **A** /'ɪmprɪnt/ *n* empreinte *f*
B /ɪm'prɪnt/ *vt* **1** (fix) graver (**on** dans)
2 (print) imprimer (**on** sur)

imprison /ɪm'prɪzn/ *vt* emprisonner

imprisonment /ɪm'prɪznmənt/ *n* emprisonnement *m*

improbable /ɪm'prɒbəbl/ *adj* (unlikely to happen) improbable; (unlikely to be true) invraisemblable

impromptu /ɪm'prɒmptjuː, (AmE) -tuː/ *adj* impromptu/-e

improper /ɪm'prɒpə(r)/ *adj* (dishonest) irrégulier/-ière; (indecent) indécent/-e; (incorrect) impropre, abusif/-ive

✓ **improve** /ɪm'pruːv/ **A** *vt* (gen) améliorer; augmenter ‹*chances*›; **to ~ one's mind** se cultiver (l'esprit)
B *vi* **1** s'améliorer
2 to ~ on améliorer ‹*score*›; renchérir sur ‹*offer*›

✓ **improvement** /ɪm'pruːvmənt/ *n*
1 amélioration *f* (**in, of, to** de); **the new edition is an ~ on the old one** la nouvelle édition est bien meilleure que l'ancienne
2 (in house) aménagement *m*; **home ~s** aménagements du domicile

improvise /'ɪmprəvaɪz/ **A** *vt* improviser; **an ~d table** une table de fortune
B *vi* improviser

impudent /'ɪmpjʊdənt/ *adj* insolent/-e, impudent/-e

impulse /'ɪmpʌls/ *n* impulsion *f*; **to have a sudden ~ to do** avoir une envie soudaine de faire; **on (an) ~** sur un coup de tête

impulse buy *n* achat *m* d'impulsion

impulsive /ɪm'pʌlsɪv/ *adj* (spontaneous) spontané/-e; (rash) impulsif/-ive

impure /ɪm'pjʊə(r)/ *adj* impur/-e

✓ **in** /ɪn/ **A** *prep* **1** (inside) dans; **~ the box** dans la boîte; **~ the newspaper** dans le journal; **~ the school/town** dans l'école/la ville; **~ school/town** à l'école/en ville; **~ the country(side)** à la campagne; **~ the photo** sur la photo; **chicken ~ a white wine sauce** du poulet à la sauce au vin blanc; **~ Rome** à Rome; **~ France/Spain** en France/Espagne; **~ Canada/the United States** au Canada/aux États-Unis
2 (showing occupation, activity) dans; **~ insurance** dans les assurances; **to be ~ politics** faire de la politique; **to be ~ the team** faire partie de l'équipe
3 (present in) chez; **it's rare ~ cats** c'est rare chez les chats; **he hasn't got it ~ him to succeed** il n'est pas fait pour réussir
4 (showing manner, medium) en; **~ Greek** en grec; **~ B flat** en si bémol; **~ a skirt** en jupe; **dressed ~ black** habillé/-e en noir; **~ pencil/ink** au crayon/à l'encre; **to speak ~ a whisper** chuchoter; **~ pairs** par deux; **~ a circle** en cercle; **~ the rain** sous la pluie
5 (as regards) **rich ~ minerals** riche en minéraux; **deaf ~ one ear** sourd/-e d'une oreille; **10 cm ~ length** 10 cm de long
6 (because of) dans; **~ his hurry** dans sa précipitation; **~ the confusion** dans la mêlée
7 (with present participle) en; **~ accepting** en acceptant; **~ doing so** en faisant cela
8 (with superlatives) de; **the tallest tower ~ the world** la plus grande tour du monde
9 (in ratios) **a gradient of 1 ~ 4** une pente de 25%; **a tax of 20 pence ~ the pound** une taxe de 20 pence par livre sterling; **to have a one ~ five chance** avoir une chance sur cinq
10 (with numbers) **she's ~ her twenties** elle a entre vingt et trente ans; **to cut sth ~ three** couper qch en trois; **the temperature was ~ the thirties** il faisait dans les trente degrés
11 (during) **~ May** en mai; **~ 1963** en 1963; **~ summer** en été; **~ the night** pendant la nuit; **~ the morning(s)** le matin; **at four ~ the morning** à quatre heures du matin; **~ the twenties** dans les années 20
12 (within) **~ ten minutes** en dix minutes; **I'll be back ~ half an hour** je serai de retour dans une demi-heure
13 (for) depuis; **it hasn't rained ~ weeks** il n'a pas plu depuis des semaines
B *adv* **1 to come ~** entrer; **to run ~** entrer en courant; **to ask** *or* **invite sb ~** faire entrer qn
2 (at home) **to be ~** être là; **to stay ~** rester à la maison
3 (arrived) **the train is ~** le train est en gare; **the ferry is ~** le ferry est à quai
4 the tide is ~ c'est marée haute
5 (Sport) **the ball is ~** la balle est bonne
6 (in supply) **we don't have any ~** nous n'en avons pas en stock; **to get some beer ~** aller chercher de la bière
C *adj* (fam) **to be ~, to be the ~ thing** être à la mode
D in and out *phr* **to come ~ and out** entrer et sortir; **to weave ~ and out of** se faufiler entre ‹*traffic, tables*›
IDIOM **he's ~ for a shock/surprise** il va avoir un choc/être surpris

inability /ˌɪnəˈbɪlətɪ/ *n* incapacité *f* (**to do** de faire)

inaccessible /ˌɪnækˈsesəbl/ *adj* (out of reach) inaccessible; (hard to understand) peu accessible (**to** à)

inaccuracy /ɪnˈækjərəsɪ/ *n* **1** (of report, estimate) inexactitude *f*
2 (error) inexactitude *f*

inaccurate /ɪnˈækjʊrət/ *adj* inexact/-e

inactive /ɪnˈæktɪv/ *adj* inactif/-ive

inadequate /ɪnˈædɪkwət/ *adj* insuffisant/-e (**for** pour)

inadvisable /ˌɪnədˈvaɪzəbl/ *adj* inopportun/-e, à déconseiller

inane /ɪˈneɪn/ *adj* ‹*person, conversation*› idiot/-e; ‹*programme*› débile (fam)

inanimate /ɪnˈænɪmət/ *adj* inanimé/-e

inappropriate /ˌɪnəˈprəʊprɪət/ *adj*
1 ‹*behaviour*› inconvenant/-e, peu convenable; ‹*remark*› inopportun/-e
2 ‹*advice, word*› qui n'est pas approprié

inarticulate /ˌɪnɑːˈtɪkjʊlət/ *adj* **1 to be ~** ne pas savoir s'exprimer
2 ‹*mumble*› inarticulé/-e; ‹*speech*› inintelligible

inasmuch /ˌɪnəzˈmʌtʃ/ *phr* (insofar as) dans la mesure où; (seeing as) vu que

inattentive /ˌɪnəˈtentɪv/ *adj* ‹*pupil*› inattentif/-ive

inaudible /ɪnˈɔːdəbl/ *adj* inaudible

inauguration /ɪˌnɔːgjʊˈreɪʃn/ *n* (of exhibition) inauguration *f*; (of president) investiture *f*

in-between *adj* intermédiaire

inbuilt /ˌɪnˈbɪlt/ *adj* intrinsèque

Inc *n abbr* (AmE) ≈ SA

incapable /ɪnˈkeɪpəbl/ *adj* incapable (**of doing** de faire)

incapacitate /ˌɪnkəˈpæsɪteɪt/ *vt* ‹*accident, illness*› immobiliser

incendiary device *n* engin *m* incendiaire

incense /ˈɪnsens/ *n* encens *m*

incensed /ɪnˈsenst/ *adj* outré/-e (**at** de, **by** par)

incentive /ɪnˈsentɪv/ *n* **1 to give sb the ~ to do** donner envie à qn de faire; **there is no ~ for people to save** rien n'incite les gens à faire des économies
2 (*also* **cash ~**) prime *f*

incentive scheme *n* système *m* de primes d'encouragement

incessant /ɪnˈsesnt/ *adj* incessant/-e

incessantly /ɪnˈsesntlɪ/ *adv* sans cesse

incest /ˈɪnsest/ *n* inceste *m*

incestuous /ɪnˈsestjʊəs, (AmE) -tʃʊəs/ *adj* incestueux/-euse

⚷ **inch** /ɪntʃ/ *n* (*pl* **~es**) **1** pouce *m* (*= 2.54 cm*)
2 ~ by ~ petit à petit; **to come within an ~ of winning** passer à deux doigts de la victoire

inch-perfect *adj* parfait/-e; **an ~ pass** une passe millimétrée

incidence /ˈɪnsɪdəns/ *n* **the ~ of** la fréquence de ‹*thefts, deaths*›; **high/low ~ of sth** taux élevé/faible de qch

⚷ **incident** /ˈɪnsɪdənt/ *n* incident *m*

incidental /ˌɪnsɪˈdentl/ *adj* ‹*detail, remark*› secondaire

incidentally /ˌɪnsɪˈdentlɪ/ *adv* (by the way) à propos; (by chance) par la même occasion

incident room *n* bureau *m* des enquêteurs

incinerate /ɪnˈsɪnəreɪt/ *vt* incinérer

incite /ɪnˈsaɪt/ *vt* **to ~ violence** inciter à la violence; **to ~ sb to do** pousser *or* inciter qn à faire

inclination /ˌɪŋklɪˈneɪʃn/ *n* inclination *f*

incline /ɪnˈklaɪn/ **A** *vt* **1** incliner ‹*head*›
2 to be ~d to do avoir tendance à faire; **if you feel so ~d** si l'envie vous en prend
B *vi* **1** (tend) **to ~ to** *or* **towards** tendre vers
2 ‹*road, tower*› s'incliner

⚷ **include** /ɪnˈkluːd/ *vt* inclure, comprendre; **all the ministers, Blanc ~d** tous les ministres, Blanc inclu; **breakfast is ~d in the price** le petit déjeuner est compris

including /ɪnˈkluːdɪŋ/ *prep* (y) compris; **£50 ~ VAT** 50 livres sterling TVA comprise; **~ service** service compris; **~ July** y compris juillet; **not ~ July** sans compter juillet

inclusive /ɪnˈkluːsɪv/ *adj* inclus/-e; ‹*price*› forfaitaire; **all-~** tout compris

incoherent /ˌɪŋkəʊˈhɪərənt/ *adj* incohérent/-e

⚷ **income** /ˈɪŋkʌm/ *n* revenus *mpl*, revenu *m*

income bracket *n* tranche *f* de revenu

income tax *n* impôt *m* sur le revenu

incoming /ˈɪnkʌmɪŋ/ *adj* ‹*call, mail*› qui vient de l'extérieur; ‹*government*› nouveau/-elle; ‹*tide*› montant/-e

incomparable /ɪnˈkɒmprəbl/ *adj* sans pareil/-eille

incompatible /ˌɪŋkəmˈpætɪbl/ *adj* incompatible

incompetent /ɪnˈkɒmpɪtənt/ *adj* ‹*doctor, government*› incompétent/-e; ‹*work, performance*› mauvais/-e *before n*

incomplete /ˌɪŋkəmˈpliːt/ *adj* **1** ‹*work, building*› inachevé/-e
2 ‹*set*› incomplet/-ète

incomprehensible /ɪnˌkɒmprɪˈhensəbl/ *adj* ‹*reason*› incompréhensible; ‹*speech*› inintelligible

inconceivable /ˌɪŋkənˈsiːvəbl/ *adj* inconcevable

inconclusive /ˌɪŋkənˈkluːsɪv/ *adj* ‹*meeting*› sans conclusion véritable; ‹*evidence*› peu concluant/-e

incongruous /ɪnˈkɒŋgrʊəs/ *adj* ‹*sight*› déconcertant/-e; ‹*appearance*›

i

surprenant/-e

inconsiderate /ˌɪŋkən'sɪdərət/ *adj* ‹*person*› peu attentif/-ive à autrui; ‹*remark*› maladroit/-e; **to be ~ towards sb** manquer d'égards envers qn

inconsistent /ˌɪŋkən'sɪstənt/ *adj* ‹*work*› inégal/-e; ‹*behaviour*› changeant/-e; ‹*argument*› incohérent/-e; ‹*attitude*› inconsistant/-e; **to be ~ with** être en contradiction avec

inconspicuous /ˌɪŋkən'spɪkjʊəs/ *adj* ‹*person*› qui passe inaperçu/-e; ‹*place, clothing*› discret/-ète

inconvenience /ˌɪŋkən'viːnɪəns/ **A** *n* 1 (trouble) dérangement *m*; **to put sb to great ~** causer beaucoup de dérangement à qn
2 (disadvantage) inconvénient *m*
B *vt* déranger

inconvenient /ˌɪŋkən'viːnɪənt/ *adj* ‹*location, arrangement*› incommode; ‹*time*› inopportun/-e

incorporate /ɪn'kɔːpəreɪt/ *vt* **1** (make part of) incorporer (**into** dans)
2 (contain) comporter
3 Smith and Brown Incorporated Smith et Brown SA

incorrect /ˌɪŋkə'rekt/ *adj* incorrect/-e (**to do** de faire)

incorrigible /ɪn'kɒrɪdʒəbl, (AmE) -'kɔːr-/ *adj* incorrigible

increase **A** /'ɪŋkriːs/ *n* **1** (in amount) augmentation *f* (**in, of** de); **a 5% ~** une augmentation de 5%
2 (in degree) accroissement *m*; **to be on the ~** être en progression
B /ɪn'kriːs/ *vt* augmenter (**by** de, **to** jusqu'à)
C /ɪn'kriːs/ *vi* augmenter (**by** de); **to ~ in value** prendre de la valeur; **to ~ in size** s'agrandir

increased *adj* ‹*demand, risk*› accru/-e

increasing *adj* ‹*number*› croissant/-e

increasingly /'ɪŋkriːsɪŋlɪ/ *adv* de plus en plus

incredible /ɪn'kredəbl/ *adj* incroyable

incredulous /ɪn'kredjʊləs, (AmE) -dʒə-/ *adj* incrédule

incriminating /ɪn'krɪmɪneɪtɪŋ/ *adj* ‹*statement, document*› compromettant/-e; ‹*evidence*› incriminant/-e

incubator /'ɪŋkjʊbeɪtə(r)/ *n* (for child) couveuse *f*; (for eggs, bacteria) incubateur *m*

incur /ɪn'kɜː(r)/ *vt* (*p prés etc* **-rr-**) contracter ‹*debts*›; subir ‹*loss*›; encourir ‹*expense, risk, wrath*›

incurable /ɪn'kjʊərəbl/ *adj* **1** ‹*disease*› incurable
2 ‹*optimist, romantic*› incorrigible

incursion /ɪn'kɜːʃn, (AmE) -ʒn/ *n* (gen) intrusion *f*; (Mil) incursion *f*

indebted /ɪn'detɪd/ *adj* **to be ~ to sb** (under an obligation) être redevable à qn; (grateful) être reconnaissant/-e à qn

indecent /ɪn'diːsnt/ *adj* **1** (improper) indécent/-e
2 (unreasonable) ‹*haste*› malséant/-e

indecent assault *n* attentat *m* à la pudeur

indecent exposure *n* outrage *m* public à la pudeur

indecisive /ˌɪndɪ'saɪsɪv/ *adj* (gen) indécis/-e (**about** quant à); ‹*battle, election*› peu concluant/-e

indeed /ɪn'diːd/ *adv* **1** (certainly) en effet, effectivement; **yes ~!** bien sûr que oui!; **'~ you can'** 'bien sûr que oui'
2 (in fact) en fait
3 (for emphasis) vraiment; **that was praise ~** c'était vraiment un compliment; **thank you very much ~** merci mille fois

indefinite /ɪn'defɪnət/ *adj* **1** (vague) vague
2 ‹*period, delay*› illimité/-e; ‹*number*› indéterminé/-e
3 the ~ article l'article *m* indéfini

indefinitely /ɪn'defɪnətlɪ/ *adv* ‹*continue, stay*› indéfiniment; ‹*postpone, ban*› pour une durée indéterminée

indelible /ɪn'deləbl/ *adj* ‹*ink, mark*› indélébile; ‹*impression*› ineffaçable

independence /ˌɪndɪ'pendəns/ *n* indépendance *f*

Independence Day *n* (AmE) fête *f* de l'Indépendance

independent /ˌɪndɪ'pendənt/ *adj* indépendant/-e (**of** de)

in-depth /ˌɪn'depθ/ **A** *adj* ‹*analysis, study*› approfondi/-e; ‹*guide*› détaillé/-e
B in depth *adv* ‹*examine, study*› en détail

indescribable /ˌɪndɪ'skraɪbəbl/ *adj* ‹*chaos, noise*› indescriptible; ‹*pleasure, beauty*› inexprimable

indestructible /ˌɪndɪ'strʌktəbl/ *adj* indestructible

index /'ɪndeks/ *n* (*pl* **~es** *ou* **-ices**) **1** (of book) index *m inv*
2 (catalogue) catalogue *m*; **card ~** fichier *m*
3 (Econ) indice *m*

index card *n* fiche *f*

index finger *n* index *m inv*

index-linked *adj* indexé/-e

India /'ɪndɪə/ *pr n* Inde *f*

Indian /'ɪndɪən/ **A** *n* **1** (from India) Indien/-ienne *m/f*
2 (Native American) Indien/-ienne *m/f* d'Amérique
B *adj* **1** (of India) indien/-ienne
2 (Native American) indien/-ienne, amérindien/-ienne

Indian Ocean *pr n* **the ~** l'océan *m* Indien

Indian summer *n* été *m* de la Saint Martin

indicate /'ɪndɪkeɪt/ **A** *vt* indiquer (**that** que, **with** de)
B *vi* ‹*driver*› mettre son clignotant; ‹*cyclist*› faire signe

indication /ˌɪndɪˈkeɪʃn/ *n* indication *f*, indice *m*

indicative /ɪnˈdɪkətɪv/ **A** *n* (in grammar) indicatif *m*
B *adj* **to be ~ of** montrer

indicator /ˈɪndɪkeɪtə(r)/ *n* **1** (pointer) aiguille *f*
2 (board) tableau *m*
3 (on car) clignotant *m*

indict /ɪnˈdaɪt/ *vt* inculper

indictment /ɪnˈdaɪtmənt/ *n* **1** (Law) acte *m* d'accusation
2 (criticism) mise *f* en accusation

indie /ˈɪndɪ/ *adj* (fam) (Mus) indépendant/-e

indifference /ɪnˈdɪfrəns/ *n* indifférence *f*

indifferent /ɪnˈdɪfrənt/ *adj* **1** (uninterested) indifférent/-e (**to, as to** à)
2 (mediocre) médiocre

indigenous /ɪnˈdɪdʒɪnəs/ *adj* indigène (**to** à)

i

indigestion /ˌɪndɪˈdʒestʃn/ *n* indigestion *f*; **to have ~** avoir des brûlures d'estomac

indignant /ɪnˈdɪgnənt/ *adj* indigné/-e (**at** de, **about, over** par)

indigo /ˈɪndɪgəʊ/ *n, adj* indigo *m inv*

indirect /ˌɪndɪˈrekt, -daɪˈr-/ *adj* indirect/-e

indirectly /ˌɪndɪˈrektlɪ, -daɪˈr-/ *adv* indirectement

indirect speech *n* discours *m* indirect

indiscreet /ˌɪndɪˈskriːt/ *adj* indiscret/-ète

indiscretion /ˌɪndɪˈskreʃn/ *n* (lack of discretion) manque *m* de discrétion; (act) indiscrétion *f*

indiscriminate /ˌɪndɪˈskrɪmɪnət/ *adj*
1 (random) sans distinction
2 ‹*person*› sans discernement

indispensable /ˌɪndɪˈspensəbl/ *adj* indispensable

indisputable /ˌɪndɪˈspjuːtəbl/ *adj* ‹*champion*› indiscuté/-e; ‹*fact*› indiscutable

indistinct /ˌɪndɪˈstɪŋkt/ *adj* ‹*sound, markings*› indistinct/-e; ‹*memory*› confus/-e; ‹*photograph*› flou/-e

🔑 **individual** /ˌɪndɪˈvɪdʒʊəl/ **A** *n* individu *m*
B *adj* **1** ‹*effort, freedom, portion*› individuel/-elle; ‹*comfort, attitude*› personnel/-elle; ‹*tuition*› particulier/-ière
2 (separate) **each ~ article** chaque article (individuellement)
3 (idiosyncratic) particulier/-ière

individuality /ˌɪndɪˌvɪdʒʊˈælətɪ/ *n* individualité *f*

individually /ˌɪndɪˈvɪdʒʊəlɪ/ *adv* (personally, in person) individuellement; (one at a time) séparément

indoctrinate /ɪnˈdɒktrɪneɪt/ *vt* endoctriner

Indonesia /ˌɪndəʊˈniːzjə/ *pr n* Indonésie *f*

indoor /ˈɪndɔː(r)/ *adj* ‹*pool, court*› couvert/-e; ‹*lavatory*› à l'intérieur; ‹*photography, shoes*› d'intérieur; ‹*sports facilities*› en salle

indoors /ˌɪnˈdɔːz/ *adv* à l'intérieur, dans la maison; **~ and outdoors** dedans et dehors; **to go ~** rentrer

induce /ɪnˈdjuːs, (AmE) -duːs/ *vt* **1** (persuade) persuader (**to do** de faire); (stronger) inciter (**to** à, **to do** à faire)
2 (bring about) provoquer

induction course *n* stage *m* d'introduction

induction loop *n* boucle *f* magnétique

indulge /ɪnˈdʌldʒ/ **A** *vt* **1** céder à ‹*whim, desire*›
2 gâter ‹*child*›; céder à ‹*adult*›
B *vi* **to ~ in** se livrer à ‹*speculation*›; se complaire dans ‹*nostalgia*›; se laisser tenter par ‹*food*›
C *v refl* **to ~ oneself** se faire plaisir

indulgence /ɪnˈdʌldʒəns/ *n* **1** (tolerance) indulgence *f* (**towards** envers, **for** pour)
2 ~ in food gourmandise *f*; **it's my one ~** c'est mon péché mignon

indulgent /ɪnˈdʌldʒənt/ *adj* indulgent/-e (**to, towards** pour, envers)

🔑 **industrial** /ɪnˈdʌstrɪəl/ *adj* (gen) industriel/-ielle; ‹*accident*› du travail

industrial action *n* (BrE) (strike) grève *f*

industrial estate *n* (BrE) zone *f* industrielle

industrialize /ɪnˈdʌstrɪəlaɪz/ *vt* industrialiser

industrial relations *npl* relations *fpl* entre les patrons et les ouvriers

industrial waste *n* déchets *mpl* industriels

industrious /ɪnˈdʌstrɪəs/ *adj* diligent/-e

🔑 **industry** /ˈɪndəstrɪ/ *n* **1** industrie *f*; **the oil ~** l'industrie du pétrole
2 (diligence) zèle *m* (au travail)

inedible /ɪnˈedɪbl/ *adj* ‹*meal*› immangeable; ‹*plants*› non comestible

ineffective /ˌɪnɪˈfektɪv/ *adj* inefficace

ineffectual /ˌɪnɪˈfektʃʊəl/ *adj* ‹*person*› incapable; ‹*policy*› inefficace; ‹*attempt*› infructueux/-euse

inefficiency /ˌɪnɪˈfɪʃnsɪ/ *n* (lack of organization) manque *m* d'organisation; (incompetence) incompétence *f*; (of machine, method) inefficacité *f*

inefficient /ˌɪnɪˈfɪʃnt/ *adj* (disorganized) mal organisé/-e; (incompetent) incompétent/-e; (not effective) inefficace

ineligible /ɪnˈelɪdʒəbl/ *adj* **to be ~** (for job) ne pas remplir les conditions pour poser sa candidature (**for** à); (for election) être inéligible; (for pension, benefit) ne pas avoir droit (**for** à)

inequality /ˌɪnɪˈkwɒlətɪ/ *n* inégalité *f*

inert /ɪˈnɜːt/ *adj* inerte

inertia /ɪˈnɜːʃə/ *n* inertie *f*

inevitable /ɪnˈevɪtəbl/ *adj* inévitable (**that** que (+ *subjunctive*))

🔑 mot clé

inexcusable /ˌɪnɪk'skjuːzəbl/ *adj* inexcusable (**that** que (+ *subjunctive*))

inexhaustible /ˌɪnɪg'zɔːstəbl/ *adj* inépuisable

inexpensive /ˌɪnɪk'spensɪv/ *adj* pas cher/chère

inexperienced /ˌɪnɪk'spɪərɪənst/ *adj* inexpérimenté/-e

inexplicable /ˌɪnɪk'splɪkəbl/ *adj* inexplicable

infallible /ɪn'fæləbl/ *adj* infaillible

infamous /'ɪnfəməs/ *adj* ‹*person*› tristement célèbre; ‹*crime*› infâme

infancy /'ɪnfənsɪ/ *n* **1** petite enfance *f* **2** (fig) débuts *mpl*; **in its ~** à ses débuts

infant /'ɪnfənt/ *n* (baby) bébé *m*; (child) petit enfant *m*

infantry /'ɪnfəntrɪ/ *n* infanterie *f*, fantassins *mpl*

infant school *n* ≈ école *f* maternelle

infatuated *adj* **to be ~ with** être entiché/-e de

infatuation /ɪnˌfætʃʊ'eɪʃn/ *n* engouement *m* (**with** pour)

infect /ɪn'fekt/ *vt* contaminer ‹*person, blood, food*›; infecter ‹*wound*›

infection /ɪn'fekʃn/ *n* infection *f*

infectious /ɪn'fekʃəs/ *adj* **1** ‹*disease*› infectieux/-ieuse; ‹*person*› contagieux/-ieuse **2** ‹*laughter*› communicatif/-ive

infer /ɪn'fɜː(r)/ *vt* (*p prés etc* **-rr-**) déduire

inferior /ɪn'fɪərɪə(r)/ **A** *n* inférieur/-e *m/f* **B** *adj* **1** ‹*goods, work*› de qualité inférieure **2** ‹*position*› inférieur/-e; **to make sb feel ~** donner un sentiment d'infériorité à qn

inferiority /ɪnˌfɪərɪ'ɒrətɪ, (AmE) -'ɔːr-/ *n* infériorité *f* (**to** vis-à-vis de)

inferiority complex *n* complexe *m* d'infériorité

inferno /ɪn'fɜːnəʊ/ *n* brasier *m*

infertile /ɪn'fɜːtaɪl, (AmE) -tl/ *adj* ‹*land*› infertile; ‹*person*› stérile

infertility /ˌɪnfə'tɪlətɪ/ *n* stérilité *f*

infest /ɪn'fest/ *vt* infester (**with** de)

infidelity /ˌɪnfɪ'delətɪ/ *n* infidélité *f*

infighting /'ɪnfaɪtɪŋ/ *n* conflits *mpl* internes

infiltrate /'ɪnfɪltreɪt/ *vt* infiltrer ‹*organization, group*›

infinite /'ɪnfɪnət/ *adj* infini/-e

infinitely /'ɪnfɪnətlɪ/ *adv* infiniment

infinitive /ɪn'fɪnətɪv/ *n* infinitif *m*; **in the ~** à l'infinitif

infinity /ɪn'fɪnətɪ/ *n* infini *m*

infinity pool *n* piscine *f* panoramique

infirmary /ɪn'fɜːmərɪ/ *n* **1** (hospital) hôpital *m* **2** (in school, prison) infirmerie *f*

inflamed /ɪn'fleɪmd/ *adj* (Med) enflammé/-e

inflammable /ɪn'flæməbl/ *adj* inflammable

inflammation /ˌɪnflə'meɪʃn/ *n* inflammation *f*

inflatable /ɪn'fleɪtəbl/ *adj* ‹*mattress, dinghy*› pneumatique; ‹*toy*› gonflable

inflate /ɪn'fleɪt/ *vt* gonfler ‹*tyre, dinghy*›

inflation /ɪn'fleɪʃn/ *n* inflation *f*

inflexible /ɪn'fleksəbl/ *adj* **1** ‹*person, attitude*› inflexible; ‹*system*› rigide **2** ‹*material*› rigide

inflict /ɪn'flɪkt/ *vt* infliger ‹*pain, presence, defeat*› (**on** à); causer ‹*damage*› (**on** à)

influence /'ɪnflʊəns/ **A** *n* influence *f*; **to be** *or* **have an ~ on** avoir une influence sur; **to drive while under the ~ of alcohol** conduire en état d'ébriété **B** *vt* influencer ‹*person*› (**in** dans); influer sur ‹*decision, choice, result*›; **to be ~d by sb/sth** se laisser influencer par qn/qch

influential /ˌɪnflʊ'enʃl/ *adj* influent/-e

influenza /ˌɪnflʊ'enzə/ *n* grippe *f*

influx /'ɪnflʌks/ *n* afflux *m*

info /'ɪnfəʊ/ *n* (fam) renseignements *mpl*, tuyaux *mpl* (fam)

inform /ɪn'fɔːm/ **A** *vt* informer, avertir (**of, about** de, **that** du fait que); **to keep sb ~ed** tenir qn informé/-e *or* au courant (**of, as to** de) **B** *vi* **to ~ on** *or* **against** dénoncer

informal /ɪn'fɔːml/ *adj* **1** ‹*person*› sans façons; ‹*manner, style*› simple; ‹*language*› familier/-ière; ‹*clothes*› de tous les jours **2** ‹*visit*› privé/-e; ‹*invitation*› verbal/-e; ‹*discussion, interview*› informel/-elle

information /ˌɪnfə'meɪʃn/ *n* **1** renseignements *mpl*, informations *fpl* (**on, about** sur); **a piece of ~** un renseignement, une information **2** (AmE) (service *m* des) renseignements *mpl*

information desk, **information office** *n* bureau *m* des renseignements

information pack *n* documentation *f*

information superhighway *n* autoroutes *fpl* de l'information

information technology, **IT** *n* informatique *f*

informative /ɪn'fɔːmətɪv/ *adj* instructif/-ive

informer /ɪn'fɔːmə(r)/ *n* indicateur/-trice *m/f*

infrared /ˌɪnfrə'red/ *adj* infrarouge

infrastructure /'ɪnfrəstrʌktʃə(r)/ *n* infrastructure *f*

infringe /ɪn'frɪndʒ/ **A** *vt* enfreindre ‹*rule*›; ne pas respecter ‹*rights*› **B** *vi* **to ~ on** *or* **upon** empiéter sur ‹*rights*›

infringement /ɪn'frɪndʒmənt/ *n* (of rule) infraction *f* (**of** à); (of rights) violation *f*

infuriating /ɪn'fjʊərɪeɪtɪŋ/ *adj* exaspérant/-e

ingenious /ɪn'dʒiːnɪəs/ *adj* ingénieux/-ieuse, astucieux/-ieuse

i

ingenuity /ˌɪndʒɪ'nju:ətɪ, (AmE) -'nu:-/ *n* ingéniosité *f*

ingenuous /ɪn'dʒenjʊəs/ *adj* ingénu/-e, candide

ingot /'ɪŋgət/ *n* lingot *m*

ingrained /ɪn'greɪnd/ *adj* ‹*dirt*› bien incrusté/-e; ‹*habit, hatred*› enraciné/-e

ingratitude /ɪn'grætɪtju:d, (AmE) -tu:d/ *n* ingratitude *f*

ingredient /ɪn'gri:dɪənt/ *n* (Culin) ingrédient *m*; (fig) élément *m* (**of** de)

inhabit /ɪn'hæbɪt/ *vt* **1** habiter ‹*house, region, planet*›
2 vivre dans ‹*fantasy world*›

inhabitant /ɪn'hæbɪtənt/ *n* habitant/-e *m/f*

inhale /ɪn'heɪl/ **A** *vt* aspirer, inhaler
B *vi* (breathe in) inspirer; (smoke) avaler la fumée

inhaler /ɪn'heɪlə(r)/ *n* inhalateur *m*

inherent /ɪn'hɪərənt, ɪn'herənt/ *adj* inhérent/-e (**to** à)

inherit /ɪn'herɪt/ *vt* hériter de ‹*money, property, title*›; **to ~ sth from sb** hériter qch de qn

inheritance /ɪn'herɪtəns/ *n* héritage *m*; **to come into an ~** faire un héritage

inhibit /ɪn'hɪbɪt/ *vt* inhiber ‹*person, reaction*›; entraver ‹*activity, progress*›

inhibited /ɪn'hɪbɪtɪd/ *adj* inhibé/-e, refoulé/-e

inhibition /ˌɪnhɪ'bɪʃn, ˌɪnɪ'b-/ *n* inhibition *f*; **to get rid of one's ~s** se libérer de ses inhibitions

inhospitable /ˌɪnhɒ'spɪtəbl/ *adj* inhospitalier/-ière

in-house /'ɪnhaʊs, -'haʊs/ *adj* interne

inhuman /ɪn'hju:mən/ *adj* inhumain/-e

inhumanity /ˌɪnhju:'mænətɪ/ *n* inhumanité *f* (**to** envers)

⚷ **initial** /ɪ'nɪʃl/ **A** *n* initiale *f*
B *adj* initial/-e; **~ letter** initiale *f*
C *vt* (*p prés etc* **-ll-** (BrE), **-l-** (AmE)) parapher, parafer

⚷ **initially** /ɪ'nɪʃəlɪ/ *adv* au départ

initiate **A** /ɪ'nɪʃɪət/ *n* initié/-e *m/f*
B /ɪ'nɪʃɪeɪt/ *vt* **1** mettre en œuvre ‹*project, reform*›; amorcer ‹*talks*›; entamer, engager ‹*proceedings*›
2 (teach) **to ~ sb into** initier qn à

⚷ **initiative** /ɪ'nɪʃətɪv/ *n* initiative *f*; **on one's own ~** de son propre chef

inject /ɪn'dʒekt/ *vt* injecter ‹*vaccine*› (**into** dans); **to ~ sb (with sth)** faire une injection *or* une piqûre (de qch) à qn

injection /ɪn'dʒekʃn/ *n* **1** (Med) piqûre *f*
2 (Tech) injection *f*

⚷ **injure** /'ɪndʒə(r)/ *vt* **1** blesser ‹*person*›; **to ~ one's hand** se blesser la main
2 nuire à, compromettre ‹*health, reputation*›

injured /'ɪndʒəd/ **A** *n* **the ~** les blessés *mpl*
B *adj* **1** (gen) blessé/-e
2 (Law) **the ~ party** la partie lésée

⚷ **injury** /'ɪndʒərɪ/ *n* blessure *f*; **head injuries** blessures à la tête

injury time *n* (BrE) (Sport) arrêts *mpl* de jeu

injustice /ɪn'dʒʌstɪs/ *n* injustice *f*

ink /ɪŋk/ *n* encre *f*; **in ~** à l'encre

inkjet printer *n* imprimante *f* à jet d'encre

inkling /'ɪŋklɪŋ/ *n* petite idée *f*; **to have an ~ that** avoir idée que

inland **A** /'ɪnlənd/ *adj* intérieur/-e
B /ˌɪn'lænd/ *adv* ‹*travel, lie*› à l'intérieur des terres

Inland Revenue *n* (BrE) service *m* des impôts britannique

in-laws *npl* (parents) beaux-parents *mpl*; (other relatives) belle-famille *f*, parents *mpl* par alliance

inmate /'ɪnmeɪt/ *n* (of mental hospital) interné/-e *m/f*; (of prison) détenu/-e *m/f*

inn /ɪn/ *n* **1** (hotel) auberge *f*
2 (pub) pub *m*

inner /'ɪnə(r)/ *adj* intérieur/-e

inner city **A** *n* **the ~** les quartiers *mpl* déshérités
B **inner-city** *n* ‹*problems*› des quartiers déshérités; ‹*area*› déshérité/-e

innermost /'ɪnəməʊst/ *adj* **sb's ~ thoughts** les pensées les plus intimes de qn

innocence /'ɪnəsns/ *n* innocence *f*

innocent /'ɪnəsnt/ *n, adj* innocent/-e *m/f*

innovation /ˌɪnə'veɪʃn/ *n* innovation *f*

innovative /'ɪnəvətɪv/ *adj* innovateur/-trice

innovator /'ɪnəveɪtə(r)/ *n* innovateur/-trice *m/f*

innuendo /ˌɪnju:'endəʊ/ *n* (*pl* **~s** *ou* **~es**) (veiled slights) insinuations *fpl*; (sexual references) allusions *fpl* grivoises

inoculation /ɪˌnɒkjʊ'leɪʃn/ *n* vaccination *f*, inoculation *f*

inoffensive /ˌɪnə'fensɪv/ *adj* inoffensif/-ive

in-patient *n* malade *mf* hospitalisé/-e

input /'ɪnpʊt/ *n* **1** (of money) apport *m*; (of energy) alimentation *f* (**of** en)
2 (contribution) contribution *f*
3 (Comput) (data) données *fpl* d'entrée *or* à traiter

inquest /'ɪŋkwest/ *n* enquête *f* (**on, into** sur)

inquire /ɪn'kwaɪə(r)/ = **enquire**

⚷ **inquiry** /ɪn'kwaɪərɪ, (AmE) 'ɪŋkwərɪ/ *n* enquête *f* (**into** sur); **murder ~** enquête criminelle; ▶ **enquiry**

inquisitive /ɪn'kwɪzətɪv/ *adj* curieux/-ieuse

insane /ɪn'seɪn/ *adj* (gen) fou/folle; (Law) aliéné/-e

insanitary /ɪn'sænɪtərɪ, (AmE) -terɪ/ *adj* insalubre, malsain/-e

insanity /ɪn'sænətɪ/ *n* (gen) folie *f*; (Law) aliénation *f* mentale

⚷ mot clé

insatiable /ɪn'seɪʃəbl/ *adj* insatiable

inscription /ɪn'skrɪpʃn/ *n* inscription *f*

insect /'ɪnsekt/ *n* insecte *m*; **~ bite** piqûre *f* d'insecte

insecticide /ɪn'sektɪsaɪd/ *n, adj* insecticide *m*

insect repellent *n* insectifuge *m*, produit *m* anti-insecte

insecure /ˌɪnsɪ'kjʊə(r)/ *adj* **1** ‹*person*› qui manque d'assurance
2 ‹*job*› précaire; ‹*investment*› risqué/-e

insecurity /ˌɪnsɪ'kjʊərətɪ/ *n* **1** (psychological) manque *m* d'assurance
2 (of position, situation) insécurité *f*

insensitive /ɪn'sensətɪv/ *adj* ‹*person*› (tactless) sans tact; (unfeeling) insensible (**to** à); ‹*remark*› indélicat/-e

inseparable /ɪn'seprəbl/ *adj* inséparable (**from** de)

insert /ɪn'sɜːt/ *vt* insérer (**in** dans)

inside **A** /'ɪnsaɪd/ *n* intérieur *m*; **to overtake on the ~** (in Europe, US) doubler à droite; (in GB, Australia) doubler à gauche; **people on the ~** les gens qui sont dans la place
B /ɪn'saɪd/ *prep* **~ of** (AmE) **1** à l'intérieur de; **~ the box** à l'intérieur de *or* dans la boîte; **to be ~ (the house)** être à l'intérieur (de la maison)
2 (under) **~ (of) an hour** en moins d'une heure
C /'ɪnsaɪd/ *adj* **1** ‹*cover, pocket*› intérieur/-e; ‹*toilet*› à l'intérieur
2 ‹*information*› de première main
3 the ~ lane (of road) (in Europe, US) la voie de droite; (in GB, Australia) la voie de gauche; (of athletics track) le couloir intérieur
D /ɪn'saɪd/ *adv* (indoors) à l'intérieur; **she's ~** elle est à l'intérieur; **to look ~** regarder à l'intérieur *or* dedans; **to go** *or* **come ~** entrer; **to bring sth ~** rentrer ‹*chairs*›
E **inside out** *phr* à l'envers; **to turn sth ~ out** retourner qch; **to know sb/sth ~ out** connaître qn/qch à fond

insider dealing *n* délit *m* d'initié

insider trading /ɪnˌsaɪdə 'treɪdɪŋ/ *n* délit *m* d'initié

insides *npl* (fam) (of human) intestin *m*, estomac *m*, boyaux *mpl* (fam)

insight /'ɪnsaɪt/ *n* **1** (glimpse, understanding) aperçu *m*, idée *f* (**into** de)
2 (intuition) perspicacité *f*, intuition *f*

insignificant /ˌɪnsɪg'nɪfɪkənt/ *adj* ‹*cost, difference*› négligeable; ‹*person, detail*› insignifiant/-e

insincere /ˌɪnsɪn'sɪə(r)/ *adj* peu sincère; **to be ~** manquer de sincérité

insinuate /ɪn'sɪnjʊeɪt/ *vt* insinuer (**that** que)

insinuation /ɪnˌsɪnjʊ'eɪʃn/ *n* insinuation *f*

insipid /ɪn'sɪpɪd/ *adj* fade

insist /ɪn'sɪst/ **A** *vt* **1** (demand) insister (**that** pour que)
2 (maintain) affirmer (**that** que)
B *vi* insister; **to ~ on** exiger ‹*punctuality, silence*›; **to ~ on doing** vouloir à tout prix faire, tenir à faire

insistent /ɪn'sɪstənt/ *adj* **to be ~** insister (**about** sur, **that** pour que (+ *subjunctive*))

insofar: **insofar as** /ˌɪnsə'fɑː(r)/ *phr* **~ as** dans la mesure où

insole /'ɪnsəʊl/ *n* semelle *f* (intérieure)

insolent /'ɪnsələnt/ *adj* insolent/-e

insomnia /ɪn'sɒmnɪə/ *n* insomnie *f*

inspect /ɪn'spekt/ *vt* examiner [qch] de près ‹*document, product*›; contrôler, vérifier ‹*accounts*›; inspecter ‹*school, factory, pitch, wiring*›; contrôler ‹*passport, ticket, baggage*›

inspection /ɪn'spekʃn/ *n* (gen) inspection *f*; (of ticket, passport) contrôle *m*; **on closer ~** en y regardant de plus près

inspector /ɪn'spektə(r)/ *n* **1** (gen) inspecteur/-trice *m/f*
2 (BrE) **police ~** inspecteur *m* de police
3 (BrE) (on bus) contrôleur/-euse *m/f*

inspiration /ˌɪnspə'reɪʃn/ *n* inspiration *f* (**for** pour)

inspire /ɪn'spaɪə(r)/ *vt* inspirer; **to be ~d by sth** s'inspirer de qch

inspired /ɪn'spaɪəd/ *adj* ‹*person*› inspiré/-e; ‹*idea*› lumineux/-euse; **an ~ guess** une heureuse inspiration

inspiring /ɪn'spaɪərɪŋ/ *adj* ‹*person, speech*› enthousiasmant/-e; ‹*thought*› exaltant/-e

install /ɪn'stɔːl/ (*also* **instal** (BrE)) *vt* **1** installer ‹*equipment, software*›; poser ‹*windows*›
2 to ~ sb in office installer qn

installation /ˌɪnstə'leɪʃn/ *n* installation *f*

instalment (BrE), **installment** (AmE) /ɪn'stɔːlmənt/ *n* versement *m* partiel; **in ~s** en plusieurs versements

instance /'ɪnstəns/ *n* exemple *m*; **for ~** par exemple

instant /'ɪnstənt/ **A** *n* instant *m*; **come here this ~!** viens ici tout de suite!
B *adj* **1** ‹*access, effect, rapport, success*› immédiat/-e; ‹*solution*› instantané/-e
2 ‹*coffee, soup*› instantané/-e

instant camera *n* polaroïd® *m*

instantly /'ɪnstəntlɪ/ *adv* immédiatement

instead /ɪn'sted/ **A** *adv* **we didn't go home—we went to the park ~** au lieu de rentrer nous sommes allés au parc; **let's take a taxi ~** prenons plutôt un taxi; **I was going to phone but wrote ~** j'allais téléphoner mais finalement j'ai écrit; **her son went ~** son fils y est allé à sa place
B **instead of** *phr* **~ of sth/of doing** au lieu de qch/de faire; **use oil ~ of butter** utilisez de l'huile à la place du beurre; **~ of sb** à la place de qn

instep /'ɪnstep/ *n* cou-de-pied *m*

instigate /'ɪnstɪgeɪt/ *vt* lancer ‹*attack*›; engager ‹*proceedings*›

instil (BrE), **instill** (AmE) /ɪn'stɪl/ *vt* (*p prés etc* **-ll-**) inculquer ‹*attitude*› (**in** à); donner ‹*confidence*› (**in** à)

instinct /'ɪnstɪŋkt/ *n* instinct *m* (**for** de)

instinctive /ɪn'stɪŋktɪv/ *adj* instinctif/-ive

⚷ **institute** /'ɪnstɪtjuːt, (AmE) -tuːt/ **A** *n* institut *m*
B *vt* instituer

⚷ **institution** /,ɪnstɪ'tjuːʃn, (AmE) -tuːʃn/ *n* **1** (gen) institution *f*; **financial ~** organisme *m* financier
2 (home, hospital) établissement *m* spécialisé

institutionalize /,ɪnstɪ'tjuːʃənəlaɪz, (AmE) -tuː-/ *vt* **1** (place in care) placer [qn] dans un établissement spécialisé; (in mental hospital) interner
2 (establish officially) institutionnaliser; **~d** ‹*racism, violence*› institutionnalisé/-e

instruct /ɪn'strʌkt/ *vt* **1 to ~ sb to do** donner l'ordre à qn de faire; **to be ~ed to do** recevoir l'ordre de faire
2 (teach) instruire; **to ~ sb in** enseigner [qch] à qn ‹*subject*›

instruction /ɪn'strʌkʃn/ *n* instruction *f*; **~s for use** mode *m* d'emploi

instruction book *n* livret *m* de l'utilisateur

instructor /ɪn'strʌktə(r)/ *n* **1** (in sports, driving) moniteur/-trice *m/f* (**in** de); (military) instructeur *m*
2 (AmE) professeur *m*

⚷ **instrument** /'ɪnstrʊmənt/ *n* instrument *m*; **to play an ~** jouer d'un instrument

instrumental /,ɪnstrʊ'mentl/ **A** *n* instrumental *m*
B *adj* **1 to be ~ in sth/in doing** contribuer à qch/à faire
2 (Mus) instrumental/-e

instrument panel *n* tableau *m* de bord

insufficient /,ɪnsə'fɪʃnt/ *adj* **there are ~ copies** il n'y a pas assez d'exemplaires; **to be ~ for** être insuffisant/-e pour

insulate /'ɪnsjʊleɪt, (AmE) -sə'l-/ *vt* isoler ‹*roof, room, wire*›

insulation /,ɪnsjʊ'leɪʃn, (AmE) -sə'l-/ *n* isolation *f*

insulin /'ɪnsjʊlɪn, (AmE) -səl-/ *n* insuline *f*

insult A /'ɪnsʌlt/ *n* insulte *f*
B /ɪn'sʌlt/ *vt* insulter

⚷ **insurance** /ɪn'ʃɔːrəns, (AmE) -'ʃʊər-/ *n* assurance *f* (**against** contre, **for** pour); **to take out ~ against sth** s'assurer contre qch

insurance policy *n* (police *f* d')assurance *f*

insure /ɪn'ʃɔː(r), (AmE) -'ʃʊər/ *vt* assurer (**against** contre)

intact /ɪn'tækt/ *adj* intact/-e

intake /'ɪnteɪk/ *n* **1** (consumption) consommation *f*
2 (Sch, Univ) (admissions) admissions *fpl*
3 an ~ of breath une inspiration *f*

intangible /ɪn'tændʒəbl/ *adj* insaisissable

integral /'ɪntɪgrəl/ *adj* intégral/-e; ‹*part*› intégrant/-e; **~ to** intrinsèque à

integrate /'ɪntɪgreɪt/ **A** *vt* **1** (incorporate, absorb) intégrer (**into** dans, **with** à)
2 (combine) combiner ‹*systems*›
B *vi* ‹*person*› s'intégrer (**with** à, **into** dans)

integration /,ɪntɪ'greɪʃn/ *n* intégration *f* (**with** à)

integrity /ɪn'tegrətɪ/ *n* intégrité *f*

intellect /'ɪntəlekt/ *n* **1** (mental capacity) intelligence *f*
2 (person) esprit *m*

intellectual /,ɪntə'lektʃʊəl/ *n, adj* intellectuel/-elle *m/f*

⚷ **intelligence** /ɪn'telɪdʒəns/ *n* **1** intelligence *f* (**to do** de faire)
2 (gen), (Mil) (information) renseignements *mpl*
3 (Mil) (secret service) services *mpl* de renseignements

intelligent /ɪn'telɪdʒənt/ *adj* intelligent/-e

intelligible /ɪn'telɪdʒəbl/ *adj* intelligible (**to** à)

⚷ **intend** /ɪn'tend/ *vt* vouloir; **to ~ to do, to ~ doing** avoir l'intention de faire; **to be ~ed for** être destiné/-e à ‹*person*›; être prévu/-e pour ‹*purpose*›

intense /ɪn'tens/ *adj* **1** (gen) intense
2 ‹*person*› sérieux/-ieuse

intensify /ɪn'tensɪfaɪ/ **A** *vt* intensifier
B *vi* s'intensifier

intensive /ɪn'tensɪv/ *adj* intensif/-ive

intensive care *n* **in ~** en réanimation

intensive care unit *n* service *m* de soins intensifs

intent /ɪn'tent/ *adj* ‹*person, expression*› absorbé/-e; **~ on doing** résolu/-e à faire
IDIOM **to all ~s and purposes** quasiment, en fait

⚷ **intention** /ɪn'tenʃn/ *n* intention *f* (**to do, of doing** de faire)

intentional /ɪn'tenʃənl/ *adj* intentionnel/-elle

intentionally /ɪn'tenʃənəlɪ/ *adv* intentionnellement, exprès

interact /,ɪntər'ækt/ *vi* ‹*two factors, phenomena*› agir l'un sur l'autre; ‹*people*› communiquer; (Comput) dialoguer

interactive /,ɪntər'æktɪv/ *adj* interactif/-ive

intercept /,ɪntə'sept/ *vt* intercepter

interchange A /'ɪntətʃeɪndʒ/ *n* **1** (road junction) échangeur *m*
2 (exchange) échange *m*
B /,ɪntə'tʃeɪndʒ/ *vt* échanger

interchangeable /,ɪntə'tʃeɪndʒəbl/ *adj* interchangeable

intercom /'ɪntəkɒm/ *n* interphone® *m*

intercourse /'ɪntəkɔːs/ *n* rapports *mpl* (sexuels)

⚷ **interest** /'ɪntrəst/ **A** *n* **1** (gen) intérêt *m*

⚷ mot clé

(in pour); **to hold sb's ~** retenir l'attention de qn; **it's in your (own) ~(s) to do** il est dans ton intérêt de faire; **to have sb's best ~s at heart** vouloir le bien de qn
2 (hobby) centre *m* d'intérêt
3 (on loan, from investment) intérêts *mpl* (**on** de)
B *vt* intéresser (**in** à)

interested /'ɪntrəstɪd/ *adj* ‹*expression, onlooker*› intéressé/-e; **to be ~ in** s'intéresser à ‹*subject, activity*›; **I am ~ in doing** ça m'intéresse de faire

interest-free *adj* sans intérêt

interesting /'ɪntrəstɪŋ/ *adj* intéressant/-e

interest rate *n* taux *m* d'intérêt

interface /'ɪntəfeɪs/ **A** *n* interface *f*
B *vt* connecter, relier

interfere /ˌɪntə'fɪə(r)/ *vi* **1 to ~ in** se mêler de ‹*affairs*›; **she never ~s** elle ne se mêle jamais de ce qui ne la regarde pas
2 (intervene) intervenir
3 to ~ with ‹*person*› toucher, traficoter (fam) ‹*machine*›
4 to ~ with ‹*activity*› empiéter sur ‹*family life*›

interference /ˌɪntə'fɪərəns/ *n* (on radio) parasites *mpl*

interfering /ˌɪntə'fɪərɪŋ/ *adj* ‹*person*› envahissant/-e

interim /'ɪntərɪm/ **A** *n* **in the ~** entre-temps
B *adj* ‹*arrangement, government*› provisoire; ‹*post, employee*› intérimaire

interior /ɪn'tɪərɪə(r)/ **A** *n* **1** intérieur *m*
2 Secretary/Department of the Interior (AmE) ministre *m* /ministère *m* de l'Intérieur
B *adj* intérieur/-e

interior decorator *n* décorateur/-trice *m/f*

interlink /ˌɪntə'lɪŋk/ *vt* **to be ~ed** être lié/-e (**with** à)

interlock /ˌɪntə'lɒk/ *vi* ‹*pipes*› s'emboîter; ‹*mechanisms*› s'enclencher; ‹*fingers*› s'entrelacer

interlude /'ɪntəluːd/ *n* (interval) intervalle *m*; (during play, concert) entracte *m*

intermediary /ˌɪntə'miːdɪərɪ, (AmE) -dɪerɪ/ *n, adj* intermédiaire *mf*

intermediate /ˌɪntə'miːdɪət/ *adj* **1** (gen) intermédiaire
2 (Sch) ‹*course*› de niveau moyen; ‹*level*› moyen/-enne

intermission /ˌɪntə'mɪʃn/ *n* entracte *m*

intern A /'ɪntɜːn/ *n* (AmE) **1** (Med) interne *mf*
2 (gen) stagiaire *mf*
B /ɪn'tɜːn/ *vt* (Mil) interner

internal /ɪn'tɜːnl/ *adj* **1** (gen) interne
2 (within country) intérieur/-e

international /ˌɪntə'næʃnəl/ *adj* international/-e

internationally /ˌɪntə'næʃnəlɪ/ *adv* ‹*known, respected*› dans le monde entier

internee /ˌɪntɜː'niː/ *n* interné/-e *m/f*

Internet /'ɪntənet/ *n* Internet *m*; **on the ~** sur Internet

Internet access *n* accès *m* Internet

Internet kiosk *n* borne *f* d'accès public à Internet

Internet service provider, ISP *n* fournisseur *m* d'accès Internet

Internet user *n* internaute *mf*

interpret /ɪn'tɜːprɪt/ **A** *vt* interpréter (**as** comme)
B *vi* faire l'interprète

interpreter /ɪn'tɜːprɪtə(r)/ *n* interprète *mf*

interrogate /ɪn'terəgeɪt/ *vt* interroger

interrogation /ɪnˌterə'geɪʃn/ *n* interrogatoire *m*

interrogative /ˌɪntə'rɒgətɪv/ *n* interrogatif *m*; **in the ~** à la forme interrogative

interrupt /ˌɪntə'rʌpt/ *vt, vi* interrompre

interruption /ˌɪntə'rʌpʃn/ *n* interruption *f*

intersect /ˌɪntə'sekt/ **A** *vt* croiser
B *vi* ‹*roads*› se croiser; **to ~ with** croiser

intersection /ˌɪntə'sekʃn/ *n* intersection *f*

interstate /ˌɪntə'steɪt/ *n* (AmE) (*also* **~ highway**) autoroute *f* (inter-États)

interval /'ɪntəvl/ *n* **1** intervalle *m*; **at regular ~s** à intervalles réguliers; **at four-hourly ~s** toutes les quatre heures; **at 100 metre ~s** à 100 mètres d'intervalle
2 (BrE) (in theatre) entracte *m*

intervene /ˌɪntə'viːn/ *vi* intervenir (**on behalf of** en faveur de)

intervention /ˌɪntə'venʃn/ *n* intervention *f* (**on behalf of** en faveur de)

interview /'ɪntəvjuː/ **A** *n* **1** (*also* **job ~**) entretien *m*
2 (in newspaper) interview *f*
B *vt* **1** faire passer un entretien à ‹*candidate*›
2 ‹*journalist*› interviewer ‹*celebrity*›; ‹*police*› interroger ‹*suspect*›

interviewee /ˌɪntəvjuː'iː/ *n* **1** (for job) candidat/-e *m/f*
2 (on TV, radio) personne *f* interviewée

interviewer /'ɪntəvjuːə(r)/ *n* **1** (for job) personne *f* faisant passer l'entretien
2 (on radio, TV, in press) intervieweur/-euse *m/f*

interwar /ˌɪntə'wɔː(r)/ *adj* **the ~ years** l'entre-deux-guerres *m*

intestine /ɪn'testɪn/ *n* intestin *m*

intimacy /'ɪntɪməsɪ/ *n* intimité *f*

intimate /'ɪntɪmət/ *adj* **1** (gen) intime; **to be on ~ terms with sb** être intime avec qn
2 ‹*knowledge*› approfondi/-e

intimidate /ɪn'tɪmɪdeɪt/ *vt* intimider

intimidating /ɪn'tɪmɪdeɪtɪŋ/ *adj* ‹*behaviour, person*› intimidant/-e; ‹*obstacle, sight, size*› impressionnant/-e; ‹*prospect*› redoutable

into /'ɪntuː, 'ɪntə/ *prep* **1** ‹*put, go, disappear*› dans ‹*place*›; **to run ~ a wall** rentrer dans un mur; **to bang ~ sb/sth** heurter qn/qch; **to go ~ town/~ the office** aller en ville/

au bureau; **to get ~ a car** monter dans une voiture; **to get ~ bed** se mettre au lit
2 ‹*transform*› en; **to change dollars ~ euros** changer des dollars en euros; **to translate sth ~ French** traduire qch en français
3 to continue ~ the 18th century continuer jusqu'au XVIIIᵉ siècle; **well ~ the afternoon** jusque tard dans l'après-midi
4 (fam) (keen on) **to be ~ sth** être fana de qch (fam); **to be ~ drugs** se droguer
5 (in division) **8 ~ 24 goes 3 times** *or* **is 3** 24 divisé par 8 égale 3

intolerable /ɪn'tɒlərəbl/ *adj* intolérable, insupportable

intolerance /ɪn'tɒlərəns/ *n* intolérance *f* (**of, towards** vis-à-vis de, **to** à)

intolerant /ɪn'tɒlərənt/ *adj* intolérant/-e (**of, towards** vis-à-vis de, **with** envers)

intoxicated /ɪn'tɒksɪkeɪtɪd/ *adj* ivre

intoxicating /ɪn'tɒksɪkeɪtɪŋ/ *adj* ‹*drink*› alcoolisé/-e; ‹*effect, substance*› toxique

intranet /'ɪntrənet/ *n* intranet *m*

intransitive /ɪn'trænsətɪv/ *adj* intransitif/-ive

intravenous /ˌɪntrə'viːnəs/ *adj* intraveineux/-euse

intravenous drug user *n* usager *m* de drogues par voie intraveineuse

in tray *n* corbeille *f* arrivée

intrepid /ɪn'trepɪd/ *adj* intrépide

intricate /'ɪntrɪkət/ *adj* ‹*mechanism, pattern, plot*› compliqué/-e; ‹*problem*› complexe

intrigue **A** /'ɪntriːg, ɪn'triːg/ *n* intrigue *f*
B /ɪn'triːg/ *vt* intriguer; **she was ~d by his story** son histoire l'intriguait

intriguing /ɪn'triːgɪŋ/ *adj* ‹*person, smile*› fascinant/-e; ‹*story*› curieux/-ieuse, intéressant/-e

🔑 **introduce** /ˌɪntrə'djuːs, (AmE) -duːs/ *vt*
1 présenter ‹*person*› (**as** comme, **to** à); **may I ~ my son?** je vous présente mon fils; **to ~ sb to** initier qn à ‹*painting, drugs*›
2 introduire ‹*law, reform, word, product, change*› (**in, into** dans)
3 (on TV, radio) présenter ‹*programme*›

🔑 **introduction** /ˌɪntrə'dʌkʃn/ *n* **1** (of person) présentation *f*; **letter of ~** lettre *f* de recommandation
2 (of liquid, system, law) introduction *f* (**into** dans)
3 (to speech, book) introduction *f*

introductory /ˌɪntrə'dʌktərɪ/ *adj* **1** ‹*speech, paragraph*› préliminaire; ‹*course*› d'initiation
2 ‹*offer*› de lancement

introvert /'ɪntrəvɜːt/ *n* introverti/-e *m/f*

intrude /ɪn'truːd/ *vi* **1 to ~ in** s'immiscer dans ‹*affairs, conversation*›
2 to ~ (on sb's privacy) être importun/-e

intruder /ɪn'truːdə(r)/ *n* intrus/-e *m/f*

intrusive /ɪn'truːsɪv/ *adj* ‹*question, cameras*› indiscret/-ète; ‹*phone call, presence*› importun/-e

intuition /ˌɪntjuː'ɪʃn, (AmE) -tuː-/ *n* intuition *f* (**about** concernant)

intuitive /ɪn'tjuːɪtɪv, (AmE) -tuː-/ *adj* intuitif/-ive

inundate /'ɪnʌndeɪt/ *vt* inonder ‹*land*›; submerger ‹*organization, market*›

invade /ɪn'veɪd/ *vt* envahir

invader /ɪn'veɪdə(r)/ *n* envahisseur/-euse *m/f*

invalid **A** /'ɪnvəliːd, 'ɪnvəlɪd/ *n* (sick person) malade *mf*; (disabled person) infirme *mf*
B /ɪn'vælɪd/ *adj* ‹*claim, passport*› pas valable; ‹*contract, marriage*› nul/nulle

invaluable /ɪn'væljʊəbl/ *adj* ‹*assistance, experience*› inestimable; ‹*person, service*› précieux/-ieuse

invasion /ɪn'veɪʒn/ *n* invasion *f*; **~ of (sb's) privacy** atteinte *f* à la vie privée (de qn)

invent /ɪn'vent/ *vt* inventer

invention /ɪn'venʃn/ *n* invention *f*

inventive /ɪn'ventɪv/ *adj* inventif/-ive

inventor /ɪn'ventə(r)/ *n* inventeur/-trice *m/f*

inventory /'ɪnvəntrɪ, (AmE) -tɔːrɪ/ *n*
1 inventaire *m*
2 (AmE) stock *m*

inverted commas /ˌɪnvɜːtɪd 'kɒməz/ *npl* (BrE) guillemets *mpl*; **in ~** entre guillemets

🔑 **invest** /ɪn'vest/ **A** *vt* investir, placer ‹*money*›; consacrer ‹*time, energy*› (**in** à)
B *vi* **1** investir; **to ~ in shares** placer son argent en valeurs
2 (buy) **to ~ in sth** s'acheter qch

🔑 **investigate** /ɪn'vestɪgeɪt/ *vt* **1** enquêter sur ‹*crime, case*›; faire une enquête sur ‹*person*›
2 (study) examiner ‹*possibility, report*›

🔑 **investigation** /ɪnˌvestɪ'geɪʃn/ *n* **1** (inquiry) enquête *f* (**of, into** sur)
2 (of accounts, reports) vérification *f*

🔑 **investment** /ɪn'vestmənt/ *n* (financial) investissement *m*, placement *m*

investment manager *n* gérant/-e *m/f* de porte-feuille

🔑 **investor** /ɪn'vestə(r)/ *n* investisseur/-euse *m/f* (**in** dans); (in shares) actionnaire *mf*

invigilate /ɪn'vɪdʒɪleɪt/ *vt* surveiller ‹*examination*›

invisible /ɪn'vɪzəbl/ *adj* invisible

invisible ink *n* encre *f* sympathique

invitation /ˌɪnvɪ'teɪʃn/ *n* invitation *f*

invitation card *n* carton *m* (d'invitation)

🔑 **invite** /ɪn'vaɪt/ *vt* inviter ‹*person*›; **to ~ sb for a drink** inviter qn à prendre un verre; **to ~ sb in** inviter qn à entrer; **to ~ sb over** *or* **round (to one's house)** inviter qn chez soi

inviting /ɪn'vaɪtɪŋ/ *adj* ‹*room*› accueillant/-e; ‹*meal*› appétissant/-e; ‹*prospect*› alléchant/-e

🔑 mot clé

invoice /ˈɪnvɔɪs/ **A** *n* facture *f*
B *vt* envoyer une facture à ‹*customer*›; **to ~ sb for sth** facturer qch à qn

involve /ɪnˈvɒlv/ *vt* **1** (entail) impliquer, nécessiter ‹*effort, travel*›; entraîner ‹*problems*›
2 (cause to participate) faire participer ‹*person*› (**in** à); **to be ~d in** participer à, être engagé/-e dans ‹*business, project*›; être mêlé/-e à ‹*scandal, robbery*›
3 (affect) concerner, impliquer ‹*person, animal, vehicle*›
4 (engross) **to get ~d in** se laisser prendre par, se plonger dans ‹*film, book, work*›
5 to get ~d with sb avoir une liaison avec qn

involved /ɪnˈvɒlvd/ *adj* **1** (complicated) ‹*explanation*› compliqué/-e
2 ‹*person, group*› (implicated) impliqué/-e; (affected) concerné/-e
3 (necessary) ‹*effort*› à fournir; **because of the expense ~** à cause de la dépense que cela entraîne

involvement /ɪnˈvɒlvmənt/ *n* **1** (in activity, task) participation *f* (**in** à); (in enterprise, politics) engagement *m* (**in** dans)
2 (with group) liens *mpl*; (with person) relations *fpl*

inward /ˈɪnwəd/ **A** *adj* ‹*satisfaction*› personnel/-elle; ‹*relief, calm*› intérieur/-e
B *adv* (*also* **inwards** (BrE)) (open, move, grow) vers l'intérieur

inward-looking *adj* replié/-e sur soi-même

inwards (BrE) /ˈɪnwədz/ = **inward B**

in-your-face *adj* (fam) agressif/-ive

iodine /ˈaɪədiːn, (AmE) -daɪn/ *n* (element) iode *m*; (antiseptic) teinture *f* d'iode

IOU *n* reconnaissance *f* de dette

IQ *n* (*abbr* = **intelligence quotient**) QI *m*

Iran /ɪˈrɑːn/ *pr n* Iran *m*

Iraq /ɪˈrɑːk/ *pr n* Iraq *m*

irate /aɪˈreɪt/ *adj* furieux/-ieuse (**about** au sujet de)

Ireland /ˈaɪələnd/ *pr n* Irlande *f*

Irish /ˈaɪərɪʃ/ **A** *n* **1** (people) **the ~** les Irlandais *mpl*
2 (language) irlandais *m*
B *adj* irlandais/-e

Irishman *n* (*pl* **-men**) Irlandais *m*

Irish Republic *pr n* République *f* d'Irlande

Irish sea *pr n* mer *f* d'Irlande

Irishwoman *n* (*pl* **-women**) Irlandaise *f*

iron /ˈaɪən, (AmE) ˈaɪərn/ **A** *n* **1** (metal) fer *m*; **scrap ~** ferraille *f*
2 (for clothes) fer *m* (à repasser)
B *vt* repasser ‹*clothes*›

ironic (*also* **ironical**) /aɪˈrɒnɪk(l)/ *adj* ironique

ironing /ˈaɪənɪŋ, (AmE) ˈaɪərn-/ *n* repassage *m*

ironing board *n* planche *f* à repasser

ironmonger /ˈaɪənmʌŋgə(r), (AmE) ˈaɪərn-/ *n* quincaillier/-ière *m/f*; **~'s (shop)** quincaillerie *f*

irony /ˈaɪərənɪ/ *n* ironie *f*

irrational /ɪˈræʃənl/ *adj* ‹*behaviour*› irrationnel/-elle; ‹*fear, hostility*› sans fondement; **he's rather ~** il n'est pas très raisonnable

irregular /ɪˈregjʊlə(r)/ *adj* **1** irrégulier/-ière
2 (AmE) ‹*merchandise*› de second choix

irregularity /ɪˌregjʊˈlærətɪ/ *n* irrégularité *f*

irrelevant /ɪˈreləvnt/ *adj* **1** ‹*remark*› hors de propos; ‹*fact*› qui n'est pas pertinent; ‹*question*› sans rapport avec le sujet
2 (unimportant) **the money's ~** ce n'est pas l'argent qui compte

irreligious /ˌɪrɪˈlɪdʒəs/ *adj* irréligieux/-ieuse

irreparable /ɪˈrepərəbl/ *adj* irréparable

irreplaceable /ˌɪrɪˈpleɪsəbl/ *adj* irremplaçable

irrepressible /ˌɪrɪˈpresəbl/ *adj* ‹*high spirits*› irrépressible; ‹*person*› infatigable

irresistible /ˌɪrɪˈzɪstəbl/ *adj* irrésistible

irrespective: **irrespective of** /ˌɪrɪˈspektɪv/ *phr* sans tenir compte de ‹*age, class*›; sans distinction de ‹*race*›

irresponsible /ˌɪrɪˈspɒnsəbl/ *adj* irresponsable

irreversible /ˌɪrɪˈvɜːsəbl/ *adj* ‹*process, decision*› irréversible; ‹*disease*› incurable

irritable /ˈɪrɪtəbl/ *adj* irritable

irritable bowel syndrome *n* colopathie *f* fonctionnelle

irritate /ˈɪrɪteɪt/ *vt* irriter

irritating /ˈɪrɪteɪtɪŋ/ *adj* irritant/-e

Islam /ˈɪzlɑːm, -læm, -ˈlɑːm/ *n* Islam *m*

Islamic /ɪzˈlæmɪk/ *adj* islamique

Islamist /ɪzləmɪst/ *adj* islamiste

island /ˈaɪlənd/ *n* **1** île *f*; (small) îlot *m*
2 (*also* **traffic ~**) refuge *m*

islander /ˈaɪləndə(r)/ *n* insulaire *mf*, habitant/-e *m/f* d'une île (*or* de l'île)

Isle of Man *pr n* île *f* de Man

isolate /ˈaɪsəleɪt/ *vt* isoler (**from** de)

isolation /ˌaɪsəˈleɪʃn/ *n* isolement *m*

Israel /ˈɪzreɪl/ *pr n* Israël *never with article*

Israeli /ɪzˈreɪlɪ/ **A** *n* Israélien/-ienne *m/f*
B *adj* israélien/-ienne

issue /ˈɪʃuː, ˈɪsjuː/ **A** *n* **1** problème *m*, question *f*; **to make an ~ (out) of** faire une histoire de; **at ~** en question
2 (of stamps, shares) émission *f*; (of book) publication *f*
3 (journal, magazine) numéro *m*; **back ~** vieux numéro
B *vt* **1** (allocate) distribuer; **to ~ sb with sth** fournir qch à qn
2 délivrer ‹*declaration*›; émettre ‹*order, warning*›
3 émettre ‹*stamps, shares*›; publier ‹*book*›

it /ɪt/ *pron* **1** (subject pronoun) il, elle; **'where is the chair?' — 'it's in the kitchen'** 'où est

la chaise?' — 'elle est dans la cuisine'; **it's a good film** c'est un bon film
2 (object pronoun) le, la l'; **I want ~** je le/la veux
3 (after a preposition) **about/from/of ~** en; **in/to ~** y; **I've heard about ~** j'en ai entendu parler; **he went to ~** il y est allé
4 (in questions) **who is ~?** qui est-ce?, qui c'est? (fam); **where is ~?** (of object) où est-il/elle?; (of place) où est-ce?, où est-ce que c'est?, c'est où? (fam); **what is ~?** (of object, noise) qu'est-ce que c'est?, c'est quoi? (fam); (what's happening?) qu'est-ce qui se passe?; (what is the matter?) qu'est-ce qu'il y a?
5 (impersonal uses) **it's raining/snowing** il pleut/neige; **~ is easy to learn English** il est facile d'apprendre l'anglais; **~ doesn't matter** ça ne fait rien; **it's time to eat** c'est l'heure de manger; **~'s me** c'est moi

IT *n* (*abbr* = **information technology**) informatique *f*

Italian /ɪ'tæljən/ **A** *n* **1** (person) Italien/-ienne *m/f*
2 (language) italien *m*
B *adj* (gen) italien/-ienne; ‹*ambassador, embassy*› d'Italie

italics *npl* italique *m*; **in ~** en italique

Italy /'ɪtəlɪ/ *pr n* Italie *f*

itch /ɪtʃ/ **A** *n* démangeaison *f*
B *vi* avoir des démangeaisons; **my back is ~ing** j'ai le dos qui me démange; **these socks make me ~** ces chaussettes me grattent

itchy /'ɪtʃɪ/ *adj* (fam) **I feel ~ all over** ça me gratte partout

IDIOM **to have ~ feet** (fam) avoir la bougeotte (fam)

✓ **item** /'aɪtəm/ *n* **1** article *m*; **~s of clothing** vêtements *mpl*; **news ~** article *m*
2 (on agenda) point *m*

itemize /'aɪtəmaɪz/ *vt* détailler; **~d bill** facture *f* le détaillée

itinerary /aɪ'tɪnərərɪ, ɪ-, (AmE) -rerɪ/ *n* itinéraire *m*

✓ **its** /ɪts/ *det* son/sa/ses

> In French, determiners agree in number and gender with the noun that follows. *its* is translated by *son* + *masculine noun*: *its nose* = son nez; by *sa* + *feminine noun*: *its tail* = sa queue; BUT by *son* + *feminine noun beginning with a vowel or mute 'h'*: *its ear* = son oreille; and by *ses* + *plural noun*: *its ears* = ses oreilles.

✓ **itself** /ɪt'self/ *pron* **1** (reflexive) se, s'; **the cat hurt ~** le chat s'est fait mal
2 (emphatic) lui-même/elle-même; **the house ~ was pretty** la maison elle-même était jolie; **he was kindness ~** c'était la bonté même *or* personnifiée
3 (after prepositions) **the heating comes on by ~** le chauffage se met en marche tout seul; **learning French is not difficult in ~** l'apprentissage du français n'est pas difficile en soi

IVF *n* (*abbr* = **in vitro fertilization**) fécondation *f* in vitro

ivory /'aɪvərɪ/ *n, adj* ivoire *m*

ivy /'aɪvɪ/ *n* lierre *m*

Jj

j, J /dʒeɪ/ *n* j, J *m*

jab /dʒæb/ **A** *n* **1** (BrE) (vaccination) vaccin *m*; (injection) piqûre *f*
2 (in boxing) direct *m*
B *vt* **to ~ sth into sth** planter qch dans qch

jabber /'dʒæbə(r)/ *vi* (chatter) jacasser; (in foreign language) baragouiner

jack /dʒæk/ *n* **1** (for car) cric *m*
2 (in cards) valet *m* (**of** de)
3 (in bowls) cochonnet *m*

IDIOM **to be a ~ of all trades** être un/-e touche-à-tout *inv*

■ **jack in** (BrE) (fam): **~ in [sth], ~ [sth] in** plaquer (fam), laisser tomber ‹*job*›

jackal /'dʒækɔːl, (AmE) -kl/ *n* chacal *m*

jackdaw *n* choucas *m*

jacket /'dʒækɪt/ *n* **1** (garment) veste *f*; (man's) veste *f*, veston *m*
2 (*also* **dust ~**) jaquette *f*
3 (AmE) (of record) pochette *f*

jacket potato *n* pomme *f* de terre en robe des champs (au four)

jack-in-the-box *n* diable *m* à ressort

jackknife /'dʒæknaɪf/ *vi* ‹*lorry*› se mettre en portefeuille

jackpot /'dʒækpɒt/ *n* **to hit the ~** (win prize) gagner le gros lot; (have great success) faire un tabac (fam)

jade /dʒeɪd/ *n* **1** (stone) jade *m*
2 (*also* **~ green**) vert *m* jade

✓ mot clé

jaded /ˈdʒeɪdɪd/ *adj* **1** (exhausted) fatigué/-e
2 (bored) ‹*person, palate*› blasé/-e

jagged /ˈdʒægɪd/ *adj* ‹*rock, cliff*› déchiqueté/-e; ‹*tooth, blade*› ébréché/-e; ‹*knife, saw*› dentelé/-e

jail /dʒeɪl/ **A** *n* prison *f*
B *vt* mettre [qn] en prison

jam /dʒæm/ **A** *n* **1** confiture *f*; **apricot ~** confiture d'abricots
2 (of traffic) embouteillage *m*
3 (in machine, system) blocage *m*
4 (fam) (difficulty) pétrin *m* (fam); **to be in a ~** être dans le pétrin (fam)
5 (*also* **~ session**) bœuf *m* (fam), jam-session *f*
B *vt* (*p prés etc* **-mm-**) **1 to ~ one's foot on the brake** freiner à bloc
2 (wedge) coincer; **the key's ~med** la clé s'est coincée
3 (block) enrayer ‹*mechanism*›; coincer ‹*lock, door, system*›
4 (*also* **~ up**) **cars ~med (up) the roads** les routes étaient embouteillées
5 (cause interference in) brouiller ‹*frequency*›
C *vi* (*p prés etc* **-mm-**) **1** ‹*mechanism*› s'enrayer; ‹*lock, door*› se coincer
2 (Mus) improviser

Jamaica /dʒəˈmeɪkə/ *pr n* Jamaïque *f*

jam-packed /ˌdʒæmˈpækt/ *adj* bondé/-e; **to be ~ with sth** être bourré/-e de qch

jangle /ˈdʒæŋgl/ **A** *n* (of bells, pots) tintement *m*; (of keys) cliquetis *m*
B *vi* ‹*bells*› tinter; ‹*bangles, keys*› cliqueter

janitor /ˈdʒænɪtə(r)/ *n* (AmE) gardien *m*

January /ˈdʒænjʊərɪ, (AmE) -jʊerɪ/ *n* janvier *m*

Japan /dʒəˈpæn/ *pr n* Japon *m*

Japanese /ˌdʒæpəˈni:z/ **A** *n* **1** (person) Japonais/-e *m/f*
2 (language) japonais *m*
B *adj* ‹*culture, food, politics*› japonais/-e; ‹*teacher, lesson*› de japonais; ‹*ambassador, embassy*› du Japon

jar /dʒɑ:(r)/ **A** *n* **1** pot *m*; (large) bocal *m*; (earthenware) jarre *f*
2 (jolt) secousse *f*, choc *m*
B *vt* (*p prés etc* **-rr-**) **1** ébranler, secouer; **to ~ one's shoulder** se cogner l'épaule
2 (AmE) **to ~ sb into action** pousser qn à agir
C *vi* (*p prés etc* **-rr-**) **1** ‹*music, voice*› rendre un son discordant; **to ~ on sb's nerves** agacer qn
2 (clash) ‹*colours*› jurer; ‹*note*› sonner faux

jargon /ˈdʒɑ:gən/ *n* jargon *m*

jasmine /ˈdʒæsmɪn, (AmE) ˈdʒæzmən/ *n* jasmin *m*

jaundice /ˈdʒɔ:ndɪs/ *n* jaunisse *f*

jaundiced /ˈdʒɔ:ndɪst/ *adj* (cynical) négatif/-ive

javelin /ˈdʒævlɪn/ *n* javelot *m*

jaw /dʒɔ:/ *n* mâchoire *f*

jawbone /ˈdʒɔ:bəʊn/ *n* mâchoire *f*

jawline *n* menton *m*

jay /dʒeɪ/ *n* geai *m*

jazz /dʒæz/ **A** *n* jazz *m*
B *adj* ‹*musician, singer*› de jazz; **~ band** jazz-band *m*
IDIOM **and all that ~** et tout le bataclan (fam)
■ **jazz up** (fam) rajeunir ‹*dress*›; égayer ‹*room*›

jazzy /ˈdʒæzɪ/ *adj* **1** ‹*colour*› voyant/-e; ‹*pattern, dress*› bariolé/-e
2 ‹*music*› jazzy *inv*

jealous /ˈdʒeləs/ *adj* jaloux/-ouse (**of** de); **to make sb ~** rendre qn jaloux

jealousy /ˈdʒeləsɪ/ *n* jalousie *f*

jeans *npl* jean *m*; **a pair of ~** un jean

Jeep® *n* jeep® *f*

jeer /dʒɪə(r)/ **A** *n* huée *f*
B *vt* huer
C *vi* se moquer; **to ~ at sb** ‹*crowd*› huer qn; ‹*individual*› railler qn

jeering /ˈdʒɪərɪŋ/ *n* huées *fpl*

jellied /ˈdʒelɪd/ *adj* en aspic; **~ eels** anguilles *fpl* en gelée

jello /ˈdʒeləʊ/ *n* (*also* **Jell-O**®) (AmE) gelée *f* de fruits

jelly /ˈdʒelɪ/ *n* **1** (savoury) gelée *f*; (sweet) gelée *f* de fruits
2 (jam) gelée *f*

jellyfish /ˈdʒelɪfɪʃ/ *n* (*pl* **~** *ou* **~es**) méduse *f*

jeopardize /ˈdʒepədaɪz/ *vt* compromettre ‹*career, plans*›; mettre [qch] en péril ‹*lives, troops*›

jeopardy /ˈdʒepədɪ/ *n* **in ~** en péril, menacé/-e

jerk /dʒɜ:k/ **A** *n* **1** (jolt) (of vehicle) secousse *f*; (of muscle, limb) tressaillement *m*, (petit) mouvement *m* brusque; **with a ~ of his head** d'un brusque mouvement de la tête
2 (fam) (idiot) abruti *m*
B *vt* tirer brusquement ‹*object*›
C *vi* ‹*person, limb, muscle*› tressaillir

jerky /ˈdʒɜ:kɪ/ **A** *n* (*also* **beef ~**) (AmE) bœuf *m* séché
B *adj* ‹*movement*› saccadé/-e; ‹*style, phrase*› haché/-e

jersey /ˈdʒɜ:zɪ/ *n* **1** (sweater) pull-over *m*
2 (for sports) maillot *m*
3 (fabric) jersey *m*

Jersey /ˈdʒɜ:zɪ/ *pr n* Jersey *f*

Jerusalem /dʒəˈru:sələm/ *pr n* Jérusalem

jest /dʒest/ **A** *n* plaisanterie *f*; **in ~** pour plaisanter
B *vi* plaisanter

jester /ˈdʒestə(r)/ *n* bouffon *m*

Jesuit /ˈdʒezjʊɪt, (AmE) ˈdʒeʒəwət/ *n, adj* jésuite *m*

Jesus /ˈdʒi:zəs/ **A** *pr n* Jésus; **~ Christ** Jésus-Christ
B *excl* (sl) **~ (Christ)!** nom de Dieu! (fam)

jet /dʒet/ **A** *n* **1** (*also* **~ plane**) jet *m*, avion *m* à réaction

2 (of water, flame) jet *m*
3 (on hob) brûleur *m*; (of engine) gicleur *m*
4 (stone) jais *m*
B *vi* **to ~ off to** s'envoler pour
jet black *adj* de jais *inv*
jet engine *n* moteur *m* à réaction, réacteur *m*
jetfoil *n* hydroglisseur *m*
jet lag *n* décalage *m* horaire
jet-lagged /ˈdʒetlægd/ *adj* **to be ~** souffrir du décalage horaire
jet setter *n* **to be a ~** faire partie du jet-set
jet-skiing *n* jet-ski *m*
jettison /ˈdʒetɪsn/ *vt* (from ship) jeter [qch] par-dessus bord; (from plane) larguer
jetty /ˈdʒetɪ/ *n* (of stone) jetée *f*; (of wood) appontement *m*
Jew /dʒuː/ *n* juif/juive *m/f*
jewel /ˈdʒuːəl/ *n* **1** (gem) pierre *f* précieuse; (piece of jewellery) bijou *m*; (in watch) rubis *m*
2 (person) perle *f*; (town, object) joyau *m*

j

jeweller (BrE), **jeweler** (AmE) /ˈdʒuːələ(r)/ *n* (person) bijoutier/-ière *m/f*; **~'s (shop)** bijouterie *f*
jewellery (BrE), **jewelry** (AmE) /ˈdʒuːəlrɪ/ *n* (gen) bijoux *mpl*; (in shop, workshop) bijouterie *f*; **a piece of ~** un bijou
Jewish /ˈdʒuːɪʃ/ *adj* juif/juive
jib /dʒɪb/ *n* **1** (sail) foc *m*
2 (of crane) flèche *f*
jibe /dʒaɪb/ *n* moquerie *f*
jiffy *n* **in a ~** en un clin d'œil
Jiffy bag® *n* enveloppe *f* matelassée
jig /dʒɪg/ *n* gigue *f*
jiggle /ˈdʒɪgl/ **A** *vt* agiter
B *vi* (*also* **~ about**, **~ around**) gigoter; (impatiently) se trémousser
jigsaw /ˈdʒɪgsɔː/ *n* **1** (*also* **~ puzzle**) puzzle *m*
2 (saw) scie *f* sauteuse
jilt /dʒɪlt/ *vt* abandonner, plaquer (fam)
jingle /ˈdʒɪŋgl/ **A** *n* **1** (of bells) tintement *m*; (of keys) cliquetis *m*
2 (verse) ritournelle *f*; (for advert) refrain *m* publicitaire, sonal *m*
B *vi* ‹*keys, coins*› cliqueter
jingoist /ˈdʒɪŋgəʊɪst/ *n, adj* chauvin/-e *m/f*
jinx /dʒɪŋks/ *n* **1** (curse) sort *m*; **to put a ~ on** jeter un sort à; **there's a ~ on me** j'ai la poisse (fam)
2 (unlucky person, object) **it's a ~** ça porte la poisse
jitters /ˈdʒɪtəz/ *npl* **to have the ~** ‹*person, stock market*› être nerveux/-euse; ‹*actor*› avoir le trac
⚷ **job** /dʒɒb/ **A** *n* **1** (employment) emploi *m*; (post) poste *m*; **to get a ~** trouver un emploi; **a teaching ~** un poste d'enseignant; **what's her ~?** qu'est-ce qu'elle fait (comme travail)?
2 (role) fonction *f*; **it's my ~ to do** c'est à moi de faire
3 (duty) travail *m*; **she's only doing her ~** elle fait son travail
4 (task) travail *m*; **to find a ~ for sb to do** trouver du travail pour qn
5 (assignment) tâche *f*
6 **to make a good ~ of sth** faire du bon travail avec qch
7 (fam) **quite a ~** toute une affaire (fam) (**to do, doing** de faire)
B *adj* ‹*advert, offer*› d'emploi; ‹*pages*› des emplois
IDIOM **that'll do the ~** ça fera l'affaire
job centre *n* (BrE) bureau *m* des services nationaux de l'emploi
job creation scheme *n* (BrE) plan *m* pour la création d'emplois
job description *n* description *f* de poste
job-hunting *n* chasse *f* à l'emploi
jobless /ˈdʒɒblɪs/ *n* **the ~** les sans-emplois *mpl*
jobseeker's allowance /ˈdʒɒbsiːkəz əˌlaʊəns/ *n* allocation *f* chômage
job-share *n* poste *m* partagé
job sharing *n* partage *m* de poste
jockey /ˈdʒɒkɪ/ *n* jockey *m*
jockey shorts *npl* (AmE) slip *m* (d'homme)
jockstrap *n* (fam) suspensoir *m*
jodhpurs /ˈdʒɒdpəz/ *npl* jodhpurs *mpl*
jog /dʒɒg/ **A** *n* **1** (with elbow) coup *m* de coude
2 **at a ~** au petit trot (fam)
3 (Sport) **to go for a ~** aller faire un jogging
4 (AmE) (in road) coude *m*
B *vt* (*p prés etc* **-gg-**) (with elbow) donner un coup de coude à; **to ~ sb's memory** rafraîchir la mémoire de qn
C *vi* (*p prés etc* **-gg-**) **to go ~ging** faire du jogging
jogger /ˈdʒɒgə(r)/ *n* joggeur/-euse *m/f*
jogging /ˈdʒɒgɪŋ/ *n* jogging *m*
⚷ **join** /dʒɔɪn/ **A** *n* raccord *m*
B *vt* **1** devenir membre de ‹*organization, team*›; adhérer à ‹*club*›; s'inscrire à ‹*library*›; entrer dans ‹*firm*›; s'engager dans ‹*army*›; **to ~ a union** se syndiquer
2 se mettre dans ‹*queue*›
3 (meet up with) rejoindre ‹*person*›; **may I ~ you?** (sit down) puis-je me joindre à vous?
4 (connect) réunir, joindre ‹*ends, pieces*›; assembler ‹*parts*›; relier ‹*points, towns*› (**to** à)
5 ‹*road*› rejoindre ‹*motorway*›; ‹*river*› se jeter dans ‹*sea*›
C *vi* **1** (become member) (of party, club) adhérer; (of group, class) s'inscrire
2 ‹*pieces*› se joindre; ‹*wires*› se raccorder; ‹*roads*› se rejoindre
■ **join in**: **A** **~ in** participer
B **~ in [sth]** participer à ‹*talks, game*›;

⚷ mot clé

prendre part à ‹*strike, demonstration, bidding*›; **to ~ in the fun** se joindre à la fête

■ **join up** **A** **~ up 1** (enlist) s'engager
2 (meet up) ‹*people*› se retrouver; ‹*roads, tracks*› se rejoindre
B **~ [sth] up** relier ‹*characters, dots*›

joiner /'dʒɔɪnə(r)/ *n* menuisier/-ière *m/f*

joint /dʒɔɪnt/ **A** *n* **1** (Anat) articulation *f*; **to be out of ~** ‹*shoulder*› être déboîté/-e
2 (in carpentry) assemblage *m*; (in metalwork) joint *m*
3 (of meat) rôti *m*
4 (fam) (place) endroit *m*; (cafe) boui-boui *m* (fam)
5 (fam) (cannabis) joint *m* (fam)
B *adj* ‹*action*› collectif/-ive; ‹*programme, session*› mixte; ‹*measures, procedure*› commun/-e; ‹*winner*› ex aequo *inv*; ‹*talks*› multilatéral/-e

joint account *n* compte *m* joint

joint effort *n* collaboration *f*

joint honours *npl* (GB) (Univ) licence *f* combinée

jointly /'dʒɔɪntlɪ/ *adv* conjointement; **to be ~ owned by** être la copropriété de

joint owner *n* copropriétaire *mf*

joint venture *n* **1** (Econ) coentreprise *f*
2 (gen) projet *m* en commun

joke /dʒəʊk/ **A** *n* **1** plaisanterie *f*, blague *f* (fam); **to tell a ~** raconter une blague; **to play a ~ on sb** jouer un tour à qn; **it's no ~ doing** ce n'est pas facile de faire
2 (person) guignol *m*; (event, situation) farce *f*
B *vi* plaisanter, blaguer (fam); **you must be joking!** tu veux rire!

joker /'dʒəʊkə(r)/ *n* **1** (prankster) farceur/-euse *m/f*
2 (in cards) joker *m*

jolly /'dʒɒlɪ/ **A** *adj* ‹*person*› enjoué/-e; ‹*tune*› joyeux/-euse
B *vt* **to ~ sb along** amadouer qn

jolt /dʒəʊlt/ **A** *n* **1** (jerk) secousse *f*
2 (shock) choc *m*
B *vt* secouer ‹*passenger*›
C *vi* ‹*vehicle*› cahoter

Jordan /'dʒɔːdn/ *pr n* (country) Jordanie *f*

jostle /'dʒɒsl/ *vi* se bousculer (**for** pour, **to do** pour faire)

jot /dʒɒt/ *v*

■ **jot down** noter ‹*ideas, names*›

journal /'dʒɜːnl/ *n* **1** (diary) journal *m*
2 (periodical) revue *f*; (newspaper) journal *m*

journalism /'dʒɜːnəlɪzəm/ *n* journalisme *m*

journalist /'dʒɜːnəlɪst/ *n* journaliste *mf*

journey /'dʒɜːnɪ/ *n* (long) voyage *m*; (short or habitual) trajet *m*; **bus ~** trajet en bus; **to go on a ~** partir en voyage

jowl /dʒaʊl/ *n* (jaw) mâchoire *f*; (fleshy fold) bajoue *f*

joy /dʒɔɪ/ *n* **1** (delight) joie *f* (**at** devant)
2 (pleasure) plaisir *m*; **the ~ of doing** le plaisir de faire

IDIOM **to be full of the ~s of spring** être en pleine forme

joyrider /'dʒɔɪraɪdə(r)/ *n* jeune chauffard *m* en voiture volée

joyriding /'dʒɔɪraɪdɪŋ/ *n* rodéo *m* à la voiture volée

joystick /'dʒɔɪstɪk/ *n* (in plane) manche *m* à balai; (for video game) manette *f*

jubilant /'dʒuːbɪlənt/ *adj* ‹*person*› exultant/-e; ‹*crowd*› en liesse; ‹*expression, mood*› réjoui/-e

jubilee /'dʒuːbɪliː/ *n* jubilé *m*

Judaism /'dʒuːdeɪɪzəm, (AmE) -dɪɪzəm/ *n* judaïsme *m*

judge /dʒʌdʒ/ **A** *n* **1** (in court) juge *m*
2 (at competition) (gen) membre *m* du jury; (Sport) juge *m*
3 to be a good ~ of character savoir juger les gens
B *vt* **1** juger ‹*person*›
2 faire partie du jury de ‹*show, competition*›
3 estimer ‹*distance, age*›; prévoir ‹*outcome, reaction*›
4 (consider) juger, estimer
C *vi* juger; **judging by** *or* **from...** à en juger d'après...

judgement, **judgment** /'dʒʌdʒmənt/ *n* jugement *m*

judicial /dʒuː'dɪʃl/ *adj* (gen) judiciaire; ‹*decision*› jurisprudentiel/-ielle

judiciary /dʒuː'dɪʃɪərɪ, (AmE) -ʃɪerɪ/ *n* **1** (system of courts) système *m* judiciaire
2 (judges) magistrature *f*

judo /'dʒuːdəʊ/ *n* judo *m*

jug /dʒʌg/ *n* **1** (BrE) (earthenware) pichet *m*; (pot-bellied) cruche *f*; (glass) carafe *f*; (for cream, milk, water) pot *m*
2 (AmE) (flagon) cruche *f*

juggernaut /'dʒʌgənɔːt/ *n* (BrE) poids *m* lourd

juggle /'dʒʌgl/ *vi* jongler (**with** avec)

juggler /'dʒʌglə(r)/ *n* jongleur/-euse *m/f*

jugular /'dʒʌgjʊlə(r)/ *n*, *adj* jugulaire *f*

juice /dʒuːs/ *n* **1** (from fruit, meat) jus *m*; **fruit ~** jus de fruit
2 (sap) suc *m*
3 gastric ~s sucs *mpl* digestifs *or* gastriques

juicy /'dʒuːsɪ/ *adj* **1** ‹*fruit*› juteux/-euse
2 (fam) ‹*story*› croustillant/-e

jukebox /'dʒuːkbɒks/ *n* juke-box *m*

July /dʒuː'laɪ/ *n* juillet *m*

jumble /'dʒʌmbl/ *n* **1** (of papers, objects) tas *m*; (of ideas) fouillis *m*; (of words) fatras *m*
2 (BrE) (items for sale) bric-à-brac *m*, vieux objets *mpl*

■ **jumble up** mélanger ‹*letters, shapes*›

jumble sale *n* (BrE) vente *f* de charité

jumbo /'dʒʌmbəʊ/ *n* (*also* **~ jet**) gros-porteur *m*

jump /dʒʌmp/ **A** *n* **1** (leap) saut *m*, bond *m*; **parachute ~** saut en parachute
2 (in horse race) obstacle *m*

3 (in price, wages) bond *m* (**in** dans)
B *vt* **1** sauter ‹*obstacle, ditch*›
2 to ~ the lights griller (fam) le feu (rouge); **to ~ the queue** (BrE) passer devant tout le monde
3 to ~ ship ne pas rejoindre son bâtiment
C *vi* **1** (leap) sauter; **to ~ across** *or* **over sth** franchir qch d'un bond; **to ~ up and down** sautiller; (in anger) trépigner de colère
2 (start in surprise) sursauter
3 ‹*prices, rate*› monter en flèche
4 to ~ at sauter sur ‹*opportunity*›; accepter [qch] avec enthousiasme ‹*offer*›
▪ **jump back** ‹*person*› faire un bond en arrière; ‹*lever*› lâcher brusquement
▪ **jump down** ‹*person*› sauter (**from** de)
▪ **jump on**: **A** **~ on [sth]** sauter dans ‹*bus, train*›; sauter sur ‹*bicycle, horse*›
B **~ on [sb]** sauter sur qn
▪ **jump out** ‹*person*› sauter; **to ~ out of** sauter par ‹*window*›; sauter de ‹*bed, train*›
▪ **jump up** ‹*person*› se lever d'un bond
jumper /'dʒʌmpə(r)/ *n* **1** (BrE) (sweater) pull *m*, pull-over *m*
2 (AmE) (pinafore) robe *f* chasuble
jump leads *npl* câbles *mpl* de démarrage
jump-start /'dʒʌmpstɑːt/ /ˌdʒʌmp'stɑːt/ *vt* faire démarrer [qch] avec des câbles ‹*car*›
jump suit *n* combinaison *f*
jumpy /'dʒʌmpɪ/ *adj* (fam) ‹*person*› nerveux/-euse; ‹*market*› instable
junction /'dʒʌŋkʃn/ *n* **1** (of two roads) carrefour *m*; (on motorway) échangeur *m*
2 (of railway lines) nœud *m* ferroviaire; (station) gare *f* de jonction
⚷ **June** /dʒuːn/ *n* juin *m*
jungle /'dʒʌŋgl/ *n* jungle *f*
junior /'dʒuːnɪə(r)/ **A** *n* **1** (younger person) cadet/-ette *m/f*
2 (low-ranking worker) subalterne *mf*
3 (BrE) (Sch) élève *mf* du primaire
4 (AmE) (Univ) ≈ étudiant/-e *m/f* de premier cycle; (in high school) ≈ élève *mf* de première
B *adj* **1** ‹*colleague, rank, position*› subalterne
2 (Sport) ‹*race, team*› des cadets; ‹*player*› jeune
3 (*also* **Junior**) **Mortimer ~** Mortimer fils *or* junior
junior high school *n* (AmE) ≈ collège *m*
junior minister *n* secrétaire *m* d'État
junior school *n* (BrE) école *f* (primaire)
junk /dʒʌŋk/ *n* **1** (rubbish) camelote *f* (fam)
2 (second-hand) bric-à-brac *m*
3 (boat) jonque *f*
junk food *n* nourriture *f* industrielle
junkie /'dʒʌŋkɪ/ *n* (fam) drogué/-e *m/f*
junk mail *n* prospectus *mpl*
junk shop *n* boutique *f* de bric-à-brac

⚷ mot clé

junkyard *n* (for scrap) dépotoir *m*; (for old cars) cimetière *f* de voitures
junta /'dʒʌntə/ *n* junte *f*
Jupiter /'dʒuːpɪtə(r)/ *pr n* Jupiter *f*
jurisdiction /ˌdʒʊərɪs'dɪkʃn/ *n* **1** (gen) compétence *f* (**over** sur)
2 (Law) juridiction *f* (**over** sur)
juror /'dʒʊərə(r)/ *n* juré *m*
jury /'dʒʊərɪ/ *n* jury *m*
jury box *n* banc *m* des jurés
jury duty (AmE), **jury service** (BrE) *n* **to do ~** faire partie d'un jury
⚷ **just¹** /dʒʌst/ **A** *adv* **1 to have ~ done** venir (juste) de faire; **he had only ~ left** il venait tout juste de partir
2 (immediately) juste; **~ before/after** juste avant/après
3 (slightly) **~ over/under 20 kg** un peu plus/moins de 20 kg
4 (only, merely) juste; **~ for fun** juste pour rire; **~ two days ago** il y a juste deux jours; **he's ~ a child** ce n'est qu'un enfant
5 (purposely) exprès; **he did it ~ to annoy us** il l'a fait exprès pour nous embêter
6 (barely) tout juste; **~ on time** tout juste à l'heure; **he's ~ 20** il a tout juste 20 ans; **I (only) ~ caught the train** j'ai eu le train de justesse
7 (simply) tout simplement; **~ tell the truth** dis la vérité, tout simplement; **she ~ won't listen** elle ne veut tout simplement pas écouter; **'~ a moment'** 'un instant'
8 (exactly) exactement; **that's ~ what I want** c'est exactement ce que je veux; **it's ~ right** c'est parfait; **she looks ~ like her father** c'est son père tout craché (fam); **it's ~ like him to forget** c'est bien de lui d'oublier
9 (possibly) **it might** *or* **could ~ be true** il se peut que ce soit vrai
10 (at this or that very moment) **to be ~ doing** être en train de faire; **to be ~ about to do** être sur le point de faire; **he was ~ leaving** il partait
11 (positively, totally) vraiment; **that's ~ wonderful** c'est vraiment merveilleux
12 (in requests) **if you could ~ hold this box** si vous pouvez tenir cette boîte
13 (equally) **~ as big as...** (tout) aussi grand que...
14 (with imperative) donc; **~ you dare!** essaie donc voir!; **~ imagine!** imagine donc!
B **just about** *phr* presque; **~ about everything** à peu près tout; **I can ~ about see it** je peux tout juste le voir
C **just as** *phr* **~ as he came** juste au moment où il est arrivé
D **just now** *phr* en ce moment; **I saw him ~ now** je viens juste de le voir
just² /dʒʌst/ *adj* ‹*person, decision*› juste; ‹*demand*› justifié/-e; ‹*claim, criticism*› légitime
⚷ **justice** /'dʒʌstɪs/ *n* **1** (fairness) justice *f*; **the**

portrait doesn't do her ~ le portrait ne l'avantage pas
2 (the law) justice *f*; **to bring sb to ~** traduire qn en justice

Justice Department *n* (AmE) ministère *m* de la justice

Justice of the Peace *n* (BrE) juge *m* de paix

justifiable /'dʒʌstɪfaɪəbl/ *adj* (that is justified) légitime; (that can be justified) justifiable

justification /ˌdʒʌstɪfɪ'keɪʃn/ *n* raison *f*; **to have some ~ for doing** avoir des raisons de faire

justified /'dʒʌstɪfaɪd/ *adj* justifié/-e; **to feel ~ in doing** se sentir en droit de faire

justify /'dʒʌstɪfaɪ/ *vt* justifier

jut /dʒʌt/ *vi* (*p prés etc* **-tt-**) (*also* **~ out**) avancer en saillie (**into** dans); ‹*balcony*› faire saillie (**over** sur)

juvenile /'dʒu:vənaɪl/ *n* (gen) jeune *mf*; (Law) mineur/-e *m/f*

juvenile delinquency *n* délinquance *f* juvénile

juvenile delinquent *n* jeune délinquant/-e *m/f*

juvenile offender *n* délinquant/-e *m/f* mineur/-e

juxtapose /ˌdʒʌkstə'pəʊz/ *vt* juxtaposer (**with** à)

Kk

k, K /keɪ/ *n* k, K *m*

kale /keɪl/ *n* (*also* **curly ~**) chou *m* frisé

kaleidoscope /kə'laɪdəskəʊp/ *n* kaléidoscope *m*

kangaroo /ˌkæŋgə'ru:/ *n* kangourou *m*

karaoke /ˌkɑrɪ'əʊkeɪ, -kɪ/ *n* karaoké *m*

karate /kə'rɑ:tɪ/ *n* karaté *m*

Kashmir /kæʃ'mɪə/ *pr n* Cachemire *m*

kayak /'kaɪæk/ *n* kayak *m*

kebab /kɪ'bæb/ *n* (*also* **shish ~**) chiche-kebab *m*

kedgeree /'kedʒəri:, ˌkedʒə'ri:/ *n* (BrE) pilaf *m* de poisson

keel /ki:l/ *n* quille *f*
■ **keel over** ‹*boat*› chavirer; ‹*person*› s'écrouler; ‹*tree*› s'abattre

keen /ki:n/ *adj* **1** (eager) ‹*artist, footballer, supporter*› enthousiaste; ‹*student*› assidu/-e; **to be ~ on** tenir à ‹*plan, project*›; être chaud/-e pour (fam) ‹*idea*›; être passionné/-e de ‹*activity*›; **to be ~ on doing** *or* **to do** tenir à faire; **to be ~ on sb** en pincer (fam) pour qn
2 ‹*appetite, interest*› vif/vive; ‹*eye, intelligence*› vif/vive; ‹*sight*› perçant/-e; ‹*hearing, sense of smell*› fin/-e
3 ‹*competition*› intense

keep /ki:p/ **A** *n* **1** pension *f*; **to pay for one's ~** payer une pension
2 (tower) donjon *m*
B *vt* (*prét, pp* **kept**) **1** (retain) garder ‹*receipt, money, letter, seat*›; **to ~ sb/sth clean** garder qn/qch propre; **to ~ sth warm** garder qch au chaud; **to ~ sb warm** protéger qn du froid; **to ~ sb waiting** faire attendre qn; **to ~ sb talking** retenir qn; **to ~ an engine running** laisser un moteur en marche
2 (detain) retenir; **I won't ~ you a minute** je n'en ai pas pour longtemps
3 tenir ‹*shop*›; élever ‹*chickens*›
4 (sustain) **to ~ [sth] going** entretenir ‹*conversation, fire*›; maintenir ‹*tradition*›; **I'll make you a sandwich to ~ you going** je te ferai un sandwich pour que tu tiennes le coup
5 (store) mettre, ranger; **where do you ~ your cups?** où rangez-vous vos tasses?
6 (support) faire vivre, entretenir ‹*family*›
7 tenir ‹*accounts, diary*›
8 to ~ sth from sb taire *or* cacher qch à qn; **to ~ sth to oneself** garder qch pour soi
9 (prevent) **to ~ sb from doing** empêcher qn de faire
10 tenir ‹*promise*›; garder ‹*secret*›; se rendre à ‹*appointment*›
11 (Mus) **to ~ time** battre la mesure
C *vi* (*prét, pp* **kept**) **1** (continue) **to ~ doing** continuer à *or* de faire, ne pas arrêter de faire; **to ~ going** ‹*person*› continuer
2 (remain) **to ~ out of the rain** se protéger de la pluie; **to ~ warm** se protéger du froid; **to ~ calm** rester calme; **to ~ silent** garder le silence
3 ‹*food*› se conserver, se garder
4 ‹*news, business*› attendre
5 'how are you ~ing?' 'comment allez-vous?'; **she's ~ing well** elle va bien
D *v refl* **to ~ oneself to oneself** ne pas être sociable
E for keeps *phr* pour de bon, pour toujours
■ **keep away**: **A ~ away** ne pas s'approcher (**from** de)

B ∼ **[sth/sb] away** empêcher [qch/qn] de s'approcher

▪ **keep back**: **A** ∼ **back** ne pas s'approcher (**from** de)

B ∼ **[sb/sth] back 1** empêcher [qn] de s'approcher ‹*crowd*› (**from** de); ‹*dam*› retenir ‹*water*›

2 (retain) garder ‹*money*›; conserver ‹*food*›

▪ **keep down**: ∼ **[sth] down**, ∼ **down [sth]** limiter ‹*number, speed, inflation*›; limiter l'augmentation de ‹*prices, unemployment*›

▪ **keep off A** ∼ **off [sth] 1** ne pas marcher sur ‹*grass*›

2 éviter ‹*alcohol*›; s'abstenir de parler de ‹*subject*›

B ∼ **[sth] off** éloigner ‹*insects*›; **this plastic sheet will** ∼ **the rain off** cette housse en plastique protège de la pluie

▪ **keep on**: **A** ∼ **on doing** continuer à faire; **to** ∼ **on about** ne pas arrêter de parler de; **to** ∼ **on at sb** harceler qn (**to do** pour qu'il fasse)

B ∼ **[sb] on** garder

▪ **keep out A** ∼ **out of [sth] 1** ne pas entrer dans ‹*house*›; **'**∼ **out!'** 'défense d'entrer'

2 rester à l'abri de ‹*sun, danger*›

3 ne pas se mêler de ‹*argument*›; **to** ∼ **out of sb's way** (not hinder) ne pas gêner qn; (avoid seeing) éviter qn

B ∼ **[sb/sth] out** ne pas laisser entrer ‹*person, animal*›

▪ **keep to** ne pas s'écarter de ‹*road*›; respecter, s'en tenir à ‹*facts*›; respecter ‹*law, rules*›

▪ **keep up**: **A** ∼ **up** ‹*car, runner, person*› suivre

B ∼ **[sth] up 1** tenir ‹*trousers*›

2 continuer ‹*attack, studies*›; entretenir ‹*correspondence, friendship*›; maintenir ‹*membership, tradition, pace*›

C ∼ **[sb] up** ‹*noise*› empêcher [qn] de dormir

▪ **keep up with 1** aller aussi vite que ‹*person*›; suivre ‹*class*›; ‹*wages*› suivre ‹*inflation*›; faire face à ‹*demand*›

2 suivre ‹*fashion, developments*›

keeper /ˈkiːpə(r)/ *n* (curator) conservateur/-trice *m/f*; (guard) gardien/-ienne *m/f*

keep fit /ˌkiːp ˈfɪt/ *n* gymnastique *f* d'entretien

keeping /ˈkiːpɪŋ/ *n* **1** (custody) **in sb's** ∼ à la garde de qn; **to put sb/sth in sb's** ∼ confier qn/qch à qn

2 (conformity) **in** ∼ **with** conforme à ‹*law, tradition*›; **to be in** ∼ **with** correspondre à ‹*image, character*›; s'harmoniser avec ‹*surroundings*›

keg /keg/ *n* (for liquid) fût *m*; (for gunpowder) baril *m*

kennel /ˈkenl/ *n* **1** (BrE) (for dog) niche *f*

2 (establishment) chenil *m*

Kenya /ˈkenjə/ *pr n* Kenya *m*; **in** ∼ au Kenya

kerb /kɜːb/ *n* (BrE) bord *m* du trottoir

kernel /ˈkɜːnl/ *n* (of nut, fruitstone) amande *f*

kerosene, **kerosine** /ˈkerəsiːn/ *n* **1** (AmE) (paraffin) pétrole *m* (lampant)

2 (fuel) kérosène *m*

kestrel /ˈkestrəl/ *n* (faucon *m*) crécerelle *f*

kettle /ˈketl/ *n* bouilloire *f*; **to put the** ∼ **on** mettre l'eau à chauffer

kettledrum *n* timbale *f*

key /kiː/ **A** *n* **1** clé *f*; **a front door** ∼ une clé de maison; **a set** *or* **bunch of** ∼**s** un jeu de clés; **under lock and** ∼ sous clé; **radiator** ∼ clavette *f* à radiateur

2 (on computer, piano) touche *f*; (on oboe, flute) clé *f*

3 (vital clue) clé *f*, secret *m* (**to** de)

4 (on map) légende *f*; (to abbreviations, symbols) liste *f*; (for code) clé *f*

5 (to test, riddle) solutions *fpl*; (Sch) corrigé *m*

6 (Mus) ton *m*, tonalité *f*; **to sing in/off** ∼ chanter juste/faux

B *adj* ‹*figure, role*› clé; ‹*point*› capital/-e

C *vt* **1** (*also* ∼ **in**) saisir ‹*data*›

2 (adapt) adapter (**to** à)

keyboard /ˈkiːbɔːd/ *n* clavier *m*

keyboards *npl* synthétiseur *m*

keyed up /ˌkiːdˈʌp/ *adj* (excited) excité/-e; (tense) tendu/-e

keyhole /ˈkiːhəʊl/ *n* trou *m* de serrure

keyhole surgery *n* chirurgie *f* endoscopique

keynote speech *n* discours *m* programme

key ring *n* porte-clés *m inv*

keyword *n* mot *m* clé

khaki /ˈkɑːkɪ/ *adj* kaki *inv*

kibbutz /kɪˈbʊts/ *n* (*pl* ∼**es** *ou* ∼**im**) kibboutz *m*

kick /kɪk/ **A** *n* **1** (of person, horse) coup *m* de pied; (of donkey, cow) coup *m* de sabot; (of swimmer) battement *m* de pieds; (of footballer) tir *m*

2 (fam) (thrill) **to get a** ∼ **out of doing** prendre plaisir à faire

3 (of firearm) recul *m*

B *vt* (once) ‹*person*› donner un coup de pied à ‹*person*›; donner un coup de pied dans ‹*door, ball, tin can*›; ‹*horse*› botter ‹*person*›; ‹*donkey, cow*› donner un coup de sabot à ‹*person*›; (repeatedly) ‹*person*› donner des coups de pied à ‹*person*›; donner des coups de pieds dans ‹*object*›; **to** ∼ **sb on the leg** ‹*person, horse*› donner à qn un coup de pied à la jambe; ‹*donkey, cow*› donner à qn un coup de sabot dans la jambe

C *vi* ‹*person*› (once) donner un coup de pied; (repeatedly) donner des coups de pied; ‹*swimmer*› faire des battements de pieds; ‹*cow*› ruer; ‹*horse*› botter

IDIOMS **to** ∼ **the habit** (fam) (of drug addiction) décrocher (fam); (of smoking) arrêter de fumer; **I could have** ∼**ed myself** je me serais donné des claques (fam)

---

mot clé

■ **kick around**, **kick about** donner des coups de pied dans, s'amuser avec ‹*ball*›
■ **kick off** **1** (Sport) donner le coup d'envoi
2 (fam) (start) commencer
■ **kick out**: **A** **~ out** ‹*animal*› ruer
B **~ [sb] out** (fam) virer (fam)

kick-off /'kɪkɒf/ *n* (Sport) coup *m* d'envoi

kick-start /'kɪkstɑ:t/ **A** *n* (*also* **~-starter**) kick *m*
B *vt* **1** faire démarrer [qch] au pied ‹*motorbike*›
2 relancer ‹*economy*›

kid /kɪd/ **A** *n* **1** (fam) (child) enfant *mf*, gosse *mf* (fam); (youth) gamin/-e *m/f* (fam)
2 (young goat) chevreau/-ette *m/f*
3 (goatskin) chevreau *m*
B *vt* (fam) (*p prés etc* **-dd-**) charrier (fam) (**about** à propos de)
C *vi* (fam) (*p prés etc* **-dd-**) rigoler (fam); **no ~ding!** sans blague! (fam)
D *v refl* (fam) **to ~ oneself** se faire des illusions

kidnap /'kɪdnæp/ *vt* (*p prés etc* **-pp-**) enlever

kidnapper /'kɪdnæpə(r)/ *n* ravisseur/-euse *m/f*

kidnapping /'kɪdnæpɪŋ/ *n* enlèvement *m*

kidney /'kɪdnɪ/ *n* **1** (Anat) rein *m*
2 (Culin) rognon *m*

kidney bean *n* haricot *m* rouge

kidney machine *n* rein *m* artificiel; **to be on a ~** être sous dialyse

kill /kɪl/ **A** *n* mise *f* à mort
B *vt* **1** tuer ‹*person, animal*›; **they ~ed each other** ils se sont entre-tués; **even if it ~s me!** (fam) même si je dois y laisser ma peau! (fam); **my feet are ~ing me** (fam) j'ai mal aux pieds
2 mettre fin à, étouffer ‹*rumour*›; ‹*editor*› supprimer ‹*story*›
3 faire disparaître ‹*pain*›; ôter ‹*appetite*›
4 (spend) **to ~ time** tuer le temps (**by doing** en faisant)
C *vi* ‹*person, animal, drug*› tuer
D *v refl* **to ~ oneself** se suicider

killer /'kɪlə(r)/ *n* (person) meurtrier *m*; (animal) tueur/-euse *m/f*; **heroin is a ~** l'héroïne tue

killer whale *n* épaulard *m*

killing /'kɪlɪŋ/ *n* (of individual) meurtre *m* (**of** de); (of animal) mise *f* à mort (**of** de)

killjoy *n* rabat-joie *mf inv*

kiln /kɪln/ *n* four *m*

kilo /'ki:ləʊ/ *n* kilo *m*

kilobyte, **KB** /'kɪləbaɪt/ *n* kilo-octet *m*, Ko *m*

kilogram /'kɪləgræm/ *n* (*also* **kilogramme**) kilogramme *m*

kilometre (BrE), **kilometer** (AmE) /kɪ'lɒmɪtə(r)/ *n* kilomètre *m*

kilowatt /'kɪləwɒt/ *n* kilowatt *m*

kind /kaɪnd/ **A** *n* **1** (sort, type) sorte *f*, genre *m*, type *m*; **this ~ of person** ce genre de personne; **all ~s of people** toutes sortes de personnes; **what ~ of dog is it?** qu'est-ce que c'est comme chien?; **what ~ of person is she?** comment est-elle?, quel genre de personne est-ce?; **this is one of a ~** il/elle est unique en son genre
2 (in vague descriptions) **a ~ of** une sorte de; **I heard a ~ of rattling noise** j'ai entendu comme un cliquetis
3 (classified type) espèce *f*, genre *m*; **one's own ~** les gens de son espèce
B *adj* ‹*person, gesture, words*› gentil/-ille; ‹*act*› bon/bonne *before n*; **to be ~ to sb** être gentil/-ille avec qn; **to be ~ to animals** bien traiter les animaux; **that's very ~ of you** c'est très gentil *or* aimable de votre part; **would you be ~ enough to pass me the salt?** auriez-vous l'amabilité de me passer le sel?
C **in kind** *phr* ‹*pay*› en nature
D **kind of** *phr* (fam) **he's ~ of cute** il est plutôt mignon; **I ~ of like him** en fait, je l'aime bien; **'is it interesting?'—'~ of'** 'est-ce que c'est intéressant?'—'assez'

kindergarten /'kɪndəgɑ:tn/ *n* jardin *m* d'enfants

kind-hearted *adj* ‹*person*› de cœur

kindle /'kɪndl/ *vt* **1** allumer ‹*fire*›
2 attiser ‹*desire, passion*›; susciter ‹*interest*›

kindly /'kaɪndlɪ/ **A** *adj* ‹*person*› gentil/-ille; ‹*smile*› bienveillant/-e
B *adv* **1** (in a kind way) avec gentillesse; **to speak ~ of sb** dire du bien de qn
2 (obligingly) gentiment; **would you ~ do/refrain from doing** auriez-vous l'amabilité de faire/de ne pas faire
3 (favourably) **to take ~ to** apprécier

kindness /'kaɪndnɪs/ *n* gentillesse *f*, bonté *f*

kindred spirit *n* âme *f* sœur

kinetics /kɪ'netɪks/ *n* cinétique *f*

king /kɪŋ/ *n* **1** (monarch) roi *m*; **King Charles** le roi Charles
2 (in chess, cards) roi *m*; (in draughts, checkers) dame *f*

kingdom /'kɪŋdəm/ *n* **1** (country) royaume *m*
2 (Bot, Zool) règne *m*; **the animal ~** le règne animal

kingfisher *n* martin-pêcheur *m*

king-size (*also* **king-sized**) /'kɪŋsaɪz(d)/ *adj* ‹*packet*› géant/-e; ‹*portion, garden*› énorme; **~ bed** grand lit *m*; **~ cigarettes** cigarettes *fpl* extra-longues

kink /kɪŋk/ *n* (in rope, tube) nœud *m*; **the hosepipe has a ~ in it** le tuyau d'arrosage est tordu

kiosk /'ki:ɒsk/ *n* **1** (stand) kiosque *m*
2 (BrE) (phone box) cabine *f*

kipper /'kɪpə(r)/ *n* (BrE) hareng *m* fumé et salé, kipper *m*

kiss /kɪs/ **A** *n* baiser *m*; **to give sb a ~** embrasser qn, donner un baiser à qn
B *vt* embrasser, donner un baiser à

‹*person*›; **to ~ sb on** embrasser qn sur ‹*cheek, lips*›; **we ~ed each other** nous nous sommes embrassés
C *vi* s'embrasser

kiss of life *n* (BrE) bouche-à-bouche *m inv*; **to give sb the ~** faire le bouche-à-bouche à qn

kit /kɪt/ *n* **1** (implements) trousse *f*
2 (gear, clothes) affaires *fpl*; **football ~** affaires de football
3 (for assembly) kit *m*
4 (Mil) paquetage *m*
■ **kit out** équiper (**with** de)

kitbag /ˈkɪtbæg/ *n* (for sport) sac *m* de sport; (for travel) sac *m* de voyage; (Mil) sac *m* de soldat

⚷ **kitchen** /ˈkɪtʃɪn/ *n* cuisine *f*

kitchen foil *n* papier *m* d'aluminium

kitchen roll *n* essuie-tout *m inv*

kitchen sink *n* évier *m*

kitchen unit *n* élément *m* de cuisine

kite /kaɪt/ *n* cerf-volant *m*; **to fly a ~** faire voler un cerf-volant

kitten /ˈkɪtn/ *n* chaton *m*

k **kitty** /ˈkɪtɪ/ *n* cagnotte *f*

kiwi fruit *n* kiwi *m*

kleptomaniac /ˌkleptəˈmeɪnɪæk/ *n, adj* kleptomane *mf*

knack /næk/ *n* **1** (dexterity) tour *m* de main (**of doing** pour faire); **to get the ~** attraper le tour de main; **to lose the ~** perdre la main
2 (talent) don *m* (**for doing** de faire)

knapsack /ˈnæpsæk/ *n* sac *m* à dos

knave /neɪv/ *n* (in cards) valet *m*

knead /niːd/ *vt* pétrir ‹*dough*›; masser ‹*flesh*›

⚷ **knee** /niː/ **A** *n* genou *m*; **on (one's) hands and ~s** à quatre pattes
B *vt* donner un coup de genou à ‹*person*›
IDIOM **to go weak at the ~s** avoir les jambes qui flageolent

kneecap /ˈniːkæp/ *n* rotule *f*

knee-deep /ˌniːˈdiːp/ *adj* **the water was ~** l'eau arrivait aux genoux

kneel /niːl/ *vi* (*also* **~ down**; *prét, pp* **kneeled, knelt**) se mettre à genoux; **to be ~ing** être à genoux

knee-length *adj* ‹*skirt*› qui s'arrête au genou; ‹*boots*› haut/-e; ‹*socks*› long/longue

knickers /ˈnɪkəz/ *npl* (BrE) petite culotte *f*

knick-knack /ˈnɪknæk/ *n* bibelot *m*

knife /naɪf/ **A** *n* (*pl* **knives**) couteau *m*
B *vt* donner un coup de couteau à; **to be ~d** recevoir un coup de couteau

knife-edge *n* **to be (living) on a ~** ‹*person*› être au bord de l'abîme

knife-point *n* **at ~** sous la menace d'un couteau

knight /naɪt/ **A** *n* (gen) chevalier *m*; (in chess) cavalier *m*
B *vt* (BrE) anoblir ‹*person*› (**for** pour)

knighthood /ˈnaɪthʊd/ *n* titre *m* de chevalier

knit /nɪt/ **A** *vt* (*prét, pp* **knitted, knit**) tricoter ‹*sweater, hat*›; **~ted** en tricot
B *vi* (*prét, pp* **knitted, knit**) **1** tricoter
2 ‹*broken bones*› se souder

knitting /ˈnɪtɪŋ/ *n* tricot *m*

knitwear *n* tricots *mpl*

knob /nɒb/ *n* **1** (of door) bouton *m*; (on bannister) boule *f*
2 (control button) bouton *m*

knobbly (BrE), **knobby** (AmE) /ˈnɒblɪ/ *adj* ‹*fingers*› noueux/-euse; ‹*knees*› saillant/-e

⚷ **knock** /nɒk/ **A** *n* **1** (blow) coup *m* (**on** sur, **with** de); **a ~ at the door** un coup à la porte; **~! ~!** toc! toc!
2 (setback) coup *m*; **to take a ~** en prendre un coup
B *vt* **1** (strike) cogner ‹*object*›; **to ~ one's head on sth** se cogner la tête contre qch; **to ~ sb unconscious** assommer qn; **to ~ sth off** *or* **out of sth** faire tomber qch de qch
2 (fam) (criticize) dénigrer
C *vi* **1** ‹*branch, engine, object*› cogner (**on, against** contre); ‹*person*› frapper (**at, on** à)
2 (collide) **to ~ into** *or* **against sth** heurter qch
■ **knock down 1** (deliberately) jeter [qn] à terre ‹*person*›; défoncer ‹*door*›; démolir ‹*building*›; (accidentally) renverser ‹*person, object*›; abattre ‹*fence*›
2 ‹*buyer*› faire baisser ‹*price*›; ‹*seller*› baisser ‹*price*›
■ **knock off**: **A ~ off** arrêter de travailler
B ~ [sb/sth] off, ~ off [sb/sth] 1 (cause to fall) faire tomber ‹*person, object*›
2 (fam) (reduce) **to ~ £10 off the price of sth** réduire le prix de qch de 10 livres
3 (fam) **~ it off!** ça suffit!
■ **knock out 1** casser ‹*tooth*›
2 (make unconscious) ‹*person, blow*› assommer; ‹*drug*› endormir; ‹*boxer*› mettre [qn] au tapis ‹*opponent*›
3 (Sport) éliminer ‹*opponent, team*›
■ **knock over** renverser ‹*person, object*›

knockabout /ˈnɒkəbaʊt/ *n* (Sport) échange *m* de balles

knock-down *adj* ‹*price*› sacrifié/-e

knocker /ˈnɒkə(r)/ *n* heurtoir *m*

knocking /ˈnɒkɪŋ/ *n* (at door) coups *mpl*; (in engine) cognement *m*

knock-kneed *adj* cagneux/-euse

knock-on effect *n* implications *fpl*

knock-out /ˈnɒkaʊt/ **A** *n* (in boxing) knock-out *m*
B *adj* **1** (Sport) ‹*competition*› avec tours éliminatoires
2 (fam) ‹*pills*› sédatif/-ive

knot /nɒt/ **A** *n* **1** nœud *m*; **to tie a ~** faire un nœud; **to tie sth in a ~** nouer qch
2 (in wood) nœud *m*

⚷ mot clé

3 (group) petit groupe *m* (**of** de)
B *vt* (*p prés etc* **-tt-**) nouer (**together** ensemble)

know /nəʊ/ **A** *vt* (*prét* **knew**, /njuː/; *pp* **known** /nəʊn/) (gen) savoir; (be acquainted or familiar with) connaître ‹*place, person, way*›; **to ~ why/how** savoir pourquoi/comment; **to ~ how to do** savoir faire; **to ~ sb by sight** connaître qn de vue; **to get to ~ sb** faire connaissance avec qn; **he ~s all about it** il est au courant; **I knew it!** j'en étais sûr!
B *vi* (*prét* **knew**, *pp* **known**) savoir; **as you ~** comme vous le savez; **to ~ about** (have information) être au courant de ‹*event*›; (have skill) s'y connaître en ‹*computing, engines*›; **to ~ of** (from experience) connaître; (from information) avoir entendu parler de; **to let sb ~ of** *or* **about** tenir qn au courant de
IDIOM **to be in the ~** être bien informé/-e

know-all *n* (BrE) (fam) je-sais-tout *mf inv*

know-how *n* (fam) savoir-faire *m inv*

knowing /ˈnəʊɪŋ/ *adj* ‹*look, smile*› entendu/-e

knowledge /ˈnɒlɪdʒ/ *n* **1** (awareness) connaissance *f*; **to my ~** à ma connaissance; **without sb's ~** à l'insu de qn
2 (factual wisdom) connaissances *fpl*; (of specific field) connaissance *f*; **technical ~** connaissances techniques

knowledgeable /ˈnɒlɪdʒəbl/ *adj* ‹*person*› savant/-e; **to be ~ about** s'y connaître en ‹*subject*›

known /nəʊn/ *adj* ‹*authority, danger*› reconnu/-e; ‹*cure*› connu/-e

knuckle /ˈnʌkl/ *n* **1** (of person) jointure *f*, articulation *f*
2 (Culin) (of lamb, mutton) manche *m* de gigot; (of pork, veal) jarret *m*
■ **knuckle down** (fam) s'y mettre (sérieusement)

knuckle-duster *n* coup-de-poing *m* américain

koala /kəʊˈɑːlə/ *n* (*also* **koala bear**) koala *m*

Koran /kəˈrɑːn/ *n* Coran *m*

Korea /kəˈrɪə/ *pr n* Corée *f*

kosher /ˈkəʊʃə(r)/ *adj* **1** ‹*food, restaurant*› casher
2 (fam) (not illegal) **it's ~** c'est réglo (fam)

Kosovan /ˈkɒsəvn/ **A** *n* Kosovar/-e *m/f*
B *adj* kosovar/-e

Kosovo /ˈkɒsəvəʊ/ *pr n* Kosovo *m*

Kurd /kɜːd/ *n* Kurde *mf*

Kurdish /ˈkɜːdɪʃ/ *adj* kurde

Kurdistan /ˌkɜːdɪˈstæn/ *pr n* Kurdistan *m*

Kuwait /kʊˈweɪt/ *pr n* Koweït *m*

Kyrgyzstan /ˌkɪəgɪˈstɑːn, kɜːgɪ-, -ˈstæn/ *pr n* Kirghizistan *m*

k

l

Ll

l, L /el/ *n* l, L *m*

lab /læb/ *n* labo *m* (fam)

lab coat *n* blouse *f* blanche

label /ˈleɪbl/ **A** *n* **1** (on clothing, jar) étiquette *f*
2 (*also* **record ~**) label *m*
3 (Comput) label *m*
B *vt* (*p prés etc* **-ll-** (BrE), **-l-** (AmE))
1 étiqueter ‹*clothing, jar*›
2 classer, étiqueter (derog) ‹*person*› (**as** comme)

labor (AmE) = **labour**

laboratory /ləˈbɒrətrɪ, (AmE) ˈlæbrətɔːrɪ/ *n* laboratoire *m*

laborer (AmE) = **labourer**

labor union *n* (AmE) syndicat *m*

labour (BrE), **labor** (AmE) /ˈleɪbə(r)/ **A** *n*
1 (work) travail *m*
2 (*also* **~ force**) main-d'œuvre *f*
3 (Med) accouchement *m*; **to be in ~** être en train d'accoucher
B *vi* travailler (**at** à, **on** sur, **to do** pour faire)
IDIOM **to ~ the point** insister lourdement

Labour /ˈleɪbə(r)/ **A** *n* (BrE) parti *m* travailliste
B *adj* travailliste

labourer (BrE), **laborer** (AmE) /ˈleɪbərə(r)/ *n* ouvrier/-ière *m/f* du bâtiment

Labour Party *n* (BrE) parti *m* travailliste

labour-saving *adj* ‹*feature, system*› qui facilite le travail; **~ device** appareil *m* ménager

labyrinth /ˈlæbərɪnθ/ *n* labyrinthe *m*, dédale *m*

lace /leɪs/ **A** *n* **1** (fabric) dentelle *f*
2 (on shoe, boot, dress) lacet *m*; (on tent) cordon *m*
B *vt* **1** lacer ‹*shoes*›
2 to ~ a drink with sth mettre qch dans une boisson

lace-up *n* (*also* **lace-up shoe**) chaussure *f* à lacet

lack /læk/ **A** *n* manque *m* (**of** de); **through ~ of** par manque de
B *vt* manquer de

C *vi* **to be ~ing** manquer; **to be ~ing in** manquer de

lacklustre (BrE), **lackluster** (AmE) *adj* terne

lacquer /'lækə(r)/ *n* **1** (for hair) laque *f*
2 (varnish) laque *f*

lacy /'leɪsɪ/ *adj* en *or* de dentelle

lad /læd/ *n* (fam) (boy) garçon *m*

ladder /'lædə(r)/ **A** *n* **1** (for climbing) échelle *f*
2 (BrE) (in stockings) échelle *f*, maille *f* filée
B *vt*, *vi* filer

laddish /'lædɪʃ/ *adj* (fam) macho *inv* (fam)

ladle /'leɪdl/ *n* (Culin) louche *f*

⚷ **lady** /'leɪdɪ/ **A** *n* (*pl* **ladies**) **1** (woman) dame *f*; **ladies and gentlemen** mesdames et messieurs; **a little old ~** une petite vieille; **she's a real ~** elle est très distinguée
2 (in titles) **Lady Churchill** Lady Churchill
B **ladies** *npl* toilettes *fpl*; (on sign) 'Dames'

ladybird *n* coccinelle *f*

ladylike /'leɪdɪlaɪk/ *adj* ‹*behaviour*› distingué/-e

lag /læg/ **A** *n* (*also* **time ~**) décalage *m*
B *vt* (*p prés etc* **-gg-**) calorifuger ‹*pipe, tank*›; isoler ‹*roof*›

■ **lag behind**: **A** **~ behind** ‹*person, prices*› être à la traîne
B **~ behind [sb/sth]** traîner derrière ‹*person*›; être en retard sur ‹*rival, product*›

lager /'lɑːgə(r)/ *n* bière *f* blonde

lager lout *n* (BrE) voyou *m* (*qui se soûle à la bière*)

lagoon /lə'guːn/ *n* lagune *f*

laid-back /ˌleɪd'bæk/ *adj* (fam) décontracté/-e

laid up *adj* **to be ~** être alité/-e

lake /leɪk/ *n* lac *m*

lamb /læm/ *n* agneau *m*; **leg of ~** gigot *m* d'agneau

lamb's wool /'læmzwʊl/ *n* laine *f* d'agneau, lambswool *m*

lame /leɪm/ *adj* boiteux/-euse

lament /lə'ment/ **A** *n* lamentation *f*
B *vt* se lamenter sur ‹*fate, misfortune*›

lamentable /'læməntəbl/ *adj* déplorable

laminated /'læmɪneɪtɪd/ *adj* ‹*plastic*› stratifié/-e; ‹*wood*› contreplaqué/-e; ‹*card*› plastifié/-e

lamp /læmp/ *n* lampe *f*

lamp post /'læmppəʊst/ *n* réverbère *m*

lampshade *n* abat-jour *m*

lance /lɑːns, (AmE) læns/ *vt* percer ‹*boil, abscess*›

⚷ **land** /lænd/ **A** *n* **1** (terrain, property) terrain *m*; (very large) terres *fpl*
2 (farmland) terre *f*
3 (country) pays *m*
4 (not sea) terre *f*; **dry ~** terre ferme; **to reach ~** toucher terre; **by ~** par voie de terre
B *vt* **1** ‹*pilot*› poser ‹*aircraft*›; faire atterrir ‹*space capsule*›
2 prendre ‹*fish*›
3 (fam) décrocher (fam) ‹*job, contract, prize*›
4 (fam) **to be ~ed with sb/sth** se retrouver avec qn/qch sur les bras
C *vi* **1** ‹*aircraft, passenger*› atterrir
2 ‹*ship*› accoster
3 ‹*person, animal, object*› atterrir; ‹*ball*› toucher le sol; **most of the paint ~ed on me** presque toute la peinture m'est tombée dessus

landing /'lændɪŋ/ *n* **1** (at turn of stairs) palier *m*; (storey) étage *m*
2 (from boat) (of people) débarquement *m*; (of cargo) déchargement *m*
3 (by plane) atterrissage *m* (**on** sur)

landing card *n* carte *f* de débarquement

landing gear *n* train *m* d'atterrissage

landing strip *n* piste *f* d'atterrissage

landlady *n* (owner) propriétaire *f*; (live-in) logeuse *f*; (of pub) patronne *f*

landlord *n* (owner) propriétaire *m*; (live-in) logeur *m*; (of pub) patron *m*

landmark /'lændmɑːk/ *n* (for bearings) point *m* de repère; (major step) étape *f* importante

land mine *n* mine *f* antipersonnel

landowner *n* propriétaire *mf* foncier/-ière

landscape /'lænskeɪp/ *n* paysage *m*

landscape gardener *n* jardinier/-ière *m/f* paysagiste

landslide /'lænslaɪd/ *n* **1** glissement *m* de terrain
2 (*also* **~ victory**) victoire *f* écrasante

lane /leɪn/ *n* **1** (in country) chemin *m*, petite route *f*; (in town) ruelle *f*
2 (of road) voie *f*, file *f*; (air, sea) couloir *m*; (Sport) couloir *m*

⚷ **language** /'læŋgwɪdʒ/ *n* **1** (system in general) langage *m*
2 (of a particular nation) langue *f*; **the French ~** la langue française
3 (of a particular group, style) langage *m*; **legal ~** langage juridique; **bad** *or* **foul ~** langage grossier
4 (Comput) langage *m*

language barrier *n* obstacle *m or* barrière *f* de la langue

language laboratory, **language lab** *n* laboratoire *m* de langues

languish /'læŋgwɪʃ/ *vi* (remain neglected) ‹*person*› languir; ‹*object*› traîner

lank /læŋk/ *adj* ‹*hair*› plat/-e

lantern /'læntən/ *n* lanterne *f*

lap /læp/ *n* **1** (of person) genoux *mpl*; **in one's ~** sur les genoux
2 (Sport) (of track) tour *m* de piste; (of racecourse) tour *m* de circuit
IDIOM **in the ~ of luxury** dans le plus grand luxe

■ **lap up 1** laper ‹*milk, water*›
2 boire [qch] comme du petit lait

⚷ mot clé

‹*compliment, flattery*›

lap belt *n* ceinture *f* ventrale

lapel /lə'pel/ *n* revers *m*

lapse /læps/ **A** *n* **1** (slip) défaillance *f*; **a ~ in concentration** un relâchement de l'attention
2 (interval) intervalle *m*, laps *m* de temps
B *vi* **1** ‹*contract, membership*› expirer; ‹*insurance*› prendre fin
2 to ~ into se mettre à parler ‹*jargon, German*›; tomber dans ‹*coma*›; prendre ‹*bad habits*›

laptop /'læptɒp/ *n* (*also* **~ computer**) portable *m*

lard /lɑːd/ *n* saindoux *m*

larder /'lɑːdə(r)/ *n* garde-manger *m inv*

large /lɑːdʒ/ **A** *adj* (gen) grand/-e *before n*; ‹*appetite, piece, person, nose*› gros/grosse *before n*; ‹*amount*› important/-e; ‹*crowd, family*› nombreux/-euse
B at large *phr* **1** ‹*prisoner, criminal*› en liberté
2 ‹*society, population*› en général, dans son ensemble
IDIOM **by and ~** en général

large-scale *adj* à grande échelle

lark /lɑːk/ *n* **1** (Zool) alouette *f*
2 (fam) (fun) **for a ~** pour rigoler (fam)

laryngitis /ˌlærɪn'dʒaɪtɪs/ *n* laryngite *f*

larynx /'lærɪŋks/ *n* larynx *m*

lasagne /lə'zænjə/ *n* lasagnes *fpl*

laser /'leɪzə(r)/ **A** *n* laser *m*
B *adj* ‹*beam, disc*› laser *inv*; ‹*printer*› à laser

laser treatment *n* thérapie *f* au laser

lash /læʃ/ **A** *n* **1** (eyelash) cil *m*
2 (whipstroke) coup *m* de fouet
B *vt* fouetter ‹*person, animal*›; ‹*rain*› cingler ‹*windows*›
■ **lash out** ‹*person*› devenir violent/-e; **to ~ out at sb** (physically) frapper qn; (verbally) invectiver qn

last /lɑːst, (AmE) læst/ **A** *pron* **the ~** le dernier/la dernière *m/f* (**to do** à faire); **the ~ but one** l'avant-dernier/-ière; **the night before ~** (evening) avant-hier soir; (night) la nuit d'avant-hier; **the week before ~** il y a deux semaines
B *adj* dernier/-ière *before n*; **~ week/year** la semaine/l'année dernière; **~ Christmas** à Noël l'an dernier; **over the ~ ten years** durant ces dix dernières années; **~ night** (evening) hier soir; (night-time) la nuit dernière
C *adv* **1 to come in ~** ‹*runner, racing car*› arriver en dernier; **the girls left ~** les filles sont parties les dernières; **to leave sth till ~** s'occuper de qch en dernier (lieu); **~ of all** en dernier lieu
2 she was ~ here in 1976 la dernière fois qu'elle est venue ici, c'était en 1976
D *vi* **1** durer; **it's too good to ~!** c'est trop beau pour que ça dure!; **he won't ~ long here** il ne tiendra pas longtemps ici
2 ‹*fabric*› faire de l'usage; ‹*perishables*› se conserver
E at last *adv* enfin

last-ditch *adj* ‹*attempt, stand*› désespéré/-e, ultime

lasting /'lɑːstɪŋ, (AmE) 'læstɪŋ/ *adj* ‹*effect, impression*› durable; ‹*relationship*› sérieux/-ieuse

lastly /'lɑːstlɪ, (AmE) 'læstlɪ/ *adv* enfin, finalement

last-minute *adj* de dernière minute

last name *n* nom *m* de famille

last rites *npl* derniers sacrements *mpl*

latch /lætʃ/ *n* (fastening) loquet *m*; (spring lock) serrure *f* (de sûreté)
■ **latch on to** (fam) s'accrocher à ‹*object, person*›; exploiter ‹*idea*›

late /leɪt/ **A** *adj* **1** ‹*arrival*› tardif/-ive; **to be ~ (for sth)** être en retard (pour qch); **to make sb ~** retarder qn; **to be ~ with the rent** payer son loyer avec du retard; **dinner will be a bit ~** le dîner sera retardé
2 ‹*hour, supper, date*› tardif/-ive; **to have a ~ night** (aller) se coucher tard; **to be in one's ~ fifties** approcher de la soixantaine; **in ~ January** (à la) fin janvier; **in the ~ 50s** à la fin des années 50
3 (deceased) feu/-e (fml); **my ~ wife** ma pauvre femme
B *adv* **1** ‹*arrive, start, finish*› en retard; **to be running ~** ‹*person*› être en retard; ‹*train, bus*› avoir du retard; **to start three months ~** commencer avec trois mois de retard
2 ‹*get up, open, close*› tard; ‹*marry*› sur le tard; **~ last night/in the evening** tard hier soir/dans la soirée

latecomer /'leɪtkʌmə(r)/ *n* retardataire *mf*

late developer *n* **to be a ~** ‹*child*› être lent/-e

lately /'leɪtlɪ/ *adv* ces derniers temps

late-night *adj* ‹*film*› dernier/-ière *before n*; ‹*session*› en nocturne; **it's ~ shopping on Thursdays** les magasins restent ouverts tard le jeudi

later **A** *adj* ‹*date*› ultérieur/-e; ‹*model, novel*› postérieur/-e
B *adv* plus tard; **~ on** plus tard; **six months ~** six mois après; **to leave no ~ than 6 am** partir au plus tard à 6 heures; **see you ~!** à tout à l'heure!

latest /'leɪtɪst/ **A** *adj* dernier/-ière *before n*
B at the latest *phr* au plus tard

latex /'leɪteks/ *n* latex *m*

lathe /leɪð/ *n* tour *m*

lather /'lɑːðə(r), 'læðə(r), (AmE) 'læð-/ *n* mousse *f*

Latin /'lætɪn, (AmE) 'lætn/ **A** *n* (language) latin *m*
B *adj* latin/-e

Latin America *pr n* Amérique *f* latine

Latin American *adj* latino-américain/-e

latitude /ˈlætɪtjuːd, (AmE) -tuːd/ *n* latitude *f*

🔑 **latter** /ˈlætə(r)/ *n* **the ~** ce dernier/cette dernière *m/f*; ces derniers/ces dernières *mpl/fpl*

Latvia /ˈlætvɪə/ *pr n* Lettonie *f*

🔑 **laugh** /lɑːf, (AmE) læf/ **A** *n* rire *m*; **to like a good ~** aimer bien rire; **to get a ~** faire rire; **for a ~** (fam) pour rigoler (fam)
B *vi* rire (**about, over** de); **to ~ at sb/sth** rire de qn/qch; **the children ~ed at the clown** le clown a fait rire les enfants; **he's afraid of being ~ed at** il a peur qu'on se moque de lui
▪ **laugh off** choisir de rire de ‹*criticism, insult*›

laughable /ˈlɑːfəbl, (AmE) ˈlæf-/ *adj* ridicule

laughing stock *n* risée *f*

laughter /ˈlɑːftə(r), (AmE) ˈlæf-/ *n* rires *mpl*

🔑 **launch** /lɔːntʃ/ **A** *n* **1** (for patrolling) vedette *f*; (for pleasure) bateau *m* de plaisance
2 (of new boat, rocket) lancement *m*; (of lifeboat) mise *f* à l'eau; (of campaign, product) lancement *m*
B *vt* **1** mettre [qch] à l'eau ‹*dinghy, lifeboat*›; lancer ‹*new ship, missile, rocket*›
2 (start) lancer ‹*campaign, career, product*›; ouvrir ‹*investigation*›

launch pad, launching pad *n* aire *f* de lancement

launder /ˈlɔːndə(r)/ *vt* **1** laver ‹*clothes*›
2 blanchir ‹*money*›

launderette (BrE), **laundromat** (AmE) /lɔːnˈdret, ˌlɔːndəˈrət/ *n* laverie *f* automatique

laundry /ˈlɔːndrɪ/ *n* **1** (place) (commercial) blanchisserie *f*; (in hotel, house) laverie *f*
2 (linen) linge *m*; **to do the ~** faire la lessive

laurel /ˈlɒrəl, (AmE) ˈlɔːrəl/ *n* laurier *m*

lava /ˈlɑːvə/ *n* lave *f*

lavatory /ˈlævətrɪ, (AmE) -tɔːrɪ/ *n* toilettes *fpl*

lavender /ˈlævəndə(r)/ *n* lavande *f*

lavish /ˈlævɪʃ/ **A** *adj* ‹*party, lifestyle*› somptueux/-euse
B *vt* prodiguer ‹*money, affection*› (**on** à)

lavishly /ˈlævɪʃlɪ/ *adv* ‹*decorated*› luxueusement; ‹*spend*› sans compter; ‹*entertain*› généreusement

🔑 **law** /lɔː/ *n* **1** (gen) loi *f*; **to obey/break the ~** respecter/enfreindre la loi; **to be against the ~** être interdit/-e; **by ~** conformément à la loi
2 (Univ) droit *m*; **to study ~** faire son droit

law-abiding *adj* respectueux/-euse des lois

law and order *n* ordre *m* public

law court *n* tribunal *m*

law firm *n* cabinet *m* d'avocats

lawful /ˈlɔːfl/ *adj* ‹*owner, strike*› légal/-e; ‹*conduct*› licite; ‹*wife, husband*› légitime

lawless /ˈlɔːlɪs/ *adj* ‹*society*› anarchique; ‹*area, town*› tombé/-e dans l'anarchie

lawn /lɔːn/ *n* pelouse *f*

lawnmower *n* tondeuse *f* (à gazon)

law school *n* faculté *f* de droit

lawsuit /ˈlɔːsuːt/ *n* procès *m*

🔑 **lawyer** /ˈlɔːjə(r)/ *n* (who practises law) avocat/-e *m/f*; (expert in law) juriste *mf*

lax /læks/ *adj* relâché/-e

laxative /ˈlæksətɪv/ *n* laxatif *m*

🔑 **lay** /leɪ/ **A** *adj* **1** (non-specialist) **~ person** profane *mf*
2 ‹*preacher, member*› laïque
B *vt* (*prét, pp* **laid**) **1** (place) poser ‹*object, card*› (**in** dans, **on** sur); (spread out) étaler ‹*rug, newspaper*› (**on** sur); (arrange) disposer (**on** sur); **to ~ the table (for)** mettre la table (pour)
2 (prepare) préparer ‹*plan, trail*›; poser ‹*basis, foundation*›; tendre ‹*trap*›
3 (Zool) pondre ‹*egg*›
C *vi* (*prét, pp* **laid**) ‹*bird*› pondre
▪ **lay down 1** coucher ‹*baby, patient*›; étaler ‹*rug, cards*›; poser ‹*book, implement*›; déposer ‹*weapon*›
2 to ~ down one's life for sacrifier sa vie pour
3 établir ‹*rule*›; poser ‹*condition*›
▪ **lay off** (temporarily) mettre [qn] en chômage technique; (permanently) licencier
▪ **lay on** prévoir ‹*meal, transport*›; organiser ‹*trip*›
▪ **lay out 1** disposer ‹*goods, food*›; étaler ‹*map, garment, fabric*›
2 concevoir ‹*building, advert*›; mettre [qch] en page ‹*letter*›; monter ‹*page*›

layabout /ˈleɪəbaʊt/ *n* (fam) fainéant/-e *m/f* (fam)

lay-by *n* (BrE) aire *f* de repos

🔑 **layer** /ˈleɪə(r)/ **A** *n* couche *f*
B *vt* **1** couper [qch] en dégradé ‹*hair*›
2 disposer [qch] en couches ‹*cheese, potatoes*›

layman /ˈleɪmən/ *n* profane *m*

lay-off /ˈleɪɒf/ *n* (permanent) licenciement *m*; (temporary) mise *f* en chômage technique

layout /ˈleɪaʊt/ *n* (of page, book, computer screen) mise *f* en page; (of advert, article) présentation *f*; (of building) agencement *m*; (of town) plan *m*; (of garden) dessin *m*

laze /leɪz/ *vi* (*also* **~ about, ~ around**) paresser

lazily /ˈleɪzɪlɪ/ *adv* ‹*move, wonder*› nonchalamment; ‹*lie, float*› mollement; ‹*flow, bob*› doucement

laziness /ˈleɪzɪnɪs/ *n* paresse *f*

lazy /ˈleɪzɪ/ *adj* ‹*person*› paresseux/-euse; ‹*day, holiday*› paisible; ‹*movement, pace*› lent/-e

🔑 **lead**[1] /liːd/ **A** *n* **1 to be in the ~** être en tête; **to go into the ~** passer en tête
2 (initiative) **to take the ~** prendre

🔑 mot clé

l'initiative; **to follow sb's ~** suivre l'exemple de qn
3 (clue) piste *f*
4 (leading role) rôle *m* principal
5 (wire) fil *m*
6 (BrE) (for dog) laisse *f*
B *adj ‹guitarist›* premier/-ière *before n*; *‹role, singer›* principal/-e
C *vt* (*prét, pp* **led**) **1** (guide, escort) mener, conduire *‹person›* (**to sth** à qch, **to sb** auprès de qn); **to ~ sb away** éloigner qn (**from** de)
2 (bring) *‹path, sign›* mener (**to** à)
3 (cause) **to ~ sb to do** amener qn à faire
4 mener *‹army, team, attack, strike›*; diriger *‹orchestra, research›*
5 (conduct, have) mener *‹active life›*; **to ~ a life of luxury** vivre dans le luxe
D *vi* (*prét, pp* **led**) **1 to ~ to** *‹path›* mener à; *‹door›* s'ouvrir sur; *‹exit, trapdoor›* donner accès à
2 (result in) **to ~ to** entraîner *‹complication, discovery, accident›*
3 *‹runner, car, company›* être en tête; *‹team, side›* mener; **to ~ by 15 seconds** avoir 15 secondes d'avance
4 (in walk) aller devant; (in action, discussion) prendre l'initiative; (in dancing) conduire
■ **lead up to 1** (precede) précéder *‹event›*
2 (build up to) amener *‹topic›*

lead[2] /led/ *n* plomb *m*; (in pencil) mine *f*

leaded petrol (BrE), **leaded gasoline** (AmE) *n* essence *f* au plomb

leader /'li:də(r)/ *n* **1** (of nation) chef *m* d'État, dirigeant/-e *m/f*; (of gang) chef *m*; (of party) leader *m*; (of trade union) secrétaire *mf*; (of strike, movement) meneur/-euse *m/f*
2 (in competition) premier/-ière *m/f*; (horse) cheval *m* de tête; (in market, field) leader *m*

leadership /'li:dəʃɪp/ *n* dirigeants *mpl*, direction *f*; **under the ~ of** sous la direction de

leadership contest, **leadership election** *n* (Pol) élection *f* à la direction du parti

leadership qualities *npl* qualités *fpl* de leader

lead-free /'ledfri:/ *adj* sans plomb

leading /'li:dɪŋ/ *adj* **1** *‹lawyer, politician›* éminent/-e, important/-e; *‹company, bank›* important/-e; *‹brand›* dominant/-e
2 *‹role›* (main) majeur/-e; (in theatre) principal/-e
3 (Sport) *‹driver, car›* en tête de course; *‹team›* en tête du classement

leading edge **A** *n* **at the ~ of** à la pointe de *‹technology›*
B **leading-edge** *adj ‹technology›* de pointe

lead story /li:d/ *n* histoire *f* à la une (fam)

leaf /li:f/ *n* (*pl* **leaves** /li:vz/) **1** (of plant) feuille *f*
2 (of book) page *f*
IDIOM **to turn over a new ~** tourner la page
■ **leaf through** feuilleter *‹papers, book›*

leaflet /'li:flɪt/ *n* (gen) dépliant *m*; (advertising) prospectus *m*

league /li:g/ *n* **1** (alliance) ligue *f*; **to be in ~ with sb** être de mèche avec qn (fam)
2 (BrE) (Sport) (competition) championnat *m*; (association) ligue *f*
3 they're not in the same ~ ils ne sont pas comparables

league table *n* classement *m*

leak /li:k/ **A** *n* fuite *f*
B *vt* divulguer *‹information, document›*
C *vi* **1** *‹container, roof›* fuir; *‹boat›* faire eau
2 *‹liquid, gas›* s'échapper (**from** de)

leaky /'li:kɪ/ *adj ‹container, pipe›* qui fuit; *‹boat›* qui prend l'eau

lean /li:n/ **A** *adj* **1** *‹body, face›* mince; *‹meat›* maigre
2 *‹year, times›* difficile
B *vt* (*prét, pp* **leaned** *ou* **leant**) appuyer (**against** contre)
C *vi* (*prét, pp* **leaned** *ou* **leant**) *‹wall, building›* pencher; **to ~ against sth** *‹bicycle, ladder›* être appuyé/-e contre qch; *‹person›* s'appuyer à qch; (with back) s'adosser à qch; **to ~ out of the window** se pencher par la fenêtre
■ **lean back** se pencher en arrière
■ **lean forward** se pencher en avant
■ **lean on**: **A** **~ on [sth]** s'appuyer sur *‹stick›*; s'accouder à *‹window sill›*
B **~ on [sb]** (as support) s'appuyer sur *‹person›*; (depend on) compter sur *‹person›*; (pressurize) faire pression sur *‹person›*
■ **lean over**: **~ over [sth]** se pencher par-dessus [qch]

leap /li:p/ **A** *n* **1** (jump) saut *m*, bond *m*
2 (step in process) bond *m* (en avant)
3 (in price) bond *m* (**in** dans)
B *vi* (*prét, pp* **leapt**, **leaped** /lept, li:pt/) **1** *‹person, animal›* bondir, sauter; **to ~ to one's feet, to ~ up** se lever d'un bond; **to ~ across** *or* **over sth** franchir qch d'un bond
2 *‹heart›* bondir (**with** de)
3 (*also* **~ up**) *‹price›* grimper (**by** de)
■ **leap at**: **~ at [sth]** sauter sur *‹chance, offer›*
■ **leap up 1** (jump to one's feet) bondir sur ses pieds
2 *‹price, rate›* grimper

leapfrog /'li:pfrɒg/ *n* saute-mouton *m*

leap year *n* année *f* bissextile

learn /lɜ:n/ **A** *vt* (*prét, pp* **learned** *ou* **learnt**) (gen) apprendre; acquérir *‹skills›* (**from** de); **to ~ (how) to do** apprendre à faire; **to ~ that** apprendre que
B *vi* (*prét, pp* **learned** *ou* **learnt**) apprendre; **to ~ about sth** apprendre qch; **to ~ from one's mistakes** tirer la leçon de ses erreurs

learned /'lɜ:nɪd/ *adj ‹person, book›* érudit/-e; *‹journal›* spécialisé/-e; *‹society›* savant/-e

learner /ˈlɜːnə(r)/ *n* (beginner) débutant/-e *m/f*; **to be a fast/slow ~** apprendre/ne pas apprendre vite

learner driver *n* élève *mf* d'auto-école

✓ **learning** /ˈlɜːnɪŋ/ *n* **1** (knowledge) érudition *f* **2** (process) apprentissage *m*

learning curve *n* courbe *f* d'apprentissage

learning difficulties *npl* (of schoolchildren) difficultés *fpl* scolaires; (of adults) difficultés *fpl* d'apprentissage

lease /liːs/ **A** *n* bail *m*
B *vt* louer [qch] à bail ‹*house*›; louer ‹*car*›

leaseholder *n* locataire *mf* à bail

leash /liːʃ/ *n* laisse *f*

leasing /ˈliːsɪŋ/ **A** *n* (by company) crédit-bail *m*; (by individual) location *f* avec option d'achat
B *adj* ‹*company, scheme*› de leasing

✓ **least** /liːst/ **A** *det* **the ~** le moins de; (in negative constructions) le *or* la moindre; **they have the ~ money** ce sont eux qui ont le moins d'argent; **I haven't the ~ idea** je n'en ai pas la moindre idée
B *pron* **the ~** le moins; **we have the ~** c'est nous qui en avons le moins; **it was the ~ I could do!** c'est la moindre des choses!
C *adv* **1** (with adjective or noun) **the ~** le/ la moins; (with plural noun) les moins; **the ~ wealthy families** les familles les moins riches
2 (with verbs) le moins *inv*; **I like that one (the) ~** c'est celui-là que j'aime le moins; **nobody liked it, ~ of all John** personne ne l'aimait, John encore moins que les autres
D **at least** *phr* (at the minimum) au moins; **she's at ~ 40** elle a au moins 40 ans; **they could at ~ have phoned!** ils auraient au moins pu téléphoner!; **he's gone to bed—at ~ I think so** il est allé se coucher—du moins, je pense
E **in the least** *phr* **not in the ~** pas du tout
IDIOM **last but not ~, last but by no means ~** enfin et surtout

leather /ˈleðə(r)/ **A** *n* cuir *m*
B *adj* ‹*garment, object*› de cuir, en cuir

✓ **leave** /liːv/ **A** *n* congé *m*; **three days' ~** trois jours de congé
B *vt* (*prét, pp* **left**) **1** (depart from) partir de ‹*house, station etc*›; (more permanently) quitter ‹*country, city etc*›; (go out of) sortir de ‹*room, building*›; **he left home early** il est parti tôt de chez lui; **to ~ school** quitter l'école
2 (forget) oublier ‹*child, object*›
3 quitter ‹*partner*›
4 laisser ‹*instructions, tip*› (**for** pour, **with** à); **to ~ sb sth** laisser qch à qn; **to ~ sb/sth in sb's care** confier qn/qch à qn
5 laisser ‹*food, drink, gap*›; **to ~ sth lying around** laisser traîner qch; **to ~ sth tidy** laisser qch en ordre
6 **to ~ sth to sb** laisser [qch] à qn ‹*job, task*›; **to ~ it (up) to sb to do** laisser à qn le soin de faire; **to ~ sb to it** laisser qn se débrouiller; **~ it to *or* with me** je m'en occupe
7 ‹*oil, wine*› faire ‹*stain*›; ‹*cup, plate*› laisser ‹*stain, mark*›
8 (postpone) laisser ‹*task, homework*›; **~ it till tomorrow** laisse ça pour demain
9 (bequeath) léguer (**to sb** à qn)
C *vi* (*prét, pp* **left**) partir (**for** pour)
■ **leave behind 1** (go faster than) distancer ‹*person, competitor*›; **to be *or* get left behind** (physically) se faire distancer; (intellectually) ne pas suivre; (in business) se laisser distancer
2 ‹*traveller*› laisser [qch] derrière soi ‹*town, country*›; ‹*person*› quitter ‹*family, husband*›; en finir avec ‹*past*›
3 (forget) oublier, laisser ‹*object, child, animal*›
■ **leave out 1** (accidentally) oublier ‹*word, ingredient, person*›; (deliberately) omettre ‹*name, fact*›; ne pas mettre ‹*ingredient, object*›; tenir [qn] à l'écart ‹*person*›; **to ~ sb out of** exclure qn de ‹*group*›
2 (outdoors) laisser [qch] dehors

leaving /ˈliːvɪŋ/ **A** *n* départ *m*
B *adj* ‹*party, present*› d'adieu

Lebanon /ˈlebənən/ *pr n* **(the) ~** (le) Liban *m*

lecherous /ˈletʃərəs/ *adj* lubrique

lectern /ˈlektɜːn/ *n* (in church) lutrin *m*; (for lecture notes) pupitre *m*

lecture /ˈlektʃə(r)/ **A** *n* conférence *f* (**on** sur); (BrE) (Univ) cours *m* magistral (**on** sur)
B *vt* **1** (BrE) (Univ) donner des cours à ‹*class*›
2 (scold) faire la leçon à ‹*person*›
C *vi* **1** (gen) donner une conférence (**on** sur)
2 (BrE) (Univ) **to ~ in sth** enseigner qch (à l'université)

lecture notes *npl* notes *fpl* de cours

lecturer /ˈlektʃərə(r)/ *n* **1** (speaker) conférencier/-ière *m/f*
2 (BrE) (Univ) enseignant/-e *m/f* (du supérieur)
3 (AmE) (Univ) ≈ chargé *m* de cours

lecture theatre *n* amphithéâtre *m*

ledge /ledʒ/ *n* **1** (shelf) rebord *m*
2 (on mountain) saillie *f* (rocheuse)

ledger /ˈledʒə(r)/ *n* registre *m* de comptabilité, grand livre *m*

leech /liːtʃ/ *n* sangsue *f*

leek /liːk/ *n* poireau *m*

leer /lɪə(r)/ *vi* **to ~ at sb/sth** lorgner qn/ qch (fam)

leeway /ˈliːweɪ/ *n* liberté *f* de manœuvre

✓ **left** /left/ **A** *n* gauche *f*; **on the ~** sur la gauche; (politically) à gauche
B *adj* **1** ‹*eye, hand, shoe*› gauche
2 (remaining) **to be ~** rester; **there are/we have five minutes ~** il reste/il nous reste cinq minutes; **I've got one ~** il m'en reste un
C *adv* ‹*go, look, turn*› à gauche

✓ mot clé

left-hand /ˌleftˈhænd/ *adj* ‹*side*› de gauche
left-hand drive *n* voiture *f* avec la conduite à gauche
left-handed /ˌleftˈhændɪd/ *adj* gaucher/-ère
left luggage *n* (*also* **left-luggage office**) (BrE) consigne *f*
left-luggage lockers *npl* (BrE) consigne *f* automatique
leftovers *npl* restes *mpl*
left wing **A** *n* **the ~** la gauche *f*
B **left-wing** *adj* ‹*attitude*› de gauche; **they are very ~** ils sont très à gauche
leg /leg/ *n* **1** (of person, horse) jambe *f*; (of other animal) patte *f*
2 (of furniture) pied *m*
3 (Culin) (of lamb) gigot *m*; (of poultry, pork, frog) cuisse *f*
4 (of trousers) jambe *f*
5 (of journey, race) étape *f*
IDIOM **to pull sb's ~** faire marcher qn
legacy /ˈlegəsɪ/ *n* **1** (Law) legs *m*
2 (fig) héritage *m*; (of war) séquelles *fpl*
legal /ˈliːgl/ *adj* **1** ‹*document, system*› juridique; ‹*costs*› de justice; **to take ~ advice** consulter un avocat
2 ‹*heir, right, separation*› légal/-e; ‹*owner, claim*› légitime
legal action *n* **to take ~ against sb** intenter un procès à qn
legal aid *n* aide *f* juridique
legal holiday *n* (AmE) jour *m* férié
legalize /ˈliːgəlaɪz/ *vt* légaliser
legally /ˈliːgəlɪ/ *adv* ‹*valid, void*› juridiquement; **this contract is ~ binding** ce contrat vous engage; ‹*act*› légalement
legal proceedings *npl* poursuites *fpl* judiciaires
legal tender *n* monnaie *f* légale
legend /ˈledʒənd/ *n* légende *f* (**of** de)
legendary /ˈledʒəndrɪ, (AmE) -derɪ/ *adj* légendaire
leggings /ˈlegɪŋz/ *npl* (for baby) collant *m*; (for woman) caleçon *m*
legible /ˈledʒəbl/ *adj* lisible
Legionnaire's disease *n* légionellose *f*
legislation /ˌledʒɪsˈleɪʃn/ *n* législation *f*
legitimate /lɪˈdʒɪtɪmət/ *adj* **1** (justifiable) ‹*action, question, request*› légitime; ‹*excuse*› valable
2 (lawful) ‹*organization*› régulier/-ière; ‹*child, heir, owner*› légitime
legitimize /lɪˈdʒɪtɪmaɪz/ *vt* (legalize) légaliser; (justify) justifier
leisure /ˈleʒə(r), (AmE) ˈliːʒə(r)/ **A** *n* loisirs *mpl*; **to do sth at (one's) ~** prendre son temps pour faire qch
B *adj* ‹*centre, facilities*› de loisirs
leisure centre /ˈleʒə ˌsentə(r)/ *n* (BrE) centre *m* de loisirs
leisure time *n* loisirs *mpl*, temps *m* libre
leisure wear *n* vêtements *mpl* de sport
lemon /ˈlemən/ *n* (fruit) citron *m*
lemonade /ˌleməˈneɪd/ *n* (fizzy) limonade *f*; (still) citronnade *f*; (AmE) (fresh) citron *m* pressé
lemon juice *n* jus *m* de citron; (BrE) (drink) citron *m* pressé
lemon tea *n* thé *m* au citron
lemon tree *n* citronnier *m*
lend /lend/ *vt* (*pp, prét* **lent**) **1** (loan) prêter ‹*object, money*›; **to ~ sb sth, to ~ sth to sb** prêter qch à qn; **to ~ a hand** donner un coup de main
2 (give) conférer ‹*quality, credibility*› (**to** à); prêter ‹*support*›; **to ~ weight to sth** donner du poids à qch
lender /ˈlendə(r)/ *n* prêteur/-euse *m/f*
lending /ˈlendɪŋ/ *n* prêt *m*
length /leŋθ/ **A** *n* **1** longueur *f*; **what ~ is the plank?** de quelle longueur est la planche?; **to be 50 cm in ~** faire 50 cm de long
2 (of book, film, list) longueur *f*; (of event, prison sentence) durée *f*; **~ of time** temps *m*
3 (piece of string, carpet, wood) morceau *m*; (of fabric) ≈ métrage *m*; (of pipe, track) tronçon *m*; **dress ~** hauteur *f* de robe
4 (Sport) longueur *f*
B **at length** *phr* longuement
IDIOM **to go to great ~s to do** se donner beaucoup de mal pour faire
lengthen /ˈleŋθən/ **A** *vt* rallonger ‹*garment*› (**by** de, par); prolonger ‹*shelf, road*› (**by** de, par); prolonger ‹*stay*›
B *vi* ‹*queue, list*› s'allonger; ‹*days*› rallonger
lengthy /ˈleŋθɪ/ *adj* long/longue
lenient /ˈliːnɪənt/ *adj* ‹*person*› indulgent/-e (**with** pour); ‹*punishment*› léger/-ère
lens /lenz/ *n* (in optical instruments) lentille *f*; (in spectacles) verre *m*; (in camera) objectif *m*; (contact) lentille *f*
lens cap *n* bouchon *m* d'objectif
Lent /lent/ *n* carême *m*
lentil /ˈlentl/ *n* lentille *f*
Leo /ˈliːəʊ/ *pr n* Lion *m*
leopard /ˈlepəd/ *n* léopard *m*
leotard /ˈliːətɑːd/ *n* justaucorps *m inv*
leper /ˈlepə(r)/ *n* lépreux/-euse *m/f*
leprosy /ˈleprəsɪ/ *n* lèpre *f*
lesbian /ˈlezbɪən/ *n* lesbienne *f*
less /les/ **A** *det* moins de; **~ beer** moins de bière; **I have ~ money than him** j'ai moins d'argent que lui
B *pron* moins; **I have ~ than you** j'en ai moins que toi; **~ than 10** moins de dix; **in ~ than three hours** en moins de trois heures; **even ~** encore moins
C *adv* moins; **I read ~ these days** je lis moins à présent; **the more I see him, the ~ I like him** plus je le vois, moins je l'aime
D *prep* moins; **~ 15% discount** moins 15% de remise; **~ tax** avant impôts
E **less and less** *phr* de moins en moins

lessen /'lesn/ *vt* diminuer ‹*influence, feelings*›; réduire ‹*cost*›; atténuer ‹*impact, pain*›

lesser /'lesə(r)/ **A** *adj* moindre; **to a ~ extent** à un moindre degré
B *adv* moins; **~ known** moins connu

⚷ **lesson** /'lesn/ *n* cours *m*, leçon *f*; **Spanish ~** cours d'espagnol; **driving ~** leçon de conduite; **I'm going to teach him a ~!** je vais lui donner une bonne leçon!

⚷ **let¹**

> When *let* is used with another verb to make a suggestion (*let's do it at once*), the first person plural of the appropriate verb can generally be used to express this in French: *faisons-le tout de suite*. (Note that the verb alone translates *let us do* and no pronoun appears in French.)
>
> In the spoken language, however, French speakers will use the much more colloquial *on + present tense* or *si on + imperfect tense*: *let's go!* = allons-y *or* on y va!; *let's go to the cinema tonight* = si on allait au cinéma ce soir?
>
> These translations can also be used for suggestions in the negative: *let's not take* or *don't let's take the bus—let's walk* = on ne prend pas le bus, on y va à pied *or* ne prenons pas le bus, allons-y à pied.
>
> When *let* is used to mean *allow*, it is generally translated by the verb *laisser*. For more examples and particular usages, see the entry below.

/let/ *vt* (*p prés* **-tt-**, *prét*, *pp* **let**) **1** (in suggestions, commands) **~'s get out of here!** sortons d'ici!; **~'s not** *or* **don't ~'s** (BrE) **talk about that!** n'en parlons pas!
2 (allow) **to ~ sb do** laisser qn faire; **~ me explain** laisse-moi t'expliquer; **don't ~ it get you down** ne te laisse pas abattre; **she wanted to go but they wouldn't ~ her** elle voulait y aller mais ils ne l'ont pas laissée faire; **to ~ one's hair grow** se laisser pousser les cheveux

■ **let down** **A** **~ [sb] down 1** (disappoint) laisser tomber; **to feel let down** être déçu/-e
2 (embarrass) faire honte à
B **~ [sth] down 1** (BrE) dégonfler ‹*tyre*›
2 rallonger ‹*garment*›

■ **let go**: **A** **~ go** lâcher prise; **to ~ go of sb/sth** lâcher qn/qch
B **~ [sb] go 1** relâcher ‹*prisoner*›
2 lâcher ‹*person, arm*›
3 licencier ‹*employee*›
4 to ~ oneself go se laisser aller
C **~ [sth] go** lâcher ‹*rope, bar*›

■ **let in**: **A** **~ [sth] in** ‹*roof, window*› laisser passer ‹*rain*›; ‹*shoes*› prendre ‹*water*›; ‹*curtains*› laisser passer ‹*light*›
B **~ [sb] in 1** (show in) faire entrer; (admit) laisser entrer
2 to ~ oneself in for aller au devant de ‹*trouble*›

■ **let off**: **A** **~ off [sth]** tirer ‹*fireworks*›; faire exploser ‹*bomb*›; faire partir ‹*gun*›
B **~ [sb] off 1** (excuse) **to ~ sb off** dispenser qn de ‹*homework*›
2 (leave unpunished) ne pas punir ‹*culprit*›

■ **let out**: **A** **~ out** (AmE) ‹*school*› finir (**at** à)
B **~ out [sth] 1** laisser échapper ‹*cry*›; **to ~ out a roar** beugler
2 (BrE) (reveal) révéler (**that** que)
C **~ [sth] out 1** faire sortir ‹*animal*›; donner libre cours à ‹*anger*›
2 élargir ‹*waistband*›
D **~ [sb] out** laisser sortir ‹*prisoner*› (**of** de); faire sortir ‹*pupils, employees*› (**of** de)

■ **let up** ‹*rain, wind*› se calmer; ‹*pressure*› s'arrêter; ‹*heat*› diminuer

let² /let/ *vt* (*p prés* **-tt-**, *prét*, *pp* **let**) (*also* **~ out** (BrE)) **'to ~'** 'à louer'

let-down /'letdaʊn/ *n* déception *f*

lethal /'li:θl/ *adj* ‹*substance, gas, dose*› mortel/-elle; ‹*weapon*› meurtrier/-ière

lethargic /lɪ'θɑ:dʒɪk/ *adj* léthargique; **to feel ~** se sentir engourdi/-e

⚷ **letter** /'letə(r)/ *n* **1** lettre *f* (**to** pour, **from** de)
2 (of alphabet) lettre *f*

letter bomb *n* lettre *f* piégée

letter box *n* boîte *f* à lettres

letterhead *n* en-tête *m*

letters page *n* courrier *m* des lecteurs

lettuce /'letɪs/ *n* salade *f*, laitue *f*

let-up /'letʌp/ *n* accalmie *f*; (respite) pause *f*

leukemia /lu:'ki:mɪə/ *n* (*also* **leukaemia**) leucémie *f*

⚷ **level** /'levl/ **A** *n* **1** (gen) niveau *m*; **to be on the same ~ as sb** être du même niveau que qn; **at street ~** au niveau de la rue
2 (of unemployment, illiteracy) taux *m*; (of spending) montant *m*; (of satisfaction, anxiety) degré *m*
3 (in hierarchy) échelon *m*
B *adj* **1** ‹*shelf, floor*› droit/-e; ‹*table*› horizontal/-e
2 ‹*ground, surface, land*› plat/-e
3 (Culin) ‹*teaspoonful*› ras/-e
4 to be ~ ‹*shoulders, windows*› être à la même hauteur; ‹*floor, building*› être au même niveau; **~ with the ground** au ras du sol
5 to remain ~ ‹*figures*› rester stable
C *adv* **to draw ~** arriver à la même hauteur (**with** que)
D *vt* (*p prés etc* **-ll-** (BrE), **-l-** (AmE))
1 (destroy) raser ‹*village*›
2 lancer ‹*accusation*› (**at** contre); adresser ‹*criticism*› (**at** à); braquer ‹*gun*› (**at** sur)
3 aplanir ‹*ground, surface*›
IDIOMS **to be ~-pegging** être à égalité; **to ~ with sb** être honnête avec qn

■ **level off** ‹*prices, curve*› se stabiliser

level crossing *n* (BrE) passage *m* à niveau

level-headed *adj* sensé/-e

lever /'li:və(r), (AmE) 'levər/ *n* (Aut, Tech) levier *m*; (small) manette *f*

levy /'levɪ/ **A** *n* taxe *f*, impôt *m*
B *vt* prélever ‹*tax, duty*›; imposer ‹*fine*›

lewd /lju:d, (AmE) 'lu:d/ *adj* ‹*joke, gesture, remark*› obscène; ‹*person*› lubrique

lexicon /'leksɪkən, (AmE) -kɒn/ *n* lexique *m*

liability /,laɪə'bɪlətɪ/ **A** *n* **1** (Law) responsabilité *f*
2 (drawback) handicap *m*
B **liabilities** *npl* passif *m*, dettes *fpl*

liable /'laɪəbl/ *adj* **1** (likely) **to be ~ to do** risquer de faire; **it's ~ to rain** il risque de pleuvoir, il se peut qu'il pleuve
2 (legally subject) **to be ~ to** être passible de ‹*fine*›; **to be ~ for tax** ‹*person, company*› être imposable; ‹*goods*› être soumis/-e à l'impôt

liaise /lɪ'eɪz/ *vi* travailler en liaison (**with** avec)

liaison /lɪ'eɪzn, (AmE) 'lɪəzɒn/ *n* liaison *f*

liar /'laɪə(r)/ *n* menteur/-euse *m/f*

libel /'laɪbl/ **A** *n* diffamation *f*
B *vt* (*p prés etc* **-ll-** (BrE), **-l-** (AmE)) diffamer

libellous (BrE), **libelous** (AmE) /'laɪbələs/ *adj* diffamatoire

liberal /'lɪbərəl/ **A** *n* libéral/-e *m/f*
B *adj* **1** (politically) libéral/-e
2 ‹*amount*› généreux/-euse; ‹*person*› prodigue (**with** de)

Liberal /'lɪbərəl/ *n* libéral/-e *m/f*

Liberal Democrat *n* (BrE) libéral-démocrate *mf*

liberalism /'lɪbərəlɪzəm/ *n* libéralisme *m*

liberalize /'lɪbərəlaɪz/ *vt* libéraliser

liberate /'lɪbəreɪt/ **A** *vt* libérer (**from** de)
B **liberated** *pp adj* ‹*lifestyle, woman*› libéré/-e
C **liberating** *pres p adj* libérateur/-trice

liberation /,lɪbə'reɪʃn/ *n* libération *f* (**from** de); **women's ~** libération de la femme

liberty /'lɪbətɪ/ *n* liberté *f*

Libra /'li:brə/ *n* Balance *f*

librarian /laɪ'breərɪən/ *n* bibliothécaire *mf*

library /'laɪbrərɪ, (AmE) -brerɪ/ *n* bibliothèque *f*; **public ~** bibliothèque municipale; **mobile ~** (BrE) bibliobus *m*

lice /laɪs/ *npl* poux *mpl*

licence (BrE), **license** (AmE) /'laɪsns/ *n* **1** (for trading) licence *f*
2 (to drive, fish) permis *m*; (for TV) redevance *f*; **to lose one's (driving) ~** se faire retirer son permis (de conduire)
3 (freedom) licence *f*

licence number *n* (of car) numéro *m* minéralogique *or* d'immatriculation

licence plate *n* plaque *f* minéralogique *or* d'immatriculation

license /'laɪsns/ **A** *n* (AmE) = **licence**
B *vt* **1** (authorize) autoriser (**to do** à faire)
2 faire immatriculer ‹*vehicle*›

licensed /'laɪsnst/ *adj* **1** ‹*restaurant*› qui a une licence de débit de boissons
2 ‹*dealer, firm, taxi*› agréé/-e; ‹*pilot*› breveté/-e; ‹*vehicle*› en règle

licensing laws *npl* (BrE) lois *fpl* réglementant la vente des boissons alcoolisées

lick /lɪk/ **A** *n* **1** coup *m* de langue
2 a ~ of paint un petit coup de peinture
B *vt* **1** lécher; **to ~ one's lips** se lécher les babines
2 (fam) écraser ‹*team, opponent*›; **to get ~ed** se faire écraser
IDIOM **to ~ one's wounds** panser ses blessures

licorice (AmE) = **liquorice**

lid /lɪd/ *n* **1** (cover) couvercle *m*
2 (eyelid) paupière *f*

lie /laɪ/ **A** *n* mensonge *m*; **to tell a ~** mentir
B *vi* **1** (*p prés* **lying**, *prét, pp* **lied**) (tell falsehood) mentir (**to sb** à qn, **about** à propos de); **he ~d about her** il a menti à son propos
2 (*p prés* **lying**, *prét* **lay**, *pp* **lain**, *also for 3 & 4*) ‹*person, animal*› (action) s'allonger; (state) être allongé/-e; ‹*objects*› être couché/-e; **he was lying on the bed** il était allongé sur le lit; **to ~ on one's back** s'allonger sur le dos; **~ still** ne bougez pas; **here ~s John Brown** ci-gît John Brown
3 (be situated) être; **to ~ open** ‹*book*› être ouvert/-e; **that's where our future ~s** c'est là qu'est notre avenir; **to ~ before sb** ‹*life, career*› s'ouvrir devant qn; **what ~s ahead?** qu'est-ce qui nous attend?; **the house lay empty for years** la maison est restée vide pendant des années
4 (can be found) résider; **their interests ~ elsewhere** leurs intérêts résident ailleurs; **to ~ in** ‹*cause, secret, talent*› résider dans; ‹*popularity, strength, fault*› venir de; **the responsibility ~s with them** ce sont eux qui sont responsables
IDIOMS **to ~ low** garder un profil bas; **to take it lying down** (fam) se laisser faire
■ **lie around** traîner; **to leave sth lying around** laisser traîner qch
■ **lie down** (briefly) s'allonger; (for longer period) se coucher

lie detector *n* détecteur *m* de mensonge

lie-in /'laɪɪn/ *n* **to have a ~** faire la grasse matinée

lieu /lju:/ **A** **in lieu** *adv phr* **one week's holiday in ~** une semaine de vacances pour compenser
B **in lieu of** *prep phr* à la place de

life /laɪf/ *n* (*pl* **lives**) **1** (gen) vie *f*; **that's ~!** c'est la vie!; **the first time in my ~** la première fois de ma vie; **a job for ~** un emploi à vie; **a friend for ~** un ami pour la vie; **for the rest of one's ~** pour le restant de ses jours; **full of ~** plein/-e de vie; **to come to ~** ‹*shy person*› sortir de sa réserve;

‹*fictional character*› prendre vie; ‹*party*› s'animer
2 (of machine, product) durée *f*
3 (Law) **to serve ~** être emprisonné/-e à vie; **to sentence sb to ~** condamner qn à perpétuité
IDIOM **to have the time of one's ~** s'amuser comme un fou/une folle

lifebelt *n* bouée *f* de sauvetage
lifeboat *n* canot *m* de sauvetage
life drawing *n* dessin *m* d'après modèle
life expectancy *n* espérance *f* de vie; (of product) durée *f* probable
lifeguard *n* surveillant/-e *m/f* de baignade
life imprisonment *n* réclusion *f* à perpétuité
life insurance *n* assurance-vie *f*
life jacket *n* gilet *m* de sauvetage
lifeless /'laɪflɪs/ *adj* ‹*body, object*› inanimé/-e; ‹*performance*› peu vivant/-e; ‹*voice*› éteint/-e
lifelike *adj* très ressemblant/-e
lifeline /'laɪflaɪn/ *n* bouée *f* de sauvetage
lifelong /'laɪflɒŋ/ *adj* ‹*friendship, fear*› de toute une vie; **to have had a ~ ambition to do** avoir toujours rêvé de faire
life-saving /'laɪfseɪvɪŋ/ *n* (gen) sauvetage *m*; (Med) secourisme *m*
life sentence *n* condamnation *f* à perpétuité
life-size *adj* grandeur nature *inv*
life span *n* durée *f* de vie
life story *n* vie *f*
lifestyle /'laɪfstaɪl/ *n* style *m* de vie
life-support machine *n* **to be on a ~** être sous assistance respiratoire
lifetime /'laɪftaɪm/ *n* vie *f*; **in her ~** de son vivant; **the chance of a ~** une chance unique; **to seem like a ~** sembler une éternité

⚷ **lift** /lɪft/ **A** *n* **1** (BrE) (elevator) ascenseur *m*; (for goods) monte-charge *m inv*
2 (ride) **she asked me for a ~** elle m'a demandé de la conduire; **can I give you a ~?** je peux te déposer quelque part?
3 (fam) (boost) **to give sb a ~** remonter le moral à qn
B *vt* **1** (pick up) soulever ‹*object, person*›; **to ~ sth out of the box** sortir qch de la boîte
2 (raise) lever ‹*arm, head*›
3 (remove) lever ‹*ban, sanctions*›
4 (boost) **to ~ sb's spirits** remonter le moral à qn
5 (fam) (steal) piquer (fam) (**from** dans)
C *vi* ‹*bad mood, headache*› disparaître; ‹*fog*› se dissiper
■ **lift off**: **A ~ off** ‹*rocket*› décoller; ‹*top, cover*› s'enlever
B ~ [sth] off enlever ‹*cover, lid*›
■ **lift up** soulever ‹*book, suitcase, lid*›; lever ‹*head, veil, eyes*›; relever ‹*jumper, coat*›

lift-off /'lɪftɒf/ *n* lancement *m*
ligament /'lɪgəmənt/ *n* ligament *m*

⚷ **light** /laɪt/ **A** *n* **1** (brightness) lumière *f*; **against the ~** à contre-jour
2 (in building, machine) lumière *f*; (in street) réverbère *m*; (on ship) feu *m*; (on dashboard) voyant *m* (lumineux)
3 (Aut) (headlight) phare *m*; (rear light) feu *m* arrière; (inside car) veilleuse *f*
4 (flame) **to set ~ to** mettre le feu à; **have you got a ~?** tu as du feu?
5 (aspect) jour *m*; **to see sth in a different ~** voir qch sous un jour différent
6 to come to *or* **be brought to ~** être découvert/-e
B lights *npl* **(traffic) ~s** feu *m*, feux *mpl*; **the ~s are red** le feu est au rouge
C *adj* **1** (bright) **to get** *or* **grow ~er** ‹*sky*› s'éclaircir; **while it's still ~** pendant qu'il fait encore jour
2 ‹*colour, wood, skin*› clair/-e; **~ blue** bleu clair *inv*
3 ‹*material, wind, clothing, meal*› léger/-ère; ‹*rain*› fin/-e; ‹*drinker*› modéré/-e; **to be a ~ sleeper** avoir le sommeil léger
4 ‹*knock, footsteps*› léger/-ère
5 ‹*work*› peu fatigant/-e; ‹*exercise*› léger/-ère
6 ‹*music*› léger/-ère; **a bit of ~ relief** un peu de divertissement; **some ~ reading** quelque chose de facile à lire
D *vt* (*prét, pp* **lit** /lɪt/ *ou* **lighted**)
1 allumer ‹*oven, cigarette, fire*›; enflammer ‹*paper*›; craquer ‹*match*›
2 ‹*torch, lamp*› éclairer
■ **light up** ‹*lamp*› s'allumer; ‹*face*› s'éclairer; ‹*eyes*› briller de joie

light bulb *n* ampoule *f*
lighten /'laɪtn/ **A** *vt* éclaircir ‹*colour, hair, skin*›; détendre ‹*atmosphere*›
B *vi* ‹*sky, hair*› s'éclaircir; ‹*atmosphere*› se détendre
light entertainment *n* variétés *fpl*
lighter /'laɪtə(r)/ *n* (for smokers) briquet *m*; (for gas cooker) allume-gaz *m inv*
lighter fuel *n* (gas) gaz *m* à briquet; (liquid) essence *f* à briquet
light-hearted /,laɪt'hɑːtɪd/ *adj* ‹*person*› enjoué/-e; ‹*book*› humoristique
lighthouse *n* phare *m*
lighting /'laɪtɪŋ/ *n* éclairage *m*
lightly /'laɪtlɪ/ *adv* **1** ‹*touch, kiss, season*› légèrement
2 ‹*undertake, dismiss*› à la légère
3 to get off ~ s'en tirer à bon compte
lightning /'laɪtnɪŋ/ **A** *n* (in sky) éclairs *mpl*; (striking sth) foudre *f*; **a flash of ~** un éclair; **struck by ~** frappé/-e par la foudre
B *adj* ‹*visit, raid*› éclair *inv*
light switch *n* interrupteur *m*
lightweight /'laɪtweɪt/ *adj* ‹*garment*› léger/-ère; ‹*champion*› des poids légers
light year *n* année-lumière *f*

⚷ mot clé

like¹ /laɪk/ **A** *prep* **1** (gen) comme; **to be ~ sb/sth** être comme qn/qch; **to look ~** ressembler à; **big cities ~ London** les grandes villes comme Londres *or* telles que Londres; **you know what she's ~!** tu sais comment elle est!; **it was just ~ a fairy tale!** on aurait dit un conte de fée!; **it looks ~ rain** on dirait qu'il va pleuvoir; **what's it ~?** c'est comment?; **what was the weather ~?** quel temps faisait-il?
2 (typical of) **it's not ~ her to be late** ça ne lui ressemble pas *or* ce n'est pas son genre d'être en retard; **that's just ~ him!** c'est bien (de) lui!
B *conj* **1** (in the same way as) comme; **~ they used to** comme ils le faisaient autrefois
2 (fam) (as if) comme si; **he acts ~ he owns the place** il se conduit comme s'il était chez lui
C *n* **fires, floods and the ~** les incendies, les inondations et autres catastrophes de ce genre; **she won't speak to the ~s of us!** (fam) elle refuse de parler à des gens comme nous!

like² /laɪk/ *vt* **1** aimer bien ‹*person*›; aimer (bien) ‹*artist, food, music, style*›; **to ~ doing** *or* **to do** aimer (bien) faire; **to ~ A best** préférer A; **how do you ~ living in London?** ça te plaît de vivre à Londres?; **she doesn't ~ to be kept waiting** elle n'aime pas qu'on la fasse attendre
2 (wish) vouloir, aimer; **I would ~ a ticket** je voudrais un billet; **I would ~ to do** je voudrais *or* j'aimerais faire; **would you ~ to come to dinner?** voudriez-vous venir dîner?; **we'd ~ her to come** nous voudrions *or* aimerions qu'elle vienne; **if you ~** si tu veux; **you can do what you ~** tu peux faire ce que tu veux

likeable /'laɪkəbl/ *adj* ‹*person*› sympathique; ‹*novel, music*› agréable

likelihood /'laɪklɪhʊd/ *n* probabilité *f*, chances *fpl*; **in all ~** selon toute probabilité

likely /'laɪklɪ/ *adj* **1** (probable) probable; ‹*explanation*› plausible; **prices are ~ to rise** les prix risquent d'augmenter; **it is** *or* **seems ~ that she'll come** il est probable qu'elle viendra; **it is hardly ~ that she'll come** il y a peu de chances qu'elle vienne; **a ~ story!** à d'autres! (fam)
2 (promising) ‹*candidate*› prometteur/-euse

like-minded /laɪk'maɪndɪd/ *adj* du même avis

liken /'laɪkən/ *vt* comparer (**to** à)

likeness /'laɪknɪs/ *n* **1** (similarity) ressemblance *f*; **family ~** air *m* de famille
2 (picture) **to be a good ~** être ressemblant/-e

likewise /'laɪkwaɪz/ *adv* (similarly) également, de même; (also) aussi, de même

liking /'laɪkɪŋ/ *n* **to take a ~ to sb** se prendre d'affection pour qn; **to be to sb's ~** plaire à qn

lilac /'laɪlək/ *n, adj* lilas *m inv*

lily /'lɪlɪ/ *n* lys *m inv*

lily of the valley *n* muguet *m*

limb /lɪm/ *n* **1** (arm, leg) membre *m*
2 (of tree) branche *f* (maîtresse)

limber /'lɪmbə(r)/ *v*
▪ **limber up** s'échauffer

limbo /'lɪmbəʊ/ *n* **1** (state) les limbes *mpl*; **to be in ~** être dans les limbes
2 (dance) limbo *m*

lime /laɪm/ *n* **1** (calcium) chaux *f*
2 (fruit) citron *m* vert
3 (*also* **~ tree**) tilleul *m*

lime green *n, adj* citron *m* vert *inv*

lime juice *n* jus *m* de citron vert

limelight /'laɪmlaɪt/ *n* vedette *f*; **to be in the ~** tenir la vedette

limestone *n* calcaire *m*

limit /'lɪmɪt/ **A** *n* limite *f*; **within ~s** dans une certaine limite; **to push sb to the ~** pousser qn à bout
B *vt* limiter (**to** à)

limitation /ˌlɪmɪ'teɪʃn/ *n* **1** (restriction) restriction *f* (**on** à)
2 (shortcoming) limite *f*; **to know one's (own) ~s** connaître ses propres limites

limited /'lɪmɪtɪd/ *adj* limité/-e

limited company *n* (BrE) société *f* anonyme

limousine /'lɪməziːn, ˌlɪmə'ziːn/ *n* limousine *f*

limp /lɪmp/ **A** *n* **to have a ~** boiter
B *adj* mou/molle
C *vi* boiter; **to ~ in/away** entrer/s'éloigner en boitant

linchpin /'lɪntʃpɪn/ *n* (essential element) **the ~ of** ‹*person*› le pilier de

line /laɪn/ **A** *n* **1** (gen), (Sport) ligne *f*; (shorter, thicker) trait *m*; (in drawing) trait *m*; **a straight ~** une ligne droite
2 (of people, cars) file *f*; (of trees) rangée *f*; **to stand** *or* **wait in ~** (AmE) faire la queue
3 (on face) ride *f*
4 (rope) corde *f*; (for fishing) ligne *f*; **to put the washing on the ~** étendre le linge
5 (electric cable) ligne *f* (électrique)
6 (phone connection) ligne *f*; **at the other end of the ~** au bout du fil; **the ~ went dead** la ligne a été coupée
7 (rail route) ligne *f* (**between** entre); (rails) voie *f*
8 (shipping company, airline) compagnie *f*
9 (in genealogy) lignée *f*
10 (in prose) ligne *f*; (in poetry) vers *m*; **to learn one's ~s** ‹*actor*› apprendre son texte
11 to fall into ~ with s'aligner sur; **to bring sb into ~** ramener qn dans le rang; **to keep sb in ~** tenir qn en main
12 (stance) **the official ~** la position officielle; **to take a firm ~ with sb** se montrer ferme avec qn
13 (type of product) gamme *f*
14 (Mil) **enemy ~s** lignes *fpl* ennemies

B *vt* doubler ‹*garment*› (**with** avec); tapisser ‹*shelf*› (**with** de); border ‹*route*›
C **in line with** *phr* en accord avec ‹*policy, trend*›; **to increase in ~ with** augmenter proportionnellement à

▪ **line up**: **A** **~ up** (side by side) se mettre en rang; (one behind the other) se mettre en file
B **~ [sth] up 1** (align) aligner (**with** sur)
2 sélectionner ‹*team*›

lined /laɪnd/ *adj* ‹*face*› ridé/-e; ‹*paper*› ligné/-e; ‹*curtains*› doublé/-e

line manager *n* responsable opérationnel/-elle *m/f*

linen /ˈlɪnɪn/ *n* **1** (fabric) lin *m*
2 (household) linge *m* de maison; (underwear) linge *m* de corps

linen basket *n* panier *m* à linge sale

linen cupboard (BrE), **linen closet** (AmE) *n* armoire *f* à linge

line of fire *n* ligne *f* de tir

line of work *n* métier *m*

liner /ˈlaɪnə(r)/ *n* paquebot *m* de grande ligne

linesman /ˈlaɪnzmən/ *n* (BrE) (in tennis) juge *m* de ligne; (in football, hockey) juge *m* de touche

l

line-up /ˈlaɪnʌp/ *n* (Sport) équipe *f*; (personnel, pop group) groupe *m*

linger /ˈlɪŋɡə(r)/ *vi* **1** ‹*person*› s'attarder; ‹*gaze*› s'attarder (**on** sur)
2 ‹*memory, smell*› persister
3 ‹*doubt, suspicion*› subsister

lingerie /ˈlænʒəriː, (AmE) ˌlɑːndʒəˈreɪ/ *n* lingerie *f*

linguist /ˈlɪŋɡwɪst/ *n* linguiste *mf*

linguistic /lɪŋˈɡwɪstɪk/ *adj* linguistique

linguistics /lɪŋˈɡwɪstɪks/ *n* linguistique *f*

lining /ˈlaɪnɪŋ/ *n* doublure *f*

🔑 **link** /lɪŋk/ **A** *n* **1** (in chain) maillon *m*
2 (connection by rail, road) liaison *f*
3 (between facts, events) rapport *m* (**between** entre); (between people) lien *m* (**with** avec)
4 (tie) relation *f*, lien *m*
5 (in TV, radio, computing) liaison *f*
B *vt* **1** ‹*road, cable*› relier ‹*places, objects*›; **to ~ A to B** *or* **A and B** relier A à B; **to ~ arms** ‹*people*› se donner le bras
2 to ~ sth to *or* **with** lier qch à ‹*inflation*›; établir un lien entre qch et ‹*fact, crime, illness*›
3 connecter ‹*terminals*›
4 (in TV, radio) établir une liaison entre ‹*places*› (**by** par)
C **linked** *pp adj* ‹*circles, symbols*› entrelacé/-e; ‹*issues, problems*› lié/-e

▪ **link up**: **A** **~ up** ‹*firms*› s'associer; **to ~ up with** s'associer avec ‹*college, firm*›
B **~ [sth] up** relier

link road *n* route *f* de raccordement

link-up /ˈlɪŋkʌp/ *n* **1** (on TV, radio) liaison *f*
2 (collaboration) association *f*

lino /ˈlaɪnəʊ/ *n* lino *m*

lint /lɪnt/ *n* tissu *m* ouaté

lion /ˈlaɪən/ *n* lion *m*

lion cub *n* lionceau *m*

lioness /ˈlaɪənes/ *n* lionne *f*

🔑 **lip** /lɪp/ *n* **1** lèvre *f*
2 (of jug) bec *m*

liposuction /ˈlaɪpəʊsʌkʃn, ˈlɪpəʊ-/ *n* liposuccion *f*

lip-read /ˈlɪpriːd/ *vi* (*prét, pp* **-read** /-red/) lire sur les lèvres de quelqu'un

lipsalve *n* baume *m* pour les lèvres

lip service *n* **to pay ~ to feminism** se dire féministe pour la forme

lipstick *n* rouge *m* à lèvres

liqueur /lɪˈkjʊə(r), (AmE) -ˈkɜːr/ *n* liqueur *f*

liquid /ˈlɪkwɪd/ *n, adj* liquide *m*

liquidate /ˈlɪkwɪdeɪt/ *vt* liquider

liquidation /ˌlɪkwɪˈdeɪʃn/ *n* liquidation *f*

liquidizer /ˈlɪkwɪdaɪzə(r)/ *n* (BrE) (Culin) mixeur *m*

liquor /ˈlɪkə(r)/ *n* alcool *m*

liquorice (BrE), **licorice** (AmE) /ˈlɪkərɪs/ *n*
1 (plant) réglisse *f*
2 (substance) réglisse *m*

liquor store *n* (AmE) magasin *m* de vins et spiritueux

Lisbon /ˈlɪzbən/ *pr n* Lisbonne

lisp /lɪsp/ *n* zézaiement *m*; **to have a ~** zézayer

🔑 **list** /lɪst/ **A** *n* liste *f* (**of** de)
B *vt* **1** (gen) faire la liste de ‹*objects, people*›; **to be ~ed in a directory** être repris/-e dans un répertoire
2 (Comput) lister
C *vi* ‹*vessel*› donner de la bande
D **listed** *pp adj* (BrE) ‹*building*› classé; ‹*company*› coté/-e en Bourse

🔑 **listen** /ˈlɪsn/ *vi* écouter; **to ~ to sb/sth** écouter qn/qch; **to ~ to reason** écouter la voix de la raison; **to ~ (out) for** guetter

▪ **listen in** écouter (par indiscrétion)

listener /ˈlɪsnə(r)/ *n* **1 to be a good ~** savoir écouter
2 (to radio) auditeur/-trice *m/f*

listeria /lɪˈstɪərɪə/ *n* (bacteria) listéria *f*; (illness) listériose *f*

listing /ˈlɪstɪŋ/ **A** *n* **1** inscription *f* (**in** dans); **Stock Exchange ~** liste *f* des sociétés cotées en Bourse
2 (Comput) listing *m*
B **listings** *npl* pages *fpl* d'informations

listless /ˈlɪstlɪs/ *adj* ‹*person*› apathique

list price *n* prix *m* au catalogue

literacy /ˈlɪtərəsɪ/ *n* (in a population) taux *m* d'alphabétisation

literal /ˈlɪtərəl/ *adj* **1** ‹*meaning*› littéral/-e
2 ‹*translation*› mot à mot

literally /ˈlɪtərəlɪ/ *adv* ‹*mean*› littéralement; ‹*translate*› mot à mot; **to take sth ~**

🔑 mot clé

prendre qch au pied de la lettre; **(quite) ~** bel et bien

literary /ˈlɪtərərɪ, (AmE) ˈlɪtərerɪ/ *adj* littéraire

literary criticism *n* critique *f* littéraire

literate /ˈlɪtərət/ *adj* **1** (able to read and write) **to be ~** savoir lire et écrire
2 (cultured) ‹*person*› cultivé/-e

literature /ˈlɪtrətʃə(r), (AmE) -tʃʊər/ *n*
1 littérature *f*; **a work of ~** une œuvre littéraire
2 (pamphlets, brochures) documentation *f*

lithe /laɪð/ *adj* leste

Lithuania /ˌlɪθjuːˈeɪnɪə/ *pr n* Lituanie *f*

litigation /ˌlɪtɪˈgeɪʃn/ *n* litiges *mpl*

litre (BrE), **liter** (AmE) /ˈliːtə(r)/ *n* litre *m*

litter /ˈlɪtə(r)/ **A** *n* **1** (rubbish) détritus *mpl*; (substantial) ordures *fpl*; (paper) papiers *mpl*
2 (of young) portée *f*; **to have a ~** mettre bas
3 (for pet tray) litière *f*
B *vt* **to be ~ed with** ‹*ground*› être jonché/-e de

litter bin (BrE) *n* poubelle *f*

little

> When *a little* is used as a pronoun and if the sentence does not specify what it refers to, the pronoun *en* (= *of it*) must be added before the verb: *I have a little left* = il m'en reste un peu.

A *adj* **1** (small) petit/-e *before n*
2 (not much) peu de; **~ chance** peu de chances; **very ~ damage** très peu de dégâts; **there's so ~ time** il y a si peu de temps
B *pron* **a ~** un peu; **I only ate a ~** je n'en ai mangé qu'un peu; **he remembers very ~** il ne se souvient pas bien; **there's ~ I can do** je ne peux pas faire grand-chose; **to do as ~ as possible** en faire le moins possible; **~ or nothing** quasiment rien
C *adv* **1** (not much) peu; **I go there very ~** j'y vais très peu; **the next results were ~ better** les résultats suivants étaient à peine meilleurs; **~ more than an hour ago** il y a à peine plus d'une heure
2 (not at all) **~ did they know that** ils étaient bien loin de se douter que
D **a little (bit)** *phr* un peu; **a ~ (bit) anxious** un peu inquiet/-iète; **a ~ less/more** un peu moins/plus; **stay a ~ longer** reste encore un peu
E **as little as** *phr* **for as ~ as 10 dollars a day** pour seulement 10 dollars par jour; **as ~ as £60** juste 60 livres sterling
IDIOM **~ by ~** petit à petit

little finger *n* petit doigt *m*, auriculaire *m*
IDIOM **to wrap** *or* **twist sb around one's ~** mener qn par le bout du nez

live¹ /lɪv/ *vi* **1** (gen) vivre; **as long as I ~...** tant que je vivrai...; **to ~ to regret sth** en venir à regretter qch; **long ~ democracy!** vive la démocratie!; **to ~ on** *or* **off** vivre de ‹*fruit, charity*›; vivre sur ‹*wage*›
2 (dwell) ‹*person*› vivre, habiter (**with** avec); ‹*animal*› vivre; **they ~ at number 7** ils habitent au numéro 7; **to ~ in** vivre dans, habiter ‹*house, apartment*›; **easy to ~ with** facile à vivre
3 (put up with) **to ~ with** accepter ‹*situation*›; supporter ‹*decor*›
IDIOM **to ~ it up** (fam) mener la grande vie
■ **live in** ‹*maid*› être logé/-e et nourri/-e
■ **live on** ‹*reputation, tradition*› se perpétuer
■ **live up to** ‹*person*› répondre à ‹*expectations*›; être à la hauteur de ‹*reputation*›

live² /laɪv/ **A** *adj* **1** (alive) vivant/-e
2 ‹*broadcast*› en direct; ‹*performance*› sur scène; ‹*album*› enregistré/-e en public; **before a ~ audience** devant un public
3 ‹*cable*› sous tension
B *adv* ‹*appear, broadcast*› en direct

live-in /ˈlɪvɪn/ *adj* ‹*maid, nanny*› qui est logé/-e et nourri/-e; **to have a ~ lover** vivre en concubinage

livelihood /ˈlaɪvlɪhʊd/ *n* gagne-pain *m*

lively /ˈlaɪvlɪ/ *adj* **1** ‹*person*› plein/-e d'entrain; ‹*place, atmosphere, conversation*› animé/-e
2 (fast) ‹*pace*› vif/vive; ‹*music, dance*› entraînant/-e

liven /ˈlaɪvn/
■ **liven up**: **A** **~ up** s'animer
B **~ [sth] up** animer ‹*event*›

liver /ˈlɪvə(r)/ *n* foie *m*

livery /ˈlɪvərɪ/ *n* **1** (uniform) livrée *f*
2 (boarding horses) **at ~** en pension

livestock /ˈlaɪvstɒk/ *n* bétail *m*

live wire /laɪv/ *n* boute-en-train *m inv*

livid /ˈlɪvɪd/ *adj* **1** (furious) furieux/-ieuse
2 (in colour) ‹*face, scar*› livide

living /ˈlɪvɪŋ/ **A** *n* **1** vie *f*; **to work for a ~** travailler pour gagner sa vie; **what do you do for a ~?** qu'est-ce que vous faites dans la vie?
2 (lifestyle) vie *f*; **easy ~** une vie facile
B *adj* vivant/-e; **within ~ memory** de mémoire d'homme

living conditions *npl* conditions *fpl* de vie

living expenses *npl* frais *mpl* de subsistance

living room *n* salle *f* de séjour, salon *m*

living standards *npl* niveau *m* de vie

living together *n* cohabitation *f*

living will *n: déclaration écrite (de l'interessé) refusant l'acharnement thérapeutique*

lizard /ˈlɪzəd/ *n* lézard *m*

llama /ˈlɑːmə/ *n* lama *m*

load /ləʊd/ **A** *n* **1** (gen) charge *f*; (on vehicle, animal) chargement *m*; (on ship, plane) cargaison *f*; (fig) fardeau *m*; **three (lorry-)~s of sand** trois camions de sable
2 (fam) (a lot) **a (whole) ~ of people** des tas (fam) de gens; **that's a ~ of nonsense** (fam) c'est vraiment n'importe quoi (fam)

B **loads** *npl* (fam) **~s of** (+ *plural nouns*) des tas (fam) de; **~s of times** plein de *or* des tas (fam) de fois; **we've got ~s of time** nous avons tout notre temps; **~s of work** un travail fou (fam)
C *vt* **1** (gen) charger ‹*vehicle, gun*› (**with** de); mettre un film dans ‹*camera*›
2 (Comput) charger ‹*program*›
3 to ~ sb with combler qn de ‹*presents, honours*›

loaded /ˈləʊdɪd/ *adj* **1** ‹*tray, lorry, gun*› chargé/-e (**with** de)
2 (fam) (rich) bourré/-e de fric (fam)
3 ‹*question*› tendancieux/-ieuse

loaf /ləʊf/ *n* (*pl* **loaves**) pain *m*; **a ~ of bread** un pain
■ **loaf about**, **loaf around** traînasser

loafer /ˈləʊfə(r)/ *n* **1** (shoe) mocassin *m*
2 (idler) flemmard/-e *m/f* (fam)

loan /ləʊn/ **A** *n* (when borrowing) emprunt *m*; (when lending) prêt *m*; **to be on ~** être prêté/-e (**to** à)
B *vt* (*also* **~ out**) prêter (**to** à)

loan shark *n* (fam) usurier/-ière *m/f*

loath /ləʊθ/ *adj* **to be ~ to do** répugner à faire

loathe /ləʊð/ *vt* détester (**doing** faire)

loathsome /ˈləʊðsəm/ *adj* répugnant/-e

lobby /ˈlɒbɪ/ **A** *n* **1** (of hotel) hall *m*; (of theatre) lobby *m*
2 (*also* **~ group**) lobby *m*
B *vi* faire pression (**for** pour obtenir)

lobbying /ˈlɒbɪɪŋ/ *n* lobbying *m*

lobe /ləʊb/ *n* lobe *m*

lobster /ˈlɒbstə(r)/ *n* homard *m*

local /ˈləʊkl/ **A** *n* **1 the ~s** les gens *mpl* du coin
2 (pub) pub *m* du coin
B *adj* (gen) local/-e; ‹*library, shop*› du quartier; ‹*radio, news*› régional/-e

local anaesthetic *n* anesthésique *m* local

local authority *n* (BrE) autorités *fpl* locales

local call *n* communication *f* téléphonique locale

local election *n* élection *f* locale

local government *n* administration *f* locale

locality /ləʊˈkælətɪ/ *n* **1** (neighbourhood) voisinage *m*
2 (place) endroit *m*

localization /ˌləʊkəlaɪˈzeɪʃn/ *n* localisation *f*

localized *adj* localisé/-e

locate /ləʊˈkeɪt, (AmE) ˈləʊkeɪt/ *vt* **1** (find) retrouver ‹*object*›; localiser ‹*fault*›
2 (position) situer ‹*site*›

location /ləʊˈkeɪʃn/ *n* endroit *m*; **on ~** ‹*filmed*› en extérieur

lock /lɒk/ **A** *n* **1** (with key) serrure *f*; (with bolt) verrou *m*; **under ~ and key** sous clé
2 (of hair) mèche *f*
3 (on canal) écluse *f*
4 (Comput) verrouillage *m*
B *vt* fermer [qch] à clé
C *vi* **1** ‹*door, drawer*› fermer à clé
2 ‹*steering wheel*› se bloquer
■ **lock in** enfermer ‹*person*›; **to ~ oneself in** s'enfermer
■ **lock out**: **~ sb out** enfermer qn dehors; **to ~ oneself out** s'enfermer dehors
■ **lock together** ‹*components, pieces*› s'emboîter
■ **lock up**: **A** **~ up** fermer
B **~ [sth] up** fermer [qch] à clé ‹*house*›
C **~ [sb] up** enfermer ‹*hostage*›; mettre [qn] sous les verrous ‹*killer*›

locker /ˈlɒkə(r)/ *n* casier *m*, vestiaire *m*

locker room *n* vestiaire *m*

locket /ˈlɒkɪt/ *n* médaillon *m*

locksmith *n* serrurier *m*

locomotive /ˌləʊkəˈməʊtɪv/ *n* locomotive *f*

locum /ˈləʊkəm/ *n* (BrE) remplaçant/-e *m/f*

lodge /lɒdʒ/ **A** *n* (small house) pavillon *m*; (for gatekeeper) loge *f* (du gardien)
B *vt* **to ~ an appeal** faire appel; **to ~ a complaint** porter plainte; **to ~ a protest** protester
C *vi* **1** ‹*person*› loger (**with** chez)
2 ‹*bullet*› se loger; ‹*small object*› se coincer

lodger /ˈlɒdʒə(r)/ *n* (room only) locataire *mf*; (with meals) pensionnaire *mf*

lodgings *npl* logement *m*

loft /lɒft, (AmE) lɔːft/ *n* **1** (attic) grenier *m*
2 (AmE) (apartment) loft *m*

loft conversion *n* aménagement *m* de grenier

log /lɒg, (AmE) lɔːg/ **A** *n* **1** (of wood) rondin *m*; (for burning) bûche *f*
2 (of ship) journal *m* de bord; (of plane) carnet *m* de vol
B *vt* (*p prés etc* **-gg-**) **1** (record) noter
2 (*also* **~ up**) avoir à son actif ‹*miles*›
IDIOM **to sleep like a ~** dormir comme une souche
■ **log in**, **log on** ouvrir une session, se connecter
■ **log off**, **log out** clore une session, se déconnecter

log book *n* (of car) ≈ carte *f* grise; (written record) registre *m*

log cabin *n* cabane *f* en rondins

log fire *n* feu *m* de bois

loggerheads /ˈlɒgəhedz/ *npl* **to be at ~** être en désaccord (**with** avec)

logic /ˈlɒdʒɪk/ *n* logique *f*

logical /ˈlɒdʒɪkl/ *adj* logique

logistics /ləˈdʒɪstɪks/ *n* logistique *f*

logo /ˈləʊgəʊ/ *n* logo *m*

log-off *n* fin *f* de connexion

log-on *n* début *m* de connexion

loin /lɔɪn/ *n* (Culin) (BrE) ≈ côtes *fpl* premières; (AmE) ≈ filet *m*

---
mot clé

loiter /'lɔɪtə(r)/ *vi* (idly) traîner; (pleasurably) flâner; (suspiciously) rôder

loll /lɒl/ *vi* ‹*person*› se prélasser; ‹*head*› tomber; ‹*tongue*› pendre

lollipop /'lɒlɪpɒp/ *n* sucette *f*

London /'lʌndən/ *pr n* Londres

Londoner /'lʌndənə(r)/ *n* Londonien/-ienne *m/f*

lone /ləʊn/ *adj* solitaire

loneliness /'ləʊnlɪnɪs/ *n* (of person) solitude *f*; (of place) isolement *m*

lonely /'ləʊnlɪ/ *adj* ‹*person*› seul/-e; ‹*life*› solitaire; ‹*place*› isolé/-e

lonely hearts' column *n* petites annonces *fpl* (*de rencontre*)

loner /'ləʊnə(r)/ *n* solitaire *mf*

lonesome /'ləʊnsəm/ *adj* (AmE) solitaire

long /lɒŋ, (AmE) lɔːŋ/ **A** *adj* (gen) long/longue; ‹*delay*› important/-e; ‹*grass*› haut/-e; **to be 20 minutes ~** durer 20 minutes; **to be 20 metres ~** avoir *or* faire 20 mètres de long; **to get ~er** ‹*days, list, queue*› s'allonger; ‹*grass, hair*› pousser; **she's been away a ~ time** elle est restée longtemps absente; **it's been a ~ time since...** ça fait longtemps que...; **to take a ~ time** ‹*person*› être lent/-e; ‹*task*› prendre longtemps; **a ~ way off** loin; **we've come a ~ way** nous avons fait beaucoup de chemin
B *adv* **1** (a long time) longtemps; **I won't be ~** je n'en ai pas pour longtemps; **how ~ will you be?** tu en as pour combien de temps?; **how ~ did it take him?** il lui a fallu combien de temps?; **how ~ is the interval?** combien de temps dure l'entracte?; **I haven't got ~** je n'ai pas beaucoup de temps; **~er than he thought** plus de temps qu'il ne pensait; **before ~** (in past) peu après; (in future) dans peu de temps; **not for ~** pas longtemps; **~ after** longtemps après; **not ~ after** peu après; **~ ago** il y a longtemps; **~ before** bien avant; **he's no ~er head** il n'est plus chef; **I can't stay any ~er** je ne peux pas rester plus longtemps
2 (for a long time) depuis longtemps; **those days are ~ gone** ce temps-là n'est plus
C *vi* **to ~ for sth** avoir très envie de qch; **to ~ to do** rêver de faire
D **as long as** *phr* (provided) du moment que (+ *indicative*), pourvu que (+ *subjunctive*)
IDIOMS **~ time no see!** (fam) ça fait une paye (fam) qu'on ne s'est pas vus!; **so ~!** (fam) salut!

long-awaited *adj* longtemps attendu/-e

long-distance *adj* ‹*runner*› de fond; ‹*telephone call*› (within the country) interurbain/-e; **~ lorry driver** (BrE) routier *m*

long-haired *adj* ‹*person*› aux cheveux longs; ‹*animal*› à poil long

longhand /'lɒŋhænd/ *n* **in ~** écrit/-e à la main

long-haul *adj* ‹*flight, aircraft*› long-courrier *inv*

longing /'lɒŋɪŋ, (AmE) 'lɔːŋɪŋ/ *n* **1** grand désir *m* (**for** de, **to do** de faire)
2 (nostalgia) nostalgie *f* (**for** de)

longitude /'lɒndʒɪtjuːd, (AmE) -tuːd/ *n* longitude *f*

long jump *n* (BrE) saut *m* en longueur

long-life *adj* ‹*milk*› longue conservation *inv*; ‹*battery*› longue durée *inv*

long-range *adj* ‹*missile*› (à) longue portée; ‹*forecast*› à long terme

long-sighted *adj* (BrE) presbyte

long-standing *adj* de longue date

long term **A** *n* **in the ~** à long terme
B **long-term** *adj, adv* à long terme

long-time *adj* de longue date

long-wave *n* grandes ondes *fpl*

long-winded *adj* verbeux/-euse

loo /luː/ *n* (BrE) (fam) vécés *mpl* (fam), toilettes *fpl*

look /lʊk/ **A** *n* **1** (glance) coup *m* d'œil; **to have *or* take a ~ at sth** jeter un coup d'œil à *or* sur qch; **to have *or* take a good ~ at** regarder [qch] de près; **to have a ~ inside/behind sth** regarder à l'intérieur de/derrière qch; **to have a ~ round** faire un tour dans ‹*park, town*›
2 (search) **to have a (good) ~** (bien) chercher
3 (expression) regard *m*; **a ~ of sadness** un regard triste; **from the ~ on his face...** à son expression...
4 (appearance) (of person) air *m*; (of building, scenery) aspect *m*
B **looks** *npl* **~s aren't everything** il n'y a pas que la beauté qui compte; **he's losing his ~s** il n'est pas aussi beau qu'autrefois
C *vi* **1** regarder (**into** dans, **over** par-dessus); **to ~ away** détourner le regard *or* les yeux; **to ~ out of the window** regarder par la fenêtre
2 (search) chercher, regarder
3 (appear, seem) avoir l'air, paraître; **you ~ cold** tu as l'air d'avoir froid; **he ~s young for his age** il fait jeune pour son âge; **that makes you ~ younger** ça te rajeunit; **the picture will ~ good in the study** le tableau ira bien dans le bureau; **it doesn't ~ right** ça ne va pas; **things are ~ing good** les choses se présentent bien; **to ~ like sb/sth** ressembler à qn/qch; **what does the house ~ like?** comment est la maison?; **it ~s like rain** on dirait qu'il va pleuvoir
D *vt* **1** (gaze at, stare at) regarder; **to ~ sb in the eye** regarder qn dans les yeux
2 (appear) **to ~ one's age** faire son âge; **she's 40 but she doesn't ~ it** elle a 40 ans mais elle ne les fait pas; **to ~ one's best** être à son avantage

■ **look after** soigner ‹*patient*›; garder ‹*child*›; s'occuper de ‹*customer, plant, finances, shop*›; surveiller ‹*class, luggage*›; entretenir ‹*car*›

■ **look around** **A** **~ around 1** (glance) regarder autour de soi
2 to ~ around for sb/sth chercher qn/qch
3 (in town) faire un tour
B **~ around [sth]** visiter ‹*church, town*›

■ **look at 1** regarder; (briefly) jeter un coup d'œil sur
2 (examine) examiner ‹*patient*›; jeter un coup d'œil à ‹*car*›; étudier ‹*problem, options*›
3 (see, view) voir ‹*life, situation*›; envisager ‹*problem*›

■ **look back 1** (turn around) se retourner (**at** pour regarder)
2 to ~ back on se tourner sur ‹*past*›; repenser à ‹*experience*›; **~ing back on it** rétrospectivement

■ **look down**: **A** **~ down** (from a height) regarder en bas
B **~ down on [sb/sth] 1** regarder [qn/qch] d'en haut
2 (condescendingly) mépriser

■ **look for** chercher ‹*person, object*›

■ **look forward to** attendre [qch] avec impatience; **she's ~ing forward to going on holiday** elle a hâte de partir en vacances; **I ~ forward to hearing from you** (in letter) j'espère avoir bientôt de tes nouvelles; (formal) dans l'attente de votre réponse, je vous prie d'agréer mes sincères salutations

■ **look into** examiner ‹*matter*›

■ **look on**: **A** **~ on** (watch) regarder; (be present) assister à
B **~ on [sb/sth]** considérer ‹*person, event*› (**as** comme, **with** avec)

■ **look onto** ‹*house*› donner sur ‹*street*›

■ **look out**: **A** **~ out** (take care) faire attention (**for** à); (be wary) se méfier (**for** de); **~ out!** attention!
B **~ out for [sb/sth]** guetter ‹*person*›; être à l'affût de ‹*bargain, new talent*›

■ **look round** **A** (look behind) se retourner; (look about) regarder autour de soi
B **~ round [sth]** visiter ‹*town*›; **to ~ round the shops** faire les magasins

■ **look through** **A** **~ through [sth]**
1 parcourir ‹*report*›; feuilleter ‹*magazine*›
2 fouiller dans ‹*belongings*›
B **~ through [sb]** faire semblant de ne pas voir

■ **look to 1** (rely on) compter sur [qn/qch]
2 (turn to) se tourner vers ‹*future, friends*›

■ **look up**: **A** **~ up** (raise eyes) lever les yeux (**from** de); **things are ~ing up for us** les choses s'arrangent pour nous
B **~ [sb/sth] up 1** chercher ‹*phone number, price*› (**in** dans)
2 passer voir ‹*acquaintance*›
C **~ up to [sb]** admirer ‹*person*›

look-alike *n* sosie *m*

look-in /ˈlʊkɪn/ *n* (BrE) **to get a ~** avoir sa chance; **to give sb a ~** donner sa chance à qn

look-out /ˈlʊkaʊt/ *n* **1 to be on the ~ for** rechercher ‹*stolen vehicle*›; être à l'affût de ‹*bargain, new talent*›; guetter ‹*visitor*›
2 (place) poste *m* d'observation

loom /luːm/ **A** *n* métier *m* à tisser
B *vi* **1** (*also* **~ up**) surgir (**out of** de, **over** au-dessus de)
2 ‹*war, crisis*› menacer; ‹*exam, interview*› être imminent/-e; **to ~ large** ‹*issue*› peser lourd

loony /ˈluːnɪ/ *adj* (fam) farfelu/-e (fam)

loop /luːp/ **A** *n* (gen), (Comput) boucle *f*
B *vt* nouer
C *vi* ‹*road, path*› faire une boucle
IDIOM **to be in/out of the ~** être/ne pas être informé

loophole /ˈluːphəʊl/ *n* lacune *f*

loose /luːs/ *adj* **1** ‹*knot, screw*› desserré/-e; ‹*handle, tooth*› branlant/-e; ‹*button*› qui se découd; ‹*thread*› décousu/-e; **to hang ~** ‹*hair*› être dénoué/-e; **~ connection** faux contact
2 (free) **to break ~** ‹*animal*› s'échapper (**from** de); **to cut sb ~** détacher qn; **to let ~** libérer ‹*animal, prisoner*›
3 ‹*page*› détaché/-e; **~ change** petite monnaie
4 ‹*jacket, trousers*› ample; ‹*collar*› lâche
5 ‹*link, weave*› lâche
6 ‹*translation, interpretation*› assez libre; ‹*wording*› imprécis/-e; ‹*connection, guideline*› vague; ‹*style*› relâché/-e
7 ‹*morals*› dissolu/-e
IDIOM **to be at a ~ end** (BrE), **to be at ~ ends** (AmE) ne pas trop savoir quoi faire

loosely /ˈluːslɪ/ *adv* **1** ‹*hold, wind, wrap*› sans serrer; **his clothes hung ~ on him** il flottait dans ses vêtements
2 ‹*connected, organized*› de façon souple
3 ‹*translate, describe*› assez librement

loosely knit *adj* ‹*group, structure*› peu uni/-e

loosen /ˈluːsn/ *vt* desserrer ‹*belt, strap, collar*›; dégager ‹*nail, post*›; relâcher ‹*grip, rope, control*›; dénouer ‹*hair*›

■ **loosen up 1** (sport) s'échauffer
2 (relax) se détendre

loot /luːt/ **A** *n* butin *m*
B *vt* piller ‹*shops*›

looter /ˈluːtə(r)/ *n* pillard/-e *m/f*

lopsided /ˌlɒpˈsaɪdɪd/ *adj* ‹*object, smile*› de travers; ‹*argument, view*› irrationnel/-elle

⚷ **lord** /lɔːd/ *n* **1** (ruler) seigneur *m* (**of** de)
2 (peer) lord *m*; **the (House of) Lords** la Chambre des Lords; **my Lord** (to noble) Monsieur le comte/duc *etc*
IDIOM **to ~ it over sb** (fam) regarder qn de haut

Lord /lɔːd/ *n* **1** (in prayers) Seigneur *m*
2 (fam) (in exclamations) **good ~!** grand Dieu!

Lord Mayor *n* lord-maire *m*

lordship /ˈlɔːdʃɪp/ *n* (*also* **Lordship**) **your/his ~** (of noble) Monsieur; (of judge)

⚷ mot clé

Monsieur le Juge

lorry /ˈlɒrɪ, (AmE) ˈlɔːrɪ/ *n* (*pl* **-ies**) (BrE) camion *m*

lorry driver *n* (BrE) routier *m*, chauffeur *m* de poids lourd

lose /luːz/ **A** *vt* (*prét*, *pp* **lost**) **1** (gen) perdre; **to ~ one's way** se perdre; **to ~ interest in sth** se désintéresser de qch
2 ‹*clock*› retarder de ‹*minutes, seconds*›
3 (get rid of) semer (fam) ‹*pursuer*›
B *vi* (*prét*, *pp* **lost**) **1** (gen) perdre
2 ‹*clock*› retarder

■ **lose out** être perdant/-e

loser /ˈluːzə(r)/ *n* (gen), (Sport) perdant/-e *m/f*

loss /lɒs, (AmE) lɔːs/ *n* perte *f* (**of** de); **to be at a ~** (puzzled) être perplexe; (helpless) être perdu/-e

lost /lɒst, (AmE) lɔːst/ *adj* **1** ‹*person, animal*› perdu/-e; **to get ~** ‹*person, animal*› se perdre; ‹*object*› s'égarer; **get ~!** (fam) fiche le camp! (fam)
2 ‹*opportunity*› manqué/-e; ‹*cause*› perdu/-e; ‹*civilization*› disparu/-e; **to be ~ on sb** passer au-dessus de la tête de qn; **to be ~ for words** être interloqué/-e; **to be ~ in** être plongé/-e dans ‹*book, thought*›

lost and found *n* objets *mpl* trouvés

lost property *n* (BrE) objets *mpl* trouvés

lot¹ /lɒt/ **A** *pron* **1** (great deal) **a ~** beaucoup; **he spent a ~** il a beaucoup dépensé, il a dépensé beaucoup d'argent; **to mean a ~ to sb** avoir beaucoup d'importance pour qn
2 (fam) **the ~** (le) tout
B *quantif* **a ~ of money/time** beaucoup d'argent/de temps; **I see a ~ of him** je le vois beaucoup
C **lots** *quantif*, *pron* (fam) **~s (and ~s) of** des tas (fam) de, beaucoup de; **~s of things** des tas (fam) de choses
D **a lot** *adv* beaucoup; **he's a ~ better/worse** il va beaucoup mieux/plus mal; **this happens quite a ~** cela arrive très souvent

lot² /lɒt/ *n* **1** (destiny) sort *m*; (quality of life) condition *f*
2 (AmE) parcelle *f* (de terrain)
3 (at auction) lot *m*
4 **to draw ~s** tirer au sort
5 (batch) fournée *f*

lotion /ˈləʊʃn/ *n* lotion *f*

lottery /ˈlɒtərɪ/ *n* loterie *f*

loud /laʊd/ **A** *adj* **1** ‹*music, voice*› fort/-e; ‹*noise, scream*› grand/-e *before n*; ‹*comment, laugh*› bruyant/-e; ‹*applause*› vif/vive
2 ‹*colour*› criard/-e; ‹*person, behaviour*› exubérant/-e
B *adv* fort; **out ~** à voix haute

loudly /ˈlaʊdlɪ/ *adv* ‹*knock, talk*› bruyamment; ‹*scream*› fort; ‹*protest*› vivement

loudspeaker *n* (for announcements) haut-parleur *m*; (for hi-fi) enceinte *f*

lounge /laʊndʒ/ *n* **1** (in house, hotel) salon *m*
2 (in airport) **departure ~** salle *f* d'embarquement
3 (*also* **cocktail ~**) (AmE) bar *m*

■ **lounge about, lounge around** paresser

lousy /ˈlaʊzɪ/ *adj* (fam) minable (fam); **a ~ trick** un sale tour

lout /laʊt/ *n* malotru *m* (fam)

loutish /ˈlaʊtɪʃ/ *adj* ‹*person*› grossier/-ière; ‹*behaviour*› de voyou

louvred (BrE), **louvered** (AmE) /ˈluːvəd/ *adj* ‹*doors*› à lamelles

lovable /ˈlʌvəbl/ *adj* ‹*person*› sympathique; ‹*child*› adorable

love /lʌv/ **A** *n* **1** amour *m*; **to be/fall in ~** être/tomber amoureux/-euse (**with** de); **to make ~** faire l'amour; **Andy sends his ~** Andy t'embrasse; **with ~ from Bob, ~ Bob** affectueusement, Bob
2 (BrE) (term of affection) mon chéri/ma chérie *m/f*
3 (in tennis) zéro *m*
B *vt* aimer; **to ~ each other** s'aimer; **to ~ doing** *or* **to do** aimer beaucoup faire; **'I'd ~ to!'** 'avec plaisir!'

IDIOM **~ at first sight** le coup de foudre

love affair *n* liaison *f* (**with** avec, **between** entre)

loved one *n* être *m* cher

love life *n* vie *f* amoureuse

lovely /ˈlʌvlɪ/ *adj* **1** (beautiful) ‹*colour, garden, woman*› beau/belle *before n*, joli/-e *before n*; **to look ~** ‹*child, dress*› être ravissant/-e
2 (pleasant) ‹*letter, person*› charmant/-e; ‹*meal, smell*› délicieux/-ieuse; ‹*idea, surprise*› bon/bonne *before n*; ‹*present, weather*› magnifique

lover /ˈlʌvə(r)/ *n* **1** (male) amant *m*; (female) maîtresse *f*; **they are ~s** ils sont amants
2 (person in love) amoureux/-euse *m/f*
3 (enthusiast) amateur *m*; **jazz ~** amateur de jazz

love-struck *adj* éperdument amoureux/-euse

loving /ˈlʌvɪŋ/ *adj* (gen) tendre; ‹*care*› affectueux/-euse

low /ləʊ/ **A** *n* **1** (in weather) dépression *f*
2 **to be at** *or* **have hit an all-time ~** être au plus bas
B *adj* **1** (gen) bas/basse; ‹*speed*› réduit/-e; ‹*number, rate*› faible *before n*; ‹*battery*› presque à plat *inv*; **in a ~ voice** tout bas; **to be ~ on staff** manquer de personnel; **to be ~ in sugar** contenir peu de sucre
2 ‹*mark, quality*› mauvais/-e *before n*
3 (depressed) déprimé/-e
4 ‹*behaviour*› ignoble
C *adv* **1** ‹*aim*› bas; ‹*bend*› très bas; ‹*fly*› à basse altitude
2 (in importance) **it's very ~ (down) on the list** c'est tout à fait secondaire
3 ‹*speak, sing*› bas; **to turn [sth] down ~** baisser ‹*heating, light*›
D *vi* ‹*cow*› meugler

low-alcohol *adj* peu alcoolisé/-e
lowbrow /ˈləʊbraʊ/ *adj* ‹*person*› peu intellectuel/-elle
low-budget *adj* à petit budget
low-calorie *adj* ‹*diet*› hypocalorique; ‹*food*› à faible teneur en calories
low-carb /ləʊˈkɑːb/ *adj* pauvre en glucides; **a ~ diet** un régime pauvre en glucides
low-cost *adj* économique, bon marché
low-cut *adj* décolleté/-e
low-down /ˈləʊdaʊn/ *n* (fam) tuyau *m* (fam)
lower **A** *adj* inférieur/-e
B *vt* **1** baisser ‹*barrier, curtain, flag*›; abaisser ‹*ceiling*›; **to ~ sb/sth** descendre qn/qch (**into** dans, **onto** sur)
2 (reduce) baisser ‹*prices, standards*›; réduire ‹*pressure, temperature*›; abaisser ‹*age limit*›; **to ~ one's voice** baisser la voix
3 affaler ‹*sail*›
C *v refl* **1 to ~ oneself** s'abaisser
2 to ~ oneself into s'asseoir précautionneusement dans ‹*bath, armchair*›
lower class /ˈləʊə(r)/ *n* (*pl* **~es**) **the ~(es)** la classe ouvrière
lower sixth /ˈləʊə(r)/ *n* (BrE) (Sch) ≈ classe *f* de première; **to be in the ~** ≈ être en première
low-fat *adj* ‹*diet*› sans matières grasses; ‹*cheese*› allégé/-e; ‹*milk*› écrémé/-e
low-income *adj* ‹*family*› à faible revenue; ‹*bracket*› des bas salaires
low-key /ˌləʊˈkiː/ *adj* ‹*approach*› discret/-ète; ‹*meeting, talks*› informel/-elle
low-level *adj* ‹*bombing*› à basse altitude; ‹*talks*› informel/-elle; ‹*radiation*› faible
low-lying *adj* à basse altitude
low-paid *adj* ‹*job*› faiblement rémunéré/-e; ‹*worker*› peu rémunéré/-e
low-priced *adj* à bas prix
low-profile *adj* discret/-ète
low-quality *adj* de qualité inférieure
low-risk *adj* à risque limité
low season *n* basse saison *f*
low-tech *adj* traditionnel/-elle
low tide *n* marée *f* basse
loyal /ˈlɔɪəl/ *adj* ‹*friend*› loyal/-e (**to** envers); ‹*customer*› fidèle (**to** à)
loyalty /ˈlɔɪəltɪ/ *n* loyauté *f* (**to, towards** envers)
loyalty card *n* carte *f* de fidélité
lozenge /ˈlɒzɪndʒ/ *n* pastille *f*
LP *n* (disque *m*) 33 tours *m*
L-plate *n* (BrE) (Aut) plaque *f* d'élève conducteur débutant accompagné
Ltd (BrE) (*abbr* = **limited liability**) ≈ SARL
lubricant /ˈluːbrɪkənt/ *n* lubrifiant *m*
lucid /ˈluːsɪd/ *adj* **1** (clear) clair/-e
2 (sane) ‹*person*› lucide; ‹*moment*› de lucidité
luck /lʌk/ *n* chance *f*; **good ~** chance *f*; **bad ~** malchance *f*; **to bring sb good/bad ~** porter bonheur/malheur à qn; **it's good ~** ça porte bonheur; **bad** *or* **hard ~!** pas de chance!; **good ~!** bonne chance!; **to be in/out of ~** avoir de la/ne pas avoir de chance
luckily /ˈlʌkɪlɪ/ *adv* heureusement (**for** pour)
lucky /ˈlʌkɪ/ *adj* **1** (fortunate) **to be ~** avoir de la chance
2 ‹*charm, colour, number*› porte-bonheur *m inv*; **it's my ~ day!** c'est mon jour de chance!
lucrative /ˈluːkrətɪv/ *adj* lucratif/-ive
ludicrous /ˈluːdɪkrəs/ *adj* grotesque
luggage /ˈlʌgɪdʒ/ *n* bagages *mpl*
luggage rack *n* porte-bagages *m inv*
lukewarm /ˌluːkˈwɔːm/ *adj* tiède
lull /lʌl/ **A** *n* (in storm, fighting) accalmie *f*; (in conversation) pause *f*
B *vt* **to ~ sb to sleep** endormir qn en le berçant; **to ~ sb into thinking that...** faire croire à qn que...; **to be ~ed into a false sense of security** se laisser aller à un sentiment de sécurité trompeur
lullaby /ˈlʌləbaɪ/ *n* berceuse *f*
lumber /ˈlʌmbə(r)/ **A** *n* (AmE) bois *m* de construction
B *vt* (BrE) (fam) **to get** *or* **be ~ed with sb/sth** se retrouver avec qn/qch sur les bras
C *vi* (*also* **~ along**) avancer d'un pas lourd; ‹*vehicle*› avancer péniblement
lumberjack *n* bûcheron/-onne *m/f*
luminous /ˈluːmɪnəs/ *adj* lumineux/-euse
lump /lʌmp/ **A** *n* **1** (gen) morceau *m*; (of soil, clay) motte *f*; (in sauce) grumeau *m*
2 (on body) (from knock) bosse *f* (**on** sur)
3 (tumour) grosseur *f* (**in, on** à)
B *vt* **to ~ X and Y together** mettre X et Y dans le même panier (fam)
IDIOM **to have a ~ in one's throat** avoir la gorge serrée
lump sum *n* versement *m* unique
lunar /ˈluːnə(r)/ *adj* ‹*landscape*› lunaire; ‹*eclipse*› de lune; ‹*landing*› sur la lune
lunatic /ˈluːnətɪk/ *n* fou/folle *m/f*
lunch /lʌntʃ/ *n* déjeuner *m*; **to have ~** déjeuner; **to take sb out for ~** emmener qn déjeuner au restaurant; **to close for ~** fermer le midi
lunch box *n* boîte *f* à sandwichs
lunch break *n* pause-déjeuner *f*
luncheon voucher, **LV** *n* ticket-repas *m*, ticket-restaurant® *m*
lunch hour *n* heure *f* du déjeuner
lunchtime /ˈlʌntʃtaɪm/ *n* heure *f* du déjeuner
lung /lʌŋ/ *n* poumon *m*
lunge /lʌndʒ/ *vi* bondir (**at** vers, **forward** en avant)

mot clé

lurch /lɜːtʃ/ *vi* ‹*person, vehicle*› tanguer; **to ~ forward** ‹*car*› faire un bond en avant
IDIOM **to leave sb in the ~** abandonner qn

lure /lʊə(r)/ **A** *n* **1** (attraction) attrait *m* (**of** de) **2** (in hunting) leurre *m*
B *vt* attirer (**into** dans, **with** avec); **they ~d him out of his house** ils ont réussi à le faire sortir de chez lui par la ruse

lurid /ˈlʊərɪd/ *adj* **1** ‹*colour*› criard/-e **2** ‹*detail, past*› épouvantable

lurk /lɜːk/ *vi* **he was ~ing in the bushes** il était tapi dans les buissons; **to ~ in the garden** rôder dans le jardin

lurker /ˈlɜːkə(r)/ *n* (Comput) observateur *m* passif/observatrice *f* passive

luscious /ˈlʌʃəs/ *adj* ‹*food*› succulent/-e; ‹*woman*› pulpeux/-euse

lush /lʌʃ/ *adj* ‹*vegetation*› luxuriant/-e; ‹*hotel, surroundings*› luxueux/-euse

lust /lʌst/ **A** *n* **1** désir *m*; (deadly sin) luxure *f* **2** (for power, blood) soif *f* (**for** de)
B *vi* **to ~ for** *or* **after sb/sth** convoiter qn/qch

luvvy /ˈlʌvɪ/ *n* (fam) acteur/-trice *m/f* prétentieux/-ieuse

Luxembourg /ˈlʌksəmbɜːg/ *pr n* Luxembourg *m*

luxurious /lʌgˈzjʊərɪəs/ *adj* ‹*apartment, lifestyle*› de luxe *never after v*; **his apartment is ~** son appartement est luxueux

luxury /ˈlʌkʃərɪ/ **A** *n* luxe *m*
B *adj* ‹*hotel, product, holiday*› de luxe

lychee /ˈlaɪtʃiː, ˌlaɪˈtʃiː/ *n* litchi *m*

lying /ˈlaɪɪŋ/ *n* mensonges *mpl*

lynch /lɪntʃ/ *vt* lyncher

lynch mob *n* lyncheurs *mpl*

lyrical /ˈlɪrɪkl/ *adj* lyrique; **to wax ~ (about sth)** disserter avec lyrisme (sur qch)

lyrics *npl* paroles *fpl*

lyric writer *n* parolier/-ière *m/f*

Mm

m, M /em/ *n* m, M *m*

MA *n* (*abbr* = **Master of Arts**) diplôme *m* supérieur de lettres

macabre /məˈkɑːbrə/ *adj* macabre

macaroni /ˌmækəˈrəʊnɪ/ *n* macaronis *mpl*

mace /meɪs/ *n* **1** (spice) macis *m* **2** (ceremonial staff) masse *f*

Macedonia /ˌmæsɪˈdəʊnɪə/ *pr n* Macédoine *f*

machete /məˈtʃetɪ, (AmE) məˈʃetɪ/ *n* machette *f*

machine /məˈʃiːn/ *n* machine *f*; **sewing ~** machine à coudre; **by ~** à la machine

machine gun *n* mitrailleuse *f*

machine-readable /məʃiːnˈriːdəbl/ *adj* ‹*data*› directement exploitable; ‹*passport*› vérifiable par ordinateur

machinery /məˈʃiːnərɪ/ *n* **1** (equipment) machines *fpl*; (working parts) mécanisme *m*, rouages *mpl*; **a piece of ~** une machine **2** (fig) dispositifs *mpl*

macho /ˈmætʃəʊ/ *adj* macho (fam)

mackerel /ˈmækrəl/ *n* maquereau *m*

mackintosh, **macintosh** /ˈmækɪntɒʃ/ *n* imperméable *m*

mad /mæd/ *adj* **1** ‹*person*› fou/folle (**with** de); ‹*dog*› enragé/-e; ‹*idea, scheme*› insensé/-e; **to go ~** devenir fou/folle; **to drive sb ~** rendre qn fou
2 (fam) (angry) furieux/-ieuse; **to be ~ at** *or* **with sb** être très en colère contre qn; **to go ~** se mettre dans une colère folle
3 (fam) (enthusiastic) **~ about** *or* **on** fou/folle de (fam) ‹*person, hobby*›
4 ‹*panic*› infernal/-e; **the audience went ~** le public s'est déchaîné
IDIOM **to work like ~** travailler comme un fou/une folle

madam /ˈmædəm/ *n* madame *f*; **Dear Madam** (in letter) Madame

mad cow disease *n* maladie *f* de la vache folle

maddening /ˈmædnɪŋ/ *adj* ‹*person*› énervant/-e; ‹*delay, situation*› exaspérant/-e

made /meɪd/ *adj* **a ~ man** un homme qui a réussi; **he's got it ~** (sure to succeed) sa réussite est assurée; (has succeeded) il n'a plus à s'en faire

Madeira /məˈdɪərə/ *pr n* Madère

made-to-measure *adj* ‹*garment*› fait/-e sur mesure

made-up /ˌmeɪdˈʌp/ *adj* **1** (wearing make-up) maquillé/-e **2** ‹*story*› fabriqué/-e

madly /ˈmædlɪ/ *adv* **1** (frantically) frénétiquement **2** ‹*jealous*› follement; **~ in love (with sb)** follement *or* éperdument amoureux/-euse (de qn)

madman *n* (fam) fou *m* (fam), malade *m* (fam)

madness /'mædnıs/ *n* folie *f*; **it is ~ to do** c'est de la folie de faire

Mafia *n* **the ~** la Mafia

🔑 **magazine** /,mægə'zi:n/ *n* **1** revue *f*; (mainly photos) magazine *m*; **fashion ~** magazine de mode; **women's ~** journal *m* féminin
2 (on radio, TV) magazine *m*
3 (of gun, camera) magasin *m*

maggot /'mægət/ *n* (in fruit) ver *m*; (for fishing) asticot *m*

magic /'mædʒık/ **A** *n* magie *f*
B *adj* magique

magical /'mædʒıkl/ *adj* magique

magic carpet *n* tapis *m* volant

magician /mə'dʒıʃn/ *n* (wizard) magicien *m*; (entertainer) illusionniste *m*

magistrate /'mædʒıstreıt/ *n* magistrat *m*

magistrate's court *n* ≈ tribunal *m* de police

magnanimous /mæg'nænıməs/ *adj* magnanime

magnate /'mægneıt/ *n* magnat *m*; **oil ~** magnat du pétrole

magnesium /mæg'ni:zıəm/ *n* magnésium *m*

magnet /'mægnıt/ *n* aimant *m*; (fig) pôle *m* d'attraction (**for** pour)

magnetic /mæg'netık/ *adj* **1** ‹*rod*› aimanté/-e; ‹*field, force, storm*› magnétique
2 ‹*appeal*› irrésistible; **to have a ~ personality** avoir du charisme

magnetism /'mægnıtızəm/ *n* magnétisme *m*

magnificent /mæg'nıfısnt/ *adj* magnifique

magnify /'mægnıfaı/ *vt* grossir

magnifying glass *n* loupe *f*

magnitude /'mægnıtju:d, (AmE) -tu:d/ *n* ampleur *f* (**of** de)

magnolia /mæg'nəʊlıə/ *n* **1** (*also* **~ tree**) magnolia *m*
2 (colour) crème *m*

magpie /'mægpaı/ *n* pie *f*

mahogany /mə'hɒgənı/ *n* acajou *m*

maid /meıd/ *n* (in house) bonne *f*; (in hotel) femme *f* de chambre

maiden /'meıdn/ **A** *n* jeune fille *f*
B *adj* ‹*flight, voyage, speech*› inaugural/-e

maiden name *n* nom *m* de jeune fille

mail /meıl/ **A** *n* **1** (postal service) poste *f*; **by ~** par la poste
2 (letters) courrier *m*
3 (email) courrier *m* électronique
B *vt* envoyer, expédier ‹*letter, parcel*› (**to** à)

mailbox /'meılbɒks/ *n* (for posting) boîte *f* aux lettres; (for delivery) boîte *f* à lettres; (for email) boîte *f* aux lettres électronique

mailing /'meılıŋ/ *n* (for advertising) publipostage *m*, mailing *m*

mailing list *n* fichier-clientèle *m*

mailman (AmE) *n* (*pl* **-men**) (AmE) facteur *m*

mail order /'meıl ɔ:də(r)/ **A** *n* **to buy (by) ~** acheter par correspondance
B *adj* ‹*business, goods*› de vente *f* par correspondance

maim /meım/ *vt* estropier

🔑 **main** /meın/ **A** *n* **1** (pipe) canalisation *f*
2 the ~s (of electricity) secteur *m*; (of water, gas) le réseau de distribution; (of sewage) le réseau d'évacuation
B *adj* principal/-e

main course *n* plat *m* principal

mainframe /'meınfreım/ *n* (*also* **~ computer**) ordinateur *m* central

mainland /'meınlənd/ *n* territoire *m* continental; **on the ~** sur le continent

main line A /,meın'laın/ *n* grande ligne *f*
B *adj* ‹*station*› de grande ligne
C mainline *vi* (fam) se piquer

🔑 **mainly** /'meınlı/ *adv* surtout, essentiellement

main road *n* (in country) route *f* principale; (in town) grande rue *f*

mainstream /'meınstri:m/ **A** *n* courant *m* dominant
B *adj* **1** (conventional) traditionnel/-elle
2 ~ jazz jazz *m* mainstream

🔑 **maintain** /meın'teın/ *vt* **1** (keep steady) maintenir
2 subvenir aux besoins de ‹*family*›; entretenir ‹*army, house, property*›
3 continuer à affirmer ‹*innocence*›; **to ~ that** soutenir que

maintenance /'meıntənəns/ *n* **1** (upkeep) entretien *m* (**of** de)
2 (BrE) (Law) (alimony) pension *f* alimentaire

maisonette /,meızə'net/ *n* duplex *m*

maize /meız/ *n* maïs *m*

majestic /mə'dʒestık/ *adj* majestueux/-euse

majesty /'mædʒəstı/ *n* **1** (grandeur) majesté *f*
2 His/Her Majesty sa Majesté

🔑 **major** /'meıdʒə(r)/ **A** *n* **1** (Mil) commandant *m*
2 (AmE) (Univ) matière *f* principale
3 (Mus) ton *m* majeur
B *adj* **1** ‹*event*› important/-e; ‹*role*› majeur/-e; ‹*significance*› capital/-e; **a ~ operation, ~ surgery** une grosse opération
2 (main) principal/-e
3 (Mus) majeur/-e; **in a ~ key** en majeur
C *vi* (AmE) (Univ) **to ~ in** se spécialiser en

Majorca /mə'jɔ:kə, mə'dʒɔ:kə/ *pr n* Majorque *f*; **in ~** à Majorque

🔑 **majority** /mə'dʒɒrətı, (AmE) -'dʒɔ:r-/ *n* majorité *f* (**of** de); **to be in a** *or* **the ~** être en majorité

🔑 **make** /meık/ **A** *n* marque *f*
B *vt* (*prét, pp* **made**) **1** (gen) faire; **to ~ the bed** faire le lit; **to ~ a noise** faire du bruit; **to ~ a rule** établir une règle; **to ~ room/the time (for sth)** trouver de la place/du temps (pour qch); **to ~ friends/enemies** se faire des amis/des ennemis; **to ~ oneself understood** se faire comprendre; **it's made**

🔑 mot clé

(out) of gold c'est en or; **made in France** fabriqué en France; **he was made treasurer** on l'a fait trésorier; **to ~ a habit/an issue of sth** faire de qch une habitude/une affaire; **it's been made into a film** on en a fait *or* tiré un film; **three and three ~ six** trois et trois font six
2 (with adjective) **to ~ sb happy/ill** rendre qn heureux/malade; **to ~ sb hungry** donner faim à qn; **to ~ sth better/bigger/worse** améliorer/agrandir/aggraver qch
3 (with infinitive) **to ~ sb cry** faire pleurer qn; **I made her smile** je l'ai fait sourire; **to ~ sb pay the bill** faire payer l'addition à qn; **to ~ sb wait** faire attendre qn; **they made me do it** ils m'ont obligé *or* forcé; **it ~s her voice sound funny** ça lui donne une drôle de voix
4 (earn) gagner ‹*salary*›; **to ~ a living** gagner sa vie; **to ~ a profit** réaliser des bénéfices; **to ~ a loss** subir des pertes
5 (reach) arriver jusqu'à ‹*place, position*›; atteindre ‹*ranking, level*›; **we'll never ~ it** nous n'y arriverons jamais; **to ~ the front page** faire la une
6 (estimate, say) **what time do you ~ it?** quelle heure as-tu?; **I ~ it five o'clock** il est cinq heures à ma montre; **let's ~ it five dollars** disons cinq dollars; **can we ~ it a bit later?** peut-on dire un peu plus tard?; **what do you ~ of it?** qu'en dis-tu?
7 (cause success of) assurer la réussite de ‹*holiday, meal*›; **it really made my day** ça m'a rendu heureux pour la journée
IDIOMS **to ~ it** (fam) (in career, life) y arriver; (to party, meeting) réussir à venir; **I can't ~ it** je ne peux pas venir
■ **make do** faire avec; **to ~ do with sth** se contenter de qch
■ **make for 1** (head for) se diriger vers
2 (help create) permettre, assurer
■ **make good**: **A ~ good** réussir
B ~ good [sth] 1 réparer ‹*damage, omission*›; rattraper ‹*lost time*›; combler ‹*deficit*›
2 tenir ‹*promise*›
■ **make out**: **A ~ out** affirmer, prétendre (**that** que)
B ~ [sb/sth] out 1 (see, distinguish) distinguer
2 (claim) **to ~ sth out to be easy/difficult** prétendre que qch est facile/difficile
3 (understand) comprendre (**if** si); **I can't ~ him out** je n'arrive pas à le comprendre
4 (write out) faire, rédiger; **to ~ out a cheque to sb** faire un chèque à qn; **it is made out to X** il est à l'ordre de X
■ **make up A ~ up 1** (after quarrel) se réconcilier (**with** avec)
2 to ~ up for rattraper ‹*lost time, lost sleep*›; compenser ‹*personal loss*›
B ~ [sth] up 1 inventer ‹*story, excuse*›
2 (prepare) faire ‹*parcel, garment, bed*›; préparer ‹*prescription*›
3 (constitute) faire; **to be made up of** être fait/-e *or* composé/-e de
4 (compensate for) rattraper ‹*loss, time*›; combler ‹*deficit*›

make-believe /ˈmeɪkbɪliːv/ *n* fantaisie *f*
makeover /ˈmeɪkəʊvə(r)/ *n* transformation *f*
maker /ˈmeɪkə(r)/ *n* (of clothes, food, appliance) fabricant *m*; (of cars, aircraft) constructeur *m*
makeshift *adj* improvisé/-e
make-up /ˈmeɪkʌp/ *n* **1** maquillage *m*; **to put on one's ~** se maquiller
2 (character) caractère *m*
make-up bag *n* trousse *f* de maquillage
make-up remover *n* démaquillant *m*
making /ˈmeɪkɪŋ/ *n* (of film, programme) réalisation *f*; (of product) fabrication *f*; (of clothes) confection *f*; **his problems are of his own ~** ses ennuis sont de sa faute; **a disaster is in the ~** une catastrophe se prépare
IDIOM **to have all the ~s of** avoir tout pour faire
maladjusted /ˌmæləˈdʒʌstɪd/ *adj* inadapté/-e
malaria /məˈleərɪə/ *n* paludisme *m*
Malaysia /məˈleɪzɪə/ *pr n* Malaisie *f*
male /meɪl/ **A** *n* **1** (animal) mâle *m*
2 (man) homme *m*
B *adj* **1** ‹*plant, animal*› mâle
2 ‹*population, role, trait*› masculin/-e; ‹*company*› des hommes; **a ~ voice** une voix d'homme; **~ student** étudiant *m*
3 ‹*plug, socket*› mâle
male chauvinism *n* machisme *m*
male chauvinist /ˌmeɪl ˈʃəʊvɪnɪst/ *n* phallocrate *m*
male model *n* mannequin *m* homme *or* masculin
malevolent /məˈlevələnt/ *adj* malveillant/-e
malformed /ˌmælˈfɔːmd/ *adj* ‹*limb, nose*› difforme; ‹*organ*› malformé/-e
malfunction /ˌmælˈfʌŋkʃn/ **A** *n* **1** (poor operation) mauvais fonctionnement *m*
2 (breakdown) défaillance *f*
B *vi* mal fonctionner
malice /ˈmælɪs/ *n* méchanceté *f* (**towards** à)
malicious /məˈlɪʃəs/ *adj* ‹*comment, person*› malveillant/-e; ‹*act*› méchant/-e; ‹*lie*› calomnieux/-ieuse
malign /məˈlaɪn/ *vt* calomnier
malignant /məˈlɪgnənt/ *adj* **1** ‹*look*› malveillant/-e; ‹*person*› malfaisant/-e
2 (Med) malin/-igne
mall /mæl, mɔːl/ *n* **1** (shopping arcade) (in town) galerie *f* marchande; (in suburbs) (AmE) centre *m* commercial
2 (AmE) (street) rue *f* piétonne
mallet /ˈmælɪt/ *n* maillet *m*
malnutrition /ˌmælnjuːˈtrɪʃn, (AmE) -nuː-/ *n* sous-alimentation *f*
malpractice /ˌmælˈpræktɪs/ *n* **1** (gen), (Law) malversations *fpl*
2 (AmE) (Med) erreur *f* médicale

malt /mɔːlt/ *n* **1** (grain) malt *m*
2 (whisky) whisky *m* pur malt
3 (AmE) (malted milk) lait *m* malté

Malta /'mɔːltə/ *pr n* Malte *f*

maltreat /ˌmæl'triːt/ *vt* maltraiter

mammal /'mæml/ *n* mammifère *m*

mammoth /'mæməθ/ **A** *n* mammouth *m*
B *adj* ‹*task*› gigantesque; ‹*organization*› géant/-e

⚷ **man** /mæn/ **A** *n* (*pl* **men**) **1** homme *m*; **an old ∼** un vieillard; **∼ to ∼** d'homme à homme; **∼ and wife** mari et femme
2 (mankind) l'humanité *f*
3 (in chess) pièce *f*; (in draughts) pion *m*
B *vt* (*p prés etc* **-nn-**) **1** tenir ‹*switchboard, desk*›
2 armer [qch] en hommes ‹*ship*›
IDIOM **every ∼ for himself** chacun pour soi

⚷ **manage** /'mænɪdʒ/ **A** *vt* **1 to ∼ to do** réussir à faire, se débrouiller (fam) pour faire
2 diriger ‹*project, finances, organization*›; gérer ‹*business, shop, hotel, estate*›; gérer ‹*money, time*›
3 (handle) savoir s'y prendre avec ‹*person, animal*›; manier ‹*tool, boat*›
B *vi* se débrouiller

manageable /'mænɪdʒəbl/ *adj* ‹*size, car*› maniable; ‹*problem*› maîtrisable; ‹*person, animal*› docile

m

⚷ **management** /'mænɪdʒmənt/ *n* **1** (system, field) gestion *f*; **bad ∼** mauvaise gestion
2 (managers) direction *f*; **top ∼** la haute direction **the ∼ team** l'équipe dirigeante

management consultant *n* conseiller *m* en gestion

management trainee *n* apprenti manager *m*

⚷ **manager** /'mænɪdʒə(r)/ *n* (of firm, bank) directeur/-trice *m/f*; (of shop) gérant/-e *m/f*; (of farm) exploitant/-e *m/f*; (of project) responsable *mf*, directeur/-trice *m/f*; (in show business) directeur/-trice *m/f* artistique; (Sport) manager *m*

manageress /ˌmænɪdʒə'res/ *n* (of firm, bank) directrice *f*; (of shop, hotel) gérante *f*; (of project) responsable *f*, directrice *f*; (in show business) directrice *f* artistique

managerial /ˌmænɪ'dʒɪərɪəl/ *adj* ‹*experience*› en gestion; ‹*decision*› de la direction; **∼ staff** les cadres *mpl*

managing director, **MD** *n* directeur/-trice *m/f* général/-e

mandarin /'mændərɪn/ *n* **1** (fruit) mandarine *f*; (tree) mandarinier *m*
2 (person) mandarin *m*

mandate /'mændeɪt/ *n* (authority) autorité *f*; (Pol) mandat *m*

mane /meɪn/ *n* crinière *f*

manger /'meɪndʒə(r)/ *n* mangeoire *f*

mangle /'mæŋgl/ *vt* mutiler ‹*body*›; broyer ‹*vehicle*›

mango /'mæŋgəʊ/ *n* (fruit) mangue *f*

mangrove /'mæŋgrəʊv/ *n* palétuvier *m*, manglier *m*

mangy /'meɪndʒɪ/ *adj* ‹*dog*› galeux/-euse

manhandle /'mænhændl/ *vt* malmener, maltraiter

manhole *n* regard *m*

manhood /'mænhʊd/ *n* **1** âge *m* d'homme
2 (masculinity) masculinité *f*

mania /'meɪnɪə/ *n* manie *f*

maniac /'meɪnɪæk/ *n* **1** (fam) fou/folle *m/f*
2 (in psychology) maniaque *mf*

manic /'mænɪk/ *adj* **1** (manic-depressive) maniaco-dépressif/-ive; (obsessive) obsessionnel/-elle
2 (fig) ‹*activity, behaviour*› frénétique

manicure /'mænɪkjʊə(r)/ **A** *n* manucure *f*
B *vt* **to ∼ one's nails** se faire les ongles

manifest /'mænɪfest/ **A** *adj* manifeste, évident/-e
B *vt* manifester

manifesto /ˌmænɪ'festəʊ/ *n* manifeste *m*, programme *m*

manipulate /mə'nɪpjʊleɪt/ *vt* manipuler

manipulative /mə'nɪpjʊlətɪv/ *adj* manipulateur/-trice

mankind *n* humanité *f*

manly /'mænlɪ/ *adj* viril/-e

man-made *adj* ‹*fibre, fabric*› synthétique; ‹*lake*› artificiel/-ielle; ‹*tools*› fait/-e à la main

⚷ **manner** /'mænə(r)/ **A** *n* **1** (way, method) manière *f*, façon *f*; **in this ∼** de cette manière *or* façon; **in a ∼ of speaking** pour ainsi dire
2 (way of behaving) attitude *f*; **she has an aggressive ∼** elle a une attitude agressive
3 (sort, kind) sorte *f*, genre *m* (**of** de)
B manners *npl* **1** manières *fpl*; **to have good/bad ∼s** avoir de bonnes/mauvaises manières; **it's bad ∼s to do** il est mal élevé de faire
2 (customs) mœurs *fpl*

mannerism /'mænərɪzəm/ *n* (habit) particularité *f*; (quirk) manie *f*

manoeuvre (BrE), **maneuver** (AmE) /mə'nuːvə(r)/ **A** *n* manœuvre *f*
B *vt* **1** manœuvrer ‹*vehicle, object*›
2 (fig) manœuvrer ‹*person*›; faire dévier ‹*discussion*› (**to** vers)
C *vi* manœuvrer

manor /'mænə(r)/ *n* (*also* **∼ house**) manoir *m*

manpower /'mænpaʊə(r)/ *n* main-d'œuvre *f*

mansion /'mænʃn/ *n* (in countryside) demeure *f*; (in town) hôtel *m* particulier

manslaughter *n* homicide *m* involontaire

mantelpiece /'mæntlpiːs/ *n* (manteau *m* de) cheminée *f*

⚷ mot clé

manual /ˈmænjʊəl/ **A** *n* manuel *m*
B *adj* ‹*labour, worker*› manuel/-elle; ‹*gearbox, typewriter*› mécanique

manufacture /ˌmænjʊˈfæktʃə(r)/ **A** *n* (gen) fabrication *f*; (of clothes) confection *f*; (of cars) construction *f*
B *vt* (gen) fabriquer; construire ‹*cars*›

⚷ **manufacturer** /ˌmænjʊˈfæktʃərə(r)/ *n* (gen) fabricant *m* (**of** de); (of cars) constructeur *m*

manure /məˈnjʊə(r)/ *n* fumier *m*; **horse ~** crottin *m* de cheval

manuscript /ˈmænjʊskrɪpt/ *n* manuscrit *m*

⚷ **many** /ˈmenɪ/ **A** *det* beaucoup de, un grand nombre de; **~ people** beaucoup de gens, un grand nombre de personnes; **~ times** de nombreuses fois, bien des fois; **for ~ years** pendant de nombreuses années; **how ~ people/times?** combien de personnes/fois?; **too ~** trop de; **I have as ~ books as you (do)** j'ai autant de livres que toi; **so ~** tant de
B *pron, quantif* (*comp* **more**, *superl* **most**) beaucoup; **not ~** pas beaucoup; **too ~** trop; **how ~?** combien?; **as ~ as you like** autant que tu veux; **I didn't know there were so ~** je ne savais pas qu'il y en avait autant; **~ (of them) were killed** beaucoup d'entre eux ont été tués

many-sided *adj* à multiples facettes

⚷ **map** /mæp/ *n* carte *f* (**of** de); (of town, underground) plan *m* (**of** de); **street ~** plan des rues
■ **map out** élaborer, mettre [qch] au point ‹*plans, strategy*›; tracer ‹*future*›

maple /ˈmeɪpl/ *n* érable *m*

mar /mɑː(r)/ *vt* (*p prés etc* **-rr-**) gâcher

marathon /ˈmærəθən, (AmE) -θɒn/ **A** *n* marathon *m*
B *adj* **1** (Sport) **~ runner** marathonien/-ienne *m/f*
2 (massive) -marathon; **a ~ session** une séance-marathon

marble /ˈmɑːbl/ *n* **1** (stone) marbre *m*
2 (Games) bille *f*; **to play ~s** jouer aux billes

march /mɑːtʃ/ **A** *n* marche *f*
B *vi* **1** (Mil) marcher au pas; **to ~ (for) 40 km** faire une marche de 40 km; **forward ~!** en avant, marche!
2 (in protest) manifester (**against** contre, **for** pour)
3 to ~ along (walk briskly) marcher d'un pas vif; **to ~ in** (angrily) entrer l'air furieux; **she ~ed up to his desk** elle s'est dirigée droit sur son bureau

⚷ **March** /mɑːtʃ/ *n* mars *m*

marcher /ˈmɑːtʃə(r)/ *n* (in demonstration) manifestant/-e *m/f*; (in procession) marcheur/-euse *m/f*

mare /meə(r)/ *n* (horse) jument *f*; (donkey) ânesse *f*

margarine /ˌmɑːdʒəˈriːn/ *n* margarine *f*

margin /ˈmɑːdʒɪn/ *n* marge *f*; **by a narrow ~** de justesse, de peu

marginal /ˈmɑːdʒɪnl/ *adj* marginal/-e

marginalize /ˈmɑːdʒɪnəlaɪz/ *vt* marginaliser

marigold /ˈmærɪgəʊld/ *n* souci *m*

marijuana /ˌmærjuːˈɑːnə/ *n* marijuana *f*

marinade /ˌmærɪˈneɪd/ *vt* (*also* **marinate**) faire mariner

marine /məˈriːn/ **A** *n* **1** (soldier) fusilier *m* marin; **the Marines** les marines *mpl*
2 (navy) **the merchant ~** la marine marchande
B *adj* ‹*mammal, biology*› marin/-e; ‹*explorer, life*› sous-marin/-e; ‹*insurance, law*› maritime

marital /ˈmærɪtl/ *adj* conjugal/-e

marital status *n* situation *f* de famille

marjoram /ˈmɑːdʒərəm/ *n* marjolaine *f*

⚷ **mark** /mɑːk/ **A** *n* **1** (gen) marque *f*; (stain) tache *f*
2 as a ~ of en signe de ‹*esteem, respect*›
3 (BrE) (Sch, Univ) note *f*
4 the high tide ~ le maximum de la marée haute; **at gas ~ 7** à thermostat 7
5 (Sport) **on your ~s!** à vos marques!
6 (*also* **Deutschmark**) deutschmark *m*
B *vt* **1** (gen) marquer; (stain) tacher
2 ‹*arrow, sign, label*› indiquer ‹*position, road*›
3 (BrE) (Sch, Univ) corriger; **to ~ sb absent** noter qn absent
4 (Sport) marquer
C *vi* **1** (BrE) ‹*teacher*› faire des corrections
2 (stain) se tacher
3 (Sport) marquer
IDIOMS **~ my words** crois-moi; **to ~ time** (Mil) marquer le pas; (fig) (wait) attendre; (wait for right moment) attendre le bon moment

marked /mɑːkt/ *adj* **1** ‹*difference, increase, contrast*› marqué/-e, net/nette *before n*; ‹*accent*› prononcé/-e
2 he's a ~ man on en veut à sa vie

marker /ˈmɑːkə(r)/ *n* **1** (pen) marqueur *m*
2 (tag) repère *m*

⚷ **market** /ˈmɑːkɪt/ **A** *n* **1** (gen), (Econ) marché *m*
2 (stock market) Bourse *f*
B *vt* **1** (sell) commercialiser, vendre
2 (promote) lancer *or* mettre [qch] sur le marché

market day *n* jour *m* du marché

market economy *n* économie *f* de marché

market forces *npl* forces *fpl* du marché

market gardening *n* culture *f* maraîchère

⚷ **marketing** /ˈmɑːkɪtɪŋ/ *n* **1** (field) marketing *m*, mercatique *f*
2 (department) service *m* de marketing

marketing strategy *n* stratégie *f* commerciale

market leader *n* (product) produit *m* vedette; (company) leader *m* du marché

marketplace /ˈmɑːkɪtpleɪs/ *n* place *f* du marché

market research *n* étude *f* de marché

market town *n* bourg *m*

market trader *n* vendeur/-euse *m/f* sur un marché

market value *n* valeur *f* marchande

markings *npl* (on animal) taches *fpl*; (on aircraft) marques *fpl*; **road ~** signalisation *f* horizontale

marksman *n* tireur *m* d'élite

marmalade /ˈmɑːməleɪd/ *n* confiture *f* or marmelade *f* d'oranges

maroon /məˈruːn/ **A** *n* bordeaux *m*
B *vt* **to be ~ed on an island** être bloqué/-e sur une île; **the ~ed sailors** les naufragés

marquee /mɑːˈkiː/ *n* **1** (BrE) (tent) grande tente *f*; (of circus) chapiteau *m*
2 (AmE) (canopy) (grand) auvent *m*

⚷ **marriage** /ˈmærɪdʒ/ *n* mariage *m* (**to** avec)

marriage certificate *n* extrait *m* d'acte de mariage

married /ˈmærɪd/ *adj* ‹*person*› marié/-e (**to** à); ‹*life*› conjugal/-e; **~ couple** couple *m*

marrow /ˈmærəʊ/ *n* **1** (in bone) moelle *f*
2 (vegetable) courge *f*; **baby ~** (BrE) courgette *f*

marrowbone /ˈmærəʊbəʊn/ *n* os *m* à moelle

⚷ **marry** /ˈmærɪ/ **A** *vt* se marier avec, épouser ‹*fiancé(e)*›; ‹*priest*› marier ‹*couple*›; **to get married** se marier (**to** avec); **will you ~ me?** veux-tu m'épouser?
B *vi* se marier

Mars /mɑːz/ *pr n* Mars *f*

marsh /mɑːʃ/ *n* (*also* **marshland**) (terrain) marécage *m*; (region) marais *m*

marshal /ˈmɑːʃl/ **A** *n* **1** (Mil) maréchal *m*
2 (at rally, ceremony) membre *m* du service d'ordre
3 (AmE) (in fire service) capitaine *m* des pompiers
B *vt* (*p prés* **-ll-** (BrE), **-l-** (AmE)) rassembler

martial /ˈmɑːʃl/ *adj* ‹*art, law*› martial/-e; ‹*spirit*› guerrier/-ière

martyr /ˈmɑːtə(r)/ **A** *n* martyr/-e *m/f*
B *vt* martyriser

martyrdom /ˈmɑːtədəm/ *n* martyre *m*

marvel /ˈmɑːvl/ **A** *n* merveille *f*
B *vi* s'étonner (**at** de), être émerveillé/-e (**at** par)

marvellous (BrE), **marvelous** (AmE) /ˈmɑːvələs/ *adj* merveilleux/-euse; **that's ~!** c'est formidable!

marzipan /ˈmɑːzɪpæn, ˌmɑːzɪˈpæn/ *n* pâte *f* d'amandes

mascot /ˈmæskət, -skɒt/ *n* mascotte *f*; **lucky ~** porte-bonheur *m inv*

masculine /ˈmæskjʊlɪn/ *adj* masculin/-e

masculinity /ˌmæskjʊˈlɪnətɪ/ *n* masculinité *f*

mash /mæʃ/ **A** *n* (for animals) pâtée *f*
B *vt* (*also* **~ up**) écraser

mashed potatoes *npl* purée *f* de pommes de terre

mask /mɑːsk, (AmE) mæsk/ **A** *n* masque *m*; (for eyes only) loup *m*
B *vt* masquer

masking tape *n* ruban *m* adhésif

masochist /ˈmæsəkɪst/ *n, adj* masochiste *mf*

mason /ˈmeɪsn/ *n* **1** (in building) maçon *m*
2 (**Mason** *also* **Free~**) franc-maçon *m*

masonry /ˈmeɪsənrɪ/ *n* maçonnerie *f*

masquerade /ˌmɑːskəˈreɪd, (AmE) ˌmæsk-/
A *n* bal *m* masqué; (fig) mascarade *f*
B *vi* **to ~ as sb/sth** se faire passer pour qn/qch

⚷ **mass** /mæs/ **A** *n* **1** masse *f* (**of** de); (of people) foule *f* (**of** de); (of details) quantité *f* (**of** de)
2 (in church) messe *f*
B **masses** *npl* **1 the ~es** les masses *fpl*
2 (BrE) (fam) **~es of work** beaucoup *or* plein (fam) de travail; **~es of people** des tas (fam) de gens
C *adj* ‹*audience, movement, meeting, tourism*› de masse; ‹*exodus, protest, unemployment*› massif/-ive; **~ hysteria** hystérie *f* collective
D *vi* ‹*troops*› se regrouper; ‹*bees*› se masser; ‹*clouds*› s'amonceler

massacre /ˈmæsəkə(r)/ **A** *n* massacre *m*
B *vt* massacrer

massage /ˈmæsɑːʒ, (AmE) məˈsɑːʒ/ **A** *n* massage *m*
B *vt* masser

mass grave *n* charnier *m*

⚷ **massive** /ˈmæsɪv/ *adj* (gen) énorme; ‹*increase, cut*› massif/-ive

mass-marketing /ˌmæsˈmɑːkɪtɪŋ/ *n* commercialisation *f* massive

mass media *n* (mass) médias *mpl*

mass murderer *n* auteur *m* d'un massacre

mass production *n* fabrication *f* en série

mast /mɑːst, (AmE) mæst/ *n* (on ship, for flags) mât *m*; (for aerial) pylône *m*

⚷ **master** /ˈmɑːstə(r), (AmE) ˈmæs-/ **A** *n* **1** (gen) maître *m*
2 (Sch) (primary) maître *m*, instituteur *m*; (secondary) professeur *m*; (BrE) (Univ) (of college) principal *m*
3 (*also* **~ copy**) original *m*
B *adj* ‹*chef, craftsman*› maître *before n*; ‹*spy*› professionnel/-elle
C *vt* **1** maîtriser ‹*subject*›; posséder ‹*art, skill*›
2 dominer ‹*feelings*›; surmonter ‹*phobia*›

master key *n* passe-partout *m inv*

masterly /ˈmɑːstəlɪ, (AmE) ˈmæs-/ *adj* magistral/-e

mastermind /ˈmɑːstəmaɪnd/ **A** *n* cerveau *m* (**of, behind** de)
B *vt* organiser ‹*robbery, event*›

Master of Arts *n* diplôme *m* supérieur de lettres

⚷ mot clé

master of ceremonies *n* (in cabaret) animateur/-trice *m/f*; (at banquet) maître *m* des cérémonies

Master of Science *n* diplôme *m* supérieur en sciences

masterpiece *n* chef-d'œuvre *m*

master plan *n* plan *m* d'ensemble

master's *n* (*also* **master's degree**) ≈ maîtrise (**in** de)

mastery /'mɑːstərɪ, (AmE) 'mæs-/ *n* maîtrise *f* (**of** de)

mat /mæt/ **A** *n* **1** (on floor) (petit) tapis *m*; (for wiping feet) paillasson *m*
2 (on table) dessous-de-plat *m inv*; **place ~** set *m* de table
B *vi* (*p prés etc* **-tt-**) ‹*hair*› s'emmêler; ‹*wool*› se feutrer; ‹*fibres*› s'enchevêtrer

match /mætʃ/ **A** *n* **1** (Sport) match *m*
2 (matchstick) allumette *f*
3 to be a ~ for sb être un adversaire à la mesure de qn; **to be no ~ for sb** être trop faible pour qn
B *vt* **1** (gen) correspondre à; ‹*colour, bag*› être assorti/-e à; **to ~ (up) the names to the photos** trouver les noms qui correspondent aux photos
2 (equal) égaler ‹*record, achievements*›
C *vi* ‹*colours, clothes, curtains*› être assortis/-ies; ‹*components*› aller ensemble; **with gloves to ~** avec des gants assortis

matchbox *n* boîte *f* d'allumettes

match point *n* balle *f* de match

matchstick /'mætʃstɪk/ *n* allumette *f*

mate /meɪt/ **A** *n* **1** (BrE) (fam) (friend) copain *m* (fam); (at work, school) camarade *mf*
2 (Zool) (male) mâle *m*; (female) femelle *f*
3 (assistant) aide *mf*
4 (in navy) second *m*
B *vt* **1** accoupler ‹*animal*› (**with** à *or* avec)
2 (in chess) faire mat
C *vi* ‹*animal*› s'accoupler (**with** à, avec)

material /mə'tɪərɪəl/ **A** *n* **1** (substance) (gen) matière *f*, substance *f*; (Tech) matériau *m*; **waste ~** déchets *mpl*
2 (fabric) tissu *m*, étoffe *f*
3 (written matter) documentation *f*; **teaching ~** matériel *m* pédagogique; **reading ~** lecture *f*
4 (potential) étoffe *f*; **she is star ~** elle a l'étoffe d'une vedette
B materials *npl* (equipment) matériel *m*; **cleaning ~s** produits *mpl* d'entretien; **building ~s** matériaux de construction
C *adj* matériel/-ielle

materialistic /məˌtɪərɪə'lɪstɪk/ *adj* matérialiste

materialize /mə'tɪərɪəlaɪz/ *vi* **1** ‹*hope, offer, plan, threat*› se concrétiser; ‹*event, situation*› se réaliser; ‹*idea*› prendre forme
2 (appear) ‹*person, object*› surgir; ‹*spirit*› se matérialiser

maternal /mə'tɜːnl/ *adj* maternel/-elle (**towards** avec)

maternity /mə'tɜːnətɪ/ *n* maternité *f*

maternity leave *n* congé *m* de maternité

maternity unit *n* service *m* d'obstétrique

maternity ward *n* maternité *f*

math /mæθ/ *n* (AmE) (fam) math *fpl* (fam)

mathematical /ˌmæθə'mætɪkl/ *adj* mathématique

mathematician /ˌmæθmə'tɪʃn/ *n* mathématicien/-ienne *m/f*

mathematics /ˌmæθə'mætɪks/ *n* mathématiques *fpl*

maths /mæθs/ *n* (BrE) (fam) maths *fpl* (fam)

matinee /'mætɪneɪ, 'mætneɪ, (AmE) ˌmætn'eɪ/ *n* matinée *f*

mating season *n* saison *f* des amours

matriculate /mə'trɪkjʊleɪt/ *vi* ‹*student*› s'inscrire

matrimony /'mætrɪmənɪ, (AmE) -məʊnɪ/ *n* mariage *m*

matrix /'meɪtrɪks/ *n* (*pl* **-trices**) matrice *f*

matron /'meɪtrən/ *n* **1** (BrE) (in hospital) infirmière *f* en chef; (in school) infirmière *f*
2 (of nursing home) directrice *f*
3 (AmE) (warder) gardienne *f*

matt (BrE), **matte** (AmE) /mæt/ *adj* ‹*paint*› mat/-e; ‹*photograph*› sur papier mat

matter /'mætə(r)/ **A** *n* **1** (affair) affaire *f*; (requiring solution) problème *m*; (on agenda) point *m*; **it will be no easy ~** cela ne sera pas (une affaire) facile; **important ~s to discuss** des choses importantes à discuter; **private ~** affaire privée; **a ~ for the police** un problème qui relève de la police; **that's another ~** c'est une autre histoire; **the fact of the ~ is that** la vérité est que
2 (question) question *f*; **a ~ of** une question de ‹*opinion, principle, taste*›; **a ~ of life and death** une question de vie ou de mort
3 (trouble) **is anything the ~?** y a-t-il un problème?; **what's the ~?** qu'est-ce qu'il y a?; **what's the ~ with Louise?** qu'est-ce qu'elle a, Louise?; **there's something the ~ with my car** ma voiture a un problème
4 (substance) matière *f*; **vegetable ~** matière végétale
5 printed ~ imprimés *mpl*; **advertising ~** publicité *f*; **reading ~** lecture *f*; **subject ~** contenu *m*
6 (Med) (pus) pus *m*
B *vi* être important/-e; **it doesn't ~** ça ne fait rien; **it doesn't ~ whether he comes or not** peu importe qu'il vienne ou pas
IDIOMS **as a ~ of course** automatiquement; **as a ~ of fact** en fait; **for that ~** d'ailleurs; **no ~ how late it is** peu importe l'heure; **no ~ what (happens)** quoi qu'il arrive; **and to make ~s worse** et pour ne rien arranger

matter-of-fact *adj* ‹*voice, tone*› détaché/-e; ‹*person*› terre à terre

mattress /'mætrɪs/ *n* matelas *m*

mature /mə'tjʊə(r), (AmE) -'tʊər/ **A** *adj* **1** ‹*plant, animal*› adulte

2 ‹*person*› mûr/-e; ‹*attitude, reader*› adulte
3 ‹*hard cheese*› fort/-e; ‹*soft cheese*› affiné/-e; ‹*whisky*› vieux/vieille
B *vi* **1** (physically) ‹*person, animal*› devenir adulte
2 (psychologically) ‹*person*› mûrir
3 ‹*wine*› vieillir; ‹*cheese*› s'affiner
4 ‹*policy*› arriver à échéance

mature student *n* personne *f* qui reprend des études (*après un temps au foyer ou dans la vie active*)

maul /mɔːl/ *vt* ‹*animal*› lacérer

mauve /məʊv/ *n, adj* mauve *m*

maverick /ˈmævərɪk/ *n, adj* nonconformiste *mf*

maxim /ˈmæksɪm/ *n* maxime *f*

maximize /ˈmæksɪmaɪz/ *vt* maximiser ‹*profit, sales*›; (Comput) agrandir

maximum /ˈmæksɪməm/ **A** *n* (*pl* **-imums, -ima**) maximum *m*
B *adj* maximum *inv*

maximum security prison *n* prison *f* de haute surveillance

⚷ **may** *modal aux* **1** (expressing possibility) **it ~ rain** il pleuvra peut-être, il se peut qu'il pleuve; **she ~ not have seen him** elle ne l'a peut-être pas vu; **'are you going to accept?'—'I ~'** 'tu vas accepter'—'peut-être'; **he ~ not come** il risque de ne pas venir; **be that as it ~** quoi qu'il en soi; **come what ~** advienne que pourra
2 (expressing permission) **you ~ sit down** vous pouvez vous asseoir; **~ I come in?** puis-je entrer?
3 (wish) **~ he rest in peace** qu'il repose en paix

⚷ **May** /meɪ/ *n* mai *m*

⚷ **maybe** /ˈmeɪbiː/ *adv* peut-être; **~ they'll arrive early** peut-être qu'ils arriveront tôt

Mayday *n* (distress signal) mayday *m*

May Day /ˈmeɪ deɪ/ *n* premier mai *m*, fête *f* du travail

mayhem /ˈmeɪhem/ *n* (chaos) désordre *m*; (violence) grabuge *m* (fam)

mayor /meə(r), (AmE) ˈmeɪər/ *n* maire *m*

mayoress /ˈmeərɪs, (AmE) ˈmeɪə-/ *n* (wife of mayor) femme *f* du maire; (lady mayor) mairesse *f*

maze /meɪz/ *n* (puzzle, in gardens) labyrinthe *m*; (of streets, corridors) dédale *m*

MBA *n* (*abbr* = **Master of Business Administration**) ≈ maîtrise *f* de gestion

MC *n* (*abbr* = **Master of Ceremonies**) (in cabaret) animateur/-trice *m/f*; (at banquet) maître *m* des cérémonies

⚷ **me** *pron* **1** me, m'; **she knows ~** elle me connaît; **he loves ~** il m'aime
2 (in imperatives, after prepositions and to be) moi; **give it to ~!** donne-le-moi!; **it's for ~** c'est pour moi; **it's ~** c'est moi

⚷ mot clé

ME *n* (*abbr* = **myalgic encephalomyelitis**) encéphalomyélite *f* myalgique

meadow /ˈmedəʊ/ *n* **1** (field) pré *m*
2 (*also* **~land**) prés *mpl*, prairies *fpl*
3 (*also* **water ~**) prairie *f* inondable

meagre (BrE), **meager** (AmE) /ˈmiːgə(r)/ *adj* maigre *before n*

⚷ **meal** /miːl/ *n* **1** repas *m*; **to go out for a ~** aller (manger) au restaurant
2 (from grain) farine *f*

⚷ **mean** /miːn/ **A** *n* moyenne *f*
B *adj* **1** ‹*person*› avare, radin/-e (fam); **he's ~ with money** il est près de ses sous
2 (unkind, vicious) méchant/-e (**to** avec); **a ~ trick** un sale tour
3 (average) ‹*weight, age*› moyen/-enne
4 that's no ~ feat! ce n'est pas un mince exploit!
C *vt* (*prét, pp* **meant**) **1** ‹*word, phrase, symbol*› signifier, vouloir dire; ‹*sign*› vouloir dire; **the name ~s nothing to me** ce nom ne me dit rien
2 (intend) **to ~ to do** avoir l'intention de faire; **to be meant for sb** être destiné/-e à qn; **I didn't ~ to do it** je ne l'ai pas fait exprès; **she meant no offence** elle ne pensait pas à mal; **he doesn't ~ you any harm** il ne te veut aucun mal; **to ~ well** avoir de bonnes intentions; **he ~s what he says** (he is sincere) il est sérieux; (he is menacing) il ne plaisante pas; **without ~ing to** par inadvertance
3 (entail) ‹*strike, law*› entraîner ‹*shortages, changes*›
4 (intend to say) vouloir dire; **what do you ~ by that remark?** qu'est-ce que tu veux dire par là?; **I know what you ~** je comprends
5 money ~s a lot to him l'argent compte beaucoup pour lui; **your friendship ~s a lot to me** ton amitié est très importante pour moi
6 (be destined) **to be meant to do** être destiné/-e à faire; **it was meant to be** *or* **happen** cela devait arriver; **they were meant for each other** ils étaient faits l'un pour l'autre
7 (be supposed to be) **he's meant to be/to be doing** il est censé être/faire

meander /mɪˈændə(r)/ *vi* ‹*river, road*› serpenter

⚷ **meaning** /ˈmiːnɪŋ/ *n* (of word, remark, action, life) sens *m*; (of symbol, film, dream) signification *f*

meaningful /ˈmiːnɪŋfl/ *adj* **1** (significant) ‹*word, statement, result*› significatif/-ive
2 (profound) ‹*relationship, comment, lyrics*› sérieux/-ieuse; ‹*experience*› riche
3 (eloquent) ‹*look, smile*› entendu/-e; ‹*gesture*› significatif/-ive

meaningless /ˈmiːnɪŋlɪs/ *adj* **1** ‹*word, phrase*› dépourvu/-e de sens
2 (pointless) ‹*act, sacrifice*› futile, vain/-e; ‹*violence*› insensé/-e

means /miːnz/ **A** *n* (*pl* ~) moyen *m* (**of doing** de faire); **a ~ of** un moyen de ‹*communication, transport*›; **by ~ of** au moyen de; **yes, by all ~** oui, certainement; **it is by no ~ certain** c'est loin d'être sûr
B *npl* moyens *mpl*, revenus *mpl*; **to live within one's ~** vivre selon ses moyens

means test *n* enquête *f* sur les ressources

meantime /'miːntaɪm/ *adv* **(in the) ~** pendant ce temps; **for the ~** pour le moment

meanwhile /'miːnwaɪl/ *adv* **1** (during this time) pendant ce temps
2 (until then) en attendant
3 (since then) entre-temps

measles /'miːzlz/ *n* rougeole *f*

measure /'meʒə(r)/ **A** *n* **1** (gen) mesure *f*; **to take ~s** prendre des mesures; **weights and ~s** les poids et mesures *mpl*
2 (measuring device) instrument *m* de mesure
B *vt* **1** mesurer; **to ~ four by five metres** mesurer quatre mètres sur cinq
2 (compare) **to ~ sth against** comparer qch à
IDIOM **for good ~** pour faire bonne mesure
■ **measure out** mesurer ‹*land, flour, liquid*›; doser ‹*medicine*›
■ **measure up** ‹*person*› avoir les qualités requises; **to ~ up to** être à la hauteur de ‹*expectations*›; soutenir la comparaison avec ‹*achievement*›

measurement /'meʒəmənt/ *n* **1** (of room, object) dimension *f*
2 (of person) **to take sb's ~s** prendre les mensurations de qn; **chest ~** tour *m* de poitrine; **leg ~** longueur *f* de jambe

measuring jug *n* verre *m* gradué

measuring tape *n* mètre *m* ruban

meat /miːt/ *n* viande *f*; **crab ~** chair *f* de crabe

meat eater /'miːtiːtə(r)/ *n* (animal) carnivore *m*; (person) **they're not great ~s** ils ne mangent pas beaucoup de viande

meaty /'miːtɪ/ *adj* **1** ‹*flavour, smell*› de viande
2 ‹*article, book*› substantiel/-ielle
3 ‹*person, hand*› épais/-aisse

Mecca /'mekə/ *pr n* La Mecque

mechanic /mɪ'kænɪk/ *n* mécanicien/-ienne *m/f*

mechanical /mɪ'kænɪkl/ *adj* mécanique

mechanical engineering *n* construction *f* mécanique

mechanics /mɪ'kænɪks/ *npl* **1** (field) mécanique *f*
2 (workings) mécanisme *m*

mechanism /'mekənɪzəm/ *n* mécanisme *m* (**of** de)

mechanization /ˌmekənaɪ'zeɪʃn, (AmE) -nɪ'z-/ *n* mécanisation *f*

medal /'medl/ *n* médaille *f*; **gold ~** médaille d'or

medallion /mɪ'dælɪən/ *n* médaillon *m*

medallist (BrE), **medalist** (AmE) /'medəlɪst/ *n* médaillé/-e *m/f*; **gold ~** médaillé/-e d'or

meddle /'medl/ *vi* **to ~ in** se mêler de ‹*affairs*›; **to ~ with** toucher à ‹*property*›

media /'miːdɪə/ **A** *n* médias *mpl*
B *adj* ‹*coverage, image, personality*› médiatique; ‹*power, reaction, report*› des médias

median *n* (*also* **median strip**) (AmE) terre-plein *m* central

media studies *npl* communication *f* et journalisme *m*

mediate /'miːdɪeɪt/ **A** *vt* négocier ‹*settlement, peace*›
B *vi* ‹*person*› arbitrer; **to ~ in/between** servir de médiateur dans/entre

mediator /'miːdɪeɪtə(r)/ *n* médiateur/-trice *m/f*

medical /'medɪkl/ **A** *n* (in school, army, for job) visite *f* médicale; (private) examen *m* médical
B *adj* médical/-e

medical insurance *n* assurance-maladie *f*

medical student *n* étudiant/-e *m/f* en médecine

medicated /'medɪkeɪtɪd/ *adj* (gen) médical/-e; ‹*shampoo*› traitant/-e

medication /ˌmedɪ'keɪʃn/ *n* médicaments *mpl*

medicinal /mɪ'dɪsɪnl/ *adj* ‹*property, use*› thérapeutique; ‹*herb*› médicinal/-e

medicine /'medsn, (AmE) 'medɪsn/ *n* **1** (field) médecine *f*
2 (drug) médicament *m* (**for** pour)

medicine cabinet, **medicine cupboard** *n* armoire *f* à pharmacie

medicine man *n* sorcier *m* guérisseur

medieval /ˌmedɪ'iːvl, (AmE) ˌmiːd- *also* mɪ'diːvl/ *adj* médiéval/-e

mediocre /ˌmiːdɪ'əʊkə(r)/ *adj* médiocre

mediocrity /ˌmiːdɪ'ɒkrətɪ/ *n* **1** (state) médiocrité *f*
2 (person) médiocre *mf*

meditate /'medɪteɪt/ *vt*, *vi* méditer

Mediterranean /ˌmedɪtə'reɪnɪən/ **A** *pr n* **1 the ~ (sea)** la (mer) Méditerranée
2 (region) **the ~** les pays méditerranéens
B *adj* méditerranéen/-éenne

medium /'miːdɪəm/ **A** *n* **1** (*pl* **-iums** *ou* **-ia**) (means) moyen *m*
2 to find *or* **strike a happy ~** trouver le juste milieu
3 (*pl* **-iums**) (spiritualist) médium *m*
B *adj* moyen/-enne

medium-dry *adj* ‹*drink*› demi-sec

medium-rare *adj* ‹*meat*› à point

medium-sized *adj* de taille moyenne

medley /'medlɪ/ *n* **1** (Mus) pot-pourri *m* (**of** de)
2 (mixture) mélange *m*

meek /miːk/ *adj* docile

meet /miːt/ **A** *n* **1** (Sport) rencontre *f* (sportive); **track ~** (AmE) rencontre d'athlétisme
2 (BrE) (in hunting) rendez-vous *m* de chasseurs
B *vt* (*prét, pp* **met**) **1** rencontrer ‹*person, team, enemy*›
2 (make acquaintance of) faire la connaissance de ‹*person*›; **have you met each other?** vous vous connaissez?
3 (await) attendre; **she went to ~ them** elle est allée les attendre *or* chercher; **to ~ sb off** (BrE) *or* **at** (AmE) **the plane** attendre qn à l'aéroport
4 répondre à, satisfaire à ‹*criteria, standards, needs*›; payer ‹*bills, costs*›; couvrir ‹*debts*›; faire face à ‹*obligations, commitments*›; remplir ‹*conditions*›
5 se montrer à la hauteur de ‹*challenge*›
C *vi* (*prét, pp* **met**) **1** ‹*people, teams*› se rencontrer; ‹*committee, parliament*› se réunir; **to ~ again** ‹*people*› se revoir
2 (by appointment) ‹*people*› se retrouver
3 (make acquaintance) ‹*people*› se connaître
4 ‹*lips, roads*› se rencontrer; **their eyes met** leurs regards se croisèrent
IDIOM **to make ends ~** joindre les deux bouts
■ **meet up** (fam) se retrouver; **to ~ up with** (fam) retrouver ‹*friend*›
■ **meet with**: **A** **~ with [sb]** rencontrer ‹*person, delegation*›
B **~ with [sth]** rencontrer ‹*opposition, success, suspicion*›; être accueilli/-e avec ‹*approval*›; subir ‹*failure*›

meeting /ˈmiːtɪŋ/ *n* **1** (official) réunion *f*; **in a ~** en réunion
2 (informal) rencontre *f*
3 (BrE) (Sport) **athletics ~** rencontre *f* d'athlétisme; **race ~** réunion *f* de courses

meeting place *n* (lieu *m* de) rendez-vous *m*

meeting point *n* point *m* de rencontre

megabyte, MB /ˈmegəbaɪt/ *n* mégaoctet *m*, Mo *m*

megalomaniac /ˌmegələˈmeɪnɪæk/ *n, adj* mégalomane *mf*

megaphone /ˈmegəfəʊn/ *n* porte-voix *m inv*

megapixel /ˈmegəpɪksl/ *n* mégapixel *m*

megastore /ˈmegəstɔː(r)/ *n* mégastore *m*

melancholy /ˈmelənkəlɪ/ **A** *n* mélancolie *f*
B *adj* ‹*person*› mélancolique; ‹*music, occasion*› triste

mellow /ˈmeləʊ/ **A** *adj* **1** ‹*wine*› moelleux/-euse; ‹*flavour*› suave; ‹*tone*› mélodieux/-ieuse
2 ‹*person*› détendu/-e; ‹*atmosphere*› serein/-e
B *vt* ‹*experience*› assagir ‹*person*›
C *vi* ‹*person, behaviour*› s'assagir

mot clé

melodrama /ˈmelədrɑːmə/ *n* mélodrame *m*

melodramatic /ˌmelədrəˈmætɪk/ *adj* mélodramatique

melody /ˈmelədɪ/ *n* mélodie *f*

melon /ˈmelən/ *n* melon *m*

melt /melt/ **A** *vt* **1** faire fondre ‹*snow, plastic, butter*›
2 attendrir ‹*heart*›
B *vi* **1** fondre; **to ~ in your mouth** fondre dans la bouche
2 to ~ into se fondre dans ‹*crowd*›

meltdown /ˈmeltdaʊn/ *n* fusion *f* du cœur d'un réacteur

melting point *n* point *m* de fusion

member /ˈmembə(r)/ *n* **1** membre *m*; **to be a ~ of** faire partie de ‹*group*›; être membre de ‹*club, committee*›; **~ of staff** (gen) employé/-e *m/f*; (Sch, Univ) enseignant/-e *m/f*; **~ of the public** (in street) passant/-e *m/f*; (in theatre, cinema) spectateur/-trice *m/f* **~ state** état *m* membre
2 (*also* **Member**) (of parliament) député *m*
3 (limb) membre *m*

Member of Congress, MC *n* (AmE) membre *m* du Congrès

Member of Parliament, MP *n* (BrE) député *m* (**for** de)

Member of the European Parliament, MEP *n* (BrE) député *m* au Parlement européen

membership /ˈmembəʃɪp/ *n* **1** (of club, organization) adhésion *f* (**of** à)
2 (fee) cotisation *f*
3 (members) membres *mpl*

membrane /ˈmembreɪn/ *n* membrane *f*

memento /mɪˈmentəʊ/ *n* (*pl* **~s** *ou* **~es**) souvenir *m* (**of** de)

memo /ˈmeməʊ/ *n* note *f* de service

memoirs /ˈmemwɑː(r)z/ *npl* mémoires *mpl*

memo pad *n* bloc-notes *m*

memorable /ˈmemərəbl/ *adj* ‹*event*› mémorable; ‹*person, quality*› inoubliable

memorial /məˈmɔːrɪəl/ **A** *n* mémorial *m* (**to** à)
B *adj* commémoratif/-ive

memorize /ˈmeməraɪz/ *vt* apprendre [qch] par cœur

memory /ˈmemərɪ/ *n* **1** mémoire *f*; **from ~** de mémoire; **to have a good ~ for faces** être physionomiste; **in (loving) ~ of** à la mémoire de
2 (recollection) souvenir *m*; **childhood memories** souvenirs d'enfance

memory stick *n* memory stick *m*

menace /ˈmenəs/ **A** *n* menace *f*
B *vt* menacer (**with** de, avec)

menacing /ˈmenəsɪŋ/ *adj* menaçant/-e

mend /mend/ **A** *n* **to be on the ~** ‹*person*› être en voie de guérison; ‹*economy*› reprendre
B *vt* réparer ‹*object, road*›; (stitch) raccommoder; (darn) repriser; **that won't ~**

matters ça n'arrangera pas les choses
C *vi* ‹*injury*› guérir; ‹*person*› se rétablir
IDIOM **to ~ one's ways** s'amender

menial /ˈmiːnɪəl/ *adj* ‹*job*› subalterne; ‹*attitude*› servile; **~ tasks** basses besognes

meningitis /ˌmenɪnˈdʒaɪtɪs/ *n* méningite *f*

menopause /ˈmenəpɔːz/ *n* ménopause *f*

men's room *n* (AmE) toilettes *fpl* pour hommes

menstruation /ˌmenstrʊˈeɪʃn/ *n* menstruation *f*

menswear /ˈmenzweə(r)/ *n* prêt-à-porter *m* pour hommes

mental /ˈmentl/ *adj* (gen) mental/-e; ‹*ability, effort, energy*› intellectuel/-elle; ‹*hospital, institution*› psychiatrique

mental block *n* blocage *m* psychologique

mentality /menˈtælətɪ/ *n* mentalité *f*

mentally /ˈmentəlɪ/ *adv* **1 ~ handicapped** handicapé/-e mental; **the ~ ill** les malades mentaux
2 ~ exhausted surmené/-e intellectuellement

mentholated /ˈmenθəleɪtɪd/ *adj* au menthol

mention /ˈmenʃn/ **A** *n* mention *f* (**of** de); **it got a ~ on the radio** on en a parlé à la radio
B *vt* **1** faire mention de ‹*person, fact*›; **please don't ~ my name** ne mentionnez pas mon nom; **to ~ sb/sth to sb** parler de qn/qch à qn; **not to ~** sans parler de; **without ~ing any names** sans nommer personne; **don't ~ it!** je vous en prie!, je t'en prie!
2 (acknowledge) citer ‹*name*›

menu /ˈmenjuː/ *n* menu *m*

menu bar *n* barre *f* de menu

MEP *n* (BrE) (*abbr* = **Member of the European Parliament**) député *m* au Parlement européen

mercenary /ˈmɜːsɪnərɪ, (AmE) -nerɪ/ **A** *n* mercenaire *mf*
B *adj* ‹*person*› intéressé/-e

merchandise /ˈmɜːtʃəndaɪz/ *n* marchandises *fpl*

merchant /ˈmɜːtʃənt/ *n* (selling in bulk) négociant *m*; (selling small quantities) marchand *m*

merchant bank *n* (BrE) banque *f* d'affaires

merchant banker *n* cadre *m* d'une banque d'affaires

merchant navy (BrE), **merchant marine** (AmE) *n* marine *f* marchande

merciful /ˈmɜːsɪfl/ *adj* **1** ‹*person*› clément/-e (**to, towards** envers); ‹*act*› charitable
2 ‹*occurrence*› heureux/-euse; **a ~ release** une délivrance

merciless /ˈmɜːsɪlɪs/ *adj* ‹*ruler, criticism*› impitoyable (**to, towards** envers); ‹*heat*› implacable

mercury /ˈmɜːkjʊrɪ/ **A** *n* mercure *m*
B **Mercury** *pr n* Mercure *f*

mercy /ˈmɜːsɪ/ *n* clémence *f*; **to have ~ on sb** avoir pitié de qn; **to beg for ~** demander grâce; **at the ~ of** à la merci de

mercy killing *n* **1** euthanasie *f*
2 (act) acte *m* d'euthanasie

mere /mɪə(r)/ *adj* **1** ‹*coincidence, nonsense*› pur/-e *before n*; ‹*formality*› simple *before n*; **he's a ~ child** ce n'est qu'un enfant; **the beach is a ~ 2 km from here** la plage n'est qu'à 2 km d'ici
2 (very) ‹*idea*› simple *before n*; **the ~ sight of her makes me nervous** rien que de la voir, ça rend nerveux

merely /ˈmɪəlɪ/ *adv* simplement, seulement

merge /mɜːdʒ/ **A** *vt* **1 to ~ sth with** fusionner qch avec ‹*company, group*›
2 mélanger ‹*colours, designs*›
B *vi* **1** (*also* **~ together**) ‹*companies, departments*› fusionner (**with** avec); ‹*roads, rivers*› se rejoindre
2 ‹*colours, sounds*› se confondre

merger /ˈmɜːdʒə(r)/ *n* fusion *f*

meringue /məˈræŋ/ *n* meringue *f*

merit /ˈmerɪt/ **A** *n* mérite *m*
B *vt* mériter

mermaid /ˈmɜːmeɪd/ *n* sirène *f*

merrily /ˈmerɪlɪ/ *adv* **1** (happily) joyeusement
2 (unconcernedly) avec insouciance

merry /ˈmerɪ/ *adj* **1** (happy) joyeux/-euse, gai/-e; **Merry Christmas!** joyeux Noël!
2 (fam) (tipsy) éméché/-e

merry-go-round /ˈmerɪgəʊraʊnd/ *n* manège *m*

mesh /meʃ/ **A** *n* **1** (netting) (of string) filet *m*; (of metal) grillage *m*
2 (net) mailles *fpl*
B *vi* (Tech) ‹*cogs*› s'engrener; **to ~ with** s'emboîter dans

mesmerize /ˈmezməraɪz/ **A** *vt* hypnotiser
B **mesmerized** *pp adj* fasciné/-e, médusé/-e

mess /mes/ **A** *n* **1** désordre *m*; **what a ~!** quel désordre!, quelle pagaille! (fam); **to make a ~** ‹*person*› mettre du désordre; **this report is a ~!** ce rapport est fait n'importe comment!; **to make a ~ on the carpet** salir la moquette; **to make a ~ of the job** massacrer (fam) le travail
2 (Mil) cantine *f*
B *vi* (fam) **1 to ~ with** toucher à ‹*drugs*›
2 don't ~ with him évite-le; **don't ~ with me** ne me cherche pas

■ **mess about** (fam), **mess around** (fam):
A **~ around** faire l'imbécile
B **~ [sb] around** traiter [qn] par-dessus la jambe (fam), prendre [qn] pour un imbécile

■ **mess up** (fam): **A** **~ up** (AmE) faire l'imbécile
B **~ [sth] up 1** semer la pagaille dans ‹*papers*›; mettre du désordre dans ‹*kitchen*›
2 (ruin) louper (fam) ‹*exam*›; gâcher ‹*chances, life*›

C ~ **[sb] up** ‹*drugs, alcohol*› détruire; ‹*experience*› faire perdre les pédales à (fam)

⚷ **message** /'mesɪdʒ/ *n* message *m* (**about** au sujet de)

message window *n* (Comput) feuille *f* de message

messaging /'mesɪdʒɪŋ/ *n* messagerie *f* électronique

messenger /'mesɪndʒə(r)/ *n* messager/-ère *m/f*; (for hotel, company) garçon *m* de courses, coursier/-ière *m/f*

messy /'mesɪ/ *adj* **1** ‹*house*› en désordre; ‹*appearance*› négligé/-e; ‹*handwriting*› peu soigné/-e
2 ‹*work, job*› salissant/-e; **he's a ~ eater** il mange comme un cochon
3 ‹*lawsuit*› compliqué/-e; **a ~ business** une sale affaire

⚷ **metal** /'metl/ **A** *n* métal *m*
B *adj* en métal

metallic /mɪ'tælɪk/ *adj* ‹*substance*› métallique; ‹*paint, finish*› métallisé/-e; ‹*taste*› de métal

metaphor /'metəfɔ:(r)/ *n* métaphore *f*

mete /mi:t/ *v*
▪ **mete out** infliger ‹*punishment*›; rendre ‹*justice*›

meteor /'mi:tɪə(r)/ *n* météore *m*

meteorite /'mi:tɪəraɪt/ *n* météorite *f*

meter /'mi:tə(r)/ **A** *n* **1** compteur *m*; **gas ~** compteur de gaz
2 (*also* **parking ~**) parcmètre *m*
3 (AmE) = **metre**
B *vt* mesurer la consommation de ‹*electricity, gas*›

⚷ **method** /'meθəd/ *n* **1** (of teaching, contraception, training) méthode *f* (**for doing** pour faire); (of payment, treatment, production) mode *m* (**of** de)
2 (orderliness) méthode *f*

methodical /mɪ'θɒdɪkl/ *adj* méthodique

Methodist /'meθədɪst/ *n, adj* méthodiste *mf*

methylated spirit *n* (*also* **methylated spirits**) alcool *m* à brûler

meticulous /mɪ'tɪkjʊləs/ *adj* méticuleux/-euse

⚷ **metre** (BrE), **meter** (AmE) /'mi:tə(r)/ *n* mètre *m*

metric /'metrɪk/ *adj* métrique

metropolitan /,metrə'pɒlɪtən/ *adj* **1** ‹*area, population*› urbain/-e; **~ New York** l'agglomération *f* de New York
2 ~ France la France métropolitaine

mettle /'metl/ *n* courage *m*; **to be on one's ~** être sur la sellette; **to put sb on his ~** amener qn à montrer de quoi il est capable

Mexico /'meksɪkəʊ/ *pr n* Mexique *m*

miaow /mi:'aʊ/ **A** *n* miaou *m*
B *vi* miauler

microbe /'maɪkrəʊb/ *n* microbe *m*

microchip /'maɪkrəʊtʃɪp/ *n* puce *f*, circuit *m* intégré

microcosm /'maɪkrəkɒzəm/ *n* microcosme *m*

microfilm /'maɪkrəʊfɪlm/ *n* microfilm *m*

microfinance /'maɪkrəʊfaɪnæns/ *n* microfinance *f*

microlighting /'maɪkrəlaɪtɪŋ/ *n* ULM *m*, ultra léger *m* motorisé

micromanage /'maɪkrəʊmænɪdʒ/ *vt* microgérer

microphone /'maɪkrəfəʊn/ *n* microphone *m*

microscope /'maɪkrəskəʊp/ *n* microscope *m*

microwave /'maɪkrəweɪv/ **A** *n* **~ (oven)** four *m* à micro-ondes
B *vt* passer [qch] au four à micro-ondes

mid- *pref* **in the ~20th century** au milieu du vingtième siècle; **~afternoon** milieu *m* de l'après-midi; **(in) ~May** (à la) mi-mai; **he's in his ~forties** il a environ quarante-cinq ans

mid-air /,mɪd'eə(r)/ **A** *adj* ‹*collision*› en plein vol
B in midair *phr* (in mid-flight) en plein vol; (in the air) en l'air

midday /,mɪd'deɪ/ *n* midi *m*

⚷ **middle** /'mɪdl/ **A** *n* **1** milieu *m*; **in the ~ of** au milieu de; **in the ~ of May** à la mi-mai; **to be in the ~ of doing** être en train de faire; **to split sth down the ~** partager qch en deux ‹*bill, work*›; diviser [qch] en deux ‹*group, opinion*›; **in the ~ of nowhere** en pleine brousse (fam)
2 (waist) taille *f*
B *adj* ‹*door, shelf*› du milieu; ‹*size, difficulty*› moyen/-enne; **there must be a ~ way** il doit y avoir une solution intermédiaire

middle-aged *adj* ‹*person*› d'âge mûr; ‹*outlook, view*› vieux jeu *inv*

Middle Ages *npl* **the ~** le Moyen Âge

middle class A *n* classe *f* moyenne
B middle-class *adj* ‹*person*› de la classe moyenne; ‹*attitude, view*› bourgeois/-e

Middle East *pr n* Moyen-Orient *m*

Middle Eastern *adj* du Moyen-Orient

middleman *n* intermédiaire *m*

middle-sized *adj* de taille moyenne

middleweight /'mɪdlweɪt/ *n* poids *m* moyen

middling /'mɪdlɪŋ/ *adj* moyen/-enne; **fair to ~** pas trop mal

midfield /,mɪd'fi:ld/ *n* milieu *m* du terrain

midge /mɪdʒ/ *n* moucheron *m*

midget /'mɪdʒɪt/ *n* nain/-e *m/f*

midnight /'mɪdnaɪt/ *n* minuit *m*

midriff /'mɪdrɪf/ *n* ventre *m*

midst /mɪdst/ *n* **in the ~ of** au beau milieu de; **in the ~ of change/war** en plein changement/pleine guerre; **in our ~** parmi nous

midsummer /,mɪd'sʌmə(r)/ *n* milieu *m* de l'été

⚷ mot clé

Midsummer Day *n* (*also* **Midsummer's Day**) la Saint-Jean
midtown /ˈmɪdtaʊn/ *n* (AmE) centre-ville *m*
midway /ˌmɪdˈweɪ/ **A** *n* (AmE) attractions *fpl* foraines
B *adj* ‹*post, position*› de mi-course; ‹*stage, point*› de mi-parcours
C *adv* ~ **between/along** à mi-chemin entre/le long de; ~ **through** au milieu de
midweek /ˌmɪdˈwiːk/ **A** *adj* de milieu de semaine
B *adv* en milieu de semaine
midwife /ˈmɪdwaɪf/ *n* (*pl* **-wives**) sage-femme *f*; **male** ~ homme *m* sage-femme
midwinter /ˌmɪdˈwɪntə(r)/ *n* milieu *m* de l'hiver
might¹ /maɪt/ *modal aux* (*prét de* **may**, *nég* **might not, mightn't**) **1** (expressing possibility) peut-être; **'will you come?'—'I ~'** 'tu viendras?'—'peut-être'; **she ~ not have heard the news** elle n'a peut-être pas entendu la nouvelle; **I ~ lose my job** je risque de perdre mon travail
2 (expressing annoyance) **you ~ have been killed!** tu aurais pu te faire tuer!; **I ~ have known!** j'aurais dû m'en douter!
3 I thought it ~ rain j'ai pensé qu'il risquait de pleuvoir; **I thought you ~ say that** je m'attendais à ce que tu dises ça; **he said you ~ be hurt** il a dit que tu serais peut-être blessé
4 ~ I make a suggestion? puis-je me permettre de faire une suggestion?; **it ~ be better to wait** ce serait peut-être mieux d'attendre
might² /maɪt/ *n* **1** (power) puissance *f*
2 (physical strength) force *f*; **with all his ~** de toutes ses forces
mighty /ˈmaɪtɪ/ *adj* puissant/-e
migrant /ˈmaɪgrənt/ **A** *n* (person) migrant/-e *m/f*; (bird) oiseau *m* migrateur; (animal) animal *m* migrateur
B *adj* ‹*labour*› saisonnier/-ière; ‹*bird, animal*› migrateur/-trice
migrate /maɪˈgreɪt, (AmE) ˈmaɪgreɪt/ *vi*
1 ‹*person*› émigrer
2 ‹*bird, animal*› migrer
mike /maɪk/ *n* (fam) micro *m* (fam)
mild /maɪld/ *adj* **1** ‹*surprise*› léger/-ère; ‹*interest, irritation*› modéré/-e
2 ‹*weather, winter*› doux/douce; ‹*climate*› tempéré/-e
3 ‹*beer, taste, tobacco*› léger/-ère; ‹*cheese*› doux/douce; ‹*curry*› peu épicé/-e
4 ‹*soap, detergent*› doux/douce
5 ‹*infection*› bénin/-igne; ‹*attack, sedative*› léger/-ère
6 ‹*person, voice*› doux/douce
mildew /ˈmɪldjuː, (AmE) -duː/ *n* moisissure *f*
mile /maɪl/ *n* **1** mile *m* (= *1,609 m*); **it's 50 ~s away** ≈ c'est à 80 kilomètres d'ici
2 to walk for ~s marcher pendant des kilomètres; **it's ~s away!** c'est au bout du monde; **to be ~s away** (daydreaming) être complètement ailleurs; **~s from anywhere** loin de tout; **to stand out a ~** sauter aux yeux
mileage /ˈmaɪlɪdʒ/ *n* **1** nombre *m* de miles
2 (done by car) kilométrage *m*
3 (miles per gallon) consommation *f*
milestone /ˈmaɪlstəʊn/ *n* borne *f* (milliaire); (fig) étape *f* importante
militant /ˈmɪlɪtənt/ **A** *n* (activist) agitateur/-trice *m/f*
B *adj* militant/-e
militarize /ˈmɪlɪtəraɪz/ *vt* militariser; **~d zone** zone *f* militarisée
military /ˈmɪlɪtrɪ, (AmE) -terɪ/ **A** *n* **the ~** (army) l'armée *f*; (soldiers) les militaires *mpl*
B *adj* militaire
military service *n* service *m* militaire
militia /mɪˈlɪʃə/ *n* milice *f*
milk /mɪlk/ **A** *n* lait *m*; **powdered ~** lait en poudre; **full-cream ~** (BrE) lait entier; **skimmed ~** (BrE) lait écrémé
B *vt* **1** traire ‹*cow*›
2 (exploit) exploiter ‹*situation, system*›; **to ~ sb dry** saigner qn à blanc
milk chocolate *n* chocolat *m* au lait
milkman /ˈmɪlkmən/ *n* laitier *m*
milkshake *n* milkshake *m*
milky /ˈmɪlkɪ/ *adj* **1** ‹*drink*› au lait
2 ‹*skin, liquid, colour*› laiteux/-euse
Milky Way *pr n* Voie *f* lactée
mill /mɪl/ **A** *n* **1** moulin *m*; **water/pepper ~** moulin à eau/à poivre
2 (factory) fabrique *f*; **steel ~** aciérie *f*
B *vt* moudre ‹*flour, pepper*›
millennium /mɪˈlenɪəm/ *n* (*pl* **-niums** *ou* **-nia**) millénaire *m*
millennium bug *n* bogue *m* de l'an 2000
milligram /ˈmɪlɪgræm/ *n* (*also* **milligramme**) milligramme *m*
millimetre (BrE), **millimeter** (AmE) /ˈmɪlɪmiːtə(r)/ *n* millimètre *m*
million /ˈmɪljən/ **A** *n* million *m*; **~s of** des millions de
B *adj* **a ~ people/pounds** un million de personnes/de livres
millionaire /ˌmɪljəˈneə(r)/ *n* millionnaire *mf*
milometer /maɪˈlɒmɪtə(r)/ *n* (BrE) ≈ compteur *m* kilométrique
mime /maɪm/ **A** *n* mime *m*; **~ show** pantomime *f*
B *vt, vi* mimer
mime artist *n* mime *mf*
mimic /ˈmɪmɪk/ **A** *n* imitateur/-trice *m/f*
B *vt* (*p prés etc* **-ck-**) imiter
mince /mɪns/ **A** *n* (BrE) viande *f* hachée; **beef ~** bœuf *m* haché
B *vt* hacher ‹*meat*›
mind /maɪnd/ **A** *n* **1** esprit *m*; **peace of ~** tranquillité *f* d'esprit; **it's all in the ~** c'est

tout dans la tête (fam); **to cross sb's ~** venir à l'esprit de qn; **to have something on one's ~** être préoccupé/-e; **to set sb's ~ at rest** rassurer qn; **nothing could be further from my ~** loin de moi cette pensée; **to take sb's ~ off sth** distraire qn de qch; **my ~'s a blank** j'ai un trou de mémoire; **I can't get him out of my ~** je n'arrive pas à l'oublier; **are you out of your ~?** (fam) tu es fou/folle? (fam)
2 (brain) intelligence *f*; **with the ~ of a two year-old** avec l'intelligence d'un enfant de deux ans
3 (opinion) avis *m*; **to my ~** à mon avis; **to make up one's ~ about/to do** se décider à propos de/à faire; **to change one's ~ about sth** changer d'avis sur qch; **to keep an open ~ about sth** réserver son jugement sur qch; **to know one's own ~** avoir des idées bien à soi; **to speak one's ~** dire ce qu'on a à dire
B *vt* **1** surveiller ‹*manners, language*›; faire attention à ‹*hazard*›
2 I don't ~ ça m'est égal, ça ne me dérange pas; **I don't ~ the cold** le froid ne me dérange pas; **I don't ~ cats, but I prefer dogs** je n'ai rien contre les chats, mais je préfère les chiens; **will they ~ us being late?** est-ce qu'ils seront fâchés si nous sommes en retard?; **would you ~ keeping my seat for me?** est-ce que ça vous ennuierait de garder ma place?; **I wouldn't ~ a glass of wine** je prendrais volontiers un verre de vin; **if you don't ~** si cela ne vous fait rien; **never ~** (don't worry) ne t'en fais pas; (it doesn't matter) peu importe; **he can't afford an apartment, never ~ a big house** il ne peut pas se permettre un appartement encore moins une grande maison
3 s'occuper de ‹*animal, children*›; tenir ‹*shop*›
C in mind *phr* **I have something in ~ for this evening** j'ai une idée pour ce soir; **to bear sth in ~** (remember) ne pas oublier qch; (take into account) prendre qch en compte
IDIOMS **to read sb's ~** lire dans les pensées de qn; **to see sth in one's ~'s eye** imaginer qch; **to have a ~ of one's own** savoir ce qu'on veut

mind-blowing *adj* (fam) époustouflant/-e (fam)

mind-boggling *adj* (fam) stupéfiant/-e

mindless /ˈmaɪndlɪs/ *adj* ‹*person, programme*› bête; ‹*work*› abrutissant/-e; ‹*vandalism*› gratuit/-e; ‹*task*› machinal/-e

mine[1] /maɪn/ *pron*

> In French, possessive pronouns reflect the gender and number of the noun they are standing for. So *mine* is translated by *le mien, la mienne, les miens, les miennes,* according to what is being referred to.

his car is red but ~ is blue sa voiture est rouge mais la mienne est bleue; **which (glass) is ~?** lequel (de ces verres) est le mien *or* est à moi?; **his children are older than ~** ses enfants sont plus âgés que les miens; **the blue car is ~** la voiture bleue est à moi; **she's a friend of ~** c'est une amie à moi; **it's not ~** ce n'est pas à moi

mine[2] /maɪn/ **A** *n* mine *f*
B *vt* **1** extraire ‹*gems, mineral*›; exploiter ‹*area*›
2 (Mil) miner ‹*area*›

minefield /ˈmaɪnfiːld/ *n* champ *m* de mines; (fig) terrain *m* miné

miner /ˈmaɪnə(r)/ *n* mineur *m*

mineral /ˈmɪnərəl/ **A** *n* (substance, class) minéral *m*; (for extraction) minerai *m*
B *adj* minéral/-e; **~ ore** minerai *m*

mineral water *n* eau *f* minérale

mingle /ˈmɪŋgl/ *vi* **1 to ~ with** se mêler à ‹*crowd, guests*›
2 ‹*sounds*› se confondre (**with** à); ‹*smells, feelings*› se mêler (**with** à)

miniature /ˈmɪnətʃə(r), (AmE) ˈmɪnɪətʃʊər/ **A** *n* miniature *f*
B *adj* (gen) miniature; ‹*dog, horse*› nain/-e

minicab /ˈmɪnɪkæb/ *n* (BrE) taxi *m* (non agréé)

minidisc /ˈmɪnɪdɪsk/ *n* minidisque *m*

minimalist /ˈmɪnɪməlɪst/ *adj* minimaliste

minimum /ˈmɪnɪməm/ **A** *n* minimum *m* (**of** de)
B *adj* minimum, minimal/-e

mining /ˈmaɪnɪŋ/ **A** *n* exploitation *f* minière
B *adj* ‹*industry, town*› minier/-ière; ‹*accident*› de mine

mini-skirt /ˈmɪnɪskɜːt/ *n* mini-jupe *f*

minister /ˈmɪnɪstə(r)/ **A** *n* **1** (Pol) ministre *m*; **~ of** *or* **for Defence, Defence ~** (BrE) ministre de la Défense
2 (clergyman) ministre *m* du culte
B *vi* **to ~ to** donner des soins à ‹*person*›; **to ~ to sb's needs** pourvoir aux besoins de qn

minister of state *n* (BrE) ministre *m* délégué

ministry /ˈmɪnɪstrɪ/ *n* ministère *m*

mink /mɪŋk/ *n* vison *m*

minor /ˈmaɪnə(r)/ **A** *n* (Law) mineur/-e *m/f*
B *adj* (gen), (Mus) mineur/-e; ‹*injury, burn*› léger/-ère; **~ road** route *f* secondaire

minority /maɪˈnɒrətɪ, (AmE) -ˈnɔːr-/ *n* minorité *f*; **to be in the ~** être en minorité

minstrel /ˈmɪnstrəl/ *n* ménestrel *m*

mint /mɪnt/ **A** *n* **1** (herb) menthe *f*
2 (sweet) bonbon *m* à la menthe
3 (for coins) hôtel *m* des Monnaies
B *adj* **in ~ condition** à l'état neuf
C *vt* **1** frapper ‹*coin*›
2 forger ‹*word, expression*›

minuet /ˌmɪnjʊˈet/ *n* menuet *m*

minus /ˈmaɪnəs/ **A** *n* **1** (in mathematics) moins *m*
2 (drawback) inconvénient *m*

mot clé

B *adj* ‹*symbol, button*› moins; ‹*number, quantity, value*› négatif/-ive; ~ **sign** signe *m* moins
C *prep* **1** moins; **what is 20 ~ 8?** combien font 20 moins 8?; **it is ~ 15 (degrees)** il fait moins 15 (degrés)
2 (without) sans

minuscule /'mɪnəskjuːl/ *adj* minuscule

minute¹ /'mɪnɪt/ **A** *n* minute *f*; **five ~s past ten** dix heures cinq; **it's five ~s' walk away** c'est à cinq minutes à pied; **the ~ I heard the news** dès que j'ai appris la nouvelle; **any ~ now** d'une minute à l'autre; **at the last ~** à la dernière minute
B **minutes** *npl* compte-rendu *m*

minute² /maɪ'njuːt, (AmE) -'nuːt/ *adj* ‹*particle*› minuscule; ‹*quantity*› infime; ‹*risk, variation*› minime

minute hand *n* aiguille *f* des minutes

miracle /'mɪrəkl/ *n* miracle *m*; **to work** *or* **perform ~s** faire des miracles

miraculous /mɪ'rækjʊləs/ *adj* **1** ‹*escape, recovery*› miraculeux/-euse
2 ‹*speed, strength*› prodigieux/-ieuse

mirror /'mɪrə(r)/ **A** *n* **1** (gen) miroir *m*, glace *f*; (Aut) rétroviseur *m*
2 (fig) reflet *m*
B *vt* refléter; **to be ~ed in** se refléter dans

mirth /mɜːθ/ *n* (laughter) hilarité *f*; (joy) joie *f*

misapprehension /ˌmɪsæprɪ'henʃn/ *n* malentendu *m*, erreur *f*; **to be (labouring) under a ~** se tromper

misappropriate /ˌmɪsə'prəʊprɪeɪt/ *vt* détourner ‹*funds*›

misbehave /ˌmɪsbɪ'heɪv/ *vi* ‹*child*› se tenir mal; ‹*adult*› se conduire mal

miscalculation /ˌmɪskælkjʊ'leɪʃn/ *n* erreur *f* de calcul; (fig) mauvais calcul *m*

miscarriage /'mɪskærɪdʒ, ˌmɪs'kærɪdʒ/ *n* **1** (Med) fausse couche *f*; **to have a ~** faire une fausse couche
2 (Law) **a ~ of justice** une grave erreur judiciaire

miscellaneous /ˌmɪsə'leɪnɪəs/ *adj* divers/-e

mischief /'mɪstʃɪf/ *n* espièglerie *f*; **to get into** *or* **make ~** faire des bêtises; **he's up to ~** il prépare quelque chose; **to be full of ~** être espiègle; **it keeps them out of ~** ça les occupe

mischievous /'mɪstʃɪvəs/ *adj* ‹*child, comedy, humour*› espiègle; ‹*smile, eyes*› malicieux/-ieuse

misconception /ˌmɪskən'sepʃn/ *n* idée *f* fausse

misdemeanour (BrE), **misdemeanor** (AmE) /ˌmɪsdɪ'miːnə(r)/ *n* délit *m*

miser /'maɪzə(r)/ *n* avare *mf*

miserable /'mɪzrəbl/ *adj* **1** ‹*person, event, expression*› malheureux/-euse; ‹*thoughts*› noir/-e; ‹*weather*› sale *before n*; **to feel ~** avoir le cafard
2 ‹*amount*› misérable; ‹*wage, life*› de misère; ‹*attempt, failure, performance*› lamentable

miserly /'maɪzəlɪ/ *adj* ‹*person*› avare; ‹*amount*› maigre

misery /'mɪzərɪ/ *n* **1** (unhappiness) souffrance *f*; (gloom) abattement *m*; **to make sb's life a ~** faire de la vie de qn un enfer
2 (misfortune) **the miseries of unemployment** le chômage et son cortège de misères
3 (BrE) (fam) (child) pleurnicheur/-euse *m/f*; (adult) rabat-joie *m inv*

misfire /ˌmɪs'faɪə(r)/ *vi* **1** ‹*gun, rocket*› faire long feu; ‹*engine*› avoir des ratés
2 ‹*plan, joke*› tomber à plat

misfit /'mɪsfɪt/ *n* marginal/-e *m/f*

misfortune /ˌmɪs'fɔːtʃuːn/ *n* (unfortunate event) malheur *m*; (bad luck) malchance *f*

misgiving /ˌmɪs'gɪvɪŋ/ *n* crainte *f*; **to have ~s about sth** avoir des craintes quant à qch; **to have ~s about sb** avoir des doutes au sujet de qn

misguided /ˌmɪs'gaɪdɪd/ *adj* ‹*strategy, attempt*› peu judicieux/-ieuse; ‹*person*› malavisé/-e

mishandle /ˌmɪs'hændl/ *vt* **1** mal conduire ‹*operation, meeting*›; mal s'y prendre avec ‹*person*›
2 (roughly) manier [qch] sans précaution ‹*object*›; malmener ‹*person, animal*›

mishap /'mɪshæp/ *n* incident *m*

mishear /ˌmɪs'hɪə(r)/ *vt* (*prét, pp* **misheard**) mal entendre

misinform /ˌmɪsɪn'fɔːm/ *vt* mal renseigner

misinterpret /ˌmɪsɪn'tɜːprɪt/ *vt* mal interpréter

misinterpretation /ˌmɪsɪntɜːprɪ'teɪʃn/ *n* interprétation *f* erronée

misjudge /ˌmɪs'dʒʌdʒ/ *vt* mal évaluer ‹*speed, distance*›; mal calculer ‹*shot*›; mal juger ‹*person*›

mislay /ˌmɪs'leɪ/ *vt* (*prét, pp* **mislaid**) égarer

mislead /ˌmɪs'liːd/ *vt* (*prét, pp* **misled**) (deliberately) tromper; (unintentionally) induire [qn] en erreur

misleading /ˌmɪs'liːdɪŋ/ *adj* ‹*impression, title, information*› trompeur/-euse; ‹*claim, statement, advertising*› mensonger/-ère

mismanage /ˌmɪs'mænɪdʒ/ *vt* mal diriger ‹*firm, project*›; mal gérer ‹*finances*›

misplace /ˌmɪs'pleɪs/ *vt* égarer

misprint /'mɪsprɪnt/ *n* coquille *f*, faute *f* typographique

mispronounce /ˌmɪsprə'naʊns/ *vt* mal prononcer

misread /ˌmɪs'riːd/ *vt* (*prét, pp* **misread** /ˌmɪs'red/) (read wrongly) mal lire; (misinterpret) mal interpréter ‹*actions*›

misrepresent /ˌmɪsˌreprɪ'zent/ *vt* présenter [qn] sous un faux jour ‹*person*›; déformer ‹*views, facts*›

m

misrepresentation /ˌmɪsˌreprɪzenˈteɪʃn/ *n* (of facts) déformation *f*

miss /mɪs/ **A** *n* **1** (in game) coup *m* manqué *or* raté
2 to give [sth] a ~ (fam) ne pas aller à ‹*film, lecture*›; se passer de ‹*dish, drink, meal*›
B *vt* **1** manquer ‹*target*›
2 rater ‹*bus, plane, event, meeting*›; laisser passer ‹*chance*›; **I ~ed the train by five minutes** j'ai raté le train de cinq minutes
3 ne pas saisir ‹*joke, remark*›
4 sauter ‹*line, class*›; manquer ‹*school*›
5 (avoid) échapper à ‹*death, injury*›; éviter ‹*traffic, bad weather, rush hour*›; **he just ~ed being caught** il a failli être pris
6 I ~ you tu me manques; **he ~ed Paris** Paris lui manquait; **I'll ~ coming to the office** le bureau va me manquer
C *vi* **1** (Games, Sport, Mil) rater son coup; **~ed!** raté!
2 ‹*engine*› avoir des ratés
■ **miss out**: **A ~ out** être lésé/-e
B ~ out on [sth] laisser passer, louper (fam)
C ~ [sb/sth] out sauter ‹*line, verse*›; omettre ‹*fact, point, person*›

Miss *n* Mademoiselle *f*; (written abbreviation) Mlle

misshapen /ˌmɪsˈʃeɪpən/ *adj* ‹*leg*› difforme; ‹*object*› déformé/-e

missile /ˈmɪsaɪl, (AmE) ˈmɪsl/ *n* **1** (Mil) missile *m*
2 (rock, bottle) projectile *m*

missing /ˈmɪsɪŋ/ *adj* **to be ~** manquer; **to go ~** ‹*person, object*› disparaître; **the ~ jewels/child** les bijoux disparus/l'enfant disparu; **there are two books ~** il manque deux livres

mission /ˈmɪʃn/ *n* mission *f*

missionary /ˈmɪʃənrɪ, (AmE) -nerɪ/ *n* missionnaire *mf*

mist /mɪst/ *n* brume *f*
■ **mist over, mist up** ‹*lens, window*› s'embuer

mistake /mɪˈsteɪk/ **A** *n* (gen) erreur *f*; (in text, spelling, typing) faute *f*; **to make a ~** se tromper; **by ~** par erreur
B *vt* (*prét* **-took**, *pp* **-taken**) **1 to ~ sth for sth else** prendre qch pour qch d'autre; **to ~ sb for sb else** confondre qn avec qn d'autre
2 mal interpréter ‹*meaning*›

mistaken /mɪˈsteɪkən/ *adj* **1 to be ~** avoir tort; **he was ~ in thinking it was over** il avait tort de croire que c'était fini
2 ‹*enthusiasm, generosity*› mal placé/-e

mistletoe /ˈmɪsltəʊ/ *n* gui *m*

mistranslation /ˌmɪstrænsˈleɪʃn/ *n* erreur *f* de traduction

mistreat /ˌmɪsˈtriːt/ *vt* maltraiter

mistress /ˈmɪstrɪs/ *n* maîtresse *f*

mistrust /ˌmɪsˈtrʌst/ **A** *n* méfiance *f* (**of** à l'égard de)
B *vt* se méfier de

misty /ˈmɪstɪ/ *adj* ‹*conditions, morning*› brumeux/-euse; ‹*lens, window*› embué/-e; ‹*photo*› flou/-e

misunderstand /ˌmɪsˌʌndəˈstænd/ *vt* (*prét, pp* **-stood**) mal comprendre; (completely) ne pas comprendre

misunderstanding /ˌmɪsˌʌndəˈstændɪŋ/ *n* malentendu *m*

misunderstood *adj* **to feel ~** se sentir incompris/-e

misuse **A** /ˌmɪsˈjuːs/ *n* (of equipment) mauvais usage *m*; (of word) usage *m* impropre; (of power, authority) abus *m*
B /ˌmɪsˈjuːz/ *vt* faire mauvais usage de ‹*equipment*›; mal employer ‹*word, resources*›; abuser de ‹*authority*›

mitigate /ˈmɪtɪgeɪt/ *vt* atténuer ‹*effects, distress, sentence*›; réduire ‹*risks*›; minimiser ‹*loss*›

mitre (BrE), **miter** (AmE) /ˈmaɪtə(r)/ *n* mitre *f*

mitten /ˈmɪtn/ *n* moufle *f*

mix /mɪks/ **A** *n* **1** (gen) mélange *m*
2 (Mus) mixage *m*, mix *m*
B *vt* **1** (gen) mélanger (**with** avec, **and** à)
2 préparer ‹*drink*›; malaxer ‹*cement, paste*›
3 (Mus) mixer
C *vi* **1** (*also* **~ together**) se mélanger (**with** avec, à)
2 (socialize) être sociable; **to ~ with** fréquenter
■ **mix up 1** (confuse) confondre; **to get two things/people ~ed up** confondre deux choses/personnes
2 (jumble up) mélanger, mêler ‹*papers, photos*›
3 to get ~ed up in se trouver mêlé/-e à

mixed /mɪkst/ *adj* **1** ‹*collection, programme, diet*› varié/-e; ‹*nuts, sweets*› assorti/-e; ‹*salad*› composé/-e; ‹*group, community*› (socially, in age) mélangé/-e; **of ~ blood** de sang mêlé
2 (for both sexes) mixte
3 ‹*reaction, feelings, reception*› mitigé/-e

mixed ability *adj* (Sch) ‹*class, teaching*› sans groupes de niveau

mixed race *n* **of ~** métis/-isse

mixer /ˈmɪksə(r)/ *n* **1** (Culin) batteur *m* électrique
2 (drink) boisson *f* nonalcoolisée

mixing /ˈmɪksɪŋ/ *n* (combining) mélange *m*; (Mus) mixage *m*

mixture /ˈmɪkstʃə(r)/ *n* mélange *m* (**of** de)

mix-up *n* confusion *f* (**over** sur)

moan /məʊn/ **A** *n* **1** (noise) gémissement *m*
2 (fam) (complaint) plainte *f* (**about** au sujet de)
B *vi* **1** (groan) gémir (**with** de)
2 (fam) (complain) râler (fam) (**about** contre)

moany /ˈməʊnɪ/ *adj* (fam) râleur/-euse

moat /məʊt/ *n* douve *f*

mob /mɒb/ **A** *n* foule *f* (**of** de)
B *vt* (*p prés etc* **-bb-**) assaillir ‹*person*›;

mot clé

envahir ‹*place*›

mobile /'məʊbaɪl, (AmE) -bl *also*-biːl/ **A** *n* mobile *m*
B *adj* **1** ‹*object, population*› mobile; ‹*canteen*› ambulant/-e
2 to be ~ (able to walk) pouvoir marcher; (able to travel) pouvoir se déplacer

mobile phone *n* (BrE) téléphone *m* portable, portable *m*

mobilization /ˌməʊbɪlaɪ'zeɪʃn, (AmE) -lɪ'z-/ *n* mobilisation *f*

mobilize /'məʊbɪlaɪz/ *vt, vi* mobiliser

mocha /'mɒkə, (AmE) 'məʊkə/ *n* **1** (coffee) moka *m*
2 (flavour) arôme *m* de café et de chocolat

mock /mɒk/ **A** *n* (BrE) (Sch) examen *m* blanc
B *adj* **1** ‹*suede, ivory*› faux/fausse *before n*; **~ leather** similicuir *m*
2 (feigned) simulé/-e; **in ~ terror** en feignant la terreur
C *vt* se moquer de ‹*person, efforts, beliefs*›
D *vi* ‹*person*› se moquer

mockery /'mɒkərɪ/ *n* moquerie *f*

mod con /ˌmɒd'kɒn/ *n* (BrE) confort *m* (moderne)

mode /məʊd/ *n* mode *m*

model /'mɒdl/ **A** *n* **1** (of car, appliance, garment) modèle *m*
2 (person) (artist's) modèle *m*; (fashion) mannequin *m*
3 (scale model) maquette *f*
4 (perfect example) modèle *m* (**of** de)
B *adj* **1** ‹*railway, soldier, village*› miniature; ‹*aeroplane, boat, car*› modèle réduit
2 ‹*husband, student, prison*› modèle
C *vt* (*p prés etc* **-ll-** (BrE), **-l-** (AmE))
1 modeler ‹*clay, wax*›
2 ‹*fashion model*› présenter ‹*garment*›
D *vi* (*p prés etc* **-ll-** (BrE), **-l-** (AmE))
1 ‹*artist's model*› poser
2 ‹*fashion model*› travailler comme mannequin

modelling (BrE), **modeling** (AmE) /'mɒdəlɪŋ/ *n* **1** (of clothes) **to take up ~** devenir mannequin; **have you done any ~?** as-tu déjà travaillé comme mannequin?
2 (Comput) modélisation *f*

modem /'məʊdem/ *n* modem *m*

moderate **A** /'mɒdərət/ *adj* **1** (not extreme) modéré/-e (**in** dans)
2 ‹*success, income*› moyen/-enne
B /'mɒdəreɪt/ *vt* modérer
C /'mɒdəreɪt/ *vi* se modérer

moderation /ˌmɒdə'reɪʃn/ *n* modération *f* (**in** dans); **in ~** avec modération

modern /'mɒdn/ *adj* moderne; **the ~ world** le monde contemporain

modernize /'mɒdənaɪz/ *vt* moderniser

modern languages *npl* langues *fpl* vivantes

modest /'mɒdɪst/ *adj* **1** modeste (**about** au sujet de)
2 ‹*gift, aim*› modeste; ‹*sum, salary*› modique

modesty /'mɒdɪstɪ/ *n* modestie *f*

modify /'mɒdɪfaɪ/ *vt* modifier

modular /'mɒdjʊlə(r), (AmE) -dʒʊ-/ *adj* modulaire

module /'mɒdjuːl, (AmE) -dʒʊ-/ *n* module *m*

mogul /'məʊgl/ *n* magnat *m*

Mohammed, **Muhammad** /məʊ'hæmɪd/ *pr n* Mahomet

moist /mɔɪst/ *adj* ‹*soil*› humide; ‹*cake*› moelleux/-euse; ‹*hands*› moite; ‹*skin*› bien hydraté/-e

moisten /'mɔɪsn/ *vt* humecter

moisture /'mɔɪstʃə(r)/ *n* humidité *f*

moisturizer /'mɔɪstʃəraɪzə(r)/ *n* (lotion) lait *m* hydratant; (cream) crème *f* hydratante

molar /'məʊlə(r)/ *n, adj* molaire *f*

mold (AmE) = **mould**

mole /məʊl/ *n* **1** (Zool) taupe *f*
2 (on skin) grain *m* de beauté

molecule /'mɒlɪkjuːl/ *n* molécule *f*

molest /mə'lest/ *vt* agresser [qn] sexuellement

mollycoddle /'mɒlɪkɒdl/ *vt* dorloter

molt (AmE) = **moult**

molten /'məʊltən/ *adj* en fusion

moment /'məʊmənt/ *n* **1** (instant) instant *m*; **in a ~** dans un instant; **at any ~** à tout instant
2 (point in time) moment *m*; **at the ~** en ce moment; **at the right ~** au bon moment

momentarily /'məʊməntrəlɪ, (AmE) ˌməʊmən'terəlɪ/ *adv* **1** (for an instant) momentanément
2 (AmE) (very soon) dans un instant; (at any moment) d'un moment à l'autre

momentary /'məʊməntrɪ, (AmE) -terɪ/ *adj* passager/-ère

momentous /mə'mentəs, məʊ'm-/ *adj* capital/-e

momentum /mə'mentəm, məʊ'm-/ *n* (gen) élan *m*; (in physics) vitesse *f*

monarch /'mɒnək/ *n* monarque *m*

monarchy /'mɒnəkɪ/ *n* monarchie *f*

monastery /'mɒnəstrɪ, (AmE) -terɪ/ *n* monastère *m*

Monday /'mʌndeɪ, -dɪ/ *n* lundi *m*

monetary union *n* union *f* monétaire

money /'mʌnɪ/ *n* argent *m*; **to make ~** ‹*person*› gagner de l'argent; ‹*business, project*› rapporter de l'argent
IDIOMS **to get one's ~'s worth, to get a good run for one's ~** en avoir pour son argent; **your ~ or your life!** la bourse ou la vie!

money belt *n* ceinture *f* porte-monnaie

money box *n* tirelire *f*

moneylender /'mʌnɪlendə(r)/ *n* prêteur/-euse *m/f*

moneymaker *n* (product) article *m* qui rapporte beaucoup; (activity) activité *f* lucrative

money order, **MO** *n* mandat *m* postal

mongrel /ˈmʌŋgrl/ *n* (chien *m*) bâtard *m*

monitor /ˈmɒnɪtə(r)/ **A** *n* (Comput, Med) moniteur *m*
B *vt* **1** surveiller ‹*results, patient, breathing*›
2 être à l'écoute de ‹*broadcast*›

monk /mʌŋk/ *n* moine *m*

monkey /ˈmʌŋkɪ/ *n* **1** (Zool) singe *m*
2 (fam) (rascal) galopin *m* (fam)

monochrome /ˈmɒnəkrəʊm/ *adj* ‹*film*› en noir et blanc; ‹*colour scheme*› monochrome

monogamous /məˈnɒgəməs/ *adj* monogame

monogamy /məˈnɒgəmɪ/ *n* monogamie *f*

monologue, **monolog** (AmE) /ˈmɒnəlɒg/ *n* monologue *m*

monopolize /məˈnɒpəlaɪz/ *vt* **1** détenir le monopole de ‹*market, supply*›
2 (fig) monopoliser

monopoly /məˈnɒpəlɪ/ *n* monopole *m*

monoski /ˈmɒnəskiː/ *vi* faire du monoski

monotonous /məˈnɒtənəs/ *adj* monotone

monotony /məˈnɒtənɪ/ *n* monotonie *f*

monsoon /mɒnˈsuːn/ *n* mousson *f*

monster /ˈmɒnstə(r)/ *n* monstre *m*

monstrous /ˈmɒnstrəs/ *adj* **1** (ugly) monstrueux/-euse; ‹*building*› hideux/-euse
2 (huge) énorme

month /mʌnθ/ *n* mois *m*; **in two ~s, in two ~s' time** dans deux mois; **every other ~** tous les deux mois; **in the ~ of June** au mois de juin

monthly /ˈmʌnθlɪ/ **A** *n* (journal) mensuel *m*
B *adj* mensuel/-elle; **~ instalment** mensualité *f*
C *adv* ‹*pay, earn*› au mois; ‹*happen, visit, publish*› tous les mois

Montreal /ˌmɒntrɪˈɔːl/ *pr n* Montréal

monument /ˈmɒnjʊmənt/ *n* monument *m*

moo /muː/ *vi* meugler

mood /muːd/ *n* **1** (humour) humeur *f*; **in a good/bad ~** de bonne/mauvaise humeur; **to be in the ~ for doing** avoir envie de faire; **to be in no ~ for doing** ne pas être d'humeur à faire
2 (bad temper) saute *f* d'humeur; **to be in a ~** être de mauvaise humeur

mood swing *n* saute *f* d'humeur

moody /ˈmuːdɪ/ *adj* **1** (unpredictable) d'humeur changeante, lunatique
2 (sulky) de mauvaise humeur

moon /muːn/ *n* lune *f*
IDIOMS **to be over the ~** être aux anges; **once in a blue ~** tous les trente-six du mois (fam); **the man in the ~** le visage de la Lune

moonlight /ˈmuːnlaɪt/ **A** *n* clair *m* de lune
B *vi* travailler au noir

moonlit /ˈmuːnlɪt/ *adj* éclairé/-e par la lune; **a ~ night** une nuit de lune

moor /mɔː(r), (AmE) mʊər/ **A** *n* lande *f*
B *vt* amarrer ‹*boat*›
C *vi* ‹*boat*› mouiller

moorings *npl* amarres *fpl*

moorland /ˈmɔːlənd, (AmE) ˈmʊər-/ *n* lande *f*

moose /muːs/ *n* (Canadian) orignal *m*; (European) élan *m*

mop /mɒp/ **A** *n* **1** (of cotton) balai *m* à franges; (of sponge) balai *m* éponge
2 ~ of hair crinière *f* (fam)
B *vt* (*p prés etc* **-pp-**) **1** laver [qch] à grande eau ‹*floor*›
2 to ~ one's face/brow s'éponger le visage/le front
▪ **mop up** éponger ‹*milk, wine*›

mope /məʊp/ *vi* se morfondre
▪ **mope about**, **mope around** traîner (comme une âme en peine)

moped /ˈməʊped/ *n* vélomoteur *m*

moral /ˈmɒrəl, (AmE) ˈmɔːrəl/ **A** *n* morale *f*
B morals *npl* moralité *f*
C *adj* moral/-e

morale /məˈrɑːl, (AmE) -ˈræl/ *n* moral *m*

morality /məˈrælətɪ/ *n* moralité *f*

moral majority *n* majorité *f* bien-pensante

morbid /ˈmɔːbɪd/ *adj* morbide

more /mɔː(r)/ **A** *adv* **1** (comparative) plus (than que); **~ expensive** plus cher/chère; **~ easily** plus facilement
2 (to a greater extent) plus, davantage; **you must rest ~** il faut que tu te reposes davantage; **he is all the ~ angry because** il est d'autant plus en colère que
3 (longer) **I don't work there any ~** je n'y travaille plus
4 (again) **once ~** une fois de plus, encore une fois
5 (else) **nothing ~** rien de plus; **something ~** autre chose
B *det* plus de; **I have ~ money than him** j'ai plus d'argent que lui; **some ~ books** quelques livres de plus; **there's no ~ bread** il n'y a plus de pain; **have some ~ beer!** reprenez de la bière!
C *pron, quantif* **1** (larger amount or number) plus; **it costs ~** il/elle coûte plus cher (**than** que); **he eats ~ than you** il mange plus que toi
2 (additional amount) davantage; **I need ~ of them** il m'en faut plus; **I need ~ of it** il m'en faut davantage
D more and more *phr* de plus en plus; **~ and ~ work** de plus en plus de travail
E more or less *phr* plus ou moins
F more than *phr* **1** (greater amount or number) plus de; **~ than 20 people** plus de 20 personnes; **~ than half** plus de la moitié; **~ than enough** plus qu'assez

mot clé

2 (extremely) **~ than generous** plus que généreux

moreover /mɔːˈrəʊvə(r)/ *adv* de plus, qui plus est

morning /ˈmɔːnɪŋ/ **A** *n* matin *m*; (with emphasis on duration) matinée *f*; **in the ~** le matin; **on Monday ~s** le lundi matin; **(on) Monday ~** lundi matin; **later this ~** plus tard dans la matinée; **yesterday/tomorrow ~** hier/demain matin
B *excl* **(good) ~!** bonjour!

morning-after pill *n* pilule *f* du lendemain

Morocco /məˈrɒkəʊ/ *pr n* Maroc *m*

Morse /mɔːs/ *n* (*also* **Morse code**) morse *m*; **in ~** en morse

morsel /ˈmɔːsl/ *n* morceau *m*

mortal /ˈmɔːtl/ *n, adj* mortel/-elle *m/f*

mortality /mɔːˈtælətɪ/ *n* mortalité *f*

mortar /ˈmɔːtə(r)/ *n* mortier *m*

mortgage /ˈmɔːgɪdʒ/ *n* emprunt-logement *m* **(on** pour)

mortgage rate *n* taux *m* de l'emprunt-logement

mortuary /ˈmɔːtʃərɪ, (AmE) ˈmɔːtʃʊerɪ/ *n* morgue *f*

mosaic /məʊˈzeɪɪk/ *n* mosaïque *f*

Moscow /ˈmɒskəʊ/ *pr n* Moscou

Moslem /ˈmɒzləm/ = **Muslim**

mosque /mɒsk/ *n* mosquée *f*

mosquito /məsˈkiːtəʊ, mɒs-/ *n* moustique *m*

mosquito repellent *n* anti-moustique *m*

moss /mɒs, (AmE) mɔːs/ *n* mousse *f*

most /məʊst/

> When used to form the superlative of adjectives, *most* is translated by *le plus* or *la plus* depending on the gender of the noun and by *les plus* with plural noun: *the most beautiful woman in the room* = la plus belle femme de la pièce; *the most expensive hotel in Paris* = l'hôtel le plus cher de Paris; *the most difficult problems* = les problèmes les plus difficiles. For examples and further uses, see the entry below.

A *det* **1** (the majority of) la plupart de; **~ people** la plupart des gens
2 (in superlatives) le plus de; **she got the ~ votes** c'est elle qui a obtenu le plus de voix
B *pron* **1** (the greatest number) la plupart (**of** de); (the largest part) la plus grande partie (**of** de); **~ of the time** la plupart du temps; **~ of us** la plupart d'entre nous; **for ~ of the day** pendant la plus grande partie de la journée; **~ of the bread** presque tout le pain
2 (all) **the ~ you can expect is...** tout ce que tu peux espérer c'est...
3 (in superlatives) le plus; **John has got the ~** c'est John qui en a le plus
C *adv* **1** (in superlatives) **the ~ beautiful château in France** le plus beau château de France; **~ easily** le plus facilement
2 (very) très, extrêmement; **~ encouraging** très *or* extrêmement encourageant; **~ probably** très vraisemblablement
3 (more than all the rest) le plus; **what annoyed him ~ (of all) was...** ce qui l'ennuyait le plus c'était que...
D **at (the) most** *phr* au maximum, au plus
E **for the most part** *phr* (most of them) pour la plupart; (most of the time) la plupart du temps; (chiefly) surtout, essentiellement
F **most of all** *phr* par-dessus tout
IDIOM **to make the ~ of** tirer le meilleur parti de ‹*situation, resources, abilities*›; profiter de ‹*opportunity, good weather*›

mostly /ˈməʊstlɪ/ *adv* **1** (chiefly) surtout, essentiellement; (most of them) pour la plupart
2 (most of the time) la plupart du temps

MOT /ˌeməʊˈtiː/ *n* (BrE) (*also* **~ test**) contrôle *m* technique des véhicules

moth /mɒθ, (AmE) mɔːθ/ *n* papillon *m* de nuit; (in clothes) mite *f*

mother /ˈmʌðə(r)/ **A** *n* mère *f*
B *vt* (coddle) dorloter

motherboard *n* carte *f* mère

motherhood /ˈmʌðəhʊd/ *n* maternité *f*

mother-in-law *n* (*pl* **mothers-in-law**) belle-mère *f*

motherly /ˈmʌðəlɪ/ *adj* maternel/-elle

mother-of-pearl /ˌmʌðərəvˈpɜːl/ *n* nacre *f*

Mother's Day *n* fête *f* des Mères

mother tongue *n* langue *f* maternelle

motion /ˈməʊʃn/ **A** *n* **1** mouvement *m*; **to set [sth] in ~** mettre [qch] en marche ‹*machine*›; mettre [qch] en route ‹*plan*›; déclencher ‹*chain of events*›
2 (proposal) motion *f*
B *vi* **to ~ to sb (to do)** faire signe à qn (de faire)

motionless /ˈməʊʃnlɪs/ *adj* immobile

motivate /ˈməʊtɪveɪt/ *vt* motiver ‹*person*›

motivated /ˈməʊtɪveɪtɪd/ *adj* **1** ‹*person, pupil*› motivé/-e
2 politically/racially ~ ‹*act*› politique/raciste

motivation /ˌməʊtɪˈveɪʃn/ *n* motivation *f*

motive /ˈməʊtɪv/ *n* (gen) motif *m* (**for, behind** de); (for crime) mobile *m* (**for** de)

motley /ˈmɒtlɪ/ *adj* ‹*crowd, gathering*› bigarré/-e; ‹*collection*› hétéroclite

motor /ˈməʊtə(r)/ **A** *n* moteur *m*
B *adj* **1** ‹*vehicle*› automobile; ‹*show*› de l'automobile
2 ‹*mower*› à moteur

motorbike *n* moto *f*

motor boat *n* canot *m* automobile

motorcycle *n* motocyclette *f*

motorcyclist *n* motocycliste *mf*

motor home *n* auto-caravane *f*

motorist /ˈməʊtərɪst/ *n* automobiliste *mf*

motor racing *n* course *f* automobile

motorway /'məʊtəweɪ/ *n* (BrE) autoroute *f*

mottled /'mɒtld/ *adj* ‹*skin, paper*› marbré/-e; ‹*hands*› tacheté/-e

motto /'mɒtəʊ/ *n* devise *f*

mould (BrE), **mold** (AmE) /məʊld/ **A** *n* **1** (Culin) (fig) moule *m*
2 (fungi) moisissure *f*
B *vt* modeler ‹*plastic, clay, shape*›; façonner ‹*character, opinions*› (**into** pour en faire)

mouldy (BrE), **moldy** (AmE) /'məʊldɪ/ *adj* moisi/-e; **to go ~** moisir

moult (BrE), **molt** (AmE) /məʊlt/ *vi* ‹*cat, dog*› perdre ses poils; ‹*bird*› muer

mound /maʊnd/ *n* **1** (hillock) tertre *m*
2 (heap) monceau *m* (**of** de)

mount /maʊnt/ **A** *vt* **1** monter sur ‹*platform, horse*›
2 monter ‹*jewel, picture, exhibit*›
3 organiser ‹*demonstration*›
B *vi* **1** ‹*person, staircase*› monter (**to** jusqu'à)
2 ‹*number, toll*› augmenter; ‹*concern*› grandir
3 (on horse) se mettre en selle

⚷ **mountain** /'maʊntɪn, (AmE) -ntn/ *n* montagne *f*

mountain bike *n* vélo *m* tout-terrain, VTT *m*

m

mountaineer /ˌmaʊntɪ'nɪə(r), (AmE) -ntn'ɪər/ *n* alpiniste *mf*

mountaineering /ˌmaʊntɪ'nɪərɪŋ, (AmE) -ntn'ɪərɪŋ/ *n* alpinisme *m*

mountainous /'maʊntɪnəs, (AmE) -ntənəs/ *adj* montagneux/-euse

mountain top *n* cime *f*

mourn /mɔːn/ **A** *vt* pleurer ‹*person, death*›
B *vi* ‹*person*› porter le deuil; **to ~ for sb/sth** pleurer qn/qch

mourning /'mɔːnɪŋ/ *n* deuil *m*

mouse /maʊs/ *n* (*pl* **mice**) (Comput, Zool) souris *f*
■ **mouse over**: **~ over [sth]** passer la souris sur

mouse mat *n* tapis *m* de souris

mouseover /'maʊsəʊvə(r)/ *n* mouse-over *m*, passage *m* de la souris; **~ ad** objet *m* publicitaire activé par le survol de la souris

mouse pointer *n* pointeur *m* de la souris

moustache, **mustache** (AmE) /mə'stɑːʃ/, *n* moustache *f*

⚷ **mouth** /maʊθ/ **A** *n* **1** (of human, horse) bouche *f*; (of other animal) gueule *f*
2 (of cave, tunnel) entrée *f*; (of river) embouchure *f*; (of volcano) bouche *f*
B *vt* articuler silencieusement
IDIOM **by word of ~** de bouche à oreille

mouthful /'maʊθfʊl/ *n* (of food) bouchée *f*; (of liquid) gorgée *f*

mouth organ *n* harmonica *m*

mouth-to-mouth resuscitation *n* bouche-à-bouche *m inv*

mouthwash *n* eau *f* dentifrice

mouth-watering /'maʊθwɔːtərɪŋ/ *adj* appétissant/-e

⚷ **move** /muːv/ **A** *n* **1** (movement) mouvement *m*; (gesture) geste *m*
2 (of residence) déménagement *m*; (of company) transfert *m*
3 (in game) coup *m*; **it's your ~** c'est ton tour
4 (step, act) manœuvre *f*; **a good/bad ~** une bonne/mauvaise idée; **to make the first ~** faire le premier pas
B *vt* **1** déplacer ‹*game piece, cursor, car, furniture*›; transporter ‹*patient, army*›; **to ~ sth (out of the way)** enlever qch
2 ‹*person*› bouger ‹*limb, head*›; ‹*wind, mechanism*› faire bouger ‹*leaf, wheel*›
3 (relocate) muter ‹*staff*›; transférer ‹*office*›; **to ~ house** déménager
4 (affect) émouvoir; **to be deeply ~d** être très ému/-e
C *vi* **1** (stir) bouger; ‹*lips*› remuer
2 (travel) ‹*vehicle*› rouler; ‹*person*› avancer; ‹*procession, army*› être en marche; **to ~ back** reculer; **to ~ forward** s'avancer; **to ~ away** s'éloigner
3 (change home, location) déménager; **to ~ to the countryside/to Japan** s'installer à la campagne/au Japon
4 (change job) être muté/-e
5 (act) agir
IDIOM **to get a ~ on** (fam) se dépêcher
■ **move about**, **move around** ‹*person*› (fidget) remuer; (move home) déménager
■ **move along**: **A** **~ along** (stop loitering) circuler; (proceed) avancer; (squeeze up) se pousser
B **~ [sb/sth] along** faire circuler ‹*onlookers, crowd*›
■ **move away** s'éloigner; (move house) déménager
■ **move in 1** (to house) emménager; **to ~ in with** s'installer avec ‹*friend, lover*›
2 (advance, attack) s'avancer (**on** sur)
■ **move on** ‹*person, traveller*› se mettre en route; ‹*vehicle*› repartir; **to ~ on to** passer à ‹*next item*›
■ **move out** (of house) déménager; **to ~ out of** quitter
■ **move over** se pousser
■ **move up 1** (make room) se pousser
2 (be promoted) être promu/-e

⚷ **movement** /'muːvmənt/ *n* mouvement *m*; (of hand, arm) geste *m*

⚷ **movie** (AmE) /'muːvɪ/ **A** *n* film *m*
B **movies** *npl* **the ~s** le cinéma

movie camera *n* caméra *f*

movie star *n* vedette *f* de cinéma

movie theater *n* (AmE) cinéma *m*

moving /'muːvɪŋ/ *adj* **1** ‹*vehicle*› en marche; ‹*parts, target*› mobile; ‹*staircase, walkway*› roulant/-e
2 ‹*scene, speech*› émouvant/-e

⚷ mot clé

mow /məʊ/ *vt* (*pp* **~ed**, **mown**) tondre ‹*grass, lawn*›

mower /ˈməʊə(r)/ *n* tondeuse *f* à gazon

MP *n* (BrE) (*abbr* = **Member of Parliament**) député *m* (**for** de)

MP3 player *n* (lecteur *m*) MP3 *m*

Mr /ˈmɪstə(r)/ *n* (*pl* **Messrs**) M., Monsieur

MRI *n* (*abbr* = **magnetic resonance imaging**) IRM *f*

Mrs /ˈmɪsɪz/ *n* Mme, Madame

Ms /mɪz, məz/ *n* ≈ Mme.

MSc *n* (*abbr* = **Master of Science**) diplôme *m* supérieur en sciences

much /mʌtʃ/ **A** *adv* beaucoup; **~ more/less** beaucoup plus/moins; **~ smaller** beaucoup plus petit; **I don't read ~** je ne lis pas beaucoup; **we'd ~ rather stay here** nous préférerions de beaucoup rester ici; **does it hurt ~?** est-ce que ça fait très mal?; **we don't go out ~** nous ne sortons pas beaucoup *or* souvent; **it's ~ the same** c'est à peu près pareil (**as** que); **too ~** trop; **very ~** beaucoup; **thank you very ~** merci beaucoup; **so ~** tellement; **as ~** autant (**as** que); **they hated each other as ~ as ever** ils se détestaient toujours autant
B *pron* beaucoup; **do you have ~ left?** est-ce qu'il vous en reste beaucoup?; **we didn't eat ~** nous n'avons pas mangé grand-chose; **I don't see ~ of them now** je ne les vois plus beaucoup maintenant; **so ~** tellement, tant; **we'd eaten so ~ that** nous avions tellement mangé que; **too ~** trop; **it costs too ~** c'est trop cher; **twice as ~** deux fois plus; **as ~ as possible** autant que possible; **how ~?** combien?; **it's not** *or* **nothing ~** ce n'est pas grand-chose; **he's not ~ to look at** il n'est pas très beau
C *det* beaucoup de; **I haven't got ~ time** je n'ai pas beaucoup de temps; **she didn't speak ~ English** elle ne connaissait que quelques mots d'anglais; **too ~ money** trop d'argent; **don't use so ~ salt** ne mets pas tant de sel; **we paid twice as ~** nous avons payé deux fois plus; **how ~ time have we got left?** combien de temps nous reste-t-il?
D **much as** *phr* bien que (+ *subjunctive*)
E **so much as** *phr* **without so ~ as an apology** sans même s'excuser; **if you so ~ as move** si tu fais le moindre mouvement

muck /mʌk/ *n* saletés *fpl*; (mud) boue *f*
■ **muck about** (fam) **muck around** (fam):
A **~ about** (fool about) faire l'imbécile; **to ~ about with** traficoter (fam) ‹*appliance*›; toucher à ‹*object*›
B **~ [sb] about** se ficher de (fam)
■ **muck in** mettre la main à la pâte (fam)

mud /mʌd/ *n* boue *f*

muddle /ˈmʌdl/ *n* **1** (mess) pagaille *f* (fam) **2** (mix-up) malentendu *m* (**over** à propos de) **3 to get into a ~** ‹*person*› s'embrouiller
■ **muddle up**: **A** **~ [sth] up** (disorder) semer la pagaille (fam) dans
B **~ [sb] up** embrouiller les idées de; **to get [sth] ~d up** s'embrouiller dans ‹*dates, names*›

muddled /ˈmʌdld/ *adj* confus/-e

muddy /ˈmʌdɪ/ *adj* ‹*hand*› couvert/-e de boue; ‹*shoe, garment*› crotté/-e; ‹*road, water*› boueux/-euse; ‹*green, yellow*› terne

mudguard *n* garde-boue *m inv*

muffle /ˈmʌfl/ *vt* assourdir ‹*bell, drum*›

muffler /ˈmʌflə(r)/ /ˈmʌflə(r)/ *n* (AmE) (for car) silencieux *m*

mug /mʌɡ/ **A** *n* **1** grande tasse *f* **2** (BrE) (fool) poire *f* (fam); **it's a ~'s game** c'est un attrape-nigaud
B *vt* (*p prés etc* **-gg-**) agresser; **to be ~ged** se faire agresser

mugger /ˈmʌɡə(r)/ *n* agresseur *m*

mugging /ˈmʌɡɪŋ/ *n* (attack) agression *f*; (crime) agressions *fpl*

muggy /ˈmʌɡɪ/ *adj* ‹*room, day*› étouffant/-e; ‹*weather*› lourd/-e

Muhammad /məˈhæmɪd/ *pr n* Mahomet

mule /mjuːl/ *n* mulet *m*, mule *f*
IDIOM **as stubborn as a ~** têtu/-e comme une mule

mull /mʌl/ *v*
■ **mull over** retourner [qch] dans sa tête

mulled wine *n* vin *m* chaud

multicultural /ˌmʌltɪˈkʌltʃərəl/ *adj* multiculturel/-elle

multidisciplinary /ˌmʌltɪdɪsɪˈplɪnərɪ, (AmE) -nerɪ/ *adj* pluridisciplinaire

multi-ethnic /ˌmʌltɪˈeθnɪk/ *adj* multi-ethnique

multi-function /ˌmʌltɪˈfʌŋkʃn/ *adj* multifonctions *inv*

multigym /ˈmʌltɪdʒɪm/ *n* appareil *m* de musculation

multilateral /ˌmʌltɪˈlætərəl/ *adj* multilatéral/-e

multimedia /ˌmʌltɪˈmiːdɪə/ *n, adj* multimédia *m inv*

multinational /ˌmʌltɪˈnæʃənl/ *adj* multinational/-e

multiple /ˈmʌltɪpl/ *n, adj* multiple *m*

multiple choice *adj* à choix multiple

multiple sclerosis, **MS** *n* sclérose *f* en plaques

multiplex /ˈmʌltɪpleks/ *n* complexe *m* multi-salles

multiply /ˈmʌltɪplaɪ/ **A** *vt* multiplier (**by** par)
B *vi* se multiplier

multipurpose /ˌmʌltɪˈpɜːpəs/ *adj* ‹*tool, gadget*› à usages multiples; ‹*area, organization*› polyvalent/-e

multipurpose vehicle, **MPV** *n* monospace *m*

multi-racial *adj* multiracial/-e

multistorey /ˌmʌltɪˈstɔːrɪ/ *adj* (BrE) ‹*car park*› à niveaux multiples; ‹*building*› à étages

m

multitrack /ˈmʌltɪtræk/ *adj* multipiste *inv*

multitude /ˈmʌltɪtjuːd, (AmE) -tuːd/ *n* multitude *f*

mum, **Mum** /mʌm/ *n* (BrE) (fam) maman *f*
IDIOM **to keep ~** ne pas piper mot

mumble /ˈmʌmbl/ *vt*, *vi* marmonner

mumbo jumbo /ˌmʌmbəʊˈdʒʌmbəʊ/ *n* (fam) charabia *m* (fam)

mummy /ˈmʌmɪ/ *n* **1** (*also* **Mummy**) (fam) maman *f*
2 (embalmed body) momie *f*

mumps /mʌmps/ *n* oreillons *mpl*

munch /mʌntʃ/ *vt* ‹*person*› mâcher; ‹*animal*› mâchonner

mundane /mʌnˈdeɪn/ *adj* terre-à-terre, quelconque

municipal /mjuːˈnɪsɪpl/ *adj* municipal/-e

mural /ˈmjʊərəl/ *n* (wall painting) peinture *f* murale; (in cave) peinture *f* rupestre

🔑 **murder** /ˈmɜːdə(r)/ **A** *n* meurtre *m*
B *vt* assassiner
IDIOM **to get away with ~** exercer ses talents en toute impunité

murderer /ˈmɜːdərə(r)/ *n* assassin *m*, meurtrier *m*

murderess /ˈmɜːdərɪs/ *n* meurtrière *f*

murderous /ˈmɜːdərəs/ *adj* ‹*look*› assassin/-e; ‹*deeds, thoughts*› meurtrier/-ière

murky /ˈmɜːkɪ/ *adj* **1** ‹*light, water, colour*› glauque
2 ‹*past*› trouble

murmur /ˈmɜːmə(r)/ **A** *n* murmure *m* (of de)
B *vt*, *vi* murmurer

🔑 **muscle** /ˈmʌsl/ *n* muscle *m*
■ **muscle in** (fam) s'imposer (**on** dans)

muscle strain *n* élongation *f*

muscular /ˈmʌskjʊlə(r)/ *adj* ‹*disease, tissue*› musculaire; ‹*person, body, limbs*› musclé/-e

museum /mjuːˈzɪəm/ *n* musée *m*

mushroom /ˈmʌʃrʊm, -ruːm/ *n* **1** (Bot, Culin) champignon *m*
2 (colour) beige *m* rosé

🔑 **music** /ˈmjuːzɪk/ *n* musique *f*

🔑 **musical** /ˈmjuːzɪkl/ **A** *n* comédie *f* musicale
B *adj* **1** ‹*person*› musicien/-ienne
2 ‹*voice, laughter*› mélodieux/-ieuse; ‹*score*› musical/-e

musical instrument *n* instrument *m* de musique

musician /mjuːˈzɪʃn/ *n* musicien/-ienne *m/f*

music video *n* clip *m* (vidéo)

musk /mʌsk/ *n* musc *m*

Muslim /ˈmʊzlɪm, (AmE) ˈmʌzləm/ **A** *n* Musulman/-e *m/f*
B *adj* musulman/-e

mussel /ˈmʌsl/ *n* moule *f*

🔑 **must** **A** *modal aux* (*nég* **must not**, **mustn't**) **1** (expressing obligation) **I ~ go** je dois partir, il faut que je parte; **he ~ sit the exam in June** il faut qu'il passe l'examen au mois de juin; **you ~ check your rear-view mirror first** il faut regarder dans le rétroviseur d'abord; **I ~ say I was impressed** je dois dire que j'ai été impressionné; **we mustn't tell anyone** il ne faut en parler à personne, nous ne devons en parler à personne
2 (making deductions) **they ~ really detest each other** ils doivent vraiment se détester; **it ~ be pleasant living there** ça doit être agréable de vivre là-bas; **he ~ have been surprised** il a dû être surpris
B *n* **it's a ~** c'est indispensable; **this film is a ~** ce film est à voir *or* à ne pas rater; **a visit to the Louvre is a ~** une visite au Louvre s'impose

mustache (AmE) = **moustache**

mustard /ˈmʌstəd/ *n* moutarde *f*

muster /ˈmʌstə(r)/ *vt* (*also* **~ up**) rassembler ‹*troops*›; rallier ‹*support*›; trouver ‹*energy, enthusiasm*›
IDIOM **to pass ~** être acceptable

musty /ˈmʌstɪ/ *adj* **to smell ~** sentir le moisi *or* le renfermé

mute /mjuːt/ *adj* (offensive) muet/-ette

mutilate /ˈmjuːtɪleɪt/ *vt* mutiler

mutiny /ˈmjuːtɪnɪ/ *n* mutinerie *f*

mutter /ˈmʌtə(r)/ *vt*, *vi* marmonner

mutton /ˈmʌtn/ *n* mouton *m*

mutual /ˈmjuːtʃʊəl/ *adj* **1** (reciprocal) réciproque; **the feeling is ~** c'est réciproque
2 ‹*friend, interests*› commun/-e; ‹*consent*› mutuel/-elle; **by ~ agreement** d'un commun accord

mutual aid *n* entraide *f*

🔑 **my** /maɪ/

> In French, determiners agree in gender and number with the noun that follows. So *my* is translated by *mon* + masculine singular noun (mon chien), *ma* + feminine singular noun (ma maison) BUT by *mon* + feminine noun beginning with a vowel or mute 'h' (mon assiette) and by *mes* + plural noun (mes enfants).
> When *my* is stressed, *à moi* is added after the noun: *MY house* = ma maison à moi.

A *det* mon/ma/mes
B *excl* **~ ~!** ça alors!

Myanmar /mjænˈmɑː(r)/ *pr n* Myanmar *m*

🔑 **myself** /maɪˈself, məˈself/ *pron* **1** (reflexive) me, m'; **I've hurt ~** je me suis fait mal
2 (emphatic) moi-même; **I saw it ~** je l'ai vu moi-même; **(all) by ~** tout seul/toute seule
3 (after prepositions) moi, moi-même; **I feel proud of ~** je suis fier de moi

🔑 mot clé

4 (expressions) **I'm not much of a dog lover ~** personnellement je n'aime pas trop les chiens; **I'm not ~ today** je ne suis pas dans mon assiette aujourd'hui

mysterious /mɪ'stɪərɪəs/ *adj* mystérieux/-ieuse

mystery /'mɪstərɪ/ *n* **1** mystère *m*
2 (book) roman *m* policier

mystify /'mɪstɪfaɪ/ *vt* laisser [qn] perplexe

myth /mɪθ/ *n* mythe *m*

mythology /mɪ'θɒlədʒɪ/ *n* mythologie *f*

Nn

n, N /en/ *n* n, N *m*

naff /næf/ *adj* (BrE) (fam) ringard/-e (fam)

nag /næg/ *vt* (*p prés etc* **-gg-**) enquiquiner (fam) (**about** au sujet de)

nagging *adj* **1 his ~ wife** sa mégère de femme
2 ‹*pain, doubt*› tenace

nail /neɪl/ **A** *n* **1** (on finger, toe) ongle *m*
2 (Tech) clou *m*
B *vt* clouer

■ **nail down**: **A ~ [sth] down** clouer
B ~ [sb] down coincer (fam) ‹*person*›

nail-biting /'neɪlbaɪtɪŋ/ *adj* ‹*match, finish*› palpitant/-e; ‹*wait*› angoissant/-e

nail brush *n* brosse *f* à ongles

nail file *n* lime *f* à ongles

nail varnish *n* vernis *m* à ongles

nail varnish remover *n* dissolvant *m*

naïve /naɪ'iːv/ *adj* naïf/naïve

naked /'neɪkɪd/ *adj* nu/-e

name /neɪm/ **A** *n* **1** (gen) nom *m*; (of book, film) titre *m*; **first ~** prénom *m*; **my ~ is Louis** je m'appelle Louis
2 (reputation) réputation *f*
3 (insult) **to call sb ~s** injurier qn
B *vt* **1** (call) appeler ‹*person, area*›; baptiser ‹*boat*›; **they ~d her after** (BrE) *or* **for** (AmE) **her mother** ils l'ont appelée comme sa mère; **a boy ~d Pascal** un garçon nommé Pascal
2 (cite) citer; **~ three American States** citez trois États américains
3 révéler ‹*sources*›; révéler l'identité de ‹*suspect*›; **to ~ ~s** donner des noms
4 (state) indiquer ‹*place, time*›; fixer ‹*price, terms*›

name-drop *vi* (*p prés etc* **-pp-**) citer des gens célèbres (*qu'on prétend connaître*)

namely /'neɪmlɪ/ *adv* à savoir

namesake *n* homonyme *m*

nanny /'nænɪ/ *n* (BrE) bonne *f* d'enfants

nanny goat *n* chèvre *f*

nanoparticle /'nænəʊpɑːtɪkl/ *n* nanoparticule *f*

nanotechnology /ˌnænəʊtek'nɒlədʒɪ/ *n* nanotechnologie *f*

nap /næp/ **A** *n* petit somme *m*; **afternoon ~** sieste *f*
B *vi* (*p prés etc* **-pp-**) sommeiller

nape /neɪp/ *n* nuque *f*; **the ~ of the neck** la nuque

napkin /'næpkɪn/ *n* serviette *f* (de table)

nappy /'næpɪ/ *n* (BrE) couche *f* (de bébé)

narcotic /nɑː'kɒtɪk/ **A** *n* (soporific) narcotique *m*; (illegal drug) stupéfiant *m*
B *adj* narcotique

narked *adj* (BrE) (fam) en rogne (fam), en boule (fam)

narration /nə'reɪʃn/ *n* récit *m*, narration *f*

narrative /'nærətɪv/ **A** *n* (account) récit *m*; (storytelling) narration *f*
B *adj* ‹*prose, poem*› narratif/-ive; ‹*skill, talent*› de conteur

narrator /nə'reɪtə(r)/ *n* narrateur/-trice *m/f*

narrow /'nærəʊ/ **A** *adj* (gen) étroit/-e; ‹*views*› étriqué/-e; ‹*majority, margin*› faible (*before n*); **to have a ~ lead** avoir une légère avance; **to have a ~ escape** l'échapper belle
B *vt* **1** (limit) limiter (**to** à); **to ~ the gap** réduire l'écart
2 rétrécir ‹*road, path, arteries*›; **to ~ one's eyes** plisser les yeux
C *vi* (gen) se rétrécir; ‹*gap, margin*› se réduire (**to** à)

■ **narrow down** réduire ‹*numbers, list, choice*› (**to** à); limiter ‹*investigation, research*› (**to** à)

narrowly /'nærəʊlɪ/ *adv* (barely) de justesse

narrow-minded /ˌnærəʊ'maɪndɪd/ *adj* borné/-e

nasal /'neɪzl/ *adj* ‹*vowel*› nasal/-e; ‹*accent, voice*› nasillard/-e

nasal spray *n* nébuliseur *m* (*pour le nez*)

nasty /'nɑːstɪ/ *adj* **1** ‹*person, expression, remark*› méchant/-e; ‹*experience, surprise, feeling, task*› désagréable; ‹*habit, smell, taste*› mauvais/-e (*before n*); ‹*trick*› sale

(*before n*); ‹*cut, bruise*› vilain/-e (*before n*); ‹*accident*› grave
2 (ugly) affreux/-euse

🔑 **nation** /'neɪʃn/ *n* nation *f*; (people) peuple *m*

🔑 **national** /'næʃənl/ **A** *n* ressortissant/-e *m/f*
B *adj* national/-e; **the ~ press** (BrE) les grands quotidiens *mpl*

national anthem *n* hymne *m* national

National Curriculum *n* (BrE) programme *m* scolaire national

National Front *n* (BrE) *parti britannique d'extrême droite*

National Health Service, **NHS** *n* (BrE) services *mpl* de santé britanniques, ≈ Sécurité *f* Sociale

National Insurance, **NI** *n* (BrE) securité *f* sociale britannique; **~ number** numéro *m* de sécurité sociale

nationalism /'næʃnəlɪzəm/ *n* nationalisme *m*

nationality /ˌnæʃə'nælətɪ/ *n* nationalité *f*

nationalize /'næʃnəlaɪz/ *vt* nationaliser ‹*industry*›

nationwide /ˌneɪʃn'waɪd/ **A** *adj* ‹*appeal, coverage, strike*› sur l'ensemble du territoire; ‹*campaign*› national/-e; ‹*survey, poll*› à l'échelle nationale
B *adv* dans tout le pays

native /'neɪtɪv/ **A** *n* autochtone *mf*; **to be a ~ of** être originaire de
B *adj* **1** ‹*land*› natal/-e; ‹*tongue*› maternel/-elle; **~ German speaker** personne *f* de langue maternelle allemande
2 ‹*flora, fauna, peoples*› indigène

Native American *n, adj* amérindien/-ienne *m/f*

Nativity /nə'tɪvətɪ/ *n* nativité *f*

NATO *n* (*abbr* = **North Atlantic Treaty Organization**) OTAN *f*

🔑 **natural** /'nætʃrəl/ *adj* **1** (gen) naturel/-elle
2 ‹*gift, talent*› inné/-e; ‹*artist, storyteller*› né/-e
3 (unaffected) simple, naturel/-elle

naturalize /'nætʃrəlaɪz/ *vt* naturaliser ‹*person*›; **to be ~d** se faire naturaliser

naturally /'nætʃrəlɪ/ *adv* **1** (obviously, of course) naturellement
2 (by nature) de nature; **politeness comes ~ to him** il est d'un naturel poli
3 ‹*behave, smile, speak*› avec naturel

🔑 **nature** /'neɪtʃə(r)/ *n* nature *f*; **let ~ take its course** laissez faire la nature; **it's not in her ~ to be aggressive** elle n'est pas agressive de nature; **it is in the ~ of things** il est dans l'ordre des choses

nature conservancy *n* protection *f* de la nature

nature reserve *n* réserve *f* naturelle

nature trail *n* sentier *m* écologique

naughty /'nɔːtɪ/ *adj* **1** (disobedient) vilain/-e
2 (rude) ‹*joke, picture, story*› coquin/-e

nausea /'nɔːsɪə, (AmE) 'nɔːʒə/ *n* nausée *f*

nauseating /'nɔːsɪeɪtɪŋ, (AmE) 'nɔːz-/ *adj* écœurant/-e

nauseous /'nɔːsɪəs, (AmE) 'nɔːʃəs/ *adj* ‹*taste, smell*› écœurant/-e; **to feel ~** avoir la nausée

nautical /'nɔːtɪkl/ *adj* nautique

naval /'neɪvl/ *adj* ‹*battle, forces, base*› naval/-e; ‹*officer, recruit, uniform, affairs*› de la marine

nave /neɪv/ *n* nef *f*

navel /'neɪvl/ *n* nombril *m*

navel ring *n* piercing *m* au nombril

navigate /'nævɪgeɪt/ **A** *vt* **1** parcourir ‹*seas*›
2 piloter ‹*plane*›; gouverner ‹*ship*›
B *vi* (in vessel, plane) naviguer; (in rally) faire le copilote; (on journey) tenir la carte

navigation /ˌnævɪ'geɪʃn/ *n* navigation *f*

navigator /'nævɪgeɪtə(r)/ *n* (in vessel, plane) navigateur/-trice *m/f*; (in car) copilote *mf*

navy /'neɪvɪ/ **A** *n* **1** (fleet) flotte *f*; (fighting force) marine *f*
2 (*also* **~ blue**) bleu *m* marine
B *adj* (*also* **~ blue**) bleu marine *inv*

Nazi /'nɑːtsɪ/ *n, adj* nazi/-e *m/f*

🔑 **near** /nɪə(r)/ **A** *adv* **1** (close) près; **to live quite ~** habiter tout près; **to move ~er** s'approcher davantage (**to** de); **to bring sth ~er** approcher qch
2 (nearly) **as ~ perfect as it could be** aussi proche de la perfection que possible; **nowhere ~ finished** loin d'être fini
B *prep* **1** près de; **~ here** près d'ici; **~ the beginning of the article** presque au début de l'article; **he's no ~er (making) a decision** il n'est pas plus décidé
2 (in time) **~er the time** quand la date approchera; **it's getting ~ Christmas** Noël approche
C *adj* proche; **in the ~ future** dans un avenir proche; **the ~est shops** les magasins les plus proches
D *vt* approcher de; **to ~ completion** toucher à sa fin
E **near enough** *phr* à peu près
F **near to** *phr* **1** (in space) près de; **~er to** plus près de
2 (on point of) au bord de ‹*tears, collapse*›
3 **to come ~ to doing** faillir faire

nearby /nɪə'baɪ/ **A** *adj* ‹*person*› qui se trouve/trouvait etc à proximité; ‹*town, village*› d'à côté
B *adv* tout près; ‹*park, stand, wait*› à proximité

🔑 **nearly** /'nɪəlɪ/ *adv* presque; **I very ~ gave up** j'ai bien failli abandonner; **not ~ as talented as** loin d'être aussi doué que

near miss *n* **to have a ~** ‹*planes*› frôler la collision; ‹*cars*› faillir se percuter

nearsighted *adj* (AmE) myope

neat /niːt/ **A** *adj* **1** ‹*person*› (in habits) ordonné/-e; (in appearance) soigné/-e;

🔑 mot clé

‹*room, house, desk*› bien rangé/-e; ‹*garden, handwriting*› soigné/-e
2 ‹*explanation, solution*› habile
3 ‹*figure*› bien fait/-e; ‹*features*› régulier/-ière
4 ‹*alcohol, spirits*› sans eau
B *adv* ‹*drink whisky*› sec, sans eau

neatly /ˈniːtlɪ/ *adv* **1** (tidily) ‹*dress, fold, arrange*› avec soin; ‹*write*› proprement
2 (perfectly) ‹*illustrate, summarize*› parfaitement; ‹*link*› habilement

necessarily /ˌnesəˈserəlɪ, ˈnesəsərəlɪ/ *adv* (definitely) forcément; (of necessity) nécessairement; **not ~** pas forcément

necessary /ˈnesəsərɪ, (AmE) -serɪ/ *adj* (gen) nécessaire; ‹*qualification*› requis/-e; **if ~, as ~** si besoin est; **it is ~ for him to do** il faut qu'il fasse

necessitate /nɪˈsesɪteɪt/ *vt* nécessiter

necessity /nɪˈsesətɪ/ *n* **1** (need) nécessité *f*; **from ~** par nécessité; **the ~ for** le besoin de
2 (essential item) **to be an absolute ~** être indispensable

neck /nek/ *n* **1** (of person) cou *m*; (of horse, donkey) encolure *f*
2 (collar) col *m*; (neckline) encolure *f*
3 (of bottle, vase, womb) col *m*
(IDIOMS) **to be ~ and ~** être à égalité; **to stick one's ~ out** (fam) prendre des risques

necklace /ˈneklɪs/ *n* collier *m*

neckline /ˈneklaɪn/ *n* encolure *f*

necktie *n* (AmE) cravate *f*

nectar /ˈnektə(r)/ *n* nectar *m*

nectarine /ˈnektərɪn/ *n* nectarine *f*, brugnon *m*

need /niːd/ **A** *modal aux* **you needn't finish it today** tu n'es pas obligé de le finir aujourd'hui; **~ he reply?** est-ce qu'il faut qu'il réponde?, est-ce qu'il doit répondre?; **I needn't have hurried** ce n'était pas la peine de me dépêcher, ce n'était pas la peine que je me dépêche
B *vt* **1** (require) **to ~ sth/to do** avoir besoin de qch/de faire; **more money is ~ed** nous avons besoin de plus d'argent; **everything you ~** tout ce qu'il vous faut; **everything you ~ to know about computers** tout ce que vous devez savoir sur les ordinateurs
2 (have to) **you'll ~ to work hard** il va falloir que tu travailles dur; **he didn't ~ to ask permission** il n'était pas obligé de demander la permission; **something ~ed to be done** il fallait faire quelque chose
C *n* **1** (necessity) nécessité *f* (**for** de); **I can't see the ~ for it** je n'en vois pas la nécessité; **to feel the ~ to do** éprouver le besoin de faire; **there's no ~ to wait** inutile d'attendre; **there's no ~ to worry** ce n'est pas la peine de s'inquiéter; **there's no ~, I've done it** inutile, c'est fait; **if ~ be** s'il le faut, si nécessaire
2 (want, requirement) besoin *m* (**for** de); **to be in ~ of sth** avoir besoin de qch
3 (poverty) **to be in ~** être dans le besoin

needle /ˈniːdl/ **A** *n* aiguille *f*
B *vt* harceler
(IDIOM) **to have pins and ~s** avoir des fourmis

needless /ˈniːdlɪs/ *adj* ‹*anxiety, suffering*› inutile; ‹*intrusion, intervention*› inopportun/-e

needlework *n* couture *f*

needy /ˈniːdɪ/ *adj* ‹*person*› nécessiteux/-euse; ‹*sector, area*› sans ressources

negate /nɪˈgeɪt/ *vt* (cancel out) réduire [qch] à néant

negative /ˈnegətɪv/ **A** *n* **1** (of photo) négatif *m*
2 (in grammar) négation *f*; **in the ~** à la forme négative
B *adj* (gen) négatif/-ive; ‹*effect, influence*› néfaste

neglect /nɪˈglekt/ **A** *n* **1** (of person) négligence *f*; (of building, garden) manque *m* d'entretien; (of health, appearance) manque *m* de soin
2 (lack of interest) indifférence *f* (**of** à l'égard de)
B *vt* **1** ne pas s'occuper de ‹*person, dog, plant*›; ne pas entretenir ‹*garden, house*›; négliger ‹*health, friend, work*›
2 (fail) **to ~ to do** négliger de faire

neglected /nɪˈglektɪd/ *adj* (gen) négligé/-e; ‹*garden, building*› mal entretenu/-e; **to feel ~** se sentir délaissé/-e

negligence /ˈneglɪdʒəns/ *n* négligence *f*

negligent /ˈneglɪdʒənt/ *adj* ‹*person, procedure*› négligent/-e; ‹*air, manner*› nonchalant/-e

negligible /ˈneglɪdʒəbl/ *adj* négligeable

negotiable /nɪˈgəʊʃəbl/ *adj* **1** ‹*rate, terms*› négociable
2 ‹*road, pass*› praticable; ‹*obstacle*› franchissable

negotiate /nɪˈgəʊʃɪeɪt/ **A** *vt* **1** (in business, diplomacy) négocier
2 négocier ‹*bend*›; franchir ‹*obstacle*›
B *vi* négocier (**with** avec, **for** pour obtenir)
C **negotiated** *pp adj* ‹*settlement, peace*› négocié/-e

negotiation /nɪˌgəʊʃɪˈeɪʃn/ *n* négociation *f*; **to be under ~** être en cours de négociations

negotiator /nɪˈgəʊʃɪeɪtə(r)/ *n* négociateur/-trice *m/f*

neigh /neɪ/ *vi* hennir

neighbour (BrE), **neighbor** (AmE) /ˈneɪbə(r)/ *n* voisin/-e *m/f*

neighbourhood (BrE), **neighborhood** (AmE) /ˈneɪbəhʊd/ *n* **1** (district) quartier *m*
2 (vicinity) **in the ~** dans le voisinage

neighbouring (BrE), **neighboring** (AmE) /ˈneɪbərɪŋ/ *adj* voisin/-e

neither /ˈnaɪðə(r), ˈniːð-/ **A** *conj* **I have ~ the time nor the money** je n'ai ni le temps

n

ni l'argent; ~ **tea, nor milk** ni (le) thé, ni (le) lait; **'I can't sleep'—'~ can I'** 'je n'arrive pas à dormir'—'moi non plus'
B *det* aucun/-e des deux; ~ **book is suitable** aucun des deux livres ne convient; ~ **girl replied** aucune des deux filles n'a répondu
C *pron, quantif* ni l'un/-e ni l'autre *m/f*; ~ **of them came** ni l'un ni l'autre n'est venu

neon /'ni:ɒn/ **A** *n* néon *m*
B *adj* ‹*light, sign*› au néon; ‹*atom*› de néon

nephew /'nevju:, 'nef-/ *n* neveu *m*

Neptune /'neptju:n/ *pr n* (planet) Neptune *f*

nerve /nɜ:v/ **A** *n* **1** (Anat) nerf *m*; (Bot) nervure *f*
2 (courage) courage *m*; **to lose one's** ~ perdre son courage
3 (fam) (cheek) culot *m* (fam); **you've got a ~!** tu as un sacré culot! (fam)
B nerves *npl* (gen) nerfs *mpl*; (stage fright) trac *m* (fam); **to get on sb's ~s** taper sur les nerfs de qn

nerve-racking *adj* (*also* **nerve-wracking**) angoissant/-e

nervous /'nɜ:vəs/ *adj* **1** ‹*person*› (fearful) timide; (anxious) angoissé/-e; (highly strung) nerveux/-euse; ‹*smile, laugh, habit*› nerveux/-euse; **to be ~ about doing** avoir peur de faire; **to feel** ~ (apprehensive) être angoissé/-e; (before performance) avoir le trac (fam); (afraid) avoir peur; (ill at ease) se sentir mal à l'aise
2 (Anat, Med) nerveux/-euse

nervous breakdown *n* dépression *f* nerveuse

nervously /'nɜ:vəslɪ/ *adv* nerveusement

nervous wreck *n* (fam) boule *f* de nerfs (fam)

nest /nest/ **A** *n* **1** (of bird, animal) nid *m*
2 ~ of tables tables *fpl* gigognes
B *vi* ‹*bird*› faire son nid

nest egg *n* magot *m* (fam)

nestle /'nesl/ *vi* **1** ‹*person, animal*› se blottir (**against** contre, **under** sous)
2 ‹*village, house*› être niché/-e

net /net/ **A** *n* (gen) filet *m*; (in football) filets *mpl*
B *adj* (*also* **nett**) (gen) net/nette; ‹*loss*› sec/sèche
C *vt* (*p prés etc* **-tt-**) **1** prendre [qch] au filet ‹*fish*›
2 (financially) ‹*person*› faire un bénéfice de; ‹*sale, export, deal*› rapporter

Net /net/ *n* Net *m*

netball *n: sport d'équipe proche du basket joué par les femmes*

net curtain *n* voilage *m*

Netherlands /'neðələndz/ *pr n* **the ~** les Pays-Bas *mpl*, la Hollande

netiquette /'netɪket/ *n* netiquette *f*

netspeak /'netspi:k/ *n* jargon *m* Internet

netting /'netɪŋ/ *n* (of rope) filet *m*; (of metal, plastic) grillage *m*; (fabric) voile *m*

nettle /'netl/ *n* (*also* **stinging ~**) ortie *f*

✓ **network** /'netwɜ:k/ **A** *n* réseau *m* (**of** de)
B *vt* (Comput) interconnecter
C *vi* tisser un réseau de relations

networking /'netwɜ:kɪŋ/ *n* **1** (Comput) interconnexion *f*
2 (establishing contacts) ~ **is important** c'est important d'avoir des contacts

network television *n* (AmE) chaîne *f* nationale

neurosis /njʊə'rəʊsɪs, (AmE) nʊ-/ *n* (*pl* **-oses**) névrose *f*

neurotic /njʊə'rɒtɪk, (AmE) nʊ-/ *adj* névrosé/-e

neuter /'nju:tə(r), (AmE) 'nu:-/ **A** *n* neutre *m*
B *adj* neutre
C *vt* châtrer ‹*animal*›

neutral /'nju:trəl, (AmE) 'nu:-/ **A** *n* (Aut) **in/into** ~ au point mort
B *adj* neutre (**about** en ce qui concerne)

neutrality /nju:'trælətɪ, (AmE) nu:-/ *n* neutralité *f*

neutralize /'nju:trəlaɪz, (AmE) 'nu:-/ *vt* neutraliser

✓ **never** /'nevə(r)/ *adv* **1** (not ever) **I ~ go to London** je ne vais jamais à Londres; **she ~ says anything** elle ne dit jamais rien; **it's now or ~** c'est le moment ou jamais; **~ again** plus jamais; **~ lie to me again!** ne me mens plus jamais!
2 (emphatic negative) **he ~ said a word** il n'a rien dit; **I ~ knew that** je ne le savais pas; **he ~ so much as apologized** il ne s'est même pas excusé

never-ending *adj* interminable

nevertheless /ˌnevəðə'les/ *adv* **1** (all the same) quand même
2 (nonetheless) pourtant, néanmoins

✓ **new** /nju:, (AmE) nu:/ *adj* nouveau/-elle *before n*; (brand new) neuf/neuve; **I bought a ~ computer** (to replace old one) j'ai acheté un nouvel ordinateur; (a brand new model) j'ai acheté un ordinateur neuf; **as good as ~** comme neuf; **to be ~ to** ne pas être habitué/-e à ‹*job, way of life*›; **we're ~ to the area** nous sommes nouveaux venus dans la région

New Age *adj* ‹*music, traveller*› New Age *inv*

newborn /'nju:bɔ:n, (AmE) 'nu:-/ *adj* nouveau-né/-née

new build *n* nouvelle construction *f*

newcomer /'nju:kʌmə(r), (AmE) 'nu:-/ *n* (in place, job, club) nouveau venu/nouvelle venue *m/f*; (in sport, theatre, cinema) nouveau/-elle *m/f*

new-found /'nju:ˌfaʊnd/ *adj* tout nouveau/toute nouvelle

new look **A** *n* nouveau style *m*
B new-look *adj* ‹*product*› nouvelle

✓ mot clé

version *inv*; ‹*car, team*› nouveau/-elle *before n*; ‹*edition, show*› remanié/-e

newly /ˈnjuːlɪ, (AmE) ˈnuː-/ *adv* ‹*arrived, built, formed, qualified*› nouvellement; ‹*washed*› fraîchement

newly-weds *npl* jeunes mariés *mpl*

⚷ **news** /njuːz, (AmE) nuːz/ *n* **1** nouvelle(s) *f(pl)*; **a piece of ~** une nouvelle; (in newspaper) une information; **have you heard the ~?** tu connais la nouvelle?
2 (on radio, TV) **the ~** les informations *fpl*, le journal *m*

news agency *n* agence *f* de presse

newsagent's *n* (BrE) magasin *m* de journaux

news bulletin (BrE), **newscast** (AmE) *n* bulletin *m* d'information

newscaster *n* présentateur/-trice *m/f* des informations

news conference *n* conférence *f* de presse

news dealer *n* (AmE) marchand *m* de journaux

news editor *n* rédacteur/-trice *m/f*

newsgroup *n* forum *m* de discussion

news headlines *npl* (on TV) titres *mpl* de l'actualité

news item *n* sujet *m* d'actualité

newsletter *n* bulletin *m*

⚷ **newspaper** /ˈnjuːspeɪpə(r), (AmE) ˈnuːz-/ *n* journal *m*

newsreader *n* (BrE) présentateur/-trice *m/f* des informations

newsreel *n* actualités *fpl*

news stand *n* kiosque *m* à journaux

New Year *n* le nouvel an *m*; **to see in the ~** fêter la Saint-Sylvestre; **Happy ~!** bonne année!

New Year's day (BrE), **New Year's** (AmE) *n* le jour *m* de l'an

New Year's Eve *n* la Saint-Sylvestre

New Zealand /ˌnjuːˈziːlənd, (AmE) ˌnuː-/ *pr n* Nouvelle-Zélande *f*

⚷ **next** /nekst/

> When *next* is used as an adjective, it is generally translated by *prochain* when referring to something which is still to come or happen and by *suivant* when it generally means *following*: *I'll be 40 next year* = j'aurai 40 ans l'année prochaine; *the next year, he went to Spain* = l'année suivante il est allé en Espagne.
> For examples and further usages see the entry below.

A *pron* **from one minute to the ~** d'un instant à l'autre; **the week after ~** dans deux semaines
B *adj* **1** prochain/-e, suivant/-e; **get the ~ train** prenez le prochain train; **he got on the ~ train** il a pris le train suivant; **'~!'** 'au suivant!'; **'you're ~'** 'c'est à vous'; **the ~ size (up)** la taille au-dessus; **~ Thursday** jeudi prochain; **he's due to arrive in the ~ 10 minutes** il devrait arriver d'ici 10 minutes; **this time ~ week** dans une semaine; **the ~ day** le lendemain
2 ‹*room, street*› voisin/-e; ‹*building, house*› voisin/-e, d'à côté
C *adv* **1** (afterwards) ensuite, après; **what happened ~?** que s'est-il passé ensuite?
2 (on a future occasion) **when I ~ go there** la prochaine fois que j'irai
3 (in order) **the ~ tallest is Patrick** ensuite c'est Patrick qui est le plus grand
D **next to** *phr* **1** (almost) presque; **~ to impossible** presque impossible; **to get sth for ~ to nothing** avoir qch pour quasiment rien; **in ~ to no time it was over** en un rien de temps c'était fini
2 (beside, close to) à côté de; **two seats ~ to each other** deux sièges l'un à côté de l'autre; **to wear silk ~ to the skin** porter de la soie à même la peau

next door **A** *adj* (*also* **next-door**) d'à côté
B *adv* ‹*live, move in*› à côté

next-door neighbour *n* voisin/-e *m/f* (d'à côté)

next of kin *n* **to be sb's ~** être le parent le plus proche de qn

NGO *n* (*abbr* = **Non-Governmental Organization**) ONG *f*

nib /nɪb/ *n* plume *f*

nibble /ˈnɪbl/ *vi* ‹*animal*› mordiller; ‹*person*› grignoter

⚷ **nice** /naɪs/ *adj* **1** ‹*drive, holiday, place*› agréable; ‹*house, picture, outfit, weather*› beau/belle *before n*; **did you have a ~ time?** tu t'es bien amusé?; **~ to have met you** ravi d'avoir fait votre connaissance; **have a ~ day!** bonne journée!; **you look very ~** tu es très chic
2 (tasty) bon/bonne *before n*; **to taste ~** avoir bon goût
3 ‹*person*› sympathique; **to be ~ to sb** être gentil/-ille avec qn
4 ‹*neighbourhood, school*› comme il faut *inv*; **it is not ~ to tell lies** ce n'est pas bien de mentir
IDIOM **~ one!** (in admiration) bravo!; (ironic) il ne manquait plus que ça!

nice-looking *adj* beau/belle *before n*

nicely /ˈnaɪslɪ/ *adv* **1** (kindly) gentiment
2 (attractively) agréablement
3 (politely) poliment
4 (satisfactorily) bien; **that'll do ~** cela fera l'affaire

niche /nɪtʃ, niːʃ/ *n* (recess) niche *f*; (fig) place *f*; (in the market) créneau *m*

niche market *n* marché *m* spécialisé

nick /nɪk/ **A** *n* encoche *f* (**in** dans)
B *vt* **1** (cut) faire une entaille dans
2 (BrE) (fam) (steal) piquer (fam)
C (BrE) (arrest) pincer (fam)
IDIOM **just in the ~ of time** juste à temps

nickel /'nɪkl/ *n* **1** (AmE) pièce *f* de cinq cents **2** (metal) nickel *m*

nickname /'nɪkneɪm/ **A** *n* surnom *m* **B** *vt* surnommer

nicotine /'nɪkətiːn/ *n* nicotine *f*

nicotine patch *n* patch *m* à la nicotine

niece /niːs/ *n* nièce *f*

niggle /'nɪgl/ (fam) **A** *n* (complaint) remarque *f*; **I've a ~ at the back of my mind** il y a quelque chose qui me travaille **B** *vt* (irritate) tracasser

niggling /'nɪglɪŋ/ *adj* ‹*doubt, worry*› insidieux/-ieuse

⚷ **night** /naɪt/ *n* nuit *f*; (before going to bed) soir *m*; **at ~** la nuit; **all ~ long** toute la nuit; **late at ~** tard le soir; **he arrived last ~** il est arrivé hier soir; **I slept badly last ~** j'ai mal dormi cette nuit *or* la nuit dernière; **the ~ before last** avant-hier soir; **on Tuesday ~s** le mardi soir; **to get an early ~** se coucher tôt; **a ~ at the opera** une soirée à l'opéra

nightclub *n* boîte *f* de nuit

nightclubbing *n* **to go ~** aller en boîte (fam)

nightdress *n* chemise *f* de nuit

nightingale /'naɪtɪŋgeɪl, (AmE) -tng-/ *n* rossignol *m*

nightlife /'naɪtlaɪf/ *n* vie *f* nocturne

nightmare /'naɪtmeə(r)/ *n* cauchemar *m*; **to have a ~** faire un cauchemar

night school *n* cours *mpl* du soir

n **night shelter** *n* asile *m* de nuit

night shift *n* (period) **to be/work on the ~** être/travailler de nuit; (workers) équipe *f* de nuit

nightshirt *n* chemise *f* de nuit (d'homme)

nightspot *n* (fam) boite *f* de nuit

night-time /'naɪttaɪm/ *n* nuit *f*; **at ~** la nuit

night watchman *n* veilleur *m* de nuit

nil /nɪl/ *n* (gen) néant *m*; (BrE) (Sport) zéro *m*

Nile /naɪl/ *pr n* Nil *m*

nimble /'nɪmbl/ *adj* ‹*person*› agile; ‹*fingers*› habile

⚷ **nine** /naɪn/ *n, pron, det* neuf *m inv*

nineteen /ˌnaɪn'tiːn/ *n, pron, det* dix-neuf *m inv*

IDIOM **to talk ~ to the dozen** (BrE) parler à n'en plus finir

nineteenth /ˌnaɪn'tiːnθ/ **A** *n* **1** (in order) dix-neuvième *mf* **2** (of month) dix-neuf *m inv* **3** (fraction) dix-neuvième *m* **B** *adj, adv* dix-neuvième

nineties *npl* **1** (era) **the ~** les années *fpl* quatre-vingt-dix **2** (age) **to be in one's ~** avoir entre quatre-vingt-dix et cent ans

ninetieth /'naɪntɪəθ/ *n, adj, adv* quatre-vingt-dixième *mf*

nine-to-five /ˌnaɪntə'faɪv/ *adj* ‹*job, routine*› de bureau

ninety /'naɪntɪ/ *n, pron, det* quatre-vingt-dix *m inv*

ninth /naɪnθ/ **A** *n* **1** (in order) neuvième *mf* **2** (of month) neuf *m inv* **3** (fraction) neuvième *m* **B** *adj, adv* neuvième

nip /nɪp/ **A** *n* (pinch) pincement *m*; (bite) morsure *f*; **there's a ~ in the air** il fait frisquet (fam) **B** *vt* (*p prés etc* **-pp-**) (pinch) pincer; (bite) donner un petit coup de dent à; (playfully) mordiller **C** *vi* (*p prés etc* **-pp-**) (bite) mordre; (playfully) mordiller

nipple /'nɪpl/ *n* mamelon *m*

nippy /'nɪpɪ/ *adj* (fam) **1** (cold) **it's a bit ~** il fait frisquet (fam) **2** (BrE) (quick) ‹*person*› vif/vive; ‹*car*› rapide

nit /nɪt/ *n* (egg) lente *f*; (larva) larve *f* de pou

nit-pick *vi* chercher la petite bête (fam), pinailler (fam)

nitrogen /'naɪtrədʒən/ *n* azote *m*

nitty-gritty /ˌnɪtɪ'grɪtɪ/ *n* (fam) **to get down to the ~** passer aux choses sérieuses

⚷ **no** /nəʊ/ **A** *particle* non; **~ thanks** non merci **B** *det* **1** (none, not any) aucun/-e; **to have ~ money** ne pas avoir d'argent; **she has ~ talent** elle n'a aucun talent; **of ~ interest** sans intérêt **2** (prohibiting) **~ smoking** défense de fumer; **~ parking** stationnement interdit; **~ talking!** silence! **3** (for emphasis) **he's ~ expert** ce n'est certes pas un expert; **this is ~ time to cry** ce n'est pas le moment de pleurer **4** (hardly any) **in ~ time** en un rien de temps **C** *adv* **it's ~ further/easier** ce n'est pas plus loin/facile; **I ~ longer work there** je n'y travaille plus; **~ later than Wednesday** pas plus tard que mercredi

no., No. (*written abbr* = **number**) n°

nobility /nəʊ'bɪlətɪ/ *n* noblesse *f*

noble /'nəʊbl/ *n, adj* noble *m*

⚷ **nobody** /'nəʊbədɪ/ **A** *pron* (*also* **no one**) personne; **~ saw her** personne ne l'a vue; **there was ~ in the car** il n'y avait personne dans la voiture; **I heard ~** je n'ai entendu personne; **~ but me** personne sauf moi **B** *n* **to be a ~** être insignifiant/-e

nocturnal /nɒk'tɜːnl/ *adj* nocturne

⚷ **nod** /nɒd/ **A** *n* **she gave him a ~** elle lui a fait un signe de (la) tête; (as greeting) elle l'a salué d'un signe de tête; (indicating assent) elle a fait oui de la tête **B** *vt* (*p prés etc* **-dd-**) **to ~ one's head** faire un signe de tête; (to indicate assent) hocher la tête **C** *vi* (*p prés etc* **-dd-**) faire un signe de tête (**to** à); (in assent) faire oui de la tête

no-go area *n* quartier *m* chaud (*où la police etc ne s'aventure plus*)

⚷ mot clé

no-hoper *n* (fam) raté/-e *m/f* (fam)

noise /nɔɪz/ *n* bruit *m*; (shouting) tapage *m*; **to make a ~** faire du bruit

noisy /'nɔɪzɪ/ *adj* ‹*person, place*› bruyant/-e; ‹*meeting, protest*› tumultueux/-euse

nomad /'nəʊmæd/ *n* nomade *mf*

nominal /'nɒmɪnl/ *adj* (gen) nominal/-e; ‹*fee, sum*› minime; ‹*fine*› symbolique

nominate /'nɒmɪneɪt/ *vt* **1** (propose) proposer; **to ~ sb for a prize** sélectionner qn pour un prix
2 (appoint) nommer (**to sth** à qch); **to ~ sb (as) chairman** nommer qn président

nomination /ˌnɒmɪ'neɪʃn/ *n* (as candidate) proposition *f* de candidat; (for award) sélection *f*; (appointment) nomination *f* (**to** à)

nominative /'nɒmɪnətɪv/ *n, adj* nominatif *m*

non-addictive /ˌnɒnə'dɪktɪv/ *adj* qui ne crée pas de dépendance

non-alcoholic /ˌnɒnælkə'hɒlɪk/ *adj* non alcoolisé/-e

non-believer /ˌnɒnbɪ'liːvə(r)/ *n* non-croyant/-e *m/f*

nonchalant /'nɒnʃələnt/ *adj* nonchalant/-e

non-committal /ˌnɒnkə'mɪtl/ *adj* évasif/-ive

non-compliance /ˌnɒnkəm'plaɪəns/ *n* (with standards) non-conformité *f* (**with** à); (with orders) non-obéissance *f* (**with** à)

nonconformist /ˌnɒnkən'fɔːmɪst/ *adj* non conformiste

non-cooperation /ˌnɒnkəʊˌɒpə'reɪʃn/ *n* refus *m* de coopération

non-denominational /ˌnɒndɪˌnɒmɪ'neɪʃənl/ *adj* ‹*church*› œcuménique; ‹*school*› laïque

nondescript /'nɒndɪskrɪpt/ *adj* ‹*person, clothes*› insignifiant/-e; ‹*building*› quelconque

non-disclosure agreement *n* (Law) accord *m* de confidentialité

none /nʌn/ *pron* **1** (not any) aucun/-e *m/f*; **~ of us/them** aucun de nous/d'entre eux; **~ of the wine was French** il n'y avait aucun vin français; **~ of the milk had been drunk** on n'avait pas touché au lait; **~ of the bread was fresh** tout le pain était rassis; **we have ~** nous n'en avons pas; **there's ~ left** il n'y en a plus; **~ of it was true** il n'y avait rien de vrai
2 (nobody) personne; **~ but him** personne sauf lui

nonentity /nɒ'nentətɪ/ *n* (person) personne *f* insignifiante

non-essentials /ˌnɒnɪ'senʃlz/ *npl* (objects) accessoires *mpl*; (details) accessoire *m sg*

nonetheless /ˌnʌnðə'les/ *adv* pourtant, néanmoins

non-existent /ˌnɒnɪg'zɪstənt/ *adj* inexistant/-e

non-fiction /ˌnɒn'fɪkʃn/ *n* œuvres *fpl* non fictionnelles

no-nonsense *adj* ‹*manner, attitude, policy*› direct/-e; ‹*person*› franc/franche

nonplussed /ˌnɒn'plʌst/ *adj* perplexe

non-profit-making /ˌnɒn'prɒfɪtmeɪkɪŋ/ *adj* ‹*organization*› à but non lucratif

non-resident /ˌnɒn'resɪdənt/ *n* non-résident/-e *m/f*

nonsense /'nɒnsns, (AmE) -sens/ *n* (foolishness) absurdités *fpl*; **to talk/write ~** dire/écrire n'importe quoi; **~!** balivernes! *fpl*; **I won't stand for this ~** j'en ai assez de ces bêtises

non-smoker /ˌnɒn'sməʊkə(r)/ *n* non-fumeur/-euse *m/f*

non-smoking *adj* non fumeur *inv*

non-starter /ˌnɒn'stɑːtə(r)/ *n* **to be a ~** ‹*plan, idea*› être voué/-e à l'échec

non-stick /ˌnɒn'stɪk/ *adj* antiadhésif/-ive

non-stop /ˌnɒn'stɒp/ **A** *adj* ‹*journey*› sans arrêt; ‹*train, flight*› direct/-e; ‹*noise*› incessant/-e
B *adv* ‹*work, talk, drive, argue*› sans arrêt; ‹*fly*› sans escale

non-taxable /ˌnɒn'taksabl/ *adj* non imposable

noodles *npl* nouilles *fpl*

nook /nʊk/ *n* coin *m*; **every ~ and cranny** tous les coins et recoins

noon /nuːn/ *n* midi *m*; **at 12 ~** à midi

no one /'nəʊ wʌn/ = **nobody A**

noose /nuːs/ *n* (loop) nœud *m* coulant; (for hanging) corde *f*

nor /nɔː(r), nə(r)/ *conj* **~ do I** moi non plus; **~ can he** lui non plus; **he was not a cruel man, ~ a mean one** il n'était ni cruel, ni méchant; **she hasn't written, ~ has she telephoned** elle n'a pas écrit, et elle n'a pas téléphoné non plus

norm /nɔːm/ *n* norme *f* (**for** pour, **to do** de faire)

normal /'nɔːml/ **A** *n* normale *f*; **above/below ~** au-dessus/en dessous de la norme
B *adj* (gen) normal/-e; ‹*place, time*› habituel/-elle

normality /nɔː'mælətɪ/ *n* normalité *f*

normally /'nɔːməlɪ/ *adv* normalement

Normandy /'nɔːməndɪ/ *pr n* Normandie *f*

north /nɔːθ/ **A** *n* **1** (compass direction) nord *m*
2 (part of world, country) **the North** le Nord
B *adj* (gen) nord *inv*; ‹*wind*› du nord; **in ~ London** dans le nord de Londres
C *adv* ‹*move*› vers le nord; ‹*lie, live*› au nord (**of** de)

North Africa *pr n* Afrique *f* du Nord

North America *pr n* Amérique *f* du Nord

north-east /ˌnɔːθ'iːst/ **A** *n* nord-est *m*
B *adj* ‹*coast, side*› nord-est *inv*; ‹*wind*› de nord-est
C *adv* ‹*move*› vers le nord-est; ‹*lie, live*› au nord-est (**of** de)

northern /'nɔːðən/ *adj* ‹*coast*› nord *inv*;

‹*town, accent*› du nord; ‹*hemisphere*› Nord *inv*; ~ **England** le nord de l'Angleterre

Northern Ireland *pr n* Irlande *f* du Nord

North Pole *pr n* pôle *m* Nord

North Sea *pr n* **the** ~ la mer du Nord

north-west /ˌnɔːθ'west/ **A** *n* nord-ouest *m*
B *adj* ‹*coast*› nord-ouest *inv*; ‹*wind*› de nord-ouest
C *adv* ‹*move*› vers le nord-ouest; ‹*lie, live*› au nord-ouest (**of** de)

Norway /'nɔːweɪ/ *pr n* Norvège *f*

Norwegian /nɔː'wiːdʒən/ **A** *n* **1** (person) Norvégien/-ienne *m/f*
2 (language) norvégien *m*
B *adj* norvégien/-ienne

⚷ **nose** /nəʊz/ *n* nez *m*
IDIOMS **to look down one's ~ at sb/sth** prendre qn/qch de haut; **to turn one's ~ up at sth** faire le dégoûté/la dégoûtée devant qch; **to poke** *or* **stick one's ~ into sth** (fam) fourrer son nez dans qch (fam)
■ **nose about, nose around** fouiner (**in** dans)

nosebleed *n* saignement *m* de nez

nose-dive /'nəʊzdaɪv/ *n* piqué *m*; **to go into a ~** ‹*plane*› faire un piqué; (fig) chuter

nose ring *n* piercing *m* au nez

nostalgia /nɒ'stældʒə/ *n* nostalgie *f*

nostalgic /nɒ'stældʒɪk/ *adj* nostalgique

nostril /'nɒstrɪl/ *n* (of person) narine *f*; (of horse) naseau *m*

nosy /'nəʊzɪ/ *adj* (fam) fouineur/-euse (fam)

⚷ **not** /nɒt/ **A** *adv* **1** (with a verb) ne...pas; **she isn't at home** elle n'est pas chez elle; **we won't need a car** nous n'aurons pas besoin d'une voiture; **hasn't he seen it?** il ne l'a pas vu alors?; **I hope ~** j'espère que non; **certainly ~** sûrement pas; **~ only** *or* **just** non seulement; **whether it rains or ~** qu'il pleuve ou non; **why ~?** pourquoi pas?; **~ everyone likes it** ça ne plaît pas à tout le monde; **it's ~ every day that** ce n'est pas tous les jours que; **~ a sound was heard** on n'entendait pas un bruit; **~ bad** pas mal
2 (in question tags) **she's English, isn't she?** elle est anglaise, n'est-ce pas?; **he likes fish, doesn't he?** il aime le poisson, n'est-ce pas?
B **not at all** *phr* (in no way) pas du tout; (responding to thanks) de rien
C **not that** *phr* **~ that I know of** pas (autant) que je sache; **if she refuses, ~ that she will...** si elle refuse, je ne dis pas qu'elle le fera...

notable /'nəʊtəbl/ *adj* ‹*person*› remarquable; ‹*event, success, difference*› notable

notably /'nəʊtəblɪ/ *adv* (in particular) notamment; (markedly) remarquablement

notch /nɒtʃ/ **A** *n* entaille *f*
B *vt* encocher ‹*stick*›
■ **notch up** (fam) remporter ‹*point, prize*›

⚷ **note** /nəʊt/ **A** *n* **1** (gen) note *f*; (short letter) mot *m*; **to take ~ of** prendre note de
2 (Mus) (sound, symbol) note *f*; (piano key) touche *f*
3 **(bank) ~** billet *m*
B *vt* noter
C **of note** *phr* ‹*person*› éminent/-e, réputé/-e; ‹*development*› digne d'intérêt
IDIOM **to compare ~s** échanger ses impressions (**with** avec)
■ **note down** noter

notebook /'nəʊtbʊk/ *n* **1** carnet *m*
2 (Comput) ordinateur *m* portable

noted *adj* ‹*intellectual, criminal*› célèbre; **to be ~ for** être réputé/-e pour

notepad *n* bloc-notes *m*

notepaper *n* papier *m* à lettres

noteworthy /'nəʊtwɜːðɪ/ *adj* remarquable

⚷ **nothing** /'nʌθɪŋ/

> When *nothing* is used alone as a reply to a question in English, it is translated by *rien*: *'what are you doing?'—'nothing'* = 'que fais-tu?'—'rien'.
>
> *Nothing* as a pronoun, when it is the subject of a verb, is translated by *rien ne* (+ verb or, in compound tenses, + auxiliary verb): *nothing changes* = rien ne change; *nothing has changed* = rien n'a changé.
>
> *Nothing* as a pronoun, when it is the object of a verb, is translated by *ne...rien*; *ne* comes before the verb, and before the auxiliary in compound tenses, and *rien* comes after the verb or auxiliary: *I see nothing* = je ne vois rien; *I saw nothing* = je n'ai rien vu.
>
> When *ne rien* is used with an infinitive, the two words are not separated: *I prefer to say nothing* = je préfère ne rien dire.
>
> For more examples and particular usages, see the entry below.

A *pron* **I knew ~ about it** je n'en savais rien; **we can do ~ (about it)** nous n'y pouvons rien; **~ much** pas grand-chose; **~ else** rien d'autre; **I had ~ to do with it!** je n'y étais pour rien!; **it's ~ to do with us** ça ne nous regarde pas; **to stop at ~** ne reculer devant rien (**to do** pour faire); **he means ~ to me** il n'est rien pour moi; **the names meant ~ to him** les noms ne lui disaient rien; **for ~** (for free) gratuitement; (pointlessly) pour rien
B *adv* **it is ~ like as difficult as** c'est loin d'être aussi difficile que; **she is** *or* **looks ~ like her sister** elle ne ressemble pas du tout à sa sœur
C **nothing but** *phr* **he's ~ but a coward** ce n'est qu'un lâche; **they've done ~ but moan** ils n'ont fait que râler (fam); **it's caused me ~ but trouble** ça ne m'a valu que des ennuis

⚷ **notice** /'nəʊtɪs/ **A** *n* **1** (written sign) pancarte *f*; (advertisement) annonce *f*; (announcing birth,

n

marriage, death) avis *m*
2 (attention) attention *f*; **to take ~** faire attention (**of** à); **to take no ~ (of)** ne pas faire attention (à)
3 (notification) préavis *m*; **one month's ~** un mois de préavis; **until further ~** jusqu'à nouvel ordre; **at short ~** à la dernière minute; **to give in one's ~** donner sa démission
B *vt* remarquer ‹*absence, mark*›; **to get oneself ~d** se faire remarquer

noticeable /'nəʊtɪsəbl/ *adj* visible

noticeboard *n* (BrE) panneau *m* d'affichage

notification /ˌnəʊtɪfɪ'keɪʃn/ *n* notification *f*; (in newspaper) avis *m*; **to receive ~ that** être avisé/-e que

notify /'nəʊtɪfaɪ/ *vt* notifier; **to ~ sb of** aviser qn de ‹*result, incident*›; avertir qn de ‹*intention*›; informer qn de ‹*birth, death*›

notion /'nəʊʃn/ *n* **1** (idea) idée *f*
2 (understanding) notion *f*

notorious /nəʊ'tɔːrɪəs/ *adj* ‹*criminal, organization*› notoire; ‹*district*› mal famé/-e; ‹*case*› tristement célèbre

notoriously /nəʊ'tɔːrɪəslɪ/ *adv* notoirement; **they're ~ unreliable** il est bien connu qu'on ne peut pas compter sur eux

notwithstanding /ˌnɒtwɪθ'stændɪŋ/ **A** *adv* néanmoins
B *prep* (in spite of) en dépit de; (excepted) exception faite de

nought /nɔːt/ *n* zéro *m*

noun /naʊn/ *n* nom *m*, substantif *m*

nourish /'nʌrɪʃ/ *vt* nourrir (**with** avec, **on** de)

nourishment /'nʌrɪʃmənt/ *n* nourriture *f*

novel /'nɒvl/ **A** *n* roman *m*
B *adj* original/-e

novelist /'nɒvəlɪst/ *n* romancier/-ière *m/f*

novelty /'nɒvəltɪ/ *n* nouveauté *f* (**of doing** de faire)

November /nə'vembə(r)/ *n* novembre *m*

novice /'nɒvɪs/ *n* débutant/-e *m/f*; (in religious order) novice *mf*

now /naʊ/ **A** *conj* **~ (that)** maintenant que
B *adv* **1** maintenant; **do it ~** fais-le maintenant; **right ~** tout de suite; **any time ~** d'un moment à l'autre; **(every) ~ and then** *or* **again** de temps en temps
2 (with preposition) **you should have phoned him before ~** tu aurais dû lui téléphoner avant; **before** *or* **until ~** jusqu'à présent; **he should be finished by ~** il devrait avoir déjà fini; **between ~ and next Friday** d'ici vendredi prochain; **between ~ and then** d'ici là; **from ~ on(wards)** dorénavant
3 (in the past) **it was ~ 4 pm** il était alors 16 heures; **by ~ it was too late** à ce moment-là, il était trop tard
4 ~ there's a man I can trust! ah! voilà un homme en qui on peut avoir confiance!; **careful ~!** attention!; **~ then, let's get back to work** bon, reprenons le travail

nowadays /'naʊədeɪz/ *adv* (these days) de nos jours; (now) actuellement

nowhere /'nəʊweə(r)/ **A** *adv* nulle part; **I've got ~ else to go** je n'ai nulle part où aller; **there's ~ to sit down** il n'y a pas d'endroit pour s'asseoir; **all this talk is getting us ~** tout ce bavardage ne nous avance à rien; **flattery will get you ~!** tu n'arriveras à rien en me flattant
B nowhere near *phr* loin de; **~ near sufficient** loin d'être suffisant/-e

noxious /'nɒkʃəs/ *adj* nocif/-ive

nozzle /'nɒzl/ *n* (of hose, pipe) ajutage *m*; (of hoover) suceur *m*; (for icing) douille *f*

nuance /'njuːɑːs, (AmE) 'nuː-/ *n* nuance *f*

nuclear /'njuːklɪə(r), (AmE) 'nuː-/ *adj* nucléaire

nuclear bomb *n* bombe *f* atomique

nuclear deterrent *n* force *f* de dissuasion nucléaire

nuclear energy, **nuclear power** *n* énergie *f* nucléaire *or* atomique

nuclear power station *n* centrale *f* nucléaire

nuclear waste *n* déchets *mpl* nucléaires

nucleus /'njuːklɪəs, (AmE) 'nuː-/ *n* (*pl* **-clei**) noyau *m*

nude /njuːd, (AmE) nuːd/ **A** *n* nu/-e *m/f*; **in the ~** nu/-e
B *adj* ‹*person*› nu/-e

nudge /nʌdʒ/ *vt* (push) pousser du coude; (accidentally) heurter; (brush against) frôler

nudist /'njuːdɪst, (AmE) 'nuː-/ *n*, *adj* nudiste *mf*

nugget /'nʌgɪt/ *n* pépite *f*

nuisance /'njuːsns, (AmE) 'nuː-/ *n* (gen) embêtement *m*; (Law) nuisance *f*; **what a ~!** que c'est agaçant!

nuisance call *n* appel *m* anonyme

null /nʌl/ *adj* (Law) **~ and void** nul et non avenu

nullify /'nʌlɪfaɪ/ *vt* invalider, annuler

numb /nʌm/ **A** *adj* **1** (from cold) engourdi/-e (**with** par); (from anaesthetic) insensible; **to go ~** s'engourdir
2 (fig) hébété/-e (**with** par)
B *vt* ‹*cold*› engourdir; (Med) insensibiliser; **to ~ the pain** endormir la douleur

number /'nʌmbə(r)/ **A** *n* **1** (gen) nombre *m*; (written figure) chiffre *m*; **a three-figure ~** un nombre à trois chiffres; **a ~ of** un certain nombre de
2 (of bus, house, page, telephone) numéro *m*; **a wrong ~** un faux numéro
3 (by performer) (act) numéro *m*; (song) chanson *f*
B *vt* **1** (allocate number to) numéroter
2 (amount to, include) compter
IDIOMS **his days are ~ed** ses jours sont comptés; **to look after ~ one** penser avant tout à son propre intérêt

n

number plate *n* (BrE) plaque *f* minéralogique *or* d'immatriculation

numeracy /'nju:mərəsɪ, (AmE) 'nu:-/ *n* aptitude *f* au calcul

numeral /'nju:mərəl, (AmE) 'nu:-/ *n* chiffre *m*

numerical /nju:'merɪkl, (AmE) 'nu:-/ *adj* numérique

🔑 **numerous** /'nju:mərəs, (AmE) 'nu:-/ *adj* nombreux/-euse

nun /nʌn/ *n* religieuse *f*, bonne sœur *f*

🔑 **nurse** /nɜ:s/ **A** *n* **1** (Med) infirmier/-ière *m/f*; **male ~** infirmier *m*
2 = **nursemaid**
B *vt* **1** soigner ‹*person, cold*›
2 allaiter ‹*baby*›
3 nourrir ‹*grievance, hope*›

nursemaid *n* nurse *f*, bonne *f* d'enfants

nursery /'nɜ:sərɪ/ *n* **1** (*also* **day ~**) crèche *f*; (in hotel, shop) garderie *f*
2 (room) chambre *f* d'enfants
3 (for plants) pépinière *f*

nursery rhyme *n* comptine *f*

nursery school *n* école *f* maternelle

nursing /'nɜ:sɪŋ/ *n* profession *f* d'infirmier/-ière

nursing home *n* **1** (old people's) maison *f* de retraite; (convalescent) maison *f* de repos
2 (BrE) (maternity) clinique *f* obstétrique

nurture /'nɜ:tʃə(r)/ *vt* **1** élever ‹*child*›; soigner ‹*plant*›
2 nourrir ‹*hope, feeling, talent*›

nut /nʌt/ *n* **1** (walnut) noix *f*; (hazel) noisette *f*; (almond) amande *f*; (peanut) cacahuète *f*
2 (Tech) écrou *m*

nutcracker *n* casse-noisettes *m inv*

nutmeg /'nʌtmeg/ *n* noix *f* de muscade

nutrition /nju:'trɪʃn, (AmE) nu:-/ *n* (process) nutrition *f*, alimentation *f*; (science) diététique *f*

nutritional /nju:'trɪʃənl, (AmE) nu:-/ *adj* ‹*value*› nutritif/-ive; ‹*composition, information*› nutritionnel/-elle

nutritious /nju:'trɪʃəs, (AmE) nu:-/ *adj* nourrissant/-e

nutshell /'nʌtʃel/ *n* **1** coquille *f* de noix *or* noisette
2 (fig) **in a ~** en un mot

nuzzle /'nʌzl/ *vt* frotter son nez contre
■ **nuzzle up**: **to ~ up against** *or* **to sb** se blottir contre qn

NVQ *n* (BrE) (*abbr* = **National Vocational Qualification**) qualification *f* nationale professionnelle (*obtenue par formation continue ou initiale*)

nylon /'naɪlɒn/ *n* nylon® *m*

nymph /nɪmf/ *n* nymphe *f*

Oo

o, O /əʊ/ *n* **1** (letter) o, O *m*
2 O (spoken number) zéro

oaf /əʊf/ *n* (clumsy) balourd/-e *m/f*; (loutish) mufle *m*

oak /əʊk/ **A** *n* chêne *m*
B *adj* de *or* en chêne

OAP *n* (BrE) (*abbr* = **old age pensioner**) retraité/-e *m/f*

oar /ɔ:(r)/ *n* rame *f*

oasis /əʊ'eɪsɪs/ *n* (*pl* **oases**) (in desert) oasis *f*; (fig) havre *m*

oat /əʊt/ *n* **~s** avoine *f*
IDIOM **to sow one's wild ~s** jeter sa gourme

oath /əʊθ/ *n* **1** serment *m*; **under ~, on ~** (BrE) sous serment
2 (swearword) juron *m*

oatmeal /'əʊtmi:l/ *n* **1** (cereal) farine *f* d'avoine
2 (AmE) (porridge) bouillie *f* d'avoine

obedience /ə'bi:dɪəns/ *n* obéissance *f* (**to** à)

obedient /ə'bi:dɪənt/ *adj* obéissant/-e

obese /əʊ'bi:s/ *adj* obèse

obesity /əʊ'bi:sətɪ/ *n* obésité *f*

obey /ə'beɪ/ **A** *vt* obéir à ‹*person, instinct*›; se conformer à ‹*instructions, law*›
B *vi* ‹*person*› obéir

obituary /ə'bɪtʃʊərɪ, (AmE) -tʃʊerɪ/ *n* (*also* **~ notice**) nécrologie *f*

🔑 **object** **A** /'ɒbdʒɪkt/ *n* **1** (item) objet *m*
2 (goal) but *m* (**of** de)
3 (focus) **to be the ~ of** être l'objet de
4 (in grammar) complément *m* d'objet
B /əb'dʒekt/ *vt* objecter (**that** que)
C /əb'dʒekt/ *vi* soulever des objections; **to ~ to** protester contre ‹*attitude, comment*›; **to ~ to doing** se refuser à faire; **I ~ to their behaviour** je trouve leur comportement inadmissible

objection /əb'dʒekʃn/ *n* objection *f* (**to** à, **from** de la part de); **I've no ~(s)** je n'y vois pas d'inconvénient

---
🔑 mot clé

objectionable /əb'dʒekʃənəbl/ *adj* ‹*remark*› désobligeant/-e; ‹*behaviour, language*› choquant/-e; ‹*person*› insupportable

objective /əb'dʒektɪv/ **A** *n* objectif *m* **B** *adj* objectif/-ive, impartial/-e

objectively /əb'dʒektɪvlɪ/ *adv* objectivement

obligation /ˌɒblɪ'geɪʃn/ *n* **1** (duty) devoir *m* (**towards, to** envers); **to be under (an) ∼ to do** être obligé/-e de faire
2 (commitment) obligation *f* (**to** envers, **to do** de faire)
3 (debt) dette *f*

obligatory /ə'blɪgətrɪ, (AmE) -tɔ:rɪ/ *adj* obligatoire (**to do** de faire)

oblige /ə'blaɪdʒ/ *vt* **1** (compel) obliger (**to do** à faire)
2 (be helpful) rendre service à
3 to be ∼d to sb être reconnaissant/-e à qn (**for** de)

obliging /ə'blaɪdʒɪŋ/ *adj* serviable

obliterate /ə'blɪtəreɪt/ *vt* effacer ‹*trace, word, memory*›; anéantir ‹*landmark, city*›

oblivion /ə'blɪvɪən/ *n* oubli *m*

oblivious /ə'blɪvɪəs/ *adj* (unaware) inconscient/-e; **to be ∼ of** *or* **to** ne pas être conscient/-e de

oblong /'ɒblɒŋ, (AmE) -lɔ:ŋ/ **A** *n* rectangle *m* **B** *adj* oblong/oblongue, rectangulaire

obnoxious /əb'nɒkʃəs/ *adj* odieux/-ieuse, exécrable

obscene /əb'si:n/ *adj* obscène

obscure /əb'skjʊə(r)/ **A** *adj* obscur/-e; (indistinct) vague
B *vt* obscurcir ‹*truth*›; cacher ‹*view*›; **to ∼ the issue** embrouiller la question

observant /əb'zɜ:vənt/ *adj* observateur/-trice

observation /ˌɒbzə'veɪʃn/ *n* observation *f* (**of** de); **to keep sb/sth under ∼** surveiller qn/qch

observe /əb'zɜ:v/ *vt* **1** (see, notice) observer (**that** que)
2 ‹*doctor, police*› surveiller
3 (remark) faire observer (**that** que)
4 observer ‹*law, custom*›

observer /əb'zɜ:və(r)/ *n* observateur/-trice *m/f* (**of** de)

obsess /əb'ses/ *vt* obséder

obsession /əb'seʃn/ *n* obsession *f*

obsessive /əb'sesɪv/ *adj* ‹*person*› maniaque; ‹*neurosis*› obsessionnel/-elle; ‹*thought*› obsédant/-e

obsolescence /ˌɒbsə'lesns/ *n* (gen) désuétude *f*; **built-in ∼** obsolescence *f* planifiée

obsolete /'ɒbsəli:t/ *adj* ‹*technology*› dépassé/-e; ‹*custom, idea*› démodé/-e; ‹*word*› désuet/-ète

obstacle /'ɒbstəkl/ *n* obstacle *m*; **to be an ∼** faire obstacle (**to** à)

obstacle course *n* (Mil) parcours *m* du combattant; (fig) course *f* d'obstacles

obstacle race *n* course *f* d'obstacles

obstetrician /ˌɒbstə'trɪʃn/ *n* obstétricien/-ienne *m/f*

obstinate /'ɒbstənət/ *adj* ‹*person*› têtu/-e (**about** en ce qui concerne); ‹*behaviour, silence, effort*› obstiné/-e; ‹*resistance*› acharné/-e

obstruct /əb'strʌkt/ *vt* cacher ‹*view*›; bloquer ‹*road*›; gêner ‹*traffic, person, progress*›; faire obstruction à ‹*player*›; entraver le cours de ‹*justice*›

obstruction /əb'strʌkʃn/ *n* **1** (to traffic, progress) obstacle *m*; (in pipe) bouchon *m*
2 (in sport) obstruction *f*

obtain /əb'teɪn/ *vt* obtenir

obtrusive /əb'tru:sɪv/ *adj* ‹*noise*› gênant/-e; ‹*person, behaviour*› importun/-e

obtuse /əb'tju:s, (AmE) -'tu:s-/ *adj* ‹*person*› obtus/-e; ‹*remark*› stupide

obvious /'ɒbvɪəs/ **A** *n* **to state the ∼** enfoncer les portes ouvertes
B *adj* évident/-e (**to** pour)

obviously /'ɒbvɪəslɪ/ **A** *adv* manifestement; **she ∼ needs help** il est évident qu'elle a besoin d'aide; **he's ∼ lying** il est clair qu'il ment
B *excl* bien sûr!, évidemment!

occasion /ə'keɪʒn/ *n* occasion *f*; **on one ∼** une fois; **to rise to the ∼** se montrer à la hauteur des circonstances; **on special ∼s** dans les grandes occasions

occasional /ə'keɪʒənl/ *adj* ‹*event*› qui a lieu de temps en temps; **the ∼ letter** une lettre de temps en temps

occasionally /ə'keɪʒənəlɪ/ *adv* de temps à autre; **very ∼** très rarement

occult /ɒ'kʌlt, (AmE) ə'kʌlt/ *n* **the ∼** les sciences *fpl* occultes

occupant /'ɒkjʊpənt/ *n* **1** (of building, bed) occupant/-e *m/f*
2 (of vehicle) passager/-ère *m/f*

occupation /ˌɒkjʊ'peɪʃn/ *n* **1** (Mil) occupation *f* (**de** of)
2 (trade) métier *m*; (profession) profession *f*
3 (activity) occupation *f*

occupational /ˌɒkjʊ'peɪʃənl/ *adj* ‹*accident*› du travail; ‹*risk*› du métier; ‹*safety*› au travail

occupational hazard *n* **it's an ∼** ça fait partie des risques du métier

occupier /'ɒkjʊpaɪə(r)/ *n* occupant/-e *m/f*

occupy /'ɒkjʊpaɪ/ *vt* occuper; **to keep oneself occupied** s'occuper (**by doing** en faisant)

occur /ə'kɜ:(r)/ *vi* (*p prés etc* **-rr-**) **1** (happen) se produire
2 (be present) se trouver
3 the idea ∼red to me that... l'idée m'est venue à l'esprit que...; **it didn't ∼ to me** ça ne m'est pas venu à l'idée

occurrence /əˈkʌrəns/ *n* **1** (event) fait *m*; **to be a rare ~** se produire rarement
2 (instance) occurrence *f*
3 (of disease, phenomenon) cas *m*

ocean /ˈəʊʃn/ *n* océan *m*

o'clock /əˈklɒk/ *adv* **at one ~** à une heure; **it's two ~** il est deux heures

octagon /ˈɒktəgən, (AmE) -gɒn/ *n* octogone *m*

octave /ˈɒktɪv/ *n* octave *f*

🔑 **October** /ɒkˈtəʊbə(r)/ *n* octobre *m*

octopus /ˈɒktəpəs/ *n* (*pl* **~es** *ou* **~**) **1** (Zool) pieuvre *f*
2 (Culin) poulpe *m*

OD /əʊdi:/ *n, vi* (fam) = **overdose**

🔑 **odd** /ɒd/ **A** *adj* **1** (strange, unusual) ‹*person, object, occurrence*› bizarre
2 ‹*socks, gloves*› dépareillés
3 (miscellaneous) **some ~ bits of cloth** quelques bouts de tissu
4 ‹*number*› impair/-e
5 to be the ~ one out ‹*person, animal, plant*› être l'exception; ‹*drawing, word*› être l'intrus; (when selecting team) être sans partenaire
B -odd *combining form* **sixty-~ people/ years** une soixantaine de personnes/ d'années

oddity /ˈɒdɪtɪ/ *n* (odd thing) bizarrerie *f*; (person) excentrique *mf*

odd job *n* (for money) petit boulot *m*; **~s** (in house, garden) petits travaux *mpl*

odd-job man *n* homme *m* à tout faire

odds /ɒdz/ *npl* **1** (in betting) cote *f* (**on** sur)
2 (chance, likelihood) chances *fpl*; **the ~ are against his winning** il y a peu de chances qu'il gagne; **to win against the ~** gagner contre toute attente
IDIOM **at ~** (in dispute) être en conflit; (inconsistent) en contradiction (**with** avec)

odds and ends *npl* (BrE) bricoles *fpl* (fam)

odour (BrE), **odor** (AmE) /ˈəʊdə(r)/ *n* odeur *f*

🔑 **of** /ɒv, əv/ *prep*

> In almost all its uses, the preposition *of* is translated by *de*. For exceptions, see the entry below.
> Remember that *de* + *le* always becomes *du* and that *de* + *les* always becomes *des*.
> When *of it* or *of them* are used for something already referred to, they are translated by *en*: *there's a lot of it* = il y en a beaucoup; *there are several of them* = il y en a plusieurs.
> Note, however, the following expressions used when referring to people: *there are six of them* = ils sont six; *there were several of them* = ils étaient plusieurs.

1 (in most uses) de; **the leg ~ the table** le pied de la table **2** (made of) en; **a ring (made) ~ gold** une bague en or **3 a friend ~ mine** un ami à moi; **that's kind ~ you** c'est très gentil de votre part *or* à vous; **some ~ us/them** quelques-uns d'entre nous/d'entre eux

🔑 **off** /ɒf, (AmE) ɔ:f/ **A** *adv* **1** (leaving) **to be ~** partir, s'en aller; **it's time you were ~** il est temps que tu partes; **I'm ~** je m'en vais
2 (at a distance) **to be 30 metres ~** être à 30 mètres; **some way ~** assez loin
3 (ahead in time) **Easter is a month ~** Pâques est dans un mois; **the exam is still several months ~** l'examen n'aura pas lieu avant plusieurs mois
B *adj* **1** (free) **Tuesday's my day ~** je ne travaille pas le mardi; **to have the morning ~** avoir la matinée libre
2 (turned off) **to be ~** ‹*water, gas*› être coupé/-e; ‹*tap*› être fermé/-e; ‹*light, TV*› être éteint/-e
3 (cancelled) ‹*match, party*› annulé/-e
4 (removed) **the lid is ~** il n'y a pas de couvercle; **with her make-up ~** sans maquillage; **25% ~** 25% de remise
5 (BrE) (fam) (bad) **to be ~** ‹*food*› être avarié/-e; ‹*milk*› avoir tourné/-e
C *prep* **1** (*also* **just ~**) juste à côté de ‹*kitchen*›; **~ the west coast** au large de la côte ouest; **just ~ the path** tout près du sentier
2 it is ~ the point là n'est pas la question
3 (fam) **to be ~ one's food** ne pas avoir d'appétit
IDIOMS **to feel a bit ~** (fam) ne pas être dans son assiette (fam); **to have an ~ day** ne pas être dans un de ses bons jours

off-centre (BrE), **off-center** (AmE) *adj* décentré/-e

off-chance /ˈɒftʃɑ:ns, (AmE) -tʃæns/ *n* **just on the ~** au cas où

off-colour *adj* (fam) (unwell) patraque (fam)

🔑 **offence** (BrE), **offense** (AmE) /əˈfens/ *n*
1 (crime) délit *m*
2 (insult) **to cause ~ to sb** offenser qn; **to take ~ (at)** s'offenser (de)
3 (Mil) offensive *f*

offend /əˈfend/ **A** *vt* offenser ‹*person*›
B *vi* commettre une infraction (**against** à)

offender /əˈfendə(r)/ *n* **1** (Law) délinquant/-e *m/f*
2 (culprit) coupable *mf*

offensive /əˈfensɪv/ **A** *n* (Mil, Sport) offensive *f*
B *adj* ‹*remark*› injurieux/-ieuse (**to** pour); ‹*behaviour*› insultant/-e; ‹*language*› grossier/-ière

🔑 **offer** /ˈɒfə(r), (AmE) ˈɔ:f-/ **A** *n* **1** offre *f* (**to do** de faire); **job ~** offre d'emploi
2 (of goods) **to be on special ~** être en promotion
B *vt* (gen) offrir; donner ‹*advice, explanation, information*›; émettre ‹*opinion*›; proposer ‹*service*›; **to ~ sb sth** offrir qch à qn; **to ~ to do** se proposer pour faire
C *vi* se proposer

🔑 mot clé

O

offering /ˈɒfərɪŋ, (AmE) ˈɔːf-/ *n* (gift) cadeau *m*; (sacrifice) offrande *f*

offhand /ˌɒfˈhænd, (AmE) ˌɔːf-/ **A** *adj* désinvolte

B *adv* **~, I don't know** comme ça au pied levé je ne sais pas

office /ˈɒfɪs, (AmE) ˈɔːf-/ *n* **1** (place) bureau *m*
2 (position) fonction *f*, charge *f*; **public ~** fonctions *fpl* officielles; **to hold ~** ‹*president, mayor*› être en fonction; ‹*political party*› être au pouvoir

office block, **office building** *n* (BrE) immeuble *m* de bureaux

officer /ˈɒfɪsə(r), (AmE) ˈɔːf-/ *n* **1** (in army, navy) officier *m*
2 (*also* **police ~**) policier *m*

office worker *n* employé/-e *m/f* de bureau

official /əˈfɪʃl/ **A** *n* fonctionnaire *mf*; (of party, union) officiel/-ielle *m/f*; (at town hall) employé/-e *m/f*

B *adj* officiel/-ielle

offing /ˈɒfɪŋ/ *n* **in the ~** en perspective

off-key *adj* faux/fausse

off-licence *n* (BrE) magasin *m* de vins et de spiritueux

off-limits *adj* interdit/-e

off-line *adj* (Comput) (not on the Internet) hors ligne; ‹*processing*› en différé

off-load /ˌɒfˈləʊd, (AmE) ˌɔːf-/ *vt* (get rid of) écouler ‹*goods*›; **to ~ the blame onto sb** rejeter la responsabilité sur qn

off-message *adj* (Pol) **to be ~** être en désaccord avec la politique gouvernementale

off-peak /ˌɒfˈpiːk, (AmE) ˌɔːf-/ *adj* ‹*electricity*› au tarif de nuit; ‹*travel*› en période creuse; ‹*call*› au tarif réduit

off-putting /ˌɒfˈpʊtɪŋ, (AmE) ˌɔːf-/ *adj* (BrE) ‹*manner*› peu engageant/-e; **it was very ~** c'était déroutant

off-road *vi* rouler en tout terrain

off-road vehicle *n* véhicule *m* tout terrain

off-season /ˌɒfˈsiːzn, (AmE) ˌɔːf-/ *adj* ‹*cruise, holiday*› hors saison

offset /ˈɒfset, (AmE) ˈɔːf-/ *vt* (*p prés* **-tt-**, *prét, pp* **offset**) compenser (**by** par); **to ~ sth against sth** mettre qch et qch en balance

offshore /ˌɒfˈʃɔː(r), (AmE) ˌɔːf-/ **A** *adj* (out to sea) au large, en mer; (towards the sea) de terre; **~ breeze** brise *f* de terre

B *adv* offshore

C *vt* délocaliser

D *vi* faire de l'offshore

offside /ˌɒfˈsaɪd, (AmE) ˌɔːf-/ **A** *n* (BrE) côté *m* conducteur

B *adj* **1** (BrE) ‹*lane*› (in France) de gauche; (in UK) de droite
2 (Sport) hors jeu *inv*

offspring /ˈɒfsprɪŋ, (AmE) ˈɔːf-/ *n* (*pl* **~**) progéniture *f*

offstage /ˌɒfˈsteɪdʒ, (AmE) ˌɔːf-/ *adj, adv* dans les coulisses

off-the-cuff *adj* ‹*remark, speech*› impromptu/-e

off-the-peg *adj* ‹*garment*› de prêt-à-porter

off-the-shelf *adj* ‹*goods*› disponible en magasin; ‹*software*› fixe

off-the-wall *adj* (fam) loufoque (fam)

off-white *adj* blanc cassé *inv*

often /ˈɒfn, ˈɒftən, (AmE) ˈɔːfn/ *adv* souvent; **as ~ as not, more ~ than not** le plus souvent; **how ~ do you meet?** vous vous voyez tous les combien?; **once too ~** une fois de trop; **every so ~** de temps en temps

oh /əʊ/ *excl* oh!; **~ dear!** oh là là!; **~ (really)?** ah bon?

oil /ɔɪl/ **A** *n* (gen) huile *f*; (petroleum) pétrole *m*; **crude ~** pétrole brut; **engine ~** huile de moteur; **heating ~** fioul *m*

B *vt* huiler

oil change *n* vidange *f*

oilcloth *n* toile *f* cirée

oilfield *n* champ *m* pétrolifère

oil painting *n* peinture *f* à l'huile

oil refinery *n* raffinerie *f* de pétrole

oil rig *n* (offshore) plate-forme *f* pétrolière offshore; (on land) tour *f* de forage

oilseed rape *n* colza *m*

oilskins *npl* (BrE) ciré *m*

oil slick *n* marée *f* noire

oil well *n* puits *m* de pétrole

oily /ˈɔɪlɪ/ *adj* ‹*cloth, food, hair*› gras/grasse; ‹*dressing, substance*› huileux/-euse

ointment /ˈɔɪntmənt/ *n* pommade *f*

okay, OK (fam) /ˌəʊˈkeɪ/ **A** *n* **to give sb/sth the ~** donner le feu vert à qn/qch

B *adj* **it's ~ by me** ça ne me dérange pas; **is it ~ if...?** est-ce que ça va si...?; **he's ~** (nice) il est sympa (fam); **to feel ~** aller bien; **I'm ~** ça va; **'how was the match?'—'~'** 'comment as-tu trouvé le match?'—'pas mal'

C *adv* ‹*cope, work out*› (assez) bien

D *particle* **1** (giving agreement) d'accord
2 (introducing topic) bien

old /əʊld/ *adj* **1** ‹*person*› vieux/vieille *before n*, âgé/-e; ‹*object, tradition, song*› vieux/vieille *before n*; **an ~ man** un vieil homme, un vieillard; **an ~ woman** une vieille femme, une vieille; **to get ~** vieillir; **how ~ are you?** quel âge as-tu?; **I'm ten years ~** j'ai dix ans; **a six year-~ boy** un garçon (âgé) de six ans; **my ~er brother** mon frère aîné; **I'm the ~est** c'est moi l'aîné/-e
2 (former, previous) ‹*address, school, job, system*› ancien/-ienne *before n*; **in the ~ days** autrefois

> The irregular form *vieil* of the adjective vieux/vieille is used before masculine nouns beginning with a vowel or a mute 'h'.

old age *n* vieillesse *f*

old-age pensioner, **OAP** *n* (BrE) retraité/-e *m/f*
old-fashioned /ˌəʊldˈfæʃnd/ *adj* ‹*person, ways*› vieux jeu *inv*; ‹*idea, attitude, garment, machine*› démodé/-e
old people's home *n* maison *f* de retraite
old wives' tale *n* conte *m* de bonne femme
olive /ˈɒlɪv/ **A** *n* **1** (fruit) olive *f*
2 (*also* ~ **tree**) olivier *m*
B *adj* ‹*dress, eyes*› vert olive *inv*; ‹*complexion*› olivâtre
olive green *n, adj* vert *m* olive *inv*
olive oil *n* huile *f* d'olive
Olympics *npl* (*also* **Olympic Games**) jeux *mpl* Olympiques
ombudsman /ˈɒmbʊdzmən/ *n* médiateur *m*
omelette /ˈɒmlɪt/ *n* omelette *f*
omen /ˈəʊmən/ *n* présage *m*
ominous /ˈɒmɪnəs/ *adj* ‹*cloud*› menaçant/-e; ‹*news*› inquiétant/-e; ‹*sign*› de mauvais augure
omission /əˈmɪʃn/ *n* omission *f*
omit /əˈmɪt/ *vt* (*p prés etc* **-tt-**) omettre (**from** de, **to do** de faire)
omnipotent /ɒmˈnɪpətənt/ *adj* omnipotent/-e
omnipresent /ˌɒmnɪˈpreznt/ *adj* omniprésent/-e

🔑 **on** /ɒn/ **A** *prep* **1** (position) sur ‹*table, coast, motorway*›; ~ **the beach** sur la plage; ~ **top of the piano** sur le piano; ~ **the floor** par terre; **there's a stain** ~ **it** il y a une tache dessus; **to live** ~ **Park Avenue** habiter Park Avenue; **a studio flat** ~ **Avenue Montaigne** un studio avenue Montaigne; **the paintings** ~ **the wall** les tableaux qui sont au mur; **I've got no small change** ~ **me** je n'ai pas de monnaie sur moi; **to have a smile** ~ **one's face** sourire; **to hang sth** ~ **a nail** accrocher qch à un clou; ~ **a string** au bout d'une ficelle
2 (about, on the subject of) sur; ~ **Africa** sur l'Afrique
3 to be ~ faire partie de ‹*team*›; être membre de ‹*committee*›
4 (in expressions of time) ~ **22 February** le 22 février; ~ **Friday** vendredi; ~ **Saturdays** le samedi; ~ **my birthday** le jour de mon anniversaire; ~ **sunny days** quand il fait beau
5 (immediately after) ~ **his arrival** à son arrivée; ~ **hearing the truth she...** quand elle a appris la vérité, elle...
6 (taking) **to be** ~ **steroids** prendre des stéroïdes; **to be** ~ **drugs** se droguer
7 (powered by) **to run** ~ **batteries** fonctionner sur piles; **to run** ~ **electricity** marcher à l'électricité
8 (indicating a medium) ~ **TV** à la télé; ~ **the news** aux informations; ~ **video** en vidéo; ~ **drums** à la batterie
9 (earning) **to be** ~ **£20,000 a year** gagner 20 000 livres sterling par an; **to be** ~ **a low income** avoir un bas salaire
10 (paid for by) **it's** ~ **me** je t'invite
11 (indicating transport) **to travel** ~ **the bus** voyager en bus; ~ **the plane** dans l'avion; **to be** ~ **one's bike** être à vélo; **to leave** ~ **the first train** prendre le premier train
B *adj* **1 while the meeting is** ~ pendant la réunion; **I've got a lot** ~ je suis très occupé; **the news is** ~ **in 10 minutes** les informations sont dans 10 minutes; **what's** ~**?** (on TV) qu'est-ce qu'il y a à la télé?; (at the cinema, theatre) qu'est-ce qu'on joue?; **there's nothing** ~ il n'y a rien de bien
2 to be ~ ‹*TV, oven, light*› être allumé/-e; ‹*dishwasher, radio*› marcher; ‹*tap*› être ouvert/-e; **the power is** ~ il y a du courant
3 to be ~ ‹*lid*› être mis/-e
C *adv* **1 to have nothing** ~ être nu/-e; **to have make-up** ~ être maquillé/-e; **with slippers** ~ en pantoufles
2 from that day ~ à partir de ce jour-là; **20 years** ~ 20 ans plus tard; **to walk** ~ continuer à marcher; **to go to Paris then** ~ **to Marseilles** aller à Paris et de là à Marseille; **a little further** ~ un peu plus loin
D on and off *phr* de temps en temps
E on and on *phr* **to go** ~ **and** ~ ‹*speaker*› parler pendant des heures; ‹*speech*› durer des heures; **to go** ~ **and** ~ **about** ne pas arrêter de parler de
IDIOM **it's just** *or* **simply not** ~ (BrE) (out of the question) c'est hors de question; (not the done thing) ça ne se fait pas; (unacceptable) c'est inadmissible

on-board /ˈɒnbɔːd/ *adj* (in-car) embarqué/-e

🔑 **once** /wʌns/ **A** *n* **just this** ~ pour cette fois; **for** ~ pour une fois
B *adv* **1** (one time) une fois; ~ **and for all** une (bonne) fois pour toutes; ~ **too often** une fois de trop; ~ **a day** une fois par jour
2 (formerly) autrefois; ~ **upon a time there was a king** il était une fois un roi
C *conj* une fois que, dès que
D at once *phr* **1** (immediately) tout de suite; **all at** ~ tout d'un coup
2 (simultaneously) à la fois

once-over /ˈwʌnsəʊvə(r)/ *n* (fam) **to give sth the** ~ jeter un rapide coup d'œil à qch; **to give sb the** ~ évaluer qn au premier coup d'œil
oncoming /ˈɒnkʌmɪŋ/ *adj* ‹*car, vehicle*› venant en sens inverse

🔑 **one** /wʌn/ **A** *det* **1** (single) un/une; ~ **car** une voiture; ~ **dog** un chien; **to raise** ~ **hand** lever la main
2 (unique, sole) seul/-e *before n*; **my** ~ **vice** mon seul vice; **my** ~ **and only tie** ma seule et unique cravate; **the** ~ **and only Edith Piaf** l'incomparable Edith Piaf
3 (same) même; **at** ~ **and the same time** en

🔑 mot clé

O

même temps
B *pron* **1** (indefinite) un/une *m/f*; **can you lend me ~?** tu peux m'en prêter un/une?; **~ of them** (person) l'un d'eux/l'une d'elles; (thing) l'un/l'une *m/f*
2 (impersonal) (as subject) on; (as object) vous; **~ never knows** on ne sait jamais
3 (demonstrative) **the grey ~** le gris/la grise; **this ~** celui-ci/celle-ci; **which ~?** lequel/laquelle?; **that's the ~** c'est celui-là/celle-là; **he's/she's the ~ who** c'est lui/elle qui
4 ~-fifty (in sterling) une livre cinquante
C *n* (number) un *m*; (referring to feminine) une *f*; **~ o'clock** une heure; **in ~s and twos** par petits groupes
D one by one *phr* un par un/une par une
IDIOMS **to be ~ up on sb** (fam) avoir un avantage sur qn; **to go ~ better than sb** faire mieux que qn; **I for ~ think that** pour ma part je crois que

one another *pron* (*also* **each other**);

one another is very often translated by using a reflexive pronoun (*nous, vous, se, s'*).

they love ~ ils s'aiment; **to help ~** s'entraider; **to worry about ~** s'inquiéter l'un pour l'autre; **kept apart from ~** séparés l'un de l'autre

one-off /ˌwʌn'ɒf/ *adj* (BrE) ‹*experiment*› unique; ‹*event, payment*› exceptionnel/-elle

one-parent family *n* famille *f* monoparentale

one-piece /'wʌnpiːs/ *adj* **~ swimsuit** maillot *m* de bain une pièce

one's /wʌnz/ *det* son/sa/ses; **~ books/friends** ses livres/amis; **to wash ~ hands** se laver les mains; **to do ~ best** faire de son mieux

oneself /ˌwʌn'self/ *pron* **1** (reflexive) se, s'; **to wash/cut ~** se laver/couper
2 (for emphasis) soi-même
3 (after prepositions) soi; **sure of ~** sûr/-e de soi; **(all) by ~** tout seul/toute seule

one-sided /ˌwʌn'saɪdɪd/ *adj* ‹*account*› partial/-e; ‹*contest*› inégal/-e; ‹*deal*› inéquitable

one-time *adj* ancien/-ienne *before n*

one-to-one /ˌwʌntə'wʌn/ *adj* ‹*talk*› en tête à tête; **~ meeting** tête-à-tête *m inv*; **~ tuition** cours *mpl* particuliers

one-way /ˌwʌn'weɪ/ *adj* **1** ‹*traffic*› à sens unique; **~ street** sens *m* unique
2 ~ ticket aller *m* simple

ongoing /'ɒngəʊɪŋ/ *adj* ‹*process*› continu/-e; ‹*battle, story*› continuel/-elle

onion /'ʌnɪən/ *n* oignon *m*

online *adj* (Comput) (on the Internet) en ligne; ‹*mode*› connecté/-e; ‹*data processing*› en direct

online dating *n* rencontre *f* en ligne

onlooker /'ɒnlʊkə(r)/ *n* spectateur/-trice *m/f*

only /'əʊnlɪ/ **A** *conj* mais, seulement; **I'd go ~ I'm too old** j'irais bien mais je suis trop vieux
B *adj* seul/-e; **~ child** enfant *m* unique
C *adv* **1** (exclusively) **~ in Italy can one...** il n'y a qu'en Italie que l'on peut...; **~ time will tell** seul l'avenir nous le dira; **'men ~'** 'réservé aux hommes'
2 (in expressions of time) **~ yesterday** pas plus tard qu'hier; **it seems like ~ yesterday** j'ai l'impression que c'était hier
3 (merely) **you ~ had to ask** tu n'avais qu'à demander; **it's ~ fair** ce n'est que justice; **he ~ grazed his knees** il s'est juste égratigné les genoux; **~ half the money** juste la moitié de l'argent
D only just *phr* **1** (very recently) **to have ~ just done** venir juste de faire
2 (barely) **~ just wide enough** juste assez large; **~ just** (narrowly) de justesse
E only too *phr* **~ too well** trop bien; **~ too pleased** trop content/-e

on-message /ɒn'mesɪdʒ/ *adj* (Pol) **to be ~** être en accord avec la politique gouvernementale

o.n.o. (BrE) (*abbr* = **or nearest offer**) à débattre

on-screen /ˌɒn'skriːn/ *adj* sur l'écran

onset /'ɒnset/ *n* début *m* (**of** de)

onside /ˌɒn'saɪd/ *adj, adv* en jeu

on-site /ˌɒn'saɪt/ *adj* sur place

onslaught /'ɒnslɔːt/ *n* attaque *f* (**on** contre)

on-target earnings, **OTE** *npl* **'~ £40,000'** 'salaire plus commission pouvant atteindre 40 000 livres sterling'

on-the-job *adj* ‹*training*› sur le lieu de travail

on the spot *adv* ‹*decide*› sur-le-champ; ‹*killed*› sur le coup; **to be ~** être sur place

onto /'ɒntuː/ *prep* (*also* **on to**) sur
IDIOM **to be ~ something** (fam) être sur une piste

onus /'əʊnəs/ *n* obligation *f*; **the ~ is on sb to do** il incombe à qn de faire

onward /'ɒnwəd/ **A** *adj* **~ flight** correspondance *f* (**to** à destination de)
B *adv* (AmE) = **onwards**

onwards /'ɒnwədz/ *adv* (*also* **onward**) **to carry ~** continuer; **from now ~** à partir d'aujourd'hui; **from that day ~** à dater de ce jour

ooze /uːz/ **A** *vt* **the wound ~d blood** du sang suintait de la blessure
B *vi* **to ~ with** ‹*person*› rayonner de ‹*charm, sexuality*›

opal /'əʊpl/ *n* opale *f*

opaque /əʊ'peɪk/ *adj* opaque

open /'əʊpən/ **A** *n* **in the ~** (outside) dehors, en plein air; **to bring sth out into the ~** mettre qch au grand jour
B *adj* **1** (gen) ouvert/-e; **to be half ~** ‹*door*› être entrouvert/-e; **the ~ air** le plein air; **in ~ country** en rase campagne; **on ~ ground** sur un terrain découvert; **the ~ road** la grand-route; **the ~ sea** la haute mer

O

2 (not covered) ‹*car, carriage*› découvert/-e, décapoté/-e
3 ~ to exposé/-e à ‹*air, wind, elements*›; **~ to attack** exposé/-e à l'attaque; **to lay oneself ~ to criticism** s'exposer (ouvertement) à la critique
4 ‹*access, competition*› ouvert/-e à tous; ‹*meeting*› public/-ique
5 (candid) ‹*person*› franc/franche (**about** à propos de)
6 (blatant) ‹*hostility, contempt*› non dissimulé/-e
7 to leave the date ~ laisser la date en suspens; **to keep an ~ mind** réserver son jugement
C *vt* (gen) ouvrir; entamer ‹*discussions*›
D *vi* **1** ‹*door, flower, curtain*› s'ouvrir; **to ~ onto sth** ‹*door, window*› donner sur qch
2 ‹*shop, bar*› ouvrir; ‹*meeting, play*› commencer (**with** par)
3 ‹*film*› sortir (sur les écrans)
■ **open up A ~ up 1** ‹*shop, branch*› ouvrir
2 ‹*gap*› se creuser
3 (fig) ‹*person*› se confier
B ~ [sth] up ouvrir

open-air /ˌəʊpən'eə(r)/ *adj* ‹*pool, stage*› en plein air

open day *n* journée *f* portes ouvertes

opener /'əʊpnə(r)/ *n* (for bottles) décapsuleur *m*; (for cans) ouvre-boîte *m*

open-heart surgery *n* (operation) opération *f* à cœur ouvert

opening /'əʊpnɪŋ/ **A** *n* **1** (start) début *m*
2 (of exhibition, shop) ouverture *f*; (of play, film) première *f*
3 (gap) trouée *f*
4 (opportunity) occasion *f* (**to do** de faire); (in market) débouché *m* (**for** pour); (for job) poste *m*
B *adj* ‹*scene, move*› premier/-ière *before n*; ‹*remarks*› préliminaire; ‹*ceremony*› d'inauguration

opening hours *npl* heures *fpl* d'ouverture

open learning *n: formule d'enseignement à distance ou dans un centre ouvert à tous*

open market *n* marché *m* libre

open-minded /ˌəʊpən'maɪndɪd/ *adj* **to be ~** avoir l'esprit ouvert

open-necked *adj* ‹*shirt*› à col ouvert

open-plan *adj* ‹*office*› paysagé/-e

open ticket *n* billet *m* ouvert

Open University, OU *n* (BrE) (Univ) *système d'enseignement universitaire par correspondance ouvert à tous*

opera /'ɒprə/ *n* opéra *m*

opera glasses *n* jumelles *fpl* de théâtre

opera house *n* opéra *m*

operate /'ɒpəreɪt/ **A** *vt* **1** faire marcher ‹*appliance, vehicle*›
2 pratiquer ‹*policy, system*›
3 (manage) gérer
B *vi* **1** (do business) opérer
2 (function) marcher
3 (run) ‹*service*› fonctionner
4 (Med) opérer; **to ~ on** opérer ‹*person*›; **to ~ on sb's leg** opérer qn à la jambe

operating instructions *npl* mode *m* d'emploi

operating room (AmE), **operating theatre** (BrE) *n* salle *f* d'opération

operating system *n* système *m* d'exploitation

operation /ˌɒpə'reɪʃn/ *n* **1** (gen), (Med) opération *f*; **to have a heart ~** se faire opérer du cœur
2 to be in ~ ‹*plan*› être en vigueur; ‹*machine*› fonctionner; ‹*oil rig, mine*› être en exploitation

operational /ˌɒpə'reɪʃənl/ *adj* **1** (ready to operate) opérationnel/-elle
2 ‹*budget, costs*› d'exploitation

operative /'ɒpərətɪv, (AmE) -reɪt-/ **A** *n* (worker) employé/-e *m/f*
B *adj* en vigueur

operator /'ɒpəreɪtə(r)/ *n* **1** (on telephone) standardiste *mf*
2 (of radio, computer) opérateur *m*
3 he's a smooth ~ il sait s'y prendre

opinion /ə'pɪnɪən/ *n* opinion *f* (**about** de), avis *m* (**about, on** sur); **to have a high/low ~ of sb/sth** avoir une bonne/mauvaise opinion de qn/qch; **in my ~** à mon avis

opinionated /ə'pɪnɪəneɪtɪd/ *adj* **to be ~** avoir des avis sur tout

opinion poll *n* sondage *m* d'opinion

opponent /ə'pəʊnənt/ *n* (in contest) adversaire *mf*; (of regime) opposant/-e *m/f* (**of** à)

opportune /'ɒpətjuːn, (AmE) -tuːn/ *adj* ‹*moment*› opportun/-e

opportunist /ˌɒpə'tjuːnɪst, (AmE) -'tuːn-/ *n, adj* opportuniste *mf*

opportunity /ˌɒpə'tjuːnətɪ, (AmE) -'tuːn-/ *n* occasion *f* (**for** de); **to take the ~ to do** profiter de l'occasion pour faire

oppose /ə'pəʊz/ **A** *vt* s'opposer à ‹*plan, bill*›; **to be ~d to sth/to doing** être contre qch/contre l'idée de faire
B opposing *pres p adj* ‹*party, team*› adverse; ‹*view, style*› opposé/-e
C as opposed to *phr* par opposition à

opposite /'ɒpəzɪt/ **A** *n* contraire *m* (**to, of** de)
B *adj* (gen) opposé/-e; ‹*building*› d'en face; ‹*page*› ci-contre; ‹*effect*› inverse; **at ~ ends of** aux deux bouts de ‹*table, street*›
C *adv* en face; **directly ~** juste en face
D *prep* en face de ‹*building, park, person*›

opposite number *n* (gen) homologue *m*; (Sport) adversaire *mf*

opposition /ˌɒpə'zɪʃn/ *n* opposition *f* (**to** à); **the Opposition** (in politics) l'opposition

oppress /ə'pres/ *vt* opprimer ‹*people, nation*›

mot clé

oppressive /ə'presɪv/ *adj* **1** ‹*law*› oppressif/-ive
2 ‹*heat, atmosphere*› oppressant/-e

opt /ɒpt/ *vi* **to ~ for sth** opter pour qch; **to ~ to do** choisir de faire
■ **opt out** décider de ne pas participer (**of** à)

optical /'ɒptɪkl/ *adj* optique

optical illusion *n* illusion *f* d'optique

optician /ɒp'tɪʃn/ *n* (selling glasses) opticien/-ienne *m/f*; (BrE) (eye specialist) optométriste *mf*

optimism /'ɒptɪmɪzəm/ *n* optimisme *m*

optimist /'ɒptɪmɪst/ *n* optimiste *mf*

optimistic /ˌɒptɪ'mɪstɪk/ *adj* optimiste (**about** quant à)

optimize /'ɒptɪmaɪz/ *vt* optimiser

optimum /'ɒptɪməm/ *n, adj* optimum *m*

option /'ɒpʃn/ *n* option *f* (**to do** de faire); **to have the ~ of doing** pouvoir choisir de faire; **I didn't have much ~** je n'avais guère le choix

optional /'ɒpʃənl/ *adj* facultatif/-ive; **~ extras** accessoires *mpl* en option

or /ɔː(r)/ *conj* **1** (gen) ou; **black ~ white?** noir ou blanc?; **either here ~ at Dave's** soit ici soit chez Dave; **whether he likes it ~ not** que cela lui plaise ou non; **in a week ~ so** dans huit jours environ; **~ should I say** ou bien devrais-je dire
2 (linking alternatives in the negative) **I can't come today ~ tomorrow** je ne peux venir ni aujourd'hui ni demain; **without food ~ lodgings** sans nourriture ni abri
3 (otherwise) sinon, autrement

oral /'ɔːrəl/ **A** *n* oral *m*
B *adj* ‹*examination, communication, contraceptive*› oral/-e; ‹*medicine*› par voie orale

orange /'ɒrɪndʒ, (AmE) 'ɔːr-/ **A** *n* **1** (fruit) orange *f*
2 (colour) orange *m*
B *adj* orange *inv*

orange juice *n* jus *m* d'orange

orbit /'ɔːbɪt/ **A** *n* orbite *f*
B *vt* décrire une orbite autour de ‹*sun, planet*›

orchard /'ɔːtʃəd/ *n* verger *m*

orchestra /'ɔːkɪstrə/ *n* orchestre *m*

orchestrate /'ɔːkɪstreɪt/ *vt* orchestrer

orchid /'ɔːkɪd/ *n* orchidée *f*

ordain /ɔː'deɪn/ *vt* **1** (decree) décréter (**that** que)
2 ordonner ‹*priest*›

ordeal /ɔː'diːl, 'ɔːdiːl/ *n* épreuve *f*

order /'ɔːdə(r)/ **A** *n* **1** (gen) ordre *m*; **in alphabetical ~** dans l'ordre alphabétique; **to restore ~** rétablir l'ordre
2 (command) ordre *m* (**to do** de faire); **to be under ~s to do** avoir (l')ordre de faire
3 (in shop, restaurant) commande *f*
4 (operational state) **in working ~** en état de marche; **to be out of ~** ‹*phone line*› être en dérangement; ‹*lift, machine*› être en panne
5 (all right) **in ~** ‹*documents*› en règle; **that remark was way out of ~** cette remarque était tout à fait déplacée
6 (*also* **religious ~**) ordre *m*
B *vt* **1** (command) ordonner; **to ~ sb to do** ordonner à qn de faire
2 commander ‹*goods, meal*›; réserver ‹*taxi*› (**for** pour)
C *vi* ‹*diner, customer*› commander
D **in order that** *phr* (with the same subject) afin de (+ *infinitive*), pour (+ *infinitive*); (when subject of verb changes) afin que (+ *subjunctive*), pour que (+ *subjunctive*)
E **in order to** *phr* pour, afin de
■ **order about, order around**: **to ~ people around** donner des ordres

order form *n* bon *m or* bulletin *m* de commande

orderly /'ɔːdəlɪ/ **A** *n* (medical) aide-soignant/-e *m/f*
B *adj* ‹*queue*› ordonné/-e; ‹*pattern, row*› régulier/-ière; ‹*mind, system*› méthodique; ‹*crowd, demonstration*› calme

ordinary /'ɔːdənrɪ, (AmE) 'ɔːrdənerɪ/ **A** *n* **to be out of the ~** sortir de l'ordinaire
B *adj* **1** (normal) ‹*family, life, person*› ordinaire; ‹*clothes*› de tous les jours
2 (average) ‹*consumer, family*› moyen/-enne
3 (uninspiring) quelconque (derog)

ore /ɔː(r)/ *n* minerai *m*; **iron ~** minerai de fer

organ /'ɔːgən/ *n* **1** (gen) organe *m*
2 (Mus) orgue *m*

organ donor *n* donneur/-euse *m/f* d'organes

organic /ɔː'gænɪk/ *adj* ‹*substance, development*› organique; ‹*produce, farming*› biologique

organism /'ɔːgənɪzəm/ *n* organisme *m*

organization /ˌɔːgənaɪ'zeɪʃn, (AmE) -nɪ'z-/ *n* **1** (group) organisation *f*; (government) organisme *m*; (voluntary) association *f*
2 (arrangement) organisation *f* (**of** de)

organize /'ɔːgənaɪz/ *vt* organiser ‹*event, time, life*›; ranger ‹*books, papers*›

organized crime *n* grand banditisme *m*

organizer /'ɔːgənaɪzə(r)/ *n* **1** (person) organisateur/-trice *m/f*
2 (*also* **personal ~**) (agenda *m*) organisateur *m*; **electronic ~** agenda électronique

organ transplant *n* transplantation *f* d'organe

orgy /'ɔːdʒɪ/ *n* orgie *f*

orient /'ɔːrɪənt/ **A** *n* **the Orient** l'Orient *m*
B *vt* (*also* **orientate**) orienter (**towards** vers)

oriental /ˌɔːrɪ'entl/ *adj* (gen) (offensive) oriental/-e; ‹*appearance, eyes*› d'Oriental; ‹*carpet*› d'Orient

orienteering /ˌɔːrɪən'tɪərɪŋ/ *n* course *f* d'orientation

🔑 **origin** /ˈɒrɪdʒɪn/ *n* origine *f*

🔑 **original** /əˈrɪdʒənl/ **A** *n* original *m*
B *adj* **1** (gen) original/-e
2 (initial) ‹*inhabitant, owner*› premier/-ière *before n*; ‹*question, site*› originel/-elle

originality /əˌrɪdʒəˈnælətɪ/ *n* originalité *f*

🔑 **originally** /əˈrɪdʒənəlɪ/ *adv* **1** (initially) au départ
2 (in the first place) à l'origine

originate /əˈrɪdʒɪneɪt/ *vi* ‹*custom, style, tradition*› voir le jour; ‹*fire*› se déclarer; **to ∼ from** ‹*goods*› provenir de

originator /əˈrɪdʒɪneɪtə(r)/ *n* **1** (of idea, rumour) auteur *m*
2 (of invention, system) créateur/-trice *m/f*

ornament /ˈɔːnəmənt/ *n* **1** (trinket) bibelot *m*
2 (ornamentation) ornement *m*

ornamental /ˌɔːnəˈmentl/ *adj* ‹*plant*› ornemental/-e; ‹*lake*› d'agrément; ‹*motif*› décoratif/-ive

ornate /ɔːˈneɪt/ *adj* richement orné/-e

ornithology /ˌɔːnɪˈθɒlədʒɪ/ *n* ornithologie *f*

orphan /ˈɔːfn/ *n* orphelin/-e *m/f*

orphanage /ˈɔːfənɪdʒ/ *n* orphelinat *m*

orthodox /ˈɔːθədɒks/ *adj* orthodoxe

orthopaedic (BrE), **orthopedic** (AmE) /ˌɔːθəˈpiːdɪk/ *adj* orthopédique

ostentatious /ˌɒstenˈteɪʃəs/ *adj* ostentatoire

osteopath /ˈɒstɪəpæθ/ *n* ostéopathe *mf*

ostracize /ˈɒstrəsaɪz/ *vt* ostraciser

ostrich /ˈɒstrɪtʃ/ *n* autruche *f*

🔑 **other** /ˈʌðə(r)/ **A** *adj* autre; **the ∼ one** l'autre; **the ∼ 25** les 25 autres; **∼ people** les autres; **he was going the ∼ way** il allait dans la direction opposée; **the ∼ day** l'autre jour; **every ∼ year** tous les deux ans; **every ∼ Saturday** un samedi sur deux
B *pron* **the ∼s** les autres; **∼s** (as subject) d'autres; (as object) les autres; **one after the ∼** l'un après l'autre; **someone or ∼** quelqu'un; **some book or ∼** un livre, je ne sais plus lequel; **somehow or ∼** d'une manière ou d'une autre
C **other than** *phr* **∼ than that** à part ça; **nobody knows ∼ than you** tu es le seul à le savoir

🔑 **otherwise** /ˈʌðəwaɪz/ **A** *adv* autrement; **no woman, married or ∼** aucune femme, mariée ou non
B *conj* sinon; **it's quite safe, ∼ I wouldn't do it** ce n'est pas dangereux du tout, sinon je ne le ferais pas

otter /ˈɒtə(r)/ *n* loutre *f*

ouch /aʊtʃ/ *excl* aïe!

ought /ɔːt/ *modal aux* **I ∼ to do/to have done** je devrais/j'aurais dû faire; **that ∼ to fix it** ça devrait arranger les choses; **oughtn't we to ask?** ne croyez-vous pas que nous devrions demander?; **we ∼ to say something** nous devrions dire quelque chose; **someone ∼ to have accompanied her** quelqu'un aurait dû l'accompagner

ounce /aʊns/ *n* once *f* (= *28.35 g*)

🔑 **our** /ˈaʊə(r), ɑː(r)/ *det* notre/nos

> In French, determiners agree in gender and number with the noun that follows. So *our* is translated by *notre* + masculine or feminine singular noun (notre chien, notre maison) and *nos* + plural noun (nos enfants).
> When *our* is stressed, *à nous* is added after the noun: *OUR house* = notre maison à nous.

ours /ˈaʊəz/ *pron*

> In French, possessive pronouns reflect the number and gender of the noun they are standing for. Thus *ours* is translated by *le nôtre, la nôtre* or *les nôtres* according to what is being referred to.

their children are older than ∼ leurs enfants sont plus âgés que les nôtres; **which tickets are ∼?** lesquels de ces billets sont les nôtres *or* à nous?; **a friend of ∼** un ami à nous; **the blue car is ∼** la voiture bleue est à nous; **it's not ∼** ce n'est pas à nous

🔑 **ourselves** /aʊəˈselvz, ɑː-/ *pron* **1** (reflexive) nous; **we've hurt ∼** nous nous sommes fait mal
2 (emphatic) nous-mêmes; **we did it ∼** nous l'avons fait nous-mêmes
3 (after prepositions) **for ∼** pour nous, pour nous-mêmes; **(all) by ∼** tout seuls/toutes seules

🔑 **out** /aʊt/

> When *out* is used as an adverb meaning *outside*, it often adds little to the sense of the phrase: *they're out in the garden* = *they're in the garden*. In such cases *out* will not usually be translated: *ils sont dans le jardin*.

A *vt* révéler l'homosexualité de ‹*person*›
B *adv* **1** (outside) dehors; **to stay ∼ in the rain** rester (dehors) sous la pluie; **∼ there** dehors
2 to go *or* **walk ∼** sortir; **I couldn't find my way ∼** je ne trouvais pas la sortie; **when the tide is ∼** à marée basse; **further ∼** plus loin; **to invite sb ∼ to dinner** inviter qn au restaurant
3 (absent) **to be ∼** être sorti/-e
4 to be ∼ ‹*book, exam results*› être publié/-e
5 to be ∼ ‹*sun, moon, stars*› briller
6 to be ∼ ‹*fire, light*› être éteint/-e
7 (Sport) **to be ∼** ‹*player*› être éliminé/-e; **'∼!'** (of ball) 'out!'
8 (over) **before the week is ∼** avant la fin de la semaine
9 (fam) **to be ∼ to do** être bien décidé/-e à faire; **he's just ∼ for what he can get** c'est l'intérêt qui le guide
C **out of** *phr* **1 to go** *or* **walk** *or* **come ∼ of**

O

🔑 mot clé

sortir de; **to jump ~ of the window** sauter par la fenêtre; **to take sth ~ of one's bag** prendre qch dans son sac
2 (expressing ratio) sur; **two ~ of every three** deux sur trois
3 hors de ‹*reach, sight*›; en dehors de ‹*city*›; à l'abri de ‹*sun*›
4 to be (right) ~ of ne plus avoir de ‹*item*›
IDIOM **to be ~ of it** (fam) être dans les vapes (fam)

out-and-out /ˌaʊtən'aʊt/ *adj* ‹*villain, liar*› fieffé/-e; ‹*supporter*› pur/-e et dur/-e; ‹*success, failure*› total/-e

outback /'aʊtbæk/ *n* **the ~** la brousse (australienne)

outboard motor *n* moteur *m* hors-bord

outbreak /'aʊtbreɪk/ *n* (of war) début *m*; (of violence, spots) éruption *f*; (of disease) déclaration *f*

outbuilding /'aʊtbɪldɪŋ/ *n* dépendance *f*

outburst /'aʊtbɜːst/ *n* accès *m*

outcast /'aʊtkɑːst, (AmE) -kæst/ *n* exclu/-e *m/f*

outcome /'aʊtkʌm/ *n* résultat *m*

outcry /'aʊtkraɪ/ *n* tollé *m* (**about, against** contre)

outdated /ˌaʊt'deɪtɪd/ *adj* ‹*idea, practice, theory*› dépassé/-e; ‹*clothing*› démodé/-e

outdo /ˌaʊt'duː/ *vt* (*prét* **outdid**, *pp* **outdone**) surpasser

outdoor /'aʊtdɔː(r)/ *adj* ‹*life, activity, sport*› de plein air; ‹*restaurant*› en plein air

outdoors /ˌaʊt'dɔːz/ *adv* ‹*sit, work, play*› dehors; ‹*live*› en plein air; ‹*sleep*› à la belle étoile; **to go ~** sortir

outer /'aʊtə(r)/ *adj* **1** (outside) extérieur/-e
2 ‹*limit*› extrême

outer space *n* espace *m* (extra-atmosphérique)

outfit /'aʊtfɪt/ *n* tenue *f*

outgoing /'aʊtgəʊɪŋ/ *adj* **1** (sociable) ouvert/-e et sociable
2 ‹*government*› sortant/-e

outgoings /'aʊtgəʊɪŋz/ *npl* (BrE) sorties *fpl* (de fonds)

outgrow /aʊt'grəʊ/ *vt* (*prét* **outgrew**, *pp* **outgrown**) **1** (grow too big for) devenir trop grand pour
2 (grow too old for) se lasser de [qch] avec le temps; **he'll ~ it** ça lui passera

outlandish /aʊt'lændɪʃ/ *adj* bizarre

outlast /ˌaʊt'lɑːst, (AmE) -læst/ *vt* durer plus longtemps que

outlaw /'aʊtlɔː/ **A** *n* hors-la-loi *m inv*
B *vt* déclarer illégal/-e ‹*practice, organization*›

outlay /'aʊtleɪ/ *n* dépenses *fpl* (**on** en)

outlet /'aʊtlet/ *n* **1** (for gas, air, water) tuyau *m* de sortie
2 retail ~ point *m* de vente
3 (for emotion, talent) exutoire *m*
4 (AmE) (socket) prise *f* de courant

outline /'aʊtlaɪn/ **A** *n* **1** (silhouette) contour *m*
2 (of plan, policy) grandes lignes *fpl*; (of essay) plan *m*
B *vt* exposer brièvement ‹*aims, plan, reasons*›

outlive /ˌaʊt'lɪv/ *vt* survivre à ‹*person*›

outlook /'aʊtlʊk/ *n* **1** (attitude) vue *f*
2 (prospects) perspectives *fpl*

outlying /'aʊtlaɪɪŋ/ *adj* (away from city centre) excentré/-e; (remote) isolé/-e

outnumber /ˌaʊt'nʌmbə(r)/ *vt* être plus nombreux/-euses que

out-of-body experience *n* **to have an ~** faire une projection hors du corps

out-of-date *adj* ‹*ticket, passport*› périmé/-e; ‹*concept*› dépassé/-e

outpatient /'aʊtpeɪʃnt/ *n* malade *mf* externe; **~'s department** service *m* de consultation

outpost /'aʊtpəʊst/ *n* avant-poste *m*

output /'aʊtpʊt/ *n* (yield) rendement *m*; (of factory) production *f*

outrage /'aʊtreɪdʒ/ **A** *n* **1** (anger) indignation *f* (**at** devant)
2 (atrocity) atrocité *f*
3 (scandal) scandale *m*
B *vt* scandaliser ‹*public*›

outrageous /aʊt'reɪdʒəs/ *adj* scandaleux/-euse; ‹*remark*› outrancier/-ière

outright /'aʊtraɪt/ **A** *adj* ‹*control, majority*› absolu/-e; ‹*ban*› catégorique; ‹*victory, winner*› incontesté/-e
B *adv* (gen) catégoriquement; ‹*killed*› sur le coup

outset /'aʊtset/ *n* **at the ~** au début; **from the ~** dès le début

outside /aʊt'saɪd, 'aʊtsaɪd/ **A** *n* **1** extérieur *m*; **on the ~** à l'extérieur
2 (maximum) **at the ~** au maximum
B *adj* extérieur/-e; **~ lane** (in GB) voie *f* de droite; (in US, Europe) voie *f* de gauche; (on athletics track) couloir *m* extérieur; **an ~ chance** une faible chance
C *adv* dehors
D *prep* (*also* **~ of**) **1** en dehors de ‹*city*›; de l'autre côté de ‹*boundary*›; à l'extérieur de ‹*building*›
2 (in front of) devant ‹*house, shop*›

outsider /ˌaʊt'saɪdə(r)/ *n* **1** (in community) étranger/-ère *m/f*
2 (Sport) outsider *m*

outsize /'aʊtsaɪz/ *adj* ‹*clothes*› grande taille

outskirts /'aʊtskɜːts/ *npl* périphérie *f*

outsource /aʊt'sɔːs/ *vt* **1** (subcontract) sous-traiter
2 (to another country for cheaper labour) externaliser

outsourcing /'aʊtsɔːsɪŋ/ *n* **1** (subcontracting) sous-traitance *f*
2 (to another country for cheaper labour) externalisation *f*

O

outspoken /ˌaʊtˈspəʊkən/ *adj* **to be ~** parler sans détour

outstanding /ˌaʊtˈstændɪŋ/ *adj*
1 (praiseworthy) remarquable
2 (striking) frappant/-e
3 ‹*bill*› impayé/-e; ‹*work*› inachevé/-e; **~ debts** créances *fpl* à recouvrer

outstay /ˌaʊtˈsteɪ/ *vt* **to ~ one's welcome** s'éterniser

outstretched /ˌaʊtˈstretʃt/ *adj* ‹*hand, arm*› tendu/-e; ‹*wings*› déployé/-e

outstrip /ˌaʊtˈstrɪp/ *vt* (*p prés etc* **-pp-**) dépasser ‹*person*›; excéder ‹*production, demand*›

outward /ˈaʊtwəd/ **A** *adj* ‹*appearance, sign*› extérieur/-e; ‹*calm*› apparent/-e; **~ journey** aller *m*
B *adv* ((BrE) *also* **outwards**) vers l'extérieur

outwardly /ˈaʊtwədlɪ/ *adv* (apparently) en apparence

outwards (BrE) /ˈaʊtwədz/ = **outward B**

outweigh /ˌaʊtˈweɪ/ *vt* l'emporter sur

outwit /ˌaʊtˈwɪt/ *vt* (*p prés etc* **-tt-**) être plus futé/-e que ‹*person*›

outworker /ˈaʊtwɜːkə(r)/ *n* travailleur/-euse *m/f* à domicile

oval /ˈəʊvl/ *n*, *adj* ovale *m*

ovary /ˈəʊvərɪ/ *n* ovaire *m*

ovation /əʊˈveɪʃn/ *n* ovation *f*; **to give sb a standing ~** se lever pour ovationner qn

oven /ˈʌvn/ *n* four *m*

oven glove *n* manique *f*

O

⚷ **over**

> *over* is often used with another preposition in English (*to*, *in*, *on*) without altering the meaning. In this case *over* is usually not translated in French: *to be over in France* = être en France; *to swim over to sb* = nager vers qn.

A *prep* **1** par-dessus; **he jumped ~ it** il a sauté par-dessus; **to wear a sweater ~ one's shirt** porter un pull par-dessus sa chemise; **a bridge ~ the Thames** un pont sur la Tamise
2 (across) **it's just ~ the road** c'est juste de l'autre côté de la rue; **~ here/there** par ici/là; **come ~ here!** viens (par) ici!
3 (above) au-dessus de; **they live ~ the shop** ils habitent au-dessus de la boutique; **children ~ six** les enfants de plus de six ans; **temperatures ~ 40°** des températures supérieures à *or* au-dessus de 40°
4 (in the course of) **~ the weekend** pendant le week-end; **~ the last few days** au cours de ces derniers jours; **~ the years** avec le temps; **~ Christmas** à Noël
5 to be ~ s'être remis/-e de ‹*illness, operation*›; **to be ~ the worst** avoir passé le pire
6 (by means of) **~ the phone** par téléphone; **~ the radio** à la radio
7 (everywhere) **all ~ the house** partout dans la maison
B *adj*, *adv* **1** (finished) **to be ~** ‹*term, meeting*› être terminé/-e; ‹*war*› être fini/-e
2 (more) **children of six and ~** les enfants de plus de six ans
3 to invite *or* **ask sb ~** inviter qn; **we had them ~ on Sunday** ils sont venus dimanche
4 (on radio, TV) **~ to you** à vous; **now ~ to our Paris studios** nous passons l'antenne à nos studios de Paris
5 (showing repetition) **five times ~** cinq fois de suite; **to start all ~ again** recommencer à zéro; **I had to do it ~** (AmE) j'ai dû recommencer; **I've told you ~ and ~ (again)...** je t'ai dit je ne sais combien de fois...

overact /ˌəʊvərˈækt/ *vi* en faire trop

⚷ **overall** **A** /ˈəʊvərɔːl/ *n* (BrE) (coat-type) blouse *f*; (child's) tablier *m*
B overalls *npl* (BrE) combinaison *f*; (AmE) salopette *f*
C *adj* ‹*cost*› global/-e; ‹*improvement*› général/-e; ‹*effect*› d'ensemble; ‹*majority*› absolu/-e
D /ˌəʊvərˈɔːl/ *adv* **1** (in total) en tout
2 (in general) dans l'ensemble

overawe /ˌəʊvərˈɔː/ *vt* intimider

overbalance /ˌəʊvəˈbæləns/ *vi* ‹*person*› perdre l'équilibre; ‹*pile of objects*› s'écrouler

overboard /ˈəʊvəbɔːd/ *adv* par-dessus bord, à l'eau

overbook /ˌəʊvəˈbʊk/ *vt*, *vi* surréserver

overcast /ˌəʊvəˈkɑːst, (AmE) -ˈkæst/ *adj* ‹*sky*› couvert/-e

overcharge /ˌəʊvəˈtʃɑːdʒ/ *vt* faire payer trop cher à

overcoat /ˈəʊvəkəʊt/ *n* pardessus *m*

overcome /ˌəʊvəˈkʌm/ **A** *vt* (*prét* **-came**, *pp* **-come**) battre ‹*opponent*›; vaincre ‹*enemy*›; surmonter ‹*dislike, fear*›; **to be ~ with despair** succomber au désespoir
B *vi* (*prét* **-came**, *pp* **-come**) triompher

overcook /ˌəʊvəˈkʊk/ *vt* trop cuire

overcrowded /ˌəʊvəˈkraʊdɪd/ *adj* ‹*train, room*› bondé/-e; ‹*city*› surpeuplé/-e; ‹*class*› surchargé/-e

overcrowding /ˌəʊvəˈkraʊdɪŋ/ *n* (in city, institution) surpeuplement *m*; (in transport) surencombrement *m*; **~ in classrooms** les classes surchargées

overdo /ˌəʊvəˈduː/ *vt* (*prét* **-did**, *pp* **-done**) **to ~ it** (when describing) exagérer; (when performing) forcer la note (fam); (when working) en faire trop (fam)

overdose, OD /ˈəʊvədəʊs/ **A** *n* (large dose) surdose *f*; (lethal dose) (of medicine) dose *f* mortelle; (of drugs) overdose *f*; **to take an ~** absorber une dose excessive de médicaments

⚷ mot clé

B *vi* (on medicine) prendre une dose mortelle de médicaments; (on drugs) faire une overdose

overdraft /ˈəʊvədrɑːft, (AmE) -dræft/ *n* découvert *m*

overdrawn *adj* à découvert

overdressed *adj* trop habillé/-e

overdrive /ˈəʊvədraɪv/ *n* **to go into ~** ‹*person*› s'activer intensivement

overdue /ˌəʊvəˈdjuː, (AmE) -ˈduː/ *adj* ‹*baby, work*› en retard (**by** de); ‹*bill*› impayé/-e; **this measure is long ~** cette mesure aurait dû être prise il y a longtemps

overeat /ˌəʊvərˈiːt/ *vi* (*prét* **-ate**, *pp* **-eaten**) manger à l'excès

overestimate /ˌəʊvərˈestɪmeɪt/ *vt* surestimer

overexcited /ˌəʊvərɪkˈsaɪtɪd/ *adj* surexcité/-e

overflow /ˌəʊvəˈfləʊ/ **A** *vt* ‹*river*› inonder ‹*banks*›
B *vi* déborder (**into** dans, **with** de)

overflow car park *n* parking *m* de délestage

overgrown /ˌəʊvəˈgrəʊn/ *adj* ‹*garden*› envahi/-e par la végétation

overhaul **A** /ˈəʊvəhɔːl/ *n* (of machine) révision *f*; (of system) restructuration *f*
B /ˌəʊvəˈhɔːl/ *vt* réviser ‹*car, machine*›; restructurer ‹*system*›

overhead **A** /ˈəʊvəhed/ *adj* ‹*cable, railway*› aérien/-ienne
B /ˌəʊvəˈhed/ *adv* **1** (in sky) dans le ciel
2 (above sb's head) au-dessus de ma/sa etc tête

overhead projector *n* rétroprojecteur *m*

overheads (BrE), **overhead** (AmE) *npl* frais *mpl* généraux

overhear /ˌəʊvəˈhɪə(r)/ *vt* (*p prés, pp* **-heard**) entendre par hasard

overheat /ˌəʊvəˈhiːt/ *vi* ‹*car, equipment*› chauffer

overindulge /ˌəʊvərɪnˈdʌldʒ/ *vi* faire des excès

overjoyed /ˌəʊvəˈdʒɔɪd/ *adj* fou/folle de joie (**at** devant)

overkill /ˈəʊvəkɪl/ *n* (excess publicity) matraquage *m*

overland /ˈəʊvəlænd/ **A** *adj* ‹*route*› terrestre; ‹*journey*› par route
B *adv* par route

overlap /ˌəʊvəˈlæp/ *vi* (*p prés etc* **-pp-**) se chevaucher

overleaf /ˌəʊvəˈliːf/ *adv* au verso

overload /ˈəʊvələʊd/ /ˌəʊvəˈləʊd/ *vt* surcharger (**with** de)

overlook /ˌəʊvəˈlʊk/ *vt* **1** ‹*building, window*› donner sur
2 (miss) ne pas voir ‹*detail, error*›; **to ~ the fact that** négliger le fait que
3 (ignore) ignorer ‹*effect, need*›

overnight **A** /ˈəʊvənaɪt/ *adj* **1** ‹*journey, train*› de nuit; ‹*stop*› pour une nuit
2 ‹*success*› immédiat/-e
B /ˌəʊvəˈnaɪt/ *adv* **1 to stay ~** passer la nuit
2 ‹*change, disappear, transform*› du jour au lendemain

overnight bag *n* petit sac *m* de voyage

overpass /ˈəʊvəpɑːs/ (AmE) /-pæs/ *n* **1** (for cars) toboggan *m*
2 (footbridge) passerelle *f*

overpopulated /ˌəʊvəˈpɒpjʊleɪtɪd/ *adj* surpeuplé/-e

overpower /ˌəʊvəˈpaʊə(r)/ *vt* **1** maîtriser ‹*thief*›; vaincre ‹*army*›
2 ‹*smell, smoke*› accabler

overpowering /ˌəʊvəˈpaʊərɪŋ/ *adj* ‹*person*› intimidant/-e; ‹*desire, urge*› irrésistible; ‹*heat*› accablant/-e; ‹*smell*› irrespirable

overpriced /ˌəʊvəˈpraɪst/ *adj* **it's ~** c'est trop cher pour ce que c'est

overqualified /ˌəʊvəˈkwɒlɪfaɪd/ *adj* surqualifié/-e

overrated /ˌəʊvəˈreɪtɪd/ *adj* ‹*person, work*› surfait/-e

overreact /ˌəʊvərɪˈækt/ *vi* réagir de façon excessive

override /ˈəʊvəraɪd/ /ˌəʊvəˈraɪd/ *vt* (*prét* **-rode**, *pp* **-ridden**) l'emporter sur ‹*consideration*›; passer outre à ‹*decision*›

overriding /ˌəʊvəˈraɪdɪŋ/ *adj* ‹*importance*› primordial/-e; ‹*priority*› numéro un

overrule /ˌəʊvəˈruːl/ *vt* **to be ~d** ‹*decision*› être annulé/-e

overrun /ˈəʊvərʌn/ /ˌəʊvəˈrʌn/ *vt* (*p prés* **-nn-**, *prét* **-ran**, *pp* **-run**) **1** (invade) envahir ‹*country, site*›
2 (exceed) dépasser ‹*time, budget*›

overseas /ˌəʊvəˈsiːz/ **A** *adj* **1** ‹*student, investor*› étranger/-ère
2 ‹*trade, market*› extérieur/-e
B *adv* à l'étranger

overshadow /ˌəʊvəˈʃædəʊ/ *vt* éclipser ‹*achievement*›

oversight /ˈəʊvəsaɪt/ *n* erreur *f*; **due to an ~** par inadvertance

oversimplify /ˌəʊvəˈsɪmplɪfaɪ/ *vt* simplifier [qch] à l'excès

oversleep /ˌəʊvəˈsliːp/ *vi* (*prét, pp* **-slept**) se réveiller trop tard

overspend /ˌəʊvəˈspend/ *vi* (*prét, pp* **-spent**) trop dépenser

overstay /ˌəʊvəˈsteɪ/ *vt* **to ~ one's visa** dépasser la limite de validité de son visa

overstep /ˌəʊvəˈstep/ *vt* (*p prés etc* **-pp-**) dépasser ‹*bounds*›; **to ~ the mark** aller trop loin

overt /ˈəʊvɜːt, (AmE) əʊˈvɜːrt/ *adj* évident/-e, manifeste

overtake /ˌəʊvəˈteɪk/ *vt, vi* (*prét* **-took**, *pp* **-taken**) dépasser

O

over-the-top, **OTT** /ˌəʊvəðəˈtɒp/ *adj* (fam) outrancier/-ière; **to go over the top** aller trop loin

overthrow /ˈəʊvəθrəʊ/ /ˌəʊvəˈθrəʊ/ *vt* (*prét* **-threw**, *pp* **-thrown**) renverser ‹*government, system*›

overtime /ˈəʊvətaɪm/ **A** *n* heures *fpl* supplémentaires
B *adv* **to work ~** ‹*person*› faire des heures supplémentaires

overtone /ˈəʊvətəʊn/ *n* sous-entendu *m*, connotation *f*

overture /ˈəʊvətjʊə(r)/ *n* ouverture *f*

overturn /ˌəʊvəˈtɜːn/ **A** *vt* **1** renverser ‹*car, chair*›; faire chavirer ‹*boat*›
2 faire annuler ‹*decision, sentence*›
B *vi* ‹*car, chair*› se renverser; ‹*boat*› chavirer

overuse **A** /ˌəʊvəˈjuːs/ *n* **1** (of word, product) abus *m*
2 (of facility) utilisation *f* excessive; **to be worn through ~** être usé d'avoir trop servi
B /ˌəʊvəˈjuːz/ *vt* trop se servir de ‹*machine*›; abuser de ‹*chemical, service*›; galvauder ‹*word*›

overweight /ˌəʊvəˈweɪt/ *adj* **1** ‹*person*› trop gros/grosse
2 ‹*suitcase*› trop lourd/-e

overwhelm /ˌəʊvəˈwelm, (AmE) -hwelm/
A *vt* **1** ‹*wave, avalanche*› submerger; ‹*enemy*› écraser
2 ‹*shame, grief*› accabler
B **overwhelmed** *pp adj* (with letters, offers, kindness) submergé/-e (**with, by** de); (with shame, work) accablé/-e (**with, by** de); (by sight, experience) ébloui/-e (**by** par)

overwhelming /ˌəʊvəˈwelmɪŋ, (AmE) -hwelm-/ *adj* ‹*defeat, victory, majority*› écrasant/-e; ‹*desire*› irrésistible; ‹*heat, sorrow*› accablant/-e; ‹*support*› massif/-ive

overwork /ˈəʊvəwɜːk/ *vi* se surmener

overworked /ˌəʊvəˈwɜːkt/ *adj* surmené/-e

owe /əʊ/ *vt* devoir; **to ~ sth to sb** devoir qch à qn

owing /ˈəʊɪŋ/ **A** *adj* à payer, dû/-e
B **owing to** *phr* en raison de

owl /aʊl/ *n* hibou *m*; (with tufted ears) chouette *f*

⚷ **own** /əʊn/ **A** *adj* propre; **her ~ car** sa propre voiture
B *pron* **my ~** le mien, la mienne; **his/her ~** le sien, la sienne; **he has a room of his ~** il a sa propre chambre *or* une chambre à lui; **a house of our (very) ~** une maison (bien) à nous
C *vt* avoir ‹*car, house, dog*›; **she ~s three shops** elle est propriétaire de trois magasins; **who ~s that house?** à qui est cette maison?
IDIOMS **to get one's ~ back** se venger (**on** sb de qn); **on one's ~** tout seul/toute seule
■ **own up** avouer

⚷ **owner** /ˈəʊnə(r)/ *n* propriétaire *mf*; **car ~** automobiliste *mf*; **home ~** propriétaire *mf*

ownership /ˈəʊnəʃɪp/ *n* propriété *f*; (of land) possession *f*

ox /ɒks/ *n* (*pl* **~en**) bœuf *m*

oxygen /ˈɒksɪdʒən/ *n* oxygène *m*

oyster /ˈɔɪstə(r)/ *n* huître *f*

ozone /ˈəʊzəʊn/ *n* ozone *m*

ozone layer *n* couche *f* d'ozone

Pp

p, **P** /piː/ *n* p, P *m*

PA *n* (*abbr* = **personal assistant**) secrétaire *mf* de direction

⚷ **pace** **A** *n* (step) pas *m*; (rate) rythme *m*; (speed) vitesse *f*; **at a fast/slow ~** vite/lentement; **at walking ~** au pas
B *vi* **to ~ up and down** (impatiently) faire les cent pas; **to ~ up and down sth** arpenter ‹*cage, room*›

pacemaker /ˈpeɪsmeɪkə(r)/ *n* **1** (Med) stimulateur *m* cardiaque
2 (athlete) lièvre *m*

Pacific /pəˈsɪfɪk/ *pr n* **the ~** le Pacifique; **the ~ Ocean** l'océan *m* Pacifique

pacifist /ˈpæsɪfɪst/ *n, adj* pacifiste *mf*

pacify /ˈpæsɪfaɪ/ *vt* apaiser ‹*person*›; pacifier ‹*country*›

⚷ **pack** /pæk/ **A** *n* **1** (box) paquet *m*; (large box) boîte *f*; (bag) sachet *m*
2 (group) bande *f*; (of hounds) meute *f*; **a ~ of lies** un tissu de mensonges
3 (in rugby) pack *m*
4 (of cards) jeu *m* de cartes
5 (backpack) sac *m* à dos
B *vt* **1** (in suitcase) mettre [qch] dans une valise ‹*clothes*›; (in box, crate) emballer

‹ornaments, books›
2 emballer *‹box, crate›*; **to ~ one's suitcase** faire sa valise
3 *‹crowd›* remplir complètement *‹church, theatre›*
4 tasser *‹snow, earth›*
C *vi* **1** *‹person›* faire ses valises
2 to ~ into *‹crowd›* s'entasser dans *‹place›*
▪ **pack up A ~ up 1** *‹person›* faire ses valises
2 (fam) (break down) *‹TV, machine›* se détraquer (fam); *‹car›* tomber en panne
B ~ [sth] up, ~ up [sth] (in boxes, crates) emballer

⚷ **package** /'pækɪdʒ/ **A** *n* **1** (parcel) paquet *m*, colis *m*
2 (of proposals, measures, aid) ensemble *m* (of de)
3 (Comput) progiciel *m*
B *vt* conditionner, emballer

package deal *n* offre *f* globale

package holiday (BrE), **package tour** *n* voyage *m* organisé

packaging /'pækɪdʒɪŋ/ *n* conditionnement *m*

packed /pækt/ *adj* comble; **~ with** plein/-e de

packed lunch *n* panier-repas *m*

packet /'pækɪt/ *n* (gen) paquet *m*; (sachet) sachet *m*

packing /'pækɪŋ/ *n* **1** (packaging) emballage *m*
2 to do one's ~ faire ses valises

pact /pækt/ *n* pacte *m*

pad /pæd/ **A** *n* **1** (of paper) bloc *m*
2 (for leg) jambière *f*
3 (of paw) coussinet *m*; (of finger) pulpe *f*
4 (*also* **launch ~**) rampe *f* de lancement
B *vt* (*p prés etc* **-dd-**) rembourrer *‹chair, shoulders, jacket›* (**with** avec); capitonner *‹walls›*
C *vi* (*p prés etc* **-dd-**) **to ~ along/around** avancer/aller et venir à pas feutrés
▪ **pad out** étoffer, délayer *‹essay, speech›*

padded envelope *n* enveloppe *f* matelassée

padding /'pædɪŋ/ *n* (stuffing) rembourrage *m*

paddle /'pædl/ **A** *n* **1** (oar) pagaie *f*
2 to go for a ~ faire trempette *f*
B *vi* **1** (row) pagayer
2 (wade) patauger
3 *‹duck, swan›* barboter

paddling pool *n* (public) pataugeoire *f*; (inflatable) piscine *f* gonflable

padlock /'pædlɒk/ **A** *n* (on door) cadenas *m*; (for bicycle) antivol *m*
B *vt* cadenasser *‹door, gate›*; mettre un antivol à *‹bicycle›*

paediatrician (BrE), **pediatrician** (AmE) *n* pédiatre *mf*

paedo (BrE), **pedo** (AmE) /'piːdəʊ/ *n* (*pl* **~s**) (fam) pédophile *nmf*

paedophile (BrE), **pedophile** (AmE) *n* pédophile *mf*

pagan /'peɪgən/ *n*, *adj* païen/païenne *m/f*

⚷ **page** /peɪdʒ/ **A** *n* **1** (in book) page *f*; **on ~ two** à la page deux
2 (attendant) groom *m*; (AmE) coursier *m*
B *vt* (on pager) rechercher; (over loudspeaker) faire appeler

pageant /'pædʒənt/ *n* (play) reconstitution *f* historique; (carnival) fête *f* à thème historique

pageboy /'peɪdʒbɔɪ/ *n* (at wedding) garçon *m* d'honneur

pager /'peɪdʒə(r)/ *n* récepteur *m* d'appel

paid /peɪd/ *adj ‹work, job›* rémunéré/-e; *‹holiday›* payé/-e; **~ assassin** tueur *m* à gages

⚷ **pain** /peɪn/ **A** *n* **1** douleur *f*; **to be in ~** souffrir; **period ~s** règles *fpl* douloureuses
2 (fam) (annoying person, thing) **he's/it's a ~** il est/c'est enquiquinant (fam); **he's a ~ in the neck** (fam) il est casse-pieds (fam)
B pains *npl* **to be at ~s to do** prendre grand soin de faire; **to take great ~s over** *or* **with sth** se donner beaucoup de mal pour qch

painful /'peɪnfl/ *adj* douloureux/-euse; *‹lesson, memory›* pénible

painkiller *n* analgésique *m*

painless /'peɪnlɪs/ *adj* **1** (pain-free) indolore
2 (trouble-free) sans peine

painstaking /'peɪnzteɪkɪŋ/ *adj* minutieux/-ieuse

⚷ **paint** /peɪnt/ **A** *n* peinture *f*
B paints *npl* couleurs *fpl*
C *vt* **1** (gen) peindre; peindre le portrait de *‹person›*; **to ~ one's nails** se vernir les ongles
2 (depict) dépeindre
D *vi* peindre

paintbox *n* boîte *f* de couleurs

paintbrush *n* pinceau *m*

painter /'peɪntə(r)/ *n* peintre *m*

⚷ **painting** /'peɪntɪŋ/ *n* **1** (activity, art form) peinture *f*
2 (work of art) tableau *m*; (unframed) toile *f*; (of person) portrait *m*
3 (decorating) peintures *fpl*

⚷ **pair** /peə(r)/ *n* **1** (gen) paire *f*; **to be one of a ~** faire partie d'une paire; **in ~s** *‹work›* en groupes de deux; **a ~ of scissors** une paire de ciseaux; **a ~ of trousers** un pantalon
2 (couple) couple *m*
▪ **pair off** (as a couple) se mettre ensemble; (for temporary purposes) se mettre par deux
▪ **pair up** *‹dancers, lovers›* former un couple; *‹competitors›* faire équipe

paisley /'peɪzlɪ/ *n* tissu *m* à motifs cachemire

pajamas (AmE) = **pyjamas**

Pakistan /ˌpɑːkɪ'stɑːn, ˌpækɪ-/ *pr n* Pakistan *m*

Pakistani /ˌpɑːkɪ'stɑːnɪ, ˌpækɪ-/ **A** *n* Pakistanais/-e *m/f*
B *adj* pakistanais/-e

palace /'pælɪs/ *n* palais *m*

p

palatable /ˈpælətəbl/ *n* ‹*food*› savoureux/-euse; ‹*solution, idea*› acceptable

palate /ˈpælət/ *n* palais *m*

pale /peɪl/ **A** *adj* (gen) pâle; ‹*light, dawn*› blafard/-e; **to turn** *or* **go ~** pâlir
B *vi* pâlir; **to ~ into insignificance** devenir dérisoire

Palestine /ˈpæləstaɪn/ *pr n* Palestine *f*

Palestinian /ˌpælɪˈstɪnɪən/ **A** *n* Palestinien/-ienne *m/f*
B *adj* palestinien/-ienne

palette /ˈpælɪt/ *n* palette *f*

pallet /ˈpælɪt/ *n* (for loading) palette *f*

pallid /ˈpælɪd/ *adj* ‹*skin, light*› blafard/-e

palm /pɑːm/ *n* **1** paume *f*; **in the ~ of one's hand** dans le creux de la main; **he read my ~** il m'a lu les lignes de la main
2 (*also* **~ tree**) palmier *m*
3 (*also* **~ leaf**) palme *f*
▪ **palm off** (fam): **to ~ sth off** faire passer qch (as pour); **to ~ sth off on sb, to ~ sb off with sth** refiler (fam) qch à qn

Palm Sunday *n* dimanche *m* des Rameaux

palmtop *n* (*also* **~ computer**) ordinateur *m* de poche

palpable /ˈpælpəbl/ *adj* ‹*fear, tension*› palpable; ‹*lie, error, nonsense*› manifeste

palpitate /ˈpælpɪteɪt/ *vi* palpiter (**with** de)

paltry /ˈpɔːltrɪ/ *adj* ‹*sum*› dérisoire; ‹*excuse*› piètre *before n*

pamper /ˈpæmpə(r)/ *vt* choyer ‹*person, pet*›

pamphlet /ˈpæmflɪt/ *n* brochure *f*; (political) tract *m*

pan /pæn/ **A** *n* (saucepan) casserole *f*
B *vt* (*p prés etc* **-nn-**) **1** (fam) (criticize) éreinter
2 (in photography) faire un panoramique de

pancake /ˈpæŋkeɪk/ *n* crêpe *f*

pancake day *n* mardi *m* gras

pandemonium /ˌpændɪˈməʊnɪəm/ *n* tohu-bohu *m*

pander /ˈpændə(r)/ *vi* **to ~ to** céder aux exigences de ‹*person*›; flatter ‹*whim*›

pane /peɪn/ *n* vitre *f*, carreau *m*; **a ~ of glass** une vitre, un carreau

⚷ **panel** /ˈpænl/ *n* **1** (of experts, judges) commission *f*; (on discussion programme) invités *mpl*; (on quiz show) jury *m*
2 (section of wall) panneau *m*
3 (of instruments, switches) tableau *m*

pang /pæŋ/ *n* **1** (emotional) serrement *m* de cœur; **a ~ of jealousy** une pointe de jalousie
2 ~s of hunger crampes *fpl* d'estomac

panhandler *n* (AmE) (fam) mendiant/-e *m/f*

panic /ˈpænɪk/ **A** *n* panique *f*, affolement *m*
B *vt* (*p prés etc* **-ck-**) affoler ‹*person, animal*›; semer la panique dans ‹*crowd*›
C *vi* (*p prés etc* **-ck-**) s'affoler

⚷ mot clé

panic buying *n* achats *mpl* par crainte de la pénurie

panic-stricken *adj* pris/-e de panique

panorama /ˌpænəˈrɑːmə/ *n* panorama *m*

pansy /ˈpænzɪ/ *n* pensée *f*

pant /pænt/ *vi* haleter

panther /ˈpænθə(r)/ *n* **1** (leopard) panthère *f*
2 (AmE) (puma) puma *m*

panties /ˈpæntɪz/ *npl* (AmE) slip *m* (de femme)

pantomime /ˈpæntəmaɪm/ *n* (BrE) spectacle *m* pour enfants

pantry /ˈpæntrɪ/ *n* garde-manger *m inv*

pants /pænts/ *npl* **1** (AmE) (trousers) pantalon *m*
2 (BrE) (underwear) slip *m*

panty hose *n* (AmE) collant *m*

panty-liner *n* protège-slip *m*

⚷ **paper** /ˈpeɪpə(r)/ **A** *n* **1** (for writing, drawing) papier *m*; **a piece of ~** (scrap) un bout de papier; (clean sheet) une feuille (de papier); (for wrapping) un morceau de papier; **writing/tissue ~** papier à lettres/de soie
2 (*also* **wall~**) papier *m* peint
3 (newspaper) journal *m*
4 article *m* (**on** sur); (lecture) communication *f* (**on** sur)
5 (exam) épreuve *f* (**on** de)
B papers *npl* (documents) papiers *mpl*
C *adj* ‹*bag, hat, handkerchief, napkin*› en papier; ‹*plate, cup*› en carton
D *vt* tapisser ‹*room, wall*›

paperback /ˈpeɪpəbæk/ *n* livre *m* de poche

paperclip *n* trombone *m*

paper knife *n* coupe-papier *m inv*

paper round *n* **he does a ~** il livre des journaux

paper shop *n* (BrE) marchand *m* de journaux

paper towel *n* essuie-tout *m inv*

paperweight *n* presse-papier *m inv*

paperwork /ˈpeɪpəwɜːk/ *n* (administration) travail *m* administratif; (documentation) documents *mpl*

par /pɑː(r)/ *n* **1 to be on a ~ with** ‹*performance*› être comparable à; ‹*person*› être l'égal/-e de; **to be up to ~** être à la hauteur; **to be below** *or* **under ~** ‹*performance*› être en dessous de la moyenne; ‹*person*› ne pas se sentir en forme
2 (in golf) par *m*

parachute /ˈpærəʃuːt/ **A** *n* parachute *m*
B *vi* descendre en parachute

parachute drop *n* parachutage *m*

parachute jump *n* saut *m* en parachute

parachuting /ˈpærəʃuːtɪŋ/ *n* parachutisme *m*

parade /pəˈreɪd/ **A** *n* **1** (procession) parade *f*
2 (Mil) défilé *m*
B *vt* (display) faire étalage de
C *vi* défiler (**through** dans); **to ~ up and down** ‹*soldier, model*› défiler; ‹*child*› parader

parade ground *n* champ *m* de manœuvres

paradise /ˈpærədaɪs/ *n* paradis *m*; **in ~** au paradis

paradox /ˈpærədɒks/ *n* paradoxe *m*

paradoxical /ˌpærəˈdɒksɪkl/ *adj* paradoxal/-e

paraffin /ˈpærəfɪn/ *n* **1** (BrE) (fuel) pétrole *m*
2 (*also* **~ wax**) paraffine *f*

paragliding /ˈpærəglaɪdɪŋ/ *n* parapente *m*

paragon /ˈpærəgən, (AmE) -gɒn/ *n* modèle *m* (of de)

paragraph /ˈpærəgrɑːf, (AmE) -græf/ *n* paragraphe *m*

parallel /ˈpærəlel/ **A** *n* **1** (gen) parallèle *m*
2 (in mathematics) parallèle *f*
B *adj* **1** (gen) parallèle (**to, with** à)
2 (similar) analogue (**to, with** à)
C *adv* **~ to, ~ with** parallèlement à

Paralympics /pærəˈlɪmpɪks/ *npl* (*also* **Paralympic Games**) jeux *mpl* paralympiques

paralyse (BrE), **paralyze** (AmE) /ˈpærəlaɪz/ *vt* paralyser

paralysis /pəˈræləsɪs/ *n* paralysie *f*

paramedic /ˌpærəˈmedɪk/ *n* auxiliaire *mf* médical/-e

parameter /pəˈræmɪtə(r)/ *n* paramètre *m*

paramilitary /ˌpærəˈmɪlɪtrɪ, (AmE) -terɪ/ **A** *n* membre *m* d'une organisation paramilitaire
B *adj* paramilitaire

paramount /ˈpærəmaʊnt/ *adj* **to be ~, to be of ~ importance** être d'une importance capitale

paranoid /ˈpærənɔɪd/ *adj* (Med) paranoïde; (gen) paranoïaque (**about** au sujet de)

paraphernalia /ˌpærəfəˈneɪlɪə/ *n* attirail *m*

paraphrase /ˈpærəfreɪz/ *vt* paraphraser

parascending /ˈpærəsendɪŋ/ *n* parachutisme *m* ascensionnel

parasite /ˈpærəsaɪt/ *n* parasite *m*

paratrooper /ˈpærətruːpə(r)/ *n* parachutiste *m*

parcel /ˈpɑːsl/ *n* paquet *m*, colis *m*
(IDIOM) **to be part and ~ of** faire partie intégrante de
■ **parcel up**: **~ up [sth], ~ [sth] up** emballer

parcel bomb *n* colis *m* piégé

parched /pɑːtʃt/ *adj* **1** (dry) desséché/-e
2 (thirsty) **to be ~** mourir de soif

parchment /ˈpɑːtʃmənt/ *n* (document) parchemin *m*; (paper) papier-parchemin *m*

pardon /ˈpɑːdn/ **A** *n* **1** (gen) pardon *m*
2 (Law) (*also* **free ~**) grâce *f*
B *excl* (what?) pardon?; (sorry!) pardon!
C *vt* **1** (gen) pardonner; **~ me!** pardon!
2 (Law) grâcier ‹*criminal*›

parent /ˈpeərənt/ *n* parent *m*

parental /pəˈrentl/ *adj* des parents, parental/-e

parent company *n* maison *f* mère

parenthood /ˈpeərənthʊd/ *n* (fatherhood) paternité *f*; (motherhood) maternité *f*

parenting /ˈpeərəntɪŋ/ *n* éducation *f* des enfants

parents' evening *n* réunion *f* pour les parents d'élèves

Paris /ˈpærɪs/ *pr n* Paris

parish /ˈpærɪʃ/ *n* **1** paroisse *f*
2 (BrE) (administrative) commune *f*

Parisian /pəˈrɪzɪən/ **A** *n* Parisien/-ienne *m/f*
B *adj* parisien/-ienne

park /pɑːk/ **A** *n* **1** (public garden) jardin *m* public, parc *m*
2 (estate) parc *m*
B *vt* garer ‹*car*›
C *vi* ‹*driver*› se garer
D **parked** *pp adj* en stationnement

park-and-ride *n* parking *m* relais

parking /ˈpɑːkɪŋ/ *n* stationnement *m*; **'No ~'** 'stationnement interdit'

parking lot *n* (AmE) parking *m*

parking meter *n* parcmètre *m*

parking place, **parking space** *n* place *f*

parking ticket *n* (fine) contravention *f*, PV *m* (fam)

parliament /ˈpɑːləmənt/ *n* parlement *m*

parliamentary /ˌpɑːləˈmentrɪ, (AmE) -terɪ/ *adj* parlementaire

parlour (BrE), **parlor** (AmE) /ˈpɑːlə(r)/ *n* petit salon *m*

parody /ˈpærədɪ/ **A** *n* parodie *f*
B *vt* parodier ‹*person, style*›

parole /pəˈrəʊl/ *n* liberté *f* conditionnelle; **on ~** en liberté conditionnelle

parrot /ˈpærət/ *n* perroquet *m*

parry /ˈpærɪ/ *vt* **1** (Sport) parer
2 éluder ‹*question*›

parsley /ˈpɑːslɪ/ *n* persil *m*

parsnip /ˈpɑːsnɪp/ *n* panais *m*

part /pɑːt/ **A** *n* **1** (of whole) partie *f*; (of country) région *f*; **to be (a) ~ of** faire partie de; **that's the best/hardest ~** c'est ça le meilleur/le plus dur; **for the most ~** dans l'ensemble
2 (Tech) (component) pièce *f*; **spare ~s** pièces détachées
3 (of serial) épisode *m*
4 (role) rôle *m* (**in** dans); **to take ~** participer (**in** à)
5 (actor's role) rôle *m* (**of** de)
6 (measure) mesure *f*
7 (behalf) **on the ~ of** de la part de; **for my ~** pour ma part
8 (AmE) (in hair) raie *f*
B *adv* en partie; **~ French, ~ Chinese** moitié français, moitié chinois
C *vt* séparer ‹*two people*›; écarter ‹*legs*›; entrouvrir ‹*lips, curtains*›; **to ~ one's hair** se faire une raie
D *vi* **1** (split up) se séparer; **to ~ from sb** quitter qn
2 ‹*crowd, clouds*› s'ouvrir

p

■ **part with** se séparer de ‹*object*›; **to ~ with money** débourser

part exchange *n* (BrE) reprise *f*; **to take sth in ~** reprendre qch

partial /'pɑːʃl/ *adj* **1** (not complete) partiel/-ielle
2 (biased) partial/-e
3 (fond) **to be ~ to** avoir un faible pour

partially sighted *n* **the ~** les malvoyants *mpl*

⚷ **participant** /pɑː'tɪsɪpənt/ *n* participant/-e *m/f* (**in** à)

⚷ **participate** /pɑː'tɪsɪpeɪt/ *vi* participer (**in** à)

participation /pɑːˌtɪsɪ'peɪʃn/ *n* participation *f* (**in** à)

participle /'pɑːtɪsɪpl/ *n* participe *m*

particle /'pɑːtɪkl/ *n* particule *f*

⚷ **particular** /pə'tɪkjʊlə(r)/ **A** *adj* **1** (gen) particulier/-ière; **for no ~ reason** sans raison particulière
2 (fussy) méticuleux/-euse; **to be ~ about** être exigeant/-e sur ‹*cleanliness, punctuality*›; prendre grand soin de ‹*appearance*›; être difficile pour ‹*food*›
B **in particular** *phr* en particulier

⚷ **particularly** /pə'tɪkjʊləlɪ/ *adv* **1** (in particular) en particulier
2 (especially) spécialement

particulars *npl* (information) détails *mpl*; (name, address) coordonnées *fpl*

parting /'pɑːtɪŋ/ *n* **1** séparation *f*
2 (BrE) (in hair) raie *f*

partisan /'pɑːtɪzæn, ˌpɑːtɪ'zæn, (AmE) 'pɑːrtɪzn/ *n* (gen), (Mil) partisan *m*

partition /pɑː'tɪʃn/ **A** *n* **1** (in room, house) cloison *f*
2 (of country) partition *f*
B *vt* **1** cloisonner ‹*area, room*›
2 diviser ‹*country*›

partly /'pɑːtlɪ/ *adv* en partie

⚷ **partner** /'pɑːtnə(r)/ *n* **1** (professional) associé/-e *m/f* (**in** dans)
2 (economic, political, sporting) partenaire *m*
3 (married) époux/-se *m/f*; (unmarried) partenaire *mf*

partnership /'pɑːtnəʃɪp/ *n* association *f*; **to go into ~ with** s'associer à

part of speech *n* partie *f* du discours

part-time /ˌpɑːt'taɪm/ *adj, adv* à temps partiel

⚷ **party** /'pɑːtɪ/ *n* **1** (social event) fête *f*; (in evening) soirée *f*; (formal) réception *f*; **to have a ~** faire une fête; **birthday ~** (fête d')anniversaire *m*; **children's ~** goûter *m* d'enfants
2 (group) groupe *m*; (Mil) détachement *m*; **rescue ~** équipe *f* de secouristes
3 (in politics) parti *m*
4 (Law) partie *f*

party dress *n* robe *f* de soirée; (for child) belle robe *f*

party line *n* **1 the ~** la ligne du parti
2 (phone line) ligne *f* commune

party political broadcast *n*: *émission dans laquelle un parti expose sa politique*

⚷ **pass** /pɑːs, (AmE) pæs/ **A** *n* **1** (permit) laisser-passer *m inv*; (for journalists) coupe-file *m inv*; **travel ~** carte *f* d'abonnement
2 (Sch, Univ) (in exam) moyenne *f* (**in** en); **to get a ~** être reçu/-e
3 (Sport) (in ball games) passe *f*; (in fencing) botte *f*
4 (in mountains) col *m*
B *vt* **1** (gen) passer ‹*plate, ball, time*›
2 passer ‹*checkpoint, customs*›; passer devant ‹*building, area*›; dépasser ‹*vehicle, level, expectation*›; **to ~ sb in the street** croiser qn dans la rue
3 ‹*person*› réussir ‹*test, exam*›; ‹*car, machine*› passer [qch] (avec succès) ‹*test*›
4 adopter ‹*bill, motion*›
5 admettre ‹*candidate*›
6 prononcer ‹*sentence*›
C *vi* (gen) passer; (in exam) réussir
IDIOM **to make a ~ at sb** faire du plat (fam) à qn

■ **pass around, pass round** (BrE) faire circuler ‹*document, photos*›; faire passer ‹*food, plates*›

■ **pass away** décéder

■ **pass by** ‹*procession*› défiler; ‹*person*› passer

■ **pass down** transmettre (**from** de, **to** à)

■ **pass off** faire passer ‹*person, incident*› (**as** pour)

■ **pass on** transmettre ‹*condolences, message*›; passer ‹*clothes, cold*› (**to** à)

■ **pass out** (faint) perdre connaissance; (fall drunk) tomber ivre mort

■ **pass through** traverser

passable /'pɑːsəbl, (AmE) 'pæs-/ *adj*
1 ‹*standard, quality*› passable; ‹*knowledge, performance*› assez bon/bonne
2 ‹*road*› praticable; ‹*river*› franchissable

passage /'pæsɪdʒ/ *n* **1** (gen) passage
2 (*also* **~way**) (indoors) corridor *m*
3 (journey) traversée *f*

⚷ **passenger** /'pæsɪndʒə(r)/ *n* (in car, plane, ship) passager/-ère *m/f*; (in train, bus, on underground) voyageur/-euse *m/f*

passer-by /ˌpɑːsə'baɪ/ *n* (*pl* **passers-by**) passant/-e *m/f*

passing /'pɑːsɪŋ, (AmE) 'pæs-/ *adj* **1** ‹*motorist, policeman*› qui passe/qui passait
2 ‹*whim*› passager/-ère
3 ‹*reference*› en passant *inv*
4 ‹*resemblance*› vague *before n*

passion /'pæʃn/ *n* passion *f*

passionate /'pæʃənət/ *adj* passionné/-e

passive /'pæsɪv/ **A** *n* **the ~** le passif, la voix passive
B *adj* passif/-ive

⚷ mot clé

pass key *n* passe *m*

pass mark *n* moyenne *f*

Passover /ˈpɑːsəʊvə(r), (AmE) ˈpæs-/ *n* Pâque *f* juive

passport /ˈpɑːspɔːt, (AmE) ˈpæs-/ *n* passeport *m*

password *n* mot *m* de passe

past /pɑːst, (AmE) pæst/ **A** *n* passé *m*; **in the ~** dans le passé
B *adj* **1** (preceding) ‹*weeks, months*› dernier/-ière *before n*; **in the ~ two years** dans les deux dernières années; **during the ~ few days** ces derniers jours
2 (former) ‹*times, problems, experience*› passé/-e; ‹*president*› ancien/-ienne *before n*; ‹*government*› précédent/-e; **in times ~** autrefois, jadis
3 summer is ~ l'été est fini; **that's all ~** c'est du passé
C *prep* **1 to walk** *or* **go ~ sb/sth** passer devant qn/qch; **to drive ~ sth** passer devant qch (en voiture)
2 (in time) **it's ~ 6** il est 6 heures passées; **twenty ~ two** deux heures vingt; **half ~ two** deux heures et demie; **he is ~ 70** il a 70 ans passés
3 (beyond) après; **~ the church** après l'église; **to be ~ caring** ne plus s'en faire
D *adv* **to go** *or* **walk ~** passer
IDIOMS **to be ~ it** (fam) avoir passé l'âge; **to be ~ its best** ‹*food*› être un peu avancé/-e; ‹*wine*› être un peu éventé/-e; **I wouldn't put it ~ him (to do)** ça ne m'étonnerait pas de lui (qu'il fasse)

pasta /ˈpæstə/ *n* pâtes *fpl* (alimentaires)

paste /peɪst/ **A** *n* **1** (glue) colle *f*
2 (mixture) pâte *f*
3 (Culin) (fish, meat) pâté *m*; (vegetable) purée *f*
B *vt* (gen), (Comput) coller (**onto** sur, **into** dans, **together** ensemble)

pastel /ˈpæstl, (AmE) pæˈstel/ **A** *n* pastel *m*
B *adj* ‹*colour, pink, shade*› pastel *inv*

pasteurize /ˈpɑːstʃəraɪz, (AmE) ˈpæst-/ *vt* pasteuriser

pastime /ˈpɑːstaɪm, (AmE) ˈpæs-/ *n* passe-temps *m inv*

pastor /ˈpɑːstə(r), (AmE) ˈpæs-/ *n* pasteur *m*

pastoral /ˈpɑːstərəl, (AmE) ˈpæs-/ *n* pastoral/-e; ‹*role, work*› de conseiller/-ère

pastrami /pæˈstrɑːmɪ/ *n* bœuf *m* fumé

pastry /ˈpeɪstrɪ/ *n* **1** (mixture) pâte *f*
2 (cake) pâtisserie *f*

past tense *n* passé *m*

pasture /ˈpɑːstʃə(r), (AmE) ˈpæs-/ *n* pré *m*, pâturage *m*

pat /pæt/ **A** *n* **1** (gentle tap) petite tape *f*
2 (of butter) noix *f*
B *vt* (*p prés etc* **-tt-**) tapoter ‹*hand*›; caresser ‹*dog*›
IDIOM **to have sth off** (BrE) *or* **down ~** connaître qch par cœur

patch /pætʃ/ **A** *n* (*pl* **~es**) **1** (in clothes) pièce *f*; (on tyre) rustine® *f*; (on eye) bandeau *m*
2 (of snow, ice) plaque *f*; (of damp, rust, sunlight) tache *f*; (of fog) nappe *f*; (of blue sky) coin *m*
3 (area of ground) zone *f*; (for planting) carré *m*; **a ~ of grass** un coin d'herbe
4 (BrE) (fam) (territory) territoire *m*
5 (fam) (period) période *f*
B *vt* rapiécer ‹*hole, trousers*›; réparer ‹*tyre*›

■ **patch up**: **A ~ up [sth], ~ [sth] up** soigner ‹*person*›; rapiécer ‹*hole, trousers*›; réparer ‹*ceiling, tyre*›; (fig) rafistoler (fam) ‹*marriage*›
B ~ up [sth] résoudre ‹*differences*›

patchy /ˈpætʃɪ/ *adj* ‹*colour, essay, quality*› inégal/-e; ‹*knowledge*› incomplet/-ète; **~ cloud** nuages *mpl* épars

pâté *n* pâté *m*; **salmon ~** terrine *f* de saumon

patent /ˈpætnt, ˈpeɪtnt, (AmE) ˈpætnt/ **A** *n* brevet *m* (**for, on** pour)
B *adj* (obvious) manifeste
C *vt* faire breveter

patent leather *n* (cuir *m*) verni *m*

paternal /pəˈtɜːnl/ *adj* paternel/-elle

paternity /pəˈtɜːnətɪ/ *n* paternité *f*

paternity leave *n* congé *m* de paternité

path /pɑːθ, (AmE) pæθ/ *n* **1** (track) (*also* **~way**) chemin *m*; (narrower) sentier *m*; (in garden) allée *f*
2 (course) (of projectile, vehicle, sun) trajectoire *f*; (of river) cours *m*; (of hurricane) itinéraire *m*
3 (option) voie *f*

pathetic /pəˈθetɪk/ *adj* **1** (moving) pathétique
2 (inadequate) misérable
3 (fam) (awful) lamentable

pathological /ˌpæθəˈlɒdʒɪkl/ *adj* ‹*fear, hatred*› pathologique; ‹*jealousy*› maladif/ive

pathology /pəˈθɒlədʒɪ/ *n* pathologie *f*

patience /ˈpeɪʃns/ *n* **1** patience *f* (**with** avec)
2 (card game) réussite *f*

patient /ˈpeɪʃnt/ **A** *n* patient/-e *m/f*
B *adj* patient (**with** avec)

patiently /ˈpeɪʃntlɪ/ *adv* avec patience, patiemment

patio /ˈpætɪəʊ/ *n* **1** (terrace) terrasse *f*
2 (courtyard) patio *m*

patio doors *npl* porte-fenêtre *f*

patriot /ˈpætrɪət, (AmE) ˈpeɪt-/ *n* patriote *mf*

patriotic /ˌpætrɪˈɒtɪk, (AmE) ˈpeɪt-/ *adj* ‹*mood, song*› patriotique; ‹*person*› patriote

patriotism /ˈpætrɪətɪzəm, (AmE) ˈpeɪt-/ *n* patriotisme *m*

patrol /pəˈtrəʊl/ **A** *n* patrouille *f*
B *vt, vi* (*p prés etc* **-ll-**) patrouiller

patrol boat, **patrol vessel** *n* patrouilleur *m*

patrol car *n* voiture *f* de police

patron /ˈpeɪtrən/ *n* **1** (of artist) mécène *m*; (of person) protecteur/-trice *m/f*; (of charity) bienfaiteur/-trice *m/f*
2 (client) client/-e *m/f* (**of** de)

patronage /ˈpætrənɪdʒ/ *n* (support) patronage *m*; **~ of the arts** mécénat *m*

p

patronize /ˈpætrənaɪz/ *vt* **1** traiter [qn] avec condescendance ‹*person*›
2 fréquenter ‹*restaurant, cinema*›

patronizing /ˈpætrənaɪzɪŋ/ *adj* condescendant/-e

patron saint *n* saint/-e *m/f* patron/-onne

patter /ˈpætə(r)/ **A** *n* **1** (of rain) crépitement *m*; **~ of footsteps** bruit *m* de pas rapides et légers
2 (talk) baratin *m*
B *vi* ‹*child, mouse*› trottiner; ‹*rain*› crépiter

🔑 **pattern** /ˈpætn/ *n* **1** (design) dessin *m*, motif *m*
2 (of behaviour) mode *m*; **weather ~s** tendances *fpl* climatiques
3 (in dressmaking) patron *m*; (in knitting) modèle *m*
4 (model, example) modèle *m*

patterned /ˈpætnd/ *adj* ‹*fabric*› à motifs

paunch /pɔːntʃ/ *n* ventre *m*

pauper /ˈpɔːpə(r)/ *n* indigent/-e *m/f*

pause /pɔːz/ **A** *n* **1** (silence) silence *m*
2 (break) pause *f*
3 (stoppage) interruption *f*
B *vi* **1** (stop speaking) marquer une pause
2 (stop) s'arrêter; **to ~ in** interrompre ‹*activity*›; **to ~ for thought** faire une pause pour réfléchir
3 (hesitate) hésiter

pave /peɪv/ *vt* paver (**with** de); **to ~ the way for sb/sth** ouvrir la voie à qn/qch

pavement /ˈpeɪvmənt/ *n* **1** (BrE) (footpath) trottoir *m*
2 (AmE) (roadway) chaussée *f*

pavement café *n* café *m* avec terrasse

pavilion /pəˈvɪlɪən/ *n* pavillon *m*

P

paving slab, **paving stone** *n* dalle *f*

paw /pɔː/ **A** *n* patte *f*
B *vt* **to ~ the ground** ‹*horse*› piaffer; ‹*bull*› frapper le sol du sabot

pawn /pɔːn/ **A** *n* pion *m*
B *vt* mettre [qch] au mont-de-piété

pawnbroker *n* prêteur/-euse *m/f* sur gages

pawnshop *n* mont-de-piété *m*

🔑 **pay** /peɪ/ **A** *n* salaire *m*
B *vt* (*prét*, *pp* **paid**) **1** payer (**for** pour); **to ~ cash** payer comptant; **to ~ sth into** verser qch sur ‹*account*›; **all expenses paid** tous frais payés
2 ‹*account*› rapporter ‹*interest*›
3 (give) **to ~ attention to** faire attention à; **to ~ a tribute to sb** rendre hommage à qn; **to ~ sb a compliment** faire des compliments à qn; **to ~ sb a visit** rendre visite à qn
4 (benefit) **it would ~ him to do** il y gagnerait à faire; **it doesn't ~ to do** cela ne sert à rien de faire
C *vi* (*prét*, *pp* **paid**) **1** ‹*person*› payer; **to ~ for sth** payer qch; **you have to ~ to get in** l'entrée est payante; **to ~ one's own way** payer sa part; **the work doesn't ~ very well** le travail est mal payé
2 ‹*business*› rapporter; ‹*activity*› payer; **to ~ for itself** ‹*business, purchase*› s'amortir

▪ **pay back** rembourser ‹*person, money*›

▪ **pay in** (BrE) déposer ‹*cheque, sum*›

▪ **pay off**: **A** **~ off** être payant/-e
B **~ [sb] off 1** (dismiss) congédier ‹*worker*›
2 (bribe) acheter le silence de ‹*person*›
C **~ [sth] off** rembourser ‹*debt*›

▪ **pay up** (fam): **~ up** payer

payable /ˈpeɪəbl/ *adj* **1** (gen) payable
2 to make a cheque ~ to faire un chèque à l'ordre de

pay cheque (BrE), **pay check** (AmE) *n* chèque *m* de paie

payday *n* jour *m* de paie

payee /peɪˈiː/ *n* bénéficiaire *mf*

pay grade *n* (Admin) échelon *m* salarial

🔑 **payment** /ˈpeɪmənt/ *n* (gen) paiement *m*; (in settlement) règlement *m*; (into account, of instalments) versement *m*; **monthly ~** mensualité *f*

pay packet *n* (BrE) enveloppe *f* de paie

payphone *n* téléphone *m* public

pay scale *n* échelle *f* salariale

payslip *n* bulletin *m* de salaire

pay television *n* télévision *f* à péage

paywall /ˈpeɪwɔːl/ *n* paywall *m* *accès payant à tout ou partie d'un site Internet*

pc, **PC** *n* (*abbr* = **personal computer**) ordinateur *m* (personnel), PC *m*

PDF *n* (*abbr* = **Portable Document Format**) PDF *m*

PE *n* (*abbr* = **physical education**) éducation *f* physique

pea /piː/ *n* pois *m*

🔑 **peace** /piːs/ *n* paix *f*; **to keep the ~** (between countries, individuals) maintenir la paix; (in town) ‹*police*› maintenir l'ordre public; **I need a bit of ~ and quiet** j'ai besoin d'un peu de calme; **to find ~ of mind** trouver la paix

peaceful /ˈpiːsfl/ *adj* **1** (tranquil) paisible
2 (without conflict) pacifique

peacefully /ˈpiːsfəlɪ/ *adv* **1** ‹*sleep*› paisiblement
2 (without violence) pacifiquement

peace-keeping forces *npl* forces *fpl* de maintien de la paix

peacemaker /ˈpiːsmeɪkə(r)/ *n* (Pol) artisan *m* de la paix; (in family) conciliateur *m*

peace process *n* processus *m* de paix

peace talks *npl* pourparlers *mpl* de paix

peacetime /ˈpiːstaɪm/ *n* temps *m* de paix

peach /piːtʃ/ *n* pêche *f*

peacock /ˈpiːkɒk/ *n* paon *m*

peak /piːk/ **A** *n* **1** (of mountain) pic *m* (**of** de)
2 (of cap) visière *f*

🔑 mot clé

3 (of inflation, demand, price) maximum *m* (**in** dans, **of** de); (on a graph) sommet *m*
4 (of career, empire) apogée *m* (**of** de); (of fitness, form) meilleur *m* (**of** de); **in the ~ of condition** en excellente santé; **to be past its** *or* **one's ~** avoir fait son temps
B *adj ‹figure, level, price›* maximum; *‹fitness›* meilleur/-e
C *vi* culminer (**at** à)
peaked /piːkt/ *adj* **1** *‹cap, hat›* à visière; *‹roof›* pointu/-e
2 (AmE) pâlot/-otte
peak period *n* période *f* de pointe
peak rate *n* (for phone calls) tarif *m* rouge
peak time *n* (on TV) heures *fpl* de grande écoute; (for switchboard, traffic) heures *fpl* de pointe
peaky /ˈpiːkɪ/ *adj* (fam) pâlot/-otte
peal /piːl/ *n* (of bells) carillonnement *m*; (of thunder) grondement *m*; **~s of laughter** éclats *mpl* de rire
peanut /ˈpiːnʌt/ *n* (nut) cacahuète *f*; (plant) arachide *f*
peanut butter *n* beurre *m* de cacahuètes
pear /peə(r)/ *n* poire *f*
pearl /pɜːl/ **A** *n* perle *f*
B *adj ‹necklace, brooch›* de perles; *‹button›* en nacre
pear tree *n* poirier *m*
peasant /ˈpeznt/ *n* paysan/-anne *m/f*
peat /piːt/ *n* tourbe *f*
pebble /ˈpebl/ *n* caillou *m*; (on beach) galet *m*
pecan /ˈpiːkən, prˈkæn, (AmE) prˈkɑːn/ *n* noix *f* de pecan
peck /pek/ **A** *n* **1** (from bird) coup *m* de bec
2 (fam) **to give sb a ~ (on the cheek)** faire une bise à qn
B *vt ‹bird›* picorer *‹food›*; donner un coup de bec à *‹person, animal›*
C *vi* **1** *‹bird›* **to ~ at** picorer *‹food›*
2 (fam) **to ~ at one's food** *‹person›* chipoter
pecking order *n* ordre *m* hiérarchique
peckish /ˈpekɪʃ/ *adj* (fam) **to be ~** avoir un petit creux (fam)
pectorals *npl* (*also* **pecs** (fam)) pectoraux *mpl*
peculiar /prˈkjuːlɪə(r)/ *adj* **1** (odd) bizarre
2 to be ~ to être particulier/-ière à *or* propre à
peculiarity /prˌkjuːlɪˈærətɪ/ *n* **1** (feature) particularité *f*
2 (strangeness) bizarrerie *f*
pedal /ˈpedl/ **A** *n* pédale *f*
B *vi* (*p prés etc* **-ll-** (BrE), **-l-** (AmE)) pédaler
pedal bin *n* (BrE) poubelle *f* à pédale
pedal boat *n* pédalo® *m*
pedantic /prˈdæntɪk/ *adj* pédant/-e
peddle /ˈpedl/ *vt* colporter *‹wares, ideas›*; **to ~ drugs** revendre de la drogue
peddler /ˈpedlə(r)/ *n* (street vendor) colporteur *m*; **drug ~** trafiquant *m*
pedestal /ˈpedɪstl/ *n* socle *m*, piédestal *m*; **to put sb on a ~** mettre qn sur un piédestal
pedestrian /prˈdestrɪən/ **A** *n* piéton *m*
B *adj ‹street, area›* piétonnier/-ière, piéton/-onne
pedestrian crossing *n* passage *m* pour piétons, passage *m* clouté
pedestrian precinct *n* (BrE) zone *f* piétonne
pediatrician /ˌpiːdɪəˈtrɪʃn/ (AmE) = **paediatrician**
pedicure /ˈpedɪkjʊə(r)/ *n* **to have a ~** se faire soigner les pieds
pedigree /ˈpedɪgriː/ **A** *n* **1** (of animal) pedigree *m*; (of person) ascendance *f*
2 (purebred animal) animal *m* avec pedigree
B *adj ‹animal›* de pure race
pee /piː/ *n* (fam) pipi *m* (fam); **to have a ~** faire pipi (fam)
peek /piːk/ *n* **to have a ~ at** jeter un coup d'œil furtif à
peel /piːl/ **A** *n* (gen) peau *f*; (of citrus fruit) écorce *f*; (of onion) pelure *f*; (peelings) épluchures *fpl*
B *vt* éplucher *‹vegetable, fruit›*; décortiquer *‹prawn›*; écorcer *‹stick›*
C *vi ‹skin›* peler; *‹fruit, vegetable›* s'éplucher
■ **peel off**: **A ~ off** *‹label›* se détacher; *‹paint›* s'écailler; *‹paper›* se décoller
B ~ [sth] off enlever *‹clothing, label›*
peeler /ˈpiːlə(r)/ *n* économe *m*
peelings *npl* épluchures *fpl*
peep /piːp/ **A** *n* **to have a ~ at sth** jeter un coup d'œil à qch; (furtively) regarder qch à la dérobée
B *vi* **1** jeter un coup d'œil (**over** par-dessus, **through** par); **to ~ at sb/sth** jeter un coup d'œil à qn/qch; (furtively) regarder qn/qch furtivement
2 *‹chick›* pépier
peephole *n* (in fence) trou *m*; (in door) judas *m*
peer /pɪə(r)/ **A** *n* **1** (equal) (in status) pair *m*; (in profession) collègue *m/f*
2 (contemporary) (adult) personne *f* de la même génération; (child) enfant *mf* du même âge
3 (BrE) (*also* **~ of the realm**) pair *m*
B *vi* **to ~ at** scruter, regarder attentivement
peerage /ˈpɪərɪdʒ/ *n* (BrE) (Pol) pairie *f*; **to be given a ~** être anobli/-e
peer group *n* **1** (of same status) pairs *mpl*
2 (contemporaries) (adults) personnes *fpl* de la même génération; (children) enfants *mpl* du même âge
peer group pressure *n* pression *f* du groupe
peg /peg/ *n* **1** (hook) patère *f*
2 (BrE) (*also* **clothes ~**) pince *f* à linge
3 (of tent) piquet *m*
4 (in carpentry) cheville *f*

pejorative /pɪ'dʒɒrətɪv, (AmE) -'dʒɔːr-/ *adj* péjoratif/-ive
Peking /ˌpiː'kɪŋ/ *pr n* Pékin
pelican /'pelɪkən/ *n* pélican *m*
pellet /'pelɪt/ *n* **1** (of paper, wax, mud) boulette *f*
2 (of shot) plomb *m*
pelmet /'pelmɪt/ *n* cantonnière *f*
pelt /pelt/ **A** *n* (fur) fourrure *f*; (hide) peau *f*
B *vt* bombarder (**with sth** de qch)
C *vi* **1** (*also* ~ **down**) ‹*rain*› tomber à verse
2 (run) **to ~ along** courir à toutes jambes
pelvis /'pelvɪs/ *n* bassin *m*, pelvis *m*
pen /pen/ *n* **1** (for writing) stylo *m*
2 (for animals) parc *m*, enclos *m*
penal /'piːnl/ *n* ‹*law, code, system*› pénal/-e; ‹*colony, institution*› pénitentiaire
penalize /'piːnəlaɪz/ *vt* pénaliser
penalty /'penltɪ/ *n* **1** (punishment) peine *f*, pénalité *f*; (fine) amende *f*
2 (fig) prix *m* (**for** de)
3 (in soccer) penalty *m*; (in rugby) pénalité *f*
pence /pens/ (BrE) ▶ **penny**
pencil /'pensl/ *n* crayon *m*; **in ~** au crayon
■ **pencil in**: **~ [sth] in, ~ in [sth]** écrire [qch] au crayon; **let's ~ in the second of May** disons le deux mai pour l'instant
pencil case *n* trousse *f* (à crayons)
pencil sharpener *n* taille-crayon *m*
pendant /'pendənt/ *n* (on necklace) pendentif *m*
pending /'pendɪŋ/ **A** *adj* **1** ‹*case*› en instance; ‹*matter*› en souffrance
2 (imminent) imminent/-e
B *prep* en attendant
pendulum /'pendjʊləm, (AmE) -dʒʊləm/ *n* pendule *m*, balancier *m*
penetrate /'penɪtreɪt/ *vt* pénétrer; percer ‹*cloud, silence, defences*›; traverser ‹*wall*›; ‹*spy*› infiltrer ‹*organization*›
penetrating /'penɪtreɪtɪŋ/ *adj* ‹*cold, eyes, question*› pénétrant/-e; ‹*sound, voice*› perçant/-e
pen friend *n* correspondant/-e *m/f*
penguin /'peŋgwɪn/ *n* pingouin *m*, manchot *m*
penicillin /ˌpenɪ'sɪlɪn/ *n* pénicilline *f*
peninsula /pə'nɪnsjʊlə, (AmE) -nsələ/ *n* péninsule *f*
penis /'piːnɪs/ *n* pénis *m*
penitent /'penɪtənt/ *n, adj* pénitent/-e *m/f*
penitentiary /ˌpenɪ'tenʃərɪ/ *n* (AmE) prison *f*
penknife *n* canif *m*
pennant /'penənt/ *n* **1** (flag) fanion *m*; (on boat) flamme *f*
2 (AmE) (Sport) championnat *m*
penniless /'penɪlɪs/ *adj* sans le sou, sans ressources

penny /'penɪ/ *n* (*pl* **-ies** *or* **pence** (BrE))
1 (BrE) penny *m*; **a five pence** *or* **five p piece** une pièce de cinq pence; **a 25p stamp** un timbre-poste à 25 pence
2 (AmE) cent *m*
IDIOMS **the ~ dropped** (fam) ça a fait tilt (fam); **not to have a ~ to one's name** être sans le sou
pension /'penʃn/ *n* (from state) pension *f*; (from employer) retraite *f*
pensioner /'penʃənə(r)/ *n* retraité/-e *m/f*
pension scheme *n* plan *m* de retraite
pentagon /'pentəgən, (AmE) -gɒn/ *n*
1 pentagone *m*
2 the Pentagon (AmE) le Pentagone *m*
Pentecost /'pentɪkɒst, (AmE) -kɔːst/ *n* Pentecôte *f*
penthouse /'penthaʊs/ *n* appartement *m* de grand standing
pent-up /ˌpent'ʌp/ *adj* ‹*energy, frustration*› contenu/-e; ‹*feelings*› réprimé/-e
penultimate /pen'ʌltɪmət/ *adj* avant-dernier/-ière
⚷ **people** /'piːpl/ **A** *n* (nation) peuple *m*
B *npl* **1** (in general) gens *mpl*; (specified or counted) personnes *fpl*; **old ~** les personnes âgées; **they're nice ~** ce sont des gens sympathiques; **there were a lot of ~** il y avait beaucoup de monde; **other ~'s property** le bien des autres
2 (of a town) habitants *mpl*; (of a country) peuple *m*
3 (citizens) **the ~** le peuple

> *gens* is masculine plural and never countable. When counting people, you must use *personnes* rather than *gens*: *three people* = trois personnes.
> When used with *gens*, some adjectives such as *vieux, bon, mauvais, petit, vilain* placed before *gens* take the feminine form: *les vieilles gens*.

people carrier *n* monospace *m*
pep /pep/ *v*
■ **pep up** remettre [qn] d'aplomb ‹*person*›; animer ‹*party, team*›
pepper /'pepə(r)/ *n* **1** (spice) poivre *m*
2 (vegetable) poivron *m*
peppercorn *n* grain *m* de poivre
pepper mill *n* moulin *m* à poivre
peppermint /'pepəmɪnt/ *n* **1** (sweet) pastille *f* de menthe
2 (plant) menthe *f* poivrée
pepper pot, **pepper shaker** *n* poivrier *m*
pep talk *n* (fam) laïus *m* (fam) d'encouragement
⚷ **per** /pɜː(r)/ *prep* par; **~ annum** par an; **~ head** par tête *or* personne; **80 km ~ hour** 80 km à l'heure; **£5 ~ hour** 5 livres sterling (de) l'heure; **as ~ your instructions** conformément à vos instructions
per capita *adj, adv* par personne
perceive /pə'siːv/ *vt* percevoir

p

⚷ mot clé

per cent /pə'sent/ *n, adv* pour cent *m*
percentage /pə'sentɪdʒ/ *n* pourcentage *m*
perceptible /pə'septəbl/ *adj* perceptible (**to** à)
perception /pə'sepʃn/ *n* **1** (by senses) perception *f*
2 (view) **my ~ of him** l'idée que je me fais de lui
3 (insight) perspicacité *f*
perceptive /pə'septɪv/ *adj* ‹*person*› perspicace; ‹*analysis*› fin/-e; ‹*article*› intelligent/-e
perch /pɜːtʃ/ **A** *n* **1** (gen) perchoir *m*
2 (fish) perche *f*
B *vi* se percher (**on** sur)
percolator /'pɜːkəleɪtə(r)/ *n* cafetière *f* à pression
percussion /pə'kʌʃn/ *n* (Mus) percussions *fpl*
perennial /pə'renɪəl/ *adj* **1** perpétuel/-elle
2 ‹*plant*› vivace
perfect **A** /'pɜːfɪkt/ *n* parfait *m*; **in the ~** au parfait
B /'pɜːfɪkt/ *adj* (gen) parfait/-e (**for** pour); ‹*moment, name, place, partner, solution*› idéal/-e (**for** pour); ‹*hostess*› exemplaire
C /pə'fekt/ *vt* perfectionner
perfection /pə'fekʃn/ *n* perfection *f* (**of** de)
perfectionist /pə'fekʃənɪst/ *n, adj* perfectionniste *mf*
perfectly /'pɜːfɪktlɪ/ *adv* **1** (totally) ‹*clear, happy*› tout à fait
2 (very well) ‹*fit, illustrate*› parfaitement
perforate /'pɜːfəreɪt/ *vt* perforer
perform /pə'fɔːm/ **A** *vt* **1** exécuter ‹*task*›; accomplir ‹*duties*›; procéder à ‹*operation*›
2 jouer ‹*play*›; chanter ‹*song*›; exécuter ‹*dance, trick*›
3 célébrer ‹*ceremony*›
B *vi* **1** ‹*actor, musician*› jouer
2 to ~ well/badly ‹*team*› bien/mal jouer; ‹*interviewee*› faire bonne/mauvaise impression; ‹*exam candidate, company*› avoir de bons/de mauvais résultats
performance /pə'fɔːməns/ *n* **1** (rendition) interprétation *f* (**of** de)
2 (concert, show, play) représentation *f* (**of** de); **to put on a ~ of Hamlet** donner une représentation d'Hamlet
3 (of team, sportsman) performance *f* (**in** à)
4 (of duties) exercice *m* (**of** de); (of task) exécution *f* (**of** de)
5 (of car, engine) performances *fpl*
performance artist *n* artiste *mf* de performances
performer /pə'fɔːmə(r)/ *n* artiste *mf*
performing arts *npl* arts *mpl* scéniques
perfume /'pɜːfjuːm, (AmE) pər'fjuːm/ **A** *n* parfum *m*
B *vt* parfumer
perhaps /pə'hæps/ *adv* peut-être; **~ she's forgotten** elle a peut-être oublié
peril /'perəl/ *n* péril *m*, danger *m*
perimeter /pə'rɪmɪtə(r)/ *n* périmètre *m*
period /'pɪərɪəd/ **A** *n* **1** (gen) période *f*; (era) époque *f*
2 (AmE) (full stop) point *m*
3 (menstruation) règles *fpl*
4 (Sch) (lesson) cours *m*, leçon *f*; **to have a free ~** ≈ avoir une heure de libre
B *adj* (of a certain era) ‹*costume, furniture*› d'époque
periodical /ˌpɪərɪ'ɒdɪkl/ *n, adj* périodique *m*
peripheral /pə'rɪfərəl/ *adj* ‹*vision, suburb*› périphérique; ‹*issue, investment*› annexe
periphery /pə'rɪfərɪ/ *n* périphérie *f*; **to remain on the ~ of** rester à l'écart de ‹*event, movement*›
periscope /'perɪskəʊp/ *n* périscope *m*
perish /'perɪʃ/ *vi* **1** (die) périr (**from** de)
2 ‹*food*› se gâter; ‹*rubber*› se détériorer
perishables /'perɪʃəblz/ *npl* denrées *fpl* périssables
perjure /'pɜːdʒə(r)/ *v refl* **to ~ oneself** faire un faux témoignage
perjury /'pɜːdʒərɪ/ *n* faux témoignage *m*
perk /pɜːk/ *n* (fam) avantage *m*
■ **perk up** ‹*person*› se ragaillardir; ‹*business, life, plant*› reprendre
perky /'pɜːkɪ/ *adj* guilleret/-ette
perm /pɜːm/ *n* permanente *f*; **to have a ~** se faire faire une permanente
permanent /'pɜːmənənt/ **A** *n* (AmE) permanente *f*
B *adj* permanent/-e
permanently /'pɜːmənəntlɪ/ *adv* ‹*happy, tired*› en permanence; ‹*employed, disabled*› de façon permanente; ‹*close, emigrate, settle*› définitivement
permeate /'pɜːmɪeɪt/ *vt* **1** ‹*liquid, gas*› s'infiltrer dans; ‹*odour*› pénétrer dans
2 ‹*ideas*› imprégner
permissible /pə'mɪsɪbl/ *adj* ‹*level, conduct*› admissible; ‹*error*› acceptable
permission /pə'mɪʃn/ *n* permission *f*; (official) autorisation *f*; **to get ~ to do** obtenir la permission *or* l'autorisation de faire
permissive /pə'mɪsɪv/ *adj* permissif/-ive
permit **A** /'pɜːmɪt/ *n* **1** permis *m*; **work ~** permis de travail
2 (AmE) (Aut) permis *m* (de conduire)
B /pə'mɪt/ *vt* (*p prés etc* **-tt-**) permettre; **to ~ sb to do** permettre à qn de faire; **smoking is not ~ted** il est interdit de fumer
C /pə'mɪt/ *vi* (*p prés etc* **-tt-**) permettre
pernickety (BrE), **persnickety** (AmE) /pə'nɪkətɪ/ *adj* (fam) **1** (detail-conscious) pointilleux/-euse (**about** sur)
2 (choosy) tatillon/-onne (**about** quant à)
peroxide blonde *n* blonde *f* décolorée
perpendicular /ˌpɜːpən'dɪkjʊlə(r)/ *adj* perpendiculaire

perpetrate /'pɜːpɪtreɪt/ *vt* perpétrer ‹*deed, fraud*›; monter ‹*hoax*›

perpetrator /'pɜːpɪtreɪtə(r)/ *n* auteur *m* (of de)

perpetual /pə'petʃʊəl/ *adj* ‹*meetings, longing, turmoil*› perpétuel/-elle; ‹*darkness, stench*› permanent/-e

perpetuate /pə'petjʊeɪt/ *vt* perpétuer

perplexed /pə'plekst/ *adj* perplexe

persecute /'pɜːsɪkjuːt/ *vt* persécuter

persecution /ˌpɜːsɪ'kjuːʃn/ *n* persécution *f*

perseverance /ˌpɜːsɪ'vɪərəns/ *n* persévérance *f*

persevere /ˌpɜːsɪ'vɪə(r)/ *vi* persévérer (**with, at** dans)

persist /pə'sɪst/ *vi* persister (**in** dans, **in doing** à faire)

persistence /pə'sɪstəns/ *n* persévérance *f*

persistent /pə'sɪstənt/ *adj* **1** (persevering) persévérant/-e; (obstinate) obstiné/-e (**in** dans)
2 ‹*rain, denial*› persistant/-e; ‹*enquiries, noise, pressure*› continuel/-elle; ‹*illness, fears, idea*› tenace

persistent offender *n* récidiviste *mf*

⚷ **person** /'pɜːsn/ *n* (*pl* **people** *ou* **~s** (formal)) personne *f*; **in ~** en personne; **to have sth about one's ~** avoir qch sur soi

personable /'pɜːsənəbl/ *adj* ‹*person*› qui présente bien

⚷ **personal** /'pɜːsənl/ **A** *n* (AmE) petite annonce *f* personnelle
B *adj* ‹*opinion, life, call, matter*› personnel/-elle; ‹*safety, choice, income, insurance*› individuel/-elle; ‹*service*› personnalisé/-e; **to make a ~ appearance** venir en personne (**at** à)

personal ad *n* petite annonce *f* personnelle

personal best *n* record *m* personnel

personal column *n* petites annonces *fpl* personnelles

personality /ˌpɜːsə'næləti/ *n* personnalité *f*

personal loan *n* emprunt *m*; (by bank etc) prêt *m* personnel

personally /'pɜːsənəli/ *adv* personnellement

personal organizer *n* ≈ agenda *m*

personal property *n* biens *mpl* personnels

personal shopper *n* acheteur/-euse *mf* personnel/-elle, personal shopper *m*

personal stereo *n* baladeur *m*

personify /pə'sɒnɪfaɪ/ *vt* incarner ‹*ideal*›

personnel /ˌpɜːsə'nel/ *n* **1** (staff, troops) personnel *m*
2 (department) service *m* du personnel

⚷ **perspective** /pə'spektɪv/ *n* perspective *f*; **to keep things in ~** garder un sens de la mesure; **to put things into ~** relativiser les choses

perspex® /'pɜːspeks/ *n* plexiglas® *m*

perspiration /ˌpɜːspɪ'reɪʃn/ *n* **1** (sweat) sueur *f*
2 (sweating) transpiration *f*

perspire /pə'spaɪə(r)/ *vi* transpirer

persuade /pə'sweɪd/ *vt* **1** (influence) persuader; **to ~ sb to do** persuader qn de faire
2 (convince) convaincre (**of** de, **that** que)

persuasion /pə'sweɪʒn/ *n* **1** (persuading) persuasion *f*
2 (religion) confession *f*
3 (political views) conviction *f*

persuasive /pə'sweɪsɪv/ *adj* ‹*person*› persuasif/-ive; ‹*argument, evidence*› convaincant/-e

pert /pɜːt/ *adj* ‹*person, manner*› espiègle; ‹*hat, nose*› coquin/-e

pertinent /'pɜːtɪnənt, (AmE) -tənənt/ *adj* pertinent/-e

perturb /pə'tɜːb/ *vt* perturber

perturbing /pə'tɜːbɪŋ/ *adj* troublant/-e

pervade /pə'veɪd/ *vt* imprégner

perverse /pə'vɜːs/ *adj* **1** (twisted) ‹*person*› retors/-e; ‹*desire*› pervers/-e
2 (contrary) ‹*refusal, attempt, attitude*› illogique; **to take a ~ pleasure in doing** prendre un malin plaisir à faire

perversion /pə'vɜːʃn, (AmE) -ʒn/ *n*
1 (deviation) perversion *f*
2 (of facts, justice) travestissement *m*

pervert **A** /'pɜːvɜːt/ *n* pervers/-e *m/f*
B /pə'vɜːt/ *vt* **1** (corrupt) corrompre
2 (misrepresent) travestir ‹*truth*›; dénaturer ‹*meaning*›; **to ~ the course of justice** entraver l'action de la justice

perverted /pə'vɜːtɪd/ *adj* (deviant) pervers/-e; (distorted) ‹*idea*› tordu/-e

pessimism /'pesɪmɪzəm/ *n* pessimisme *m*

pessimist /'pesɪmɪst/ *n* pessimiste *mf*

pessimistic /ˌpesɪ'mɪstɪk/ *adj* pessimiste

pest /pest/ *n* **1** (animal) animal *m* nuisible; (insect) insecte *m* nuisible
2 (fam) (person) enquiquineur/-euse *m/f* (fam)

pester /'pestə(r)/ *vt* harceler

pesticide /'pestɪsaɪd/ *n* pesticide *m*

pet /pet/ **A** *n* **1** (animal) animal *m* de compagnie
2 (favourite) chouchou/chouchoute *m/f* (fam)
B *adj* **1** (favourite) favori/-ite
2 ~ dog chien *m*
C *vt* (*p prés etc* **-tt-**) caresser ‹*animal*›
D *vi* (*p prés etc* **-tt-**) ‹*people*› échanger des caresses

petal /'petl/ *n* pétale *m*

peter /'piːtə(r)/ *v*

■ **peter out** ‹*conversation*› tarir; ‹*supplies*› s'épuiser

⚷ mot clé

pet food *n* aliments *mpl* pour chiens et chats

pet hate *n* (BrE) bête *f* noire

petition /pə'tɪʃn/ **A** *n* pétition *f*
B *vt* adresser une pétition à ‹*person, body*›
C *vi* **to ~ for divorce** demander le divorce

pet name *n* petit nom *m*

pet project *n* enfant *m* chéri (fig)

petrified /'petrɪfaɪd/ *adj* pétrifié/-e

petrol /'petrəl/ *n* (BrE) essence *f*; **to fill up with ~** faire le plein (d'essence)

petrol can *n* (BrE) bidon *m* à essence

petroleum /pə'trəʊlɪəm/ *n* pétrole *m*

petrol station *n* (BrE) station *f* d'essence

pet shop (BrE), **pet store** (AmE) *n* animalerie *f*

petticoat /'petɪkəʊt/ *n* (full slip) combinaison *m*; (half slip) jupon *m*

petty /'petɪ/ *adj* ‹*person, squabble*› mesquin/-e; ‹*detail*› insignifiant/-e

petty cash *n* petite caisse *f*

petty crime *n* petite délinquance *f*

petty officer *n* ≈ maître *m*

petty theft *n* larcin *m*

pew /pjuː/ *n* banc *m* (d'église)

pewter /'pjuːtə(r)/ *n* étain *m*

PGCE *n* (BrE) (*abbr* = **postgraduate certificate in education**) diplôme *m* de spécialisation dans l'enseignement

pharmaceutical /ˌfɑːmə'sjuːtɪkl, (AmE) -'suː-/ *adj* pharmaceutique

pharmacist /'fɑːməsɪst/ *n* pharmacien/-ienne *m/f*

pharmacy /'fɑːməsɪ/ *n* pharmacie *f*

phase /feɪz/ **A** *n* phase *f*; **it's just a ~ (he's/they're going through)** ça lui/leur passera
B *vt* échelonner (**over** sur)
■ **phase in** introduire [qch] progressivement
■ **phase out** supprimer [qch] peu à peu

PhD *n* (*abbr* = **Doctor of Philosophy**) doctorat *m*

pheasant /'feznt/ *n* faisan/-e *m/f*

phenomenal /fə'nɒmɪnl/ *adj* phénoménal/-e

phenomenon /fə'nɒmɪnən/ *n* (*pl* **-na**) phénomène *m*

phew /fjuː/ *excl* (in relief) ouf!; (when too hot) pff!

philanthropist /fɪ'lænθrəpɪst/ *n* philanthrope *mf*

philistine /'fɪlɪstaɪn/ *n* béotien/-ienne *m/f*

philosopher /fɪ'lɒsəfə(r)/ *n* philosophe *mf*

philosophic /ˌfɪlə'sɒfɪk(l)/ *adj* (*also* **philosophical**) **1** ‹*knowledge, question*› philosophique
2 (calm, stoical) philosophe (**about** à propos de)

philosophy /fɪ'lɒsəfɪ/ *n* philosophie *f*

phishing /'fɪʃɪŋ/ *n* (Comput) hameçonnage *m*

phobia /'fəʊbɪə/ *n* phobie *f*

phone /fəʊn/ **A** *n* téléphone *m*; **to be on the ~** (be talking) être au téléphone (**to sb** avec qn); (be subscriber) avoir le téléphone
B *vt* (*also* **~ up**) passer un coup de fil à (fam), téléphoner à, appeler
C *vi* (*also* **~ up**) téléphoner; **to ~ for a taxi** appeler un taxi

phone book *n* annuaire *m* (téléphonique)

phone booth, **phone box** (BrE) *n* cabine *f* téléphonique

phone call *n* coup *m* de fil (fam); (more formal) communication *f* (téléphonique)

phone card *n* (BrE) télécarte *f*

phone hacking /'fəʊn hækɪŋ/ *n* piratage *m* de téléphone

phone-in *n* émission *f* à ligne ouverte

phone link *n* liaison *f* téléphonique

phone number *n* numéro *m* de téléphone

phoney /'fəʊnɪ/ (fam) **A** *n* **1** (affected person) poseur/-euse *m/f*
2 (impostor) charlatan *m*
B *adj* ‹*address, accent*› faux/fausse *before n*; ‹*company, excuse*› bidon *inv* (fam); ‹*emotion*› simulé/-e

phoney war *n* **the ~** la drôle de guerre

phosphates *npl* phosphates *mpl*

photo /'fəʊtəʊ/ = **photograph A**

photo album *n* album *m* de photos

photo booth *n* photomaton® *m*

photo-call *n* séance *f* de photos

photocopier /'fəʊtəʊkɒpɪə(r)/ *n* photocopieuse *f*

photocopy /'fəʊtəʊkɒpɪ/ **A** *n* photocopie *f*
B *vt* photocopier

photogenic /ˌfəʊtəʊ'dʒenɪk/ *adj* photogénique

photograph /'fəʊtəgrɑːf, (AmE) -græf/ **A** *n* (*also* **photo**) photo *f*; **in the ~** sur la photo; **to take a ~ of sb/sth** prendre qn/qch en photo
B *vt* photographier, prendre [qn/qch] en photo

photographer /fə'tɒgrəfə(r)/ *n* photographe *mf*

photography /fə'tɒgrəfɪ/ *n* photographie *f*

photo opportunity *n* séance *f* de photos

photo session *n* séance *f* de photos

phrase /freɪz/ **A** *n* expression *f*
B *vt* formuler ‹*question, speech*›

phrase book *n* manuel *m* de conversation

physical /'fɪzɪkl/ **A** *n* (check-up) bilan *m* de santé
B *adj* physique

physical fitness *n* forme *f* physique

physically handicapped *adj* **to be ~** être handicapé/-e *m/f* physique

physicist /'fɪzɪsɪst/ *n* physicien/-ienne *m/f*

physics /'fɪzɪks/ *n* physique *f*

physiology /ˌfɪzɪ'ɒlədʒɪ/ *n* physiologie *f*

physiotherapy /ˌfɪzɪəʊ'θerəpɪ/ *n* kinésithérapie *f*

p

physique /fɪ'zi:k/ *n* physique *m*
pianist /'pɪənɪst/ *n* pianiste *mf*
piano /pɪ'ænəʊ/ *n* piano *m*
⚷ **pick** /pɪk/ **A** *n* **1** (tool) pioche *f*, pic *m*; (of climber) piolet *m*
2 (choice) choix *m*; **to have one's ~ of** avoir le choix parmi; **take your ~** choisis
3 the ~ of the bunch (singular) le meilleur/la meilleure du lot
B *vt* **1** (choose) choisir (**from** parmi); (in sport) sélectionner ‹*player*› (**from** parmi); **to ~ a fight** chercher à se bagarrer (fam) (**with** avec); (quarrel) chercher querelle (**with** à)
2 to ~ one's way through avancer avec précaution parmi ‹*rubble, litter*›
3 cueillir ‹*fruit, flowers*›
4 gratter ‹*spot, scab*›; **to ~ sth from** *or* **off** enlever qch de; **to ~ one's teeth/nose** se curer les dents/le nez
C *vi* choisir
■ **pick at 1** ‹*person*› manger [qch] du bout des dents ‹*food*›; gratter ‹*spot, scab*›
2 ‹*bird*› picorer ‹*crumbs*›
■ **pick on** harceler, s'en prendre à ‹*person*›
■ **pick out 1** (select) choisir; (single out) repérer
2 distinguer ‹*landmark*›; reconnaître ‹*person in photo*›; repérer ‹*person in crowd*›
■ **pick up**: **A ~ up** ‹*business*› reprendre; ‹*weather, health*› s'améliorer; ‹*ill person*› se rétablir
B ~ [sb/sth] up 1 (lift up) ramasser ‹*object, litter, toys*›; relever ‹*person*›; **to ~ up the receiver** décrocher le téléphone; **to ~ oneself up** se relever
2 prendre ‹*passenger, cargo*›; passer prendre ‹*ticket, keys*›; prendre, acheter ‹*milk, paper*›; **could you ~ me up?** est-ce que tu peux venir me chercher?
3 apprendre ‹*language*›; prendre ‹*habit, accent*›; développer ‹*skill*›; **you'll soon ~ it up** tu t'y mettras vite
4 trouver ‹*trail, scent*›; ‹*radar*› détecter la présence de ‹*aircraft, person, object*›; ‹*radio receiver*› capter ‹*signal*›
5 gagner ‹*point*›; acquérir ‹*reputation*›; **to ~ up speed** prendre de la vitesse
6 (resume) reprendre ‹*conversation, career*›
7 ramasser ‹*partner, prostitute*›
pickaxe (BrE), **pickax** (AmE) *n* pioche *f*
picket /'pɪkɪt/ **A** *n* piquet *m* (de grève)
B *vt* installer un piquet de grève aux portes de ‹*factory*›
picking /'pɪkɪŋ/ **A** *n* (of crop) cueillette *f*
B pickings *npl* (rewards) gains *mpl*
pickle /'pɪkl/ **A** *n* **1** (preserves) conserves *fpl* au vinaigre
2 (gherkin) cornichon *m*
B *vt* (in vinegar) conserver [qch] dans du vinaigre
IDIOM **to be in a ~** être dans le pétrin (fam)
pick-me-up *n* remontant *m*
pickpocket *n* voleur *m* à la tire

⚷ mot clé

pickup truck *n* (BrE) pick-up *m inv*
picnic /'pɪknɪk/ *n* pique-nique *m*; **to go for** *ou* **on a ~** aller faire un pique-nique, pique-niquer
⚷ **picture** /'pɪktʃə(r)/ **A** *n* **1** (painting) peinture *f*, tableau *m*; (drawing) dessin *m*; (in book) illustration *f*; (in mind) image *f*
2 (description) description *f*
3 (snapshot) photo *f*, photographie *f*
4 I get the ~ je vois; **to put sb in the ~** mettre qn au courant
5 (film) film *m*
6 (on TV screen) image *f*
B *vt* s'imaginer
picture card *n* figure *f* (*carte*)
picture frame *n* cadre *m*
picture hook *n* crochet *m* (à tableaux)
picturesque /ˌpɪktʃə'resk/ *adj* pittoresque
pie /paɪ/ *n* tourte *f*; **meat ~** tourte à la viande
⚷ **piece** /pi:s/ *n* **1** (gen) morceau *m*; (of string, ribbon) bout *m*; **a ~ of furniture** un meuble; **a ~ of luggage** une valise; **a ~ of advice** un conseil; **a ~ of information** un renseignement; **a ~ of luck** un coup de chance; **£20 a ~** 20 livres sterling pièce; **to fall to ~s** ‹*object*› tomber en morceaux; ‹*argument*› s'effondrer; **to go to ~s** (from shock) s'effondrer; (emotionally) craquer (fam); (in interview) paniquer complètement
2 (of jigsaw, machine, model) pièce *f*; **to take sth to ~s** démonter qch
3 (article) article *m* (**on** sur)
4 (coin) **a 50p ~** une pièce de 50 pence
5 (in chess) pièce *f*
IDIOM **to give sb a ~ of one's mind** dire ses quatre vérités à qn
■ **piece together**: **~ [sth] together, ~ together [sth]** reconstituer ‹*vase, letter*›; assembler ‹*puzzle*›; reconstituer ‹*facts*›
piecemeal /'pi:smi:l/ **A** *adj* (random) fragmentaire; (at different times) irrégulier/-ière
B *adv* petit à petit
pie chart *n* diagramme *m* circulaire sectorisé, camembert *m* (fam)
pier /pɪə(r)/ *n* (at seaside) jetée *f* (sur pilotis); (landing stage) embarcadère *f*
pierce /pɪəs/ *vt* (make hole in) percer; (penetrate) transpercer
piercing /pɪəsɪŋ/ *adj* ‹*scream, eyes*› perçant/-e; ‹*light*› intense; ‹*wind*› glacial/-e, pénétrant/-e
pig /pɪg/ *n* **1** (animal) porc *m*, cochon *m*
2 (fam) ‹*person*› (greedy) goinfre *m* (fam); (dirty) cochon/-onne *m/f* (fam); (nasty) sale type *m* (fam)
■ **pig out** (fam) se goinfrer (fam), s'empiffrer (fam) (**on** de)
pigeon /'pɪdʒɪn/ *n* pigeon *m*
pigeonhole /'pɪdʒɪnhəʊl/ (BrE) **A** *n* casier *m*
B *vt* étiqueter, cataloguer

P

pigeon-toed *adj* **to be ~** marcher les pieds en dedans

piggyback *n* (*also* **piggyback ride**) **to give sb a ~** porter qn sur son dos *or* sur ses épaules

piggy bank *n* tirelire *f*

pig-headed /ˌpɪgˈhedɪd/ *adj* entêté/-e, obstiné/-e

piglet /ˈpɪglɪt/ *n* porcelet *m*, petit cochon *m*

pigment /ˈpɪgmənt/ *n* pigment *m*

pigpen (AmE) = **pigsty**

pigskin /ˈpɪgskɪn/ *n* peau *f* de porc

pigsty, **pigpen** (AmE) *n* (*pl* **-sties**) porcherie *f*

pigtail /ˈpɪgteɪl/ *n* natte *f*

pike /paɪk/ *n* (fish) brochet *m*

pile /paɪl/ **A** *n* **1** (heap) tas *m* (**of** de); (stack) pile *f* (**of** de); **in a ~** en tas *or* en pile
2 (of fabric, carpet) poil *m*
3 (fam) **~s of** des tas (fam) de ‹*books, letters*›; **~s of money** plein d'argent (fam)
B piles *npl* hémorroïdes *fpl*
C *vt* entasser (**on** sur, **into** dans)
▪ **pile up** ‹*debts, problems, work*› s'accumuler

pile-up *n* carambolage *m*

pilfer /ˈpɪlfə(r)/ **A** *vt* dérober (**from** dans)
B *vi* commettre des larcins

pilgrim /ˈpɪlgrɪm/ *n* pèlerin *m* (**to** de)

pilgrimage /ˈpɪlgrɪmɪdʒ/ *n* pèlerinage *m*

pill /pɪl/ *n* **1** (gen) comprimé *m*, cachet *m*
2 (contraceptive) **the ~** la pilule

pillage /ˈpɪlɪdʒ/ *vt*, *vi* piller

pillar /ˈpɪlə(r)/ *n* pilier *m*

pillar box *n* (BrE) boîte *f* aux lettres

pillion /ˈpɪlɪən/ **A** *n* (*also* **~ seat**) siège *m* de passager
B *adv* **to ride ~** monter en croupe

pillow /ˈpɪləʊ/ *n* oreiller *m*

pillowcase *n* taie *f* d'oreiller

pilot /ˈpaɪlət/ **A** *n* pilote *m*
B *adj* **1** ‹*project, study*› pilote; ‹*series*› expérimental/-e
2 ‹*error*› de pilotage

pilot light *n* veilleuse *f*; (electric) voyant *m* lumineux

pilot scheme *n* projet-pilote *m*

pimp /pɪmp/ *n* proxénète *m*

pimple /ˈpɪmpl/ *n* bouton *m*

pimply /ˈpɪmplɪ/ *adj* boutonneux/-euse

pin /pɪn/ **A** *n* **1** (for cloth, paper) épingle *f*
2 three-~ plug prise *f* à trois fiches
3 (for wood, metal) goujon *m*
4 (Med) broche *f*
5 (brooch) barrette *f*
B *vt* (*p prés etc* **-nn-**) **1** épingler ‹*dress, hem, curtain*› (**to** à)
2 (trap) **to ~ sb to** coincer qn contre ‹*wall, floor*›
3 (fam) **to ~ sth on sb** mettre qch sur le dos de qn ‹*theft*›
▪ **pin down A ~ [sb] down 1** (physically) immobiliser (**to** à)
2 (fig) coincer; **to ~ sb down to a definite date** arriver à fixer une date ferme avec qn
B ~ [sth] down identifier ‹*concept, feeling*›
▪ **pin up** accrocher ‹*poster, notice*› (**on** à)

PIN *n* (*abbr* = **personal identification number**) (*also* **PIN number**) code *m* confidentiel (pour carte bancaire)

pinafore /ˈpɪnəfɔː(r)/ *n* **1** (apron) tablier *m*
2 (dress) robe-chasuble *f*

pinball *n* flipper *m*

pincers *npl* tenailles *fpl*

pinch /pɪntʃ/ **A** *n* **1** pincement *m*; **to give sb a ~** pincer qn
2 (of salt, spice) pincée *f*
B *vt* **1** (on arm, leg) pincer
2 ‹*shoe*› serrer
3 (fam) (steal) faucher (fam) (**from** à)
C *vi* ‹*shoe*› serrer
IDIOM **to feel the ~** avoir de la peine à joindre les deux bouts

pine /paɪn/ **A** *n* pin *m*
B *adj* ‹*furniture*› en pin
C *vi* ‹*person*› languir (**for** après); ‹*animal*› s'ennuyer (**for** de)

pineapple /ˈpaɪnæpl/ *n* ananas *m*

pine cone *n* pomme *f* de pin

ping-pong® /ˈpɪŋpɒŋ/ *n* ping-pong® *m*

pink /pɪŋk/ **A** *n* **1** (colour) rose *m*
2 (flower) œillet *m* mignardise
B *adj* rose; **to go** *or* **turn ~** rosir; (blush) rougir (**with** de)

pinnacle /ˈpɪnəkl/ *n* **1** (on building) pinacle *m*
2 (of rock) cime *f* (**of** de)
3 (fig) apogée *m* (**of** de)

pinpoint /ˈpɪnpɔɪnt/ *vt* indiquer ‹*problem, causes, location, site*›; déterminer ‹*time*›

pinstripe /ˈpɪnstraɪp/ *adj* (*also* **pinstriped**) ‹*fabric, suit*› à fines rayures

pint /paɪnt/ *n* pinte *f* ((BrE) = *0.57 l*, (AmE) = *0.47 l*); **a ~ of milk** ≈ un demi-litre de lait; **a ~ (of beer)** un demi

pin-up /ˈpɪnʌp/ *n* (woman) pin-up *f* (fam); (poster of star) affiche *f* de vedette; (star) idole *f*

pioneer /ˌpaɪəˈnɪə(r)/ **A** *n* pionnier *m* (**of, in** de)
B *vt* **to ~ the use of** être le premier/la première à utiliser

pious /ˈpaɪəs/ *adj* pieux/pieuse

pip /pɪp/ *n* **1** (seed) pépin *m*
2 (on radio) top *m*
IDIOM **to be ~ped at** *or* **to the post** (BrE) se faire souffler la victoire

pipe /paɪp/ **A** *n* **1** (for gas, water) tuyau *m*; (underground) conduite *f*
2 (smoker's) pipe *f*
B pipes *npl* (Mus) cornemuse *f*
C *vt* **water is ~d across/to** l'eau est acheminée par canalisation à travers/jusqu'à
▪ **pipe down** (fam) faire moins de bruit

p

■ **pipe up** ‹*voice*› se faire entendre
pipe dream *n* chimère *f*
pipeline /'paɪplaɪn/ *n* oléoduc *m*; **to be in the ~** être prévu/-e
piping hot *adj* fumant/-e
pique /pi:k/ *n* dépit *m*; **a fit of ~** un accès de dépit
pirate /'paɪərət/ **A** *n* pirate *m*
B *adj* ‹*video, tape, radio*› pirate *after n*; ‹*ship*› de pirates
C *vt* pirater ‹*tape, video, software*›
pirouette /ˌpɪrʊ'et/ *n* pirouette *f*
Pisa /'pi:zə/ *pr n* Pise
Pisces /'paɪsi:z/ *n* Poissons *mpl*
pistol /'pɪstl/ *n* pistolet *m*
piston /'pɪstən/ *n* piston *m*
pit /pɪt/ **A** *n* **1** (in ground, in garage) fosse *f*; **gravel ~** carrière *f* de gravier
2 (mine) mine *f*
3 (in theatre) parterre *m*; **orchestra ~** fosse *f* d'orchestre
4 (AmE) (in fruit) noyau *m*
B *vt* (*p prés etc* **-tt-**) **to ~ sb against** opposer qn à ‹*opponent*›; **to ~ one's wits against sb** se mesurer à qn
IDIOM **it's the ~s!** (fam) c'est l'horreur!
pit bull terrier *n* pit bull *m*
pitch /pɪtʃ/ **A** *n* **1** (BrE) (sportsground) terrain *m*; **football ~** terrain de foot(ball)
2 (of note, voice) hauteur *f*; (in music) ton *m*
3 (highest point) comble *m*
4 (sales talk) boniment *m*
5 (for street trader) emplacement *m*
B *vt* **1** (throw) jeter (**into** dans); (Sport) lancer
2 adapter ‹*campaign, speech*› (**at** à)
3 ‹*singer*› trouver ‹*note*›
4 planter ‹*tent*›; **to ~ camp** établir un camp
C *vi* **1** ‹*boat*› tanguer
2 (AmE) (in baseball) lancer (la balle)
■ **pitch in** (fam) (eat) attaquer (fam); (help) donner un coup de main (fam)
pitch-black *adj* tout/-e noir/-e
pitcher /'pɪtʃə(r)/ *n* **1** (jug) cruche *f*
2 (AmE) (Sport) lanceur *m*
pitchfork /'pɪtʃfɔ:k/ *n* fourche *f*
pitfall /'pɪtfɔ:l/ *n* écueil *m* (**of** de)
pith /pɪθ/ *n* **1** (of fruit) peau *f* blanche
2 (of plant) moelle *f*
pitiful /'pɪtɪfl/ *adj* ‹*cry, sight*› pitoyable; ‹*state*› lamentable; ‹*amount*› ridicule
pitiless /'pɪtɪlɪs/ *adj* impitoyable
pittance /'pɪtns/ *n* **to live on/earn a ~** vivre avec/gagner trois fois rien
pity /'pɪtɪ/ **A** *n* **1** (compassion) pitié *f* (**for** pour); **out of ~** par pitié; **to take ~ on sb** avoir pitié de qn
2 (shame) dommage *m*; **what a ~!** quel dommage!
B *vt* plaindre

⚷ mot clé

pivot /'pɪvət/ **A** *vt* faire pivoter ‹*lever*›; orienter ‹*lamp*›
B *vi* **1** ‹*lamp, device*› pivoter (**on** sur)
2 (fig) ‹*outcome, success*› reposer (**on** sur)
pixel /'pɪksl/ *n* pixel *m*
pizza /'pi:tsə/ *n* pizza *f*
placard /'plækɑ:d/ *n* (at protest march) pancarte *f*; (on wall) affiche *f*
⚷ **place** /pleɪs/ **A** *n* **1** (location, position) endroit *m*; **in ~s** ‹*hilly, damaged, worn*› par endroits; **~ of birth/work** lieu *m* de naissance/travail; **~ of residence** domicile *m*; **to be in the right ~ at the right time** être là où il faut quand il le faut; **to lose/find one's ~** (in book) perdre/retrouver sa page; (in paragraph, speech) perdre/retrouver le fil; **all over the ~** (everywhere) partout
2 (home) **at Isabelle's ~** chez Isabelle; **your ~ or mine?** chez toi ou chez moi?
3 (on bus, at table, in queue) place *f*
4 (on team, with firm, on course) place *f* (**on** dans, **as** comme)
5 (in competition, race) place *f*; **to finish in first ~** terminer premier/-ière *or* à la première place; **in the first ~** (firstly, when listing) premièrement; (most importantly, most notably) tout d'abord, pour commencer
6 (correct position) **everything is in its ~** tout est bien à sa place; **to hold sth in ~** maintenir qch en place; **in ~** ‹*law, system, scheme*› en place; **to put sb in his/her ~** remettre qn à sa place
7 (personal level or position) **it's not my ~ to do** ce n'est pas à moi de faire; **in his ~** à sa place
8 (moment) moment *m*; **in ~s** ‹*funny, boring, silly*› par moments
B *vt* **1** (gen) placer
2 passer ‹*order*›; **to place a bet** parier (**on** sur)
3 (in competition, exam) classer
4 (identify) situer ‹*person*›; reconnaître ‹*accent*›
C **out of place** *phr* déplacé/-e; **to look out of ~** ‹*building, person*› détonner
place mat *n* set *m* de table
placement /'pleɪsmənt/ (*also* **work ~**) *n* stage *m*
place name /'pleɪsneɪm/ *n* nom *m* de lieu
placid /'plæsɪd/ *adj* placide
plagiarize /'pleɪdʒəraɪz/ *vt*, *vi* plagier
plague /pleɪg/ **A** *n* **1** (bubonic) peste *f*
2 (epidemic) épidémie *f*
3 (of ants, locusts) invasion *f*
4 (fig) plaie *f*
B *vt* **1 to be ~d by** être en proie à ‹*doubts, difficulties*›
2 (harass) harceler
plaice /pleɪs/ *n* (*pl* **~**) plie *f*, carrelet *m*
plaid /plæd/ *adj* écossais/-e
plain /pleɪn/ **A** *n* plaine *f*
B *adj* **1** (simple) simple
2 (of one colour) uni/-e; ‹*envelope*› sans

p

inscription; a ~ **blue dress** une robe toute bleue
3 ‹*woman*› quelconque
4 (obvious) évident/-e, clair/-e; **it's ~ to see** ça saute aux yeux
5 ‹*common sense*› simple *before n*; ‹*ignorance*› pur/-e et simple *after n*
6 ‹*yoghurt, rice*› nature *inv*

plain chocolate *n* chocolat *m* à croquer

plain clothes *adj* ‹*policeman*› en civil

plainly /'pleɪnlɪ/ *adv* **1** (obviously) manifestement
2 ‹*see, remember*› clairement
3 ‹*speak*› franchement
4 ‹*dress, eat*› simplement; ‹*furnished*› sobrement

plait /plæt/ *n* natte *f*

plan /plæn/ **A** *n* (gen) plan *m*; (definite aim) projet *m* (**for** de, **to do** pour faire); **to go according to ~** se passer comme prévu
B *vt* (*p prés etc* **-nn-**) **1** (prepare, organize) planifier ‹*future*›; organiser, préparer ‹*timetable, meeting, expedition*›; organiser ‹*day*›; faire un plan de ‹*career*›; faire le plan de ‹*essay, book*›; préméditer ‹*crime*›
2 (intend, propose) projeter ‹*visit, trip*›; **to ~ to do** projeter de faire
3 (design) concevoir
C *vi* (*p prés etc* **-nn-**) prévoir; **to ~ for sth** prévoir qch; **to ~ on doing** compter faire
■ **plan ahead** (vaguely) faire des projets; (look, think ahead) prévoir

plane /pleɪn/ *n* **1** (aircraft) avion *m*
2 (in geometry) plan *m*
3 (tool) rabot *m*
4 (*also* ~ **tree**) platane *m*

planet /'plænɪt/ *n* planète *f*

plank /plæŋk/ *n* planche *f*

planner /'plænə(r)/ *n* planificateur/-trice *m/f*; (in town planning) urbaniste *mf*

planning /'plænɪŋ/ *n* **1** (of industry, economy, work) planification *f*; (of holiday, party) organisation *f*
2 (in town) urbanisme *m*; (out of town) aménagement *m* du territoire

planning permission *n* permis *m* de construire

plant /plɑːnt, (AmE) plænt/ **A** *n* **1** (Bot) plante *f*
2 (factory) usine *f*
B *vt* **1** planter ‹*seed, bulb, tree*›
2 placer ‹*bomb, spy*›; **to ~ drugs on sb** cacher de la drogue sur qn pour l'incriminer
C *v refl* **to ~ oneself between/in front of** se planter entre/devant

plantation /plæn'teɪʃn/ *n* plantation *f*

plaque /plɑːk, (AmE) plæk/ *n* **1** (on wall, monument) plaque *f*
2 (on teeth) plaque *f* dentaire

plasma TV /plæzmə tiː'viː/ *n* télé *f* fà écran plasma

plaster /'plɑːstə(r), (AmE) 'plæs-/ **A** *n* **1** (gen) plâtre *m*
2 (BrE) (*also* **sticking ~**) sparadrap *m*
B *vt* **1** faire les plâtres de ‹*house*›
2 (cover) couvrir (**with** de)

plaster cast *n* plâtre *m*

plasterer /'plɑːstərə(r), (AmE) 'plæst-/ *n* plâtrier *m*

plastic /'plæstɪk/ **A** *n* plastique *m*; (credit cards) cartes *fpl* de crédit
B *adj* ‹*bag, toys, container*› en plastique

plastic surgeon *n* chirurgien *m* esthétique

plastic surgery *n* chirurgie *f* plastique

plate /pleɪt/ **A** *n* **1** (dish) (for eating) assiette *f*; (for serving) plat *m*
2 (sheet of metal) plaque *f*, tôle *f*
3 (number plate) plaque *f* minéralogique
4 (illustration) planche *f*
5 (in dentistry) dentier *m*
6 (in earth's crust) plaque *f*
B **-plated** *combining form* **gold/silver-~d** plaqué/-e or/argent

plate glass *n* verre *m* à vitre

platform /'plætfɔːm/ *n* **1** (for performance) estrade *f*; (at public meeting) tribune *f*
2 (in scaffolding) plate-forme *f*
3 (in politics) plate-forme *f* électorale
4 (at station) quai *m*
5 (Comput) plate-forme *f*

platform shoes *npl* chaussures *fpl* à plateforme

platinum /'plætɪnəm/ *n* platine *m*

platinum blonde *n* blonde *f* platine *or* platinée

platonic *adj* platonique

platoon /plə'tuːn/ *n* (of soldiers, police, firemen) section *f*; (in cavalry) peloton *m*

platter /'plætə(r)/ *n* (dish) plat *m*

plausible /'plɔːzəbl/ *adj* plausible, vraisemblable

play /pleɪ/ **A** *n* **1** (in theatre) pièce *f* (**about** sur)
2 (recreation) jeu *m*
3 (Sport) (game) partie *f*; **out of ~/in ~** ‹*ball*› hors jeu/en jeu
4 (movement, interaction) jeu *m*; **to come into ~** entrer en jeu; **a ~ on words** un jeu de mots
B *vt* **1** jouer à ‹*game, cards*›; jouer ‹*card*›; **to ~ hide and seek** jouer à cache-cache; **to ~ a joke on sb** jouer un tour à qn
2 jouer de ‹*instrument*›; jouer ‹*tune, symphony, chord*›; jouer à ‹*venue*›
3 (in theatre) interpréter, jouer ‹*role*›
4 mettre ‹*tape, video, CD*›
C *vi* jouer

IDIOM **to ~ for time** essayer de gagner du temps

■ **play along**: **to ~ along with sb** entrer dans le jeu de qn
■ **play down** minimiser ‹*effects, disaster*›
■ **play out**: **~ out [sth]** vivre ‹*fantasy*›
■ **play up** (fam) ‹*computer, person*› faire des siennes (fam)

p

play-acting /ˈpleɪæktɪŋ/ *n* comédie *f*, simagrées *fpl*

playboy *n* playboy *m*

⚷ **player** /ˈpleɪə(r)/ *n* (in sport, music) joueur/-euse *m/f*; (actor) comédien/-ienne *m/f*; **tennis ~** joueur/-euse de tennis

playful /ˈpleɪfl/ *adj* ‹*remark*› taquin/-e; ‹*child, kitten*› joueur/-euse

playground /ˈpleɪɡraʊnd/ *n* cour *f* de récréation

playgroup *n* ≈ halte-garderie *f*

playhouse *n* théâtre *m*

playing card *n* carte *f* à jouer

playing field *n* terrain *m* de sport

playlist *n* liste *f* d'écoute

play-off /ˈpleɪɒf/ *n* (BrE) prolongation *f*; (AmE) match *m* crucial

playroom *n* salle *f* de jeux

playschool *n* ≈ halte-garderie *f*

plaything /ˈpleɪθɪŋ/ *n* jouet *m*

playtime *n* récréation *f*

playwright *n* auteur *m* dramatique

plaza /ˈplɑːzə, (AmE) ˈplæzə/ *n* **1** (square) place *f*; **shopping ~** centre *m* commercial
2 (AmE) péage *m*

plc, **PLC** *n* (BrE) (*abbr* = **public limited company**) SA

plea /pliː/ *n* **1** (gen) appel *m* (**for** à); (for money, food) demande *f* (**for** de)
2 (Law) **to enter a ~ of guilty/not guilty** plaider coupable/non coupable

plead /pliːd/ **A** *vt* (*prét*, *pp* **pleaded** (BrE), **pled** (AmE)) plaider
B *vi* (*prét*, *pp* **pleaded** (BrE), **pled** (AmE))
1 to ~ with sb supplier qn
2 (Law) plaider

pleasant /ˈpleznt/ *adj* agréable

⚷ **please** /pliːz/ **A** *adv* s'il vous plaît; **'may I?'—'~ do'** 'je peux?'—'oui, je vous en prie'
B *vt* faire plaisir à ‹*person*›; **she is hard to ~** elle est difficile (à contenter)
C *vi* plaire; **do as you ~** fais comme il te plaira, fais comme tu veux

pleased /pliːzd/ *adj* content/-e (**that** que (+ *subjunctive*), **about, at** de, **with** de); **to look ~ with oneself** avoir l'air content de soi; **I am ~ to announce that...** j'ai le plaisir d'annoncer que...; **~ to meet you** enchanté

pleasing /ˈpliːzɪŋ/ *adj* ‹*appearance, colour, voice*› agréable; ‹*manner, personality*› avenant/-e; ‹*effect, result*› heureux/-euse

pleasurable /ˈpleʒərəbl/ *adj* agréable

pleasure /ˈpleʒə(r)/ *n* plaisir *m* (**of** de, **of doing** de faire); **for ~** par plaisir; **my ~** (replying to request for help) avec plaisir; (replying to thanks) je vous en prie

pleat /pliːt/ *n* pli *m*

pleated *adj* ‹*skirt*› plissé/-e; ‹*trousers*› à plis *after n*

pledge /pledʒ/ **A** *n* **1** (promise) promesse *f*
2 (money promised to charity) promesse *f* de don
B *vt* promettre ‹*allegiance, aid, support*› (**to** à); **to ~ one's word** donner sa parole

plentiful /ˈplentɪfl/ *adj* abondant/-e

⚷ **plenty** /ˈplentɪ/ *quantif, pron* **~ of** beaucoup de; **~ to do** beaucoup à faire

pliable /ˈplaɪəbl/ *adj* ‹*twig, plastic*› flexible; ‹*person*› malléable

pliers /ˈplaɪəz/ *npl* pinces *fpl*; **a pair of ~s** des pinces

plight /plaɪt/ *n* **1** (dilemma) situation *f* désespérée
2 (suffering) détresse *f*

plimsoll /ˈplɪmsəl/ *n* (BrE) chaussure *f* de tennis

plod /plɒd/ *v*
▪ **plod along** ‹*walk*› avancer d'un pas lent
▪ **plod away** ‹*work*› travailler ferme, bosser (fam)

plodder /ˈplɒdə(r)/ *n* bûcheur/-euse *m/f* (fam)

plonk /plɒŋk/ (fam) **A** *n* (wine) vin *m* ordinaire, pinard *m* (pop)
B *vt* (*also* **~ down**) planter ‹*plate, bottle, box*› (**on** sur)

⚷ **plot** /plɒt/ **A** *n* **1** (conspiracy) complot *m*
2 (of novel, film, play) intrigue *f*
3 ~ of land parcelle *f* de terre; **a vegetable ~** un carré de légumes
4 (building site) terrain *m* à bâtir
B *vt* (*p prés etc* **-tt-**) **1** (plan) comploter ‹*murder, attack, return*›; fomenter ‹*revolution*›
2 (chart) relever [qch] sur une carte ‹*course*›
3 (on graph) tracer [qch] point par point ‹*curve, graph*›
C *vi* (*p prés etc* **-tt-**) conspirer (**against** contre)

plough (BrE), **plow** (AmE) /plaʊ/ **A** *n* charrue *f*
B *vt* **1** labourer ‹*land, field*›; creuser ‹*furrow*›
2 (invest) **to ~ money into** investir beaucoup d'argent dans ‹*project, company*›
▪ **plough back**: **~ [sth] back, ~ back [sth]** réinvestir ‹*profits, money*› (**into** dans)
▪ **plough through** avancer péniblement dans ‹*mud, snow*›; ramer sur (fam) ‹*book*›

ploy /plɔɪ/ *n* stratagème *m* (**to do** pour faire)

pluck /plʌk/ **A** *n* courage *m*, cran *m* (fam)
B *vt* **1** cueillir ‹*flower, fruit*›
2 plumer ‹*chicken*›
3 (in music) pincer ‹*strings*›; pincer les cordes de ‹*guitar*›
4 to ~ one's eyebrows s'épiler les sourcils
IDIOM **to ~ up one's courage** prendre son courage à deux mains

plucky /ˈplʌkɪ/ *adj* courageux/-euse

plug /plʌɡ/ **A** *n* **1** (on appliance) prise *f* (de courant)
2 (in bath, sink) bonde *f*

⚷ mot clé

3 (*also* **spark ~**) bougie *f*
4 (in advertising) pub *f* (fam), publicité *f* (**for** pour)
B *vt* (*p prés etc* **-gg-**) **1** boucher ‹*hole*› (**with** avec)
2 (fam) (promote) faire de la publicité pour ‹*book, show, product*›
3 to ~ sth into brancher qch à
■ **plug in**: **A** **~ in** se brancher
B **~ [sth] in** brancher ‹*appliance*›
plug and play *n* plug and play *m* (*on branche et ça marche*)
plughole /'plʌghəʊl/ *n* (BrE) bonde *f*
plum /plʌm/ **A** *n* prune *f*
B *adj* **1** (colour) prune *inv*
2 (fam) **to get a ~ job** décrocher un boulot en or (fam)
plumb /plʌm/ **A** *adv* **1** (AmE) ‹*crazy*› complètement
2 (fam) **~ in the middle** en plein milieu
B *vt* sonder ‹*depths*›; **to ~ the depths of** toucher le fond de ‹*despair, misery*›
plumber /'plʌmə(r)/ *n* plombier *m*
plumbing /'plʌmɪŋ/ *n* plomberie *f*
plummet /'plʌmɪt/ *vi* chuter, dégringoler (fam)
plump /plʌmp/ *adj* ‹*person, arm, leg*› potelé/-e; ‹*cheek, face*› rond/-e, plein/-e
plunge /plʌndʒ/ **A** *vt* plonger (**into** dans)
B *vi* ‹*road, cliff, waterfall*› plonger; ‹*bird, plane*› piquer; ‹*person*› (dive) plonger; (fall) tomber (**from** de); ‹*rate, value*› chuter
IDIOM **to take the ~** se jeter à l'eau
plunger /'plʌndʒə(r)/ *n* ventouse *f*
plural /'plʊərəl/ **A** *n* pluriel *m*; **in the ~** au pluriel
B *adj* ‹*noun, adjective*› au pluriel; ‹*form, ending*› du pluriel
plus /plʌs/ **A** *n* avantage *m*
B *adj* **the ~ side** le côté positif; **50 ~** plus de 50; **the 65-~ age group** les personnes qui ont 65 ans et plus
C *prep* plus; **15 ~ 12** 15 plus 12
D *conj* et; **bedroom ~ bathroom** chambre et salle de bains
plus fours *npl* culotte *f* de golf
plus sign *n* signe *m* plus
Pluto /'plu:təʊ/ *pr n* (planet) Pluton *f*
plutonium /plu:'təʊnɪəm/ *n* plutonium *m*
ply /plaɪ/ **A** *vt* **1** vendre ‹*wares*›; **to ~ one's trade** exercer son métier
2 to ~ sb with food/drink ne cesser de remplir l'assiette/le verre de qn
B *vi* ‹*boat, bus*› faire la navette (**between** entre)
plywood /'plaɪwʊd/ *n* contreplaqué *m*
pm *adv* (*abbr* = **post meridiem**) **two ~** deux heures de l'après-midi; **nine ~** neuf heures du soir
pneumatic drill *n* marteau *m* piqueur
pneumonia /nju:'məʊnɪə, (AmE) nu:-/ *n* pneumonie *f*
poach /pəʊtʃ/ **A** *vt* **1** chasser [qch] illégalement ‹*game*›
2 (Culin) faire pocher
B *vi* braconner
poacher /'pəʊtʃə(r)/ *n* braconnier *m*
PO Box *n* boîte *f* postale
pocket /'pɒkɪt/ **A** *n* **1** (in garment) poche *f*
2 (in billiards) bourse *f*
B *adj* ‹*diary, dictionary, edition*› de poche
C *vt* empocher
pocketbook /'pɒkɪtbʊk/ *n* (AmE) (wallet) portefeuille *m*; (handbag) sac *m* à main
pocketknife *n* couteau *m* de poche
pocket money *n* argent *m* de poche
podcast /'pɒdkɑ:st, (AmE) /-kæst/ **A** *n* podcast *m* (*fichier m numérique téléchargeable audio ou vidéo*)
B *vt* podcaster (*mettre à disposition sur un site internet des fichiers téléchargeables audio ou vidéo*)
podgy /'pɒdʒɪ/ *adj* (fam) grassouillet/-ette
podium /'pəʊdɪəm/ *n* (*pl* **-iums, -ia**) (for speaker, conductor) estrade *f*; (for winner) podium *m*
poem /'pəʊɪm/ *n* poème *m*
poet /'pəʊɪt/ *n* poète *m*
poetic /pəʊ'etɪk/ *adj* poétique
poetry /'pəʊɪtrɪ/ *n* poésie *f*; **to write/read ~** écrire/lire des poèmes
poignant /'pɔɪnjənt/ *adj* poignant/-e
point /pɔɪnt/ **A** *n* **1** (of knife, needle, pencil) pointe *f*
2 (location, position on scale) point *m*; (less specific) endroit *m*
3 (extent, degree) point *m*; **up to a ~** jusqu'à un certain point
4 (moment) (precise) moment *m*; (stage) stade *m*; **to be on the ~ of doing** être sur le point de faire; **at this ~ in her career** à ce stade(-là) de sa carrière; **at some ~ in the future** plus tard; **at one ~** à un moment donné
5 (question, idea) point *m*; **to make the ~ that** faire remarquer que; **you've made your ~** vous vous êtes exprimé; **to make a ~ of doing** (as matter of pride) mettre un point d'honneur à faire; (do deliberately) faire exprès
6 (central idea) point *m* essentiel; **to come straight to the ~** aller droit au fait; **to keep** *or* **stick to the ~** rester dans le sujet; **to miss the ~** ne pas comprendre; **that's beside the ~** là n'est pas la question; **to get the ~** comprendre; **that's not the ~** il ne s'agit pas de cela
7 (purpose) objet *m*; **what's the ~ of doing...?** à quoi bon faire...?; **there's no ~ in doing** ça ne sert à rien de faire; **I don't see the ~ of doing** je ne vois pas l'intérêt de faire
8 (feature, characteristic) point *m*, côté *m*; **her strong ~** son point fort
9 (in scoring) point *m*; **match ~** (in tennis) balle *f* de match

10 (decimal point) virgule *f*
11 (headland) pointe *f*
B *vt* **1** (aim, direct) **to ~ sth at sb** braquer qch sur qn ‹*camera, gun*›; **to ~ one's finger at sb** montrer qn du doigt
2 (show) **to ~ the way to** indiquer la direction de
3 (in ballet, gym) **to ~ one's toes** faire des pointes
C *vi* **1** (indicate) indiquer *or* montrer (du doigt); **to ~ at sb/sth** montrer qn/qch du doigt
2 ‹*signpost, arrow, compass*› indiquer; **to be ~ing at sb** ‹*gun, camera*› être braqué/-e sur qn
▪ **point out** **A** montrer ‹*place, person*› (**to** à) **B** faire remarquer ‹*fact, discrepancy*›

point-blank /ˌpɔɪnt'blæŋk/ *adv* **1** ‹*shoot*› à bout portant
2 ‹*refuse, deny*› catégoriquement

pointed /'pɔɪntɪd/ *adj* **1** ‹*hat, stick, chin*› pointu/-e
2 ‹*remark*› qui vise quelqu'un

pointer /'pɔɪntə(r)/ *n* **1** (piece of information) indication *f*
2 (on projector screen) flèche *f*
3 (Comput) pointeur *m*

pointless /'pɔɪntlɪs/ *adj* ‹*request, activity*› absurde; **it's ~ to do/for me to do** ça ne sert à rien de faire/que je fasse

point of view *n* point *m* de vue

poise /pɔɪz/ *n* **1** (confidence) assurance *f*
2 (physical elegance) aisance *f*

poised /pɔɪzd/ *adj* **1** (self-possessed) plein/-e d'assurance
2 (elegant) plein/-e d'aisance
3 (on the point of) **to be ~ to do** être sur le point de faire

poison /'pɔɪzn/ **A** *n* poison *m*
B *vt* empoisonner ‹*person, environment, relationship*›; ‹*fumes*› intoxiquer ‹*person*›

poisoning /'pɔɪzənɪŋ/ *n* empoisonnement *m*

poisonous /'pɔɪzənəs/ *adj* **1** ‹*chemicals, gas*› toxique; ‹*mushroom, berry*› vénéneux/-euse; ‹*snake, insect, bite*› venimeux/-euse
2 ‹*rumour, propaganda*› pernicieux/-ieuse

poke /pəʊk/ *vt* **1** (jab, prod) pousser [qn] du bout du doigt ‹*person*›; donner un coup dans ‹*pile, substance*›; tisonner ‹*fire*›
2 (push, put) **to ~ sth into** enfoncer qch dans ‹*hole, pot*›; **to ~ one's head out of the window** passer la tête par la fenêtre
▪ **poke around, poke about** farfouiller (in dans)
▪ **poke out**: **A** **~ out** ‹*elbow, toe, blade*› dépasser
B **~ out [sth], ~ [sth] out** sortir ‹*head, nose, tongue*›

poker /'pəʊkə(r)/ *n* **1** (for fire) tisonnier *m*
2 (card game) poker *m*
IDIOM (as) **stiff as a ~** raide comme la justice

poker-faced /'pəʊkəfeɪst/ *adj* ‹*person*› impassible

Poland /'pəʊlənd/ *pr n* Pologne *f*

polar /'pəʊlə(r)/ *adj* polaire

pole /pəʊl/ *n* **1** (stick) perche *f*; (for tent, flag) mât *m*; (for skiing) bâton *m*
2 (of earth's axis) pôle *m*

Pole /pəʊl/ *n* Polonais/-e *m/f*

pole dancing *n* pole dancing *m*

pole star /'pəʊlstɑː(r)/ *n* étoile *f* polaire

pole vault /'pəʊlvɔːlt/ *n* saut *m* à la perche

⚷ **police** /pə'liːs/ **A** *n* **1** (police force) **the ~** la police
2 (policemen) policiers *mpl*
B *vt* maintenir l'ordre dans ‹*area*›

police constable, PC *n* agent *m* de police

Police Department, PD *n* (AmE) services *mpl* de police (d'une ville)

police force *n* police *f*

policeman *n* (*pl* **-men**) agent *m* de police

police officer *n* policier *m*

police station *n* poste *m* de police; (larger) commissariat *m*

policewoman *n* (*pl* **-women**) femme *f* policier

policing /pə'liːsɪŋ/ *n* **1** (maintaining law and order) maintien *m* de l'ordre
2 (of demonstration, match) organisation *f* du service d'ordre
3 (of measures) contrôle *m* de l'application

⚷ **policy** /'pɒləsɪ/ *n* **1** (plan, rule) politique *f* (**on** sur)
2 (in insurance) (cover) contrat *m*; (document) police *f*

policyholder *n* assuré/-e *m/f*

policy unit *n* comité *m* de conseillers politiques

polio /'pəʊlɪəʊ/ *n* poliomyélite *f*

polish /'pɒlɪʃ/ **A** *n* **1** (for wood, floor) cire *f*; (for shoes) cirage *m*; (for brass, silver) pâte *f* à polir; (for car) lustre *m*
2 (shiny surface) éclat *m*
3 (of manner, performance) élégance *f*
B *vt* **1** cirer ‹*shoes, furniture*›; astiquer ‹*leather, car, glass, brass*›; polir ‹*stone*›
2 (refine) soigner ‹*performance, image*›; affiner ‹*style*›
▪ **polish off** (fam) expédier (fam) ‹*food, job*›

Polish /'pəʊlɪʃ/ **A** *n* (language) polonais *m*
B *adj* polonais/-e

polished /'pɒlɪʃt/ *adj* **1** ‹*surface, wood*› poli/-e; ‹*floor, shoes*› ciré/-e
2 ‹*manner*› raffiné/-e
3 ‹*performance*› (bien) rodé/-e

polite /pə'laɪt/ *adj* poli/-e (**to** avec)

politeness /pə'laɪtnɪs/ *n* politesse *f*

⚷ **political** /pə'lɪtɪkl/ *adj* politique

politically correct, PC *adj* politiquement correct/-e

⚷ mot clé

political prisoner *n* prisonnier/-ière *m/f* politique

politician /ˌpɒlɪˈtɪʃn/ *n* homme/femme *m/f* politique

politicize /pəˈlɪtɪsaɪz/ *vt* politiser

politics /ˈpɒlətɪks/ *n* **1** (gen) politique *f*
2 (subject) sciences *fpl* politiques
3 (views) opinions *fpl* politiques

poll /pəʊl/ **A** *n* **1** (vote casting) scrutin *m*, vote *m*; (election) élections *fpl*; **to go to the ~s** se rendre aux urnes
2 (survey) sondage *m* (**on** sur)
B *vt* **1** obtenir ‹*votes*›
2 (canvass) interroger ‹*group*›

pollen /ˈpɒlən/ *n* pollen *m*

polling booth *n* isoloir *m*

polling day *n* jour *m* des élections

polling station *n* bureau *m* de vote

poll tax *n* (BrE) ≈ impôts *mpl* locaux

pollutant /pəˈluːtənt/ *n* polluant *m*

pollute /pəˈluːt/ *vt* polluer

polluter /pəˈluːtə(r)/ *n* pollueur/-euse *m/f*

pollution /pəˈluːʃn/ *n* pollution *f*

polo /ˈpəʊləʊ/ *n* polo *m*

polo neck *n* (BrE) col *m* roulé

poltergeist /ˈpɒltəgaɪst/ *n* esprit *m* frappeur

poly /ˈpɒlɪ/ **A** *n* (BrE) (Hist) (fam) (*abbr* = **polytechnic**) établissement *m* d'enseignement supérieur
B **poly-** *pref* poly-

polystyrene /ˌpɒlɪˈstaɪriːn/ *n* polystyrène *m*

polytechnic /ˌpɒlɪˈteknɪk/ *n* (BrE) (Hist) (*also* **poly**) établissement *m* d'enseignement supérieur

polythene /ˈpɒlɪθiːn/ *n* (BrE) polyéthylène *m*

pomegranate /ˈpɒmɪgrænɪt/ *n* grenade *f*

pompom, **pompon** /ˈpɒmpɒm/ *n* pompon *m*

pompous /ˈpɒmpəs/ *adj* ‹*person*› plein/-e de suffisance; ‹*air, speech, style*› pompeux/-euse

pond /pɒnd/ *n* (large) étang *m*; (smaller) mare *f*; (in garden) bassin *m*

ponder /ˈpɒndə(r)/ *vi* réfléchir (**on** à); (more deeply) méditer (**on** sur)

pontiff /ˈpɒntɪf/ *n* pontife *m*

pontoon /pɒnˈtuːn/ *n* **1** (pier) ponton *m*
2 (BrE) (Games) vingt-et-un *m*

pony /ˈpəʊnɪ/ *n* poney *m*

ponytail /ˈpəʊnɪteɪl/ *n* queue *f* de cheval

poodle /ˈpuːdl/ *n* caniche *m*

pool /puːl/ **A** *n* **1** (pond) étang *m*; (artificial) bassin *m*
2 (*also* **swimming ~**) piscine *f*
3 (of water, light) flaque *f*; **a ~ of blood** une mare de sang
4 (kitty) cagnotte *f*; (in cards) mises *fpl*
5 (of money, resources) pool *m*; (of ideas, experience) réservoir *m*
6 (billiards) billard *m* américain
B **pools** *npl* (BrE) (*also* **football ~s**) ≈ loto *m* sportif
C *vt* mettre [qch] en commun

pool table *n* table *f* de billard américain

poor /pɔː(r), (AmE) pʊər/ *adj* **1** ‹*person, country*› pauvre (**in** en)
2 ‹*quality, work, planning, weather, visibility*› mauvais/-e *before n*; ‹*attendance*› faible
3 (deserving pity) pauvre *before n*; **~ you!** mon/ma pauvre!
4 ‹*attempt, excuse*› piètre *before n*

poorly /ˈpɔːlɪ, (AmE) ˈpʊərlɪ/ *adv* **1** ‹*live, dress, dressed*› pauvrement
2 ‹*written, lit, paid*› mal

pop /pɒp/ **A** *n* **1** (sound) pan *m*; **to go ~** faire pan
2 (fam) (drink) soda *m*
3 (music) musique *f* pop
4 (fam) (each) **tickets were £5 a ~** les tickets étaient 5 livres sterling pièce
B *adj* ‹*concert, group, music, song*› pop; ‹*record, singer*› de pop
C *vt* (*p prés etc* **-pp-**) **1** faire éclater ‹*balloon, bubble*›
2 faire sauter ‹*cork*›
3 (fam) (put) **to ~ sth in(to)** mettre qch dans ‹*oven, cupboard, mouth*›
D *vi* (*p prés etc* **-pp-**) **1** ‹*balloon*› éclater; ‹*cork, buttons*› sauter
2 ‹*ears*› se déboucher brusquement; **her eyes were ~ping out of her head** les yeux lui sortaient de la tête
3 (BrE) (fam) (go) **to ~ into town/the bank** faire un saut (fam) en ville/à la banque
■ **pop in** (BrE) (fam) passer
■ **pop out** (BrE) (fam) sortir
■ **pop round**, **pop over** (BrE) passer

pope /pəʊp/ *n* pape *m*; **Pope Paul VI** le Pape Paul VI

poplar /ˈpɒplə(r)/ *n* peuplier *m*

poppy /ˈpɒpɪ/ *n* pavot *m*; **wild ~** coquelicot *m*

pop sock *n* mi-bas *m*

popular /ˈpɒpjʊlə(r)/ *adj* **1** ‹*actor, politician*› populaire (**with, among** parmi); ‹*hobby, sport*› répandu/-e (**with, among** chez); ‹*food, dish*› prisé/-e (**with, among** par); ‹*product, resort, colour, design*› en vogue (**with, among** chez); **John is very ~** John a beaucoup d'amis
2 (of or for the people) ‹*music, movement, press*› populaire; ‹*entertainment*› grand public *inv*; ‹*science, history*› de vulgarisation

popularity /ˌpɒpjʊˈlærətɪ/ *n* popularité *f* (**of** de, **with** auprès de)

popularize /ˈpɒpjʊləraɪz/ *vt* (make fashionable) généraliser; (make accessible) vulgariser

population /ˌpɒpjʊˈleɪʃn/ *n* population *f*

pop-up /ˈpɒpʌp/ **A** *adj* **1** (Comput) pop-up; **~ menu** menu *m* surgissant, menu *m* pop-up; **~ window** pop-up *f*, fenêtre *f* pop-up
2 (of shop, venue) éphémère; **~ store** magasin

m éphémère, pop-up store *m*
B *n* (Comput) pop-up *f*

pop-up menu *n* menu *m* déroulant *or* contextuel

pop-up window *n* fenêtre *m* popup

porcelain /ˈpɔːsəlɪn/ *n* porcelaine *f*

porch /pɔːtʃ/ *n* **1** (of house, church) porche *m*
2 (AmE) (veranda) véranda *f*

porcupine /ˈpɔːkjʊpaɪn/ *n* porc-épic *m*

pore /pɔː(r)/ *n* pore *m*

■ **pore over** être plongé/-e dans ‹*book*›; étudier soigneusement ‹*map*›

pork /pɔːk/ *n* (viande *f* de) porc *m*

pornographic /ˌpɔːnəˈgræfɪk/ *adj* pornographique

pornography /pɔːˈnɒgrəfɪ/ *n* pornographie *f*

porpoise /ˈpɔːpəs/ *n* marsouin *m*

porridge /ˈpɒrɪdʒ, (AmE) ˈpɔːr-/ *n* porridge *m* (*bouillie de flocons d'avoine*)

port /pɔːt/ *n* **1** (harbour) port *m*; **in ~** au port; **~ of call** escale *f*; (fig) arrêt *m*
2 (drink) porto *m*
3 (Comput) port *m*

portable /ˈpɔːtəbl/ *adj* portable

portable media player *n* tourniquet *m*

porter /ˈpɔːtə(r)/ *n* **1** (in station, airport, hotel) porteur *m*; (in hospital) brancardier *m*
2 (BrE) (doorman) (of hotel) portier *m*; (of apartment block) gardien/-ienne *m/f*
3 (AmE) (steward) employé *m* des wagons-lits

portfolio /pɔːtˈfəʊlɪəʊ/ *n* **1** (case) porte-documents *m inv*; (for drawings) carton *m* (à dessins)
2 (sample) portfolio *m*
3 (in politics, finance) portefeuille *m*

P

porthole *n* hublot *m*

portion /ˈpɔːʃn/ *n* **1** (of house, machine, document, country) partie *f* (**of** de)
2 (share) (of money, blame) part *f* (**of** de)
3 (at meal) portion *f*

portrait /ˈpɔːtreɪt, -trɪt/ *n* portrait *m*

portray /pɔːˈtreɪ/ *vt* **1** (depict) décrire ‹*place, era, event*›; présenter ‹*person, situation*›
2 ‹*actor*› interpréter ‹*character*›
3 ‹*artist*› peindre ‹*person*›; ‹*picture, artist*› représenter ‹*scene*›

Portugal /ˈpɔːtʃʊgl/ *pr n* Portugal *m*

Portuguese /ˌpɔːtʃʊˈgiːz/ **A** *n* **1** (person) Portugais/-e *m/f*
2 (language) portugais *m*
B *adj* portugais/-e

pose /pəʊz/ **A** *vt* poser ‹*problem*› (**for** pour); présenter ‹*challenge*› (**to** à); représenter ‹*threat, risk*› (**to** pour); soulever ‹*question*› (**about** de)
B *vi* **1** ‹*artist's model*› poser; ‹*performer*› prendre des poses
2 to ~ as se faire passer pour
3 (posture) frimer (fam)

poser /ˈpəʊzə(r)/ *n* (fam) **1** (person) frimeur/-euse *m/f* (fam)
2 (puzzle) colle *f* (fam)

posh /pɒʃ/ *adj* (fam) ‹*person*› huppé/-e (fam); ‹*house, area, clothes, car*› chic; ‹*voice*› distingué/-e

🔑 **position** /pəˈzɪʃn/ **A** *n* **1** (gen) position *f*; **to be in ~** (in place) être en place; (ready) être prêt/-e
2 (situation, state) situation *f*; **to be in a ~ to do** être en mesure de faire
3 (Sport) poste *m*; **what ~ does he play?** quel est son poste?
4 (job) poste *m*
B *vt* poster ‹*policemen, soldiers*›; disposer ‹*object*›

🔑 **positive** /ˈpɒzətɪv/ *adj* **1** (affirmative) ‹*answer, reaction, result*› positif/-ive
2 (optimistic) ‹*message, person, feeling, tone*› positif/-ive
3 (constructive) ‹*contribution, effect, progress*› positif/-ive; ‹*advantage, good*› réel/réelle *before n*
4 (sure) ‹*identification, proof*› formel/-elle; ‹*fact*› indéniable; **to be ~** être sûr/-e (**about** de, **that** que)
5 (forceful) ‹*action*› catégorique
6 (in mathematics, science) positif/-ive
7 (extreme) ‹*pleasure*› pur/-e *before n*; ‹*disgrace, outrage, genius*› véritable *before n*

positive discrimination *n* mesures *fpl* antidiscriminatoires

possess /pəˈzes/ *vt* **1** posséder ‹*property, weapon, proof, charm*›; avoir ‹*power, advantage*›; (illegally) détenir ‹*arms, drugs*›
2 (take control of) ‹*anger, fury*› s'emparer de ‹*person*›; ‹*devil*› posséder ‹*person*›; **what ~ed you to do that?** qu'est-ce qui t'a pris de faire ça?

possession /pəˈzeʃn/ **A** *n* **1** (gen) possession *f*
2 (Law) (illegal) détention *f* (**of** de)
B possessions *npl* biens *mpl*

possessive /pəˈzesɪv/ **A** *n* (in grammar) possessif *m*
B *adj* possessif/-ive (**towards** à l'égard de, **with** avec)

🔑 **possibility** /ˌpɒsəˈbɪlətɪ/ *n* **1** (chance, prospect) possibilité *f*
2 (eventuality) éventualité *f*

🔑 **possible** /ˈpɒsəbl/ *adj* possible; **he did as much as ~** il a fait tout son possible; **as far as ~** dans la mesure du possible; **as quickly as ~** le plus vite possible; **as soon as ~** dès que possible

🔑 **possibly** /ˈpɒsəblɪ/ *adv* **1** (maybe) peut-être
2 (for emphasis) **how could they ~ understand?** comment donc pourraient-ils comprendre?; **we can't ~ afford it** nous n'en avons absolument pas les moyens

🔑 **post** /pəʊst/ **A** *n* **1** (job) poste *m* (**as, of** de); **to hold a ~** occuper un poste
2 (BrE) (postal system) poste *f*; (letters) courrier

🔑 mot clé

m; (delivery) distribution *f*; **by return of ~** par retour du courrier; **it was lost in the ~** cela s'est égaré dans le courrier
3 (Mil) poste *m*
4 (pole) poteau *m*
B **post-** *pref* post-; **in ~-1992 Europe** dans l'Europe d'après 1992
C *vt* **1** (BrE) (send by post) poster, expédier [qch] (par la poste); (put in letterbox) mettre [qch] à la poste
2 (stick up) afficher ‹*notice, poster*›; annoncer ‹*details, results*›
3 (gen), (Mil) (send abroad) affecter (**to** à)
4 (station) poster ‹*guard, sentry*›

postage /ˈpəʊstɪdʒ/ *n* affranchissement *m*; **including ~ and packing** frais *mpl* d'expédition inclus; **~ free** franc de port **~ paid** pré-affranchi

postal /ˈpəʊstl/ *adj* ‹*charges, district*› postal/-e; ‹*application*› par la poste

postal order, **PO** *n* (BrE) mandat *m* (**for** de)

postbox *n* (BrE) boîte *f* aux lettres

postcard *n* carte *f* postale

post code *n* (BrE) code *m* postal

post-date /ˌpəʊstˈdeɪt/ *vt* postdater

poster /ˈpəʊstə(r)/ *n* (for information) affiche *f*; (decorative) poster *m*

posterity /pɒˈsterətɪ/ *n* postérité *f*

poster paint *n* gouache *f*

postgraduate /ˌpəʊstˈgrædʒʊət/ **A** *n* ≈ étudiant/-e *m/f* de troisième cycle
B *adj* ≈ de troisième cycle

posthumous /ˈpɒstjʊməs, (AmE) ˈpɒstʃəməs/ *adj* posthume

postman *n* facteur *m*

postmark /ˈpəʊstmɑːk/ *n* cachet *m* de la poste

post-mortem /ˌpəʊstˈmɔːtəm/ *n* autopsie *f*

post-natal /ˌpəʊstˈneɪtl/ *adj* post-natal/-e

post office, **PO** *n* poste *f*

postpone /pəˈspəʊn/ *vt* reporter, remettre (**until** à, **for** de)

postscript /ˈpəʊsskrɪpt/ *n* (in letter) post-scriptum *m inv* (**to** à); (to book) postface *f* (**to** à)

posture /ˈpɒstʃə(r)/ **A** *n* **1** (pose) posture *f*; (fig) (stance) position *f*
2 (bearing) maintien *m*; **to have good/bad ~** se tenir bien/mal
B *vi* poser, prendre des poses

post-viral syndrome *n* (*also* **post-viral fatigue syndrome**) encéphalomyélite *f* myalgique

post-war /ˌpəʊstˈwɔː(r)/ *adj* d'après-guerre

pot /pɒt/ **A** *n* **1** (container) pot *m*
2 (teapot) théière *f*; (coffee pot) cafetière *f*
3 **~s and pans** casseroles *fpl*
4 (piece of pottery) poterie *f*
B *vt* (*p prés etc* **-tt-**) **1** mettre [qch] en pot ‹*jam*›
2 (in billiards) blouser ‹*ball*›
3 mettre [qch] en pot ‹*plant*›
C **potted** *pp adj* **1** ‹*plant*› en pot
2 ‹*biography, history*› bref/brève *before n*
IDIOMS **to go to ~** ‹*person*› se laisser aller; ‹*situation*› aller à vau-l'eau; **to take ~ luck** (for meal) (BrE) manger à la fortune du pot; (gen) prendre ce que l'on trouve

potassium /pəˈtæsɪəm/ *n* potassium *m*

potato /pəˈteɪtəʊ/ *n* (*pl* **-es**) pomme *f* de terre

potato chips (AmE), **potato crisps** (BrE) *npl* chips *fpl*

potato peeler *n* épluche-légumes *m inv*

pot belly *n* bedaine *f*

potent /ˈpəʊtnt/ *adj* **1** ‹*symbol, drug*› puissant/-e; ‹*drink*› fort/-e
2 (sexually) viril/-e

potential /pəˈtenʃl/ **A** *n* potentiel *m* (**as** en tant que, **for** de); **the ~ to do** les qualités *fpl* nécessaires pour faire; **to fulfil one's ~** montrer de quoi on est capable
B *adj* ‹*buyer, danger, energy, market, victim*› potentiel/-ielle; ‹*champion, rival*› en puissance; ‹*investor*› éventuel/-elle

pothole /ˈpɒthəʊl/ *n* fondrière *f*, nid *m* de poule

potholing *n* (BrE) spéléologie *f*

pot plant *n* plante *f* d'appartement

potter /ˈpɒtə(r)/ *n* potier *m*
■ **potter about, potter around** (BrE) (do odd jobs) bricoler (fam); (go about daily chores) suivre son petit train-train (fam)

pottery /ˈpɒtərɪ/ *n* poterie *f*

potting compost *n* terreau *m*

potty /ˈpɒtɪ/ (fam) **A** *n* pot *m* (d'enfant)
B *adj* (BrE) ‹*person*› dingue (fam); ‹*idea*› farfelu/-e (fam); **to be ~ about** être toqué/-e de (fam)

pouch /paʊtʃ/ *n* **1** (bag) petit sac *m*; (for tobacco) blague *f* (à tabac); (for ammunition) étui *m* (à munitions)
2 (of marsupials) poche *f* ventrale

poultry /ˈpəʊltrɪ/ *n* (birds) volailles *fpl*; (meat) volaille *f*

pounce /paʊns/ *vi* bondir; **to ~ on** ‹*animal*› bondir sur ‹*prey, object*›; ‹*person*› se jeter sur ‹*victim*›

pound /paʊnd/ **A** *n* **1** (weight measurement) livre *f* (= *453.6 g*); **two ~s of apples** ≈ un kilo de pommes
2 (unit of currency) livre *f*
3 (for dogs, cars) fourrière *f*
B *vt* **1** (Culin) piler ‹*spices, grain*›; aplatir ‹*meat*›
2 ‹*waves*› battre ‹*shore*›
3 ‹*artillery*› pilonner ‹*city*›
C *vi* **1** **to ~ on** marteler ‹*door, wall*›
2 ‹*heart*› battre
3 **to ~ up/down the stairs** monter/descendre l'escalier d'un pas lourd
4 **my head is ~ing** j'ai l'impression que ma tête va éclater

pour /pɔː(r)/ **A** *vt* **1** verser ‹*liquid*›; couler ‹*cement, metal, wax*›

p

2 (*also* ~ **out**) servir ‹*drink*›
3 to ~ money into investir des sommes énormes dans
B *vi* **1** ‹*liquid*› couler (à flots); **to ~ into** ‹*water, liquid*› couler dans; ‹*smoke, fumes*› se répandre dans; ‹*light*› inonder ‹*room*›; **tears ~ed down her face** les larmes ruisselaient sur son visage
2 to ~ into ‹*people*› affluer dans; **to ~ out of** ‹*people, cars*› sortir en grand nombre de
C *v impers* **it's ~ing (with rain)** il pleut à verse

- **pour away** vider
- **pour in** ‹*people*› affluer; ‹*letters, money*› pleuvoir; ‹*water*› entrer à flots
- **pour out**: **A ~ out** ‹*liquid, smoke, crowd*› se déverser; ‹*people*› sortir en grand nombre **B ~ [sth] out 1** verser, servir ‹*coffee, wine*› **2** rejeter ‹*fumes, sewage*›; **to ~ out one's troubles** *or* **heart to sb** s'épancher auprès de qn

pout /paʊt/ *vi* faire la moue

poverty /ˈpɒvətɪ/ *n* pauvreté *f*; (more severe) misère *f*

poverty line *n* seuil *m* de pauvreté

poverty-stricken *adj* dans la misère

POW *n* (*abbr* = **prisoner of war**) prisonnier/-ière *m/f* de guerre

powder /ˈpaʊdə(r)/ **A** *n* poudre *f*
B *vt* **to ~ one's face** se poudrer le visage

powdered *adj* ‹*egg, milk, coffee*› en poudre

powdery /ˈpaʊdərɪ/ *adj* ‹*snow*› poudreux/-euse; ‹*stone*› friable

⚷ **power** /ˈpaʊə(r)/ **A** *n* **1** (control) pouvoir *m*; **to be in/come to ~** être/accéder au pouvoir; **to be in sb's ~** être à la merci de qn
2 (influence) influence *f* (**over** sur)
3 (capability) pouvoir *m*; **to do everything in one's ~** faire tout ce qui est en son pouvoir (**to do** pour faire)
4 (*also* **~s**) (authority) attributions *fpl*
5 (physical force) (of person, explosion) force *f*; (of storm) violence *f*
6 (Tech) énergie *f*; (current) courant *m*; **to switch on the ~** mettre le courant
7 (of vehicle, plane) puissance *f*; **to be running at full/half ~** fonctionner à plein/mi-régime
8 (in mathematics) **6 to the ~ of 3** 6 puissance 3
9 (country) puissance *f*
B *adj* ‹*drill, cable*› électrique; ‹*brakes*› assisté/-e
C *vt* faire marcher ‹*engine*›; propulser ‹*plane, boat*›
IDIOMS **to do sb a ~ of good** faire à qn un bien fou; **the ~s that be** les autorités

powerboat *n* hors-bord *m inv*

power cut *n* coupure *f* de courant

⚷ **powerful** /ˈpaʊəfl/ *adj* ‹*person, engine, computer*› puissant/-e; ‹*smell, emotion, voice, government*› fort/-e; ‹*argument*› solide

powerless /ˈpaʊəlɪs/ *adj* impuissant/-e (**against** face à); **to be ~ to do** ne pas pouvoir faire

power line *n* ligne *f* à haute tension

power of attorney *n* procuration *f*

power plant (AmE), **power station** *n* centrale *f* (électrique)

power sharing *n* partage *m* du pouvoir

power steering *n* direction *f* assistée

power user *n* (Comput) utilisateur/-trice *mf* avancé/-e

PR *n* **1** (*abbr* = **public relations**) relations *fpl* publiques
2 (*abbr* = **proportional representation**)

practical /ˈpræktɪkl/ **A** *n* (exam) épreuve *f* pratique; (lesson) travaux *mpl* pratiques
B *adj* **1** (gen) pratique
2 ‹*plan*› réalisable

practicality /ˌpræktɪˈkælətɪ/ *n* **1** (of person) esprit *m* pratique; (of equipment) facilité *f* d'utilisation
2 (of scheme, idea, project) aspect *m* pratique

practical joke *n* farce *f*

practically /ˈpræktɪklɪ/ *adv* **1** (almost) pratiquement
2 (in practical way) d'une manière pratique

⚷ **practice** /ˈpræktɪs/ **A** *n* **1** (exercises) exercices *mpl*; (experience) entraînement *m*; **to have had ~ in** *or* **at sth/in** *or* **at doing sth** avoir déjà fait qch; **to be out of ~** être rouillé/-e (fam)
2 (for sport) entraînement *m*; (for music, drama) répétition *f*
3 (procedure) pratique *f*, usage *m*; **it's standard ~ to do** il est d'usage de faire; **business ~** usage en affaires
4 (habit) habitude *f*
5 (custom) coutume *f*
6 (business of doctor, lawyer) cabinet *m*
7 (not theory) pratique *f*; **in ~** en pratique
B *adj* ‹*game, match*› d'essai; ‹*flight*› d'entraînement
C *vt, vi* (AmE) = **practise**
IDIOM **~ makes perfect** c'est en forgeant qu'on devient forgeron (Proverb)

practise (BrE), **practice** (AmE) /ˈpræktɪs/
A *vt* **1** travailler ‹*song, speech, French*›; s'exercer à ‹*movement, shot*›; répéter ‹*play*›; **to ~ the piano** travailler le piano; **to ~ doing** *or* **how to do** s'entraîner à faire
2 (use) pratiquer ‹*restraint, kindness*›; utiliser ‹*method*›
3 exercer ‹*profession*›
4 (observe) pratiquer ‹*custom, religion*›
B *vi* **1** (at instrument) s'exercer; (for sports) s'entraîner; (for play, concert) répéter
2 (work) exercer; **to ~ as** exercer la profession de ‹*doctor, lawyer*›

practising (BrE), **practicing** (AmE) /ˈpræktɪsɪŋ/ *adj* ‹*Christian, Muslim*› pratiquant/-e; ‹*doctor, lawyer*› en exercice;

⚷ mot clé

‹*homosexual*› actif/-ive

practitioner /præk'tɪʃənə(r)/ *n* practicien/-enne *m/f*; **dental ~** dentiste *mf*

pragmatic /præg'mætɪk/ *adj* pragmatique

pragmatist /'prægmətɪst/ *n* pragmatiste *mf*

prairie /'preərɪ/ *n* plaine *f* (herbeuse)

praise /preɪz/ **A** *n* éloges *mpl*, louanges *fpl*
B *vt* **1** faire l'éloge de ‹*person, book*› (**as** en tant que)
2 louer ‹*God*› (**for** pour)

praiseworthy /'preɪzwɜ:ðɪ/ *adj* digne d'éloges

pram /præm/ *n* (BrE) landau *m*

prance /prɑ:ns, (AmE) præns/ *vi* ‹*horse*› caracoler; ‹*person*› sautiller

prank /præŋk/ *n* farce *f*

prattle /'prætl/ *vi* bavarder; ‹*children*› babiller; **to ~ on about sth** parler de qch à n'en plus finir

prawn /prɔ:n/ *n* crevette *f* rose, bouquet *m*

pray /preɪ/ *vi* prier (**for** pour)

prayer /'preə(r)/ *n* prière *f*; **to say one's ~s** faire sa prière

preach /pri:tʃ/ **A** *vt* prêcher (**to** à)
B *vi* prêcher (**to** à); (fig) sermonner
IDIOM **to practise what one ~es** prêcher d'exemple

preacher /'pri:tʃə(r)/ *n* prédicateur *m*; (clergyman) pasteur *m*

prearrange /ˌpri:ə'reɪndʒ/ *vt* fixer [qch] à l'avance

precarious /prɪ'keərɪəs/ *adj* précaire

precaution /prɪ'kɔ:ʃn/ *n* précaution *f* (**against** contre)

precautionary /prɪ'kɔ:ʃənərɪ, (AmE) -nerɪ/ *adj* préventif/-ive

precede /prɪ'si:d/ *vt* précéder

precedence /'presɪdəns/ *n* **1** (in importance) priorité *f* (**over** sur)
2 (in rank) préséance *f* (**over** sur)

precedent /'presɪdənt/ *n* précédent *m*; **to set a ~** créer un précédent

preceding /prɪ'si:dɪŋ/ *adj* précédent/-e

precinct /'pri:sɪŋkt/ *n* **1** (BrE) (*also* **shopping ~**) quartier *m* commerçant
2 (BrE) (*also* **pedestrian ~**) zone *f* piétonne
3 (AmE) (administrative district) circonscription *f*

precious /'preʃəs/ *adj* **1** (valuable) précieux/-ieuse
2 (held dear) ‹*person*› cher/chère (**to** à)
3 (affected) précieux/-ieuse, affecté/-e

precipice /'presɪpɪs/ *n* précipice *m*

precis /'preɪsi:, (AmE) preɪ'si:/ *n* résumé *m*

precise /prɪ'saɪs/ *adj* **1** (exact) précis/-e
2 ‹*person, mind*› méticuleux/-euse

precisely /prɪ'saɪslɪ/ *adv* **1** (exactly) exactement, précisément; **at ten o'clock ~** à dix heures précises
2 (accurately) ‹*describe, record*› avec précision

precision /prɪ'sɪʒn/ *n* précision *f*

preclude /prɪ'klu:d/ *vt* exclure ‹*possibility*›; empêcher ‹*action*›

precocious /prɪ'kəʊʃəs/ *adj* précoce

preconceived /ˌpri:kən'si:vd/ *adj* préconçu/-e

preconception /ˌpri:kən'sepʃn/ *n* opinion *f* préconçue

precondition /ˌpri:kən'dɪʃn/ *n* condition *f* requise

precursor /ˌpri:'kɜ:sə(r)/ *n* (person) précurseur *m*; (sign) signe *m* avant-coureur

predate /ˌpri:'deɪt/ *vt* antidater ‹*cheque*›; ‹*discovery, building*› être antérieur/-e à

predator /'predətə(r)/ *n* prédateur *m*

predecessor /'pri:dɪsesə(r), (AmE) 'predə-/ *n* prédécesseur *m*

predetermine /ˌpri:dɪ'tɜ:mɪn/ *vt* déterminer d'avance

predicament /prɪ'dɪkəmənt/ *n* situation *f* difficile

✓ **predict** /prɪ'dɪkt/ *vt* prédire

predictable /prɪ'dɪktəbl/ *adj* prévisible

prediction /prɪ'dɪkʃn/ *n* prédiction *f* (**that** selon laquelle)

predispose /ˌpri:dɪ'spəʊz/ *vt* prédisposer

predominant /prɪ'dɒmɪnənt/ *adj* prédominant/-e

predominantly /prɪ'dɒmɪnəntlɪ/ *adv* principalement

predominate /prɪ'dɒmɪneɪt/ *vi* prédominer

pre-eminent /ˌpri:'emɪnənt/ *adj* éminent/-e

pre-empt /ˌpri:'empt/ *vt* **1** anticiper ‹*question, decision, move*›; devancer ‹*person*›
2 (thwart) contrecarrer ‹*action, plan*›

pre-emptive /ˌpri:'emptɪv/ *adj* préventif/-ive

preen /pri:n/ *v refl* **to ~ oneself** ‹*bird*› se lisser les plumes; ‹*person*› se pomponner

prefab /'pri:fæb, (AmE) ˌpri:'fæb/ *n* (bâtiment *m*) préfabriqué *m*

preface /'prefɪs/ *n* (to book) préface *f*; (to speech) préambule *m*

prefect /'pri:fekt/ *n* (BrE) (Sch) élève *m/f* chargé/-e de la surveillance

✓ **prefer** /prɪ'fɜ:(r)/ *vt* **1** (like better) préférer, aimer mieux; **I ~ painting to drawing** je préfère la peinture au dessin; **to ~ it if** aimer mieux que (+ *subjunctive*)
2 (Law) **to ~ charges** ‹*police*› déférer [qn] au parquet

preferable /'prefrəbl/ *adj* préférable (**to** à)

preferably /'prefrəblɪ/ *adv* de préférence

preference /'prefrəns/ *n* préférence *f* (**for** pour)

preferential /ˌprefə'renʃl/ *adj* préférentiel/-ielle

prefigure /ˌpri:'fɪgə(r), (AmE) -gjər/ *vt* ‹*event*› préfigurer; ‹*person*› être le précurseur de

p

prefix /ˈpriːfɪks/ *n* (*pl* **-es**) préfixe *m*
pregnancy /ˈpregnənsɪ/ *n* (gen) grossesse *f*; (Zool) gestation *f*
pregnant /ˈpregnənt/ *adj* (gen) enceinte; (Zool) pleine; **to get sb ~** (fam) faire un enfant à qn (fam)
preheat /ˌpriːˈhiːt/ *vt* préchauffer ‹*oven*›
prehistoric /ˌpriːhɪˈstɒrɪk, (AmE) -tɔːrɪk/ *adj* préhistorique
prejudice /ˈpredʒʊdɪs/ **A** *n* préjugé *m*; **racial/political ~** préjugés raciaux/en matière de politique
B *vt* **1** (bias) influencer; **to ~ sb against/in favour of** prévenir qn contre/en faveur de
2 porter préjudice à ‹*claim, case*›; léser ‹*person*›; compromettre ‹*chances*›
prejudiced /ˈpredʒʊdɪst/ *adj* ‹*person*› plein/-e de préjugés; ‹*account*› partial/-e; ‹*opinion*› préconçu/-e
preliminary /prɪˈlɪmɪnərɪ, (AmE) -nerɪ/ **A** *n*
1 (gen) **as a ~ to** en prélude à
2 (Sport) épreuve *f* éliminatoire
B **preliminaries** *npl* préliminaires *mpl* (to à)
C *adj* préliminaire
prelude /ˈpreljuːd/ *n* prélude *m* (**to** à)
premarital /ˌpriːˈmærɪtl/ *adj* avant le mariage
premature /ˈpremətjʊə(r), (AmE) ˌpriːməˈtʊər/ *adj* ‹*baby, action*› prématuré/-e; ‹*ejaculation, menopause*› précoce
premeditate /ˌpriːˈmedɪteɪt/ *vt* préméditer
premier /ˈpremɪə(r), (AmE) ˈpriːmɪər/ **A** *n* premier ministre *m*
B *adj* premier/-ière *before n*
premiere /ˈpremɪeə(r), (AmE) ˈpriːmɪər/ **A** *n* première *f*
B *vt* donner [qch] en première ‹*film, play*›
premises *npl* locaux *mpl*; **on the ~** sur place; **off the ~** à l'extérieur; **to leave the ~** quitter les lieux
premium /ˈpriːmɪəm/ *n* **1** (extra payment) supplément *m*
2 (on stock exchange) prime *f* d'émission
3 (in insurance) prime *f* (d'assurance)
4 to be at a ~ valoir de l'or; **to set a (high) ~ on sth** mettre qch au (tout) premier plan
premium bond *n* (BrE) obligation *f* à lots
premonition /ˌpriːməˈnɪʃn, ˌpre-/ *n* prémonition *f*
prenatal /ˌpriːˈneɪtl/ *adj* prénatal/-e
prenuptial agreement *n* contrat *m* prénuptial
preoccupation /ˌpriːɒkjʊˈpeɪʃn/ *n* préoccupation *f*
preoccupied /ˌpriːˈɒkjʊpaɪd/ *adj* préoccupé/-e
preoccupy /ˌpriːˈɒkjʊpaɪ/ *vt* (*prét, pp* **-pied**) préoccuper

prepaid /ˌpriːˈpaɪd/ *adj* payé/-e d'avance; **~ envelope** enveloppe *f* affranchie pour la réponse
preparation /ˌprepəˈreɪʃn/ *n* préparation *f*; **~s** préparatifs *mpl*; **in ~ for sth** en vue de qch
preparatory /prɪˈpærətrɪ, (AmE) -tɔːrɪ/ *adj* ‹*training, course, drawing*› préparatoire; ‹*meeting, report, investigations*› préliminaire
preparatory school *n* **1** (BrE) école *f* primaire privée
2 (AmE) lycée *m* privé
🔑 **prepare** /prɪˈpeə(r)/ **A** *vt* préparer; **to ~ to do** se préparer à faire; **to ~ sb for** préparer qn à
B *vi* **to ~ for** se préparer à ‹*trip, talks, exam, war*›; se préparer pour ‹*party, ceremony, game*›; **to ~ oneself** se préparer
🔑 **prepared** /prɪˈpeəd/ *adj* **1** (willing) **to be ~ to do** être prêt/-e à faire
2 (ready) **to be ~ for** être prêt/-e pour ‹*event*›; **to come ~** venir bien préparé/-e; **to be ~ for the worst** s'attendre au pire
preposition /ˌprepəˈzɪʃn/ *n* préposition *f*
preposterous /prɪˈpɒstərəs/ *adj* grotesque
prerequisite /ˌpriːˈrekwɪzɪt/ *n* **1** (gen) préalable *m* (**of** de, **for** à)
2 (AmE) (Univ) unité *f* de valeur
prerogative /prɪˈrɒgətɪv/ *n* (official) prérogative *f*; (personal) droit *m*
preschool /ˌpriːˈskuːl/ **A** *n* (AmE) école *f* maternelle
B *adj* préscolaire
prescribe /prɪˈskraɪb/ *vt* **1** (Med) (fig) prescrire (**for sb** à qn, **for sth** pour qch)
2 imposer ‹*rule*›
prescription /prɪˈskrɪpʃn/ *n* ordonnance *f*; **repeat ~** ordonnance renouvelable
prescription charges *npl* frais *mpl* d'ordonnance
🔑 **presence** /ˈprezns/ *n* présence *f*
presence of mind *n* présence *f* d'esprit
🔑 **present** **A** /ˈpreznt/ *n* **1** (gift) cadeau *m*; **to give sb a ~** offrir un cadeau à qn
2 the ~ le présent; **for the ~** pour le moment, pour l'instant
3 (*also* **~ tense**) présent *m*
B /ˈpreznt/ *adj* **1** (attending) présent/-e; **to be ~ at** assister à
2 (current) actuel/-elle; **up to the ~ day** jusqu'à ce jour
C /prɪˈzent/ *vt* **1** (gen) présenter; offrir ‹*chance, opportunity*›; **to be ~ed with a choice** se trouver face à un choix
2 remettre ‹*prize, certificate*› (**to** à)
D *v refl* **to ~ oneself** se présenter; **to ~ itself** ‹*opportunity, thought*› se présenter
E **at present** *phr* (at this moment) en ce moment; (nowadays) actuellement
presentable /prɪˈzentəbl/ *adj* présentable
🔑 **presentation** /ˌprezənˈteɪʃn/ *n* **1** (gen)

🔑 mot clé

présentation *f*
2 (talk) exposé *m*
3 (of gift, award) remise *f* (**of** de)
4 (portrayal) représentation *f*

present-day *adj* actuel/-elle

presenter /prɪ'zentə(r)/ *n* présentateur/-trice *m/f*

presently /'prezəntlɪ/ *adv* (currently) à présent; (soon, in future) bientôt

present perfect *n* passé *m* composé

preservation /ˌprezə'veɪʃn/ *n* (of building, wildlife, peace) préservation *f* (**of** de); (of food) conservation *f* (**of** de); (of life) protection *f* (**of** de)

preservative /prɪ'zɜːvətɪv/ *n* (for food) agent *m* de conservation; (for wood) revêtement *m* (protecteur)

preserve /prɪ'zɜːv/ **A** *n* **1** (Culin) (jam) confiture *f*; (pickle) conserve *f*
2 (territory) chasse *f* gardée (**of** de)
B *vt* **1** (save) préserver ‹*land, building, tradition*› (**for** pour); entretenir ‹*wood, leather, painting*›
2 (maintain) préserver ‹*peace, standards, rights*›; maintenir ‹*order*›; garder ‹*humour, dignity, health*›
3 conserver ‹*food*›

preset /ˌpriː'set/ *vt* (*prét, pp* **-set**) régler (à l'avance) ‹*timer, cooker*›; programmer ‹*video*›

preside /prɪ'zaɪd/ *vi* présider; **to ~ at sth** présider qch; **to ~ over** présider ‹*conference, committee*›

presidency /'prezɪdənsɪ/ *n* présidence *f*

president /'prezɪdənt/ *n* **1** président/-e *m/f*; **to run for ~** être candidat/-e à la présidence
2 (AmE) (managing director) président-directeur *m* général

presidential /ˌprezɪ'denʃl/ *adj* présidentiel/-ielle

press /pres/ **A** *n* **1 the ~, the Press** la presse *f*; **to get a good/bad ~** avoir bonne/mauvaise presse
2 (*also* **printing ~**) presse *f*
3 (device for flattening) presse *f*
B *vt* **1** (push) appuyer sur; **to ~ sth in** enfoncer qch; **to ~ one's nose against sth** coller son nez contre qch
2 (squeeze) presser ‹*fruit, flower*›; serrer ‹*arm, hand, person*›
3 (iron) repasser ‹*clothes*›
4 (urge) faire pression sur ‹*person*›; mettre [qch] en avant ‹*issue*›; **to ~ sb to do** presser qn de faire; **to ~ a point** insister
C *vi* **1 to ~ (down)** appuyer
2 ‹*crowd, person*› se presser (**forward** vers l'avant)
D *v refl* **to ~ oneself against** se plaquer contre ‹*wall*›; se presser contre ‹*person*›

■ **press for** faire pression pour obtenir ‹*change, release*›; **to be ~ed for** ne pas avoir beaucoup de ‹*time, cash*›

■ **press on** continuer; **to ~ on with** faire avancer ‹*reform, plan*›

press agency *n* agence *f* de presse

press conference *n* conférence *f* de presse

pressing /'presɪŋ/ *adj* **1** (urgent) urgent/-e
2 ‹*invitation*› pressant/-e

press release *n* communiqué *m* de presse

press stud *n* (BrE) (bouton-)pression *m*

press-up *n* pompe *f* (fam)

pressure /'preʃə(r)/ *n* **1** (gen) pression *f*; **to put ~ on sb** faire pression sur qn; **to do sth under ~** faire qch sous la contrainte
2 (of traffic, tourists) flux *m*

pressure cooker *n* cocotte-minute® *f*

pressure group *n* groupe *m* de pression

pressurize /'preʃəraɪz/ *vt* **1** pressuriser ‹*cabin, suit, gas*›
2 faire pression sur ‹*person*›; **he was ~d into going** on a fait pression sur lui pour qu'il y aille

prestige /pre'stiːʒ/ *n* prestige *m*

prestigious /pre'stɪdʒəs/ *adj* prestigieux/-ieuse

presumably /prɪ'zjuːməblɪ, (AmE) -'zuːm-/ *adv* sans doute

presume /prɪ'zjuːm, (AmE) -'zuːm/ *vt*
1 (suppose) supposer, présumer
2 (dare) **to ~ to do** se permettre de faire

presumptuous /prɪ'zʌmptʃʊəs/ *adj* présomptueux/-euse, arrogant/-e

presuppose /ˌpriːsə'pəʊz/ *vt* présupposer (**that** que)

pre-tax /ˌpriː'tæks/ *adj* avant impôts *inv*

pretence (BrE), **pretense** (AmE) /prɪ'tens/ *n* faux-semblant *m*; **to make a ~ of sth** feindre qch; **to make a ~ of doing** faire semblant de faire

pretend /prɪ'tend/ **A** *vt* **to ~ that** faire comme si; **to ~ to do** faire semblant de faire
B *vi* faire semblant

pretension /prɪ'tenʃn/ *n* prétention *f*

pretentious /prɪ'tenʃəs/ *adj* prétentieux/-ieuse

preterite /'pretərət/ *n* prétérit *m*

pretext /'priːtekst/ *n* prétexte *m*

pretty /'prɪtɪ/ **A** *adj* joli/-e; **it was not a ~ sight** ce n'était pas beau à voir
B *adv* (fam) (very) vraiment; (fairly) assez; **~ good** pas mal du tout

prevail /prɪ'veɪl/ *vi* **1** (win) prévaloir (**against** contre)
2 (be common) prédominer

■ **prevail upon** persuader ‹*person*›

prevailing /prɪ'veɪlɪŋ/ *adj* ‹*attitude, style*› qui prévaut; ‹*rate*› en vigueur; ‹*wind*› dominant/-e

prevalent /'prevələnt/ *adj* **1** (widespread) répandu/-e
2 (ruling) qui prévaut

P

prevaricate /prɪˈværɪkeɪt/ *vi* se dérober

⚷ **prevent** /prɪˈvent/ *vt* prévenir ‹*fire, illness, violence*›; éviter ‹*conflict, disaster, damage*›; faire obstacle à ‹*marriage*›; **to ~ sb from doing** empêcher qn de faire

preventable /prɪˈventəbl/ *adj* évitable

prevention /prɪˈvenʃn/ *n* prévention *f*; **crime ~** lutte *f* contre la délinquance

preventive /prɪˈventɪv/ *adj* préventif/-ive

preview /ˈpriːvjuː/ *n* (of film, play) avant-première *f*

⚷ **previous** /ˈpriːvɪəs/ *adj* précédent/-e; (further back in time) antérieur/-e

⚷ **previously** /ˈpriːvɪəslɪ/ *adv* (before) auparavant, avant; (already) déjà

prewar /ˌpriːˈwɔː(r)/ *adj* d'avant-guerre *inv*

prey /preɪ/ *n* proie *f*

▪ **prey on 1** (hunt) chasser
2 (worry) **to ~ on sb's mind** préoccuper qn
3 (exploit) exploiter ‹*fears, worries*›

⚷ **price** /praɪs/ **A** *n* **1** (cost) prix *m*; **to go up in ~** augmenter; **to pay a high ~ for sth** payer qch cher; **at any ~** à tout prix
2 (value) valeur *f*; **to put a ~ on** évaluer ‹*object, antique*›
B *vt* fixer le prix de (**at** à)

price cut *n* baisse *f* du prix

price freeze *n* blocage *m* des prix

priceless /ˈpraɪslɪs/ *adj* **1** (extremely valuable) inestimable
2 (fam) (amusing) impayable (fam)

price list *n* (in shop, catalogue) liste *f* des prix; (in bar, restaurant) tarif *m*

price rise *n* hausse *f* des prix

price tag *n* (label) étiquette *f*

price war *n* guerre *f* des prix

prick /prɪk/ **A** *n* (of needle) piqûre *f*
B *vt* piquer; **to ~ one's finger** se piquer le doigt
C *vi* piquer

▪ **prick up**: **to ~ up one's ears** ‹*person*› dresser l'oreille; **the dog ~ed up its ears** le chien a dressé les oreilles

prickle /ˈprɪkl/ **A** *n* (of hedgehog, plant) piquant *m*
B *vi* ‹*hairs*› se hérisser (**with** de)

prickly /ˈprɪklɪ/ *adj* **1** ‹*bush, leaf*› épineux/-euse; ‹*animal*› armé/-e de piquants; ‹*thorn*› piquant/-e
2 (itchy) qui gratte
3 (fam) (touchy) irritable (**about** à propos de)

pride /praɪd/ **A** *n* **1** fierté *f*; **to take ~ in** être fier/fière de ‹*ability, achievement*›; soigner ‹*appearance, work*›; **to be sb's ~ and joy** être la (grande) fierté de qn
2 (self-respect) amour-propre *m*; (excessive) orgueil *m*
3 (of lions) troupe *f*
B *v refl* **to ~ oneself on sth/on doing** être fier/fière de qch/de faire

IDIOM **to have ~ of place** occuper la place d'honneur

priest /priːst/ *n* prêtre *m*; **parish ~** curé *m*

priesthood /ˈpriːsthʊd/ *n* (calling) prêtrise *f*; **to enter the ~** entrer dans les ordres

prig /prɪg/ *n* bégueule *mf*

prim /prɪm/ *adj* (*also* **~ and proper**) ‹*person, manner, appearance*› guindé/-e; ‹*expression*› pincé/-e; ‹*voice*› affecté/-e; ‹*clothing*› très convenable

primarily /ˈpraɪmərəlɪ, (AmE) praɪˈmerəlɪ/ *adv* (chiefly) essentiellement; (originally) à l'origine

⚷ **primary** /ˈpraɪmərɪ, (AmE) -merɪ/ **A** *n* (AmE) (*also* **~ election**) primaire *f*
B *adj* **1** (main) principal/-e; ‹*sense, meaning, stage*› premier/-ière; **of ~ importance** de première importance
2 (Sch) ‹*teaching, education*› primaire
3 ‹*industry, products*› de base

primary colour (BrE), **primary color** (AmE) *n* couleur *f* primaire

primary school *n* école *f* primaire

primary teacher *n* (*also* **primary school teacher**) (BrE) instituteur/-trice *m/f*

primate /ˈpraɪmeɪt/ *n* **1** (mammal) primate *m*
2 (archbishop) primat *m* (**of** de)

prime /praɪm/ **A** *n* **in one's ~** (professionally) à son apogée; (physically) dans la fleur de l'âge; **in its ~** à son apogée; **to be past its ~** avoir connu des jours meilleurs
B *adj* **1** (chief) principal/-e; ‹*importance*› primordial/-e
2 (good quality) ‹*site*› de premier ordre; ‹*meat, cuts*› de premier choix; **of ~ quality** de première qualité
3 (classic) ‹*example*› excellent/-e (*before n*)
C *vt* **1** (brief) préparer; **to ~ sb about** mettre qn au courant de; **to ~ sb to say** souffler à qn de dire
2 (Mil, Tech) amorcer

⚷ **prime minister**, **PM** *n* Premier ministre *m*

prime mover *n* (person) promoteur/-trice *m/f*

prime number *n* nombre *m* premier

prime time *n* heures *fpl* de grande écoute *m*

primeval /praɪˈmiːvl/ *adj* primitif/-ive

primitive /ˈprɪmɪtɪv/ **A** *n* primitif *m*
B *adj* primitif/-ive

primrose /ˈprɪmrəʊz/ *n* primevère *f* (jaune)

prince /prɪns/ *n* prince *m*

princess /prɪnˈses/ *n* princesse *f*

principal /ˈprɪnsəpl/ **A** *n* (of senior school) proviseur *m*; (of junior school, college) directeur/-trice *m/f*
B *adj* principal/-e

⚷ **principle** /ˈprɪnsəpl/ *n* principe *m*; **in ~** en principe; **on ~** par principe

print /prɪnt/ **A** *n* **1** (typeface) caractères *mpl*; **the small *or* fine ~** les détails; **in ~** disponible en librairie; **out of ~** épuisé/-e

---
⚷ mot clé

2 (etching) estampe *f*; (engraving) gravure *f*
3 (of photo) épreuve *f*
4 (of finger, hand, foot) empreinte *f*; (of tyre) trace *f*
5 (fabric) tissu *m* imprimé
B *vt* **1** imprimer ‹*book, banknote, pattern, design*›
2 (publish) publier
3 faire développer ‹*photos*›
4 (write) écrire [qch] en script

■ **print off** tirer ‹*copies*›
■ **print out** imprimer

printer /'prɪntə(r)/ *n* (person, firm) imprimeur *m*; (machine) imprimante *f*

printout /'prɪntaʊt/ *n* sortie *f* sur imprimante; (perforated) listing *m*

print preview /prɪnt'priːvjuː/ *vt* prévisualiser

prior /'praɪə(r)/ **A** *adj* **1** (previous) préalable; **~ notice** préavis *m*
2 (more important) prioritaire
B **prior to** *phr* avant

priority /praɪ'ɒrətɪ, (AmE) -'ɔːr-/ *n* priorité *f*

priory /'praɪərɪ/ *n* prieuré *m*

prise /praɪz/ *v*
■ **prise apart** séparer ‹*layers, people*›
■ **prise off** enlever [qch] en forçant ‹*lid*›
■ **prise open** ouvrir [qch] en forçant ‹*door*›

prism /'prɪzəm/ *n* prisme *m*

prison /'prɪzn/ *n* prison *f*; **to put sb in ~** emprisonner qn

prison camp *n* camp *m* de prisonniers

prisoner /'prɪznə(r)/ *n* prisonnier/-ière *m/f*; (in jail) détenu/-e *m/f*

prison officer *n* surveillant/-e *m/f* de prison

prison sentence *n* peine *f* de prison

pristine /'prɪstiːn, 'prɪstaɪn/ *adj* immaculé/-e

privacy /'prɪvəsɪ, 'praɪ-/ *n* **1** (private life) vie *f* privée; **to invade sb's ~** s'immiscer dans la vie privée de qn
2 (solitude) intimité *f* (**of** de)

private /'praɪvɪt/ **A** *n* simple soldat *m*
B *adj* **1** ‹*property, vehicle, meeting, life*› privé/-e; ‹*letter, phone call*› personnel/-elle; ‹*sale*› de particulier à particulier; ‹*place*› tranquille; **room with ~ bath** chambre avec salle de bains particulière; **a ~ joke** une plaisanterie pour initiés
2 ‹*sector, education, school, hospital*› privé/-e; ‹*accommodation, lesson*› particulier/-ière
C **in private** *phr* en privé

private eye *n* (fam) détective *m* privé

privately /'praɪvɪtlɪ/ *adv* **1** (in private) en privé
2 (not in public sector) dans le privé; **~-owned** privé/-e

privatization /ˌpraɪvɪtaɪ'zeɪʃn, (AmE) -tɪ'z-/ *n* privatisation *f*

privatize /'praɪvɪtaɪz/ *vt* privatiser

privilege /'prɪvəlɪdʒ/ *n* privilège *m*

privileged /'prɪvəlɪdʒd/ *adj* ‹*minority, life*› privilégié/-e; ‹*information*› confidentiel/-ielle

prize /praɪz/ **A** *n* **1** (award) prix *m*; (in lottery) lot *m*; **first ~** premier prix; (in lottery) gros lot
2 (valued object) trésor *m*; (reward for effort) récompense *f*
B *adj* **1** ‹*vegetable, bull*› primé/-e; ‹*pupil*› hors-pair *inv*
2 ‹*possession*› précieux/-ieuse
3 ‹*idiot, example*› parfait/-e *before n*

prize draw *n* (for charity) tombola *f*; (for advertising) tirage *m* au sort

prize-giving *n* remise *f* des prix

prize money *n* argent *m* du prix

prizewinner *n* (in lottery) gagnant/-e *m/f*; (of award) lauréat/-e *m/f*

pro /prəʊ/ **A** *n* **1** (fam) (professional) pro *mf* (fam)
2 (advantage) **the ~s and cons** le pour et le contre; **the ~s and cons of sth** les avantages et les inconvénients de qch
B *prep* (in favour of) pour

proactive /prəʊ'æktɪv/ *adj* ‹*approach, role*› dynamique

probability /ˌprɒbə'bɪlətɪ/ *n* (of desirable event) chances *fpl*; (of unwelcome event) risques *mpl*

probable /'prɒbəbl/ *adj* probable

probably /'prɒbəblɪ/ *adv* probablement

probation /prə'beɪʃn, (AmE) prəʊ-/ *n* **1** (for adult) sursis *m* avec mise à l'épreuve; (for juvenile) mise *f* en liberté surveillée
2 (trial period) période *f* d'essai

probationary /prə'beɪʃnrɪ, (AmE) prəʊ'beɪʃənerɪ/ *adj* (trial) ‹*period, year*› d'essai; (training) ‹*period*› probatoire

probation officer *n* (for juveniles) délégué/-e *m/f* à la liberté surveillée; (for adults) agent *m* de probation

probe /prəʊb/ **A** *n* **1** (investigation) enquête *f*
2 (instrument) sonde *f*
B *vt* (Med, Tech) sonder (**with** avec)

probing /'prəʊbɪŋ/ *adj* ‹*look*› inquisiteur/-trice; ‹*question*› pénétrant/-e; ‹*examination*› très poussé/-e

problem /'prɒbləm/ **A** *n* problème *m*
B *adj* ‹*child*› difficile; ‹*family*› à problèmes

problematic /ˌprɒblə'mætɪk/ *adj* (*also* **problematical**) problématique

problem page *n* courrier *m* du cœur

procedure /prə'siːdʒə(r)/ *n* procédure *f*

proceed /prə'siːd, prəʊ-/ *vi* **1** (set about) procéder; **to ~ with** poursuivre
2 (be in progress) ‹*project, work*› avancer; ‹*interview, talks, trial*› se poursuivre
3 ‹*person, road*› continuer; ‹*vehicle*› avancer

proceedings *npl* **1** (meeting) réunion *f*; (ceremony) cérémonie *f*; (discussion) débats *mpl*
2 (Law) poursuites *fpl*

proceeds /'prəʊsiːdz/ *npl* (of sale) produit *m*; (of event) recette *f*

⚷ **process** /ˈprəʊses, (AmE) ˈprɒses/ **A** *n* **1** (gen) processus *m* (**of** de); **to be in the ~ of doing** être en train de faire; **in the ~** en même temps
2 (method) procédé *m*
B *vt* **1** traiter ‹*applications, data*›
2 traiter ‹*raw materials, chemicals, waste*›
3 développer ‹*film*›
4 (Culin) (mix) mixer; (chop) hacher

processing /ˈprəʊsesɪŋ, (AmE) ˈprɒ-/ *n* traitement *m*; **the food ~ industry** l'industrie *f* alimentaire

procession /prəˈseʃn/ *n* (of demonstration, carnival) défilé *m*; (formal) cortège *m*; (religious) procession *f*

processor /ˈprəʊsesə(r), (AmE) ˈprɒ-/ *n* (Comput) unité *f* centrale

proclaim /prəˈkleɪm/ *vt* proclamer (**that** que)

proclamation /ˌprɒkləˈmeɪʃn/ *n* proclamation *f*

procrastinate /prəʊˈkræstɪneɪt/ *vi* atermoyer

procure /prəˈkjʊə(r)/ *vt* procurer; **to ~ sth for sb** procurer qch à qn; **to ~ sth for oneself** se procurer qch

prod /prɒd/ **A** *n* **1** (poke) petit coup *m*
2 (fam) (reminder) **to give sb a ~** secouer (fam) qn
B *vt* (*p prés etc* **-dd-**) (*also* **~ at**) (with foot, instrument, stick) donner des petits coups à; (with finger) toucher

prodigy /ˈprɒdɪdʒɪ/ *n* prodige *m*

⚷ **produce A** /ˈprɒdju:s, (AmE) -du:s/ *n* produits *mpl*
B /prəˈdju:s, (AmE) -ˈdu:s/ *vt* **1** (cause) produire ‹*result, effect*›; provoquer ‹*reaction, change*›
2 ‹*region, farmer, company*› produire (**from** à partir de); ‹*worker, machine*› fabriquer
3 (generate) produire ‹*heat, sound, energy*›; rapporter ‹*profits*›
4 (present) produire ‹*passport, report*›; fournir ‹*evidence, argument, example*›; **to ~ sth from** sortir qch de ‹*pocket, bag*›
5 produire ‹*show, film*›; mettre [qch] en scène ‹*play*›
6 (put together) préparer ‹*meal*›; mettre au point ‹*timetable, package, solution*›; éditer ‹*brochure, guide*›

⚷ **producer** /prəˈdju:sə(r), (AmE) -ˈdu:s-/ *n* **1** (of produce) producteur *m*; (of machinery, goods) fabricant *m*
2 (of film) producteur/-trice *m/f*; (of play) metteur *m* en scène

⚷ **product** /ˈprɒdʌkt/ *n* produit *m*

⚷ **production** /prəˈdʌkʃn/ *n* **1** (of crop, foodstuffs, metal) production *f* (**of** de); (of machinery, furniture, cars) fabrication (**of** de)
2 (output) production *f*
3 (of film, opera) production *f* (**of** de); (of play) mise *f* en scène (**of** de)

production line *n* chaîne *f* de fabrication

productive /prəˈdʌktɪv/ *adj* ‹*factory, land, day*› productif/-ive; ‹*system, method, use*› efficace; ‹*discussion*› fructueux/-euse

productivity /ˌprɒdʌkˈtɪvətɪ/ *n* productivité *f*

profane /prəˈfeɪn, (AmE) prəʊˈfeɪn/ *adj*
1 (blasphemous) impie
2 (secular) profane

profession /prəˈfeʃn/ *n* profession *f*

⚷ **professional** /prəˈfeʃənl/ **A** *n* professionnel/-elle *m/f*
B *adj* professionnel/-elle

professionalism /prəˈfeʃənəlɪzəm/ *n* (of person, organization) professionnalisme *m*; (of performance, work) (haute) qualité *f*

professionally /prəˈfeʃənəlɪ/ *adv* **1** (expertly) ‹*designed*› par un professionnel
2 (in work situation) dans un cadre professionnel
3 ‹*play sport*› en professionnel/-elle; **he sings ~** il est chanteur professionnel
4 (to a high standard) de manière professionnelle

⚷ **professor** /prəˈfesə(r)/ *n* **1** (Univ) (chair holder) professeur *m* d'Université
2 (AmE) (Univ) (teacher) professeur *m*

proficiency /prəˈfɪʃnsɪ/ *n* (practical) compétence *f* (**in, at** en); (academic) niveau *m* (**in** en)

proficient /prəˈfɪʃnt/ *adj* compétent/-e

profile /ˈprəʊfaɪl/ *n* (of face) profil *m*; (of body) silhouette *f*; **in ~** de profil; **to have/maintain a high ~** occuper/rester sur le devant de la scène

profiling *n* (gen), (Med) typage *m*

⚷ **profit** /ˈprɒfɪt/ **A** *n* **1** bénéfice *m*, profit *m*; **gross/net ~** bénéfice brut/net
2 (fig) profit *m*
B *vt* profiter à ‹*person, group*›
C *vi* **to ~ by** *or* **from sth** tirer profit de qch

profitable /ˈprɒfɪtəbl/ *adj* rentable; (fig) fructueux/-euse

profit margin *n* marge *f* bénéficiaire

profit sharing *n* intéressement *m* des salariés aux bénéfices

profound /prəˈfaʊnd/ *adj* profond/-e

profuse /prəˈfju:s/ *adj* ‹*praise, thanks*› profus/-e; ‹*bleeding*› abondant/-e

profusely /prəˈfju:slɪ/ *adv* ‹*sweat, bleed*› abondamment; **to apologize ~** se confondre en excuses

prognosis /prɒgˈnəʊsɪs/ *n* **1** (Med) pronostic *m* (**on, about** sur)
2 (prediction) pronostics *mpl*

⚷ **program** /ˈprəʊgræm, (AmE) -grəm/ **A** *n*
1 (Comput) programme *m*
2 (AmE) (on radio, TV) émission *f*
B *vt, vi* programmer (**to do** pour faire)

⚷ **programme** (BrE), **program** (AmE) /ˈprəʊgræm, (AmE) -grəm/ **A** *n* **1** (broadcast)

p

⚷ mot clé

émission *f* (**about** sur)
2 (schedule) programme *m*
3 (for play, opera) programme *m*
B *vt* programmer ‹*machine*› (**to do** pour faire)

programmer /'prəʊgræmə(r), (AmE) -grəm-/ *n* programmeur/-euse *m/f*

progress **A** /'prəʊgres, (AmE) 'prɒgres/ *n* **1** (advances) progrès *m*; **to make ~** ‹*person*› faire des progrès
2 (of person, inquiry) progression *f*; (of talks, disease, career) évolution *f*; **to be in ~** ‹*discussions, exam*› être en cours
B /prə'gres/ *vi* progresser

progression /prə'greʃn/ *n* **1** (evolution) évolution *f*
2 (improvement) progression *f*
3 (series) suite *f*

progressive /prə'gresɪv/ *adj* **1** (gen) progressif/-ive
2 (forward-looking) ‹*person, policy*› progressiste; ‹*school*› parallèle

progress report *n* (on construction work) rapport *m* sur l'état des travaux; (on project) rapport *m* sur l'état du projet; (on patient) bulletin m de santé

prohibit /prə'hɪbɪt, (AmE) prəʊ-/ *vt* interdire; **to ~ sb from doing** interdire à qn de faire

prohibition /ˌprəʊhɪ'bɪʃn, (AmE) ˌprəʊə'bɪʃn/ *n* interdiction *f* (**on, against** de)

prohibitive /prə'hɪbətɪv, (AmE) prəʊ-/ *adj* prohibitif/-ive

project **A** /'prɒdʒekt/ *n* **1** (scheme) projet *m* (**to do** pour faire)
2 (Sch) dossier *m* (**on** sur); (Univ) mémoire *m* (**on** sur); **research ~** programme *m* de recherches
3 (AmE) (state housing) (large) ≈ cité *f* HLM; (small) ≈ lotissement *m* HLM
B /prə'dʒekt/ *vt* **1** envoyer ‹*missile*›; faire porter ‹*voice*›
2 projeter ‹*guilt, anxiety*› (**onto** sur)
3 (estimate) prévoir
4 projeter ‹*image, slides*›

projecting /prə'dʒektɪŋ/ *adj* saillant/-e

projector /prə'dʒektə(r)/ *n* projecteur *m*

pro-life /ˌprəʊ'laɪf/ *adj* contre l'avortement

proliferate /prə'lɪfəreɪt, (AmE) prəʊ-/ *vi* proliférer

prolific /prə'lɪfɪk/ *adj* (gen) prolifique; ‹*decade*› fécond/-e; ‹*growth*› rapide

prologue /'prəʊlɒg, (AmE) -lɔːg/ *n* prologue *m* (**to** de)

prolong /prə'lɒŋ, (AmE) -'lɔːŋ/ *vt* prolonger

promenade /ˌprɒmə'nɑːd, (AmE) -'neɪd/ *n* (path) promenade *f*; (by sea) front *m* de mer

prominent /'prɒmɪnənt/ *adj* **1** ‹*figure, campaigner*› très en vue; ‹*artist*› éminent/-e; **to play a ~ part in sth** jouer un rôle de premier plan dans qch
2 ‹*place, feature*› proéminent/-e; ‹*ridge, cheekbone*› saillant/-e; ‹*eye*› exorbité/-e

promiscuity /ˌprɒmɪ'skjuːətɪ/ *n* (sexual) vagabondage *m* sexuel

promiscuous /prə'mɪskjʊəs/ *adj* ‹*person*› aux mœurs légères

promise /'prɒmɪs/ **A** *n* promesse *f*; **to break one's ~** manquer à sa promesse; **she shows great ~** elle promet beaucoup
B *vt* **to ~ to do** promettre de faire; **to ~ sb sth** promettre qch à qn
C *vi* promettre; **do you ~?** c'est promis?

promising /'prɒmɪsɪŋ/ *adj* ‹*situation, result, future*› prometteur/-euse; ‹*artist, candidate*› qui promet

promote /prə'məʊt/ *vt* **1** (in rank) promouvoir (**to** à)
2 (advertise) faire de la publicité pour; (market) promouvoir
3 (encourage) promouvoir
4 (BrE) (in football) **to be ~d from the fourth to the third division** passer de quatrième en troisième division

promotion /prə'məʊʃn/ *n* promotion *f*

promotional video *n* vidéo *f* publicitaire

prompt /prɒmpt/ **A** *adj* rapide; **to be ~ to do** être prompt/-e à faire
B *vt* **1** provoquer ‹*reaction, decision*›; susciter ‹*concern, comment*›; **to ~ sb to do** inciter qn à faire
2 (remind) souffler à ‹*actor*›

prompter /'prɒmptə(r)/ *n* **1** (in theatre) souffleur/-euse *m/f*
2 (AmE) (teleprompter) téléprompteur *m*

promptly /'prɒmptlɪ/ *adv* **1** (immediately) immédiatement
2 (without delay) rapidement
3 (punctually) à l'heure; **~ at six o'clock** à six heures précises

prone /prəʊn/ *adj* **1 to be ~ to** être sujet/-ette à ‹*colds*›; être enclin/-e à ‹*depression*›
2 to lie ~ être allongé/-e face contre terre

pronoun /'prəʊnaʊn/ *n* pronom *m*

pronounce /prə'naʊns/ *vt* prononcer
■ **pronounce on** se prononcer sur ‹*case, matter*›

pronounced /prə'naʊnst/ *adj* ‹*accent, tendency*› prononcé/-e; ‹*change, increase*› marqué/-e

pronunciation /prəˌnʌnsɪ'eɪʃn/ *n* prononciation *f*

proof /pruːf/ *n* **1** (evidence) preuve *f*; **~ of identity** pièce *f* d'identité
2 (in printing, photography) épreuve *f*
3 (of alcohol) **to be 70% ~** ≈ titrer 40° d'alcool

proof of purchase *n* justificatif *m* d'achat

proofread /'pruːfriːd/ *vt* (*prét, pp* **-read** /red/) corriger les épreuves de

prop /prɒp/ **A** *n* étai *m*
B **props** *npl* accessoires *mpl*
C *vt* (*p prés etc* **-pp-**) **1** (*also* **~ up**) étayer

2 to ~ sb/sth against sth appuyer qn/qch contre qch

propaganda /ˌprɒpəˈgændə/ *n* propagande *f*

propagate /ˈprɒpəgeɪt/ *vi* se propager

propel /prəˈpel/ *vt* (*p prés etc* **-ll-**) propulser

propeller /prəˈpelə(r)/ *n* hélice *f*

🔑 **proper** /ˈprɒpə(r)/ *adj* **1** (right) ‹*term, spelling*› correct/-e; ‹*order, tool, response*› bon/bonne *before n*; ‹*clothing*› qu'il faut; **everything is in the ~ place** tout est à sa place
2 (adequate) ‹*recognition, facilities*› convenable; ‹*education, training*› bon/bonne *before n*; ‹*care*› requis/-e
3 (respectable) ‹*person*› correct/-e; ‹*upbringing*› convenable
4 (real, full) ‹*doctor, holiday, job*› vrai/-e *before n*
5 (actual) **in the village ~** dans le village même

🔑 **properly** /ˈprɒpəlɪ/ *adv* **1** (correctly) correctement
2 (fully) complètement; **I didn't have time to thank you ~** je n'ai pas eu le temps de vous remercier
3 (adequately) convenablement

proper name, **proper noun** *n* nom *m* propre

🔑 **property** /ˈprɒpətɪ/ *n* **1** (belongings) propriété *f*, biens *mpl*
2 (real estate) biens *mpl* immobiliers
3 (house) propriété *f*
4 (characteristic) propriété *f*

property developer *n* promoteur *m* immobilier

property owner *n* propriétaire *mf*

prophecy /ˈprɒfəsɪ/ *n* prophétie *f*

prophet /ˈprɒfɪt/ *n* prophète *m*

🔑 **proportion** /prəˈpɔːʃn/ **A** *n* **1** (of group, population) proportion *f* (**of** de); (of income, profit, work) part *f* (**of** de)
2 (ratio) proportion *f*
3 (harmony) **out of/in ~** hors de/en proportion
4 (perspective) **to get sth out of all ~** faire tout un drame de qch; **to be out of all ~** être tout à fait disproportionné/-e (**to** par rapport à)
B proportions *npl* dimensions *fpl*

proportional /prəˈpɔːʃənl/ *adj* proportionnel/-elle

proportional representation, **PR** *n* représentation *f* proportionnelle

🔑 **proposal** /prəˈpəʊzl/ *n* **1** (suggestion) proposition *f*
2 (of marriage) demande *f* en mariage

🔑 **propose** /prəˈpəʊz/ **A** *vt* proposer ‹*course of action, solution*›; présenter ‹*motion*›
B *vi* faire sa demande en mariage (**to** à)
C proposed *pp adj* ‹*action, reform*› envisagé/-e

🔑 mot clé

proposition /ˌprɒpəˈzɪʃn/ **A** *n* **1** (suggestion) proposition *f*
2 (assertion) assertion *f*
B *vt* faire une proposition à ‹*person*›

proprietor /prəˈpraɪətə(r)/ *n* propriétaire *mf* (**of** de)

propriety /prəˈpraɪətɪ/ *n* **1** (politeness) correction *f*
2 (morality) décence *f*

proscribe /prəˈskraɪb, (AmE) prəʊ-/ *vt* proscrire

prose /prəʊz/ *n* **1** prose *f*
2 (BrE) (translation) thème *m*

prosecute /ˈprɒsɪkjuːt/ **A** *vt* poursuivre [qn] en justice
B *vi* engager des poursuites

prosecution /ˌprɒsɪˈkjuːʃn/ *n* (Law)
1 (accusation) poursuites *fpl* (judiciaires)
2 the ~ le/les plaignant/-s; (state, Crown) le ministère public

prosecutor /ˈprɒsɪkjuːtə(r)/ *n* (Law) procureur *m*

🔑 **prospect** /ˈprɒspekt/ **A** *n* **1** (hope) espoir *m*, chance *f*
2 (outlook) perspective *f*
B prospects *npl* perspectives *fpl*

prospective /prəˈspektɪv/ *adj* ‹*buyer, candidate*› potentiel/-ielle; ‹*husband, wife*› futur/-e *before n*

prospectus /prəˈspektəs/ *n* brochure *f*

prosper /ˈprɒspə(r)/ *vi* prospérer

prosperity /prɒˈsperətɪ/ *n* prospérité *f*

prosperous /ˈprɒspərəs/ *adj* prospère

prostate /ˈprɒsteɪt/ *n* (*also* **~ gland**) prostate *f*

prostitute /ˈprɒstɪtjuːt, (AmE) -tuːt/ **A** *n* prostituée *f*; **male ~** prostitué *m*
B *vt* prostituer ‹*person, talent*›

prostitution /ˌprɒstɪˈtjuːʃn, (AmE) -tuːt-/ *n* prostitution *f*

prostrate /ˈprɒstreɪt/ *adj* **to lie ~** être allongé/-e de tout son long; **~ with grief** accablé/-e de chagrin

protagonist /prəˈtægənɪst/ *n* protagoniste *mf*

🔑 **protect** /prəˈtekt/ *vt* (gen) protéger (**against** contre, **from** de, contre); défendre ‹*consumer, interests*› (**against** contre)

🔑 **protection** /prəˈtekʃn/ *n* protection *f*

protection factor *n* indice *m* de protection

protection racket *n* racket *m*

protective /prəˈtektɪv/ *adj* protecteur/-trice

protein /ˈprəʊtiːn/ *n* protéine *f*

🔑 **protest A** /ˈprəʊtest/ *n* **1** protestation *f*; **in ~** en signe de protestation
2 (demonstration) manifestation *f*
B /prəˈtest/ *vt* **1 to ~ that** protester que; **to ~ one's innocence** protester de son innocence
2 (AmE) (complain about) protester contre

(to auprès de)
C /prəˈtest/ *vi* **1** (complain) protester
2 (demonstrate) manifester (**against** contre)

Protestant /ˈprɒtɪstənt/ *n, adj* protestant/-e *m/f*

protester /prəˈtestə(r)/ *n* manifestant/-e *m/f*

protocol /ˌprəʊtəˈkɒl, (AmE) -kɔːl/ *n* protocole *m*

prototype /ˈprəʊtətaɪp/ *n* prototype *m* (of de)

protrude /prəˈtruːd, (AmE) prəʊ-/ *vi* (gen) dépasser; ‹*teeth*› avancer

protruding /prəˈtruːdɪŋ, (AmE) prəʊ-/ *adj* ‹*rock*› en saillie; ‹*eyes*› globuleux/-euse; ‹*ears*› décollé/-e; ‹*ribs*› saillant/-e; ‹*chin*› en avant

proud /praʊd/ *adj* **1** fier/fière (**of** de); ‹*owner*› heureux/-euse *before n*
2 ‹*day, moment*› grand/-e *before n*

prove /pruːv/ **A** *vt* prouver; (by demonstration) démontrer; **to ~ a point** montrer qu'on a raison
B *vi* **to ~ to be** s'avérer être
C *v refl* **to ~ oneself** faire ses preuves; **to ~ oneself (to be)** se révéler

proverb /ˈprɒvɜːb/ *n* proverbe *m*

provide /prəˈvaɪd/ *vt* **1** (supply) fournir ‹*opportunity, evidence, jobs, meals*› (**for** à); apporter ‹*answer, support*› (**for** à); assurer ‹*service, access, training, shelter*› (**for** à)
2 ‹*clause, law*› prévoir (**that** que)
■ **provide for 1** envisager ‹*eventuality, expenses*›
2 subvenir aux besoins de ‹*family*›; **to be well ~d for** être à l'abri du besoin

provided, **providing** /prəˈvaɪdɪd/ *conj* (*also* **~ that**) à condition que (+ *subjunctive*)

province /ˈprɒvɪns/ *n* province *f*; **in the ~s** en province

provincial /prəˈvɪnʃl/ *adj* **1** ‹*newspaper, town*› de province; ‹*life*› provincial/-e
2 (narrow) provincial/-e

provision /prəˈvɪʒn/ **A** *n* **1** (of goods, equipment) fourniture *f* (**of** de, **to** à); (of service) prestation *f*; **~ of food/supplies** approvisionnement *m* (**to** de)
2 (for future) dispositions *fpl*
3 (in agreement) clause *f*; (in bill, act) disposition *f*
B provisions *npl* (supplies) provisions *fpl*

provisional /prəˈvɪʒənl/ *adj* provisoire

provocative /prəˈvɒkətɪv/ *adj* **1** ‹*dress, remark*› provocant/-e
2 ‹*book*› qui fait réfléchir

provoke /prəˈvəʊk/ *vt* **1** (annoy) provoquer
2 (cause) susciter ‹*anger, complaints*›; provoquer ‹*laughter, reaction*›

prow /praʊ/ *n* proue *f*

prowess /ˈpraʊɪs/ *n* **1** (skill) prouesses *fpl*
2 (bravery) vaillance *f*

prowl /praʊl/ **A** *vt* **to ~ the streets** rôder dans les rues
B *vi* ‹*animal, person*› rôder

proximity /prɒkˈsɪmətɪ/ *n* proximité *f*

proxy /ˈprɒksɪ/ *n* **1** (person) mandataire *mf*
2 by ~ par procuration

prudent /ˈpruːdnt/ *adj* prudent/-e

prudish /ˈpruːdɪʃ/ *adj* pudibond/-e, prude

prune /pruːn/ **A** *n* (Culin) pruneau *m*
B *vt* (cut back) tailler; (thin out) élaguer

pry /praɪ/ *vi* **to ~ into** mettre son nez dans

PS *n* (*abbr* = **postscript**) PS *m*

psalm /sɑːm/ *n* psaume *m*

pseudonym /ˈsjuːdənɪm, (AmE) ˈsuːd-/ *n* pseudonyme *m*

psych /saɪk/ *v*
■ **psych up** (fam): **to ~ oneself up** se préparer (psychologiquement) (**for** pour)

psychiatric /ˌsaɪkɪˈætrɪk/ *adj* psychiatrique

psychiatrist /saɪˈkaɪətrɪst, (AmE) sɪ-/ *n* psychiatre *mf*

psychiatry /saɪˈkaɪətrɪ, (AmE) sɪ-/ *n* psychiatrie *f*

psychic /ˈsaɪkɪk/ *n* médium *m*, voyant/-e *m/f*

psychoanalysis /ˌsaɪkəʊəˈnæləsɪs/ *n* psychanalyse *f*

psychological /ˌsaɪkəˈlɒdʒɪkl/ *adj* psychologique

psychologist /saɪˈkɒlədʒɪst/ *n* psychologue *mf*

psychology /saɪˈkɒlədʒɪ/ *n* psychologie *f*

psychopath /ˈsaɪkəʊpæθ/ *n* psychopathe *mf*

psychotherapist /ˌsaɪkəʊˈθerəpɪst/ *n* psychothérapeute *mf*

PTO (*abbr* = **please turn over**) TSVP

pub /pʌb/ *n* (BrE) pub *m*

puberty /ˈpjuːbətɪ/ *n* puberté *f*

public /ˈpʌblɪk/ **A** *n* **the ~** le public
B *adj* (gen) public/-ique; ‹*library, amenity*› municipal/-e; ‹*duty, spirit*› civique; **to be in the ~ eye** occuper le devant de la scène
C in public *phr* en public

public address *n* (*also* **public address system**) (système *m* de) sonorisation *f*

public assistance *n* (AmE) aide *f* sociale

publication /ˌpʌblɪˈkeɪʃn/ *n* publication *f*

public company *n* société *f* anonyme par actions

public convenience *n* (BrE) toilettes *fpl*

public holiday *n* jour *m* férié

publicity /pʌbˈlɪsətɪ/ *n* publicité *f*; **to attract ~** attirer l'attention des médias

publicity campaign *n* (to sell product) campagne *f* publicitaire; (to raise social issue) campagne *f* de sensibilisation

publicity stunt *n* coup *m* publicitaire

publicize /ˈpʌblɪsaɪz/ *vt* **1** attirer l'attention du public sur ‹*issue, problem*›
2 rendre [qch] public ‹*information, facts*›
3 faire de la publicité pour ‹*show*›

p

publicly /'pʌblɪklɪ/ *adv* publiquement

public opinion *n* opinion *f* publique

public prosecutor *n* procureur *m* général

public relations, **PR** *n* relations *fpl* publiques

public school *n* (BrE) école *f* privée; (AmE) école *f* publique

public sector *n* secteur *m* public

public transport *n* transports *mpl* en commun

publish /'pʌblɪʃ/ *vt* publier ‹*book, letter, guide*›; éditer ‹*newspaper, magazine*›

publisher /'pʌblɪʃə(r)/ *n* **1** (person) éditeur/-trice *m/f*
2 (*also* **publishing house**) maison *f* d'édition

publishing /'pʌblɪʃɪŋ/ *n* édition *f*

pudding /'pʊdɪŋ/ *n* **1** (BrE) (dessert course) dessert *m*
2 (cooked dish) pudding *m*
3 (BrE) (sausage) **black/white ~** boudin *m* noir/blanc

puddle /'pʌdl/ *n* flaque *f*

puff /pʌf/ **A** *n* (of air, smoke, steam) bouffée *f*; (of breath) souffle *m*
B *vt* tirer sur ‹*pipe*›
C *vi* **1 to ~ at** tirer des bouffées de ‹*cigarette, pipe*›
2 (pant) souffler

■ **puff out 1** gonfler ‹*cheeks*›; ‹*bird*› hérisser ‹*feathers*›
2 to ~ out smoke lancer des bouffées de fumée

■ **puff up**: **A ~ up** ‹*feathers*› se hérisser; ‹*eye*› devenir bouffi/-e; ‹*rice*› gonfler
B ~ [sth] up hérisser ‹*feathers, fur*›; **~ed up with pride** rempli/-e d'orgueil

puff pastry *n* pâte *f* feuilletée

puffy /'pʌfɪ/ *adj* bouffi/-e

pull /pʊl/ **A** *n* **1** (tug) coup *m*; **to give sth a ~** tirer sur qch
2 (attraction) force *f*; (fig) attrait *m* (**of** de)
3 (fam) (influence) influence *f* (**over, with** sur)
B *vt* **1** (gen) tirer; tirer sur ‹*cord, rope*›; **to ~ sb/sth through** faire passer qn/qch par ‹*hole, window*›; **to ~ sth out of** tirer qch de ‹*pocket, drawer*›; **to ~ sb out of** retirer qn de ‹*wreckage*›; sortir qn de ‹*river*›
2 (fam) sortir ‹*gun, knife*›; **to ~ a gun on sb** menacer qn avec un pistolet
3 appuyer sur ‹*trigger*›
4 se faire une élongation à ‹*muscle*›
5 to ~ a face faire la grimace
C *vi* tirer (**at, on** sur)

■ **pull apart 1** (dismantle) démonter
2 (destroy) ‹*child*› mettre en pièces; ‹*animal*› déchiqueter

■ **pull away**: **A ~ away** ‹*car*› démarrer
B ~ [sb/sth] away éloigner ‹*person*›; retirer ‹*hand*›; **to ~ sb/sth away from** écarter qn/qch de ‹*window, wall*›

■ **pull back 1** ‹*troops*› se retirer (**from** de)
2 ‹*car, person*› reculer

■ **pull down** démolir ‹*building*›; baisser ‹*blind, trousers*›

■ **pull in** ‹*car, bus, driver*› s'arrêter

■ **pull off 1** ôter ‹*coat, sweater*›; enlever ‹*shoes, lid, sticker*›
2 conclure ‹*deal*›; réaliser ‹*feat*›

■ **pull out A ~ out 1** ‹*car, truck*› déboîter; **to ~ out of sth** quitter qch ‹*station, drive*›
2 ‹*troops, participants*› se retirer (**of** de)
B ~ [sth] out 1 extraire ‹*tooth*›; enlever ‹*splinter*›; arracher ‹*weeds*›
2 (from pocket) sortir

■ **pull over**: **A ~ over** ‹*motorist, car*› s'arrêter (sur le côté)
B ~ [sb/sth] over ‹*police*› forcer [qn/qch] à se ranger sur le côté

■ **pull through** ‹*accident victim*› s'en tirer

■ **pull together**: **A ~ together** faire un effort
B ~ oneself together se ressaisir

■ **pull up**: **A ~ up** s'arrêter
B ~ up [sth], ~ [sth] up 1 (uproot) arracher
2 lever ‹*anchor*›; remonter ‹*trousers, socks*›; prendre ‹*chair*›
C ~ [sb] up 1 (lift) hisser
2 (reprimand) réprimander
3 arrêter ‹*driver*›

pull-down menu *n* (Comput) menu *m* déroulant

pulley /'pʊlɪ/ *n* poulie *f*

pullover /'pʊləʊvə(r)/ *n* pull-over *m*

pulp /pʌlp/ **A** *n* (soft centre) pulpe *f*; (crushed mass) pâte *f*
B *vt* écraser ‹*fruit, vegetable*›; réduire [qch] en pâte ‹*wood, cloth*›; mettre [qch] au pilon ‹*newspapers, books*›

pulp fiction *n* littérature *f* de gare

pulpit /'pʊlpɪt/ *n* chaire *f*

pulse /pʌls/ *n* pouls *m*

pulse rate *n* pouls *m*

pulverize /'pʌlvəraɪz/ *vt* pulvériser

pump /pʌmp/ **A** *n* **1** (for air) pompe *f*; **bicycle ~** pompe à vélo
2 (plimsoll) chaussure *f* de sport; (BrE) (flat shoe) ballerine *f*; (AmE) (shoe with heel) chaussure *f* à talon
B *vt* **1** pomper ‹*air, gas, water*› (**out of** de)
2 (fam) (question) cuisiner (fam) ‹*person*›
3 (Med) **to ~ sb's stomach** faire un lavage d'estomac à qn
C *vi* ‹*heart*› battre violemment

■ **pump up** gonfler ‹*tyre, air bed*›

pumpkin /'pʌmpkɪn/ *n* citrouille *f*

pun /pʌn/ *n* jeu *m* de mots, calembour *m*

punch /pʌntʃ/ **A** *n* **1** (blow) coup *m* de poing
2 (of style, performance) énergie *f*
3 (drink) punch *m*
B *vt* **1** donner un coup de poing à ‹*person*›; **to ~ sb in the face** donner un coup de poing dans la figure de qn
2 perforer ‹*cards, tape*›; (manually) poinçonner ‹*ticket*›

mot clé

Punch and Judy show *n* ≈ (spectacle *m* de) guignol *m*
punchbag *n* (BrE) sac *m* de sable
punch line *n* chute *f*
punch-up *n* (BrE) (fam) bagarre *f*
punctual /ˈpʌŋktʃʊəl/ *adj* ponctuel/-elle
punctually /ˈpʌŋktʃʊəlɪ/ *adv* ‹*start, arrive, leave*› à l'heure
punctuation /ˌpʌŋktʃʊˈeɪʃn/ *n* ponctuation *f*
punctuation mark *n* signe *m* de ponctuation
puncture /ˈpʌŋktʃə(r)/ **A** *n* crevaison *f*; **we had a ~ on the way** on a crevé en chemin
B *vt* crever ‹*tyre, balloon, air bed*›; **to ~ a lung** se perforer un poumon
puncture kit *n* (*also* **puncture repair kit**) boîte *f* de rustines®
pundit /ˈpʌndɪt/ *n* expert/-e *m/f*
pungent /ˈpʌndʒənt/ *adj* ‹*flavour*› relevé/-e; ‹*smell*› fort/-e; ‹*gas, smoke*› âcre
punish /ˈpʌnɪʃ/ *vt* punir
punishment /ˈpʌnɪʃmənt/ *n* punition *f*; (stronger) châtiment *m*
punitive /ˈpjuːnətɪv/ *adj* punitif/-ive
punk /pʌŋk/ **A** *n* **1** (music) punk *m*
2 (punk rocker) punk *mf*
3 (AmE) (fam) voyou *m*
B *adj* punk *inv*
punnet /ˈpʌnɪt/ *n* (BrE) barquette *f*
punt /pʌnt/ *n* **1** (boat) barque *f* (à fond plat)
2 (Irish pound) livre *f* irlandaise
puny /ˈpjuːnɪ/ *adj* ‹*person, body*› chétif/-ive
pup /pʌp/ *n* **1** (*also* **puppy**) chiot *m*
2 (seal, otter) petit *m*
♂ **pupil** /ˈpjuːpɪl/ *n* **1** (Sch) élève *mf*
2 (in eye) pupille *f*
puppet /ˈpʌpɪt/ *n* marionnette *f*
♂ **purchase** /ˈpɜːtʃəs/ **A** *n* achat *m*
B *vt* acheter
purchasing power *n* pouvoir *m* d'achat
pure /pjʊə(r)/ *adj* pur/-e
purée /ˈpjʊəreɪ, (AmE) pjʊəˈreɪ/ *n* purée *f*
purely /ˈpjʊəlɪ/ *adv* purement
purge /pɜːdʒ/ **A** *n* purge *f*
B *vt* purger ‹*party, system*› (**of** de); expier ‹*sin*›
purify /ˈpjʊərɪfaɪ/ *vt* (gen) purifier; épurer ‹*water, chemical*›
purist /ˈpjʊərɪst/ *n, adj* puriste *mf*
purity /ˈpjʊərətɪ/ *n* pureté *f*
purple /ˈpɜːpl/ **A** *n* violet *m*
B *adj* (bluish) violet/-ette; (reddish) pourpre
♂ **purpose** /ˈpɜːpəs/ **A** *n* **1** (aim) but *m*; **for the ~ of doing** dans le but de faire
2 (*also* **strength of ~**) résolution *f*
B **on ~** *phr* exprès
purposely /ˈpɜːpəslɪ/ *adv* exprès, intentionnellement
purpose-made *adj* fait/-e spécialement (**for** pour)
purr /pɜː(r)/ **A** *n* (of cat, engine) ronronnement *m*
B *vi* ‹*cat, engine*› ronronner
purse /pɜːs/ *n* (for money) porte-monnaie *m inv*; (AmE) (handbag) sac *m* à main
IDIOM **to hold the ~ strings** tenir les cordons de la bourse
purser /ˈpɜːsə(r)/ *n* commissaire *m* de bord
♂ **pursue** /pəˈsjuː, (AmE) -ˈsuː-/ *vt* **1** (chase) poursuivre
2 poursuivre ‹*aim, ambition, studies*›; mener ‹*policy*›; se livrer à ‹*occupation, interest*›; **to ~ a career** faire carrière (**in** dans)
pursuer /pəˈsjuːə(r), (AmE) -ˈsuː-/ *n* poursuivant/-e *m/f*
pursuit /pəˈsjuːt, (AmE) -ˈsuː-/ *n* **1** poursuite *f*; **in ~ of** à la poursuite de; **in hot ~** à vos/ses etc trousses
2 (hobby) passe-temps *m inv*; **artistic ~s** activités *fpl* artistiques
♂ **push** /pʊʃ/ **A** *n* poussée *f*; **to give sb/sth a ~** pousser qn/qch
B *vt* **1** pousser ‹*person, car, pram*›; appuyer sur ‹*button, switch*›; **to ~ sb/sth away** repousser qn/qch; **she ~ed him down the stairs** elle l'a poussé dans l'escalier; **to ~ sb aside** écarter qn; **to ~ sb too far** pousser qn à bout
2 (fam) (promote) promouvoir ‹*policy, theory*›
3 (fam) (sell) vendre ‹*drugs*›
C *vi* pousser; **to ~ past sb** bousculer qn
IDIOMS **at a ~** (BrE) s'il le faut; **to ~ one's luck** aller un peu trop loin
■ **push around** (fam) (bully) bousculer ‹*person*›
■ **push for** faire pression en faveur de ‹*reform*›
■ **push in**: **A** **~ in** resquiller
B **~ [sth] in** enfoncer ‹*button, door, window*›
■ **push over**: **A** **~ over!** (fam) pousse-toi!
B **~ [sb/sth] over** renverser ‹*person, table, car*›
■ **push through** faire voter ‹*bill, legislation*›; faire passer ‹*deal*›
push-button /ˈpʊʃbʌtn/ *adj* ‹*telephone*› à touches
pushchair *n* (BrE) poussette *f*
pusher /ˈpʊʃə(r)/ *n* (fam) (*also* **drug ~**) revendeur/-euse *m/f* de drogue
push-start /ˌpʊʃˈstɑːt/ *vt* pousser [qch] pour le/la faire démarrer ‹*vehicle*›
push-up *n* (Sport) pompe *f* (fam)
pushy /ˈpʊʃɪ/ *adj* (fam) (ambitious) arriviste; **she's very ~** (assertive) elle s'impose
♂ **put** /pʊt/ *vt* (*p prés* **-tt-**, *prét, pp* **put**)
1 (place) mettre ‹*object, person*› (**in** dans, **on** sur); **to ~ sth through** glisser qch dans ‹*letterbox*›; **to ~ sb through** envoyer qn à ‹*university*›; faire passer qn par ‹*ordeal*›; faire passer [qch] à qn ‹*test*›; **to ~ one's**

P

hand to porter la main à ‹*mouth*›
2 (devote, invest) **to ~ money/energy into sth** investir de l'argent/son énergie dans qch; **to ~ a lot into** s'engager à fond pour ‹*work, project*›; sacrifier beaucoup à ‹*marriage*›
3 to ~ money towards donner de l'argent pour ‹*gift*›; **~ it towards some new clothes** sers-t'en pour acheter des vêtements; **to ~ tax on sth** taxer qch
4 (express) **to ~ it bluntly** pour parler franchement; **let me ~ it another way** laissez-moi m'exprimer différemment
IDIOM **I wouldn't ~ it past him!** ça ne m'étonnerait pas de lui!
■ **put across** communiquer ‹*idea, case*›
■ **put away 1** (tidy away) ranger
2 (save) mettre [qch] de côté
3 (fam) avaler ‹*food*›; descendre (fam) ‹*drink*›
■ **put back 1** (return) remettre; **to ~ sth back where it belongs** remettre qch à sa place
2 remettre ‹*meeting*› (**to** à, **until** jusqu'à); repousser ‹*date*›
3 retarder ‹*clock, watch*›
■ **put down** **A** **~ [sth] down 1** poser ‹*object*›
2 réprimer ‹*rebellion*›
3 (write down) mettre (par écrit)
4 to ~ sth down to mettre qch sur le compte de; **to ~ sth down to the fact that** imputer qch au fait que
5 (by injection) piquer ‹*animal*›
6 to ~ down a deposit verser des arrhes; **to ~ £50 down on sth** verser 50 livres sterling d'arrhes sur qch
B **~ [sb] down 1** déposer ‹*passenger*›
2 (humiliate) rabaisser
■ **put forward 1** (propose) avancer ‹*theory, name*›; soumettre ‹*plan*›; présenter la candidature de ‹*person*›
2 (in time) avancer ‹*meeting, date, clock*› (**by** de, **to** à)
■ **put in** **A** **~ in 1** ‹*ship*› faire escale (**at** à, **to** dans)
2 to ~ in for postuler pour ‹*job, promotion, rise*›; demander ‹*transfer*›
B **~ [sth] in 1** installer ‹*heating, units*›
2 (make) faire ‹*request, claim*›; **to ~ in an appearance** faire une apparition
3 passer ‹*time*›
4 (insert) mettre
■ **put off** **A** **~ [sth] off 1** (delay, defer) remettre [qch] (à plus tard)
2 (turn off) éteindre ‹*light, radio*›
B **~ [sb] off 1** décommander ‹*guest*›; dissuader ‹*person*›; **to be easily put off** se décourager facilement
2 (repel) ‹*appearance, smell*› dégoûter; ‹*manner, person*› déconcerter
■ **put on 1** mettre ‹*garment, make-up*›
2 allumer ‹*light, heating*›; mettre ‹*record, music*›; **to ~ the kettle on** mettre de l'eau à chauffer
3 prendre ‹*weight, kilo*›
4 (produce) monter ‹*play, exhibition*›
5 (adopt) prendre ‹*accent, expression*›; **he's ~ting it on** il fait semblant
■ **put out 1** (extend) tendre ‹*hand*›; **to ~ out one's tongue** tirer la langue
2 éteindre ‹*fire, cigarette*›
3 sortir ‹*bin, garbage*›; faire sortir ‹*cat*›
4 diffuser ‹*warning, statement*›
5 mettre ‹*food, towels*›
6 (dislocate) se démettre ‹*shoulder*›
7 (inconvenience) déranger ‹*person*›; (annoy) contrarier ‹*person*›
■ **put through 1** (implement) faire passer ‹*bill, reform*›
2 passer ‹*caller*› (**to** à)
■ **put together 1** (assemble) assembler ‹*pieces, parts*›; **to ~ sth back together** reconstituer qch
2 (place together) mettre ensemble
3 établir ‹*list*›; faire ‹*film, programme*›
4 construire ‹*argument*›
■ **put up**: **A** **~ up [sth]** opposer ‹*resistance*›; **to ~ up a fight** combattre
B **~ [sth] up 1** hisser ‹*flag, sail*›; relever ‹*hair*›; **to ~ up one's hand** lever la main
2 mettre ‹*sign, plaque*›; afficher ‹*list*›
3 dresser ‹*fence, tent*›
4 augmenter ‹*rent, prices, tax*›; faire monter ‹*temperature*›
5 (provide) fournir ‹*money*›
C **~ [sb] up 1** (lodge) héberger
2 to ~ sb up to sth pousser qn à qch
■ **put up with** supporter ‹*person, situation*›
put-down /ˈpʊtdaʊn/ *n* remarque *f* humiliante
putt /pʌt/ **A** *n* putt *m*
B *vi* putter
putty /ˈpʌtɪ/ *n* mastic *m*
puzzle /ˈpʌzl/ **A** *n* **1** (mystery) mystère *m*
2 (game) casse-tête *m inv*
B *vt* déconcerter
puzzle book *n* livre *m* de jeux
puzzled /ˈpʌzld/ *adj* perplexe
PVC *n* (*abbr* = **polyvinyl chloride**) PVC *m*
pygmy /ˈpɪgmɪ/ *n* pygmée *mf*
pyjamas (BrE), **pajamas** (AmE) *npl* pyjama *m*; **a pair of ~** un pyjama
pylon /ˈpaɪlən, -lɒn/ *n* pylône *m*
pyramid /ˈpɪrəmɪd/ *n* pyramide *f*
python /ˈpaɪθn, (AmE) ˈpaɪθɒn/ *n* python *m*

Qq

q, **Q** /kjuː/ *n* q, Q *m*

QE *n* = **quantitative easing**

quack /kwæk/ **A** *n* **1** (of duck) coin-coin *m inv*
2 (BrE) (fam) (doctor) toubib *m* (fam)
3 (impostor) charlatan *m*
B *vi* cancaner

quadrangle /ˈkwɒdræŋgl/ *n* **1** (shape) quadrilatère *m*
2 (courtyard) cour *f* carrée

quadruple **A** /ˈkwɒdrʊpl, (AmE) kwɒˈdruːpl/ *n*, *adj* quadruple *m*
B /kwɒˈdruːpl/ *vt*, *vi* quadrupler

quadruplet /ˈkwɒdrʊplət, (AmE) kwɒˈdruːp-/ *n* quadruplé/-e *m/f*

quagmire /ˈkwɒgmaɪə(r), ˈkwæg-/ *n* bourbier *m*

quail /kweɪl/ **A** *n* (*pl* **~s** *ou collect* **~**) caille *f*; **~'s egg** œuf *m* de caille
B *vi* trembler

quaint /kweɪnt/ *adj* **1** (pretty) pittoresque
2 (old-world) au charme vieillot
3 (odd) bizarre

quake /kweɪk/ *vi* trembler

qualification /ˌkwɒlɪfɪˈkeɪʃn/ *n* **1** (diploma, degree) diplôme *m* (**in** en); (experience, skills) qualification *f*
2 (restriction) restriction *f*; **without ~** sans réserves

qualified /ˈkwɒlɪfaɪd/ *adj* **1** (for job) (having diploma) diplômé/-e; (having experience, skills) qualifié/-e
2 (competent) (having authority) qualifié/-e (**to do** pour faire); (having knowledge) compétent/-e (**to do** pour faire)
3 (modified) nuancé/-e, mitigé/-e

qualifier /ˈkwɒlɪfaɪə(r)/ *n* (contestant) qualifié/-e *m/f*; (match) éliminatoire *f*

✓ **qualify** /ˈkwɒlɪfaɪ/ **A** *vt* **1** (modify) nuancer ‹*approval, opinion*›; préciser ‹*statement, remark*›
2 (entitle) **to ~ sb to do** donner à qn le droit de faire
B *vi* **1** (get diploma, degree) obtenir son diplôme (**as** de, en)
2 (be eligible) remplir les conditions (requises); **to ~ for** avoir droit à ‹*membership, legal aid*›; **to ~ to do** avoir le droit de faire
3 (Sport) se qualifier

qualitative /ˈkwɒlɪtətɪv, (AmE) -teɪt-/ *adj* qualitatif/-ive

✓ **quality** /ˈkwɒlətɪ/ **A** *n* qualité *f*
B *adj* de qualité

quality control *n* contrôle *m* de qualité

qualm /kwɑːm/ *n* scrupule *m*

quandary /ˈkwɒndərɪ/ *n* embarras *m*; (serious) dilemme *m*

quantifiable /ˌkwɒntɪˈfaɪəbl/ *adj* facile à évaluer

quantify /ˈkwɒntɪfaɪ/ *vt* quantifier

quantitative /ˈkwɒntɪtətɪv, (AmE) -teɪt-/ *adj* quantitatif/-ive

quantitive easing /ˈkwɒntɪtɪv iːzɪŋ/ *n* assouplissement *m* quantitatif

quantity /ˈkwɒntətɪ/ *n* quantité *f*; **in ~** en grande quantité

quantity surveyor *n* (BrE) métreur *m*

quantum leap *n* saut *m* quantique; (fig) bond *m* prodigieux

quarantine /ˈkwɒrəntiːn, (AmE) ˈkwɔːr-/ **A** *n* quarantaine *f*; **in ~** en quarantaine
B *vt* mettre [qn/qch] en quarantaine

quarrel /ˈkwɒrəl, (AmE) ˈkwɔːrəl/ **A** *n* dispute *f* (**between** entre, **over** au sujet de); **to have a ~** se disputer
B *vi* (*p prés etc* **-ll-** (BrE), **-l-** (AmE)) **1** (argue) se disputer
2 (sever relations) se brouiller
3 to ~ with contester ‹*claim, idea*›; se plaindre de ‹*price, verdict*›

quarrelling (BrE), **quarreling** (AmE) /ˈkwɒrəlɪŋ, (AmE) ˈkwɔː-/ *n* disputes *fpl*

quarrelsome /ˈkwɒrəlsəm, (AmE) ˈkwɔː-/ *adj* ‹*person*› querelleur/-euse; ‹*remark*› agressif/-ive

quarry /ˈkwɒrɪ, (AmE) ˈkwɔːrɪ/ **A** *n* **1** (in ground) carrière *f*
2 (prey) proie *f*; (in hunting) gibier *m*
B *vt* extraire ‹*stone*›

quarry tile *n* carreau *m* de terre cuite

quart /kwɔːt/ *n* (BrE) = *1.136 l* (AmE) = *0.946 l*

✓ **quarter** /ˈkwɔːtə(r)/ **A** *n* **1** (one fourth) quart *m*; **in a ~ of an hour** dans un quart d'heure
2 (three months) trimestre *m*
3 (district) quartier *m*
B **quarters** *npl* (Mil) quartiers *mpl*; (gen) logement *m*
C *pron* **1** (25%) quart *m*; **only a ~ passed** seul le quart a réussi
2 (in time phrases) **at (a) ~ to 11** (BrE), **at a ~ of 11** (AmE) à onze heures moins le quart; **an hour and a ~** une heure et quart
D *adj* **a ~ century** un quart de siècle

q

E *adv* a ~ **full** au quart plein; ~ **the price** quatre fois moins cher
F *vt* couper [qch] en quatre ‹*cake, apple*›
G at close quarters *phr* de près

quarter-final *n* quart *m* de finale

quarterly /ˈkwɔːtəlɪ/ **A** *adj* trimestriel/-ielle
B *adv* tous les trois mois

quartermaster *n* (in army) intendant *m*; (in navy) maître *m* de timonerie

quartet /kwɔːˈtet/ *n* quatuor *m*; **jazz** ~ quartette *m*

quartz /kwɔːts/ *n* quartz *m*

quash /kwɒʃ/ *vt* rejeter ‹*proposal*›; réprimer ‹*rebellion*›

quasi *pref* (*also* **quasi-**) quasi (+ *adj*), quasi- (+ *n*)

quaver /ˈkweɪvə(r)/ **A** *n* **1** (BrE) (Mus) croche *f*
2 (trembling) tremblement *m* (**in** dans)
B *vi* trembloter

quay /kiː/ *n* quai *m*; **on the** ~ sur le quai

quayside /ˈkiːsaɪd/ *n* quai *m*

queasiness /ˈkwiːzɪnɪs/ *n* nausée *f*

queasy /ˈkwiːzɪ/ *adj* **to be** *or* **feel** ~ avoir mal au cœur

Quebec /kwɪˈbek/ *pr n* Québec *m*; **in** ~ (city) à Québec; (province) au Québec

queen /kwiːn/ *n* **1** (gen) reine *f*
2 (in cards) dame *f*

queen bee *n* reine *f* des abeilles

queen mother *n* Reine mère *f*

Queen's Counsel, **QC** *n* (BrE) (Law) avocat *m* éminent

queer /kwɪə(r)/ *adj* **1** (strange) étrange, bizarre
2 (suspicious) louche, suspect

quell /kwel/ *vt* étouffer ‹*anger, anxiety, revolt*›

quench /kwentʃ/ *vt* étancher ‹*thirst*›; étouffer ‹*desire*›

querulous /ˈkwerʊləs/ *adj* grincheux/-euse

query /ˈkwɪərɪ/ **A** *n* question *f* (**about** au sujet de); **a** ~ **from sb** une question venant de qn
B *vt* mettre en doute; **to** ~ **whether** demander si

quest /kwest/ *n* quête *f*; **the** ~ **for sb/sth** la recherche de qn/qch

question /ˈkwestʃən/ **A** *n* **1** (gen) question *f* (**about** sur); **to ask sb a** ~ poser une question à qn; **it's a** ~ **of doing** il s'agit de faire; **that's another** ~ c'est une autre affaire; **there was never any** ~ **of you paying** il n'a jamais été question que tu paies; **the person in** ~ la personne en question; **it's out of the** ~ **for him to leave** il est hors de question qu'il parte
2 (doubt) doute *m*; **to call sth into** ~ mettre qch en doute; **it's open to** ~ cela se discute
B *vt* **1** (interrogate) questionner ‹*suspect, politician*›
2 (cast doubt upon) mettre en doute ‹*tactics, methods*›

questionable /ˈkwestʃənəbl/ *adj*
1 (debatable) discutable
2 (dubious) douteux/-euse

questioner /ˈkwestʃənə(r)/ *n* interrogateur/-trice *m/f*

questioning /ˈkwestʃənɪŋ/ *n* (of person) interrogation *f*; **to bring sb in for** ~ amener qn pour interrogatoire

question mark *n* point *m* d'interrogation

questionnaire /ˌkwestʃəˈneə(r)/ *n* questionnaire *m* (**on** sur)

queue /kjuː/ **A** *n* (BrE) (of people) queue *f*, file *f* (d'attente); (of vehicles) file *f*; **to stand in a** ~ faire la queue; **to join the** ~ ‹*person*› se mettre à la queue; ‹*car*› se mettre dans la file; **to jump the** ~ (fam) passer avant son tour
B *vi* (*also* ~ **up**) ‹*people*› faire la queue (**for** pour); ‹*taxis*› attendre en ligne

queue-jump *vi* resquiller, passer avant son tour

quibble /ˈkwɪbl/ *vi* chicaner (**about, over** sur)

quick /kwɪk/ **A** *n* **to bite one's nails to the** ~ se ronger les ongles jusqu'au sang
B *adj* **1** (speedy) ‹*pace, reply, profit, meal*› rapide; ‹*storm, shower*› bref/brève *before n*; **to have a** ~ **coffee** prendre un café en vitesse; **to have a** ~ **wash** faire une toilette rapide; **she's a** ~ **worker** elle travaille vite; **the** ~**est way to do** le meilleur moyen de faire; **to make a** ~ **recovery** se rétablir vite; **be** ~ **(about it)!** dépêche-toi!
2 (clever) ‹*child, student*› vif/vive d'esprit
3 (prompt) ‹*reaction*› vif/vive; **to be a** ~ **learner** apprendre vite
C *adv* ~! vite!; ~ **as a flash** avec la rapidité de l'éclair
IDIOM **to cut** *or* **sting sb to the** ~ piquer qn au vif

quicken /ˈkwɪkən/ **A** *vt* accélérer ‹*pace*›; stimuler ‹*interest*›
B *vi* ‹*pace*› s'accélérer; ‹*anger*› s'intensifier

quick-fire *adj* rapide

quicklime *n* chaux *f* vive

quickly /ˈkwɪklɪ/ *adv* (rapidly) vite, rapidement; (without delay) sans tarder; **(come)** ~! (viens) vite!

quick march *n* (Mil) ≈ pas *m* cadencé

quicksand *n* sables *mpl* mouvants; (fig) bourbier *m*

quicksilver /ˈkwɪksɪlvə(r)/ *n* mercure *m*

quick-tempered *adj* coléreux/-euse

quick time *n* (AmE) marche *f* rapide

quid /kwɪd/ *n* (*pl* ~) (BrE) (fam) livre *f* (sterling)

quiet /ˈkwaɪət/ **A** *n* **1** (silence) silence *m*
2 (peace) tranquillité *f*
3 (fam) (secret) **on the** ~ discrètement

mot clé

B *adj* **1** (silent) ‹*church, person, room*› silencieux/-ieuse; **to keep ~** garder le silence; **to go ~** se taire; **to keep [sb] ~** faire taire ‹*dog, child*›; **be ~** (stop talking) tais-toi; (make no noise) ne fais pas de bruit
2 (not noisy) ‹*voice*› bas/basse; ‹*engine*› silencieux/-ieuse; ‹*music*› doux/douce; **in a ~ voice** à voix basse; **to keep the children ~** ‹*activity*› tenir les enfants tranquilles
3 (discreet) discret/-ète; **to have a ~ word with sb** prendre qn à part pour lui parler
4 (calm) ‹*village, holiday, night, life*› tranquille
5 ‹*meal*› intime; ‹*wedding*› célébré/-e dans l'intimité
6 (secret) **to keep [sth] ~** ne pas divulguer ‹*plans*›; garder [qch] secret/-ète ‹*engagement*›

■ **quiet down** (AmE) ▶ **quieten down**

quieten /ˈkwaɪətn/ *vt* **1** (calm) calmer ‹*person, animal*›
2 (silence) faire taire ‹*critics, children*›

■ **quieten down** (BrE) **A ~ down 1** (become calm) ‹*person, activity*› se calmer
2 (fall silent) se taire
B ~ [sb/sth] down 1 (calm) calmer
2 (silence) faire taire

quietly /ˈkwaɪətlɪ/ *adv* **1** (not noisily) ‹*move*› sans bruit; ‹*cough, speak*› doucement
2 (silently) ‹*play, read, sit*› en silence
3 (calmly) calmement

quietness /ˈkwaɪətnɪs/ *n* **1** (silence) silence *m*
2 (of voice) faiblesse *f*
3 (of place) tranquillité *f*

quiff /kwɪf/ *n* (BrE) (on forehead) toupet *m*; (on top of head) houppe *f*

quill /kwɪl/ *n* **1** (feather) penne *f*; (stem of feather) tuyau *m* de plume
2 (on porcupine) piquant *m*
3 (*also* **~ pen**) plume *f* d'oie

quilt /kwɪlt/ **A** *n* **1** (BrE) (duvet) couette *f*
2 (bed cover) dessus *m* de lit
B *vt* matelasser

quinine /kwɪˈniːn, (AmE) ˈkwaɪnaɪn/ *n* quinine *f*

quintuplet /ˈkwɪntjuːplet, (AmE) kwɪnˈtuːplɪt/ *n* quintuplé/-e *m/f*

quip /kwɪp/ **A** *n* trait *m* d'esprit
B *vi* (*p prés etc* **-pp-**) plaisanter

quirk /kwɜːk/ *n* (of person) excentricité *f*; (of fate, nature) caprice *m*

quit /kwɪt/ **A** *vt* (*p prés* **-tt-**, *prét, pp* **quitted** *ou* **quit**) démissionner de ‹*job*›; quitter ‹*place, person, profession*›
B *vi* (*p prés* **-tt-**, *prét, pp* **quitted** *ou* **quit**)
1 (give up) arrêter (**doing** de faire)
2 (resign) démissionner

quite /kwaɪt/ *adv* **1** (completely) ‹*new, ready, understand*› tout à fait; ‹*alone, empty, exhausted*› complètement; ‹*impossible*› totalement; ‹*extraordinary*› vraiment; **I ~ agree** je suis tout à fait d'accord; **you're ~ right** vous avez entièrement raison; **it's ~ all right** c'est sans importance; **are you ~ sure?** en êtes-vous certain?; **~ clearly** ‹*see*› très clairement
2 (exactly) **not ~** pas exactement; **I don't ~ know** je ne sais pas du tout
3 (rather) ‹*big, easily, often*› assez; **it's ~ small** ce n'est pas très grand; **it's ~ warm today** il fait bon aujourd'hui; **it's ~ likely that** il est très probable que; **I ~ like Chinese food** j'aime assez la cuisine chinoise; **~ a few** un bon nombre de ‹*people, examples*›; **~ a lot of money** pas mal d'argent; **I've thought about it ~ a bit** j'y ai pas mal réfléchi
4 (as intensifier) **~ simply** tout simplement; **~ a difference** une différence considérable; **that will be ~ a change for you** ce sera un grand changement pour toi; **she's ~ a woman!** quelle femme!
5 (expressing agreement) **~ (so)** c'est sûr

quits /kwɪts/ *adj* (fam) **to be ~** être quitte (**with sb** envers qn)

quiver /ˈkwɪvə(r)/ **A** *n* **1** tremblement *m*
2 (for arrows) carquois *m*
B *vi* ‹*voice, lip, animal*› trembler (**with** de); ‹*leaves*› frémir; ‹*flame*› vaciller

quiz /kwɪz/ **A** *n* (*pl* **~zes**) **1** (game) jeu *m* de questions-réponses, quiz *m*; (written, in magazine) questionnaire *m* (**about** sur)
2 (AmE) (Sch) interrogation *f*
B *vt* (*p prés etc* **-zz-**) questionner (**about** au sujet de)

quiz game, **quiz show** *n* jeu *m* de questions-réponses

quizzical /ˈkwɪzɪkl/ *adj* interrogateur/-trice

quota /ˈkwəʊtə/ *n* **1** (prescribed number, amount) quota *m* (**of, for** de)
2 (share) part *f* (**of** de); (officially allocated) quote-part *f*

quotation /kwəʊˈteɪʃn/ *n* **1** (quote) citation *f*
2 (estimate) devis *m*

quotation marks *npl* (*also* **quotes**) guillemets *mpl*; **in ~** entre guillemets

quote /kwəʊt/ **A** *n* **1** (quotation) citation *f* (**from** de)
2 (statement to journalist) déclaration *f*
3 (estimate) devis *m*
B quotes *npl* = **quotation marks**
C *vt* **1** citer ‹*person, passage, proverb*›; rapporter ‹*words*›; rappeler ‹*reference number*›; **she was ~d as saying that...** elle aurait dit que...
2 (state) indiquer ‹*price, figure*›; **they ~d us £200** dans leur devis, ils ont demandé £200 sterling
3 (on stock exchange) coter ‹*share, price*› (**at** à)
4 (in betting) **to be ~d 6 to 1** être coté/-e 6 contre 1
D *vi* (from text, author) faire des citations; **to ~ from Keats** citer Keats

Rr

r, R /ɑː(r)/ *n* r, R *m*

rabbi /'ræbaɪ/ *n* rabbin *m*

rabbit /'ræbɪt/ *n* lapin *m*

rabid /'ræbɪd, (AmE) 'reɪbɪd/ *adj* **1** (with rabies) enragé/-e
2 (fanatical) fanatique

rabies /'reɪbiːz/ *n* rage *f*

race /reɪs/ **A** *n* **1** (gen), (Sport) course *f*; **to have a ~** faire la course
2 (ethnic group) race *f*
B *vt* faire la course avec ‹*person, car, horse*› (**to** jusqu'à)
C *vi* **1** (gen), (Sport) courir; **to ~ in/away** entrer/partir en courant
2 (hurry) se dépêcher (**to do** de faire)
3 ‹*heart*› battre précipitamment; ‹*engine*› s'emballer

racehorse *n* cheval *m* de course

racer /'reɪsə(r)/ *n* (bike) vélo *m* de course

race relations *npl* relations *fpl* interraciales

racetrack /'reɪstræk/ *n* (for horses) champ *m* de courses; (for cars) circuit *m*; (for dogs, cycles) piste *f*

racial /'reɪʃl/ *adj* racial/-e

racing /'reɪsɪŋ/ *n* courses *fpl*

racing car *n* voiture *f* de course

racing cyclist *n* coureur/-euse *m/f* cycliste

racing driver *n* coureur/-euse *m/f* automobile

racism /'reɪsɪzəm/ *n* racisme *m*

racist /'reɪsɪst/ *n, adj* raciste *mf*

rack /ræk/ **A** *n* **1** (for plates) égouttoir *m*; (for clothes) portant *m*; (for bottles) casier *m*
2 = **roof rack**
3 (torture) chevalet *m*
B *vt* **~ed with** torturé/-e par ‹*guilt*›
IDIOM **to ~ one's brains** se creuser la cervelle (fam)

racket /'rækɪt/ *n* **1** (*also* **racquet**) (Sport) raquette *f*
2 (fam) (noise) vacarme *m*
3 (swindle) escroquerie *f*

racketeering /ˌrækə'tɪərɪŋ/ *n* racket *m*

racquetball /'rækɪtbɔːl/ *n* (AmE) ≈ squash *m*

racy /'reɪsɪ/ *adj* **1** (lively) plein/-e de verve
2 (risqué) osé/-e

radar /'reɪdɑː(r)/ *n* radar *m*

radiant /'reɪdɪənt/ *adj* radieux/-ieuse

radiate /'reɪdɪeɪt/ *vt* **1** rayonner de ‹*happiness*›; déborder de ‹*confidence*›
2 émettre ‹*heat*›

radiation /ˌreɪdɪ'eɪʃn/ *n* (medical, nuclear) radiation *f*; (rays) radiations *fpl*

radiation exposure *n* irradiation *f*

radiation sickness *n* maladie *f* des rayons

radiator /'reɪdɪeɪtə(r)/ *n* radiateur *m*

radical /'rædɪkl/ *n, adj* radical/-e *m/f*

radio /'reɪdɪəʊ/ **A** *n* (*pl* **~s**) radio *f*; **on the ~** à la radio
B *adj* ‹*signal*› radio *inv*; ‹*programme*› de radio
C *vt* (3e *pers sg prés* **~s**, *prét, pp* **~ed**) **to ~ sth (to sb)** communiquer qch par radio (à qn)
D *vi* (3e *pers sg prés* **~s**, *prét, pp* **~ed**) **to ~ for help** appeler au secours par radio

radioactive *adj* radioactif/-ive

radio alarm *n* radio-réveil *m*

radio announcer *n* speaker/-erine *m/f*

radio cassette *n* (*also* **radio cassette recorder**) radiocassette *f*

radiology /ˌreɪdɪ'ɒlədʒɪ/ *n* radiologie *f*

radio station *n* (channel) station *f* de radio; (installation) station *f* émettrice

radiotherapy *n* radiothérapie *f*

radish /'rædɪʃ/ *n* radis *m*

radius /'reɪdɪəs/ *n* (*pl* **-dii** *ou* **-diuses**) rayon *m*

raffle /'ræfl/ *n* tombola *f*

raft /rɑːft, (AmE) ræft/ *n* radeau *m*

rafter /'rɑːftə(r), (AmE) 'ræftə(r)/ *n* chevron *m*

rag /ræg/ *n* **1** (cloth) chiffon *m*
2 (fam) (newspaper) torchon *m* (fam)

rage /reɪdʒ/ **A** *n* **1** rage *f*, colère *f*; **to fly into a ~** entrer dans une colère noire
2 (fam) **to be (all) the ~** faire fureur
B *vi* **1** ‹*storm, battle*› faire rage
2 ‹*person*› tempêter (**at, against** contre)

ragged /'rægɪd/ *adj* **1** ‹*garment*› en loques; ‹*cuff, collar*› effiloché/-e; ‹*person*› dépenaillé/-e
2 ‹*outline*› déchiqueté/-e

raging /'reɪdʒɪŋ/ *adj* **1** ‹*passion, argument*› violent/-e; ‹*thirst, pain*› atroce; **a ~ toothache** une rage de dents
2 ‹*blizzard, sea*› déchaîné/-e

rags *npl* loques *fpl*; **in ~** en haillons

raid /reɪd/ **A** *n* raid *m* (**on** sur); (on bank) hold-up *m* (**on** de); (by police, customs) rafle *f* (**on** dans)

mot clé

r

B *vt* ‹*military*› faire un raid sur; ‹*police*› faire une rafle dans; ‹*criminals*› attaquer ‹*bank*›

raider /ˈreɪdə(r)/ *n* **1** (thief) pillard *m*
2 (*also* **corporate ~**) raider *m*

rail /reɪl/ *n* **1** (on balcony) balustrade *f*; (on tower) garde-fou *m*; (handrail) rampe *f*
2 (for curtains) tringle *f*
3 (for train) rail *m*; **by ~** par chemin de fer

railing /ˈreɪlɪŋ/ *n* (*also* **~s**) grille *f*

railroad /ˈreɪlrəʊd/ *n* (AmE) **1** (network) chemin *m* de fer
2 (*also* **~ track**) voie *f* ferrée

railroad car *n* (AmE) wagon *m*

railway /ˈreɪlweɪ/ *n* (BrE) **1** (network) chemin *m* de fer
2 (*also* **~ line**) ligne *f* de chemin de fer
3 (*also* **~ track**) voie *f* ferrée

railway carriage *n* (BrE) wagon *m*

railway station *n* (BrE) gare *f*

rain /reɪn/ **A** *n* pluie *f*; **in the ~** sous la pluie
B *v impers* pleuvoir; **it's ~ing (hard)** il pleut (à verse)

rainbow /ˈreɪnbəʊ/ *n* arc-en-ciel *m*

raincoat *n* imperméable *m*

raindrop *n* goutte *f* de pluie

rainfall /ˈreɪnfɔːl/ *n* niveau *m* de précipitations

rainforest *n* forêt *f* tropicale

rainy /ˈreɪnɪ/ *adj* ‹*afternoon, climate*› pluvieux/-ieuse

rainy season *n* saison *f* des pluies

raise /reɪz/ **A** *n* (AmE) (pay rise) augmentation *f*
B *vt* **1** (lift) lever ‹*baton, barrier, curtain*›; hisser ‹*flag*›; soulever ‹*lid*›; renflouer ‹*sunken ship*›; **to ~ one's hand/head** lever la main/tête
2 (increase) augmenter ‹*price, offer, salary*› (**from** de, **to** à); élever ‹*standard*›; reculer ‹*age limit*›; **to ~ one's voice** (to be heard) parler plus fort; (in anger) hausser le ton; **to ~ the bidding** (in gambling) monter la mise; (at auction) monter l'enchère
3 (cause) faire naître ‹*fears*›; soulever ‹*dust*›
4 (mention) soulever ‹*issue, objection*›
5 (bring up) élever ‹*child, family*›
6 (breed) élever ‹*livestock*›
7 (find) trouver ‹*capital*›
8 (collect) lever ‹*tax*›; ‹*person*› collecter ‹*money*›
9 (end) lever ‹*ban*›
10 (give) **to ~ the alarm** donner l'alarme

raised /reɪzd/ *adj* ‹*platform, jetty*› surélevé/-e; **~ voices** des éclats de voix

raisin /ˈreɪzn/ *n* raisin *m* sec

rake /reɪk/ **A** *n* râteau *m*
B *vt* ratisser ‹*grass, leaves*›
■ **rake up**: **~ up [sth], ~ [sth] up** ressusciter ‹*grievance*›; remuer ‹*past*›

rally /ˈrælɪ/ **A** *n* **1** (meeting) rassemblement *m*
2 (race) rallye *m*
3 (in tennis) échange *m*
B *vt* rassembler ‹*support, troops*›
C *vi* **1** ‹*people*› se rallier (**to** à)
2 (recover) ‹*patient*› se rétablir

rallying call *n* cri *m* de ralliement

ram /ræm/ **A** *n* bélier *m*
B *vt* (*p prés etc* **-mm-**) **1** (crash into) rentrer dans, heurter
2 (push) enfoncer

RAM /ræm/ *n* (Comput) (*abbr* = **random access memory**) RAM *f*

ramble /ˈræmbl/ *n* randonnée *f*, balade *f*
■ **ramble on** discourir (**about** sur)

rambler /ˈræmblə(r)/ *n* randonneur/-euse *m/f*

rambling /ˈræmblɪŋ/ *adj* **1** ‹*house*› plein/-e de coins et de recoins
2 ‹*talk, article*› décousu/-e

ramification /ˌræmɪfɪˈkeɪʃn/ *n* ramification *f*

ramp /ræmp/ *n* rampe *f*; (BrE) (to slow traffic) ralentisseur *m*; (up to plane) passerelle *f*; (AmE) (slip road) bretelle *f*

rampage /ˈræmpeɪdʒ/ *n* **to be** *or* **go on the ~** tout saccager

rampant /ˈræmpənt/ *adj* ‹*crime, disease*› endémique

rampart /ˈræmpɑːt/ *n* rempart *m*

ram raid **A** *n* casse *f* à la voiture bélier
B *vt* dévaliser [qch] à l'aide d'une voiture bélier

ramshackle /ˈræmʃækl/ *adj* délabré/-e

ranch /rɑːntʃ, (AmE) ræntʃ/ *n* ranch *m*

rancid /ˈrænsɪd/ *adj* rance; **to go ~** rancir

random /ˈrændəm/ *adj* (fait/-e) au hasard

range /reɪndʒ/ **A** *n* **1** (of prices, products) gamme *f*; (of activities) éventail *m*, choix *m*; (of radar, weapon) portée *f* (**of** de)
2 (AmE) (prairie) prairie *f*
3 (of mountains) chaîne *f*
4 (stove) (wood) fourneau *m*
5 (*also* **shooting ~**) champ *m* de tir
B *vi* **1** (vary) varier (**between** entre)
2 (cover) **to ~ over sth** couvrir qch

ranger /ˈreɪndʒə(r)/ *n* garde-forestier *m*

rank /ræŋk/ **A** *n* **1** (gen) rang *m*; (in military, police) grade *m*; **to break ~s** ‹*soldiers*› rompre les rangs; **to close ~s** serrer les rangs
2 (BrE) **taxi ~** station *f* de taxis
B *adj* **1** ‹*outsider, beginner*› complet/-ète
2 ‹*odour*› fétide
C *vt* classer (**among** parmi)
D *vi* se classer (**among** parmi)

rank and file /ˌræŋkənˈfaɪl/ *n* **the ~** la base *f*

ranking /ˈræŋkɪŋ/ *n* classement *m*

rankle /ˈræŋkl/ *vi* **it still ~s** je ne l'ai pas encore digéré (fam)

ransack /ˈrænsæk, (AmE) rænˈsæk/ *vt* fouiller ‹*drawer*› (**for** pour trouver); mettre [qch] à sac ‹*house*›

r

ransom /'rænsəm/ *n* rançon *f*; **to hold sb to** (BrE) *or* **for** (AmE) ~ garder qn en otage

rant /rænt/ *vi* déclamer; **to ~ and rave** tempêter

rap /ræp/ **A** *n* **1** (tap) coup *m* sec
2 (music) rap *m*
B *vt* (*p prés etc* **-pp-**) frapper sur ‹*table, door*›

rape /reɪp/ **A** *n* **1** (attack) viol *m*
2 (plant) colza *m*
B *vt* violer

rapid /'ræpɪd/ *adj* rapide

rapidly /'ræpɪdlɪ/ *adv* rapidement

rapids /'ræpɪdz/ *npl* rapides *mpl*

rapist /'reɪpɪst/ *n* violeur *m*

rapper /'ræpə(r)/ *n* (Mus) rappeur/-euse *m/f*

rapport /ræ'pɔː(r), (AmE) -'pɔːrt/ *n* bons rapports *mpl*

rapture /'ræptʃə(r)/ *n* ravissement *m*; **to go into ~s about sth** s'extasier sur qch

rapturous /'ræptʃərəs/ *adj* ‹*delight*› extasié/-e; ‹*applause*› frénétique

rare /reə(r)/ *adj* **1** (uncommon) rare
2 ‹*steak*› saignant/-e

rarely /'reəlɪ/ *adv* rarement

raring /'reərɪŋ/ *adj* **to be ~ to do** être très impatient/-e de faire; **to be ~ to go** piaffer d'impatience

rarity /'reərətɪ/ *n* **1 to be a ~** ‹*occurrence*› être rare; ‹*plant*› être une plante rare; ‹*collector's item*› être une pièce rare
2 (rareness) rareté *f*

rascal /'rɑːskl, (AmE) 'ræskl/ *n* coquin/-e *m/f*

rash /ræʃ/ **A** *n* **1** (on skin) rougeurs *fpl*
2 (fig) vague *f* (**of** de)
B *adj* irréfléchi/-e

rasher /'ræʃə(r)/ *n* tranche *f*

raspberry /'rɑːzbrɪ, (AmE) 'ræzberɪ/ *n* framboise *f*

rasping *adj* ‹*voice, sound*› râpeux/-euse

rat /ræt/ *n* rat *m*

rate /reɪt/ **A** *n* **1** (speed) rythme *m*; **at this ~** (fig) à ce train-là
2 (level) taux *m*; **the interest ~** le taux d'intérêt
3 (charge, fee) tarif *m*
4 (in foreign exchange) cours *m*
B rates *npl* (BrE) impôts *mpl* locaux; **business ~s** ≈ taxe *f* professionnelle
C *vt* **1** (classify) **to ~ sb as sth** considérer qn comme qch; **to ~ sb among** classer qn parmi
2 estimer ‹*honesty, friendship, person*›
IDIOM **at any ~** en tout cas

ratepayer *n* (BrE) contribuable *m/f*

rather /'rɑːðə(r)/ *adv* **1** plutôt (**than** que); **I ~ like him** je le trouve plutôt sympathique; **it's ~ like an apple** ça ressemble un peu à une pomme
2 (preferably) **I would (much) ~ do** je préférerais (de loin) faire (**than do** que faire); **I'd ~ not** j'aimerais mieux pas

ratify /'rætɪfaɪ/ *vt* ratifier

rating /'reɪtɪŋ/ *n* cote *f*

ratings *npl* indice *m* d'écoute, audimat® *m*

ratio /'reɪʃɪəʊ/ *n* proportion *f*, rapport *m*

ration /'ræʃn/ **A** *n* ration *f*
B *vt* rationner ‹*food*› (**to** à); limiter la ration de ‹*person*› (**to** à)

rational /'ræʃənl/ *adj* ‹*approach, argument*› rationnel/-elle; ‹*person*› sensé/-e

rationale /ˌræʃə'nɑːl, (AmE) -'næl/ *n*
1 (reasons) raisons *fpl* (**for** pour, **for doing** de faire)
2 (logic) logique *f* (**behind** de)

rationalize /'ræʃnəlaɪz/ *vt* **1** (justify) justifier
2 (BrE) (streamline) rationaliser

rationing /'ræʃnɪŋ/ *n* rationnement *m*

rat race *n* foire *f* d'empoigne

rat run *n: petite rue servant de raccourci*

rattle /'rætl/ **A** *n* **1** (of bottles, cutlery, chains) cliquetis *m*; (of window, engine) vibrations *fpl*
2 (baby's) hochet *m*
B *vt* ‹*wind*› faire vibrer ‹*window*›; ‹*person*› s'acharner sur ‹*handle*›
C *vi* ‹*bottles, cutlery, chains*› s'entrechoquer; ‹*window*› vibrer

rattlesnake /'rætlsneɪk/ *n* serpent *m* à sonnette, crotale *m*

raucous /'rɔːkəs/ *adj* ‹*laugh*› éraillé/-e; ‹*person*› bruyant/-e

raunchy /'rɔːntʃɪ/ *adj* (fam) ‹*performer, voice, song*› torride

ravage /'rævɪdʒ/ *vt* ravager

rave /reɪv/ **A** *n* (BrE) (fam) (party) bringue *f* (fam) (branchée)
B *adj* (fam) ‹*review*› dithyrambique
C *vi* (enthusiastically) parler avec enthousiasme (**about** de); (when fevered) délirer

ravenous /'rævənəs/ *adj* ‹*animal*› vorace; **to be ~** avoir une faim de loup

ravine /rə'viːn/ *n* ravin *m*

raving /'reɪvɪŋ/ *adj* (fanatical) enragé/-e; **a ~ lunatic** un fou furieux/une folle furieuse

ravioli /ˌrævɪ'əʊlɪ/ *n* ravioli *mpl*

ravishing /'rævɪʃɪŋ/ *adj* ravissant/-e

raw /rɔː/ *adj* **1** ‹*food*› cru/-e; ‹*rubber, sugar, data*› brut/-e; ‹*sewage*› non traité/-e
2 (without skin) ‹*patch*› à vif
3 (cold) ‹*weather*› froid/-e et humide
4 (inexperienced) inexpérimenté/-e
IDIOM **to get a ~ deal** (fam) être défavorisé/-e

raw material *n* matière *f* première

ray /reɪ/ *n* rayon *m*; **a ~ of** une lueur de ‹*hope*›

raze /reɪz/ *vt* raser

razor /'reɪzə(r)/ *n* rasoir *m*

razor blade *n* lame *f* de rasoir

re[1] /reɪ/ *n* (Mus) ré *m*

mot clé

re² /riː/ *prep* (*abbr* = **with reference to**) (about) au sujet de; (in letterhead) 'objet'

RE *n* (Sch) (*abbr* = **Religious Education**) éducation *f* religieuse

reach /riːtʃ/ **A** *n* portée *f*; **out of ~** hors de portée; **within (arm's) ~** à portée de (la) main; **within easy ~** ‹*place*› tout près
B *vt* **1** atteindre ‹*place, person, object, switch*›; ‹*sound, news, letter*› parvenir à ‹*person, place*›
2 (come to) arriver à ‹*decision, understanding*›; **to ~ a verdict** (Law) rendre un verdict
3 toucher ‹*audience, market*›
4 (in height, length) arriver à ‹*floor, ceiling*›
C *vi* **1 to ~ up/down** lever/baisser le bras; **to ~ out** tendre le bras
2 (extend) **to ~ (up/down) to** arriver jusqu'à

reaches *npl* **the upper/lower ~** (of river) la partie supérieure/inférieure

react /rɪ'ækt/ *vi* réagir (**to** à, **against** contre)

reaction /rɪ'ækʃn/ *n* réaction *f*

reactionary /rɪ'ækʃənrɪ, (AmE) -ənerɪ/ *n, adj* réactionnaire *mf*

reactor /rɪ'æktə(r)/ *n* réacteur *m*

read /riːd/ **A** *vt* (*prét, pp* **read** /red/) **1** (gen) lire; **to ~ sb's mind** lire dans les pensées de qn
2 (at university) faire des études de ‹*history, French*›
3 relever ‹*meter*›
B *vi* (*prét, pp* **read** /red/) lire (**to sb** à qn)
▪ **read out** lire [qch] à haute voix
▪ **read up**: **to ~ up on sth/sb** étudier qch/qn à fond

readable /'riːdəbl/ *adj* **1** (legible) lisible
2 (enjoyable) agréable à lire

reader /'riːdə(r)/ *n* lecteur/-trice *m/f*

readily /'redɪlɪ/ *adv* **1** (willingly) sans hésiter
2 (easily) facilement

reading /'riːdɪŋ/ *n* **1** lecture *f*
2 (on meter) relevé *m* (**on** de); (on instrument) indication *f* (**on** de)
3 (interpretation) interprétation *f* (**of** de)

reading glasses *npl* lunettes *fpl* (pour lire)

reading list *n* liste *f* d'ouvrages recommandés

readjust /ˌriːə'dʒʌst/ **A** *vt* régler [qch] de nouveau
B *vi* ‹*person*› se réadapter (**to** à)

re-advertise /riː'ædvətaɪz/ *vt* refaire paraître une annonce pour ‹*post, item*›

ready /'redɪ/ *adj* **1** (prepared) prêt/-e (**for** pour, **to do** à faire); **to get ~** se préparer; **to get sth ~** préparer qch; **~, steady, go** à vos marques, prêts, partez!
2 (willing) prêt/-e (**to do** à faire)

ready-made /ˌredɪ'meɪd/ *adj* ‹*clothes*› de confection; ‹*excuse*› tout/-e fait/-e

ready-to-wear *adj* ‹*garment*› prêt-à-porter

real /rɪəl/ *adj* **1** (not imaginary) véritable, réel/réelle; **in ~ life** dans la réalité
2 (genuine) ‹*diamond, flower, leather*› vrai/-e *before n*, authentique
3 (proper) ‹*holiday, rest*› véritable, vrai/-e *before n*
4 (for emphasis) ‹*charmer, pleasure*› vrai/-e *before n*

real estate *n* **1** (property) biens *mpl* immobiliers
2 (AmE) (profession) immobilier *m*

realism /'riːəlɪzəm/ *n* réalisme *m*

realist /'riːəlɪst/ *n, adj* réaliste *mf*

realistic /ˌrɪə'lɪstɪk/ *adj* réaliste

reality /rɪ'ælətɪ/ *n* réalité *f* (**of** de)

reality TV *n* télé *f* réalité

realization /ˌrɪəlaɪ'zeɪʃn, (AmE) -lɪ'z-/ *n* prise *f* de conscience

realize /'rɪəlaɪz/ *vt* **1** se rendre compte de; **to ~ that** se rendre compte que; **to make sb ~ sth** faire comprendre qch à qn
2 réaliser ‹*idea, dream, goal*›; **to ~ one's potential** développer ses capacités

reallocate /riː'æləˌkeɪt/ *vt* réattribuer

really /'rɪəlɪ/ **A** *adv* **1** (gen) vraiment
2 (in actual fact) en fait, réellement; **~?** (expressing disbelief) c'est vrai?
B *excl* (*also* **well ~!**) franchement!

real time *n* (Comput) temps *m* réel

realtor /'riːəltə(r)/ *n* (AmE) agent *m* immobilier

reap /riːp/ *vt* **1** moissonner ‹*corn*›
2 récolter ‹*benefits*›

reappear /ˌriːə'pɪə(r)/ *vi* reparaître

reappearance /ˌriːə'pɪərəns/ *n* réapparition *f*

reapply /ˌriːə'plaɪ/ *vi* reposer sa candidature (**for** à)

reappraise /ˌriːə'preɪz/ *vt* réexaminer ‹*question*›; réévaluer ‹*writer, work*›

rear /rɪə(r)/ **A** *n* **1** (of building, car, room) arrière *m*; (of procession, train) queue *f*
2 (of person) derrière *m* (fam)
B *adj* **1** ‹*door, garden*› de derrière
2 (of car) ‹*light, seat, wheel*› arrière *inv*
C *vt* élever ‹*child, animals*›; cultiver ‹*plants*›
D *vi* (*also* **~ up**) ‹*horse*› se cabrer

rearmament /ˌriː'ɑːməmənt/ *n* réarmement *m*

rearrange /ˌriːə'reɪndʒ/ *vt* réaménager ‹*room*›; modifier ‹*plans*›; changer ‹*appointment*›

rear-view mirror *n* rétroviseur *m*

reason /'riːzn/ **A** *n* **1** (cause) raison *f* (**for, behind** de); **for no (good) ~** sans raison valable; **to have ~ to do** avoir des raisons de faire; **the ~ why...** la raison pour laquelle...; **I'll tell you the ~ why** je vais te *or* vous dire pourquoi; **to have every ~ to do** avoir tout lieu de faire; **with good ~** à juste titre
2 (common sense) raison *f*; **to listen to** *or* **see**

r

~ entendre raison; **it stands to ~ that** il va sans dire que; **within ~** dans la limite du raisonnable
B *vi* **to ~ with sb** raisonner qn

⚷ **reasonable** /'ri:znəbl/ *adj* **1** (sensible) raisonnable
2 (moderately good) convenable

reasonably /'ri:znəblɪ/ *adv* **1** (sensibly) raisonnablement
2 (rather) assez

reasoning /'ri:znɪŋ/ *n* raisonnement *m*

reassert /ˌri:ə'sɜ:t/ *vt* réaffirmer ‹*authority, claim*›

reassess /ˌri:ə'ses/ *vt* réexaminer, reconsidérer

reassurance /ˌri:ə'ʃɔ:rəns, (AmE) -'ʃʊər-/ *n* **1** (comfort) réconfort *m*
2 (guarantee) garantie *f*

reassure /ˌri:ə'ʃɔ:(r), (AmE) -'ʃʊər-/ *vt* rassurer ‹*person*› (**about** sur)

reassuring /ˌri:ə'ʃɔ:rɪŋ, (AmE) -'ʃʊər-/ *adj* rassurant/-e

rebate /'ri:beɪt/ *n* remboursement *m*

rebel **A** /'rebl/ *n* rebelle *mf*
B /rɪ'bel/ *vi* (*p prés etc* **-ll-**) se rebeller

rebellion /rɪ'belɪən/ *n* rébellion *f*, révolte *f*

rebellious /rɪ'belɪəs/ *adj* rebelle, insoumis/-e

rebuff /rɪ'bʌf/ **A** *n* rebuffade *f*
B *vt* rabrouer ‹*person*›; repousser ‹*advances*›

rebuild /ˌri:'bɪld/ *vt* (*prét, pp* **rebuilt** /ri:'bɪlt/) reconstruire

rebuke /rɪ'bju:k/ **A** *n* réprimande *f*
B *vt* réprimander (**for** pour)

rebut /rɪ'bʌt/ *vt* (*p prés etc* **-tt-**) réfuter

⚷ **recall** **A** /'ri:kɔ:l/ *n* (memory) mémoire *f*
B /rɪ'kɔ:l/ *vt* **1** (remember) se souvenir de
2 (summon back) rappeler

recapitulate /ˌri:kəpɪtʃʊleɪt/ *vt, vi* récapituler

recapture /ˌri:'kæptʃə(r)/ *vt* recapturer ‹*prisoner, animal*›; reprendre ‹*town*›; recréer ‹*period, atmosphere*›

recede /rɪ'si:d/ *vi* (gen) s'éloigner; ‹*hope, memory*› s'estomper

receding *adj* ‹*chin*› fuyant/-e; **he has a ~ hairline** son front se dégarnit

receipt /rɪ'si:t/ **A** *n* **1** reçu *m*, récépissé *m*; (from till) ticket *m* de caisse
2 (act of receiving) réception *f*
B **receipts** *npl* (takings) recette *f* (**from** de)

⚷ **receive** /rɪ'si:v/ **A** *vt* **1** (gen) recevoir; receler ‹*stolen goods*›
2 (greet) accueillir, recevoir ‹*visitor, proposal, play*› (**with** avec); **to be well ~d** être bien reçu/-e
B **received** *pp adj* ‹*ideas, opinions*› reçu/-e

receiver /rɪ'si:və(r)/ *n* **1** (telephone) combiné *m*
2 (radio or TV) (poste *m*) récepteur *m*

receivership /rɪ'si:vəʃɪp/ *n* (BrE) **to go into ~** être placé/-e sous administration judiciaire

receiving /rɪ'si:vɪŋ/ *n* (crime) recel *m*

⚷ **recent** /'ri:snt/ *adj* ‹*event, change, arrival, film*› récent/-e; ‹*acquaintance, development*› nouveau/-elle *before n*; **in ~ years** au cours des dernières années

⚷ **recently** /ri:'sntlɪ/ *adv* récemment; **until ~** jusqu'à ces derniers temps

reception /rɪ'sepʃn/ *n* **1** (*also* **~ desk**) réception *f*
2 (gathering) réception *f* (**for sb** en l'honneur de qn, **for sth** à l'occasion de qch)
3 (welcome) accueil *m* (**for** de)
4 (on radio, TV) réception *f* (**on** sur)

receptionist /rɪ'sepʃənɪst/ *n* réceptionniste *mf*

receptive /rɪ'septɪv/ *adj* réceptif/-ive (**to** à)

recess /rɪ'ses, (AmE) 'ri:ses/ *n* **1** (in parliament) (holiday) vacances *fpl*
2 (AmE) (break) (in school) récréation *f*; (during meeting) pause *f*
3 (alcove) alcôve *f*, recoin *m*

recession /rɪ'seʃn/ *n* récession *f*

recharge /ˌri:'tʃɑ:dʒ/ *vt* recharger

rechargeable /ˌri:'tʃɑ:dʒəbl/ *adj* rechargeable

recipe /'resəpɪ/ *n* recette *f* (**for** de)

recipient /rɪ'sɪpɪənt/ *n* (of letter) destinataire *mf*; (of benefits, aid, cheque) bénéficiaire *mf*; (of prize, award) lauréat/-e *m/f*

reciprocal /rɪ'sɪprəkl/ *adj* réciproque

reciprocate /rɪ'sɪprəkeɪt/ **A** *vt* retourner ‹*compliment*›; payer [qch] de retour ‹*love*›; rendre ‹*affection*›
B *vi* rendre la pareille

recital /rɪ'saɪtl/ *n* récital *m*

recite /rɪ'saɪt/ *vt, vi* réciter

reckless /'reklɪs/ *adj* imprudent/-e

recklessly /'reklɪslɪ/ *adv* ‹*act*› avec imprudence; ‹*promise, spend*› de manière inconsciente

reckon /'rekən/ *vt* **1** (judge) considérer (**that** que)
2 (fam) (think) **to ~ (that)** croire que
3 calculer ‹*amount*›

▪ **reckon on** (fam): **A** **~ on [sb/sth]** compter sur
B **~ on doing** compter faire

▪ **reckon with** compter avec

reckoning /'rekənɪŋ/ *n* (estimation) estimation *f*; (accurate calculation) calculs *mpl*

reclaim /rɪ'kleɪm/ *vt* **1** reconquérir ‹*coastal land*›; assécher ‹*marsh*›; défricher ‹*forest*›; récupérer ‹*glass, metal*›
2 récupérer ‹*deposit, money*›

reclaimable /rɪ'kleɪməbl/ *adj* ‹*waste product*› récupérable

recline /rɪ'klaɪn/ *vi* ‹*person*› s'allonger; ‹*seat*› s'incliner

⚷ mot clé

reclining /rɪˈklaɪnɪŋ/ *adj* **1** ‹*figure*› allongé/-e **2** ‹*seat*› inclinable; ‹*chair*› réglable

recluse /rɪˈkluːs/ *n* reclus/-e *m/f*

recognition /ˌrekəgˈnɪʃn/ *n* reconnaissance *f*; **in ~ of** en reconnaissance de

recognizable /ˌrekəgˈnaɪzəbl, ˈrekəgnaɪzəbl/ *adj* reconnaissable

recognize /ˈrekəgnaɪz/ *vt* reconnaître (**by** à)

recoil /rɪˈkɔɪl/ *vi* reculer (**from** devant)

recollect /ˌrekəˈlekt/ **A** *vt* se souvenir de, se rappeler
B *vi* se souvenir

recollection /ˌrekəˈlekʃn/ *n* souvenir *m*

recommend /ˌrekəˈmend/ *vt* **1** (commend) recommander
2 (advise) conseiller, recommander

recommendation /ˌrekəmenˈdeɪʃn/ *n* recommandation *f*; **to give sb a ~** recommander qn

recommended reading *n* livres *mpl* conseillés *or* recommandés

recompense /ˈrekəmpens/ *n* **1** (reward) récompense *f* (**for** de)
2 (compensation) dédommagement *m* (**for** pour)

reconcile /ˈrekənsaɪl/ *vt* **1** réconcilier ‹*people*›
2 concilier ‹*attitudes, views*›
3 to become ~d to sth se résigner à qch

reconnaissance /rɪˈkɒnɪsns/ *n* reconnaissance *f*

reconnoitre (BrE), **reconnoiter** (AmE) /ˌrekəˈnɔɪtə(r)/ **A** *vt* reconnaître
B *vi* faire une reconnaissance

reconsider /ˌriːkənˈsɪdə(r)/ **A** *vt* réexaminer
B *vi* réfléchir

reconstruct /ˌriːkənˈstrʌkt/ *vt* **1** (rebuild) reconstruire ‹*building*›
2 ‹*police*› faire une reconstitution de ‹*crime*›

reconstruction /ˌriːkənˈstrʌkʃn/ *n* **1** (of building) reconstruction *f*
2 (of crime) reconstitution *f*

record A /ˈrekɔːd, (AmE) ˈrekərd/ *n* **1** (of events) compte-rendu *m*; (of official proceedings) procès-verbal *m*; **to keep a ~ of sth** noter qch; **to say sth off the ~** dire qch en privé; **to set the ~ straight** mettre les choses au clair
2 (data) **~s** (historical, public) archives *fpl*; (personal, administrative) dossier *m*
3 (history) (of individual) passé *m*; (of organization, group) réputation *f*
4 (*also* **criminal ~**) casier *m* judiciaire
5 (Mus) disque *m*
6 (of athlete) record *m* (**for, in** de)
B *adj* **1** ‹*company, label*› de disques
2 ‹*sales, time*› record *after n*; **to be at a ~ high/low** être à son niveau le plus haut/bas
C /rɪˈkɔːd/ *vt* **1** (note) noter ‹*detail, idea, opinion*›
2 (on disc, tape) enregistrer
3 ‹*instrument*› enregistrer ‹*temperature, rainfall*›

record book *n* livre *m* des records

recorded /rɪˈkɔːdɪd/ *adj* (on tape) enregistré/-e; (documented) ‹*case, sighting*› connu/-e

recorded delivery *n* (BrE) **to send sth ~** envoyer qch en recommandé

recorder /rɪˈkɔːdə(r)/ *n* (Mus) flûte *f* à bec

record holder /ˈrekɔːdhəʊldə(r), (AmE) ˈrekərd-/ *n* recordman/recordwoman *m/f*

recording /rɪˈkɔːdɪŋ/ *n* enregistrement *m*

record player *n* tourne-disque *m*

recourse /rɪˈkɔːs/ *n* recours *m* (**to** à)

recover /rɪˈkʌvə(r)/ **A** *vt* **1** retrouver, récupérer ‹*money, vehicle*›; récupérer ‹*territory*›; (from water) repêcher, retrouver ‹*body, wreck*›; **to ~ one's strength** reprendre des forces
2 (recoup) réparer, compenser ‹*losses*›
B *vi* **1** (from illness) se remettre (**from** de); (from defeat) se ressaisir (**from** après)
2 ‹*economy*› se redresser

recovery /rɪˈkʌvərɪ/ *n* **1** (getting better) rétablissement *m*, guérison *f*
2 (of economy, company, market) reprise *f*
3 (getting back) (of vehicle) rapatriement *m*; (of money) récupération *f*

recovery vehicle *n* camion *m* de dépannage

recreate /ˈrekrɪeɪt, ˌriːkrɪˈeɪt/ *vt* recréer

recreation /ˌrekrɪˈeɪʃn/ *n* **1** (leisure) loisirs *mpl*
2 (playtime) récréation *f*

recreational drug *n: drogue que l'on prend de façon occasionnelle*

recreational vehicle *n* (*also* **RV**) camping-car *m*

recrimination /rɪˌkrɪmɪˈneɪʃn/ *n* récrimination *f*

recruit /rɪˈkruːt/ **A** *n* recrue *f*
B *vt* recruter (**from** dans)

recruiting officer *n* officier *m* recruteur

recruitment /rɪˈkruːtmənt/ *n* recrutement *m*

rectangle /ˈrektæŋgl/ *n* rectangle *m*

rectangular /rekˈtæŋgjʊlə(r)/ *adj* rectangulaire

rectify /ˈrektɪfaɪ/ *vt* rectifier

rector /ˈrektə(r)/ *n* pasteur *m*

recuperate /rɪˈkuːpəreɪt/ *vi* se rétablir (**from** de), récupérer

recur /rɪˈkɜː(r)/ *vi* (*p prés etc* **-rr-**) ‹*event, error*› se reproduire; ‹*illness*› réapparaître; ‹*theme*› revenir

recurrence /rɪˈkʌrəns/ *n* (of illness) récurrence *f*; (of symptom) réapparition *f*

recurrent /rɪˈkʌrənt/ *adj* récurrent/-e

recycle /ˌriːˈsaɪkl/ *vt* recycler ‹*paper, waste*›

recycling /ˌriːˈsaɪklɪŋ/ *n* recyclage *m*

red /red/ **A** *n* **1** (colour) rouge *m*; **in ~** en rouge
2 to be in the ~ ‹*person, account*› être à

découvert; ‹*company*› être en déficit
B *adj* rouge (**with** de); ‹*hair*› roux/rousse; **to go** *or* **turn ~** rougir
IDIOM **to be caught ~-handed** être pris/-e la main dans le sac (fam)

red alert *n* alerte *f* rouge

Red Crescent *n* Croissant-Rouge *m*

Red Cross *n* Croix-Rouge *f*

redcurrant /ˌred'kʌrənt/ *n* groseille *f*

redden /'redn/ *vt, vi* rougir

redecorate /ˌriː'dekəreɪt/ *vt* repeindre et retapisser, refaire

redeem /rɪ'diːm/ *vt* **1** retirer ‹*pawned goods*›; rembourser ‹*debt*›
2 racheter ‹*sinner*›; **her one ~ing feature is...** ce qui la rachète, c'est...

redeploy /ˌriːdɪ'plɔɪ/ *vt* redéployer ‹*troops*›; réaffecter ‹*staff*›

redevelop /ˌriːdɪ'veləp/ *vt* réaménager ‹*site, town*›

red-faced /ˌred'feɪst/ *adj* (embarrassed) penaud/-e

redhead *n* roux/rousse *m/f*

red herring *n* faux problème *m*

red-hot /ˌred'hɒt/ *adj* ‹*metal, coal*› chauffé/-e au rouge

redial /ˌriː'daɪəl/ **A** *vt* refaire ‹*number*›
B *vi* recomposer le numéro

redial facility *n* rappel *m* du dernier numéro composé

redirect /ˌriːdɪ'rekt/ *vt* canaliser ‹*resources*›; dévier ‹*traffic*›; réexpédier ‹*mail*›

rediscover /ˌriːdɪ'skʌvə(r)/ *vt* redécouvrir

red light area *n* quartier *m* chaud

redo /ˌriː'duː/ *vt* (3ᵉ *pers sg prés* **redoes**, *prét* **redid**, *pp* **redone**) refaire

red pepper *n* poivron *m* rouge

redress /rɪ'dres/ *vt* **to ~ the balance** rétablir l'équilibre

red tape *n* paperasserie *f*

🔑 **reduce** /rɪ'djuːs, (AmE) -'duːs/ *vt* **1** réduire ‹*inflation, number, pressure, sentence*› (**by** de); baisser ‹*prices, temperature*›; **to ~ speed** ralentir; **to ~ sb to tears** faire pleurer qn; **to be ~d to begging** en être réduit/-e à la mendicité
2 (in cooking) faire réduire ‹*sauce, stock*›

🔑 **reduction** /rɪ'dʌkʃn/ *n* **1** (in inflation, pressure, number) réduction *f* (**in** de); (of weight, size) diminution *f* (**in** de)
2 (discount) réduction *f*, rabais *m*

redundancy /rɪ'dʌndənsɪ/ *n* (BrE)
1 (unemployment) chômage *m*
2 (dismissal) licenciement *m*

redundant /rɪ'dʌndənt/ *adj* **1** (BrE) (dismissed) licencié/-e; (out of work) au chômage; **to be made ~** être licencié/-e
2 (not needed) superflu/-e

reed /riːd/ *n* **1** (plant) roseau *m*
2 (Mus) anche *f*

reef /riːf/ *n* récif *m*, écueil *m*

reek /riːk/ *vi* **to ~ (of sth)** puer (qch)

reel /riːl/ **A** *n* bobine *f*; (for fishing) moulinet *m*
B *vi* (sway) ‹*person*› tituber; **the blow sent him ~ing** le coup l'a projeté en arrière
■ **reel off** débiter ‹*list, names*›

re-elect /ˌriːɪ'lekt/ *vt* réélire

re-emerge /ˌriːɪ'mɜːdʒ/ *vi* ‹*person, sun*› réapparaître; ‹*problem*› resurgir

re-examine /ˌriːɪg'zæmɪn/ *vt* réexaminer

refectory /rɪ'fektrɪ, 'refɪktrɪ/ *n* réfectoire *m*

🔑 **refer** /rɪ'fɜː(r)/ **A** *vt* (*p prés etc* **-rr-**) renvoyer ‹*task, problem*› (**to** à); **to ~ sb to** ‹*person*› envoyer qn à ‹*department*›
B *vi* (*p prés etc* **-rr-**) **1** (allude to) **to ~ to** parler de, faire allusion à ‹*person, topic, event*›
2 (relate, apply) **to ~ to** ‹*number, date, term*› se rapporter à
3 (consult) **to ~ to** consulter ‹*notes, article*›

referee /ˌrefə'riː/ **A** *n* **1** arbitre *m*
2 (BrE) (giving job reference) personne *f* pouvant fournir des références
B *vt, vi* arbitrer

🔑 **reference** /'refərəns/ **A** *n* **1** (allusion) référence *f* (**to** à), allusion *f* (**to** à)
2 (consultation) **without ~ to sb/sth** sans consulter qn/qch; **for future ~** pour information
3 (in book, letter) référence *f*
4 (testimonial) références *fpl*
B with reference to *phr* **with ~ to your letter** suite à votre lettre

reference book *n* ouvrage *m* de référence

reference number *n* numéro *m* de référence

referendum /ˌrefə'rendəm/ *n* (*pl* **-da**) référendum *m*

referral /rɪ'fɜːrəl/ *n* (of matter, problem) renvoi *m* (**to** à)

refill A /'riːfɪl/ *n* (for ballpoint, lighter, perfume) recharge *f*
B /ˌriː'fɪl/ *vt* recharger ‹*pen, lighter*›; remplir [qch] à nouveau ‹*glass, bottle*›

refine /rɪ'faɪn/ *vt* **1** raffiner ‹*oil, sugar*›
2 (improve) peaufiner ‹*theory*›

refined /rɪ'faɪnd/ *adj* raffiné/-e

refinement /rɪ'faɪnmənt/ *n* (elegance) raffinement *m*

refinery /rɪ'faɪnərɪ/ *n* raffinerie *f*

🔑 **reflect** /rɪ'flekt/ **A** *vt* **1** refléter ‹*image*›; **to be ~ed in sth** se refléter dans qch
2 renvoyer, réfléchir ‹*light, heat*›
3 (think) se dire
B *vi* **1** (think) réfléchir (**on, upon** à)
2 to ~ well/badly on sb faire honneur/du tort à qn

reflection /rɪ'flekʃn/ *n* **1** (image) reflet *m* (**of** de), image *f* (**of** de)
2 (thought) réflexion *f*; **on ~** à la réflexion

🔑 mot clé

reflector /rɪ'flektə(r)/ *n* (on vehicle) catadioptre *m*

reflex /'ri:fleks/ **A** *n* réflexe *m*
B *adj* réflexe; **a ~ action** un réflexe

reflexive verb *n* verbe *m* pronominal réfléchi

reform /rɪ'fɔ:m/ **A** *n* réforme *f*
B *vt* réformer

reformation /ˌrefə'meɪʃn/ *n* réforme *f*; **the Reformation** la Réforme

refrain /rɪ'freɪn/ **A** *n* refrain *m*
B *vi* se retenir; **to ~ from doing** s'abstenir de faire

refresh /rɪ'freʃ/ *vt* ‹*bath, drink*› rafraîchir; ‹*rest*› reposer; **to ~ sb's memory** rafraîchir la mémoire à qn

refresher course *n* cours *m* de recyclage

refreshing /rɪ'freʃɪŋ/ *adj* ‹*drink, shower*› rafraîchissant/-e; ‹*rest*› réparateur/-trice

refreshments *npl* (drinks) rafraîchissements *mpl*; **light ~** repas *m* léger

refrigerate /rɪ'frɪdʒəreɪt/ *vt* frigorifier

refrigerator /rɪ'frɪdʒəreɪtə(r)/ *n* réfrigérateur *m*, frigidaire® *m*

refuel /ˌri:'fjʊəl/ *vi* (*p prés etc* **-ll-** (BrE), **-l-** (AmE)) se ravitailler en carburant

refuge /'refju:dʒ/ *n* **1** (shelter, protection) refuge *m* (**from** contre); **to take ~ from** s'abriter de ‹*storm*›
2 (hostel) foyer *m*

refugee /ˌrefjʊ'dʒɪ, (AmE) 'refjʊdʒi:/ *n* réfugié/-e *m/f*

refugee camp *n* camp *m* de réfugiés

refund **A** /'ri:fʌnd/ *n* remboursement *m*
B /ˌri:'fʌnd/ *vt* rembourser

refurbish /ˌri:'fɜ:bɪʃ/ *vt* rénover

refusal /rɪ'fju:zl/ *n* refus *m* (**to do** de faire); (to application) réponse *f* négative

refuse¹ /rɪ'fju:z/ **A** *vt* refuser (**to do** de faire)
B *vi* refuser

refuse² /'refju:s/ *n* (BrE) (household) ordures *fpl*; (industrial) déchets *mpl*; (garden) déchets *mpl* de jardinage

refuse collector *n* (BrE) éboueur *m*

refute /rɪ'fju:t/ *vt* réfuter

regain /rɪ'geɪn/ *vt* retrouver ‹*health, strength, sight, composure*›; reconquérir ‹*power, seat*›; reprendre ‹*lead, control*›; **to ~ consciousness** reprendre connaissance

regal /'ri:gl/ *adj* royal/-e

regale /rɪ'geɪl/ *vt* régaler (**with** de)

regalia /rɪ'geɪlɪə/ *npl* insignes *mpl*

regard /rɪ'gɑ:d/ **A** *n* **1** (consideration) égard *m*; **out of ~ for** par égard pour
2 (esteem) estime *f* (**for** pour); **to hold sb/sth in high ~** avoir beaucoup d'estime pour qn/qch
3 with *or* **in ~ to** en ce qui concerne; **in this ~** à cet égard
B *vt* considérer (**as** comme)

regarding /rɪ'gɑ:dɪŋ/ *prep* concernant

regardless /rɪ'gɑ:dlɪs/ **A** *prep* **~ of** sans tenir compte de
B *adv* malgré tout

regards *npl* amitiés *fpl*; **give them my ~** transmettez-leur mes amitiés

regatta /rɪ'gætə/ *n* régate *f*

regent /'ri:dʒənt/ *n* régent/-e *m/f*

reggae /'regeɪ/ *n* reggae *m*

regime, **régime** /reɪ'ʒi:m, 'reʒi:m/ *n* régime *m*

regiment /'redʒɪmənt/ *n* régiment *m*

region /'ri:dʒən/ *n* région *f*; **(somewhere) in the ~ of £300** environ 300 livres sterling

regional /'ri:dʒənl/ *adj* régional/-e

register /'redʒɪstə(r)/ **A** *n* registre *m*; (at school) cahier *m* des absences
B *vt* **1** déclarer ‹*birth, death*›; faire immatriculer ‹*vehicle*›; faire enregistrer ‹*luggage, company*›; déposer ‹*trademark, complaint*›
2 ‹*instrument*› indiquer ‹*speed, temperature*›; ‹*person*› exprimer ‹*anger, disapproval*›
3 envoyer [qch] en recommandé ‹*letter*›
C *vi* (for course, school, to vote) s'inscrire; (at hotel) se présenter

registered /'redʒɪstəd/ *adj* **1** ‹*voter*› inscrit/-e; ‹*vehicle, student*› immatriculé/-e; ‹*charity*› ≈ agréé/-e
2 ‹*letter*› recommandé/-e; **by ~ post** en recommandé

registered trademark *n* marque *m* déposée

registrar /ˌredʒɪs'trɑ:(r), 'redʒ-/ *n* **1** (BrE) (gen) officier *m* d'état civil; (medical) adjoint *m*
2 (academic) responsable *mf* du bureau de la scolarité

registration /ˌredʒɪ'streɪʃn/ *n* (of person) inscription *f*; (of trademark, patent) dépôt *m*; (of birth, death, marriage) déclaration *f*

registration number *n* (BrE) numéro *m* d'immatriculation

registry office *n* (BrE) bureau *m* de l'état civil; **to get married in a ~** se marier civilement

regress /'ri:gres/ *vi* régresser (**to** au stade de)

regret /rɪ'gret/ **A** *n* regret *m* (**about** à propos de); **to have no ~s about doing** ne pas regretter d'avoir fait
B *vt* (*p prés etc* **-tt-**) regretter (**that** que (+ *subjunctive*)); **to ~ doing** regretter d'avoir fait; **I ~ to inform you that** j'ai le regret de vous informer que

regretfully /rɪ'gretfəlɪ/ *adv* à regret

regrettable /rɪ'gretəbl/ *adj* regrettable (**that** que + subjunctive)

regular /'regjʊlə(r)/ **A** *n* **1** (client, visitor) habitué/-e *m/f*
2 (AmE) (petrol) ordinaire *m*
B *adj* **1** (gen) régulier/-ière; **to take ~ exercise** faire de l'exercice régulièrement

2 (usual) ‹*activity, customer, visitor*› habituel/-elle; ‹*viewer, listener*› fidèle
3 ‹*army, soldier*› de métier

regularity /ˌregjʊˈlærətɪ/ *n* régularité *f*

regularly /ˈregjʊləlɪ/ *adv* régulièrement

regulate /ˈregjʊleɪt/ *vt* **1** (gen), (Econ) réguler
2 (adjust) régler ‹*mechanism*›

🔑 **regulation** /ˌregjʊˈleɪʃn/ **A** *n* **1** (gen) règlement *m*; (for safety, fire) consigne *f*; **under the (new) ~s** selon la (nouvelle) réglementation; **against the ~s** contraire au règlement *or* aux normes
2 (controlling) réglementation *f*
B *adj* ‹*width, length, uniform*› réglementaire

regurgitate /rɪˈgɜːdʒɪteɪt/ *vt* régurgiter; (fig) ressortir

rehabilitate /ˌriːəˈbɪlɪteɪt/ *vt* réinsérer ‹*disabled person, ex-prisoner*›; réhabiliter ‹*addict, area*›

rehabilitation centre (BrE), **rehabilitation center** (AmE) *n* (for disabled people) centre *m* de rééducation; (for addicts etc) centre *m* de réinsertion

rehearsal /rɪˈhɜːsl/ *n* répétition *f* (**of** de)

rehearse /rɪˈhɜːs/ **A** *vt* répéter ‹*scene*›; préparer ‹*speech, excuse*›
B *vi* répéter (**for** pour)

reheat /ˌriːˈhiːt/ *vt* réchauffer

rehouse /ˌriːˈhaʊz/ *vt* reloger

reign /reɪn/ **A** *n* règne *m*
B *vi* régner (**over** sur)

reimburse /ˌriːɪmˈbɜːs/ *vt* rembourser

rein /reɪn/ *n* rêne *f*

reincarnation /ˌriːɪnkɑːˈneɪʃn/ *n* réincarnation *f*

reindeer /ˈreɪndɪə(r)/ *n* (*pl* ~) renne *m*

reinforce /ˌriːɪnˈfɔːs/ *vt* renforcer

reinforced concrete *n* béton *m* armé

reinforcement /ˌriːɪnˈfɔːsmənt/ *n* (support) renfort *m*; **~s** (Mil) renforts

reinstate /ˌriːɪnˈsteɪt/ *vt* réintégrer ‹*employee*›

reiterate /riːˈɪtəreɪt/ *vt* réitérer

🔑 **reject A** /ˈriːdʒekt/ *n* marchandise *f* de deuxième choix
B /rɪˈdjekt/ *vt* rejeter ‹*advice, application, person, transplant*›; refuser ‹*candidate, manuscript*›; démentir ‹*claim, suggestion*›

rejection /rɪˈdʒekʃn/ *n* (gen) rejet *m*; (of candidate, manuscript) refus *m*

rejection letter *n* lettre *f* de refus

rejoice /rɪˈdʒɔɪs/ *vi* se réjouir (**at, over** de)

rejuvenate /rɪˈdʒuːvɪneɪt/ *vt* rajeunir

rekindle /ˌriːˈkɪndl/ *vt* ranimer

relapse A /ˈrilæps/ *n* rechute *f*
B /rɪˈlæps/ *vi* (Med) rechuter (gen) **to ~ into** retomber dans

🔑 mot clé

🔑 **relate** /rɪˈleɪt/ **A** *vt* **1** (connect) faire le rapprochement entre
2 raconter ‹*story*› (**to** à)
B *vi* **to ~ to** (have connection) se rapporter à; (communicate) s'entendre avec

🔑 **related** /rɪˈleɪtɪd/ *adj* **1** ‹*person*› apparenté/-e (**by, through** par, **to** à)
2 (connected) ‹*area, idea, incident*› lié/-e (**to** à); **drug-~** lié/-e à la drogue

🔑 **relation** /rɪˈleɪʃn/ **A** *n* **1** (relative) parent/-e *m/f*; **my ~s** ma famille
2 (connection) rapport *m*
B relations *npl* (dealings) relations *fpl* (**with** avec)

🔑 **relationship** /rɪˈleɪʃnʃɪp/ *n* **1** (between people) relations *fpl*; (with colleagues) rapports *mpl*
2 (connection) rapport *m* (**to, with** avec)

🔑 **relative** /ˈrelətɪv/ **A** *n* parent/-e *m/f*; **my ~s** ma famille
B *adj* **1** (gen) relatif/-ive
2 (respective) respectif/-ive

🔑 **relatively** /ˈrelətɪvlɪ/ *adv* relativement; **~ speaking** toutes proportions gardées

🔑 **relax** /rɪˈlæks/ **A** *vt* décontracter ‹*muscle*›; assouplir ‹*restrictions, discipline*›; détendre ‹*body*›; relâcher ‹*efforts, grip, concentration*›
B *vi* **1** ‹*person*› se détendre
2 ‹*grip*› se relâcher; ‹*jaw, muscle*› se décontracter

relaxation /ˌriːlækˈseɪʃn/ *n* **1** (of person) détente *f*
2 (of restrictions, discipline) assouplissement *m* (**in** de)

relaxed /rɪˈlækst/ *adj* détendu/-e, décontracté/-e

relaxing /rɪˈlæksɪŋ/ *adj* ‹*atmosphere, activity*› délassant/-e; ‹*holiday*› reposant/-e

relay A *n* /ˈriːleɪ/ **1** (of workers) équipe *f* (de relais)
2 (*also* ~ **race**) course *f* de relais
B *vt* /ˈriːleɪ, riˈleɪ/ (*prét, pp* **~ed**) transmettre ‹*message*› (**to** à)

🔑 **release** /rɪˈliːs/ **A** *n* **1** (liberation) libération *f*
2 (relief) soulagement *m*
3 (for press) communiqué *m*
4 (of film) sortie *f*
5 (film, video, record) (*also* **new ~**) nouveauté *f*
B *vt* **1** libérer ‹*prisoner*›; dégager ‹*accident victim*›; relâcher ‹*animal*›; **to ~ sb from** dégager qn de ‹*promise*›
2 faire jouer ‹*catch, clasp*›; déclencher ‹*shutter*›; desserrer ‹*handbrake*›; larguer ‹*bomb*›
3 (let go) lâcher ‹*object, arm, hand*›
4 faire sortir ‹*film, record*›

relegate /ˈrelɪgeɪt/ *vt* **1** reléguer ‹*person, object*› (**to** à)
2 (BrE) (Sport) reléguer (**to** en)

relegation /ˌrelɪˈgeɪʃn/ *n* relégation *f*

relent /rɪ'lent/ *vi* céder

relentless /rɪ'lentlɪs/ *adj* ‹*pressure*› implacable; ‹*noise, activity*› incessant/-e; ‹*attack*› acharné/-e

relevant /'reləvənt/ *adj* **1** ‹*issue, facts, point*› pertinent/-e; ‹*information*› utile; **to be ~ to** avoir rapport à
2 (appropriate) ‹*chapter*› correspondant/-e; ‹*period*› en question

reliable /rɪ'laɪəbl/ *adj* ‹*friend, witness*› digne de confiance, fiable; ‹*employee, firm*› sérieux/-ieuse; ‹*car, memory, account*› fiable; ‹*information, source*› sûr/-e

reliant /rɪ'laɪənt/ *adj* **to be ~ on** être dépendant/-e de

relic /'relɪk/ *n* relique *f*

relief /rɪ'li:f/ *n* **1** (from pain, distress) soulagement *m*
2 (aid) aide *f*, secours *m*
3 (in sculpture, geography) relief *m*

relief agency *n* organisation *f* humanitaire

relief fund *n* fonds *m* de secours

relief supplies *npl* secours *mpl*

relief work *n* travail *m* humanitaire

relief worker *n* secouriste *mf*

relieve /rɪ'li:v/ *vt* **1** soulager ‹*pain, suffering, tension*›; dissiper ‹*boredom*›; remédier à ‹*poverty, famine*›; **to be ~d** être soulagé/-e
2 to ~ sb of débarrasser qn de ‹*coat, bag*›; soulager qn de ‹*burden*›
3 (help) secourir ‹*troops, population*›
4 relever ‹*worker, sentry*›

religion /rɪ'lɪdʒən/ *n* religion *f*

religious /rɪ'lɪdʒəs/ *adj* (gen) religieux/-ieuse; ‹*person*› croyant/-e; ‹*war*› de religion

relinquish /rɪ'lɪŋkwɪʃ/ *vt* renoncer à ‹*claim, right*› (**to** en faveur de); céder ‹*task, power*› (**to** à)

relish /'relɪʃ/ **A** *n* **1 with ~** ‹*eat, drink*› avec un plaisir évident
2 (Culin) condiment *m*
B *vt* savourer ‹*food*›; se réjouir de ‹*prospect*›

relocate /ˌri:ləʊ'keɪt, (AmE) ˌri:'ləʊkeɪt/ **A** *vt* muter
B *vi* ‹*company*› déménager; (for cheaper labour) délocaliser; ‹*employee*› être muté/-e

relocation /ˌri:ləʊ'keɪʃn/ *n* délocalisation *f*

reluctance /rɪ'lʌktəns/ *n* réticence *f* (**to do** à faire)

reluctant /rɪ'lʌktənt/ *adj* ‹*person*› peu enthousiaste; **to be ~ to do** être peu disposé/-e à faire

reluctantly /rɪ'lʌktəntlɪ/ *adv* à contrecœur

rely /rɪ'laɪ/ *vi* **1** (be dependent) **to ~ on** dépendre de ‹*person, aid, industry*›; reposer sur ‹*method, technology, exports*›
2 (count) **to ~ on sb/sth** compter sur qn/qch (**to do** pour faire)

remain /rɪ'meɪn/ *vi* rester; **to ~ silent** garder le silence

remainder /rɪ'meɪndə(r)/ *n* reste *m* (**of** de)

remains /rɪ'meɪnz/ *npl* restes *mpl*

remand /rɪ'mɑ:nd, (AmE) rɪ'mænd/ **A** *n* **on ~** (in custody) en détention provisoire; (on bail) en liberté sous caution
B *vt* **to be ~ed in custody** être placé/-e en détention provisoire

remand centre *n* (BrE) centre *m* de détention (provisoire)

remark /rɪ'mɑ:k/ **A** *n* remarque *f*
B *vt* **1** (comment) faire remarquer (**that** que, **to** à)
2 (notice) remarquer (**that** que)

remarkable /rɪ'mɑ:kəbl/ *adj* remarquable

remarry /ˌri:'mærɪ/ *vi* se remarier

remedial /rɪ'mi:dɪəl/ *adj* (Sch) ‹*class*› de rattrapage

remedy /'remədɪ/ **A** *n* remède *m* (**for** à, contre)
B *vt* remédier à

remember /rɪ'membə(r)/ **A** *vt* **1** (recall) se souvenir de, se rappeler ‹*fact, name, place, event*›; se souvenir de ‹*person*›; **to ~ doing** se rappeler avoir fait, se souvenir d'avoir fait
2 (not forget) **to ~ to do** penser à faire, ne pas oublier de faire
B *vi* se souvenir

remind /rɪ'maɪnd/ *vt* rappeler; **to ~ sb of sb/sth** rappeler qn/qch à qn; **to ~ sb to do** rappeler à qn de faire

reminder /rɪ'maɪndə(r)/ *n* rappel *m* (**of** de, **that** du fait que)

reminisce /ˌremɪ'nɪs/ *vi* évoquer ses souvenirs (**about** de)

reminiscent /ˌremɪ'nɪsnt/ *adj* **to be ~ of sb/sth** faire penser à qn/qch

remiss /rɪ'mɪs/ *adj* négligent/-e

remission /rɪ'mɪʃn/ *n* **1** (of sentence, debt) remise *f*
2 (Med) rémission *f*

remit /'ri:mɪt/ *n* attributions *fpl*

remnant /'remnənt/ *n* (gen) reste *m*; (of building, past) vestige *m*; (of fabric) coupon *m*

remorse /rɪ'mɔ:s/ *n* remords *m* (**for** de)

remote /rɪ'məʊt/ *adj* **1** ‹*area, village*› isolé/-e; ‹*ancestor, country*› éloigné/-e
2 (aloof) ‹*person*› distant/-e
3 (slight) ‹*chance*› vague, infime

remote control *n* télécommande *f*

remote-controlled *adj* télécommandé/-e

remotely /rɪ'məʊtlɪ/ *adv* ‹*resemble*› vaguement; **he's not ~ interested** ça ne l'intéresse pas du tout

removal /rɪ'mu:vl/ *n* **1** (of furniture, parcel, rubbish) enlèvement *m*; (Med) ablation *f*; **stain ~** détachage *m*
2 (change of home) déménagement *m* (**from** de, **to** à)

remove /rɪ'mu:v/ *vt* **1** (gen), (Med) enlever

(**from** de); enlever, ôter ‹*clothes, shoes*›; supprimer ‹*threat*›; chasser ‹*doubt*›; **cousin once ~d** cousin/-e *m/f* au deuxième degré
2 to ~ sb from office démettre qn de ses fonctions

remover /rɪ'muːvə(r)/ *n* déménageur *m*

remuneration /rɪˌmjuːnə'reɪʃn/ *n* rémunération *f*

Renaissance /rɪ'neɪsns, (AmE) 'renəsɑːns/ *n* **the ~** la Renaissance

render /'rendə(r)/ *vt* rendre

rendezvous /'rɒndɪvuː/ **A** *n* (*pl* ~) rendez-vous *m inv*
B *vi* **to ~ with sb** rejoindre qn

renegade /'renɪgeɪd/ *n* renégat/-e *m/f*

renew /rɪ'njuː, (AmE) -'nuː/ *vt* (gen) renouveler; renouer ‹*acquaintance*›; raviver ‹*courage*›; faire prolonger ‹*library book*›

renewal /rɪ'njuːəl, (AmE) -'nuːəl/ *n* (of contract, passport) renouvellement *m*; (of hostilities) reprise *f*; (of interest) regain *m*

renewed *adj* ‹*interest, optimism*› accru/-e; ‹*attack, call*› renouvelé/-e

renounce /rɪ'naʊns/ *vt* (gen) renoncer à; renier ‹*faith, friend*›

renovate /'renəveɪt/ *vt* rénover ‹*building*›

renovation /ˌrenə'veɪʃn/ *n* rénovation *f*; **~s** travaux *mpl* de rénovation

renowned /rɪ'naʊnd/ *adj* célèbre (**for** pour)

rent /rent/ **A** *n* loyer *m*; **for ~** à louer
B *vt* louer

rental /'rentl/ *n* (of car, premises, equipment) location *f*; (of phone line) abonnement *m*

rent boy *n* jeune prostitué *m*

reoffend /riːə'fend/ *vi* récidiver

reopen /ˌriː'əʊpən/ *vt, vi* rouvrir

reorganize /ˌriː'ɔːgənaɪz/ *vt* réorganiser

rep /rep/ *n* représentant/-e *m/f* (de commerce)

repair /rɪ'peə(r)/ **A** *n* réparation *f*; **to be (damaged) beyond ~** ne pas être réparable; **to be in good/bad ~** être en bon/mauvais état
B *vt* réparer

repairman *n* réparateur *m*

repatriate /riː'pætrɪeɪt, (AmE) -'peɪt-/ *vt* rapatrier

repatriation /ˌriːpætrɪ'eɪʃn, (AmE) -peɪt-/ *n* rapatriement *m*

repay /rɪ'peɪ/ *vt* (*prét, pp* **repaid**) rembourser ‹*person, sum*›; rendre ‹*hospitality, favour*›

repayment /rɪ'peɪmənt/ *n* remboursement *m* (**on** de)

repeal /rɪ'piːl/ **A** *n* abrogation *f* (**of** de)
B *vt* abroger

⚷ **repeat** /rɪ'piːt/ **A** *n* (gen) répétition *f*; (on radio, TV) rediffusion *f*; (Mus) reprise *f*
B *vt* (gen) répéter; (Sch) redoubler ‹*year*›; rediffuser ‹*programme*›

repeated /rɪ'piːtɪd/ *adj* ‹*warnings, requests, attempts*› répété/-e; ‹*setbacks*› successif/-ive

repeatedly /rɪ'piːtɪdlɪ/ *adv* plusieurs fois, à plusieurs reprises

repel /rɪ'pel/ *vt* (*p prés etc* **-ll-**) repousser

repellent /rɪ'pelənt/ *adj* repoussant/-e

repent /rɪ'pent/ *vi* se repentir

repercussion /ˌriːpə'kʌʃn/ *n* répercussion *f*

repertoire /'repətwɑː(r)/ *n* répertoire *m*

repetition /ˌrepɪ'tɪʃn/ *n* répétition *f*

repetitive /rɪ'petɪtɪv/ *adj* répétitif/-ive

repetitive strain injury, RSI *n* microtraumatismes *mpl* répétés

⚷ **replace** /rɪ'pleɪs/ *vt* **1** (put back) remettre ‹*lid, cork*›; remettre [qch] à sa place ‹*book, ornament*›
2 (provide replacement for) remplacer (**with** par)

replacement /rɪ'pleɪsmənt/ *n* **1** (person) remplaçant/-e *m/f* (**for** de)
2 (act) remplacement *m*
3 (spare part) pièce *f* de rechange

replay **A** /'riːpleɪ/ *n* (Sport) match *m* rejoué
B /ˌriː'pleɪ/ *vt* rejouer

replenish /rɪ'plenɪʃ/ *vt* reconstituer ‹*stocks*›

replica /'replɪkə/ *n* réplique *f*, copie *f* (**of** de)

⚷ **reply** /rɪ'plaɪ/ **A** *n* réponse *f*
B *vt, vi* répondre

⚷ **report** /rɪ'pɔːt/ **A** *n* **1** (written account) rapport *m* (**on** sur); (verbal account, minutes) compte-rendu *m*; (in media) communiqué *m*; (longer) reportage *m*
2 (BrE) (Sch) (*also* **school ~**) bulletin *m* scolaire; (AmE) (Sch) (review) critique *f*
B *vt* **1** signaler ‹*fact, event, theft, accident*›; **to ~ sth to sb** transmettre qch à qn ‹*result, decision, news*›
2 (make complaint about) signaler ‹*person*›; se plaindre de ‹*noise*›
C *vi* **1 to ~ on** faire un compte-rendu sur ‹*talks, progress*›; ‹*reporter*› faire un reportage sur ‹*events*›; ‹*committee, group*› faire son rapport sur
2 (present oneself) se présenter; **to ~ for duty** prendre son service
3 to ~ to être sous les ordres (directs) de ‹*manager, superior*›

report card *n* (AmE) bulletin *m* scolaire

⚷ **reporter** /rɪ'pɔːtə(r)/ *n* journaliste *mf*, reporter *mf*

repose /rɪ'pəʊz/ *n* repos *m*; **in ~** au repos

repossess /ˌriːpə'zes/ *vt* ‹*bank*› saisir ‹*house*›; ‹*creditor*› reprendre possession de ‹*property*›

repossession /ˌriːpə'zeʃn/ *n* saisie *f* immobilière

reprehensible /ˌreprɪ'hensɪbl/ *adj* répréhensible

⚷ **represent** /ˌreprɪ'zent/ *vt* **1** (gen) représenter
2 (present) présenter ‹*person, event*› (**as** comme)

⚷ mot clé

representation /ˌreprɪzenˈteɪʃn/ *n*
1 représentation *f* (**of** de, **by** par)
2 to make ~s to sb faire des démarches *fpl* auprès de qn

representative /ˌreprɪˈzentətɪv/ **A** *n*
1 représentant/-e *m/f*
2 (AmE) (politician) député *m*
B *adj* représentatif/-ive (**of** de), typique (**of** de)

repress /rɪˈpres/ *vt* réprimer ‹*reaction, smile*›; refouler ‹*feelings*›

reprieve /rɪˈpriːv/ **A** *n* **1** (Law) remise *f* de peine
2 (delay) sursis *m*
3 (respite) répit *m*
B *vt* accorder une remise de peine à ‹*prisoner*›

reprimand /ˈreprɪmɑːnd, (AmE) -mænd/ **A** *n* réprimande *f*
B *vt* réprimander

reprisal /rɪˈpraɪzl/ *n* représailles *fpl*

reproach /rɪˈprəʊtʃ/ **A** *n* reproche *m*; **beyond ~** irréprochable
B *vt* reprocher à ‹*person*›; **to ~ sb with** *or* **for sth** reprocher qch à qn

reprocessing plant *n* (*also* **nuclear ~**) usine *f* de retraitement (des déchets nucléaires)

reproduce /ˌriːprəˈdjuːs, (AmE) -ˈduːs/ **A** *vt* reproduire
B *vi* se reproduire

reproduction /ˌriːprəˈdʌkʃn/ *n* reproduction *f*

reproduction furniture *n* meubles *mpl* de style

reproductive /ˌriːprəˈdʌktɪv/ *adj* reproducteur/-trice

reproof /rɪˈpruːf/ *n* réprimande *f*

reprove /rɪˈpruːv/ *vt* réprimander (**for doing** de faire)

reptile /ˈreptaɪl, (AmE) -tl/ *n* reptile *m*

republic /rɪˈpʌblɪk/ *n* république *f*

republican /rɪˈpʌblɪkən/ **A** *n* républicain/-e *m/f*; **Republican** (AmE) Républicain/-e *m/f*
B *adj* (*also* **Republican**) républicain/-e

repudiate /rɪˈpjuːdɪeɪt/ *vt* rejeter

repugnant /rɪˈpʌgnənt/ *adj* répugnant/-e

repulse /rɪˈpʌls/ *vt* repousser

repulsion /rɪˈpʌlʃn/ *n* répulsion *f*

repulsive /rɪˈpʌlsɪv/ *adj* repoussant/-e

reputable /ˈrepjʊtəbl/ *adj* de bonne réputation

reputation /ˌrepjʊˈteɪʃn/ *n* réputation *f* (**as** de)

repute /rɪˈpjuːt/ *n* **of ~** réputé/-e

reputed /rɪˈpjuːtɪd/ *adj* (gen) réputé/-e; (Law) putatif/-ive; **he is ~ to be very rich** à ce que l'on dit il serait très riche

request /rɪˈkwest/ **A** *n* **1** demande *f* (**for** de), **to** à, requête *f* (**for** de, **to** à); **on ~** sur demande
2 (on radio) dédicace *f*
B *vt* demander (**from** à); **to ~ sb to do** demander à qn de faire

require /rɪˈkwaɪə(r)/ *vt* **1** (need) avoir besoin de
2 (necessitate) ‹*job, situation*› exiger ‹*funds, qualifications*›; **to be ~d to do** être tenu/-e de faire

requirement /rɪˈkwaɪəmənt/ *n* **1** (need) besoin *m*
2 (condition) condition *f*
3 (obligation) obligation *f* (**to do** de faire)
4 (AmE) (Univ) matière *f* obligatoire

requisite /ˈrekwɪzɪt/ *adj* exigé/-e, requis/-e

requisition /ˌrekwɪˈzɪʃn/ *vt* réquisitionner

reschedule /ˌriːˈʃedjuːl, (AmE) -ˈskedʒʊl/ *vt* (change time) changer l'heure de; (change date) changer la date de

rescue /ˈreskjuː/ **A** *n* **1** (aid) secours *m*; **to come/go to sb's ~** venir/aller au secours de qn; **to come to the ~** venir à la rescousse
2 (operation) sauvetage *m* (**of** de)
B *vt* **1** (save) sauver
2 (aid) porter secours à
3 (release) libérer

rescue worker *n* secouriste *mf*

research /rɪˈsɜːtʃ, ˈriːsɜːtʃ/ **A** *n* recherche *f* (**into, on** sur)
B *vt* faire des recherches sur ‹*topic*›; préparer ‹*book, article*›

research and development, **R&D** *n* recherche-développement *f*, recherche *f* et développement *m*

researcher /rɪˈsɜːtʃə(r), ˈriːsɜːtʃə(r)/ *n* chercheur/-euse *m/f*; (in TV) documentaliste *mf*

resemblance /rɪˈzembləns/ *n* ressemblance *f* (**between** entre, **to** avec)

resemble /rɪˈzembl/ *vt* ressembler à; **to ~ each other** se ressembler

resend /riːˈsend/ *vt* envoyer de nouveau, renvoyer

resent /rɪˈzent/ *vt* en vouloir à ‹*person*› (**for doing** d'avoir fait); ne pas aimer ‹*tone*›

resentful /rɪˈzentfl/ *adj* plein/-e de ressentiment (**of sb** envers qn)

resentment /rɪˈzentmənt/ *n* ressentiment *m*

reservation /ˌrezəˈveɪʃn/ *n* **1** (doubt) réserve *f*; **without ~** sans réserve; **to have ~s about sth** avoir des doutes sur qch
2 (booking) réservation *f*
3 (AmE) **(Indian) ~** réserve *f* (indienne)

reservation desk *n* bureau *m* des réservations

reserve /rɪˈzɜːv/ **A** *n* **1** (stock) réserve *f*; **to keep sth in ~** tenir qch en réserve
2 (reticence) réserve *f*
3 (Mil) **the ~(s)** la réserve
4 (Sport) remplaçant/-e *m/f*
5 réserve *f*; **wildlife ~** réserve naturelle
B *vt* réserver

reserved /rɪˈzɜːvd/ *adj* réservé/-e

r

reservoir /ˈrezəvwɑː(r)/ *n* réservoir *m*
reset /ˌriːˈset/ *vt* (*p prés* **-tt-**, *prét*, *pp* **reset**) régler ‹*machine*›; remettre [qch] à l'heure ‹*clock*›
reshuffle /ˌriːˈʃʌfl/ *n* remaniement *m*
reside /rɪˈzaɪd/ *vi* résider, habiter (**with** avec)
residence /ˈrezɪdəns/ *n* résidence *f*
residence permit *n* permis *m* de séjour
⚷ **resident** /ˈrezɪdənt/ **A** *n* (gen) résident/-e *m/f*; (of street) riverain/-e *m/f*; (of guest house) pensionnaire *mf*
B *adj* ‹*population*› local/-e; ‹*staff, tutor*› à demeure
residential /ˌrezɪˈdenʃl/ *adj* ‹*area*› résidentiel/-ielle; ‹*staff*› à demeure; ‹*course*› en internat; **to be in ~ care** être pris en charge par une institution
residue /ˈrezɪdjuː, (AmE) -duː/ *n* résidu *m* (**of** de)
resign /rɪˈzaɪn/ **A** *vt* démissionner de ‹*post, job*›
B *vi* démissionner (**as** du poste de, **from** de)
C *v refl* **to ~ oneself** se résigner (**to** à)
resignation /ˌrezɪɡˈneɪʃn/ *n* **1** (from post) démission *f* (**from** de, **as** du poste de)
2 (patience) résignation *f*
resigned /rɪˈzaɪnd/ *adj* résigné/-e (**to** à)
resilient /rɪˈzɪlɪənt/ *adj* (morally) déterminé/-e; (physically) résistant/-e
resin /ˈrezɪn, (AmE) ˈrezn/ *n* résine *f*
resist /rɪˈzɪst/ **A** *vt* résister à
B *vi* résister
⚷ **resistance** /rɪˈzɪstəns/ *n* résistance *f* (**to** à)
Resistance /rɪˈzɪstəns/ *n* **the ~** la Résistance
resistance fighter *n* résistant/-e *m/f*
resistant /rɪˈzɪstənt/ *adj* **1 heat-~** résistant/-e à la chaleur; **water-~** imperméable
2 (opposed) **~ to** réfractaire à
r
resit /ˌriːˈsɪt/ *vt* (*prét*, *pp* **resat**) (BrE) repasser ‹*exam, test*›
reskill /riːˈskɪl/ *vt* recycler
resolute /ˈrezəluːt/ *adj* ‹*person*› résolu/-e
⚷ **resolution** /ˌrezəˈluːʃn/ *n* résolution *f*; **to make a ~ to do** prendre la résolution de faire
⚷ **resolve** /rɪˈzɒlv/ **A** *n* détermination *f*
B *vt* **1** (gen) résoudre
2 (decide) **to ~ that** décider que; **to ~ to do** résoudre de faire
resonant /ˈrezənənt/ *adj* ‹*voice*› sonore
resort /rɪˈzɔːt/ **A** *n* **1** recours *m*; **as a last ~** en dernier recours
2 seaside ~ station *f* balnéaire; **ski ~** station *f* de ski
B *vi* **to ~ to** recourir à
resound /rɪˈzaʊnd/ *vi* **1** ‹*noise*› retentir (**through** dans)
2 ‹*place*› retentir (**with** de)
resounding /rɪˈzaʊndɪŋ/ *adj* ‹*cheers*› retentissant/-e; ‹*success*› éclatant/-e
⚷ **resource** /rɪˈsɔːs, -ˈzɔːs, (AmE) ˈriːsɔːrs/ *n* ressource *f*
resource centre (BrE), **resource center** (AmE) *n* centre *m* de documentation
resourceful /rɪˈsɔːsfl, -ˈzɔːsfl, (AmE) ˈriːsɔːrsfl/ *adj* plein/-e de ressources, débrouillard/-e (fam)
⚷ **respect** /rɪˈspekt/ **A** *n* **1** (gen) respect *m*; **out of ~** par respect (**for** pour); **with (all due) ~** sauf votre respect; **with ~ to** par rapport à
2 (aspect) égard *m*; **in many ~s** à bien des égards
B respects *npl* respects *mpl*; **to pay one's ~s to sb** présenter ses respects à qn
C *vt* respecter
respectable /rɪˈspektəbl/ *adj* **1** ‹*person, family*› respectable
2 (adequate) ‹*amount*› respectable; ‹*performance*› honorable
respectful /rɪˈspektfl/ *adj* respectueux/-euse
respective /rɪˈspektɪv/ *adj* respectif/-ive
respiration /ˌrespɪˈreɪʃn/ *n* respiration *f*
respirator /ˈrespɪreɪtə(r)/ *n* respirateur *m*
respiratory /rɪˈspɪrətrɪ, (AmE) -tɔːrɪ/ *adj* respiratoire
respite /ˈrespaɪt, ˈrespɪt/ *n* répit *m* (**from** dans)
⚷ **respond** /rɪˈspɒnd/ *vi* **1** (answer) répondre (**to** à, **with** par)
2 (react) réagir (**to** à)
⚷ **response** /rɪˈspɒns/ *n* **1** (answer) réponse *f* (**to** à); **in ~ to** en réponse à
2 (reaction) réaction *f* (**to** à, **from** de)
⚷ **responsibility** /rɪˌspɒnsəˈbɪlətɪ/ *n* responsabilité *f* (**for** de); **to take ~ for sth** prendre la responsabilité de qch
⚷ **responsible** /rɪˈspɒnsəbl/ *adj* **1** (to blame) responsable (**for** de)
2 (in charge) **~ for doing** chargé/-e de faire
3 (trustworthy) responsable
4 ‹*job*› à responsabilités
responsive /rɪˈspɒnsɪv/ *adj* réceptif/-ive
⚷ **rest** /rest/ **A** *n* **1** (remainder) **the ~** le reste (**of** de); **for the ~ of my life** pour le restant de mes jours
2 (other people) **the ~ (of them)** les autres
3 (repose) repos *m*; (break) pause *f*; **to have a ~** se reposer
B *vt* **1** (lean) **to ~ sth on** appuyer qch sur
2 reposer ‹*legs*›; ne pas utiliser ‹*injured limb*›
C *vi* **1** se reposer; **to ~ easy** être tranquille; **to let the matter ~** en rester là
2 (be supported) **to ~ on** reposer sur
3 to ~ on ‹*decision*› reposer sur ‹*assumption*›
■ **rest with**: **~ with [sb/sth]** être entre les mains de

⚷ mot clé

restart /ˈriːstɑːt/ /ˌriːˈstɑːt/ *vt* **1** reprendre ‹*talks*›
2 remettre [qch] en marche ‹*engine*›

restaurant /ˈrestrɒnt, (AmE) -tərənt/ *n* restaurant *m*

restaurant car *n* (BrE) wagon-restaurant *m*

restaurant owner *n* restaurateur/-trice *m/f*

restful /ˈrestfl/ *adj* ‹*holiday*› reposant/-e; ‹*place*› paisible

restless /ˈrestlɪs/ *adj* ‹*person*› nerveux/-euse; ‹*patient, sleep*› agité/-e

restock /ˌriːˈstɒk/ *vt* regarnir ‹*shelf*› (**with** en); réapprovisionner ‹*shop*› (**with** en)

restoration /ˌrestəˈreɪʃn/ *n* restauration *f*

restore /rɪˈstɔː(r)/ *vt* **1** restituer ‹*property*› (**to** à)
2 rétablir ‹*health, peace, monarchy*›; rendre ‹*faculty*›; **to ∼ sb to power** ramener qn au pouvoir
3 (repair) restaurer

restrain /rɪˈstreɪn/ **A** *vt* retenir ‹*person*›; contenir ‹*crowd*›; maîtriser ‹*animal*›
B *v refl* **to ∼ oneself** se retenir

restrained /rɪˈstreɪnd/ *adj* ‹*manner*› calme; ‹*reaction*› modéré/-e; ‹*person*› posé/-e

restraint /rɪˈstreɪnt/ *n* **1** (moderation) modération *f*
2 (restriction) restriction *f*; **wage ∼** contrôle *m* des salaires
3 (constraint) contrainte *f*

restrict /rɪˈstrɪkt/ *vt* limiter ‹*activity, choice, growth*› (**to** à); restreindre ‹*freedom*›; réserver ‹*access, membership*› (**to** à)

restricted /rɪˈstrɪktɪd/ *adj* ‹*growth, movement*› limité/-e; ‹*document*› confidentiel/-ielle; ‹*parking*› réglementé/-e

restriction /rɪˈstrɪkʃn/ *n* limitation *f*

re-string /ˌriːˈstrɪŋ/ *vt* (*prét, pp* **re-strung**) changer les cordes de ‹*guitar*›; recorder ‹*racket*›; renfiler ‹*necklace*›

rest room *n* (AmE) toilettes *fpl*

result /rɪˈzʌlt/ **A** *n* résultat *m* (**of** de); **as a ∼ of** à la suite de; **as a ∼** en conséquence
B *vi* résulter; **to ∼ in** avoir pour résultat

resume /rɪˈzjuːm, (AmE) -ˈzuːm/ *vt, vi* reprendre

résumé /ˈrezjuːmeɪ, (AmE) ˌrezʊˈmeɪ/ *n*
1 (summary) résumé *m*
2 (AmE) (CV) curriculum vitae *m inv*

resumption /rɪˈzʌmpʃn/ *n* reprise *f* (**of** de)

resurface /ˌriːˈsɜːfɪs/ **A** *vt* refaire (la surface de) ‹*road*›
B *vi* ‹*submarine*› faire surface; ‹*person*› refaire surface

resurrect /ˌrezəˈrekt/ *vt* ressusciter

resurrection /ˌrezəˈrekʃn/ *n* résurrection *f*; **the Resurrection** la Résurrection

resuscitate /rɪˈsʌsɪteɪt/ *vt* (Med) réanimer

resuscitation /rɪˌsʌsɪˈteɪʃn/ *n* réanimation *f*

retail /ˈriːteɪl/ **A** *n* vente *f* au détail
B *adv* au détail
C *vi* **to ∼ at** se vendre au détail à

retailer /ˈriːteɪlə(r)/ *n* détaillant *m*

retail price *n* prix *m* de détail

retail sales *npl* ventes *fpl* au détail

retail trade *n* commerce *m* de détail

retain /rɪˈteɪn/ *vt* garder ‹*control, identity*›; conserver ‹*heat, title*›; retenir ‹*water, fact*›

retaliate /rɪˈtælɪeɪt/ *vi* réagir

retaliation /rɪˌtælɪˈeɪʃn/ *n* représailles *fpl* (**for** de)

retarded /rɪˈtɑːdɪd/ *adj* (offensive) retardé/-e

retch /retʃ/ *vi* avoir des haut-le-cœur

rethink /ˈriːθɪŋk/ *n* **to have a ∼** y repenser

reticent /ˈretɪsnt/ *adj* réticent/-e; **to be ∼ about sth** être discret/-ète sur qch

retina /ˈretɪnə, (AmE) ˈretənə/ *n* rétine *f*

retinue /ˈretɪnjuː, (AmE) ˈretənuː/ *n* escorte *f*

retire /rɪˈtaɪə(r)/ *vi* **1** (from work) prendre sa retraite
2 (withdraw) se retirer (**from** de)

retired *adj* retraité/-e

retirement /rɪˈtaɪəmənt/ *n* retraite *f*

retirement age *n* âge *m* de la retraite

retirement home *n* maison *f* de retraite

retiring /rɪˈtaɪərɪŋ/ *adj* (shy) réservé/-e

retort /rɪˈtɔːt/ **A** *n* riposte *f*
B *vt* rétorquer (**that** que)

retrace /riːˈtreɪs/ *vt* **to ∼ one's steps** revenir sur ses pas

retract /rɪˈtrækt/ **A** *vt* rétracter ‹*statement, claws*›; escamoter ‹*landing gear*›
B *vi* ‹*landing gear*› s'escamoter

retrain /ˌriːˈtreɪn/ **A** *vt* recycler ‹*staff*›
B *vi* ‹*person*› se recycler

retraining /ˌriːˈtreɪnɪŋ/ *n* recyclage *m*

retreat /rɪˈtriːt/ **A** *n* retraite *f*
B *vi* ‹*person*› se retirer (**into** dans, **from** de); ‹*army*› se replier (**to** sur); ‹*flood water*› reculer; **to ∼ into a dream world** se réfugier dans un monde imaginaire

retrial /ˌriːˈtraɪəl/ *n* nouveau procès *m*

retrieve /rɪˈtriːv/ *vt* récupérer ‹*object*›; redresser ‹*situation*›; extraire ‹*data*›

retrograde /ˈretrəgreɪd/ *adj* rétrograde

retrospect /ˈretrəʊspekt/ **in retrospect** *phr* rétrospectivement

retrospective /ˌretrəˈspektɪv/ **A** *n* (*also* **∼ exhibition** *or* **∼ show**) rétrospective *f*
B *adj* **1** (gen) rétrospectif/-ive
2 (Law) rétroactif/-ive

return /rɪˈtɜːn/ **A** *n* **1** (gen) retour *m* (**to** à, **from** de, **of** de); **by ∼ of post** par retour du courrier
2 (on investment) rendement *m* (**on** de)
B *vt* **1** (give back) rendre; (pay back) rembourser; **to ∼ sb's call** rappeler qn
2 (bring back) rapporter (**to** à)
3 (put back) remettre
4 (send back) renvoyer; **'∼ to sender'** 'retour à l'expéditeur'

5 (reciprocate) répondre à ‹*love*›
6 (Mil) riposter à ‹*fire*›
7 (Law) prononcer ‹*verdict*›
8 rapporter ‹*profit*›
C *vi* **1** (come back) revenir (**from** de); retourner (**to** à); (get back from abroad) rentrer (**from** de); (get back home) rentrer chez soi
2 (resume) **to ~ to** reprendre ‹*activity*›; **to ~ to power** revenir au pouvoir
3 (recur) ‹*symptom, doubt*› réapparaître
D **in return** *phr* en échange (**for** de)
IDIOM **many happy ~s!** bon anniversaire!

return fare *n* prix *m* d'un billet aller-retour

return flight *n* vol *m* de retour

return ticket *n* billet *m* aller-retour

return trip *n* retour *m*

reunification /ˌriːjuːnɪfɪˈkeɪʃn/ *n* réunification *f*

reunion /ˌriːˈjuːnɪən/ *n* réunion *f*

reunite /ˌriːjuːˈnaɪt/ *vt* réunir ‹*family*›; réunifier ‹*party*›

reuse /ˌriːˈjuːz/ *vt* réutiliser

rev /rev/ *vt* (fam) (*p prés etc* **-vv-** *also* **~ up**) monter le régime de ‹*engine*›

revalue /ˌriːˈvæljuː/ *vt* réévaluer

revamp /ˌriːˈvæmp/ *vt* rajeunir ‹*image*›; réorganiser ‹*company*›; retaper (fam) ‹*building*›

⚷ **reveal** /rɪˈviːl/ *vt* (gen) révéler; dévoiler ‹*truth, plan*›; **to ~ sth to sb** révéler qch à qn

revealing /rɪˈviːlɪŋ/ *adj* **1** ‹*remark*› révélateur/-trice
2 ‹*blouse*› décolleté/-e

revel /ˈrevl/ *vi* (*p prés etc* **-ll-** (BrE), **-l-** (AmE)) **to ~ in sth/in doing** se délecter de qch/à faire

revelation /ˌrevəˈleɪʃn/ *n* révélation *f*

revenge /rɪˈvendʒ/ **A** *n* vengeance *f*; **to get one's ~** se venger (**for** de, **on** sur)
B *v refl* **to ~ oneself** se venger

r ⚷ **revenue** /ˈrevənjuː, (AmE) -ənuː/ *n* revenus *mpl*

reverberate /rɪˈvɜːbəreɪt/ *vi* résonner (**with** de, **through** dans, par); (fig) se propager

revere /rɪˈvɪə(r)/ *vt* révérer

reverence /ˈrevərəns/ *n* profond respect *m*

Reverend /ˈrevərənd/ *n* **1** (Protestant) pasteur *m*
2 (as title) **the ~ Jones** le révérend Jones; **~ Mother** Révérende Mère

reverent /ˈrevərənt/ *adj* ‹*hush*› religieux/-ieuse; ‹*expression*› de respect

reverie /ˈrevərɪ/ *n* rêverie *f*

reversal /rɪˈvɜːsl/ *n* (of policy, roles) renversement *m*; (of order, trend) inversion *f*; (of fortune) revers *m*

reverse /rɪˈvɜːs/ **A** *n* **1** (opposite) **the ~** le contraire
2 (back) **the ~** (of coin) le revers; (of banknote) le verso; (of fabric) l'envers *m*
3 (Aut) (*also* **~ gear**) marche *f* arrière
B *adj* **1** ‹*effect*› contraire; **in ~ order** ‹*answer questions*› en commençant par le dernier/la dernière; ‹*list*› en commençant par la fin
2 (Aut) **~ gear** marche *f* arrière
C *vt* inverser ‹*trend, process*›; renverser ‹*roles*›; faire rouler [qch] en marche arrière ‹*car*›; **to ~ the charges** (BrE) appeler en PCV
D *vi* ‹*driver*› faire marche arrière
E **in reverse** *phr* en sens inverse

reverse charge call *n* (BrE) appel *m* en PCV

reversible /rɪˈvɜːsəbl/ *adj* réversible

revert /rɪˈvɜːt/ *vi* **to ~ to** reprendre ‹*habit, name*›; redevenir ‹*wilderness*›

⚷ **review** /rɪˈvjuː/ **A** *n* **1** (reconsideration) révision *f* (**of** de); (report) rapport *m* (**of** sur)
2 (of book, film) critique *f* (**of** de)
3 (magazine) revue *f*
4 (Mil) revue *f*
5 (AmE) (Sch, Univ) révision *f*
B *vt* **1** reconsidérer ‹*situation*›; réviser ‹*attitude, policy*›; passer [qch] en revue ‹*troops*›
2 faire la critique de ‹*book, film*›
3 (AmE) (Sch, Univ) réviser

reviewer /rɪˈvjuːə(r)/ *n* critique *m*

revise /rɪˈvaɪz/ **A** *vt* **1** (alter) réviser, modifier ‹*estimate, figures*›; **to ~ one's opinion of sb/sth** réviser son jugement sur qn/qch
2 (BrE) (for exam) réviser ‹*subject*›
3 (correct) revoir, réviser ‹*text*›
B *vi* (BrE) ‹*student*› réviser

revision /rɪˈvɪʒn/ *n* révision *f*

revitalize /riːˈvaɪtəlaɪz/ *vt* revitaliser

revival /rɪˈvaɪvl/ *n* (of economy) reprise *f*; (of interest) regain *m*; (of custom, language) renouveau *m*

revive /rɪˈvaɪv/ **A** *vt* **1** ranimer ‹*person*›
2 raviver ‹*custom*›; ranimer ‹*interest, hopes*›; relancer ‹*movement, fashion*›; revigorer ‹*economy*›
B *vi* **1** ‹*person*› reprendre connaissance
2 ‹*economy*› reprendre

revoke /rɪˈvəʊk/ *vt* révoquer ‹*will*›; annuler ‹*decision*›

revolt /rɪˈvəʊlt/ **A** *n* révolte *f* (**against** contre)
B *vt* dégoûter, révolter
C *vi* se révolter (**against** contre)

revolting /rɪˈvəʊltɪŋ/ *adj* **1** (physically) répugnant/-e; (morally) révoltant/-e
2 (fam) ‹*food*› infect/-e; ‹*person*› affreux/-euse

revolution /ˌrevəˈluːʃn/ *n* **1** révolution *f* (**in** dans)
2 (Aut, Tech) tour *m*

revolutionary /ˌrevəˈluːʃənərɪ, (AmE) -nerɪ/ *n, adj* révolutionnaire *mf*

revolutionize /ˌrevəˈluːʃənaɪz/ *vt* révolutionner

⚷ mot clé

revolve /rɪ'vɒlv/ *vi* **1** (turn) tourner (**around** autour de)
2 to ~ around (be focused on) être axé/-e sur

revolving /rɪ'vɒlvɪŋ/ *adj* ‹*chair*› pivotant/-e; ‹*stage*› tournant/-e; **~ door** porte *f* à tambour

revue /rɪ'vju:/ *n* revue *f*

revulsion /rɪ'vʌlʃn/ *n* dégoût *m*

reward /rɪ'wɔ:d/ **A** *n* récompense *f*; **a £50 ~** 50 livres sterling de récompense
B *vt* récompenser (**for** de, pour)

rewarding /rɪ'wɔ:dɪŋ/ *adj* ‹*experience*› enrichissant/-e; ‹*job*› gratifiant/-e

rewind /ˌri:'waɪnd/ *vt* (*prét*, *pp* **rewound**) rembobiner ‹*tape, film*›

rewind button *n* bouton *m* de retour en arrière

rewire /ˌri:'waɪə(r)/ *vt* refaire l'installation électrique de ‹*building*›

reword /ˌri:'wɜ:d/ *vt* reformuler

rework /ˌri:'wɜ:k/ *vt* retravailler ‹*theme, metal*›

rewrite /ˌri:'raɪt/ *vt* (*prét* **rewrote**, *pp* **rewritten**) ré(é)crire ‹*story, history*›

rhapsody /'ræpsədɪ/ *n* rhapsodie *f*

rhetoric /'retərɪk/ *n* rhétorique *f*

rhetorical /rɪ'tɒrɪkl, (AmE) -'tɔ:r-/ *adj* rhétorique

rheumatism /'ru:mətɪzəm/ *n* rhumatisme *m*

Rhine /raɪn/ *pr n* Rhin *m*

rhinoceros /raɪ'nɒsərəs/ *n* (*pl* **-eroses**, **-eri** *ou* **~**) rhinocéros *m*

rhubarb /'ru:bɑ:b/ *n* rhubarbe *f*

rhyme /raɪm/ **A** *n* **1** (gen) rime *f*
2 (poem) vers *mpl*; (children's) comptine *f*
B *vi* rimer (**with** avec)

rhythm /'rɪðəm/ *n* rythme *m*

rhythmic /'rɪðmɪk(l)/ *adj* (*also* **rhythmical**) rythmique

rib /rɪb/ *n* **1** (Anat, Culin) côte *f*
2 (in umbrella) baleine *f*; (in plane, building) nervure *f*

ribbon /'rɪbən/ *n* ruban *m*

rib cage *n* cage *f* thoracique

rice /raɪs/ *n* riz *m*

rich /rɪtʃ/ **A** *n* **the ~** les riches *mpl*
B *adj* riche; **to grow** *or* **get ~** s'enrichir; **to make sb ~** enrichir qn

riches *npl* richesses *fpl*

richness /'rɪtʃnɪs/ *n* richesse *f*

rickety /'rɪkətɪ/ *adj* branlant/-e

rickshaw /'rɪkʃɔ:/ *n* pousse-pousse *m inv*

ricochet /'rɪkəʃeɪ, (AmE) ˌrɪkə'ʃeɪ/ *vi* (*prét*, *pp* **ricocheted**, **ricochetted** /-ʃeɪd/) ricocher (**off** sur)

rid /rɪd/ **A** *vt* (*p prés* **-dd-**, *prét*, *pp* **rid**) **to ~ sb/sth of** débarrasser qn/qch de
B *pp adj* **to get ~ of** se débarrasser de ‹*old car, guests*›; éliminer ‹*poverty*›

riddance /'rɪdns/ *n*
IDIOM **good ~ (to bad rubbish)!** bon débarras! (fam)

riddle /'rɪdl/ **A** *n* **1** (puzzle) devinette *f*
2 (mystery) énigme *f*
B *vt* **to be ~d with** être criblé/-e de ‹*bullets*›; être rongé/-e par ‹*disease, guilt*›

ride /raɪd/ **A** *n* **1** (in vehicle, on bike) trajet *m* (**in, on** en, à); (for pleasure) tour *m*, promenade *f*; **to go for a ~** aller faire un tour; **to give sb a ~** (AmE) emmener qn (en voiture)
2 (on horse) promenade *f* à cheval
B *vt* (*prét* **rode**, *pp* **ridden**) **1** rouler à ‹*bike*›; **to ~ a horse** monter à cheval; **can you ~ a bike?** sais-tu faire du vélo?
2 (AmE) prendre ‹*bus, subway*›; parcourir ‹*range*›
3 chevaucher ‹*wave*›
C *vi* (*prét* **rode**, *pp* **ridden**) (go horse-riding) faire du cheval; **to ~ in** *or* **on** (AmE) prendre ‹*bus*›
IDIOM **to take sb for a ~** rouler qn (fam)
■ **ride out** surmonter ‹*crisis*›; survivre à ‹*recession*›; **to ~ out the storm** surmonter la crise
■ **ride up 1** ‹*rider*› s'approcher (**to** de)
2 ‹*skirt*› remonter

rider /'raɪdə(r)/ *n* **1** (on horse) cavalier/-ière *m/f*; (on motorbike) motocycliste *mf*; (on bike) cycliste *mf*
2 (to document) annexe *f*

ridge /rɪdʒ/ *n* **1** (along mountain top) arête *f*, crête *f*
2 (on rock, metal surface) strie *f*; (in ploughed land) crête *f*
3 (on roof) faîte *m*, faîtage *m*

ridicule /'rɪdɪkju:l/ **A** *n* ridicule *m*
B *vt* tourner [qn/qch] en ridicule

ridiculous /rɪ'dɪkjʊləs/ *adj* ridicule

riding /'raɪdɪŋ/ *n* équitation *f*; **to go ~** faire de l'équitation

riding school *n* centre *m* équestre

rife /raɪf/ *adj* **to be ~** être répandu/-e

riff-raff /'rɪfræf/ *n* populace *f*

rifle /'raɪfl/ **A** *n* (firearm) fusil *m*
B *vt* vider ‹*wallet, safe*›
■ **rifle through** fouiller dans

rift /rɪft/ *n* **1** (disagreement) désaccord *m*; (permanent) rupture *f*
2 (in rock) fissure *f*; (in clouds) trouée *f*

rig /rɪg/ **A** *n* (for oil) (on land) tour *f* de forage; (offshore) plate-forme *f* pétrolière offshore
B *vt* (*p prés etc* **-gg-**) truquer ‹*election, result*›
■ **rig up** installer ‹*equipment*›; improviser ‹*clothes line, shelter*›

rigging /'rɪgɪŋ/ *n* **1** (on ship) gréement *m*
2 (of election, competition, result) truquage *m*

right /raɪt/ **A** *n* **1** (side, direction) droite *f*; **on** *or* **to your ~** à votre droite
2 (in politics) (*also* **Right**) **the ~** la droite
3 (morally) bien *m*; **~ and wrong** le bien et le mal
4 (just claim) droit *m*; **to have a ~ to sth** avoir

r

droit à qch; **civil ~s** droits civils
B *adj* **1** (not left) droit/-e, de droite
2 (morally) bien; **it is only ~ and proper** ce n'est que justice; **to do the ~ thing** faire ce qu'il faut
3 (correct) ‹*choice, direction, size, answer*› bon/bonne *before n*; ‹*word*› juste; ‹*time*› exact/-e; **to be ~** ‹*person*› avoir raison; ‹*answer*› être juste
4 (suitable) qui convient; **the ~ person for the job** la personne qu'il faut pour le poste; **to be in the ~ place at the ~ time** être là où il faut au bon moment
5 (in good order) **the engine isn't quite ~** le moteur ne fonctionne pas très bien; **I don't feel quite ~ these days** je ne me sens pas très bien ces jours-ci
6 to put *or* **set ~** corriger ‹*mistake*›; réparer ‹*injustice*›; arranger ‹*situation*›; réparer ‹*machine*›
7 ‹*angle*› droit/-e; **at ~ angles to** à angle droit avec, perpendiculaire à
C *adv* **1** (not left) à droite; **to turn/look ~** tourner/regarder à droite
2 (directly) droit, directement; **it's ~ in front of you** c'est droit *or* juste devant toi; **I'll be ~ back** je reviens tout de suite
3 (exactly) **~ in the middle of the room** en plein milieu de la pièce; **~ now** (immediately) tout de suite; (AmE) (at this point in time) en ce moment
4 (correctly) juste, comme il faut; **you're not doing it ~** tu ne fais pas ça comme il faut; **to guess ~** deviner juste
5 (completely) tout; **go ~ back to the beginning** revenez tout au début; **~ at the bottom** tout au fond; **to turn the central heating ~ up** mettre le chauffage central à fond
6 (very well) bon; **~, let's have a look** bon, voyons ça
D *vt* redresser
(IDIOM) **by ~s** normalement, en principe

r

right angle *n* angle *m* droit
right away *adv* tout de suite
righteous /ˈraɪtʃəs/ *adj* vertueux/-euse
rightful /ˈraɪtfl/ *adj* légitime
right-hand /ˈraɪthænd/ *adj* du côté droit; **on the ~ side** sur la droite
right-hand drive *n* conduite *f* à droite
right-handed *adv* ‹*person*› droitier/-ière; ‹*blow*› du droit
right-hand man *n* bras *m* droit
rightly /ˈraɪtlɪ/ *adv* **1** (accurately) correctement
2 (justifiably) à juste titre; **~ or wrongly** à tort ou à raison
3 (with certainty) au juste; **I don't ~ know** je ne sais pas au juste
right-of-centre *adj* (Pol) centre-droite *inv*
right of way *n* **1** (Aut) priorité *f*
2 (over land) droit *m* de passage; **'no ~'** 'entrée *f* interdite'
right-on /ˌraɪtˈɒn/ *adj* (fam) **they're very ~** ils s'appliquent à être idéologiquement corrects sur tout
right-thinking *adj* bien-pensant/-e
right wing A *n* **the ~** la droite
B right-wing *adj* ‹*attitude*› de droite; **they are very ~** ils sont très à droite
rigid /ˈrɪdʒɪd/ *adj* ‹*rules, person, material*› rigide; ‹*controls, timetable*› strict/-e
rigidly /ˈrɪdʒɪdlɪ/ *adv* ‹*oppose*› fermement; ‹*control*› rigoureusement; ‹*stick to, apply*› strictement
rigorous /ˈrɪgərəs/ *adj* rigoureux/-euse
rigour (BrE), **rigor** (AmE) /ˈrɪgə(r)/ *n* rigueur *f*
rim /rɪm/ *n* bord *m*; (on wheel) jante *f*
rind /raɪnd/ *n* **1** (on cheese) croûte *f*; (on bacon) couenne *f*
2 (on fruit) peau *f*
✓ **ring** /rɪŋ/ **A** *n* **1** anneau *m*; (with stone) bague *f*; **a diamond ~** une bague de diamants; **a wedding ~** une alliance
2 (circle) cercle *m*; **to have ~s under one's eyes** avoir les yeux cernés
3 (at door) coup *m* de sonnette; (of phone) sonnerie *f*
4 (in circus) piste *f*; (in boxing) ring *m*
5 (of smugglers, spies) réseau *m*
6 (on cooker) (electric) plaque *f*; (gas) brûleur *m*
B *vt* (*prét* **rang**, *pp* **rung**) **1** sonner ‹*church bells*›; **to ~ the doorbell** *or* **bell** sonner
2 (BrE) (*also* **~ up**) appeler
C *vi* (*prét* **rang**, *pp* **rung**) **1** ‹*bell, phone, person*› sonner; **the doorbell rang** on a sonné à la porte
2 ‹*footsteps, laughter*› résonner; **to ~ true** sonner vrai
3 (BrE) (phone) téléphoner; **to ~ for** appeler ‹*taxi*›
▪ **ring off** (BrE) raccrocher
▪ **ring out** ‹*voice, cry*› retentir; ‹*bells*› sonner
ring binder *n* classeur *m* à anneaux
ringing /ˈrɪŋɪŋ/ *n* **1** (of bell, alarm) sonnerie *f*
2 (in ears) bourdonnement *m*
ringleader *n* meneur/-euse *m/f*
ringlet /ˈrɪŋlɪt/ *n* anglaise *f*
ring road /ˈrɪŋrəʊd/ *n* (BrE) périphérique *m*
ringtone *n* sonnerie *f*
rinse /rɪns/ **A** *n* rinçage *m*
B *vt* rincer; (wash) laver
riot /ˈraɪət/ **A** *n* **1** émeute *f*, révolte *f*; **prison ~** mutinerie *f*
2 a ~ of une profusion de ‹*colours*›
B *vi* ‹*crowd, demonstrators*› se soulever; ‹*prisoners*› se mutiner
(IDIOM) **to run ~** ‹*crowd*› se déchaîner; ‹*imagination*› se débrider; ‹*plant*› proliférer
rioter /ˈraɪətə(r)/ *n* émeutier/-ière *m/f*; (in prison) mutin *m*

✓ mot clé

riot gear *n* tenue *f* antiémeutes

rioting /'raɪətɪŋ/ *n* émeutes *fpl*, bagarres *fpl*

riot police *n* forces *fpl* antiémeutes

rip /rɪp/ **A** *vt* (*p prés etc* **-pp-**) déchirer; **to ~ sth out** arracher qch
B *vi* (*p prés etc* **-pp-**) ‹*fabric*› se déchirer
■ **rip off** **A** **~ off [sth], ~ [sth] off** **1** arracher ‹*garment, roof*›
2 (fam) (steal) rafler (fam) ‹*idea, design*›
B **~ [sb] off** arnaquer (pop)
■ **rip through**: **~ through [sth]** ‹*bomb blast*› défoncer ‹*building*›

RIP (*abbr* = **rest in peace**) qu'il/elle repose en paix

ripe /raɪp/ *adj* ‹*fruit*› mûr/-e; ‹*cheese*› fait/-e

ripen /'raɪpən/ **A** *vt* mûrir ‹*fruit*›; affiner ‹*cheese*›
B *vi* ‹*fruit*› mûrir; ‹*cheese*› se faire

rip-off *n* (fam) arnaque *f* (pop)

ripple /'rɪpl/ **A** *n* ondulation *f*
B *vi* **1** ‹*water*› se rider; (making noise) clapoter
2 ‹*hair, corn*› onduler; ‹*muscles*› saillir

rise /raɪz/ **A** *n* **1** (increase) augmentation *f* (**in** de); (in prices, pressure) hausse *f* (**in** de); (in temperature) élévation *f* (**in** de)
2 (of person) ascension *f*; (of empire) essor *m*
3 (slope) montée *f*
B *vi* (*prét* **rose**, *pp* **risen**) **1** ‹*water, tension*› monter; ‹*price, temperature*› augmenter; ‹*voice*› devenir plus fort/-e; ‹*hopes*› grandir
2 (get up) ‹*person*› se lever; **to ~ from the dead** ressusciter; **to ~ to the occasion** se montrer à la hauteur
3 ‹*road*› monter; ‹*cliff*› s'élever
4 ‹*sun, moon*› se lever
5 ‹*dough*› lever
IDIOM **to give ~ to** donner lieu à ‹*rumours*›; causer ‹*problem*›

rising /'raɪzɪŋ/ **A** *n* soulèvement *m*
B *adj* (gen) en hausse; ‹*tension*› grandissant/-e; ‹*sun, moon*› levant/-e

risk /rɪsk/ **A** *n* risque *m*; **to run a ~** courir un risque; **to take ~s** prendre des risques; **at ~** menacé/-e
B *vt* risquer; **to ~ doing** courir le risque de faire

risky /'rɪskɪ/ *adj* ‹*decision, undertaking*› risqué/-e; ‹*share, investment*› à risques

risqué /'ri:skeɪ, (AmE) rɪ'skeɪ/ *adj* osé/-e

rite /raɪt/ *n* rite *m*

ritual /'rɪtʃʊəl/ **A** *n* rituel *m*, rites *mpl*
B *adj* rituel/-elle

rival /'raɪvl/ **A** *n* (person) rival/-e *m/f*; (company) concurrent/-e *m/f*
B *adj* ‹*team, business*› rival/-e; ‹*claim*› opposé/-e
C *vt* (*p prés etc* **-ll-** (BrE), **-l-** (AmE)) rivaliser avec (**in** de)

rivalry /'raɪvlrɪ/ *n* rivalité *f* (**between** entre)

river /'rɪvə(r)/ *n* (flowing into sea) fleuve *m*; (tributary) rivière *f*

riverbank /'rɪvəbæŋk/ *n* berge *f*; **along the ~** le long de la rivière

riverside /'rɪvəsaɪd/ **A** *n* berges *fpl*
B *adj* ‹*pub*› au bord de la rivière

rivet /'rɪvɪt/ **A** *n* rivet *m*
B *vt* **1** (Tech) riveter
2 to be ~ed by être captivé/-e par; **to be ~ed to the spot** être cloué/-e sur place

riveting /'rɪvɪtɪŋ/ *adj* fascinant/-e

Riviera /ˌrɪvɪ'eərə/ *n* **the Italian ~** la Riviera; **the French ~** la Côte d'Azur

road /rəʊd/ *n* **1** route *f*; **the ~ to Leeds** la route de Leeds
2 (street) rue *f*
3 (fig) voie *f* (**to** de); **to be on the right ~** être sur la bonne voie

roadblock /'rəʊdblɒk/ *n* barrage *m* routier

road hump *n* ralentisseur *m*

road rage *n* violence *f* au volant

roadshow /'rəʊdʃəʊ/ *n* (play, show) spectacle *m* de tournée; (publicity tour) tour *m* promotionnel

roadside /'rəʊdsaɪd/ *n* bord *m* de la route

road sign *n* panneau *m* de signalisation

road tax disc *n* (BrE) vignette *f*

roadworks *npl* travaux *mpl* (routiers)

roadworthy *adj* en état de rouler

roam /rəʊm/ *vt* parcourir ‹*countryside*›; faire le tour de ‹*shops*›; traîner dans ‹*streets*›
■ **roam around** ‹*person*› vadrouiller (fam)

roaming /'rəʊmɪŋ/ *n* (mobile phone) itinérance *f*

roar /rɔ:(r)/ **A** *n* (of lion) rugissement *m*; (of person) hurlement *m*; (of engine) vrombissement *m*; (of traffic) grondement *m*; **a ~ of laughter** un éclat de rire
B *vi* ‹*lion*› rugir; ‹*person*› hurler; ‹*sea, wind*› mugir; ‹*fire*› ronfler; ‹*engine*› vrombir

roaring /'rɔ:rɪŋ/ *adj* **1** ‹*engine, traffic*› grondant/-e; **a ~ fire** une belle flambée
2 ‹*success*› fou/folle

roast /rəʊst/ **A** *n* (Culin) rôti *m*; (AmE) barbecue *m*
B *adj* ‹*meat, potatoes*› rôti/-e; **~ beef** rôti *m* de bœuf, rosbif *m*
C *vt* rôtir ‹*meat, potatoes*›; (faire) griller ‹*chestnuts*›; torréfier ‹*coffee beans*›

rob /rɒb/ *vt* (*p prés etc* **-bb-**) voler ‹*person*›; dévaliser ‹*bank, train*›; **to ~ sb of sth** voler qch à qn; (fig) priver qn de qch

robber /'rɒbə(r)/ *n* voleur/-euse *m/f*

robbery /'rɒbərɪ/ *n* vol *m*

robe /rəʊb/ *n* **1** (ceremonial garment) robe *f*
2 (AmE) (bath robe) peignoir *m*

robin /'rɒbɪn/ *n* (*also* **~ redbreast**) rouge-gorge *m*

robot /'rəʊbɒt/ *n* robot *m*

r

robust /rəʊ'bʌst/ *adj* robuste

rock /rɒk/ **A** *n* **1** (substance) roche *f*; **solid ~** roche dure
2 (boulder) rocher *m*
3 (*also* **~ music**) rock *m*
B *vt* **1** balancer ‹*cradle*›; bercer ‹*baby, boat*›
2 ‹*tremor*› secouer ‹*town*›; ‹*scandal*› ébranler ‹*government*›
C *vi* ‹*person*› se balancer; **to ~ back and forth** se balancer d'avant en arrière
IDIOMS **on the ~s** ‹*drink*› avec des glaçons; **to be on the ~s** ‹*marriage*› aller à vau-l'eau

rock and roll /ˌrɒkən'rəʊl/ *n* (*also* **rock 'n' roll**) rock and roll *m*

rock bottom /ˌrɒk'bɒtəm/ *n* **to hit ~** toucher le fond

rock climber *n* varappeur/-euse *m/f*

rock climbing *n* varappe *f*

rockery /'rɒkərɪ/ *n* (BrE) rocaille *f*

rocket /'rɒkɪt/ **A** *n* **1** (gen), (Mil) fusée *f*
2 (salad) roquette *f*
B *vi* ‹*price, profit*› monter en flèche

rock face *n* paroi *f* rocheuse

rockfall *n* chute *f* de pierres

rocking chair *n* fauteuil *m* à bascule

rocking horse *n* cheval *m* à bascule

rock star *n* rock-star *f*

rocky /'rɒkɪ/ *adj* **1** ‹*beach, path, road*› rocailleux/-euse; ‹*coast*› rocheux/-euse
2 ‹*relationship, period*› difficile; ‹*business*› précaire

Rocky Mountains *pr n pl* (*also* **Rockies**) **the ~** les montagnes *fpl* Rocheuses

rod /rɒd/ *n* **1** (gen), (Tech) tige *f*; **curtain/stair ~** tringle *f* à rideaux/de marche
2 (for punishment) baguette *f*
3 (for fishing) canne *f* à pêche

rodent /'rəʊdnt/ *n* rongeur *m*

roe /rəʊ/ *n* œufs *mpl* (de poisson)

roe deer /ˌrəʊ'dɪə(r)/ *n* (male) chevreuil *m*; (female) chevrette *f*

rogue /rəʊg/ *n* **1** (rascal) coquin *m*
2 (animal) solitaire *m*

role /rəʊl/ *n* rôle *m* (**of** de); **title ~** rôle-titre *m*

role model *n* modèle *m*

role-play /'rəʊlpleɪ/ *n* (Sch) jeu *m* de rôle; (for therapy) psychodrame *m*

roll /rəʊl/ **A** *n* **1** (of paper, cloth) rouleau *m*; (of banknotes) liasse *f*; (of flesh) bourrelet *m*; **a ~ of film** une pellicule
2 (bread) petit pain *m*; **cheese ~** sandwich *m* au fromage
3 (of dice) lancer *m*
4 (register) liste *f*; **to call the ~** faire l'appel
B *vt* **1** (gen) rouler; faire rouler ‹*dice*›; **to ~ [sth] into a ball** faire une boulette de ‹*paper*›; faire une boule de ‹*clay, dough*›
2 étirer ‹*dough*›
C *vi* **1** ‹*person, animal*› rouler (**onto** sur); ‹*car, plane*› faire un tonneau; ‹*ship*› tanguer
2 ‹*thunder*› gronder; ‹*drum*› rouler
3 ‹*camera, press*› tourner
■ **roll about** (BrE), **roll around** ‹*animal, person*› se rouler; ‹*marbles, tins*› rouler
■ **roll down** baisser ‹*blind, sleeve*›
■ **roll over** se retourner
■ **roll up** enrouler ‹*rug, poster*›; **to ~ up one's sleeves** retrousser ses manches

roller /'rəʊlə(r)/ *n* **1** (gen) rouleau *m*
2 (curler) bigoudi *m*

rollerblade /'rəʊləbleɪd/ **A** *n* patin *m* en ligne; roller *m*
B *vi* faire du patin en ligne; roller

roller blind *n* store *m*

roller coaster *n* montagnes *fpl* russes

roller-skate /'rəʊləskeɪt/ *n* patin *m* à roulettes

roller-skating /'rəʊləskeɪtɪŋ/ *n* patinage *m* à roulettes; **to go ~** faire du patin à roulettes

rolling pin *n* rouleau *m* à pâtisserie

roll-neck *n* col *m* roulé

ROM /rɒm/ *n* (*abbr* = **read-only memory**) ROM *f*, mémoire *f* morte

Roman /'rəʊmən/ **A** *n* Romain/-e *m/f*
B *adj* romain/-e

Roman Catholic *n*, *adj* catholique *mf*

romance /rəʊ'mæns/ *n* **1** (of era, place) charme *m*; (of travel) côté *m* romantique
2 (love affair) histoire *f* d'amour; (love) amour *m*
3 (novel) roman *m* d'amour; (film) film *m* d'amour

Romania /rəʊ'meɪnɪə/ *pr n* Roumanie *f*

Romanian /rəʊ'meɪnɪən/ **A** *n* **1** (person) Roumain/-e *m/f*
2 (language) roumain *m*
B *adj* roumain/-e

romantic /rəʊ'mæntɪk/ **A** *n* romantique *mf*
B *adj* **1** ‹*setting, story, person*› romantique
2 ‹*attachment*› sentimental/-e
3 ‹*novel, film*› d'amour

romantic fiction *n* (genre) romans *mpl* d'amour

romanticize /rəʊ'mæntɪsaɪz/ *vt* idéaliser

Romany /'rɒmənɪ/ *n* Tzigane *mf*, Romani *mf*

romp /rɒmp/ **A** *n* ébats *mpl*
B *vi* s'ébattre

rompers /'rɒmpəz/ *npl* (*also* **romper suit**) barboteuse *f*

roof /ru:f/ *n* **1** (on building) toit *m*
2 (Anat) **the ~ of the mouth** la voûte du palais
IDIOM **to go through** *or* **hit the ~** ‹*person*› sauter au plafond (fam); ‹*prices*› battre tous les records

roof rack *n* galerie *f*

rooftop /'ru:ftɒp/ *n* toit *m*

rook /rʊk/ *n* **1** (bird) (corbeau *m*) freux *m*
2 (in chess) tour *f*

room /ru:m, rʊm/ **A** *n* **1** pièce *f*; (bedroom)

chambre *f*; (for working) bureau *m*; (for meetings, teaching, operating) salle *f*
2 (space) place *f*; **to make ~** faire de la place
B *vi* (AmE) loger (**with** chez)

room-mate /ˈruːmmeɪt/ *n* **1** (in same room) camarade *mf* de chambre
2 (AmE) (flatmate) compagnon/compagne *m/f* d'appartement

room service *n* service *m* de chambre

room temperature *n* température *f* ambiante; **at ~** ‹*wine*› chambré/-e

roomy /ˈruːmɪ/ *adj* ‹*car, house*› spacieux/-ieuse; ‹*garment*› ample; ‹*bag, cupboard*› grand/-e *before n*

roost /ruːst/ **A** *n* perchoir *m*
B *vi* (in trees) percher (pour la nuit); (in attic) se nicher
IDIOM **to rule the ~** faire la loi

rooster /ˈruːstə(r)/ *n* coq *m*

root /ruːt/ **A** *n* **1** racine *f*; **to take ~** ‹*plant*› prendre racine; ‹*idea, value*› s'établir; ‹*industry*› s'implanter
2 (of problem) fond *m*; (of evil) origine *f*
B *vt* **to be ~ed in** être ancré/-e dans; **deeply-~ed** bien enraciné/-e; **~ed to the spot** figé/-e sur place
■ **root around**, **root about** fouiller (**in** dans)
■ **root out** traquer ‹*corruption*›; déloger ‹*person*›

rootless /ˈruːtlɪs/ *adj* sans racines

rope /rəʊp/ **A** *n* (gen), (Sport) corde *f*; (of pearls) rang *m*
B *vt* attacher ‹*victim, animal*› (**to** à); encorder ‹*climber*›
IDIOM **to know the ~s** connaître les ficelles (fam)
■ **rope in** (fam): **~ [sb] in**, **~ in [sb]** (to help with task) embaucher (fam)

rope ladder *n* échelle *f* de corde

rosary /ˈrəʊzərɪ/ *n* (prayer) rosaire *m*; (beads) chapelet *m*

rose /rəʊz/ *n* rose *f*

rosebud /ˈrəʊzbʌd/ *n* bouton *m* de rose

rose bush *n* rosier *m*

rosemary /ˈrəʊzmərɪ, (AmE) -merɪ/ *n* romarin *m*

rose-tinted *adj*
IDIOM **to see the world through ~ spectacles** voir la vie en rose

rosette /rəʊˈzet/ *n* (for winner) cocarde *f*

roster /ˈrɒstə(r)/ *n* (*also* **duty ~**) tableau *m* de service

rostrum /ˈrɒstrəm/ *n* (*pl* **-trums** *ou* **-tra**) estrade *f*

rosy /ˈrəʊzɪ/ *adj* ‹*cheek, light*› rose; **to paint a ~ picture** peindre un tableau favorable

rot /rɒt/ **A** *n* pourriture *f*
B *vt* (*p prés etc* **-tt-**) pourrir
C *vi* (*p prés etc* **-tt-**) (*also* **~ away**) pourrir

rota /ˈrəʊtə/ *n* (BrE) tableau *m* de service

rotary /ˈrəʊtərɪ/ *adj* rotatif/-ive

rotate /rəʊˈteɪt, (AmE) ˈrəʊteɪt/ **A** *vt* faire tourner ‹*blade*›
B *vi* ‹*blade, handle, wings*› tourner

rotation /rəʊˈteɪʃn/ *n* rotation *f*

rote /rəʊt/ *n* **by ~** par cœur

rotten /ˈrɒtn/ *adj* **1** ‹*produce*› pourri/-e; ‹*teeth*› gâté/-e; ‹*smell*› de pourriture
2 (corrupt) pourri/-e (fam)
3 (fam) (bad) ‹*weather*› pourri/-e; ‹*cook, driver*› exécrable

rouble /ˈruːbl/ *n* rouble *m*

rough /rʌf/ **A** *adj* **1** ‹*material*› rêche; ‹*hand, skin, surface, rock*› rugueux/-euse; ‹*terrain*› cahoteux/-euse
2 ‹*person, behaviour, sport*› brutal/-e, violent/-e; ‹*landing*› brutal/-e; ‹*area*› dur/-e
3 ‹*description, map*› sommaire; ‹*figure, idea, estimate*› approximatif/-ive
4 (difficult) dur, difficile; **a ~ time** une période difficile
5 (crude) grossier/-ière
6 (harsh) ‹*voice, taste, wine*› âpre
7 (stormy) ‹*sea, crossing*› agité/-e
B *adv* **to sleep ~** dormir à la dure
IDIOM **to ~ it** vivre à la dure

roughage /ˈrʌfɪdʒ/ *n* fibres *fpl*

rough-and-ready /ˌrʌfənˈredɪ/ *adj* ‹*person, manner*› fruste; ‹*conditions*› rudimentaire; ‹*method, system*› sommaire

roughen /ˈrʌfn/ *vt* rendre [qch] rêche *or* rugueux

roughly /ˈrʌflɪ/ *adv* **1** ‹*calculate*› grossièrement; **~ speaking** en gros; **~ 10%** à peu près 10%
2 ‹*treat, hit*› brutalement
3 ‹*make*› grossièrement

rough paper *n* feuille *f* de brouillon

roulette /ruːˈlet/ *n* roulette *f*

round /raʊnd/ **A** *adv* (BrE) **1 all ~** tout autour; **whisky all ~!** du whisky pour tout le monde!; **to go all the way ~** faire tout le tour; **to go ~ and ~** tourner en rond
2 (to place, home) **to go ~ to sb's house** passer chez qn; **to ask sb ~** dire à qn de passer à la maison; **to invite sb ~ for lunch** inviter qn à déjeuner (chez soi)
3 all year ~ toute l'année; **this time ~** cette fois-ci
B *prep* (BrE) **1** autour de ‹*table*›; **to sit ~ the fire** s'asseoir au coin du feu
2 to go ~ the corner tourner au coin de la rue; **just ~ the corner** tout près; **to go ~ an obstacle** contourner un obstacle
3 her sister took us ~ Oxford sa sœur nous a fait visiter Oxford; **to go ~ the shops** faire les magasins
C *n* **1** (of competition) manche *f*; (of golf, cards) partie *f*; (in boxing) round *m*; (in showjumping) parcours *m*; (in election) tour *m*; (of talks) série *f*; **a ~ of drinks** une tournée; **a ~ of ammunition** une cartouche; **a ~ of applause** une salve d'applaudissements; **a ~ of toast** un toast

r

2 **to do one's ~s** ‹*postman, milkman*› faire sa tournée; ‹*doctor*› visiter ses malades; ‹*guard*› faire sa ronde; **to go** *or* **do the ~s** ‹*rumour, flu*› circuler
3 (shape) rondelle *f*
D *adj* **1** rond/-e; **in ~ figures, that's £100** si on arrondit, ça fait 100 livres sterling; **a ~ dozen** une douzaine exactement
2 **to have ~ shoulders** avoir le dos voûté
E *vt* contourner ‹*headland*›; **to ~ the corner** tourner au coin; **to ~ a bend** prendre un virage
F **round about** *phr* **1** (approximately) à peu près, environ
2 (vicinity) **the people ~ about** les gens des environs
■ **round off** **1** finir ‹*meal, evening*› (**with** par); conclure ‹*speech*›
2 arrondir ‹*corner, figure*›
■ **round on**: **~ on [sb]** attaquer violemment; **she ~ed on me** elle m'est tombée dessus (fam)
■ **round up** **1** regrouper ‹*people*›; rassembler ‹*livestock*›
2 arrondir [qch] au chiffre supérieur ‹*figure*›

roundabout /ˈraʊndəbaʊt/ **A** *n* (BrE) (in fairground) manège *m*; (in playground) tourniquet *m*; (for traffic) rond-point *m*
B *adj* **to come by a ~ way** faire un détour; **by ~ means** par des moyens détournés; **a ~ way of saying** une façon détournée de dire

rounders /ˈraʊndəz/ *n* (BrE) ≈ baseball *m*

round-neck sweater *n* (*also* **round-necked sweater**) pull-over *m* ras-de-cou *inv*

round-the-clock *adj* 24 heures sur 24

round-the-world *adj* autour du monde

round trip *n* aller-retour *m*

roundup /ˈraʊndʌp/ *n* **1** (herding) rassemblement *m* (**of** de)
2 (by police) rafle *f*

rouse /raʊz/ *vt* réveiller ‹*person*›; susciter ‹*anger, interest*›

rousing /ˈraʊzɪŋ/ *adj* ‹*speech*› galvanisant/-e; ‹*music*› exaltant/-e

rout /raʊt/ **A** *n* déroute *f*, défaite *f*
B *vt* (Mil) mettre en déroute; (fig) battre à plates coutures

🔑 **route** /ruːt, (AmE) raʊt/ **A** *n* chemin *m*, itinéraire *m*; (in shipping) route *f*; (in aviation) ligne *f*; (fig) (to power) voie *f* (**to** de); **bus ~** ligne d'autobus
B *vt* expédier, acheminer ‹*goods*›

router /ˈruːtə(r), (AmE) ˈraʊtə(r)/ *n* (Comput) routeur *m*

routine /ruːˈtiːn/ **A** *n* **1** routine *f*
2 (act) numéro *m*
B *adj* **1** ‹*enquiry, matter*› de routine
2 (uninspiring) routinier/-ière

routinely /ruːˈtiːnlɪ/ *adv* **1** ‹*check, review*› systématiquement
2 ‹*tortured, abused*› régulièrement

routing number /ˈraʊtɪŋnʌmbər/ *n* (AmE) code *m* d'agence

🔑 **row¹** /rəʊ/ **A** *n* **1** (of people, plants, stitches) rang *m* (**of** de); (of houses, seats, books) rangée *f* (**of** de)
2 (succession) **six times in a ~** six fois de suite; **the third week in a ~** la troisième semaine d'affilée
B *vt* **to ~ a boat up the river** remonter la rivière à la rame
C *vi* (gen) ramer; (Sport) faire de l'aviron; **to ~ across** traverser [qch] à la rame ‹*lake*›

row² /raʊ/ **A** *n* **1** (quarrel) dispute *f* (**about** à propos de); (public) querelle *f*; **to have a ~ with** se disputer avec
2 (noise) tapage *m*
B *vi* se disputer (**with** avec, **about, over** à propos de)

rowboat *n* (AmE) bateau *m* à rames

rowdy /ˈraʊdɪ/ *adj* (noisy) tapageur/-euse; (in class) chahuteur/-euse

rowing /ˈrəʊɪŋ/ *n* aviron *m*

rowing boat *n* (BrE) bateau *m* à rames

🔑 **royal** /ˈrɔɪəl/ *adj* royal/-e

royal blue *n, adj* bleu *m* roi *inv*

Royal Highness *n* **His ~** Son Altesse *f* royale; **Your ~** Votre Altesse *f*

royalty /ˈrɔɪəltɪ/ *n* **1** (persons) membres *mpl* d'une famille royale
2 (to author, musician) droits *mpl* d'auteur; (on patent) royalties *fpl*

rub /rʌb/ **A** *n* **1** (massage) friction *f*
2 (polish) coup *m* de chiffon
B *vt* (*p prés etc* **-bb-**) se frotter ‹*chin, eyes*›; frotter ‹*stain, surface*›; frictionner ‹*sb's back*›; **to ~ sth into the skin** faire pénétrer qch dans la peau
C *vi* (*p prés etc* **-bb-**) frotter
(IDIOM) **to ~ sb up the wrong way** prendre qn à rebrousse-poil (fam)
■ **rub out** (erase) effacer
■ **rub in**: **~ [sth] in, ~ in [sth]** faire pénétrer ‹*lotion*›; **there's no need to ~ it in!** (fam) inutile d'en rajouter! (fam)

rubber /ˈrʌbə(r)/ **A** *n* **1** (substance) caoutchouc *m*
2 (BrE) (eraser) gomme *f*
B *adj* de *or* en caoutchouc

rubber band *n* élastique *m*

rubber glove *n* gant *m* en *or* de caoutchouc

rubber plant *n* caoutchouc *m*

rubber stamp *n* tampon *m*

rubber tree *n* hévéa *m*

rubbish /ˈrʌbɪʃ/ **A** *n* **1** (refuse) déchets *mpl*; (domestic) ordures *fpl*; (on site) gravats *mpl*
2 (inferior goods) camelote *f* (fam); **this book is ~!** (fam) ce livre est nul! (fam)
3 (nonsense) bêtises *fpl*

🔑 mot clé

B *vt* (BrE) descendre [qn/qch] en flammes

rubbish bin *n* (BrE) poubelle *f*

rubbish dump *n* (BrE) décharge *f* (publique)

rubbish heap *n* tas *m* d'ordures

rubble /'rʌbl/ *n* (after explosion) décombres *mpl*; (on site) gravats *mpl*

ruby /'ru:bɪ/ **A** *n* **1** (gem) rubis *m*
2 (*also* ~ **red**) rouge *m* rubis
B *adj* **1** ‹*liquid, lips*› vermeil/-eille; ~ **wedding** noces *fpl* de vermeil
2 ‹*bracelet, necklace*› de rubis

rucksack /'rʌksæk/ *n* sac *m* à dos

rudder /'rʌdə(r)/ *n* (on boat) gouvernail *m*; (on plane) gouverne *f*

ruddy /'rʌdɪ/ *adj* ‹*cheeks*› coloré/-e

rude /ru:d/ *adj* **1** (impolite) ‹*comment*› impoli/-e; ‹*person*› mal élevé/-e; **to be ~ to sb** être impoli/-e envers qn
2 (indecent) ‹*joke*› grossier/-ière; **a ~ word** un gros mot

rudimentary /ˌru:dɪ'mentrɪ/ *adj* rudimentaire

rudiments /'ru:dɪmənts/ *npl* rudiments *mpl* (**of** de)

rueful /'ru:fl/ *adj* ‹*smile, thought*› triste

ruff /rʌf/ *n* (of lace) fraise *f*; (of fur, feathers) collier *m*

ruffle /'rʌfl/ **A** *n* (at sleeve) manchette *f*; (at neck) ruche *f*; (on shirt front) jabot *m*
B *vt* **1** ébouriffer ‹*hair, fur*›; hérisser ‹*feathers*›; rider ‹*water*›
2 (disconcert) énerver; (upset) froisser

rug /rʌg/ *n* **1** tapis *m*; (by bed) descente *f* de lit
2 (BrE) (blanket) couverture *f*

rugby /'rʌgbɪ/ *n* rugby *m*

rugby league *n* rugby *m* à 13

rugby shirt *n* polo *m* rugby

rugby union *n* rugby *m* à 15

rugged /'rʌgɪd/ *adj* **1** ‹*landscape*› accidenté/-e; ‹*coastline*› déchiqueté/-e
2 ‹*man, features*› rude

ruin /'ru:ɪn/ **A** *n* ruine *f*
B *vt* **1** ruiner ‹*economy, career*›; **to ~ one's eyesight** s'abîmer la vue
2 gâcher ‹*holiday, meal*›; abîmer ‹*clothes*›
IDIOM **to go to rack and ~** se délabrer

ruined /'ru:ɪnd/ *adj* **1** (derelict) en ruines
2 (spoilt) ‹*holiday, meal*› gâché/-e; ‹*clothes, furniture*› abîmé/-e; ‹*reputation*› ruiné/-e; (financially) ruiné/-e

rule /ru:l/ **A** *n* **1** (of game, language) règle *f*; (of school, organization) règlement *m*; **against the ~s** contraire aux règles *or* au règlement (**to do** de faire); **~s and regulations** réglementation *f*; **as a ~** généralement
2 (authority) domination *f*, gouvernement *m*
3 (for measuring) règle *f*
B *vt* **1** ‹*ruler, law*› gouverner; ‹*monarch*› régner sur; ‹*party*› diriger; ‹*army*› commander
2 ‹*factor*› dicter ‹*strategy*›; **to be ~d by** ‹*person*› être mené/-e par ‹*passions, spouse*›
3 (draw) faire, tirer ‹*line*›
4 ‹*court, umpire*› **to ~ that** décréter que
C *vi* **1** ‹*monarch, anarchy*› régner
2 ‹*court, umpire*› statuer
▪ **rule out 1** exclure ‹*possibility, candidate*› (**of** de); **to ~ out doing** exclure de faire
2 interdire ‹*activity*›

ruler /'ru:lə(r)/ *n* **1** (leader) dirigeant/-e *m/f*
2 (measure) règle *f*

ruling /'ru:lɪŋ/ **A** *n* décision *f*
B *adj* **1** (in power) dirigeant/-e
2 (dominant) dominant/-e

rum /rʌm/ *n* rhum *m*

rumble /'rʌmbl/ **A** *n* (of thunder, artillery, trucks) grondement *m*; (of stomach) gargouillement *m*
B *vi* ‹*thunder, artillery*› gronder; ‹*stomach*› gargouiller

ruminate /'ru:mɪneɪt/ *vi* **1** (think) **to ~ on** *or* **about** ruminer sur
2 (Zool) ruminer

rummage /'rʌmɪdʒ/ *vi* fouiller (**through** dans)

rummy /'rʌmɪ/ *n* rami *m*

rumour (BrE), **rumor** (AmE) /'ru:mə(r)/ *n* rumeur *f*, bruit *m*

rumoured (BrE), **rumored** (AmE) /'ru:məd/ *adj* **it is ~ that** il paraît que, on dit que

rump /rʌmp/ *n* **1** (*also* ~ **steak**) rumsteck *m*
2 (of animal) croupe *f*

rumple /'rʌmpl/ *vt* ébouriffer ‹*hair*›; froisser ‹*clothes, sheets, papers*›

run /rʌn/ **A** *n* **1** course *f*; **a two-mile ~** une course de deux miles; **to go for a ~** aller courir; **to break into a ~** se mettre à courir
2 (flight) **on the ~** en fuite; **to make a ~ for it** fuir, s'enfuir
3 (series) (of successes, failures) série *f*; (in printing) tirage *m*; **to have a ~ of luck** être en veine
4 (trip, route) trajet *m*
5 (in cricket, baseball) point *m*
6 (for rabbit, chickens) enclos *m*
7 (in tights) échelle *f*
8 (for skiing) piste *f*
9 (in cards) suite *f*
B *vt* (*prét* **ran**, *pp* **run**) **1** courir ‹*distance, marathon*›; **to ~ a race** faire une course
2 (drive) **to ~ sb to the station** conduire qn à la gare
3 (pass, move) **to ~ one's hand over** passer la main sur; **to ~ one's eye(s) over** parcourir rapidement
4 (manage) diriger; **a well-/badly-run organization** une organisation bien/mal dirigée
5 (operate) faire fonctionner ‹*machine*›; faire tourner ‹*motor*›; exécuter ‹*program*›; entretenir ‹*car*›; **to ~ tests on** effectuer des tests sur
6 (organize, offer) organiser ‹*competition,*

course›; mettre [qch] en place ‹*bus service*›
7 faire couler ‹*bath*›; ouvrir ‹*tap*›
8 (enter) faire courir ‹*horse*›; présenter ‹*candidate*›
C *vi* (*prét* **ran**, *pp* **run**) **1** ‹*person, animal*› courir; **to ~ across/down sth** traverser/descendre qch en courant; **to ~ for the bus** courir pour attraper le bus; **to come ~ning** accourir (**towards** vers)
2 (flee) fuir, s'enfuir; **to ~ for one's life** s'enfuir pour sauver sa peau (fam)
3 (fam) (rush off) filer (fam)
4 (function) ‹*machine*› marcher; **to leave the engine ~ning** laisser tourner le moteur
5 (continue, last) ‹*contract, lease*› être valide
6 ‹*play, musical*› tenir l'affiche (**for** pendant)
7 (pass) **to ~ past/through** ‹*road, frontier, path*› passer/traverser; **to ~ (from) east to west** aller d'est en ouest
8 (move) ‹*sledge*› glisser; ‹*curtain*› coulisser
9 ‹*bus, train*› circuler
10 (flow) couler; **tears ran down his face** les larmes coulaient sur son visage; **my nose is ~ning** j'ai le nez qui coule
11 ‹*dye, garment*› déteindre; ‹*make-up*› couler
12 (as candidate) se présenter; **to ~ for president** être candidat/-e à la présidence
IDIOMS **in the long ~** à long terme; **in the short ~** à brève échéance
▪ **run about**, **run around** courir
▪ **run away**: **A** **~ away** s'enfuir; **to ~ away from home** ‹*child*› faire une fugue
B **~ away with [sb/sth] 1** (flee) partir avec
2 rafler (fam) ‹*prize, title*›
▪ **run down**: **A** **~ down** ‹*battery*› se décharger; ‹*watch*› retarder
B **~ [sb/sth] down 1** (in vehicle) renverser
2 réduire ‹*production, defences*›; user ‹*battery*›
3 (disparage) dénigrer
▪ **run into 1** heurter, rentrer dans (fam) ‹*car, wall*›
2 (encounter) rencontrer ‹*person, difficulty*›
3 (amount to) s'élever à ‹*hundreds, millions*›
▪ **run off** partir en courant
▪ **run out** **A** **~ out 1** ‹*supplies, oil*› s'épuiser; **time is ~ning out** le temps manque
2 ‹*pen, machine*› être vide
3 ‹*contract, passport*› expirer
B **~ out of** ne plus avoir de ‹*petrol, time, money, ideas*›; **to be ~ning out of** n'avoir presque plus de ‹*petrol, time, money, ideas*›
▪ **run over** (in vehicle) (injure) renverser; (kill) écraser
▪ **run through** parcourir ‹*list, article*›; répéter ‹*scene, speech*›
▪ **run up** accumuler ‹*debt*›
▪ **run up against** se heurter à ‹*difficulty*›

runaway /ˈrʌnəweɪ/ *adj* ‹*teenager*› fugueur/-euse; ‹*slave*› fugitif/-ive; ‹*horse*› emballé/-e

rundown /ˈrʌnˌdaʊn/ *n* récapitulatif *m* (**on** de)

run-down /ˌrʌnˈdaʊn/ *adj* **1** (exhausted) fatigué/-e, à plat (fam)
2 (shabby) décrépit/-e

rung /rʌŋ/ *n* **1** (of ladder) barreau *m*
2 (in hierarchy) échelon *m*

run-in *n* (fam) prise *f* de bec (fam)

runner /ˈrʌnə(r)/ *n* **1** (person, animal) coureur *m*
2 (horse) partant/-e *m/f*
3 (messenger) estafette *f*
4 (for door, seat) glissière *f*; (for drawer) coulisseau *m*; (on sled) patin *m*
5 (on stairs) chemin *m* d'escalier

runner bean *n* (BrE) haricot *m* d'Espagne

runner up /ˌrʌnərˈʌp/ *n* (*pl* **~s up**) second/-e *m/f* (**to** après)

running /ˈrʌnɪŋ/ **A** *n* **1** (sport, exercise) course *f* à pied
2 (management) direction *f* (**of** de)
B *adj* **1** ‹*water*› courant/-e; ‹*tap*› ouvert/-e
2 five days ~ cinq jours de suite
IDIOM **to be in/out of the ~** être/ne plus être dans la course (**for** pour)

running battle *n* éternel conflit *m*

running commentary *n* commentaire *m* ininterrompu

running total *n* total *m* cumulé

runny /ˈrʌnɪ/ *adj* ‹*jam, sauce*› liquide; ‹*butter*› fondu/-e; ‹*omelette*› baveux/-euse; **to have a ~ nose** avoir le nez qui coule

run-of-the-mill *adj* ordinaire, banal/-e

runt /rʌnt/ *n* **1** (of litter) le plus faible de la portée
2 (weakling) avorton *m*

run-up /ˈrʌnʌp/ *n* **1** (for a jump) course *f* d'élan; **to take a ~** prendre son élan pour sauter
2 (preceding period) **the ~ to** la dernière ligne droite avant

runway *n* piste *f* d'aviation

rupee /ruːˈpiː/ *n* roupie *f*

rupture /ˈrʌptʃə(r)/ *n* rupture *f*

⚷ **rural** /ˈrʊərəl/ *adj* (country) rural/-e; (pastoral) champêtre

ruse /ruːz/ *n* stratagème *m*

⚷ **rush** /rʌʃ/ **A** *n* **1** (surge) ruée *f* (**to do** pour faire); **to make a ~ for sth** ‹*crowd*› se ruer vers qch; ‹*individual*› se précipiter vers qch
2 (hurry) **to be in a ~** être pressé/-e (**to do** de faire); **to leave in a ~** partir en vitesse
3 (of liquid, adrenalin) montée *f*; (of air) bouffée *f*
4 (plant) jonc *m*
B *vt* **1 to ~ sth to** envoyer qch d'urgence à; **to be ~ed to the hospital** être emmené/-e d'urgence à l'hôpital
2 expédier ‹*task, speech*›
3 (hurry) bousculer ‹*person*›
4 (charge at) sauter sur ‹*person*›; prendre d'assaut ‹*building*›
C *vi* ‹*person*› (hurry) se dépêcher (**to do**

⚷ mot clé

de faire); (rush forward) se précipiter (**to do** pour faire); **to ~ out of the room** se précipiter hors de la pièce; **to ~ down the stairs/past** descendre l'escalier/passer à toute vitesse

■ **rush into**: **A** **to ~ into marriage/a purchase** se marier/acheter sans prendre le temps de réfléchir
B **~ [sb] into doing** bousculer [qn] pour qu'il/elle fasse

■ **rush out**: **~ out** sortir en vitesse

■ **rush through**: **A** **~ through [sth]** expédier ‹*task*›
B **~ [sth] through** adopter en vitesse ‹*legislation*›; traiter en priorité ‹*order, application*›

rushed /rʌst/ *adj* ‹*attempt, letter*› expédié/-e

rush hour /'rʌʃaʊə(r)/ *n* heures *fpl* de pointe

rusk /rʌsk/ *n* biscuit *m* pour bébés

russet /'rʌsɪt/ *adj* roussâtre

Russia /'rʌʃə/ *pr n* Russie *f*

Russian /'rʌʃn/ **A** *n* **1** (person) Russe *mf*
2 (language) russe *m*
B *adj* ‹*culture, food, politics*› russe; ‹*teacher, lesson*› de russe; ‹*ambassador, embassy*› de Russie

rust /rʌst/ **A** *n* rouille *f*
B *vt* rouiller ‹*metal*›
C *vi* ‹*metal*› se rouiller

rustic /'rʌstɪk/ *adj* rustique

rustle /'rʌsl/ **A** *n* (of paper, dry leaves) froissement *m*; (of leaves, silk) bruissement *m*
B *vt* froisser ‹*papers*›

rusty /'rʌstɪ/ *adj* rouillé/-e

rut /rʌt/ *n* **1** (in ground) ornière *f*
2 (routine) **be in a ~** être enlisé/-e dans la routine
3 (Zool) **the ~** le rut

rutabaga /ˌruːtə'beɪgə/ *n* (AmE) rutabaga *m*

ruthless /'ruːθlɪs/ *adj* impitoyable (**in** dans)

RV *n* (AmE) (*abbr* = **recreational vehicle**) camping-car *m*, autocaravane *f*

Rwanda /rʊ'ændə/ *pr n* Rwanda *m*

rye /raɪ/ *n* **1** (cereal) seigle *m*
2 (AmE) (*also* **~ whiskey**) whisky *m* à base de seigle

rye bread *n* pain *m* de seigle

Ss

s, S /es/ *n* s, S *m*

sabbath /'sæbəθ/ *n* (*also* **Sabbath**) (Jewish) sabbat *m*; (Christian) jour *m* du seigneur

sabbatical /sə'bætɪkl/ *n* congé *m* sabbatique

sabotage /'sæbətɑːʒ/ **A** *n* sabotage *m*
B *vt* saboter

saboteur /ˌsæbə'tɜː(r)/ *n* saboteur/-euse *m/f*

sabre (BrE), **saber** (AmE) /'seɪbə(r)/ *n* sabre *m*

sachet /'sæʃeɪ, (AmE) sæ'ʃeɪ/ *n* sachet *m*

sack /sæk/ **A** *n* **1** sac *m*
2 (BrE) **to get the ~** se faire mettre à la porte (fam)
B *vt* **1** (BrE) (fam) mettre [qn] à la porte (fam) ‹*employee*›
2 mettre [qch] à sac ‹*town*›

sacrament /'sækrəmənt/ *n* sacrement *m*

sacred /'seɪkrɪd/ *adj* sacré/-e (**to** pour)

sacrifice /'sækrɪfaɪs/ **A** *n* sacrifice *m* (**to** à, **of** de)
B *vt* **1** (gen) sacrifier (**to** à)
2 (to the gods) offrir [qch] en sacrifice (**to** à)
C *v refl* **to ~ oneself** se sacrifier (**for** pour)

sacrilege /'sækrɪlɪdʒ/ *n* sacrilège *m*

sacrosanct /'sækrəʊsæŋkt/ *adj* sacro-saint/-e

sad /sæd/ *adj* triste (**that** que + *subjunctive*); **it makes me ~** cela me rend triste

sadden /'sædn/ *vt* attrister

saddle /'sædl/ **A** *n* selle *f*
B *vt* **1** seller ‹*horse*›
2 **to ~ sb with** mettre [qch] sur les bras de qn ‹*responsibility, task*›

saddle bag *n* sacoche *f*

sadist /'seɪdɪst/ *n* sadique *mf*

sadistic /sə'dɪstɪk/ *adj* sadique

sadness /'sædnɪs/ *n* tristesse *f*

sae *n* (*abbr* = **stamped addressed envelope**) enveloppe *f* timbrée à votre/son etc adresse

safari /sə'fɑːrɪ/ *n* safari *m*

safari park *n* parc *m* zoologique (*où les animaux vivent en semi-liberté*)

safe /seɪf/ **A** *n* coffre-fort *m*
B *adj* **1** (after ordeal, risk) ‹*person*› sain et sauf/saine et sauve; ‹*object*› intact/-e; **~ and sound** sain et sauf/saine et sauve
2 (free from threat, harm) **to be ~** ‹*person*› être en sécurité; ‹*document, valuables*› être en lieu sûr; ‹*company, job, reputation*› ne pas être menacé/-e; **is the bike ~ here?** est-ce

qu'on peut laisser le vélo ici sans risque?; **have a ~ journey!** bon voyage!
3 (risk-free) ‹*toy, level, method*› sans danger; ‹*place, vehicle*› sûr/-e; ‹*structure, building*› solide; **it's not ~** c'est dangereux
4 (prudent) ‹*investment*› sûr/-e; ‹*choice*› prudent/-e
5 (reliable) **to be in ~ hands** être en bonnes mains
IDIOMS **better ~ than sorry!** mieux vaut prévenir que guérir!; **just to be on the ~ side** simplement par précaution

safe bet *n* **it's a ~** c'est quelque chose de sûr

safe conduct /ˌseɪfˈkɒndʌkt/ *n* laissez-passer *m inv*

safe-deposit box *n* coffre *m* (à la banque)

safeguard /ˈseɪfgɑːd/ **A** *n* garantie *f* (**for** pour, **against** contre)
B *vt* protéger (**against, from** contre)

safe house *n* refuge *m*

safekeeping /ˌseɪfˈkiːpɪŋ/ *n* **in sb's ~** à la garde de qn

safely /ˈseɪflɪ/ *adv* **1** ‹*come back*› (of person) sans encombre; (of parcel, goods) sans dommage; (of plane) ‹*land, take off*› sans problème; **I arrived ~** je suis bien arrivé
2 we can ~ assume that... nous pouvons être certains que...
3 ‹*locked, hidden*› bien

safe sex *n* rapports *mpl* sexuels sans risque

⚷ **safety** /ˈseɪftɪ/ *n* sécurité *f*; **in ~** en (toute) sécurité; **to reach ~** parvenir en lieu sûr

safety belt *n* ceinture *f* de sécurité

safety net *n* filet *m* (de protection); (fig) filet *m* de sécurité

safety pin *n* épingle *f* de sûreté

sag /sæg/ *vi* (*p prés etc* **-gg-**) **1** ‹*beam, mattress*› s'affaisser; ‹*tent, rope*› ne pas être bien tendu/-e
2 ‹*breasts*› pendre; ‹*flesh*› être flasque

saga /ˈsɑːgə/ *n* saga *f*

S

sage /seɪdʒ/ *n* **1** (herb) sauge *f*
2 (wise person) sage *m*

Sagittarius /ˌsædʒɪˈteərɪəs/ *n* Sagittaire *m*

Sahara /səˈhɑːrə/ *pr n* Sahara *m*; **the ~ desert** le désert du Sahara

sail /seɪl/ **A** *n* **1** (of boat) voile *f*; **to set sail** prendre la mer; **a ship in full ~** un navire toutes voiles dehors
2 (of windmill) aile *f*
B *vt* **1** piloter ‹*ship, yacht*›
2 traverser [qch] en bateau ‹*ocean, channel*›
C *vi* **1** ‹*person*› voyager en bateau; **to ~ around the world** faire le tour du monde en bateau
2 ‹*ship*› **to ~ across** traverser ‹*ocean*›; **the boat ~s at 10 am** le bateau part à 10 h
3 (as hobby) **to go ~ing** faire de la voile
■ **sail through** gagner [qch] facilement ‹*match*›; **to ~ through an exam** réussir un examen les doigts dans le nez (fam)

sailboard *n* planche *f* à voile

sailboarder *n* véliplanchiste *mf*

sailboat *n* (AmE) bateau *m* à voiles

sailing /ˈseɪlɪŋ/ *n* voile *f*

sailing boat *n* bateau *m* à voiles

sailing ship *n* voilier *m*

sailor /ˈseɪlə(r)/ *n* marin *m*

saint /seɪnt, snt/ *n* saint/-e *m/f*; **Saint Mark** saint Marc

sake /seɪk/ *n* **1 for the ~ of clarity** pour la clarté; **for the ~ of argument** à titre d'exemple; **to kill for the ~ of killing** tuer pour le plaisir de tuer; **for old times' ~** en souvenir du bon vieux temps
2 (benefit) **for the ~ of sb, for sb's ~** par égard pour qn; **for God's/heaven's ~!** pour l'amour de Dieu/du ciel!

salad /ˈsæləd/ *n* salade *f*; **ham ~** salade au jambon

salad bar *n* buffet *m* de crudités

salad bowl *n* saladier *m*

salad dressing *n* sauce *f* pour salade

salami /səˈlɑːmɪ/ *n* saucisson *m* sec

salary /ˈsælərɪ/ *n* salaire *m*

⚷ **sale** /seɪl/ *n* **1** (gen) vente *f* (**of** de, **to** à); **for sale** à vendre; **on ~** en vente
2 (at cut prices) solde *f*; **the sales** les soldes; **in the ~(s)** (BrE), **on ~** (AmE) en solde

sale price *n* prix *m* soldé

sales assistant *n* (BrE) vendeur/-euse *m/f*

sales executive *n* cadre *m* commercial

salesman /ˈseɪlzmən/ *n* (*pl* **-men**) (rep) représentant *m*; (in shop) vendeur *m*

sales pitch *n* baratin *m* (fam) publicitaire

sales rep, **sales representative** *n* représentant/-e *m/f*

saleswoman *n* (*pl* **-women**) (rep) représentante *f*; (in shop) vendeuse *f*

saliva /səˈlaɪvə/ *n* salive *f*

salivate /ˈsælɪveɪt/ *vi* saliver

sallow /ˈsæləʊ/ *adj* cireux/-euse

salmon /ˈsæmən/ *n* (*pl* **~**) saumon *m*

salmonella /ˌsælməˈnelə/ *n* (*pl* **-æ** *ou* **-as**) salmonelle *f*

salon /ˈsælɒn, (AmE) səˈlɒn/ *n* salon *m*

saloon /səˈluːn/ *n* **1** (BrE) (*also* **~ car**) berline *f*
2 (AmE) saloon *m*, bar *m*
3 (on boat) salon *m*

salt /sɔːlt/ **A** *n* sel *m*
B *vt* saler ‹*meat, fish, road, path*›

salt cellar *n* salière *f*

salty /ˈsɔːltɪ/ *adj* ‹*water, food, flavour*› salé/-e

salutary /ˈsæljʊtrɪ, (AmE) -terɪ/ *adj* salutaire

salute /səˈluːt/ **A** *n* salut *m*
B *vt, vi* saluer

⚷ mot clé

salvage /ˈsælvɪdʒ/ **A** *n* **1** (rescue) sauvetage *m* (**of** de)
2 (goods rescued) biens *mpl* récupérés
B *vt* **1** sauver ‹*cargo, materials, belongings*› (**from** de); effectuer le sauvetage de ‹*ship*›
2 sauver ‹*marriage, reputation, game*›
3 (for recycling) récupérer ‹*metal, paper*›

salvation /sælˈveɪʃn/ *n* salut *m*

Salvation Army *n* Armée *f* du Salut

salve /sælv, (AmE) sæv/ **A** *n* baume *m*
B *vt* **to ~ one's conscience** soulager sa conscience

Samaritan /səˈmærɪtən/ *n* **the Good ~** le bon Samaritain; **the ~s** les Samaritains *mpl*

same /seɪm/ **A** *adj* même (**as** que); **to be the ~** être le/la même; **to look the ~** être pareil/-eille; **to be the ~ as sth** être comme qch; **it amounts** *or* **comes to the ~ thing** cela revient au même; **it's all the ~ to me** ça m'est complètement égal; **if it's all the ~ to you** si ça ne te fait rien; **at the ~ time** en même temps; **to remain** *or* **stay the ~** ne pas changer
B the same *pron* la même chose (**as** que); **I'll have the ~** je prendrai la même chose; **to do the ~ as sb** faire comme qn; **the ~ to you!** (in greeting) à toi aussi, à toi de même!; (of insult) toi-même! (fam)
C the same *adv* ‹*act, dress*› de la même façon; **to feel the ~ as sb** penser comme qn
IDIOMS **all the ~..., just the ~,...** tout de même,...; **thanks all the ~** merci quand même

same-day *adj* ‹*service*› effectué/-e dans la journée

same-sex /seɪmseks/ /seɪmseks/ *adj* de même sexe

sample /ˈsɑːmpl, (AmE) ˈsæmpl/ **A** *n* **1** (of product, fabric) échantillon *m*
2 (for analysis) prélèvement *m*
B *vt* **1** (taste) goûter (à) ‹*food, wine*›
2 (test) essayer ‹*products*›; sonder ‹*opinion, market*›

sanatorium (BrE), **sanitarium** (AmE) /ˌsænəˈtɔːrɪəm/ *n* (*pl* **-riums** *ou* **-ria** (BrE)) sanatorium *m*

sanctimonious /ˌsæŋktɪˈməʊnɪəs/ *adj* supérieur/-e

sanction /ˈsæŋkʃn/ **A** *n* sanction *f*; **to impose ~s** prendre des sanctions
B *vt* (permit) autoriser; (approve) sanctionner

sanctity /ˈsæŋktətɪ/ *n* sainteté *f*

sanctuary /ˈsæŋktʃʊərɪ, (AmE) -tʃʊerɪ/ *n*
1 (safe place) refuge *m*
2 (holy place) sanctuaire *m*
3 (for wildlife) réserve *f*; (for mistreated pets) refuge *m*

sand /sænd/ **A** *n* sable *m*
B *vt* **1** (*also* **~ down**) poncer ‹*floor*›; frotter [qch] au papier de verre ‹*woodwork*›
2 sabler ‹*icy road*›

sandal /ˈsændl/ *n* sandale *f*

sandcastle *n* château *m* de sable

sand dune *n* dune *f*

sandpaper /ˈsændpeɪpə(r)/ **A** *n* papier *m* de verre
B *vt* poncer

sandpit /ˈsændpɪt/ *n* (quarry) sablière *f*; (BrE) (for children) bac *m* à sable

sandstone /ˈsændstəʊn/ *n* grès *m*

sandwich /ˈsænwɪdʒ, (AmE) -wɪtʃ/ **A** *n* sandwich *m*; **cucumber ~** sandwich au concombre
B *vt* **to be ~ed between** ‹*car, building, person*› être pris/-e en sandwich entre

sandwich bar *n* sandwich bar *m*

sandwich course *n* (BrE) cours *m* avec stage pratique

sandy /ˈsændɪ/ *adj* **1** ‹*beach*› de sable; ‹*path, soil*› sablonneux/-euse
2 ‹*hair*› blond roux *inv*; ‹*colour*› sable *inv after n*

sane /seɪn/ *adj* **1** ‹*person*› sain/-e d'esprit
2 ‹*policy, judgement*› sensé/-e

sanitarium (AmE) = **sanatorium**

sanitary /ˈsænɪtrɪ, (AmE) -terɪ/ *adj*
1 ‹*engineer, installations*› sanitaire
2 (hygienic) hygiénique; (clean) propre

sanitary towel (BrE), **sanitary napkin** (AmE) *n* serviette *f* hygiénique *or* périodique

sanitation /ˌsænɪˈteɪʃn/ *n* installations *fpl* sanitaires

sanity /ˈsænətɪ/ *n* équilibre *m* mental

Santa /ˈsæntə (klɔːz)/ *pr n* (*also* **Santa Claus**) le père Noël

sap /sæp/ **A** *n* sève *f*
B *vt* (*p prés etc* **-pp-**) saper ‹*strength, courage, confidence*›

sapling /ˈsæplɪŋ/ *n* jeune arbre *m*

sapphire /ˈsæfaɪə(r)/ *n* **1** (stone) saphir *m*
2 (colour) bleu *m* saphir

sarcasm /ˈsɑːkæzəm/ *n* sarcasme *m*

sarcastic /sɑːˈkæstɪk/ *adj* sarcastique

sardine /sɑːˈdiːn/ *n* sardine *f*

Sardinia /sɑːˈdɪnɪə/ *pr n* Sardaigne *f*

sardonic /sɑːˈdɒnɪk/ *adj* ‹*laugh, look*› sardonique; ‹*person, remark*› acerbe

SARS /sɑːz/ *n* (*abbr* = **severe acute respiratory syndrome**) SRAS *m*

SAS *n* (BrE) (*abbr* = **Special Air Service**) commandos *mpl* britanniques aéroportés

sash /sæʃ/ *n* (round waist) large ceinture *f*; (ceremonial) écharpe *f*

sassy /ˈsæsɪ/ *adj* (AmE) (fam) culotté (fam)

Satan /ˈseɪtn/ *pr n* Satan

satanic /səˈtænɪk/ *adj* ‹*rites*› satanique; ‹*pride, smile*› démoniaque

satchel /ˈsætʃəl/ *n* cartable *m* (à bandoulière)

satellite /ˈsætəlaɪt/ *n* satellite *m*

satellite dish *n* antenne *f* parabolique

satellite TV *n* télévision *f* par satellite
satin /'sætɪn, (AmE) 'sætn/ **A** *n* satin *m*
B *adj* ‹*garment, shoe*› de satin; **with a ~ finish** satiné/-e
satire /'sætaɪə(r)/ *n* satire *f* (**on** sur)
satiric /sə'tɪrɪk(l)/ *adj* (*also* **satirical**) satirique
satirize /'sætəraɪz/ *vt* faire la satire de
satisfaction /ˌsætɪs'fækʃn/ *n* satisfaction *f*
satisfactory /ˌsætɪs'fæktərɪ/ *adj* satisfaisant/-e
satisfied /'sætɪsfaɪd/ *adj* **1** (pleased) satisfait/-e (**with, about** de)
2 (convinced) convaincu/-e (**by** par, **that** que)
🔑 **satisfy** /'sætɪsfaɪ/ *vt* **1** satisfaire ‹*person, need, desires, curiosity*›; assouvir ‹*hunger*›
2 (persuade) convaincre ‹*person, public opinion*› (**that** que)
3 (meet) satisfaire à ‹*demand, requirements, conditions*›
satisfying /'sætɪsfaɪɪŋ/ *adj* **1** ‹*meal*› substantiel/-ielle
2 ‹*job*› qui apporte de la satisfaction
3 ‹*result, progress*› satisfaisant/-e
satnav /'sætnæv/ *n* GPS *m*
satphone *n* téléphone *m* satellite
saturate /'sætʃəreɪt/ *vt* saturer (**with** de)
saturated /'sætʃəreɪtɪd/ *adj* (wet) ‹*person, clothes*› trempé/-e; ‹*ground*› détrempé/-e
saturation point *n* point *m* de saturation; **to reach ~** arriver à saturation
🔑 **Saturday** /'sætədeɪ, -dɪ/ *n* samedi *m*; **he has a ~ job** il a un petit boulot (fam) le samedi
Saturn /'sætən/ *pr n* (planet) Saturne *f*
sauce /sɔːs/ *n* sauce *f*
saucepan /'sɔːspən/ *n* casserole *f*
saucer /'sɔːsə(r)/ *n* soucoupe *f*
Saudi Arabia *pr n* Arabie *f* saoudite
sauna /'sɔːnə, 'saʊnə/ *n* sauna *m*
saunter /'sɔːntə(r)/ *vi* (*also* **~ along**) marcher d'un pas nonchalant; **to ~ off** s'éloigner d'un pas nonchalant
S
sausage /'sɒsɪdʒ, (AmE) 'sɔːs-/ *n* saucisse *f*
sausage roll *n* feuilleté *m* à la chair à saucisse
savage /'sævɪdʒ/ **A** *n* sauvage *mf*
B *adj* (gen) féroce; ‹*blow, beating*› violent/-e; ‹*attack*› sauvage; ‹*criticism*› virulent/-e
C *vt* ‹*dog*› attaquer [qn/qch] sauvagement; ‹*lion*› déchiqueter
🔑 **save** /seɪv/ **A** *n* (Sport) arrêt *m* de but
B *vt* **1** (rescue) sauver (**from** de); **to ~ sb's life** sauver la vie à qn
2 (put by, keep) mettre [qch] de côté ‹*money, food*› (**to do** pour faire); garder ‹*goods, documents*› (**for** pour); sauvegarder ‹*data, file*›; **to have money ~d** avoir de l'argent de côté; **to ~ sth for sb, to ~ sb sth** garder qch pour qn
3 (economize on) économiser ‹*money*› (**by doing** en faisant); gagner ‹*time, space*› (**by doing** en faisant); **to ~ one's energy** ménager ses forces; **you'll ~ money** vous ferez des économies; **to ~ sb/sth (from) having to do** éviter à qn/qch de faire
4 (Sport) arrêter
C *vi* **1** (put money by) = **save up**
2 (economize) économiser, faire des économies; **to ~ on** faire des économies de ‹*energy, paper*›
■ **save up** faire des économies; **to ~ up for** mettre de l'argent de côté pour s'acheter ‹*car, house*›; mettre de l'argent de côté pour s'offrir ‹*holiday*›
saver /'seɪvə(r)/ *n* épargnant/-e *m/f*
saving grace *n* bon côté *m*; **it's his ~** c'est ce qui le sauve
savings *npl* économies *fpl*
savings account *n* (BrE) compte *m* d'épargne; (AmE) compte *m* rémunéré
savings bank *n* caisse *f* d'épargne
saviour (BrE), **savior** (AmE) /'seɪvɪə(r)/ *n* sauveur *m*
savour (BrE), **savor** (AmE) /'seɪvə(r)/ **A** *n* saveur *f*
B *vt* savourer
savoury (BrE), **savory** (AmE) /'seɪvərɪ/ *adj* (not sweet) salé/-e; (appetizing) appétissant/-e
saw /sɔː/ **A** *n* scie *f*
B *vt* (*prét* **sawed**, *pp* **sawn** (BrE), **sawed** (AmE)) scier; **to ~ through/down/off** scier
sawdust *n* sciure *f* (de bois)
sawn-off shotgun *n* (BrE) fusil *m* à canon scié
saxophone /'sæksəfəʊn/ *n* saxophone *m*
🔑 **say** /seɪ/ **A** *n* **to have one's ~** dire ce qu'on a à dire (**on** sur); **to have a ~/no ~ in sth** avoir/ne pas avoir son mot à dire sur qch; **to have no ~ in the matter** ne pas avoir voix au chapitre
B *vt* (*prét, pp* **said**) **1** (gen) dire (**to** à); **'hello,' he said** 'bonjour,' dit-il; **to ~ (that)** dire que; **they ~ she's very rich, she is said to be very rich** on dit qu'elle est très riche; **to ~ sth about sb/sth** dire qch au sujet de qn/qch; **to ~ sth to oneself** se dire qch; **let's ~ no more about it** n'en parlons plus; **it goes without ~ing that** il va sans dire que; **that is to ~** c'est-à-dire; **let's ~ there are 20** mettons *or* supposons qu'il y en ait 20; **how high would you ~ it is?** à ton avis, quelle en est la hauteur?; **I'd ~ she was about 25** je lui donnerais environ 25 ans
2 ‹*sign, clock, dial, gauge*› indiquer
C *vi* (*prét, pp* **said**) **stop when I ~** arrête quand je te le dirai; **he wouldn't ~** il n'a pas voulu le dire
IDIOMS **it ~s a lot for sb/sth** c'est tout à l'honneur de qn/qch; **there's a lot to be said for that method** cette méthode est très intéressante à bien des égards; **when all is**

🔑 mot clé

said and done tout compte fait, en fin de compte

saying /'seɪɪŋ/ *n* dicton *m*

scab /skæb/ *n* croûte *f*

scaffolding /'skæfəldɪŋ/ *n* échafaudage *m*

scald /skɔ:ld/ *vt* ébouillanter

scalding /'skɔ:ldɪŋ/ *adj* brûlant/-e

scale /skeɪl/ **A** *n* **1** (gen) échelle *f*; **pay ~, salary ~** échelle des salaires; **on a ~ of 1 to 10** sur une échelle allant de 1 à 10
2 (extent) (of disaster, success, violence) étendue *f* (**of** de); (of defeat, recession, task) ampleur *f* (**of** de); (of activity, operation) envergure *f* (**of** de)
3 (on ruler, gauge) graduation *f*
4 (for weighing) balance *f*
5 (Mus) gamme *f*
6 (on fish, insect) écaille *f*
B **scales** *npl* balance *f*
C *vt* **1** escalader ‹*wall, mountain*›
2 écailler ‹*fish*›
■ **scale down**: **~ [sth] down, ~ down [sth]** réduire l'échelle de ‹*drawing*›; réduire ‹*activity*›

scale drawing *n* dessin *m* à l'échelle

scale model *n* maquette *f* à l'échelle

scallop, **scollop** /'skɒləp/ *n* coquille *f* Saint-Jacques

scalp /skælp/ **A** *n* cuir *m* chevelu
B *vt* scalper

scam /skæm/ *n* (fam) escroquerie *f*

scamper /'skæmpə(r)/ *vi* **to ~ about** *or* **around** ‹*child, dog*› gambader; ‹*mouse*› trottiner

scan /skæn/ **A** *n* (Med) (CAT) scanner *m*; (ultrasound) échographie *f*
B *vt* (*p prés etc* **-nn-**) **1** lire rapidement ‹*page, newspaper*›
2 (examine) scruter ‹*face, horizon*›
3 ‹*beam of light, radar*› balayer
4 (Med) faire un scanner de ‹*organ*›

scandal /'skændl/ *n* scandale *m*

scandalize /'skændəlaɪz/ *vt* scandaliser

scandalous /'skændələs/ *adj* scandaleux/-euse

Scandinavia /ˌskændɪ'neɪvɪə/ *pr n* Scandinavie *f*

scanner /'skænə(r)/ *n* (Comput, Med) scanner *m*; (for bar codes) lecteur *m* optique

scanty /'skæntɪ/ *adj* ‹*meal, supply*› maigre *before n*; ‹*information*› sommaire; ‹*knowledge*› rudimentaire; ‹*swimsuit*› minuscule

scapegoat /'skeɪpgəʊt/ *n* bouc *m* émissaire (**for** de)

scar /skɑ:(r)/ **A** *n* cicatrice *f*; (on face from knife) balafre *f*
B *vt* (*p prés etc* **-rr-**) marquer; (on face with knife) balafrer; **to ~ sb for life** laisser à qn une cicatrice permanente; (fig) marquer qn pour la vie

scarce /skeəs/ *adj* rare; **to become ~** se faire rare

scarcely /'skeəslɪ/ *adv* à peine; **~ anybody believes it** presque personne ne le croit

scare /skeə(r)/ **A** *n* **1** peur *f*; **to give sb a ~** faire peur à qn
2 (alert) alerte *f*; **bomb ~** alerte à la bombe
B *vt* faire peur à
■ **scare away**, **scare off** faire fuir ‹*animal, attacker*›; (fig) dissuader

scarecrow /'skeəkrəʊ/ *n* épouvantail *m*

scared /skeəd/ *adj* ‹*animal, person*› effrayé/-e; ‹*look*› apeuré/-e; **to be** *or* **feel ~** avoir peur; **to be ~ stiff** (fam) avoir une peur bleue (fam)

scaremongering *n* alarmisme *m*

scarf /skɑ:f/ *n* (*pl* **scarves**) (long) écharpe *f*; (square) foulard *m*

scarlet /'skɑ:lət/ *n, adj* écarlate *f*

scarlet fever *n* scarlatine *f*

scary /'skeərɪ/ *adj* (fam) qui fait peur

scathing /'skeɪðɪŋ/ *adj* ‹*remark, tone, wit*› cinglant/-e; ‹*criticism*› virulent/-e

scatter /'skætə(r)/ **A** *vt* **1** (*also* **~ around, ~ about**) répandre ‹*seeds, earth*›; éparpiller ‹*books, papers, clothes*›
2 disperser ‹*crowd, herd*›
B *vi* ‹*people, animals, birds*› se disperser

scatter-brained *adj* ‹*person*› étourdi/-e; ‹*idea*› farfelu/-e (fam)

scattered /'skætəd/ *adj* ‹*houses, trees, population, clouds*› épars/-e; ‹*books, litter*› éparpillé/-e; ‹*support, resistance*› clairsemé/-e

scatty /'skætɪ/ *adj* (BrE) (fam) étourdi/-e

scavenge /'skævɪndʒ/ *vi* **to ~ for food** ‹*bird, animal*› chercher de la nourriture

scavenger /'skævɪndʒə(r)/ *n* **1** (animal) charognard *m*
2 (person) (for food) faiseur *m* de poubelles; (for objects) récupérateur *m*

scenario /sɪ'nɑ:rɪəʊ, (AmE) -'nær-/ *n* (*pl* **~s**) (gen) cas *m* de figure; (of film, play) scénario *m*

scene /si:n/ *n* **1** (gen) scène *f*; **behind the ~s** dans les coulisses *fpl*; **you need a change of ~** tu as besoin de changer de décor
2 (of crime, accident) lieu *m*; **at** *or* **on the ~** sur les lieux
3 (image, sight) image *f*
4 (view) vue *f*

scenery /'si:nərɪ/ *n* **1** (landscape) paysage *m*
2 (in theatre) décors *mpl*

scent /sent/ **A** *n* **1** (smell) odeur *f*
2 (perfume) parfum *m*
3 (of animal) fumet *m*; (in hunting) piste *f*
B *vt* **1** flairer ‹*prey, animal*›
2 pressentir ‹*danger, trouble*›
3 (perfume) parfumer ‹*air*›

sceptic (BrE), **skeptic** (AmE) /'skeptɪk/ *n* sceptique *mf*

sceptical (BrE), **skeptical** (AmE) /'skeptɪkl/ *adj* sceptique

scepticism (BrE), **skepticism** (AmE) /'skeptɪsɪzəm/ *n* scepticisme *m*

schedule /'ʃedjuːl, (AmE) 'skedʒʊl/ **A** *n*
1 (of work, events) programme *m*; (timetable) horaire *m*; **to be ahead of/behind ~** être en avance/en retard; **to arrive on/ahead of ~** ‹*bus, train, plane*› arriver à l'heure/en avance
2 (list) liste *f*
B *vt* (plan) prévoir; (arrange) programmer

scheduled flight *n* vol *m* régulier

⚷ **scheme** /skiːm/ **A** *n* **1** projet *m*, plan *m* (**to do, for doing** pour faire); **pension ~** régime *m* de retraite
2 (plot) combine *f* (**to do** pour faire)
B *vi* comploter

scheming /'skiːmɪŋ/ *n* machinations *fpl*

schizophrenic /ˌskɪtsəʊ'frenɪk/ *adj* schizophrénique

scholar /'skɒlə(r)/ *n* érudit/-e *m/f*

scholarship /'skɒləʃɪp/ *n* bourse *f* (**to** pour)

⚷ **school** /skuːl/ **A** *n* **1** école *f*; **at ~** à l'école
2 (AmE) (university) université *f*
3 (of fish) banc *m*
B *adj* ‹*holiday, outing, trip, uniform, year*› scolaire

school bag *n* sac *m* de classe

schoolboy /'skuːlbɔɪ/ *n* (pupil) élève *m*; (primary) écolier *m*; (secondary) collégien *m*

schoolchild *n* écolier/-ière *m/f*

school fees *npl* frais *mpl* de scolarité

school friend *n* camarade *mf* de classe

schoolgirl /'skuːlgɜːl/ *n* (pupil) élève *f*; (primary) écolière *f*; (secondary) collégienne *f*

schooling /'skuːlɪŋ/ *n* scolarité *f*

school-leaver *n* (BrE) jeune *mf* ayant fini sa scolarité

school leaving age *n* âge *m* de fin de scolarité

school lunch *n* repas *m* de la cantine scolaire

school report (BrE), **school report card** (AmE) *n* bulletin *m* scolaire

schoolteacher /'skuːltiːtʃə(r)/ *n* enseignant/-e *m/f*; (primary) instituteur/-trice *m/f*; (secondary) professeur *m*

schoolwork /'skuːlwɜːk/ *n* travail *m* de classe

⚷ **science** /'saɪəns/ **A** *n* science *f*; **to study ~** étudier les sciences
B *adj* ‹*exam, subject*› scientifique; ‹*teacher, textbook*› de sciences

science fiction *n* science-fiction *f*

⚷ **scientific** /ˌsaɪən'tɪfɪk/ *adj* scientifique

⚷ **scientist** /'saɪəntɪst/ *n* scientifique *mf*

scissors /'sɪzəz/ *npl* ciseaux *mpl*

scoff /skɒf, (AmE) skɔːf/ **A** *vt* (BrE) (fam) (eat) engloutir (fam), bouffer (fam)
B *vi* se moquer (**at** de)

scold /skəʊld/ *vt* gronder (**for doing** pour avoir fait)

⚷ mot clé

scoop /skuːp/ **A** *n* **1** (for measuring) mesure *f*
2 (of ice cream) boule *f*
3 (in journalism) exclusivité *f*
B *vt* (fam) décrocher (fam) ‹*prize, sum of money, story*›

scooter /'skuːtə(r)/ *n* **1** (child's) trottinette *f*
2 (motorized) scooter *m*

scope /skəʊp/ *n* **1** (opportunity) possibilité *f* (**for** de)
2 (of inquiry, report, book) portée *f*; (of plan) envergure *f*
3 (of person) compétences *fpl*

scorch /skɔːtʃ/ **A** *n* (*also* **~ mark**) légère brûlure *f*
B *vt* ‹*fire*› brûler; ‹*sun*› dessécher ‹*grass, trees*›; griller ‹*lawn*›; ‹*iron*› roussir ‹*fabric*›

scorching /'skɔːtʃɪŋ/ *adj* (fam) (*also* **~ hot**) ‹*day*› torride; ‹*weather*› caniculaire

⚷ **score** /skɔː(r)/ **A** *n* **1** (Sport) score *m*; (in cards) marque *f*; **to keep (the) ~** marquer les points; (in cards) tenir la marque
2 (in exam, test) note *f*, résultat *m*
3 (Mus) (written music) partition *f*; (for film) musique *f* (de film)
4 (twenty) **a ~** vingt *m*, une vingtaine *f*
5 on this *or* **that ~** à ce sujet
B *vt* **1** marquer ‹*goal, point*›; remporter ‹*victory, success*›; **to ~ 9 out of 10** avoir 9 sur 10
2 (cut) entailler
C *vi* (gain point) marquer un point; (obtain goal) marquer un but
IDIOM to settle a ~ régler ses comptes

scoreboard *n* tableau *m* d'affichage

scorn /skɔːn/ **A** *n* mépris *m* (**for** pour)
B *vt* (despise) mépriser; (reject) accueillir avec mépris ‹*claim, suggestion*›

scornful /'skɔːnfl/ *adj* méprisant/-e

Scorpio /'skɔːpɪəʊ/ *n* Scorpion *m*

Scot /skɒt/ *n* Écossais/-e *m/f*

Scotch /skɒtʃ/ **A** *n* (*also* **~ whisky**) whisky *m*, scotch *m*
B *adj* écossais/-e

Scotch tape® *n* (AmE) scotch® *m*

scot-free /ˌskɒt'friː/ *adj* **to get off ~** (unpunished) s'en tirer sans être inquiété/-e; (unharmed) s'en sortir indemne

Scotland /'skɒtlənd/ *pr n* Écosse *f*

Scottish /'skɒtɪʃ/ *adj* écossais/-e

scour /'skaʊə(r)/ *vt* **1** (scrub) récurer
2 (search) parcourir ‹*area, list*› (**for** à la recherche de)

scourer /'skaʊərə(r)/ *n* tampon *m* à récurer

scourge /skɜːdʒ/ *n* fléau *m*

scout /skaʊt/ *n* **1** (*also* **boy ~**) scout *m*
2 (Mil) éclaireur *m*
3 (*also* **talent ~**) découvreur/-euse *m/f* de nouveaux talents
■ **scout around** explorer; **to ~ around for sth** rechercher qch

scowl /skaʊl/ **A** *n* air *m* renfrogné
B *vi* prendre un air renfrogné

scramble /'skræmbl/ **A** *n* **1** (rush) course *f* (**for** pour, **to do** pour faire)
2 (climb) escalade *f*
B *vt* brouiller ‹*signal*›
C *vi* **to ~ up** escalader; **to ~ down** dégringoler

scrambled egg *n* (*also* **~s**) œufs *mpl* brouillés

scrambling /'skræmblɪŋ/ *n* (Sport) motocross *m*

scrap /skræp/ **A** *n* **1** (of paper, cloth) petit morceau *m*; (of news, information) fragment *m*
2 (old iron) ferraille *f*
B **scraps** *npl* (of food) restes *mpl*; (from butcher's) déchets *mpl*
C *vt* (*p prés etc* **-pp-**) **1** (fam) abandonner ‹*idea, plan, system*›
2 détruire ‹*aircraft, equipment*›

scrapbook *n* album *m*

scrap dealer *n* ferrailleur *m*

scrape /skreɪp/ **A** *n* **to get into a ~** (fam) s'attirer des ennuis
B *vt* **1** (clean) gratter ‹*vegetables, shoes*›
2 érafler ‹*car, paintwork, furniture*›; **to ~ one's knees** s'écorcher les genoux
C *vi* **to ~ against sth** (rub) frotter contre qch; (scratch) érafler qch
■ **scrape by** (financially) s'en sortir à peine; (in situation) s'en tirer de justesse
■ **scrape in** (to university, class) entrer de justesse
■ **scrape out**: **~ out [sth]**, **~ [sth] out** nettoyer [qch] en grattant ‹*saucepan*›
■ **scrape through**: **A** **~ through** s'en tirer de justesse
B **~ through [sth]** réussir de justesse à ‹*exam, test*›

scrap heap /'skræp hiːp/ *n* **to be thrown on the ~** être mis/-e au rebut

scrap iron, **scrap metal** *n* ferraille *f*

scrap paper *n* papier *m* brouillon

scrap yard /'skræp jɑːd/ *n* chantier *m* de ferraille, casse *f*

scratch /skrætʃ/ **A** *n* **1** (on skin) égratignure *f*; (from a claw, fingernail) griffure *f*
2 (on metal, furniture) éraflure *f*; (on record, glass) rayure *f*
3 (sound) grattement *m*
4 (fam) **he/his work is not up to ~** il/son travail n'est pas à la hauteur
5 to start from ~ partir de zéro
B *vt* **1 to ~ one's initials on sth** graver ses initiales sur qch
2 ‹*cat, person*› griffer ‹*person*›; ‹*thorns, rose bush*› égratigner ‹*person*›; érafler ‹*car, wood*›; rayer ‹*record*›; ‹*cat*› se faire les griffes sur ‹*furniture*›; ‹*person*› **to ~ sb's eyes out** arracher les yeux à quelqu'un
3 to ~ sb's back gratter le dos de qn
C *vi* se gratter

scratch card *n* jeu *m* de grattage

scrawl /skrɔːl/ **A** *n* gribouillage *m*
B *vt*, *vi* gribouiller

scrawny /'skrɔːnɪ/ *adj* ‹*person, animal*› décharné/-e

scream /skriːm/ **A** *n* (of person, animal) cri *m* (perçant); (stronger) hurlement *m*; (of brakes) grincement *m*; (of tyres) crissement *m*
B *vt* crier
C *vi* crier; (stronger) hurler

screech /skriːtʃ/ **A** *n* (of person, animal) cri *m* strident; (of tyres) crissement *m*
B *vi* ‹*person, animal*› pousser un cri strident; ‹*tyres*› crisser

screen /skriːn/ **A** *n* **1** (on TV, VDU, at cinema) écran *m*
2 (furniture) paravent *m*
3 (AmE) (in door) grille *f*
B *vt* **1** (at cinema) projeter; (on TV) diffuser
2 (conceal) cacher; (protect) protéger (**from** de)
3 (test) examiner le cas de ‹*applicants, candidates*›; contrôler ‹*baggage*›; **to ~ sb for cancer** faire passer à qn des tests de dépistage du cancer

screening /'skriːnɪŋ/ *n* **1** (showing) projection *f*; (on TV) diffusion *f*
2 (of patients) examens *mpl* de dépistage
3 (vetting) filtrage *m*

screenplay *n* scénario *m*

screen saver *n* économiseur *m* d'écran

screenwriter *n* scénariste *mf*

screw /skruː/ **A** *n* vis *f*
B *vt* visser (**into** dans, **onto** sur)
■ **screw up 1** froisser ‹*piece of paper, material*›; **to ~ up one's eyes** plisser les yeux; **to ~ up one's face** faire la grimace
2 (fam) faire foirer (fam) ‹*plan, task*›

screwdriver /'skruːdraɪvə(r)/ *n* **1** (tool) tournevis *m*
2 (cocktail) vodka-orange *f*

scribble /'skrɪbl/ *vt*, *vi* griffonner, gribouiller

scrimp /skrɪmp/ *vi* économiser; **to ~ and save** se priver de tout

script /skrɪpt/ *n* **1** (for film, radio, TV) script *m*; (for play) texte *m*
2 (BrE) (Sch, Univ) copie *f* (d'examen)

scripture /'skrɪptʃə(r)/ *n* (*also* **Holy Scripture**, **Holy Scriptures**) (Christian) Écritures *fpl*; (other) textes *mpl* sacrés

scriptwriter *n* scénariste *mf*

scroll /skrəʊl/ *n* rouleau *m*
■ **scroll down**: **A** **~ down** ‹*person*› faire défiler de haut en bas
B **~ down [sth]** faire défiler [qch] de haut en bas ‹*document*›
■ **scroll up**: **A** **~ up** ‹*person*› faire défiler de bas en haut
B **~ up [sth]** faire défiler [qch] de bas en haut ‹*document*›

scroll bar *n* barre *f* de défilement

scrounge /skraʊndʒ/ *vt* (fam) **to ~ sth off sb** piquer (fam) qch à qn ‹*cigarette*›; taper (fam) qn de ‹*money*›

scrounger /'skraʊndʒə(r)/ *n* (fam) parasite *m*

scrub /skrʌb/ **A** *n* **1** (clean) **to give sth a (good) ~** (bien) nettoyer qch
2 (Bot) broussailles *fpl*
B *vt* (*p prés etc* **-bb-**) frotter ‹*back, clothes*›; récurer ‹*pan, floor*›; nettoyer ‹*vegetable*›; **to ~ one's nails** se brosser les ongles
■ **scrub up** ‹*doctor*› se stériliser les mains

scrubbing brush (BrE), **scrub brush** (AmE) *n* brosse *f* de ménage

scruff /skrʌf/ *n* **by the ~ of the neck** par la peau du cou

scruffy /ˈskrʌfɪ/ *adj* ‹*clothes, person*› dépenaillé/-e; ‹*flat, town*› délabré/-e

scrum, **scrummage** /skrʌm/ *n* (in rugby) mêlée *f*

scrunchie *n* chouchou *m*

scruple /ˈskru:pl/ *n* scrupule *m* (**about** vis-à-vis de)

scrupulous /ˈskru:pjʊləs/ *adj* scrupuleux/-euse

scrutinize /ˈskru:tɪnaɪz, (AmE) -tənaɪz/ *vt* scruter ‹*face, motives*›; examiner [qch] minutieusement ‹*document, plan*›; vérifier ‹*accounts, votes*›

scrutiny /ˈskru:tɪnɪ, (AmE) ˈskru:tənɪ/ *n* examen *m*

scuba diving *n* plongée *f* sous-marine

scuff /skʌf/ **A** *n* (*also* **~ mark**) (on floor, furniture) rayure *f*; (on leather) éraflure *f*
B *vt* érafler ‹*shoes*›; rayer ‹*floor, furniture*›

scuffle /ˈskʌfl/ *n* bagarre *f*

sculpt /skʌlpt/ *vt, vi* sculpter

sculptor /ˈskʌlptə(r)/ *n* sculpteur *m*

sculpture /ˈskʌlptʃə(r)/ *n* sculpture *f*

scum /skʌm/ *n* **1** (on pond) écume *f*
2 (on liquid) mousse *f*
3 they're the ~ of the earth c'est de la racaille

scuttle /ˈskʌtl/ **A** *vt* **1** saborder ‹*ship*›
2 faire échouer ‹*talks, project*›
B *vi* **to ~ away** *or* **off** filer

scythe /saɪð/ *n* faux *f inv*

S

⚷ **sea** /si:/ **A** *n* mer *f*; **beside** *or* **by the ~** au bord de la mer; **the open ~** le large; **by ~** ‹*travel*› en bateau; ‹*send*› par bateau
B *adj* ‹*air, breeze*› marin/-e; ‹*bird, water*› de mer; ‹*crossing, voyage*› par mer; ‹*battle*› naval/-e; ‹*power*› maritime

seafood /ˈsi:fu:d/ *n* fruits *mpl* de mer

seafront /ˈsi:frʌnt/ *n* front *m* de mer

seagull *n* mouette *f*

sea horse *n* hippocampe *m*

seal /si:l/ **A** *n* **1** (Zool) phoque *m*
2 (stamp) sceau *m*
3 (on container) plomb *m*; (on package, letter) cachet *m*; (on door) scellés *mpl*
B *vt* **1** cacheter ‹*document*›
2 fermer, cacheter ‹*envelope*›
3 fermer [qch] hermétiquement ‹*jar, tin*›; rendre [qch] étanche ‹*window frame*›
4 sceller ‹*alliance, friendship*› (**with** par); **to ~ sb's fate** décider du sort de qn
■ **seal off** isoler ‹*ward*›; boucler ‹*area, building*›; barrer ‹*street*›

sea lion *n* lion *m* de mer

seam /si:m/ *n* (of garment) couture *f*

seamless /ˈsi:mlɪs/ *adj* ‹*transition*› sans heurts; ‹*process, whole*› continu/-e

seaplane *n* hydravion *m*

⚷ **search** /sɜ:tʃ/ **A** *n* **1** (for person, object) recherches *fpl* (**for sb/sth** pour retrouver qn/qch); **in ~ of** à la recherche de
2 (of place) fouille *f* (**of** de)
3 (Comput) recherche *f*
B *vt* **1** fouiller ‹*area, building*›; fouiller dans ‹*cupboard, drawer, memory*›
2 examiner (attentivement) ‹*map, records*›
C *vi* **1** chercher; **to ~ for** *or* **after sb/sth** chercher qn/qch; **to ~ through** fouiller dans ‹*cupboard, bag*›; examiner ‹*records, file*›
2 (Comput) **to ~ for** rechercher ‹*data, file*›
■ **search out**: **~ [sb/sth] out, ~ out [sb/sth]** découvrir

search engine *n* moteur *m* de recherche

searching /ˈsɜ:tʃɪŋ/ *adj* ‹*look, question*› pénétrant/-e

searchlight *n* projecteur *m*

search party *n* équipe *f* de secours

search warrant *n* mandat *m* de perquisition

sea salt *n* sel *m* de mer

seashell *n* coquillage *m*

seashore /ˈsi:ʃɔ:(r)/ *n* (part of coast) littoral *m*; (beach) plage *f*

seasick /ˈsi:sɪk/ *adj* **to feel ~** avoir le mal de mer

seaside /ˈsi:saɪd/ **A** *n* **the ~** le bord de la mer
B *adj* ‹*hotel*› en bord de mer; ‹*town*› maritime; **~ resort** station *f* balnéaire

⚷ **season** /ˈsi:zn/ **A** *n* saison *f*; **strawberries are in/out of ~** c'est/ce n'est pas la saison des fraises; **the holiday ~** la période des vacances; **Season's greetings!** Joyeuses fêtes!
B *vt* (with spices) relever; (with condiments) assaisonner

seasonal /ˈsi:zənl/ *adj* ‹*work, change*› saisonnier/-ière; ‹*fruit, produce*› de saison

seasoned /ˈsi:znd/ *adj* ‹*soldier*› aguerri/-e; ‹*traveller*› grand/-e *before n*; ‹*campaigner, performer*› expérimenté/-e; ‹*dish*› assaisonné/-e; **highly ~** relevé/-e, épicé/-e

seasoning /ˈsi:znɪŋ/ *n* assaisonnement *m*

season ticket *n* (for travel) carte *f* d'abonnement; (for theatre, matches) abonnement *m*

⚷ **seat** /si:t/ **A** *n* **1** (chair) siège *m*; (bench-type) banquette *f*
2 (place) place *f*; **take** *or* **have a ~** asseyez-

⚷ mot clé

vous; **to book a ~** réserver une place
3 (of trousers) fond *m*
B *vt* **1** placer ‹*person*›
2 the car ~s five c'est une voiture à cinq places; **the table ~s six** c'est une table de six couverts

seat belt /ˈsiːtbelt/ *n* ceinture *f* (de sécurité)

-seater /ˈsiːtə(r)/ *combining form* **a two~** (plane) un avion à deux places; (car) un coupé; (sofa) un (canapé) deux places

seating /ˈsiːtɪŋ/ *n* places *fpl* assises; **I'll organize the ~** je placerai les gens

sea urchin *n* oursin *m*

sea view *n* vue *f* sur la mer

seaweed *n* algue *f* marine

seaworthy /ˈsiːwɜːðɪ/ *adj* en état de naviguer

secateurs /ˌsekəˈtɜːz/ *npl* (BrE) sécateur *m*

secluded /sɪˈkluːdɪd/ *adj* retiré/-e

seclusion /sɪˈkluːʒn/ *n* isolement *m* (**from** à l'écart de)

second /ˈsekənd/ **A** *n* **1** (in order) deuxième *mf*, second/-e *m/f*
2 (unit of time) seconde *f*; (instant) instant *m*
3 (of month) deux *m inv*
4 (Aut) (*also* **~ gear**) deuxième *f*, seconde *f*
5 (defective article) article *m* qui a un défaut
6 (*also* **~-class honours degree**) (BrE) (Univ) ≈ licence *f* avec mention bien
B *adj* deuxième, second/-e; **to have a ~ helping (of sth)** reprendre (de qch); **to have a ~ chance to do sth** avoir une nouvelle chance de faire
C *adv* **1** (in second place) deuxième; **to come** *or* **finish ~** arriver deuxième; **the ~ biggest building** le deuxième bâtiment de par sa grandeur
2 (*also* **secondly**) deuxièmement
D *vt* (in debate) appuyer ‹*proposal*›
IDIOMS **to be ~ nature** être automatique; **to be ~ to none** être sans pareil; **on ~ thoughts** à la réflexion; **to have ~ thoughts** avoir quelques hésitations *or* doutes

secondary /ˈsekəndrɪ, (AmE) -derɪ/ *adj* secondaire

secondary school *n* ≈ école *f* secondaire

second class **A** *adv* ‹*travel*› en deuxième classe; ‹*send*› au tarif lent
B **second-class** *adj* **1** ‹*post, stamp*› au tarif lent
2 ‹*carriage, ticket*› de deuxième classe
3 (second-rate) de qualité inférieure

second hand /ˈsekəndhænd/ **A** *n* (on watch, clock) trotteuse *f*
B **second-hand** *adj* ‹*clothes, car*› d'occasion; ‹*news, information*› de seconde main
C *adv* ‹*buy*› d'occasion; ‹*find out, hear*› indirectement

secondly /ˈsekəndlɪ/ *adv* deuxièmement

second name *n* (surname) nom *m* de famille; (second forename) deuxième prénom *m*

second-rate *adj* de second ordre

seconds *npl* (fam) rab *m* (fam)

secrecy /ˈsiːkrəsɪ/ *n* secret *m*

secret /ˈsiːkrɪt/ **A** *n* secret *m*; **to tell sb a ~** confier un secret à qn
B *adj* secret/-ète
C **in secret** *phr* en secret

secretarial /ˌsekrəˈteərɪəl/ *adj* ‹*skills, work*› de secrétaire; ‹*college*› de secrétariat

secretary /ˈsekrətrɪ, (AmE) -rəterɪ/ *n*
1 (assistant) secrétaire *mf* (**to sb** de qn)
2 Foreign Secretary (BrE), **Secretary of State** (AmE) ministre *m* des Affaires étrangères

secretive /ˈsiːkrətɪv/ *adj* ‹*person, organization*› secret/-ète; **to be ~ about sth** faire un mystère de qch

secretly /ˈsiːkrɪtlɪ/ *adv* secrètement

secret weapon *n* arme *f* secrète

sect /sekt/ *n* secte *f*

section /ˈsekʃn/ *n* **1** (of train, aircraft, town, book) partie *f*; (of pipe, tunnel, road) tronçon *m*; (of object, kit) élément *m*; (of fruit) quartier *m*; (of population) tranche *f*
2 (of company, department) service *m*; (of library, shop) rayon *m*
3 (of act, bill, report) article *m*; (of newspaper) rubrique *f*

sector /ˈsektə(r)/ *n* secteur *m*

secular /ˈsekjʊlə(r)/ *adj* ‹*politics, society, education*› laïque; ‹*belief, music*› profane

secure /sɪˈkjʊə(r)/ **A** *adj* **1** ‹*job, marriage, income*› stable; ‹*basis, base*› solide
2 ‹*hiding place*› sûr/-e
3 ‹*padlock, knot*› solide; ‹*structure, ladder*› stable; ‹*rope*› bien attaché/-e; ‹*door, window*› bien fermé/-e; ‹*line*› sécurisé/-e
4 to feel ~ se sentir en sécurité
B *vt* **1** obtenir ‹*promise, release, right, victory*›
2 bien attacher ‹*rope*›; bien fermer ‹*door, window*›; stabiliser ‹*ladder*›
3 protéger ‹*house*›; assurer ‹*position, future*›
4 garantir ‹*loan, debt*› (**against, on** sur)

secure unit *n* (in children's home) *section surveillée dans une maison de rééducation*; (in psychiatric hospital) quartier *m* de haute sécurité

securities /sɪˈkjʊərətɪz/ *npl* titres *mpl*

security /sɪˈkjʊərətɪ/ **A** *n* **1** sécurité *f*; **job ~** sécurité de l'emploi; **national ~** sûreté *f* de l'État
2 (guarantee) garantie *f* (**on** sur)
B *adj* ‹*camera, check, measures*› de sécurité; ‹*firm, staff*› de surveillance

security code *n* code *m* de sécurité

security guard *n* garde *m* sécurité, vigile *m*

security leak *n* fuite *f* (*d'information*)

S

sedate /sɪ'deɪt/ **A** *adj* ‹*person*› posé/-e; ‹*lifestyle, pace*› tranquille
B *vt* mettre [qn] sous calmants ‹*patient*›

sedation /sɪ'deɪʃn/ *n* sédation *f*; **under ~** sous calmants

sedative /'sedətɪv/ *n* sédatif *m*, calmant *m*

seduce /sɪ'djuːs, (AmE) -'duːs/ *vt* séduire

seductive /sɪ'dʌktɪv/ *adj* ‹*person*› séduisant/-e; ‹*smile*› aguicheur/-euse

🔑 **see** /siː/ **A** *vt* (*prét* **saw**, *pp* **seen**) **1** voir; **can you ~ him?** est-ce que tu le vois?; **I can't ~ him** je ne le vois pas; **to ~ the sights** faire du tourisme; **~ you next week!** à la semaine prochaine!; **to ~ sb as** considérer qn comme ‹*friend, hero*›; **it remains to be seen whether** *or* **if** reste à voir si
2 (make sure) **to ~ (to it) that** veiller à ce que (+ *subjunctive*); **~ (to it) that the children are in bed by nine** veillez à ce que les enfants soient couchés à neuf heures
3 (accompany) **to ~ sb to the station** accompagner qn à la gare; **to ~ sb home** raccompagner qn chez lui/elle
B *vi* (*prét* **saw**, *pp* **seen**) voir; **I can't ~** je ne vois rien; **I'll go and ~** je vais voir; **we'll just have to wait and ~** il ne nous reste plus qu'à attendre; **let's ~, let me ~** voyons (un peu)

■ **see off**: **to ~ sb off** dire au revoir à qn

■ **see out**: **to ~ sb out** raccompagner qn à la porte

■ **see through**: **A ~ through [sth]** déceler ‹*deception, lie*›
B ~ through [sb] percer [qn] à jour
C ~ [sth] through mener [qch] à bonne fin

■ **see to** s'occuper de ‹*arrangements*›

🔑 **seed** /siːd/ *n* **1** (gen) graine *f*; (fruit pip) pépin *m*; (for sowing) semences *fpl*; **to go to ~** ‹*plant*› monter en graine; ‹*person*› se ramollir; ‹*organization, country*› être en déclin
2 (Sport) tête *f* de série

seedling /'siːdlɪŋ/ *n* plant *m*

seedy /'siːdɪ/ *adj* ‹*person*› louche; ‹*area, club*› mal famé/-e

🔑 **seek** /siːk/ *vt* (*prét, pp* **sought**) **1** chercher ‹*agreement, refuge, solution*›; demander ‹*advice, help, permission*›
2 ‹*police, employer*› rechercher ‹*person*›

■ **seek out** aller chercher, dénicher

🔑 **seem** /siːm/ *vi* sembler; **it ~s that** il semble que (+ *subjunctive*); **it ~s to me that** il me semble que (+ *indicative*); **he ~s happy/disappointed** il a l'air heureux/déçu; **it ~s odd (to me)** ça (me) paraît bizarre; **he ~s to be looking for someone** on dirait qu'il cherche quelqu'un

seep /siːp/ *vi* suinter; **to ~ away** s'écouler; **to ~ through sth** ‹*water, gas*› s'infiltrer à travers qch; ‹*light*› filtrer à travers qch

seesaw /'siːsɔː/ **A** *n* tapecul *m*
B *vi* ‹*price, rate*› osciller

seethe /siːð/ *vi* **1 to ~ with rage** bouillir de colère; **he was seething** il était furibond
2 (teem) grouiller; **the streets were seething with tourists** les rues grouillaient de touristes

see-through *adj* transparent/-e

segment /'segmənt/ *n* segment *m*; (of orange) quartier *m*

segregate /'segrɪgəɪt/ *vt* **1** (separate) séparer (**from** de)
2 (isolate) isoler (**from** de)

segregated /'segrəgeɪtɪd/ *adj* ‹*education, society*› ségrégationniste; ‹*area, school*› où la ségrégation raciale (*or* religieuse) est en vigueur

segregation /ˌsegrɪ'geɪʃn/ *n* ségrégation *f* (**from** de)

seize /siːz/ *vt* **1** saisir; **to ~ hold of** se saisir de ‹*person*›; s'emparer de ‹*object*›
2 s'emparer de ‹*territory, prisoner, power*›; prendre ‹*control*›

■ **seize up** ‹*engine*› se gripper; ‹*limb*› se bloquer

seizure /'siːʒə(r)/ *n* **1** (of territory, power) prise *f*; (of arms, drugs, property) saisie *f*
2 (Med) attaque *f*

seldom /'seldəm/ *adv* rarement

🔑 **select** /sɪ'lekt/ **A** *adj* ‹*group*› privilégié/-e; ‹*hotel*› chic, sélect/-e; ‹*area*› chic, cossu/-e
B *vt* sélectionner (**from, from among** parmi)

🔑 **selection** /sɪ'lekʃn/ *n* sélection *f*

selective /sɪ'lektɪv/ *adj* ‹*memory, recruitment*› sélectif/-ive; ‹*admission, education*› basé/-e sur la sélection; ‹*account*› tendancieux/-ieuse

🔑 **self** /self/ *n* (*pl* **selves**) moi *m*; **he's back to his old ~ again** il est redevenu lui-même

self-addressed envelope, SAE *n* enveloppe *f* à mon/votre etc adresse

self-adhesive *adj* autocollant/-e

self-assembly *adj* en kit

self-assured /ˌselfə'ʃɔːd, (AmE) -'ʃʊərd/ *adj* plein/-e d'assurance

self-catering /ˌself'keɪtərɪŋ/ *adj* ‹*flat*› avec cuisine; **~ holiday** vacances *fpl* en location

self-centred (BrE), **self-centered** (AmE) *adj* égocentrique

self-confessed *adj* avoué/-e

self-confidence *n* assurance *f*

self-confident *adj* ‹*person*› sûr/-e de soi; ‹*attitude*› plein/-e d'assurance

self-conscious /ˌself'kɒnʃəs/ *adj* **1** (shy) timide; **to be ~ about sth/about doing** être gêné/-e par qch/de faire
2 ‹*style*› conscient/-e

self-contained /ˌselfkən'teɪnd/ *adj* ‹*flat*› indépendant/-e

self-control /ˌselfkən'trəʊl/ *n* sang-froid *m*

self-defence (BrE), **self-defense** (AmE) /ˌselfdɪ'fens/ *n* (gen) autodéfense *f*; (Law)

🔑 mot clé

légitime défense *f*
self-destructive *adj* autodestructeur/-trice
self-determination *n* autodétermination *f*
self-disciplined *adj* autodiscipliné/-e
self-effacing *adj* effacé/-e
self-employed /ˌselfɪm'plɔɪd/ *adj* indépendant/-e; **to be ~** travailler à son compte
self-esteem *n* amour-propre *m*
self-evident *adj* évident/-e
self-explanatory *adj* explicite
self-expression /ˌselfɪk'spreʃn/ *n* expression *f* de soi/de lui-même etc
self-governing *adj* autonome
self-image *n* image *f* de soi-même/de lui-même etc
self-important *adj* suffisant/-e
self-induced *adj* auto-infligé/-e
self-indulgent *adj* complaisant/-e
self-interested *adj* intéressé/-e
selfish /'selfɪʃ/ *adj* égoïste (**to do** de faire)
selfishness /'selfɪʃnɪs/ *n* égoïsme *m*
selfless /'selflɪs/ *adj* ‹*person*› dévoué/-e; ‹*devotion*› désintéressé/-e
self-pity *n* apitoiement *m* sur soi-même
self-portrait *n* autoportrait *m*
self-raising flour (BrE), **self-rising flour** (AmE) *n* farine *f* à gâteau
self-reliant *adj* autosuffisant/-e
self-respect *n* respect *m* de soi
self-respecting *adj* ‹*teacher, journalist, comedian*› qui se respecte
self-righteous *adj* satisfait/-e de soi-même
self-rule *n* autonomie *f*
self-sacrifice *n* abnégation *f*
self-satisfied *adj* satisfait/-e de soi-même
self-service /ˌself'sɜːvɪs/ **A** *n* libre-service *m* **B** *adj* ‹*cafeteria*› en libre-service
self-sufficient *adj* autosuffisant/-e
self-taught *adj* autodidacte
sell /sel/ **A** *vt* (*prét, pp* **sold**) **1** vendre; **to ~ sth to sb, to ~ sb sth** vendre qch à qn; **to ~ sth for £5** vendre qch 5 livres sterling
2 (promote sale of) faire vendre
3 faire accepter ‹*idea, image, policy, party*›
B *vi* (*prét, pp* **sold**) **1** ‹*person, shop, dealer*› vendre (**to sb** à qn)
2 ‹*goods, product, house, book*› se vendre
■ **sell off**: **~ [sth] off, ~ off [sth]** liquider; (in sale) solder
■ **sell out 1** ‹*merchandise*› se vendre; **we've sold out of tickets** tous les billets ont été vendus; **we've sold out** nous avons tout vendu; **the play has sold out** la pièce affiche complet
2 (fam) (betray one's principles) retourner sa veste (fam)
sell-by date *n* date *f* limite de vente
seller's market *n* marché *m* à la hausse
selling /'selɪŋ/ **A** *n* vente *f* **B** *adj* ‹*price*› de vente
Sellotape® /'seləʊteɪp/ (BrE) **A** *n* scotch® *m* **B** *vt* scotcher
sellout /'selaʊt/ **A** *n* **the show was a ~** le spectacle affichait complet **B** *adj* ‹*performance*› à guichets fermés
semen /'siːmən/ *n* sperme *m*
semester /sɪ'mestə(r)/ *n* (AmE) semestre *m*
semi-automatic *n, adj* semi-automatique *m*
semibreve *n* (BrE) (Mus) ronde *f*
semicircle *n* demi-cercle *m*
semicolon *n* point-virgule *m*
semi-conscious *adj* à peine conscient/-e
semi-darkness *n* pénombre *f*, demi-jour *m*
semi-detached *n* (*also* **semi-detached house**) maison *f* jumelée
semi-final *n* demi-finale *f*
semi-finalist *n* demi-finaliste *mf*
seminar /'semɪnɑː(r)/ *n* séminaire *m* (**on** sur)
semi-skimmed *adj* (BrE) ‹*milk*› demi-écrémé/-e
senate /'senɪt/ *n* sénat *m*
senator /'senətə(r)/ *n* sénateur *m* (**for** de)
send /send/ *vt* (*prét, pp* **sent**) **1** envoyer; **to ~ sth to sb, to ~ sb sth** envoyer qch à qn; **to ~ sb home** (from school, work) renvoyer qn chez lui/elle; **to ~ sb to prison** mettre qn en prison; **~ her my love!** embrasse-la de ma part; **~ them my regards** transmettez-leur mes amitiés
2 to ~ shivers down sb's spine donner froid dans le dos à qn; **to ~ sb to sleep** endormir qn; **it sent him into fits of laughter** ça l'a fait éclater de rire
IDIOM **to ~ sb packing** (fam) envoyer balader qn (fam)
■ **send away**: **A ~ away for [sth]** commander [qch] par correspondance
B ~ [sb/sth] away faire partir
C to ~ an appliance away to be mended envoyer un appareil chez le fabricant pour le faire réparer
■ **send for** appeler ‹*doctor, plumber*›; demander ‹*reinforcements*›
■ **send in** envoyer ‹*letter, form, troops*›; faire entrer ‹*visitor*›; **to ~ in one's application** poser sa candidature
■ **send off**: **A ~ off for [sth]** commander [qch] par correspondance
B ~ [sth] off envoyer, expédier ‹*letter*›
C ~ [sb] off (Sport) expulser
■ **send on** expédier [qch] à l'avance ‹*baggage*›; faire suivre ‹*letter, parcel*›
■ **send out 1** émettre ‹*light, heat*›
2 faire sortir ‹*pupil*›
■ **send up** (BrE) (fam) (parody) parodier

sender /'sendə(r)/ *n* expéditeur/-trice *m/f*

send-off /'sendɒf/ *n* adieux *mpl*

send-up *n* (BrE) (fam) parodie *f*

senile /'si:naɪl/ *adj* sénile

senile dementia *n* démence *f* sénile

⚷ **senior** /'si:nɪə(r)/ **A** *n* **1** (gen) aîné/-e *m/f*; **to be sb's ~** être plus âgé/-e que qn
2 (BrE) (Sch) élève *mf* dans les grandes classes; (AmE) (Sch) élève *mf* de terminale
B *adj* **1** (older) ‹*person*› plus âgé/-e
2 ‹*civil servant*› haut/-e *before n*; ‹*partner*› principal/-e; ‹*officer, job, post*› supérieur/-e

senior citizen *n* personne *f* du troisième âge

senior high school *n* (AmE) (Sch) ≈ lycée *m*

seniority /,si:nɪ'ɒrətɪ, (AmE) -'ɔ:r-/ *n* (in years) âge *m*; (in rank) statut *m* supérieur; (in years of service) ancienneté *f*

senior management *n* direction *f*

senior school *n* lycée *m*

sensation /sen'seɪʃn/ *n* sensation *f*; **to cause** *or* **create a ~** faire sensation

sensational /sen'seɪʃənl/ *adj* sensationnel/-elle

sensationalist /sen'seɪʃənəlɪst/ *adj* ‹*headline, story, writer*› à sensation

sensationalize /sen'seɪʃənəlaɪz/ *vt* faire un reportage à sensation sur ‹*event, story*›

⚷ **sense** /sens/ **A** *n* **1** (faculty, ability) sens *m*; **a ~ of humour/direction** le sens de l'humour/de l'orientation; **~ of hearing** ouïe *f*; **~ of sight** vue *f*; **~ of smell** odorat *m*; **~ of taste** goût *m*; **~ of touch** toucher *m*; **to lose all ~ of time** perdre toute notion du temps
2 (feeling) **a ~ of identity** un sentiment d'identité; **a ~ of purpose** le sentiment d'avoir un but
3 (common) ~ bon sens *m*; **to have the ~ to do** avoir le bon sens de faire
4 (meaning) sens *m*; (reason) **there's no ~ in doing** cela ne sert à rien de faire; **to make ~ of sth** comprendre qch; **I can't make ~ of this article** je ne comprends rien à cet article; **to make ~** ‹*sentence, film*› avoir un sens
B senses *npl* **to come to one's senses** revenir à la raison
C *vt* **1** deviner (**that** que); **to ~ danger** sentir un danger
2 ‹*machine*› détecter
(IDIOMS) **to see ~** entendre raison; **to talk ~** dire des choses sensées

senseless /'senslɪs/ *adj* **1** ‹*violence*› gratuit/-e; ‹*discussion*› absurde; ‹*act, waste*› insensé/-e
2 to knock sb ~ faire perdre connaissance à qn

sensible /'sensəbl/ *adj* ‹*person, attitude*› raisonnable; ‹*decision, solution*› judicieux/-ieuse; ‹*garment*› pratique; ‹*diet*› intelligent/-e

sensitive /'sensətɪv/ *adj* **1** (gen) sensible (**to** à)
2 ‹*person*› (easily hurt) sensible, susceptible (**to** à)
3 ‹*situation*› délicat/-e; ‹*issue*› difficile; ‹*information*› confidentiel/-ielle

sensitivity /,sensə'tɪvətɪ/ *n* sensibilité *f* (**to** à)

sensor /'sensə(r)/ *n* détecteur *m*

sensual /'senʃʊəl/ *adj* sensuel/-elle

⚷ **sentence** /'sentəns/ **A** *n* **1** (Law) peine *f*; **to serve a ~** purger une peine
2 (in grammar) phrase *f*
B *vt* condamner (**to** à, **to do** à faire, **for** pour)

sentiment /'sentɪmənt/ *n* **1** (feeling) sentiment *m* (**for** pour, **towards** envers)
2 (opinion) opinion *f*

sentimental /,sentɪ'mentl/ *adj* sentimental/-e

sentry /'sentrɪ/ *n* sentinelle *f*

⚷ **separate A** /'sepərət/ *adj* **1** (independent, apart) ‹*piece, section*› à part; **she has a ~ room** elle a une chambre à part; **the flat is ~ from the rest of the house** l'appartement est indépendant du reste de la maison; **keep the knives ~** rangez les couteaux séparément; **keep the knives ~ from the forks** séparez les couteaux des fourchettes
2 (different) ‹*sections, problems*› différent/-e; ‹*organizations, agreements*› distinct/-e; **they have ~ rooms** ils ont chacun leur chambre; **they asked for ~ bills** (in restaurant) ils ont demandé chacun leur addition
B /'sepəreɪt/ *vt* **1** séparer (**from** de)
2 (sort out) répartir ‹*people*›; trier ‹*objects, produce*›
C /'sepəreɪt/ *vi* se séparer (**from** de)

separately /'sepərətlɪ/ *adv* séparément

separates *npl* (garments) coordonnés *mpl*

separation /,sepə'reɪʃn/ *n* séparation *f* (**from** de)

separatist /'sepərətɪst/ *n, adj* séparatiste *mf*

⚷ **September** /sep'tembə(r)/ *n* septembre *m*

septic /'septɪk/ *adj* infecté/-e; **to go** *or* **turn ~** s'infecter

septic tank *n* fosse *f* septique

sequel /'si:kwəl/ *n* suite *f* (**to** à)

sequence /'si:kwəns/ *n* **1** (series) série *f*
2 (order) ordre *m*; **in ~** dans l'ordre
3 (in film) séquence *f*

Serbia /'sɜ:bɪə/ *pr n* Serbie *f*

Serb, Serbian A *n* Serbe *mf*
B *adj* serbe

serene /sɪ'ri:n/ *adj* serein/-e

sergeant /'sɑ:dʒənt/ *n* **1** (BrE) (Mil) sergent *m*
2 (AmE) (Mil) caporal-chef *m*
3 (in police) ≈ brigadier *m*

serial /'sɪərɪəl/ *n* feuilleton *m*; **TV ~** feuilleton télévisé

⚷ mot clé

S

serialize /ˈsɪərɪəlaɪz/ *vt* adapter [qch] en feuilleton

serial killer *n* tueur *m* en série

serial number *n* numéro *m* de série

series /ˈsɪəriːz/ *n* (*pl* ~) série *f*; **a drama ~** une série de fiction

serious /ˈsɪərɪəs/ *adj* ‹*person, expression, discussion, offer*› sérieux/-ieuse; ‹*accident, crime, crisis, problem*› grave; ‹*literature, actor*› de qualité; ‹*attempt, concern*› réel/réelle; **to be ~ about sth** prendre qch au sérieux; **to be ~ about doing** avoir vraiment l'intention de faire

seriously /ˈsɪərɪəslɪ/ *adv* **1** ‹*speak, think*› sérieusement; **to take sb/sth ~** prendre qn/qch au sérieux
2 ‹*ill, injured*› gravement; ‹*underestimate*› vraiment

seriousness /ˈsɪərɪəsnɪs/ *n* **1** (of person, film, study) sérieux *m*; (of tone, occasion, reply) gravité *f*; **in all ~** sérieusement
2 (of illness, problem, situation) gravité *f*

sermon /ˈsɜːmən/ *n* sermon *m*

serrated /sɪˈreɪtɪd, (AmE) ˈsereɪtɪd/ *adj* dentelé/-e; **~ knife** couteau-scie *m*

serum /ˈsɪərəm/ *n* sérum *m*

servant /ˈsɜːvənt/ *n* domestique *mf*

serve /sɜːv/ **A** *n* (Sport) service *m*
B *vt* **1** servir ‹*country, cause, public*›; travailler au service de ‹*employer, family*›
2 servir ‹*customer, guest, meal, dish*›; **to ~ sb with sth** servir qch à qn
3 (provide facility) ‹*power station, reservoir*› alimenter; ‹*public transport, library, hospital*› desservir
4 (satisfy) servir ‹*interests*›; satisfaire ‹*needs*›
5 to ~ a purpose être utile; **to ~ the** *or* **sb's purpose** faire l'affaire
6 purger ‹*prison sentence*›
7 (Law) délivrer ‹*injunction*› (**on sb** à qn); **to ~ a summons on sb** citer qn à comparaître
8 (Sport) servir
C *vi* **1** (in shop) servir; (at table) faire le service
2 to ~ on être membre de ‹*committee, jury*›
3 to ~ as sth servir de qch
4 (Mil) servir (**as** comme, **under** sous)
5 (Sport) servir (**for** pour); **Bruno to ~** au service, Bruno
IDIOM **it ~s you right!** ça t'apprendra!

server /ˈsɜːvə(r)/ *n* (Sport, Comput) serveur *m*

service /ˈsɜːvɪs/ **A** *n* **1** (gen) service *m*; **(accident and) emergency ~** service des urgences; **'out of ~'** (on machine) 'en panne'
2 (overhaul) révision *f*
3 (ceremony) office *m*; **Sunday ~** office du dimanche; **marriage ~** cérémonie *f* nuptiale
B services *npl* (BrE) **1** (*also* **~ area**) aire *m* de services
2 (Mil) **the Services** les armées *fpl*
C *vt* faire la révision de ‹*vehicle*›; entretenir ‹*machine, boiler*›; **to have one's car ~d** faire réviser sa voiture

service centre (BrE), **service center** (AmE) *n* centre *m* de service après-vente

service charge *n* **1** (in restaurant) service *m*; **what is the ~?** le service est de combien?
2 (in banking) frais *mpl* de gestion de compte

service engineer *n* technicien *m* de maintenance

serviceman *n* (*pl* **-men**) militaire *m*

service provider *n* fournisseur *m* d'accès

service station *n* station-service *f*

servicewoman *n* (*pl* **-women**) femme *f* soldat

serving /ˈsɜːvɪŋ/ *n* portion *f*

serving dish *n* plat *m* (de service)

serving spoon *n* cuillère *f* de service

session /ˈseʃn/ *n* **1** (gen) séance *f*
2 (of parliament) session *f*
3 (AmE) (Sch) (term) trimestre *m*; (period of lessons) cours *mpl*

set /set/ **A** *n* **1** (of keys, tools) jeu *m*; (of golf clubs, chairs) série *f*; (of cutlery) service *m*; (of rules, instructions, tests) série *f*; **a new ~ of clothes** des vêtements neufs; **they're sold in ~s of 10** ils sont vendus par lots de 10; **a ~ of fingerprints** des empreintes digitales; **a ~ of traffic lights** des feux *mpl* (de signalisation); **a chess ~** un jeu d'échecs; **a ~ of false teeth** un dentier
2 (Sport) (in tennis) set *m*
3 TV *or* **television ~** poste *m* de télévision
4 (scenery) (for play) décor *m*; (for film) plateau *m*
5 (BrE) (Sch) groupe *m*
6 (hair-do) mise *f* en plis
B *adj* **1** ‹*pattern, procedure, rule, task*› bien déterminé/-e; ‹*time, price*› fixe; ‹*menu*› à prix fixe; **~ phrase** expression *f* consacrée; **to be ~ in one's ways** avoir ses habitudes
2 ‹*expression, smile*› figé/-e
3 (Sch, Univ) ‹*text*› au programme
4 (ready) prêt/-e (**for** pour, **to do** à faire)
5 to be (dead) ~ against sth/doing être tout à fait contre qch/l'idée de faire; **to be ~ on doing** tenir absolument à faire
6 ‹*jam, jelly, honey*› épais/épaisse; ‹*cement*› dur/-e; ‹*yoghurt*› ferme
C *vt* (*p prés* **-tt-**, *prét*, *pp* **set**) **1** (place) placer ‹*object*› (**on** sur); monter ‹*gem*› (**in** dans); **a house ~ among the trees** une maison située au milieu des arbres; **to ~ the record straight** mettre les choses au point; **his eyes are ~ very close together** ses yeux sont très rapprochés
2 mettre ‹*table*›; tendre ‹*trap*›
3 fixer ‹*date, deadline, price, target*›; lancer ‹*fashion, trend*›; donner ‹*tone*›; établir ‹*precedent, record*›; **to ~ a good/bad example to sb** montrer le bon/mauvais exemple à qn; **to ~ one's sights on** viser

S

4 mettre [qch] à l'heure ‹*clock*›; mettre ‹*alarm clock, burglar alarm*›
5 (start) **to ~ sth going** mettre qch en marche ‹*machine*›; **to ~ sb laughing/thinking** faire rire/réfléchir qn
6 donner ‹*homework, essay*›; **to ~ an exam** préparer les sujets d'examen
7 (in fiction, film) situer; **the film is ~ in Munich** le film se passe à Munich
8 to ~ sth to music mettre qch en musique
9 (Med) immobiliser ‹*broken bone*›
10 to have one's hair ~ se faire faire une mise en plis
D *vi* (*p prés* **-tt-**, *prét*, *pp* **set**) **1** ‹*sun*› se coucher
2 ‹*jam, concrete*› prendre; ‹*glue*› sécher
3 (Med) ‹*fracture*› se ressouder

■ **set about** se mettre à ‹*work*›; **to ~ about (the job** *or* **task of) doing** commencer à faire
■ **set apart** distinguer (**from** de)
■ **set aside** réserver ‹*area, room, time*› (**for** pour); mettre [qch] de côté ‹*money, stock*›
■ **set back**: **A** **~ back [sth], ~ [sth] back** (delay) retarder
B **~ [sb] back** coûter les yeux de la tête à (fam)
■ **set down** **~ down [sth], ~ [sth] down**
1 (establish) fixer ‹*conditions*›
2 (record) enregistrer ‹*fact*›
■ **set in** ‹*infection*› se déclarer; ‹*depression*› s'installer
■ **set off**: **A** **~ off** partir (**for** pour); **to ~ off on a journey** partir en voyage
B **~ [sth] off 1** faire partir ‹*firework*›; faire exploser ‹*bomb*›; déclencher ‹*riot, panic, alarm*›
2 (enhance) mettre [qch] en valeur ‹*garment*›
3 to ~ sth off against profits/debts déduire qch des bénéfices/des dettes
C **~ [sb] off** faire pleurer ‹*baby*›; **she laughed and that ~ me off** elle a ri et ça m'a fait rire à mon tour
■ **set on**: **A** **~ on [sb]** attaquer
B **~ [sth] on sb** lâcher [qch] contre qn ‹*dog*›
■ **set out**: **A** **~ out** se mettre en route (**for** pour, **to do** pour faire); **to ~ out to do** ‹*person*› entreprendre de faire
B **~ [sth] out 1** disposer ‹*goods, chairs, food*›; préparer ‹*board game*›
2 présenter ‹*ideas, proposals*›; formuler ‹*objections, terms*›
■ **set up**: **A** **to ~ up on one's own** s'établir à son compte; **to ~ up in business** monter une affaire
B **~ [sth] up 1** monter ‹*stand, stall*›; assembler ‹*equipment, easel*›; ériger ‹*roadblock*›; **to ~ up home** s'installer
2 préparer ‹*experiment*›; (Sport) préparer ‹*goal, try*›
3 créer ‹*business, company*›; implanter ‹*factory*›; former ‹*support group, charity*›; constituer ‹*committee*›
4 organiser ‹*meeting*›; mettre [qch] en place ‹*procedures*›
C **~ [sb] up 1 she ~ her son up (in business) as a gardener** elle a aidé son fils à s'installer comme jardinier
2 that deal has ~ her up for life grâce à ce contrat elle n'aura plus à se soucier de rien
3 (BrE) (fam) ‹*police*› tendre un piège à ‹*criminal*›; ‹*friend*› monter un coup contre ‹*person*›

setback /ˈsetbæk/ *n* revers *m* (**for** pour)
settee /seˈtiː/ *n* canapé *m*
setting /ˈsetɪŋ/ *n* **1** (location) cadre *m*
2 (in jewellery) monture *f*
3 (position on dial) position *f* (de réglage)
setting-up /ˌsetɪŋˈʌp/ *n* (of scheme, business) création *f*; (of factory) implantation *f*
settle /ˈsetl/ **A** *vt* **1** installer ‹*person, animal*›
2 calmer ‹*stomach, nerves*›
3 régler ‹*matter, business, dispute*›; mettre fin à ‹*conflict, strike*›; régler, résoudre ‹*problem*›; décider ‹*match*›; **that's ~d** voilà qui est réglé
4 fixer ‹*arrangements, price*›
5 to ~ one's affairs mettre de l'ordre dans ses affaires
6 régler ‹*bill, debt, claim*›
B *vi* **1** ‹*dust*› se déposer; ‹*bird, insect*› se poser
2 (in new home) s'installer
3 ‹*contents, ground*› se tasser
4 ‹*weather*› se mettre au beau fixe
5 (Law) régler; **to ~ out of court** parvenir à un règlement à l'amiable
■ **settle down 1** (get comfortable) s'installer (**on** sur, **in** dans)
2 (calm down) ‹*person*› se calmer
3 (marry) se ranger
■ **settle for**: **~ for sth** se contenter de qch
■ **settle in 1** (move in) s'installer
2 (become acclimatized) s'adapter
■ **settle up** (pay) payer

settlement /ˈsetlmənt/ *n* **1** (agreement) accord *m*
2 (Law) règlement *m*
3 (dwellings) village *m*; (colonial) territoire *m*
set-top box /setˌtɒp bɒks/ *n* décodeur *m*
seven /ˈsevn/ *n, pron, det* sept *m inv*
seventeen /ˌsevnˈtiːn/ *n, pron, det* dix-sept *m inv*
seventeenth /ˌsevnˈtiːnθ/ **A** *n* **1** (in order) dix-septième *mf*
2 (of month) dix-sept *m inv*
3 (fraction) dix-septième *m*
B *adj, adv* dix-septième
seventh /ˈsevnθ/ **A** *n* **1** (in order) septième *mf*
2 (of month) sept *m inv*
3 (fraction) septième *m*
B *adj, adv* septième
seventies /ˈsevntɪz/ *npl* **1** (era) **the ~** les années *fpl* soixante-dix
2 (age) **to be in one's ~** avoir plus de

mot clé

soixante-dix ans

seventieth /ˈsevntɪəθ/ *n, adj, adv* soixante-dixième *mf*

seventy /ˈsevntɪ/ *n, pron, det* soixante-dix *m inv*

sever /ˈsevə(r)/ *vt* **1** sectionner ‹*limb, artery*›; couper ‹*rope, branch*›
2 rompre ‹*link, relations*›; couper ‹*communications*›

⚷ **several** /ˈsevrəl/ **A** *quantif* **~ of you/us** plusieurs d'entre vous/d'entre nous
B *det* plusieurs; **~ books** plusieurs livres

⚷ **severe** /sɪˈvɪə(r)/ *adj* **1** ‹*problem, damage, shortage, injury, depression, shock*› grave; ‹*weather, cold, winter*› rigoureux/-euse
2 (harsh) sévère (**with sb** avec qn)
3 ‹*haircut, clothes*› austère

severely /sɪˈvɪəlɪ/ *adv* ‹*damage*› sévèrement; ‹*affect, shock*› durement; ‹*disabled*› gravement; ‹*injured*› grièvement; ‹*beat*› violemment

severity /sɪˈverətɪ/ *n* (of problem, illness) gravité *f*; (of punishment, treatment) sévérité *f*; (of climate) rigueur *f*

sew /səʊ/ **A** *vt* (*prét* **sewed**, *pp* **sewn**, **sewed**) coudre
B *vi* (*prét* **sewed**, *pp* **sewn**, **sewed**) coudre, faire de la couture
■ **sew up** recoudre ‹*hole, tear*›; faire ‹*seam*›; (re)coudre ‹*wound*›

sewage /ˈsuːɪdʒ, ˈsjuː-/ *n* eaux *fpl* usées

sewer /ˈsuːə(r), ˈsjuː-/ *n* égout *m*

sewing /ˈsəʊɪŋ/ *n* (activity) couture *f*; (piece of work) ouvrage *m*

sewing machine *n* machine *f* à coudre

⚷ **sex** /seks/ **A** *n* **1** (gender) sexe *m*; **the opposite ~** le sexe opposé
2 (intercourse) (one act) rapport *m* sexuel; (repeated) rapports *mpl* sexuels
B *adj* sexuel/-elle

sex change *n* **to have a ~** changer de sexe

sex discrimination *n* discrimination *f* sexuelle

sex education *n* éducation *f* sexuelle

sexism /ˈseksɪzəm/ *n* sexisme *m*

sexist /ˈseksɪst/ *n, adj* sexiste *mf*

sex object *n* objet *m* érotique

sex offender *n* délinquant/-e *m/f* sexuel/-elle

⚷ **sexual** /ˈsekʃʊəl/ *adj* sexuel/-elle

sexual abuse *n* violence *f* sexuelle

sexual harassment *n* harcèlement *m* sexuel

sexuality /ˌsekʃʊˈælətɪ/ *n* sexualité *f*

sexually transmitted disease, **STD** *n* maladie *f* sexuellement transmissible, MST *f*

sexy /ˈseksɪ/ *adj* (fam) ‹*person, clothing*› sexy *inv* (fam); ‹*book*› érotique

shabby /ˈʃæbɪ/ *adj* ‹*person*› habillé/-e de façon miteuse; ‹*room, furnishings, clothing*› miteux/-euse; ‹*treatment*› mesquin/-e

shack /ʃæk/ *n* cabane *f*

shade /ʃeɪd/ **A** *n* **1** (shadow) ombre *f*; **in the ~** à l'ombre (**of** de)
2 (of colour) ton *m*
3 (*also* **lamp ~**) abat-jour *m inv*
4 (AmE) (*also* **window ~**) store *m*
B *vt* donner de l'ombre à; **to ~ one's eyes (with one's hand)** s'abriter les yeux de la main
IDIOMS **to put sb in the ~** éclipser qn; **to put sth in the ~** surpasser *or* surclasser qch

shadow /ˈʃædəʊ/ **A** *n* ombre *f*; **to have ~s under one's eyes** avoir les yeux cernés
B *vt* filer ‹*person*›

shadow cabinet *n* (BrE) cabinet *m* fantôme

shadowy /ˈʃædəʊɪ/ *adj* (dark) sombre; (indistinct) ‹*outline*› flou/-e; ‹*form*› indistinct/-e

shady /ˈʃeɪdɪ/ *adj* **1** ‹*place*› ombragé/-e
2 ‹*deal, businessman*› véreux/-euse

shaft /ʃɑːft, (AmE) ʃæft/ *n* **1** (of tool) manche *m*; (of arrow) tige *f*; (in machine) axe *m*
2 (passage, vent) puits *m*
3 **~ of light** rai *m*; **~ of lightning** éclair *m*

shaggy /ˈʃægɪ/ *adj* ‹*hair, beard, eyebrows*› en broussailles; ‹*animal*› poilu/-e

⚷ **shake** /ʃeɪk/ **A** *n* **1** **to give sb/sth a ~** secouer qn/qch
2 (*also* **milk-~**) milk-shake *m*
B *vt* (*prét* **shook**, *pp* **shaken**) **1** (gen) secouer; **to ~ one's head** (in dismay) hocher la tête; (to say no) faire non de la tête; **to ~ hands with sb, to ~ sb's hand** serrer la main de qn, donner une poignée de main à qn
2 ébranler ‹*confidence, faith, resolve*›; ‹*event, disaster*› secouer ‹*person*›
C *vi* (*prét* **shook**, *pp* **shaken**) **1** trembler; **to ~ with** trembler de ‹*fear, cold, emotion*›; se tordre de ‹*laughter*›
2 (shake hands) **'let's ~ on it!'** 'serrons-nous la main!'
■ **shake off** se débarrasser de ‹*cold, depression, habit, person*›; se défaire de ‹*feeling*›
■ **shake up 1** agiter ‹*bottle, mixture*›
2 ‹*experience, news*› secouer ‹*person*›

shaken /ˈʃeɪkən/ *adj* (shocked) choqué/-e

shake-up *n* réorganisation *f*; (Pol) remaniement *m*

shaky /ˈʃeɪkɪ/ *adj* **1** ‹*chair, ladder*› branlant/-e; **I feel a bit ~** je me sens un peu flageolant
2 ‹*relationship, position*› instable; ‹*evidence, argument*› peu solide; ‹*knowledge, memory*› peu sûr/-e; ‹*regime*› chancelant/-e; **my French is a bit ~** mon français est un peu hésitant

⚷ **shall** /ʃæl, ʃəl/ *modal aux* **1** (in future tense) **I ~ *or* I'll see you tomorrow** je vous verrai demain; **we ~ not *or* shan't have a reply before Friday** nous n'aurons pas de réponse

S

avant vendredi
2 (in suggestions) **~ I set the table?** est-ce que je mets la table?; **~ we go to the cinema tonight?** et si on allait au cinéma ce soir?; **let's buy some peaches, ~ we?** et si on achetait des pêches?

shallot /ʃəˈlɒt/ *n* **1** (BrE) échalote *f*
2 (AmE) cive *f*

shallow /ˈʃæləʊ/ *adj* ‹*container, water, grave*› peu profond/-e; ‹*breathing, character, response*› superficiel/-ielle

shallows *npl* bas-fonds *mpl*

sham /ʃæm/ **A** *n* **1** (person) imposteur *m*
2 it's (all) a ~ c'est de la comédie
B *adj* ‹*event*› prétendu/-e *before n*; ‹*object, building, idea*› factice; ‹*activity, emotion*› feint/-e
C *vi* (*p prés etc* **-mm-**) faire semblant

shambles /ˈʃæmblz/ *n* (fam) pagaille *f* (fam)

shame /ʃeɪm/ **A** *n* **1** (gen) honte *f*
2 it's a (real) shame c'est (vraiment) dommage; **it was a ~ (that) she lost** c'est dommage qu'elle ait perdu
B *vt* **1** (embarrass) faire honte à
2 (disgrace) déshonorer (**by doing** en faisant)

shameful /ˈʃeɪmfl/ *adj* honteux/-euse

shameless /ˈʃeɪmlɪs/ *adj* ‹*person*› éhonté/-e; ‹*attitude*› effronté/-e; ‹*negligence*› scandaleux/-euse

shampoo /ʃæmˈpuː/ **A** *n* shampooing *m*
B *vt* (*prés* **-poos**, *prét*, *pp* **-pooed**) faire un shampooing à; **to ~ one's hair** se faire un shampooing

shamrock /ˈʃæmrɒk/ *n* trèfle *m*

shandy (BrE), **shandygaff** (AmE) /ˈʃændɪ(gæf)/ *n* panaché *m*

shanty town *n* bidonville *m*

🔑 **shape** /ʃeɪp/ **A** *n* forme *f*; **a square ~** une forme carrée; **what ~ is the room?** quelle forme a la pièce?; **to take ~** prendre forme; **to be in/out of ~** ‹*person*› être/ne pas être en forme; **to get in ~** se mettre en forme; **to knock sth into ~** mettre qch au point ‹*project, idea, essay*›
B *vt* **1** modeler ‹*clay*›; sculpter ‹*wood*›
2 ‹*person, event*› déterminer ‹*future, idea*›; modeler ‹*character*›
■ **shape up 1** (develop) ‹*person*› s'en sortir
2 (meet expectations) être à la hauteur

-shaped *combining form* **star/V~** en forme d'étoile/de V

shapeless /ˈʃeɪplɪs/ *adj* sans forme, informe

shapely /ˈʃeɪplɪ/ *adj* ‹*woman*› bien fait/-e; ‹*ankle*› fin/-e; ‹*leg*› bien galbé/-e

🔑 **share** /ʃeə(r)/ **A** *n* **1** part *f* (**of** de); **to pay one's (fair) ~** payer sa part
2 (in stock market) action *f*
B *vt* partager (**with** avec); **we ~ an interest in animals** nous aimons tous les deux les animaux
C *vi* **to ~ in** prendre part à
■ **share out** (amongst selves) partager ‹*food*›; (amongst others) répartir ‹*food*› (**among, between** entre)

shared /ʃeəd/ *adj* ‹*house, interest*› partagé/-e; ‹*facilities*› commun/-e

shareholder /ˈʃeəhəʊldə(r)/ *n* actionnaire *mf*

share option scheme *n* plan *m* de participation par achat d'actions

shareware *n* shareware *m*, logiciel *m* contributif

shark /ʃɑːk/ *n* requin *m*

🔑 **sharp** /ʃɑːp/ **A** *adj* **1** ‹*razor*› tranchant/-e; ‹*edge*› coupant/-e; ‹*blade, scissors, knife*› bien aiguisé/-e
2 ‹*tooth, fingernail, end, needle*› pointu/-e; ‹*pencil*› bien taillé/-e; ‹*features*› anguleux/-euse
3 ‹*angle*› aigu/aiguë; ‹*bend*› brusque; ‹*drop, incline*› fort/-e; ‹*fall, rise*› brusque, brutal/-e
4 ‹*taste, smell*› âcre; ‹*fruit*› acide
5 ‹*pain, cold*› vif/vive; ‹*cry*› aigu/aiguë; ‹*blow*› sévère; ‹*frost*› intense
6 ‹*tongue*› acéré/-e; ‹*tone*› acerbe
7 ‹*person, mind*› vif/vive; ‹*eyesight*› perçant/-e
8 ‹*businessman*› malin/-igne; **~ operator** filou *m*
9 ‹*image*› net/nette; ‹*contrast*› prononcé/-e
10 (Mus) ‹*note*› dièse *inv*; (too high) aigu/aiguë
B *adv* **1** ‹*stop*› net; **to turn ~ left** tourner brusquement vers la gauche
2 (fam) **at 9 o'clock ~** à neuf heures pile (fam)
3 (Mus) ‹*sing, play*› trop haut

sharpen /ˈʃɑːpən/ *vt* aiguiser, affûter ‹*blade, scissors*›; tailler ‹*pencil*›

sharpener /ˈʃɑːpənə(r)/ *n* taille-crayon *m*

sharply /ˈʃɑːplɪ/ *adv* **1** ‹*turn, rise, fall*› brusquement, brutalement
2 ‹*speak*› d'un ton brusque

shatter /ˈʃætə(r)/ **A** *vt* fracasser ‹*window, glass*›; rompre ‹*peace, silence*›; briser ‹*hope*›; démolir ‹*nerves*›
B *vi* ‹*window, glass*› voler en éclats

shattered /ˈʃætəd/ *adj* **1** ‹*dream*› brisé/-e; ‹*life, confidence*› anéanti/-e
2 ‹*person*› (devastated) effondré/-e; (tired) (fam) crevé/-e (fam), épuisé/-e

shave /ʃeɪv/ **A** *n* **to have a ~** se raser
B *vt* (*pp* **~d** *ou* **shaven**) ‹*barber*› raser ‹*person*›; **to ~ one's beard off** se raser la barbe; **to ~ one's legs** se raser les jambes
C *vi* (*pp* **~d** *ou* **shaven**) se raser
IDIOM **that was a close ~!** je l'ai/il l'a etc échappé belle!

shaver /ˈʃeɪvə(r)/ *n* (*also* **electric ~**) rasoir *m* électrique

shaving /ˈʃeɪvɪŋ/ **A** *n* **1** (action) rasage *m*
2 ~s (of wood, metal) copeaux *mpl*
B *adj* ‹*cream, foam*› à raser

🔑 mot clé

shaving brush *n* blaireau *m*

shaving mirror *n* petit miroir *m*

shawl /ʃɔːl/ *n* châle *m*

she /ʃiː, ʃɪ/ *pron* elle; **~'s not at home** elle n'est pas chez elle; **here ~ is** la voici; **there ~ is** la voilà; **~'s a beautiful woman** c'est une belle femme

sheaf /ʃiːf/ *n* (*pl* **sheaves**) (of corn, flowers) gerbe *f*; (of papers) liasse *f*

shear /ʃɪə(r)/ *vt* (*prét* **sheared**, *pp* **shorn**) tondre ‹*grass, sheep*›

shears /ʃɪərz/ *npl* **1** (for garden) cisaille *f* **2** (for sheep) tondeuse *f*

shed /ʃed/ **A** *n* (in garden) remise *f*, abri *m*; (at factory site, port) hangar *m*
B *vt* (*prét, pp* **shed**) **1** verser ‹*tears*›; perdre ‹*leaves, weight, antlers*›; ‹*lorry*› déverser ‹*load*›; verser ‹*blood*›; **to ~ skin** muer
2 répandre ‹*light, happiness*›

sheep /ʃiːp/ *n* (*pl* **~**) mouton *m*; (ewe) brebis *f*; **black ~** brebis galeuse

sheep dog *n* chien *m* de berger

sheepish /ˈʃiːpɪʃ/ *adj* penaud/-e

sheepskin /ˈʃiːpskɪn/ *n* peau *f* de mouton

sheer /ʃɪə(r)/ *adj* **1** ‹*boredom, hypocrisy, stupidity*› pur/-e *before n*
2 ‹*cliff*› à pic
3 ‹*fabric*› léger/-ère, fin/-e; ‹*stockings*› extra-fin/-e

sheet /ʃiːt/ *n* **1** (of paper, stamps) feuille *f*; (of metal, glass) plaque *f*
2 (for bed) drap *m*; **dust ~** housse *f*
3 fact ~ bulletin *m* d'informations
4 (of ice) couche *f*; (of flame) rideau *m*

sheet lightning *n* éclair *m* en nappe

sheet metal *n* tôle *f*

sheik /ʃeɪk, (AmE) ʃiːk/ *n* cheik *m*

shelf /ʃelf/ *n* (*pl* **shelves**) **1** étagère *f*; (in oven) plaque *f*; (in shop, fridge) rayon *m*; **(a set of) shelves** une étagère
2 (in rock, ice) corniche *f*

shelf life /ˈʃelflaɪf/ *n* (of product) durée *f* de conservation; (of technology, pop music) durée *f* de vie

shell /ʃel/ **A** *n* **1** (of egg, nut, snail) coquille *f*; (of crab, tortoise, shrimp) carapace *f*; **to come out of one's ~** sortir de sa coquille
2 (bomb) obus *m*; (cartridge) cartouche *f*
3 (of building) carcasse *f*
B *vt* **1** (Mil) pilonner ‹*town, installation*›
2 (Culin) écosser ‹*peas*›; décortiquer ‹*prawn, nut*›
■ **shell out** (fam): **~ out [sth]** débourser ‹*sum*› (**for** pour)

shellfish /ˈʃelfɪʃ/ *npl* **1** (Zool) crustacés *mpl*; (mussels, oysters) coquillages *mpl*
2 (Culin) fruits *mpl* de mer

shelter /ˈʃeltə(r)/ **A** *n* **1** abri *m*; **to take ~ from** s'abriter de ‹*weather*›
2 (for homeless) refuge *m* (**for** pour); (for refugee) asile *m*
B *vt* **1** (against weather) abriter (**from, against** de); (from truth) protéger (**from** de)
2 donner refuge *or* asile à ‹*refugee*›
C *vi* se mettre à l'abri; **to ~ from the storm** s'abriter de l'orage

sheltered accommodation *n* foyer-résidence *m*

shelving /ˈʃelvɪŋ/ *n* (at home) étagères *fpl*; (in shop) rayons *mpl*

shepherd /ˈʃepəd/ *n* berger *m*

shepherd's pie *n* hachis *m* Parmentier

sheriff /ˈʃerɪf/ *n* shérif *m*

sherry /ˈʃerɪ/ *n* xérès *m*, sherry *m*

Shia(h) **A** *n* chiisme *m*
B *adj* chiite

shield /ʃiːld/ **A** *n* **1** (Mil) bouclier *m*
2 (on machine) écran *m* de protection; (around gun) pare-balles *m inv*
3 (AmE) (policeman's badge) insigne *m*
B *vt* protéger; **to ~ one's eyes** se protéger les yeux

shift /ʃɪft/ **A** *n* **1** (change) changement *m* (**in** de), modification *f* (**in** de)
2 (at work) période *f* de travail; (group of workers) équipe *f*; **to work an eight-hour ~** faire les trois-huit
B *vt* **1** déplacer ‹*furniture, vehicle*›; bouger, remuer ‹*arm*›; changer ‹*theatre scenery*›
2 faire partir, enlever ‹*stain, dirt*›
3 rejeter ‹*blame, responsibility*› (**onto** sur); **to ~ attention away from a problem** détourner l'attention d'un problème
4 (AmE) (Aut) **to ~ gear** changer de vitesse
C *vi* (*also* **~ about**) ‹*load*› bouger; **to ~ from one foot to the other** se dandiner d'un pied sur l'autre

shift key *n* touche *f* de majuscule

shiftless /ˈʃɪftlɪs/ *adj* paresseux/-euse, apathique

shift work *n* travail *m* posté

shifty /ˈʃɪftɪ/ *adj* louche, sournois/-e

Shiism *n* chiisme *m*

Shiite /ˈʃiːaɪt/ **A** *n* chiite *m*
B *adj* chiite

shimmer /ˈʃɪmə(r)/ *vi* **1** ‹*jewels, water*› scintiller; ‹*silk*› chatoyer
2 (in heat) ‹*landscape*› vibrer

shin, **shin bone** /ʃɪn/ *n* tibia *m*

shine /ʃaɪn/ **A** *n* lustre *m*
B *vt* **1** (*prét, pp* **shone**) braquer ‹*headlights, spotlight, torch*› (**on** sur)
2 (*prét, pp* **shined**) faire reluire ‹*silver*›; cirer ‹*shoes*›
C *vi* (*prét, pp* **shone**) **1** ‹*hair, light, sun*› briller; ‹*brass, floor*› reluire; **the light is shining in my eyes** j'ai la lumière dans les yeux
2 ‹*eyes*› briller (**with** de); ‹*face*› rayonner (**with** de)
3 (excel) briller; **to ~ at** être brillant/-e en

S

‹*science, languages*›
IDIOM **to take a ~ to sb** (fam) s'enticher de qn (fam)
■ **shine through** ‹*talent*› éclater au grand jour

shingle /'ʃɪŋgl/ **A** *n* **1** (on beach) galets *mpl*
2 (on roof) bardeau *m*
B shingles *npl* (Med) zona *m*

shining /'ʃaɪnɪŋ/ *adj* **1** ‹*hair, metal, eyes*› brillant/-e
2 ‹*face*› radieux/-ieuse
3 ‹*example*› parfait/-e *before n*

shiny /'ʃaɪnɪ/ *adj* **1** ‹*metal, surface, hair*› brillant/-e
2 ‹*shoes, wood*› bien ciré/-e

✐ **ship** /ʃɪp/ **A** *n* navire *m*; (smaller) bateau *m*; **passenger ~** paquebot *m*
B *vt* (*p prés etc* **-pp-**) transporter [qch] par mer

shipment /'ʃɪpmənt/ *n* cargaison *f*

ship owner *n* armateur *m*

shipping /'ʃɪpɪŋ/ *n* navigation *f*, trafic *m* maritime

shipping company *n* compagnie *f* maritime

shipwreck /'ʃɪprek/ **A** *n* (event) naufrage *m*; (ship) épave *f*
B *vt* **to be ~ed** faire naufrage; **a ~ed sailor** un marin naufragé

shipyard /'ʃɪpjɑːd/ *n* chantier *m* naval

shirk /ʃɜːk/ *vt* esquiver ‹*task, duty*›; fuir ‹*responsibility*›

✐ **shirt** /ʃɜːt/ *n* (man's) chemise *f*; (woman's) chemisier *m*; (for sport) maillot *m*

shirt-sleeve /'ʃɜːtsliːv/ *n* manche *f* de chemise; **in one's ~s** en manches de chemise

shirty /'ʃɜːtɪ/ *adj* (BrE) (fam) **to get ~** prendre la mouche (fam)

shit /ʃɪt/ *excl* (sl) merde! (pop)

shiver /'ʃɪvə(r)/ **A** *n* frisson *m*; **to give sb the ~s** donner froid dans le dos à qn
B *vi* (with cold) grelotter (**with** de); (with fear) frémir (**with** de); (with disgust) frissonner (**with** de)

shoal /ʃəʊl/ *n* (of fish) banc *m*

✐ **shock** /ʃɒk/ **A** *n* **1** choc *m*; **to get** *or* **have a ~** avoir un choc; **to give sb a ~** faire un choc à qn; **to be in ~** être en état de choc
2 (electrical) décharge *f*; **to get a ~** prendre une décharge
3 (of collision) choc *m*; (of explosion) souffle *m*
4 a ~ of red hair une tignasse rousse
B *vt* (distress) consterner; (scandalize) choquer

shock absorber *n* amortisseur *m*

shocking /'ʃɒkɪŋ/ *adj* ‹*sight*› consternant/-e; ‹*news*› choquant/-e

shock wave *n* remous *mpl*; **to send ~s through the stock market** provoquer des remous à la Bourse

shoddy /'ʃɒdɪ/ *adj* ‹*product*› de mauvaise qualité; ‹*work*› mal fait/-e

✐ **shoe** /ʃuː/ **A** *n* chaussure *f*; (for horse) fer *m*
B *vt* (*p prés* **shoeing**, *prét, pp* **shod**) ferrer ‹*horse*›

shoelace /'ʃuːleɪs/ *n* lacet *m* de chaussure

shoe polish *n* cirage *m*

shoe shop *n* magasin *m* de chaussures

shoe size *n* pointure *f*

shoestring /'ʃuːstrɪŋ/ *n* (AmE) lacet *m* de chaussure
IDIOM **on a ~** (fam) avec peu de moyens

shoo /ʃuː/ *vt* (*also* **~ away**) chasser

✐ **shoot** /ʃuːt/ **A** *n* (Bot) pousse *f*
B *vt* (*prét, pp* **shot**) **1** tirer ‹*bullet, arrow*› (**at** sur); lancer ‹*missile*› (**at** sur)
2 tirer sur ‹*person, animal*›; (kill) abattre ‹*person, animal*›; **she shot him in the leg** elle lui a tiré dans la jambe; **to ~ sb dead** abattre qn; **to ~ oneself** se tirer une balle
3 to ~ questions at sb bombarder qn de questions
4 (film) tourner ‹*film, scene*›; prendre [qch] (en photo) ‹*subject*›
5 mettre ‹*bolt*›
6 to ~ the rapids franchir les rapides
7 (AmE) jouer à ‹*pool*›
C *vi* (*prét, pp* **shot**) **1** tirer (**at** sur)
2 to ~ forward s'élancer à toute vitesse; **the car shot past** la voiture est passée en trombe
3 (Sport) tirer, shooter
■ **shoot down** abattre, descendre (fam) ‹*plane, pilot*›
■ **shoot up A** ‹*flames, spray*› jaillir; ‹*prices, profits*› monter en flèche
B ~ up [sth], ~ [sth] up (fam) (inject) se shooter à (fam) ‹*heroin*›

shooting /'ʃuːtɪŋ/ **A** *n* **1** (killing) meurtre *m* (par arme à feu)
2 (shots) coups *mpl* de feu, fusillade *f*
B *adj* ‹*pain*› lancinant/-e

shooting range *n* stand *m* de tir

shooting star *n* étoile *f* filante

shoot-out *n* (fam) fusillade *f*

✐ **shop** /ʃɒp/ **A** *n* **1** magasin *m*; (small, fashionable) boutique *f*; **to go to the ~s** aller faire les courses
2 (AmE) (in department store) rayon *m*
3 (workshop) atelier *m*
B *vi* (*p prés etc* **-pp-**) **to go ~ping** aller faire des courses; (browse) aller faire les magasins
IDIOM **to talk ~** parler boutique
■ **shop around** (compare prices) faire le tour des magasins (**for** pour trouver); (compare courses, services etc) bien chercher

shopaholic /ʃɒpə'hɒlɪk/ *n* (fam) accro *mf* (fam) du shopping

shop assistant *n* (BrE) vendeur/-euse *m/f*

shopkeeper *n* commerçant/-e *m/f*

shoplifter *n* voleur/-euse *m/f* à l'étalage

✐ mot clé

shoplifting *n* vol *m* à l'étalage
shopping /ˈʃɒpɪŋ/ *n* courses *fpl*
shopping bag *n* sac *m* à provisions
shopping cart *n* (AmE) (in shop) caddie® *m*, chariot *m*; (online) panier *m*
shopping centre (BrE), **shopping mall** (AmE) *n* centre *m* commercial
shopping trolley *n* (BrE) caddie® *m*
shop-soiled *adj* (BrE) ‹*garment*› sali/-e
shop steward *n* représentant/-e *m/f* syndical/-e
shop window *n* vitrine *f*
shopworn *adj* (AmE) ‹*garment*› sali/-e
shore /ʃɔː(r)/ *n* (of sea) côte *f*, rivage *m*; (of lake) rive *f*; **on ~** à terre
short /ʃɔːt/ **A** *n* **1** (drink) alcool *m* fort
2 (film) court métrage *m*
B **shorts** *npl* short *m*; (underwear) caleçon *m*
C *adj* **1** ‹*stay, memory, period*› court/-e *before n*; ‹*course*› de courte durée; ‹*conversation, speech, chapter*› bref/brève *before n*; ‹*walk*› petit/-e *before n*; **the days are getting ~er** les jours diminuent *or* raccourcissent
2 ‹*hair, dress, distance, stick*› court/-e *before n*
3 ‹*person*› petit/-e *before n*
4 to be in ~ supply être difficile à trouver; **time is getting ~** le temps presse
5 (lacking) **he is ~ of sth** il lui manque qch; **to be ~ on** ‹*person*› manquer de ‹*talent, tact*›; **to run ~ of** manquer de ‹*clothes, money, food*›
6 Tom is ~ for Thomas Tom est le diminutif de Thomas
7 (abrupt) **to be ~ with sb** être brusque avec qn
8 ‹*pastry*› brisé/-e
D *adv* ‹*stop*› net; **to stop ~ of doing** se retenir pour ne pas faire
E **in short** *phr* bref
F **short of** *phr* **~ of doing** à moins de faire
(IDIOMS) **to sell oneself ~** se sous-estimer; **to make ~ work of sth/sb** expédier qch/qn
shortage /ˈʃɔːtɪdʒ/ *n* pénurie *f*, manque *m* (of de)
shortbread, **shortcake** *n* sablé *m*
short-change *vt* ne pas rendre toute sa monnaie à
short circuit /ʃɔːtˈsɜːkɪt/ **A** *n* court-circuit *m*
B **short-circuit** *vt* court-circuiter
C **short-circuit** *vi* faire court-circuit
shortcomings *npl* points *mpl* faibles
shortcut *n* raccourci *m*; **keyboard ~** raccourci clavier
shorten /ˈʃɔːtn/ **A** *vt* abréger ‹*visit, life*›; raccourcir ‹*garment, talk*›; réduire ‹*time, list*›
B *vi* ‹*days*› diminuer
shortfall /ˈʃɔːtfɔːl/ *n* (in budget, accounts) déficit *m*; (in earnings, exports) manque *m*
shorthand /ˈʃɔːthænd/ *n* sténographie *f*, sténo *f* (fam)
shorthand typist *n* sténo-dactylo *f*
shortlist /ˈʃɔːtlɪst/ **A** *n* liste *f* des candidats sélectionnés
B *vt* sélectionner ‹*applicant*› (**for** pour)
short-lived /ʃɔːtˈlɪvd/ *adj* **to be ~** ne pas durer longtemps
shortly /ˈʃɔːtlɪ/ *adv* **1** ‹*return*› bientôt; ‹*be published*› prochainement
2 ~ after(wards)/before peu (de temps) après/avant
3 (crossly) sèchement
short-sighted /ʃɔːtˈsaɪtɪd/ *adj* **1** myope
2 (fig) ‹*person*› peu clairvoyant/-e; ‹*policy, decision*› à courte vue
short-sleeved *adj* à manches courtes
short-staffed /ʃɔːtˈstɑːft, (AmE) -stæft/ *adj* **to be ~** manquer de personnel
short story *n* nouvelle *f*
short term **A** *n* **in the ~** dans l'immédiat
B **short-term** *adj* à court terme
short wave *n* ondes *fpl* courtes
shot /ʃɒt/ **A** *n* **1** (from gun) coup *m* (de feu)
2 (Sport) (in tennis, golf, cricket) coup *m*; (in football) tir *m*
3 (snapshot) photo *f* (**of** de)
4 (in film-making) plan *m* (**of** de); **action ~** scène *f* d'action
5 (injection) piqûre *f* (**of** de)
6 to have a ~ at doing essayer de faire
7 (person) **a good ~** un bon tireur
B *adj* ‹*silk*› changeant/-e
shotgun /ˈʃɒtgʌn/ *n* fusil *m*
shot put *n* (Sport) lancer *m* de poids
should /ʃʊd, ʃəd/ *modal aux* (*conditional of* **shall**) **1 ~ I call the doctor?** est-ce que je devrais faire venir le médecin?; **why shouldn't I do it?** pourquoi est-ce que je ne le ferais pas?; **she ~ learn to drive** elle devrait apprendre à conduire; **shouldn't you be at school?** tu ne devrais pas être à l'école?
2 it shouldn't be difficult ça ne devrait pas être difficile; **she ~ have been here hours ago** elle aurait dû arriver il y a plusieurs heures déjà; **it shouldn't have cost so much** ça n'aurait pas dû coûter si cher
3 I ~ think she's about 40 à mon avis, elle doit avoir à peu près 40 ans; **I shouldn't be surprised** cela ne m'étonnerait pas
4 ~ you require any further information, please contact... si vous souhaitez plus de renseignements, adressez-vous à...
5 I ~ think so! je l'espère!; **I ~ think not!** j'espère bien que non!; **how ~ I know?** comment veux-tu que je le sache?; **flowers? you shouldn't have!** des fleurs? il ne fallait pas!
shoulder /ˈʃəʊldə(r)/ **A** *n* épaule *f*
B *vt* se charger de ‹*burden, expense, task*›; endosser ‹*responsibility*›
(IDIOM) **to rub ~s with sb** côtoyer qn

shoulder blade *n* omoplate *f*
shoulder-length *adj* ‹*hair*› mi-long/-ue
shoulder pad *n* épaulette *f*
shout /ʃaʊt/ **A** *n* cri *m* (**of** de)
B *vt* crier; (stronger) hurler
C *vi* crier; **to ~ at sb** crier après qn; **he was ~ing to me** il me criait quelque chose
■ **shout out** pousser un cri
shouting /ˈʃaʊtɪŋ/ *n* cris *mpl*
shove /ʃʌv/ **A** *n* **to give sb/sth a ~** pousser qn/qch
B *vt* **1** (push) pousser (**against** contre); **to ~ sth into sth** fourrer qch dans qch
2 (jostle) bousculer ‹*person*›
C *vi* pousser
■ **shove up** (fam) se pousser
shovel /ˈʃʌvl/ **A** *n* pelle *f*
B *vt* (*p prés etc* **-ll** (BrE), **-l-** (AmE)) enlever [qch] à la pelle ‹*leaves, snow*› (**off** de)
show /ʃəʊ/ **A** *n* **1** spectacle *m*; (in cinema) séance *f*; (on radio, TV) émission *f*; (of slides) projection *f*
2 (exhibition) exposition *f*; (of cars, boats) salon *m*; (of fashion) défilé *m*; **flower/dog ~** exposition florale/canine
3 (of feelings) semblant *m* (**of** de); (of strength) démonstration *f* (**of** de); (of wealth) étalage *m* (**of** de); **he made a ~ of concern** il a affiché sa sollicitude; **to be just for ~** être de l'esbroufe (fam)
B *vt* (*prét* **showed**, *pp* **shown**)
1 montrer ‹*person, object, photo, feelings*› (**to** à); présenter ‹*ticket*› (**to** à); ‹*TV channel, cinema*› passer ‹*film*›; ‹*garment*› laisser voir ‹*underclothes, stain*›; indiquer ‹*time, direction*›; **to ~ sb sth** montrer qch à qn; **that carpet ~s the dirt** cette moquette est salissante
2 (exhibit) présenter ‹*animal*›; exposer ‹*flower, vegetables*›
3 (prove) démontrer ‹*truth, guilt*›
4 to ~ sb to their seat placer qn; **to ~ sb to their room** accompagner qn à sa chambre; **to ~ sb to the door** reconduire qn
C *vi* (*prét* **showed**, *pp* **shown**) **1** ‹*stain, label*› se voir; ‹*emotion*› se voir; (in eyes) se lire
2 ‹*film*› passer
IDIOM **to have nothing to ~ for sth** ne rien avoir tiré de qch
■ **show in**: **~ [sb] in** faire entrer
■ **show off**: **A ~ off** faire le fier/la fière
B ~ [sb/sth] off faire admirer ‹*skill*›; exhiber ‹*baby, car*›
■ **show out**: **~ [sb] out** accompagner [qn] à la porte
■ **show round**: **~ [sb] round** faire visiter
■ **show up**: **A ~ up** (fam) (arrive) se montrer (fam)
B ~ up [sth] révéler ‹*fault, mark*›
C ~ [sb] up faire honte à ‹*person*›
show business *n* industrie *f* du spectacle

showcase /ˈʃəʊkeɪs/ *n* (for paintings, ideas) vitrine *f*; (for new artist etc) tremplin *m*
showdown *n* confrontation *f*
shower /ˈʃaʊə(r)/ **A** *n* **1** douche *f*; **to take a ~** prendre une douche
2 (of rain) averse *f*
B *vt* **to ~ sb with [sth]** couvrir qn de ‹*gifts, compliments, praise*›
C *vi* ‹*person*› prendre une douche
show house *n* maison-témoin *f*
showjumping *n* saut *m* d'obstacles
show-off *n* (fam) m'as-tu-vu *mf inv* (fam)
show of hands *n* vote *m* à mains levées
showroom /ˈʃəʊruːm, -rʊm/ *n* exposition *f*; **to look at cars in a ~** regarder les voitures exposées
shrapnel /ˈʃræpnl/ *n* éclats *mpl* d'obus
shred /ʃred/ **A** *n* **1** (of paper, fabric) lambeau *m*
2 (of evidence, truth) parcelle *f*
B *vt* (*p prés etc* **-dd-**) déchiqueter ‹*paper*›; râper ‹*vegetables*›
shredder /ˈʃredə(r)/ *n* (for paper) déchiqueteuse *f*
shrewd /ʃruːd/ *adj* ‹*person*› habile; ‹*move, investment*› astucieux/-ieuse
shriek /ʃriːk/ **A** *n* **1** (of pain, fear) cri *m* perçant, hurlement *m*; (of delight) cri *m*; **~s of laughter** éclats *mpl* de rire
2 (of bird) cri *m*
B *vi* crier, hurler (**in, with** de)
shrill /ʃrɪl/ *adj* ‹*voice, cry, laugh*› perçant/-e; ‹*whistle, tone*› strident/-e
shrimp /ʃrɪmp/ *n* crevette *f* grise; (AmE) (prawn) crevette *f* rose
shrine /ʃraɪn/ *n* **1** (place) lieu *m* de pèlerinage
2 (building) chapelle *f*
3 (tomb) tombeau *m*
shrink /ʃrɪŋk/ **A** *vt* (*prét* **shrank**, *pp* **shrunk** *ou* **shrunken**) faire rétrécir ‹*fabric*›; contracter ‹*wood*›
B *vi* (*prét* **shrank**, *pp* **shrunk** *ou* **shrunken**) **1** ‹*fabric*› rétrécir; ‹*timber*› se contracter; ‹*dough, meat*› réduire; ‹*sales*› être en recul; ‹*resources*› s'amenuiser; ‹*old person, body*› se tasser
2 to ~ from se dérober devant ‹*conflict, responsibility*›; **to ~ from doing** hésiter à faire
shrinking /ˈʃrɪŋkɪŋ/ *adj* ‹*population, market*› en baisse; ‹*audience*› qui s'amenuise
shrink-wrap /ˈʃrɪŋkræp/ *vt* (*p prés etc* **-pp-**) emballer [qch] sous film plastique
shrivel /ˈʃrɪvl/ **A** *vt* ‹*sun, heat*› flétrir ‹*skin*›; dessécher ‹*plant, leaf*›
B *vi* (*p prés etc* **-ll-** (BrE), **-l-** (AmE)) (*also* **~ up**) ‹*fruit, vegetable*› se ratatiner; ‹*skin*› se flétrir; ‹*plant, meat*› se dessécher
shroud /ʃraʊd/ **A** *n* linceul *m*
B *vt* envelopper (**in** dans)
Shrove Tuesday *n* mardi *m* gras

mot clé

shrub /ʃrʌb/ *n* arbuste *m*
shrubbery /ˈʃrʌbərɪ/ *n* massif *m* d'arbustes
shrug /ʃrʌg/ **A** *n* haussement *m* d'épaules
B *vt* (*p prés etc* **-gg-**) **to ∼ one's shoulders** hausser les épaules
■ **shrug off** ignorer ‹*problem, rumour*›
shudder /ˈʃʌdə(r)/ **A** *n* **1** (of person) frisson *m* (**of** de)
2 (of vehicle) secousse *f*
B *vi* **1** ‹*person*› frissonner (**with** de)
2 ‹*vehicle*› **to ∼ to a halt** avoir quelques soubresauts et s'arrêter
shuffle /ˈʃʌfl/ *vt* **1** battre ‹*cards*›
2 brasser ‹*papers*›
3 to ∼ one's feet traîner les pieds
shun /ʃʌn/ *vt* (*p prés etc* **-nn-**) fuir ‹*people, publicity, temptation*›; dédaigner ‹*work*›
shunt /ʃʌnt/ **A** *vt* aiguiller ‹*wagon, engine*› (**into** sur)
B *vi* ‹*train*› changer de voie
shut /ʃʌt/ **A** *adj* fermé/-e; **her eyes were ∼** elle avait les yeux fermés; **to slam the door ∼** claquer la porte (pour bien la fermer); **to keep one's mouth ∼** (fam) se taire
B *vt* (*p prés* **-tt-**, *prét*, *pp* **shut**) fermer
C *vi* (*p prés* **-tt-**, *prét*, *pp* **shut**) **1** ‹*door, book, box, mouth*› se fermer
2 ‹*office, factory*› fermer
■ **shut down**: **A ∼ down** ‹*business*› fermer; ‹*machinery*› s'arrêter
B ∼ [sth] down fermer ‹*business*›; arrêter ‹*machinery*›
■ **shut in**: **∼ [sb/sth] in** enfermer
■ **shut off**: **∼ [sth] off**, **∼ off [sth]** couper ‹*supply, motor*›
■ **shut out 1** laisser [qn/qch] dehors ‹*animal, person*›; éliminer ‹*noise*›; **to be ∼ out** être à la porte
2 empêcher [qch] d'entrer ‹*light*›
■ **shut up**: **A ∼ up** (fam) se taire (**about** au sujet de)
B ∼ [sb] up 1 (fam) (silence) faire taire ‹*person*›
2 (confine) enfermer ‹*person, animal*› (**in** dans)
C ∼ [sth] up, **∼ up [sth]** fermer ‹*house*›
shutdown *n* fermeture *f*
shutter /ˈʃʌtə(r)/ *n* **1** (wooden, metal) volet *m*; (on shop front) store *m*
2 (on camera) obturateur *m*
shuttle /ˈʃʌtl/ **A** *n* **1** navette *f*
2 (*also* **∼cock**) volant *m*
B *vt* transporter ‹*passengers*›
shuttle service *n* service *m* de navette
shy /ʃaɪ/ **A** *adj* ‹*person*› timide (**with, of** avec); ‹*animal*› farouche (**with, of** avec)
B *vi* ‹*horse*› faire un écart (**at** devant)
■ **shy away** se tenir à l'écart (**from** de)
Siberia /saɪˈbɪərɪə/ *pr n* Sibérie *f*
sibling /ˈsɪblɪŋ/ *n* frère/sœur *m/f*
Sicily /ˈsɪsɪlɪ/ *pr n* Sicile *f*
sick /sɪk/ *adj* **1** (ill) malade; **worried ∼** malade d'inquiétude
2 (nauseous) **to be ∼** vomir; **to feel ∼** avoir mal au cœur
3 ‹*joke, mind*› malsain/-e
4 (disgusted) écœuré/-e, dégoûté/-e
5 (fam) **to be ∼ of sb/sth** en avoir assez *or* marre (fam) de qn/qch
sickbay *n* infirmerie *f*
sick building syndrome *n* syndrome *m* causé par un milieu de travail insalubre
sicken /ˈsɪkən/ **A** *vt* (disgust) écœurer
B *vi* **to be ∼ing for sth** couver qch
sickening /ˈsɪkənɪŋ/ *adj* ‹*sight*› qui soulève le cœur; ‹*smell, cruelty*› écœurant/-e
sickie /ˈsɪkɪ/ *n* (BrE) (fam) **to throw/pull/chuck a ∼** se faire porter pâle (fam)
sick leave *n* congé *m* de maladie
sickly /ˈsɪklɪ/ *adj* **1** ‹*person, plant*› chétif/-ive
2 ‹*smell, taste*› écœurant/-e; ‹*colour*› fadasse; **∼ sweet** douceâtre
sickness /ˈsɪknɪs/ *n* **1** (illness) maladie *f*
2 (nausea) nausée *f*; **bouts of ∼** vomissements *mpl*
sick note *n* (fam) (for school) mot *m* d'excuse; (for work) certificat *m* médical
sick pay *n* indemnité *f* de maladie
sickroom *n* infirmerie *f*
side /saɪd/ **A** *n* **1** (gen) côté *m*; (of animal's body, hill) flanc *m*; (of lake, road) bord *m*; **on one's/its ∼** sur le côté; **∼ by ∼** côte à côte; **at** *or* **by the ∼ of** au bord de ‹*lake, road*›; à côté de ‹*building*›
2 to take ∼s prendre position; **to change ∼s** changer de camp
3 (Sport) (team) équipe *f*
B *adj* ‹*door, window, entrance, view*› latéral/-e
C on the side *phr* **with salad on the ∼** avec de la salade; **to work on the ∼** (in addition) travailler à côté; (illegally) travailler au noir
■ **side with** se mettre du côté de ‹*person*›
sideboard *n* buffet *m*
sideboards (BrE), **sideburns** *npl* pattes *fpl*
side effect *n* (of drug) effet *m* secondaire; (of action) répercussion *f*
side impact bars *npl* (Aut) renforts *mpl* latéraux
sideline /ˈsaɪdlaɪn/ *n* **1 as a ∼** comme à-côté
2 (Sport) ligne *f* de touche; **on the ∼s** sur la touche
sidelong *adj* ‹*look*› oblique
side plate *n* petite assiette *f*
side-saddle *adv* en amazone
sideshow *n* attraction *f*
sidestep /ˈsaɪdstep/ *vt* (*p prés etc* **-pp-**) éviter ‹*opponent*›; éluder ‹*issue*›
side street *n* petite rue *f*
side stroke *n* brasse *f* indienne
sidetrack /ˈsaɪdtræk/ *vt* fourvoyer ‹*person*›; **to get ∼ed** se fourvoyer

sidewalk *n* (AmE) trottoir *m*

sideways /ˈsaɪdweɪz/ **A** *adj* ‹*look, glance*› de travers
B *adv* ‹*move*› latéralement; ‹*look at*› de travers

siding /ˈsaɪdɪŋ/ *n* voie *f* de garage

siege /siːdʒ/ *n* siège *m*; **to lay ~ to sth** assiéger qch

siesta /sɪˈestə/ *n* sieste *f*; **to have a ~** faire la sieste

sieve /sɪv/ **A** *n* (for draining) passoire *f*; (for sifting) tamis *m*
B *vt* tamiser ‹*flour*›

sift /sɪft/ *vt* **1** tamiser, passer [qch] au tamis ‹*flour*›
2 passer [qch] au crible ‹*information*›
■ **sift through** trier ‹*applications*›; fouiller (dans) ‹*ashes*›

⚷ **sigh** /saɪ/ **A** *n* soupir *m*
B *vi* soupirer, pousser un soupir; **to ~ with relief** pousser un soupir de soulagement

⚷ **sight** /saɪt/ **A** *n* **1** vue *f*; **at first ~** à première vue; **to catch ~ of sb/sth** apercevoir qn/qch; **to lose ~ of sb/sth** perdre qn/qch de vue; **I can't stand the ~ of him!** je ne peux pas le voir (fam) (en peinture)!; **to be in ~** ‹*land, border*› être en vue; ‹*peace, freedom*› être proche; **to be out of ~** être caché/-e; **don't let her out of your ~!** ne la quitte pas des yeux!
2 (scene) spectacle *m*; **it was not a pretty ~!** ce n'était pas beau à voir!
B **sights** *npl* **1** attractions *fpl* touristiques (of de); **to see the ~s** faire du tourisme
2 (on rifle, telescope) viseur *m*
3 **to set one's ~s on sth** viser qch

sightseeing /ˈsaɪtsiːɪŋ/ *n* tourisme *m*; **to go ~** faire du tourisme

sightseer /ˈsaɪtsiːə(r)/ *n* touriste *mf*

⚷ **sign** /saɪn/ **A** *n* **1** (gen) signe *m*; **the pound ~** le symbole de la livre sterling
2 (road sign) panneau *m* (**for** pour); (smaller) pancarte *f*; (outside shop) enseigne *f*
B *vt, vi* signer
■ **sign on 1** (BrE) (for benefit) pointer au chômage
2 (for course) s'inscrire (**for** à, dans)
■ **sign up 1** (in forces) s'engager
2 (for course) s'inscrire (**for** à, dans)

⚷ **signal** /ˈsɪgnl/ **A** *n* signal *m* (**for** de)
B *vt* (*p prés etc* **-ll-** (BrE), **-l-** (AmE)) **to ~ (to sb) that** faire signe (à qn) que
C *vi* (*p prés etc* **-ll-** (BrE), **-l-** (AmE))
1 (gesture) faire des signes
2 (in car) mettre son clignotant

signature /ˈsɪgnətʃə(r)/ *n* signature *f*

signature tune *n* indicatif *m*

significance /sɪgˈnɪfɪkəns/ *n* **1** (importance) importance *f*
2 (meaning) signification *f*

⚷ **significant** /sɪgˈnɪfɪkənt/ *adj* ‹*amount, impact*› considérable; ‹*event, role*› important/-e; ‹*name*› significatif/-ive

signify /ˈsɪgnɪfaɪ/ *vt* indiquer

sign language *n* code *m or* langage *m* gestuel

signpost /ˈsaɪnpəʊst/ *n* panneau *m* indicateur

Sikh /siːk/ *n, adj* sikh *mf*

⚷ **silence** /ˈsaɪləns/ **A** *n* silence *m*; **in ~** en silence
B *vt* faire taire

silencer /ˈsaɪlənsə(r)/ *n* (BrE) (for car) silencieux *m*

⚷ **silent** /ˈsaɪlənt/ *adj* **1** silencieux/-ieuse; **to be ~** se taire
2 ‹*disapproval, prayer*› muet/muette
3 ‹*film*› muet/muette

silhouette /ˌsɪluːˈet/ *n* silhouette *f*

silicon chip *n* puce *f* électronique

silk /sɪlk/ *n* soie *f*

silky /ˈsɪlkɪ/ *adj* soyeux/-euse

sill /sɪl/ *n* (of window) (interior) rebord *m*; (exterior) appui *m*

silly /ˈsɪlɪ/ **A** *adj* ‹*person*› idiot/-e; ‹*question, game*› stupide; ‹*behaviour, clothes*› ridicule
B *adv* **to drink oneself ~** s'abrutir d'alcool; **to bore sb ~** assommer qn

silo /ˈsaɪləʊ/ *n* (*pl* **~s**) silo *m*

silt /sɪlt/ *n* limon *m*, vase *f*

silver /ˈsɪlvə(r)/ **A** *n* **1** (metal, colour) argent *m*
2 (silverware) argenterie *f*
3 (medal) médaille *f* d'argent
B *adj* ‹*ring, coin*› en argent

silver birch *n* bouleau *m* argenté

silver foil *n* (BrE) papier *m* d'aluminium

silverware *n* argenterie *f*

SIM card /ˈsɪm kɑːd/ *n* carte *f* SIM

⚷ **similar** /ˈsɪmɪlə(r)/ *adj* similaire, analogue; **~ to** analogue à, comparable à

similarity /ˌsɪmɪˈlærətɪ/ *n* ressemblance *f* (**to, with** avec)

similarly /ˈsɪmɪləlɪ/ *adv* de la même façon

simmer /ˈsɪmə(r)/ *vi* **1** ‹*soup*› cuire à feu doux, mijoter; ‹*water*› frémir
2 ‹*person*› bouillonner (**with** de); ‹*revolt, violence*› couver

⚷ **simple** /ˈsɪmpl/ *adj* **1** (gen) simple; ‹*dress, style*› sobre
2 (offensive) (dimwitted) simplet/-ette (fam), simple d'esprit

simplicity /sɪmˈplɪsətɪ/ *n* simplicité *f*

simplify /ˈsɪmplɪfaɪ/ *vt* simplifier

simplistic /sɪmˈplɪstɪk/ *adj* simpliste

⚷ **simply** /ˈsɪmplɪ/ *adv* **1** ‹*write, dress, live*› simplement, avec simplicité; **to put it ~...** en deux mots...
2 (merely) simplement

simulate /ˈsɪmjʊleɪt/ *vt* (feign) simuler ‹*anger, illness*›; affecter ‹*interest*›; (reproduce) simuler

simulator /ˈsɪmjʊleɪtə(r)/ *n* simulateur *m*

S

⚷ mot clé

simultaneous /ˌsɪml'teɪnɪəs, (AmE) ˌsaɪm-/ *adj* simultané/-e

sin /sɪn/ **A** *n* péché *m*, crime *m*
B *vi* (*p prés etc* **-nn-**) pécher (**against** contre)

since /sɪns/ **A** *prep* depuis; **I haven't seen him ~ then** je ne l'ai pas vu depuis; **I haven't been feeling well ~ Monday** je ne me sens pas bien depuis lundi; **I had been waiting ~ 9 o'clock** j'attendais depuis 9 heures
B *conj* **1** (from the time when) depuis que; **~ he's been away** depuis qu' il est absent; **ever ~ I married him** depuis que nous nous sommes mariés, depuis notre mariage; **I've known him ~ I was 12** je le connais depuis que j'ai 12 ans *or* depuis l'âge de 12 ans; **it's 10 years ~ we last met** cela fait 10 ans que nous ne nous sommes pas revus
2 (because) comme; **~ you're so clever, do it yourself!** puisque tu es tellement malin, fais-le toi-même!
C *adv* **she has ~ qualified** depuis elle a obtenu son diplôme; **I haven't phoned her ~** je ne lui ai pas téléphoné depuis

sincere /sɪn'sɪə(r)/ *adj* sincère

sincerely /sɪn'sɪəlɪ/ *adv* sincèrement; **Yours ~, Sincerely yours** (AmE) Veuillez agréer, Monsieur/Madame, l'expression de mes sentiments les meilleurs

sincerity /sɪn'serətɪ/ *n* sincérité *f*

sinew /'sɪnju:/ *n* tendon *m*

sing /sɪŋ/ **A** *vt* (*prét* **sang**, *pp* **sung**) chanter; **to ~ sb's praises** chanter les louanges de qn
B *vi* (*prét* **sang**, *pp* **sung**) chanter

Singapore /ˌsɪŋə'pɔ:(r)/ *pr n* Singapour *f*

singe /sɪndʒ/ *vt* (*p prés* **singeing**) brûler [qch] légèrement ‹*hair, clothing*›; (with iron) roussir ‹*clothes*›

singer /'sɪŋə(r)/ *n* chanteur/-euse *m/f*

singing /'sɪŋɪŋ/ *n* chant *m*

single /'sɪŋgl/ **A** *n* **1** (BrE) (*also* **~ ticket**) aller *m* simple
2 (*also* **~ room**) chambre *f* pour une personne
3 (record) 45 tours *m*
B *adj* **1** (sole) seul/-e *before n*
2 (for one) ‹*sheet, bed, person*› pour une personne
3 (unmarried) célibataire
4 every ~ day tous les jours sans exception; **every ~ one of those people** chacune de ces personnes
■ **single out** choisir ‹*person*›

single cream *n* (BrE) ≈ crème *f* fraîche liquide

single currency *n* monnaie *f* unique

single file *adv* en file indienne

single-handed /ˌsɪŋgl'hændɪd/ *adv* (*also* **single-handedly**) tout seul/toute seule

single market *n* marché *m* unique

single-minded /ˌsɪŋgl'maɪndɪd/ *adj* tenace, résolu/-e

single mother *n* mère *f* qui élève ses enfants seule

single-parent *adj* ‹*family*› monoparental/-e

singles /'sɪŋglz/ *npl* (Sport) **the women's/men's ~** le simple dames/messieurs

singles bar *n* bar *m* de rencontres pour célibataires

singles charts *npl* palmarès *m* des 45 tours

single-sex *adj* non mixte

singlet /'sɪŋglɪt/ *n* (BrE) **1** (Sport) maillot *m*
2 (vest) maillot *m* de corps

singular /'sɪŋgjʊlə(r)/ **A** *n* singulier *m*
B *adj* singulier/-ière

sinister /'sɪnɪstə(r)/ *adj* sinistre

sink /sɪŋk/ **A** *n* (in kitchen) évier *m*; (in bathroom) lavabo *m*
B *vt* (*prét* **sank**, *pp* **sunk**) **1** couler ‹*ship*›
2 forer ‹*oil well, shaft*›; creuser ‹*foundations*›; enfoncer ‹*post, pillar*› (**into** dans); **the dog sank its teeth into my arm** le chien a planté ses crocs dans mon bras
C *vi* (*prét* **sank**, *pp* **sunk**) **1** ‹*ship, object, person*› couler
2 ‹*sun*› baisser; ‹*cake*› redescendre; **to ~ to the floor** s'effondrer; **to ~ into a chair** s'affaler dans un fauteuil; **to ~ into a deep sleep** sombrer dans un profond sommeil
3 ‹*building, wall*› s'effondrer; **to ~ into** s'enfoncer dans ‹*mud*›; sombrer dans ‹*anarchy, obscurity*›
■ **sink in** ‹*news*› faire son chemin

sinner /'sɪnə(r)/ *n* pécheur/-eresse *m/f*

sinus /'saɪnəs/ *n* (*pl* **~es**) sinus *m inv*

sip /sɪp/ **A** *n* petite gorgée *f*
B *vt* (*p prés etc* **-pp-**) boire [qch] à petites gorgées

siphon /'saɪfn/ **A** *n* siphon *m*
B *vt* (*also* **~ off**) siphonner ‹*petrol, water*›

sir /sɜ:(r)/ *n* **1** Monsieur; **Dear Sir** Monsieur
2 (BrE) (in titles) **Sir James** Sir James

siren /'saɪərən/ *n* sirène *f*

sirloin /'sɜ:lɔɪn/ *n* aloyau *m*

sister /'sɪstə(r)/ *n* **1** (gen) sœur *f*
2 (BrE) (nurse) infirmière *f* chef

sister-in-law *n* (*pl* **sisters-in-law**) belle-sœur *f*

sit /sɪt/ **A** *vt* (*prét*, *pp* **sat**) (BrE) se présenter à, passer ‹*exam*›
B *vi* (*prét*, *pp* **sat**) **1** s'asseoir (**at** à, **in** dans, **on** sur); **to be sitting** être assis/-e; **to ~ still** se tenir tranquille
2 ‹*committee, court*› siéger
3 to ~ on faire partie de ‹*committee, jury*›
4 ‹*hen*› **to ~ on** couver ‹*eggs*›
■ **sit about, sit around** rester assis à ne rien faire
■ **sit down** s'asseoir (**at** à, **in** dans, **on** sur)
■ **sit in** ‹*observer*› assister (**on** à)
■ **sit up** se redresser; **to be ~ing up** être assis/-e; **~ up straight!** tiens-toi droit!

sitcom /ˈsɪtkɒm/ *n* (fam) sitcom *m*

🔑 **site** /saɪt/ *n* **1** (*also* **building ~**) (before building) terrain *m*; (during building) chantier *m*
2 (for tent) emplacement *m*; **caravan ~** (BrE) terrain *m* de caravaning
3 (archaeological) site *m*

sitting /ˈsɪtɪŋ/ *n* **1** (session) séance *f*
2 (in canteen) service *m*

sitting room *n* salon *m*

sitting target *n* cible *f* facile

situate /ˈsɪtjʊeɪt, (AmE) ˈsɪtʃʊeɪt/ *vt* situer; **to be ~d** être situé/-e, se trouver

🔑 **situation** /ˌsɪtjʊˈeɪʃn, (AmE) ˌsɪtʃʊ-/ *n* situation *f*

sit-ups /ˈsɪtʌps/ *npl* abdominaux *mpl*

🔑 **six** /sɪks/ *n, pron, det* six *m inv*

sixteen /ˌsɪkˈstiːn/ *n, pron, det* seize *m inv*

sixteenth /sɪkˈstiːnθ/ **A** *n* **1** (in order) seizième *mf*
2 (of month) seize *m inv*
3 (fraction) seizième *m*
B *adj, adv* seizième

sixth /sɪksθ/ **A** *n* **1** (in order) sixième *mf*
2 (of month) six *m inv*
3 (fraction) sixième *m*
B *adj, adv* sixième

sixth form *n* (BrE) (Sch) (lower) ≈ classes *fpl* de première; (upper) ≈ classes *fpl* de terminale

sixth form college *n* (BrE) lycée *m* (*n'ayant que des classes de première et terminale*)

sixth sense *n* sixième sens *m*

sixties /ˈsɪkstɪz/ *npl* **1** (era) **the ~** les années *fpl* soixante
2 (age) **to be in one's ~** avoir entre soixante et soixante-dix ans

sixtieth /ˈsɪkstɪəθ/ *n, adj, adv* soixantième *mf*

sixty /ˈsɪkstɪ/ *n, pron, det* soixante *m inv*

🔑 **size** /saɪz/ *n* (of person, paper, clothes) taille *f*; (of container, room, building, region) grandeur *f*; (of apple, egg, book, parcel) grosseur *f*; (of carpet, bed, machine) dimensions *fpl*; (of population, audience) importance *f*; (of class, company) effectif *m*; (of shoes, gloves) pointure *f*
IDIOM **to cut sb down to ~** remettre qn à sa place, rabattre le caquet à qn (fam)
■ **size up** se faire une opinion de ‹*person*›; évaluer ‹*situation*›; mesurer ‹*problem*›

sizeable /ˈsaɪzəbl/ *adj* ‹*amount*› assez important/-e; ‹*house, field, town*› assez grand/-e

sizzle /ˈsɪzl/ *vi* grésiller

skate /skeɪt/ **A** *n* **1** (ice) patin *m* à glace; (roller) patin *m* à roulettes
2 (fish) raie *f*
B *vi* patiner (**on, along** sur)

skateboard /ˈskeɪtbɔːd/ *n* skateboard *m*, planche *f* à roulettes

skateboarder *n* skateur/-euse *m/f*

skater /ˈskeɪtə(r)/ *n* patineur/-euse *m/f*

skating /ˈskeɪtɪŋ/ *n* patinage *m*

skating rink *n* (ice) patinoire *f*; (roller-skating) piste *f* de patins à roulettes

skeleton /ˈskelɪtn/ *n* squelette *m*

skeleton key *n* passe-partout *m inv*

skeptic (AmE) = **sceptic**

skeptical (AmE) = **sceptical**

skepticism (AmE) = **scepticism**

sketch /sketʃ/ **A** *n* **1** (drawing, draft) esquisse *f*; (hasty outline) croquis *m*; **rough ~** ébauche *f*
2 (comic scene) sketch *m*
B *vt* faire une esquisse de; (hastily) faire un croquis de

sketchbook *n* carnet *m* à croquis

sketch pad *n* bloc *m* à dessin

sketchy /ˈsketʃɪ/ *adj* ‹*information, details*› insuffisant/-e; ‹*memory*› vague

skewer /ˈskjuːə(r)/ **A** *n* (for kebab) brochette *f*; (for joint) broche *f*
B *vt* embrocher

ski /skiː/ **A** *n* ski *m*
B *vi* (*prét, pp* **skied**) faire du ski; **to ~ down a slope** descendre une pente à skis

ski boot *n* chaussure *f* de ski

skid /skɪd/ **A** *n* dérapage *m*
B *vi* (*p prés etc* **-dd-**) déraper (**on** sur)

skier /ˈskiːə(r)/ *n* skieur/-ieuse *m/f*

skiing /ˈskiːɪŋ/ *n* ski *m*; **to go ~** faire du ski

skiing holiday *n* vacances *fpl* de neige

ski jumping *n* saut *m* à skis

skilful (BrE), **skillful** (AmE) /ˈskɪlfl/ *adj* habile, adroit/-e

ski lift *n* remontée *f* mécanique

🔑 **skill** /skɪl/ **A** *n* **1** (intellectual) habileté *f*, adresse *f*; (physical) dextérité *f*
2 (special ability) (acquired) compétence *f*, capacités *fpl*; (practical) technique *f*
B skills *npl* (training) connaissances *fpl*

skilled /skɪld/ *adj* **1** (trained) ‹*labour, work*› qualifié/-e
2 (talented) consommé/-e

skim /skɪm/ **A** *vt* (*p prés etc* **-mm-**) **1** (remove cream) écrémer; (remove scum) écumer
2 ‹*plane, bird*› raser, frôler ‹*surface, treetops*›
3 to ~ stones faire des ricochets avec des cailloux
B *vi* (*p prés etc* **-mm-**) **to ~ through** parcourir ‹*book, article*›; **to ~ over** passer rapidement sur ‹*event, facts*›

skim milk *n* (*also* **skimmed milk**) lait *m* écrémé

skimp /skɪmp/ *vi* **to ~ on** lésiner sur

skimpy /ˈskɪmpɪ/ *adj* ‹*garment*› minuscule; ‹*portion, allowance, income*› maigre *before n*

🔑 **skin** /skɪn/ **A** *n* peau *f*; (of onion) pelure *f*
B *vt* (*p prés etc* **-nn-**) **1** écorcher ‹*animal*›
2 to ~ one's knee s'écorcher le genou
IDIOMS **to have a thick ~** être insensible; **to be** *or* **get soaked to the ~** être trempé/-e

---

🔑 mot clé

jusqu'aux os (fam); **by the ~ of one's teeth** de justesse

skin-deep /ˌskɪnˈdiːp/ *adj* superficiel/-ielle

skin diving *n* plongée *f* sous-marine

skinhead /ˈskɪnhed/ *n* (BrE) (youth) skin(head) *m*

skinny /ˈskɪnɪ/ *adj* (fam) maigre

skint /skɪnt/ *adj* (BrE) (fam) fauché/-e (fam)

skintight *adj* moulant/-e

skip /skɪp/ **A** *n* **1** (jump) petit bond *m*
2 (BrE) (container) benne *f*
B *vt* (*p prés etc* **-pp-**) sauter ‹*page, lunch, school*›
C *vi* (*p prés etc* **-pp-**) **1** (once) bondir; (several times) sautiller
2 (with rope) sauter à la corde

ski pants *n* fuseau *m* (de ski)

ski pass *n* forfait-skieur *m*

skipper /ˈskɪpə(r)/ *n* (of ship) capitaine *m*; (of fishing boat) patron *m*; (of yacht) skipper *m*

skipping rope *n* (BrE) corde *f* à sauter

ski resort *n* station *f* de ski

skirt /skɜːt/ **A** *n* jupe *f*
B *vt* **1** contourner ‹*wood, village, city*›
2 esquiver ‹*problem*›

skirting board *n* (BrE) plinthe *f*

ski slope *n* piste *f*

ski suit *n* combinaison *f* de ski

skittle /ˈskɪtl/ **A** *n* quille *f*
B **skittles** *npl* (jeu *m* de) quilles *fpl*

skive /skaɪv/ *vi* (BrE) (fam) (*also* ~ **off**) (shirk) tirer au flanc (fam); (be absent) (from school) sécher l'école (fam); (from work) ne pas aller au boulot (fam)

skulk /skʌlk/ *vi* rôder; **to ~ out/off** sortir/s'éloigner furtivement

skull /skʌl/ *n* crâne *m*

skunk /skʌŋk/ *n* moufette *f*

sky /skaɪ/ *n* ciel *m*

skydiving *n* parachutisme *m* (en chute libre)

sky-high /ˌskaɪˈhaɪ/ *adj* ‹*prices, rates*› exorbitant/-e

skyjacker *n* (fam) pirate *m* de l'air

skylight *n* fenêtre *f* à tabatière

skyline *n* (in countryside) ligne *f* d'horizon; (in city) ligne *f* des toits

sky marshal *n* garde *m* armé (*à bord d'un avion*)

skyscraper *n* gratte-ciel *m inv*

slab /slæb/ *n* (of stone, wood, concrete) dalle *f*; (of meat, cheese, cake) pavé *m*; (of chocolate) tablette *f*

slack /slæk/ **A** *n* (in rope, cable) mou *m*
B *adj* **1** ‹*worker*› peu consciencieux/-ieuse; ‹*work*› peu soigné/-e
2 ‹*period*› creux/creuse *after n*; ‹*demand, sales*› faible
3 ‹*cable, rope, body*› détendu/-e
C *vi* ‹*worker*› se relâcher dans son travail
■ **slack off** ‹*business, trade*› diminuer; ‹*rain*› se calmer

slacken /ˈslækən/ **A** *vt* **1** donner du mou à ‹*rope*›; lâcher ‹*reins*›
2 réduire ‹*pace*›
B *vi* **1** ‹*rope*› se relâcher
2 ‹*activity, pace, speed, business*› ralentir

slalom /ˈslɑːləm/ *n* slalom *m*

slam /slæm/ **A** *vt* (*p prés etc* **-mm-**) ‹*person*› claquer ‹*door*›; ‹*wind*› faire claquer ‹*door*›; **to ~ the door in sb's face** claquer la porte au nez de qn; **to ~ the ball into the net** renvoyer brutalement la balle dans le filet
B *vi* (*p prés etc* **-mm-**) ‹*door*› claquer (**against** contre); **to ~ shut** se refermer en claquant

slander /ˈslɑːndə(r), (AmE) ˈslæn-/ *n* (gen) calomnie *f* (**on** sur); (Law) diffamation *f* orale

slang /slæŋ/ *n* argot *m*

slangy /ˈslæŋɪ/ *adj* (fam) argotique

slant /slɑːnt, (AmE) slænt/ **A** *n* **1** (perspective) point *m* de vue (**on** sur)
2 (bias) tendance *f*
3 (slope) pente *f*
B *vi* ‹*floor, ground*› être en pente; ‹*handwriting*› pencher (**to** vers)

slanting *adj* ‹*roof*› en pente; **~ eyes** yeux *mpl* bridés

slap /slæp/ **A** *n* tape *f* (**on** sur); (stronger) claque *f* (**on** sur); **a ~ in the face** une gifle
B *vt* (*p prés etc* **-pp-**) donner une tape à ‹*person, animal*›; **to ~ sb in the face** gifler qn

slap bang /ˌslæpˈbæŋ/ *adv* (fam) **he ran ~ into the wall** il s'est cogné en plein dans le mur en courant; **~ in the middle (of)** au beau milieu (de)

slapdash /ˈslæpdæʃ/ *adj* (fam) ‹*person*› brouillon/-onne (fam); **in a ~ way** à la va-vite

slash /slæʃ/ **A** *n* **1** (wound) balafre *f* (**on** à)
2 (in fabric, seat, tyre) lacération *f*; (in painting) entaille *f*; (in skirt) fente *f*
3 (in printing) barre *f* oblique
B *vt* **1** balafrer ‹*cheek*›; faire une balafre à ‹*person*›; couper ‹*throat*›; ‹*knife*› entailler ‹*face*›; **to ~ one's wrists** se tailler les veines
2 taillader ‹*painting, fabric, tyres*›; trancher ‹*cord*›
3 (reduce) réduire [qch] (considérablement) ‹*amount, spending*›; sacrifier ‹*prices*›

slat /slæt/ *n* (of shutter, blind) lamelle *f*; (of bench, bed) lame *f*

slate /sleɪt/ **A** *n* ardoise *f*
B *vt* **1** couvrir [qch] d'ardoises ‹*roof*›
2 (BrE) (fam) (criticize) taper sur (fam) (**for** pour)
IDIOM **to wipe the ~ clean** faire table rase

slaughter /ˈslɔːtə(r)/ **A** *n* **1** (in butchery) abattage *m*
2 (massacre) massacre *m*, boucherie *f* (fam)
B *vt* **1** abattre ‹*animal*›

S

2 massacrer ‹*people*›
3 (fam) (defeat) écraser
slaughterhouse *n* abattoir *m*
Slav /slɑːv, (AmE) slæv/ **A** *n* Slave *mf*
B *adj* slave
slave /sleɪv/ **A** *n* esclave *mf*
B *vi* (*also* ~ **away**) travailler comme un forçat, trimer (fam)
slaver *vi* ‹*person, animal*› baver
slavery /ˈsleɪvərɪ/ *n* esclavage *m*
slaw /slɔː/ (AmE) = **coleslaw**
slay /sleɪ/ *vt* (*prét* **slew**, *pp* **slain**) faire périr ‹*enemy*›; pourfendre ‹*dragon*›
sleaze /sliːz/ *n* (fam) (pornography) pornographie *f*; (corruption) corruption *f*
sleazy /ˈsliːzɪ/ *adj* (fam) ‹*club, area, character*› louche; ‹*story, aspect*› scabreux/-euse; ‹*café, hotel*› borgne
sled, **sledge** (BrE) /sled/ **A** *n* luge *f*; (sleigh) traîneau *m*
B *vi* (*p prés etc* **-dd-**) faire de la luge
sledgehammer /ˈsledʒhæmə(r)/ *n* masse *f*
sleek /sliːk/ *adj* **1** ‹*hair*› lisse et brillant/-e; ‹*animal*› au poil lisse et brillant
2 ‹*shape*› élégant/-e; ‹*figure*› mince et harmonieux/-ieuse
🔑 **sleep** /sliːp/ **A** *n* sommeil *m*; **to go to ~** s'endormir; **to go back to ~** se rendormir; **to send** *or* **put sb to ~** endormir qn; **to have a ~** dormir; **my leg has gone to ~** (fam) j'ai la jambe engourdie; **to put an animal to ~** faire piquer un animal
B *vi* (*prét*, *pp* **slept**) dormir; **to ~ at a friend's house** coucher chez un ami
IDIOM **to ~ like a log** *or* **top** dormir comme une souche *or* un loir
■ **sleep in** (stay in bed late) faire la grasse matinée; (oversleep) dormir trop tard
■ **sleep on**: **to ~ on a decision** attendre le lendemain pour prendre une décision
sleeping bag *n* sac *m* de couchage
sleeping car *n* voiture-lit *f*, wagon-lit *m*
sleeping pill *n* somnifère *m*
sleepless /ˈsliːplɪs/ *adj* **to have a ~ night** passer une nuit blanche
sleepover /ˈsliːpəʊvə(r)/ *n* **she's having a ~** elle invite des amies à coucher chez elle
sleepwalk *vi* marcher en dormant, être somnambule
sleepy /ˈsliːpɪ/ *adj* ‹*voice, village*› endormi/-e, somnolent/-e; **to feel** *or* **be ~** avoir envie de dormir, avoir sommeil; **to make sb ~** ‹*fresh air*› donner envie de dormir à qn; ‹*wine*› endormir qn, assoupir qn
sleet /sliːt/ *n* neige *f* fondue
sleeve /sliːv/ *n* **1** (of garment) manche *f*
2 (of record) pochette *f*
3 (Tech) (inner) chemise *f*; (outer) gaine *f*
IDIOM **to have something up one's ~** avoir quelque chose en réserve

sleeveless /ˈsliːvlɪs/ *adj* sans manches
sleigh /sleɪ/ *n* traîneau *m*
sleight of hand /ˌslaɪtəvˈhænd/ *n*
1 (dexterity) dextérité *f*
2 (trick) tour *m* de passe-passe
slender /ˈslendə(r)/ *adj* **1** ‹*person*› mince; ‹*waist*› fin/-e
2 ‹*income, means*› modeste, maigre *before n*
sleuth /sluːθ/ *n* limier *m*, détective *m*
slew /sluː/ *vi* ‹*vehicle*› déraper; ‹*mast*› pivoter
slice /slaɪs/ **A** *n* **1** (of bread, meat) tranche *f*; (of cheese) morceau *m*; (of pie, tart) part *m*; (of lemon, cucumber, sausage) rondelle *f*
2 (of profits) part *f*; (of territory, population) partie *f*
3 (utensil) spatule *f*
B *vt* **1** couper [qch] (en tranches) ‹*loaf, roast*›; couper [qch] en rondelles ‹*lemon, cucumber*›
2 fendre ‹*air*›
3 (Sport) slicer, couper ‹*ball*›
C *vi* **to ~ through** fendre ‹*water, air*›; trancher ‹*timber, rope, meat*›
sliced bread *n* pain *m* en tranches
slice of life *n* tranche *f* de vie
slick /slɪk/ **A** *n* (*also* **oil ~**) (on water) nappe *f* de pétrole; (on shore) marée *f* noire
B *adj* **1** ‹*production*› habile; ‹*operation*› mené/-e rondement
2 (superficial) qui a un éclat plutôt superficiel
3 ‹*person*› roublard/-e (fam); ‹*answer*› astucieux/-ieuse; ‹*excuse*› facile
4 (AmE) (slippery) ‹*road, surface*› glissant/-e; ‹*hair*› lissé/-e
slide /slaɪd/ **A** *n* **1** (in playground) toboggan *m*
2 (photographic) diapositive *f*
3 (microscope plate) lame *f* porte-objet
4 (BrE) (*also* **hair ~**) barrette *f*
5 (decline) baisse *f* (**in** de)
B *vt* (*prét*, *pp* **slid**) faire glisser
C *vi* (*prét*, *pp* **slid**) **1** ‹*car, person*› glisser, partir en glissade (**into** dans, **on** sur); **to ~ in and out** ‹*drawer*› coulisser
2 ‹*prices, shares*› baisser
slide projector *n* projecteur *m* de diapositives
slide rule (BrE), **slide ruler** (AmE) *n* règle *f* à calcul
slide show *n* (at exhibition) diaporama *m*; (at lecture, at home) séance *f* de projection
sliding /ˈslaɪdɪŋ/ *adj* ‹*door*› coulissant/-e; ‹*roof*› ouvrant/-e
sliding scale *n* échelle *f* mobile
slight /slaɪt/ **A** *n* affront *m* (**on** à, **from** de la part de)
B *adj* **1** (gen) léger/-ère *before n*; ‹*risk, danger*› faible *before n*; ‹*pause, hesitation*› petit/-e *before n*; **not to have the ~est difficulty** ne pas avoir la moindre difficulté
2 (in build) mince
C *vt* **1** (offend) offenser; (stronger) humilier
2 (AmE) (underestimate) sous-estimer

🔑 mot clé

slightly /'slaɪtlɪ/ *adv* ‹*fall, change*› légèrement; ‹*different, more, less*› un peu

slim /slɪm/ **A** *adj* ‹*person, figure*› mince; ‹*ankle, leg*› fin/-e, mince; ‹*watch, calculator*› plat/-e
B *vi* (*p prés etc* **-mm-**) (BrE) maigrir; **I'm ~ming** je fais un régime amaigrissant

slime /slaɪm/ *n* dépôt *m* gluant *or* visqueux; (of slug, snail) bave *f*

sling /slɪŋ/ **A** *n* **1** (Med) écharpe *f*
2 (for carrying baby) porte-bébé *m*; (for carrying load) élingue *f*
B *vt* (*prét, pp* **slung**) lancer ‹*object, insult*› (**at** à)

slip /slɪp/ **A** *n* **1** (error) erreur *f*; **~ of the tongue** lapsus *m*
2 (receipt) reçu *m*; (for salary) bulletin *m*; **~ of paper** bout *m* de papier
3 (stumble) faux pas *m*
4 (petticoat) (full) combinaison *f*; (half) jupon *m*
B *vt* (*p prés etc* **-pp-**) **1** (gen) glisser (**into** dans); **she ~ped the shirt over her head** (put on) elle a enfilé sa chemise; (take off) elle a retiré sa chemise
2 ‹*dog*› se dégager de ‹*leash*›; ‹*boat*› filer ‹*moorings*›; **it had ~ped my mind (that)** j'avais complètement oublié (que); **to let ~ a remark** laisser échapper une remarque
3 (Med) **to ~ a disc** se déplacer une vertèbre
C *vi* (*p prés etc* **-pp-**) **1 to ~ into** passer ‹*dress, costume*›; tomber dans ‹*coma*›
2 to ~ into/out of se glisser dans/hors de ‹*room, building*›
3 ‹*person, vehicle*› glisser (**on** sur, **off** de); ‹*knife, razor, pen*› glisser, déraper; **to ~ through sb's fingers** ‹*money, opportunity*› filer entre les doigts de qn
4 (Aut) ‹*clutch*› patiner

slip knot *n* nœud *m* coulant

slip-on *n* (*also* **slip-on shoe**) mocassin *m*

slipped disc *n* hernie *f* discale

slipper /'slɪpə(r)/ *n* pantoufle *f*

slippery /'slɪpərɪ/ *adj* glissant/-e

slip road *n* (BrE) bretelle *f* d'accès

slipshod *adj* ‹*person*› négligent/-e; ‹*appearance, work*› négligé/-e, peu soigné/-e

slip-up *n* (fam) bourde *f* (fam)

slit /slɪt/ **A** *n* fente *f* (**in** dans)
B *adj* ‹*eyes*› bridé/-e; ‹*skirt*› fendu/-e
C *vt* (*prét, pp* **slit**) (on purpose) faire une fente dans; (by accident) déchirer; **to ~ sb's throat** égorger qn; **to ~ one's wrists** s'ouvrir les veines

slither /'slɪðə(r)/ *vi* glisser

sliver /'slɪvə(r)/ *n* (of glass) éclat *m*; (of food) mince tranche *f*

slob /slɒb/ *n* (fam) (lazy) flemmard/-e *m/f* (fam)

slog /slɒg/ *vi* (fam) (*p prés etc* **-gg-**) (*also* **~ away**) travailler dur, bosser (fam)

slogan /'sləʊgən/ *n* slogan *m*

slop /slɒp/ **A** *vt* renverser ‹*liquid*›
B *vi* (*also* **~ over**) ‹*liquid*› déborder

slope /sləʊp/ **A** *n* pente *f*
B *vi* être en pente (**towards** vers); ‹*writing*› pencher (**to** vers)

sloping /'sləʊpɪŋ/ *adj* ‹*ground, roof*› en pente; ‹*ceiling*› incliné/-e; ‹*writing*› penché/-e

sloppy /'slɒpɪ/ *adj* **1** (fam) ‹*appearance*› débraillé/-e; ‹*work*› peu soigné/-e
2 (fam) (over-emotional) sentimental/-e

slot /slɒt/ **A** *n* **1** (for coin, ticket) fente *f*; (for letters) ouverture *f*; (groove) rainure *f*
2 (in timetable, schedule) créneau *m*
B *vt* (*p prés etc* **-tt-**) **to ~ sth into a machine** insérer qch dans une machine
C *vi* (*p prés etc* **-tt-**) **to ~ into sth** ‹*coin, piece*› s'insérer dans qch; **to ~ into place** *or* **position** s'encastrer
■ **slot together** s'emboîter

sloth /sləʊθ/ *n* (Zool) paresseux *m*

slot machine *n* (game) machine *f* à sous; (vending machine) distributeur *m* automatique

slouch /slaʊtʃ/ *vi* être avachi/-e

Slovakia /slə'vækɪə/ *pr n* Slovaquie *f*

Slovenia /slə'vi:nɪə/ *pr n* Slovénie *f*

slovenly /'slʌvnlɪ/ *adj* négligé/-e

slow /sləʊ/ **A** *adj* **1** (gen) lent/-e
2 ‹*business, market*› stagnant/-e
3 (dull-witted) lent/-e (d'esprit)
4 to be ~ ‹*clock, watch*› retarder; **to be 10 minutes ~** retarder de 10 minutes
B *adv* lentement
C *vt, vi* (*also* **~ down**) ralentir

slowly /'sləʊlɪ/ *adv* lentement

slow motion *n* ralenti *m*; **in ~** au ralenti

slow-moving *adj* lent/-e

sludge /slʌdʒ/ *n* **1** (*also* **sewage ~**) eaux *fpl* usées
2 (mud) vase *f*

slug /slʌg/ *n* limace *f*

sluggish /'slʌgɪʃ/ *adj* **1** ‹*person, animal*› léthargique; ‹*circulation*› lent/-e
2 ‹*market, trade*› qui stagne

sluice /slu:s/ *n* **1** (*also* **~ gate**) vanne *f*
2 (*also* **~way**) canal *m*

slum /slʌm/ *n* **1** (area) quartier *m* pauvre
2 (dwelling) taudis *m*

slumber /'slʌmbə(r)/ **A** *n* sommeil *m*
B *vi* sommeiller

slump /slʌmp/ **A** *n* (in trade, prices) effondrement *m* (**in** de)
B *vi* **1** ‹*demand, trade, price*› chuter (**from** de, **to** à, **by** de); ‹*economy, market*› s'effondrer; ‹*popularity*› être en forte baisse
2 ‹*person, body*› s'affaler (fam)

slur /slɜ:(r)/ **A** *n* **1** (in speech) marmonnement *m*
2 (Mus) liaison *f*

3 (aspersion) calomnie *f*
B *vi* (*p prés etc* **-rr-**) avoir du mal à articuler
C **slurred** *pp adj* ‹*voice, speech*› inarticulé/-e

slush /slʌʃ/ *n* neige *f* fondue

slush fund *n* caisse *f* noire

sly /slaɪ/ *adj* ‹*person, animal*› rusé/-e; ‹*remark, smile*› entendu/-e
IDIOM **on the ~** en douce (fam), en cachette

smack /smæk/ **A** *n* claque *f*; (on face) gifle *f*
B *vt* (on face) gifler ‹*person*›; taper ‹*object*› (**on** sur, **against** contre); **she ~ed him on the bottom** elle lui a donné une tape sur les fesses
C *vi* **to ~ of** sentir

small /smɔːl/ **A** *n* **the ~ of the back** le creux du dos
B *adj* **1** (gen) petit/-e *before n*; ‹*quantity, amount*› faible *before n*
2 to feel ~ être dans ses petits souliers (fam); **to make sb feel** *or* **look ~** humilier qn
C *adv* ‹*write*› petit

small ad *n* (BrE) petite annonce *f*

small change *n* petite monnaie *f*

small talk *n* banalités *fpl*; **to make ~** faire la conversation

smart /smɑːt/ **A** *adj* **1** (elegant) ‹*person, clothes*› élégant/-e; ‹*restaurant, hotel, street*› chic
2 (clever) malin/-e
3 ‹*blow*› vif/vive; ‹*rebuke*› cinglant/-e; **to walk at a ~ pace** marcher à vive allure
4 (Comput) intelligent/-e
B *vi* ‹*cut, cheeks*› brûler; **his eyes were ~ing from the smoke** la fumée lui brûlait les yeux

smart bomb *n* bombe *f* intelligente

smart card *n* carte *f* à puce

smarten /ˈsmɑːtn/ *v*
■ **smarten up** embellir ‹*room*›; **to ~ oneself up** se faire beau

smartphone /ˈsmɑːtfəʊn/ *n* smartphone *m*, ordiphone *m*, téléphone *m* intelligent

smash /smæʃ/ **A** *n* **1** (fam) (*also* **~-up**) (accident) collision *f*
2 (fam) (*also* **~ hit**) tube *m* (fam)
3 (in tennis) smash *m*
4 (sound) fracas *m*
B *vt* **1** briser ‹*glass, door, car*›; (more violently) fracasser
2 démanteler ‹*drugs ring, gang*›
3 (Sport) **to ~ the ball** faire un smash
C *vi* se briser, se fracasser

smashing /ˈsmæʃɪŋ/ *adj* (BrE) formidable (fam)

smattering /ˈsmætərɪŋ/ *n* notions *fpl* (**of** de); **to have a ~ of Russian** avoir quelques connaissances en russe

mot clé

smear /smɪə(r)/ **A** *n* **1** (spot) tache *f*; (streak) traînée *f*
2 (defamation) propos *m* diffamatoire
3 (*also* **~ test**) (Med) frottis *m*
B *vt* **1** faire des taches sur ‹*glass, window*›; **her face was ~ed with jam** elle avait le visage barbouillé de confiture
2 (spread) étaler ‹*butter, paint*›; appliquer ‹*lotion*› (**on** sur)
C *vi* ‹*ink, paint*› s'étaler; ‹*lipstick, make-up*› couler

smell /smel/ **A** *n* **1** odeur *f*
2 (sense) odorat *m*
B *vt* (*prét, pp* **smelled**, **smelt** (BrE)) ‹*person*› sentir; ‹*animal*› renifler, sentir; **I can ~ burning** ça sent le brûlé
C *vi* (*prét, pp* **smelled**, **smelt** (BrE)) sentir; **that ~s nice/horrible** ça sent bon/très mauvais; **to ~ of sth** sentir qch

smelling salts *npl* sels *mpl*

smelly /ˈsmelɪ/ *adj* malodorant/-e, qui sent mauvais

smile /smaɪl/ **A** *n* sourire *m*
B *vi* sourire (**at sb** à qn)
■ **smile on**: **~ on [sb/sth]** ‹*fortune, weather*› sourire à; ‹*person*› être favorable à

smiley /ˈsmaɪlɪ/ *n* (fam) souriant *m*, smiley *m* (fam)

smirk /smɜːk/ **A** *n* (self-satisfied) petit sourire *m* satisfait; (knowing) sourire *m* en coin
B *vi* (in a self-satisfied way) avoir un petit sourire satisfait; (knowingly) avoir un sourire en coin

smithereens /ˌsmɪðəˈriːnz/ *npl* **in ~** en mille morceaux; **to smash sth to ~** faire voler qch en éclats

smock /smɒk/ *n* blouse *f*, sarrau *m*

smog /smɒg/ *n* smog *m*

smoke /sməʊk/ **A** *n* fumée *f*
B *vt, vi* fumer

smoke alarm *n* détecteur *m* de fumée

smoked *adj* fumé/e

smoker /ˈsməʊkə(r)/ *n* fumeur/-euse *m/f*

smoke screen *n* (Mil) écran *m* de fumée; (fig) diversion *f*

smoking /ˈsməʊkɪŋ/ **A** *n* **~ and drinking** le tabac et l'alcool; **to give up ~** arrêter de fumer; **'no ~'** 'défense de fumer'
B *adj* ‹*compartment, section*› fumeurs *after n*

smoking-related *adj* ‹*disease*› associé/-e au tabac

smoky /ˈsməʊkɪ/ *adj* ‹*room*› enfumé/-e; ‹*cheese, bacon*› fumé/-e

smooth /smuːð/ **A** *adj* **1** ‹*stone, surface, skin, fabric*› lisse; ‹*curve, breathing*› régulier/-ière; ‹*sauce*› homogène; ‹*crossing, flight*› sans heurts; ‹*movement*› aisé/-e
2 ‹*taste, wine, whisky*› moelleux/-euse
3 (suave) ‹*person*› mielleux/-euse; ‹*manners, appearance*› onctueux/-euse; **to be a ~**

talker être enjôleur/-euse
B *vt* **1** (flatten out) lisser; (get creases out of) défroisser
2 faciliter ‹*transition, path*›
■ **smooth over**: ~ **over [sth]** atténuer ‹*differences*›; aplanir ‹*difficulties, problems*›; **to ~ things over** arranger les choses

smooth-running *adj* ‹*organization, event*› qui marche bien

smother /ˈsmʌðə(r)/ *vt* étouffer

smoulder (BrE), **smolder** (AmE) /ˈsməʊldə(r)/ *vi* **1** ‹*cigarette, fire*› se consumer
2 ‹*hatred, jealousy*› couver; **to ~ with** être consumé/-e de

SMS *n* (*abbr* = **Short Message Service**) SMS *m*

smudge /smʌdʒ/ **A** *n* trace *f*
B *vt* étaler ‹*make-up, print, ink, paint*›; faire des traces sur ‹*paper, paintwork*›
C *vi* ‹*make-up, print, ink, paint*› s'étaler

smug /smʌg/ *adj* suffisant/-e

smuggle /ˈsmʌgl/ *vt* faire du trafic de ‹*arms, drugs*›; faire passer [qch] en contrebande ‹*watches, alcohol, cigarettes*›; **to ~ sb/sth in** faire entrer qn/qch clandestinement

smuggler /ˈsmʌglə(r)/ *n* contrebandier/-ière *m/f*; **drug/arms ~** passeur/-euse *m/f* de drogue/d'armes

smuggling /ˈsmʌglɪŋ/ *n* contrebande *f*; **drug/arms ~** trafic *m* de drogue/d'armes

smutty /ˈsmʌtɪ/ *adj* **1** (crude) grivois/-e
2 (dirty) ‹*face*› noir/-e; ‹*mark*› noirâtre

snack /snæk/ **A** *n* **1** (small meal) repas *m* léger; (instead of meal) casse-croûte *m inv*
2 (crisps, peanuts) **~s** amuse-gueule *m inv*
B *vi* grignoter, manger légèrement

snag /snæg/ *n* **1** (hitch) inconvénient *m* (**in** de)
2 (tear) accroc *m* (**in** à)

snail /sneɪl/ *n* escargot *m*

snail mail *n* (fam) courrier *m* postal

snake /sneɪk/ *n* serpent *m*

snap /snæp/ **A** *n* **1** (of branch) craquement *m*; (of fingers, elastic) claquement *m*
2 (fam) (photograph) photo *f*
3 (game) ≈ bataille *f*
B *adj* ‹*decision, judgement, vote*› rapide
C *vt* (*p prés etc* **-pp-**) **1** faire claquer ‹*fingers, jaws, elastic*›
2 (break) (faire) casser net
3 (say crossly) dire [qch] hargneusement
D *vi* (*p prés etc* **-pp-**) **1** (break) se casser
2 (speak sharply) parler hargneusement
■ **snap at 1** (speak sharply) parler sèchement à
2 ‹*dog*› essayer de mordre
■ **snap up** sauter sur ‹*bargain*›

snappy /ˈsnæpɪ/ *adj* ‹*rhythm, reply*› rapide; ‹*advertisement*› accrocheur/-euse

snapshot *n* photo *f*

snare /sneə(r)/ **A** *n* piège *m*
B *vt* prendre [qn/qch] au piège

snarl /snɑːl/ *vi* ‹*animal*› gronder férocement; ‹*person*› grogner

snarl-up *n* (in traffic) embouteillage *m*; (in distribution network) blocage *m*

snatch /snætʃ/ **A** *n* (*pl* **~es**) **1** (of conversation) bribe *f*; (of tune) quelques notes *fpl*
2 (theft) vol *m*
B *vt* **1** (grab) attraper ‹*book, key*›; **to ~ sth from sb** arracher qch à qn
2 (fam) (steal) voler ‹*handbag*› (**from** à)

sneak /sniːk/ *vi* **to ~ in/out** entrer/sortir furtivement; **to ~ up on sb/sth** s'approcher sans bruit de qn/qch

sneaker /ˈsniːkə(r)/ *n* (AmE) basket *f*, (chaussure *f* de) tennis *f*

sneaking /ˈsniːkɪŋ/ *adj* ‹*suspicion*› vague

sneaky /ˈsniːkɪ/ *adj* sournois/-e

sneer /snɪə(r)/ **A** *n* sourire *m* méprisant
B *vi* sourire avec mépris

sneeze /sniːz/ **A** *n* éternuement *m*
B *vi* éternuer

snide /snaɪd/ *adj* sournois/-e

sniff /snɪf/ **A** *n* reniflement *m*
B *vt* ‹*dog*› flairer; ‹*person*› sentir ‹*food*›; inhaler ‹*glue, cocaine*›
C *vi* renifler

snigger /ˈsnɪgə(r)/ **A** *n* ricanement *m*
B *vi* ricaner

snip /snɪp/ *vt* (*p prés etc* **-pp-**) découper (à petits coups de ciseaux) ‹*fabric, paper*›; tailler ‹*hedge*›
■ **snip off** couper

sniper /ˈsnaɪpə(r)/ *n* tireur *m* embusqué

snippet /ˈsnɪpɪt/ *n* (of conversation, information) bribes *f*; (of text, fabric, music) fragment *m*

snivel /ˈsnɪvl/ *vi* (*p prés etc* **-ll-** (BrE), **-l-** (AmE)) pleurnicher

snob /snɒb/ *n* snob *mf*

snobbery /ˈsnɒbərɪ/ *n* snobisme *m*

snobbish /ˈsnɒbɪʃ/ *adj* snob

snog /snɒg/ **A** *n* bécotage *m* (fam)
B *vt, vi* (*p prés etc* **-gg-**) se bécoter (fam)

snooker /ˈsnuːkə(r)/ **A** *n* (game) snooker *m*
B *vt* **1** (Sport) (fig) coincer ‹*player, person*›
2 (AmE) (deceive) avoir (fam) ‹*person*›

snoop /snuːp/ (fam) **A** *n* fouineur/-euse *m/f*
B *vi* fouiner, fureter

snooze /snuːz/ (fam) **A** *n* petit somme *m*
B *vi* sommeiller

snore /snɔː(r)/ **A** *n* ronflement *m*
B *vi* ronfler

snorkel /ˈsnɔːkl/ *n* tuba *m*

snorkelling /ˈsnɔːklɪŋ/ *n* plongée *f* avec tuba

snort /snɔːt/ **A** *vi* ‹*person, pig*› grogner; ‹*horse, bull*› s'ébrouer
B *vt* sniffer ‹*drugs*›

snout /snaʊt/ *n* museau *m*; (of pig) groin *m*

snow /snəʊ/ **A** *n* neige *f*
B *v impers* neiger; **it's ~ing** il neige

snowball /ˈsnəʊbɔːl/ **A** *n* boule *f* de neige
B *vi* faire boule de neige

snowboard /ˈsnəʊbɔːd/ **A** *n* surf *m* des neiges
B *vi* faire du surf des neiges
snowdrift *n* congère *f*
snowdrop *n* perce-neige *m inv*
snowfall *n* chute *f* de neige
snowflake *n* flocon *m* de neige
snowman *n* bonhomme *m* de neige
snow mobile *n* motoneige *f*
snow plough (BrE), **snow plow** (AmE) *n* chasse-neige *m inv*
snow shoe *n* raquette *f*
snub /snʌb/ **A** *n* rebuffade *f*
B *vt* (*p prés etc* **-bb-**) rembarrer
snub-nosed *adj* au nez retroussé
snuff /snʌf/ *n* tabac *m* à priser
snug /snʌg/ *adj* ‹*bed, room*› douillet/-ette; ‹*coat*› chaud/-e
snuggle /ˈsnʌgl/ *vi* se blottir
⚷ **so** /səʊ/ **A** *adv* **1** (to such an extent) si, tellement; ~ **happy/quickly** si *or* tellement heureux/vite; ~ **much noise/many things** tant de bruit/de choses
2 (in such a way) ~ **arranged/worded that** organisé/rédigé d'une telle façon que; **and ~ on and ~ forth** et ainsi de suite; ~ **be it!** soit!
3 (thus) ainsi; (therefore) donc; ~ **that's the reason** voilà donc pourquoi; ~ **you're going are you?** alors tu y vas?
4 (true) **is that** ~? c'est vrai?; **if (that's)** ~ si c'est vrai
5 (also) aussi; ~ **is she** elle aussi; ~ **do I** moi aussi
6 (fam) (thereabouts) environ; **20 or** ~ environ 20
7 (other uses) **I think/don't think** ~ je crois/ne crois pas; **I'm afraid** ~ j'ai bien peur que oui *or* si; ~ **it would appear** c'est ce qu'il semble; ~ **to speak** si je puis dire; **I told you** ~ je te l'avais bien dit; ~ **I see** je le vois bien; **who says** ~? qui dit ça?; **only more** ~ mais encore plus; **he dived and as he did** ~... il a plongé et en le faisant...; **'it's broken'—'~ it is'** 'c'est cassé'—'je le vois bien!'; ~ **(what)?** et alors?
B **so (that)** *phr* (in order that) pour que (+ *subjunctive*)
C **so as** *phr* pour; ~ **as to attract attention** pour attirer l'attention
D **so much** *phr* tellement; **she worries ~ much** elle s'inquiète tellement; **she taught me ~ much** elle m'a tant appris; **thank you ~ much** merci beaucoup
IDIOMS ~ **much the better** tant mieux; ~ ~ comme ci comme ça
soak /səʊk/ **A** *vt* **1** ‹*rain*› tremper ‹*person, clothes*›
2 ‹*person*› faire tremper ‹*clothes, foods*›
B *vi* **1** ‹*clothes, foods*› tremper
2 ‹*liquid*› **to ~ into** être absorbé/-e par; **to ~ through** traverser
■ **soak up**: **A** ~ **[sth] up**, ~ **up [sth]** absorber
B ~ **up [sth]** s'imprégner de ‹*atmosphere*›; **to ~ up the sun** faire le plein (fam) de soleil
soaked *adj* trempé/-e; **to be ~ through** *or* ~ **to the skin** être trempé/-e jusqu'aux os
soaking /ˈsəʊkɪŋ/ *adj* trempé/-e
soap /səʊp/ *n* savon *m*; **a bar of ~** un savon
soap opera *n* feuilleton *m*
soap powder *n* lessive *f* (en poudre)
soar /sɔː(r)/ *vi* **1** ‹*ball*› filer; ‹*bird, plane*› prendre son essor
2 (glide) planer
3 ‹*price, temperature, costs*› monter en flèche; ‹*hopes*› grandir considérablement
4 ‹*tower, cliffs*› se dresser
soaring /ˈsɔːrɪŋ/ *adj* ‹*inflation, demand*› en forte progression; ‹*prices, temperatures*› en forte hausse
sob **A** *n* sanglot *m*
B *vi* (*p prés etc* **-bb-**) sangloter
sober /ˈsəʊbə(r)/ **A** *adj* **1 I'm ~** (not drunk) je n'ai pas bu d'alcool; (in protest) je ne suis pas ivre
2 (no longer drunk) dessoûlé/-e
3 (serious) ‹*person*› sérieux/-ieuse; ‹*mood*› grave
4 ‹*colour, suit*› sobre
B *vt* ‹*news, reprimand*› calmer
■ **sober up** dessoûler
sob story *n* (fam) mélo *m* (fam)
soccer /ˈsɒkə(r)/ *n* football *m*
sociable /ˈsəʊʃəbl/ *adj* ‹*person*› sociable; ‹*evening*› agréable
⚷ **social** /ˈsəʊʃl/ *adj* **1** (gen) social/-e
2 ‹*call, visit*› amical/-e
social climber *n* (still rising) arriviste *mf*; (at his/her peak) parvenu/-e *mf*
social club *n* club *m*
social gathering *n* réunion *f* entre amis
socialism /ˈsəʊʃəlɪzəm/ *n* socialisme *m*
socialist /ˈsəʊʃəlɪst/ *n, adj* (*also* **Socialist**) socialiste *mf*
socialite /ˈsəʊʃəlaɪt/ *n* mondain/-e *m/f*
socialize /ˈsəʊʃəlaɪz/ *vi* rencontrer des gens; **to ~ with sb** fréquenter qn
social life *n* (of person) vie *f* sociale; (of town) vie *f* culturelle
social media *n* médias *mpl* sociaux
social mobility *n* mobilité *f* sociale
social network *n* (Comput) réseau *m* social
social networking site *n* (Comput) site *m* de réseau social
social science *n* science *f* sociale
social security *n* aide *f* sociale; **to be on ~** recevoir l'aide sociale
Social Services *npl* (BrE) services *mpl* sociaux
social work *n* travail *m* social

⚷ mot clé

social worker *n* travailleur/-euse *m/f* social/-e

society /sə'saɪətɪ/ *n* **1** (gen) société *f* **2** (club) société *f*; (for social contact) association *f* **3** (*also* **high ~**) haute société *f*

sociologist /ˌsəʊsɪ'ɒlədʒɪst/ *n* sociologue *mf*

sociology /ˌsəʊsɪ'ɒlədʒɪ/ *n* sociologie *f*

sock /sɒk/ *n* (*pl* **~s** *ou* **sox** (AmE)) chaussette *f*

socket /'sɒkɪt/ *n* **1** (for plug) prise *f* (de courant); (for bulb) douille *f* **2** (of joint) cavité *f* articulaire; (of eye) orbite *f*

soda /'səʊdə/ *n* **1** (chemical) soude *f* **2** (*also* **washing ~**) soude *f* ménagère **3** (*also* **~ water**) eau *f* de seltz; **whisky and ~** whisky *m* soda **4** (*also* **~ pop** (AmE)) soda *m*

sodden /'sɒdn/ *adj* ‹*towel, clothing*› trempé/-e; ‹*ground*› détrempé/-e

sofa /'səʊfə/ *n* canapé *m*

sofa bed *n* canapé-lit *m*

soft /sɒft, (AmE) sɔːft/ *adj* **1** (gen) doux/douce; ‹*ground*› meuble; ‹*bed, cushion*› moelleux/-euse; ‹*brush, hair*› souple; ‹*dough, butter*› mou/molle; ‹*impact, touch*› léger/-ère; ‹*eyes, heart*› tendre; ‹*fold*› souple **2** (lenient) ‹*parent, teacher*› (trop) indulgent/-e

soft cheese *n* fromage *m* à pâte molle

soft drink *n* boisson *f* non alcoolisée

soft drug *n* drogue *f* douce

soften /'sɒfn, (AmE) 'sɔːfn/ **A** *vt* **1** adoucir ‹*skin, water, light, outline*›; ramollir ‹*butter*› **2** atténuer ‹*blow, shock, pain*› **B** *vi* **1** ‹*light, outline, music, colour*› s'adoucir; ‹*skin*› devenir plus doux; ‹*substance*› se ramollir **2** ‹*person*› s'assouplir (**towards sb** vis-à-vis de qn)

■ **soften up**: **A** **~ up** amollir **B** **~ [sb] up** affaiblir ‹*enemy, opponent*›; attendrir ‹*customer*›

softly /'sɒftlɪ, (AmE) 'sɔːft-/ *adv* ‹*speak, touch, blow*› doucement; ‹*fall*› en douceur

soft option *n* **to take the ~** choisir la facilité

soft porn *n* (fam) soft *m* (fam)

soft skills *npl* compétences *fpl* douces

soft spot *n* (fam) **to have a ~ for sb** avoir un faible (fam) pour qn

soft-top *n* décapotable *f*

soft touch *n* (fam) poire *f* (fam)

soft toy *n* peluche *f*

software /'sɒftweə(r), (AmE) 'sɔːft-/ *n* logiciel *m*

software house *n* fabricant *m* de logiciels

software package *n* progiciel *m*

software piracy *n* piratage *m* de logiciels

soggy /'sɒgɪ/ *adj* ‹*ground*› détrempé/-e; ‹*food*› ramolli/-e

soil /sɔɪl/ **A** *n* sol *m*, terre *f* **B** *vt* salir

soiled /sɔɪld/ *adj* **1** (dirty) sali/-e **2** (*also* **shop-~**) vendu/-e avec défaut

solace /'sɒləs/ **A** *n* (feeling of comfort) consolation *f*; (source of comfort) réconfort *m* **B** *vt* consoler (**for** de)

solar /'səʊlə(r)/ *adj* solaire

solar eclipse *n* éclipse *f* de soleil

solar energy *n* énergie *f* solaire

solar farm *n* ferme *f* solaire

solar panel *n* panneau *m* solaire

solar power *n* énergie *f* solaire

solder /'səʊldə(r), 'sɒ-, (AmE) 'sɒdər/ *vt, vi* souder (**onto, to** à)

soldier /'səʊldʒə(r)/ *n* soldat *m*

■ **soldier on** persévérer malgré tout

sole /səʊl/ **A** *n* **1** (fish) sole *f* **2** (of foot) plante *f*; (of shoe, sock) semelle *f* **B** *adj* **1** (single) seul/-e *before n*, unique *before n* **2** ‹*agent, right*› exclusif/-ive; ‹*trader*› indépendant

solely /'səʊlɪ/ *adv* (wholly) entièrement; (exclusively) uniquement

solemn /'sɒləm/ *adj* ‹*occasion, person, voice*› solennel/-elle; ‹*duty, warning*› formel/-elle

solicit /sə'lɪsɪt/ **A** *vt* solliciter ‹*information, help, money, votes*›; rechercher ‹*business, investment, orders*› **B** *vi* ‹*prostitute*› racoler

soliciting /sə'lɪsɪtɪŋ/ *n* racolage *m*

solicitor /sə'lɪsɪtə(r)/ *n* (BrE) (for documents, oaths) ≈ notaire *m*; (for court and police work) ≈ avocat/-e *m/f*

solid /'sɒlɪd/ **A** *n* solide *m* **B** *adj* **1** (gen) solide; **to go** *or* **become ~** se solidifier **2** ‹*gold, marble*› massif/-ive; **the gate was made of ~ steel** le portail était tout en acier; **cut through ~ rock** taillé dans la roche **3** ‹*crowd*› compact/-e; ‹*line*› continu/-e; **five ~ days, five days ~** cinq jours entiers **4** ‹*advice, worker*› sérieux/-ieuse; ‹*investment*› sûr/-e **5** ‹*freeze*› complètement; **to be packed ~** ‹*hall*› être bondé/-e; **the play is booked ~** la pièce affiche complet

solidarity /ˌsɒlɪ'dærətɪ/ *n* solidarité *f*

solidify /sə'lɪdɪfaɪ/ **A** *vt* solidifier **B** *vi* ‹*liquid*› se solidifier; ‹*honey, oil*› se figer

solitary /'sɒlɪtrɪ, (AmE) -terɪ/ *adj* **1** (unaccompanied) ‹*occupation, walker*› solitaire **2** (lonely) ‹*person*› très seul/-e; ‹*farm, village*› isolé/-e **3** (single) seul/-e

solitary confinement *n* isolement *m* cellulaire

solo /ˈsəʊləʊ/ **A** *n* solo *m*
B *adj, adv* en solo

soloist /ˈsəʊləʊɪst/ *n* soliste *mf*

solstice /ˈsɒlstɪs/ *n* solstice *m*

soluble /ˈsɒljʊbl/ *adj* soluble

⚷ **solution** /səˈluːʃn/ *n* solution *f*

⚷ **solve** /sɒlv/ *vt* résoudre ‹*equation, problem*›; élucider ‹*crime*›; trouver la solution de ‹*mystery*›; trouver la solution à ‹*clue, crossword*›; trouver une solution à ‹*crisis, poverty, unemployment*›

solvent /ˈsɒlvənt/ **A** *n* solvant *m*
B *adj* (in funds) solvable

sombre (BrE), **somber** (AmE) /ˈsɒmbə(r)/ *adj* sombre

⚷ **some** /sʌm/

> When *some* is used to mean an unspecified amount of something, it is translated by *du, de l'* (before a vowel or mute 'h'), *de la* or *des* according to the gender and number of the noun that follows: *I'd like some bread* = je voudrais du pain; *have some water* = prenez de l'eau; *we've bought some beer* = nous avons acheté de la bière; *they've bought some peaches* = ils ont acheté des pêches.
>
> But note that when a plural noun is preceded by an adjective in French, *some* is translated by *de* alone: *some pretty dresses* = de jolies robes.
>
> When *some* is used as a pronoun, it is translated by *en* which is placed before the verb in French: *would you like some?* = est-ce que vous en voulez?; *I've got some* = j'en ai.
>
> For further examples, see the entry below.

A *det* **1** (an unspecified amount or number) du/de l'/de la/des; **~ old socks** de vieilles chaussettes; **~ red socks** des chaussettes rouges; **I need ~ help** j'ai besoin d'aide
2 (certain) certain/-e *before n*; **~ people say that** certaines personnes disent que; **to ~ extent** dans une certaine mesure
3 (a considerable amount or number) **his suggestion was greeted with ~ hostility** sa suggestion a été accueillie avec hostilité; **it will take ~ doing** ça ne va pas être facile à faire; **we stayed there for ~ time** nous sommes restés là assez longtemps
4 (a little, a slight) **the meeting did have ~ effect** la réunion a eu un certain effet; **you must have ~ idea where the house is** tu dois avoir une idée de l'endroit où se trouve la maison
5 (an unknown) **he's doing ~ course** il suit des cours; **a car of ~ sort, ~ sort of car** une voiture quelconque
B *pron, quantif* **1** (an unspecified amount or number) en; **he took ~ of it/of them** il en a pris un peu/quelques-uns; **(do) have ~!** servez-vous!
2 (certain ones) certain/-e; **~ (of them) are blue** certains sont bleus; **~ (of them) arrived early** certains d'entre eux sont arrivés tôt
C *adv* **1** (approximately) environ; **~ 20 people** environ 20 personnes
2 (AmE) (fam) un peu

⚷ **somebody** /ˈsʌmbədɪ/ *pron* (*also* **someone**) quelqu'un; **~ famous** quelqu'un de célèbre

⚷ **somehow** /ˈsʌmhaʊ/ *adv* **1** (*also* **~ or other**) (of future action) d'une manière ou d'une autre; (of past action) je ne sais comment; **we'll get there ~** on y arrivera d'une manière ou d'une autre; **we managed it ~** nous avons réussi je ne sais comment
2 (for some reason) **~ it doesn't seem very important** en fait, ça ne semble pas très important

⚷ **someone** /ˈsʌmwʌn/ = **somebody**

somersault /ˈsʌməsɒlt/ **A** *n* (of gymnast) roulade *f*; (of child) galipette *f*; (accidental) culbute *f*
B *vi* ‹*gymnast*› faire une roulade; ‹*vehicle*› faire un tonneau

⚷ **something** /ˈsʌmθɪŋ/ **A** *pron* quelque chose; **~ interesting** quelque chose d'intéressant; **~ to do** quelque chose à faire; **there's ~ wrong** il y a un problème; **~ or other** quelque chose; **in nineteen-sixty-~** en mille neuf cent soixante et quelques; **she's gone shopping or ~** elle est allée faire les courses ou quelque chose comme ça
B **something of** *phr* **she is ~ of an expert on...** elle est assez experte en...; **it was ~ of a surprise** c'était assez étonnant

sometime /ˈsʌmtaɪm/ *adv* **we'll have to do it ~** il va falloir qu'on le fasse un jour ou l'autre; **I'll tell you about it ~** je te raconterai ça un de ces jours; **I'll phone you ~ next week** je te téléphonerai dans le courant de la semaine prochaine

⚷ **sometimes** /ˈsʌmtaɪmz/ *adv* parfois, quelquefois

⚷ **somewhat** /ˈsʌmwɒt/ *adv* (with adjective) plutôt; (with verb, adverb) un peu

⚷ **somewhere** /ˈsʌmweə(r)/ *adv* (some place) quelque part; **~ hot** un endroit chaud; **~ or other** je ne sais où; **~ between 50 and 100 people** entre 50 et 100 personnes

⚷ **son** /sʌn/ *n* fils *m*

sonata /səˈnɑːtə/ *n* sonate *f*

⚷ **song** /sɒŋ/ *n* chanson *f*; (of bird) chant *m*

songwriter /ˈsɒŋraɪtə(r)/ *n* (of words) parolier/-ière *m/f*; (of words and music) auteur-compositeur *m* de chansons

sonic /ˈsɒnɪk/ *adj* sonore

sonic boom *n* bang *m*

son-in-law *n* (*pl* **sons-in-law**) gendre *m*

sonnet /ˈsɒnɪt/ *n* sonnet *m*

⚷ mot clé

soon /suːn/ *adv* **1** (in a short time) bientôt; **see you ~!** à bientôt!
2 (quickly) vite
3 (early) tôt; **the ~er the better** le plus tôt sera le mieux; **as ~ as possible** dès que possible; **as ~ as you can** dès que tu pourras; **as ~ as he has finished** dès qu'il aura fini; **~er or later** tôt ou tard
4 (not long) **~ afterwards** peu après; **no ~er had I finished than...** j'avais à peine fini que...

soot /sʊt/ *n* suie *f*

soothe /suːð/ *vt* calmer ‹*pain, nerves, person*›; apaiser ‹*sunburn*›

soothing /ˈsuːðɪŋ/ *adj* ‹*music, voice*› apaisant/-e; ‹*cream, effect*› calmant/-e; ‹*words*› rassurant/-e

sophisticated /səˈfɪstɪkeɪtɪd/ *adj* **1** ‹*person*› (cultured) raffiné/-e; (affected) sophistiqué/-e; (elegant) chic; ‹*restaurant*› chic
2 ‹*taste*› raffiné/-e; ‹*civilization*› évolué/-e
3 ‹*equipment, technology*› sophistiqué/-e

soporific /ˌsɒpəˈrɪfɪk/ *adj* soporifique

soprano /səˈprɑːnəʊ, (AmE) -ˈpræn-/ *n* (*pl* **~s**) (person) soprano *mf*; (voice, instrument) soprano *m*

sorcerer /ˈsɔːsərə(r)/ *n* sorcier *m*

sordid /ˈsɔːdɪd/ *adj* sordide

sore /sɔː(r)/ **A** *n* plaie *f*
B *adj* **1** ‹*eyes, gums*› irrité/-e; ‹*muscle, arm, foot*› endolori/-e; **to have a ~ throat** avoir mal à la gorge
2 ‹*subject, point*› délicat/-e

sorrow /ˈsɒrəʊ/ *n* chagrin *m*

sorrowful /ˈsɒrəʊfl/ *adj* ‹*look*› affligé/-e; ‹*voice*› triste

sorry /ˈsɒrɪ/ **A** *adj* **1** désolé/-e; **I'm terribly ~** je suis vraiment désolé, je suis navré; **I'm ~ I'm late** je suis désolé d'être en retard; **to be ~ about sth** s'excuser de qch; **to say ~** s'excuser; **to be ~ to do** regretter de faire
2 (pitying) **to be** *or* **feel ~ for sb** plaindre qn; **to feel ~ for oneself** s'apitoyer sur soi-même
3 ‹*state, sight, business*› triste; ‹*person*› minable
B *excl* **1** (apologizing) pardon!, désolé!
2 (pardon) **~?** pardon?

sort /sɔːt/ **A** *n* sorte *f*, genre *m*; **books, records—that ~ of thing** des livres, des disques, ce genre de choses; **I'm not that ~ of person** ce n'est pas mon genre; **some ~ of computer** une sorte d'ordinateur
B *vt* classer ‹*data, files, stamps*›; trier ‹*letters, apples, potatoes*›; **to ~ books into piles** ranger des livres en piles
C (**of sorts, of a sort**) *phr* **a duck of ~s** *or* **of a ~** une sorte de canard; **progress of ~s** un semblant de progrès
D **sort of** *phr* (fam) **~ of cute** plutôt mignon/-onne; **I ~ of understand** je comprends plus ou moins; **~ of blue-green** dans les bleu-vert; **it just ~ of happened** c'est arrivé comme ça
IDIOMS **to be** *or* **feel out of ~s** (ill) ne pas être dans son assiette; (grumpy) être de mauvais poil (fam); **it takes all ~s (to make a world)** il faut de tout pour faire un monde
■ **sort out 1** régler ‹*problem, matter*›
2 s'occuper de ‹*details, arrangements*›; **I'll ~ it out** je m'en occuperai
3 ranger ‹*cupboard, desk*›; classer ‹*files, documents*›; mettre de l'ordre dans ‹*finances, affairs*›; clarifier ‹*ideas*›
4 trier ‹*photos, clothes*›

sort code *n* code *m* d'agence

SOS *n* SOS *m*

so-so /ˌsəʊˈsəʊ/ (fam) **A** *adj* moyen/-enne
B *adv* comme ci comme ça (fam)

sought-after /ˈsɔːtɑːftə(r), (AmE) -æf-/ *adj* ‹*person, skill*› demandé/-e, recherché/-e; ‹*job, brand, area*› prisé/-e

soul /səʊl/ *n* **1** (gen) âme *f*
2 (*also* **~ music**) soul *m*

soul-destroying *adj* abrutissant/-e

soulmate *n* âme *f* sœur

soul-searching /ˈsəʊlsɜːtʃɪŋ/ *n* débat *m* intérieur

sound /saʊnd/ **A** *n* **1** (gen) son *m*; (noise) bruit *m* (**of** de); **to turn the ~ up/down** augmenter/baisser le volume; **the ~ of voices** un bruit de voix; **a grating** *or* **rasping ~** un grincement; **without a ~** sans bruit
2 (fig) **by the ~ of it, we're in for a rough crossing** d'après ce qu'on a dit, la traversée va être mauvaise
3 (Med) sonde *f*
4 (strait) détroit *m*
B *adj* **1** ‹*heart, constitution*› solide; ‹*health*› bon/bonne *before n*; **to be of ~ mind** être sain/-e d'esprit
2 ‹*basis, argument*› solide; ‹*judgement*› sain/-e; ‹*advice, investment*› bon/bonne *before n*, sûr/-e
C *vt* faire retentir ‹*siren, foghorn*›; **to ~ one's horn** klaxonner; **to ~ the alarm** sonner l'alarme
D *vi* **1** (seem) sembler; **it ~s as if he's really in trouble** il semble qu'il ait vraiment des ennuis; **it ~s like it might be dangerous** ça a l'air dangereux; **to ~ boring** paraître ennuyeux; **it ~s like a flute** on dirait une flûte
2 ‹*alarm, buzzer, bugle*› sonner
E *adv* **to be ~ asleep** dormir à poings fermés
■ **sound out** sonder, interroger ‹*person*›

sound barrier *n* mur *m* du son

sound bite *n: bref extrait d'une interview enregistrée*

sound card *n* (Comput) carte *f* son

sound effect *n* effet *m* sonore

soundly /ˈsaʊndlɪ/ *adv* ‹*sleep*› à poings fermés; ‹*defeat*› à plates coutures

soundproof *adj* insonorisé/-e

sound system *n* (hi-fi) stéréo *f* (fam); (for disco etc) sono *f* (fam)

S

soundtrack *n* (of film) bande *f* sonore; (on record) bande *f* originale
soup /suːp/ *n* soupe *f*, potage *m*
soup kitchen *n* soupe *f* populaire
soup plate *n* assiette *f* creuse
soup spoon *n* cuillère *f* à soupe
sour /ˈsaʊə(r)/ **A** *adj* **1** aigre; **to go ~** ‹*milk*› tourner
2 (bad-tempered) revêche
B *vt* gâter ‹*relations, atmosphere*›
⚷ **source** /sɔːs/ *n* source *f*; **at ~** à la source; **~ of** source de ‹*anxiety, resentment, satisfaction*›; cause *f* de ‹*problem, error, infection, pollution*›
sourdough *n* (AmE) levain *m*
⚷ **south** /saʊθ/ **A** *n* **1** (compass direction) sud *m*
2 (part of world, country) **the South** le Sud
B *adj* (gen) sud *inv*; ‹*wind*› du sud; **in ~ London** dans le sud de Londres
C *adv* ‹*move*› vers le sud; ‹*lie, live*› au sud (**of** de)
South Africa *pr n* Afrique *f* du Sud
South America *pr n* Amérique *f* du Sud
south-east /ˌsaʊθˈiːst/ **A** *n* sud-est *m*
B *adj* ‹*coast, side*› sud-est *inv*; ‹*wind*› de sud-est
C *adv* ‹*move*› vers le sud-est; ‹*lie, live*› au sud-est (**of** de)
⚷ **southern** /ˈsʌðən/ *adj* ‹*coast*› sud *inv*; ‹*town, accent*› du sud; ‹*hemisphere*› Sud *inv*; **~ England** le sud de l'Angleterre
South Pole *pr n* pôle *m* Sud
south-west /ˌsaʊθˈwest/ **A** *n* sud-ouest *m*
B *adj* ‹*coast*› sud-ouest *inv*; ‹*wind*› de sud-ouest
C *adv* ‹*move*› vers le sud-ouest; ‹*lie, live*› au sud-ouest (**of** de)
souvenir /ˌsuːvəˈnɪə(r), (AmE) ˈsuːvənɪər/ *n* souvenir *m*
sovereign /ˈsɒvrɪn/ **A** *n* **1** (monarch) souverain/-e *m/f*
2 (coin) souverain *m*
B *adj* souverain/-e *after n*
sovereign debt *n* dette *f* souveraine
sovereignty /ˈsɒvrəntɪ/ *n* souveraineté *f*
Soviet Union *pr n* Union *f* soviétique
sow¹ /saʊ/ *n* truie *f*
sow² /səʊ/ *vt* (*prét* **sowed**, *pp* **sowed, sown**) **1** semer ‹*seeds, corn*›
2 ensemencer ‹*field, garden*› (**with** de)
3 (fig) semer
soya (BrE), **soy** (AmE) /ˈsɔɪə/ *n* soja *m*
soya sauce, **soy sauce** *n* sauce *f* soja
spa /spɑː/ *n* **1** (town) station *f* thermale
2 (AmE) (health club) club *m* de remise en forme
⚷ **space** /speɪs/ **A** *n* **1** (*also* **outer ~**) espace *m*
2 (room) place *f*, espace *m*
3 (gap) espace *m* (**between** entre); (on form) case *f*
4 (interval of time) intervalle *m*; **in the ~ of five minutes** en l'espace de cinq minutes
5 (area of land) espace *m*; **open ~s** espaces libres
B *adj* ‹*programme, rocket*› spatial/-e
C *vt* espacer
■ **space out** espacer ‹*words, objects*›; échelonner ‹*payments*›
space bar *n* barre *f* d'espacement
spaced out *adj* (fam) **he's completely ~** il plane (fam) complètement
spaceship *n* vaisseau *m* spatial
space station *n* station *f* orbitale
spacesuit *n* combinaison *f* spatiale
spacing /ˈspeɪsɪŋ/ *n* espacement *m*; (of payments) échelonnement *m*; **in single/double ~** en simple/double interligne
spacious /ˈspeɪʃəs/ *adj* spacieux/-ieuse
spade /speɪd/ *n* **1** (implement) bêche *f*, pelle *f*
2 (in cards) pique *m*
spaghetti /spəˈgetɪ/ *n* spaghetti *mpl inv*
Spain /speɪn/ *pr n* Espagne *f*
spamming /ˈspæmɪŋ/ *n* (Internet) envoi *m* de publicités à l'ensemble des connectés
span /spæn/ **A** *n* **1** (of time) durée *f*
2 (of bridge) travée *f*; **(wing)~** envergure *f*
B *vt* (*p prés etc* **-nn-**) **1** ‹*bridge, arch*› enjamber
2 (fig) s'étendre sur
Spaniard /ˈspænjəd/ *n* Espagnol/-e *m/f*
spaniel /ˈspænjəl/ *n* épagneul *m*
Spanish /ˈspænɪʃ/ **A** *n* **1** (people) **the ~** les Espagnols *mpl*
2 (language) espagnol *m*
B *adj* (gen) espagnol/-e; ‹*teacher, lesson*› d'espagnol; ‹*embassy, ambassador*› d'Espagne
spank /spæŋk/ *vt* donner une fessée à
spanner /ˈspænə(r)/ *n* (BrE) clé *f* (de serrage)
spar /spɑː(r)/ *vi* (*p prés etc* **-rr-**) ‹*boxers*› échanger des coups
spare /speə(r)/ **A** *n* (part) pièce *f* de rechange; (wheel) roue *f* de secours
B *adj* **1** ‹*cash*› restant/-e; ‹*seat*› disponible; ‹*copy*› en plus; **I've got a ~ ticket** j'ai un ticket en trop; **a ~ moment** un moment de libre
2 ‹*part*› de rechange; ‹*wheel*› de secours
3 ‹*person, build*› élancé/-e
C *vt* **1 to have sth to ~** avoir qch de disponible; **to catch the train with five minutes to ~** prendre le train avec cinq minutes d'avance; **can you ~ a minute?** as-tu un moment?
2 (treat leniently) épargner; **to ~ sb sth** épargner qch à qn
3 (manage without) se passer de ‹*person*›
IDIOM **to ~ no effort** faire tout son possible
spare part *n* pièce *f* de rechange
spare room *n* chambre *f* d'amis
spare time *n* loisirs *mpl*

⚷ mot clé

spare tyre (BrE), **spare tire** (AmE) *n* pneu *m* de rechange

sparingly /'speərɪŋlɪ/ *adv* ‹*use, add*› en petite quantité

spark /spɑːk/ **A** *n* étincelle *f*
B *vt* (*also* ~ **off** (BrE)) provoquer ‹*reaction, panic*›; être à l'origine de ‹*friendship, affair*›

sparkle /'spɑːkl/ **A** *n* scintillement *m*; (in eye) éclair *m*
B *vi* ‹*flame, light*› étinceler; ‹*jewel, frost, metal, water*› scintiller; ‹*eyes*› briller; ‹*drink*› pétiller

sparkler /'spɑːklə(r)/ *n* cierge *m* magique

sparkling /'spɑːklɪŋ/ *adj* **1** ‹*eyes*› brillant/-e
2 ‹*wit*› plein/-e de brio
3 ‹*drink*› pétillant/-e

spark plug *n* bougie *f*

sparrow /'spærəʊ/ *n* moineau *m*

sparse /spɑːs/ *adj* clairsemé/-e

sparsely /'spɑːslɪ/ *adv* peu; ~ **wooded** peu boisé/-e; ~ **populated** à faible population

spasm /'spæzəm/ *n* (of pain) spasme *m* (**of** de); (of panic, rage) accès *m* (**of** de)

spate /speɪt/ *n* **1 in full** ~ (BrE) ‹*river*› en pleine crue; ‹*person*› en plein discours
2 a ~ **of** une série de ‹*incidents*›

spatula /'spætʃʊlə/ *n* spatule *f*

speak /spiːk/ **A** *vt* (*prét* **spoke**, *pp* **spoken**) **1** parler ‹*language*›; **can you ~ English?** parlez-vous (l')anglais?
2 dire ‹*truth*›; prononcer ‹*word, name*›; **to ~ one's mind** dire ce qu'on pense
B *vi* (*prét* **spoke**, *pp* **spoken**) parler (**to, with** à, **about, of** de); **who's ~ing?** (on phone) qui est à l'appareil?; **(this is) Eileen ~ing** c'est Eileen; **generally ~ing** en règle générale; **roughly ~ing** en gros; **strictly ~ing** à proprement parler
■ **speak out** se prononcer
■ **speak up 1** (louder) parler plus fort
2 (dare to speak) intervenir

speaker /'spiːkə(r)/ *n* **1** (person talking) personne *f* qui parle; (public speaker) orateur/-trice *m/f*
2 a French ~ un/-e francophone; **a Russian ~** un/-e russophone
3 (on stereo system) haut-parleur *m*

-speaking *combining form* **English/French~** anglophone/francophone; **Welsh~** ‹*person*› qui parle le gallois

spear /'spɪə(r)/ *n* lance *f*

spearhead /'spɪəhed/ *vt* mener ‹*campaign, revolt, reform*›

spearmint *n* menthe *f* verte

special /'speʃl/ *adj* (gen) spécial/-e; ‹*case, reason, treatment*› particulier/-ière; ‹*friend*› très cher/chère

special effect *n* effet *m* spécial

specialist /'speʃəlɪst/ *n* spécialiste *mf* (**in** de)

speciality (BrE), **specialty** (AmE) /ˌspeʃɪ'ælətɪ/ *n* spécialité *f*

specialize /'speʃəlaɪz/ *vi* se spécialiser

specially /'speʃəlɪ/ *adv* **1** (specifically) spécialement; **I made it ~ for you** je l'ai fait exprès pour toi
2 (particularly) particulièrement; ‹*like, enjoy*› surtout

special needs *npl* (Sch) difficultés *fpl* d'apprentissage scolaire

special school *n* établissement *m* médico-éducatif pour enfants handicapés

species /'spiːʃiːz/ *n* (*pl* ~) espèce *f*

specific /spə'sɪfɪk/ *adj* précis/-e

specifically /spə'sɪfɪklɪ/ *adv* **1** (specially) spécialement
2 (explicitly) explicitement
3 (in particular) en particulier

specify /'spesɪfaɪ/ **A** *vt* stipuler; ‹*person*› préciser
B specified *pp adj* ‹*amount, date, day*› spécifié/-e

specimen /'spesɪmən/ *n* (of rock, urine, handwriting) échantillon *m*; (of blood, tissue) prélèvement; (of species, plant) spécimen *m*

speck /spek/ *n* (of dust, soot) grain *m*; (of dirt, mud, blood) petite tache *f*; (of light) point *m*

spectacle /'spektəkl/ **A** *n* spectacle *m*
B spectacles *npl* lunettes *fpl*

spectacular /spek'tækjʊlə(r)/ *adj* spectaculaire

spectator /spek'teɪtə(r)/ *n* spectateur/-trice *m/f*

spectre (BrE), **specter** (AmE) /'spektə(r)/ *n* spectre *m*

spectrum /'spektrəm/ *n* (*pl* **-tra, -trums**)
1 (of colours) spectre *m*
2 (range) gamme *f*

speculate /'spekjʊleɪt/ **A** *vt* **to ~ that** supposer que
B *vi* spéculer (**on** sur, **about** à propos de)

speculation /ˌspekjʊ'leɪʃn/ *n* **1** (conjecture) spéculations *fpl*
2 (financial) spéculation *f* (**in** sur)

speech /spiːtʃ/ *n* **1** discours *m* (**on** sur, **about** à propos de); **to give a ~** faire un discours
2 (faculty) parole *f*
3 (language) langage *m*

speech day *n* (BrE) (Sch) (jour *m* de la) distribution *f* des prix

speech impediment *n* défaut *m* d'élocution

speechless /'spiːtʃlɪs/ *adj* muet/-ette (**with** de); **to be ~ with** rester muet de; **I was ~ at the news** la nouvelle m'a laissé sans voix

speed /spiːd/ **A** *n* **1** vitesse *f*; (of response, reaction) rapidité *f*; **at top ~** à toute vitesse
2 (fam) (drug) amphétamines *fpl*
B *vt* (*prét*, *pp* **sped** *ou* **speeded**) hâter ‹*process, recovery*›
C *vi* (*prét*, *pp* **sped**) **1 to ~ along** ‹*driver, car*› rouler à toute allure; **to ~ away** s'eloigner à toute allure
2 (drive too fast) conduire trop vite

S

▪ **speed up**: **A** ~ **up** ‹*walker*› aller plus vite; ‹*athlete, driver, car*› accélérer; ‹*worker*› travailler plus vite
B ~ **[sth] up** accélérer

speedboat *n* hors-bord *m*

speed bump *n* ralentisseur *m*

speed camera *n* ≈ cinémomètre *m*

speed dating *n* speed dating *m*, rencontres *fpl* rapides

speed dial *n* composition *f* abrégée

speeding /'spiːdɪŋ/ *n* excès *m* de vitesse

speed limit *n* limitation *f* de vitesse

speedometer /spɪ'dɒmɪtə(r)/ *n* compteur *m* (de vitesse)

spell /spel/ **A** *n* **1** (period) moment *m*, période *f*; **sunny** ~ éclaircie *f*
2 (magic words) formule *f* magique; **to be under a** ~ être envoûté/-e; **to cast** *or* **put a** ~ **on sb** jeter un sort à qn; **to be under sb's** ~ être sous le charme de qn
B *vt* (*pp, prét* **spelled** *ou* **spelt**) **1** écrire ‹*word*›
2 signifier ‹*danger, disaster*›
C *vi* (*pp, prét* **spelled** *ou* **spelt**) **he can't/can** ~ il a une mauvaise/bonne orthographe

▪ **spell out 1** épeler ‹*word*›
2 (explain) expliquer [qch] clairement

spellbound /'spelbaʊnd/ *adj* envoûté/-e (**by** par)

spellcheck *vt* effectuer une correction orthographique sur ‹*document*›

spellchecker *n* correcteur *m* orthographique

spelling /'spelɪŋ/ *n* orthographe *f*

⚷ **spend** /spend/ **A** *vt* (*prét, pp* **spent**)
1 dépenser ‹*money, salary*› (**on** en)
2 passer ‹*time*› (**doing** à faire)
B *vi* (*prét, pp* **spent**) dépenser

spending cut *n* réduction *f* des dépenses; (Pol) restriction *f* budgétaire

spending power *n* pouvoir *m* d'achat

spending spree *n* folie *f* (fam) (de dépense); **to go on a** ~ faire des folies (fam)

spendthrift /'spendθrɪft/ *adj* ‹*person*› dépensier/-ière

sperm /spɜːm/ *n* sperme *m*

sperm donor *n* donneur *m* de sperme

spew /spjuː/ *vt* vomir

sphere /sfɪə(r)/ *n* **1** (shape) sphère *f*
2 (field) domaine *m* (**of** de); ~ **of influence** sphère *f* d'influence

spherical /'sferɪkl/ *adj* sphérique

spice /spaɪs/ *n* (Culin) épice *f*; (fig) piment *m*

spick and span *adj* impeccable

spicy /'spaɪsɪ/ *adj* **1** ‹*food*› épicé/-e
2 ‹*detail*› croustillant/-e

spider /'spaɪdə(r)/ *n* araignée *f*

spiderweb *n* (AmE) toile *f* d'araignée

⚷ mot clé

spike /spaɪk/ **A** *n* pointe *f*
B *vt* (fam) corser ‹*drink*› (**with** de)

spiky /'spaɪkɪ/ *adj* ‹*hair*› en brosse *inv*; ‹*branch*› piquant/-e; ‹*object*› acéré/-e

spill /spɪl/ **A** *vt* (*prét, pp* **spilt** *ou* ~**ed**) renverser ‹*drink*› (**on, over** sur)
B *vi* (*prét, pp* **spilt** *ou* ~**ed**) se répandre (**onto** sur, **into** dans)

▪ **spill over** déborder; **to** ~ **over into** dégénérer en ‹*looting, hostility*›

spin /spɪn/ **A** *n* **1** (of wheel) tour *m*; (of dancer, skater) pirouette *f*
2 to go into a ~ ‹*plane*› descendre en vrille
3 to go for a ~ (in car) aller faire un tour
B *vt* (*p prés* **-nn-**, *prét, pp* **spun**) **1** lancer ‹*top*›; faire tourner ‹*globe, wheel*›
2 filer ‹*wool, thread*›
3 ‹*spider*› tisser ‹*web*›
C *vi* (*p prés* **-nn-**, *prét, pp* **spun**) tourner; ‹*weathercock, top*› tournoyer; ‹*dancer*› pirouetter; **my head is** ~**ning** j'ai la tête qui tourne

▪ **spin out** prolonger ‹*visit*›; faire traîner [qch] en longueur ‹*speech*›; faire durer ‹*work, money*›

▪ **spin round**: **A** ~ **round** ‹*person*› se retourner rapidement; ‹*dancer, skater*› pirouetter; ‹*car*› faire un tête-à-queue
B ~ **[sb/sth] round** faire tourner ‹*wheel*›

spinach /'spɪnɪdʒ, (AmE) -ɪtʃ/ *n* (Culin) épinards *mpl*

spinal cord *n* moelle *f* épinière

spindly /'spɪndlɪ/ *adj* grêle

spin doctor *n* (Pol) consultant *m* en communication attaché à un parti politique

spin drier, **spin dryer** *n* essoreuse *f*

spine /spaɪn/ *n* **1** (Anat) colonne *f* vertébrale
2 (on hedgehog, cactus) piquant *m*
3 (of book) dos *m*

spineless /'spaɪnlɪs/ *adj* mou/molle

spin-off /'spɪnɒf/ *n* **1** (incidental benefit) retombée *f* favorable
2 (by-product) sous-produit *m*

spinster /'spɪnstə(r)/ *n* célibataire *f*; (derog) vieille fille *f*

spiral /'spaɪərəl/ **A** *n* spirale *f*
B *adj* ‹*structure*› en spirale
C *vi* (*p prés etc* **-ll-** (BrE), **-l-** (AmE)) ‹*prices, costs*› monter en flèche
D (**spiralling** (BrE), **spiraling** (AmE)) *pres p adj* qui monte en flèche

spiral staircase *n* escalier *m* en colimaçon

spire /'spaɪə(r)/ *n* flèche *f*

⚷ **spirit** /'spɪrɪt/ **A** *n* **1** (gen) esprit *m*
2 (courage, determination) courage *m*
B spirits *npl* **1** (alcohol) spiritueux *mpl*
2 to be in good ~**s** être de bonne humeur; **to be in high** ~**s** être d'excellente humeur; **to keep one's** ~**s up** garder le moral

spirited /'spɪrɪtɪd/ *adj* ‹*horse, debate, reply*› fougueux/-euse; ‹*attack, defence*› vif/vive

spirit level *n* niveau *m* à bulle
spiritual /ˈspɪrɪtʃʊəl/ **A** *n* spiritual *m*
B *adj* spirituel/-elle
spit /spɪt/ **A** *n* **1** (saliva) salive *f*
2 (Culin) broche *f*
B *vt* (*p prés* **-tt-**, *prét*, *pp* **spat**) ‹*person*› cracher; ‹*pan*› projeter ‹*oil*›
C *vi* (*p prés* **-tt-**, *prét*, *pp* **spat**) ‹*cat, person*› cracher (**at, on** sur); ‹*oil, sausage*› grésiller; ‹*logs, fire*› crépiter
D *v impers* (*p prés* **-tt-**, *prét*, *pp* **spat**) **it's ~ting (with rain)** il bruine
IDIOM **to be the ~ting image of sb** être le portrait tout craché de qn
spite /spaɪt/ **A** *n* rancune *f*
B *vt* faire du mal à; (less strong) embêter
C **in spite of** *phr* malgré; **in ~ of the fact that** bien que
spiteful /ˈspaɪtfl/ *adj* ‹*person*› rancunier/-ière; ‹*remark*› méchant/-e
splash /splæʃ/ **A** *n* **1** (sound) plouf *m*
2 (of mud) tache *f*; (of water, oil) éclaboussure *f*; (of colour) touche *f*; (of tonic, soda) goutte *f*
B *vt* éclabousser; **to ~ water on to one's face** s'asperger le visage d'eau
C *vi* faire des éclaboussures
■ **splash out** (fam) faire des folies (fam); **to ~ out on sth** se payer qch
splay /spleɪ/ *vt* écarter ‹*feet, fingers*›
spleen /spliːn/ *n* (Anat) rate *f*
splendid /ˈsplendɪd/ *adj* splendide; ‹*idea, holiday, performance*› merveilleux/-euse
splendour (BrE), **splendor** (AmE) /ˈsplendə(r)/ *n* splendeur *f*
splice /splaɪs/ *vt* coller ‹*tape, film*›; épisser ‹*ends of rope*›
splint /splɪnt/ *n* (for injury) attelle *f*
splinter /ˈsplɪntə(r)/ **A** *n* éclat *m*
B *vi* ‹*glass, windscreen*› se briser; ‹*wood*› se fendre; ‹*alliance*› se scinder
splinter group *n* groupe *m* dissident
split /splɪt/ **A** *n* **1** (in fabric) déchirure *f*; (in rock, wood) fissure *f*
2 (in party, alliance) scission *f* (**in** de)
B **splits** *npl* **to do the ~s** faire le grand écart
C *adj* ‹*fabric*› déchiré/-e; ‹*seam*› défait/-e; ‹*log, lip*› fendu/-e
D *vt* (*p prés* **-tt-**, *prét*, *pp* **split**) **1** fendre ‹*log, rock*› (**in, into** en); déchirer ‹*garment*›
2 diviser ‹*party*›
3 (share) partager (**between** entre)
E *vi* (*p prés* **-tt-**, *prét*, *pp* **split**) **1** ‹*wood, log, rock*› se fendre (**in, into** en); ‹*fabric, garment*› se déchirer
2 ‹*party*› se diviser
■ **split up**: **A** **~ up** ‹*couple, band*› se séparer
B **~ [sth] up** diviser (**into** en)
split second *n* fraction *f* de seconde
splutter /ˈsplʌtə(r)/ *vi* ‹*person*› bafouiller; ‹*fire, fat*› grésiller
spoil /spɔɪl/ **A** *vt* (*pp* **~ed** *ou* **~t** (BrE)) **1** (mar) gâcher ‹*event, view, game*›; gâter ‹*place, taste, effect*›; **to ~ sth for sb** gâcher qch à qn
2 (ruin) abîmer ‹*garment, crops*›
3 (pamper) gâter ‹*child, pet*›
B *vi* (*pp* **~ed** *ou* **~t** (BrE)) ‹*product, foodstuff*› s'abîmer
spoiled, **spoilt** (BrE) /spɔɪlt/ *adj* ‹*child, dog*› gâté/-e; **a ~ brat** un gamin pourri (fam)
spoiler /ˈspɔɪlə(r)/ *n* (Aut) becquet *m*
spoils *npl* (of war) butin *m* (**of** de)
spoilsport /ˈspɔɪlspɔːt/ *n* (fam) **to be a ~** être un rabat-joie
spoke /spəʊk/ *n* rayon *m*
spokesman *n* (*pl* **-men**) porte-parole *m inv*
spokeswoman *n* (*pl* **-women**) porte-parole *m inv*
sponge /spʌndʒ/ **A** *n* **1** éponge *f*
2 (*also* **~ cake**) génoise *f*
B *vt* éponger ‹*material, stain, face*›
C *vi* (fam) **to ~ off** *or* **on** vivre sur le dos de ‹*family, state*›
sponge bag *n* (BrE) trousse *f* de toilette
sponsor /ˈspɒnsə(r)/ **A** *n* **1** (advertiser, backer) sponsor *m*
2 (patron) mécène *m*
B *vt* sponsoriser ‹*event, team*›; financer ‹*student*›; parrainer ‹*child*›
sponsorship /ˈspɒnsəʃɪp/ *n* sponsorat *m*
spontaneous /spɒnˈteɪnɪəs/ *adj* spontané/-e
spontaneously /spɒnˈteɪnɪəslɪ/ *adv* spontanément
spoof /spuːf/ *n* (fam) (parody) parodie *f* (**on** de)
spooky /ˈspuːkɪ/ *adj* (fam) ‹*house, atmosphere*› sinistre; ‹*story*› qui fait froid dans le dos
spool /spuːl/ *n* bobine *f*
spoon /spuːn/ *n* cuillère *f*; (teaspoon) petite cuillère *f*
spoonful /ˈspuːnfʊl/ *n* (*pl* **-fuls** *ou* **-sful**) cuillerée *f*, cuillère *f*
sporadic /spəˈrædɪk/ *adj* sporadique
sport /spɔːt/ *n* **1** sport *m*
2 **he's a good ~** (good loser) il est beau joueur
sporting /ˈspɔːtɪŋ/ *adj* **1** ‹*fixture, event*› sportif/-ive
2 (fair, generous) généreux/-euse; **to have a ~ chance of doing** avoir de bonnes chances de faire
sports car *n* voiture *f* de sport
sports centre (BrE), **sports center** (AmE) *n* centre *m* sportif
sports club *n* club *m* sportif
sports ground *n* (large) stade *m*; (in school, club) terrain *m* de sports
sports jacket *n* veste *f* en tweed
sportsman *n* (*pl* **-men**) sportif *m*
sports star *n* vedette *f* sportive

sportswear *n* vêtements *mpl* de sport

sportswoman *n* (*pl* **-women**) sportive *f*

sporty /ˈspɔːtɪ/ *adj* (fam) sportif/-ive

🔑 **spot** /spɒt/ **A** *n* **1** (on animal) tache *f*; (on fabric) pois *m*; (on dice, domino) point *m*
2 (stain) tache *f*
3 (pimple) bouton *m*
4 (place) endroit *m*; **on the ~** sur place; **to decide on the ~** décider sur-le-champ
5 (fam) (small amount) **a ~ of** un peu de
6 (fam) **to be in a (tight) ~** être dans une situation embêtante
B *vt* (*p prés etc* **-tt**) **1** apercevoir ‹*person*›; repérer ‹*difference, mistake*›
2 (stain) tacher

spot check *n* contrôle *m* surprise

spotless /ˈspɒtlɪs/ *adj* impeccable

spotlight /ˈspɒtlaɪt/ *n* **1** (light) projecteur *m*; (in home) spot *m*
2 (focus of attention) **to be in** *or* **under the ~** ‹*person*› être sur la sellette; **the ~ is on Aids** le sida fait la une; **to turn** *or* **put the ~ on sb/sth** attirer l'attention sur qn/qch

spotted /ˈspɒtɪd/ *adj* ‹*fabric*› à pois; ‹*fur, dog*› tacheté/-e

spotty /ˈspɒtɪ/ *adj* (pimply) ‹*skin*› boutonneux/-euse; **he's very ~** il est plein de boutons; (patterned) à pois *after n*

spouse /spaʊz, (AmE) spaʊs/ *n* époux/épouse *m/f*

spout /spaʊt/ **A** *n* (of kettle, teapot) bec *m* verseur
B *vt* **1** (spurt) faire jaillir ‹*water*›
2 (recite) débiter ‹*poetry, statistics*›
C *vi* ‹*liquid*› jaillir (**from, out of** de)

sprain /spreɪn/ **A** *n* entorse *f*
B *vt* **to ~ one's ankle** se faire une entorse à la cheville; (less severely) se fouler la cheville

sprawl /sprɔːl/ **A** *n* (of suburbs, buildings) étendue *f*
B *vi* s'étaler

spray /spreɪ/ **A** *n* **1** (seawater) embruns *mpl*; (other) nuages *mpl* de (fines) gouttelettes
2 (container) (for perfume) vaporisateur *m*; (can) bombe *f*; (for inhalant, throat, nose) pulvérisateur *m*
3 (of flowers) (bunch) gerbe *f*; (single branch) rameau *m*
B *vt* vaporiser ‹*liquid*›; asperger ‹*person*› (**with** de); **to ~ sth onto sth** (onto fire) projeter qch sur qch ‹*foam, water*›; (onto surface, flowers) vaporiser qch sur qch ‹*paint, water*›

spray can *n* bombe *f*, aérosol *m*

🔑 **spread** /spred/ **A** *n* **1** (of disease, drugs) propagation *f*; (of news, information) diffusion *f*
2 (Culin) pâte *f* à tartiner
B *vt* (*prét, pp* **spread**) **1** (unfold) étaler, étendre ‹*cloth, newspaper, map*› (**on, over** sur); ‹*bird*› déployer ‹*wings*›
2 étaler ‹*butter, jam, glue*› (**on, over** sur)
3 (distribute) disperser ‹*troops*›; répartir ‹*workload, responsibility*›
4 (*also* **~ out**) étaler, échelonner ‹*payments, meetings*› (**over** sur)
5 propager ‹*disease, fire*›; semer ‹*confusion, panic*›; faire circuler ‹*rumour, story*›
C *vi* (*prét, pp* **spread**) **1** ‹*butter, jam, glue*› s'étaler
2 ‹*forest, drought*› s'étendre (**over** sur); ‹*disease, fear, fire*› se propager; ‹*rumour, story*› circuler; ‹*stain, damp*› s'étaler

■ **spread out**: **A** **~ out** ‹*group*› se disperser (**over** sur); ‹*wings, tail*› se déployer
B **~ [sth] out** étaler, étendre ‹*cloth, map, rug*› (**on, over** sur)

spread betting *n* spread betting *m forme de pari ou de spéculation consistant à pronostiquer par rapport à une fourchette fixée par le bookmaker*

spread-eagled *adj* bras et jambes écartés

spreadsheet *n* tableur *m*

spree /spriː/ *n* **to go on a ~** (drinking) faire la bringue (fam); **to go on a shopping ~** aller faire des folies dans les magasins

sprig /sprɪg/ *n* (of holly) petite branche *f*; (of parsley) brin *m*

sprightly /ˈspraɪtlɪ/ *adj* alerte, gaillard

🔑 **spring** /sprɪŋ/ **A** *n* **1** (season) printemps *m*; **in ~** au printemps
2 (of wire) ressort *m*
3 (leap) bond *m*
4 (water source) source *f*
B *vt* (*prét* **sprang**, *pp* **sprung**)
1 déclencher ‹*trap, lock*›
2 **to ~ a leak** ‹*tank, barrel*› commencer à fuir
3 **to ~ sth on sb** annoncer qch de but en blanc à qn ‹*news, plan*›
C *vi* (*prét* **sprang**, *pp* **sprung**) **1** (jump) bondir (**onto** sur)
2 (originate) **to ~ from** venir de

■ **spring up** ‹*new building*› apparaître

spring-clean *vt* nettoyer [qch] de fond en comble ‹*house*›

spring onion *n* (BrE) ciboule *f*

springtime /ˈsprɪŋtaɪm/ *n* printemps *m*

springy /ˈsprɪŋɪ/ *adj* ‹*mattress, seat*› élastique

sprinkle /ˈsprɪŋkl/ *vt* **to ~ sth with** saupoudrer qch de ‹*salt, sugar*›; parsemer qch de ‹*herbs*›; **to ~ sth with water** humecter qch

sprinkler /ˈsprɪŋklə(r)/ *n* **1** (for lawn) arroseur *m*
2 (to extinguish fires) diffuseur *m*

sprint /sprɪnt/ **A** *n* (race) sprint *m*, course *f* de vitesse
B *vi* (in athletics) sprinter; (to catch bus) courir (à toute vitesse)

sprout /spraʊt/ **A** *n* (*also* **Brussels ~**) chou *m* de Bruxelles

🔑 mot clé

B *vi* ‹*seed, shoot*› germer; ‹*grass, weeds*› pousser

spruce /spruːs/ **A** *n* (*also* ~ **tree**) épicéa *m*
B *adj* ‹*person*› soigné/-e; ‹*house, garden*› bien tenu/-e

▪ **spruce up** astiquer ‹*house*›; nettoyer ‹*garden*›; **to ~ oneself up** se faire beau/belle

spry /spraɪ/ *adj* alerte, leste

spun /spʌn/ *adj* ‹*glass, gold, sugar*› filé/-e

spur /spɜː(r)/ **A** *n* **1** (for horse) éperon *m*; (fig) aiguillon *m*
2 (of rock) contrefort *m*
B *vt* (*p prés etc* **-rr-**) (*also* ~ **on**) éperonner ‹*horse*›; aiguillonner ‹*person*›; **to ~ sb to do** inciter qn à faire
IDIOM **on the ~ of the moment** sur une impulsion

spurn /spɜːn/ *vt* refuser [qch] (avec mépris)

spurt /spɜːt/ **A** *n* **1** (gush) (of water, oil, blood) giclée *f*; (of flame) jaillissement *m*
2 (of activity) regain *m*; (of energy) sursaut *m*; (in growth) poussée *f*; **to put on a ~** ‹*runner, cyclist*› pousser une pointe de vitesse
B *vi* (*also* ~ **out**) jaillir (**from, out of** de)

spy /spaɪ/ **A** *n* espion/-ionne *m/f*
B *vt* remarquer, discerner ‹*figure, object*›
C *vi* **to ~ on sb/sth** espionner qn/qch

spying /ˈspaɪɪŋ/ *n* espionnage *m*

squabble /ˈskwɒbl/ *vi* se disputer, se chamailler (fam)

squad /skwɒd/ *n* (Mil) escouade *f*; (Sport) sélection *f*

squad car *n* voiture *f* de police

squadron /ˈskwɒdrən/ *n* escadron *m*

squalid /ˈskwɒlɪd/ *adj* sordide

squall /skwɔːl/ *n* (wind) bourrasque *f*, rafale *f*; (at sea) grain *m*

squalor /ˈskwɒlə(r)/ *n* (filth) saleté *f* repoussante; (wretchedness) misère *f* (noire)

squander /ˈskwɒndə(r)/ *vt* gaspiller

square /skweə(r)/ **A** *n* **1** (shape) carré *m*
2 (in town) place *f*
3 (in game, crossword) case *f*; (of glass, linoleum) carreau *m*
4 (fam) (person) ringard/-e *m/f* (fam)
B *adj* **1** (in shape) carré/-e; **four ~ metres** quatre mètres carrés
2 (quits) **to be ~** ‹*people*› être quitte
C *vt* **1 to ~ one's shoulders** redresser les épaules
2 (settle) régler ‹*account, debt*›
IDIOM **to go back to ~ one** retourner à la case départ

▪ **square up** (settle accounts) régler ses comptes

square bracket *n* crochet *m*; **in ~s** entre crochets

square root *n* racine *f* carrée

squash /skwɒʃ/ **A** *n* **1** (Sport) squash *m*
2 (drink) sirop *m*
3 (vegetable) courge *f*
B *vt* écraser

▪ **squash up** (fam) se serrer (**against** contre)

squat /skwɒt/ **A** *adj* ‹*person, structure, object*› trapu/-e
B *vi* (*p prés etc* **-tt-**) **1** (crouch) s'accroupir
2 to ~ in squatter ‹*building*›

squatter /ˈskwɒtə(r)/ *n* squatter *m*

squawk /skwɔːk/ *vi* ‹*hen*› pousser des gloussements; ‹*duck, parrot*› pousser des cris rauques

squeak /skwiːk/ **A** *n* (of door, wheel, chalk) grincement *m*; (of mouse, soft toy) couinement *m*; (of furniture, shoes) craquement *m*
B *vi* ‹*door, wheel, chalk*› grincer; ‹*mouse, soft toy*› couiner; ‹*shoes, furniture*› craquer (**on** sur)

squeaky /ˈskwiːkɪ/ *adj* ‹*voice*› aigu/aiguë; ‹*gate, hinge, wheel*› grinçant/-e

squeal /skwiːl/ *vi* ‹*person, animal*› pousser des cris aigus

squeamish /ˈskwiːmɪʃ/ *adj* impressionnable, sensible

squeeze /skwiːz/ **A** *n* **1** (on credit, finances) resserrement *m* (**on** de)
2 (fam) (crush) **it will be a tight ~** ce sera un peu juste
B *vt* **1** presser ‹*lemon, bottle, tube*›; serrer ‹*arm, hand*›; appuyer sur ‹*trigger*›; percer ‹*spot*›; **to ~ water out of** essorer, tordre ‹*cloth*›
2 (fig) réussir à obtenir ‹*money*› (**out of** de); **to ~ the truth out of sb** arracher la vérité à qn
3 (fit) **to ~ sth into sth** entasser qch dans qch

▪ **squeeze in**: **A** ~ **in** ‹*person*› se glisser
B ~ **sb in** ‹*doctor etc*› faire passer qn entre deux rendez-vous

▪ **squeeze past** ‹*car, person*› se passer

squelch /skweltʃ/ *vi* ‹*water, mud*› glouglouter; **to ~ along** avancer en pataugeant

squid /skwɪd/ *n* calmar *m*, encornet *m*

squiggle /ˈskwɪgl/ *n* gribouillis *m*

squint /skwɪnt/ **A** *n* strabisme *m*; **to have a ~** loucher
B *vi* **1** (look) plisser les yeux
2 (have eye condition) loucher

squire /ˈskwaɪə(r)/ *n* ≈ châtelain *m*

squirm /skwɜːm/ *vi* (wriggle) se tortiller; ‹*person*› (in pain) se tordre; (with embarrassment) être très mal à l'aise

squirrel /ˈskwɪrəl, (AmE) ˈskwɜːrəl/ *n* écureuil *m*

squirt /skwɜːt/ **A** *vt* faire gicler ‹*liquid*›
B *vi* ‹*liquid*› jaillir (**from, out of** de)

stab /stæb/ **A** *n* **1** (act) coup *m* de couteau; **a ~ in the back** (fig) un coup en traître
2 (of pain) élancement *m* (**of** de)
B *vt* (*p prés etc* **-bb-**) poignarder ‹*person*›

stabbing /ˈstæbɪŋ/ *n* agression *f* au couteau

stability /stəˈbɪlətɪ/ *n* stabilité *f*

stabilize /ˈsteɪbəlaɪz/ **A** *vt* stabiliser
B *vi* se stabiliser

stable /ˈsteɪbl/ **A** *n* écurie *f*; **riding ~s** manège *m*

S

B *adj* **1** (steady) stable
2 (psychologically) équilibré/-e

stack /stæk/ **A** *n* (pile) pile *f*; (of hay, straw) meule *f*
B *vt* **1** (*also* ~ **up**) ‹*pile*› empiler
2 (fill) remplir ‹*shelves*›
3 mettre [qch] en attente ‹*planes, calls*›

stadium /ˈsteɪdɪəm/ *n* (*pl* **-iums** *ou* **-ia**) stade *m*

🔑 **staff** /stɑːf, (AmE) stæf/ *n* (*pl* ~) (of company) personnel *m*; (of a school, college) personnel *m* enseignant

staff meeting *n* réunion *f* du personnel enseignant

staffroom *n* salle *f* des professeurs

stag /stæg/ *n* cerf *m*

🔑 **stage** /steɪdʒ/ **A** *n* **1** (phase) (of illness, career, life) stade *m* (**of, in** de); (of project, process, plan) phase *f* (**of, in** de); (of journey, negotiations) étape *f* (**of, in** de)
2 (raised platform) estrade *f*; (in theatre) scène *f*
B *vt* **1** (organize) organiser ‹*event, rebellion, strike*›
2 (fake) simuler ‹*quarrel, scene*›
3 (in theatre) monter ‹*play*›

stagecoach *n* diligence *f*

stage fright *n* trac *m*

stage manager *n* régisseur/-euse *m/f*

stagger /ˈstægə(r)/ **A** *vt* **1** (astonish) stupéfier, abasourdir
2 échelonner ‹*holidays, payments*›
B *vi* (from weakness) chanceler; (drunkenly) tituber

staggering /ˈstægərɪŋ/ *adj* ‹*amount, increase*› prodigieux/-ieuse; ‹*news*› renversant/-e; ‹*achievement, contrast*› stupéfiant/-e; ‹*success*› étourdissant/-e

stagnant /ˈstægnənt/ *adj* stagnant/-e

stagnate /stægˈneɪt, (AmE) ˈstægneɪt/ *vi* stagner

stag night, **stag party** *n* soirée *f* pour enterrer une vie de garçon

staid /steɪd/ *adj* guindé/-e

stain /steɪn/ **A** *n* **1** (mark) tache *f*
2 (dye) teinture *f*
B *vt* **1** (soil) tacher ‹*clothes, carpet, table*›
2 teindre ‹*wood*›

stained glass *n* verre *m* coloré

stained glass window *n* vitrail *m*

stainless steel *n* acier *m* inoxydable

stain remover *n* détachant *m*

stair /steə(r)/ **A** *n* (step) marche *f* (d'escalier)
B **stairs** *npl* **the** ~**s** l'escalier; **to fall down the** ~**s** tomber dans l'escalier

staircase, **stairway** *n* escalier *m*

stake /steɪk/ **A** *n* **1** (amount risked) enjeu *m*; **to be at** ~ être en jeu
2 (investment) participation *f* (**in** dans)
3 (post) pieu *m*
B *vt* miser ‹*money, property*›; risquer ‹*reputation*›
■ **stake out**: ~ **out [sth]**, ~ **[sth] out** surveiller ‹*place*›

stale /steɪl/ *adj* ‹*bread, cake*› rassis/-e; ‹*beer*› éventé/-e; ‹*smell*› de renfermé; ‹*ideas*› éculé/-e

stalemate /ˈsteɪlmeɪt/ *n* **1** (in chess) pat *m*
2 (deadlock) impasse *f*

stalk /stɔːk/ **A** *n* (on plant, flower) tige *f*; (of leaf, apple) queue *f*; (of mushroom) pied *m*
B *vt* ‹*hunter, murderer*› traquer ‹*prey, victim*›; ‹*animal*› chasser ‹*prey*›

stall /stɔːl/ **A** *n* **1** (at market) éventaire *m*
2 (in stable) stalle *f*
B **stalls** *npl* (BrE) orchestre *m*
C *vt* caler ‹*engine, car*›
D *vi* **1** ‹*car*› caler
2 (play for time) temporiser

stallholder *n* marchand/-e *m/f*

stallion /ˈstælɪən/ *n* étalon *m*

stalwart /ˈstɔːlwət/ *adj* loyal/-e

stamina /ˈstæmɪnə/ *n* résistance *f*, endurance *f*

stammer /ˈstæmə(r)/ **A** *n* bégaiement *m*
B *vi* bégayer

stamp /stæmp/ **A** *n* **1** (for envelope) timbre *m*
2 (on passport, document) cachet *m*
3 (marker) (rubber) tampon *m*; (metal) cachet *m*
B *vt* **1** apposer [qch] au tampon ‹*date, name*› (**on** sur); tamponner ‹*ticket, book*›; viser ‹*document, passport*›
2 to ~ **one's foot** (in anger) taper du pied
C *vi* ‹*horse*› piaffer; **to** ~ **on** écraser (du pied) ‹*toy, foot*›; piétiner ‹*soil, ground*›

stamp collecting *n* philatélie *f*

stamped addressed envelope, **sae** *n* (BrE) enveloppe *f* timbrée à votre/son etc adresse

stampede /stæmˈpiːd/ **A** *n* débandade *f*
B *vi* s'enfuir (pris d'affolement)

stance /stɑːns, (AmE) stæns/ *n* position *f*

🔑 **stand** /stænd/ **A** *n* **1** (support, frame) support *m*; (for coats) portemanteau *m*
2 (stall) (in market) éventaire *m*; (kiosk) kiosque *m*; (at exhibition, trade fair) stand *m*
3 (in stadium) tribunes *fpl*
4 (witness box) barre *f*
5 (stance) **to take a** ~ **on sth** prendre position sur qch
6 (to make) a last ~ (livrer) une dernière bataille
B *vt* (*prét, pp* **stood**) **1** (place) mettre ‹*person, object*› (**against** contre, **in** dans, **on** sur)
2 (bear) supporter ‹*cold, weight*›; tolérer ‹*nonsense, bad behaviour*›; **I can't** ~ **him** je ne peux pas le supporter *or* le sentir; **I can't** ~ **this town** je déteste cette ville; **I can't** ~ **doing** je déteste faire
3 (fam) **to** ~ **sb a drink** payer un verre à qn
4 to ~ **trial** passer en jugement

S

C *vi* (*prét, pp* **stood**) **1** (*also* ~ **up**) se lever
2 (be upright) ‹*person*› se tenir debout; ‹*object*› tenir debout; **to remain ~ing** rester debout
3 ‹*building, village*› se trouver, être
4 (step) **to ~ on** marcher sur ‹*insect, foot*›
5 (be) **as things ~...** étant donné l'état actuel des choses...; **the total ~s at 300** le total est de 300; **to ~ in sb's way** (fig) faire obstacle à qn
6 (remain valid) ‹*offer, agreement*› rester valable
7 (be a candidate) se présenter (**as** comme); **to ~ for election** se présenter aux élections

■ **stand back** ‹*person, crowd*› reculer (**from** de); (fig) prendre du recul (**from** par rapport à)
■ **stand by**: **A** ~ **by** ‹*doctor, army*› être prêt/-e à intervenir
B ~ **by [sb/sth]** soutenir ‹*person*›; s'en tenir à ‹*principles, decision*›
■ **stand down** démissionner
■ **stand for 1** (represent) représenter; ‹*initials*› vouloir dire
2 (tolerate) tolérer
■ **stand in**: **to ~ in for sb** remplacer qn
■ **stand out** ‹*person*› sortir de l'ordinaire; ‹*work, ability*› être remarquable
■ **stand up A** ~ **up 1** (rise) se lever
2 (stay upright) se tenir debout
3 ‹*theory, story*› tenir debout
4 to ~ up to tenir tête à ‹*person*›
5 to ~ up for défendre ‹*person, rights*›
B ~ **[sth] up** redresser ‹*object*›
C ~ **[sb] up** poser un lapin à (fam)

standard /'stændəd/ **A** *n* **1** (level) niveau *m*; **not to be up to ~** ne pas avoir le niveau requis
2 (official specification) norme *f* (**for** de)
3 (banner) étendard *m*
B *adj* ‹*size, rate, pay*› standard *inv*; ‹*procedure*› habituel/-elle; ‹*image*› traditionnel/-elle; **it's ~ practice** c'est l'usage

Standard Assessment Task *n* (BrE) (Sch) test *m* d'aptitude scolaire (*par tranches d'âge*)

standardize /'stændədaɪz/ *vt* normaliser, standardiser

standard lamp *n* (BrE) lampadaire *m*

standard of living *n* niveau *m* de vie

standby /'stændbaɪ/ *n* (person) remplaçant/-e *m/f*; **to be on ~** ‹*army, emergency services*› être prêt/-e à intervenir; (for airline ticket) être en stand-by

stand-in /'stændɪn/ *n* remplaçant/-e *m/f*

standing /'stændɪŋ/ **A** *n* **1** (reputation) réputation *f*, rang *m* (**among** parmi, **with** chez)
2 (length of time) **of long ~** de longue date
B *adj* **1** ‹*army, committee, force*› actif/-ive
2 ‹*invitation*› permanent/-e

standing charge *n* frais *mpl* d'abonnement

standing order *n* (BrE) virement *m* automatique

stand-off /'stændɒf/ *n* impasse *f*

standpoint *n* point *m* de vue

standstill /'stændstɪl/ *n* **to be at a ~** ‹*traffic*› être à l'arrêt; ‹*factory, port*› être au point mort; ‹*work*› être arrêté/e; ‹*talks*› être arrivé/-e à une impasse; **to come to a ~** ‹*person, car*› s'arrêter

stand-up /'stændʌp/ **A** *n* (*also* ~ **comedy**) one man show *m* comique
B *adj* ~ **comedian** comique *mf*

Stanley knife® /'stænlɪnaɪf/ *n* cutter *m*

staple /'steɪpl/ **A** *n* **1** (for paper) agrafe *f*
2 (basic food) aliment *m* de base
B *adj* ‹*product, food, diet*› de base
C *vt* agrafer (**to** à, **onto** sur)

stapler /'steɪplə(r)/ *n* agrafeuse *f*

star /stɑː(r)/ **A** *n* **1** (in sky) étoile *f*
2 (celebrity) vedette *f*, star *f*
3 (asterisk) astérisque *m*
4 (ranking) **a three-~ hotel** un hôtel (à) trois étoiles
B *vi* (*p prés etc* **-rr-**) ‹*actor*› jouer le rôle principal (**in** dans)
C *vt* (*p prés etc* **-rr-**) ‹*film, play*› avoir [qn] pour vedette ‹*actor*›

starch /stɑːtʃ/ *n* **1** (carbohydrate) féculents *mpl*
2 (for clothes) amidon *m*

stardom /'stɑːdəm/ *n* célébrité *f*; **to rise to ~** devenir une vedette

stare /steə(r)/ **A** *n* regard *m* fixe
B *vi* **to ~ at sb/sth** regarder fixement qn/qch

starfish *n* étoile *f* de mer

stark /stɑːk/ *adj* ‹*landscape*› désolé/-e; ‹*room, decor*› nu/-e; **in ~ contrast to** en opposition totale avec
(IDIOM) ~ **naked** tout/-e nu/-e

starry /'stɑːrɪ/ *adj* ‹*night, sky*› étoilé/-e

starry-eyed *adj* ébloui/-e (**about** par)

star sign *n* signe *m* astrologique

star-studded *adj* ‹*cast, line-up*› avec de nombreuses vedettes

start /stɑːt/ **A** *n* **1** (beginning) début *m*
2 (in sport) (advantage) avantage *m*; (in time, distance) avance *f*; (departure line) ligne *f* de départ
3 (movement) **with a ~** en sursaut
B *vt* **1** (begin) commencer; entamer ‹*bottle, packet*›; **to ~ doing** commencer à faire
2 (cause, initiate) déclencher ‹*quarrel, war*›; lancer ‹*fashion, rumour*›
3 faire démarrer ‹*car*›; mettre [qch] en marche ‹*machine*›
C *vi* **1** (begin) commencer (**by doing** par faire); **to ~ again** recommencer
2 ‹*car, engine, machine*› démarrer
3 (depart) partir
4 (jump nervously) sursauter (**in** de)
D to start with *phr* **1** (firstly) d'abord, premièrement

S

2 (at first) au début
■ **start off** **A** ~ **off** **1** (set off) ‹*train, bus*› démarrer; ‹*person*› partir
2 (begin) ‹*person*› commencer; ‹*business, employee*› débuter (**as** comme, **in** dans)
B ~ **[sth] off** **1** commencer ‹*visit, talk*› (**with** par)
2 mettre [qch] en marche ‹*machine*›
■ **start out** (on journey) partir
■ **start over** recommencer (à zéro)
■ **start up**: **A** ~ **up** ‹*engine*› démarrer
B ~ **[sth] up** faire démarrer ‹*car*›; ouvrir ‹*shop*›; créer ‹*business*›

starter /ˈstɑːtə(r)/ *n* **1** (of race) starter *m*
2 (on menu) hors-d'œuvre *m inv*
(IDIOM) **for ~s** (fam) pour commencer

startle /ˈstɑːtl/ *vt* **1** (take aback) surprendre
2 (alarm) effrayer

startling /ˈstɑːtlɪŋ/ *adj* saisissant/-e

starvation /ˌstɑːˈveɪʃn/ *n* famine *f*; **to die of ~** mourir de faim

starve /stɑːv/ **A** *vt* affamer; (fig) priver (**of** de); **to ~ oneself** se sous-alimenter; **to be ~d of** être en mal de ‹*company, conversation*›
B *vi* mourir de faim

starving /ˈstɑːvɪŋ/ *adj* (hungry) **to be ~** mourir de faim; (hunger-stricken) affamé/-e

🔑 **state** /steɪt/ **A** *n* **1** état *m*; **he's not in a fit ~ to drive** il n'est pas en état de conduire
2 (*also* **State**) (government, nation) État *m*
B **States** *npl* **the States** les États-Unis *mpl*
C *adj* **1** ‹*school, sector*› public/-ique; ‹*enterprise, pension*› d'État; ‹*subsidy*› de l'État
2 ‹*occasion*› d'apparat; ‹*visit*› officiel/-ielle
D *vt* **1** (declare) exposer ‹*fact, opinion*›; indiquer ‹*age, income*›; **to ~ that** ‹*person*› déclarer que
2 (specify) spécifier ‹*amount, time, terms*›; exprimer ‹*preference*›
(IDIOM) **to be in a ~** être dans tous ses états

State Department *n* (AmE) ministère *m* des Affaires étrangères

state-funded *adj* subventionné/-e par l'État

stateless /ˈsteɪtlɪs/ *adj* apatride

stately /ˈsteɪtlɪ/ *adj* imposant/-e

stately home *n* (BrE) château *m*

🔑 **statement** /ˈsteɪtmənt/ *n* **1** déclaration *f*; (official) communiqué *m*
2 (*also* **bank ~**) relevé *m* de compte

state-of-the-art *adj* ‹*equipment*› ultramoderne; ‹*technology*› de pointe

statesman /ˈsteɪtsmən/ *n* (*pl* **-men**) homme *m* d'État

static /ˈstætɪk/ **A** *n* **1** (*also* **~ electricity**) électricité *f* statique
2 (interference) parasites *mpl*
B *adj* **1** (stationary) ‹*image*› fixe; ‹*traffic*› bloqué/-e
2 (stable) ‹*population, prices*› stationnaire

🔑 **station** /ˈsteɪʃn/ **A** *n* **1** (*also* **railway ~** (BrE)) gare *f*
2 (radio, TV) station *f*
3 (*also* **police ~**) commissariat *m*; (small) poste *m* de police
B *vt* poster ‹*officer, guard*›; stationner ‹*troops*›

stationary /ˈsteɪʃənrɪ, (AmE) -nerɪ/ *adj* immobile, à l'arrêt

stationer /ˈsteɪʃnə(r)/ *n* (*also* **~'s**) papeterie *f*

stationery /ˈsteɪʃnərɪ, (AmE) -nerɪ/ *n* fournitures *fpl* de bureau; (writing paper) papier *m* à lettres

station wagon *n* (AmE) break *m*

statistic /stəˈtɪstɪk/ *n* statistique *f*; **~s show that...** d'après les statistiques...

statistical /stəˈtɪstɪkl/ *adj* statistique

statue /ˈstætʃuː/ *n* statue *f*

stature /ˈstætʃə(r)/ *n* **1** (height) taille *f*
2 (status) envergure *f*

🔑 **status** /ˈsteɪtəs/ *n* (*pl* **-uses**) **1** (position) position *f*
2 (prestige) prestige *m*
3 (legal, professional) statut *m* (**as** de); **financial ~** situation *f* financière

status quo *n* statu quo *m*

status symbol *n* signe *m* de prestige

statute /ˈstætʃuːt/ *n* texte *m* de loi; **by ~** par la loi

statutory /ˈstatʃʊtərɪ, (AmE) -tɔːrɪ/ *adj* légal/-e

staunch /stɔːntʃ/ *adj* ‹*supporter, defence*› loyal/-e; ‹*Catholic, communist*› fervent/-e

stave /steɪv/ *n* (Mus) portée *f*
■ **stave off** tromper ‹*hunger, fatigue*›; écarter ‹*threat*›

🔑 **stay** /steɪ/ **A** *n* **1** (visit) séjour *m*
2 **~ of execution** sursis *m*
B *vi* **1** (remain) rester; **to ~ for lunch** rester (à) déjeuner
2 (have accommodation) loger; **to ~ in a hotel/with a friend** loger à l'hôtel/chez un ami; **to ~ overnight** passer la nuit
3 (visit) passer quelques jours (**with** chez)
■ **stay in** rester à la maison
■ **stay out**: **to ~ out late/all night** rentrer tard/ne pas rentrer de la nuit; **to ~ out of trouble** éviter les ennuis
■ **stay up** **1** (waiting for sb) veiller
2 (as habit) se coucher tard
3 (not fall down) tenir

staying power *n* endurance *f*

steadfast /ˈstedfɑːst, (AmE) -fæst/ *adj* tenace

steadily /ˈstedɪlɪ/ *adv* **1** (gradually) progressivement
2 ‹*work, rain*› sans interruption

steady /ˈstedɪ/ **A** *adj* **1** (continual) ‹*stream, increase*› constant/-e; ‹*rain*› incessant/-e; ‹*breathing, progress*› régulier/-ière
2 (stable) stable; **to hold [sth] ~** bien tenir ‹*ladder*›

🔑 mot clé

S

3 ‹*voice, hand*› ferme; ‹*gaze*› calme
4 (reliable) ‹*job*› stable; ‹*relationship*› durable
B *vt* **to ~ one's nerves** se calmer les nerfs

steak /steɪk/ *n* (of beef) steak *m*; (of fish) darne *f*

steal /sti:l/ **A** *vt* (*prét* **stole**, *pp* **stolen**) voler (**from sb** à qn)
B *vi* (*prét* **stole**, *pp* **stolen**) **1** (thieve) voler
2 (creep) **to ~ into/out of a room** entrer/quitter une pièce subrepticement

stealing /ˈsti:lɪŋ/ *n* vol *m*

stealthy /ˈstelθɪ/ *adj* ‹*step, glance*› furtif/-ive

steam /sti:m/ **A** *n* vapeur *f*
B *vt* faire cuire [qch] à la vapeur ‹*vegetables*›
C *vi* fumer, dégager de la vapeur
IDIOMS **to run out of ~** s'essouffler; **to let off ~** décompresser
■ **steam up** ‹*window, glasses*› s'embuer

steam engine *n* locomotive *f* à vapeur

steamer /ˈsti:mə(r)/ *n* (boat) (bateau *m* à) vapeur *m*

steamroller /ˈsti:mrəʊlə(r)/ *n* rouleau *m* compresseur

steamy /ˈsti:mɪ/ *adj* **1** ‹*window*› embué/-e; ‹*climate*› chaud/-e et humide
2 (fam) (erotic) torride

steel /sti:l/ **A** *n* acier *m*
B *v refl* **to ~ oneself** s'armer de courage

steelworks, **steelyard** *n* installations *fpl* sidérurgiques

steep /sti:p/ **A** *adj* **1** ‹*slope, stairs*› raide; ‹*street, path*› escarpé/-e; ‹*roof*› en pente raide
2 (sharp) ‹*rise, fall*› fort/-e *before n*
3 (fam) ‹*price*› exorbitant/-e
B *vt* **to ~ sth in** faire tremper qch dans

steeple /ˈsti:pl/ *n* (tower) clocher *m*; (spire) flèche *f*

steer /stɪə(r)/ **A** *n* (animal) bouvillon *m*
B *vt* **1** piloter ‹*ship, car*›
2 (guide) diriger ‹*person*›
C *vi* (in car) piloter; (in boat) gouverner
IDIOM **to ~ clear of sb/sth** se tenir à l'écart de qn/qch

steering lock *n* blocage *m* de direction

steering wheel *n* volant *m*

stem /stem/ **A** *n* **1** (of flower, leaf) tige *f*; (of fruit) queue *f*
2 (of glass) pied *m*
B *vt* (*p prés etc* **-mm-**) arrêter ‹*flow*›; enrayer ‹*advance, tide*›
C *vi* (*p prés etc* **-mm-**) **to ~ from** provenir de

stem cell /stem sel/ *n* cellule *f* mère, cellule *f* souche

stencil /ˈstensɪl/ **A** *n* pochoir *m*
B *vt* décorer [qch] au pochoir ‹*fabric, surface*›

stenography /steˈnɒgrəfɪ/ *n* (AmE) sténographie *f*

step /step/ **A** *n* **1** (pace) pas *m*
2 (measure) mesure *f*; **to take ~s** prendre des mesures
3 (stage) étape *f* (**in** dans)
4 (stair) marche *f*; **~s** (small ladder) escabeau *m*
B *vi* (*p prés etc* **-pp-**) marcher (**in** dans, **on** sur); **to ~ into** entrer dans ‹*lift*›; monter dans ‹*dinghy*›; **to ~ off** descendre de ‹*pavement*›; **to ~ over** enjamber ‹*fence*›
IDIOM **one ~ at a time** chaque chose en son temps
■ **step back** (fig) prendre du recul (**from** par rapport à)
■ **step down** se retirer; (as electoral candidate) se désister
■ **step in** intervenir (**and do** pour faire)
■ **step up** accroître ‹*production*›; intensifier ‹*campaign*›

step aerobics *n* step *m*

stepbrother *n* demi-frère *m*

step-by-step **A** *adj* ‹*guide*› complet/-ète
B **step by step** *adv* ‹*explain*› étape par étape

stepchild *n* beau-fils/belle-fille *m/f*

stepdaughter *n* belle-fille *f*

stepfather *n* beau-père *m*

stepladder *n* escabeau *m*

stepmother *n* belle-mère *f*

stepping stone *n* pierre *f* de gué; (fig) tremplin *m*

stepsister *n* demi-sœur *f*

stepson *n* beau-fils *m*

stereo /ˈsterɪəʊ/ *n* **1** (sound) stéréo *f*; **in ~** en stéréo
2 (*also* **~ system**) chaîne *f* stéréo; **personal ~** baladeur *m*

stereotype /ˈsterɪətaɪp/ *n* stéréotype *m*

sterile /ˈsteraɪl, (AmE) ˈsterəl/ *adj* stérile

sterilize /ˈsterəlaɪz/ *vt* stériliser

sterling /ˈstɜ:lɪŋ/ *n* livre *f* sterling *inv*

stern /stɜ:n/ **A** *n* (of ship) poupe *f*
B *adj* sévère

steroid /ˈstɪərɔɪd, ˈste-/ *n* stéroïde *m*

stew /stju:, (AmE) stu:/ **A** *n* ragoût *m*
B *vt* cuire [qch] en ragoût ‹*meat*›; faire cuire ‹*fruit*›; **~ed apples** compote *f* de pommes

steward /ˈstjʊəd, (AmE) ˈstu:ərd/ *n* (on plane, ship) steward *m*; (of club) intendant/-e *m/f*; (at races) organisateur *m*

stewardess /ˈstjʊədes, (AmE) ˈstu:ərdəs/ *n* (on plane) hôtesse *f* (de l'air)

stick /stɪk/ **A** *n* **1** (of wood, chalk, dynamite) bâton *m*
2 (*also* **walking ~**) canne *f*
3 (in hockey) crosse *f*
B *vt* (*prét*, *pp* **stuck**) **1 to ~ sth into sth** planter qch dans qch
2 (fam) (put) mettre
3 (fix in place) coller ‹*poster, stamp*› (**on** sur, **to** à)
C *vi* (*prét*, *pp* **stuck**) **1 the thorn stuck in my finger** l'épine m'est restée dans le doigt
2 ‹*stamp, glue*› coller; **to ~ to the pan**

‹*sauce, rice*› attacher (fam)
3 ‹*drawer, door, lift*› se coincer
4 (remain) rester; **to ~ in sb's mind** rester gravé dans la mémoire de qn
■ **stick at**: **~ at [sth]** persévérer dans ‹*task*›
■ **stick out**: **A** **~ out** ‹*nail, sharp object*› dépasser (**of** de); **his ears ~ out** il a les oreilles décollées
B **~ [sth] out: to ~ out one's hand/foot** tendre la main/le pied; **to ~ one's tongue out** tirer la langue
■ **stick to** **1** (keep to) s'en tenir à ‹*facts, point*›; maintenir ‹*story, version*›
2 (follow) suivre ‹*river, road*›
■ **stick together** **1** ‹*pages*› se coller
2 (fam) (be loyal) être solidaires
3 (fam) (not separate) rester ensemble
■ **stick up** (project) se dresser; **to ~ up for sb** défendre qn
sticker /'stɪkə(r)/ *n* autocollant *m*
sticking plaster *n* pansement *m* adhésif, sparadrap *m*
sticky /'stɪkɪ/ *adj* **1** ‹*floor, fingers*› poisseux/-euse; ‹*label*› adhésif/-ive
2 (sweaty) ‹*hand, palm*› moite
sticky tape *n* (fam) Scotch® *m*, ruban *m* adhésif
stiff /stɪf/ **A** *adj* **1** raide; (after sport, sleeping badly) courbaturé/-e; **~ neck** torticolis *m*; **to have ~ legs** (after sport) avoir des courbatures dans les jambes
2 ‹*lever, handle*› dur/-e à manier
3 ‹*manner, style*› compassé/-e
4 (tough) ‹*sentence*› sévère; ‹*exam, climb*› difficile; ‹*competition*› rude
5 (high) ‹*charge, fine*› élevé/-e
6 a ~ drink un remontant
B *adv* (fam) **to bore sb ~** ennuyer qn à mourir; **to be scared ~** avoir une peur bleue
stiffen /'stɪfn/ **A** *vt* renforcer ‹*card*›; empeser ‹*fabric*›
B *vi* **1** ‹*person*› se raidir
2 ‹*egg white*› devenir ferme; ‹*mixture*› prendre de la consistance
stifle /'staɪfl/ *vt* étouffer
stigma /'stɪgmə/ *n* (*pl* **-mas** *ou* **-mata**) stigmate *m*
stigmatize /'stɪgmətaɪz/ *vt* stigmatiser
stile /staɪl/ *n* échalier *m*
stiletto /stɪ'letəʊ/ *n* (*pl* **-tos**) (*also* **~ heel**) (shoe, heel) talon *m* aiguille
✓ **still[1]** /stɪl/ *adv* **1** encore, toujours; **he's ~ as crazy as ever!** il est toujours aussi fou!; **they're ~ in town** ils sont encore en ville
2 (referring to the future) encore; **I have four exams ~ to go** j'ai encore quatre examens à passer
3 (nevertheless) quand même
4 (with comparatives) encore; **better/worse ~** encore mieux/pire

✓ mot clé

still[2] /stɪl/ **A** *n* **1** (for making alcohol) alambic *m*
2 (photograph) photo *f* de plateau
B *adj* **1** (motionless) ‹*air, water*› calme; ‹*hand, person*› immobile
2 (peaceful) ‹*countryside, streets*› tranquille
3 ‹*drink*› non gazeux/-euse
C *adv* ‹*lie, stay*› immobile; **to sit ~** se tenir tranquille; **to stand ~** ne pas bouger
still life *n* (*pl* **-lifes**) nature *f* morte
stilted /'stɪltɪd/ *adj* guindé/-e
stimulant /'stɪmjʊlənt/ *n* stimulant *m* (**to** de)
stimulate /'stɪmjʊleɪt/ *vt* stimuler
stimulating /'stɪmjʊleɪtɪŋ/ *adj* stimulant/-e
stimulus /'stɪmjʊləs/ *n* (*pl* **-li**) **1** (physical) stimulus *m*
2 (boost) impulsion *f*
3 (incentive) stimulant *m*
sting /stɪŋ/ **A** *n* **1** (part of insect) aiguillon *m*
2 (result of being stung) piqûre *f*
B *vt* (*prét, pp* **stung**) **1** ‹*insect*› piquer
2 ‹*wind*› cingler
C *vi* (*prét, pp* **stung**) (gen) piquer; ‹*cut*› cuire
stingy /'stɪndʒɪ/ *adj* radin/-e (fam)
stink /stɪŋk/ **A** *n* (mauvaise) odeur *f*
B *vi* (*prét* **stank**, *pp* **stunk**) puer
stint /stɪnt/ **A** *n* **to do a three-year ~** travailler trois ans
B *vi* **to ~ on** lésiner sur ‹*drink, presents*›
stipulate /'stɪpjʊleɪt/ *vt* stipuler (**that** que)
stir /stɜː(r)/ **A** *n* **to cause (quite) a ~** faire sensation
B *vt* (*p prés etc* **-rr-**) **1** remuer ‹*liquid, sauce*›; mélanger ‹*paint, powder*›; **to ~ sth into sth** incorporer qch à qch
2 ‹*breeze*› agiter ‹*leaves, papers*›
C *vi* (*p prés etc* **-rr-**) **1** ‹*leaves, papers*› trembler; ‹*curtains*› remuer
2 (budge) bouger
■ **stir up** provoquer ‹*trouble*›; attiser ‹*hatred, unrest*›; exciter ‹*crowd*›
stir-fry /'stɜːfraɪ/ **A** *n* sauté *m*
B *vt* (*prét, pp* **-fried**) faire sauter ‹*beef, vegetables*›
stirring /'stɜːrɪŋ/ *adj* ‹*story*› passionnant/-e; ‹*music, speech*› enthousiasmant/-e
stirrup /'stɪrəp/ *n* étrier *m*
stitch /stɪtʃ/ **A** *n* **1** (in sewing, embroidery) point *m*; (in knitting, crochet) maille *f*
2 (in wound) point *m* de suture
3 (pain) point *m* de côté
B *vt* coudre (**to, onto** à); recoudre ‹*wound*›
stoat /stəʊt/ *n* hermine *f*
✓ **stock** /stɒk/ **A** *n* **1** (supply) stock *m*; **we're out of ~** nous n'en avons plus
2 (descent) souche *f*, origine *f*
3 (Culin) bouillon *m*
4 (livestock) bétail *m*
B **stocks** *npl* **1** (BrE) (in finance) valeurs *fpl*, titres *mpl*; **~s and shares** valeurs *fpl* mobilières

2 (AmE) actions *fpl*
3 the ~s le pilori
C *adj* ‹*size*› courant/-e; ‹*answer*› classique; ‹*character*› stéréotypé/-e
D *vt* **1** (sell) avoir, vendre
2 remplir ‹*fridge*›; garnir ‹*shelves*›; approvisionner ‹*shop*›
IDIOM **to take ~** faire le point (**of** sur)
■ **stock up** s'approvisionner (**with, on** en)

stockbroker *n* agent *m* de change

stock cube *n* bouillon-cube® *m*

stock exchange *n* **the ~** la Bourse

Stockholm /'ʃtɒkhəʊm/ *pr n* Stockholm

stocking /'stɒkɪŋ/ *n* bas *m*

stock market /'stɒkmɑːkɪt/ *n* **1** (stock exchange) Bourse *f* (des valeurs)
2 (prices, trading activity) marché *m* (des valeurs)

stockpile /'stɒkpaɪl/ *vt* stocker ‹*weapons*›; faire des stocks de ‹*food, goods*›

stock room *n* magasin *m*

stock-still /ˌstɒk'stɪl/ *adv* **to stand ~** rester cloué/-e sur place

stocktaking /'stɒkteɪkɪŋ/ *n* inventaire *m*

stocky /'stɒkɪ/ *adj* trapu/-e

stodgy /'stɒdʒɪ/ *adj* ‹*food*› bourratif/-ive

stoical /'stəʊɪkl/ *adj* stoïque

stoke /stəʊk/ *vt* (*also* **~ up**) alimenter ‹*fire, furnace*›

stolid /'stɒlɪd/ *adj* ‹*person, character*› flegmatique

stomach /'stʌmək/ **A** *n* estomac *m*; (belly) ventre *m*
B *vt* supporter ‹*person, attitude*›

stomach ache *n* **to have (a) ~** avoir mal au ventre

stone /stəʊn/ **A** *n* **1** pierre *f*; (pebble) caillou *m*
2 (in fruit) noyau *m*
3 (BrE) (weight) = *6.35 kg*
B *vt* dénoyauter ‹*peach*›

Stone Age *n* âge *m* de pierre

stone circle *n* enceinte *f* de monolithes, cromlech *m*

stone-cold /ˌstəʊn'kəʊld/ *adj* glacé/-e

stonemason *n* tailleur *m* de pierre

stonewall /ˌstəʊn'wɔːl/ *vi* faire de l'obstruction

stone-washed *adj* délavé/-e

stony /'stəʊnɪ/ *adj* **1** (rocky) pierreux/-euse
2 ‹*look, silence*› glacial/-e

stool /stuːl/ *n* tabouret *m*

stoop /stuːp/ **A** *n* **to have a ~** avoir le dos voûté
B *vi* être voûté/-e; (bend down) se baisser; **to ~ so low as to do** s'abaisser jusqu'à faire

stop /stɒp/ **A** *n* **1** (gen) arrêt *m*; **to come to a ~** ‹*vehicle, work, progress*› s'arrêter; **to put a ~ to** mettre fin à
2 (in telegram) stop *m*
B *vt* (*p prés etc* **-pp-**) **1** (cease) arrêter; (temporarily) interrompre ‹*activity*›; **to ~ doing** arrêter de faire
2 (prevent) empêcher; **to ~ sb (from) doing** empêcher qn de faire
3 supprimer ‹*allowance*›; **to ~ a cheque** faire opposition à un chèque
4 (plug) boucher ‹*gap, hole, bottle*›
C *vi* (*p prés etc* **-pp-**) **1** s'arrêter
2 (stay) rester; **to ~ for dinner** rester dîner; **I can't ~** je n'ai vraiment pas le temps
D *v refl* (*p prés etc* **-pp-**) **to ~ oneself** se retenir
■ **stop off** (on journey) faire un arrêt
■ **stop up**: **~ [sth] up, ~ up [sth]** boucher ‹*hole*›

stopgap /'stɒpgæp/ *n* bouche-trou *m*

stop-off *n* (quick break) arrêt *m*; (longer) halte *f*

stopover *n* escale *f*

stoppage /'stɒpɪdʒ/ *n* (strike) arrêt *m* de travail

stopper /'stɒpə(r)/ *n* (for flask, jar) bouchon *m*

stop sign *n* (panneau *m* de) stop *m*

stopwatch *n* chronomètre *m*

storage /'stɔːrɪdʒ/ **A** *n* (of food, fuel) stockage *m* (**of** de); **to be in ~** ‹*furniture*› être au garde-meuble
B *adj* ‹*space*› de rangement

storage heater *n* radiateur *m* électrique à accumulation

store /stɔː(r)/ **A** *n* **1** (shop) magasin *m*; (smaller) boutique *f*
2 (supply) provision *f*
3 (place) (for food, fuel) réserve *f*; (for furniture) garde-meuble *m*
4 what does the future have in ~ for us? qu'est-ce que l'avenir nous réserve?
B *vt* **1** conserver ‹*food, information*›; ranger ‹*furniture*›
2 (Comput) mémoriser ‹*data*›

storekeeper *n* (AmE) commerçant/-e *m/f*

storeroom *n* (in house, school, office) réserve *f*; (in factory, shop) magasin *m*

storey (BrE), **story** (AmE) /'stɔːrɪ/ *n* (*pl* **-reys** (BrE), **-ries** (AmE)) étage *m*; **on the third ~** au troisième étage (BrE), au quatrième étage (AmE)

stork /stɔːk/ *n* cigogne *f*

storm /stɔːm/ **A** *n* tempête *f*; (thunderstorm) orage *m*
B *vt* prendre [qch] d'assaut ‹*citadel, prison*›
C *vi* **he ~ed off in a temper** il est parti furibond

stormy /'stɔːmɪ/ *adj* orageux/-euse; **~ scenes** éclats *mpl*

story /'stɔːrɪ/ *n* **1** (gen) histoire *f* (**about, of** de); **a true ~** une histoire vécue; **a ghost ~** une histoire de fantômes
2 (in newspaper) article *m* (**on, about** sur)
3 (rumour) rumeur *f* (**about** sur); **the ~ goes that** on raconte que
4 (AmE) (floor) étage *m*

storybook /'stɔːrɪbʊk/ *n* livre *m* de contes

S

storyteller /'stɔːrɪtelə(r)/ *n* conteur/-euse *m/f*
stout /staʊt/ *adj* **1** (fat) corpulent/-e
2 (strong) ‹*wall*› épais/-aisse
stove /stəʊv/ *n* **1** (cooker) cuisinière *f*
2 (heater) poêle *m*
stovetop *n* (AmE) (on cooker) table *f* de cuisson
stow /stəʊ/ *vt* ranger ‹*baggage*›
stowaway *n* passager/-ère *m/f* clandestin/-e
straddle /'strædl/ *vt* enfourcher ‹*horse, bike*›; s'asseoir à califourchon sur ‹*chair*›
straggle /'strægl/ *vi* **1** ‹*houses, villages*› être disséminé/-e (**along** le long de)
2 (dawdle) traîner
straggler /'stræglə(r)/ *n* traînard/-e *m/f*
straggly /'stræglɪ/ *adj* ‹*hair, beard*› en désordre
straight /streɪt/ **A** *adj* **1** ‹*line, nose, road*› droit/-e; ‹*hair*› raide; **in a ~ line** en ligne droite
2 (level, upright) bien droit/-e; **the picture isn't ~** le tableau est de travers
3 (tidy, in order) en ordre
4 (clear) **to get sth ~** comprendre qch; **to set the record ~** mettre les choses au clair
5 (honest, direct) ‹*person*› honnête, droit/-e; ‹*answer, question*› clair/-e; **to be ~ with sb** jouer franc-jeu avec qn
6 ‹*choice*› simple
7 ‹*spirits, drink*› sec, sans eau
8 ‹*actor, role*› sérieux/-ieuse
B *adv* **1** droit; **stand up ~!** tenez-vous droit!; **to go/keep ~ ahead** aller/continuer tout droit; **to look ~ ahead** regarder droit devant soi
2 (without delay) directement; **to go ~ back to Paris** rentrer directement à Paris
3 (frankly) tout net; **I'll tell you ~** je vous le dirai tout net; **~ out** carrément
4 (neat) ‹*drink*› sec, sans eau
IDIOM **to keep a ~ face** garder son sérieux
straightaway /'streɪtəweɪ/ *adv* tout de suite
straighten /'streɪtn/ *vt* tendre ‹*arm, leg*›; redresser ‹*picture, teeth*›; ajuster ‹*tie, hat*›; défriser ‹*hair*›
■ **straighten out**: **to ~ things out** (resolve) arranger les choses
■ **straighten up**: **A ~ up** ‹*person*› se redresser
B ~ [sth] up (tidy) ranger ‹*objects, room*›
straightforward /ˌstreɪt'fɔːwəd/ *adj* ‹*answer, person*› franc/franche; ‹*account*› simple
straight-laced *adj* collet-monté *inv*
strain /streɪn/ **A** *n* **1** (force) effort *m* (**on** sur)
2 (pressure) (on person) stress *m*; (in relations) tension *f*
3 (of virus, bacteria) souche *f*
B *vt* **1 to ~ one's eyes** (to see) plisser les yeux; **to ~ one's ears** tendre l'oreille
2 (try) mettre [qch] à rude épreuve ‹*patience*›
3 (injure) **to ~ a muscle** se froisser un muscle; **to ~ one's eyes** se fatiguer les yeux; **to ~ one's back** se faire un tour de reins
4 (sieve) passer ‹*sauce*›; égoutter ‹*vegetables, pasta, rice*›
C *vi* **to ~ at** tirer sur ‹*leash, rope*›
strained /streɪnd/ *adj* (tense) tendu/-e; (injured) ‹*muscle*› froissé/-e
strainer /'streɪnə(r)/ *n* passoire *f*
strait /streɪt/ *n* détroit *m*
IDIOM **to be in dire ~s** être aux abois
straitjacket /'streɪtdʒækɪt/ *n* camisole *f* de force
strand /strænd/ **A** *n* (gen) fil *m*; (of hair) mèche *f*
B *vt* **to be ~ed** être bloqué/-e; **to leave sb ~ed** laisser qn en rade (fam)
strange /streɪndʒ/ *adj* **1** (unfamiliar) inconnu/-e; **a ~ man** un inconnu
2 (odd) bizarre; **it is ~ (that)** il est bizarre que (+ *subjunctive*)
strangely /'streɪndʒlɪ/ *adj* ‹*behave, react*› d'une façon étrange; ‹*quiet, empty*› étrangement; **~ enough,...** chose étrange,...
stranger /'streɪndʒə(r)/ *n* (from elsewhere) étranger/-ère *m/f*; (unknown person) inconnu/-e *m/f*
strangle /'stræŋgl/ *vt* étrangler
stranglehold /'stræŋglhəʊld/ *n* (control) mainmise *f*
strap /stræp/ **A** *n* (on shoe) bride *f*; (on case, harness) courroie *f*; (on watch) bracelet *m*; (on handbag) bandoulière *f*; (on dress, bra) bretelle *f*
B *vt* (*p prés etc* **-pp-**) attacher (**to** à)
strapless /'stræplɪs/ *adj* sans bretelles
strapped /stræpt/ *adj* (fam) **to be ~ for** être à court de ‹*cash, staff*›
strapping /'stræpɪŋ/ *adj* costaud/-e
stratagem /'strætədʒəm/ *n* stratagème *m*
strategic /strə'tiːdʒɪk/ *adj* stratégique
strategy /'strætədʒɪ/ *n* stratégie *f*
straw /strɔː/ *n* paille *f*
IDIOMS **to clutch at ~s** se raccrocher à n'importe quoi; **the last ~** la goutte qui fait déborder le vase
strawberry /'strɔːbrɪ, (AmE) -berɪ/ **A** *n* fraise *f*; **strawberries and cream** fraises à la crème
B *adj* ‹*tart*› aux fraises; ‹*ice cream*› à la fraise; ‹*jam*› de fraises
straw poll *n* sondage *m* non-officiel
stray /streɪ/ **A** *n* (dog) chien *m* errant; (cat) chat *m* vagabond
B *adj* ‹*dog*› errant/-e; ‹*cat*› vagabond/-e; ‹*bullet*› perdu/-e; ‹*tourist*› isolé/-e
C *vi* **1** (wander) s'égarer; **to ~ from the road**

mot clé

s'écarter de la route
2 ‹*eyes, mind*› errer

streak /stri:k/ **A** *n* **1** (in character) côté *m*
2 (period) **a winning/losing ~** une bonne/ mauvaise passe
3 (of paint) traînée *f*; **~ of lightning** éclair *m*
4 (in hair) mèche *f*
B *vt* **1** strier ‹*sea, sky*›
2 to get one's hair ~ed se faire faire des mèches
C *vi* **to ~ past** passer comme une flèche

streaky bacon *n* (BrE) bacon *m* entrelardé

stream /stri:m/ **A** *n* **1** (brook) ruisseau *m*
2 a ~ of un flot de ‹*traffic, questions*›; **a ~ of abuse** un torrent d'insultes
B *vi* **1** (flow) ruisseler; **sunlight was ~ing into the room** le soleil entrait à flots dans la pièce; **people ~ed out of the theatre** un flot de gens sortait du théâtre
2 ‹*banners, hair*› **to ~ in the wind** flotter au vent
3 ‹*eyes, nose*› couler

streamer /'stri:mə(r)/ *n* (of paper) banderole *f*

streaming /'stri:mɪŋ/ *adj* **1** (of a cold) **a ~ cold** gros rhume *m*
2 (Comput) streaming; **~ video** vidéo *f* en streaming

streamline /'stri:mlaɪn/ *vt* **1** (in design) caréner
2 (make more efficient) rationaliser ‹*distribution, production*›
3 (cut) dégraisser ‹*company*›

streamlined /'stri:mlaɪnd/ *adj* **1** ‹*cooker, furniture*› aux lignes modernes; ‹*hull, body*› caréné/-e
2 ‹*production, system*› simplifié/-e

street /stri:t/ *n* rue *f*; **in** *or* **on the ~** dans la rue

street cred /ˌstri:t 'kred/ *n* (fam) **to have ~** être dans le coup (fam)

street lamp *n* (old gas-lamp) réverbère *m*; (modern) lampadaire *m*

street market *n* marché *m* en plein air

street plan *n* indicateur *m* des rues

street value *n* valeur *f* à la revente

streetwise *adj* (fam) dégourdi/-e (fam)

strength /streŋθ/ *n* (of wind, person, government, bond, argument) force *f*; (of lens, magnet, voice, army) puissance *f*; (of structure, equipment) solidité *f*; (of material) résistance *f*; (of feeling) intensité *f*

strengthen /'streŋθn/ *vt* renforcer ‹*building, argument, love, position*›; consolider ‹*bond, links*›; affirmer ‹*power, role*›; fortifier ‹*muscles*›; raffermir ‹*dollar*›

strenuous /'strenjʊəs/ *adj* ‹*exercise*› énergique; ‹*activity, job*› ardu/-e

stress /stres/ **A** *n* **1** (nervous) tension *f*, stress *m*; **mental ~** tension nerveuse; **to be under ~** être stressé/-e
2 (emphasis) accent *m* (**on** sur); **to lay ~ on** insister sur ‹*fact, problem*›
3 (in physics) effort *m*
4 (in pronouncing) accent *m*
B *vt* mettre l'accent sur, insister sur; **to ~ the importance of sth** souligner l'importance *f* de qch; **to ~ (that)** souligner que
■ **stress out** (fam): **~ [sb] out** stresser

stressed /strest/ *adj* **1** (*also* **~ out**) stressé/-e
2 ‹*syllable*› accentué/-e

stressful /'stresfl/ *adj* stressant/-e

stretch /stretʃ/ **A** *n* **1** (of road, track) tronçon *m*; (of coastline, river) partie *f*
2 (of water, countryside) étendue *f*
3 (period) période *f*; **to work for 12 hours at a ~** travailler 12 heures d'affilée
B *adj* ‹*cover, fabric, waist*› extensible
C *vt* **1** (extend) tendre ‹*rope, net*›; étirer ‹*arms, legs*›; **to ~ one's legs** (fig) se dégourdir les jambes
2 étirer ‹*elastic*›; élargir ‹*shoe*›
3 déformer ‹*truth*›
4 utiliser [qch] au maximum ‹*budget, resources*›
D *vi* **1** ‹*person*› s'étirer
2 ‹*road, track*› s'étaler (**for, over** sur); ‹*beach, moor*› s'étendre (**for** sur)
3 ‹*elastic*› s'étendre; ‹*shoe*› s'élargir
■ **stretch out**: **A ~ out** s'étendre
B ~ [sth] out tendre ‹*hand, foot*› (**towards** vers); étendre ‹*arm, leg*›; étaler ‹*nets, sheet*›

stretcher /'stretʃə(r)/ *n* brancard *m*

strew /stru:/ *vt* (*prét* **strewed**, *pp* **strewed** *ou* **strewn**) éparpiller ‹*litter, paper*› (**on** sur); **~n with** jonché/-e de

stricken /'strɪkən/ *adj* **1** ‹*face*› affligé/-e; ‹*area*› sinistré/-e; **~ by** frappé/-e de ‹*illness*›; pris/-e de ‹*fear*›; accablé/-e de ‹*guilt*›
2 ‹*plane, ship*› en détresse

strict /strɪkt/ *adj* ‹*person*› strict/-e (**about** sur); ‹*view*› rigide; ‹*silence*› absolu/-e; ‹*Methodist, Catholic*› de stricte observance; **in ~ confidence** à titre strictement confidentiel; **in ~ secrecy** dans le plus grand secret

strictly /'strɪktlɪ/ *adv* **1** ‹*treat*› avec sévérité
2 ‹*confidential, prohibited*› strictement; **~ speaking** à proprement parler

stride /straɪd/ **A** *n* enjambée *f*
B *vi* (*prét* **strode**, *pp* (rare) **stridden**) **to ~ out/in** sortir/entrer à grands pas; **to ~ across sth** enjamber qch
IDIOM **to take sth in one's ~** prendre qch calmement

strife /straɪf/ *n* conflits *mpl*

strike /straɪk/ **A** *n* **1** grève *f*; **on ~** en grève
2 (attack) attaque *f*
B *vt* (*prét, pp* **struck**) **1** (hit) frapper ‹*person, vessel*›; heurter ‹*rock, tree, pedestrian*›; **he struck his head on the table** il s'est cogné la tête contre la table; **to be struck by lightning** être frappé/-e par la foudre

S

2 (afflict) frapper ‹*area, people*›
3 ‹*idea, thought*› venir à l'esprit de ‹*person*›; ‹*resemblance*› frapper; **to ~ sb as odd** paraître étrange à qn
4 (fam) (find) tomber sur (fam) ‹*oil, gold*›
5 (achieve) conclure ‹*deal, bargain*›; **to ~ a balance** trouver le juste milieu (**between** entre)
6 frotter ‹*match*›
7 ‹*clock*› sonner
C *vi* (*prét, pp* **struck**) **1** (gen) frapper
2 ‹*workers*› faire (la) grève
■ **strike down** terrasser ‹*person*›
■ **strike off**: **A** ~ **[sth] off**, ~ **off [sth]** (delete) rayer
B ~ **[sb] off** radier ‹*doctor*›
C ~ **[sb/sth] off** sth rayer [qn/qch] de ‹*list*›
■ **strike out**: **A** ~ **out** (hit out) frapper; **to ~ out at** attaquer ‹*adversary*›; s'en prendre à ‹*critics*›
B ~ **[sth] out** rayer
■ **strike up**: ~ **up** ‹*orchestra*› commencer à jouer;
~ **up [sth] to ~ up a conversation with** engager la conversation avec; **to ~ up a friendship with** se lier d'amitié avec

strike-breaker *n* briseur/-euse *m/f* de grève

strike-breaking *n* retour *m* au travail

strike force *n* force *f* d'intervention

striker /'straɪkə(r)/ *n* **1** (person on strike) gréviste *mf*
2 (in football) attaquant/-e *m/f*

striking /'straɪkɪŋ/ *adj* ‹*person*› (good-looking) beau/belle *before n*; ‹*design, contrast*› frappant/-e

string /strɪŋ/ **A** *n* **1** (twine) ficelle *f*; **a piece of ~** un bout de ficelle
2 (on bow, racket) corde *f*; (on puppet) fil *m*
3 (series) **a ~ of** un défilé de ‹*visitors*›; une succession de ‹*successes, awards*›
4 (set) ~ **of pearls** collier *m* de perles
B strings *npl* (Mus) **the ~s** les cordes *fpl*
C *vt* (*prét, pp* **strung**) enfiler ‹*beads, pearls*› (**on** sur)
IDIOM **to pull ~s** faire jouer le piston (fam)
■ **string along**: **A** ~ **along** suivre
B ~ **sb along** mener qn en bateau (fam)
■ **string together** aligner ‹*words*›

string bean *n* haricot *m* à écosser

stringed instrument *n* instrument *m* à cordes

stringent /'strɪndʒənt/ *adj* rigoureux/-euse

strip /strɪp/ **A** *n* bande *f* (**of** de)
B *vt* (*p prés etc* **-pp-**) **1** déshabiller ‹*person*›; vider ‹*house, room*›; défaire ‹*bed*›; **to ~ sb of** dépouiller qn de ‹*belongings, rights*›
2 (remove paint from) décaper
3 (dismantle) démonter
C *vi* (*p prés etc* **-pp-**) se déshabiller

strip cartoon *n* bande *f* dessinée

stripe /straɪp/ *n* **1** (on fabric, wallpaper) rayure *f*
2 (on animal) (isolated) rayure *f*; (one of many) zébrure *f*

striped *adj* rayé/-e

strip lighting *n* éclairage *m* au néon *m*

stripper /'strɪpə(r)/ *n* strip-teaseur/-euse *m/f*

strive /straɪv/ *vi* (*prét* **strove**, *pp* **striven**) s'efforcer (**to do** de faire)

stroke /strəʊk/ **A** *n* **1** (gen) coup *m*; **at a single ~** d'un seul coup; **a ~ of luck** un coup de chance; **a ~ of genius** un trait de génie
2 (in swimming) mouvement *m* des bras; (particular style) nage *f*
3 (of pen) trait *m*; (of brush) touche *f*
4 (Med) congestion *f* cérébrale
B *vt* caresser

stroll /strəʊl/ **A** *n* promenade *f*, tour *m*
B *vi* se promener; (aimlessly) flâner

stroller /'strəʊlə(r)/ *n* (AmE) (pushchair) poussette *f*

⚷ **strong** /strɒŋ, (AmE) strɔːŋ/ *adj* **1** (powerful) ‹*arm, person, current, wind*› fort/-e; ‹*army, swimmer, country*› puissant/-e
2 ‹*heart, fabric, table*› solide; ‹*candidate, argument*› de poids
3 ‹*tea, medicine, glue*› fort/-e; ‹*coffee*› serré/-e
4 ‹*smell, taste*› fort/-e
5 ‹*desire, feeling*› profond/-e
6 ‹*chance, possibility*› fort/-e *before n*
IDIOMS **to be still going ~** ‹*person*› se porter toujours très bien; ‹*relationship*› aller toujours bien; **it's not my ~ point** ce n'est pas mon fort

strongbox *n* coffre-fort *m*

stronghold /'strɒŋhəʊld, (AmE) 'strɔːŋ-/ *n* forteresse *f*; (fig) fief *m*

⚷ **strongly** /'strɒŋlɪ, (AmE) 'strɔːŋlɪ/ *adv*
1 ‹*oppose, advise*› vivement; ‹*protest, deny*› énergiquement; ‹*suspect*› fortement; ‹*believe*› fermement; **I feel ~ about this** c'est quelque chose qui me tient à cœur
2 (solidly) solidement

strongroom *n* chambre *f* forte

strong-willed *adj* obstiné/-e

structural damage *n* dégâts *mpl* matériels

⚷ **structure** /'strʌktʃə(r)/ **A** *n* **1** (organization) structure *f*
2 (building) construction *f*
B *vt* structurer ‹*argument, essay, novel*›; organiser ‹*day, life*›

⚷ **struggle** /'strʌgl/ **A** *n* (gen) lutte *f*; (scuffle) rixe *f*
B *vi* **1** (put up a fight) se débattre (**to do** pour faire); (tussle, scuffle) se battre
2 (try hard) lutter (**to do** pour faire, **for** pour)

struggling /'strʌglɪŋ/ *adj* ‹*writer, artist*› qui essaie de percer

strum /strʌm/ *vt* (*p prés etc* **-mm-**) (carelessly) gratter ‹*guitar, tune*›; (gently) jouer doucement de ‹*guitar*›

⚷ mot clé

strung out /ˌstrʌŋˈaʊt/ *adj* **to be ~ on** être accro (fam) à ‹*drug*›; **to be ~** (from drugs) être en état de manque

strut /strʌt/ **A** *n* montant *m*
B *vi* (*p prés etc* **-tt-**) (*also* **~ about, ~ around**) se pavaner

stub /stʌb/ **A** *n* (of pencil) bout *m*; (of cheque, ticket) talon *m*; (of cigarette) mégot *m*
B *vt* (*p prés etc* **-bb-**) **to ~ one's toe** se cogner l'orteil
■ **stub out** écraser ‹*cigarette*›

stubble /ˈstʌbl/ *n* **1** (straw) chaume *m*
2 (beard) barbe *f* de plusieurs jours

stubborn /ˈstʌbən/ *adj* ‹*person, animal*› entêté/-e; ‹*behaviour*› obstiné/-e; ‹*refusal*› opiniâtre; ‹*stain*› rebelle

stuck /stʌk/ *adj* **1** (jammed, trapped) coincé/-e; **to get ~ in** rester coincé/-e dans ‹*lift*›; s'enliser dans ‹*mud*›
2 to be ~ for an answer ne pas savoir quoi répondre

stuck-up /ˌstʌkˈʌp/ *adj* (fam) bêcheur/-euse (fam)

stud /stʌd/ *n* **1** (on jacket) clou *m*; (on door) clou *m* à grosse tête; (on boot) crampon *m*
2 (stallion) étalon *m*; (horse farm) haras *m*
3 (earring) clou *m* d'oreille

student /ˈstjuːdnt, (AmE) ˈstuː-/ *n* (university) étudiant/-e *m/f*; (AmE) ((high) school) élève *mf*

student grant *n* bourse *f* d'études

student ID card *n* carte *f* d'étudiant

student nurse *n* élève *mf* infirmier/-ière

student teacher *n* enseignant/-e *m/f* stagiaire

student union *n* (building) maison *f* des étudiants

studio /ˈstjuːdɪəʊ, (AmE) ˈstuː-/ *n* (*pl* **~s**) (gen) studio *m*; (of painter) atelier *m*

studious /ˈstjuːdɪəs, (AmE) ˈstuː-/ *adj* studieux/-ieuse

study /ˈstʌdɪ/ **A** *n* **1** (work, research) étude *f* (**of, on** de)
2 (room) bureau *m*
B *npl* études *fpl*; **computer studies** informatique *f*; **social studies** sciences *fpl* humaines
C *adj* ‹*leave, group, visit*› d'étude; **~ trip** voyage *m* d'études
D *vt* étudier
E *vi* faire ses études

study aid *n* outil *m* pédagogique (destiné à l'élève)

stuff /stʌf/ **A** *n* (things) choses *fpl*, trucs *mpl* (fam); (personal belongings) affaires *fpl*; (rubbish, junk) bazar *m* (fam); (substance) truc *m* (fam)
B *vt* **1** rembourrer ‹*cushion*› (**with** de); bourrer ‹*suitcase, room*› (**with** de)
2 (shove) fourrer (fam) (**in, into** dans)
3 (Culin) farcir ‹*turkey, chicken*›
4 empailler ‹*dead animal, bird*›

stuffed *adj* ‹*turkey, chicken*› farci/-e; ‹*toy animal*› en peluche; ‹*bird, fox*› empaillé/-e

stuffing /ˈstʌfɪŋ/ *n* **1** (Culin) farce *f*
2 (of furniture, pillow) rembourrage *m*

stuffy /ˈstʌfɪ/ *adj* **1** (airless) étouffant/-e
2 (staid) guindé/-e

stumble /ˈstʌmbl/ *vi* **1** (trip) trébucher (**against** contre, **on, over** sur)
2 (in speech) hésiter
■ **stumble across** tomber par hasard sur ‹*rare find*›

stumbling block /ˈstʌmblɪŋblɒk/ *n* obstacle *m*

stump /stʌmp/ **A** *n* (of tree) souche *f*; (of candle, pencil, cigar) bout *m*; (of tooth) chicot *m*; (part of limb, tail) moignon *m*
B *vt* (fam) **to be ~ed by sth** être en peine d'expliquer qch; **I'm ~ed!** (in quiz) je sèche! (fam); (nonplussed) aucune idée!
■ **stump up** (BrE) (fam) débourser (**for** pour)

stun /stʌn/ *vt* (*p prés etc* **-nn-**) **1** (daze) assommer
2 (amaze) stupéfier

stunned /stʌnd/ *adj* **1** (dazed) assommé/-e
2 (amazed) ‹*person*› stupéfait/-e; ‹*silence*› figé/-e

stunning /ˈstʌnɪŋ/ *adj* (beautiful) sensationnel/-elle

stunt /stʌnt/ **A** *n* **1** (for attention) coup *m* organisé, truc *m* (fam)
2 (in film) cascade *f*
B *vt* empêcher ‹*development*›; nuire à ‹*plant growth*›

stunted /ˈstʌntɪd/ *adj* rabougri/-e

stuntman *n* cascadeur *m*

stupefying /ˈstjuːpɪfaɪɪŋ, (AmE) ˈstuː-/ *adj* stupéfiant/-e

stupendous /stjuːˈpendəs, (AmE) stuː-/ *adj* prodigieux/-ieuse

stupid /ˈstjuːpɪd, (AmE) ˈstuː-/ *adj* bête, stupide; **I've done something ~** j'ai fait une bêtise

stupidity /stjuːˈpɪdətɪ, (AmE) stuː-/ *n* bêtise *f*

stupor /ˈstjuːpə(r), (AmE) ˈstuː-/ *n* stupeur *f*; **in a drunken ~** hébété/-e par l'alcool

sturdy /ˈstɜːdɪ/ *adj* robuste, solide

stutter /ˈstʌtə(r)/ *vt, vi* bégayer

St Valentine's Day *n* la Saint-Valentin

sty /staɪ/ *n* **1** (for pigs) porcherie *f*
2 (*also* **stye**) orgelet *m*

style /staɪl/ **A** *n* **1** (manner) style *m*
2 (elegance) classe *f*; **to do things in ~** faire les choses en grand
3 (design) (of car, clothing) modèle *m*; (of house) type *m*
4 (fashion) mode *f*
B *vt* couper ‹*hair*›

styling /ˈstaɪlɪŋ/ **A** *n* **1** (design) conception *f*
2 (in hairdressing) coupe *f*
B *adj* ‹*gel, mousse, product*› coiffant/-e

stylish /ˈstaɪlɪʃ/ *adj* ‹*car, coat, person*› élégant/-e; ‹*resort, restaurant*› chic

stylist /ˈstaɪlɪst/ *n* **1** (hairdresser) coiffeur/-euse *m/f*

2 (designer) concepteur/-trice *m/f*
stylistic /staɪ'lɪstɪk/ *adj* stylistique
stylus /'staɪləs/ *n* (*pl* **-li** *ou* **-luses**) pointe *f* de lecture
suave /swɑːv/ *adj* ‹*person*› mielleux/-euse
subconscious /ˌsʌb'kɒnʃəs/ **A** *n* **the ~** le subconscient
B *adj* inconscient/-e
subcontinent /ˌsʌb'kɒntɪnənt/ *n* sous-continent *m*
subcontract /ˌsʌbkən'trækt/ *vt* sous-traiter (**out to** à)
subcontracting /ˌsʌbkən'træktɪŋ/ *n* sous-traitance *f*
subcontractor /ˌsʌbkən'træktə(r)/ *n* sous-traitant *m*
subdivide /ˌsʌbdɪ'vaɪd/ *vt* subdiviser
subdue /səb'djuː, (AmE) -'duː/ *vt* soumettre ‹*people, nation*›
subdued /səb'djuːd, (AmE) -'duːd/ *adj* ‹*person*› silencieux/-ieuse; ‹*excitement*› contenu/-e; ‹*lighting*› tamisé/-e
subheading /'sʌbhedɪŋ/ *n* sous-titre *m*
🔑 **subject A** /'sʌbdʒɪkt/ *n* **1** (topic) sujet *m*; **to change the ~** parler d'autre chose
2 (at school, college) matière *f*; (for research, study) sujet *m*
3 to be the ~ of an inquiry faire l'objet d'une enquête
4 (citizen) sujet/-ette *m/f*
B /'sʌbdʒɪkt/ *adj* **1** (liable) **to be ~ to** être sujet/-ette à ‹*flooding, fits*›; être passible de ‹*tax*›
2 (dependent) **to be ~ to** dépendre de ‹*approval*›; être soumis/-e à ‹*law*›
C /səb'dʒekt/ *vt* **to ~ sb to sth** faire subir qch à qn
subject heading *n* sujet *m*
subjective /səb'dʒektɪv/ *adj* subjectif/-ive
subjugate /'sʌbdʒʊgeɪt/ *vt* subjuguer ‹*country, people*›
subjunctive /səb'dʒʌŋktɪv/ *n* subjonctif *m*
sublet /'sʌblet/ /ˌsʌb'let/ *vt, vi* (*p prés* **-tt-**, *prét, pp* **-let**) sous-louer
sublime /sə'blaɪm/ *adj* ‹*beauty, genius*› sublime; ‹*indifference*› suprême
subliminal /səb'lɪmɪnl/ *adj* subliminal/-e
sub-machine gun /ˌsʌbmə'ʃiːn/ *n* mitraillette *f*
submarine /ˌsʌbmə'riːn, (AmE) 'sʌb-/ *n* sous-marin *m*
submerge /səb'mɜːdʒ/ *vt* ‹*sea, flood*› submerger; ‹*person*› immerger (**in** dans)
🔑 **submission** /səb'mɪʃn/ *n* soumission *f* (**to** à)
submissive /səb'mɪsɪv/ *adj* ‹*person*› soumis/-e; ‹*behaviour*› docile
🔑 **submit** /səb'mɪt/ **A** *vt* (*p prés etc* **-tt-**) soumettre ‹*report, plan, script*› (**to** à); présenter ‹*bill, application*›
B *vi* (*p prés etc* **-tt-**) se soumettre; **to ~ to** subir ‹*indignity, injustice*›; céder à ‹*will, demand*›
subnormal /sʌb'nɔːml/ *adj* ‹*person*› arriéré/-e
subordinate /sə'bɔːdɪnət, (AmE) -dənət/ *n, adj* subalterne *mf*
subpoena /sə'piːnə/ *vt* (*3e pers sg prés* **~s**, *prét, pp* **~ed**) assigner [qn] à comparaître
sub-prime mortgages *npl* crédits *mpl* immobiliers à risque
subscribe /səb'skraɪb/ *vi* **1 to ~ to** partager ‹*view, values*›
2 to ~ to être abonné/-e à ‹*magazine*›
subscriber /səb'skraɪbə(r)/ *n* abonné/-e *m/f* (**to** de)
subscription /səb'skrɪpʃn/ *n* abonnement *m* (**to** à)
subsequent /'sʌbsɪkwənt/ *adj* (in past) ultérieur/-e; (in future) à venir
subsequently /'sʌbsɪkwəntlɪ/ *adv* par la suite
subservient /səb'sɜːvɪənt/ *adj* servile (**to** envers)
subside /səb'saɪd/ *vi* **1** ‹*storm, wind, noise*› s'apaiser; ‹*emotion*› se calmer; ‹*fever, excitement*› retomber
2 ‹*building, land*› s'affaisser
subsidiary /səb'sɪdɪərɪ, (AmE) -dɪerɪ/ **A** *n* (*also* **~ company**) filiale *f*
B *adj* secondaire (**to** par rapport à)
subsidize /'sʌbsɪdaɪz/ *vt* subventionner
subsidy /'sʌbsɪdɪ/ *n* subvention *f* (**to, for** à)
subsist /səb'sɪst/ *vi* subsister
subsistence /səb'sɪstəns/ *n* subsistance *f*
subsistence level *n* niveau *m* minimum pour vivre
substance /'sʌbstəns/ *n* **1** (gen) substance *f*
2 (of argument, talks) essentiel *m*; (of claim, accusation) fondement *m*
substance abuse *n* abus *m* de substances toxiques
substandard /ˌsʌb'stændəd/ *adj* de qualité inférieure
🔑 **substantial** /səb'stænʃl/ *adj* **1** (considerable) considérable; ‹*sum, quantity*› important/-e; ‹*meal*› substantiel/-ielle
2 (solid) ‹*proof, lock*› solide
substantiate /səb'stænʃɪeɪt/ *vt* justifier ‹*allegation*›; appuyer [qch] par des preuves ‹*statement*›
substitute /'sʌbstɪtjuːt, (AmE) -tuːt/ **A** *n*
1 (person) remplaçant/-e *m/f*
2 (product, substance) succédané *m*
B *vt* substituer (**for** à)
subtitle /'sʌbtaɪtl/ *n* sous-titre *m*
subtitled *adj* sous-titré/-e
subtle /'sʌtl/ *adj* (gen) subtil/-e; ‹*change*› imperceptible; ‹*hint*› voilé/-e; ‹*lighting*› tamisé/-e

🔑 mot clé

subtlety /'sʌtltɪ/ *n* subtilité *f*
subtotal /'sʌbtəʊtl/ *n* sous-total *m*
subtract /səb'trækt/ *vt* soustraire (**from** de)
subtraction /səb'trækʃn/ *n* soustraction *f*
suburb /'sʌbɜːb/ **A** *n* banlieue *f*; **inner ~** faubourg *m*
B **suburbs** *npl* **the ~s** la banlieue
suburban /sə'bɜːbən/ *adj* ‹*street, shop, train*› de banlieue; (AmE) ‹*shopping mall*› à l'extérieur de la ville
suburbia /sə'bɜːbɪə/ *n* la banlieue *f*
subversive /səb'vɜːsɪv/ **A** *n* élément *m* subversif
B *adj* subversif/-ive
subway /'sʌbweɪ/ *n* **1** (BrE) (for pedestrians) passage *m* souterrain
2 (AmE) (underground railway) métro *m*
sub-zero /ˌsʌb'zɪərəʊ/ *adj* inférieur/-e à zéro
succeed /sək'siːd/ **A** *vt* succéder à ‹*person*›
B *vi* réussir; **to ~ in doing** réussir à faire
succeeding /sək'siːdɪŋ/ *adj* qui suit, suivant/-e
success /sək'ses/ *n* succès *m*, réussite *f*; **to be a ~** ‹*party*› être réussi/-e; ‹*film, person*› avoir du succès
successful /sək'sesfl/ *adj* ‹*attempt, operation*› réussi/-e; ‹*plan, campaign*› couronné/-e de succès; ‹*film, book, writer*› (profitable) à succès; (well regarded) apprécié/-e; ‹*businessman*› prospère; ‹*career*› brillant/-e; **to be ~** réussir (**in doing** à faire)
successfully /sək'sesfəlɪ/ *adv* avec succès
succession /sək'seʃn/ *n* **1** (sequence) série *f* (**of** de); **in ~** de suite; **in close ~** coup sur coup
2 (inheriting) succession *f* (**to** à)
successive /sək'sesɪv/ *adj* successif/-ive; ‹*day, week*› consécutif/-ive
successor /sək'sesə(r)/ *n* successeur *m*
success rate *n* taux *m* de réussite
success story *n* réussite *f*
succinct /sək'sɪŋkt/ *adj* succinct/-e
succulent /'sʌkjʊlənt/ *adj* succulent/-e
succumb /sə'kʌm/ *vi* succomber (**to** à)
such /sʌtʃ/ **A** *det* tel/telle; (similar) pareil/-elle; **~ a situation** une telle situation; **in ~ a situation** dans une situation pareille; **some ~ remark** quelque chose comme ça; **there's no ~ thing** ça n'existe pas; **you'll do no ~ thing!** il n'en est pas question!; **in ~ a way that** d'une telle façon que; **~ money as I have** le peu d'argent *or* tout l'argent que j'ai
B *adv* (with adjectives) si, tellement; (with nouns) tel/telle; **in ~ a persuasive way** d'une façon si convaincante; **~ a nice boy!** un garçon si gentil!; **~ good quality** une telle qualité; **I hadn't seen ~ a good film for years** je n'avais pas vu un aussi bon film depuis des années; **~ a lot of problems** tant de problèmes; **there were (ever (**fam**)) ~ a lot of people** il y avait beaucoup de monde
C **such as** *phr* comme, tel/telle que; **a house ~ as this** une maison comme celle-ci; **a person ~ as her** une personne comme elle; **have you ~ a thing as a screwdriver?** auriez-vous un tournevis par hasard?
such and such *det* tel/telle; **on ~ a topic** sur tel ou tel sujet
suck /sʌk/ **A** *vt* sucer ‹*thumb, fruit, lollipop, pencil*›; (drink in) aspirer ‹*liquid, air*›
B *vi* **to ~ at** sucer; **to ~ on** tirer sur ‹*pipe*›
■ **suck up**: **A** (fam) **~ up** faire de la lèche (fam); **to ~ up to sb** cirer les pompes à qn (fam)
B **~ [sth] up** pomper ‹*liquid*›; aspirer ‹*dirt*›
sucker /'sʌkə(r)/ *n* **1** (fam) (dupe) bonne poire *f* (fam)
2 (on plant) surgeon *m*
3 (pad) ventouse *f*
suction /'sʌkʃn/ *n* succion *f*
suction pad *n* ventouse *f*
sudden /'sʌdn/ *adj* (gen) soudain/-e; ‹*movement*› brusque; **all of a ~** tout à coup
sudden death play-off *n: penalties pour départager deux équipes*
suddenly /'sʌdnlɪ/ *adv* ‹*die, grow pale*› subitement; ‹*happen*› tout à coup
sudoku /suːˌdəʊkuː/ *n* sudoku *m*
suds /sʌdz/ *npl* (*also* **soap ~**) (foam) mousse *f* (de savon); (soapy water) eau *f* savonneuse
sue /suː, sjuː/ **A** *vt* intenter un procès à; **to ~ sb for divorce** demander le divorce à qn; **to ~ sb for damages** réclamer à qn des dommages-intérêts
B *vi* intenter un procès
suede /sweɪd/ **A** *n* daim *m*
B *adj* ‹*shoe, glove*› en daim
suffer /'sʌfə(r)/ **A** *vt* subir ‹*loss, consequences, defeat*›; **to ~ a heart attack** avoir une crise cardiaque
B *vi* **1** souffrir; **to ~ from** souffrir de ‹*rheumatism, heat*›; avoir ‹*headache, high blood pressure, cold*›; **to ~ from depression** être dépressif/-ive
2 (do badly) ‹*company, profits*› souffrir; ‹*health, quality, work*› s'en ressentir
sufferer /'sʌfərə(r)/ *n* victime *f*; **leukaemia ~s** les leucémiques *mpl*
suffering /'sʌfərɪŋ/ **A** *n* souffrances *fpl* (**of** de)
B *adj* souffrant/-e
sufficient /sə'fɪʃnt/ *adj* suffisamment de, assez de; **to be ~** suffire
sufficiently /sə'fɪʃntlɪ/ *adv* suffisamment, assez
suffocate /'sʌfəkeɪt/ **A** *vt* ‹*smoke, fumes*› asphyxier; ‹*person, anger*› étouffer
B *vi* **1** (by smoke, fumes) être asphyxié/-e; (by pillow) être étouffé/-e
2 (fig) suffoquer

suffocating /'sʌfəkeɪtɪŋ/ *adj* ‹*smoke*› asphyxiant/-e; ‹*atmosphere, heat*› étouffant/-e

suffrage /'sʌfrɪdʒ/ *n* (right) droit *m* de vote; (system) suffrage *m*

sugar /'ʃʊgə(r)/ *n* sucre *m*; **brown ~** sucre roux

sugar beet *n* betterave *f* à sucre

sugar cane *n* canne *f* à sucre

sugar-free *adj* sans sucre

sugar lump *n* morceau *m* de sucre

🔑 **suggest** /sə'dʒest, (AmE) səg'dʒ-/ *vt* suggérer; **they ~ed that I (should) leave** ils m'ont suggéré de partir

🔑 **suggestion** /sə'dʒestʃn, (AmE) səg'dʒ-/ *n* **1** (gen) suggestion *f*; **at sb's ~** sur le conseil de qn
2 (hint) soupçon *m* (**of** de); (of smile) pointe *f*

suggestive /sə'dʒestɪv, (AmE) səg'dʒ-/ *adj* suggestif/-ive

suicidal /ˌsu:ɪ'saɪdl, ˌsju:-/ *adj* suicidaire

🔑 **suicide** /'su:ɪsaɪd, 'sju:-/ *n* (action) suicide *m*; (person) suicidé/-e *m/f*; **to commit ~** se suicider

suicide attack *n* attentat *m* suicide

🔑 **suit** /su:t, sju:t/ **A** *n* **1** (man's) costume *m*; (woman's) tailleur *m*; **a ~ of armour** une armure (complète)
2 (lawsuit) procès *m*
3 (in cards) couleur *f*
B *vt* **1** ‹*colour, outfit*› aller à ‹*person*›
2 ‹*date, climate, arrangement*› convenir à
C *vi* convenir
D *v refl* **to ~ oneself** faire comme on veut

suitable /'su:təbl, 'sju:-/ *adj* ‹*accommodation, clothing, employment*› adéquat/-e; ‹*candidate*› apte; ‹*gift, gesture*› approprié/-e; ‹*moment*› opportun/-e; **to be ~ for** convenir à ‹*person*›; bien se prêter à ‹*climate, activity, occasion*›

suitably /'su:təblɪ, 'sju:-/ *adv* convenablement

suitcase /'su:tkeɪs, 'sju:-/ *n* valise *f*

suite /swi:t/ *n* **1** (gen) suite *f*
2 (furniture) mobilier *m*

suited /'su:tɪd, 'sju:-/ *adj* **to be ~ to** ‹*place, clothes*› être commode pour; ‹*game, style*› convenir à; ‹*person*› être fait/-e pour

sulk /sʌlk/ *vi* bouder (**about, over** à cause de)

sulky /'sʌlkɪ/ *adj* boudeur/-euse; **to look ~** faire la tête

sullen /'sʌlən/ *adj* ‹*person, expression*› renfrogné/-e; ‹*day, sky, mood*› maussade

sulphur (BrE), **sulfur** (AmE) /'sʌlfə(r)/ *n* soufre *m*

sulphuric acid *n* acide *m* sulfurique

sultana /sʌl'tɑ:nə, (AmE) -'tænə/ *n* (Culin) raisin *m* de Smyrne

sultry /'sʌltrɪ/ *adj* **1** ‹*day*› étouffant/-e; ‹*weather*› lourd/-e
2 ‹*look, smile*› sensuel/-elle

sum /sʌm/ *n* **1** (of money) somme *f*
2 (calculation) calcul *m*

■ **sum up**: **A** **~ up** récapituler
B **~ up [sth]** résumer

summarize /'sʌməraɪz/ *vt* résumer ‹*book, problem*›; récapituler ‹*argument, speech*›

summary /'sʌmərɪ/ *n* résumé *m*

🔑 **summer** /'sʌmə(r)/ **A** *n* été *m*; **in ~** en été
B *adj* ‹*evening, resort, clothes*› d'été

summer camp *n* (AmE) colonie *f* de vacances

summer holiday (BrE), **summer vacation** (AmE) *n* (gen) vacances *fpl* (d'été); (Sch, Univ) grandes vacances *fpl*

summer house *n* pavillon *m* (de jardin)

summer school *n* université *f* d'été

summertime /'sʌmətaɪm/ *n* été *m*

summit /'sʌmɪt/ *n* sommet *m*

summon /'sʌmən/ *vt* **1** (gen) faire venir
2 (Law) citer

■ **summon up** rassembler ‹*energy, strength*› (**to do** pour faire)

summons /'sʌmənz/ **A** *n* **1** (Law) citation *f*
2 (gen) injonction *f* (**from** de, **to** à)
B *vt* citer (**to** à, **to do** à faire, **for** pour)

sumptuous /'sʌmptʃʊəs/ *adj* somptueux/-euse

sum total *n* (of money) montant *m* total; (of achievements) ensemble *m*

🔑 **sun** /sʌn/ *n* soleil *m*; **in the ~** au soleil

sunbathe /'sʌnbeɪð/ *vi* se faire bronzer

sunbed *n* (lounger) chaise *f* longue; (with sunlamp) lit *m* solaire

sunblock *n* crème *f* écran total

sunburn *n* coup *m* de soleil

sunburned, **sunburnt** /'sʌnbɜ:nt/ *adj* (burnt) brûlé/-e par le soleil; (tanned) (BrE) bronzé/-e; **to get ~** attraper un coup de soleil

🔑 **Sunday** /'sʌndeɪ, -dɪ/ *n* dimanche *m*

Sunday best *n* **(dressed) in one's ~** endimanché/-e

Sunday trading *n* commerce *m* dominical

sundial *n* cadran *m* solaire

sundress *n* robe *f* bain de soleil

sundries *npl* articles *mpl* divers

sundry /'sʌndrɪ/ *adj* divers/-e; **(to) all and ~** (à) tout le monde

sunflower /'sʌnflaʊə(r)/ *n* tournesol *m*

sunglasses *npl* lunettes *fpl* de soleil

sun hat *n* chapeau *m* de soleil

sunken /'sʌŋkən/ *adj* **1** ‹*treasure, wreck*› immergé/-e
2 ‹*cheek*› creux/creuse; ‹*eye*› cave
3 ‹*bath*› encastré/-e; ‹*garden*› en contrebas

sunlamp *n* lampe *f* à bronzer

sunlight /'sʌnlaɪt/ *n* lumière *f* du soleil

Sunni /'sʌnɪ/ *n* **1** (religion) sunnisme
2 (adherent) sunnite *mf*

🔑 mot clé

sunny /'sʌnɪ/ *adj* **1** ensoleillé/-e; **it's going to be ~** il va faire (du) soleil
2 ‹*child, temperament*› enjoué/-e

sunrise *n* lever *m* du soleil

sunroof *n* toit *m* ouvrant

sunset /'sʌnset/ *n* coucher *m* du soleil

sunshade *n* parasol *m*

sun shield *n* pare-soleil *m inv*

sunshine /'sʌnʃaɪn/ *n* soleil *m*

sunstroke /'sʌnstrəʊk/ *n* insolation *f*

suntan /'sʌntæn/ *n* bronzage *m*; **to get a ~** bronzer

suntan lotion *n* lotion *f* solaire

suntanned *adj* bronzé/-e

suntan oil *n* huile *f* solaire

super /'su:pə(r), 'sju:-/ *adj, excl* (fam) formidable

superb /su:'pɜ:b, sju:-/ *adj* superbe

supercilious /ˌsu:pə'sɪlɪəs, ˌsju:-/ *adj* dédaigneux/-euse

superficial /ˌsu:pə'fɪʃl, ˌsju:-/ *adj* superficiel/-ielle

superfluous /su:'pɜ:flʊəs, sju:-/ *adj* superflu/-e

superimpose /ˌsu:pərɪm'pəʊz, ˌsju:-/ *vt* superposer (**on** à)

superintendent /ˌsu:pərɪn'tendənt, ˌsju:-/ *n*
1 (supervisor) responsable *mf*
2 (*also* **police ~**) ≈ commissaire *m* de police
3 (AmE) (for apartments) concierge *mf*
4 (*also* **school ~**) (AmE) inspecteur/-trice *m/f*

superior /su:'pɪərɪə(r), sju:-, sʊ-/ **A** *n* supérieur/-e *m/f*
B *adj* **1** supérieur/-e (**to** à, **in** en); ‹*product*› de qualité supérieure
2 (condescending) condescendant/-e

superiority /su:ˌpɪərɪ'ɒrətɪ, sju:-, (AmE) -'ɔ:r-/ *n* supériorité *f*

superlative /su:'pɜ:lətɪv, sju:-/ **A** *n* superlatif *m*
B *adj* ‹*performance, service*› superbe

superman /'su:pəmæn, 'sju:-/ *n* (*pl* **-men**) surhomme *m*

supermarket /'su:pəmɑ:kɪt, 'sju:-/ *n* supermarché *m*

supermodel /'su:pəmɒdl, 'sju:-/ *n* top model *m*

supernatural /ˌsu:pə'nætʃrəl, ˌsju:-/ **A** *n* surnaturel *m*
B *adj* surnaturel/-elle

superpower /'su:pəpaʊə(r), 'sju:-/ *n* superpuissance *f*

supersede /ˌsu:pə'si:d, ˌsju:-/ *vt* remplacer

supersonic /ˌsu:pə'sɒnɪk, ˌsju:-/ *adj* supersonique

superstar /'su:pəstɑ:(r), 'sju:-/ *n* superstar *f*

superstition /ˌsu:pə'stɪʃn, ˌsju:-/ *n* superstition *f*

superstitious /ˌsu:pə'stɪʃəs, ˌsju:-/ *adj* superstitieux/-ieuse

superstore /'su:pəstɔ:(r), 'sju:-/ *n* (large supermarket) hypermarché *m*; (specialist shop) grande surface *f*

supervise /'su:pəvaɪz, 'sju:-/ *vt* superviser ‹*activity, staff*›; surveiller ‹*child, patient*›

supervision /ˌsu:pə'vɪʒn, ˌsju:-/ *n* **1** (of staff, work) supervision *f*
2 (of child, patient) surveillance *f*

supervisor /'su:pəvaɪzə(r), 'sju:-/ *n* **1** (for staff) responsable *m*
2 (BrE) (for thesis) directeur/-trice *m/f* de thèse
3 (AmE) (Sch) directeur/-trice *m/f* d'études

supper /'sʌpə(r)/ *n* (evening meal) dîner *m*; (late snack) collation *f* (du soir); (after a show) souper *m*; **the Last Supper** la Cène *f*

supple /'sʌpl/ *adj* souple

supplement **A** /'sʌplɪmənt/ *n* **1** (fee) supplément *m*
2 (to diet, income) complément *m* (**to** à)
3 (in newspaper) supplément *m*
B /'sʌplɪment/ *vt* compléter ‹*diet, resources, training*› (**with** de); augmenter ‹*income, staff*› (**with** de)

supplementary /ˌsʌplɪ'mentrɪ, (AmE) -terɪ/ *adj* supplémentaire

supplier /sə'plaɪə(r)/ *n* fournisseur *m* (**of, to** de)

supply /sə'plaɪ/ **A** *n* **1** (stock) réserves *fpl*; **in short ~** difficile à obtenir; **to get in a ~ of sth** s'approvisionner en qch
2 (source) (of fuel, gas, oxygen) alimentation *f*; (of food) approvisionnement *m*; (of equipment) fourniture *f*
B **supplies** *npl* **1** (equipment) réserves *fpl*; **food supplies** ravitaillement *m*
2 (for office) fournitures *fpl*
C *vt* (provide) fournir, approvisionner (**to, for** à); approvisionner ‹*factory, company*› (**with** en); (with fuel, food) ravitailler ‹*town, area*› (**with** en)

supply and demand *n* l'offre *f* et la demande

supply teacher *n* (BrE) suppléant/-e *m/f*

support /sə'pɔ:t/ **A** *n* **1** (moral, financial, political) soutien *m*, appui *m*; **to give sb/sth (one's) ~** apporter son soutien à qn/qch; **means of ~** (financial) moyens *mpl* de subsistance
2 (physical, for weight) support *m*
3 (person) soutien *m*; **to be a ~ to sb** aider qn
B *vt* **1** (morally, financially) soutenir ‹*person, cause, organization, currency*›; donner à ‹*charity*›
2 (physically) supporter ‹*weight*›; soutenir ‹*person*›
3 confirmer ‹*argument, theory*›
4 (maintain) ‹*breadwinner, farm*› subvenir aux besoins de

supporter /sə'pɔ:tə(r)/ *n* (gen) partisan *m*; (Sport) supporter *m*; (of political party)

S

sympathisant/-e *m/f*

support group *n* groupe *m* de soutien

supporting /sə'pɔːtɪŋ/ *adj* **∼ actor/actress** second rôle masculin/féminin; **the ∼ cast** les seconds rôles *mpl*

supportive /sə'pɔːtɪv/ *adj* ‹*person, organization*› d'un grand secours; ‹*role, network*› de soutien

🗝 **suppose** /sə'pəʊz/ *vt* **1** (assume) supposer (**that** que); **I ∼ so/not** je suppose que oui/non
2 (think) **to ∼ (that)** penser *or* croire que

supposed *adj* **to be ∼ to do/be** être censé/-e faire/être; **it's ∼ to be a good hotel** il paraît que c'est un bon hôtel

supposing /sə'pəʊzɪŋ/ *conj* **∼ (that) he says no?** et s'il dit non?; **∼ your income is X** supposons que ton revenu soit de X

suppress /sə'pres/ *vt* supprimer ‹*evidence, information*›; réprimer ‹*smile, urge, rebellion*›; étouffer ‹*scandal, yawn*›; dissimuler ‹*truth*›

supreme /suː'priːm, sjuː-/ *adj* suprême

surcharge /'sɜːtʃɑːdʒ/ *n* supplément *m*

🗝 **sure** /ʃɔː(r), (AmE) ʃʊər/ **A** *adj* (gen) sûr/-e (**about, of** de); **I'm not ∼ when he's coming** je ne sais pas trop quand il viendra; **we'll be there tomorrow for ∼!** on y sera demain sans faute!; **nobody knows for ∼** personne ne (le) sait au juste; **to make ∼ that** (ascertain) s'assurer que; (ensure) faire en sorte que; **he's ∼ to fail** il va sûrement échouer; **to be ∼ of oneself** être sûr/-e de soi
B *adv* **'∼!'** (of course) 'bien sûr!'; **∼ enough** effectivement

sure-fire *adj* (fam) garanti/-e

sure-footed *adj* agile

🗝 **surely** /'ʃɔːlɪ, (AmE) 'ʃʊərlɪ/ *adv* sûrement, certainement

surf /sɜːf/ **A** *n* (waves) vagues *fpl* (déferlantes); (foam) écume *f*
B *vt* **to ∼ the Internet** naviguer *or* surfer sur Internet
C *vi* **1** (Sport) faire du surf
2 (Comput) naviguer *or* surfer sur Internet

🗝 **surface** /'sɜːfɪs/ **A** *n* **1** surface *f*; **on the ∼** (of liquid) à la surface; (of solid) sur la surface
2 (of solid, cube) côté *m*
3 (worktop) plan *m* de travail
B *vi* **1** ‹*person, object*› remonter à la surface; ‹*submarine*› faire surface
2 ‹*problem*› se manifester

surface area *n* superficie *f*

surfboard *n* planche *f* de surf

surfer *n* **1** (on water) surfeur/-euse *m/f*
2 (Comput) internaute *mf*

surfing /'sɜːfɪŋ/ *n* surf *m*

surge /sɜːdʒ/ **A** *n* **1** (of water, blood, energy) montée *f* (**of** de); (of anger, desire) accès *m* (**of** de)
2 (in prices, unemployment) hausse *f* (**in** de); (in demand) accroissement *m* (**in** de)
B *vi* **1** ‹*water, waves*› déferler; ‹*blood, energy, emotion*› monter; **to ∼ forward** ‹*crowd*› s'élancer en avant
2 ‹*prices, demand*› monter en flèche

surgeon /'sɜːdʒən/ *n* chirurgien *m*

🗝 **surgery** /'sɜːdʒərɪ/ *n* **1** (operation) chirurgie *f*; **to have ∼** se faire opérer
2 (BrE) (Med) (premises) cabinet *m*

surgical /'sɜːdʒɪkl/ *adj* ‹*instrument*› chirurgical/-e; ‹*boot, stocking*› orthopédique

surgical spirit *n* alcool *m* (à 90 degrés)

surly /'sɜːlɪ/ *adj* revêche

surname /'sɜːneɪm/ *n* nom *m* de famille

surpass /sə'pɑːs, (AmE) -pæs/ **A** *vt* surpasser (**in** en); dépasser ‹*expectations*›
B *v refl* **to ∼ oneself** se surpasser

surplus /'sɜːpləs/ **A** *n* (*pl* **∼es**) surplus *m*; (in business) excédent *m*
B *adj* (gen) en trop; (in business) excédentaire

🗝 **surprise** /sə'praɪz/ **A** *n* surprise *f*; **to take sb by ∼** (gen) prendre qn au dépourvu; (Mil) surprendre qn
B *vt* **1** surprendre, étonner; **it ∼d them that no one came** ils ont été surpris que personne ne vienne
2 surprendre ‹*intruder*›; attaquer [qch] par surprise ‹*garrison*›

surprised /sə'praɪzd/ *adj* étonné/-e; **I'm not ∼** ça ne m'étonne pas

surprising /sə'praɪzɪŋ/ *adj* étonnant/-e, surprenant/-e

surprisingly /sə'praɪzɪŋlɪ/ *adv* ‹*well, quickly*› étonnamment; **∼ frank** d'une franchise étonnante

surreal /sə'rɪəl/ *adj* surréaliste

surrealist /sə'rɪəlɪst/ *n, adj* surréaliste *mf*

surrender /sə'rendə(r)/ **A** *n* **1** (of army) capitulation *f* (**to** devant); (of soldier, town) reddition *f* (**to** à)
2 (of territory, rights) abandon *m* (**to** à); (of weapons, document) remise *f* (**to** à)
B *vt* **1** livrer ‹*town*› (**to** à); céder ‹*weapons*› (**to** à)
2 racheter ‹*insurance policy*›; rendre ‹*passport*› (**to** à)
C *vi* ‹*army, soldier*› se rendre (**to** à); ‹*country*› capituler (**to** devant)

surrogate /'sʌrəgeɪt/ **A** *n* substitut *m* (**for** de)
B *adj* de substitution

surrogate mother *n* mère *f* porteuse

🗝 **surround** /sə'raʊnd/ *vt* (gen) entourer; ‹*police*› encercler ‹*building*›; cerner ‹*person*›

surrounding /sə'raʊndɪŋ/ *adj* environnant/-e; **the ∼ area** les environs *mpl*

🗝 mot clé

S

surroundings /sə'raʊndɪŋz/ *npl* cadre *m*; (of town) environs *mpl*; **natural ~** milieu *m* naturel

surveillance /sɜː'veɪləns/ *n* surveillance *f*

survey **A** /'sɜːveɪ/ *n* **1** (of trends, prices) enquête *f* (**of** sur); (by questioning people) sondage *m*; (study) étude *f* (**of** de)
2 (BrE) (of house) expertise *f* (**on** de)
3 (of land) étude *f* topographique; (map) levé *m* topographique
B /sə'veɪ/ *vt* **1** faire une étude de ‹*market, trends*›
2 (BrE) faire une expertise de ‹*house*›
3 faire l'étude topographique de ‹*area*›
4 contempler ‹*scene, landscape*›

surveyor /sə'veɪə(r)/ *n* **1** (BrE) (in housebuying) expert *m* (en immobilier)
2 (for map-making) topographe *mf*

survival /sə'vaɪvl/ *n* (of person, animal) survie *f* (**of** de); (of custom, belief) survivance *f* (**of** de)

survive /sə'vaɪv/ **A** *vt* **1** survivre à ‹*winter, heart attack*›; réchapper de ‹*accident*›; surmonter ‹*crisis*›
2 survivre à ‹*person*›
B *vi* survivre; **to ~ on sth** vivre de qch

surviving /sə'vaɪvɪŋ/ *adj* survivant/-e

survivor /sə'vaɪvə(r)/ *n* **1** (of accident, attack) rescapé/-e *m/f*
2 (Law) survivant/-e *m/f*

susceptible /sə'septəbl/ *adj* sensible (**to** à)

suspect **A** /'sʌspekt/ *n* suspect/-e *m/f*
B /'sʌspekt/ *adj* suspect/-e
C /sə'spekt/ *vt* **1** (believe) soupçonner ‹*murder, plot*›; **to ~ that** penser que
2 (doubt) douter de ‹*truth, motives*›
3 (have under suspicion) soupçonner ‹*person*›

suspend /sə'spend/ *vt* **1** (gen) suspendre
2 exclure [qn] temporairement ‹*pupil*› (**from** de)

suspended sentence *n* condamnation *f* avec sursis

suspender belt *n* (BrE) porte-jarretelles *m inv*

suspenders /sə'spendəz/ *npl* **1** (BrE) (for stockings) jarretelles *fpl*
2 (AmE) (braces) bretelles *fpl*

suspense /sə'spens/ *n* (in film, novel) suspense *m*; **to leave sb in ~** laisser qn dans l'expectative

suspension /sə'spenʃn/ *n* **1** (gen), (Aut) suspension *f*
2 (of pupil) exclusion *f* temporaire

suspicion /sə'spɪʃn/ *n* méfiance *f* (**of** de); **to arouse ~** éveiller des soupçons; **to have ~s about sb/sth** avoir des doutes *mpl* sur qn/qch

suspicious /sə'spɪʃəs/ *adj* **1** (wary) méfiant/-e; **to be ~ of sth** se méfier de qch
2 ‹*person, object*› suspect/-e; ‹*behaviour, activity*› louche

sustain /sə'steɪn/ *vt* **1** (maintain) maintenir ‹*interest, success*›
2 (Mus) soutenir ‹*note*›
3 (support) soutenir; (physically) donner des forces à; **to ~ life** rendre la vie possible
4 recevoir ‹*injury, burn*›; éprouver ‹*loss*›

sustainable /səs'teɪnəbl/ *adj* ‹*development, forestry*› durable; ‹*resource*› renouvelable; ‹*growth*› viable

sustenance /'sʌstɪnəns/ *n* nourriture *f*

swab /swɒb/ *n* (Med) tampon *m*

swagger /'swægə(r)/ *vi* **1** (walk) se pavaner
2 (boast) fanfaronner

swallow /'swɒləʊ/ **A** *n* **1** (bird) hirondelle *f*
2 (gulp) gorgée *f*
B *vt* **1** (eat) avaler
2 ravaler ‹*pride*›
3 (fam) (believe) avaler (fam)
C *vi* avaler; (nervously) avaler sa salive

swamp /swɒmp/ **A** *n* marais *m*, marécage *m*
B *vt* inonder

swan /swɒn/ *n* cygne *m*

swap /swɒp/ (fam) **A** *n* échange *m*
B *vt* (*p prés etc* **-pp-**) échanger; **to ~ sth for sth** échanger qch contre qch; **to ~ places** changer de place

swarm /swɔːm/ **A** *n* (of bees) essaim *m*; (of flies) nuée *f*
B *vi* ‹*bees*› essaimer; **to be ~ing with** grouiller de ‹*people, maggots*›

swarthy /'swɔːðɪ/ *adj* basané/-e

swastika /'swɒstɪkə/ *n* croix *f* gammée, svastika *m*

swat /swɒt/ *vt* (*p prés etc* **-tt-**) écraser ‹*fly, wasp*› (**with** avec)

sway /sweɪ/ **A** *n* **to hold ~** avoir une grande influence; **to hold ~ over** dominer
B *vt* **1** (influence) influencer
2 (rock) osciller
C *vi* ‹*tree, bridge*› osciller; ‹*person*› chanceler; (to music) se balancer

swear /sweə(r)/ **A** *vt* (*prét* **swore**, *pp* **sworn**) jurer (**to do** de faire); **to ~ sb to secrecy** faire jurer le secret à qn
B *vi* (*prét* **swore**, *pp* **sworn**) **1** (curse) jurer
2 (attest) **to ~ to having done** jurer avoir fait
▪ **swear by** (fam): **~ by [sth/sb]** ne jurer que par ‹*remedy, expert*›
▪ **swear in**: **~ in [sb]**, **~ [sb] in** faire prêter serment à

swearing /'sweərɪŋ/ *n* jurons *mpl*

swear word *n* juron *m*, gros mot *m*

sweat /swet/ **A** *n* sueur *f*; **to break out into a ~** se mettre à suer; **to be in a cold ~ about sth** avoir des sueurs froides à l'idée de qch
B **sweats** *npl* (AmE) survêtement *m*
C *vi* ‹*person, horse*› transpirer, suer; ‹*hands, feet, cheese*› transpirer

sweatband *n* bandeau *m*

sweater /'swetə(r)/ *n* pull *m*

S

sweat pants *npl* (AmE) pantalon *m* de survêtement

sweatshirt *n* sweatshirt *m*

sweatshop *n* atelier *m* où on exploite le personnel

sweaty /ˈswetɪ/ *adj* ‹*person*› en sueur; ‹*hand, palm*› moite

swede /swi:d/ *n* (BrE) rutabaga *m*

Swede /swi:d/ *n* Suédois/-e *m/f*

Sweden /ˈswi:dn/ *pr n* Suède *f*

Swedish /ˈswi:dɪʃ/ **A** *n* (language) suédois *m*
B *adj* suédois/-e

sweep /swi:p/ **A** *n* **1 to give sth a ~** donner un coup de balai à qch
2 (movement) **with a ~ of his arm** d'un grand geste du bras
3 (of land, woods) étendue *f*
4 (*also* **chimney ~**) ramoneur *m*
B *vt* (*prét, pp* **swept**) **1** balayer ‹*floor, path*›; ramoner ‹*chimney*›
2 (push) **to ~ sth off the table** faire tomber qch de la table (d'un grand geste de la main); **to ~ sb off his/her feet** (fig) faire perdre la tête à qn
3 ‹*beam, searchlight*› balayer
C *vi* (*prét, pp* **swept**) **1** (clean) balayer
2 to ~ in/out (majestically) entrer/sortir majestueusement
■ **sweep aside** écarter ‹*person, objection*›
■ **sweep up** balayer

sweeping /ˈswi:pɪŋ/ *adj* **1** ‹*change, review*› radical/-e
2 ~ generalization généralisation *f* à l'emporte-pièce

⚷ **sweet** /swi:t/ **A** *n* (BrE) **1** (candy) bonbon *m*
2 (dessert) dessert *m*
B *adj* **1** (gen) doux/douce; ‹*food, tea, taste*› sucré/-e; **to have a ~ tooth** aimer les sucreries
2 (kind) ‹*person*› gentil/-ille
3 (cute) ‹*baby, cottage*› mignon/-onne
C *adv* **to taste ~** avoir un goût sucré; **to smell ~** sentir bon

sweet-and-sour *adj* aigre-doux/-douce

sweetcorn *n* maïs *m*

sweeten /ˈswi:tn/ *vt* **1** (Culin) sucrer (**with** avec)
2 rendre [qch] plus tentant ‹*offer*›
■ **sweeten up** amadouer ‹*person*›

sweetener /ˈswi:tnə(r)/ *n* **1** (in food) édulcorant *m*
2 (fam) (bribe) incitation *f*; (illegal) pot-de-vin *m*

sweetheart /ˈswi:thɑ:t/ *n* (boyfriend) petit ami *m*; (girlfriend) petite amie *f*

sweetly /ˈswi:tlɪ/ *adv* ‹*say, smile*› gentiment

sweet potato *n* patate *f* douce

sweet-talk /ˈswi:ttɔ:k/ *vt* (fam) baratiner (fam)

swell /swel/ **A** *n* (of waves, sea) houle *f*
B *vt* (*prét* **swelled**, *pp* **swollen** *ou* **swelled**) gonfler ‹*crowd, funds*›; grossir ‹*river*›
C *vi* (*prét* **swelled**, *pp* **swollen** *ou* **swelled**) ‹*balloon, tyre, stomach*› se gonfler; ‹*wood*› gonfler; ‹*ankle, gland*› enfler; ‹*river*› grossir; ‹*crowd*› s'accroître

swelling /ˈswelɪŋ/ *n* (on limb, skin) enflure *f*; (on head) bosse *f*

sweltering /ˈsweltərɪŋ/ *adj* (fam) torride

swerve /swɜ:v/ *vi* faire un écart; **to ~ off the road** sortir de la route

swift /swɪft/ **A** *n* martinet *m*
B *adj* rapide, prompt/-e

swill /swɪl/ *n* pâtée *f* (des porcs)

swim /swɪm/ **A** *n* baignade *f*; **to go for a ~** (in sea, river) aller se baigner; (in pool) aller à la piscine
B *vt* (*p prés* **-mm-**, *prét* **swam**, *pp* **swum**) nager ‹*distance, stroke*›
C *vi* (*p prés* **-mm-**, *prét* **swam**, *pp* **swum**) **1** nager; **to ~ across sth** traverser qch à la nage
2 to be ~ming in baigner dans ‹*sauce, oil*›
3 ‹*scene, room*› tourner

swimmer /ˈswɪmə(r)/ *n* nageur/-euse *m/f*

swimming /ˈswɪmɪŋ/ *n* natation *f*

swimming costume *n* (BrE) maillot *m* de bain

swimming pool *n* piscine *f*

swimming trunks *npl* slip *m* de bain

swimsuit *n* maillot *m* de bain

swindle /ˈswɪndl/ **A** *n* escroquerie *f*
B *vt* escroquer; **to ~ sb out of sth** escroquer qch à qn

swindler /ˈswɪndlə(r)/ *n* escroc *m*

swine flu /ˈswaɪn flu:/ *n* grippe *f* A

swing /swɪŋ/ **A** *n* **1** (of pendulum, needle) oscillation *f*; (of hips, body) balancement *m*
2 (in public opinion) revirement *m* (**in** de); (in prices, economy) fluctuation *f* (**in** de); (in mood) saute *f* (**in** de)
3 (in playground) balançoire *f*
B *vt* (*prét, pp* **swung**) (to and fro) balancer; **to ~ sb round and round** faire tournoyer qn
C *vi* (*prét, pp* **swung**) **1** (to and fro) se balancer; ‹*pendulum*› osciller
2 to ~ open s'ouvrir; **the car swung into the drive** la voiture s'est engagée dans l'allée; **to ~ around** ‹*person*› se retourner (brusquement)
3 (change) **to ~ from optimism to despair** passer de l'optimisme au désespoir; **the party swung towards the left** le parti a basculé vers la gauche
IDIOMS **to get into the ~ of things** se mettre dans le bain (fam); **to be in full ~** battre son plein (fam)

swing door (BrE), **swinging door** (AmE) *n* porte *f* battante

swipe card *n* carte *f* à piste magnétique

swirl /swɜ:l/ *vi* tourbillonner

S

⚷ mot clé

Swiss /swɪs/ **A** *n* Suisse *mf*
B *adj* suisse; ‹*embassy*› de Suisse

switch /swɪtʃ/ **A** *n* **1** (change) changement *m* (**in** de)
2 (for light) interrupteur *m*; (on radio, appliance) bouton *m*
B *vt* **1** reporter ‹*attention*› (**to** sur); **to ~ flights** changer de vol
2 intervertir ‹*objects, roles*›; **I've ~ed the furniture round** j'ai changé la disposition des meubles
C *vi* changer
■ **switch off** éteindre ‹*appliance, light, engine*›; couper ‹*supply*›
■ **switch on** allumer ‹*appliance, light, engine*›
■ **switch over** (on TV) changer de chaîne

switchblade /'swɪtʃbleɪd/ *n* (AmE) (couteau *m* à) cran *m* d'arrêt

switchboard /'swɪtʃbɔ:d/ *n* standard *m*

switchboard operator *n* standardiste *mf*

switchover /'swɪtʃəʊvə(r)/ *n* passage *m* (**from** de, **to** à)

Switzerland /'swɪtzəlænd/ *pr n* Suisse *f*

swivel /'swɪvl/ *vt* (*p prés etc* **-ll-** (BrE), **-l-** (AmE)) faire pivoter ‹*chair, camera*›; tourner ‹*head, body*›
■ **swivel round** pivoter

swivel chair, **swivel seat** *n* fauteuil *m* tournant, chaise *f* tournante

swollen /'swəʊlən/ *adj* ‹*ankle, gland*› enflé/-e; ‹*eyes*› gonflé/-e; ‹*river*› en crue

swoop /swu:p/ *vi* **1** ‹*bird, bat, plane*› plonger; **to ~ down** descendre en piqué; **to ~ down on** fondre sur
2 ‹*police, raider*› faire une descente

sword /sɔ:d/ *n* épée *f*

swordfish *n* espadon *m*

sworn /swɔ:n/ *adj* **1** ‹*statement*› fait/-e sous serment
2 ‹*enemy*› juré/-e; ‹*ally*› pour la vie

swot /swɒt/ (BrE) (fam) **A** *n* bûcheur/-euse *m/f* (fam)
B *vi* (*p prés etc* **-tt-**) bûcher (fam)

sycamore /'sɪkəmɔ:(r)/ *n* (*also* **~ tree**) sycomore *m*

syllable /'sɪləbl/ *n* syllabe *f*

syllabus /'sɪləbəs/ *n* (*pl* **-buses** *ou* **-bi**) programme *m*

symbol /'sɪmbl/ *n* symbole *m* (**of, for** de)

symbolic /sɪm'bɒlɪk(l)/ *adj* symbolique (**of** de)

symbolism /'sɪmbəlɪzəm/ *n* symbolisme *m*

symbolize /'sɪmbəlaɪz/ *vt* symboliser (**by** par)

symmetric /sɪ'metrɪk(l)/ *adj* (*also* **symmetrical**) symétrique

sympathetic /ˌsɪmpə'θetɪk/ *adj* (compassionate) compatissant/-e (**to, towards** envers); (understanding) compréhensif/-ive; (kindly) gentil/-ille; (well disposed) bien disposé/-e (**to, towards** à l'égard de)

sympathize /'sɪmpəθaɪz/ *vi* **1** témoigner de la sympathie (**with** à); **I ~ with you in your grief** je compatis à votre douleur
2 (support) **to ~ with** souscrire à ‹*aims, views*›

sympathizer /'sɪmpəθaɪzə(r)/ *n* sympathisant/-e *m/f* (**of** de)

sympathy /'sɪmpəθɪ/ *n* **1** (compassion) compassion *f*
2 (solidarity) solidarité *f*

symphony /'sɪmfənɪ/ *n* symphonie *f*

symphony orchestra *n* orchestre *m* symphonique

symptom /'sɪmptəm/ *n* symptôme *m*

synagogue /'sɪnəgɒg/ *n* synagogue *f*

synchronize /'sɪŋkrənaɪz/ *vt* synchroniser

syndicate /'sɪndɪkət/ *n* (gen) syndicat *m*; (of companies) consortium *m*

syndrome /'sɪndrəʊm/ *n* syndrome *m*

synonymous /sɪ'nɒnɪməs/ *adj* synonyme (**with** de)

synopsis /sɪ'nɒpsɪs/ *n* (*pl* **-ses**) (of play) synopsis *m*; (of book) résumé *m*

syntax /'sɪntæks/ *n* syntaxe *f*

synthesis /'sɪnθəsɪs/ *n* (*pl* **-ses**) synthèse *f*

synthesizer /'sɪnθəsaɪzə(r)/ *n* synthétiseur *m*

synthetic /sɪn'θetɪk/ *adj* synthétique

syringe /sɪ'rɪndʒ/ **A** *n* seringue *f*
B *vt* **to have one's ears ~d** se faire déboucher les oreilles (avec une seringue)

syrup /'sɪrəp/ *n* sirop *m*

system /'sɪstəm/ *n* système *m* (**for doing, to do** pour faire); **road ~** réseau *m* routier; **reproductive ~** appareil *m* reproducteur; **to get sth out of one's ~** oublier qch

systematic /ˌsɪstə'mætɪk/ *adj* **1** (efficient) méthodique
2 (deliberate) systématique

systematically /ˌsɪstə'mætɪklɪ/ *adv* ‹*work, list*› méthodiquement; ‹*arrange, destroy*› systématiquement

systems analyst *n* analyste *mf* (de) systèmes

Szechuan /se'tʃwɑ:n/ (AmE) 'seʒ-/ *adj* sichuanais

Tt

t, **T** /tiː/ *n* t, T *m*

tab /tæb/ *n* **1** (loop) attache *f*
2 (on can) languette *f*
3 (label) étiquette *f*
IDIOM **to keep ~s on sb** (fam) tenir qn à l'œil (fam)

tabby /ˈtæbɪ/ *n* (*also* **tabby cat**) chat/chatte *m/f* tigré/-e

⚷ **table** /ˈteɪbl/ **A** *n* **1** table *f*; **to set the ~** mettre le couvert
2 (list) table *f*, tableau *m*
B *vt* **1** (BrE) (present) présenter
2 (AmE) (postpone) ajourner

tablecloth *n* nappe *f*

table manners *npl* **to have good/bad ~** savoir/ne pas savoir se tenir à table

table mat *n* (under plate) set *m* de table; (under serving-dish) dessous-de-plat *m inv*

tablespoon /ˈteɪblspuːn/ *n* **1** (object) cuillère *f* de service
2 (*also* **~ful**) cuillerée *f* à soupe

tablet /ˈtæblɪt/ *n* comprimé *m* (**for** pour)

table tennis *n* tennis *m* de table, ping-pong® *m*

tabloid /ˈtæblɔɪd/ **A** *n* tabloïde *m*; **the ~s** la presse populaire
B *adj* ‹*journalism, press*› populaire

taboo /təˈbuː/ *n, adj* tabou *m*

tacit /ˈtæsɪt/ *adj* tacite

tack /tæk/ **A** *n* **1** (nail) clou *m*
2 (AmE) (drawing pin) punaise *f*
3 (Naut) bordée *f*
4 (tactic) tactique *f*
B *vt* **1** (nail) **to ~ sth to** clouer qch à
2 (in sewing) bâtir
C *vi* ‹*sailor*› faire une bordée; ‹*yacht*› louvoyer
■ **tack on**: **~ [sth] on, ~ on [sth]** ajouter [qch] après coup ‹*clause, ending, building*› (**to** à)

tackle /ˈtækl/ **A** *n* **1** (in soccer, hockey) tacle *m*; (in rugby, American football) plaquage *m*
2 (for fishing) articles *mpl* de pêche
3 (on ship) gréement *m*; (for lifting) palan *m*
B *vt* **1** s'attaquer à ‹*task, problem*›
2 (confront) **to ~ sb about** parler à qn de
3 (in soccer, hockey) tacler; (in rugby, American football) plaquer

tacky /ˈtækɪ/ *adj* **1** (sticky) collant/-e
2 (fam) (cheap) tocard/-e (fam)

tact /tækt/ *n* tact *m*

tactful /ˈtæktfl/ *adj* ‹*person, letter*› plein/-e de tact; ‹*enquiry*› discret/-ète

tactical /ˈtæktɪkl/ *adj* tactique; **~ voting** vote *m* utile

tactics *npl* tactique *f*

tactless /ˈtæktlɪs/ *adj* ‹*person, question, suggestion*› indélicat/-e; **to be ~** ‹*person, remark*› manquer de tact

tadpole /ˈtædpəʊl/ *n* têtard *m*

tag /tæg/ *n* (label) étiquette *f*; (on cat, dog) plaque *f*; (on file) onglet *m*
■ **tag along** suivre

tail /teɪl/ *n* queue *f*
■ **tail off 1** ‹*figures, demand*› diminuer
2 ‹*voice*› s'éteindre

tailback *n* bouchon *m*

tailgate /ˈteɪlgeɪt/ *n* hayon *m*

tail-off *n* diminution *f*

tailor /ˈteɪlə(r)/ **A** *n* tailleur *m*
B *vt* **to ~ sth to** adapter qch à ‹*needs, person*›

tailor-made /ˌteɪləˈmeɪd/ *adj* ‹*garment*› fait/-e sur mesure; (fig) conçu/-e spécialement

tails *npl* **1** (tailcoat) habit *m*
2 (of coin) pile *f*; **heads or ~?** pile ou face?

tainted /ˈteɪntɪd/ *adj* ‹*food*› avarié/-e; ‹*water, air*› pollué/-e (**with** par); ‹*reputation*› entaché/-e

⚷ **take** /teɪk/ **A** *n* **1** (in film-making) prise *f* (de vues); (Mus) enregistrement *m*
2 (AmE) (takings) recette *f*
B *vt* (*prét* **took**, *pp* **taken**) **1** (gen) prendre; **he took the book off the shelf** il a pris le livre sur l'étagère; **she took a chocolate from the box** elle a pris un chocolat dans la boîte; **he took a pen out of his pocket** il a sorti un stylo de sa poche; **to ~ an exam** passer un examen; **to ~ a shower** prendre une douche; **to ~ sb/sth seriously** prendre qn/qch au sérieux
2 (carry with one) emporter, prendre ‹*object*›; (carry to a place) emporter, porter ‹*object*›; **to ~ sb sth, to ~ sth to sb** apporter qch à qn; **he took his umbrella with him** il a emporté son parapluie; **to ~ a letter to the post office** porter une lettre à la poste; **to ~ the car to the garage** emmener la voiture au garage; **to ~ sth upstairs/downstairs** monter/descendre qch
3 (accompany, lead) emmener ‹*person*›; **to ~ sb to** ‹*bus*› emmener qn à ‹*place*›; ‹*road*› conduire *or* mener qn à ‹*place*›; **I'll ~ you to your room** je vais vous conduire à votre chambre; **he took her home** il l'a raccompagnée; **to ~ a dog/a child for a walk**

⚷ mot clé

promener un chien/emmener un enfant faire une promenade
4 (accept) ‹*person*› accepter ‹*job, bribe*›; ‹*shop*› accepter ‹*credit card, cheque*›; ‹*person*› supporter ‹*pain, criticism*›; **she can't ~ a joke** elle ne comprend pas la plaisanterie; **I can't ~ any more!** je n'en peux plus!
5 (require) demander, exiger ‹*patience, skill, courage*›; **it ~s patience to do** il faut de la patience pour faire; **it ~s three hours to get there** il faut trois heures pour y aller; **it won't ~ long** ça ne prendra pas longtemps; **it took her ten minutes to repair it** elle a mis dix minutes pour le réparer; **to have what it ~s** avoir tout ce qu'il faut (**to do** pour faire)
6 (assume) **I ~ it that** je suppose que
7 (hold) ‹*hall, bus*› pouvoir contenir ‹*50 people*›; ‹*tank, container*› avoir une capacité de ‹*quantity*›
8 (wear) **what size do you ~?** (in clothes) quelle taille faites-vous?; (in shoes) quelle pointure faites-vous?; **I ~ a size 10** (in clothes) je m'habille en 36; **I ~ a size 5** (in shoes) je chausse du 38
9 (subtract) soustraire ‹*number, quantity*› (**from** de)
C *vi* (*prét* **took**, *pp* **taken**) ‹*drug*› faire effet; ‹*dye, plant*› prendre
IDIOMS **that's my last offer, ~ it or leave it!** c'est ma dernière proposition, c'est à prendre ou à laisser!; **to ~ a lot out of sb** fatiguer beaucoup qn
▪ **take aback** interloquer; **to be ~n aback** rester interloqué/-e
▪ **take after** tenir de ‹*person*›
▪ **take apart** démonter ‹*car, machine*›
▪ **take away 1** (carry away) emporter
2 (remove) enlever ‹*object*›; emmener ‹*person*›
3 (subtract) soustraire ‹*number*›; **that doesn't ~ anything away from his achievement** ça n'enlève rien à ce qu'il a accompli
▪ **take back 1** (to shop) rapporter ‹*goods*›
2 retirer ‹*statement, words*›
3 (accompany) ramener ‹*person*›
4 (accept again) reprendre
▪ **take down 1** enlever ‹*picture, curtains*›; démonter ‹*tent, scaffolding*›
2 noter ‹*name, details*›
▪ **take hold** ‹*disease, epidemic*› s'installer; ‹*idea, ideology*› se répandre; **to ~ hold of** prendre ‹*object, hand*›
▪ **take in 1** (deceive) tromper; **I wasn't taken in by him** je ne me suis pas laissé prendre à son jeu
2 recueillir ‹*refugee*›; prendre ‹*lodger*›
3 (understand) saisir, comprendre ‹*situation*›
4 (observe) noter ‹*detail*›
5 (encompass) inclure
6 (absorb) absorber ‹*nutrients, oxygen*›
7 ‹*boat*› prendre ‹*water*›
8 (in sewing) reprendre ‹*garment*›
▪ **take off** **A** **~ off 1** ‹*plane*› décoller
2 ‹*idea, fashion*› prendre
B **~ [sth] off 1 to ~ £10 off (the price)** réduire le prix de 10 livres sterling
2 to ~ two days off prendre deux jours de congé
C **~ off [sth], ~ [sth] off** enlever ‹*clothing, shoes, lid*›
D **~ [sb] off** (imitate) imiter ‹*person*›
▪ **take on 1** (employ) embaucher ‹*staff, worker*›
2 jouer contre ‹*team, player*›; (fight) se battre contre ‹*person*›
3 (accept) prendre ‹*responsibilities, work*›
▪ **take out** **A** **~ [sth] out 1** sortir ‹*object*› (**from, of** de); extraire ‹*tooth*›; enlever ‹*appendix*›; retirer ‹*money*›
2 to ~ [sth] out on sb passer [qch] sur qn ‹*anger, frustration*›; **to ~ it out on sb** s'en prendre à qn
B **~ [sb] out** sortir avec ‹*person*›; **to ~ sb out to dinner** emmener qn dîner
▪ **take over** **A** **~ over 1** ‹*army, faction*› prendre le pouvoir
2 (be successor) ‹*person*› prendre la suite; **to ~ over from** remplacer ‹*predecessor*›
B **~ over [sth]** prendre le contrôle de ‹*town, region*›; reprendre ‹*business*›
▪ **take part** prendre part; **to ~ part in** participer à
▪ **take place** avoir lieu
▪ **take to 1** se prendre de sympathie pour ‹*person*›
2 (begin) **to ~ to doing** se mettre à faire
3 (go) se réfugier dans ‹*forest, hills*›; **to ~ to the streets** descendre dans la rue
▪ **take up**: **A** **to ~ up with** s'attacher à ‹*person, group*›
B **~ up [sth] 1** (lift) enlever ‹*carpet, pavement*›
2 (start) se mettre à ‹*golf, guitar*›; prendre ‹*job*›; **to ~ up one's duties** entrer dans ses fonctions
3 (continue) reprendre ‹*story, cry, refrain*›
4 (accept) accepter ‹*offer, invitation*›; relever ‹*challenge*›
5 to ~ sth up with sb soulever qch avec qn ‹*matter*›
6 (occupy) prendre ‹*space, time, energy*›
7 prendre ‹*position, stance*›
8 (shorten) raccourcir ‹*skirt, curtains*›
C **~ sb up on 1** reprendre qn sur ‹*point, assertion*›
2 to ~ sb up on an offer accepter l'offre de qn

take-away /'teɪkəweɪ/ *n* (BrE) **1** (meal) repas *m* à emporter
2 (restaurant) restaurant *m* qui fait des plats à emporter

take-home pay *n* salaire *m* net

taken /'teɪkən/ *adj* **1 to be ~** ‹*seat, room*› être occupé/-e
2 (impressed) **to be ~ with** être emballé/-e (fam) par ‹*idea, person*›

take-off /'teɪkɒf/ *n* **1** (by plane) décollage *m*
2 (fam) (imitation) imitation *f* (**of** de)

take-out /ˈteɪkaʊt/ *adj* (AmE) ‹*food*› à emporter

takeover /ˈteɪkəʊvə(r)/ *n* (of company) rachat *m*; (of political power) prise *f* de pouvoir

takeover bid *n* offre *f* publique d'achat, OPA *f*

taker /ˈteɪkə(r)/ *n* preneur/-euse *m/f*

takings *npl* recette *f*

talc, **talcum (powder)** /tælk/ *n* talc *m*

tale /teɪl/ *n* (story) histoire *f*; (fantasy story) conte *m*; (narrative, account) récit *m*

🔑 **talent** /ˈtælənt/ *n* talent *m*

talent contest *n* concours *m* de jeunes talents *or* d'amateurs

talented /ˈtæləntɪd/ *adj* doué/-e, talentueux/-euse

talisman /ˈtælɪzmən, ˈtælɪs-/ *n* talisman *m*

🔑 **talk** /tɔːk/ **A** *n* **1** (talking, gossip) propos *mpl*; **they are the ~ of the town** on ne parle que d'eux
2 (conversation) conversation *f*, discussion *f*
3 (speech) exposé *m* (**about, on** sur); (more informal) causerie *f*
B **talks** *npl* négociations *fpl*; (political) pourparlers *mpl*; **peace ~** pourparlers de paix
C *vt* parler; **to ~ business** parler affaires; **to ~ nonsense** raconter n'importe quoi; **to ~ sb into/out of doing** persuader/dissuader qn de faire; **he ~ed his way out of it** il s'en est tiré grâce à son bagout (fam)
D *vi* parler; **to ~ to oneself** parler tout seul/toute seule

talkative /ˈtɔːkətɪv/ *adj* bavard/-e

talking /ˈtɔːkɪŋ/ **A** *n* **I'll do the ~** c'est moi qui parlerai; **'no ~!'** 'silence!'
B *adj* ‹*bird, doll*› qui parle

talking book *n* livre *m* enregistré (*à l'usage des non-voyants*)

talking-to /ˈtɔːkɪŋtuː/ *n* réprimande *f*

talk show *n* talk-show *m*

🔑 **tall** /tɔːl/ *adj* ‹*person*› grand/-e; ‹*building, tree, chimney*› haut/-e; **he's six feet ~** ≈ il mesure un mètre quatre-vingts; **to grow ~er** grandir

tally /ˈtælɪ/ **A** *n* compte *m*
B *vi* concorder

tambourine /ˌtæmbəˈriːn/ *n* tambourin *m*

tame /teɪm/ **A** *adj* **1** ‹*animal*› apprivoisé/-e
2 ‹*story, party*› sage; ‹*reform*› timide
B *vt* **1** apprivoiser ‹*bird, wild animal*›; dompter ‹*lion, tiger*›
2 soumettre ‹*person*›

tamper /ˈtæmpə(r)/ *vi* **to ~ with** tripoter ‹*machinery, lock*›; trafiquer ‹*accounts, evidence*›

tampon /ˈtæmpɒn/ *n* tampon *m*

tan /tæn/ **A** *n* **1** (*also* **sun~**) bronzage *m*
2 (colour) fauve *m*
B *adj* fauve
C *vt* (*p prés etc* **-nn-**) **1** bronzer ‹*skin*›
2 tanner ‹*animal hide*›
D *vi* (*p prés etc* **-nn-**) ‹*skin, person*› bronzer

tandem /ˈtændəm/ *n* tandem *m*; **in ~** en tandem

tang /tæŋ/ *n* (taste) goût *m* acidulé; (smell) odeur *f* piquante

tangent /ˈtændʒənt/ *n* tangente *f*; **to go off on a ~** partir dans une digression

tangerine /ˈtændʒəriːn/ *n* tangerine *f*

tangible /ˈtændʒəbl/ *adj* tangible

tangle /ˈtæŋgl/ **A** *n* (of hair, string, wires) enchevêtrement *m*; (of clothes, sheets) fouillis *m*
B *vi* ‹*hair, string, cable*› s'emmêler

■ **tangle up**: **A** **~ up** s'embrouiller
B **to get ~d up** ‹*hair, string, wires*› s'emmêler

tangy /ˈtæŋɪ/ *adj* acidulé/-e

tank /tæŋk/ *n* **1** (gen), (Aut) réservoir *m*; (for oil) cuve *f*; (for water) citerne *f*; (for fish) aquarium *m*
2 (Mil) char *m* (de combat)

tankard /ˈtæŋkəd/ *n* chope *f*

tanker /ˈtæŋkə(r)/ *n* **1** (ship) navire-citerne *m*; **oil ~** pétrolier *m*
2 (lorry) camion-citerne *m*

tanned /tænd/ *adj* (*also* **sun~**) bronzé/-e

Tannoy® /ˈtænɔɪ/ *n* (BrE) **the ~** le système de haut-parleurs

tantalizing /ˈtæntəlaɪzɪŋ/ *adj* ‹*suggestion*› tentant/-e; ‹*possibility*› séduisant/-e; ‹*glimpse*› excitant/-e

tantamount /ˈtæntəmaʊnt/ *adj* **to be ~ to** équivaloir à, être équivalent/-e à

tantrum /ˈtæntrəm/ *n* crise *f* de colère; **to throw a ~** piquer une crise (fam)

tap /tæp/ **A** *n* **1** (BrE) (for water, gas) robinet *m*
2 (blow) petit coup *m*
B *vt* (*p prés etc* **-pp-**) **1** (knock) taper (doucement); (repeatedly) tapoter
2 mettre [qch] sur écoute ‹*telephone*›
3 inciser ‹*rubber tree*›; exploiter ‹*resources*›

■ **tap in**: **~ [sth] in, ~ in [sth]** enfoncer ‹*nail*›; taper ‹*information, number*›

tap dance *n* (*also* **~ dancing**) claquettes *fpl*

tape /teɪp/ **A** *n* **1** bande *f* (magnétique); (cassette) cassette *f*; (video) cassette *f* vidéo; (recording) enregistrement *m*
2 (*also* **adhesive ~**) scotch® *m*
B *vt* **1** (record) enregistrer
2 (stick) **to ~ sth to** coller qch à ‹*surface, door*›

tape deck *n* platine *f* cassette

tape measure *n* mètre *m* ruban

taper /ˈteɪpə(r)/ *vi* ‹*sleeve, trouser leg*› se resserrer; ‹*column, spire*› s'effiler

tape recorder *n* magnétophone *m*

tapestry /ˈtæpəstrɪ/ *n* tapisserie *f*

🔑 mot clé

tapeworm *n* ver *m* solitaire, ténia *m*
tap water *n* eau *f* du robinet
tar /tɑː(r)/ *n* goudron *m*; (on roads) bitume *m*
target /'tɑːgɪt/ **A** *n* **1** (in archery, shooting) cible *f*; (Mil) objectif *f*
2 (butt) cible *f*; **to be the ~ of abuse** être insulté/-e
3 (goal) objectif *m*
B *adj* ‹*date, figure*› prévu/-e; ‹*audience, group*› visé/-e, ciblé/-e
C *vt* **1** diriger ‹*weapon, missile*›; prendre [qch] pour cible ‹*city, site*›
2 (in marketing) viser ‹*group, sector*›
target language *n* langue *f* cible
tariff /'tærɪf/ *n* **1** (price list) tarif *m*
2 (customs duty) droit *m* de douane
tarmac /'tɑːmæk/ *n* **1** (*also* **Tarmac**®) macadam *m*
2 (BrE) (of airfield) piste *f*
tarnish /'tɑːnɪʃ/ **A** *vt* ternir
B *vi* se ternir
tarpaulin /tɑː'pɔːlɪn/ *n* (material) toile *f* de bâche; (sheet) bâche *f*
tarragon /'tærəgən/ *n* estragon *m*
tart /tɑːt/ *n* (small) tartelette *f*; (large) tarte *f*
■ **tart up** (BrE) (fam): **A** **~ [sth] up, ~ up [sth]** retaper (fam) ‹*house, room*›
B **~ oneself up** se pomponner (fam)
tartan /'tɑːtn/ *adj* écossais/-e
task /tɑːsk, (AmE) tæsk/ *n* tâche *f*; **a hard ~** une lourde tâche
task bar *n* (Comput) barre *f* de tâches
task force *n* (Mil) corps *m* expéditionnaire; (committee) groupe *m* de travail
taskmaster /'tɑːskmɑːstə(r), (AmE) 'tæsk-/ *n* tyran *m*; **to be a hard ~** être très exigeant/-e
tassel /'tæsl/ *n* gland *m*
taste /teɪst/ **A** *n* **1** (gen) goût *m*; **that's a matter of ~** ça dépend des goûts; **to be in bad ~** être de mauvais goût
2 (brief experience) expérience *f*; (foretaste) avant-goût *m*
B *vt* **1** (try) goûter ‹*food, drink*›
2 I can ~ the brandy in this coffee je sens le (goût du) cognac dans ce café
3 (experience) goûter à ‹*freedom, success*›
C *vi* **to ~ sweet** avoir un goût sucré; **to ~ horrible** avoir mauvais goût; **to ~ like sth** avoir le goût de qch; **to ~ of** avoir un goût de
taste bud *n* papille *f* gustative
tasteful /'teɪstfl/ *adj* de bon goût
tasteless /'teɪstlɪs/ *adj* **1** ‹*remark, joke*› de mauvais goût
2 ‹*food, drink*› insipide
tasty /'teɪstɪ/ *adj* ‹*food*› succulent/-e
tatters /'tætəz/ *npl* **to be in ~** ‹*clothing*› être en lambeaux; ‹*career, reputation*› être en ruines
tattoo /tə'tuː, (AmE) tæ'tuː/ **A** *n* tatouage *m*
B *vt* tatouer (**on** sur)
tatty /'tætɪ/ *adj* (fam) ‹*carpet, garment*› miteux/-euse; ‹*book, shoes*› en mauvais état
taunt /tɔːnt/ *vt* railler ‹*person*›
Taurus /'tɔːrəs/ *n* Taureau *m*
taut /tɔːt/ *adj* tendu/-e
tauten /'tɔːtn/ **A** *vt* tendre
B *vi* se tendre
tax /tæks/ **A** *n* (on goods, services, property) taxe *f*; (on income, profits) impôt *m*
B *vt* **1** imposer ‹*earnings, person*›; taxer ‹*luxury goods*›
2 mettre [qch] à l'épreuve ‹*patience*›
taxation /tæk'seɪʃn/ *n* **1** (imposition of taxes) imposition *f*
2 (revenue from taxes) impôts *mpl*
tax bracket *n* tranche *f* d'imposition du revenu
tax collector *n* percepteur *m*
tax disc *n* (BrE) vignette *f* (automobile)
tax evasion *n* fraude *f* fiscale
tax exile *n*: *personne qui s'est expatriée pour raisons fiscales*
tax-free *adj* exempt/-e d'impôt
tax haven *n* paradis *m* fiscal
taxi /'tæksɪ/ *n* taxi *m*; **by ~** en taxi
taxing /'tæksɪŋ/ *adj* épuisant/-e
taxi rank (BrE), **taxi stand** *n* station *f* de taxis
tax office *n* perception *f*
taxpayer *n* contribuable *mf*
tax return *n* **1** (form) feuille *f* d'impôts
2 (declaration) déclaration *f* de revenus
TB *n* (*abbr* = **tuberculosis**) tuberculose *f*
tea /tiː/ *n* **1** (drink) thé *m*
2 (BrE) (afternoon meal) thé *m*; (for children) goûter *m*; (evening meal) dîner *m*
tea bag *n* sachet *m* de thé
tea break *n* (BrE) pause-café *f*
teach /tiːtʃ/ **A** *vt* enseigner à ‹*children, adults*›, enseigner ‹*subject*›; **to ~ sb** enseigner [qch] à qn ‹*academic subject*›; apprendre [qch] à qn ‹*practical skill*›; **to ~ school** (AmE) être instituteur/-trice; **to ~ sb a lesson** ‹*person*› donner une bonne leçon à qn; ‹*experience*› servir de leçon à qn
B *vi* enseigner
teacher /'tiːtʃə(r)/ *n* (in general) enseignant/-e *m/f*; (secondary) professeur *m*; (primary) instituteur/-trice *m/f*; (special needs) éducateur/-trice *m/f*
teacher training *n* formation *f* pédagogique
teaching /'tiːtʃɪŋ/ **A** *n* enseignement *m*
B *adj* ‹*post*› d'enseignant; ‹*method, qualification*› pédagogique; ‹*staff*› enseignant/-e
teaching hospital *n* centre *m* hospitalo-universitaire, CHU *m*
teacup /'tiːkʌp/ *n* tasse *f* à thé
teak /tiːk/ *n* teck *m*

t

✓ **team** /tiːm/ *n* équipe *f*
team member *n* équipier/-ière *m/f*
team spirit *n* esprit *m* d'équipe
teamwork *n* collaboration *f*
teapot /ˈtiːpɒt/ *n* théière *f*
tear¹ /teə(r)/ **A** *n* (gen) accroc *m*; (Med) déchirure *f*
B *vt* (*prét* **tore**, *pp* **torn**) déchirer ‹*garment, paper*›; **to ~ sth out of** arracher qch de ‹*book, notepad*›
C *vi* (*prét* **tore**, *pp* **torn**) **1** (rip) se déchirer
2 (rush) **to ~ out/off** sortir/partir en trombe
■ **tear apart 1** mettre [qch] en pièces ‹*prey*›; déchirer ‹*country*›
2 (separate) séparer
3 (criticize) descendre [qn] en flammes
■ **tear off** (carefully) détacher; (violently) arracher
■ **tear open** ouvrir [qch] en le/la déchirant
■ **tear out** détacher ‹*coupon, cheque*›; arracher ‹*page*›
■ **tear up** déchirer ‹*letter, document*›
✓ **tear²** /tɪə(r)/ *n* larme *f*; **to burst into ~s** fondre en larmes
tearful /ˈtɪəfl/ *adj* ‹*person, face*› en larmes; ‹*voice*› larmoyant/-e
tear gas *n* gaz *m* lacrymogène
tease /tiːz/ *vt* taquiner ‹*person*› (**about** à propos de); tourmenter ‹*animal*›
teasing /ˈtiːzɪŋ/ *n* taquineries *fpl*
teaspoon *n* petite cuillère *f*, cuillère *f* à café
teaspoonful *n* cuillerée *f* à café
teat /tiːt/ *n* **1** (of cow, goat, ewe) trayon *m*
2 (BrE) (on baby's bottle) tétine *f*
teatime *n* l'heure *f* du thé
tea towel *n* (BrE) torchon *m* (à vaisselle)
✓ **technical** /ˈteknɪkl/ *adj* technique
technical college *n* institut *m* d'enseignement technique
technical drawing *n* dessin *m* industriel
technical hitch *n* incident *m* technique
technicality /ˌteknɪˈkælətɪ/ *n* **1** (technical detail) détail *m* technique (**of** de)
2 (minor detail) point *m* de détail
3 (technical nature) technicité *f*
technically /ˈteknɪklɪ/ *adv* **1** (strictly speaking) théoriquement
2 (technologically) techniquement
technician /tekˈnɪʃn/ *n* technicien/-ienne *m/f*
✓ **technique** /tekˈniːk/ *n* technique *f*
techno /ˈteknəʊ/ **A** *n* techno *f*
B *adj* techno *inv*
technological /ˌteknəˈlɒdʒɪkl/ *adj* technologique
✓ **technology** /tekˈnɒlədʒɪ/ *n* technologie *f*; **information ~** informatique *f*
technology park *n* parc *m* technologique

✓ mot clé

t

technology transfer *n* transfert *m* de technologie
teddy /ˈtedɪ/ *n* (*also* **~ bear**) ours *m* en peluche
tedious /ˈtiːdɪəs/ *adj* ennuyeux/-euse
teem /tiːm/ *vi* **to be ~ing with** grouiller de ‹*people*›
teenage /ˈtiːneɪdʒ/ *adj* ‹*son, daughter*› qui est adolescent/-e; ‹*singer, player*› jeune *before n*; ‹*fashion*› des adolescents
teenager /ˈtiːneɪdʒə(r)/ *n* jeune *mf*, adolescent/-e *m/f*
teens /tiːnz/ *npl* adolescence *f*; **to be in one's ~** être adolescent/-e
tee shirt /ˈtiːʃɜːt/ *n* tee-shirt *m*, T-shirt *m*
teeter /ˈtiːtə(r)/ *vi* vaciller
teethe /tiːð/ *vi* faire ses dents
teething troubles *npl* difficultés *fpl* initiales
teetotal /tiːˈtəʊtl, (AmE) ˈtiːtəʊtl/ *adj* **I'm ~** je ne bois jamais d'alcool
teetotaller (BrE), **teetotaler** (AmE) /tiːˈtəʊtələ(r)/ *n* personne *f* qui ne boit jamais d'alcool
TEFL /ˈtefl/ *n* (*abbr* = **Teaching of English as a Foreign Language**) enseignement *m* de l'anglais langue étrangère
telecommunications /ˌtelɪkəˌmjuːnɪˈkeɪʃnz/ *npl* télécommunications *fpl*
telecommuting /ˌtelɪkəˈmjuːtɪŋ/ *n* télétravail *m*
teleconference /ˈtelɪkɒnfərəns/ *n* téléconférence *f*
telegram /ˈtelɪgræm/ *n* télégramme *m*
telegraph /ˈtelɪgrɑːf, (AmE) -græf/ **A** *n* télégraphe *m*
B *vt* télégraphier
telegraph pole *n* poteau *m* télégraphique
telemarketer /telɪˈmɑːkɪtə(r)/ *n* téléprospecteur/-trice *m/f*
telemarketing /ˈtelɪmɑːkɪtɪŋ/ *n* télémarketing *m*
telepathy /tɪˈlepəθɪ/ *n* télépathie *f*
telephone /ˈtelɪfəʊn/ **A** *n* téléphone *m*; **to be on the ~** (connected) avoir le téléphone; (talking) être au téléphone
B *vt* téléphoner à ‹*person*›; téléphoner ‹*instructions*›; **to ~ France** appeler la France
C *vi* appeler, téléphoner
telephone banking *n* transactions *fpl* bancaires télématiques
telephone booth, **telephone box** (BrE) *n* cabine *f* téléphonique
telephone call *n* appel *m* téléphonique
telephone directory *n* annuaire *m* (du téléphone)
telephone number *n* numéro *m* de téléphone
telephone operator *n* standardiste *mf*

telephonist /tɪ'lefənɪst/ *n* (BrE) standardiste *mf*

telephoto lens /'telɪfəʊtəʊ lenz/ *n* téléobjectif *m*

telesales /'telɪseɪlz/ *n* télévente *f*

telescope /'telɪskəʊp/ *n* télescope *m*

teleshopping /'telɪʃɒpɪŋ/ *n* téléachat *m*

teletext /'telɪtekst/ *n* télétexte *m*

televise /'telɪvaɪz/ *vt* téléviser

television /'telɪvɪʒn, -'vɪʒn/ *n* **1** (medium) télévision *f*; **on ~** à la télévision
2 (set) téléviseur *m*

television licence *n* redevance *f* télévision

television programme *n* émission *f* de télévision

television set *n* téléviseur *m*, poste *m* de télévision

teleworking *n* télétravail *m*

telex /'teleks/ **A** *n* télex *m*
B *vt* télexer

tell /tel/ **A** *vt* (*prét, pp* **told**) **1** (gen) dire; raconter ‹*joke, story*›; prédire ‹*future*›; **to ~ sb about sth** parler de qch à qn; **to ~ sb to do** dire à qn de faire; **to ~ sb how to do/ what to do** expliquer à qn comment faire/ ce qu'il faut faire; **to ~ the time** ‹*clock*› indiquer *or* marquer l'heure; ‹*person*› lire l'heure; **can you ~ me the time, please?** peux-tu me dire l'heure (qu'il est), s'il te plaît?; **I was told that...** on m'a dit que...; **I told you so!** je te l'avais bien dit!
2 (deduce) **you can ~ (that) he's lying** on voit bien qu'il ment; **I can ~ (that) he's disappointed** je sais qu'il est déçu
3 (distinguish) distinguer; **can you ~ the difference?** est-ce que vous voyez la différence?; **how can you ~ them apart?** comment peut-on les distinguer l'un de l'autre?
B *vi* (*prét, pp* **told**) **1** (reveal secret) **don't ~!** ne le répète pas!
2 (know) savoir; **as far as I can ~** pour autant que je sache; **how can you ~?** comment le sais-tu?
3 (show effect) **her age is beginning to ~** elle commence à faire son âge
■ **tell off** réprimander ‹*person*›
■ **tell on 1** dénoncer ‹*person*› (**to** à)
2 the strain is beginning to ~ on him on commence à voir sur lui les effets de la fatigue

telling /'telɪŋ/ *adj* ‹*remark, omission*› révélateur/-trice

tell-tale A *n* rapporteur/-euse *m/f*
B *adj* ‹*sign*› révélateur/-trice

telly /'telɪ/ *n* (BrE) (fam) télé *f* (fam)

temp /temp/ (BrE) (fam) **A** *n* intérimaire *mf*
B *vi* travailler comme intérimaire

temper /'tempə(r)/ **A** *n* **1** (mood) humeur *f*; **to be in a good/bad ~** être de bonne/ mauvaise humeur
2 to be in a ~ être en colère; **to lose one's ~** se mettre en colère (**with** contre)
3 (nature) caractère *m*
B *vt* **1** (moderate) tempérer
2 tremper ‹*steel*›

temperament /'temprəmənt/ *n* **1** (nature) tempérament *m*
2 (excitability) humeur *f*

temperamental /ˌtemprə'mentl/ *adj* (volatile) capricieux/-ieuse

temperate /'tempərət/ *adj* ‹*climate, zone*› tempéré/-e; ‹*person, habit*› modéré/-e

temperature /'temprətʃə(r), (AmE) 'tempərtʃʊər/ *n* température *f*; **to have a ~** avoir de la température *or* de la fièvre

temper tantrum *n* caprice *m*

tempest /'tempɪst/ *n* tempête *f*

tempestuous /tem'pestʃʊəs/ *adj* turbulent/-e

template /'templeɪt/ *n* gabarit *m*; (Comput) modèle *m*

temple /'templ/ *n* **1** (building) temple *m*
2 (Anat) tempe *f*

temporarily /'tempərəlɪ, (AmE) -pərerɪlɪ/ *adv* (for a limited time) temporairement; (provisionally) provisoirement

temporary /'temprərɪ, (AmE) -pərerɪ/ *adj* ‹*job, contract*› temporaire; ‹*manager, secretary*› intérimaire; ‹*arrangement, accommodation*› provisoire

tempt /tempt/ *vt* tenter; **to be ~ed to do** être tenté/-e de faire

temptation /temp'teɪʃn/ *n* tentation *f*

tempting /'temptɪŋ/ *adj* ‹*offer*› alléchant/-e; ‹*food, smell*› appétissant/-e; ‹*idea*› tentant/-e

ten /ten/ *n, pron, det* dix *m inv*

tenacious /tɪ'neɪʃəs/ *adj* tenace

tenancy /'tenənsɪ/ *n* location *f*

tenant /'tenənt/ *n* locataire *mf*

tend /tend/ **A** *vt* soigner ‹*patient*›; entretenir ‹*garden*›; s'occuper de ‹*stall, store*›
B *vi* **to ~ to do** avoir tendance à faire

tendency /'tendənsɪ/ *n* tendance *f* (**to do** à faire)

tender /'tendə(r)/ **A** *n* soumission *f*
B *adj* **1** ‹*meat*› tendre
2 ‹*kiss, love, smile*› tendre
3 ‹*bruise, skin*› sensible
C *vt* présenter ‹*apology, fare*›; donner ‹*resignation*›

tendon /'tendən/ *n* tendon *m*

tendril /'tendrəl/ *n* vrille *f*

tenement /'tenəmənt/ *n* immeuble *m* ancien

tenner /'tenə(r)/ *n* (BrE) (fam) (note) billet *m* de dix livres

tennis /'tenɪs/ *n* tennis *m*

tennis court *n* court *m* de tennis, tennis *m inv*

tenor /'tenə(r)/ *n* (Mus) ténor *m*

tenpin bowling (BrE), **tenpins** (AmE) *n* bowling *m* (à dix quilles)

tense /tens/ **A** *n* temps *m*; **the present ~** le présent; **in the past ~** au passé
B *adj* ‹*person, atmosphere, conversation*› tendu/-e; ‹*moment*› de tension; **to make sb ~** rendre qn nerveux
C *vt* tendre ‹*muscle*›; raidir ‹*body*›
■ **tense up** ‹*person*› se crisper

tension /'tenʃn/ *n* **1** (gen), (Tech) tension *f*
2 (suspense) suspense *m*

tent /tent/ *n* tente *f*

tentacle /'tentəkl/ *n* tentacule *m*

tentative /'tentətɪv/ *adj* ‹*smile, suggestion*› timide; ‹*conclusion, offer*› provisoire

tenterhooks /'tentəhʊks/ *npl*
IDIOMS **to be on ~** être sur des charbons ardents; **to keep sb on ~** faire languir qn

tenth /tenθ/ **A** *n* **1** (in order) dixième *mf*
2 (of month) dix *m inv*
3 (fraction) dixième *m*
B *adj, adv* dixième

tenuous /'tenjʊəs/ *adj* ‹*link*› ténu/-e; ‹*distinction, theory*› mince

tepid /'tepɪd/ *adj* tiède

⚷ **term** /tɜːm/ **A** *n* **1** (period of time) (gen) période *f*, terme *m*; (Sch, Univ) trimestre *m*; **autumn/spring/summer ~** (Sch, Univ) premier/deuxième/troisième trimestre; **the president's first ~ of office** le premier mandat du président
2 (word, phrase) terme *m*
B terms *npl* **1** (conditions) termes *mpl*; (of financial arrangement) conditions *fpl* de paiement
2 to come to ~s with assumer ‹*identity, past, disability*›; accepter ‹*death, defeat, failure*›; affronter ‹*issue*›
3 (relations) termes *mpl*; **to be on good ~s with** être en bons termes avec
C *vt* appeler, nommer
D in terms of *phr* du point de vue de, sur le plan de

terminal /'tɜːmɪnl/ **A** *n* **1** (at station) terminus *m*; (in airport) aérogare *f*; **ferry ~** gare *f* maritime
2 (Comput) terminal *m*
3 (for electricity) borne *f*
B *adj* ‹*stage*› terminal/-e; ‹*illness*› (incurable) incurable; (at final stage) en phase terminale

terminate /'tɜːmɪneɪt/ **A** *vt* mettre fin à ‹*meeting, phase, relationship*›; résilier ‹*contract*›; annuler ‹*agreement*›; interrompre ‹*pregnancy*›
B *vi* se terminer

termination /ˌtɜːmɪ'neɪʃn/ *n* **1** (of contract) résiliation *f*; (of service) interruption *f*
2 (Med) interruption *f* de grossesse

terminology /ˌtɜːmɪ'nɒlədʒɪ/ *n* terminologie *f*

⚷ mot clé

terminus /'tɜːmɪnəs/ *n* (*pl* **-ni** *ou* **-nuses**) (BrE) terminus *m*

terrace /'terəs/ **A** *n* **1** (patio) terrasse *f*
2 (row of houses) alignement *m* de maisons
B terraces *npl* (BrE) (in stadium) gradins *mpl*

terrace house *n* (*also* **terraced house**) maison *f* (*située dans un alignement de maisons identiques et contiguës*)

terracotta /ˌterə'kɒtə/ *n* **1** (earthenware) terre *f* cuite
2 (colour) ocre brun *m*

terrain /'tereɪn/ *n* terrain *m*

terrible /'terəbl/ *adj* **1** ‹*pain, noise, sight*› épouvantable; ‹*accident, fight*› terrible; ‹*mistake*› grave
2 (fam) ‹*food, weather*› affreux/-euse

terribly /'terəblɪ/ *adv* **1** (very) ‹*pleased, obvious*› très; ‹*clever*› extrêmement; **I'm ~ sorry** je suis navré
2 (badly) ‹*suffer*› horriblement; ‹*sing, drive*› affreusement mal

terrific /tə'rɪfɪk/ *adj* **1** (huge) ‹*amount*› énorme; ‹*noise*› épouvantable; ‹*speed*› fou/folle; ‹*accident, shock*› terrible
2 (fam) (wonderful) formidable

terrifically /tə'rɪfɪklɪ/ *adv* extrêmement

terrified /'terɪfaɪd/ *adj* terrifié/-e; **to be ~ of** avoir une peur folle de

terrify /'terɪfaɪ/ *vt* terrifier

terrifying /'terɪfaɪɪŋ/ *adj* (frightening) terrifiant/-e; (alarming) effroyable

territorial /ˌterə'tɔːrɪəl/ *adj* territorial/-e

⚷ **territory** /'terətrɪ, (AmE) 'terɪtɔːrɪ/ *n* territoire *m*; (fig) domaine *m*

terror /'terə(r)/ **A** *n* terreur *f*
B *adj* ‹*tactic*› d'intimidation; **a ~ campaign** une vague terroriste

⚷ **terrorism** /'terərɪzəm/ *n* terrorisme *m*

⚷ **terrorist** /'terərɪst/ *n* terroriste *mf*

terrorize /'terəraɪz/ *vt* terroriser

terry /'terɪ/ *n* (*also* **~ towelling** (BrE), **~ cloth** (AmE)) tissu *m* éponge

terse /tɜːs/ *adj* ‹*style*› succinct/-e; ‹*person, statement*› laconique

tertiary /'tɜːʃərɪ, (AmE) -ʃɪerɪ/ *adj* ‹*sector*› tertiaire; ‹*education*› supérieur/-e

⚷ **test** /test/ **A** *n* **1** (gen) test *m*; (Sch, Univ) (written) contrôle *m*; (oral) épreuve *f* orale; **to put sb/sth to the ~** mettre qn/qch à l'épreuve
2 (of equipment, machine, new model) essai *m*
3 (Med) (of blood, urine) analyse *f*; (of organ) examen *m*; (to detect virus, cancer) test *m* de dépistage; **to have a blood ~** se faire faire une analyse de sang
4 (*also* **driving ~**) (Aut) examen *m* du permis de conduire
B *vt* **1** (gen) évaluer ‹*intelligence, efficiency*›; (Sch) (in classroom) interroger (**on** en); (at exam time) contrôler
2 essayer ‹*new model, product*›; (Med)

analyser ‹*blood, sample*›; expérimenter ‹*new drug*›; **to have one's eyes ~ed** se faire faire un examen des yeux
3 mettre [qch] à l'épreuve ‹*strength, patience*›

testament /'testəmənt/ *n* **1** (proof) témoignage *m*; **to be a ~ to sth** témoigner de qch
2 the Old/the New Testament l'Ancien/le Nouveau Testament

test ban *n* interdiction *f* d'essais nucléaires

test case *n* procès *m* qui fait jurisprudence

test-drive /'testdraɪv/ *vt* faire un essai de route à, essayer

testicle /'testɪkl/ *n* testicule *m*

testify /'testɪfaɪ/ **A** *vt* témoigner (**that** que)
B *vi* témoigner; **to ~ to** témoigner de

testimony /'testɪmənɪ, (AmE) -məʊnɪ/ *n* témoignage *m*, déposition *f*

testing /'testɪŋ/ *n* (of drug, cosmetic) expérimentation *f*; (of blood, water etc) analyse *f*; (Sch) contrôles *mpl*

test paper *n* (Sch) interrogation *f* écrite

test tube *n* éprouvette *f*

test-tube baby *n* bébé-éprouvette *m*

tetanus /'tetənəs/ *n* tétanos *m*

tether /'teðə(r)/ **A** *n* longe *f*
B *vt* attacher (**to** à)
IDIOM **to be at the end of one's ~** être au bout du rouleau (fam)

text /tekst/ **A** *n* **1** (document) texte *m*
2 (SMS) texto *m*
B *vt* envoyer un texto à ‹*person*›

textbook /'tekstbʊk/ **A** *n* manuel *m* (**about, on** sur)
B *adj* ‹*case*› exemplaire; ‹*example*› parfait/-e

textile /'tekstaɪl/ *n* textile *m*

textphone *n* textphone *m*

texture /'tekstʃə(r)/ *n* texture *f*

Thames /temz/ *pr n* **the (river) ~** la Tamise

than /ðæn, ðən/ **A** *prep* **1** (in comparisons) que; **he's taller ~ me** il est plus grand que moi; **he has more ~ me** il en a plus que moi
2 (expressing quantity, degree, value) de; **more/less ~ 100** plus/moins de 100; **more ~ half** plus de la moitié; **temperatures lower ~ 30 degrees** des températures de moins de 30 degrés
B *conj* **1** (in comparisons) que; **he's older ~ I am** il est plus âgé que moi; **it took us longer ~ we expected** ça nous a pris plus de temps que prévu
2 (expressing preferences) **I'd sooner** *or* **rather go to Rome ~ go to Venice** je préférerais aller à Rome que d'aller à Venise, j'aimerais mieux aller à Rome qu'à Venise
3 (when) **hardly** *or* **no sooner had he left ~ the phone rang** à peine était-il parti que le téléphone a sonné
4 (AmE) **to be different ~ sth** être différent/-e de qch

thank /θæŋk/ *vt* remercier ‹*person*›; **~ God!** Dieu merci!

thankful /'θæŋkfl/ *adj* (grateful) reconnaissant/-e; (relieved) soulagé/-e

thankfully /'θæŋkfəlɪ/ *adv* **1** (luckily) heureusement
2 (with relief) avec soulagement; (with gratitude) avec gratitude

thankless /'θæŋklɪs/ *adj* ‹*task, person*› ingrat/-e

thanks /θæŋks/ **A** *npl* remerciements *mpl*; **with ~** avec mes/nos remerciements
B *excl* (fam) merci; **~ a lot** merci beaucoup; **no ~** non merci
C **thanks to** *phr* grâce à

Thanksgiving *n* (*also* **Thanksgiving Day**) (AmE) jour *m* d'Action de Grâces

thank you /'θæŋkju:/ **A** *n* (*also* **thank-you, thankyou**) merci; **to say ~ to sb** dire merci à qn
B *adj* ‹*letter, gift*› de remerciement
C *excl* merci; **~ for coming** merci d'être venu; **~ very much** merci beaucoup

that

> **As a determiner**
> In French, determiners agree in gender and number with the noun that follows; *that* is translated by *ce* + masculine singular noun (*ce monsieur*), by *cet* + masculine singular noun beginning with a vowel or mute 'h' (*cet arbre, cet homme*) and by *cette* + feminine singular noun (*cette femme*). The plural form *those* is translated by *ces*.
> Note, however, that the above translations are also used for the English *this* (plural *these*). So when it is necessary to insist on *that* as opposed to others of the same sort *-là* is added to the noun: *I prefer* THAT *version* = je préfère cette version-là.
> **As a pronoun** (*meaning that one*)
> In French, pronouns reflect the gender and number of the noun they are standing for. So *that* (meaning *that one*) is translated by *celui-là* for a masculine noun, *celle-là* for a feminine noun; *those* (meaning *those ones*) is translated by *ceux-là* for a masculine plural noun and *celles-là* for a feminine plural noun.

A /ðæt/ *det* ce/cet/cette/ces; **~ chair** cette chaise; **those chairs** ces chaises; **at ~ moment** à ce moment-là; **at ~ time** à cette époque-là; **you can't do it ~ way** tu ne peux pas le faire comme ça; **he went ~ way** il est allé par là; **~ lazy son of yours** ton paresseux de fils
B /ðæt/ *dem pron* (*pl* **those**) **1** (that one) celui-/celle-/ceux-/celles-là
2 (that thing, that person) **what's ~?** qu'est-ce que c'est que ça?; **who's ~?** qui est-ce?; (on phone) qui est à l'appareil?; **is ~ Françoise?** c'est Françoise?; **who told you ~?** qui t'a dit ça?; **~'s how he did it** c'est comme ça qu'il

t

l'a fait; **what did he mean by ~?** qu'est-ce qu'il entendait par là?; **~'s the kitchen** ça, c'est la cuisine
C /ðət/ *rel pron* **1** (as subject) qui; (as object) que; **the day ~ she arrived** le jour où elle est arrivée
2 (as subject) lequel, laquelle, lesquels, lesquelles; **the chair ~ I was sitting on** la chaise sur laquelle j'étais assis
3 (with prepositions, translated by *à*) auquel, à laquelle, auxquels, auxquelles; **the girls ~ I was talking to** les filles auxquelles je parlais
4 (with prepositions, translated by *de*) dont; **the people ~ I've talked about** les personnes dont j'ai parlé
D /ðət/ *conj* que; **he said ~ he had finished** il a dit qu'il avait fini
E /ðæt/ *adv* **it's about ~ thick** c'est à peu près épais comme ça; **I can't do ~ much work in one day** je ne peux pas faire autant de travail dans une journée; **he can't swim ~ far** il ne peut pas nager aussi loin
IDIOMS **~ is (to say)...** c'est-à-dire...; **~'s it!** (that's right) c'est ça!; (that's enough) ça suffit!; **I don't want to see you again and ~'s ~!** je ne veux pas te revoir point final!

thatched cottage *n* chaumière *f*

thatched roof *n* toit *m* de chaume

thaw /θɔː/ **A** *n* dégel *m*
B *vt* faire fondre ‹*ice, snow*›; décongeler ‹*frozen food*›
C *vi* **1** ‹*snow*› fondre; ‹*ground, frozen food*› dégeler
2 (fig) se détendre

🔑 **the** /ðiː, ðɪ, ðə/ *det* le/la/l'/les

> In French, determiners agree in gender and number with the noun that follows. So *the* is translated by *le* or *l'* + masculine singular noun (*le chien, l'ami*), by *la* or *l'* + feminine singular noun (*la chaise, l'amie*) and by *les* + plural noun (*les chaussures*).
> When *the* is used with a preposition that translates by *de* in French *de* + *le* + masculine singular noun = *du* (*du fromage*) and *de* + *les* + plural noun = *des* (*des crayons*).
> When *the* is used with a preposition that translates by *à* in French *à* + *le* + masculine singular noun = *au* (*au cinéma*) and *à* + *les* + plural noun = *aux* (*aux enfants*).

two chapters of ~ book deux chapitres du livre; **I met them at ~ supermarket** je les ai rencontrés au supermarché; **~ French** les Français; **~ wounded** les blessés; **she buys only ~ best** elle n'achète que ce qu'il y a de mieux; **~ more I learn ~ less I understand** plus j'apprends moins je comprends; **~ longer he waits ~ harder it will be** plus il attendra plus ce sera difficile; **~ sooner ~ better** le plus tôt sera le mieux; **~ fastest train** le train le plus rapide; **~ prettiest house in the village** la plus jolie maison du village; THE **book of the year** le meilleur livre de l'année; **do you mean** THE **Charlie Parker?** tu veux dire le célèbre Charlie Parker?; **Charles ~ First** Charles 1er *or* Premier; **~ Smiths** les Smith

🔑 **theatre** (BrE), **theater** (AmE) /'θɪətə(r)/ *n* **1** théâtre *m*; **to go to the ~** aller au théâtre
2 (AmE) (cinema) cinéma *m*

theatregoer *n* amateur *mf* de théâtre

theatrical /θɪ'ætrɪkl/ *adj* théâtral/-e; ‹*group*› de théâtre

theft /θeft/ *n* vol *m* (**of** de)

🔑 **their** /ðeə(r)/ *det* leur/leurs

> In French, determiners agree in gender and number with the noun that follows. So *their* is translated by *leur* + masculine or feminine singular noun (*leur chien, leur maison*) and by *leurs* + plural noun (*leurs enfants*).
> When *their* is stressed, *à eux* is added after the noun: *THEIR house* = leur maison à eux.

theirs /ðeəz/ *pron*

> In French, possessive pronouns reflect the gender and number of the noun they are standing for; *theirs* is translated by *le leur, la leur, les leurs*, according to what is being referred to.

my car is red but ~ is blue ma voiture est rouge mais la leur est bleue; **my children are older than ~** mes enfants sont plus âgés que les leurs; **which house is ~?** c'est laquelle leur maison?; **the money wasn't ~ to give away** ils/elles n'avaient pas à donner cet argent

🔑 **them** /ðem, ðəm/ *pron* **1** (direct object) les; **I've seen ~** je les ai vus; **catch ~!** attrape-les!; **don't eat ~!** ne les mange pas!
2 (indirect object) leur; **I gave it to ~** je le leur ai donné; **write to ~!** écris-leur!
3 (with prepositions, with être) eux, elles; **with ~** avec eux/elles; **it's ~** c'est eux/elles; **both of ~** tous/toutes les deux; **both of ~ work in London** ils/elles travaillent à Londres tous/toutes les deux; **some of ~** quelques-uns d'entre eux/quelques-unes d'entre elles

🔑 **theme** /θiːm/ *n* thème *m*

theme park *n* parc *m* d'attractions (à thème)

theme song, **theme tune** *n* (of film) musique *f*; (of radio, TV programme) indicatif *m*

🔑 **themselves** /ðəm'selvz/ *pron*

> When used as a reflexive pronoun, direct and indirect, *themselves* is translated by *se* (or *s'* before a vowel or mute 'h').
> When used for emphasis, the translation is *eux-mêmes* in the masculine and *elles-mêmes* in the feminine: *they did it themselves* = ils l'ont fait eux-mêmes/elles l'ont fait elles-mêmes.

After a preposition, the translation is *eux* or *elles* or *eux-mêmes* or *elles-mêmes*: *they bought the painting for themselves* = (*masculine or mixed gender*) ils ont acheté le tableau pour eux *or* pour eux-mêmes; (*feminine gender*) elles ont acheté le tableau pour elles *or* pour elles-mêmes.

1 (reflexive) se, s'; **they washed ~** ils se sont lavés **2** (emphatic) eux-mêmes/elles-mêmes **3** (after preposition) eux/elles, eux-mêmes/elles-mêmes; **(all) by ~** tout seuls/toutes seules

then /ðen/ *adv* **1** (at that time) alors, à ce moment-là; (implying more distant past) en ce temps-là; **I was working in Oxford ~** je travaillais alors à Oxford; **since ~** depuis **2** (afterwards, next) puis, ensuite **3** (in that case, so) alors **4** (therefore) donc **5** (in addition, besides) puis, aussi

thence /ðens/ *adv* de là

theology /θɪ'ɒlədʒɪ/ *n* théologie *f*

theorem /'θɪərəm/ *n* théorème *m*

theoretical /ˌθɪə'retɪkl/ *adj* théorique

theoretically /ˌθɪə'retɪklɪ/ *adv* théoriquement; **~ speaking** en théorie

theory /'θɪərɪ/ *n* théorie *f*; **in ~** en théorie

therapeutic /ˌθerə'pju:tɪk/ *adj* thérapeutique

therapist /'θerəpɪst/ *n* thérapeute *mf*

therapy /'θerəpɪ/ *n* thérapie *f*

there /ðeə(r)/

there is generally translated by *là* after prepositions (*near there* = près de là) and when emphasizing the location of an object/a point etc visible to the speaker: *put them there* = mettez-les là.

Voilà is used to draw attention to a visible place/object/person: *there's my watch* = voilà ma montre, whereas *il y a* is used for generalizations: *there's a village nearby* = il y a un village tout près.

There, when unstressed with verbs such as *aller* and *être*, is translated by *y*: *we went there last year* = nous y sommes allés l'année dernière, but not where emphasis is made: *it was there that we went last year* = c'est là que nous sommes allés l'année dernière.

For examples of the above and further uses, see the entry below.

A *pron* **~ is/are** il y a; **~ isn't any room** il n'y a pas de place; **~ are many reasons** il y a beaucoup de raisons; **~ are two** il y en a deux; **~ is some left** il en reste; **~ seems to be** il semble y avoir

B *adv* **1** là; **up to ~, down to ~** jusque là; **put it in ~** mettez-le là-dedans; **stand ~** mettez-vous là; **go over ~** va là-bas; **will she be ~ now?** est-ce qu'elle y est maintenant? **2** (to draw attention) (to person, activity) voilà; **~ you are** (seeing somebody arrive) vous voilà; (giving object) tenez, voilà; (that's done) et voilà; **~'s a bus coming** voilà un bus; **that paragraph ~** ce paragraphe

C *excl* **~ ~!** allez! allez!; **~, I told you!** voilà, je te l'avais bien dit!; **~, you've woken the baby!** c'est malin, tu as réveillé le bébé!

D **there again** *phr* (on the other hand) d'un autre côté

thereabouts (BrE), **thereabout** (AmE) /ðeərəbaʊts/ *adv* **1** (in the vicinity) par là **2** (roughly) **100 dollars or ~** 100 dollars environ

thereby /ðeə'baɪ, 'ðeə-/ *conj* ainsi

therefore *adv* donc, par conséquent

thermal /'θɜ:ml/ *adj* thermique; ‹*spring*› thermal/-e; ‹*garment*› en thermolactyl®

thermal imaging *n* thermographie *f*

thermometer /θə'mɒmɪtə(r)/ *n* thermomètre *m*

Thermos® /'θɜ:məs/ *n* (*also* **~ flask**) bouteille *f* thermos®

thermostat /'θɜ:məstæt/ *n* thermostat *m*

thesaurus /θɪ'sɔ:rəs/ *n* (*pl* **-ri** *ou* **-ruses**) dictionnaire *m* analogique

these /ði:z/ ▶ **this**

thesis /'θi:sɪs/ *n* (*pl* **theses**) **1** (Univ) (doctoral) thèse *f*; (master's) mémoire *m* **2** (theory) thèse *f*

they /ðeɪ/ *pron*

they is translated by *ils* (masculine) or *elles* (feminine). For a group of people or things of mixed gender, *ils* is always used. The emphatic form is *eux* (masculine) or *elles* (feminine).

~ have already gone (masculine or mixed) ils sont déjà partis; (feminine) elles sont déjà parties; **here ~ are!** les voici!; **there ~ are!** les voilà!

thick /θɪk/ **A** *adj* **1** (gen) épais/épaisse; ‹*forest, vegetation, fog*› dense, épais/épaisse; **to be 6 cm ~** faire 6 cm d'épaisseur **2** (fam) (stupid) bête

B *adv* **don't spread the butter on too ~** ne mets pas trop de beurre; **the snow lay ~ on the ground** il y avait une épaisse couche de neige sur le sol

IDIOM **to be in the ~ of** être au beau milieu de

thicken /'θɪkən/ **A** *vt* épaissir **B** *vi* s'épaissir; ‹*voice*› s'enrouer

thicket /'θɪkɪt/ *n* fourré *m*

thickly /'θɪklɪ/ *adv* ‹*spread*› en une couche épaisse; ‹*cut*› en morceaux épais

thickness /'θɪknɪs/ *n* épaisseur *f*

thickset *adj* trapu/-e

thick-skinned *adj* insensible

thief /θi:f/ *n* (*pl* **thieves**) voleur/-euse *m/f*

thieve /θi:v/ *vt, vi* voler

thigh /θaɪ/ *n* cuisse *f*

thimble /'θɪmbl/ *n* dé *m* à coudre

⚷ **thin** /θɪn/ **A** *adj* **1** ‹*nose, lips, wall*› mince; ‹*line, stripe, wire, paper*› fin/-e; ‹*slice, layer*› fin/-e, mince; ‹*fabric, mist*› léger/-ère
2 ‹*mixture*› liquide; ‹*soup, sauce*› clair/-e
3 ‹*person, body*› maigre; **to get ~** maigrir
4 to wear ~ ‹*joke, excuse*› être usé/-e
B *vt* (*p prés etc* **-nn-**) diluer ‹*paint*›; allonger ‹*sauce, soup*›
C *vi* (*p prés etc* **-nn-**) (*also* **~ out**) ‹*hair*› se clairsemer

⚷ **thing** /θɪŋ/ **A** *n* **1** (object) chose *f*, truc *m* (fam); (action, task, event) chose *f*; **the best ~ (to do) would be to go and see her** le mieux serait d'aller la voir; **I couldn't hear a ~ (that) he said** je n'ai rien entendu de ce qu'il a dit; **the ~ is, (that)...** ce qu'il y a, c'est que...; **the only ~ is,...** la seule chose, c'est que...
2 (person, animal) **she's a pretty little ~** c'est une jolie petite fille; **you lucky ~!** (fam) veinard/-e! (fam)
B things *npl* **1** (personal belongings, equipment) affaires *fpl*
2 (situation, circumstances, matters) les choses *fpl*; **how are ~s with you?** comment ça va?; **all ~s considered** tout compte fait
IDIOMS **for one ~... (and) for another ~...** premièrement... et deuxièmement...; **I must be seeing ~s!** je dois avoir des visions!

⚷ **think** /θɪŋk/ **A** *vt* (*prét*, *pp* **thought**)
1 (believe) croire, penser; **I ~ so** je crois; **I don't ~ so** je ne crois pas; **what do you ~ it will cost?** combien ça va coûter à ton avis?
2 (imagine) imaginer, croire
3 (have opinion) **to ~ a lot/not much of** penser/ne pas penser beaucoup de bien de; **what do you ~ of him?** que penses-tu de lui?
B *vi* (*prét*, *pp* **thought**) **1** penser; (carefully) réfléchir; **to ~ about** *or* **of sb/sth** penser à qn/qch; **I'll have to ~ about it** il faudra que j'y réfléchisse; **to ~ hard** bien réfléchir; **to be ~ing of doing** envisager de faire; **to ~ about doing** penser à faire
2 (consider) **to ~ of sb as** considérer qn comme
3 (remember) **to ~ of** se rappeler
■ **think again** (reflect more) se repencher sur la question; (change mind) changer d'avis
■ **think ahead** bien réfléchir (à l'avance)
■ **think back** se reporter en arrière (**to** à)
■ **think over**: **~ over [sth], ~ [sth] over** réfléchir à
■ **think through** bien réfléchir à ‹*proposal, action*›; faire le tour de ‹*problem, question*›

thinking /ˈθɪŋkɪŋ/ *n* (reflection) réflexion *f*; **current ~ is that...** la tendance actuelle de l'opinion est que...; **to my way of ~** à mon avis

think tank *n* groupe *m* de réflexion

thinly /ˈθɪnlɪ/ *adv* ‹*slice*› en tranches fines; ‹*spread*› en couche mince; **~ disguised** à peine déguisé/-e

thinner /ˈθɪnə(r)/ *n* diluant *m*

⚷ **third** /θɜːd/ **A** *n* **1** (in order) troisième *mf*
2 (of month) trois *m inv*
3 (fraction) tiers *m*
4 (*also* **~-class honours degree**) (BrE) (Univ) ≈ licence *f* avec mention passable
5 (*also* **~ gear**) (Aut) troisième *f*
B *adj* troisième
C *adv* **1** ‹*come, finish*› troisième
2 (*also* **thirdly**) troisièmement

third-class /ˌθɜːdˈklɑːs/ *adj* de troisième classe

third degree /ˌθɜːdəˈgriː/ *n* (fam) **to give sb the ~** ‹*parent, teacher*› soumettre qn à une interrogation

third party /ˌθɜːdˈpɑːtɪ/ *n* tiers *m*

third sector /ˈθɜːd ˌsektə(r)/ /ˈθɜːd ˌsektə(r)/ *n* troisième secteur *m*

Third Way *n* (BrE) (Pol) troisième voie *f*

Third World /ˌθɜːd ˈwɜːld/ *n* tiers-monde *m*

thirst /θɜːst/ *n* soif *f* (**for** de)

thirsty /ˈθɜːstɪ/ *adj* assoiffé/-e; **to be ~** avoir soif; **to make sb ~** donner soif à qn

thirteen /ˌθɜːˈtiːn/ *n*, *pron*, *det* treize *m inv*

thirteenth /ˌθɜːˈtiːnθ/ **A** *n* **1** (in order) treizième *mf*
2 (of month) treize *m inv*
3 (fraction) treizième *m*
B *adj*, *adv* treizième

thirties *npl* **1** (era) **the ~** les années *fpl* trente
2 (age) **to be in one's ~** avoir entre trente et quarante ans

thirtieth /ˈθɜːtɪəθ/ **A** *n* **1** (in order) trentième *mf*
2 (of month) trente *m inv*
3 (fraction) trentième *m*
B *adj*, *adv* trentième

thirty /ˈθɜːtɪ/ *n*, *pron*, *det* trente *m inv*

thirty-first **A** *n* (of month) trente et un *m*
B *adj* trente et unième

thirty something *n*: *jeune cadre de plus de trente ans qui s'installe, fonde une famille etc*

⚷ **this** /ðɪs/

As a determiner

In French, determiners agree in gender and number with the noun that follows; *this* is translated by *ce* + masculine singular noun (*ce monsieur*), BUT by *cet* + masculine singular noun beginning with a vowel or mute 'h' (*cet arbre*, *cet homme*) and by *cette* + feminine singular noun (*cette femme*). The plural form *these* is translated by *ces* (*ces livres*, *ces histoires*).

Note, however, that the above translations are also used for the English *that* (plural *those*). So when it is necessary to insist on *this* as opposed to another or others of the same sort, the adverbial tag *-ci* (*this one here*) is added to the noun:

⚷ mot clé

I prefer THIS *version* = je préfère cette version-ci.

As a pronoun (*meaning this one*)

In French, pronouns reflect the gender and number of the noun they are standing for. So *this* (meaning *this one*) is translated by *celui-ci* for a masculine noun, *celle-ci* for a feminine noun; *those* (meaning *those ones*) is translated by *ceux-ci* for a masculine plural noun, *celles-ci* for a feminine plural noun: *of all the dresses this is the prettiest one* = de toutes les robes celle-ci est la plus jolie.

For other uses of *this*, see the entry below.

A *det* **~ paper** ce papier; **~ lamp** cette lampe; **do it ~ way not that way** fais-le comme ça et pas comme ça
B *pron* **what's ~?** qu'est-ce que c'est?; **who's ~?** qui est-ce?; (on telephone) qui est à l'appareil?; **whose is ~?** à qui appartient ceci?; **~ is the dining room** voici la salle à manger; **~ is my sister Moira** (introduction) voici ma sœur Moira; (on photo) c'est ma sœur, Moira; **~ is not the right one** ce n'est pas le bon; **who did ~?** qui a fait ça?; **~ is what happens when...** voilà ce qui se passe quand...
C *adv* **it's ~ big** c'est grand comme ça
IDIOM **to talk about ~ and that** parler de tout et de rien

thistle /ˈθɪsl/ *n* chardon *m*

thong /θɒŋ/ *n* **1** (on whip) lanière *f*
2 (on shoe, garment) lacet *m*
3 (underwear) string *m* ficelle

thorn /θɔːn/ *n* épine *f*

thorough /ˈθʌrə, (AmE) ˈθʌrəʊ/ *adj* **1** (detailed) ‹*analysis, knowledge*› approfondi/-e; ‹*search, work*› minutieux/-ieuse
2 (meticulous) minutieux/-ieuse

thoroughbred /ˈθʌrəbred/ **A** *n* pur-sang *m*
B *adj* de pure race

thoroughfare /ˈθʌrəfeə(r)/ *n* rue *f*; **'no ~'** 'passage interdit'

thoroughly /ˈθʌrəlɪ, (AmE) ˈθʌrəʊlɪ/ *adv* **1** (meticulously) ‹*clean, examine, read*› à fond; ‹*check, search*› minutieusement
2 (completely) ‹*clean, reliable, dangerous*› tout à fait; ‹*agree*› parfaitement; ‹*recommend*› chaleureusement

those /ðəʊs/ ▶ **that**

though /ðəʊ/ **A** *conj* bien que (+ *subjunctive*); **a foolish ~ courageous act** un acte stupide quoique courageux
B *adv* quand même, pourtant; **it's very expensive, ~** c'est très cher, pourtant

thought /θɔːt/ *n* **1** (idea) idée *f*, pensée *f*
2 (reflection) pensée *f*; **deep in ~** plongé dans ses pensées
3 (consideration) considération *f*; **to give ~ to sth** considérer qch

thoughtful /ˈθɔːtfl/ *adj* **1** (reflective) pensif/-ive
2 (considerate) ‹*person, gesture*› prévenant/-e; ‹*letter*› gentil/-ille

thoughtless /ˈθɔːtlɪs/ *adj* irréfléchi/-e

thought out /ˌθɔːtˈaʊt/ *adj* **well/badly ~** bien/mal conçu/-e

thought-provoking /ˌθɔːtprəˈvəʊkɪŋ/ *adj* qui fait réfléchir

thousand /ˈθaʊznd/ *n, pron, det* mille *m inv*; **a ~ and two** mille deux; **about a ~** un millier; **four ~ pounds** quatre mille livres sterling; **~s of** des milliers de

thousandth /ˈθaʊzndθ/ *n, adj, adv* millième *mf*

thrash /θræʃ/ *vt* **1** (whip) rouer [qn] de coups
2 (Mil, Sport) écraser
■ **thrash about, thrash around** se débattre
■ **thrash out** venir à bout de ‹*problem*›; réussir à élaborer ‹*plan*›

thrashing /ˈθræʃɪŋ/ *n* raclée *f*

thread /θred/ **A** *n* **1** (for sewing) fil *m*
2 (of screw) filetage *m*
3 (of story, argument) fil *m*
B *vt* enfiler ‹*bead, needle*›

threadbare *adj* usé/-e jusqu'à la corde

threat /θret/ *n* menace *f* (**to** pour)

threaten /ˈθretn/ **A** *vt* menacer; **to ~ to do** ‹*person*› menacer de faire; ‹*event, thing*› risquer de faire; **to be ~ed with extinction** risquer de disparaître
B *vi* menacer

three /θriː/ *n, pron, det* trois *m inv*

three-dimensional *adj* en trois dimensions

threefold /ˈθriːfəʊld/ **A** *adj* triple
B *adv* triplement; **to increase ~** tripler

three-piece suit *n* (costume *m*) trois-pièces *m inv*

three-piece suite *n* salon *m* trois pièces

three-quarters /ˌθriːˈkwɔːtəz/ *n* trois-quarts *mpl*; **~ of an hour** trois-quarts d'heure

thresh /θreʃ/ *vt* battre

threshold /ˈθreʃəʊld, -həʊld/ *n* seuil *m*

thrift /θrɪft/ *n* économie *f*

thrifty /ˈθrɪftɪ/ *adj* ‹*person*› économe (**in** dans)

thrill /θrɪl/ **A** *n* **1** (sensation) frisson *m*
2 (pleasure) plaisir *m*
B *vt* transporter [qn] de joie
C *vi* frissonner (**at, to** à)

thrilled *adj* ravi/-e; **~ed with** enchanté/-e de

thriller /ˈθrɪlə(r)/ *n* thriller *m*

thrilling /ˈθrɪlɪŋ/ *adj* ‹*adventure, match, story*› palpitant/-e; ‹*concert, moment, sensation*› exaltant/-e

thrive /θraɪv/ *vi* (*prét* **throve** *ou* **thrived**, *pp* **thriven** *ou* **thrived**) ‹*person*› se porter bien; ‹*plant*› pousser bien; ‹*business, community*› prospérer

thriving /ˈθraɪvɪŋ/ *adj* ‹*business, community*› florissant/-e; ‹*plant, animal*› en pleine santé

throat /θrəʊt/ *n* gorge *f*; **to have a sore ~** avoir mal à la gorge

throb /θrɒb/ *vi* (*p prés etc* **-bb-**) **1** ‹*heart, pulse*› battre; **my head is ~bing** ça me lance dans la tête
2 ‹*motor*› vibrer; ‹*music, building*› résonner

throbbing /ˈθrɒbɪŋ/ *adj* ‹*pain, ache, music*› lancinant/-e

throne /θrəʊn/ *n* trône *m*

throng /θrɒŋ, (AmE) θrɔːŋ/ **A** *n* foule *f* (of de)
B *vt* envahir ‹*street, town*›

throttle /ˈθrɒtl/ *n* (accelerator) accélérateur *m*

🔑 **through** /θruː/ **A** *prep* **1** (from one side to the other) à travers; **the nail went right ~ the wall** le clou a traversé le mur
2 (via, by way of) **to go ~ the town centre** passer par le centre-ville; **to look ~** regarder avec ‹*telescope*›; regarder par ‹*hole, window*›; **it was ~ her that I got this job** c'est par son intermédiaire que j'ai eu ce travail
3 (past) **to go ~** brûler ‹*red light*›; **to get** *or* **go ~** passer à travers ‹*barricade*›; passer ‹*customs*›; **she's been ~ a lot** elle en a vu des vertes et des pas mures (fam)
4 (because of) **~ carelessness** par négligence; **~ illness** pour cause de maladie
5 (until the end of) **all** *or* **right ~ the day** toute la journée
6 (up to and including) jusqu'à; **from Friday ~ to Sunday** de vendredi jusqu'à dimanche
B *adj* **1** ‹*train, ticket, route*› direct/-e; ‹*freight*› à forfait; **'no ~ road'** 'voie sans issue'
2 (successful) **to be ~ to the next round** être sélectionné/-e pour le deuxième tour
3 (fam) (finished) fini/-e; **are you ~ with the paper?** as-tu fini de lire le journal?
C *adv* **the water went ~** l'eau est passée à travers; **to let sb ~** laisser passer qn; **to read sth right ~** lire qch jusqu'au bout
D **through and through** *phr* **English ~ and ~** anglais jusqu'au bout des ongles

🔑 **throughout** /θruːˈaʊt/ **A** *prep* **1** (all over) **~ France** dans toute la France; **~ the world** dans le monde entier
2 (for the duration of) tout au long de; **~ his life** toute sa vie; **~ history** à travers l'histoire
B *adv* (in every part) partout; (the whole time) tout le temps

throughway *n* (AmE) voie *f* rapide *or* express

🔑 **throw** /θrəʊ/ **A** *n* (in football) touche *f*; (of javelin) lancer *m*; (in judo, wrestling) jeté *m*; (of dice) coup *m*
B *vt* (*prét* **threw**, *pp* **thrown**) **1** (with careful aim) lancer; (downwards) jeter; (with violence) projeter; **to ~ sth at sb** lancer qch à qn; **to ~ a six** (in dice) faire un six
2 ‹*horse*› désarçonner ‹*rider*›
3 lancer ‹*punch*›; jeter ‹*glance*›; projeter ‹*light, shadow*› (**on** sur)
4 (disconcert) désarçonner
5 to ~ a party faire une fête (fam)
6 (in pottery) tourner
C *vi* (*prét* **threw**, *pp* **thrown**) lancer
▪ **throw away** jeter ‹*paper, old clothes*›; gâcher ‹*chance, life*›
▪ **throw back** rejeter ‹*fish*›; relancer ‹*ball*›
▪ **throw in**: **~ in [sth]**, **~ [sth] in** (give free) faire cadeau de; (add) ajouter
▪ **throw out 1** jeter ‹*rubbish*›; expulser ‹*person*› (**of** de)
2 rejeter ‹*application, decision*›
▪ **throw together**: **A** **~ [sb] together** réunir ‹*people*›
B **~ [sth] together** improviser
▪ **throw up**: **A** **~ up** vomir
B **~ [sth] up 1** lever ‹*arms, hands*›; lancer ‹*ball*›
2 (abandon) laisser tomber ‹*job*›

throwaway /ˈθrəʊəweɪ/ *adj* (discardable) jetable; ‹*society*› de consommation; ‹*remark*› désinvolte

throwback *n* survivance *f* (**to** de)

thrush /θrʌʃ/ *n* (Zool) grive *f*

thrust /θrʌst/ **A** *n* **1** (gen), (Mil, Tech) poussée *f*; **sword ~** coup *m* d'épée
2 (of argument) portée *f*
B *vt* (*prét, pp* **thrust**) **to ~ sth towards** *or* **at sb** mettre brusquement qch sous le nez de qn; **to ~ sth into sth** enfoncer qch dans qch

thud /θʌd/ **A** *n* bruit *m* sourd
B *vi* (*p prés etc* **-dd-**) faire un bruit sourd

thug /θʌg/ *n* voyou *m*

thumb /θʌm/ **A** *n* pouce *m*
B *vt* **1** (*also* **~ through**) feuilleter ‹*book, magazine*›
2 (fam) **to ~ a lift** faire du stop (fam)
IDIOM **to be under sb's ~** être sous la domination de qn

thumbs down /ˌθʌmzˈdaʊn/ *n* (fam) **to give sb/sth the ~** rejeter qn/qch; **to get the ~** être rejeté/-e

thumbs up /ˌθʌmzˈʌp/ *n* (fam) **to give sb/sth the ~** (approve) approuver qn/qch; **start the car when I give you the ~** démarre quand je te fais signe

thumbtack /ˈθʌmtæk/ *n* (AmE) punaise *f*

thump /θʌmp/ **A** *n* **1** (blow) (grand) coup *m*
2 (sound) bruit *m* sourd
B *vt* taper sur; **he ~ed me** il m'a tapé dessus
C *vi* ‹*heart*› battre violemment; ‹*music, rhythm*› résonner

thunder /ˈθʌndə(r)/ **A** *n* **1** tonnerre *m*; **a peal of ~** un roulement de tonnerre
2 (of hooves) fracas *m*; (of applause) tonnerre *m*
B *v impers* tonner

🔑 mot clé

thunderbolt *n* foudre *f*

thunderclap *n* coup *m* de tonnerre

thunderstorm *n* orage *m*

thunderstruck *adj* abasourdi/-e

Thursday /ˈθɜːzdeɪ, -dɪ/ *n* jeudi *m*

thus /ðʌs/ *adv* ainsi; **~ far** jusqu'à présent

thwart /θwɔːt/ *vt* contrarier ‹*plan*›; contrecarrer les desseins de ‹*person*›

thyme /taɪm/ *n* thym *m*

thyroid /ˈθaɪrɔɪd/ *n* (*also* **~ gland**) thyroïde *f*

tiara /tɪˈɑːrə/ *n* (woman's) diadème *m*; (Pope's) tiare *f*

Tibet /tɪˈbet/ *pr n* Tibet *m*

tick /tɪk/ **A** *n* **1** (of clock) tic-tac *m*
2 (mark) coche *f*
3 (Zool) tique *f*
B *vt* cocher ‹*box, name, answer*›
C *vi* ‹*bomb, clock, watch*› faire tic-tac

■ **tick off** cocher ‹*name, item*›

ticket /ˈtɪkɪt/ *n* **1** (for plane, train, cinema, exhibition) billet *m* (**for** pour); (for bus, underground, cloakroom, left-luggage) ticket *m*; (for library) carte *f*; (label) étiquette *f*
2 (Aut) (fam) (for fine) PV *m* (fam)
3 (AmE) (of political party) liste *f* (électorale)

ticket office *n* (office) bureau *m* de vente (des billets); (booth) guichet *m*

tickle /ˈtɪkl/ **A** *n* chatouillement *m*
B *vt* **1** ‹*person, feather*› chatouiller; ‹*wool, garment*› gratter
2 (fam) (gratify) chatouiller ‹*palate, vanity*›
3 (amuse) amuser
C *vi* chatouiller

tidal wave *n* raz-de-marée *m inv*

tide /taɪd/ *n* marée *f*; (fig) (of emotion) vague *f*; (of events) cours *m*

tidy /ˈtaɪdɪ/ **A** *adj* **1** ‹*house, room, desk*› bien rangé/-e; ‹*garden, work, appearance*› soigné/-e; ‹*habits, person*› ordonné/-e; ‹*hair*› bien coiffé/-e
2 (fam) ‹*amount*› beau/belle *before n*
B *vt, vi* = **tidy up**

■ **tidy up**: **A** **~ up** faire du rangement; **to ~ up after** ranger derrière ‹*person*›
B **~ up [sth]** ranger ‹*house, room, objects*›; arranger ‹*appearance, hair*›

tie /taɪ/ **A** *n* **1** (piece of clothing) cravate *f*
2 (bond) lien *m*
3 (constraint) contrainte *f*
4 (draw) match *m* nul
B *vt* (*p prés* **tying**) **1** attacher ‹*label, animal*› (**to** à); ligoter ‹*hands*›; ficeler ‹*parcel*› (**with** avec); nouer ‹*scarf, cravat*›; attacher ‹*laces*›; **to ~ a knot in sth** faire un nœud à qch
2 (link) associer (**to** à)
3 to be ~d to être rivé/-e à ‹*job*›; être cloué/-e à (fam) ‹*house*›
C *vi* (*p prés* **tying**) **1** (fasten) s'attacher
2 (draw) (in match) faire match nul; (in race) être ex aequo; (in vote) obtenir le même nombre de voix

■ **tie back** nouer [qch] derrière ‹*hair*›

■ **tie down**: **she feels ~d down** elle se sent coincée (fam); **he doesn't want to be ~d down** il ne veut pas perdre sa liberté; **to ~ sb down to sth** (limit) imposer qch à qn

■ **tie in with** concorder avec ‹*fact, event*›

■ **tie up 1** ligoter ‹*prisoner*›; ficeler ‹*parcel*›; attacher ‹*animal*›
2 (freeze) immobiliser ‹*capital*›
3 to be ~d up (busy) être pris/-e
4 (finalize) conclure ‹*deal*›; **to ~ up the loose ends** régler les derniers détails

tie break *n* (*also* **tie breaker**) (in tennis) tie-break *m*; (in quiz) question *f* subsidiaire

tier /tɪə(r)/ *n* (of cake, sandwich) étage *m*; (of system) niveau *m*; (of seating) gradin *m*

tiff /tɪf/ *n* (petite) querelle *f*

tiger /ˈtaɪgə(r)/ *n* tigre *m*

tight /taɪt/ **A** *adj* **1** ‹*grip*› ferme; ‹*knot*› serré/-e; ‹*rope, voice*› tendu/-e
2 ‹*space*› étroit/-e; ‹*clothing*› serré/-e; (closefitting) ‹*jacket, shirt*› ajusté/-e; **my shoes are too ~** mes chaussures me serrent
3 (strict) ‹*security, deadline*› strict/-e; ‹*budget, credit, schedule*› serré/-e
B *adv* ‹*hold, grip*› fermement; **hold ~!** cramponne-toi!; **sit ~!** ne bouge pas!

tighten /ˈtaɪtn/ **A** *vt* serrer ‹*lid, screw*›; resserrer ‹*grip*›; renforcer ‹*security, restrictions*›
B *vi* ‹*lips*› se serrer; ‹*muscle*› se contracter

tight-fisted *adj* (fam) radin/-e (fam)

tight-fitting *adj* ajusté/-e

tight-knit *adj* uni/-e

tightly /ˈtaɪtlɪ/ *adv* ‹*grasp, hold*› fermement; ‹*embrace*› bien fort; ‹*fastened*› bien

tightrope /ˈtaɪtrəʊp/ *n* corde *f* raide

tightrope walker *n* funambule *mf*

tights *npl* (BrE) collant *m*

tile /taɪl/ **A** *n* (for roof) tuile *f*; (for floor, wall) carreau *m*
B *vt* poser des tuiles sur ‹*roof*›; carreler ‹*floor, wall*›

till¹ /tɪl/ = **until**

till² /tɪl/ *n* caisse *f*

tiller /ˈtɪlə(r)/ *n* barre *f*

till receipt *n* ticket *m* (de caisse)

tilt /tɪlt/ **A** *vt* pencher ‹*table, sunshade*›; incliner ‹*head*›; rabattre ‹*hat, cap*›
B *vi* (slant) pencher

timber /ˈtɪmbə(r)/ *n* (for building) bois *m* (de construction); (trees) arbres *mpl*; (beam) poutre *f*

time /taɪm/ **A** *n* **1** temps *m*; **as ~ goes/went by** avec le temps; **you've got plenty of ~** tu as tout ton temps; **a long ~** longtemps; **a long ~ ago** il y a longtemps; **in five days' ~** dans cinq jours
2 (hour of the day, night) heure *f*; **what ~ is it?**, **what's the ~?** quelle heure est-il?; **10 am French ~** 10 heures, heure française; **this ~**

last week il y a exactement huit jours; **on ~** à l'heure; **the train ~s** les horaires *mpl* des trains; **it's ~ for bed** c'est l'heure d'aller au lit; **it's ~ we started** il est temps de commencer; **about ~ too!** ce n'est pas trop tôt!; **in ~ for Christmas** à temps pour Noël
3 (era, epoch) époque *f*; **at the ~** à l'époque; **in former ~s** autrefois; **it's just like old ~s** c'est comme au bon vieux temps
4 (moment) moment *m*; **at ~s** par moments; **at the right ~** au bon moment; **this is no ~ for jokes** ce n'est pas le moment de plaisanter; **at all ~s** à tout moment; **any ~ now** d'un moment à l'autre; **by the ~ I finished the letter the post had gone** le temps de finir ma lettre et le courrier était parti; **some ~ next month** dans le courant du mois prochain; **for the ~ being** pour le moment
5 (occasion) fois *f*; **nine ~s out of ten** neuf fois sur dix; **three ~s a month** trois fois par mois; **three at a ~** trois à la fois; **from ~ to ~** de temps en temps
6 (experience) **to have a hard ~ doing** avoir du mal à faire; **he's having a hard ~** il traverse une période difficile; **we had a good ~** on s'est bien amusés
7 (Mus) mesure *f*
8 ten ~s longer/stronger dix fois plus long/plus fort; **eight ~s as much** huit fois autant
9 (in mathematics) fois *f*
B *vt* **1** (schedule) prévoir ‹*holiday, visit, attack*›; fixer ‹*appointment, meeting*›
2 (judge) calculer ‹*blow, shot*›
3 chronométrer ‹*athlete, cyclist*›
IDIOMS **all in good ~** chaque chose en son temps; **only ~ will tell** l'avenir nous le dira; **to have ~ on one's hands** (for brief period) avoir du temps devant soi; (longer) avoir beaucoup de temps libre

time bomb *n* bombe *f* à retardement
time-consuming /ˌtaɪmkən'sjuːmɪŋ, (AmE) -'suː-/ *adj* qui prend du temps
time difference *n* décalage *m* horaire
time frame *n* (period envisaged) calendrier *m*; (period allocated) délai *m*
timeless /'taɪmlɪs/ *adj* éternel/-elle
time limit /'taɪmlɪmɪt/ *n* **1** (deadline) date *f* limite
2 (maximum duration) durée *f* maximum
timely /'taɪmlɪ/ *adj* opportun/-e
time management *n* gestion *f* du temps
time off /ˌtaɪm 'ɒf/ *n* (leave) congé *m*; (free time) temps *m* libre
timer /'taɪmə(r)/ *n* (on light) minuterie *f*; (for cooking) minuteur *m*
timeshare /'taɪmʃeə(r)/ *n* (house) maison *f* en multipropriété; (apartment) appartement *m* en multipropriété
time sheet *n* feuille *f* de présence
time span /'taɪmspæn/ *n* durée *f*

timetable /'taɪmteɪbl/ **A** *n* (Sch) emploi *m* du temps; (for plans, negotiations) calendrier *m*; (for buses, trains) horaire *m*
B *vt* fixer l'heure de ‹*class*›; fixer la date de ‹*meeting*›
time zone *n* fuseau *m* horaire
timid /'tɪmɪd/ *adj* timide; ‹*animal*› craintif/-ive
timing /'taɪmɪŋ/ *n* **1** (gen) **the ~ of the announcement was unfortunate** le moment choisi pour la déclaration était inopportun
2 (Aut) réglage *m* de l'allumage
3 (Mus) sens *m* du rythme
tin /tɪn/ *n* **1** (metal) étain *m*
2 (BrE) (can) boîte *f* (de conserve)
3 (for biscuits, cake) boîte *f*; (for paint) pot *m*; (for baking) moule *m*; (for roasting) plat *m* (à rôtir)
tin can *n* boîte *f* en fer-blanc
tinfoil *n* papier *m* (d')aluminium
tinge /tɪndʒ/ **A** *n* nuance *f*
B *vt* teinter (with de)
tingle /'tɪŋgl/ **A** *n* (physical) picotement *m*; (psychological) frisson *m*
B *vi* (physically) picoter; (psychologically) frissonner
tinker /'tɪŋkə(r)/ *vi* **to ~ with** bricoler ‹*car*›; faire des retouches à ‹*document*›
tinkle /'tɪŋkl/ **A** *n* tintement *m*
B *vi* tinter
tinned *adj* (BrE) ‹*meat, fruit*› en boîte, en conserve
tinny /'tɪnɪ/ *adj* ‹*sound*› grêle; (badly made) de camelote (fam)
tin opener *n* (BrE) ouvre-boîtes *m inv*
tinsel /'tɪnsl/ *n* guirlandes *fpl*
tint /tɪnt/ *n* (trace) nuance *f*; (pale colour) teinte *f*; (hair colour) shampooing *m* colorant
tinted *adj* ‹*glass, spectacles*› fumé/-e; ‹*hair*› teint/-e
✓ **tiny** /'taɪnɪ/ *adj* tout/-e petit/-e
tip /tɪp/ **A** *n* **1** (of stick, sword, pen, shoe, spire) pointe *f*; (of branch, leaf, shoot, tail, feather) extrémité *f*; (of finger, nose, tongue) bout *m*
2 (gratuity) pourboire *m*
3 (practical hint) truc *m* (fam), conseil *m*; (in betting) tuyau *m* (fam)
B *vt* (*p prés etc* **-pp-**) **1** (tilt) incliner; (pour) verser; (dump) déverser ‹*waste, rubbish*›
2 (predict) **to ~ sb/sth to win** prédire que qn/qch va gagner
3 donner un pourboire à ‹*waiter, driver*›
C *vi* (*p prés etc* **-pp-**) (tilt) s'incliner
■ **tip off**: **~ off [sb], ~ [sb] off** avertir
■ **tip over** faire basculer ‹*chair*›; renverser ‹*bucket, pile*›
tip-off /'tɪpɒf/ *n* dénonciation *f*
tiptoe /'tɪptəʊ/ **A** *n* **on ~** sur la pointe des pieds
B *vi* marcher sur la pointe des pieds
tire /'taɪə(r)/ **A** *n* (AmE) pneu *m*
B *vt* fatiguer

✓ mot clé

C *vi* **1** (get tired) se fatiguer
2 (get bored) **to ~ of** se lasser de
■ **tire out** épuiser ‹*person*›; **to be ~d out** être éreinté/-e

tired /'taɪəd/ *adj* **1** (weary) ‹*person, face, legs*› fatigué/-e; ‹*voice*› las/lasse
2 (bored) **to be ~ of sth/of doing** en avoir assez de qch/de faire; **to grow ~ of sth/of doing** se lasser de qch/de faire

tiredness /'taɪədnɪs/ *n* fatigue *f*

tireless /'taɪəlɪs/ *adj* ‹*person*› inlassable, infatigable; ‹*efforts*› constant/-e

tiresome /'taɪəsəm/ *adj* ‹*person, habit*› agaçant/-e; ‹*problem, duty*› fastidieux/-ieuse

tiring /'taɪərɪŋ/ *adj* fatigant/-e (**to do** de faire)

tissue /'tɪʃuː/ *n* **1** (handkerchief) mouchoir *m* en papier
2 (*also* **~ paper**) papier *m* de soie
3 (Anat, Bot) tissu *m*

tit /tɪt/ *n* (Zool) mésange *f*
IDIOM **~ for tat** un prêté pour un rendu

titbit /'tɪtbɪt/ *n* (BrE) (of food) gâterie *f*; (of gossip) cancan *m* (fam)

title /'taɪtl/ **A** *n* titre *m*
B **titles** *npl* (in film) générique *m*
C *vt* intituler ‹*book, play*›

title bar *n* (Comput) barre *f* de titre

title-holder *n* tenant/-e *m/f* du titre

title role *n* rôle *m* titre

titter /'tɪtə(r)/ **A** *n* ricanement *m*
B *vi* ricaner

tizzy /'tɪzɪ/ *n* (fam) **to be in a ~** être dans tous ses états

to /tə, *before a vowel* tʊ, tuː, *emphat.* tuː/

> Remember that when *to* is translated by *à* then *à* + *le* = *au* and *à* + *les* = *aux*.

A *infinitive particle* **1** (expressing purpose) pour; **to do sth ~ impress one's friends** faire qch pour impressionner ses amis
2 (linking consecutive acts) **he looked up ~ see...** en levant les yeux, il a vu...
3 (after superlatives) à; **the youngest ~ do** le *or* la plus jeune à faire
4 (avoiding repetition of verb) **'did you go?'—'no I promised not ~'** 'tu y es allé?'—'non j'avais promis de ne pas le faire'; **'are you staying?'—'I want ~ but...'** 'tu restes?'—'j'aimerais bien mais...'
5 (following impersonal verb) **it is difficult ~ do** il est difficile de faire; **it's difficult ~ understand** c'est difficile à comprendre; **it's easy ~ read her writing** il est facile de lire son écriture
B *prep* **1** (in direction of) à ‹*shops, school*›; (with purpose of visiting) chez ‹*doctor's*›; **she's gone ~ Mary's** elle est partie chez Mary; **~ Paris** à Paris; **~ Spain** en Espagne; **~ town** en ville; **the road ~ the village** la route qui mène au village; **turned ~ the wall** tourné vers le mur
2 (up to) jusqu'à; **~ the end/this day** jusqu'à la fin/ce jour
3 (in telling time) **ten (minutes) ~ three** trois heures moins dix; **it's five ~** il est moins cinq
4 (introducing direct or indirect object) ‹*give, offer*› à; (to + *personal pronoun*) me/te/lui/nous/vous/leur; **give the book ~ Sophie** donne le livre à Sophie; **be nice ~ your brother** sois gentil avec ton frère; **~ me it's just a minor problem** pour moi ce n'est qu'un problème mineur; **she gave it ~ them/him** elle le leur/lui a donné
5 (in toasts, dedications) à; **~ prosperity** à la prospérité; **~ our dear son** (on tombstone) à notre cher fils
6 (in accordance with) **is it ~ your taste?** c'est à ton goût?; **to dance ~ the music** danser sur la musique
7 (in relationships, comparisons) **to win by three goals ~ two** gagner par trois buts à deux; **next door ~ the school** à côté de l'école
8 (showing accuracy) **three weeks ~ the day** trois semaines jour pour jour; **~ scale** à l'échelle
9 (showing reason) **to invite sb ~ dinner** inviter qn à dîner; **~ this end** à cette fin
10 (belonging to) de; **the key ~ the safe** la clé du coffre; **a room ~ myself** une chambre pour moi tout seul; **personal assistant ~ the director** assistant du directeur
11 ‹*tied*› à; ‹*pinned*› à ‹*noticeboard*›; sur ‹*lapel, dress*›
12 (showing reaction) à; **~ his surprise/dismay** à sa grande surprise/consternation

toad /təʊd/ *n* crapaud *m*

toadstool *n* champignon *m* vénéneux

to and fro /ˌtuː ən 'frəʊ/ *adv* ‹*swing*› d'avant en arrière; **to go ~** ‹*person*› aller et venir

toast /təʊst/ **A** *n* **1** (bread) toast *m*; **a slice of ~** un toast
2 (drink) toast *m*; **to drink a ~** lever son verre
B *vt* **1** faire griller ‹*bread*›
2 porter un toast à ‹*person, success*›

toaster /'təʊstə(r)/ *n* grille-pain *m inv*

tobacco /tə'bækəʊ/ *n* (*pl* **~s**) tabac *m*

toboggan /tə'bɒgən/ *n* luge *f*, toboggan *m*

today /tə'deɪ/ **A** *n* aujourd'hui *m*; **~ is Monday** (aujourd'hui) nous sommes lundi
B *adv* aujourd'hui; (nowadays) de nos jours; **~ week** dans une semaine aujourd'hui; **a week ago ~** il y a une semaine aujourd'hui; **later ~** plus tard dans la journée

toddler /'tɒdlə(r)/ *n* très jeune enfant *m*

toe /təʊ/ *n* **1** (Anat) orteil *m*; **big/little ~** gros/petit orteil
2 (of sock, shoe) bout *m*
IDIOMS **to ~ the line** marcher droit; **from top to ~** de la tête aux pieds

toehold /'təʊhəʊld/ *n* (in climbing) prise *f*; **to get** *or* **gain a ~ in** s'introduire dans ‹*market, organization*›

toffee /'tɒfɪ, (AmE) 'tɔːfɪ/ *n* caramel *m* (au beurre)

⚷ **together** /tə'geðə(r)/ **A** *adv* **1** ensemble; **to get back ~ again** se remettre ensemble; **to be close ~** être rapprochés/-es; **she's cleverer than all the rest of them put ~** elle est plus intelligente que tous les autres réunis; **they belong ~** (objects) ils vont ensemble; (people) ils sont faits l'un pour l'autre; **the talks brought the two sides closer ~** les négociations ont rapproché les deux parties
2 (at the same time) à la fois
B together with *phr* (as well as) ainsi que; (in the company of) avec
IDIOM **to get one's act ~** s'organiser

togetherness /tə'geðənɪs/ *n* (in team, friendship) camaraderie *f*; (in family, couple) intimité *f*

toil /tɔɪl/ **A** *n* labeur *m*
B *vi* **1** (*also* **toil away**) ‹*work*› peiner
2 (struggle) **to ~ up the hill** monter péniblement la côte

toilet /'tɔɪlɪt/ *n* toilettes *fpl*; **public ~(s)** toilettes publiques

toilet bag *n* trousse *f* de toilette

toilet paper, **toilet tissue** *n* papier *m* hygiénique

toiletries /'tɔɪlɪtrɪz/ *npl* articles *mpl* de toilette

toilet roll *n* (roll) rouleau *m* de papier toilette; (tissue) papier *m* toilette

token /'təʊkən/ **A** *n* **1** (for machine, phone) jeton *m*
2 (voucher) bon *m*; **book/record ~** chèque-cadeau *m* pour livre/pour disque
3 témoignage *m*; **as a ~ of** en signe de
B *adj* symbolique; **to make a ~ gesture** faire un geste pour la forme

tolerable /'tɒlərəbl/ *adj* (bearable) tolérable; (adequate) acceptable

tolerance /'tɒlərəns/ *n* (gen), (Med) tolérance *f*

tolerant /'tɒlərənt/ *adj* tolérant/-e

tolerate /'tɒləreɪt/ *vt* (permit) tolérer; (put up with) supporter

toll /təʊl/ **A** *n* **1 death ~** nombre *m* de victimes (**from** de)
2 (levy) (on road, bridge) péage *m*
3 (of bell) son *m*; (for funeral) glas *m*
B *vt*, *vi* sonner

toll call *n* (AmE) communication *f* interurbaine

tomato /tə'mɑːtəʊ, (AmE) tə'meɪtəʊ/ **A** *n* (*pl* **~es**) tomate *f*
B *adj* ‹*purée*› de tomate; ‹*juice, salad*› de tomates; ‹*soup*› à la tomate

tomato sauce *n* sauce *f* tomate

tomb /tuːm/ *n* tombeau *m*

⚷ mot clé

tomboy /'tɒmbɔɪ/ *n* garçon *m* manqué

tombstone *n* pierre *f* tombale

tomcat /'tɒmkæt/ *n* matou *m*

⚷ **tomorrow** /tə'mɒrəʊ/ **A** *n* demain *m*; **I'll do it by ~** je le ferai d'ici demain
B *adv* demain; **see you ~!** à demain!; **~ week** demain en huit; **a week ago ~** il y aura une semaine demain

tomorrow afternoon *n*, *adv* demain après-midi

tomorrow evening *n*, *adv* demain soir

tomorrow morning *n*, *adv* demain matin

ton /tʌn/ *n* **1** (in weight) (BrE) (*also* **gross ~** *or* **long ~**) tonne *f* britannique (= *1.1016 kg*); (AmE) (*also* **net ~** *or* **short ~**) tonne *f* américaine (= *907 kg*); **metric ~** tonne *f*
2 (fam) (a lot) **~s of** des tas de (fam) ‹*food, paper, bands*›

⚷ **tone** /təʊn/ **A** *n* **1** (gen) ton *m*; **his ~ of voice** son ton; **to set the ~** donner le ton (**for** à)
2 (Mus) timbre *m*; (on phone) tonalité *f*
3 (of muscle) tonus *m*
B *vt* (*also* **~ up**) tonifier ‹*body, muscles*›
C *vi* (*also* **~ in**) (blend) ‹*colours*› s'harmoniser
■ **tone down** atténuer ‹*colours, criticism*›; adoucir le ton de ‹*letter, statement*›

tone-deaf /ˌtəʊn'def/ *adj* **to be ~** ne pas avoir l'oreille musicale

tongs /tɒŋz/ *npl* (for coal) pincettes *fpl*; (in laboratory, for sugar) pince *f*

tongue /tʌŋ/ *n* **1** (gen) langue *f*; **to stick one's ~ out at sb** tirer la langue à qn; **to lose one's ~** (fig) avaler sa langue
2 (on shoe) languette *f*
IDIOMS **I have his name on the tip of my ~** j'ai son nom sur le bout de la langue; **a slip of the ~** un lapsus

tongue-in-cheek /ˌtʌŋɪn'tʃiːk/ *adj*, *adv* au deuxième degré

tongue stud *n* piercing *m* de la langue

tongue-tied *adj* muet/-ette

tongue-twister *n* phrase *f* difficile à dire

tonic /'tɒnɪk/ *n* **1** (*also* **~ water**) eau *f* tonique; **a gin and ~** un gin tonic
2 (Med) remontant *m*

⚷ **tonight** /tə'naɪt/ **A** *n* ce soir
B *adv* (this evening) ce soir; (after bedtime) cette nuit

tonne /tʌn/ *n* tonne *f*

tonsil /'tɒnsl/ *n* amygdale *f*; **to have one's ~s out** se faire opérer des amygdales

tonsillitis /ˌtɒnsɪ'laɪtɪs/ *n* amygdalite *f*

⚷ **too** /tuː, tʊ, tə/ *adv* **1** (also) aussi; **have you been to India ~?** (like me) est-ce que toi aussi tu es allé en Inde?; (as well as other countries) est-ce que tu es allé en Inde aussi?
2 (excessively) trop; **~ big** trop grand/-e; **~ many/~ few people** trop de/trop peu de gens; **I ate ~ much** j'ai trop mangé; **you're**

~ **kind!** vous êtes trop aimable!; **I'm not ~ sure about that** je n'en suis pas si sûr

tool /tuːl/ *n* outil *m*

toolbar *n* (Comput) barre *f* d'outils

toolbox *n* boîte *f* à outils

toolkit *n* trousse *f* à outils

tooth /tuːθ/ *n* (*pl* **teeth**) dent *f*

toothache /ˈtuːθeɪk/ *n* mal *m* de dents; **to have ~** (BrE) *or* **a ~** avoir mal aux dents

toothbrush *n* brosse *f* à dents

toothpaste *n* dentifrice *m*

toothpick *n* cure-dents *m inv*

top /tɒp/ **A** *n* **1** (of page, ladder, stairs, wall) haut *m*; (of list) tête *f*; (of mountain, hill) sommet *m*; (of garden, field) (autre) bout *m*; (of vegetable) fane *f*; (of box, cake) dessus *m*; (surface) surface *f*; **at the ~ of** en haut de ‹*page, stairs, street, scale*›; au sommet de ‹*hill*›; en tête de ‹*list*›; **at the ~ of the building** au dernier étage de l'immeuble; **at the ~ of the table** à la place d'honneur; **to be at the ~ of the agenda** être une priorité
2 (highest position) **to aim for the ~** viser haut; **to get to** *or* **make it to the ~** réussir; **to be ~ of the class** être le premier/la première de la classe; **to be ~ of the bill** être la tête d'affiche
3 (cap, lid) (of pen) capuchon *m*; (of bottle) bouchon *m*; (with serrated edge) capsule *f*; (of paint-tin, saucepan) couvercle *m*
4 (item of clothing) haut *m*
5 (toy) toupie *f*
B *adj* **1** (highest) ‹*step, storey*› dernier/-ière *before n*; ‹*bunk*› de haut; ‹*button, shelf*› du haut; ‹*layer, lip*› supérieur/-e; ‹*speed*› maximum; ‹*concern, priority*› majeur/-e; **in the ~ left-hand corner** en haut à gauche; **to get ~ marks** (BrE) (Sch) avoir dix sur dix *or* vingt sur vingt
2 (furthest away) ‹*field, house*› du bout
3 (leading) ‹*adviser, politician*› de haut niveau; ‹*job*› élevé/-e; ‹*wine, restaurant*› haut de gamme
C *vt* (*p prés etc* **-pp-**) **1** être en tête de ‹*charts, polls*›
2 (exceed) dépasser ‹*sum, figure*›
3 (finish off) compléter (**with** par); (Culin) recouvrir ‹*cake*›
D on top of *phr* **1** (on) sur ‹*cupboard, fridge, layer*›
2 (in addition to) en plus de ‹*salary, workload*›
IDIOMS **on ~ of all this, to ~ it all** par-dessus le marché (fam); **from ~ to bottom** de fond en comble; **to be over the ~, to be OTT** (fam) ‹*behaviour, reaction*› être exagéré/-e; **to feel on ~ of the world** être aux anges; **to shout at the ~ of one's voice** crier à tue-tête
■ **top up** remplir (à nouveau) ‹*tank, glass*›; recharger ‹*mobile phone*›

topaz /ˈtəʊpæz/ *n* topaze *f*

top hat *n* haut-de-forme *m*

top-heavy /ˌtɒpˈhevɪ/ *adj* lourd/-e du haut

topic /ˈtɒpɪk/ *n* (of conversation, conference) sujet *m*; (of essay, research) thème *m*

topical /ˈtɒpɪkl/ *adj* d'actualité

topless /ˈtɒplɪs/ *adj* ‹*model*› aux seins nus

top-level *adj* ‹*talks, negotiations*› au plus haut niveau

top management *n* (haute) direction *f*

top of the range *adj* haut de gamme *inv*

topping /ˈtɒpɪŋ/ *n* (of jam, cream) nappage *m*

topple /ˈtɒpl/ **A** *vt* renverser
B *vi* (sway) ‹*vase, pile of books*› vaciller; (fall) (*also* **~ over**) ‹*vase, person*› basculer; ‹*pile of books*› s'effondrer

top-ranking *adj* important/-e

top secret *adj* ultrasecret/-ète

topsy-turvy /ˌtɒpsɪˈtɜːvɪ/ *adj, adv* (fam) sens dessus dessous

top-up card *n* (for mobile phone) carte *f* de recharge

torch /tɔːtʃ/ *n* **1** (BrE) (flashlight) lampe *f* de poche
2 (burning) flambeau *m*, torche *f*

torment **A** /ˈtɔːment/ *n* supplice *m*
B /tɔːˈment/ *vt* tourmenter

tormentor /tɔːˈmentə(r)/ *n* persécuteur/-trice *m/f*

torn /tɔːn/ *adj* déchiré/-e

tornado /tɔːˈneɪdəʊ/ *n* (*pl* **~es** *ou* **~s**) tornade *f*

torpedo /tɔːˈpiːdəʊ/ *n* torpille *f*

torrent /ˈtɒrənt, (AmE) ˈtɔːr-/ *n* torrent *m*; (fig) flot *m*

torrential /təˈrenʃl/ *adj* torrentiel/-ielle

torrid /ˈtɒrɪd, (AmE) ˈtɔːr-/ *adj* torride

torso /ˈtɔːsəʊ/ *n* (*pl* **~s**) torse *m*

tortoise /ˈtɔːtəs/ *n* tortue *f*

tortoiseshell /ˈtɔːtəsʃel/ *n* (shell) écaille *f*

tortuous /ˈtɔːtʃʊəs/ *adj* tortueux/-euse

torture /ˈtɔːtʃə(r)/ **A** *n* torture *f*; (fig) supplice *m*
B *vt* torturer; (fig) tourmenter

Tory /ˈtɔːrɪ/ *n* (BrE) Tory *mf*, conservateur/-trice *m/f*

toss /tɒs/ **A** *n* (*pl* **~es**) **1** (throw) jet *m*; **a ~ of the head** un mouvement brusque de la tête
2 to decide sth on the ~ of a coin décider qch à pile ou face
B *vt* **1** (throw) lancer ‹*ball, stick, dice*›; faire sauter ‹*pancake*›; tourner ‹*salad*›; **to ~ a coin** jouer à pile ou face
2 ‹*animal*› secouer ‹*head, mane*›; **to ~ one's head** ‹*person*› rejeter la tête en arrière
3 ‹*horse*› désarçonner ‹*rider*›
4 ‹*wind*› agiter ‹*branches, leaves*›
C *vi* **1** ‹*person*› se retourner; **I ~ed and turned all night** je me suis tourné et retourné toute la nuit
2 (flip a coin) tirer à pile ou face; **to ~ for first turn** tirer le premier tour à pile ou face

t

■ **toss off** (fam): **~ [sth] off, ~ off [sth]** expédier

■ **toss out**: **A** **~ [sth] out, ~ out [sth]** jeter ‹*newspaper, empty bottles*›
B **~ [sb] out** éjecter (**from** de)

tot /tɒt/ *n* **1** (fam) (toddler) tout/-e petit/-e enfant *m/f*
2 (BrE) (of whisky, rum) petite dose *f*

✓ **total** /ˈtəʊtl/ **A** *n* total *m*; **in ~** au total
B *adj* **1** ‹*cost, amount, profit*› total/-e
2 (complete) ‹*effect*› global/-e; ‹*disaster, eclipse*› total/-e; ‹*ignorance*› complet/-ète
C *vt* (*p prés etc* **-ll-** (BrE), **-l-** (AmE)) **1** (add up) additionner ‹*figures*›
2 ‹*bill*› se monter à ‹*sum*›

totalitarian /ˌtəʊtælɪˈteərɪən/ *n, adj* totalitaire *mf*

✓ **totally** /ˈtəʊtəlɪ/ *adv* ‹*blind, deaf*› complètement; ‹*unacceptable, convinced*› totalement; ‹*agree, change, new, different*› entièrement

totem /ˈtəʊtəm/ *n* (pole) totem *m*; (symbol) symbole *m*

totter /ˈtɒtə(r)/ *vi* ‹*person, regime, government*› chanceler; ‹*drunk person*› tituber; ‹*baby*› trébucher; ‹*pile of books, building*› chanceler

✓ **touch** /tʌtʃ/ **A** *n* **1** contact *m* (physique); **the ~ of her hand** le contact de sa main
2 (sense) toucher *m*
3 (style, skill) (of artist, writer) touche *f*; (of musician) toucher *m*; **to lose one's ~** perdre la main; **that's a clever ~!** ça, c'est génial!
4 (little) **a ~** un petit peu
5 (communication) **to get/stay in ~ with** se mettre/rester en contact avec; **he's out of ~ with reality** il est déconnecté de la réalité
6 (Sport) touche *f*
B *vt* **1** toucher; (interfere with) toucher à; **to ~ sb on the shoulder** toucher l'épaule de qn; **I never ~ alcohol** je ne prends jamais d'alcool
2 (affect) toucher; (adversely) affecter; (as matter of concern) concerner; **we were most ~ed** nous avons été très touchés
C *vi* se toucher

IDIOMS **to be a soft ~** être un pigeon (fam); **it's ~ and go whether he'll make it through the night** il risque fort de ne pas passer la nuit

■ **touch down 1** ‹*plane*› atterrir
2 (Sport) (in rugby) marquer un essai

■ **touch (up)on** effleurer ‹*topic*›

touchdown /ˈtʌtʃdaʊn/ *n* **1** (by plane) atterrissage *m*
2 (Sport) essai *m*

touched /tʌtʃt/ *adj* **1** (emotionally) touché/-e
2 (fam) (mad) dérangé/-e (fam)

touching /ˈtʌtʃɪŋ/ *adj* touchant/-e

touchline *n* ligne *f* de touche

touchpad *n* tablette *f* tactile

touch screen *n* écran *m* tactile

touch-tone *adj* ‹*telephone*› à touches

touch-type *vi* taper au toucher

touchy /ˈtʌtʃɪ/ *adj* susceptible (**about** sur la question de)

✓ **tough** /tʌf/ **A** *adj* **1** ‹*businessman*› coriace; ‹*criminal*› endurci/-e; ‹*policy, measure, law*› sévère; ‹*opposition, competition*› rude; **a ~ guy** un dur (fam)
2 (difficult) difficile
3 (robust) ‹*person, animal*› robuste; ‹*plant, material*› résistant/-e
4 ‹*meat*› coriace
5 (rough) ‹*area, school*› dur/-e
B *excl* (fam) tant pis pour toi!

toughen /ˈtʌfn/ *vt* **1** renforcer ‹*leather, plastic*›; tremper ‹*glass, steel*›; durcir ‹*skin*›
2 (*also* **~ up**) endurcir ‹*person*›; renforcer ‹*law*›

toupee /ˈtuːpeɪ, (AmE) tuːˈpeɪ/ *n* postiche *m*

✓ **tour** /tʊə(r), tɔː(r)/ **A** *n* **1** (of country) circuit *m*; (of city) tour *m*; (of building) visite *f*; (trip in bus) excursion *f*
2 (by team, band, theatre company) tournée *f*
B *vt* **1** visiter ‹*building, country, gallery*›
2 ‹*band, team*› être en tournée en ‹*country*›; ‹*theatre production*› tourner en ‹*country*›
C *vi* ‹*orchestra, play, team*› être en tournée

touring /ˈtʊərɪŋ, ˈtɔːr-/ *n* **1** (by tourist) tourisme *m*
2 (by team, theatre company, band) tournée *f*

tourism /ˈtʊərɪzəm, ˈtɔːr-/ *n* tourisme *m*

✓ **tourist** /ˈtʊərɪst, ˈtɔːr-/ *n* touriste *mf*

tourist class *n* (on flight) classe *f* touriste

tourist office *n* (*also* **tourist information office**) (in town) syndicat *m* d'initiative; (national organization) office *m* du tourisme

tourist trap *n* piège *m* à touristes

touristy /ˈtʊərɪstɪ, ˈtɔːr-/ *adj* (fam) envahi/-e par les touristes

tournament /ˈtɔːnəmənt, (AmE) ˈtɜːrn-/ *n* tournoi *m*

tousle /ˈtaʊzl/ *vt* ébouriffer ‹*hair*›

tousled *adj* ‹*hair*› ébouriffé/-e; ‹*person, appearance*› débraillé/-e

tout /taʊt/ *n* **1** (BrE) (selling tickets) revendeur *m* de billets au marché noir
2 (soliciting custom) racoleur/-euse *m/f*
3 (racing) vendeur *m* de tuyaux

tow /təʊ/ **A** *n* (Aut) **to be on ~** être en remorque
B *vt* remorquer, tracter ‹*trailer, caravan*›

■ **tow away**: **~ away [sth], ~ [sth] away** ‹*police*› emmener [qch] à la fourrière; ‹*recovery service*› remorquer

✓ **towards** (BrE), **toward** (AmE) *prep*

When *towards* is used to talk about direction or position, it is generally translated by *vers*: *she ran toward(s) him* = elle a couru vers lui.

> When *toward(s)* is used to mean *in relation to*, it is translated by *envers*: *his attitude toward(s) his parents* = son attitude envers ses parents. For further examples, see the entry below.

1 vers; **~ the east** vers l'est; **he was standing with his back ~ me** il me tournait le dos; **~ evening** vers le soir; **~ the end of** vers la fin de ‹*month, life*› **2** envers; **to be friendly/hostile ~ sb** se montrer cordial/hostile envers qn **3** (as contribution) **the money will go ~ a new car** l'argent servira à payer une nouvelle voiture

towel /'taʊəl/ *n* serviette *f* (de toilette)

towelling /'taʊəlɪŋ/ *n* (cloth) tissu *m* éponge

tower /'taʊə(r)/ **A** *n* **1** (structure) tour *f* **2** (Comput) boîtier *m* vertical, tour *f*
B *vi* **to ~ above** *or* **over** dominer
IDIOM **to be a ~ of strength** être solide comme un roc

tower block *n* (BrE) tour *f* (d'habitation)

towering /'taʊərɪŋ/ *adj* imposant/-e

town /taʊn/ *n* ville *f*; **to go into ~** aller en ville
IDIOMS **to go to ~ on** ne pas lésiner sur ‹*decor, catering*›; exploiter [qch] à fond ‹*story, scandal*›; **he's the talk of the ~** on ne parle que de lui

town and country planning *n* aménagement *m* du territoire

town centre (BrE), **town center** (AmE) *n* centre-ville *m*

town council *n* (BrE) conseil *m* municipal

town hall *n* mairie *f*

town house *n* petite maison *f* en centre ville; (mansion) hôtel *m* particulier

town planning *n* (BrE) urbanisme *m*

township /'taʊnʃɪp/ *n* commune *f*; (in South Africa) township *m*

towpath *n* chemin *m* de halage

tow truck *n* dépanneuse *f*

toxic /'tɒksɪk/ *adj* toxique

toxin /'tɒksɪn/ *n* toxine *f*

toy /tɔɪ/ **A** *n* jouet *m*
B *vi* **to ~ with** jouer avec ‹*object, feelings*›; caresser ‹*idea*›; **to ~ with one's food** chipoter

toy boy *n* (BrE) (fam) gigolo *m*

toyshop *n* magasin *m* de jouets

trace /treɪs/ **A** *n* trace *f*
B *vt* **1** (locate) retrouver ‹*person, weapon, car*›; dépister ‹*fault*›; déterminer ‹*cause*›; **the call was ~d to a London number** on a pu établir que le coup de téléphone venait d'un numéro à Londres
2 (*also* **~ back**) faire remonter ‹*origins, ancestry*› (**to** à)
3 (draw) tracer; (copy) décalquer ‹*map, outline*›

tracing paper *n* papier-calque *m*

track /træk/ **A** *n* **1** (print) (of animal, person, vehicle) traces *fpl*
2 (course, trajectory) (of person) trace *f*; (of missile, aircraft, storm) trajectoire *f*; **to keep ~ of** ‹*person*› se tenir au courant de ‹*developments, events*›; suivre le fil de ‹*conversation*›; ‹*police*› suivre les mouvements de ‹*criminal*›; **to lose ~ of** perdre de vue ‹*friend*›; perdre la trace de ‹*document, aircraft, suspect*›; perdre le fil de ‹*conversation*›; **to lose ~ of (the) time** perdre la notion du temps
3 (path, road) sentier *m*, chemin *m*; (Sport) piste *f*
4 (railtrack) voie *f* ferrée; (AmE) (platform) quai *m*; **to leave the ~(s)** ‹*train*› dérailler
5 (on record, tape, CD) morceau *m*
6 (of tank, tractor) chenille *f*
7 (AmE) (Sch) (stream) groupe *m* de niveau
B *vt* suivre la trace de ‹*person, animal*›; suivre la trajectoire de ‹*rocket, plane*›
■ **track down** retrouver ‹*person, object*›

tracker ball *n* boule *f* de commande

tracker dog *n* chien *m* policier

track record *n* **to have a good ~** avoir de bons antécédents

track shoe *n* chaussure *f* de course à pointes

tracksuit *n* survêtement *m*

tract /trækt/ *n* **1** (of land) étendue *f* **2** (pamphlet) pamphlet *m*

tractor /'træktə(r)/ *n* tracteur *m*

trade /treɪd/ **A** *n* **1** (activity) commerce *m*; **to do a good ~** faire de bonnes affaires
2 (sector of industry) industrie *f*
3 (profession) (manual) métier *m*; (intellectual) profession *f*; **by ~** de métier
B *vt* échanger (**for** contre)
C *vi* faire du commerce
■ **trade in**: **he ~d in his old car for a new one** on lui a repris sa vieille voiture et il en a acheté une nouvelle

trade fair *n* salon *m*

trade-in /'treɪdɪn/ *n* reprise *f* (*d'un article usagé à l'achat d'un article neuf*)

trademark /'treɪdmɑːk/ *n* marque *f* déposée

trade name *n* nom *m* (de marque)

trade-off /'treɪdɒf/ *n* compromis *m*

trader /'treɪdə(r)/ *n* **1** (shopkeeper, stallholder) commerçant/-e *m/f*
2 (at stock exchange) opérateur/-trice *m/f* (en Bourse)

tradesman's entrance *n* entrée *f* de service

Trades Union Congress, TUC *n* (BrE) Confédération *f* des syndicats (britanniques)

trade union *n* syndicat *m*

trade union member *n* syndiqué/-e *m/f*

trading /'treɪdɪŋ/ *n* **1** (business) commerce *m* **2** (at stock exchange) transactions *fpl* (boursières)

trading estate *n* (BrE) zone *f* industrielle

🔑 **tradition** /trə'dɪʃn/ *n* tradition *f*

🔑 **traditional** /trə'dɪʃənl/ *adj* traditionnel/-elle

traditionalist /trə'dɪʃənəlɪst/ *n, adj* traditionaliste *mf*

🔑 **traffic** /'træfɪk/ **A** *n* **1** (on road) circulation *f*; (air, sea, rail) trafic *m*
2 (in drugs, arms, slaves, goods) trafic *m* (**in** de)
B *vi* (*p prés etc* **-ck-**) **to ~ in** faire du trafic de ‹*drugs, arms, stolen goods*›

traffic calming *n* mesures *fpl* pour ralentir la circulation

traffic jam *n* embouteillage *m*

trafficker /'træfɪkə(r)/ *n* trafiquant/-e *m/f* (in de)

traffic lights *npl* feux *mpl* (de signalisation)

traffic warden *n* (BrE) contractuel/-elle *m/f*

tragedy /'trædʒədɪ/ *n* tragédie *f*

tragic /'trædʒɪk/ *adj* tragique

trail /treɪl/ **A** *n* **1** (path) chemin *m*, piste *f*
2 (of blood, dust, slime) traînée *f*, trace *f*
3 (trace) trace *f*, piste *f*
B *vt* **1** (follow) ‹*animal, person*› suivre la piste de; ‹*car*› suivre
2 (drag) traîner
C *vi* **1** ‹*skirt, scarf*› traîner; ‹*plant*› pendre
2 (shuffle) **to ~ in/out** entrer/sortir en traînant les pieds
3 (lag) traîner; **our team were ~ing by 3 goals to 1** notre équipe avait un retard de 2 buts

trail bike *n* moto *f* tout terrain

trailblazer *n* pionnier/-ière *m/f*

trailer /'treɪlə(r)/ *n* **1** (vehicle, boat) remorque *f*
2 (AmE) (caravan) caravane *f*
3 (for film) bande-annonce *f*

trailer park *n* (AmE) terrain *m* de caravaning

🔑 **train** /treɪn/ **A** *n* **1** (means of transport) train *m*; (underground) rame *f*; **a ~ to Paris** un train pour Paris; **to go to Paris by ~** aller à Paris en train
2 (succession) (of events) série *f*; **my ~ of thought** le fil de mes pensées
3 (procession) (of animals, vehicles, people) file *f*; (of mourners) cortège *m*
4 (of dress) traîne *f*
B *vt* **1** former ‹*staff, worker, musician*›; entraîner ‹*athlete, player*›; dresser ‹*circus animal, dog*›
2 (aim) braquer ‹*gun, binoculars*› (**on** sur)
C *vi* **1** (for profession) être formé/-e, étudier; **he's ~ing to be/he ~ed as a doctor** il suit/il a reçu une formation de docteur
2 (Sport) s'entraîner

trained /treɪnd/ *adj* ‹*staff*› qualifié/-e; ‹*professional*› diplômé/-e; ‹*voice, eye, ear*› exercé/-e; ‹*singer, actor*› professionnel/-elle; ‹*animal*› dressé/-e

trainee /treɪ'niː/ *n* stagiaire *mf*

trainer /'treɪnə(r)/ *n* **1** (of athlete, horse) entraîneur/-euse *m/f*; (of circus animal, dogs) dresseur/-euse *m/f*
2 (BrE) (shoe) (high) basket *f*; (low) tennis *m*

🔑 **training** /'treɪnɪŋ/ *n* **1** (gen) formation *f*; (less specialized) apprentissage *m*
2 (Mil, Sport) entraînement *m*

training college *n* (BrE) école *f* professionnelle; (for teachers) centre *m* de formation pédagogique

training course *n* stage *m* de formation

trainspotter *n* passionné/-e *m/f* de trains

trait /treɪ, treɪt/ *n* trait *m*

traitor /'treɪtə(r)/ *n* traître/traîtresse *m/f* (to à)

tram /træm/ *n* (BrE) tramway *m*

tramp /træmp/ *n* (rural) vagabond *m*; (urban) clochard/-e *m/f*

trample /'træmpl/ *vt* piétiner

trampoline /'træmpəliːn/ *n* trampoline *m*

trance /trɑːns, (AmE) træns/ *n* transe *f*; (fig) état *m* second; **to go into a ~** entrer en transe

tranquil /'træŋkwɪl/ *adj* tranquille

tranquillizer (BrE), **tranquilizer** (AmE) /'træŋkwɪlaɪzə(r)/ *n* tranquillisant *m*

transaction /træn'zækʃn/ *n* transaction *f*

transatlantic /ˌtrænzət'læntɪk/ *adj* ‹*crossing, flight*› transatlantique; ‹*accent*› d'outre-atlantique *inv*

transcend /træn'send/ *vt* (gen) transcender; (surpass) surpasser

transcribe /træn'skraɪb/ *vt* transcrire

transcript /'trænskrɪpt/ *n* **1** (copy) transcription *f*
2 (AmE) (Sch) duplicata *m* de livret scolaire

🔑 **transfer** **A** /'trænsfɜː(r)/ *n* **1** (gen) transfert *m*; (of property, debt) cession *f*; (of funds) virement *m*; (of employee) mutation *f*
2 (BrE) (on skin, china, paper) décalcomanie *f*; (on T-shirt) transfert *m*
B /træns'fɜː(r)/ *vt* (*p prés etc* **-rr-**)
1 transférer ‹*data, baggage*›; virer ‹*money*›; céder ‹*property, power*›; reporter ‹*allegiance, support*›; **I'm ~ring you to reception** je vous passe la réception
2 (relocate) transférer ‹*office, prisoner, player*›; muter ‹*employee*›
C /træns'fɜː(r)/ *vi* (*p prés etc* **-rr-**) **1** ‹*player, passenger*› être transféré/-e; ‹*employee*› être muté/-e
2 ‹*traveller*› changer d'avion

transferable /træns'fɜːrəbl/ *adj* (gen) transmissible; (in finance) négociable

transfer passenger *n* passager/-ère *m/f* en transit

transferred charge call *n* appel *m* en PCV

transfixed *adj* (fascinated) fasciné/-e; (horrified) paralysé/-e d'horreur

🔑 mot clé

t

⚷ **transform** /træns'fɔːm/ *vt* transformer

transformation /ˌtrænsfə'meɪʃn/ *n* transformation *f*

transformer /træns'fɔːmə(r)/ *n* transformateur *m*

transfusion /træns'fjuːʒn/ *n* transfusion *f*

transgender /trænz'dʒendə(r)/ *adj* transgenre *inv*

transgenic /træns'dʒenɪk/ *adj* transgénique

transient /'trænzɪənt, (AmE) 'trænʃnt/ *adj* ‹*phase*› transitoire; ‹*emotion, beauty*› éphémère; ‹*population*› de passage

transistor /træn'zɪstə(r), -'sɪstə(r)/ *n* transistor *m*

transit /'trænzɪt, -sɪt/ *n* transit *m*; **in ~** en transit

transition /træn'zɪʃn, -'sɪʃn/ *n* transition *f*

transitional /træn'zɪʃənl, -'sɪʃənl/ *adj* ‹*arrangement, measure*› transitoire; ‹*period*› de transition

transitive /'trænzətɪv/ *adj* transitif/-ive

translate /trænz'leɪt/ **A** *vt* traduire
B *vi* **1** ‹*person*› traduire
2 ‹*word, phrase, text*› se traduire

translation /trænz'leɪʃn/ *n* traduction *f*; (school exercise) version *f*

translator /trænz'leɪtə(r)/ *n* traducteur/-trice *m/f*

transmission /trænz'mɪʃn/ *n* transmission *f*

transmit /trænz'mɪt/ **A** *vt* (*p prés etc* **-tt-**) transmettre
B *vi* (*p prés etc* **-tt-**) émettre

transmitter /trænz'mɪtə(r)/ *n* (in radio, TV) émetteur *m*; (in telecommunications) capsule *f* microphonique

transparency /træns'pærənsɪ/ *n* (slide) diapositive *f*; (for overhead projector) transparent *m*

transparent /træns'pærənt/ *adj* transparent/-e

transplant /træns'plɑːnt, (AmE) -'plænt/ **A** *n* (operation) transplantation *f*; (organ, tissue transplanted) transplant *m*
B *vt* transplanter

⚷ **transport** /træns'pɔːt/ **A** *n* (*also* **transportation** (AmE)) **air/road ~** transport *m* aérien/par route; **to travel by public ~** utiliser les transports en commun
B *vt* transporter

transportation /ˌtrænspɔː'teɪʃn/ *n* transport *m*

transpose /træn'spəʊz/ *vt* transposer

transsexual /trænz'sekʃʊəl/ *n, adj* transsexuel/-elle *m/f*

transvestite /trænz'vestaɪt/ *n* travesti/-e *m/f*

trap /træp/ **A** *n* **1** (snare) piège *m*
2 (vehicle) cabriolet *m*
B *vt* (*p prés etc* **-pp-**) **1** (snare) prendre [qn/qch] au piège
2 (catch) coincer ‹*person, finger*›; retenir ‹*heat*›

trapdoor *n* trappe *f*

trash /træʃ/ *n* **1** (AmE) (refuse) (in streets) déchets *mpl*; (from household) ordures *fpl*
2 (fam) (low-grade goods) camelote *f* (fam)
3 (fam) (nonsense) âneries *fpl*; **the film is (absolute) ~** le film est (complètement) nul (fam)

trash can *n* (AmE) poubelle *f*

trashy /'træʃɪ/ *adj* (fam) ‹*novel, film*› nul/nulle (fam); ‹*goods*› de pacotille

trauma /'trɔːmə, (AmE) 'traʊ-/ *n* (*pl* **-as, -ata**) traumatisme *m*

traumatic /trɔː'mætɪk, (AmE) traʊ-/ *adj* (psychologically) traumatisant/-e; (Med) traumatique

traumatize /'trɔːmətaɪz, (AmE) 'traʊ-/ *vt* traumatiser

⚷ **travel** /'trævl/ **A** *n* voyages *mpl*; **foreign ~** voyages à l'étranger
B *vt* (*p prés etc* **-ll-** (BrE), **-l-** (AmE)) parcourir ‹*country, road, distance*›
C *vi* (*p prés etc* **-ll-** (BrE), **-l-** (AmE))
1 (journey) voyager; **he ~s widely** il voyage beaucoup; **to ~ abroad/to Brazil** aller à l'étranger/au Brésil
2 (move) ‹*person, object, plane, boat*› aller; ‹*car, train*› aller, rouler; ‹*light, sound*› se propager; **to ~ back in time** remonter le temps
3 to ~ well ‹*cheese, wine*› supporter le transport

travel agency *n* agence *f* de voyages

travel agent *n* agent *m* de voyages

travel card *n* carte *f* de transport

travel insurance *n* assurance *f* voyage

traveller (BrE), **traveler** (AmE) /'trævlə(r)/ *n* **1** (voyager) voyageur/-euse *m/f*
2 (BrE) (gypsy) nomade *mf*

traveller's cheque (BrE), **traveler's check** (AmE) *n* chèque-voyage *m*

travelling (BrE), **traveling** (AmE) /'trævlɪŋ/ **A** *n* (touring) voyages *mpl*; (on single occasion) voyage *m*; **to go ~** partir en voyage; **the job involves ~** le poste exige des déplacements
B *adj* **1** ‹*actor, company, circus*› itinérant/-e
2 ‹*companion, rug*› de voyage; ‹*conditions*› (on road) de route
3 ‹*allowance, expenses*› de déplacement

travelling salesman *n* voyageur *m* de commerce

travel-sick /'trævlsɪk/ *adj* **to be** *or* **get ~** souffrir du mal des transports

trawler /'trɔːlə(r)/ *n* chalutier *m*

tray /treɪ/ *n* plateau *m*

treacherous /'tretʃərəs/ *adj* traître/traîtresse

treachery /'tretʃərɪ/ *n* traîtrise *f*

treacle /'triːkl/ *n* (BrE) (black) mélasse *f*; (golden syrup) mélasse *f* raffinée

t

tread /tred/ **A** *n* (of tyre) (pattern) sculptures *fpl*; (outer surface) chape *f*
B *vt* (*prét* **trod**, *pp* **trodden**) fouler ‹*street, path, area*›; **to ~ water** nager sur place
C *vi* (*prét* **trod**, *pp* **trodden**) marcher; **to ~ on** (walk) marcher sur; (squash) piétiner; **to ~ carefully** (fig) être prudent/-e

treason /ˈtriːzn/ *n* trahison *f*; **high ~** haute trahison

treasure /ˈtreʒə(r)/ **A** *n* trésor *m*
B *vt* **1** (cherish) chérir ‹*person, gift*›
2 (prize) tenir beaucoup à ‹*friendship*›

treasurer /ˈtreʒərə(r)/ *n* **1** (on committee) trésorier/-ière *m/f*
2 (AmE) (in company) directeur *m* financier

Treasury /ˈtreʒərɪ/ *n* (*also* **~ Department**) ministère *m* des finances

treat /triːt/ **A** *n* (pleasure) (petit) plaisir *m*; (food) gâterie *f*; **I took them to the museum as a ~** je les ai emmenés au musée pour leur faire plaisir; **it's my ~** (fam) c'est moi qui paie
B *vt* **1** (gen), (Med) traiter; **to ~ sb well/badly** bien traiter/maltraiter qn; **to ~ sb/sth with care** prendre soin de qn/qch; **they ~ the house like a hotel** ils prennent la maison pour un hôtel
2 (pay for) **to ~ sb to sth** payer *or* offrir qch à qn; **to ~ oneself to** s'offrir ‹*holiday, hairdo*›

treatment /ˈtriːtmənt/ *n* traitement *m*

treaty /ˈtriːtɪ/ *n* traité *m*

treble /ˈtrebl/ **A** *adj* triple
B *vt, vi* tripler

tree /triː/ *n* arbre *m*; **an apple/a cherry ~** un pommier/un cerisier

tree stump *n* souche *f*

treetop *n* cime *f* (d'un arbre)

tree trunk *n* tronc *m* d'arbre

trek /trek/ **A** *n* (long journey) randonnée *f*; (laborious) randonnée *f* pénible
B *vi* (*p prés etc* **-kk-**) **to ~ across** traverser péniblement ‹*desert*›

trekking /ˈtrekɪŋ/ *n* **to go ~** faire de la randonnée pédestre

tremble /ˈtrembl/ *vi* trembler

tremendous /trɪˈmendəs/ *adj* ‹*effort, improvement, amount*› énorme; ‹*pleasure*› immense; ‹*storm, explosion*› violent/-e; ‹*success*› fou/folle (fam)

tremor /ˈtremə(r)/ *n* **1** (in voice) tremblement *m*
2 (in earthquake) secousse *f*

trench /trentʃ/ *n* tranchée *f*

trench coat *n* imperméable *m*, trench-coat *m*

trend /trend/ *n* **1** (tendency) tendance *f*
2 (fashion) mode *f*; **to set a new ~** lancer une nouvelle mode

trendsetter /ˈtrendsetə(r)/ *n* innovateur/-trice *m/f*; **to be a ~** lancer des modes

trendy /ˈtrendɪ/ *adj* (fam) branché/-e (fam)

trespass /ˈtrespəs/ *vi* s'introduire illégalement; **'no ~ing'** 'défense d'entrer'

trespasser /ˈtrespəsə(r)/ *n* intrus/-e *m/f*

trial /ˈtraɪəl/ **A** *n* **1** (Law) procès *m*; **to go on ~, to stand ~** passer en jugement
2 (test) (of machine, vehicle) essai *m*; (of drug, new product) test *m*; **on ~** à l'essai; **by ~ and error** ‹*learn*› par l'expérience; ‹*proceed*› par tâtonnements
3 (Sport) épreuve *f*
4 (trouble) épreuve *f*; (less strong) difficulté *f*
B *adj* ‹*period, separation*› d'essai; **on a ~ basis** à titre expérimental

trial run *n* essai *m*; **to take a car for a ~** essayer une voiture

triangle /ˈtraɪæŋgl/ *n* triangle *m*

tribe /traɪb/ *n* tribu *f*

tribunal /traɪˈbjuːnl/ *n* tribunal *m*

tributary /ˈtrɪbjʊtərɪ, (AmE) -terɪ/ *n* affluent *m*

tribute /ˈtrɪbjuːt/ *n* hommage *m*; **to pay ~ to** rendre hommage à; **floral ~** (spray) gerbe *f*; (wreath) couronne *f*

trick /trɪk/ **A** *n* **1** (to deceive) tour *m*, combine *f*; **to play a ~ on sb** jouer un tour à qn; **a ~ of the light** un effet de lumière
2 (by magician, conjurer, dog) tour *m*; **to do a ~** faire un tour
3 (knack, secret) astuce *f*
4 (in cards) pli *m*; **to take** *or* **win a ~** faire un pli
B *adj* ‹*photo, shot*› truqué/-e
C *vt* duper, rouler (fam); **to ~ sb into doing sth** amener qn à faire qch par la ruse
IDIOMS **the ~s of the trade** les ficelles du métier; **that'll do the ~** ça fera l'affaire

trickle /ˈtrɪkl/ **A** *n* (of liquid) filet *m*; (of powder, sand) écoulement *m*; (of investment, orders) petite quantité *f*; (of people) petit nombre *m*
B *vi* **to ~ down** dégouliner le long de ‹*pane, wall*›; **to ~ into** ‹*liquid*› s'écouler dans ‹*container*›; ‹*people*› entrer petit à petit ‹*hall*›
■ **trickle away** ‹*water*› s'écouler lentement; ‹*people*› s'éloigner lentement

trick question *n* question *f* piège

tricky /ˈtrɪkɪ/ *adj* **1** ‹*decision, task*› difficile; ‹*problem*› épineux/-euse; ‹*situation*› délicat/-e
2 (wily) malin/-igne

tricycle /ˈtraɪsɪkl/ *n* (cycle) tricycle *m*

trifle /ˈtraɪfl/ **A** *n* **1** (BrE) (Culin) ≈ diplomate *m*
2 (triviality) bagatelle *f*
B *vi* **to ~ with** jouer avec ‹*feelings, affections*›; **to ~ with sb** traiter qn à la légère

trifling /ˈtraɪflɪŋ/ *adj* ‹*sum, cost, detail*› insignifiant/-e

trigger /ˈtrɪgə(r)/ *n* **1** (on gun) gâchette *f*
2 (on machine) manette *f*
■ **trigger off** déclencher

trilogy /ˈtrɪlədʒɪ/ *n* trilogie *f*

---
mot clé

trim /trɪm/ **A** *n* **1** (of hair) coupe *f* d'entretien
2 (good condition) **to keep oneself in ~** se maintenir en bonne forme physique
B *adj* ‹*garden*› soigné/-e; ‹*boat, house*› bien tenu/-e; ‹*figure*› svelte; ‹*waist*› fin/-e
C *vt* (*p prés etc* **-mm-**) **1** (cut) couper ‹*hair, grass, material*›; tailler ‹*beard, hedge*›
2 (reduce) réduire (**by** de)
3 (Culin) dégraisser ‹*meat*›
4 (decorate) décorer ‹*tree, furniture*›; border ‹*dress, handkerchief*›

trimming /ˈtrɪmɪŋ/ *n* (on clothing) garniture *f*; **~s** (Culin) (with dish) accompagnements *mpl* traditionnels

trinket /ˈtrɪŋkɪt/ *n* babiole *f*

trio /ˈtriːəʊ/ *n* trio *m* (**of** de)

trip /trɪp/ **A** *n* **1** (journey) (abroad) voyage *m*; (excursion) excursion *f*; **business ~** voyage d'affaires
2 (fam) trip *m* (fam)
B *vt* (*p prés etc* **-pp-**) (*also* **~ over, ~ up**) faire trébucher; (with foot) faire un croche-pied à
C *vi* (*p prés etc* **-pp-**) **1** (*also* **~ over, ~ up**) (stumble) trébucher, faire un faux pas; **to ~ on** *or* **over** trébucher sur ‹*step, rock*›; se prendre les pieds dans ‹*scarf, rope*›
2 (walk lightly) **to ~ along** ‹*child*› gambader; ‹*adult*› marcher d'un pas léger

triple /ˈtrɪpl/ *adj* triple

triplet /ˈtrɪplɪt/ *n* (child) triplé/-e *m/f*

triplicate: **in ~** /ˈtrɪplɪkət/ *phr* en trois exemplaires

tripod /ˈtraɪpɒd/ *n* trépied *m*

triumph /ˈtraɪʌmf/ **A** *n* triomphe *m*
B *vi* triompher (**over** de)

triumphant /traɪˈʌmfnt/ *adj* ‹*person, team*› triomphant/-e; ‹*return, success*› triomphal/-e

trivia /ˈtrɪvɪə/ *npl* futilités *fpl*

trivial /ˈtrɪvɪəl/ *adj* ‹*matter, scale, film*› insignifiant/-e; ‹*error, offence*› léger/-ère *before n*; ‹*conversation, argument, person*› futile

trivialize /ˈtrɪvɪəlaɪz/ *vt* banaliser; minimiser ‹*role*›

trolley /ˈtrɒlɪ/ *n* **1** (BrE) (for food, drinks, luggage, shopping) chariot *m*
2 (AmE) tramway *m*

trolleybus *n* (BrE) trolleybus *m*

trolley car *n* (AmE) tramway *m*, tram *m*

troop /truːp/ *n* troupe *f*

trooper /ˈtruːpə(r)/ *n* **1** (Mil) homme *m* de troupe
2 (AmE) (policeman) policier *m*

trophy /ˈtrəʊfɪ/ *n* trophée *m*

tropic /ˈtrɒpɪk/ *n* tropique *m*; **in the ~s** sous les tropiques

tropical /ˈtrɒpɪkl/ *adj* tropical/-e

trot /trɒt/ **A** *n* trot *m*; **at a ~** au trot
B *vi* (*p prés etc* **-tt-**) ‹*animal, rider*› trotter; ‹*person*› courir, trotter; ‹*child*› trottiner
IDIOM **on the ~** (one after the other) coup sur coup; (continuously) d'affilée
■ **trot out** (fam): **~ out [sth]** débiter ‹*excuse, explanation*›

trouble /ˈtrʌbl/ **A** *n* **1** (problems) problèmes *mpl*; (personal) ennuis *mpl*; (difficulties) difficultés *fpl*; **to be in** *or* **get into ~** ‹*person*› avoir des ennuis; ‹*company*› avoir des difficultés; **to get sb into ~** créer des ennuis à qn; **back ~** mal *m* de dos; **what's the ~?** qu'est-ce qui ne va pas?; **to have ~ doing** avoir du mal à faire; **to get sb out of ~** tirer qn d'affaire
2 (effort, inconvenience) peine *f*; **it's not worth the ~** cela n'en vaut pas la peine; **to take the ~ to do, to go to the ~ of doing** se donner la peine de faire; **to save sb the ~ of doing** épargner à qn la peine de faire; **to go to a lot of ~** se donner beaucoup de mal
B troubles *npl* soucis *mpl*; **money ~s** problèmes *mpl* d'argent
C *vt* **1** (disturb, inconvenience) déranger ‹*person*›; **may** *or* **could I ~ you to...** puis-je vous demander de...
2 (bother) **to be ~d by** être incommodé/-e par ‹*cough, pain*›
3 (worry) tracasser ‹*person*›; **don't let that ~ you** ne te tracasse pas pour cela

troubled /ˈtrʌbld/ *adj* ‹*person, expression*› soucieux/-ieuse; ‹*mind*› inquiet/-iète; ‹*sleep, times, area*› agité/-e

trouble-free /ˌtrʌblˈfriː/ *adj* sans problèmes

troublemaker *n* fauteur/-trice *m/f* de troubles

troubleshooter /ˈtrʌblʃuːtə(r)/ *n* consultant/-e *m/f* en gestion des entreprises

troublesome /ˈtrʌblsəm/ *adj* ‹*person*› ennuyeux/-euse; ‹*problem*› gênant/-e; ‹*cough, pain*› désagréable

trouble spot *n* point *m* chaud

trough /trɒf, (AmE) trɔːf/ *n* **1** (for drinking) abreuvoir *m*; (for animal feed) auge *f*
2 (between waves, hills, on graph) creux *m*
3 (in weather) zone *f* dépressionnaire

trousers *npl* (BrE) pantalon *m*; **short ~** culotte *f* courte

trout /traʊt/ *n* (*pl* **~**) truite *f*

trowel /ˈtraʊəl/ *n* **1** (for cement) truelle *f*
2 (for gardening) déplantoir *m*

truancy /ˈtruːənsɪ/ *n* absentéisme *m*

truant /ˈtruːənt/ *n* **to play ~** faire l'école buissonnière

truce /truːs/ *n* trêve *f*

truck /trʌk/ *n* **1** (lorry) camion *m*
2 (rail wagon) wagon *m* de marchandises

truck driver, **trucker** (fam) *n* routier *m*

trudge /trʌdʒ/ *vi* marcher d'un pas lourd; **to ~ through the snow** marcher péniblement dans la neige

true /truː/ **A** *adj* **1** (based on fact, not a lie) ‹*news, fact, story*› vrai/-e; (from real life)

t

‹*story*› vécu/-e
2 (real, genuine) vrai/-e *before n*; ‹*identity, age*› véritable *before n*; **to come ~** se réaliser
3 (heartfelt, sincere) ‹*feeling, understanding*› sincère; **~ love** le véritable amour
4 (accurate) ‹*copy*› conforme; ‹*assessment*› correct, juste
5 (faithful, loyal) fidèle (**to** à)
6 (Mus) ‹*note, instrument*› juste
B *adv* ‹*aim, fire*› juste

true-life *adj* ‹*adventure, story*› vécu/-e

truffle /ˈtrʌfl/ *n* truffe *f*

🔑 **truly** /ˈtruːlɪ/ *adv* **1** (gen) vraiment; **well and ~** bel et bien
2 (in letter) **yours ~** je vous prie d'agréer l'expression de mes sentiments distingués (fml)

trump /trʌmp/ *n* atout *m*
IDIOM **to come up ~s** sauver la situation

trumped up /ˌtrʌmptˈʌp/ *adj* ‹*charge*› forgé/-e de toutes pièces

trumpet /ˈtrʌmpɪt/ *n* **1** (instrument, player) trompette *f*
2 (elephant call) barrissement *m*
IDIOM **to blow one's own ~** vanter ses propres mérites

trumpeter /ˈtrʌmpɪtə(r)/ *n* trompettiste *mf*

truncheon /ˈtrʌntʃən/ *n* matraque *f*

trunk /trʌŋk/ *n* **1** (of tree, body) tronc *m*
2 (of elephant) trompe *f*
3 (for travel) malle *f*
4 (AmE) (car boot) coffre *m*

trunks *npl* slip *m* de bain

truss /trʌs/ *n* (Med) bandage *m* herniaire
■ **truss up** brider, trousser ‹*chicken*›; ligoter ‹*person*›

🔑 **trust** /trʌst/ **A** *n* **1** (faith) confiance *f*; **to put one's ~ in** se fier à
2 (Law) (arrangement) fidéicommis *m*; (property involved) propriété *f* fiduciaire
B *vt* **1** (believe) se fier à ‹*person, judgement*›
2 (rely on) faire confiance à
3 (entrust) **to ~ sb with sth** confier qch à qn
C *vi* **to ~ in** faire confiance à ‹*person*›; croire en ‹*God, fortune*›; **to ~ to luck** se fier au hasard
D *v refl* **to ~ oneself to do** être sûr de pouvoir faire

trust company *n* société *f* fiduciaire

trusted *adj* ‹*friend*› fidèle

trusted third party, TTP *n* tierce partie *f* de confiance, TPC *f*

trustee /trʌsˈtiː/ *n* **1** (who administers property in trust) fiduciaire *m*
2 (of company) administrateur/-trice *m/f* (**of** de)

trust fund *n* fonds *m* en fidéicommis

trusting /ˈtrʌstɪŋ/ *adj* ‹*person*› qui fait facilement confiance aux gens

🔑 mot clé

trustworthy /ˈtrʌstwɜːðɪ/ *adj* ‹*staff, firm*› sérieux/-ieuse; ‹*friend, lover*› digne de confiance

🔑 **truth** /truːθ/ *n* (real facts) **the ~** la vérité; **there is some ~ in it** il y a du vrai dans cela

truthful /ˈtruːθfl/ *adj* ‹*person*› honnête; ‹*account, version*› vrai/-e

🔑 **try** /traɪ/ **A** *n* (*pl* **tries**) **1** (attempt) essai *m*; **to have a ~** essayer (**at doing** de faire)
2 (Sport) essai *m*
B *vt* (*prét*, *pp* **tried**) **1** (attempt) essayer de répondre à ‹*exam question*›; **to ~ doing** *or* **to do** essayer de faire; **to ~ hard to do** faire de gros efforts pour faire; **to ~ one's best to do** faire tout son possible pour faire
2 (test out) essayer ‹*tool, product, method, activity*›; prendre [qn] à l'essai ‹*person*›; ‹*thief*› essayer d'ouvrir ‹*door, window*›; tourner ‹*door knob*›; **to ~ one's hand at sth** s'essayer à qch
3 (taste) goûter ‹*food*›
4 (consult) demander à ‹*person*›; consulter ‹*book*›; **~ the library** demandez à la bibliothèque
5 (subject to stress) **to ~ sb's patience** pousser qn à bout
6 (Law) juger ‹*case, criminal*›
C *vi* (*prét*, *pp* **tried**) essayer; **to ~ again** (to perform task) recommencer; (to see somebody) repasser; (to phone) rappeler; **to ~ for** essayer d'obtenir ‹*loan, university place*›; essayer de battre ‹*world record*›; essayer d'avoir ‹*baby*›; **keep ~ing!** essaie encore!
■ **try on** essayer ‹*hat, dress*›
■ **try out**: **~ [sth] out, ~ out [sth]** essayer

trying /ˈtraɪɪŋ/ *adj* ‹*person*› pénible; ‹*experience*› éprouvant/-e

T-shirt *n* T-shirt *m*

tub /tʌb/ *n* **1** (for flowers, water) bac *m*; (of ice cream, pâté) pot *m*
2 (AmE) (bath) baignoire *f*

tubby /ˈtʌbɪ/ *adj* (fam) grassouillet/-ette (fam)

tube /tjuːb, (AmE) ˈtuːb/ *n* **1** (cylinder, container) tube *m*
2 (BrE) **the ~** le métro (londonien)
3 (AmE) (fam) (TV) télé *f* (fam)
4 (in TV set) tube *m* cathodique
5 (in tyre) chambre *f* à air

tuberculosis /tjuːˌbɜːkjʊˈləʊsɪs, (AmE) ˈtuː-/ *n* tuberculose *f*

tuck /tʌk/ **A** *n* (in sewing) pli *m*
B *vt* (put) glisser; **to ~ one's shirt into one's trousers** rentrer sa chemise dans son pantalon
■ **tuck away** (put away) ranger; **the house was ~ed away in the wood** la maison se cachait *or* était cachée dans le bois
■ **tuck in** rentrer ‹*garment, shirt*›; border ‹*bedclothes, person*›

🔑 **Tuesday** /ˈtjuːzdeɪ, -dɪ, (AmE) ˈtuː-/ *n* mardi *m*

tuft /tʌft/ *n* touffe *f*

t

tug /tʌg/ **A** *n* **1** (pull) secousse *f*; **to give sth a ~** tirer sur qch
2 (*also* **tug boat**) remorqueur *m*
B *vt* (*p prés etc* **-gg-**) (pull) tirer
C *vi* (*p prés etc* **-gg-**) **to ~ at** *or* **on** tirer sur ‹*rope, hair*›

tug-of-love /ˌtʌgəvˈlʌv/ *n: lutte entre les parents pour la garde de l'enfant*

tug of war /ˌtʌgəvˈwɔː(r)/ *n* (Sport) gagne-terrain *m*

tuition /tjuːˈɪʃn, (AmE) tuː-/ *n* cours *mpl*

tuition fees *npl* frais *mpl* pédagogiques

tulip /ˈtjuːlɪp, (AmE) ˈtuː-/ *n* tulipe *f*

tumble /ˈtʌmbl/ **A** *n* **1** (fall) chute *f*; **to take a ~** ‹*person*› faire une chute
2 (of clown, acrobat) culbute *f*
B *vi* **1** (fall) ‹*person, object*› tomber (**off, out of** de)
2 ‹*price, share, currency*› chuter
3 ‹*clown, acrobat, child*› faire des culbutes
■ **tumble down** ‹*wall, building*› s'écrouler

tumble drier, **tumble dryer** *n* sèche-linge *m inv*

tumble-dry /ˌtʌmblˈdraɪ/ *vt* sécher (en machine)

tumbler /ˈtʌmblə(r)/ *n* verre *m* droit

tummy /ˈtʌmɪ/ *n* (fam) ventre *m*

tumour (BrE), **tumor** (AmE) /ˈtjuːmə(r), (AmE) ˈtuː-/ *n* tumeur *f*

tumult /ˈtjuːmʌlt, (AmE) ˈtuː-/ *n* **1** (noise) tumulte *m*
2 (disorder) agitation *f*

tuna /ˈtjuːnə, (AmE) ˈtuː-/ *n* (*also* **~fish**) thon *m*

tune /tjuːn, (AmE) tuːn/ **A** *n* air *m*; **to be in/out of ~** ‹*instrument*› être/ne pas être en accord; **to sing in/out of ~** chanter juste/faux
B *vt* accorder ‹*musical instrument*›; régler ‹*engine, radio, TV*›
■ **tune in**: **A** **~ in** mettre la radio; **to ~ in to** se mettre à l'écoute de ‹*programme*›; régler sur ‹*channel*›
B **~ [sth] in** régler (**to** sur)

tunic /ˈtjuːnɪk, (AmE) ˈtuː-/ *n* (for gym) tunique *f*; (for nurse, schoolgirl) blouse *f*; (for soldier) vareuse *f*

tuning fork *n* diapason *m*

tunnel /ˈtʌnl/ **A** *n* tunnel *m*
B *vt, vi* (*p prés etc* **-ll-** (BrE), **-l-** (AmE)) creuser

tunnel vision *n* **to have ~** (fig) avoir des œillères

turbine /ˈtɜːbaɪn/ *n* turbine *f*

turbo /ˈtɜːbəʊ/ *n* (engine) turbo *m*; (car) turbo *f*

turbocharged /ˌtɜːbəʊˈtʃɑːdʒd/ *adj* turbo *inv*

turbot /ˈtɜːbət/ *n* turbot *m*

turbulent /ˈtɜːbjʊlənt/ *adj* **1** ‹*water*› agité/-e
2 ‹*times, situation*› agité/-e; ‹*career, history*› mouvementé/-e; ‹*passions, character, faction*› turbulent/-e

tureen /təˈriːn/ *n* soupière *f*

turf /tɜːf/ **A** *n* (*pl* **~s, turves**) (grass) gazon *m*; (peat) tourbe *f*
B *vt* gazonner ‹*lawn, pitch*›
■ **turf out**: **~ out [sb/sth]**, **~ [sb/sth] out** virer (fam)

Turk /tɜːk/ *n* Turc/Turque *m/f*

turkey /ˈtɜːkɪ/ *n* **1** (bird) dinde *f*
2 (AmE) (fam) (flop) bide *m* (fam); (bad film) navet *m* (fam)

Turkey /ˈtɜːkɪ/ *pr n* Turquie *f*

Turkish /ˈtɜːkɪʃ/ **A** *n* (language) turc *m*
B *adj* turc/turque

Turkish delight *n* loukoum *m*

turmoil /ˈtɜːmɔɪl/ *n* désarroi *m*

turn /tɜːn/ **A** *n* **1** (in games, sequence) tour *m*; **whose ~ is it?** c'est à qui le tour?; **to be sb's ~ to do** être le tour de qn de faire; **to take ~s at sleeping, to take it in ~s to sleep** dormir à tour de rôle; **by ~s** tour à tour; **to speak out of ~** commettre un impair
2 (circular movement) tour *m*; **to give sth a ~** tourner qch; **to do a ~** ‹*dancer*› faire un tour
3 (in vehicle) virage *m*; **to make** *or* **do a left/right ~** tourner à gauche/à droite
4 (bend, side road) tournant *m*, virage *m*; **take the next right ~, take the next ~ on the right** prenez la prochaine (rue) à droite
5 (change, development) tournure *f*; **to take a ~ for the better** ‹*things, events, situation*› prendre une meilleure tournure; **to take a ~ for the worse** ‹*situation*› se dégrader; ‹*health*› s'aggraver
6 (BrE) (fam) (attack) crise *f*; **a dizzy ~** un vertige; **it gave me quite a ~, it gave me a nasty ~** ça m'a fait un coup (fam)
7 (act) numéro *m*
B *vt* **1** (rotate) ‹*person*› tourner ‹*wheel, handle*›; serrer ‹*screw*›; ‹*mechanism*› faire tourner ‹*cog, wheel*›
2 (turn over, reverse) retourner ‹*mattress, soil, steak, collar*›; tourner ‹*page*›; **it ~s my stomach** ça me soulève le cœur
3 (change direction of) tourner ‹*chair, head, face, car*›
4 (focus direction of) **to ~ [sth] on sb** braquer [qch] sur qn ‹*gun, hose, torch*›
5 (transform) **to ~ sth white/black** blanchir/noircir qch; **to ~ sth opaque** rendre qch opaque; **to ~ sth into** transformer qch en ‹*office, car park, desert*›; **to ~ a book into a film** adapter un livre pour le cinéma; **to ~ sb into** ‹*magician*› changer qn en ‹*frog*›; ‹*experience*› faire de qn ‹*extrovert, maniac*›
6 (deflect) détourner ‹*person, conversation*› (**towards** vers, **from** de)
7 (fam) (pass the age of) **he has ~ed 50** il a 50 ans passés; **she has just ~ed 30** elle vient d'avoir 30 ans
8 (on lathe) tourner ‹*wood, piece*›

t

C *vi* **1** (change direction) ‹*person, car, plane, road*› tourner; ‹*ship*› virer; **to ~ down** *or* **into** tourner dans ‹*street, alley*›; **to ~ towards** tourner en direction de ‹*village, mountains*›
2 (reverse direction) ‹*person, vehicle*› faire demi-tour; ‹*tide*› changer; ‹*luck*› tourner
3 (revolve) ‹*key, wheel, planet*› tourner; ‹*person*› se tourner
4 (hinge) **to ~ on** ‹*argument*› tourner autour de ‹*point, issue*›; ‹*outcome*› dépendre de ‹*factor*›
5 (spin round angrily) **to ~ on sb** ‹*dog*› attaquer qn; ‹*person*› se retourner contre qn
6 (resort to) **to ~ to** se tourner vers ‹*person, religion*›; **to ~ to drink/drugs** se mettre à boire/se droguer; **I don't know where to ~** je ne sais plus où donner de la tête (fam)
7 (change) **to ~ into** ‹*person, tadpole*› se transformer en ‹*frog*›; ‹*sofa*› se transformer en ‹*bed*›; ‹*situation, evening*› tourner à ‹*farce, disaster*›; **to ~ to** ‹*substance*› se changer en ‹*ice, gold*›; ‹*fear, surprise*› faire place à ‹*horror, relief*›
8 (become by transformation) devenir ‹*pale, cloudy, green*›; **to ~ white/black/red** blanchir/noircir/rougir; **the weather is ~ing cold/warm** le temps se rafraîchit/se réchauffe
9 (fam) (become) devenir ‹*Conservative, Communist*›; **businessman ~ed politician** ex-homme d'affaires devenu homme politique
10 (go sour) ‹*milk*› tourner
11 ‹*trees, leaves*› jaunir
D **in turn** *phr* ‹*answer, speak*› à tour de rôle; **she spoke to each of us in ~** elle nous a parlé chacun à notre tour
IDIOM **to do sb a good ~** rendre un service à qn

■ **turn against**: **A** **~ against [sb/sth]** se retourner contre
B **~ [sb] against** retourner [qn] contre

■ **turn around** **A** **~ around 1** (to face other way) ‹*person*› se retourner; ‹*bus, vehicle*› faire demi-tour
2 (revolve, rotate) ‹*object, windmill, dancer*› tourner
B **~ [sth] around** tourner [qch] dans l'autre sens ‹*object*›

■ **turn aside** se détourner (**from** de)

■ **turn away**: **A** **~ away** se détourner
B **~ [sb] away** refuser ‹*spectator, applicant*›; ne pas laisser entrer ‹*salesman, caller*›

■ **turn back** **A** **~ back 1** (on foot) rebrousser chemin; **there's no ~ing back** il n'est pas question de revenir en arrière
2 (in book) revenir
B **~ [sth] back** reculer ‹*dial, clock*›
C **~ [sb] back** refouler ‹*people, vehicles*›

■ **turn down 1** (reduce) baisser ‹*volume, radio, gas*›
2 (fold over) rabattre ‹*sheet, collar*›; retourner ‹*corner of page*›
3 (refuse) refuser ‹*person, request*›; rejeter ‹*offer, suggestion*›

■ **turn off** **A** **~ off 1** ‹*driver, walker*› tourner
2 ‹*motor, fan*› s'arrêter
B **~ [sth] off** éteindre ‹*light, oven, TV, radio*›; fermer ‹*tap*›; couper ‹*water, gas, engine*›
C **~ off [sth]** (leave) quitter ‹*road*›
D **~ [sb] off** (fam) rebuter

■ **turn on 1** allumer ‹*light, oven, TV, radio, gas*›; ouvrir ‹*tap*›
2 (fam) exciter ‹*person*›

■ **turn out** **A** **~ out 1** (be eventually) **to ~ out well/badly** bien/mal se terminer; **it depends how things ~ out** cela dépend de la façon dont les choses vont tourner; **to ~ out to be wrong/easy** se révéler faux/facile; **it ~s out that they know each other already** il se trouve qu'ils se connaissent déjà
2 (come out) ‹*crowd, people*› venir
B **~ [sth] out 1** (turn off) éteindre ‹*light*›
2 (empty) vider ‹*pocket, bag*›; (Culin) démouler ‹*mousse*›
3 (produce) fabriquer ‹*goods*›; former ‹*scientists, graduates*›
C **~ [sb] out** (evict) mettre [qn] à la porte

■ **turn over** **A** **~ over 1** (roll over) ‹*person, vehicle*› se retourner
2 (turn page) tourner la page
3 ‹*engine*› se mettre en marche
B **~ [sb/sth] over 1** (turn) tourner ‹*page, paper*›; retourner ‹*card, object, mattress, soil, patient*›
2 (hand over) remettre ‹*object, money, find, papers*›; livrer ‹*person*› (**to** à); remettre la succession de ‹*company*›

■ **turn round** (BrE) = **turn around**

■ **turn up** **A** **~ up 1** (arrive, show up) arriver, se pointer (fam); **don't worry—it will ~ up** ne t'inquiète pas—tu finiras par le retrouver
2 (present itself) ‹*opportunity, job*› se présenter
3 (point up) ‹*corner, edge*› être relevé/-e
B **~ [sth] up 1** (increase, intensify) augmenter ‹*heating, volume, gas*›; mettre [qch] plus fort ‹*TV, radio, music*›
2 (point up) relever ‹*collar*›

turnaround /ˈtɜːnəraʊnd/ *n* (in attitude) revirement *m*; (of fortune) revirement *m* (**in** de); (for the better) redressement *m* (**in** de)

turning /ˈtɜːnɪŋ/ *n* (BrE) (in road) virage *m*

turning point *n* tournant *m* (**in, of** de)

turnip /ˈtɜːnɪp/ *n* navet *m*

turnoff /ˈtɜːnɒf/ *n* **1** (in road) embranchement *m*
2 (fam) (person) **to be a real ~** être vraiment repoussant/-e

turn of mind *n* tournure *f* d'esprit

turn of phrase *n* (expression) expression *f*

t

turnout /ˈtɜːnaʊt/ *n* (to vote, strike, demonstrate) taux *m* de participation; **there was a magnificent ~ for the parade** beaucoup de gens sont venus voir le défilé

turnover /ˈtɜːnəʊvə(r)/ *n* **1** (of company) chiffre *m* d'affaires
2 (of stock) rotation *f*; (of staff) taux *m* de renouvellement

turnpike *n* (tollgate) barrière *f* de péage; (AmE) (toll expressway) autoroute *f* à péage

turnstile *n* (gate) tourniquet *m*; (to count number of visitors) compteur *m* pour entrées

turntable /ˈtɜːnteɪbl/ *n* (on record player) platine *f*

turn-up /ˈtɜːnʌp/ *n* (BrE) (of trousers) revers *m*

turpentine, /ˈtɜːpəntaɪn/, **turps** (fam) *n* térébenthine *f*

turret /ˈtʌrɪt/ *n* tourelle *f*

turtle /ˈtɜːtl/ *n* (BrE) tortue *f* marine; (AmE) tortue *f*

turtle dove *n* tourterelle *f*

turtleneck *n* (*also* **turtleneck sweater**) pull-over *m* à col cheminée

Tuscany /ˈtʌskənɪ/ *pr n* Toscane *f*

tusk /tʌsk/ *n* défense *f*

tussle /ˈtʌsl/ *n* empoignade *f* (**for** pour)

tutor /ˈtjuːtə(r), (AmE) tuː-/ *n* **1** (private teacher) professeur *m* particulier
2 (BrE) (Univ) chargé/-e *m/f* de travaux dirigés
3 (AmE) (Univ) assistant/-e *m/f*

tutorial /tjuːˈtɔːrɪəl, (AmE) tuː-/ *n* (Univ) (group) classe *f* de travaux dirigés; (private) cours *m* privé

tuxedo /tʌkˈsiːdəʊ/ *n* (*pl* **~es** *ou* **~s**) (AmE) smoking *m*

TV *n* (fam) (*abbr* = **television**) télé *f* (fam)

TV dinner *n* plateau *m* télé

TV screen *n* écran *m* télé

twang /twæŋ/ *n* (of string, wire) vibration *f*; (of tone) ton *m* nasillard

tweak /twiːk/ *vt* tordre ‹*ear, nose*›; tirer ‹*hair, moustache*›

tweet /twiːt/ **A** *n* **1** (of bird) gazouillis *m*
2 (on Twitter) tweet *m*
B *vi* (of bird) gazouiller
C *vt* (on Twitter) twitter; **she ~ed a picture of him and his friends** elle a tweeté une photo de lui et ses copains

tweezers /ˈtwiːzəz/ *npl* pincettes *fpl*; (for eyebrows) pince *f* à épiler

twelfth /twelfθ/ **A** *n* **1** (in order) douzième *mf*
2 (of month) douze *m inv*
3 (fraction) douzième *m*
B *adj, adv* douzième

twelve /twelv/ *n, pron, det* douze *m inv*

twenties *npl* **1** (era) **the ~** les années *fpl* vingt
2 (age) **to be in one's ~** avoir entre vingt et trente ans

twentieth /ˈtwentɪəθ/ **A** *n* **1** (in order) vingtième *mf*
2 (of month) vingt *m*
3 (fraction) vingtième *m*
B *adj, adv* vingtième

twenty /ˈtwentɪ/ *n, pron, det* vingt *m inv*

twice /twaɪs/ *adv* deux fois; **~ a day** *or* **daily** deux fois par jour; **she's ~ his age** elle a le double de son âge; **~ as much, ~ as many** deux fois plus

twiddle /ˈtwɪdl/ *vt* tripoter; **to ~ one's thumbs** se tourner les pouces

twig /twɪg/ *n* brindille *f*

twilight /ˈtwaɪlaɪt/ *n* crépuscule *m*

twilight zone *n* zone *f* d'ombre

twin /twɪn/ **A** *n* jumeau/-elle *m/f*
B *adj* **1** ‹*brother, sister*› jumeau/-elle
2 ‹*masts, propellers, beds*› jumeaux/-elles *after n*; ‹*speakers*› jumelés
C *vt* (*p prés etc* **-nn-**) jumeler ‹*town*› (**with** avec)

twine /twaɪn/ *n* ficelle *f*

twinge /twɪndʒ/ *n* (of pain) élancement *m*; (of conscience, doubt) accès *m*; (of jealousy) pointe *f*

twinkle /ˈtwɪŋkl/ *vi* ‹*light, star, jewel*› scintiller; ‹*eyes*› pétiller

twin town *n* ville *f* jumelle

twirl /twɜːl/ **A** *n* tournoiement *m*
B *vt* faire tournoyer ‹*baton, partner*›; entortiller ‹*ribbon, vine*›
C *vi* ‹*dancer*› tournoyer; **to ~ round** (turn round) se retourner brusquement

twist /twɪst/ **A** *n* **1** (in rope, cord, wool) tortillon *m*; (in road) zigzag *m*; (in river) coude *m*
2 (in play, story) coup *m* de théâtre; (in events) rebondissement *m*
3 (small amount) (of yarn, thread, hair) torsade *f*; **a ~ of lemon** une tranche de citron
B *vt* **1** (turn) tourner ‹*knob, handle*›; (open) dévisser ‹*cap, lid*›; (close) visser ‹*cap, lid*›
2 (wind) enrouler; **to ~ threads together** torsader des fils
3 (bend, distort) tordre ‹*metal, rod, branch*›; déformer ‹*words, facts, meaning*›; **his face was ~ed with pain** son visage était tordu de douleur
4 (injure) **to ~ one's ankle/wrist** se tordre la cheville/le poignet; **to ~ one's neck** attraper un torticolis
C *vi* **1** ‹*person*› **to ~ round** (turn round) se retourner; **he ~ed around in his chair** il s'est retourné dans son fauteuil
2 ‹*rope, flex, coil*› s'entortiller; **to ~ and turn** ‹*road, path*› serpenter

twisted /ˈtwɪstɪd/ *adj* ‹*wire, metal*› tordu/-e; ‹*cord*› entortillé/-e; ‹*ankle, wrist*› tordu/-e; ‹*sense of humour*› malsain/-e

twit /twɪt/ *n* (fam) idiot/-e *m/f*

twitch /twɪtʃ/ **A** *n* **1** (tic) tic *m*
2 (spasm) soubresaut *m*
B *vt* tirer sur [qch] d'un coup sec ‹*fabric, curtain*›

C *vi* ‹*person*› avoir des tics; ‹*mouth*› trembler; ‹*eye*› cligner nerveusement; ‹*limb, muscle*› tressauter

twitchy /ˈtwɪtʃɪ/ *adj* agité/-e

twitter /ˈtwɪtə(r)/ *vi* ‹*bird*› gazouiller

🔑 **two** /tuː/ *n, det, pron* deux *m inv*; **in ~s and threes** par deux ou trois, deux ou trois à la fois; **to break sth in ~** casser qch en deux
IDIOMS **to be in ~ minds about doing** hésiter à faire; **to put ~ and ~ together** faire le rapprochement

two-faced *adj* hypocrite, fourbe

twofold /ˈtuːfəʊld/ **A** *adj* double
B *adv* doublement; **to increase ~** doubler

two-piece /ˌtuːˈpiːs/ *n* (*also* **~ suit**) (woman's) tailleur *m*; (man's) costume *m* (deux-pièces)

two-seater /ˌtuːˈsiːtə(r)/ *n* (car) voiture *f* à deux places; (plane) avion *m* à deux places

two-tier *adj* ‹*society, health service*› à deux vitesses

two-time /ˈtuːtaɪm/ *vt* (fam) être infidèle envers, tromper ‹*partner*›

two-way /ˌtuːˈweɪ/ *adj* ‹*street*› à double sens; ‹*traffic*› dans les deux sens; ‹*communication, exchange*› bilatéral/-e

two-way mirror *n* glace *f* sans tain

two-way radio *n* émetteur-récepteur *m*

tycoon /taɪˈkuːn/ *n* magnat *m*

🔑 **type** /taɪp/ **A** *n* **1** (variety, kind) type *m*, genre *m* (of de)
2 (in printing) caractères *mpl*
B *vt* taper (à la machine) ‹*word, letter*›; **a ~d letter** une lettre dactylographiée
C *vi* taper (à la machine)

typecast *vt* (*prét, pp* **-cast**) cataloguer ‹*person*›

typeface *n* police *f* (de caractères)

typewriter /ˈtaɪpraɪtə(r)/ *n* machine *f* à écrire

typhoid /ˈtaɪfɔɪd/ *n* typhoïde *f*

typhoon /taɪˈfuːn/ *n* typhon *m*

🔑 **typical** /ˈtɪpɪkl/ *adj* ‹*case, example, day, village*› typique; ‹*generosity, compassion*› caractéristique; **it's ~ of him to be late** cela ne m'étonne pas de lui qu'il soit en retard

typically /ˈtɪpɪklɪ/ *adv* ‹*react, behave*› (of person) comme à mon/ton etc habitude; **~ English** ‹*place, behaviour*› typiquement anglais; **she's ~ English** c'est l'Anglaise type

typify /ˈtɪpɪfaɪ/ *vt* ‹*feature, behaviour*› caractériser; ‹*person, institution*› être le type même de

typing /ˈtaɪpɪŋ/ *n* dactylo *f*

typist /ˈtaɪpɪst/ *n* dactylo *mf*

typographic /ˌtaɪpəˈgræfɪk(l)/ *adj* (*also* **typographical**) typographique

typography /taɪˈpɒgrəfɪ/ *n* typographie *f*

tyrannize /ˈtɪrənaɪz/ *vt* tyranniser

tyranny /ˈtɪrənɪ/ *n* tyrannie *f* (**over** sur)

tyrant /ˈtaɪərənt/ *n* tyran *m*

tyre (BrE), **tire** (AmE) /ˈtaɪə(r)/ *n* pneu *m*; **spare ~** (for car) pneu de rechange; (fat) bourrelet *m*

tyre pressure *n* pression *f* des pneus

Uu

u, U /juː/ *n* u, U *m*

udder /ˈʌdə(r)/ *n* pis *m*

UFO *n* (*abbr* = **unidentified flying object**) ovni *m inv*

ugly /ˈʌglɪ/ *adj* **1** ‹*person, building*› laid/-e
2 ‹*situation*› dangereux/-euse

UK *pr n* (*abbr* = **United Kingdom**) Royaume-Uni *m*

Ukraine /juːˈkreɪn/ *pr n* **the ~** l'Ukraine *f*

ulcer /ˈʌlsə(r)/ *n* ulcère *m*

ulterior /ʌlˈtɪərɪə(r)/ *adj* **without any ~ motive** sans arrière-pensée

ultimate /ˈʌltɪmət/ **A** *n* **the ~ in** le nec plus ultra de ‹*comfort, luxury*›
B *adj* ‹*result, destination*› final/-e; ‹*sacrifice*› ultime *before n*

🔑 **ultimately** /ˈʌltɪmətlɪ/ *adv* en fin de compte, au bout du compte

ultimatum /ˌʌltɪˈmeɪtəm/ *n* (*pl* **~s** *ou* **-mata**) ultimatum *m*

ultramarine /ˌʌltrəməˈriːn/ *n, adj* outremer *m inv*

ultrasound /ˈʌltrəsaʊnd/ *n* ultrasons *mpl*

ultrasound scan *n* échographie *f*

ultraviolet /ˌʌltrəˈvaɪələt/ *adj* ultraviolet/-ette

umbilical cord *n* cordon *m* ombilical

umbrella /ʌmˈbrelə/ *n* parapluie *m*

umpire /ˈʌmpaɪə(r)/ *n* arbitre *m*

UN *n* (*abbr* = **United Nations**) **the ~** l'ONU *f*

🔑 mot clé

unable /ʌnˈeɪbl/ *adj* **to be ~ to do** (lacking means or opportunity) ne pas pouvoir faire; (lacking knowledge or skill) ne pas savoir faire; (incapable, not qualified) être incapable de faire

unabridged /ˌʌnəˈbrɪdʒd/ *adj* intégral/-e

unacceptable /ˌʌnəkˈseptəbl/ *adj* ‹*proposal*› inacceptable; ‹*behaviour*› inadmissible

unaccompanied /ˌʌnəˈkʌmpənɪd/ *adj* **1** ‹*child, baggage*› non accompagné/-e; ‹*man, woman*› seul/-e **2** (Mus) sans accompagnement

unaccounted /ˌʌnəˈkaʊntɪd/ *adj* **to be ~ for** (gen) être introuvable; **two of the crew are still ~ for** deux membres de l'équipage sont toujours portés disparus

unaccustomed /ˌʌnəˈkʌstəmd/ *adj* **to be ~ to sth/to doing** ne pas avoir l'habitude de qch/de faire

unaffected /ˌʌnəˈfektɪd/ *adj* **1 to be ~** ne pas être affecté/-e (**by** par) **2** (natural) tout simple

unafraid /ˌʌnəˈfreɪd/ *adj* ‹*person*› sans peur

unaided /ʌnˈeɪdɪd/ *adv* ‹*stand, sit, walk*› sans aide

unambiguous /ˌʌnæmˈbɪgjʊəs/ *adj* sans équivoque

unanimous /juːˈnænɪməs/ *adj* unanime

unanimously /juːˈnænɪməslɪ/ *adv* ‹*agree, condemn*› unanimement; ‹*vote*› à l'unanimité

unannounced /ˌʌnəˈnaʊnst/ *adv* ‹*arrive, call*› sans prévenir

unanswered /ʌnˈɑːnsəd, (AmE) ʌnˈæn-/ *adj* ‹*letter, question*› resté/-e sans réponse

unappetizing /ʌnˈæpɪtaɪzɪŋ/ *adj* peu appétissant/-e

unappreciative /ˌʌnəˈpriːʃətɪv/ *adj* ‹*person, audience*› ingrat/-e

unapproachable /ˌʌnəˈprəʊtʃəbl/ *adj* inaccessible

unarmed /ʌnˈɑːmd/ *adj* ‹*person*› non armé/-e; ‹*combat*› sans armes

unashamedly /ˌʌnəˈʃeɪmɪdlɪ/ *adv* ouvertement

unasked /ʌnˈɑːskt, (AmE) ʌnˈæskt/ *adv* ‹*come, attend*› sans être invité/-e; **to do sth ~** faire qch spontanément

unassuming /ˌʌnəˈsjuːmɪŋ, (AmE) ˌʌnəˈsuː-/ *adj* modeste

unattached /ˌʌnəˈtætʃt/ *adj* **1** ‹*part, element*› détaché/-e **2** (single) ‹*person*› célibataire

unattainable /ˌʌnəˈteɪnəbl/ *adj* inaccessible

unattractive /ˌʌnəˈtræktɪv/ *adj* ‹*person*› peu attirant/-e; ‹*proposition*› peu intéressant/-e (**to** pour)

unauthorized /ʌnˈɔːθəraɪzd/ *adj* fait/-e sans autorisation

unavailable /ˌʌnəˈveɪləbl/ *adj* **to be ~** ‹*person*› ne pas être disponible

unavoidable /ˌʌnəˈvɔɪdəbl/ *adj* inévitable

unaware /ˌʌnəˈweə(r)/ *adj* **1** (not informed) **to be ~ that** ignorer que **2** (not conscious) **to be ~ of sth** ne pas être conscient/-e de qch

unawares /ˌʌnəˈweəz/ *adv* **to catch** *or* **take sb ~** prendre qn au dépourvu

unbearable /ʌnˈbeərəbl/ *adj* insupportable

unbeatable /ʌnˈbiːtəbl/ *adj* imbattable

unbeknown /ˌʌnbɪˈnəʊn/ *adv* **~ to sb** à l'insu de qn

unbelievable /ˌʌnbɪˈliːvəbl/ *adj* incroyable

unbending /ʌnˈbendɪŋ/ *adj* inflexible

unbiased /ʌnˈbaɪəst/ *adj* (*also* **unbiassed**) impartial/-e

unblock /ʌnˈblɒk/ *vt* déboucher ‹*pipe, sink*›; désimlocker ‹*mobile phone*›

unborn /ʌnˈbɔːn/ *adj* ‹*child*› à naître; **her ~ child** l'enfant qu'elle porte/portait etc

unbreakable /ʌnˈbreɪkəbl/ *adj* incassable

unbroken /ʌnˈbrəʊkən/ *adj* **1** ‹*sequence, silence, view*› ininterrompu/-e **2** ‹*pottery*› intact/-e

unbuckle /ʌnˈbʌkl/ *vt* déboucler ‹*belt*›; défaire la boucle de ‹*shoe*›

unbutton /ʌnˈbʌtn/ *vt* déboutonner

uncalled-for /ʌnˈkɔːldfɔː(r)/ *adj* ‹*remark*› déplacé/-e

uncanny /ʌnˈkænɪ/ *adj* ‹*resemblance*› étrange; ‹*accuracy*› étonnant/-e; ‹*silence*› troublant/-e

uncaring /ʌnˈkeərɪŋ/ *adj* ‹*world*› indifférent/-e

uncertain /ʌnˈsɜːtn/ **A** *adj* **1** (unsure) incertain/-e; **to be ~ about** ne pas être certain/-e de **2** (changeable) ‹*temper*› instable; ‹*weather*› variable
B in no ~ terms *phr* ‹*state*› en termes on ne peut plus clairs

uncertainty /ʌnˈsɜːtntɪ/ *n* incertitude *f*

unchallenged /ˌʌnˈtʃælɪndʒd/ *adj* incontesté/-e; **to go ~** ‹*statement, decision*› ne pas être récusé/-e

unchanged /ʌnˈtʃeɪndʒd/ *adj* inchangé/-e

uncharacteristic /ˌʌnkærɪktəˈrɪstɪk/ *adj* ‹*generosity*› peu habituel/-elle; **it was ~ of him to...** ce n'est pas son genre de...

uncharitable /ʌnˈtʃærɪtəbl/ *adj* peu charitable

unchecked /ʌnˈtʃekt/ *adv* de manière incontrôlée

uncivilized /ʌnˈsɪvɪlaɪzd/ *adj* **1** (inhumane) ‹*treatment, conditions*› inhumain/-e **2** (uncouth, rude) grossier/-ière **3** (barbarous) ‹*people, nation*› non civilisé/-e

uncle /ˈʌŋkl/ *n* oncle *m*

unclear /ʌnˈklɪə(r)/ *adj* **1** ‹*motive, reason*› peu clair/-e; **it is ~ how/whether...** on ne sait pas très bien comment/si... **2** ‹*instructions, voice*› pas clair/-e; ‹*answer*› peu clair/-e; ‹*handwriting*› difficile à lire

uncomfortable /ʌn'kʌmftəbl, (AmE) -fərt-/ *adj* **1** ‹*shoes, garment, seat*› inconfortable; ‹*journey, heat*› pénible; **you look ~ in that chair** tu n'as pas l'air à l'aise dans ce fauteuil
2 ‹*feeling, silence, situation*› pénible; **to make sb (feel) ~** mettre qn mal à l'aise

uncommon /ʌn'kɒmən/ *adj* rare

uncommunicative /ˌʌnkə'mjuːnɪkətɪv/ *adj* peu communicatif/-ive

uncomplimentary /ˌʌnkɒmplɪ'mentrɪ, (AmE) -terɪ/ *adj* peu flatteur/-euse

uncompromising /ʌn'kɒmprəmaɪzɪŋ/ *adj* intransigeant/-e

unconcerned /ˌʌnkən'sɜːnd/ *adj* (uninterested) indifférent/-e (**with** à); (not caring) insouciant/-e; (untroubled) imperturbable

unconditional /ˌʌnkən'dɪʃənl/ *adj* ‹*obedience, support, love*› inconditionnel/-elle; ‹*offer, surrender*› sans condition

unconfirmed /ˌʌnkən'fɜːmd/ *adj* non confirmé/-e

unconnected /ˌʌnkə'nektɪd/ *adj* ‹*incidents, facts*› sans lien entre eux/elles; **to be ~ with** ‹*event, fact*› n'avoir aucun rapport avec; ‹*person*› n'avoir aucun lien avec

unconscious /ʌn'kɒnʃəs/ **A** *n* **the ~** l'inconscient *m*
B *adj* **1** (insensible) sans connaissance; **to knock sb ~** assommer qn
2 (unaware) **to be ~ of sth** ne pas être conscient/-e de qch
3 ‹*bias, hostility*› inconscient/-e

unconstitutional /ˌʌnkɒnstɪ'tjuːʃənl/ *adj* inconstitutionnel/-elle

uncontested /ˌʌnkən'testɪd/ *adj* ‹*leader, fact*› incontesté/-e; ‹*seat*› non disputé/-e

uncontrollable /ˌʌnkən'trəʊləbl/ *adj* ‹*emotion*› incontrôlable; ‹*tears*› qu'on ne peut retenir

uncontrollably /ˌʌnkən'trəʊləblɪ/ *adv* ‹*laugh, sob*› sans pouvoir se contrôler

unconventional /ˌʌnkən'venʃənl/ *adj* peu conventionnel/-elle

unconvincing /ˌʌnkən'vɪnsɪŋ/ *adj* peu convaincant/-e

uncooked /ʌn'kʊkt/ *adj* non cuit/-e

uncooperative /ˌʌnkəʊ'ɒpərətɪv/ *adj* peu coopératif/-ive

uncoordinated /ˌʌnkəʊ'ɔːdɪneɪtɪd/ *adj* ‹*efforts, service*› désordonné/-e; **to be ~** ‹*person*› manquer de coordination

uncouth /ʌn'kuːθ/ *adj* ‹*person*› grossier/-ière; ‹*accent*› peu raffiné/-e

uncover /ʌn'kʌvə(r)/ *vt* dévoiler ‹*scandal*›; découvrir ‹*evidence, body*›

uncritical /ʌn'krɪtɪkl/ *adj* peu critique

unctuous /'ʌŋktjʊəs/ *adj* onctueux/-euse, mielleux/-euse

uncut /ʌn'kʌt/ *adj* **1** ‹*film, version*› intégral/-e
2 ‹*gem*› non taillé/-e

undamaged /ʌn'dæmɪdʒd/ *adj* ‹*crops*› non endommagé/-e; ‹*building, reputation*› intact/-e

undecided /ˌʌndɪ'saɪdɪd/ *adj* ‹*person*› indécis/-e; ‹*outcome*› incertain/-e

undemanding /ˌʌndɪ'mɑːndɪŋ, (AmE) -'mænd-/ *adj* ‹*task*› peu fatigant/-e; ‹*person*› peu exigeant/-e

undemocratic /ˌʌndemə'krætɪk/ *adj* antidémocratique

undemonstrative /ˌʌndɪ'mɒnstrətɪv/ *adj* peu démonstratif/-ive

undeniable /ˌʌndɪ'naɪəbl/ *adj* indéniable

⚷ **under** /'ʌndə(r)/ **A** *prep* **1** sous; **~ the bed** sous le lit; **~ it** en dessous; **it's ~ there** c'est là-dessous; **~ letter D** sous la lettre D
2 (less than) **~ £10** moins de 10 livres sterling; **children ~ five** les enfants de moins de cinq ans *or* au-dessous de cinq ans; **a number ~ ten** un nombre inférieur à dix; **temperatures ~ 10°C** des températures inférieures à *or* au-dessous de 10°C
3 (according to) **~ the law** selon la loi
4 (subordinate to) sous; **I have 50 people ~ me** j'ai 50 employés sous mes ordres
B *adv* **1** ‹*crawl, sit, hide*› en dessous; **to go ~** ‹*diver, swimmer*› disparaître sous l'eau
2 (less) moins; **£10 and ~** 10 livres sterling et moins; **children of six and ~** des enfants de six ans et au-dessous
3 (anaesthetized) **to put sb ~** endormir qn

underachieve /ˌʌndərə'tʃiːv/ *vi* (Sch) ne pas obtenir les résultats dont on est capable

underachiever /ˌʌndərə'tʃiːvə(r)/ *n* (Sch) sous-performant/-e *m/f*

under-age /ˌʌndər'eɪdʒ/ *adj* **~ drinking** la consommation d'alcool par les mineurs; **to be ~** être mineur/-e

undercarriage *n* train *m* d'atterrissage

underclass *n* classe *f* sous-prolétariat

underclothes *npl* sous-vêtements *mpl*

undercoat /'ʌndəkəʊt/ *n* couche *f* de fond

undercooked *adj* pas assez cuit/-e; **the meat is ~** la viande n'est pas assez cuite

undercover /ˌʌndə'kʌvə(r)/ *adj* ‹*activity, group*› clandestin/-e; ‹*agent*› secret/-ète

undercurrent /'ʌndəkʌrənt/ *n* (in water) courant *m* profond; (in sea) courant *m* sous-marin; (fig) courant *m* sous-jacent

undercut /ˌʌndə'kʌt/ *vt* (*p prés* **-tt-**, *prét, pp* **-cut**) concurrencer ‹*prices*›

underdeveloped /ˌʌndədɪ'veləpt/ *adj* ‹*country*› sous-développé/-e; ‹*negative*› pas assez développé/-e

underdog /'ʌndədɒg, (AmE) -dɔːg/ *n* (in society) opprimé/-e *m/f*; (in game, contest) perdant/-e *m/f*

⚷ mot clé

underdone /ˌʌndəˈdʌn/ *adj* ‹*food*› pas assez cuit/-e; ‹*steak*› (BrE) saignant/-e

underestimate /ˌʌndərˈestɪmeɪt/ *vt* sous-estimer

underexpose /ˌʌndərɪkˈspəʊz/ *vt* sous-exposer

underfed /ˌʌndəˈfed/ *adj* sous-alimenté/-e

underfoot /ˌʌndəˈfʊt/ *adv* sous les pieds; **the ground was wet ~** le sol était humide

underfunded /ˌʌndəˈfʌndɪd/ *adj* insuffisamment financé/-e

undergo /ˌʌndəˈgəʊ/ *vt* (*prét* **-went**, *pp* **-gone**) subir ‹*change, test, operation*›; suivre ‹*treatment, training*›; **to ~ surgery** subir une intervention chirurgicale

undergraduate /ˌʌndəˈgrædʒʊət/ *n* étudiant/-e *m/f*

underground **A** /ˈʌndəgraʊnd/ *n* **1** (BrE) (subway) métro *m*; **on the ~** dans le métro
2 the ~ (political) la clandestinité; (artistic) l'underground *m*
B /ˈʌndəgraʊnd/ *adj* **1** (below ground) souterrain/-e
2 (secret) clandestin/-e
3 (artistic) underground *inv*
C /ˌʌndəˈgraʊnd/ *adv* **1** (below ground) sous terre
2 (secretly) **to go ~** passer dans la clandestinité

underground train *n* rame *f* (de métro)

undergrowth /ˈʌndəgrəʊθ/ *n* sous-bois *m*

underhand /ˌʌndəˈhænd/ *adj* (*also* **underhanded** (AmE)) ‹*person, method*› sournois/-e; **~ dealings** magouilles *fpl* (fam)

underline /ˌʌndəˈlaɪn/ *vt* souligner

underling /ˈʌndəlɪŋ/ *n* subordonné/-e *m/f*

underlying /ˌʌndəˈlaɪɪŋ/ *adj* ‹*problem*› sous-jacent/-e

undermine /ˌʌndəˈmaɪn/ *vt* saper ‹*foundations, authority, efforts*›; ébranler ‹*confidence, position*›

underneath /ˌʌndəˈniːθ/ **A** *n* dessous *m*
B *adv* dessous, en dessous
C *prep* sous, au-dessous de; **from ~ a pile of books** de dessous une pile de livres

undernourished /ˌʌndəˈnʌrɪʃt/ *adj* sous-alimenté/-e

underpants /ˈʌndəpænts/ *npl* slip *m*; **a pair of ~** un slip

underpass /ˈʌndəpɑːs, (AmE) -pæs/ *n* (for traffic) voie *f* inférieure; (for pedestrians) passage *m* souterrain

underpay /ˌʌndəˈpeɪ/ *vt* (*prét, pp* **-paid**) sous-payer ‹*employee*›

underprivileged /ˌʌndəˈprɪvəlɪdʒd/ *adj* défavorisé/-e

underrate /ˌʌndəˈreɪt/ *vt* sous-estimer

under-secretary /ˌʌndəˈsekrətrɪ, (AmE) -terɪ/ *n* (*also* **~ of state** (BrE)) sous-secrétaire *mf* d'État

undersell /ˌʌndəˈsel/ **A** *vt* (*prét, pp* **-sold**) vendre moins cher que ‹*competitor*›
B *v refl* (*prét, pp* **-sold**) **to ~ oneself** se dévaloriser

undershirt /ˈʌndəʃɜːt/ *n* (AmE) maillot *m* de corps

understaffed /ˌʌndəˈstɑːft, (AmE) -ˈstæft/ *adj* **to be ~** manquer de personnel

understand /ˌʌndəˈstænd/ **A** *vt* (*prét, pp* **-stood**) **1** (gen) comprendre; **to make oneself understood** se faire comprendre
2 (believe) **to ~ that** croire que
B *vi* (*prét, pp* **-stood**) comprendre (**about** à propos de)

understandable /ˌʌndəˈstændəbl/ *adj* compréhensible; **it's ~** ça se comprend

understandably /ˌʌndəˈstændəblɪ/ *adv* naturellement

understanding /ˌʌndəˈstændɪŋ/ **A** *n*
1 (grasp of subject, issue) compréhension *f*
2 (arrangement) entente *f* (**about** sur, **between** entre)
3 (sympathy) compréhension *f*
4 (powers of reason) entendement *m*
B *adj* ‹*tone*› bienveillant/-e; ‹*person*› compréhensif/-ive

understatement /ˈʌndəsteɪtmənt/ *n* litote *f*

understudy /ˈʌndəstʌdɪ/ *n* doublure *f* (**to** de)

undertake /ˌʌndəˈteɪk/ *vt* (*prét* **-took**, *pp* **-taken**) **1** entreprendre ‹*search, study, trip*›; se charger de ‹*mission, offensive*›
2 to ~ to do s'engager à faire

undertaker /ˈʌndəteɪkə(r)/ *n* (BrE) (person) entrepreneur *m* de pompes funèbres; (company) entreprise *f* de pompes funèbres

undertaking /ˌʌndəˈteɪkɪŋ/ *n* **1** (venture) entreprise *f*
2 (promise) garantie *f*

under-the-counter *adj* ‹*goods, trade*› illicite; ‹*payment*› sous le manteau

undertone /ˈʌndətəʊn/ *n* **1** (low voice) voix *f* basse
2 (hint) nuance *f*

undervalue /ˌʌndəˈvæljuː/ *vt* **1** (financially) sous-évaluer
2 sous-estimer ‹*person, quality*›

underwater /ˌʌndəˈwɔːtə(r)/ **A** *adj* ‹*cable, exploration*› sous-marin/-e; ‹*lighting*› sous l'eau
B *adv* sous l'eau

under way /ˌʌndəˈweɪ/ *adj* **to get ~** ‹*vehicle*› se mettre en route; ‹*season*› commencer

underwear /ˈʌndəweə(r)/ *n* sous-vêtements *mpl*

underweight /ˌʌndəˈweɪt/ *adj* trop maigre

underworld /ˈʌndəwɜːld/ *n* milieu *m*, pègre *f*

undesirable /ˌʌndɪˈzaɪərəbl/ *adj* ‹*aspect, habit, result*› indésirable; ‹*influence*› néfaste; ‹*friend*› peu recommandable

undetected /ˌʌndɪˈtektɪd/ *adv* ‹*break in, listen*› sans être aperçu/-e; **to go ~** ‹*person*› rester inaperçu/-e; ‹*cancer*› rester non décelé/-e; ‹*crime*› rester non découvert/-e

undeterred /ˌʌndɪ'tɜːd/ *adj* **to be ~ by sb/sth** ne pas se laisser démonter par qn/qch

undeveloped /ˌʌndɪ'veləpt/ *adj* ‹*person, organ, idea*› non développé/-e; ‹*land*› inexploité/-e; ‹*country*› sous-développé/-e

undignified /ʌn'dɪgnɪfaɪd/ *adj* indigne

undisciplined /ʌn'dɪsɪplɪnd/ *adj* indiscipliné/-e

undiscovered /ˌʌndɪs'kʌvəd/ *adj* ‹*secret*› non révélé/-e; ‹*land*› inexploré/-e; ‹*crime, document*› non découvert/-e

undiscriminating /ˌʌndɪ'skrɪmɪneɪtɪŋ/ *adj* sans discernement

undisguised /ˌʌndɪs'gaɪzd/ *adj* non déguisé/-e

undisputed /ˌʌndɪ'spjuːtɪd/ *adj* incontesté/-e

undisturbed /ˌʌndɪ'stɜːbd/ *adj* ‹*sleep*› paisible, tranquille; **to leave sb/sth ~** ne pas déranger qn/qch

undivided /ˌʌndɪ'vaɪdɪd/ *adj* **to give sb one's ~ attention** accorder à qn toute son attention

undo /ʌn'duː/ *vt* (*3ᵉ pers sg prés* **-does**, *prét* **-did**, *pp* **-done**) **1** défaire ‹*button, lock*›; ouvrir ‹*parcel*›
2 annuler ‹*good, effort*›

undocumented /ʌn'dɒkjʊmentɪd/ *adj*
1 (immigrant) sans papiers
2 (Comput) non documenté/-e

undone /ʌn'dʌn/ *adj* défait/-e; **to come ~** ‹*parcel, button*› se défaire

undoubtedly /ʌn'daʊtɪdlɪ/ *adv* indubitablement

undress /ˌʌn'dres/ **A** *vt* déshabiller
B *vi* se déshabiller

undrinkable /ʌn'drɪŋkəbl/ *adj* (unpleasant) imbuvable; (dangerous) non potable

undue /ʌn'djuː, (AmE) -'duː/ *adj* excessif/-ive

unduly /ˌʌn'djuːlɪ, (AmE) -'duːlɪ/ *adv* ‹*optimistic, surprised*› excessivement; ‹*neglect, worry*› outre mesure

unearthly /ʌn'ɜːθlɪ/ *adj* ‹*light, landscape*› surnaturel/-elle; ‹*cry, silence*› étrange; **at an ~ hour** à une heure indue

uneasily /ʌn'iːzɪlɪ/ *adv* **1** (anxiously) avec inquiétude
2 (uncomfortably) avec gêne

uneasiness /ʌn'iːzɪnɪs/ *n* (worry) appréhension *f* (**about** au sujet de); (dissatisfaction) malaise *m*

uneasy /ʌn'iːzɪ/ *adj* **1** ‹*person*› inquiet/-iète (**about, at** au sujet de); ‹*conscience*› pas tranquille
2 ‹*compromise*› difficile; ‹*peace*› boiteux/-euse; ‹*silence*› gêné/-e
3 ‹*sleep*› agité/-e

uneconomical /ˌʌnˌiːkə'nɒmɪkl, -ˌekə-/ *adj* (wasteful) pas économique; (not profitable) pas rentable

uneducated /ʌn'edʒʊkeɪtɪd/ *adj* **1** ‹*person*› sans instruction
2 ‹*person, speech*› inculte; ‹*accent, tastes*› commun/-e

unemotional /ˌʌnɪ'məʊʃənl/ *adj* ‹*person*› impassible; ‹*account, reunion*› froid/-e

unemployed /ˌʌnɪm'plɔɪd/ **A** *n* **the ~** les chômeurs *mpl*
B *adj* au chômage, sans emploi

unemployment /ˌʌnɪm'plɔɪmənt/ *n* chômage *m*

unemployment benefit (BrE), **unemployment compensation** (AmE) *n* allocations *fpl* de chômage

unemployment rate *n* taux *m* de chômage

unenthusiastic /ˌʌnɪnˌθjuːzɪ'æstɪk, (AmE) -ˌθuːz-/ *adj* peu enthousiaste

unenviable /ʌn'envɪəbl/ *adj* peu enviable

unequal /ʌn'iːkwəl/ *adj* ‹*amounts, contest, pay*› inégal/-e

unequivocal /ˌʌnɪ'kwɪvəkl/ *adj* ‹*person, declaration*› explicite; ‹*answer, support*› sans équivoque

unethical /ʌn'eθɪkl/ *adj* (gen) contraire à la morale; (Med) contraire à la déontologie

uneven /ʌn'iːvn/ *adj* ‹*hem, teeth*› irrégulier/-ière; ‹*contest, surface*› inégal/-e

uneventful /ˌʌnɪ'ventfl/ *adj* ‹*day, life, career*› ordinaire; ‹*journey, period*› sans histoires

unexciting /ˌʌnɪk'saɪtɪŋ/ *adj* sans intérêt

unexpected /ˌʌnɪk'spektɪd/ *adj* ‹*arrival, success*› imprévu/-e; ‹*ally, outcome*› inattendu/-e; ‹*death*› inopiné/-e

unexpectedly /ˌʌnɪk'spektɪdlɪ/ *adv* ‹*happen*› à l'improviste; ‹*large, small, fast*› étonnamment

unexplored /ˌʌnɪk'splɔːd/ *adj* inexploré/-e

unfailing /ʌn'feɪlɪŋ/ *adj* ‹*support*› fidèle; ‹*optimism*› à toute épreuve; ‹*efforts*› constant/-e

unfair /ʌn'feə(r)/ *adj* injuste (**to, on** envers, **to do** de faire); ‹*play, tactics*› irrégulier/-ière; ‹*trading*› frauduleux/-euse

unfair dismissal *n* licenciement *m* abusif

unfairness /ʌn'feənɪs/ *n* injustice *f*

unfaithful /ʌn'feɪθfl/ *adj* infidèle (**to** à)

unfamiliar /ˌʌnfə'mɪlɪə(r)/ *adj* **1** ‹*face, name, place*› inconnu/-e (**to** à); ‹*concept, feeling, situation*› inhabituel/-elle (**to** à)
2 to be ~ with sth ne pas connaître qch

unfashionable /ʌn'fæʃənəbl/ *adj* qui n'est pas à la mode

unfasten /ʌn'fɑːsn/ *vt* défaire ‹*clothing, button*›; ouvrir ‹*bag*›

unfavourable (BrE), **unfavorable** (AmE) /ʌn'feɪvərəbl/ *adj* défavorable

unfinished /ʌn'fɪnɪʃt/ *adj* ‹*work*› inachevé/-e; **to have ~ business** avoir des choses à régler

unfit /ʌn'fɪt/ *adj* **1** (out of condition) qui n'est pas en forme
2 ‹*housing*› inadéquat/-e; ‹*pitch, road*› impraticable (**for** à); **~ for human consumption** impropre à la consommation humaine

unflattering /ʌn'flætərɪŋ/ *adj* peu flatteur/-euse

unfold /ʌn'fəʊld/ **A** *vt* déplier ‹*paper, map, deckchair*›; déployer ‹*wings*›; décroiser ‹*arms*›
B *vi* **1** ‹*leaf*› s'ouvrir
2 ‹*scene*› se dérouler; ‹*mystery*› se dévoiler

unforeseeable /ˌʌnfɔː'siːəbl/ *adj* imprévisible

unforeseen /ˌʌnfɔː'siːn/ *adj* imprévu/-e

unforgettable /ˌʌnfə'getəbl/ *adj* inoubliable

unforgivable /ˌʌnfə'gɪvəbl/ *adj* impardonnable

unforgiving /ˌʌnfə'gɪvɪŋ/ *adj* impitoyable

unfortunate /ʌn'fɔːtʃənət/ *adj* **1** (pitiable) malheureux/-euse
2 (regrettable) ‹*incident, choice*› malencontreux/-euse; ‹*remark*› fâcheux/-euse
3 (unlucky) malchanceux/-euse

unfortunately /ʌn'fɔːtʃənətlɪ/ *adv* malheureusement

unfounded /ʌn'faʊndɪd/ *adj* sans fondement

unfriendly /ʌn'frendlɪ/ *adj* ‹*person, attitude, reception*› peu amical/-e; ‹*place*› inhospitalier/-ière

unfulfilled /ˌʌnfʊl'fɪld/ *adj* ‹*ambition*› non réalisé/-e; ‹*desire, need*› inassouvi/-e; **to feel ~** se sentir insatisfait/-e

unfurnished /ʌn'fɜːnɪʃt/ *adj* non meublé/-e

ungracious /ʌn'greɪʃəs/ *adj* désobligeant/-e (**of** de la part de)

ungrammatical /ˌʌngrə'mætɪkl/ *adj* incorrect/-e

ungrateful /ʌn'greɪtfl/ *adj* ingrat/-e (**of** de la part de, **towards** envers)

unhappily /ʌn'hæpɪlɪ/ *adv* **1** (miserably) d'un air malheureux
2 (unfortunately) malheureusement
3 (inappropriately) malencontreusement

unhappiness /ʌn'hæpɪnɪs/ *n* **1** (misery) tristesse *f*
2 (dissatisfaction) mécontentement *m*

unhappy /ʌn'hæpɪ/ *adj* **1** ‹*person, childhood, situation*› malheureux/-euse; ‹*face, occasion*› triste
2 (dissatisfied) mécontent/-e; **to be ~ with sth** ne pas être satisfait/-e de qch
3 (concerned) inquiet/-iète

unharmed /ʌn'hɑːmd/ *adj* ‹*person*› indemne; ‹*object*› intact/-e

unhealthy /ʌn'helθɪ/ *adj* **1** ‹*person*› maladif/-ive; ‹*diet*› malsain/-e; ‹*conditions*› insalubre
2 (unwholesome) malsain/-e

unheard-of /ʌn'hɜːdɒv/ *adj* **1** (shocking) inouï/-e
2 ‹*price*› record; ‹*actor*› inconnu/-e

unheeded /ʌn'hiːdɪd/ *adj* **to go ~** ‹*warning, plea*› rester vain/-e

unhelpful /ʌn'helpfl/ *adj* ‹*employee*› peu serviable; ‹*attitude*› peu obligeant/-e

unhindered /ʌn'hɪndəd/ *adj* **~ by** sans être entravé/-e par ‹*rules*›; sans être encombré/-e par ‹*luggage*›

unhook /ʌn'hʊk/ *vt* dégrafer ‹*skirt*›; décrocher ‹*picture*› (**from** de)

unhurried /ʌn'hʌrɪd/ *adj* ‹*person*› posé/-e; ‹*pace, meal*› tranquille

unhygienic /ˌʌnhaɪ'dʒiːnɪk/ *adj* ‹*conditions*› insalubre; ‹*way, method*› peu hygiénique

unidentified /ˌʌnaɪ'dentɪfaɪd/ *adj* non identifié/-e

unification /ˌjuːnɪfɪ'keɪʃn/ *n* unification *f* (**of** de)

uniform /'juːnɪfɔːm/ **A** *n* uniforme *m*
B *adj* identique; ‹*temperature*› constant/-e

unify /'juːnɪfaɪ/ *vt* unifier

unilateral /ˌjuːnɪ'lætrəl/ *adj* unilatéral/-e

unimaginative /ˌʌnɪ'mædʒɪnətɪv/ *adj* ‹*style*› sans originalité; **to be ~** manquer d'imagination

unimpeded /ˌʌnɪm'piːdɪd/ *adj* ‹*access, influx*› libre

unimportant /ˌʌnɪm'pɔːtnt/ *adj* sans importance

unimpressed /ˌʌnɪm'prest/ *adj* **to be ~ by** être peu impressionné/-e par ‹*person, performance*›; n'être guère convaincu/-e par ‹*argument*›

uninhabitable /ˌʌnɪn'hæbɪtəbl/ *adj* inhabitable

uninhabited /ˌʌnɪn'hæbɪtɪd/ *adj* inhabité/-e

uninhibited /ˌʌnɪn'hɪbɪtɪd/ *adj* ‹*person*› sans complexes (**about** en ce qui concerne)

uninitiated /ˌʌnɪ'nɪʃɪeɪtɪd/ *n* **the ~** les profanes

uninjured /ʌn'ɪndʒəd/ *adj* indemne

uninspired /ˌʌnɪn'spaɪəd/ *adj* ‹*approach*› terne; ‹*performance*› honnête; **to be ~** ‹*person*› manquer d'inspiration; ‹*strategy*› manquer d'imagination

unintelligible /ˌʌnɪn'telɪdʒəbl/ *adj* incompréhensible

unintended /ˌʌnɪn'tendɪd/ *adj* ‹*slur, irony*› involontaire; ‹*consequence*› non voulu/-e

unintentional /ˌʌnɪn'tenʃənl/ *adj* involontaire

uninterested /ʌn'ɪntrəstɪd/ *adj* indifférent/-e (**in** à)

uninteresting /ʌn'ɪntrəstɪŋ/ *adj* sans intérêt

uninvited /ˌʌnɪn'vaɪtɪd/ *adj* ‹*attentions*› non sollicité/-e; ‹*remark*› gratuit/-e; **~ guest** intrus/-e *m/f*

uninviting /ˌʌnɪnˈvaɪtɪŋ/ *adj* ‹*place*› rébarbatif/-ive; ‹*food*› peu appétissant/-e

⚷ **union** /ˈjuːnɪən/ *n* **1** (*also* **trade ~**) syndicat *m*
2 (uniting) union *f*; (marriage) union *f*, mariage *m*

Unionist /ˈjuːnɪənɪst/ *n, adj* unioniste *mf*

Union Jack *n* drapeau *m* du Royaume-Uni

⚷ **unique** /juːˈniːk/ *adj* **1** (sole) unique; **to be ~ to** être particulier/-ière à
2 (remarkable) unique, exceptionnel/-elle

unisex /ˈjuːnɪseks/ *adj* unisexe

unison /ˈjuːnɪsn, ˈjuːnɪzn/ *n* **in ~** à l'unisson

⚷ **unit** /ˈjuːnɪt/ *n* **1** (gen) unité *f*
2 (group) groupe *m*; (in army, police) unité *f*
3 (department) (gen), (Med) service *m*
4 (piece of furniture) élément *m*

unite /juːˈnaɪt/ **A** *vt* unir (**with** à)
B *vi* s'unir (**with** à)

⚷ **united** /juːˈnaɪtɪd/ *adj* ‹*group, front*› uni/-e (**in** dans); ‹*effort*› conjoint/-e

United Kingdom *pr n* Royaume-Uni *m*

United Nations *n* (*also* **United Nations Organization**) (Organisation *f* des) Nations *fpl* unies

United States *pr n* (*also* **United States of America**) États-Unis *mpl* (d'Amérique)

unit trust *n* ≈ société *f* d'investissement à capital variable, SICAV *f*

unity /ˈjuːnətɪ/ *n* unité *f*

universal /ˌjuːnɪˈvɜːsl/ *adj* ‹*acclaim, reaction*› général/-e; ‹*education*› pour tous; ‹*principle, truth*› universel/-elle

universally /ˌjuːnɪˈvɜːsəlɪ/ *adv* ‹*believed*› par tous, universellement; ‹*known, loved*› de tous

universe /ˈjuːnɪvɜːs/ *n* univers *m*

⚷ **university** /ˌjuːnɪˈvɜːsətɪ/ *n* université *f*

unjust /ʌnˈdʒʌst/ *adj* injuste (**to** envers)

unjustified /ʌnˈdʒʌstɪfaɪd/ *adj* injustifié/-e

unkempt /ʌnˈkempt/ *adj* ‹*appearance*› négligé/-e; ‹*hair*› ébouriffé/-e; ‹*beard*› peu soigné/-e

unkind /ʌnˈkaɪnd/ *adj* ‹*person, thought, act*› pas très gentil/-ille; ‹*remark*› désobligeant/-e; **to be ~ to sb** (by deed) ne pas être gentil/-ille avec qn; (verbally) être méchant/-e avec qn

unknown /ʌnˈnəʊn/ **A** *n* **1 the ~** l'inconnu *m*
2 (person) inconnu/-e *m/f*
B *adj* inconnu/-e

unlace /ʌnˈleɪs/ *vt* délacer

unlawful /ʌnˈlɔːfl/ *adj* ‹*activity*› illégal/-e; ‹*detention*› arbitraire; **~ killing** meurtre *m*

unlawfully /ʌnˈlɔːfəlɪ/ *adv* illégalement

unleaded petrol (BrE), **unleaded gasoline** (AmE) *n* essence *f* sans plomb

unleavened /ʌnˈlevnd/ *adj* sans levain

⚷ **unless** /ənˈles/ *conj* à moins que (+ *subjunctive*), à moins de (+ *infinitive*); **he won't come ~ you invite him** il ne viendra pas à moins que tu (ne) l'invites; **she can't take the job ~ she finds a nanny** elle ne peut pas accepter le poste à moins de trouver une nourrice

⚷ **unlike** /ʌnˈlaɪk/ *prep* **1** (in contrast to) contrairement à, à la différence de; **~ me, he...** contrairement à moi, il...
2 (different from) différent/-e de
3 (uncharacteristic of) **it's ~ her (to be so rude)** ça ne lui ressemble pas (d'être aussi impolie)

⚷ **unlikely** /ʌnˈlaɪklɪ/ *adj* **1** (unexpected) improbable, peu probable; **it is ~ that** il est peu probable que (+ *subjunctive*)
2 ‹*partner, choice, situation*› inattendu/-e
3 ‹*story*› invraisemblable

unlimited /ʌnˈlɪmɪtɪd/ *adj* illimité/-e; ‹*access*› libre *before n*

unlined /ʌnˈlaɪnd/ *adj* **1** ‹*garment, curtain*› sans doublure
2 ‹*paper*› non réglé

unload /ʌnˈləʊd/ **A** *vt* **1** décharger ‹*goods, vessel, gun, camera*›
2 (get rid of) se décharger de ‹*feelings*› (**on(to)** sur); se débarrasser de ‹*goods*›
B *vi* ‹*truck, ship*› décharger

unlock /ʌnˈlɒk/ *vt* ouvrir ‹*door*›; **to be ~ed** ne pas être fermé/-e à clé

unluckily /ʌnˈlʌkɪlɪ/ *adv* malheureusement (**for** pour)

unlucky /ʌnˈlʌkɪ/ *adj* **1** ‹*person*› malchanceux/-euse; ‹*event*› malencontreux/-euse; ‹*day*› de malchance
2 ‹*number, colour*› néfaste, maléfique; **it's ~ to do** ça porte malheur de faire

unmade /ʌnˈmeɪd/ *adj* ‹*bed*› défait/-e

unmanageable /ʌnˈmænɪdʒəbl/ *adj* ‹*child, dog*› difficile; ‹*system*› ingérable; ‹*hair*› rebelle

unmarried /ʌnˈmærɪd/ *adj* célibataire

unmistakable /ˌʌnmɪˈsteɪkəbl/ *adj*
1 (recognizable) caractéristique (**of** de)
2 (unambiguous) sans ambiguïté
3 (marked) net/nette

unmotivated /ʌnˈməʊtɪveɪtɪd/ *adj* ‹*act*› gratuit/-e; ‹*person*› non motivé/-e

unmoved /ʌnˈmuːvd/ *adj* (unconcerned) indifférent/-e (**by** à); (emotionally) insensible (**by** à)

unnamed /ʌnˈneɪmd/ *adj* (name not divulged) ‹*company, source*› dont le nom n'a pas été divulgué; (without name) **as yet ~** encore à la recherche d'un nom

unnatural /ʌnˈnætʃrəl/ *adj* **1** (odd) anormal/-e; **it is ~ that** ce n'est pas normal que (+ *subjunctive*)
2 ‹*style, laugh*› affecté/-e
3 ‹*silence, colour*› insolite

⚷ mot clé

unnecessarily /ˌʌn'nesəsərəlɪ, (AmE) ˌʌnˌnesə'serəlɪ/ *adv* inutilement

unnecessary /ʌn'nesəsrɪ, (AmE) -serɪ/ *adj* **1** (not needed) inutile; **it is ~ to do** il est inutile de faire; **it is ~ for you to do** il est inutile que tu fasses
2 (uncalled for) déplacé/-e

unnerve /ʌn'nɜːv/ *vt* décontenancer, rendre [qn] nerveux/-euse

unnoticed /ʌn'nəʊtɪst/ *adj* inaperçu/-e

unobstructed /ˌʌnəb'strʌktɪd/ *adj* ‹*view, exit, road*› dégagé/-e

unobtainable /ˌʌnəb'teɪnəbl/ *adj* ‹*supplies*› impossible à se procurer; ‹*number*› impossible à obtenir

unobtrusive /ˌʌnəb'truːsɪv/ *adj* ‹*person*› effacé/-e; ‹*site, object, noise*› discret/-ète

unoccupied /ʌn'ɒkjʊpaɪd/ *adj* ‹*house, shop*› inoccupé/-e; ‹*seat*› libre

unofficial /ˌʌnə'fɪʃl/ *adj* ‹*figure*› officieux/-ieuse; ‹*candidate*› indépendant/-e; ‹*strike*› sauvage

unorthodox /ʌn'ɔːθədɒks/ *adj* peu orthodoxe

unpack /ʌn'pæk/ *vt* défaire ‹*suitcase*›; déballer ‹*belongings*›

unpaid /ʌn'peɪd/ *adj* ‹*bill, tax*› impayé/-e; ‹*debt*› non acquitté/-e; ‹*work*› non rémunéré/-e; **~ leave** congé *m* sans solde

unpalatable /ʌn'pælətəbl/ *adj* **1** ‹*truth, statistic*› inconfortable; ‹*advice*› dur/-e à avaler
2 ‹*food*› qui n'a pas bon goût

unparalleled /ʌn'pærəleld/ *adj* **1** ‹*strength, luxury*› sans égal; ‹*success*› hors pair
2 (unprecedented) sans précédent

unpasteurized /ʌn'pɑːstʃəraɪzd/ *adj* ‹*milk*› cru/-e; ‹*cheese*› au lait cru

unperturbed /ˌʌnpə'tɜːbd/ *adj* imperturbable

unplanned /ʌn'plænd/ *adj* ‹*stoppage, increase*› imprévu/-e; ‹*pregnancy, baby*› non prévu/-e

unpleasant /ʌn'pleznt/ *adj* désagréable

unpleasantness /ʌn'plezntnɪs/ *n*
1 (of odour, experience, remark) caractère *m* désagréable
2 (bad feeling) dissensions *fpl* (**between** entre)

unplug /ʌn'plʌg/ *vt* (*p prés etc* **-gg-**) débrancher ‹*appliance*›; déboucher ‹*sink*›

unpopular /ʌn'pɒpjʊlə(r)/ *adj* impopulaire

unprecedented /ʌn'presɪdentɪd/ *adj* sans précédent

unpredictable /ˌʌnprɪ'dɪktəbl/ *adj* ‹*event*› imprévisible; ‹*weather*› incertain/-e; **he's ~** on ne sait jamais à quoi s'attendre avec lui

unpremeditated /ˌʌnpriː'medɪteɪtɪd/ *adj* non prémédité/-e

unprepared /ˌʌnprɪ'peəd/ *adj* **1** ‹*person*› pas préparé/-e (**for** pour)
2 ‹*speech*› improvisé/-e; ‹*translation*› non préparé/-e

unprepossessing /ˌʌnˌpriːpə'zesɪŋ/ *adj* peu avenant/-e

unpretentious /ˌʌnprɪ'tenʃəs/ *adj* sans prétention

unproductive /ˌʌnprə'dʌktɪv/ *adj* improductif/-ive

unprofessional /ˌʌnprə'feʃənl/ *adj* peu professionnel/-elle

unprofitable /ʌn'prɒfɪtəbl/ *adj* non rentable

unprotected /ˌʌnprə'tektɪd/ *adj* ‹*person, sex, area*› sans protection (**from** contre)

unprovoked /ˌʌnprə'vəʊkt/ *adj* ‹*attack, aggression*› délibéré/-e

unqualified /ʌn'kwɒlɪfaɪd/ *adj* **1** ‹*person*› non qualifié/-e
2 ‹*support, respect*› inconditionnel/-elle; ‹*success*› grand/-e *before n*

unquestionable /ʌn'kwestʃənəbl/ *adj* incontestable

unravel /ʌn'rævl/ **A** *vt* (*p prés etc* **-ll-** (BrE), **-l-** (AmE)) défaire ‹*knitting*›; démêler ‹*thread, mystery*›
B *vi* (*p prés etc* **-ll-** (BrE), **-l-** (AmE)) ‹*knitting*› se défaire; ‹*mystery, thread*› se démêler; ‹*plot*› se dénouer

unreal /ʌn'rɪəl/ *adj* **1** (not real) irréel/-éelle
2 (fam) (unbelievable) incroyable

unrealistic /ˌʌnrɪə'lɪstɪk/ *adj* irréaliste, peu réaliste

unreasonable /ʌn'riːznəbl/ *adj*
1 ‹*behaviour, expectation*› qui n'est pas raisonnable; **he's being very ~ about it** il n'est vraiment pas raisonnable
2 ‹*price, demand*› excessif/-ive

unrecognizable /ʌn'rekəgnaɪzəbl/ *adj* méconnaissable

unrelated /ˌʌnrɪ'leɪtɪd/ *adj* **1** (not connected) sans rapport (**to** avec)
2 (as family) **to be ~** ne pas avoir de lien de parenté

unrelenting /ˌʌnrɪ'lentɪŋ/ *adj* ‹*heat, stare, person*› implacable; ‹*pursuit, zeal*› acharné/-e

unreliable /ˌʌnrɪ'laɪəbl/ *adj* ‹*evidence*› douteux/-euse; ‹*method, employee*› peu sûr/-e; ‹*equipment*› peu fiable; **she's very ~** on ne peut pas compter sur elle

unrepentant /ˌʌnrɪ'pentənt/ *adj* impénitent/-e

unrequited /ˌʌnrɪ'kwaɪtɪd/ *adj* ‹*love*› sans retour

unresolved /ˌʌnrɪ'zɒlvd/ *adj* irrésolu/-e

unrest /ʌn'rest/ *n* **1** (dissatisfaction) malaise *m*
2 (agitation) troubles *mpl*

unrestricted /ˌʌnrɪ'strɪktɪd/ *adj* ‹*access*› libre *before n*; ‹*power*› illimité/-e

unrewarding /ˌʌnrɪ'wɔːdɪŋ/ *adj* (unfulfilling) peu gratifiant/-e; (thankless) ingrat/-e

unripe /ʌn'raɪp/ *adj* ‹*fruit*› pas mûr/-e

unrivalled /ʌn'raɪvld/ *adj* sans égal

unroll /ʌn'rəʊl/ *vt* dérouler

unruffled /ʌn'rʌfld/ *adj* **1** (calm) imperturbable
2 ‹*hair*› lisse

unruly /ʌn'ruːlɪ/ *adj* indiscipliné/-e

unsafe /ʌn'seɪf/ *adj* **1** ‹*environment*› malsain/-e; ‹*drinking water*› non potable; ‹*goods, working conditions*› dangereux/-euse
2 (threatened) **to feel ~** ne pas se sentir en sécurité

unsaid /ʌn'sed/ *adj* **to leave sth ~** passer qch sous silence

unsatisfactory /ˌʌnsætɪs'fæktərɪ/ *adj* insatisfaisant/-e

unsatisfied /ʌn'sætɪsfaɪd/ *adj* ‹*person*› insatisfait/-e; ‹*need*› inassouvi/-e

unsatisfying /ʌn'sætɪsfaɪɪŋ/ *adj* peu satisfaisant/-e

unsavoury (BrE), **unsavory** (AmE) /ʌn'seɪvərɪ/ *adj* ‹*individual*› louche, répugnant/-e

unscathed /ʌn'skeɪðd/ *adj* indemne

unscheduled /ʌn'ʃedjuːld, (AmE) ʌn'skedʒʊld/ *adj* ‹*appearance, speech*› surprise *after n*; ‹*flight*› supplémentaire; ‹*stop*› qui n'a pas été prévu

unscrew /ʌn'skruː/ *vt* dévisser

unscrupulous /ʌn'skruːpjʊləs/ *adj* ‹*person*› sans scrupules; ‹*tactic*› peu scrupuleux/-euse

unseat /ʌn'siːt/ *vt* désarçonner ‹*rider*›

unseen /ʌn'siːn/ *adv* ‹*escape, slip away*› sans être vu/-e

unselfconscious /ˌʌnself'kɒnʃəs/ *adj* **1** (natural) naturel/-elle
2 (uninhibited) sans complexes

unselfish /ʌn'selfɪʃ/ *adj* ‹*person*› qui pense aux autres; ‹*act*› désintéressé/-e

unsentimental /ˌʌnsentɪ'mentl/ *adj* ‹*account, film*› qui ne donne pas dans la sensiblerie; ‹*person*› qui ne fait pas de sentiment

unsettled /ʌn'setld/ *adj* **1** ‹*weather, climate*› instable; ‹*person*› perturbé/-e
2 ‹*account*› impayé/-e

unsettling /ʌn'setlɪŋ/ *adj* ‹*question, experience*› troublant/-e; ‹*work of art*› dérangeant/-e

unshaken /ʌn'ʃeɪkən/ *adj* ‹*person*› imperturbable (**by** devant); ‹*belief*› inébranlable

unshaven /ʌn'ʃeɪvn/ *adj* pas rasé/-e

unskilled /ʌn'skɪld/ *adj* ‹*worker, labour*› non qualifié/-e; ‹*job, work*› qui n'exige pas de qualification professionnelle

unsociable /ʌn'səʊʃəbl/ *adj* peu sociable

unsocial /ʌn'səʊʃl/ *adj* **to work ~ hours** travailler en dehors des heures normales

✓ mot clé

unsolicited /ˌʌnsə'lɪsɪtɪd/ *adj* non sollicité/-e

unsophisticated /ˌʌnsə'fɪstɪkeɪtɪd/ *adj* ‹*person*› sans façons; ‹*mind*› simple; ‹*analysis*› simpliste

unspeakable /ʌn'spiːkəbl/ *adj* **1** (dreadful) ‹*pain, sorrow*› inexprimable; ‹*act*› innommable
2 (inexpressible) indescriptible ‹*joy*›

unspoiled, **unspoilt** /ʌn'spɔɪld/ *adj* ‹*landscape, town*› préservé/-e intact

unspoken /ʌn'spəʊkən/ *adj* **1** (secret) inexprimé/-e
2 (implicit) tacite

unstable /ʌn'steɪbl/ *adj* instable

unsteady /ʌn'stedɪ/ *adj* ‹*steps, legs, voice*› chancelant/-e; ‹*ladder*› instable; ‹*hand*› tremblant/-e; **to be ~ on one's feet** marcher de façon mal assurée

unstoppable /ʌn'stɒpəbl/ *adj* ‹*force, momentum*› irrésistible; ‹*athlete, leader*› imbattable

unstuck /ʌn'stʌk/ *adj* **to come ~** ‹*stamp*› se décoller; ‹*person*› connaître un échec

unsubscribe /ʌnsəbˌskraɪb/ *vi* (Comput) se désabonner

unsubstantiated /ˌʌnsəb'stænʃɪeɪtɪd/ *adj* non corroboré/-e

unsuccessful /ˌʌnsək'sesfl/ *adj* **1** ‹*attempt, campaign*› infructueux/-euse; ‹*novel, film*› sans succès; ‹*effort, search*› vain/-e; **to be ~** ‹*attempt*› échouer
2 ‹*candidate*› (for job) malchanceux/-euse; (in election) malheureux/-euse; ‹*businessperson*› malchanceux/-euse; ‹*artist*› inconnu/-e; **to be ~ in doing** ne pas réussir à faire

unsuccessfully /ˌʌnsək'sesfəlɪ/ *adv* ‹*try*› en vain; ‹*challenge, bid*› sans succès

unsuitable /ʌn'suːtəbl/ *adj* ‹*location, clothing, accommodation, time*› inapproprié/-e; ‹*moment*› inopportun/-e; **to be ~** ne pas convenir (**for sb** à qn); **to be ~ for a job** ne pas convenir pour un travail

unsupervised /ʌn'suːpəvaɪzd/ *adj* ‹*activity*› non encadré/-e; ‹*child*› laissé/-e sans surveillance

unsure /ʌn'ʃɔː(r), (AmE) -'ʃʊər/ *adj* peu sûr/-e (**of** de); **to be ~ about how/why/where** ne pas savoir très bien comment/pourquoi/où; **to be ~ of oneself** manquer de confiance en soi

unsuspecting /ˌʌnsə'spektɪŋ/ *adj* ‹*person*› naïf/-ïve; ‹*public*› non averti/-e

unsweetened /ʌn'swiːtnd/ *adj* sans sucre, non sucré/-e

unsympathetic /ˌʌnsɪmpə'θetɪk/ *adj* **1** (uncaring) ‹*person, attitude, tone*› peu compatissant/-e
2 (unattractive) ‹*person, character*› antipathique

untaxed /ʌn'tækst/ *adj* ‹*goods*› non taxé/-e; ‹*car*› sans vignette

untenable /ʌn'tenəbl/ *adj* ‹*position*› intenable; ‹*claim, argument*› indéfendable

unthinkable /ʌn'θɪŋkəbl/ *adj* impensable

untidily /ʌn'taɪdɪlɪ/ *adv* ‹*scattered, strewn*› en désordre; ~ **dressed** habillé/-e de façon débraillée

untidy /ʌn'taɪdɪ/ *adj* ‹*person*› (in habits) désordonné/-e; (in appearance) peu soigné/-e; ‹*habits, clothes*› négligé/-e; ‹*room*› en désordre

untie /ʌn'taɪ/ *vt* (*p prés* **-tying**) défaire, dénouer ‹*knot, rope, laces*›; défaire ‹*parcel*›; délier ‹*hands, hostage*›

until, *also* **till** /ən'tɪl/

When used as a preposition in positive sentences, *until* is translated by *jusqu'à*: *they're staying until Monday* = ils restent jusqu'à lundi.

Remember that *jusqu'à* + *le* becomes *jusqu'au* and *jusqu'à* + *les* becomes *jusqu'aux*: *until the right moment* = jusqu'au bon moment; *until the exams* = jusqu'aux examens.

In negative sentences, *not until* is translated by *ne...pas avant*: *I can't see you until Friday* = je ne peux pas vous voir avant vendredi.

When used as a conjunction in positive sentences, *until* is translated by *jusqu'à ce que* + *subjunctive*: *we'll stay here until Maya comes back* = nous resterons ici jusqu'à ce que Maya revienne.

In negative sentences where the two verbs have different subjects, *not until* is translated by *ne...pas avant que* + *subjunctive*: *we won't leave until Maya comes back* = nous ne partirons pas avant que Maya revienne.

In negative sentences where the two verbs have the same subject, *not until* is translated by *pas avant de* + *infinitive*: *we won't leave until we've seen Claire* = nous ne partirons pas avant d'avoir vu Claire.

For more examples and particular usages, see the entry below.

A *prep* jusqu'à; (after negative verb) avant; ~ **Tuesday** jusqu'à mardi; ~ **the sixties** jusqu'aux années soixante; ~ **now** jusqu'à présent; ~ **then** jusqu'à ce moment-là, jusque-là; **(up)** ~ **1901** jusqu'en *or* jusqu'à 1901; **valid (up)** ~ **April 2006** valable jusqu'en avril 2006; **to work from Monday** ~ **Saturday** travailler du lundi au samedi **B** *conj* jusqu'à ce que (+ *subjunctive*); (in negative constructions) avant que (+ *subjunctive*), avant de (+ *infinitive*); **we'll stay** ~ **a solution is reached** nous resterons jusqu'à ce que nous trouvions une solution; **let's watch TV** ~ **he's ready** regardons la télévision en attendant qu'il soit prêt; **I'll wait** ~ **I get back** j'attendrai d'être rentré (**before doing** pour faire); **she waited** ~ **they were alone** elle a attendu qu'ils soient seuls

untimely /ʌn'taɪmlɪ/ *adj* ‹*arrival, announcement*› inopportun/-e; ‹*death*› prématuré/-e

untold /ʌn'təʊld/ *adj* (not quantifiable) ~ **millions** des millions et des millions; ~ **damage** d'énormes dégâts; (endless) indicible

untrained /ʌn'treɪnd/ *adj* ‹*worker*› sans formation; ‹*eye*› inexercé/-e; **to be** ~ n'avoir aucune formation

untranslatable /ˌʌntrænz'leɪtəbl/ *adj* intraduisible (**into** en)

untroubled /ʌn'trʌbld/ *adj* ‹*face, life*› paisible; **to be** ~ (by news) ne pas être troublé/-e (**by** par)

untrue /ʌn'tru:/ *adj* faux/fausse

untrustworthy /ʌn'trʌstwɜ:ðɪ/ *adj* ‹*information*› douteux/-euse; ‹*person*› indigne de confiance

unused[1] /ʌn'ju:st/ *adj* **to be** ~ **to sth/to doing** ne pas être habitué/-e à qch/à faire

unused[2] /ʌn'ju:zd/ *adj* ‹*machine, building*› inutilisé/-e; ‹*stamp*› neuf/neuve

unusual /ʌn'ju:ʒl/ *adj* ‹*colour, animal, flower*› peu commun/-e; ‹*feature, occurrence, skill*› peu commun/-e, inhabituel/-elle; ‹*dish, dress, person*› original/-e; **it is** ~ **to find/see** il est rare de trouver/voir; **there's nothing** ~ **about it** cela n'a rien d'extraordinaire

unusually /ʌn'ju:ʒəlɪ/ *adv* exceptionnellement

unwanted /ʌn'wɒntɪd/ *adj* ‹*goods, produce*› superflu/-e; ‹*pet*› abandonné/-e; ‹*visitor*› indésirable; ‹*child*› non souhaité/-e; **to feel** ~ se sentir de trop

unwarranted /ʌn'wɒrəntɪd, (AmE) -'wɔ:r-/ *adj* injustifié/-e

unwary /ʌn'weərɪ/ *n* **the** ~ les imprudents *mpl*

unwelcome /ʌn'welkəm/ *adj* ‹*visitor, interruption*› importun/-e; ‹*news*› fâcheux/-euse

unwell /ʌn'wel/ *adj* souffrant/-e; **he is feeling** ~ il ne se sent pas très bien

unwilling /ʌn'wɪlɪŋ/ *adj* ‹*attention, departure*› forcé/-e; **he is** ~ **to do it** il n'est pas disposé à le faire; (stronger) il ne veut pas le faire

unwillingness /ʌn'wɪlɪŋnɪs/ *n* réticence *f* (**to do** à faire)

unwind /ʌn'waɪnd/ **A** *vt* (*prét, pp* **-wound**) dérouler ‹*cable, bandage, scarf*› **B** *vi* (*prét, pp* **-wound**) **1** ‹*tape, cable, scarf*› se dérouler **2** (relax) se relaxer

unwise /ʌn'waɪz/ *adj* ‹*choice, loan, decision*› peu judicieux/-ieuse; ‹*person*› imprudent/-e

u

unwisely /ʌn'waɪzlɪ/ *adv* imprudemment

unwittingly /ʌn'wɪtɪŋlɪ/ *adv* (innocently) innocemment; (without wanting to) involontairement

unworthy /ʌn'wɜːðɪ/ *adj* indigne (**of** de)

unwrap /ʌn'ræp/ *vt* (*p prés etc* **-pp-**) déballer ‹*parcel*›

unwritten /ʌn'rɪtn/ *adj* ‹*rule, agreement*› tacite

unzip /ʌn'zɪp/ *vt* (*p prés etc* **-pp-**) **1** (open) défaire la fermeture à glissière de ‹*garment, bag*›
2 (Comput) dézipper, décomprimer

up /ʌp/ **A** *adj* **1** (out of bed) **she's ~** elle est levée; **we were ~ very late last night** nous nous sommes couchés très tard hier soir; **they were ~ all night** ils ont veillé toute la nuit; **I was still ~ at 2 am** j'étais toujours debout à 2 heures du matin
2 (higher in amount, level) **sales are ~ (by 10%)** les ventes ont augmenté (de 10%); **numbers of students are ~** le nombre d'étudiants est en hausse
3 (fam) (wrong) **what's ~?** qu'est-ce qui se passe?; **what's ~ with him?** qu'est-ce qu'il a?
4 (erected, affixed) **the notice is ~ on the board** l'annonce est affichée sur le panneau; **is the tent ~?** est-ce que la tente est déjà montée?; **he had his hand ~ for five minutes** il a gardé la main levée pendant cinq minutes
5 (open) **the blinds were ~** les stores étaient levés; **when the lever is ~ the machine is off** si le levier est vers le haut la machine est arrêtée
6 (finished) **'time's ~!'** 'c'est l'heure!'; **when the four days were ~** à la fin des quatre jours
7 (facing upwards) **'this side ~'** 'haut'; **she was floating face ~** elle flottait sur le dos
8 (pinned up) **her hair was ~** elle avait les cheveux relevés
B *adv* **1 ~ here/there** là-haut; **~ on the wardrobe** sur l'armoire; **~ in the tree/the clouds** dans l'arbre/les nuages; **~ in London** à Londres; **~ to/in Scotland** en Écosse; **~ North** au Nord; **four floors ~ from here** quatre étages au-dessus; **on the second shelf ~** sur la deuxième étagère en partant du bas
2 (ahead) d'avance; **to be four points ~ (on sb)** avoir quatre points d'avance (sur qn)
3 (upwards) **T-shirts from £2 ~** des T-shirts à partir de deux livres
C *prep* **~ the tree** dans l'arbre; **the library is ~ the stairs** la bibliothèque se trouve en haut de l'escalier; **he ran ~ the stairs** il a monté l'escalier en courant; **he lives just ~ the road** il habite juste à côté; **to walk/drive ~ the road** remonter la rue; **he put it ~ his sleeve** il l'a mis dans sa manche
D up above *phr* au-dessus; **~ above sth** au-dessus de qch
E up against *phr* contre ‹*wall*›; **to come ~ against** rencontrer ‹*opposition*›
F up and about *phr* debout; **to be ~ and about again** être de nouveau sur pied
G up and down *phr* **1** (to and fro) **to walk ~ and down** aller et venir, faire les cent pas
2 (throughout) **~ and down the country** dans tout le pays
H up to *phr* **1** (to particular level) jusqu'à; **~ to here/there** jusqu'ici/jusque là
2 (as many as) jusqu'à, près de; **~ to 20 people/50 dollars** jusqu'à 20 personnes/50 dollars
3 (until) jusqu'à; **~ to 1964** jusqu'en 1964; **~ to 10.30 pm** jusqu'à 22 h 30; **~ to now** jusqu'à maintenant
4 I'm not ~ to it (not capable) je n'en suis pas capable; (not well enough) je n'en ai pas la force; (can't face it) je n'en ai pas le courage
5 it's ~ to him to do c'est à lui de faire; **it's ~ to you!** c'est à toi de décider!
6 (doing) **what is he ~ to?** qu'est-ce qu'il fait?; **they're ~ to something** ils mijotent quelque chose (fam)
IDIOMS **to be one ~ on sb** faire mieux que qn; **to be (well) ~ on** s'y connaître en ‹*art, history*›; être au courant de ‹*news*›; **the ~s and downs** les hauts et les bas (**of** de)

up and coming *adj* prometteur/-euse

upbeat /'ʌpbiːt/ *adj* optimiste

upbringing /'ʌpbrɪŋɪŋ/ *n* éducation *f*

update /ˌʌp'deɪt/ *vt* **1** (revise) mettre *or* remettre [qch] à jour ‹*database, information*›; actualiser ‹*price, value*›
2 (modernize) moderniser
3 (inform) mettre [qn] au courant (**on** de)

upfront /ˌʌp'frʌnt/ *adj* (fam) **1** (frank) franc/franche
2 ‹*money*› payé/-e d'avance

upgrade **A** /'ʌpgreɪd/ *n* (new version) nouvelle version *f*, mise *f* à jour; (in tourism) surclassement *m*
B /ˌʌp'greɪd/ *vt* **1** (modernize) moderniser; (improve) améliorer
2 (Comput) améliorer ‹*software, hardware*›
3 (raise) promouvoir ‹*person*›; revaloriser ‹*job*›

upheaval /ˌʌp'hiːvl/ *n* **1** (disturbance) bouleversement *m*
2 (instability) (political, emotional) bouleversements *mpl*; (physical) remue-ménage *m inv*

uphill /ˌʌp'hɪl/ **A** *adj* **1** ‹*road*› qui monte; **~ slope** côte *f*, montée *f*
2 ‹*task*› difficile
B *adv* **to go/walk ~** monter

uphold /ˌʌp'həʊld/ *vt* (*prét, pp* **-held**) soutenir ‹*right*›; faire respecter ‹*law*›; confirmer ‹*decision*›

upholstery /ˌʌp'həʊlstərɪ/ *n* **1** (covering) revêtement *m*
2 (stuffing) rembourrage *m*

mot clé

u

upkeep /ˈʌpkiːp/ *n* **1** (of property) entretien *m* (**of** de)
2 (cost) frais *mpl* d'entretien

uplifting /ˌʌpˈlɪftɪŋ/ *adj* tonique

upload /ˈʌpləʊd/ *vt* **to ~ sth to a server** télécharger qch vers un serveur

upmarket *adj* ‹*car, hotel*› haut de gamme; ‹*area*› riche

upon /əˈpɒn/ *prep* **1** (on) sur
2 (linking two nouns) **thousands ~ thousands of people** des milliers et des milliers de personnes

upper /ˈʌpə(r)/ **A** *n* (of shoe) empeigne *f*
B *adj* **1** ‹*shelf, cupboard*› du haut; ‹*floor, deck, lip*› supérieur/-e; ‹*teeth*› du haut
2 (in rank, scale) supérieur/-e
3 the ~ limit la limite maximale (**on** de)
IDIOM **to have/get the ~ hand** avoir/prendre le dessus

upper case *adj* **~ letters** (lettres *fpl*) majuscules *fpl*

upper class *n* (*pl* **~es**) **the ~, the ~es** l'aristocratie *f* et la haute bourgeoisie

uppermost /ˈʌpəməʊst/ *adj* **1** (highest) ‹*branch*› le plus haut/la plus haute; (in rank) ‹*echelon*› le plus élevé/la plus élevée
2 to be ~ in sb's mind être au premier plan des préoccupations de qn

upper sixth *n* (BrE) (Sch) ≈ (classe *f*) terminale *f*

upright /ˈʌpraɪt/ **A** *adj* **1** (physically) droit/-e; **to stay ~** ‹*person*› rester debout
2 (morally) droit/-e
B *adv* **to stand ~** se tenir droit; **to sit ~** (action) se redresser

uprising /ˈʌpraɪzɪŋ/ *n* soulèvement *m* (**against** contre)

uproar /ˈʌprɔː(r)/ *n* (noise) tumulte *m*; (protest) protestations *fpl*

uproot /ˌʌpˈruːt/ *vt* déraciner

upset **A** /ˈʌpset/ *n* **1** (surprise, setback) revers *m*
2 (upheaval) bouleversement *m*
3 (distress) peine *f*
4 to have a stomach ~ avoir l'estomac détraqué
B *adj* **to be** *or* **feel ~** (distressed) être très affecté/-e; (annoyed) être contrarié/-e; **to get ~** (angry) se fâcher (**about** pour); (distressed) se tracasser (**about** pour)
C /ˌʌpˈset/ *vt* (*p prés* **-tt-**, *prét, pp* **-set**)
1 (distress) ‹*sight, news*› bouleverser; ‹*person*› faire de la peine à
2 (annoy) contrarier
3 bouleverser ‹*plan*›; déjouer ‹*calculations*›
4 (destabilize) rompre ‹*balance*›
5 (Med) rendre [qn] malade ‹*person*›; perturber ‹*digestion*›

upsetting /ˌʌpˈsetɪŋ/ *adj* (distressing) navrant/-e; (annoying) contrariant/-e

upside down /ˌʌpsaɪd ˈdaʊn/ **A** *adj* à l'envers
B *adv* à l'envers; **to turn the house ~** mettre la maison sens dessus dessous

upstage /ˌʌpˈsteɪdʒ/ *vt* éclipser

upstairs /ˌʌpˈsteəz/ **A** *n* haut *m*
B *adj* ‹*room*› du haut; **an ~ bedroom** une chambre à l'étage
C *adv* en haut; **to go ~** monter (l'escalier)

upstart /ˈʌpstɑːt/ *n, adj* arriviste *mf*

upstream /ˌʌpˈstriːm/ *adv* ‹*travel*› vers l'amont; **~ from here** en amont d'ici

uptake /ˈʌpteɪk/ *n*
IDIOM **to be quick/slow on the ~** (fam) comprendre/ne pas comprendre vite

uptight /ˌʌpˈtaɪt/ *adj* (fam) **1** (tense) tendu/-e
2 (inhibited) coincé/-e (fam)

up-to-date /ˌʌptəˈdaɪt/ *adj* **1** ‹*music, clothes*› à la mode; ‹*equipment*› moderne
2 ‹*records, timetable*› à jour; ‹*information*› récent/-e
3 (informed) ‹*person*› au courant (**with** de)

up-to-the-minute *adj* ‹*information*› dernier/-ière

upward /ˈʌpwəd/ **A** *adj* ‹*push, movement*› vers le haut; ‹*path, road*› qui monte; ‹*trend*› à la hausse
B *adv* (*also* **upwards**) **to go** *or* **move ~** monter; **from £10 ~** à partir de 10 livres sterling

upwardly mobile *adj* en pleine ascension sociale

upwards /ˈʌpwədz/ = **upward B**

uranium /jʊˈreɪnɪəm/ *n* uranium *m*

Uranus /ˈjʊərənəs, jʊˈreɪnəs/ *pr n* Uranus *f*

urban /ˈɜːbən/ *adj* urbain/-e

urban planning *n* urbanisme *m*

urban sprawl *n* mitage *m*

urchin /ˈɜːtʃɪn/ *n* gamin *m*

Urdu /ˈʊəduː/ *n* urdu *m*

urge /ɜːdʒ/ **A** *n* forte envie *f*, désir *m* (**to do** de faire)
B *vt* conseiller vivement, préconiser ‹*caution, restraint, resistance*›; **to ~ sb to do** conseiller vivement à qn de faire; (stronger) pousser qn à faire

urgency /ˈɜːdʒənsɪ/ *n* (of situation, appeal, request) urgence *f*; (of voice, tone) insistance *f*; **a matter of ~** une affaire urgente

urgent /ˈɜːdʒənt/ *adj* **1** (pressing) ‹*case, need*› urgent/-e, pressant/-e; ‹*message, demand*› urgent/-e; ‹*meeting, measures*› d'urgence
2 ‹*request, tone*› insistant/-e

urgently /ˈɜːdʒəntlɪ/ *adv* ‹*request*› d'urgence; ‹*plead*› instamment

urinal /jʊəˈraɪnl, ˈjʊərɪnl/ *n* (place) urinoir *m*; (fixture) urinal *m*

urinate /ˈjʊərɪneɪt/ *vi* uriner

urine /ˈjʊərɪn/ *n* urine *f*

URL *n* (*abbr* = **Unified Resource Locator**) adresse *f* URL

urn /ɜːn/ *n* urne *f*

us /ʌs, əs/ *pron* nous; **she knows ~** elle nous connaît; **both of ~** tous/toutes les deux; **every single one of ~** chacun/-e d'entre nous; **some of ~** quelques-uns/-unes d'entre nous; **she's one of ~** elle est des nôtres

US *pr n* (*abbr* = **United States**) USA *mpl*

USA *pr n* (*abbr* = **United States of America**) USA *mpl*

USB key *n* clé *f* USB

🔑 **use** **A** /juːs/ *n* **1** (act of using) (of substance, object, machine) emploi *m*, utilisation *f* (**of** de); (of word, expression) emploi *m*, usage *m* (**of** de); **for the ~ of** à l'usage de ‹*customer, staff*›; **for my own ~** pour mon usage personnel; **to make ~ of sth** utiliser qch; **to put sth to good ~** tirer parti de qch; **while the machine is in ~** lorsque la machine est en service *or* en fonctionnement; **to have the ~ of** avoir l'usage de ‹*house, car, kitchen*›; avoir la jouissance de ‹*garden*›; **to lose the ~ of one's legs** perdre l'usage de ses jambes
2 (way of using) (of resource, object, material) utilisation *f*; (of term) emploi *m*; **to have no further ~ for sb/sth** ne plus avoir besoin de qn/qch
3 (usefulness) **to be of ~** être utile (**to** à); **to be (of) no ~** ‹*object*› ne servir à rien; ‹*person*› n'être bon/bonne à rien; **what's the ~ of crying?** à quoi bon pleurer?; **it's no ~ (he won't listen)** c'est inutile (il n'écoutera pas)
B /juːz/ *vt* **1** se servir de, utiliser ‹*object, car, room, money*›; employer ‹*method, word*›; profiter de, saisir ‹*opportunity*›; faire jouer ‹*influence*›; avoir recours à ‹*blackmail*›; utiliser ‹*knowledge, talent*›; **to ~ sb/sth as** se servir de qn/qch comme; **to ~ sth to do** se servir de qch pour faire
2 (consume) consommer ‹*fuel, food*›; utiliser ‹*water, leftovers*›
3 (exploit) se servir de ‹*person*›
C **used** *pp adj* ‹*car*› d'occasion; ‹*envelope*› qui a déjà servi

■ **use up** finir ‹*food*›; dépenser ‹*money*›; épuiser ‹*supplies*›

used

> To translate *used to do*, use the imperfect tense in French: *he used to live in York* = il habitait York.
> To emphasize a contrast between past and present, you can use *avant*: *I used to love sport* = avant, j'adorais le sport.

A /juːst/ *modal aux* **I ~ to read a lot** je lisais beaucoup; **she ~ to smoke, didn't she?** elle fumait avant, non?; **she doesn't smoke now, but she ~ to** elle ne fume plus maintenant, mais elle fumait avant; **there ~ to be a pub here** il y avait un pub ici (dans le temps)
B /juːst/ *adj* **to be ~ to sth** avoir l'habitude de qch, être habitué/-e à qch; **to get ~ to** s'habituer à; **I'm not ~ to it** je n'ai pas l'habitude; **you'll get ~ to it** tu t'y habitueras

🔑 **useful** /ˈjuːsfl/ *adj* utile

useless /ˈjuːslɪs/ *adj* **1** (not helpful) inutile
2 (not able to be used) inutilisable
3 (fam) (incompetent) incapable, nul/nulle (fam)

🔑 **user** /ˈjuːzə(r)/ *n* (of public service) usager *m*; (of product, machine) utilisateur/-trice *m/f*

user-friendly *adj* (Comput) convivial/-e; (gen) facile à utiliser

user group *n* groupe *m* d'utilisateurs

username *n* (Comput) nom *m* d'utilisateur

usher /ˈʌʃə(r)/ *vt* conduire, escorter; **to ~ sb in/out** faire entrer/sortir qn

usherette /ˌʌʃəˈret/ *n* ouvreuse *f*

USSR *pr n* (*abbr* = **Union of Soviet Socialist Republics**) URSS *f*

🔑 **usual** /ˈjuːʒl/ *adj* (gen) habituel/-elle; ‹*word, term*› usuel/-elle; **it is ~ for sb to do** c'est normal pour qn de faire; **it is ~ to do** il est d'usage de faire; **as ~** comme d'habitude; **more/less than ~** plus/moins que d'habitude

🔑 **usually** /ˈjuːʒəlɪ/ *adv* d'habitude, normalement

utensil /juːˈtensl/ *n* ustensile *m*

uterus /ˈjuːtərəs/ *n* utérus *m*

utility /juːˈtɪlətɪ/ **A** *n* **1** (usefulness) utilité *f*
2 (*also* **public ~**) (service) service *m* public
B **utilities** *npl* (AmE) factures *fpl*

utility bill /juːˈtɪlɪtɪ bɪl/ *n* facture *f* de services publics

utility company *n* société *f* chargée d'assurer un service public

utmost /ˈʌtməʊst/ **A** *n* **to do** *or* **try one's ~ to do** faire tout son possible pour faire; **to the ~ of one's abilities** au maximum de ses capacités
B *adj* ‹*caution, ease, secrecy*› le plus grand/la plus grande *before n*; ‹*limit*› extrême; **it is of the ~ importance that** il est extrêmement important que (+ *subjunctive*)

Utopia /juːˈtəʊpɪə/ *n* utopie *f*

utter /ˈʌtə(r)/ **A** *adj* ‹*disaster, boredom, despair*› total/-e; ‹*honesty, sincerity*› absolu/-e; ‹*fool, stranger*› parfait/-e *before n*
B *vt* prononcer ‹*word, curse*›; pousser ‹*cry*›; émettre ‹*sound*›

utterly /ˈʌtəlɪ/ *adv* complètement; ‹*condemn*› avec vigueur

U-turn *n* demi-tour *m*; (fig) volte-face *f inv*

UV *adj* (*abbr* = **ultraviolet**) ‹*light, ray, radiation*› ultraviolet/-ette

🔑 mot clé

Vv

v, **V** /viː/ *n* **1** (letter) v, V *m*
2 v (*abbr* = **versus**) contre

vacancy /ˈveɪkənsɪ/ *n* **1** (room) **'vacancies'** 'chambres libres'; **'no vacancies'** 'complet'
2 (unfilled job) poste *m* à pourvoir, poste *m* vacant

vacant /ˈveɪkənt/ *adj* **1** ‹*flat, room, seat*› libre, disponible; ‹*office, land*› inoccupé/-e
2 ‹*job, post*› vacant/-e, à pourvoir
3 ‹*look, stare*› absent/-e; ‹*expression*› vide

vacant possession *n* jouissance *f* immédiate

vacate /vəˈkeɪt, (AmE) ˈveɪkeɪt/ *vt* quitter ‹*house, premises, job*›

vacation /veɪkeɪʃn/ *n* (AmE) vacances *fpl*; **on ~** en vacances

vacationer /vəˈkeɪʃənə(r), (AmE) veɪ-/ *n* (AmE) vacancier/-ière *m/f*

vaccinate /ˈvæksɪneɪt/ *vt* vacciner (**against** contre)

vaccination /ˌvæksɪˈneɪʃn/ *n* vaccination *f* (**against** contre)

vaccine /ˈvæksiːn, (AmE) vækˈsiːn/ *n* vaccin *m* (**against** contre)

vacillate /ˈvæsəleɪt/ *vi* hésiter

vacuum /ˈvækjʊəm/ **A** *n* **1** (gen) vide *m*
2 (*also* **~ cleaner**) aspirateur *m*
B *vt* passer [qch] à l'aspirateur ‹*carpet*›; passer l'aspirateur dans ‹*room*›

vacuum pack *vt* emballer [qch] sous vide

vagrant /ˈveɪgrənt/ *n*, *adj* vagabond/-e *m/f*

vague /veɪg/ *adj* **1** (gen) vague; **to be ~ about** rester vague sur *or* évasif/-ive au sujet de ‹*plans, past*›
2 (distracted) ‹*person, expression*› distrait/-e

vaguely /ˈveɪglɪ/ *adv* **1** (gen) vaguement
2 (distractedly) ‹*smile, gaze*› d'un air distrait *or* vague

vain /veɪn/ **A** *adj* **1** (conceited) vaniteux/-euse, vain/-e *after n*
2 (futile) ‹*attempt, promise, hope*› vain/-e *before n*
B **in vain** *phr* en vain

valentine card *n* carte *f* de la Saint-Valentin

Valentine Day *n* (*also* **Valentine's Day**) la Saint-Valentin

valet /ˈvælɪt, -leɪ/ *n* **1** (employee) valet *m* de chambre
2 (AmE) (rack) valet *m* de nuit

valet parking *n* service *m* de voiturier

valiant /ˈvælɪənt/ *adj* ‹*soldier*› vaillant/-e; ‹*attempt*› courageux/-euse

valid /ˈvælɪd/ *adj* **1** ‹*passport, licence*› valide; ‹*ticket, offer*› valable (**for** pour)
2 ‹*argument, excuse*› valable; ‹*complaint*› fondé/-e; ‹*point, comment*› pertinent/-e

validate /ˈvælɪdeɪt/ *vt* **1** prouver le bien-fondé de ‹*claim, theory*›
2 valider ‹*document, passport*›

valley /ˈvælɪ/ *n* (*pl* **~s**) vallée *f*; (small) vallon *m*

valour (BrE), **valor** (AmE) /ˈvælə(r)/ *n* bravoure *f*

valuable /ˈvæljʊəbl/ *adj* **1** ‹*object, asset*› de valeur; **to be ~** avoir de la valeur; **a very ~ ring** une bague de grande valeur
2 ‹*advice, information, lesson, member*› précieux/-ieuse

valuables /ˈvæljʊəblz/ *npl* objets *mpl* de valeur

valuation /ˌvæljʊˈeɪʃn/ *n* (of house, land, company) évaluation *f*; (of antique, art) expertise *f*; **to have a ~ done on sth** faire évaluer qch

value /ˈvæljuː/ **A** *n* valeur *f*; **novelty ~** caractère *m* nouveau; **to be good ~** avoir un bon rapport qualité-prix; **to get ~ for money** en avoir pour son argent
B *vt* **1** évaluer ‹*house, asset, company*› (**at** à); expertiser ‹*antique, jewel, painting*›
2 (appreciate) apprécier ‹*person, friendship, opinion, help*›; tenir à ‹*independence, life*›

value pack *n* lot *m* économique

valve /vælv/ *n* **1** (in machine, engine) soupape *f*; (on tyre, football) valve *f*
2 (Anat) valvule *f*

van /væn/ *n* **1** (small, for deliveries) fourgonnette *f*, camionnette *f*; (larger, for removals) fourgon *m*
2 (AmE) (camper) auto-caravane *f*, camping-car *m*

vandal /ˈvændl/ *n* vandale *mf*

vandalism /ˈvændəlɪzəm/ *n* vandalisme *m*

vandalize /ˈvændəlaɪz/ *vt* vandaliser

van driver *n* chauffeur *m* de camionnette

vanguard /ˈvængɑːd/ *n* avant-garde *f*; **in the ~** à l'avant-garde

vanilla /vəˈnɪlə/ *n* vanille *f*

vanish /ˈvænɪʃ/ *vi* disparaître (**from** de); **to ~ into thin air** se volatiliser

vanity /ˈvænətɪ/ *n* vanité *f*

vantage point *n* point *m* de vue, position *f* élevée

vaporizer /ˈveɪpəraɪzə(r)/ *n* vaporisateur *m*

vapour (BrE), **vapor** (AmE) /'veɪpə(r)/ *n* vapeur *f*

vapour trail *n* traînée *f* de condensation, traînée *f* d'avion

variable /'veərɪəbl/ *n, adj* variable *f*

variance /'veərɪəns/ *n* **to be at ~ with** ne pas concorder avec ‹*evidence, facts*›

variant /'veərɪənt/ *n* variante *f* (**of** de, **on** par rapport à)

🔑 **variation** /ˌveərɪ'eɪʃn/ *n* **1** (change) variation *f*, différence *f* (**in, of** de)
2 (new version) variante *f* (**of** de); (in music) variation *f* (**on** sur)

varied /'veərɪd/ *adj* varié/-e

🔑 **variety** /və'raɪətɪ/ *n* **1** (diversity, range) variété *f* (**in, of** de); **for a ~ of reasons** pour diverses raisons; **a ~ of sizes/colours** un grand choix de tailles/de coloris
2 (type) type *m*; (of plant) variété *f*

variety show *n* spectacle de variétés

🔑 **various** /'veərɪəs/ *adj* **1** (different) différents/-es *before n*
2 (several) divers/-es

varnish /'vɑːnɪʃ/ **A** *n* vernis *m*
B *vt* vernir ‹*woodwork*›; **to ~ one's nails** se vernir les ongles

🔑 **vary** /'veərɪ/ **A** *vt* varier ‹*menu, programme*›; faire varier ‹*temperature*›; changer de ‹*method, pace, route*›
B *vi* varier (**with, according to** selon); **it varies from one town to another** cela varie d'une ville à l'autre

varying /'veərɪɪŋ/ *adj* variable

vase /vɑːz, (AmE) veɪs, veɪz/ *n* vase *m*; **flower ~** vase à fleurs

🔑 **vast** /vɑːst, (AmE) væst/ *adj* **1** ‹*amount, sum, improvement, difference*› énorme; **the ~ majority** la très grande majorité
2 ‹*room, area, plain*› vaste *before n*, immense

vat /væt/ *n* cuve *f*; **beer/wine ~** cuve à bière/vin

VAT *n* (BrE) (*abbr* = **value-added tax**) TVA *f*, taxe *f* à la valeur ajoutée

Vatican /'vætɪkən/ *pr n* Vatican *m*; **~ City** cité *f* du Vatican

vault /vɔːlt/ **A** *n* **1** (roof) voûte *f*
2 (*also* **~s**) (of bank) chambre *f* forte; (for safe-deposit boxes) salle *f* des coffres; (of house, for wine) cave *f*
B *vt* sauter par-dessus ‹*fence, bar*›
C *vi* sauter (**over** par-dessus)

VCR *n* (*abbr* = **video cassette recorder**) magnétoscope *m*

VD *n* (*abbr* = **venereal disease**) MST *f*

VDU *n* (*abbr* = **visual display unit**) écran *m* de visualisation

veal /viːl/ *n* veau *m*

veer /vɪə(r)/ *vi* ‹*ship*› virer (*also* **~ off**) ‹*person, road*› tourner; **to ~ off course** dévier de sa route

vegan /'viːgən/ *n, adj* végétalien/-ienne *m/f*

veganism /'viːgənɪzəm/ *n* végétalisme *m*

Vegeburger® /'vedʒɪbɜːgə(r)/ ▶ **veggie burger**

vegetable /'vedʒtəbl/ **A** *n* légume *m*
B *adj* ‹*soup, patch*› de légumes; ‹*fat, oil*› végétal/-e; **~ garden** potager *m*

vegetarian /ˌvedʒɪ'teərɪən/ *n, adj* végétarien/-ienne *m/f*

vegetarianism /ˌvedʒɪ'teərɪənɪzəm/ *n* végétarisme *m*

vegetate /'vedʒɪteɪt/ *vi* végéter

vegetation /ˌvedʒɪ'teɪʃn/ *n* végétation *f*

veggie burger *n* croquette *f* pour végétariens

vehement /'viːəmənt/ *adj* véhément/-e

🔑 **vehicle** /'vɪəkl, (AmE) 'viːhɪkl/ *n* véhicule *m*

veil /veɪl/ **A** *n* (gen, fig) voile *m*; (on hat) voilette *f*
B *vt* ‹*mist, cloud*› voiler

veiled *adj* voilé/-e

vein /veɪn/ *n* (blood vessel) veine *f*; (on insect wing, leaf) nervure *f*; (in cheese) veinure *f*; (of ore) veine *f*

velocity /vɪ'lɒsətɪ/ *n* vélocité *f*

velour /və'lʊə(r)/ *n* (*also* **velours**) velours *m*

velvet /'velvɪt/ *n* velours *m*; **crushed ~** velours frappé

velvety /'velvətɪ/ *adj* velouté/-e

vending machine *n* distributeur *m* automatique

vendor /'vendə(r)/ *n* **1** (in street, kiosk) marchand/-e *m/f*
2 (as opposed to buyer) vendeur/-euse *m/f*

veneer /vɪ'nɪə(r)/ *n* placage *m*; (fig) vernis *m*

venereal disease *n* maladie *f* vénérienne

venetian blind *n* store *m* vénitien

Venezuela /ˌvenɪ'zweɪlə/ *pr n* Venezuela *m*

vengeance /'vendʒəns/ *n* vengeance *f*; **with a ~** de plus belle

Venice /'venɪs/ *pr n* Venise

venison /'venɪsn, -zn/ *n* (viande *f* de) chevreuil *m*

venom /'venəm/ *n* venim *m*

venomous /'venəməs/ *adj* venimeux/-euse

vent /vent/ **A** *n* (outlet for gas, pressure) bouche *f*, conduit *m*; **air ~** bouche d'aération; **to give ~ to** décharger ‹*anger, feelings*›
B *vt* décharger ‹*anger, frustration*› (**on** sur)

ventilate /'ventɪleɪt/ *vt* aérer ‹*room*›

ventilation /ˌventɪ'leɪʃn/ *n* **1** (gen) aération *f*, ventilation *f*
2 (of patient) ventilation *f* artificielle

ventilator /'ventɪleɪtə(r)/ *n* (for patient) respirateur *m* artificiel

ventriloquist /ven'trɪləkwɪst/ *n* ventriloque *mf*

🔑 mot clé

venture /ˈventʃə(r)/ **A** *n* **1** (undertaking) aventure *f*, entreprise *f*; **a commercial ~** une entreprise commerciale
2 (experiment) essai *m*
B *vt* hasarder ‹*opinion, suggestion*›; **to ~ to do** se risquer à faire
C *vi* **to ~ into** s'aventurer dans ‹*place, street, city*›; **to ~ out(doors)** s'aventurer dehors

venture capital *n* capital-risque *m*

venue /ˈvenjuː/ *n* lieu *m*

Venus /ˈviːnəs/ *pr n* Vénus *f*

verb /vɜːb/ *n* verbe *m*

verbal /ˈvɜːbl/ *adj* verbal/-e

verbatim /vɜːˈbeɪtɪm/ **A** *adj* ‹*report, account*› textuel/-elle
B *adv* ‹*describe, record*› mot pour mot

verbose /vɜːˈbəʊs/ *adj* verbeux/-euse

verdict /ˈvɜːdɪkt/ *n* **1** (Law) verdict *m*; **a ~ of guilty/not guilty** un verdict positif/négatif
2 (fig) (opinion) verdict *m*; **well, what's the ~?** (fam) eh bien, qu'est-ce que tu en penses?

verge /vɜːdʒ/ *n* **1** (BrE) (by road) accotement *m*, bas-côté *m*
2 (brink) **on the ~ of** au bord de ‹*tears*›; au seuil de ‹*adolescence, death*›; **on the ~ of doing** sur le point de faire
■ **verge on** friser ‹*panic, stupidity, contempt*›

verification /ˌverɪfɪˈkeɪʃn/ *n* vérification *f*

verify /ˈverɪfaɪ/ *vt* vérifier

vermicelli /ˌvɜːmɪˈselɪ, -ˈtʃelɪ/ *n* vermicelles *mpl*

vermilion /vəˈmɪlɪən/ *n, adj* vermillon *m inv*

vermin /ˈvɜːmɪn/ *n* **1** (rodents) animaux *mpl* nuisibles
2 (lice, insects) vermine *f*

verruca /vəˈruːkə/ *n* (*pl* **-cae** *ou* **-cas**) verrue *f* plantaire

versatile /ˈvɜːsətaɪl/ *adj* **1** ‹*person*› plein/-e de ressources, aux talents divers *after n*; ‹*mind*› souple
2 ‹*vehicle*› polyvalent/-e; ‹*equipment*› à usages multiples

verse /vɜːs/ *n* **1** (poems) poésie *f*
2 (form) vers *mpl*; **in ~** en vers
3 (part of poem) strophe *f*; (of song) couplet *m*

version /ˈvɜːʃn, (AmE) -ʒn/ *n* version *f* (**of** de)

versus /ˈvɜːsəs/ *prep* contre

vertebra /ˈvɜːtɪbrə/ *n* (*pl* **-brae**) vertèbre *f*

vertebrate /ˈvɜːtɪbrət/ *n* vertébré *m*

vertical /ˈvɜːtɪkl/ *adj* vertical/-e; **a ~ drop** un à-pic

vertigo /ˈvɜːtɪgəʊ/ *n* (*pl* **-goes** *ou* **-gines**) vertige *m*; **to get ~** avoir le vertige

verve /vɜːv/ *n* brio *m*, verve *f*

very /ˈverɪ/ **A** *adj* **1** (actual) même *after n*; **this ~ second** immédiatement
2 (ideal) **the ~ person I need** exactement la personne qu'il me faut
3 (ultimate) tout/-e; **from the ~ beginning** depuis le tout début; **at the ~ front** tout devant; **on the ~ edge** à l'extrême bord
4 (mere) ‹*mention, thought, word*› seul/-e *before n*; **the ~ idea!** quelle idée!
B *adv* **1** (extremely) très; **I'm ~ sorry** je suis vraiment désolé; **~ well** très bien; **that's all ~ well but who's going to pay for it?** c'est bien beau, tout ça, mais qui va payer?; **~ much** beaucoup; **I didn't eat ~ much** je n'ai pas mangé grand-chose
2 (absolutely) **the ~ best/worst thing** de loin la meilleure/pire chose; **at the ~ latest** au plus tard; **at the ~ least** tout au moins; **the ~ next day** le lendemain même; **a car of your ~ own** ta propre voiture

vessel /ˈvesl/ *n* **1** (ship) vaisseau *m*
2 (Anat) **blood ~** vaisseau *m* sanguin
3 (container) vase *m*

vest /vest/ *n* **1** (BrE) (underwear) maillot *m* de corps
2 (for sport, fashion) débardeur *m*
3 (AmE) (waistcoat) gilet *m*

vested interest *n* **to have a ~** être personnellement intéressé/-e (**in** dans)

vestige /ˈvestɪdʒ/ *n* vestige *m*

vet /vet/ **A** *n* **1** (*abbr* = **veterinary surgeon**) vétérinaire *mf*
2 (AmE) (fam), (Mil) ancien combattant *m*, vétéran *m*
B *vt* (*p prés etc* **-tt-**) mener une enquête approfondie sur ‹*person*›; passer [qch] en revue ‹*plan*›; approuver ‹*publication*›

veteran /ˈvetərən/ **A** *n* vétéran *m*
B *adj* ‹*sportsman, politician*› chevronné/-e

veterinarian /ˌvetərɪˈneərɪən/ *n* (AmE) vétérinaire *mf*

veterinary surgeon *n* vétérinaire *mf*

veterinary surgery *n* clinique *f* vétérinaire

veto /ˈviːtəʊ/ **A** *n* (*pl* **-toes**) **1** (practice) veto *m*
2 (right) droit *m* de veto (**over, on** sur)
B *vt* (*prés* **-toes**, *prét*, *pp* **-toed**) mettre *or* opposer son veto à

vetting /ˈvetɪŋ/ *n* contrôle *m*

vex /veks/ *vt* (annoy) contrarier; (worry) tracasser

vexed /vekst/ *adj* **1** (annoyed) mécontent/-e (**with** de)
2 ‹*question, issue*› épineux/-euse

VHF *n* (*abbr* = **very high frequency**) VHF

via /ˈvaɪə/ *prep* **1** (by way of) (on ticket, timetable) via; (other contexts) en passant par; **we came ~ Paris** nous sommes venus en passant par Paris
2 (by means of) par

viability /vaɪəˈbɪlətɪ/ *n* (of company) viabilité *f*; (of project, idea) validité *f*

viable /ˈvaɪəbl/ *adj* ‹*company, government, farm*› viable; ‹*project, idea, plan*› réalisable, valable

viaduct /ˈvaɪədʌkt/ *n* viaduc *m*

vibrant /ˈvaɪbrənt/ *adj* ‹*person, place, personality*› plein/-e de vie; ‹*colour*› éclatant/-e

vibrate /vaɪˈbreɪt, (AmE) ˈvaɪbreɪt/ *vi* vibrer (**with** de)

vibration /vaɪˈbreɪʃn/ *n* vibration *f*

vicar /ˈvɪkə(r)/ *n* pasteur *m*

vicarage /ˈvɪkərɪdʒ/ *n* presbytère *m*

vicarious /vɪˈkeərɪəs, (AmE) vaɪˈk-/ *adj* ‹*pleasure*› indirect/-e

vice /vaɪs/ *n* **1** vice *m*; (amusing weakness) faiblesse *f*
2 (*also* **vise** (AmE)) (tool) étau *m*

vice-captain *n* capitaine *m* en second

vice-chancellor *n* président/-e *m/f* d'Université

vice-president *n* vice-président/-e *m/f*

vice squad *n* brigade *f* des mœurs

vicinity /vɪˈsɪnətɪ/ *n* voisinage *m*; **in the (immediate) ~ of Oxford** à proximité (immédiate) d'Oxford

vicious /ˈvɪʃəs/ *adj* ‹*animal*› malfaisant/-e; ‹*speech, attack*› brutal/-e; ‹*rumour, person, lie*› malveillant/-e

vicious circle *n* cercle *m* vicieux

⚷ **victim** /ˈvɪktɪm/ *n* victime *f*

victimization /ˌvɪktɪmaɪˈzeɪʃn/ *n* persécution *f*

victimize /ˈvɪktɪmaɪz/ *vt* persécuter

victor /ˈvɪktə(r)/ *n* vainqueur *m*

Victorian /vɪkˈtɔːrɪən/ *adj* victorien/-ienne

victorious /vɪkˈtɔːrɪəs/ *adj* victorieux/-ieuse (**over** sur)

⚷ **victory** /ˈvɪktərɪ/ *n* victoire *f*

⚷ **video** /ˈvɪdɪəʊ/ **A** *n* (*pl* **~s**) **1** (*also* **~ recorder**) magnétoscope *m*
2 (*also* **~ cassette**) cassette *f* vidéo; **on ~** en vidéo
3 (*also* **~ film**) vidéo *f*
B *adj* vidéo *inv*
C *vt* (*prés* **~s**, *prét, pp* **~ed**) **1** (from TV) enregistrer
2 (on camcorder) filmer [qch] en vidéo

video camera *n* caméra *f* vidéo

video card *n* (Comput) carte *f* vidéo

video clip *n* (from film) extrait *m*; (Mus) clip *m*

videoconference *n* vidéoconférence *f*

videoconferencing *n* vidéoconférence *f*

videodisc *n* vidéodisque *m*

video game *n* jeu *m* vidéo

video jock *n* (fam) vidéo jockey *mf*

video nasty *n* vidéo *f* représentant des violences véritables

videophone *n* vidéophone *m*, visiophone *m*

video shop (BrE), **video store** (AmE) *n* vidéoclub *m*

videotape /ˈvɪdɪəʊteɪp/ *n* bande *f* vidéo

vie /vaɪ/ *vi* (*p prés* **vying**) rivaliser (**with** avec, **for** pour, **to do** pour faire)

Vienna /vɪˈenə/ *pr n* Vienne

⚷ **view** /vjuː/ **A** *n* **1** (gen) vue *f*; **in (full) ~ of sb** devant qn, sous les yeux de qn; **to disappear from ~** disparaître
2 (personal opinion, attitude) avis *m*, opinion *f*; **point of ~** point *m* de vue; **in his ~** à son avis
B *vt* **1** (consider) considérer; (envisage) envisager
2 (look at) voir ‹*scene, building, collection, exhibition*›; visiter ‹*house, castle*›; regarder ‹*programme*›
3 (Comput) visualiser
C **in view of** *phr* (considering) vu, étant donné
D **with a view to** *phr* **with a ~ to doing** en vue de faire, afin de faire

viewer /ˈvjuːə(r)/ *n* **1** (of TV) téléspectateur/-trice *m/f*
2 (of property) visiteur/-euse *m/f*
3 (on camera) visionneuse *f*

viewfinder *n* viseur *m*

viewing /ˈvjuːɪŋ/ **A** *n* (of exhibition, house) visite *f*; (of film) projection *f*; (of new range) présentation *f*
B *adj* ‹*habits, preferences*› des téléspectateurs; **~ figures** taux *m* d'écoute

viewpoint *n* (all contexts) point *m* de vue

vigil /ˈvɪdʒɪl/ *n* (gen) veille *f*; (by sickbed) veillée *f*; (by demonstrators) manifestation *f* silencieuse

vigilant /ˈvɪdʒɪlənt/ *adj* vigilant/-e

vigilante /ˌvɪdʒɪˈlæntɪ/ *n* membre *m* d'un groupe d'autodéfense

vigorous /ˈvɪgərəs/ *adj* vigoureux/-euse

vigour (BrE), **vigor** (AmE) /ˈvɪgə(r)/ *n* vigueur *f*

vile /vaɪl/ *adj* ‹*smell*› infect/-e; ‹*weather*› abominable; ‹*place, colour*› horrible; ‹*mood*› exécrable

villa /ˈvɪlə/ *n* (in town) pavillon *m*; (in country, for holiday) villa *f*

⚷ **village** /ˈvɪlɪdʒ/ *n* village *m*

village green *n* terrain *m* communal

village hall *n* salle *f* des fêtes

villager /ˈvɪlɪdʒə(r)/ *n* villageois/-e *m/f*

villain /ˈvɪlən/ *n* (in book, film) méchant *m*; (child) coquin/-e *m/f*; (criminal) bandit *m*

vindicate /ˈvɪndɪkeɪt/ *vt* justifier

vindictive /vɪnˈdɪktɪv/ *adj* vindicatif/-ive

vindictiveness /vɪnˈdɪktɪvnɪs/ *n* esprit *m* de vengeance

vine /vaɪn/ *n* **1** (grapevine) vigne *f*
2 (climbing plant) plante *f* grimpante

vinegar /ˈvɪnɪgə(r)/ *n* vinaigre *m*

vineyard /ˈvɪnjəd/ *n* vignoble *m*

vintage /ˈvɪntɪdʒ/ **A** *n* (wine) millésime *m*
B *adj* **1** ‹*wine, champagne*› millésimé/-e; ‹*port*› vieux/vieille

⚷ mot clé

V

2 ‹*comedy*› classique
3 ‹*clothes*› vintage

vintage car *n* voiture *f* d'époque

vinyl /'vaɪnl/ **A** *n* vinyle *m*
B *adj* en vinyle; ‹*paint*› vinylique

viola *n* (violon *m*) alto *m*

violate /'vaɪəleɪt/ *vt* **1** violer ‹*law, agreement, rights*›
2 profaner ‹*sacred place*›; troubler ‹*peace*›

violation /ˌvaɪə'leɪʃn/ *n* violation *f*; **traffic ~** infraction *f* au code de la route

violence /'vaɪələns/ *n* violence *f*

violent /'vaɪələnt/ *adj* **1** ‹*crime, behaviour, film, storm, emotion*› violent/-e
2 ‹*contrast*› brutal/-e
3 ‹*colour*› criard/-e

violently /'vaɪələntlɪ/ *adv* ‹*attack, react, shake*› violemment; ‹*brake, swerve*› brusquement

violet /'vaɪələt/ **A** *n* **1** (flower) violette *f*
2 (colour) violet *m*
B *adj* violet/-ette

violin /ˌvaɪə'lɪn/ *n* violon *m*

violinist /ˌvaɪə'lɪnɪst/ *n* violoniste *mf*

VIP (*abbr* = **very important person**) **A** *n* personnalité *f* (en vue)
B *adj* ‹*area, lounge*› réservé/-e aux personnalités; **~ guest** hôte *mf* de marque; **to give sb (the) ~ treatment** recevoir qn en hôte de marque

viper /'vaɪpə(r)/ *n* vipère *f*

virgin /'vɜːdʒɪn/ *n, adj* vierge *f*

Virgo /'vɜːgəʊ/ *n* Vierge *f*

virile /'vɪraɪl, (AmE) 'vɪrəl/ *adj* viril/-e

virtual /'vɜːtʃʊəl/ *adj* **1** (gen) quasi-total/-e; **he was a ~ prisoner** il était pratiquement prisonnier
2 (Comput) virtuel/-elle

virtually /'vɜːtʃʊəlɪ/ *adv* pratiquement, presque; **it's ~ impossible** c'est quasiment (fam) impossible

virtual reality *n* réalité *f* virtuelle

virtue /'vɜːtʃuː/ **A** *n* **1** (goodness) vertu *f*
2 (advantage) avantage *m*
B by virtue of *phr* en raison de

virtuoso /ˌvɜːtjʊ'əʊsəʊ, -zəʊ/ *n* (*pl* **-sos** *ou* **-si**) virtuose *mf* (**of** de)

virtuous /'vɜːtʃʊəs/ *adj* vertueux/-euse

virus /'vaɪərəs/ *n* virus *m*

virus checker *n* (Comput) logiciel *m* antivirus

visa /'viːzə/ *n* visa *m*; **tourist ~** visa de touriste

vis-à-vis /ˌviːzɑː'viː/ *prep* (in relation to) par rapport à; (concerning) en ce qui concerne

visibility /ˌvɪzə'bɪlətɪ/ *n* visibilité *f*

visible /'vɪzəbl/ *adj* **1** (able to be seen) visible; **clearly ~** bien visible
2 (concrete) ‹*improvement, sign*› évident/-e

visibly /'vɪzəblɪ/ *adv* ‹*moved, shocked*› manifestement

vision /'vɪʒn/ *n* **1** (idea, mental picture, hallucination) vision *f*
2 (ability to see) vue *f*
3 (foresight) sagacité *f*

visionary /'vɪʒənrɪ, (AmE) 'vɪʒənerɪ/ *n, adj* visionnaire *mf*

visit /'vɪzɪt/ **A** *n* (gen) visite *f*; (stay) séjour *m*; **a state ~** une visite officielle; **to pay a ~ to sb, to pay sb a ~** aller voir qn; (more formal) rendre visite à qn
B *vt* **1 to ~ Paris** (see) visiter Paris; (stay) faire un séjour à Paris, aller passer quelques jours à Paris; **to ~ sb** (call) aller voir qn; (more formal) rendre visite à qn; (stay with) aller (passer quelques jours) chez qn
2 (AmE) **to ~ with sb** aller voir qn

visiting card *n* (BrE) carte *f* de visite

visiting hours *npl* heures *fpl* de visite

visitor /'vɪzɪtə(r)/ *n* **1** (caller) invité/-e *m/f*
2 (tourist) visiteur/-euse *m/f*

visitor centre *n* centre *m* d'accueil et d'information des visiteurs

visitors' book *n* (in exhibition) livre *m* d'or; (in hotel) registre *m*

visor /'vaɪzə(r)/ *n* visière *f*

vista /'vɪstə/ *n* panorama *m*; (fig) perspective *f*

visual /'vɪʒʊəl/ *adj* visuel/-elle

visual aid *n* support *m* visuel

visual arts *npl* arts *mpl* plastiques

visualize /'vɪʒʊəlaɪz/ *vt* **1** (picture) s'imaginer
2 (envisage) envisager

visually impaired *n* **the ~** les malvoyants *mpl*

vital /'vaɪtl/ *adj* **1** (essential) (gen) primordial/-e; ‹*match, point, support, factor*› décisif/-ive; ‹*service, help*› indispensable; ‹*treatment, organ, force*› vital/-e; **of ~ importance** d'une importance capitale
2 ‹*person*› plein/-e de vie

vitality /vaɪ'tælətɪ/ *n* vitalité *f*

vitally /'vaɪtəlɪ/ *adv* ‹*important*› extrêmement; ‹*needed*› absolument

vital statistics *n* (of woman) mensurations *fpl*

vitamin /'vɪtəmɪn, (AmE) 'vaɪt-/ *n* vitamine *f*

viva **A** /'vaɪvə/ *n* oral *m*
B /viːvə/ *excl* vive!

vivacious /vɪ'veɪʃəs/ *adj* plein/-e de vivacité

vivid /'vɪvɪd/ *adj* **1** (bright) ‹*colour, light*› vif/vive
2 (graphic) ‹*imagination*› vif/vive; ‹*memory, picture*› (très) net/nette; ‹*dream, impression, description*› frappant/-e

vividly /'vɪvɪdlɪ/ *adv* ‹*describe, illustrate*› de façon très vivante; ‹*remember, recall*› très bien

vivisection /ˌvɪvɪ'sekʃn/ *n* vivisection *f*

vixen /'vɪksn/ *n* **1** (fox) renarde *f*
2 (woman) mégère *f*

viz /vɪz/ *adv* (*abbr* = **videlicet**) à savoir

V-neck *n* **1** (neck) encolure *f* en V
2 (sweater) pull *m* en V

vocabulary /və'kæbjʊlərɪ, (AmE) -lerɪ/ *n* vocabulaire *m*

vocal /'vəʊkl/ *adj* **1** (concerning speech) vocal/-e
2 (vociferous) ‹*person*› qui se fait entendre

vocalist /'vəʊkəlɪst/ *n* chanteur/-euse *m/f* (*dans un groupe pop*)

vocals *npl* chant *m*; **to do the backing ~** faire les chœurs

vocation /vəʊ'keɪʃn/ *n* vocation *f*

vocational /vəʊ'keɪʃənl/ *adj* professionnel/-elle

vocational course *n* stage *m* de formation professionnelle

vociferous /və'sɪfərəs, (AmE) vəʊ-/ *adj* ‹*person, protest*› véhément/-e

vogue /vəʊg/ *n* vogue *f* (**for** de)

🔑 **voice** /vɔɪs/ **A** *n* voix *f*; **in a loud ~** à haute voix; **in a low ~** à voix basse; **in a cross ~** d'une voix irritée; **to have lost one's ~** (when ill) être aphone; **at the top of one's ~** à tue-tête
B *vt* exprimer ‹*concern, grievance*›

voicemail /vɔɪsmeɪl/ *n* messagerie *f* vocale

voice-over *n* voix-off *f*

voice recognition *n* reconnaissance *f* vocale

void /vɔɪd/ **A** *n* vide *m*; **to fill the ~** combler le vide
B *adj* **1** (Law) ‹*contract, agreement*› nul/nulle; ‹*cheque*› annulé/-e
2 (empty) vide; **~ of** dépourvu/-e de

volatile /'vɒlətaɪl, (AmE) -tl/ *adj* ‹*situation*› explosif/-ive; ‹*person*› lunatique; ‹*market, exchange rate*› instable

volcano /vɒl'keɪnəʊ/ *n* (*pl* **-es** *ou* **-s**) volcan *m*

volley /'vɒlɪ/ **A** *n* **1** (in tennis) volée *f*
2 (of gunfire) salve *f* (**of** de)
3 (series) **a ~ of** un feu roulant de ‹*questions*›; une bordée de ‹*insults, oaths*›
B *vt* (in tennis) prendre [qch] de volée ‹*ball*›
C *vi* (in tennis) jouer à la volée

volleyball /'vɒlɪbɔːl/ *n* volley(-ball) *m*

volt /vəʊlt/ *n* volt *m*

voltage /'vəʊltɪdʒ/ *n* tension *f*

🔑 **volume** /'vɒljuːm, (AmE) -jəm/ *n* **1** (gen) volume *m* (**of** de); (of container) capacité *f*
2 (book) volume *m*; (part of set) tome *m*

volume control *n* (bouton *m* de) réglage *m* du volume

voluntarily /'vɒləntrəlɪ/ *adv* de plein gré, volontairement

voluntary /'vɒləntrɪ, (AmE) -terɪ/ *adj* **1** (gen) volontaire
2 (unpaid) bénévole

voluntary redundancy *n* départ *m* volontaire

volunteer /ˌvɒlən'tɪə(r)/ **A** *n* **1** (offering to do sth) volontaire *mf*
2 (unpaid worker) bénévole *mf*
B *vt* **1** (offer) offrir; **to ~ to do** offrir de faire, se porter volontaire pour faire
2 fournir [qch] spontanément ‹*information*›
C *vi* **1** se porter volontaire (**for** pour)
2 (as soldier) s'engager comme volontaire

voluptuous /və'lʌptʃʊəs/ *adj* voluptueux/-euse

vomit /'vɒmɪt/ **A** *n* vomi *m*
B *vt, vi* vomir

voodoo /'vuːduː/ *n* vaudou *m*

voracious /və'reɪʃəs/ *adj* vorace

vortex /'vɔːteks/ *n* (*pl* **~es** *ou* **-tices**) tourbillon *m*

🔑 **vote** /vəʊt/ **A** *n* **1** (gen) vote *m*
2 (franchise) **the ~** le droit de vote
B *vt* **1** (gen) voter; **to ~ sb into/out of office** élire/ne pas réélire qn
2 (fam) (propose) proposer
C *vi* voter (**on** sur, **for sb** pour qn, **against** contre); **let's ~ on it** mettons-le aux voix; **to ~ to strike** voter la grève

vote of confidence *n* vote *m* de confiance (**in** en)

vote of thanks *n* discours *m* de remerciement

🔑 **voter** /'vəʊtə(r)/ *n* électeur/-trice *m/f*

voting /'vəʊtɪŋ/ *n* scrutin *m*

voting age *n* majorité *f* électorale

vouch /vaʊtʃ/ *v*
■ **vouch for 1** (informally) répondre de ‹*person*›; témoigner de ‹*fact*›
2 (officially) se porter garant de

voucher /'vaʊtʃə(r)/ *n* bon *m*

vow /vaʊ/ **A** *n* (religious) vœu *m*; (of honour) serment *m*; **marriage** *or* **wedding ~s** promesses *fpl* du mariage
B *vt* faire vœu de ‹*love, revenge, allegiance*›; **to ~ to do** jurer de faire

vowel /'vaʊəl/ *n* voyelle *f*

voyage /'vɔɪɪdʒ/ *n* voyage *m*

V-sign /'viːsaɪn/ *n* **1** (victory sign) V *m* de la victoire
2 (BrE) (offensive gesture) geste *m* obscène

VSO *n* (*abbr* = **Voluntary Service Overseas**) (BrE) coopération *f* civile

vulgar /'vʌlgə(r)/ *adj* **1** (tasteless) ‹*furniture, clothes*› de mauvais goût; ‹*taste*› douteux/-euse; ‹*person*› vulgaire
2 (rude) grossier/-ière

vulnerable /'vʌlnərəbl/ *adj* vulnérable (**to** à)

vulture /'vʌltʃə(r)/ *n* vautour *m*

🔑 mot clé

Ww

w, W /ˈdʌbljuː/ *n* w, W *m*

wad /wɒd/ *n* **1** (of banknotes, paper) liasse *f* (of de)
2 (of cotton wool, padding) boule *f* (of de)

waddle /ˈwɒdl/ *vi* ‹*duck, person*› se dandiner

wade /weɪd/ *vi* **1** (in water) **to ~ into the water** entrer dans l'eau; **to ~ ashore** marcher dans l'eau jusqu'au rivage; **to ~ across** traverser à gué
2 he was wading through 'War and Peace' il lisait 'Guerre et Paix', mais ça avançait lentement

waders /ˈweɪdəz/ *npl* cuissardes *fpl*

wafer /ˈweɪfə(r)/ *n* (Culin) gaufrette *f*

wafer-thin *adj* ‹*slice*› ultrafin/-e

waffle /ˈwɒfl/ **A** *n* **1** (Culin) gaufre *f*
2 (fam) (empty words) verbiage *m*
B *vi* (*also* **~ on**) (speaking) bavasser (fam); (writing) faire du remplissage

waft /wɒft, (AmE) wæft/ *vi* **to ~ towards** flotter vers; **to ~ up** monter

wag /wæg/ **A** *vt* (*p prés etc* **-gg-**) remuer ‹*tail*›
B *vi* (*p prés etc* **-gg-**) ‹*tail*› remuer, frétiller; **tongues will ~** ça va faire jaser

wage /weɪdʒ/ **A** *n* (*also* **~s** *pl*) salaire *m*
B *vt* mener ‹*campaign*›; **to ~ (a) war against sb/sth** faire la guerre contre qn/qch

wage earner *n* **1** (person earning a wage) salarié/-e *m/f* (hebdomadaire)
2 (breadwinner) soutien *m* de famille

wage packet *n* **1** (envelope) enveloppe *f* de paie
2 (money) paie *f*

wager /ˈweɪdʒə(r)/ *n* pari *m*; **to make** *or* **lay a ~** parier, faire un pari

wage slip *n* feuille *f* de paie

waggon (BrE), **wagon** *n* **1** (horse-drawn) chariot *m*
2 (BrE) (on rail) wagon *m* (de marchandises)
IDIOM **to be on the ~** (fam) être au régime sec

wail /weɪl/ **A** *n* (of person) gémissement *m*; (of siren) hurlement *m*; (of musical instrument) son *m* plaintif
B *vi* ‹*person, wind*› gémir; ‹*siren*› hurler; ‹*music*› pleurer

waist /weɪst/ *n* taille *f*

waistband *n* ceinture *f*

waistcoat *n* (BrE) gilet *m*

waistline *n* taille *f*

waist measurement *n* tour *m* de taille

wait /weɪt/ **A** *n* attente *f*; **an hour's ~** une heure d'attente
B *vt* **1** attendre ‹*one's turn*›
2 (AmE) **to ~ table** servir à table
C *vi* attendre; **to keep sb ~ing** faire attendre qn; **to ~ for sb/sth** attendre qn/qch; **to ~ for sb/sth to do** attendre que qn/qch fasse; **to ~ to do** attendre de faire; **I can't ~ to do** j'ai hâte de faire; (stronger) je meurs d'impatience de faire; **you'll have to ~ and see** attends et tu verras
IDIOM **to lie in ~ for sb** guetter qn
■ **wait around, wait about** attendre
■ **wait behind** attendre un peu; **to ~ behind for sb** attendre qn
■ **wait on** servir ‹*person*›; **to ~ on sb hand and foot** être aux petits soins pour qn
■ **wait up 1** (stay awake) veiller; **to ~ up for sb** veiller jusqu'au retour de qn
2 (AmE) **~ up!** attends!

waiter /ˈweɪtə(r)/ *n* serveur *m*; **'~!'** 'monsieur!'

waiting game *n* **to play a ~** attendre son heure; (in politics) faire de l'attentisme

waiting list *n* liste *f* d'attente

waiting room *n* salle *f* d'attente

waitress /ˈweɪtrɪs/ *n* serveuse *f*; **'~!'** 'madame!','mademoiselle!'

waive /weɪv/ *vt* déroger à ‹*rule*›; renoncer à ‹*claim, right*›; supprimer ‹*fee*›

wake /weɪk/ **A** *vt* (*also* **~ up**, *prét* **woke**, **waked**†, *pp* **woken**, **waked**†) réveiller; **to ~ sb from a dream** tirer qn d'un rêve
B *vi* (*also* **~ up**, *prét* **woke**, **waked**†, *pp* **woken**, **waked**†) se réveiller
■ **wake up**: **A ~ up** se réveiller; **~ up!** réveille-toi!; (to reality) ouvre les yeux!
B ~ [sb] up réveiller

wake-up call *n* **1** réveil *m* téléphoné
2 (fig) piqûre *f* de rappel

Wales /weɪlz/ *pr n* pays *m* de Galles

walk /wɔːk/ **A** *n* **1** promenade *f*; (shorter) tour *m*; (hike) randonnée *f*; **it's about ten minutes' ~** c'est à environ dix minutes à pied; **to go for a ~** (aller) faire une promenade
2 (gait) démarche *f*
3 (pace) pas *m*
4 (path) allée *f*
5 (Sport) épreuve *f* de marche
B *vt* **1** faire [qch] à pied ‹*distance, path, road*›
2 conduire ‹*horse*›; promener ‹*dog*›; **to ~ sb home** raccompagner qn chez lui/elle
C *vi* (in general) marcher; (for pleasure) se

promener; (not run) aller au pas; **it's not very far, let's ~** ce n'est pas très loin, allons-y à pied; **he ~ed up/down the road** il a remonté/descendu la rue (à pied)

> *à pied* is often omitted with movement verbs if we already know that the person is on foot. If it is surprising or ambiguous, *à pied* should be included.

■ **walk around**: **A** **~ around** se promener; (aimlessly) traîner
B **~ around [sth]** (to and fro) faire un tour dans; (make circuit of) faire le tour de

■ **walk away 1** s'éloigner (**from** de)
2 (refuse to face) **to ~ away from** se désintéresser de ‹*problem*›
3 (survive unscathed) sortir indemne (**from** de)
4 (win easily) **to ~ away with** gagner [qch] haut la main ‹*game, tournament*›; remporter [qch] haut la main ‹*election*›; décrocher ‹*prize, honour*›

■ **walk back** revenir sur ses pas (**to** jusqu'à); **we ~ed back (home)** nous sommes rentrés à pied

■ **walk in** entrer; **I'd just ~ed in when...** je venais à peine d'entrer quand...

■ **walk into ~ into [sth] 1** (enter) entrer dans
2 tomber dans ‹*trap*›; se fourrer dans ‹*tricky situation*›
3 (bump into) rentrer dans ‹*door, person*›

■ **walk off** **A** **~ off 1** partir brusquement
2 to ~ off with sth (innocently) partir avec qch; (as theft) filer (fam) avec qch
B **~ [sth] off** se promener pour faire passer ‹*hangover, large meal*›

■ **walk out 1** sortir (**of** de)
2 (desert) partir; **to ~ out on** laisser tomber (fam) ‹*lover*›; rompre ‹*contract, undertaking*›
3 (as protest) partir en signe de protestation; (on strike) se mettre en grève

■ **walk over**: **A** **~ over** s'approcher (**to** de)
B **~ over [sb]** (fam) **1** (defeat) battre [qn] à plates coutures
2 (humiliate) marcher sur les pieds de

■ **walk round**: **A** **~ round** faire le tour
B **~ round [sth]** (round edge of) faire le tour de; (visit) visiter ‹*town*›

■ **walk through** traverser ‹*house, forest*›; passer ‹*door*›; parcourir ‹*streets*›; marcher dans ‹*snow, mud, grass*›

■ **walk up**: **to ~ up to** s'approcher de

walker /ˈwɔːkə(r)/ *n* (for pleasure) promeneur/-euse *m/f*; (for exercise) marcheur/-euse *m/f*

walkie-talkie /ˌwɔːkɪˈtɔːkɪ/ *n* talkie-walkie *m*

walking /ˈwɔːkɪŋ/ *n* (for pleasure) promenades *fpl* à pied; (for exercise) marche *f* à pied

walking boots *npl* chaussures *fpl* de marche

walking distance *n* **to be within ~** être à quelques minutes de marche (**of** de)

walking pace *n* pas *m*; **at a ~** au pas

walking stick *n* canne *f*

Walkman® *n* (*pl* **-mans**) walkman® *m*, baladeur *m*

walkout /ˈwɔːkaʊt/ *n* (strike) grève *f* surprise

walkover *n* victoire *f* facile (**for** pour)

walkway *n* allée *f*

⚷ **wall** /wɔːl/ *n* **1** (construction) mur *m*
2 (of cave, tunnel) paroi *f*
3 (Anat) paroi *f*

wall chart *n* affiche *f*

walled /wɔːld/ *adj* ‹*city*› fortifié/-e; ‹*garden*› clos/-e

wallet /ˈwɒlɪt/ *n* (for notes) portefeuille *m*; (for documents) porte-documents *m inv*

wallflower /ˈwɔːlflaʊə(r)/ *n* giroflée *f* jaune
IDIOM **to be a ~** faire tapisserie

wall light *n* applique *f* murale

wall-mounted *adj* fixé/-e au mur

wallow /ˈwɒləʊ/ *vi* **to ~ in** se vautrer dans ‹*mud, luxury*›; se complaire dans ‹*self-pity, nostalgia*›

wallpaper /ˈwɔːlpeɪpə(r)/ **A** *n* **1** (for walls) papier *m* peint
2 (Comput) fond *m* d'écran
B *vt* tapisser ‹*room*›

walnut /ˈwɔːlnʌt/ *n* **1** (nut) noix *f*
2 (tree, wood) noyer *m*

walrus /ˈwɔːlrəs/ *n* morse *m*

waltz /wɔːls, (AmE) wɔːlts/ **A** *n* valse *f*
B *vi* danser la valse (**with** avec)

wand /wɒnd/ *n* baguette *f*

wander /ˈwɒndə(r)/ **A** *vt* parcourir; **to ~ the streets** traîner dans la rue
B *vi* **1** (walk, stroll) se promener; **to ~ around town** se balader en ville
2 (stray) errer; **to ~ away** *or* **off** s'éloigner (**from** de)
3 ‹*eyes, hands*› errer (**over** sur); ‹*attention*› se relâcher; **her mind is ~ing** elle divague

■ **wander about**, **wander around** (stroll) se balader; (when lost) errer

wane /weɪn/ *vi* ‹*moon*› décroître; ‹*enthusiasm, popularity*› diminuer

wangle /ˈwæŋgl/ **A** *n* (fam) combine *f* (fam)
B *vt* soutirer ‹*money, promise*›; se débrouiller pour avoir ‹*leave*›; **to ~ sth for sb** se débrouiller pour faire avoir qch à qn

wannabe /ˈwɒnəbiː/ *n* (*also* **wannabee**) (fam) *personne qui rêve d'être célèbre*

⚷ **want** /wɒnt/ **A** *n* **1** (need) besoin *m*
2 (lack) défaut *m*; **for ~ of** à défaut *or* faute de; **it's not for ~ of trying** ce n'est pas faute d'avoir essayé
B *vt* **1** (desire) vouloir; **I ~** (as general statement) je veux; (would like) je voudrais; (am seeking) je souhaite; **I don't ~ to** je n'en ai pas envie; (flat refusal) je ne veux pas; **to ~ to do** vouloir faire; **to ~ sb to do** vouloir que qn fasse
2 (fam) (need) avoir besoin de
3 (require presence of) demander; **if anyone**

W

⚷ mot clé

~s me si quelqu'un me demande; **you're ~ed on the phone** on vous demande au téléphone; **to be ~ed by the police** être recherché/-e par la police
C *vi* **to ~ for** manquer de

wanting /'wɒntɪŋ/ *adj* **to be ~** faire défaut; **to be ~ in** manquer de; **to be found ~** s'avérer décevant/-e

wanton /'wɒntən, (AmE) 'wɔːn-/ *adj* ‹*cruelty, damage, waste*› gratuit/-e; ‹*disregard*› délibéré/-e

war /wɔː(r)/ *n* guerre *f*; **in the ~** à la guerre; **to wage ~ on** faire la guerre contre; (fig) mener une lutte contre

ward /wɔːd/ *n* **1** (in hospital) (unit) service *m*; (room) unité *f*; (separate building) pavillon *m*; **maternity ~** service de maternité; **hospital ~** salle *f* d'hôpital
2 (electoral) circonscription *f* électorale
3 (*also* **~ of court**) (Law) pupille *m*
■ **ward off** chasser ‹*evil, predator*›; faire taire ‹*accusations, criticism*›; écarter ‹*attack, threat*›; éviter ‹*disaster*›

warden /'wɔːdn/ *n* (of institution, college) directeur/-trice *m/f*; (of park, estate) gardien/-ienne *m/f*

warder /'wɔːdə(r)/ *n* (BrE) gardien/-ienne *m/f*

wardrobe /'wɔːdrəʊb/ *n* **1** (furniture) armoire *f*
2 (set of clothes) garde-robe *f*; (for theatre) costumes *mpl*

warehouse /'weəhaʊs/ *n* entrepôt *m*

wares *npl* marchandise *f*, marchandises *fpl*

warfare /'wɔːfeə(r)/ *n* guerre *f*

war game *n* jeu *m* de stratégie (militaire)

warhead *n* ogive *f*

warlike /'wɔːlaɪk/ *adj* ‹*people*› guerrier/-ière; ‹*mood, words*› belliqueux/-euse

warm /wɔːm/ **A** *adj* **1** ‹*place, food, temperature, water, day, clothing*› chaud/-e; **to be ~** ‹*person*› avoir chaud; **it's ~** il fait bon *or* chaud
2 (affectionate) ‹*person, atmosphere, welcome*› chaleureux/-euse; ‹*admiration, support*› enthousiaste
3 ‹*colour*› chaud/-e
B *vt* chauffer ‹*plate, food, water*›; réchauffer ‹*implement, bed*›; **to ~ oneself** se réchauffer; **to ~ one's hands** se réchauffer les mains
C *vi* ‹*food, liquid, object*› chauffer
■ **warm to, warm towards** se prendre de sympathie pour ‹*person*›; se faire à ‹*idea*›; prendre goût à ‹*task*›
■ **warm up A ~ up 1** ‹*person, room, house*› se réchauffer; ‹*food, liquid, engine*› chauffer
2 (become lively) s'animer
3 ‹*athlete*› s'échauffer; ‹*singer*› s'échauffer la voix; ‹*orchestra, musician*› se préparer
B ~ [sth] up réchauffer ‹*room, bed, person*›; faire réchauffer ‹*food*›

warm-hearted *adj* chaleureux/-euse

warmly /'wɔːmlɪ/ *adv* ‹*smile, thank, recommend*› chaleureusement; ‹*speak, praise*› avec enthousiasme

warmth /wɔːmθ/ *n* chaleur *f*

warm-up /'wɔːmʌp/ *n* échauffement *m*

warn /wɔːn/ **A** *vt* avertir, prévenir; **to ~ sb about** *or* **against sth** mettre qn en garde contre qch; **to ~ sb to do** conseiller *or* dire à qn de faire; **to ~ sb not to do** déconseiller à qn de faire
B *vi* **to ~ of sth** annoncer qch

warning /'wɔːnɪŋ/ *n* avertissement *m*; (by an authority) avis *m*; (by light, siren) alerte *f*; **to give sb ~** avertir qn (**of** de); **advance ~** préavis *m*; **health ~** mise *f* en garde; **flood ~** avis de crue

warning light *n* voyant *m* lumineux

warning shot *n* coup *m* de semonce

warning sign *n* (on road) panneau *m* d'avertissement; (of illness, stress) signe *m* annonciateur

warning triangle *n* (Aut) triangle *m* de présignalisation

warp /wɔːp/ **A** *vt* **1** déformer ‹*metal, wood, record*›
2 pervertir ‹*mind, personality*›
B *vi* se déformer

warped /wɔːpt/ *adj* **1** ‹*metal, wood, record*› déformé/-e
2 ‹*mind, humour*› tordu/-e; ‹*personality, sexuality*› perverti/-e; ‹*account, view*› faussé/-e

warplane *n* avion *m* militaire

warrant /'wɒrənt, (AmE) 'wɔːr-/ **A** *n* (Law) mandat *m*
B *vt* justifier ‹*action, measure*›

warranty /'wɒrəntɪ, (AmE) 'wɔːr-/ *n* garantie *f*

warren /'wɒrən, (AmE) 'wɔːrən/ *n* **1** (rabbits') garenne *f*
2 (building, maze of streets) labyrinthe *m*

warring /'wɔːrɪŋ/ *adj* en conflit

warrior /'wɒrɪə(r), (AmE) 'wɔːr-/ *n* guerrier/-ière *m/f*

Warsaw /'wɔːsɔːw/ *pr n* Varsovie

warship *n* navire *m* de guerre

wart /wɔːt/ *n* verrue *f*

wartime /'wɔːtaɪm/ *n* **in ~** en temps de guerre

war-torn *adj* déchiré/-e par la guerre

war veteran *n* ancien combattant *m*

wary /'weərɪ/ *adj* **1** (cautious) prudent/-e; **to be ~** montrer de la circonspection (**of** vis-à-vis de); **to be ~ of doing** hésiter à faire
2 (distrustful) méfiant/-e; **to be ~** se méfier (**of** de)

wash /wɒʃ/ **A** *n* **1** (clean) **to have a ~** se laver; **to give [sth] a ~** laver ‹*window, floor*›; nettoyer ‹*object*›; lessiver ‹*paintwork, walls*›; **to give [sb] a ~** débarbouiller ‹*child*›
2 (laundry process) lavage *m*; **weekly ~** lessive *f* hebdomadaire; **in the ~** (about to be cleaned) au sale; (being cleaned) au lavage
3 (from boat) remous *m*
B /wɒʃ, (AmE) wɔːʃ/ *vt* laver ‹*person, clothes,*

W

floor›; nettoyer ‹*object, wound*›; lessiver ‹*paintwork, surface*›; **to get ~ed** se laver; **to ~ one's hands/face** se laver les mains/le visage; **to ~ the dishes** faire la vaisselle
C *vi* **1** ‹*person*› se laver, faire sa toilette; ‹*animal*› faire sa toilette
2 (do laundry) faire la lessive
■ **wash away** emporter ‹*structure, debris, person*›
■ **wash up** **A** **~ up 1** (BrE) (do dishes) faire la vaisselle
2 (AmE) (clean oneself) faire un brin de toilette (fam)
B **~ [sth] up 1** (clean) laver ‹*plate*›; nettoyer ‹*pan*›
2 ‹*tide*› rejeter ‹*debris*›

washable /ˈwɒʃəbl, (AmE) ˈwɔːʃ-/ *adj* lavable
washbasin *n* lavabo *m*
washbowl *n* (AmE) lavabo *m*
washcloth *n* (AmE) lavette *f*
washed-out /ˌwɒʃtˈaʊt, (AmE) ˌwɔːʃ-/ *adj* **1** (faded) délavé/-e
2 (tired) épuisé/-e, lessivé/-e (fam)
washed-up /ˌwɒʃtˈʌp, (AmE) ˌwɔːʃ-/ *adj* (fam) fichu/-e (fam)
washer /ˈwɒʃə(r), (AmE) ˈwɔːʃər/ *n* (Tech) (as seal) joint *m*
washer-dryer *n* lave-linge/sèche-linge *m inv*
washing /ˈwɒʃɪŋ, (AmE) ˈwɔːʃɪŋ/ *n* (laundry) (to be cleaned) linge *m* sale; (when clean) linge *m*; **to do the ~** faire la lessive
washing line *n* corde *f* à linge
washing machine *n* machine *f* à laver
washing powder *n* (BrE) lessive *f* (en poudre)
washing-up *n* (BrE) vaisselle *f*
washing-up liquid *n* (BrE) liquide *m* (à) vaisselle
washout *n* **1** (fam) (project, system) fiasco *m*
2 (fam) (person) nullité *f* (fam)
3 (game, camp) fiasco *m* dû à la pluie
washroom *n* toilettes *fpl*
wash-stand *n* (AmE) lavabo *m*
wasp /wɒsp/ *n* guêpe *f*
waspish /ˈwɒspɪʃ/ *adj* acerbe
wastage /ˈweɪstɪdʒ/ *n* **1** (of money, resources, talent) gaspillage *m*; (of heat, energy) déperdition *f*
2 (*also* **natural ~**) élimination *f* naturelle
waste /weɪst/ **A** *n* **1** (of food, money, energy) gaspillage *m* (**of** de); (of time) perte *f* (**of** de); **a ~ of effort** un effort inutile; **that car is such a ~ of money!** cette voiture, c'est vraiment de l'argent jeté par les fenêtres!; **to let sth go to ~** gaspiller qch
2 (detritus) (*also* **wastes** (AmE)) déchets *mpl* (**from** de)
B **wastes** *npl* **1** (wilderness) étendues *fpl* sauvages
2 (AmE) = **A2**
C *adj* **1** ‹*heat, energy*› gaspillé/-e; ‹*water*› usé/-e; **~ materials** déchets *mpl*
2 ‹*land*› inculte
3 to lay ~ to dévaster
D *vt* **1** (squander) gaspiller ‹*food, resources, energy, money, talents*›; perdre ‹*time, opportunity*›; user ‹*strength*›
2 (make thinner) décharner; (make weaker) atrophier
wastebasket *n* corbeille *f* à papier
wastebin *n* (BrE) (for paper) corbeille *f* à papier; (for rubbish) poubelle *f*
wasted /ˈweɪstɪd/ *adj* **1** ‹*effort, life, vote*› inutile; ‹*energy, years*› gaspillé/-e
2 (fleshless) ‹*body, limb*› décharné/-e; (weak) ‹*body, limb*› atrophié/-e
waste disposal *n* traitement *m* des déchets
waste-disposal unit *n* (BrE) broyeur *m* d'ordures
wasteful /ˈweɪstfl/ *adj* ‹*product, machine*› qui consomme beaucoup; ‹*method, process*› peu économique; ‹*person*› gaspilleur/-euse
wasteland *n* (urban) terrain *m* vague; (rural) terre *f* à l'abandon
waste paper *n* papier *m or* papiers *mpl* à jeter
waste-paper basket, **waste-paper bin** *n* (BrE) corbeille *f* à papier
waste pipe *n* tuyau *m* de vidange
wasting /ˈweɪstɪŋ/ *adj* ‹*disease*› débilitant/-e
🔑 **watch** /wɒtʃ/ **A** *n* **1** (timepiece) montre *f*
2 (surveillance) surveillance *f* (**on** sur); **to keep ~** monter la garde; **to keep (a) ~ on sb/sth** surveiller qn/qch
B *vt* **1** (look at) regarder; (observe) observer
2 (monitor) suivre ‹*career, development*›; surveiller ‹*situation*›
3 (keep under surveillance) surveiller ‹*person, movements*›
4 (pay attention to) faire attention à ‹*obstacle, dangerous object, money*›; surveiller ‹*language, manners, weight*›; **to ~ one's step** (fig) faire attention
5 (look after) garder ‹*person, property*›
C *vi* regarder (**from** de)
■ **watch for** guetter ‹*person, chance*›; surveiller l'apparition de ‹*symptom*›
■ **watch out** (be careful) faire attention (**for** à); (keep watch) guetter; **~ out!** attention!
■ **watch over** veiller sur ‹*person*›; veiller à ‹*interests, rights, welfare*›
watchable /ˈwɒtʃəbl/ *adj* qui se laisse regarder
watch band *n* (AmE) bracelet *m* de montre
watchdog /ˈwɒtʃdɒg/ *n* **1** (dog) chien *m* de garde
2 (organization) organisme *m* de surveillance
watchmaker *n* horloger/-ère *m/f*
watchman /ˈwɒtʃmən/ *n* (guard) gardien *m*
watch strap *n* bracelet *m* de montre

🔑 mot clé

watchword *n* slogan *m*

water /ˈwɔːtə(r)/ **A** *n* eau *f*
B *vt* arroser ‹*lawn, plant*›; irriguer ‹*crop, field*›; abreuver ‹*livestock*›
C *vi* **the smell of cooking makes my mouth ~** l'odeur de cuisine me fait venir l'eau à la bouche; **the smoke made her eyes ~** la fumée l'a fait pleurer
■ **water down 1** couper [qch] d'eau ‹*beer, wine*›; diluer ‹*syrup*›
2 atténuer ‹*effect, plans, policy*›; édulcorer ‹*description, story*›

water bed *n* matelas *m* d'eau

water bird *n* oiseau *m* aquatique

water birth *n* accouchement *m* aquatique

water bottle *n* (for cyclist) bidon *m*

water cannon *n* canon *m* à eau

watercolour (BrE), **watercolor** (AmE) /ˈwɔːtəkʌlə(r)/ *n* (paint) peinture *f* pour aquarelle; (painting) aquarelle *f*

watercress *n* cresson *m* (de fontaine)

waterfall *n* cascade *f*

water filter *n* filtre *m* à eau

waterfront /ˈwɔːtəfrʌnt/ *n* (on harbour) front *m* de mer; (by lakeside, riverside) bord *m* de l'eau

water heater *n* chauffe-eau *m inv*

watering can *n* arrosoir *m*

water jump *n* rivière *f*

water level *n* niveau *m* d'eau

water lily *n* nénuphar *m*

waterlogged *adj* ‹*ground, pitch*› détrempé/-e

water main *n* canalisation *f* d'eau

watermark /ˈwɔːtəmɑːk/ *n* (of sea) laisse *f*; (of river) ligne *f* des hautes eaux; (on paper) filigrane *m*

watermelon *n* pastèque *f*

water power *n* énergie *f* hydraulique

waterproof /ˈwɔːtəpruːf/ *adj* ‹*coat*› imperméable; ‹*make-up*› résistant/-e à l'eau

waterproofs *npl* vêtements *mpl* imperméables

water-resistant *adj* qui résiste à l'eau

watershed /ˈwɔːtəʃed/ *n* **1** (AmE) (area) bassin *m* hydrographique
2 (BrE) (line) ligne *f* de partage des eaux; (fig) point *m* décisif

water-ski /ˈwɔːtəskiː/ **A** *n* ski *m* nautique
B *vi* faire du ski nautique

water-skiing /ˈwɔːtəskiːɪŋ/ *n* ski *m* nautique

water slide *n* toboggan *m* de piscine

water sport *n* sport *m* nautique

water supply *n* (in an area) approvisionnement *m* en eau; (to a building) alimentation *f* en eau

watertight /ˈwɔːtətaɪt/ *adj* **1** ‹*container, seal*› étanche
2 ‹*argument, case*› incontestable; ‹*alibi*› irréfutable

water tower *n* château *m* d'eau

water trough *n* abreuvoir *m*

waterway *n* voie *f* navigable

water wings *npl* bracelets *mpl* de natation

watery /ˈwɔːtərɪ/ *adj* **1** ‹*sauce, paint*› trop liquide; ‹*coffee*› trop léger/-ère
2 ‹*colour, smile*› pâle

watt /wɒt/ *n* watt *m*

wave /weɪv/ **A** *n* **1** (of hand) signe *m* (de la main)
2 (of water) vague *f*; **to make ~s** ‹*wind*› faire des vagues; (cause a stir) faire du bruit; (cause trouble) créer des histoires (fam)
3 (outbreak, surge) vague *f* (**of** de)
4 (of light, radio) onde *f*
5 (in hair) cran *m*
B *vt* **1** agiter ‹*flag, ticket, banknote*›; brandir ‹*umbrella, stick, gun*›
2 to ~ goodbye to sb faire au revoir de la main à qn
C *vi* **1** (with hand) **to ~ to** *or* **at sb** saluer qn de la main
2 ‹*branches*› être agité/-e par le vent; ‹*corn*› ondoyer; ‹*flag*› flotter au vent

waveband *n* bande *f* de fréquence

wave farm *n* ferme *f* hydrolienne

wavelength /ˈweɪvleŋθ/ *n* (on radio) longueur *f* d'onde
IDIOM **to be on the same ~ as sb** être sur la même longueur d'onde que qn

waver /ˈweɪvə(r)/ *vi* **1** (weaken) ‹*person*› vaciller; ‹*courage, love*› faiblir; ‹*voice*› trembler
2 (hesitate) hésiter (**between** entre, **over** sur)

wavy /ˈweɪvɪ/ *adj* ‹*hair, line*› ondulé/-e

wax /wæks/ **A** *n* (for candle, seal) cire *f*; (for skis) fart *m*; (in ear) cérumen *m*
B *vt* **1** cirer ‹*floor*›; lustrer ‹*car*›; farter ‹*ski*›
2 (depilate) épiler [qch] à la cire ‹*legs*›
C *vi* ‹*moon*› croître

waxed jacket *n* ciré *m*

wax paper *n* papier *m* paraffin

waxwork *n* personnage *m* en cire

waxworks *n* musée *m* de cire

waxy /ˈwæksɪ/ *adj* cireux/-euse

way /weɪ/ **A** *n* **1** (route, road) chemin *m* (**from** de, **to** à); **the quickest ~ to town** le chemin le plus court pour aller en ville; **to ask the ~ to the station** demander le chemin pour aller à la gare; **there is no ~ around the problem** il n'y a pas moyen de contourner le problème; **on the ~ back** sur le chemin du retour; **on the ~ back from the meeting** en revenant de la réunion; **the ~ in** l'entrée (**to** de); **the ~ out** la sortie (**of** de); **a ~ out of our difficulties** un moyen de nous sortir de nos difficultés; **the ~ up** la montée; **on the ~** en route; **to be out of sb's ~** ‹*place*› ne pas être sur le chemin de qn; **don't go out of your ~ to do** ne te donne pas de mal

W

pour faire; **out of the ~** (isolated) isolé/-e; (unusual) extraordinaire; **by ~ of** (via) en passant par; **to make one's ~ towards** se diriger vers; **to make one's ~ along** avancer le long de; **to make one's own ~ there** y aller par ses propres moyens
2 (direction) direction *f*, sens *m*; **which ~ did he go?** dans quelle direction est-il parti?; **he went that ~** il est parti par là; **come this ~** suivez-moi, venez par ici; **'this ~ up'** 'haut'; **to look the other ~** (to see) regarder de l'autre côté; (to avoid seeing unpleasant thing) détourner les yeux; (to ignore wrongdoing) fermer les yeux; **the other ~ up** dans l'autre sens; **the right ~ up** dans le bon sens; **the wrong ~ up** à l'envers; **to turn sth the other ~ around** retourner qch; **I didn't ask her, it was the other ~ around** ce n'est pas moi qui le lui ai demandé, c'est l'inverse; **the wrong/right ~ around** dans le mauvais/bon sens
3 (space in front, projected route) passage *m*; **to be in sb's ~** empêcher qn de passer; **to be in the ~** gêner le passage; **to get out of the ~** s'écarter (du chemin); **to get out of sb's ~** laisser passer qn; **to keep out of the ~** rester à l'écart; **to keep out of sb's ~** éviter qn; **to make ~** s'écarter; **to make ~ for sb/sth** faire place à qn/qch
4 (distance) distance *f*; **it's a long ~** c'est loin (to jusqu'à); **to go all the ~ to China** aller jusqu'en Chine
5 (manner) façon *f*, manière *f*; **do it this/that ~** fais-le comme ceci/cela; **to do another ~** faire autrement; **the French ~** à la française; **to write sth the right/wrong ~** écrire qch bien/mal; **try to see it my ~** mets-toi à ma place; **in his/her/its own ~** à sa façon; **to have a ~ with words** savoir manier les mots; **to have a ~ with children** savoir s'y prendre avec les enfants; **a ~ of doing** (method) une façon *or* manière de faire; (means) un moyen de faire; **I like the ~ he dresses** j'aime la façon dont il s'habille; **either ~, she's wrong** de toute façon, elle a tort; **one ~ or another** d'une façon ou d'une autre; **I don't care one ~ or the other** ça m'est égal; **you can't have it both ~s** on ne peut pas avoir le beurre et l'argent du beurre; **no ~!** (fam) pas question! (fam); **~ of life** mode de vie
6 (respect, aspect) sens *m*; **in a ~ it's sad** en un sens c'est triste; **in a ~ that's true** dans une certaine mesure c'est vrai; **in many ~s** à bien des égards; **in some ~s** à certains égards; **in no ~, not in any ~** aucunement
7 (custom, manner) coutume *f*, manière *f*; **that's the modern ~** c'est ce qui se fait de nos jours; **I know all her little ~s** je connais toutes ses petites habitudes; **that's just his ~** il est comme ça; **it's the ~ of the world** c'est la vie
8 (will, desire) **to get one's ~, to have one's own ~** faire à son idée; **she likes (to have) her own ~** elle aime n'en faire qu'à sa tête; **if I had my ~** si cela ne tenait qu'à moi; **have it your (own) ~** comme tu voudras
B *adv* **we went ~ over budget** le budget a été largement dépassé; **to be ~ out** (in guess, estimate) être loin du compte; **that's ~ out of order** je trouve ça un peu fort
C by the way *phr* en passant; **by the ~,...** à propos,...; **what time is it, by the ~?** quelle heure est-il, au fait?

waylay /ˌweɪˈleɪ/ *vt* (*prét, pp* **-laid**) ‹*attacker*› attaquer; ‹*beggar, friend*› arrêter, harponner (fam)

waymark *n* balise *f*

way-out /ˌweɪˈaʊt/ *adj* (fam) excentrique

wayside /ˈweɪsaɪd/ *n*
IDIOM **to fall by the ~** (stray morally) quitter le droit chemin; (fail, not stay the course) abandonner en cours de route; (be cancelled, fall through) tomber à l'eau

wayward /ˈweɪwəd/ *adj* ‹*person, nature*› difficile; ‹*husband, wife*› volage

we /wiː, wɪ/ *pron* nous

> In standard French, *we* is translated by *nous* but in informal French, *on* is frequently used: *we're going to the cinema* = nous allons au cinéma *or more informally* on va au cinéma.
> *On* is also used in correct French to refer to a large, vaguely defined group: *we shouldn't lie to our children* = on ne devrait pas mentir à ses enfants.

~ saw her yesterday nous l'avons vue hier; **~ left at six** nous sommes partis à six heures; (informal) on est partis (fam) à six heures; **~ Scots like the sun** nous autres Écossais, nous aimons le soleil; WE **didn't say that** nous, nous n'avons pas dit cela; (fam) nous, on n'a pas dit ça (fam); **~ all make mistakes** tout le monde peut se tromper

weak /wiːk/ *adj* **1** ‹*person, animal, muscle, limb*› faible; ‹*health, ankle, heart, nerves*› fragile; ‹*stomach*› délicat/-e; ‹*intellect*› médiocre; ‹*chin*› fuyant/-e; **to be ~ with** *or* **from hunger** être affaibli/-e par la faim; **to grow** *or* **become ~(er)** ‹*person*› s'affaiblir; ‹*pulse, heartbeat*› faiblir
2 ‹*beam, support*› peu solide; ‹*structure*› fragile
3 (lacking authority, strength) ‹*government, team, pupil, president*› faible; ‹*parent, teacher*› (not firm) qui manque de fermeté; (poor) piètre *before n*; ‹*plot*› mince; ‹*actor, protest, excuse, argument*› peu convaincant/-e; **~ link** *or* **spot** point *m* faible
4 (faint) ‹*light, current, concentration, sound*› faible; ‹*tea, coffee*› léger/-ère
5 ‹*economy, dollar*› faible (**against** par rapport à)

weaken /ˈwiːkən/ **A** *vt* **1** (through illness, damage) affaiblir ‹*person, heart, structure*›;

W

mot clé

diminuer ‹*resistance*›; rendre [qch] moins solide ‹*joint, bank, wall*›
2 (undermine) nuire à l'autorité de ‹*government, president*›; affaiblir ‹*team, company, authority, defence*›; amoindrir ‹*argument, power*›; nuire à ‹*morale*›
3 (dilute) diluer
B *vi* **1** (physically) s'affaiblir
2 ‹*government, resolve*› fléchir; ‹*support, alliance*› se relâcher
3 (Econ) ‹*economy, currency*› être en baisse

weakling /'wiːklɪŋ/ *n* (physically) gringalet *m*; (morally) mauviette *f*

weakness /'wiːknɪs/ *n* **1** (weak point) point *m* faible
2 (liking) faible *m* (**for** pour)
3 (physical, moral) faiblesse *f*
4 (lack of authority) faiblesse *f*; (of evidence, position) fragilité *f*
5 (of light, current, sound) faiblesse *f*; (of tea, solution) légèreté *f*
6 (of economy, currency) faiblesse *f*

weak-willed /ˌwiːk'wɪld/ *adj* **to be ~** manquer de fermeté

wealth /welθ/ *n* **1** (possessions) fortune *f*
2 (state) richesse *f*
3 (large amount) **a ~ of** une mine de ‹*information*›; une profusion de ‹*detail*›; énormément de ‹*experience, talent*›

wealthy /'welθɪ/ *adj* riche

wean /wiːn/ *vt* sevrer ‹*baby*›; **to ~ sb away from** *or* **off sth** détourner qn de qch

weapon /'wepən/ *n* arme *f*; **~s of mass destruction** armes de destruction massive

weaponry /'wepənrɪ/ *n* matériel *m* de guerre

wear /weə(r)/ **A** *n* **1** (clothing) **children's/sports ~** vêtements *mpl* pour enfants/de sport
2 (use) **for everyday ~** de tous les jours; **for summer ~** pour l'été
3 (damage) usure *f* (**on** de); **~ and tear** usure; **to be the worse for ~** (drunk) être ivre; (tired) être épuisé/-e
B *vt* (*prét* **wore**, *pp* **worn**) **1** (be dressed in) porter; **to ~ blue** s'habiller en bleu; **to ~ one's hair long/short** avoir les cheveux longs/courts
2 (put on, use) mettre; **I haven't got a thing to ~** je n'ai rien à me mettre; **to ~ make-up** se maquiller
3 (display) **he wore a puzzled frown** il fronçait les sourcils d'un air perplexe
4 (damage by use) user; **to ~ a hole in** trouer ‹*garment, sheet*›
C *vi* (*prét* **wore**, *pp* **worn**) ‹*carpet, shoes*› s'user; **my patience is ~ing thin** je commence à être à bout de patience
■ **wear away** ‹*inscription*› s'effacer; ‹*tread, cliff, facade*› s'user
■ **wear down**: **A ~ down** s'user; **to be worn down** être usé/-e
B ~ [sth] down user ‹*steps*›; saper ‹*resistance, resolve*›
C ~ [sb] down épuiser
■ **wear off 1** ‹*drug, effect*› se dissiper; ‹*sensation*› passer
2 (come off) s'effacer
■ **wear out**: **A ~ out** s'user
B ~ [sth] out user
C ~ [sb] out épuiser
■ **wear through** ‹*elbow, trousers*› se trouer; ‹*sole, metal, fabric*› se percer

weariness /'wɪərɪnɪs/ *n* lassitude *f*

wearing /'weərɪŋ/ *adj* (exhausting) fatigant/-e; (irritating) pénible

weary /'wɪərɪ/ **A** *adj* ‹*person, smile, sigh, voice*› las/lasse; ‹*eyes, limbs, mind*› fatigué/-e; **to grow ~** se lasser (**of** de, **of doing** de faire)
B *vi* se lasser (**of** de, **of doing** de faire)

weasel /'wiːzl/ *n* **1** (Zool) belette *f*
2 (sly person) sournois/-e *m/f*

weather /'weðə(r)/ **A** *n* temps *m*; **what's the ~ like?** quel temps fait-il?; **the ~ here is hot** il fait chaud ici; **in hot/cold ~** quand il fait chaud/froid; **~ permitting** si le temps le permet; **in all ~s** par tous les temps
B *vt* survivre à ‹*crisis, upheaval*›; **to ~ the storm** (fig) surmonter la crise
IDIOM **to be under the ~** ne pas se sentir bien

weather-beaten /'weðəbiːtn/ *adj* ‹*face*› hâlé/-e; ‹*rocks, landscape*› battu/-e par les vents

weathercock *n* girouette *f*

weather forecast *n* bulletin *m* météorologique

weather forecaster *n* (on TV) présentateur/-trice *m/f* de la météo; (specialist) météorologue *mf*, météorologiste *mf*

weatherproof /'weðəpruːf/ *adj* ‹*garment, shoe*› imperméable; ‹*shelter, door*› étanche

weave /wiːv/ **A** *vt* (*prét* **wove** *ou* **weaved**, *pp* **woven** *ou* **weaved**) **1** tisser ‹*rug, fabric*›
2 tresser ‹*cane, basket, wreath*›
B *vi* (*prét* **wove** *ou* **weaved**, *pp* **woven** *ou* **weaved**) **to ~ in and out** se faufiler (**of** entre); **to ~ towards sth** (drunk) s'approcher en titubant de qch

weaving /'wiːvɪŋ/ *n* tissage *m*

web /web/ *n* **1** (*also* **spider's ~** (BrE), **spiderweb** (AmE)) toile *f* (d'araignée)
2 (network) **a ~ of** un réseau de ‹*ropes, lines*›; **a ~ of lies** un tissu de mensonges

Web /web/ *n* **the ~** le Web *m*, la Toile *f*

webbing /'webɪŋ/ *n* (material) sangles *fpl*

Webcam *n* Webcam *f*

web foot *n* (*pl* **web feet**) patte *f* palmée

webinar /'webɪnɑː(r)/ *n* webinaire *m*

webmaster *n* Webmestre *m*, Webmaster *m*

Web page *n* page *f* Web
Web server *n* serveur *m* Web
website *n* site *m* Web
webspace *n* espace *m* Web
wed /wed/ *n* **the newly ~s** les jeunes mariés *mpl*
wedding /'wedɪŋ/ *n* mariage *m*; **a church ~** un mariage religieux
wedding anniversary *n* anniversaire *m* de mariage
wedding day *n* jour *m* des noces
wedding dress, **wedding gown** *n* robe *f* de mariée
wedding reception *n* repas *m* de mariage
wedding ring *n* alliance *f*
wedge /wedʒ/ **A** *n* **1** (to insert in rock, wood) coin *m*; (to hold sth in position) cale *f*; (in rock climbing) piton *m*
2 (of cake, pie, cheese) morceau *m*
B *vt* **1 to ~ sth in place** caler qch; **to ~ a door open** caler une porte pour la tenir ouverte
2 (jam) **to ~ sth into** enfoncer qch dans; **to be ~d between** être coincé/-e entre
IDIOM **that's the thin end of the ~** c'est le commencement de la fin
⚷ **Wednesday** /'wenzdeɪ, -dɪ/ *n* mercredi *m*
wee /wi:/ *vi* (BrE) faire pipi (fam)
weed /wi:d/ **A** *n* mauvaise herbe *f*; (in water) herbes *fpl* aquatiques
B *vt, vi* désherber
■ **weed out**: **A ~ [sb] out, ~ out [sb]** (gen) éliminer; se débarrasser de ‹*employee*›
B ~ [sth] out, ~ out [sth] se débarrasser de ‹*stock, items*›
weedkiller *n* désherbant *m*, herbicide *m*
weedy /'wi:dɪ/ *adj* (fam) ‹*person, build*› malingre; ‹*character, personality*› faible
⚷ **week** /wi:k/ *n* semaine *f*; **last/next ~** la semaine dernière/prochaine; **this ~** cette semaine; **the ~ before last** il y a deux semaines; **the ~ after next** dans deux semaines; **every other ~** tous les quinze jours; **twice a ~** deux fois par semaine; **~ in ~ out** toutes les semaines; **a ~ today/on Monday** (BrE), **today/Monday ~** aujourd'hui/lundi en huit; **a ~ yesterday** (BrE), **a ~ from yesterday** (AmE) il y a eu huit jours *or* une semaine hier; **in three ~s' time** dans trois semaines; **the working *or* work** (AmE) **~** la semaine de travail
weekday /'wi:kdeɪ/ *n* jour *m* de (la) semaine; **on ~s** en semaine

⚷ **weekend** /ˌwi:k'end, (AmE) 'wi:k-/ *n* week-end *m*; **at the ~** (BrE), **on the ~** (AmE) pendant le week-end; **at ~s** (BrE), **on ~s** (AmE) le week-end
weekend bag *n* petit sac *m* de voyage
weekend cottage *n* résidence *f* secondaire

weekly /'wi:klɪ/ **A** *n* (newspaper) journal *m* hebdomadaire; (magazine) (revue *f*) hebdomadaire *m*
B *adj* hebdomadaire; **on a ~ basis** à la semaine
C *adv* ‹*pay*› à la semaine; ‹*meet, visit*› une fois par semaine
weep /wi:p/ *vi* (*prét, pp* **wept**) **1** (cry) pleurer (**over** sur)
2 (ooze) suinter
weepy /'wi:pɪ/ *adj* ‹*mood, film*› larmoyant/-e; **to feel ~** avoir envie de pleurer
weigh /weɪ/ **A** *vt* **1** (on scales) peser; **to ~ 10 kilos** peser 10 kilos; **how much *or* what do you ~?** combien pèses-tu?; **to ~ oneself** se peser
2 (assess) évaluer ‹*arguments, advantages, options*›; peser ‹*consequences, risks, words*›
B *vi* **to ~ on sb** peser sur qn; **to ~ on sb's mind** préoccuper qn
■ **weigh down**: **A ~ down on [sb/sth]** peser sur
B ~ [sb/sth] down surcharger ‹*vehicle, boat*›; faire plier ‹*branches*›; ‹*responsibility, debt*› accabler; **to be ~ed down with** crouler sous le poids de ‹*luggage*›; être accablé/-e de ‹*worry, guilt*›
■ **weigh in** ‹*boxer, wrestler*› se faire peser; ‹*jockey*› aller au pesage
■ **weigh out** peser ‹*ingredients, quantity*›
■ **weigh up** évaluer ‹*prospects, situation*›; juger ‹*person*›; mettre [qch] en balance ‹*options, benefits, risks*›
weighing machine /'weɪɪŋ məʃi:n/ *n* (for people) balance *f*; (for luggage, freight) bascule *f*
⚷ **weight** /weɪt/ **A** *n* poids *m*; **to put on/lose ~** prendre/perdre du poids
B *vt* lester ‹*net, arrow*›
IDIOMS **not to carry much ~** ne pas peser lourd (**with** pour); **to be a ~ off one's mind** être un grand soulagement; **to pull one's ~** faire sa part de travail; **to throw one's ~ about *or* around** faire l'important/-e *m/f*
weightlessness /'weɪtlɪsnɪs/ *n* (in space) apesanteur *f*
weight-lifter *n* haltérophile *m*
weight-lifting *n* haltérophilie *f*
weight problem *n* problème *m* de poids
weight training *n* musculation *f* (en salle)
weighty /'weɪtɪ/ *adj* **1** (serious) de grand poids
2 (heavy) lourd/-e
weir /wɪə(r)/ *n* barrage *m*
weird /wɪəd/ *adj* (strange) bizarre; (eerie) mystérieux/-ieuse
⚷ **welcome** /'welkəm/ **A** *n* accueil *m*; **to give sb a warm ~** faire un accueil chaleureux à qn
B *adj* **1** bienvenu/-e; **to be ~** être le bienvenu/la bienvenue *m/f*; **to make sb ~** (on arrival) réserver un bon accueil à qn

---
⚷ mot clé

2 'thanks'—'you're ~' 'merci'—'de rien'
C *excl* (to respected guest) soyez le bienvenu/la bienvenue chez nous!; (greeting friend) entre donc!; **~ back!**, **~ home!** je suis content que tu sois de retour!
D *vt* accueillir ‹*person*›; se réjouir de ‹*news, decision, change*›; être heureux/-euse de recevoir ‹*contribution*›; accueillir favorablement ‹*initiative, move*›

welcoming /ˈwelkəmɪŋ/ *adj* ‹*atmosphere, person*› accueillant/-e; ‹*ceremony, committee*› d'accueil

weld /weld/ *vt* (*also* **~ together**) souder; **to ~ sth on** *or* **to** souder qch à

welfare /ˈwelfeə(r)/ **A** *n* **1** (well-being) bien-être *m inv*; (interest) intérêt *m*
2 (state assistance) assistance *f* sociale; (money) aide *f* sociale
B *adj* ‹*system*› de protection sociale; (AmE) ‹*meal*› gratuit/-e

welfare benefit *n* prestation *f* sociale

welfare services *npl* services *mpl* sociaux

welfare spending *n* dépenses *fpl* sociales

welfare state *n* (as concept) État-providence *m*; (stressing state assistance) protection *f* sociale

well¹ /wel/ **A** *adj* (*comp* **better**, *superl* **best**) bien; **to feel ~** se sentir bien; **are you ~?** vous allez bien?/tu vas bien?; **she's not ~ enough to travel** elle n'est pas en état de voyager; **to get ~** se rétablir; **that's all very ~, but...** tout ça c'est bien beau, mais...; **it would be just as ~ to check** il vaudrait mieux vérifier; **it would be as ~ for you not to get involved** tu ferais mieux de ne pas t'en mêler; **the flight was delayed, which was just as ~** le vol a été retardé, ce qui n'était pas plus mal
B *adv* (*comp* **better**, *superl* **best**) bien; **to do ~ at school** être bon/bonne élève; **mother and baby are both doing ~** la mère et l'enfant se portent bien; **the operation went ~** l'opération s'est bien passée; **~ done!** bravo!; **you may ~ be right** il se pourrait bien que tu aies raison; **we may as ~ go home** on ferait aussi bien de rentrer; **it was ~ worth waiting for** ça valait vraiment la peine d'attendre; **to wish sb ~** souhaiter beaucoup de chance à qn
C *excl* (expressing astonishment) eh bien!; (expressing indignation, disgust) ça alors!; (expressing disappointment) tant pis!; (qualifying statement) enfin; **~, you may be right** après tout, tu as peut-être raison; **~, that's too bad** c'est vraiment dommage; **~ then, what's the problem?** alors, quel est le problème?; **very ~ then** très bien
D **as well** *phr* aussi
E **as well as** *phr* aussi bien que; **they have a house in the country as ~ as an apartment in Paris** ils ont à la fois une maison à la campagne et un appartement à Paris

IDIOMS **to be ~ in with sb** (fam) être bien avec qn (fam); **to be ~ up in sth** s'y connaître en qch; **to leave ~ alone** (BrE) *or* **~ enough alone** (AmE) ne pas s'en mêler

well² /wel/ *n* (sunk in ground) puits *m*; (pool) source *f*

well-balanced *adj* équilibré/-e

well-behaved *adj* ‹*child*› sage; ‹*dog*› bien dressé/-e

well-being *n* bien-être *m inv*

well-defined /ˌweldɪˈfaɪnd/ *adj* ‹*outline*› net/nette; ‹*role, boundary*› bien défini/-e

well-disposed /ˌweldɪˈspəʊzd/ *adj* **to be ~ towards** être bien disposé/-e envers ‹*person*›; être favorable à ‹*regime, idea, policy*›

well done *adj* ‹*steak*› bien cuit/-e; ‹*task*› bien fait/-e

well-educated *adj* (having a good education) instruit/-e; (cultured) cultivé/-e

well-heeled *adj* (fam) riche

well-informed /ˌwelɪnˈfɔːmd/ *adj* bien informé/-e (**about** sur); **he's very ~** il est très au courant de l'actualité

wellington /ˈwelɪŋtən/ *n* (*also* **wellington boot**) (BrE) botte *f* de caoutchouc

well-kept *adj* ‹*house, garden, village*› bien entretenu/-e

well-known /ˌwelˈnəʊn/ *adj* ‹*person, place*› célèbre; **to be ~ to sb** être connu/-e de qn; **it is ~ that, it is a ~ fact that** il est bien connu que

well-liked /ˌwelˈlaɪkt/ *adj* très apprécié/-e

well-made *adj* bien fait/-e

well-meaning *adj* ‹*person*› bien intentionné/-e; ‹*advice*› qui part d'une bonne intention

well-meant /ˌwelˈment/ *adj* **his offer was ~** sa proposition partait d'une bonne intention

well-off **A** *n* **the ~** les gens *mpl* aisés; **the less ~** les plus défavorisés *mpl*
B *adj* (wealthy) aisé/-e; **to be ~ for** avoir beaucoup de ‹*space, provisions*›

well-read *adj* cultivé/-e

well-respected /ˌwelrɪˈspektɪd/ *adj* très respecté/-e

well-rounded /ˌwelˈraʊndɪd/ *adj* ‹*education, programme*› complet/-ète; ‹*individual*› qui a reçu une éducation complète

well-thought-out *adj* bien élaboré/-e

well-timed /ˌwelˈtaɪmd/ *adj* qui tombe/tombait à point; **that was well timed!** (of entrance, phone call etc) c'est bien tombé!

well-to-do *adj* aisé/-e

well-wisher /ˈwelwɪʃə(r)/ *n* personne *f* qui veut témoigner sa sympathie

well-worn /ˌwelˈwɔːn/ *adj* ‹*carpet, garment*› élimé/-e; ‹*steps*› usé/-e; ‹*joke*› rebattu/-e

Welsh /welʃ/ **A** *n* **1** (people) **the ~** les Gallois *mpl*
2 (language) gallois *m*
B *adj* gallois/-e

welt /welt/ *n* (on skin) marque *f* (de coup)

welterweight /ˈweltəweɪt/ *n* poids *m* welter

⚷ **west** /west/ **A** *n* **1** (compass direction) ouest *m*
2 the West l'Occident *m*, l'Ouest *m*; (part of country) l'Ouest *m*; (political entity) l'Occident *m*
B *adj* (gen) ouest *inv*; ‹*wind*› d'ouest
C *adv* ‹*move*› vers l'ouest; ‹*lie, live*› à l'ouest (**of** de)

West Bank *pr n* Cisjordanie *f*

western /ˈwestən/ **A** *n* (film) western *m*
B *adj* **1** ‹*coast*› ouest *inv*; ‹*town, accent*› de l'ouest; **~ France** l'ouest de la France
2 (Pol) occidental/-e

westerner /ˈwestənə(r)/ *n* Occidental/-e *m/f*

westernize /ˈwestənaɪz/ *vt* occidentaliser; **to become ~d** s'occidentaliser

west-facing *adj* exposé/-e à l'ouest

West Indian /ˌwest ˈɪndɪən/ **A** *n* Antillais/-e *m/f*
B *adj* antillais/-e

West Indies /ˌwest ˈɪndiːz/ *pr npl* Antilles *fpl*

wet /wet/ **A** *adj* **1** (damp) ‹*hair, clothes, grass, surface*› mouillé/-e; **to get ~** se faire mouiller; **to get one's feet ~** se mouiller les pieds; **to get the floor ~** tremper le sol; **~ through** trempé/-e
2 (freshly applied) ‹*cement, varnish*› humide; **'~ paint'** 'peinture fraîche'
3 (rainy) ‹*weather, day, night*› pluvieux/-ieuse; ‹*season*› des pluies; **when it's ~** quand il pleut
4 (BrE) ‹*person*› qui manque de caractère
B *vt* (*p prés* **-tt-**, *prét, pp* **~**) **1** mouiller ‹*floor, object, clothes*›
2 to ~ one's pants/the bed ‹*adult*› mouiller sa culotte/le lit; ‹*child*› faire pipi (fam) dans sa culotte/dans son lit

wet blanket *n* (fam) rabat-joie *mf inv*

wet-look /ˈwetlʊk/ *adj* luisant/-e

wetsuit *n* combinaison *f* de plongée

whack /wæk, (AmE) hwæk/ **A** *n* (blow) (grand) coup *m*
B *excl* paf!
C *vt* **1** (hit) battre ‹*person, animal*›; frapper ‹*ball*›
2 (BrE) (defeat) piler (fam)

W

whacked /wækt, (AmE) hwækt/ *adj* (fam) (tired) vanné/-e (fam)

whacky /ˈwækɪ, (AmE) ˈhwækɪ/ *adj* (fam) ‹*person*› dingue (fam); ‹*sense of humour*› farfelu/-e (fam)

whale /weɪl, (AmE) hweɪl/ **A** *n* **1** (Zool) baleine *f*
2 (fam) **to have a ~ of a time** s'amuser comme un fou
B *vt* (AmE) (fam) (thrash) donner une raclée à (fam)

whale-watching *n* observation *f* des baleines

whaling /ˈweɪlɪŋ, (AmE) ˈhweɪlɪŋ/ *n* pêche *f* à la baleine

wharf /wɔːf, (AmE) hwɔːf/ *n* (*pl* **wharves**) quai *m*

⚷ **what** /wɒt, (AmE) hwɒt/

> **As a pronoun**
> When used in questions as an object pronoun *what* is translated by *qu'est-ce que* (*qu'est-ce qu'* in front of a vowel or mute 'h'): *what did you say?* qu'est-ce que tu as dit? Alternatively you can use *que* (*qu'* before a vowel or mute 'h'), but note that subject and verb are reversed and a hyphen is inserted before a pronoun: *what did you say?* qu'as-tu dit?
> As a subject pronoun in questions *what* is translated by *qu'est-ce qui*: *what is happening?* qu'est-ce qui se passe? Alternatively *que* can be used and the subject and verb are reversed and the subject becomes *il*: *what is happening?* que se passe-t-il?
> When *what* is used to introduce a clause it is translated by *ce que* (*ce qu'*) as the object of the verb: *I don't know what you want* je ne sais pas ce que tu veux. As the subject of the verb it is translated by *ce qui*: *what matters is that...* ce qui compte c'est que...

A *pron* **with ~?** avec quoi?; **and ~ else?** et quoi d'autre?; **~ for?** (why) pourquoi?; (about what) à propos de quoi?; **~'s the matter?** qu'est-ce qu'il y a?; **~'s her telephone number?** quel est son numéro de téléphone?; **~'s that button for?** à quoi sert ce bouton?; **~'s it like?** comment c'est?; **do ~ you want** fais ce que tu veux; **take ~ you need** prends ce dont tu as besoin; **~ I need is...** ce dont j'ai besoin c'est...; **and ~'s more** et en plus; **and ~'s worse** et en plus; **he did ~?** il a fait quoi?; **George ~?** George comment?
B *det* quel/quelle/quels/quelles; **do you know ~ train he took?** est-ce que tu sais quel train il a pris?; **~ a nice dress/car!** quelle belle robe/voiture!; **~ a strange thing to do!** quelle drôle d'idée!; **~ use is that?** à quoi ça sert?; **~ money he earns he spends** tout ce qu'il gagne, il le dépense; **~ few friends she had** les quelques amis qu'elle avait
C what about *phr* **1** (to draw attention) **~ about the children?** et les enfants (alors)?
2 (to make suggestion) **~ about a meal out?** et si on dînait au restaurant?; **~ about Tuesday?** qu'est-ce que tu dirais de mardi?
D what if *phr* et si; **~ if I bring the dessert?** et si j'apportais le dessert?

⚷ mot clé

E *excl* quoi!, comment!

IDIOM **~ with one thing and another** avec ceci et cela

whatever /wɒt'evə(r), (AmE) hwɒt-/ **A** *pron* **1** (that which) (as subject) ce qui; (as object) ce que; **to do ~ one can** faire ce qu'on peut **2** (anything that) (as subject) tout ce qui; (as object) tout ce que; **do ~ you like** fais tout ce que tu veux; **~ you say** (as you like) tout ce qui vous plaira **3** (no matter what) quoi que (+ *subjunctive*); **~ happens** quoi qu'il arrive; **~ she says, ignore it** quoi qu'elle dise n'en tiens pas compte; **~ it costs it doesn't matter** quel que soit le prix, ça n'a pas d'importance **4** (what on earth) (as subject) qu'est-ce qui; (as object) qu'est-ce que; **~'s that?** qu'est-ce c'est que ça?

B *det* **1** (any) **they eat ~ food they can get** ils mangent tout ce qu'ils trouvent à manger **2** (no matter what) **~ their arguments** quels que soient leurs arguments; **~ the reason** quelle que soit la raison; **for ~ reason** pour je ne sais quelle raison

C *adv* (*also* **whatsoever**) **to have no idea ~** ne pas avoir la moindre idée; **'any petrol?'—'none ~'** 'il y a de l'essence?'—'pas du tout'

wheat /wi:t, (AmE) hwi:t/ *n* blé *m*

wheatgerm *n* germe *m* de blé

wheatmeal *n* farine *f* complète

wheedle /'wi:dl, (AmE) 'hwi:dl/ *vt* **to ~ sth out of sb** soutirer qch à qn par la cajolerie

wheel /wi:l, (AmE) hwi:l/ **A** *n* **1** (on vehicle) roue *f*; (on trolley, piece of furniture) roulette *f* **2** (for steering) (in vehicle) volant *m*; (on boat) roue *f* (de gouvernail); **to be at** *or* **behind the ~** être au volant **3** (in watch, mechanism, machine) rouage *m* **4** (for pottery) tour *m*

B *vt* pousser ‹*bicycle, barrow*›; **they ~ed me into the operating theatre** ils m'ont emmené dans la salle d'opération sur un chariot

C *vi* (*also* **~ round**) ‹*person, regiment*› faire demi-tour; ‹*car, motorbike*› braquer fortement; ‹*ship*› virer de bord

IDIOM **to ~ and deal** magouiller (fam)

wheelbarrow *n* brouette *f*

wheelchair *n* fauteuil *m* roulant

wheel clamp /'wi:lklæmp, (AmE) 'hwi:l-/ *n* (Aut) sabot *m* de Denver

wheeler dealer *n* (fam) magouilleur/-euse *m/f* (fam)

wheelie bin /'wi:lɪ bɪn/ *n* (BrE) poubelle *f* à roulettes

wheeze /wi:z, (AmE) hwi:z/ *vi* avoir la respiration sifflante

wheezy /'wi:zɪ, (AmE) 'hwi:zɪ/ *adj* ‹*voice, cough*› rauque; **to have a ~ chest** avoir la respiration sifflante

when /wen, (AmE) hwen/

> *when* in questions is usually translated by *quand*.
>
> Note that there are three ways of asking questions using *quand*: *when did she leave?* = quand est-ce qu'elle est partie?, elle est partie quand?, quand est-elle partie?
>
> When talking about future time, *quand* will be used with the future tense of the verb: *tell him when you see him* = dis-lui quand tu le verras.

A *adv* **1** (in questions) quand; **~ are we leaving?** quand est-ce qu'on part?; **~ is the concert?** c'est quand le concert?; **I wonder ~ the film starts** je me demande à quelle heure commence le film; **say ~** dis-moi stop **2** (whenever) quand; **he's only happy ~ he's moaning** il n'est content que quand il rouspète; **~ I eat ice cream, I feel ill** quand *or* chaque fois que je mange de la glace, j'ai mal au cœur

B *rel pron* où; **the week ~ it all happened** la semaine où tout cela s'est produit; **there are times ~ it's too stressful** il y a des moments où c'est trop stressant

C *conj* **1** (expressing time) quand; **~ he was at school** quand il était à l'école, lorsqu'il était à l'école; **~ I am 18** quand j'aurai 18 ans; **~ he arrives, I'll let you know** quand il arrivera *or* dès qu'il arrivera, je te le dirai **2** (expressing contrast) alors que; **why buy their products ~ ours are cheaper?** pourquoi acheter leurs produits alors que les nôtres sont moins chers?

D *pron* quand; **until/since ~?** jusqu'à/depuis quand?; **1982, that's ~ I was born** 1982, c'est l'année où je suis né; **that's ~ I found out** c'est à ce moment-là que j'ai su

whenever /wen'evə(r), (AmE) hwen-/ *adv* **1** (no matter when) **~ you want** quand tu veux; **I'll come ~ it is convenient** je viendrai quand cela vous arrangera **2** (every time that) chaque fois que; **~ I see a black cat, I make a wish** chaque fois que je vois un chat noir, je fais un vœu

where /weə(r), (AmE) hweər/

> *where* in questions is usually translated by *où*: *where are the plates?* = où sont les assiettes?; *I don't know where the plates are* = je ne sais pas où sont les assiettes; *do you know where he is?* = est-ce que tu sais où il est?; *do you know where Paul is?* = est-ce que tu sais où est Paul?
>
> Note that *où* + *est-ce que* does not require a change in word order: *where did you see her?* = où est-ce que tu l'as vue?

A *adv* où; **~ is my coat?** où est mon manteau?; **~ do you work?** où est-ce que vous travaillez; **ask him ~ he went** demande-lui où il est allé; **do you know ~ she's going?** est-ce tu sais où elle va?; **sit ~ you like** asseyez-vous où vous voulez;

W

it's cold ~ we live il fait froid là où nous habitons; **~ necessary** si nécessaire; **~ possible** dans la mesure du possible
B *pron* **from ~?** d'où?; **that's ~ I fell** c'est là que je suis tombé; **that is ~ he is mistaken** c'est là qu'il se trompe

whereabouts *npl* **do you know his ~?** savez-vous où il est?

⚷ **whereas** /ˌweər'æz, (AmE) ˌhweər-/ *conj* **she likes dogs ~ I prefer cats** elle aime les chiens mais moi je préfère les chats; **he chose to stay quiet ~ I would have complained** il a choisi de ne rien dire alors que moi je me serais sûrement plaint

whereby /weə'baɪ, (AmE) hweər-/ *conj* **a system ~ all staff will carry identification** un système qui prévoit que tous les membres du personnel auront une carte

wherever /weər'evə(r), (AmE) hweər-/ *adv*
1 (in questions) **~ has he got to?** où est-ce qu'il a bien pu passer?
2 (anywhere) **~ she goes I'll go** où qu'elle aille, j'irai; **~ you want** où tu veux; **we'll meet ~'s convenient for you** nous nous retrouverons là où ça t'arrange
3 (whenever) **~ necessary** quand c'est nécessaire; **~ possible** dans la mesure du possible

whet /wet, (AmE) hwet/ *vt* (*p prés etc* **-tt-**) **to ~ the appetite** stimuler l'appétit; **the books ~ted his appetite for travel** les livres lui donnèrent envie de voyager

⚷ **whether** /'weðə(r), (AmE) 'hweðər/ *conj*

> When *whether* is used to mean *if*, it is translated by *si*: *I wonder whether she got my letter* = je me demande si elle a reçu ma lettre.
> In *whether... or not* sentences, *whether* is translated by *que* and the verb that follows is in the subjunctive.

1 (when outcome is uncertain) si; **I wasn't sure ~ to answer or not** je ne savais pas s'il fallait répondre; **can you check ~ it's cooked?** est-ce que tu peux vérifier si c'est cuit? **2** (no matter if) **you're coming ~ you like it or not!** tu viendras que cela te plaise ou non!; **~ you have children or not, this book should interest you** que vous ayez des enfants ou non, ce livre devrait vous intéresser

whew /fju:/ *excl* (in relief) ouf!; (in hot weather) pff!; (in surprise) hein!

⚷ **which** /wɪtʃ, (AmE) hwɪtʃ/ **A** *pron* **1** (in questions) lequel/laquelle/lesquels/lesquelles; **there are three peaches, ~ do you want?** il y a trois pêches, laquelle veux-tu?; **show her ~ you mean** montre-lui celui/celle etc dont tu parles; **I don't mind ~** ça m'est égal; **can you tell ~ is ~?** peux-tu les distinguer?
2 (relative pronoun) (as subject) qui; (as object) que; (with a preposition) lequel/laquelle/lesquels/lesquelles; (with a preposition translated by *de*) dont; **the book ~ is on the table** le livre qui est sur la table; **the book ~ I am reading** le livre que je lis; **the contract ~ he's spoken about** le contrat dont il a parlé; **~ reminds me...** ce qui me fait penser que...
3 (with a superlative adjective) quel/quelle/quels/quelles; **~ is the biggest?** (of masculine objects) quel est le plus gros?
B *det* quel/quelle/quels/quelles; **~ books?** quels livres?; **she asked me ~ coach was leaving first** elle m'a demandé lequel des cars allait partir le premier; **~ one of the children...?** lequel/laquelle des enfants...?; **you may wish to join, in ~ case...** vous voulez peut-être vous inscrire, auquel cas...

whichever /wɪtʃ'evə(r), (AmE) hwɪtʃ-/
A *pron* **1** (the one that) (as subject) celui qui, celle qui; (as object) celui *m* que, celle *f* que; **'which restaurant?'—'~ is nearest'** 'quel restaurant?'—'celui qui est le plus proche'; **come at 2 or 2.30, ~ suits you best** viens à 14 h ou 14 h 30, comme cela te convient le mieux
2 (no matter which one) (as subject) quel que soit celui qui, quelle que soit celle qui; (as object) quel que soit celui que, quelle *f* que soit celle que; **'do you want the big piece or the small piece?'—'~'** 'est-ce que tu veux le gros ou le petit morceau?'—'n'importe'
B *det* **1** (the one that) **let's go to ~ station is nearest** allons à la gare la plus proche
2 (no matter which) **I'll be happy ~ horse wins** quel que soit le cheval qui gagne je serai content

whiff /wɪf, (AmE) hwɪf/ *n* (of perfume, food) odeur *f*; (of smoke, garlic) bouffée *f*

⚷ **while** /waɪl, (AmE) hwaɪl/ **A** *conj* (*also* **whilst**) **1** (during the time that) pendant que; **he made a sandwich ~ I phoned** il s'est fait un sandwich pendant que je téléphonais; **~ in Spain, I visited Madrid** pendant que j'étais en Espagne, j'ai visité Madrid; **I fell asleep ~ watching TV** je me suis endormi en regardant la télé; **close the door ~ you're at it** ferme la porte pendant que tu y es
2 (although) bien que (+ *subjunctive*), quoique (+ *subjunctive*)
3 (whereas) alors que, tandis que; **she likes dogs ~ I prefer cats** elle aime les chiens mais moi je préfère les chats
B *n* **a ~ ago** il y a quelque temps; **a ~ later** quelque temps plus tard; **for a good ~** pendant longtemps; **a short ~ ago** il y a peu de temps; **it will take a ~** cela va prendre un certain temps; **after a (short) ~** au bout d'un moment; **once in a ~** de temps en temps

■ **while away** tuer ‹*time*› (**doing, by doing** en faisant)

whilst /waɪlst, (AmE) hwaɪlst/ = **while A**

whim /wɪm, (AmE) hwɪm/ *n* caprice *m*; **on a ~** sur un coup de tête

W

⚷ mot clé

whimper /ˈwɪmpə(r), (AmE) ˈhwɪm-/ **A** *n* gémissement *m* (**of** de)
B *vi* **1** ‹*person, animal*› gémir
2 (whinge) ‹*person*› pleurnicher

whimsical /ˈwɪmzɪkl, (AmE) ˈhwɪm-/ *adj* ‹*person*› fantasque; ‹*play, tale, manner, idea*› saugrenu/-e

whine /waɪn, (AmE) hwaɪn/ *vi* (complain) se plaindre (**about** de); (snivel) pleurnicher; ‹*dog*› gémir

whinge /wɪndʒ/ *vi* (fam) râler

whining /ˈwaɪnɪŋ, (AmE) ˈhwaɪn-/ **A** *n* (complaints) jérémiades *fpl*; (of dog) gémissements *mpl*
B *adj* ‹*voice*› geignard/-e; ‹*child*› pleurnicheur/-euse

whinny /ˈwɪnɪ, (AmE) ˈhwɪnɪ/ *vi* ‹*horse*› hennir doucement

whip /wɪp, (AmE) hwɪp/ **A** *n* **1** (for punishment) fouet *m*; (for horse) cravache *f*
2 (Culin) mousse *f*
B *vt* (*p prés etc* **-pp-**) **1** (beat) fouetter
2 (Culin) fouetter ‹*cream*›; battre [qch] en neige ‹*egg whites*›
3 (fam) **to ~ sth out** sortir qch brusquement; (remove quickly) **he ~ped the plates off the table** il a prestement retiré les assiettes de la table; **I ~ped the key out of his hand** je lui ai arraché la clé des mains; **to ~ the crowd up into a frenzy** mettre la foule en délire

whiplash injury *n* (Med) coup *m* du lapin

whip-round *n* (BrE) (fam) collecte *f*

whirl /wɜːl, (AmE) hwɜːl/ **A** *n* **1** (of activity, excitement) tourbillon *m* (**of** de)
2 (spiral motif) spirale *f*
B *vi* ‹*dancer*› tournoyer; ‹*blade, propeller*› tourner; ‹*snowflakes, dust, thoughts*› tourbillonner
IDIOM **to give sth a ~** (fam) essayer qch
■ **whirl round** ‹*person*› se retourner brusquement; ‹*blade, clock hand*› tourner brusquement

whirlpool *n* tourbillon *m*

whirlpool bath *n* bain *m* bouillonnant

whirlwind *n* tourbillon *m*

whirr /wɜː(r), (AmE) hwɜːr/ *vi* ‹*motor*› vrombir; ‹*camera, fan*› tourner; ‹*insect*› bourdonner; ‹*wings*› bruire

whisk /wɪsk, (AmE) hwɪsk/ **A** *n* (*also* **egg ~**) (manual) fouet *m*; (electric) batteur *m*
B *vt* **1** (Culin) battre
2 (transport quickly) **he was ~ed off to meet the president** on l'a emmené sur le champ rencontrer le président; **she was ~ed off to hospital** elle a été emmenée d'urgence à l'hôpital

whisker /ˈwɪskə(r), (AmE) ˈhwɪ-/ **A** *n* (of animal) poil *m* de moustache
B **whiskers** *npl* (of animal) moustaches *fpl*; (of man) (beard) barbe *f*; (moustache) moustache *f*

whisper /ˈwɪspə(r), (AmE) ˈhwɪs-/ **A** *n* chuchotement *m*; **to speak in a ~** *or* **in ~s** parler à voix basse
B *vt* chuchoter (**to** à); **to ~ sth to sb** chuchoter qch à qn; **'she's asleep', he ~ed** 'elle dort', dit-il en chuchotant
C *vi* chuchoter; **to ~ to sb** parler à voix basse à qn

whistle /ˈwɪsl, (AmE) ˈhwɪ-/ **A** *n* **1** (object) sifflet *m*; **to blow the** *or* **one's ~** donner un coup de sifflet
2 (sound) (through mouth) sifflement *m*; (by referee) coup *m* de sifflet; (of bird, train) sifflement *m*
B *vt* siffler; (casually) siffloter
C *vi* siffler; **to ~ at sb/sth** siffler qn/qch; **to ~ for** siffler ‹*dog*›
IDIOM **to blow the ~ on sb** dénoncer qn

white /waɪt, (AmE) hwaɪt/ **A** *n* **1** (gen) blanc *m*
2 (*also* **White**) (Caucasian) Blanc/Blanche *m/f*
3 (in chess, draughts) blancs *mpl*
B *adj* **1** blanc/blanche; **bright ~ teeth** dents *mpl* d'un blanc éclatant; **to go** *or* **turn ~** devenir blanc, blanchir; **to paint sth ~** peindre qch en blanc
2 ‹*race, child, skin*› blanc/blanche; ‹*area*› habité/-e par des Blancs; ‹*culture, prejudice*› des Blancs; **a ~ man/woman** un Blanc/une Blanche
3 (pale) pâle (**with** de); **to go** *or* **turn ~** pâlir (**with** de)

whitebait /ˈwaɪtbeɪt, (AmE) ˈhwaɪt-/ *n* (raw) blanchaille *f*; (fried) petite friture *f*

whiteboard *n* tableau *m* blanc

white coffee *n* (at home) café *m* au lait; (in café) (café *m*) crème *m*

white-collar /ˌwaɪtˈkɒlə(r), (AmE) ˌhwaɪt-/ *adj* ‹*job, work*› d'employé de bureau; ‹*staff*› de bureau; **~ worker** col *m* blanc, employé/-e *m/f* de bureau

white elephant *n* **1** (item, knicknack) bibelot *m*
2 (public project) réalisation *f* coûteuse et peu rentable

white goods *npl* (appliances) gros électro-ménager *m*

white horses *npl* (waves) moutons *mpl*

White House *n* **the ~** la Maison Blanche

white-knuckle ride *n* tour *m* de manège qui fait peur

white lie *n* pieux mensonge *m*

whitener /ˈwaɪtnə(r), (AmE) ˈhwaɪt-/ *n* **1** (for clothes) agent *m* blanchissant
2 (for shoes) produit *m* pour blanchir
3 (for coffee, tea) succédané *m* de lait en poudre

whiteness /ˈwaɪtnɪs, (AmE) ˈhwaɪt-/ *n* blancheur *f*

white spirit *n* white-spirit *m*

whitewash /ˈwaɪtwɒʃ, (AmE) ˈhwaɪt-/ **A** *n* **1** (for walls) lait *m* de chaux
2 (fig) (cover-up) mise *f* en scène
B *vt* **1** blanchir [qch] à la chaux ‹*wall*›

2 (*also* ~ **over**) blanchir ‹*facts*›

white water *n* eau *f* vive

white water rafting *n* rafting *m* en eau vive

white wedding *n* mariage *m* en blanc

Whitsun /ˈwɪtsn, (AmE) hwɪ-/ *n* (*also* **Whitsuntide**) Pentecôte *f*

Whit Sunday *n* Pentecôte *f*

whittle /ˈwɪtl, (AmE) ˈhwɪt-/ *vt* tailler [qch] au couteau; **to ~ sth away** *or* **down** réduire qch (**to** à)

whizz /wɪz, (AmE) hwɪz/ *vi* **to ~ by** *or* **past** ‹*arrow, bullet*› passer en sifflant; ‹*car*› passer à toute allure; ‹*person*› passer rapidement

whizz-kid *n* (fam) jeune prodige *m*

who /huː/ *pron*

> Note that there are three ways of asking questions using *qui* as the object of the verb: *who did he call?* = qui est-ce qu'il a appelé?, qui a-t-il appelé?, il a appelé qui?

1 (in questions) (as subject) qui (est-ce qui); (as object) qui (est-ce que); (after prepositions) qui; **~ knows the answer?** qui connaît la réponse?; **~'s going to be there?** qui sera là?; **~ did you invite?** qui est-ce que tu as invité?, qui as-tu invité?; **~ was she with?** avec qui était-elle?; **~ did you buy it for?** pour qui l'as-tu acheté?; **~ did you get it from?** qui te l'a donné? **2** (relative) (as subject) qui; (as object) que; (after prepositions) qui; **his friend, ~ lives in Paris** son ami, qui habite Paris; **his friend ~ he sees once a week** l'ami qu'il voit une fois par semaine
3 (whoever) **bring ~ you like** tu peux amener qui tu veux; **~ do you think you are?** tu te prends pour qui?

whodunit *n* (*also* **whodunnit**) polar *m* (fam), roman *m* policier

whoever /huːˈevə(r)/ *pron* **1** (the one that) **~ wins the election** celui ou celle qui gagnera les élections
2 (anyone that) (as subject) quiconque; (as object) qui; **~ saw the accident should contact us** quiconque a assisté à l'accident devrait nous contacter; **invite ~ you like** invite qui tu veux
3 (no matter who) **~ you are** qui que vous soyez

whole /həʊl/ **A** *n* **1** (total unit) tout *m*; **as a ~** (not in separate parts) en entier; (overall) dans l'ensemble
2 (all) **the ~ of** tout/-e; **the ~ of the weekend/August** tout le week-end/mois d'août; **the ~ of London is talking about it** tout Londres en parle; **nearly the ~ of Berlin was destroyed** Berlin a été presque entièrement détruit
B *adj* **1** (entire) tout/-e, entier/-ière; (more emphatic) tout entier/-ière; **a ~ hour** une heure entière; **a ~ day** toute une journée; **for three ~ weeks** pendant trois semaines entières; **his ~ life** toute sa vie, sa vie entière; **the ~ truth** toute la vérité; **the most beautiful city in the ~ world** la plus belle ville du monde
2 (emphatic use) **a ~ new way of life** un mode de vie complètement différent; **that's the ~ point of the exercise** c'est tout l'intérêt de l'exercice
3 (intact) intact/-e
C *adv* ‹*swallow, cook*› tout entier
D on the whole *phr* dans l'ensemble

wholefood *n* (BrE) produits *mpl* biologiques

wholehearted /ˌhəʊlˈhɑːtɪd/ *adj* ‹*approval, support*› sans réserve; **to be in ~ agreement with** être en accord total avec

wholeheartedly *adv* sans réserve

wholemeal *adj* (BrE) (*also* **wholewheat**) complet/-ète

whole milk *n* lait *m* entier

wholesale /ˈhəʊlseɪl/ **A** *adj* **1** ‹*business*› de gros
2 (large-scale) ‹*destruction*› total/-e; ‹*acceptance, rejection*› en bloc; ‹*attack*› sur tous les fronts
B *adv* **1** ‹*buy, sell*› en gros
2 ‹*accept, reject*› en bloc

wholesaler /ˈhəʊlseɪlə(r)/ *n* grossiste *mf*, marchand/-e *m/f* en gros

wholesome /ˈhəʊlsəm/ *adj* **1** (healthy) sain/-e
2 (decent) ‹*person, appearance*› bien propre; ‹*entertainment*› innocent/-e

wholewheat = **wholemeal**

wholly /ˈhəʊllɪ/ *adv* entièrement, tout à fait

whom /huːm/ *pron* **1** (in questions) qui (est-ce que); (after prepositions) qui; **~ did she meet?** qui a-t-elle rencontré?, qui est-ce qu'elle a rencontré?; **to ~ are you referring?** à qui est-ce que vous faites allusion?
2 (relative) que; (after prepositions) qui; **the person to ~/of ~ I spoke** la personne à qui/dont j'ai parlé

whooping cough *n* coqueluche *f*

whopper /ˈwɒpə(r), (AmE) ˈhwɒpər/ *n* (fam) (large thing) monstre *m*

whopping /ˈwɒpɪŋ, (AmE) ˈhwɒpɪŋ/ *adj* (fam) (*also* **~ great**) monstre (fam)

whorl /wɜːl, (AmE) hwɜːl/ *n* (of cream, chocolate) spirale *f*; (on fingerprint) volute *f*; (shell pattern) spire *f*; (of petals) verticille *m*

whose /huːz/ **A** *pron* **1** (in questions) à qui; **~ is this?** à qui est ceci?
2 (relative) dont; **the boy ~ dog was killed** le garçon dont le chien a été tué; **the man ~ daughter he was married to** l'homme dont il avait épousé la fille
B *det* **~ pen is that?** à qui est ce stylo?; **do you know ~ car was stolen?** est-ce que tu sais à qui appartenait la voiture volée?; **~ coat did you take?** tu as pris le manteau de qui?

W

why /waɪ, (AmE) hwaɪ/

> Note that there are three ways of asking questions using *why*:
> *Why did you go?* = pourquoi est-ce que tu y es allé?, pourquoi y es-tu allé?, tu y es allé pourquoi?

A *adv* **1** (in questions) pourquoi; **~ do you ask?** pourquoi est-ce que tu me poses la question?, pourquoi me poses-tu la question?; **~ bother?** pourquoi se tracasser?; **~ the delay?** pourquoi ce retard?; **~ not?** pourquoi pas?; **'tell them'—'~ should I?'** 'dis-le-leur'—'et pourquoi (est-ce que je devrais le faire)?'
2 (making suggestions) pourquoi; **~ don't we go away for the weekend?** pourquoi ne pas partir quelque part pour le week-end?; **~ don't I invite them for dinner?** et si je les invitais à manger?
B *conj* pour ça; **that is ~ they came** c'est pour ça qu'ils sont venus; **I need to know the reason ~** j'ai besoin de savoir pourquoi

wick /wɪk/ *n* mèche *f*

wicked /'wɪkɪd/ *adj* **1** (evil) ‹*person*› méchant/-e; ‹*heart, deed*› cruel/-elle; ‹*plot*› pernicieux/-ieuse; ‹*intention*› mauvais/-e *before n*
2 ‹*grin, humour*› malicieux/-ieuse; ‹*thoughts*› pervers/-e
3 (vicious) ‹*wind*› méchant/-e; ‹*weapon*› redoutable; **to have a ~ tongue** être mauvaise langue

wicker /'wɪkə(r)/ **A** *n* (*also* **wickerwork**) osier *m*
B *adj* ‹*basket, furniture*› en osier

wide /waɪd/ **A** *adj* **1** (broad) ‹*river, opening, mouth*› large; ‹*margin*› grand/-e; **how ~ is your garden?** quelle est la largeur de votre jardin?; **it's 30 cm ~** il fait 30 cm de large; **the river is 1 km across at its ~st** le fleuve fait *or* atteint 1 km à son point le plus large; **her eyes were ~ with fear** ses yeux étaient agrandis par la peur
2 (immense) ‹*ocean, desert, expanse*› vaste *before n*
3 (extensive) ‹*variety, choice*› grand/-e *before n*; **a ~ range of opinions** une grande variété d'opinions; **a ~ range of products** une vaste gamme de produits
4 (Sport) ‹*ball, shot*› perdu/-e
B *adv* **to open one's eyes ~** ouvrir grand les yeux; **to open the door/window ~** ouvrir la porte/la fenêtre en grand; **his eyes are (set) ~ apart** il a les yeux très écartés; **his legs were ~ apart** il avait les jambes écartées; **to be ~ of the mark** ‹*ball, dart*› être à côté; ‹*guess*› être loin de la vérité

wide-angle lens *n* objectif *m* à grand angle

wide awake *adj* complètement éveillé/-e

wide-eyed *adj* **1** (with surprise, fear) **he was ~** il ouvrait de grands yeux; **~ with fear/surprise** les yeux écarquillés de peur/surprise; **she stared/listened ~** elle regardait/écoutait les yeux écarquillés
2 (naïve) ‹*person, innocence*› ingénu/-e

widely /'waɪdlɪ/ *adv* **1** (commonly) ‹*accepted, used*› largement; **this product is now ~ available** on trouve maintenant ce produit partout
2 ‹*spaced, planted*› à de grands intervalles; ‹*travel, differ, vary*› beaucoup

widely read /ˌwaɪdlɪ'red/ *adj* ‹*student*› qui a beaucoup lu; ‹*author*› très lu/-e

widen /'waɪdn/ **A** *vt* élargir ‹*road, gap*›; étendre ‹*powers*›; **this has ~ed their lead in the opinion polls** ceci a renforcé leur position dominante dans les sondages
B *vi* s'élargir

widening *adj* ‹*division*› de plus en plus grand/-e; ‹*gap*› qui s'élargit de plus en plus

wide open *adj* **1** ‹*door, window, eyes, mouth*› grand/-e ouvert/-e
2 the race is ~ l'issue de la course est indécise

wide-ranging /ˌwaɪd'reɪndʒɪŋ/ *adj* ‹*reforms*› de grande envergure; ‹*interests*› très variés

wide screen *n* grand écran *m*

wide-screen TV *n* téléviseur *m* à grand écran

widespread /'waɪdspred/ *adj* ‹*epidemic*› généralisé/-e; ‹*devastation*› étendu/-e; ‹*belief*› très répandu/-e

widow /'wɪdəʊ/ **A** *n* veuve *f*
B *vt* **to be ~ed** devenir veuf/veuve *m/f*

widower /'wɪdəʊə(r)/ *n* veuf *m*

width /wɪdθ, wɪtθ/ *n* **1** largeur *f*; **it is 30 metres in ~** il fait *or* mesure 30 mètres de large
2 (of fabric) lé *m*

wield /wi:ld/ *vt* **1** brandir ‹*weapon, tool*›
2 exercer ‹*power*› (**over** sur)

wife /waɪf/ *n* (*pl* **wives**) femme *f*; (more formally) épouse *f*; **the baker's/farmer's ~** la boulangère/la fermière

Wi-Fi® /waɪfaɪ/ /waɪfaɪ/ *n* (*abbr* = **Wireless Fidelity**) Wi-Fi® *m*

wig /wɪg/ *n* (whole head) perruque *f*; (partial) postiche *m*

wiggle /'wɪgl/ (fam) **A** *n* **a ~ of the hips** un roulement des hanches
B *vt* faire bouger ‹*tooth, wedged object*›; **to ~ one's hips** rouler les hanches; **to ~ one's fingers/toes** remuer les doigts/orteils
C *vi* ‹*snake, worm*› se tortiller

wild /waɪld/ **A** *n* **in the ~** ‹*conditions, life*› en liberté; **to grow in the ~** pousser à l'état sauvage; **the call of the ~** l'appel de la nature
B *adj* **1** ‹*animal, plant*› sauvage; **the pony is still quite ~** le poney est encore assez farouche
2 ‹*landscape*› sauvage
3 ‹*wind*› violent/-e; ‹*sea*› agité/-e; **it was a**

~ night c'était une nuit de tempête
4 ‹*party, laughter, person*› fou/folle; ‹*imagination*› délirant/-e; ‹*applause*› déchaîné/-e; **to go ~** se déchaîner
5 (fam) (furious) furieux/-ieuse; **he'll go** *or* **be ~!** ça va le mettre hors de lui!
6 (fam) (enthusiastic) **to be ~ about** être un/une fana (fam) de; **I'm not ~ about him/it** il/ça ne m'emballe (fam) pas
7 (outlandish) ‹*idea, plan*› fou/folle; ‹*claim, promise, accusation*› extravagant/-e; ‹*story*› farfelu/-e (fam)
C *adv* ‹*grow*› à l'état sauvage; **the garden had run ~** le jardin était devenu une vraie jungle; **those children are allowed to run ~!** on permet à ces enfants de faire n'importe quoi!; **to let one's imagination run ~** laisser libre cours à son imagination

wild boar *n* sanglier *m*

wilderness /'wɪldənɪs/ *n* étendue *f* sauvage et désolée

wild-eyed *adj* au regard égaré

wildfire /'waɪldfaɪə(r)/ *n* **to spread like ~** se répandre comme une traînée de poudre

wild flower *n* fleur *f* des champs, fleur *f* sauvage

wild goose chase /ˌwaɪld'guːs tʃeɪs/ *n* **it turned out to be a ~** ça n'a abouti à rien; **to lead sb on a ~** mettre qn sur une mauvaise piste

wildlife *n* (animals) faune *f*; (animals and plants) faune *f* et flore *f*

wildlife park, **wildlife reserve**, **wildlife sanctuary** *n* réserve *f* naturelle

wildly /'waɪldlɪ/ *adv* **1** ‹*invest, spend, talk*› de façon insensée; ‹*fire, shoot*› au hasard; **to hit out/run ~** envoyer des coups/courir dans tous les sens
2 ‹*wave, gesture*› de manière très agitée; ‹*applaud*› à tout rompre; **to fluctuate ~** subir des fluctuations violentes; **to beat ~** ‹*heart*› battre à tout rompre
3 ‹*enthusiastic, optimistic*› extrêmement

wilds *npl* **to live in the ~ of Arizona** habiter au fin fond de l'Arizona

Wild West *n* Far West *m*

wilful (BrE), **willful** (AmE) /'wɪlfl/ *adj*
1 ‹*person, behaviour*› volontaire
2 ‹*damage, disobedience*› délibéré/-e

wilfully (BrE), **willfully** (AmE) /'wɪlfəlɪ/ *adv*
1 (in headstrong way) obstinément
2 (deliberately) délibérément

W

⚷ **will¹** /wɪl, əl/ **A** *modal aux* **1** (expressing the future) **I'll see you tomorrow** je te verrai demain; **it won't rain** il ne pleuvra pas; **~ there be many people?** est-ce qu'il y aura beaucoup de monde?; **they'll come tomorrow** ils vont venir demain; **what ~ you do now?** qu'est-ce que tu vas faire maintenant?
2 (expressing willingness or intention) **~ you help me?** est-ce que tu m'aideras?; **we won't stay too long** nous ne resterons pas trop longtemps; **he won't cooperate** il ne veut pas coopérer
3 (in requests, commands) **~ you pass the salt, please?** est-ce que tu peux me passer le sel, s'il te plaît; **~ you please be quiet!** est-ce que tu vas te taire?; **wait a minute, ~ you!** attends un peu!
4 (in invitations) **~ you have some tea?** est-ce que vous voulez du thé?; **won't you join us for dinner?** est-ce que tu veux dîner avec nous?; **what ~ you have to drink?** qu'est-ce que tu prends?
5 (in assumptions) **he'll be about 30 now** il doit avoir 30 ans maintenant; **you'll be tired, I expect** tu dois être fatigué, je suppose
6 (indicating sth predictable or customary) **they ~ ask for a deposit** ils demandent une caution; **these things ~ happen** ce sont des choses qui arrivent; **you ~ keep contradicting her!** il faut toujours que tu la contredises!
7 (in short answers and tag questions) **you'll come again, won't you?** tu reviendras, n'est-ce pas?; **you won't forget, ~ you?** tu n'oublieras pas, n'est-ce pas?; **that'll be cheaper, won't it?** ça sera moins cher, non?; **'they won't be ready'—'yes, they ~'** 'ils ne seront pas prêts'—'(bien sûr que) si'; **'~ you call me?'—'yes, I ~'** 'est-ce que tu me téléphoneras?'—'bien sûr que oui'; **'she'll be furious'—'no, she won't!'** 'elle sera furieuse'—'bien sûr que non!'; **'I'll do it'—'no you won't!'** 'je le ferai'—'il n'en est pas question!'
B *vt* **1** (urge mentally) **to ~ sb to do** supplier mentalement qn de faire; **to ~ sb to live** prier pour que qn vive
2 (wish, desire) vouloir
3 (Law) léguer (**to** à)

will² /wɪl/ **A** *n* **1** volonté *f* (**to do** de faire); **to have a ~ of one's own** n'en faire qu'à sa tête; **against my ~** contre mon gré; **to do sth with a ~** faire de bon cœur; **to lose the ~ to live** ne plus avoir envie de vivre
2 (Law) testament *m*; **to leave sb sth in one's ~** léguer qch à qn
B **at will** *phr* ‹*select, take*› à volonté; **they can wander about at ~** ils peuvent se promener comme ils veulent

⚷ **willing** /'wɪlɪŋ/ *adj* **1** (prepared) **to be ~ to do** être prêt/-e à faire
2 (eager) ‹*pupil, helper*› de bonne volonté; ‹*slave*› consentant/-e; ‹*recruit, victim*› volontaire; **to show ~** faire preuve de bonne volonté

willingly /'wɪlɪŋlɪ/ *adv* ‹*accept, help*› volontiers; ‹*work*› avec bonne volonté

willingness /'wɪlɪŋnɪs/ *n* (readiness) volonté *f* (**to do** de faire)

willow /'wɪləʊ/ *n* (*also* **~ tree**) saule *m*

⚷ mot clé

willpower *n* volonté *f* (**to do** de faire)

willy-nilly /ˌwɪlɪˈnɪlɪ/ *adv* **1** (regardless of choice) bon gré mal gré
2 (haphazardly) au hasard

wilt /wɪlt/ *vi* **1** ‹*plant, flower*› se faner
2 ‹*person*› (from heat, fatigue) se sentir faible; (at daunting prospect) perdre courage

wimp /wɪmp/ *n* (fam) (ineffectual) lavette *f* (fam); (fearful) poule *f* mouillée (fam)

win /wɪn/ **A** *n* victoire *f* (**over** sur)
B *vt* (*p prés* **-nn-**, *prét, pp* **won**) **1** gagner ‹*match, bet, battle, money*›; remporter ‹*election*›
2 (acquire) obtenir ‹*delay, reprieve*›; gagner ‹*friendship, heart*›; s'attirer ‹*sympathy*›; s'acquérir ‹*support*› (**of** de); **to ~ sb's love/respect** se faire aimer/respecter de qn
C *vi* (*p prés* **-nn-**, *prét, pp* **won**) gagner; **to ~ against sb** l'emporter sur qn

▪ **win back**: **~ [sth] back, ~ back [sth]** récupérer ‹*support, votes*› (**from sb** sur qn); regagner ‹*affection, respect*›; reprendre ‹*prize, territory*› (**from** à)

▪ **win over, win round** convaincre ‹*person*›

wince /wɪns/ **A** *n* grimace *f*
B *vi* grimacer, faire une grimace

winch /wɪntʃ/ **A** *n* treuil *m*
B *vt* **to ~ sth down/up** descendre/hisser qch au treuil

wind¹ /wɪnd/ **A** *n* **1** vent *m*; **the ~ is blowing** il y a du vent; **which way is the ~ blowing?** d'où vient le vent?
2 (breath) **to knock the ~ out of sb** couper le souffle à qn; **to get one's ~** reprendre souffle
3 (flatulence) vents *mpl*; **to break ~** lâcher un vent
B *vt* (*prét, pp* **winded**) **1** (make breathless) ‹*blow, punch*› couper la respiration à; ‹*climb*› essouffler
2 faire faire son rot à ‹*baby*›

wind² /waɪnd/ **A** *vt* (*prét, pp* **wound**)
1 (coil up) enrouler ‹*hair, rope, wire*› (**on, onto** sur, **round** autour de)
2 (*also* **~ up**) remonter ‹*clock, toy*›
3 donner un tour de ‹*handle*›
4 to ~ its way ‹*procession, road, river*› serpenter
B *vi* (*prét, pp* **wound**) ‹*road, river*› serpenter (**along** le long de); ‹*stairs*› tourner

▪ **wind down A ~ down 1** ‹*organization*› réduire ses activités; ‹*activity, production*› toucher à sa fin; ‹*person*› se détendre
2 ‹*clockwork*› être sur le point de s'arrêter
B ~ [sth] down 1 baisser ‹*car window*›
2 mettre fin à ‹*activity, organization*›

▪ **wind up A ~ up** (fam) **1** (finish) ‹*event*› se terminer (**with** par); ‹*speaker*› conclure
2 (end up) finir, se retrouver
B ~ [sth] up 1 liquider ‹*business*›; mettre fin à ‹*debate, meeting, project*›
2 remonter ‹*clock, car window*›
C ~ [sb] up 1 (tease) faire marcher ‹*person*›
2 (make tense) énerver

wind chimes *npl* carillon *m* éolien

wind energy *n* énergie *f* éolienne

windfall /ˈwɪndfɔːl/ *n* fruit *m* tombé par terre; (fig) aubaine *f*

windfall profit *n* profit *m* inattendu

wind farm *n* ferme *f* éolienne

winding /ˈwaɪndɪŋ/ *adj* ‹*road, river*› sinueux/-euse; ‹*stairs*› en spirale

wind instrument *n* instrument *m* à vent

windmill /ˈwɪndmɪl/ *n* moulin *m* à vent

window /ˈwɪndəʊ/ *n* **1** (of house) fenêtre *f*; (of shop, public building) vitrine *f*; (of vehicle) (gen) vitre *f*; (of plane) hublot *m*; (stained glass) vitrail *m*; **to look out of** *or* **through the ~** regarder par la fenêtre
2 (for service at bank or post office) guichet *m*

window blind *n* store *m*

window box *n* jardinière *f*

window cleaner *n* laveur/-euse *m/f* de carreaux

window display *n* vitrine *f*

window ledge *n* appui *m* de fenêtre

windowpane *n* carreau *m*

window seat *n* **1** (in room) banquette *f*
2 (in plane, bus, train) place *f* côté vitre

window-shopping *n* **to go ~** faire du lèche-vitrines *m inv* (fam)

window sill *n* rebord *m* de fenêtre

windpipe *n* trachée-artère *f*

wind power *n* énergie *f* éolienne

windscreen (BrE), **windshield** (AmE) *n* pare-brise *m inv*

windscreen wiper *n* (BrE) essuie-glace *m inv*

windshield (AmE) = **windscreen**

windsurf *vi* faire de la planche à voile

windsurfer *n* (person) véliplanchiste *mf*; (board) planche *f* à voile

windswept *adj* venteux/-euse

windy /ˈwɪndɪ/ *adj* ‹*place*› venteux/-euse; ‹*day*› de vent; **it was very ~** il faisait beaucoup de vent

wine /waɪn/ *n* **1** (drink) vin *m*
2 (colour) lie-de-vin *m*

wine bar *n* bar *m* à vin

wine box *n* ≈ cubitainer® *m*

wine cellar *n* cave *f*

wine glass *n* verre *m* à vin

wine grower *n* viticulteur/-trice *m/f*

wine growing A *n* viticulture *f*
B *adj* ‹*region*› vinicole

wine list *n* carte *f* des vins

wine rack *n* casier *m* à bouteilles

wine shop *n* marchand *m* de vin

wine tasting *n* dégustation *f* de vins

wine vinegar *n* vinaigre *m* de vin

wine waiter *n* sommelier/-ière *m/f*

⚷ **wing** /wɪŋ/ **A** *n* aile *f*
B **wings** *npl* (in theatre) **the ~s** les coulisses *fpl*; **to be waiting in the ~s** (fig) attendre son heure

winger /ˈwɪŋə(r)/ *n* (BrE) ailier *m*

wing nut *n* écrou *m* à oreilles

wink /wɪŋk/ **A** *n* clin *m* d'œil; **we didn't get a ~ of sleep all night** nous n'avons pas fermé l'œil de la nuit
B *vi* cligner de l'œil; **to ~ at sb** faire un clin d'œil à qn

⚷ **winner** /ˈwɪnə(r)/ *n* **1** (victor) gagnant/-e *m/f*
2 (success) **to be a ~** ‹*film, book, song*› avoir un gros succès

winning /ˈwɪnɪŋ/ *adj* **1** (victorious) gagnant/-e
2 ‹*smile*› engageant/-e; **to have ~ ways** avoir du charme

winning post *n* poteau *m* d'arrivée

winnings *npl* gains *mpl*

winning streak *n* **to be on a ~** être dans une bonne période

⚷ **winter** /ˈwɪntə(r)/ **A** *n* hiver *m*; **in ~** en hiver
B *adj* ‹*sports, clothes, weather*› d'hiver
C *vi* passer l'hiver

wintertime *n* hiver *m*

wipe /waɪp/ **A** *n* **1 to give sth a ~** (clean, dust) donner un coup de chiffon à qch; (dry) essuyer qch
2 (for face, baby) lingette *f*
B *vt* essuyer ‹*table, glass*› (**on** sur, **with** avec); **to ~ one's hands/feet** s'essuyer les mains/les pieds; **to ~ one's nose** se moucher; **to ~ a baby's bottom** essuyer (les fesses d')un bébé; **to ~ the dishes** essuyer la vaisselle
■ **wipe away** essuyer ‹*tears, sweat*›; faire partir ‹*dirt, mark*›
■ **wipe out 1** nettoyer ‹*container, cupboard*›
2 annuler ‹*inflation*›; anéantir ‹*species, enemy, population*›
■ **wipe up**: **A ~ up** essuyer la vaisselle
B ~ [sth] up essuyer

wipe-clean *adj* facile à nettoyer

wire /ˈwaɪə(r)/ **A** *n* **1** fil *m*; **electric/telephone ~** fil électrique/téléphonique
2 (AmE) (telegram) télégramme *m*
B *vt* **1 to ~ a house** installer l'électricité dans une maison; **to ~ a plug/a lamp** connecter une prise/une lampe
2 (telegraph) télégraphier à ‹*person*›; télégraphier ‹*money*›

wireless /ˈwaɪəlɪs/ **A** *n* (BrE) (Hist) radio *f*
B *adj* sans fil

wiring /ˈwaɪərɪŋ/ *n* (in house) installation *f* électrique; (in appliance) circuit *m* (électrique)

wiry /ˈwaɪərɪ/ *adj* **1** ‹*person, body*› mince et nerveux/-euse
2 ‹*hair*› rêche

wisdom /ˈwɪzdəm/ *n* sagesse *f*

wisdom tooth *n* dent *f* de sagesse

wise /waɪz/ **A** *adj* ‹*person, words, precaution, saying*› sage; ‹*choice, investment*› judicieux/-ieuse; ‹*smile, nod*› avisé/-e; **a ~ man** un sage; **a ~ move** une décision judicieuse; **to be none the ~r** (understand no better) ne pas être plus avancé/-e; (not realize) ne s'apercevoir de rien
B **-wise** *combining form* **1** (direction) dans le sens de; **length-~** dans le sens de la longueur
2 (with regard to) pour ce qui est de; **work-~** pour ce qui est du travail

wisecrack /ˈwaɪzkræk/ *n* vanne *f* (fam)

wise guy *n* (fam) gros malin *m* (fam)

wisely /ˈwaɪzlɪ/ *adv* judicieusement

⚷ **wish** /wɪʃ/ **A** *n* **1** (request) souhait *m* (**for** de); **to make a ~** faire un vœu; **her ~ came true** son souhait s'est réalisé
2 (desire) désir *m* (**for** de, **to do** de faire); **to go against sb's ~es** aller contre la volonté de qn
B **wishes** *npl* vœux *mpl*; **good** *or* **best ~es** meilleurs vœux; (ending letter) bien amicalement; **best ~es on your birthday** meilleurs vœux pour votre anniversaire; **please give him my best ~es** je vous prie de lui faire toutes mes amitiés
C *vt* **1** (expressing longing) **I ~ he were here/had been here** si seulement il était ici/avait été ici; **he ~ed he had written** il regrettait de ne pas avoir écrit
2 (express congratulations, greetings) souhaiter; **I ~ you good luck/a happy birthday** je vous souhaite bonne chance/un bon anniversaire; **I ~ him well** je souhaite que tout aille bien pour lui
3 (want) souhaiter, désirer
D *vi* **1** (desire) vouloir; **just as you ~** comme vous voudrez
2 (make a wish) faire un vœu

wishful thinking /ˌwɪʃfl ˈθɪŋkɪŋ/ *n* **that's ~** c'est prendre ses désirs pour des réalités

wishy-washy /ˈwɪʃɪwɒʃɪ/ *adj* (fam) ‹*colour*› délavé/-e; ‹*person*› incolore et inodore (fam)

wisp /wɪsp/ *n* (of hair) mèche *f*; (of straw) brin *m*; (of smoke, cloud) volute *f*

wispy /ˈwɪspɪ/ *adj* ‹*hair, beard*› fin/-e; ‹*cloud, smoke*› léger/-ère

wisteria /wɪˈstɪərɪə/ *n* glycine *f*

wistful /ˈwɪstfl/ *adj* (sad) mélancolique; (nostalgic) nostalgique

wit /wɪt/ **A** *n* **1** (sense of humour) esprit *m*
2 (witty person) personne *f* spirituelle
B **to wit** *phr* à savoir

witch /wɪtʃ/ *n* sorcière *f*

witchcraft *n* sorcellerie *f*

witch doctor *n* shaman *m*

witch-hunt *n* chasse *f* aux sorcières

⚷ **with** /wɪð, wɪθ/ *prep* **1** (gen) avec; **a meeting ~ sb** une réunion avec qn; **to hit sb ~ sth**

⚷ mot clé

frapper qn avec qch; **~ difficulty/pleasure** avec difficulté/plaisir; **to be patient ~ sb** être patient/-e avec qn; **delighted ~ sth** ravi/-e de qch; **to travel ~ sb** voyager avec qn; **to live ~ sb** (in one's own house) vivre avec qn; (in their house) vivre chez qn; **I'll be ~ you in a second** je suis à vous dans un instant; **take your umbrella ~ you** emporte ton parapluie; **bring the books back ~ you** rapporte les livres
2 (in descriptions) à; **a girl ~ black hair** une fille aux cheveux noirs; **the boy ~ the broken leg** le garçon à la jambe cassée; **a boy ~ a broken leg** un garçon avec une jambe cassée; **a TV ~ remote control** une télévision avec télécommande; **furnished ~ antiques** meublé/-e avec des meubles anciens; **covered ~ mud** couvert/-e de boue; **to lie ~ one's eyes closed** être allongé/-e les yeux fermés; **to stand ~ one's arms folded** se tenir les bras croisés; **filled ~ sth** rempli/-e de qch
3 (according to) **to increase ~ time** augmenter avec le temps; **to vary ~ the temperature** varier selon la température
4 (owning, bringing) **passengers ~ tickets** les passagers munis de billets; **people ~ qualifications** les gens qualifiés; **somebody ~ your experience** quelqu'un qui a ton expérience; **have you got the report ~ you?** est-ce que tu as (amené) le rapport?
5 (as regards) **how are things ~ you?** comment ça va?; **what's up ~ you?** qu'est-ce que tu as?; **what do you want ~ another car?** qu'est-ce que tu veux faire d'une deuxième voiture?
6 (because of) **sick ~ worry** malade d'inquiétude; **he can see better ~ his glasses on** il voit mieux avec ses lunettes; **I can't do it ~ you watching** je ne peux pas le faire si tu me regardes
7 (suffering from) **people ~ Aids/leukaemia** les personnes atteintes du sida/de leucémie; **to be ill ~ flu** avoir la grippe
8 (employed by, customer of) **a reporter ~ the Gazette** un journaliste de la Gazette; **he's ~ the UN** il travaille pour l'ONU; **I'm ~ Chemco** je travaille chez Chemco; **we're ~ the National Bank** nous sommes à la National Bank
9 (in the same direction as) **to sail ~ the wind** naviguer dans le sens du vent; **to drift ~ the tide** dériver avec le courant

withdraw /wɪð'drɔː, wɪθ'd-/ **A** *vt* (*prét* **-drew**, *pp* **-drawn**) retirer ‹*hand, money, application, permission, troops*›; renoncer à, retirer ‹*claim*›; rétracter ‹*accusation, statement*›
B *vi* (*prét* **-drew**, *pp* **-drawn**) **1** (gen) se retirer (**from** de)
2 (psychologically) se replier sur soi-même

withdrawal /wɪð'drɔːəl, wɪθ'd-/ *n* **1** (of money, troops) retrait *m* (**of, from** de)
2 (psychological reaction) repli *m* sur soi
3 (of drug addict) état *m* de manque

withdrawal symptoms *npl* symptômes *mpl* de manque; **to be suffering from ~** être en état de manque

withdrawn /wɪð'drɔːn, wɪθ'd-/ *adj* ‹*person*› renfermé/-e, replié/-e sur soi-même

wither /'wɪðə(r)/ **A** *vt* flétrir
B *vi* se flétrir

withering /'wɪðərɪŋ/ *adj* ‹*look*› plein/-e de mépris; ‹*contempt, comment*› cinglant/-e

withhold /wɪð'həʊld/ *vt* (*prét*, *pp* **-held**) différer ‹*payment*›; retenir ‹*tax, grant, rent*›; refuser ‹*consent, permission*›; ne pas divulguer ‹*information*›

within /wɪ'ðɪn/ **A** *prep* **1** (inside) **~ the city walls** dans l'enceinte de la ville; **~ the party** au sein du parti; **it's a play ~ a play** c'est une pièce dans la pièce
2 (in expressions of time) **I'll do it ~ the hour** je le ferai en moins d'une heure; **15 burglaries ~ a month** 15 cambriolages en (moins d')un mois; **they died ~ a week of each other** ils sont morts à une semaine d'intervalle
3 (not more than) **to be ~ several metres of sth** être à quelques mètres seulement de qch; **it's accurate to ~ a millimetre** c'est exact au millimètre près
4 to live ~ one's income vivre selon ses moyens
B *adv* à l'intérieur; **from ~** de l'intérieur

without /wɪ'ðaʊt/ **A** *prep* sans; **~ a key** sans clé; **~ any money** sans argent; **she left ~ it** elle est partie sans; **they left ~ me** ils sont partis sans moi; **~ looking** sans regarder; **it goes ~ saying** cela va de soi
B *adv* à l'extérieur; **from ~** de l'extérieur

withstand /wɪð'stænd/ *vt* (*prét*, *pp* **-stood**) résister à

witness /'wɪtnɪs/ **A** *n* **1** (gen), (Law) (person) témoin *m*; **she was a ~ to the accident** elle a été témoin de l'accident; **~ for the prosecution/the defence** témoin à charge/à décharge
2 (testimony) témoignage *m*; **to be** *or* **bear ~ to sth** témoigner de qch
B *vt* **1** (see) être témoin de, assister à ‹*incident, attack*›
2 servir de témoin lors de la signature de ‹*will, treaty*›; être témoin à ‹*marriage*›

witness box (BrE), **witness stand** (AmE) *n* barre *f* des témoins

wits *npl* (intelligence) intelligence *f*; (presence of mind) présence *f* d'esprit; **to collect** *or* **gather one's ~** rassembler ses esprits; **to frighten sb out of their ~** faire une peur épouvantable à qn; **to live by one's ~** vivre d'expédients; **a battle of ~** une joute verbale
IDIOM **to be at one's ~ end** ne plus savoir quoi faire

witticism /'wɪtɪsɪzəm/ *n* bon mot *m*

witty /'wɪtɪ/ *adj* spirituel/-elle

wizard /'wɪzəd/ *n* **1** (magician) magicien *m*
2 (expert) **to be a ~ at chess/computing** être

un as (fam) aux échecs/en informatique

wizened /ˈwɪznd/ *adj* ratatiné/-e

wobble /ˈwɒbl/ *vi* ‹*table, chair*› branler; ‹*pile of books, plates*› osciller; ‹*jelly*› trembloter; ‹*person*› (on bicycle) osciller; (on ladder, tightrope) chanceler

wobbly /ˈwɒblɪ/ *adj* ‹*table, chair*› bancal/-e; ‹*tooth*› branlant/-e

woe /wəʊ/ *n* malheur *m*; **a tale of ~** une histoire pathétique

wolf /wʊlf/ *n* (*pl* **wolves**) loup *m*; **she-~** louve *f*

IDIOM **to cry ~** crier au loup

wolf-whistle /ˈwʊlfwɪsl, (AmE) -hwɪ-/ **A** *n* sifflement *m*
B *vi* siffler

⚷ **woman** /ˈwʊmən/ *n* (*pl* **women**) femme *f*; **a ~ Prime Minister** une femme premier ministre; **he's always criticizing women drivers** il est toujours en train de critiquer les femmes au volant

woman friend *n* amie *f*

womanizer /ˈwʊmənaɪzə(r)/ *n* coureur *m* (de jupons)

womb /wuːm/ *n* (Anat) uterus *m*

women's refuge *n* foyer *m* pour femmes battues

women's studies *npl* études *fpl* féministes

⚷ **wonder** /ˈwʌndə(r)/ **A** *n* **1** (miracle) merveille *f*; **to do** *or* **work ~s** faire des merveilles (**for** pour, **with** avec); **(it's) no ~ that he's late** (ce n'est) pas étonnant qu'il soit en retard
2 (amazement) émerveillement *m*
B *vt* (ask oneself) se demander; **I ~ how/why/whether** je me demande comment/pourquoi/si; (as polite request) **I ~ if you could help me?** pourriez-vous m'aider?; **it makes you ~ why** c'est à se demander pourquoi
C *vi* **1** (think) **to ~ about sth/about doing sth** penser à qch/à faire qch; **it makes you ~** cela donne à penser
2 (be surprised) **to ~ at sth** s'étonner de qch; (admiringly) s'émerveiller de qch

⚷ **wonderful** /ˈwʌndəfl/ *adj* ‹*book, film, meal, experience, holiday*› merveilleux/-euse; ‹*musician, teacher*› excellent/-e

wonderfully /ˈwʌndəfəlɪ/ *adv* ‹*funny, exciting, clever*› très; ‹*work, cope, drive*› admirablement

wonky /ˈwɒŋkɪ/ *adj* (fam) (crooked) de traviole (fam); (wobbly) ‹*furniture*› bancal/-e

wont /wəʊnt, (AmE) wɔːnt/ *adj* **to be ~ to do** avoir coutume de faire; **as is his/their ~** comme à son/leur habitude

woo /wuː/ *vt* courtiser

⚷ **wood** /wʊd/ **A** *n* bois *m*
B **woods** *npl* bois *mpl*
C *adj* ‹*fire, smoke*› de bois; **~ floor** plancher *m*

⚷ mot clé

IDIOMS **touch ~!** (BrE), **knock on ~!** (AmE) touchons du bois!; **we are not out of the ~s yet** on n'est pas encore sorti de l'auberge

wooden /ˈwʊdn/ *adj* **1** ‹*furniture, object, house*› en bois; ‹*leg, spoon*› de bois
2 ‹*expression*› figé/-e

woodland /ˈwʊdlənd/ *n* bois *m*

woodpecker *n* pic *m*

wood pigeon *n* pigeon *m* ramier

woodwind /ˈwʊdwɪnd/ *npl* bois *mpl*

woodwork /ˈwʊdwɜːk/ *n* **1** (carpentry) menuiserie *f*
2 (doors, windows) boiseries *fpl*

woodworm /ˈwʊdwɜːm/ *n* ver *m* du bois

wool /wʊl/ *n* laine *f*; **pure (new) ~** pure laine (vierge)

IDIOM **to pull the ~ over sb's eyes** duper qn

woollen (BrE), **woolen** (AmE) /ˈwʊlən/ **A** *n* (garment) lainage *m*
B *adj* ‹*garment*› de laine

woolly (BrE), **wooly** (AmE) /ˈwʊlɪ/ **A** *n* lainage *m*
B *adj* **1** ‹*garment*› de laine; ‹*animal coat, hair*› laineux/-euse; ‹*cloud*› cotonneux/-euse
2 ‹*thinking*› flou/-e

⚷ **word** /wɜːd/ **A** *n* **1** mot *m*; **to have the last ~** avoir le dernier mot; **I couldn't get a ~ in** je n'ai pas pu placer un mot; **in other ~s** en d'autres termes; **a ~ of warning** un avertissement; **a ~ of advice** un conseil; **too sad for ~s** trop triste; **I believed every ~ he said** je croyais tout ce qu'il me disait; **I mean every ~ of it** je pense ce que je dis; **a man of few ~s** un homme peu loquace; **not a ~ to anybody** pas un mot à qui que ce soit; **I don't believe a ~ of it** je n'en crois pas un mot
2 (information) nouvelles *fpl* (**about** concernant); **there is no ~ of the missing climbers** on est sans nouvelles des alpinistes disparus; **~ got out that...** la nouvelle a transpiré que...; **to bring/send ~ that** annoncer/faire savoir que
3 (promise, affirmation) parole *f*; **he gave me his ~** il m'a donné sa parole; **to keep/break one's ~** tenir/ne pas tenir parole; **to take sb's ~ for it** croire qn sur parole; **take my ~ for it!** crois-moi!
4 (rumour) **~ has it that he's a millionaire** on dit qu'il est millionnaire; **~ got around that...** le bruit a couru que...
5 (command) ordre *m*; **to give the ~ to do** donner l'ordre de faire
B **words** *npl* (of play) texte *m*; (of song) paroles *fpl*
C *vt* formuler ‹*reply, letter, statement*›

IDIOMS **my ~!** (in surprise) ma parole!; **right from the ~ go** dès le départ; **to have a ~ with sb about sth** parler à qn à propos de qch; **to have ~s with sb** s'accrocher avec qn; **to put in a good ~ for sb** glisser un mot en faveur de qn

word for word *adv* ‹*copy, translate*› mot à mot; ‹*repeat*› mot pour mot

W

wording /ˈwɜːdɪŋ/ *n* formulation *f*

word list *n* liste *f* de mots

word-of-mouth **A** *adj* verbal/-e
B **by word of mouth** *phr* verbalement

word processing, **WP** *n* traitement *m* de texte

word processor *n* machine *f* à traitement de texte

work /wɜːk/ **A** *n* **1** (physical or mental activity) travail *m* (**on** sur); **it was hard ~ doing** ça a été dur de faire; **to be hard at ~** travailler dur; **it's thirsty ~** ça donne soif
2 (occupation) travail *m*; **to be in ~** avoir du travail *or* un emploi; **place of ~** lieu *m* de travail; **to be off ~** (on holiday) être en congé; **to be off ~ with flu** être en arrêt de travail parce qu'on a la grippe; **to be out of ~** être au chômage
3 (place of employment) **to go to ~** aller au travail
4 (building, construction) travaux *mpl* (**on** sur)
5 (essay, report) travail *m*; (artwork, novel, sculpture) œuvre *f* (**by** de); (study) ouvrage *m* (**by** de, **on** sur); (research) recherches *fpl* (**on** sur); **a ~ of reference** un ouvrage de référence; **a ~ of fiction** une œuvre de fiction; **the ~s of Racine** l'œuvre *m* de Racine; **this attack is the ~ of professionals** l'attaque est l'œuvre de professionnels
B **works** *npl* **1** (factory) usine *f*
2 (building work) travaux *mpl*
3 (fam) (everything) **the (full** *or* **whole) ~s** toute la panoplie (fam)
C *vt* **1** (drive) **to ~ sb hard** surmener qn
2 (labour) **to ~ days/nights** travailler de jour/de nuit; **to ~ a 40 hour week** faire la semaine de 40 heures; **he ~ed his way through college** il a travaillé pour payer ses études
3 (operate) se servir de ‹*computer, machine*›
4 (exploit commercially) exploiter ‹*mine, seam*›
5 (bring about) **to ~ wonders** *or* **miracles** faire des merveilles
6 (use to one's advantage) **to ~ the system** exploiter le système
7 (fashion) travailler ‹*clay, metal*›
8 (manoeuvre) **to ~ sth into** introduire qch dans ‹*slot, hole*›; **to ~ a lever up and down** actionner un levier
9 (exercise) faire travailler ‹*muscles*›
10 (move) **to ~ one's way through** se frayer un passage à travers ‹*crowd*›; **to ~ one's way along** avancer le long de ‹*ledge, window sill*›; **to ~ one's hands free** se libérer les mains; **it ~ed its way loose, it ~ed itself loose** cela s'est desserré peu à peu
D *vi* **1** (do a job) travailler (**doing** à faire); **to ~ for a living** gagner sa vie
2 (strive) lutter (**against** contre, **for** pour, **to do** pour faire); **to ~ towards** aller vers ‹*solution*›; s'acheminer vers ‹*compromise*›; négocier ‹*agreement*›
3 (function) fonctionner; **to ~ on electricity** marcher *or* fonctionner à l'électricité; **the washing machine isn't ~ing** la machine à laver est en panne
4 (act, operate) **it doesn't** *or* **things don't ~ like that** ça ne marche pas comme ça; **to ~ in sb's favour** tourner à l'avantage de qn; **to ~ against sb** jouer en la défaveur de qn
5 (be successful) ‹*treatment*› avoir de l'effet; ‹*detergent, drug*› agir (**against** contre, **on** sur); ‹*plan*› réussir; ‹*argument, theory*› tenir debout; **flattery won't ~ with me** la flatterie ne marche pas avec moi
6 ‹*face, features*› se contracter
IDIOMS **to ~ one's way up** gravir tous les échelons; **to ~ one's way up the company** faire son chemin dans l'entreprise
■ **work in**: **~ in [sth]**, **~ [sth] in 1** glisser ‹*joke*›; mentionner ‹*fact, name*›
2 (Culin) incorporer
■ **work off 1** (remove) retirer ‹*lid*›
2 (repay) travailler pour rembourser ‹*loan, debt*›
3 (get rid of) se débarrasser de ‹*excess weight*›; dépenser ‹*excess energy*›; passer ‹*anger, frustration*›
■ **work on**: **A** **~ on** continuer à travailler
B **~ on [sb]** travailler (fam) ‹*person*›
C **~ on [sth]** travailler à ‹*book, report*›; travailler sur ‹*project*›; s'occuper de ‹*case, problem*›; chercher ‹*cure, solution*›; examiner ‹*idea, theory*›
■ **work out** **A** **~ out 1** (exercise) s'entraîner
2 (go according to plan) marcher
3 (add up) **to ~ out at** (BrE) *or* **to** (AmE) s'élever à
B **~ [sth] out 1** (calculate) calculer ‹*amount*›
2 (solve) trouver ‹*answer, reason, culprit*›; résoudre ‹*problem*›; comprendre ‹*clue*›
3 (devise) concevoir ‹*plan, scheme*›; trouver ‹*route*›
C **~ [sb] out** comprendre ‹*person*›
■ **work up**: **A** **~ up [sth]** développer ‹*interest*›; accroître ‹*support*›; **to ~ up the courage to do** trouver le courage de faire; **to ~ up some enthusiasm for** s'enthousiasmer pour; **to ~ up an appetite** s'ouvrir l'appétit
B **~ up to [sth]** se préparer à ‹*confrontation, announcement*›
C **~ [sb] up 1** (excite) exciter ‹*child, crowd*›
2 (annoy) **to get ~ed up, to ~ oneself up** s'énerver

workable /ˈwɜːkəbl/ *adj* **1** ‹*idea, plan, suggestion*› réalisable; ‹*system*› pratique; ‹*arrangement, compromise*› possible
2 ‹*land, mine*› exploitable; ‹*cement*› maniable

workaholic /ˌwɜːkəˈhɒlɪk/ *n* (fam) bourreau *m* de travail

workbook *n* (blank) cahier *m*; (with exercises) livre *m* d'exercices

worker /ˈwɜːkə(r)/ *n* (in manual job) ouvrier/-ière *m/f*; (in white-collar job) employé/-e *m/f*

work experience *n* stage *m*

workforce *n* (in industry) main-d'œuvre *f*; (in service sector) effectifs *mpl*

working /'wɜːkɪŋ/ *adj* **1** ‹*parent, woman*› qui travaille; ‹*conditions, environment, methods*› de travail; ‹*population, life*› actif/-ive; ‹*breakfast, lunch, day*› de travail; **during ~ hours** (in office) pendant les heures de bureau; (in shop) pendant les heures d'ouverture
2 (provisional) ‹*document*› de travail; ‹*definition, title*› provisoire
3 (functional) ‹*model*› qui fonctionne; ‹*farm, mine*› en exploitation; **in full ~ order** en parfait état de marche

working class **A** *n* classe *f* ouvrière; **the ~es** les classes *fpl* laborieuses
B **working-class** *adj* ‹*area, background, family, life*› ouvrier/-ière; ‹*culture, London*› prolétarien/-ienne; ‹*person*› de la classe ouvrière

workings *npl* rouages *mpl*

workload /'wɜːkləʊd/ *n* charge *f* de travail

workman /'wɜːkmən/ *n* ouvrier *m*

workmanship /'wɜːkmənʃɪp/ *n* **a carpenter famous for sound ~** un menuisier connu pour la qualité de son travail; **furniture of the finest ~** des meubles d'une belle facture; **a piece of poor** *or* **shoddy ~** du travail mal fait *or* bâclé

workmate *n* collègue *mf* de travail

work of art *n* œuvre *f* d'art

workout *n* séance *f* de mise en forme

work pack *n* fiches *fpl* de travail

work permit *n* permis *m* de travail

workplace /'wɜːkpleɪs/ *n* lieu *m* de travail

work-sharing *n* partage *m* du travail

worksheet *n* (Sch) feuille *f* de questions

workshop /'wɜːkʃɒp/ *n* atelier *m*

workstation *n* poste *m* de travail

worktop *n* (BrE) plan *m* de travail

work to rule *n* grève *f* du zèle

world /wɜːld/ **A** *n* monde *m*; **throughout the ~** dans le monde entier; **to go round the ~** faire le tour du monde; **the biggest in the ~** le plus grand du monde; **more than anything in the ~** plus que tout au monde; **to go up in the ~** faire du chemin; **to go down in the ~** déchoir; **the Eastern/Western ~** les pays de l'Est/occidentaux; **the ancient ~** l'antiquité; **he lives in a ~ of his own** il vit dans un monde à part
B *adj* ‹*events, market, leader, politics, rights, scale*› mondial/-e; ‹*record, tour, championship*› du monde; ‹*cruise*› autour du monde
IDIOMS **to be on top of the ~** être aux anges; **to get the best of both ~s** gagner sur les deux tableaux; **a man/woman of the ~** un homme/une femme d'expérience; **out of this ~** extraordinaire; **there's a ~ of difference** il y a une différence énorme; **it did him the** *or* **a ~ of good** ça lui a fait énormément de bien; **to think the ~ of sb** penser le plus grand bien de qn; **what/where/who in the ~?** que/où/qui diable?; **~s apart** diamétralement opposé

world-class *adj* de niveau mondial

World Cup *n* Coupe *f* du Monde

World Fair *n* Exposition *f* universelle

world-famous *adj* mondialement connu/-e

world leader *n* **1** (politician) chef *m* d'État
2 (athlete) meilleur/-e *m/f* du monde; (company) leader *m* mondial

worldly /'wɜːldlɪ/ *adj* **1** (not spiritual) matériel/-ielle
2 (experienced) ‹*person*› avisé/-e, qui a de l'expérience

worldly-wise *adj* avisé/-e, qui a de l'expérience

world music *n* musiques *fpl* du monde

world power *n* puissance *f* mondiale

world view *n* vision *f* du monde

world war *n* guerre *f* mondiale; **the First/Second World War** la Première/Seconde Guerre mondiale

world-wide **A** *adj* mondial/-e
B *adv* dans le monde entier

World Wide Web *n* **the ~** la Toile *f* mondiale, le Web *m*

worm /wɜːm/ *n* ver *m*

worn /wɔːn/ *adj* ‹*carpet, clothing, shoe, tyre*› usé/-e; ‹*stone*› abîmé/-e; ‹*tread*› lisse

worn-out /ˌwɔːn'aʊt/ *adj* **1** ‹*carpet, brake*› complètement usé/-e
2 ‹*person*› épuisé/-e

worried /'wʌrɪd/ *adj* ‹*person, face*› inquiet/-iète; **to be ~ about sb/sth** se faire du souci *or* s'inquiéter pour qn/qch; **I'm ~ (that) he might get lost** j'ai peur qu'il ne se perde

worrier /'wʌrɪə(r)/ *n* anxieux/-ieuse *m/f*

worry /'wʌrɪ/ **A** *n* **1** (anxiety) soucis *mpl* (**about, over** à propos de)
2 (problem) souci *m* (**about, over** au sujet de)
B *vt* **1** (concern) inquiéter; **I ~ that he won't come** j'ai peur qu'il ne vienne pas; **it worried him that he couldn't find the keys** ça l'a inquiété de ne pas trouver les clés
2 (bother) ennuyer; **would it ~ you if I opened the window?** est-ce que ça vous ennuierait que j'ouvre la fenêtre?
3 ‹*dog*› harceler ‹*sheep*›
C *vi* (be anxious) s'inquiéter; **to ~ about** *or* **over sb/sth** s'inquiéter *or* se faire du souci pour qn/qch; **don't ~!** ne t'inquiète pas!; **there's nothing to ~ about** il n'y a pas lieu de s'inquiéter
D *v refl* **to ~ oneself** s'inquiéter, se faire du souci (**about sb** au sujet de qn, **about sth** à propos de qch); **to ~ oneself sick over sth** se ronger les sangs (fam) au sujet de qch
■ **worry at** ‹*dog*› mordiller, jouer avec ‹*toy*›;

mot clé

W

‹*person*› retourner [qch] dans tous les sens ‹*problem*›

worry beads *npl* chapelet *m* antistress

worrying /ˈwʌrɪɪŋ/ *adj* inquiétant/-e

worse /wɜːs/ **A** *adj* (*comparative of* **bad**) pire (**than** que); **to get ~** ‹*pressure, noise*› augmenter; ‹*conditions, weather*› empirer; ‹*illness, conflict*› s'aggraver; **he's getting ~** (in health) il va plus mal; **the cough is getting ~** la toux empire; **to feel ~** (more ill) se sentir plus malade; (more unhappy) aller moins bien; **and what is ~...** et le pire, c'est que...; **and to make matters ~, he lied** et pour ne rien arranger, il a menti
B *n* **there is ~ to come** ce n'est pas encore le pire; **to change for the ~** empirer
C *adv* (*comparative of* **badly**) ‹*play, sing*› moins bien (**than** que); **to behave ~** se conduire plus mal; **she could do ~ than follow his example** ce ne serait pas si mal si elle suivait son exemple

worsen /ˈwɜːsn/ **A** *vt* aggraver ‹*situation, problem*›
B *vi* ‹*condition, health, weather, situation*› se détériorer; ‹*problem, crisis, shortage, flooding*› s'aggraver

worsening /ˈwɜːsnɪŋ/ **A** *n* aggravation *f* (**of** de)
B *adj* ‹*situation*› en voie de détérioration; ‹*problem, shortage*› en voie d'aggravation

worse off *adj* **1** (less wealthy) **to be ~** avoir moins d'argent (**than** que); **I'm £10 a week ~** j'ai dix livres de moins par semaine
2 (in a worse situation) **to be ~** être dans une situation pire

worship /ˈwɜːʃɪp/ **A** *n* **1** (religious devotion) culte *m*; **sun/ancestor ~** culte du soleil/des ancêtres; **place of ~** lieu *m* de culte
2 (veneration) vénération *f*
B **W~** *pr n* (BrE) **Your Worship** (to judge) Monsieur le juge; (to mayor) Monsieur le maire
C *vt* (*p prés etc* **-pp-**) **1** (venerate) vénérer ‹*God, Buddha*›; (give praise to) rendre hommage à
2 adorer, avoir un culte pour ‹*person*›; avoir le culte de ‹*money, success*›
D *vi* (*p prés etc* **-pp-**) pratiquer sa religion

worshipper /ˈwɜːʃɪpə(r)/ *n* fidèle *mf*

worst /wɜːst/ **A** *n* **1** (most difficult, unpleasant) **the ~** le/la pire *m/f*; **if the ~ came to the ~** (in serious circumstances) dans le pire des cas; (involving fatality) si le pire devait arriver
2 (most negative trait) **to bring out the ~ in sb** mettre à jour ce qu'il y a de plus mauvais chez qn
3 (of the lowest standard, quality) **the ~** le plus mauvais/la plus mauvaise *m/f*; **he's one of the ~** c'est un des plus mauvais; **to be the ~ at French** être le plus mauvais en français
B *adj* (*superlative of* **bad**) **1** (most unsatisfactory, unpleasant) pire, plus mauvais/-e; **the ~ book I've ever read** le plus mauvais livre que j'aie jamais lu; **the ~ thing about the film is...** ce qu'il y a de pire dans le film c'est...
2 (most serious) plus grave; **one of the ~ recessions** une des crises les plus graves
C *adv* **the children suffer (the) ~** ce sont les enfants qui souffrent le plus; **they were (the) ~ hit by the strike** ce sont eux qui ont été les plus touchés par la grève; **~ of all,...** le pire de tout, c'est que...

worth /wɜːθ/ **A** *n* **1** (quantity) **five pounds' ~ of sth** pour cinq livres de qch; **thousands of pounds' ~ of damage** des milliers de livres de dégâts; **a week's ~ of supplies** une semaine de provisions; **to get one's money's ~** en avoir pour son argent
2 (value) valeur *f*; **of great ~** de grande valeur; **of no ~** sans valeur
B *adj* **1** (of financial value) **to be ~ sth** valoir qch; **how much is it ~?** combien cela vaut-il?; **the pound was ~ 10 francs then** à l'époque, la livre valait 10 francs
2 (of abstract value) **to be ~ sth** valoir qch; **to be ~ it** (en) valoir la peine; **the book isn't ~ reading** le livre ne vaut pas la peine d'être lu; **that's ~ knowing** cela est bon à savoir; **those little pleasures that make life ~ living** ces petits plaisirs qui rendent la vie agréable
IDIOMS **for all one is ~** de toutes ses forces; **for what it's ~** pour ce que cela vaut; **to be ~ sb's while** valoir le coup

worthless /ˈwɜːθlɪs/ *adj* sans valeur; **he's ~** c'est un bon à rien

worthwhile /wɜːθˈwaɪl/ *adj* ‹*discussion, undertaking, visit*› qui en vaut la peine; ‹*career, project*› intéressant/-e; **to be ~ doing** valoir la peine de faire

worthy /ˈwɜːðɪ/ *adj* **1** (deserving) **to be ~ of sth** mériter qch, être digne de qch; **~ of note** digne d'intérêt; **to be ~ of doing** ‹*person*› être digne de faire
2 (admirable) ‹*cause*› noble; ‹*citizen, friend*› digne

would /wʊd, wəd/ *modal aux* **1** (expressing the conditional) **it ~ be nice if everyone were there, wouldn't it?** ce serait bien si tout le monde était là, n'est-ce pas?; **if he had more money, he'd buy a car** s'il avait plus d'argent il achèterait une voiture; **we ~ have missed the train if we had left later** si nous étions partis plus tard, nous aurions raté le train; **we wouldn't have succeeded without him** nous n'aurions pas réussi sans lui
2 (in indirect statements or questions) **we thought he'd forget** nous pensions qu'il oublierait; **did she say she ~ be coming?** est-ce qu'elle a dit qu'elle viendrait?; **I wish he ~ be quiet!** il ne pourrait pas se taire!
3 (expressing willingness to act) **she wouldn't listen to me** elle ne voulait pas m'écouter; **he wouldn't do a thing to help us** il n'a rien voulu faire pour nous aider; **they asked me to leave but I wouldn't** ils m'ont demandé

de partir mais j'ai refusé; **of course you ~ contradict him!** bien sûr il a fallu que tu le contredises!
4 (in requests) **~ you give her the message?** est-ce que vous voulez bien lui transmettre le message?; **switch off the radio, ~ you?** éteins la radio, tu veux bien?; **~ you excuse me for a moment?** excusez-moi un instant
5 (expressing one's wishes) **~ you like something to eat?** désirez-vous *or* voulez-vous manger quelque chose?; **I ~ like a beer** je voudrais une bière; **we ~ like to stay another night** nous aimerions rester une nuit de plus; **she'd have liked to stay here** elle aurait aimé rester ici; **I wouldn't mind another slice of cake** je prendrais bien un autre morceau de gâteau
6 (offering advice) **if I were you, I wouldn't say anything** à ta place, je ne dirais rien; **it ~ be better to write** il vaudrait mieux écrire; **it ~ be a good idea to wait** ce serait une bonne idée d'attendre; **you ~ do well to check the timetable** tu ferais bien de vérifier l'horaire
7 (in assumptions) **I ~ have been 12** je devais avoir 12 ans; **it ~ have been about midday** il devait être à peu près midi
8 (used to) **she ~ talk for hours** elle parlait pendant des heures

would-be /'wʊdbiː/ *adj* **1** (desirous of being) **~ emigrants/investors** personnes *fpl or* ceux qui désirent émigrer/investir
2 (so-called) **~ intellectuals** les soi-disant intellectuels *mpl*
3 (having intended to be) **the ~ thieves were arrested** les voleurs ont été arrêtés avant qu'ils aient pu passer à l'acte

wound **A** *n* **1** (injury) blessure *f*; (cut) plaie *f*; **bullet ~** blessure par balle; **knife ~** coup *m* de couteau; **a ~ to** *or* **in the head** une blessure à la tête
2 (fig) blessure *f*
B *vt* blesser
IDIOMS **to lick one's ~s** panser ses blessures; **to rub salt into the ~** remuer le couteau dans la plaie

wounded /'wuːndɪd/ **A** *n* **the ~** les blessés/blessées *m/fpl*
B *adj* blessé/-e; **~ in the arm** blessé au bras

wrangle /'ræŋgl/ **A** *n* querelle *f*
B *vi* se quereller (**over, about** sur, à propos de, **with** avec)

🔑 **wrap** /ræp/ **A** *n* (shawl) châle *m*; (stole) étole *f*
B *vt* (*p prés etc* **-pp-**) (in paper) emballer (**in** dans); (in blanket, garment) envelopper (**in** dans); **to be ~ped in** être emmitouflé/-e dans ‹*blanket*›; être enveloppé/-e dans ‹*newspaper*›; être enveloppé/-e de ‹*mystery*›
IDIOM **to keep sth/to be under ~s** garder qch/être secret/-ète
■ **wrap up**: **A** **~ up** se couvrir; **~ up well** *or* **warm!** couvre-toi bien!
B **~ [sth] up 1** faire ‹*parcel*›; envelopper ‹*gift, purchase*›; emballer ‹*rubbish*›
2 to be ~ped up in ne s'occuper que de ‹*person, child*›; être absorbé/-e dans ‹*activity, work*›; **they are completely ~ped up in each other** ils ne vivent que l'un pour l'autre
3 dissimuler ‹*meaning, facts, ideas*› (**in** derrière)

wraparound *adj* ‹*window, windscreen*› panoramique; ‹*skirt*› portefeuille

wraparound sunglasses *npl* lunettes *fpl* de soleil enveloppantes

wrap-over *adj* ‹*skirt*› portefeuille; ‹*dress*› croisé/-e

wrapper /'ræpə(r)/ *n* (of sweet) papier *m*

wrapping /'ræpɪŋ/ *n* emballage *m*

wrapping paper *n* (brown) papier *m* d'emballage; (decorative) papier *m* cadeau

wreak /riːk/ *vt* assouvir ‹*revenge*› (**on** sur); **to ~ havoc** *or* **damage** infliger des dégâts; **to ~ havoc** *or* **damage on sth** dévaster qch

wreath /riːθ/ *n* couronne *f*; **to lay a ~** déposer une gerbe

wreck /rek/ **A** *n* **1** (car, plane) (crashed) épave *f*; (burnt out) carcasse *f*
2 (sunken ship) épave *f*
3 (person) épave *f*
B *vt* **1** ‹*explosion, fire, vandals*› dévaster ‹*building, machinery*›; ‹*person, driver, impact*› détruire ‹*vehicle*›
2 ruiner ‹*career, chances, health, life, marriage*›; gâcher ‹*holiday, weekend*›

wreckage /'rekɪdʒ/ *n* **1** (of plane, car, ship) épave *f*; (of building) décombres *mpl*
2 (of hopes, plans) naufrage *m*

wrecked /rekt/ *adj* **1** ‹*car, plane*› accidenté/-e; ‹*ship*› naufragé/-e; ‹*building*› démoli/-e
2 ‹*life, career, marriage*› ruiné/-e

wren /ren/ *n* roitelet *m*

wrench /rentʃ/ **A** *n* **1** (BrE) (adjustable spanner) tourne-à-gauche *m inv*; (AmE) (spanner) clé *f* de serrage
2 (emotional upheaval) déchirement *m*
B *vt* tirer violemment sur ‹*handle*›; **to ~ one's ankle/knee** se tordre la cheville/le genou; **to ~ sth from sb** arracher qch à qn; **to ~ sth away from sth** arracher qch de qch

wrestle /'resl/ **A** *vt* **to ~ sb for sth** lutter contre qn pour qch; **to ~ sb to the ground** terrasser qn
B *vi* **1** (Sport) faire du catch
2 (struggle) **to ~ with** se débattre avec ‹*person, problem, homework, conscience*›; se battre avec ‹*controls, zip, suitcase*›; lutter contre ‹*temptation*›

wrestler /'reslə(r)/ *n* catcheur/-euse *m/f*

wrestling /'reslɪŋ/ *n* catch *m*

wretched /'retʃɪd/ *adj* ‹*person*› infortuné/-e; ‹*existence, appearance, conditions*› misérable; ‹*weather*›

🔑 mot clé

affreux/-euse; ‹*accommodation*› minable; ‹*amount*› dérisoire

wriggle /ˈrɪgl/ **A** *vt* **to ~ one's toes/fingers** remuer les orteils/doigts; **to ~ one's way out of sth** se sortir de qch
B *vi* ‹*person*› s'agiter, gigoter; ‹*snake, worm*› se tortiller; ‹*fish*› frétiller; **to ~ out of** se défiler devant ‹*duty, task*›

wring /rɪŋ/ *vt* (*prét, pp* **wrung**) **1** (*also* **~ out**) essorer ‹*clothes, cloth*›
2 (extract) arracher ‹*confession, money*› (**from, out of** à)
3 (twist) **to ~ sb's/sth's neck** tordre le cou à qn/qch; **to ~ one's hands** se tordre les mains; (fig) se lamenter

wrinkle /ˈrɪŋkl/ **A** *n* (on skin) ride *f*; (in fabric) pli *m*
B *vt* **1** rider ‹*skin*›; **to ~ one's nose** faire la grimace (**at** devant)
2 froisser ‹*fabric*›
C *vi* ‹*skin*› se rider; ‹*fabric*› se froisser; ‹*wallpaper*› gondoler

wrist /rɪst/ *n* poignet *m*

wristband *n* (for tennis, on sleeve) poignet *m*

wristwatch *n* montre-bracelet *f*

writ /rɪt/ *n* assignation *f* (**for** pour); **to issue** *or* **serve a ~ against sb, to serve sb with a ~** assigner qn en justice

write /raɪt/ **A** *vt* (*pp* **written**) **1** écrire ‹*letter, poem, novel*› (**to** à); composer ‹*song, symphony*›; rédiger ‹*business letter, article, report, prescription*›; faire ‹*cheque*›; écrire ‹*software, program*›; élaborer ‹*legislation*›; **he wrote me a cheque for £100** il m'a fait un chèque de 100 livres sterling; **I wrote home** j'ai écrit à ma famille
2 (AmE) écrire à ‹*person*›
B *vi* (*pp* **written**) écrire (**to sb** à qn)
■ **write back** répondre (**to** à)
■ **write down** noter ‹*details, name*›; mettre [qch] par écrit ‹*ideas, suggestions*›; consigner [qch] par écrit ‹*information, findings*›
■ **write off**: **A ~ off** écrire une lettre (**to** à); **to ~ off for** écrire pour demander
B ~ [sth] off 1 (wreck) bousiller complètement (fam) ‹*car*›
2 (in bookkeeping) passer [qch] aux pertes et profits ‹*bad debt, loss*›; amortir ‹*capital*›
3 (end) annuler ‹*debt, project, operation*›
■ **write out 1** (put down on paper) écrire
2 (copy) copier

write-off /ˈraɪtɒf/ *n* **1** (AmE) (in taxation) somme *f* déductible de la déclaration des revenus
2 (wreck) épave *f*

write protect *n* (Comput) protection *f* en mode écriture

writer /ˈraɪtə(r)/ *n* (author) (professional) écrivain *m*; (non-professional) auteur *m*

writer's block *n* l'angoisse *f* de la page blanche

write-up /ˈraɪtʌp/ *n* **1** (review) critique *f*
2 (account) rapport *m* (**of** sur)

writhe /raɪð/ *vi* (*also* **~ about, ~ around**) se tortiller; **to ~ in agony** se tordre de douleur

writing /ˈraɪtɪŋ/ *n* **1** (activity) **~ is her life** écrire, c'est sa vie
2 (handwriting) écriture *f*; **his ~ is poor/good** il écrit mal/bien
3 (words and letters) écriture *f*; **to put sth in ~** mettre qch par écrit
4 (literature) littérature *f*

writing pad *n* bloc *m* de papier à lettres

writing paper *n* papier *m* à lettres

writing table *n* bureau *m*

written /ˈrɪtn/ *adj* ‹*reply, guarantee, proof*› écrit/-e; **he failed the ~ paper** il a échoué à l'écrit; **~ evidence** *or* **proof** (Law) preuves *fpl* écrites; **the ~ word** l'écriture *f*

wrong /rɒŋ, (AmE) rɔːŋ/ **A** *n* **1** (evil) mal *m*
2 (injustice) tort *m*; **to right a ~** réparer un tort
B *adj* **1** (incorrect) faux/fausse *before n*; (ill-chosen) mauvais/-e *before n*; **he took the ~ key** il a pris la mauvaise clé; **it's the ~ glue for the purpose** ce n'est pas la colle qu'il faut; **to go the ~ way** se tromper de chemin; **I dialled the ~ number** je me suis trompé de numéro, j'ai fait un faux *or* mauvais numéro; **you've got the ~ number** vous faites erreur
2 (reprehensible, unjust) **it is ~ to cheat** c'est mal de tricher; **she hasn't done anything ~** elle n'a rien fait de mal; **it was ~ of me to do** je n'aurais pas dû faire; **it is ~ that** c'est injuste que; **there's nothing ~ with** *or* **in sth** il n'y a pas de mal à qch; **(so) what's ~ with that?** où est le mal?
3 (mistaken) **to be ~** ‹*person*› avoir tort, se tromper; **to be ~ about** se tromper sur; **she was ~ about him** elle s'est trompée sur son compte; **to prove sb ~** donner tort à qn
4 (not as it should be) **there is something (badly) ~** il y a quelque chose qui ne va pas (du tout); **there's something ~ with this computer** il y a un problème avec cet ordinateur; **the wording is all ~** la formulation ne va pas du tout; **what's ~ with your arm?** qu'est-ce que tu as au bras?; **what's ~ with you?** (to person suffering) qu'est-ce que tu as?; (to person behaving oddly) qu'est-ce qui t'arrive?; **your clock is ~** votre pendule n'est pas à l'heure
C *adv* **to get [sth] ~** se tromper de ‹*date, time, details*›; se tromper dans ‹*calculations*›; **I think you've got it ~** je pense que tu te trompes; **to go ~** ‹*person*› se tromper; ‹*machine*› ne plus marcher
D *vt* faire du tort à ‹*person, family*›
IDIOMS **to be in the ~** être dans mon/ton etc tort; **to get on the ~ side of sb** se faire mal voir de qn; **to go down the ~ way** ‹*food, drink*› passer de travers

wrongdoer *n* malfaiteur *m*

wrong-foot *vt* (Sport) prendre [qn] à contre-pied; (fig) prendre [qn] au dépourvu

wrongly /ˈrɒŋlɪ, (AmE) ˈrɔːŋ-/ *adv* mal; **he concluded, ~, that...** il a conclu, à tort, que...; **rightly or ~** à tort ou à raison
wrought /rɔːt/ *adj* ‹*silver, gold*› travaillé/-e
wrought iron *n* fer *m* forgé
wry /raɪ/ *adj* ‹*smile, look, humour*› narquois/-e; **to have a ~ sense of humour** être pince-sans-rire
WTO (*abbr* = **World Trade Organization**) OMC *f*

Xx

x, X /eks/ *n* **1** (letter) x, X *m*
2 (standing for number, name) **for x people** pour x personnes; **Ms X** Mme X; **X marks the spot** l'endroit est marqué d'une croix
3 (kisses ending letter) grosses bises
X certificate *adj* ‹*film*› interdit/-e aux moins de 18 ans
xenophobia /ˌzenəˈfəʊbɪə/ *n* xénophobie *f*
xerox® /ˈzɪərɒks/ *vt* photocopier
Xmas *n* Noël *m*
X-rated *adj* ‹*film, video*› interdit/-e aux moins de 18 ans
X-ray /ˈeksreɪ/ **A** *n* **1** (ray) rayon *m* X
2 (photo) radiographie *f*, radio *f* (fam); **to have an ~** se faire radiographier; **to give sb an ~** faire une radiographie à qn
B *vt* radiographier
X-ray unit *n* service *m* de radiologie

Yy

y, Y /waɪ/ *n* y, Y *m*
yacht /jɒt/ *n* yacht *m*
yachting /ˈjɒtɪŋ/ *n* yachting *m*; **to go ~** faire du yachting
yachtsman *n* yachtman *m*
yahoo /jəˈhuː/ **A** *n* abruti/-e *m* (fam)
B *excl* hourra!
yak /jæk/ *n* yack *m*
Yale lock® *n* serrure *f* de sûreté
yam /jæm/ *n* igname *f*
yank /jæŋk/ **A** *n* (derog) coup *m* sec; **to give sth a ~** tirer qch d'un coup sec
B *vt* tirer ‹*person, rope*›
▪ **yank out** arracher
Yank /jæŋk/ *n* yankee *mf*
Yankee /ˈjæŋkɪ/ *n* (derog) yankee *m*
yap /jæp/ **A** *n* jappement *m*
B *vi* ‹*dog*› japper (**at** après)
yapping /ˈjæpɪŋ/ **A** *n* jappements *mpl*
B *adj* ‹*dog*› jappeur/-euse
🔑 **yard** /jɑːd/ *n* **1** yard *m* (= *0.9144 m*)
2 (of house, farm, prison, hospital) cour *f*
3 (AmE) (garden) jardin *m*
4 (for storage) dépôt *m*; (for construction) chantier *m*; **builder's ~** dépôt *m* de matériaux de construction
yardarm *n* bout *m* de vergue
yardstick *n* (fig) critères *mpl*
yarn /jɑːn/ *n* **1** (fibre) fibre *f* textile; (wool) laine *f*
2 (tale) histoire *f*; **to spin a ~** raconter des histoires
yashmak /ˈjæʃmæk/ *n* voile *m* islamique
yawn /jɔːn/ **A** *n* bâillement *m*; **to give a ~** bâiller
B *vi* **1** ‹*person*› bâiller
2 ‹*abyss, chasm*› béer
🔑 **yeah** /jeə/ *particle* (fam) ouais (fam), oui; **oh ~?** vraiment?
🔑 **year** /jɪə(r), jɜː(r)/ **A** *n* **1** (period of time) an *m*; (with emphasis on duration) année *f*; **in the ~ 1789/2000** en 1789/l'an 2000; **two ~s ago** il y a deux ans; **all (the) ~ round** toute

🔑 mot clé

l'année; **every ~** tous les ans; **over the ~s** au cours des ans *or* des années; **the ~ before last** il y a deux ans; **every ~** tous les ans; **they have been living in Paris for ~s** ils habitent Paris depuis des années; **for the first time in ~s** pour la première fois depuis des années; **it's a ~ since I heard from him** je n'ai plus de ses nouvelles depuis un an; **they lived in Paris for ~s** ils ont habité Paris pendant des années; **to earn £30,000 a ~** gagner 30 000 livres sterling par an
2 (indicating age) **to be 19 ~s old** *or* **19 ~s of age** avoir 19 ans; **a two-~-old child** un enfant de deux ans
3 (pupil) **first/second-~** ≈ élève *mf* de sixième/cinquième
B **~s** *npl* (fam) (a long time) **that would take ~s!** ça prendrait une éternité!; **it's ~s since we last met!** ça fait un siècle qu'on ne s'est pas vus!
IDIOM **this job has put ~s on me!** ce travail m'a vieilli de 10 ans!

yearbook /'jɪəbʊk, 'jɜː-/ *n* **1** (directory) annuaire *m*
2 (AmE) album *m* de promotion

year-long *adj* ‹*stay, course, absence*› d'un an, d'une année

yearly /'jɪəlɪ, 'jɜː-/ **A** *adj* ‹*visit, account, income*› annuel/-elle
B *adv* annuellement

yearn /jɜːn/ *vi* **1 to ~ for** désirer (avoir) ‹*child*›; aspirer à ‹*freedom, unity*›; attendre ‹*season, event*›; **to ~ to do** avoir très envie de faire
2 (miss) **she ~s for her son** son fils lui manque terriblement

yearning /'jɜːnɪŋ/ **A** *n* désir *m* ardent (**for** de, **to do** de faire)
B **yearnings** *npl* aspirations *fpl*
C *adj* ‹*expression*› plein/-e de désir

year out *n: année d'interruption des études entre le lycée et l'université*

year tutor *n: professeur responsable de toutes les classes d'un même niveau*

yeast /jiːst/ *n* levure *f*

yell /jel/ **A** *n* (shout) cri *m*; (of rage, pain) hurlement *m*
B *vt* crier ‹*warning*›; (louder) hurler ‹*insults*›
C *vi* crier; **to ~ at sb** crier après qn

yelling /'jelɪŋ/ *n* cris *mpl*

yellow /'jeləʊ/ **A** *n* jaune *m*
B *adj* **1** (in colour) jaune; **to go** *or* **turn ~** jaunir
2 (fam) (cowardly) trouillard/-e (fam)
C *vi* jaunir

yellow-belly *n* (fam) trouillard/-e *m/f* (fam)

yellow card *n* (Sport) carton *m* jaune

yellowish /'jeləʊwɪʃ/ *adj* tirant sur le jaune; (unpleasantly) jaunâtre

Yellow Pages® *npl* pages *fpl* jaunes

yelp /jelp/ **A** *n* glapissement *m*
B *vi* glapir

Yemen /'jemən/ *pr n* Yémen *m*

yen /jen/ *n* **1** (currency) yen *m*
2 (fam) (craving) **to have a ~ for sth/to do** avoir grande envie de qch/de faire

yeoman /'jəʊmən/ *n* (*pl* **-men**) (*also* **~ farmer**) franc tenancier *m*

yeoman of the guard *n* (BrE) membre *m* de la garde royale

yep, yup /jep/ *particle* (AmE) (fam) ouais (fam), oui

yes /jes/ *particle* oui; (in reply to negative question) si

> *yes* is translated by *oui*, except when used in reply to a negative question in which case the translation is *si* or, more emphatically, *mais si*: *'did you see him?'—'yes (I did)'* = 'est-ce que tu l'as vu?'—'oui (je l'ai vu)'; *'you're not hungry, are you?'—'yes I am'* = 'tu n'as pas faim?'—'si (j'ai faim)'.
> Note that there are no direct equivalents in French for tag questions and short replies such as *yes I did, yes I am*.
> For some suggestions on how to translate these, see **do**.

yes-man /'jesmæn/ *n* (*pl* **-men**) (fam) lèche-bottes *m inv*

yesterday /'jestədeɪ, -dɪ/ **A** *n* hier *m*; **~'s newspaper** le journal d'hier; **~ was a sad day for all of us** la journée d'hier a été triste pour nous tous; **~ was the fifth of April** hier nous étions le cinq avril; **the day before ~** avant-hier
B *adv* hier; **only ~** pas plus tard qu'hier; **all day ~** toute la journée d'hier

yesterday afternoon *n, adv* hier après-midi

yesterday evening *n, adv* hier soir

yesterday morning *n, adv* hier matin

yesteryear /'jestəjɪə(r)/ *n* temps *m* jadis; **the fashions of ~** la mode d'antan *or* du temps jadis

yes vote *n* oui *m*

yet /jet/ **A** *conj* pourtant
B *adv* **1** (up till now, so far) encore; (in questions) déjà; (with superlatives) jusqu'ici; **it's not ready ~** ce n'est pas encore prêt; **has he arrived ~?** est-il (déjà) arrivé?; **not ~** pas encore, pas pour l'instant; **it's the best ~** jusqu'ici, c'est le meilleur
2 (*also* **just ~**) tout de suite, encore; **don't start ~** ne commence pas tout de suite
3 (still) encore; **they may ~ come** ils pourraient encore arriver; **he'll finish it ~** il va le finir; **he won't come for hours ~** il ne viendra pas avant quelques heures
4 (even, still) encore; **~ more cars** encore plus de voitures; **~ another attack** encore une autre attaque; **~ again** encore une fois

yew /juː/ *n* (*also* **~ tree**) if *m*

Y-fronts *npl* (BrE) slip *m* ouvert

YHA *n* (BrE) (*abbr* = **Youth Hostels Association**) association *f* des auberges de jeunesse

yield /jiːld/ **A** *n* rendement *m*
B *vt* **1** (produce) produire
2 (provide) donner, fournir ‹*result, meaning*›; fournir ‹*clue*›
3 (surrender) céder (**to** à); **to ~ ground** (fig) céder du terrain
C *vi* **1** (to person, temptation, pressure, threats) céder (**to** à)
2 (under weight, physical pressure) céder (**under** sous)
3 (be superseded) **to ~ to** ‹*technology, phenomenon*› céder le pas à
4 (AmE) (driving) céder le passage

yob, **yobbo** /ˈjɒb/ *n* (BrE) loubard *m* (fam), voyou *m*

yodel /ˈjəʊdl/ *vi* (*p prés etc* **-ll-** (BrE), **-l-** (AmE)) jodler, iodler

yoga /ˈjəʊɡə/ *n* yoga *m*

yoghurt /ˈjɒɡət, (AmE) ˈjəʊɡərt/ *n* yaourt *m*, yoghourt *m*

yo-heave-ho /jəʊhiːvˈhəʊ/ *excl* oh! hisse!

yoke /jəʊk/ **A** *n* joug *m*
B *vt* (*also* **~ up**) atteler

yokel /ˈjəʊkl/ *n* péquenaud/-e *m/f* (fam), plouc *mf* (fam)

yolk /jəʊk/ *n* jaune *m* (d'œuf)

yonks /jɒŋks/ *npl* (BrE) (fam) **I haven't seen him for ~** ça fait une éternité que je ne l'ai pas vu

⚷ **you** /juː, jʊ/ *pron*

> In French *you* has two forms: *tu* and *vous*. The usual word to use to anyone you do not know very well is *vous*, also called the polite form: *can I help you?* = est-ce que je peux vous aider? The more informal *tu* (plural *vous*) is used between close friends and family members, within groups of children and young people, and by adults when talking to children: *there's a biscuit for you* = il y a un biscuit pour toi. If in doubt, use the *vous* form.

1 (subject) tu, vous; (object) te, t', vous; (with prepositions, for emphasis) toi, vous; you **would never do that** (polite) vous, vous ne feriez jamais cela; (informal) toi, tu ne ferais jamais ça; **~ English** vous autres Anglais; **~ idiot!** (fam) espèce d'imbécile! (fam); **~ two can stay** vous deux, vous pouvez rester **2** (as indefinite pronoun) (subject) on; (object, indirect object) vous, te; **~ never know!** on ne sait jamais!; **it makes ~ sleepy** ça fait dormir

you-know-what *pron* (fam) vous-savez-quoi/tu-sais-quoi

you-know-who *pron* (fam) qui-vous-savez/qui-tu-sais

⚷ **young** /jʌŋ/ **A** *n* **1** (young people) **the ~** les jeunes *mpl*, la jeunesse *f*
2 (animal's offspring) petits *mpl*
B *adj* (not very old) jeune; **to be ~ at heart** avoir l'esprit jeune; **she is ten years ~er than him** elle a dix ans de moins que lui; **I feel ten years ~er** j'ai l'impression d'avoir rajeuni de dix ans; **~ lady** jeune femme *f*; **~ people** jeunes gens *mpl*; **~ person** jeune *m*; **the ~er generation** la jeune génération; **her ~er brother** son frère cadet; **I'm not as ~ as I used to be** je n'ai plus 20 ans

young blood *n* sang *m* neuf

youngish /ˈjʌŋɪʃ/ *adj* assez jeune

young-looking *adj* **to be ~** faire (très) jeune

young offender *n* délinquant/-e *m/f*

young professional *n* jeune salarié/-e *m/f*

youngster /ˈjʌŋstə(r)/ *n* **1** (young person) jeune *m*
2 (child) enfant *mf*

⚷ **your** /jɔː(r), jʊə(r)/

> For a full note on the use of the *vous* and *tu* forms in French, see the entry **you**.
> In French, determiners agree in gender and number with the noun that follows: *your* + masculine singular noun = *ton, votre* (*your dog* ton/votre chien); *your* + feminine singular noun = *ta, votre* (*your house* ta/votre maison); *your* + plural noun = *tes, vos* (*your parents* tes/vos parents).

det **1** votre/vos; (more informally) ton/ta/tes
2 (used impersonally) son, sa, ses; **you buy ~ tickets at the door** on prend ses billets à l'entrée; **smoking is bad for ~ health** le tabac est mauvais pour la santé
3 (for emphasis) à vous, à toi; **your house** votre maison à vous/ta maison à toi

yours /jɔːz, (AmE) jʊərz/ *pron*

> For a full note on the use of the *vous* and *tu* forms in French, see the boxed note for the entry **you**.
> In French, possessive pronouns reflect the gender and number of the noun they are standing for. When *yours* is referring to only one person, it is translated by *le vôtre, la vôtre, les vôtres*, or more informally *le tien, la tienne, les tiens, les tiennes*. When *yours* is referring to more than one person, it is translated by *le vôtre, la vôtre, les vôtres*.

my car is red but ~ is blue ma voiture est rouge mais la vôtre/la tienne est bleue; **her children are older than ~** ses enfants sont plus âgés que les vôtres *or* les tiens; **which house is ~?** votre/ta maison c'est laquelle?; **he's a colleague of ~** c'est un de vos/tes collègues; **it's not ~** ce n'est pas à vous/toi; **the money wasn't ~ to give away** vous n'aviez pas à donner cet argent

⚷ **yourself** /jɔːˈself, (AmE) jʊərˈself/ *pron*

> For a full note on the use of the *vous* and *tu* forms in French, see the entry **you**.
> When used as a reflexive pronoun, direct and indirect, *yourself* is translated by *vous*

y

or familiarly *te* (or *t'* before a vowel or mute 'h'): *you've hurt yourself* = vous vous êtes fait mal/tu t'es fait mal.
In imperatives, the translation is *vous* or *toi*: *help yourself* = servez-vous/sers-toi. (Note the hyphens).
When used for emphasis, the translation is *vous-même/toi-même*: *you yourself don't know* = vous ne savez pas vous-même/tu ne sais pas toi-même.

1 (reflexive) vous, te, t'; **have you hurt ~?** est-ce que tu t'es fait mal? **2** (in imperatives) vous, toi **3** (emphatic) vous-même, toi-même; **you ~ said that...** vous avez dit vous-même que.../tu as dit toi-même que... **4** (after prepositions) vous, vous-même, toi, toi-même **5** (expressions) **(all) by ~** tout seul/toute seule; **you're not ~ today** tu n'as pas l'air dans ton assiette aujourd'hui

yourselves /-'selvz/ *pron*

When used as a reflexive pronoun, direct and indirect, *yourselves* is translated by *vous*: *help yourselves* = servez-vous.
When used for emphasis, the translation is *vous-mêmes*: *do it yourselves* = faites-le vous-mêmes.

1 (reflexive) vous; **help ~** servez-vous **2** (emphatic) vous-mêmes **3** (after prepositions) vous, vous-mêmes; **all by ~** tous seuls/toutes seules

✓ **youth** /ju:θ/ *n* (*pl* **~s** /ju:ðz/) **1** (young man) jeune homme *m*; **a gang of ~s** une bande de jeunes gens
2 (period, state of being young) jeunesse *f*; **because of his ~** à cause de son jeune âge
3 (young people) jeunes *mpl*

youth club *n* centre *m* de jeunes

youthful /'ju:θfl/ *adj* **1** (young) jeune **2** (typical of youth) **his ~ looks** son air jeune

youth hostel *n* auberge *f* de jeunesse

youth hostelling *n* logement *m* en auberge de jeunesse

youth work *n* travail *m* social auprès des jeunes

youth worker *n* éducateur/-trice *m/f*

yowl /jaʊl/ *vi* ‹*person, dog*› hurler; ‹*cat*› miauler; ‹*baby*› brailler

yo-yo *n* yo-yo *m*

yuck /jʌk/ *excl* (BrE) berk (fam) !

yucky /'jʌkɪ/ *adj* (BrE) dégoûtant/-e

Yugoslavia /ju:gəʊ'slɑ:vɪə/ *pr n* Yougoslavie *f*

Yule log *n* bûche *f* de Noël

yummy /'jʌmɪ/ (fam) **A** *adj* délicieux/-ieuse **B** *excl* miam-miam (fam)

yuppie /'jʌpɪ/ **A** *n* jeune cadre *m* dynamique
B *adj* ‹*image, style, fashion*› de jeune cadre dynamique

Zz

z, Z /zed, (AmE) zi:/ *n* z, Z *m*

zany /'zeɪnɪ/ *adj* loufoque (fam)

zap /zæp/ (fam) **A** *excl* paf!
B *vt* (*p prés etc* **-pp-**) **1** (destroy) détruire ‹*town*›; tuer ‹*person, animal*›
2 (fire at) tirer sur ‹*person*›
3 (delete from computer screen) supprimer
C *vi* (*p prés etc* **-pp-**) **to ~ into town/a shop** faire un saut (fam) en ville/dans un magasin; **to ~ from channel to channel** zapper (fam)

zapper /'zæpə(r)/ *n* (fam) (TV remote control) télécommande *f*

zeal /zi:l/ *n* **1** (fanaticism) zèle *m*; (religious) ferveur *f*
2 (enthusiasm) ardeur *f*, zèle *m*

zealot /'zelət/ *n* fanatique *mf*

zebra /'zebrə, 'zi:-/ *n* zèbre *m*

zebra crossing *n* (BrE) passage *m* (protégé) pour piétons

zenith /'zenɪθ/ *n* (fig) apogée *m*

zero /'zɪərəʊ/ **A** *n* zéro *m*
B *adj* ‹*altitude, growth, inflation, voltage*› zéro *inv*; ‹*confidence, interest, involvement, development*› nul/nulle; **sub-~ temperatures** des températures *fpl* en dessous de zéro
■ **zero in**: **to ~ in on [sth]** (Mil) viser ‹*target*›; (fig) cerner ‹*problem*›; foncer droit sur ‹*person*›; repérer ‹*place*›

zero-carbon *adj* sans émission de CO2; **~ homes** logements *mpl* sans émission de CO2

zero-emission *adj* propre, sans émission de co2; **~ car** voiture *f* propre

zero hour *n* heure *f* H

zest /zest/ *n* (enthusiasm) entrain *m*; **his ~ for life** sa joie *f* de vivre

zigzag /'zɪgzæg/ **A** *n* zigzag *m*
B *adj* ‹*design, pattern*› à zigzags; ‹*route, road*› en zigzag
C *vi* (*p prés etc* **-gg-**) ‹*person, vehicle, road*›

zigzaguer; ‹*river, path*› serpenter; **to ~ up/down** monter/descendre en zigzag

zilch /zɪltʃ/ *n* (fam) que dalle (pop)

Zimmer® /'zɪmə(r)/ *n* déambulateur *m*

zing /zɪŋ/ *n* (fam) (energy) entrain *m*

zip /zɪp/ **A** *n* **1** (*also* **~ fastener**, **~per** (AmE)) fermeture *f* à glissière, fermeture *f* éclair®; **to do up/undo a ~** tirer/défaire une fermeture à glissière
2 (fam) (energy) tonus *m*
3 (*also* **~ code**) (AmE) code *m* postal
B *vt* (*p prés etc* **-pp-**) **1** (close) **to ~ sth shut** fermer qch en tirant la fermeture à glissière
2 (Comput) zipper, comprimer
C *vi* (*p prés etc* **-pp-**) **to ~ along, to ~ past** filer à toute allure; **to ~ past sb/sth** dépasser qn/qch à toute allure

■ **zip through** (fam): **to ~ through a book** lire un livre en diagonale (fam)

■ **zip up**: **A** **~ up** ‹*garment, bag*› se fermer par une fermeture à glissière
B **~ [sth] up** remonter la fermeture à glissière de

zipper /'zɪpə(r)/ (AmE) = **zip A1**

zip pocket *n* poche *f* à fermeture à glissière

zodiac /'zəʊdɪæk/ *n* zodiaque *m*

zombie /'zɒmbɪ/ *n* zombi(e) *m*; (fig) abruti/-e *m/f* (fam)

⚷ **zone** /zəʊn/ **A** *n* zone *f*
B *vt* (divide) diviser [qch] en zones

zonked /zɒŋkt/ (*also* **zonked out**) *adj* (fam) (tired) crevé/-e (fam)

zoo /zu:/ *n* zoo *m*

zookeeper *n* gardien/-ienne *m/f* de zoo

zoologist /zəʊ'ɒlədʒɪst/ *n* zoologue *mf*, zoologiste *mf*

zoology /zəʊ'ɒlədʒɪ/ *n* zoologie *f*

zoom /zu:m/ **A** *n* (*also* **~ lens**) zoom *m*
B *vi* **1** (fam) (move quickly) **to ~ past** passer en trombe; **to ~ around [sth]** passer à toute vitesse dans; **he's ~ed off to Paris** il a foncé (fam) à Paris
2 (fam) (rocket) ‹*prices, profits*› monter en flèche

zucchini /zu:'ki:nɪ/ *n* (*pl* **~** *ou* **~s**) (AmE) courgette *f*

⚷ mot clé

Summary of French grammar

Grammar provides a description of the rules by which a language functions. Many of these rules are complex and there are many exceptions to them. The following pages offer a summary of some of the most important features of French grammar.

1 Nouns and Gender

All French nouns are either masculine or feminine. The gender of nouns is shown by the definite and indefinite articles. Most nouns relating to male people are masculine and most relating to female people are feminine. Inanimate objects can be either gender and other nouns may be a particular gender for no clear reason, *une personne* = a person. A few have different genders according to their sense: *le mode* = method; *la mode* = fashion.

1.1 The definite article (= *the*)

	Singular	Plural
Masculine	*le*	*les*
Feminine	*la*	*les*

- *le* and *la* are reduced to *l'* before:
  a singular noun starting with a vowel: *école* → *l'école*
  a singular noun starting with a silent *h*: *hôtel* → *l'hôtel*
- *les* is the plural in all cases: *les écoles*, *les hôtels*
- The preposition *à* + *le* become *au*: *au café* = at the café. Similarly *à* + *les* become *aux*

Note: Unlike in English, articles are rarely omitted, *les enfants aiment les bonbons* = children like sweets

1.2 The indefinite article (= *a* or *an*; plural = *some*)

	Singular	Plural
Masculine	*un*	*des*
Feminine	*une*	*des*

- *un* and *une* also indicate the number 1 in counting: *un couteau* = one knife; *une pomme* = one apple
- *des* is the plural form for both masculine and feminine nouns: *des couteaux*, *des pommes*

But when specifying someone's occupation or profession, the article is dropped:

il est boucher = he is a butcher *ma sœur est avocat* = my sister is a lawyer

The article *le* is used to specify the day of the month:

aujourd'hui, c'est le six septembre = today is the 6th of September
c'est le mardi deux juillet = it's Tuesday 2 July

2 Nouns and Number

Nouns can be *singular* or *plural*, and this is referred to as *number*. This is an important consideration when choosing verb forms or adjectival agreements. Most nouns add an ending to form the plural.

2.1 Typical nouns:

Most nouns add *-s* in the plural:

chaise → *chaises* (= chairs) *chien* → *chiens* (= dogs)
voiture → *voitures* (= cars) *chat* → *chats* (= cats)

2.2 Nouns ending in *-au*, *-eu* or *-eau* usually add *-x* in the plural:

tuyau → *tuyaux* (= pipes) *jeu* → jeux (= games)
neveu → *neveux* (= nephews) *bureau* → *bureaux* (= desks)

2.3 Nouns ending in *-ail* usually add *-s*:

détail → *détails* (= details)

But there are exceptions:

travail → *travaux* (= works)

2.4 Nouns ending in *-al* usually change from *-al* to *-aux*:

rival → *rivaux* (= rivals) *cheval* → *chevaux* (= horses)

But there are exceptions:

bal → *bals* (= dances)

2.5 Nouns ending in *-ou*:

These nouns usually add -s in the plural. But there are six common exceptions which add *-x*:

bijou → *bijoux* (= jewels) *genou* → *genoux* (= knees)
caillou → *cailloux* (= pebbles) *hibou* → *hiboux* (= owls)
chou → *choux* (= cabbages) *joujou* → *joujoux* (= toys)

2.6 Some nouns have unusual plurals and these have to be learnt individually:

ciel → *cieux* (= skies) *œil* → *yeux* (= eyes)

Note the plurals in the group: *monsieur* → *messieurs*; *madame* → *mesdames*; *mademoiselle* → *mesdemoiselles*: *mon-*, *ma-* in these words meant 'my' originally (as in 'my lord', 'my lady').

Surnames are not used in the plural in phrases such as: *les Dupont* = the Duponts; names of dynasties do however take *-s* in the plural: *les Bourbons* = the Bourbons.

2.7 Hyphenated nouns

The plurals of this group of nouns vary and depend on how the word is formed, ADJECTIVE + NOUN, VERB + NOUN, etc. In cases where there is an ADJECTIVE + NOUN, it is normal for both words in the compound to change:

beau-père → *beaux-pères* (= fathers-in-law)
chou-fleur → *choux-fleurs* (= cauliflowers)

If an element of a compound is neither a noun nor an adjective, it does not change in the plural.

le tire-bouchon = corkscrew → *les tire-bouchons* (*tire* is part of the verb *tirer*)
un passe-partout = skeleton key → *des passe-partout* (no noun: *passe* is a verb, *partout* is an adverb)

If in doubt it can be helpful to translate the compound word for word and find which element would logically become plural in English:

arc-en-ciel (= rainbow) → *arcs-en-ciel* (= rainbows)
(literally 'arc in the sky' → 'arcs in the sky')

2.8 Nouns which do not change in the plural

Nouns already ending in *-s*: *bois* → *bois* (= woods)
Nouns already ending in *-x*: *voix* → *voix* (= voices)
Nouns ending in *-z*: *nez* → *nez* (= noses)

3 *De* and expressions of quantity

De is used in many expressions of quantity. In many cases, it is translated in English by *some* or *any*.

Note how *de* is used with articles before nouns and how it may change:

de + le → du	*le pain* → *du pain* = some bread
de + la → de la	*la crème* → *de la crème* = some cream
de + l' → de l'	*l'huile* → *de l'huile* = some oil
de + les → des	*les oranges* → *des oranges* = some oranges

Note that after a negative the article is dropped and *de* alone is used:

j'ai du pain = I have some bread
je n'ai pas de pain = I don't have any bread
avez-vous de la crème = do you have (some) cream?
nous n'avons pas de crème = we do not have any cream

If *de* comes before a vowel or a silent *h*, it is written *d'*:

achetez des oranges/de l'huile = buy some oranges/oil
n'achetez pas d'oranges/d'huile = don't buy any oranges/oil

There is more on Negatives in section 11.

If *de* comes before an adjective which qualifies a noun, it often remains *de* or *d'* rather than *des*:

de jolies fleurs = some pretty flowers
d'énormes problèmes = enormous problems
d'autres amis = other friends

Expressions of quantity. The following always use *de* or *d'* before a vowel or silent 'h'.

un verre de vin = a glass of wine
un kilo de haricots verts = a kilo of French beans
deux kilos de pommes = two kilos of apples
beaucoup de farine = a lot of flour
beaucoup de cerises = a lot of cherries
peu de mots = few words
peu d'habitants = not many inhabitants

But note the following:

encore du pain, s'il vous plaît = some more bread, please

4 Pronouns

4.1 Subject pronouns

Pronouns such as *I*, *we*, *they*, etc replace nouns as the subjects of sentences, and can refer to people or things. Subject pronouns determine the choice of endings for verbs, *je chante* = I sing, *tu chantes* = you sing, *nous chantons* = we sing, *vous chantez* = you (plural) sing.

Singular	Plural
je = I	*nous* = we
tu = you	*vous* = you
il = he/it	*ils* = they [masculine or masculine + feminine]
elle = she/it	*elles* = they [feminine]
on = one*	

- *tu* is used to speak to a child or someone who is well known
- *vous* is used in polite speech or to more than one person
- *ils* means 'they' referring to a male group, or a mixed male and female group

**on* is used as a less specific subject pronoun to mean 'one', 'you', 'we', 'people', 'they'. It always takes the endings of the third person singular, see the verb tables.

on mange ici? = shall we eat here? *on n'aime pas refuser* = one doesn't like to refuse

4.2 Object pronouns

4.2.a Direct object pronouns

Direct object pronouns in French, the equivalent of *it*, *her*, *him*, *us*, etc are used to replace noun objects. They can refer to people or things and can only be used with transitive verbs, marked *vtr* in this dictionary. Transitive verbs are those which affect or act on someone or something.

frapper *vtr* to hit: hit the ball; go on, hit it! = frappe la balle; allez, frappe-la!

French	English	French	English
me/m'	me	*nous*	us
te/t'	you [*singular*]	*vous*	you [*plural*]
le/l'	him /it	*les*	them
la/l'	her/it	*se/s'*	themselves
se/s'	himself/herself/itself		

- *m'/t'/l'/s'* are used if the word that follows begins with a vowel or a silent h:

  ils l'aiment = they love her
  elle l'héberge gratuitement = she puts him up for free

- Object pronouns can affect the endings of past participles in compound tenses if the object is feminine or plural:

  elle a poli la table → *elle l'a polie* (+e for feminine singular = she polished it)
  elle a poli les tables → *elle les a polies* (+es for feminine plural = she polished them)

4.2.b Indirect object pronouns

Indirect object pronouns in French, the equivalent of *to it*, *to her*, *to him*, *to us*, etc are used to replace indirect noun objects. They can refer to people or things and are indirectly affected by the action of the verb.

donnez-lui la balle! = give the ball to him/to her
il m'a montré la photo = he showed me the photo
donne-le-leur! = give them that!/give that to them!

French	English	French	English
me/m'	(to) me	*nous*	(to) us
te/t'	(to) you [*singular*]	vous	(to) you [*plural*]
lui	(to) him or it	*leur*	(to) them
lui	(to) her or it		

4.2.c Indirect object pronouns *y* and *en*

y is used in sentences with verbs which govern a preposition, e.g. *s'intéresser à*, *s'opposer à*, *penser à*

il ne s'y intéresse pas = he's not interested in it
je m'y oppose = I'm against it
j'y pense = I'm thinking about it

The indirect object pronoun referring to a quantity is: *en* = of it, of them, some

j'en voudrais trois = I'd like three (of them)
offrez-leur-en = offer them some

It is also used in sentences such as:

nous en parlerons ce soir = we'll talk about it this evening

4.3 Order of object pronouns in the sentence

Object pronouns come before most verb parts:

elle leur rend les livres = she is returning the books to them

Object pronouns come before an infinitive:

elle va leur rendre les livres = she is going to return the books to them

Object pronouns come before the first part of the compound tenses conjugated with *avoir* and *être*: see Verbs section 10.1.f

elle leur a rendu les livres = she returned the books to them
il y est allé = he went there

Object pronouns follow the imperative form of the verb and are linked to it by a hyphen:

rends-leur les livres! = give the books back to them!

Object pronouns return to normal order, object pronoun before verb, in imperative sentences if they are in the negative:

ne les rendez pas! = don't give them back!

Order of Object Pronouns (see 4.2 for meanings):

When more than one object pronouns occur in the same sentence, they keep a fixed sequence as follows:

me	*le*	*lui*	*y*	*en*
te	*la*	*leur*		
se	*les*			
nous				
vous				
se				

- any combination of object pronouns will follow the above order:
  nous le lui avons envoyé = we sent it to her/him
  ils le leur ont expliqué = they explained it to them
  elle leur en donne = she gives them some
  nous nous y opposons = we're against it
- *me*, *te*, *nous*, *vous* can be both direct and indirect objects. They are also used with reflexive verbs [see Verbs section 10.1]
- *se* means: (to) himself, (to) herself, (to) oneself, (to) themselves, and is used with reflexive verbs

4.4 Emphatic or disjunctive pronouns

moi	= me	*nous*	= us
toi	= you	*vous*	= you [plural or formal usage]
lui	= him	*eux*	= them
elle	= her	*elles*	= them [all female]

The emphatic pronouns are used in the following situations:

- after prepositions:
  avec moi = with me   *sans elle* = without her
  je pense à elle = I'm thinking of her
- after *que* or *qu'* in comparative sentences [see Comparison section 8.1]:
  plus petit que lui = smaller than him   *plus grand que toi* = bigger than you
- to emphasize the subject:
  lui, il n'aime pas le vin rouge mais elle, elle adore ça = he doesn't like red wine but she loves it
- with *c'est*, *ce sont*
  c'est moi! = it's me!   *ce sont eux* = it's them
- with *même* meaning 'self' (myself, yourself, etc.):
  toi-même = yourself   *vous-mêmes* = yourselves

Note: -*s* is added to *même* in the plural

Note: *moi* and *toi* are used in imperatives when pronouns follow the verb:

donnez-le-moi! = give it to me! *mets-toi là!* = sit yourself there!

5 Adjectives

Adjectives are listed alphabetically according to the masculine form in this dictionary. In those cases where the feminine form is the same as the masculine, no further information is given. When the feminine is formed by adding an ending to the masculine, this is shown by the symbol ~ followed immediately by the ending: **lent, ~e** *adj* slow. If the change involves a spelling change to the masculine form, this is clearly shown: **langoureux**, **-euse** *adj*. Many determiners *ce, mon, tout* etc (= *this, my, all* etc) are adjectival and therefore must also agree with the nouns they qualify

5.1 Common adjectival endings:

Adjectives which add *-e* to form the feminine:

une jupe courte = a short skirt

Adjectives which add *-s* to form the masculine plural:

des voyages intéressants = interesting journeys

All adjectives follow this pattern in the plural unless the ending is *-x*, *curieux* → masculine plural *curieux*, or there is already a final *-s*, *bas* → masculine plural *bas*

Adjectives which add *-s* to the feminine to form the feminine plural

des histoires amusantes = funny stories

5.2 Adjectives ending in -e

These are unchanged in the feminine: *aimable* → feminine *aimable*

-s is added in the normal way to form the plural for both masculine and feminine adjectives of this type: *aimable* → plural *aimables*

Note: If the adjective ends in *-é*, then the feminine form adds *-e*:

aimé → feminine *aimée* plural: *aimés* → feminine *aimées*

5.3 Table of adjective endings and their typical feminine variants:

The following double the last letter and add an *-e*

Typical ending	Adjective	Feminine	English
-as	*bas*	*basse*	low
-eil	*pareil*	*pareille*	similar
-el	*mortel*	*mortelle*	fatal
-en	*ancien*	*ancienne*	ancient
-et*	*muet*	*muette*	mute
-on	*bon*	*bonne*	good
-ul	*nul*	*nulle*	no good

*Note that some adjectives ending in *-et* follow a different pattern: *inquiet* → *inquiète* = anxious

The following add a final *-e* and add an accent or change a consonant or consonant group

Typical ending	Adjective	Feminine	English
-er	*premier*	*première*	first
-ef	*bref*	*brève*	brief
-if	*actif*	*active*	active
-eux	*fameux*	*fameuse*	infamous
-eur	*menteur*	*menteuse*	untruthful
-nc	*blanc*	*blanche*	white
-ic	*public*	*publique*	public
-gu	*aigu*	*aiguë*	acute

The following are examples of irregular adjectives which show additional variations

doux → *douce* (= sweet)
favori → *favorite* (= favourite)
gentil → *gentille* (= kind)
malin → *maligne* (= cunning)
sot → *sotte* (= silly)
faux → *fausse* (= false)
frais → *fraîche* (= fresh)
jaloux → *jalouse* (= jealous)
roux → *rousse* (= red)

5.4 Position of adjectives

In French most adjectives follow the noun:

un chocolat chaud (= a hot chocolate)
un homme grand (= a tall man)
un stylo noir (= a black pen)

Some adjectives go before the noun. These are usually common adjectives: ***bon*** = good, ***gros*** = big, ***joli*** = pretty, ***nouveau*** = new, ***grand*** = big, ***petit*** = small

These may almost become part of the noun as a compound:

un jeune homme (= a young man)

They become part of a compound when they're joined to the noun by a hyphen:

les petits-enfants (= the grandchildren)

Some adjectives radically change their meaning depending on whether they precede or follow the noun, compare:

la pauvre fille (= the poor girl)
la mauvaise clé (= the wrong key)
un grand homme = a great man
la fille pauvre (= the girl with little money)
un animal mauvais (= a vicious animal)
un homme grand = a tall man

5.5 Adjectives which always precede the noun

The following classes of adjective always come before the nouns they qualify:

Numbers, cardinal and ordinal:

les trois filles = the three girls
la troisième fois = the third time

Possessive and demonstrative adjectives:

mon parapluie = my umbrella   *cette église* = this church

Indefinite adjectives such as:

chaque = each, *tel* = such, *autre* = other
chaque enfant = each child   *une telle personne* = such a person

beau, nouveau, vieux

These adjectives form a group because they have a variant spelling:

Masculine	Masculine with vowel*	Plural	Feminine	Plural	English
beau	*bel*	*beaux*	*belle*	*belles*	beautiful
nouveau	*nouvel*	*nouveaux*	*nouvelle*	*nouvelles*	new
vieux	*vieil*	*vieux*	*vieille*	*vieilles*	old

une belle femme (= a beautiful woman)
de nouveaux livres (= new books)
de vieilles histoires (= old stories)

*The variant spelling is used if the noun following is masculine and begins with a vowel or a silent *h*:

arbre → *un bel arbre* (= a lovely tree)

6 Possession

6.1 Expressing possession

Possession is commonly expressed by *de*, meaning of.

le chien de Paul (= literally: the dog of Paul) = Paul's dog
les vêtements de Sophie (= literally: the clothes of Sophie) = Sophie's clothes

6.2 Possessive adjectives

The possessive adjectives are the equivalents of *my*, *your*, *his*, *her* etc.

POSSESSIVE ADJECTIVES

Masculine	Feminine	Plural	English
mon	*ma*	*mes*	my
ton	*ta*	*tes*	your
son	*sa*	*ses*	his/her/its/one's
notre	*notre*	*nos*	our
votre	*votre*	*vos*	your
leur	*leur*	*leurs*	their

- The possessive adjective matches the gender and number of what is possessed NOT the possessor:

  ma sœur = my sister (the speaker may be male)   *sa femme* = his wife

- the feminine forms *ma*, *ta*, and *sa* end in vowels and are not used before a vowel. Instead the masculine form is used:

  son élève = his or her student   *son obligation* = her or his obligation

6.3 Possessive Pronouns

These are the equivalents of English *mine*, *yours*, *ours* etc. In French they reflect the gender and number of what is possessed:

POSSESSIVE PRONOUNS

Masculine	Feminine	Masculine Plural	Feminine Plural	English
le mien	*la mienne*	*les miens*	*les miennes*	mine
le tien	*la tienne*	*les tiens*	*les tiennes*	yours
le sien	*la sienne*	*les siens*	*les siennes*	his/hers/its
le nôtre	*la nôtre*	*les nôtres*	*les nôtres*	ours
le vôtre	*la vôtre*	*les vôtres*	*les vôtres*	yours
le leur	*la leur*	*les leurs*	*les leurs*	theirs

ce n'est pas sa veste, c'est la mienne = it's not his jacket, it's mine (the speaker may be male)

ce ne sont pas ses chaussures, ce sont les miennes = these are not his shoes, they're mine

7 Adverbs

Adverbs usually give additional information about a verb: i.e. they say 'how' (= in what way or manner), 'when', or 'where' something happens

Most French adverbs are formed from the feminine adjective by adding *-ment*

heureux → *heureuse* → *heureusement* (= happily, fortunately)
égal → *égale* → *également* (= equally)

Exceptions include:

7.1 masculine adjectives ending in a vowel

The adverb is formed from the masculine adjective rather than the feminine:

hardi → *hardiment* (= robustly) *résolu* → *résolument* (= resolutely)

7.2 adjectives ending in *-ant* or *-ent*

The *-nt* is dropped and the *-m-* is doubled:

constant → *constamment* (= constantly) *intelligent* → *intelligemment* (= intelligently)

Note however *lent* → *lentement* (= slowly). Some adverbs are irregular in their formation:

bon = good → *bien* = well
gentil = kind → *gentiment* = kindly
bref = brief → *brièvement* = briefly
mauvais = bad → *mal* = badly

8 Comparison

8.1 Comparative of adjectives and adverbs

The comparative of adjectives and adverbs in English is usually expressed by:

'more...'	*more interesting – adjective; more interestingly* – adverb
'as...'	*as easy – adjective; as easily* – adverb
'less...'	*less intelligent – adjective; less intelligently* – adverb

The comparative of adjectives and adverbs in French is expressed in most cases by:

'plus...	*plus intéressant – adjective; plus facilement* – adverb
aussi...'	*aussi grand – adjective (= as big); aussi facilement* – adverb (= as easily)
'moins...'	*moins intelligent – adjective (= less intelligent); moins facilement* – adverb (= less easily)

Comparative adjectives and adverbs are followed by *que* (or *qu'* before a vowel or silent *h*) to translate 'than' or 'as' in English.

plus intéressant que = more interesting than
aussi facilement que = as easily as
moins intelligent que = less intelligent than

The comparative adjective reflects the gender and number of the noun described:

il est plus grand que toi = he is taller than you
cette rue est moins longue que celle-là = this road is shorter than that one

SOME IRREGULAR:

ADJECTIVE COMPARATIVES			ADVERB COMPARATIVES		
Adjective	**Comparative**	**English**	**Adverb**	**Comparative**	**English**
bon = good	*meilleur*	better	*beaucoup* = much	plus	more
mauvais = bad	*pire*	worse	*bien* = well	*mieux*	better
			mal = badly	*pis*	worse
			peu = little	*moins*	less

8.2 Superlative of adjectives and adverbs

The superlative of adjectives and adverbs in English is expressed by 'most...'

most interesting – adjective, *most interestingly* – adverb

The superlative adjective in French is expressed in most cases by:

'le/la/les plus + *adjective*' le plus intéressant

The article is repeated reflecting the gender and number of the noun described:

la ville la plus belle = the most beautiful city

Note how *de* (or *du*) following the superlative in French is translated by *in* or *of* in English in sentences like:

la ville la plus belle du monde = the most beautiful city in the world
le meilleur épisode de la série = the best episode of the series

The superlative of adverbs in French closely resembles the adjective, but the article is always *le* (never: *la* or *les*): *le plus facilement* = the most easily

9 Time

Time phrases in French begin with *il est...* (= it is...) and the French equivalent of 'o'clock' is *heures*, except for 'one o'clock' *une heure*. The 24 hour clock is often used to distinguish between a.m. and p.m.

The number of hours is stated first and any minutes 'past' the hour are simply added to the end of the phrase:

il est sept heures dix = it's ten minutes past seven

'quarter past' is expressed by *et quart*:

il est sept heures et quart = it's quarter past seven *or* seven fifteen.

minutes 'to' the hour follow the word *moins* (= minus):

il est quatre heures moins cinq = it's five to four

'quarter to' is expressed by *moins le quart*:

il est quatre heures moins le quart = it's quarter to four

'half past' is expressed by *et demie*:

il est trois heures et demie = it's half past three

Note: *midi* (= midday) and *minuit* (= midnight) are masculine; therefore *et demie* changes to *et demi* with these two words:

il est midi/minuit et demi = it's half past twelve (midday)/midnight

Examples:

1.00 = il est une heure
2.00 = il est deux heures
2.10 = il est deux heures dix
2.15 = il est deux heures et quart *or* il est deux heures quinze
2.30 = il est deux heures et demie *or* il est deux heures trente
2.35 = il est trois heures moins vingt-cinq *or* il est deux heures trente-cinq

10 Verbs

The infinitive is the basic form of the verb and the one you look up in the dictionary. Verbs are described as being *transitive* or *intransitive*. Transitive verbs, marked *vtr* in the dictionary, take an object. In *he kicks the ball*, 'kick' is the verb and 'the ball' is the object. Intransitive verbs, marked *vi*, function without objects; verbs like 'to die', 'to sleep', 'to live' are intransitive.

The tenses are the forms of the verb which convey the time at which something acts, happens, exists, etc. They are called the present tense, the future tense, the past tense etc. Verbs which follow the same pattern as others and make up a recognizable group are called regular verbs. Verbs which deviate from the general pattern or are unique in their verb forms are called irregular verbs. In the French-English section of the dictionary every French verb is cross-referenced to the verbs section by a number in square brackets, **déplacer** /deplase/ [12] ... This means that the relevant information will be found in table 12 of the section *French verbs*.

10.1 Verb patterns

In French there are three major groupings of regular verbs identified by their infinitive endings, *-er*, *-ir*, and *-re*. There are also many irregular verbs which don't follow the same patterns. Some verbs are reflexive which means that the object of the verb is the same as its subject.

je me lave = I wash myself [see Pronouns section 4.3]

10.1.a Present tense

The present tense describes what is happening now (*it is raining*) or what regularly happens (*he plays football on Tuesdays*) or a current truth (*she loves chips*)

parler 'to speak'	AN EXAMPLE OF AN -ER VERB
je parle = I speak	*nous parlons* = we speak
tu parles = you speak	*vous parlez* = you speak
il parle = he speaks	*ils parlent* = they speak (*masculine*)
elle parle = she speaks	*elles parlent* = they speak (*feminine*)

- the translation *I speak*, etc., may also be *I am speaking* and *I do speak*

finir 'to finish'	AN EXAMPLE OF AN -IR VERB
je finis = I finish	*nous finissons* = we finish
tu finis = you finish	*vous finissez* = you finish
il finit = he finishes	*ils* (*masc*) *finissent* = they finish
elle finit = she finishes	*elles* (*fem*) *finissent* = they finish

- note the lengthened stem *-iss-* in the plural

vendre 'to sell'	AN EXAMPLE OF AN -RE VERB
je vends = I sell	*nous vendons* = we sell
tu vends = you sell	*vous vendez* = you sell
il vend = he sells	*ils* (*masc*) *vendent* = they sell
elle vend = she sells	*elles* (*fem*) *vendent* = they sell

- note the dropped verb ending with *il* and *elle*

10.1.b Imperative

The imperative is the form of the verb for giving orders. Three parts of the present tense are used: *tu*, *nous*, *vous*

The *-s* is dropped from the *tu* part of the verb:

parle! (= talk!); *parlons!* (= let's talk!); *parlez!* (= talk!)

But there are exceptions [see Verb Tables]:

aie! (= have!); *ayons!* (= let's have!); *ayez!* (= have!)
sois! (= be!); *soyons!* (= let's be!); *soyez!* (= be!)
sache! (= know!); *sachons!* (= let's know!); *sachez!* (= know!)

10.1.c Imperfect tense

The imperfect tense describes what was happening in the past (*it was raining*) or what used to be a fact or a regular occurrence (*he used to like chocolate; he used to go to classes*)

il jouait au football tous les jeudis = he played football/used to play football every Tuesday

Imperfect tense endings	
-ais	*-ions*
-ais	*-iez*
-ait	*-aient*
-ait	*-aient*

These endings apply to all verbs and are added to the verb stem. The stem is taken from the *nous* form of the present tense, *nous finiss-ons* → *finiss-* → *je finissais*

The only irregular stem is *ét-* from *être*: *j'étais* (= I was), tu *étais* (= you were)... etc.

10.1.d Future tense

The future tense describes what will happen (*it will rain*) or what is expected to be a fact (*it will be easy*):

Future tense endings	
-ai	*-ons*
-as	*-ez*
-a	*-ont*
-a	*-ont*

These endings apply to all verbs and are added to the infinitive, which acts as the 'stem' for most verbs in the future tense:

finir → *je finirai* (= I shall finish)

But *-re* verbs drop the final *-e* of the infinitive:

vendre → *je vendrai* (= I shall sell)

The future may also be expressed by: the verb *aller* + Infinitive

je vais finir... (= I am going to finish...)

Table of irregular future verb stems

Infinitive	Future Stem		Infinitive	Future Stem	
avoir	*j'aurai*	= I shall have	*tenir*	*je tiendrai*	= I shall hold
être	*je serai*	= I shall be	*vouloir*	*je voudrai*	= I shall want
faire	*je ferai*	= I shall make	*pouvoir*	*je pourrai*	= I shall be able
savoir	*je saurai*	= I shall know	*recevoir*	*je recevrai*	= I shall get
voir	*je verrai*	= I shall see	*devoir*	*je devrai*	= I shall have to
envoyer	*j'enverrai*	= I shall send	*courir*	*je courrai*	= I shall run
venir	*je viendrai*	= I shall come	*mourir*	*je mourrai*	= I shall die

Compounds of the above verbs take the same the same stem as the basic verb:

retenir (= to hold back) → *je retiendrai* *défaire* (= to undo) → *je déferai*

10.1.e Conditional tense

The conditional tense describes what would happen (*it would make him angry*) or what would be a fact (*it would be easy*). Conditionals are often preceded or followed by a phrase introduced by *si* (= if).

Formation: The conditional is made up of the Future Stem + Imperfect Endings. This applies to all verbs.

il commencerait (= he would begin)
tu devrais (= you ought to)
il le ferait si tu le lui demandais = he'd do it if you asked him

10.1.f Perfect tense

The perfect tense describes what has happened (*it has snowed; they have written*). In French it is also used for what happened and remained the case until a specific point in time (*ils y sont restés jusqu'à mardi* = they stayed there until Tuesday) or to state an action as part of a series, each action being complete in itself (*je me suis approché de la maison, j'ai sonné à la porte...* = I went up to the house, rang the doorbell...)

Formation of the perfect tense:

Two common verbs are important in the formation of the perfect tense: *avoir* and *être*

avoir = to have		être = to be	
j'ai	*nous avons*	*je suis*	*nous sommes*
tu as	*vous avez*	*tu es*	*vous êtes*
il a	*ils ont*	*il est*	*ils sont*
elle a	*elles ont*	*elle est*	*elles sont*

There are three elements in the perfect tense:

SUBJECT + *avoir*/*être* + PAST PARTICIPLE

The past participle of regular verbs is formed by removing the last syllable of the infinitive (*regarder*, *choisir*, *rendre*) and by replacing it with *-é*, *-i*, *-u* respectively:

-ER verbs: *regarder* → *regardé* → *j'ai regardé* (= I have looked)
-IR verbs: *choisir* → *choisi* → *tu as choisi* (= you have chosen)
-RE verbs: *rendre* → *rendu* → *il a rendu* (= he has given back)

But some past participles are unique and have to be learnt by heart

Table of common irregular past participles following the auxiliary verb *avoir*:

Infinitive	Past Participle		Infinitive	Past Participle	
avoir	*j'ai eu*	= I have had	croire	*j'ai cru*	= I have believed
être	*j'ai été*	= I have been	savoir	*j'ai su*	= I have known
faire	*j'ai fait*	= I have made	voir	*j'ai vu*	= I have seen
boire	*j'ai bu*	= I have drunk	pleuvoir	*il a plu*	= it has rained
pouvoir	*j'ai pu*	= I have been able	dire	*j'ai dit*	= I have said
devoir	*j'ai dû*	= I have had to	écrire	*j'ai écrit*	= I have written
lire	*j'ai lu*	= I have read	mettre	*j'ai mis*	= I have put
vouloir	*j'ai voulu*	= I have wanted	prendre	*j'ai pris*	= I have taken

- the past participle does not change its spelling after *avoir* unless there is a direct object preceding it: *j'ai vendu la table* (= I sold the table). No preceding direct object, no change to the past participle *vendu*. But in *tu l'as vendue* (= you've sold it), *l'* (referring to *la table*, feminine) makes *vendu* take the feminine ending *-e*.

Most verbs form their perfect tense with *avoir*. The exceptions are reflexive verbs and a small group of verbs of 'motion'. These take *être* and the past participle functions like an adjective qualifying the subject.

1 Reflexive verb: *se laver* = to get washed/to wash oneself

je me suis lavé(e) = I got washed	*nous nous sommes lavé*(e)*s* = we got washed
tu t'es lavé(e) = you got washed	*vous vous êtes lavé*(e)(s) = you got washed
il s'est lavé = he got washed	*ils se sont lavés* = they got washed
elle s'est lavée = she got washed	*elles se sont lavées* = they got washed

- The alternatives in brackets depend on gender (masculine or feminine) and number (singular or plural) of the subject: *je*, *tu*, *elle*, *nous*, etc

2 Verbs of motion which take *être*

aller	*je suis allé*(e)	= I went	partir	*je suis parti*(e)	= I left
arriver	*je suis arrivé*(e)	= I arrived	rester	*je suis resté*(e)	= I stayed
descendre	*je suis descendu*(e)	= I went down	retourner	*je suis retourné*(e)	= I returned
entrer	*je suis entré*(e)	= I entered	revenir	*je suis revenu*(e)	= I came back
monter	*je suis monté*(e)	= I went up	sortir	*je suis sorti*(e)	= I went out
mourir	*je suis mort*(e)	= I died	tomber	*je suis tombé*(e)	= I fell
naître	*je suis né*(e)	= I was born	venir	*je suis venu*(e)	= I came

- compounds of the above also take *être*: *devenir* (= to become) → *je suis devenu*(*e*)

10.1.g Pluperfect tense

The pluperfect tense describes what had happened (*it had snowed*; *they had written*) or what had been the case (*it had been easy*).

Formation: = Imperfect Tense of *avoir* or *être* + PAST PARTICIPLE

Examples:

j'avais fini = I had finished
nous avions vendu l'appartement = we had sold the flat
elle s'était réveillée = she had woken up
nous étions partis = we had left

- As with the perfect tense, past participles after *être* function like adjectives. They qualify the subject of the verb and reflect its gender and number.

10.1.h Future perfect tense

The future perfect tense describes what will have happened (*he will have arrived*) or what will have been the case (*it will not have been easy*)

Formation: = Future Tense of *avoir* or *être* + PAST PARTICIPLE

Examples:

j'aurai fini = I shall have finished
nous aurons vendu la voiture = we shall have sold the car
nous serons descendus = we shall have gone down

- As with the perfect tense, past participles after *être* function like adjectives. They qualify the subject of the verb and reflect its gender and number.

11 Negatives

Negative is the idea expressed by words such as *no*, *never*, *nobody*, *nothing*, etc in English and *non*, *jamais*, *personne*, *rien*, etc in French. The negative of French verbs is formed by using *ne* before the verb, and *pas*, *jamais*, *plus*, etc after the verb according to the sense required.

ne ... pas (= not)	ne ... jamais (= never)
ne ... personne (= nobody, no one)	ne ... plus (= no longer)
ne ... que (= only)	ne ... rien (= nothing)

In simple sentences *ne* is placed before the verb and *pas*, *jamais*, *plus* etc after it.

je ne lis pas = I am not reading

If there are pronouns before the verb, *ne* comes before them.

je ne le lui donne jamais = I never give it to him

If an auxiliary verb is used in a compound tense, it comes within *ne* ... *pas*, *jamais*, *plus* etc.

il n'a rien mangé = he didn't eat anything

If an infinitive is used in the sentence, it comes after *ne* ... *pas*, *jamais*, *plus* etc.

il ne veut pas manger = he doesn't want to eat

Neither ... nor is expressed by *ni* ... *ni*:

ni *Jean* ni *Luc ne voulaient venir* = neither Jean nor Luc wanted to come

If pronoun objects are used in the sentence they take the emphatic form.

ni lui *ni sa femme n'étaient là* = neither he nor his wife was there

If *personne* (= nobody) *or rien* (= nothing) is the subject it is followed only by *ne*:

personne ne vous dérangera = no one will disturb you
rien n'est impossible = nothing is impossible

Note also the following usage:

qui a frappé? – personne = who knocked? nobody
qu'est-ce qui se passe? – rien = what's going on? nothing

The use of the adjective *aucun/aucune* (= no) is very common; *aucun* is used with *ne* before the verb.

il n'a aucun talent = he has no talent
elle n'avait aucune nouvelle de lui = she hadn't heard from him

French verbs

Standard verb endings

		-er	-ir	-r, -re
Present				
Singular	**1**	-e	-is	-s *or* -e
	2	-es	-is	-s *or* -es
	3	-e	-it	-t *or* -e
Plural	**1**	-ons	-(iss)ons	-ons
	2	-ez	-(iss)ez	-ez
	3	-ent	-(iss)ent	-ent

		-er	-ir	-r, -re
Imperfect				
Singular	**1**	-ais	-(iss)ais	-ais
	2	-ais	-(iss)ais	-ais
	3	-ait	-(iss)ait	-ait
Plural	**1**	-ions	-(iss)ions	-ions
	2	-iez	-(iss)iez	-iez
	3	-aient	-(iss)aient	-aient

		-er	-ir	-r, -re
Past historic				
Singular	**1**	-ai	-is	-s
	2	-as	-is	-s
	3	-a	-it	-t
Plural	**1**	-âmes	-îmes	-mes
	2	-âtes	-îtes	-tes
	3	-èrent	-irent	-rent

		-er	-ir	-r, -re
Future				
Singular	**1**	-erai	-irai	-rai
	2	-eras	-iras	-ras
	3	-era	-ira	-ra
Plural	**1**	-erons	-irons	-rons
	2	-erez	-irez	-rez
	3	-eront	-iront	-ront

	-er	-ir	-r, -re
Present	-er	-ir	-r *or* -re

		-er	-ir	-r, -re
Present				
Singular	**1**	-e	-(iss)e	-e
	2	-es	-(iss)es	-es
	3	-e	-(iss)e	-e
Plural	**1**	-ions	-(iss)ions	-ions
	2	-iez	-(iss)iez	-iez
	3	-ent	-(iss)ent	-ent

		-er	-ir	-r, -re
Imperfect				
Singular	**1**	-asse	-isse	-sse
	2	-asses	-isses	-sses
	3	-ât	-ît	-ît *or* -ût
Plural	**1**	-assions	-issions	-ssions
	2	-assiez	-issiez	-ssiez
	3	-assent	-issent	-ssent

		-er	-ir	-r, -re
Present				
Singular	**1**			
	2			
	3	-e	-is	-s
Plural	**1**	-ons	-(iss)ons	-ons
	2	-ez	-(iss)ez	-ez

		-er	-ir	-r, -re
Present				
Singular	**1**	-erais	-irais	-rais
	2	-erais	-irais	-rais
	3	-erait	-irait	-rait
Plural	**1**	-erions	-irions	-rions
	2	-eriez	-iriez	-riez
	3	-eraient	-iraient	-raient

	-er	-ir	-r, -re
Present	-ant	-(iss)ant	-ant
Past	-é	-i	-i *or* -u

1 aimer

Indicative

Present

j'	aim**e**
tu	aim**es**
il	aim**e**
nous	aim**ons**
vous	aim**ez**
ils	aim**ent**

Imperfect

j'	aim**ais**
tu	aim**ais**
il	aim**ait**
nous	aim**ions**
vous	aim**iez**
ils	aim**aient**

Past historic

j'	aim**ai**
tu	aim**as**
il	aim**a**
nous	aim**âmes**
vous	aim**âtes**
ils	aim**èrent**

Future

j'	aim**erai**
tu	aim**eras**
il	aim**era**
nous	aim**erons**
vous	aim**erez**
ils	aim**eront**

Perfect

j'	ai	**aimé**
tu	as	**aimé**
il	a	**aimé**
nous	avons	**aimé**
vous	avez	**aimé**
ils	ont	**aimé**

Pluperfect

j'	avais	**aimé**
tu	avais	**aimé**
il	avait	**aimé**
nous	avions	**aimé**
vous	aviez	**aimé**
ils	avaient	**aimé**

Imperative

Present	aim**e**	
	aim**ons**	
	aim**ez**	
Past	aie	**aimé**
	ayons	**aimé**
	ayez	**aimé**

Subjunctive

Present

(que) j'	aim**e**
(que) tu	aim**es**
(qu')il	aim**e**
(que) nous	aim**ions**
(que) vous	aim**iez**
(qu')ils	aim**ent**

Perfect

(que) j'	aie	**aimé**
(que) tu	aies	**aimé**
(qu')il	ait	**aimé**
(que) nous	ayons	**aimé**
(que) vous	ayez	**aimé**
(qu')ils	aient	**aimé**

Pluperfect

(que) j'	eusse	**aimé**
(que) tu	eusses	**aimé**
(qu')il	eût	**aimé**
(que) nous	eussions	**aimé**
(que) vous	eussiez	**aimé**
(qu')ils	eussent	**aimé**

Conditional

Present

j'	aim**erais**
tu	aim**erais**
il	aim**erait**
nous	aim**erions**
vous	aim**eriez**
ils	aim**eraient**

Past I

j'	aurais	**aimé**
tu	aurais	**aimé**
il	aurait	**aimé**
nous	aurions	**aimé**
vous	auriez	**aimé**
ils	auraient	**aimé**

Participle

Present	aim**ant**
Past	aim**é, -e**
	ayant **aimé**

Infinitive

Present	aim**er**
Past	avoir aimé

2 plier

Indicative

Present

je	pli**e**
tu	pli**es**
il	pli**e**
nous	pli**ons**
vous	pli**ez**
ils	pli**ent**

Imperfect

je	pli**ais**
tu	pli**ais**
il	pli**ait**
nous	pli**ions**
vous	pli**iez**
ils	pli**aient**

Past historic

je	pli**ai**
tu	pli**as**
il	pli**a**
nous	pli**âmes**
vous	pli**âtes**
ils	pli**èrent**

Future

je	pli**erai**
tu	pli**eras**
il	pli**era**
nous	pli**erons**
vous	pli**erez**
ils	pli**eront**

Perfect

j'	ai	**plié**
tu	as	**plié**
il	a	**plié**
nous	avons	**plié**
vous	avez	**plié**
ils	ont	**plié**

Pluperfect

j'	avais	**plié**
tu	avais	**plié**
il	avait	**plié**
nous	avions	**plié**
vous	aviez	**plié**
ils	avaient	**plié**

Imperative

Present	pli**e**	
	pli**ons**	
	pli**ez**	
Past	aie	**plié**
	ayons	**plié**
	ayez	**plié**

Subjunctive

Present

(que) je	pli**e**
(que) tu	pli**es**
(qu')il	pli**e**
(que) nous	pli**ions**
(que) vous	pli**iez**
(qu')ils	pli**ent**

Perfect

(que) j'	aie	**plié**
(que) tu	aies	**plié**
(qu')il	ait	**plié**
(que) nous	ayons	**plié**
(que) vous	ayez	**plié**
(qu')ils	aient	**plié**

Pluperfect

(que) j'	eusse	**plié**
(que) tu	eusses	**plié**
(qu')il	eût	**plié**
(que) nous	eussions	**plié**
(que) vous	eussiez	**plié**
(qu')ils	eussent	**plié**

Conditional

Present

je	pli**erais**
tu	pli**erais**
il	pli**erait**
nous	pli**erions**
vous	pli**eriez**
ils	pli**eraient**

Past I

j'	aurais	**plié**
tu	aurais	**plié**
il	aurait	**plié**
nous	aurions	**plié**
vous	auriez	**plié**
ils	auraient	**plié**

Participle

Present	pli**ant**
Past	pli**é, -e**
	ayant **plié**

Infinitive

Present	pli**er**
Past	avoir **plié**

3 finir

Indicative

Present

je	fin**is**
tu	fin**is**
il	fin**it**
nous	fin**issons**
vous	fin**issez**
ils	fin**issent**

Imperfect

je	fin**issais**
tu	fin**issais**
il	fin**issait**
nous	fin**issions**
vous	fin**issiez**
ils	fin**issaient**

Past historic

je	fin**is**
tu	fin**is**
il	fin**it**
nous	fin**îmes**
vous	fin**îtes**
ils	fin**irent**

Future

je	fin**irai**
tu	fin**iras**
il	fin**ira**
nous	fin**irons**
vous	fin**irez**
ils	fin**iront**

Perfect

j'	ai	fin**i**
tu	as	fin**i**
il	a	fin**i**
nous	avons	fin**i**
vous	avez	fin**i**
ils	ont	fin**i**

Pluperfect

j'	avais	fin**i**
tu	avais	fin**i**
il	avait	fin**i**
nous	avions	fin**i**
vous	aviez	fin**i**
ils	avaient	fin**i**

Imperative

Present	fin**is**	
	fin**issons**	
	fin**issez**	
Past	aie	fin**i**
	ayons	fin**i**
	ayez	fin**i**

Subjunctive

Present

(que) je	fin**isse**
(que) tu	fin**isses**
(qu')il	fin**isse**
(que) nous	fin**issions**
(que) vous	fin**issiez**
(qu')ils	fin**issent**

Perfect

(que) j'	aie	fin**i**
(que) tu	aies	fin**i**
(qu')il	ait	fin**i**
(que) nous	ayons	fin**i**
(que) vous	ayez	fin**i**
(qu')ils	aient	fin**i**

Pluperfect

(que) j'	eusse	fin**i**
(que) tu	eusses	fin**i**
(qu')il	eût	fin**i**
(que) nous	eussions	fin**i**
(que) vous	eussiez	fin**i**
(qu')ils	eussent	fin**i**

Conditional

Present

je	fin**irais**
tu	fin**irais**
il	fin**irait**
nous	fin**irions**
vous	fin**iriez**
ils	fin**iraient**

Past I

j'	aurais	fin**i**
tu	aurais	fin**i**
il	aurait	fin**i**
nous	aurions	fin**i**
vous	auriez	fin**i**
ils	auraient	fin**i**

Participle

Present	fin**issant**
Past	fin**i, -e**
	ayant fin**i**

Infinitive

Present	fin**ir**
Past	avoir fin**i**

4 offrir

Indicative

Present

j'	off**re**
tu	off**res**
il	off**re**
nous	off**rons**
vous	off**rez**
ils	off**rent**

Imperfect

j'	offr**ais**
tu	offr**ais**
il	offr**ait**
nous	offr**ions**
vous	offr**iez**
ils	offr**aient**

Past historic

j'	offr**is**
tu	offr**is**
il	offr**it**
nous	offr**îmes**
vous	offr**îtes**
ils	offr**irent**

Future

j'	offr**irai**
tu	offr**iras**
il	offr**ira**
nous	offr**irons**
vous	offr**irez**
ils	offr**iront**

Perfect

j'	ai	offert
tu	as	offert
il	a	offert
nous	avons	offert
vous	avez	offert
ils	ont	offert

Pluperfect

j'	avais	offert
tu	avais	offert
il	avait	offert
nous	avions	offert
vous	aviez	offert
ils	avaient	offert

Imperative

Present	off**re**	
	off**rons**	
	off**rez**	
Past	aie	offert
	ayons	offert
	ayez	offert

Subjunctive

Present

(que) j'	off**re**
(que) tu	off**res**
(qu')il	off**re**
(que) nous	offr**ions**
(que) vous	offr**iez**
(qu')ils	off**rent**

Perfect

(que) j'	aie	offert
(que) tu	aies	offert
(qu')il	ait	offert
(que) nous	ayons	offert
(que) vous	ayez	offert
(qu')ils	aient	offert

Pluperfect

(que) j'	eusse	offert
(que) tu	eusses	offert
(qu')il	eût	offert
(que) nous	eussions	offert
(que) vous	eussiez	offert
(qu')ils	eussent	offert

Conditional

Present

j'	offr**irais**
tu	offr**irais**
il	offr**irait**
nous	offr**irions**
vous	offr**iriez**
ils	offr**iraient**

Past I

j'	aurais	offert
tu	aurais	offert
il	aurait	offert
nous	aurions	offert
vous	auriez	offert
ils	auraient	offert

Participle

Present	offr**ant**
Past	offert, -e
	ayant offert

Infinitive

Present	offr**ir**
Past	avoir offert

5 recevoir

Indicative

Present
je reç**ois**
tu reç**ois**
il reç**oit**
nous rec**evons**
vous rec**evez**
ils reç**oivent**

Imperfect
je rec**evais**
tu rec**evais**
il rec**evait**
nous rec**evions**
vous rec**eviez**
ils rec**evaient**

Past historic
je reç**us**
tu reç**us**
il reç**ut**
nous reç**ûmes**
vous reç**ûtes**
ils reç**urent**

Future
je rec**evrai**
tu rec**evras**
il rec**evra**
nous rec**evrons**
vous rec**evrez**
ils rec**evront**

Perfect
j' ai reç**u**
tu as reç**u**
il a reç**u**
nous avons reç**u**
vous avez reç**u**
ils ont reç**u**

Pluperfect
j' avais reç**u**
tu avais reç**u**
il avait reç**u**
nous avions reç**u**
vous aviez reç**u**
ils avaient reç**u**

Imperative

Present
reç**ois**
rec**evons**
rec**evez**

Past
aie reç**u**
ayons reç**u**
ayez reç**u**

Subjunctive

Present
(que) je reç**oive**
(que) tu reç**oives**
(qu')il reç**oive**
(que) nous rec**evions**
(que) vous rec**eviez**
(qu')ils reç**oivent**

Perfect
(que) j' aie reç**u**
(que) tu aies reç**u**
(qu')il ait reç**u**
(que) nous ayons reç**u**
(que) vous ayez reç**u**
(qu')ils aient reç**u**

Pluperfect
(que) j' eusse reç**u**
(que) tu eusses reç**u**
(qu')il eût reç**u**
(que) nous eussions reç**u**
(que) vous eussiez reç**u**
(qu')ils eussent reç**u**

Conditional

Present
je rec**evrais**
tu rec**evrais**
il rec**evrait**
nous rec**evrions**
vous rec**evriez**
ils rec**evraient**

Past I
j' aurais reç**u**
tu aurais reç**u**
il aurait reç**u**
nous aurions reç**u**
vous auriez reç**u**
ils auraient reç**u**

Participle

Present rec**evant**

Past reç**u, -e**
ayant reç**u**

Infinitive

Present rec**evoir**

Past avoir reç**u**

6 rendre

Indicative

Present
je rend**s**
tu rend**s**
il rend
nous rend**ons**
vous rend**ez**
ils rend**ent**

Imperfect
je rend**ais**
tu rend**ais**
il rend**ait**
nous rend**ions**
vous rend**iez**
ils rend**aient**

Past historic
je rend**is**
tu rend**is**
il rend**it**
nous rend**îmes**
vous rend**îtes**
ils rend**irent**

Future
je rend**rai**
tu rend**ras**
il rend**ra**
nous rend**rons**
vous rend**rez**
ils rend**ront**

Perfect
j' ai rend**u**
tu as rend**u**
il a rend**u**
nous avons rend**u**
vous avez rend**u**
ils ont rend**u**

Pluperfect
j' avais rend**u**
tu avais rend**u**
il avait rend**u**
nous avions rend**u**
vous aviez rend**u**
ils avaient rend**u**

Imperative

Present
rends
rendons
rendez

Past
aie rendu
ayons rendu
ayez rendu

Subjunctive

Present
(que) je rend**e**
(que) tu rend**es**
(qu')il rend**e**
(que) nous rend**ions**
(que) vous rend**iez**
(qu')ils rend**ent**

Perfect
(que) j' aie rend**u**
(que) tu aies rend**u**
(qu')il ait rend**u**
(que) nous ayons rend**u**
(que) vous ayez rend**u**
(qu')ils aient rend**u**

Pluperfect
(que) j' eusse rend**u**
(que) tu eusses rend**u**
(qu')il eût rend**u**
(que) nous eussions rend**u**
(que) vous eussiez rend**u**
(qu')ils eussent rend**u**

Conditional

Present
je rend**rais**
tu rend**rais**
il rend**rait**
nous rend**rions**
vous rend**riez**
ils rend**raient**

Past I
j' aurais rend**u**
tu aurais rend**u**
il aurait rend**u**
nous aurions rend**u**
vous auriez rend**u**
ils auraient rend**u**

Participle

Present rend**ant**

Past rend**u, -e**
ayant rend**u**

Infinitive

Present rend**re**

Past avoir rend**u**

7 être

Indicative

Present

je	suis
tu	es
il	est
nous	sommes
vous	êtes
ils	sont

Imperfect

j'	étais
tu	étais
il	était
nous	étions
vous	étiez
ils	étaient

Past historic

je	fus
tu	fus
il	fut
nous	fûmes
vous	fûtes
ils	furent

Future

je	serai
tu	seras
il	sera
nous	serons
vous	serez
ils	seront

Perfect

j'	ai	été
tu	as	été
il	a	été
nous	avons	été
vous	avez	été
ils	ont	été

Pluperfect

j'	avais	été
tu	avais	été
il	avait	été
nous	avions	été
vous	aviez	été
ils	avaient	été

Imperative

Present sois
soyons
soyez

Past aie été
ayons été
ayez été

Subjunctive

Present

(que) je	sois
(que) tu	sois
(qu')il	soit
(que) nous	soyons
(que) vous	soyez
(qu')ils	soient

Perfect

(que) j'	aie	été
(que) tu	aies	été
(qu')il	ait	été
(que) nous	ayons	été
(que) vous	ayez	été
(qu')ils	aient	été

Pluperfect

(que) j'	eusse	été
(que) tu	eusses	été
(qu')il	eût	été
(que) nous	eussions	été
(que) vous	eussiez	été
(qu')ils	eussent	été

Conditional

Present

je	serais
tu	serais
il	serait
nous	serions
vous	seriez
ils	seraient

Past I

j'	aurais	été
tu	aurais	été
il	aurait	été
nous	aurions	été
vous	auriez	été
ils	auraient	été

Participle

Present étant

Past été (invariable)
ayant été

Infinitive

Present être

Past avoir été

8 avoir

Indicative

Present

j'	ai
tu	as
il	a
nous	avons
vous	avez
ils	ont

Imperfect

j'	avais
tu	avais
il	avait
nous	avions
vous	aviez
ils	avaient

Past historic

j'	eus
tu	eus
il	eut
nous	eûmes
vous	eûtes
ils	eurent

Future

j'	aurai
tu	auras
il	aura
nous	aurons
vous	aurez
ils	auront

Perfect

j'	ai	eu
tu	as	eu
il	a	eu
nous	avons	eu
vous	avez	eu
ils	ont	eu

Pluperfect

j'	avais	eu
tu	avais	eu
il	avait	eu
nous	avions	eu
vous	aviez	eu
ils	avaient	eu

Imperative

Present aie
ayons
ayez

Past aie eu
ayons eu
ayez eu

Subjunctive

Present

(que) j'	aie
(que) tu	aies
(qu')il	ait
(que) nous	ayons
(que) vous	ayez
(qu')ils	aient

Perfect

(que) j'	aie	eu
(que) tu	aies	eu
(qu')il	ait	eu
(que) nous	ayons	eu
(que) vous	ayez	eu
(qu')ils	aient	eu

Pluperfect

(que) j'	eusse	eu
(que) tu	eusses	eu
(qu')il	eût	eu
(que) nous	eussions	eu
(que) vous	eussiez	eu
(qu')ils	eussent	eu

Conditional

Present

j'	aurais
tu	aurais
il	aurait
nous	aurions
vous	auriez
ils	auraient

Past I

j'	aurais	eu
tu	aurais	eu
il	aurait	eu
nous	aurions	eu
vous	auriez	eu
ils	auraient	eu

Participle

Present ayant

Past eu, -e
ayant eu

Infinitive

Present avoir

Past avoir eu

9 aller

Indicative

Present

je	vais
tu	vas
il	va
nous	allons
vous	allez
ils	vont

Imperfect

j'	allais
tu	allais
il	allait
nous	allions
vous	alliez
ils	allaient

Past historic

j'	allai
tu	allas
il	alla
nous	allâmes
vous	allâtes
ils	allèrent

Future

j'	irai
tu	iras
il	ira
nous	irons
vous	irez
ils	iront

Perfect

je	suis	allé
tu	es	allé
il	est	allé
nous	sommes	allés
vous	êtes	allés
ils	sont	allés

Pluperfect

j'	étais	allé
tu	étais	allé
il	était	allé
nous	étions	allés
vous	étiez	allés
ils	étaient	allés

Imperative

Present	va	
	allons	
	allez	
Past	sois	allé
	soyons	allés
	soyez	allés

Subjunctive

Present

(que) j'	aille
(que) tu	ailles
(qu')il	aille
(que) nous	allions
(que) vous	alliez
(qu')ils	aillent

Perfect

(que) je	sois	allé
(que) tu	sois	allé
(qu')il	soit	allé
(que) nous	soyons	allés
(que) vous	soyez	allés
(qu')ils	soient	allés

Pluperfect

(que) je	fusse	allé
(que) tu	fusses	allé
(qu')il	fût	allé
(que) nous	fussions	allés
(que) vous	fussiez	allés
(qu')ils	fussent	allés

Conditional

Present

j'	irais
tu	irais
il	irait
nous	irions
vous	iriez
ils	iraient

Past I

je	serais	allé
tu	serais	allé
il	serait	allé
nous	serions	allés
vous	seriez	allés
ils	seraient	allés

Participle

Present	allant
Past	allé, -e
	étant allé

Infinitive

Present	aller
Past	être allé

10 faire

Indicative

Present

je	fais
tu	fais
il	fait
nous	faisons
vous	faites
ils	font

Imperfect

je	faisais
tu	faisais
il	faisait
nous	faisions
vous	faisiez
ils	faisaient

Past historic

je	fis
tu	fis
il	fit
nous	fîmes
vous	fîtes
ils	firent

Future

je	ferai
tu	feras
il	fera
nous	ferons
vous	ferez
ils	feront

Perfect

j'	ai	fait
tu	as	fait
il	a	fait
nous	avons	fait
vous	avez	fait
ils	ont	fait

Pluperfect

j'	avais	fait
tu	avais	fait
il	avait	fait
nous	avions	fait
vous	aviez	fait
ils	avaient	fait

Imperative

Present	fais	
	faisons	
	faites	
Past	aie	fait
	ayons	fait
	ayez	fait

Subjunctive

Present

(que) je	fasse
(que) tu	fasses
(qu')il	fasse
(que) nous	fassions
(que) vous	fassiez
(qu')ils	fassent

Perfect

(que) j'	aie	fait
(que) tu	aies	fait
(qu')il	ait	fait
(que) nous	ayons	fait
(que) vous	ayez	fait
(qu')ils	aient	fait

Pluperfect

(que) j'	eusse	fait
(que) tu	eusses	fait
(qu')il	eût	fait
(que) nous	eussions	fait
(que) vous	eussiez	fait
(qu')ils	eussent	fait

Conditional

Present

je	ferais
tu	ferais
il	ferait
nous	ferions
vous	feriez
ils	feraient

Past I

j'	aurais	fait
tu	aurais	fait
il	aurait	fait
nous	aurions	fait
vous	auriez	fait
ils	auraient	fait

Participle

Present	faisant
Past	fait, -e
	ayant fait

Infinitive

Present	faire
Past	avoir fait

Infinitive	Rules	**Indicative** Present	Imperfect	Past Historic	Future
11 *créer*	*always* é	je crée, -es, -e, -ent nous créons, -ez	je créais …	je créai …	je créerai …
12 *placer*	c	je place, -es, -e, -ez, -ent	nous placions, -iez	ils placèrent	je placerai …
	ç *before* a *and* o	nous plaçons	je plaçais, -ais, -ait, -aient	je plaçai, -as, -a, -âmes, -âtes	
13 *manger*	g	je mange, -es, -e, -ez, -ent	nous mangions, -iez	ils mangèrent	je mangerai …
	ge *before* a *and* o	nous mangeons	je mangeais, -eais, -eait, -eaient	je mangeai, -as, -a, -âmes, -âtes	
14 *céder*	è *before silent final syllable*	je cède, -es, -e, -ent			
	é	nous cédons, -ez	je cédais …	je cédai …	je céderai …
15 *assiéger*	è *before silent final syllable*	j'assiège, -es, -e, -ent			
	ge *before* a *and* o	nous assiégeons	j'assiégeais, -eais, -eait, -eaient	j'assiégeai	
	é *before silent syllable*				j'assiégerai …
16 *lever*	è *before silent syllable*	je lève, -es, -e, -ent			je lèverai …
	e	nous levons, -ez	je levais …	je levai …	
17 *geler*	è *before silent syllable*	je gèle, -es, -e, -ent			je gèlerai …
	e	nous gelons, -ez	je gelais …	je gelai …	
18 *acheter*	è *before silent syllable*	j'achète, -es, -e, -ent			j'achèterai …
	e	nous achetons, -ez	j'achetais …	j'achetai …	
19 *appeler*	ll *before mute* e	j'appelle, -es, -e, -ent			j'appellerai …
	l	nous appelons, -ez	j'appelais …	j'appelai …	
20 *jeter*	tt *before mute* e	je jette, -es, -e, -ent			je jetterai …
	t	nous jetons, -ez	je jetais …	je jetai …	
21 *payer*	i *before mute* e	je paie, -es, -e, -ent			je paierai …
	or y	je paye, -es, -e, -ent nous payons, -ez	je payais …	je payai …	je payerai …

Conditional *Present*	Subjunctive *Present*	Imperative	Participle *Present*	 *Past*	
je créerais ...	que je crée ...	crée créons, -ez	créant	créé, -e	*11*
je placerais ...	que je place ...	place, -ez plaçons	plaçant	placé, -e	*12*
je mangerais ...	que je mange ...	mange, -ez mangeons	mangeant	mangé, -e	*13*
je céderais ...	que je cède, -es, -e, -ent que nous cédions, -iez	cède cédons, -ez	cédant	cédé, -e	*14*
j'assiégerais ...	que j'assiège ... que nous assiégions, -iez	assiège assiégeons	assiégeant	assiégé, -e	*15*
je lèverais ...	que je lève, -es, -e, -ent que nous levions, -iez	lève levons, -ez	levant	levé, -e	*16*
je gèlerais ...	que je gèle, -es, -e, -ent que nous gelions, -iez	gèle gelons, -ez	gelant	gelé, -e	*17*
j'achèterais ...	que j'achète, -es, -e, -ent que nous achetions, -iez	achète achetons, -ez	achetant	acheté, -e	*18*
j'appellerais ...	que j'appelle, -es, -e, -ent que nous appelions, -iez	appelle appelons, -ez	appelant	appelé, -e	*19*
je jetterais ...	que je jette, -es, -e, -ent que nous jetions, -iez	jette jetons, -ez	jetant	jeté, -e	*20*
je paierais ... je payerais ...	que je paie, -es, -e, -ent que je paye, -es, -e, -ent que nous payions, -iez	paie paye payons, -ez	payant	payé, -e	*21*

Infinitive		**Indicative**			
	Rules	*Present*	*Imperfect*	*Past Historic*	*Future*
22 essuyer	i *before mute* e	j'essuie, -es, -e, -ent			j'essuierai ...
	y	nous essuyons, -ez	j'essuyais ...	j'essuyai ...	
23 employer	i *before mute* e	j'emploie, -es, -e, -ent			j'emploierai ...
	y	nous employons, -ez	j'employais ...	j'employai ...	
24 envoyer	i *before mute* e	j'envoie, -es, -e, -ent			
	y	nous envoyons, -ez	j'envoyais ...	j'envoyai ...	
	err				j'enverrai ...
25 haïr	i	je hais, -s, -t			
	ï	nous haïssons, -ez, -ent	je haïssais ...	je haïs ... (haïmes, haïtes)	je haïrai ...
26 courir		je cours ...	je courais ...	je courus ...	je courrai ...
27 cueillir		je cueille, -es, -e, nous cueillons ...	je cueillais ...	je cueillis ...	je cueillerai ...
28 assaillir		j'assaille, -es, -e, nous assaillons, -ez, -ent	j'assaillais ...	j'assaillis ...	j'assaillirai ...
29 fuir	i *before consonants and* e	je fuis, -s, -t, -ent		je fuis ...	je fuirai ...
	y before a, ez, i, o	nous fuyons, -ez	je fuyais ...		
30 partir	*without* t	je pars ...			
	with t	il part ...	je partais ...	je partis ...	je partirai ...
31 bouillir	ou	je bous, s, t			
	ouill	nous bouillons ...	je bouillais ...	je bouillis ...	je bouillirai ...
32 couvrir		je couvre, -es, -e, nous couvrons ...	je couvrais ...	je couvris ...	je couvrirai ...
33 vêtir		je vêts ...	je vêtais ...	je vêtis ...	je vêtirai ...
34 mourir	eur	je meurs, -s, -t, -ent			
	our	nous mourons, -ez	je mourais ...	je mourus ...	je mourrai ...
35 acquérir	quier	j'acquiers, -s, -t, -ièrent			
	quér	nous acquérons -ez	j'acquérais ...		j'acquerrai ...
	qu			j'acquis ...	
36 venir	i	je viens, -s, -t, -nent		je vins ... ils vinrent	je viendrai ...
	e	nous venons, -ez	je venais ...		

Conditional	Subjunctive	Imperative	Participle		
Present	*Present*		*Present*	*Past*	
j'essuierais ...	que j'essuie, -es, -e, -ent que nous essuyions, -iez	essuie essuyons, -ez	essuyant	essuyé, e	22
j'emploierais ...	que j'emploie, -es, -e, -ent que nous employions, -iez	emploie employons, -ez	employant	employé, -e	23
j'enverrais ...	que j'envoie, -es, -e, -ent que nous envoyions, -iez	envoie envoyons, -ez	envoyant	envoyé, -e	24
je haïrais ...	que je haïsse, qu'il haïsse	hais haïssons, haïssez	haïssant	haï, -e	25
je courrais ...	que je coure ...	cours, courons, -ez	courant	couru, -e	26
je cueillerais ...	que je cueille ...	cueille cueillons, -ez	cueillant	cueilli, -e	27
j'assaillirais ...	que j'assaille ...	assaille assaillons, -ez	assaillant	assailli, -e	28
je fuirais ...	que je fuie, -es, -e, -ent que nous fuyions, -iez	fuis fuyons, -ez	fuyant	fui, -e	29
je partirais ...	que je parte ...	pars partons, -ez	partant	parti, -e	30
je bouillirais ...	que je bouille ...	bous bouillons, -ez	bouillant	bouilli, -e	31
je couvrirais ...	que je couvre, -es, -e, que nous couvrions ...	couvre couvrons, -ez	couvrant	couvert, -e	32
je vêtirais ...	que je vête ...	vêts vêtons, vêtez	vêtant	vêtu, -e	33
je mourrais ...	que je meure ...	meurs mourons, -ez	mourant	mort, -e	34
j'acquerrais ...	que j'acquière, -es, -e, -ent que nous acquérions, -iez	acquiers acquérons, -ez	acquérant	acquis, -e	35
je viendrais ...	que je vienne, -es, -e, -ent que nous venions, -iez	viens venons, -ez	venant	venu, -e	36

Infinitive	Rules	Present	Imperfect	Past Historic	Future
		Indicative			
37 gésir	Defective (only exists in certain tenses)	je gis, tu gis, il gît, nous gisons, -ez, -ent	je gisais …		
38 ouïr	Archaic	j'ois … nous oyons …	j'oyais …	j'ouïs …	j'ouïrai …
39 pleuvoir		il pleut ils pleuvent	il pleuvait ils pleuvaient	il plut ils plurent	il pleuvra ils pleuvront
40 pourvoir	i	je pourvois, -s, -t, -ent			je pourvoirai …
	y	nous pourvoyons, -ez	je pourvoyais …		
	u			je pourvus …	
41 asseoir	ie	j'assieds, -ds, -d			j'assiérai …
	ey	nous asseyons, -ez, -ent	j'asseyais …		
	i			j'assis …	
asseoir (oi/oy replace ie/ey)	oi	j'assois, -s, -t, -ent			j'assoirai …
	oy	nous assoyons, -ez	j'assoyais …		
42 prévoir	oi	je prévois, -s, -t, -ent			je prévoirai …
	oy	nous prévoyons, -ez	je prévoyais …		
	i/u			je prévis …	
43 mouvoir	eu	je meus, -s, -t, -vent			
	ou	nous mouvons, -ez	je mouvais …		je mouvrai …
	u			je mus, -s, -t, -(û)mes, -(û)tes, -rent	
44 devoir	û in the past participle masc. sing.	je dois, -s, -t -vent nous devons, -ez	je devais …	je dus …	je devrai …
45 valoir	au, aille	je vaux, -x, -t			je vaudrai …
	al	nous valons, -ez, -ent	je valais …	je valus …	
prévaloir					
46 voir	oi	je vois, -s, -t, -ent			
	oy	nous voyons, -ez	je voyais …		
	i/e/u			je vis …	je verrai …
47 savoir	5 forms	je sais, -s, -t, nous savons, -ez, -ent	je savais …	je sus …	je saurai …

Conditional	Subjunctive	Imperative	Participle		
Present	*Present*		*Present*	*Past*	
			gisant		*37*
j'ouïrais ...	que j'oie ... que nous oyions ...	ois oyons, -ez	 oyant	ouï, -e	*38*
il pleuvrait ils pleuvraient	qu'il pleuve qu'ils pleuvent		pleuvant	plu	*39*
je pourvoirais ...	que je pourvoie, -es, -e, -ent que nous pourvoyions, -iez	pourvois pourvoyons, -ez	 pourvoyant	pourvu, -e	*40*
j'assiérais ...	que j' asseye ... que nous asseyions ...	assieds asseyons, -ez	 asséyant	assis, -e	*41*
j'assoirais ...	que j'assoie, -es, -e, -ent que nous assoyions, -iez	assois assoyons, -ez	 assoyant		
je prévoirais ...	que je prévoie, -es, -e, -ent que ns prévoyions, -iez	prévois prévoyons, -ez	 prévoyant	prévu, -e	*42*
je mouvrais ...	que je meuve, -es, -e, -ent que nous mouvions, -iez	meus mouvons, -ez	 mouvant	mû, mue	*43*
je devrais ...	que je doive, -es, -e, -ent que nous devions, -iez	dois devons, -ez	 devant	dû, due	*44*
je vaudrais ...	que je vaille, -es, -e, -ent que nous valions, -iez	vaux valons, -ez	 valant	valu, -e	*45*
	que je prévale, -es, -e				
je verrais ...	que je voie, -es, -e, -ent que nous voyions, -iez	vois voyons, -ez	 voyant	vu, -e	*46*
je saurais ...	que je sache ...	sache, -ons, -ez	sachant	su, -e	*47*

Infinitive	*Rules*	**Indicative** *Present*	*Imperfect*	*Past Historic*	*Future*
48 *vouloir*	veu/veuil	je veux, -x, -t, veulent			
	voul/voudr	nous voulons, -ez	je voulais …	je voulus …	je voudrai …
49 *pouvoir*	eu/u(i)	je peux, -x, -t, peuvent		je pus …	
	ouv/our	nous pouvons, -ez	je pouvais …		je pourrai …
50 *falloir*	*Impersonal*	il faut	il fallait	il fallut	il faudra
51 *déchoir*	choir *and* échoir *are defective* (only exist in certain tenses)	je déchois, -s, -t, -ent nous déchoyons, -ez	je déchoyais …	je déchus …	je décherrai …
52 *prendre*	prend	je prends, -ds, -d			je prendrai …
	pren	nous prenons, -ez ils prennent	je prenais …		
	pri(s)			je pris …	
53 *rompre*		je romps, -ps, -pt, nous rompons …	je rompais …	je rompis …	je romprai …
54 *craindre*	ain/aind	je crains, -s, -t			je craindrai …
	aign	nous craignons, -ez, -ent	je craignais …	je craignis …	
55 *peindre*	ein	je peins, -s, -t			je peindrai …
	eign	nous peignons, -ez, -ent	je peignais …	je peignis …	
56 *joindre*	oin/oind	je joins, -s, -t			je joindrai …
	oign	nous joignons, -ez, -ent	je joignais …	je joignis …	
57 *vaincre*	ainc	je vaincs, -cs, -c			je vaincrai …
	ainqu	nous vainquons, -ez, -ent	je vainquais …	je vainquis …	
58 *traire*	i	je trais, -s, -t, -ent		(obsolete)	je trairai …
	y	nous trayons, -ez	je trayais …		
59 *plaire*	ai	je plais, tu plais, il plaît (but il tait) nous plaisons …	je plaisais …		je plairai …
	u			je plus …	
60 *mettre*	met	je mets, nous mettons	je mettais …		je mettrai …
	mis			je mis …	
61 *battre*	t	je bats, -ts, -t			
	tt	nous battons …	je battais …	je battis …	je battrai …
62 *suivre*	ui	je suis, -s, -t			
	uiv	nous suivons …	je suivais …	je suivis …	je suivrai …

Conditional	Subjunctive	Imperative	Participle		
Present	*Present*		*Present*	*Past*	
	que je veuille, -es, -e, -ent	veux (veuille)			*48*
je voudrais …	que nous voulions, -iez	voulons, -ez (veuillez)	voulant	voulu, -e	
	que je puisse …	(obsolete)		pu	*49*
je pourrais …			pouvant		
il faudrait	qu'il faille	(no form)	(obsolete)	fallu	*50*
	que je déchoie, -es, -e, -ent	déchois	(no form but échéant)		*51*
je décherrais …	que nous déchoyions, -iez	déchoyons, -ez		déchu, -e	
je prendrais …		prends			*52*
	que je prenne …	prenons, -ez	prenant		
				pris, -e	
je romprais …	que je rompe …	romps -pons, -pez	rompant	rompu, -e	*53*
je craindrais …		crains		craint, -e	*54*
	que je craigne …	craignons, -ez	craignant		
je peindrais …		peins		peint, -e	*55*
	que je peigne …	peignons, -ez	peignant		
je joindrais …		joins		joint, -e	*56*
	que je joigne …	joignons, -ez	joignant		
je vaincrais …		vaincs		vaincu, -e	*57*
	que je vainque …	vainquons, -ez	vainquant		
je trairais …	que je traie, -es, -e, -ent	trais		trait, -e	*58*
	que nous trayions,	trayons, -ez	trayant		
je plairais …	que je plaise …	plais plaisons, -ez	plaisant		*59*
				plu	
je mettrais …	que je mette …	mets mettons, -ez	mettant		*60*
				mis, -e	
		bats			*61*
je battrais …	que je batte …	battons, -ez	battant	battu, -e	
		suis			*62*
je suivrais …	que je suive …	suivons, -ez	suivant	suivi, -e	

Infinitive		Indicative			
	Rules	Present	Imperfect	Past Historic	Future
63 *vivre*	vi/viv	je vis, -s, -t, nous vivons …	je vivais …		je vivrai …
	véc			je vécus …	
64 *suffire*		je suffis, -s, -t, nous suffisons …	je suffisais …	je suffis …	je suffirai …
65 *médire*		je médis, -s, -t, nous médisons, vous médisez (but vous dites, redites)	je médisais …	je médis …	je médirai …
66 *lire*	i	je lis, -s, -t			je lirai …
	is	nous lisons, -ez, -ent	je lisais …		
	u			je lus …	
67 *écrire*	i	j'écris, -s, -t			j'écrirai …
	iv	nous écrivons, -ez, -ent	j'écrivais …	j'écrivis …	
68 *rire*		je ris, -s, -t, nous rions …	je riais … nous riions, -iez	je ris … nous rîmes …	je rirai …
69 *conduire*		je conduis …	je conduisais …	je conduisis…	je conduirai …
70 *boire*	oi	je bois, -s, -t, -vent			je boirai …
	u(v)	nous buvons, -ez	je buvais …	je bus …	
71 *croire*	oi	je crois, -s, -t, ils croient			je croirai …
	oy	nous croyons, -ez	je croyais …		
	u			je crus …	
72 *croître*	oî	je croîs, -s, -t			je croîtrai …
	oiss	nous croissons, -ez, -ent	je croissais …		
	û			je crûs …	
73 *connaître*		je connais, -s, -ssons, -ssez, -ssent	je connaissais …	je connus …	
	î before t	il connaît			je connaîtrai …
74 *naître*		je nais, nais,			
	î before t	naît			je naîtrai …
	naisse	nous naissons, -ez, -ent	je naissais …		
	naqu			je naquis …	

Conditional	**Subjunctive**	**Imperative**	**Participle**		
Present	*Present*		*Present*	*Past*	
je vivrais ...	que je vive ...	vis vivons, -ez	vivant	vécu, -e	*63*
je suffirais ...	que je suffise ...	suffis suffisons, -ez	suffisant	suffi (but confit, déconfit, frit, circoncis)	*64*
je médirais ...	que je médise ... que nous médisions, -iez	médis médisons médisez (but dites, redites)	médisant	médit	*65*
je lirais ...	que je lise ...	lis lisons, -ez	lisant	lu, -e	*66*
j'écrirais ...	que j'écrive ...	écris écrivons, -ez	écrivant	écrit, -e	*67*
je rirais ...	que je rie ... que nous riions, -iez	ris, rions, riez	riant	ri	*68*
je conduirais ...	que je conduise ...	conduis conduisons, -ez	conduisant	conduit, -e (but lui, nui)	*69*
je boirais ...	que je boive, -es, -e, -ent que nous buvions, -iez	bois buvons, -ez	buvant	bu, -e	*70*
je croirais ...	que je croie ...	crois croyons, -ez	croyant	cru, -e	*71*
je croîtrais...	que je croisse ...	croîs croissons, -ez	croissant	crû, crue (but accru, -e)	*72*
je connaîtrais ...	que je connaisse ...	connais, -ssons, -ssez	connaissant	connu, -e	*73*
je naîtrais ...	que je naisse ...	nais naissons, -ez	naissant	né, -e	*74*

Infinitive		**Indicative**			
	Rules	*Present*	*Imperfect*	*Past Historic*	*Future*
75 résoudre	ou ol/olv olu	je résous, -s, -t nous résolvons, -ez, -ent	je résolvais ...	(absoudre and dissoudre have no past historic) je résolus ...	je résoudrai...
76 coudre	oud ous	je couds, -ds, -d nous cousons, -ez, -ent	je cousais ...	je cousis ...	je coudrai ...
77 moudre	moud moul	je mouds, -ds, -d nous moulons, -ez, -ent	je moulais ...	je moulus ...	je moudrai ...
78 conclure		je conclus, -s, -t, nous concluons, -ez, -ent	je concluais ...	je conclus ...	je conclurai ...
79 clore	Defective (only exists in certain tenses)	je clos, -os, -ôt ils closent	(obsolete)	(obsolete)	je clorai ...
80 maudire		je maudis, -s, -t nous maudissons, -ez, -ent	je maudissais ...	je maudis ...	je maudirai ...

Conditional	Subjunctive	Imperative	Participle		
Present	*Present*		*Present*	*Past*	
je résoudrais ...	que je résolve ...	résous résolvons, -ez	résolvant	(absous, -oute; dissous, -oute) résolu, -e	*75*
je coudrais ...	que je couse ...	couds cousons, -ez	cousant	cousu, -e	*76*
je moudrais ...	que je moule ...	mouds moulons, -ez	moulant	moulu, -e	*77*
je conclurais ...	que je conclue ...	conclus concluons, -ez	concluant	conclu, -e (but inclus, -e)	*78*
je clorais ...	que je close ...	clos	closant	clos, -e	*79*
je maudirais ...	que je maudisse qu'il maudisse	maudis -ssons, -ssez	maudissant	maudit, -e	*80*

Numbers

Cardinal numbers

0 zéro*
1 un†
2 deux
3 trois
4 quatre
5 cinq
6 six
7 sept
8 huit
9 neuf
10 dix
11 onze
12 douze
13 treize
14 quatorze
15 quinze
16 seize
17 dix-sept
18 dix-huit
19 dix-neuf
20 vingt
21 vingt et un
22 vingt-deux
30 trente
40 quarante
50 cinquante
60 soixante
70 soixante-dix
71 soixante et onze
80 quatre-vingts§
81 quatre-vingt-un¶
82 quatre-vingt-deux
90 quatre-vingt-dix
91 quatre-vingt-onze
92 quatre-vingt-douze
99 quatre-vingt-dix-neuf
101 cent un†
102 cent deux
110 cent dix
187 cent quatre-vingt-sept
200 deux cents
250 deux cent◊ cinquante
1 000 mille∞
1 001 mille un†
1 002 mille deux
1 020 mille vingt
1 200 mille** deux cents
2 000 deux mille††
10 000 dix mille
100 000 cent mille
102 000 cent deux mille
1 000 000 un million‡‡
1 264 932 un million deux cent soixante-quatre mille neuf cent trente-deux
1 000 000 000 un milliard‡‡
1 000 000 000 000 un billion‡‡

* In English 0 may be called *nought*, *zero* or even nothing; French is always *zéro*: **a nought** = **un zéro**.

† **one** is **une** in French when it agrees with a feminine noun, so *un crayon* but *une table*, *une des tables*, *vingt et une tables*, etc.

§ Note that when *80* is used as a page number it has no *s*: **page eighty** = **page quatre-vingt**.

¶ **vingt** has no *s* when it is in the middle of a number. The only exception to this rule is when *quatre-vingts* is followed by *millions*, *milliards* or *billions*, eg **quatre-vingts millions, quatre-vingts billions** etc.

◊ **cent** does not take an *s* when it is in the middle of a number. The only exception to this rule is when it is followed by *millions*, *milliards* or *billions*, eg **trois cents millions, six cents billions** etc. It has a normal plural when it modifies other nouns: **200 inhabitants** = **deux cents habitants.**

∞ Where English would have a comma, French has simply a space. A full stop (period) can be used, e.g. **1.000**. As in English, there is no separation in dates between thousands and hundreds: **in 2004** = **en 2004**.

** In dates, the spelling **mil** is preferred to **mille**, i.e. **en 1200** = **en mil deux cents.** However, when the year is a round number of thousands, the spelling is always **mille**, so **en l'an mille, en l'an deux mille** etc.

†† **mille** is invariable; it never takes an *s*.

‡‡ The French words **million, milliard** and **billion** are nouns, and when written out in full they take **de** before another noun, eg **a million inhabitants** = **un million d'habitants**. However, when written in figures, **1,000,000 inhabitants** = **1 000 000 habitants**, but is still spoken as *un million d'habitants*. When **million** etc. is part of a complex number, **de** is not used before the nouns, eg **6,000,210 people** = **six millions deux cent dix personnes**.

Ordinal numbers§

1st	1er‡	premier (*fem.* première)
2nd	2e	second (*fem.* seconde) *or* deuxième
3rd	3e	troisième
4th	4e	quatrième
5th	5e	cinquième
6th	6e	sixième
7th	7e	septième
8th	8e	huitième
9th	9e	neuvième
10th	10e	dixième
11th	11e	onzième
12th	12e	douzième
13th	13e	treizième
14th	14e	quatorzième
15th	15e	quinzième
16th	16e	seizième
17th	17e	dix-septième
18th	18e	dix-huitième
19th	19e	dix-neuvième
20th	20e	vingtième
21st	21e	vingt et unième
22nd	22e	vingt-deuxième
23rd	23e	vingt-troisième
24th	24e	vingt-quatrième
25th	25e	vingt-cinquième
30th	30e	trentième
31st	31e	trente et unième
40th	40e	quarantième
50th	50e	cinquantième
60th	60e	soixantième
70th	70e	soixante-dixième
71st	71e	soixante et onzième
72nd	72e	soixante-douzième
73rd	73e	soixante-treizième
74th	74e	soixante-quartorzième
75th	75e	soixante-quinzième
79th	79e	soixante-dix-neuvième
80th	80e	quatre-vingtième
81st	81e	quatre-vingt-unième
90th	90e	quatre-vingt-dixième
91st	91e	quatre-vingt-onzième
99th	99e	quatre-vingt-dix-neuvième
100th	100e	centième
101st	101e	cent et unième
102nd	102e	cent-deuxième
200th	200e	deux centième
1,000th	1 000e	millième
2,000th	2 000e	deux millième
1,000,000th	1 000 000e	millionième

Like English, French makes nouns by adding the definite article:

the first .... = le premier (or la première, or les premiers *m pl* or les premières *f pl*)

the second .... = le second (or la seconde etc)

the first three ...... = les trois premiers *or* les trois premières

Note the French word order in:

the third richest country in the world = le troisième pays le plus riche du monde

§ All the ordinal numbers in French behave like ordinary adjectives and take normal plural endings where appropriate.

‡ This is the masculine form; the feminine is **1re** and the plural **1ers** (m) or **1res** (f). All the other abbreviations of ordinal numbers are invariable.

Use of en

Note the use of ***en*** in the following examples:

there are six .... = il y en a six

I've got a hundred .... = j'en ai cent

en must be used when the thing you are talking about is not expressed (the French says literally *there of them are six, I of them have a hundred* etc.). However, ***en*** is not needed when the object is specified:

there are six apples...... = il y a six pommes

Decimals in French

Note that French uses a comma where English has a decimal point.

written as	*spoken as*
0,25	zéro virgule vingt-cinq
0,05	zéro virgule zéro cinq
3,45	trois virgule quarante-cinq
8,195	huit virgule cent quatre-vingt-quinze

Approximate numbers

When you want to say 'about ...', remember the French ending *-aine*:

about ten .... = une dizaine
about ten books .... = une dizaine de livres
about fifteen .... = une quinzaine
about fifteen people .... = une quinzaine de personnes

Similarly *une trentaine, une quarantaine, une cinquantaine, une soixantaine* and *une centaine* (and *une douzaine* means *a dozen*). For other numbers, use ***environ*** (*about*):

about thirty-five .... = environ trente-cinq
hundreds of books .... = des centaines de livres
thousands of books .... = des milliers de livres
I've got thousands .... = j'en ai des milliers

Percentages in French

written as	*spoken as*
25%	vingt-cinq pour cent
50%	cinquante pour cent
100%	cent pour cent
200%	deux cents pour cent
365%	trois cent soixante-cinq pour cent
4,25%	quatre virgule vingt-cinq pour cent

Phrases

numbers up to ten .... = les nombres jusqu'à dix
to count up to ten .... = compter jusqu'à dix
almost ten .... = presque dix
less than ten .... = moins de dix
more than ten .... = plus de dix
all ten of them .... = tous les dix
all ten boys .... = les dix garçons
my last ten pounds .... = mes dix dernières livres
the next twelve weeks .... = les douze prochaines semaines
the other two .... = les deux autres
the last four .... = les quatre derniers

Calculations in French

$10 + 3 = 13$	dix et trois font *or* égalent treize
$10 - 3 = 7$	trois ôté de dix il reste sept *or* dix moins trois égale sept
$10 \times 3 = 30$	dix fois trois égalent trente
$30 : 3 = 10$ ($30 \div 3 = 10$)	trente divisé par trois égale dix
5^2	cinq au carré
5^3	cinq puissance trois
$\sqrt{12}$	racine carrée de douze

Fractions in French

in figures	*in words*
$^1/_2$	un demi*
$^1/_3$	un tiers
$^1/_4$	un quart
$^1/_5$	un cinquième
$^1/_6$	un sixième
$^1/_7$	un septième
$^1/_8$	un huitième
$^1/_9$	un neuvième
$^1/_{10}$	un dixième
$^1/_{11}$	un onzième
$^1/_{12}$	un douzième (*etc*)

in figures	*in words*
$^2/_3$	deux tiers†
$^2/_5$	deux cinquièmes
$^3/_4$	trois quarts
$^3/_{10}$	trois dixièmes
$1\,^1/_2$	un et demi
$1\,^1/_3$	un (et) un tiers
$1\,^1/_4$	un et quart
$1\,^1/_5$	un (et) un cinquième
$5\,^2/_3$	cinq (et) deux tiers
$5\,^3/_4$	cinq (et) trois quarts

* Note that **half**, when not a fraction, is translated by the noun **moitié** or the adjective **demi**; see the dictionary entry.

† Note the use of **les** and **d'entre** when these fractions are used about a group of people or things: **two-thirds of them = les deux tiers d'entre eux**.